Congress and the Nation

Volume VI
1981-1984

A Review of Government and Politics

Congressional Quarterly Inc.
Washington, D.C.

Congressional Quarterly Inc.

Congressional Quarterly Inc., an editorial research service and publishing company, serves clients in the fields of news, education, business and government. It combines Congressional Quarterly's specific coverage of Congress, government and politics with the more general subject range of an affiliated service, Editorial Research Reports.

Congressional Quarterly publishes the *Congressional Quarterly Weekly Report* and a variety of books, including college political science textbooks under the CQ Press imprint and public affairs paperbacks designed as timely reports to keep journalists, scholars and the public abreast of developing issues and events. CQ also publishes information directories and reference books on the federal government, national elections and politics, including the *Guide to Congress*, the *Guide to the U.S. Supreme Court*, the *Guide to U.S. Elections* and *Politics in America*. The *CQ Almanac*, a compendium of legislation for one session of Congress, is published each year. *Congress and the Nation*, a record of government for a presidential term, is published every four years.

CQ publishes *The Congressional Monitor*, a daily report on current and future activities of congressional committees, and several newsletters including *Congressional Insight*, a weekly analysis of congressional action, and *Campaign Practices Reports*, a semimonthly update on campaign laws.

The online delivery of CQ's Washington Alert Service provides clients with immediate access to Congressional Quarterly's institutional information and expertise.

Library of Congress Catalog Number: 65-22351

ISBN: 0-87187-334-6

Editor: Mary W. Cohn
Associate Editor: Colleen McGuiness
Major Contributors: Tom Arrandale, Barbara Coleman, Patricia Ann O'Connor, Margaret Thompson, Elder Witt, Michael D. Wormser
Contributing Editors: James R. Ingram, John L. Moore, David R. Tarr
Contributors: Nancy Blanpied, Mary Ames Booker, Christopher Conte, John Felton, Martha V. Gottron, Anne Meadows, Mary McNeil, Alan Murray, Patricia Russotto, Donald Smith, William Sweet, Amy Stern, Pat Towell
Editorial Assistants: Gail Harris, C. Keith Head, Sheri Kroskie, Judith E. Leckrone, Jodean Marks, Neal Santelmann
Index: Jan Danis
Graphics: Richard A. Pottern, Robert Redding, Kathleen Ossenfort
Proofreaders: William L. Bonn, Eugene J. Gabler, Dave Kaplan, Guy Lamolinara, Gabriel Shapiro

Congressional Quarterly Inc.

Eugene Patterson   *Editor and President*
Wayne P. Kelley   *Publisher*
Peter A. Harkness   *Deputy Publisher and Executive Editor*
Robert C. Hur   *General Manager*
Robert E. Cuthriell   *Director, Research and Development*
I. D. Fuller   *Production Manager*
Maceo Mayo   *Assistant Production Manager*
Sydney E. Garriss   *Computer Services Manager*

Book Department

David R. Tarr   *Director*
Joanne D. Daniels   *Director, CQ Press*
John L. Moore   *Assistant Director*
Kathryn C. Suárez   *Book Marketing Manager*
Mary W. Cohn   *Associate Editor*
Nola Healy Lynch   *Developmental Editor, CQ Press*
Nancy Blanpied   *Project Editor*
Carolyn Goldinger   *Project Editor*
Carolyn McGovern   *Project Editor*
Colleen McGuiness   *Project Editor*
Susanna Spencer   *Project Editor*
Bryan Daves   *Editorial Assistant*
Linda M. Pompa   *Editorial Assistant*
Renee S. Reiner   *Editorial Assistant*
Maria J. Sayers   *Editorial Assistant*
Sheri Kroskie   *Secretary*

Editor's Note

Congress and the Nation Vol. VI continues a series launched by Congressional Quarterly in 1965 with the publication of *Congress and the Nation Vol. I*, a 2,000-page reference book covering national government and politics from 1945 through 1964. Each of the succeeding volumes has covered governmental action during a four-year presidential term: *Congress and the Nation Vol. II*, 1965-68; *Congress and the Nation Vol. III*, 1969-72; *Congress and the Nation Vol. IV*, 1973-76; *Congress and the Nation Vol. V*, 1977-80.

With the publication of this volume, librarians, historians, political scientists, journalists and students now have six volumes spanning the 40 years of Congressional Quarterly's reporting on public policy.

In compiling *Congress and the Nation Vol. VI*, Congressional Quarterly has condensed its legislative, presidential and political coverage during the 1981-84 period into a 1,200-page volume. Readers are given both an overview of the four-year period and detailed chronologies of governmental action in every major subject area.

This volume chronicles an upheaval in government policy as dramatic as any since the Great Depression of the 1930s. President Reagan took office in 1981 promising to reduce the scope of the federal government after half a century of massive growth. To further that goal, Reagan called for deep cuts both in federal spending, especially for domestic social programs, and in individual and business taxes. At the same time the new president embarked on an unprecedented peacetime military buildup and edged the nation toward a more assertive foreign policy.

Congress swiftly approved Reagan's spending and tax cuts, but the severe recession that followed prompted second thoughts about his program. Federal deficits skyrocketed, and Congress and the White House became locked in a conflict over deficit reduction that found no resolution.

Reagan's confrontational approach to foreign policy also led to some disputes with Congress. A bipartisan majority applauded the U.S. invasion of Grenada, but American involvement in Lebanon and Central America led Congress to demand a greater policy-making role in those areas. After Congress blocked funds to produce the MX intercontinental missile and the House came within one vote of approving a nuclear freeze resolution, Reagan agreed to soften his stance on arms control negotiations with the Soviet Union.

Notable legislation enacted during the four-year period included measures to ensure the financial stability of the ailing Social Security system and to extend the Voting Rights Act for 25 years. But Congress was unable to reach agreement on immigration reform, or on proposals to reshape Depression-era farm and banking programs. Reagan-backed measures to permit school prayer, end abortion and court-ordered busing, and require a balanced federal budget failed to win approval.

Congress and the Nation Vol. VI is a record of these and other congressional activities — from momentous events to routine extensions of programs. Researchers can find the pertinent facts on issues and legislation, descriptions of proposals and bills, succinct accounts of legislative, executive and lobbying action, key votes and provisions of legislation.

How to Use This Book

The **Summary Table of Contents** following this editor's note shows the overall organization of the volume. The detailed **Table of Contents** *(p. ix)* provides an outline of each chapter, as well as a listing of all of the stories contained in a particular chapter. For a specific topic within a story, the reader should consult the **Index** *(p. 1125)*. For example, a reader who is interested in congressional action on the defense budget would find in the Table of Contents that there are stories on this issue in the Defense Policy chapter. A reader who needs more specific information, such as details of executive and legislative action on individual missile programs, could consult the Index and find a number of page references for separate missile programs.

The first chapter, Politics and National Issues, gives a legislative summary of each session of the 97th and 98th Congresses and a discussion of the 1982 and 1984 elections. The chapter forms a framework for the legislative chapters that follow.

Note the organization of the legislative chapters — Economic Policy, Foreign Policy, Defense Policy, etc. Each opens with an introduction providing the reader with an overview of the four-year period. That is followed by a chronology of legislative action from 1981 through 1984.

The final chapter on the Reagan presidency assesses the president's relations with Congress during his first term and gives a summary of how legislation Reagan supported or opposed fared in Congress.

The **Appendix** *(p. 859)* contains a variety of supplementary material, including Senate and House key votes (identified in boldface in the legislative chapters) during the four-year period, with a chart showing how each member voted; a glossary of congressional terms and an explanation of how a bill becomes law; lists of committee and subcommittee chairmen; biographical data on members of Congress in 1981-84; profiles of Cabinet members and other senior officials; controversial nominations; presidential vetoes; major presidential speeches and messages to Congress; and political charts, including presidential election returns for 1980 and 1984 and House, Senate and gubernatorial election returns for 1982 and 1984.

Mary W. Cohn
August 1985

Summary Table of Contents

Chapter	*1*	Politics and National Issues	1
Chapter	*2*	Economic Policy	25
Chapter	*3*	Foreign Policy	121
Chapter	*4*	Defense Policy	199
Chapter	*5*	Commerce and Communications	259
Chapter	*6*	Transportation Policy	287
Chapter	*7*	Energy Policy	331
Chapter	*8*	Environmental Policy	401
Chapter	*9*	Agricultural Policy	483
Chapter	*10*	Health, Education and Welfare	517
Chapter	*11*	Housing and Urban Aid	627
Chapter	*12*	Labor and Pension Policy	641
Chapter	*13*	Law and Justice	673
Chapter	*14*	General Government	769
Chapter	*15*	Inside Congress	795
Chapter	*16*	The Reagan Presidency	841
Appendix			859
Index			1125

Table of Contents

Chapter 1 — Politics and National Issues

Introduction 3

1981 Chronology 5
The Legislative Year 5
The Political Year 7
1982 Chronology 7
The Legislative Year 7
The Political Year 9

1983 Chronology 12
The Legislative Year 12
The Political Year 14

1984 Chronology 15
The Legislative Year 15
The Political Year 17

Chapter 2 — Economic Policy

Introduction 27
Federal Reserve Monetary Policy 28

The Federal Budget
Introduction 33
Congressional Budget Process 34
Presidents, Congress and the Budget 36
1981 Chronology 37
Reagan Budget 37
Fiscal 1982 Budget Targets 38
Fiscal 1981 Revisions 40
Reconciliation Cuts 40
Debt Ceiling 42
Binding 1982 Budget Levels 44
Fiscal 1982 Appropriations 45
1982 Chronology 45
Reagan Budget 46
Fiscal 1983 Budget Resolution 46
Fiscal 1982 Revisions 48
Reconciliation Cuts 48
Fiscal 1983 Appropriations 50
1983 Chronology 50
Reagan Budget 51
Fiscal 1984 Budget Resolution 51
Balanced Budget Drive 52
Fiscal 1983 Revisions 54
Deficit Reduction 54
Fiscal 1984 Appropriations 56

1984 Chronology 56
Reagan Budget 56
Deficit Reduction 56
Fiscal 1985 Budget Resolution 59
Fiscal 1984 Revisions 60
Fiscal 1984 Reconciliation Cuts 60
Fiscal 1985 Appropriations 61

Tax Policy
Introduction 63
1981 Chronology 65
Reagan Tax Cuts 65
Miscellaneous Tax Law Changes 71
1982 Chronology 72
Tax Increase 72
Gas Tax Increase 76
Cruise Ships 76
Subchapter S Taxation 76
Miscellaneous Revenue Bill 76
Technical Corrections 77
Periodic Payments, Miscellany 77
Computer Donations 77
1983 Chronology 77
Tax Increase Efforts 77
Cap on Reagan Tax Cut 78
Interest, Dividend Withholding 78
Social Security Taxes 78
Tuition Tax Credits 78

1984 Chronology......................78
Tax Increases 79
Education Fringe Benefits................82
Legal Service Benefits, Imputed Interest....82

Financial Regulation

Introduction...........................83
1981-82 Chronology..................87
'All Savers' Certificates 87
Financial Regulation......................87
Interest and Dividend Withholding.........90
Export Trading Companies................90
1983-84 Chronology..................90
Interest Withholding Repeal..............90
Financial Regulation.....................92
IMF Funding Increase 93
Mortgage Lending.......................93

International Economic Policy

Introduction...........................95
1981 Chronology.....................99
Overseas Investment Agency..............99
Export Control Enforcement..............99
Foreign Bribery Statute..................100
Export Trading Companies...............100
Trade Adjustment Aid...................100
Embargo Loans 100
1982 Chronology....................100
Export Trading Companies..............101
Reagan Caribbean Trade Plan...........102
Auto Domestic Content 102
Trade 'Reciprocity' 102

Romania Trade Status 103
Soviet Economic Sanctions 103
1983 Chronology....................103
IMF Funding 104
Export-Import Bank....................105
Reagan Caribbean Trade Plan...........106
Favored Nation Trade 107
Export Controls Extension 107
Auto Domestic Content 108
Trade 'Reciprocity' 109
1984 Chronology....................109
Omnibus Trade Bill 109
Export Controls Extension 111
Energy Trade 111
Industrial Policy 111
Export Subsidies 111
Textile Labeling........................112

Fiscal Assistance

Introduction..........................113
1981 Chronology....................115
Economic Development Aid 115
Defense Production.....................115
1982 Chronology....................115
Economic Development Aid 115
Defense Production/Stimulus 116
Enterprise Zones 117
1983 Chronology....................117
Revenue Sharing 117
Economic Development Aid 118
Defense Production/Stimulus 119
1984 Chronology....................119
Defense Production.....................119
Industrial Policy 119
Enterprise Zones 119

Chapter 3 — Foreign Policy

Introduction 123
Secretaries of State: Haig, Shultz 127
1981 Chronology....................129
AWACS Sale to Saudi Arabia 129
Development Banks 131
Foreign Aid Authorization...............132
F-16 Sale to Pakistan...................133
Foreign Aid Appropriations..............136
Non-Proliferation Policy 138
Latin Nuclear Arms Treaty..............139
Intelligence Authorization 139
Agent Identity Disclosure 140

Sinai Peacekeeping Force 140
Lefever and Human Rights..............141
Casey, Hugel Controversies..............141
Richard Allen Resignation...............142
Czech Claims Agreement................142
Infant Formula Marketing...............142
U.S.-Iran Claims 143
State Department Authority.............143
Canada Maritime Treaty................143
Wallenberg Citizenship..................144
1982 Chronology....................144
Soviet Economic Sanctions 144
Foreign Aid Authorization...............145

Foreign Aid Appropriations............... 146
State Department Authority............. 148
Caribbean Basin Initiative............. 149
Development Banks Funding 150
Radio Marti Authorization 150
Cuba Resolution........................ 150
Agent Identity Disclosure 151
Intelligence Authorization 152
Japanese Defense Spending.............. 153
BIB Supplemental Funds 153
U.N. Warning on Israel 153
Arms Sales to India 153
U.S.-China Communiqué 154
African Development Fund 154
Shultz Confirmation 155
Spanish Entry Into NATO 155

1983 Chronology..................... 155
Lebanon Policy, War Powers 156
Aid to Lebanon 158
Foreign Aid............................ 159
Nicaragua Covert Aid................... 162
U.S. Aid to Guatemala................. 163

El Salvador Aid 165
Stone Confirmation..................... 165
Radio Marti Authorization 166
State Department Authorization 167
U.S.-Vatican Relations 167
Development Banks, IMF Funds.......... 168
Intelligence Authorization 168
Grenada Invasion....................... 169
Korean Airliner Downing................ 169

1984 Chronology..................... 169
Foreign Aid............................ 170
U.S. Aid to El Salvador................ 174
Aid to Nicaraguan Rebels 175
U.S. Presence in Honduras 176
Central America Aid Plan............... 177
Food Aid for Africa.................... 178
Aid for Afghan Rebels 179
Embassy Security 179
Intelligence Agencies.................. 179
Genocide Treaty........................ 179

Special Report: Central America...... 181
Special Report: Middle East.......... 191

Chapter 4 — Defense

Introduction 201

1981 Chronology..................... 205
1982 Defense Authorization............. 205
1982 Defense Appropriations 208
1981 Supplemental Funds 211
1981 Supplemental Authorization 211
1982 Military Construction 212
Military Pay Increase.................. 214
Nuclear Weapons Programs 215
Strategic Materials Stockpile 216
Arms Agency Authority 217
Defense Production Act................. 217

1982 Chronology..................... 217
1983 Defense Authorization............. 217
Draft Registration 218
1983 Defense Appropriations 219
Nuclear Freeze......................... 221

1983 Military Construction 222
Arms Agency Authority 224
Military Pay 224
Joint Chiefs Reorganization 224
Nuclear Weapons Programs 225

1983 Chronology..................... 225
1984 Defense Authorization............. 225
1984 Defense Appropriations 228
Nuclear Freeze......................... 230
1984 Military Construction 231
Adelman Nomination 233
Joint Chiefs Reorganization 233

1984 Chronology..................... 234
1985 Defense Authorization............. 235
1985 Defense Appropriations 245
1985 Military Construction 246
Military Construction Funding.......... 247

Special Report: Arms Control 249

Chapter 5 — Commerce and Communications

Introduction 261

1981 Chronology..................... 263
Broadcast Licenses 263

Public Broadcasting 264
AT&T Deregulation 265
New Western Union Service.............. 265
Small Business Loans................... 265

Small Business Research Funds...........266
Minority Businesses 266
Tourism Promotion....................266
Consumer Product Safety 267
Consumer Cooperative Bank.............268
FTC Used-Car Rule Veto 268
Cash Discount Ban 269
Product Liability Insurance..............269
Daylight-Saving Time...................269

1982 Chronology....................269
AT&T Deregulation 270
FCC Lottery Rules 272
Broadcast Deregulation 273
Public Broadcasting 273
Small Business Research Funds..........273
FTC Used-Car Rule Veto 273
FTC Regulation of Doctors.............274

1983 Chronology....................274
Phone Rate Hike......................275
Broadcast Deregulation 275
Cable Television Deregulation 275
Television Rerun Rights.................275
Public Broadcasting 275
Insider Trading Curbs 276

Small Business Contract Aid 276
Minority Businesses 276
FTC Authorization 276
FTC Funeral Rule......................277
Consumer Product Safety 277
Credit Card Surcharges, Fraud...........277
Daylight-Saving Time...................277

1984 Chronology....................278
Phone Rate Hike......................278
Cable Television Deregulation 279
Broadcast Deregulation 281
Broadcast Freedom 281
Television Rerun Rights.................282
Public Broadcasting 282
Insider Trading Curbs 283
Corporate Takeover Reforms 283
Small Business Programs................283
Unisex Insurance......................284
Credit Card Surcharges 284
Recall of Dangerous Toys 285
Product Liability......................285
'Fire-Safe' Cigarettes..................285
Park Ride Inspections 285
Odometer Fraud Bill...................285
Election Projections 285

Chapter 6 — Transportation Policy

Introduction 289

1981 Chronology....................291
Conrail................................291
Amtrak................................295
Highway Authorizations.................297
Airport Development 298
Maritime Subsidy Programs 299
Maritime Transfer......................299
Mass Transit Programs 299
Bus Deregulation......................300
Transportation Safety..................300
Hazardous Transport 300
Coast Guard Authorizations 300
Pipeline Safety........................301
Rock Island Railroad 301

1982 Chronology....................301
Gas Tax, Highway/Transit Aid 301
Truck Size.............................307
Airport Development Aid 308
Airline Pact...........................310
Bus Deregulation......................310
Rail Strike............................314
Alaska Railroad 314
Coal Slurry Pipelines 315
Port User Fees........................315
Maritime Subsidy Programs 316

Maritime Antitrust Immunity............316
Coast Guard Authorizations 316
Drunken Driving 316
Highway Safety Agency 317

1983 Chronology....................317
Maritime Antitrust Immunity............317
Coal Slurry Pipelines 319
Highway Aid..........................320
Maritime Authorization 320
Amtrak................................320
Transportation Safety Board 321

1984 Chronology....................321
Highway Aid..........................321
Air Bag Rule..........................322
Drunken Driving 322
Auto Theft Bill 323
Truck Size.............................324
Maritime Antitrust Immunity...........324
Maritime Authorization 324
CAB Consumer Powers Transfer........325
Amtrak................................326
Conrail................................326
Hazardous Transport 328
Pipeline Safety........................328
Coast Guard Authorizations 328
Boating, Fishing Taxes.................328
Puerto Rico Cruises 329
Railroad Issues........................329

Chapter 7 — Energy Policy

Introduction 333

Mineral Leasing

1981-82 Chronology.................339
Wilderness Leasing 339
Watt Contempt Citation 341
Oil and Gas Royalties...................344
Naval Petroleum Reserves...............346
Outer Continental Shelf.................347
Pauley Group Leases 349
Offshore Revenue Sharing...............350
Watershed Leasing 350
Coal Leasing...........................351

1983-84 Chronology.................351
Coal Leasing Moratorium 352
Offshore Leasing Bans 357
Offshore Leasing: State Powers 358
Offshore Revenue Sharing...............359

Nuclear Power

1981-82 Chronology.................361
Radioactive Wastes 361
NRC Authorization 366
Three Mile Island 369
Clinch River Reactor 370

1983-84 Chronology.................371
Clinch River Reactor 371
'Whoops' Rescue Attempt 372
NRC Authorization 373
Power Plant Construction Costs 374

Oil and Gas Regulation

1981-82 Chronology.................375
Oil Price Decontrol 375
Standby Oil Allocation Authority 376
Antitrust Exemption....................378
Strategic Petroleum Reserve.............379
Oil Company Mergers...................382
Natural Gas Deregulation 382
Power Plant Conversion.................383
Alaska Gas Pipeline 384

1983-84 Chronology.................386
Natural Gas Deregulation 387
Energy Preparedness...................390
Strategic Petroleum Reserve.............390
Oil Company Mergers...................390
Antitrust Exemption Extension 390

Research and Development

1981-82 Chronology.................393
1981 Energy Reconciliation..............393
Fiscal 1982 Appropriations 395
Fiscal 1983 Appropriations 396
Department of Energy 397

1983-84 Chronology.................397
Synfuels Funding Cutback 397
Fiscal 1984-85 Appropriations............399
Energy Audits..........................400

Chapter 8 — Environmental Policy

Introduction 403
Watt Role at Interior 406

Clean Air

1981-82 Chronology.................411
Clean Air Act Revisions.................411
Steel Cleanup Delay 417

1983-84 Chronology.................420
Clean Air/Acid Rain 420
EPA Sanctions Moratorium 422

Federal Water Policy

1981-82 Chronology.................425
Sewer Grants 425
Water Policy Planning 428
Dam Repair Funds 430
Reclamation Law Revision 431
Water Project Appropriations............433
Administration Power Rate Study........434
Papago Indian Water Rights.............435
Ocean Dumping 436
Seabed Mining 437
Oil Spill Liability.......................437

Marine Sanctuaries 438
Project Deauthorizations 438
Urgent Reclamation Repairs............. 438
WEB Pipeline........................... 438

1983-84 Chronology................. 438
Clean Water 439
Safe Drinking Water.................... 440
Water Projects/Cost Sharing............. 440
Water Project Appropriations........... 442
Western Dam Repairs................... 444
Hoover Dam Power Pricing.............. 445
Water Research Veto Override........... 446
Ocean Dumping 446
Colorado River Salinity 447
High Plains Groundwater 447

EPA Pollution Control Programs

1981-82 Chronology................. 449
Gorsuch Contempt/Superfund 449
Council on Environmental Quality 451
Hazardous Waste Disposal 452
EPA Research Veto..................... 453
Toxic Substances Control 453
Noise Control 454
Risk Analysis 454

1983-84 Chronology................. 454
Burford/Superfund Controversy.......... 454
Hazardous Waste Controls 457
Superfund Renewal..................... 459
Research Authorizations................. 461

Federal Land Management

1981-82 Chronology................. 463

National Park Expansion................. 463
Forest Wilderness System 465
National Parks Protection............... 467
National Park Repairs 467
Barrier Islands Development............. 467
Strip-Mining Regulation 468
Payments in Lieu of Taxes.............. 469
Mount St. Helens Monument............ 469
National Trails Legislation 469

1983-84 Chronology................. 470
Forest Wilderness System 470
Wild and Scenic Rivers 472
Forest Timber Contract Relief........... 473
Alaska Parks Hunting Debate 474
Parks Protection Bill 475
Critical Materials Council 475
National Trails Legislation 475
Truman Home Site...................... 476
Oregon Land Tracts 476

Wildlife Protection

1981-82 Chronology................. 477
Endangered Species Act................. 477
Sikes Act Extension 478
Marine Mammal Protection 479
Fur Seal Treaty Extension 479
Illegal Wildlife Trade 480

1983-84 Chronology................. 480
Wetlands Protection Program............ 480
Marine Mammal Protection 481
Striped Bass Conservation............... 481
Pribilof Seal Harvest 481
Matagorda Island Accord................ 482

Chapter 9 — Agricultural Policy

Introduction 519

1981 Chronology..................... 487
Omnibus Farm Bill..................... 487
Dairy Price Supports 493
Reconciliation Changes.................. 494
Grain Embargo, Loans 495
Crop Insurance......................... 495

1982 Chronology..................... 496
Farm Program Cuts 496
Tobacco Bill 497
PIK Bills.............................. 498
Commodity Futures..................... 499
Pesticide Law Revisions................. 501

FmHA Authorization 502
Migrant Farm Worker Relief 502
Western Water Reclamation............. 503
Firearms for Border Patrols 503
Government Gasohol..................... 503

1983 Chronology..................... 503
Dairy, Tobacco Programs................ 504
PIK Plan.............................. 508
PIK Cotton Program 508
Farm 'Recession Relief' 509
Pesticide Reauthorization 509
Tobacco Price Support Lid............... 509
Target Price Freeze..................... 510
Specialty Cotton Program 510

Wheat Program Announcements 510
'Sodbuster' Conservation Bill 511
Export Subsidy Program 511

1984 Chronology 511
Target Price Freeze 511

REA Loan Repayments 514
'Sodbuster' Conservation Bill 515
Grain, Cotton Inspection 515
Farm Disaster Loans 516
Honey Promotion 516
Central Kitchen Inspections 516

Chapter 10 — Health, Education and Welfare

Introduction 519

Health Policy

Introduction 521

1981 Chronology 523
Health Block Grants, Funding Cuts 523
Medicaid, Medicare Cuts 527
Health Manpower Programs 530
Saccharin Ban Deferral 530
PHS Hospital Funding 531
Koop Nomination 531
Health Planning System 531
Federal Aid to HMOs 532

1982 Chronology 532
Medicaid, Medicare Cuts 532
'Orphan Drugs' 536
National Institutes of Health 537
Alcohol, Drug Abuse Research 537
Health Planning System 537
Health Promotion 538
FTC Regulation of Doctors 538

1983 Chronology 538
Medicare Cuts 538
Abortion Curbs 540
Saccharin Ban Deferral 541
Alcohol, Drug Abuse Research 541
Health Emergency Fund 542
Hospice Payments 542
Jobless Health Insurance 542
Medicaid Child Health Plan 543
National Institutes of Health . . . . : . . . 543
Cigarette Warning Labels 543
Health Planning System 543

1984 Chronology 543
Medicare Cuts 544
Medicaid Child Health Care 546
Generic Drugs 547
Cigarette Warning Labels 548
Organ Transplant System 549
NIH Bill Veto 550
Health Professions Aid Veto 551

Alcohol, Drug Abuse Research 551
Health Leadership 552
Preventive Health 552
Health Promotion 552
Family Life Programs 552
'Baby Doe' Bill 553
Hospice Payments 553
Heroin for Cancer Patients 553
Computer Tampering 554

Education Policy

Introduction 555

1981 Chronology 557
College Student Aid 557
Elementary, Secondary Aid 559
Impact Aid Cut 560

1982 Chronology 561
College Student Aid 562
Draft Registration Rule 562
Education Regulations 563
Tuition Tax Credit 564
Education Bill Vetoes 564
School Busing 565
Science Education 565
Education Department Dismantlement 565

1983 Chronology 565
College Student Aid 566
Handicapped, Rehabilitation Aid 567
Tuition Tax Credit 567
Elementary, Secondary Aid 568
Education Spending Hike 568
Endowment Aid 569
Tribal Colleges 569
Desegregation Aid 569
Math-Science Education 570
Educational Summit 570
Peace Academy 570
Close Up, Law Programs 570
Sex Discrimination 570

1984 Chronology 570
Math-Science Education 571

School Prayer........................572
Access for Religious Groups.............572
Omnibus Education Bill................573
Draft Registration Ruling.............574
College Student Aid...................575
Vocational Education..................576
Library Aid..........................578
Close Up, Law Programs...............578
Education Leadership..................579
Peace Institute......................579
Teacher Scholarships.................579
School Improvement Aid...............579
Foreign Language Aid.................580
New GI Bill..........................580
Sex Discrimination...................580

Welfare Policy

Introduction........................581

1981 Chronology....................583
Food Stamp Legislation................583
Welfare Benefits.....................586
Social Services, Energy Aid..............588
Anti-Poverty Programs.................590
Child Nutrition Programs..............591
Older Americans Act...................593

1982 Chronology....................594
Food Stamp Program...................594
Welfare Benefits.....................596

1983 Chronology....................598
Relief, Food Aid Bills.................598
Social Services Funds.................602
SSI Benefits.........................602
VISTA Authorization..................602
Vocational Rehabilitation..............602
Child Support Enforcement.............603
Older Americans Act...................603

1984 Chronology....................603
Social Services, Energy Aid..............603
Child Support Enforcement.............605

Child Abuse, 'Baby Doe'...............606
Child Abuse Funds....................608
'Latch-Key' Children Aid..............608
Vocational Rehabilitation..............608
Developmental Disabilities.............609
Older Americans Act..................609
VISTA Authorization..................610
SSI, AFDC Benefits...................611
Food Aid Bills.......................611
Social Welfare Leadership..............611

Veterans

Introduction........................613

1981 Chronology....................615
Veterans' Health Care................615
Veterans' Benefit Cuts................616
Disability Benefit Increase.............616
POW Benefits........................616
New GI Bill..........................616

1982 Chronology....................617
Veterans' Benefits Increase.............617
Veterans' Health Care................617
New GI Bill Proposals.................618
Pell Grant Eligibility.................618
Reconciliation Changes................618

1983 Chronology....................618
Veterans' Health Care................618
Emergency Job Training...............619
Disability Benefit Increase.............620
Mortgage Aid........................620
New GI Bill..........................620

1984 Chronology....................620
Agent Orange Compensation............620
New GI Bill..........................621
Disability Benefits Increase............622
Disability, Education Benefits..........623
Veterans Leadership..................623
Veterans' Health Care................624
Veterans' Job Preference..............625
Veterans' Group Charter...............625

Chapter 11 — Housing and Urban Aid

Introduction........................629

1981 Chronology....................631
Housing Authorization................631

1982 Chronology....................633
Emergency Mortgage Aid...............633
Housing Authorization................634
Mortgage Assumption Plan.............634
FHA Insurance Premiums..............635
Enterprise Zones.....................635

1983 Chronology....................635
Housing Authorization................635
Mortgage Aid........................638
Mortgage Revenue Bonds..............638

1984 Chronology....................638
Housing Funds.......................638
Mortgage Revenue Bonds..............638
Mortgage-Backed Securities............638
Enterprise Zones.....................639
Community Development Funds.........639

Chapter 12 — Labor and Manpower

Introduction 643

1981 Chronology 645
  Social Security Financing 645
  Unemployment Benefits................. 647
  CETA Jobs Programs.................. 648
  CETA Youth Jobs Programs 648
  Railroad Retirement System.............. 648
  Black Lung Trust Fund................. 649
  Trade Adjustment Aid 650

1982 Chronology 651
  Anti-Recession Jobs Plans.............. 652
  Unemployment Benefits................. 654
  Job Training Program 655
  Donovan Investigation 656
  Disability Benefits.................... 656
  Conservation Corps.................... 657
  Racketeering, Longshore Bills........... 657
  Social Security Financing 658
  Jobs for Older Americans 658
  Trade Adjustment Aid 658

Domestic Content 658
Migrant Farm Workers 658

1983 Chronology 658
  Social Security Rescue Plan 659
  Jobs and Recession Relief.............. 663
  'Phase II' Jobs Bills 664
  Jobless Aid Extension................. 665
  Trade Adjustment Aid 665
  Railroad Retirement 666
  Labor Reform Measures................ 666
  Social Security Disability............... 667
  Pension Equity....................... 667
  Conservation Corps 667

1984 Chronology 667
  Social Security Disability............... 667
  Pension Equity....................... 669
  Social Security COLAs................. 670
  Conservation Corps Veto 671
  Longshore Compensation................ 671
  Targeted Jobs Tax Credit 672
  Trade Adjustment Aid 672

Chapter 13 — Law and Justice

Law and Law Enforcement

Introduction 675

1981 Chronology 677
  Legal Services Corporation 677
  Justice Authorization 677
  Immigration Law...................... 677
  National Guard Torts.................. 677
  Bankruptcy Bill 677
  Voting Rights 678
  Criminal Code Revision 678
  Civil Rights Commission 678
  Patent Matters....................... 678
  Tris Reimbursement 678
  Pretrial Services..................... 678
  Foreign Antitrust Suits 678
  Aliens in Virgin Islands 678
  Constitutional Convention Procedures 679
  Drug Programs....................... 680
  Record, Tape, Film Piracy 680

1982 Chronology 680
  Voting Rights 680
  Special Prosecutor Law 681
  Equal Rights Amendment 682

Legal Services Corporation 683
Protecting Public Officials............... 683
Supreme Court Police................... 683
Victims and Witnesses 685
Pretrial Services...................... 685
Arson 685
Theft of Nuclear Materials 685
Missing Children 686
Record, Tape, Film Piracy 686
Copyright Clause 686
Patent Fees.......................... 686
Trademark Amendments 686
New Appeals Court.................... 686
Law Enforcement Leaders............... 687
Federal Jurors 688
Foreign Antitrust Suits 688
Tris Reimbursement 688
Service of Process 688
Aliens in Virgin Islands 688
'Amerasian' Immigration 689
Refugee Resettlement.................. 689
False Identification 689
Employee Claims...................... 689
Crime Control Veto.................... 689
Anti-Abortion Efforts 690

Criminal Code Revision 692
Immigration Reform 692
Extradition Revision 692
Bankruptcy Impasse 692
Antitrust Damages. 693
Justice Authorization 693
Electronic Surveillance. 693
Court Jurisdiction 693
State Justice Institute 693
Patent Extension 693
Cable TV 694
Surplus Property 694

1983 Chronology 694
Civil Rights Commission 694
Legal Services Corporation 695
Military Justice 695
Air Treaty Rejection 696
Anti-Tampering Act 696
Constitutional Bicentennial 696
Equal Rights Amendment 696
Women's Economic Equity Bills 697
Immigration 697
Refugee Programs 697
Anti-Crime Package 697
Anti-Crime Grants. 697
Drug Treatment. 697
Child Pornography 697
Bankruptcy Courts 697
Record Copyrights. 697
Justice Authorization 698

1984 Chronology 698
Crime Control Package. 698
Balanced Budget Amendment 700
Pharmacy Robberies 701
Child Pornography 701
Drug Treatment. 702
Criminal Fine Collection 702
Airplanes and Drugs. 702
Bankruptcy Courts 702
School Prayer 703
Legal Services Corporation 705

School Busing. 705
Cities and Antitrust 705
Semiconductor Chips 706
Joint Research Ventures 706
Meese Nomination. 707
Record Copyrights. 707
Patent Law. 708
Immigration Reform 708
Refugee Programs 708
Civil Rights. 708
Capital Punishment. 709
Exclusionary Rule 709
Habeas Corpus 709
Supreme Court Jurisdiction 709
Justice Authorization 709
Constitutional Convention Procedures 709
Attorneys' Fee Bill 709

The Supreme Court

Introduction 711
Supreme Court Decisions, 1980-84 . 715
Criminal Law 715
Individual and Civil Rights. 725
First Amendment Rights 735
Election Laws. 740
Business Law 741
Labor Law. 748
Energy and Environment. 752
State Powers. 755
Interstate Relations. 760
Powers of the President. 761
Powers of Congress 761
Federal Courts 762
Official Immunity 765
Government Employees 766
Freedom of Information. 766
Social Security, Health. 766
Suits Against the United States. 767
Miscellaneous 768

Chapter 14 — General Government

Introduction 771

1981 Chronology 773
Reagan Block Grants 773
Federal Pay, Pensions 774
Postal Service Reductions 775
Regulatory Reform 776
Freedom of Information Act. 776
NASA Authorization. 776
Science Authorization. 776

Arts, Humanities Funding. 776
Federal Debt Collection 776
Federal Building Policy 777
Virgin Islands Constitution 777
Cost Estimates 777
King Memorial. 777

1982 Chronology 777
'New Federalism'. 777
Regulatory Reform 777
Freedom of Information Act. 778

Federal Pay, Pensions 779
Flexitime Extension 780
Debt Collection Act.................... 780
Mail Fraud 780
Indian Claims......................... 781
Contract Disputes Veto 781
NASA Authorization................... 781
Science Authorization.................. 782
NOAA Authorization.................. 782
Earthquake Hazards Reduction 782
Uniform Relocation Act................. 782
Roosevelt Memorial.................... 782
Prompt Pay Act....................... 783
Waste, Fraud Control.................. 783
Reports to Congress 783
OMB Funds Study 783
Surplus Property Donation 783
Tax-Exempt Aid for Brady.............. 783
Capitol Historical Society 783
Olympic Coins 783
Smithsonian Museum 784
King Memorial........................ 784

1983 Chronology..................... 784
Federal Workers' Social Security......... 784
Federal Pay, Pensions 785
Government Ethics Office 785
Martin Luther King Holiday 786
NASA/Weather Satellites............... 786
Science Authorization.................. 786
Procurement Policy Office............... 786
Mail Fraud 787

Federal Debt Collection.................. 787
OPM Personnel Rules 787
Indian Land Claim Veto 787
School Tax Leasing Veto................ 787
Relocation Assistance 787
Federal Election Commission 788
Paperwork Reduction 788
Bureau of Standards Funding 788
Freedom of Information 788
Earthquake Hazards Reduction 788

1984 Chronology..................... 788
Freedom of Information 788
NASA Authorization................... 789
Landsat Sale.......................... 789
Space Launch Licensing................ 789
Arts, Humanities Funding.............. 789
Bureau of Standards Veto.............. 789
NOAA Veto........................... 790
National Archives 790
Government Reorganization 790
Procurement Costs 790
Indian Legislation 790
Grace Commission Recommendations...... 791
Earthquake Hazards Reductions 792
Federal Pay, COLAs.................... 792
Whistleblower Awards 792
Former Spouse Benefits................ 792
National Party Conventions 792
Polling Place Accessibility.............. 792
D.C. Home Rule....................... 793
Presidential Libraries 793
Infrastructure Study................... 793

Chapter 15 — Inside Congress

Introduction 797

Members and Procedures

1981 Chronology..................... 801
Organization 801
Senate Subpoena Power................ 802
Abscam Scandal....................... 802
Special-Interest Caucus 802
Spellman Vacancy..................... 802
Capitol Hill Area Development 803
Hinson Resignation.................... 804

1982 Chronology..................... 804
Williams Resignation 804
Richmond Resignation 809
Congressional Pages 809
Senate Television..................... 810
House Chaplain Vote 811
House Bicentennial Office............... 812

1983 Chronology..................... 812
Organization 812
Bomb Explosion in Capitol.............. 813
Study of Senate Operations 813
House Sex Scandal 813
Transcript Alterations 814
House Drug Investigation 815
West Front Restoration 815
Senate Day-Care Program.............. 815

1984 Chronology..................... 816
House Television Dispute 816
President's Pocket-Veto Power........... 817
Senate TV Coverage 818
Congressional Ethics Violations 818
Williams' Campaign Funds 819

Pay and Benefits

1981 Chronology..................... 821
Congressional Pay 821

State Tax Exemption 823
House Earned Income Limit 823
House Expense Allowances 824
Franking Privilege 826

1982 Chronology 827
House Members' Pay Hike 827
Senate Earned Income Limit 829
Members' Expense Allowances 829
Repeal of 1981 Tax Deduction 829

1983 Chronology 830
Congressional Pay 830
Social Security Coverage 831
Franking Privilege 831

1984 Chronology 832
Congressional Pay 832
Pay Commission Proposal 832

Special Report: Legislative Veto . . . 833

Chapter 16 — The Reagan Presidency

First-Term Review 843
Reagan Profile 844

Assassination Attempt 847
Bush Profile 854

Appendix

Glossary of Congressional Terms 861
The Legislative Process in Brief 873

Key Votes

1981 Key Votes 879
1982 Key Votes 895
1983 Key Votes 911
1984 Key Votes 927

Congress and Its Members

Membership Lists 945
Members of Congress, 1981-85 953
Congressional Committees 963
Post-Election Sessions 975
Senate Cloture Votes, 1917-84 977
Text of Legislative Veto Opinions 981

Congressional Reapportionment

Redistricting for the 1980s 995
Reapportionment History 999

The Presidency

Reagan Appointments to Major Posts . . . 1017
Presidential Vetoes, 1981-84 1031
Selected Presidential Messages 1033

Political Charts

Winning Party in Presidential Races 1089
Presidential Elections, 1860-1984 1090
1980 Presidential Election 1092
1984 Presidential Election 1093
1984 Electoral Votes by States 1094
Republican Convention Balloting 1095
Democratic Convention Balloting 1096
Political Parties in Congress, Presidency . 1098
House Election Results, 1944-84 1100
House Seats and Electoral Votes 1102
97th Congress Special Elections 1103
1982 Election Results 1104
98th Congress Special Elections 1113
1984 Election Results 1115
Governors, 1980-84 1122

Index 1125

Congress and the Nation

Volume VI
1981-1984

1

Politics and National Issues

Introduction   *3*
1981 Chronology   *5*
1982 Chronology   *7*
1983 Chronology   *12*
1984 Chronology   *15*

Politics and National Issues

The state of the economy propelled Ronald Reagan into the White House in 1981, and it dominated the congressional agenda throughout the president's first term. In that period, the new Republican president led Congress to enact what has been called the greatest shift in federal spending priorities since the New Deal, the nation experienced the worst recession since the Great Depression, and the federal deficit more than doubled to nearly $200 billion a year, a level that affected virtually every action of Congress.

When Ronald Reagan took the oath of office on Jan. 20, 1981, Americans were beginning to feel good again about themselves and their country. The 52 Americans held hostage by the Iranian government for more than a year were set free just as the new president completed his inaugural speech. And although Americans were still suffering from double-digit inflation and interest rates and more than 7 percent of the work force was unemployed, most voters believed Reagan's promise that he could bring the country a new prosperity.

In stark contrast to President Jimmy Carter, who appeared not to know what to do to right the economy, Reagan promised to stimulate economic growth by cutting taxes and overall federal spending. He said he would build up the nation's defenses and cut back the amount of regulation coming from Washington. And he promised to balance the federal budget, then running an almost $60 billion deficit, by the end of his first term.

Taking full advantage of his landslide election momentum, a little used congressional budget procedure and his skillful use of television to appeal to the public, Reagan pushed the largest tax and spending cuts in history through Congress in less than eight months. Congress reduced personal income taxes by 25 percent over three years, accelerated business depreciation allowances and cut dozens of domestic social programs by a total of $130.6 billion over four years. At the same time it approved most of Reagan's defense spending requests.

But that was the last time during Reagan's first term that Congress and the president reached such broad accord on the federal budget. By the end of Reagan's first year, the country had plunged into the worst recession in 50 years. Reagan blamed it on his predecessor, but fears over the soaring federal deficit also fueled the slump. Revenues already lowered by the tax cut fell even more as the unemployment rate climbed above 10 percent. And recession-related federal spending increased. Despite an unexpectedly strong economic rebound in 1983, the deficit for the fiscal year ending Sept. 30, 1983, hit a record $195.4 billion.

By the end of his first term, Reagan had fulfilled part of his 1980 campaign promise. The gross national product, a key measure of economic growth, had risen 6.8 percent in 1984, the biggest gain since 1951. Inflation had been held to 4 percent, the lowest rate since 1967. But while the unemployment rate had fallen considerably from its recession high of 10.7 percent, it remained above 7 percent, about the same as it was when Reagan took office. And instead of balancing the federal budget, Reagan was presiding over the largest deficits in the nation's history.

Setting Priorities

The struggle to lower the federal deficit tested both Congress and its budget-setting procedures as the political costs of federal spending reductions began to be felt on Capitol Hill. Allegations that the 1981 reductions were hurting primarily the poor and near-poor were coupled with the realization that further substantial cuts could be made only in programs that affected middle-income voters. Democrats and Republicans alike refused to approve further domestic spending cuts unless defense spending also was slowed and taxes raised. With great reluctance, Reagan agreed to tax increases in 1982 and 1984.

The president also was forced to accept less than he wanted for defense. In 1982, 1983 and 1984, Congress cut at least $15 billion from the proposed defense budget. Rather than saving money by killing any major weapons programs, however, Congress made modest cuts in a lot of programs and thus did not drastically alter the direction of Reagan's arms buildup. The only weapons program Congress refused to fund was a new type of lethal nerve gas weapon.

The strain of negotiating annual budget packages that would win the support of a majority of members in both chambers stretched the traditional congressional comity to the breaking point. To much of the public, Congress often appeared chaotic, indecisive and unable to solve the nation's problems.

In the Democratic-controlled House, a coalition of conservative Southern Democrats known as "Boll Weevils" voted with the Republicans on many budget issues in 1981 and 1982, giving the minority party the balance of power. The 1982 elections added 26 Democrats, most of them moderate or liberal, to the House, restoring power to the Democratic leadership. But without Reagan's support, House Speaker Thomas P. O'Neill Jr., D-Mass., was reluctant to push for tax increases that could expose the Democrats to 1984 election campaign charges that they belonged to the party of high taxes and federal spending.

Politics and National Issues

Although Republicans controlled the Senate, they were divided into two camps on budget issues: those who sided with the president's "supply-side" approach to the economy, which emphasized tax cuts, and those who wanted a more balanced package of spending cuts and tax increases. Under Majority Leader Howard H. Baker Jr., R-Tenn., the Senate's tradition of acceding to the individual at the expense of the majority at times nearly brought that chamber to a standstill because of filibusters or other obstructionist tactics.

Security and Foreign Policy

Reagan's conduct of the nation's foreign and national security policy was as confrontational as his approach to the federal budget. He clearly and loudly branded the Soviet Union and its supporters as the enemy and sought to re-establish the United States as the undisputed leader of the free world. His approach led to frequent disputes with members of Congress who thought Reagan was too quick to seek military solutions to diplomatic problems. By and large Reagan prevailed.

A solid majority of both houses applauded the U.S. invasion of Grenada in October 1983 to rid the Caribbean island of a Soviet-backed Marxist regime. Reagan also won bipartisan congressional support for stationing Marines as a peacekeeping force in Lebanon until the terrorist killing of 241 Americans at Beirut's airport made withdrawal of the U.S. military presence from Lebanon the only political option.

For the most part, foreign policy focused on Central America, where Reagan vigorously supported El Salvador's attempts to wipe out a leftist insurgency and just as vigorously worked to undermine the leftist Sandinista government in Nicaragua. Although congressional opponents may have moderated Reagan's policies somewhat, Congress rejected outright only one military campaign: the funding of guerrilla "contras" fighting to overthrow the Sandinistas.

Congressional opposition to Reagan's militaristic approach to nuclear arms control did have a demonstrable moderating effect. A nuclear freeze campaign came within one vote of victory in the House in 1982, and in December of that year Congress blocked funds to produce the MX intercontinental missile. To save the missile Reagan bargained with moderates in Congress, essentially agreeing to changes in his arms control negotiating stance that helped lead to renewed negotiations with the Soviets in early 1985.

Other Legislation

Congressional preoccupation with the federal budget left little time or political will to tackle other legislation. Instead of enacting new measures, members spent much of their time trying to protect existing programs from budget cuts. Apart from budget/tax matters and appropriations, the major bills Congress approved during the four-year period were overshadowed by the legislation it did not pass.

High on the congressional list of achievements were measures to revitalize the financially faltering Social Security system and to extend the Voting Rights Act for 25 years. But Congress was unable to reach agreement on immigration reform or a measure to overturn a Supreme Court decision that narrowed the protection of several federal anti-discrimination laws. Proposals to reshape Depression-era farm and banking programs remained on hold.

Congress also could not come to grips with several environmental protection bills. It approved nuclear and hazardous waste measures and, breaking an impasse with the administration, added 8.3 million acres to the federal wilderness system. But political and policy disagreements held up reauthorization of the Clean Air and Clean Water acts and the "superfund" measure to clean up abandoned toxic waste dumps.

Congress rejected much of the president's legislative agenda. Measures to permit school prayer, end abortion and court-ordered busing and require a balanced federal budget were all defeated in one or the other chamber. Conservatives criticized the president, saying that at least one or two of these measures would have passed had Reagan lobbied harder for them. Also falling by the wayside was Reagan's enterprise zone plan that would have given tax breaks to businesses that created jobs in depressed areas. His "New Federalism" proposal, which would have radically changed the relationship between the federal government and the states, was never even seriously debated.

In the wake of a 1983 Supreme Court ruling striking down the legislative veto, Congress tested other ways to ensure that the executive branch carried out the laws as Congress intended. Legislative vetoes had been written into more than 200 laws over half a century to enable lawmakers to overrule executive branch orders or regulations.

Politics

Reagan was one of the most personally popular presidents of modern times. Frustrated political foes talked about the "Teflon presidency" in which adverse events that would have politically damaged others seemed to roll off Reagan, leaving him unblemished.

But Reagan's success with the voters did not extend to other races. Instead of solidifying their control in the Senate, the Republicans lost a net of one seat over the four-year period. They began Reagan's first term with a 54-46 edge; they started his second with a 53-47 lineup. In 1982, when the Democrats — who were defending 19 of the 33 seats at stake — might have been relegated to minority status for many years to come, the lineup held steady. Democrats, however, were not totally pleased with their performance; many of them had predicted they would regain control of the Senate in the 1984 elections.

Reagan's coattails were even shorter in the House. In 1982 the Democrats picked up 26 House seats, giving them a 103-vote edge. The Republican defeat was partly a result of partisan redistricting in several Democratic-controlled states. But it also indicated voter dissatisfaction with Reagan's economic program, which many voters blamed for the recession the country was just beginning to escape. Republicans picked up 14 seats in the 1984 elections, but the balance of power was not expected to change much.

The one bright spot for the GOP was a significant gain in state legislatures. While the average number of legislatures the Republicans controlled did not change as a result of the 1984 elections, the numbers of GOP legislators increased in several states. After the 1984 elections the Republicans controlled both chambers in 11 states and one chamber in another 10. Continued increases could give the party control in several states and possibly influence the course of the redistricting that was to occur after the 1990 Census.

1981

The Legislative Year

Dominated by Republicans for the first time in 2½ decades and guided by a forceful and popular president, Congress took bold steps in 1981 toward reducing the federal government's scope. Following the wishes of President Reagan, the 97th Congress slashed government spending, cut taxes for individuals and businesses, slimmed down federal regulatory activities and generally sought to dispel the notion that people and institutions should rely on Washington to solve their problems.

In giving Reagan most of what he asked for, Congress was acting under the belief that it was responding to the mandate of the 1980 elections. That political tide not only swept a conservative Republican into the White House, but also floated the GOP into its first Senate majority (53-47) since January 1955. The change in control in the Senate meant that the entire committee leadership shifted to the Republicans and that the Democrats were relegated to minority leadership. The new Senate majority leader was Howard H. Baker Jr., R-Tenn.

In the House, the Democrats, under the leadership of Thomas P. O'Neill Jr., D-Mass., were still in the majority, though by a slimmer margin (243-192) than they enjoyed in the previous Congress. And the conservative leanings of many of their numbers made the Democratic leadership's grasp on House proceedings tentative at times.

Reagan's Economic Triumph

In all, the first session of the 97th Congress was a great personal triumph for Reagan. Congressional approval of his plan was due largely to his own efforts and strength. When Reagan entered office in January, he laid out what appeared to some to be contradictory goals for his presidency. To revitalize the economy and strengthen the nation, he said, he would cut federal spending yet increase spending for defense, reduce taxes yet balance the budget. Many traditional Republicans in Congress were uneasy with this "supply-side" economic approach. But the GOP leaders in both houses proved to be effective and loyal lieutenants for their president.

Reagan himself was the administration's best lobbyist. He promised that his plan, if approved, would have immediate results. The mere expectation of the changes to be wrought by his recovery program would spur the economy, he said. As the first session drew to a close in December, the returns on the Reagan program were not all in, but the results were at best mixed.

Congress had enacted $35.2 billion in fiscal 1982 program reductions, cut nearly $4 billion more from appropriations, approved a cut in individual and business taxes totaling $749 billion over a five-year period, and added about $18 billion to the fiscal 1982 defense budget drafted by President Carter the year before.

But the federal deficit for the year appeared to be heading over the $100 billion mark, and the economy was in recession. And in the process of getting his program enacted, Reagan exhausted his winning coalition, stretched congressional procedures out of shape and bruised sensitive legislative egos.

Almost all the sweeping budget cuts Congress approved were made in one package, the budget "reconciliation" bill. The use of the reconciliation method in such a massive way — more ambitious than Congress had contemplated in 1974 when it invented the legislative device to carry out its fiscal goals — was criticized by some members as an abuse of the budget process.

The one budget bill touched on virtually every federal activity except defense. Included in it were a multitude of changes in existing law, including provisions to tighten eligibility for food stamps and public assistance, cut funds for subsidized housing programs, reduce school lunch subsidies, impose a needs test for guaranteed student loans and cut Medicaid payments to the states.

Distorted Loyalties

In a sense, Congress did work its will on Reagan's economic proposals — by passing even more generous tax cuts for business and high-income investors than he ini-

---

Congressional Leadership 1981-84

Senate

President Pro Tempore — Strom Thurmond, R-S.C.
Majority Leader — Howard H. Baker Jr., R-Tenn.
Majority Whip — Ted Stevens, R-Alaska
Republican Conference Chairman — James A. McClure, R-Idaho
Republican Conference Secretary — Jake Garn, R-Utah

Minority Leader — Robert C. Byrd, D-W.Va.
Minority Whip — Alan Cranston, D-Calif.
Democratic Conference Secretary — Daniel K. Inouye, D-Hawaii

House

Speaker — Thomas P. O'Neill Jr., D-Mass.
Majority Leader — Jim Wright, D-Texas
Majority Whip — Thomas S. Foley, D-Wash.
Caucus Chairman — Gillis W. Long, D-La.

Minority Leader — Robert H. Michel, R-Ill.
Minority Whip — Trent Lott, R-Miss.
Chairman of the Conference — Jack F. Kemp, R-N.Y.
Policy Committee Chairman — Dick Cheney, R-Wyo.

tially had asked for. Ironically, Democrats abetted this turn of events by engaging in a fruitless bidding war for interest groups' support.

Traditional party interests and loyalties were distorted in other ways as well. Republicans were able to win their twin economic victories only with the help of Democratic defectors in the House, mostly a group of Southern conservatives calling themselves "Boll Weevils." Such defections led House Democratic leaders to threaten discipline of such errant colleagues in the future.

In September, when Reagan proposed a second package of $13 billion in further spending cuts and $3 billion in unspecified revenue increases for 1982, the president's coalition began to crumble. Even members who had worked hard for Reagan's first round of cuts had no stomach for a second in a single year.

Moderate House Republicans threatened to desert him unless he shielded their pet programs. Conservative Democrats threatened to bail out over the growing deficit, and the Reagan team was split over the question of tax increases.

The president maintained symbolic pressure on Congress to make additional spending cuts — even bringing the government to a halt for a day in late November by vetoing a temporary funding resolution. But Congress was unwilling to make the cuts he demanded. The appropriations process ground to a halt, and the government limped through the end of the year on a series of temporary funding resolutions.

The appropriations logjam ended just five days before the session's end, when the president announced he would sign any individual appropriations bills that came in under the ceilings set in the stopgap funding measure that cleared Congress on Dec. 11.

Defense, Foreign Affairs

On defense, Congress granted Reagan's request for significant spending increases. The $200 billion fiscal 1982 defense appropriation was the largest peacetime appropriations bill ever approved. After eight months of deliberation, the administration killed the mobile version of the MX missile but deferred a final decision on how to base the controversial weapon until 1984. Efforts to block the $2 billion in the budget to continue MX development were rejected in both houses. Reagan also won congressional approval to begin production of the B-1 bomber that President Carter had canceled four years before.

Following a dramatic lobbying effort by the president, the Senate narrowly voted to permit the sale to Saudi Arabia of sophisticated radar planes and other arms, a victory Reagan said was essential to his conduct of foreign policy.

In another example of Reagan's persuasive powers, Congress cleared its first foreign aid appropriations bill since 1978. Earlier bills had fallen victim to partisan differences in Congress over the proper ratio of military to economic aid. The same issue had kept the fiscal 1982 bill in limbo all year. But at the last minute Reagan rallied a sufficient number of Republicans to push the measure through a reluctant Congress.

Both houses of Congress voted to impose conditions on U.S. arms aid to the ruling centrist junta in El Salvador even though the Reagan administration, in a "white paper" on the conflict in the tiny Central American nation, declared a leftist insurgency to be a "textbook case of indirect

Congress in 1981

Working late into the night on several major pieces of legislation, the first session of the 97th Congress completed its legislative business on Dec. 16, 1981. The Senate adjourned *sine die* at 10:28 p.m. and the House, after rejecting an earlier motion to adjourn, followed suit at 11:22 p.m.

The session, which convened at noon on Jan. 5, 1981, lasted 346 days and tied with the first session of the 95th Congress and the second session of the 76th Congress as the 14th longest in history. The third session of the 76th Congress, from Jan. 3, 1940, to Jan. 3, 1941, was the longest on record.

The Senate met for 165 days during the year, the House for 163 days. A total of 8,719 bills and resolutions (2,478 Senate and 6,241 House) were introduced during the session, an increase of 4,296 from 1980 but fewer than the 10,171 bills and resolutions introduced during the first session of the 96th Congress.

President Reagan signed into law 145 public bills that were cleared during the session. In 1980 President Carter signed 426 public bills into law. Reagan vetoed two bills. Neither veto was overridden. *(Public laws, box, p. 11; presidential vetoes, p. 1031)*

During 1981 the House took 353 recorded votes, substantially below the record-setting 834 votes taken in 1978, and the fewest since 1972. The Senate's 483 recorded votes fell 205 below the record 688 taken in 1976 and were the fewest since 1971. *(Record votes, box, p. 10)*

armed aggression by communist powers through Cuba." The conditions were designed to help win a negotiated settlement and protect human rights.

Domestic Programs

In the fields of health, education and the social services, Congress approved the transformation of many domestic aid programs into block grants that transferred power from the federal government to the states and localities — although Reagan did not get all he asked for in that area. Congress refused the administration's request to put a cap on federal payments for Medicaid, the health care program for the poor and disabled, but it did reduce those payments.

Congress approved a new four-year farm bill that came close to Reagan's requested spending cuts in subsidy programs. The measure continued most existing price support and other farm programs with moderate increases except for the dairy program, whose support rates were reduced sharply. It included a one-year extension of food stamps with new enforcement authority to discourage fraud and abuse.

Despite the sweeping changes Congress made, several important controversies remained unresolved. In an embarrassment for the president, Congress refused to even consider his proposal to overhaul the Social Security system, and Reagan subsequently withdrew it. He proposed instead the formation of a bipartisan panel to come up with recommendations to solve the Social Security funding problem. Legislators then abandoned their own efforts to achieve a comprehensive reform of the retirement system, opting instead to seek a temporary solution.

A scheduled reauthorization of the Clean Air Act also became mired in controversy and was put off. The House approved by a wide margin legislation to extend the 1965 Voting Rights Act, but the bill got nowhere in the Senate during 1981. Legislation to deregulate the telecommunications industry and to restructure the American Telephone & Telegraph Co. cleared the Senate but was still pending in the House.

Congress debated proposals to permit school prayer, curb busing and ban abortions. But at year's end, these volatile social issues remained to be resolved.

A constitutional amendment giving the states and Congress joint authority to restrict abortion was approved by a Senate Judiciary subcommittee and was pending before the full committee at adjournment. Also pending before the Senate panel was a bill declaring that human life begins at conception and allowing states to pass anti-abortion laws.

The Senate adopted a far-reaching curb on the use of court-ordered busing for racial balance as an amendment to a Justice Department reauthorization bill, but the measure subsequently became enmeshed in a filibuster. A filibuster also stymied efforts to enact legislation allowing voluntary school prayer.

Congress never acted on Reagan campaign promises to deregulate natural gas and abolish the Education and Energy departments because the administration never formally proposed them.

Muted Boasts

At session's end, Republican legislators hailed the year's accomplishments in glowing terms. "We helped define a new direction for national government and national politics in this country," said House Minority Leader Robert H. Michel, R-Ill., following Congress' Dec. 16 adjournment.

But the leaders conceded that considerable challenges still faced the GOP in 1982. "This situation wasn't created in a year. We can't clean it up in a year," said Senate Majority Whip Ted Stevens, R-Alaska.

For the Democrats, House Chief Deputy Majority Whip Bill Alexander, D-Ark., said, "it was necessary to fight each round, but it was fortunate that we did not win. Had we won and changed Ronald Reagan's economic plan, the president could have pointed to us and accused us of being responsible for the mess we find ourselves in today."

The Political Year

Voter uneasiness over President Reagan's economic program helped Democrats in several 1981 off-year elections, although Republican losses were too few to be considered a significant trend. Of the five House special elec-

tions, Democrats picked up one GOP seat and came close to winning a second.

In the Virginia gubernatorial contest, animosity toward Reaganomics produced a sizable black turnout that helped sweep Democrat Charles S. Robb into office, ending a 12-year Republican occupancy. And in New Jersey Republican Thomas H. Kean won an extremely close gubernatorial election that was decided only after a recount. The close vote showed that Reagan policies were disliked by many blue-collar Democrats who had voted Republican in the 1980 presidential election. But the unpopularity of the outgoing Democratic administration and Kean's ability to distance himself from the parts of the Reagan plan voters disliked helped the Republican win in the Garden State.

The GOP loss in the House occurred when Democrat Wayne Dowdy triumphed by turning out a large black vote in a Mississippi district that was almost half non-white. Dowdy supported renewal of the Voting Rights Act, which his opponent wanted to terminate. The Democrats were also buoyed in midsummer when their candidate almost won an Ohio rural district with Republican ties. Although Republican Michael Oxley took pains to disassociate himself from Reagan's plans to cut back Social Security benefits, Democrat Dale Locker used the issue with unexpected benefit, losing by only 341 votes.

The outcomes of elections to fill seats in Michigan, Maryland and Pennsylvania surprised no one. The Michigan seat was firmly Republican, the other two were just as firmly Democratic, and traditional voting patterns remained unaltered. At year's end the partisan breakdown in the House stood at 242 Democrats and 192 Republicans. The one vacancy, a longtime Democratic seat in Connecticut, stayed with the Democrats in early 1982 voting.

1982

The Legislative Year

Congress grew increasingly independent of the White House in 1982. The legislators adhered to President Reagan's general course of restraining domestic programs while increasing military spending, but they rejected many of the president's specific proposals.

They substantially rewrote Reagan's fiscal 1983 budget and convinced the president to support a large tax increase only a year after passing his three-year tax cut plan. For the first time, in September, Congress overrode Reagan's veto of an appropriations bill, a measure the president had labeled a "budget-buster."

Reagan's problems with the 97th Congress seemed to increase after the Nov. 2 elections, when 26 incumbent House Republicans were defeated and some GOP senators found themselves in much tighter races than they had anticipated. A lame-duck session left members dispirited and disgruntled.

The 97th's Record

While modifying or rejecting many of Reagan's requests, Congress did not originate much of its own legisla-

Congress in 1982

By using all-night sessions, holding a rare Saturday meeting and finally breaking a filibuster against the president's gasoline tax increase proposal, the second session of the 97th Congress was able to complete its business on Dec. 23, 1982. The Senate adjourned *sine die* at 1:13 p.m. that day. The House had adjourned on Dec. 21 at 9:56 p.m.

The session, which convened at noon on Jan. 25, 1982, lasted 333 days. It was the shortest since the second session of the 95th Congress (1978) but still ranked as the 23rd longest in history. The Senate met for 147 days during the year, the House for 140 days. There were 4,520 bills and resolutions introduced during the session, compared with 8,719 in 1981.

A total of 328 public bills became law in 1984, bringing the total for the entire 97th Congress to 473, the smallest since the 470 enacted during the 66th Congress (1919-21). Reagan vetoed 12 public bills in 1982. Two of these vetoes were overridden and the bills enacted into law without his signature. *(Public laws, box, p. 11; presidential vetoes, p. 1031)*

During 1982 the House took 459 recorded votes, substantially fewer than the record-setting 834 votes taken in 1978, but 106 more than in 1981. The Senate took 465 recorded votes, well below that chamber's record of 688 taken in 1976 and 18 fewer than in 1981. *(Recorded votes, box, p. 10)*

tion in 1982. Faced with soaring federal deficits, members spent a lot of their time defending existing programs from budget cuts rather than trying to create new ones. In addition, Congress packaged many bills into a few omnibus measures.

The budget almost totally dominated the congressional schedule. The first six months of the session were spent on lengthy budget negotiations, drafting sessions and floor consideration of the first fiscal 1983 budget resolution. The exercise proved so painful that members decided to sidestep action on the second budget resolution, and as the year ended members of both parties were considering changes in the budget process they had set up less than a decade earlier to give them some control over setting federal spending priorities.

A major achievement of the session was a tax increase bill, enacted as part of Congress' deficit reduction efforts, that was designed to raise $98 billion over the following three years. To it Congress added several other measures ranging from authorizing money for airport development to limiting Medicare and Medicaid payments to hospitals and doctors. Also in the tax bill, Congress established a supplemental unemployment benefits program to help about two million jobless workers who had exhausted benefits pro-

vided under existing law.

Other notable achievements included a 25-year extension of the Voting Rights Act and passage of a nuclear waste disposal bill. Congress also passed bills deregulating the inter-city bus industry, blocking a strike by railroad workers and updating antiquated laws governing the use of federal irrigation water in the West.

Although rising unemployment — resulting from the worst recession since the 1930s — made Congress increasingly sympathetic to direct federal jobs programs, Reagan stoutly resisted such proposals. But the president eventually endorsed, and Congress in its lame-duck session approved, legislation raising the federal gasoline tax to finance highway and mass transit improvements. Reagan insisted the measure was not a jobs bill, but supporters maintained it would create 300,000 jobs.

Unfinished Business

Among the specific proposals that Congress rejected in 1982 was the president's call for a constitutional amendment requiring a balanced federal budget. The Senate killed a Reagan-backed proposal designed to ban most abortions, and it laid aside a measure intended to return prayer to the public schools. The Senate did approve language that would have ended court-ordered school busing, but the bill never emerged from the House.

Congress also turned down most of Reagan's ambitious efforts at reducing the scope of the federal government and failed to pass his proposals to reform the regulatory process, revamp clean air and water laws, abolish the departments of Energy and Education and establish new financial relationships with the 50 states.

The major foreign policy initiatives Reagan had sought from Congress both died in the Senate. A bill to create Radio Marti, which would beam American propaganda to Cuba, was buried in a filibuster. And a bill containing the trade portions of Reagan's Caribbean Basin Initiative also died in the Senate, stalled behind other bills that were being filibustered. Congress seemed increasingly impatient with the methods and results of Reagan's policies in Central America, especially El Salvador. But aside from refusing to increase military aid to El Salvador, the lawmakers took no action to force a dramatic change in administration policies.

A late-session presidential request to set up a new farm program, paying farmers in grain as well as cash for keeping land out of production, died in the Senate. In January 1983 the administration announced it would implement the payment-in-kind (PIK) program administratively. An immigration reform bill sought by the administration passed the Senate but died under a fusillade of amendments from House opponents.

Congress agreed to much of the defense spending increase Reagan sought but rejected his request to begin procurement of two major nuclear weapons — the MX and Pershing missiles. A nuclear weapons freeze resolution also failed.

Other important bills that did not make it through included measures rewriting federal pesticide laws, reauthorizing hazardous waste disposal laws, setting up the urban "enterprise zones" sought by the president and strengthening federal health warnings on cigarette packages. Congress did not meet a Supreme Court deadline for legislation to straighten out the federal bankruptcy court system, and it did not take any action on regulation of

natural gas prices and supplies or on restructuring the telecommunications industry.

Congress also put off dealing with the financial woes of the ailing Social Security system. Apart from a spate of partisan rhetoric at election time, legislators managed to skirt this controversial issue throughout the year.

Lame-Duck Session

The 97th Congress finally adjourned Dec. 23, when the Senate cleared the gas tax/highway repair legislation. Senators left town feeling bitter toward a handful of their colleagues who had staged a last-ditch filibuster on the gas tax bill. The normally gentlemanly Senate turned into a collection of 100 tired men and women complaining about each others' bad behavior.

The House adjourned Dec. 21, but many representatives had departed several days before. When the House approved the conference agreement on the gas tax bill Dec. 21, only 267 members remained to vote.

Against the wishes of the Senate and House leadership, Reagan in September had called the lame-duck session, which began Nov. 29. It was requested primarily to deal with the 10 fiscal 1983 appropriations bills Congress had not finished before recessing Oct. 1 for the midterm elections.

Congress eventually cleared four additional appropriations bills during the lame-duck session, packaging the remaining six into the stopgap, continuing appropriations resolution. It added a host of special interest amendments to the continuing resolution, including a pay raise for House members. Breaking with tradition, senators did not take the raise, but the Senate did eliminate strict ceilings on outside income that would have gone into effect in 1983.

The Political Year

The 1982 election produced major change in the House of Representatives but left the Senate comparatively untouched. A combination of redistricting and recession produced a huge crop of 81 House freshmen — 57 of them Democrats. In the previous 30 years only three other elections had brought in that many new Democrats.

In the Senate the party ratio remained 54-46 Republican. Only two incumbents were defeated, giving the Senate a stability that it had lacked throughout the 1970s when turnover was much higher. In addition to their gains in the House, Democrats won a net of seven governors' offices from the Republicans.

House Elections

Democrats scored a 26-seat gain in the House on Nov. 2, as voters expressed antipathy toward President Reagan's economic program but stopped short of repudiating it altogether. The outcome revealed an unusual degree of voter frustration with a party only two years into national power. The electorate is usually kinder to a party facing its first midterm election after capturing the White House.

Jimmy Carter's Democratic Party lost only 11 House seats in the 1978 midterm election. Republicans under Richard M. Nixon dropped 12 in 1970. The Republican loss in 1982 was the worst suffered by any party at the two-year

point in 60 years — since the GOP under Warren G. Harding lost 75 seats in 1922.

Democrats won 269 seats to 166 seats for the GOP, giving the Democrats a 103-seat advantage. This total included Colorado's 6th District, whose newly elected GOP representative, Jack Swigert, died Dec. 27, and two districts in Georgia where redistricting problems forced postponement of the election until Nov. 30. Both Georgia seats were retained by incumbent Democrats. Swigert's seat remained in GOP hands after a special election in 1983.

Going into the 1982 election, Democrats held 241 seats and Republicans 192, with vacancies in two districts formerly occupied by Democrats. Twenty-six Republican incumbents and three sitting Democrats were beaten, nearly a mirror image of the 1980 election, in which the GOP lost three incumbents and unseated 28 Democratic members. Democrats scored a net gain of two in the 36 districts left open by the retirement, primary defeat or death of an incumbent.

The Redistricting Factor

Redistricting played a major role in 1982. This was the election in which reapportionment, the rise of the Sun Belt and the decline of the Frost Belt were supposed to catch up with the Democrats, setting in motion a decade of conservative and Republican advance of power in the House. But it did not work out that way.

The Sun Belt proved the Republicans' greatest disappointment. The nationwide shift in population away from the industrial North gave Southern and Western states 17 new districts, and the GOP at one time hoped to take at least a dozen of them. But Democratic legislative cartography and unfriendly federal court action got in the way, and in the end Democrats won 10 of the 17.

Democrats also managed to sidestep the brunt of district losses in the Northeast and Midwest. Legislative map makers eliminated Republican seats in Illinois and New Jersey, even though the population decline had been in urban, Democratic areas. On Nov. 2, anti-Republican economic resentments took over, bringing victory to several Democrats in new districts that were nominally Democratic but had been voting conservatively in recent years. In all, in the 10 Northern states that lost districts, Republicans came out 18 seats short of where they stood before the election.

In most of the 11 states that gained seats, the GOP seemed the natural heir to demographic changes. All 11 were carried by Ronald Reagan in the 1980 presidential race, and eight went for Republican Gerald R. Ford in 1976. Nonetheless, legislatures or courts in six of the states drew new districts favoring or leaning to Democrats. And contrary to prediction, not one of these new constituencies nominated a conservative Democrat. As a result, liberals (including four Hispanics) made up a large portion of the Sun Belt's new House contingent.

The Democrats' greatest boost came in California, where Democratic Rep. Phillip Burton masterminded a remap that dissolved three GOP-held seats and diluted a fourth enough to fatally weaken the incumbent. And although population gains entitled California to only two additional districts, Burton managed to give his party five new seats while strengthening its grip on most of the districts it already held.

Republicans expected to win at least one of the three new Texas districts, but instead they were shut out. Demo-

crats also won new seats in New Mexico, Arizona and Tennessee.

Republicans' biggest gains came in Florida, where two of the state's four new seats were placed firmly in GOP hands. The GOP also picked up one seat each in Colorado, Nevada, Oregon, Utah and Washington. None of those gains came at the expense of Democratic seats, however, as some Republican legislators had initially planned; Democrats still held a majority of the delegations of Washington and Oregon, and the partisan balance was even in Nevada and Colorado.

In the Northeast and Midwest, Democrats used redistricting and the national Democratic tide to deny Republicans their apparent advantages of population shift. In Illinois and New Jersey, where population losses forced the removal of two seats and one seat, respectively, Democratic legislatures dissolved existing GOP districts to bring delegation sizes down. They also left several Republican incumbents weaker. In New Jersey, GOP Rep. Harold C. Hollenbeck lost his seat in a 9th District that had gained several Democratic towns; in Illinois, GOP Rep. Paul Findley was evicted from a 20th District that had picked up three traditionally Democratic counties and lost Republican territory.

Even in Northern states where Republicans controlled the redistricting process, Democrats managed to post gains or cut their losses. In Indiana, which lost one seat, the GOP-dominated Legislature drew a map designed to cost Democrats two or three seats; however, the new map not only galvanized Democrats in other states to work to offset those losses, it ended up costing Democrats only one seat even in Indiana.

Only in Ohio did a change in a district prove fatal to a Democratic incumbent facing a challenger. In the 12th District, freshman Rep. Bob Shamansky saw his constituency lose Democratic portions of Columbus and gain rural and conservative territory. Shamansky was unseated by New Right Republican John R. Kasich.

Regional Wrapup

In a year when voters obviously were concerned that Reagan was charting a course that veered too sharply to the right, an unusual number of the defeated incumbents were moderate Eastern Republicans, some of whom had sharply questioned the president's policies.

The worst news for Republicans came from Pennsylvania, where four of the party's incumbents lost. One of these was Eugene V. Atkinson who had left the Democratic Party in 1981 to signal his belief that Reagan policies would bring economic recovery to the steel-producing 4th District. Prominent national politicians from both parties campaigned in this contest where more than the usual amount of pride was at stake. In the end, Atkinson lost decisively to state Rep. Joe Kolter.

One of the biggest upsets was the defeat of freshman Rep. Lawrence J. DeNardis, the moderate Republican incumbent in Connecticut's 3rd District. Another moderate Eastern Republican who lost was Margaret M. Heckler of Massachusetts. Redistricting paired the 15-year veteran against liberal Democratic incumbent Barney Frank, who managed to focus voters' attention on Heckler's support of Reagan's economic program. Reagan later tapped Heckler to head the Department of Health and Human Services.

Oddly enough, some of the most impressive Republican showings came in pockets of the industrial Northeast

Recorded Vote Totals

Following are the recorded congressional vote totals between 1947 and 1984. The 95th Congress (1977-79) took 2,691 recorded votes, the highest number for an entire Congress. The high for a single year was in 1978 when 1,350 recorded votes were taken. That year also was the high mark for recorded votes in the House — 834. The high for the Senate was 688 recorded votes in 1976.

Year	House	Senate	Total
1984	408	275	683
1983	498	371	869
1982	459	465	924
1981	353	483	836
1980	604	531	1,135
1979	672	497	1,169
1978	834	516	1,350
1977	706	635	1,341
1976	661	688	1,349
1975	612	602	1,214
1974	537	544	1,081
1973	541	594	1,135
1972	329	532	861
1971	320	423	743
1970	266	422	688
1969	177	245	422
1968	233	281	514
1967	245	315	560
1966	193	235	428
1965	201	258	459
1964	113	305	418
1963	119	229	348
1962	124	224	348
1961	116	204	320
1960	93	207	300
1959	87	215	302
1958	93	200	293
1957	100	107	207
1956	73	130	203
1955	76	87	163
1954	76	171	247
1953	71	89	160
1952	72	129	201
1951	109	202	311
1950	154	229	383
1949	121	227	348
1948	79	189	268
1947	84	138	222

where economic conditions were bad, but where resourceful GOP candidates managed to prevent the opposition from saddling them with the blame. Republican Nancy L. Johnson took the Connecticut seat being vacated by Democrat Toby Moffett, a Senate candidate, and John R. McKernan Jr. eked out a narrow win in Maine's 1st. The departing

incumbent was a Republican, but a return to Democratic control had been expected. And in Pennsylvania's 21st, where GOP Rep. Marc L. Marks decided to retire after a close escape in 1980, Republican Thomas J. Ridge was a surprise winner by fewer than 1,000 votes.

Evidence of Middle America's skepticism over Reaganomics was clearly seen in Illinois, where Democrats picked up two GOP seats and frightened several other Republican incumbents. Voters in Illinois' 18th District gave the White House one of its worst scares: 13-term Republican Robert H. Michel, the House minority leader, nearly lost to 31-year-old labor lawyer G. Douglas Stephens. Reagan campaigned personally for Michel; in a speech after the ballots were counted, Michel interpreted his narrow margin as a signal that some adjustments in the president's programs were necessary.

Elsewhere in the Midwest, Democratic state Rep. Alan Wheat scored a landmark victory for blacks in Missouri's 5th District, which included Kansas City and some of its suburbs. Wheat defeated Republican state Rep. John A. Sharp to become the first black in modern times to win a district that was neither predominantly black nor overwhelmingly liberal.

In some economically troubled regions of the Midwest, though, Republican incumbents held on better than expected. This was largely due to the strength of young GOP members who took over in 1980 and applied the usual formula of tireless constituent service and aggressive self-promotion.

Resurgence of traditional Democratic voting habits in five Southern and border states — Virginia, West Virginia, North Carolina, South Carolina and Tennessee — produced a gain of nine Democratic seats, more than one-third of the party's nationwide net gain of 26 districts.

The GOP scored some scattered gains in the South. In Mississippi's open 2nd District, Republican Webb Franklin defeated state Rep. Robert G. Clark, who was the first black since Reconstruction to win a Democratic congressional primary in Mississippi. Thanks to redistricting, the GOP also took two newly created seats in Florida.

Republicans also picked up five newly created seats in the West and gained a seat in Arizona as party-switching Bob Stump won his first election as a Republican. These wins helped cushion the impact of the California remap. Before the election, the Democrats had a one seat advantage in the state's delegation, 22-21. Afterwards Democrats controlled the lineup, 28-17.

Senate Elections

The only thing remarkable about the 1982 Senate results was the sheer absence of change. Not only did the party ratio remain the same — 54 Republicans and 46 Democrats — but 95 of the 100 senators returned to Washington. The class of five newcomers was the smallest such group in the 68-year history of popular Senate elections.

That sort of stability was itself a dramatic reversal of recent election trends. During the past decade a Senate seat had been one of the most difficult offices in U.S. politics to hold. While re-election rates for House incumbents regularly had run above 85 percent, senators were struggling against well-financed challengers and effective special interest groups.

In both 1976 and 1978 less than 65 percent of the Senate incumbents running for re-election won. In 1980 the

Public Laws

Following is a list of the number of bills cleared by Congress that became public laws each year since 1967:

Year	Public Laws	Year	Public Laws
1984	408	1975	205
1983	215	1974	404
1982	328	1973	247
1981	145	1972	383
1980	426	1971	224
1979	187	1970	505
1978	410	1969	190
1977	223	1968	391
1976	383	1967	249

rate tumbled to 55 percent as a conservative, anti-incumbent tide swept Democratic senators from office across the country.

But there was no national tide visible in Senate contests in 1982, and the cry of "throw the bums out" was barely audible. Of 30 incumbents who sought re-election, all but two — Republican Harrison "Jack" Schmitt of New Mexico and Democrat Howard W. Cannon of Nevada — won re-election. And Cannon lost by only 6,000 votes.

Three members of the tiny freshman class were Republicans: former Nevada state Sen. Chic Hecht, 53, who ousted Cannon; San Diego Mayor Pete Wilson, 49, who defeated California Gov. Edmund G. Brown Jr. for the seat of retiring GOP Sen. S. I. "Sam" Hayakawa; and U.S. Rep. Paul S. Trible Jr., 35, who edged out Virginia Lt. Gov. Richard J. Davis for the seat that was vacated by Harry F. Byrd Jr., who ran as an independent but caucused with Senate Democrats.

The two new Democratic senators were New Mexico state Attorney General Jeff Bingaman, 39, who retired Schmitt, and New Jersey computer executive Frank R. Lautenberg, 58, who defeated Rep. Millicent Fenwick. The New Jersey contest was for the seat formerly held by Democratic Sen. Harrison A. Williams Jr. but occupied by Republican Nicholas F. Brady, who was appointed as a caretaker after Williams' resignation in March.

The Senate outcome was neither the "ratifying" election that Republicans had hoped for after their sweep of 1980 nor the "correcting" election that Democrats had wanted. But there were favorable results for both parties. Republicans kept their beachhead on Capitol Hill, ensuring that Ronald Reagan would be the first Republican president since Herbert Hoover to have a GOP Senate majority throughout his four-year term.

Democrats broke even in an election that could have relegated them to minority status in the Senate for a long time. Of the 33 seats that were contested in 1982, the Democrats were defending 19 (not including Byrd's seat). They ended up winning 60.6 percent of the races — a figure almost identical to the one in the House, where Democrats

took just over 61 percent.

Democrats came closer to regaining a Senate majority than the final partisan tally indicated. While the Democrats held nearly all their 19 seats with solid majorities, Republicans retained theirs by much smaller margins. The GOP lost only two of the 13 seats that it was defending, but in six others Republican candidates struggled to victory with no more than 53 percent of the vote.

State Races

Hurt by losses in the economically distressed Midwest, Republicans saw their hold on the nation's governorships dwindle to 16 in the Nov. 2 election. The Democrats controlled statehouses in 34 states.

The GOP's net loss of seven statehouses — they dropped nine and picked up two — ended a comeback in the party's gubernatorial fortunes. Republicans had been posting gains since 1977, when they hit a low point of 12 governors' chairs.

Of the Republican governors' seats that switched to the Democrats, five were in the Midwest, where the recession had been most acute, hitting both manufacturing and farming. Michigan, Minnesota, Nebraska, Ohio and Wisconsin opted for Democrats. Republican incumbents were retiring in all these states except Nebraska, where Gov. Charles Thone was turned out by about 10,000 votes.

The Illinois governor, Republican James R. Thompson, won by the smallest of margins in a tight contest against former Democratic Sen. Adlai E. Stevenson III (1970-81). The outcome of the Illinois race was certified Nov. 22, but the results were the subject of continued legal wrangling through December. South Dakota's William J. Janklow, the other Midwestern GOP governor who sought re-election, enjoyed a comfortable victory.

Republicans also encountered a setback in their progress in the South. They held four of the region's 13 governorships in 1982; in 1983, they had just two. Frank D. White of Arkansas and William Clements of Texas were ousted. Only Tennessee's Lamar Alexander won re-election.

In addition, Democrats took over GOP statehouses in Alaska and Nevada. Republicans assumed power in California, where George Deukmejian edged Democrat Tom Bradley and in New Hampshire, where GOP challenger John H. Sununu unseated Democratic incumbent Hugh Gallen. Each party had six open seats at stake. Democrats held all theirs except for California. Republicans managed to retain only Iowa.

Democrats also turned the tables on the GOP in state legislative elections, regaining most of the chambers taken by the Republicans in the past two elections and ending a six-year decline in the number of legislatures under Democratic control.

Aided by a strong showing in congressional and gubernatorial elections across the country — and, in some instances, redrawn legislative districts — the Democrats raised from 28 to 34 the number of states in which they controlled both houses. When most legislatures reconvened in January 1983, the GOP controlled both houses in 11 states — a net loss of four from the end of the 1982 legislative session. In four states neither party controlled both chambers, down from six before the elections. Nebraska maintained its unique non-partisan, unicameral system.

Democrats reclaimed four of the five chambers captured by the GOP in 1980, winning back the lower houses in Illinois, Montana and Washington and picking up two seats to establish a tenuous one-seat edge in the Ohio Senate. Although the GOP held on to the Pennsylvania Senate, a shift of two seats returned the Democrats to power in Pennsylvania's lower house after four years of Republican control.

Republicans did manage to add one new legislature to their column. Gaining one seat in Alaska's upper house, Republicans broke the tie that resulted from the 1980 election and resumed control of the chamber. An additional five-seat gain enabled them to capture the House. However, GOP strength was undercut somewhat by the election of Democrat Bill Sheffield as Alaska's governor. Republican gains brought them to within one seat of the Democrats in Wisconsin's upper chamber; they trailed by a mere two seats in the upper houses in Michigan and New Mexico.

1983

The Legislative Year

Congress and President Reagan generally kept to their own turf in 1983 — each branch going about business with little involvement from the other side.

Unlike the first two years of the Reagan administration, when the president essentially wrote the economic script, Congress conducted its 1983 debate on deficits without Reagan's overt participation. And while Congress tried to assert itself on foreign policy, Reagan consistently called the global shots.

There were important bipartisan agreements in 1983: on Social Security, jobs legislation, the War Powers Resolution and fiscal 1984 appropriations bills. But these were rare commodities in a year in which political motivations ranked above policy considerations.

The prime example of this dilemma was the way Congress and Reagan reacted to massive federal deficits. No matter how many experts said soaring deficits hurt the economy, few people were willing to take the politically risky steps needed to cure the problem. Reagan made a calculated decision to stay out of the deficit debate, thereby ducking any responsibility for tax increases his advisers viewed as a 1984 election liability.

Anti-deficit rhetoric was a constant refrain among legislators, but Congress took little decisive action on the issue. For the first time since passage of the Congressional Budget Act in 1974, Congress failed to enact deficit reduction measures required by its own budget plan. Nor did either chamber approve any of the tax increases that plan required.

"The structural deficit is rapidly becoming out of control, and very little was accomplished to reduce deficits," lamented James R. Jones, D-Okla., House Budget Committee chairman. "The leadership, starting with the president, avoided all the tough problems and basically took the politically safe approach," he said.

The reason for the stalemate, according to many mem-

bers, was the early onset of presidential politics. "I don't remember a presidential election starting so early," Rep. Bill Gradison, R-Ohio, said.

1984 Positioning

Reagan was clearly thinking about the elections when he analyzed Congress' deeds in 1983. "The greatest contribution of the Congress was not what it did for us, but what it didn't do to us," the president said in a radio speech Nov. 19, returning to the anti-Washington theme that helped bring him into office.

House Speaker Thomas P. O'Neill Jr., D-Mass., also took a political outlook when he summed up the session Nov. 17. "If the elections were held tomorrow," O'Neill said, "the polls show that Democrats would [gain] 35 to 50 seats. In the eyes of the American people, we're doing something right."

O'Neill told reporters that 1983 was "very gratifying." One reason had to be the Democrats' increased numerical strength. The 1982 elections gave Democrats an extra 26 House seats, allowing O'Neill to wrest control away from the coalition of Republicans and conservative "Boll Weevil" Democrats that dominated the 97th Congress.

When the 98th Congress settled down to business Jan. 25, Democrats held a 267-165 lead in the House, with three vacancies. (Republicans retained their 54-46 edge in the Senate.)

Reagan and Senate Majority Leader Howard H. Baker Jr., R-Tenn., recognized this new alignment and the need for compromise. With O'Neill, they pressed a plan to revitalize the Social Security system. The rescue plan, based on recommendations of a bipartisan presidential commission and pushed through both chambers in little more than a month, was one of the biggest overhauls of Social Security since the program began in 1937. Another major compromise resulted in a $4.6 billion emergency jobs and recession relief measure.

Bipartisanship also produced unusual progress in the passage of fiscal 1984 appropriations bills. Congress sent Reagan 10 of the 13 regular 1984 spending bills, its best performance in years. Reagan had threatened to veto any money bills that exceeded his budget targets. But constant give-and-take between Congress and the White House produced bills that Reagan signed.

On other subjects, though, partisan sniping took over. O'Neill hammered away all year at the "fairness" issue, charging that Reagan's economic policies had unjustly hurt many Americans. He pushed through the House a cap on the third year of Reagan's 1981 tax cut plan and a series of bills to aid the unemployed. But the Republican-controlled Senate never approved them.

The Democratic attack on Reaganomics also lost steam as the economy perked up. "As the recovery got started, the attitude was: Let's not rock the boat," Gradison observed.

While partisanship was rampant, party unity did not always flourish. O'Neill had a 100-vote Democratic margin during most of the year, but he could not always keep his troops in line. In early November, for example, restless freshman Democrats made a symbolic protest against rising deficits and helped kill a spending bill important to their leaders.

In the Senate, Baker no longer could get Republicans to march in lock step, as they often had in the 97th Congress. In May moderate Republican senators defied GOP

Congress in 1983

Lacking consensus on how to reduce soaring federal deficits, members of Congress called an end to the first session of the 98th Congress Nov. 18 and left Washington for a nine-week vacation before reconvening Jan. 23, 1984. The Senate adjourned *sine die* at 10:04 p.m. The House had adjourned at 7:34 p.m.

Convened at noon on Jan. 3, the session lasted 320 days. It was the shortest non-election year session since the first session of the 89th Congress in 1965, yet it ranked as the 28th longest in history.

The Senate met for 150 days during the year, the House for 146. There were 8,434 bills and resolutions introduced during the session compared with 4,520 in 1982 and 8,719 in 1981, the first session of the 97th Congress.

The total of 215 public bills that became law in 1983 was 113 fewer than in 1982, but 70 more than in 1981. Reagan signed 214 bills and vetoed seven in 1983, one of which was overridden and enacted into law without his signature. (*Public laws, box, p. 11; presidential vetoes, p. 1031*)

During 1983 the House took 498 recorded votes, 39 more than in 1982. The Senate took 371 recorded votes, 94 fewer than in 1982. (*Recorded votes, box, p. 10*)

---

leaders when they helped pass a budget calling for increased taxes and domestic spending while slowing the defense buildup.

Foreign Policy, Defense

One major change from Reagan's first two years was that Congress was far more concerned about foreign affairs during 1983. There were several showdowns over key foreign policy issues. But Congress repeatedly bowed to Reagan's wishes, however reluctantly. This was partly due to O'Neill's adherence to the adage that "politics should end at the water's edge."

Standing behind Reagan, O'Neill in September helped push through a measure allowing the president to keep U.S. troops in Lebanon for up to 18 months. In backing Reagan on Lebanon, Congress for the first time invoked major parts of the 1973 War Powers Resolution. On Oct. 23, 241 U.S. Marines, sailors and soldiers and 58 French paratroopers were killed by a terrorist truck bomb in Beirut. Subsequent efforts to revise or revoke the measure keeping troops in Lebanon failed in both houses. Under congressional pressure, Reagan announced in February 1984 that he had ordered the troop withdrawal.

Congress reluctantly continued to back Reagan's policy in Nicaragua and El Salvador. The House twice voted to force Reagan to stop backing rightist forces that were fighting to overthrow the leftist government of Nicaragua.

When the Senate refused to go along, a compromise was reached limiting aid to the rebels and requiring Reagan to seek explicit approval from Congress for additional aid. The president also had to invoke all of his persuasive powers — including a rare speech to a joint session of Congress — to win increased financial backing for the government of El Salvador.

Reagan won widespread approval in both chambers for the Oct. 25 invasion of the Caribbean island of Grenada. The president said the invasion, which he called a "rescue mission," was necessary to protect some 1,000 Americans, mostly medical students, from civil strife that erupted following the overthrow and murder of Marxist Prime Minister Maurice Bishop.

Members also quickly passed a resolution condemning the Soviet Union's downing of a Korean Air Lines passenger plane over Soviet territory on Sept. 1. Rep. Larry P. McDonald, D-Ga., was among the 269 passengers killed in the incident.

Reagan was victorious in most of his defense fights with Congress. He won the go-ahead for production of the MX missile, although the House came within a handful of votes of killing funding for the project. And he staved off a congressional endorsement of a nuclear freeze proposal. The House passed a freeze resolution, but the Senate rejected a similar measure.

Congress refused, however, to go along with Reagan's plan to resume nerve gas production after a 14-year moratorium. And in the military appropriations bill for fiscal 1984, Congress allowed roughly a 4 percent real-dollar increase in total defense spending, compared with the 10 percent boost that Reagan sought.

Age Structure of Congress

(Average ages at start of first session)

	House	Senate	Congress
1949	51.0	58.5	53.8
1951	52.0	56.6	53.0
1953	52.0	56.6	53.0
1955	51.4	57.2	52.2
1957	52.9	57.9	53.8
1959	51.7	57.1	52.7
1961	52.2	57.0	53.2
1963	51.7	56.8	52.7
1965	50.5	57.7	51.9
1967	50.8	57.7	52.1
1969	52.2	56.6	53.0
1971	51.9	56.4	52.7
1973	51.1	55.3	52.0
1975	49.8	55.5	50.9
1977	49.3	54.7	50.3
1979	48.8	52.7	49.5
1981	48.4	52.5	49.2
1983	45.5	53.4	47.0
1985	49.7	54.2	50.5

Other Issues

The Supreme Court shook Congress June 23 when it ruled that the legislative veto device was unconstitutional. The ruling invalidated a tool that Congress had used over the past 50 years to overturn executive branch regulations or orders. The decision — a victory for the executive branch and a potential blow to congressional power — sent lawmakers scrambling for a constitutional replacement.

A constitutional confrontation between Congress and Reagan was eased when the House effectively dropped its contempt of Congress citation against Anne M. Burford, who had resigned earlier in the year as administrator of the Environmental Protection Agency. The citation had been issued late in 1982 when Burford, acting on Reagan's orders, refused to provide materials a House subcommittee sought in its investigation of EPA's relations with some of the industries it regulated.

Despite a last-minute spurt of activity, Congress left town Nov. 18 with a long list of unfinished business. Among the major pieces of legislation left for 1984 were bills affecting telephone rates, natural gas decontrol, immigration reform, criminal code changes and revisions in the Clean Air and Clean Water acts.

The Political Year

Despite the popularity of President Reagan in the South and the party's successes in congressional elections there, the GOP continued to lose control of statehouses in the region. The defeat in November 1983 of Louisiana's incumbent governor, Republican David C. Treen, left the GOP with only one governor in the region, Lamar Alexander of Tennessee.

Treen lost to Democrat Edwin W. Edwards, who had served two terms as Louisiana governor, from 1972 to 1980. Two other Democrats, Kentucky Lt. Gov. Martha Layne Collins and Mississippi Attorney General Bill Allain, also were elected governors of their states in the 1983 elections.

The electoral clout of the Democrats in Southern state-level contests was underscored by the somewhat unusual character of the gubernatorial winners and the size of their victories. All three Democratic candidates were outside the conventional mode — Collins was the first woman governor of her state, Allain allegedly was involved in homosexual escapades, and Edwards was a flamboyant wheeler-dealer dogged by accusations of corruption. Each was elected with a substantial majority.

The GOP's loss of Southern governorships paralleled its decline in statehouses nationally. The party entered the 1982 elections with 23 governors' chairs; by the end of 1983 it had only 15, compared with the Democrats' 35.

Off-year elections did not reveal any clear trends. Of the six special elections to the House, only one changed the partisan breakdown: Phil Gramm's election as a Republican to the Texas House seat from which he had resigned as a Democrat. At the end of 1983 there were 267 Democrats and 167 Republicans in the House, and one vacant seat.

In the other special elections, Democratic state Sen. Gary L. Ackerman replaced the late Rep. Benjamin S. Rosenthal, D-N.Y.; GOP state Sen. Daniel L. Schaefer won the Colorado seat left vacant by the death of former astronaut Jack Swigert, R; Sala Burton won the San Francisco House seat left empty with the death of her husband, Rep. Phillip Burton; Georgia state Rep. George W. "Buddy"

Number of Black Members In Congress 1947-85

Listed below by Congress is the number of black members of the Senate and House of Representatives from the 80th Congress through the opening of the 99th Congress. The figures do not include the nonvoting delegate from the District of Columbia.

Congress	Senate	House
99th (1985-87)	0	19
98th (1983-85)	0	20
97th (1981-83)	0	17
96th (1979-81)	0	16
95th (1977-79)	1	16
94th (1975-77)	1	16
93rd (1973-75)	1	15
92nd (1971-73)	1	12
91st (1969-71)	1	9
90th (1967-69)	1	5
89th (1965-67)		6
88th (1963-65)		5
87th (1961-63)		4
86th (1959-61)		4
85th (1957-59)		4
84th (1955-57)		3
83rd (1953-55)		2
82nd (1951-53)		2
81st (1949-51)		2
80th (1947-49)		2

Number of Women Members In Congress 1947-85

Listed below by Congress is the number of women members of the Senate and House of Representatives from the 80th Congress through the beginning of the 99th Congress. The figures include women appointed to office as well as those chosen by voters in general elections and special elections.

Congress	Senate	House
99th (1985-87)	2	22
98th (1983-85)	2	22
97th (1981-83)	2	21
96th (1979-81)	1	16
95th (1977-79)	2	18
94th (1975-77)	0	19
93rd (1973-75)	0	16
92nd (1971-73)	2	13
91st (1969-71)	1	10
90th (1967-69)	1	11
89th (1965-67)	2	10
88th (1963-65)	2	11
87th (1961-63)	2	17
86th (1959-61)	1	16
85th (1957-59)	1	15
84th (1955-57)	1	16
83rd (1953-55)	3	12
82nd (1951-53)	1	10
81st (1949-51)	1	9
80th (1947-49)	1	7

Darden, D, replaced Rep. Larry P. McDonald who died aboard the Korean Air Lines jet shot down by the Soviets, and Democrat Charles A. Hayes replaced Rep. Harold Washington who was elected mayor of Chicago.

The 1983 elections had a much more significant impact on the Senate. The death of veteran Washington Democratic Sen. Henry M. Jackson (1953-83) led to the appointment by the state's GOP governor of Republican Daniel J. Evans to fill the vacant seat. Evans went on to defeat Democratic Rep. Mike Lowry in the November special election, thus earning the right to serve the five years remaining in Jackson's term. Evans' appointment and election victory fixed the Senate partisan ratio at 55-45, a one-seat gain in the Republicans' control of the chamber.

In a major redistricting development the Supreme Court by a 5-4 vote ruled that states must adhere as closely as possible to the "one man, one vote" standard of reapportionment and bear the burden of proving that deviations from precise population equality were made in pursuit of a legitimate goal. The ruling upheld a lower court decision to overturn the New Jersey district map. The lower court found that the 0.69 percent deviation between the state's most and least populous districts was too great, violating the "one man, one vote" principle.

1984

The Legislative Year

A year of politics and procrastination on Capitol Hill left many members of the 98th Congress disappointed with their track record and a long list of unsolved problems for the new Congress to address. Nearly two years after opening on a harmonious note with the passage of a Social Security rescue plan, the 98th Congress ended in partisan discord Oct. 12. The only way lawmakers could wind up their business was to bump the most controversial issues onto the 1985 calendar.

Left for members of the 99th Congress to decide were whether to continue MX missile production, test anti-satellite weapons and provide aid to Nicaraguan rebels. By deferring these matters until 1985, members avoided votes

that could have damaged their re-election chances. And each party hoped to return with an election mandate that would allow it to work its will in 1985.

One of the biggest problems shoved onto 1985's agenda was the massive federal deficit. Although Congress took actions designed to reduce the deficit by $149 billion over three years, the tax increases and spending cuts were viewed as a mere "down payment" on a larger remedy.

Several other contentious issues were almost resolved in 1984, but compromises fell apart in the final days of the session. These failed efforts included legislation to overhaul the nation's immigration laws, a bill releasing Interstate highway funds to the states and a renewal of the Export Administration Act, which permitted the president to restrict U.S. shipments abroad for national security or other reasons. Also lost in the rush to adjourn was a civil rights measure to overturn a Supreme Court decision that narrowed the reach of major anti-discrimination laws.

Other measures were abandoned even earlier. The Senate passed banking deregulation legislation, but the House did not. The House passed a renewal of the "superfund" program to clean up toxic wastes and a reauthorization of the nation's main water pollution control law, but the Senate did not. Neither house passed bills to decontrol natural gas prices or extend the Clean Air Act.

There were, however, several notable achievements in 1984. Congress sent President Reagan measures that revamped the nation's bankruptcy courts, pressured states to raise their minimum drinking age to 21, established a national policy for cable television franchising and created more wilderness areas than Congress had approved in 20 years.

Worried about the influence of the gender gap on the elections, Congress approved bills of special interest to women, including one expanding pension coverage for women and another enforcing child support payments.

There also was substantial progress in health legislation. Congress cleared a bill to place stronger health warnings on cigarette packages. It also approved measures making low-cost generic drugs more widely available to consumers and creating a national computer network to match patients who needed organ transplants with donors.

'The Money Game'

One of the biggest frustrations for members of the 98th Congress was their absorption with budget issues throughout the year. "All we do is play the money game," griped Sen. Dave Durenberger, R-Minn. "We're not dealing with peace to the world, with feeding the hungry. We just sit around and play with numbers."

Despite its preoccupation with money, Congress was able to clear only five of the 13 regular appropriations bills for fiscal 1985. The major roadblock was a standoff between Reagan and House Democrats over the military budget. "For five months we were tied up because the damn administration wanted a 13 percent increase on defense and the House wanted 3 percent," Durenberger said. In the end, the administration relented, settling for a 5 percent inflation-adjusted increase over current spending, a compromise between the House level of 3.5 percent and the Senate-passed 7.8 percent increase.

But the lengthy standoff created a legislative backlog as Congress tried to adjourn in early October. Members fought to attach their favorite bills to the last two "must-pass" items — the 1985 continuing spending resolution and

Congress in 1984

The second session of the 98th Congress ended Oct. 12 when the Senate adjourned *sine die* at 3:17 p.m. The House had adjourned at 3:05 p.m.

Convened at noon on Jan. 23, the session lasted 264 days. Although it was the shortest election-year session since the second session of the 94th Congress in 1976, it ranked as the 43rd-longest in history.

The Senate met for 131 days in 1984, the House for 120 days. There were 3,764 bills and resolutions introduced during the session, compared with 8,434 in 1983 and 4,520 in 1982, the second session of the 97th Congress.

A total of 408 public bills became law in 1984, 193 more than in 1983 and 80 more than in 1982. Reagan signed 407 public bills into law and vetoed 17 in 1984; one veto was overridden and enacted into law without his signature. (*Public laws, box, p. 11; presidential vetoes, p. 1031*)

During 1984 the House took 408 recorded votes, 90 fewer than in 1983. The Senate took 275 recorded votes, 96 fewer than in 1983. (*Recorded votes, box, p. 10*)

a measure to increase the debt limit — and their battles stalled the passage of both urgent measures.

The late approval of the continuing resolution led to a half-day shutdown of federal government offices. And the delays in increasing the debt limit cost the government $400 million in higher interest costs, according to the Treasury Department.

While legislators spent much of 1984 talking about the evils of the swelling federal deficit, they only took a first step toward a cure. Instead, many members figured they would deal with the problem in 1985 — after the November elections.

Reagan's Record

Unlike his first two years in office, Reagan did not seek sweeping changes in economic policy during the 98th Congress. And he often was forced to adjust his goals in the face of congressional opposition.

On domestic issues, Reagan met many disappointments on Capitol Hill in 1984. The president could not persuade Congress to approve his social agenda, which featured constitutional amendments to ban abortion and allow school prayer. Nor did Congress adopt his plan to give tuition tax credits to parents who sent their children to private schools, or his enterprise zone system to provide tax relief to businesses that created jobs in depressed areas.

Congress did not consider Reagan's proposal to lower the minimum wage for teenagers. And it did not act on his call for constitutional amendments requiring a balanced budget and giving the president a veto over individual items in appropriations bills. Members also reversed some

earlier Reagan policies, restoring budget cuts in social welfare programs, such as college student aid and maternal and child health programs.

Reagan did, however, win approval of his anti-crime package, which included new sentencing procedures and insanity plea restrictions. And while Congress rejected his school prayer amendment, it did agree to an "equal access" proposal, allowing student religious groups to meet in school facilities on the same terms as other extracurricular clubs.

Most of the squabbling between Congress and the president concerned national security issues. The year started on a dissonant note when members challenged Reagan's actions in Lebanon. By the time Reagan pulled troops out of Beirut in February, he and Congress were arguing about who was to blame for the policy failures in the Middle East.

On Central America, Reagan's policies had mixed success on Capitol Hill. Successful presidential elections in El Salvador quieted congressional debate about that country, enabling Reagan to win approval for most of the military aid he sought for fiscal years 1984 and 1985. But Congress barred the president from providing further aid to anti-government rebels in Nicaragua through Feb. 28, 1985, and said that Reagan must bring a new request to Congress in March if he wanted to continue direct U.S. involvement in the war to oust Nicaragua's leftist government.

Congress also deferred decisions on two major military matters. Although about $2.5 billion was appropriated to build another 21 MX missiles (in addition to 21 funded in fiscal 1984), the new money could not be spent unless Congress passed two separate resolutions in March 1985 approving more MX production. Congress also imposed a moratorium until March on tests of the anti-satellite missile. And it pared more than 20 percent from the first installment of Reagan's "Strategic Defense Initiative" to develop space-based defenses against nuclear missiles.

Internal Politics

Partisan warfare was not limited in 1984 to battles between the White House and Congress. Much of the political strife took place within the confines of the Capitol building. In the Senate, filibuster threats and drawn-out negotiations slowed work on almost every major piece of legislation considered during the session.

Pre-election partisanship was heightened in the House by the aggressive floor tactics of junior Republicans who were angry that the Democratic leadership would not bring up their conservative agenda. Almost daily these Republicans attacked the Democrats in speeches aimed largely at the growing cable television audience watching live broadcasts of House sessions.

In May the simmering dispute erupted into a shouting match between Speaker Thomas P. O'Neill Jr., D-Mass., and Newt Gingrich, R-Ga., one of the leaders of the Republican barrage. The partisan fighting eventually quieted down, but some Democrats predicted it would recur in 1985.

Both chambers were handicapped in 1984 by lame-duck leaders. The impending retirement of Senate Majority Leader Howard H. Baker Jr., R-Tenn., put him in a less persuasive position with his rambunctious colleagues. And the announcement by House Speaker O'Neill that he would retire by the end of 1986 opened the door for more rebellions against his leadership.

The Political Year

There was never much doubt that Ronald Reagan, one of the most personally popular presidents in American history, would win re-election to a second term in 1984. And it would be hard to imagine a vote more decisive than the balloting that gave him his victory. Reagan's win was about as sweeping as they come. He drew 59 percent of the popular vote — just shy of the 61 percent standard established by President Lyndon B. Johnson in 1964. Reagan won all but one state, a feat performed previously only by Richard Nixon in 1972, and he won a record 525 electoral votes. That left 13 electoral votes for his Democratic opponent, former Vice President Walter F. Mondale, who carried his home state of Minnesota and the District of Columbia.

Despite the size of Reagan's victory, its meaning remained unclear. The vote clearly exposed the Democrats' limited appeal in presidential elections. On the other hand, Democrats held their own in other elections. In the Senate, instead of gaining as most presidents do, Reagan lost two seats, reducing the Republican majority to 53-47. In the House of Representatives, the president's party gained 14 seats, far short of the historical average for landslides. The GOP gained one governor for a lineup of 16 Republicans and 34 Democrats. Only in the state legislatures did the GOP make gains that could be considered significant.

Presidential Election

The focus in the early months of the presidential election was not on Reagan but on the Democratic candidates seeking their party's nomination. Sen. Alan Cranston of California was the first to toss his hat in the ring formally, announcing his candidacy Feb. 2, 1983. But Mondale had informally started his campaign shortly after he and President Jimmy Carter lost to Reagan and George Bush in 1980, putting in operation a strategy that would allow him to take full advantage of the party's nomination rules. These provided for a new class of uncommitted party and elected officials, most of whom supported Mondale, more caucuses than in 1980 and a delegate distribution system in the large primary states that gave extra delegates for winning.

But Mondale was never particularly popular with the voters. His public personality and speaking style were bland, his traditional "New Deal" Democratic message seemed stale and, to many, ineffective, and his identification as a candidate of the special interests led voters to look closely and often approvingly at Mondale's competitors.

Before the primaries began, Mondale's main opponent seemed to be John Glenn, the senator from Ohio and former astronaut. Political analysts thought Glenn might draw the Democratic center and right, many of whom had voted for Reagan in 1980. But the first delegate selection event of the season — the Iowa precinct caucuses of Feb. 20 — were disastrous for Glenn as well as two other conservative Democrats in the race, South Carolina Sen. Ernest F. Hollings and former Florida Gov. Reubin Askew. Together these three drew less than 10 percent of the vote. In New Hampshire a week later, the result for Glenn, Hollings and Askew was just as discouraging. Hollings and Askew withdrew from the race, as did Cranston.

New Hampshire was also the first serious setback for

Mondale. Campaigning on a theme of "new ideas" for the Democrats and the country, Colorado Sen. Gary Hart won that primary, propelling himself out of "dark horse" status and placing Mondale's "front runner" image in jeopardy.

Hart continued his romp through "Super Tuesday" March 13, winning the Florida, Massachusetts and Rhode Island primaries and five of the seven caucuses held that day. Although Mondale won only the Alabama and Georgia primaries, he continued to hold a clear lead in the delegate count. But his limited appeal and base of support were more apparent than ever.

Glenn and George McGovern, the former South Dakota senator whose losing 1972 presidential campaign Hart had managed, withdrew from the race after Super Tuesday. That left in contention Mondale, Hart and the Rev. Jesse Jackson, the first black to pursue seriously the presidential nomination of either major political party. Jackson himself held few illusions about actually winning the nomination; he sought instead to establish his "rainbow coalition" as a major influence in the Democratic Party. It was unclear what long-term impact Jackson's candidacy would have on the party. He was not supported by many of the politicians in the black establishment and, while he increased voter registration and turnout among blacks in many areas of the country, it was uncertain how many of these new voters would stay in the political process.

Hart's momentum was blunted almost as quickly as it began. In the week after Super Tuesday, he ran behind Mondale in six of seven delegate selection events. Then Mondale got a much-needed boost by winning the New York and Pennsylvania primaries. But his chance to eliminate Hart evaporated when Hart won Ohio and Indiana. Mondale continued to lead in the number of delegates committed to him, and with his win in New Jersey June 5 he had enough delegates to win the nomination. But his campaign ended on the same lackluster note that had characterized most of the last four months; the same day Mondale claimed the nomination, Hart won three other primaries including California's.

Democratic Convention

Despite the difficult, sometimes bitter, primary season campaign, Democrats mustered a display of party unity at their convention and made a historic vice presidential choice. The Democratic National Convention, held July 16-19 in San Francisco, picked Mondale to be the party standard bearer against President Reagan. As in much of his drive for the nomination, Mondale was almost overshadowed again, this time by the attention generated by his selection of Rep. Geraldine A. Ferraro to be his running mate. Ferraro, a three-term House member from Queens, New York, was the first woman ever chosen for the national ticket by a major party.

Mondale finished the convention balloting with nearly 1,000 votes more than Hart, his closest competitor, yet he was by no means the overwhelming choice. He polled 2,191 votes — about 55 percent of a possible 3,933.

Although the convention ended on a unified note, it did not begin that way. A last-minute imbroglio over Mondale's attempt to oust California lawyer Charles T. Manatt as chairman of the Democratic National Committee (DNC) proved embarrassing to the Mondale campaign. While the candidate's decision to name Georgia state party Chairman Bert Lance to replace Manatt never seriously jeopardized Mondale's chances of nomination, it raised doubts about

his political judgment. Just before the convention began, Mondale agreed under pressure to retain Manatt and named Lance as general campaign chairman. Lance, who was President Carter's budget director, had resigned that post under fire over his banking practices in Georgia.

Despite fears that radical and homosexual elements in San Francisco would stage confrontations in the streets outside the convention center — evoking memories of the party's 1968 catastrophe in Chicago — there were no violent incidents.

Pre-convention accommodations helped prevent any fights over the reports from the credentials and party rules. Future party rules would be considered by a new rules review commission that would meet after the election.

Potential division over five minority proposals to the platform was averted after a meeting among the three major candidates on July 16 resulted in an eventual compromise package. In general, the proposals approved by the convention gave something to both the Hart and Jackson camps but showed Mondale forces in solid control on key points.

Jackson offered four minority planks; three, on a nuclear freeze, defense spending and runoff elections, were defeated. The fourth, on affirmative action, was adopted after a reference to quotas was deleted. Hart's sole minority plank outlined conditions for the use of U.S. military force. Mondale backers originally had opposed the plank, fearing it might hinder a president's flexibility in a crisis, but they finally agreed to back the proposal.

The emotional highlights of the first days belonged to New York Gov. Mario M. Cuomo, who gave the convention's keynote address July 16 and to Jesse Jackson who spoke July 17. Cuomo's eloquent appeal for Democratic unity, family values and compassion for the poor helped set the tone for the rest of the convention. Speaking forcefully but without dramatic oratorical flourishes, Cuomo's speech combined an appeal to Democratic traditions with specific attacks on the domestic and foreign policies of the Reagan administration.

Jackson's address followed the platform debate. At first he spoke almost haltingly, his voice cracking with emotion or exhaustion. But as he went on his tone became more forceful, encouraged by the repeated call-and-response chanting from black delegates. Some of Jackson's speech represented the standard Democratic litany against Reagan, attacking the administration for its economic and foreign policies. But other themes also emerged and seemed to represent a kind of emotional catharsis for the candidate and his supporters. One was a pledge to support the Democratic nominee, ending speculation that Jackson might refuse to back the ticket if he did not get what he wanted from the party.

The following night, Hart took the podium before the balloting for the presidential nomination began, hoping that a dramatic speech on the night of balloting would sway enough Mondale delegates to deny the Minnesotan a first ballot majority. That did not happen. In addition to Mondale, Jackson and Hart, George McGovern was also nominated. Mondale quickly moved into a solid lead over Hart and Jackson in the balloting. But because some large states passed when their names were first called, Mondale had not reached the required 1,967 votes by the time all delegations had been recognized. New Jersey cast its strategic 115 votes for Mondale as the second round was called. The final vote was 2,191 for Mondale, 1,200.5 for Hart and 465.5 for Jackson. There were 40 abstentions.

Presidential Vote by Regions

The 1984 vote in this chart is based on the virtually complete but unofficial Associated Press tally for Reagan and Mondale. The 1980 vote is based on official returns and does not add to 100 percent because third-party candidates are not included. The winner's percentage in each region is noted in bold type.

	1984			1980			
	Turnout (in millions)	Reagan	Mondale	Turnout (in millions)	Reagan	Carter	Anderson
East	22.8	**55%**	45%	21.9	**47%**	43%	9%
Midwest	25.1	**58**	42	25.2	**51**	41	7
South	25.4	**63**	37	23.1	**52**	44	3
West	17.0	**60**	40	16.3	**54**	34	9
Total	90.4	**59%**	41%	86.5	**51%**	41%	7%

Ferraro's nomination for vice president on July 19 provided the convention with one of its most emotional moments. If male delegates seemed pleased by the possible political benefits to be gained by having a woman on the ticket, women seemed filled with joy and pride by the chance that one of their sisters might attain the nation's second-highest office.

Mondale had announced his selection of Ferraro July 12, and approval of her by the party was never in doubt. Her formal nomination was accomplished with dispatch. Her name was placed in nomination by fellow House member Barbara B. Kennelly of Connecticut, who said that Democrats were "breaking down another barrier to full equality and justice" with her selection. Ferraro was nominated by acclamation.

Republican Nomination

President Reagan enjoyed the smoothest road to re-nomination that any presidential candidate could have. The president launched his re-election campaign Jan. 29 against the weakest primary field that any incumbent president of either party had encountered since 1956 when President Dwight D. Eisenhower went through the primary season without any declared opponent appearing on the ballot.

The only two Republicans with any public following to challenge Reagan were former Minnesota Gov. Harold E. Stassen, a perennial candidate who mounted a serious challenge for the nomination in 1948 but had last won a convention delegate in 1968, and Ben Fernandes, a California businessman who ran in 1980 as the nation's first Hispanic presidential aspirant.

Reagan swept all 24 Republican primaries held in 1984, winning each with at least 86 percent of the vote. In many primaries he was literally unopposed — even by minor candidates, a "no preference" line or write-in votes for someone else.

Republican Convention

Brimming with confidence that President Reagan and Vice President George Bush would be "the winning team" in November, a jubilant Republican Party held its convention in Dallas Aug. 20-23. With the ticket's renomination certain beforehand, the 33rd Republican National Convention was more a celebration for GOP activists than a business meeting. Criticisms from the party's shrinking band of moderates, worried by the strongly conservative tone of the platform, did little to dispel the optimistic mood of delegates, who looked forward with confidence to Reagan's easy re-election victory.

Along with showering praise on Reagan and his administration, Republican leaders also sought to use the convention to advance a long-range goal — persuading conservative Democrats to shift to the GOP. Throughout the week speakers made attacks on the current leadership of the Democratic Party a key theme of the convention.

Reagan, too, emphasized criticisms of the Democrats in his 55-minute acceptance speech Aug. 23. "The choices this year are not just between two different personalities or between two political parties," Reagan said. "They are between two different visions of the future, two fundamentally different ways of governing — their government of pessimism, fear and limits . . . or ours of hope, confidence and growth."

Convention speakers also sought repeatedly to link Democratic presidential nominee Walter F. Mondale with the Carter administration, in which he served as vice president. "Carter-Mondale" became their shorthand for a list of evils: inflation, high interest rates, foreign policy failures and sagging national spirit. On Aug. 20 United Nations Representative Jeane J. Kirkpatrick delivered a strongly worded foreign policy speech, loaded with harsh words for her fellow Democrats. Kirkpatrick joined the Republican Party in 1985.

The party adopted the platform for the 1984 campaign on Aug. 21 with no debate. During the week of Aug. 13, the

106-member platform committee had worked over the campaign document and delivered to delegates a statement that conformed to the themes Reagan had stressed in his first term.

There had been spirited fights over language in the platform, principally over tax increases, criticism of the autonomous Federal Reserve Board, the refusal to endorse the Equal Rights Amendment and opposition to abortion. Despite heavy White House lobbying, the platform contained strong language opposing tax boosts — stronger than administration officials wanted. Reagan's operatives also were unable to soften the language critical of the Federal Reserve Board, but they declined to press the issue for fear of producing a backlash that would have made the language harsher.

On the evening of Aug. 22, delegates renominated Reagan and Bush, following first lady Nancy Reagan's appeal to "make it one more for the Gipper." Nevadan Paul Laxalt, the president's closest friend in the Senate, put Reagan's name in nomination. Although the outcome came as no surprise, there was a state-by-state roll call on the nominations. On an unusual joint roll call, Reagan received 2,233 votes, with two delegates, from Illinois and Pennsylvania, abstaining.

Bush received 2,231 votes; his name had been placed in nomination by Calif. Gov. George Deukmejian. In addition to the two abstentions, Kirkpatrick received one vote from a delegate in Alabama, and Kemp got one vote from Nebraska.

Fall Campaign

As the final stretch of the long campaign got under way, it seemed in many instances that the candidates were just going through the motions. Since late summer the pollsters had been predicting a massive Reagan sweep, and most voters seemed to have made up their minds long before Election Day. Bets were not on how many states Reagan would carry but whether he would take all 50.

Highlights of the fall campaign were the two presidential debates. The first, held Oct. 7, was focused on domestic issues. Mondale made a strong showing, which lessened his negative image. Equally important was the perception that Reagan turned in a poor performance; the 73-year-old president seemed tired and disorganized, leading journalists and Democrats to suggest that age was finally catching up with Reagan.

The second debate on Oct. 21, this one focusing on foreign affairs, was a draw in the opinion of most analysts. The debate was not a significant boost to Mondale's campaign, and it allowed Reagan to ease concerns about his age and competence raised by his performance during the first debate. The vice presidential candidates also held a nationally televised debate, on Oct. 11. Most analysts viewed its impact as a draw or gave a slight edge to Bush.

Almost every thrust Mondale made was effectively parried by his Republican opponents. Mondale's efforts to draw attention to the massive budget deficits run up during Reagan's first term by promising a tax increase did not stand a chance against Reagan's promise not to raise taxes. Similarly Mondale's attempts to paint Reagan as a man who favored the rich over the poor, the majority over the minority, did not overcome charges that Mondale was a tool of the special interests. Even the novelty of the first woman nominated by a major party ticket and Ferraro's confident style were somewhat offset by questions about

the completeness of her financial disclosure reports and her husband's real estate dealings.

In the end, perhaps no Democrat could have defeated Ronald Reagan in 1984. For one thing, most voters thought they were better off than they were four years earlier when Reagan first asked that question during his 1980 run against Carter and Mondale. Perhaps more important, voters seemed to respond to Reagan's upbeat attitude and his promise of continued peace and prosperity.

Turnout and Vote Analysis

The Democrats' efforts to register millions of new voters, many of them black, were successful, but fell short of their hopes. Instead of the 100 million voters the Democrats had pushed for, about 93 million people voted. That total was large enough to end the 20-year decline in the presidential-year voter turnout rate, which had slumped to 52.6 percent of the voting age population in 1980.

Census Bureau interviews conducted two weeks after the election revealed that higher voting rates among women, blacks and Hispanics accounted for the increased turnout. Sixty-one percent of women 18 or older voted, up 2 percentage points from 1980. The bureau put the turnout for men at 59 percent, the same as in 1980. Fifty-six percent of blacks voted, and among blacks aged 65 and above, 68 percent cast ballots. Blacks aged 18 to 34 also voted in greater numbers — 47 percent in 1984, compared with 39 percent in 1980.

But the increased turnout was not large enough to do Mondale much good. While his national popular vote total was about one million votes higher than Carter's in 1980, Reagan's soared upward by nearly 10 million votes. Reagan became the first candidate to win more than 50 million votes in a presidential election.

Although the Democrats are known as a coalition party, it was Reagan who put together the grand coalition in 1984. He led in all sociological categories of voters except blacks, Hispanics, Jews, union members and people with low incomes. Of political groups, Reagan led among Republicans and independents; he led overwhelmingly among conservatives and fairly substantially among moderates. He trailed only among self-designated Democrats and liberals. The categories in which Reagan enjoyed greater support than his national average of 59 percent included white Protestants (73 percent), born-again Christians (80 percent), Southerners (63 percent), self-designated Republicans (92 percent) and self-designated conservatives (81 percent).

As in 1980, Reagan swept most of the suburbs, small towns and villages throughout the country, as well as the bulk of the high-growth population centers of the Sun Belt, a number of academic communities and many areas dominated by blue-collar voters. And to that large coalition he added virtually all of the rural white South, where Carter had maintained a toehold four years earlier.

The president ran unusually well among young voters (aged 18-29), taking more than 55 percent of their ballots, according to an ABC News-*Washington Post* poll. Youth had been a weak link for the GOP in the past, supporting Democratic presidential candidates more loyally than any other age group. There was no corresponding swing to the Democrats among older voters.

Democratic efforts to exploit the gender gap failed. Even with Ferraro on the Democratic ticket, women preferred Reagan over Mondale. According to a *New York*

Times/CBS exit poll, 56 percent of women voted for Reagan. (Sixty-two percent of men voted for Reagan.)

The best news for the Democrats may have been that in most states Mondale was able to draw about 35 to 40 percent of the vote. There was no region where the party's presidential vote consistently collapsed below 30 percent, as it did for McGovern in the South in 1972 and for Carter in much of the West in 1980. Mondale was unable to reach out beyond the traditional Democratic base. According to the ABC News-*Washington Post* poll, he won nine out of every 10 black votes, while winning with smaller majorities the support of Jews, union households, the unemployed and least educated. Although GOP voters were nearly unanimous in their support for Reagan, nearly one out of every four Democrats deserted Mondale to back the incumbent. Among them were a large share of blue-collar, ethnic voters.

Regional Breakdown

Mondale drew consistently strong support from only two significant voting areas, the declining cities of the Frost Belt and the black-majority counties of the South. And even in the cities, there was evidence of splintering Democratic alliance, with minorities voting in large numbers for the Democratic ticket but with white ethnic neighborhoods registering a larger-than-usual Republican vote. The once-reliable base that Democrats had among blue-collar workers in older suburbs and smaller industrial centers provided Mondale little help. The votes generally divided in a way that reflected local economic conditions.

Rural America was a triumph for Reagan. The big falloff in the rural Democratic vote was in the South. Democrats had hoped to carry several Southern states in 1984 by constructing a biracial coalition of "have-nots." But the vote instead was extremely polarized, with whites voting decisively for Reagan and blacks for Mondale. Because whites held the majority in every state, the result was a string of Reagan victories across the South. In the South, race tended to override economic considerations.

Reagan's emphasis on conservative religious issues helped him lock up the Southern white vote, but Democrats hoped that it would produce a backlash elsewhere. If it did, it was in the West, where the Democratic ticket showed its biggest gains from 1980. There Mondale apparently won the bulk of the sizable vote that went for independent John B. Anderson in 1980.

The Democratic presidential vote rose dramatically in a number of the more liberal Western population centers, running well ahead of Carter's 1980 total in the counties surrounding San Francisco, Denver, Seattle and Portland, Ore. Still, in most of the high-growth, vote-rich territory of the West and Southwest, Reagan was awesome: He won at least 62 percent of the vote in the counties that are home to Dallas, Houston and Phoenix, and 75 percent of the vote in suburban Orange County, Calif.

Reagan was able to reclaim the support of many moderate Republicans who had shown signs of drifting away from the GOP in 1980. Yankee Republicans in particular seem to have returned to the fold. At the same time, five of the states in which Mondale drew his highest percentages were the Northeast Corridor: Maryland, Massachusetts, New York, Pennsylvania and Rhode Island.

Unemployment was a decisive factor for many Midwestern voters. In areas of the industrial Frost Belt suffering double-digit jobless rates, the Democratic presidential vote tended to go up. But in "smokestack" areas where economic conditions were better than they had been four years earlier, blue-collar voters continued their movement away from the national Democratic ticket.

Senate Elections

Neither the Republicans nor the Democrats came away with quite what they wanted from the 1984 struggle for control of the Senate. Democrats had hoped to regain the majority they lost in 1980 when Republicans won a Senate majority for the first time since the 1954 elections. Republicans hoped that President Reagan's march to re-election would bring about a modest reprise of 1980, making the GOP hold on the Senate more secure.

But this election, Reagan was no trailblazer: Democrats retained 13 of the 14 seats they were defending, and a trio of Democratic House members captured Republican seats: Illinois Rep. Paul Simon edged out three-term veteran Sen. Charles H. Percy, chairman of the Foreign Relations Committee; Iowa Rep. Tom Harkin defeated Sen. Roger W. Jepsen; and Tennessee Rep. Albert Gore Jr. crushed state Sen. Victor Ashe to take the seat being vacated by Senate Majority Leader Howard H. Baker Jr. Countering that good news for the Democrats was an unexpected outcome in Kentucky — the defeat of two-term Democratic Sen. Walter D. Huddleston at the hands of Jefferson County (Louisville) Judge Mitch McConnell.

Thus Democrats won a net gain of two Senate seats, shifting the party ratio to 53 Republicans and 47 Democrats. That standing was an improvement over the pre-election ratio of 55-45 but a comedown from the Democrats' 1983 prediction that the party could recapture Senate control by picking up a number of Republican seats Democrats regarded as shaky.

As it turned out, Democrats failed to win most of the GOP seats in the "at risk" category. The biggest Democratic disappointment came in North Carolina, where GOP incumbent Jesse Helms narrowly won his bitter battle with Democratic Gov. James B. Hunt Jr. It was the most expensive Senate contest ever, with the campaigns spending a total of about $22 million, eclipsing the $12.5 million spent in the 1982 California Senate contest.

In four other key states where Democrats had hoped to pull upsets, Republicans prevailed easily: Mississippi Sen. Thad Cochran, who was elected with only 45 percent in 1978, won 61 percent against former Gov. William Winter; Sen. Gordon J. Humphrey, once regarded as a staunch conservative, moderated his image and won a second term with 59 percent in New Hampshire; Texas Rep. Phil Gramm, who switched parties in 1983, also polled 59 percent to earn the right to replace retiring GOP Sen. John Tower; and Sen. Rudy Boschwitz took 58 percent in Minnesota, encountering no problems with Mondale's coattails because the Democratic presidential nominee barely carried his home state.

Although the Senate freshman class of 1984 was not large, it was a politically experienced group of activists likely to make a mark in Senate affairs quickly. Each of the four representatives who won promotion — Simon, Harkin, Gore and Gramm — had served three terms or more in Congress; McConnell was in his eighth year as county executive in Kentucky's most populous county; Democrat John D. Rockefeller IV of West Virginia, who won the seat of retiring Democratic Sen. Jennings Randolph, was finish-

Reagan and Past Landslides

Landslides are not unusual in presidential contests. In nearly one out of every three elections since a national popular vote tally became commonplace around 1824, the winner had received at least 55 percent of the total vote. Most of the big winners, like President Reagan, had been incumbents seeking re-election.

In the following chart, incumbents are indicated with an asterisk (*). The number in parentheses is the winning candidate's percentage of the electoral vote. Reagan and his 1984 totals, which are based on complete and official returns, are highlighted in bold type.

	Year	Percentage of Popular Vote	Electoral Vote	States Won
Lyndon B. Johnson (D) *	1964	61.1	486 (90.3%)	44
Franklin D. Roosevelt (D) *	1936	60.8	523 (98.5%)	46
Richard M. Nixon (R) *	1972	60.7	520 (96.7%)	49
Warren G. Harding (R)	1920	60.3	404 (76.1%)	37
Ronald Reagan (R) *	**1984**	**58.8**	**525 (97.6%)**	**49**
Herbert Hoover (R)	1928	58.2	444 (83.6%)	40
Franklin D. Roosevelt (D)	1932	57.4	472 (88.9%)	42
Dwight D. Eisenhower (R) *	1956	57.4	457 (86.1%)	41
Theodore Roosevelt (R) *	1904	56.4	336 (70.6%)	33
Andrew Jackson (D)	1828	56.0	178 (68.2%)	14
Ulysses S. Grant (R) *	1872	55.6	286 (78.1%)	31
Dwight D. Eisenhower (R)	1952	55.1	442 (83.2%)	39
Abraham Lincoln (R) *	1864	55.0	212 (90.6%)	22

ing his second term as governor. Democrat John Kerry of Massachusetts, who succeeded retiring Democratic Sen. Paul E. Tsongas, was in his first term as lieutenant governor.

House Elections

For the second time in a little over a decade, Republicans watched with disappointment as their presidential standard bearer swept triumphantly across the nation followed by a threadbare retinue of new U.S. House members.

The Nov. 6, 1984, elections revealed considerable hesitation nationwide over an all-out endorsement of Republican policies, as voters in district after district stopped short of backing GOP challengers who campaigned on their loyalty to Ronald Reagan.

After several closely contested battles were decided, Republicans had gained 14 seats, falling well short of making up the 26 seats they lost in the 1982 midterm elections. One race was still undecided at year's end; it eventually remained Democratic.

The results were reminiscent of the 1972 elections when Richard M. Nixon racked up overwhelming margins around the country, but carried only 12 fellow Republicans into the House behind him. Similarly skimpy coattails accompanied a strong re-election showing by Republican Dwight D. Eisenhower in 1956, when he won a second term by a stunning margin but the GOP lost two seats in the House.

Not counting the undecided seat, Democrats retained control of the House with 252 members to the GOP's 182.

That was nine more seats than the Democrats had after the banner GOP election year in 1980.

Going into the election, Democrats held 266 seats and Republicans 167, with vacancies in a New Jersey district previously held by a Republican and in a Kentucky district held by a Democrat. Those seats stayed in their respective parties' hands and were filled for the remainder of the term in special elections. As a result of the election there were 43 House freshmen in 1985, a small class, due mostly to the relatively low number of open seats in 1984. There were 81 freshmen after the 1982 elections.

Of the members elected in 1982, four Democrats were defeated in 1984, a figure fairly close to the norm for freshmen. On average, their Democratic colleagues in the class of 1982 ran 3.9 percentage points ahead of their showings two years earlier, while Republicans seeking their first re-election surged a full 10 points.

Although Reagan's strength in the election was crucial to Republican victories in most of the districts the GOP took from the Democrats, his coattails proved half as strong against Democratic incumbents as they were in 1980, when the GOP lost three incumbents but unseated 28 Democratic members.

In 1984 three Republican incumbents were defeated, but only 13 Democratic incumbents lost their seats. Among the defeated Democrats were six subcommittee chairmen: California's Jerry M. Patterson, Maryland's Clarence D. Long, Donald J. Albosta of Michigan, Georgia's Elliott H. Levitas, Joseph G. Minish of New Jersey, and North Carolina's Ike Andrews.

Democrats got some welcome news in California, where voters rejected by a 10-point margin an initiative

pushed by Republican Gov. George Deukmejian that would have redrawn the state's congressional districts. The existing map heavily favored Democrats, and party leaders feared that a new one would cut severely into their House delegation.

Republicans scored a net gain of four in the 27 districts left open by the retirement, primary defeat or death of an incumbent, winning five formerly Democratic seats but losing an Arkansas district to the opposition.

Close Contests

The outcomes in several districts were especially close. The closest was in Indiana's 8th District, where Democratic incumbent Frank McCloskey faced a challenge from Republican Richard D. McIntyre. McIntyre was certified the winner by the Indiana secretary of state, but McCloskey claimed the seat was his on the basis of a later recount. The House early in 1985 declared the seat vacant, pending an investigation. After the House Administration Committee concluded April 23 that Democrat McCloskey had won by four votes, the House on a series of partisan votes first refused to call a special election and then voted to seat the Democrat. Debate over the issue had grown so rancorous that Republicans walked out of the House chamber just as the Democrats were preparing to swear in McCloskey.

In Illinois the successor to 22nd District Democrat Paul Simon, who gave up his seat for a successful Senate bid, was former Democratic Rep. Kenneth J. Gray (1955-74), although his 1,200-vote margin prompted his opponent to consider requesting a recount.

Three Republican-held seats also were in doubt for days after the election. Embattled incumbent George Hansen eventually lost to challenger Richard Stallings by 170 votes in Idaho's 2nd District. In North Carolina's open 9th District, Republican J. Alex McMillan defeated attorney D. G. Martin by 321 votes.

And in Utah's 2nd District, which GOP Rep. Dan Marriott gave up in an unsuccessful bid for the governorship, Democratic state Sen. Frances Farley lost to Lt. Gov. David S. Monson by 496 votes.

Voting Patterns

The modest nature of the GOP's House gains came despite a vigorous pre-election effort by the party's national election apparatus to give Reagan as much company on Capitol Hill as possible. In the days before the election, Vice President George Bush campaigned for Republican challengers, and the GOP's House campaign committee aired advertisements and sent out mailings encouraging voters to cast straight Republican ballots. Some Republicans, including House Minority Leader Robert H. Michel, Ill., contended that, had Reagan paid more attention to close contests, his popularity would have helped GOP candidates over the top.

If the House results failed to satisfy Republicans hoping for a major congressional realignment to match their recent presidential strength, they still gave some signs that the party was picking up steam in traditionally Democratic territory. Regionally, the GOP made most of its gains where Democrats historically had been strongest — the South, where eight Democratic seats went Republican, and the East, where five shifted into the GOP column. Equally important, the party picked up three heavily blue-collar seats and showed enough potency in others to mark them

as potential future battlegrounds.

The Republicans' best gains came in Texas and North Carolina, where bitterly fought Senate contests brought out huge numbers of voters whose unalloyed loyalty to Reagan proved devastating to Democrats lower down on the ticket. The results were especially striking in Texas, where the GOP won 10 of 27 seats — its best showing ever and a sign of remarkable growth for a party that a scant 10 years earlier controlled only a trio of seats.

Elsewhere in the South, the Democratic Party's growing reliance on black voters was brought home with special force. In districts with sizable black populations where Democratic incumbents faced credible Republican challengers — such as South Carolina's 6th and Mississippi's 4th — the incumbents won with little trouble.

But in North Carolina, where voter turnout was unusually high, three incumbent Democrats with relatively small numbers of black voters in their districts were defeated, and two others almost lost to weak opponents. Democrats in the more heavily black eastern districts of the state had little trouble in the election.

The Democrats' three pickups included two in districts where the Republican incumbents had been weakened by scandal. In Idaho's 2nd District, Republican Hansen had suffered recurring electoral difficulties since allegations concerning false campaign finance reports and questionable personal debts first surfaced in 1975. This election, after his conviction for filing false financial disclosure statements, his constituents apparently had enough, giving the seat to challenger Stallings.

In Illinois' 19th District, Republican Daniel B. Crane, censured by the House in 1983 for sexual misconduct with a female congressional page, lost his seat to state Sen. Terry L. Bruce. Bruce put together an overwhelming margin in Champaign County, where Crane had never been popular, and matched Crane in the usually Republican rural counties to the south.

State Races

The 1984 gubernatorial elections did little to dent the 2-1 advantage the Democratic Party had in governorships it controlled. Republicans notched victories in North Carolina, Rhode Island, Utah and West Virginia, where the statehouses were left vacant in 1984 by departing Democratic incumbents.

But the Democrats captured three seats, toppling Republican incumbents in North Dakota and Washington and picking up the seat left open by retiring GOP Gov. Richard A. Snelling in Vermont.

Republicans thus scored a net gain of one seat, boosting the total governorships under their control from 15 to 16 and reducing the number of states in the Democratic column from 35 to 34. The GOP's showing represented an improvement over 1982, when the party suffered a net loss of seven seats. Republicans still remained a long way, however, from capturing a majority of governorships — a feat they last accomplished in 1969.

While their gain in governorships may have been meager, the GOP scored an impressive string of victories in state legislative contests. The election results did not dramatically affect the overall legislative dominance of the Democrats, who now controlled both chambers in 28 states. But further Republican advances in several states could pose a long-range danger to the Democratic majority in the

Politics and National Issues

U.S. House because the legislatures would control the congressional redistricting process following the 1990 Census.

The GOP did not gain control of any additional state legislatures as a result of the elections; it controlled 11. But the Republicans achieved a net gain of five states in which they controlled one chamber, bringing to 10 the number of legislatures where party control was divided.

One state, Nebraska, had a non-partisan, unicameral Legislature.

Many of the Republican pickups were in states with heavy Democratic majorities, particularly in the South, so the figures on party control did not fully reflect Republican gains. Republicans added nearly 300 seats nationwide.

By far the most striking legislative change came in Connecticut, where Republicans took control of both chambers from the Democrats. Aided by a Reagan landslide in the state and divisions within the Democratic Party, Connecticut Republicans won an additional 11 seats in the Senate and 23 seats in the House.

Republicans also picked up control of one legislative chamber each in Delaware, Minnesota, Nevada, New Mexico and Ohio. Idaho Republicans added significantly to their existing majorities, gaining enough votes to override any future vetoes by Democratic Gov. John V. Evans. Perhaps more important in the long run, however, were the Republican gains in traditionally Democratic Southern states. Significant GOP pickups came in Florida (six seats in the two chambers combined), North Carolina (25 seats), South Carolina (9) and Texas (17).

Democrats were not without some offsetting gains of their own, however. In Alaska, the party ended Republican legislative dominance by winning a bare majority in the House. Vermont Democrats pulled off a similar feat, taking control of the Senate by a four-seat margin.

2

Economic Policy

Introduction   *27*
The Federal Budget   *33*
Tax Policy   *63*
Financial Regulation   *83*
International Economics   *95*
Fiscal Assistance   *113*

Economic Policy

When Ronald Reagan captured the presidency in 1980, he mounted the most serious assault on federal spending and tax policies in nearly 50 years.

The "Reagan Revolution" challenged the trend, begun in the 1930s and extended almost continually until the 1970s, toward growing government intervention in the economy. Reagan, calling for steep cuts both in taxes and domestic social spending, sought to curtail the government's role as economic manager and guarantor of social equity.

Congress initially went along with the president's program. Lawmakers as well as the president had received a clear signal to do something about economic conditions. The stagnant, inflation-ridden economy that had hung on since the mid-1970s had not only helped Reagan evict Jimmy Carter from the White House. It had contributed to a Republican takeover of the Senate and a diminished Democratic majority in the House.

Reagan's novel formulation of economic policy pulled together disparate elements in the Republican Party — traditional fiscal conservatives, tax-cutting neo-conservative activists and free market theorists — into a ruling coalition that enabled him to achieve changes in policy many had thought impossible.

The president's strength was not unlimited, however. For some of his key victories, he relied on defectors from Democratic Party ranks. After scoring big wins during his first year in office, the going got tougher in Congress, and the president had to spend much of the remainder of his first term defending his accomplishments rather than trying to extend them.

Nonetheless, by the end of his first term Reagan had changed the terms of debate about economic policy in Washington. He had brought the nation through a recession without significant emergency spending legislation. And he had so cut federal revenues that new spending programs were unthinkable. Indeed, further spending cuts were in prospect.

As Reagan began his second term in 1985, re-elected by an overwhelming majority, Democrats continued to control the House by a wide margin, and Republicans felt far from secure in their hold on the Senate. While the economy had managed to weather the worst recession since the Great Depression of the 1930s, more than eight million people remained unemployed. Inflation had subsided and interest rates were falling, but worrisome deficits and deteriorating U.S. competitiveness in international markets clouded the economic future. *(Key economic indicators, chart, p. 31)*

Foundations

To a large degree Reagan won the presidency because traditional economic policies were not working to bring about growth without inflation. Based on the teachings of British economist John Maynard Keynes, post-World War II economic theory had assigned to the government an ever-larger role in regulating the pace of economic activity.

Keynes maintained that government could bring about optimal economic performance by controlling the level of total demand for goods and services in the economy. He said unemployment results from inadequate demand for goods and services. To cure that, he recommended increasing people's income, either by cutting taxes or raising government spending.

Inflation, according to Keynesian theory, results when demand exceeds the economy's capacity. To cure inflation, the theory recommended taking steps to reduce income, either by raising taxes or cutting spending.

As the postwar era wore on, Keynesian prescriptions worked well against unemployment. But they increasingly fell short in controlling inflation.

Presidents and Congresses generally found it easier to pursue policies that were likely to result in inflation than to risk producing the social conflict that comes with high unemployment. That may be because unemployment, although it affects fewer people, causes more severe hardship than fairly modest inflation spread out among most people.

Both Democrats and Republicans found it difficult to restrain demand. Inflationary pressures grew in the late 1960s, when President Lyndon B. Johnson and Congress balked at raising taxes or cutting back "Great Society" spending to pay for the Vietnam War. Later, President Richard M. Nixon overheated the economy to help assure his re-election in 1972.

Moreover, beginning in the 1970s, the economy began to experience a new kind of inflation, which Keynesian

References

Discussion of economic policy for the years 1945-64 may be found in *Congress and the Nation Vol. I*, pp. 335-458; for the years 1965-68, *Congress and the Nation Vol. II*, pp. 119-182, 253-305; for the years 1969-72, *Congress and the Nation Vol. III*, pp. 51-145; for the years 1973-76, *Congress and the Nation Vol. IV*, pp. 49-149; for the years 1977-80, *Congress and the Nation Vol. V*, pp. 205-287.

Federal Reserve's Tight Money Strategy ...

President Reagan's first term in office saw the Federal Reserve Board achieve unprecedented primacy in the nation's economic life.

Since 1979 the Fed had assumed the leading role in combating inflation, sharply restricting growth in the money supply. Even when that pushed the economy into the most severe recession since the 1930s, the central bank managed to deflect criticism from Congress and the Reagan administration until inflation abated substantially.

Fighting Inflation

The Federal Reserve's anti-inflation crusade stemmed from the failure of federal fiscal policy since the mid-1960s to deal with inflationary pressures. Although the Fed began its fight against inflation before President Reagan's election, he gave it important support after he took office.

Relations between the central bank and the White House had been shaky in the final years of President Carter's term. The White House demurred when, on Oct. 6, 1979, the Fed revamped its operating procedures to give precedence to fighting inflation. Previously the Fed tried mainly to control the federal funds rate, the key interest rate banks charge on overnight loans to each other. Under the new policy it concentrated on slowing the growth of the money supply, even at the expense of letting interest rates rise and fluctuate dramatically. *(Interest rate changes, chart, p. 31)*

The Fed has several ways to influence the money supply, but its key device is "open market operations," the buying and selling of government securities in the open market. If the Fed wants to increase the money supply, it buys government securities from banks. That puts new cash in the hands of the banks, which they in turn can lend out. Conversely, if the Fed wants to cut the money supply, it sells government securities, thus draining cash out of the banking system. Money is said to be "tight," and loans become more costly.

Hoping to cool inflation without driving interest rates up, President Carter persuaded a reluctant Fed in March 1980 to join him in imposing credit controls on the economy. But that policy backfired, sending the economy reeling into an alarmingly steep recession, and within months the controls were dropped.

When it became clear that inflation remained untamed, the Fed returned to its tight money policy. By the 1980 election, interest rates again were rising and a new recession appeared imminent. *(Congress and the Nation Vol. V, p. 206)*

President Reagan's economic philosophy was more compatible with the Fed's strategy. Advocating free market policies, he opposed credit controls as government meddling. And, accepting the views of monetarist economists, he supported the Fed's basic policy of clamping down on money growth.

In mid-1981 high interest rates induced by tight money again tipped the economy into a recession. The new president blamed the economic decline on inflationary excesses of previous administrations.

Friction

Relations between the White House and the Fed resembled a marital dispute in 1981 and 1982. While philosophically committed to the tight money strategy for beating inflation, the White House also had promised that substantial cuts in income tax rates would generate rapid economic growth. Many economists warned that the two policies were in conflict — a view that was confirmed when high interest rates induced by the Fed's anti-inflation policy thwarted the strong economic recovery Reagan promised.

The administration had hoped interest rates would drop quickly once inflation abated. When they failed to do so, despite the severity of the recession, the White House grew increasingly nervous. Many economists attributed lingering high rates to financial market fears that large federal deficits eventually would rekindle inflation, but the administration sought to shift blame to the Fed, saying that "erratic" implementation of monetary policy unnerved the markets and kept interest rates high.

Fed Chairman Paul A. Volcker, for his part, welcomed the administration's resolve to bring down inflation. But he worried that the administration's tax cut would undermine public support for the Fed's

economics had not considered. Poor harvests pushed up food prices. Then, the Arab oil embargo sent oil prices soaring, and that drove up prices for a myriad of related goods.

Economic policy makers were at a loss to deal with these problems. If they did nothing, higher energy prices would reduce purchasing power. And the resulting fall in demand would lead to a rise in unemployment. But if they tried to offset the loss in income by pumping more dollars into the economy, they ran the risk of fostering inflation because there then would be more dollars available to buy the same limited supply of goods.

Most economists preferred bolstering income rather than letting the increase in oil prices touch off a potentially severe recession. Even if that produced more inflation, they said it was a price worth paying.

A variety of factors reduced the incentive to deal with inflation as a political issue. Cost-of-living adjustments

... Tames Inflation, Triggers Deep Recession

anti-inflation policy. He feared that massive deficits would force the federal government to compete increasingly with private borrowers for credit, driving interest rates much higher than needed to combat inflation. Volcker feared that would generate pressure on the Fed to increase the money supply.

While warning about the dangers of large deficits, Volcker avoided a direct confrontation with the White House by steadfastly refusing to oppose the tax cuts or to recommend specifically how Congress and the administration should bring the budget closer to balance.

Democratic Opposition

Congressional Democrats, unlike the White House, directly challenged the central bank's policy of concentrating on controlling the money supply. Their challenge reflected an historic tension between Democrats — and farmers and small-business men — who wanted to keep interest rates low, and Republicans and monetarists who wanted to fight inflation at all costs. It was another in a long succession of efforts to make monetary policy subject to congressional oversight.

Democrats in both houses pressed legislation in 1982 to force fundamental changes in Fed policy. In the Senate, Democrats proposed directing the Fed to keep short-term interest rates a few percentage points above the rate of inflation. Since inflation was declining, the Senate bill (S 2807) would have forced the central bank to engineer a reduction in interest rates — a policy that many economists warned would cause renewed inflation over the long run.

House Democrats took another approach. They proposed requiring the Fed to target long-term interest rates, with no adjustment for inflation. Their bill (HR 6967) gave the Fed more flexibility than the Senate Democrats' approach, but it still challenged the core of the Fed's anti-inflation policy.

Reflecting Democratic frustration that the Reagan administration was escaping blame for the recession by ceding to monetary policy the key role in fighting inflation, the House bill also included a provision requiring the president to take a public position on Fed decisions.

Perhaps because of the differences between House and Senate approaches, the Democratic challenge to the Fed did not reach the floor in either chamber in 1982. One other Democratic proposal — to renew the president's authority to impose credit controls, which had lapsed in July 1982 — won House Banking Committee approval (HR 6124 — H Rept 97-774). But it was opposed by the Reagan administration and the Fed, and it went no further. *(Credit controls, Congress and the Nation Vol. V, p. 229)*

Although it shied away from firm directives to the Fed, Congress did attempt to link Fed monetary policy to fiscal policy through vague, non-binding language included in its annual budget resolutions.

Easing Up

While political opposition alone did not deter the Fed, the slowdown in inflation, the continued recession and growing strains in the domestic and international financial system finally convinced it to ease up in October 1982. That month it announced that it was abandoning its strict focus on the money supply in favor of a more flexible approach.

By November the economy was recovering. The next year, 1983, brought vigorous growth with little inflation. Volcker enjoyed the strong support of the nation's financial community. Recognizing the importance of maintaining that confidence, Reagan in July nominated him to a second four-year term as Fed chairman. The Senate confirmed him, 84-16.

Relations between the Fed and the administration were not entirely peaceful, despite the recovery. As strong economic growth generated new fears of inflation, the Fed tightened monetary growth again in mid-1983. The White House, concerned that the recovery would slow before the 1984 elections, grew critical of the central bank.

Despite such "Fed-bashing," Volcker kept a tight grip until the economy showed signs of slowing in September 1984. Then the Fed relaxed the money reins a bit. On election day President Reagan could boast that the economy was growing, unemployment was down and inflation was stilled.

eased the pain from inflation for workers and retirees. Inflation in housing prices benefited homeowners. And steadily rising federal tax revenues permitted Congress to create new programs without raising taxes to pay for them.

"There's no sense in shooting ourselves in the foot to show how much we care about inflation," said economist Arthur M. Okun in 1979. "Inflation is a terribly serious problem, but it's not going to be cured by deep recession. Or if it is, the cost may not be worth it."

Setting the Stage. By the late 1970s the economy seemed badly out of balance. Years of stimulative economic policy, coupled with an accommodative approach to oil shocks, had produced ever-worsening inflation. The unpredictable rise in prices undermined voters' confidence at home and sent the dollar plummeting in international money markets.

Moreover, the rate of new capital investment in the United States was lagging behind that of most Western

industrial nations — also partly the result of inflation, which encouraged consumption over investment. The investment lag was especially worrisome because high energy prices made investment doubly important by rendering obsolete many plants and production processes that relied on cheap energy.

"The new reality ... is the re-emergence during the 1970s of the economics of scarcity — a progressive imbalance between the demands we have been placing on our economy and our capacity to satisfy them," wrote Alfred Kahn, a Cornell University economist who served as President Carter's inflation adviser.

Carter gradually came to the conclusion that inflation — which surged 12.4 percent during his final year in office — was the nation's primary economic problem. But he could turn only to conventional medicine — a bitter dose of austerity, slow growth and stagnant or declining standards of living. "There is no way we can avoid a decline in our standard of living," Kahn said in 1979. "All we can do is adapt to it."

That view proved politically unpalatable. "To materially reduce standards of living as compelled by low productivity is unthinkable for a democratic government in peacetime," declared Sen. Jacob K. Javits, R-N.Y. (1957-81).

'Reaganomics'

Reagan picked up the banner of prosperity just as Democrats gloomily were telling Americans they had to settle for a lower standard of living. He said the nation could fight inflation and achieve greater prosperity at the same time. The key, he said, was to diminish the role of government in the economy.

"The people have not created this disaster in our economy," he said in announcing his candidacy for president in 1979. "The federal government has. It has outspent, overestimated and overregulated. It has failed to deliver services within the revenues it should be allowed to raise from taxes."

After his election, the new president directly challenged the postwar faith in government intervention in the economy. The American economic system, he said, "has never failed us." But we have failed it "through a lack of confidence and sometimes through a belief we could fine-tune the economy and get a tune to our liking."

"Reaganomics," as the new president's economic views came to be known, rested on several principles: taxes and government spending should be cut sharply; the government should focus on creating a healthy long-term economic environment rather than trying to smooth every swing of the business cycle; wages and prices should be set by market forces — meaning that any suggestion of using wage and price controls to rein in inflation should be dropped, and that deregulation of transportation, banking and other industries should be continued; and finally, price stability should be assured through firm control of the money supply.

Supply-Side Economics. Supply-side economics, an untested new doctrine popular among some young conservatives, provided the rationale for cutting taxes despite the fear of inflation. Supply-siders argued that Keynesian tax cuts had mistakenly concentrated on increasing consumers' purchasing power. They said cuts should be designed instead to create incentives to save and invest, producing an increase in the supply of goods and services that would avert price increases.

The fulcrum of economic activity, according to supply-siders, is the marginal rate of taxation, the rate on the last dollar earned. The higher the marginal tax rate, the less incentive a person has to work rather than be idle, or to save rather than consume, they maintained. By reducing marginal tax rates, supply-siders concluded, the government could encourage more work and savings, in the process increasing output without inflation.

Reagan economists said the effects of a cut in marginal tax rates would be felt at all levels of income. But they said the cut in marginal rates would be effective because the biggest benefits would go to people in the upper income brackets, who can afford to save and invest more. Tax cuts that redistribute income to poor people are more likely to increase consumption because people in low tax brackets cannot afford to save, they said.

Liberals said that argument merely rationalized a program designed to benefit the well-to-do. But Reagan replied that the nation had grown tired of Democratic programs designed to redistribute income. "The taxing power of the government must be used to provide revenues for legitimate government purposes," he said. "It must not be used to regulate the economy or bring about social change."

Conservative Activism. Reagan also tapped traditional conservative objections to heavy domestic spending. Rep. David A. Stockman (R-Mich., 1977-81), who was to become Reagan's budget director, complained in 1980 that the federal budget had become "an automatic coast-to-coast soup line that dispenses remedial aid with almost reckless abandon."

That sentiment struck a responsive chord with an American public facing the threat of economic stagnation and declining living standards. While federal programs to help the most needy maintained a fair level of support, others that aided the working poor — people with some job but very low income — proved particularly vulnerable.

Significantly, Reagan heeded a group of young neo-conservatives who said tax cuts should take priority over spending reductions, though. Young conservatives such as Republican Jack Kemp of New York complained that the Republicans in the past had consigned themselves to the status of political outsiders because they placed too much emphasis on balancing the budget rather than on cutting taxes. The defeat four years earlier of President Gerald R. Ford, who made spending reductions a prerequisite to tax cuts, underscored Republican frustration.

"As Republicans, we must rid ourselves of the perceived political idolatry of balanced budgets," Kemp said. "Republicans must not be bookkeepers for Democratic deficits."

The same idea was advanced by Irving Kristol, a popular conservative polemicist. "When in office, liberals ... will always spend generously, regardless of budgetary considerations, until the public permits the conservatives an interregnum in which to clean up the mess — but with liberals retaining their status as the activist party, the party of the 'natural majority,' " he wrote. "The neo-conservatives have decided that two can play at this game — and must, since it is the only game in town.... They vigorously advocate [increased defense spending and] tax cuts, with the budget remaining a secondary consideration."

Monetarism. Reagan embraced one other idea that had been outside the mainstream of economic thinking for much of the postwar period — monetarism.

Key Measures of the Economy

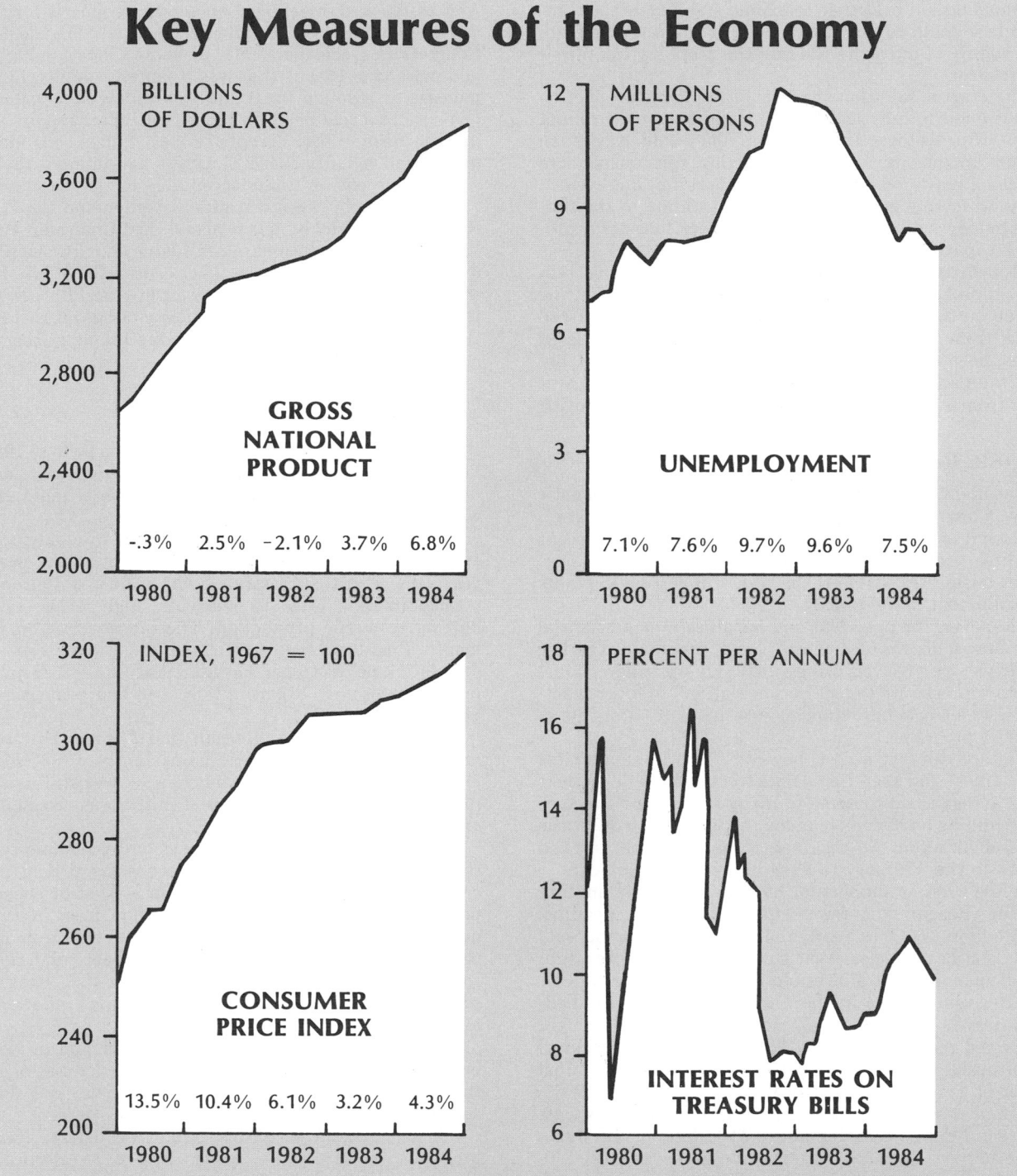

BILLIONS OF DOLLARS

GROSS NATIONAL PRODUCT

-.3%   2.5%   -2.1%   3.7%   6.8%

1980   1981   1982   1983   1984

MILLIONS OF PERSONS

UNEMPLOYMENT

7.1%   7.6%   9.7%   9.6%   7.5%

1980   1981   1982   1983   1984

INDEX, 1967 = 100

CONSUMER PRICE INDEX

13.5%   10.4%   6.1%   3.2%   4.3%

1980   1981   1982   1983   1984

PERCENT PER ANNUM

INTEREST RATES ON TREASURY BILLS

1980   1981   1982   1983   1984

Gross National Product: Measures total national output of goods and services. Line plots growth in current dollars. Inset figures show average annual rate of change after adjustment for inflation.

Unemployment: Measures unemployment in the civilian labor force of persons age 16 and over. Line plots number of persons unemployed. Inset figures show average annual unemployment rate.

Consumer Price Index: Measures price changes for fixed market baskets of essential goods and services purchased by all urban consumers. Line plots increases in consumer prices. Inset figures show average annual rate of change after adjustment for inflation.

Interest Rates: Line plots interest rates on three-month Treasury bills.

SOURCE: Joint Economic Committee, *Economic Indicators,* April 1985

Developed by conservative economist Milton Friedman, monetarism held that economic stability without inflation best could be assured by holding the rate of growth in the supply of money to the rate the economy can physically achieve.

Monetarists said that the level of economic production is determined by physical factors the government cannot greatly influence over the long run. They said Keynesian attempts to increase demand by giving consumers more purchasing power might work in the short run but eventually would merely produce inflation by adding to the supply of money without being able to affect long-term productive capacity.

Monetarism had important effects on Reagan's economic approach. It put prime responsibility for fighting inflation on the Federal Reserve Board. Moreover, it freed Reagan from traditional Republican worries about large deficits, because monetarists held that deficits would not cause inflation, so long as the Fed prevented the supply of money from increasing faster than the economy's potential.

1981-82: Reagan Ascendancy

President Reagan's first year in office was a dramatic success. Congress approved the centerpiece of his program — personal income tax rate reductions totaling 25 percent over three years and accelerated depreciation allowances that let businesses write off the cost of investing in plants and equipment more quickly.

Moreover, the president and his allies won substantial reductions in dozens of domestic social programs. The key to their victory involved using a little-known congressional budgetary procedure called "reconciliation" to force enactment — in a single bill requiring just one vote — of cuts in dozens of programs.

Victory came at a cost, however. To win support for the tax cut — and keep Democrats from claiming it as their own — Reagan had to agree to many expensive "sweeteners," including provisions to index the tax code to offset the effects of inflation. All together, these provisions swelled the loss to the Treasury to $749 billion over five years.

While winning support for his big increases in military spending, Reagan won fewer cuts in domestic spending, $130.6 billion over four years, than he originally proposed.

It soon became clear that steep tax cuts and less substantial spending restraint would result in growing deficits. Federal revenues were further undermined when the Federal Reserve's return to strict monetary restraint brought on renewed recession in July 1981. The economy declined precipitously, at a 4.9 percent annual rate in the final quarter of 1981, 4.6 percent in the first quarter of 1982.

Coupled with projections that the Reagan tax cuts would send deficits soaring above $100 billion, the recession unnerved financial markets. Reagan was forced to return to Congress in September 1981 with a package of additional budget cuts and "revenue enhancements" — a euphemism for tax increases.

Lawmakers, stung by heavy administration pressure for the initial tax and budget bills, rejected the new proposals in 1981. But in 1982 they passed an administration-supported bill to raise almost $100 billion in revenues by closing tax loopholes and beefing up tax compliance.

True to his word, Reagan resisted stopgap spending measures to pull the country out of recession. Although the unemployment rate surged — peaking at 10.7 percent in November and December 1982 — the president let CETA,

the Democratic public jobs program of the 1970s, expire. And he blocked sweeping Democratic proposals for public works spending. Reagan did endorse legislation, cleared by Congress in December 1982, to boost funds for highways and mass transit, but that was financed completely by an increase in gasoline taxes and was widely seen more as a response to a real need for roads and bridge repairs. Early in 1983 Reagan also accepted a $4.6 billion jobs and humanitarian relief package; Congress had tailored the measure to stay within limits acceptable to the president.

Relations between the administration and the Federal Reserve were prickly, but peaceful. Fed Chairman Paul A. Volcker said the administration's large deficits contributed to driving up interest rates. That caused the White House some embarrassment. But Volcker, carefully avoiding treading on more sensitive political ground, refused to tell Congress whether it should reduce red ink by raising taxes or cutting spending. *(Monetary policy, box, p. 28)*

1983-84: Recovery

The recession hurt Republicans at the polls in 1982. In his 1983 budget message to Congress, the president admitted that the promised supply-side miracle of rapid growth without inflation had not materialized.

Although the Consumer Price Index rose only 3.9 percent during 1982, down from 8.9 percent in the previous year, the Fed's successful fight against inflation had pushed interest rates to unusually high levels, severely hurting economic production. The interest rate on three-month Treasury bills, a benchmark for short-term rates, did not fall below 10 percent until August 1982. A runup of interest rates that began in late 1980 had peaked at 16.3 percent in May 1981.

Relations between Reagan and Capitol Hill turned nastier in 1983. Democratic gains in the 1982 elections made Congress less pliable, but Reagan was still in a position to block actions he opposed. Little was accomplished on the legislative front in 1983.

Meanwhile, high interest rates and economic stagnation had sent the value of the dollar soaring, driving up the cost of U.S. exports and bringing in a flood of cheap imports. Pressures mounted for protection from imports in numerous industries. Moreover, many developing countries neared the brink of default on their debt, undermining confidence in the U.S. banking system. U.S. banks also suffered severe loan losses as the slowdown of inflation sent many businesses into bankruptcy.

These developments worried the Fed, and in November 1982, with inflation significantly slowed, it began easing the monetary reins. By mid-1983 the economy was surging, and growth for the year wound up at 3.7 percent.

When Reagan eased his assault on federal spending programs in 1984 — a move derided as election-year maneuvering — lawmakers rejected his proposals and adopted a three-year, $150 billion deficit reduction plan. It included $50 billion in tax increases.

That barely put a dent in deficits projected to total about $600 billion through fiscal 1987. But at least by 1984 the economic picture had brightened. Unemployment was down to 7.5 percent, inflation was running at 4 percent and interest rates — though still high by historical standards — were easing. One sour note was trade: American factories continued to lose ground to foreign competitors, and the U.S. merchandise trade deficit ballooned to $123 billion for the year, up from $69 billion in 1983.

The Federal Budget

The specter of "$200 billion deficits as far as the eye can see" — the catch phrase of the period — dominated debates on the budget during most of President Reagan's first term in office.

Deficits were running at less than a third that level when Reagan took office in 1981; the budget had been in balance only once in the past 20 years. In his inaugural address the president warned that continuing decades of deficit spending would "guarantee tremendous social, cultural, political and economic upheavals." And he called for a radical shift in fiscal policy that he said would permit him to balance the budget in fiscal 1984, as he had pledged in his 1980 campaign.

Reagan promptly launched a dramatic assault on the budget by proposing massive across-the-board cuts in all areas of domestic spending except defense. At the same time, as part of his supply-side prescription for economic growth, Reagan proposed the largest tax cut in the nation's history.

Within seven months Reagan had succeeded beyond most observers' expectations. Seizing control of Congress' own budget-making procedures, the president forced the Democratic House to join the Republican Senate in accepting his economic plan. Congress slashed $130.6 billion from projected federal spending over fiscal 1982-84, and it cut personal and corporate income taxes by an estimated $280.3 billion over the same period.

The president had hoped his economic program would revitalize the sagging economy, but recession took hold instead. As deficit projections mounted following enactment of his tax cuts, Reagan retreated from his pledge to balance the budget by 1984. That had been only a goal, he said.

The important factor, administration officials maintained, was that the deficit as a percentage of gross national product (GNP) was on a downward trend. In fact, however, the deficit had begun an upward surge that was to take it from 2 percent of GNP in fiscal 1981 to 6.1 percent in 1983, before easing to 4.9 percent the following year.

The actual deficit never reached the threatened $200 billion level during Reagan's first term, but it came close. The deficit ballooned from $57.9 billion in fiscal 1981 to a peak of $195.4 billion in 1983, reflecting recession-induced declines in revenues and increases in spending. Although it fell back to $175.4 billion in fiscal 1984, Congress in mid-1985 forecast a shortfall of $209.8 billion for fiscal 1985. Like all budget forecasts, the congressional projections were built on shifting sands: They depended on uncertain assumptions about future economic behavior — unemployment, inflation, growth in GNP and other factors — that could radically alter federal spending and revenue patterns.

Persisting deficits of the magnitude projected could pose serious problems for the economy, many economists warned, ranging from higher interest rates and loss of export markets to a runaway accumulation of federal debt.

Fears of uncontrolled deficits notwithstanding, a campaign for a constitutional amendment to require balanced budgets made little headway in 1981-84. A proposed balanced budget amendment stalled in Congress, despite pressure from President Reagan and mounting state calls for a constitutional convention to consider the issue. Congress dismissed another Reagan proposal for a constitutional amendment giving him authority to veto individual items in appropriations bills.

Congress and the Budget

Congress was consumed by the budget throughout Reagan's first term. Lawmakers routinely dismissed the budgets sent to Capitol Hill by the president in 1982-84, yet they found it nearly impossible to develop fiscal plans of their own that also were acceptable to Reagan.

Members went along with the president in 1981 when he proposed sharp increases in the defense budget while slashing spending for social programs. But they became less willing to support Reagan's defense buildup and more protective of social spending in subsequent years.

Budget negotiations repeatedly were stalemated by two key players' rigid stands: Reagan's refusal to consider rescinding any personal tax cuts granted in 1981 and the adamant opposition of House Speaker Thomas P. O'Neill Jr., D-Mass., to any cutbacks in Social Security benefits. The standoff on Social Security illustrated the difficulties

References

Discussion of federal budget policy for the years 1945-64 may be found in *Congress and the Nation Vol. I*, pp. 387-395; for the years 1965-68, *Congress and the Nation Vol. II*, pp. 127-140; for the years 1969-72, *Congress and the Nation Vol. III*, pp. 63-75; for the years 1973-76, *Congress and the Nation Vol. IV*, pp. 57-81; for the years 1977-80, *Congress and the Nation Vol. V*, pp. 211-230.

Budget Process: Reconciling Spending, Taxes

In enacting the Congressional Budget and Impoundment Control Act of 1974 (PL 93-344), Congress attempted to regain some measure of control over the federal budget, which it had forfeited to the president over the years. To that end the law established a procedure enabling Congress to relate its individual taxing and spending decisions to overall budget levels it also had set.

Under the provisions of the 1974 act, each spring Congress would review the president's budget proposals for the fiscal year that was to begin the following Oct. 1 and then set spending and revenue goals of its own. These non-binding goals would be incorporated in a first budget resolution to be adopted by May 15. Congress would then spend the summer and early fall enacting the regular appropriations bills for the coming fiscal year. By Sept. 15 it would adopt a second, and binding, budget resolution setting final spending and revenue figures. The budget resolutions also would establish non-binding limits for the public debt and for federal credit activity.

To reconcile spending and revenue requirements with the levels set out in the budget resolutions, Congress could direct its authorizing and appropriating committees to recommend legislative changes in programs already on the books. Their proposals would be packaged in an omnibus bill for floor action in each chamber. In devising this "reconciliation" procedure, the authors of the 1974 act reckoned that lawmakers would find it easier to vote for a package of budget savings than for a number of separate spending cut measures. Congress first used the reconciliation process in 1980 to achieve modest cuts in the fiscal 1981 deficit. *(Background, Congress and the Nation Vol. IV, p. 71; Congress and the Nation Vol. V, p. 228)*

The Reagan Years

Reconciliation assumed a new importance when Ronald Reagan entered the White House in 1981. The incoming Republican administration seized control of the congressional budget process to carry out Reagan's sweeping spending and tax cut program. Congress endorsed his controversial plan in its first fiscal 1982 budget resolution, then went on to enact reconciliation legislation providing the massive spending cuts required by that measure.

Later in the year Congress approved a second fiscal 1982 budget resolution that merely reaffirmed the first.

President Reagan proved unable to repeat his 1981 triumph, and throughout the remainder of his first term Congress took the lead in setting budget priorities. But lawmakers engaged in protracted struggles with the White House that made a mockery of the statutory budget deadlines. The appropriations process lagged far behind schedule, and much of the government had to be funded each year under omnibus spending bills hastily approved at session's end.

Institutional conflicts also intensified, prompting calls for revision of the 1974 act. The budget process bred resentment among Senate and House authorizing and appropriating committees, whose powers had been curtailed by the law. And many members protested that reconciliation abused normal congressional procedures.

Budget Act Changes

Although efforts to rewrite the 1974 act made little headway, some revisions in the budget process were achieved informally.

Congress agreed, starting in 1982, to tie reconciliation to the first annual budget resolution and to bypass a second resolution altogether. Final revisions were folded into the next year's budget resolution the following spring.

In a further change, the Senate in 1984 refused to consider a fiscal 1985 budget resolution before passage of deficit reduction legislation. As a result, the budget resolution — which did not clear until Oct. 1 — was little more than a footnote to the deficit reduction measure.

After two years of study, the House Rules Committee in 1984 approved a bill (HR 5247 — H Rept 98-1152) to make modest changes in the congressional budget process. The bill's main feature was a compressed timetable for drafting and acting on the budget. Congress would not have been allowed to leave for its July 4th recess until it had completed work on all 13 regular annual appropriations bills. There was no further action on the measure.

Likewise, the Senate took no action on a proposal that the Budget Committee be abolished and its duties taken over by the Appropriations and Finance committees jointly. That step was recommended in 1983 by a study group led by former Sens. Abraham A. Ribicoff, D-Conn. (1963-81), and James B. Pearson, R-Kan. (1962-68).

One de facto change in the 1974 budget act resulted from a 1983 Supreme Court decision outlawing the legislative veto. That decision knocked out impoundment provisions of the 1974 act under which a single house of Congress could overrule a presidential decision to defer spending temporarily. The decision did not affect an alternative procedure under which appropriations could be rescinded, or canceled permanently, through legislation passed by both houses and signed by the president. *(Legislative veto, p. 833)*

in trimming automatic increases in middle-class entitlement benefits, which many experts viewed as crucial to long-term spending control. *(Entitlements, box, p. 38)*

Meanwhile federal deficits continued to rise in spite of major deficit-cutting measures voted in 1981, 1982 and 1984. Servicing costs on the mounting federal debt more than doubled over fiscal 1980-84, perpetuating the deficit spiral. Net interest costs accounted for $111 billion of total federal spending of $842 billion in fiscal 1984. They would double again by fiscal 1990, according to Congressional Budget Office (CBO) projections.

Strains in Process

Conflicts over the deficit in 1981-84 imposed grave strains on the budget process, which Congress had created in 1974 as a mechanism for establishing its own budget priorities. Under the 1974 law, Congress each year adopted resolutions setting spending and revenue goals. The law also established a "reconciliation" procedure for bringing existing tax and spending laws into conformity with the budget resolutions. *(Budget process, box, p. 34)*

In its early years congressional budget making was largely a process of accommodation. House and Senate leaders, anxious to keep the process going, steered away from proposing budget resolutions that would force legislative and appropriations committees to compete openly for budget resources. The House and Senate Budget committees first considered spending needs for each budget category before setting an overall total, not the other way around.

As long as Congress remained in an expansive mood, the House and Senate were able to construct in a piecemeal fashion budgets that satisfied the particular interests of various committees and groups. But when Congress tried to shift toward fiscal austerity in mid-1979, it encountered much rougher going. *(Background, Congress and the Nation Vol. V, p. 211)*

The budget battles of the early 1980s played havoc with congressional operations and clouded the future of the fiscal control procedures established in 1974. Budget deadlines fell by the wayside, and lengthy deficit reduction efforts blocked action on other urgent measures. Much of each year's legislation was folded into a few omnibus measures — reconciliation bills incorporating the deficit-cutting recommendations of legislative committees, or massive continuing appropriations resolutions providing funding for scores of federal agencies.

As deficits continued to mount, the usefulness of the budget process was called into question, especially by Senate and House committees whose powers it had curtailed. Champions of the process acknowledged its weaknesses but argued that deficits were much lower than they would have been without Congress' annual exercises in fiscal discipline.

Impact on Deficit

There was some support for that view. While no definitive assessment was possible, a CBO study released early in 1985 offered one hypothetical measure of the effect of the congressional budget process in keeping deficits from rising even higher. The non-partisan CBO was created by the 1974 budget act to provide technical support for Congress on budget matters. One of its major functions was to prepare analyses of alternative fiscal and economic policies.

According to CBO estimates, deficits would have de-

Stockman's Stewardship

The steward of administration deficit reduction efforts during President Reagan's first term was David A. Stockman, director of the White House Office of Management and Budget (OMB).

Stockman was a two-term representative from Michigan when Reagan tapped him for the budget post in January 1981. He had caught Reagan's eye during the 1980 presidential campaign while playing the role of independent candidate John B. Anderson in a practice debate. Reagan was particularly impressed with Stockman's knowledge of economics, and Stockman's November 1980 "manifesto" on how the new Republican administration could avoid an "economic Dunkirk" recommended him to the president.

Stockman was credited with being the main architect of the massive 1981 tax and budget cuts that he and others in the administration said would lower inflation, spur economic growth and eventually eliminate the deficit.

In the following three years he helped steer several deficit reduction measures through Congress. Stockman's almost singular drive to reduce the federal deficit was often at odds with other White House goals. While overseeing dramatic cutbacks in domestic spending, Stockman pushed unsuccessfully within the administration for further restraint in the growth of defense spending. He also argued for new revenues, despite Reagan's adamant opposition to tax increases.

Frustrated by his inability to bring the deficit down, Stockman began publicly to voice his doubts about Reagan's economic policies. Those doubts had first surfaced in a December 1981 *Atlantic Monthly* article that led to his chastisement by Reagan.

Stockman resigned in mid-1985 to join the New York investment banking firm of Salomon Brothers Inc. *(Stockman background, p. 1025)*

clined steadily and the budget would have shifted to a small surplus by fiscal 1989 if policies in effect in January 1981, just before the Reagan administration took office, had been followed without change. But CBO early in 1985 projected deficits rising steadily to $290 billion by fiscal 1990 if current policies were not changed. This rise resulted from tax cuts, defense spending increases and climbing interest costs since 1981, CBO said. The projected deficits would be even bigger, according to CBO, if non-defense expenditures had not been cut substantially below the path they were on in 1981.

CBO estimated these reductions in the growth of non-defense spending at $38 billion in fiscal 1985 and more than $400 billion cumulatively over six years, fiscal 1985 through 1990.

Presidents, Congress and the Budget, 1980-85

(In billions of dollars)

	Budget Authority	Outlays	Revenues	Deficit
Fiscal Year 1980				
Carter Budget	615.5	531.6	502.6	−29.0
First Resolution	604.4	532.0	509.0	−23.0
Second Resolution	638.0	547.6	517.8	−29.8
Revised Second Resolution	658.9	572.65	525.7	−46.95
Actual	658.8	576.7	517.1	−59.6
Fiscal Year 1981				
Carter Budget	696.1	615.8	600.0	−15.8
Carter Revisions	691.3	611.5	628.0	+16.5
First Resolution	697.2	613.6	613.8	+ 0.2
Second Resolution	694.6	632.4	605.0	−27.4
Revised Second Resolution	717.5	661.35	603.3	−58.05
Actual	718.4	657.2	599.3	−57.9
Fiscal Year 1982				
Carter Budget	809.8	739.3	711.8	−27.5
Reagan Revision	772.4	695.3	650.3	−45.0
First Resolution[1]	770.9	695.45	657.8	−37.65
Revised Second Resolution	777.67	734.10	628.4	−105.7
Actual	779.9	728.4	617.8	−110.6
Fiscal Year 1983				
Reagan Budget	801.9	757.6	666.1	−91.5
First Resolution[2]	822.39	769.82	665.9	−103.92
Revised Resolution	877.2 } * 883.36 } *	807.4 } * 812.85 } *	604.3	−203.1 } * −208.55 } *
Actual	866.7	795.97	600.56	−195.4
Fiscal Year 1984				
Reagan Budget	900.1	848.5	659.7	−188.8
First Resolution[2]	919.5 } * 928.73 } *	849.5 } * 858.93 } *	679.6	−169.9 } * −179.33 } *
Revised Resolution	918.9	845.6	672.9	−172.7
Actual	927.4	841.8	666.5	−175.36
Fiscal Year 1985				
Reagan Budget	1,006.5	925.5	745.1	−180.4
First Resolution[2]	1,021.35	932.05	750.9	−181.15
Revised Resolution	1,062.1	946.3	736.5	−209.8

[1] Second resolution merely reaffirmed figures in first resolution.
[2] First resolution became binding at beginning of fiscal year Oct. 1.

* Larger figure assumed enactment of 10 programs included in a special $8.5 billion reserve fund.

SOURCES: Federal budgets, congressional budget resolutions.

Chronology
Of Action
On the Budget

1981

Innovative use of the congressional budget process enabled President Reagan during his first year in office to achieve a dramatic about-face in the direction of government and an abrupt slowdown in the growth of federal spending.

But enactment of his program failed to revitalize the sluggish U.S. economy as Reagan had promised, and the nation sank into its second recession in two years.

In keeping with his supply-side economic approach, the new president asked Congress March 10 to cut $48.6 billion from projected fiscal 1982 spending and to reduce taxes by $53.9 billion. That would lead to increased investment, higher productivity and a decline in inflation, the administration said.

Because military spending would increase sharply under the president's plan, domestic social programs would bear the brunt of the proposed cuts. Reagan nonetheless maintained that his program was "evenhanded" and could be accomplished "without harm to government's legitimate purpose or to our responsibility to all who need our benevolence."

Congress moved swiftly to approve Reagan's plan. By August it had completed action on both the first fiscal 1982 budget resolution, which endorsed major elements of the president's proposals, and sweeping reconciliation and tax cut bills, which gave them force.

Reagan's success in achieving $35.2 billion in budget cuts for fiscal 1982 — $130.6 billion over fiscal 1982-84 — stemmed in part from the administration's use of reconciliation, a budget-cutting tool designed to help Congress meet its fiscal goals. The reconciliation vehicle permitted a variety of politically difficult budget cuts to be sheltered in one bill and sent to the floor for a single, up-or-down vote in each chamber.

The administration billed it as a vote on the Reagan economic program — a program that was the mandate of the 1980 election. The strategy worked. With solid Republican backing and help from a group of Southern conservative Democrats, who called themselves "Boll Weevils," the administration was able to seize control of the Democratic House on key budget votes. In the Senate, where Republicans enjoyed a majority for the first time in a quarter-century, Reagan found overwhelming support.

Within weeks after enactment of the budget cuts and the companion tax reduction measure the administration was forced to acknowledge that its economic program was not giving the economy the psychological lift Reagan had predicted. Interest rates soared and stock prices dropped in response to projections that the fiscal 1982 deficit would far exceed the president's revised $42.5 billion estimate. Reagan responded Sept. 24 by proposing a package of $13 billion in additional budget cuts and $3 billion in tax

increases, but Congress — still smarting from the earlier battles — rebuffed the president's plan. In the end Reagan won only $4 billion in appropriations cuts.

The controversy over the president's second-round cuts delayed action on the second — and supposedly binding — budget resolution for the fiscal year. With many Republicans unwilling to adopt a resolution that showed the gravity of the deficit outlook, Congress Dec. 10 approved a pro forma resolution that simply reaffirmed the budget it had adopted in May. The $37.65 billion deficit forecast by that measure was far below levels projected by the time Congress took up the second resolution.

Meanwhile — as the recession took hold in the fall, pushing deficit forecasts to $100 billion for fiscal 1982 and to even higher levels in subsequent years — the president began to backpedal on his 1980 campaign pledge to balance the budget by fiscal 1984. Acknowledging that he probably would not be able to carry out that pledge, Reagan said balancing the budget had been only a "goal." The important factor, administration officials maintained, was that the deficit as a percentage of total output was on a downward trend.

Reagan Budget

In his fiscal 1982 budget proposals, submitted to Congress March 10, President Reagan issued a blunt warning to lawmakers to adopt his sweeping spending and tax cuts or risk angering voters who had instructed Washington in November 1980 to put "America's economic house in order."

The president maintained that his program would slash inflation, currently running about 12 percent, to 6 percent by year's end. At the same time, economic growth would jump and productivity would increase.

Reagan proposed sharp cuts in the fiscal 1982 budget submitted by President Carter before he left office in January. Carter had recommended $739.3 billion in spending and $711.8 billion in revenues, with a $27.5 billion deficit. (Carter budget message, p. 1033)

Through comprehensive revisions of the Carter budget, Reagan proposed that federal spending be held to $695.3 billion and revenues to $650.3 billion in fiscal 1982, with a resulting deficit of $45 billion. His fiscal plan would reduce projected federal spending by $48.6 billion and lower taxes by $53.9 billion, Reagan said. Combined with a "stable" monetary policy and a rollback in regulations, the budget reductions would result in a quick drop in inflation and a "return to prosperity."

Reagan's broad spending cuts, which spared only military and certain basic social programs, would reduce the growth of federal spending to 6.2 percent in fiscal 1982, down from the 11.6 percent rate proposed by outgoing President Carter in his final budget Jan. 15. Reagan proposed a $26 billion increase, to $222 billion, in Carter's fiscal 1982 defense budget, plus sharp increases in fiscal 1981 defense funding.

The new president's ambitious plan to scale back individual tax rates by 30 percent over three years and to speed up depreciation write-offs for businesses would cut revenue growth from 17.2 percent to 8.3 percent.

Because military spending would jump under Reagan's economic program, the broad budget cuts he proposed would slash the government's role in hundreds of programs established during the past two decades of social reform.

Entitlements: The Uncontrollable Problem

Discussions of deficit reduction during 1981-84 often focused on entitlement programs, which accounted for nearly half of all federal spending when President Reagan took office in 1981.

Federal programs are entitlements if they provide benefits for which the recipients have a legally enforceable right. They include programs as diverse as Social Security, public assistance and farm price supports.

Each entitlement is a benefit some past Congress deemed so important that it bound the federal government to pay it, with the threat of judicial action if necessary to force Uncle Sam to write the check. Entitlements are not totally uncontrollable; Congress can change the basic laws that set them up. However, such changes generally entail a long and politically difficult process.

Some programs, while not technically entitlements, are considered as such because benefits are provided as if required by law. One example is food stamps, for which Congress always has appropriated enough money to cover all benefits to eligible recipients.

Rapid Growth

Following several decades of rapid growth — in the number of programs, the number of recipients and costs — entitlements in fiscal 1971 displaced defense as the major obligation of federal taxpayers. Spending for entitlements grew from $33.7 billion in fiscal 1963 to $400.3 billion in fiscal 1983, according to a Congressional Budget Office (CBO) study. Payments expanded from 5.8 percent of the gross national product (GNP) to 12.4 percent of GNP over the 20-year period, before dropping back to $395.6 billion, or 11 percent of GNP, in fiscal 1984.

The bulk of federal entitlement payments went to the middle class, which vigorously resisted attempts to curtail them. Most entitlement benefits, ranging from Social Security to farm price supports, were paid regardless of beneficiaries' incomes. But some programs, such as Medicaid and food stamps, imposed income limits — known as "means tests" — on eligibility.

Inflation Adjustments

The rapid growth in entitlement spending stemmed in large part from Congress' efforts to protect recipients against inflation. Starting in the early 1960s, Congress began authorizing automatic increases in benefits by "indexing" — gearing benefit payments under many programs to the Consumer Price Index (CPI). By 1980 benefits that rose automatically with the inflation rate — known as cost-of-living adjustments, or COLAs — accounted for 30 percent of total federal outlays.

One of the biggest ongoing battles in the 1981-84 deficit reduction campaign involved efforts to limit COLAs, especially for Social Security beneficiaries. While lawmakers did agree to delay Social Security COLAs, as part of a bipartisan 1983 plan to ensure the solvency of the giant pension system, they shied away from further action that might alienate 36 million elderly voters. The political sensitivity of the issue was highlighted during the 1984 election campaign when President Reagan demanded and Congress approved legislation to guarantee Social Security recipients a COLA on Jan. 1, 1985, even if the inflation rate fell below a threshold level established in 1983. *(Social Security, p. 659)*

"While recognizing the need for bold action," Reagan said, "we have ensured that the impact of spending reductions will be shared widely and fairly.... Also, we have, as pledged, maintained this society's basic social safety net, protecting programs for the elderly and others who rely on government for their very existence."

Reagan said enactment of his economic plan would permit him to balance the budget in fiscal 1984.

Fiscal 1982 Budget Targets

Congress May 21 approved a fiscal 1982 target budget drawn to President Reagan's blueprint — a plan that called for deep cuts in social programs, increased defense spending and a three-year individual tax cut.

Endorsing the most sweeping redirection of federal programs in a generation, the resolution (H Con Res 115) recommended $695.45 billion in outlays, $657.8 billion in revenues and a $37.65 billion deficit for fiscal 1982. It forecast a budget surplus of $1.5 billion in fiscal 1984.

The measure proposed $770.9 billion in new spending authority, including $226.3 billion for defense, not all of which would be spent in fiscal 1982. Actual defense spending for the year was set at $188.8 billion.

In calling for a $51.3 billion reduction in fiscal 1982 revenues, H Con Res 115 assumed enactment of the full $53.9 billion tax cut sought by Reagan, partially offset by $2.6 billion in additional user fees. *(Reagan budget, p. 37; tax cut, p. 65)*

To meet the budget targets, the measure included reconciliation instructions requiring Senate and House committees to alter existing programs to achieve about $36 billion in fiscal 1982 spending cuts. *(Reconciliation, p. 40; second budget resolution, p. 44)*

"The blueprint contained in this resolution is ... unequivocal," said Senate Budget Committee Chairman Pete V. Domenici, R-N.M. "It responds directly to the mandate

of the American people and the requests of our president."

The Senate, with its new Republican majority, moved swiftly to approve the president's requests. Even before taking up its fiscal 1982 budget resolution, the Senate Budget Committee drafted — and the Senate approved — a measure (S Con Res 9) ordering $36.9 billion in spending cuts sought by Reagan.

The House went along with the president's plan only after a momentous floor battle that overturned an alternative Democratic budget strategy. A coalition of Republicans and conservative Democrats frustrated efforts of Democratic leaders to modify the Reagan budget priorities.

Committee Action

House. House Democratic leaders drew up their own budget plan that scaled back both Reagan's spending cuts and his companion proposal for three-year tax reductions. Assuming a leadership role for the first time was newly elected Budget Committee Chairman James R. Jones, D-Okla. With the votes of conservative Southern Democrats, Jones earlier in the year had defeated liberal Rep. David R. Obey, D-Wis., for the post.

As reported by the Budget Committee April 16, H Con Res 115 (H Rept 97-23) called for $714.55 billion in spending and $688.95 billion in revenues in fiscal 1982, with a resulting $25.6 billion deficit. The committee approved the measure by a 17-13 vote April 9.

Reconciliation instructions included in the Democratic budget required House and Senate committees to recommend program changes that would save $15.8 billion in fiscal 1982 and $61.3 billion over fiscal 1982-84.

Approval of the stringent 1982 budget represented a major rightward shift by the majority party in the House. The Democrats did alter many of Reagan's spending proposals. They disagreed with him on the size of his tax reduction, providing for only a one-year, $38 billion tax cut — almost $16 billion under Reagan's request. But they acceded to his request for an overall cutback in government spending and accepted to the letter a majority of the budget cuts drafted by the Office of Management and Budget (OMB) under the leadership of Reagan's budget director, former Rep. David A. Stockman, R-Mich. (1977-81).

Stockman nonetheless decried the committee plan as "unacceptable" to the White House. Jones had hoped to win bipartisan support for the budget, but the administration instructed Republicans not to compromise.

Consistently voting against his fellow Democrats was Phil Gramm, D-Texas. The conservative Gramm, working closely with the Reagan administration, offered a substitute that would have cut deeper into spending in order to lower the $25.6 billion deficit in the committee plan. Gramm, whose role was sharply criticized by his fellow Democrats, switched parties and won re-election as a Republican in 1983.

The Gramm substitute, which was cosponsored by Delbert L. Latta, R-Ohio, ranking minority member on the panel, failed 13-17. Latta's bid to replace the Democratic budget with Reagan's numbers was defeated on a similar vote.

Senate. The Senate Budget Committee April 28 approved a Reagan-backed fiscal 1982 budget resolution (S Con Res 19 — S Rept 97-49) that showed a balanced budget in 1984.

By making mostly cosmetic changes and assuming deeper, unspecified spending cuts, the Republican majority

wooed back three GOP conservatives who had voted against an earlier version because of its continuing high deficits. The Republicans also won three Southern Democrats, sealing their 15-6 victory.

The committee-approved changes trimmed the fiscal 1982 deficit from the committee's original $53.8 billion to $48.8 billion. In fiscal 1983 the deficit would drop to $21.4 billion from the earlier version's $52.3 billion. In fiscal 1984 the budget would be balanced instead of showing a $44.7 billion deficit.

Total fiscal 1982 spending under the Senate resolution, which generally reflected administration requests, was set at $699.1 billion. Revenues totaled $650.3 billion, allowing for a $51.3 billion cut.

The committee April 9 had scuttled the initial version of the resolution by an 8-12 vote. On that vote conservative GOP Sens. William L. Armstrong, Colo., Charles E. Grassley, Iowa, and Steven D. Symms, Idaho, abandoned their Republican colleagues because they believed the resolution's deficits for fiscal 1981-84 broke faith with Republican pledges to balance the budget.

Unlike its House counterpart, S Con Res 19 did not include reconciliation instructions. S Con Res 9, a separate measure requiring $36.9 billion in fiscal 1982 spending cuts, had been adopted April 2 by a **key 88-10 vote (R 51-1; D 37-9)**. In reporting S Con Res 9 (S Rept 97-28) March 23, the Budget Committee had virtually rubber-stamped Reagan's savings proposals. *(1981 key votes, p. 879)*

Floor Action

House. In a stunning victory for the president, the House May 7 overturned the Democratic plan reported by the Budget Committee, replacing it with a Reagan-backed proposal sponsored by Gramm and Latta. Sixty-three Democrats joined all of the House Republicans to substitute the Reagan budget plan on a **key vote of 253-176 (R 190-0; D 63-176)**. The House went on to pass the resolution 270-154.

As passed, the Gramm-Latta measure called for $688.8 billion in outlays, $657.8 billion in revenues and a $31 billion deficit in fiscal 1982. The Gramm-Latta plan ordered House authorizing panels to make $36.6 billion worth of reconciliation cuts in fiscal 1982. The Democratic plan had called for only $15.8 billion in authorization savings.

Senate. After four days of debate, the Senate May 12 approved a $700.8 billion fiscal 1982 budget resolution.

Only two Senate Republicans — Lowell P. Weicker Jr., Conn., and Gordon J. Humphrey, N.H. — opposed the Reagan-backed budget on the 78-20 vote.

Democrats tried in vain to restore money to S Con Res 19 for education, job training and veterans' programs, and to trim the size of the anticipated three-year tax cut.

The Senate agreed to only one amendment, easing committee-approved delays in cost-of living adjustments (COLAs) for federal civilian and military retirees. That boosted outlays and the deficit by $1.7 billion.

Conference

By the time the conferees met to work out the differences between the Senate- and House-passed versions of the fiscal 1982 spending plan, many Democrats seemed resigned to their defeat.

"I don't think it is any secret," said Rep. Leon E. Panetta, D-Calif., head of the House reconciliation task

force, "that what we're embarking upon is a gamble. We're testing a theory on the American people. I don't think it's going to work — but it's a theory Congress wants to test."

The disagreements between the House and Senate versions were fairly narrow. Close to $8 billion of the difference between the Senate's $700.8 billion spending figure and the House's $688.8 billion resulted from differences in economic assumptions — chiefly differences in assumptions about interest rate levels for the year. Conferees forecast a 10.5 percent interest rate, which the Democrats said was overly optimistic.

The Senate accepted the House measure's more optimistic growth rates for the remainder of fiscal 1981 and fiscal 1982, as well as the House's higher revenue figures. Both helped lower the anticipated deficit.

In actual spending areas, the most touchy issue involved Social Security cuts. The Senate had agreed to cut nearly $6 billion from Social Security spending by changing the formula for calculating COLAs and delaying the benefit increase three months in fiscal 1982. Several attempts to delete the provision failed.

But in the uproar that greeted Social Security cuts proposed by the administration May 12, conferees agreed to drop the savings assumed by the Senate's COLA changes. That still left Senate outlays for income security programs, including Social Security, $3 billion below the House figure. Conferees agreed to split the difference. (Social Security, p. 645)

With little debate, the House approved the conference report on the resolution (H Rept 97-46) May 20 by a 244-155 vote. The Senate completed the first round of budget action the next day when it approved the measure 76-20.

Fiscal 1981 Revisions

As part of its first budget resolution for fiscal 1982 (H Con Res 115), cleared May 21, Congress revised previously established binding budget levels for the fiscal year ending Sept. 30, 1981. The revised measure reflected changes in economic forecasts and spending estimates, as well as actual and anticipated congressional action. Major increases were provided to cover rising interest costs and additional defense funding sought by President Reagan.

The resolution boosted the fiscal 1981 spending limit to $661.35 billion, a $28.9 billion increase, and cut revenues to $603.3 billion, a $1.7 billion decrease, for a resulting deficit of $58.05 billion.

A year earlier, in its first fiscal 1981 budget resolution, Congress had forecast a small surplus for the year. That forecast was replaced by a $27.4 billion deficit projection in the second fiscal 1981 budget resolution approved in November 1980.

The actual deficit for the fiscal year wound up at $57.9 billion. (Previous action, Congress and the Nation Vol. V, p. 227; budget totals compared, box, p. 36)

Reconciliation Cuts

Congress July 31 approved a sweeping package of reconciliation budget cuts (HR 3982 — PL 97-35) that sharply curtailed the scope and shape of many government programs.

Final action on what House Budget Committee Chairman James R. Jones, D-Okla., called "clearly the most

Reconciliation Stories

For a detailed accounting of major provisions of the Omnibus Reconciliation Act of 1981 (PL 97-35), see stories on the following pages:

Agriculture
Farm credit............................. 494
Commerce and Communications
Consumer Cooperative Bank.............. 268
Consumer Product Safety Board.......... 267
Public broadcasting...................... 264
Radio-TV licenses 263
Small-business loans..................... 265
Defense
Strategic materials stockpile.............. 216
Economic Policy/Fiscal Assistance
Economic Development Administration.... 115
Energy
Power plant conversion 383
Research and development 393
Strategic Petroleum Reserve.............. 379
Environment
Barriers islands development 467
National park expansion 463
Payments in lieu of taxes 469
Foreign Policy
International development banks.......... 131
General Government
Arts funds.............................. 776
Block grant transition................... 773
Federal employees' pay, COLAs........... 774
Postal reductions........................ 775
Health, Education and Welfare
AFDC benefits 586
Anti-poverty programs 590
College student aid...................... 557
Elementary, secondary aid................ 559
Food stamps 583
Health funding, block grants 523
Health maintenance organizations........ 532
Health manpower 530
Health planning......................... 531
Medicaid, Medicare..................... 527
Public Health Service.................... 531
School meal subsidies.................... 591
Social services, emergency assistance 588
Veterans' benefits 616
Housing and Urban Aid
Housing authorization 631
Labor and Pension Policy
Public service jobs....................... 648
Railroad retirement...................... 648
Social Security cuts...................... 645
Trade adjustment assistance.............. 650
Unemployment compensation............. 647
Transportation
Airport aid 298
Amtrak................................. 295
Conrail................................. 291
Maritime subsidies 299
Mass transit 299

monumental and historic turnaround in fiscal policy that has ever occurred" came just two days after both the House and Senate approved the other major element of President Reagan's economic recovery program, a three-year tax relief package. *(Tax cuts, p. 65)*

As signed into law Aug. 13, the Omnibus Reconciliation Act of 1981 revised existing federal programs to slash nearly $35.2 billion from the $740 billion spending level projected by the Congressional Budget Office (CBO) for fiscal 1982.

Included in the bill's 27 titles were provisions to tighten income eligibility for food stamps and public assistance, eliminate minimum Social Security benefits, cut funds requested for subsidized housing programs, reduce school lunch subsidies, institute a "needs test" for guaranteed student loans, cut federal Medicaid payments to the states and consolidate various health and education programs into block grants.

Other provisions of the bill terminated public service employment programs, limited pay raises for federal workers, increased interest rates in lending programs for farmers and small businesses, set conditions for sale of the Conrail freight system, provided longer terms for radio and TV licenses, reauthorized the Consumer Product Safety Commission, and made a multitude of other charges in existing law. *(Index to stories, box, p. 40)*

By making program cuts in advance of the appropriations process, the bill preordained the actions of the Appropriations committees in drafting fiscal 1982 funding bills.

The Republican Senate gave easy approval to the sweeping reconciliation measure, which was mandated by the first fiscal 1982 budget resolution. The House passed the bill only after a coalition of Republicans and conservative Southern Democrats overturned a version drafted by Democratic leaders.

Swift Enactment

Enactment of HR 3982 ended a remarkably swift journey that began in late February, when Reagan and Republican leaders in Congress announced they wanted to use reconciliation as the tool to cut expected spending by $48.6 billion in fiscal 1982 and close to $200 billion through the end of fiscal 1984.

The idea of using reconciliation to carry through Reagan's pledge to trim federal spending had been advanced by David A. Stockman, director of the Office of Management and Budget (OMB). Stockman, a former House member (R-Mich., 1977-81), was responsible for a highly publicized "black book" that formed the basis for the administration's sweeping budget cut proposals.

Reconciliation had been used only once before — in 1980. But the 1980 reconciliation bill was far more modest in scale and limited in purpose than Reagan's assault on federal spending, which included widespread and permanent changes in numerous program authorizations.

In 1981, as in 1980, reconciliation became a part of the budget process in conjunction with the first annual budget resolution, instead of the second resolution as envisioned in the 1974 Congressional Budget Act (PL 93-344). *(Background, box, p. 34)*

The final version of the bill provided an estimated $130.6 billion in reconciliation savings for fiscal 1982-84, a total that fell somewhat short of the instructions given House and Senate authorizing committees by the first budget resolution in May. *(Resolution, p. 38)*

Institutional Impact

For members deeply involved in the budget process the swift enactment of massive budget cuts was such a noteworthy achievement that they played down the importance of the severely truncated legislative process used to consider the bill. Others, however, expressed concern that Congress was abandoning its responsibilities and abdicating its powers to the executive branch.

"This is the most excessive use of presidential power and license," said House Rules Committee Chairman Richard Bolling, D-Mo. "And reconciliation is the most brutal and blunt instrument used by a president in an attempt to control the congressional process since [President Richard M.] Nixon used impoundment." *(Background, Congress and the Nation Vol. IV, p. 60)*

Within Congress, reconciliation greatly enhanced the power of the Budget committees, especially in the Senate where the Budget panel played a large role in shaping the reconciliation package and shepherding it through Congress. Reconciliation circumscribed the powers of authorizing and appropriating committees, by forcing them to meet stringent budget requirements they had had little role in developing.

Reconciliation Instructions

The budget resolution's reconciliation instructions required 14 Senate and 15 House authorizing committees to cut or alter existing programs to meet the $36 billion savings requirement for fiscal 1982. The instructions applied to both authorizations and direct spending — that is, spending to which the government was committed whether or not the appropriations were provided in advance. Direct spending embraced entitlement payments, such as Social Security benefits and veterans' compensation, and interest on the public debt, as well as contract authority and authority to incur indebtedness. *(Entitlements, box, p. 38)*

Although the reconciliation instructions required legislative committees to achieve specific savings objectives, the program reductions on which the savings were based were not binding — legislative committees retained the right to make the cuts in other programs if they chose. In fact, however, some committees had little discretion, given the magnitude of their spending reductions.

The panels were required to report their savings measures to the Budget committees by June 12. The Budget committees then were to consolidate the various measures into omnibus bills for House and Senate floor consideration.

The reconciliation bills fell under special rules that limited floor debate to 20 hours.

Cuts were calculated from a baseline figure established by the Congressional Budget Office that reflected anticipated fiscal 1982 spending adjusted for inflation.

Committee Action

Senate. The Republican-controlled Senate Budget Committee met June 16 and routinely packaged the $39.6 billion in reconciliation cuts recommended by Senate authorizing committees. Its bill was reported the next day (S 1377 — S Rept 97-139).

The chief concern over the Senate bill was the inclusion of "extraneous" legislation that had no budgetary impact. Committees had buried within their reconciliation recommendations a wide variety of unrelated legislation.

Debt Ceiling Almost Doubles During 1981-84 ...

Congress nearly doubled the public debt ceiling during President Reagan's first term, increasing the government's borrowing authority from $935.1 billion when Reagan took office in 1981 to $1.824 trillion by the time of his re-election in 1984.

Throughout the four-year period debt limit hikes were linked to efforts to control federal spending. For years conservative Republicans had used debt limit bills as vehicles to attack "fiscal irresponsibility." Democrats delighted in turning the tables once Reagan took office, putting responsibility for passage of the administration's debt limit requests on their GOP colleagues. But most members on both sides of the aisle recognized that they had no practical alternative. "To vote against a debt ceiling after we have voted for spending is a sham," said Rep. Bill Frenzel, R-Minn.

Nonetheless, a vote to increase the ceiling had been used over the years by conservatives to campaign against more liberal opponents. House defeat of many debt bills led in 1979 to adoption of a new procedure that permitted the House to approve debt ceiling increases as part of the congressional budget resolutions, without voting on separate bills. *(Background, Congress and the Nation Vol. V, p. 226)*

To ease the pressure on debt limit hikes, Congress in 1983 eliminated an existing distinction between "permanent" and "temporary" debt ceilings. Previously the debt ceiling dropped to a permanent level of $400 billion barring periodic action by Congress. Any increases above that level were considered temporary. But since the government would be unable to function at such a low level, the ceiling always had to be raised, and urgent debt bills routinely became targets for controversial amendments.

1981: To $1.08 Trillion

Congress enacted debt ceiling increases twice during 1981, ultimately boosting the temporary ceil-

ing above the trillion-dollar mark for the first time. Had Congress failed to act, the debt limit would have fallen to its permanent $400 billion level, leaving the government unable to meet its borrowing needs.

The first bill (HR 1553 — PL 97-2), cleared Feb. 6, boosted the ceiling from $935.1 billion to $985 billion through Sept. 30, 1981. The increase was requested by President Reagan as one of his first official acts and sailed through Congress under regular procedures with unaccustomed Republican support. The House passed the bill (H Rept 97-1) by a **key vote of 305-104 (R 150-36; D 155-68)**; Senate passage came on a **73-18 key vote (R 46-3; D 27-15)**. Republicans who had voted against previous debt limit bills voted for the increase, claiming it was leftover business from the Carter administration. *(1981 key votes, p. 879)*

The second measure (H J Res 265 — PL 97-49), cleared Sept. 29, provided a further increase to $1,079,800,000,000 through Sept. 30, 1982. In considering that increase, Congress used the shortcut procedures established in 1979: Upon approval of the first fiscal 1982 budget resolution (H Con Res 115), the debt limit level in that measure was incorporated in H J Res 265 and sent to the Senate without a separate House vote. The Senate passed the bill without change Sept. 29. Action came on a 64-34 vote following an all-night filibuster by William Proxmire, D-Wis., who sought to hold the debt ceiling below $1 trillion. Proxmire's speech, running 16 hours and 12 minutes, was the fourth longest in Senate history. *(Longest speeches, Guide to Congress Third Edition, p. 92)*

1982: To $1.29 Trillion

Congress approved two debt limit increases in 1982, ultimately boosting the temporary limit to $1.29 trillion through Sept. 30, 1983.

In approving the final version of the fiscal 1983

House. The House Budget Committee reported its reconciliation bill (HR 3982 — H Rept 97-158) June 19, providing fiscal 1982 spending cuts totaling $37.76 billion.

By law the Budget committees had no authority to touch the reconciliation cuts made by the authorizing committees. The Energy and Commerce Committee had deadlocked over reconciliation, however, so the Budget panel included in its package the recommendations of the Energy Committee's Democratic majority.

Another crisis had been averted when Education and Labor Committee Democrats pushed through a proposal that basically met their $12.1 billion reconciliation goal. "We are meeting with a gun pointed at our heads," protested Chairman Carl D. Perkins, D-Ky. "The majority of

this committee does not want to make these drastic cutbacks."

The administration and House GOP leaders complained that the Democratic package did not make deep enough cuts in entitlements and did not go far enough in folding separate social programs into block grants.

Republicans and some conservative Democrats therefore decided to push an alternative package on the House floor. Backers said the Republican/conservative Democratic alternative — known as "Gramm-Latta II" for the sponsors of the House-passed fiscal 1982 budget resolution — would save an additional $5.1 billion in major programs in fiscal 1982, $20 billion by fiscal 1984. But it also would restore money for some popular programs.

... Nears $2 Trillion As Reagan Ends First Term

budget resolution (S Con Res 92), the House June 22 automatically approved an increase in the debt limit to $1.14 trillion through the remainder of fiscal 1982, and to $1.29 trillion through fiscal 1983. Those increases were packaged in separate House joint resolutions and sent directly to the Senate.

The Senate June 23 approved the fiscal 1982 increase (H J Res 519 — PL 97-204), thereby clearing the short-term measure for the president's signature.

A week before the fiscal 1982 ceiling was set to expire, the Senate Sept. 23 completed action on the fiscal 1983 measure (H J Res 520 — PL 97-270) — finally unencumbered by extraneous amendments and debate over social issues that had burdened the legislation for five weeks. The bill had been on the Senate floor since Aug. 16.

1983: To $1.49 Trillion

Two debt limit increases in 1983 brought the ceiling to $1.49 trillion, an amount expected to meet the Treasury's borrowing needs until April 1984.

The initial increase (HR 2990 — PL 98-34) raised the debt ceiling to $1.389 trillion. The new ceiling had no statutory cutoff date because the bill eliminated the existing distinction between temporary and permanent ceilings.

The measure was passed by the House (H Rept 98-121) May 18, on a surprise voice vote in a nearly empty chamber, and cleared by the Senate on a 51-41 vote May 25. House leaders had warned against any Senate changes that would force further action on the bill, saying House approval was unlikely the second time around.

The second increase (H J Res 308 — PL 98-161) became embroiled in Senate maneuvering over deficit reduction measures and cleared only hours before Congress adjourned Nov. 18. It was enacted after the Senate first trimmed and then rejected by a **39-56 key vote (R 28-25; D 11-31)** a $1.6 trillion

House-passed version, drawn from the budget resolution, to which it had attached various non-germane amendments. Upon reconsideration, the Senate passed its $1.45 trillion version on a 58-40 vote Nov. 16. Senate-House conferees (H Rept 98-566) stripped the bill of all Senate amendments and settled on a $1.49 trillion debt ceiling. *(1983 key votes, p. 911)*

1984: To $1.82 Trillion

In three rounds of action to keep pace with Treasury borrowing needs, Congress in 1984 increased the debt ceiling to $1.824 trillion.

The first bill (HR 5692 — PL 98-302), cleared May 24, raised the ceiling to $1.52 trillion. The House passed the bill on a 211-198 vote May 24, two days after rejecting a previous version (HR 5665 — H Rept 98-785) 150-262. The Senate passed the bill by voice vote later in the day, after deleting a House-approved June 22 expiration date for the increase. The House accepted the Senate change.

A month later House Democrats tried unsuccessfully to force action on the military budget by refusing to raise the debt ceiling a second time. After defeating two debt limit bills June 28, enough Democrats backed off to allow passage June 29 of a measure (HR 5953 — H Rept 98-878) raising the ceiling to $1.573 trillion. Following the 208-202 House vote, the Senate cleared the bill (PL 98-342) by voice vote later in the day.

The third bill (H J Res 654 — PL 98-475), boosting the ceiling to $1.824 trillion, was approved Oct. 12, clearing the way for the 98th Congress to adjourn. Final action came when the Senate reconsidered and by a 37-30 vote passed the measure it had rejected just 14 hours earlier.

Some senators already had left Washington and had to be flown back to ensure final passage. The House had approved the increase as part of the fiscal 1985 budget resolution.

Floor Action

Senate. The Senate approved its version of the reconciliation measure June 25 by an 80-15 vote.

While the Senate made some minor revisions in its $39.6 billion reconciliation package, the significant elements remained the same as those drafted by the Senate authorizing committees and put together by the Budget Committee. Final fiscal 1982 savings tally: $38.1 billion.

Before passing the omnibus spending cut package, the Senate agreed to delete many of its extraneous provisions — those having no budgetary impact. But then, on separate votes, members put some of them back.

House. In a replay of their earlier triumph on the budget resolution, a coalition of Republicans and conserva-

tive Democrats overturned the Budget Committee's reconciliation package on the House floor June 26. The House adopted the Reagan-backed Gramm-Latta II alternative by a **key vote of 217-211 (R 188-2; D 29-209)**. *(1981 key votes, p. 879)*

The House then passed the bill, providing $37.3 billion in fiscal 1982 savings, on a 232-193 vote. The Reagan victory followed two days of often acrimonious debate and intense lobbying by the president.

The outcome had been foreshadowed June 25 when Republicans, with the help of 29 dissident Democrats, won adoption of a rule governing floor debate that permitted a single up-or-down vote on their alternative budget package. Democrats had sought to force separate votes on pain-

ful spending cuts supported by the administration.

Republicans decided not to challenge the Democratic Energy and Commerce Committee provisions, which remained in the bill by default.

Most of the details of the Gramm-Latta proposal were not available until hours before the House vote, a circumstance decried by members of both parties.

Leon E. Panetta, D-Calif., protested that "we are dealing with over 250 programs with no committee consideration, no hearings, no debate and no opportunity to offer amendments."

"This has been a terrible way to legislate, but we have no alternatives," lamented Barber B. Conable Jr., R-N.Y.

Conference Action

More than 250 members of Congress participated in the conference, which split up into 58 subgroups to consider various sections of the legislation. The Senate had cleared the way for a conference July 13, when it passed HR 3982 after substituting its provisions for those of the House-passed bill.

Conferees faced a number of difficult issues, even though the House-passed Gramm-Latta II was a nearly complete reflection of the Reagan administration's budget-cutting program and the Senate bill contained only minor differences from the Reagan plan. Conferees finally filed their report (H Rept 97-208) July 29.

Reagan lost more than he gained in conference. Deeper cuts than he sought were made in the food stamp program and several other areas. But conferees refused to place a "cap" on federal contributions to the states for Medicaid and declined to create some of the block grants Reagan wanted. In addition, funding was continued for several programs — such as the Economic Development Administration and the non-highway programs of the Appalachian Regional Commission — that Reagan wanted to eliminate.

The House approved the conference report by voice vote July 31, with the Senate concurring by a vote of 80-14 a few hours later.

For one frenetic day the fate of the bill had been jeopardized as Democrats staged a last-ditch effort to restore a minimum Social Security benefit that had been eliminated in the conference agreement. The issue was resolved by allowing two separate House votes — one on the reconciliation conference report and one on a bill to reinstate the minimum benefit. Legislation to restore the minimum benefit cleared Congress Dec. 16. *(Minimum benefit, p. 645)*

Binding 1982 Budget Levels

Congress Dec. 10 adopted what members acknowledged was a meaningless second budget resolution for fiscal 1982 (S Con Res 50). The measure simply reaffirmed the first resolution, adopted in May, which called for a $37.65 billion deficit for fiscal 1982 and predicted a slight surplus by 1984. By December those figures were totally out of line with current, more pessimistic projections. In 1982 Congress raised the fiscal 1982 deficit forecast to $105.7 billion. *(First resolution, p. 38; revisions, p. 48)*

The Senate, which in the past had approved budget resolutions by wide margins, narrowly adopted S Con Res 50 by a largely party-line vote of 49-48. The House approved it 206-200. By law Congress was required to adopt a

second budget resolution before adjourning for the year.

The final version of the resolution included Senate language calling for cuts in all programs and tax increases to achieve a balanced budget in fiscal 1984. It also urged President Reagan to submit "as soon as possible" his own plan for balancing the budget.

By the time Congress took up the second resolution, the Reagan administration had retreated from its pledge to balance the budget in 1984. And it had blocked attempts to cut too deeply into defense or some entitlements, especially Social Security, or to raise taxes.

However, Reagan had shifted some of the blame for budgetary problems to Congress, which resisted the further budget cuts he requested in September. The resolution was, in part, congressional self-defense.

Reagan Second-Round Cuts

Within weeks after enactment of its budget reconciliation bill (HR 3982 — PL 97-35), which chopped $35.2 billion from the fiscal 1982 deficit, and its massive tax cut legislation (HR 4242 — PL 97-34), which reduced revenues by $37.7 billion, the administration was forced to acknowledge that the Reagan economic program was not delivering on its promises. *(Reconciliation bill, p. 40; tax cuts, p. 65)*

Approval of the program had seriously shaken the financial markets, which feared runaway federal deficits that would perpetuate inflation and high interest rates. As deficit expectations mounted, the stock market plunged.

Responding to the crisis on Wall Street, the administration decided to seek a new round of deficit reduction measures. "The president is determined to show them [investors] that he can balance the budget," said White House Director of Communications David Gergen.

Accordingly, Reagan asked Congress Sept. 24 to save $13 billion by paring fiscal 1982 appropriations measures and making changes in non-discretionary entitlement programs such as Medicaid. He also called for $3 billion in new taxes, euphemistically described as "revenue enhancements."

Congressional response was negative, especially among Republicans. GOP members of the Senate Appropriations Committee said they could not cut more than $5 billion from fiscal 1982 appropriations. And House Republicans said they would not attempt to raise taxes — not with an election approaching and not in a recession. Reagan ultimately agreed to settle for $4 billion in cuts and to postpone his entitlement and tax proposals. *(Appropriations, p. 45)*

Committee Action

House. The House Budget Committee — its members irritated by lack of direction from the White House on specific budget cuts — agreed by voice vote Nov. 12 to adopt a second fiscal 1982 budget resolution that was simply a carbon copy of the first resolution Congress had approved in May. That measure (H Con Res 115) called for deficits of $37.65 billion in fiscal 1982 and $19.05 billion in fiscal 1983, with a $1.05 billion surplus in fiscal 1984.

The proposal to extend the first resolution was offered by ranking minority member Delbert L. Latta, R-Ohio.

The Budget Committee did not formally report the second resolution until Dec. 8 (H Con Res 230 — H Rept 97-369).

Senate. Calling it a "sham," a "travesty" and the

"height of irresponsibility," the Senate Budget Committee grudgingly followed its House counterpart and voted out a second resolution (S Con Res 50 — S Rept 97-279) that merely reaffirmed the first.

Conceding that its figures were too optimistic, the committee ordered the measure reported without recommendation Nov. 19. The vote was 13-7.

Office of Management and Budget (OMB) figures showed that without the Sept. 24 budget reductions called for by President Reagan, outlays for fiscal 1982 would reach $722.3 billion, revenues $663.2 billion and the deficit $59.1 billion.

The Budget Committee included in S Con Res 50 "sense of Congress" language noting that "large deficits in the range of $76-$92 billion in fiscal 1982, $95-$136 billion in fiscal 1983 and $103-$165 billion in fiscal 1984" would occur if no further action was taken. It called upon the president to "submit a plan as soon as possible" to lower interest rates, decrease unemployment, reduce inflation and balance the budget by 1984.

Floor Action

Senate. Before passing S Con Res 50 by a 49-48 vote Dec. 9, the Senate added language calling for a revised resolution in March 1982 that would achieve a balanced budget in fiscal 1984 by cutting all programs, including defense and entitlement programs, and by increasing taxes. It excluded from such increases the individual income tax cuts and business depreciation measures in the 1981 tax law (PL 97-34).

The non-binding amendment, which also called for the 1984 outlays to equal no more than 20.5 percent of the gross national product, was offered by Budget Chairman Pete V. Domenici, R-N.M., and adopted by a largely party-line vote of 50-47.

For Senate Republicans, the Dec. 8-9 debate on S Con Res 50 coincided with some embarrassing developments:

● New OMB estimates showed a combined $423 billion deficit for fiscal 1982-84 — about $242 billion higher than its September projections.

● Members of President Reagan's Council of Economic Advisers (CEA) told an American Enterprise Institute gathering Dec. 8 that such large deficits were not necessarily a problem.

"In general, concern about the deficit has been misplaced," CEA member William A. Niskanen was quoted as saying. He added there was no direct evidence that deficits caused inflation or high interest rates.

Even though White House spokesmen later denied that the remarks reflected administration policy, stunned Senate Republicans took the occasion of debate on the budget resolution to denounce the CEA comments as "incredible," "disheartening" and "foolish."

The Republicans already had been disconcerted by publication of a magazine article that quoted OMB Director David A. Stockman as saying the main objective of the administration's supply-side economic plan was to cut tax rates for top income brackets. Stockman also observed that "none of us really understands what's going on with these numbers." Stockman offered his resignation Nov. 12, but President Reagan asked the OMB director to remain on his "team."

House. As in the Senate, House members had clear disclaimers for the resolution, which they took up Dec. 10.

"There should be no confusion that this will get us

through the year," said Budget Committee Chairman James R. Jones, D-Okla. "But this is the only thing upon which we can reach agreement."

The Senate measure was substituted for the House committee version by unanimous consent as soon as floor debate began. The resolution itself was adopted 206-200.

Fiscal 1982 Appropriations

The coalition that supported President Reagan's initial budget offensive deserted the president when he called Sept. 24 for a second round of spending cuts as part of a $16 billion deficit reduction plan. *(Reagan proposals, above; social program cuts, p. 589)*

The spending cut controversy stalled action on fiscal 1982 appropriations bills, and most of the government was funded under short-term continuing appropriations resolutions during the early weeks of the fiscal year.

Negotiations between the White House and congressional Republicans finally cleared the way for approval Dec. 11 of a catchall funding measure (H J Res 370 — PL 97-92). H J Res 370 met Reagan's minimum demand for $4 billion in savings, largely through a 4 percent across-the-board cut in most domestic programs.

On Nov. 23 Reagan had vetoed an earlier version (H J Res 357) providing savings estimated at less than $2 billion. In doing so, he forced a temporary shutdown in many government functions.

Agreement on the catchall measure was followed by resumption of action on long-stalled regular fiscal 1982 appropriations bills. By session's end Congress had completed action on 10 of the 13 regular bills. H J Res 370 funded programs covered by the three remaining bills through March 31, 1982. Congress in 1982 extended the funding through the remainder of the fiscal year (H J Res 409 — PL 97-161).

Congress had approved the first major component of Reagan's economic program in a supplemental fiscal 1981 appropriations bill (HR 3512 — PL 97-12), cleared June 4. The bill provided an additional $11.8 billion for defense programs, reflecting the defense buildup proposed by the new president, and rescinded $14.3 billion in previous appropriations, chiefly for social and environmental programs.

1982

With the 1982 elections at hand, Congress unequivocally rejected the $91.5 billion deficit proposed by President Reagan in his fiscal 1983 budget. But lawmakers took months to come up with an alternative budget strategy.

In the end Congress did no better than Reagan in holding down the deficit. Nonetheless, it succeeded in setting priorities in its own way. Reagan agreed to accept some modest cuts in the defense buildup he wanted. More significantly, the president was persuaded to accept $18 billion in tax increases in fiscal 1983 — $98.3 billion over the next three years.

The compromise budget plan, which forecast a $103.9 billion deficit for fiscal 1983, was incorporated in the first fiscal 1983 budget resolution cleared June 23. To hold the

deficit to that level, the resolution called for legislation to provide $20.9 billion in increased revenues and $6.57 billion in spending cuts for fiscal 1983.

The measure also included language that would automatically convert the budget targets it set into binding budget levels should Congress fail to approve a second resolution by Oct. 1, 1982, the beginning of the new fiscal year.

By Oct. 1, with unemployment at a post-World War II peak and recovery not yet in sight, the budget outlook had grown significantly worse. Under the combined pressures of the sagging economy and the impending midterm elections, Congress decided to avoid another round of difficult budget votes. Thus the first budget resolution became binding, even though its budget projections generally were regarded as unreasonably optimistic.

By the time the 97th Congress adjourned in December, officials were talking about a fiscal 1983 deficit approaching $200 billion, nearly double the level projected in the budget resolution approved six months earlier.

That sharp increase occurred even though Congress carried out the deficit reduction measures required by the budget resolution in two reconciliation bills cleared in mid-August. The bills were expected to raise $98.3 billion in additional revenues and cut anticipated spending by $30.8 billion over fiscal 1983-85.

When combined, the measures were expected to reduce projected federal deficits by about $130 billion by fiscal 1985. The budget resolution had called for $125.5 billion in deficit reductions over the three-year period.

Reagan Budget

Asking Congress to "persevere, to stay the course, to shun defeat," President Reagan Feb. 8 proposed a fiscal 1983 budget showing record deficit even with sharp new cuts in domestic programs. *(Text of message, p. 1050)*

Reagan did not propose any major tax increases, although critics charged that his 1981 tax cuts were in large part responsible for the mushrooming deficits. Nor did he take the scalpel to his proposed defense budget, $221 billion for fiscal 1983. *(Tax cuts, p. 65)*

Supporting this position in his budget message to Congress, the president said, "... Our incentive-minded tax policy and our security-based defense programs are right and necessary for long-run peace and prosperity, and must not be tampered with in a vain attempt to cure deficits in the short run."

Instead, the administration proposed a $55.9 billion "deficit reduction plan" that would cut domestic spending (including both mandatory entitlements and discretionary programs), impose user fees, revise some tax benefits and institute so-called "management initiatives."

Even if this plan were adopted in its entirety, the fiscal 1983 deficit would hit $91.5 billion, according to White House estimates. Outlays would total $757.6 billion, revenues $666.1 billion.

The White House estimated the fiscal 1984-85 deficits at $82.9 billion and $71.9 billion, respectively.

The president's plan was criticized almost universally among members of Congress. Reagan had asked Congress to make what most members considered Draconian cuts in domestic spending while sharply increasing the military budget. He made his request in the midst of a severe recession and only months before the 1982 elections.

To avert a budget stalemate, White House Chief of Staff James A. Baker III began a series of private — and ultimately unsuccessful — negotiations with congressional leaders March 25. The compromise efforts ran into two major stumbling blocks: the president's unwillingness to repeal part of the personal tax cut enacted in 1981 and the reluctance of House Speaker Thomas P. O'Neill Jr., D-Mass., to trim Social Security benefits.

The talks of the White House-congressional negotiating team — dubbed the "Gang of 17" — collapsed in a final meeting between Reagan and O'Neill in the Capitol April 28. The Senate Budget Committee began drafting a budget resolution the following day.

Fiscal 1983 Budget Resolution

Congress completed action on the first fiscal 1983 budget resolution (S Con Res 92) June 23, nearly six weeks after the statutory May 15 deadline. It had taken five frustrating months to win approval of the measure, which projected deficits above the politically critical $100 billion mark — $103.92 billion in fiscal 1983 and $105.7 billion in fiscal 1982.

Senate-House conferees were able to get the figures that low only by accepting controversial accounting practices used by House Republicans to pass their version of the resolution on the House floor June 10.

The final version of S Con Res 92 called for outlays of $769.82 billion and revenues of $665.9 billion for fiscal 1983. The resolution continued the previous year's pattern of cutting back the size of domestic programs while providing massive increases in military spending. Defense programs accounted for nearly $253.6 billion of the $822.4 billion in spending authority contemplated by the measure; defense outlays were nearly $214 billion. The resolution called for deficit reduction measures amounting to $76.8 billion in fiscal 1983 and $378.5 billion over fiscal 1983-85.

As its primary means of enforcing the budget targets, the measure relied on the reconciliation procedure that was used during 1981 to enact President Reagan's fiscal 1982 budget cuts. Under this process, the resolution included specific instructions ordering congressional committees to draft legislation making the actual spending cuts and revenue increases. *(1981 action, p. 38)*

The reconciliation instructions ordered $6.57 billion in spending cuts and $20.9 billion in revenue increases in fiscal 1983; the rest of the assumed 1983 savings were to be achieved through management savings, lower interest payments and other sources over which Congress had little control. *(Reconciliation action, p. 48)*

The resolution estimated the deficit would drop from $103.9 billion in fiscal 1983 to $60 billion by fiscal 1985. The Congressional Budget Office (CBO) calculated, however, that the measure would produce a $116.4 billion deficit in fiscal 1983, declining to $92.7 billion in fiscal 1985. Spending for fiscal 1983, according to CBO, would be $775.5 billion, instead of the $769.8 billion contained in the resolution.

Included in the resolution was a provision stipulating that the budget targets set in that measure automatically would become binding if Congress did not approve a second resolution by Oct. 1, the beginning of the fiscal year.

Although the validity of the figures in S Con Res 92 was widely questioned, the House and Senate Budget committees put off until the 98th Congress any effort to revise

or update them. Thus, the preliminary targets set in S Con Res 92 became binding limits on fiscal 1983 spending decisions. In updating those figures in 1983, Congress nearly doubled the deficit estimates. *(Fiscal 1983 revisions, p. 54)*

Senate Action

Committee. The Senate Budget Committee began markups April 29, following the collapse of White House–congressional budget negotiations. On May 6 the panel adopted, by a 12-8 party-line vote, a newly drafted fiscal plan that was embraced by Reagan.

As reported May 10, S Con Res 92 (S Rept 97-385) called for $95 billion in tax increases and $40 billion in savings in Social Security programs over fiscal 1983-85.

The Budget Committee's plan targeted outlays at $779.1 billion and revenues at $667.0 billion in fiscal 1983. That reduced the projected deficit for the fiscal year to $106.1 billion, compared with $182 billion if current policy remained unchanged.

The committee's budget figures were calculated from a baseline budget that had been accepted earlier by administration and congressional negotiators. The baseline budget was an estimate of spending and revenue under current law, plus defense spending increases proposed by Reagan.

Approval of the plan came after the committee unanimously turned down Reagan's February budget and the White House re-entered the budget negotiations to forestall any change in the third year of Reagan's 1981 tax plan. In return, the president agreed to accept cuts in Social Security. As in 1981, domestic programs bore the largest cuts. Reagan's proposed increases in defense spending escaped relatively unscathed.

The package's deficit reduction plans were intended to save $75.9 billion in fiscal 1983, $147 billion in 1984 and $193 billion in 1985.

Floor. The Senate made substantial modifications in the resolution before approving a $784.3 billion fiscal 1983 spending plan May 21 by a near party-line **key vote of 49-43 (R 46-2; D 3-41).** *(1982 key votes, p. 895)*

Acceding to pressure from moderate Republican senators and to partisan sniping from Democrats, Senate GOP leaders decided to remove the $40 billion in Social Security cuts from the committee-approved resolution. The modified resolution called for three-year tax increases of $101.2 billion, plus $6 billion in user fees.

Once the modifications were agreed to, in a closed-door Republican caucus, Senate Republicans successfully fended off most Democratic amendments — including two that were directed at eliminating the third year of the 1981 personal tax cut.

The deletion of Social Security savings plus additional funds for domestic programs increased the fiscal 1983 deficit under the modified Senate resolution from $106.1 billion to $115.4 billion. By fiscal 1985 the deficit would drop to $64.4 billion under the plan.

House Action

Committee. The House Budget Committee May 13 approved its version of the resolution (H Con Res 345 — H Rept 97-521), which envisioned a $103.85 billion deficit in fiscal 1983, dropping to $34.65 billion in fiscal 1985.

The House plan called for $147 billion in new revenues, plus $6 billion in user fees, over fiscal 1983-85. It cut

$47 billion from projected defense spending and $47 billion from discretionary domestic spending and entitlements.

Initial Floor Defeat. During a session that extended into the early hours of May 28, the House defeated seven budget alternatives before rejecting H Con Res 345 by a 159-265 vote.

In addition to rejecting all of the budget options before it, the House agreed to amendments that eliminated the only enforcement teeth in the resolution: the ability to hold back appropriations bills that exceeded the budget's spending allocation targets pending adoption of a second resolution.

Following the House defeat, Minority Leader Robert H. Michel, R-Ill., told members it was clear to him that for a budget to pass it would have to move "several degrees to the right."

Michel had cosponsored a Reagan-backed budget that was defeated 192-235. A moderate-bipartisan alternative, offered by Les Aspin, D-Wis., failed 137-289, and the committee plan, offered by Budget Chairman James R. Jones, D-Okla., was defeated 171-253. The Michel plan took a smaller bite out of defense spending increases and called for smaller revenue increases than either of the other plans.

Michel attributed defeat of the Reagan-backed plan to an amendment, offered by Mary Rose Oakar, D-Ohio, to restore Medicare funding in fiscal 1983 to current services levels while taking an equivalent amount out of defense. The Oakar amendment was added to the Reagan-backed substitute by a **228-196 key vote (R 64-125; D 164-71).** *(1982 key votes, p. 895)*

All of the three major budget alternatives included cuts in Medicare funding. But the Reagan-backed plan cut the deepest — $23.3 billion over three years, compared with $9.3 billion in the committee and moderate-bipartisan plans.

Democrats seized on the Oakar amendment as an opportunity to embarrass the Republicans on a clear-cut guns vs. butter issue. "You have a choice of choosing between our older and disabled people in the country and the price of a cost overrun of a helicopter," Oakar told her colleagues.

In earlier action, the House May 22 defeated four other alternative budgets:

● A "pay as you go" plan, offered by George Miller, D-Calif., that would have frozen all spending at existing levels was rejected 181-225. Under this plan any increase in spending would have required offsetting increases in taxes or cuts in other spending areas. *(1984 action, p. 59)*

● A liberal plan, offered by David R. Obey, D-Wis., that would have provided additional funds for various domestic programs while dramatically increasing taxes — $233 billion over the next three years — was defeated 152-268.

● A package put together by the Congressional Black Caucus was rejected 86-322. This plan also would have increased funding for domestic programs, to be offset by large increases in new taxes.

● A conservative Republican plan calling for a balanced budget in fiscal 1983 was rejected 182-242. The plan, proposed by California Reps. John H. Rousselot and William E. Dannemeyer, would have cut domestic spending by $113.9 billion in fiscal 1983.

Passage. By squeezing the deficit below $100 billion and maintaining party discipline, the Republican leadership finally won House approval of a budget June 10. The victory came on a GOP-sponsored amendment to a revised measure reported by the Budget Committee June 7 (H Con

Res 352 — H Rept 97-597).

Following the defeat of H Con Res 345 on the House floor May 28, the Budget Committee had met June 3 and agreed to report the president's February budget, to be used as a vehicle for House votes on two alternative plans, drafted by the Republicans and the Democrats. If both alternatives failed, the House would have to vote on the Reagan budget. That was a prospect the Republicans clearly did not relish, since there was virtually no support for the president's original blueprint.

The Republican victory June 10 came on a **key 220-207 vote** on what was called the Latta plan after its primary sponsor, ranking Budget Committee Republican Delbert L. Latta, Ohio. Forty-six Democrats voted with 174 Republicans in favor of the amendment, while only 15 Republicans voted against their party's plan. Twenty-five Democrats and eight Republicans who had voted against the earlier GOP budget voted for the new one. *(1982 key votes, p. 895)*

Budget Chairman Jones once again was the shepherd for a losing Democratic budget, defeated 202-225.

As passed on a 219-206 vote, the House resolution envisioned a $99.27 billion deficit, while the version approved by the Senate showed a deficit just under $116 billion.

The House resolution directed the Ways and Means Committee to come up with $20.9 billion in new revenues for fiscal 1983. And it required seven committees to draft legislation providing fiscal 1983 outlay savings of $8.1 billion.

Like the Senate resolution, the House measure called for further cuts in entitlement and discretionary domestic spending while allowing sizable increases for defense and maintaining the third year of the 1981 individual tax cuts.

The House budget called for $7.4 billion in entitlement savings in fiscal 1983, $32.6 billion over fiscal 1983-85. It cut $7.85 billion from the defense spending increase sought by Reagan for fiscal 1983, compared with $5 billion in the Senate measure. Over three years the House budget would cut $28.45 billion from his defense increase, the Senate's plan $22 billion.

Conference Action

Conferees, dominated by Republicans · from both chambers, June 17 approved a conference agreement on the resolution (H Rept 97-614) that envisioned budget deficits of $103.92 billion in fiscal 1983 and $105.7 billion in 1982.

The agreement, based on a compromise drafted behind closed doors by Senate and House Republicans and modified slightly by the full conference, called for fiscal 1983 revenues of $665.9 billion, including $20.9 billion in revenue increases, and outlays of $769.82 billion.

Democrats criticized the figures in the final resolution because Republicans had departed from budget assumptions previously agreed upon by House, Senate and White House representatives and calculated by the Congressional Budget Office. "I feel very strongly we are underestimating where the deficit is going to be," said House Budget Chairman Jones.

The conference agreement moved toward the House position in several program areas. It accepted the House provisions on the defense budget, and it cut foreign aid deeply below the Senate level, which dissenters said would cripple U.S. military aid efforts. Democrats had most success in softening the impact of the GOP compromise pro-

posal on domestic programs, although they emphasized that the final product still was unacceptable to most in their party.

As its primary means of enforcing the budget targets, the compromise resolution included reconciliation instructions ordering congressional committees to come up with $6.57 billion in spending cuts and $20.9 billion in revenue increases.

The resolution retained Senate language, also included in the House committee version and the House Republican substitute, telling the Federal Reserve to reconsider its tight money policy as deficits were reduced.

Congress completed action on the resolution June 23, when the Senate adopted the conference report by a 54-45 vote. The House had approved the report a day earlier, 210-208.

Fiscal 1982 Revisions

The fiscal 1983 budget resolution (S Con Res 92), cleared June 23, forced Congress finally to acknowledge the dimensions of the mounting deficit crisis.

In revising budget levels for the year ending Sept. 30, 1982, lawmakers boosted the fiscal 1982 spending limit to $734.1 billion and lowered revenues to $628.4 billion. The revisions, reflecting the deep recession that followed enactment of President Reagan's 1981 economic program, brought the projected deficit for fiscal 1982 to a record $105.7 billion, nearly three times the $37.65 billion forecast by the first fiscal 1982 budget resolution a year earlier. Congress had sidestepped a second round of deficit reduction measures late in 1981 and approved a second resolution that merely reaffirmed the figures in the first.

When the books finally were closed on fiscal 1982, the deficit stood at $110.6 billion, nearly $5 billion more than Congress had projected in S Con Res 92. *(1981 action, p. 38; budget totals compared, box, p. 36)*

Reconciliation Cuts

Congress completed action in August on two reconciliation bills designed to carry out the deficit reduction instructions in the first fiscal 1983 budget resolution.

● The Omnibus Reconciliation Act of 1982 (HR 6955 — PL 97-253), cleared Aug. 18, cut anticipated federal spending by $13.3 billion over fiscal 1983-85. The measure tightened spending on government pensions, farm programs, food stamps, federal home loans and veterans' benefits.

● The Tax Equity and Fiscal Responsibility Act of 1982 (HR 4961 — PL 97-248), cleared Aug. 19, aimed to provide $98.3 billion in increased revenues and cut $17.5 billion from projected spending for Medicare, Medicaid, welfare and savings bond programs over fiscal 1983-85.

When combined, the measures were expected to reduce the federal deficit by about $130 billion by fiscal 1985. The budget resolution Congress cleared June 23 (S Con Res 92) had directed Senate and House committees to come up with about $125.5 billion in deficit reductions over the three-year period.

The budget resolution assumed total deficit reductions of $378.5 billion over fiscal 1983-85, only part of which was to be achieved through reconciliation. Less than $27.5 billion of the $76.8 billion assumed for fiscal 1983 was required by the reconciliation instructions, for example. The

rest of the assumed fiscal 1983 savings were to come from a variety of sources, including nearly $28.2 billion over which Congress had almost no control: $13.7 billion in management savings and $14.5 billion in lower interest payments. *(Budget resolution, reconciliation instructions, p. 46)*

The budget cuts were measured against spending estimates for the coming year. The savings were calculated from a baseline established by the Congressional Budget Office (CBO), which projected spending for programs as they existed under current law and then adjusted the figures to take into account anticipated inflation.

Responsibility for making the spending cuts fell most heavily on the Senate Finance and House Ways and Means committees, which had jurisdiction over the bulk of federal entitlement programs. Entitlements, such as Social Security, guaranteed a certain level of benefits to everyone who met the requirements set by law. The two committees also were charged with finding $98.3 billion in new revenues over fiscal 1983-85. *(Entitlements, box, p. 38)*

Tax Reconciliation Bill

HR 4961, the Tax Equity and Fiscal Responsibility Act of 1982, cleared Congress Aug. 19 with the belated backing of the Reagan administration. Most of the measure's $98.3 billion in fiscal 1983-85 revenue increases were achieved by closing loopholes and clamping down on tax evasion. The bill's $17.5 billion spending reduction included cuts in major income support programs for the poor, as well as savings of $13.3 billion in Medicare, the health care program for the elderly, and $1.9 billion resulting from payment of variable interest rates on U.S. savings bonds. *(Details of action, tax provisions, p. 72; Medicare-Medicaid cuts, p. 532; welfare, p. 596)*

The bill had an irregular legislative history. Although the Constitution stipulates that revenue legislation must originate in the House, the Democratic-controlled Ways and Means Committee chose to sit back and let the Republican-controlled Senate sweat out a politically unpopular tax increase package on its own. As a result, the tax/spending reconciliation measure was put together in the Senate Finance Committee and then attached to HR 4961, a miscellaneous tax bill that had been passed by the House in 1981.

The Finance Committee reported the bill July 12 (S Rept 97-494), and the Senate passed it July 23 by a largely party-line **key vote of 50-47 (R 49-3; D 1-44)**. The bill met the Finance panel's spending and revenue requirements under the fiscal 1983 budget resolution. *(1982 key votes, p. 895)*

On July 28 the House agreed, on a **208-197 key vote (R 44-137; D 164-60)**, to go directly to conference on the Senate-passed bill, bypassing action by the Ways and Means Committee and House floor debate. The conference version (H Rept 97-760), which closely mirrored the Senate bill, won the endorsement of both President Reagan and House Speaker Thomas P. O'Neill Jr., D-Mass. The House approved the conference report Aug. 19, 226-207, and the Senate went on to clear the measure, 52-47.

Omnibus Reconciliation Bill

HR 6955, the omnibus 1982 reconciliation bill, was a three-year, $13.3 billion package of spending cuts drafted by other Senate and House committees.

The bill's most significant provision, with three-year

savings of $4.1 billion, limited inflation adjustments for certain federal retirees. Budget leaders claimed the move was a first step toward controlling automatic increases in federal benefits. Other major elements of the bill included cuts of $4.2 billion in dairy price supports and $1.9 billion in food stamps during the next three years.

Although the administration disputed the savings figures, officials backed the measure as a key to lower deficits, eased interest rates and economic recovery.

Senate. The Senate passed its version of the omnibus bill (S 2774 — S Rept 97-504) by a 72-24 vote Aug. 5. The measure, reported by the Budget Committee July 26, aimed to reduce projected spending by $12.6 billion over three years.

The package included reductions in agriculture, veterans' and banking programs, as well as a 4 percent cap on cost-of-living adjustments (COLAs) for federal civilian and military retirees. Savings provided by the measure amounted to $2.5 billion in fiscal 1983.

During floor debate the Senate rejected a number of amendments to retain various spending programs.

A proposal to eliminate the cap on COLAs for federal and military retirees — with the exception of members of Congress — failed on a **key 48-51 vote (R 10-44; D 38-7)**. Adoption of the amendment would have eliminated nearly half of the bill's three-year savings, $5 billion. *(1982 key votes, p. 895)*

The Senate approved a proposal to pay farmers for not growing wheat, corn and feed grains. While costing the government money in the first year, the program would save $400 million over three years.

House. The House initially handled its reconciliation requirements in a number of separate measures. The piecemeal approach was part of a Democratic strategy to force Republicans into a series of painful election-year votes on budget cuts. Republicans, who had hoped to accomplish the cuts in an omnibus bill, charged the Democrats with subverting the budget process.

After passing four separate bills, the House Aug. 10 folded them into an omnibus measure (HR 6955), which it passed by voice vote.

Earlier the House took these actions on the individual bills:

● Veterans (HR 6782). The bill was reported by the Veterans' Affairs Committee July 23 (H Rept 97-660) and passed by the House July 27 on a 400-0 vote. Savings under the bill's reconciliation provisions totaled $550 million over fiscal 1983-85.

● Housing (HR 6812). In reporting the bill July 29 (H Rept 97-683), the Banking Committee rejected its reconciliation instructions by approving only $5 million in fiscal 1983 savings.

Before passing HR 6812 by voice vote Aug. 5, the House adopted, 337-69, an amendment to provide $2.1 billion in additional savings over three years by requiring home buyers to pay a lump-sum premium for Federal Housing Administration (FHA) mortgage insurance.

● Federal Pensions (HR 6862). As passed by the House Aug. 3, 268-128, HR 6862 was a token reconciliation bill that reduced federal pensions by only $113 million during fiscal 1983-85.

The House refused to clamp a 4 percent lid on COLAs for federal retirees, defying its instructions to slash $3.2 billion from pension payments over the three-year period. The Post Office and Civil Service Committee, which drafted the bill, also had rejected the 4 percent COLA cap.

Although the House action directly affected only civil service retirees, the decision would have a domino effect on military, foreign service and other federal retirees.

● **Agriculture (HR 6892).** The agriculture reconciliation bill was reported by the Agriculture Committee Aug. 2 (H Rept 97-687) and passed by the House Aug. 10 by a 268-121 vote. Three-year savings in farm and food stamp programs totaled $4.6 billion.

Conference. Conferees wrapped up their work the night of Aug. 16, and House Budget Committee Chairman James R. Jones, D-Okla., brought the conference report (H Rept 97-759) to the House floor the next day.

After deleting non-germane language involving congressional pay, the House adopted the conference report by a 243-176 vote Aug. 18. The Senate then cleared the measure 67-32.

Omnibus Bill Provisions

As signed into law Sept. 8, HR 6955 (PL 97-253) included the following major provisions:

Agriculture. The bill made two major changes in farm policies. One required new payments to farmers for not growing major crops; the other froze dairy price supports at current levels. HR 6955 also curbed inflation adjustments in food stamp benefits and tightened eligibility for the food stamp program. The changes were expected to cut $6.6 billion from projected spending in fiscal 1983-85. *(Details of agriculture action, p. 496; food stamp cuts, p. 594)*

Federal Pensions. The bill reduced inflation adjustments in pensions for federal retirees under age 62 in fiscal 1983-85. It delayed by one month the effective date of COLAs for all federal retirees in each of the three years. Three-year savings from these changes were estimated at $4.1 billion. *(Details, p. 779)*

FHA Insurance Premiums. The bill required home buyers to pay a lump-sum premium for FHA mortgage insurance, instead of spreading payments over the life of a mortgage.

Conferees included House provisions requiring refunds of the premium if a home was sold in the early years of the mortgage, and proof by the secretary of housing and urban development that the advance premium program was sound.

Early collection of the fees was expected to save about $2 billion during the next three years.

Veterans' Affairs. Instead of making $387 million in cuts as ordered by the budget resolution, conferees slashed spending by about $552 million for the three fiscal years.

To save costs, the bill imposed a new user fee on Veterans Administration-backed home loans equal to .5 percent of the amount guaranteed. It also delayed payment of certain compensation and pension benefits, rounded benefit checks to the next lower dollar and changed the effective date for benefit reductions caused by a change in dependency status. *(Story, p. 616)*

Regulatory Agencies. The Federal Communications Commission was to be reduced to five members from its authorized level of seven by July 1, 1983. Conferees estimated resulting savings of $100,000 in fiscal 1983 and $500,000 annually thereafter.

The Interstate Commerce Commission was to be reduced to five members from its authorized level of 11 on a phased basis to be completed by Dec. 31, 1985. A member's term would be reduced to five years, from seven. Savings were estimated at $475,000 annually. The commission had not had a full complement of members in recent years.

Fiscal 1983 Appropriations

Because the budget struggle consumed so much time in 1982, the appropriation process lagged far behind schedule. When fiscal 1983 began Oct. 1, only two of the 13 regular annual appropriations bills had been signed into law.

Two omnibus continuing appropriations resolutions were needed to keep the government running. The second of these resolutions (H J Res 631 — PL 97-377) provided $379 billion in full-year funding for agencies covered by the six regular appropriations bills that did not clear before adjournment — including the giant Defense and Labor-Health and Human Services-Education measures. Congress completed action on the omnibus measure Dec. 20 after Senate-House conferees bowed to President Reagan's veto threats by dropping money for emergency jobs programs that both chambers had included in the bill. Reagan signed the resolution Dec. 20, four days after much of the government technically had run out of funds.

Congress and the president engaged in two long battles over supplemental funding bills for fiscal 1982.

Congress handed Reagan his first big budget defeat Sept. 10 when it overrode his veto of a $14.2 billion supplemental bill (HR 6863 — PL 97-257). The president wanted more for defense and less for social programs than the bill provided, but his attempts to portray the measure as a "budget-buster" backfired as Congress insisted on its right to help set spending priorities. The House voted to override Sept. 9 on a **key vote of 301-117 (R 81-104; D 220-13).** The Senate completed the override effort the following day on a **key vote of 60-30 (R 21-26; D 39-4).** *(1982 key votes, p. 895)*

Earlier in the year Congress spent 16 weeks fashioning an "urgent" supplemental that the president would sign (HR 6685 — PL 97-216). Reagan vetoed two previous versions (HR 5922, HR 6682) because of money added for an emergency housing bailout and other programs. The House failed to override the vetoes. *(Housing funds, p. 633)*

1983

Debate over federal deficits dominated economic policy making during 1983 as Republicans and Democrats jockeyed for advantage in the 1984 election campaigns.

Congress gave short shrift to President Reagan's fiscal 1984 budget with its $188.8 billion projected deficit. Democrats and Republicans alike looked askance at the administration's priorities: a 10 percent real growth rate for defense spending coupled with a freeze on domestic spending. A White House proposal for a standby tax, to take effect in fiscal 1986 if the deficit were too large, was dead on arrival on Capitol Hill.

In the House, where Democrats had gained an additional 26 seats in the 1982 elections, the balance of power shifted back to the more liberal politics of pre-Reagan

days. Splintering of the coalition of Republicans and conservative Southern Democrats that had pushed through budgets in 1981 and 1982 made it easy for the House to adopt a budget resolution that was, in effect, the Democrats' economic manifesto.

The 1982 elections had their impact on the Republican-controlled Senate as well. A number of moderate GOP senators narrowly won re-election and were able to do so, in part, because they distanced themselves from Reagan's economic policies. These lessons were not lost on their colleagues. But far from simplifying the Senate's handling of the budget, the elections and their aftermath helped divide Republican members into two camps — those who were willing to attack future deficits with tax increases, and those who favored only spending cuts. After several abortive attempts, the Senate finally adopted a budget plan that had almost no constituency and was approved primarily to keep the budget process from collapsing altogether.

Congress eventually approved a compromise fiscal 1984 budget resolution June 23, but the measure proved impossible to implement. Lawmakers did hold the level of appropriations bills at or below the targets set out in the resolution. But the budget's deficit reduction strategy — to raise $73 billion in additional revenues and cut $12 billion from projected spending over fiscal 1984-86 — remained unfulfilled at year's end.

The spending reductions mandated by the resolution, mostly adjustments in cost-of-living increases for federal retirement programs, were approved with relative ease by House and Senate committees. The House easily passed a three-year, $10.3 billion spending cut package; the Senate approved the bill in 1984.

Finding $73 billion in new taxes over fiscal 1984-86 proved considerably more difficult. The House Ways and Means and Senate Finance committees drafted tax increase legislation that raised only a fraction of the revenues required by the budget. Neither house voted on the tax increase bills until 1984.

As in 1982, Congress made no effort to shape a second budget resolution, and the first measure became binding when fiscal 1984 began Oct. 1.

Lawmakers' failure to deliver the deficit reduction measures promised in the budget resolution spurred demands for revision of the nine-year-old budget process. Although Congress made no changes in the 1974 Congressional Budget and Impoundment Control Act, the Supreme Court, in its June 23 decision outlawing the legislative veto, invalidated provisions under which either chamber could force the president to spend appropriated funds. *(Budget process, box, p. 34; legislative veto, p. 833)*

Reagan Budget

As submitted to Congress Jan. 31, President Reagan's budget called for $848.5 billion in spending and $659.7 billion in revenues in fiscal 1984. The president proposed a 10 percent increase in defense spending, after adjustment for inflation, within the framework of an overall spending freeze. *(Text of message, p. 1063)*

Although Reagan called for $43 billion in budget savings, he still forecast a fiscal 1984 deficit of $188.8 billion. The budget included a contingency tax plan to take effect in fiscal 1986 if deficits remained very high. Reagan projected a $147.7 billion deficit for that year.

While striking a note for bipartisanship and accommo-

dation, the president did not swerve from the basic policies he set down at the outset of his administration. Military spending would continue its upward spiral. Discretionary spending for social programs would continue to be whittled away. And the personal and business tax cuts enacted in 1981 would stay firmly in place.

Reagan's contingency tax plan did provide for a 5 percent surcharge on individual and corporate income taxes, as well as a $5-per-barrel oil import fee, to be triggered Oct. 1, 1985, if deficit reduction efforts proved ineffective.

Fiscal 1984 Budget Resolution

Congress completed action June 23 on the first fiscal 1984 budget resolution (H Con Res 91). The measure, designed to set preliminary budget guidelines for fiscal 1984, established higher tax and domestic spending targets and called for lower military funding than President Reagan wanted. In the process it made substantial reductions in the administration's deficit projections for fiscal 1984-86. Acknowledging the unlikelihood of action on another budget resolution in 1983, H Con Res 91 included a provision that converted its targets into binding budget levels when Congress failed to approve a second resolution by Oct. 1.

Final action on the measure concluded nearly five months of tortuous negotiations during which the future of the congressional budget process often seemed in doubt. Brushing aside the austere budget submitted by Reagan in January, House Democratic leaders won easy passage March 23 of a budget resolution that constituted a Democratic policy statement. Passage came harder in the Senate, where moderate Republicans and Democrats bent on deficit reduction narrowly won approval May 19 of a budget blueprint that was unacceptable both to Senate GOP leaders and to the president. It took another month for Senate-House conferees to patch together the final compromise plan. Both chambers approved the compromise June 23, nearly six weeks after the statutory May 15 deadline for final action on the budget.

As cleared, H Con Res 91 called for fiscal 1984 spending of $849.5 billion, rising to as much as $858.93 billion if Congress approved 10 anti-recession programs set aside in a special reserve fund. It granted only half of the 10 percent increase in defense funding the president sought, calling for $268.6 billion in budget authority and $240 billion in outlays. Even so, the congressional spending targets were at least $5.6 billion above revised budget estimates released by the administration April 12; revenues, at $679.6 billion, were $25.9 billion higher. The fiscal 1984 deficit was forecast at $179.33 billion with the reserve fund amounts; without the reserve fund, $169.9 billion.

The creation of the reserve fund was a way for Senate-House conferees to accommodate the desire of many House Democrats to provide recession relief money and at the same time appease members intent on controlling the deficit. Congress approved only two of the 10 programs.

The resolution included reconciliation instructions directing congressional committees to approve deficit reduction measures designed to meet the budget's targets. Authorizing committees were required to approve $2.8 billion in program savings in fiscal 1984 and $12.3 billion over fiscal 1984-86. The House Ways and Means and Senate Finance committees were directed to raise $12 billion in

Balanced Budget Drive Stalls in Congress

A proposed constitutional amendment to require balanced federal budgets made little headway in Congress during 1981-84. The Senate adopted a balanced budget amendment in 1982, but the House rejected a similar proposal. Balanced budget amendments never reached the floor in either chamber thereafter despite pressure from President Reagan and mounting state calls for a constitutional convention to consider the issue.

Since 1975 the National Taxpayers Union had been leading a campaign in state legislatures to force Congress to call a constitutional convention to consider a balanced budget amendment. Under Article V of the Constitution, Congress must call a constitutional convention if two-thirds of the states (34) request one. *(Background, Congress and the Nation Vol. V, p. 221)*

The convention approach had never been tried. All existing amendments to the Constitution had been developed under an alternative system that required approval by two-thirds of each house of Congress. Both systems required ratification by three-fourths (38) of the states.

No procedures existed for determining what was a valid state call for a constitutional convention, nor for actually running one. Many members believed a constitutional convention would be disastrous and could range far beyond the balanced budget issue to other contentious matters such as abortion and school busing.

By 1984 32 states had passed resolutions demanding that Congress convene a constitutional convention to consider a balanced budget amendment: Alabama; Alaska; Arizona; Arkansas; Colorado; Delaware; Florida; Georgia; Idaho; Indiana; Iowa; Kansas; Louisiana; Maryland; Mississippi; Missouri; Nebraska; Nevada; New Hampshire; New Mexico; North Carolina; North Dakota; Oklahoma; Oregon; Pennsylvania; South Carolina; South Dakota; Tennessee; Texas; Utah; Virginia; Wyoming.

But during the year state courts declared unconstitutional ballot initiatives aimed at forcing the legislatures in California and Montana to petition for a constitutional convention.

The twin court actions effectively took the steam out of efforts by supporters of a balanced budget amendment to force House and Senate votes on the proposal. Once members were assured that there was no way the tally of state convention calls could reach 34, they proved less than eager to confront the issue.

Legislative History

1981-82. When the Republicans took over the Senate in January 1981, Judiciary Committee Chairman Strom Thurmond, R-S.C., and Sen. Orrin G. Hatch, R-Utah, chairman of the Judiciary Subcommittee on the Constitution, made the balanced budget proposal a priority item. The committee reported a balanced budget amendment (S J Res 58 — S Rept 97-151) July 10, 1981.

The Senate approved the measure Aug. 4, 1982, by a **key vote of 69-31 (R 47-7; D 22-24)**, two more than the two-thirds majority required. A Democratic amendment to require the president to submit a balanced budget was rejected, 45-53. *(1982 key votes, p. 895)*

The House took up a balanced budget amendment (H J Res 350) Oct. 1, 1982, after supporters gathered 218 signatures on a discharge petition forcing the proposal out of the Judiciary Committee. The measure failed on a **236-187 key vote (R 167-20; D 69-167)**, which was 46 short of the necessary two-thirds.

Generally, both the Senate and House proposals required Congress to adopt a balanced federal budget every year, except in time of war, unless a three-fifths majority voted to allow a deficit.

1984. Congress took no further action on the balanced budget amendment until the closing weeks of the 98th Congress.

The Senate Judiciary Committee reported such an amendment (S J Res 5 — PL 98-628) Sept. 20, 1984, but the measure went no further.

In an election-year maneuver, the Democratic-controlled House Oct. 2 passed a bill (HR 6300) requiring the president to submit a balanced budget. The Republican Senate ignored that measure.

The Senate Judiciary Committee approved a bill (S 119 — S Rept 98-594) May 17 establishing procedures for holding a constitutional convention. The Senate did not act on the bill. *(Details of legislation, p. 709)*

Line-Item Veto

The balanced budget proposal was one of two constitutional amendments President Reagan sought to help cut federal deficits. In 1984 he also requested a constitutional amendment permitting the president to veto individual "line items" in appropriations bills.

That also failed to win Congress' endorsement.

Line-item veto authority would allow a president to reject spending for specific programs in an appropriations bill without having to veto the entire measure. It would take a two-thirds vote of each chamber to override the veto.

The president said 43 of the nation's governors had line-item veto power, and that he himself had found it a "powerful tool" against wasteful spending when he was governor of California.

new revenues in fiscal 1984 and a total of $73 billion over fiscal 1984-86. Congress failed to approve any of these savings in 1983. It did enact deficit reduction legislation in 1984. *(1983 reconciliation, p. 54; 1984 action, p. 60)*

The lengthy legislative struggle over H Con Res 91 imposed severe strains on the nine-year-old congressional budget process. In an ironic turnabout, the Reagan administration displayed growing disenchantment with the process, which the president had used as the vehicle for implementing his economic program in 1981 and 1982.

As lawmakers whittled away at Reagan's proposed military spending increase, Defense Secretary Caspar W. Weinberger reportedly suggested to the president that the administration might be better off without a congressional budget. That way, Weinberger reasoned, Reagan might be able to get more money for defense in the appropriations process, and he would be able to veto appropriations bills for other programs if he thought they were too high.

Weinberger's view was sharply disputed by Office of Management and Budget Director David A. Stockman, who warned the president that without the discipline of a budget resolution there would be $200 billion deficits "as far as the eye can see."

But many Republicans seemed willing to tolerate big deficits in order to maintain both the costly military build-up and Reagan's tax policy, which included the third installment of the 1981 personal tax cut, due July 1, and the indexing of tax rates to offset inflation, scheduled to take effect in 1985. Reagan remained obdurately opposed to any budget resolution that called for 1984 tax increases. *(1981 tax bill, p. 65)*

House Action

Committee. The entire Democratic membership of the House helped formulate the budget resolution reported by the House Budget Committee March 21 (H Con Res 91 — H Rept 98-41).

The Democratic Caucus held several meetings to discuss the budget, and House Democrats were asked to complete a multiple-choice form detailing their budget preferences. When the Budget Committee sat down March 17 and in one whirlwind day approved a fiscal 1984 budget, the outcome was a foregone conclusion. The committee approved the measure on a straight 20-11 party-line vote.

The panel called for fiscal 1984 outlays of $863.55 billion and revenues totaling $689.1 billion, with a $174.45 billion deficit.

While cutting $14.3 billion from the president's deficit forecast for fiscal 1984, the Democrats' budget would increase domestic spending by approximately $33 billion, with much of the money earmarked for human needs programs that were significantly cut in the fiscal 1982 and 1983 budgets.

The plan also repudiated Reagan's proposal for further major escalation in defense spending. It called for a 4 percent growth rate after adjustment for inflation, far below the 10 percent administration request.

Finally, in order to arrive at a deficit figure lower than the administration's, the House Democrats called for $30 billion in additional revenues in fiscal 1984 — a goal that probably would require elimination of the third installment of the 1981 personal income tax cut. And in 1985, when $40 billion in new revenues would be required under the Democrats' plan, the indexing provision of the 1981 tax bill probably would have to be dropped.

Committee Republicans were rebuffed in every attempt to bring the plan back in line with the president's budget. "... This is the most irresponsible budget that has ever been proposed during my four years in Congress," asserted a newly minted Republican, Phil Gramm of Texas, who had served as the Democratic point man for Reagan's budgets in 1981 and 1982. Gramm switched parties in 1983.

The Democrats argued that their budget was a "truly Democratic" one that addressed their traditional concerns — education, health and help for the disadvantaged. Reflecting the gain of 26 House seats in the 1982 elections, their strategy was markedly different from the one employed by Democrats in 1981 and 1982, when their budgets were only a notch to the left of the Republicans'.

Floor. The House passed H Con Res 91 March 23 by a **229-196 key vote (R 4-160; D 225-36)**. The ground rules for floor debate permitted one floor amendment, in the form of a Republican substitute. But the Republicans did not offer one, and the committee-reported resolution was adopted without change. *(1983 key votes, p. 911)*

The Democratic leadership let it be known, especially to the freshmen, that they were expected to stick by the budget when it came to a vote. And stick they did. Fifty-two of the 58 Democratic freshmen voted for the Budget Committee plan. Of the 50 sitting Democrats who voted with Reagan on his first budget in 1981, 23 stuck with their party in 1983.

Democrats lost a total of 36 votes but picked up four Republicans on the final tally. The GOP defectors were Claudine Schneider, R.I.; Bill Green, N.Y.; James M. Jeffords, Vt.; and Matthew J. Rinaldo, N.J.

The Republicans, on the other hand, could not agree on an alternative budget. And because many Republicans did not want to vote for it, the GOP did not want to offer the president's original budget plan. The vacuum left by the Republicans' refusal to offer a substitute made it easier for many conservative "Boll Weevil" Democrats to return to the party fold.

Senate Action

Committee. Defying President Reagan, the Republican-controlled Senate Budget Committee April 21 approved a Democratic-inspired budget that called for more than $30 billion in new taxes in fiscal 1984 and provided only half the increase in defense spending authority the president sought.

Committee Chairman Pete V. Domenici, R-N.M., and three other Republicans joined with nine of the panel's 10 Democrats to report out the budget resolution 13-4, breaking a deadlock that had prevented the committee from acting the week before. Voting against the resolution were Republicans William L. Armstrong, Colo.; Charles E. Grassley, Iowa; and Dan Quayle, Ind.; and Democrat Ernest F. Hollings, S.C., who supported a budget freeze.

As reported April 24, the resolution (S Con Res 27 — S Rept 98-63) called for fiscal 1984 spending of $848.8 billion, revenues of $686.7 billion and a $162 billion deficit.

The committee's budget was born more out of frustration than belief. Domenici and others argued that it was more important to keep the budget process moving than to insist on any particular numbers. "The time has come to get a budget resolution," Domenici declared after weeks of fruitless efforts to achieve an accommodation with the White House. The committee had begun its markups March 9.

But Domenici vowed he would do his utmost to change the revenue numbers on the Senate floor, as well as fight to increase the resolution's 5 percent real growth rate for defense.

Domenici's decision to push through a resolution — even a Democratic one — came one day after he, Majority Leader Howard H. Baker Jr., R-Tenn., and White House advisers failed to convince all the Republicans on the Budget panel to support a compromise offered by Reagan.

Floor. Moderate Senate Republicans and Democrats defied President Reagan and the GOP leadership May 19 by approving a fiscal 1984 budget that increased taxes and domestic spending while slowing the defense buildup.

Unwilling to torpedo the budget process, the Senate approved its budget plan by a **50-49 key vote (R 21-32; D 29-17)** at the end of a grueling session. During the course of the day the Senate twice rejected a leadership plan that had the reluctant endorsement of the president, and initially turned down the budget it ultimately accepted. *(1983 key votes, p. 911)*

The message of the vote was clear: Big deficits were less tolerable than increased taxes. And in a striking demonstration of political and philosophical role reversal, a small band of moderate Republicans led the quest for deficit reduction.

As approved by the Senate, S Con Res 27 contained a fiscal 1984 deficit of $178.6 billion, compared with a $193 billion deficit in the leadership plan and $185 billion in the president's own budget.

Perhaps more important, the plan — drafted by Slade Gorton, R-Wash. — showed declining deficits through fiscal 1988. Projecting the leadership budget to fiscal 1988, the deficit would climb to $220 billion.

The final Senate budget called for fiscal 1984 spending of $849.7 billion and revenues totaling $671.1 billion. The resolution proposed a 6 percent inflation-adjusted growth rate for defense and recommended tax increases of $9.9 billion in fiscal 1984.

Approval of the resolution ended a three-week ordeal during which the Senate rejected a succession of plans offered by the Republican leadership and the moderate Republican group, plus an assortment of other plans. At one point the resolution was returned to the Budget Committee, but the sharply divided panel was unable to draw up a winning proposal.

In an impassioned speech before the leadership plan went down for the last time, Domenici said: "It's insanity for the U.S. Senate not to vote in a budget resolution.... There's nothing wrong with the budget process. What's wrong is that these are extremely difficult economic times. It's the facts we don't want to vote on, so we blame the budget process." Domenici opposed the Gorton plan but voted for it anyway to move the budget debate into conference.

Conference Action

Conferees reached agreement on the resolution June 20 (H Rept 98-248). The three touchiest issues dividing the House and Senate were resolved as follows:

Taxes. The House resolution called for $30 billion in fiscal 1984 revenue increases, excluding $5.2 billion in Social Security increases voted earlier in the year; the Senate, $9.9 billion. Conferees finally settled on $12 billion.

Defense Spending. Splitting the difference between the 4 percent increase allowed by the House and the 6 percent increase proposed by the Senate, conferees provided a 5 percent inflation-adjusted growth rate for defense spending. Budget authority was set at $268.6 billion, outlays at $240 billion.

Domestic Spending. Domestic spending was about $33 billion more than Reagan requested in the House resolution, $12.6 billion more in the Senate version. Chief differences involved money the House provided for new initiatives — such as mortgage foreclosure relief and health insurance for the unemployed — that the Senate did not include. Conferees agreed to establish a special $8.5 billion reserve fund to accommodate 10 new spending initiatives that might or might not become law.

Later in the year Congress enacted two of the 10 programs. That added $1.5 billion for supplemental unemployment compensation benefits and $150 million for job training for veterans.

The reconciliation instructions included in the conference agreement directed Senate committees and House committees to cut existing programs to achieve outlay savings totaling $2.8 billion in fiscal 1984 and $12.3 billion over fiscal 1984-86. In addition, the Ways and Means and Finance committees were directed to come up with $73 billion in new revenues over the three-year period.

The conferees modified Senate and House provisions on monetary policy. The final language requested the House and Senate Banking committees to report a resolution expressing the sense of Congress as to the need for coordination of Federal Reserve monetary policy with the fiscal policy set out in the budget resolution. Such a measure was reported in the Senate but did not reach the floor (S Con Res 73 — S Rept 98-263).

The House June 23 adopted the conference report by a 239-186 vote. The Senate then went on to clear the resolution by a comfortable 51-43 margin after defeating an effort by Finance Committee Chairman Robert Dole, R-Kan., to reduce the tax increase required by the resolution's reconciliation instructions.

Fiscal 1983 Revisions

As part of its fiscal 1984 budget resolution (H Con Res 91), cleared June 23, Congress updated its budget for the ongoing fiscal year to take account of revised economic forecasts, new spending estimates and additional legislation affecting fiscal 1983 spending.

Under H Con Res 91, fiscal 1983 spending could go as high as $812.85 billion, depending on enactment of 10 antirecession programs set aside in a special reserve fund. Revenues were set at $604.3 billion, with a resulting deficit of up to $208.55 billion. That was more than double the deficit Congress initially had forecast in 1982.

The actual deficit for fiscal 1983 turned out somewhat lower than predicted, however: A booming economic recovery held the shortfall to $195.4 billion. *(1982 action, p. 46; budget totals compared, p. 36)*

Deficit Reduction

After months of decrying the evils of threatened $200 billion deficits "as far as the eye can see," Congress adjourned Nov. 18 without meeting its own mandate to approve $85.3 billion in deficit reduction measures over fiscal 1984-86.

Defeated, or left in limbo, was every major deficit reduction designed to put Congress in compliance with its own fiscal 1984 budget resolution, adopted in June. It was the first time since passage of the 1974 Congressional Budget Act (PL 93-344) that Congress failed to enact any of the deficit reduction measures required by its budget process. By adjourning without having met its budget's mandate, Congress disregarded one of the key budget control provisions of the 1974 act. *(Budget control, box, p. 34)*

"As we leave Washington, word of our impotence will precede us . . .," said Rep. Dan Rostenkowski, D-Ill., chairman of the House Ways and Means Committee. "We have confessed to an already doubting nation that we are ruled by political fear rather than economic courage."

Rostenkowski's comment came after the House, on a 204-214 vote, refused to consider an $8 billion tax increase bill (HR 4170) drafted by the Ways and Means Committee.

Following the House vote, the Senate suspended action on a $28 billion reconciliation package (S 2062), containing an estimated $13.4 billion in tax increases and $14.6 billion in spending cuts. The House had approved a $10.3 billion spending cut package (HR 4169) in October.

Members cited a long list of scapegoats for their deficit-cutting failures. Republicans blamed Democrats. Democrats blamed Republicans. House Speaker Thomas P. O'Neill Jr., D-Mass., and President Reagan were repeatedly faulted for not leading the assault on the deficit. Throughout the year the president and his chief economic spokesman, Treasury Secretary Donald T. Regan, had played down the significance of the deficits and their impact on the economy.

Background

The fiscal 1984 budget resolution (H Con Res 91), cleared June 23, included reconciliation instructions calling for $85.3 billion in deficit reductions over fiscal 1984-86. *(Budget resolution, p. 51)*

The reconciliation instructions directed Senate and House committees to cut existing programs to achieve outlay savings of $2.8 billion in fiscal 1984 and $12.3 billion over fiscal 1984-86. In addition, the Ways and Means and Finance committees were directed to come up with $73 billion in new revenues over the three-year period.

While most reconciliation cuts easily won committee approval, required savings in Medicare proved controversial. And the Finance and Ways and Means committees showed no stomach for approving $73 billion in three-year revenue increases in light of President Reagan's vow to veto any tax increase measure.

Deficit reduction efforts remained on the back burner for several months following adoption of the budget resolution. The economy's recovery from the 1981-82 recession exceeded earlier forecasts, causing short-term deficit projections to decline. Many economists nonetheless warned that tax increases and spending cuts were necessary to keep the recovery going. The Congressional Budget Office said Aug. 20 that failure to enact the reconciliation measures required by the budget resolution would result in budget deficits "on the order of $200 billion for years to come."

By autumn pressure began building for meaningful action to cut the fiscal 1984-86 deficits. Republicans in both chambers spoke of giving the president new powers to control spending if Congress failed to meet its deficit reduction goals.

House Democrats, pressured by their freshman members, caucused Sept. 22 and agreed that deficit reduction was imperative, although they could not agree on how to proceed. Democratic leaders feared the political consequences of getting out front on the tax issue. Ways and Means Chairman Rostenkowski insisted it was futile to try to raise taxes without the cooperation and support of the White House. Reagan had said repeatedly he would not lend his support to any deficit reduction effort that involved tax increases.

House Action

Spending Cut Bill. As the stalemate over tax increases dragged on, the House Oct. 25 took one step toward deficit reduction when it gave voice vote approval to a reconciliation bill (HR 4169 — H Rept 98-425) that would reduce spending by an estimated $10.3 billion over fiscal 1984-86.

The bill was reported Oct. 20 by the Budget Committee, which had packaged the spending cuts of various authorizing committees in a single piece of legislation. It did not include Medicare savings that the Ways and Means Committee was considering in conjunction with tax measures.

The bulk of the savings in HR 4169 would come from delaying cost-of-living adjustments (COLAs) for federal retirees' benefits and veterans' compensation, limiting and delaying a scheduled federal civilian pay raise, and limiting farmers' eligibility for small-business disaster loans. The Senate cleared the bill in 1984. *(Senate action, provisions, p. 60)*

Tax Increases. Despite Democratic reluctance to take the lead on taxes, the Ways and Means Committee reported legislation Oct. 21 (HR 4170 — H Rept 98-432) that would raise about $8 billion over fiscal 1984-86, mostly by closing loopholes. The total was far below the $73 billion reconciliation requirement.

HR 4170 was stalled for nearly a month as House leaders struggled to defuse opposition to the legislation. But on Nov. 17, the day before Congress' scheduled adjournment, the House rejected the rule for floor consideration of the Ways and Means package by a **204-214 key vote (R 13-149; D 191-65)**. *(1983 key votes, p. 911)*

Congress completed action on the bill in 1984 as part of a three-year, $149.2 billion deficit reduction package. *(Details, p. 56)*

Senate Action

The Senate never voted on its $28 billion reconciliation package (S 2062 — S Rept 98-300), which contained spending cuts similar to those approved by the House, plus major savings in the Medicare program.

Three-year spending savings amounted to $14.6 billion, $2.3 billion more than the budget resolution required. Revenue increases totaled only $13.4 billion, however, far below the $73 billion goal.

The bill was brought to the floor Nov. 16, but action was suspended after the Senate sidetracked an amendment offered by Budget Committee leaders that would have brought the total deficit reduction to $87.6 billion.

During the final weeks of the session Finance Committee Chairman Robert Dole, R-Kan., tried in vain to win agreement on a $150 billion deficit reduction plan, equally divided between tax increases and spending cuts. Finance members voted Nov. 18 to try again in 1984.

Fiscal 1984 Appropriations

By the time it adjourned Nov. 18, Congress had cleared 10 of the 13 regular annual appropriations bills for fiscal 1984. All were scaled to stay within limits acceptable to President Reagan, who had threatened to veto measures that exceeded his budget proposals. Programs covered by the three remaining bills were funded through Sept. 30, 1984, by a catchall continuing appropriations resolution (H J Res 413 — PL 98-151) cleared Nov. 12.

The House had rejected an earlier version of the continuing resolution (H J Res 403) after Democratic leaders succeeded in adding nearly $1 billion for social programs. Reagan adamantly opposed the extra money, which the House approved on a **254-155 key vote (R 22-134; D 232-21)**. The resolution itself was rejected 203-206, as rebellious freshman Democrats, angry over Congress' stalemate on deficit reduction legislation, voted against the measure. *(Details, p. 54; 1983 key votes, p. 911)*

In other action, Congress March 24 cleared a $4.6 billion jobs and anti-recession relief package as part of a $15.6 billion supplemental appropriations bill for fiscal 1983 (HR 1718 — PL 98-8). The jobs portion of the bill represented a Senate-House compromise fashioned to fall within a $5 billion limit set by the president.

And in one of their final acts before adjourning for the year, lawmakers approved a fiscal 1984 supplemental (HR 3959 — PL 98-181) after attaching a $15.6 billion housing authorization sought by House Democrats and an $8.4 billion U.S. contribution to the International Monetary Fund sought by the Reagan administration.

1984

Efforts to cut federal budget deficits, estimated to remain near $200 billion annually through 1989, occupied Congress for most of 1984. After months of negotiations among administration officials, Democratic leaders in the House and Republican leaders in the Senate, lawmakers completed a plan to cut projected deficits by $149.2 billion over fiscal 1984-87.

The final elements of the four-year plan were reflected in the fiscal 1985 budget resolution cleared Oct. 1: $50.8 billion from increased tax revenues; $58.3 billion from limiting increases in the defense budget; $12.2 billion from savings in entitlements and other mandatory benefit programs; $3.9 billion from reductions in non-defense discretionary spending; $18.3 billion from net interest savings; and $5.7 billion from offsetting receipts, such as revenues from the use of federal property.

As a "down payment" on that plan, Congress in June cleared legislation providing about $50 billion in tax increases and $13 billion in spending cuts through fiscal 1987. But a stalemate on Pentagon spending was not resolved until the closing weeks of the session, holding up approval of the budget resolution.

In other action, the Senate in April cleared an $8.2 billion deficit reduction bill carried over from 1983. That bill provided reconciliation savings required by the fiscal 1984 budget resolution.

Congress' annual fiscal argument was complicated in 1984 by the strategy adopted by the administration and Republican leaders in the Senate. Reversing the procedures established by the 1974 Congressional Budget Act (PL 93-344), the Senate refused to consider a fiscal 1985 budget resolution before it enacted legislation mandating deficit reductions.

The House followed the traditional route outlined in the Budget Act. First it approved a budget resolution that set overall spending and revenue goals. Then it passed legislation providing tax increases and spending cuts to carry out its fiscal blueprint.

Although legislative action to cut deficits preceded adoption of the $932 billion fiscal 1985 spending plan, the congressional budget process continued to provide the framework for the deficit debate.

Reagan Budget

The fiscal 1985 budget submitted by President Reagan Feb. 1 was rejected out of hand by both political parties because it did not go far enough to reduce anticipated deficits. *(Text of message, p. 1076)*

The president proposed a budget in which total outlays of $925.5 billion would greatly outweigh projected revenues of $745.1 billion, leaving a deficit of $180.4 billion. Although Reagan proposed three-year spending reductions and cost savings of $73 billion and tax increases of $33.5 billion, deficits would hover around $180 billion for each year through fiscal 1987.

While calling for a freeze on discretionary domestic spending, Reagan proposed a 13 percent increase in spending authority for defense. He sought to achieve $106 billion in deficit reductions over three years by cutting Medicare and other programs and imposing modest tax hikes. There was no retreat from the big tax cut Reagan pushed through in 1981. *(1981 tax cut, p. 65)*

Even before submitting his budget, the president had asked Congress to join him in a bipartisan effort to craft a deficit down payment that would reduce the federal deficit by $100 billion through fiscal 1987. But those negotiations stalled over defense spending almost immediately.

Meanwhile, the House moved ahead with its budget resolution, which aimed to slash deficits by $182 billion. And the Senate GOP leadership concocted the "Rose Garden plan," which contained $150 billion in deficit reductions — later reduced to $140 billion. The plan was so named because President Reagan endorsed it March 15 at a ceremony in the White House Rose Garden. Defense growth was held at 5.1 percent under the plan.

At the center of the Senate's deficit-cutting plan were two spending caps — one for defense and one for all non-military discretionary spending. The administration and the GOP leadership insisted on putting the caps in deficit reduction legislation, thus giving them the force of law, rather than in the non-binding budget resolution.

The caps were employed to convince both Reagan and conservative Republicans that they could count on long-term efforts to increase military spending and restrain domestic spending. In exchange, Reagan and the conservatives agreed to support a relatively modest tax hike.

Deficit Reduction

With relative ease and little fanfare, Congress gave final approval June 27 to a $63 billion deficit reduction package. The bill (HR 4170 — PL 98-369) — the first

installment of the deficit down payment requested by President Reagan — was expected to generate about $50 billion in new taxes and cut government spending by about $13 billion through fiscal 1987. *(Reagan budget, deficit negotiations, p. 56)*

Although the president had warned earlier that he would not accept tax hikes until more spending restraints were in place, Reagan changed course and sent a letter to members before the final vote pledging to sign HR 4170.

Most of the tax increases came from provisions designed to shut down a wide range of tax loopholes and shelters. A few sweeteners were hidden in the package, including a tax break for investors and an increase in the earned income tax credit for poor working families.

The largest spending reductions were made in Medicare, the nation's health care program for the elderly and disabled. The legislation increased out-of-pocket costs for beneficiaries and imposed a 15-month freeze on physician fees reimbursed by Medicare.

Changes also were made in cost-of-living increases for military retirees, and salaries of federal judges were increased 4 percent.

Committee Action

Working in the shadow of the White House-congressional deficit negotiations, the House Ways and Means and Senate Finance committees forged ahead with their own deficit-cutting measures.

Ways and Means March 1 approved a package of tax increases estimated at $49.2 billion for fiscal 1984-87. The package (H Rept 98-432, Part II) was attached to HR 4170, which the committee initially had reported in 1983.

The Senate committee March 21 approved a package to increase taxes $48 billion through fiscal 1987. The committee also agreed to $25.8 billion in spending savings. The package included $21.4 billion in tax increases and $3.8 billion in funding cuts that also were contained in a budget reconciliation bill (S 2062) on which the Senate had suspended action in 1983. *(1983 action, p. 54)*

Tax Increases. There were surprisingly few differences between the House and Senate committees over how to raise taxes.

Both packages included proposals from the administration's fiscal 1985 budget to curtail a wide range of tax shelters. Both also raised liquor taxes, extended telephone excise taxes, revamped taxation of the life insurance industry, restricted the use of tax-exempt industrial development bonds and reduced scheduled tax hikes for large trucks.

In part, the consensus on taxes formed because both committees steered clear of proposals that would threaten what was most dear to the Reagan administration: across-the-board income tax cuts enacted in 1981 and indexing of tax brackets to offset inflation, scheduled to go into effect in 1985. *(Details of tax action, p. 79; 1981 tax cut bill, p. 65)*

Medicare/Medicaid Cuts. The Senate bill called for a variety of Medicare and Medicaid spending cuts not included in HR 4170.

The Ways and Means Committee originally approved approximately $1.8 billion in Medicare spending cuts through fiscal 1987 as part of HR 4170. But that section of the bill later was transferred to a separate entitlement-cutting measure (HR 5394), which the House passed April 12.

The Senate committee package went much further, calling for approximately $12 billion in Medicare and Medicaid savings through fiscal 1987, including a hike in premiums paid by Medicare beneficiaries. The Finance Committee also agreed to a freeze on doctors' fees in Medicare cases and penalties for physicians who refused to accept "assignment" of Medicare fees.

Floor Action

House. The House passed HR 4170 on a 318-97 vote April 11 after little more than three hours of debate.

The following day the House passed HR 5394 on a 261-152 vote. The provisions of the entitlement cut bill subsequently were folded into HR 4170.

As HR 5394 was presented to the House, including the Medicare provisions stripped from HR 4170 during Ways and Means Committee consideration of the tax legislation, the measure shaved about $4.8 billion from 1985-87 deficits by cuts in a variety of domestic programs. But bowing to pressure from the American Medical Association, the House refused to agree to a one-year freeze on physicians' fees paid by Medicare and a requirement forcing doctors to accept set fees for hospital services.

Elimination of those provisions cut the savings in HR 5394 to $3.9 billion.

Despite the deficit reduction aim of the reconciliation package, it also called for new spending in several areas: on welfare and agriculture programs and on the proposed Child Health Assurance Program (CHAP), which expanded Medicaid coverage for maternal and pediatric care.

A Republican motion to recommit the bill with instructions to eliminate all of its spending increases and to impose the Medicare physician pay freeze failed on a **172-242 key vote (R 157-2; D 15-240).** *(1984 key votes, p. 927)*

Senate. The Senate passed HR 4170 by a 74-23 vote May 17 after substituting its own tax and spending provisions for those of the House-passed bill. A budget resolution conforming to the deficit package was routinely approved the following day. *(Story, p. 59)*

The Senate had spent four weeks considering deficit reduction proposals as amendments to a minor House-passed tariff bill (HR 2163). It adopted its $47 billion tax increase package by a 76-5 vote early April 13, after cutting $1 billion from the committee-approved plan. The critical spending part of the plan did not win approval until May 17, when the Senate adopted the entire $140 billion tax increase/spending cut package on a **65-32 key vote (R 53-0; D 12-32).**

On the eve of the bill's passage, Majority Leader Howard H. Baker Jr., R-Tenn., joined with other Republican leaders and White House officials in striking a deal with GOP dissidents on a $2 billion increase over three years in domestic spending programs. The compromise preserved the defense spending level that Baker had described as essential for Reagan's continued support.

Under the three-year spending caps in the plan, military spending authority totaled $299 billion in fiscal 1985, $333.7 billion in fiscal 1986 and $372 billion in fiscal 1987, while the budget for other discretionary spending was $139.8 billion in fiscal 1985, $144.3 billion in fiscal 1986 and $151.5 billion in fiscal 1987. The tax portion increased revenues by $47.7 billion.

The caps were one of the most divisive factors during the Senate debate. The defense spending authority cap

allowed an average 7 percent inflation-adjusted growth rate through fiscal 1987. Under the other cap, all remaining discretionary spending was held to a 2 percent growth rate in fiscal 1985 and a slightly higher increase in fiscal 1986 and 1987. The Republican leadership narrowly fended off, on a 48-46 vote, an attempt by GOP moderates to merge the two caps, which would have given the Appropriations Committee the leeway to take money from defense, if it felt other programs warranted additional money.

A Democratic proposal, offered by Lawton Chiles, D-Fla., the senior Democrat on the Budget Committee, to reduce the deficit $204 billion over fiscal 1984-87 drew six Republican defectors, but failed May 8 on a 49-49 tie. Instead of the 7 percent growth in defense proposed in the Republican leaders' plan, the Democrats sought a 4 percent rise. They also called for a two-year delay in tax indexing scheduled to take effect in 1985 and a $17.4 billion reduction in non-defense spending.

Conference

The House-Senate conference on HR 4170 began June 6. The conferees were split into 12 subconferences, each assigned a specific section of the bill. Conferees on the tax provisions made rapid progress, approving items to raise about $40 billion in three short sessions June 6-8. But negotiations on the remaining tax provisions and sensitive spending issues dragged on for more than two weeks.

Conferees reached agreement on the bulk of the deficit reduction package after a marathon session that started at 8:30 a.m. June 22 and ended at 5:15 a.m. the following day.

The administration's insistence that the bill contain mandatory spending caps through fiscal 1987 on domestic and defense spending was finessed when negotiators agreed to substitute non-binding language for the ceilings.

The final version of HR 4170 contained "sense of the House" language calling for a $182 billion deficit reduction through fiscal 1987. It also contained "sense of the Senate" language that said the Senate would abide by its domestic and military caps in fashioning appropriations bills for fiscal 1985. Neither chamber was bound by the other's "sense" language.

In the end, conferees agreed to drop several contentious provisions, including a proposed increase in the cigarette excise tax passed by the House and the administration's plan to set up so-called "enterprise zones" to encourage development of economically distressed areas.

An impasse over spending cuts affecting the poor and tax breaks for the wealthy and the middle class was broken after the House agreed to the physician fee freeze and the Senate, after getting the go-ahead from the White House, dropped approximately $5 billion in tax breaks included in its version of the deficit reduction plan. These included the tax credits to promote energy conservation and business research and an administration proposal to expand the use of Individual Retirement Accounts (IRAs) for non-working spouses.

The conference report (H Rept 98-861) was filed June 23. The House adopted the report by a 268-155 vote June 27. The Senate then cleared the bill, 83-15.

Final Provisions

As signed into law July 18, the Deficit Reduction Act of 1984 (HR 4170 — PL 98-369) contained the following major provisions (cost estimates are for fiscal 1984-87 un-less otherwise noted):

Taxes. Provided an estimated $50.8 billion in additional revenues through fiscal 1987, largely by closing loopholes and other steps to beef up taxpayer compliance. *(Details, p. 79)*

Medicare. Reduced projected spending for Medicare by more than $6.5 billion through fiscal 1987. Among other things, the legislation increased out-of-pocket medical costs for the elderly and imposed a 15-month freeze on physician fees reimbursed by the program. *(Details, p. 544)*

Medicaid. Increased projected spending for Medicaid by $270 million by requiring states to provide Medicaid assistance to certain needy women and children not receiving coverage in some states.

The bill also made additional changes in Medicaid and other health aid programs. *(Details, p. 546)*

Public Assistance. Raised the assets a needy aged, blind or disabled person could have and still qualify for Supplemental Security Income (SSI) benefits. The existing $1,500 limit ($2,250 for couples) was gradually increased to $2,000 ($3,000 for couples) by 1989, at a cost of $65 million.

The bill also limited, in some cases substantially, the amount an individual's SSI payments could be reduced by the government in an effort to recoup past overpayments.

● Made several changes in the Aid to Families with Dependent Children (AFDC) program to help families who were thrown off the rolls, or were subject to removal from the rolls, as a result of changes made to the program in 1981. These included allowing up to 15 months of additional Medicaid coverage to those who lost AFDC benefits because they had taken low-paying jobs.

The bill also expanded AFDC eligibility to families with higher incomes than existing law allowed.

Other Provisions. Implemented several recommendations of the President's Private Sector Survey on Cost Control, also known as the Grace commission, for estimated savings of $3.2 billion.

The changes accelerated the deposit and collection of federal non-tax receipts, such as customs duties; allowed the Treasury Department, in limited cases, to deduct from an individual's tax refund uncollected government debts — such as student loan repayments; and increased the use of tax returns and other government records to verify an individual's eligibility for public assistance. *(Grace commission, p. 791)*

● Eliminated by the end of 1984 a scheme used by the Puerto Rican government to collect a tax rebate from the Treasury for liquor diverted from the U.S. mainland to the island for redistribution in the United States. The bill also limited repayments to Puerto Rico for taxes collected on liquor distilled on the island to $10.50 for a gallon of 100 proof liquor. Estimated savings: $757 million.

● Moved the date for payment of cost-of-living adjustments for federal military retirees from Dec. 1, 1985, to Jan. 1, 1986. Estimated reduction in outlays from this one-time bookkeeping change: $1.6 billion. *(Federal pay story, p. 792)*

● Provided a 4 percent pay raise for federal judges retroactive to Jan. 1, 1984. Estimated cost: $1.7 million over one year.

● Increased the contributions credit unions must make to the federal agency that insured them, saving about $1 billion.

● Tightened requirements on federal procurement procedures and established a legal requirement for "full and open" competition for all contracts. *(Story, p. 790)*

• Extended for one year, until Oct. 1, 1987, provisions of the fiscal 1984 reconciliation bill (HR 4169 — PL 98-270) that required farmers to seek disaster loans from the Farmers Home Administration before they could be considered eligible for Small Business Administration loans. Estimated savings: about $200 million. *(Disaster loans, p. 516)*

• Eliminated retroactive awards of veterans' non-service-connected disability pensions for the period between the date of disability and the date of application for a pension unless the veteran's disability prevented him from applying for a pension for at least 30 days, beginning on the date of the disability. Also increased the fee for veterans' home loans. Combined savings: about $721 million. *(Veterans' disability benefits, p. 622)*

• Rescinded $2 billion from the spending authority of the Synthetic Fuels Corporation. This rescission allowed overall budget authority for domestic spending programs to increase by that amount.

Fiscal 1985 Budget Resolution

Winding up a session-long struggle over deficit reduction, Congress Oct. 1 cleared its fiscal 1985 budget resolution (H Con Res 280). Final action on the measure was anticlimactic, since most critical budget decisions had been made earlier in the year during consideration of a $63 billion deficit reduction bill (HR 4170). A deadlock over defense spending held up conference agreement on H Con Res 280 until the final weeks of the session. *(Deficit reduction, p. 56)*

H Con Res 280 assumed $149.2 billion in deficit reductions through fiscal 1987: $50.8 billion from increased tax revenues; $58.3 billion from limiting increases in the defense budget; $12.2 billion from savings in entitlements and other mandatory benefit programs; $3.9 billion from reductions in non-defense discretionary spending; $18.3 billion from net interest savings; and $5.7 billion from offsetting receipts.

The resolution projected that the deficit would rise to $207.6 billion in fiscal 1987 in spite of these reductions. For fiscal 1985, the measure set spending at $932 billion and revenues at $750.9 billion, with a deficit of $181.1 billion.

In addressing its 1985 fiscal plan, Congress reversed the decade-old budget process, which required lawmakers to adopt a budget resolution before acting on spending and revenue bills for any year. Republican leaders in the Senate and Reagan administration officials opted early in 1984 for a strategy that would commit Congress to deficit-cutting legislation before it adopted a fiscal 1985 budget resolution. *(Budget process, box, p. 34)*

Following that strategy, the Senate first passed a $140 billion deficit reduction bill that was dubbed the "Rose Garden" plan because President Reagan endorsed it in the White House Rose Garden. The Senate then adopted a budget resolution (S Con Res 106) that mirrored the deficit reduction measure.

The House followed the route outlined in the 1974 Congressional Budget Act, first setting overall spending and revenue goals in a budget resolution and then passing deficit reduction legislation required by its fiscal plan.

House Action

Committee. The leaders of the Democratic-controlled House spent several weeks in February and March forging a consensus among their colleagues on the shape of the fiscal 1985 budget. The leadership, working with House Budget Committee Chairman James R. Jones, D-Okla., eventually endorsed a proposal based on a "pay-as-you-go" concept, which required any new spending to be offset by either increases in taxes or spending cuts in other areas.

The pay-as-you-go plan had been championed since 1982 by Rep. George Miller, D-Calif., and was adopted with liberal Democratic support. Other members argued unsuccessfully for a budget "freeze," continuing taxes and spending at fiscal 1984 levels. Still others called for a $200 billion deficit reduction instead of the $100 billion cut proposed by President Reagan. *(Reagan budget, p. 56)*

The budget blueprint adopted by the committee March 28 on a party-line 19-9 vote (H Con Res 280) envisioned deficit reductions of $182 billion during fiscal years 1985-87. Defense was limited to a 3.5 percent increase after adjustment for inflation, and domestic spending was reduced about $15 billion through 1987. The resolution also called for $49.8 billion in tax hikes. Fiscal 1985 outlays were set at $918.1 billion, revenues at $742.45 billion.

To appease junior Democrats who wanted to force a floor vote on a pay-as-you-go amendment, the committee also reported a second resolution (H Con Res 282 — H Rept 98-645) that did not include that feature. However, House leaders decided to take up H Con Res 280 instead.

The three-year deficit reduction totals in the Democratic budget plan broke down as follows: $31.35 billion in 1985; $63.35 billion in 1986; and $87.65 billion in 1987. The budget would be in deficit $174.45 billion in 1985, $172.3 billion in 1986 and $182 billion in 1987.

The resolution required $12.35 billion in entitlement savings over the three years. However, the House already had approved some of this amount in 1983 as part of the fiscal 1984 reconciliation bill (HR 4169). *(1984 reconciliation bill, p. 60)*

Floor. The House adopted its pay-as-you-go budget resolution April 5 on a **250-168 key vote (R 21-139; D 229-29)** after rejecting a Republican plan and six other alternative budgets. *(1984 key votes, p. 927)*

The chief challenge was not from the Republicans' deficit reduction package, but from a modified freeze proposal offered by Florida Democrats Buddy MacKay and Bill Nelson that would have reduced deficits $234 billion over fiscal 1985-87. Despite heavy support from freshman Democrats, the plan was defeated 108-310.

A $205 billion GOP deficit reduction plan that would have frozen discretionary spending for three years and included additional administrative savings was rejected 107-311.

Senate Action

Committee. As the full Senate was debating deficit-reduction legislation, the Senate Budget Committee April 11 endorsed by a single vote a budget plan, backed by the GOP leadership and President Reagan, to slice $143.7 billion off the deficit through fiscal 1987. The plan received no Democratic votes. Though only one Republican defected from the party's ranks to vote against it — Mark Andrews, N.D. — a number of others expressed misgivings.

The committee-approved resolution (S Con Res 106 — S Rept 98-399) followed the Rose Garden plan negotiated in March by Senate Republicans and the administration. Three-year deficit reductions included $48.3 billion from tax increases, $40.2 billion from cutbacks in Reagan's de-

fense buildup and $37.4 billion from reductions in non-defense spending programs. Military spending would rise at an inflation-adjusted rate of slightly more than 7 percent over three years, compared with 3.5 percent under the House resolution.

The committee settled for the Reagan-backed plan only after five other plans that would have achieved larger deficit reductions failed to attract a majority. The biggest challenge came from a bipartisan proposal sponsored by Nancy Landon Kassebaum, R-Kan.; Charles E. Grassley, R-Iowa; and Joseph R. Biden Jr., D-Del. The plan, rejected 7-13, called for a one-year spending freeze on all federal programs, for three-year deficit reductions of $241.8 billion.

The most vociferous opponent of the plan was Armed Services Chairman John Tower, R-Texas, who also served on the Budget panel. The freeze on defense spending, Tower charged, would "almost be tantamount to unilateral disarmament."

Committee Chairman Pete V. Domenici, R-N.M., cautioned members that if they voted for the plan they were voting against such things as Social Security increases scheduled for January 1985. Although the plan had a great deal of appeal, it was highly unlikely it would ever be implemented, he said.

The Democratic alternative, which would have cut deficits $150 billion over fiscal years 1985-87, was defeated 10-11. Andrews was the only Republican who voted for it.

Floor. The Republican leadership held up floor action on the budget resolution pending Senate passage of HR 4170, the administration-backed deficit reduction bill. On May 18, one day after passage of HR 4170, the Senate adopted the committee-approved budget resolution after substituting its text for that of the House measure.

The Senate resolution called for $933.1 billion in spending and $750.9 billion in revenues in fiscal 1985, with a resulting deficit of $182.2 billion. The deficit would rise to $193.9 billion in fiscal 1986 and $212.5 billion in fiscal 1987 under the Senate plan.

Conference, Final Action

The conference on the budget resolution was delayed by the Senate's determination to force agreement on deficit reduction legislation before adopting a final budget guideline. The key obstacle was the Senate's insistence on including spending "caps" in the deficit reduction measure that would set funding levels for defense and non-defense spending for three years.

HR 4170 cleared Congress June 27, after Senate conferees agreed to non-binding language that allowed each chamber to follow its own budget in setting appropriations levels.

Budget conferees quickly settled most of their spending differences, but negotiations deadlocked over defense spending. Following marching orders issued by the White House, Senate Republicans refused to budge from the average 7 percent inflation-adjusted growth rate through fiscal 1987 agreed to by the president in the Rose Garden plan.

Initially, it appeared that the Republicans wanted to use the conference on the defense authorization bill (HR 5167) as the basis for a budget agreement. The defense level in the House authorization bill — assuming a 6 percent real growth rate — was significantly higher than the 3.5 percent inflation-adjusted growth rate assumed in the House budget resolution. The Senate's authorization mea-

sure provided a 7.8 percent inflation-adjusted growth rate for military programs. But the conference on the defense authorization bill also was stalled — at least in part because Senate Republicans did not want any specific defense number that could be used to lower the final defense appropriations level. *(Defense authorization, p. 235)*

As the stalemate continued, the Budget Committee's ranking Democrat, Lawton Chiles, D-Fla., attempted to force final action on the budget resolution by objecting to consideration of fiscal 1985 appropriations bills. The 1974 Congressional Budget Act barred consideration of the funding bills prior to adoption of the budget resolution, which should have been in pace by May 15. *(Appropriations, p. 61)*

To keep the appropriations process moving, Majority Leader Howard H. Baker Jr., R-Tenn., on Aug. 10 accepted Chiles' suggestion that Republican and Democratic leaders convene a budgetary "summit" meeting to fashion a defense spending compromise. House Speaker Thomas P. O'Neill Jr., D-Mass., also agreed.

Negotiating sessions between Baker and O'Neill centered on the MX missile. A compromise reached Sept. 20 set fiscal 1985 defense spending at about 5 percent over 1984 levels, after taking inflation into account. The agreement also set conditions on spending for the MX.

Once the defense logjam was broken, conferees moved quickly to wrap up the budget resolution. Conferees finished work Sept. 25. The Senate approved the conference report on the budget resolution (H Rept 98-1079) the next day by voice vote. The House approved the report Oct. 1 on a 232-162 vote.

Fiscal 1984 Revisions

Caught up in a yearlong dispute over deficit reduction, Congress' revisions of its fiscal 1984 budget did not clear until Oct. 1, one day after the close of the fiscal year.

The revisions, which were included in the fiscal 1985 budget resolution (H Con Res 280), reflected changes in economic conditions, re-estimates of spending and legislative action by Congress since approval of the initial 1984 resolution in June 1983.

The revised resolution lowered fiscal 1984 spending to $845.6 billion, nearly $4 billion below the minimum figure Congress originally had allowed. Revenues also dropped, to $672.9 billion from $679.6 billion, leaving a deficit of $172.7 billion under the congressional plan.

The actual deficit for the year wound up at $175.36 billion. Spending totaled $841.8 billion; revenues, $666.5 billion. *(1983 action, p. 51; budgets compared, p. 36)*

Fiscal 1984 Reconciliation Cuts

Congress in early April cleared a budget reconciliation bill left hanging from fiscal 1984.

By a 67-26 vote, the Senate April 5 passed a measure (HR 4169 — PL 98-270) providing $8.2 billion in budget savings over fiscal 1984-87. The Senate made no changes in the bill, which the House had passed in October 1983. However, the delay in enactment trimmed $2.1 billion from the $10.3 billion House-approved savings figure. The savings were mandated by the fiscal 1984 budget resolution (H Con Res 91). The House passed HR 4169 in October 1983. *(1983 action, p. 54)*

Most of the savings in HR 4169 came from delaying cost-of-living adjustments (COLAs) for federal retirees.

The bill also gave white-collar federal employees and members of Congress a retroactive 4 percent pay raise in 1984 instead of the 3.5 percent increase that took effect in January. Although several senators were unhappy about the backdoor pay raise for themselves, Budget Committee Chairman Pete V. Domenici, R-N.M., said he did not want to change the House-passed version of HR 4169, go to conference and risk missing an April 30 deadline necessary to achieve the federal retiree savings.

The Senate April 5 by voice vote passed a separate bill (S 2539) to hold the pay increase to 3.5 percent, but the House did not act and the 4 percent raise was awarded. This boosted congressional salaries from $72,200 a year to $72,600. *(Story, p. 832)*

Before sending the reconciliation bill to the president, the Senate and House approved a concurrent resolution (S Con Res 102) striking provisions that would have given disabled veterans a 4.1 percent COLA in April. Congress had approved a 3.5 percent COLA in a separate bill (S 1388) cleared Feb. 9. *(Story, p. 622)*

Provisions

As signed into law April 18, HR 4169 (PL 98-270):

COLAs. Delayed the effective date of civil service retirement and disability COLAs until December, with payments due in January 1985.

The COLA change also affected military, foreign service, Coast Guard and public health retirement systems, which were linked to civil service retirement under existing law.

Disaster Loans. Extended for three years, until Sept. 30, 1986, a requirement that farmers seek disaster loans from the Farmers Home Administration before seeking more favorable loans from the Small Business Administration (SBA).

This requirement was extended for an additional year by the Deficit Reduction Act of 1984 (HR 4170 — PL 98-369) cleared June 27. *(Deficit reduction, p. 56; disaster loans, p. 516)*

● Reduced interest rates on SBA disaster loans, imposing a ceiling of 4 percent on loans to homeowners and businesses who could not find credit elsewhere and 8 percent on loans to those who could.

● Made eligible for SBA disaster assistance businesses adversely affected by the payment-in-kind (PIK) farm acreage reduction program or by the devaluation of the Mexican peso.

● Limited direct loans for physical disasters to $500 million annually in fiscal 1984-86. Non-physical disasters were limited to $100 million annually during that period.

Federal, Congressional Pay Raise. Gave white-collar federal employees and members of Congress a 4 percent pay raise in 1984 instead of the 3.5 percent increase that took effect in January. The extra half a percentage point was retroactive to January, and cost $249 million in 1984.

Fiscal 1985 Appropriations

Deficit and election-year politics stalled the regular appropriations process in 1984. As a result, most funding for fiscal 1985 was enacted as part of the largest catchall continuing appropriations bill ever adopted by Congress.

The mammoth $470 billion funding bill (H J Res 648 — PL 98-473), which cleared Congress Oct. 11, contained money for programs in nine of the 13 regular appropriations measures Congress considered each year.

Overall, Congress approved less spending than the administration had originally requested for discretionary programs. According to the Office of Management and Budget, total spending authority for fiscal 1985 was $563.5 billion, compared with $572.9 billion requested by President Reagan in his February 1984 budget submission.

The lower funding levels were achieved, in part, by limiting spending increases for most programs to 2 percent. Senate Republicans agreed to this formula early in the year as part of the "Rose Garden" deficit reduction negotiations, and later the full Senate endorsed it. House Republicans successfully pushed through across-the-board percentage cuts during floor action on five appropriations bills. *(Deficit reduction, p. 56)*

Appropriations action was complicated by the year-long debate over deficit reduction, which delayed final action on the fiscal 1985 budget resolution until Oct. 1 — long past the May 15 deadline. The 1974 Congressional Budget Act required Congress to approve a budget resolution setting spending and revenue goals before taking up the annual appropriations bills. Over the years each chamber had waived that provision for individual appropriations measures, but in 1984 the entire appropriations process fell within the Budget Act restriction. *(Budget process, box, p. 34)*

The House May 22 approved a blanket Budget Act waiver for all fiscal 1985 appropriations bills, and by the Independence Day recess it had approved eight of the 13 measures.

The Senate was working its way through appropriations bills as well, waiving the Budget Act bill by bill. That practice continued until Aug. 1 when Lawton Chiles, D-Fla., objected to a waiver for the agriculture funding bill (HR 5743). Chiles, the Budget Committee's ranking Democrat, hoped to force final action on the budget resolution, which was stalled by a dispute over defense spending.

Backed by fellow Democrats, Chiles filibustered until Aug. 8, when the Senate cut him off by invoking cloture on a 68-30 vote. An earlier attempt to invoke cloture had failed Aug. 6 on a **54-31 key vote (R 46-3; D 8-28)**, six short of the 60 votes required. *(1984 key votes, p. 927)*

Although the vote was reversed two days later, Chiles' obstructionist tactics eventually persuaded Senate Majority Leader Howard H. Baker Jr., R-Tenn., to accept Chiles' suggestion for a high-level summit on defense spending.

The defense impasse was resolved, but not until Sept. 20, 11 days before the start of the fiscal year. By then Congress had little choice but to lump the nine remaining appropriations bills in a continuing resolution.

Tax Policy

Discussion of tax policy during President Reagan's first term seldom strayed far from the package of individual and business tax cuts that Reagan had espoused in his 1980 election campaign.

Reagan's tax plan, one of the twin pillars of his supply-side economic program, called for a three-year, 30 percent cut in individual income tax rates and faster depreciation write-offs for business investments. According to supply-side theory, such deep cuts would encourage individuals to invest savings and thus set off a spiral that would result in higher productivity and lower inflation. To help control inflation, and to narrow the government's role, Reagan also proposed significant cuts in scores of federal domestic spending programs.

Reagan's plan was widely attacked as unworkable and unrealistic. Many economists warned that the large-scale tax cuts could trigger an increase in spending rather than savings; that would push already worrisome inflation to even higher levels, they said. Some cautioned that the revenues lost to the Treasury through the tax cuts would lead to skyrocketing federal budget deficits. Congressional Democrats objected that the president's tax cuts were inequitable: Because rates were to be cut across the board, they would benefit primarily the well-to-do. Democrats were to raise this "fairness" issue repeatedly in the years ahead.

The president had a clear electoral mandate for his economic program, however, and within seven months after he took office Congress had voted the largest tax cut in history, along with a $35.2 billion spending cut measure. The tax bill, which reduced personal and corporate income taxes by an estimated $37.7 billion in fiscal 1982 alone, was to have a devastating impact on future federal deficits.

To win congressional approval Reagan was forced to accept some modifications in his plan. Individual rate cuts were scaled back to 25 percent over three years, and the final package also provided that tax brackets would be indexed to offset the effects of inflation, beginning in 1985. The indexing provisions were designed to prevent "bracket creep," by which taxpayers were pushed into higher tax brackets as their income increased because of inflation. Reagan had wanted to defer action on indexing, which was a central element in the Kemp-Roth tax bill from which his own proposals were drawn.

Republicans and conservative Southern Democrats banded together to push the bill through Congress. But the coalition fell apart later in the year when Reagan sought $3 billion worth of tax increases, euphemistically styled "revenue enhancements." Lawmakers took no action on that request, part of a larger budget-cutting plan intended to soothe public concern about rising federal deficits. Meanwhile the economy failed to pick up upon enactment of Reagan's economic program, as the president had predicted it would; instead the nation plunged into its most severe recession since the 1930s.

Democratic Repeal Efforts

"We have set in place a fundamental reorientation of our tax laws," Reagan boasted in his 1982 economic report to Congress. "Rather than using the tax system to redistribute existing income, we have significantly restructured it to encourage people to work, save and invest more."

That approach was the antithesis of traditional Democratic thinking on tax policy. Democrats generally focused their tax cuts on lower-income groups; they tried unsuccessfully in 1981 to skew more tax relief to low- and middle-income taxpayers than Reagan's plan would provide.

During the remainder of Reagan's first term congressional Democrats mounted a succession of efforts to repeal or limit the 1981 tax cuts. Those efforts, though unsuccessful, gave the Democrats repeated opportunities to attack Reagan on the fairness issue and to press their campaign for tax increases to reduce the budget deficits.

Reagan remained unswervingly opposed to any plan to tamper with the 1981 personal tax cuts. But the president ultimately endorsed three major tax increase bills, after saying he would oppose them:

● In 1982 Reagan reluctantly accepted deficit reduction legislation that modified some of the business tax cuts enacted in 1981 and imposed new excise taxes on individuals, for an estimated revenue gain of $98 billion over three years.

● Later in 1982 Reagan approved a bill that increased the federal gasoline tax to pay for mass transit and highway repairs. The bill, pushed by Democrats as an anti-recession jobs measure, was expected to yield about $5.5 billion annually.

References

Discussion of tax policy for the years 1945-64 may be found in *Congress and the Nation Vol. I*, pp. 397-442; for the years 1965-68, *Congress and the Nation Vol. II*, pp. 141-182; for the years 1969-72, *Congress and the Nation Vol. III*, pp. 77-96; for the years 1973-76, *Congress and the Nation Vol. IV*, pp. 83-106; for the years 1977-80, *Congress and the Nation Vol. V*, pp. 231-251.

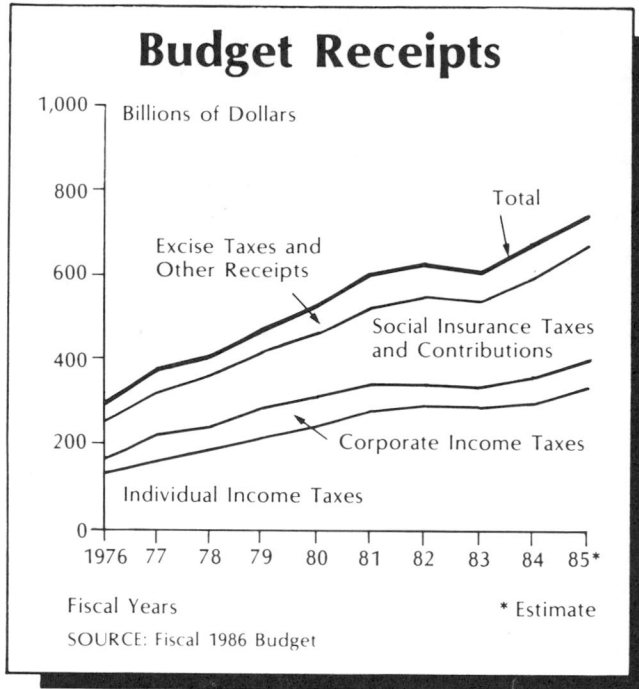

Budget Receipts

Billions of Dollars

Total

Excise Taxes and
Other Receipts

Social Insurance Taxes
and Contributions

Corporate Income Taxes

Individual Income Taxes

1976 77 78 79 80 81 82 83 84 85*

Fiscal Years   * Estimate

SOURCE: Fiscal 1986 Budget

● In 1984 the president signed legislation designed to raise taxes $50 billion through fiscal 1987, mostly by closing loopholes and increasing taxpayer compliance. The bill was the first installment of a $149.2 billion deficit reduction plan negotiated by Congress and Reagan early in the year.

In other major tax action, Reagan in 1983 endorsed payroll tax increases recommended by an advisory commission on Social Security reform. And he grudgingly agreed to repeal of a requirement for tax withholding on interest and dividend income that Congress had voted in 1982.

Impact of Tax Changes

Reagan had said he would reduce the federal government's tax bite on the economy, and he made good on his word. Partly as a result of his 1981 tax cuts and partly because of poor economic conditions, revenues as a percentage of gross national product (GNP) declined from a peak of 20.8 percent in fiscal 1981 to 18.6 percent in fiscal 1984. The White House Council of Economic Advisers estimated that revenues would have risen to 22 percent of GNP in 1984 in the absence of the 1981-84 tax law changes, given actual economic conditions.

The tax measures also had long-term implications. In its fiscal 1986 budget, released early in 1985, the administration estimated that tax law changes during Reagan's first term would cause a net loss in federal revenues of nearly $650 billion over fiscal 1984-88. A $1 trillion loss from the tax cuts enacted in 1981 would be partially offset by more than $400 billion in subsequent tax increases.

A substantial portion of the expected revenue loss was attributable to indexing, first effective in the 1985 tax year. Proponents viewed indexing as a brake on federal programs, because it forced members of Congress to vote tax increases if they wanted to augment spending. Previously, new spending could be financed through automatic increases in revenues that resulted from inflation. But indexing remained an attractive target for deficit reduction efforts. The Congressional Budget Office estimated early in 1985 that repeal of indexing would boost federal revenues by $149.3 billion over fiscal 1986-90. *(Indexing, box, p. 67)*

The 1984 Campaign

Democrats hammered at the fairness issue in the 1984 presidential election campaign. Reagan's tax cuts had helped the rich, they charged, while his spending cuts hit mainly the working poor. That view was supported in a 1984 study by the Urban Institute. The study said the Reagan tax cuts had not helped the poor at all, but that they raised after-tax income by 2.8 percent for the middle class and by 6 percent for the wealthy.

Polls indicated that many Americans considered the tax system riddled with loopholes and unfair. Both Reagan and Democratic presidential candidate Walter F. Mondale called for overhaul of the tax code to make it simpler and more equitable, but neither endorsed specific reform proposals.

Mondale made raising taxes a cornerstone of his campaign. He charged that Reagan was not being honest with the electorate if he did not admit the need for higher taxes to help reduce federal deficits. Reagan, however, said he would oppose a tax increase — except as a "last resort." His overwhelming electoral victory in November appeared to confirm the political wisdom of that stand.

As the year ended, President Reagan was weighing a tax reform plan prepared by the Treasury Department at his request. The Treasury plan, which recommended eliminating most special-interest tax breaks while lowering tax rates for individuals, pleased Democrats who had been pressing such changes for years.

Reagan was less enthusiastic. The president said he would "listen to the comments and suggestions of all Americans, especially those from Congress" before presenting his own tax proposals in 1985.

Chronology
Of Action
On Taxes

1981

President Reagan scored a legislative triumph in 1981 with the passage of the largest tax reduction bill in history.

The legislation, a central feature of the new president's supply-side economic program, cut individual income tax rates by 25 percent over three years. It also sharply cut business taxes to encourage new investment in plant and equipment. The bill was expected to reduce federal revenues by approximately $749 billion over the following five years. However, that figure was partially offset by increases in Social Security taxes over the period. *(Social Security, p. 645)*

Reagan promised that his tax plan would bring economic recovery as businesses realized a larger return on investments and individuals were encouraged by lower tax rates to work harder and to save more of their earnings.

But the economy did not quickly begin to improve as predicted. Instead, the large tax reductions and concern over a runaway federal deficit shook the financial markets. Interest rates rose and Wall Street sought action to close the deficit gap.

In September Reagan asked Congress to approve $3 billion in revenue-raising measures as part of a $16 billion deficit reduction package for fiscal 1982. But lawmakers were unwilling to raise taxes so soon after cutting them, and Reagan decided to defer action until 1982.

Reagan Tax Cuts

In a stunning endorsement of President Reagan's economic policies, Congress Aug. 4 completed action on legislation providing a $37.7 billion tax cut in fiscal 1982. The action came only four days after the House and Senate gave final approval to a $35.2 billion package of fiscal 1982 reconciliation spending cuts — the other major item in Reagan's economic program. *(Reconciliation, p. 40)*

The Economic Recovery Tax Act (ERTA) of 1981 was expected to put $749 billion — more money than the federal government planned to spend in fiscal 1982 — back in the hands of business and individual taxpayers over the next five years.

The final version of the bill (HR 4242 — PL 97-34) reflected a wide range of concessions made to ensure enactment of Reagan's revolutionary tax cut policies. But it retained the essence of the Reagan supply-side plan: across-the-board reductions in individual income taxes and faster write-offs for capital investment to spur productivity and economic growth.

Congress added one feature the president had hoped to defer. The bill called for indexation of individual income tax brackets to offset the effects of inflation, beginning in 1985. The aim was to eliminate "bracket creep," through which inflation pushed taxpayers into higher income levels subject to stiffer tax rates. *(Indexing, box, p. 67)*

Bowing to the realities of politics, the president had reshaped the package several times, giving in on some details while standing firm on the central theme. By doing so, he forced Democrats, intent on passing their own alternative tax plan, to move closer and closer to the administration position.

"This is President Reagan's economic tax recovery plan," Treasury Secretary Donald T. Regan told reporters Aug. 1 after a conference agreement was reached on the two versions of the bill passed by the House and Senate earlier in the week. Regan boasted that the administration received "95 percent" of what it had sought.

Democrats were more than happy to shift all responsibility for the economic consequences to Reagan. "Make no mistake about it," Rep. Dan Rostenkowski, D-Ill., chairman of the House Ways and Means Committee, told colleagues before the final vote. "This is the president's bill. It outlines a bold — and risky — economic strategy. Only time will tell whether the risks involved ... were worth taking."

The Reagan bill was a radical departure from the tax legislation produced by a generation of Democratic-dominated Congresses. Democratic tax bills tended to be relatively more generous to people at the low end of the income scale. And they generally placed emphasis on closing "loopholes" — limiting the special treatment afforded certain kinds of income. That approach culminated in the Tax Reform Act of 1976 (PL 94-455). In 1978, however, Congress repealed some prized liberal "reforms" and voted individual cuts skewed toward the upper end of the income scale. The Revenue Act of 1978 (PL 95-600) was a harbinger of the Reagan tax cuts three years later. *(Congress and the Nation Vol. IV, p. 99; Congress and the Nation Vol. V, p. 238)*

Democrats fought in vain against the 1981 Reagan tax plan. The Senate, with its new Republican majority, passed the bill with predictable ease. In the House, where a coalition of Republicans and conservative Democrats had assumed effective control of the chamber, a Democratic tax measure that would have provided additional tax relief to low- and middle-income taxpayers fell before the president's plan.

Throughout the remainder of Reagan's first term, Democrats waged a guerrilla campaign against the tax program they had been unable to block initially. While they won some changes in the 1981 legislation, the Democrats never succeeded in scaling back its critical elements: a three-year, 25 percent reduction in personal tax cuts, followed by indexing of taxes for inflation. *(Subsequent action, pp. 72, 78, 79)*

Background

Reagan's 1981 tax legislation originated with a bill first introduced in 1977 by Rep. Jack F. Kemp, R-N.Y., and Sen. William V. Roth Jr., R-Del. The Kemp-Roth bill called for a three-year average income tax cut of approximately 30 percent, future indexing of taxes for inflation and reductions in business taxes. The proposal was not given serious attention until the Republican Party and Reagan himself endorsed Kemp-Roth during the 1980 campaign. *(Congress and the Nation Vol. V, p. 231)*

Following through on his campaign pledge, on Feb. 18, 1981, President Reagan asked Congress to approve individ-

ual and business tax cuts totaling $53.9 billion in fiscal 1982.

In line with the Kemp-Roth plan, Reagan proposed to cut marginal tax rates by 10 percent a year for three years. The Kemp-Roth indexing proposal was dropped, however.

Under existing law, the maximum marginal tax rate — the rate imposed on the last dollar of an individual's income — was 70 percent. But that rate affected only unearned or investment income, such as interest and dividends, because the tax code imposed a maximum rate of 50 percent on earned income, such as wages, salaries and fees.

As a result of the personal rate cuts, once the top marginal rate dropped to 50 percent the distinction between earned income and unearned income would be eliminated. Reagan also proposed cutting the preferential tax rate on capital gains, profits earned by selling stocks, real estate or other assets.

Reagan also proposed a simplified depreciation system for business investments, called the Accelerated Cost Recovery System (ACRS). The depreciation schedule, to be phased in over five years, would provide businesses with $9.7 billion for investment in fiscal 1982 rising to $44.2 billion in fiscal 1985, with parallel revenue losses to the Treasury.

If the tax cuts were not enacted, the administration said, federal taxes would consume a rapidly increasing share of the national income — rising to 23.4 percent of gross national product (GNP) after 1985. Under the president's program, the Treasury Department said, tax receipts would drop to 20.4 percent of GNP in 1982 and 19.3 percent by 1985. Individual rate reductions would cost the Treasury $44.2 billion in fiscal 1982, rising to $162.4 billion in fiscal 1986.

Although the congressional response to his Feb. 18 tax proposals was unenthusiastic, the president spurned all compromise suggestions for several months. On June 4, however, Reagan finally proposed major changes in his original plan. The revised proposal reduced the initial individual rate reduction to 5 percent and delayed it three months until Oct. 1, 1981. To build congressional support, Reagan also added some popular "sweeteners," including savings incentives, a tuition tax credit and tax relief to ease the "marriage penalty" on two-earner married couples.

Senate Action

Committee. Pressuring the House Ways and Means Committee to act quickly on tax legislation, the Senate Finance Committee June 25 adopted by a 19-1 vote a package almost identical to that requested by Reagan.

It attached its tax cut package to a House-passed debt limit measure (H J Res 266), a maneuver designed to circumvent the constitutional mandate that all revenue-raising measures originate in the House. The committee reported its bill July 6 (S Rept 97-144).

The panel approved by a 15-4 vote the core of Reagan's plan: a three-year, 25 percent across-the-board cut in individual income tax rates and an accelerated depreciation plan for business. And it accepted administration proposals to ease the marriage penalty and to increase deductions for contributions to retirement plans set up by individuals and the self-employed. Other provisions reduced estate and gift taxes, increased tax relief for American workers overseas, and increased tax credits for the rehabilitation of old buildings and for small oil royalty owners subject to the windfall profits tax.

The committee also added several items to the Reagan proposal, including a one-year "all-savers" plan, promoted by savings and loan institutions to counter dwindling deposits. The provision would allow banks, credit unions and savings and loans to issue one-year certificates that would earn 70 percent of the yield on a one-year Treasury bill. Individuals could exclude up to $1,000 of the certificate interest from their incomes (couples up to $2,000).

The provision would cut government revenues by an estimated $4.6 billion by 1984. To offset the cost, the panel agreed to allow the current $200 ($400 for a joint return) exclusion for dividend and interest income to revert to prior law — a $100 ($200 for a joint return) exclusion for dividend income. *(Repeal, p. 90)*

The committee also approved, 9-5, an indexing plan under which individual income, capital gains and estate and gift taxes would be adjusted to reflect increases in the Consumer Price Index, beginning in 1985. The indexing provisions were to be offered as a committee amendment to the Finance bill, requiring a separate vote on the Senate floor.

Floor. The Senate took its bill to the floor July 15 and approved its provisions July 29. On July 31 the Senate substituted its bill for the text of HR 4242, which the House had passed two days earlier.

The decisive Senate vote came July 29 when the Finance Committee's version as amended on the floor was approved 89-11. Thirty-seven of the Senate's 47 Democrats voted for the bill; only one Republican voted against it.

During 12 days of debate, the Senate considered 118 amendments and adopted 80.

On July 16 members approved by a **key 57-40 vote (R 43-8; D 14-32)** the committee amendment requiring the indexation of individual income taxes starting in 1985, the year after the proposed 25 percent rate cut would be in full effect. According to the Joint Committee on Taxation, indexation could cut revenues by $12.6 billion in fiscal 1985 and $37.4 billion in 1986. *(1981 key votes, p. 879)*

Opponents argued that indexation would take away congressional ability to target future tax reductions, result in bloated budget deficits and prove inflationary by giving taxpayers more take-home pay during times of high inflation. But supporters countered that the plan would put a hold on government spending and force Congress to go on record when it needed to increase taxes, instead of allowing inflation to do the job more painlessly.

In earlier action the Senate July 23 rejected a Democratic alternative to the Reagan tax plan on a **26-71 key vote (R 0-51; D 26-20)**. The amendment, offered by Ernest F. Hollings, D-S.C., would have provided only a one-year, 10 percent cut in individual income taxes, with much of the relief targeted to those earning less than $50,000.

In other major action, the Senate:

● Adopted 56-40 an administration-backed substitute for the committee's all-savers plan that extended the program to 15 months and revised the interest exclusion plan. The revised plan was attached to an amendment, subsequently approved 86-10, that required institutions issuing the certificates to use 75 percent of the additional savings income for home or farm loans.

● Tabled 61-38 an amendment to exempt 1,000 barrels of oil a day for independent producers and 10 barrels a day for royalty owners from the federal "windfall profits" tax on rising oil prices. *(Windfall profits tax, Congress and the Nation Vol. V, p. 503)*

Indexing for Inflation: Tax Policy Watershed

Although slipped in almost as an afterthought, the indexing provisions of the 1981 tax law (PL 97-34) marked a major shift in revenue policy.

The indexing plan called for automatic adjustment of individual income taxes to offset inflation, beginning in 1985. It was designed to prevent taxpayers from being pushed into higher tax brackets if their income rose solely because of inflation.

Indexing halted such "bracket creep" by revising income tax brackets, the personal exemption and the zero bracket amount (that amount of income on which there is no tax) to reflect, and offset, yearly increases in inflation as measured by the Consumer Price Index.

Those who pushed the indexing provision said inflation had given liberal Congresses a relatively painless way to amass funding for new government programs. They said it was time for Congress to be more "honest" about its spending and tax policies.

Opponents charged that indexing would lock the government into perpetual deficits or a succession of painful spending cuts and would prevent Congress from reforming the tax system through periodic tax reduction. They also said indexing would weaken the nation's will to fight inflation by shielding more people from its destructive effects.

Adoption of Plan

Indexing was not included in President Reagan's original tax cut proposal, even though the president supported the concept. The administration wanted to steer clear of any proposals that might bog down the primary elements of Reagan's tax plan: a three-year, 25 percent rate reduction for individuals and an accelerated depreciation system for businesses.

Congressional support for indexing was strong, however. During floor debate on the Reagan tax bill, the Senate adopted, 57-40, an indexing provision approved by its Finance Committee. The Senate action encouraged backers in the House, where an indexing bill had 223 cosponsors. They urged the administration to add indexing to its tax plan to ensure defeat of a Democratic alternative measure. The administration agreed, and indexing was included in the final version of the tax package, cleared July 31.

Impact on Tax Policy

Indexing advocates viewed the proposal as a way to rein in runaway federal spending. They charged that recent Congresses had used the extra tax revenues brought in by inflation to finance questionable government programs. Indexing would force spending restraint, they said.

And, as indexing curtailed government revenues,

Congress no longer would be able to bestow periodic tax "cuts" on constituents. Thus members no longer would receive credit for cutting taxes when they really were only stopping them from getting any larger.

Indexing proponents also argued for permanent tax rules. "I think the economy will be better off if we set the rules of the game. It will make it much easier for businesses and individuals to make decisions over the long run," said House Ways and Means Committee member Bill Gradison, R-Ohio.

But setting the rules also deprived Congress of the ability to change the tax code, possibly for the better, countered Sen. Russell B. Long, D-La. Long, ranking minority member of the Senate Finance Committee, argued during floor debate on the indexing provision that President Reagan's far-reaching tax program would not have been possible if such a system were in place in 1981.

Long and others claimed that indexing would tie Congress to the current tax system and leave little leeway for making changes to adjust to fluid economic conditions.

Indexing advocates wrote off such statements as the bitter replies of Democrats who had built their careers on government growth.

Impact on Budget

Both proponents and opponents of indexing conceded that the provision would put a great deal of pressure on the federal budget.

Before Senate adoption of the indexing proposal, Budget Committee Chairman Pete V. Domenici, R-N.M., warned that indexing would push the budget "sharply into deficit" in 1985. He chastised his colleagues for setting the nation on such an uncharted course during a time of economic uncertainty.

"What we are really saying with management by formula is that we cannot trust ourselves, the policy makers, to make the hard decisions on tax and spending policy without being bolstered by a formula," he said.

Even some supporters of indexing doubted that it would be permitted to take effect in 1985.

Indexing "is a very good idea, but I think we'll never see it," said Rudolph G. Penner, director of tax policy for the American Enterprise Institute. Penner pointed out that other countries, such as Australia, had suspended their indexing programs when budgetary pressures became too great. "And I think we'll suspend ours," he said.

Penner, who became director of the Congressional Budget Office in 1983, had to eat his words. Indexing took effect as scheduled in 1985, even though the budget deficit had tripled since 1981.

● Adopted 97-1 an amendment to allow those who did not itemize deductions on their tax returns to take a deduction for charitable contributions. The measure was expected to cut revenues by about $4.8 billion over the next five years.

House Action

Committee. Despite prodding by the Senate and the administration, the House panel did not approve its tax cut bill (HR 4242 — H Rept 97-201) until July 23.

After rejecting the president's individual tax cut plan, the committee July 14 approved a two-year, 15 percent proposal by a 22-13 vote, basically along party lines.

The Ways and Means plan cut average individual income tax rates by 5 percent Oct. 1, 1981, and by an additional 10 percent July 1, 1982. It skewed the cuts to favor those earning less than $50,000.

Including tax breaks for low-income families, reductions in the marriage penalty and other provisions, the committee's individual tax package was expected to lower revenues by $419 billion over fiscal 1982-86, compared with $500 billion for individual cuts in the Finance Committee bill.

The committee approved a business tax plan that gradually lowered the top corporate income tax rate paid by companies with annual incomes over $100,000 from the current 46 percent to 34 percent. Business would be allowed to expense, or write off, the entire cost of machinery and equipment in the year of its purchase, instead of depreciating its cost over a period of time.

All told, the committee business tax plan was expected to equal the cost of the administration's business proposal, estimated by the Joint Taxation Committee at $485 billion through 1990.

The panel agreed to several tax relief measures to encourage savings and investment. It accepted an administration proposal to increase deductions for contributions to retirement plans set up by the self-employed, known as Keogh plans, and to individual retirement accounts (IRAs). It also adopted a savings certificate plan similar to that approved by the Senate.

In addition, the committee approved several provisions designed to help small businesses, expected to cost almost $10 billion over the next five years.

Before reporting the bill, the panel at 2 a.m. July 22 adopted by an 18-17 vote a provision allowing the exemption of 500 barrels of oil a day from the windfall profits tax, at a cost to the Treasury of approximately $7 billion over the next five years.

The oil "sweetener" emerged from days of negotiation among Democrats anxious to hold the votes of conservative party members — many of whom came from oil-producing states — when the tax bill reached the House floor.

But not to be outbid, the White House and House Republicans hastily revised Reagan's 25 percent, across-the-board tax cut and crafted a new package expected to cost over $730 billion through fiscal 1986.

Added to Reagan's individual rate cuts and accelerated depreciation plans were tax breaks for oil producers, annual indexation of tax rates to offset inflation, relief from estate and gift taxes, increased charitable deductions and a host of other measures designed, for the most part, to win a handful of swing votes.

Both Republicans and Democrats admitted their bills were more products of a political bidding war than blueprints for sound economic policy.

Floor. Reagan's tax cut triumph was assured July 29 when the Democratic House substituted his tax package for the Ways and Means Committee version before passing the bill, 323-107.

Forty-eight Democrats, mostly Southern conservatives known as "Boll Weevils," defected to Reagan in the crucial showdown as the House adopted the administration substitute by a **key 238-195 vote (R 190-1; D 48-194)**. Only one Republican broke ranks. *(1981 key votes, p. 879)*

The House vote was touted by some as a test, after Reagan's budget victory a month earlier, of who had true control of the House — the Democratic majority or administration-backed Republicans in coalition with conservative Democrats.

"If we accept the president's substitute, we accept his dominance of our House for the months ahead," warned Rostenkowski, in his first floor battle as Ways and Means Committee chairman. "We surrender to the political and economic whim of his White House."

The vote was a painful loss for Rostenkowski. Earlier in the year he had tried to compromise with the White House on a bipartisan bill, but the talks quickly broke down. Some Democrats criticized Rostenkowski for trying to "out-Republican" the Republicans in an attempt to win votes. They argued that Democrats should have constructed a traditional Democratic tax bill aimed at helping the poor over the wealthy, even if that meant going down to defeat.

A day before the vote, both sides labeled the outcome too close to call. But as debate was about to begin, House Speaker Thomas P. O'Neill Jr., D-Mass., all but conceded the battle was lost — largely as a result of heavy lobbying by the president, his aides and voters mobilized by Reagan in a televised appeal July 27. "We are experiencing a telephone blitz like this nation has never seen," O'Neill said. "It's had a devastating effect."

Conference Action

The conference agreement on the bill (H Rept 97-215) was the product of an all-night session July 31.

The Senate accepted House provisions to give oil royalty owners more generous exemptions from the windfall profits tax and to totally exempt "stripper" wells — those that produced 10 barrels or less of oil a day — from the tax after 1982. The two measures were expected to cost $8.4 billion through fiscal 1986.

House plans to freeze the oil depletion allowance at 22 percent and to allow a tax credit for wood-burning stoves were dropped, as was a Senate provision to give tax credits for home heating costs. Both measures reduced the windfall profits tax on newly discovered oil from 30 percent to 15 percent by 1986, a $3.2 billion tax break.

The House accepted Senate-passed child-care credits, increased tax benefits for employee stock ownership plans and stricter curbs on the commodity tax straddle, a tax shelter technique involving the purchase of offsetting futures contracts. The Senate accepted House-passed tax breaks for homes sold, but it rejected a provision to reduce to six months from one year the holding period for capital gains. That change was approved in 1984 deficit reduction legislation. *(Story, p. 79)*

The Senate gave its final approval to the measure Aug. 3 by a 67-8 vote. The House cleared the package the following day, 282-95.

Major Provisions

As signed into law Aug. 13, the Economic Recovery Tax Act of 1981 (HR 4242 — PL 97-34) included the following major provisions:

Individual Tax Cuts

Rate Cuts. Reduced all individual income tax rates by 5 percent Oct. 1, 1981, 10 percent July 1, 1982, and an additional 10 percent July 1, 1983. Each cut was to be applied to marginal tax rates, or those rates imposed on the last dollar of income. The changes were to be reflected in lower withholding in paychecks beginning Oct. 1.

The 1981 cut was just over 1 percent for the entire year because the 5 percent rate change was in effect only for the last three months of the year. The cuts averaged 10 percent for 1982, 19 percent for 1983 and 23 percent for 1984, when the program was fully phased in. The final cut was only 23 percent instead of 25 percent because the rate reductions each succeeding year were applied to a smaller base.

Investment Income. Reduced the top rate on investment, or "unearned," income from 70 percent to 50 percent, the existing maximum for earned income.

● Reduced the maximum rate on capital gains — which were taxed at 40 percent of the investment income rate — from 28 percent to 20 percent, effective June 10, 1981.

Indexing. Increased individual income tax brackets, the zero bracket amount and the personal exemption to reflect annual increases in the Consumer Price Index, beginning with the 1985 tax year. The tax rates would remain the same.

Marital Deductions. Allowed two-earner married couples filing joint returns in 1982 to deduct 5 percent of up to $30,000 (a maximum deduction of $1,500) of the lesser of their two incomes. The deduction would increase to 10 percent (a maximum of $3,000) in 1983 and after.

Child Care. Increased to 30 percent from 20 percent the tax credit for child and dependent day-care expenses in connection with the taxpayer's employment, for those earning $10,000 or less. The credit would be reduced one percentage point for each $2,000 in additional income, up to $28,000. Those earning more than $28,000 would be eligible for a 20 percent credit.

● Increased the maximum amount of expenses eligible for the credit from $2,000 to $2,400 for one dependent and from $4,000 to $4,800 for two or more dependents.

Charitable Contributions. Allowed individuals who did not itemize deductions on their tax returns to deduct charitable contributions as follows: up to 25 percent of contributions of $100 or less (a $25 maximum deduction) in 1982 and 1983; 25 percent of up to $300 in 1984 (a $75 maximum); 50 percent with no cap in 1985; and 100 percent in 1986. The provision would expire after 1986.

Sale of Residence. Extended from 18 months to 24 months the period an individual was allowed to defer taxes on proceeds from the sale of a primary residence if that money was used to buy another home at the same or greater cost.

● Increased from $100,000 to $125,000 the one-time exclusion from tax of capital gains from the sale of a home by those aged 55 and over.

Foreign Earned Income. Allowed an individual working overseas to exclude from tax up to $75,000 of foreign earned income in 1982. The exclusion would increase $5,000 each year over the next four years to $95,000 in 1986 and after. The provision, if elected by the taxpayer, would replace current tax breaks for the excess living costs of those working abroad.

Business Tax Cuts

Accelerated Depreciation. Replaced the complex existing system for depreciating assets over their "useful" lives with a simplified approach called the Accelerated Cost Recovery System (ACRS). Under ACRS, investments in plant and equipment would be grouped in four classes, each having a standard schedule of deductions that could be taken over a fixed recovery period. Businesses could write off the value of an asset over three, five, 10 or 15 years at an accelerated rate.

Assets were classified as follows:

Three years: Automobiles, light trucks, equipment used in research and development, certain racehorses, and machinery and equipment that under existing law had a depreciation range of up to four years. A one-time, 6 percent investment tax credit would be allowed.

Five years: All other machinery and equipment, public utilities with a current depreciation range of 18 years or less, single-use farm structures (such as hen houses) and some petroleum storage facilities. A 10 percent investment tax credit would be allowed.

Ten years: Public utility property with a current depreciation range from 18.5 years to 25 years, railroad tank cars, some mobile homes and other structures (such as theme parks). A 10 percent investment credit would be allowed.

Fifteen years: Public utility property with a current depreciation range of more than 25 years and all other buildings. A 10 percent investment tax credit would be available for public utility property. *(1984 change, p. 79)*

Small Business Depreciation. Allowed expensing — the immediate deduction — by small businesses of the cost of new or used machinery and equipment, of up to $5,000 in 1982 and 1983, $7,500 in 1984 and 1985, and $10,000 after 1985.

Credit Carryover. Extended from seven to 15 years the period over which businesses could carry forward unused tax credits and offset them against future tax liability.

Leasing. Liberalized leasing laws to make it easier to transfer investment tax credit and accelerated depreciation benefits from businesses that were not profitable enough to use such benefits to businesses that could use them.

Congress in 1982 voted new restrictions on leasing to halt "abuses" of the 1981 provisions. *(Story, p. 72)*

Rehabilitation of Old Buildings. Increased the current 10 percent investment tax credit for the rehabilitation of old buildings to 15 percent for buildings 30-39 years old, 20 percent for buildings 40 years and older and 25 percent for certified historic structures.

Research and Development. Allowed, through Dec. 31, 1985, a 25 percent tax credit for new spending on research and development above and beyond the average annual amount spent on such activities over the three preceding years.

Shareholder Size. Increased from 15 to 25 the maximum number of shareholders a small business could have and still retain the option of having its individual shareholders, not both the corporation and the shareholders, taxed on income.

Small Business Accounting. Simplified the use of "last in, first out" (LIFO) accounting. LIFO is generally an

attractive accounting method to use during times of high inflation, but, under existing law, had been considered too complex for small businesses to undertake.

Corporate Rate Reductions. Reduced the lowest corporate income tax rates from 17 percent on the first $25,000 of income to 16 percent in 1982 and 15 percent in 1983, and from 20 percent on the next $25,000 to 19 percent in 1982 and 18 percent in 1983.

'Incentive' Stock Options. Created so-called "incentive" stock options for employees to buy their employer's stock and for which the employee would be taxed only when the stock purchased under the option was sold. Under existing law, employees were taxed on ordinary income at the time they were granted such options.

Targeted Jobs Tax Credit. Extended for one year the targeted jobs tax credit program created by the 1978 tax bill (PL 95-600), which was due to expire at the end of 1981, and expanded the group of disadvantaged workers for which employers could receive the credit. *(Congress and the Nation Vol. V, p. 243, subsequent extensions, pp. 76, 79, 672)*

Energy Provisions

Royalty Owners. Increased from $1,000 to $2,500 the tax credit allowed small oil royalty owners to offset the windfall profits tax in 1981. *(Windfall profits tax, Congress and the Nation Vol. V, p. 503)*

● Provided an exemption from the windfall profits tax on oil production of two barrels a day for 1982-84 and three barrels of oil a day for 1985 and after.

'Stripper' Oil. Exempted from the windfall profits tax all independently produced oil from "stripper" wells — those that produce an average of 10 barrels of oil a day or less. The provision would begin in 1983.

Newly Discovered Oil. Reduced gradually from 30 percent to 15 percent by 1986 the windfall profits tax on newly discovered oil.

Savings Incentives

Individual Retirement Accounts (IRAs). Increased to the lesser of $2,000 or 100 percent of compensation (from $1,500 or 15 percent of compensation) the amount an individual could deduct for annual contributions to an IRA.

● Increased from $1,750 to $2,250 the deduction for contributions to "spousal" IRAs, those set up by a working spouse for both himself, or herself, and a non-working spouse. A requirement that contributions must be equally divided between the two spouses was dropped.

● Allowed deductible IRA contributions both for those not covered and for those covered by an employer-sponsored plan. In cases where an individual was covered by an employer-sponsored plan, voluntary contributions to that plan would be deductible up to $2,000.

● Permitted divorced spouses to contribute at least $1,125 a year to an IRA that had been set up for them by the other spouse. Under existing law, such persons could no longer contribute to such an IRA after divorce.

Self-Employed Retirement Plans (Keogh). Increased from $7,500 to $15,000 the amount a self-employed individual could deduct for contributions to his or her own retirement plan.

Interest and Dividend Exclusion. Repealed as of Jan. 1, 1982, the current $200 exclusion ($400 for couples) allowed for interest and dividend income, and reinstated a previous $100 ($200 for couples) exclusion for dividend income only.

● Allowed taxpayers, beginning in 1985, to exclude 15 percent of up to $3,000 ($6,000 for couples) of interest income.

Savings Certificates. Allowed banks, savings and loans, credit unions and other depository institutions to issue, from Oct. 1, 1981, through Dec. 31, 1982, one-year savings certificates that would yield 70 percent of the yield on one-year Treasury bills.

● Permitted individuals to exclude up to $1,000 of the interest on such certificates; couples could exclude up to $2,000.

● Required institutions, other than credit unions, issuing the certificates to make at least 75 percent of their net new savings available for home or agricultural loans.

Employee Stock Ownership Plans (ESOPs). Replaced the existing additional 1 percent investment tax credit allowed employers for contributions to tax credit ESOPs with a payroll-based tax credit. The new credit would be phased in gradually up to .75 percent of compensation of employees covered by the plan in 1985. The provision would expire Dec. 31, 1987.

● Increased from 15 percent of payroll to 25 percent the tax deductions allowed employers for contributions to an ESOP that borrowed money to buy stock in the company, provided the contribution was used to pay off the loan.

Legal Service Plans. Extended for three years, through Dec. 31, 1984, the existing exclusion from employee income of employer contributions to, and the value of benefits received from, a prepaid legal service plan for employees. *(1984 extension, p. 82)*

Estate and Gift Taxes

Exemption. Increased gradually from $175,625 to $600,000 by 1987 the total amount of estate and gift transfers that would be exempt from estate and gift taxes. By 1987 less than 1 percent of all estates would be taxed.

Rate Reduction. Reduced the top estate and gift tax rate from the existing 70 percent to 50 percent by 1985. When fully phased in, the top rate would apply to gifts and estates over $2.5 million. *(1984 change, p. 81)*

Marital Deduction. Repealed existing limits on tax-free estate and gift transfers between spouses.

Gift Tax. Increased the annual gift tax exclusion from $3,000 to $10,000 per donee, with an unlimited exclusion for tuition and medical expenses; allowed gift taxes to be paid on an annual rather than quarterly basis.

Other Provisions

Commodity Tax Straddles. Restricted the use of the commodity tax straddle by imposing a maximum 32 percent tax on the net gain of an individual's commodity futures holdings as of the last day of a tax year, even if the gain had yet to be realized. The straddle, which involved the purchase of offsetting futures contracts, had been used widely to avoid or defer taxes.

Railroad Retirement Taxes. Increased Railroad Retirement System taxes 2.25 percentage points for rail management and two percentage points for employees to keep the troubled fund from going broke. *(Story, p. 648)*

State Legislators. Allowed state legislators to deduct per diem expenses during legislative sessions, even if

1981 Tax Bill's Estimated Revenue Impact

(Fiscal years, in millions of dollars)

Provisions	1981	1982	1983	1984	1985	1986
Individual Income Taxes	$ −39	$−26,929	$−71,098	$−114,684	$−148,237	$−196,143
Business Tax Cuts	−1,562	−10,657	−18,599	− 28,275	− 39,269	− 54,468
Energy Taxes	——	−1,320	−1,742	−2,242	−2,837	−3,619
Savings Incentives	——	−247	−1,797	−4,208	−5,740	−8,375
Estate and Gift Taxes	——	−204	−2,114	−3,218	−4,248	−5,568
Tax Straddles	37	623	327	273	249	229
Administrative Provisions	——	1,182	2,048	1,856	718	592
Miscellaneous Provisions	−1	−104	243	535	53	−275
Total	$−1,565	$−37,656	$−92,732	$−149,963	$−199,311	$−267,627

SOURCE: Joint Committee on Taxes

---

they did not stay overnight in the state capital, provided they lived more than 50 miles away. The provision was made retroactive to Jan. 1, 1976.

Fringe Benefits. Extended the current prohibition on the taxation of fringe benefits until Dec. 31, 1983. *(1984 action, p. 79)*

Campaign Committees. Reduced taxes on the income, such as interest income, of a congressional candidate's principal campaign committee. Under existing law, all such income was taxed at 46 percent; under the bill, it would be taxed at the graduated corporate rate, from 15 percent to 46 percent.

Mass Transit. Allowed use of tax-exempt industrial development bonds for any bus, subway car, rail car or similar equipment leased to a public mass transit system.

Telephone Excise Tax. Extended the telephone excise tax at 1 percent through 1984. *(1984 extension, p. 79)*

Employee Awards. Allowed employees a deduction of up to $400 per item for awards given by their company for length of service, productivity or safety.

Adoption Expenses. Allowed a deduction of up to $1,500 for expenses incurred in the adoption of a disadvantaged or hard-to-place child.

Miscellaneous Tax Law Changes

Several miscellaneous changes in tax law cleared Congress Dec. 16 as part of a bill (HR 5159 — PL 97-119) to overhaul the black lung disability benefits program for coal miners.

These included provisions allowing members of Congress to deduct the cost of maintaining a home in Washington, D.C., and requiring firms that sold unused tax credits to report such transactions to the Internal Revenue Service.

The Senate added the unrelated provisions to the black lung bill before passing the measure late Dec. 15, 63-30. The House accepted the Senate changes the following day, 363-47.

In the final hours before it adjourned Dec. 16, Congress attempted to push through more than two dozen other tax changes, but time ran out before a conference could be arranged to work out a final House-Senate agreement on the bills (HR 4961, HR 4717).

Congress completed action on the measures in 1982. HR 4961 became the vehicle for $98.3 billion in tax increases over three years. *(Story, p. 72; black lung provisions, p. 649)*

Provisions. As signed into law Dec. 29, the miscellaneous tax provisions of the black lung bill (HR 5159 — PL 97-119):

● Required businesses involved in so-called safe-harbor leasing transactions, in which unprofitable firms could effectively sell unused tax credits to profitable ones, to report such transactions to the Internal Revenue Service within 30 days. *(Subsequent action, p. 72)*

● Delayed for two years, until Jan. 1, 1984, the effective date of a provision in the 1976 Tax Reform Act that would limit the carry-over of net operating losses for firms with substantial ownership changes. *(Congress and the Nation Vol. IV, p. 99)*

● Allowed taxpayers to deduct the costs of maintaining a second home for business purposes when it was also used as a residence. While applying to all taxpayers, the primary beneficiaries of this provision would be members of Congress, who under existing law could not deduct such expenses if their families resided with them in Washington.

● Directed the Treasury secretary to determine the "appropriate" amount a member of Congress could deduct for business expenses while Congress was in session without having to substantiate them. *(Details of action on congressional deductions, pay, p. 821)*

● Allowed certain deductions for a residence that was used as a person's primary place of work for a second job.

● Liberalized rules governing business deductions in cases where a residence was rented to a relative at a fair market rate.

1982

Confronted by a deteriorating economy and mounting deficits, President Reagan reluctantly backed legislation designed to raise $98.3 billion in taxes over three years. The bill, cleared Aug. 19, was part of a deficit reduction effort undertaken by Congress through the budget reconciliation process.

Although much of the revenue was to be raised by closing loopholes and clamping down on tax evasion, the issue was a tough one for members facing re-election. In the House, mainstream Democrats and Republicans joined to win approval of the bill, after conservative Republicans balked at the party line. They charged that the measure ran counter to Reagan's own supply-side belief that high taxes would hinder economic growth.

The bill did not touch the 1981 individual tax cut that Reagan considered the centerpiece of his economic program, however. Democrats pushed hard for repeal or delay of the July 1983 installment of that cut, but Republicans and the president refused to budge.

Late in the year, with unemployment setting post-World War II records, Congress and the administration agreed on a 5-cent-a-gallon increase in the federal gasoline tax to finance highway and mass transit repairs. The increase, to run through fiscal 1988, was expected to yield $5.5 billion in additional revenues annually.

Tax Increases

President Reagan continued his unbroken winning streak on fiscal issues when Congress gave final approval Aug. 19 to a $98.3 billion tax increase and $17.5 billion spending reduction package over three years.

But the victory came at a price. Faced with large budget deficits, Reagan was forced to retreat from his tax-cutting philosophy of the previous year in an effort to raise the much-needed revenue.

The final package (HR 4961 — PL 97-248) did not alter the core of Reagan's 1981 tax cut program: a three-year, across-the-board reduction in individual income taxes. Instead, the new bill — the Tax Equity and Fiscal Responsibility Act (TEFRA) of 1982 — was labeled a reform and focused on closing tax loopholes and increasing taxpayer compliance with laws already on the books. It did, however, repeal some business tax breaks enacted in 1981 and it imposed new excise taxes on individuals.

Election-year politics required the president's strong, though grudging, support for the legislation. Members of both parties who found themselves in close re-election battles feared the wrath of the electorate if they voted for the tax increase without the backing of the popular president.

Besides, Democrats were reluctant to hand Republicans a legislative victory without forcing Reagan to share in the blame. House Speaker Thomas P. O'Neill Jr., D-Mass., and his Democratic lieutenants were critical to the final 226-207 House vote to approve the tax increase. Without the support of 123 Democrats, the conference report on the tax/spending bill would have gone down in defeat.

But House Republican unity — the hallmark of the president's earlier successes — was broken by the tax bill fight. Conservative Republicans, led by staunch supply-sider Jack F. Kemp, R-N.Y., bolted from the party line. They argued that the middle of a recession was not the time to repudiate the 1980 election mandate to cut taxes and spending. Only 103 Republicans voted for the measure; 89 voted against it.

In the GOP-controlled Senate 11 Republicans defected on the Aug. 19 52-47 tally that cleared the bill for the president's signature. Nine Democrats voted for the measure.

HR 4961 was the last piece of the deficit reduction plan mandated by reconciliation instructions included in the fiscal 1983 budget resolution (S Con Res 92). In addition to its tax provisions, the measure revised Medicare, Medicaid and welfare programs to cut projected spending by $17.5 billion in fiscal 1983-85. Other provisions authorized additional unemployment benefits for workers who had exhausted their benefits under existing law and extended authorizations for airport development and air traffic control programs. *(Reconciliation details, p. 48; Medicare, Medicaid, p. 532; welfare, p. 596; unemployment benefits, p. 654; airport programs, p. 308)*

Background

By early 1982 it was apparent that spending cuts alone would not be sufficient to hold the fiscal 1983 deficit below $100 billion, an administration goal. Democrats called for repeal or delay of Reagan's 1981 personal tax cut program, but the president held firm.

In his State of the Union address Jan. 26 Reagan said he would not retreat from his original plan or "balance the budget on the backs of the American taxpayers." Instead, Reagan vowed to "plug unwarranted tax loopholes" and strengthen the law requiring corporations to pay a minimum income tax. He also called for improved tax collection, including a requirement for faster corporate tax payments. *(Text, p. 1046)*

The dimensions of the 1982 tax bill were decided in May, when Reagan and Senate Budget Committee Republicans settled on a $95 billion revenue increase over fiscal 1983-85. But Reagan did not specify how that revenue target would be met, and insisted the money could be raised without altering the personal income tax cuts enacted the previous year.

The agreement found its way into the fiscal 1983 budget resolution (S Con Res 92). That measure, cleared June 23, required the Senate Finance and House Ways and Means committees to come up with $98.3 billion in new taxes over three years. *(Resolution, p. 46)*

Senate Action

Committee. The Senate Finance Committee July 2 approved a package of approximately $98 billion in new taxes and other revenue raisers for fiscal years 1983-85. The straight party-line vote of 11-9 came at the end of a 15-hour markup session, following several days of closed-door negotiations among committee Republicans and administration officials.

The committee circumvented the constitutional requirement that all revenue-raising measures originate in the House by attaching its package to HR 4961, a minor tax bill passed by the House in 1981.

The final plan, reported July 12 (S Rept 97-494), differed greatly from the tax increases proposed by Reagan

earlier in the year. It would raise approximately $21 billion in fiscal 1983, $34 billion in fiscal 1984 and $43 billion in fiscal 1985 — meeting the committee's budget reconciliation requirements.

The proposed tax increases affected both individuals and businesses and included higher taxes on cigarettes and airplane tickets, a minimum tax for high-income individuals and restrictions on deductions for pensions and health costs. Unexpectedly, it included a controversial Reagan proposal to withhold taxes from interest and dividends.

The bill also cut back some of the business tax breaks approved the previous year, including the controversial leasing provisions, and took steps to improve taxpayer compliance. It left intact the personal tax cuts voted in 1981.

Floor. The Senate passed the bill early July 23 by a **key vote of 50-47 (R 49-3; D 1-44).** Despite strong pressure from lobbyists and general unwillingness among members to raise taxes during an election year, the package put together by the Finance Committee was kept largely intact during the lengthy session that began July 22. *(1982 key votes, p. 895)*

An amendment to delete the interest and dividend withholding plan, and strengthen interest and dividend reporting instead, was defeated earlier by a 48-49 vote. Republican leaders considered the provision essential because it would raise more than $12 billion over fiscal 1983-85 and there was little prospect for finding another tax increase that large to replace it. It was feared that rejection of the withholding plan could mean collapse of the carefully crafted bill.

The biggest symbolic challenge came from Democrats who charged that the large tax-increase package was made necessary by overly generous tax cuts enacted in 1981 and by the failure of the Reagan administration's economic recovery program.

They proposed that, instead of cutting spending for health care and raising taxes on individuals, the Senate delay scheduled individual income tax cuts — but only for the wealthy — until the federal budget was balanced. The Democratic alternative was defeated by a largely party-line vote of 45-54.

Shortly before the 4:30 a.m. final vote, the Senate agreed 70-25 to delete an unpopular provision requiring employers to report employee tip income. The move left the package some $2.8 billion short of the committee's revenue target, threatening final passage. But Finance Chairman Robert Dole, R-Kan., offered an amendment to allow deductions for only half the cost of business — so-called "three-martini" — lunches, covering the entire $2.8 billion shortfall. Adoption of the amendment, in apparent retaliation for the restaurant industry's strong opposition to the tip provision, paved the way for final passage.

House Action

Committee. Unable to agree in closed-door negotiations what should go into a revenue-raising package, the House Ways and Means Committee voted July 28 to forgo writing its own tax bill and to go straight to conference on HR 4961. Later that day, the full House agreed by a **key 208-197 vote (R 44-137; D 164-60)** to go along with the Ways and Means Committee plan. *(1982 key votes, p. 895)*

The action meant that the House had little hand in shaping the legislation. It was a chore many election-minded House members were not sorry to miss, and one Democrats were glad to unload on Republicans.

Republicans charged during floor debate that Democrats were shirking their constitutional duty so that they could blame the GOP for the controversial tax and spending legislation.

But Democrats, and some Republicans, insisted that the House bypass was the only practical way to get tax increases enacted quickly in an election year.

Conference Action

Report. The conference agreement, reported Aug. 17 (H Rept 97-760), was crafted over eight grueling days of meetings. The outlines of the conference report mirrored closely the bill approved by the Finance Committee and passed by the Senate.

Early in the deliberations conferees agreed to one of the most controversial tax increases — the withholding of taxes on income from interest and dividends. Most remaining tax decisions, however, were delayed until conferees resolved major philosophical differences on the spending cut side — principally in the welfare area.

Chief among the tax-hike difficulties were the business tax increases contained in the Senate-passed bill. Even with the aid of several major business lobbying groups, House Republicans were unable to make major changes in the business tax provisions, although several were softened slightly.

Conferees dropped Senate provisions that liberalized the treatment of capital gains by reducing the holding period that distinguished long-term from short-term capital gains and losses from one year to six months. They also dropped a Senate floor amendment that would have indexed long-term capital gains taxation to account for inflation after Dec. 31, 1984.

The six-month holding period for capital gains won approval in 1984. *(Story, p. 79)*

Conferees agreed to go along with a provision requiring restaurants to report employee tip income. The provision had been replaced on the Senate floor by an amendment to limit deductions on business meals. Restaurateurs had lobbied heavily and successfully in the Senate against the tip reporting requirement, but they found the business meal provision even more distasteful, and it was dropped in conference.

The conferees went beyond the Senate bill in strengthening the minimum tax on wealthy individuals, nearly tripling the revenue increase to $1.3 billion over the next three years.

Final Action. The House adopted the conference report on the bill Aug. 19 by a 226-207 vote after narrowly rejecting, 220-210, an effort to force separate votes on the bill's provisions. The Senate then cleared the measure 52-47.

Warned that passage was impossible without presidential backing, Reagan pulled out all the stops in the final days before the vote on the conference report. Scores of members visited with him at the White House and the Camp David, Md., presidential retreat.

To assuage Democrats' fears that a vote for the tax increase might be used against them in the coming election campaign, Reagan promised personal letters thanking members who supported the bill. The Republican National Committee committed $400,000 to solicit grass-roots support for the measure.

Estimated Revenue Impact of 1982 Tax Increase Bill

(Fiscal years, in millions of dollars)

Provisions	1983	1984	1985	1986	1987
Individual Income Tax Provisions	$ 272	$ 3,113	$ 3,106	$ 3,336	$ 3,556
Business Tax Provisions	5,422	13,292	16,497	28,042	40,116
Compliance Provisions	3,365	8,869	8,660	10,174	11,217
Pension Provisions	194	780	870	970	1,058
Life Insurance and Annuities	1,942	2,155	2,920	3,138	3,370
Employment Tax Provisions	1,904	3,083	3,577	2,853	2,572
Excise Tax Provisions	2,798	4,009	4,702	2,054	1,472
Miscellaneous Provisions	−38	−37	−34	−32	−30
Subtotal	15,859	35,264	40,298	50,535	63,331
Revenue gain resulting from additional IRS enforcement personnel	2,100	2,400	2,400	1,300	600
Total, all tax provisions	$17,959	$37,664	$42,698	$51,835	$63,931

SOURCE: Joint Committee on Taxation

Final Provisions

As signed into law Sept. 3, the Tax Equity and Fiscal Responsibility Act of 1982 (HR 4961 — PL 97-248) included the following revenue-raising provisions (effective Jan. 1, 1983, unless otherwise noted):

Business Taxes

Accelerated Depreciation, Investment Tax Credit. Required that taxpayers subtract half the value of any tax credits — for regular investment, historic rehabilitation or energy — before computing depreciation deductions for a new asset. Previously, taxpayers could depreciate the full value of the asset, even if they had received a 10 percent investment tax credit.

● Limited regular and rehabilitation tax credits to 85 percent of the liability in excess of $25,000 instead of the current 90 percent.

● Repealed provisions in the Economic Recovery Tax Act of 1981 (PL 97-34) that would have increased the benefits from accelerated depreciation in 1985 and again in 1986 by allowing greater deductions in the early years of an investment.

Corporate Tax Payments. Speeded up collection of corporate tax payments by raising from 80 percent to 90 percent the amount of estimated tax liability a firm must pay during its tax year to avoid penalty. However, any company whose tax payments through the year ended up between 80 and 90 percent of actual tax liability would be assessed only 75 percent of the penalty. The bill also moved up the deadline for final tax payments and increased the amount of estimated tax payment required of certain large corporations.

Possessions Tax Break. Limited a tax break for certain corporations earning income in Puerto Rico and U.S. possessions — mostly pharmaceutical firms — by disallowing credits for income from intangibles such as patents, copyrights and trade names. In general, companies would still be allowed to shelter investment income earned in Puerto Rico.

Foreign Oil and Gas Income. Repealed a tax break allowing oil and gas companies to shelter income through the use of credits and losses from foreign oil and gas extraction. *(Background, Congress and the Nation Vol. IV, pp. 88, 91)*

Corporate Tax Preferences. Reduced several business tax breaks by 15 percent, including special deductions for mining exploration and development, interest on debt used to purchase or carry tax-exempt securities, tax breaks for depletion of coal and iron ore, excess bad debt reserves, rapid write-off of pollution control facilities, certain tax breaks for selling structures, and subsidies for U.S. exporting firms.

● Reduced from 90 percent to 85 percent the amount of tax liability that could be offset by the 10 percent investment tax credit. Full tax breaks for intangible drilling costs could be taken, but would have to be spread over a five-year period for major oil producers, with most of the benefits in the first year.

These changes, imposed in addition to existing corporate minimum taxes, were an alternative to the administration's plan for a new minimum corporate tax.

Construction Deductions. Required corporations to amortize over 10 years interest and property taxes incurred during construction of non-residential real property.

Insurance Tax Breaks. Repealed an existing law allowing life insurance companies to shelter much of their

income through a process called "modco," through which firms transferred some of their policyholder risks to other insurance companies and thus paid lower taxes. But in a concession to the life insurance industry — which had complained that, without modco, tax burdens would grow too large — the bill made other changes reducing industry taxes. *(1984 insurance tax changes, p. 79)*

Multi-Year Contracts. Instructed the Treasury Department to tighten up regulations governing firms involved in long-term contracts — such as those in the construction and aerospace industries — that could defer tax payments through special accounting procedures. Contractors with annual gross receipts below $25 million for the three preceding years and contracts expected to be completed in less than three years were exempt.

Leasing. Restricted, and eliminated as of Jan. 1, 1984, the use of so-called "safe-harbor leasing" provisions in the 1981 tax bill that allowed firms to sell unused tax breaks. The new provision attempted to eliminate many of the "abuses" of the controversial 1981 provision by limiting to 50 percent the amount of tax liability that could be offset through purchase of such tax breaks and by not allowing leasing to be used to offset tax payments from previous years. In addition, the amount of property that could be leased and the length of the lease term were restricted.

The measure allowed companies to use 150 percent declining balance depreciation, deducting 15 percent of the undepreciated value of an investment each year, for lease transactions. But companies were required to take the investment tax credit over a five-year period compared with three years in the Senate bill.

As of 1984, the bill also would liberalize the use of traditional "leverage" leasing — transactions in which a company transfers tax breaks in reduced lease payments. This type of leasing transaction, however, would have to comply with restrictions that applied to safe-harbor leasing.

Corporate Mergers. Changed current law governing corporate mergers and acquisitions to prevent such actions from being taken only for tax advantages and to limit certain tax abuses. Most of the changes went into effect Sept. 1, 1982.

Payments to Foreign Officials. Allowed a business expense deduction for any payments to foreign officials or agents of a foreign government as long as the payment was legal under the Foreign Corrupt Practices Act.

Restaurant Tips. Required restaurants with more than 10 employees to take 8 percent of their gross income and allocate a share to each employee. The restaurant was required to report that amount under the employee's name to the Internal Revenue Service (IRS) each year. IRS would use the amount reported as a bench mark to measure the accuracy of the amount of tip income reported by the employee. This provision was to take effect April 1, 1983.

Individual Taxes

Medical and Casualty Deductions. Repealed the current deduction for one-half of health insurance premiums up to $150. The bill also allowed deductions for medical expenses exceeding 5 percent of a taxpayer's adjusted gross income, compared with the current 3 percent. After 1983 the provision allowing deductions for prescription drug costs greater than 1 percent of income was to be repealed. Casualty losses were to be deductible only if they exceeded 10 percent of adjusted gross income.

Pension Contributions. Restricted deductions for contributions to corporate pension plans, many of which had been used as tax shelters for wealthy individuals.

The bill lowered the limits on tax-deductible contributions to such plans and increased the allowable annual contribution for self-employed, or Keogh, retirement plans. For corporate, defined contribution benefit plans the maximum dollar limit on contributions was dropped to $30,000 a year from $45,475. For defined benefit plans, or those that allowed contributions necessary to produce a specified benefit level at retirement, the maximum benefit was cut from $136,425 to $90,000. The maximum tax-deferred pension contribution for the self-employed was doubled to $30,000 after 1983.

Federal Employees. Required federal employees to pay the 1.3 percent Federal Insurance Contributions Act (FICA) tax for Medicare coverage. Even though federal workers had not paid the tax previously, about 80 percent of retired federal employees over age 65 had been covered by Medicare because of previous non-government employment or through their spouses.

Individual Minimum Tax. Replaced existing minimum taxes on wealthy individuals with a more comprehensive "alternative" minimum tax that would prevent taxpayers from wiping out their tax liability with large deductions. Such taxpayers were required to increase their taxable income by the amount of certain tax breaks, called preference items, and pay a 20 percent tax on income above $30,000 for individuals, or 20 percent on income above $40,000 for couples filing joint returns.

The minimum tax was to be payable only to the extent that it exceeded regular taxes.

Tax Collection

Compliance. Beefed up compliance with existing tax law by requiring additional reporting of income, by increasing penalties for non-compliance and by strengthening IRS enforcement powers.

● Required the withholding of taxes from pension payments unless taxpayers requested otherwise and increased requirements for reporting tip income.

● Included provisions to improve tax compliance by so-called independent contractors and extended a congressional moratorium on IRS regulations dealing with independent contractors — which expired June 30 — to Jan. 1, 1983.

Interest and Dividend Withholding. Required withholding of 10 percent of interest and dividend payments, with exceptions for payments to certain low-income and elderly individuals, to tax-exempt institutions and to corporations. This provision would not become effective until July 1, 1983. *(Repeal, p. 90)*

● Allowed the Treasury to issue regulations giving financial institutions a chance to earn income on the withheld funds to cover administrative costs and to exempt certain small institutions from the requirements.

Other

Airport and Airway Trust Fund. Raised $2.8 billion in various taxes for the Airport and Airway Trust Fund by making changes that included: increasing the passenger ticket tax from 5 percent to 8 percent; raising the general

aviation gasoline tax from 4 cents a gallon to 12 cents a gallon; imposing a 14-cent-a-gallon tax on jet fuel; and reinstating the 5 percent air freight waybill and $3 international departure ticket taxes. All the airport and airway taxes would expire after four years unless extended by Congress. The new taxes would go into effect Sept. 1, 1982.

● Authorized expenditures from the trust fund for airport development and air traffic control modernization. *(Story, p. 308)*

Unemployment Insurance. Raised net unemployment taxes from .7 percent of the first $6,000 of wages to .8 percent of the first $7,000, for an increase of $6.4 billion for fiscal 1983-85. The increase was expected to cost approximately $1.20 a month for each employee. The federal tax rate was to be increased further in 1985 with the likely effect of pushing up state unemployment taxes.

● Increased the portion of unemployment compensation payments subject to the federal personal income tax in order to finance new supplemental unemployment benefits included in the bill. The income threshold was lowered from $20,000 to $12,000 for single taxpayers and from $25,000 to $18,000 for couples filing joint returns.

Telephone. Raised the current 1 percent telephone excise tax to 3 percent on Jan. 1, 1983. It would stay at that level for three years and then drop to zero after 1985. *(1984 extension, p. 79)*

Cigarettes. Doubled the excise tax on cigarettes from 8 cents to 16 cents a pack through Sept. 30, 1985.

Industrial Development Bonds. Restricted the use of tax-exempt industrial development bonds (IDBs) issued by state and local governments. The bill required public hearings and official approval of all IDBs, and required private users in most cases to forgo depreciation benefits enacted in 1981. No tax-exempt IDBs could be issued after Dec. 1, 1986. The bill also loosened limits on the use of tax-free mortgage subsidy bonds imposed by Congress in 1980. These changes generally would be effective after July 1, 1982. *(1980 action on mortgage bonds, Congress and the Nation Vol. V, p. 249; 1984 action on IDBs, p. 79)*

Other Bonds. Changed the tax treatment of so-called "original issue discount bonds" to limit tax breaks for issuers and tax penalties for those who purchase such bonds. The bill also limited tax advantages of bonds stripped of coupons.

Targeted Jobs Tax Credit. Extended the targeted jobs tax credit program for two more years, through 1984. The credit, last extended in 1981, also was expanded to encourage summer employment of disadvantaged youths. *(1984 extension, p. 672)*

Debt Management. Allowed the Treasury to offer variable interest rates on U.S. savings bonds and increased the ceiling for long-term bonds from $70 billion to $110 billion.

Windfall Profits. Repealed special windfall profits tax provisions for oil produced at Prudhoe Bay in Alaska. *(Windfall tax, Congress and the Nation Vol. V, p. 503)*

Other Tax Measures

Gas Tax Increase

The federal gasoline tax was increased from 4 cents to 9 cents under legislation cleared Dec. 23 (HR 6211 — PL 97-424). The increase, expected to yield about $5.5 billion

annually, was earmarked for repair of deteriorating roads and mass transit systems. Supporters claimed the bill would create more than 300,000 jobs. *(Details of action, p. 301)*

Cruise Ships

A measure to allow certain business tax deductions for conventions aboard U.S. cruise ships was cleared by Congress Dec. 23 as part of the gas tax and highway authorization measure (HR 6211 — PL 97-424). *(Authorization, p. 301)*

The provision, attached on the Senate floor to the highway bill, allowed such deductions as long as the cruise ships stopped at U.S. ports or those of U.S. possessions. The deduction was limited to $2,000 for an individual.

The House passed similar legislation (HR 3191 — H Rept 97-828) Dec. 16 by a 227-172 vote.

Congress voted major restrictions on deductions for all foreign business travel in 1976, because of a proliferation of overseas conventions that many in Congress viewed as thinly veiled vacation trips. But the law was liberalized in 1980 to allow special exemptions for conventions held in Mexico and Canada. *(Business deductions, Congress and the Nation Vol. IV, p. 103)*

Subchapter S Taxation

Legislation (HR 6055 — PL 97-354) cleared Oct. 1 simplified tax laws governing so-called Subchapter S corporations — firms whose shareholders elected to be taxed as individuals rather than as corporations.

Businesses chose to incorporate under Subchapter S so they could take advantage of certain legal protections allowed corporations, while still enjoying tax advantages similar to those of a partnership.

Shareholders in a Subchapter S firm reported their share of the firm's income, and deducted a share of the losses, on individual tax returns, instead of having a corporate tax imposed directly on the firm's profits and additional taxes placed on shareholder dividends.

HR 6055 increased from 25 to 35 the number of shareholders a firm could have and still elect Subchapter S treatment. In addition, it liberalized requirements that such firms receive not more than 20 percent of their gross receipts from "passive" sources — such as patents — and loosened other eligibility standards for the special tax status. It also made certain changes allowing Subchapter S tax treatment to conform more closely with that of a partnership.

The House originally passed the bill (H Rept 97-826) Sept. 20. The Senate passed its version (S Rept 97-640) Sept. 30. The House accepted the Senate-passed bill Oct. 1.

Miscellaneous Revenue Bill

Congress in 1982 completed action on HR 4717 (PL 97-362), a miscellaneous tax measure that had been in conference for almost 10 months.

The House originally passed the bill (H Rept 97-405) Dec. 15, 1981. The Senate passed it the following day. Both chambers adopted the conference report on the legislation (H Rept 97-929) Oct. 1, 1982.

As cleared by Congress, HR 4717 deferred for one year the scheduled Jan. 1, 1982, effective date for regulations governing the taxation of "last in, first out" (LIFO) inven-

tories of liquidating companies. The effective date change applied only to the first $1 million of a company's LIFO reserves.

The measure also extended from three years to 10 years the period over which the Federal National Mortgage Association could carry back net operating losses to offset taxes, and shortened the period over which such losses could be carried forward. The change gave the association tax advantages already allowed other financial institutions.

Additional provisions expanded the type of oil shale equipment that could qualify for a 10 percent energy investment tax credit in 1981 and 1982 and reduced excise taxes on legal betting operations and their employees.

Numerous other provisions of HR 4717, added by the Senate in 1981, were deleted from the final package because they had been enacted earlier in 1982 as part of the tax reconciliation bill (PL 97-248). *(Story, p. 72)*

Technical Corrections

Congress Dec. 21 approved legislation (HR 6056 — PL 97-448) making technical corrections in the Tax Equity and Fiscal Responsibility Act of 1982 (PL 97-248), the Economic Recovery Tax Act of 1981 (PL 97-34), the Crude Oil Windfall Profit Tax Act of 1980 (PL 96-471) and other tax legislation. *(Background, 1982 Tax Equity and Fiscal Responsibility Act, p. 72; 1981 Economic Recovery Tax Act, p. 65; 1980 Crude Oil Windfall Profit Tax Act, Congress and the Nation Vol. V, p. 503)*

The House passed the measure Sept. 14 and the Senate followed suit Sept. 30, first adding a number of controversial amendments.

Differences were cleared up during a conference held in the post-election session (H Rept 97-986). Conferees dropped the most controversial provisions, including one to give certain troubled airlines a special tax break in the event of bankruptcy.

Periodic Payments, Miscellany

Congress Dec. 21 cleared a bill (HR 5470 — PL 97-473) that put into law current Internal Revenue Service (IRS) rulings that damages paid to individuals for personal injury or sickness would be tax exempt, whether paid periodically or in a lump sum.

The legislation also included several miscellaneous tax provisions added by the Senate Finance Committee (S Rept 97-646) that:

● Excluded from income all payments made to individuals for care of a foster child, including special payments for handicapped children.

● Gave tax breaks to Indian tribal governments similar to those enjoyed by states.

● Exempted certain multiple-employer welfare arrangements and the Hawaii Prepaid Health Care Act from the Employee Retirement Income Security Act of 1974.

Not included in the final measure was a Senate amendment to allow the Virgin Islands to lower a tax the Island government was required to withhold from certain investment income generated there, but paid to U.S. individuals or corporations. It was struck in conference because the provision was adopted as part of a separate disability measure (HR 7093). *(Disability, p. 656)*

The House originally passed the bill (H Rept 97-832) Sept. 20, and the Senate passed its version Oct. 1. The conference report (H Rept 97-984) was approved Dec. 21.

Computer Donations

A proposed tax break for companies that donated computers to primary and secondary schools did not survive the 97th Congress.

A bill (HR 5573) designed primarily to help the Apple computer firm, which had plans to give every school in the country its own computer, was approved by both the House and the Senate Finance Committee.

But by the time the measure was ready for Senate floor action, it had been so changed that even the main beneficiary — Apple — no longer supported the legislation.

The House passed its version of HR 5573 (H Rept 97-836) Sept. 22 by a vote of 323-62.

Under existing law, firms donating such equipment could deduct only their own costs, not the fair market value of the donated machines.

While the House bill would have allowed Apple — or any other computer company meeting certain restrictions — to deduct up to twice their cost, the Finance version (S Rept 97-647) limited the deduction to 1.5 times the cost and broadened the bill to permit more firms to take advantage of the tax break.

1983

Soaring deficits intensified calls for tax increases during 1983, but Congress adjourned Nov. 18 without approving new revenue measures.

In adopting its fiscal 1984 budget resolution June 23, Congress agreed in principle to raise $73 billion in new taxes over three years. But neither chamber voted on tax increases until 1984. And legislation drafted by House and Senate committees in 1983 provided only a fraction of the revenues required by the budget.

Without President Reagan's support, House Democrats were reluctant to step out front on tax increases. After the House refused to consider a modest tax bill Nov. 17, House Speaker Thomas P. O'Neill Jr., D-Mass., said, "Today's vote once again proves that we cannot reduce the deficit with the president sitting on the sidelines."

Reagan adamantly opposed any deficit reduction effort that included tax increases. He said members of Congress should "start doing what they were elected to do — get spending under control once and for all. We do not face large deficits because Americans aren't taxed enough. We face those deficits because Congress still spends too much."

There was some disagreement within the administration on taxes, however. The chairman of the Council of Economic Advisers, Martin S. Feldstein, rankled a number of administration officials by publicly calling for tax increases as a necessary element in urgent deficit reduction efforts. Without such efforts, he warned, federal borrowing to finance the deficit would "crowd out" private borrowing, causing interest rates to rise. And the deficit would mushroom as federal borrowing costs increased.

Tax Increase Efforts

Leery of raising taxes without President Reagan's support, Congress in 1983 shirked the revenue mandate of its fiscal 1984 budget resolution.

The resolution (H Con Res 91), cleared June 23, called for $73 billion in new revenues as part of a three-year, $85.3 billion deficit reduction plan. *(Budget resolution, p. 51; deficit reduction action, p. 54)*

The House Ways and Means Committee reported an $8 billion tax increase bill (HR 4170 — H Rept 98-432) Oct. 21, but the House Nov. 17 defeated the rule for floor consideration of the measure on a **204-214 key vote (R 13-149; D 191-65)**. *(1983 key votes, p. 911)*

Following the House vote the Senate suspended action on its $28.3 billion deficit reduction bill, which included $13.4 billion in tax increases. That measure (S 2062 — S Rept 98-300) had been reported Nov. 4.

Congress completed action on HR 4170 in 1984. The final version of the bill was expected to yield $50.8 billion in additional revenues through fiscal 1987. *(Details of 1983-84 action, p. 79)*

Cap on Reagan Tax Cut

During the fight over fiscal 1984 spending, Democrats tried unsuccessfully to score some political points by limiting the third installment of President Reagan's three-year tax cut plan.

The House June 23 passed legislation (HR 1183) placing a $720 per family "cap" on the 10 percent cut in individual income taxes scheduled to take effect July 1, but the measure was killed easily in the Senate six days later. President Reagan had vowed to veto the bill.

The July 1 tax cut was the final portion of a three-stage, across-the-board cut in individual income taxes that was a key element of Reagan's 1981 economic program. *(1981 tax bill, p. 65)*

While the defeat of HR 1183 was no surprise, Democratic leaders in both houses used the legislation to brand the Reagan tax cut as benefiting those in the high-income brackets. It was a theme the party used repeatedly during the year in an attempt to discredit Reagan's economic policies.

House Action. House Democrats were not united on the tax cap issue. But armed with a survey of caucus members showing a majority supported the cap, the House leadership decided to push ahead with the bill. The leadership was prodded on by House freshmen, many of whom had been elected because of their criticism of the Reagan tax cut program.

The Ways and Means Committee reluctantly reported HR 1183 (H Rept 98-252) June 21, and the House passed it June 23 by a 229-191 vote. No Republicans voted for the bill, and 29 Democrats voted against it, despite the strong urgings of the party leadership.

Democrats defended the cap as the most equitable way to cut the deficit, noting that the cap would largely affect those in the high-income brackets who had benefited most from the first two years of Reagan's tax cut program.

But Republicans countered that Democrats were engaged in little more than a futile political exercise aimed at the voters back home. They charged that the tax cap would not only affect wealthy taxpayers but would permanently raise taxes for millions of middle-income families.

Senate. The tax cap issue was laid to rest June 29 when the Republican-controlled Senate defeated HR 1183 on a near party-line vote of 45-55.

Only three Republicans voted for the Democratic proposal; four Democrats voted against the bill.

Other Tax Measures

Interest, Dividend Withholding

Bowing to months of intense public pressure, Congress July 28 cleared legislation (HR 2973 — PL 98-67) to repeal a new requirement for 10 percent withholding of taxes on interest and dividend income.

The withholding requirement, approved in 1982 tax legislation, had been scheduled to take effect July 1, 1983. *(Details, p. 90)*

Social Security Taxes

Congress early in the year approved substantial increases in payroll taxes as part of a plan to assure the solvency of the financially troubled Social Security system. The legislation (HR 1900 — PL 98-21) was expected to raise about $165 billion over seven years. *(Details, p. 659)*

Tuition Tax Credits

The Senate Nov. 16 overwhelmingly rejected President Reagan's proposal to provide tax credits for parents who sent their children to private elementary and secondary schools. The Senate defeat came on a 59-38 vote to table a tuition tax credit amendment offered at Reagan's behest. *(Details, p. 567)*

1984

Congress and the president in 1984 finally achieved the agreement on tax increases that had eluded them in 1983.

The House and Senate June 27 approved $50 billion in new revenues as part of a bill designed to cut projected deficits by $63 billion over four years. Closing of loopholes and other taxpayer compliance steps accounted for most of the revenue gain.

President Reagan had pledged to sign the measure, which was drawn from a $140 billion deficit reduction plan drafted by Senate Republican leaders and endorsed by the president in March. In a letter to members before the final vote, Reagan noted that the bill did not increase individual tax rates that had been cut 25 percent under his 1981 tax plan.

Taxes became a central issue in the 1984 presidential campaign after Democratic candidate Walter F. Mondale asserted that they would be raised in 1985 no matter who was elected president. "Mr. Reagan will raise taxes and so will I," Mondale said in his July 19 acceptance speech. "He won't tell you. I just did."

Reagan denied that he had a secret plan to raise taxes. In January he had asked the Treasury to study and suggest ways to make the tax code more simple and fair, but its report was not due until after the election.

The Treasury plan, which was released Nov. 27, called for elimination of most special interest tax breaks while lowering tax rates for individuals and businesses. It received a noticeably lukewarm reception from Reagan, who said he would "listen to the comments and suggestions of

all Americans, especially those from Congress," before presenting his own tax simplification and reform plan.

There was no shortage of alternative proposals for overhauling the tax code. Perhaps the most prominent was a plan pushed by Sen. Bill Bradley, D-N.J., and Rep. Richard A. Gephardt, D-Mo., that also called for lower tax rates and the elimination of most tax credits, deductions and exemptions.

Tax Increases

Congress completed action June 27 on legislation (HR 4170 — PL 98-369) that was expected to provide about $50 billion in increased revenues through fiscal 1987. The bill, which also provided $13 billion in spending cuts, was the first installment of a $149.2 billion deficit reduction plan that occupied legislators throughout the year. *(Deficit reduction, p. 56)*

Although President Reagan had warned earlier that he would not accept tax hikes until more spending restraints were in place, Reagan changed course and sent a letter to members before the final vote pledging to sign HR 4170. The president signed the measure July 18.

Most of the tax increases were contained in provisions designed to shut down a wide range of tax loopholes and shelters. A few sweeteners were hidden in the package, including a tax break for investors and an increase in the earned income tax credit for poor working families.

1983 Action

The 1984 deficit reduction bill stemmed from a modest, $8 billion tax increase measure reported by the House Ways and Means Committee Oct. 21, 1983 (HR 4170 — H Rept 98-432). The House Nov. 17, 1983, rejected the rule for floor consideration of that measure by a **204-214 key vote (R 13-149; D 191-65)**. Floor consideration was blocked because of objections to restrictions on industrial development bonds (IDBs) and controversy over Medicare spending cuts that also were included in the bill. *(1983 key votes, p. 911)*

Following the House vote, the Senate suspended action on a deficit reduction bill (S 2062 — S Rept 98-300) that included a $13.4 billion tax increase package drafted by its Finance Committee.

Thus Congress adjourned for the year without approving any of the $73 billion in three-year revenue increases required by its fiscal 1984 budget resolution (H Con Res 91). *(1983 action, p. 77)*

1984 Action

Committee. The House Ways and Means Committee March 1 approved a package of tax increases estimated at $49.2 billion for fiscal 1984-87. The package (H Rept 98-432, Part II) was attached to HR 4170, which the committee initially had reported in 1983.

The Senate Finance Committee March 21 approved a measure to increase taxes $48 billion through fiscal 1987, including $21.4 billion in tax increases from S 2062.

In contrast to past years, a consensus emerged among the House, the Senate and the administration on how much revenue to raise and, for the most part, on who should pay. The "Rose Garden" deficit reduction plan, devised by Senate GOP leaders and endorsed by President Reagan March

15, included $48 billion in specific tax hikes culled from the House and Senate bills.

Both packages included proposals from the administration's fiscal 1985 budget to curtail a wide range of tax shelters. Both also raised liquor taxes and extended telephone excise taxes, revamped taxation of the life insurance industry, restricted the use of tax-exempt industrial development bonds and reduced scheduled tax hikes for large trucks.

In part, the consensus on taxes formed because both committees steered clear of proposals that would threaten what was most dear to the Reagan administration: across-the-board income tax cuts enacted in 1981 and indexing of tax brackets to offset inflation, scheduled to go into effect in 1985. *(1981 legislation, p. 65)*

Floor Action. The tax measures were approved in both houses with little argument. The House passed HR 4170 April 11 on a 318-97 vote after little more than three hours of debate. No floor amendments were permitted to the bill.

The Senate approved its $47 billion tax increase package early April 13 by a 76-5 vote. The package was first adopted as an amendment to a minor House-passed tariff bill (HR 2163). It finally passed May 17 as part of an overall deficit reduction plan that the Senate substituted for the House version of HR 4170.

During floor action on the tax provisions, the Senate adopted various amendments that cut $1 billion from the $48 billion in tax increases approved by the Finance Committee.

Responding to lobbying by the real estate industry, the Senate weakened a Finance Committee provision that would have increased from 15 to 20 years the minimum time period over which a building could be depreciated, or written off against taxes. By a **62-19 key vote (R 37-8; D 25-11)**, the Senate agreed instead to a depreciation life of 20 years in 1984, 19 years in 1985 and 18 years thereafter. To offset the loss in expected revenues, the Senate reduced the investment tax credits available for rehabilitation of old buildings. *(1984 key votes, p. 927)*

An attempt to delay tax indexing for three years was tabled on a **57-38 key vote (R 46-7; D 11-31)**.

Conference

The conference report on HR 4170 (H Rept 98-861) was filed June 23.

Conferees agreed to drop several contentious provisions, including a proposed increase in the cigarette excise tax passed by the House and the administration's plan to set up "enterprise zones" to encourage development of economically distressed areas. *(Story, p. 119)*

Finance Committee Chairman Robert Dole, R-Kan., said the White House had to be convinced to sacrifice its enterprise zone initiative to keep the entire conference agreement from falling apart. The House would agree to drop its cigarette excise tax hike only if the zone proposal, opposed by Ways and Means Chairman Dan Rostenkowski, D-Ill., was withdrawn, he said. If retained in the final conference report, the cigarette provision likely would have run into stiff opposition from Sen. Jesse Helms, R-N.C., who was up for re-election in his tobacco-growing state.

In a surprise move, the House accepted a Senate provision reducing from one year to six months the length of time an asset must be held before the proceeds from its sale could qualify for preferred capital gains tax treatment. The

HR 4170 Revenue Provisions: Estimated Impact

(Fiscal years, in millions of dollars)

Provisions	1984	1985	1986	1987	1984-87
Tax Freeze; Tax Reform Generally	$ 1,467	$10,546	$18,071	$24,123	$54,201
Life Insurance Tax Provisions	−80	−315	−375	−469	−1,239
Private Foundation Provisions;					
Exempt Organizations		−33	−46	−47	−126
Tax Simplification Provisions	99	924	175	208	1,406
Provisions Relating to Employers and					
Employees and to Retirement	31	149	265	274	719
Tax-Exempt Obligations	−73	−231	−359	−536	−1,199
Technical Corrections					
Foreign Sales Corporations		−62	−62	19	−105
Highway Revenue Provisions	−152	−102	19	−32	−267
Miscellaneous Revenue Provisions	−82	−268	−1,143	−1,067	−2,560
Other Tax-Related Provisions	−67	−16	−12	−6	−101
Total	$ 1,143	$10,592	$16,533	$22,467	$50,735

SOURCE: Joint Committee on Taxation

move was unexpected because Rostenkowski had rejected identical Senate provisions in conferences on two previous tax bills. *(Stories, pp. 65, 72)*

In exchange, the maximum tax credit available to working-poor families was increased from $500 to $550.

The conferees also reached last-minute agreement on restrictions on the use by state and local governments of industrial development bonds and changes in real estate depreciation.

They resolved the IDB issue by crafting a compromise to give states the option of choosing the greater of a $150 per capita limit or an overall $200 million ceiling on the amount of IDBs issued annually within a state. And they agreed to increase from 15 years to 18 years the write-off period for new investment in real estate. The House had instructed its conferees not to accept any lengthening of the write-off period.

Conferees also:

● Retained existing law allowing certain tax credits for the rehabilitation of old and historic buildings.

● Retained existing law allowing energy tax credits for residences and businesses to expire at the end of 1985.

● Allowed the 25 percent tax credit for new research and development expenses to expire at the end of 1985.

● Dropped a Senate provision that allowed retirees to exclude tax-exempt income in calculating whether their Social Security benefits were subject to tax.

An impasse over spending cuts affecting the poor and tax breaks for the wealthy and the middle class was broken after the House agreed to a Medicare physician fee freeze and the Senate, after getting the go-ahead from the White House, dropped approximately $5 billion in tax breaks included in its version of the deficit reduction plan. These included the tax credits to promote energy conservation and business research and an administration proposal to expand the use of Individual Retirement Accounts for non-working spouses.

Final Action

The House adopted the conference report on HR 4170 by a 268-155 vote June 27. The Senate adopted the conference report several hours later, 83-15, clearing the bill.

There was a last-minute dispute over a provision to penalize those who helped finance the sale of their homes or businesses by offering loans at below-market interest rates. Both buyer and seller could reap tax benefits from such an arrangement.

The bill raised the minimum interest rate a seller could charge without incurring a penalty. It also increased the tax penalty for sellers who charged a lower rate, by permitting the Internal Revenue Service to apply a higher interest rate to calculate their tax liability. The so-called "imputed interest" provision was included in the bill to combat tax shelter schemes by ensuring that transactions were taxed as if prevailing mortgage rates applied.

Only after both houses had adopted the conference report on HR 4170, but before it was sent to the president, did the real estate and housing interests rally to oppose the imputed interest section. They complained that the limits on seller-financed deals, which were to take effect Jan. 1, 1985, would hurt the housing market.

The House hurriedly passed a separate measure (H Con Res 328) to make "technical" corrections in HR 4170 that would exempt most residences and small farms from the interest rate provision.

But in the Senate, the resolution was held up by some Democrats, led by John Melcher, D-Mont., who wanted to

expand the exemptions to include larger farms and small businesses. The Senate finally voted to exempt all farms, but not small businesses, and the House agreed June 29. Before adjourning in October, Congress agreed to postpone the imputed interest penalty for six months. *(Imputed interest, p. 82)*

Final Provisions

As signed into law July 18, the Deficit Reduction Act of 1984 (HR 4170 — PL 98-369) contained the following major tax provisions:

Individual Taxes

Liquor. Increased the $10.50 tax on a gallon of 100 proof liquor to $12.50, effective Oct. 1, 1985.

Telephones. Extended for two years the 3 percent telephone excise tax, due to expire at the end of 1985.

Income Averaging. Restricted the use of income averaging, a tax-calculating technique that lowered taxes for individuals who had large increases in income from one year to the next.

Interest Exclusion. Repealed a provision in existing law allowing taxpayers, after 1984, to exclude from taxes 15 percent of their net interest income.

Estate and Gift. Delayed for three years a scheduled reduction in the maximum estate and gift tax. The maximum rate would be 55 percent through 1987 and 50 percent thereafter.

The bill also closed a loophole that allowed housing bonds issued under the Housing Act of 1937 to be exempt from estate and gift taxes.

Foreign Income. Froze for four years the $80,000 maximum exclusion for income earned abroad. The exclusion would increase to $95,000 by 1990.

Capital Gains. Reduced from one year to six months the length of time an asset had to have been held before proceeds from its sale could qualify for special capital gains tax treatment. The change was effective for assets acquired between June 22, 1984, and Jan. 1, 1988.

Earned-Income Tax Credit. Increased from $500 to $550 the maximum credit allowed for low-income wage earners with dependent children, effective Jan. 1, 1985. The credit was completely phased out for those earning more than $11,000 per year.

Mileage Deduction. Raised from 9 cents to 12 cents the mileage tax deduction allowed for individuals who used their automobiles while performing charitable work, effective Jan. 1, 1985.

Estimated Tax. Required that individuals liable for the alternative minimum tax — usually those who took large deductions — make quarterly estimated tax payments during the course of the tax year.

Business Taxes

'Luxury' Cars. Limited business tax deductions for automobiles that cost more than $16,000.

Personal Use Equipment. Restricted business tax breaks for equipment, such as home computers, boats and airplanes, that was used for business 50 percent or less of the time. Taxpayers were required to keep a detailed log of business use of such equipment, including automobiles. In addition, use of such property had to be a requirement of employment, not a convenience for the employee, to qual-

ify for a deduction. Congress repealed the record-keeping requirements in 1985, following widespread complaints that they were unnecessary and burdensome.

Sale/Leaseback. Clamped down on the use of so-called "sale/leaseback" arrangements used by non-profit organizations and governmental entities to benefit indirectly from tax breaks they could not use directly. The bill prevented those involved in such leasing plans from benefiting from the generous business tax breaks that made such arrangements worthwhile. However, a number of exceptions were made for ongoing projects.

Truck Taxes. Reduced scheduled tax hikes on heavy trucks enacted in 1982 and effective July 1, 1984. Trucks that weighed less than 55,000 pounds were exempted from the highway use tax. Those weighing more than 55,000 pounds would pay $100, plus $22 for every 1,000 pounds above 55,000. Trucks weighing more than 75,000 pounds would pay a maximum tax of $550.

To pay for the truck tax change, the excise tax on diesel fuel was increased from 9 cents to 15 cents a gallon.

Leasing. Delayed for four years, until 1988, the effective date of liberalized rules governing business leasing of equipment. The rules, designed primarily to help unprofitable firms, were enacted in 1982 to replace so-called "safe-harbor" leasing that allowed firms to sell unused tax breaks. *(1982 action, p. 72)*

Life Insurance. Overhauled taxation of the life insurance industry to eliminate different treatment of two segments of the industry, the mutual insurance companies and the stock companies.

Corporate Tax Rates. Phased out benefits of graduated corporate tax rates for companies with taxable income in excess of $1 million.

Golden Parachutes. Clamped down on the use of so-called "golden parachute" agreements, generous severance payments to executives displaced by a corporate merger. The bill imposed a 20 percent excise tax on payments in excess of 300 percent of the executive's usual annual salary, and prevented the business from taking a deduction for the excess payment.

Windfall Profits. Delayed a scheduled reduction in the top tax rate on newly discovered oil. The bill kept the existing 22.5 percent tax through 1987; it would then drop to 20 percent in 1988 and 15 percent thereafter.

Small Business. Froze for four years a law allowing small businesses to write off, in one year, assets worth less than $5,000, instead of depreciating them over a longer period. The $5,000 limit was scheduled to rise to $7,500 in 1984 and 1985 and $10,000 thereafter.

Corporate 'Preferences.' Reduced from 85 percent to 80 percent the value of certain business tax deductions, called "preference items" — such as some accelerated depreciation benefits.

Tax Straddles. Restricted a tax avoidance scheme involving stock options "straddles" through which investors deferred income from one year to the next. However, the top tax rate on such transactions was lowered from about 50 percent to 32 percent.

Foreign Withholding. Repealed the existing 30 percent withholding tax on interest paid to foreign investors.

Foreign Sales Corporations. Set up, at the administration's request, a new export subsidy program involving Foreign Sales Corporations to replace existing Domestic International Sales Corporations (DISCs). The change was made because of objections raised by U.S. trading partners about the DISC subsidy.

Foreign Tax Shelter. Prevented firms from sheltering income from the sale of foreign trade receivables (promises to pay for goods).

Accounting. Made several accounting changes primarily aimed at preventing companies or individuals from taking deductions before expenses were required to be paid.

Freddie Mac. Repealed a tax exemption for the Federal Home Loan Bank Mortgage Corporation, or Freddie Mac, a federally backed corporation that bought and sold mortgages and mortgage-backed securities. Removal of the exemption put Freddie Mac on a more competitive footing with private mortgage firms.

Other Changes

Fringe Benefits. Exempted from taxes most common employee fringe benefits, such as parking spaces, airline tickets, employee discounts and college tuition. To qualify for the exemption such benefits had to be available to all employees on a non-discriminatory basis, with the exception of parking spaces.

Faculty Housing. Extended for two years, through 1985, a moratorium on the issuance of regulations by the Treasury Department on taxation of on-campus housing benefits for faculty members.

Industrial Development Bonds. Limited the amount of IDBs and student loan bonds that could be issued annually within a state to the greater of $150 per capita or $200 million (for less populous states). The $150 per capita limit was to be lowered to $100 in 1986.

Exceptions were made for bonds used to finance multi-family housing and publicly owned airports, docks, wharves, mass transit facilities and convention or trade show facilities. Exceptions also were made for hundreds of specific projects already in the works.

Taxable Bonds. Closed a number of loopholes used by investors in taxable bonds, such as savings bonds and Treasury bills, to reduce their tax liability.

Mortgage Revenue Bonds. Allowed state and local governments to issue tax-exempt mortgage revenue bonds, through 1987, to help finance low- and moderate-income housing. The authority had expired Dec. 31, 1983.

Real Estate. Increased from 15 years to 18 years the length of time over which a building could be depreciated. Exceptions were made for low-income housing.

Welfare Benefit Plans. Restricted several potential tax abuses involving voluntary employee beneficiary associations, trusts used to fund employee health and welfare benefits.

'Cafeteria Plans.' Restricted the use of new benefit plans that the Internal Revenue Service (IRS) feared were used to avoid taxes. The plans offered employees a choice of fringe benefits. The bill permitted the plans to offer only non-taxable fringe benefits.

Employee Stock Ownership Plans (ESOPs). Repealed scheduled increases in a tax credit for employer contributions to ESOPs, while making a number of other changes to encourage the use of such plans. The .5 percent tax credit was to expire after Dec. 31, 1987. ESOPs are stock bonus plans often used to encourage employee interest in a company's success.

Tax Shelters. Made a number of changes to eliminate tax shelters involving partnerships. The bill also required registrations of tax shelters with the IRS and higher penalties for promotion of "abusive" tax shelters.

Charitable Deductions. Required individuals who claimed a deduction for a charitable contribution of property worth more than $5,000 to have the property appraised to determine its value.

Interest-Free Loans. Provided guidelines for taxing benefits from interest-free loans or below-market interest rate loans, including those between family members. The lender would pay income taxes on the interest forgone, but the borrower could deduct the same amount. The provision generally did not apply to loans under $100,000 unless they were made solely to avoid taxes.

Targeted Jobs. Extended for one year the 1978 targeted jobs tax credit, due to expire at the end of 1984. The credit was designed to encourage employment of disadvantaged youth, the handicapped and Vietnam veterans.

Social Security. Allowed churches a one-time option to drop out of the retirement system. If they did so, the churches' employees were required to pay higher payroll taxes, as though they were self-employed.

Other Tax Measures

Education Fringe Benefits

In the rush of last-minute business before adjournment, the Senate Oct. 11 cleared a bill (HR 2568 — PL 98-611) to continue through 1985 the tax-free status of employer-provided education fringe benefits. The House had passed the bill Oct. 1 (H Rept 98-1049).

The existing law that allowed for tax-free educational aid expired at the end of 1983. The new measure made the tax exclusion retroactive to Jan. 1, 1984, but it also imposed a new $5,000 limit on the amount of such benefits an individual could receive tax-free in a year.

Many in Congress and the administration were concerned that the growth of fringe benefits in place of direct employee compensation was eroding the income tax base, leading to a loss of potential tax revenues.

Some restrictions on the tax-free status of fringe benefits were enacted earlier in 1984 as part of the Deficit Reduction Act of 1984 (PL 98-369). *(Story, p. 79)*

Legal Service Benefits, Imputed Interest

Congress Oct. 11 cleared a measure (HR 5361 — PL 98-612) extending through 1985 the tax-free status of employer contributions to group legal service plans.

HR 5361 also included a compromise agreement on a disputed real estate tax provision of the Deficit Reduction Act of 1984 (PL 98-369). Intended to limit tax-avoiding real estate schemes, the so-called "imputed interest" provision in the earlier law imposed a tax penalty on sellers who financed certain sales at below-market interest rates. The imputed interest penalty was strongly opposed by the real estate industry. *(Deficit reduction details, p. 79)*

Following extensive negotiations among the House, the Senate, real estate lobbyists and the administration, both chambers agreed to delay the effective date of the imputed interest penalty for six months — until July 1, 1985 — but only for sales involving mortgages of $2 million or less.

As originally passed by the House Oct. 1, HR 5361 (H Rept 98-1050) dealt only with legal services plans. Before passing the bill Oct. 11, the Senate added an imputed interest amendment that had threatened to hold up passage of unrelated debt ceiling legislation.

Financial Regulation

Banks and other financial institutions were whipsawed by economic upheaval and regulatory disarray during President Reagan's first term. By 1984 government policy toward banking institutions could best be described as confused.

Rapid inflation and high interest rates had started undermining time-honored regulatory controls on banks during the late 1970s. Government responded in fits and starts, moving haltingly toward deregulation. But often it was paralyzed by conflicts between financial companies and within its own ranks.

Congress, meanwhile, deadlocked in its efforts to overhaul banking laws dating back to the 1930s. Although lawmakers approved an interim measure in 1982, Rep. Fernand J. St Germain, D-R.I., the anti-deregulation chairman of the House Banking Committee, and his pro-deregulation counterpart, Senate Banking Committee Chairman Jake Garn, R-Utah, were unable to bridge their differences over broader financial legislation. They vowed to try again in 1985.

Adding to the difficulties Congress faced in dealing with deregulation issues were sharp territorial disputes among banks, savings and loan (S&L) institutions, insurance companies and securities companies.

Signs of Trouble

Strains in the nation's financial system were readily apparent. In 1980 Bache Group Inc., a securities firm, floundered because of loans it had made to the Hunt brothers, whose huge investments in silver were jeopardized by plunging silver values. In 1982 Drysdale Government Securities Inc. collapsed, causing huge losses to Chase Manhattan Bank and numerous securities firms, which had loaned it large sums.

Also that year Penn Square Bank of Oklahoma City went belly up, the victim of an energy lending spree run awry. That collapse weakened several other banks — including Chicago-based Continental Illinois Corp., Seafirst Corp. in Seattle and Chase Manhattan — which had bought large quantities of bad Penn Square loans.

The next year, 1983, brought more troubles. Baldwin-United Corp., an insurance and financial services company, filed for bankruptcy. Seafirst, unable to right itself after the Penn Square debacle, had to merge with giant Bankamerica Corp. And the failure of United American Bank of Knoxville, Tenn., led to the closing of nine related banks in that state.

Perhaps the biggest shock came in 1984, when federal regulators and major banks had to piece together a $7.5 billion rescue package for Continental Illinois, the nation's eighth largest bank. The package cost the Federal Deposit Insurance Corp. (FDIC) an estimated $4.5 billion over three years, and left it holding preferred stock equal to 80 percent of Continental's equity — leading some to characterize the rescue as the first nationalization of a major U.S. bank.

Roots of the Problem

Financial strains were rooted in dramatic economic changes. Rising inflation in the late 1970s had begun boosting interest rates. When the Federal Reserve jammed on the monetary brakes in 1979, sharply restricting growth in the money supply, interest rates soared to unprecedented levels. Moreover, changes in Fed policy led to dramatic swings in interest rates, causing financial institutions tremendous difficulty in matching their assets and liabilities. *(Monetary policy, box, p. 28)*

Savings and loan associations were hit especially hard. For years they had used short-term deposits to finance billions of dollars in low, fixed-rate, long-term mortgages. That worked well, so long as the government imposed low ceilings on deposit interest rates. But with rising market rates, depositors began pulling their money out of S&Ls in search of a better return.

Non-bank companies quickly responded to growing consumer demands for higher rates of return. Money market funds, which pooled small deposits to buy short-term government and corporate securities, offered small depositors market rates at relatively little risk. Depositors turned to them in droves, even though money market funds were not backed by federal deposit insurance.

References

Discussion of financial regulation legislation for the years 1945-64 may be found in *Congress and the Nation Vol. I*, pp. 337-386; for the years 1965-68, *Congress and the Nation Vol. II*, pp. 253-279; for the years 1969-72, *Congress and the Nation Vol. III*, pp. 135-145; for the years 1973-76, *Congress and the Nation Vol. IV*, pp. 107-117; for the years 1977-80, *Congress and the Nation Vol. V*, pp. 253-265.

Financial Regulation

Unwilling to clamp down on money market funds because that would deny savers the chance to earn market rates, regulators had little choice but to remove controls on bank and S&L deposit rates so they could compete for deposits. That helped avert a liquidity crunch for scores of S&Ls, but it still squeezed their earnings severely by driving their costs near or above what they were earning on mortgage loans.

The transition from a high-inflation to a low-inflation economy also hit many banks. Economic slowdown made marginal loans turn sour. In some areas real estate loans went bad as land prices suddenly stabilized and, in some cases, even fell. As the Penn Square collapse demonstrated, an energy lending bubble burst when worldwide economic recession and increased oil production led to an oil glut.

International economic woes also left many U.S. banks saddled with huge amounts of questionable foreign loans. When oil prices soared in the 1970s, U.S. banks had pumped vast quantities of loans overseas, helping many countries meet staggering energy costs and finance development. World recession made many of those loans look doubtful, and worries grew that an international default could ripple through the U.S. financial system. *(International economic policy, p. 95)*

Competitive Pressures

Financial institutions tried to adapt to changing circumstances by diversifying. Merrill Lynch & Co. Inc.; Sears, Roebuck & Co.; and other companies formed "financial supermarkets" that offered increasingly sophisticated consumers one-stop shopping for banking, insurance, securities and real estate services.

Banks, however, felt restricted in meeting such competition by a web of government restrictions that had kept them out of many non-banking financial activities. As pressures mounted, they began poking loopholes in these restrictions. One of the most popular was the "non-bank bank loophole" in the 1956 Bank Holding Company Act (PL 84-511). *(Background, Congress and the Nation Vol. I, p. 448; Congress and the Nation Vol. II, p. 265; Congress and the Nation Vol. III, p. 139)*

Bank holding companies are organizations that control stock in one or more banks. The act generally prohibited them from owning non-bank subsidiaries, or from owning affiliates in more than one state unless allowed by state law. The law defined a bank as an institution that both accepted demand deposits (checking accounts) and made commercial loans. A firm could escape the legal prohibitions on bank holding companies by engaging in just one of those activities, even though it still could receive a bank charter and thus qualify for federal deposit insurance.

Securities firms had exploited the loophole first, forming non-bank bank affiliates that would take deposits but refrain from making commercial loans. They hoped that way to be able to offer deposits insured by the government, and thus regain some of the competitive edge they lost in 1982 when Congress finally authorized banks to pay competitive interest rates on short-term deposits. Banks fought back by using the same loophole to form non-bank bank affiliates across state lines, effectively skirting the ban on interstate banking.

That was not the only loophole banks tried to use to gain greater competitive freedom. Since the Bank Holding Company Act applied only to banks that belonged to the Federal Reserve System, some sought to use state-chartered affiliates to engage in activities prohibited by federal law. New York-based Citicorp acquired a state-chartered affiliate in South Dakota and began using it to sell insurance nationwide. South Dakota, seeing a chance to generate in-state jobs, obliged with enabling legislation. That became known as the "South Dakota loophole."

Soon such moves reopened a fissure within the banking industry. Medium-sized banks in some regions, fearing the encroachment of big New York banks, tried to band together to keep out their big city rivals. Seizing on the Bank Holding Company Act provision that allowed states to sanction cross-border banking, banks in New England and elsewhere began pushing for compacts that would allow interstate banking only within their region. Large national banks with territorial ambitions complained that such arrangements were an unconstitutional interference with interstate commerce.

Disputes Over Regulation

Bank regulators disagreed how best to cope with these difficulties. One school of thought held that government should loosen its regulatory reins and let banks gain strength through diversification.

Reagan appointees advanced this view with considerable success. Treasury Secretary Donald T. Regan pushed for speedy decontrol of bank and thrift deposit interest rates. Richard T. Pratt, chairman of the Federal Home Loan Bank Board, played a key role in convincing Congress to broaden S&L lending powers in response to their financial problems. And C. Todd Conover, comptroller of the currency, encouraged banks and other financial institutions to exploit the non-bank bank loophole.

The Federal Reserve Board held to a more traditional view. Fed Chairman Paul A. Volcker argued that banks play too central a role in the economy to be unfettered. Although he conceded that some post-Depression restrictions on banks could legitimately be relaxed, he battled Conover over non-bank banks and urged Congress to reinforce a crumbling barrier separating banking and commerce.

Frustrated by the Fed's conservative stance, deregulation-minded regulators pressed to strip the central bank of many of its regulatory powers. They took their case to a financial regulatory reform task force chaired by Vice President George Bush. The powerful American Bankers Association (ABA), frustrated by the Fed's reluctance to let banks branch into new lines of financial service, supported them.

For a while the task force appeared ready to recommend taking away most of the Fed's regulatory and bank examination functions, and to propose vesting these instead in a new federal banking agency that would consolidate many of the powers of the Fed, the comptroller and the FDIC. But Volcker counterattacked, arguing that the Fed needed to retain its direct supervisory powers over banks to assure the smooth operation of monetary policy. When he threatened to oppose even modest banking deregulation, ABA support for the assault on the Fed quickly faded.

After months of wrangling the task force finally issued its recommendations in early 1984. They called for the new federal banking agency to assume the comptroller of the currency's regulatory authority over federally chartered banks. The new agency would also take over much of the Fed's supervision of bank holding companies. But, bowing

Financial Industry Ups and Downs

Banks and savings and loan (S&L) institutions were buffeted by changing economic conditions in the 1970s and 1980s. After World War II and until the 1970s, prosperity and bankers' conservatism combined to keep failure rates negligible.

Then came years of high inflation mixed with recessions. Institutions began taking more risks and opening more branches, helped along by liberalized state laws. Competitive pressures increased.

In the 1980s, Congress phased out the caps on interest rates for savers' deposits. Increasingly, banks and S&Ls competed not only among themselves but also with non-banking firms that offered alternative, high-interest investments.

As these charts show, many financial institutions did not weather the recession of 1973-75, and failure rates went up in 1975 and 1976.

Several relatively stable years followed. Then, as the 1970s closed, spiraling interest rates and the recession of 1981-82 doomed record numbers of banks and S&Ls. S&Ls were hit especially hard, since they held long-term mortgage loans with low interest but had to pay high interest to draw deposits.

Congressional aid in 1982 helped some S&Ls survive until interest rates briefly came back down. But when interest rates again inched upward, their futures were back in doubt again.

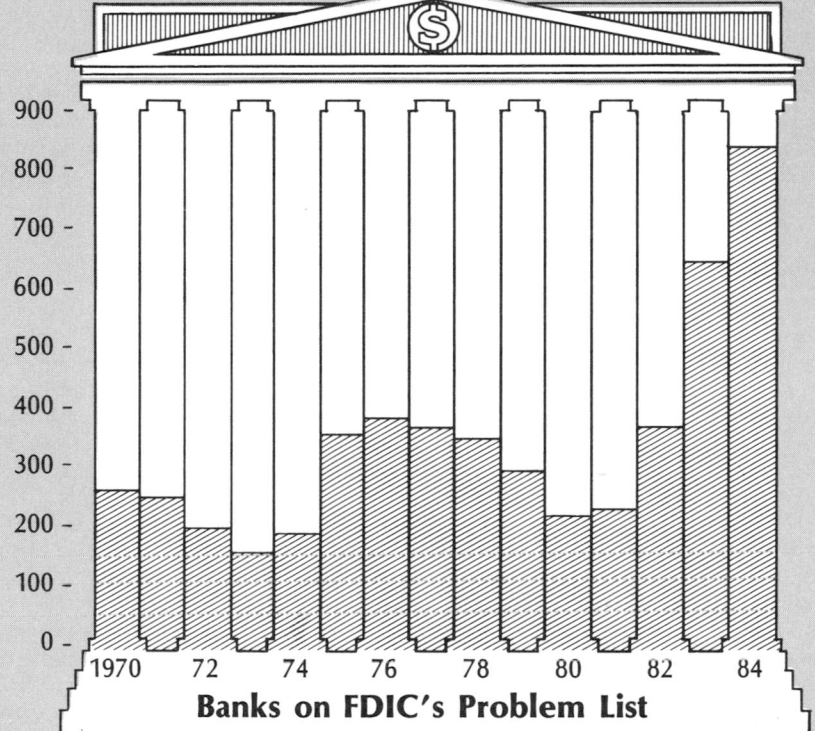

Banks on FDIC's Problem List

SOURCE: Federal Deposit Insurance Corp.

The Federal Deposit Insurance Corp's (FDIC) "problem bank" list told much the same story. The identities of those banks, whose finances merited regulator's extra attention, were guarded carefully because disclosure could ignite a run by depositors. By Dec. 31, 1984, 828 banks were on the list — almost four times the total (217) of 1980.

Insured Bank Failures

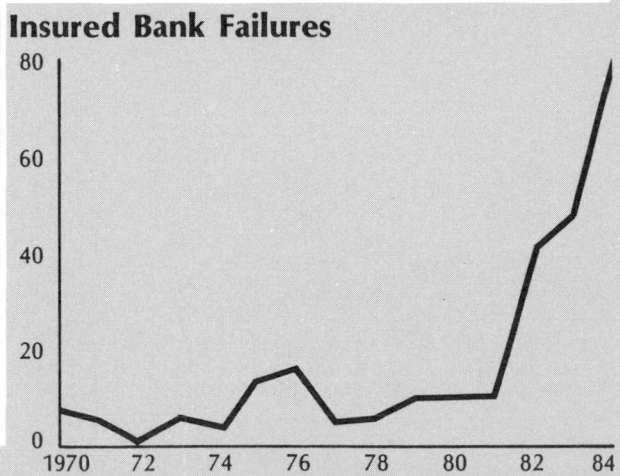

The last bank failure of 1984 occurred Dec. 22, when the First Security Bank of Sandwich, Ill., with $10.4 million in deposits, closed. The bank was reopened Dec. 24 as the First National Bank of Sandwich, a subsidiary of Union Bankcorp in Illinois. There were 79 failures in 1984.

SOURCE: Federal Deposit Insurance Corp.

Savings and Loan Casualties

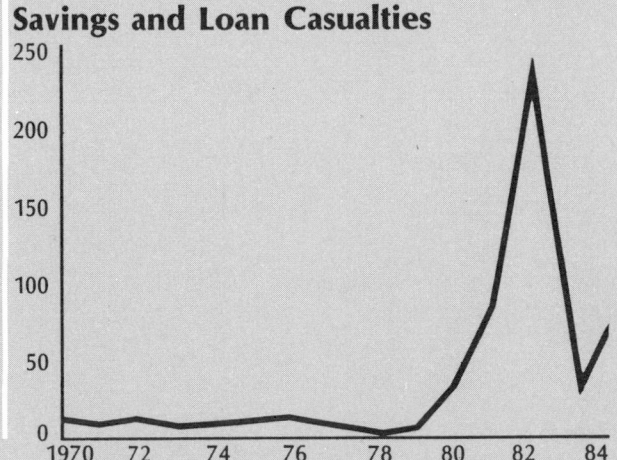

The total of 70 includes troubled S&Ls that did not close but merged with healthy institutions, with or without FLIC financial assistance. Regulators do not consider such supervised mergers as failures, though industry analysts do.

SOURCE: Federal Home Loan Bank Board

to Volcker, the task force recommended letting the Fed continue regulating the parents of the 50 largest federally chartered banks.

And, while the task force proposed giving the new banking agency the Fed's former control over deciding permissible diversifications for bank holding companies, it recommended letting the Fed veto any of these it considered a threat to the soundness and safety of the banking system.

Most observers considered the task force's recommendations a decisive victory for Volcker and the Fed. The proposals quickly dropped from sight, as Congress showed no interest in revising the bank regulatory structure. *(Regulatory system, p. 88)*

Unresolved Questions

Faced with substantial uncertainties and conflicting pressures, government policies grew increasingly murky during President Reagan's first term. In 1981 and 1982 Congress and regulators tried a good measure of deregulation, in part through 1982 legislation that accelerated a modest deregulation plan lawmakers had approved in 1980. But continuing bank and S&L failures and financial instability raised doubts in 1983 and 1984 about continuing down that path.

Regulators themselves became unsettled that the tremendous interdependence of financial institutions made it difficult to contain failures. The Penn Square Bank failure demonstrated that problems in one financial institution could easily spread to others as a result of the widespread practice of selling loans between institutions.

Other developments added to regulators' headaches. FDIC Chairman William M. Isaac warned that the appearance of "money brokers" meant banks and thrifts could raise large sums of money almost instantaneously, possibly pumping it into bad loans much faster than regulators could keep pace. And S&L regulators voiced concerns that while deregulation gave thrift institutions enormous freedom, federal deposit insurance insulated them almost entirely from the costs of imprudence.

Proponents of deregulation reasoned that the discipline of the market could replace government controls and keep banks in line. Chairman Isaac of the FDIC pushed for greater public disclosure of bank and S&L problems, and he toyed with the idea of setting variable deposit insurance premiums according to each institution's "risk" of failure. He also warned big depositors — those with deposits above the $100,000 federal insurance limit — to scrutinize the financial health of banks where they kept their funds.

It was not clear that approach worked, though rhetoric made big money handlers nervous. When rumors spread about trouble at Continental Illinois, large uninsured deposits rapidly fled, precipitating the crisis. The resulting federal bailout demonstrated that the costs to the economy of a major financial failure were greater than regulators would allow. But some said so long as the government would not allow failure, there could be no true market discipline.

At the end of Reagan's first term, many voices called for tighter regulation. They argued that the economic importance of banks, confirmed by federal insurance on deposits, required special restraints. But deregulators, noting how the government-imposed reliance on home mortgage lending had almost sunk the S&L industry, still pushed for decontrol. Those two forces awaited a second Reagan term, and watched to see whether economic developments would ease or worsen the outlook.

Chronology
Of Action
On Financial Regulation

1981-82

Interest rates climbed sharply in late 1980 and early 1981, putting a squeeze on savings and loan (S&L) association earnings. The House in 1981 passed a short-term emergency measure authorizing federal regulators to provide expanded aid to troubled S&Ls and to arrange for interstate mergers for failing S&Ls, but the Senate deferred action until 1982. Lawmakers did approve a tax law amendment authorizing S&Ls, banks and credit unions to issue tax-exempt certificates as a way of attracting low-cost deposits.

In 1982 Congress approved legislation accelerating the deregulation of the financial industry that began in 1980, while providing emergency assistance to troubled S&Ls.

The legislation, a product of two years of jockeying among different segments of the financial services industry, freed traditional deposit-taking institutions to compete head-on with money market funds. It also strengthened the hand of federal regulators to deal with failing financial institutions, and it further loosened the savings and loan industry's traditional role as a home mortgage lender.

'All Savers' Certificates

Congress in 1981 showed its willingness to support the distressed thrift industry by including in its massive tax cut bill (HR 4242 — PL 97-34) a provision authorizing depository institutions to issue one-year, tax-exempt savings certificates. Dubbed "all savers" certificates, they could yield 70 percent of the yield on one-year Treasury bills. Individuals could exclude up to $1,000 of the interest on such certificates from income subject to federal taxes. Couples could exclude up to $2,000. The certificates could be issued only for a 15-month period ending Dec. 31, 1982. *(Tax bill, p. 65)*

Savings and loan (S&L) institutions devised the idea as a way of attracting low-cost deposits. Critics, though, argued that it merely gave upper-income people a tax break without resolving the long-term problems that got thrift institutions into trouble in the first place.

By granting the tax break, the federal government in effect subsidized the interest S&Ls paid on the certificates. For savers in high tax brackets, the tax advantage would make all-savers certificates return more than most money market funds, even though the cost to S&Ls would fall below market levels.

To widen support for the certificates, Congress authorized other deposit-taking institutions to offer them too. But it said institutions, other than credit unions, issuing the certificates would have to make at least 75 percent of their net new deposits available for home or agricultural loans.

Financial Regulation

The continuing crisis in the savings and loan (S&L) industry prompted Congress in 1982 to enact the second major law in three years restructuring financial services providers. The bill (HR 6267 — PL 97-320) cleared Oct. 1.

In 1980 lawmakers had attempted to ease financial industry problems by enacting the Depository Institutions Deregulation and Monetary Control Act (PL 96-221). Major provisions of that act ordered the elimination over six years of federal ceilings on interest rates for bank and thrift accounts, authorized federally insured financial institutions to offer interest-bearing checking (NOW) accounts, gave S&Ls new consumer lending powers and required all depository institutions to maintain reserves as directed by the Federal Reserve Board. *(Congress and the Nation Vol. V, p. 261)*

But even before the effects of that law could be felt, the S&L industry's plight grew worse as interest rates soared to record levels in 1981. In July 1981 Federal Home Loan Bank Board Chairman Richard T. Pratt told the House Banking Committee that one-third of the nation's S&Ls were not "viable under today's conditions."

Ideas about how to deal with the problem varied widely. S&Ls, with strong support from House Banking Committee Chairman Fernand J. St Germain, D-R.I., sought federal backing until they could get back on their feet. Regulators, fearing the costs of a simple bailout, asked for sweeping authority to merge ailing S&Ls with healthier institutions. And Senate Banking Committee Chairman Jake Garn, R Utah, with Reagan administration support, said the answer was a heavy new dose of deregulation for both banks and S&Ls.

The search for a solution was complicated by sharp rivalries among financial institutions. Commercial banks resisted proposals that would allow S&Ls to strengthen their financial condition by diversifying their lending activities beyond making home mortgages. When Garn tried to placate the banks by letting them invade the traditional turf of securities firms, the securities industry howled. The insurance industry also fought to keep banks out of its traditional turf. *(Background, p. 83)*

After months of wrangling, lawmakers finally settled on a compromise that gave each group something of what it wanted. S&Ls got emergency financial backing from the federal government — though not as much as they originally sought. Regulators' powers to deal with failing thrifts were significantly expanded. And banks won the ability to compete with money market funds for deposits, though their bid for broader powers otherwise was scrubbed.

1981 Action

House Action. On Oct. 28, 1981, the House passed, by a 371-46 vote, a short-term emergency measure (HR 4603 — H Rept 97-272) expanding the authority of federal regulators to aid S&Ls.

Banking Committee Chairman St Germain argued that regulators needed more flexibility to deal with troubled thrifts. The Federal Deposit Insurance Corp. (FDIC) and the Federal Savings & Loan Insurance Corp. (FSLIC) feared that too many bank or thrift failures might deplete their deposit insurance funds and shake public confidence. So they wanted authority to provide stopgap assistance to avert widespread failures.

The bill expanded regulators' authority to arrange

Bank Regulatory System: Depression Legacy

The nation's existing bank regulatory system was a legacy of the 1930s. In their competition to attract depositors, banks in the years leading up to the Great Depression made risky investments to get high returns and thus be able to raise the interest rates paid to depositors. The gamble often failed.

In the absence of any deposit insurance, lack of confidence by depositors quickly spread after the stock market crash of 1929, leading to a general run on the nation's banks that left 9,000 banks closed by 1933. In March of that year President Franklin D. Roosevelt took the unprecedented step of closing all the nation's banks for four days in an effort to stop the run.

The System

Congress responded to the financial crisis by dividing the industry by function and submitting each type of financial institution to the oversight of at least one regulatory agency.

The Banking Act of 1933 severely limited the ways in which commercial banks could compete for depositors. Interest payments were no longer allowed on demand deposits, or checking accounts, and the Federal Reserve was authorized to set ceilings on interest paid for savings deposits by banks belonging to the Federal Reserve System.

The Glass-Steagall Act of 1933 effectively separated the banking and securities industries and prohibited banks and brokers from engaging in each other's activities. To shore up the confidence of small depositors and prevent the kind of widespread bank runs that had devastated the industry, it established the Federal Deposit Insurance Corp. (FDIC), funded by premiums paid by commercial banks and most mutual savings banks on their deposits. In 1934 the Federal Savings and Loan Insurance Corp. (FSLIC) was set up under the Federal Home Loan Bank Board to insure the deposits of all federal savings and loans. A prohibition on interstate banking had been erected previously under the McFadden Act of 1927.

The financial system that emerged from the Depression was composed of several kinds of institutions, each with well-defined functions. Commercial banks offered checking accounts to depositors desiring ready access to their funds and provided loans, excluding mortgage loans, to both individuals and businesses. Savings and loan associations offered savings accounts and were engaged primarily in mortgage lending, while mutual savings banks offered consumer loans as well. Securities firms and investment banks catered to large investors and large corporate borrowers.

That system endured largely intact through the 1970s. The drive to liberalize banking regulation be-gan building in 1971, with the recommendations of the President's Commission on Financial Structure and Regulation — also known as the Hunt commission after its chairman, Reed O. Hunt. But it was not until 1980 that many of the commission's recommendations were enacted into law.

The Regulators

Following is a brief description of the federal regulatory agencies for financial institutions. In addition, all 50 states had regulatory agencies for state-chartered financial institutions.

The Office of the Comptroller of the Currency had primary responsibility for regulating 4,800 federally chartered national banks. The comptroller's office was set up in 1863 as a quasi-independent arm of the U.S. Treasury. It approved all applications for bank charters, branch offices, mergers and new services, such as discount brokerages.

The Federal Reserve Board was the primary regulator for bank holding companies, organizations with controlling stock interests in one or more commercial banks. The seven-member board of governors also regulated 1,000 state-chartered banks that were voluntary members of the Federal Reserve System; it had some jurisdiction over national banks.

The Fed, the nation's central bank, was established in 1913 to act as lender of last resort for banks, provide a check-clearing facility and control monetary policy. There were 12 regional Federal Reserve Banks, which were the superbanks for Fed members.

The Federal Deposit Insurance Corp., established in 1933 to guarantee deposits, was chief regulator for state-chartered banks that were not members of the Fed but whose deposits were insured, up to a certain amount, by the FDIC's insurance fund. Also, the FDIC was the receiver, handling the property settlements, for national banks and some state banks that failed. Both the FDIC and the Federal Home Loan Bank Board supervised federal savings banks. The FDIC had a three-member board.

FDIC insurance, from a fund financed through assessments on banks, was required for federally chartered institutions but voluntary for state banks that were not Fed members.

The Federal Home Loan Bank Board regulated more than 3,000 federally and state-chartered savings and loan associations. Formed in 1932, the three-member board supervised Federal Home Loan Banks in 12 districts, from which the thrift institutions could borrow money to finance residential mortgages, much as commercial banks drew from the Federal Reserve System's district banks. Also, the board operated the FSLIC, which was similar to the banks' FDIC but was not independent.

mergers for failing thrifts into healthier ones or into commercial banks — across state lines, if necessary. But to limit interstate mergers and those combining commercial banks and thrifts, the House bill required regulators first to try to select for a merger an institution of the same type within the same state. Next in priority was an institution of the same type in a different state, then an institution of a different type within the same state and, finally, a different institution in a different state.

The bill also expanded the circumstances under which the FDIC and the FSLIC could provide financial aid to insured banks and S&Ls. It allowed the two agencies to purchase the securities of insured institutions or make contributions to them. In cases where a significant number of institutions were threatened, it authorized the agencies to provide aid in order to help prevent insolvency and thus reduce losses to the insurance funds.

Regulators had preferred more sweeping powers, but they endorsed the House bill. The Reagan administration, though, opposed it on the grounds it did not address the thrift industry's "long-term structural difficulties" — namely, its reliance on volatile, short-term deposits to finance fixed-rate, long-term mortgage loans.

Senate Inaction. In the Senate, Banking Committee Chairman Garn decided against acting on the House bill. Instead, he announced plans to move forward in 1982 on a broader measure making long-range structural changes in the financial services industry. He suggested that the bill could form the basis for negotiations among the many financial industry interests.

The major elements of the Garn bill would:

● Authorize the FSLIC to approve interstate and cross-industry mergers when severe financial conditions threatened the stability of a significant number of S&Ls.

● Authorize the FDIC under the same "severe financial conditions" test to make loans, investments or deposits in distressed insured banks.

● Give S&Ls many of the powers enjoyed by commercial banks, including authority to offer checking accounts, make commercial loans and invest in real estate and in corporate debt instruments.

● Authorize banks and thrift institutions to operate, manage and sell interests in mutual funds.

● Authorize national banks to deal in and underwrite municipal revenue bonds.

● Pre-empt state laws that prohibited banks from enforcing due-on-sale clauses in mortgage contracts.

● Pre-empt state consumer usury ceilings, but give states a three-year period to override the pre-emptions. (The 1980 banking deregulation law lifted state usury ceilings on most other loans, including agriculture and business loans above $25,000.)

● Generally prohibit insurance activities by bank holding companies.

1982 Action

House Action. In 1982 the House again sought to bolster the sick thrift industry. In return, it demanded that S&Ls maintain their commitment to home lending.

The House May 20 approved, 272-91, the Net Worth Guarantee Act (HR 6267 — H Rept 97-550) allowing the Treasury to guarantee the net worth of savings and loan associations, mutual savings banks, commercial banks and credit unions if their net worth (value of assets minus liabilities) dropped below 2 percent of assets.

The legislation would establish an $8.5 billion fund to back the net worth of these institutions, although no money would change hands unless the bank or S&L failed.

Because the bill's sponsors viewed it as a way to strengthen the housing market, the legislation involved two important conditions: At least 20 percent of a qualifying institution's loan portfolio was required to be in residential real estate; and a thrift receiving aid had to earmark at least 60 percent of its new deposits for home mortgages.

Senate Action. Garn's lengthy interest group negotiations dragged on until August, when the Senate Banking Committee finally reported a stripped-down compromise version (S 2879 — S Rept 97-536) of the chairman's ambitious 1981 proposal. The full Senate approved the compromise by voice vote Sept. 24.

Significantly, the bill required the Depository Institutions Deregulation Committee, no later than 60 days after enactment, to authorize for banks and thrifts a new account that would compete with money market funds. The committee had been established under the 1980 deregulation law.

Savings and loans were buoyed by the measure, even though it offered less federal backing to them than the House bill. It would allow a thrift institution whose net worth fell below a certain level to exchange capital notes with the FDIC or FSLIC. The agency's note would boost the institution's net worth, enabling it to continue operating. If it later failed, the insurance agency would have to honor the note in paying off the institution's creditors. If the institution recovered, it would return the agency's capital note — receiving back, in turn, a promissory note it had given the agency.

The bill imposed several conditions before the assistance could be provided. And, rather than fully restore an institution's net worth, it provided aid equal to only a portion of the losses.

The bill also expanded the lending authority of S&Ls. In all, the legislation freed S&Ls to put as much as 90 percent of their assets into commercial and consumer loans. But because it thus reduced the distinction between commercial banks and thrifts, it ordered the Depository Institutions Deregulation Committee to phase out all interest rate differentials by July 1, 1982.

Much to the bitter disappointment of commercial banks, the committee dropped provisions authorizing them to offer mutual funds and underwrite revenue bonds. Indeed, while its general thrust was to give financial institutions greater freedom, in one area it actually reduced bank powers: Under intense insurance industry lobbying, lawmakers agreed to prohibit banks from selling casualty and property insurance. The American Bankers Association called the bill "a sweetheart savings and loan bill that leaves the commercial banking community at a greater disadvantage than before."

The banks were mollified by floor amendments that expanded the authority of bank service corporations and restricted S&Ls to offering checking accounts to their own business customers. Most important, banks said, was the provision authorizing depository institutions to offer market rate accounts.

Final Action. Working quickly to complete action before the election recess, conferees reached agreement (H Rept 97-899) on the complex legislation Sept. 29. The final version of HR 6267 generally followed the Senate bill. The Senate adopted the conference report Sept. 30, and the House cleared the bill the following day.

Major Provisions

As signed into law Oct. 15, 1982, the Garn-St Germain Depository Institutions Act of 1982 (HR 6267 — PL 97-320):

● Established a three-year program allowing ailing federally insured financial institutions to bolster their net worth by exchanging capital notes with the FDIC and FSLIC.

● Allowed institutions with net worth of 3 to 2 percent, 2 to 1 percent and 1 to .5 percent of assets to receive federal notes equal to 50 percent, 60 percent and 70 percent, respectively, of their losses during the two preceding quarters.

● Required that institutions have a net worth of at least .5 percent, have incurred losses during the two previous quarters and have 20 percent of their loans in mortgages to qualify for assistance.

Regulation. Expanded the powers of both the FDIC and the FSLIC to arrange mergers for failing banks and thrift institutions. Rather than wait until a financial institution actually failed, regulators could arrange a merger if they determined an institution had net worth of less than .5 percent and would exhaust its net worth entirely in six months. Regulators also could arrange mergers between banks and savings and loans, and they could arrange interstate combinations for failing thrifts.

● Gave priority to mergers between institutions of the same type in the same state, followed by those between the same type in different states, different types in the same state and, finally, different types in different states.

Deposit Powers. Gave the Depository Institutions Deregulation Committee two months to authorize an insured account for thrift institutions and banks that would be "directly equivalent to and competitive with" money market funds. The minimum balance was not to exceed $5,000.

(The account, called the "money market deposit account," became available Dec. 14. The deregulation committee set a $2,500 minimum balance requirement.)

● Required that all interest rate differentials between banks and thrift institutions be phased out no later than Jan. 1, 1984. Under existing law, thrifts could pay a quarter percentage point more on certain deposits.

● Allowed S&Ls to offer checking accounts to commercial customers.

Thrift Lending Powers. Increased to 40 percent from 20 percent the amount of assets S&Ls could invest in non-residential real estate.

● Increased to 30 percent from 20 percent the amount of assets S&Ls could invest in consumer lending and permitted thrifts to make inventory and floor plan loans.

● Removed limitations on thrift investments in municipal and state securities.

● Authorized S&Ls to invest up to 10 percent of assets in personal property such as furniture, vehicles and manufactured homes and to engage in consumer and corporate leasing.

● Prohibited commercial banks from selling casualty and property insurance. Banks could still sell credit-related insurance.

● Overrode state laws barring enforcement of due-on-sale clauses in home mortgage contracts, except for mortgages originated or assumed during a "window period" specified in the bill. *(Details of action on due-on-sale issue, p. 634)*

Other Legislation

Interest and Dividend Withholding

The 1981 tax cut bill (HR 4242 — PL 97-34) required banks and other financial institutions to withhold for income taxes 10 percent of all interest and dividend payments as of July 1, 1983. However, Congress repealed the requirement in 1983, and it never took effect. *(Details, below)*

Export Trading Companies

As part of an effort to increase U.S. exports, Congress in 1982 approved legislation (S 734 — PL 97-290) permitting banking institutions to be active partners in export trading companies.

Banking traditionally was separated from commerce to ensure the financial soundness of banking institutions. But the export trading law authorized bank holding companies to invest up to 5 percent of their capital and to loan an additional 10 percent to trading companies, subject to supervision by the Federal Reserve Board. *(Details, p. 101)*

1983-84

Financial strains and severe competitive pressures continued to buffet banks in 1983-84. But sharp philosophical differences among lawmakers prevented Congress from devising a blueprint for the future of financial institutions.

Banks, trying to fight back against an invasion of their turf by non-bank firms, sought ways to skirt traditional prohibitions keeping them from engaging in insurance and securities activities. Their cause was championed by the Reagan administration and Senate Banking Committee Chairman Jake Garn, R-Utah. But their attempts at further banking deregulation were shot down by House Banking Committee Chairman Fernand J. St Germain, D-R.I., who argued that financial instability pointed to the need for tighter — not looser — controls on banks.

The differences between Garn and St Germain were too wide to be resolved, and no new legislation emerged.

In other action, depository institutions showed in 1983 that they could be an overwhelming lobbying force when united. Despite the strong opposition by the congressional leadership and President Reagan, banks and savings and loan associations won repeal of a 1982 law that would have required 10 percent witholding of taxes on interest and dividend income.

Interest Withholding Repeal

Bowing to months of pressure, Congress in 1983 approved legislation (HR 2973 — PL 98-67) to repeal a requirement for 10 percent withholding of taxes on interest and dividend income.

Congress had approved tax withholding for interest and dividend income in 1982, as part of the Tax Equity and Fiscal Responsibility Act (PL 97-248). Treasury Department studies had shown that income tax compliance on

interest and dividends, for which there was no withholding, was much lower than on wages. Employers deducted federal income taxes on wages from most employees' paychecks and passed the tax payments on directly to the Internal Revenue Service (IRS). *(1982 tax bill, p. 72)*

Financial institutions that year were distracted from the withholding issue by major financial restructuring legislation. But in 1983 they mounted one of the most massive mail-in campaigns in Capitol Hill history, calling for repeal.

The 1982 law would have required them to withhold taxes from depositors' accounts beginning July 1. Bank and thrift officials charged that withholding would be an administrative and financial nightmare for them and their customers, as well as an invasion of customer privacy. The Reagan administration and congressional supporters of withholding complained that financial institutions unfairly drummed up support for repeal by misleading their customers into thinking the law increased taxes, rather than simply clamping down on tax cheaters.

Although President Reagan vowed repeatedly that he would veto any repeal measure, he signed HR 2973 Aug. 5.

Initial Senate Action

The 1983 drive to repeal interest and dividend tax withholding began in the Senate. On April 21 it voted 91-5 in favor of a bill effectively scuttling the 1982 law.

Senate Finance Committee Chairman Robert Dole, R-Kan., vehemently opposed repeal. But when proponents of repeal threatened to attach it to important jobs and Social Security legislation, the Senate leadership agreed to allow it to be offered as an amendment to an unrelated trade bill (S 144). Even then, Dole prepared to filibuster against the amendment, but he retreated when he learned he only had 28 votes — not enough to prevent cloture on the amendment or to uphold an expected presidential veto. It took sixty votes to invoke cloture to cut off a filibuster; a two-thirds majority was needed to override a veto.

The Senate amendment postponed withholding until July 1, 1987. In the meantime it called for beefed-up compliance by toughening requirements that individuals and financial institutions report interest and dividend income. It also set higher penalties for tax cheating and imposed a "backup" withholding rate of 20 percent for those who failed to file a proper tax return or under-reported interest and dividend income by more than $50.

The amendment said withholding could be implemented in 1987 only if the General Accounting Office (GAO) found that those measures did not increase compliance to at least 95 percent by 1985. But even if the GAO found that compliance was lower, the bill required affirmative votes by both houses of Congress to implement withholding.

The House did not act on S 144, protesting that it violated the constitutional prerogative of the House to originate all revenue bills.

House Action

As in the Senate, backers of repeal had to defy their leadership to force a bill through the House. Their key victory came May 4, when a majority of House members signed a discharge petition forcing a repeal bill out of the Ways and Means Committee and onto the floor. Since discharge petitions were first allowed in 1910, they had been used to force bills to the floor only 26 times.

The Ways and Means Committee reluctantly sent a simple repeal bill (HR 2973 — H Rept 98-120) to the floor May 12 "without recommendation." Despite arguments from the committee's chairman, Rep. Dan Rostenkowski, D-Ill., that withholding was "the most effective means of collecting" taxes, the full House approved the bill May 17 by a 382-41 vote.

Senate Passage

On May 25 the Senate Finance Committee agreed to a plan — similar to the one approved by the full Senate the previous month — to block withholding. But this time it loaded the package with a number of unrelated amendments, some of which were intended to make the bill more palatable to the administration. These included the administration's Caribbean Basin and "enterprise zone" initiatives, a "reciprocity" trade bill and extension of tax-exempt mortgage revenue bonds.

On June 16 the full Senate approved the committee's package, offered as a committee substitute for the House-passed version of HR 2973, by a 48-41 vote. It then passed the bill, 86-4.

The biggest challenge to the package came from ranking Finance Democrat Russell B. Long, D-La., who argued that the extraneous provisions would drag down the entire bill in conference. But Republicans, in a face-saving gesture to President Reagan, blocked Long's motion to table the committee amendment on an almost straight party-line vote of 46-51.

Conference Agreement

In a conference report filed July 27 (H Rept 98-325), House-Senate conferees accepted compliance provisions less stringent than those passed by the Senate, and they approved tax incentives for Caribbean nations. But they dropped other extraneous Senate provisions, including those involving mortgage revenue bonds, enterprise zones and trade reciprocity.

Both the House and Senate accepted the conference version on July 28. The Senate acted on a **90-7 key vote (R 51-2; D 39-5)**; the House also approved the measure by a wide margin, 392-18. *(1983 key votes, p. 911)*

In its final form the legislation was expected to yield only $2.4 billion for fiscal 1983-88, assuming $300 million offsetting appropriations for the IRS to beef up its compliance capabilities. The original withholding law had been expected to raise about $13.4 billion in uncollected revenues during that period.

Major Provisions

As signed into law Aug. 5, HR 2973 (PL 98-67):

● Repealed provisions of the 1982 tax increase law that required banks and other financial institutions to withhold for income taxes 10 percent of all interest and dividend payments as of July 1, 1983.

● Required "backup" withholding at a rate of 20 percent on interest and dividend payments for all taxpayers who either had interest and dividend income and failed to file a return, or under-reported interest and dividend income by a certain threshold amount.

● Required IRS to set a secret threshold amount of under-reported income that would trigger backup withholding. Once the threshold was determined, IRS would

identify individuals under-reporting or failing to report and notify institutions to begin backup withholding.

● Made taxpayers who under-reported interest and dividend income subject to stricter negligence penalties than previous law.

Taxpayers were not required to attach to their tax returns duplicate 1099 forms they received from financial institutions that reported their interest and dividend income. However, banks and financial institutions were required to send a 1099 form to the taxpayer with a note warning that interest and dividend was taxable.

Financial Regulation

By early 1984 it appeared that accelerating change in the financial services industry and growing anomalies in government regulation would prompt Congress to revise banking laws.

First, securities firms and other non-bank institutions moved to exploit the "non-bank bank" loophole in the 1956 Bank Holding Company Act (PL 84-511). The law defined a bank as an institution that both accepted demand deposits and made commercial loans. By engaging in only one of those activities a firm could evade longstanding bans against mingling securities and banking activities and against interstate banking. *(Bank Holding Company Act, Congress and the Nation Vol. I, p. 448; Congress and the Nation Vol. II, p. 265)*

Then, Citicorp devised the "South Dakota loophole" — using a state-chartered affiliate to market insurance nationwide despite rules prohibiting national banks from selling insurance. And banks in several regions began organizing regional interstate compacts in a move decried by some critics as "Balkanization" of the nation's banking system. *(Background, introduction, p. 83)*

Comptroller of the Currency C. Todd Conover, the primary regulator for nationally chartered banks, encouraged establishment of non-bank banks. The Federal Reserve Board, which shared regulatory authority, opposed them. Bowing to congressional pressure, Conover in April 1983 imposed a moratorium on granting new non-bank bank charters. He extended it twice, the last time in May 1984, when he said he would wait until the end of the year to give Congress time to approve new banking legislation.

House Legislation

Following a series of hearings that were generally critical of deregulation, House Banking Committee Chairman Fernand J. St Germain, D-R.I., in May introduced legislation to close some of the growing loopholes in bank regulation and attempt to restore the traditional barriers between financial companies.

The bill redefined bank to close the non-bank bank loophole and require banks and non-banks to divest themselves of 61 of these hybrid affiliates within two years of the bill's enactment.

To plug the South Dakota loophole, it prohibited state-chartered banks that provided non-banking services not permitted under federal law from offering such services outside their home states. It also extended the prohibition against mingling banking and securities functions to banks that did not belong to the Federal Reserve System, and to thrift institutions.

Reversing the 1982 relaxation of controls on savings

and loan (S&L) associations, it also required that at least 65 percent of S&L assets be related to home mortgages.

The House committee reported St Germain's bill (HR 5916 — H Rept 98-889) on July 12.

A New Garn Bill

Meanwhile, Senate Banking Committee Chairman Jake Garn, R-Utah, renewed his painstaking attempts to build a consensus among competing financial interests in support of broader legislation. As in 1982, he argued that banks needed deregulation so they could compete on a "level playing field" with their non-bank financial competitors.

After months of controversy, the Senate Sept. 13 approved a new, trimmed-down Garn deregulation bill (S 2851 — S Rept 98-560) by an 89-5 vote. As passed, Garn's bill allowed bank holding companies to form subsidiaries to underwrite mortgage-backed securities, municipal revenue bonds and commercial paper, and to provide limited brokerage services at a discount.

Mortgage-backed securities are investments of home loans that are pooled together. Commercial paper is a kind of corporate IOU that major companies issue to raise funds instead of taking out a bank loan. And municipal revenue bonds are securities issued by state and local governments to pay for projects — bridges or roads, for example. They are repaid with proceeds, such as tolls, generated by the project.

Bowing to forceful lobbying groups, Garn voluntarily dropped from the bill provisions permitting banks to enter the insurance and real estate businesses. He described the remaining provisions as modest. But even they generated controversy. The securities industry especially fought to keep banks out of the potentially lucrative mortgage-backed securities and municipal bond markets.

Sen. John Heinz, R-Pa., agreeing with securities industry leaders, fought to drop all but the discount brokerage provisions from the Garn bill. He argued that federal deposit insurance and other protections would give bank affiliates an unfair advantage competing against securities firms.

"Right now the securities industry is free from government support," he said. "We don't subsidize them. We don't bail them out. . . . But the same can't be said of the banking industry."

Like St Germain's bill, the Senate bill redefined bank in federal law to plug the non-bank bank loophole. Despite strong opposition from New York's senators on behalf of Citibank and Chase Manhattan Bank, it sanctioned regional interstate banking compacts. Many states had entered regional compacts to permit interstate banking in their areas, fencing out big New York banks.

The insurance industry again flexed its muscle on the new Garn bill, winning approval of a provision nullifying the South Dakota loophole. The bill originally had provided, much as the proposed House bill did, that a bank holding company's state-chartered affiliate could market insurance only in the affiliate's home state. But in a close committee vote during markup, Christopher J. Dodd, D-Conn., won approval of an amendment — pushed by the insurance lobby — that prohibited bank holding company affiliates from marketing insurance at all, including interstate.

During floor action the Senate removed a provision that would have obliged the Federal Reserve to pay banks

interest on certain funds they were required to keep on reserve with the Fed. It also approved amendments prohibiting lenders from raising interest on adjustable rate mortgages by more than 5 percentage points over the life of a loan, and requiring banks to disclose fees charged to customers.

Stalemate

Prospects for a banking bill in 1984 died a week after Senate passage of Garn's bill, when St Germain announced that he would not proceed with any legislation.

"I regret that it is not possible to move the loophole-closing legislation in this session, but it is obvious the Senate will not consider it unless we buy off on new and greatly expanded powers for banks and other financial institutions," he said. "There is no question in my mind but that the Senate package — or even a diluted conference version — would fail overwhelmingly in the House."

With Congress stalemated, Comptroller Conover on Nov. 1 began approving applications to establish non-bank banks. Conover evidently figured that creation of numerous such institutions nationwide soon would make divestiture politically impossible.

The Federal Reserve, which had opposed creation of the loophole banks, reluctantly began accepting them in face of the congressional impasse. On Nov. 1 it approved five applications forwarded earlier by Conover. Fed Chairman Paul A. Volcker renewed his plea that Congress plug the loophole.

In early 1985 applications remained on hold pending court challenges by rival banks.

Other Legislation

IMF Funding Increase

Lawmakers in 1983 approved legislation (HR 3959 — PL 98-181) increasing the U.S. contribution to the International Monetary Fund, despite claims by opponents that it amounted to a "bailout" for big banks that had imprudently lent billions of dollars to countries burdened with debt. *(Story, p. 104)*

Mortgage Lending

In 1984 Congress cleared a measure (S 2040 — PL 98-440) that removed some of the regulatory impediments faced by private companies that tried to buy mortgages from banks and to sell securities backed by them. *(Story, p. 638)*

International Economic Policy

International economic issues caused sharp tensions between Congress and the White House during President Reagan's first term.

Mounting trade deficits fueled protectionist sentiment on Capitol Hill, prompting repeated challenges to the free trade philosophy espoused by the president. Protectionism found its most dramatic expression in legislation that would have required high proportions of U.S. parts and labor in foreign cars sold in the United States. Aimed chiefly at Japanese imports, this "domestic content" legislation was passed twice by the House but died in the Republican Senate.

Congress and the White House also tangled over support for international lending agencies. Lawmakers in 1983 approved an increase in the U.S. contribution to the International Monetary Fund (IMF) — but only after an epic, yearlong battle in which Republican members opposed their president's request for additional funding. The IMF's role in warding off a world debt crisis had persuaded Reagan to reverse his previous views on IMF support. Reagan had entered office planning to reduce U.S. contributions to the organization.

Administration Policy

The best international economic policy is a good domestic economic policy. That, in a phrase, was the philosophy the Reagan administration brought to Washington in 1981. Reagan officials discarded the idealistic efforts of the Carter years to increase international cooperation and coordination of economic policies, and decided instead to go it alone. They had a plan to get the United States' house in order, and they pursued that plan with little regard to its effects on the rest of the world.

The basic tenets of the new international economic policy were these:

A monetary and fiscal policy that ignored international implications. The Reagan admnistration's economic policy had two principal aims: to eradicate inflation and to reduce the size of the federal government. Reagan pursued the first goal, at least in the early months of his administration, by encouraging the Federal Reserve's tight money policies. He tackled the second goal by curtailing federal spending and pushing through a huge tax cut that ensured pressure would remain on Congress to keep spending down. The results of these policies were sharp increases in interest rates, on top of skyrocketing rates in 1980, which foreign leaders complained led the world into its deepest recession since the 1930s and drove the international financial system to the brink of collapse.

A strong commitment to free trade. The Reagan administration believed markets should be allowed to operate free of government influence, both at home and abroad. Although in the end the administration's record was marred by a variety of protectionist blemishes, few people questioned the strength of the president's ideological commitment to maintaining uninhibited international trade.

A reluctance to intervene in international currency markets. High interest rates resulting from U.S. domestic economic policies attracted record amounts of foreign capital to this country, and pushed up the value of the dollar by more than 50 percent between 1980 and 1984. Currency markets became increasingly volatile. But the Reagan Treasury Department largely resisted the pleas of the Europeans — and at times of Federal Reserve Board Chairman Paul A. Volcker — to intervene in those markets to influence currency rates.

Decreased emphasis on international economic institutions. To the new administration, institutions like the World Bank and the International Monetary Fund carried an aura of international socialism. The Reagan team set out from the first to reduce its contributions to both, and to cut back grants aimed at redistributing world income. The administration also tried to pressure the institutions into encouraging market-oriented growth policies.

This new set of international economic policies not only created tensions with U.S. trading partners; it often left the administration at odds with Congress as well. And at times the separate policies seemed to conflict with each other, or with national security goals.

By the end of his first four years, President Reagan had been forced to compromise his tough position on each of these policies. But they set the tone for debates between

References

Discussion of international economic action for the years 1945-64 may be found in *Congress and the Nation Vol. I*, pp. 187-207; for the years 1965-68, *Congress and the Nation Vol. II*, pp. 49-116; for the years 1969-72, *Congress and the Nation Vol. III*, pp. 119-134; for the years 1973-76, *Congress and the Nation Vol. IV*, pp. 125-137; for the years 1977-80, *Congress and the Nation Vol. V*, pp. 267-276.

the White House and Congress, and between the United States and its allies, throughout Reagan's first term.

International Trade

In July 1981 the administration sent to Congress a white paper outlining its support for international free trade. The document served notice to U.S. industries hard hit by imports that President Reagan would not support protectionist measures to ease their pain. Instead, the new administration intended to rely on market forces to bring about any adjustments needed in the economy.

At the same time it was preparing that policy paper, however, the administration was pursuing economic policies that would make it increasingly difficult to adhere to a free trade line. Interest rates rose in response to Reagan's tight monetary and loose fiscal policies, luring foreigners to put their money into U.S. assets and bid up the dollar's value. The strong dollar made imports cheaper, and made U.S. exports increasingly expensive on world markets. Largely as a result, the U.S. trade deficit ballooned to more than $123 billion in 1984 from $36 billion in 1980.

Battered by complaints from constituents who had lost their jobs or lost business because of the nation's trade problems, members of Congress grew increasingly concerned. They had 40 years earlier ceded much of their role in trade policy to the executive branch, fearing a repeat of the protectionist legislative binge that had helped plunge the world into the Great Depression of the 1930s. But faced with high unemployment, soaring trade deficits and an administration ideologically wedded to free trade, members decided it was time for Congress to reassert itself.

Congressional ire, like that of the public, was largely aimed at the Japanese, whose manufacturers were best able to exploit the benefits of the strong dollar with a wide array of attractive products.

In Detroit bumper stickers commanded drivers to "Remember Pearl Harbor." In West Virginia a charity raised money by selling sledgehammer hits on a Japanese-made Toyota automobile. Throughout the country politicians courted votes by promising to "get tough" with Japan.

Public sentiment was amplified in Congress, where the declining industries hit hardest by imports also happened to have the most political clout. "While Japanese cars invade our highways, American workers pay for the defense of Japan," complained Democratic Rep. Donald Pease, whose Ohio district depended on the ailing auto and steel industries. And even Sun Belt representatives such as California Republican Duncan Hunter raised complaints: "In effect, we work our tail off so that the Japanese can have a stable international economic environment which they use to put Americans out of work."

The clamor in Congress had a noticeable effect on the administration. Trade officials first tried to avoid protectionist pressure by "Japan bashing" — complaining that Japanese markets were closed to many U.S. products. Eager to maintain their access to the U.S. market, the Japanese government tried to oblige with a series of "market-opening packages." But some Japanese trade barriers, as in the United States, were backed by politically powerful interest groups. More importantly, no action by the Japanese government could have offset the effects of the strong dollar; therefore, no action could have been sufficient to stop the outcry in the United States.

Bowing to pressure, the Reagan administration negotiated a so-called "voluntary restraint agreement" with the Japanese, requiring that nation's automakers to limit their exports to the United States. (The agreement expired early in 1985.) The administration also restricted imports of Japanese motorcycles. But such measures still were not enough to stop the outrage in Congress. Egged on by labor union leaders, the House of Representatives passed domestic content legislation in late 1982 — and again in 1983 — that would have required automakers to use fixed levels of U.S. labor and parts in the cars they sold in this country. The most protectionist measure to make headway in Congress in years, that bill never gained support in the Republican Senate. But it was a striking symbol of congressional concern over the nation's trade problems.

Even moderate Republicans joined in the effort to boost trade restrictions. Sen. John C. Danforth, R-Mo., for instance, championed the push for "reciprocity" legislation. His proposal would have strengthened the president's power to retaliate against foreign trading practices that he considered unfair, and it would have provided new authority to retaliate against countries that restricted investment by U.S. companies within their borders.

Industrial Policy

Frustrated by Reagan's faithful adherence to free trade principles in the face of a rising trade deficit and double-digit unemployment, the Democrats in late 1982 began to consider the merits of advocating a national industrial policy. It was a vague concept, which often seemed to mean different things to different people. For a period, nevertheless, industrial policy seemed to be in vogue on Capitol Hill.

The interest in industrial policy stemmed from the perception that other governments, particularly the Japanese, had enjoyed some success in encouraging the develop-

---

Merchandise Trade Deficit

The nation's merchandise trade deficit more than tripled during President Reagan's first term in office, as a strong dollar made U.S. products expensive on the world market, while letting foreign goods sell at bargain prices in the United States.

The merchandise trade deficit reached the following levels in 1981-84 *(in millions of dollars)*:

Year	Trade Deficit
1980 *	$ −36,354
1981 *	−39,675
1982	−42,691
1983	−69,392
1984	−123,312

* Data include trade of the U.S. Virgin Islands.

SOURCE: Economic Report of the President, February 1985

ment of their export industries. An unusual trade petition filed by Houdaille Industries, a Florida-based machine tool maker, attempted to document with more than 1,000 pages of supporting evidence the wide range of government policies that had been used by the Japanese government to promote development of computerized machine tools. Government bureaucrats encouraged mergers, established and subsidized research cartels, provided generous tax benefits and even prodded other industries to buy computerized machine tools. It was such industrial policy efforts, the Houdaille petition said, that enabled Japan to become the world's leading producer, consumer and exporter of computerized machine tools and to capture half the U.S. market in those products.

Faced with these examples of success, Democratic legislators toyed with the idea of promoting similar policies in the United States. "Our economy has historically worked the best when we have had cooperation between the public and private sector," said Rep. Timothy E. Wirth, D-Colo., citing the canal projects of the 1830s, the railroads of the mid-1800s, the Eisenhower Interstate highway program and the Kennedy space program. "We have had that kind of cooperation over and over again, and we have to find the mechanism to do it again."

Wirth's idea was to create an economic cooperation council, made up of government, business and labor leaders, to devise a strategy for industrial growth. Senate Minority Leader Robert C. Byrd, D-W.Va., proposed resurrecting the Depression-era Reconstruction Finance Corp., to make long-term, low-cost loans for modernizing basic industries such as steel, autos, coal and heavy manufacturing. Democratic presidential candidates Walter F. Mondale and Sen. Gary Hart, Colo., expressed interest in the idea.

But the surprising strength of the economic recovery in 1983 and 1984 dampened enthusiasm for schemes to inject the government into industrial decision making. The source of the economy's strength seemed to be small, entrepreneurial businesses that flourished best in a free market atmosphere. Industrial policy plans faded. The final nail was put in their coffin in November 1984 when Reagan, still espousing his free market faith, trounced Democratic opponent Mondale and was re-elected for a second term.

Reagan's re-election, however, by no means put an end to the nation's trade problems. The trade deficit continued to grow. By the fall of 1984 the flood of imports seemed to have brought manufacturing growth to a halt. Protectionist sentiment began to rise again in Congress, setting the stage for a second term in which it seemed the administration's free trade stance might come under even heavier attack.

International Finance

While high interest rates were an irritant to the United States and its industrialized trading partners, for many developing nations they proved to be devastating.

During the late 1970s, banks, flush with deposits from newly rich oil nations, cultivated business with the more advanced developing nations such as Brazil, Argentina and Mexico. Heated competition among bankers, combined with rising inflation, resulted in very low "real" interest rates. (Real interest rates are the actual rate minus inflation, and represent the true cost of a loan to a borrower.) Banks were virtually giving loans away. Eager to expand their economies, developing countries welcomed the gifts.

Bankers felt safe lending to sovereign nations because they believed the chances of default were slim. The total

The Rise of the Dollar

The index figures below show changes in the value of the dollar, measured against a composite "basket" of major foreign currencies. The basket is weighted according to the importance of each nation's trade with the United States. The index takes the value of the dollar in March 1973 as 100. Thus, the dollar's average value in 1980, at 87.4, was 12.6 percent below its March 1973 value, and its value in 1984, at 138.2, was 38.2 percent above its March 1973 value.

March 1973	100
1980	84.8
1981	100.8
1982	111.7
1983	117.3
1984	128.7

SOURCE: Economic Report of the President, February 1985

foreign debt of developing nations skyrocketed from $100 billion in 1973 to more than $500 billion, with most of the lending concentrated among a small group of countries.

The binge ended in 1981 when the U.S. Federal Reserve tightened its grip on credit, which pushed up interest rates and reduced inflation. That caused real interest rates to jump from levels of 1 percent or less to between 5 percent and 10 percent. Many of the loans to developing countries had variable interest rates, so the cost of servicing developing country debt soared.

At the same time the slump in the world economy caused commodity prices to drop, cutting severely the export incomes of the most heavily indebted nations such as Brazil, Mexico, Argentina and Venezuela. As their debt costs rose, their ability to pay interest on that debt plummeted. In mid-1982 the total annual payments of interest and principal facing Argentina were 79 percent higher than its expected export earnings. Mexico and Brazil also faced debt service that far exceeded their ability to pay. The nations teetered on the verge of default, and threatened to bring down a number of major U.S. banks with them.

The IMF stepped in to manage the crisis. It offered new funds to the troubled nations, and pressured private banks to keep lending. In return the indebted nations agreed to accept IMF austerity programs, designed to increase exports and reduce imports. Working with the IMF, the banks managed to survive the worst of the crisis and the troubled nations were kept afloat.

But the incident had profound effects on administration policy. Fearing a financial crisis, the Federal Reserve — with the administration's blessing — reversed course in mid-1982 and began pumping new money into the economy. And, recognizing the critical role the IMF had played in avoiding an international disaster, the Reagan administration also did an about-face and began lobbying for a more than $8 billion increase in U.S. support for the inter-

national agency. Ironically, the president had to rely on Democratic votes to win that request, since a majority of Republican legislators continued to hold to the early Reagan view that the IMF was an unnecessary intrusion into the world market.

The debt crisis, along with the continuing high flight of the dollar, led some to question whether the international financial system was in need of an overhaul. "What once were arcane subjects studied only by bankers and professors have become objects of intense political interest," said Sen. Bill Bradley, D-N.J. Bradley and others argued that the problems of international money and credit were not nearly so distant from the New Jersey worker as they had once seemed. A strong dollar could cause auto workers and steel workers to lose their jobs because of imports. And debt problems in Mexico could bring unemployment in South Florida and Texas, or perhaps even a nationwide banking crisis.

Rep. Jack Kemp, R-N.Y., and some of his supply-side colleagues even argued that the problems necessitated a return to a gold standard, the last vestiges of which had been dropped a decade earlier. Kemp called for a new monetary conference like that held in 1944 at Bretton Woods, N.H., where the postwar international monetary system was designed. His call was echoed by repeated requests from the French government, which felt buffeted by volatile exchange rates and wanted to consider ways to stabilize those rates.

Such pleas for massive overhaul of the international monetary system, however, made little progress inside the administration. The Treasury did back off, to a limited degree, from its refusal to intervene in currency markets. But for the most part the administration stuck to its conviction that there was no reasonable alternative to free-floating exchange rates, and therefore no good reason to discuss overhauling the financial system.

Export Restrictions

One of the greatest challenges to the administration's free trade policy came not from outside, but from within the administration itself. Ever-worried about the Soviet threat, Reagan defense officials on numerous occasions found it in their interest to advocate limiting U.S. exports.

During his first year in office, President Reagan imposed trade sanctions to protest Soviet pressure on the communist government of Poland, which had declared martial law and imprisoned leaders of the independent Solidarity trade union. The action came eight months after Reagan lifted an embargo on grain sales to the Soviets that had been imposed by President Carter in 1979 following the Soviet invasion of Afghanistan.

Under the new restrictions, U.S. companies and their foreign subsidiaries and affiliates were prohibited from exporting equipment or technology that could be used to help build the natural gas pipeline from Siberia to Western Europe. That raised an uproar in Europe, and also upset many U.S. manufacturers. Some companies claimed the sanctions caused them to lose many millions of dollars of business to overseas competitors.

The controversial sanctions were finally lifted in November 1982. But the conflict between national security interests and international trade goals did not go away. Indeed, the expiration of the Export Administration Act in 1983 provided the stage for a fierce debate that lasted through the end of President Reagan's first term.

The rapid growth of the U.S. high-tech industry during the 1970s had caused the Defense Department and its network of contractors to lose their once-privileged position at the forefront of new technology. Products on the shelf at Radio Shack had become as sophisticated as those under development in Pentagon research laboratories. "It is the commercial sector, the private sector, that is now the cutting edge of technological development," Commerce Department Under Secretary Lionel H. Olmer said in 1983.

That fact of high-tech life posed a difficult problem for the Reagan administration and for members of Congress. In the name of national security they felt compelled to constrain the flow of technology to the Soviet Union. But for the sake of the nation's economic health they had an obligation to promote the export of high-tech products.

"This is a genuine dilemma for both the legislative branch and the executive branch," said Rep. Don Bonker, D-Wash. "We have to be more competitive. We must increase export opportunities if we are going to have economic recovery. But we have certain national security and foreign policy objectives which are responsibilities of the United States as a world power."

Efforts to restrict high-tech exports were led by Defense Assistant Secretary Richard N. Perle, who told Congress the previous decade had witnessed "a virtual hemorrhage of strategic technology to the Soviet bloc countries.

"In certain applications, the Soviet bloc has narrowed its technology gap with the West from 10 years to within two years," Perle claimed. He wanted the Pentagon to have a broad role in deciding what products could be exported, not only to Soviet bloc countries, but also to U.S. allies. Even the allies, he contended, were often guilty of re-exporting high-tech U.S. products to the Soviet Union.

On the other hand, Commerce Department officials, such as Under Secretary Olmer, were concerned that such controls could severely hamper trade. During the 1970s, they noted, exports of U.S. goods and services had grown from 6 percent to more than 10 percent of the nation's total output of goods and services. Estimates were circulated suggesting that 80 percent of the manufacturing jobs created between 1979 and 1981 were due to expanded trade. The United States, they argued, desperately needed exports to keep growing. Yet businessmen were complaining that export controls were damaging their success overseas. Export licenses were usually granted after Commerce Department and Defense Department review, they conceded. But for many products the wait could be a half year or longer. That often meant lost business.

The debate in the administration was echoed in Congress. Senate Banking Committee Chairman Jake Garn, R-Utah, argued that billions of dollars worth of defense spending could have been saved in recent years if U.S. export controls had been tighter. "We cannot preserve our national interests and keep defense costs down while supplying our adversaries with the means to threaten those interests."

Opposing Garn were an array of members whose principal concern was to promote exports, such as Republican Rep. Ed Zschau of California. A former Silicon Valley entrepreneur who was elected to Congress in 1982, Zschau argued effectively that export controls "aren't a problem that kills a company. But on the other hand, they're just one more roadblock. And you have to ask the question, why? Why are we doing this to ourselves?"

In spite of many hours of debate, that question remained unanswered through the end of 1984.

Chronology
Of Action
On International
Economic Policy

1981

Preoccupied with President Reagan's sweeping budget and tax cut plans, lawmakers took little action on international economic legislation in 1981. Congress reauthorized the Overseas Private Investment Corp., a government corporation that insured American investors in foreign countries against political risks. And the Senate passed a measure to encourage the formation of export trading companies to help U.S. firms market their goods abroad. The bill cleared in 1982.

President Reagan's commitment to free trade was put to the test as various industries — automobiles, steel, footwear, textiles and others — pleaded for relief from import competition. The administration responded by negotiating or extending a number of "voluntary" import quotas and other restrictions. A voluntary quota on Japanese automobile imports was negotiated early in 1981 and periodically extended thereafter. It finally expired March 31, 1985.

Overseas Investment Agency

Congress Oct. 2 approved legislation (HR 3136 — PL 97-65) expanding the activities of the Overseas Private Investment Corp. (OPIC), a government corporation that insured American investors in foreign countries against political risks.

The bill extended for four years, through Sept. 30, 1985, OPIC's authority to issue new insurance and added civil strife to the risks against which the agency could insure. It also removed restrictions on OPIC activities in 18 countries.

In addition, the legislation required the corporation to reimburse taxpayers for $106 million appropriated for start-up costs in the corporation's early years. Since 1974 OPIC had been operating on a self-sustaining basis without federal appropriations.

The Reagan administration supported OPIC's extension. But it opposed a House provision, retained in the final bill, that continued the OPIC direct loan program for small businesses.

Background

OPIC was created in 1969 (PL 91-175) and went into full operation in 1971. It was designed to encourage private U.S. business ventures in developing countries by providing insurance against the risks of war, expropriation and non-convertibility of currency. In 1978 Congress extended OPIC's lending authority through Sept. 30, 1981 (PL 95-268). *(Congress and the Nation Vol. V, p. 268)*

According to the House Foreign Affairs Committee, OPIC had insured or helped finance 337 investment projects in 58 countries since 1978, resulting in a total U.S. investment of $4.6 billion. The projects were expected to generate more than $3.4 billion in direct U.S. exports during the first five years of their operation.

OPIC had reserves and capital of almost $700 million, and fiscal 1980 net income was $65 million, the panel said.

Legislative History

The House passed its version of the bill (H Rept 97-195) Sept. 22 by voice vote. The ease of passage contrasted with the difficulty that OPIC's renewal had faced in 1977. House supporters then were forced to withdraw legislation from the floor after active labor opposition developed. Labor contended that OPIC aggravated U.S. economic problems by encouraging firms to invest abroad rather than at home. The House finally approved the extension on a second try the following year.

The Senate originally included OPIC extension in its broader foreign aid bill (S 1196 — S Rept 97-83). But on Sept. 25 it substituted the OPIC provisions of S 1196 for HR 3136.

Differences between the House and Senate versions of the bill were resolved without a formal conference. The bill cleared Oct. 2 when the House accepted a Senate amendment that brought OPIC's direct loan program for small businesses under the appropriations process.

Provisions

As signed into law Oct. 16, HR 3136 (PL 97-65):
- Extended for four years, through Sept. 30, 1985, OPIC's authority to issue foreign investment political risk insurance and loan guarantees.
- Expanded the OPIC board of directors to 15 members from 13 and required the appointment of a Labor Department official.
- Added civil strife as a political risk that could be covered by OPIC insurance.
- Mandated the continued transfer of OPIC revenues to the Direct Investment Fund (DIF) to provide direct loans for small-business projects.
- Repealed specific restrictions on OPIC support for projects involving copper, palm oil, sugar and citrus.
- Required OPIC to reimburse the Treasury over an indefinite period for the $106 million that the corporation had received in appropriations.

Export Control Enforcement

Legislation designed to improve federal enforcement of controls on exports was cleared by Congress Dec. 16. The bill (HR 3567 — PL 97-145) raised fines for criminal violation of controls placed on exports for national security purposes to $1 million for corporations and $250,000 for individuals, both up from $100,000.

Sen. John Heinz, R-Pa., floor manager of the Senate bill, said the higher penalties would improve U.S. defenses against increasing efforts by the Soviet Union to obtain high technology American goods.

HR 3567 also authorized more than $19 million for federal export control programs in fiscal 1982 and 1983. Specific funding authorizations for those years had not

been included in a four-year extension of the Export Administration Act passed in 1979 (PL 96-72). *(Background, Congress and the Nation Vol. V, p. 274)*

Congress was unable to agree on a further reauthorization bill in 1983-84; President Reagan used stopgap legislation and emergency powers to maintain control of U.S. shipments abroad. *(1983-84 action, pp. 107, 111)*

Legislative History

The House originally passed HR 3567 June 8 (H Rept 97-57). The Senate passed its version of the measure (S 1112 — S Rept 97-91) Nov. 12.

Conferees filed their report on the bill on Dec. 11 (H Rept 97-401). They dropped several Senate-passed provisions, including one requiring congressional approval for any selective embargo on agricultural exports ordered by the president, starting Jan. 21, 1985.

The embargo amendment was a response to President Carter's embargo on grain sales to the Soviet Union following the Soviet invasion of Afghanistan in 1979. President Reagan lifted the grain embargo April 24. A similar embargo provision was contained in the 1981 omnibus farm bill (S 884 — PL 97-98), conferees noted. *(Farm bill, p. 487)*

The conference compromise did include a House provision barring food embargoes if they would result in malnutrition, except under limited circumstances. It also included a modified version of a Senate amendment stating that there should be an embargo on all U.S. trade to Russia if the Soviet Union or its allies engaged in direct military action against Poland.

The Senate agreed to the conference report on the bill Dec. 15 by a 67-27 vote. The House adopted it by voice vote Dec. 16.

Provisions

As signed into law Dec. 29, HR 3567 (PL 97-145):

● Authorized $9,659,000 in each of fiscal 1982 and 1983 for federal export control programs.

● Increased fines for willful violations of export controls established for national security purposes to $1 million per violation for corporations and $250,000 for individuals, from $100,000. The maximum civil penalty was increased to $100,000, from $10,000.

● Barred a food embargo if it would result in measurable malnutrition, unless the president determined that the embargo was necessary for U.S. security interests or that the food would not reach needy persons.

● Made clear that existing export control law (PL 96-72) could not be construed to prohibit export embargoes in response to military action by the Soviet Union or its allies against Poland.

Foreign Bribery Statute

The Senate by voice vote Nov. 23 passed a bill (S 708) to ease a law prohibiting U.S. companies from bribing foreign officials.

However, the House never acted on the measure, and the bill died at the end of the 97th Congress. Softening the law was a goal of the Reagan administration.

S 708, reported by the Senate Banking Committee Oct. 9 (S Rept 97-209), would have limited prosecutions to companies or corporate officials who "knowingly" falsified records or directly ordered a bribe offer to be made. It also would have permitted companies to keep less strict records than mandated by existing law.

Under the Foreign Corrupt Practices Act of 1977 (PL 95-213), corporate officers could be liable if they had "reason to believe" bribes were being made. They could be punished if loose accounting standards resulted in bribes going undetected. *(Congress and the Nation Vol. V, p. 48)*

Congress passed the 1977 act after the Securities and Exchange Commission uncovered large-scale foreign bribery involving the secret slush funds of more than 400 U.S. corporations. In 1975 and 1976, for instance, the Lockheed Corp. paid more than $106 million in "commissions" to boost its foreign sales. That included a large payment to Prince Bernhard of the Netherlands to influence his recommendation on Dutch fighter plane purchases.

The proponents of S 708 argued that the existing law discouraged exports, especially by small American companies uneasy about the law's strictness. Proponents of the bill said that some payments were, by custom, necessary in foreign lands. Outlawing them for American firms put the United States at a competitive disadvantage, they said.

Other Legislation

Export Trading Companies

The Senate April 8 passed a bill (S 734 — S Rept 97-27) to promote the formation of export trading companies to help U.S. firms market their goods abroad. The legislation cleared in 1982. *(Story, p. 101)*

Trade Adjustment Aid

The trade adjustment assistance program, designed to help those who lost their jobs as a result of competition from imports, was trimmed back substantially as part of the budget reconciliation package (HR 3982 — PL 97-35), cleared July 31. The bill extended the program through Sept. 30, 1983. In 1983 the program was extended for another two years. *(Stories, pp. 650, 665)*

Embargo Loans

Less than a year after approving certain interest-free loans for farmers to compensate for the embargo of grain sales to the Soviet Union, Congress reinstated the interest charges. President Reagan signed the legislation (S 1395 — PL 97-24) July 23.

The bill ended a mandatory interest waiver established in December 1980 on loans for 1980 and 1981 grain crops stored in the farmer-held reserve. *(Details, p. 495)*

1982

A rising trade deficit and double-digit unemployment intensified protectionist pressures on the House and Senate in 1982.

The House passed a bill to require foreign auto companies either to build more of their cars in the United States

or to reduce sales here. It substantially weakened the "domestic content" measure, however, by accepting an amendment that would nullify the bill if it were found to violate the General Agreement on Tariffs and Trade (GATT). The measure, promoted by the United Auto Workers union, was directed principally at Japanese penetration of the U.S. auto market.

Watered-down versions of bills seeking "reciprocity" in trade relations were reported by congressional committees but did not reach the Senate or House floor in 1982. The bills, designed to stiffen the U.S. response to trade barriers imposed by foreign countries, gathered substantial support, particularly in the Senate, and sponsors promised to revive them in 1983.

Before leaving for its election recess, Congress completed action on legislation designed to encourage the formation of export trading companies to help U.S. firms market their goods abroad.

Export Trading Companies

Congress Oct. 1 cleared legislation to encourage formation of export trading companies to help small- and medium-sized U.S. businesses sell their goods and services abroad.

The measure (S 734 — PL 97-290) set up a mechanism for federal officials to grant export trading firms limited immunity from U.S. antitrust laws. For the first time it allowed bank holding companies and certain banking institutions — but not commercial banks themselves — to take advantage of their international connections by participating in trading companies.

President Reagan supported the legislation. He and other proponents said the bill would result in the creation of several hundred thousand jobs.

The Senate had passed a similar bill in 1980, but a companion measure never reached the House floor. (Congress and the Nation Vol. V, p. 276)

Export trading companies had been slow to develop in the United States, partly because of the uncertainties caused by antitrust laws and problems in banking regulation. Banking was traditionally separated from commerce to ensure the financial soundness of banking institutions.

1981 Action

The Senate passed its version in 1981. S 734 was reported by the Senate Banking Committee March 18, 1981 (S Rept 97-27), and passed by the Senate on a 93-0 vote April 8.

The legislation permitted banks for the first time to participate as active partners in export trading companies. It also eased existing antitrust barriers that had inhibited joint exporting activities.

The committee report said banks "appear to be the best intermediary between the potential U.S. exporter and the foreign buyer because they already have offices (branches) at both ends of the chain and are already communicating with business people on both ends."

1982 Action

Action in the House was slowed because three committees had overlapping jurisdiction. The bill consisted of a measure reported by the Foreign Affairs and Judiciary committees (HR 1799 — H Rept 97-637, Parts I and II) as amended by a separate measure reported by the Banking Committee (HR 6016 — H Rept 97-629). After passing each bill by voice vote July 27, the House combined them as a substitute for S 734 and requested a conference with the Senate.

The compromise legislation, reported by the conferees Oct. 1 (H Rept 97-924), tilted toward the House version, which supporters said provided stronger protections against possible antitrust abuses.

The measure permitted the secretary of commerce to issue a certificate providing limited antitrust immunity for a trading company — but only if the attorney general concurred. The Senate bill had provided a certification process that required the secretary to consult with the attorney general, while the House bill placed the certification process in the Justice Department.

The compromise followed the House measure in excluding commercial banks from investing in trading companies, which the Senate bill would have allowed. But it permitted participation by bank holding companies under Federal Reserve Board regulation.

Both chambers adopted the conference report Oct. 1, completing congressional action on the bill.

Provisions

As signed into law Oct. 8, S 734 (PL 97-290):

● Directed the secretary of commerce to establish an office to promote the formation of export trading companies.

● Defined export trading companies as organizations engaged primarily in exporting U.S. goods or services, such as communications, construction, insurance and architecture; or providing export trade services, such as consulting, marketing, trade documentation or processing foreign orders.

● Authorized bank holding companies, banker's banks and Edge Act corporations that were subsidiaries of bank holding companies to invest in trading companies, subject to Federal Reserve Board regulation under the Bank Holding Company Act of 1956. (A banker's bank does business solely with other banks and is owned primarily by the banks with which it does business. Edge Act corporations are those formed to aid overseas operations of U.S. banks.)

● Provided guidelines for regulations by the Federal Reserve Board to promote the creation of trading companies with broad enough powers to enable them to compete with similar foreign-owned institutions and to foster participation by smaller and regional banking institutions in trading companies. The bill also directed the Federal Reserve Board to facilitate the formation of joint venture export trading companies between eligible banking institutions and exporters.

● Limited a banking institution's investments in a trading company to 5 percent of the institution's capital and surplus. An additional 10 percent could be loaned to the trading company.

● Authorized the Export-Import Bank to establish a program to provide loan guarantees to trading companies.

● Created a certification process that would provide a limited immunity from the antitrust laws to trading companies. The commerce secretary, with the attorney general's concurrence, would approve the certificate.

The certificate could be issued if the company's proposed conduct would not substantially lessen competition within the United States, unreasonably enhance or depress

prices within the United States, constitute unfair methods of competition or result in the resale in the United States of goods or services exported by the applicant.

Reagan Caribbean Trade Plan

As part of his Central American policy, President Reagan Feb. 24 proposed a three-part Caribbean Basin Initiative (CBI) that included U.S. trade concessions to Central American nations. The House passed the trade proposal in 1982, but the Senate did not act before adjournment.

The trade portion of the package provided duty-free entry into the United States for products of the nations of the Caribbean basin and Central America. Reagan put heavy emphasis on the measure, saying it would help stabilize the impoverished region and prevent the spread of communism.

The House approved the trade bill (HR 7397) Dec. 17 by a 260-142 vote. In an unexpected boost for the president's plan, Ways and Means Chairman Dan Rostenkowski, D-Ill., had pushed it through his committee, which reported the measure Dec. 10 (H Rept 97-958). Rostenkowski had switched from a skeptic to an ardent supporter of the measure while on a trip to the Caribbean during the fall election recess.

Following House passage, the Senate Finance Committee approved the bill in an impromptu session Dec. 20. But the full Senate did not take up the measure before adjourning Dec. 23, and the bill died.

The trade legislation was enacted in 1983. *(Details, 1983 action, p. 106)*

Congress in 1982 approved only one part of the three-part CBI: $350 million in emergency economic aid for fiscal 1982. A third part, tax benefits for U.S. companies that invested in the region, never was seriously considered in either house. *(Economic aid, p. 149)*

Auto Domestic Content

In a largely symbolic action, the House Dec. 15 passed a bill (HR 5133) that would have forced major Japanese automakers to purchase from the United States as much as 75 percent of the parts and labor used to make automobiles sold in this country. The bill, passed on a **215-188 key vote (R 44-130; D 171-58)**, was reported Sept. 21 by the House Energy and Commerce Committee (H Rept 97-842).

Neither the sponsors nor the opponents of the measure expected it to be considered by the Senate in the few remaining days of the lame-duck session. But supporters said the House vote would send a "clear signal" to Japan to change its trading practices. *(1982 key votes, p. 895)*

That signal, however, was made considerably less clear after an unexpected amendment by lame-duck Rep. Millicent Fenwick, R-N.J., seriously weakened the bill. Fenwick's amendment said the measure should not "supersede" any "treaty, international convention or agreement on tariffs and trade." The provision would enable U.S. courts to invalidate the measure for violating regulations of the General Agreement on Tariffs and Trade (GATT). *(GATT box, p. 103)*

"We just gutted the bill," gloated Phil Gramm, D-Texas, an opponent of the House measure, after the Fenwick amendment was adopted by a narrow 195-194 vote.

Lobbyists for the United Auto Workers (UAW) union, who lined the halls outside the House chamber throughout the debate, were clearly surprised and angered when they learned of the Fenwick amendment. The survival of the bill could be attributed almost solely to the UAW, which had pushed tirelessly for the measure since late 1981. The AFL-CIO also had worked for its passage in hopes that it would help restore the more than one million jobs lost by workers in automobile and related industries since 1978.

Opposing the measure was a much longer list of business, agriculture, exporting and public interest groups, who feared retaliation by other nations in response to domestic content legislation. Automobile dealers, longshoremen and other port-related workers who would suffer from a decline in imports also lobbied against the bill, as did General Motors and the Ford Motor Co.

The Reagan administration also opposed the domestic content measure, which U.S. Trade Representative William E. Brock III called "the worst piece of economic legislation since the 1930s."

Despite the breadth of opposition, the bill did not die easily. House supporters made another unsuccessful attempt to enact the legislation in 1983. *(Story, p. 108)*

Trade 'Reciprocity'

Watered-down versions of bills seeking "reciprocity" in trade relations were reported by congressional committees but did not reach the Senate or House floor in 1982. However, limited reciprocity provisions were included in omnibus trade legislation enacted in 1984. *(1983-84 action, p. 109)*

The reciprocity concept would require retaliatory action against nations that did not provide American firms with access to markets equal to that afforded foreign firms by the United States. Pressure for reciprocity legislation reflected increasing congressional frustration over the nation's mounting trade deficit, especially with Japan, and with foreign practices and policies that had caused difficulties for U.S. businesses.

The Reagan administration opposed any bill that would identify non-reciprocity as an independent cause for trade action against another country or require equal access on a product-by-product basis.

The Senate Finance Committee June 30 reported a bill (S 2094 — S Rept 97-483) that won the endorsement of administration trade negotiators. The measure would have strengthened procedures for enforcing violations of existing trade law and required the government to seek international agreements on trade in investment and services (such as banking) as well as trade in high technology products, such as computers and semiconductors. Existing international rules applied mainly to merchandise.

The administration was seeking the negotiating authority before the ministerial meeting of the General Agreement on Tariffs and Trade (GATT) Nov. 24-29. GATT was a multilateral treaty that had provided a framework for liberalizing world trade since 1948. *(GATT conference, box, p. 103)*

After discussions with the administration, the committee's bill was softened to require the United States to demand "fair and equitable" market opportunities, rather than the stricter formula of "substantially equivalent market access" as originally drafted.

The Finance Committee Sept. 21 attached the measure to an unrelated House-passed tariff bill (HR 4566),

GATT Talks

International trade talks held in Geneva Nov. 24-29, 1982, made little progress toward resolving pressing trade issues. The United States went to Geneva with an ambitious agenda. But the communiqué signed by members of the 88-nation General Agreement on Tariffs and Trade (GATT) contained few U.S. proposals.

The administration and congressional advocates of free trade originally had hoped they would be able to use a GATT agreement to fight protectionist legislation in Congress. But the flimsy accord signed in Geneva did not dampen the surge of protectionism in the United States and abroad. Highlights of the GATT meeting:

Agricultural Subsidies. The United States failed completely in its attempt to get a freeze and then a gradual rollback of the heavy subsidies that the European Community (EC) was using to gain a growing share of the world's agricultural export markets. The Europeans — particularly France — were intransigent.

Dispute Settlement. The United States' major victory at the conference — an agreement on the dispute settlement process — was a thin one. U.S. trade officials were anxious to improve the way in which disputes between nations were settled under the GATT structure. Existing procedures made obstruction easy, and allowed a nation that lost a dispute simply to veto a GATT finding.

The agreement did not eliminate that veto power, but it did commit members to avoid "obstruction" in the dispute settlement process.

GATT Expansion. The U.S. delegation convinced the GATT conference to take a very preliminary look at the problems of trade in services, such as banking, insurance and data processing. But it could obtain no agreement for a study of high technology trade or of trade-distorting investment requirements.

The services agreement called on member nations "with an interest in services" to study and exchange information on the issue.

Safeguards. The United States had hoped for an agreement to improve the "safeguard" measures nations could take to protect domestic industry from severe damage caused by import competition. It was hoped this would reduce the proliferation of protective actions taken outside the GATT framework — such as the "voluntary" restraint agreement that restricted Japanese automobile imports to the United States.

Other Issues. There was no agreement on an approach for negotiations between the industrial and "developing" nations to reduce tariff and non-tariff barriers. No progress was made on the problem of counterfeit production of trade goods.

but the reciprocity provisions were dropped from HR 4566 in the final days of the lame-duck session.

In the House, the Energy and Commerce Committee Aug. 19 reported a narrower measure (HR 5519 — H Rept 97-766) that would have provided negotiating authority for agreements covering trade in services and set procedures for retaliating against service firms of foreign nations that unfairly restricted access of U.S. companies to their markets. The House did not act on the bill.

Romania Trade Status

Congress in August effectively quashed protests by conservatives against President Reagan's renewal of "most-favored-nation" (MFN) status for Romania. The designation was routinely given to all U.S. trading partners, except communist nations, allowing them to export goods to the United States at reduced tariff rates.

The House Ways and Means Committee Aug. 12 reported H Res 521 (H Rept 97-743) and recommended that it be rejected by the House because it would deny the renewal. The House killed the measure Aug. 18 by postponing action on it indefinitely.

The Senate Finance Committee rejected a resolution that called for denial of the renewal and on Aug. 13 reported its own measure (S Res 445 — S Rept 97-522) that, in effect, approved the president's action. The full Senate did not act on the issue before leaving Washington for its Labor Day recess.

Either house could have blocked the one-year extension by adopting a resolution before Sept. 1 — a procedure known as a legislative veto.

There were no moves in Congress in 1982 to block most-favored-nation status for Hungary and China. Poland also lost its MFN status in 1982. *(Background, 1983 action, p. 107; Poland, p. 144)*

Soviet Economic Sanctions

By a **206-203 key vote (R 124-57; D 82-146)** the House Sept. 29 gutted a bill (HR 6838) that would have forced President Reagan to lift economic sanctions against the Soviet Union imposed in December 1981 and June 1982 in response to the imposition of martial law in Poland. One goal of the sanctions was to prevent the Soviet Union from using U.S. technology to build a natural gas pipeline from Siberia to Western Europe.

Opponents of the sanctions charged that they resulted in lost jobs for Americans at a time of high unemployment and irritated America's NATO allies.

The closeness of the House vote demonstrated the depth of congressional opposition to the sanctions. Responding to the pressure, Reagan lifted the sanctions Nov. 13. *(Details, p. 144; 1982 key votes, p. 895)*

1983

Congress battled all year over boosting the U.S. contribution to the International Monetary Fund, ultimately approving an $8.4 billion increase on the final day of the session. President Reagan lobbied vigorously for the mea-

sure, warning that failure to act could cause a global "economic nightmare."

Conservative opponents of the bill viewed it as a bailout for banks that had made huge loans to debt-ridden nations.

Earlier in the year a whittled-down version of Reagan's Caribbean trade plan won approval from Congress. The measure was designed to promote economic development in the region by providing duty-free entry into the United States for certain Caribbean exports.

The House and Senate failed to complete action on legislation to reauthorize the Export Administration Act, but Congress temporarily extended the president's authority to control exports under the expiring law. Lawmakers were again unable to reach agreement in 1984.

An unexpectedly robust economic recovery failed to dampen pressure for protectionist legislation in 1983. As the U.S. merchandise trade deficit surged to a record $69.4 billion, the House for the second year in a row approved a "domestic content" measure that would require fixed levels of U.S. labor and parts in foreign cars sold in this country. And the Senate passed a "reciprocity" bill to expand the president's authority to retaliate against unfair trading practices by other countries and require the administration to seek new international agreements on trade in services and high technology.

Limited reciprocity legislation cleared in 1984 as part of omnibus trade legislation.

IMF Funding

After a yearlong struggle, Congress on Nov. 18 cleared legislation (HR 3959 — PL 98-181) increasing the U.S. contribution to the International Monetary Fund (IMF) by $8.4 billion, a shot in the arm the fund's proponents said it desperately needed to maintain world economic stability. The authorization was attached to the conference report on a fiscal 1984 supplemental appropriations bill.

The IMF measure also included a three-year extension of the Export-Import Bank and authorized funding for the Inter-American Development Bank, the Asian Development Bank and the African Development Fund. *(Export-Import Bank, p. 105; development banks, p. 168)*

Opponents claimed that the increase in the U.S. fund quota represented a "big-bank bailout," a rescue operation for banking institutions that had imprudently lent billions to countries burdened with debt. But the Reagan administration supported the IMF, and opponents were unable to block the increase.

IMF backers viewed the bill as a necessary, if not particularly palatable, measure. The fund had played a key role in keeping afloat debt-ridden nations, but it was expected to run out of money as early as January 1984, increasing the danger of a worldwide economic crisis.

Background

The IMF was established in 1944 to help member nations meet temporary balance of payments deficits. Nations borrowing from the fund were usually required to adopt adjustment programs, designed to increase export earnings and decrease spending on imports in order to reduce the deficits. The United States provided roughly 20 percent of the IMF's funds.

The IMF was used by both developing and developed nations, but recently had concentrated on newly industrialized countries like Mexico and Brazil that borrowed heavily from private banks in the 1970s. Hit by a combination of low world commodity prices and high interest rates, these nations were unable to meet their obligations.

The 146 IMF member nations agreed early in 1983 to increase their fund contributions by 47 percent, or nearly $32 billion, thus boosting total IMF resources to about $94.5 billion. All member nations increased their contributions, called quotas, by approximately the same percentage.

The $8.4 billion U.S. contribution to the IMF was not a direct government expenditure and did not increase the federal budget deficit. The government traded its dollars for Special Drawing Rights (SDRs), an international currency used in transactions between nations. The United States collected interest on the dollars it contributed.

Senate Action

The Senate version of the IMF increase (S 695) was reported by the Foreign Relations Committee March 24 (S Rept 98-35) and the Banking Committee May 16 (S Rept 98-122). It passed the Senate by a 55-34 vote June 8, after numerous attempts by conservative Republicans to restrict the fund's activities were defeated.

Jesse Helms, R-N.C., who had cast the sole dissenting vote in the Foreign Relations Committee, said the bill was designed to "bail out the international banks that have made bad loans and now want the taxpayers to back them up."

The bill was strongly supported by President Reagan, who sent a letter to the Senate June 6 saying that "passage of this legislation is of the utmost importance to the world economy, to the strength of the recovery and to the U.S. position of leadership in world affairs."

Despite the president's plea, however, 24 members of his own party voted against Senate passage of the measure.

House Action

The House Banking Committee reported a package May 16 (HR 2957 — H Rept 98-175) that combined measures to authorize the IMF funding increase, reauthorize the Export-Import Bank and provide additional funding to the multilateral development banks. The package was approved by a 27-14 vote.

As reported, the IMF measure required banks to establish special reserves to offset loans to nations that had been unable to repay according to the original terms of those loans. That stricture would apply to loans to most of the Third World borrowers, which had been forced to renegotiate or "reschedule" their foreign debt payments.

The House took up HR 2957 July 25 and passed the measure Aug. 3 by a **217-211 key vote (R 72-94; D 145-117)**. *(1983 key votes, p. 911)*

Led by a coalition of conservative Republicans and populist Democrats, opponents tagged the bill as a big-bank bailout and a foreign aid giveaway. Armed with more than 60 amendments, they threatened to prolong floor proceedings indefinitely.

Big banks were not alone in taking heat from the House during the IMF debate. The fund itself was saddled with restrictions imposed by House committee and floor amendments. A measure forcing the United States to vote against IMF loans to "communist dictatorships," offered by Phil Gramm, R-Texas, was adopted 242-185 Aug. 3.

That measure was the conservatives' answer to a provision adopted in the Banking Committee prohibiting loans to countries that practiced apartheid, or racial segregation.

The Gramm amendment was opposed by many of the IMF bill's principal supporters, including President Reagan, House Republican leader Robert H. Michel, Ill., and Chalmers P. Wylie, Ohio, the ranking GOP member of the Banking Committee. Those members argued that the IMF, whose purpose was to preserve the stability of the international monetary system, should not be turned into a political institution.

Noting that the IMF had 103 million ounces of gold, valued at $40 billion, Ron Paul, R-Texas, and others offered amendments to force the IMF to sell its gold reserves, return the gold to fund members or re-establish a gold standard. The proposals were defeated without difficulty.

House Stalemate

The IMF legislation remained stalled for three months following House passage because of a series of press releases sent out by the Republican Congressional Campaign Committee. The releases attacked Democrats who had voted against the Gramm amendment opposing IMF loans to communist dictatorships. House Democratic leaders were angry that they had to provide most of the support for the president on the IMF bill, while a majority of members from the president's own party voted against the legislation.

In another complication, Banking Chairman Fernand J. St Germain, D-R.I., said he would hold up the conference on the IMF bill until passage of a housing authorization bill.

Conference, Final Action

In the final week of the session, the housing authorization sought by House Democrats was mated to the IMF increase sought by the administration. The unusual combination — put together by the administration and key members of Congress — was then attached to the conference report on HR 3959 (H Rept 98-551), a non-controversial supplemental appropriations bill, and presented to members in a take-it-or-leave-it package. They took it.

The Senate added the new provisions to the supplemental on a 67-30 vote Nov. 17, and the House agreed the following day, 226-186.

Major Provisions

As signed into law Nov. 30, the IMF section of the fiscal 1984 supplemental appropriations bill (HR 3959 — PL 98-181):

● Increased the United States' quota in the IMF by approximately $5.8 billion and provided a $2.6 billion increase in the U.S. contribution to the General Arrangements to Borrow (GAB), a contingency fund established by 11 industrialized nations for use when the international financial system was threatened. The dollar figures were not exact because the authority was denominated in Special Drawing Rights, whose dollar value fluctuated daily. The bill also appropriated the $8.4 billion required by increased fund participation.

● Required the Treasury secretary to consult with Congress 30 days in advance of any additional increases in the U.S. quota.

● Required the U.S. representative to the IMF to oppose loans to any country that practiced apartheid or was ruled by a communist dictatorship. Loans to such nations were permitted if the Treasury secretary notified Congress 30 days before the IMF vote on the loans and ensured that the loan was in the best interests of a majority of the citizens of the recipient nation.

● Instructed the U.S. representative to the IMF to promote exchange rate stability and avoid manipulation of exchange rates. Directed the representative to back changes in IMF policy to convert the liabilities of debtor nations from short-term, high-interest loans to long-term loans at lower rates of interest.

● Mandated that the federal banking agencies require banks to set aside reserves for international loans when, over a period of time, debtor nations failed to abide by the terms of IMF loans or when it appeared unlikely that repayment would proceed in a timely fashion.

Export-Import Bank

In one of its final acts before adjournment, Congress approved a three-year extension of the Export-Import Bank, through Sept. 30, 1986.

The extension was included in International Monetary Fund legislation that was attached to a supplemental appropriations bill (HR 3959 — PL 98-181) cleared Nov. 18. *(Details of action, p. 104)*

The House Aug. 3 had passed a combined IMF and Ex-Im Bank bill (HR 2957 — H Rept 98-175). The Senate Sept. 23 had approved a two-year extension of the Ex-Im Bank (S 869 — S Repts 98-111, 98-183).

Background

The Export-Import Bank, a government institution providing low-interest loans for the purchase of U.S. goods by foreign nations and companies, was last extended in 1978. *(Congress and the Nation Vol. V, p. 63)*

Ex-Im concentrated its efforts on big-ticket items — airplanes and power plants, for example — and did far less for smaller capital goods exports that could get adequate financing, although at higher rates, from commercial banks.

The bank, a federally chartered independent corporation, did not receive appropriations from Congress. Rather, it borrowed money from the Federal Financing Bank (FFB), which in turn borrowed from the Treasury; the Treasury raised its funds by the sale of government securities. Because the interest the Treasury had to pay on the securities it sold was generally lower than commercial loan rates, Ex-Im could make loans somewhat below market rates.

The agency had long been subject to complaints that the vast majority of its subsidized loans benefited only a handful of huge U. S. corporations. But by early 1983, with the nation's unemployment rate exceeding 10 percent, subsidized export credit no longer was seen simply as bounty for big business. It was viewed as a way to keep and create jobs.

Many traditional economists — including the three members of President Reagan's Council of Economic Advisers — argued that export subsidies could not create new jobs. Nonetheless there was growing sentiment that foreign governments' export subsidies had cost the United States

jobs, and similar subsidies here might win those jobs back.

Reagan, who attempted to cut the Export-Import Bank's operations in his first two annual budgets, supported a modest expansion of its lending authority in 1983.

Provisions. As signed into law Nov. 30, HR 3959 (PL 98-181) contained the following Ex-Im Bank provisions:

● Extended the Export-Import Bank for three years, through Sept. 30, 1986. The bill also mandated that, while the bank should consider the cost of money in setting interest rates on loans, all Ex-Im programs should be competitive with the export promotion programs of other nations.

● Established a "tied aid" credit program for U.S. exports that would permit foreign nations to receive a combination of Ex-Im Bank credits and foreign aid, resulting in very generous credit terms.

● Specified that the bank could provide financing for the export of services, such as insurance, as it did for exports of manufactured products, equipment and other capital goods.

● Mandated special treatment for small business by setting aside percentages of total Ex-Im Bank loans, insurance and guarantees for small businesses — rising from 6 percent in 1984 to 10 percent in 1986.

● Required the Ex-Im board of directors to include at least one small-business representative. The bill changed the terms for board members by providing for staggered terms of four years.

Reagan Caribbean Trade Plan

Congress July 28 handily endorsed the Reagan administration's proposal to provide special trade incentives to aid troubled Central American and Caribbean nations.

The measure (HR 2973 — PL 98-67) was designed to promote economic development in the region by providing duty-free entry into the United States for certain Caribbean exports, and by allowing U.S. businessmen to take tax deductions for the expense of attending conventions in the region.

Passage of the trade plan fulfilled a promise that President Reagan made to the nations of Central America and the Caribbean in his February 1982 Caribbean Basin Initiative. The House that December passed legislation nearly identical to the 1983 bill, but it died at the end of the session when the Senate failed to act. *(Story, p. 102)*

The Reagan administration had envisioned a broader program of trade and tax benefits. But Congress, concerned about heavy unemployment in the United States, whittled away at the bill until only a modest package of incentives remained. Less than 10 percent of the region's exports were to receive new duty-free treatment under the bill.

The administration campaigned energetically for the bill to prove to the politically unstable nations of the Caribbean region that the United States was a reliable friend.

The Caribbean trade plan was attached to tax withholding legislation that was opposed by President Reagan, who nevertheless signed the bill Aug. 5. The Senate had added the trade measure to the tax bill after the House passed a separate version. *(Withholding, p. 90)*

Legislative History

House Action. The Ways and Means Committee approved the initial version of the Caribbean trade bill (HR 2769 — H Rept 98-266) June 21, and the House passed the bill July 14 by a 289-129 vote, despite heavy labor opposition.

Opponents complained the bill would add to U.S. unemployment. "Jobs will be lost in the American workplace," said James L. Oberstar, D-Minn. "They will be replaced by jobs in the Caribbean, but those will be subsistence-type jobs. The workers will have no health benefit plan, no retirement plan, no vacation pay, no overtime, nothing."

Supporters countered that the bill would create jobs in both the Caribbean and the United States. U.S. exports to Caribbean nations totaled more than $6 billion in 1982, they said, and an improvement in the economies of those nations would push exports even higher.

Many members also argued that the economic package would contribute to political stability in the troubled region. "We have made many promises to the people of the Caribbean," said Ways and Means Chairman Dan Rostenkowski, D-Ill. "If we turn them away, they are likely to seek assistance from others who will promise them easy answers and offer political stability from the barrel of a gun."

Senate, Final Action. The Senate Finance Committee May 12 approved its version of the Caribbean trade plan, 15-3, and the full Senate June 16 attached it to HR 2973, the tax withholding bill.

Conferees filed their report on the bill (H Rept 98-325) July 27. The report was approved July 28 by the Senate, 90-7, and the House, 392-18.

Following the Senate bill, the final version contained provisions to protect the U.S. Virgin Islands rum industry from Caribbean competition.

Provisions

As signed into law Aug. 5, the Caribbean trade provisions of HR 2973 (PL 98-67):

Eligibility. Stipulated that the bill's provisions were applicable to the 27 nations in Central America and the Caribbean as well as Guyana and Surinam, but not Cuba. A nation would be eligible for benefits if it:

● Was not a communist country.

● Had not nationalized, expropriated or otherwise seized ownership of U.S. property, and had not repudiated contracts, patents or trademarks of U.S. citizens.

● Had not failed to act in good faith on the results of binding arbitration in favor of U.S. citizens.

● Did not provide preferential trade treatment to the products of countries other than the United States, to the detriment of U.S. commerce.

● Had not broadcast U.S. copyrighted material without the consent of the owners.

● Cooperated with the United States to prevent drug traffic.

● Had signed an extradition agreement with the United States.

Beneficiary nations wishing to export beef and sugar to the United States must also implement "stable food production plans" to ensure that land needed to provide food for the nations' citizens was not converted to export crops.

Beneficiary nations were to be designated by the president after notification to Congress. A decision to terminate beneficiary status required 60 days' notice to Congress.

Benefits. Provided, through Sept. 30, 1995, duty-free entry into the U.S. market for Caribbean products except: textiles and apparel, petroleum products, footwear, hand-

bags, luggage, flat goods (wallets, eyeglass cases, etc.), work gloves, leather wearing apparel, tuna, and watches or watch parts. Sugar would be duty free but subject to quotas.

- Stipulated that products eligible for duty-free status must be imported directly from a beneficiary country. At least 35 percent of the products' value must consist of Caribbean parts and labor, but U.S. parts and labor could account for up to 15 percent of that 35 percent. Items that were not the product of a beneficiary country and were simply combined, packaged or diluted in the Caribbean would not be eligible for duty-free status.

Duty-free status for any Caribbean export could be suspended through existing import relief procedures. An emergency relief procedure was provided for "perishable" agricultural products.

Under existing procedures, established by the Trade Act of 1974 (PL 93-618), the Senate and House could require the president to grant import relief in certain cases through adoption of a concurrent resolution. This device, called a legislative veto, was ruled unconstitutional by the Supreme Court in 1983. *(1974 Trade Act, Congress and the Nation Vol. IV, p. 131; Legislative veto, p. 833)*

- Allowed U.S. citizens to take the same tax deduction for conventions held in eligible Caribbean nations as allowed for U.S. conventions, provided the nation had entered into a tax treaty with the United States. That provision was expected to cost the government about $5 million in lost tax revenues per year.

Puerto Rico, Virgin Islands. Included provisions to compensate Puerto Rico and the Virgin Islands for the increased competition they would face in the U.S. market from Caribbean competition.

Favored Nation Trade

As in previous years, Congress in 1983 sidetracked legislation to deny most-favored-nation (MFN) trading status to China, Hungary and Romania. In 1982 Congress had rejected resolutions to remove MFN status for Romania. *(Story, p. 103)*

The House Aug. 1 postponed indefinitely — effectively killing — resolutions to block President Reagan's renewal of the favorable trading status for the three communist countries. The House postponed a resolution (H Res 256) rejecting the trade status for Romania by a 279-126 vote and postponed resolutions on China and Hungary (H Res 257, 258) by voice votes. The Ways and Means Committee had recommended their rejection (H Repts 98-315, 98-316, 98-317).

The Senate Finance Committee rejected a related resolution on Romania (S Res 171) July 29.

Jackson-Vanik Amendment

The resolutions were offered under the Jackson-Vanik amendment to the 1974 Trade Act (PL 93-618), which allowed either house of Congress to deny most-favored-nation status to communist countries by adopting a simple resolution. That "one-house veto" provision was invalidated by the Supreme Court's June 23 ruling on legislative vetoes. *(Legislative veto, p. 833; Jackson-Vanik, Congress and the Nation Vol. IV, p. 131)*

Reagan on June 3 had waived the Jackson-Vanik amendment to allow China, Hungary and Romania access to most-favored-nation benefits.

Export Controls Extension

The Senate and House did not complete action in 1983 on legislation to reauthorize the Export Administration Act, which expired Sept. 30. Instead, Congress temporarily extended the president's authority to control exports under the expiring law and put off further action on its replacement until the following year. However, Congress again failed to reach agreement on a reauthorization measure in 1984.

Background

The United States had restricted exports for national security or foreign policy reasons since the 1940s. The Export Administration Act dated from 1969 and had last been extended in 1979 (PL 96-72). *(Congress and the Nation Vol. V, p. 274)*

Under the act exports could be controlled for three purposes: to protect national security, to achieve foreign policy goals, or to prevent the depletion of goods in short supply.

The act was administered by the Office of Export Administration in the Department of Commerce. That office maintained the Commodity Control List, and items on that list could not be exported without a license.

Most of the goods on the control list were there for national security reasons and required a validated export license regardless of their destination. If the goods were to be exported to a communist country, the secretary of defense could ask to review the license application.

The United States coordinated export controls with its allies through a Coordinating Committee (COCOM), which included the NATO nations (minus Iceland and Spain) and Japan. But the U.S. government was a more ardent controller of exports than its allies, and it restricted many products not on the COCOM list.

Foreign policy controls had been imposed by the Reagan administration and previous administrations for a variety of reasons. Certain products, for instance, were controlled to countries such as Vietnam, Cuba, Cambodia, Libya and South Africa. Foreign policy controls also had been used against the Soviet Union to protest events in Afghanistan and Poland.

In April 1981 Reagan lifted an unpopular embargo on grain sales to the Soviets that his predecessor had established in 1980 to protest the 1979 Soviet invasion of Afghanistan. And in November 1982 Reagan lifted sanctions he had imposed in December 1981 to protest Soviet pressure on the communist government of Poland. *(Details, pp. 103, 144)*

Short supply controls affected petroleum and certain agricultural products. Under the 1979 export control act, the export of Alaskan crude oil also was prohibited.

1983 Action

House. The House Oct. 27 approved a two-year extension of the act (HR 3231) that encouraged increased export trade by lessening the president's authority to impose controls for national security and foreign policy reasons. The major change in controls made by the legislation allowed exporters to forgo licensing for shipments to Japan and U.S. allies in Western Europe.

The House passed HR 3231 by voice vote, but only after reversing itself on a key provision of the complex

measure. During consideration of the bill Oct. 18, members had deleted, by a 239-171 vote, a restriction on the president's power to control exports of high-technology products to U.S. allies. Before final passage of the bill Oct. 27, however, the House took a separate vote on the amendment and rejected it, 188-223.

The House bill differed in large part from the measure originally reported by the Foreign Affairs Committee June 22 (H Rept 98-257, Part I). Pro-control members added an amendment on the House floor to strike a provision calling for automatic decontrol of any product that was controlled only by the United States and that had been consistently approved for export over a one-year period.

Another amendment barred all new investments by U.S. individuals and firms in South Africa. It was designed to censure the government for its practice of apartheid, the policy of segregating the races. The bill also required U.S. firms operating in South Africa to institute fair employment practices. And it prohibited the importation of Krugerrands and other gold coins from South Africa.

Senate Committee. A six-year export control bill reported by the Senate Banking Committee May 23 (S 979 — S Rept 98-170) did not receive floor consideration until 1984. The Senate bill retained tight national security controls and was more to the liking of the Reagan administration, which wanted no relaxation.

The Senate measure, however, contained a "contract sanctity" provision that pleased pro-export forces. It prohibited the president from imposing foreign policy controls that would force exporters to break contracts. The House bill's contract sanctity provision allowed the president to disregard contracts upon Congress' approval or in reaction to terrorism, human rights violations, nuclear weapons tests or imminent acts of aggression. A similar contract sanctity measure for agriculture exports was contained in a commodity futures trading bill (PL 97-444) that cleared in 1982. *(Story, p. 499)*

Temporary Extensions. When it became clear that the Senate and House would not complete action on reauthorizing legislation before the existing act expired Sept. 30, Congress provided a temporary extension of the president's authority to control exports until Oct. 14 (HR 3962 — PL 98-108). Upon expiration of that measure, President Reagan invoked emergency powers to prevent controls from lapsing. A second bill (HR 4476 — PL 98-207), cleared in the last hours before adjournment Nov. 18, extended the president's export control authority until Feb. 29, 1984. When that bill ran out, Congress provided a further stopgap extension, ending March 30, 1984 (HR 4956 — PL 98-222).

1984 Action

Senate. The Senate passed S 979 March 1, 1984, by voice vote.

The Senate measure was a carefully crafted compromise between those who pushed for strict limits on the use of export controls for foreign policy purposes and those who sought tighter controls to protect national security.

Bill sponsors successfully parried attempts to change key provisions that might have upset the balance between foreign policy and national security concerns. But the Senate adopted amendments to tighten controls over nuclear-related exports and to curtail the president's authority to impose embargoes on the overseas sale of U.S. farm products.

Conference. House and Senate conferees tried unsuccessfully to meld the two chambers' bills during 14 conference sessions and countless hours of informal negotiations between April and October 1984. Especially hard-fought were a Senate plan to boost Defense Department controls on licenses for certain high-technology exports and a House-backed proposal to ban new U.S. commercial bank loans to the South African government.

Final Effort. In a last-ditch attempt to renew the act, Senate backers Oct. 10 offered a five-year extension of controls (HR 4230) that included many of the compromises that had been reached in the conference. The bill, which excluded the increased Pentagon controls and the South African loan ban, was passed by voice vote. The House had passed it in 1983.

But the House Oct. 11 reinstated the prohibition on bank loans, which effectively killed the bill's Senate chances. The House action came on a **269-62 key vote (R 96-50; D 173-12).** *(1984 key votes, p. 927)*

Auto Domestic Content

For the second year in a row, the House Nov. 3 approved a "domestic content" measure that would require fixed levels of U.S. labor and parts in foreign cars sold in the United States. There was no further action on the measure. *(1982 action, p. 102)*

The bill (HR 1234) was approved 219-199 with the strong backing of industrial-state Democrats and a sprinkling of Republicans who claimed that foreign car imports, primarily from Japan, were taking jobs away from U.S. autoworkers and employees in such related industries as rubber and steel. Domestic content had become an important symbolic issue for labor-backed Democrats in Congress, who were anxious to demonstrate their concern about imports and continuing high unemployment in the auto industry and related industries. The administration opposed the measure, which President Reagan described as a "cruel hoax."

The House-passed content bill would cover foreign auto manufacturers that sold more than 100,000 cars a year in the United States, beginning in 1985.

Depending upon the number of cars sold, the domestic content requirement would range from 3.3 percent to 30 percent during the first year the law was in effect. The content level would rise to a maximum of 90 percent on companies selling more than 900,000 autos in the United States in 1987 and beyond.

By comparison, five Japanese car companies in 1982 had a domestic content level of 5 percent each for the cars they sold in the United States.

House approval of the domestic content bill came despite a Nov. 1 announcement that Japan would restrict U.S. exports to 1.85 million cars for the year beginning in April 1984. While that figure was up from the limit of 1.68 million cars in effect for the past three years, U.S. and Japanese trade negotiators had hoped the announcement would reduce protectionist sentiment in Washington.

Committee Action. The bill sparked a power struggle between the Energy and Commerce Committee, which had jurisdiction over interstate commerce, and the Ways and Means Committee — a bulwark of free trade in the House — which had jurisdiction over trade. The Energy and Commerce Committee favorably reported the bill June 30 (H Rept 98-287, Part I), but the Ways and Means

Committee reported the bill unfavorably Sept. 21 (H Rept 98-287, Part II).

Trade 'Reciprocity'

The Senate April 21 by voice vote passed "reciprocity" trade legislation (S 144) that would expand the president's authority to retaliate against unfair trading practices by other countries and require the administration to seek new international agreements on trade in services and high technology. Passage came after the Senate added to the bill a controversial measure repealing a requirement for tax withholding on interest and dividend income. The reciprocity bill had been reported unanimously by the Senate Finance Committee on March 14 (S Rept 98-24).

The House never acted on the Senate bill. It passed a separate withholding measure instead and returned S 144 to the Senate, protesting that the bill violated the constitutional prerogative of the House to originate all revenue legislation. The Ways and Means Committee reported a modified reciprocity bill Sept. 27 (HR 1571 — H Rept 98-383, Part I), but there was no further action on the measure. *(Withholding, p. 90)*

Reciprocity legislation had generated considerable controversy in the 97th Congress. It was reported by committees in both chambers but never came to a vote. Watered-down provisions cleared in 1984 as part of an omnibus trade package. *(Story, this page)*

1984

Facing election-year pressures and a merchandise trade deficit nearly double that for the previous year, Congress provided aid for a number of import-sensitive industries in a massive trade package cleared shortly before adjournment. But in the final bill Congress dropped or weakened the most strongly protectionist proposals to avoid a presidential veto.

As cleared, the bill's most controversial provisions included free-trade talks with Israel, preferred treatment of goods from developing nations and import relief for the steel and wine industries. President Reagan in September had rejected tariffs and quotas on steel imports but had endorsed negotiations to limit shipments of steel to the United States. Steel imports accounted for about 25 percent of the U.S. market in 1984.

For the second year in a row lawmakers were unable to agree on legislation reauthorizing the Export Administration Act, and the administration was forced to continue to rely on emergency powers to control U.S. shipments abroad.

Omnibus Trade Bill

Congress Oct. 9 cleared an omnibus trade bill (HR 3398 — PL 98-573) that was an amalgam of more than 100 measures. The vast majority of the bill's provisions involved import relief for particular products.

Faced with a possible presidential veto, legislators cut or softened most of the strongest protectionist measures in the bill. The legislation that emerged from lengthy, infor-

mal negotiations and a heated House-Senate conference won administration praise for its "pro-trade" slant.

Among other things, the bill:

● Extended for eight and one-half years the Generalized System of Preferences (GSP), which lifted duties on some imports from some developing countries. The bill linked benefits for the first time to recipients' steps to open markets to U.S. trade, honor copyrights and other intellectual property and respect worker rights. It also cut benefits for countries with an annual per capita gross national product of more than $8,500.

● Approved duties to offset "upstream subsidies" — through foreign government aid such as financing — that unfairly lowered the export price of goods countries shipped to U.S. markets. This provision originally was part of a trade remedies bill (HR 4784) passed by the House July 26. Other remedies in that bill were dropped.

● Gave the president authority to enforce voluntary restraints on steel imports, which President Reagan had recommended Sept. 18. The authority was linked to steelmakers' steps to modernize equipment and retrain workers. The bill also asked the president to reduce steel imports to between 17 percent and 20.2 percent of the domestic market, and instructed the administration to negotiate voluntary copper import reductions with major foreign copper producers.

● Granted the president authority to negotiate to lower or eliminate barriers on most trade between Israel and the United States, and extended the president's powers to negotiate free-trade agreements with other countries, subject to congressional review.

● Asked, but did not require, the president to negotiate reduced barriers to U.S. wine trade. The provision was a watered-down version of so-called wine "equity" legislation meant to prevent U.S. wine makers from being shut out of European markets by high tariffs or substantially losing domestic sales to foreign imports. The bill also allowed grape growers to bring unfair-trade complaints to the U.S. International Trade Commission.

● Extended to service industries many of the same remedies for unfair foreign trade practices that already applied to goods. The bill authorized the president to negotiate lowered barriers to trade in high-technology items, U.S. investment abroad and services such as banking.

Legislative History

Senate. HR 3398 started out as a routine tariff bill, passed by the House June 28, 1983. In reporting the bill Nov. 10, 1983 (S Rept 98-308), the Senate Finance Committee added trade "reciprocity" provisions that had been dropped from an unrelated tax measure in 1983. The provisions aimed to strengthen the president's authority to retaliate against unfair trading practices by other nations and require the administration to seek new international agreements on trade in services and high technology. *(Reciprocity, this page)*

The Senate passed the bill Sept. 20, 1984, 96-0, after attaching a package of committee-approved amendments, including provisions to encourage U.S.-Israel free trade and a 10-year GSP extension. Floor managers succeeded in fending off a number of strongly protectionist amendments aimed at aiding import-sensitive domestic industries.

House. In the House, meanwhile, the Ways and Means Committee Sept. 26 approved a trade package that included a Democratic alternative to President Reagan's steel import decision, as well as measures on U.S.-Israel

free trade, expanded import relief for domestic wine makers and a five-year extension of the GSP.

In addition, the bill sought to extend for two years the trade adjustment assistance program, which targeted government aid to workers who lost their jobs because of foreign competition. The program had last been extended in 1983. *(Story, p. 665)*

The House Oct. 3 attached these and other parts of its trade package to HR 3398 and sent the bill to conference. The House package included the U.S.-Israel free-trade arrangement, steel import stabilization, wine equity, GSP, service industries commercial development, the trade remedies bill the House had passed July 26 and other measures.

The trade remedies bill (HR 4784 — H Rept 98-725), which had passed by a 259-95 vote, strengthened the Commerce Department's power to act against several foreign practices not currently defined by international agreement as export subsidies or unfair trade practices. Designated eligible for U.S. retaliation were government support for natural resource and energy prices and imports made with subsidized components. The measure also addressed "downstream dumping," the practice of adding subsidized components made in one country to exports assembled in another country. Under HR 4784, proof of downstream dumping would trigger anti-dumping duties.

The bill required an in-depth study of trading partners' methods of targeting: a government practice to coordinate antitrust, tax and other policies to bolster selected industries. It originally had called for protection against targeting, but Trade Representative William E. Brock III argued that trading partners could claim the U.S. computer, semiconductor and other industries received unfair help from Washington. Bowing to industry and administration pressure, the bill's supporters agreed to modify the legislation to call for a study.

Before sending HR 3398 to conference, the House rejected on a **174-233 key vote (R 14-142; D 160-91)** an amendment that would have dropped Taiwan, Hong Kong and South Korea from the GSP program. The three countries received more than half of the U.S. benefits under the program. *(1984 key votes, p. 927)*

Conference. House and Senate conferees moved quickly as adjournment neared. Although major components of the package — free trade with Israel, aid to domestic steel producers, import relief procedures for domestic wine makers and the GSP extension — threatened to hang up the conference, conferees finished work Oct. 5.

After painstaking negotiations, most provisions opposed by the Reagan administration were dropped or softened by the conference.

Conferees agreed to authorize the president to negotiate a free-trade agreement with Israel. But the final agreement included additional, more restrictive, language authorizing free-trade negotiations with other countries.

The conference agreement also instructed the president to work to reduce steel imports to 17-20.2 percent of the domestic market. His enforcement of any negotiated limit was tied to the industry's efforts to reinvest earnings to modernize their operations. Most domestic steel producers also were required to spend 1 percent of net cash-flow for worker retraining.

A House provision extending the Trade Adjustment Assistance Act, which aided workers who lost their jobs when imports caused domestic plant closings, was dropped.

The final version of HR 3398 excluded three intricate proposals that would have extended the range of foreign actions eligible for trade remedies. Lawmakers cut a provision, strongly opposed by the administration because it feared retaliation, to allow duties on imports made with natural resources heavily subsidized by foreign governments.

Also removed from the bill was a controversial provision to assess duties on unfairly priced exports from countries, such as China, whose economies were government-controlled. The administration strongly opposed the provision, which would have set a new standard for judging whether government-set prices were fair.

In addition, lawmakers dropped a proposal that would extend protection to U.S. producers against illegally priced exports shipped from one country but manufactured with another country's unfairly subsidized or priced parts.

In other major action, conferees:

● Extended the Generalized System of Preferences for 8.5 years. The conference tightened eligibility requirements for GSP privileges, but less severely than the House bill would have done.

● Adopted a weakened wine equity provision instructing the U.S. trade representative to consult with major foreign wine producers to promote U.S. wine trade. Conferees also agreed to allow grape growers to join wine makers in bringing unfair trade practices cases.

● Asked the president to negotiate voluntary import restraints with leading foreign copper producers.

● Granted the president authority to negotiate reduced barriers to trade in services and investments abroad.

● Voted to extend to service industries the same remedies for some unfair foreign trade practices as already applied to goods.

Final Action. The conference report on HR 3398 (H Rept 98-1156) was filed Oct. 5. The House adopted the report Oct. 9 on a 386-1 vote. The Senate then approved it by voice vote.

Major Provisions

As signed into law Oct. 30, the Trade and Tariff Act of 1984 (HR 3398 — PL 98-573):

● Extended the Generalized System of Preferences for eight and one-half years, through July 4, 1993. For the first time, Congress tied GSP benefits to countries' steps to open markets to exports from the United States, honor patents and other intellectual property rights and respect workers' rights. The program, established by the Trade Act of 1974, had been scheduled to expire in January 1985. *(Congress and the Nation Vol. IV, p. 131)*

The bill denied GSP benefits to countries with annual per capita incomes of more than $8,500.

● Permitted administration officials to pursue talks with Israel on the establishment of a free-trade agreement between the two nations.

HR 3398 also approved a limited version of powers, long desired by the Office of the U.S. Trade Representative, to negotiate free-trade area agreements with other countries.

● Expanded administration authority to respond to other nations' trade practices. The trade reciprocity provisions authorized negotiations to reduce or remove barriers against trade in high-technology products, U.S. investment abroad and trade in services, such as banking. It also permitted the elimination of duties on some high-tech items for up to five years.

• Clarified the application of trade remedies enjoyed by goods to the service industries.

• Permitted the government to charge duties on unfairly priced goods exported to the United States made with various kinds of government-subsidized assistance, such as financing.

• Requested the administration to remove or reduce barriers to U.S. wine trade.

At the prompting of California grape growers, members also approved a proposal, opposed by the administration, to let grape growers join wine makers in filing unfair-trade complaints. The provision allowing growers to ask for relief expired in 1986.

• Instructed the president to negotiate voluntary copper import reductions with major foreign copper producers.

• Gave the president authority to enforce the voluntary restraints on steel imports he recommended Sept. 18. That authority was to be linked to steelmakers' commitment to modernizing operations and retraining workers.

Lawmakers also merged House and administration steel proposals, asking the president to reduce steel imports to between 17 percent and 20.2 percent of the U.S. market.

• Granted the U.S. Customs Service more power to confiscate property during drug-smuggling investigations.

Export Controls Extension

The 98th Congress Oct. 11 gave up efforts to extend the Export Administration Act, forcing the president to continue to rely indefinitely on emergency powers to control U.S. shipments abroad.

Because of a standoff between the two chambers, hard-won agreements reached during six months of stop-and-start House-Senate conferences were scrapped. And government controls over exports remained largely under the umbrella of the International Emergency Economic Powers Act of 1977 (PL 95-223).

The previous authorization of the Export Administration Act expired Sept. 30, 1983. The House had approved a two-year extension (HR 3231) Oct. 27, 1983, but the Senate did not act on the reauthorization until March 1, 1984, when it approved a six-year extension by voice vote. As Congress considered reauthorizing the measure, the executive branch relied on the emergency powers and temporary extensions of the act. *(1983-84 action, p. 107)*

Energy Trade

Congress in 1984 approved legislation (HR 3169 — PL 98-370) designed to help domestic manufacturers of renewable energy technology compete in the international market.

The measure cleared June 29 when the House accepted an amendment adopted by the Senate June 28. The House had passed HR 3169 (H Rept 98-537) by voice vote Nov. 16, 1983. After approving a technical amendment, the Senate passed the measure (S Rept 98-508), also by voice vote, on June 28. The bill was signed by the president July 18 (PL 98-370).

As enacted, HR 3169 required the commerce secretary to establish a government program aimed at promoting the export of U.S.-made renewable energy products. The measure also directed the commerce secretary to evaluate the status of the domestic renewable energy industry and its ability to compete in international markets and report his findings to Congress before May 31, 1985. And the legislation established a federal interagency working group, chaired by the secretary of energy, to recommend government actions.

Sponsored by Rep. Ron Wyden, D-Ore., the legislation was in response to growing international competition in the renewable energy technology business.

Such technology included photovoltaics (solar energy cells) and wind energy turbines. Because foreign governments actively promoted and subsidized the export of renewable energy products made in their countries, the share of the international market held by United States firms declined.

Industrial Policy

Legislation to establish a national industrial policy was approved by two House committees but went no further in 1984.

A measure (HR 4360) to establish a Bank for Industrial Competitiveness, a Council for Industrial Competitiveness and a Federal Industrial Mortgage Association (FIMA) won the approval of both the House Banking Committee and the House Energy and Commerce Committee. The bank was designed to make loan guarantees and purchase stock to help finance industrial modernization. It was slated to receive $8.5 billion in federal funds over 10 years. The council was to have been a board of government, business and labor leaders to coordinate government industrial policy, while FIMA would establish a wider market for industrial mortgages to help small and medium-sized firms that needed capital. HR 4360 was approved by the Banking Committee April 24 and the Energy and Commerce panel June 6 (H Rept 98-697, Parts I and II).

A second industrial policy measure (HR 4361 — H Rept 98-693, Part I) was reported by the Banking Committee, also on April 24. It called for a $500 million authorization over four years for an Advanced Technology Foundation to fund applied scientific research.

In 1983 the Senate Governmental Affairs Committee had attached industrial policy provisions to a bill to establish a new Department of International Industry and Trade (S 121 — S Rept 98-374). But there was no further action on the bill.

Other Legislation

Export Subsidies

The deficit reduction bill (HR 4170 — PL 98-369) cleared June 27 set up a new export subsidy program under which existing Domestic International Sales Corporations (DISCs) would be replaced by Foreign Sales Corporations. The change was made at the administration's request because of objections to DISCs raised by U.S. trading partners.

DISCs in most cases were paper companies, with no employees and no real operations, which served as conduits for a company's exports. A certain portion of the company's export earnings could be attributed to the DISC and were sheltered from taxes.

The DISC plan, enacted in 1971, was long a target of

Democratic tax "reform" efforts. *(Background, Congress and the Nation Vol. IV, p. 99)*

Under HR 4170 U.S. exporters retained the tax advantage they had under existing law.

But companies would have to direct export earnings to offshore subsidiaries rather than domestic trading subsidiaries. *(HR 4170, p. 79)*

Textile Labeling

Major drug legislation (S 1538 — PL 98-417) cleared Sept. 12 included an unrelated provision requiring that clothing sold in the United States be conspicuously labeled to show country of origin and that mail-order and other catalogs indicate whether clothing was manufactured in the United States or imported. *(Generic drugs, p. 547)*

Fiscal Assistance

President Reagan took office in 1981 determined to scale back the federal government's role in managing the economy.

Reagan sought to eliminate economic development assistance programs initiated by Democratic administrations of the past and to encourage a greater degree of self-reliance among individuals, businesses and state and local governments. He spoke feelingly of the rewards of "hard work and risk taking" that would result from "limiting government spending to those functions which are the proper sphere of government."

The president soon found it was not easy to abolish existing programs of fiscal assistance, each of which had a vocal and powerful constituency. Congress, its resistance stiffened by the recession that began in mid-1981, rebuffed the president's plans to eliminate revenue sharing and other programs that helped states and local communities. But lawmakers agreed to hold down funding for several programs and turned aside efforts to refocus them on anti-recession aid.

Reagan, for his part, was unable to sell Congress on his chief economic development initiative — a plan to provide tax breaks for businesses that located in designated "enterprise zones" in inner cities and rural areas.

The president had more success in heading off new programs intended to revitalize the sagging economy.

Confronted with the worst recession since the Great Depression of the 1930s, Democratic members of Congress found themselves unable to win passage of sweeping jobs and counter-cyclical aid programs patterned after those enacted in the 1970s. Budget stringencies and the opposition of a popular Republican president foreclosed that possibility, although Democratic leaders continued to offer such plans with maximum fanfare.

Revenue Sharing

Congress in 1983 voted a three-year extension of the general revenue sharing program of grants to local governments after Senate conferees forced their House colleagues to back off from a plan to increase funding. The final legislation mandated the same $4.6 billion annual spending level that Congress had provided in fiscal 1981-83.

The Reagan administration had threatened to veto any bill authorizing an increase. As part of his New Federalism plan to transfer certain programs to state and local governments, Reagan originally had recommended creation of a local block grant that would merge revenue sharing with Community Development Block Grants. Those grants gave cities a lump sum to use for activities such as housing rehabilitation, slum clearance or the construction of public buildings. They were reauthorized separately for three years, at $3.5 billion annually. Separate funding also was continued for Urban Development Action Grants, a related program intended to help local governments stimulate private development; Reagan wanted to phase out the action grants.

Congress sidestepped efforts to include anti-recession aid in the revenue sharing extension legislation. Revenue sharing had been linked with anti-recession aid since 1976, when Congress enacted a counter-cyclical aid program for state and local governments to pump in more federal money when the economy flagged. The program, triggered by high unemployment, funneled $3.7 billion to states and localities for accelerated public works construction and for payments to ease the burden that national economic problems placed on government budgets. Counter-cyclical aid was dropped from the 1980 extension bill.

Economic Development Aid

From the time he took office in 1981, President Reagan sought to abolish the Economic Development Administration (EDA). The agency, a relic of President Johnson's Great Society program, was established in 1965 to provide economic and community development aid to depressed areas.

The most telling criticism of the economic development program was that Congress gradually had expanded its jurisdiction until almost all of the country was eligible for assistance that was supposed to be reserved for impoverished communities.

References

Discussion of fiscal assistance for the years 1945-64 may be found in *Congress and the Nation Vol. I*, pp. 337-386; for the years 1965-68, *Congress and the Nation Vol. II*, pp. 281-304; for the years 1969-72, *Congress and the Nation Vol. III*, pp. 97-117, 177-187; for the years 1973-76, *Congress and the Nation Vol. IV*, pp. 119-125, 137-146; for the years 1977-80, *Congress and the Nation Vol. V*, pp. 277-287.

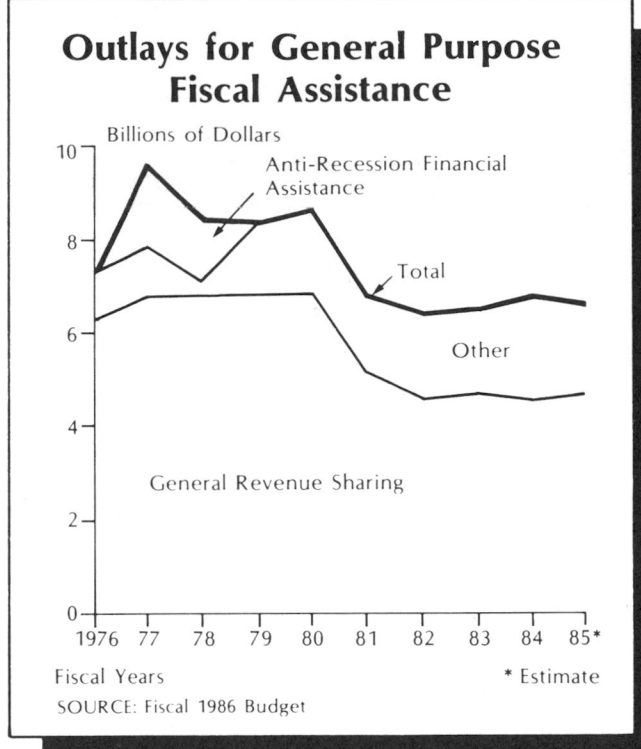

Outlays for General Purpose Fiscal Assistance

Billions of Dollars

Anti-Recession Financial Assistance

Total

Other

General Revenue Sharing

Fiscal Years   * Estimate

SOURCE: Fiscal 1986 Budget

Especially after it became the vehicle for a separate $6 billion public works program pushed by congressional Democrats to combat the 1974-75 recession, EDA was attacked as fostering wasteful pork barrel projects. The symbol of that criticism was the use of EDA funds to build a replica of the Great Pyramid in southern Indiana.

Congress throughout Reagan's first term insisted on continued funding for the agency, although at sharply reduced levels. Another economic development agency, the Appalachian Regional Commission, also suffered cuts in funding, but Congress rejected Reagan's efforts to abolish its social service programs.

Anti-Recession Aid

Lawmakers had only limited success in pushing new measures to fight the recession.

In 1982 Congress, with Reagan's backing, did enact legislation providing a five-cent-a-gallon increase in the federal gasoline tax to finance highway and mass transit improvements throughout the country. And early in 1983 it enacted a scaled-down Democratic anti-recession jobs program, including funds for public works, general construction and water projects. Reagan also backed that program, which had been trimmed to stay within limits acceptable to him. *(Anti-recession bills, labor, p. 663)*

But an unexpectedly strong rebound from the recession during 1983 eased pressure for counter-cyclical measures, and the Democrats were unable win congressional support for further legislation that would have put the long-term unemployed to work repairing public facilities in areas of high unemployment.

Industrial Policy

At times in 1983 "industrial policy" appeared likely to become a rallying cry for the Democrats and a focal point of the 1984 presidential election campaign. Instead it remained largely a collection of ideas looking for supporters.

In general, industrial policy involved enlarging the government's role in promoting particular industries. Supporters, citing Japan's success in encouraging the development of its export industries, urged adoption of a national industrial policy as a way to curb mounting U.S. trade deficits.

The concept was greeted warily by Republicans, who viewed it as an intrusion into the free enterprise system. Even many Democrats were uneasy about advancing central planning. In particular, Democrats split in their support for a Bank for Industrial Competitiveness, which would lend money and promote stock purchases to finance industrial modernization.

Industrial policy legislation never reached the floor in either chamber, although the concept influenced several trade bills in 1984. *(Trade bills, international economic policy, p. 95)*

Chronology
Of Action
On Fiscal Assistance

1981

Economic Development Aid

As part of its budget-cutting 1981 reconciliation bill (HR 3982 — PL 97-35), Congress authorized fiscal 1982 funding for two economic assistance programs that President Reagan wanted to eliminate or scale back.

Congress declined to go along with Reagan's proposal to abolish the Economic Development Administration (EDA), a Commerce Department agency created in 1965 to provide economic and community development aid to depressed areas.

Although lawmakers agreed to spare the agency, they reduced its fiscal 1982 authorization to $290 million. Congress in 1980 had extended EDA through fiscal 1982, with authorizations of $1 billion annually. Reagan had sought only $50 million to close down EDA programs.

The reconciliation bill authorized $215 million for the Appalachian Regional Commission (ARC) in fiscal 1982. The commission fostered anti-poverty and highway programs in 13 states.

Of the total authorization, $165 million was earmarked for highways and $50 million for other projects. President Reagan had sought to terminate funding for the non-highway programs. *(Previous authorizations, Congress and the Nation Vol. V, p. 286)*

Congress continued to provide limited funding for both EDA and ARC throughout Reagan's first term. *(Background, 1982 action, this page; 1983, p. 118)*

As requested, the reconciliation measure repealed a network of eight regional planning commissions authorized under Title V of the Public Works and Economic Development Act of 1965 (PL 89-136).

Defense Production

Congress Sept. 24 completed action on a bill (HR 2903 — PL 97-47) extending the provisions of the Defense Production Act for one year, through Sept. 30, 1982. The bill cleared when the House accepted an unrelated amendment added by the Senate Sept. 22. The House originally passed the bill July 13.

The administration had asked for a five-year extension of the act, which gave the president various powers to guarantee the health of defense-related industries. *(Congress and the Nation Vol. V, p. 139)*

Following a succession of short-term extensions, Congress in 1984 reauthorized the act through Sept. 30, 1986. *(Story, p. 119)*

Economic Development Aid

Legislation to extend the Economic Development Administration (EDA) and the Appalachian Regional Commission (ARC) failed to clear Congress in 1982.

The existing authorization for both programs expired Sept. 30, but Congress provided $168.5 million in fiscal 1983 funding for EDA through a continuing appropriations resolution (PL 97-377) cleared Dec. 20. ARC was funded at $165.1 million.

While not a large program — spending over the years for its public works development totaled about $5 billion — the Commerce Department's EDA provided a good example of the limbo into which many Great Society programs had fallen under the Reagan administration. From the time he took office, President Reagan had sought to abolish the EDA. *(1981 action, this page; 1983, p. 118)*

The idea behind the program was that communities afflicted with poverty or high unemployment lacked the resources to pay for the infrastructure of public facilities needed to support economic growth. Funds had gone for everything from sewer construction to renovation of old market buildings for new stores.

In calling for the abolition of EDA, Reagan administration officials attacked its program as being too thinly spread around the country, too costly and too slow to do much good. When the EDA was established in 1965, about 12 percent of the country was eligible for aid. Projects were supposed to be limited to areas with particularly severe economic problems. By 1982 eligibility for the program had expanded to include 80 percent of the population.

The Appalachian Regional Commission, established in 1965, fostered anti-poverty and highway programs in 13 states. It had powerful allies in Congress, notably Sen. Jennings Randolph, D-W.Va., ranking Democrat on the Environment and Public Works Committee.

Background

The basic legislation (PL 89-136) establishing EDA was passed by Congress in 1965. Backed by the Johnson administration, the legislation expanded a smaller area redevelopment program set up in 1962. ARC was established under a separate 1965 law (PL 89-4). *(Congress and the Nation Vol. II, p. 290)*

Over the years Congress repeatedly reauthorized both the EDA and ARC programs. Twice during the Nixon administration Congress tried to transform the EDA program into a counter-cyclical program to combat joblessness. President Nixon successfully vetoed both bills. Nixon then tried to abolish the EDA in 1973 and transfer its functions to other agencies. Congress did not buy the idea, however, and continued reauthorizing the program at two- or three-year intervals. *(Congress and the Nation Vol. III, p. 178; Congress and the Nation Vol. IV, p. 144)*

In 1976 and 1977 Congress approved $6 billion in counter-cyclical public works projects, to be spent by EDA. The first year the aid was approved over President Ford's

veto; the second year with President Carter's support. Carter later sought to expand EDA's lending power, as part of his urban policy, but the proposal died in Congress after Reagan's election in 1980. *(Background, Congress and the Nation Vol. IV, p. 708; Congress and the Nation Vol. V, pp. 286, 401)*

By 1982 EDA was operating a number of different programs for distressed areas. Grants were given to eligible areas that could show that federally funded projects would aid their overall economic development. In addition, the agency provided loans to developing businesses and financed planning and technical assistance to help areas plan their economic development.

The Appalachian Regional Commission funded both social service programs, such as health facilities and vocational training, and construction of highways in the Appalachian region.

New York City Turnaround

Bolstered by federal loan guarantees, New York City in the early 1980s emerged from a fiscal crisis that had brought it to the brink of bankruptcy in the previous decade.

Congress in 1978 authorized $1.65 billion in 15-year Treasury guarantees for bonds sold by the city government. New York City, which had been unable to borrow in the credit markets because of lagging investor confidence, used the full $1.65 billion before the loan guarantee authority expired on June 30, 1982. By that time the city was able once again to borrow on its own credit.

The loan guarantee program was the final step in a two-stage federal rescue effort for New York City. In 1975 Congress had provided $2.3 billion a year in short-term direct loans as part of a package of federal, state and city measures that kept the city from defaulting on outstanding loans. *(1978 legislation, Congress and the Nation Vol. V, p. 279; 1975 action, Congress and the Nation Vol. IV, p. 494)*

Renewed strength in the credit markets permitted the city in 1985 to accelerate retirement of its federally guaranteed loans, thus speeding the end of state financial controls that had been imposed on the city in connection with the rescue program. In April 1985 Mayor Edward I. Koch announced a $588 million bond sale to pay off nearly all of the city's federally guaranteed bonds.

"Seven years ago financial experts ... said that if the federal government guaranteed loans for the City of New York, those guarantees were certain to be called upon," Koch said. "Seven years later, however, not only are we about to repay these loans without using the guarantees, but we are repaying them eight years ahead of schedule."

Legislative Action

House. By a 281-95 vote, the House Aug. 12 passed a bill (HR 6100 — H Rept 97-540) authorizing three years of development assistance, at $500 million a year.

Responding to criticisms of the existing EDA program, HR 6100 focused eligibility for aid on areas with severe problems. The bill, which was drafted by the Public Works and Transportation Committee, also extended the authorization for the Appalachian Regional Commission. ARC funding was to be gradually reduced, until the non-highway programs were terminated by 1987.

Only 41 percent of the population would be eligible for EDA assistance under the bill. Aid would be limited to areas with continuing high unemployment or low per capita income. Areas would be required to show how they would use federal funds, as part of an overall economic strategy, to achieve their goals.

The legislation would end direct federal involvement with loan and loan guarantee programs to businesses. Instead, it would allow areas to apply for grants of up to $1 million, to establish revolving funds for loans to small businesses.

Senate. The Senate Environment and Public Works Committee three times during the 97th Congress voted against recommending funds for EDA.

However, the Senate did not go along with the Reagan administration in its efforts to do away immediately with the non-highway programs of the ARC. A bill (S 2144 — S Rept 97-452) to provide a one-year extension of the ARC passed by voice vote June 9.

Stalemate. The Senate rejected House efforts to hold a conference on S 2144 and the broader House measure, and both bills died when Congress adjourned.

Defense Production/Stimulus

House Democrats' efforts to establish a $6.75 billion economic stimulus program blocked 1982 action on a five-year extension of the Defense Production Act. The act, first passed in 1950, gave the president various economic powers to ensure defense-related production during times of national emergency. Congress early Oct. 2 approved a six-month extension (S 2375 — PL 97-336), through March 31, 1983. *(1981 extension, p. 115; 1984, p. 119)*

The House Sept. 23 had considered the five-year reauthorization as part of a bill called the Defense Industrial Base Revitalization Act (HR 5540), which would have established a $6.75 billion, five-year program of grants and loans for small business and job training aid. But the bill was pulled from the schedule after Republicans won a key vote on an amendment to limit loan authority under the new program.

Critics of the measure argued that it was nothing but a massive subsidy to businesses largely unrelated to national defense. The Reagan administration opposed the bill.

HR 5540 sought to help ailing industries by making loans and payments to small businesses struggling against foreign competition and other economic problems. The bill also would have established a new vocational education program, and provided high-technology equipment to colleges and universities for use in professional training.

The legislation had backing from a majority of Republicans on the Banking Committee, which along with the Education and Labor Committee reported the measure May 17 (H Rept 97-530, Parts I, II and III).

Enterprise Zones

President Reagan's only new proposal to help cities — his plan to create "enterprise zones" to revive decaying urban areas — made little headway in Congress in 1982.

The plan, presented to Congress March 23, aimed to revitalize blighted areas by providing federal tax and regulatory relief to businesses that invested in economically depressed inner cities and rural towns.

A modified version of the proposal was approved Sept. 28 by the Senate Finance Committee as part of an unrelated tax bill (HR 7094). But there was no further action, and the measure died when Congress adjourned.

The enterprise zone plan also failed in the 98th Congress. *(Story, p. 119)*

1983

Revenue Sharing

Congress in 1983 voted a three-year extension of the federal revenue sharing program of aid to local governments.

The measure (HR 2780 — PL 98-185) entitled local governments to $4.6 billion in revenue sharing grants annually over fiscal 1984-86. The bill cleared Nov. 17 after House conferees yielded to Senate insistence that funding be maintained at the level authorized for fiscal 1980-83. The House had sought a $450 million increase, to $5.02 billion. The Reagan administration had threatened a veto of any bill authorizing an increase.

The administration earlier in the year opposed any multi-year extension of revenue sharing unless it was melded with Community Development Block Grants as part of the administration's New Federalism initiative. But Treasury Secretary Donald T. Regan said in May that a simple, three-year extension would be acceptable.

Background

Revenue sharing was first enacted in 1972 as part of President Nixon's New Federalism. The idea was to transfer money — and thus power — to state and local governments to spend as they pleased. Congress extended the program in 1976 and again in 1980. *(Congress and the Nation Vol. V, p. 284)*

By the time HR 2780 expired in 1986, the program would have distributed more than $78 billion in federal funds to states and localities. States had not participated in the program since 1980; they were formally excluded under the 1983 extension. *(Total payments, box, this page)*

More than 39,000 local governments benefited from the program. They used revenue sharing money to pay police and fire personnel, provide health care to residents, buy library books, build and repair highways, support education and for dozens of other purposes.

Legislative History

House. The House Government Operations Committee reported HR 2780 May 16 (H Rept 98-179). As ap-

Revenue Sharing

Following are the federal revenue sharing funds distributed within each state in fiscal 1985 and the total that governments within each state would have received over the 14-year life of the program, ending Sept. 30, 1986:

	Fiscal 1985	Total
Alabama	$ 77,185,121	$1,290,582,888
Alaska	22,469,662	244,935,759
Arizona	55,735,988	873,537,196
Arkansas	46,397,074	797,997,809
California	509,755,233	8,631,871,740
Colorado	54,316,472	871,773,791
Connecticut	54,742,162	982,235,836
Delaware	13,389,898	238,179,493
District of Columbia	17,695,946	328,820,081
Florida	168,107,790	2,485,419,664
Georgia	111,069,380	1,738,089,470
Hawaii	21,885,974	367,332,466
Idaho	19,615,760	307,847,501
Illinois	212,839,880	3,900,961,185
Indiana	86,683,853	1,584,244,792
Iowa	54,879,670	998,360,767
Kansas	38,867,164	703,894,995
Kentucky	75,125,815	1,289,367,562
Louisiana	84,472,447	1,690,231,580
Maine	28,751,730	486,010,537
Maryland	88,450,992	1,545,252,874
Massachusetts	130,514,401	2,452,100,763
Michigan	193,875,196	3,254,577,952
Minnesota	90,196,697	1,555,123,688
Mississippi	60,964,814	1,161,751,490
Missouri	80,670,856	1,443,627,251
Montana	20,372,209	306,648,207
Nebraska	31,013,526	523,536,569
Nevada	14,460 906	201,560,447
New Hampshire	14,377,323	256,236,985
New Jersey	148,020,394	2,502,566,175
New Mexico	32,483,058	518,720,063
New York	467,838,096	8,562,124,002
North Carolina	122,294,022	1,995,925,390
North Dakota	13,182,202	240,898,295
Ohio	193,370,351	3,138,226,538
Oklahoma	58,084,169	910,461,945
Oregon	55,392,995	858,081,215
Pennsylvania	222,123,584	3,984,921 484
Rhode Island	20,464,592	343,688,007
South Carolina	69,605,536	1,101,347,334
South Dakota	14,845,508	286,248,333
Tennessee	84,080,262	1,467,300,086
Texas	242,439,322	3,900,638,512
Utah	36,473,566	499,990,058
Vermont	12,159,675	226,903,619
Virginia	99,921,884	1,632,558,816
Washington	74,760,736	1,149,719,157
West Virginia	45,172,107	742,249,240
Wisconsin	109,046,379	1,862,075,445
Wyoming	15,871,415	164,264,237
TOTAL	**$4,616,513,792**	**$78,601,019,289**

SOURCE: U.S. Office of Revenue Sharing

proved by the committee on a 37-2 vote May 11, the bill extended revenue sharing assistance to local governments through fiscal 1988 and increased funding by more than $730 million a year to $5.3 billion.

Ted Weiss, D-N.Y., chairman of the Intergovernmental Relations Subcommittee, argued that the "modest" funding increase was needed to make up for inflationary erosion of the federal aid program since it began in 1972.

The House passed HR 2780 Aug. 2 by a 381-85 vote. Before passing the bill, the House trimmed two years from the five-year extension reported by the Government Operations Committee and cut annual authorizations to $5.02 billion from the $5.03 billion committee-approved figure. Proposals to target aid to areas hardest hit by the recession were turned aside.

Senate. The Senate Finance Committee reported a three-year extension bill (S 1426 — S Rept 98-189) July 20.

The Senate passed HR 2780 Sept. 21, 87-6, after substituting its $4.6 billion-a-year reauthorization for fiscal 1984-86 and rejecting moves to increase funding for the program.

Conference. Senate conferees refused to accept any increase in the Reagan-approved $4.6 billion funding level, and the House gave in. Conferees filed their report (H Rept 98-550) Nov. 15.

Both chambers approved the conference report Nov. 17 by voice votes.

Major Provisions

As signed into law Nov. 30, HR 2780 (PL 98-185):

● Extended general revenue sharing grants to local governments for three years, from Oct. 1, 1983, through Sept. 30, 1986.

● Set mandatory, or entitlement, funding for the program at $4.57 billion a year.

● Eliminated the previous authorization allowing state governments to receive revenue sharing funds on a case-by-case basis if specifically appropriated by Congress.

● Permanently extended authority for each state to develop, subject to certain constraints, its own formula for allocating revenue sharing funds to local governments within its borders.

● Provided that a local government whose tax base fell by 20 percent or more due to a plant closing or other economic hardship would not have its revenue sharing allocation cut for at least a year.

Economic Development Aid

Legislation to reauthorize the Economic Development Administration (EDA) bogged down in Congress for the second year in a row. EDA operated programs to encourage economic growth in many areas of the country.

The House July 12 voted 306-113 to extend EDA through fiscal 1986 as part of a broader bill (HR 10 — H Rept 98-52, Parts I and II) that also extended the Appalachian Regional Commission (ARC), an organization that promoted anti-poverty and highway programs in 13 states.

The Senate did not act on a substantially different economic development measure (S 724 — S Rept 98-94) that also authorized funding for youth jobs programs. *(Youth jobs, p. 667)*

The Reagan administration had tried since taking office to abolish EDA. Legal authority for the agency had expired Sept. 30, 1982, but Congress nonetheless provided funds to keep it operating. *(Previous action, p. 115)*

Funding

Although the 98th Congress never completed action on EDA reauthorization legislation, Congress in 1984 included $228.5 million for the agency in a fiscal 1985 appropriations bill (PL 98-411) for the Commerce Department and other agencies. Other fiscal 1985 appropriations legislation (PL 98-360) provided $49 million for ARC regional development programs, which Reagan wanted to abolish, and $100 million for the Appalachian highway system.

Chrysler Success Story

Proponents of a national industrial policy cited Chrysler Corp.'s remarkable turnaround as proof that the government has a useful role to play in industry.

At the end of 1979 the company was on the verge of collapse. The sharp increase in gasoline prices that followed the Iranian oil embargo had saddled it with an enormous unsold inventory of big, gas-guzzling cars. It was projecting cash shortfalls of more than $2 billion.

Enter Congress, which agreed to guarantee $1.5 billion in loans for the ailing firm, provided certain conditions were met. The United Auto Workers Union had to give up $462 million in pay raises, company suppliers chipped in $180 million, state and local governments gave $250 million, and the company's banks provided $500 million in new loans and negotiated debt. *(Congress and the Nation Vol. V, p. 280)*

The package was unprecedented in the history of federal assistance to private companies, both because of its size and because of the stringent and detailed conditions it included. In 1971 Congress had approved up to $250 million in federal loan guarantees to help Lockheed Aircraft Corp., a major defense contractor, avoid bankruptcy. *(Lockheed guarantee, Congress and the Nation Vol. III, p. 233)*

The plan enabled Chrysler Chairman Lee A. Iacocca to conduct a massive reorganization without going into bankruptcy courts. The company cut its work force almost in half, cut its productive capacity by a third, cut costs, and concentrated its energy on a new line of small, fuel-efficient cars.

So successful was the rescue effort that a leaner Chrysler was able to pay off its federally backed loans in 1983, seven years before they were due. The company posted a record $700.9 million profit for the year.

Defense Production/Stimulus

Unable to complete action on Defense Production Act reauthorization legislation, Congress in 1983 enacted two stopgap extensions of the law, which gave the president various powers to ensure the health of defense-related industries.

The first extension (HR 2112 — PL 98-12), cleared March 24, renewed the act for six months, through Sept. 30, 1983. Congress had voted a previous stopgap extension in 1982.

A further six-month extension, until March 30, 1984, was included in a complex supplemental appropriations bill (HR 3959 — PL 98-181) cleared Nov. 18.

That temporary extension of the Defense Production Act became necessary when the Senate and House failed to reach agreement on a longer-term measure (S 1852) passed by the Senate Sept. 30 and the House Oct. 6. Congress completed action on S 1852 in 1984. *(1984 action, below)*

Earlier in the year the House Banking Committee included a three-year extension of the Defense Production Act in a $2.9 billion defense-related economic stimulus bill reported in May (HR 2782 — H Rept 98-110, Parts I and II).

There was no further action on the stimulus bill, a scaled-down version of a measure that had run into trouble in 1982. *(1982 action, p. 116)*

1984

Defense Production

Congress April 10 cleared a bill (S 1852 — PL 98-265) reauthorizing the Defense Production Act through Sept. 30, 1986. A previous extension expired March 30.

Under the act the president had the power to offer financial incentives to ensure adequate supplies of material and minerals vital to defense production.

S 1852 gave Congress new oversight authority over the president's powers to authorize loans and loan guarantees to defense-related industries. And, for the first time since the law was enacted in 1950, the president was required to determine that defense projects covered by the act were essential to national defense. In addition, the legislation required 60 days' notice to Congress before new projects went forward.

The administration had sought a five-year extension of the existing law without the added restrictions.

Congress completed action on S 1852 April 10, when the House adopted the conference report (H Rept 98-651) on the bill. The Senate had approved the report April 5. Both chambers originally had passed the bill in 1983. *(1983 action, this page; 1981-82, pp. 115, 116)*

Industrial Policy

Legislation to establish a national industrial policy was approved by two House committees but went no further in the 98th Congress.

A measure (HR 4360) to establish a Bank for Industrial Competitiveness, a Council for Industrial Competitiveness and a Federal Industrial Mortgage Association (FIMA) won the approval of both the House Banking Committee and the House Energy and Commerce Committee in 1984. The legislation had been the subject of hearings held in November 1983.

The bank was designed to make loan guarantees and purchase stock to help finance industrial modernization. It was slated to receive $8.5 billion in federal funds over 10 years. The council was to have been a board of government, business and labor leaders to coordinate government industrial policy, while FIMA would establish a wider market for industrial mortgages to help small and medium-sized firms that needed capital. HR 4360 was approved by the Banking Committee April 24 and the Commerce Committee June 6 (H Rept 98-697, Parts I and II).

A second industrial policy measure (HR 4361 — H Rept 98-693, Part I) was reported by the Banking Committee, also on April 24. It called for a $500 million authorization over four years for an Advanced Technology Foundation to fund applied scientific research.

Industrial policy legislation had been reported in the Senate in 1983, but no further action was taken.

Although industrial policy legislation made little headway in the 98th Congress, the concept influenced several trade bills, including a steel plan enacted as part of omnibus 1984 trade legislation (HR 3398 — PL 98-573). That plan linked the president's authority to enforce voluntary restraints on steel imports with steel makers' efforts to modernize and retrain workers. *(Trade bill, p. 109)*

Enterprise Zones

President Reagan's proposal to provide tax breaks for businesses that located in designated "enterprise zones" in inner cities and rural areas failed to become law for the third year in a row.

The plan, intended to bring jobs and development to decaying areas, had been included by the Senate in its version of 1984 deficit reduction legislation (HR 4170 — PL 98-369). It was dropped in conference with the House. The proposal would have authorized the secretary of housing and urban development to name up to 25 zones for three years; businesses locating in the zones would be eligible for a variety of tax and regulatory relief. *(Deficit reduction, p. 56)*

Senate Finance Committee Chairman Robert Dole, R-Kan., reintroduced the proposal as a separate bill (S 2914), but it did not reach the floor before adjournment.

Reagan, charging that House Democrats had refused to consider the plan, wrote House Minority Whip Trent Lott, R-Miss., in September asking the House to consider enterprise zones. Lott, however, was unable to bring it to the House floor.

Although he first proposed creating an enterprise zone program in 1982, Reagan had been unable to persuade Congress to enact it. The Senate twice before had approved legislation. In 1983 it attached the plan to an interest withholding bill, but the provision was dropped in conference with the House. In 1982 the Senate included it in a tax bill that died. *(Previous action, p. 117)*

The House Ways and Means Committee held hearings but never acted on the plan, which was opposed by some

majority members of the panel and its chairman.

Critics doubted that the tax incentives would create new jobs in the zones, a point also raised by a Congressional Research Service evaluation of the proposal.

And they questioned the propriety of giving businesses tax breaks that would reduce federal revenues at a time of high deficits. According to the Senate Finance Committee, the tax breaks would cost $1.3 billion in lost revenues over three years.

To the president, enterprise zones represented a break with the old-line federal programs of heavy subsidies and central planning. It was the ideal urban program, from the administration's point of view, entailing minimum federal involvement and maximum private sector incentives.

Many urban groups backed the plan. However, they warned that it would not make up for administration cuts in housing, job and economic development programs.

The Senate-passed plan would have required potential sites to be nominated by state and local governments according to criteria of economic distress and population. Also, local governments would be required to make a commitment to remove impediments to economic development, such as cutting red tape or making street improvements.

Businesses that located in zones would be eligible for tax relief, including extra investment credit for capital costs.

3

Foreign Policy

Introduction   *123*
1981 Chronology   *129*
1982 Chronology   *144*
1983 Chronology   *155*
1984 Chronology   *169*
Central America   *181*
Middle East   *191*

Foreign Policy

President Reagan entered office in 1981 proclaiming that the Soviet Union was the root of much of the world's troubles, and that containing Soviet misdeeds required firm U.S. resolve backed up by renewed military strength.

Reagan discovered in his first term that not all evil could be traced directly to Moscow, and that tough talk and an unprecedented peacetime military buildup by Washington did not guarantee peace and stability.

Nevertheless, Reagan was able to get the United States through four years with only one major foreign policy disaster — the retreat from Lebanon in the wake of terrorist bombings. Considering the failures of his recent predecessors, ranging from Vietnam to Iran, that was no mean accomplishment. The president and his aides proudly proclaimed that no country went communist or was invaded by the Soviet Union during his watch — a direct reference to the Nicaraguan revolution and invasion of Afghanistan during Jimmy Carter's sole term in office.

Neither did Reagan score any major foreign policy successes, measured in the usual manner of significant treaties signed or diplomatic chills thawed. The United States brokered only one important international agreement — the May 1983 troop pullout accord between Israel and Lebanon. But Lebanon abrogated that agreement a year later when Syria shouldered aside the United States as the leading outside influence in Lebanon.

A certain, if unmeasurable, accomplishment was the renewal of a clear sense of purpose for most U.S. policies in the world. Allies and adversaries alike seemed to appreciate Reagan's forthright stand on most issues and his eagerness to assert the U.S. leadership of the non-communist world.

The tangible success of which Reagan seemed proudest was the invasion of Grenada in October 1983. Advertised as a "rescue mission" to save American medical students from the internecine battles of a Marxist regime, the invasion was Reagan's clearest possible statement that the United States would act decisively to root out communism whenever it cropped up in the Western Hemisphere.

As Grenada demonstrated, Reagan did not flinch from using military force to achieve foreign policy objectives — an attitude that brought mixed reactions from Congress.

A clear majority on Capitol Hill backed the stationing of Marines in Lebanon (until the loss of life became unacceptable) and the invasion of Grenada. Congress also made no move to halt Reagan's escalation of U.S. arms sales throughout the world or his use of large-scale military exercises to harass the Nicaraguan government; arms sales and exercises did not involve actual fighting.

Congress directly challenged Reagan on only one military campaign: the funding of guerrillas, called "contras," who were battling to oust the leftist government of Nicaragua. Reagan at first portrayed U.S. backing of the contras as a limited tactic to block Nicaragua's arms shipments to leftist guerrillas in neighboring El Salvador. But when it became clear that the administration was using the contras to rid itself of an unpleasant government in Nicaragua, Congress balked and, in 1984, cut off U.S. involvement in that war.

The debate over the use of force raged as much within the administration as between the White House and Capitol Hill. As an outgrowth of the Lebanon experience, Secretary of State George P. Shultz and Defense Secretary Caspar W. Weinberger disputed the conditions under which the military should be sent into combat. Shultz appeared to argue for a liberal use of the military to support diplomatic missions, as in Lebanon. But Weinberger, in November 1984, suggested strict conditions that should be met for the use of force overseas; most seemed to apply the lessons of Vietnam and Lebanon.

The Reagan administration also seemed divided on how to respond to terrorism. The talk in Washington was tough: Reagan said the United States would never surrender to terrorist threats, and Shultz suggested the need for pre-emptive strikes against terrorists, even if innocent civilians could be hurt. But the United States was able to respond with little more than rhetoric to three brutal terrorist attacks on U.S. installations in Lebanon. And Reagan's February 1984 retreat from Lebanon was in recognition of the powers the terrorists held.

The administration's rhetoric and deeds were more consistent on human rights, an issue that had been at the forefront of Carter's foreign policy. Reagan said the United States would use "quiet diplomacy" to promote respect for human rights in authoritarian societies, in contrast to Carter's loud denunciations of dictatorships of both the right and left.

References

Discussion of foreign policy for the years 1945-64 may be found in *Congress and the Nation Vol. I*, pp. 91-232; for the years 1965-68, *Congress and the Nation Vol. II*, pp. 52-116; for the years 1969-72, *Congress and the Nation Vol. III*, pp. 853-948; for the years 1973-76, *Congress and the Nation Vol. IV*, pp. 847-912; for the years 1977-80, *Congress and the Nation Vol. V*, pp. 31-95.

Foreign Policy

True to his word, Reagan's human rights diplomacy was quiet — when aimed at countries whose governments were friendly to the United States, such as Chile, South Africa, the Philippines, South Korea, El Salvador and Guatemala. Reagan was less restrained toward communist countries, speaking of the Soviet Union as the "evil empire" and of the Sandinista-led regime in Nicaragua as a "brutal dictatorship."

Congressional Role

During the first Reagan term Congress never lacked for something to do in its role of reacting to presidential foreign policy initiatives. Reagan's activist approach to the world's troubles meant that Congress was constantly responding to new initiatives. Reagan's policies were especially controversial in Congress because most seemed to involve the use of military force, either directly, as with the stationing of Marines in Lebanon, or indirectly, as with the U.S.-financed guerrilla war against Nicaragua.

Congress picked at the Reagan program but was unable to force any fundamental changes of direction. By curbing some of Reagan's options, Congress may have had a moderating influence on his actions, particularly in Central America. The congressional cuts in military aid for El Salvador and hesitation in funding the Nicaraguan contras forced the administration to curb its expectations for quick military victories and may have forced a greater use of diplomacy.

Reagan repeatedly complained about congressional restraints, but few were imposed that prevented him from doing what he wanted. When Congress made its annual cuts in military aid to El Salvador, Reagan often responded by invoking his own presidential powers to give the aid anyway. When Congress balked at aid for the contras, Reagan kept coming back for more and then encouraged private aid through conservative activist groups.

Congress forced Reagan to back away from a confrontation only once, in April 1984, when he withdrew a proposed arms sale to Jordan. But that surrender appeared motivated largely by election-year politics and by the administration's unhappiness with anti-U.S. statements by Jordan's King Hussein. Reagan almost certainly could have rammed the sale through Congress if he wanted; no president had ever lost a battle with Congress on such an issue.

The Supreme Court's 1983 ruling striking down legislative vetoes appeared to herald a shift in the structural balance of power between Congress and the executive branch. In the field of foreign policy, the ruling took away Congress' right to veto arms sales and to force the withdrawal of U.S. armed forces from foreign hostilities. But in the immediate wake of the court decision, the loss of the legislative veto made no discernible difference in Congress' impact on foreign policy. Congress had never used the veto power, other than as a threat to extract concessions for the president, and Reagan was able to get what he wanted from Congress without provoking confrontations in which the legislative veto could have come into play.

Reagan also gave de facto recognition to the congressional role in the stationing of U.S. forces overseas by signing a resolution in September 1983 authorizing him to keep Marines in a Lebanese peacekeeping force for up to 18 months. That was the first real use of the War Powers Resolution since its enactment in 1973; it came just three months after the Supreme Court invalidated Congress' right, under the resolution, to withdraw troops from foreign hostilities by passing a concurrent resolution.

One of the congressional restraints that Reagan complained about most often actually was imposed by his own administration. In 1981, in response to concern on Capitol Hill about the potential for a U.S. military escalation in El Salvador, the Pentagon set a limit of 55 military trainers there. Congress never put the limit in law, and it was unclear whether a move to do so would have made it through Congress and past a likely presidential veto. Nevertheless, the administration abided by the 55-trainer limit as if it were in law and and made no move to change it.

Central America

With brief interludes, Central America was the dominant U.S. foreign policy issue during the first Reagan term. In no other part of the world did Reagan move with such vigor, and in no other area did his policies encounter such sustained opposition from Congress and the public.

The basic elements of Reagan's policies were simple: firm support for pro-U.S. governments in El Salvador, Costa Rica, Honduras and Guatemala, and unrelenting opposition to the leftist government of Nicaragua, which Reagan charged was the key to instability in the region. But the tools that Reagan used to implement his policies were many and complex, and to the extent those tools symbolized the policies, they served as the ground for executive-congressional battles.

Within weeks of entering office, Reagan took two steps that set the course for his actions in Central America. Using his executive authority, he shipped $20 million in military aid to El Salvador to prop up the military-civilian junta against a rapidly growing leftist insurgency, and he cut off the final installments of the Carter administration's program of economic aid to Nicaragua.

By the end of Reagan's first term, U.S. aid to Central America exceeded $1 billion per year, and the United States was the key supporter of a 15,000-man guerrilla force that was seeking to overthrow the Nicaraguan government.

Reagan's critics had little argument with his ultimate aims of promoting peace and democracy in the region. Few in Congress openly supported the Salvadoran guerrillas or were sympathetic toward the Sandinistas in Nicaragua. There also was little disagreement with the president's contention that Cuba and the Soviet Union were using Nicaragua to foment unrest in the rest of Central America, especially El Salvador.

The opposition to Reagan policy was founded on several beliefs: that the United States no longer could or should attempt to shape Central America in its own image; that the region's troubles were more likely to be resolved over the long term through negotiation than through war; and that Reagan was more interested in backing the old Latin elites (landowners and the military) than in promoting true democracy and economic reform.

Emboldening the congressional critics were public opinion polls showing that Americans opposed Reagan's interventionist policies out of fear that Central America might become another Vietnam.

Because Congress had little control over the fundamental direction of U.S. policies, opponents in Congress resorted to fighting a guerrilla war against foreign aid and other tools that Reagan used to carry out his policies. At times debates in Congress centered not so much on broad U.S. goals in the region as on such questions as whether El

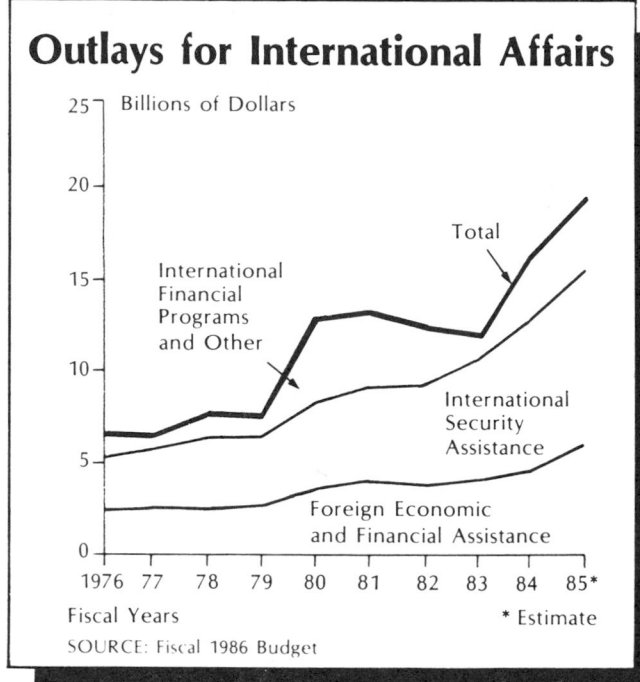

Outlays for International Affairs

Billions of Dollars

25 —
20 —
15 —
10 —
5 —
0 —

Total

International Financial Programs and Other

International Security Assistance

Foreign Economic and Financial Assistance

1976 77 78 79 80 81 82 83 84 85*

Fiscal Years   * Estimate

SOURCE: Fiscal 1986 Budget

Salvador should receive an additional $40 million or $70 million in military aid. Congress' lack of faith in the administration resulted in the drafting of restrictions on El Salvador's aid that were the most detailed in the history of the U.S. foreign aid program.

During the first three years of the Reagan administration, El Salvador was the key Central American issue in Washington. Reagan offered unqualified backing to a succession of reformist governments, all of which were under attack from mountain-based guerrillas on the left and shadowy death squads on the right.

As the policy evolved, the administration developed the concept that the United States needed to give military aid to the Salvadoran government as a "shield" against guerrilla attack. At the same time the United States would quietly encourage economic and political reforms that would improve the stability and legitimacy of the government in the eyes of the Salvadoran people.

Reagan flatly opposed all suggestions that the United States press for negotiations between the Salvadoran government and the guerrillas — especially negotiations that would give the guerrillas a share of power without their having participated in elections.

The administration also was decidedly cool toward broader negotiations to resolve Central America's troubles. It refused direct involvement in talks sponsored by Colombia, Mexico, Panama and Venezuela (the four "Contadora" countries, named after the Panamanian island where the talks began in 1983). In September 1984, when the Contadora countries presented a draft agreement calling for a regionwide demilitarization, the administration objected that the burden would fall unfairly on pro-U.S. countries, leaving Nicaragua to dominate its neighbors.

Reagan's critics attacked his El Salvador policy at its weakest point: the administration's reluctance to admit that successive governments in San Salvador were unwilling or unable to control human rights abuses by military and paramilitary forces. Starting in late 1981 Congress

barred U.S. military aid to El Salvador unless the president certified that the government was curtailing the death squads and taking other steps to protect human rights. The certification reports became semiannual events in 1982 and 1983, with human rights groups charging that little had changed in El Salvador and the administration claiming dramatic reductions in the number of civilians killed, kidnapped or injured by security forces.

The human rights reports fueled the annual struggles between Congress and the administration over the amount of military aid to be provided in El Salvador. Reagan dramatically escalated his requests for aid. When Congress made cuts, Reagan used his executive authority to give El Salvador what he wanted or returned to Congress with follow-up requests that kept the cycle going.

In 1984 El Salvador held its first free presidential elections in 50 years; the winner was José Napoleón Duarte, a centrist who reportedly had won presidential elections in 1972 only to be denied office by the military. Duarte defeated Roberto d'Aubuisson, a rightist widely alleged to have close ties to the death squads.

With Duarte's election, and his subsequent appeals for U.S. support, congressional resistance to aiding El Salvador all but vanished. In a series of steps after the election, Congress for the first time voted nearly all the aid Reagan had requested for that country and imposed only symbolic restrictions on how it could be spent.

Even as El Salvador was fading as an issue, the U.S.-backed guerrilla war against Nicaragua was becoming a more serious point of contention between Reagan and Congress.

Reagan launched the war in November 1981, authorizing the CIA to recruit and train some 500 Nicaraguan exiles to harass the government and attempt to block arms shipments from Nicaragua to the rebels in El Salvador. By 1982 the "covert action" had mushroomed into a full-scale war involving several thousand guerrillas. Inevitably, the U.S. role became public knowledge when the guerrillas invited reporters and television crews along on their campaigns.

Congressional concern about the scope and management of the war escalated almost as rapidly as the fighting itself. In 1982 Congress barred the CIA from attempting to overthrow the Nicaraguan regime. In 1983, after the House voted twice to suspend U.S. aid to the contras, Congress set a $24 million limit on the aid — about half of what Reagan wanted to spend. And in 1984, when Reagan sought to have the $24 million cap lifted, Congress instead halted all aid to the contras.

The aid cutoff was spurred by revelations in February 1984 that the CIA had supervised the mining of several Nicaraguan harbors, and had not notified the Senate and House Intelligence committees in advance.

Reagan's one bold gamble to silence congressional criticism of his Central American policies fell flat on its face. In 1983, at the suggestion of Sen. Henry M. Jackson, D-Wash., and other moderates, Reagan named a commission to study the region's problems and suggest options for U.S. policy. Former Secretary of State Henry A. Kissinger was named chairman.

The commission's report, delivered in January 1984, failed to quiet the debate, largely because the commission itself was divided. Although the report backed the general goals of U.S. policy toward the region, individual members differed sharply on such key issues as the war in Nicaragua and the best way of promoting human rights in El Salvador. Congress enacted only minor parts of the commission's

bold $8.8 billion, six-year plan for economic and development aid to Central America.

Middle East

Reagan appeared to have no clear goals or established agenda for the other conflict-ridden area of the world — the Middle East.

His administration went through periods of frantic involvement in Middle East issues, followed by interludes of passivity and seeming unconcern about the region. When the administration chose to intervene in the Middle East, it did so in a big way, prompting two of its greatest foreign policy struggles with Congress, on the sale of AWACS radar planes to Saudi Arabia and the assignment of Marines to a peacekeeping force in Lebanon.

The AWACS battle was the highlight in a period, from January 1981 to mid-1982, of U.S. detachment from the struggles of the Middle East. Reagan declined, during that period, to follow President Carter's lead in actively promoting peace talks between Israel and Arab nations.

As part of a campaign for "strategic consensus" in the region, Reagan did carry out Carter's implied promise to sell the Saudis five sophisticated AWACS planes, along with equipment to upgrade F-15 warplanes that Carter had sold in 1978.

After a fierce lobbying campaign, Reagan pushed the AWACS sale through Congress in October 1981, defeating the powerful pro-Israel lobby in the Senate by only four votes.

Reagan then turned his attention away from the Middle East, only to have it abruptly shifted back by the Israeli invasion of Lebanon in June 1982.

With Israel occupying southern Lebanon, Reagan twice sent Marines to Beirut as part of multinational peacekeeping forces. The first time was for a few weeks in August and September 1982, when the role of the outsiders was to monitor the evacuation from Beirut of thousands of guerrilla fighters belonging to the Palestine Liberation Organization.

The second assignment of Marines to Lebanon was originated by one tragedy and ended by the aftermath of another.

On Sept. 16, 1982, shortly after the Marines were withdrawn from their first assignment, rightist Christian forces entered two Palestinian refugee camps in Beirut and slaughtered hundreds of men, women and children. Reagan immediately sent some 1,200 Marines back to Lebanon, along with special forces from Great Britain, France and Italy. That mission was peaceful for nearly a year, and the United States launched a massive aid program to bolster the government of Lebanese President Amin Gemayal.

In August and September 1983 radical Moslem militia groups began isolated attacks on the Marines, prompting calls in Congress for Reagan to withdraw from the peacekeeping force.

The president refused but, under pressure from Democrats in the House, did agree to passage of a congressional resolution invoking the War Powers act and authorizing him to keep the Marines in Lebanon for 18 months. Speaker Thomas P. O'Neill Jr., D-Mass., personally pushed that resolution through the House, telling his colleagues that supporting the president on the issue was their patriotic duty. The resolution barely made it through the Senate, where Democrats overwhelmingly opposed it as a blank check that allowed Reagan to keep the Marines in indefensible positions with no clear military mission.

On Oct. 23, 1983, a terrorist driving a truck packed with thousands of pounds of explosives plowed into Marine headquarters at the Beirut airport, setting off a blast that killed more than 240 Americans. From that moment congressional support for Reagan's policy in Lebanon was shattered, and it was only a matter of time before the president would be forced to reverse course.

In February 1984, with House Democrats readying to pass a resolution calling for the prompt withdrawal of the Marines and with Moslem militiamen seizing control of West Beirut, Reagan suddenly ordered the Marines "redeployed" to offshore ships. Within a few months, the Marines and the ships were withdrawn entirely from Lebanon and the United States ended its experiment in building a cohesive government in Lebanon.

Perhaps more than any other issue, the Lebanon experience illustrated Reagan's primary strength in dealing with Congress: He fought relentlessly for his position but, when faced with strong opposition, would suddenly agree to a compromise or switch tactics, thereby confusing his opponents and appearing to demonstrate leadership.

By withdrawing the Marines before Congress forced him to do so, Reagan defused a politically dangerous issue and could take credit for acting boldly. Although the Lebanon episode was widely described as the worst disaster for U.S. foreign policy since the Iranian hostage crisis of 1979-80, public opinion polls later showed that few Americans blamed Reagan for what had happened to the Marines.

U.S.-Soviet Relations

As the most anti-communist president in recent history, Reagan excoriated the Soviet Union almost daily. But Reagan's actions were not as consistent as his words, and he allowed domestic and international politics to override his ideological inclination for Kremlin-bashing.

One of Reagan's first major actions as president was to lift the grain embargo that President Carter had imposed on the Soviet Union after the invasion of Afghanistan. He had opposed the embargo in a 1980 campaign promise to farmers. And, under pressure from the European allies and Congress, Reagan in 1982 abandoned an effort to deny the Soviet Union equipment for construction of a huge natural gas pipeline.

According to his rhetoric, Reagan should have been the foremost American advocate of "linkage" — the practice of punishing the Soviet Union for misbehavior and rewarding it for actions approved by the United States. But Reagan avoided putting action behind the rhetoric of linkage. He took no steps to punish the Soviets for the occupation of Afghanistan, other than boosting U.S. aid to fundamentalist Moslem rebels there, and he never did follow through on an early pledge by Secretary of State Alexander M. Haig Jr. to "go to the source" of Soviet-inspired revolutions in Central America. When the Soviet Union employed its own linkage — breaking off nuclear arms control talks in 1983 following the deployment of U.S. missiles in Europe — Reagan did not retaliate.

Aside from the ideological gulf, the greatest stumbling block to U.S.-Soviet relations was the fact that for much of Reagan's first term Moscow's leadership was in transition. President Leonid I. Brezhnev died in November 1982, after a long illness, and was succeeded by Yuri V. Andropov, who himself became ill in late 1983 and died in February 1984. Andropov's successor, Konstantin U. Chernenko, appeared to have little impact; he died in March 1985.

First-Term Secretaries of State: Haig, Shultz

In selecting the two men who served as secretary of state in his first administration, President Reagan turned to old Washington hands.

His initial choice was Alexander M. Haig Jr., a retired general and former NATO commander who had served as a top aide in the Nixon White House. When Haig resigned abruptly in mid-1982, Reagan tapped George P. Shultz, a former Nixon Cabinet official and veteran foreign policy adviser.

Alexander M. Haig Jr.

Reagan's choice of Haig was controversial from the start. Haig's reputation as a brilliant public servant had been clouded with questions about his role in Vietnam, wiretapping during the Nixon administration and the Watergate affair. *(Haig background, p. 1023)*

During five days of confirmation hearings before the Senate Foreign Relations Committee, Haig forcefully defended his conduct under Nixon and demonstrated a broad grasp of foreign policy issues. The Senate, with little dissent, confirmed his nomination to be secretary of state on Jan. 21, 1981. The vote was 93-6.

Haig resigned on June 25, 1982, after serving less than a year and a half in the post. In his resignation letter he complained that the administration was "shifting" from what he described as a "careful course" of foreign policy.

The volatile Haig had fought a long series of battles with other high administration officials, particularly Defense Secretary Caspar W. Weinberger, over foreign policy issues. A week before Haig's resignation Weinberger won a long intramural dispute over economic sanctions against the Soviet Union. Reagan decided to toughen the sanctions in an effort to delay construction of a pipeline from Siberia to Western Europe. Haig reportedly opposed the decision, saying it would merely alienate European allies and would do little to actually block construction of the pipeline.

Haig also had been forced to the mat to secure congressional approval, over the opposition of Senate conservatives, of several key State Department appointees.

Early in his tenure, Haig's actions in the aftermath of the March 30, 1981, assassination attempt on Reagan raised questions about his future role in the administration and about whether his effectiveness as the administrations's foreign policy spokesman had been compromised. Haig added to the initial confusion about who was running the country in the hours after the shooting by making a nationally televised statement in which he said, "As of now, I am in control here at the White House, pending return of

the vice president, and in close touch with him." *(Assassination attempt, p. 847)*

George P. Shultz

President Reagan chose Shultz, an informal foreign policy adviser, to succeed Haig. Acting rapidly because of crises in the Middle East and U.S.-European relations, the Senate unanimously confirmed Shultz on July 15, 1982.

Shultz had served as secretary of the Treasury, secretary of labor and director of the Office of Management and Budget in the Nixon administration. At Treasury he was the top U.S. official in trade matters. Shultz served Reagan as campaign adviser on economics in 1980 and was a member of the economic policy team during the transition period after the 1980 election. He was president of Bechtel Group Inc., a worldwide construction and engineering firm at the time of his nomination. *(Shultz background, p. 1024)*

During confirmation hearings before the Senate Foreign Relations Committee, Shultz' calm, secure approach contrasted sharply with Haig's combative, mercurial manner. Shultz proposed no dramatic departures from policies Haig pursued, but he set out and defended his views in a judicious style that clearly soothed committee Democrats who were uneasy with Haig.

Shultz cast himself as a modest team player. Haig claimed to be Reagan's foreign policy "vicar," and was famed for jealous jousting over policy turf with other administration officials.

Shultz pledged that his views on the Middle East would not be colored by his experience at Bechtel, which he had joined in 1974. One of Bechtel's major clients was Saudi Arabia, and Shultz had developed a reputation for his expertise in Middle East affairs. Some senators had feared his years with Bechtel would lead him to favor the Arabs over Israel.

During his tenure as secretary of state Shultz gained influence among the president's advisers. Reports indicated a growing tension between Shultz and Defense Secretary Weinberger. Shultz and Weinberger at times seemed to be speaking for different administrations: the secretary of state advocating an activist approach to Third World conflicts and the secretary of defense counseling caution on the use of troops overseas.

Shultz led administration policy makers advocating the use of military troops in Lebanon and Grenada. Weinberger was reluctant to send troops to those areas. The two advisers reportedly differed on other issues as well, including arms control, the treatment of NATO allies and the extent of U.S. intervention in Central America.

Foreign Aid

Although Reagan represented a branch of the Republican Party that long had opposed foreign aid as a giveaway of the taxpayers' money, his conservative administration presided over the biggest onslaught of foreign aid spending since the postwar Marshall Plan.

Reagan played down the humanitarian and economic development aspects of foreign aid and emphasized its virtue as a relatively inexpensive means of advancing U.S. foreign policy and national security interests.

The most useful purpose of foreign aid, Reagan and his aides told Congress on numerous occasions, was to help strengthen the economies and armed forces of countries friendly to the United States. In his 1985 State of the Union address, Reagan said that "dollar for dollar, our security assistance contributes as much to global security as our own defense budget."

In 1981 Reagan's strategy succeeded in getting Congress for the first time in several years to pass both foreign aid authorization and appropriations bills. While Congress failed to pass regular foreign aid bills in each of the next three years, it did approve huge increases in aid as part of omnibus continuing appropriations resolutions.

Between 1981 and 1985 the total foreign aid budget increased by a third, from $10.6 billion to $14.3 billion. Nearly all of the increase was in direct military aid, used to help foreign countries buy U.S. weapons and military services, and in military-related aid that bolstered the economies of friendly countries with heavy defense burdens. The increases were most dramatic in countries such as El Salvador, but the upward trend extended even to countries in Africa and South America that traditionally had received little U.S. military aid.

At the same time Reagan pared back aid for long-term development programs — building schools, hospitals, bridges and the like — except in Central America, where he used development aid as a form of government support. The president also sought to shift the United States away from heavy contributions to the international development banks, such as the World Bank, in spite of a report prepared by his Treasury Department in 1982 that praised those institutions.

Politically, Reagan's aid buildup benefited from the virtual collapse after 1981 of the congressional process for writing foreign aid legislation.

When Congress passed separate foreign aid bills, as it was supposed to do, opponents often forced roll-call votes that highlighted individual issues and the amount of money that was being voted. But putting foreign aid in omnibus spending bills reduced its visibility and enabled the administration to focus its lobbying efforts on a handful of key members of the two Appropriations committees. The administration also was able to skirt the two aid authorizing committees, Senate Foreign Relations and House Foreign Affairs, which were dominated by liberals and moderates eager to make their own mark on U.S. foreign policy through the foreign aid process.

Chronology
Of Action
On Foreign Policy

1981

In their first year in office, President Reagan and his team delivered what they had implicitly promised — an America unafraid to upset adversaries and allies alike in the name of gaining renewed respect.

The administration assumed power vowing to get tough with the Soviet Union and other of America's nemeses, notably Cuba and Libya. It did — and U.S. relations with each of those nations became more and more testy as time went by.

But the price for confronting America's foes often proved to be discomfort or protest on the part of U.S. allies, many of whom did not share the Reagan view that the world's major problems flowed from communist or Libyan mischief.

Even relations with Israel declined as Prime Minister Menachem Begin, uneasy with administration efforts to woo Arab states into a "strategic consensus" against the Soviet Union, pursued increasingly aggressive policies that embarrassed the United States.

On the issue of human rights, the new administration rejected Carter's dedication to holding anti-communist authoritarian governments publicly accountable for their human rights records by withholding aid to those with unsuitable ones. Reagan said he would promote human rights through "quiet diplomacy" instead, relying on the carrot rather than the stick to foster liberty and justice.

The policy shift was greeted with suspicion by the president's critics and contributed to one of Reagan's few defeats in Congress — the withdrawal under pressure of his nominee as assistant secretary of state for human rights, Ernest W. Lefever.

In advocating large increases in military aid and arms sales to friendly nations early in the year, Reagan was charged with failing to develop his own guidelines and goals on arms transfers before dropping Carter's, which had attempted to discourage them.

Reagan's political opponents were galvanized by administration plans to step up military aid to El Salvador and to sell sophisticated Airborne Warning and Control System (AWACS) radar planes to Saudi Arabia.

Congress stopped short of undercutting Reagan's support for the centrist junta in El Salvador, in the end doing nothing more than setting conditions on further U.S. aid.

The opposition was far stronger on the AWACS sale, which led to a bitter battle in Congress that Reagan barely won. A congressional veto of the plan to sell AWACS to the Saudis was avoided only through Reagan's personal lobbying of the Senate.

The president won another foreign policy victory when he invested his prestige in a fight to get two foreign aid bills through Congress. His efforts helped win passage of the first regular aid appropriations bill since 1978.

AWACS Sale to Saudi Arabia

President Reagan narrowly won the first major test of his authority in foreign policy Oct. 28 when the Senate, in a **key 48-52 vote (R 12-41; D 36-11)**, rejected a resolution to disapprove the sale to Saudi Arabia of five Airborne Warning and Control System (AWACS) radar planes and other arms.

A majority of each house would have had to approve the veto resolution (H Con Res 194) for it to take effect under a 1976 law that gave Congress the right to veto major arms sales. Congress had 30 days after receiving formal notice of the $8.5 billion sale on Oct. 1 to do so. On Oct. 14, by a **key 301-111 vote (R 108-78; D 193-33)**, the House had overwhelmingly adopted the resolution of disapproval. *(1981 key votes, p. 879)*

The Senate vote to allow the sale preserved Congress' record of never having used its arms sale veto power, though the threat of a veto had forced previous administrations to alter the terms of other weapons deals. In 1983 the Supreme Court held that legislative veto provisions were unconstitutional. *(Story, p. 833)*

The Senate vote on AWACS was a stunning victory for Reagan because 50 senators — one less than the majority needed to block the sale — had cosponsored the resolution of disapproval. In the end, Reagan won by persuading seven first-term GOP senators among those cosponsors to switch their positions.

The debate, which began in earnest in the spring, had centered on fears that Saudi Arabia might use the AWACS against Israel in concert with other Arab nations or might fail to guard the AWACS' secrets from falling into unfriendly hands.

Israel strongly opposed the AWACS sale, viewing it as a threat to Israeli air superiority in the region. The American Jewish community campaigned vigorously against the sale, and many members of Congress opposed it as a threat to Israel.

But in the final days before the issue was decided, the White House relentlessly portrayed the question as a matter of presidential power and prestige, arguing that Reagan would lose his credibility in Saudi Arabia and other foreign lands if the Senate scotched the deal.

That aspect was especially important because the AWACS sale had become the most visible symbol of Reagan's policy in the Middle East. The policy rested in large part on the U.S. ability to hold together a "strategic consensus" among nations that opposed Soviet adventurism in the region.

But in order to gain his victory, the president was forced at the eleventh hour to spend large amounts of political capital wooing senators whose support might have been gained much earlier. *(Lobbying, box, p. 130)*

Background

The AWACS sale had its origins in a study of Saudi military needs conducted by the U.S. Defense Department in 1974. Partly as a result of that study — coupled with the U.S. desire to develop closer ties with its largest supplier of imported oil — the United States began selling Saudi Arabia large quantities of weapons and weapons-related services.

From 1974 to mid-1981, Saudi Arabia contracted to buy $32.1 billion worth of weapons and services from the United States. Of that amount, $8.6 billion was for weap-

Administration Faulted on AWACS Lobbying

Although it won a victory on the Saudi arms sale, the Reagan administration was faulted for its lobbying tactics by a number of observers who said the White House, by maladroit handling of the issue, gave opponents of the sale a large head start, then had to invest precious political capital to catch up.

Specific criticisms ranged from the initial conception of the arms package to allegations, heatedly denied, of small favors bestowed on wavering senators.

But the most common objection was that the administration unnecessarily let the sale become a divisive referendum on Reagan's ability to conduct foreign policy.

"I know of no one on either side who does not think this has been grossly mishandled," said Sen. John Glenn, D-Ohio, who voted against the sale after unsuccessful efforts to negotiate a compromise.

Critics faulted the administration's conduct of the AWACS campaign on a number of points:

Conception. Many senators, including a number who supported the sale, said the administration failed from the outset to recognize the repercussions of the sale or to establish its place in an overall Mideast policy.

I. M. Destler, director of the Carnegie Endowment's Project on Executive-Congressional Relations in Foreign Policy, said that where the Saudi-U.S. relationship required nuance and delicacy, Reagan's decision to sell AWACS led to a massive public confrontation that "contradicts or cuts into the whole way we ought to be managing our relations with the Saudis."

Consultation. Several senators complained that the administration neglected to inform or consult with Congress as the deal was hatched.

"This whole exercise could have been prevented had there been proper consultation with the Congress," said AWACS opponent Sen. Claiborne Pell, D-R.I.

Coordination. Changes in the chairmanship of the interdepartmental committee handling the AWACS and bickering among the various departments hindered the administration's lobbying effort.

Timing. Rumors that AWACS would be sold to the Saudis circulated in March. The administration confirmed them in April. Months passed — and opposition hardened — before the administration did any lobbying on the package.

By the time Reagan himself became aggressively involved, in September, opponents of the sale had more than half of the Senate publicly on record as critical of the package. Moreover, several senators said, the president was not well-versed in particulars of the sale in his first few meetings with senators.

Bargaining. When Israeli Prime Minister Menachem Begin visited Reagan in September, the White House offered to establish a closer military partnership in the Mideast. Though the proposal was designed to mitigate Israeli objections to the AWACS sale, Reagan neglected to link the two issues. Begin promptly went to the press and renewed his attack on the Saudi sale.

Anti-Semitism Issue. Administration officials spoke of Jewish opposition to AWACS in ways that many Jews, and some senators, found offensive. The administration also raised the specter of Israeli meddling in U.S. policy and, more indirectly, the possibility of an anti-Jewish backlash if the sale failed.

Hyman Bookbinder, Washington representative for the American Jewish Committee, called such statements "tragic, poisonous," and said the administration "probably lost half of the new Jewish support they picked up in 1980."

Side Deals. Some critics said the deliberations were demeaned by a last-minute aura of horse-trading and news reports of instances where administration favors were bestowed on marginal senators. However, Reagan himself said that "there have been no deals made."

---

ons, ammunition, spare parts and equipment; the remaining $23.5 billion was for services, such as design and construction supervision of several new air, naval and army bases.

In 1978 Congress agreed after a bruising political battle to allow the sale to Saudi Arabia of 60 F-15 fighters, costing $2.5 billion; that was the first sale of the advanced warplanes to any country other than a close U.S. ally. The sale was part of a package, which included 50 F-5E planes for Egypt and 15 F-15s and 150 F-16 fighters for Israel. During debate on that sale, the Carter administration promised Congress that Saudi Arabia would not be sold sophisticated air surveillance aircraft, such as the E-2C

"Hawkeye" or the E-3A AWACS. *(Congress and the Nation Vol. V, p. 63)*

In October 1980, following the outbreak of war between Iran and Iraq, Carter sent four AWACS planes to Saudi Arabia, their mission to detect threats to the Saudi oil fields. Manned by American crews, those planes remained in Saudi Arabia through the rest of 1980 and all of 1981.

Reagan Proposals, Israeli Opposition

On Feb. 26, 1981, Reagan administration officials told congressional committees that the United States had

agreed to sell the Saudis advanced AIM-9L Sidewinder air-to-air missiles and long-range fuel tanks for their F-15s. The United States also had agreed "in principle" to sell Saudi Arabia tanker planes for mid-air refueling of the F-15s and a radar surveillance plane, possibly the AWACS. Those decisions were made public on March 6 by the State Department.

Opposition to the sale immediately mounted in Congress. Between March 24 and April 7, 44 senators and 78 House members made floor speeches denouncing the proposal.

During a Middle East trip April 3-9, Secretary of State Alexander M. Haig Jr. discussed the sale in Saudi Arabia and Israel. In an attempt to reduce Israeli opposition, Haig promised Israel an extra $300 million annually in military aid for fiscal years 1983 and 1984. That was to be in addition to the $1.4 billion in military grants and loans Israel already was receiving each year.

But Israeli Prime Minister Menachem Begin spurned Haig's arguments that the sale would not jeopardize Israel's security. Begin publicly told Haig April 6 that allowing Saudi Arabia to buy AWACS planes would present "a very serious threat to Israel."

Begin's statement prompted several American Jewish groups to start lobbying against the sale.

Nevertheless, on April 21 the White House announced that the United States would sell Saudi Arabia five AWACS planes in addition to the other equipment.

Under standard procedures for major arms sales, the administration officially notified Congress of the AWACS package sale in two steps: On Aug. 24, the Defense Department sent Congress an "informal notice" with details of the sale; that was followed Oct. 1 with the formal notice, which kicked off the 30-day period in which Congress could veto the sale.

The $8.5 billion package included the five AWACS planes, 101 sets of conformal fuel tanks for the Saudi F-15s, six to eight KC-707 fuel tanker aircraft, and 1,177 AIM-9L Sidewinder air-to-air missiles.

Defending the sale, administration officials said the AWACS planes were needed to improve Saudi Arabia's ability to defend its oil fields, to preserve Western access to Persian Gulf oil supplies, to guard against Soviet intrusions in the area, to show U.S. resolve to guarantee the region's security and to cement U.S.-Saudi ties.

Opponents responded that selling advanced weapons to the Saudis would aggravate regional tensions, forcing Israel to buy more arms. They said the Saudis did not need the AWACS for their own defense.

House Action

The administration sustained its first formal defeat on the issue Oct. 7 when the House Foreign Affairs Committee, by a 28-8 vote, approved H Con Res 194 (H Rept 97-268) to disapprove the entire AWACS sale package.

The committee vote demonstrated the difficulty of trying to gauge how members of Congress would approach the issue. The panel's chairman, Democrat Clement J. Zablocki, Wis., voted against the resolution, while ranking Republican William S. Broomfield, Mich., voted for it.

On Oct. 14, following a debate that repeated arguments that had been made for or against the sale for months, the House voted 301-111 to adopt the resolution disapproving the sale. The administration had made little effort to avert a defeat in that chamber.

Senate Action

The stage was set Oct. 15 for a Senate showdown on the issue, as the Senate Foreign Relations Committee adopted its disapproval resolution (S Con Res 37 — S Rept 97-249) by a 9-8 vote.

Despite the adverse vote for Reagan, there was evidence that White House lobbying and the president's pleas for support were having the desired effect on some senators. The committee vote was closer than many observers had expected.

The Foreign Relations Committee's action followed by a few hours the Senate Armed Services Committee's approval, on a 10-5 vote, of a report declaring the AWACS sale to be in the U.S. interest and no threat to Israel. Armed Services had no official role in considering the sale, but Chairman John Tower, R-Texas, wanted his panel to be on record favoring it.

The 48-52 Senate vote rejecting the resolution to veto the AWACS sale came at 5 p.m. on Oct. 28, following eight hours of debate.

As late as about two hours before the roll call, opponents, led by Republican Bob Packwood, Ore., and Democrat Alan Cranston, Calif., believed they could get the 51 votes needed to win. But a number of last-minute vote switches gave Reagan his foreign policy victory.

Development Banks

Authorizations for U.S. contributions to four international development banks and their affiliates were included in the omnibus reconciliation bill (HR 3982 — PL 97-35) that cleared Congress in July. The House Banking Committee had attached authorizations for the development banks, such as the World Bank, to the budget-cutting reconciliation bill in a political maneuver. Committee members argued that bank funding might not pass as a separate bill and that the only way to get the funding through Congress was to attach it to legislation certain to be passed. *(Reconciliation, p. 40)*

The World Bank and other multilateral development banks had been traditional targets of many Republicans, especially in the House, where conservative opposition killed one bank funding bill and substantially reduced another one in 1980. Moreover, conservative GOP members had reviled Democrats for years for supporting U.S. donations to multilateral banks, which they disliked on a variety of counts. During political campaigns, Democrats who had voted to contribute to the banks, or for other foreign aid, often were charged by Republican opponents with being spendthrift.

IDA, World Bank Funding

The international development banks posed an ironic political problem for the Reagan administration. As had happened previously, Republican President Reagan found himself asking conservative GOP members of Congress to alter their stance on one of their pet issues.

The major question was a proposed $3.24 billion authorization for the International Development Association (IDA). Known as the "soft loan window" of the World Bank, IDA was established to make loans at no interest to the poorest nations to help them develop their economies. IDA's donors had replenished its capital five times since it was founded in 1960.

In December 1979, after 18 months of negotiations, the United States agreed with 32 other donor nations to a sixth replenishment of $12 billion, known as IDA VI. The U.S. share of $3.24 billion was to have been made in three installments of $1.08 billion each. IDA VI was to have gone into effect on July 1, 1980, but Congress failed to authorize the U.S. share. The agreement could not go into effect without the United States.

Rather than let IDA run out of funds, other donors tided the bank over with a $1.6 billion "bridging arrangement," but those advance contributions were exhausted in April 1981.

The Reagan administration, intent on cutting federal spending, in March proposed stretching out the U.S. payments over fiscal 1981-83. The amounts in the annual appropriations could be altered without abrogating the U.S. commitment to IDA. But the $3.24 billion total pledge could not be cut without either breaching or renegotiating IDA VI.

The conference agreement (H Rept 97-208) on the reconciliation bill reduced the fiscal 1981 IDA contribution to $500 million, from the Reagan request of $540 million, and placed limits on future appropriations of $850 million in fiscal 1982 and $945 million in fiscal 1983. That meant that, at a minimum, a fourth installment of $945 million would be necessary to complete the $3.24 billion payment.

The reconciliation measure also authorized $8 billion for the U.S. share of a $40 billion General Capital increase (GCI) for the International Bank for Reconstruction and Development (IBRD), the World Bank agency that made loans at near-market interest rates. Under a January 1980 agreement, the GCI was to double — from $40 billion to $80 billion — the capital available to the IBRD. The intention was to allow the bank to increase its lending by 5 percent in real terms, after inflation, during the 1980s.

The U.S. share was to be 21.95 percent of the GCI, or $8,807,561,350. Only 7.5 percent of that amount, or $658.3 million, had to be appropriated as "paid-in capital." Reagan in March proposed appropriating that amount in six equal installments of $109.7 million each, beginning in fiscal 1982.

The remaining amount was "callable capital," similar to a loan guarantee. A separate appropriation would be required before any of that sum could be called.

If Congress had failed to authorize the U.S. pledge, the United States would have lost its veto over changes in the World Bank's charter.

Congressional debate on the issue came during a period of transition for the bank. Robert S. McNamara, bank president since 1968, retired in April, and was succeeded by A. W. Clausen, former president of BankAmerica Corp. *(1980 action on development banks, Congress and the Nation Vol. V, p. 87)*

Other Development Banks

Other development bank authorizations included in the reconciliation bill were:

● $360 million, the Reagan request, for a U.S. subscription to the African Development Bank.

● $275 million to restore a 10 percent cut Congress made in 1980 in a requested $2.7 billion U.S. donation to an $8 billion replenishment of the Inter-American Development Bank (IADB).

● $70 million to restore a 10 percent cut Congress made in 1980 in a requested $700 million U.S. donation to the

IADB's concessional lending facility, the Fund for Special Operations (FSO). The bill also authorized $15.7 million for fiscal 1982 to cover part of the $600 million U.S. share of a previous FSO replenishment.

● $67 million to make up a 15 percent cut Congress made in 1980 in a $445 million U.S. donation to the second replenishment of the Asian Development Fund, the concessional arm of the Asian Development Bank. The bill also authorized $14 million as partial payment of an overdue donation of $56 million to the fund's first replenishment, to which the United States pledged $180 million.

Foreign Aid Authorization

President Reagan won broadened control over U.S. foreign aid in a fiscal 1982 aid authorization bill (S 1196 — PL 97-113) cleared by Congress Dec. 16, but Congress refused simply to drop the controls on aid that gave it a policy-making role.

In an unusual two-year authorization, the bill provided $5.9 billion for fiscal 1982 and $5.96 billion for fiscal 1983. The president had requested $6.7 billion for fiscal 1982.

In S 1196, Reagan won a modified victory on one of his most urgent foreign policy initiatives — improving U.S. relations with Pakistan by embarking on a six-year, $3.2-billion economic and military aid program for that nation.

But the administration had to give up on another priority when it was forced to abandon its plea for the repeal of a law banning covert aid to warring factions in Angola. It did so to get Democrats to go along with lifting bans on arms sales or military aid to Argentina and Chile.

Although the administration's ambitious requests early in the year for large increases in military aid were whittled down substantially in the final version of S 1196, the bill took two steps toward reducing congressional involvement in reviewing overseas arms sales.

First, it doubled the thresholds for reporting individual arms sales to Congress. Under the bill, sales made through U.S. government channels had to be reported to Congress if they exceeded $14 million for a single item or $50 million for a package of items. Previous thresholds, established in 1976, had been $7 million and $25 million respectively.

The bill also reduced from 30 to 15 days the time Congress had to review and veto U.S. arms sales to NATO and its member countries, Japan, New Zealand and Australia. The provision also applied to sales of U.S. arms among those countries and transfers of U.S. equipment from those countries to other countries. In 1983 the Supreme Court ruled that the legislative veto device was unconstitutional. *(Story, p. 833)*

Senate, House Committee Reports

As reported by the Senate Foreign Relations Committee May 15 (S Rept 97-83), S 1196 authorized appropriations of $5.778 billion for fiscal 1982 bilateral foreign aid. The House committee bill (HR 3566 — H Rept 97-58), reported May 19, authorized spending $6.027 billion in fiscal 1982 and $6.216 billion in fiscal 1983.

Both bills generally approved the Reagan administration's emphasis on military-related aid at the expense of development assistance. And both bills substantially boosted the foreign aid authorization over the fiscal 1981 figure of $4.982 billion.

While each measure paid tribute to Reagan requests for greater executive control over the foreign aid dollar, each also reflected a continued congressional determination to keep a hand on the foreign policy tiller.

For example, both committees approved a Reagan request for repeal of a law prohibiting military aid or sales to Argentina. But each panel also said future aid or sales to that nation should be made only if the president could certify that the military government of Argentina had met certain conditions to atone in part for its poor human rights record.

Both panels placed conditions on military aid to El Salvador.

The two committees also reacted coolly to Reagan requests for foreign aid contingency funds unencumbered by congressional spending instructions. Each committee cut those requests; despite its Republican majority, the Senate committee was the more severe, deleting them.

Each committee also approved strict new controls over the president's power to lease defense equipment or services to foreign countries.

However, each also agreed to requests to ease controls on certain arms sales to major U.S. allies.

Senate Floor Action

The Senate broadly endorsed the Reagan administration view that more U.S. foreign aid must be spent to beef up America's allies militarily and less must go to help poor nations develop their economies.

In passing the foreign aid bill Oct. 22 by a 40-33 vote, the Senate also went along in general with administration insistence that the president needed a freer hand to use U.S. aid dollars as a policy tool.

While the Senate imposed conditions on U.S. aid to El Salvador, it gave the president broad leeway to decide whether those conditions had been met. Similarly, while providing for continued congressional participation in U.S. policy toward Angola, Argentina, Chile and Pakistan, the Senate agreed to lift bans imposed in the 1970s on U.S. military aid to those countries.

Moreover, the Senate agreed without debate to double the dollar thresholds at which arms sales must be reported to Congress and become subject to congressional veto. The Senate also doubled, from $50 million to $100 million, the value of military equipment the president could take from U.S. stocks and give to a foreign country in an emergency.

Despite sharp disagreements within the Senate over U.S. policy in a number of troubled regions of the world, the debate on S 1196 was less than contentious on most issues. Foreign Relations Committee Chairman Charles H. Percy, R-Ill., won compromises on many amendments that allowed them to be handled by voice vote.

House Floor Action

Heeding the pleas of their party's president and secretary of state, House Republicans who had been key foes of foreign aid in the past reluctantly helped pass the two-year foreign aid authorization bill Dec. 9. The vote was 222-184, with 97 Republicans joining 125 Democrats to form the majority.

Foreign aid authorization bills had been passed by the House in recent years only after bitter and lengthy debate. But in 1981, despite the underlying partisan tension, House leaders succeeded early on in their quest to glide over

F-16 Sale to Pakistan

Many foreign policy specialists and observers had seen in the administration's proposal to sell 40 F-16 warplanes to Pakistan the potential for a major battle between President Reagan and Congress.

The F-16s, costing $1.1 billion, were related to a $3.2 billion package of military and economic aid designed to bolster Pakistan in the wake of the Soviet occupation of neighboring Afghanistan.

Under the Arms Export Control Act (PL 94-329), Congress could have blocked the F-16 sale by adopting a concurrent resolution of disapproval within 30 days after formal notice of the sale was delivered on Oct. 23.

But the F-16 issue came on the heels of the debate over selling AWACS radar planes to Saudi Arabia, and many observers agreed that Congress had little taste for yet another confrontation with the president on arms sales. *(AWACS, p. 129)*

The F-16 sale won congressional approval when the Senate Foreign Relations and House Foreign Affairs committees rejected veto resolutions (S Con Res 48 and H Con Res 211, respectively).

The Senate panel voted against S Con Res 48 by a 7-10 vote Nov. 17. The same day, two House Foreign Affairs subcommittees disapproved H Con Res 211 but sent it to the full committee anyway. On Nov. 19, the full committee failed to approve the measure on a 13-13 tie vote.

James L. Buckley, under secretary of state for security assistance, had given Senate and House panels identical reasons why the administration thought it wise to sell Pakistan the F-16s.

Some members of Congress feared the administration's willingness to sell the planes to Pakistan and other nations would lead additional countries to expect the United States to sell the aircraft to them as well.

The administration was wary of that, Buckley said, but Pakistan should be an exception to a general policy of encouraging potential customers to buy other aircraft. He said the threat to Pakistan posed by the Soviet troops in Afghanistan warranted the sale. Buckley rejected arguments that the F-16 was a more sophisticated aircraft than Pakistan required to meet the Soviet threat in Afghanistan.

Critics of the sale also worried that it would upset the balance of power between Pakistan and India, which had been enemies ever since Pakistan was created by the 1947 partition of India in which India gained its independence from Britain. Pakistan and India were at war as recently as 1971. Buckley assured the panels that the balance of power would not be affected.

conflicts on the issues raised by the bill, and the spirit of comity seemed to gain momentum as the debate proceeded.

The measure was boosted by Secretary of State Alexander M. Haig Jr., who made an unusual appearance Dec. 8 before the House Republican Conference and urged GOP members to swallow their qualms and vote for foreign aid.

To stress the administration's interest, President Reagan had delivered the same message the previous evening at a White House meeting of 14 House Republican leaders.

Both Reagan and Haig portrayed foreign aid, especially military aid, as part of a needed U.S. defense build-up.

Conference, Final Action

After meeting Dec. 11 and Dec. 14, conferees filed their report (H Rept 97-413) on the aid bill Dec. 15. The Senate adopted the conference report Dec. 15 on a 55-42 vote, with 30 Republicans and 25 Democrats supporting it. The House cleared the bill by voice vote Dec. 16.

Pakistan. The administration's Pakistan aid package could not go forward without amendments to U.S. nuclear non-proliferation laws and was a major issue in the conference on S 1196.

Reagan proposed the aid program for Pakistan as a means of countering the Soviet presence in Afghanistan, which the Soviet Union had occupied since December 1979.

But aid to Pakistan had been barred since 1979 under a U.S. law that prohibited aid to nations dealing in nuclear fuel enrichment technology — which could be used to build nuclear weapons — outside international safeguards.

The law permitted the president to waive the aid ban if he could certify that he had "reliable assurances" the nation in question was not trying to develop nuclear weapons, but the administration had said it could not make that certification for Pakistan.

Conferees agreed to allow the president to waive the law banning aid to nations dealing in enrichment technology for Pakistan alone and only until Sept. 30, 1987 — the life of the six-year administration aid program. *(Arms sales to Pakistan, box, p. 133)*

Angola. The administration had wanted Congress to repeal a 1976 ban on covert aid to factions in the African nation of Angola — a law known as the Clark amendment.

The Senate had granted the request, but Democrats on the House Foreign Affairs Committee had refused to go along, arguing that it would raise the specter of U.S. intervention in Angola and torpedo sensitive negotiations for a peaceful settlement of the conflict in neighboring Namibia.

House Republicans, anxious to get the aid authorization bill through the House, had declined to raise the issue on the floor but pledged to seek the Clark amendment's repeal in conference. However, facing the deadline of impending adjournment, the Republican conferees decided to drop the matter so as to expedite a conference agreement.

El Salvador. After lengthy negotiations conferees agreed on final wording of the conditions that must be met by the ruling junta of El Salvador and certified by the president before the junta could receive further U.S. military aid.

Major Provisions

As signed into law Dec. 29, S 1196 (PL 97-113) authorized funds for both fiscal 1982 and 1983. The fiscal 1982

authorizations were limited to $5,901,070,000. Fiscal 1983 authorizations were limited to $5,960,570,000.

Major provisions of the bill:

Pakistan, Nuclear Curbs. Allowed the president to waive for Pakistan, until Sept. 30, 1987, the so-called Symington amendment in PL 94-329 banning aid to nations dealing in nuclear enrichment technology. For any other country dealing in unsafeguarded enrichment technology, the president could use the authority in PL 94-329 to waive the aid ban only if he certified to Congress that he had "reliable assurances" that the nation was not seeking to develop nuclear weapons.

● Banned economic or military aid to any country that transferred a nuclear device to a non-nuclear weapons state, and to any non-nuclear weapons state that received a nuclear device from another country. Non-nuclear weapons states were defined as nations that were not known to possess nuclear weapons.

● Gave Congress the right to veto, by passing a concurrent resolution of disapproval within 30 days, any presidential waiver of an aid ban imposed under the non-proliferation laws on dealings in enrichment and reprocessing equipment.

● Allowed the president to waive an aid ban imposed against a nation that transferred, received or exploded a nuclear device, but provided that the ban would be automatically reimposed unless Congress authorized further aid by passing a joint resolution within 30 days.

● Required a secret report to Congress from the president on his reasons if he chose to waive an aid ban for a nation dealing in enrichment or reprocessing equipment.

El Salvador. Stated that "Congress recognizes that the efforts of the government of El Salvador to achieve [a peaceful settlement of the conflict in that nation] are affected by the activities of forces beyond its control."

● Established conditions that the government of El Salvador must meet in order to receive U.S. aid. *(Conditions, box, p. 135)*

Argentina, Chile. Allowed U.S. aid or arms sales to Argentina if the president certified to Congress that the government of Argentina had made significant progress in complying with internationally recognized principles of human rights and that providing aid or sales was in the U.S. national interest. Congress had imposed the ban in the mid-1970s.

● Allowed U.S. aid or arms sales to Chile if the president certified to Congress that the government of Chile had made significant progress in complying with internationally recognized principles of human rights; that providing aid or sales was in the U.S. national interest; and that the Chilean government was not aiding or abetting international terrorism and had taken steps to cooperate in the U.S. investigation of the 1976 slaying in Washington, D.C., of former Chilean Ambassador Orlando Letelier.

Military Aid. Authorized $800 million in Foreign Military Sales (FMS) loans that did not have to be repaid: $550 million for Israel, $200 million for Egypt and $50 million for the Sudan.

● Authorized $3,269,525,000 in regular FMS loans. Of that amount, $280 million was earmarked for Greece.

● Authorized special repayment terms on FMS loans for Egypt, Greece, Turkey, the Sudan and Somalia: 30 years to repay the loans, with an initial 10-year grace period on repayment of principal. Regular FMS loans required repayment within 20 years.

● Authorized $238.5 million in Military Assistance Pro-

gram (MAP) grants, including $38.5 million to phase out previous MAP grant programs; and the remainder to be divided among countries selected by the administration for concessional aid.

● Authorized $42 million for the International Military Education and Training program, under which foreign officers received U.S. training.

● Authorized $19 million for the U.S. share of United Nations peacekeeping operations.

● Required sales of weapons, military equipment or defense services made through U.S. government channels to be reported to Congress if they exceeded $14 million for a single item or $50 million for a package of items.

● Allowed Congress 15 days to review U.S. arms sales to NATO and its member countries, Japan, New Zealand and Australia. The provision also applied to sales of U.S. arms among those countries and transfers of U.S. equipment from those countries to other countries.

● Placed Defense Department leases of defense equipment to foreign nations under the same congressional controls and scrutiny as U.S. government arms sales. Proposed leases of equipment valued at $14 million or more (or $50 million or more for a package of items) had to be reported to Congress 30 days in advance and could be disapproved by Congress within the 30-day period.

● Allowed the president to override Congress' right to veto a defense lease by certifying that there was an emergency requiring the lease and that U.S. national security interests required it. Congressional review of leases would not apply to NATO or its members, Japan, Australia or New Zealand.

● Required the president in each case of a defense lease to determine that there were "compelling foreign policy and national security reasons" for leasing rather than selling the equipment. In most cases, the president also would have to certify that the United States would recover all its costs in connection with a lease.

● Set at $75 million the value of Defense Department arms, equipment or services the president could provide to a foreign country in an emergency in any one year.

● Repealed a $100 million limit on individual sales of arms or military equipment abroad that could be made through private channels. Under the previous limit, individual sales over that amount had to be made through the U.S. government.

● Directed the secretary of defense to establish a revolving Special Defense Acquisition Fund, to be used for advance purchases of weapons and equipment frequently ordered by U.S. arms loan recipients. The fund was limited to $300 million in fiscal 1982 and to $600 million in fiscal 1983 and afterwards. The fund was to be replenished with a portion of payments made to the United States from the FMS program. The president was required to report to Congress by Dec. 31 of each year on the use of the funds.

Economic Aid. Authorized up to $75 million in fiscal 1982 for a Special Requirements Fund under the Economic Support Fund (ESF) program. The money could be used to provide emergency aid to nations. The president was required to notify the House Foreign Affairs, Senate Foreign Relations and House and Senate Appropriations committees 15 days before spending any of the fund. (The related aid appropriations bill, HR 4559, reduced the fund to $25 million in fiscal 1982.)

● Authorized the president to transfer, or "reprogram," up to $75 million each year among accounts to provide emergency aid to foreign countries "when the national

---

El Salvador Certification

The 1981 foreign aid authorization bill (PL 97-113) established a number of requirements that had to be met before U.S. aid could be given to El Salvador. The bill:

● Required that the junta in El Salvador be "achieving substantial control" over its armed forces in order to receive U.S. aid.

● Permitted aid to the government of El Salvador if it had "demonstrated its good faith efforts to begin discussions with all major political factions in El Salvador" who had shown themselves willing to find an "equitable political solution" — the solution to include a renunciation of military or paramilitary operations.

● Required the president, before providing military aid or arms sales to El Salvador, to certify to Congress that the government of that nation was making a concerted and significant effort to comply with internationally recognized human rights.

The president would have to make his certification to Congress within 30 days of enactment of the bill and every 180 days thereafter. If he did not make a certification, he would have to suspend all U.S. aid and arms shipments to El Salvador initiated after enactment of the bill and withdraw all U.S. military advisers from the country.

The president also was required to certify that the Salvadoran government had made good faith efforts to investigate the murders of six U.S. citizens in El Salvador in December 1980 and January 1981.

● Called on the government of El Salvador to reform its human rights practices, to seek to control its own armed forces, to continue economic and political reforms, to conduct free elections as soon as possible and to end extremist violence on all sides.

● Stated that economic assistance to El Salvador should emphasize revitalizing the private sector.

---

interests of the United States urgently require economic support to promote economic or political stability." In using this authority, the president could transfer up to 5 percent from the funds earmarked for any one country.

● Earmarked the following amounts in ESF for both fiscal 1982 and 1983: Israel, $785 million; Egypt, $750 million; Pakistan, $100 million; Cyprus, $15 million; Tunisia, $5 million; Costa Rica, $15 million; Lebanon, $5 million; Poland, $5 million.

● Authorized all ESF money for Israel and Egypt as grants; for Turkey, ESF aid was to be two-thirds grant and one-third loan.

● Prohibited new ESF aid to Syria.

● Stated the sense of Congress that $7 million should be

Peace Corps Independence

Ten years after President Nixon placed the Peace Corps under the ACTION agency, Congress undid the deed by making the corps an independent agency. *(Congress and the Nation Vol. III, p. 878)*

The independence move came in spite of opposition from some conservatives, who saw it as a slap at the Reagan administration's ACTION director, Thomas W. Pauken. The Senate confirmed Pauken's nomination May 7. Pauken was a former Army intelligence officer who served in Vietnam in the late 1960s.

Proponents of separating the agencies feared Pauken's background would taint the Peace Corps' reputation for being free of involvement in intelligence activities.

The foreign aid authorization bill (S 1196 — PL 97-113) made the Peace Corps' independence effective upon enactment.

In an effort to prevent the Reagan administration from reducing the independence of the Peace Corps, conferees adopted a modified House provision stating that its director must continue to exercise all functions in effect on Dec. 14, 1981 — the date of the conference agreement on the bill.

made available in fiscal 1982 and 1983 for relief programs in Lebanon.

● Prohibited the use of ESF money to construct, maintain, operate or supply fuel to any nuclear facility abroad unless the president certified to Congress that such spending was "indispensable to the achievement of non-proliferation objectives which are uniquely significant and of paramount importance to the United States."

Nicaragua. Earmarked $20 million in ESF aid to Nicaragua in fiscal years 1982 and 1983. In providing the aid, the president was directed to take into account the Nicaraguan government's respect for human rights, its role in international terrorism and its commitment to the Organization of American States. The aid also was to be targeted to the private sector "to the maximum extent feasible." The president was directed to report to Congress every six months on the use of the Nicaraguan aid.

Development Aid. Prohibited the use of U.S. Agency for International Development (AID) funds to perform abortions or to carry out research concerning abortion.

International Organizations. Earmarked funds for several programs under the "international organizations" account, but stated that the president could spend either the amount proposed by Congress or a percentage of the total international organizations account, whichever was less. The earmarked programs were: UNICEF, $45 million, or 19.6 percent of the international organizations account; United Nations Development Program, $134.5 million, or 59.5 percent; United Nations Environment Fund, $10 million, or 4.4 percent; United Nations Trust Fund for Southern Africa, $400,000, or .159 percent; United Nations Institute for Training and Research, $500,000, or .196 percent.

● Earmarked $500,000 under a separate account for the United Nations Decade for Women. (The funds subsequently were dropped from the appropriations bill.)

Food for Peace. Required the president, before entering into agreements to provide Food for Peace aid, to consider whether a recipient country had undertaken programs to reduce illiteracy and improve the health of the rural poor.

● Beginning in fiscal 1983, prohibited any one country from receiving more than 30 percent of the total dollar amount of financing made available under Title I of the Food for Peace program.

● Required that, of the 1.7 million metric tons of agricultural commodities that must be distributed under Title II of the Food for Peace program, 1.2 million tons must be distributed through non-profit voluntary agencies and the World Food Program.

Peace Corps. Established the Peace Corps as an independent agency, effective upon enactment of the bill, and provided for the transfer to the control of the Peace Corps of personnel, assets, liability, contracts, personnel records and unexpended balances primarily used by the Peace Corps. The Peace Corps had been placed under the ACTION agency in 1971. *(Box, this page)*

Marijuana Spraying. Repealed a 1978 ban on the use of U.S. foreign aid to spray the herbicide paraquat on marijuana. The bill directed the secretary of state to inform the secretary of health and human services if funds were used for that purpose, and the latter official was to monitor the impact of paraquat spraying on the health of marijuana users. The bill also earmarked $100,000 for research on substances that would leave a mark on marijuana or other illicit crops if sprayed on those crops along with herbicides.

Foreign Aid Appropriations

Congress Dec. 16 cleared HR 4559 (PL 97-121), making appropriations for foreign aid programs in fiscal 1982. It was the first regular foreign aid spending bill to be enacted since 1978.

The bill contained $7.495 billion in new budget authority for foreign aid programs. In addition, it set $13.6 billion in limits on Export-Import Bank loans and operations (including $4.4 billion for direct loans) and a $3.1 billion limit on arms loans to foreign countries.

The bill had been held up by conflict over arms aid and the U.S. contribution to the International Development Association (IDA). Those issues had been a principal reason for Congress' failure to pass a foreign aid appropriations bill in each of the previous two years. Foreign aid programs had been funded instead under continuing resolutions that also funded a multitude of other government programs. *(Congress and the Nation Vol. V, p. 85)*

Along with the foreign aid authorization (S 1196 — PL 97-113), the aid spending bill was enmeshed all year in partisan disputes that threatened to kill both measures, leaving President Reagan without increases he wanted in the arms aid so integral to his foreign policy. But the bills were rushed through Congress in the final days before it

adjourned after the president rallied GOP support for them. *(Authorization bill, p. 132)*

The situation was turned around when Reagan and Secretary of State Alexander M. Haig Jr. issued personal appeals to their party early in December to get the Reagan foreign aid program, as embodied in both bills, through Congress.

Committee, Floor Action

The House Appropriations Committee reported HR 4559 (H Rept 97-245) Sept. 22 after weeks of dispute within its Foreign Operations Subcommittee over the IDA and military aid questions. But it was not until Dec. 11 that the full chamber passed the politically unpopular measure on a **key 199-166 vote (R 84-87; D 115-79)**. *(1981 key votes, p. 879)*

The Senate Appropriations Committee normally would await House action on an appropriations bill before taking up such a measure itself. However, acknowledging that House action on HR 4559 was stalled, the Senate panel reported its own bill (S 1802 — S Rept 97-266) Nov. 3, and the full Senate — breaking with tradition and risking a fight with the House — passed it Nov. 17 by a 57-33 vote.

The House and Senate bills dramatized the fundamental philosophical and partisan divisions in Congress on how U.S. aid should be spent.

The two bills provided similar amounts for U.S. aid programs in fiscal 1982: $7,594,280,064 under the House bill and $7,250,083,804 under the Senate measure. (Reagan had requested $7,650,098,683.)

But that similarity masked basic disputes over how much of the foreign aid budget should go for military aid given directly to U.S. allies and how much should go toward underwriting IDA.

Most Democrats generally favored less military aid than did most Republicans. Thus, with Democrats in the majority, the House committee approved $923.5 million for military aid spending in HR 4559 — $172.9 million less than the $1.096 billion the Republican-controlled Senate panel approved in S 1802.

A central issue in the struggles over the aid bill was an $850 million donation to the IDA for the second installment on a U.S. pledge to give $3.24 billion to IDA's sixth replenishment (called IDA VI). The IDA was an arm of the World Bank that made no-interest loans to the globe's poorest nations.

Conservatives in Congress — mainly Republicans — had been waging a campaign to stretch out the scheduled U.S. donations to IDA VI. Liberals — most of them Democrats — had been fighting to maintain a Reagan administration plan for graduated IDA VI payments.

Reflecting this division, the Senate committee approved only $532 million for the fiscal 1982 payment to IDA VI, while the House committee approved $850 million — the amount President Reagan requested in March. Reagan revised his budget requests in September and reduced his fiscal 1982 IDA VI request to $820 million.

When the bill came to the House floor, however, representatives voted 281-114 to adopt an amendment cutting the fiscal 1982 contribution to $725 million.

The U.S. pledge to IDA was authorized in the omnibus budget reconciliation bill (HR 3982 — PL 97-35). *(Story, p. 40)*

Conference Action

Conferees filed their report (H Rept 97-416) on the bill Dec. 16. Congress completed action later that day when the House adopted the conference report on a 217-201 vote and the Senate followed suit by a 55-34 vote.

Much of the conference committee meeting was consumed by heated arguments and complex negotiations over the central issue that had held up HR 4559 all year: the proper ratio of military to development aid.

The development aid issue fell under two major items in the bill: the fiscal 1982 U.S. payment to IDA and the combined total of bilateral development aid administered by the U.S. Agency for International Development (AID). The key to the conference was striking a balance between the two forms of aid.

After rejecting several formulas that split the difference in various ways, conferees finally settled on $700 million for IDA, $1.295 billion for AID and $965 million for military aid. Those figures represented a cut of $25 million from the House amount for IDA, the full House amount for AID development programs and an increase of $41.5 million over the House military aid figure.

Military Aid Programs. Conferees later agreed to the following breakdown of the $965 million approved for military aid:

● $38.5 million for the international military education and training (IMET) program, a 50-50 split between the $35 million in the House bill and the $41.9 million in the Senate bill.

● $176.5 million in Military Assistance Program (MAP) grants. Of that amount, $38.5 million was to complete previously authorized grants, and $138 million was to be divided among 14 countries for whom Reagan requested concessional arms aid, not including Israel and Egypt. Reagan originally had requested $582 million for special grants to the 14 countries but in September reduced that request to $265 million.

● $750 million in Foreign Military Sales (FMS) program loans that did not have to be repaid: $550 million for Israel and $200 million for Egypt.

In addition, conferees settled on a $3.084 billion limit, the Senate figure, for regular FMS loans to foreign countries that had to be repaid. The House had approved a $2.846 billion limit. The limit on FMS loans did not count as new budget authority in the appropriations bill.

Special FMS Fund. The administration lost one of its priority requests at the last minute when the conference deleted $250 million that had been provided in both bills for a Special Defense Acquisition Fund (SDAF).

Reagan had requested the SDAF to allow the Pentagon to order in advance those items, such as M-16 rifles, most frequently requested by nations buying U.S. military equipment with FMS credits.

The fund was approved under the foreign aid authorization bill but was dropped from the appropriations bill because the Congressional Budget Office (CBO) had ruled that the $250 million would be charged against the limit on budget authority imposed on that measure under the second fiscal 1982 budget resolution (S Con Res 50).

The conference decided to drop the SDAF for fear the CBO ruling, which effectively added $250 million to the total of HR 4559, might threaten House and Senate approval of the conference report.

Economic Support Fund. The next most contentious debate occurred when House Democrats sought to

trade off a high-priority Reagan request for $100 million in Economic Support Fund (ESF) aid for Pakistan against another $75 million request for an unallocated ESF Special Requirements Fund. The fund would be available to the president to use at his discretion to give friendly nations quick injections of aid any time during the fiscal year. In the end, conferees approved the full $100 million for Pakistan and only $25 million for the ESF Special Requirements Fund. *(Pakistan aid, box, p. 133)*

Provisions

As signed into law Dec. 29, the legislative provisions of the fiscal 1982 foreign aid appropriations bill (HR 4559 — PL 97-121):

Military Aid. Earmarked $550 million for Israel and $200 million for Egypt for Foreign Military Sales loans that did not have to be repaid.

Multilateral Aid. Limited the salaries of U.S. representatives to the international development banks to no more than level IV of the federal Executive Schedule ($52,750 per year in 1981, increasing to $58,500 as of Jan. 1, 1982).

● Instructed the U.S. representative to the IDA to press for a "more efficient distribution" of IDA lending, including a reduction in the maximum loans provided to any individual nation.

● Prohibited U.S. donations to the World Health Organization Special Programme of Research, Development, and Research Training in Human Reproduction.

● Prohibited the use of funds for the United Nations Fund for Science and Technology.

● Prohibited the use of funds for the United Nations Decade for Women. Funds had been authorized for the project in the aid authorization bill.

● Earmarked $126,750,000 for the United Nations Development Program.

● Limited contributions to the United Nations Childrens Fund to $41.5 million.

● Limited contributions to the United Nations Environment Program to $7,850,000.

Bilateral Aid. Earmarked $10 million of the $27 million international disaster assistance account for the relief of earthquake victims in southern Italy.

● Prohibited expenditure of money under the Special Requirements Fund of the Economic Support Fund without the prior written approval of the House and Senate Appropriations committees.

● Earmarked the following amounts under the Economic Support Fund: $806 million for Israel, $771 million for Egypt, $100 million for the Sudan, $20 million for Costa Rica, $15 million for Cyprus, $5 million for Poland, $5 million for Tunisia.

● Earmarked $30 million in the migration and refugee assistance account for use by the Agency for International Development for resettlement services and facilities for refugees and displaced persons in Africa.

● Limited administrative expenses for the Office of Refugee Programs to $7,426,000.

General Provisions. Prohibited the use of any funds in the bill to "lobby for abortion."

● Added Libya, Iraq and South Yemen to a list of nations barred from directly receiving "any assistance or reparations" from the United States. Nations previously on the list were Angola, Cambodia, Cuba, Laos, Vietnam and Syria.

Non-Proliferation Policy

President Reagan July 16 announced his policy on steps the United States would take to restrict the spread of nuclear weapons.

The next day, both houses of Congress unanimously passed resolutions calling on Reagan to take more sweeping and specific nuclear non-proliferation actions than his policy embraced.

Sen. John Glenn, D-Ohio, and Rep. Dennis E. Eckart, D-Ohio, had introduced the resolutions prior to Reagan's announcement, saying they hoped to prod the president into stating his long-delayed non-proliferation policy.

Immediately following Reagan's announcement, Glenn and Eckart pushed for passage of the resolutions in order to persuade the president to raise non-proliferation issues at the July 20-21 economic summit meeting of industrialized nations in Ottawa, Canada. The final summit communiqué, issued July 21, mentioned non-proliferation only in passing.

Reagan Policy

Although most of its points were vaguely worded, the Reagan policy added up to a sharp change in emphasis from former President Carter's non-proliferation policy.

Carter had emphasized U.S. restrictions on exports of nuclear material and equipment that could be used to build weapons. In asking other countries to restrict nuclear exports, the United States should set an example by restricting its own exports, Carter said.

Reliable Supplier. The Reagan policy emphasized the opposite: By improving its reputation as a reliable supplier of nuclear technology to other countries, the United States could win back some of the nuclear business it lost under Carter and would be in a better position to enforce non-proliferation standards, the president said.

Critics of Carter's policy, especially the nuclear industry, argued that restricting U.S. nuclear exports reduced the U.S. leverage over other countries. Since other nations could no longer rely on the United States for nuclear supplies, they turned to other suppliers, such as France, which did not impose the same restrictions, the critics said.

Reprocessing Technology. Reagan's most direct break with Carter concerned exports of reprocessing and breeder reactor technology, which could be used to create weapons-grade plutonium. Carter had banned exports of those items and halted reprocessing and breeder reactor plants in the United States.

Reagan said the administration would not inhibit reprocessing and breeder reactor development "in nations with advanced nuclear power programs where it does not constitute a proliferation risk." He did not set specific standards for determining what nations would be permitted to buy that technology. However, congressional aides said Reagan's policy was directed at allowing exports of those items to Japan.

Reagan also did not set out a policy covering exports of uranium enrichment technology, which could convert natural uranium into highly enriched fuel capable of making atomic weapons.

Safeguards. Reagan also put greater reliance than did Carter on international inspections (called "safeguards") of nuclear facilities to detect nuclear weapons-building efforts.

Before entering into "any significant new nuclear sup-

ply commitment" with another nation, Reagan said, the United States would require that the nation accept international safeguards on all its nuclear facilities (called "full-scope safeguards").

Reagan's statement did not say whether the United States would continue to press for adoption of full-scope safeguards by nations that already had nuclear agreements with the United States but which had refused to accept the safeguards. Those nations included India, South Africa, Argentina, Brazil and Spain.

Neither Reagan's two-page statement nor an accompanying four-page "fact sheet" mentioned the Nuclear Non-proliferation Act (NNPA), the 1978 law (PL 95-242) that established U.S. non-proliferation policy. (Congress and the Nation Vol. V, p. 147)

The law placed strict controls on all nuclear exports and prohibited exports after March 1980 to countries that refused to accept full-scope safeguards. The president could waive that prohibition, but Congress could override his approval of an export.

Spokesmen for the nuclear industry had complained that the law was too rigid and placed too many hurdles in the way of nuclear exports.

Reagan said he would direct U.S. agencies to expedite export requests that met conditions of the law.

Congressional Resolutions

The Senate and House July 17 adopted similar resolutions on the non-proliferation issue.

The strongest and most specific resolution was S Res 179, adopted by the Senate 88-0, that called on the president to work to strengthen international safeguards and to formulate a "clear" U.S. policy on nuclear trade. The resolution also called for a temporary worldwide moratorium on transfers of uranium enrichment and reprocessing equipment to "sensitive areas, such as the Middle East and South Asia"; a limit on the size of research reactors, eliminating the use of weapons-grade uranium in those reactors and requiring importing nations to return spent nuclear fuel to the nations that supplied the original fuel. S Res 179 stated that the United States should make nuclear exports only to nations that accepted safeguards on all their nuclear facilities (only the United States and Canada required those safeguards) and should impose sanctions on nations that violated safeguards.

The House resolution (H Res 177) also called for non-proliferation steps beyond Reagan's policy. It was adopted 365-0, with two members — Larry P. McDonald, D-Ga., and Ron Paul, R-Texas — voting "present."

The resolution asked the president to "develop and implement a United States nuclear non-proliferation policy which aggressively and creatively strengthens the political, institutional and technical barriers to the further spread of nuclear weapons," including "concrete methods for achieving restraint on the part of all nuclear suppliers."

It called for "credible" sanctions against nations that misused nuclear material and said the president should fully implement the Nuclear Nonproliferation Act.

Latin Nuclear Arms Treaty

The Senate Nov. 13 approved, on a 79-0 vote, Protocol I to the Treaty for the Prohibition of Nuclear Weapons in Latin America, known as the Treaty of Tlatelolco. The treaty had been ratified by 22 Latin American nations.

Under the protocol the United States agreed not to base nuclear weapons in Latin America. The full treaty established a nuclear-free zone in Latin America, with nations of the region agreeing not to make, test, use, store, deploy or possess nuclear weapons.

Although not a direct party to the treaty, the United States was invited to participate through Protocol I, which applied to nations possessing territories in Latin America. U.S. territories in the region were Puerto Rico, the Virgin Islands and the Guantanamo Naval Base in Cuba.

The United States signed the protocol May 26, 1977, and President Carter sent it to the Senate a year later. The Senate Foreign Relations Committee held hearings in August 1978, but delayed action because of questions about whether the agreement would affect the U.S. right to transport ships and planes armed with nuclear weapons in Latin America.

In urging approval of the protocol, the Reagan administration insisted the United States was not prohibited from transporting nuclear weapons in the region. In its report (Exec Rept 97-21), the Senate Foreign Relations Committee added an understanding to that effect.

Intelligence Authorization

The House and Senate Nov. 18 cleared for the president a fiscal 1982 intelligence authorization bill (HR 3454 — PL 97-89) approving secret amounts of spending by the Central Intelligence Agency (CIA) and other U.S. spy services. The bill also contained a secret, supplemental fiscal 1981 authorization for intelligence agency spending.

While spending authorized by HR 3454 was secret, Edward P. Boland, D-Mass., chairman of the House Intelligence Committee, said Senate-House conferees had given the Reagan administration "almost everything that it asked for."

When the House passed HR 3454 on July 13, Boland had said the House bill contained a "net reduction" from President Reagan's request, compared with a "substantial addition" to Reagan's request by the Senate Intelligence Committee.

Legislative Action. The House Intelligence Committee approved HR 3454 (H Rept 97-101, Part I) May 7. The bill also was referred to the House Armed Services Committee, which reported it (H Rept 97-101, Part II) June 12 without amendment. It passed the House July 13 by voice vote.

The Senate passed the bill by voice vote July 16 after substituting the version reported by the Senate Intelligence Committee May 6 (S 1127 — S Rept 97-57).

The House approved the conference report on HR 3454 (H Rept 97-332) by a 379-22 vote Nov. 18. The Senate approved the report by voice vote with only perfunctory discussion of it.

Conference action was delayed because amounts for military intelligence had to be considered in conjunction with the fiscal 1982 defense authorization bill, which in turn was delayed for several months while the administration deliberated on its strategic weapons policies. (Defense authorization, p. 205)

Provisions. The provisions of the bill that were made public:

● Authorized $13.6 million and 220 personnel for the staff of the director of central intelligence. The director

Intelligence Order

Seeking to "remove the aura of suspicion and mistrust that can hobble our nation's intelligence efforts," President Reagan Dec. 4 issued Executive Order 12333 expanding the information-gathering authority of the CIA and other intelligence organizations.

The order, which had the force of law, loosened restrictions that President Carter had imposed on U.S. intelligence agencies in Executive Order 12036, issued Jan. 24, 1978. *(Congress and the Nation Vol. V, p. 150)*

Specifically, the Reagan order permitted the CIA and other agencies besides the FBI to collect "significant foreign intelligence" within the United States, provided the effort was not aimed at monitoring domestic activities of American citizens and corporations.

In addition, the order allowed the CIA to conduct domestic or foreign operations approved by the president, if they were undertaken to further "national foreign policy objectives abroad" and "not intended to influence United States political processes, public opinion, policies, or media." Carter had prohibited domestic covert operations.

Congressional Criticisms. Members of Congress had criticized three earlier drafts of the order for going too far in easing the Carter safeguards. Members of the House and Senate Intelligence committees had been concerned that Reagan would not adequately limit CIA operations within the United States.

After the final order was issued, some members still had reservations. Sen. Daniel Patrick Moynihan, D-N.Y., said there still were "a very few provisions" that could "pose problems" if they were "misinterpreted or stretched beyond the legitimate intent of their authors."

The White House had accepted 15 of the 18 major changes to earlier drafts that had been proposed by the Senate Intelligence Committee. Deleted, for example, was a provision that would have allowed the CIA to infiltrate domestic organizations without a court warrant.

Oversight Panel. In a separate order (Executive Order 12334), also issued Dec. 4, Reagan continued the Intelligence Oversight Board begun by Carter and recommissioned the 19-member Foreign Intelligence Advisory Board, which Carter had disbanded. Composed of three private citizens appointed by the president, the Oversight Board was authorized to inform the president of any "intelligence activities" that any member believed was "in violation of the Constitution or laws of the United States, executive orders or presidential directives."

supervised all intelligence agencies and also was director of the CIA.

● Authorized $11.9 million for a Federal Bureau of Investigation domestic counterintelligence program, which the Senate had not included in its version of the bill.

● Established a senior cryptologic executive service within the National Security Agency (NSA) similar to the senior executive service for other federal employees, and a senior executive service for civilian personnel in the Defense Intelligence Agency.

● Permitted the director of the NSA to make grants for research into cryptology, which involves writing and breaking coded messages.

● Prohibited unauthorized persons from using the names, initials or seals of the CIA and NSA for commercial or improper purposes, and gave those agencies authority to seek U.S. district court injunctions to halt such activities. (A similar provision for the Defense Intelligence Agency was enacted in 1982. *(Story, p. 152)*)

● Barred use of funds authorized in the bill for purposes other than those for which they were proposed unless the House and Senate Intelligence committees were notified at least 15 days in advance.

● Allowed CIA personnel to carry firearms to perform authorized CIA duties. (Conferees stipulated that such authority would be limited within the United States to the protection of classified materials, training CIA personnel to use firearms, maintaining security at CIA installations or other property, and protecting CIA personnel, defectors and their families or foreign visitors in the United States under the auspices of the CIA.)

● Authorized $84.6 million for the CIA Retirement and Disability System.

● Provided that the NSA could establish a cryptologic linguist reserve of persons who could make and break codes in foreign languages.

● Made allowances and benefits for CIA employees comparable to those offered members of the Foreign Service, as well as special travel allowances.

Agent Identity Disclosure

Legislation (HR 4) to make it a federal crime to expose the names of U.S. secret agents passed the House Sept. 23, but a companion bill (S 391) did not make it to the Senate floor in 1981 because of a threatened filibuster by Sen. Bill Bradley, D-N.J.

Congress completed action on the agent identity legislation in 1982. *(1981-82 action, p. 151)*

Sinai Peacekeeping Force

Congress Dec. 16 cleared a joint resolution (S J Res 100 — PL 97-132) authorizing the president to send up to 1,200 U.S. soldiers and to spend $125 million in fiscal 1982 to support a new 2,500-member peacekeeping force in the Sinai Peninsula.

The force was to be established under the Egyptian-Israeli peace treaty of 1979, which required that Israel completely withdraw from the Sinai by April 25, 1982. Israeli forces had occupied parts of the peninsula since the 1967 Arab-Israeli war. *(Congress and the Nation Vol. V, p. 105)*

Golan Heights. But even before Congress had approved that key element of the Camp David accords, an angry dispute erupted between Israel and the United States over Israel's annexation of the Golan Heights, shaking the foundations of the Camp David peace process.

At the urging of Prime Minister Menachem Begin, the Israeli Knesset voted Dec. 14 in effect to annex the Golan Heights — captured from Syria by Israel in the six-day war of 1967 — by extending Israeli law to the region.

On Dec. 17 the United Nations Security Council unanimously adopted a resolution calling Israel's action "null and void" and demanding that it be reversed.

Legislative History. The Senate passed its version (S Rept 97-197) of the Sinai resolution Oct. 7. That resolution authorized U.S. participation in the peacekeeping force but placed few restrictions on the U.S. role.

The House adopted a more restrictive version (H J Res 349 — H Rept 97-310) Nov. 19, on a 368-13 vote. H J Res 349 placed a limit of 1,200 on the number of U.S. military personnel that could be assigned to the force. Administration officials had told Congress that the U.S. force would include an 800-man infantry battalion, a 350-man logistics unit and about 50 civilian observers.

The bill also authorized the U.S. share of the costs of the Sinai mission: $125 million in fiscal 1982. In addition, the United States was to pay an estimated $35 million a year to run the force starting in fiscal 1983.

The Senate accepted the House language with minor changes Dec. 16; the House agreed.

Lefever and Human Rights

President Reagan's first major congressional defeat on a foreign policy issue came June 5, when the Senate Foreign Relations Committee voted 13-4 to recommend that the Senate reject the nomination of Ernest W. Lefever as assistant secretary of state for human rights and humanitarian affairs. Hours after the vote, Lefever asked that his nomination be withdrawn.

On Oct. 30 Reagan nominated Elliott Abrams to the position; Abrams was confirmed by the Senate Nov. 20 without controversy. A former assistant to Democratic Sens. Daniel Patrick Moynihan, N.Y., and Henry M. Jackson, Wash., Abrams had been serving as assistant secretary of state for international organizations.

Background. The vote against Lefever came after several weeks of bitter controversy over Lefever's commitment to human rights and his truthfulness with the committee. The vote was a setback for Reagan because the president strongly backed Lefever until the very end.

Lefever had spent most of his life as a scholar of ethics and foreign policy, holding teaching or research positions at several universities in the Washington, D.C., area. Since 1976 Lefever had been president of the Ethics and Public Policy Center, a non-profit foundation established under the auspices of Georgetown University but later separated from the school.

Earlier in his career, Lefever was an active and orthodox liberal idealist, according to testimony given the committee. But his philosophy evolved over the years toward conservatism. His statements and writings on the Carter human rights policy earned him conservative admiration and liberal enmity.

Even before his nomination was announced in February, the rumor that he would be named led some 35 groups, including church and liberal foreign-policy interest groups, to form an Ad Hoc Committee of the Human Rights Community to fight the nomination. This group and other opponents charged that Lefever was at best indifferent to human rights concerns and therefore unqualified for the post.

Lefever's foes raised various other charges against him, questioning his integrity and that of his Ethics and Public Policy Center, for example, by alleging that the foundation had received financial support from the government of South Africa — a charge Lefever denied during his hearings.

Committee Action. Lefever's troubles heightened after *The Washington Post* reported May 22 that the Ethics and Public Policy Center had received $25,000 from the Nestlé Corp., makers of infant formula, and later reprinted and distributed an article favoring infant formula exports. Lefever's involvement in the issue was especially controversial because on May 21 the United States cast the lone dissenting vote against a World Health Organization code calling for a worldwide ban on advertising and promotion of baby formula. Lefever denied that his center's support for infant formula makers was in exchange for the Nestlé contribution. *(Infant formula, p. 142)*

The committee vote to recommend that Lefever be rejected, thought to be unprecedented in committee history, occurred the day after Lefever appeared before the committee in a closed session lasting more than five and a half hours, defending his views on the role of human rights in foreign policy and further explaining his dealings with the Nestlé Corp.

The committee voted against Lefever's nomination June 5 without debate.

Human Rights Issues. For all the criticism of Lefever personally, the root issue was the Reagan human rights policy in general.

Lefever and other critics of the Carter policy complained that it alienated friendly authoritarian regimes, such as Argentina's, while overlooking greater human rights abuses by totalitarian communist nations such as the Soviet Union.

These critics, including Reagan, said abuses in anti-communist authoritarian regimes could be reduced most readily by offering their leaders the security of U.S. friendship and quietly using the influence thus gained.

Advocates of the Carter policy contended it saved lives and prevented torture in many cases by focusing world attention on specific rights abuses. They said the "quiet diplomacy" policy would mean ignoring human rights abuses by anti-communist U.S. allies while publicly condemning abuses only in Marxist nations.

Casey, Hugel Controversies

The Senate Intelligence Committee concluded after a four-month investigation that CIA Director William J. Casey had been lax in complying with ethics laws but that "no basis has been found for concluding that Mr. Casey is unfit to hold office as director of Central Intelligence."

Committee Report. The report (S Rept 97-285), issued Dec. 1, said Casey failed to disclose more than $250,000 in investments and almost $500,000 in personal debts and contingent liabilities. The disclosures should have been made in a financial disclosure statement required of presidential appointees, the committee said.

Casey also failed to list more than 70 legal clients he represented during the four years before he became CIA director, the existence of four civil suits to which he was a party, and his services as a member of the board of directors of several corporations and foundations.

Sen. Joseph R. Biden Jr., D-Del., took exception to the report's central finding, saying he had lost faith in Casey because of Casey's "consistent pattern of omissions, misstatements and contradictions in his dealings with this and other committees of Congress."

But other members of the committee — eight Republicans and six Democrats — approved the report.

An intelligence officer in World War II, Casey was named CIA director after serving as President Reagan's 1980 campaign manager. He was unanimously confirmed by the Senate Jan. 28.

Hugel Controversy. The Intelligence Committee in July began its investigation into allegations of financial misconduct on Casey's behalf, after similar charges toppled Max C. Hugel, Casey's deputy for covert operations.

Senate Majority Leader Howard H. Baker Jr., R-Tenn., an *ex-officio* member of the committee, said July 16 the panel had ordered its staff to review "the whole package" of allegations against Casey and Hugel.

Hugel resigned July 14, hours after *The Washington Post* published a lengthy article detailing charges by two stockbrokers that Hugel had engaged in insider trading and manipulation of the stock of Brother International Corp., an export-import firm he headed in the early 1970s. Hugel denied the charges.

Richard Allen Resignation

President Reagan's national security adviser, Richard V. Allen, resigned Jan. 4, 1982, in the wake of misconduct charges that had dogged him in 1981.

Allen's resignation came the same day the White House counsel's office cleared him of allegations of misconduct that had led him to take a leave of absence Nov. 29, 1981. Among other charges, Allen had come under fire for his receipt of a $1,000 "honorarium" from a Japanese magazine when one of its reporters interviewed Mrs. Reagan in the White House Jan. 21, 1981. Allen said he had told his secretary to turn the money over to the proper authorities, but the secretary apparently forgot to do so. The Justice Department said Allen had violated no laws in the matter.

National Security Post

Reagan promptly replaced Allen with Deputy Secretary of State William P. Clark — a foreign policy novice but a longtime Reagan confidant. The White House national security apparatus was reorganized to provide the national security adviser frequent and assured access to the president, implying greater power and prestige for Clark than Allen had enjoyed.

Clark later became known as a quick study who reportedly worked well with Secretary of State Alexander M. Haig Jr. Rivalry between Allen and Haig had brought rebukes from Reagan.

The national security adviser post was not subject to Senate confirmation, but some members of Congress had advocated legislation to make it so because holders of the office historically had clashed with secretaries of state. The Senate passed such a provision in 1979.

Czech Claims Agreement

Congress Dec. 16 approved an agreement between the United States and Czechoslovakia settling claims dating from the end of World War II (S 1946 — PL 97-127).

The two governments had reached an accord on Nov. 6 to return about 8.5 metric tons of Czech gold held by the United States after the communists seized power in Czechoslovakia in 1948.

Under the Nov. 6 agreement, the United States was to return the gold to Czechoslovakia, and that country in turn was to pay $81.5 million to the United States for claims of U.S. citizens, plus interest. In addition, Czechoslovakia agreed to pay the United States $8 million for surplus Army equipment that Czechoslovakia bought in 1946 but never paid for, and to return $1 million in U.S. bank accounts in Czechoslovakia that had been frozen.

The Senate originally passed S 1946 Dec. 11, and the House passed its bill (HR 5125) Dec. 15. Both chambers approved a compromise version of S 1946 Dec. 16.

As cleared, the Czechoslovakian Claims Settlement Act of 1981 approved the Nov. 6 agreement and set priorities for distribution of the $81.5 million. The bill required the State Department to carry out the agreement within 60 days of enactment, with a possible 30-day extension.

Infant Formula Marketing

Both houses of Congress in June overwhelmingly approved resolutions criticizing the Reagan administration's stand against a voluntary international code to restrict the promotion of infant formula.

The United States was the only one of 119 countries to vote against the code at the World Health Organization (WHO) assembly May 21 in Geneva.

Infant formulas are powdered-milk substitutes used instead of breast-feeding. The code was aimed at preventing marketing techniques such as salespeople dressing as nurses and ads suggesting that good health depended on formula, as opposed to breast milk. The code, which suggested rules for each nation to adopt individually, was directed primarily at developing countries where unsanitary practices such as preparation of formula with contaminated water had contributed, health experts said, to as many as a million infant deaths a year.

Although the Reagan administration agreed that breast-feeding was preferable to formula, officials argued that the code would infringe on the constitutional guarantees of freedom of speech. However, the emotionalism associated with "motherhood" issues, combined with the isolation of the U.S. position, prompted even administration supporters to question whether principle was being applied too rigidly. Sen. Robert Dole, R-Kan., suggested that an abstention would have been more appropriate.

Administration critics were more forceful. "How often have we placed the profits of the giant international drug firms above saving the lives of dying children?" asked Sen. Edward M. Kennedy, D-Mass. "The answer is never — until this administration's vote in Geneva."

Republicans were as eager as Democrats to distance themselves from the unpopular administration stand. However, the slap at President Reagan was tempered by the mild wording of the two different, non-binding resolutions. The House expressed "dismay" at the action; the Senate voiced "concern."

U.S.-Iran Claims

A July 2 Supreme Court decision upholding the hostage release agreement with Iran allowed the United States to follow through on steps already taken to implement the accords.

The court's decision also relieved Congress of any necessity to approve the agreement.

President Reagan agreed Feb. 18 to honor the agreement.

In addition to releasing the hostages Jan. 20, Iran agreed to arbitration before a joint Iran-United States Claims Tribunal of any claims by U.S. nationals against Iran and by Iranian nationals against the United States.

The 52 Americans released by Iran on Inauguration Day were among the 66 Americans — most of them State Department employees — taken hostage in the U.S. Embassy in Tehran on Nov. 4, 1979. Thirteen hostages were released later in November 1979, and another, Richard I. Queen, was released in July 1980. *(Background, Congress and the Nation Vol. V, p. 111)*

The United States agreed to return portions of $12 billion in Iranian assets President Carter had frozen in retaliation on Nov. 14, 1979.

In the House, almost half the Republicans and most of the Democrats voted June 16 for a sense-of-Congress resolution (H J Res 287) opposing the administration's stand. The resolution was approved 301-100; 85 Republicans and all but seven Democrats voted for it.

In the Senate, only two members — John P. East, R-N.C., and Steven D. Symms, R-Idaho — voted against the resolution, offered June 18 as an amendment to the State Department authorization bill (S 1193) by Dave Durenberger, R-Minn. The vote was 89-2.

In clearing the State Department authorization bill in 1982, Congress included a provision expressing concern over the administration's opposition to the infant formula code. *(Story, p. 148)*

State Department Authority

Congress failed in 1981 to enact an authorization bill for the State Department, in large part because House Republicans helped defeat the bill the first time it reached the House floor.

The pivotal action came Sept. 17, when 131 House Republicans were joined by 95 Democrats in rejecting the bill (HR 3518 — H Rept 97-102, Parts I, II), authorizing $3 billion in fiscal 1982 and $3.1 billion in fiscal 1983 for State Department operations and for payments to the United States and other international organizations.

The Senate Foreign Relations Committee had reported its version of the legislation May 15 (S 1193 — S

Rept 97-71). The bill was passed by the Senate on June 18.

Later, on Oct. 29, the House passed a revised version of S 1193 that met administration requests for $2.9 billion in fiscal 1982 and $2.8 billion in fiscal 1983. But House-Senate conferees did not work out a compromise measure in time for action before adjournment. The bill finally cleared in August 1982. *(Details, p. 148)*

Canada Maritime Treaty

A treaty designed to resolve an East Coast maritime boundary dispute between the United States and Canada was approved by the Senate April 29 by a vote of 91-0.

In the treaty (Exec U, 96th Cong, 1st Sess), the two countries agreed to submit the dispute to the World Court for binding arbitration. The disagreement involved jurisdiction over fishing and oil leasing in 5,000 square miles of the Georges Bank off Cape Cod, one of the world's richest fishing grounds.

Overlapping claims had resulted in the mid-1970s when both countries claimed control over the seas within 200 miles of their coasts.

The World Court Oct. 12, 1984, awarded five-sixths of the Georges Bank to the United States, the remaining sixth to Canada.

Treaties' Terms

The treaty was one of two agreements (Exec U, V; 96th Cong, 1st Sess) signed March 29, 1979, after nearly two years of active negotiation. *(Congress and the Nation Vol. V, p. 94)*

The Maritime Boundary Settlement Treaty provided for World Court binding arbitration of the dispute.

In addition to determining fishing grounds, the treaty aimed to resolve conflicting claims over offshore oil fields in the Georges Bank. Both countries already had taken steps to claim the area for oil production. The United States had issued leases for drilling in the area, prompting outcries from fishermen and environmentalists.

Under the boundary treaty, the two countries agreed to ask the International Court of Justice (the World Court) to appoint a special five-member panel to arbitrate the conflicting claims. If the court failed to appoint such a panel within six months after the treaty took effect, the two countries could jointly appoint a five-member panel to arbitrate the dispute.

State Department officials said the arbitration process could take several years. In the meantime, Reagan said the United States would allow Canadians to fish in all areas claimed by Canada.

A companion East Coast Fisheries Agreement would have established conservation guidelines for North Atlantic fishing grounds. Its most controversial provisions would have set shares of various fish species that could be caught by U.S. and Canadian fishermen. Reagan, however, ordered a review of the treaty shortly after taking office and decided to withdraw it. "After examining the matter, it is clear to me that the fishery treaty cannot be ratified in a form that would be acceptable to Canada," Reagan said.

Senate Action

In submitting the treaties to the Senate in 1979, Carter said they were fair to both countries and "an important

contribution to good relations" between them. Delay in approving the accords could lead to "serious irritants" in relations, he said.

But the Senate did delay action on the treaties. The Foreign Relations Committee did not hold hearings on them until April 1980. Following the hearings, administration officials attempted to work out a compromise acceptable to both Canada and the New England fishermen.

While the Senate delayed, Canadian officials fumed. Mark MacGuigan, Canada's secretary of state for external affairs, said the dispute over the treaty "is not only the most serious bilateral issue we have with the United States. It is the most serious bilateral issue we have with any country."

The Foreign Relations Committee finally reported the boundary treaty April 1, 1981 (Exec Rept 97-5), with technical amendments removing references to the fishing treaty.

Wallenberg Citizenship

On Oct. 5, in large part because of efforts by the Hungarian-born Rep. Tom Lantos, D-Calif., Raoul Wallenberg became the second person in modern American history to be awarded honorary citizenship. The first was former British Prime Minister Winston Churchill, in 1963.

Wallenberg, a Swedish diplomat operating in Hungary toward the end of World War II, was instrumental in getting Lantos and his wife Annette safely out of Nazi-controlled Hungary. Shortly afterward, Wallenberg was arrested by the invading Russians and had not been seen since. For several years, Annette Lantos, founder of the International Free Raoul Wallenberg Committee, worked for his release. Jewish groups credited Wallenberg with saving the lives of at least 100,000 Hungarian Jews facing extermination by the Nazis.

In making Wallenberg an honorary citizen, Congress instructed the president to ascertain from the Soviet Union Wallenberg's whereabouts.

A resolution (S J Res 65 — PL 97-54) making Wallenberg an honorary citizen, was passed by the Senate Aug. 3 and the House Sept. 22. President Reagan signed it Oct. 5.

1982

Mutual skepticism characterized the relationship between Congress and the executive branch on foreign policy issues in 1982.

There were no intense foreign policy struggles during the year, such as the highly emotional 1981 battle over the sale of AWACS planes to Saudi Arabia.

Congress did challenge President Reagan on a few foreign policy items, including economic sanctions against the Soviet Union, aid to El Salvador, covert action against Nicaragua and foreign aid spending. But none of those challenges produced dramatic fights; instead, the administration and its disparate critics on Capitol Hill tried to outmaneuver each other and wound up making compromises that merely postponed decisions on the basic issues.

Toward the end of 1982 leaders of the Senate Foreign Relations and House Foreign Affairs committees expressed concern that Reagan was evading requirements of the War Powers Resolution (PL 93-148) by refusing to seek congressional approval for his decision to station U.S. Marines in Lebanon as part of a multinational peacekeeping force. However, most members of Congress seemed less interested in guarding the sanctity of the War Powers Resolution than in avoiding any action that might upset the chances for a peaceful settlement in Lebanon.

Secretary of State Alexander M. Haig Jr. abruptly stepped down June 25, citing policy conflicts. Haig, the first Reagan Cabinet member to resign, was replaced by George P. Shultz. *(Box, p. 127)*

Soviet Economic Sanctions

The House on Sept. 29 narrowly rejected a bipartisan move to force President Reagan to lift economic sanctions against the Soviet Union. On a **key 206-203 vote (R 124-57; D 82-146)**, members gutted a bill (HR 6838) that would have lifted the sanctions. The weakened measure never was formally considered by the Senate. *(1982 key votes, p. 895)*

Conservatives as well as liberals complained that the sanctions hurt American workers and businesses more than the Soviets. The sanctions prohibited American companies, their foreign subsidiaries and foreign companies using U.S. licenses from selling to the Soviet Union equipment or technology for the transmission or refining of oil and natural gas. One goal of the sanctions was to prevent the U.S.S.R. from using U.S. technology to build a 2,600-mile natural gas pipeline from Siberia to Western Europe.

Reagan himself lifted the pipeline-related sanctions on Nov. 13, saying they had accomplished the purpose of demonstrating U.S. concern over Soviet pressure on Poland. Reagan also said the United States and its Western allies had agreed to conduct a study of ways to limit future trade that bolstered the Soviet economy. The president's announcement came just three days after the death of Soviet President Leonid Brezhnev and one day after the Polish martial law government announced that it was freeing Lech Walesa, leader of the outlawed trade union, Solidarity. (Walesa had been held in detention since December 1981. He was released Nov. 14.)

Although he lifted the pipeline sanctions, Reagan in 1982 maintained and even expanded similar economic sanctions he had imposed directly on Poland. On Oct. 28, three weeks after the Polish government disbanded Solidarity, Reagan suspended indefinitely Poland's "most favored nation" (MFN) trading status that guaranteed favorable tariff treatment. Poland had held the trade status for 22 years.

To justify his suspension of the trading status, Reagan declared that Poland had failed since 1978 to meet its obligations under the General Agreement on Tariffs and Trade (GATT) to increase the total value of imports from other GATT member nations by at least 7 percent per year. GATT governed the general terms of trade among most nations.

Background

Reagan issued the sanctions against Moscow Dec. 29, 1981, and June 22, 1982, to protest imposition of martial

law in Poland and the crackdown on Solidarity, for which he blamed the Soviet Union.

Among other things, the Dec. 29 sanctions required U.S. firms to obtain government licenses for sales to the Soviet Union of equipment or technology for the transmission or refining of oil and natural gas. The sanctions also applied to equipment and technical data for two Soviet truck plants. To put teeth into the sanctions, Reagan ordered the Commerce Department to stop processing all applications for the licenses.

Reagan complained that the natural gas pipeline would make Western Europe overly dependent on the Soviet Union for energy supplies and would provide billions of dollars in hard currency to prop up the ailing Soviet economy.

The president raised the international political stakes June 22 by prohibiting foreign subsidiaries of U.S. firms from selling the same equipment and technology and prohibiting overseas firms from selling the Soviets those products made under U.S. licenses.

Administration attempts to enforce the June 22 sanctions brought bitter protests from European leaders, who complained that Reagan was attempting to use American law to force non-American companies to break valid contracts. Great Britain, France and Italy ordered their firms to proceed with their Soviet contracts and West Germany encouraged its firms to do the same.

Reagan's action came only a few weeks after a Western summit meeting at Versailles, France. European leaders reportedly left that meeting with the understanding that the United States would take no further unilateral actions affecting their trade.

House Action

In an unusually bold demonstration of its willingness to challenge the president on foreign policy, the House Foreign Affairs Committee on Aug. 10 voted 22-12 to approve legislation lifting the sanctions. The committee filed its report on the bill (H Rept 97-762) on Aug. 18.

HR 6838 was widely viewed as symbolic because it had almost no chance of taking legal effect. Even if it had been passed by the Senate, the bill would have been vetoed by Reagan. And even if the bill somehow had been enacted over a veto, Reagan would have been free to restore the sanctions under his own authority provided by the 1979 Export Administration Act (PL 96-72). *(Congress and the Nation Vol. V, p. 274)*

Nevertheless, supporters portrayed the bill as an effort to help Reagan back away from the sanctions. They said the sanctions had irritated the NATO allies and failed either to stop construction of the pipeline or to ease repression in Poland.

The administration lobbied hard against the committee action. Secretary of State George P. Shultz sent all committee members a letter the morning of the vote saying passage of the bill "would severely cripple the president's ability" to carry out foreign policy. The letter admitted that the sanctions had hurt American firms, but it argued that "unfortunate sacrifice" was needed to continue pressure on the Soviet Union.

The administration's effort apparently paid off: The House essentially gutted the committee's bill on Sept. 29, when, on the 206-203 key vote, it inserted a clause saying the sanctions would be repealed only if Reagan certified to Congress that the Soviet Union was not using slave labor

on the natural gas pipeline project. Because Reagan realistically could not make such a certification, the sanctions would remain in effect. The House then passed the amended bill by a 209-197 vote.

The sanctions issue was particularly difficult for House Republicans, many of whom had to choose between supporting their president and voting for a measure that seemed to promise the restoration of jobs for Americans.

Some Sanctions Continued

Reagan's Nov. 13 decision to lift some of the sanctions left in place a 1980 licensing requirement for exports to the Soviet Union of oil and gas exploration and production equipment. Administration officials said those licenses would be processed on a "case-by-case basis." The government also required licenses for exports to the Soviet Union of "high-technology" items, such as computers, that could be used for military purposes. *(1983 story, p. 107)*

Also left intact were licensing requirements for exports of parts and equipment for two Soviet truck plants.

The president's action did not affect a companion series of moves that he took during late 1981 to protest Soviet pressure on Poland. Those actions, which were to remain in effect, were: suspension of service to the United States by Aeroflot, the Soviet airline; imposition of a new series of controls on access to U.S. ports by all Soviet ships; closing of the Soviet Purchasing Commission office in New York City, and postponement of negotiations for a new U.S.-Soviet maritime agreement.

A State Department official said those sanctions were kept because they had had "a heavier short-term economic effect on the Soviet Union" than the pipeline sanctions.

Foreign Aid Authorization

Congress failed in 1982 to complete work on legislation authorizing additional funding for foreign aid programs in fiscal 1983.

The House Foreign Affairs and Senate Foreign Relations committees reported bills in May, but neither received floor consideration. The legislation was doomed by two major factors: a philosophical disagreement over the balance between military and development aid, and the traditional reluctance of Congress to deal with foreign aid issues in an election year.

Because the fiscal 1982 aid bill had authorized funding for two years, the fiscal 1983 bills were supplementals, authorizing less than $1 billion each rather than the full foreign aid budget of around $7 billion. President Reagan already was authorized to spend $5.96 billion on aid in fiscal 1983 under the 1981 law (PL 97-113). *(Story, p. 132)*

As a result, the House bill (HR 6370 — H Rept 97-547) for fiscal 1983, reported May 17 by the Foreign Affairs Committee, authorized only an additional $778 million, for a total of $6.739 billion. The Senate version (S 2608 — S Rept 97-464), reported May 28 by the Foreign Relations Committee, authorized an additional $786 million, for a total aid budget of $6.748 billion. Reagan had requested an increase of $1.221 billion — $975 million of it in military aid.

Although the fiscal 1983 bills were comparatively small, they consisted almost entirely of additional authority for military aid. Because many Democrats favored development and economic aid over arms assistance, the

fragile coalition that got foreign aid through Congress in 1981 was shattered in 1982, thus dooming the chances for the supplementals.

Appropriations for foreign aid programs were included in the fiscal 1983 continuing resolution (PL 97-377). In writing that legislation, the two Appropriations committees followed the lead of the authorizing committees on such issues as military aid and the levels of aid to El Salvador and Israel. *(Foreign aid funding, below)*

Foreign Aid Appropriations

Although Congress failed to clear a foreign aid authorization bill, funds for the programs were provided in the foreign aid portion of a fiscal 1983 continuing resolution (H J Res 631 — PL 97-377) cleared Dec. 20.

Neither chamber took up a regular foreign aid appropriations bill for fiscal 1983. The House Appropriations Committee never wrote such a measure. The Senate committee approved a separate aid bill (S 3075) Dec. 2, and the Senate incorporated the bulk of that measure into its version of H J Res 631 Dec. 16.

As cleared, the continuing resolution included $11.2 billion for "foreign operations" in fiscal 1983, of which $8.1 billion was for foreign economic, military and development aid programs. For budget purposes those amounts did not count several billion dollars for guaranteed loans.

The remainder of the foreign operations category of H J Res 631 was accounted for by the Export-Import Bank. The bank was authorized $13.4 billion in fiscal 1983, but for technical reasons only $3.1 billion of that amount counted as part of the $11.2 billion total in the bill.

House-Senate conferees on the measure warned the administration not to return with new requests for the money that had been denied.

Any request for additional money "must be in response to serious emergency needs," the conferees said in their report on H J Res 631 (H Rept 97-980). "A simple re-requesting of those items which the conferees have provided under the regular fiscal 1983 budget estimates will not be considered genuine needs resulting from real foreign policy problems."

Aid to Israel

Over the opposition of the Reagan administration, Congress increased military aid to Israel for fiscal 1983. But the increase was substantially less than what Israel and its staunchest allies in Congress had wanted.

The issue of aid to Israel crept up on Congress in 1982. During the spring, the House Foreign Affairs and Senate Foreign Relations committees quietly voted increases in grants for Israel as part of the fiscal 1983 foreign aid authorization bills (HR 6370, S 2608). Neither of those bills ever reached the floor. *(Authorization, p. 145)*

But Israel's June 1982 invasion and subsequent occupation of Lebanon led many members of Congress to argue that it was time to hold the line on aid to Israel. Supporters of Israel, however, continued to work for an aid increase.

Senate Committee Action. Their chance came early in December, when the Senate Appropriations Subcommittee on Foreign Operations finally began work on a fiscal 1983 foreign aid bill. With the backing of Chairman Bob Kasten, R-Wis., and ranking Democrat Daniel K. Inouye, Hawaii, the subcommittee boosted economic aid for

Israel in fiscal 1983 to $910 million, from the $785 million requested by Reagan and provided in 1982.

The full Appropriations Committee approved the same amount in S 3075, its $11.6 billion funding bill reported Dec. 3 (S Rept 97-672).

Lobbying. The Appropriations Committee action capped a week of furious lobbying that pitted the administration against the pro-Israel lobby in an unusual debate over Israel's policies and U.S. support for them.

In letters sent to Capitol Hill Dec. 1 and 9, the State Department said increasing aid to Israel would require cuts in aid for other countries and would undercut the Middle East peace process. The letters first said countries such as Spain, Portugal, Turkey and Pakistan would suffer if aid to Israel were increased.

On the second issue, the letters referred by implication to Israeli Prime Minister Menachem Begin and his policies toward Lebanon and the occupied West Bank of the Jordan River. "By appearing to endorse and reward Israel's policies," they said, increasing aid "could strengthen the hand of those who are content with the status quo, while calling into question among others the U.S. commitment to an equitable outcome."

The letters were countered by the American Israel Public Affairs Committee, the pro-Israel lobby. It claimed Reagan had sought an aid cut that would "send a dangerous signal of abandonment [of Israel] to Israel's enemies."

Israeli officials bitterly complained about the administration's opposition to increased aid. Foreign Minister Yitzhak Shamir on Dec. 4 called it "an unfriendly act" that "endangers the peace process."

House, Conference Action. The House version of the continuing resolution, passed Dec. 14, struck a middle line on aid to Israel. It put direct military grants for Israel at $750 million, compared to the $500 million administration request and the $850 million included in the Senate version, passed Dec. 19. And the House bill kept economic aid for Israel at the $785 million request level, but decreed that all of it would be a grant; Reagan had requested that only about two-thirds of the economic aid be a grant.

To avoid ruffling Egypt's feathers, the House bill added $25 million for military grants to Egypt, bringing that nation's total to $425 million.

The final bill increased economic and military aid to Israel for fiscal 1983 by $300 million over fiscal 1982, including an additional $200 million in military grants. But the bill also gave Israel $225 million less in military and economic grants than the Senate had approved.

Conferees adopted all the House figures for Israel and Egypt.

From the Reagan administration's point of view, the final bill was an important victory because it basically maintained a rough balance between Israel and Egypt in the amount of U.S. aid they were to receive. Nevertheless, a State Department official said the administration was reluctant to accept any increases over Reagan's request for Israel.

Arms vs. Development

Although it kept a basic balance between aid to Israel and Egypt, the continuing resolution did little toward maintaining the politically important balance between military and development aid.

Military Aid. The bill provided $1.2 billion of the $2.3 billion in additional military aid that Reagan had

El Salvador Certified Eligible for U.S. Aid

The Reagan administration certified to Congress twice in 1982 that the government of El Salvador was making progress in protecting human and civil rights.

Both certifications brought cries of protest from critics of President Reagan's policy of providing military arms and advisers to the Salvadoran government. The critics insisted that little progress had been made by either government in power in 1982: the moderate, civilian junta that ruled from October 1979 until May 1982, or the rightist regime that took over after May 28 elections for a new Constituent Assembly.

The certifications were required by the fiscal 1982 foreign aid authorization bill (PL 97-113), which cleared Congress in December 1981. That measure established conditions on further military aid to El Salvador and required the president to certify by Jan. 29 and each 180 days afterward that the conditions had been met. President Reagan in 1983 vetoed a similar certification bill. *(Background on El Salvador, p. 181; PL 97-113, p. 132; certification conditions, box, p. 135; 1983 certification reports, p. 165; 1983 veto, p. 165)*

January Certification

The strife in El Salvador already had made headlines in the days before the president's Jan. 28 certification, when the American Civil Liberties Union charged the junta with continuing repression, including 12,501 murders in 1981, and urged Reagan to decline to make his certification. A January report by Amnesty International also charged "a systematic and brutal policy of government-sponsored intimidation and repression" in El Salvador in 1981 and "massive" abuses that "constitute a gross and consistent pattern of human rights abuses."

Nonetheless, in a six-page "Justification" accompanying the formal certification to the Foreign Relations and Foreign Affairs committees, the administration explained how it found that El Salvador had met the conditions on U.S. aid.

The administration said the junta had banned a rightist paramilitary organization known as ORDEN, adopted a code of conduct for the military in October 1980 to prohibit armed forces members from violating human rights and removed or reassigned officers sympathetic to the violent right.

It added that one of the "principal missions of our military trainers in El Salvador is to increase the professionalism of the armed forces and improve the system of military discipline and command and control, thus reducing the abuses suffered in the past by the civilian population at the hands of the armed forces."

"These efforts are beginning to have a positive effect," the justification said. "The level of violence — and particularly the number of deaths — is difficult to quantify, but statistics compiled by our embassy in San Salvador indicate a declining level of violence over the past year and a decrease in alleged abuses by security forces." It said there was "a definite trend in this regard."

The justification admitted that "ultra-rightist ad hoc groups still operate without official sanction." It warned that "all abuses will not end in the immediate future."

The justification said land reform was progressing despite being "targeted by extremists of the right and left" and disrupted by rightist assassinations of agrarian reform officials and intimidation of the peasants being given the land.

The administration said the junta was committed to "free and fair constituent assembly elections in March 1982 and presidential elections in 1983" and had "invited all parties that renounce violence to participate," offering amnesty to guerrillas and freedom for political parties to campaign. But it said the political-guerrilla coalition had "denounced the elections and rejected the government's standing invitation" to discuss election issues.

July Certification

The administration's July 27 certification report acknowledged that violence was continuing in El Salvador but said there were "tangible signs of progress" by the new government in curbing human rights abuses and pursuing land reform and other economic and political changes desired by Congress.

Consequently, the report said, administration officials "believe a firm base has been established for further progress in the months ahead."

It blamed leftist guerrilla attacks for violence that "continues to result in reports of violations of basic human rights committed by leftist guerrillas, right-wing terrorists and members of the government security forces."

The report also acknowledged that the land reform program was slowed by changes made by the Constituent Assembly that had led to "confusion" and illegal evictions of peasants from land already distributed. But the administration maintained that the land reform program had been "relaunched" and the "new government has already undertaken substantial steps to ensure continued progress in human rights" protection.

The report said the most promising development since the Jan. 28 certification was the March 28 election of a 60-member Constituent Assembly, which set up the interim government under President Alvaro Magaña.

requested for fiscal 1983, while holding the line on economic and development aid programs at near-1982 levels. Total military aid came to $5.273 billion, about halfway between the Senate and House amounts.

Of the total, $3.638 billion was for arms loans that carried market interest rates and were guaranteed by the U.S. government, and $1.5 billion was for several grant programs.

The bill kept a lid on the Economic Support Fund (ESF), a program of grants and loans that bolstered the economies of key U.S. allies and friends. The ESF program was part of the administration's "security assistance" package and was generally considered an adjunct of military aid.

The bill included $2.661 billion for that program — $85 million above fiscal 1982 and $225 million less than Reagan had requested. Most of the aid, $1.5 billion, was earmarked for Israel and Egypt.

Development Aid. On the other side of the ledger, H J Res 631 kept a tight rein on programs aimed at developing the economies of poor countries.

The bill provided $3.9 billion for U.S. contributions to international development banks, such as the World Bank, and organizations such as the United Nations; $1.5 billion of that amount was counted as new budget authority and the rest was for loan guarantees. The total was about $84 million above fiscal 1982 and $235 million less than Reagan's request.

Included in the $3.9 billion was $700 million, the same as fiscal 1982, for the fiscal 1983 U.S. contribution to the International Development Association (IDA), the World Bank agency that made low-interest loans to the world's poorest countries. Reagan had requested $945 million, but the administration made little effort to win approval for that amount.

President Carter in 1979 promised to contribute $3.24 billion to IDA over fiscal years 1981-83; Reagan in 1981 stood by the overall amount but decided to make the contribution in four, rather than three, years. As of the end of fiscal 1982, the United States had contributed $1.2 billion. Thus, with the 1983 appropriation, the U.S. contribution over the three years came to $1.9 billion. *(1981 action, p. 131)*

H J Res 631 also held the line on bilateral U.S. development aid programs, including those administered by the Agency for International Development (AID). AID programs were funded at $1.298 billion, the administration request, which was only $3 million above fiscal 1982.

State Department Authority

After a year's hiatus, the House Aug. 11 cleared for the president's signature a bill (S 1193 — PL 97-241) authorizing fiscal 1982-83 funds for the State Department and other agencies. The Senate had adopted the conference report on the bill Aug. 9.

The normally routine bill, stalled in a House-Senate conference committee since October 1981, had been the focus of a revolt in the House on Sept. 17, 1981, when House Republicans shocked the Reagan administration by voting down the first version of the bill. Republicans charged at the time that the bill exceeded the administration request for fiscal 1983, and Democrats refused to vote for the bill because the Republicans were not supporting a bill advocated by their own administration.

1981 Legislative History

As reported by the Senate Foreign Relations Committee May 15, 1981 (S Rept 97-71), S 1193 cut Reagan's fiscal 1982 request by $26 million and his fiscal 1983 request by $32 million. The full chamber passed the bill by a vote of 88-4 on June 18.

In contrast to the Senate's action, the bill reported by the House Foreign Affairs Committee May 19 (HR 3518 — H Rept 97-102, Part I) increased the Reagan request to $3.7 billion for fiscal 1983. But when the bill came to the floor Sept. 17, the House first cut $496 million out of the fiscal 1983 State Department budget that the committee had recommended. Then 131 House Republicans were joined by 95 Democrats in flatly rejecting the bill, 165-226.

Five weeks later, however, the House took up S 1193 and on Oct. 29 passed a trimmed-down bill that cut $171.4 million in fiscal 1982 and $251 million in fiscal 1983 from the floor-amended version of HR 3518. As passed, the new bill matched the administration's revised requests, which were made in September.

Failure to clear the legislation did not force the State Department to close its doors when the new fiscal year began Oct. 1, since its appropriations were included in an omnibus continuing resolution (H J Res 325 — PL 97-51).

Conference, Final Provisions

The conference report on S 1193 (H Rept 97-693) was filed Aug. 3, 1982. The bill authorized $2.87 billion in fiscal 1982 and $2.92 billion in 1983 for the State Department, the International Communication Agency (ICA), the Board for International Broadcasting (BIB) and the Inter-American Foundation. The State Department was to receive the bulk of the authorization, $2.28 billion in fiscal 1982 and $2.25 billion in 1983.

United Nations. The bill prohibited funding of U.N. projects whose primary purpose was to provide political benefits to the Palestine Liberation Organization. However, conferees said the prohibition was not a ban on U.S. contributions to projects whose primary purpose was to provide humanitarian, educational, developmental and other non-political benefits to the Palestinian people.

Conferees expressed opposition to efforts by the United Nations Educational, Scientific and Cultural Organization (UNESCO) to "regulate the world press and license journalists," through its call for a New World Information Order. The "order" was an effort by some developing nations to change what they said was a bias against them in the world press.

To back up that opposition, the bill prohibited authorized funds from being used to pay the U.S. assessed contribution to UNESCO if UNESCO "implements any policy which has the effect of licensing journalists or their publications, restricting the free flow of information within or among countries, or imposing mandatory codes of journalistic practice or ethics."

S 1193 required the president to report to Congress on his assessment of the relationship between U.S. contributions to UNESCO and the U.S. national interest. (In September 1983 the State Department announced that the United States intended to withdraw from UNESCO in 1984. The U.S. withdrawal took place as planned.)

Refugee Aid. The bill provided $29.4 million in fiscal 1982 and 1983 for the resettlement in Israel of refugees from the Soviet Union and Eastern Europe. The measure

also extended aid to refugees from Ethiopia and Iran and urged the executive branch to use all appropriate diplomatic means to help Ethiopian Falasha and Iranian Jews to emigrate to Israel.

The conferees said part of the earmarked money, along with contributions from other donors, should go to the 1.5 million ethnic Somali refugees who had fled fighting in the Ogaden region of Ethiopia.

Consulates. The bill reprogrammed $400,000 in 1982 to reopen and maintain seven U.S. consulates closed by President Carter in an economy move in 1980. Congress ordered the consulates reopened in the fiscal 1980-81 State Department authorization bill (PL 96-60), but neither the Carter nor Reagan administrations had complied. The offices were in Turin, Italy; Salzburg, Austria; Goteborg, Sweden; Bremen, West Germany; Nice, France; Mandalay, Burma; and Brisbane, Australia.

USIA. The bill renamed the International Communication Agency as the United States Information Agency (USIA). The agency's name was changed to ICA in April 1978. The change back to USIA was to take effect on the date of enactment. Some critics had complained that the acronym ICA was easily confused with that of the Central Intelligence Agency (CIA), reducing the credibility of American communications programs around the world.

The bill authorized $86.5 million in 1982 and $98.3 million in 1983 for the Board for International Broadcasting and authorized a merger of the board with the board of Radio Free Europe (RFE) and Radio Liberty (RL). Conferees said the merger was intended to facilitate efficient management of the stations. *(BIB authorization dispute, p. 153)*

Other Provisions. In other provisions, the measure:
● Stated a concern over the lone U.S. vote on May 21, 1981, against the World Health Organization International Code of Marketing Breastmilk Substitutes. The committee urged the president and the U.S. infant formula manufacturing industry to re-examine their positions regarding support for the code. *(Story, p. 142)*
● Extended the validity of U.S. passports from five to 10 years. The bill also authorized the secretary of state to set passport and visa fees.

The fee for passports for adults was to be increased to $42, from $15.
● Stated that any U.S. government broadcasts directed to Cuba should be called "Radio Marti," after the Cuban patriot José Marti. *(Action on Radio Marti authorization, pp. 150, 166)*

Caribbean Basin Initiative

Congress in 1982 enacted into law only one of the three parts of President Reagan's Caribbean Basin Initiative (CBI).

In its fiscal 1982 supplemental appropriations bill (HR 6863 — PL 97-257), Congress voted $350 million in emergency economic aid for nations in the Caribbean and Central American region. Neither house gave serious consideration to a second Reagan proposal, extending the investment tax credit to Caribbean nations. The third part of the package, providing duty-free entry for Caribbean imports to the United States, passed the House in 1982 and was cleared in 1983. *(Legislative action on CBI trade bill, p. 106)*

Reagan Proposal

Reagan Feb. 24 formally announced his Caribbean Basin Initiative, which he said was designed to help stabilize an area of "vital interest" to the United States. In an address to the Organization of American States in Washington, he said the plan would help Caribbean and Central American nations "make use of the magic of the market of the Americas to earn their own way toward self-sustaining growth."

The key elements of the Reagan plan were proposals to:
● Remove for 12 years duties on Caribbean imports to the United States — with the politically important exception of textiles and with limits on duty-free sugar imports.
● Enact federal tax credits or other incentives to induce U.S. firms to invest in Caribbean nations.
● Develop a variety of programs using U.S. agencies and businesses and international organizations such as the World Bank to encourage private investment and production in Caribbean nations.
● Appropriate $60 million in supplemental fiscal 1982 military aid and $350 million in economic aid for the Economic Support Fund (ESF), a program of loans and grants that was the primary means of economic and political support for countries friendly to the United States. Administration officials said most of the additional ESF aid would be used to finance imports of U.S. goods by private businesses in recipient nations.

The supplemental would boost fiscal 1982 ESF aid to the region to $490 million. Congress already had approved $211.3 million in traditional development aid to the region.

In his separate foreign aid request, Reagan also asked for $326 million in ESF aid and $217.6 million in development assistance for the region in fiscal 1983.

Although there was broad support in Congress for an economic, rather than military, approach to the problems of the Caribbean and Central America, Reagan's program was widely viewed as an attempt to disguise increased U.S. aid to El Salvador. Both Republicans and Democrats expressed concern that one-third of the "emergency" economic aid would go to El Salvador, where the administration was backing an embattled regime against leftist guerrillas. And although the economic aid itself was relatively non-controversial, some members expressed concern about boosting foreign aid when domestic programs were being sharply cut. *(Central America special report, p. 181)*

Congressional Action

The House Foreign Affairs Committee July 15 approved by voice vote the $350 million in fiscal 1982 economic aid under the CBI plan, but added restrictions on the money's use. The committee filed its report (HR 5900 — H Rept 97-665, Part I) on July 26.

The Senate Foreign Relations Committee reported its $350 million authorization bill Sept. 10 (S 2899 — S Rept 97-541). It also placed various restrictions on the money's use.

Although the authorization bills never made it to the floor of either chamber, Congress included the CBI economic aid in HR 6863, the omnibus fiscal 1982 supplemental funding bill cleared Aug. 20. Reagan Aug. 28 vetoed the $14.2 billion funding measure, which included nearly $1 billion more than he wanted for various social programs. But Congress overrode his veto Sept. 10, and the bill became law without his signature.

Development Banks Funding

The Reagan administration proposed in 1982 to limit future U.S. contributions to the World Bank and pressed the bank to place tighter conditions on its loans to developing nations.

The future cutbacks were proposed in a report to Congress, issued Feb. 18 by the Treasury Department, assessing the U.S. role in the World Bank and three other multilateral development banks serving Africa, Asia and Latin America. The underlying theme of the report was to play down the development role of official agencies such as the banks and to emphasize the role of private markets.

The report was initiated at the urging of several of the banks' critics in Congress, who said the United States should reconsider whether to continue supporting the banks. Authorizations for the U.S. contribution to the banks had been the subject of considerable debate in 1981. *(Story, p. 131)*

Although proposing reduced U.S. contributions to the multilateral banks in the future and demanding several changes, the report generally endorsed the banks' goals and operations. Even with the cutbacks, the report suggested continued large contributions to the International Development Association (IDA), the most controversial arm of the World Bank.

The report provided encouragement for both critics and supporters of the development banks. Critics in Congress were pleased that the report proposed substantial reductions in U.S. contributions to the banks and demanded some changes in bank policies. Supporters of the banks saw their views vindicated in the report's endorsement of most of the banks' operations and policies.

Radio Marti Authorization

A Senate filibuster in the December lame-duck session killed legislation (HR 5427) authorizing the establishment of a U.S. government radio station to broadcast to Cuba. The bill finally cleared in 1983. *(Details, p. 166)*

The House had passed the legislation on Aug. 10.

The station was to be named Radio Marti after José Marti, a Cuban who led the fight for the island's independence from Spain in 1898.

The White House proposed Radio Marti in 1981 as part of its effort to counter Cuban influence in Central America and the Caribbean. Administration officials said Cubans, insulated from the outside world, needed accurate information about their government and its interference in other nations' affairs.

The House Foreign Affairs Committee reported HR 5427 April 2 (H Rept 97-479, Part I); the House Energy and Commerce Committee ordered the bill reported (H Rept 97-479, Part II) July 13. The Senate Foreign Relations Committee approved an amended version of the bill Sept. 9 (S Rept 97-544).

Cuba Resolution

Congress in 1982 adopted a watered-down version of a resolution reaffirming a 1962 threat to use force to stop Cuban subversion or the use of Cuba by the Soviet Union as a base for nuclear weapons.

The original version of the Cuba resolution, sponsored by Sen. Steven D. Symms, R-Idaho, was at first rejected by the Senate in April, amid confusion about the Reagan administration's position on the issue. But, with administration support, it was amended and included in the fiscal 1982 supplemental appropriations bill (HR 6863 — PL 97-257). The supplemental was enacted into law over President Reagan's veto, which concerned funding levels, Sept. 10.

Mixed Signals. The Senate foreign policy establishment barely defeated a challenge from anti-communist conservatives April 14 as the Senate narrowly rejected the Symms resolution, which was offered as an amendment to an unrelated measure (S Res 20).

The 41-39 vote came on a motion by Charles H. Percy, R-Ill., chairman of the Foreign Relations Committee, to table — or kill — Symms' amendment reaffirming a 1962 law (PL 87-733) authorizing the president to use force to stop Cuban subversion in the Western Hemisphere or a buildup of Soviet offensive weapons in Cuba.

Despite its anti-Cuban rhetoric, the administration itself seemed at the time to be divided on the issue. A State Department lobbyist at one point produced a letter saying the measure was not "helpful." But higher State Department officials later retracted that stand and said the administration supported the Symms amendment.

The measure said the United States would "prevent by whatever means may be necessary, including the use of arms," Cuban aggression or subversion or an "externally supported" Cuban military buildup endangering the United States. It pledged to "work with the Organization of American States and with freedom-loving Cubans" for Cuban self-determination.

Adoption of Amendment. With the administration backing Symms, the Senate adopted the measure as an amendment to the supplemental appropriations bill by a 68-28 vote Aug. 11. Several hours later, the Senate adopted, 97-2, an amendment by Dale Bumpers, D-Ark., to clarify that the Symms amendment would not authorize the president to use U.S. armed forces outside the limits of the War Powers Resolution (PL 93-148).

But inclusion of the amendment in the final version of the bill nevertheless was reported by newspapers and television as a strong message to Cuba, which Symms had said was its central purpose.

The Symms resolution was worded as a restriction on the use of $350 million in economic aid for Caribbean and Central American nations. The aid was the only portion of President Reagan's Caribbean Basin Initiative to be passed by Congress in 1982. The Caribbean Basin Initiative was a three-part plan designed to help stabilize an area of "vital interest" to the United States. *(Caribbean Basin Initiative, p. 149)*

Agent Identity Disclosure

A bill to outlaw what had come to be known as "naming names" — the practice of exposing U.S. intelligence agents to disrupt their work — was signed into law (HR 4 — PL 97-200) June 23, concluding a legislative struggle of several years.

A House-Senate conference report (H Rept 97-580) on the bill was filed in each house May 20 after nearly two months of private negotiations.

The House adopted the conference report June 3, on a 315-32 vote. The Senate adopted it June 10, 81-4.

The House had passed its version of the legislation Sept. 23, 1981. The Senate Judiciary Committee had voted Oct. 6, 1981, to report a names-of-agents bill, but a threatened filibuster prevented Senate leaders from taking up the measure in the final days of the congressional rush to adjournment, and it was not until March 18, 1982, that the full Senate acted.

Similar legislation had died in 1980, when bills reported by the Intelligence and Judiciary committees of both houses failed to reach the floor of either house because of the crush of business. *(Congress and the Nation Vol. V, p. 174)*

Background

The CIA and its allies in Congress had pressed for the names-of-agents bill for several years as a way to stop CIA critics from trying to hamper agency operations by exposing agents. Intelligence agency advocates claimed the practice had led to the assassination of at least one agent and had endangered the lives of many others.

Civil libertarians and other opponents of the "names-of-agents" bill had argued that such a law would be unconstitutional under First Amendment guarantees of free speech and free press because it would apply even to disclosures of names gleaned from public sources.

Legislation to protect the identities of agents got a boost June 29, 1981, when the Supreme Court, in *Haig v. Agee,* denied a former CIA agent's claim of a First Amendment right to uncover his erstwhile colleagues. Among the court's findings in its decision against expatriate former CIA agent Philip Agee was that Agee's practice of disclosing the names of alleged CIA agents was action, not just speech, and "clearly not protected by the Constitution." *(Decision, p. 736)*

Supporters of the names-of-agents legislation maintained that it would stop disclosures by CIA critics such as Agee and the editors of *Covert Action Information Bulletin* (a Washington-based pamphlet that regularly listed alleged CIA agents) without affecting "legitimate journalists" who might name an agent incidentally in the course of writing a "legitimate" story about the CIA or another intelligence agency.

But the American Civil Liberties Union, the Society of Professional Journalists/Sigma Delta Chi and other press groups argued that it was impossible for Congress to pass such a law without putting orthodox journalists in danger of prosecution and thus chilling public debate over the activities of U.S. intelligence agencies.

Legislative History

House Action. The House Intelligence Committee July 22, 1981, approved its version of the names-of-agents

legislation (HR 4 — H Rept 97-221) after adopting a subcommittee amendment narrowing the bill to make it more palatable to House critics.

As reported by the Intelligence Committee Sept. 10, HR 4 required proof that a defendant had exposed an agent "with the intent to impair or impede" U.S. intelligence "by the fact of" the exposure. Intelligence Committee leaders warned against relaxing that standard. They said some constitutional scholars believed that without a specific "intent" standard, the courts might rule the law an unconstitutional abridgment of First Amendment rights to free speech and free press.

But in passing the bill Sept. 23, the House expanded it — over Intelligence Committee protests — to cover negligent as well as malicious disclosures. The amendment, offered by John M. Ashbrook, R-Ohio, would enable a prosecutor to convict a private citizen who had exposed an agent by proving the defendant merely had "reason to believe" the exposure might "impair or impede" U.S. intelligence.

Senate Action. The Senate Judiciary Committee, however, reversed the House's action. As originally introduced in 1981, the standard of proof required to convict a private citizen under the Senate bill (S 391) was the same as that passed by the House: A prosecutor would only have to prove a defendant had exposed U.S. agents "with reason to believe" the disclosure would harm U.S. intelligence.

But by a 9-8 vote Oct. 6, 1981, the panel adopted an amendment to require instead that a prosecutor prove the defendant had exposed U.S. agents "with the intent to impair or impede" U.S. intelligence "by the fact of such identification" — the standard the House Intelligence Committee had approved and the House had rejected.

In its report (S Rept 97-201), the committee said: "S 391 strikes a proper and constitutional balance between the needs of a free society for information that might contribute to informed debate on public policy issues and the compelling concerns of the men and women who serve our nation's intelligence agencies at great risk and sacrifice."

But the full Senate dismissed warnings that the First Amendment was at risk, and on March 17, 1982, scrapped its committee's recommendation, voting 55-39 to adopt an amendment that would imprison and/or fine journalists or other private persons who exposed U.S. agents with "reason to believe" U.S. intelligence might be hurt. The Senate passed the bill the following day.

Conference Agreement. Both chambers had resolved the major issue — the standard of proof to be required to convict private citizens of "naming names" — in identical fashion. Under HR 4 as passed by the House and Senate, a private citizen without access to official secrets could be convicted of exposing a U.S. intelligence agent if he had engaged in a "pattern of activities intended to identify and expose covert agents" and had "reason to believe" the exposure would harm U.S. intelligence.

But that provision continued to be controversial in conference. Arguments between the House and Senate Intelligence committee staffs delayed agreement on conference report language for weeks, and several members refused to sign the report.

Among the criticisms was fear that the bill would have a "chilling effect" on legitimate reporting of spy agency failures and abuses — especially under the "reason to believe" standard of proof, which the Justice Department had said could cover "negligent" disclosures of agent identities.

It was this central concern that led conferees to agree on report language spelling out what should be considered a crime under the bill. "A journalist writing stories about the CIA would not be engaged in the requisite 'pattern of activities,' even if the stories he wrote included the names of one or more covert agents, unless the government proved that there was an intent to identify and expose agents," the conference report said.

To be committing a crime, the report said, "a discloser must be engaged in a purposeful enterprise of revealing identities — he must, in short, be in the business of 'naming names.' "

Provisions

As signed into law June 23, the Intelligence Identities Protection Act (HR 4 — PL 97-200):

● Provided a fine of up to $50,000 and/or a prison term of up to 10 years for anyone who, having had authorized access to U.S. government secrets identifying covert agents, divulged the identity of an agent to anyone not authorized to receive it.

● Provided a fine of up to $25,000 and/or a prison term of up to five years for anyone who, having had authorized access to any U.S. government secrets, disclosed the identity of a covert agent to anyone not authorized to know it.

● Provided a fine of up to $15,000 and/or a prison term of up to three years for anyone who disclosed the identity of a covert agent after engaging in "a pattern of activities intended to identify and expose covert agents" and "with reason to believe" the disclosure would "impair or impede the foreign intelligence activities of the United States." This provision would apply to persons who had not had authorized access to government secrets.

● Provided that a defendant could escape conviction by proving that, before he disclosed the agent's identity, the government had "publicly acknowledged or revealed" the agent's "intelligence relationship" to the United States.

● Provided that a defendant could be convicted of conspiracy to identify an agent only if he had engaged in a "pattern of activities intended to identify and expose covert agents and with reason to believe" the exposure would harm U.S. intelligence.

A conspiracy conviction also could be obtained against someone who had had authorized access to classified information.

● Exempted from prosecution disclosures made directly to the House and Senate Intelligence committees. The bill did not specify whether the exemption was limited to government officials or extended to private citizens as well.

● Exempted from prosecution an agent's disclosure of his own identity.

● Required the president to submit an annual report to the Intelligence committees on measures taken to protect the identities of covert agents and on any related matters.

● Extended the jurisdiction of the law to disclosures made overseas by U.S. citizens or by permanent resident aliens of the United States.

● Provided that nothing in the act was to be construed as justification for withholding information from Congress.

● Defined "covert agent" to mean: any officer or employee of a U.S. intelligence agency, or any member of the armed services assigned to an intelligence agency, whose identity was an official secret and who was serving or within five years had served outside the United States; any U.S. citizen abroad who had a secret "intelligence relation-

ship" with the United States, including work as an agent, informant or "source of operational assistance" to U.S. intelligence; anyone else who had an existing or former secret intelligence relationship with the United States.

● Defined "intelligence agency" to include the CIA, any military intelligence agency or the foreign counterintelligence or foreign counterterrorism arms of the FBI.

● Defined "pattern of activities" as requiring "a series of acts with a common purpose or objective."

The conference report said a pattern of activities "must involve much more than merely restating that which is in the public domain" but could include: efforts to gain unauthorized access to official secrets, physical or electronic surveillance of intelligence agents or "other techniques of espionage," or simply "systematically collecting, collating and analyzing information from documentary sources" in order to divine agent identities.

The report also noted that a pattern of activities did not refer to a pattern of disclosures. It said a "single, first disclosure" was punishable if the other elements of the crime were proven.

Intelligence Authorization

Congress Sept. 10 cleared a bill (HR 6068 — PL 97-269) authorizing fiscal 1983 and supplemental fiscal 1982 spending by U.S. intelligence agencies.

Major agencies included in the bill were the Central Intelligence Agency (CIA), the Defense Intelligence Agency (DIA), the National Security Agency and the Army, Navy and Air Force intelligence branches. In writing the measure, the House and Senate Intelligence committees stuck by the practice of keeping spy agency spending secret.

Legislative History. The House Intelligence Committee approved HR 6068 on April 5 (H Rept 97-486, Part I), and the House passed the bill May 19. The Senate passed HR 6068 June 30 after substituting the version reported by its Intelligence Committee May 5 (S 2487 — S Rept 97-379).

House-Senate conferees Aug. 19 filed their report on the Intelligence Authorization Act (H Rept 97-779). The House adopted the report by voice vote Sept. 8, and the Senate followed suit Sept. 10. President Reagan signed HR 6068 Sept. 27 (PL 97-269).

Provisions. Provisions of the bill that were made public:

● Changed the laws on CIA retirement and survivors' benefits to give a share of such benefits to former spouses of CIA employees who had served at least five years overseas.

● Barred unauthorized commercial uses of the Defense Intelligence Agency's name, initials or insignia, and authorized the attorney general to seek a court injunction to halt them. Similar provisions protecting CIA insignia were passed by Congress in 1981. (Story, p. 139)

● Authorized $12.1 million for FBI counterterrorism programs in fiscal 1983.

● Authorized $15.4 million to fund a staff of 210 persons for William J. Casey, the director of central intelligence.

● Authorized $91.3 million for the CIA Retirement and Disability Fund in fiscal 1983.

● Provided that the CIA director could increase civilian personnel at his agency in fiscal 1982 by up to 2 percent, permitting him to hire persons who otherwise could not be hired until fiscal 1983 began Oct. 1, 1982.

Japanese Defense Spending

The Senate on Dec. 21 passed by voice vote a resolution (S Con Res 46) stating that Japan should "immediately increase" its spending on defense and should "assume a significantly larger share" of the U.S. costs of defending Japan.

The resolution was one of the strongest formal expressions in recent years of congressional dissatisfaction with the Japanese defense efforts. There was no House action on the measure.

Sen. Carl Levin, D-Mich., was the main sponsor of an earlier version of the resolution. "An America gripped by 10.8 percent unemployment and staggering federal deficits will remain unconvinced when the Japanese government pleads that its own debt-financing situation problems prevent increased defense investments," he said.

The resolution had been approved on Dec. 14 by the Senate Foreign Relations Committee, whose members warned that Congress would take stronger steps in the future if Japan did not heed the call for increased defense spending. The resolution included two key statements:

● That Japan "should immediately increase its annual defense expenditures to the levels required for its forces to deploy fully by 1990 an effective conventional self-defense capability, including the capability to carry out its policy, announced by the prime minister [former Prime Minister Zenko Suzuki] in May 1981 of defending its sea lanes of communication."

● That Japan should assume "a significantly larger share of the total annual overall operating costs of the U.S. forces in Japan and should contribute to meeting the U.S. costs currently incurred in Japan for operations, maintenance, repair and overhaul of U.S. ships and aircraft operating in Japan's security interests in the Pacific Ocean region."

In his statement, Levin said achieving those goals would require Japan to spend an average of 1.5 to 2 percent of its gross national product on defense each year through the rest of the 1980s.

BIB Supplemental Funds

A dispute over the salary to be paid to the new head of Radio Free Europe and Radio Liberty helped sidetrack routine legislation (HR 7367, S 3052) making a $13.3 million supplemental fiscal 1983 authorization for the Board for International Broadcasting (BIB), which supervised the stations.

The request itself was non-controversial, but Sen. Edward Zorinsky, D-Neb., used it to launch an attack on the board's decision to pay about $200,000 in salary and benefits to its new president, former Sen. James L. Buckley, R-N.Y. (1971-77). "People who are without jobs just can't understand these types of salaries," Zorinsky said.

Zorinsky delayed Senate Foreign Relations Committee action on the Senate bill long enough to kill its chances of passage in the lame-duck session. The House Foreign Affairs Committee approved its version of the bill Dec. 14, but it, too, did not reach the floor before adjournment.

U.N. Warning on Israel

Both houses of Congress adopted resolutions warning the U.N. General Assembly against any attempt to expel Israel. The resolutions were a reaction to a Feb. 5 resolution adopted by the General Assembly, which declared that Israel "is not a peace-loving state."

The Senate acted first, on April 14 adopting S Con Res 68. The resolution stated the sense of Congress that if the U.N. General Assembly "illegally" expelled or suspended Israel from either the General Assembly or specialized U.N. agencies, the United States should withhold its assessed contribution to the United Nations or suspend its own participation in the General Assembly or agency in question.

S Con Res 68 noted that a nation could be expelled from the General Assembly, or any U.N. agency, only upon the recommendation of the U.N. Security Council. The United States — Israel's closest ally — had a veto in the Security Council.

The House on May 12 adopted an identical resolution (H Con Res 322) by a 401-3 vote, and the Senate also approved that measure Dec. 1.

In September the United States suspended its participation in the International Atomic Energy Agency (IAEA) after that U.N.-related body voted to deny Israel's credentials. A similar move in October to expel Israel from the International Telecommunications Union was averted.

The U.N. General Assembly on Oct. 27 rejected an attempt by Iran to expel Israel. The vote on a procedural move to halt debate on Iran's motion was 75-9, with 31 abstentions. Earlier, 49 countries, including Iran, had signed a letter criticizing Israel's U.N. membership on the grounds that it was not "a peace-loving state."

Arms Sale to India

Congress Dec. 13 cleared for the president a bill (HR 6758 — PL 97-392) lifting legal hurdles facing a Pennsylvania firm that was seeking to make the first major U.S. arms sale to India in nearly 20 years.

The bill enabled the firm, Bowen-McLaughlin-York Corp., to buy U.S. government-made parts for about 200 howitzers that the firm wanted to sell to India. The company would assemble the howitzers at its York, Pa., plant and sell them directly to India. Under previous law, government-made parts could be sold to foreign countries only by the U.S. government. There were estimates that the sale could mean up to $1 billion for the firm, its contractors and the government.

Background

India had not bought major U.S. weapons since 1965, when a war between India and Pakistan led the United States to impose an arms embargo on both countries. The United States lifted the embargo in 1975 but said it would not make a sale to either nation that might disrupt the military balance between the two.

Although it had the world's fourth largest military force, India had bought only about $10 million worth of weapons from the United States in each of the previous five years. Most of the sales involved communications gear, ammunition and other small items.

The Soviet Union had been India's largest weapons supplier since the mid-1960s, but India in the 1970s built up its own armaments industry and bought advanced fighter planes from Britain and France and submarines from West Germany.

U.S.-China Communiqué

President Reagan infuriated his hard-line conservative backers in Congress Aug. 17 by issuing a joint communiqué with the communist People's Republic of China (PRC) declaring an accommodation on the issue of U.S. arms sales to Taiwan. The People's Republic, which considered Taiwan a province, had long demanded an end to U.S. arms sales to the anti-communist Republic of China on Taiwan, which claimed to be the legitimate government of the mainland Chinese.

The communiqué, produced after 10 months of secret talks, said the United States would hold the quantity and quality of future arms sales to Taiwan below 1979-82 levels and intended "to reduce gradually its sales of arms to Taiwan, leading over a period of time to a final resolution." It did not define "final resolution."

A Taiwan government spokesman called the communiqué a "serious mistake" and said Taiwan had "reason to be angry." U.S. press reports from Peking said the communiqué was described there as a triumph for Chinese diplomacy but a "minimum" U.S. concession. The PRC had threatened for months to downgrade diplomatic relations with the United States unless a deadline for an end to U.S. arms sales to Taiwan was set.

To soften the blow to Taiwan, the administration Aug. 19 sent Congress formal notice of a decision to extend an agreement permitting Taiwan to co-produce 30 F-5E and 30 F-5F fighters, at a total price of $622 million over four years.

Conservatives called the communiqué a violation of the Taiwan Relations Act (PL 96-8), a 1979 law governing relations with Taiwan after U.S. relations with China were normalized. The act declared that sales would continue at whatever levels the president and Congress decided would meet Taiwan's "legitimate" needs. *(Background, Congress and the Nation Vol. V, pp. 65, 97)*

The United States had placed a moratorium on sales to Taiwan in 1979 after breaking relations with the island, but sold Taiwan about $830 million worth of arms in 1980.

In 1980 and 1981 the State Department reported to Congress that India was expected to buy U.S. artillery and anti-tank missiles, in part because India wanted to diversify its sources of arms. But in both years, India backed away from ordering the weapons, reportedly because the terms were not acceptable.

Legislative History

House. The House passed the Indian arms sale measure July 19 by voice vote.

In briefly describing HR 6758 to the House, sponsor Bill Goodling, R-Pa., and other backers did not say that a potential sale to India was the main reason for the speedy action on the bill. (Bowen-McLaughlin-York was located in the district represented by Goodling.) A House aide said the members were concerned that publicity about the sale could disrupt negotiations with India.

Foreign Relations Committee Chairman Clement J. Zablocki, D-Wis., described the bill as a non-controversial measure that "is not designed to stimulate or significantly increase commercial arms sales." His committee had approved the bill July 15 with no public debate and did not issue a report on it.

In his fiscal 1983 foreign aid request, President Reagan had asked Congress to make the same change in the arms sales law that Goodling's bill made. The House committee approved the request in HR 6370, the foreign aid authorization bill. But Goodling told the House that separate legislation on the issue was necessary because the foreign aid bill "may be stalled for some time." *(Authorization bill, p. 145)*

Senate. The Senate Oct. 1 passed HR 6758 by voice vote, after adopting amendments recommended by the General Accounting Office (GAO) and incorporated in the Foreign Relations Committee version reported Sept. 24 (S Rept 97-586). Sen. John Glenn, D-Ohio, had asked the GAO to examine how the change would affect the flow of arms overseas.

Both the GAO and administration officials expressed concern that the House-passed bill would enable arms contractors to expand sales with little government control. The GAO report's basic criticism was that HR 6758 as passed by the House did not invoke the 1968 Arms Export Control Act (PL 90-629) in authorizing the transfer of government-supplied equipment to private contractors. The 1968 law gave government agencies and Congress the right to review and approve most overseas arms sales.

Final Action. Because its bill contained technical errors, the Senate passed a corrected version Dec. 8. The House accepted the Senate measure Dec. 13.

Provisions

As signed into law Dec. 29, HR 6758 (PL 97-392):

• Authorized the U.S. government to sell military equipment to U.S. companies for the purpose of incorporating it into items to be sold overseas. Military services also could be sold to U.S. companies, but only if they were performed in the United States. Such sales were to be subject to all restrictions of the Arms Export Control Act (PL 90-629).

• Stipulated that U.S. government equipment and services could be sold to a U.S. company only if the eventual overseas recipient was a "friendly country" or an international organization. U.S. companies also were required to pay the government the replacement cost of equipment and the actual cost of services.

• Required the president to report to Congress on any sale that "could have a significant adverse effect on the combat readiness" of U.S. armed forces.

African Development Fund

Congress failed in 1982 to complete action on a bill authorizing money for the African Development Fund, forcing the Reagan administration to default on its com-

mitment of support for the multilateral program. The fund, a concessional lending facility associated with the African Development Bank, provided low-interest loans for development projects in the poorest countries of Africa.

The administration had asked Congress to authorize $150 million for the fund, with appropriations to be spread over fiscal 1983-85. The money was required for the third replenishment of the fund under an international agreement reached in February 1982. The United States had provided $175 million to the fund since 1976.

The Senate Foreign Relations Committee approved the legislation (S 2398 — S Rept 97-391) May 6, and the full chamber passed the bill May 24 by voice vote with no debate.

The House Banking Committee reported its version (HR 6149 — H Rept 97-513) May 13. But the bill was delayed for months and did not reach the House floor until the last week of the lame-duck session.

Rep. Jerry M. Patterson, D-Calif., chairman of the Banking Committee's International Development Subcommittee, asked the full House to consider the bill Dec. 21. But his request required unanimous consent, and Rep. Hank Brown, R-Colo., objected.

"This certainly is one good cause among many," said Brown, "but we as a country have been unwilling and unable to say 'no' to good causes.... It seems to me that to place the priority of the African Development Bank [sic] above the urgent needs of the poor of our country is a mistake."

Money for the African Development Fund was appropriated in the continuing resolution (PL 97-377), which cleared Dec. 21, but that money could not be transferred to the fund until an authorization bill was enacted. Authorizing legislation was enacted in 1983. *(Story, p. 168)*

Spanish Entry Into NATO

The Senate, by a standing vote, on March 16 approved a protocol (Treaty Doc 97-22) authorizing the entry of Spain into NATO.

Spain officially became the 16th member of the NATO alliance on May 30, after all other members ratified the treaty. It was the first new member since West Germany joined in 1955.

Shultz Replaces Haig

The Senate July 15, 1982, confirmed the nomination of George P. Shultz as secretary of state, replacing Alexander M. Haig Jr., who resigned June 25. Haig, flamboyant and contentious, had come under increasing criticism from other administration officials, particularly Defense Secretary Caspar W. Weinberger. Shultz, an economist and former Nixon Cabinet official, was confirmed 97-0. *(First-term secretaries of state, box, p. 127)*

The United States maintained two active Air Force bases in Spain (at Torregon and Zaragoza). The two countries ratified a military and economic cooperation treaty in 1976.

1983

After two years of sparring, Congress and the Reagan administration slugged it out on foreign policy issues in 1983. Throughout the year the legislative and executive branches were at odds on the direction of U.S. policy in Central America. And as the year progressed, Congress became less and less willing to accept President Reagan's rationale for keeping U.S. Marines in Lebanon.

The root of nearly every dispute between Congress and Reagan was use of military muscle to address foreign policy questions. Whether the issue was military aid, arms sales or the introduction of U.S. troops into hostilities abroad, Congress was quick to attack administration actions that seemed to emphasize a military approach.

After lengthy negotiations between the administration and House Democratic leaders, Congress Sept. 29 approved a compromise measure allowing Reagan to keep U.S. troops in Lebanon for up to 18 months; in the process lawmakers invoked for the first time key provisions of the 1973 War Powers Resolution. However, the Lebanon compromise quickly fell apart after a truck bombing Oct. 23 killed 241 U.S. servicemen in Beirut, and by year's end Reagan was coming under increasing pressure to withdraw the Marines.

U.S. "covert" aid to anti-government guerrillas in Nicaragua was the issue upon which the House Democratic leadership made its stand in opposition to Reagan's foreign policies. The House voted on July 28 and again on Oct. 20 to force the president to end his support of rightist forces that were fighting to overthrow the leftist Sandinista regime of Nicaragua. When the Senate refused to go along with the House, the issue had to be compromised by two conference committees.

Reagan invoked all the persuasive powers of his presidency — including a rare speech to a joint session of Congress on April 27 — to win increased financial backing for El Salvador. He found Congress willing to go along, for the most part.

The president also won widespread approval in Congress for the U.S. invasion of Grenada on Oct. 25. Reagan said the invasion, which he called a "rescue mission," was necessary to protect some 1,000 Americans from civil strife that erupted following the overthrow and eventual murder of Marxist Prime Minister Maurice Bishop.

Congressional conservatives expressed unhappiness with the Reagan administration's response to the Soviet Union's destruction of a Korean Air Lines commercial plane Sept. 1, killing all 269 passengers and crew. While the White House backed a resolution strongly condemning the Soviet action, it did not go far enough for conservatives, who saw the incident as an opportunity to strengthen anti-Soviet attitudes in the United States and the rest of the world.

The regular legislative procedure for handling foreign aid collapsed in 1983. Congress and the administration found it more convenient, for political and tactical reasons, to deal with foreign aid on a stopgap basis. For the first time in a decade Congress failed to pass legislation making

statutory authorizations for foreign aid programs. And for the fourth time in five years, Congress failed to pass the annual bill providing appropriations for those programs.

Lebanon Policy, War Powers

President Reagan's 1982 dispatch of a contingent of Marines to Lebanon to take part in a multinational peace-keeping force evolved during 1983 into a far larger commitment, and a major foreign policy dilemma for Congress.

Congress insisted on injecting itself into the peace-keeping effort. In September it passed a resolution (S J Res 159 — PL 98-119) authorizing the president to keep U.S. forces in Lebanon for as long as 18 months, or until April 1985. Earlier in the year Congress had passed legislation (S 639 — PL 98-43) requiring the president to seek congressional authorization for any "substantial expansion" of the number of U.S. troops stationed in Lebanon. *(Story, p. 158)*

But the spirit of compromise that had led to congressional approval of a Marine presence for another 18 months soon soured as a terrorist bomb killed 241 U.S. servicemen on Oct. 23 and U.S. naval and air forces clashed with Syrian forces in eastern Lebanon, inflicting more U.S. casualties and provoking fears of a war with Soviet-backed Syria that would risk a superpower confrontation.

Public and congressional concern over Reagan's policy mounted throughout the fall, building pressure on Reagan to withdraw U.S. forces from Lebanon or show more convincingly why they should stay. Demands for a withdrawal gained momentum in December when a House subcommittee and a Pentagon-appointed panel of military experts issued reports faulting both the military and political conduct of U.S. policy.

Reagan March 30, 1984, announced that the Marine contingent had accomplished its mission in Lebanon and formally notified Congress that he was ending all U.S. participation in the peacekeeping force. Reagan acted as the House was preparing to adopt a resolution calling for the "prompt and orderly withdrawal" of the Marines. *(Lebanon involvement, special report on Middle East policy, p. 191)*

Legislative Background

As it emerged in September, the Lebanon resolution was founded on a desire among members both to limit Reagan's use of U.S. armed forces and to assert Congress' right to do so under the 1973 War Powers Resolution (PL 93-148). *(War Powers Resolution, Congress and the Nation Vol. IV, p. 849)*

The War Powers Resolution proscribed the deployment of U.S. forces in hostile situations for more than 90 days without congressional authorization. But like presidents before him, Reagan had refused to concede the law's constitutionality and had sidestepped it.

On Aug. 30 Reagan formally notified Congress that two Marines had been killed and 14 others wounded in Beirut on Aug. 29. But in his letter Reagan refused to cite the section of the 1973 War Powers Resolution that would have enabled Congress to force a withdrawal.

Under section 4(a)(1) of the act, Congress could, by passing a concurrent resolution, force the president to withdraw U.S. troops from overseas if he had reported that they were sent "into hostilities or into situations where imminent involvement in hostilities is clearly indicated by the circumstances." While acknowledging that the Marines were engaged in "sporadic fighting," Reagan refused to say they were actually involved in "hostilities."

U.S. officials, including Secretary of State George P. Shultz, said they believed the Moslem attacks were directed at the Lebanese army, not at the Marines.

Reagan told Congress that using U.S. forces in Lebanon was "essential to the objective of helping to restore the territorial integrity, sovereignty and political independence of Lebanon." He said it was "not possible to predict the duration of the presence of these forces in Lebanon. We will continue to assess this question in the light of progress toward this objective."

Several congressional leaders publicly urged Reagan to invoke section 4(a)(1) of the War Powers Resolution and were upset when he refused.

House Foreign Affairs Committee Chairman Clement J. Zablocki, D-Wis., said in the days following the Marine deaths that Reagan was "unnecessarily risking a confrontation with Congress" by "persisting in trying to exclude the Congress from fulfilling its constitutional responsibilities."

Zablocki's Senate counterpart, Charles H. Percy, R-Ill., chairman of the Foreign Relations Committee, agreed that Congress should be involved in the decision making under terms of the War Powers Resolution.

Senate Minority Leader Robert C. Byrd, D-W.Va., wrote Reagan Aug. 31 saying: "American forces are clearly involved in hostilities within the meaning of section 4(a)(1) of the War Powers Resolution" and that Reagan should invoke that section to "assure the fullest possible cooperation" between Congress and the executive.

None of those leaders suggested that Congress would or should attempt to force withdrawal of the Marines. But members who had been critical of Reagan's decision to send the Marines to Beirut in the first place advocated a withdrawal.

Compromise

The lengthy negotiations that led to the eventual compromise were initiated by Zablocki, with the backing of Speaker Thomas P. O'Neill Jr., D-Mass. Zablocki's aim was to preserve the War Powers Resolution — of which he had been a primary author — and at the same time head off legislative attempts to force an immediate withdrawal of the Marines.

Administration negotiators at first rejected a Zablocki resolution that supported U.S. policy in Lebanon and invoked the War Powers act. The administration wanted congressional support but rejected any limit on how long the Marines could remain in Lebanon.

After Senate Democrats introduced S J Res 163, raising the prospect of a direct vote on the War Powers issue, Reagan's aides held talks with Senate Majority Leader Howard H. Baker Jr., R-Tenn., and House leaders. A compromise setting an 18-month limit on deployment of the Marines was reached Sept. 19 and agreed to by both sets of negotiators the next day. Senate Democrats were left out of the final negotiations — ensuring their opposition to the compromise agreement.

In essence, the compromise required Reagan to sign a joint resolution invoking the War Powers Resolution and imposing an 18-month limit on troop deployment. In return, the president could declare in writing that he did not recognize the War Powers act's constitutionality and that

he retained his constitutional authority as commander in chief to deploy U.S. forces.

Zablocki insisted that the compromise was a victory for Congress. "This will be the first administration that has acknowledged the War Powers act," he said. Yet both sides said the value of the compromise was its avoidance of a confrontation over whether Congress had the power to force the president to withdraw U.S. troops from hostilities overseas.

Committee Action

The amended resolutions incorporating the compromise were approved by the House Foreign Affairs Committee on Sept. 22 (H J Res 364 — H Rept 98-385) and by the Senate Foreign Relations Committee Sept. 23 (S J Res 159 — S Rept 98-242).

The House panel approved the compromise 30-6, though many members expressed serious misgivings. The measure squeezed through the Senate committee thanks to pressure exerted by Majority Leader Baker on a party-line vote of 9-7. Initially a substitute limiting the Marine deployment to six months had been adopted by a vote of 9-8, with Charles McC. Mathias Jr., R-Md., voting with the eight committee Democrats. But under pressure from Baker, Mathias later switched and voted with his fellow Republicans to reconsider the substitute. The panel then adopted the original compromise, with Mathias voting "aye."

Before the compromise could be considered by the House and Senate, it was challenged in the House Appropriations Committee. During action Sept. 21 on a stopgap fiscal 1984 funding measure (H J Res 367), that panel adopted an amendment to cut off all funds for the Marines in Lebanon in 60 days unless the president submitted a report to Congress invoking the War Powers act.

The committee's action, taken by a 20-16 vote, angered Speaker O'Neill. He said it would sabotage the compromise with the White House if allowed to stand, and he ordered H J Res 367 referred to the Foreign Affairs Committee, where the measure died. Appropriations Chairman Jamie L. Whitten, D-Miss., drafted a new funding bill (H J Res 368) on Sept. 22 without the Lebanon amendment.

Floor Action

The House passed H J Res 364 on Sept. 28 by a **270-161 key vote (R 140-27; D 130-134)**. The Senate passed S J Res 159 on Sept. 29 by a **54-46 key vote (R 52-3; D 2-43)**. Only two Democrats — George J. Mitchell, Maine, and Edward Zorinsky, Neb. — favored it; three Republicans — Mark O. Hatfield, Ore., William V. Roth Jr., Del., and Lowell P. Weicker Jr., Conn. — opposed it. Several Republicans voted for the resolution only after last-minute arm-twisting by Majority Leader Baker. *(1983 key votes, p. 911)*

House Debate. The major challenge to the compromise in the House was embodied in an amendment that would have forced the president to pull the Marines out of Lebanon before the end of 1983 unless he submitted to Congress a report, as required by the War Powers Resolution, concerning hostilities in Lebanon or certified to Congress that a cease-fire was in effect and "significant progress" was being made in negotiations to broaden the base of the Lebanese government.

The amendment, rejected 158-272, was as close as

House members came to an opportunity to vote to reduce the time period for the Marine deployment.

Two minor changes in the resolution were adopted. One was a requirement that the president report to Congress every 60 days, rather than every six months. The report was to include such information as the cost of maintaining the Marines and the military rules under which the U.S. force was operating. The second put Congress on record as opposing any partition of Lebanon, parts of which Syria claimed.

Speaker O'Neill had worked with the Republican leadership in arranging the compromise and made it a test of party loyalty. Speaking just before the key vote, O'Neill defended the resolution as an affirmation of the validity of the War Powers Resolution. That act, he said, "is doing what it was intended to do." It "clearly limits the scope and role of the U.S. forces in Lebanon so that the danger of a Vietnam-type escalation is avoided," he told the House. "This resolution, believe me, is not a blank check, as some have asserted."

Senate Debate. The major test for the compromise in the Senate came on an amendment offered by Minority Leader Byrd that sought to force the president to withdraw the Marines before the end of 1983 unless Reagan gave Congress the specific reports called for in the War Powers Resolution. But the amendment was tabled, and thus killed, on a straight party-line vote of 55-45.

Senate Democrats were united in their opposition partly because they had been left out of the negotiations between the administration and the House Democratic leadership that arranged the compromise.

The Democrats used the debate to question the administration's goals in Lebanon and the use of the Marines to promote them. Several Democrats argued that the resolution appeared to commit the United States to goals beyond reach: the removal of all foreign forces, Lebanese government control over its territory and progress toward national reconciliation among Lebanon's religious factions.

But Foreign Relations Committee Chairman Percy said there was a distinction between the administration's broad goals and the mission of the Marines. S J Res 159, he said, authorized the Marines to remain in Lebanon for the limited purpose of keeping peace. Reagan accepted a limited mission for the Marines, other Republican senators emphasized. But Democrats noted that the resolution also permitted U.S. forces to take "such protective measures as may be necessary to ensure the safety" of the peacekeeping force. Democrats said that language created a loophole that could enable Reagan to escalate the fighting.

Since Reagan refused to comply with the reporting requirement in the War Powers Resolution, Democrats charged, the resolution had little meaning.

The Senate rejected three other amendments offered by Democrats in hope of tightening the language of S J Res 159.

Final Action

By a 253-156 vote just hours after the Senate acted, the House accepted the minor differences in the Senate version and cleared S J Res 159 for the president.

The House had accepted the Senate position after Reagan promised to make such reports each 60 days anyway.

Reagan praised the "bipartisan spirit" of Congress, but it was clear that his policy lacked genuinely bipartisan

support. A majority of Democrats in both houses had voted against the resolution, many charging that it gave Reagan a "blank check" amounting to another Tonkin Gulf Resolution, which Presidents Johnson and Nixon had used to claim congressional backing for the war in Vietnam.

Baker said he had opposed Reagan's decision to send the Marines to Lebanon and still had "grave doubts" about using U.S. military force in the Middle East. But Baker said he had been obliged to support S J Res 159 because the Marines were "under fire, and I think it would be a mistake of tragic proportions if this Congress were to withdraw them. . . ."

Provisions

As signed into law Oct. 12, S J Res 159 (PL 98-119):

● Stated that the removal of all foreign forces from Lebanon was "an essential United States foreign policy objective in the Middle East."

● Stated that the United States was participating in the multinational peacekeeping force in Lebanon "in order to restore full control by the government of Lebanon over its own territory."

● Stated that U.S. armed forces participating in the multinational force were "now in hostilities requiring authorization of their continued presence under the War Powers Resolution."

● Stated that Congress "determines" that the requirements of section 4(a)(1) of the War Powers Resolution came into effect on Aug. 29, 1983, when two Marines were killed in Lebanon.

● Authorized the president, "for the purposes of" section 5(b) of the War Powers Resolution, to continue participation by U.S. armed forces in the multinational force in Lebanon, subject to the limitations contained in letters exchanged Sept. 25, 1982, between the Lebanese and U.S. governments. The letters stated that 1,200 U.S. armed personnel were to serve in the Beirut area only for peacekeeping and were not to engage in combat.

● Authorized U.S. forces to engage in "such protective measures as may be necessary to ensure the safety of the multinational force. . . ."

● Authorized U.S. forces to remain part of the multinational force in Lebanon "until the end of the 18-month period" beginning on the date of enactment of the joint resolution, which was Oct. 12, 1983. The authorization was to expire before the end of that 18-month period if all foreign forces were withdrawn from Lebanon, unless the president certified to Congress that troops should remain, or if the United Nations or the Lebanese government assumed the duties of the multinational force, or if other "effective security arrangements" had been implemented, or if all other countries had withdrawn from participation in the multinational peacekeeping force.

● Required the president to report to Congress at least every three months on the status of U.S. forces in Lebanon. (Reagan agreed informally to submit such reports every 60 days.) The reports were to include statements on the activities being performed by the multinational force; the composition, responsibilities and areas of deployment of the force; the results of efforts to reduce and eventually eliminate the force; how continued U.S. participation in the force was advancing U.S. foreign policy interests in the Middle East; and what progress had occurred toward political reconciliation among all groups in Lebanon.

● Stated that Congress believed it should be U.S. policy to continue to promote discussions with Israel, Syria and Lebanon on the removal of all foreign forces from Lebanon.

● Stated the sense of Congress that not later than one year after enactment of the resolution, and at least annually thereafter, the United States should discuss with other members of the U.N. Security Council the establishment of a U.N. force to assume the responsibilities of the multinational force in Lebanon.

● Stated that nothing in the resolution precluded the president from withdrawing U.S. forces from Lebanon if circumstances warranted, and nothing precluded Congress by joint resolution from directing such a withdrawal.

● Stated that the resolution did not modify or supersede the War Powers Resolution or the Lebanese Emergency Assistance Act of 1983 (PL 98-43), which required congressional authorization before there could be "any substantial expansion in the number or role of United States Armed Forces in Lebanon."

● Established priority procedures in both houses of Congress for the consideration of any joint resolution or bill to amend or repeal the resolution.

Aid to Lebanon

The Senate June 15 cleared legislation (S 639 — PL 98-43) authorizing $251 million in economic and military aid to Lebanon in fiscal 1983.

The aid included $150 million in Economic Support Fund loans and grants, $100 million in Foreign Military Sales loans and $1 million in military training aid. The administration had requested the aid in the wake of Israel's June 1982 invasion of Lebanon.

Congress backed off attempts to require the president to obtain permission from Congress before sending more Marines into Lebanon. But the bill did require the president to seek congressional authorization for any "substantial expansion" of the number of U.S. troops stationed in Lebanon as part of a multinational peacekeeping force. That provision, however, applied only to stationing U.S. troops in Lebanon in conjunction with agreements providing for withdrawal of all foreign occupying forces in Lebanon. The United States had more than 1,200 Marines stationed in Lebanon.

Congressional action followed a bombing of the U.S. Embassy in Beirut April 18 that resulted in the deaths of 63 people.

The bill's language dealing with the Marine deployment stated:

"The president shall obtain statutory authorization from the Congress with respect to any substantial expansion in the number or role in Lebanon of United States Armed Forces, including any introduction of United States Armed Forces into Lebanon in conjunction with agreements providing for the withdrawal of all foreign troops from Lebanon and for the creation of a new multinational peacekeeping force in Lebanon.

"Nothing in this section is intended to modify, limit, or suspend any of the standards and procedures prescribed by the War Powers Resolution of 1973 [PL 93-148]." *(War Powers, Congress and the Nation Vol. IV, p. 849)*

Legislative Action

The Senate Foreign Relations Committee held three sessions on the bill April 19 and 20. The administration

strongly objected to a Democratic initiative that would have placed the Marines under a provision of the War Powers Resolution declaring them to be facing "imminent hostilities." In that status Congress had the right under the 1973 act to withdraw U.S. troops from overseas combat in certain circumstances. Also opposed was a proposal requiring congressional approval before additional Marines could be sent to Lebanon.

As a result of the administration's adamant position, the committee approved milder language stating that the president must obtain congressional approval for "any substantial expansion in the number or role of United States Armed Forces in Lebanon or for the creation of a new, expanded or extended multinational peacekeeping force in Lebanon."

The bill was reported May 5 (S Rept 98-72) and passed by the Senate May 20 by voice vote without amendment.

The House Foreign Affairs Committee approved with little debate language requiring the president to get approval from Congress "with respect to the introduction of United States Armed Forces into Lebanon in conjunction with agreements providing for the withdrawal of all foreign troops from Lebanon and for the creation of a new, more permanent multinational peacekeeping force in Lebanon." The committee had substituted that version for a measure approved April 12 by the panel's Middle East subcommittee that would have required prior approval before any more troops were sent to Lebanon. The language had been modified because of administration opposition, and subcommittee Chairman Lee H. Hamilton, D-Ind., said the final version of the provision would not preclude the president from increasing the U.S. force already in Lebanon.

The House committee's version was reported May 19 (HR 2532 — H Rept 98-208).

The House passed S 639 June 2 by a 276-76 vote, after substituting the text of its own bill. The Senate accepted the House version June 15.

Foreign Aid

President Reagan's rapid expansion of U.S. military aid to friendly countries continued to make headway in 1983. Congress passed two measures that included significant increases in foreign military aid: an omnibus fiscal 1983 supplemental appropriations bill and a fiscal 1984 continuing appropriations resolution.

Congress failed to pass regular authorization and appropriations bills for foreign aid in fiscal 1984 and instead approved those programs in the continuing resolution, which included funds for all foreign economic development and military programs. The bulk of the funds went to military and related programs.

Earlier in the year, as part of the fiscal 1983 supplemental funding measure, Congress gave Reagan an extra $689 million in military and military-related aid, bringing that year's total for those programs to $8.6 billion — a 16 percent increase over the previous year.

Fiscal 1983 Supplemental

The fiscal 1983 supplemental appropriations bill (HR 3069 — PL 98-63), cleared July 29, provided about two-thirds of the $1 billion-plus that Reagan had requested for "security assistance." Security assistance included military

aid, such as loans and grants to help foreign governments buy U.S. arms, and economic aid.

The bill also included a $245 million request for the International Development Association, an arm of the World Bank. That sum was in addition to $945 million previously approved by Congress.

HR 3069 was passed by the House May 25 (H Rept 98-207) and the Senate June 16 (S Rept 98-148). Conferees filed their report (H Rept 98-308) July 20. Major foreign aid provisions:

Security Aid. HR 3069 appropriated $689 million of $1.067 billion requested for security assistance programs. The major items were:

● $301.3 million for the Economic Support Fund (ESF), which bolstered the economies of countries friendly to the United States. Reagan had requested $354 million.

● $293.5 million for Foreign Military Sales (FMS) market-rate loans that helped friendly countries buy U.S. weapons. Reagan had requested $525 million.

● $93.3 million for Military Assistance Program (MAP) grants, which also helped foreign countries buy U.S. arms. Reagan had requested $187 million.

Congress gave Reagan virtually complete discretion in allocating the security aid among the more than 30 countries for which money was requested. There were three exceptions to that rule: Lebanon, El Salvador and Somalia.

The bill earmarked $251 million for Lebanon — $150 million in ESF aid, $100 million in FMS loans and $1 million in military training aid.

The El Salvador money was one of the most controversial issues. Reagan had requested an additional $50 million in fiscal 1983 for military grants to El Salvador as part of a $110 million boost in military aid announced in March. The House Appropriations Committee had rejected the $50 million request and the Senate committee had approved it. The final bill contained $25 million.

A limit of $25 million on military aid for El Salvador was not written into the bill itself, and thus was not legally binding, but Reagan accepted it. Combined with $26.3 million previously appropriated and $30 million reprogrammed from other countries, the $25 million put military aid to El Salvador in fiscal 1983 at $81.3 million.

Another informal limit, of $2 million, was placed on FMS loans to Somalia, which was engaged in a border dispute with Ethiopia. Reagan asked for $4 million in loans and $5 million in military grants for Somalia.

Other Provisions. Other major foreign aid provisions of HR 3069 were:

● A flat prohibition on additional FMS loans for Jordan. Reagan had requested $35 million in supplemental loans for Jordan, largely to encourage King Hussein to participate in Middle East peace negotiations. Congress previously had approved $51.5 million. But Hussein had shied away from direct negotiations, prompting moves in Congress to cut Jordan's aid.

● A prohibition on all forms of aid to Guatemala except for development projects conducted by private voluntary organizations. *(Guatemala, box, p. 163)*

● A similar requirement that economic aid for Zaire be used only to fund development projects sponsored by private organizations.

Fiscal 1984 Authorization

Neither chamber acted on foreign aid authorization bills reported by House and Senate committees in May.

House Foreign Affairs Committee Chairman Clement J. Zablocki, D-Wis., pointed out three obstacles to congressional passage of a foreign aid authorization: The House bill contained controversial provisions the administration opposed; the administration never lobbied for the aid bills; and leaders of both parties showed no enthusiasm for devoting days of floor time to the politically difficult issues posed by foreign aid.

The Foreign Affairs Committee reported its aid bill (HR 2992 — H Rept 98-192) on May 17. The Senate Foreign Relations panel reported its version (S 1347 — S Rept 98-146) May 23. The two panels cut Reagan's request for military aid for El Salvador and imposed conditions on what they did approve. *(El Salvador, p. 165; Central America special report, p. 181)*

Foreign Aid Assessment

A commission appointed by Secretary of State George P. Shultz took Congress to task for engaging in "unproductive" debates that endangered foreign aid legislation.

Headed by Frank C. Carlucci, former deputy secretary of defense, the foreign aid commission called on the president and congressional leaders to issue a joint statement endorsing foreign aid as an "essential and integral part of the foreign policy of the United States."

The commission released its report Nov. 21, following six months of hearings and studies. Nine of its 24 members were members of Congress.

Among the commission's recommendations, the most controversial were suggestions that the United States provide more of its overseas military aid as grants (and less as loans) and that foreign aid agencies be reorganized into a Mutual Development and Security Administration because the existing system was "procedurally and organizationally fragmented."

In calling for increased military grants, the commission noted that several countries, including Turkey, Egypt and the Sudan, had built up large debts in U.S. military loans at the same time that the United States was providing them economic aid.

"Thus, the one program is adding to the debt problems of these countries, while the other is seeking to alleviate them through favorable financial terms and economic improvements," the report stated.

Several members of the panel opposed an increase in military grants on the grounds that developing countries needed economic aid grants more than military aid. They noted that the administration was in the process of reducing U.S. contributions to such agencies as the International Development Association, which made interest-free loans to the world's poorest countries.

Both bills continued Reagan's policy of rapidly expanding U.S. military aid programs, although Democrats charged (as they had in the past) that the emphasis came at the expense of economic and development aid. In fiscal 1982 the total authorization for the four major military aid programs was $4.1 billion; for fiscal 1984 the committees approved $6.3 billion, an increase of more than 50 percent. Reagan had wanted even more — $6.45 billion.

Israel, Egypt. Both committees increased military aid for Israel by substantial amounts above the administration request. A total of $1.7 billion in various types of military aid was recommended, along with $910 million under the Economic Support Fund. Egypt was to get $1.36 billion in economic aid and $750 million in ESF grants.

Greece, Turkey. The two committees adhered to the traditional practice of protecting military aid for Greece while cutting and imposing conditions on assistance to Turkey. The actions of the committees had the effect of retaining a traditional aid "balance" under which Greece received $7 in U.S. military aid for every $10 that Turkey received. The 7-10 ratio also was contained in the aid appropriations legislation.

Latin America. In addition to the strings it attached to aid for El Salvador, the House committee imposed conditions on military aid to or U.S. military involvement in six other countries in Latin America: Guatemala, Honduras, Argentina, Chile, Paraguay and Uruguay.

The Senate committee changed the aid request for Honduras but did not impose conditions on aid for any of the countries.

Economic, Development Aid. The Senate committee took a small step toward reversing the Reagan administration's emphasis on military over economic aid. By a 10-7 vote on May 5, the committee approved an amendment to shift $76 million from the Military Assistance Program and ESF accounts into several economic development aid programs. But the committee later had second thoughts about cutting the ESF aid and restored most of the money it had cut. ESF aid was included under the administration's "security assistance" budget but was not used directly for military purposes.

Both committees voted substantial increases over Reagan's requests for population and health programs administered by the U.S. Agency for International Development (AID).

Both committees approved the administration's request for authority to establish a revolving fund that would finance AID's programs to encourage investments in developing countries by private businesses. The administration requested a $20 million authorization for the fund in each of the 1984-86 fiscal years.

Fiscal 1984 Appropriations

Because it failed to complete action on the foreign aid authorization bill, Congress lumped together authorizations and appropriations for the programs in the fiscal 1984 continuing appropriations resolution (H J Res 413 — PL 98-151) cleared Nov. 12.

H J Res 413 appropriated $11.468 billion for foreign aid in fiscal 1984, of which $8.881 billion was for traditional military, economic and development programs. The remainder represented the impact on the budget of Export-Import Bank loans.

President Reagan had requested $11.637 billion in new budget authority for fiscal 1984, including $9.1 billion for

military and economic aid and $2.5 billion for the Export-Import Bank.

Putting foreign aid appropriations in a continuing resolution was not unusual: Congress had done so for fiscal years 1980, 1981 and 1983. But since 1973 Congress regularly had passed a separate authorization bill for foreign aid. Its failure to do so in 1983 forced congressional leaders to put stopgap authorization language in the funding resolution.

Because foreign aid was an unpopular subject, especially in election years, Congress had not passed either an authorization bill or an appropriations measure since 1981, when it approved an authorization measure covering fiscal years 1982-83 and an appropriations bill for fiscal 1982. In 1982 and 1984 foreign aid funding also had to be included in a catchall appropriations bill. *(Stories, pp. 132, 136, 146, 170)*

H J Res 413 was passed by the House Nov. 10 and the Senate Nov. 11. Both chambers adopted the conference report (H Rept 98-540) Nov. 12, and Reagan signed the bill Nov. 14 (PL 98-151).

As H J Res 413 was working its way through the legislative process, both Senate Foreign Relations Committee Chairman Charles H. Percy, R-Ill., and House Foreign Affairs Committee Chairman Zablocki tried to use it to preserve at least some of their influence over foreign aid.

Percy on Nov. 10 sought to force action on his committee's authorization bill by placing an amendment in the continuing resolution to prevent foreign aid spending after April 15, 1984, unless it had been authorized. The Senate approved that amendment by voice vote with little debate.

Zablocki simply pared his committee's complex bill down to the minimum necessary to authorize the funds in H J Res 413. The House adopted Zablocki's limited authorizations amendment on Nov. 8. The final version of H J Res 413 contained the bulk of Zablocki's amendment.

El Salvador. El Salvador was a major issue in foreign aid discussions at the House-Senate conference on the continuing resolution.

The bill set a $64.8 million limit on military aid for El Salvador, a cut of $21.5 million from Reagan's request. The $64.8 million limit was the first statutory cap that Congress had imposed on aid to El Salvador.

However, conferees made a significant concession to Reagan by not stipulating the accounts under which the aid would be provided. That gave Reagan a free hand to dispense much of the military aid on a grant basis.

The continuing resolution mandated the toughest conditions yet imposed by Congress on aid to El Salvador.

One provision withheld expenditure of 30 percent of the military aid until the Salvadoran government completed its investigation into the murders of four U.S. churchwomen in December 1980, brought the accused murderers to trial and obtained a verdict. Five former national guardsmen had been charged, but their trial was delayed repeatedly.

The bill did not state who would determine when those conditions had been met. In the past critics had accused the administration of overlooking the shortcomings of the Salvadoran government and the judicial process in a rush to certify its eligibility for U.S. aid.

Another condition withheld 10 percent of El Salvador's military aid until the president certified to Congress that the government had taken no actions that would "modify, alter, suspend or terminate" the two key parts of its land reform program in a manner that would undermine the rights of those who were intended to benefit from the program. The president also had to certify that the government "continues to make documented progress" in the land reform program.

Although the bill placed conditions on a total of 40 percent of the military aid, conferees nevertheless stipulated that withheld aid for El Salvador would be limited to 30 percent.

The bill did not restrict economic and development aid to El Salvador — an issue that had generated little controversy in Congress. Reagan had requested $120 million in economic aid and $38 million in development aid in 1984.

Military vs. Development Aid. The continuing appropriations resolution represented a substantial victory for the administration's effort to boost military aid to friendly countries.

Counting all forms of aid, the bill increased military aid programs by 15 percent over fiscal 1983. By contrast, total funding for economic and development aid programs was cut by 5.6 percent from fiscal 1983 levels.

The largest single increase in the bill was for military assistance grants. When Reagan entered office in 1981, the Military Assistance Program provided $110 million in grants to help economically strapped nations buy U.S. weapons. By fiscal 1983 it had grown to $383 million; H J Res 413 provided $510 million.

For Foreign Military Sales loans, the bill had the effect of giving Reagan slightly more than he requested. By shifting $300 million of Israel's $1.7 billion in military aid from loans to FMS grants, the bill as enacted contained $3.551 billion in arms loans to other countries, $45 million more than Reagan had requested.

The bill gave Reagan much more freedom to allocate military aid among countries than any president had had in recent years. Traditionally, amounts for most countries were specified in foreign aid bills or in the reports issued by congressional committees.

But H J Res 413 specified amounts for only a few countries and allowed Reagan to shift the remaining military aid among countries, so long as he notified Congress in advance and stayed within his original budget requests, submitted in January and February.

U.S. foreign military and related aid were embodied in two other programs: International Military Education and Training loans and grants and Economic Support Fund loans and grants.

Israel, Egypt. The bill's $1.7 billion in military aid for Israel was the same amount provided in fiscal 1983. Fully half was designated as a forgiven loan (the same as a grant), a $100 million increase over 1983; the remainder was a regular FMS loan, to be repaid at market rates. The bill also gave Israel $910 million in ESF grants, an increase of $125 million over 1983.

The bill provided $1.365 billion in military aid for Egypt, Israel's partner in the 1979 Middle East Peace Treaty, of which $900 million was in loans to be repaid, and $750 million in ESF grants.

International Banks. The bill included $1.3 billion in direct U.S. contributions and $2.1 billion in so-called "callable capital" (similar to loan guarantees) for the World Bank and other international development banks. The final version cut the administration's request for direct contributions by $280.3 million and callable capital by $794.5 million.

As in previous years, the most controversial item was the U.S. contribution to the International Development

Association (IDA), the World Bank agency that made interest-free, long-term loans to the world's poorest countries. Conservatives in Congress for years had criticized IDA's lending policies and had strongly opposed U.S. funding of the agency. *(1981 action, p. 131)*

Reagan requested $1.1 billion in fiscal 1984 for the final payment on the U.S. pledge of $3.24 billion to the sixth replenishment of IDA resources. The final bill provided $945 million.

The bill also reduced Reagan's requests for the U.S. contributions to the main arm of the World Bank, the International Bank for Reconstruction and Development. That agency made loans at near-market rates to middle-income developing countries, such as Mexico and Brazil.

Reagan had requested $109.7 million in direct contributions to that agency and $1.4 billion in callable capital. Congress cut those amounts to $79.7 million and $983.2 million, respectively.

Greece, Turkey. The bill appeared to give Reagan a free hand to provide Turkey all of the $755 million in military aid he had proposed. However, Congress unofficially cut that aid by $35 million.

While the funding resolution itself set no limits on aid to either Greece or Turkey, the House-Senate conference report that accompanied the final version of the bill directed the administration to adhere to a 7-10 ratio in military aid to those countries.

Under congressional pressure, Reagan in March agreed to increase aid to Greece to $500 million, from the $280 million he originally proposed, if Greece renewed an agreement providing for several U.S. military bases on Greek soil. Greece and the United States signed a five-year bases agreement in September.

Adhering to the 7-10 ratio, the administration in December allocated $500 million in FMS loans to Greece and $715 million in aid to Turkey (including $585 million in FMS loans and $130 million in MAP grants).

Other Provisions. In a move unusual for its directness, H J Res 413 withdrew some $80 million in previously appropriated economic aid to Syria and shifted $15 million of that money to Grenada and $10 million to Italy. *(Grenada invasion, p. 169)*

The bill appropriated $1.4 billion for development assistance programs of the Agency for International Development.

It prohibited all military, economic and development aid to Guatemala, except for economic development projects conducted through private voluntary organizations. A similar prohibition was contained in the supplemental appropriations bill.

Nicaragua Covert Aid

Congress and the Reagan administration managed to find a compromise in 1983 that resolved — but only temporarily — the issue of "covert" U.S. aid to anti-government rebels in Nicaragua. The issue was to surface again in 1984, particularly after disclosures of U.S. participation in the mining of Nicaraguan harbors in February and March. *(1984 action, p. 175; background, special report, p. 181)*

Cleared by Congress on Nov. 18 after months of debate, the Nicaragua compromise gave neither side all it wanted. President Reagan got $24 million to continue aiding some 10,000 rebels seeking to overthrow the leftist government of Nicaragua; congressional opponents received assurances that they would get a better chance to block the program in mid-1984. The compromise was contained in both the fiscal 1984 defense appropriations (HR 4185 — PL 98-212) and intelligence agencies authorization (HR 2968 — PL 98-215) bills.

Rep. C. W. Bill Young, R-Fla., and other supporters of the president's policy praised the compromise for continuing the formerly "covert" aid to the Nicaraguan rebels for another nine months. Democrats, who twice in 1983 were able to kill the aid in the House, said they were disappointed for the same reason.

Temporary Solution

As with many compromises, the 1983 Nicaragua agreement postponed rather than resolved the issue.

Reagan apparently had planned to give the rebels $35 million-$50 million in military aid. Congressional leaders said that $24 million would enable the CIA to continue providing arms and other aid to the Nicaraguan rebels through June 1984, at the 1983 rate of spending. Once the money ran out, Reagan would have to seek more from Congress or terminate the aid.

House Intelligence Committee Chairman Edward P. Boland, D-Mass., who led the opposition to Reagan's covert aid requests, told the House Nov. 18 that the compromise was the best deal he could negotiate with the Republican-controlled Senate. The only alternative, he said, was to rely on stopgap funding measures that "would mean no limitation on this program."

Boland and his Democratic colleagues in the House stood almost alone in opposition to the program.

The Republican leadership in both chambers was solidly behind Reagan's Nicaragua policies. And most Senate Democrats, many of whom were skeptical of the covert aid, chose not to challenge it head-on. In contrast to the House, where the U.S. covert action was a major topic of debate for months, only a handful of senators took to the floor to discuss the issue.

Instead, senators of both parties demanded that Reagan narrow the scope of the aid. Twice, on May 6 and Sept. 21, the Senate Intelligence Committee voted 13-2 to allow the aid to continue, with changes.

Background

Detailed press reports in 1983 prompted intense congressional scrutiny of CIA support for Honduras-based rebels, who in 1982 invaded Nicaragua with the declared aim of overthrowing the government. U.S. officials, however, refused publicly to confirm or deny reports of U.S. covert operations in Central America.

Faced with mounting congressional challenges not only on his Nicaragua policy but on other aspects of his Central America policy as well, Reagan April 27 addressed a joint session of Congress to defend his Central America policy.

The president devoted much of his speech to a harsh attack on the leftist government of Nicaragua, saying it "has treated us as an enemy."

In his only direct reference to U.S. activities against Nicaragua, Reagan said the United States was merely trying to prevent the flow of Soviet- and Cuban-supplied arms through Nicaragua to the guerrillas in El Salvador.

"We do not seek [the government's] overthrow," he said. "Our interest is to ensure that it does not infect its neighbors through the export of subversion and violence."

U.S. Aid to Guatemala Blocked by Congress

Acting sometimes in concert and sometimes at odds, Congress and the Reagan administration in 1983 bluntly warned the Guatemalan government to improve its performance on human rights issues.

With little fanfare, Congress blocked all U.S. aid to the Guatemalan government, and the administration halted a long-pending sale of helicopter spare parts and other equipment for that country's army.

The administration, which had promoted the sale and other military aid, went along with congressional critics of aid to Guatemala after a hard-line general overthrew one who appeared to be easing repression.

The warnings produced no immediate results. The United States had been complaining about human rights abuses by right-wing governments in Guatemala since 1977, with little noticeable effect. Guatemala had been ruled by military and authoritarian governments since 1954, when a CIA-financed coup overthrew a left-leaning government that irritated the Eisenhower administration.

Proposed Arms Sales. In January 1983 the Reagan administration offered a major political carrot to the government of Gen. Efrain Rios Montt, agreeing to sell the Guatemalan army $6.4 million worth of helicopter parts and other items that could be used for military purposes. The State Department said the sale was justified because Guatemala under Rios Montt had taken "significant steps" to improve respect for human rights.

The administration's offer was protested by human rights groups and congressional critics, who said there was not enough evidence that Rios Montt had made the improvements the administration claimed.

The sale never was consummated. Guatemala said it could not afford to pay cash for the equipment, and Congress did not approve any U.S. aid to help finance the sale.

In August 1983 Defense Minister Oscar Mejia Victores, a hard-line anti-communist army general, overthrew Rios Montt. The new government, accord-ing to administration officials, was ready to buy just spare parts and repair work for its three UH-1H helicopters, valued at more than $2 million.

Word of plans for the smaller sale brought new protests from Capitol Hill. On Nov. 9, 51 House members, most of them liberal Democrats, wrote Reagan asking him not to sell Guatemala any equipment "which may be used for offensive military purposes." They also said there was "no evidence" that the Mejia Victores government "constitutes an improvement over its predecessors."

The administration did not formally respond to that letter, but State Department officials said Nov. 28 the sale was being held in abeyance because of an upsurge in political violence in Guatemala.

Congress had no automatic power to veto the Guatemala military equipment sale, which fell well below the $50 million threshold for congressional review of overseas arms sale packages.

U.S. Aid Ban. In a related development, Congress in November flatly banned all U.S. military, economic and development aid that would directly benefit the Guatemalan government.

An omnibus funding bill (H J Res 413 — PL 98-151), cleared Nov. 12, barred aid to Guatemala "except for economic development projects through private voluntary organizations."

That provision generated no controversy in Congress and was not actively opposed by the administration. Reagan signed H J Res 413 Nov. 14 without commenting on the Guatemala provision.

A similar provision was contained in a fiscal 1983 supplemental appropriations bill (HR 3069 — PL 98-63) cleared July 29. *(Aid funds, p. 159)*

In his fiscal 1984 budget, Reagan had requested $10 million in military loans, $40 million in economic aid and $26.6 million in other aid for Guatemala.

The United States had provided small amounts of development and food aid to Guatemala, but after 1977 had given no military or economic aid that might imply active U.S. support for the government.

Covert Aid Ban

Boland and Intelligence Committee member Clement J. Zablocki, D-Wis., April 27 introduced HR 2760, to end all U.S. support for military groups in Nicaragua. The bill had the support of the Intelligence Committee Democrats and the House Democratic leadership.

Earlier, on April 13, the committee agreed to demand that the Reagan administration explain what it was doing in Nicaragua. Boland said he believed the administration was violating the 1982 Boland amendment, which prohibited U.S. covert actions "for the purpose of" overthrowing the Sandinista regime or provoking a military conflict between Nicaragua and Honduras. The amendment had been attached to fiscal 1983 intelligence authorization (PL 97-269) and defense appropriations (PL 97-377) legislation. *(Stories, pp. 152, 219)*

On May 3 the House Intelligence Committee approved HR 2760 (H Rept 98-122, Part I), with all Democrats supporting it and all five Republicans opposing it.

In similar fashion, the House Foreign Affairs Committee split nearly along party lines in approving, 20-14, HR 2760 (H Rept 98-122, Part II) on June 7. The bill had to be considered by Foreign Affairs because it also authorized $30 million in fiscal 1983 and $50 million in 1984 to help "friendly" Central American countries (primarily El Salva-

dor and Honduras) monitor and prevent use of their territory for transport of Cuban- or Nicaraguan-supplied military equipment.

The Foreign Affairs Committee's action occurred as U.S.-Nicaragua relations deteriorated in the wake of Nicaragua's June 6 expulsion of three American diplomats, and, in retaliation, the Reagan administration's expulsion of 21 Nicaraguan diplomats the next day. Each side claimed the ousted diplomats of the other side were guilty of spying.

The House passed the bill July 28 by a **228-195 key vote (R 18-145; D 210-50)**. House debate on the issue was intensely partisan, with Republicans repeatedly accusing Democrats of abandoning U.S. friends in Central America. Three questions about the U.S. covert operations dominated the debate: whether it was legal under U.S. law, whether it had accomplished its objectives, and whether it was hindering or promoting the cause of peace in Central America. *(1983 key votes, p. 911)*

The chamber held an extraordinary four-hour closed session July 19. According to members who were present, the session was highlighted by presentations by senior members of the Intelligence Committee.

When public debate began on July 27, Republicans filed more than a dozen amendments to the bill, most of which had the effect of allowing the covert activity to continue indefinitely. None of these was adopted.

There was no Senate action on HR 2760.

Intelligence Agency Authorization

When HR 2760 became bottled up in the Senate Intelligence Committee following House passage, the focus of Capitol Hill action on covert aid shifted to other legislation, including the annual authorization bill for U.S. intelligence agencies. In most years that bill was routine legislation that attracted little attention. Most of its provisions were secret. But in 1983 the committees inserted provisions affecting the Nicaragua operation in their respective bills.

Committee Action. The Senate Intelligence Committee, on a 13-2 vote in closed session May 6, adopted a compromise provision in its authorization bill (S 1230 — S Rept 98-77) that enabled the CIA to continue its activities in Nicaragua for the remaining five months of fiscal 1983. But the committee voted to require the president to provide a new plan for those covert actions during fiscal 1984. That agreement was a compromise between those who would have given Reagan free rein to continue the covert action and those who would have voted to end it quickly.

The compromise proposed to change the existing procedure for approving covert actions in two respects, at least in the Nicaragua situation. For the first time money for a covert action was to be earmarked in the CIA's reserve fund by the Intelligence committees, rather than by the administration. Secondly, the administration was required to get explicit approval from one or both Intelligence committees before that money could be spent.

The administration plan, presented in September and approved by the panel Sept. 22 by a 13-2 vote, included a $19 million authorization for covert action in the first half of 1984, $10 million in leftover fiscal 1983 funds and an unspecified amount from the CIA contingency fund. Together, these amounts could have brought the total to as much as $50 million.

In drafting a companion intelligence authorization bill (HR 2968 — H Rept 98-189, Part I) approved May 11, the House Foreign Affairs panel incorporated a key section of HR 2760, suspending the covert action at a secret date during the remainder of fiscal year 1983. Although the bill contained no specific dollar amounts for covert aid, it effectively authorized the administration's $19 million covert action request. However, it did not allow the CIA to spend leftover fiscal 1983 funds or its contingency funds for covert aid.

Floor Action. Setting up a confrontation with the Senate and the Reagan administration, the House on Oct. 20 reaffirmed its opposition to U.S. backing for rebels fighting against the Nicaraguan government. On a 227-194 party-line vote, the House added the key covert action language in HR 2760 to the intelligence authorization measure.

In place of covert aid, the measure provided $50 million for an "overt" program in Central America during fiscal 1984 to help friendly countries in the region combat cross-border arms shipments.

The Senate took a stance directly opposite to that of the House Nov. 3 when it passed HR 2968 by voice vote, flatly opposing the House demand for a legal date for terminating the covert action to Nicaragua. Passage of the intelligence authorization bill amounted to an endorsement of Reagan's program of aiding the rebels in Nicaragua. As approved by the Senate, the bill authorized $29 million for covert aid. That included $19 million specifically authorized for fiscal 1984 and $10 million to be carried over from unspent funds from fiscal 1983. Once the $29 million ran out, the Senate bill allowed the CIA director to dip into his contingency fund to continue the aid unless both Intelligence committees objected.

Senate Democrats who opposed the covert action chose not to contest it on the floor. They said the covert action probably would have been approved by the Republican-controlled Senate on a direct vote, thus giving its Senate proponents a stronger hand in conference with the House.

Defense Authorization, Funding

Even as the House was acting on the intelligence bill Oct. 20, the House Appropriations Committee was moving to delete funding for the Nicaraguan rebels from another bill. By a 22-24 recorded vote and later by voice vote, the committee rejected attempts to drop a provision of the 1984 defense appropriations bill (HR 4185) that cut out all funds for covert operations in Nicaragua. That provision took effect upon the enactment of an intelligence bill, or on April 1, 1984, if no intelligence bill had been enacted. Appropriations for the intelligence agencies were hidden in the defense bill.

The appropriations bill was reported on Oct. 20 (H Rept 98-427) and passed by the House Nov. 2. The Senate Nov. 8 passed the bill with amendments backing the funding of Nicaraguan rebels. *(Defense bill, p. 228)*

On Nov. 17 a House-Senate conference committee on the defense bill reached agreement (H Rept 98-567) on the Nicaragua issue. The next day conferees on the intelligence authorization bill (HR 2968) adopted the compromise (H Rept 98-569).

Both bills were cleared Nov. 18.

The compromise dropped the 1982 Boland amendment, the first congressional attempt to rein in U.S. covert action in Nicaragua. The provision, barring the United States from aiding any groups trying to overthrow the Nicaraguan government, expired Sept. 30, 1983.

Compromise Provisions

As contained in the final version of the fiscal 1984 defense and intelligence bills (PL 98-212, PL 98-215), the Nicaragua compromise stated:

"During fiscal year 1984, not more than $24,000,000 of the funds available to the Central Intelligence Agency, the Department of Defense, or any other agency or entity of the United States involved in intelligence activities may be obligated or expended for the purpose or which would have the effect of supporting, directly or indirectly, military or paramilitary operations in Nicaragua by any nation, group, organization, movement or individual."

The bills included no date for terminating the covert action, as had been approved by the House.

The compromise also gave Reagan three options for the covert aid, rather than the single cutoff option the House had voted. He could continue the aid at the 1983 rate and allow it to expire when the funds run out; he could continue the program at the 1983 rate and return to Congress for more money in mid-1984; or he could reduce the size of the program to make the $24 million last throughout fiscal 1984.

The 1984 intelligence authorization bill also included most of the provisions of the House-passed amendment — originally added to HR 2760 — directing the president to seek intervention by the Organization of American States (OAS) to review Nicaragua's compliance with the OAS chapter and to resolve conflicts in Central America.

The amendment also said the United States should support actions by the OAS and the so-called "Contadora group" to end terrorism, subversion and other activities aimed at the violent overthrow of governments in the region. Panama, Colombia, Venezuela and Mexico comprised the Contadora group.

The president was directed to report to Congress by March 15, 1984, on the results of his efforts to achieve peace in Central America and his recommendations for further action. *(Central America aid plan, p. 177)*

El Salvador Aid

For the third year in a row Congress and the president in 1983 battled to a draw over U.S. policy toward El Salvador.

As it had done in previous years, Congress used its control over the foreign aid budget to moderate the administration's requests for military aid to the Salvadoran government, which had been fighting leftist guerrillas since 1980. Nevertheless, Congress refused to cut off the aid, thus generally allowing President Reagan's activist, anti-communist policies in Central America to continue.

The essential political reality in Congress was that there were not enough votes either to give Reagan full backing on El Salvador or to force an immediate withdrawal of U.S. aid from that country. The compromise position was to provide limited aid, but to attach conditions that addressed congressional concerns about human rights and other issues in El Salvador.

Under sustained administration pressure, Congress approved $81.3 million in military aid for El Salvador in fiscal 1983. The total included $25 million provided in a supplemental appropriations bill (HR 3069 — PL 98-63) cleared July 29, as well as funds voted in 1982 and transfers from other programs. Reagan's various requests for fiscal 1983 had totaled $136.3 million.

For fiscal 1984, a continuing appropriations resolution cleared Nov. 12 (H J Res 413 — PL 98-151) limited El Salvador's military aid to $64.8 million; Reagan had requested $86.3 million. The resolution also contained new restrictions aimed at encouraging progress on land reform and in the trial of those accused of murdering four American churchwomen in December 1980. Lawmakers approved without debate Reagan's requests for economic and development aid for El Salvador: $170 million in fiscal 1983 and $158 million in fiscal 1984.

Certification Bill Veto

At the very end of the session Congress approved a bill (HR 4042) continuing a requirement that the president certify twice each year that El Salvador was making sufficient progress on human rights and other issues to warrant receiving U.S. aid.

Reagan pocket-vetoed the measure, which had been passed by the House Sept. 30 and the Senate Nov. 17. By not signing HR 4042 by Nov. 30, after Congress had adjourned, Reagan allowed the bill to die. Originally enacted in 1981 (PL 97-113), the certification requirement was in effect for fiscal years 1982 and 1983. *(Box, p. 135)*

Stone Confirmation

The Senate May 25, 1983, confirmed former Sen. Richard B. Stone, D-Fla. (1975-80), as President Reagan's ambassador-at-large for Central America.

Reagan appointed Stone largely in response to a demand by Rep. Clarence D. Long, D-Md., for a U.S. "special negotiator" to settle the civil war in El Salvador. Long, chairman of the House Appropriations Committee's Foreign Operations Subcommittee, which handled the foreign aid program, made the appointment of such a negotiator a condition for his approval of additional military aid to the Salvadoran government.

Stone traveled throughout the region and successfully arranged meetings between Salvadoran government officials and political representatives of its leftist opposition. But his efforts were overshadowed by the workings of the "Contadora group," composed of Mexico, Panama, Venezuela and Colombia. In October that group published a list of 21 points for a regional agreement. In January 1984 the Contadora countries and the five nations of Central America signed a limited agreement calling for a peaceful settlement of the region's conflicts.

Stone resigned the post early in 1984. He was replaced by Harry W. Shlaudeman, former U.S. ambassador to Argentina. Shlaudeman had been executive director to the Kissinger commission on Central America. *(Kissinger commission, p. 188)*

1983 Certification Reports

The State Department in 1983 sent Congress two reports on El Salvador's progress in human rights, land reform and other areas.

January Report. The 67-page report backing up the Jan. 21 certification was tougher than its two predecessors in its criticisms of the Salvadoran government. The report complained of the "systematic ineffectiveness" of the criminal justice system, "particularly in cases originating in political violence." U.S. officials had said the major obstacle to certification was El Salvador's failure to bring to justice those responsible for political murders, especially the murders of eight Americans in 1980 and 1981.

While conceding that "human rights abuses continue," the State Department said the human rights criterion had been met because "political violence" was diminishing and the government was moving to protect its citizens' rights.

The State Department cited some success in the Salvadoran land reform program.

Of all the certification standards, the report cited the greatest progress in the movement toward free elections. A Constituent Assembly was elected in March 1982, and presidential and municipal elections were held in the spring of 1984.

The report labeled as a "setback" the October 1982 kidnappings of 17 opposition leaders, including labor union officials and several leaders of the Democratic Revolutionary Front, the political arm of the guerrilla movement. The government acknowledged holding eight of the 17.

July Report. The State Department's fourth report, sent to Congress July 20, was by far the most negative one yet given Congress. The report was signed by Secretary of State George P. Shultz, who said El Salvador had met the standards of the 1981 law but added: "It is evident that the record falls far short of the broad and sustained progress which both the Congress and the administration believe is necessary for the evolution of a just and democratic society in El Salvador."

The State Department reported that leaders of the Salvadoran armed forces had attempted to promote respect for human rights. But it acknowledged that military personnel continued to be involved in "right wing paramilitary activity."

On a brighter note, the report said El Salvador in the first half of 1983 had "made clear progress in strengthening democratic institutions." The State Department noted that the Constituent Assembly, whose members were elected in March 1982, was functioning as "El Salvador's primary organ for political decision and debate."

The report said El Salvador's land reform program "remains on track and is moving forward."

Radio Marti Authorization

Congress Sept. 29 cleared legislation (S 602 — PL 98-111) authorizing creation of a Voice of America (VOA) service, called Radio Marti, to broadcast news and information to Cuba.

The Reagan administration and other proponents wanted Radio Marti to be separate from the Voice of America, but opponents had blocked that plan for more than a year.

The sponsors had sought a Latin version of Radio Free Europe, but many members feared the project would do more harm than good. Some opponents argued that the station would be used by exiles to irritate Cuban Premier Fidel Castro. Others feared that U.S. commercial radio stations would be affected if Castro jammed Radio Marti broadcasts. Midwest broadcasters warned that Cuban interference could be costly for domestic broadcasters.

Passage came almost two years after the Reagan administration proposed Radio Marti as a way to counter Cuban influence in Central America and the Caribbean. Authorizing legislation had been passed by the House on Aug. 10, 1982, but was killed by a Senate filibuster in the December 1982 lame-duck session. *(Previous action, p. 150)*

Reagan revised the proposal to avoid Cuban jamming that would interfere with domestic broadcasts in the United States. The administration's original proposal was for Radio Marti to broadcast on 1040 AM, which was used by WHO in Des Moines, Iowa. S 602, introduced in 1983, offered the option of using the Voice of America frequency (1180 AM) and facilities in Marathon, Fla.

Legislative History

The revised Radio Marti plan survived challenges in both the Senate Foreign Relations and House Foreign Affairs committees in June.

The committees rejected efforts to put Radio Marti under the Voice of America. Sponsors of a VOA proposal said it would prevent Radio Marti from being used for propaganda purposes since the Voice of America was mandated by law to be an "objective" news source.

Both committees went on to approve legislation authorizing the establishment of Radio Marti as an independent station under the supervision of the Board for International Broadcasting, which ran Radio Free Europe and Radio Liberty.

The Foreign Relations Committee approved its bill (S 602 — S Rept 98-156) by a 13-4 vote on June 8, and the Foreign Affairs Committee approved a companion bill (HR 2453 — H Rept 98-284, Part I) by a 19-8 vote the next day.

The House Energy and Commerce Committee, which had jurisdiction over communications issues, adopted an amendment that tightened restrictions in HR 2453 banning Radio Marti from commercial AM and FM frequencies (H Rept 98-284, Part II). The station could operate only on shortwave frequencies, or on the 1180 AM frequency used by the Voice of America for limited broadcasts to Cuba.

The Senate passed a compromise version of S 602 by voice vote Sept. 13. The bill was less than the administration sought, but it won the support of a coalition that had blocked the legislation for more than a year.

The Senate bill, placing Radio Marti under the Voice of America, was the result of negotiations among key Senate sponsors and opponents of the radio station. VOA already was broadcasting about five and one-half hours a day to Latin America, including Cuba. Sponsors of the compromise said the new station should send 14½ hours daily to Cuba.

The House passed S 602 Sept. 29 without change by a 302-109 vote, completing congressional action.

Major Provisions

As signed into law Oct. 4, the Radio Broadcasting to Cuba Act (S 602 — PL 98-111):

● Established the Cuba Service, or Radio Marti, within

the United States Information Agency (USIA), as part of the Voice of America — incorporating VOA standards. VOA was already broadcasting to Cuba, but its programs were not prepared specifically for Cuban consumption.

● Authorized $14 million in fiscal 1984 and $11 million in fiscal 1985 for the station's operations. Also authorized was an additional $54.8 million in each year for modernization of VOA facilities. The figures represented concessions by Radio Marti opponents, who accepted higher amounts in return for putting the Cuba Service under VOA auspices.

● Required that transmissions be part of Voice of America broadcasts to Cuba, in accordance with VOA standards; namely, "programs which are objective, accurate, balanced and which present a variety of views."

● Required Radio Marti to use facilities at Marathon, Fla., and the 1180 AM frequency used by the VOA. Other non-commercial AM frequencies also could be used, although they had to be frequencies used for other VOA broadcasts to Cuba.

● Permitted non-governmental shortwave radio stations to carry the Cuba Service if at least 30 percent of the remaining programs were regular VOA broadcasts.

● Stipulated that if Radio Marti broadcasts on the 1180 AM frequency were jammed 25 percent or more than VOA broadcasts were jammed in the year preceding Sept. 1, 1983, USIA could lease time on commercial or non-commercial AM-band radio stations.

● Authorized the director of USIA to establish a separately administered Cuba Service, with a separate staff.

● Permitted USIA to compensate U.S. radio stations for technical expenses incurred as a result of Cuban interference. Procedures for such claims would be established by the Federal Communications Commission. The bill authorized $5 million for USIA, effective Oct. 1, 1984, to pay for such compensation.

● Authorized USIA to arrange an independent evaluation of Radio Marti programming, with the first report due in 18 months, then annually for three years.

● Specified that the programs were to be designated "Voice of America: Cuba Service," or "Voice of America: Radio Marti Program." A previously enacted law (PL 97-241) stipulated that any U.S. broadcast to Cuba be called Radio Marti, after the Cuban patriot José Marti.

State Department Authorization

Disputes over secondary issues delayed action in 1983 on normally routine legislation authorizing funds for the State Department and related agencies.

Congress finally cleared the measure (HR 2915 — PL 98-164) Nov. 18, authorizing $3.2 billion in fiscal 1984 and $3.5 billion in fiscal 1985 for the State Department, U.S. Information Agency (USIA), Board for International Broadcasting and other programs.

Committee Action

The House Foreign Affairs Committee reported HR 2915 (H Rept 98-130) May 16, and the Senate Foreign Relations Committee reported its version (S 1342 — S Rept 98-143) May 23.

In drafting their respective bills, the committees devoted much of their attention to President Reagan's proposal for a Project Democracy to promote democratic val-

U.S.-Vatican Relations

Over the objections of a number of religious groups, Congress in November quietly agreed to repeal an 1867 law that prohibited the use of federal funds to maintain a diplomatic mission to the Vatican.

The action came on an amendment that was added by the Senate to legislation (HR 2915 — PL 98-164) authorizing funds in fiscal 1984 and 1985 for the State Department and related agencies. *(State Department authorization bill, this page)*

The Reagan administration announced Jan. 10, 1984, that it would establish full diplomatic ties with the Vatican. A day later, Reagan nominated William A. Wilson, who had been serving as his personal envoy to the Vatican, to become the U.S. ambassador.

The Senate on March 7, 1984, confirmed the nomination by a vote of 81-13.

Political Role

Members of Congress who supported U.S.-Vatican relations said the move was justified because of Pope John Paul II's emergence as a political as well as religious leader. Sen. Richard G. Lugar, R-Ind., sponsor of the amendment to repeal the 1867 law, argued that by formalizing relations with the Vatican the United States would be recognizing the pope not as the head of the Catholic Church but rather as leader of a sovereign state that was playing an increasingly important role in world affairs.

The Vatican in 1983 maintained diplomatic relations with 107 nations, including Great Britain, which established such ties in 1980 after a 448-year lapse. The Vatican also was represented in all major United Nations organizations and had permanent observers to the European Common Market and the Organization of American States.

Although the Vatican did not have a formal diplomatic presence in Washington, an apostolic delegate to the American church, Archbishop Pio Laghi, served in an unofficial diplomatic capacity. After diplomatic relations were established, Laghi's position was elevated to papal nuncio, the title of the permanent representative of the pope serving in foreign countries.

Despite objections from various Protestant denominations, administration officials contended there were no legal barriers to the move because the U.S. government was recognizing the Vatican as an independent state and was not conferring any special status on the Roman Catholic religion.

Catholic officials in the United States said they were neutral on the sensitive Vatican issue.

ues around the world. Rather than put such a program under government auspices, as Reagan had proposed, the committees voted to finance it through four private foundations run by the Democratic and Republican parties, the AFL-CIO and the Chamber of Commerce of the United States. That approach had been recommended in April by a private commission, called the Democracy Program, composed of representatives of those organizations.

The committee reports included blistering attacks on USIA operations during the first two years of the Reagan administration. The House panel said USIA had "arguably violated the letter and spirit of its charter" by using its grantmaking and personnel policies for partisan political purposes. The Senate committee said USIA was "an agency financially out of control." The panel specifically complained about the hiring "of friends and relatives of high administration officials without apparent regard for qualifications."

Floor Action

The House passed HR 2915 June 9 by voice vote after gutting the proposed National Endowment for Democracy by deleting grants of $5 million each to the institutes to be established by the Republican and Democratic parties.

The Senate passed its version of the bill Oct. 20. The Senate adopted 65 amendments, many of which subsequently were dropped.

The Senate was more receptive than the House to the proposed National Endowment for Democracy, rejecting two attempts, by 26-68 and 42-49 votes, to cut funding for the agency.

Other Senate amendments included a proposal, adopted by a 66-23 vote, to cut about $500 million from the U.S. contributions to the United Nations and related agencies over the next four years.

Final Action

After an extended series of meetings, a House-Senate conference committee Nov. 17 reached agreement on HR 2915 (H Rept 98-563). Both chambers gave final approval to the bill on Nov. 18.

As cleared, the bill froze total U.S. contributions to the United Nations for 1984 at the 1983 level. It placed no similar restriction on 1985 contributions. It retained a Senate amendment calling for a thorough review of U.S. participation in the United Nations.

The bill included a sweeping provision designed to encourage Pakistan, Thailand and other countries to crack down on the production and export of illicit narcotics, especially opium and cocaine. While not naming any of those countries, the provision threatened suspension of U.S. aid to any nation that failed to take adequate steps on the issue. U.S. representatives to international financial institutions, such as the World Bank, also were to vote against loans for such countries. The Senate Oct. 19 had adopted an amendment suspending aid to countries that failed to meet projected reductions in narcotics production.

HR 2915 included provisions allowing the State Department to give special pay supplements to diplomats in areas of potential danger even if members of their families were stationed with them. Previously, the State Department had refused to give danger pay to diplomats who were accompanied by their families to such strife-torn areas as El Salvador and Lebanon.

The final bill retained a Senate amendment repealing an 1867 law that had prohibited the establishment of a U.S. diplomatic mission at the Vatican. In January 1984 Reagan formally established diplomatic relations with the Vatican. *(Box, p. 167)*

The bill included a Senate provision opposing all exports of nuclear supplies and equipment to Argentina, India and South Africa until those countries forswore any attempt to build nuclear weapons and accepted international controls on all their nuclear facilities. The provision stated the sense of Congress on the issue; it did not directly ban any sales to those countries. The bill included an escape clause saying the president could authorize exports of equipment for India's Tarpur reactor if he determined the equipment was necessary for humanitarian reasons and was not available from another supplier.

Development Banks, IMF Funds

In one of its last acts before adjournment, Congress approved fiscal 1984 authorizations for the Inter-American Development Bank (IADB), the Asian Development Bank and the African Development Bank. The authorizations were attached to the conference report (H Rept 98-551) on a supplemental appropriations bill (HR 3959 — PL 98-181) cleared Nov. 18. The bill authorized $5.2 billion for the IADB, $1.3 billion for the Asian Development Bank and $150 million for the African Development Fund. *(Previous action, p. 154)*

HR 3959 also authorized and appropriated $8.4 billion to increase the U.S. contribution to the International Monetary Fund. *(IMF increase, p. 104)*

Intelligence Authorization

Congress Nov. 18 completed action on legislation (HR 2968 — PL 98-215) authorizing fiscal 1984 funding for the CIA, the National Security Agency, the Defense Intelligence Agency and other intelligence services.

Controversy over covert aid to Nicaraguan rebels had delayed final action on the bill, which had been passed by the House Oct. 20 (H Rept 98-189, Parts I and II) and the Senate Nov. 3. The Senate Intelligence Committee had reported its version May 6 (S 1230 — S Rept 98-77). *(Nicaragua aid action, provisions, p. 162)*

Provisions

As in previous years, most funding items in the bill were kept secret. In published provisions, the final version of HR 2968 (H Rept 98-569):

● Authorized $75.5 million for construction of a new building at CIA headquarters in Langley, Va.

● Authorized $13.8 million for counter-terrorism activities by the FBI.

● Authorized $18.5 million and 215 employees for CIA's "intelligence community staff." Provided that a commissioned military officer serving as director of the staff would serve under the same terms and conditions as a civilian and would not be subject to direct supervision by the Defense Department.

● Tightened restrictions on the CIA director's authority to "reprogram," or transfer, funds from one account to another.

Grenada Invasion

President Reagan won widespread approval in both houses of Congress for the Oct. 25 U.S. invasion of Grenada. Reagan said the invasion, which he called a "rescue mission," was necessary to protect some 1,000 Americans from civil strife that erupted following the overthrow and eventual murder of the Caribbean island's Marxist prime minister. About 600 American medical students were airlifted from the island.

While Congress passed no legislation directly concerning the invasion, it did approve $15 million in economic aid for Grenada in a fiscal 1984 continuing appropriations resolution (H J Res 413 — PL 98-151). *(Foreign aid, p. 159)*

Invasion. Reagan had declared Grenada a sore spot in March, when he said its anti-American, Marxist regime was permitting Cuba to build military airfields there.

The island was thrown into turmoil Oct. 12 when an even harder-line Marxist group staged a coup d'état, killed the previous regime's Marxist leader, Maurice Bishop, and his top officials, and imposed a 24-hour "shoot-on-sight" curfew.

The administration said it launched the invasion, which left 18 U.S. soldiers killed and 115 wounded, following a request for American help from neighboring island nations in the Organization of Eastern Caribbean States (OECS).

The chairman of the OECS, Prime Minister Eugenia Charles of Dominica, and Reagan jointly announced the invasion on Oct. 25. The OECS nations, lacking military forces, contributed 300 constables to the force.

At the height of the invasion, some 7,300 U.S. Marines, Army Rangers and paratroopers were on Grenada. By Dec. 12 all "combat" troops were withdrawn, leaving about 300 U.S. military support personnel on the island.

War Powers. Some members of Congress sought to emphasize the need for an early withdrawal, and at the same time assert a right to have a hand in decisions to use military force, by trying to invoke the 1973 War Powers Resolution (PL 93-148). *(Congress and the Nation Vol. IV, p. 849)*

The House Foreign Affairs Committee Oct. 27 approved, 32-2, a bill (H J Res 402) to declare under a provision of the 1973 act that the U.S. forces must be withdrawn within 90 days unless extended by Congress. On Nov. 1 the full House passed the resolution, 403-23.

The Senate had adopted the same language Oct. 28, voting 64-20 to attach it to an unrelated debt ceiling bill (H J Res 308). That amendment later died, and Majority Leader Howard H. Baker Jr., R-Tenn., blocked Senate action on the House measure.

Korean Airliner Downing

Lawmakers spoke with one voice in condemning the Soviet Union's Sept. 1 destruction of a South Korean commercial airliner, which killed all 269 people aboard.

Congress Sept. 15 unanimously approved a joint resolution (H J Res 353 — PL 98-98) calling it a "cold-blooded barbarous attack . . . [and] one of the most infamous and reprehensible acts in history."

Rep. Larry P. McDonald, R-Ga., was one of 61 American passengers killed in the crash of Korean Air Lines flight 007, which was shot down by a Soviet jet fighter when it strayed into Soviet territory. Soviet officials later said they did not know that the plane was a civilian airliner when it was shot down, and they insisted that the plane was spying on sensitive military installations on Sakhalin Island. On Sept. 12 the Soviet Union vetoed a resolution in the United Nations Security Council that deplored the shooting down of flight 007.

H J Res 353, drafted by the White House and congressional leaders, did not go far enough for conservatives, who saw the incident as an opportunity to strengthen anti-Soviet attitudes in the United States and the rest of the world. But when the resolution came to the Senate floor Sept. 15, the administration fended off efforts by Jesse Helms, R-N.C., and others to "put some teeth" in the measure. The House had adopted the resolution Sept. 14.

1984

For the third year in a row Central America was the focal point of foreign policy battles between President Reagan and Congress in 1984. Both Reagan and his congressional critics scored political victories on foreign policy, but on only one issue — aid to El Salvador — did the president end the year in measurably better shape. By sidestepping confrontations on Lebanon, Middle East arms sales and other issues, Reagan avoided outright defeats in Congress and gave himself running room for the future.

Successful presidential elections in El Salvador guaranteed, at least temporarily, that Congress would accept the president's request for military as well as economic aid for the new government of José Napoleón Duarte. Along with winning some $132 million of the $179 million in military aid requested, the White House convinced Congress not to attach the tough human rights conditions that were tied to the El Salvador aid in 1981-83.

On the other hand, Democrats in Congress prevailed decisively over the president on Nicaragua, blocking aid to the guerrillas, or contras, who were fighting the leftist Sandinista regime in that country.

On Honduras, the third leg of Reagan's policy of massive buildup of U.S. military involvement in Central America, Congress adopted some conditions on aid but did not do anything to block U.S. military involvement there.

In a gamble to quash the debate over Central America, Reagan in 1983 had created a bipartisan presidential commission, chaired by former Secretary of State Henry A. Kissinger, to recommend solutions. But Congress in 1984 never approved enough of the panel's recommendations, most of which the president accepted, to give Reagan the broad political endorsement he sought.

In the Middle East, President Reagan pulled out the Marines he had sent to Lebanon in 1982 before Congress could pass legislation that might have limited his foreign policy powers in the region or at least embarrassed his Lebanon policy. By pulling U.S. Marines from their "peacekeeping" role there, and then by reneging on proposed arms sales to Jordan and Saudi Arabia in the face of strong opposition in Congress, Reagan reduced the active U.S. presence that had been an important feature of Middle East politics for a dozen years. The retreat diminished U.S. prestige in the region, guaranteed that ethnic and religious factions would continue to brutalize Lebanon, and enabled Syria to boast that it had prevailed over the United States.

As in 1982 and 1983, foreign aid authorization legislation bogged down in Congress, and fiscal 1985 funding for the aid programs was folded into an omnibus appropriations measure.

Foreign Aid

For the third year in a row, Congress failed to enact regular authorization and appropriations bills for foreign aid programs. Instead, $18.2 billion worth of foreign aid and related spending for fiscal 1985 was included in an omnibus continuing appropriations resolution (H J Res 648 — PL 98-473) cleared on Oct. 11. *(1981-83 action, pp. 132, 136, 145, 146, 159)*

The House passed a separate aid authorization bill May 10, but the Senate never took up its companion measure because of disputes over aid to Central America and because neither the Reagan administration nor the Foreign Relations Committee was able to drum up enough support for the bill.

A last-minute attempt to attach a full authorization bill to the continuing resolution failed when several Senate Democrats complained that the move was being made behind their backs. Some provisions of the House-passed bill, however, were included in the resolution.

Fiscal 1984 Authorizations

Committee Action. The House and Senate foreign policy committees were torn by partisan fighting over U.S. aid to Central America and the administration's policies in El Salvador, Nicaragua and Honduras. Unable to reach a compromise, the panels reported their foreign aid bills without any funding or policy provisions on Central America. *(Central America aid, p. 177)*

House Foreign Affairs reported its authorization bill (HR 5119 — H Rept 98-628) on March 21. Senate Foreign Relations reported its version (S 2582 — S Rept 98-400) on April 18.

In keeping with past practice and political realities, both committees boosted aid to Israel. They accepted the administration's request for $1.4 billion in military aid, but they increased its $850 million economic aid request: the House to $1.1 billion and the Senate to $1.2 billion.

At the other end of the political spectrum, Egypt and Jordan, two "moderate" Arab nations, suffered rebukes at the hands of the House committee. The panel added to its bill a series of statements about and conditions on aid to those countries.

The committees approved $15 million in military aid requested for Lebanon, but the Senate panel balked at providing $20 million requested for economic aid, noting that the administration had been unable to spend all of the $150 million in emergency aid Congress had authorized for Lebanon in 1983.

Both committees approved, but with conditions, the president's so-called economic policy initiative in Africa that was intended to bolster capitalist economies. Reagan planned to reward countries that made economic "reforms" such as eliminating price controls that discouraged farm production.

The House committee also imposed conditions on regular U.S. economic and military aid programs to several African countries, but the restrictions were less severe than those it had proposed in 1982 and 1983.

After dropping all requests for Central America, both committees approved the bulk of the president's military aid requests. Reagan had sought $6.05 billion in fiscal 1985, not counting Central America. The Senate panel approved $6.25 billion and the House committee $5.73 billion. In reaction to the administration's increasing use of arms sales as a foreign policy tool, both committees adopted amendments that sought to pressure Reagan on the issue.

Reagan had requested $538.5 million for a new "concessional" program enabling 16 countries to buy U.S. weapons and defense services with loans bearing a 5 percent interest rate, rather than the 12 percent currently prevailing for standard Foreign Military Sales (FMS) loans. The House committee approved $358.5 million in concessional loans to 11 countries; the Senate panel approved $478.5 million to 12 countries. Central America was excluded.

Because of the aid increases voted for Israel, both panels approved substantial boosts in Economic Support Fund (ESF) assistance. Reagan requested $2.797 billion for fiscal 1985 — more than half of it for Israel and Egypt. The House committee voted $3.236 billion and the Senate committee approved $3.071 billion, plus $171 million authorized for 1984 but made available for 1985.

House Floor Action. The House passed its $10.95 billion foreign aid authorization bill May 10 by a 211-206 vote, after handing the president an important victory in his three-year struggle for congressional backing of U.S. involvement in Central America.

The House approved a Republican-sponsored amendment that gave Reagan most of the military aid he had requested for El Salvador, free of the stringent conditions sought by many House Democrats. The Republican plan authorized $1.21 billion for military, economic, development and other aid programs in El Salvador in 1985. But unlike Reagan's recommendations stemming from an advisory commission's proposals on Central America, the GOP plan did not include authorizations for aid after 1985.

The Republican plan also authorized $281 million in supplemental aid for fiscal 1984, with most of that amount going for economic aid ($119 million) and military aid ($129.35 million).

The amendment was approved by a **212-208 key vote (R 156-8; D 56-200)**. Majority Leader Jim Wright, D-Texas, splitting with Speaker Thomas P. O'Neill Jr., D-Mass., and other House leaders, led 55 fellow Democrats in backing Reagan's plan. *(1984 key votes, p. 927)*

The House vote came four days after presidential elections in El Salvador that the administration had portrayed to Congress as a victory for democracy. Twice in 1983 the House had rejected aid to Nicaraguan guerrillas. But before May 10 it never had voted directly on aid to the government of El Salvador.

A major floor fight over aid to Turkey was averted when the administration agreed to provide $250 million in special economic aid to Cyprus, the Mediterranean island that was partially occupied by Turkey. As part of the agreement, $85 million was cut from Reagan's request for $755 million in military aid to Turkey.

Fiscal 1985 Appropriations

In spite of election-year politics and disputes over Central America, Congress approved the bulk of President Reagan's requests for funding for foreign aid programs in fiscal 1985.

An omnibus continuing appropriations resolution (H J

Res 648 — PL 98-473), cleared Oct. 11, included a record $18.2 billion for foreign aid and related programs, just $81 million less than Reagan had requested.

Congress rejected only one major Reagan request: a multi-year, $8 billion authorization for economic and development aid to Central American countries recommended by the Kissinger commission in January. However, Congress did give Reagan most of the Central America aid he sought for fiscal 1985. *(Kissinger commission plan, p. 188)*

The foreign aid provisions in H J Res 648 generally caused little controversy, largely because El Salvador was no longer a major political issue in Congress. Congress approved most of Reagan's requests for aid to help that country's government fight leftist guerrillas after José Napoleón Duarte, a centrist, was elected president in May.

The continuing resolution provided $5.9 billion in military assistance, on which Reagan had placed a premium since taking office. With Reagan pushing it, military aid had shot up dramatically during his presidency. In fiscal 1981, the last budget year for which the administration of President Carter was largely responsible, the United States provided $3.2 billion to foreign governments through the major military aid programs.

Senate Committee Action. The Senate Appropriations Committee June 26 reported a $13.8 billion foreign aid appropriations bill (S 2793 — S Rept 98-531). S 2793 provided Reagan with all but about $91.4 million of his aid requests for fiscal 1985.

S 2793 included $1.2 billion for Central America: $962.6 million in economic development aid and $255.9 million in military aid. The panel made no changes from Reagan's request, which included such controversial issues as military aid to El Salvador, the beginning of a new guarantee program for Export-Import Bank loans to the region and the resumption of military aid to the military dictatorship in Guatemala.

The bill provided the full $132.5 million in military aid requested for El Salvador, without the conditions on how the money could be spent that Congress had imposed in the past. It provided $210 million for economic aid to El Salvador but imposed several conditions aimed at ensuring that the money was not diverted illegally and that Congress would be informed how it was being used.

Besides Central America, S 2793 appropriated direct economic, military and development aid to about 70 countries, and indirect aid to dozens of countries through international agencies such as the World Bank.

The committee rejected a request for $75 million for Reagan's new economic policy initiative for Africa.

House Committee Action. The House Appropriations Committee Sept. 13 reported a $17.8 billion foreign aid spending measure (HR 6237 — H Rept 98-1021).

In providing $123.5 million in military aid for El Salvador, the House committee imposed conditions on how the money could be used. It accepted $180 million of Reagan's $210 million request for economic aid for that country; it also cut the request for development aid.

Military aid for other Central American countries was cut as well. The panel also cut economic and development aid to the region by more than $200 million, including the elimination of a $136.6 million request for regional economic programs that were to be earmarked for reviving a Central American free trade zone. Also eliminated was $35 million Reagan had requested for Guatemala.

Aid to Greece and Turkey remained a politically sensitive issue. The panel slashed Reagan's request for $755 million in military aid to Turkey to $540 million. Much of this request was intended to allow Turkey to buy U.S.-built F-16 fighter planes. The request for $175 million for economic aid to Turkey was approved in full, as was the president's $500 million request for military aid to Greece.

The committee made one significant change in the bill approved by its Foreign Operations Subcommittee Aug. 8, adding $319.6 million in grants to international financial agencies, such as the World Bank.

Continuing Resolution. On Sept. 14 the House Appropriations Committee inserted its foreign aid package into H J Res 648 (H Rept 98-1030). The House passed H J Res 648 Sept. 25, after voting a 2 percent cut in foreign aid, except aid to Israel and Egypt.

The Senate also folded its foreign aid package into H J Res 648, after the Senate Appropriations Committee approved an amendment guaranteeing for five years that economic support provided to Israel would not drop below the annual debt repayments Israel made to the United States. The committee also cut $40 million from the $755 million requested for military aid to Turkey.

The Senate passed H J Res 648 Oct. 4, following a dispute over military aid to the guerrillas, known as the contras, fighting the leftist government of Nicaragua. The House version barred all aid to the contras; the Senate measure provided $28 million. *(Nicaragua, p. 175)*

Under intense pressure from the administration, the Senate Oct. 3 rejected, 42-57, an amendment that sought to "wind down" the Nicaraguan war. The amendment would have barred further military aid to help the rebels fight but would have provided $2 million to help them get out of Nicaragua and $4 million to resettle them elsewhere.

The Senate also rejected, 45-53, an amendment that would have barred the contras from using U.S. money to engage in "terrorist" activities.

The administration headed off two major challenges to its military aid program. The Senate tabled, 51-46, an amendment that would have cut $215 million from the bill's $715 million in military grants to Turkey. The amendment, adopted earlier by the Foreign Relations Committee, would have barred the grants unless Turkey relinquished control of the town of Famagusta on Cyprus. The proposal was backed by the politically influential "Greek lobby," and State Department officials argued that it would disrupt Turkey's military modernization.

The Senate also turned back, 46-54, an amendment that would have cut the Military Assistance Program (MAP) by $211.5 million, to $705.5 million.

Final Action. A House-Senate compromise on foreign aid spending was incorporated in the conference report (H Rept 98-1159) on H J Res 648, filed Oct. 10.

Aid to the Nicaraguan contras continued to be a hotly contested issue, delaying final agreement on the aid section of the omnibus funding bill. Both sides linked resolution of the aid question to a related provision in H J Res 648 preventing the president from using U.S. armed forces to fight in Central America. The Reagan administration and Senate Republicans were willing to delete the $28 million in the bill for Nicaraguan contras if the House agreed to drop a ban on CIA use of its contingency fund to help the contras and if the House also agreed to drop the prohibition on using U.S. forces in the region. The conference compromise cut aid for the contras to $14 million from $28 million but stipulated that none of it could be used before Feb. 28, 1985. And before using the $14 million, the president would have to submit a report to Congress certifying

that the money was needed to combat expansionism by the Nicaraguan regime. Both chambers would have to approve any request to use the money, effectively giving either house a veto.

An attempt by members of the Senate Foreign Relations and House Foreign Affairs committees to insert a full-scale foreign aid authorization bill into H J Res 648 was blocked by Senate Democrats. Ironically, their objections had the effect of eliminating several Central America human rights and land reform provisions that Democrats had sought.

Both the House and the Senate approved H J Res 648, containing the foreign aid compromise, on Oct. 11, completing congressional action.

Final Funding Levels

As signed into law Oct. 12, H J Res 648 (PL 98-473) appropriated $18.2 billion for foreign aid and related programs for fiscal 1985. That was $4.7 billion more than Congress approved for fiscal 1984 in various aid bills (PL 98-151, PL 98-332 and PL 98-396). Because of a bookkeeping change in the way military aid was counted for fiscal 1985, however, the actual increase in spending on aid programs over 1984 was only $311 million.

Military Aid. H J Res 648 appropriated $5.9 billion for military assistance in fiscal 1985, a slight drop from 1984 ($6.5 billion). In part this reflected a new program in which about 16 countries were given smaller loans than in the past but under better terms. Interest rates for those nations were expected to be about 5 percent rather than the 10-12 percent charged for standard military aid loans.

Military aid for Israel also was reduced, to $1.4 billion from $1.7 billion in fiscal 1984. But Israel received all of its 1985 aid as a grant, whereas in past years it had to pay back half of U.S. aid.

In a reform that was called a step toward "honest budgeting," Congress and the administration agreed to count all military aid as part of the federal budget, starting in 1985. In the past only about one-fourth of all military aid dollars showed up in the budget as actual appropriations; the rest was in Foreign Military Sales guaranteed loans that were counted as "off-budget."

The fastest growing part of the aid budget was the Military Assistance Program, which provided grants to help foreign countries buy U.S. weapons and military services. The MAP program soared from $110 million in fiscal 1981 to $805 million in fiscal 1985.

El Salvador. Congress provided $128.25 million of Reagan's $132.5 million request for military aid in fiscal 1985 for El Salvador. Of that amount, $111.75 million was in MAP grants, $15 million was in FMS low-interest loans, and $1.5 million was for military training.

Congress put three major restrictions on El Salvador's military aid in fiscal 1985:

● Only half of the MAP money could be spent before March 1, 1985, unless the president sought approval from the House and Senate Appropriations committees to spend it at a faster rate. Before he could spend the second half, the president would have to report to the committees that the Salvadoran government had made "substantial progress" in several areas, including curbing killings by so-called "death squads," eliminating government corruption, improving the performance of the military and conducting discussions with the leftist opposition about ending the civil war.

● $5 million was held in escrow until the Salvadoran government conducted a trial and obtained a verdict in the case of two Americans, Mark Pearlman and Michael Hammer, and a Salvadoran, José Rodolfo Viera, who were killed in January 1981. The three men worked for El Salvador's land reform program.

● All aid to El Salvador would have to be suspended if the elected president of El Salvador was deposed by a military coup or decree.

H J Res 648 also provided $195 million in Economic Support Fund aid to bolster El Salvador's overall economy, a slight cut from Reagan's $210 million request.

An additional $6 million was included for improvements in the judicial system.

Central America. Reagan had asked for $1.2 billion in appropriations for economic, development and military aid to Central America in fiscal 1985. He also requested authorizations for at least $1.2 billion annually in fiscal years 1986-89, in accordance with the Kissinger commission's recommendations for multi-year aid to the region. Congress approved about $1.1 billion for 1985, but rejected the request for follow-up authorizations.

The resolution included authorizations and appropriations for a new "trade credit insurance" program to guarantee $300 million worth of loans made by the Export-Import Bank for high-risk exports of goods to Central America.

Congress set a $225 million limit on development aid programs in Central America — a cut of $48 million from Reagan's requests.

For the second year in a row, Congress rejected Reagan's request to resume aid for Guatemala to buy weapons from the United States. Reagan requested $10 million in FMS loans for Guatemala in fiscal years 1984 and 1985, but Congress banned the aid because of continuing repression by the rightist government. H J Res 648 lifted, for 1985, a related ban on aid to train Guatemalan military officers.

The bill also pared, to $12.5 million, Reagan's $35 million request for economic aid to Guatemala, and required that the money be spent on programs "aimed directly at improving the lives of the poor."

Reagan also had requested $40 million for development aid to Guatemala — an amount that would be subject to cuts resulting from the $225 million Central America limit imposed in H J Res 648.

Congress put restraints on administration plans to build a large regional military training center in Honduras. H J Res 648 barred the president from spending any money on the center unless certain conditions were met. *(Honduras, box, p. 176)*

Aside from El Salvador and Guatemala, the legislation did not set specific aid levels for Central American countries. Overall funding in the bill, however, provided enough military aid to meet the president's requests of $10 million for Costa Rica and $62.5 million for Honduras.

Middle East. Israel, faced with severe economic problems, won a bonanza of aid concessions from the administration and Congress — and the promise of more in the future.

● Israel was to receive all of its military aid as a grant, rather than half-grant, half-loan as in the past. In fiscal 1985 Israel was to get a $1.4 billion grant — worth more, administration aides said, than the $1.7 billion grant and loan it got in fiscal 1984.

● Israel would be able to use $400 million of its arms aid to develop and build its new warplane, the Lavi. Of that amount, $150 million would have to be spent in the United

States and $250 million in Israel. Congress had approved $550 million for the plane in fiscal 1984, setting a precedent for allowing Israel to spend U.S. aid on the Lavi.

● Israel was to get $1.2 billion in Economic Support Fund (ESF) grants in fiscal 1985 — an increase of $290 million over fiscal 1984 and of $350 million over Reagan's 1985 request.

● In a concession with long-term implications, H J Res 648 stated that it was U.S. "policy and intention" to give Israel at least as much economic aid each year as Israel owed the United States annually on past loans. The resolution said that guarantee was being made because "an economically and militarily secure Israel serves the security interests of the United States." At the end of 1984 Israel owed the United States about $9.6 billion, on which it was making annual interest and principal payments of about $1.1 billion.

● H J Res 648 exempted Israel — and possibly Lebanon and Turkey — from a 1980 law (PL 96-533) that banned construction and engineering firms in "advanced developing countries" from competing for work on U.S. foreign aid-financed projects. Under this exemption, Israeli firms could compete on U.S. aid projects anywhere.

● $2 million under the Agency for International Development's energy aid program was set aside for overseas development programs carried out in cooperation between the United States and Israel. Israel, a provider of technical aid to several countries, mostly in Africa, had sought $20 million in U.S. support for those efforts.

Congress also awarded increased aid to Egypt: $1.175 billion in military aid and $815 million in economic aid, all as a grant. The arms aid was the same as Reagan's request, but Congress added $65 million to the economic aid request as a partial balance to its much bigger boost in Israel aid.

In fiscal 1984 Egypt received $1.365 billion in military aid, of which it had to repay $900 million, and $750 million in economic aid grants.

In addition, $100 million of the 1985 economic aid was to be provided as a no-strings-attached cash transfer to the Egyptian government, instead of the normal procedure under which all economic aid funds were allocated for specific programs.

In a mild rebuke to Egypt, Congress stated that U.S. aid was based "in great measure upon the continued participation of Egypt" in the 1978 Camp David accords and the 1979 Egyptian-Israeli peace treaty. Egypt recalled its ambassador to Israel in 1982 to protest the Israeli invasion of Lebanon. Some members of Congress charged that Egypt's refusal to return an envoy violated its treaty commitments to Israel.

Enshrining in law a U.S. policy in effect since 1975, H J Res 648 barred any official of the U.S. government from recognizing or negotiating with the Palestine Liberation Organization (PLO) as long as that group continued to refuse to recognize Israel's right to exist, refused to accept U.N. Resolutions 242 and 338 on the Middle East and failed to renounce terrorism.

The bill included language stating that the United States should not sell "sophisticated weaponry" to Jordan until Amman had committed itself to recognize Israel and begin "serious peace negotiations." A formal ban on advanced arms sales to Jordan had been added to the unfinished fiscal 1985 foreign aid bill. Reagan had threatened to veto any legislation containing a ban.

Greece, Turkey. Pressured by pro-Greek lobbying, the House and Senate foreign policy committees recom-

mended major cuts and restrictions on U.S. aid to Turkey. The administration strongly protested that cuts would damage U.S. ties with a country that was vital to NATO and hosted several U.S. military and intelligence installations. Reagan had sought $755 million for Turkey, an increase of $40 million over the previous year.

After a long deadlock between the administration and Congress and between the House and Senate, lawmakers settled on a $700 million compromise: $215 million in MAP grants and $485 million in FMS loans. Turkey also received $175 million in economic aid, which was not controversial.

Congress provided Greece with $500 million in arms aid. Both countries were to get loans at a special 5 percent interest rate. Cyprus received $15 million in economic aid.

Africa. H J Res 648 provided most of the $1.2 billion requested for various aid programs for Africa in fiscal 1985. However, some major changes were made in how the aid was allocated.

Congress killed the administration's request for a new economic policy initiative intended to reward African countries that moved away from socialist policies and toward private enterprise. Reagan asked for $75 million for the program in fiscal 1985 as the first installment of a five-year, $500 million commitment. Instead, Congress diverted the $75 million into the Economic Support Fund, a government program that bolstered the economies of friendly countries.

Congress specified that Africa should get at least as much in no-interest loans from the International Development Association (IDA) during the next three years as it did during the previous three years. The move was made to protect Africa from the administration's decision to cut the U.S. contribution to IDA, which contributed to a projected drop in IDA's lending pool from $12 billion to $9 billion in fiscal 1985-88.

Lawmakers also earmarked $42 million for health and development assistance, approved $97.5 million for the Sahel Development Fund, a program that since the mid-1970s had helped drought-stricken western Africa, and gave about $68 million in direct contributions to the African Development Bank and Fund.

Congress pared both economic and military aid to Zaire. Economic aid was set at $10 million, $5 million below Reagan's request, and arms aid was set at $4 million, $6 million below the request.

AID Programs. Congress appropriated $1.7 billion for development programs run by the Agency for International Development, earmarking funds to boost health care in poor countries, especially for children. Funds also were approved for overseas family planning programs run by the U.S. government and the United Nations.

International Financial Institutions. After months of controversy that threatened to scuttle some funds earmarked for affiliates of the World Bank, Congress agreed to appropriate a total of $1.3 billion for international financial institutions.

Especially hard fought was the contribution for the International Development Association, which loaned money to the poorest Third World countries. As in past years, a lengthy debate on the politically unpopular program was skirted by approving IDA funding through the omnibus appropriations measure, thereby avoiding a specific vote on the issue in the House and Senate. As cleared by Congress, H J Res 648 approved the administration's request of $2.25 billion for fiscal 1985-87 as the U.S. share of IDA's international lending pool. That amount was 31

percent lower than the previous U.S. pledge and brought the total IDA fund to $9 billion, $7 billion less than the World Bank initially requested.

In addition to the $2.25 billion pledge, H J Res 648 contained a $750 million appropriation for the first year of the three-year commitment, and $150 million for the final installment of a previous pledge.

To hold down appropriations in the resolution, Congress cut $44 million from the Asian Development Fund's proposed $144 million appropriation, and the U.S. direct contribution to the Inter-American Development Bank was reduced by $20 million, to $38 million. Other appropriations for the international banks were: $109.7 million for the World Bank, $72.5 million for the Inter-American Development Bank's Fund for Special Operations, $113.2 million for the Asian Development Bank, $50 million for the African Development Fund and $17.9 million for the African Development Bank.

Other Provisions. H J Res 648 also:

• Shifted $45 million in military aid to the Philippines to economic aid, as a symbolic congressional protest against the authoritarian regime of President Ferdinand E. Marcos. Reagan had requested $180 million for the Philippines, in connection with a new agreement for the operation of U.S. military bases there. He sought $60 million in military aid loans, $25 million in military aid grants and $95 million in economic aid. The resolution allowed the full $180 million, but shifted the mix to $15 million in military aid loans, $25 million in military grants and $140 million in economic aid.

• Established a $50 million fund requested by the president to provide emergency aid to relieve "severe food shortages" overseas. *(Africa food aid, p. 178)*

• Barred all military aid to Haiti, and permitted economic and development aid up to $54.7 million only if the president reported to Congress every six months that the Haitian government was continuing to cooperate with efforts to halt illegal emigration to the United States, was cooperating with U.S. efforts to improve the management of aid programs there, and was making progress toward respecting human rights and reforming its political system.

• Barred U.S. aid to any country found by the president to be "failing to take adequate measures" to prevent narcotic drugs produced in its territory from entering the United States.

• Barred U.S. aid to any country more than one year in default on past obligations to the United States.

U.S. Aid to El Salvador

After three years of bitter debate between Congress and President Reagan over U.S. policy toward El Salvador, the Central American country faded as a major political issue in 1984. Lawmakers gave the president most of the additional military aid he requested for fiscal 1984, as well as his fiscal 1985 request to help the Salvadoran government battle leftist guerrillas.

The changed attitude in Congress resulted largely from the election May 6 of José Napoleón Duarte as president of El Salvador in a U.S.-backed election that was boycotted by leftist politicians and their guerrilla allies. Duarte, of the center-left Christian Democratic Party, was viewed as a centrist figure who would try to negotiate with the guerrillas for an end to the four-year-old civil war and would try to move the country toward greater democratization and respect for human rights.

Duarte had won the presidency in a runoff election against Roberto d'Aubuisson, who had been linked to right-wing "death squads." An initial election March 25 had produced no clear-cut winner.

Within weeks of his election, Duarte visited Capitol Hill and made more progress in winning congressional support for increased aid for his country than the Reagan administration had been able to accomplish in more than three years. His direct, low-key appeal for aid in May and July meetings with congressional leaders helped ensure the approval of $131.75 million in military aid for fiscal 1984, in addition to $64.8 million previously voted. Congress also gave the president most of the military aid he requested for El Salvador in fiscal 1985.

The favorable response in Congress to Duarte's election broke a political stalemate that had developed between Congress and the Reagan administration over El Salvador.

Critics of administration policy, mostly House Democrats, had argued that increased military aid merely bolstered Salvadoran right-wing extremists in the military and security police; such extremists were suspected in the deaths of thousands of civilians and in other human rights abuses. Despite Reagan administration objections, Congress since 1981 had treated human rights as a priority issue for continuing U.S. aid to Central America.

Congress used its control over the foreign aid budget to impose conditions on the distribution of aid to El Salvador. The conditions were intended to force progress by the Salvadoran government to end human rights abuses. The president requested increased military aid with no conditions attached.

Conditions on Aid

Congress in 1984 continued to insist that the distribution of aid to El Salvador be conditioned on progress in respect for human rights by the Salvadoran authorities and on land reform. One of the most controversial issues between the administration and its Democratic critics in Congress was the certification process that had governed U.S. aid to El Salvador in 1982 and 1983. That law (PL 98-113) expired Sept. 30, 1983, and President Reagan vetoed a bill that would have reinstated it. *(1983 action, p. 165)*

In a move to win congressional approval of further military aid for fiscal 1984, however, Reagan agreed to meet his congressional critics part way by offering to impose human rights conditions on the military aid, as long as there was no threat of an aid cutoff.

Congress nonetheless included a new certification requirement in an "urgent" supplemental appropriations bill cleared June 26, 1984. Complying with that law, the State Department issued a report in July. For the first time in two years the administration and its most persistent critics agreed that the Salvadoran regime had made significant progress in curtailing killings of civilians by the so-called death squads.

Fiscal 1984 Aid Increases

Congress in 1984 voted two increases in military aid to El Salvador for fiscal 1984: $61.75 million in the urgent supplemental appropriations bill (H J Res 492 — PL 98-332) cleared June 26 and $70 million in a further supplemental bill (HR 6040 — PL 98-396) cleared Aug. 10. The

administration in February had requested $178.7 million in supplemental funding.

Enactment of the supplementals brought total fiscal 1984 appropriations for military aid to El Salvador to $196.55 million, more than twice the level for fiscal 1983. Reagan had requested $243.5 million.

Urgent Supplemental. Following a bold administration strategy to bypass opposition by House Democrats, the Senate Appropriations Committee agreed to attach $92.7 million in additional military aid for El Salvador to H J Res 492, a House-passed measure providing $150 million in emergency food aid for Africa. The committee made the El Salvador aid contingent on reports by the president every 60 days that the country was improving its record on human rights and democratic reforms. The panel reported the bill March 14 (S Rept 98-365).

When H J Res 492 reached the Senate floor, it became the vehicle for an extended debate on U.S. policy in Central America. The Senate finally passed the resolution April 5, after cutting the El Salvador aid figure to $61.75 million. The reduction reflected a compromise between Senate leaders and the Reagan administration.

Opponents of the aid, led by Sen. Edward M. Kennedy, D-Mass., were able to delay floor action until after El Salvador's March 25 election. They argued against appropriating additional money until the United States knew who would be in charge of the government. When a clear-cut winner did not emerge, Kennedy offered an amendment reducing the aid to $21 million, to last through the May runoff election. He lost on a **25-63 key vote (R 2-48; D 23-15)**. *(1984 key votes, p. 927)*

The Senate did adopt an amendment that would cut off funds to El Salvador in the event of a successful military coup against the newly elected Duarte government. And opponents of the aid secured a pledge from the Senate Intelligence Committee to probe possible Central Intelligence Agency involvement in Salvadoran death squad activity.

During debate on H J Res 492, the Senate April 4 tabled on a **59-36 key vote (R 49-5; D 10-31)** an amendment that would have required the president to seek congressional authorization before sending combat troops into or over El Salvador, unless such action was necessary to evacuate U.S. citizens.

House Democrats delayed further action on H J Res 492 until after the May 6 election runoff in El Salvador. Conferees filed their report (H Rept 98-792) May 17; the El Salvador aid remained in disagreement. On May 24 the House agreed by a 267-154 vote to the $61.75 million the Senate had added to H J Res 492; several Democratic critics of the administration's Central America policy backed the aid to El Salvador, apparently swayed by Salvadoran President-elect Duarte, who visited Capitol Hill during the week.

The final version of H J Res 492, cleared June 26, included the following provisions related to El Salvador:

● Appropriated $61.75 million in military aid for El Salvador for fiscal 1984.

● Required the president to report every 60 days, during the remainder of fiscal 1984, on the following issues in El Salvador: elections, the administration of justice, freedom of association, government actions to curtail death squads, the development of a medical evacuation and training system, the training of the armed forces, the status of ammunition and supplies for the military, and land reform.

● Required the president to submit a report to Congress on the whereabouts of military equipment sent since 1980 to El Salvador, and the location of military personnel trained with U.S. funds.

● Required the immediate cutoff of military aid in the event of a military coup in El Salvador.

● Stated the sense of the Senate that the United States should provide military equipment to El Salvador to suppress guerrilla terrorism.

Additional Supplemental Aid. Continuing to press for the full $178.7 million it requested in February, the administration asked Congress to provide an additional $117 million in HR 6040, an omnibus fiscal 1984 supplemental bill.

The House version of HR 6040 (H Rept 98-916), passed Aug. 1, contained no military aid for El Salvador, although it provided $25 million in economic aid as part of a $131 million aid appropriation for Central America.

The Senate Appropriations Committee, in reporting HR 6040 (S Rept 98-570) Aug. 2, provided the full $117 million requested for military aid to El Salvador for fiscal 1984 as part of its $565 million Central America aid package. The Senate passed HR 6040 Aug. 8, after decisively rejecting Democratic efforts to cut or sharply restrict funding.

The final version of the bill, cleared Aug. 10, provided the Duarte government with another $70 million in military aid. Senate-House conferees had been unable to reach agreement on the El Salvador aid, which remained in dispute when the conference report (H Rept 98-977) was filed Aug. 10. The issue was resolved later that day when the House accepted, 234-161, a $70 million compromise that previously had been rejected by the House conferees. The Senate went along with the House figure.

Fiscal 1985 Funding

Congress provided $128.25 million in military aid and $195 million in economic aid for El Salvador in fiscal 1985 as part of an omnibus continuing appropriations resolution (H J Res 648 — PL 98-473) cleared Oct. 11. The money was included in the omnibus measure because lawmakers had not completed action on separate bills authorizing and appropriating funds for foreign aid for fiscal 1985.

Because of controversy over President Reagan's policies, Central America aid provisions had been omitted from authorization bills (HR 5119, S 2582) reported by the Senate Foreign Relations and House Foreign Affairs committees early in 1984. During floor debate on HR 5119, the House adopted, by a **212-208 key vote (R 156-8; D 56-200)**, a Republican amendment authorizing $1.21 billion for military and other aid programs in El Salvador. The House passed HR 5119 May 10, but the Senate never acted and the bill died. *(1984 key votes, p. 927)*

Foreign aid funding provisions drafted by the House and Senate Appropriations committees subsequently were incorporated in the continuing resolution. The final military aid appropriation was $4 million less than Reagan had requested. *(Details, foreign aid action, p. 170)*

Aid to Nicaraguan Rebels

House Democrats in 1984 persuaded Congress to reject President Reagan's request for additional support for guerrillas who were trying to oust the leftist government of Nicaragua.

U.S. Presence in Honduras

While playing down the extent of direct U.S. military involvement in Central America, the Reagan administration considerably expanded the U.S. presence in the region, especially in Honduras.

The Pentagon May 8 revealed "tentative plans" for U.S. military exercises in Honduras through 1988. It also said the Pentagon would store military equipment and supplies in Honduras in case U.S. troops were needed to defend U.S. allies in the region.

Democratic critics of President Reagan's policies in Central America charged that the Pentagon used a series of "exercises" as a facade for the establishment of a permanent military presence in Honduras. At any one time 5,000 or more U.S. troops participated in two series of war games in the country that ran from March 1983 to February 1984. All the exercises in Honduras were accompanied by naval maneuvers in the region.

The administration had plans to build a large Regional Military Training Center in northern Honduras to replace a makeshift camp it had been using near Trujillo for training Honduran and Salvadoran soldiers. But the Honduran government announced it would no longer permit Salvadorans to be trained at the camp.

Congressional Action

At the same time, Congress added a provision to the omnibus funding resolution (H J Res 648 — PL 98-473) for fiscal 1985 to bar the president from spending any money on the Honduran training facility until certain conditions were met. *(Foreign aid, p. 170)*

The Pentagon also was forced in 1984 to withdraw a request to Congress for $4.4 million for construction projects at two bases in Honduras. The Pentagon pulled back the request June 8 to avert a floor fight over the funding during Senate debate on military construction authorizations for fiscal 1985.

The General Accounting Office (GAO), an investigatory arm of Congress, reported that the Defense Department had used "improper" funding sources in building several military facilities, training Honduran troops and providing medical and other humanitarian services for Honduran civilians.

Conferees on the military construction authorization bill (HR 5604) Aug. 7 approved (H Rept 98-962) without comment an additional $4.3 million for Honduran facilities for a U.S. Army air reconnaissance unit. *(Military construction, p. 246)*

Under a compromise reached during the final days of the session, Congress appropriated $14 million for the guerrilla operation but barred the president from spending the money until after Feb. 28, 1985 — and then only if both chambers of Congress agreed. The compromise was included in a fiscal 1985 omnibus continuing appropriations resolution (H J Res 648 — PL 98-473) and a fiscal 1985 authorization bill for the CIA and other intelligence agencies (HR 5399 — PL 98-618).

The aid compromise ended a stalemate that had threatened to delay Congress' adjournment for the 1984 election campaign. Earlier in the year House conferees had succeeded in blocking additional aid for the guerrillas that the Senate had included in a fiscal 1984 supplemental appropriations bill (H J Res 492).

Congressional Democrats had been trying to cut off aid to the Nicaraguan guerrillas, known as "contras," since 1982. Their efforts gained support early in 1984 following an administration decision to mine several harbors in Nicaragua without telling the Senate Intelligence Committee beforehand. When the mines went off, committee Chairman Barry Goldwater, R-Ariz., castigated the CIA for sidestepping his panel. Both chambers adopted non-binding statements condemning the mining. *(Previous action, p. 162; summary, p. 184)*

The furor over the mining was followed in the fall by news stories about CIA involvement in the production of a manual that appeared to advocate the kidnapping and killing of Nicaraguan government officials by the guerrillas. The administration attributed the manual to low-level agency employees and disavowed any connection with political assassinations in Nicaragua.

By cutting off U.S. involvement in the war in Nicaragua, which began when the Reagan administration took office, Congress for the first time in eight years halted an overseas "covert" activity by the CIA. In 1976 Congress had banned aid to anti-Marxist rebels in Angola. *(Congress and the Nation Vol. IV, p. 878)*

Fiscal 1984 Supplemental

Early in the year President Reagan requested $21 million in additional fiscal 1984 funding for the contras, on top of $24 million appropriated by Congress in 1983. The Senate Appropriations Committee added the money to a House-passed supplemental appropriations bill (H J Res 492 — S Rept 98-365) reported March 14, and the Senate passed the bill April 5.

An amendment to delete the contra aid funds, offered by Edward M. Kennedy, D-Mass., was defeated 30-61, after Majority Leader Howard H. Baker Jr., R-Tenn., read a letter from President Reagan saying the United States did "not seek to destabilize or overthrow the government of Nicaragua."

Further congressional action on H J Res 492 was complicated April 6 when the press reported that the CIA was involved in the mining of Nicaraguan harbors, triggering recriminations on Capitol Hill by members who charged they had not been notified in advance. The Senate April 10 attached a non-binding condemnation of the mining to an unrelated tax bill (HR 2163) by an 84-12 vote. Two days later the House adopted a resolution (H Con Res 290) condemning the mining by a 281-111 vote.

Despite administration efforts, including a televised speech by Reagan May 9, House conferees on H J Res 492 refused to accept the Senate's $21 million appropriation for

the contras. On May 24 the disagreement moved to the House floor, where the aid for the contras was rejected May 24 by a **241-177 (R 24-132; D 217-45) key vote.** *(1984 key votes, p. 927)*

The administration finally was persuaded to give up the fight for the money in H J Res 492, and on June 25 the Senate voted 88-1 to delete the $21 million from the bill.

Fiscal 1985 Funds

Congress also resisted the administration's request for $28 million for the contras in fiscal 1985.

The House Intelligence Committee inserted a flat prohibition on further aid to the contras in its fiscal 1985 intelligence agencies authorization bill (HR 5399 — H Rept 98-743, Part I), reported May 10.

The full $28 million was authorized in the Senate version of the authorization bill, reported by the Senate Intelligence Committee May 24 (S 2713 — S Rept 98-481). But the Senate bill stipulated that the president could spend the $28 million only if he reported that the rebels were not trying to overthrow the Sandinista government. The bill also required the CIA to report to the committee in writing whenever it or the contras began a new military campaign.

Support for the administration's position on the covert aid to the contras continued to wane in June. On June 18 the Senate rejected an amendment to the fiscal 1985 defense authorization bill (S 2723) that would have prohibited U.S. assistance to the anti-government guerrillas in 1985. But the **key vote of 58-38 (R 48-6; D 10-32)** disguised a sharp drop in support among crucial Democrats at a time when the administration was waging an uphill battle to continue subsidizing the contras. Four Democrats on the Intelligence Committee who earlier had backed Reagan's policy of arming the Nicaraguan rebels bolted on the vote, depriving the administration of strong bipartisan support.

The House again rejected the idea of continued support for the contras by approving the ban on such aid in HR 5399. The House passed the measure Aug. 2 by a 294-118 vote, after Republican leaders decided not to mount a challenge to the Nicaragua provision.

The legislation remained stymied until the last days of the session, when a compromise was struck to clear the way for passage of H J Res 648, an omnibus continuing appropriations measure. The House version of H J Res 648, passed Sept. 25, contained a flat prohibition on any U.S. support for paramilitary activities in Nicaragua, while the version passed by the Senate Oct. 4 approved Reagan's full $28 million request.

The White House and Senate Republicans were willing to delete the $28 million from H J Res 648 if the House agreed to drop a ban on the CIA's use of its contingency fund to help the contras and also drop a prohibition on the use of U.S. forces in the region.

House conferees finally compromised by appropriating $14 million but barring the president from spending it until after Feb. 28, 1985. If the president decided that he wanted to spend the money, he would have to submit a report certifying that the funds were needed to combat Sandinista expansionism. Both chambers would have to approve any request, effectively giving either chamber a veto.

The final version of H J Res 648 containing the compromise (H Rept 98-1159) was adopted by the House Oct. 10 and by the Senate Oct. 11.

The compromise also was included in the intelligence authorization bill, which was passed by the Senate Oct. 11 and cleared by the House the following day.

Central America Aid Plan

Congress in 1984 enacted only pieces of a sweeping $8.8 billion, six-year program of aid for Central America, recommended in January by a presidential commission headed by former Secretary of State Henry A. Kissinger.

Congress approved most of the $1 billion-plus in economic and development aid that the commission recommended for fiscal 1985, as well as additional funding for fiscal 1984, but it rejected a plan to authorize follow-up aid for fiscal years 1986-89. The multi-year aspect was at the heart of the commission's recommendations.

The Kissinger commission recommendations suffered their biggest setback in the Republican-controlled Senate, where liberal Democrats and Jesse Helms, R-N.C., joined in an unusual coalition to help block the fiscal 1985 foreign aid authorization bill.

President Reagan had appointed the Kissinger panel, formally the National Bipartisan Commission on Central America, in July 1983 in hopes of getting a broad consensus behind his program of supporting El Salvador against leftist guerrillas while pressuring Nicaragua to drop its pro-Soviet stance. Kissinger was secretary of state in 1973-77.

Commission Report

The Kissinger commission's report, released Jan. 11, endorsed the thrust of Reagan's approach toward Central America. It called for more than $8 billion in economic aid to the region through 1989 and for firm U.S. resistance to the expansion of Soviet and Cuban influence.

The Soviet-Cuban advance affected the global balance of power, the commission said. Forced to "defend against security threats near our borders," the United States "would either have to assume a permanently increased defense burden, or see our capacity to defend distant trouble-spots reduced, and as a result have to reduce important commitments elsewhere in the world." The result would be a "strategic coup" for the Soviet Union.

The commission endorsed a "substantial" increase in military aid for El Salvador and backed indirectly Reagan's program of "covert" aid to anti-government rebels, called "contras," fighting the Sandinista government in Nicaragua. The commission also called on Reagan and Central American leaders to meet to decide on a plan for long-range economic development in the region.

The commission did not recommend using U.S. military forces to fight in Central America. But it said the United States should consider force against the Nicaraguan government as a "last resort" if it refused to agree to stop supporting guerrilla movements in other countries.

Reflecting congressional initiatives, the commission recommended one major departure from Reagan's policy. It advised conditioning military aid to El Salvador and Guatemala on progress on such human rights concerns as curbing the activities of so-called "death squads."

Foreign Aid Bill Action

Congress considered Reagan's requests primarily in conjunction with foreign aid. *(Authorization legislation, p. 170)*

House. In its consideration of the fiscal 1985 foreign aid authorization bill (HR 5119), the House Foreign Affairs Committee on March 14 dropped the broad Central America provisions. Democrats on the committee were united in their opposition to almost all of the Kissinger commission's recommendations. And members of both parties were leery of committing Congress to more aid for El Salvador until after that country's presidential election, scheduled March 25. A runoff election was held May 6.

After dropping the Reagan long-term plan for the region, committee Democrats drafted an alternative aid package, authorizing $250 million in aid for fiscal 1985 only. And they decided to impose new restrictions on several major aspects of Reagan's policies in the region. In particular, Democrats imposed a series of conditions on aid to El Salvador.

When the bill reached the House floor, however, Reagan gained a dramatic victory. The House May 10, on a **212-208 key vote (R 156-8; D 56-200)**, approved a Republican substitute for the committee's watered-down Central America aid package. *(1984 key votes, p. 927)*

The Republican substitute authorized $1.21 billion for military, economic, development and other aid programs for Central America in fiscal 1985. But the substitute did not include authorizations for aid after 1985, a feature that Kissinger commission members said was one of the most important of the initiative.

The substitute also authorized $281 million in supplemental aid for fiscal 1984, with the bulk going for economic aid ($119 million) and military aid ($129.35 million). The amendment did not specify amounts for individual countries in either 1984 or 1985.

After several attempts to revise or kill the Republican substitute failed, the House approved HR 5119 by a vote of 211-206.

Senate. The full Senate never considered its fiscal 1985 foreign aid authorization bill (S 2582), killing President Reagan's long-term aid package for Central America.

In drafting the 1985 foreign aid legislation, the Senate Foreign Relations Committee in early April split along partisan and ideological lines when it considered Reagan's Central America aid proposals. On April 11 the deadlocked Senate committee followed the House committee's example and approved a foreign aid bill for fiscal 1985 without the Central America provisions. That action, by a panel widely seen as receptive to the Kissinger commission's recommendations, was a major setback for Reagan's plan. The vote to report the stripped-down S 2582 was 16-2.

On May 9, while the House was debating HR 5119, the Senate Foreign Relations Committee reached an informal agreement on a compromise Central America aid package that would be incorporated in the Senate's aid authorization bill. But the agreement fell apart the next day over the question of how much aid each country in the region would receive.

Controversy over Central America aid and other foreign aid issues continued to stall Senate action on the aid authorization bill. Finally, in early August, the Republican leadership decided to give up on the measure.

Continuing Appropriations Resolution

Proponents of the Kissinger commission's plan also had hoped to attach it to a fiscal 1985 omnibus appropriations resolution (H J Res 648 — PL 98-473), which was cleared by Congress Oct. 11. But the key components of the Central America package died in the struggle over passage of H J Res 648, the largest stopgap funding bill Congress had ever approved.

Instead of giving the White House the multi-year aid program for Central America advocated by the commission, Congress in H J Res 648 provided $1.1 billion for the region for fiscal 1985. No funding was approved for fiscal years 1986-89. *(Details, p. 188)*

Congress Aug. 10 provided $498 million in additional fiscal 1984 aid to Central America as part of a supplemental appropriations bill (HR 6040 — PL 98-396).

Food Aid for Africa

Moved by starvation and death in Africa, Congress and the Reagan administration in 1984 approved an unprecedented amount of emergency food assistance to drought-stricken countries on that continent.

U.S. efforts to respond to Africa's food problems focused on two approaches: emergency assistance — food and seeds, and trucks to deliver them — and long-term aid to help countries develop their economies to avert food shortages in the future.

Appropriations

Congress provided $90 million in emergency food aid to Africa in a supplemental appropriations bill for fiscal 1984 (H J Res 493 — PL 98-248), cleared March 27. The bill also made available $90 million from Commodity Credit Corp. food stocks for sale to Africa. The African food aid was attached to the conference version of the bill when a separate measure (H J Res 492) containing $150 million in aid became embroiled in a dispute over El Salvador. Another $60 million remained in H J Res 492, which did not clear until June 26 (PL 98-332). Because time was running out in fiscal 1984, the $60 million was programmed for fiscal 1985.

A further fiscal 1984 supplemental appropriations measure (HR 6040 — PL 98-396), cleared Aug. 10, provided $16 million for other emergency needs — trucks, blankets and seeds.

Congress also provided about $1.2 billion for foreign aid and food assistance to Africa in fiscal 1985 in an omnibus continuing appropriations resolution (H J Res 648 — PL 98-473), cleared Oct. 11. The bulk of the money was for ongoing economic development programs.

Administration Steps

The Agency for International Development (AID) approved some $172 million in emergency aid in fiscal 1984. Then, when the famine continued to spread during the year, AID approved an additional $200 million for the first 45 days of fiscal 1985, which began Oct. 1, 1984. About $100 million went to Ethiopia, the most severely affected by the famine. Other major recipients included Kenya, the Sudan, Mauritania and Mozambique.

The administration announced Nov. 28 that it also intended, for the first time, to release wheat from the U.S. emergency reserve to needy African countries. Reagan agreed to release 300,000 tons, the maximum amount allowed under the 1980 law establishing the reserve. *(Congress and the Nation Vol. V, p. 388)*

Apart from increasing emergency food aid, the admin-

istration offered two approaches to bolster aid to Africa. Both had only limited success on Capitol Hill in 1984.

● Reagan sought $75 million as a first installment on a five-year, $500 million plan to provide extra aid to promote changes in African countries' economic systems.

The Senate Foreign Relations and House Foreign Affairs committees approved the $75 million as part of their foreign aid authorization bills (HR 5119, S 2582). The House Appropriations Committee also approved the program, but it was sidetracked in the Senate and ultimately died in conference on H J Res 648. Conferees on that bill diverted the $75 million into the Economic Support Fund, a program bolstering the economies of friendly countries.

● The president unveiled a five-point food aid program at a White House ceremony July 10 marking the 30-year anniversary of the Food for Peace program. Congress in H J Res 648 authorized $50 million for one element of the plan, a presidential fund for severe food emergencies, but it appropriated no new money.

Aid for Afghan Rebels

Some three years after the issue was first publicly raised, Congress Oct. 4 approved a resolution (S Con Res 74) calling on the administration "to effectively support" rebels who were fighting the Soviet occupation forces in Afghanistan. The Senate adopted S Con Res 74 on Oct. 3, and the House adopted it the following day. The administration had opposed the original version of the resolution on the grounds that it might focus attention on Pakistan, through which most supplies for the rebels flowed.

Congress also appropriated $50 million to support the rebels in a supplemental spending bill (HR 6040 — PL 98-396) for fiscal 1984.

Precise amounts of U.S. aid going to the rebels, Moslem mujahideen, were secret. The authorization for the aid, administered by the CIA, was contained in the fiscal 1985 intelligence authorization bill (HR 5399 — PL 98-618).

In the past all aid to the Afghans had been hidden within dozens of accounts in the "classified" portion of the Defense Department's regular budget, and the covert aid appropriations approved by Congress hidden in the defense appropriations bill. The $50 million in HR 6040 was disclosed inadvertently.

The mujahideen had inflicted heavy casualties on the 100,000-plus Soviet troops who had occupied Afghanistan since December 1979.

Embassy Security

Congress Oct. 5 cleared a bill (HR 6311 — PL 98-533) authorizing $355.5 million to bolster security at U.S. embassies overseas.

The bill, the most important of four "anti-terrorism" measures Reagan had proposed in April 1984, remained in limbo until after the Sept. 20, 1984, terrorist bombing of a U.S. Embassy annex near Beirut, killing two Americans and a dozen others. Congress moved ahead on the bill in a bitter climate of bickering between Democrats and the administration over responsibility for security lapses at the embassy annex. *(Lebanon developments, special report, p. 181)*

In addition to authorizing funds, HR 6311 established a new $10 million program of rewards for information

about terrorist activities in the United States and overseas. The bill was passed by the House Oct. 1 and the Senate Oct. 5.

Congress appropriated $110.2 million for the program in an omnibus continuing appropriations resolution (H J Res 648 — PL 98-473) for fiscal 1985, cleared Oct. 11.

Intelligence Agencies

Congress Oct. 11 cleared legislation authorizing funds for the CIA and other U.S. intelligence agencies. The bill (HR 5399 — PL 98-618) was held up because of a controversy over CIA covert aid to guerrillas who were fighting the leftist Sandinista regime in Nicaragua.

HR 5399 (H Rept 98-743, Parts I and II) was passed by the House Aug. 2, and a companion bill was reported (S 2713 — S Rept 98-481) by the Senate Intelligence Committee May 24. The Senate passed HR 5399 Oct. 11, after incorporating a Senate-House compromise on the Nicaragua aid issue. The House accepted the Senate-passed version, completing action on the bill. *(Nicaragua aid details, p. 184)*

Most of the intelligence provisions of HR 5399 were classified, but intelligence sources said the bill authorized about $9 billion for the CIA and other intelligence agencies.

In other provisions, the bill:

● Exempted the Defense Intelligence Agency, during fiscal years 1985-86, from standard civil service rules for classification of civilian employees. This provision allowed the agency to set its own salary schedules.

● Authorized $114.5 million to complete a $190 million two-year authorization for design and construction of a new building at CIA headquarters in Langley, Va.

● Stated the sense of Congress that the numbers and treatment of diplomats in the United States from hostile countries should not exceed the numbers and treatment of U.S. diplomats in those countries.

● Required the president to submit an annual report to Congress, beginning in November 1985, stating the number and treatment of diplomats in the United States from hostile countries, and the number of U.S. diplomats in those countries. The president also was required to report on any actions the United States might take to correct any "imbalance."

● Allowed either the director or the deputy director of the Office of Foreign Missions in the State Department to be either a foreign service officer or a representative of intelligence agencies. Previously the director was required to be a foreign service officer. The office was responsible for ensuring that embassies and other diplomatic missions in the United States complied with U.S. laws.

Genocide Treaty

Despite overwhelming support among senators and the belated backing of President Reagan, a handful of conservatives blocked Senate approval of a United Nations treaty outlawing genocide.

Drafted in 1947-48 with the help of the United States, the treaty (Exec O, 81st Cong, 1st Sess) called on signatories to take steps to prevent and punish a number of acts described as genocide. The treaty had been stalled in the Senate for 35 years. *(Background, Congress and the Nation Vol. III, p. 888)*

The Senate began debate on the genocide pact Oct. 10, but the treaty was withdrawn when Jesse Helms, R-N.C., and other conservatives threatened to throw up procedural barriers to its approval. They argued that the treaty, which the Foreign Relations Committee had approved Sept. 19, might undermine U.S. sovereignty.

In lieu of the treaty, the Senate on Oct. 11 adopted, 87-2, a resolution (S Res 478) commending the treaty's principles and pledging to act "expeditiously" on it during the first session of the 99th Congress.

The resolution was so broadly worded that it attracted the votes of two of the four senators who recently had spoken publicly against the genocide treaty: Helms and Orrin G. Hatch, R-Utah. Two other treaty opponents, John P. East, R-N.C., and Steven D. Symms, R-Idaho, cast the two "nay" votes on S Res 478.

The genocide treaty defined genocide as the intentional destruction of any national, racial, ethnic or religious group by killing its members, causing them serious physical or mental harm, imposing living conditions intended to bring about their destruction, or preventing births.

Reagan, who had ordered a review of the treaty after taking office in 1981, announced his support on Sept. 5. Several Democrats privately voiced suspicion that Reagan backed the treaty just two months before the presidential election as a way of courting favor with Jewish groups. But Sen. William Proxmire, D-Wis., a longtime advocate of the treaty, praised Reagan for giving it the push that was needed to get it to the Senate floor.

Despite Reagan's endorsement, however, the administration made little effort to overcome opposition by conservatives in the Senate.

Special Report: Central America

The United States sharply altered its relationship with its Central American and Caribbean neighbors in the early 1980s. The Reagan administration, alarmed about the future of U.S. interests and its allies in the region, developed a strategy based on military aid and intervention to protect those interests.

Military and related aid, rather than the development assistance that the United States had been providing, were the weapons used by the administration to bolster rightist or centrist governments and to oppose Soviet or Cuban encroachment in the region.

President Reagan summed up the administration's policy in an April 27, 1983, speech to a joint session of Congress in which he said the problems of Central America directly affected the security and well-being of the United States. He said two-thirds of all U.S. foreign trade and oil shipments passed through the Panama Canal and the Caribbean Sea.

The main threat to the region, Reagan said, was communist "adventurism" promoted by the Soviet Union, Cuba and Nicaragua. *(Text of address, p. 1069)*

Democrats in Congress were not persuaded by the president's arguments. Throughout Reagan's first term, House Democrats fought his requests for military aid to El Salvador in its war against leftist guerrillas and to rebel insurgents in Nicaragua who were fighting the leftist government there. Reagan's critics charged that the administration's emphasis on military solutions ignored the area's pressing economic difficulties and encouraged repressive regimes to continue human rights violations. Congressional critics also feared the United States was being drawn into direct military action similar to its involvement in Vietnam in the 1960s and 1970s. *(Details of 1981-84 legislative action, p. 129)*

In response to the charges that he had only a military strategy for Central America, Reagan in 1982 proposed a three-point program called the Caribbean Basin Initiative. The program, announced in a speech to the Organization of American States, called for tax incentives, trade concessions and $350 million in emergency economic aid.

In another response to critics of his Central American policies, Reagan in 1983 established a Bipartisan Commission on Central America to develop long-range recommendations for the region. Known as the Kissinger commission for its chairman, former Secretary of State Henry A. Kissinger, the panel sought to balance concern for U.S. political interests in the region with attention to long-range economic development needs.

Reagan incorporated most of the Kissinger commission recommendations in a six-year, $8.8 billion proposal he sent to Congress in the spring of 1984. Congress gave the president most of what he requested for fiscal 1985, the first full year of the program, but rejected his proposal for follow-up (fiscal 1986-89) authorizations.

Neither the Caribbean Basin Initiative nor the Kissinger commission recommendations slowed the administration's military escalation in the region, however. By the end of 1984 the Nicaraguan government was charging that the United States planned to invade the country. At the same time, the administration charged the Soviet Union with creating another "Cuban missile crisis" by shipping MiG fighters to the Nicaraguans.

The most dramatic demonstration of the Reagan administration emphasis on military solutions in the Caribbean region came in October 1983 when the United States invaded Grenada. The United States sent more than 7,000 troops into Grenada as part of a "rescue mission" for about 600 Americans studying at a U.S.-run medical school on the island.

Although the Grenadian invasion was a startling example of the administration's increasing reliance on military solutions to problems in the Caribbean, it only temporarily overshadowed the ongoing controversy over U.S. involvement in El Salvador and Nicaragua.

Meanwhile, four Latin American countries tried to develop a process that would lead to negotiated settlements of the conflicts in Central America. While the governments "agreed in principle" to a 21-point list of objectives for a peaceful settlement, nothing concrete was achieved through 1984. *('Contadora' negotiations, box, p. 185)*

Background

In both Nicaragua and El Salvador, coups in 1979 brought in new governments. In Nicaragua, a leftist coup ousted the Somoza family, which had ruled Nicaragua for 40 years. The government was taken over by "Sandinistas" — leftists who took their name from Augusto Sandino, the national hero who battled the U.S. Marine occupation of Nicaragua in the early 1930s.

Soon after taking office, Reagan charged that the Sandinistas were trying to establish a Marxist state under the influence of Cuba and the Soviet Union. Reagan suspended a Carter administration program of economic aid to Nicaragua.

The action was the first of a series of moves by the administration against the Sandinista government. Later in 1981 the president reportedly authorized U.S. military support, through the Central Intelligence Agency (CIA), for Nicaraguan exiles in Honduras who were fighting the Sandinistas. The insurgent forces, called "contras," grew in strength as a result of U.S. military assistance and training.

Although House Democrats fought the president on requests for "covert" aid to the contras, they were blocked by administration supporters in the Senate. But after Congress learned in the spring of 1984 that the CIA had directed the mining of Nicaraguan harbors, the Senate joined the House in refusing further administration requests for the covert aid.

By the end of 1984 relations between the United States and Nicaragua had deteriorated to the point where the Sandinista government had put the country on nationwide alert, claiming that a U.S. invasion was imminent.

Equally controversial was the administration's unswerving support of the government of El Salvador, where American power was directed toward protecting and stabilizing the government against leftist guerrilla forces. The 1979 coup in El Salvador led to the establishment of a moderate civilian junta, but civil war continued to rage throughout the country. Elections for a new Constituent Assembly in 1982 resulted in the establishment of an interim government dominated by rightist forces.

Congressional Democrats, joined by some Republicans, opposed administration requests for increased military and economic support for El Salvador as long as the government failed to advance land reform, negotiate with rebel forces or control rightist "death squads" accused of torturing and killing thousands of civilians.

However, the election in May 1984 of a moderate president, José Napoleón Duarte, and the initiation of talks between Duarte and rebel leaders later that year, helped Reagan gain more support in Congress for administration aid requests.

Reagan also escalated U.S. military involvement in the Central American region by conducting a series of military maneuvers and training exercises in Honduras. At various times U.S. aircraft carrier task forces were stationed off both the Atlantic and Pacific coasts of Central America. *(U.S. presence in Honduras, p. 176)*

The administration was much less successful in attempting to restore U.S. military ties to Guatemala. Under the Carter administration the United States had cut off military aid and arms sales to Guatemala because of alleged human rights abuses by its military government. When the Reagan administration moved in late 1982 and early 1983 to restore U.S. military ties, liberals in Congress protested that human rights violations had not ceased. Provisions attached to appropriations for fiscal 1983 and 1984 banned all U.S. aid to Guatemala except for humanitarian assistance provided through private voluntary organizations. Congressional opposition also forced the administration to shelve a sale to Guatemala of helicopter spare parts and other equipment that had both military and civilian uses. *(Box, p. 163)*

Declining Economies

The five nations of Central America — Guatemala, El Salvador, Honduras, Nicaragua and Costa Rica — together had a population of about 22 million in 1983 and a gross national product of under $20 billion.

Annual per capita income in the region ranged in 1981 from a low of $600 in Honduras to a high of $1,430 in Costa Rica, according to the World Bank. On a per capita basis, the region had suffered a decline in production every year since 1979; in 1982 per capita production dropped by 6.5 percent.

Some countries were hit harder than others by the economic decline. Twenty-five percent of El Salvador's productive facilities, ranging from farms to factories, had been destroyed by guerrilla warfare since 1979.

In the 1950s and 1960s the Central American economies were among the most robust in the hemisphere, growing at rates in excess of 5 percent a year. But a number of factors slowed the growth in the 1970s: the Arab oil embargo, soaring oil prices, reduced demand in industrialized countries for the products of Central America, higher interest rates and less trade between countries in the region itself. Rapidly deteriorating economic conditions helped spawn military coups, revolutions and other threats to stability.

The Reagan administration came into office stressing the importance of fostering democratic regimes in the region. Deputy Secretary of State Kenneth W. Dam said in a December 1983 speech that administration policy was "to actively support democracy, reform and human freedom against dictators and would-be dictators of both left and right."

U.S. Invasion of Grenada

When the United States sent armed American soldiers to Grenada on Oct. 25, 1983, it was the first time the United States had intervened militarily in the Caribbean since it sent troops to the Dominican Republic in 1965. *(Congress and the Nation Vol. II, p. 66)*

The intervention was the consequence of political developments on the tiny Caribbean island that began in March 1979, when a coup put into power a leftist government under Prime Minister Maurice Bishop. Bishop built strong ties with Cuba and the Soviet Union, and a Soviet-Cuban military presence was established.

Of particular concern to the United States was the construction of an airport with a landing strip long enough, the Pentagon claimed, to serve as a forward base for Cuban MiG fighters and for refueling transport planes ferrying arms and supplies from Soviet-bloc countries to Central America. President Reagan referred to the airstrip in a March 1983 televised speech to the National Association of Manufacturers and in his April 27 address to a joint session of Congress.

Bishop unexpectedly was deposed and placed under house arrest on Oct. 13, 1983, by a hard-line leftist group led by Deputy Prime Minister Bernard Coard. A "Revolutionary Military Council" under the army chief, Gen. Hudson Austin, took over control of Grenada.

Bishop was freed by his supporters Oct. 19, but was recaptured and executed the same day by the Grenadian Army. A 24-hour "shoot on sight" curfew was imposed.

Four Caribbean islands that belonged to the Organization of Eastern Caribbean States (OECS) — Dominica, Antigua, St. Lucia and St. Vincent — asked for U.S. military assistance. They were joined by Jamaica and Barbados. U.S. intervention was opposed by some other Caribbean countries — Trinidad and Tobago, the Bahamas, Belize and Guyana.

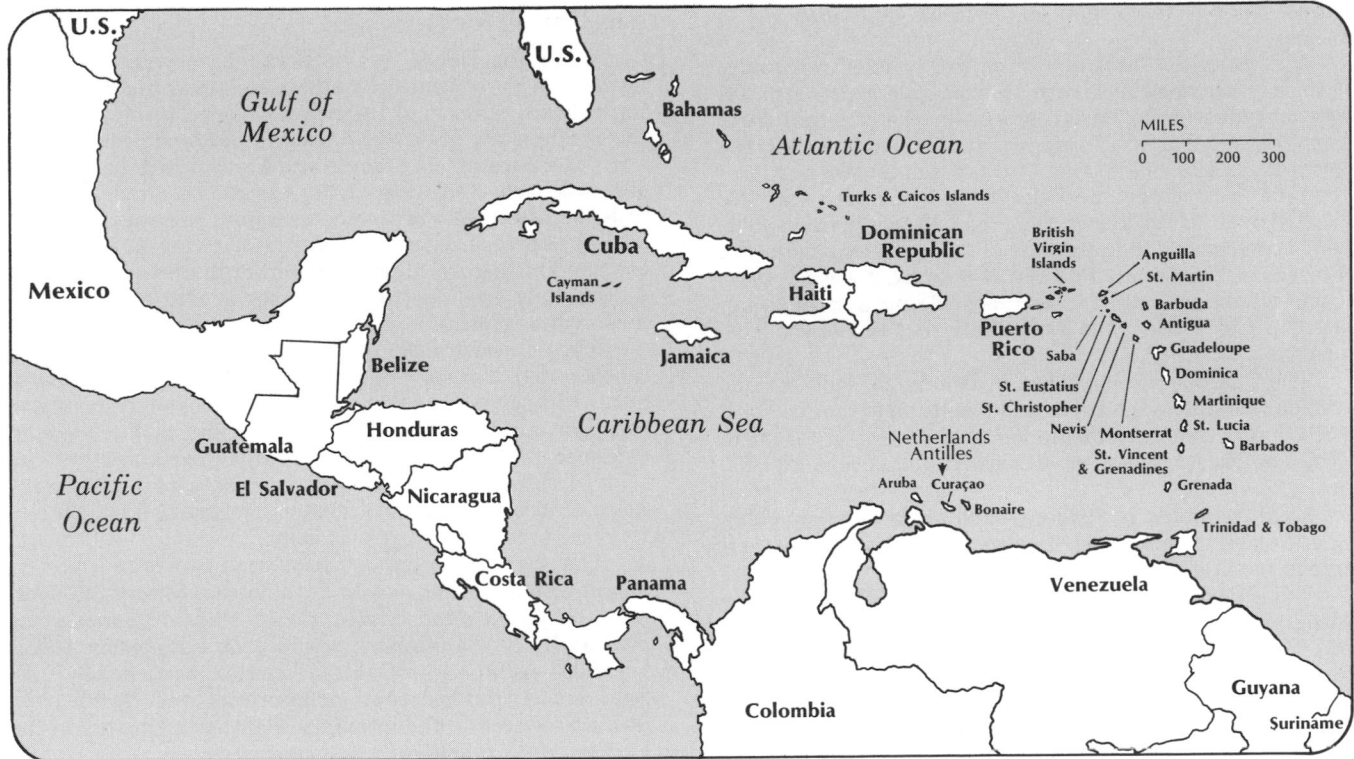

The chairman of the OECS, Prime Minister Eugenia Charles of Dominica, on Oct. 25 announced jointly with Reagan that the United States had intervened. The OECS nations, lacking military forces, contributed 300 constables to the American force of 7,300 U.S. Marines, Army Rangers and paratroopers.

President Reagan said the invasion was necessary to protect the lives of the 1,000 Americans there, most of whom were students attending St. George's Medical College, and because the OECS had requested the assistance.

Eighteen U.S. soldiers were killed and 115 wounded in the attack. U.S. forces captured more than 700 Cubans within a few days of the invasion. By Dec. 12 all U.S. combat troops had been withdrawn, leaving some 300 U.S. military support personnel on the island.

U.S. troops uncovered tons of military equipment and turned up documents that revealed secret agreements between Grenada and Cuba, the Soviet Union and North Korea that covered the delivery of arms and supplies through the end of 1985. Pentagon analysts said the Soviets and Cubans had been building an arsenal on the island that could have been used to destabilize governments elsewhere in the eastern Caribbean.

The U.S. intervention was viewed with alarm in Latin America. The United Nations General Assembly voted 108-9, with 27 abstentions, in favor of a resolution that "deeply deplored" the invasion and called it a "flagrant violation of international law." But there was substantial support for the action in the United States. The U.S. ambassador to the United Nations, Jeane J. Kirkpatrick, summed up the message of the invasion that Americans seemed to approve: "I think it does communicate to the Soviets that we are willing under certain narrowly defined circumstances, where there are American nationals' lives at stake, where there is a collective security arrangement with the countries who request our cooperation, to act in defense of self-

determination and law and our own national security."

Congress debated whether to invoke the War Powers Resolution (PL 93-148), which required the withdrawal of all U.S. forces within 90 days unless an extension was authorized by Congress. A resolution to apply the 1973 act was passed by the House Oct. 27, but was blocked in the Republican-dominated Senate.

Some Democrats had misgivings about the legality of the invasion under international and U.S. laws. Others complained that Reagan had used the American medical students as a pretext to oust the pro-Cuban regime in Grenada. However, the favorable public reaction to the invasion, the testimony of the medical students about the danger they believed they were in and the evidence of the stockpiles of Soviet-made arms blunted these criticisms. Most Democrats eventually supported the president.

Grenada held its first elections in eight years on Dec. 2, 1984, voting for a 15-member House of Representatives. The New National Party, whose leader was Herbert Blaize, won a majority of the seats. Blaize had been chief minister under British colonial rule before Grenadian independence in 1974.

Aid to Nicaraguan 'Contras'

The United States began providing covert military assistance to the rebels fighting the Sandinista government of Nicaragua soon after Reagan took office. Nicaraguan dictator Anastasio Somoza was ousted in July 1979 in a broadly based revolution led by leftists, who later took full control of the government. Anti-Sandinista rebels, called "contras," organized in Honduras under the banner of the Nicaraguan Democratic Force.

According to press reports, some of the key military leaders of the contras were members of Somoza's national

guard, believed to have been involved in human rights abuses.

U.S. activities in support of the contras reportedly began in December 1981 with an executive order from the president authorizing covert actions by the CIA to disrupt arms shipments into Nicaragua and to harass what the executive order called the "Cuban-Sandinista support" structure in Nicaragua and elsewhere in Central America.

Although it was known that the CIA was giving equipment and training to thousands of troops belonging to the Nicaraguan Democratic Force in Honduras, it was not clear if the intelligence agency also was aiding a rival group based in Costa Rica, the Democratic Revolutionary Alliance.

The CIA operations, based in Honduras, soon became an open secret through press and television accounts. With U.S. support the guerrilla forces grew, totaling 15,000 in 1984. The Nicaraguan army was estimated at about 26,000 men.

By the summer of 1983 guerrilla units were launching air and naval attacks that damaged major Nicaraguan oil storage facilities.

The Nicaraguan government denounced U.S. action aiding the contras, saying it amounted to "undeclared war." The Sandinistas took their case to the U.N. Security Council in March 1983 and to the World Count in April 1984. The Security Council took no action after a week of debate, but the World Court in November 1984 agreed to hear Nicaragua's case. *(Details, box, p. 187)*

Critics of administration policy feared the United States was expanding its role in Nicaragua to include the ouster of an internationally recognized government of a foreign country, in violation of both U.S. and international laws. Administration officials argued they were not trying to overthrow the Sandinista government, merely trying to stop the flow of Soviet- and Cuban-supplied arms to leftists in El Salvador.

Democrats in the House repeatedly tried to cut off the covert aid to the contras. In 1982 they succeeded in adding to a CIA authorization measure and to a defense appropriations bill an amendment prohibiting CIA operations aimed specifically at overthrowing the Nicaraguan government. The provision was known as the Boland amendment for its sponsor, House Intelligence Committee Chairman Edward P. Boland, D-Mass.

In the spring of 1983 House Democrats renewed their attack on the aid to the rebels, contending the administration was violating the Boland amendment.

President Reagan mounted a strong campaign for his policies in an April 27, 1983, address to Congress. Although the address dealt with overall policy toward Central America, it included a harsh attack on the Sandinista government.

The United States did not seek the overthrow of the Sandinista government, Reagan said. "Our interest is to ensure that it does not infect its neighbors through the export of subversion and violence."

Reagan assured Congress that there was "no thought of sending American combat troops to Central America; they are not needed."

House Democrats made four attempts in 1983 and 1984 to end U.S. aid to the anti-Sandinista rebels. Though their attempts initially were blocked in the Republican Senate, a compromise eventually was reached on contra aid for fiscal 1984. And Democrats succeeded in blocking an administration request for additional aid in 1984.

Aid Ban Efforts

While the House was debating the covert aid issues, Democrats were lobbied by administration officials and by top political officials of the two main rebel groups fighting the Sandinistas. They were Adolfo Calero and Lucia Salazar of the Nicaraguan Democratic Force, which had openly acknowledged receiving CIA assistance, and Alfonso Robelo Callejas of the Democratic Revolutionary Alliance.

The three insisted they were not trying to overthrow the Sandinista government, but rather to pressure the Sandinistas into keeping 1979 promises of free elections and democratic reforms.

The administration argued that cutting off aid to the rebels would "virtually destroy" the prospects that Nicaragua might agree to reciprocal and verifiable agreements to end assistance to guerrilla forces in the region. Reagan defended the use of covert action. In a press conference he said: "I think covert actions have been a part of government, and a part of government's responsibilities, for as long as there's been a government."

One tactic the administration used to avert a total ban on aid to the contras was to develop the concept of "symmetry": The United States would stop supporting the contras if the Sandinistas would stop supporting leftist guerrillas elsewhere in Central America, particularly in El Salvador. An amendment incorporating the "symmetry" idea was offered to the intelligence authorization bill in the House, but it failed by a 20-vote margin.

The compromise reached by Congress in 1983 was incorporated in both the intelligence authorization and defense appropriations bills. The administration could spend a maximum of $24 million for covert aid in fiscal 1984, but the president would have to return to Congress for more funds if he wanted to continue the aid into fiscal 1985. Although the $24 million enabled support to the contras to continue, it was short of the $35 million to $50 million the president reportedly planned to spend on the effort.

Stiffening Opposition

In early 1984 the president asked Congress for another $21 million. On April 6, 1984, a story appeared in *The Wall Street Journal* reporting direct CIA involvement in the mining of Nicaraguan harbors. The tone of the congressional debate grew more harsh, and many Republicans joined the Democrats for the first time in opposition to the aid.

The Senate Intelligence Committee previously had laid down restrictions on covert aid: The United States was not to support attacks on the Nicaraguan economy. The attacks on Nicaraguan oil supplies and ports, with CIA assistance, were seen as violating the restriction.

In addition, members of the Senate Intelligence Committee said the CIA had been involved in the mining for two months without giving detailed notice to the committee, as required. Although administration officials said the Intelligence committees had been briefed on "all U.S. activities in the Central American region," CIA Director William J. Casey later apologized to the Senate committee for failing to "fully inform" members about the agency's involvement in the mining.

Reagan tried to salvage the covert aid program and other aid requests for El Salvador with a nationwide television address May 9, 1984. Reagan called congressional critics of his policies "new isolationists" who "would yield to

'Contadora' Group Seeks Negotiated Solutions

Four Latin American countries began working in 1983 to develop a negotiated solution to the conflicts in Central America. The four — Colombia, Mexico, Panama and Venezuela — came to be known as the "Contadora" group, for the Panamanian island where the countries' foreign ministers first met for talks on collective diplomacy in January 1983. The group held several joint sessions with the foreign ministers of Guatemala, Honduras, El Salvador, Nicaragua and Costa Rica.

In September 1983 the Contadora countries agreed to a 21-point "Document of Objectives," which outlined "principles for the peaceful settlement of Central American disputes." Among the principles were demilitarization of Central America, more economic aid from outside countries and moves toward democracy. The document stressed the need for economic development of the region, protection of human rights and establishment of "democratic representative and pluralistic systems."

The military points called for the phasing out of foreign arms shipments, the removal of foreign military advisers and the closing of foreign military bases and limits on the size of each nation's military force.

The nine countries agreed "in principle" to implement the objectives in meetings on Jan. 8 and May 1, 1984, but the agreements contained few specifics. Contadora negotiators said they hoped to produce treaties requiring each Central American country to abide by the 21 points.

While endorsing the Contadora process, the United States did not participate directly in the talks. Administration officials said the talks needed to be a regional effort, not an adjunct of U.S. policy. The negotiations would fail, the officials said, if leaders in the region thought the United States was attempting to use the talks to impose its own will.

Congressional Democrats and some Latin American leaders charged that the administration was giving only rhetorical backing to the talks while actively pursuing a military buildup in Central America.

In a March 15, 1984, report to Congress, Secretary of State George P. Shultz said Nicaragua, not the United States, was thwarting progress in the Contadora negotiations. Nicaragua's Sandinista leaders were "clearly uncomfortable" with some of the Contadora objectives, "particularly those calling for respect for basic human rights and national reconciliation through democratic pluralism," Shultz said.

Shultz said Nicaragua tried to bypass the Contadora process when it submitted four draft bilateral treaties to the United States in October 1983. Those treaties, Shultz said, "disregarded many of the 21 points and renewed the Sandinista push for bilateral and piecemeal agreements. Thus, while paying lip service to the aims of Contadora, the Sandinistas were still far from eager participants and actively sought to change the direction of the process."

One of the Contadora leaders, Mexican President Miguel de la Madrid, met with President Reagan on May 15, 1984, to urge Reagan to support the negotiations more actively and to curtail military exercises in the region.

Venezuelan President Jaime Lusinchi met President Reagan in December 1984 to discuss the effort to work out a draft peace treaty acceptable to all the countries. Although Lusinchi was rumored to have presented new proposals from Nicaragua to the president, the White House denied having any knowledge of such proposals.

---

temptation to do nothing" in the face of aggression. The president called the Sandinista rule "a communist reign of terror." The government had broken its 1979 promise to hold elections, he said, had repressed its critics and had tried to "wipe out an entire culture" — the Miskito Indians in northeast Nicaragua.

The United States had a "moral duty," Reagan said, to support the Nicaraguan guerrillas, whom he called "freedom fighters."

But Congress refused to grant the president the additional $21 million for fiscal 1984. Immediately after that defeat, the administration sought $28 million to continue the covert aid in fiscal 1985. For the fourth time the House banned the aid. Eventually it reached a compromise with the Senate approving $14 million. But none of the $14 million could be spent before Feb. 28, 1985, and it could be spent by the administration only if the president submitted a report to Congress, certifying that the money was needed to combat Sandinista expansionism. Both houses of Congress would have to approve any request to spend the

funds.

Adolfo Calero of the Nicaraguan Democratic Force in November 1984 said the contras were able to continue their war against the Sandinistas with the aid of $3 million raised from private American and foreign sources. The rebel effort also had been helped, he said, by a rapid devaluation of Nicaraguan currency on the local black market and by rebel captures of government ammunition from raids inside Nicaragua.

Elections were held in Nicaragua on Nov. 4, 1984. Apart from the ruling Sandinista National Liberation Front, whose leader, Daniel Ortega, became president, only minor parties participated. Ortega was the coordinator of the three-member junta of the Government of National Reconstruction.

That same month the Sandinistas and the Reagan administration engaged in a war of words about whether Nicaragua was receiving advanced warplanes from the Soviet Union and engaging in a military buildup. The Nicaraguans alleged that the United States was preparing to

invade their country. Each side denied the other's charges.

On Nov. 6 an unnamed U.S. official said there was "credible evidence" that a Soviet freighter was carrying MiG-21 warplanes to Nicaragua. For three days administration spokesmen seemed to encourage speculation that the United States would take military action should the MiGs turn up in Nicaragua. On Nov. 9 U.S. officials said it appeared the Soviet ship had not unloaded MiGs, although other Soviet ships were delivering attack helicopters.

Aid to El Salvador

President Reagan and Democrats in Congress also tangled over administration policy toward El Salvador. Reagan sought increased military and economic aid to support the Salvadoran government, which had been battling leftist guerrillas since 1980. The administration hoped that a centrist government would be installed that could win the loyalty of the population as well as the war against the guerrillas. Although Congress used its control over the foreign aid budget to moderate the administration's requests for military aid, the aid was never totally cut off. The result was that the administration was able generally to pursue its policies in El Salvador.

Administration officials revived the Vietnam-era "domino theory" as the rationale for providing military aid to El Salvador. If El Salvador fell under Marxist influence, administration officials said, other nations in Central America would inevitably be threatened as well.

In a May 1984 nationally televised speech, Reagan said: "If we do nothing or if we continue to provide too little help, our choice will be a communist Central America with additional communist military bases on the mainland of this hemisphere, and communist subversion spreading southward and northward."

His critics in Congress were skeptical of the president's arguments for increasing U.S. aid. They claimed that despite the extensive aid the United States had provided the country in the early 1980s, the Salvadoran economy continued to deteriorate, and the guerrillas continued to score military gains against the government. *(U.S. aid, below)*

Before Reagan took office, leftist rebels attempted a "final offensive" to topple the centrist military-civilian

---

U.S. Aid to El Salvador

The following chart shows the growth of U.S. aid to El Salvador during fiscal years 1981-85 *(in millions of dollars)*:

	Military Aid	Non-Military Aid
1981	$ 35.50	$106.6
1982	82.00	192.5
1983	81.30	245.5
1984	196.50	329.3
1985	128.25	326.1

---

junta that had assumed power in 1979. (The junta had appointed José Napoleón Duarte as president in 1980.) But the guerrillas were not successful, and the Reagan administration immediately moved to shore up the Salvadoran government by sending military aid and U.S. military advisers.

Reagan's first secretary of state, Alexander M. Haig Jr., said the United States would "draw the line" in El Salvador against communist interference in Central America. Haig solicited support for the policy on Capitol Hill by showing key members evidence that communist nations were supplying arms to the guerrillas.

Congressional critics charged that building up the military strength of the government, which had not been willing or able to stamp out the rightist "death squads," would only encourage continued repression and violence in the country. They argued that the Reagan policy had done nothing to encourage negotiations between the government and the guerrillas.

Before Duarte lost the presidency in 1982 elections, administration supporters in Congress said Duarte offered the only hope for a democratic future in El Salvador. An end to U.S. aid, they said, would encourage communist nations and the leftist insurgents to intensify their efforts to win control of the government.

Aid Restrictions

Although the Democrats were unable to block the administration's aid requests, they did succeed in attaching conditions to the aid aimed at pressuring the Salvadoran government to curb human rights abuses and institute political and economic reforms. As a condition for releasing the aid money, the president had to certify to Congress twice a year that the Salvadoran government was "making a concerted and significant effort to comply with internationally recognized human rights" and was "achieving substantial control over all elements of its own armed forces. . . ."

The certification requirements were included in a 1981 foreign aid authorization bill and became the source of twice-yearly disputes between the administration and critics of administration policy over the extent of progress by El Salvador in meeting the conditions. Each time the administration certified that El Salvador was moving toward improvements in human rights and democratization, organizations monitoring human rights overseas would issue contradictory reports of events in El Salvador. These organizations included the American Civil Liberties Union, Amnesty International and Americas Watch.

Typical of the debate were the accounts of the number of civilians killed. In January 1983 the certification report issued by the State Department said civilian deaths attributed to political causes had "declined significantly." The report referred to Salvadoran press reports that such deaths had not exceeded 200 per month in the second half of 1982 compared with a monthly average of nearly 500 in 1981. Human rights groups, on the other hand, cited reports by two Catholic Church-related legal aid offices in El Salvador that more than 5,000 civilians had been killed in 1982.

In 1982 elections were held in El Salvador for a 60-member Constituent Assembly, which set up an interim government under President Alvaro Magana. The Assembly was to write a new constitution and prepare for the election of a permanent government.

Salvadorans turned out to vote in large numbers in the May 28 elections, despite leftist attempts to disrupt the balloting. Although the elections generally were viewed as free and fair, the left did not participate; rightist parties won control of the Assembly. The Assembly was headed by Roberto d'Aubuisson, head of the right-wing ARENA party. A former U.S. ambassador to El Salvador had charged d'Aubuisson, a former army major, with complicity in political murders. U.S. officials had hoped for a victory by moderate Christian Democrats under Duarte. The rightists were persuaded, however, to give a share of power to the Christian Democrats.

The Assembly was composed of many conservatives who opposed a government program to turn over land from large estates to peasants. Progress toward land reform was one of the conditions Congress had attached to the distribution of military aid.

The Reagan administration's July 1982 certification report said foes of land reform in the Assembly "took advantage of an effort to correct some of the program's genuine shortcomings to pass ambiguous legislation which cast doubt on the future of the program and contributed to a surge in illegal evictions."

The hopes raised by the election were dashed by other events as well. The political and military situation in El Salvador deteriorated sharply in 1983. The Salvadoran military was performing poorly, and paralysis was developing in the Constituent Assembly. Presidential elections scheduled for November 1983 had to be postponed.

The tone of the two administration certification reports in 1983 reflected administration frustration with events in El Salvador. The administration was harsher in its criticisms of the Salvadoran government, citing failures in military discipline and in the criminal justice system. The United States was particularly critical of El Salvador's failure to bring to justice those responsible for political murders, particularly the murders of Americans. The administration concluded, nonetheless, that El Salvador was "making progress" in several areas and was meeting the standards of the certification process. Congressional critics said the administration was going to certify "regardless of the circumstances." Human rights groups continued to maintain that murder, abduction and torture for political reasons were "routine practice" by the Salvadoran security forces.

Reagan vetoed a bill in December 1983 that would have extended the requirement for the semiannual certifications, but the administration voluntarily submitted a report in January 1984. Congress continued, however, to attach to appropriations bills specific conditions the Salvadorans had to meet before aid could be released. For example, the fiscal 1984 omnibus continuing appropriations resolution contained a provision making 30 percent of the military aid in the bill conditional on progress in the trial of five former Salvadoran national guardsmen accused of murdering four U.S. churchwomen in December 1980. The repeated delays in that case had come to symbolize El Salvador's failure to protect human rights. (The national guardsmen were convicted on all counts on May 24, 1984.)

Duarte Election

The attitude in Congress toward aid for El Salvador changed dramatically after Duarte in May 1984 became El Salvador's first freely elected president. In an initial election in March, Duarte had won 44 percent of the vote to 30

Nicaragua in World Court

In its attempt to portray the United States as a violator of international law because of its support of military actions against Nicaragua, the ruling Sandinista government of Nicaragua filed a suit with the International Court of Justice, the World Court, at The Hague, Netherlands, on April 9, 1984.

The Sandinistas demanded a halt to all U.S. assistance to the anti-government rebels and compensation for the damage caused by the guerrillas.

Three days before Nicaragua filed its suit, the United States informed the U.N. secretary general that the United States would not accept the court's jurisdiction in any cases involving Central America. The State Department said the action was taken to prevent Nicaragua from using the court for propaganda purposes. But the court said the agreement signed by the United States in 1946 accepting the court's compulsory jurisdiction required six months' notice if the United States wanted to terminate the agreement.

The World Court was established by the United Nations Charter after World War II, but its authority was recognized by only 45 of the more than 160 states that signed that charter.

In May the World Court issued an interim ruling that called on the United States to "cease and desist" in all military activity against Nicaragua. On Nov. 26, 1984, the court decided unanimously to accept Nicaragua's suit after rejecting, by a 15-1 vote, the U.S. argument that the court did not hold proper jurisdiction to try the case. The judgment opened the way for further hearings.

State Department officials said the United States had presented "compelling arguments why this is not the appropriate forum for resolving complex conflicts in Central America." The counsel for the Nicaraguan government said the United States would be regarded as an "international delinquent" if it refused to abide by the findings of the court.

It was not clear what position the United States would ultimately take.

percent for d'Aubuisson, forcing a runoff election May 6. Duarte won the runoff with 53.6 percent of the vote. D'Aubuisson charged the United States with rigging the election in Duarte's favor. (The White House denied taking sides in the election. However, the CIA later admitted supplying aid to Duarte, but not to his opponent. The CIA supposedly gave more than $360,000 to Duarte's party and more than $100,000 to the conservative National Conciliation Party, which also opposed d'Aubuisson.)

After his election Duarte visited Washington twice, on May 22 and July 23. In his meetings with congressional

leaders, Duarte made substantial progress in winning support for his country.

Urging approval of $61.75 million in military aid pending in an "urgent" supplemental appropriations bill, Duarte said he believed "the people in the United States understand the dream that the people of my country have for democracy, justice and liberty."

Although Duarte won grudging respect from opponents of administration policy, he left many Democrats still skeptical that he could wrest control of the country from the long-dominant military. Duarte promised to create a commission under his personal control to investigate killings attributed to the death squads, including the 1980 assassination of San Salvador Archbishop Oscar Romero.

Duarte said he wanted to negotiate with the leftist guerrillas, but he vowed not to accept "any position in which the solution is through arms, through killing people. I will not negotiate with rifles over the table."

Social and economic problems were the root causes of El Salvador's civil war, Duarte said. "We have to solve the problem by solving the causes and not by attacking only the symptoms. Guerrillas are symptoms, not causes."

Duarte opened peace talks with rebel commanders in mid-October 1984, which led to the guerrillas agreeing to take part in a joint commission to hold further talks. Another meeting was held in early December.

Although the fighting continued, by the end of 1984 there was optimism in both El Salvador and the United States that peace could be achieved.

The encouraging political events in El Salvador in 1984 pretty much brought to a close congressional disputes with the president over aid. After having approved $64.8 million for fiscal 1984, congressional Democrats resisted requests by Reagan for additional military assistance in fiscal 1984. But following the presidential elections and Duarte's visits to Washington, Congress approved another $61.75 million in June and $70 million in August, for a fiscal 1984 total of $196.55 million. This was more than twice the previous year's level. Of the $132.5 million in military aid the president requested in February 1984 for fiscal 1985, Congress pared only slightly more than $4 million.

Through 1984 Reagan had asked Congress for $412 million in military aid for El Salvador and Congress approved $310 million. The president used another $85 million on his own authority, without asking congressional approval. (El Salvador aid, chart, p. 186)

Kissinger Commission

In July 1983 President Reagan established a 12-member National Bipartisan Commission on Central America, headed by former Secretary of State Kissinger. Reagan predicted the commission would "lay the foundation for a long-term unified national approach to the freedom and independence of the countries of Central America."

After five months of closed hearings, meetings and travels to the region, the commission issued its report on Jan. 11, 1984. The report generally endorsed the thrust of Reagan's policies. It said there was a "crisis" in Central America that was "real and acute" and the United States must "act to meet it, and act boldly."

The commission's mandate was to report to the president on "the elements of a long-term United States policy that will best respond to the challenges of social, economic and democratic development in the region, and to internal and external threats to its security and stability." Reagan also asked the commission to give advice "on means of building a national consensus on a comprehensive United States policy for the region."

The commission proposed an $8.8 billion program of economic aid to Central America over fiscal 1984-89, and it said the United States should act to resist the expansion of Soviet and Cuban influence. Without giving a specific dollar figure, the commission endorsed a "substantial" increase in military aid for El Salvador and backed indirectly Reagan's program of covert aid to the contras in Nicaragua. It also called on Reagan and Central American leaders to meet to decide on a plan for long-range economic development in the region.

A majority of the commission members agreed that military assistance to El Salvador should be conditioned on progress toward democracy, establishment of rules of law and an end to death squads. The conditions should be "seriously enforced," the commission said. However, Kissinger, joined by two other members, cautioned against cutting off military aid to El Salvador. The "conditionality" clause, they said, should not lead to a "Marxist-Leninist victory . . . damaging vital American interests and risking a larger war."

The commission did not recommend using U.S. military forces to fight in Central America. But it did say the United States should consider force against the Nicaraguan government as a "last resort" if it refused to agree to stop supporting guerrilla movements in other countries.

The commission also proposed the creation of a new agency — a Central American Development Organization (CADO) — to be run by representatives of Latin American countries. One-fourth of all U.S. development aid for the region would go through CADO. (The Justice Department later said that giving a foreign-dominated board control over expenditures of U.S. tax dollars would be unconstitutional.)

In testimony before congressional committees, Kissinger said the Central American countries needed the aid to improve their economies as well as their security. Withholding economic aid until the wars in the region stopped, he said, "gives a veto to the most intransigent elements" in Central America. Efforts to improve living conditions and achieve peace had to proceed simultaneously, he said.

Reagan's Aid Proposals

In February 1984 President Reagan unveiled the details of an aid package that reflected the Kissinger commission recommendations.

Reagan requested money for four of the five countries in Central America, excluding only Nicaragua. A State Department official said Nicaragua was "potentially eligible" for U.S. assistance, but he did not spell out what kind of aid or the conditions under which it might be granted. The administration said it would try to ensure that Nicaragua would not get direct benefits from some regional efforts, such as loans to bolster the Central America Common Market, a free trade zone of which Nicaragua was a member.

Although the legislative package called for a six-year program of economic, development and related aid totaling $8.8 billion, Reagan asked for specific amounts for only two years, fiscal 1984 and 1985. For 1984 he requested $400 million in supplemental economic and development aid,

which would have nearly doubled, to $830.1 million, the amount of aid Congress had already approved for the region. For 1985 Reagan requested $1.1 billion in direct aid as well as $600 million in loan guarantees.

For fiscal years 1986-89, Reagan proposed $1.2 billion in each year for economic and development aid and $40 million in each year in housing loan guarantees. Reagan also requested $200 million in fiscal 1984 for U.S. export guarantees.

Of the $2.1 billion budgeted for fiscal 1984-85, $931 million was earmarked for the Economic Support Fund (ESF), the main program used by the United States to shore up the economies of friendly countries.

On the military aid side, Reagan requested an additional $259 million for fiscal 1984 and $256 million for 1985. The bulk of each year's amount was to go to El Salvador.

The Central American aid package also included the Kissinger commission recommendation for a Central American Development Organization, but in an altered form. The proposed legislation set out "a series of principles to guide the negotiations" among the United States and other countries that would lead to the creation of CADO. CADO would not have direct control over any U.S. aid, but could make general recommendations on aid programs in the region and veto up to 25 percent of the economic aid allocated by the United States for any country in the region.

The request for authorizations beyond fiscal 1985 was one of the most controversial parts of the package since Congress traditionally authorized foreign aid funds for only one or two years at a time; a longer-term authorization could undermine congressional control over the aid programs.

Congress' Response

By the end of 1984 Congress had provided about $1.1 billion for fiscal 1985 — plus $498 million in additional economic and military aid for fiscal 1984 — but it had rejected any funds for fiscal 1986-89. Other parts of the aid package that failed to secure congressional approval included authority for U.S. participation in a new multinational agency; a new $20 million program to improve the administration of justice in Central American countries; exemption of Central America from a 1974 law banning aid to foreign police forces; and a new program of scholarships to enable 10,000 Latin American students to attend U.S. colleges through 1989.

The 1984 legislation did not include authorizations and appropriations for a new "trade credit insurance" program to guarantee $300 million worth of loans made by the U.S. Export-Import Bank for high-risk exports of goods to Central America.

Although Congress rejected Reagan's request to resume military aid for Guatemala to permit that country to buy weapons from the United States, a related ban on aid to train Guatemalan military officers was lifted. Reagan had also requested $35 million for economic aid to Guatemala, but Congress cut that amount to $12.5 million.

Special Report: The Middle East

American prestige and power in the Middle East suffered a sharp decline in the early 1980s after major diplomatic and military efforts by the Reagan administration to bring peace to war-torn Lebanon ended in failure.

Almost from its first days in office, the Reagan administration was forced by events to focus on Lebanon, a country that had suffered nearly 10 years of civil war and occupation by Syrian and Israeli troops and the forces of the Palestine Liberation Organization (PLO). *(Background, Congress and the Nation Vol. V, p. 105)*

The administration initially undertook a mediating role among the rival religious factions in Lebanon to help bring stability to the Christian-led government, while it also tried to persuade the Syrians and Palestinians, and later the Israelis, to withdraw their forces from the country.

By 1983 that diplomatic role had been considerably altered by the stationing of 1,800 U.S. Marines in Lebanon. The Marines were increasingly drawn into the Lebanese civil war, coming under fire and shelling. Public pressure to withdraw the U.S. forces grew after 241 Americans were killed by a terrorist attack on Marine headquarters in Beirut. In February 1984 President Reagan announced that the Marines would be pulled out of Lebanon.

Other events also eroded U.S. influence and contributed to turmoil and violence in the region. Continued hostility toward Israel by the Arab states wiped out the optimism engendered by the 1979 peace treaty between Israel and Egypt. The 1981 assassination of Egyptian President Anwar Sadat removed from the scene America's most loyal and understanding ally in the Arab world. The fate of the Palestinians residing in Israeli-occupied territories remained a basic cause of instability in the region. The Iran-Iraq war that began in September 1980 escalated by 1984 to threaten shipping in the Persian Gulf, the key transportation link for much of Europe's and Japan's oil supplies.

Meanwhile, the political consensus at home on the policies the United States should pursue in the region disintegrated. As the administration moved from diplomacy and mediation to increased reliance on military solutions, through use of American troops and large arms sales to moderate Arab states, the administration and Congress clashed repeatedly. *(1981-84 legislative action, p. 129)*

Lebanon

The first major diplomatic effort by the Reagan administration in Lebanon took place soon after the administration took office. In April 1981 Syria moved Soviet-supplied surface-to-air missiles into Lebanon's Bekaa Valley after Israel shot down Syrian aircraft over Lebanon. At about the same time, Israel and the PLO stepped up their interminable border crossing raids and hit-and-run attacks against each other. President Reagan dispatched special envoy Philip C. Habib to intercede in the crisis, and Habib's efforts produced a general cease-fire in Lebanon on July 24, 1981.

Mounting Crisis

Habib was sent back to Lebanon in June 1982 after Israeli armed forces invaded Lebanon, over U.S. objections, with the stated purpose of creating a 25-mile-wide buffer zone in southern Lebanon free of Palestinian guerrillas. But the Israelis continued their advance until they reached the outskirts of Beirut and surrounded thousands of PLO guerrillas in West Beirut. Habib negotiated an agreement for the evacuation of the PLO forces that was monitored by a multinational peacekeeping force of American, French and Italian troops.

The Marines left Lebanon Sept. 10 after the PLO eviction was completed. But only weeks later Lebanon's president-elect, Bashir Gemayel, was assassinated and, in apparent retaliation, hundreds of Palestinian civilians in two refugee camps near Beirut were massacred. Reagan sent a contingent of about 1,200 Marines back into Lebanon Sept. 29, again as part of a multinational peacekeeping force.

The president's action drew fire from members of Congress who thought Reagan was evading the requirements of the War Powers Resolution (PL 93-148) by refusing to seek congressional approval for the deployment of the troops in Lebanon. The War Powers Resolution proscribed the use of U.S. forces in hostile situations for more than 90 days without congressional authorization.

Behind the debate over the War Powers Resolution appeared to be concern that the United States was jeopardizing its position as a mediator by intervening militarily to prop up the existing Lebanese government. That concern grew when the U.S. Embassy in Beirut on April 18, 1983, became the target of a terrorist attack that gutted the embassy and killed 63 persons, including 17 Americans.

By autumn the Marine contingent had grown to 1,800, and two Marines had been killed by artillery fire from Druse Moslem forces fighting the U.S.-backed Christian government. In the wake of that incident pressure quickly mounted in Congress to force the president to invoke the War Powers Resolution.

Dispute Over War Powers

Reagan Aug. 30, 1983, formally notified Congress that two Marines had been killed and 14 others wounded in Beirut on Aug. 29. But in his letter Reagan refused to cite the section of the 1973 War Powers Resolution that would have enabled Congress to force a withdrawal. Reagan said the U.S. forces were "essential to the objective of helping to restore the territorial integrity, sovereignty and political independence of Lebanon." It was not possible to predict how long the Marines would have to stay in Lebanon, he said.

On Sept. 1 the Pentagon announced that about 2,000 Marines were being sent to join a U.S. naval task force stationed in the eastern Mediterranean off the Lebanese coast. That move was widely seen as a warning that the United States would retaliate for further attacks on the Marines. On Sept. 5 two Marines were killed by rocket fire, and on Sept. 8 a U.S. warship fired for the first time on Moslem artillery positions believed responsible for attacking the Marines.

With a confrontation on the issue clearly building, the administration and key congressional leaders began negotiating to head off a constitutional clash between the executive and legislative branches. Congressional leaders of both parties insisted the president acknowledge the right of Congress to share in setting the terms of the Marine deployment. House Democrats, led by Speaker Thomas P. O'Neill Jr., D-Mass., and Foreign Affairs Committee Chairman Clement J. Zablocki, D-Wis., proposed that Congress pass a joint resolution invoking the War Powers Resolution but authorizing Reagan to keep the Marines in Lebanon for at least another 18 months. The president resisted this approach, but Senate Democrats forced his hand by introducing a resolution that simply would have triggered the War Powers act, giving Congress legal control over how long the Marines stayed.

A compromise was reached that required Reagan to sign a joint resolution invoking the War Powers Resolution and imposing an 18-month limit on the Marine deployment. In turn, the president declared in writing that he did not recognize the constitutionality of the War Powers Resolution and that he retained his constitutional authority as commander in chief to deploy U.S. forces.

Both sides said the value of the compromise was its avoidance of a confrontation over whether Congress had the power to force the president to withdraw U.S. troops from hostilities overseas.

The joint resolution was approved by Congress Sept. 29 and signed (PL 98-119) by Reagan Oct. 12, 1983.

Withdrawal of Marines

Events in Lebanon quickly shattered the importance of the compromise on the War Powers act. On Oct. 23 a terrorist truck bombing at the Marine headquarters killed 241 Americans. About the same time a car laden with explosives rammed into a Beirut building occupied by French members of the peacekeeping unit, killing 58 French soldiers.

The deaths of the Marines appeared to erase what support had existed for a long-term commitment of U.S. troops in Lebanon. Those who publicly continued to support the Marines' deployment said they did so only because to withdraw them after the bombing would be to encourage the terrorists who had conceived the act.

Among those who said the United States had to hold its ground was the man perhaps most responsible for enactment of the compromise — Speaker O'Neill. On Oct. 25 he said withdrawing the Marines "would say to the fanatics and terrorists of the world that they have achieved what they set out to do."

A previously unknown group calling itself the Islamic Revolutionary Movement claimed responsibility for the Marine barracks attack. But the president saw it as an extension of the East-West conflict, blaming Russia for assisting and encouraging violence and providing direct support "through a network of surrogates and terrorists."

The president laid much of the responsibility for Lebanon's troubles on Soviet-backed Syria, which he said had reneged on promises to withdraw its troops from Lebanon. Reagan said Syria had "become a home for 7,000 Soviet advisers and technicians who man a massive amount of Soviet weaponry, including SS-21 ground-to-ground missiles capable of reaching vital areas of Israel." Reagan suggested that U.S. abandonment of Lebanon might lead to a Middle East "incorporated into the Soviet bloc."

Some members of Congress argued that the president appeared to be shifting his reasons for U.S. involvement in Lebanon. Sen. Patrick J. Leahy, D-Vt., said the U.S. role originally "was a peacekeeping mission" but, as explained by Reagan, had become an effort "to stop the spread of communism."

Questions also were raised about the adequacy of security, with members skeptical of administration claims that everything possible had been done to protect Americans in Lebanon. The administration position was undercut by the findings of a blue-ribbon Pentagon panel. In its December 1983 report, the panel concluded that the Marines could not perform their avowed role of neutral peacekeepers, partly because warring Lebanese factions no longer saw the Marines as "even-handed and neutral" because of the gradual involvement of U.S. military units in direct combat assistance of the Lebanese armed forces controlled by President Amin Gemayel, a Maronite Christian, who had succeeded his slain brother. The government's military force was seen by rival religious factions as an arm of the right-wing Maronite Christian "Phalange" faction in the struggle for power, the commission said.

The panel called for "a re-examination of alternative means of achieving U.S. objectives ... [including] a more vigorous and demanding approach to pursuing diplomatic alternatives."

By year's end, after other American servicemen had been killed in the first direct military clash between U.S. and Syrian forces in Lebanon, Congress was rapidly backing away from its September agreement to keep the Marines in Lebanon through mid-1985.

Reagan, however, said in his January 1984 State of the Union address that the September resolution was "serving the cause of peace." The president maintained there was still hope "for a free, independent and sovereign Lebanon. We must have courage to give peace a chance."

House Democrats reached general agreement Feb. 1, 1984, on a non-binding resolution calling on Reagan to order the "prompt and orderly withdrawal" of the Marines, a move Senate Democrats endorsed the next day. The president continued to argue that if the United States were to "get out," it would mean the end of Lebanon.

But on Feb. 7 Reagan announced that some 1,600 Marines would be moved in stages to ships offshore. In a March 30 letter to Congress, the president said he was

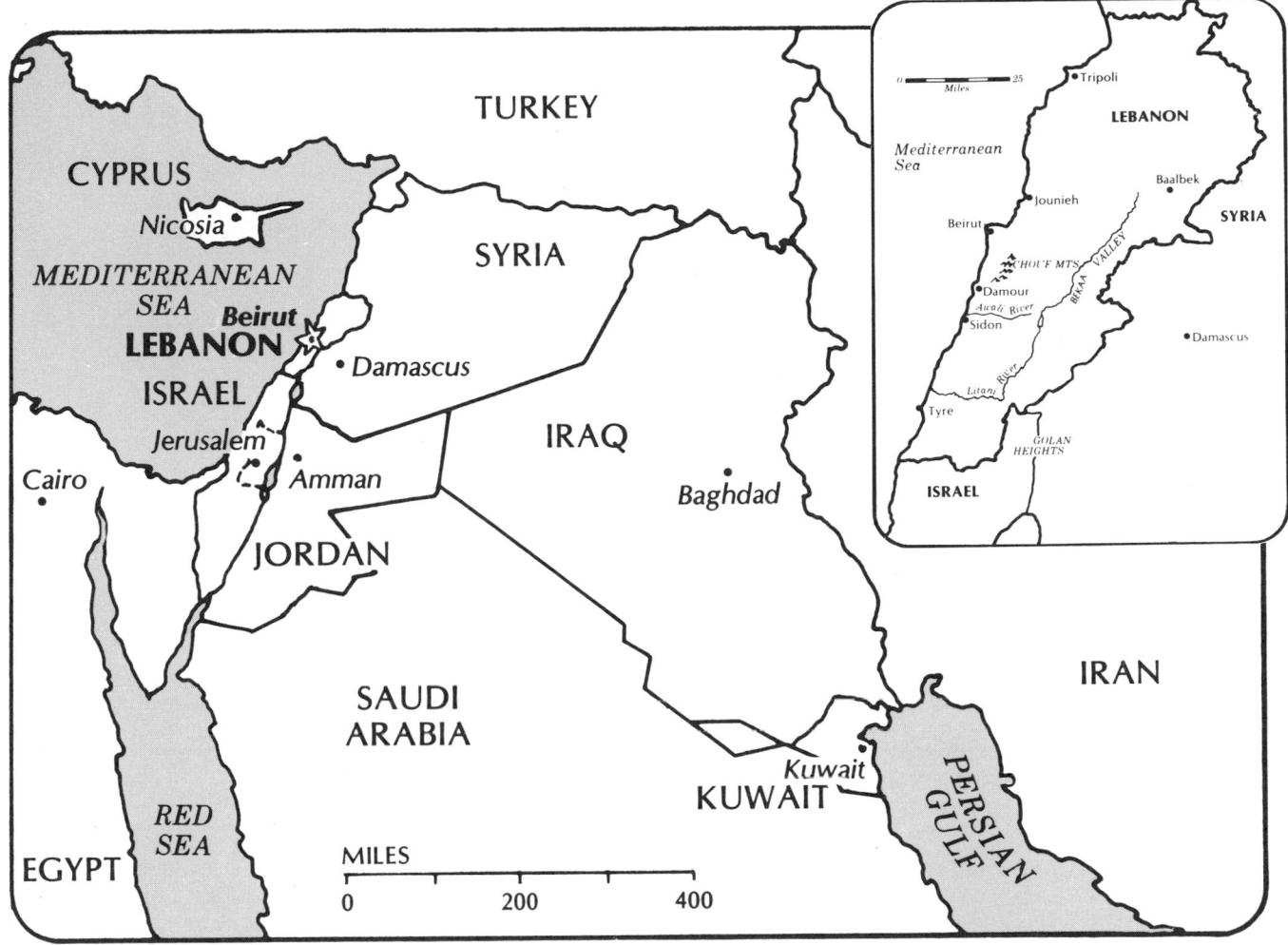

ending all U.S. participation in the peacekeeping force in Lebanon.

With the departure of the Marines and the near-collapse of the Gemayel government, Syria emerged once again as the dominant force in Lebanon. In return for its assistance in negotiating a new coalition government in Lebanon, Syria pressured Gemayel into scrapping a U.S.-mediated agreement on troop withdrawal that he had signed with Israel in May 1983. A side letter to the agreement had stipulated that Israeli forces were not required to withdraw from Lebanon until Syrian forces had left.

Israel

The euphoria and optimism resulting from President Carter's successful negotiation of the Camp David peace accords between Egypt and Israel died in the early days of the Reagan administration.

The administration was accused by its critics of failing to push Egypt and Israel to make progress on Palestinian autonomy provided under the peace treaty. Relations between the United States and Israel became strained when the Israelis objected to proposed U.S. weapons sales to Saudi Arabia and when the Reagan administration became alarmed by various Israeli military moves against Iraq, Syria and the PLO.

The first sign of trouble between the United States and Israel came in February 1981 when the White House announced that it would sell five AWACS radar planes to Saudi Arabia. Israel strongly opposed the plan and lobbied members of Congress to veto it, but Reagan persuaded Congress to approve the sale.

The AWACS dispute was only the beginning. On June 7, 1981, Israel bombed a nuclear reactor being built in Iraq, using U.S.-supplied F-16 jet fighters. The Iraq raid was defended by Israel Prime Minister Menachem Begin as "an act of supreme legitimate self-defense."

Reagan responded to the attack by delaying delivery of four more F-16s already bought by Israel. On July 17 an Israeli raid on PLO headquarters in Beirut killed more than 200 civilians. The Beirut raid occurred on the very day the State Department had been prepared to release the F-16s that were being withheld. Instead, on July 20, Reagan extended the suspension of F-16 deliveries to six additional planes. Reagan lifted the suspension Aug. 17 and the planes were later delivered.

After the AWACS issue was resolved, the administration sought Israeli agreement to a plan for "strategic cooperation" to include special arrangements with Israel regarding the use of U.S. military aid. That agreement was threatened in December 1981, however, when Begin surprised the United States by getting the Israeli parliament, the Knesset, to vote to extend Israeli law to the Golan

193

Economic and Military Assistance to Israel

Following are State Department figures on U.S. economic and military aid to Israel. Military aid is under the Foreign Military Sales program; economic aid is under the Economic Support Fund.

(Fiscal years, in millions of dollars)

	1978	1979	1980	1981	1982	1983	1984	1985
MILITARY								
Aid	$1,000	$4,000[2]	$1,000	$1,400	$1,400	$1,700	$1,700	$1,400
% Forgiven loans[1]	50	33	50	36	39	44	50	100
ECONOMIC								
Aid	$792	$790	$786	$764	$806	$785	$910	$1,200
% Grants	66	66	100	100	100	100	100	100

[1] Until fiscal 1985, all of Israel's annual military aid was provided as a loan, but a specified portion did not have to be repaid, and thus was considered a "forgiven" loan.

[2] For fiscal 1979, in conjunction with the Israeli-Egyptian peace treaty, the United States provided Israel $3 billion in special military aid ($2.2 billion in regular loans and $800 million in forgiven loans), in addition to the then-normal $1 billion annual military aid (equally divided between regular loans and forgiven loans).

Heights, strategic territory captured from Syria in the 1967 Arab-Israeli war.

Friction between the United States and Israel intensified when Israel invaded Lebanon in 1982. Israel argued that it had to protect its northern border from hostile attack and would withdraw its forces only if Syria pulled out its troops at the same time. However, Israel began withdrawing from Lebanon early in 1985.

U.S. Policy Shift

When George P. Shultz replaced Alexander M. Haig Jr. as secretary of state in June 1982, he shifted the focus of U.S. policy in the Middle East away from the East-West conflict and toward resolution of the Arab-Israeli dispute. Shultz was widely credited with being the principal architect of Reagan's Sept. 1, 1982, Middle East policy initiative that reaffirmed U.S. support for Israel but called for Palestinian self-government on the West Bank of the Jordan River "in association with" Jordan. Reagan demanded that Israel halt further construction of Jewish settlements on the West Bank and proposed an association between Palestinians and Jordan to govern the West Bank. But he also called for further negotiations to determine the final legal status of the West Bank and of Jerusalem. *(Reagan plan, box, p. 195)*

Begin rejected the plan immediately; Israel opposed any participation by PLO members.

The Reagan administration in 1982 actively opposed a move in Congress to increase aid to Israel beyond the president's request, which was another source of irritation between the two countries. Administration officials wrote letters to Congress complaining that an aid increase would upset other countries in the Middle East (especially Egypt and Jordan) and would be seen as a reward to Israel for politics the United States had opposed. Israeli officials bitterly complained about the administration's opposition to increased aid, calling it "an unfriendly act" that endangered the peace process.

Congress eventually compromised on the issue, giving Israel an increase in military aid that was substantial but fell far short of what Israel had sought.

Although the bitterness that developed between the United States and Israel quickly evaporated after Begin resigned in September 1983, renewed cooperation between the two countries was limited by political turmoil in Israel itself. Begin was succeeded by his foreign minister, Yitzhak Shamir, but elections in 1984 gave a narrow edge to the opposition Labor Party under Shimon Peres. A coalition government resulted, with Peres as prime minister and Shamir as deputy prime minister; they were to switch positions in two years.

Peres made his first trip to Washington in October 1984, seeking a huge increase in U.S. aid: an additional $800 million for fiscal 1985, on top of $2.6 billion already allocated, plus $4.05 billion for fiscal 1986. The requests were geared at stabilizing Israel's economy and maintaining its military preparedness. The country was facing the most serious economic crisis in its 36-year history, with inflation approaching 500 percent and the heaviest foreign debt on a per capita basis in the world.

The Reagan administration said any increases in economic aid would be delayed "pending the adoption of an effective Israeli economic stabilization program."

U.S. Aid to Israel

United States aid to Israel accounted for 12 percent of the Israeli government budget; in the 1980s the United States was subsidizing one-fourth to one-third of Israel's defense spending.

As a Jewish state in the midst of hostile Arab neighbors, Israel had had to devote a disproportionate share of its resources to defense — up to a third of the government budget. Israel maintained one of the world's most sophisticated defense establishments at an annual cost of about $5.5 billion. From 1973 to 1985 the United States had provided $18.5 billion to Israel for defense spending. Israel's $4.05 billion request for fiscal 1986 amounted to about a quarter of all American foreign aid.

The 1973 Arab-Israeli conflict cost Israel some $12 billion and stunted economic growth. The United States poured military aid into Israel, but half of it was in loans that in the 1980s cost Israel more than $1 billion a year to repay. Israel also claimed an $8 billion cost from its 1979 peace treaty with Egypt, and a heavy toll from the 1982 invasion, and subsequent occupation, of Lebanon.

Defense spending was a major cause of Israel's economic problems, but domestic policies contributed as well. The Begin government, which took office in 1977, implemented policies that spurred inflation and encouraged Israelis to make highly speculative investments and to import luxury consumer goods. Because of heavy government spending and foreign borrowing by citizens and government, Israel owed the rest of the world more than $23 billion. A third of that debt was owed to the United States on loans for weapons purchases since the 1973 war.

For fiscal years 1981, 1982 and 1983, Reagan had asked that Israel's economic aid be divided into one-third loan and two-thirds grant. Each year Congress approved a full grant. Congress also voted major boosts in economic aid for fiscal years 1984 and 1985. For 1984, Reagan requested $785 million for Israel and Congress approved $910 million. For 1985, Reagan requested $850 million and Congress approved $1.2 billion. *(Box, p. 194)*

In one of its most far-reaching steps on foreign aid, Congress in 1984 approved a statement that Israel should receive at least as much economic aid each year as Israel had to pay to the United States on past loans. That provision was one reason Congress boosted Israel's aid to $1.2 billion in fiscal 1985, during which Israel had to pay the United States about $1.1 billion on past debts.

Egypt

The hopes for peace in the Middle East engendered by the 1979 Egyptian-Israeli peace treaty had already begun to evaporate when Egyptian President Anwar Sadat was gunned down by extremists on Oct. 6, 1981. Although Sadat's successor, Hosni Mubarak, pledged to adhere to the 1979 pact and continue Sadat's foreign policy, Egypt's relations with Israel cooled. Egypt recalled its ambassador to Israel in September 1982, following the massacre of civilians at two Palestinian refugee camps in Israeli-held territory in Lebanon. By 1984 Egypt actively was seeking accommodation with its former Arab allies and playing down its relations with Israel.

As the only Arab nation officially at peace with Israel, Egypt received the second-largest amount of U.S. aid — $2 billion in economic and military support — and expected proportionate increases to keep pace with Israel.

Reagan Mideast Peace Plan

In 1982 President Reagan attempted to revitalize the Arab-Israeli peace process that began at Camp David in 1978.

However, Reagan's Middle East peace initiative, launched in a televised speech Sept. 1, made little headway. The plan departed only slightly from various other statements of U.S. views on Palestinian autonomy and related issues, but it was significant for staking out U.S. views firmly and putting forth concrete proposals.

Reagan said the United States would support self-government for Palestinians on the West Bank of the Jordan River and in the Gaza Strip in association with Jordan but not in an independent state nor under Israeli sovereignty.

He also called upon Israel to "freeze" further Jewish settlement in the West Bank and Gaza, which Israel had held since the 1967 Arab-Israeli war, as a prelude to resuming negotiations under the 1978 Camp David accords.

The president pledged U.S. fealty to the Camp David plan for an interim agreement to provide self-government for the Palestinians in the West Bank and Gaza for five years while the ultimate status of the territories was negotiated by Israel, Egypt, the United States and Jordan.

"The final status of these lands must, of course, be reached through the give and take of negotiations," Reagan said. "But it is the firm view of the United States that self-government by the Palestinians of the West Bank and Gaza in association with Jordan offers the best chance for a durable, just and lasting peace."

Reagan said the U.S. position was based on the principle "that the Arab-Israeli conflict should be resolved through negotiations involving an exchange of territory for peace" as set out in United Nations Security Council Resolution 242 of 1967. He said the resolution's call for Israel to withdraw from "territories occupied in the recent conflict" clearly applied to the West Bank and Gaza.

The president took pains to reaffirm the U.S. commitment to Israel, and he urged that Israel's enemies recognize Israel's right to exist.

"Finally," Reagan said, "we remain convinced that Jerusalem must remain undivided, but its final status should be decided through negotiations."

Israel promptly repudiated the Reagan plan. Jordan's King Hussein initially gave cautious support to the plan and opened talks with Yasir Arafat, chairman of the Palestine Liberation Organization (PLO). But Hussein failed to secure permission from the PLO to negotiate on behalf of West Bank Palestinians, and by April 1983 he had backed away from any further involvement.

But its lack of progress toward normalization of relations with Israel drew increasing criticism from members of Congress. Lawmakers in 1984 implicitly rebuked Egypt by attaching to fiscal 1985 foreign aid legislation a statement that U.S. aid was based "in great measure upon the continued participation of Egypt" in the 1979 peace treaty.

Saudi Arabia, Jordan

One of the major foreign policy goals of the Reagan administration in the Middle East was to bolster moderate Arab governments to block Soviet advances in the region. Key to that strategy were arms sales to Saudi Arabia and Jordan.

Saudi Arabia

From 1974 to mid-1981 Saudi Arabia contracted to buy $32.1 billion worth of weapons and services from the United States. Of that amount, $8.6 billion was for weapons, ammunition, spare parts and equipment; the remaining $23.5 billion was for services, such as design and construction supervision of several new air, naval and army bases.

The United States first provided Saudi Arabia with AWACS in April 1979, when President Carter sent two of the planes to Saudi Arabia during a border war between North and South Yemen. In October 1980, following the outbreak of war between Iran and Iraq, Carter sent four AWACS planes to Saudi Arabia, their mission to detect threats to the Saudi oil fields. Manned by American crews, those planes remained in Saudi Arabia through the rest of 1980 and all of 1981.

In 1981 a Reagan proposal to send five AWACS to Saudi Arabia drew heavy opposition in Congress, but the president narrowly won on the issue when the Senate, in a dramatic **48-52 key vote (R 12-41; D 36-11)** Oct. 28, rejected a resolution to disapprove the sale of the planes. The White House relentlessly portrayed the question as a matter of presidential power and prestige, arguing that Reagan would lose his credibility in Saudi Arabia and other foreign lands if Congress blocked the sale. *(1981 key votes, p. 879; details of action, p. 129)*

Further arms sales proposals ran into stronger resistance from Congress in 1984.

Reagan had proposed in early 1984 to sell Saudi Arabia 1,200 Stinger missiles and 400 launchers to reinforce Saudi air defenses against threats from Iran and other radical Arab states.

After the Iran-Iraq war threatened Persian Gulf shipping in May, President Reagan used emergency authority to send 400 of the anti-aircraft missiles to Saudi Arabia. By invoking emergency powers, Reagan avoided a 30- to 50-day review by Congress of the sale.

The portable missiles and 200 launchers for them, plus training and support equipment, were to cost the Saudis a total of $40 million. Saudi Arabia became the first country outside the North Atlantic Treaty Organization or Japan to get Stingers.

Reagan on May 30 sent Congress a formal notification of the sale along with a justification for using his emergency powers, while administration officials sought to reassure Congress that safeguards would prevent terrorists from getting the missiles.

Jordan

The administration also sought improved ties with Jordan as a counterweight to other, more radical, Arab states and as a means of advancing President Reagan's September 1982 Middle East peace initiative. The peace plan had called on Israel to give up control of the West Bank of the Jordan River to an "association" of Jordan and the Palestinians who lived there.

Reagan offered Jordan's King Hussein financial aid and military equipment and training for a Jordanian rapid deployment force that could respond to military crises in the region.

In 1983 Congress rejected the idea of arming and supporting two brigades of the Jordanian army as a rapid deployment strike force in the Middle East. Congressional opposition also prevented the administration from even proposing to sell Jordan advanced fighter planes and anti-aircraft systems.

The strike force plan called for U.S. training of Jordanian units in rapid-reaction tactics, such as responding to a military threat to oil facilities in the Persian Gulf. The units were to be equipped with C-130 transport planes, anti-aircraft and anti-tank missiles, tanks, communications equipment and other supplies.

Reagan submitted the plan to Congress in secret. Administration officials asked Congress not to reveal the proposal, saying that King Hussein feared that publicity would undermine his standing in the Arab world.

With few members knowing about it, Congress secretly authorized $220 million for the plan when it cleared the fiscal 1984 defense authorization bill Sept. 15.

But in mid-October press reports about the plan (originating in Israel) created an uproar in Congress, leading the two Appropriations committees to reject funds for the plan.

The administration then renamed its proposal the Joint Logistics Planning Program and to dilute opposition dropped a plan to give Jordan 58 Stingers. In May 1984, however, the administration withdrew the request for funding for the plan.

Part of the difficulty in persuading Congress to approve weapons sales and provide military aid to Jordan had to do with King Hussein and his position toward Israel and the peace process in the Middle East. Some members thought Jordan should not receive advanced U.S. weapons and military aid until it recognized Israel and agreed to negotiate directly with Israel under the terms of United Nations Security Council resolutions on the Middle East and the 1978 Camp David accords. Hussein angered many members in April 1983 when he abandoned his six-month-long effort to secure the consent of other Arab nations and the PLO to his entry into Middle East peace talks. Members complained that Hussein had given the PLO a veto over his participation in peace talks.

In late February 1984 President Reagan proposed selling 1,613 Stinger missiles and 315 launchers to Jordan, at a cost of $133 million. Only a few weeks later, however, the president withdrew the proposal when faced with overwhelming opposition in Congress, caused partly by anti-U.S. statements by Hussein. In an interview published March 15 in *The New York Times*, Hussein said the United States could no longer serve as a mediator between Israel and Arab neighbors. "You obviously have made your choice, and your choice is Israel," Hussein said. "Therefore, there is no hope of achieving anything."

In subsequent interviews with U.S. television networks, Hussein repeatedly attacked the United States as a major stumbling block to peace in the Middle East.

Persian Gulf

U.S. concern about the security of Persian Gulf oil supplies developed after the 1979 revolution in Iran that replaced America's ally, Shah Mohammed Reza Pahlavi, with an anti-American Islamic revolutionary regime.

Although America got less than 5 percent of its total oil from the region, other countries such as Japan, France, Great Britain and West Germany were much more dependent on gulf oil supplies. About 20 percent of the noncommunist world's oil was shipped through the gulf.

One of the first Reagan initiatives involved an $8.5 billion arms sale for Saudi Arabia, which the president defended on the grounds that the Saudis and OPEC (Organization of Petroleum Exporting Countries) were providing the bulk of energy in the Western world.

Safeguarding shipping in the gulf became a major issue in 1984 when Iran and Iraq expanded their four-year-old war into attacks on the shipping of other nations, including Saudi Arabia. President Reagan repeatedly said the United States would take the necessary steps to ensure that the gulf remained open to shipping, but he also denied that the United States was planning to take unilateral military action.

Reagan sent a letter to the Saudis in May 1984, reportedly offering direct U.S. military action if it was needed and requested. One source said the letter noted that the United States could land a squadron of F-15 jets on Saudi territory within 48 hours of getting a request for aid. While administration officials did not state publicly who they expected to attack Saudi facilities, they made it clear that Iran posed the major threat.

On June 5 Saudi Arabia for the first time used U.S.-supplied weapons to successfully defend its air space against Iranian attack. The action prompted warnings from some members of Congress, who cautioned against direct U.S. involvement in the gulf conflict. "Do we really want to get into a full-scale war with Iran?" asked Sen. Alfonse M. D'Amato, R-N.Y.

4

Defense Policy

Introduction   *201*
1981 Chronology   *205*
1982 Chronology   *217*
1983 Chronology   *225*
1984 Chronology   *234*
Arms Control   *249*

Defense Policy

National security policy was a bone of incessant contention between Congress and the White House during Ronald Reagan's first presidential term.

Even if the Reagan team had been just another Republican administration, along the lines of Gerald R. Ford's, there would have been major battles with the Democratic-controlled House.

In a climate of rising public skepticism of the Pentagon, Democrats who cut their political teeth on opposition to the Vietnam War were gaining greater influence in the party's congressional caucuses. The process had been accelerated by mid-1970s procedural reforms that reined in senior members more inclined to view national security issues as a presidential preserve.

Those post-Vietnam Democrats would have challenged any imaginable GOP administration on grounds that it overemphasized force as an instrument of international policy and allocated too large a share of the national effort to military preparedness at the cost of domestic programs.

But the Reagan team tried to go beyond the old Republican line, thus raising the stakes and broadening the scope of its battles with the 97th and 98th Congresses over the defense budget and strategic arms policy. Even the GOP-controlled Senate became a battleground for the administration.

Break With the Past

Particularly at the outset, Reagan and Defense Secretary Caspar W. Weinberger described their budget requests as dramatic breaks from the past, ending a "decade of neglect" by Republican as well as Democratic administrations.

But in reality Reagan's defense budgets were not particularly radical, when viewed in isolation. They called for hefty increases over the budgets of Jimmy Carter, but the increases were at the margin — modernizing the existing force or slightly expanding it, rather than fundamentally changing the shape of the U.S. military or the strategy guiding its planning and deployment.

What put a special edge on the debate over defense budgets was the context of Reagan's sharp tax cuts and wholesale efforts to end or sharply curtail the federal role in wide areas of national life.

Viewed as a part of that process, Reagan's Pentagon budget was radical enough. Not only the president but also his congressional critics couched much of the debate over the budget — and over the national security portion of it — in philosophically sweeping terms.

But when it came to action Congress dealt with the defense budget the same way it usually handled spending issues: as a series of margins to be pared or added to; as so many differences to be split rather than as a set of fundamental ideological choices.

For three years in a row — beginning in 1982 — Congress trimmed Reagan's defense requests by more than $15 billion annually. Yet, each time, it was done by making relatively minor cuts in hundreds of programs. The only major weapons program Congress flatly refused to fund was a new type of lethal nerve gas weapon — so-called binary munitions — that evoked an extraordinary degree of congressional revulsion.

By contrast with its overall defense budget, the Republican administration's strategic arms policy clearly was divergent, at least in part. The segment of it that was conventional, in the first few years of Reagan's term, was the choice of weapons. Reagan's initial purchasing list for strategic weapons marked no basic departure from the plans of Ford and Carter before him.

Reagan's radical break came on the question of arms control strategy. He had campaigned for office on the claim that a decade of U.S.-Soviet arms control negotiations had coincided with a tilt in Moscow's favor of the balance of nuclear power. Well into 1982, he was adamant that the only arms control agreement worth having was one that would achieve significant reductions in both countries' nuclear arsenals — particularly in land-based ballistic missiles that make up the backbone of the Soviet nuclear force.

Since prospects for Soviet acceptance of such an agreement seemed nil, many observers suspected that Reagan's position was a charade — an excuse for supporting no feasible arms control agreement.

The administration's stance aroused strong and widespread public alarm, which liberal activists and congressional Democrats shaped into a political movement that

References

Discussion of defense policy for the years 1945-64 may be found in *Congress and the Nation Vol. I*, pp. 233-334; for the years 1965-68, *Congress and the Nation Vol. II*, pp. 825-890; for the years 1969-72, *Congress and the Nation Vol. III*, pp. 189-252; for the years 1973-76, *Congress and the Nation Vol. IV*, pp. 153-197; for the years 1977-80, *Congress and the Nation Vol. V*, pp. 125-176.

threatened several times in 1982-84 to repudiate Reagan's arms control approach.

So by the time Reagan faced former Vice President Walter F. Mondale in the 1984 election he was striking a very different tone on nuclear arms control than he had in 1981. While still demanding a deeper reduction than any arms control agreement had achieved in the 1970s, Reagan policy no longer talked in terms of seeking a radical change in the balance of nuclear power — not immediately.

Conservatives who hoped for a fundamental transformation of the U.S.-Soviet balance of power were unhappy with that shift. But they took heart from another facet of Reagan policy: the Strategic Defense Initiative (SDI) or "Star Wars" plan to develop an exotic, space-based defense against Soviet missiles.

In 1984, the first political test of the program, the SDI budget was cut by almost 25 percent — from $1.7 billion to $1.3 billion. But no deployment of such defenses would occur until the 1990s at the earliest, and it was too soon to tell whether Congress would challenge the underlying policy of SDI or would merely pick away at it as part of its overall budget-reduction effort.

How Much Is Enough?

Reagan's initial, long-term defense plan called for spending $1.46 trillion in fiscal 1982-86, an increase of nearly $200 billion over the budgets projected by Jimmy Carter in January 1981.

According to Reagan and Weinberger, this was a sharp break from the austerity imposed on the Pentagon throughout the 1970s in the wake of the Vietnam War. In fact, when allowance was made for the cost of inflation, the Defense Department's purchasing power declined in real terms each year from 1968 through 1975. But the trend had turned around at least four years before Reagan took office.

By the end of his first year as president, Carter was publicly committed to requesting annual "real" increases of 3 percent in the defense budget — though his requests for new budget authority repeatedly fell short of that. Late in 1979, under strong pressure from conservative Democrats threatening to oppose the SALT II nuclear arms treaty with Moscow, Carter agreed with evident reluctance to seek annual real defense increases of 5 percent.

When the Reagan team was preparing to take office late in 1980, conservative think tanks proposed several alternative national security programs, each calling for structural change in the U.S. defense establishment: hefty increases in the number of combat units and very rapid modernization of the entire U.S. arsenal.

But the incoming Reagan team did not adopt those proposals — evidently because of their projected cost. Reagan outlined instead a slower modernization — though one that would proceed more rapidly than Carter's plan — and expansion of U.S. forces on a selective basis. Only the Navy would be enlarged dramatically. Highlights of Reagan's program included:

● Across-the-board modernization of the nuclear arsenal, including production of a new land-based missile (MX), two new bombers (B-1 and the so-called "stealth" bomber) and a new missile-launching submarine (Trident). The only element that had not been in Carter's plan was the B-1, which Carter had argued would be rendered obsolete by the stealth plane after only a few years' service.

● Expansion to a "600-ship Navy," which — like production of the B-1 — had been a theme of Reagan's 1980 presidential campaign. In large part, this amounted to increasing the fleet of aircraft carriers from 12 to 15, equipping four mothballed battleships with modern cruise missiles and building enough additional escort ships to protect those large vessels.

● Across-the-board modernization of the Army, which had largely forgone the deployment of new equipment for 15 years: in the late 1960s because of the expense of fighting the Vietnam War, and in the early 1970s because of the low defense budgets that were a political result of controversy over the war.

● Enlargement of the fleet of ships and planes to ferry troops and equipment overseas. Carter had begun this in the wake of the radical takeover of the U.S. Embassy in Iran in November 1979. But Reagan planned a bigger buildup and — unlike Carter — proposed expanding the fleet of amphibious landing ships, designed to let the Marine Corps fight its way ashore against armed opponents.

● Rapid increases in stockpiles of spare parts and ammunition to improve the combat readiness of forces in the field, and to give them the resources to fight longer, once a war began.

Budget Minuets

By the end of his first year in office, Reagan's initial defense budget plan was under strong political pressure from both ends of the political spectrum.

Most liberals opposed in principle his emphasis on military power and his efforts to cut domestic programs. But as Reagan's first term wore on those ideological opponents of the administration found partial allies on the political right. Conservative critics of the Reagan spending plan saw defense cuts as a way to pare the projected $200 billion deficits. More important, many of the conservatives also believed it would be politically impossible to cut popular domestic programs unless reductions were distributed across the federal budget in what seemed to be an equitable way.

For four years, Reagan and his aides argued that defense should be treated differently from other federal programs because it was driven by the actions of hostile governments. But whatever that argument's philosophical merit, it was politically stillborn.

Reagan easily dominated congressional action on his budget through late summer of 1981, but from August of that year onward he encountered serious opposition. This resistance began to emerge as the prospect of a huge fiscal 1982 deficit compelled the administration to revise its March 1981 budget request. Reagan's budget chief David A. Stockman and other senior White House aides called for cuts of up to $30 billion in the defense request.

Reagan agreed to a cut only about half that size, and Congress ultimately made only minor reductions in his revised request. But the extensively publicized debate within the administration seemed to galvanize latent malcontents into vigorous Pentagon critics. By late 1982 a de facto compromise had emerged: Annual real increases of 5 percent seemed to be about the best Reagan could hope for from Capitol Hill.

But despite widespread belief that a "5 percent solution" had become the norm after Reagan's first year, it took a long time to get there during the rest of his first term. Each year from 1982 through 1984 the administration proposed a defense budget with a real growth rate

exceeding 10 percent and the Democratic House countered with a first concurrent resolution on the budget allowing real increases of 3 percent or less. Each time, the widely expected compromise — a 5 percent real growth rate — emerged after some political sparring, though in 1984 this did not come until September.

The administration's explanation for the prolonged posturing was that House Democrats would use the legislative process to whittle away at any defense figure agreed to by Reagan — whether it was his initial request or a budget agreement negotiated with Congress in May, regardless of how big or how little an increase the president sought. Administration allies cited as an example the 1983 battle when Congress approved a budget resolution allowing a real increase of 5 percent, but then trimmed appropriations to allow a real growth of only 3.7 percent.

But this view was challenged by some congressional defense specialists who supported the Reagan buildup. They repeatedly warned the administration that it was squandering political capital by its adamant insistence on budgets Congress clearly would not approve.

It was a common theme of many critics on both the right and the left that cuts in the Reagan budget ought to be concentrated in the weapons procurement account, which was growing more rapidly than other parts of the budget. Each year, as the Armed Services and Defense Appropriations panels worked out the details of bringing Pentagon budgets under the overall limit set by the congressional budget resolution, the proponderance of reductions were made in the weapons accounts.

But contrary to the critics' hopes, no major weapons programs actually were killed off. Instead, the cuts came in relatively modest slowdowns of hundreds of programs.

Rooting Out Waste

Beginning in 1982, highly publicized instances of evident waste in weapons program management fueled congressional unhappiness over defense spending. But the "horror stories" of $400 hammers and $7,000 wrenches also provided members with opportunities to take firm stands against waste without having to slog through the details of the Pentagon budget and without battling military officials over the technical merits of specific programs.

The result was a series of amendments to the defense funding bills in 1983-84 aimed at making the Pentagon a more careful customer in the military marketplace. Many of the reforms tried to force the Defense Department to rely more heavily on competitive bidding to select its contractors, in hopes of driving down weapons' price tags.

Increased competition was the goal of a series of changes enacted in 1984 in procedures for buying spare parts. Some of the most celebrated allegations of Pentagon mismanagement involved small parts — many of them commercially available for a few dollars or less — for which contractors had charged the Pentagon hundreds or thousands of dollars.

Other congressionally mandated reforms included:
- Appointment of senior military officers as "competition advocates" to require justification of any purchases that were not made on a competitive basis.
- Requirement that manufacturers warrant their products against material defects or performance shortfalls.
- Establishment of an independent office to test new weapons under combatlike conditions before they were approved for production.

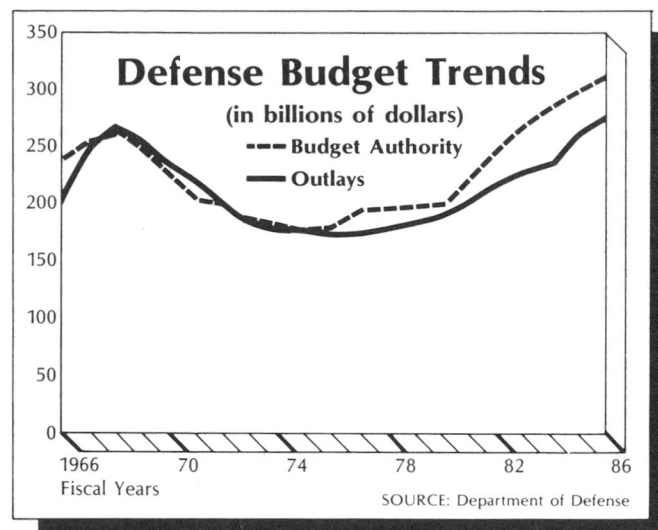

Defense Budget Trends
(in billions of dollars)
- - - Budget Authority
—— Outlays

1966   70   74   78   82   86
Fiscal Years

SOURCE: Department of Defense

Each of these reforms had encountered stiff opposition, which heightened suspicion that mismanagement was rife in the defense establishment.

Arms Control

Substantively, the administration and the most prominent advocates of orthodox arms control were at loggerheads over three issues at the start of Reagan's first term:

Arms Control Impact. Some administration officials and other conservatives viewed arms control negotiations with Moscow as intrinsically disadvantageous to the United States. According to this view, public hopes for an agreement translated into political pressure on a U.S. administration to make concessions to Moscow. No such countervailing domestic pressure was felt by the Soviet government, the conservatives complained.

By contrast, it had long been a fundamental premise of arms control advocates that the proliferation of increasingly powerful weapons fueled international tensions quite apart from any underlying political conflicts. According to this argument, the common U.S. and Soviet interest in controlling that buildup was more important than any other facet of the U.S.-Soviet relationship, and should be pursued under nearly any circumstances.

Land-Based Missiles. Reagan officials saw accurate, land-based ballistic missiles, which predominated in the Soviet nuclear arsenal, as far more potent than other nuclear arms — such as the missile-firing submarines and bombers in which the United States had invested more heavily.

For that reason, the administration regarded Moscow's virtual monopoly on large, accurate land-based missiles as intolerable: The Soviet missile force must be drastically reduced, if possible, or matched, if necessary, according to this view. By the same token, the only arms control agreements worth reaching were those that substantially reduced the Soviet land-based missile force.

Land-based missiles were much more accurate than existing submarine-launched missiles. And they could strike within minutes, in contrast to the hours it would take for manned bombers to reach their targets. In the jargon of nuclear strategists, they were "prompt hard-tar-

get killers" — able to threaten almost immediate destruction of heavily armored military targets, such as underground command posts and missile launchers. According to the administration argument, what mattered was not the likelihood that Moscow ever would attempt a first strike to disable the U.S. nuclear force, but the mere theoretical possibility that it could do so while facing no corresponding threat from the United States.

But the arms controllers saw Reagan's emphasis on land-based missiles as dangerous. Any alleged Soviet advantage in land-based missiles was illusory, they argued: Land-based missiles could not hit the missile-launching submarines that could retaliate for a Soviet first strike, so the existing nuclear balance was acceptable.

But the arms controllers also warned against a U.S. effort to match the Soviet land-based missile force: If each country's missiles were vulnerable to destruction by the other country's missiles, both forces might be placed on a hair trigger during international crises. According to this view, each government would be dangerously quick to decide that it had to "use them or lose them."

'Bargaining Chips.' Besides disagreeing over the merits of arms control in general and over the specific goals negotiations should pursue, the Reagan team and liberal arms control advocates also were at odds over negotiating tactics.

On a range of arms control issues, the administration position was that Moscow would surrender alleged advantages only if it faced the concrete prospect that, failing a negotiated agreement, a similar U.S. weapon would be deployed. This was a large part of Reagan's public rationale for:

● The MX missile, which the administration said was needed to give Moscow an incentive to sharply cut back its own arsenal of large, accurate, land-based missiles.

● The Pershing II missile, designed to reach Soviet targets from launchers in West Germany. This was to match the Soviet SS-20, a triple-warhead missile able to reach any target in Western Europe from Soviet sites.

● The anti-satellite (ASAT) guided missile, intended to respond to a much more cumbersome Soviet ASAT that had been tested (with middling results) since the late 1960s.

● Binary munitions, a new generation of artillery shells and aerial bombs to disperse lethal nerve gas. For years, the Pentagon had warned of Moscow's heavy investment in chemical weapons forces.

Viewed in isolation, Reagan's bargaining-chip rationale was not far different from that embraced by the Carter administration, which had cited similar arguments in favor of the MX, the Pershing II and ASAT.

Many liberal arms controllers had reluctantly tolerated Carter's position, partly on the grounds that developing new weapons might be an acceptable political price for achieving new arms control agreements, and partly in the belief that Carter would, in good faith, try to bargain the chips away.

But on Reagan's lips the bargaining-chip argument was a fraud, they insisted — one intended merely to rationalize the piling up of more weapons while arms negotiations stagnated because of the administration's far-reaching demands for Soviet concessions.

More fundamentally, the liberals simply did not buy the bargaining-chip logic. In their view, the arms buildups

of the 1970s were a history of bargaining chips that had become central features of the U.S. arsenal, never to be bargained away.

Pushing Reagan to the Middle

Arms control policy was put on the political front burner not by the substance of this debate but by the style in which the administration presented its case to the public. The stage was set by the generally confrontational tone toward Moscow, taken by Reagan and his aides from the start of the administration.

Against that background, several comments by the president and his aides about the possibility of "limited" nuclear war were widely interpreted as bespeaking an overly casual attitude toward the risk of nuclear conflict.

Reagan's ideological opponents channeled much of the resulting alarm into a campaign for a "freeze" on the testing, production and deployment of nuclear weapons. Insisting that he too was for arms control, only of a more comprehensive sort than had been achieved in the 1970s, Reagan had begun negotiations with Moscow on intermediate-range nuclear arms in November 1981 and on strategic arms in May 1982. But this won him only a temporary political respite on the issue.

By late summer of 1982, the administration had to use a tremendous amount of political capital to eke out a bare one-vote victory over the nuclear freeze campaign in the House of Representatives.

In November of that year, eight states endorsed freeze referendums. In December Congress blocked the initial request for production funds for the MX intercontinental missile, the first such defeat suffered by a president on a major nuclear arms vote.

As 1983 began Reagan clearly was on the political defensive on nuclear arms. For help in saving MX, he turned to the bipartisan national security establishment that his conservative backers had denounced for years on grounds of flaccidity in the face of Soviet challenges.

In January 1983 he appointed a blue-ribbon panel, heavy with veterans of the Nixon, Ford and Carter administrations, to recommend an approach to winning support for MX. The commission was chaired by retired Lt. Gen. Brent Scowcroft, who had been Gerald R. Ford's national security adviser.

The recommendations of the Scowcroft panel were embraced by a small group of influential defense specialists in Congress led by Sen. Sam Nunn, D-Ga., and Rep. Les Aspin, D-Wis. Through 1983-84, these two led a group of self-styled congressional moderates who bargained with Reagan over MX and the future of the administration's arms control policy. Essentially, they offered their support for the beleaguered missile in return for shifts in the administration's arms control negotiating stance that, in the moderates' view, would increase the prospects for agreement with Moscow. For the most part, these changes required less drastic reductions in the Soviet land-based missile forces than did Reagan's original positions.

Despite intense pressure from House Democratic leaders, the basic bargain between Reagan and the moderates held through 1984. By the end of that year, although the arms controllers were geared up for one last effort to kill the MX early in 1985, the nuclear arms debate was moving into a new phase that would focus on the role of defensive weapons.

Chronology
Of Action
On Defense

1981

Congress in 1981 enthusiastically supported the defense buildup demanded by President Reagan during the 1980 presidential election campaign.

With the $26 billion he initially added to President Carter's last (fiscal 1982) defense budget request, Reagan embarked on a program to accelerate the rate at which existing forces would be modernized with new tanks and warplanes. The Reagan plan incorporated two substantial additions to the Carter program: the B-1 bomber as a replacement for the fleet of B-52s, and a bigger Navy with more nuclear-powered aircraft carriers.

After months of delay, Reagan on Oct. 2 announced a broad-gauged plan for modernizing U.S. nuclear weaponry. The most controversial elements of the program were his decisions to begin production of the B-1 bomber and to scrap the very expensive mobile basing version for the new MX intercontinental ballistic missile (ICBM), long espoused by the Air Force and endorsed by Carter in 1979 with evident reluctance. Reagan proposed instead to deploy the first few dozen missiles in existing missile silos, which were to be reinforced with additional concrete armor. A permanent plan for deploying subsequent MX missiles would be selected by Reagan by 1984.

The only dramatic congressional challenge in 1981 to Reagan's defense program resulted from the Senate Armed Services Committee's outrage at the MX decision. Critics complained that the initial deployment of a few dozen missiles in existing silos made no sense because they would be vulnerable to a Soviet attack, even if the silos were strengthened. The Senate seconded that judgment by overwhelmingly approving an amendment to the fiscal 1982 defense appropriations bill that strongly discouraged — but did not flatly prohibit — the so-called superhardening plan. The provision was incorporated in the final bill.

Otherwise, Congress approved the administration's defense requests with no more than the usual quibbles over specific programs. By late August, however, it was evident that "Reaganomics" was not having the predicted psychological impact on the economy. Faced with projections of soaring deficits, Reagan announced Sept. 11 that his planned increase in defense outlays for fiscal 1982-84 would be pared by $13 billion, $2 billion of which would come out of the revised fiscal 1982 budget. Reagan refused to consider further cuts in his defense plan, despite calls by several senior Republican members of Congress for additional defense cuts.

In the end, most of the president's complaining congressional allies acceded. In acting on the two major Pentagon appropriations bills in mid-December (Defense Department and military construction projects), Congress cut less than $1.5 billion from Reagan's total request of $208.2 billion.

1982 Defense Authorization

Defense programs were spared the budget-cutting fervor that swept Congress and the administration in 1981. Although President Reagan announced Sept. 11 that he was trimming his March defense budget request as part of an overall spending reduction package, the defense authorization bill cleared by Congress Nov. 17 (S 815 — PL 97-86) authorized a record $130.7 billion for defense programs in fiscal 1982, $419.4 million above Reagan's revised request. *(Reagan requests, box, p. 207; major weapons programs, arms control special report, p. 249)*

The bill contained a provision allowing Congress to veto Reagan's controversial Oct. 2 decisions to begin production of the B-1 bomber and to temporarily base MX intercontinental ballistic missiles (ICBMs) in reinforced Minuteman silos instead of shuttling them among multiple protective shelters, which President Carter had recommended. The veto could be exercised by passing a concurrent resolution within 60 days of the president's decision. But the House Armed Services Committee was able to thwart use of the veto by holding up final approval of the bill until just before the Nov. 18 deadline for Congress to exercise that option. *(MX basing plan, p. 252)*

Showdown votes on both programs occurred on the defense appropriations bills in both houses. *(Story, p. 208)*

In contrast to their far-reaching disagreements with President Carter's defense budgets, the Senate and House Armed Services committees strongly endorsed the Reagan administration's general approach to defense and the need to beef up the U.S. military arsenal.

The fiscal 1982 authorization bill was the first one to encompass the budget request for operations and maintenance (O&M) expenses. The Armed Services panels in 1981 decided to extend their authority over O&M so they could review training, maintenance and fuel budgets that affected the combat readiness of units in the field.

The bill also covered manpower levels.

Senate Committee Action

As reported May 6 by the Senate Armed Services Committee (S Rept 97-58), S 815 authorized $136.52 billion for weapons procurement, military research, O&M and civil defense — $29.86 million more than Reagan requested.

The panel warmly endorsed the president's pledge of a sustained buildup in U.S. weaponry that was to be substantially more rapid than the one Carter agreed to toward the end of his administration. But it warned that the buildup might come under heavy political pressure as the administration continued its drive to restrain other federal spending. The committee emphasized that it expected the administration to stick to its defense program even if it meant asking for more money later on.

Strategic Forces. In addition to authorizing continued MX development, the committee added $53.7 million to continue production of the Mark 12A ICBM warhead. Three Mark 12As were being put on each of 300 Minuteman III missiles (to replace smaller Mark 12s); each MX would carry 10 of the warheads. The added funds would buy warheads to convert an additional 150 Minuteman IIIs and would keep the production line running until it was time to begin producing Mark 12As for the MX.

In 1982, however, the administration requested — and Congress concurred — that the Mark 12As be replaced with a new, more accurate warhead. *(Fiscal 1983 Defense*

Department authorization, p. 217)

Continued production of Trident I submarine-launched missiles was approved as requested: $783.2 million for 72 missiles. But the committee refused the request for $1.1 billion to build a 10th Trident-launching submarine, citing continued delays in delivery of the first of those ships.

The administration request for $2.4 billion to develop a new long-range bomber was approved, but with the proviso that Congress could block the president's choice of the plane.

The committee approved Reagan's request for nearly half a billion dollars for research on anti-ballistic missile defense. But it refused to increase the administration's request for research on powerful laser-armed space satellites that some scientists argued could destroy attacking ICBMs — a decision subsequently overturned on the Senate floor.

In its farthest-reaching change in the administration's strategic war budget, the committee recommended an additional $341.6 million for various improvements in the electronic systems that would warn of an impending enemy attack and on which policy makers would rely for control of U.S. forces during a nuclear war.

Ground Combat Forces. The committee basically supported the administration plan to modernize heavily armored U.S. units assigned to defend Europe against Soviet attack. The panel approved requests for the M-1 tank, a new troop carrier and the first 14 copies of a new tank-hunting helicopter.

A $20 million request was approved to equip a factory to make new nerve gas artillery shells, called binary munitions. Money for the project had been deleted from the 1981 defense appropriations bill. However, the fiscal 1981 supplemental appropriations bill (PL 97-12) contained $20 million for the program. *(Fiscal 1981 funding, p. 211; 1980 action, Congress and the Nation Vol. V, p. 165)*

Naval Forces. Reagan's pledge to build a larger Navy with at least 15 large carriers (instead of the 12 then in service) won strong committee support.

Except for reactivation of the *Oriskany,* the committee approved all funds requested for combat ships. The committee also approved the request for additional funds to modernize and reactivate the battleships *New Jersey* and *Iowa.* Funds for those ships also had been contained in the fiscal 1981 supplemental appropriations bill.

RDF Airlift and Sealift. The committee approved only $1 million of the requested $245.7 million to develop a new intercontinental transport plane. However, the panel authorized the requested amount ($722.4 million) to buy nine fast commercial cargo ships that could carry U.S. troops to distant regions as part of the Rapid Deployment Force (RDF) program, under which the Pentagon was trying to increase its capacity to send U.S. forces to distant areas, such as the Persian Gulf, where there were no U.S. bases or facilities. Also approved was a request for $392 million for ships to store arms and equipment for U.S. troops near potential trouble spots.

Senate Floor Action

The Senate passed the bill 92-1 on May 14, with Mark O. Hatfield, R-Ore., casting the "no" vote. Conservatives and liberals alike used the measure to try to nudge Reagan toward their respective theories of how to handle nuclear weapons.

The more aggressive tack was taken by a group composed primarily of Western conservatives who tried to push the Pentagon toward a radical new strategic policy. These senators proposed to deter nuclear attack by developing a capability to shoot down attacking Soviet missiles and bombers, rather than by threatening a retaliatory strike. Reagan himself was to emphasize that strategy two years later in his Strategic Defense Initiative, labeled "Star Wars" by liberal critics. *(Details, box, p. 253)*

That so-called "defense dominance" school won only limited victories during debate on S 815; some $50 million was added to accelerate research on lasers that might be used for a satellite-based anti-missile defense.

The only solace for traditional arms control supporters was adoption of an amendment by Gary Hart, D-Colo., expressing the Senate's support for eventual resumption of arms control talks.

House Committee Action

The House Armed Services Committee reported its version on May 19 (HR 3519 — H Rept 97-71, Part I). The committee authorized $136,046,036,000 for weapons procurement, military research, operations and maintenance and civil defense. That was $445.2 million less than Reagan's March request.

Strategic Forces. The panel indicated its support for a version of the B-1 as the bomber of the future by approving $2.24 billion to continue development and begin production of the B-1 bomber. The committee required congressional consent by concurrent resolution if the president decided on some course other than a B-1 version.

The committee approved the $2.4 billion requested to continue development of the MX.

To improve the accuracy of Minuteman III missiles, the panel added $5.5 million; it also added $44.6 million to continue production of the Mark 12A nuclear warhead.

The committee agreed with its Senate counterpart not to approve the $1.1 billion requested for construction of a 10th large submarine to launch Trident missiles, citing production delays in the program. But the House panel added $100 million to buy components for the ship. The Senate had approved $75 million for the same purpose. Funds for the 10th submarine subsequently were made available in the fiscal 1983 appropriations bill. *(Story, p. 219)*

Unlike the Senate, the committee refused to authorize any funds to accelerate development of laser-armed space satellites.

Naval Forces. The committee approved the $658 million requested for components for a sixth nuclear-powered aircraft carrier. An appropriation of nearly $3 billion was requested in fiscal 1983 for the carrier itself.

The panel also approved $364 million requested to reactivate the *Oriskany,* although that project was opposed by the Senate Armed Services and both Appropriations committees; Reagan subsequently dropped the project in his September budget revisions.

Funds to begin equipping the battleships *New Jersey* and *Iowa* with cruise missiles and returning them to service were approved as requested ($246 million).

RDF Airlift and Sealift. The committee continued its support of the Rapid Deployment Force program but approved only $20 million of the $245.7 million requested for developing the C-17 cargo plane.

The committee approved various supply ships to sup-

Reagan Boosts Carter's Defense Budget

Carrying out his campaign pledge to boost military spending, President Reagan in March 1981 added $32.6 billion to President Carter's proposed Defense Department budgets for fiscal years 1981 and 1982.

Reagan's additions included $6.8 billion in new budget authority that was incorporated in a supplemental fiscal 1981 appropriations bill. Along with a $6.3 billion supplemental requested by Carter in January 1981, just before he left office, Reagan's addition brought total planned defense spending for fiscal 1981 to $178 billion.

For fiscal 1982, Reagan asked for an additional $25.8 billion; Carter had requested $195.7 billion.

Overall, Reagan initially proposed $1.638 trillion in defense budget authority for defense in fiscal years 1981 through 1986, compared with Carter's proposed $1.447 trillion.

In September 1981, bowing to the fiscal reality of ballooning budget deficits, Reagan reluctantly agreed to trim his plans for increased defense spending.

Congress accepted most of Reagan's defense spending proposals, his dramatic increases made in March as well as the September cuts, which were formally submitted to Congress in October.

In several fiscal 1982 defense appropriations bills passed in 1981, Congress appropriated a total of $211.6 billion in new budget authority — $1.4 billion less than Reagan's $213 billion request. These figures included the appropriations in HR 4995 (PL 97-114), covering most Defense Department operations; HR 4241 (PL 97-106), covering military construction projects; and HR 4144 (PL 97-88), covering nuclear weapons programs by the Department of Energy.

March Increases

Most of Reagan's $32.6 billion addition to the Defense Department budget for fiscal years 1981 and 1982 was earmarked for projects that the Pentagon would have bought anyway if it had been given the extra money by the Carter administration.

Some of Reagan's conservative advisers had called for much larger defense budgets to pay for a crash program of new nuclear weapons and expanded conventional forces. But, except for advocating a larger Navy and a new manned bomber, Reagan concentrated on modernizing the equipment and improving the combat-readiness of forces the Pentagon already had.

The only definite force enlargement budgeted by Reagan was for the Navy, which Reagan had pledged to increase from 450 to 600 ships. Reagan added $4.2 billion to Carter's shipbuilding budget, including the down payment on a $3.7 billion nuclear aircraft carrier and funds to refurbish a smaller carrier and two battleships in mothballs.

About $2.5 billion was earmarked for the Rapid Deployment Force and related programs to increase U.S. military capability in the Persian Gulf area. This nearly doubled the amounts requested by Carter in the 1981 supplemental and the 1982 budget for that purpose. Reagan also sought $2.5 billion to continue developing a new strategic bomber to replace the B-52.

September Cutbacks

As the nation's economic problems worsened — and as projections for the fiscal 1982 deficit soared — the Reagan administration came under increasing pressure to pare back the defense budget.

On Sept. 11 Reagan announced he had agreed to cut $13 billion in defense outlays over three years: $2 billion in fiscal 1982, $5 billion in 1983 and $6 billion in 1984. The specific cuts were submitted to Congress Oct. 9.

To cut outlays by $2 billion in fiscal 1982, Reagan had to propose $8 billion worth of cuts in budget authority, only part of which was spent in a single year.

Two items accounted for the bulk of Reagan's proposed $2 billion fiscal 1982 cut in strategic arms programs:

● A cut of $965 million reflected Reagan's cancellation of the multiple launch-site version of the MX intercontinental missile endorsed by President Carter.

● An additional $960.8 million reflected postponement of the request for a 10th Trident missile-launching submarine. Both Armed Services committees had opposed the funding.

The administration also proposed cutting $98.6 million (including some fiscal 1981 money) from two programs aimed at improving the existing force of Minuteman intercontinental missiles.

A net total of $416 million was cut from the budget by the administration's abandonment of plans to reactivate the mothballed aircraft carrier *Oriskany*. Of the congressional defense panels, only the House Armed Services Committee had shown enthusiasm for the plan to equip the ship with small Marine Corps bombers.

Among other proposed cuts was more than $1.3 billion for programs related to the Rapid Deployment Force and U.S. military reinforcements in the Middle East. Reagan ended the policy, dating from January 1980, of keeping two aircraft carrier task forces in the Indian Ocean full time. A proposed reduction of $200.8 million meant that there would be one carrier task force in the Indian Ocean at all times, with a second carrier force there about half the time.

port the RDF, among them the construction of one new prepositioning ship ($195 million) as requested.

In an attempt to push the administration to enlarge the amphibious landing fleet, the committee added $427.3 million to build a ship (called an LSD-41) designed to launch landing barges carrying tanks and other large equipment.

House Floor Action

The House passed the defense bill July 16 on a 354-63 vote.

The House Armed Services Committee swept from the board nearly all its ideological and institutional opponents during the seven-day debate on the bill. The only change in the committee's authorization amounts was a $65 million increase the committee recommended at the Pentagon's request.

Only one amendment involving a major defense issue was adopted over Armed Services' objection. The House adopted by voice vote an amendment identical to one contained in the Senate version that would give Congress a chance to block Reagan's final choice of a basing technique for the MX. But it rejected by a margin of only six votes (201-207) an amendment that would have required congressional concurrence in the president's decision within 60 days. Another amendment that would have killed the MX entirely was rejected 96-316.

Conference Action

House and Senate conferees on the authorization bill met in October after Reagan had submitted his revised budget requests. In their Nov. 3 report (H Rept 97-311) on S 815, conferees emphasized that the amounts initially approved by the Senate and House "more nearly reflect the long-term requirements for achieving the marked improvement in national defense posture that is needed." Any deeper cuts, they insisted, "would seriously compromise the absolute necessity to revitalize our military forces."

The conferees agreed on $2.1 billion for the B-1 bomber program, cutting $100 million from the procurement request and $51 million earmarked for spare parts. The request and authorization figures for the "stealth" bomber were classified.

Of the $1.95 billion requested for development of the MX, conferees approved $1.875 billion. The conference report did not account for the $75 million difference, but it appeared to reflect most conferees' intense disagreement with Reagan's Oct. 2 decision to cancel the Carter administration's shuttle system for basing the MX missile.

The bill included $34.3 million to complete previously planned production of the Mark 12A nuclear warhead. But efforts by both houses to fund production of additional Mark 12A warheads were dropped.

To accelerate work on an anti-ballistic missile defense system the Army had under development, the conferees authorized $336.7 million. That amount included $35 million of the $52 million Reagan requested in submitting his October budget revision.

The more exotic kind of anti-missile defenses favored by some conservative senators fared poorly. The final bill authorized only $5 million of the $50 million added by the Senate to accelerate development of laser-armed anti-missile satellites.

The final version authorized 63 Navy F/A-18s ($2.13

billion, plus $343 million for spare parts), 36 Air Force F-15s ($1.08 billion, plus $71 million for spare parts) and 120 Air Force F-16s ($1.82 billion, plus $394 million for spare parts).

The conferees dropped authorizations to reactivate the *Oriskany* — Reagan had rescinded the request — but authorized $237 million to reactivate and modernize the *New Jersey.*

Conferees approved the request for two nuclear-powered submarines designed to hunt enemy ships and submarines ($1.1 billion). They also authorized $397.9 million to buy components for three submarines that would be funded in fiscal 1983 and another three in fiscal 1984.

The conference report authorized $1.42 billion for the purchase of 665 M-1 tanks — $200 million less than had been budgeted. Savings uncovered during negotiations on the fiscal 1981 tank contract made the reduction possible, according to the report.

Conferees approved the amount requested to buy 96 UH-60 troop-carrying helicopters ($545.2 million) and $438.4 million to build the first 14 AH-64 tank-hunting helicopters.

Conferees accepted the administration's revised recommendation setting the Army manpower ceiling at 780,300, just 300 more than the fiscal 1981 limit but 6,000 fewer than had been requested in March (at an estimated savings of $62.3 million). The bill retained relatively tough Senate-sponsored limits on the number of men who were not high school graduates the Army would be allowed to enlist: no more than 35 percent of its fiscal 1982 inductees.

To help the Selective Service System identify 18-year-old men who had not registered for the draft, as required by law, conferees included a House-passed provision requiring the secretary of health and human services to make available to the draft agency the names and addresses of Social Security registrants who met the requirements for registration. Twice in the previous year the Senate had dropped similar riders from defense bills under filibuster threats from anti-draft crusader Sen. Hatfield. *(Draft registration, box, p. 218)*

Conferees accepted the administration's proposal to keep only one aircraft carrier in the Indian Ocean full time, with one additional carrier in the region about half the time, for a savings of $74.6 million. The conferees turned down most other administration recommendations to pare back operating tempos or maintenance plans.

The Senate adopted the conference report Nov. 5. The House followed suit Nov. 17, clearing the bill for the president.

1982 Defense Appropriations

Congress in 1981 handed President Reagan a $199.7 billion defense appropriations bill (HR 4995 — PL 97-114) that funded essentially the military program he requested for fiscal 1982. Total funding, including transfers from previous appropriations, fell just $979 million short of Reagan's request, as revised in October. *(Reagan requests, box, p. 207)*

The issue of the defense budget's size was nearly submerged by battles over Reagan's strategic arms policies, particularly the MX missile and B-1 bomber, and the combat readiness of U.S. ground forces. Nonetheless, a number of influential Republicans joined Democrats in complaining about the Pentagon's relative immunity from the aus-

terity imposed on most domestic programs. *(Major weapons programs, arms control special report, p. 249)*

House Action

Committee. As reported by the House Appropriations Committee Nov. 6 (H Rept 97-333), HR 4995 appropriated $196,607,809,000 for defense programs, $4.27 billion less than the administration's revised budget request.

Characteristically, the committee's cut was accounted for by hundreds of reductions, many of a few million dollars. None of the changes involved dramatic policy disputes with the administration. Many involved relatively technical issues and some of the largest were intended to rectify what the committee insisted was "waste, fraud and abuse."

The panel approved the general outlines of Reagan's strategic weapons plan, which called for production of the B-1 bomber and an interim basing system for MX intercontinental missiles using existing Minuteman silos. *(Basing plan, p. 252)*

The Defense Appropriations Subcommittee had voted Oct. 28 by a one-vote margin to cancel the MX missile. But that decision was overridden by the full committee, which voted 25-23 on Nov. 16 to restore $1.9 billion for development of the MX. The panel placed no restrictions on the use of basing research funds.

The committee recommended $2.092 billion of the $2.423 billion requested for the B-1 bomber program. Part of the reduction ($151 million for procurement) had been allocated in the authorization bill (S 815 — PL 97-86). *(Story, p. 205)*

In its report the committee warned that plans to deploy U.S. forces near the Persian Gulf — the Rapid Deployment Force (RDF) — depended too heavily on uncertain assumptions that countries in the area would allow U.S. use of their facilities. The administration had been reluctant to pressure nations such as Egypt to sign formal agreements that might create political problems for their leaders. However, such agreements had been negotiated with Oman, Kenya and Somalia.

Floor. The House passed HR 4995 on Nov. 18. No major funding changes were made in the bill. President Reagan's nuclear arms reduction proposal, announced the same day, dominated House debate on the strategic nuclear weapons funded in HR 4995. Reagan offered to cancel U.S. plans to deploy intermediate-range nuclear weapons (Pershing IIs and ground-launched cruise missiles) in Europe if the Soviet Union would dismantle its equivalent missiles. Negotiations on the so-called "theater nuclear force" missiles had begun in Geneva Nov. 30.

Jack Edwards, R-Ala., senior Republican on the Defense Subcommittee, summarized the administration's argument. "[Reagan] must go to the bargaining table with chips in his pocket to deal with. We simply cannot at this time consider cutting back or terminating or doing away with or slowing down the MX, . . . the B-1, . . . the Pershing II's . . . and the ground-launched cruise missiles."

Defense Appropriations Subcommittee Chairman Joseph P. Addabbo, D-N.Y., who tried to delete the production funds for the B-1 bomber and Pershing missiles as well as the research money for the MX, countered that each of them would be seen by Soviet negotiators as a hollow threat because of their respective inadequacies.

"What is a bargaining chip?" he demanded. "A bargaining chip is something that can be used. The Russians know what can be used and what cannot be used. An MX for which we have no basing mode cannot be used and therefore is not much of a bargaining chip."

Presenting his amendment to remove $1.8 billion in procurement money for the B-1, Addabbo warned that it would not be able to penetrate Soviet air defenses for very long but would drain funds from development of a "stealth" bomber. "This country cannot afford to develop both the B-1 and the stealth," he said.

The House, however, rejected Addabbo's B-1 amendment on a **142-263 key vote (R 21-157; D 121-106)**. Addabbo's MX amendment was rejected by a slightly larger margin than his B-1 amendment, on a **139-264 key vote (R 27-151; D 112-113)**. *(1981 key votes, p. 879)*

With the bargaining chip argument dominating discussion, the House also rejected, by voice vote, an Addabbo amendment that would have deleted $218.9 million to begin procurement of Pershing II missiles.

Before passing HR 4995, the House rejected, 197-202, an amendment to cut 2 percent from funds for weapons procurement, research and development.

Senate Action

Committee. As reported Nov. 17, the Senate Appropriations Committee's version (S 1857 — S Rept 97-273) provided $208.5 billion for defense. That was $7.641 billion more than Reagan's revised budget and $11.1 billion more than the amount approved by the House.

Reviewing the deep cuts the committee had made in domestic programs, Appropriations Committee Chairman Mark O. Hatfield, R-Ore., protested that nearly three-fourths of the savings would be offset by the Defense Appropriations Subcommittee's $7.5 billion addition to the Reagan request. Subcommittee Chairman Ted Stevens, R-Alaska, countered that most of the increase simply reflected predictable cost increases not included in the budget. Moreover, he argued, a higher Senate appropriation was needed to give the Senate bargaining leverage against the lower House-passed figure in the conference on the bill.

The committee bill essentially funded nuclear war programs — the MX, B-1 and improvements in the existing Minuteman intercontinental ballistic missile fleet — at the requested levels.

The panel's recommendations for procurement of tanks (including the M-1) and most other Army combat equipment conformed to the authorization bill, as did funding levels for most fighter planes and light bombers.

Floor. Before passing the bill on a 84-5 vote on Dec. 4, the Senate engaged in a weeklong debate on Reagan's strategic policies and the combat readiness of ground forces.

Seconding the judgment of most of its defense specialists, the Senate signaled an overwhelming lack of confidence in Reagan's proposal to temporarily deploy the first few dozen MX missiles in existing silos.

By a vote of 90-4, the Senate adopted an amendment cosponsored by Armed Services Committee members William S. Cohen, R-Maine, and Sam Nunn, D-Ga., that discouraged — but did not flatly prohibit — Reagan's plan.

The sponsors' intent — echoed by several of the Senate's defense specialists — was to make the administration concentrate its effort on a permanent, more survivable basing method. Cohen and Nunn argued that using existing silos, even if reinforced, would not appreciably improve the chances of their surviving a Soviet missile attack,

In addition to the MX, the B-1 came under critical scrutiny on the Senate floor. On a **key 28-66 vote (R 5-43; D 23-23)**, the Senate rejected an amendment by Ernest F. Hollings, D-S.C., that would have deleted the entire $2.4 billion for the B-1 program and would have redistributed $1.8 billion of that amount to a long list of conventional weapons and combat-readiness improvements. Several of the additions previously had been offered by Democrats as separate amendments.

Proponents of the amendment argued that the B-1 was less essential than improvements in the preparedness of conventional forces and development of other new strategic weapons such as the stealth bomber. They cited Reagan's October cuts in his earlier defense requests as evidence that the B-1's cost would starve those other programs.

The Senate also tabled, by a 51-40 vote, an amendment by Minority Leader Robert C. Byrd, D-W.Va., that would have added $250 million to the classified amount in the bill for development of the stealth bomber. Republicans argued that the bill funded stealth research at the fastest prudent pace.

Conference, Final Action

House-Senate conferees filed their report on HR 4995 Dec. 15 (H Rept 97-410). Both the House and Senate adopted the conference report the same day, clearing the measure for the president. Liberal Democrats predominated among the "nay" votes cast in both chambers.

Strategic Forces. The final bill provided the $1.913 billion requested for developing the MX but denied $95.5 million added by the Senate in anticipation of a 3 percent increase in costs that was not included in the budget. The bill also incorporated the Cohen-Nunn amendment designed to discourage the administration from going ahead with its proposal to reinforce, or "superharden," existing missile silos. The amendment stipulated that $334 million of the $354 million requested for development of the interim basing technique could be used only for existing silos that were not superhardened.

MX funds included $10 million to develop a system that would launch MXs from large airplanes, one of the proposals for solving the permanent basing question. The defense authorization bill had provided $38.5 million for that option.

To improve the existing force of Minuteman ICBMs, the conferees added the following amounts to the budget request:

● $5 million to replace 50 single-warhead Minuteman IIs with triple-warhead Minuteman IIIs.

● $22.3 million to continue production of the Mark 12A warhead for the Minuteman III. A year later, however, the Mark 12A was dropped in favor of a new, more accurate warhead. *(Story, p. 218)*

As was done with the MX funding, conferees dropped the Senate's 3 percent cost-growth cushion for the B-1 bomber. They also accepted House-approved reductions in B-1 procurement and research funds totaling $329.3 million. For the B-1 program, the final bill appropriated $2,092,900,000.

The total amount appropriated for development of the stealth bomber was not disclosed in the bill. But the conferees retained a Senate floor amendment prohibiting any reduction in that amount in fiscal 1982.

The final bill contained $330.7 million for components of future Trident missile-launching submarines to be funded in subsequent years.

Ground Combat Forces. The bill appropriated $1.348 billion as requested to purchase 665 M-1 tanks. The Senate had provided an additional $76.3 million to buy 720 tanks, the number requested by Reagan before he revised the budget.

The bill provided the $484.6 million requested to buy 96 UH-60 troop-carrying helicopters and $438 million for 14 AH-64 tank-hunting helicopters.

Conferees retained two House-passed provisions that could complicate U.S. relations with other NATO members. In providing only $155.7 million for payment of damage claims against the Pentagon, the House denied $39.8 million requested to pay claims filed by West German citizens for damage caused by U.S. units on maneuvers.

The other provision directed the Pentagon to store enough tanks and other equipment in Europe to equip four Army divisions that would be used on the continent as reinforcements in case of an international crisis. The Pentagon had planned to store enough equipment for six divisions.

Naval Forces. The two versions of the bill were in basic agreement on the shipbuilding request. Relatively minor funding disagreements were resolved in favor of the lower House-passed figures:

● $475 million for components for a sixth nuclear-powered aircraft carrier to be funded in a future budget at an approximate cost of $3 billion.

● $2.909 billion for three cruisers equipped with the Aegis missile system designed to protect U.S. carrier task forces against the large Soviet arsenal of anti-ship cruise missiles.

● $926 million for three missile-armed escort frigates. The administration had requested $748 million for two ships.

For anti-submarine helicopters, the final bill approved $559 million.

The bill contained $237 million to complete renovation of the battleship *New Jersey* and $90 million to buy materials for the *Iowa*.

Rapid Deployment Force. Both Appropriations committees had expressly told the Air Force to stop trying to develop a new wide-body, long-range transport plane, the C-17, to haul U.S. ground units to small overseas airstrips. Both versions of the bill denied the $169.7 million requested for the plane and appropriated instead $50 million to begin purchasing existing wide-body transports. Some funds for the C-17 were contained in the fiscal 1983 defense appropriations bill that cleared in December 1982. *(Story, p. 219)*

For two high-speed cargo ships and modification of six others bought in 1980 to transport an Army division, the bill provided $307.6 million in new funds plus $102.4 million appropriated but not spent in earlier years. The administration had requested $668.4 million.

To beef up the Navy's shrinking amphibious fleet, the conferees added three items to the budget:

● $301 million for an LSD 41-class landing ship.

● $45 million for components of a helicopter carrier that would haul troop-carrying helicopters.

● $15 million to design the new type of helicopter carrier.

Tactical Aircraft. For Air Force fighters, the final bill provided $980.2 million for 36 F-15s and $1.27 billion for 120 F-16s. For Navy carrier-launched planes, the bill provided $888.7 million for 30 F-14 fighters, $1.89 billion for 63 F-18 fighters and $269 million for 16 A-6E bombers.

Both houses had rejected an administration proposal in October to cut the budget by retiring the 70-odd oldest B-52s — the D model planes — several years earlier than had been planned. Both chambers added $81 million to continue operating the planes.

Personnel Costs. The Senate had added to the bill more than $200 million for new bonuses and special pay established by the military pay raise bill (PL 97-60) enacted in October. The conferees approved only $44.4 million, which was intended for certain bonuses paid to members of the Army and Navy. *(Pay raise, p. 214)*

1981 Supplemental Funds

A supplemental appropriations bill (HR 3512 — PL 97-12) for fiscal 1981, which cleared Congress June 4, contained $11.801 billion for defense, $514.2 million more than President Reagan requested to cover higher-than-estimated inflation in defense operations and maintenance, shipbuilding and military pay.

The total included $4.7 billion for a military pay raise that took effect Oct. 1, 1980, and $227.3 million for military construction projects.

House Action

In drafting the supplemental bill, the House Appropriations Committee cut $1.78 billion from the Reagan request of $12.7 billion. Only a handful of changes were flat challenges to administration policy.

The largest change based on a policy disagreement was the committee's addition of $482 million to offset what it said was the Reagan administration's underestimate of inflation.

In another policy dispute, the committee opposed a $139 million request to recommission the aircraft carrier *Oriskany*, a request the administration later dropped.

Consistent with its refusal to risk money on the MX intercontinental missile until a final basing plan was chosen, the committee denied a $36.2 million request to speed development of an anti-ballistic missile defense for MX bases.

The committee also deleted $35.1 million from MX missile-related design and construction projects and recommended that Congress block further expenditure of $92 million already appropriated for MX construction until final decisions were made on whether to go ahead with the new missile and how to deploy it.

In passing HR 3512 on May 13 by a 329-70 vote, the House made no changes in the defense provisions of the supplemental appropriations bill recommended by the committee.

Senate Action

As reported by Senate Appropriations May 14 (S Rept 97-67), HR 3512 appropriated $13.075 billion for defense programs, $325 million more than the president's request. As with the House, the largest single change in the Reagan request was the addition of $1.656 billion to offset inflation (other than fuel price increases), which the committee argued would be higher than assumed by the administration.

The Senate panel also endorsed the House action denying funds for the MX missile until a basing mode had been selected.

Like the House bill, the Senate committee version approved in general the administration policy of preparing to deploy more U.S. military units to the Middle East; but it disapproved several specific requests.

The committee concurred with a House decision to cut $5 million from the $70.2 million requested to keep warships operating in the Indian Ocean. (Reagan in September decided to keep only one aircraft carrier, instead of the existing two, in the area.) For construction of military facilities in the Indian Ocean region, the committee approved $43 million of the $68 million requested. It told the Army to use previously appropriated funds to design facilities at the Egyptian Red Sea port of Ras Banas, where combat gear would be stored for use by U.S. troops flown to the Middle East in a crisis. *(1982 action on Ras Banas, p. 223)*

Before passing the bill May 21, the Senate dealt with two controversial weapons programs:

• The Senate voted 61-34 to appropriate funds for modernizing two mothballed battleships — the *New Jersey* and the *Iowa*.

• The Senate refused to delay the next step toward producing a new nerve gas weapon. The decision to go ahead with the program was made by a margin of only two votes (48-50). The program was vigorously backed by Defense Secretary Caspar W. Weinberger and Secretary of State Alexander M. Haig Jr.

In all, the Senate version provided just under $13 billion for defense programs and made few substantive departures from President Reagan's request. In one change, however, the Senate went along with the House in deleting $139 million for reactivating the *Oriskany*.

Conference Action

Conferees filed a report (H Rept 97-124) on the bill June 3. They recommended a total of $11.801 billion for defense programs — $1.1 billion below the Senate-approved amount and $881 million above the House-passed figure.

Conferees denied all requests associated with the MX because Reagan had not yet decided how to base the missile.

Over the strong objection of Senate Appropriations Defense Subcommittee Chairman Ted Stevens, R-Alaska, the conferees approved the $89 million requested to begin modernizing the *New Jersey*.

Conferees approved $59.2 million, the Senate figure, to cover cost increases in the ground-launched cruise missile to be based in Europe.

A request for $20 million to buy equipment for a plant to manufacture binary nerve gas weapons was not at issue in conference because both houses had accepted it. But the conferees ordered the administration to inform Congress of the total long-term cost of deploying the weapons and of the policies of other NATO nations toward those weapons. Funds for the project subsequently were deleted from the fiscal 1983 and 1984 defense authorization bills. *(Stories, pp. 217, 225)*

1981 Supplemental Authorization

Congress Aug. 4 cleared a $2.7 billion defense supplemental authorization (S 694 — PL 97-39) for fiscal 1981. The funding was in addition to the $58.3 billion authorized

by the regular fiscal 1981 defense authorization and military construction bills cleared in 1980. Approval of S 694 came two months after Congress completed action on the supplemental appropriations bill for fiscal 1981 (HR 3512 — PL 97-12). *(Story, p. 211)*

House and Senate conferees on the bill challenged as overly optimistic the administration's claim that a rapid drop in inflation would allow large savings to be made in the 1981 defense budget.

The final bill cut two-thirds of the $655 million Reagan wanted to slice from 1981 defense programs. Reagan had said the 1981 budget could be reduced by that amount because his estimate of 10 percent inflation for the fiscal year was lower than President Carter's 10.4 percent. Members of both Armed Services committees questioned that assumption, but the Senate panel approved the full Reagan cut. House Armed Services cut $435.7 million, and the conferees accepted the House version.

Although the administration requested funds to renovate the battleship *New Jersey* ($89 million in fiscal 1981) and the mothballed aircraft carrier *Oriskany* ($139 million), conferees noted that the regular fiscal 1981 authorization (PL 96-342) already authorized those programs and that a new authorization was not needed. *(Congress and the Nation Vol. V, p. 161)*

Legislative Action

Senate. In reporting S 694 (S Rept 97-35) on April 1, the Senate Armed Services Committee authorized $2.8 billion for additional weapons procurement and military research, $238.2 million less than the administration requested.

The Senate approved S 694 April 7 after tabling by a 69-23 vote an amendment that would have barred use of any money in the bill to reactivate the *New Jersey*.

In its first vote on the MX intercontinental missile issue since late 1979, the Senate, by a **79-15 key vote (R 44-6; D 35-9)**, tabled an amendment that would have deleted $7 million for research related to the MX. The administration was in the process of re-examining alternative approaches to basing the missile in a way that would protect it from Soviet attack. Reagan announced an interim basing plan in October. *(Details, this page; 1981 key votes, p. 879)*

House. The House Armed Services Committee reported its version (HR 2614 — H Rept 97-20) April 9. The bill authorized $2.6 billion for weapons procurement, research and military construction — $401.1 million less than the administration requested. The difference did not represent a reduction in programs because the panel said new authorization was not needed for some of the projects dropped from the bill. The House passed the bill June 23.

Conference Action. House-Senate conferees filed their report on S 694 July 27 (H Rept 97-204). The final version authorized $2,741,602,000 for weapons procurement, military research and construction in fiscal 1981.

Conferees approved $20 million requested to begin updating the equipment on B-52 bombers so it would not be damaged by the electronic effects of a nuclear explosion. But conferees insisted that, before spending the money, the president adopt a comprehensive program for modernizing the bomber fleet. In mid-1981 Defense Secretary Caspar W. Weinberger was in the process of deciding whether to begin building the proposed B-1 bomber or the stealth bomber. The House bill had denied the B-52 funds because

Reagan had not yet explained his overall bomber plan.

The conferees also approved $41.4 million requested to meet unexpected cost increases in developing the ground-launched cruise missile, designed to hit Soviet targets with nuclear warheads from bases in Europe. The House had proposed shifting $41.2 million of that amount to speed production of a ship-launched version of the cruise missile.

Conferees essentially accepted the House position to accelerate production of two tactical fighter planes. First, they approved a request for $95.9 million to meet unexpected cost increases in the F-18 program so that the 60 budgeted could be purchased.

Conferees also approved a House initiative to buy enough components in 1981 to build 180 F-16s in fiscal 1982 instead of the 120 planes for which components were budgeted. Compared with the $65.7 million added to the bill for this purpose in the House, the conference report added $51.1 million and told the Pentagon to make up the difference with already-enacted budget authority.

The House had cut by 10 percent the $605.2 million requested for Air Force spare parts. Conferees approved $573.1 million and told the Air Force to use existing authority for the other $32.1 million.

The conferees approved the amounts requested to meet cost overruns for the M-1 tank ($337.5 million) and for the M-2 armored troop carrier ($158.5 million). The House had made small reductions in the two programs. The conference report blocked expenditure of $278.1 million of the M-1 funds until the Pentagon certified that the tank's transmission demonstrated adequate durability.

The Senate adopted the conference report on the measure July 30; the House adopted it Aug. 4.

1982 Military Construction

President Reagan in 1981 obtained almost all of what he requested for military construction projects. But in passing the annual military construction authorization and appropriations bills (HR 3455 — PL 97-99, HR 4241 — PL 97-106), Congress renewed its demand that other NATO allies and Japan pay for a larger share of U.S. efforts to defend their interests in Western Europe and in the oil-rich Persian Gulf.

RDF. Congress authorized and appropriated funds for construction related to the Rapid Deployment Force (RDF). RDF was the umbrella concept under which the Pentagon was trying to increase its capacity to send U.S. forces to distant areas where there were no U.S. bases or facilities. Initial planning for the RDF emphasized deployments to the Persian Gulf or nearby territory on the rim of the Indian Ocean.

MX Basing Plan. Funds related to construction of MX intercontinental ballistic missile bases were originally included in the bills. But the House and Senate appropriation and authorization committees held up, altered or deleted funds for the program, partly because Reagan announced a new plan for deploying the MX.

The Carter administration had recommended, and senior military officers still preferred, a design called Multiple Protective Structures (MPS) in which 200 MX missiles would be shuttled among 4,600 covered launch sites in Nevada and Utah. The plan had drawn intense opposition, especially in those two states, and was reviewed by a blue-ribbon panel appointed by Defense Secretary Caspar W. Weinberger. Reagan in October scrapped the very expen-

sive MPS plan and decided instead to temporarily base MX missiles in existing silos pending studies on a permanent basing system.

Burden Sharing. The burden-sharing issue dominated much of the debate on the bills. Since 1978 NATO members had been committed to annual real growth rates in defense spending of 3 percent, though few countries consistently met that goal.

Congressional anger was fueled in part by the belief that Western Europe and Japan derived a competitive advantage over U.S. industry as a result. Rep. Ralph Regula, Ohio, senior Republican on the House Appropriations Military Construction Subcommittee, summarized the argument during a hearing on RDF facilities in the Middle East: "You can build a lot of Toyotas with the money they don't spend on the security of [the Persian Gulf] but we do."

The conference report on the military construction authorization bill contained an unusually blunt warning on the politics of burden sharing. Because Washington was paying the total cost of the RDF and Persian Gulf forces, House-Senate conferees argued, it was imperative that other NATO members pay some of the costs of certain U.S. facilities in Europe.

Authorization

House Action. Nearly all of President Reagan's $7 billion request was approved by the House Armed Services Committee in its version of the fiscal 1982 military construction authorization bill (HR 3455 — H Rept 97-44) on May 15.

Acting before Reagan made his MX announcement, the committee insisted on congressional approval of any change made in the MX basing system recommended by Carter.

It approved RDF projects without major modifications, including authorizations to enlarge the U.S. base on the British-owned island of Diego Garcia in the Indian Ocean ($237.74 million) and to build facilities in Oman ($78.48 million) and Somalia ($24 million), where supplies and equipment would be stored for U.S. forces. The Oman and Somalia facilities were to remain under local sovereignty but would be available to U.S. units under agreements negotiated with those countries.

A similar agreement had been negotiated for naval facilities in Kenya, but the committee approved only $4 million of the $26 million requested for the project, saying that other funds were available to the Pentagon to make up the difference.

The House passed the bill June 4, after reaffirming its 1980 authorization for a factory to build a new nerve gas weapon (binary munitions — artillery shells containing two chemicals that produce a lethal gas when mixed).

By a vote of 135-220 the House rejected an amendment that would have rescinded a fiscal 1981 appropriation of $3.15 million to build the binary plant. The House reversed itself in 1982, 1983 and 1984, denying funds for the project. *(1980 authorization, Congress and the Nation Vol. V, p. 166; 1982-84 action, pp. 219, 228, 229, 237)*

The House also adopted an amendment giving Congress 60 days to block by concurrent resolution Reagan's choice of a basing technique for the MX.

Senate Action. The Senate Armed Services Committee reported its version of the construction bill (S 1408 — S Rept 97-141) June 22. Insisting that U.S. European allies

pay more of the cost of NATO's defense, the Senate committee cut the Pentagon's European construction budget for the fourth consecutive year.

The panel deleted $42 million for Army and Air Force projects intended to improve the combat readiness of U.S. units. The panel endorsed the projects on their merits but insisted that the allies should pay a substantial part of the cost. The size of the reduction was relatively small only because the Pentagon had not asked for many projects of the type that NATO had funded in the past.

The committee approved the request for $366 million to begin construction of the MX MPS basing system, but the funds later were dropped in conference after Reagan announced his decision to deploy the missiles temporarily in existing Minuteman silos.

Also authorized was $65 million requested for the first installment of an estimated $1.25 billion to build a base at King's Bay, Ga., for Trident missile-launching submarines.

The committee approved $500.2 million of the $531.2 million request to support the Rapid Deployment Force.

The committee bill included a provision exempting military construction projects from the 1931 Davis-Bacon Act, which required contractors to pay locally prevailing wages on federally funded construction. Business allies in Congress charged that the act artificially inflated construction wages, partly by imposing union-scale wages in areas that were not heavily unionized. But organized labor rejected those arguments and fiercely defended the Davis-Bacon Act.

Labor won when the bill went to the Senate floor. On Nov. 5 the Senate voted 55-42 to delete the waiver from the construction funding measure. The Senate then passed the bill.

Conference Action. A conference report on HR 3455 was filed Dec. 7 (H Rept 97-362). Both chambers approved the final version Dec. 8, completing congressional action.

As signed into law Dec. 23, HR 3455 (PL 97-99) authorized $6,546,810,000 for military construction programs in fiscal 1982. That was $62.9 million less than President Reagan's budget requests, as revised in October. The bill authorized all but $34 million of the $531.2 million requested for projects related to the RDF and other U.S. deployments in the Persian Gulf region.

The final bill contained all but $3 million of the $49.57 million requested for projects at Lajes Air Force Base in the Portuguese-owned Azores Islands, used by the United States as a staging point for planes flying to the Middle East. Funding for the base was cut in the fiscal 1983 military construction authorization and appropriations bills.

Also authorized was the full $70.4 million Air Force request for construction of a base at Ras Banas on Egypt's Red Sea coast. The project was dropped in 1983.

Because Reagan's decision on the MX intercontinental missile killed the mobile basing plan, the conferees dropped the $366 million budgeted for that purpose.

Appropriations

Acting on the basis of Reagan's original March request for $8.02 billion, the House Sept. 16 passed the version of the fiscal 1982 military construction appropriations bill reported by the Appropriations Committee on July 23 (HR 4241 — H Rept 97-193). The bill provided $6.89 billion for military construction programs.

By the time the Senate passed its version on Dec. 4 (S

Rept 97-271), Reagan had cut $715.6 million from his request: $492 million from construction for the MX MPS basing system, $24 million from other Air Force projects and $199.6 million from various Army projects.

The Senate version of the bill provided about $15.4 million more than Reagan's revised $7.3 billion request.

A House-Senate compromise, embodied in a conference report filed Dec. 11 (H Rept 97-400), contained $241.35 million less than the administration's October request. The final version contained $440.7 million of the $545.6 million requested for RDF projects. Of $120.7 million requested for Army and Air Force construction at Ras Banas, the conferees approved only $14.3 million earmarked for planning and design "because of the preliminary nature of the construction program." The entire $240.5 million requested for construction at Diego Garcia was approved, as was most other RDF-related construction.

Both chambers adopted the conference report on Dec. 15, completing congressional action on HR 4241 (PL 97-106).

Military Pay Increase

Congress Oct. 7 cleared a $4.5 billion military pay raise bill (S 1181 — PL 97-60).

Bowing to Senate insistence that senior enlisted personnel should receive larger raises than new recruits, House-Senate conferees on S 1181 drafted a compromise that ranged from a 10 percent increase in pay for recruits to 17 percent for senior sergeants. The raises took effect Oct. 1, 1981.

The differential between ranks covered only about half the range of the Senate-passed version, which went from 7 percent for privates to 22 percent for some sergeants major.

The increase in the raise for lower ranks reflected a partial victory for the House, which had backed an administration proposal for a 14.3 percent across-the-board pay hike.

The House position prevailed on officer pay. The Senate bill had authorized raises of 9 percent to 11 percent for new officers, 12 percent for senior officers and 14 percent to 16.5 percent for most mid-career officers.

Also in line with House conferees' concern for attracting high-quality enlistees, the bill authorized enlistment bonuses of up to $8,000. The Senate bill had raised the bonus ceiling to $7,500 from the existing $5,000, and many Senate conferees were unhappy even with that increase.

Background

The Reagan administration came to Washington promising to support an adequate level of military compensation to give the all-volunteer system, inaugurated in 1972, a better chance to work — a chance President Reagan maintained had been stifled by President Carter's tight military budgets. When the system was established, low-ranking personnel immediately received large pay raises. However, a 1967 law (PL 90-206) tied military pay raises to pay hikes for federal civil service employees, which, in turn, were linked to annual surveys of private sector pay raises for professional, administrative, technical and clerical workers (called PATC). *(All-volunteer Army legislation, Congress and the Nation Vol. III, p. 225)*

In 1975, 1978 and 1979, Presidents Ford and Carter set a cap on all federal pay raises, including those of the military, at levels below those called for by the PATC surveys.

Senior military officers and advocates of the all-volunteer Army had long argued for restoring military pay to the level of purchasing power relative to private sector pay that prevailed in 1972. Reagan advisers generally agreed that a catch-up raise was needed and that future pay hikes should not be capped. There also was support for more generous compensation policies than Carter had advocated. Congress in 1980 had enacted a military pay raise that was higher than Carter sought. *(Congress and the Nation Vol. V, p. 171)*

The disagreement between the House and Senate approaches to the military pay raise issue centered on the basic question of which problem needed the greater attention: recruitment, especially for the all-volunteer Army, or retention of senior enlisted personnel.

Military careerists complained that the ratio of senior personnel pay to that of junior personnel had steadily narrowed since the big 1972 boost in recruit pay. The resulting "compression" of the pay table reduced the incentive for enlisted personnel to seek promotions and make the service a career, it was argued.

According to Senate Armed Services Committee member Sam Nunn, D-Ga., between 1972 and 1981 the average annual compensation of a typical recruit increased by 225 percent (to $16,620 from $5,116). Over the same period, the average compensation of a typical sergeant major — the Army's highest enlisted rank — increased by 92 percent (to $29,026 from $15,121), 19 percent less than the increase in the cost of living.

Pentagon critics blamed the compression, in part, for the services' shortage of senior enlisted personnel — more than 20,000 short in the Navy and about 5,000 in the Army.

In the early months of fiscal 1981, the services came close to enlisting their planned number of recruits while complying with congressionally imposed limits on recruits' educational and test score qualifications.

House Action

The pay bill reported by the House Armed Services Committee on May 19 (HR 3380 — H Rept 97-109, Part I), set a 14.3 percent across-the-board pay hike. In explaining its reason for not targeting the raise, the panel said, "If the all-volunteer force is to be afforded a realistic chance of succeeding, a reasonably adequate level of entry pay must be provided. To short-change the pay for those initially entering military service runs counter to our efforts to recruit volunteers."

Even with the full increase for recruit pay and the higher enlistment bonuses authorized in HR 3380, the committee warned, the Army stood only a 50-50 chance of meeting congressionally mandated standards on recruit quality in fiscal 1982 and probably would fall short in fiscal 1983.

The committee also attacked the assumption that pay of higher and lower enlisted ranks had become "compressed."

HR 3380 was referred sequentially to the Appropriations Committee because of budgeting considerations. In its June 11 report (H Rept 97-109, Part II), the committee objected to the portion of the pay raise intended to restore military pay to the level of comparability with civilian pay in 1972. That base line was purely arbitrary, the committee

said in its report on the bill.

The House passed HR 3380 on Sept. 15, incorporating the administration's request for a 14.3 percent across-the-board hike in the basic pay of all military ranks.

Senate Action

The Senate Armed Services Committee July 8 reported S 1181 (S Rept 97-146). The Senate bill focused on rectifying the so-called pay compression problem. S 1181 included pay raises for enlisted personnel ranging from 7 percent for recruits to 22 percent for some senior sergeants major. Most persons in the top four sergeant grades would receive raises of 19-20 percent.

Some supporters of the all-volunteer Army discounted the negative recruiting impact of only a 7 percent pay hike for recruits, arguing that enlistees remained in the lowest pay grades for a relatively brief period.

The Senate passed S 1181 on Sept. 11. The Senate debated but did not vote on an amendment that would have slightly increased recruit pay at the expense of officers' increases.

Conference Action

House-Senate conferees reached agreement on S 1181 Oct. 6. The conference report (H Rept 97-265) underscored the conflict between personnel specialists of the Senate and House Armed Services committees on the pay issue.

Given the irreconcilable disagreement over the recruiting vs. officer retention issue, House conferees seized on a "targeting" proposal by Defense Secretary Caspar W. Weinberger as a reasonable compromise and rejected efforts by Senate members to tilt the pay raise more toward senior enlisted personnel.

Both the House and Senate approved the conference report Oct. 7, clearing the bill for the president.

Major Provisions

As signed into law Oct. 14, S 1181 (PL 97-60) authorized:

● Pay raises, effective Oct. 1, 1981, ranging from 10 percent for recruits to 14.3 percent for officers and up to 17 percent for the three senior sergeant grades.

● A 14.3 percent increase in the food and housing allowance for personnel who did not live in barracks.

● Enlistment bonuses of up to $8,000.

● Addition of three jobs to the list of hazardous duties for which personnel received extra pay. Eligibility was extended to persons working on aircraft carrier flight decks, in laboratories handling viruses or bacteria and in laboratories handling toxic fuels.

● Extra pay for weapons control officers on AWACS radar-warning and command planes and increased extra pay for some aviators.

● Payment of sea-duty bonuses to the two crews of a ballistic missile-launching submarine. To increase the amount of time the missile subs were at sea and within range of Soviet targets, they had two crews, which made alternate patrols. The provision gave both crews sea-duty pay for the entire period they were assigned to the ship, whether they were on patrol or ashore.

● Payment of a $3,000 bonus to naval officers who volunteered for service on nuclear-powered surface ships, an amount already paid to volunteers for nuclear-powered submarines.

● A re-enlistment bonus of up to $3,000 a year for officers trained as engineers or scientists.

● 5,000 new Navy and Air Force ROTC scholarships.

Nuclear Weapons Programs

Congress Nov. 19 cleared a bill (HR 3413 — PL 97-90) authorizing $5.12 billion in fiscal 1982 for nuclear weapons programs administered by the Department of Energy (DOE). That amount was $123.8 million more than President Reagan had requested.

The bill represented a substantial boost in funding for Energy Department nuclear weapons programs. The amount was 29 percent larger than the $3.97 billion approved for fiscal 1981.

The Energy Department conducted all nuclear research and nuclear weapons production for the Pentagon. The annual authorization bill covered development of nuclear weapons and naval power plants, and manufacture and testing of nuclear weapons.

For the first time in several years, the so-called neutron bomb was not a major issue in congressional consideration of the nuclear weapons bill. The neutron warhead was intended to allow nuclear attacks against any Soviet tank columns that might invade densely populated parts of Western Europe, without causing widespread property damage.

In April 1978 President Carter deferred indefinitely a decision to deploy the new radiation warheads for short-range Lance missiles and 8-inch artillery pieces in Europe. He ordered the design of new nuclear warheads for the weapons, which could quickly be converted to radiation weapons after they had been deployed. *(Background, Congress and the Nation Vol. V, p. 146)*

In 1980 the Senate Armed Services Committee complained that it would take months or years to carry out the conversion unless the high-radiation components were manufactured and stockpiled. The fiscal 1981 authorization bill for Energy Department military programs ordered that production of the components begin immediately. *(Congress and the Nation Vol. V, p. 171)*

President Reagan Aug. 6 announced his decision to begin manufacturing the neutron warheads, but to base them in the United States, rather than in Europe. The decision to keep the warheads in the United States was made to avoid disputes in Europe, where the weapon was highly controversial. The weapons could be transferred to Europe in a matter of hours in the event of a Soviet attack, Defense Secretary Caspar W. Weinberger said.

Legislative History

House. Reagan's budget for military nuclear programs was the first one in years to meet with the overall approval of the House Armed Services Committee. During the Carter administration, the panel regularly had charged that the military nuclear budget was too low. It warned that the Energy Department's weapons development and production complex was deteriorating to a point where it would be unable to produce new weapons planned for deployment in the mid-1980s.

But in its May 15 report on the fiscal 1982 nuclear weapons authorization bill (H Rept 97-45), the committee called Reagan's request "more in line with committee expectations."

The committee's $5.06 billion authorization was accepted by the House, which passed HR 3413 on June 11. As it had done several times in the previous four years, the House, before passing the bill, also went on record as overwhelmingly in favor of producing the neutron bomb. By a vote of 88-293, the House rejected an amendment to bar use of any authorized funds for the development or production of the enhanced radiation weapon.

Senate. Like its House counterpart, the Senate Armed Services Committee applauded Reagan's 25 percent increase in the budget for nuclear weapons. "For the first time in several years, the committee feels comfortable that the requested amount for these defense programs is more nearly at the level that it should be," the panel said in its July 30 report (S Rept 97-173) on S 1549, its version of the fiscal 1982 nuclear weapons authorization bill.

However, the panel recommended $168.7 million more than Reagan requested and warned that "significant real increases" would be needed in future budgets to pay for planned new weapons and for modernization of weapons already in the U.S. stockpile.

Some of the modernizations were designed to render the warheads harmless in case they were seized by terrorists; others were intended to reduce the risk that a fire or other disaster would set off their high-explosive "triggers," thus scattering radioactive material.

The Senate passed its version of the authorization bill Nov. 3.

Conference Action

A conference report (H Rept 97-342) on HR 3413 was filed Nov. 18. Both houses approved the conference version Nov. 19.

Conferees split the difference between the House and Senate bills, recommending a total authorization of $5,120,200,000. The amount included an undisclosed sum to continue production of the neutron bomb.

The administration did not recommend cuts for DOE nuclear programs in its autumn budget reductions.

Conferees authorized $142.3 million, $106 million more than the Reagan request, for research on the inertial confinement fusion process. Inertial confinement fusion was a process intended to simulate in the laboratory the kinds of explosions produced by a hydrogen bomb. The process could be used to test nuclear weapons designs. More than $1 billion had been spent since 1977 on the process.

Conferees said a shortage of fuel for nuclear weapons "may occur between 1985 and 1990 unless additional measures are taken to remedy the problem of declining production of the aging reactors" in Richland, Wash., and Savannah River, S.C.

Conferees added $10 million — not requested by the administration — for studies of a new reactor to produce weapons-grade nuclear materials.

Conferees also approved $30 million — $8.2 million more than the administration request — for research on a technique to separate weapons-grade plutonium from spent nuclear fuel. The technique was called laser isotope separation. The process also could be used to clean up nuclear wastes and to produce special isotopes for other purposes.

The conferees said they were cutting the administration's request for funds to decontaminate some 500 sites formerly used for mining or processing nuclear materials because the Energy Department and other agencies had not adequately explained the costs and benefits of a massive cleanup. The administration requested $10.2 million for decontamination and decommissioning; the final bill contained only $4 million.

Conferees approved $38.6 million to continue the Waste Isolation Pilot Plant in New Mexico. The Reagan administration had requested $6.8 million. The plant was designed as a demonstration project to dispose of nuclear wastes produced by defense facilities. *(Background, Congress and the Nation Vol. V, p. 501)*

Strategic Materials Stockpile

The Senate and House Armed Services committees in 1981 used the budget reconciliation process to make one more move in their long campaign to force the executive branch to rejuvenate the national stockpile of strategic and critical materials.

The Office of Management and Budget (OMB) and the House and Senate Budget committees had suggested the sale of surplus silver from the stockpile to collect $572 million of the $966 million by which the Armed Services panels were directed to cut defense spending in fiscal 1982. But Senate conferees on the budget-cutting reconciliation bill (HR 3982 — PL 97-35) basically accepted a House decision to substitute other surplus commodities for some of the silver and to reduce the amount of the sale to $535 million. The conferees also incorporated into the reconciliation bill "management reforms" for the stockpile that would force the Reagan administration to carry out its announced plans to buy additional commodities that were intended to keep the U.S. economy going for three years in the event of a war. *(Budget reconciliation legislation, p. 40)*

The Armed Services committees had complained repeatedly that presidents routinely tried to use the stockpiled commodities, worth about $9 billion in 1981, as a pool of potentially liquid assets to be converted by sale whenever the budget needed a few hundred million dollars. Presidents also had reduced the period for which stockpiled commodities were supposed to suffice. Congress in 1979 enacted legislation — PL 96-41 — mandating that the supply of strategic raw materials be sufficient to last three years. *(Background, 1979 legislation, Congress and the Nation Vol. V, p. 158)*

To make up for the $37 million reduction in the stockpile sale proceeds, the conferees accepted a House initiative to create a one-year open-enrollment period for the Survivor Benefit Plan, under which a military careerist could contribute to a fund from which his or her survivors would be paid an annuity after the military member's death. The maximum annuity was 55 percent of the military member's retired pay, and smaller annuities — with proportionately smaller contributions — could be chosen.

During the open enrollment period, military members who had passed the period when they were eligible to join the benefit plan could join, and personnel already contributing could increase the size of their annuity.

For at least the first five years after the open enrollment, the new contributions to the benefit plan would give the Treasury a net income. At some point, as the newly eligible annuitants began drawing money from the plan, the change would begin to cost the Treasury money. However, precise figures on the ultimate cost were not available.

The House-passed provision had provided that if a

military member died within one year of taking advantage of the open enrollment period, his or her survivors would receive only the amount contributed to the plan. In conference, the Senate insisted that the moratorium be extended to two years.

Both the House and Senate agreed that the remaining mandated $394 million budget cut would come from giving cost-of-living adjustments to military retirees annually instead of every six months. Both houses had made the change contingent on a similar change in benefits for retired civilian government workers. The change for civilians also was included in the reconciliation bill. *(Story, p. 40)*

Other Legislation

Arms Agency Authority

Congress in 1981 failed to enact the biennial authorization, covering fiscal 1982 and 1983, for the Arms Control and Disarmament Agency (ACDA).

The House passed an ACDA bill (HR 3467 — H Rept 97-55) June 8, but the Senate did not act on the measure until 1982, when the bill cleared. *(Story, p. 224)*

A stopgap authorization for ACDA activities in fiscal 1982 was contained in the omnibus budget reconciliation bill (HR 3982 — PL 97-35) that was cleared by Congress July 31. The bill authorized $18.3 million for the agency, an increase of $1.5 million above the administration request.

Defense Production Act

Congress Sept. 24 cleared legislation (HR 2903 — PL 97-47) extending the provisions of the Defense Production Act for one year, through Sept. 30, 1982. The law, first enacted in 1950, gave the president various powers to guarantee the economic health of defense-related industries. *(Details, p. 115; subsequent action on extensions, pp. 116, 119)*

1982

The political momentum of President Reagan's defense buildup was partly checked by Congress in 1982.

His $258 billion Pentagon budget request was pared significantly (although his defense programs were not revised in any basic way). The chilling prospect of massive budget deficits led Congress to make an unprecedentedly large reduction of nearly $19 billion in budget authority, a cut of 7.27 percent.

Further, congressional refusal to approve initial production funds for the MX intercontinental missile in late December marked the first time the legislature had ever denied funds for a major nuclear weapon requested by a president, though the action was a deferral rather than an outright cancellation of the missile.

In early August the House fell two votes shy of calling for a nuclear arms freeze that the administration adamantly opposed. This followed by only two weeks a House vote against production of a new form of lethal chemical weapons, called binary munitions, after a debate in which arms control advocates led the charge against the highly controversial weapons.

In each of those battles some Republicans and conservative Democrats, who typically had been bedrock supporters of a hard line on defense issues, defected from the administration.

A key factor in the defections was the seeming incongruity of Reagan's call for continued defense spending increases — in a period when deficits were reaching record-high levels — while at the same time calling for greater domestic austerity. Another factor was the administration's occasional insensitivity to the fine line between "toughness" in the international arena and politically unpalatable bellicosity.

For the most part, Reagan and his aides managed to avoid the sort of provocative statements on nuclear war that had created alarm in 1981. But the political burden of those earlier statements lingered through 1982. And the apprehension was widespread in Washington and among U.S. European allies that the administration's rigidity would preclude any nuclear arms limitation agreement with the Soviet Union.

Compounding the administration's political problems was an apparently widespread suspicion that neither Reagan nor Defense Secretary Caspar W. Weinberger had a firm personal grip on the details of defense policy. That belief was linked to complaints that there was no underlying purpose to the administration's defense buildup — that the armed services simply had been allowed to go on uncoordinated buying sprees.

1983 Defense Authorization

Congress Aug. 18 cleared a $177.9 billion fiscal 1983 defense authorization bill (S 2248 — PL 97-252) that reduced Reagan's request by $5.6 billion but made little substantial change in the president's defense program.

The authorizing bill, however, was cleared before the administration and Congress began serious negotiations over the defense budget. Those battles were dominated by a concern for reducing the projected federal deficit, and the defense spending skirmishes were fought primarily over outlays, which represented actual spending, rather than budget authority, which set the total funding levels for programs. The outcome of those struggles led to a revised request by Reagan in November and passage of appropriations bills that trimmed almost $17.6 billion from Reagan's initial defense plans.

One of the primary victims of the spending cuts was the MX missile. Congress refused to approve initial production funds for the missile. *(Defense appropriations, p. 219; major weapons programs, arms control special report, p. 249)*

About a third of the reduction in the defense authorization bill came from strategic weapons programs. Among the cuts were:

• $699 million associated with approval of only one of two additional Trident missile-launching submarines requested.

• $414 million from the MX program, partly because procurement of five missiles was authorized instead of the requested nine. (Congress subsequently dropped all funding for MX.)

• $350 million of $727 million requested for development of an anti-ballistic missile system.

• $100 million of $254 million requested for civil defense

planning for fiscal 1983.

S 2248 also cut Reagan's budget by $638 million through essentially bookkeeping changes that did not reduce the size of the defense program. Those changes included lower-than-estimated fuel prices and increases in the value of the dollar against some foreign currencies.

The only major weapon denied by Congress during debate on S 2248 was a new class of lethal nerve gas bombs and artillery shells, called binary munitions. By a 3-2 margin, the House denied the $54 million requested to begin production of the new weapons, and the conferees reluctantly concurred. The program also was dropped from the defense funding legislation.

Committee Action

The Senate Armed Services Committee reported S 2248 April 13 (S Rept 97-330); the companion House Armed Services Committee bill (HR 6030 — H Rept 97-482) was reported the same day.

Both panels agreed that the Reagan defense buildup, which was estimated to cost $1.6 trillion over the next five years, was both affordable and essential.

Strategic Forces. The two panels reiterated previous endorsements of the general thrust of Reagan's strategic force modernization plan announced Oct. 2, 1981. They were in substantial disagreement, however, over several components of the package, including the president's refusal to build the shuttle-based version of the MX, endorsed by the Air Force and by President Carter, as well as the Reagan administration's proposals for defending the United States against a Soviet nuclear attack.

The Senate panel opposed Reagan's plan to base the MX temporarily in existing hardened silos, rejecting the $715 million requested for silo basing. At the same time, the committee increased funding for development of a long-term basing plan by $255 million, for a total of $565 million. The panel also dropped the $1.497 billion requested to begin MX production, arguing that production would not be needed until fiscal 1984 to meet the new deadline for a survivable basing method. Overall, the Senate committee cut MX funding to $2.277 billion.

The House Armed Services Committee, though as unhappy as the Senate panel over Reagan's cancellation of the MX shuttle plan, concluded that MX in the silos sooner was better than a survivable MX later, for international political reasons.

The House committee approved the bulk of the administration's $3.751 billion MX request.

The two panels approved the administration's decision to develop a new re-entry vehicle to carry the nuclear warheads of the MX. Compared with the existing Mark 12A re-entry vehicles (which Congress had funded in 1982), the new Advanced Ballistic Re-entry Vehicle (ABRV) was more accurate and could produce either a larger nuclear blast for the same amount of nuclear fuel, or the same size blast with less fuel.

The panels disagreed on the treatment of Reagan's proposals to step up efforts to defend the United States against a Soviet nuclear attack. The House committee reduced administration requests for anti-ballistic missile defenses, while the Senate panel approved them.

Both committees reiterated their enthusiastic support for an improved B-1 bomber, approving the entire request for $4 billion to buy the first seven bombers and their spare parts, and $753.5 million to continue development of the

<hr>

Draft Registration Kept

Reversing a stand he took during the 1980 presidential election campaign, President Reagan on Jan. 7, 1982, ordered the continuation of mandatory draft registration for 18-year-old men. The registration requirement had been reinstated by President Carter in January 1980, ostensibly as a response to the Soviet invasion of Afghanistan.

During the campaign Reagan had cited estimates that peacetime registration would reduce by only a few days the time needed to call up draftees in case of war. But presidential counselor Edwin Meese III cited new estimates that registration could speed the start of conscription by about six weeks.

In a statement Meese read to reporters, Reagan said the decision "does not foreshadow a return to the draft."

<hr>

plane. They also apparently approved secret amounts requested to continue development of the so-called "stealth" bomber designed to evade enemy radar. But they emphasized their opposition to gambling on the plane as a future replacement for the B-1.

The committees also approved requests for two additional Trident missile-launching submarines and for Pershing II medium-range ballistic missiles and ground-launched cruise missiles (GLCMs). The Pershings and GLCMs were designed to reach Soviet territory from Western Europe.

Naval Forces. The Armed Services panels were in general agreement with Reagan's proposed naval buildup and the goal of 600 ships, a hallmark of the administration's non-nuclear war strategy.

The heart of the administration program — a package deal for two *Nimitz*-class nuclear powered aircraft carriers ($6.795 billion) — was approved by both committees.

Modernization of the mothballed battleship *Iowa*, to be armed with cruise missiles, was approved, as was the request to modernize the battleship *Missouri*. The *New Jersey*, first of the battleships to be modernized, rejoined the fleet in 1983.

Rapid Deployment. The committees were in similar agreement on programs to equip the Rapid Deployment Force (RDF) for action in the Persian Gulf and to shift U.S. troops rapidly anywhere around the globe.

The Senate panel praised the administration for, according to the committee, shifting its emphasis to forces designed to cope with local threats to U.S. interests without relying on local basing rights, instead of concentrating on dealing with a Soviet ground invasion. A local threat was far more likely to arise, the panel said.

Ground Combat Forces. In the main the committees concurred in administration plans to equip U.S. forces to deal with the Soviet Union's huge tank divisions and its growing air attack force.

The M-1 tank, a favorite target of defense critics be-

cause of problems in earlier tests, won strong endorsement by the panels, which said the Army had mastered the earlier cost and performance problems.

Floor Action

The Senate passed the defense authorization bill on May 14 after the Armed Services Committee had turned back most serious threats to the measure.

Splitting basically along liberal-conservative lines, the Senate voted 49-45 to table an amendment by Gary Hart, D-Colo., banning production of binary munitions weapons. And by a vote of 65-29 the Senate tabled an amendment to scrap the MX missile and begin development of a missile that could more easily be protected against Soviet missile attack.

Except for the emotionally charged issue of chemical warfare, Reagan's defense programs emerged essentially unscathed during House action on the defense bill. The House version was approved July 29.

But unhappiness with defense spending was highlighted by a symbolic swipe at the overall authorization total. The House adopted a provision limiting to $175.3 billion the amount that actually could be spent under the bill — in effect a 1 percent across-the-board reduction. That cut subsequently was dropped in conference, however.

The majority of the House was unwilling to challenge specific defense programs. There appeared to be little support for the argument that the United States should not build weapons that could threaten a surprise attack on Soviet command posts and missile launchers. For example, an effort to cancel development of the Trident II submarine-launched missile was easily rejected, 89-312. A move to kill the Pershing II missile on the same grounds lost by a similar vote.

An amendment that would have removed $1.14 billion for MX production was killed by passage, 212-209, of a substitute that held up use of the money until the president had presented Congress with his new basing method. That provision was retained in the final bill. Reagan did not announce his "dense pack" basing plan until November 1982.

Republicans contributed substantially to the margin by which the House rejected an administration request for $54 million to begin production of the so-called binary munitions. An amendment by Clement J. Zablocki, D-Wis., that deleted the funds was approved by a 251-159 vote. But the real test came minutes earlier, when the House rejected, by a **192-225 key vote (R 112-72; D 80-153)**, an administration-approved substitute that would have allowed production of binary weapons if one existing chemical weapon was dismantled for each new weapon produced. The House was to repeat its action denying the binary weapons program in both 1983 and 1984. *(1982 key votes, p. 895)*

Opponents laid heavy emphasis on the argument that the 13-year-old U.S. ban on chemical weapons production provided valuable propaganda leverage, particularly in the face of evidence that the Soviet Union and its clients had used chemical weapons in Afghanistan and Southeast Asia.

Conference, Final Action

A House-Senate conference compromise on the defense authorization bill was approved by the Senate Aug. 17 and by the House Aug. 18, completing congressional action.

According to the conference report (H Rept 97-749), the request for $54 million to begin production of binary munitions was denied "without prejudice." Conferees accepted a Senate provision expressing the support of Congress for negotiations toward a "complete, effective and verifiable prohibition of the development, production and stockpiling" of chemical weapons.

For major weapons programs, the bill authorized:

● $830 million for the first five production-line MX missiles and $158 million for support equipment.

● $337.1 million of the $727.3 million requested to develop an anti-missile missile system, called LoADS, intended to protect MX missiles against Soviet missile attack. For research on more exotic anti-missile programs that might use laser-armed satellites or other "directed-energy weapons" to shoot down Soviet missiles, the bill provided $81.7 million of the $122.3 million requested.

● $1.5 billion for the 10th Trident missile-firing submarine.

● $3.9 billion as requested to begin procurement of the B-1B bomber and $753.5 million for research and development. Also approved was an additional, unspecified amount for development of the stealth bomber intended to penetrate Soviet defenses in the 1990s.

● $847.5 million to buy the first C-5B wide-body cargo plane.

● $795 million for the fiscal 1983 share of a multi-year contract to buy 44 KC-10 tanker planes and $435.6 million to continue replacing obsolete engines on some 600 Air Force KC-135 tanker planes.

● $1.56 billion to buy 855 M-1 tanks, of which $198.2 million was authorized but not spent in prior years.

● $710 million for 48 Apache (AH-64) anti-tank helicopters and $115 million for components to be used in fiscal 1984.

● $1.24 billion for the purchase of 39 F-15 fighters and $162 million for advance procurement of F-15 components; $1.711 billion for 120 F-16s and $323 million for components; and $140.6 million for two E-3A (AWACS) radar warning and command planes, along with $25.7 million for components.

● $6.795 billion for two aircraft carriers, $1.027 billion for two attack submarines, $3.1 billion for three Aegis cruisers and $323 million to modernize and recommission the battleship *Iowa*.

● $558.4 million for the purchase of 27 LAMPS III anti-submarine helicopters.

1983 Defense Appropriations

Despite growing concern about the level of defense spending in an era of mounting federal budget deficits, Congress cut only 7 percent from the president's fiscal 1983 defense budget request of $249.6 billion. Lawmakers Dec. 20 approved $232 billion for defense as part of a fiscal 1983 continuing appropriations resolution (H J Res 631 — PL 97-377).

Although the $17.585 billion defense cut was the biggest since the early 1970s, the bulk of the reduction came from routine congressional efforts to tighten bureaucratic belts. For example, a $2.3 million reduction was made in the size of the annual pay hike for Pentagon employees, an austerity measure imposed on all federal agencies.

And Congress was able to slice $833 million in fuel purchase funds, reflecting a continuing decline in petroleum prices.

Just over half the total reduction — $8.9 billion — came from weapons procurement accounts, although some of the cut came from production slowdowns rather than the cancellation of arms programs.

The bill took three major swipes at Reagan's defense program: It deleted funds for production of the MX missile and directed Reagan to come up with a better plan for basing the MX than the "dense pack" system he had proposed Nov. 22, 1982; it cut funds for production of the Pershing II missile, which was to be deployed in Western Europe beginning in December 1983; and it included provisions that were bound to irritate U.S. allies in Europe. *(Major weapons programs, arms control special report, p. 249)*

Rejection of the entire $988 million Reagan requested for MX production marked the first time Congress ever had denied production of a major nuclear weapon requested by a president. The resolution retained $2.5 billion in funds to continue development of the MX and its basing method, but $560 million of that amount could not be spent before Congress approved a specific basing method. The president was directed to recommend a basing method on or after March 1, 1983; the plan would be subject to congressional approval through adoption of a concurrent resolution under expedited procedures. *(Subsequent action, pp. 228, 231, 238, 241, 244, 245)*

Otherwise, the bill included funds for nearly all the major weapons programs requested by the president, including the B-1 bomber, one additional Trident submarine (two originally had been requested), two nuclear-powered *Nimitz*-class aircraft carriers, two *Los Angeles*-class attack submarines and reactivation of the battleship *Iowa*. One major exception was Reagan's $54 million request for production of a new family of chemical weapons, called binary munitions. That request had been denied during action on the defense authorization bill (S 2248 — PL 97-252). *(Authorization bill, p. 217)*

Legislative History

House. The House Appropriations Committee reported the fiscal 1983 defense appropriations bill (HR 7355 — H Rept 97-943) on Dec. 2. The committee recommended an appropriation of $231.1 billion, an $18 billion cut in Reagan's November revised request of $249.6 billion.

Despite the size of its reduction, the committee proposed few changes in Reagan's planned defense program. The trouble-plagued Pershing II missile was the only major weapons program for which the panel flatly refused to approve production funds. The MX survived in the committee on a 26-26 vote Dec. 2.

However, in a major symbolic defeat for the president, the full chamber on a **245-176 key vote (R 50-138; D 195-38)** Dec. 7 dropped $988 million requested to purchase the first five production-line versions of the MX. *(1982 key votes, p. 895)*

The House passed the $231 billion defense bill Dec. 8.

Senate. The $233.4 billion defense funding bill reported Sept. 23 by the Senate Appropriations Committee (S 2951 — S Rept 97-580) was about 5 percent below Reagan's request, but it funded all major weapons programs, most of them at or near the budgeted levels.

During committee action on the bill, the B-1 bomber

never was challenged, and an effort to fund only one nuclear-powered aircraft carrier, rather than two, was overwhelmingly rejected.

The Defense Subcommittee had tentatively deferred initial procurement of MX missiles but quickly reversed itself when the administration warned that such action would undermine the U.S. bargaining position in arms control talks with the U.S.S.R.

The Appropriations Committee incorporated most provisions of S 2951 into the emergency fiscal 1983 funding measure, H J Res 631. The committee included the MX procurement money in H J Res 631 but barred its expenditure until Congress approved an MX basing method by adopting a concurrent resolution.

The full Senate backed that position by a **56-42 key vote (R 41-12; D 15-30)** Dec. 17, but added language to guarantee prompt congressional action on the basing issue. As passed, H J Res 631 required action on a concurrent resolution within 45 days of the time the president submitted a report to Congress on dense pack and various alternative basing methods.

The Senate passed H J Res 631 Dec. 19.

Conference. A House-Senate compromise on defense funding, included as part of H J Res 631 (H Rept 97-980), was reached Dec. 20, and the bill was approved by both chambers the same day, completing congressional action.

Reagan's request of $3.5 billion for MX programs was the most heatedly contested defense issue in the House-Senate conference committee. The conferees accepted the House amendment deleting the $988 million that Reagan requested for production of the first five MXs. However, Congress approved $2.509 billion for research and development on the MX and its basing system. And conferees retained the Senate-passed provision requiring the president to report to Congress on his choice of a basing system on or after March 1, 1983.

A presidentially appointed commission released its report April 11, 1983, concurring with Reagan's interim basing plan to deploy the missiles in existing silos. The president endorsed the panel's recommendations. *(Details, box, p. 227)*

Conferees also adopted a Senate provision prohibiting any MX flight testing until both houses of Congress had approved expenditures for the MX basing mode.

Conferees accepted the House provision deleting $493.3 million for production of Pershing II nuclear-tipped missiles. The funds were restored in 1983, however. *(Story, p. 228)*

The final bill contained a modified version of a Senate Appropriations Committee provision limiting the number of active-duty U.S. military personnel stationed onshore in Europe to 315,600, the level authorized at the end of fiscal 1982. But the president was allowed to waive that limitation if he declared to Congress that "overriding national security requirements" made such action necessary.

The final version took several actions bound to irritate U.S. allies in Europe. For the most part, the provisions were aimed at signaling congressional dissatisfaction with the level of European defense spending, a complaint expressed in previous years. The provisions reduced U.S. funding for various NATO-related programs, implying that European nations would have to make up the difference if they wanted to retain them.

Conferees retained an existing ban on storing equipment in Europe for more than four U.S. Army divisions. The Pentagon wanted to store enough tanks and other

heavy equipment for six divisions that could be flown to Europe in case of an international crisis.

Major Weapons Funding

As signed into law Dec. 21, H J Res 631 (PL 97-377) appropriated for major weapons programs:

- $2.509 billion for research and development on the MX missile; $560 million of that amount was designated for full-scale engineering development of the basing system and could not be spent without approval by Congress.
- $4.6 billion for procurement of the first seven production-line versions of the B-1 bomber and for continued development of the plane.
- $532.2 million to modernize existing B-52 bombers.
- $548.2 million for procurement of cruise missiles.
- $1.462 billion for a 10th Trident missile-launching submarine, $633.7 million for 66 Trident I submarine missiles and $366.7 million as requested for development of the larger and more powerful Trident II.
- $1.36 billion for procurement of 855 new M-1 tanks.
- $695.3 million for 48 Apache (AH-64) anti-tank helicopters, $357.3 million for 20 A-10 anti-tank planes and $134.7 million for 12,000 TOW anti-tank guided missiles.
- $779.1 million for 376 Patriot long-range missiles and $214.6 million for 2,256 Stinger portable short-range missiles.
- $800 million to begin purchasing 50 more giant C-5 transport planes; $94 million to buy used, wide-body transports from U.S. airlines; $60 million to continue development of the C-17 wide-body transport; and $915 million for procurement of KC-10 aircraft, a version of the DC-10 jetliner modified to haul cargo and to refuel other planes in midair.
- $379.2 million to procure an additional LSD-41 class ship, designed to carry combat vehicles and landing barges to haul them ashore.
- $6.6 billion for two nuclear-powered aircraft carriers, $300.8 million to modernize the battleship *Iowa* and $2.9 billion for three cruisers intended to protect the carriers against Soviet cruise missiles.
- $1.004 billion for two *Los Angeles*-class nuclear-powered submarines designed to hunt other subs, $646.3 million for two escort frigates designed to protect convoys against submarine attack and $576.1 million for 27 Seahawk small sub-hunting helicopters (formerly called LAMPS III).
- $1.24 billion for 39 F-15 fighter planes, $1.71 billion for 120 smaller F-16s, $235.2 million for 8 A-6E bombers, $875 million for 24 F-14 fighters, $2.136 billion for 84 F-18 fighters, $702 million for 21 Harrier (vertical-takeoff bombers used by the Marine Corps) and $100 million to continue developing LANTIRN, a combined radar and infrared viewing system to allow fighters to fly low and find ground targets at night.

Nuclear Freeze

The House Aug. 5 narrowly rejected an immediate "freeze" on U.S. and Soviet nuclear weapons, a proposal strongly opposed by the Reagan administration.

Discarding a freeze resolution (H J Res 521) reported by the Foreign Affairs Committee, the House replaced it with an administration-backed substitute that linked a freeze to an agreement on arms reduction through the Strategic Arms Reduction Talks (START) proposed by President Reagan May 9.

The Senate Foreign Relations Committee also rejected the freeze proposal. Instead, the committee reported an alternative arms control resolution (S J Res 212) that called on the United States to refrain from actions that would "undercut" SALT II, the unratified Strategic Arms Limitation Treaty Reagan had opposed as a candidate for president in 1980.

S J Res 212 never reached the Senate floor, largely because the Republican leadership did not want to open up a potentially divisive debate in which the administration would come under attack both from liberals who favored the freeze and hard-line conservatives who argued that the administration was not taking a tough enough stance on strategic arms issues.

The House in 1983 adopted a milder version of the freeze resolution, which the Senate again rejected. *(1983 action, p. 230; background, arms control special report, p. 255)*

House Action

Committee. The House Foreign Affairs Committee reported H J Res 521 on July 19 (H Rept 97-640). The key vote in committee came on an amendment to incorporate the freeze concept, which was adopted 26-11. The language in the resolution said the United States and the Soviet Union "should immediately begin the strategic arms reduction talks" having the following objectives:

- "Pursuing a complete halt to the nuclear arms race";
- "Deciding when and how to achieve a mutual verifiable freeze on the testing, production and further deployment of nuclear warheads, missiles and other delivery systems";
- "Giving special attention to destabilizing weapons whose deployment would make such a freeze more difficult to achieve";
- "Proceeding from this mutual and verifiable freeze, pursuing substantial, equitable and verifiable reductions" in the U.S. and Soviet arsenals.

The committee majority said it based its support for a freeze on the assumption that "nuclear parity presently describes the overall nuclear balance between the two superpowers." The majority rejected the administration's position that Moscow had a dangerous margin of superiority in land-based intercontinental ballistic missiles (ICBMs). The larger and more powerful Soviet missile force was offset by U.S. advantages in long-range bombers and submarine-launched missiles, the committee asserted.

H J Res 521 stipulated that the freeze-oriented START talks should give special attention to destabilizing weapons. In its report the panel described such destabilizing weapons as "those which have the capability of destroying the other side's strategic nuclear weapons, thereby reducing confidence in their deterrent value."

The committee declared that "testing and deployment of Soviet systems can be effectively verified by U.S. national technical means" (reconnaissance satellites and other electronic intelligence equipment that did not require the cooperation of the country being spied on). But committee members noted that Soviet agreement to allow on-site inspection of alleged freeze violations would improve the verifiability of a freeze.

The majority rejected the administration's contention that unless development of new weapons continued, particularly the MX missile and B-1 bomber, the Soviets

would not have any incentive to agree to reduce their nuclear arsenal.

Floor. The House passed H J Res 521 Aug. 5 after substituting an administration-backed alternative for the committee-approved freeze proposal. The House adopted the substitute, sponsored by William S. Broomfield, R-Mich., by a **204-202 key vote (R 151-27; D 53-175)**. *(1982 key votes, p. 895)*

Although both versions were ambiguous, the committee's language called for "a mutual [and] verifiable" freeze, to be followed by arms reductions; the GOP substitute, on the other hand, implicitly rejected the need for an immediate freeze and instead proposed an arms freeze, at "equal and substantially reduced levels," to be realized through Reagan's START negotiations with the U.S.S.R.

Confidence in the administration's commitment to serious arms control negotiations, more than the merits of any specific U.S. arms policy, was the central theme of the debate over H J Res 521. Widespread public concern over the pace of Reagan's negotiations with the Soviets had boosted the freeze movement to national prominence in the first place. And by accounts on both sides of the freeze debate, the administration's most effective argument in winning over the last few votes for the GOP substitute was the argument that a freeze would jeopardize arms reduction talks between the superpowers.

House Minority Leader Robert H. Michel, R-Ill., said he had never seen a legislative issue "so clouded by emotion, so fraught with danger, so unexamined in its consequences, so seemingly plausible, so attractive on the surface, yet so surely wrong and so ultimately deadly to our national survival as H J Res 521."

In addition to the Broomfield substitute, other major amendments considered during the debate involved efforts by freeze backers to widen the resolution's appeal among House members. For example, amendments were adopted that loosened the resolution's link with the unratified SALT II agreement prepared by the Carter administration; reaffirmed the need for "equivalence in overall nuclear capabilities"; added a section providing that, consistent with the "overriding objective of an immediate freeze," the resolution did not preclude the United States from pursuing other "complementary" arms control proposals; and emphasized that negotiators, in giving special attention in the START talks to destabilizing weapons, should focus on weapons already deployed, such as the Soviet ICBMs, in addition to those still on the drawing board, such as the U.S. MX and Trident II missiles.

Over the opposition of some freeze sponsors, the House approved another amendment adding to the list of goals for START "providing for cooperative measures of verification, including provision for on-site inspection."

Senate Action

The Senate Foreign Relations Committee rejected a freeze proposal in July. Instead, the panel on July 12 reported a resolution (S J Res 212 — S Rept 97-493) giving the force of law to the policy that the United States "shall not . . . undercut" the restrictions embodied in the unratified 1979 SALT II treaty. The administration opposed the mandatory character of the resolution, although Reagan May 31 announced that the United States would not undercut the terms of the treaty. Reagan insisted he did not want to be legally bound by the treaty, but he never spelled out the provisions from which the administration desired

some relief. Administration officials said the committee resolution went far beyond their position on SALT II.

In its report the committee majority praised the nuclear freeze movement "for catalyzing public debate throughout the United States on arms control." But it then listed various reasons why it rejected an arms freeze as a policy. Some questioned the verifiability of a freeze. Others worried that it would set in concrete the existing Soviet monopoly on long-range, land-based nuclear missiles. However, the report did not specifically endorse the administration's contention that the Soviets currently enjoyed superiority in land-based missiles.

The resolution called for a START agreement to be negotiated and ratified in at least two stages. The first would require reductions in the number of missiles held by both countries; the second would cover missile "throw-weight," or warhead capacity.

Pending negotiation of a START treaty, the resolution stipulated that the United States "shall continue to refrain from actions which would undercut the SALT I and SALT II agreements, provided the Soviet Union shows equal restraint." The committee rejected, on a 7-10 vote, a Democratic-sponsored amendment that would have added the gist of the freeze proposal.

There was no further action in 1982 on the freeze measure.

1983 Military Construction

The 1982 debate on military construction legislation focused, as in 1981, on congressional efforts to pressure U.S. allies to pay more of the cost of the common defense.

Congress appropriated slightly more than $7 billion for military construction projects for fiscal 1983 in legislation (HR 6968 — PL 97-323) cleared Oct. 1. The funds, about $1 billion less than the president requested, had been authorized in a separate bill (S 2586 — PL 97-321) cleared Sept. 29.

The Reagan administration — like the Carter administration before it — generally agreed with Congress that U.S. allies in Europe and Japan ought to carry more of the burden of common defense. But the Reagan team resisted congressional efforts to deny funds for projects that one or another of the congressional defense committees thought should be funded by America's allies.

NATO Construction. Despite the sentiment on Capitol Hill that the Europeans were not bearing their fair share of defense costs, Congress agreed to authorize improvements at NATO airfields and military facilities in West Germany.

The authorization measure included $28 million for aircraft parking ramps and supply dumps at six European-owned airfields that would harbor U.S. combat planes flown to the continent as wartime reinforcements. But in the appropriations measure Congress rejected the request and said NATO should pay for the improvements.

Congress, however, included $37.2 million for projects at Vilseck and Wildflecken in West Germany, where the U.S. Army planned to move three combat battalions that were stationed about a hundred miles farther back from the East German and Czechoslovakian borders.

The House had insisted that West Germany pay for this re-stationing plan. The final version of the authorization measure took basically the same position as the Senate, authorizing the requested money but barring its ex-

penditure until the United States and West Germany reached a cost-sharing agreement.

In the construction appropriations bill, Congress insisted that before the $26.5 million budgeted for Vilseck could be spent, the Pentagon would have to notify the Appropriations panels that West Germany had agreed to "substantially assume the cost of the restationing plan."

MX Missile Construction. Congress denied funds for construction of any basing plan for the MX intercontinental ballistic missile. It authorized only $40 million of the $207 million related to construction of a deployment method. The $40 million was for testing and supply facilities that would be required regardless of the basing method selected for the new missile.

The related appropriations bill further reduced the MX figure to $16.7 million. Those funds were for logistic facilities at Newark, Ohio, and Hill Air Force Base in Utah. Both would be needed to service the missile no matter how it was based.

Honduras Airfield. To extend the runway and build storage facilities at the airfield in Comayagua, Honduras, Congress approved $13 million. An additional $8 million for similar improvements at another Honduras airfield was authorized, but that appropriation was deferred until 1983. Under an agreement with Honduras concluded May 7, 1983, U.S. forces would be entitled to use the bases in return for the improvements. *(U.S. military activities in Honduras, box, p. 176)*

Persian Gulf, Rapid Deployment Force. Congress indicated its support for U.S. efforts to develop military options in the Persian Gulf region, funding all projects sought by the administration. Congress, however, complained in the construction authorization bill that "neither our NATO allies nor Japan, who import 70 percent of their oil from the Persian Gulf, have taken sufficient steps to support facility construction in the region or to develop other types of offsets to the large U.S. investment."

In contrast to the support for reinforcing the U.S. presence in the Persian Gulf, Congress sharply pared back the administration's plans for facilities at Ras Banas, a port at the southern end of Egypt's Red Sea coast. Lawmakers approved $91 million of the $125.6 million requested for Air Force facilities and none of the $53 million requested for Army facilities. The Pentagon wanted to use the site as a staging area and supply base for ground and air forces flown from the United States as part of the Rapid Deployment Force (RDF).

Deletion of the funds marked the third congressional setback for the Ras Banas plan in two years. In the fiscal 1982 military construction appropriations bill (PL 97-106), Congress rejected all but $14.3 million of the $120.7 million requested for facilities at Ras Banas. The Ras Banas money also was eliminated from the fiscal 1982 supplemental appropriations bill (PL 97-257) cleared by Congress Aug. 20. In 1983 Congress dropped funding for the project because the administration said the plans had fallen through. *(Story, p. 232)*

Congress denied a request for new facilities at the air base at Lajes in the Portuguese-owned Azores Islands because negotiations with Lisbon over U.S. rights to use the base had not been completed.

Authorization

As cleared Sept. 29, S 2586 cut $33.6 million from the requested fiscal 1983 authorization of $7.8 billion by apply-ing an 8.5 percent across-the-board cut to the total authorization of each service (excluding their family housing accounts).

Senate Action. The Senate passed S 2586 June 30, making no significant change in the version of the bill reported by its Armed Services Committee May 27 (S Rept 97-440).

The committee, as part of its effort to cut Reagan's overall defense budget by 5 percent, reduced the Pentagon's construction budget by nearly 20 percent. The panel approved $6.4 billion of Reagan's $7.8 billion request.

More than half of the $1.4 billion reduction came from two decisions deferring whole categories of projects deemed not essential to combat readiness.

The committee also shaved more than $300 million from the request because of policy disagreements with the administration. About $70 million of that cut reflected a growing congressional insistence that U.S. allies in Europe and Japan offset more of the cost of defending alliance interests in Europe and the Persian Gulf region.

Another $167 million was cut from the request for construction related to the MX missile because of Congress' rejection of the administration's plan to put the first 40 MXs in existing missile silos.

House Action. The House version of the bill, reported by the Armed Services Committee May 17 (HR 6214 — H Rept 97-525), recommended several program reductions or deferrals that had a common theme: avoiding expenditures on construction that might have to be abandoned because of possible policy changes by the United States or its allies. However, the committee did approve the requested $375 million annual U.S. contribution to the NATO fund for constructing facilities of mutual benefit. Before passing the bill Aug. 11, the House rejected an amendment to withhold the U.S. contribution by a vote of 151-245.

The bill as passed authorized $7,515,167,000 for Pentagon construction projects, including $18.3 million for a plant to manufacture binary munitions. Those funds subsequently were dropped from the construction appropriations bill and from the fiscal 1983 defense authorization bill.

Final Action. House-Senate conferees filed their report Sept. 28 (H Rept 97-880). The Senate approved the conference report the same day, and the House cleared it Sept. 29.

Appropriations

Congressional efforts to pressure U.S. allies to pay more of the cost of the common defense were turned up another notch during debate on HR 6968, the $7 billion military construction appropriations bill for fiscal 1983.

Besides paring the Ras Banas base funds, the bill barred use of any funds until the secretary of defense certified that negotiations were under way seeking support from Japan and the NATO allies for the U.S. military buildup in the Persian Gulf region.

Congress also refused to finance some airfield improvements in Europe, which the Air Force insisted were vital but which lawmakers said should be paid for by NATO.

Congress approved funds requested to restation U.S. troops in West Germany. But it barred use of those funds until the Bonn government agreed to pay for most of the relocation costs.

The House Appropriations Committee reported HR 6968 Aug. 11 (H Rept 97-726). The full chamber passed the bill Aug. 19, after rejecting an amendment that would have reduced appropriations in the bill by 30.8 percent.

The Senate Appropriations Committee reported its version of HR 6968 Sept. 22 (S Rept 97-572). The Senate passed the bill Sept. 27.

The committee complained that the Pentagon was sacrificing needed construction projects to protect weapons programs, which were covered in the separate Defense Department appropriations bill for fiscal 1983, in the face of congressional insistence on budget cuts.

The administration had offered to give up $1.4 billion of its $8.2 billion military construction request during negotiations with Congress on budget cuts for fiscal 1983. But, the Appropriations Committee warned, "without the docks for the ships, without the runways and hangars for the planes, without the maintenance facilities for wheeled and tracked vehicles, and without the launching sites for missiles, all of the funds spent on these systems would be of no use."

A House-Senate conference compromise on HR 6968 (H Rept 97-913), reached Sept. 30, appropriated $7.043 billion for military construction projects, including the construction and operation of military family housing units. The final amount was $1.17 billion less than President Reagan's request.

Both houses gave the bill final approval on Oct. 1.

Arms Agency Authority

After a year in limbo, legislation authorizing funds for the Arms Control and Disarmament Agency (ACDA) was cleared by Congress Oct. 1.

The bill (HR 3467 — PL 97-339) authorized $18,268,000 in fiscal 1982 and $19,893,852 in fiscal 1983 for ACDA. The final bill incorporated a provision sought by the administration allowing the arms control agency to accept security clearances awarded by the departments of State and Defense for officials of those agencies who were temporarily assigned to ACDA. Existing law required the Office of Personnel Management to conduct full-scale security investigations of such persons, regardless of any clearances they already held — a process that could take months.

The bill also incorporated a Senate-passed provision, sponsored by Larry Pressler, R-S.D., adding anti-satellite activities to the list of arms control problems the agency should study. The Soviet Union reportedly already had — and the United States was developing — a limited capability to destroy space satellites on which the other superpower relied for military communication and warning of enemy attack.

A House-passed provision that would have dropped the word "disarmament" from the agency's name was not included in the final version of the bill. The Foreign Affairs Committee had advocated the change to remove what the panel called an "inaccurate and unfounded impression that the agency was in some way involved in unilateral disarmament at the expense of our national security."

Legislative History

The bill was reported (H Rept 97-55) May 19, 1981, and passed by the House June 8, 1981. The bill authorized $1.5 million more for the agency in fiscal 1982 than the administration had requested.

The Senate Foreign Relations Committee reported an amended version on May 26, 1982 (S Rept 97-430). The panel retained the House-passed authorization levels, but dropped the name change and added the Pressler amendment on anti-satellite activities.

In its report the committee complained that ACDA was the only federal agency dealing with national security policy whose budget was going down under the Reagan administration.

The Senate passed HR 3467 without further amendment Oct. 1. The House accepted the Senate amendments Oct. 1, thus clearing the bill for the president.

Military Pay

Congress in 1982 failed to pass legislation dealing specifically with military pay, but most pay issues were handled in other defense bills or by the administration under terms negotiated with Congress. Moreover, Reagan already had the authority to initiate pay hikes for military and civilian employees, so legislation was not absolutely required.

After proposing raises of 8 percent for military employees and 5 percent for civilian employees in fiscal 1983, Reagan and Congress agreed to across-the-board federal raises of only 4 percent.

Military pay had been raised by 11.4 percent in fiscal 1981 and by an average of 14.3 percent in fiscal 1982. *(1981 bill, p. 214)*

The House Armed Services Committee reported a pay bill (HR 6317 — H Rept 97-552) May 17, but the full chamber on Sept. 22 failed to pass the bill. A redrafted version (HR 7166) was approved Sept. 29.

Both bills would have extended through fiscal 1987 the Pentagon's authority to continue paying enlistment and re-enlistment bonuses. The bonus authority had been scheduled to expire Oct. 1, but it was extended by a stopgap fiscal 1983 continuing appropriations measure (H J Res 631 — PL 97-377).

The Senate never acted on a military pay raise bill (S 2936 — S Rept 97-565) reported by its Armed Services Committee on Sept. 21.

Joint Chiefs Reorganization

Legislation aimed at giving the chairman of the Joint Chiefs of Staff (JCS) a stronger hand in challenging the parochial interests of the armed services was passed by the House in 1982, but the bill (HR 6954) died in the Senate.

The House passed a similar bill (HR 3718) in 1983, but again the Senate did not act. *(Story, p. 233)*

Senate Armed Services Committee Chairman John Tower, R-Texas, displayed little enthusiasm for proposals to reorganize the Joint Chiefs. His committee held hearings but took no steps to draft legislation on the issue.

The five-member Joint Chiefs of Staff consisted of a chairman and the head of each of the four services — the chiefs of staff of the Army and Air Force, the chief of naval operations and the Marine Corps commandant.

Strictly speaking, the JCS did not command U.S. forces in the field. All combat units were organized into nine major commands, to which the Joint Chiefs merely

transmitted orders from the secretary of defense.

Six of these were "unified" commands, which included components from more than one armed service, such as the European command. The other three major commands, called "specified" commands, were Air Force units: the Strategic Air Command, the Military Airlift Command and the Aerospace Defense Command.

The Joint Chiefs' incentive to bargain in search of unanimity in their recommendations came from the fact that, by law, they had to report to the secretary of defense any issue on which they could not reach agreement.

Congressional debate on the question of reorganizing the military hierarchy had been prompted by former JCS Chairman Gen. David C. Jones, who was Air Force chief of staff from 1974 to 1978 and JCS chairman from 1978 until the end of June 1982. Jones had spent most of his last five months in office campaigning for reorganization of the Joint Chiefs.

Jones' thesis was that the JCS organization too often made policy by accommodating the bureaucratic interests of the individual services. He proposed several steps to strengthen the hand of the JCS chairman — the only member of the group not simultaneously responsible for heading one of the military branches.

House Action

The Armed Services Committee reported HR 6954 (H Rept 97-744) on Aug. 12, and the House passed the measure Aug. 16. Although the bill was intended to strengthen the role of the JCS chairman, it stopped short of Jones' proposal to correspondingly reduce the clout of the individual services in deliberations on issues of fundamental policy.

The bill expressly authorized the Joint Chiefs chairman to provide military advice "in his own right" to the president and secretary of defense. It also created the post of deputy chairman, to be filled by a full general or full admiral from a service other than the chairman's.

The Joint Staff was charged by the bill with assisting the chairman, as well as the Joint Chiefs as a corporate body. And the measure directed the secretary of defense to organize the Joint Staff to ensure its independence and its effectiveness in helping the Joint Chiefs provide unified strategic direction and operation of U.S. forces under unified command.

But the bill left untouched the existing ban on the Joint Staff's functioning as a "general staff" in overall direction of the armed forces.

Nuclear Weapons Programs

Congress in 1982 failed to complete action on legislation authorizing fiscal 1983 funding for nuclear weapons programs carried out by the Energy Department.

The House passed its version of the authorization bill (HR 6329 — H Rept 97-551) Dec. 1, but the Senate did not act on a companion bill reported by the Senate Armed Services Committee on Aug. 5 (S 2812 — S Rept 97-517).

Appropriations for the Energy Department weapons programs were included in a fiscal 1983 continuing appropriations resolution (H J Res 631 — PL 97-377).

In its report on S 2812, the Senate committee challenged the contention of many proponents of a nuclear weapons "freeze" that the U.S. nuclear arsenal had steadily increased over the years and would increase further under Reagan. *(Freeze background, p. 255)*

Though the specific number of nuclear weapons in the U.S. stockpile at any time was secret, the committee said it had peaked in the mid-1960s at "a few tens of thousands of weapons." Despite some fluctuations, the overall trend in stockpile size had been downward since then.

1983

Two broad themes dominated the 1983 congressional debate on defense policy: the pace and scope of Ronald Reagan's planned military buildup and the administration's nuclear weapons policy.

The major outlines of Reagan's original policies remained intact. Nevertheless, by year's end, defense hard-liners lamented that Reagan had yielded on crucial points in battles over both issues.

The president's request for a fiscal 1984 defense budget 10 percent larger than the fiscal 1983 amount in "real" terms — that is, in addition to the cost of inflation — was trimmed by Congress to a 5 percent real increase. By the time it finished action on the fiscal 1984 appropriations bills, Congress actually had provided a real increase of about 4 percent — a reduction from the January budget request by about $18 billion.

Under intense pressure at home from a Congress threatening to kill production of the MX intercontinental ballistic missile and abroad from European allies apprehensive about his confrontational style, Reagan recast his major arms control offers to Moscow so they would require less sweeping reductions in existing Soviet forces.

Overall, however, the president gained much more than he lost on nuclear issues during the year. The B-1 bomber, the Pershing II intermediate-range missile and several versions of the cruise missile handily won congressional approval. Congress also endorsed initial production of the controversial MX, despite a close shave in the House. The administration's only major defeat — and it was more symbolic than substantive — was the House's adoption of a resolution calling for a mutual and verifiable freeze on and reduction in nuclear weapons.

Along with the victories in Congress, there was a definite shift in the administration's rhetoric on nuclear arms issues. The hard-nosed willingness to talk of "protracted" nuclear wars in which the United States would try to "prevail" was replaced by discussion of nuclear war only as something to be deterred at all cost.

The change in rhetoric was accompanied by a search for political allies on nuclear arms issues in the political center and in Washington's bipartisan defense establishment, which Reagan had come to office condemning for having presided over a decline in U.S. power.

In contrast to the budget struggle, which was resolved for all practical purposes by early summer, the confrontation over nuclear arms continued throughout the session.

1984 Defense Authorization

Even before powerful anti-Soviet sentiments were aroused by the Soviet destruction of a South Korean passenger jet on Sept. 1, Congress was firmly on the road

toward approving a fiscal 1984 defense authorization bill (S 675 — PL 98-94) that retained the overall shape of President Reagan's military buildup. The $187.5 billion bill, which had been drafted at the start of the August recess, was approved in mid-September by hefty margins. The final authorization was $10.5 billion less than Reagan had requested.

The measure included hotly disputed authorizations for the MX missile and a new type of lethal chemical weapon. Funds for the nerve gas project, however, subsequently were rejected by Congress. (Appropriations, p. 229)

House Action

In reporting the defense authorization bill May 11 (HR 2969 — H Rept 98-107), the House Armed Services Committee allocated $4.54 billion to begin procurement of MX missiles and $250 million to start work on a much smaller, single-warhead intercontinental ballistic missile (ICBM) that could be deployed in the 1990s. In approving research on the smaller missile, the committee accepted the recommendation of a White House advisory commission, chaired by former presidential adviser Brent Scowcroft.

The Scowcroft panel, in a report made public April 11, linked MX deployment to a long-term arms control policy aimed at a more stable nuclear balance through abolition of large, multi-warhead missiles, such as the MX and Soviet ICBMs. (Commission report highlights, box, p. 227)

The Armed Services Committee praised the Scowcroft commission's linkage of "modernization of our ICBM force and arms control. In a democracy, such linkage is a critical ingredient to developing and maintaining a public consensus in support of such efforts."

The committee underscored its insistence that the administration pursue the entire Scowcroft package — not just the MX deployment — by barring the use of any funds authorized for MX until the Pentagon submitted a detailed schedule for development and deployment of the proposed small missile.

The administration's $6.18 billion procurement request for the B-1 bomber program was approved by the committee without change. The authorization covered the purchase of 10 planes with spare parts and components for planes scheduled for purchase in fiscal 1985.

The bill included a secret amount for development of the "stealth" bomber to be designed to evade detection by Soviet radar.

Reflecting a change in Pentagon plans, the committee authorized $464 million for 240 air-launched cruise missiles (called ALCM-Bs), designed to be fired from B-1s and existing B-52 bombers. In January the Pentagon had planned no further production of the ALCM-B, partly because of its potential vulnerability to a new Soviet anti-aircraft missile, called the SA-10. But in April the Pentagon decided to continue ALCM-B production for at least one more year as a hedge against any major problems that might arise in developing a second-generation cruise missile.

For the 11th in a class of submarines designed to fire Trident missiles, the committee authorized $1.45 billion. Also approved without change were the requests to purchase the final increment of Trident I missiles and to continue development of the larger Trident II missile.

More than $1 billion was approved without change for 95 Pershing II and 120 ground-launched cruise missiles

designed to reach Soviet territory from launchers in Western Europe.

The committee approved only $238 million of the $538.4 million requested to develop a "conventional" anti-ballistic missile (ABM) system — one using anti-missile missiles instead of more exotic technologies such as laser beams. The panel approved essentially the amount requested to develop various kinds of lasers and other "directed-energy" weapons that might be used for the kind of countrywide ABM defense — popularly labeled "Star Wars" — Reagan called for in a March 23 televised address. (Box, p. 253)

In other actions, the committee authorized 840 additional M-1 tanks instead of the 720 tanks requested. The committee approved without change the number of Navy and Marine combat planes requested, 22 of the 23 ships requested for the Navy and several air- and sea-lift programs intended to speed the movement of U.S. combat units abroad.

The House passed a $187.4 billion fiscal 1984 defense authorization bill in the session that began July 26 by a vote of 305-114. Passage came on the eighth day of a debate that spanned more than two months, largely because of delays occasioned by the politics of the MX missile issue and by strong objections to chemical warfare funding.

For the second year in a row, the House rejected a Reagan administration effort to begin production of binary munitions. It approved, 256-161, an amendment deleting $114.6 million to gear up for production of binary chemical weapons or their components. On the deciding vote of the battle, nerve gas opponents won by a much narrower margin. A proposal that would have retained the binary munitions authorization in the bill was rejected 202-216.

As it had done each year since Reagan revived the B-1 bomber in 1981, the House backed production of the plane by a hefty margin, rejecting by 164-255 an amendment that would have deleted procurement funds. Also defeated was an amendment that would have denied $19.4 million to begin buying parts for a missile that would be launched from F-15 fighter planes to destroy low-flying Soviet space satellites. A move to delete all funds for the Pershing II similarly was rejected.

Senate Action

In reporting its version of the authorization bill July 5 (S 675 — S Rept 98-174), the Senate Armed Services Committee authorized $4.6 billion to deploy 100 MXs in existing missile silos, as recommended by the Scowcroft commission, which also called on the administration to develop a new, small single-warhead missile for future deployment. The authorization approved would buy 27 MXs and continue development of the smaller missile.

The committee approved requests for air-launched cruise missiles, an 11th Trident submarine, Trident II missiles, Pershing II missiles, ground-launched cruise missiles and most of the Navy's shipbuilding budget.

The panel trimmed $227 million from the request for M-1 tanks and adjusted the planned procurement rates of several Navy and Air Force combat planes.

When the bill came to the Senate, Reagan's plan for the MX retained its numerically comfortable but politically tenuous Senate majority. A motion to delete the MX procurement authorization was rejected 41-58.

The administration's closest shave on a major weapons issue came on an amendment to delete $131 million ear-

Scowcroft Panel Backs MX, Midgetman

An influential endorsement for developing the controversial MX intercontinental missile was given April 11, 1983, when a presidential commission recommended that the United States build 100 of the huge nuclear weapons and deploy them in existing missile silos.

The blue-ribbon panel urged the Pentagon to begin developing a new, smaller missile that could become the keystone of a radical new approach to stabilizing the nuclear balance between U.S. and Soviet nuclear forces.

President Reagan appointed the commission Jan. 3, after Congress in December 1982 turned down the administration's "dense pack" MX basing proposal.

Similarly, the Carter administration had been unable to gain congressional approval of its plan to base the MX in a "race track" configuration covering hundreds of miles in lightly populated areas of the West. *(Congress and the Nation Vol. V, p. 156)*

Chaired by Brent Scowcroft, former national security adviser to Presidents Nixon and Ford, the President's Commission on Strategic Forces was made up of 10 members and seven "senior consultants," including four former secretaries of defense and two former secretaries of state. Efforts were made to devise a politically acceptable plan for deploying the 100-ton, multi-warhead missile.

President Reagan April 19 endorsed the plan as "absolutely essential both for maintaining an effective deterrent [to a Soviet attack] and for achieving successful arms reductions." Congress approved the recommendations in May.

Report Highlights

The Scowcroft commission acknowledged that silo-based MXs would be as vulnerable to Soviet missiles as the Minuteman missiles housed in silos. So after nearly a decade in which the public debate over MX had been dominated by the search for a basing method invulnerable to Soviet attack, Reagan's advisory commission abandoned the argument for MX as being a more "survivable" successor to Minuteman.

Instead, it justified MX on grounds of its military potency and political symbolism — as a counterweight to several hundred existing Soviet missiles, some with even more destructive power than MX. With 10 warheads, more accurate and potentially more powerful than the three warheads on the existing Minuteman III missile, MX was designed to destroy armored underground targets, such as command centers and silos housing intercontinental ballistic missiles (ICBMs).

By most estimates, some 600 Soviet ICBMs, carrying 6-10 warheads each, possessed such so-called "hard-target kill capability."

The proposed small, single-warhead U.S. missile — dubbed "Midgetman" — would deal with the survivability problem over the long run, the commission argued. Because the new missile would weigh about 30,000 pounds — compared with 192,000 pounds for MX — its launchers could be made to be much more mobile than MX launchers, thus thwarting a Soviet attack.

As a third component of its package, linked to Midgetman, the panel held out the hope of inducing Moscow to join the United States in gradually shifting land-based missile forces to single-warhead weapons. The commission said this would restore a degree of stability to the nuclear balance that had been lost with the advent of missiles that could carry accurate MIRVs — multiple warheads.

It was widely agreed that accurate MIRVs made the strategic balance "unstable" because, while both superpowers owned roughly similar numbers of missiles, MIRVs conferred at least a theoretical advantage to whichever side fired its missiles first. Because each attacking multiple-warhead missile could destroy several of the opponent's not-yet-launched missiles, an aggressor could obliterate his opponent's missile force while retaining most of his own missiles.

The commission said its plan would cost $19.9 billion through fiscal 1988, compared with an estimated $22.9 billion for dense pack. (Amounts were in fiscal 1982 dollars.)

Hill Reaction

By divorcing MX from the quest for ICBM survivability, the commission forced out of the closet what long had been a key issue among defense and arms control specialists: whether the United States needed missiles that were militarily and symbolically equivalent to the Soviets'.

Rather than bog down in discussions of basing methods, the commission argued for MX using the public position taken by administrations since at least 1974: Deterrence of Soviet aggression depended on the technical plausibility of a U.S. attack that would disrupt Soviet military power without causing so many civilian casualties that retaliation against U.S. cities would be inevitable.

Only MX offered that plausibility, the commission said. It argued in addition that "Canceling the MX when it is ready for flight testing, when over $5 billion have already been spent on it, and when its importance has been stressed by our last four presidents, does not communicate to the Soviets that we have the will essential to deterrence," the panel warned. "Quite the contrary."

marked for production of binary chemical munitions. A motion to table the amendment was agreed to on a **50-49 key vote (R 35-17; D 14-32)**. Vice President George Bush, exercising his constitutional role as president of the Senate, cast the tie-breaking vote July 13 after the senators present tied 49-49. Bush was to do so again on Nov. 8 — once more breaking a tie to save nerve gas funding — during debate on the defense appropriations bill. *(Story, p. 229; 1983 key votes, p. 911)*

As in the House, the B-1 bomber easily survived an attempt to kill the plane. The Senate rejected, 68-30, an amendment to delete the $6.9 billion earmarked for procurement of 10 bombers and further development of the plane.

The Senate passed the bill July 26.

Conference Action

House-Senate conferees reached agreement (S Rept 98-213) Aug. 15. The final bill authorized $10.5 billion less than Reagan's $198 billion defense request but left it up to the Pentagon to allocate nearly 15 percent of the cuts.

Conferees tried to mollify House opponents of the binary munitions program by barring final assembly of the nerve gas shells before Oct. 1, 1985, to give U.S. and Soviet negotiators two years to seek a ban on the weapons. Conferees also adopted a provision requiring that one existing chemical shell be scrapped for each new one produced.

Opponents were not appeased and they would try to defeat the conference report in the House. But when the House took up the conference report Sept. 15, supporters insisted the bill needed a strong "yea" vote to reinforce a resolution adopted the day before that condemned the Soviet Union for downing a South Korean airliner. The conference report was easily adopted, 266-152, completing congressional action.

Nerve gas opponents made no effort to beat the conference report in the Senate, which approved the bill Sept. 13 by an 83-8 vote.

The final bill authorized $2.1 billion to purchase 21 MX missiles. To begin development of the new small missile and various technologies that might be used in its basing method, conferees approved $604 million.

The bill authorized $6.2 billion for procurement of 10 B-1 bombers and a classified amount to continue development of the stealth bomber. The bill contained a Senate-passed provision barring the Pentagon from diverting any of the classified bomber funds to other projects.

Other provisions authorized:

● $1.4 billion for the 11th Trident submarine, $587.2 million for 52 Trident I missiles and $1.5 billion for development of the larger and more accurate Trident II missile.

● $407 million for 95 Pershing II missiles and $563.8 million for 120 ground-launched cruise missiles. (Also included was an authorization to purchase 124 seaborne versions of the missile, called the Tomahawk.)

● $1.35 billion for 840 M-1 tanks; $1.2 billion for 112 AH-64 Apache helicopters and $17.8 million for components to be used in Cobra helicopters, both to be armed with laser-guided Hellfire and anti-tank missiles, and $75 million to purchase Copperhead laser-guided artillery shells for the Army.

● $122.5 million to develop an airborne radar to locate enemy tanks and $80.1 million to develop missiles equipped with dozens of warheads designed to home in on tanks.

● $200 million for anti-aircraft missiles to protect U.S. air bases in Europe.

● $1.7 billion for three nuclear-powered, submarine-hunting subs, $57.7 million for components to modernize a third battleship and equip it with cruise missiles and $447 million for 21 LAMPS III sub-hunting helicopters.

● $1.3 billion for 36 Air Force F-15s, $2.3 billion for 144 F-16s, $2.3 billion for 84 F-18 Navy fighters, $792 million for 24 F-14s, $435 million for 8 A-6E electronic warfare planes and $777 million for 27 AV-8B Harriers (small, vertical-takeoff jet bombers).

● $1.3 billion to buy 50 C-5 transport planes, $759 million to buy 44 KC-10 midair refueling tankers, $27 million to continue development of the C-17 transport plane, $100 million to modify commercial airliners for rapid conversion to haul military cargo in wartime, $1.5 billion for a large helicopter carrier ship that could haul 2,000 Marines, $327 million for a smaller ship designed to carry the Marines' tanks, combat vehicles and landing barges, and $182 million for future purchases of the ship.

The bill authorized a 4 percent pay raise for all Pentagon civilian workers and military personnel except recruits in their first four months of service. The bill established an office of weapons testing that would have authority to approve or disapprove any plan for operational testing of a new weapon.

1984 Defense Appropriations

Congress Nov. 18 approved a fiscal 1984 defense appropriations bill (HR 4185 — PL 98-212) containing $249.8 billion in new budget authority to continue President Reagan's defense buildup and most of the major weapons programs backed by the administration.

While the final appropriation was $11.1 billion below Reagan's revised budget request, it was $17.3 billion above the fiscal 1983 level. That was roughly a 4 percent increase, after adjustment for inflation.

Reagan's January budget request called for a "real," or inflation-adjusted, growth rate of 10 percent in defense funding.

The reductions made in HR 4185 were distributed across the board without imposing fundamental changes in Reagan defense policy. In addition to providing $2.1 billion to prepare the first 21 MX missiles and $2 billion to continue development of the missile, the bill earmarked $407.7 million to procure 95 intermediate-range Pershing II missiles. Under a 1979 NATO decision, the first nine Pershing IIs were to be deployed in West Germany in December 1983.

The administration justified the MX and Pershing missiles by arguing that the Soviet Union would give up its monopoly of similar weapons only when faced with the prospect of a matching U.S. deployment.

For more than a year, political support for the MX had dimmed steadily on Capitol Hill, partly in reaction to a seeming lack of urgency by the Reagan administration in its approach to nuclear arms control negotiations with Moscow. But the political threat to MX faded. For one thing, members wanted to take a tougher anti-Soviet stance in the wake of the destruction of a South Korean airliner by Soviet forces Sept. 1, 1983. Moreover, Reagan struck a more conciliatory arms control tone in 1983, partly as a result of negotiations with a bipartisan congressional group that demanded a more flexible arms negotiating

posture as the price for its support of MX. *(MX, arms control, story, p. 249; Korean airliner, p. 169)*

Also contained in the final bill was $279 million to develop Midgetman, a small, single-warhead intercontinental ballistic missile (ICBM), and $75 million to develop an armored mobile launcher for Midgetman.

House Action

The House Appropriations Committee cut $14 billion out of President Reagan's request of $261 billion for programs funded in the fiscal 1984 defense appropriations bill. Viewed from the standpoint of the administration's defense policy, the cuts were mostly marginal. Major programs were trimmed but not reshaped in the bill reported Oct. 20 (H Rept 98-427).

The committee voted to restrain two controversial new weapons proposals despite administration contentions that they were needed to offset similar Soviet arms. Dropped from the bill were $19.4 million to begin production of antisatellite missiles and $61.5 million to set up production lines for binary chemical munitions.

The panel, though, refused to block the Pershing II or MX missile programs, both of which stood at the center of the battle over U.S. nuclear arms policy. An attempt to delete all funds in the bill for procurement of the Pershing was easily defeated, but the MX ran into substantial opposition in the committee. An amendment by Defense Subcommittee Chairman Joseph P. Addabbo, D-N.Y., to cut the entire $2.1 billion in HR 4185 to procure the first 21 of the expensive intercontinental missiles was rejected by only a six-vote margin, 23-29.

The committee also approved a provision that would bar after April 1, 1984, any U.S.-funded covert military operations against the government of Nicaragua unless a U.S. intelligence agencies authorization bill for fiscal 1984 became law before that date. An effort to delete the ban was rejected 22-24. *(Nicaragua aid, p. 162)*

The House passed a $247 billion defense appropriations bill Nov. 2.

An amendment to cut off funds for U.S. participation in the multinational peacekeeping force in Beirut was rejected 153-274. Clarence D. Long, D-Md., and Samuel S. Stratton, D-N.Y., had drafted the amendment after a bomb attack in the early hours of Oct. 23 killed 241 Americans. The amendment would have forced the withdrawal of 1,600 Marines from Lebanon after March 1, 1984. *(Background, special report, p. 191)*

During three days of debate, the House approved amendments making a net addition of $292.7 million to the bill. An effort by Addabbo to delete all funds for the Pershing II was rejected by voice vote.

Reflecting the closely divided sentiment in the committee, the MX missile barely survived in the full House. On a **208-217 key vote (R 18-145; D 190-72)**, representatives rejected another amendment by Addabbo to delete the entire $2.1 billion. *(1983 key votes, p. 911)*

The House also turned back, 175-247, an Addabbo amendment to delete $438.7 million to begin multi-year procurement of B-1 bombers. The amendment would not have affected B-1 funds for fiscal 1984 and 1985.

Senate Action

The Senate Appropriations Subcommittee on Defense approved essentially all major weapons programs. The only major battle involved subcommittee Chairman Ted Stevens', R-Alaska, unsuccessful effort to delete $57.7 million to begin equipping a World War II-era battleship with cruise missiles, a modernization already funded for two sister ships.

The subcommittee approved the battleship funds by a 10-6 vote.

As reported by the Appropriations Committee Nov. 1, S 2039 (S Rept 98-292) provided $251.7 billion in new appropriations for military programs in fiscal 1984.

The committee deleted $124 million earmarked for facilities to manufacture the controversial nerve gas weapon.

The Senate passed HR 4185 on Nov. 8.

On Nov. 7, by a **37-56 key vote (R 6-46; D 31-10)**, the Senate had rejected an amendment identical to that rejected in the House to delete the $2.1 billion earmarked for the MX missile.

But the contest was much closer on an amendment expressing the sense of the Senate that President Reagan should propose to the Soviet Union a mutual moratorium on flight tests of ICBMs with multiple warheads (MIRVs) for the duration of U.S.-Soviet Strategic Arms Reduction Talks. Such a ban would block further flight tests of the MX as well as a new Soviet missile designated by the United States as the SS-24 and improved versions of the already-deployed Soviet SS-18 and SS-19 missiles.

The amendment was rejected, 42-50.

The Senate approved an administration request for $124.4 million related to production of binary chemical weapons by a one-vote margin: 47-46, with Vice President Bush casting the deciding vote.

Conference Action

A House-Senate conference compromise on HR 4185 (H Rept 98-567) was reached Nov. 18, the final day of the session.

Only two issues involving broad national policy differences were at issue between the House and Senate, and both of them, in dollar terms, were marginal to the $250 billion bill.

Only $124 million was at stake in the battle over whether to begin production of binary munitions. At the insistence of House conferees, the funds were dropped.

Although a majority of House conferees had voted for funding of binary chemical munitions, the full House voted decisively against the weapons Nov. 15, approving by a **key 258-166 vote (R 60-103; D 198-63)** a motion to instruct its conferees to oppose binary funds.

The fight over the well-publicized but formally "covert" U.S. aid to Nicaraguan rebels, though central to U.S. policy in Latin America, involved only $24 million of the large, secret amount in the bill for U.S. intelligence agencies.

There was no controversy over $5.6 billion earmarked to buy 10 B-1 bombers and to begin a multi-year contract on some 80 additional copies of the plane.

The bill also included a secret amount to develop the so-called "stealth" bomber, intended to evade detection by enemy radars.

For 240 of the long-range air-launched cruise missiles (ALCMs) designed to be launched from U.S. bombers beyond the reach of Soviet air defenses, the bill provided $407 million.

For the 11th of the huge Trident missile-launching

submarines, the bill provided $1.398 billion. The bill contained $55.3 million for the last 52 Trident I missiles and $1.5 billion for development of a larger Trident II missile.

The bill provided $19.4 million for components of the first production-line versions of anti-satellite weapons designed to shoot down Soviet military satellites.

Other provisions of the bill appropriated:

- $1.31 billion for 840 M-1 tanks.
- $792.8 million for 600 Bradley armored infantry carriers.
- $1.2 billion for 112 Apache anti-tank helicopters.
- $75 million to continue production of the Copperhead laser-guided artillery shell, for use in tank warfare.
- $60.1 million to develop missiles that would home in on attacking tank formations and $63 million to develop a radar that would locate targets for the missile and guide it toward them.
- $132.5 million to buy 172 large armored cars that could be hauled to remote locations more easily than conventional tanks and armored troop carriers.
- $541.5 million for 130 Sergeant York anti-aircraft tanks and $23.1 million for components.
- $200 million to buy anti-aircraft missile batteries that German troops would man to defend U.S. air bases in West Germany.
- $1.3 billion for 36 Air Force F-15s.
- $2 billion for 144 Air Force F-16s.
- $792.4 million for 24 Navy F-14s.
- $2.1 billion for 84 Navy F-18s.
- $435.1 million for eight EA-6B carrier-based radar jamming planes.
- $42.7 million to develop an improved version of the Navy's F-14, one that might use the new engine selected by the Air Force.
- $370.9 million for so-called HARM missiles, designed to be fired from U.S. planes against hostile anti-aircraft radars.
- $57.7 million as a down payment on the modernization in fiscal 1985 of a third battleship (due to cost nearly $590 million by 1984 estimates).
- $95.9 million for components to rebuild the 25-year-old aircraft carrier *Independence*, a project due to cost an additional $800 million in the fiscal 1985 budget.
- $3.28 billion for three cruisers that would use the Aegis defense system to protect U.S. fleets against anti-ship missiles.
- $79 million for equipment that would be used in the first of a fleet of destroyers built to carry smaller versions of the Aegis system.
- $1.68 billion for three *Los Angeles*-class attack submarines, designed to hunt other subs.
- $397.9 million for 21 LAMPS III anti-sub helicopters, the type scheduled to be stationed on most of the Navy's newer surface warships.
- $116.4 million for construction of one additional ship in the large class of guided-missile escort frigates built since the mid-1970s.
- $325.5 million for an LSD-41-type amphibious landing ship.
- $127.6 million for six air-cushion landing barges (or LCACs) designed to carry tanks from landing ships onto beaches at nearly 60 mph, four times the speed of conventional landing barges.
- $104.3 million to develop an airplane/helicopter to replace the aging transport helicopters used by the Marines.

The House and Senate approved the conference version of the bill Nov. 18, clearing the measure for the president.

Nuclear Freeze

The House May 4 adopted a much-amended resolution calling for an immediate, mutual and verifiable freeze on the production of nuclear weapons by the United States and the Soviet Union. Five months later, the Senate voted down a similarly worded measure. In 1982 the House had narrowly rejected a stronger freeze resolution, adopting instead an administration-backed substitute. *(1982 action, p. 221)*

Final approval of the resolution (H J Res 13), which the Reagan administration vigorously opposed, came only after adoption of an amendment that voided a freeze agreement unless it led to mutual arms reductions within a specified period. That change was pushed by administration backers and allowed both sides in the long debate to claim victory.

Freeze supporters argued that the administration's position was merely a ruse to permit Reagan's nuclear arms buildup since Moscow was unlikely to abandon its existing numerical advantage in intercontinental nuclear missiles. *(Background on freeze movement, special report, p. 255)*

Although a joint resolution, if signed by the president, has the force of law, H J Res 13 merely expressed the sense of the Congress that a mutual freeze should be an objective in arms control negotiations. It did not compel the administration to take any particular actions, even if the measure had been passed by both houses and enacted over the president's veto.

The Senate Oct. 31 tabled a similar freeze proposal (S J Res 2) urging an immediate nuclear weapons freeze. The Senate also considered but took no action on a proposal for a weapons "build-down" agreement that would have required the United States and the Soviet Union to retire an average of two nuclear weapons for each new one deployed.

The vote rejecting a freeze came as no surprise. Freeze proponents had discounted any prospect of winning in the GOP-controlled Senate. Their goal, they said, was simply to force all senators to take a public stand on the freeze before the 1984 elections.

House Action

The House Foreign Affairs Committee reported the original version of H J Res 13 on March 14 (H Rept 98-31). It had won approval in committee on March 3 by a vote of 27-9.

As reported, the measure expressed the sense of Congress that U.S.-Soviet arms negotiations should include among their objectives "deciding when and how to achieve a mutual and verifiable freeze on testing, production and deployment" of nuclear weapons.

Proponents of a freeze tried to counter administration contentions that their effort would undermine U.S. arms control talks. "It is not an exercise in congressional boat-rocking," said committee Chairman Clement J. Zablocki, D-Wis. Since Congress would have to approve any arms control agreement, he argued, it had an obligation to signal to the president its views.

Opponents argued that a freeze would destroy any chance of persuading the Soviet Union to substantially reduce its forces. The committee adopted an amendment stating that the primacy assigned by H J Res 13 to a

nuclear freeze did not preclude other "concurrent and complementary arms control proposals" that might emerge.

Also adopted was an amendment declaring that the freeze negotiations would be a U.S. objective "consistent with the maintenance of essential equivalence in overall nuclear capabilities." According to the administration, however, nuclear equivalence required deployment of several new weapons, including the MX missile and Trident I submarine, which the freeze campaign vehemently opposed.

The House passed H J Res 13 May 4 by a **key vote of 278-149 (R 60-106; D 218-43)** after rejecting, 175-247, a motion to recommit the bill, which would have killed it for the session. *(1983 key votes, p. 911)*

The resolution was debated for more than 40 hours spread over six days from March 16 to May 4.

A central theme of the House debate and of the amendments offered by freeze opponents was whether an immediate arms freeze or mutual arms reductions should have priority in the negotiations with the Soviets.

President Reagan had charged that a freeze was a "very dangerous fraud ... merely the illusion of peace. A freeze at current levels of weapons would remove any incentive for the Soviets to negotiate seriously and virtually end our chances to achieve the major arms reductions which we have proposed."

Freeze backers shared the view of House Speaker Thomas P. O'Neill Jr., D-Mass., that "The freeze comes first [before reductions]." This sequence — a freeze first, followed by reductions — was at the heart of the resolution's implicit criticism of the president's policy. Reagan maintained that the U.S.S.R. held important military advantages and would agree to arms reductions only if faced with the imminent prospect of a U.S. nuclear buildup to offset the Soviet edge.

Freeze backers were forced to accept some compromises as the price of winning House approval. In particular, the House adopted, after a series of procedural votes, an amendment written by Elliott H. Levitas, D-Ga., that required suspension of a freeze agreement with the Soviets if it were not followed within a certain period by mutual arms reductions. The crucial vote came when freeze backers offered their own amendment rewording Levitas' language so that the primacy of an arms freeze, without any direct requirement for arms reductions, was restored. But their amendment lost, 210-214, and the original Levitas language was eventually adopted by votes of 221-203 and 225-191.

Freeze proponents were able to turn back other attempts to revise the resolution's language calling for a freeze first. They did this by retaining the upper hand, except in the debate on the Levitas amendment, during the parliamentary maneuvering and numerous recorded votes taken during the debate.

Supporters of a freeze accepted some amendments offered by administration backers, if they did not jeopardize the main thrust of the resolution. An amendment to require that a negotiated nuclear arms freeze make provision for verification of on-site inspection, for example, was adopted unanimously. And an anti-freeze amendment stating that nothing in H J Res 13 would prevent modernization of U.S. nuclear forces was successfully changed on the House floor by a further amendment stating that, consistent with the overriding goal of a nuclear arms freeze, nothing in the resolution would prevent maintenance of U.S. nuclear forces.

The administration came close to toppling the freeze measure on several votes. For example, an amendment that would have sanctioned the Reagan administration's insistence on reductions of U.S. and Soviet nuclear arsenals to equal, lower levels — instead of trying to negotiate an immediate freeze — lost by only 209-215.

A so-called build-down proposal, which had substantial support in the Senate in 1983, lost by a 190-229 vote. Instead of a freeze, the build-down approach required each superpower to retire two currently deployed nuclear warheads for each new warhead deployed. It would have allowed deployment of some new weapons, such as the Pershing II and the MX missile.

Senate Action

The Senate Foreign Relations Committee Sept. 20 rejected a nuclear weapons freeze resolution as well as the proposal for a weapons build-down. The committee reported both measures to the Senate unfavorably on Oct. 24 (S Rept 98-276).

The freeze resolution (S J Res 2) was rejected by the committee on a 7-10 vote.

The build-down resolution, which would have endorsed a U.S.-Soviet agreement that each country retire a larger number of existing nuclear warheads than the number of new ones it deployed, was rejected on a tie vote of 8-8. Although the build-down approach reportedly had the backing of many Senate moderates, the administration refused to back it, so there was little pressure on the committee to approve it.

The Senate freeze resolution, offered as an amendment to an unrelated debt ceiling bill (H J Res 308), was tabled by a **key vote of 58-40 (R 46-7; D 12-33)** on Oct. 31.

After parliamentary maneuvering on the build-down proposal, the measure was withdrawn, so there was no direct test of Senate support for it.

Senate debate on the two resolutions highlighted a fundamental issue dividing those senators backing the freeze and those favoring the build-down alternative: whether there was a rough nuclear balance between the superpowers and whether U.S. security required substantial modernization of strategic nuclear forces. Those supporting the freeze said the two nations already were in "a situation of essential equivalence," in the words of Edward M. Kennedy, D-Mass.

But William S. Cohen, R-Maine, a cosponsor of the build-down initiative, said a freeze failed to take into account the need to modernize U.S. strategic forces because many American nuclear weapons were nearing the end of their operational life, while the U.S. Minuteman ICBMs were becoming more vulnerable to accurate Soviet missile warheads.

1984 Military Construction

Congress trimmed the Pentagon's fiscal 1984 military construction budget request by $1.55 billion, to $7.1 billion.

Some $417.8 million was cut from President Reagan's January budget request for construction related to the MX intercontinental missile. But the administration had initiated $377 million of that reduction when it proposed a new MX basing method three months after the budget was submitted. *(Background on MX, p. 252)*

As in previous years, the issue of allied defense burden

sharing figured prominently in congressional consideration of the construction authorization and appropriations bills. In 1983 this concern was focused on the cost of NATO facilities in Western Europe associated with the deployment of ground-launched cruise missiles (GLCMs). GLCM deployment was planned for West Germany, Italy, Great Britain, Belgium and the Netherlands. In 1979 NATO had agreed to deploy 464 GLCMs and 108 Pershing II intermediate-range missiles in Europe unless U.S.-Soviet arms control talks resulted in a ban on those weapons and similar Soviet missiles, which were already deployed and targeted on Western Europe.

Most of the GLCM-related cuts were for facilities to support families of U.S. personnel assigned to GLCM bases. As in 1982, the congressional defense committees agreed to fund only the most essential facilities at the GLCM bases in case U.S.-Soviet arms control talks reached some agreement to reduce the scale of the planned deployment.

Authorization

Congress completed action on the military construction authorization bill (HR 2972 — PL 98-115) Sept. 27. The final authorization totaled $7.35 billion.

Congress authorized only $79.2 million of the $207.6 million requested for facilities in Europe for the GLCMs. The reduction included the entire $34 million earmarked to begin construction in the Netherlands, the only one of the five NATO countries that had not formally approved a specific basing plan for the missiles.

House Action. In reporting HR 2972 May 16 (H Rept 98-166), the House Armed Services Committee cut $978 million from the $8.5 billion request; this was partly offset by additions of some $400 million.

Besides reducing the MX-related construction budget in line with the administration's revised MX basing plan, the committee cut nearly half the GLCM-related budget request.

The committee authorized $15.5 million to build fuel and ammunition dumps at European-owned air bases to be used by U.S. planes flown to the continent as reinforcements in case of war. For years senior military officers had cited these bases as among the highest construction priorities in Europe. But they had fallen victim to congressional insistence that the NATO allies pay a greater share of their cost.

These facilities were eligible for money from NATO's common fund for facilities benefiting all members. But the Pentagon wanted to begin work on the projects quickly, hoping to recoup the costs once NATO funds became available. The committee authorized the $15.5 million reluctantly, noting the delay in recouping funds from NATO for these bases.

The House passed HR 2972 on June 21.

Senate Action. The Senate Armed Services Committee July 5 authorized $7.3 billion in military construction funding (S 675 — S Rept 98-174). In what had become a routine congressional stance in recent years, the committee condemned U.S. allies for not paying more of the cost of keeping U.S. forces in Europe and other overseas sites — deployments that, it contended, contributed to the defense of those allies.

The panel threatened to begin requiring U.S. material and labor in construction projects for U.S. forces in Europe as a way to reduce the dollar outflow.

The Senate approved the construction authorization bill July 26 without amendment.

Conference Action. A House-Senate conference report (H Rept 98-359) on HR 2972 was filed Sept. 19. The House adopted the conference version of the bill Sept. 22, and the Senate Sept. 27, completing congressional action.

Conferees authorized $66 million, as requested by the administration, to upgrade two Turkish airfields to be used by U.S. planes in case of war. A provision was attached barring expenditure of the funds for the Turkish air bases or for any other pre-financed project until the secretary of defense gave Congress a projection of the schedule on which NATO would repay the funds.

Although they approved $17 million, of $19.9 million requested, for the U.S. share of improvements at Japan's Misawa air base, where U.S. F-16 fighter planes were to be based, conferees stipulated that the funds could not be spent until the Japanese government had contributed its agreed-upon share.

Appropriations

Cleared by Congress Sept. 28, the fiscal 1984 military construction appropriations bill (HR 3263 — PL 98-116) contained $7.1 billion in new budget authority.

The bill provided $31.2 million for MX missile-related construction, compared with $69.3 million requested. And only $50 million of $150 million requested was approved for the annual U.S. contribution to NATO, reflecting once more congressional irritation over European allies' refusal to increase their share of the costs of the alliance.

At the Defense Department's request, conferees deleted $96.4 million that originally was in the bill for construction at Ras Banas on Egypt's Red Sea coast. Plans for the United States to build a base there, which would remain under Egyptian control, had "fallen through."

The House Appropriations Committee had fought Pentagon plans for Ras Banas for two years. The base would protect oil routes most critical to U.S. allies, who would incur none of the direct cost. In addition, the Egyptian government was loath to sign a formal agreement guaranteeing U.S. access to the site. The Senate Appropriations Committee, on the other hand, supported the plan.

House Action. In reporting the construction funding bill June 9 (H Rept 98-238), the House Appropriations Committee rekindled congressional concern over continued increases in U.S. military deployments abroad. The panel asked rhetorically whether the pattern of expanded commitments abroad reflected a coherent strategy or merely "a series of isolated responses to separate emergent situations." And it warned that unilateral U.S. actions might undermine allied willingness to share more of the burden of the common defense.

The committee approved full funding for overseas projects only at sites where construction already was under way or where the host government had helped to pay for the project.

Pentagon plans for construction in Western Europe bore the brunt of the committee's unhappiness. The panel approved only $100 million of the $150 million requested for NATO. And it approved only $18 million of $44.1 million requested to build fuel and ammunition dumps at European-owned air bases.

Protection of oil routes from the Persian Gulf to Western Europe and Japan was another burden that had been taken on by the United States without commensurate al-

lied financial help, the committee asserted. With nearly $1 billion already committed to air and naval bases near the gulf or at critical points on the route thereto, the panel approved most of the requests to continue or complete these projects.

This included $90 million for the Indian Ocean base on the island of Diego Garcia, $28.6 million to improve airfields in Oman and $25 million for aircraft refueling facilities in Morocco.

On June 21 the House passed HR 3263 without further amendment.

Senate Action. In reporting the bill July 14 (S Rept 98-180), the Senate Appropriations Committee cut nearly in half (to $78.3 million) the $147.9 million requested to build bases in Western Europe for ground-launched cruise missiles.

The committee denied the $44 million requested for fuel and ammunition storage facilities in NATO countries, and it approved only $50 million of the $150 million requested for NATO's common alliance projects.

The Senate passed HR 3263 July 27 with only minor amendments.

Conference Action. The House-Senate conference version of the bill (H Rept 98-378) was filed Sept. 22. The House adopted it Sept. 27, the Senate Sept. 28, clearing the bill for the president.

In addition to cutting funds for MX-related construction and for NATO, the bill provided only $29.3 million of $66 million requested for improvements at two air bases in Turkey. Congress barred use of any of the money until the Turkish share of the projects had been funded, and it told the Pentagon to seek NATO funding of the rest of the work.

Congress approved only $6.4 million of $44.1 million requested for payments in advance for the construction of fuel and ammunition storage dumps at NATO bases. For ground-launched cruise missile bases in Europe, Congress appropriated $74.5 million, slightly less than had been authorized.

For the U.S. F-16 fighter plane base at Misawa, Japan, Congress approved $17 million on the same terms as that contained in the authorization bill: funds could not be used until Japan allocated its agreed-upon share.

As requested, $8 million was approved to improve an air base at La Cieba, Honduras, to which U.S. forces would have access in case of a regional crisis. The funds could not be used until the House and Senate Appropriations panels reviewed a Pentagon report on all U.S. facilities planned for Central America.

Adelman Nomination

After a three-month debate, the Senate April 14 confirmed Kenneth L. Adelman as director of the Arms Control and Disarmament Agency (ACDA). The vote on the nomination was 57-42.

Confirmation of Adelman became, in effect, a vote of confidence on the administration's approach to arms control negotiations with the Soviet Union.

Adelman, 36, had been named to succeed Eugene V. Rostow as ACDA director. Rostow had been fired following months of turmoil in which foreign policy hard-liners in the Defense Department and on Capitol Hill had charged that Rostow too eagerly compromised U.S. bargaining positions in arms control talks with the Soviet Union.

Legislative Action

Adelman, nominated Jan. 12, came under challenge Jan. 27 from Senate Foreign Relations Committee members of both political parties, who charged that he had neither the strong personal commitment to arms control nor the political stature required to make him an effective arms control advocate within the administration.

Several members doubted that Adelman would be a match for the conservative critics both within the administration and on Capitol Hill of past arms control initiatives who had opposed Rostow's positions.

Following a Feb. 24 hearing, the committee rejected, 8-9, a motion to report Adelman's nomination to the Senate with a favorable recommendation. The committee then voted 14-3 to report the Adelman nomination to the Senate with an unfavorable recommendation, that is, a recommendation that he not be confirmed. Although it was a clear rebuff to Adelman and President Reagan, the committee action did represent a victory of sorts for both men.

In a meeting before the votes, Senate Majority Leader Howard H. Baker Jr., R-Tenn., had convinced most of the opponents of the nomination in the committee to compromise by reporting the nomination to the Senate with a negative recommendation.

Vigorous lobbying by top administration officials, including the president, bore fruit April 14 when the Senate confirmed Adelman's nomination.

All but four voting Republicans supported the nomination. Eight Democrats also voted for the nomination, with 38 Democrats voting "nay."

Several senators who backed Adelman said that rejection of Adelman would only create further delay in the search for agreements to control nuclear weapons. Others stressed the heavy burden on the administration to prove its commitment to achieving significant arms control agreements if it hoped to hold on to moderate GOP support for its arms control policy.

Another factor that made it easier for senators to support the nomination was administration assurances that Secretary of State George P. Shultz, who would be Adelman's immediate superior, would take a much firmer hand in shaping arms control policy.

Joint Chiefs Reorganization

The House Oct. 17 passed legislation giving the Joint Chiefs of Staff more stature as an independent military counsel to the president. The Senate did not act on the bill (HR 3718) in 1983 or 1984, and the measure died at the end of the 98th Congress.

In 1982 the House approved a similar bill, but the Senate also withheld action on that measure. *(Background, 1982 action, p. 224)*

The House Armed Services Committee — which usually backed the military in battles to boost defense programs — drafted the bill partly in hopes of giving military advice more impact on national decision making.

Clear-cut, realistic, feasible and prudent professional military advice often was not available to civilian leaders, the panel complained in its Sept. 27 report (H Rept 98-382) on HR 3718.

The administration opposed the bill, warning that some provisions might undermine "the fundamental principle of civilian control over the military."

1984

For the third consecutive year, congressional debate on President Reagan's defense policy focused on two general themes: the pace of the administration's planned military buildup and the White House approach to arms control, particularly as it related to nuclear weapons.

The upshot of both battles in 1984 was the same as the outcomes in the earlier years of the Reagan presidency. Although the president suffered some substantial defeats, the fundamental shape of his defense program survived.

On the arms control front, Congress took numerous actions designed to nudge Reagan toward new initiatives. Most of these had only marginal immediate impact, but two came close to upsetting his nuclear defense plans:

● Congress put off until March 1985 a decision on whether to continue production of the MX intercontinental missile, although it indicated its unwillingness to kill the program outright. (Congress had approved production of 21 MXs in 1983, and in March 1985 it voted to procure another 21.)

● For the first time, Congress blocked, though only for a few months, testing of a new weapon in the hope that negotiations with the Soviets would lead to a ban on all such weapons. At stake was the anti-satellite missile (ASAT).

As in past years, Reagan's initial fiscal 1985 budget request went far beyond virtually all assessments of what Congress would be willing to approve. The president sought a military budget 13.3 percent higher than the previous year's appropriation, in addition to the cost of inflation. The priorities also were the same as in the earlier years:

● Modernization of all three parts of the so-called nuclear triad — the fleets of bombers, land-based missiles and submarine-launched missiles. Reagan's budget continued production of the MX missile, the Trident submarine missile and the B-1 bomber, while allocating billions to the development of wholly new weapons in each of the three classes. While the Pentagon's nuclear arsenal continued to absorb only about 15 percent of the annual defense budget, it was consuming a much larger share of the weapons procurement budget than it did during the 1970s.

● Expansion of the fleet to reach the "600-ship Navy" touted by Reagan during his 1980 presidential campaign. The slogan was shorthand for a fleet built around 15 big aircraft carriers and their escorts. The last of the new carriers had been funded in fiscal 1983, but expensive new escort ships would be budgeted for years to come. The expansion was aimed, in part, at building new ships equipped with the Aegis system to shoot down anti-ship cruise missiles.

● Modernization of the Army's front-line units. The financial drain in the 1970s of fighting the Vietnam War and the reduced defense budgets in the immediate post-Vietnam years had delayed the introduction of new weapons that could deal with Soviet forces in Europe. Accordingly, the Army was replacing older weapons with M-1 tanks, anti-tank helicopters armed with Apache missiles, Bradley armored troop carriers and other new arms.

● Expansion of the fleet of ships and planes that could haul U.S. forces overseas in time of war or international tension.

Negotiations on the fiscal 1985 military budget dragged on throughout the summer. Finally, on Sept. 20, House Speaker Thomas P. O'Neill Jr., D-Mass., and Senate Majority Leader Howard H. Baker Jr., R-Tenn., with the

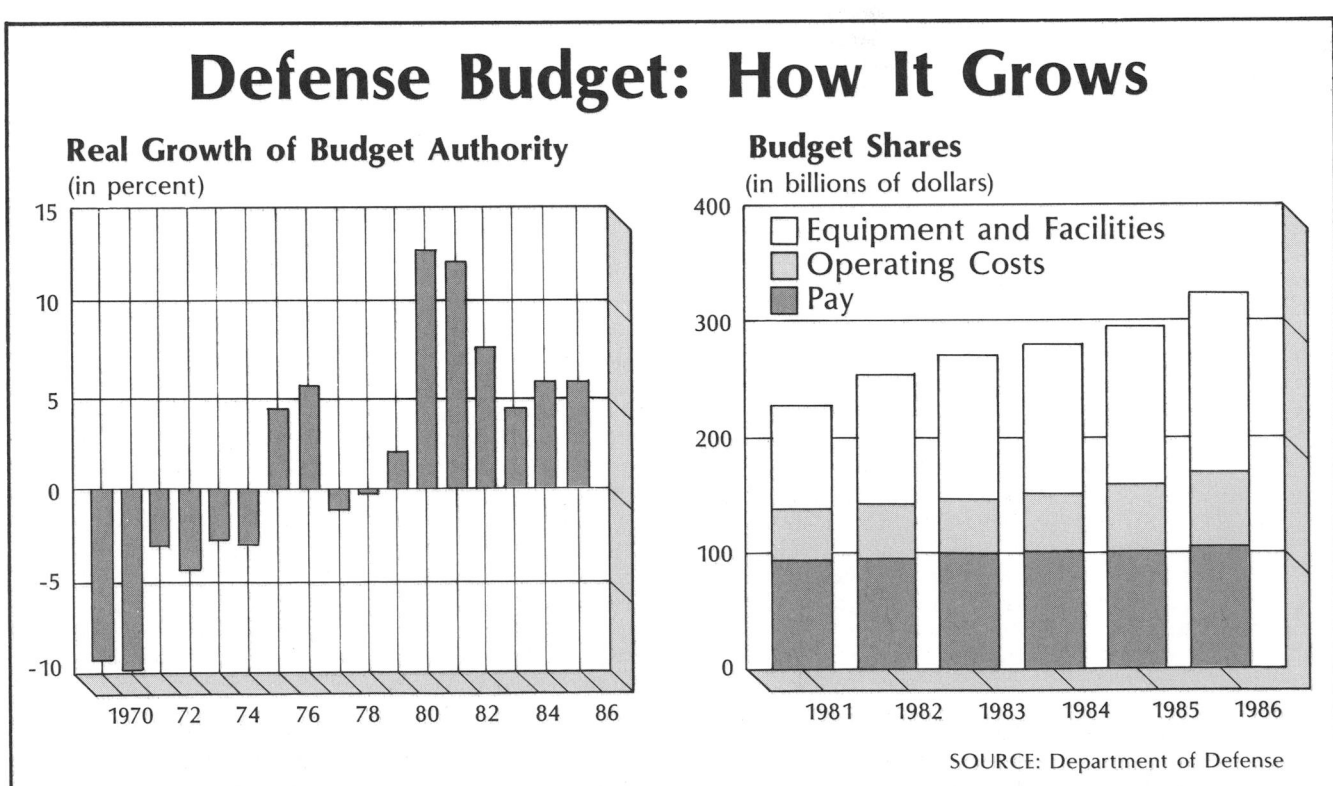

Defense Budget: How It Grows

Real Growth of Budget Authority
(in percent)

Budget Shares
(in billions of dollars)

□ Equipment and Facilities
▨ Operating Costs
▉ Pay

SOURCE: Department of Defense

concurrence of the White House, negotiated a defense agreement, subsequently agreed to by both chambers, that settled on an appropriation of $292.9 million for the Pentagon in 1985 — a "real" (after inflation) increase over fiscal 1984 of 5 percent.

As in 1983, the 1984 debate in Congress over nuclear arms crystallized around Reagan's request to continue production of MX missiles. Pro-arms-control lawmakers took issue with the president on two fundamental issues: whether land-based ballistic missiles were uniquely threatening, even if only in symbolic terms, among the array of weapons in the nuclear arsenal, and whether new, more powerful U.S. nuclear weapons would encourage Moscow to agree to an acceptable arms control treaty, or whether the Soviets would start work on new weapons of their own to match the U.S. programs.

The administration argued that land-based missiles were uniquely potent, and that Soviet advantages in the number and destructive power of ICBMs and their weapons deployed in Eastern Europe, such as the SS-20 missile, were unacceptable. Such weapons' speed and accuracy would make it theoretically possible for Moscow to destroy much of the U.S. nuclear force in a surprise attack.

The arms controllers dismissed these "war-fighting" scenarios as implausible and argued that nuclear war would not remain the relatively limited and orderly minuet that administration strategists were assuming. They contended that nuclear weapons were so destructive that the two superpowers would "use" them only passively, as threats to deter a rival from using them. For that role, the arms controllers maintained, U.S. advantages in bombers and missile-launching submarines offset Soviet advantages in the number and power of ICBMs.

As to the "bargaining-chip" issue, the administration viewed the MX partly as a lever to induce the Russians to move away from the large, multi-warhead ICBMs that made up the bulk of their nuclear arsenal. If such weapons became vulnerable to new U.S. missiles, the reasoning went, the Soviets would see its ICBMs as a "wasting asset" that would have to be replaced. But the administration's critics saw the history of bargaining chips as a sequence of new weapons that accelerated the arms race.

In budgetary terms, Reagan's victory on MX — not completely secured until March 1985 — meant an additional $2.35 billion for the program in fiscal 1985.

Reagan's no-less-important 1984 victories in the first round of the battle over space weaponry, which was likely to replace the MX as the key arms control issue for the rest of the century, resulted in new appropriations for fiscal 1985 totaling $1.65 billion. This included $1.4 billion for the president's Strategic Defense Initiative, ridiculed by arms control supporters as "Star Wars," and $254 million for his anti-satellite missile program.

1985 Defense Authorization

In approving a defense authorization bill (HR 5167 — PL 98-525) for fiscal 1985, Congress continued to back the fundamental shape of President Reagan's military buildup. In so doing, however, it insisted on cutting the cost.

The legislation authorized $211.7 billion for various military weapons procurement, development and research programs and much of the operations and maintenance cost of administering the U.S. armed forces. Also authorized were the nuclear weapons development programs

conducted for the Defense Department by the Energy Department. Normally covered by separate legislation, this $7.4 billion authorization was incorporated in HR 5167.

The legislation authorized military programs covering approximately 70 percent of the overall Pentagon budget. Military personnel costs, for example, did not have to be authorized in advance of actual funding. When combined with these and other defense programs not covered by the authorization bill, HR 5167 produced a total defense budget for fiscal 1985 of $297 billion. Actual defense spending for the year as approved by Congress was some $4.1 billion less, or $292.9 billion. *(Military appropriations, pp. 245, 246)*

For those programs contained in the authorization legislation, cleared Sept. 27, the Reagan administration had requested roughly $225 billion. Congress made hundreds of modest reductions in trimming the bill. Very few of the cuts posed substantial challenges to the administration's defense policies or threatened major weapons programs. About two-thirds ($8.5 billion) of the overall cut came from the $107.6 billion the president requested for weapons purchases. Another $2.5 billion had little real impact on Pentagon programs, reflecting fuel price declines and similar shifts in defense costs.

Disagreement on the fate of the MX intercontinental missile, centerpiece of Reagan's strategic defense program, stalled final action on HR 5167 for weeks. That dispute, and the dollar amount for the military, were resolved only by the intervention of congressional leaders and the administration. Essentially, Congress postponed a decision on whether to go ahead with the missile's development until after the November election. It was agreed to resolve the issue through two sets of House and Senate votes in the spring. (In March 1985 the House and Senate voted to authorize procurement of 21 MX missiles and to appropriate $1.5 billion in fiscal 1985.)

Reagan Defense Request

The administration's original budget request for the military in fiscal 1985 was $313 billion. This included the $225 billion considered by Congress in the authorization bill, a separate amount for military construction projects, the funds for military programs that did not have to be authorized and those conducted by the Energy Department.

On May 3, 1984, under intense pressure from Congress to reduce the budget deficit, the Pentagon proposed a $13.9 billion cut in its defense programs, lowering the request to $299 billion. The cutback was part of a deficit reduction package negotiated between the White House and Senate Republican leaders. The Pentagon whittled away at dozens of programs instead of drastically reshaping its original request. No major weapons systems were killed.

Many of the specific recommendations mirrored changes already proposed in April by the House Armed Services Committee in its version of HR 5167. None of the major strategic weapons programs — the MX and Trident II missiles, the B-1 bomber and Reagan's Strategic Defense Initiative (SDI) to develop space-based anti-missile weapons — were to be cut.

House Committee Action

As reported by the House Armed Services Committee on April 19 (H Rept 98-691), HR 5167 authorized $208.1

billion for military programs requiring authorization. The amount represented a cut of $16.4 billion in the president's original defense budget request submitted Feb. 1.

MX Missile. In its report on the bill, the House committee cut Reagan's $2.9 billion MX production request by $450 million, resulting in a reduction from 40 missiles to 30.

Midgetman. The committee approved $405.2 million to develop a small, single-warhead ICBM, informally dubbed Midgetman, to supplement the multi-warhead MX. The panel dropped money requested for a controversial plan to equip Midgetman with maneuverable warheads (called MARV).

Anti-Missile Defense. The panel endorsed the general thrust of Reagan's call for research into the feasibility of developing large-scale anti-missile defenses (Star Wars).

The panel complained, however, that the administration's projected five-year $24 billion research program was ill-defined. Armed Services cut $407 million — about 23 percent — from the president's fiscal 1985 request for $1.78 billion, charging that amount was too high, given budgetary constraints, and that there was too much overlap among different projects under the strategic defense umbrella.

The committee also strongly endorsed the administration's request to begin production of the ASAT anti-satellite guided missile. ASAT was intended to be launched from an F-15 fighter to destroy an orbiting space satellite. The $84.5 million requested to begin ASAT production was approved, as was $120 million of the $143 million sought for development of the weapon.

Strategic Bombers. A classified amount estimated at $1 billion was included in the bill for the so-called "stealth" bomber, designed to avoid enemy radar. The panel cut about $350 million from the request.

Trident Submarine. Of the $1.49 billion requested for the 12th Trident missile-firing submarine, the panel authorized $1.15 billion, plus $265.5 million requested for components of two more Trident subs. For the advanced Trident II missile for the sub, some $2.05 billion was approved.

Ground Combat. The only major weapon for which the panel increased the procurement recommendation was for the M-1 tank. The administration requested 720 in fiscal 1985; the House panel insisted on buying 840.

The committee approved conditionally the administration's request for $95 million for binary chemical nerve gas components and for the weapon's assembly line. The committee bill sought to require the president to assemble a bipartisan commission to recommend whether the weapon should be produced. Actual production could begin only after the president reviewed the findings and certified that binary production was dictated by national security. Congress formally had to endorse the decision.

Tactical Air Combat. The committee cut the Air Force's $5.6 billion request for 198 of its front-line fighter planes (48 F-15s and 150 F-16s) by 20 percent. But the only change in the number of planes sought was a reduction to 40 of the more expensive F-15s. That reflected the committee's view that the Air Force should abandon plans to increase the F-15 production rate to 96 planes a year. This was part of the service's plan to expand from 36 fighter wings to 40 within five years.

The committee deemed such expansion unrealistic in light of budget constraints and directed the Air Force to plan on 38 fighter wings with an annual F-15 production rate of 42 planes.

The requests for the Navy's carrier-based combat planes were approved without substantial change. The total request came to more than $5 billion for: 24 F-14 fighters, 84 F-18 fighters/light bombers, 6 A-6E medium bombers and 32 AV-8B vertical-takeoff light bombers for the Marine Corps.

Navy Ships. The $13.1 billion shipbuilding request was cut by $1.25 billion without canceling a single major combat ship requested by the administration. For the most part, the trims were achieved by paying for ships with funds appropriated in earlier years, but not spent.

The planned modernization of the carrier *Independence* was approved without change ($583.2 million). The modernization of the battleship *Missouri* to carry long-range cruise missiles also was approved but without providing any of the requested $422.6 million in new budget authority. Unspent funds from earlier appropriations would be enough to cover the cost.

Approved without change was the $532 million request for 180 Tomahawk cruise missiles — similar to the Air Force ground-launched cruise missiles. The Tomahawks would let the renovated battleships and most other large warships strike at ships and land targets hundreds of miles distant.

The panel approved four ships intended to protect U.S. fleets against Soviet cruise missile attack with the Aegis anti-aircraft system: the 14th, 15th and 16th Aegis cruisers ($3.1 billion), and the $1.2 billion DDG-51 — the *Arleigh Burke*, first of a new class of destroyers intended to replace some 30 ships due for retirement around 1990.

Four *Los Angeles*-class nuclear submarines, designed chiefly to hunt Soviet subs, were approved as requested ($2.3 billion), as were components for four more of the ships in each of the next two years ($617.8 million).

The panel also approved $174 million to begin developing a new submarine, but on condition that the Navy certify that the new vessel could defeat projected Soviet subs. This requirement reflected the committee's unhappiness that new Soviet submarines were faster and could dive deeper than U.S. subs.

Operating Costs. The committee cut $2.7 billion from the Pentagon's request for operations and maintenance of the services, recommending $78.3 billion in fiscal 1985. Almost $500 million came from various cuts intended to underscore the committee's desire that certain wasteful practices exposed by Pentagon auditors be stopped.

House Floor Action

The House passed HR 5167 on June 1 by a 298-98 vote after several days of debate. As passed, the bill authorized $208 billion for the military in fiscal 1985.

Floor action on the bill was marked by cliffhanger votes on the MX missile, resulting in new controls on the weapon that represented a dramatic setback for Reagan. *(Crucial votes on MX, box, p. 238)*

The House also made clear its suspicion that the administration was not trying hard enough to reach arms control agreements with the Soviet Union. Members adopted, over strong White House opposition, amendments:

● Deleting funds aimed at resuming production of chemical weapons.

● Barring tests of an anti-satellite missile unless the Soviet Union tests its own version first.

By a vote of 212-218 May 16, after intensive lobbying

by the administration and timely parliamentary maneuvering by MX backers, the House rejected an amendment that would have blocked production of any MX missiles in fiscal 1985.

The position on the MX that won the day in the House had been devised by a centrist group led by Rep. Les Aspin, D-Wis. Under that plan, 15 missiles were authorized, at a cost of $1.8 billion, under certain conditions: No money could be spent until April 1, 1985, and then only if the president determined that the Soviets were not indicating a willingness to bargain in good faith for limits on ICBMs such as the MX. If they were willing to bargain, the ban would continue. The Aspin policy on MX was accepted on a 229-199 vote.

However, after a concerted drive by the House Democratic leadership, the House on May 31 voted to further tighten congressional controls on the 15 MX missiles. On each of three votes on MX, the House affirmed by margins of no more than three votes an amendment insisting that Congress, not the president, would have the last say on whether to proceed with procurement of the 15 MXs. The decision, under the amendment, was to be made by joint resolution of Congress. The amendment did not affect the 21 MX missiles Congress approved in 1983 and contained in the fiscal 1984 budget. *(1983 action on MX, p. 217)*

In a replay of action taken by the House in 1982 and 1983, lawmakers rejected production funds for the beginning stage in manufacturing binary chemical nerve gas weapons. The 1984 vote, taken May 17, was 247-179 to delete the $95 million authorization in the bill. *(1982 and 1983 congressional rejection of nerve gas weapons, pp. 219, 229)*

The House voted to continue for a year a moratorium on tests of an ASAT missile, so long as the Soviet Union did likewise. The freeze on testing was approved by a 238-181 vote. An amendment to allow the administration to continue limited testing in 1985 lost on votes of 178-236 and 186-228. A related amendment allowing testing in 1985 if the president initiated plans for seeking a U.S.-Soviet ASAT ban was rejected 186-229.

In other major floor votes on HR 5167, the House rejected amendments that would have denied funding to begin setting up the production line for the Trident II submarine-launched missile and halted further deployment in fiscal 1985 of Pershing II and cruise missiles. A related amendment, also rejected, would have temporarily blocked procurement of 70 Pershing II missiles that already were authorized.

On May 23 the House adopted an amendment barring use of U.S. combat troops in El Salvador and Nicaragua except with Congress' approval or if there was a clear threat of attack on the United States, U.S. personnel or a U.S. embassy. *(Related action on El Salvador, Nicaragua, pp. 174, 175)*

A proposal to require the Pentagon to cut about $4.5 billion from the bill's authorization for weapons procurement was rejected 173-250.

Senate Committee Action

The Senate Armed Services Committee reported its defense authorization bill (S 2723) on May 31 (S Rept 98-500). The bill authorized $213.5 billion, or about $6 billion more than the House approved. However, the Senate panel's bill, unlike the House version, contained $16.6 billion for two programs the House authorized in separate legisla-

tion: construction of military facilities (HR 5604) and programs conducted for the Defense Department by the Energy Department.

As reported, the bill authorized real growth in defense spending of 6.9 percent, the rate agreed to by Reagan and the Senate Republican leadership in a budget deficit reduction package. As a result of the agreement, the Pentagon in May cut $14.4 billion from its original defense budget request submitted in February.

Strategic Weaponry. The committee halved the number of MX missiles to be purchased in fiscal 1985, authorizing $2.4 billion for 21 missiles instead of the 40 requested. A move to bar any MX procurement was rejected 7-11.

The committee accepted a cut of $47.3 million in the single-warhead Midgetman missile program proposed by the administration in May as part of its fiscal 1985 budget compromise, authorizing $358.3 million.

For 34 additional B-1 bombers and related equipment, the panel accepted without change the $7.7 billion requested. The overall B-1 procurement goal of the Defense Department was 100 planes. Also agreed to was the amount requested — which was classified — to develop the stealth bomber.

In related action, the committee recommended $597.8 million of $626.8 million requested for modifications to the existing fleet of aging B-52 bombers, plus $77.3 million for missile launchers for the B-52s, B-1s or the stealth bombers.

The request for a 12th Trident missile-launching submarine was approved without change, at a cost of $1.5 billion. Also approved were most of the requested funds for continued development of the Trident II missile and to begin procurement of Trident II components.

The committee revived a program, cut by the administration in its May budget revisions, to develop a plane with new, highly sensitive antennas for communicating with submerged submarines.

The committee provided the president with a $1.65 billion authorization for initial development of Reagan's SDI program, which was to include such weapons as laser-armed space satellites. An attempt to cut an additional $200 million from the program was rejected 7-11.

Ground Combat. Democrats on the committee lost in an attempt to increase the number of M-1 tanks purchased from 720 to 840. The lower number, costing $1.3 billion, was approved by a 10-7 vote. (In May the administration trimmed its tank request from 720 to 600 for fiscal 1985.)

The Senate committee rejected an administration proposal to cut back production of missile-launching anti-tank helicopters. Instead, it affirmed the original request to buy 144 so-called Apache planes, which cost about $14 million apiece. The goal was procurement of 515 by the late 1980s.

The committee bill also included authorizations for development of new missile warheads that could pierce Soviet tanks. And the committee went along with the House panel in authorizing funds for new radar-guided missiles that could disrupt a Soviet ground attack by smashing targets up to 200 miles behind enemy lines. The program was seen as a way for NATO to offset the numerical advantages in Central Europe of the Soviet-led Warsaw Pact forces.

Additional funds were authorized for anti-aircraft defenses, such as Sergeant York anti-aircraft tanks, at $438.5 million, and long-range anti-aircraft missiles.

MX Missile Survives Third Year . . .

The MX intercontinental missile, the center-piece of President Reagan's strategic defense program, survived a third year of crucial tests on Capitol Hill. Congress approved 21 of the controversial missiles for fiscal 1985, the same number as it approved in fiscal 1984.

There was a major difference, however. Congress in 1984 put new strings on the MX program. It appropriated $2.35 billion for the second batch of 21 missiles but barred the spending of any of that money until after March 1985, when Congress was to vote twice on whether to reaffirm its intent to produce the additional missiles. (In the 1985 votes, March 26 and 28, Congress gave the go-ahead to production of the 21 missiles.)

The 1984 fight over the MX became a symbolic vote of confidence in President Reagan's nuclear arms policy. There were cliffhanger votes on the floor of each chamber of Congress, which contributed to a stalemate in the ensuing House-Senate conference that met to negotiate a compromise on the defense authorization bill (HR 5167 — PL 98-525).

The deadlock over MX was broken only after talks between congressional leaders and the White House.

Lawmakers disagreed over MX's effectiveness as a weapon and its role in arms control efforts. The administration contended that land-based ballistic missiles like the MX were needed to offset unacceptable advantages the Soviet Union had in such weapons. Liberal arms controllers argued that ICBMs worked only in limited-war scenarios and that other kinds of nuclear weapons would counter the Soviet threat more effectively.

MX opponents disputed the administration's contention that the missile would be a bargaining chip in arms control negotiations. They continued their effort, begun in 1983, to convince House Democrats that a vote for MX represented an endorsement of the president's nuclear arms policy. Well-organized lobbying among members and at the grass-roots level brought the arms control coalition to within a hair's breadth of victory in the House in mid-May. Speaker Thomas P. O'Neill Jr., D-Mass., and the House Democratic leadership then threw their organizational resources into the fray and eked out the few votes needed to win a symbolic victory on May 31.

In the Senate, too, there was a change in the political dynamic of the MX fight. Members who opposed the missile gained some support from more conservative Democrats, led by Lawton Chiles, D-Fla., who saw MX largely as a budget issue. Together, those two groups produced a tie vote that the administration won only by Vice President George Bush's vote.

First House Test

MX foes in the House, led by Charles E. Bennett, D-Fla., and Nicholas Mavroules, D-Mass., pushed an amendment to deny all production funding for the MX. Reagan had requested $2.9 billion to build 40 additional missiles in fiscal 1985. The House Armed Services Committee recommended 30 missiles and authorized $2.45 billion. The amendment did not touch some $1.7 billion to continue development of the missile.

Centrist members of the House, led by Les Aspin, D-Wis., saved the day for the administration on May 16 by arranging a compromise that allowed 15 missiles to be produced, at a cost of $1.8 billion, under certain conditions:

● No money would be spent until April 1, 1985.

● It would be spent only if, in the president's judgment, the Soviets were not indicating a willingness to bargain in good faith for limits on ICBMs. If they were willing to bargain, the ban would continue.

In the May 16 voting, the centrists' legislative craftsmanship and strong White House lobbying prevailed over the anti-MX lobby, which had honed its skills in two years of legislative battles against the MX and for a nuclear freeze resolution.

While rallying "swing" members looking for a middle position, Aspin's proposal won the support of members who backed the full Reagan request but knew it had no chance of passage. Aspin and Joel Pritchard, R-Wash., credited Minority Leader Robert H. Michel, R-Ill., and other GOP leaders for bringing along conservative Republicans.

The showdown between the MX opponents and the Aspin team took place in a dramatic, seven-hour-long debate in which rhetorical eloquence took a back seat to parliamentary maneuvering. After the jockeying was over, the Bennett-Mavroules team got a roll-call vote on their "no-MX" amendment. When the seesaw vote was over, the MX opponents had lost, 212-218. The Aspin position was then approved on a 229-199 vote.

Second House Test

Before the dust had settled on the May 16 victory for the MX, the Democratic leadership began girding for a rematch. This was made necessary because Congress separately had to appropriate the funds for MX production. The first round merely authorized the building of 21 more missiles.

Although various anti-MX groups intensified their lobbying of Congress, what really changed the political equation was Speaker O'Neill's commitment of the House leadership and other influential Democrats behind the anti-MX drive. This task force was

... Of Crucial Votes on Its Future

led by Richard A. Gephardt, Mo., and Democratic Congressional Campaign Committee Chairman Tony Coelho, Calif. Others in the group were Marty Russo, Ill.; Mavroules; Les AuCoin, Ore.; Thomas J. Downey, N.Y.; Mike Synar, Okla.; Mike Lowry, Wash.; and Peter H. Kostmayer, Pa.

The Gephardt group accepted the basic premise of Aspin's amendment — that 15 new missiles would be authorized in 1985, but that production would not begin before April 1985 and would not begin at all if the Soviets resumed arms talks. The Gephardt group added the wrinkle that it would be up to Congress, not the president, to decide whether to release production funds.

With MX backers confining their tactical planning to procedural moves, rather than political persuasion, the MX opponents won out in a series of tight votes on May 31. The MX backers decided to force the issue by offering an amendment that restated the position that the House had adopted on May 16. It was agreed to 203-182. But then Bennett offered his amendment requiring congressional votes in 1985 before the MX production money could be spent. This time the action ended in the MX foes' favor, on a **199-197 key vote (R 17-141; D 182-56)**. *(1984 key votes, p. 927)*

Two other votes were forced on the Bennett amendment by MX backers, but the anti-MX forces held their troops together, sealing their victory on votes of 198-197 and 199-196.

Close Call in Senate

Two weeks later, on June 14, the Republican-controlled Senate gave the administration a scare. A 48-48 tie vote on an amendment to bar funding of 21 more MX missiles in fiscal 1985 had to be broken by Vice President Bush.

The close call on that amendment, offered by Chiles, reflected several factors in addition to the general sensitivity about nuclear arms programs. Support of MX had been lukewarm ever since Reagan had abandoned the search for a basing method that would guarantee protection of the big missile against Soviet attack. Chiles' reputation as a moderate who was "strong" on defense offered senators a way to register unhappiness with the MX.

The Senate Armed Services Committee had trimmed the number of missiles for fiscal 1985 from 40 to 21. The Senate committee had rejected conditions on the program, dismissing them as providing "the Soviets with veto power over such an important U.S. program."

Chiles, in looking for an MX position different from the one taken by that panel, came up with an alternative that he said would give the United States

the bargaining chip of MX without paying full price for it.

Under the amendment, no new missiles would be built in fiscal 1985, but the production line for the missile's production would be kept ready to start cranking them out on short notice. The amendment also appropriated $596 million to keep the production line intact, $200 million to test the 21 missiles authorized and funded for fiscal 1984, and $200 million that would be needed if Congress decided subsequently to deploy the 21 MXs authorized for fiscal 1985. In all, the Chiles amendment would have trimmed $1.9 billion from the Senate committee's recommendation for ICBM-related programs, a point made by Chiles and cosponsor J. Bennett Johnston, D-La., in the Senate debate.

Opponents of the Chiles amendment complained about the mechanics of a "hot" production line that was not producing anything and warned that stopping MX production would reward Soviet intransigence on arms control.

The vote on Chiles' proposal came on a motion by Armed Services Chairman John Tower, R-Texas, to table the amendment. The vote ended in a 48-48 tie, which Vice President Bush broke in the administration's favor. With Bush voting "yea," the amendment was tabled on a **49-48 key vote (R 43-10; D 5-38)**.

The Senate June 14 also had defeated an amendment that would have killed the MX outright. The vote tabling that version was 55-41.

In the House-Senate negotiations over MX in the conference on the defense bill, the two chambers were apart, first of all, on the number of missiles to be produced: the House's 15 or the Senate's 21. But the real sticking point was the House's stipulation that the money could not be spent until April 1, 1985, and then only if Congress voted its approval by concurrent resolution.

The dispute over what role Congress would have in releasing the funds after the delay ended held up final action on the defense bill throughout the summer. With congressional adjournment set for early October, O'Neill and Senate Majority Leader Howard H. Baker Jr., R-Tenn., held two weeks of talks to resolve the impasse.

The outcome, announced Sept. 20, gave Reagan $2.35 billion for procurement of the 21 MX missiles in fiscal 1985. *(Details of agreement, legislative action, p. 244)*

The Sept. 20 agreement freed up the authorization bill, which was cleared by Congress on Sept. 27. The compromise language also was folded into the defense appropriations section of the omnibus funding resolution for fiscal 1985 (H J Res 648 — PL 98-473), which was cleared on Oct. 11.

Defense

As the House panel had done, the Senate committee reduced the authorization sought for a missile program designed to nullify short-range Soviet ballistic missiles with non-nuclear, chemical warheads that might be launched against Western Europe in a surprise attack. The panel cautioned the Army not to expand the program in such a way as to threaten long-range missiles in contravention of the 1972 ABM treaty.

Tactical Air Combat. The Senate committee cut $790 million from the overall request for the U.S. fleet of jet fighters. Most of the reduction was related to the Pentagon's selection of a new jet engine for its F-16 fighters. The request was for $6.4 billion for procurement and $472 million for research in fiscal 1985. All 150 F-16s and 42 F-15s requested were approved. The committee also approved more than $200 million for a program to develop a radar and infrared television system that would let pilots attack ground targets at night.

For Navy carrier-based aircraft, including F-14 fighters, F-18 small bombers and AV-8B vertical-takeoff Harriers, the committee approved the administration's request with only minor changes. Also approved were authorizations for additional A-6E medium bombers and for an improved version of the bomber.

Also in the Senate bill were authorizations for various short- and long-range air-to-air missiles, including the 100-mile-range Phoenix, at a cost of $357 million.

Naval Warfare. Administration plans were approved for the two largest warships in the fiscal 1985 budget: renovation of the 25-year-old carrier *Independence* ($583 million) and modernization of the World War II battleship *Missouri* to carry cruise missiles.

Four ships that would carry the Aegis anti-aircraft system designed to protect U.S. fleets against cruise missile attack were approved as requested: three *Ticonderoga*-class cruisers ($3.1 billion) and the *Arleigh Burke*, the first of the new class of destroyers ($1.2 billion). The Navy said it would need more than 30 of the new destroyers to replace anti-aircraft escort ships due for retirement around 1990.

The administration was overruled in its proposal to drop one of the four *Los Angeles*-class submarines requested in February but then trimmed in May. The authorization for four subs came to $2.3 billion. The Navy's goal was to build 100 of the attack submarines, to be used through the 1990s. The committee also authorized funds for a new attack sub to replace the *Los Angeles* class. In addition, the bill contained authorizations for sub-hunting helicopters ($466.5 million), amphibious assault ships, including LSDs ($406 million), and a large assortment of cargo ships and planes.

Personnel. Instead of the requested 5.5 percent, across-the-board pay raise effective Jan. 1, 1985, the committee approved a 4 percent raise for all personnel except new recruits, the same raise Congress had approved for fiscal 1984.

The committee added to the bill a provision lifting the deadline of Dec. 31, 1989, for the use of education benefits earned by military personnel under the so-called "Vietnam-era GI Bill."

The new provision gave eligible beneficiaries 10 years after they left military service in which to use their benefits. Without this change, the committee warned, up to 400,000 service personnel would have faced the alternative of leaving the service to go to school or giving up their GI Bill benefits.

Also in the bill approved by the committee were various policy directives related to defense contractors' performances in weapons specifications and quality control. One gave the Pentagon greater latitude in carrying out a 1983 law requiring manufacturers' warranties on all weapons.

Military Construction Projects. The Senate committee cut military construction in fiscal 1985 by $1.2 billion — actually a little less than the administration had suggested in its revised budget. The amount authorized — $9.3 billion — was the same as that approved by the House committee in separate legislation (HR 5604). *(Military construction legislation, p. 246)*

On the controversial issue of U.S. aid to Central America, the Senate panel narrowly approved a $4.4 million authorization for two facilities to store U.S. military equipment and ammunition in Honduras. A motion to delete those funds lost on a 9-9 tie vote.

Senate Floor Action

The Senate passed the defense authorization bill June 21 after a two-week debate. The bill as passed authorized $213.5 billion for weapons research, development, procurement and operations and maintenance of the military. It did not include authorizations for defense-related nuclear weapons programs conducted by the Energy Department or military construction programs. These were deleted and then added to separate bills. The bill (S 2459) containing the nuclear programs of the Energy Department also was passed by the Senate on June 21, but there was no further action on that measure. *(Military construction legislation, p. 246)*

As in the House debate, the MX issue was the hardest fought in the Senate. Ultimately, senators approved 21 of the 40 missiles requested by Reagan. But the administration won only on the strength of Vice President George Bush's tie-breaking vote June 14 that killed an amendment that would have blocked all funding for additional MX procurement in fiscal 1985. The **key vote was 49-48 (R 43-10; D 5-38)**. *(1984 key votes, p. 927)*

The close call on the MX, despite strong White House lobbying, reflected several factors in addition to congressional sensitivity on nuclear arms programs. For one thing, support for MX had been tepid, even among its Senate supporters, ever since the administration abandoned the search for a basing method to protect the big missile against Soviet attack. That did not translate into Senate willingness to kill the missile outright, however. An amendment to that end was rejected 55-41.

Also narrowly rejected was an amendment to cut $100 million from Reagan's SDI program to develop space-based anti-missile defenses. The amendment was tabled, and thus killed, by a **47-45 key vote (R 40-10; D 7-35)**.

Facing a close Senate vote on the anti-satellite missile program, the administration elected instead to seek a compromise. During a secret Senate session June 12, a compromise was reached that barred ASAT target tests until 30 days after the president had certified to Congress that "The United States is endeavoring to negotiate in good faith the strictest possible [ASAT] limitations ... consistent with the national security interests." The compromise was adopted easily, 61-28, following unsuccessful attempts to modify and kill it.

By a 49-45 vote, the Senate killed an amendment that would have provided a 5.5 percent military pay raise for all ranks, beginning in 1985, instead of the Armed Services Committee's 4 percent recommendation for all ranks with

the exception of recruits.

Widespread unhappiness with U.S. allies was underscored June 7 when the Senate adopted, 91-3, an amendment dealing with the sensitive subject of defense burden-sharing among the United States, its NATO allies and Japan. The non-binding amendment affirmed an earlier pledge by the allies to increase defense spending by at least 3 percent above the cost of inflation in 1984 and 1985. Subsequently, the issue was more strongly underscored when Sam Nunn, D-Ga., offered an amendment that could have removed up to 90,000 of the 326,000 U.S. troops stationed in Europe if other NATO members did not carry out defense improvements. Though the proposal was tabled, 55-41, there was general agreement that the allies were not paying their share of the cost of defending Western Europe.

The Senate indicated its support for a broad revival of the GI Bill June 13, then reversed itself and approved a less sweeping measure offering educational aid to certain recruits once they completed their military service. On a 72-20 vote, the Senate voted to establish a four-year test program offering $500 a month for three years in educational benefits as a recruiting incentive. The broader plan reviving the GI Bill by granting everyone in the military who completed three years of active military duty a fully funded educational program was tabled 47-45.

Adopted without opposition was an amendment to bar the administration from diverting to any other program the secret amount in the bill for the stealth bomber program. The House version had cut as much as $350 million from the administration's request of about $1 billion. Some senators had warned that certain Pentagon officials might wish to prolong production of the B-1 bomber by delaying development of the stealth plane, due to replace the B-1.

The Senate, rejecting a proposal to end U.S. support for anti-government guerrillas in Nicaragua, on June 18 handed Reagan a nominal victory in his Central America policy. But the **58-38 key vote (R 48-6; D 10-32)** disguised a sharp drop in support among key Democrats at a time when the administration was waging an uphill battle to continue subsidizing the civil war in Nicaragua. *(Related story, p. 175)*

Earlier, the Senate rejected an amendment that sought to prohibit the introduction of U.S. combat troops into Central America, except under several narrow conditions. That amendment was tabled, 63-31.

Also on Central America, the administration averted what could have become a contentious debate by agreeing to drop $4.4 million to build two storage sites in Honduras for ammunition and equipment intended for use by U.S. forces. *(Honduras issue, p. 246)*

A non-binding amendment calling on the president to seek ratification of two nuclear test ban treaties and to resume negotiations on a comprehensive treaty banning all nuclear tests was adopted, 77-22. A move to kill the amendment first was turned back, 34-65.

At issue was a treaty signed in 1974 banning underground nuclear weapons tests with a power of more than 150 kilotons — the so-called "threshold test ban treaty" — and one signed in 1976 setting a similar ceiling on the size of underground peaceful nuclear explosions. The Ford and Carter administrations, husbanding their political capital for other fights, had left the two treaties on the shelf.

President Carter began negotiations with the Russians for a comprehensive test ban treaty. But those talks were suspended, along with all other U.S.-Soviet arms control efforts, in early 1980 after the Soviet invasion of Afghanistan.

In 1983 the Reagan administration announced it would not seek ratification of the threshold and peaceful explosions treaties, unless procedures for verifying compliance with the limits were renegotiated. The Russians rejected several requests to reopen those issues, maintaining they would be willing to talk about verification methods after the treaties were ratified.

Another Senate battle erupted over a related issue: U.S. policy toward certain weapons limits contained in the unratified Strategic Arms Limitation Treaty (SALT II). An amendment was introduced calling on the president to continue the current policy of complying with SALT II, which was scheduled to expire Dec. 31, 1985. To accommodate conservatives, the amendment's sponsors agreed to a modification that required a presidential report by September 1984 on Soviet compliance with the policy of not undercutting the treaty, called on the president to "carefully consider" the implications of any change in the U.S. approach to the SALT limits and required the president to consult Congress before making any changes. As modified, the amendment was adopted 82-17.

Agreed to in modified form was an amendment requesting the president to discuss with the Soviets means by which nuclear sea-launched cruise missile (SLCM) limitations could be verified. Because the new SLCMs were so small, and because there was no external difference between nuclear and non-nuclear versions, arms controllers had warned for years that limitations on the nuclear version would become impossible once the missiles were deployed. Arms controllers originally had sought adoption of a non-binding amendment urging a mutual U.S.-Soviet moratorium on nuclear SLCM deployment pending negotiation of a ban on such weapons.

Conference Action

A House-Senate compromise version of the defense authorization bill was reached Sept. 25, and a conference report (H Rept 98-1080) on HR 5167 was filed Sept. 26. The House adopted the conference report the same day and the Senate followed suit Sept. 27, completing congressional action.

Chief obstacles to a final agreement were the MX missile, U.S. involvement in Central America and the total dollar level of the authorization bill. Conference negotiations had begun in June soon after the Senate passed the bill. The May agreement between Reagan and Senate Republican leaders, setting an overall defense budget for fiscal 1985 of $299 billion, made GOP conferees on HR 5167 particularly resistant to House demands for a lower authorization level. Finally, after weeks of stalemate, the issue was resolved in a carefully crafted bargain between House Speaker O'Neill and Senate Majority Leader Baker on budget levels and the MX.

Under the Sept. 20 agreement, Congress would authorize $297 billion for defense, and appropriate $292.9 billion. That appropriation would provide a real increase in defense spending, beyond the cost of inflation, of 5 percent. Reagan initially had sought a 13 percent after-inflation increase.

Because some parts of the defense budget were not covered by the annual authorization bill, the amount actually authorized in the conference report on HR 5167 was $219.7 billion.

Congress Places Test Restrictions ...

Congress set new restrictions on testing of the anti-satellite missile (ASAT) in fiscal 1985, limiting the number of tests and barring a trial search for a target in space until after March 1, 1985.

The battle over ASAT represented a test of support for the "new" arena of President Reagan's defense strategy: space weaponry. In much the same way, the fight over the MX missile posed a vote of confidence in the "old" arms race issue of nuclear missiles. *(MX, ASAT authorization, funding, pp. 235, 245)*

To some degree, conservatives saw in space weaponry a way to break out of the Earth-based nuclear stalemate by rendering the Soviet Union's missiles obsolete. But liberal arms controllers argued that such technology was just another attempt to surpass the Soviets, rather than negotiate with them.

The ASAT, a 19-foot-long missile to be fired from an F-15 fighter plane, was designed to destroy Soviet satellites by homing in on their heat and ramming them. Technically, the ASAT was not part of the president's Strategic Defense Initiative (SDI) to develop anti-missile space weapons. But ASAT became a test case on the whole panoply of space weaponry in 1984.

1983: Opposition Develops

ASAT opponents argued that it was foolhardy for the United States to try out its version of the weapon. Once actual testing began, they insisted, the United States and the U.S.S.R. could not achieve a mutual ban on the weapon. This was because the American weapon was so small, in contrast to the huge ICBM-launched Soviet ASAT, that Moscow could not be sure the U.S. ASAT had not been secretly developed and produced. Reagan defense officials disagreed, maintaining that any effort to deploy the ASAT covertly would be quickly exposed.

In 1983 a group of House members led by Democrats Joe Moakley, Mass., George E. Brown Jr., Calif., and John F. Seiberling, Ohio, joined forces with the Federation of American Scientists (FAS) and the Union of Concerned Scientists (UCS), two liberal groups that emphasized a technical approach to arms control issues.

Staffers for those two organizations, the three lawmakers and other parties began meeting weekly. Out of these sessions came the first congressional vote on space weapons issues: Brown's amendment to the fiscal 1984 defense authorization bill (PL 98-94) to delete the $19.4 million requested to begin ASAT production. Though the House rejected it, 177-243, the amendment drew more support than liberal arms control moves usually did.

In the Senate, Armed Services Committee lead-ers and proponents of a moratorium on space weapons tests negotiated a compromise that was agreed to, 91-0. The amendment, offered by Paul E. Tsongas, D-Mass., barred ASAT tests against targets in space unless the president certified that he was trying to negotiate a ban with the Soviet Union on such weapons. The amendment was enacted into law.

When the focus of action shifted to the defense appropriations bill, FAS and UCS lobbyists found allies on the House Appropriations Committee in Matthew F. McHugh, D-N.Y., Lawrence Coughlin, R-Pa., and Norman D. Dicks, D-Wash. Their amendment, accepted with modification by the committee, dropped the $19.4 million in ASAT production money and required a report on administration plans to seek arms control agreements dealing with ASAT weapons. The money was restored in the House-Senate conference on the bill, but the requirement for the report was retained.

1984: Tests Limited

Preparing for the 1984 space weapons policy battles, the FAS and UCS brought several of the arms control and other liberal lobby groups into the coalition against ASAT. Meanwhile, Brown, Moakley and Seiberling and their allies announced that they would seek a mutual ASAT moratorium.

On March 31 the administration submitted, as required under the fiscal 1984 appropriations bill, its report to Congress on an ASAT ban. The administration, while not ruling out curbs on certain types of ASAT activity, concluded that a total ban:

- Could not be verified, even if existing Soviet ASAT weapons were destroyed. In part, the administration argued, this was because the Soviets could use other weapons and space vehicles as substitute ASATs.

- Would prevent production of the U.S. ASAT. To deter Soviet attacks on U.S. satellites, the administration argued, it would be necessary to threaten retaliation against Soviet satellites.

- Would make outer space a sanctuary from which Soviet reconnaissance satellites could guide Soviet attacks on U.S. and allied military targets.

House Position. In its April 19, 1984, report on the fiscal 1985 defense authorization bill (HR 5167), the House Armed Services Committee strongly endorsed the administration's request to begin ASAT production. The panel approved Reagan's request for $84.5 million to begin production, plus $120 million of the $143 million requested for further development. The committee cited arguments, made during the Carter administration, that since the Soviet Union had its own ASAT a U.S. counterpart might "encourage good faith ASAT negotiations."

... On Proposed Anti-Satellite Missile

When members debated the issue in the House May 23, ASAT opponents had lined up enough votes to adopt a moratorium on testing so long as the Soviet Union did likewise. The amendment, offered by Brown, was needed to head off an ASAT race between the two superpowers, Moakley and other members argued.

ASAT backers rallied behind a counter-amendment by Beverly B. Byron, D-Md., that would have allowed the United States as many tests of the weapon as the Soviets had conducted. (As of that date, the Soviets had conducted 20 tests, nine of which were reported to have been successful.)

Backers of Brown's amendment were more concerned, however, about a "middle ground" amendment offered by Dave McCurdy, D-Okla., that would have barred an ASAT target test until March 31, 1985, but would have allowed testing if the president submitted to Congress a plan seeking a U.S.-Soviet ban and had actively sought to resume negotiations with Moscow.

The Brown forces, through a parliamentary maneuver, succeeded in having the House vote first on their amendment, which prevailed on a **238-181 key vote (R 39-122; D 199-59)**. *(1984 key votes, p. 927)*

The House then rejected the Byron amendment twice, on votes of 178-236 and 181-229. McCurdy's amendment was then rejected 196-228.

Senate Position. The defense authorization bill approved by the Senate Armed Services Committee May 31 set the stage for a potential floor fight. That panel's version gutted the 1983 Tsongas amendment barring ASAT flight testing pending presidential certification of administration willingness to negotiate with the Soviets. Ultimately, a floor fight was averted after the White House chose to seek a compromise.

Under the Senate panel's bill, an ASAT flight test would be banned unless the president certified that continued testing was essential to achieving an ASAT arms control agreement.

Meanwhile, Senate ASAT opponents had lowered their sights, realizing that the administration probably could stave off a flat ban on testing. They revised a measure sponsored by Sen. Larry Pressler, R-S.D., dropping the call for a test moratorium. The new version called on the president to resume talks for "a ban or strict limitations" on ASAT testing and to seek a mutual ban on all space weapons. The sponsors intended the new language to amount to a Senate vote of no confidence in Reagan's plan for a space-based anti-missile defense.

Although he cosponsored the Pressler amendment, Tsongas still hoped to salvage as much as possible of his original amendment. Abandoning the goal of a total ASAT ban, Tsongas instead sought to bar an ASAT flight test until the president certified a willingness to negotiate with the Soviets "the strictest possible limitations" on ASATs.

John W. Warner, R-Va., became the interlocutor between the administration and the Tsongas group. Sam Nunn, D-Ga., was part Tsongas ally and part independent player in the bargaining with the administration. Nunn wanted to allow target testing so long as it was linked to serious efforts to limit future ASAT weapons.

When the Senate took up the ASAT issue June 12, Pressler beat Tsongas to the punch and offered his revised measure as an amendment to the defense bill. But before the Senate voted it went into a secret session, at Warner's insistence, to receive a briefing on Soviet anti-satellite capabilities. When the Senate reopened its doors, Pressler withdrew his amendment. Warner offered in its place a compromise, barring ASAT tests until 30 days after the president had certified to Congress that he was trying to negotiate strict limitations on the weapons. The president would have to describe the limitations he was prepared to negotiate. And the certification would have to include recommendations to decrease the vulnerability of U.S. satellites to Soviet ASATs.

The deal was harshly attacked by conservatives, who denounced it as one more effort to "make people comfortable" by holding out hope of arms control agreements while forcing the administration to give ground to Soviet negotiating positions.

A conservative-backed amendment to amend the compromise by stating that nothing in the provision would prevent the president from acting "in the national security interest" was rejected, 45-48. The compromise was adopted, 61-28.

Final Compromise. House-Senate conferees on the defense bill agreed to limit tests of the ASAT missile during fiscal 1985 to two "successful" tests against target satellites. They warned the Pentagon against trying to circumvent the two-test limit by aiming the ASAT to miss the target narrowly.

The final bill authorized the full $144 million requested for ASAT development and $84.5 million for ASAT procurement. HR 5167 was cleared by Congress on Sept. 27.

The bill providing fiscal 1985 appropriations for the Pentagon — a section of the 1985 omnibus appropriations resolution (H J Res 648 — PL 98-473) — contained even tougher restrictions on ASAT: tests would be delayed until March 1, 1985, at the earliest, and no more than three tests — successful or unsuccessful — would be allowed in fiscal 1985. The bill appropriated $254.1 million for the program.

The omnibus bill containing the ASAT funding and test restrictions was cleared by Congress Oct. 11.

The MX Deal. Never at issue in the conference was the $1.7 billion each chamber had approved to continue MX development. Most leaders of the anti-MX coalition wanted to kill the program outright. However, the MX foes had for the most part taken the more moderate public stance opposing production of the missile while supporting its development as a bargaining chip for arms control negotiations with Moscow.

The battle focused on procurement funds, of which the administration requested nearly $3.2 billion, including $233 million for spare parts. As had been agreed to by the White House and Capitol Hill leaders, the authorization conferees approved $2.5 billion for MX procurement, $148 million of which was earmarked for spares. The remaining $2.352 billion could be used for deployment of the fiscal 1984 missiles and production of up to 21 of the 40 additional missiles Reagan had requested.

Midgetman. The two houses had made similar, small trims in the $724.5 million request to develop future ICBMs that would be less vulnerable to attack than the MX. The conferees agreed on $701.8 million to develop the small single-warhead missile and to test new basing methods.

Because of budgetary limits, the authorization for Pershing II ballistic missiles had been trimmed by both chambers from 93 missiles to 70, for which the conferees authorized $375 million.

'Star Wars.' For research on Reagan's proposal to develop a space-based defense against nuclear missiles, the conferees agreed to the Senate-passed figure of $1.63 billion.

The conferees authorized $32 million to modify the Patriot anti-aircraft missile so it could intercept short-range Soviet missiles in Europe.

Submarine Missiles. Conferees trimmed $16 million from the $2.1 billion requested to develop a new Trident II submarine-launched missile, intended — like MX and Midgetman — to be accurate enough to destroy armored Soviet missile launchers.

For the 12th huge submarine designed to launch Trident missiles, the conference authorized $1.7 billion, all but $47 million of the request.

The final bill contained a $60 million authorization for the Navy to develop an airborne radio station to communicate with submerged missile submarines.

Bombers, Cruise Missiles. The final bill authorized $7.1 billion for 34 B-1 bombers, $149 million for B-52 modifications and the entire $116 million requested for the FB-111 bomber. Most of the secret amount in the bill for the stealth bomber was authorized as well as the amount sought for a new, bomber-launched cruise missile.

Conferees approved various provisions added by each house intended to promote various arms control policies, but which imposed only modest limitations on ongoing weapons programs. One provision limited tests of the ASAT missile in fiscal 1985 to two "successful" tests against target satellites. The $144 million requested for ASAT development was agreed to, and the bill contained another $84.5 million for procurement.

The final bill retained the Senate provision stating that Reagan should seek Senate consent to ratification of two treaties limiting underground nuclear explosions that were signed in the mid-1970s but never ratified.

The final bill also required the president to report to Congress on several related issues:

● The impact of Reagan's anti-missile defense plan on the 1972 anti-ballistic missile treaty.

● The feasibility of reducing NATO's reliance on short-range nuclear weapons, such as artillery shells.

● The implications for U.S. nuclear strategy of the proposed procurement of extremely accurate nuclear missiles, including the MX, Midgetman and Trident II missiles.

● The theory that a nuclear war would create a "nuclear winter" because of the soot and debris blown into the atmosphere.

● A method for distinguishing nuclear-armed sea-launched cruise missiles aboard warships from conventionally armed ones. Conferees dropped a House provision that would have barred deployment of the nuclear-armed U.S. Tomahawk missile unless the Soviets deployed a similar one.

Ground Combat. The final bill authorized 840 M-1 tanks, costing $1.7 billion, anti-tank helicopters ($1.3 billion), armored troop carriers with anti-tank missiles ($992 million), and authorizations for laser-guided artillery shells, TOW guided missiles and mortar shells, also used against tanks.

Procurement and development of various expensive anti-aircraft weapons, including the long-range Patriot anti-aircraft missile, were approved, at an overall authorization level of about $1.74 billion.

Navy Ships. Congress cut about $1 billion from the $13 billion requested for Navy ships, but without dropping a single major warship. The bill authorized $3.1 billion for three cruisers and the first of a new class of small destroyers to carry a version of the cruisers' Aegis anti-missile defense system. Arms controllers opposed the bill's inclusion of $10 million to develop a nuclear warhead for the Navy's Standard anti-aircraft missile.

All $423 million requested to refurbish the mothballed World War II battleship *Missouri* was available from unspent money appropriated in previous years and did not require a new authorization in HR 5167.

Lawmakers agreed to authorize some $2.7 billion for four additional nuclear-powered sub-hunting submarines and $213 million for new anti-submarine torpedoes. And for 24 more Navy anti-submarine helicopters, $458 million was authorized. Those sub-hunters were carried on most modern classes of cruisers, destroyers and frigates.

Tactical Air Combat. The final bill authorized the procurement of an additional 42 F-15 fighters and 150 F-16s. These amounts reflected the Air Force's plans for a rapid buildup of its fighter-plane fleet.

For Navy combat planes, the bill authorized procurement of 24 F-14 fighters, 84 F-18 fighters and six A-6E bombers, at a total cost of almost $3.3 billion. Congress also agreed to purchase air-to-air and air-to-ground missiles, authorizing more than $700 million.

Operations and Maintenance. The final bill cut the Pentagon's $80.9 billion request for operations and maintenance of the armed forces by $2.6 billion or 3 percent. The cut, however, did not jeopardize any defense programs or combat readiness.

Personnel Issues. Conferees accepted the Senate position on the annual military pay hike. The final version of HR 5167 approved a 4 percent raise, effective Jan. 1, 1985, for all uniformed personnel except recruits in service less than four months.

For the first time since 1976, a large-scale program of education benefits for all military recruits was authorized. A voluntary three-year test program was established. A separate program was established for enlistees in the Na-

tional Guard or reserve forces who met certain criteria and enlisted for six years.

HR 5167 also contained policy provisions aimed at reducing the costs of spare parts and modifying a 1983 law requiring warranties on all major weapons. It omitted a proposal in the House to substantially increase the powers of the chairman of the Joint Chiefs of Staff.

The bill set a ceiling of 326,414 on the number of U.S. military personnel that could be stationed in Europe. It also called on the president to seek commitments from other NATO members to increase their contributions to the alliance. The authorization measure set the manpower ceiling for the U.S. active-duty military at 2,152,470, which was 13,330 fewer than the Pentagon had requested.

Central America. A provision that the House adopted overwhelmingly in May, barring the introduction of combat troops into El Salvador or Nicaragua without prior congressional approval, was turned into a non-binding expression of the "sense of Congress."

The conference report on HR 5167 also asked the secretary of defense to consider regulations that would bar National Guard or reserve force members from fighting as private parties in foreign wars. That plea was brought on by the death in Nicaragua Sept. 1, 1984, of two U.S. reservists who were participating in a guerrilla attack on a Nicaraguan installation.

1985 Defense Appropriations

Congress approved spending on defense totaling $274.4 billion in fiscal 1985 as part of an omnibus appropriations resolution. That measure (H J Res 648 — PL 98-473) was cleared by Congress Oct. 11.

The Sept. 20 agreement on the companion defense authorization bill, which resolved the contentious issues of the MX missile and the overall spending level for defense, also paved the way for congressional agreement on the appropriations measure.

Under that agreement — between the White House and the Senate and House leadership — the total defense appropriation for the year was set at $292.9 billion, of which the $274.4 billion that would normally have been included in the main defense appropriations bill was incorporated in H J Res 648. The resolution deferred a decision on continued production of the controversial MX missile.

That amount did not include $1.5 billion for production of a second batch of 21 MX missiles (in addition to the 21 MXs already paid for by the fiscal 1984 budget). As part of the September agreement, the 1985 money for MX could be spent only if Congress adopted two resolutions in the spring of 1985. *(Agreements on defense spending level, MX, see defense authorization, p. 244)*

Besides MX, Congress added restrictions or made substantial spending cuts in several other key defense programs and policies pushed by the Reagan administration:

● Tests of the anti-satellite (ASAT) missile were delayed until March 1, 1985, at the earliest, with no more than three tests permitted in fiscal 1985. The provision marked a novel action by Congress: imposing a test moratorium on a new weapon.

● The $1.78 billion requested by President Reagan for development of a space-based anti-missile defense — the program dubbed "Star Wars" by arms control advocates — was trimmed to $1.40 billion.

● New limitations were placed on funding for the rebels,

called "contras," who were battling the leftist Sandinista government of Nicaragua. *(Details, Foreign Policy chapter, p. 175)*

Legislative Action

The Appropriations committees' markup of the defense appropriations legislation fell victim to the political deadlock that had stalled action on the authorization measure (HR 5167), which typically precedes the appropriations bill. On Sept. 26 the two Appropriations panels reported separate versions of a defense funding bill (HR 6329 — H Rept 98-1086, S 3026 — S Rept 98-636). However, provisions of those bills were considered by the House and Senate only as part of the omnibus appropriations resolution.

The Republican-controlled Senate panel's bill was the higher of the two, appropriating $278 billion of an overall defense budget request of $297 billion.

The House Appropriations Committee approved a $268 billion defense bill. By a vote of 24-21, the House panel cut to $1.09 billion the budget for developing Reagan's Star Wars anti-missile weapons program.

Reagan called for the program to make nuclear weapons "impotent and obsolete." But traditional arms control lobbyists maintained that a "leak-proof" defense would be technically impossible and would simply extend the arms race to outer space.

These activists canvassed the committee for support of an amendment that would have cut the program to $1.1 billion. They assumed that the Defense Subcommittee would recommend a $1.37 billion appropriation, the amount approved by the House version of the authorization bill.

To the lobbyists' pleasant surprise, the subcommittee recommended a figure $200 million lower than the House-passed authorization. The Star Wars opponents then decided to seek a further reduction to $1.09 billion, which would amount to a real increase for the program of 5 percent over the fiscal 1984 budget.

This was the first vote taken in the House on Reagan's Star Wars proposal. Arms control lobbyists had decided not to try to reduce the program during the authorization debate in May.

With the MX issue settled by the Sept. 20 agreement between Reagan and the congressional leadership, the only issue in the defense part of H J Res 648 that provoked much floor debate in either house was the administration's request to fund the guerrillas' activities against Nicaragua's Sandinista government.

In the defense portion of the House-Senate conference compromise (H Rept 98-1159) on H J Res 648, conferees agreed to a defense budget for fiscal 1985 of $274,398,173,000 in new budget authority.

Opponents of the administration's ASAT missile decided to try limiting tests of the weapon rather than trying to block its production. That strategy's partial success was embodied in a conference agreement that barred until March 1985 any ASAT tests against a target in space and allowed only three such tests for the rest of fiscal 1985.

Both houses had approved the $65.2 million requested to begin full-scale ASAT production. However, the House denied an additional $38.7 million scattered through various accounts to prepare for continued ASAT production and eventual deployment. The Senate had approved this request.

Defense

The House approved $157.4 million of the $195.5 million request for research and development associated with ASAT. The Senate had approved the entire request. In each case, the two chambers split the difference, approving $18.5 million for procurement and $170.4 million for research and development related to ASAT.

The companion authorization bill (HR 5167) had trimmed the active-duty manpower ceiling to 2,152,470, which was 13,330 fewer than the budget request. The conferees translated this into a reduction of $209 million in the military personnel account and $26 million in the operations and maintenance account.

Conferees trimmed $14.5 million from Air Force travel costs, in keeping with Senate opposition to increasing the number of Air Force personnel stationed in Europe.

1985 Military Construction

Congress approved a $9.13 billion authorization for military construction projects in fiscal 1985. As part of the legislation (HR 5604 — PL 98-407) cleared Aug. 9, Congress warned U.S. allies that they should pay more toward the cost of stationing American troops in Europe.

President Reagan initially requested $10.5 billion for such programs, roughly $1.36 billion higher than the amount finally authorized. However, Reagan in May trimmed his request to $8.5 billion as part of an overall $13.9 billion cut in defense to reduce the federal budget deficit.

In a separate omnibus appropriations resolution (H J Res 648 — PL 98-473), Congress provided $8.4 billion for military construction in fiscal 1985. (Details, p. 247)

House Committee Action

The House Armed Services Committee reported HR 5604 (H Rept 98-765) on May 15. The panel cut $1.2 billion from the $10.5 billion requested, with the bulk of the reduction, about $1 billion, coming from essentially book-keeping adjustments. For example, the committee said it could cut $387 million because of the more favorable bidding climate in the job-hungry construction industry. And the strength of the dollar overseas allowed the committee to cut about $47 million from the U.S. contribution to NATO's common fund for building projects of the alliance. The panel authorized $250 million as the U.S. share.

U.S. Facilities in Honduras. The committee denied an administration request for $8.7 million to construct various military facilities in Honduras. It complained that the Pentagon had not yet supplied Congress with a comprehensive report on U.S. military construction plans for Central America, as required by the previous year's construction appropriations legislation (PL 98-116). The panel's action deleted $1.5 million for a munitions storage area at Palmerola, Honduras, $4.3 million for a maintenance hangar and barracks there and $2.9 million for a warehouse, ammunition storage area and fuel tank at San Lorenzo.

Military construction in Honduras, a neighbor country to strife-torn El Salvador and Nicaragua, came under close congressional scrutiny after an unprecedented number of U.S. servicemen participated in joint military exercises there. Critics charged that the administration was trying to circumvent Congress and establish a permanent presence in Honduras. (Box, p. 176)

Cruise Missiles and NATO. The House committee recommended ending a two-year delay in authorizing construction of facilities for U.S. dependents at European bases where ground-launched cruise missiles (GLCMs) were being deployed.

At the same time, it recommended a $96.2 million reduction in Reagan's request for the GLCM facilities. In December 1983 NATO began deploying 464 of these small, drone jet planes and 108 Pershing II ballistic missiles, both of which could strike Soviet territory from launchers in Western Europe.

Since U.S.-Soviet negotiations to ban these and other intermediate-range nuclear force (INF) missiles had begun in late 1981, Congress had insisted that construction at the missile bases be held down to minimize the loss in case the deployment was stopped at the bargaining table.

The INF talks broke off in late 1983, when the Soviets walked out to protest the imminent deployment of the cruise and Pershing II missiles. In light of the stalled negotiations, the committee approved $94.8 million requested for dependent-related facilities at Greenham Common in the United Kingdom and Cosimo in Sicily.

In all, the panel approved $159 million of the $254 million requested for missile facilities. It deferred for one year $52.2 million requested for dependents' facilities at the base under construction in Florennes, Belgium. It also approved only $35 million of the $79 million requested for cruise missile installations at Woensdrecht, the Netherlands, and provided that none of the funds could be spent until the Dutch Parliament ratified the deployment decision. The Dutch government announced June 1, 1984, that it would accept cruise missiles but not until 1988, two years later than the date set by NATO.

In other construction authorizations in Europe, the panel approved $9.7 million for Army facilities in Greece but rejected $3.95 million requested for Navy communications facilities, citing the Greeks' stated intention to eventually close down U.S. bases in that country. And it denied $8.3 million for construction at a U.S. Navy base in Italy, insisting that NATO should pay for it.

In other actions, the committee:

● Cut $77 million for facilities in a secret Mideast location that would be used by the Rapid Deployment Force, the umbrella organization that would command U.S. forces sent to the Middle East or Indian Ocean regions.

● Approved $26.9 million for Air Force projects in Oman, but denied $15.1 million requested to build bombproof airplane shelters in that country.

● Approved $232 million for various projects at the Atlantic coast base for Trident missile submarines at Kings Bay, Ga.

● Approved $96 million for facilities in connection with the first B-1 bomber squadrons in South Dakota and Texas.

● Approved $44 million for construction at the prospective MX missile base near Cheyenne, Wyo.

● Approved $16.5 million for facilities at Langley Air Force Base, Va., to handle the anti-satellite (ASAT) missile.

House Floor Action

The House passed HR 5604 June 22 by a 312-49 vote, authorizing $9.2 billion for construction projects. Of several amendments adopted, the most noteworthy deleted $35 million earmarked for ground-launched cruise missile facil-

ities in the Netherlands. The cut reflected the Dutch government's deferral of a final decision on whether to allow GLCM deployment.

Senate Committee Action

The Senate Armed Services Committee reported its construction authorization bill (S 2723) on May 31 (S Rept 98-500). Unlike the House bill, the Senate bill also included the fiscal 1985 authorizations for weapons procurement, research, operations and maintenance as well as the nuclear weapons programs conducted on behalf of the Defense Department by the Department of Energy. *(Defense procurement authorization bill, p. 235)*

As reported, the Senate committee's bill authorized $9.3 billion for the military construction portion of the defense authorization.

Compared with its House counterpart, the Senate panel made substantially larger cuts. These included:

• $420 million that would not be needed since the committee expected contractors to submit lower-than-anticipated bids.

• $100.6 million to be replaced by funds left over from the fiscal 1984 construction appropriation because of low bids.

• $165 million (of the $296.7 million requested) for the U.S. contribution to NATO's fund for building facilities of common benefit.

On the other hand, the Senate committee approved the entire amounts requested for two new military hospitals at Fort Lewis, Wash. ($353 million), and at Travis Air Force Base, Calif. ($201 million).

Military Facilities in Honduras. The Senate committee approved a $4.4 million authorization for the two facilities sought by the Pentagon for storing U.S. military equipment and ammunition in Honduras. During markup, a move to delete the authorization lost on a 9-9 tie vote. The funds "represent the first step toward committing American forces to combat in Central America," charged Sen. Jeff Bingaman, D-N.M., who offered the motion to drop the funds.

Senate Floor Action

The Senate-passed version, incorporated initially in the Defense Department authorization bill (HR 5167), authorized $9.3 billion for military construction. On June 26, the construction authorization was added as an amendment to HR 5604.

A floor fight over the military base in Honduras was averted when the administration agreed June 1 to drop the $4.4 million it had requested for construction.

A controversial issue that did surface in the debate was the question of U.S. European allies' share of the defense burden in NATO. Widespread unhappiness with the allies was underscored June 7 when the Senate voted 91-3 to adopt a non-binding amendment expressing the sense of Congress that the president should "insist" that:

• Major NATO members meet their earlier pledges to increase defense spending by at least 3 percent above the cost of inflation in 1984 and 1985.

• Japan "further increase its defense spending." Because of domestic anti-militarist political pressures since World War II, the Japanese government had held its defense budget to less than 1 percent of the Japanese gross national product.

But by a vote of 76-16 the Senate rejected an amendment that was intended to limit the rate of increase in spending for U.S. forces in Europe to the rate at which NATO countries increased their defense budgets.

With Congress confronting the options of higher taxes, higher deficits, stark reductions in domestic programs or a slowdown in Reagan's proposed defense buildup, the argument that the allies should do more offered a way for members to seek lower defense spending without seeming to endorse a weaker U.S. military position.

Just how far congressional sentiment had come was underscored June 20, when Sen. Sam Nunn, D-Ga., introduced an amendment that would have trimmed U.S. troop strength in Europe by almost 30 percent unless the other NATO members began following through on certain agreed-to defense improvements. The amendment was rejected, 55-41, but only after heavy lobbying by the White House. In the end, the administration carried the day because tight party discipline prevailed and because of concern on the part of some senators that the timing was wrong for a hard-nosed approach to the allies.

Conference Action

A conference report on HR 5604 (H Rept 98-962) was filed Aug. 7. The final bill settled on a $9.1 billion authorization for military construction projects in fiscal 1985.

In their report, House-Senate conferees warned that the refusal of European allies to pay a greater share of the cost of keeping U.S. forces in Europe was "becoming a major issue with the American people. Unless the allies are more forthcoming in their support for U.S. forces, there will be ever increasing pressure to bring U.S. forces home."

The conferees singled out West Germany for special criticism. In the 1970s, the Bonn government had paid for several construction projects to support U.S. units. But now, the conferees complained, West Germany was refusing to pay for the so-called "master restationing plan." Under that plan, three battalions were to be moved from their current billets to new facilities a hundred miles closer to the defensive positions along the East German border that U.S. forces would be expected to hold in case of war. Congress had insisted for years that West Germany pay for the move. The repositioning plan was stalled because of the funding deadlock.

The conference compromise accepted the Senate figure of $131.7 million as the annual U.S. contribution to NATO's fund for jointly financed construction projects. The administration had requested $296.7 million.

Although the administration had abandoned its $4.4 million request for two facilities in Honduras, the administration also requested $4.3 million for a U.S. Army air reconnaissance unit in Honduras. The Senate, but not the House, had approved that authorization, and conferees went along with the Senate.

The House adopted the conference report Aug. 8 and the Senate followed suit the next day, completing congressional action.

Military Construction Funding

Congress appropriated $8.4 billion for military construction programs in fiscal 1985. The funds were contained in the omnibus appropriations resolution (H J Res 648 — PL 98-473) cleared by Congress Oct. 11.

Defense

House Action

The House Appropriations Committee drafted its own funding bill for construction projects (HR 5898), which was reported (H Rept 98-850) on June 20. The panel cut almost $2 billion from the Defense Department's $10.3 billion request. Approximately $140 million of the overall cut came from projects the panel said should be paid for by U.S. allies, once again underscoring congressional frustration over the burden-sharing issue.

In its report, the committee criticized the Pentagon for "going it alone" to meet military threats, regardless of whether U.S. allies were willing to do more for their own military security. The report added that unilateral U.S. efforts had a pernicious side effect. "As the trend toward U.S. willingness to proceed unilaterally continues, our allies have shown less and less willingness to contribute a fair share."

Projects in Europe that the committee insisted should be paid for by the NATO alliance (or by the host country for the facilities) included:

- $38 million for improvements to an Army airfield at Ansbach, West Germany.
- $29 million to support equipment of Army units in West Germany with the DIVAD anti-aircraft tank.
- $13 million for improvements to existing facilities so Air Force units could continue operating in the event of attack by chemical weapons.

The panel refused to provide funds to build ammunition and fuel dumps and maintenance shops at non-U.S. air bases in Europe that 1,500 U.S. fighter planes would use in the event of a NATO mobilization.

The committee also dropped funds for improvements at bases in Britain ($16.7 million) and Turkey ($24.5 million). In each case, the committee insisted that NATO pay for the construction through its common fund.

In addition, the committee demanded that non-NATO countries help pay for military construction projects that improved defenses in those countries. The panel refused to appropriate $15.8 million for a storage facility in South Korea and $7.2 million for improvements at an airfield in Japan. The panel also deleted $8.7 million requested for three projects in Honduras, on the ground they had not yet been authorized. *(Honduras projects, authorization bill, p. 246)*

The committee added language requiring the secretary of defense to inform the panel of any military exercise in which more than $100,000 was expected to be spent on construction projects. And the committee complained that it had not been informed of construction plans associated with previous U.S. training exercises in Honduras.

The House passed HR 5898 on June 28. Before passage, the House adopted, 218-180, an amendment that cut the bill by $25 million.

Senate Action

The Senate Appropriations Committee reported its version of HR 5898 on July 26 (S Rept 98-567).

The Senate panel's funding recommendations reflected concern that the House had gone too far in cutting funds for overseas projects in the hope that the NATO allies would pick up the tab. The bill as reported provided $8.5 billion in appropriations, about $277 million more than the House-passed version. Though the Senate side also felt U.S. allies were not paying their fair share, the committee restored $114 million of the House cuts. Some of the projects were too vital to allow them to become hostage to dickering among the allies, it maintained.

The committee added language expressing the sense of Congress that the allies should adhere to their 1973 agreement to boost defense budgets at an annual rate of 3 percent.

The panel restored the funds cut by the House for facilities in South Korea and Japan but agreed with the House in denying a $37.9 million request for Air Force facilities in Oman.

Also restored by the committee were funds for various Air Force facilities, improvements at an airfield in Turkey, new personnel facilities in Germany in connection with the plan to restation U.S. Army units closer to the East German border, and facilities to house Apache tank-hunting helicopters and personnel at Ansbach, Germany.

The Senate approved funds for military construction, which were incorporated in the omnibus funding resolution, on Oct. 4.

Conference Action

In the Oct. 10 conference report on H J Res 648 (H Rept 98-1159), the section on military construction contained some, but not all, of the major projects in the NATO countries and Japan that had become issues in the 1985 defense burden-sharing disputes.

Conferees approved $19 million for facilities at Ansbach, saying they were urgently needed. But they refused to appropriate another $25 million for facilities in Germany. However, conferees dropped a 1982 embargo Congress had placed on spending $23.5 million in connection with the allied restationing plan.

The final bill included funds for construction in Japan, but not in South Korea. And conferees said NATO should provide the $24.5 million to improve an air base in Turkey that U.S. forces would use in time of war.

Of the $29.3 million Reagan had requested for construction related to MX missile deployment at Warren Air Force Base near Cheyenne, Wyo., the conference committee approved $16.6 million. This would be enough to deploy the first 10 MXs.

Construction related to another controversial weapon — the ASAT missile — was placed on hold. The Air Force had requested $16.5 million for facilities at Langley Air Force Base near Newport News, Va., where the weapons first would be deployed.

The conference committee version of H J Res 648 was approved by the House Oct. 10 and by the Senate Oct. 11, completing action.

Special Report: Arms Control

Ronald Reagan assumed the presidency in an era of increased military spending and distrust between the superpowers. Jimmy Carter's Strategic Arms Limitation Treaty (SALT II) remained unratified, its doom sealed by the Soviet invasion of Afghanistan. Congressional and public support for arms control had waned. Détente was dead.

As a presidential candidate Reagan had denounced SALT II. He agreed with defense hard-liners that the nuclear balance had tipped dangerously to the Soviet Union's advantage because previous administrations of both parties had placed too much faith in arms control agreements as a response to the Soviet military buildup. Reagan believed the United States had to accelerate its own buildup to avoid having to negotiate from a position of nuclear inferiority.

His opponents claimed existing U.S. and Soviet arsenals were more than sufficient to ensure that a nuclear attack by either side would result in the annihilation of both countries. To build more weapons, therefore, would only waste money and resources. Moreover, the administration's critics maintained, the weapons Reagan sought — including the MX, Pershing II and cruise missiles — would induce the Soviets to speed up their buildup, destabilize East-West relations and increase the likelihood of nuclear war.

Arms control negotiations in Reagan's first term focused on achieving essential equivalence and overall reductions in the two superpowers' strategic and theater nuclear forces. The United States and the Soviet Union held talks on intercontinental and intermediate-range nuclear forces but neither approached the point where agreements were serious possibilities.

Public Skepticism

Many Democrats and moderate Republicans, NATO allies and the general public complained that the administration's arms control proposals offered little promise for agreement because they would require far greater reductions in Soviet forces than in U.S. forces. Reagan seemed unable or unwilling to make arms control proposals that stood some realistic chance of being accepted by the Soviets, and his occasional use of bellicose rhetoric raised questions about whether he fully appreciated the dangers of nuclear war and the nuclear arms race. Doubts became especially acute in early 1983, when Reagan fired the head of the Arms Control and Disarmament Agency (ACDA) and replaced him with an inexperienced critic of arms control. Congress delayed appropriations for the MX missile, in part because of pressure from an increasingly sophisticated peace movement, and seriously considered a nuclear freeze to prod Reagan into being more flexible at the bargaining table.

Public opinion and congressional pressure succeeded in shifting the administration's arms control policies somewhat toward the center, but the East-West negotiations produced no arms control agreements in Reagan's first term. The Soviets suspended the talks as the United States, late in 1983, began deploying Pershing II and cruise missiles in Western Europe. Almost immediately the Soviets began deploying SS-22 missiles in East Germany.

SALT II

The failure of SALT II to win Senate approval set the tone for U.S. arms control efforts of the early 1980s.

President Carter and Soviet President Leonid I. Brezhnev signed the treaty at a summit meeting in Vienna June 18, 1979. But senators, even members of Carter's own party, showed little enthusiasm for SALT II. And after the Soviet Union invaded Afghanistan in late 1979 Carter formally asked the Senate to defer action, knowing the pact could not win the necessary two-thirds Senate majority. *(Background, Congress and the Nation Vol. V, p. 193)*

Although he continued to express support for the treaty, Carter in 1980 substantially increased his budget requests for defense spending in response to what he termed "the steady military buildup by the Soviets, and their growing inclination to rely on military power to exploit turbulent situations."

Both the United States and the Soviet Union pledged to honor the unratified SALT II agreement. President Reagan continued to criticize the treaty, but he agreed informally not to violate its provisions if the Soviets abided by them.

SALT II set basic numerical limits on intercontinental missiles and bombers to be in effect until 1985:

● Of 2,250 weapons allowed each country (after 1982), no more than 1,320 could be missiles with multiple warheads (MIRVs) or bombers carrying long-range cruise missiles.

● Of those 1,320, no more than 1,200 could be missiles.

● Of those 1,200, no more than 820 could be land-based missiles (ICBMs).

Additional restrictions on mobile land-based missiles and cruise missiles launched from land or ships were to run only until 1982.

The Strategic Balance

In the post-Vietnam War era, the Soviet Union's strategic capabilities grew while members of the NATO alliance, including the United States, adopted a policy of arms restraint and reduced military spending. By the early or mid-1970s Moscow had gained the lead in the number of missiles deployed and in the size of the ICBMs' payload.

By the late 1970s technological advances threatened to undermine the foundations of arms control and heighten the peril of nuclear war. Generally, as nuclear weapons systems became more compact, easily concealed, accurate and effective, they destabilized the strategic balance. By making it seem possible to undertake a pre-emptive first strike or the limited use of nuclear weapons to promote military objectives, the technological advances made such events more likely, according to arms control proponents. Deemed particularly destabilizing were extremely accurate weapons — such as the Soviet SS-20 and the U.S. MX, Pershing II and cruise missiles — that could threaten or seem to threaten the adversary's nuclear arsenal. (Weapons at issue, box, p. 252)

Although the 1980 annual report of the Defense Department acknowledged that the concept of "mutual assured destruction" (MAD) remained the "bedrock of nuclear deterrence," the Pentagon called for flexibility to respond at appropriate levels to smaller-scale nuclear attacks.

The European Theater

One arena in which a limited nuclear war seemed possible was Europe. In 1977 the Soviet Union began to deploy SS-20 intermediate-range ballistic missiles (IRBMs), each armed with three highly accurate warheads. By 1983 more than two-thirds of the Soviet force of some 350 SS-20 mobile, reloadable launchers were pointed toward Western Europe. Older additional IRBMs on stationary launchers and a fleet of medium-range Backfire bombers carrying nuclear missiles supplemented the SS-20s.

To counter the Soviet threat the NATO alliance in 1979 agreed to pursue a two-track policy of modernizing its theater nuclear forces while encouraging negotiations to limit such forces. U.S. Pershing II intermediate-range missiles and ground-launched cruise missiles (GLCMs) were to be deployed beginning in December 1983. (The United States alone would control the Pershing IIs, as NATO allies chose not to share the cost.)

A principal argument for deploying Pershing IIs and cruise missiles in Europe was to prevent the "decoupling" of the United States from its NATO allies through Soviet pressure. So long as the allies had no weapons that could match the Soviet missiles, Moscow might think it could avoid retaliation by striking Western Europe while sparing the United States.

The Reagan administration saw the Pershing II as a powerful bargaining lever because the Soviets viewed the missile as having first-strike potential. Moscow warned that deployment of the Pershing IIs would force it to adopt an "instantaneous" retaliatory posture of launch-on-warning.

'Window of Vulnerability'

The Reagan administration generally agreed with its predecessor that maintaining essential equivalence with the Soviet Union in nuclear forces was crucial for ensuring the nation's security. But Reagan and his advisers viewed the existing nuclear balance as much more favorable to Moscow than did Carter.

Like Carter, Reagan pursued a strategic policy based on developing the most advanced land-based nuclear missiles. Both administrations placed particular importance on the theoretical ability of Moscow's increasingly accurate MIRVed (multiple warhead) ICBMs to destroy America's land-based missiles during a period in which U.S. forces, according to some analysts, posed no equivalent threat to heavily protected Soviet missile silos embedded in tons of concrete and rock.

Reagan decried this disparity as a "window of vulnerability" that might encourage Moscow to step up political confrontations and even risk military actions threatening vital interests of the United States and its allies.

Some defense experts, including Reagan administration officials, were skeptical that the window was as large as Reagan and others claimed. Among the skeptics were members of the Presidential Commission on Strategic Forces, appointed in January 1983 at the urging of congressional defense specialists to recommend an adequate (survivable) MX basing plan in light of the existing strategic balance. Retired Lt. Gen. Brent Scowcroft, who had been President Gerald R. Ford's national security adviser, chaired the commission. Other members were veterans of the Nixon, Ford and Carter administrations, including Carter's defense secretary, Harold Brown. The panel concluded that some MX missiles were needed but that, viewed in its entirety, the U.S. strategic system of ICBMs, submarine-launched ballistic missiles (SLBMs) and long-range bombers continued to provide an effective deterrent to a successful Soviet attack. (Scowcroft report highlights, box, p. 227)

The Carter administration took measures to enhance U.S. capability to fight a nuclear war, but Reagan went even further. Throughout his first two years in office, Reagan emphasized the need to modernize and strengthen the U.S. strategic nuclear triad of land-, air- and sea-based weapons.

Reagan characterized his strategic policy as "peace through strength." But many observers perceived instead a gradual return to the Cold War climate of East-West confrontation and a growing paranoia, accompanied by provocative rhetoric on both sides. In 1981 Reagan spoke casually of "limited" nuclear war without linking it to deterrence or expressing much discomfort at the prospect of a nuclear exchange.

With public and congressional demands increasing for presidential action to contain the arms race, however, Reagan initiated efforts to eliminate nuclear weapons throughout Europe and to reduce the superpowers' arsenal of intercontinental nuclear weapons.

Reagan's Approach to Arms Control

Reagan insisted that any arms agreement would have to preserve an "equitable" balance between the two superpowers. His goal was to reduce the deployment of nuclear weapons without endangering U.S. security.

The administration's approach rested on two fundamental premises: 1) that peace depended on a nearly symmetrical balance of U.S. and Soviet forces, especially in land-based ICBMs; and 2) that the Soviet Union would reduce its nuclear arsenals only if confronted with unequiv-

ocal indications that the United States would match Soviet military advances in the absence of an arms control agreement.

Reagan initially appointed longtime defense analysts to key arms control posts. To head the Arms Control and Disarmament Agency (ACDA), the president chose Eugene V. Rostow, who had been chairman of the Committee on the Present Danger, the most influential anti-SALT group in the Ford and Carter years. Paul H. Nitze, former staff director for the Committee on the Present Danger, became the U.S. negotiator on medium-range missiles in Europe. Reagan's choice for START negotiator was retired general Edward L. Rowny, who had resigned from Carter's SALT II delegation in protest against concessions made to the Soviet Union. Despite the appointees' conservative credentials, some hard-line critics viewed the group as suspiciously "soft" on the basic notion of arms control.

From other quarters, concern about the administration's commitment to halting the arms race grew steadily. Early in 1983 Reagan had three major conflicts with critics of his arms control policy.

The first came in January, after Reagan dismissed Rostow as ACDA director. Rostow claimed he was fired for favoring too much flexibility in the arms control negotiations, but others contended his arrogance cost him his job. Rostow's replacement was Kenneth L. Adelman, a 36-year-old member of the U.S. delegation to the United Nations who had little background in the technicalities of arms control.

At his confirmation hearing before the Senate Foreign Relations Committee, Adelman gave noncommittal answers to several questions, saying, for example, that he had never thought much about whether a nuclear war was winnable. Committee Democrats charged that Reagan had shown his indifference toward arms control by naming an ACDA director without the experience, enthusiasm or political stature to be an effective advocate for arms control. Adelman's confirmation did not come until three months after Reagan nominated him. (Details, p. 233)

Liberals again assailed the president after a March 23 televised address in which Reagan called for a new emphasis on developing anti-missile defenses, possibly including satellites armed with laser weapons, to render nuclear weapons "impotent and obsolete." The suggestion, which the news media quickly dubbed a "Star Wars" scheme, drew harsh words from arms control advocates, who warned that it would undermine the deterrent balance between the superpowers.

Some administration members moved quickly to remove the rhetorical wrapping from Reagan's proposal. They emphasized that decades would pass before such weapons would be available and stressed the importance of accelerating existing research and development programs — if only to keep abreast of Soviet activity.

The third confrontation in 1983 was another round in the congressional battle to use defense appropriations and the substantial support of the nuclear freeze movement to make Reagan less rigid in arms control talks with the Soviet Union.

The Geneva Talks

In November 1981 Reagan announced his first arms control initiatives. He sought talks on intermediate-range nuclear forces (INF) in the European theater and talks on intercontinental nuclear forces. Unlike SALT II, which he said would have allowed both countries to continue expanding their strategic forces, Reagan's goal was to reduce existing nuclear arsenals substantially. To reinforce this difference, he called the negotiations on intercontinental missiles and bombers START, for Strategic Arms Reduction Talks.

INF Talks

As a basis for the INF talks, which began Nov. 30, 1981, the president proposed a "zero option" for intermediate-range nuclear forces: If the Soviet Union would decommission its SS-20 missiles (and some older, shorter-range weapons directed at the West), the United States would suspend plans to deploy 108 Pershing II ballistic missiles and 464 ground-launched cruise missiles in Europe.

Although the Soviets expressed a willingness to give up some of their intermediate-range weapons, they rejected Reagan's proposal, saying it had been designed to be non-negotiable. One sticking point, they claimed, was that the proposal gave the West unfair advantages.

For years Moscow had insisted that any limitation of nuclear forces in Europe take account of all arms capable of reaching Soviet territory, including British and French missile-launching submarines and many warplanes of the NATO countries. Reagan's proposal, however, did not meet that demand.

Each side made a number of formal and informal proposals, but progress was slow. In February 1982 Reagan rejected an informal Soviet proposal that would have allowed deployment of Soviet SS-20 missiles, but not U.S. Pershing IIs or cruise missiles. Although the West European NATO allies also rejected the Soviet proposal, they let it be known that they preferred a more flexible negotiating position than Reagan's zero option plan. Although they found the Soviet monopoly of intermediate-range nuclear weapons unacceptable, many European officials contended that Moscow would never accept the zero option plan without modifications.

The following month, when the Soviet Union announced a unilateral halt in deployment of new Soviet missiles in Europe, the Reagan administration dismissed it as a propaganda ploy. Secretary of State Alexander M. Haig Jr. rejected the freeze concept and ruled out a U.S. declaration of "no first use" of nuclear weapons.

Nitze Initiative Rejected. Reagan also rejected an informal compromise chief U.S. negotiator Nitze worked out in July 1982 with his Soviet counterpart, Yuli A. Kvitsinsky, even though Nitze told the president that the basic U.S. negotiating position was unrealistic. The so-called "walk in the woods" agreement would have prohibited the deployment of Pershing II missiles and would have limited the number of SS-20 and cruise missile launchers to 75 each. Because each SS-20 launcher held only three warheads, compared with four for each cruise missile launcher, the agreement would have given the United States an advantage — as compensation for giving up development of the Pershing IIs.

The Soviets also rejected the agreement suggested by Nitze and Kvitsinsky.

The United States, France and Britain rejected a December 1982 offer by the Soviets to reduce their nuclear weapons aimed at Europe to 162, the number deployed by France and Britain.

Weapons at Issue in Reagan Defense Plan ...

President Reagan's defense modernization program called for upgrading or augmentation of the forces that provide the U.S. deterrent against nuclear attack. Following are brief descriptions of the most controversial weapons systems in the Reagan plan.

Strategic Forces

The strategic arms reduction talks (START) process applied to intercontinental ballistic missiles (ICBMs), submarine-launched ballistic missiles (SLBMs), air-to-surface ballistic missiles (ASBMs) and intercontinental bombers.

MX Missile

Among nuclear weapons systems, the proposed MX intercontinental missile consumed the most congressional attention during President Reagan's first term. The MX (missile experimental) was mobile and much larger than the increasingly vulnerable, immobile Minuteman III, which still formed the core of the U.S. ICBM force.

The MX carried 10 MIRV warheads — each more powerful than the three on the existing Minuteman III and accurate to within 100 yards of a target — that could destroy the most heavily fortified Soviet installation.

The central issues in Congress were 1) whether to go ahead with production despite MX's high cost and 2) how to base or deploy the missiles so they could not be destroyed before they were launched in a retaliatory attack.

Congress barred most funds appropriated in fiscal 1982 for Reagan's interim plan to "superharden" existing silos, ordered the administration to select a long-term MX basing mode by July 1983 and denied funding for an air-launch plan.

Reagan next proposed what became known as the "dense pack" scheme. One hundred MXs would be deployed 1,800 feet apart in a column 14 miles long at Warren Air Force Base near Cheyenne, Wyo. In theory the blast effect created by the first few attacking missiles would destroy or disable all the other incoming Soviet missiles. But the MXs would be far enough apart that a Soviet warhead could destroy only one of them.

Proponents argued that if the MXs were hit simultaneously most would survive and be usable for a counterattack. Soviet warheads aimed at the surviving MXs would be neutralized by the first Soviet warheads to explode. Debris thrown up by the first explosions would deflect any later warheads. Before a second Soviet attack was possible, the surviving MXs could be launched.

The Reagan administration worked hard to overcome congressional objections to dense pack's cost, its effect on the arms race and its uncertain feasibility. There was also some concern that it might violate SALT II and the 1972 Anti-Ballistic Missile (ABM) treaty.

In December 1982 the House blocked funds for the first five MXs. The Senate restored the funds but said they could not be spent until Congress approved an MX basing system.

In April 1983 the Presidential Commission on Strategic Nuclear Forces recommended deploying 100 MX missiles in existing silos while the United States developed a new, smaller single-warhead mobile missile (Midgetman) that would be invulnerable to Soviet attack. The commission cited four main arguments for producing the MX: leverage in the START negotiations; deterrence; righting the strategic imbalance; and modernizing the ICBM force.

Congress in May 1983 approved funds to begin implementing the MX basing plan and to produce the first 21 missiles. In June 1984 the administration narrowly staved off an attempt to bar funds for additional MX production, but Congress withheld the go-ahead for the 21 additional missiles until March 1985. *(Details, p. 238)*

B-1 Bomber vs. 'Stealth'

Like the MX, the long-range bomber force had been the focus of protracted, loud debate. President Carter in 1977 emphatically rejected the B-1 bomber and Congress eventually went along after a tough battle. Carter favored modernizing the B-52 with air-launched cruise missiles.

But supporters of the B-1 — which brought jobs to hundreds of congressional districts — seized on a 1979 Strategic Air Command (SAC) study that showed the United States dropping below the Soviets in nuclear capability and staying there until the MX was ready in the late 1980s. SAC commander Richard H. Ellis said that only a new bomber could quickly overcome the problem.

When the House Armed Services Committee cited the SAC study as proof the B-1 was needed, Ellis argued that it would be cheaper and faster to enlarge the F-111 fighters already in service. Ellis also feared the B-1 program would shift money away from development of the then-secret "stealth" bomber, which was being designed with non-metallic surfaces and a smooth shape to make it a smaller target for enemy radar.

In 1982 Congress agreed to procure the first 100 B-1s but the battle continued, with Sen. Sam Nunn, D-Ga., and others warning that the B-1 inevitably would compete for funds with the stealth bomber.

... Range from Cruise Missile to 'Star Wars'

Theater Nuclear Weapons

The intermediate-range nuclear forces (INF) talks concerned weapons with a range of less than 5,500 kilometers (km.), called theater nuclear weapons or intermediate-range weapons.

Pershing II Missile

The Pershing II's extreme accuracy, and its ability to hit targets in the western Soviet Union within some 10-12 minutes after being launched, caused the missile to be particularly destabilizing, arms control supporters contended. If the Soviets feared a surprise attack, they might put their own missiles on a hair trigger, such as "launch on warning."

Attempts in Congress to cut funding for Pershing II had been unsuccessful. As the scheduled date of deployment drew near, freeze leaders unsuccessfully sought a delay. Subsequently, Rep. Edward J. Markey, D-Mass., and some 30 other members of Congress wrote to Reagan urging a six-month delay in the European deployment if the Soviet Union agreed to an immediate, verifiable 20 percent reduction in the 243 SS-20s aimed at Western Europe. More than 110 House members signed a second letter calling on Reagan to defer deployment. But the administration went ahead and the first missiles were deployed in late 1983, as scheduled.

Cruise Missile

A small, pilotless drone jet, the cruise was designed to fly at very low altitudes and follow the contours of the terrain to minimize detection by radar. Cruise missiles could be air-, ground- or sea-launched and could carry conventional or nuclear warheads. The cruise missile's deployment in Western Europe began along with that of the Pershing II.

Because of its slow speed, the cruise missile was considered inappropriate for use in a surprise "first-strike" attack. Its accuracy and its ability to evade radar, however, made it a formidable weapon. Critics in the arms control community worried that deployment of cruise missiles would lead to serious verification problems. The drones were hard to detect, and it was virtually impossible to distinguish those with nuclear warheads from those without them.

Strategic Defense Initiative

In 1983 President Reagan proposed development of defensive weapons that could destroy Soviet missiles before they reached the United States. He called on the scientific community to undertake a "long-term [missile defense] research and development program to begin to achieve our ultimate goal." Administration officials acknowledged that the Strategic Defense Initiative (SDI), called "Star Wars" by its detractors, would take decades to reach fruition, with no guarantee of success. Its feasibility was not expected to be known until the early 1990s.

Reagan said SDI would strengthen deterrence because Moscow would have little incentive to build weapons that the United States could render impotent. Reagan offered to share SDI technology with the Soviet Union. If both sides constructed viable strategic defenses, he said, perhaps both would then dismantle their nuclear arsenals.

SDI would constitute a "layered defense," using different technologies to destroy attacking missiles during each phase of the ballistic trajectory. An ICBM could be destroyed during its "boost phase" shortly after launch, during the "post-boost phase" before the warheads were released, in the "mid-course phase" while the released warheads were soaring through space or during the "terminal phase" as they re-entered the atmosphere. The system would use space- and Earth-based lasers and mirrors.

SDI overtook the MX as the most controversial element of the administration's defense modernization program.

In its five-year preliminary research phase alone, SDI was expected to cost $26 billion; some estimates put its final figure at $1 trillion.

In addition, many arms control advocates in Congress feared that deploying a strategic defense system in space would set off a new arms race, with the Soviet Union trying to devise offensive weapons that could penetrate SDI and the United States trying to build even more elaborate defenses.

Some physicists believed the plan to be feasible. But others said SDI would pose grave dangers, even if it were possible to extend a nuclear umbrella over the United States.

A Union of Concerned Scientists study said that "If the president's vision is pursued, outer space could become a battlefield."

The Soviets charged that SDI would make a pre-emptive first strike more likely. Moscow insisted that preventing the militarization of space was the most important issue to be addressed when the Geneva talks resumed in 1985.

Testing and deploying SDI would possibly violate the 1972 ABM treaty, under which each party agreed "not to deploy ABM systems for a defense of the territory of its country." Critics charged that the Reagan administration accused the Soviet Union of violating the ABM treaty at least in part because it wanted to be free of the treaty for SDI.

Modified Zero Option

As the call for U.S. flexibility grew at home and in Europe, Reagan gave up his insistence that the Soviets abandon their entire force of SS-20s. Although the zero option remained his ultimate goal, as an interim step he offered to consider any Soviet proposal that would limit to equal numbers the U.S. and Soviet warheads deployed on intermediate-range ballistic missiles.

Congress and NATO leaders reacted favorably to Reagan's new offer, taking it as a sign the administration was willing to negotiate. The Soviets were unhappy with the plan, however, because it ignored other types of intermediate-range nuclear weapons and American bombers deployed in Europe and expanded the scope of the bargain to include Soviet missiles aimed at Asia.

In May 1983 the new Soviet leader, Yuri V. Andropov, announced that Moscow was prepared to reach an agreement with the United States limiting the number of nuclear warheads, as well as launchers, to the existing NATO levels (including those of French and British forces) in the European theater. Andropov added that Moscow would "be compelled to take measures in reply" if the United States went ahead with its planned European deployment of Pershing II missiles.

Reagan called Andropov's proposal encouraging, and the Soviets continued to be conciliatory during the summer. In September, however, positions hardened after Soviet pilots downed a commercial South Korean airliner. Soviet leaders, announcing that they would not make arms control concessions to temper world opinion, backed off from previous offers.

In December 1983 the Soviet Union suspended all arms control talks after the United States began deploying Pershing II and cruise missiles in Western Europe. The Soviets announced their intention to deploy medium-range missiles in East Germany and Czechoslovakia, and in January 1984 U.S. intelligence sources confirmed that deployment of a new missile, the SS-22, had begun in East Germany.

START

Reagan's START plan focused on restricting each country's total number of ballistic missile warheads as well as the number of deployed missiles. His initial proposal set limits to be reached over a period of five to 10 years:

● No more than about 5,000 warheads on ICBMs and submarine-launched missiles. (Administration officials said there were about 7,500 such warheads in each country's arsenal as of 1982.)

● No more than about 850 ICBMs and SLBMs. (The administration placed inventories at about 2,500 for the Soviet Union and 1,700 for the United States.)

● No more than 2,500 ICBM warheads on each side. (The administration placed inventories at about 5,500 for the Soviet Union and 2,152 for the United States.)

Although the proposal did not set ceilings on bombers and cruise missiles, Secretary of State Haig told the Senate Foreign Relations Committee a first-phase START treaty might contain them. In the meantime the United States would proceed with development of the B-1 bomber and the so-called "stealth" plane. The Pentagon was also working to improve cruise missiles.

As a second step in the START process, Reagan intended to seek equal limits on total throw weight — weapons-carrying capacity of long-range missiles — at a lower level than the existing U.S. total. Hard-line U.S. defense analysts had condemned the SALT II treaty for limiting the number of weapons launchers rather than missile throw weight, a measure by which Moscow enjoyed nearly a 3-to-1 advantage over the United States.

Strategic weapons not covered by the first phase of START would have equal limits for the two superpowers under the second phase.

Reactions to START

Reagan's proposal received a generally favorable reception in Congress. Nevertheless, START encountered many of the same objections raised against SALT II.

Opponents said Moscow would retain an advantage in missile throw weight and warhead power, at least in the first phase, even if there were equal ceilings on the ICBM arsenals. The disparity would result because existing Soviet ICBMs were larger than the U.S. Minuteman missiles, and the Soviet SS-18 was larger than the projected MX.

Critics also complained that START would limit the number of deployed missiles, rather than the total missile stockpile, giving an advantage to the Soviets because their missile launchers were reusable. Secretary Haig, however, said "mutual understandings" would bar large stockpiles under START.

Some defense experts objected to START (and to SALT before it) because they felt the underlying assessment of the nuclear balance was misleading. These critics said the accuracy and invulnerability of missiles mattered more than the number of warheads and the throw weight.

The Soviets did not summarily reject Reagan's START plan as they had Carter's initial proposal, but they made it clear they would not accept START as proposed.

Phase two would require the Soviet Union to abandon nearly two-thirds of its land-based missile power, the strongest component of its nuclear force. ICBMs constituted about 75 percent of Soviet strategic capability, about 70 percent of Soviet strategic warheads and more than 80 percent of Soviet nuclear explosive power. By contrast, ICBMs accounted for about 40 percent of U.S. strategic capability, about half of U.S. strategic launchers, about one quarter of U.S. strategic warheads and about 40 percent of the U.S. arsenal's explosive power.

Administration officials maintained that it was in the Soviet Union's interest to shift away from reliance on ICBMs because technological advances in strategic warheads would make land-based missiles increasingly vulnerable in both countries.

Congress engaged the administration in a protracted struggle over defense appropriations and approval of the MX missile, which the president viewed as essential to his nuclear strategy. In May 1983, shortly before important votes to release funds for further MX development, Reagan wrote to influential members of Congress giving his blessing in general terms to a build-down approach — in which each country would scrap a certain number of warheads for each new warhead it deployed. Reagan formally committed himself to the build-down approach in October of that year.

Applying his new approach to START, Reagan abandoned his demand for low ceilings on ICBMs, thus requiring a less radical cut in the existing Soviet missile force, and offered to limit the number of bomber-launched cruise missiles his administration was planning to build. Within six months, however, START was suspended when the

European deployment of Pershing II and cruise missiles began.

The Nuclear Freeze

A wave of protest washed over Europe after NATO agreed in December 1979 to deploy Pershing II and cruise missiles in Germany, England, Italy, the Netherlands and Belgium. The anti-nuclear sentiment soon reached American shores and buoyed a grass-roots movement for a freeze on nuclear weapons. Winning endorsements from numerous church groups, political candidates, state and local legislative bodies, the United Nations General Assembly and the U.S. House of Representatives, the freeze — or the threat of one — helped persuade President Reagan to take a more flexible approach to arms control negotiations.

European Anti-Missile Protests

Even before NATO's decision to deploy intermediate-range missiles in Western Europe, many Europeans were disturbed by the lack of progress in arms control and by the vast amount of overkill in the superpowers' nuclear arsenals.

And Europeans grew particularly alarmed when Reagan administration officials talked openly about the possibility of prevailing in nuclear combat. Europeans feared that the superpowers might try to fight a nuclear war on European soil. Some even said they believed Reagan was seriously contemplating a nuclear attack on the Soviet Union.

Reagan himself contributed to anti-American sentiment abroad when he remarked to a group of newspaper editors in October 1981 that he "could see where you could have the exchange of tactical weapons against troops in the field [in Europe] without it bringing either one of the major powers to pushing the button." The statement was widely interpreted in Europe as a reflection of U.S. indifference to the fate of its allies.

Nearly two decades had elapsed between the last European "ban-the-bomb" rallies and the Carter administration's announced policy to deploy neutron bombs in Western Europe. Because the neutron bomb was designed to kill combatants but spare civilians near the battlefield, it was easy for its opponents to describe the "enhanced radiation warhead" as a weapon to kill people but spare property.

In the fall of 1981 massive demonstrations against the deployment of additional nuclear weapons took place in many European cities. Although protestors often took care to emphasize their opposition to all nuclear weapons, they generally left little doubt that they found U.S. arms policies even more distasteful than the Soviet Union's.

The U.S. Freeze Movement

Concern about nuclear war was also growing in the United States. In January 1980 scholar Randall Forsberg, who had served an apprenticeship researching and writing about nuclear weapons for the Stockholm International Peace Research Institute, persuaded representatives of leading U.S. peace groups to join in a campaign for a bilateral freeze on the development, testing, production and deployment of new nuclear weapons.

Although Forsberg's proposals for a ban on the production of fissionable material (plutonium and highly en-

riched uranium) for weapons and a comprehensive nuclear test ban were staples of the arms control agenda, her proposal for a freeze on new weapons systems represented a fresh approach.

One criticism of Forsberg's proposal was that prohibiting further development and deployment would bar replacement of existing delivery systems, dooming the superpowers to total disarmament by obsolescence. If replacements were allowed, however, drawing the line between replacing old weapons and developing essentially new ones might present difficulties.

Critics also charged that compliance with a freeze would not be verifiable. Freeze supporters disagreed, saying that detailed technical means to monitor compliance with a comprehensive test ban had already been worked out in negotiations. Although some weapons, such as cruise missiles and howitzer shells, might be difficult to monitor, that would be true in the context of any arms control agreement, proponents of a nuclear freeze argued. They also pointed out that a total ban would be easier to verify than a partial ban because any evidence of a barred weapon would indicate that a violation had occurred.

Support for the Freeze

American peace groups, which previously had operated on shoestring budgets, found it much easier to raise money. New groups rapidly gained members, financial support and attention in the news media.

The media did much to highlight the horrors of nuclear war. A 1981 CBS television series on U.S. defense policy opened with the simulated nuclear destruction of Omaha, Neb. In 1983 ABC aired a two-hour drama, "The Day After," which portrayed the efforts of survivors to cope with the devastating effects of a nuclear attack. *Parade* magazine featured a cover story by scientist Carl Sagan forecasting that even a small nuclear war would produce a "nuclear winter" as fallout and debris in the atmosphere blotted out the sun for months. Sagan said a major nuclear war could make the human species extinct.

Documentary films such as "Atomic Cafe" and "Dark Circle" satirized the notion that nuclear war could be won and depicted the peacetime health consequences of radiation exposure experienced by military personnel and the workers and neighbors of nuclear weapons factories.

Reagan's provocative rhetoric also contributed to the growing public concern about the possibility of nuclear war. In a 1983 speech he called the U.S.S.R. an "evil empire." In 1984 he joked that he had "just signed legislation which outlaws Russia forever" and that "we begin bombing in five minutes."

The idea of a nuclear freeze garnered considerable support among arms control specialists but, from the beginning, churches were the most ardent supporters. Endorsements came from the United Presbyterian Church, the United Methodist Church, the Episcopal Church, the American Baptist Churches, the Unitarian Universalist Association, the Union of American Hebrew Congregations, the Rabbinical Assembly and others.

Many of the churches adopted extensive statements on nuclear weapons. The most influential was the pastoral letter the U.S. Conference of Catholic Bishops adopted in May 1983. The bishops called nuclear war immoral, rejected first use of nuclear weapons and endorsed the doctrine of nuclear deterrence "strictly conditional" on the pursuit of serious arms reduction.

Opposition to the Freeze

During the second year of the Catholic Church's deliberations about nuclear war, the Reagan administration made a concerted effort to influence the bishops. In an August 1982 speech to the Supreme Council of the Knights of Columbus, Reagan asked Catholics to reject the freeze. William P. Clark, then Reagan's national security adviser, wrote to the bishops taking issue with the second draft of the pastoral letter. When he praised the third draft as substantially improved, the bishops resented the implication that they had bowed to political pressure. They later restored some of the original, tougher language.

The president also sought Protestant support for his nuclear policies. In a March 1983 speech to the Association of Evangelicals, which represented 3.5 million evangelical Christians, Reagan appealed for their support "against those who would place the United States in a position of military and moral inferiority" against communist countries, which he referred to as "the focus of evil in the modern world." Although the audience gave the president a standing ovation, they declined to endorse his nuclear weapons policies and adopted a centrist position instead.

The Freeze and Politics

By the spring of 1982 doubts about the sincerity of Reagan's commitment to arms control were widespread, and the freeze campaign was thriving. In June more than 500,000 people turned out in New York City's Central Park to demonstrate against the arms race. Later the U.N. General Assembly called for a nuclear test ban and freeze.

Initially freeze supporters hoped merely to slow or stop development of some nuclear arms programs and to speed up Reagan's arms control efforts. But the burgeoning grassroots movement quickly became sophisticated. Besides holding vigils and handing out leaflets, peace groups began working to put freeze initiatives on state ballots, forming political action committees (PACs) and channeling money and support to defeat arms control foes and elect profreeze candidates.

In 1982 voters in eight states, 11 state legislatures, more than 400 town meetings and 195 city councils had passed referendums and similar initiatives calling for a nuclear freeze. Freeze activists claimed credit for helping to defeat a few House members, including Don H. Clausen, R-Calif., and Jim Coyne, R-Pa.

In 1984 a chief target was Sen. Roger W. Jepsen, R-Iowa, whom the Council for a Livable World called a "superhawk" in fund-raising letters it sent on behalf of Jepsen's opponent, Democratic Rep. Tom Harkin. SANE (the Committee for a Sane Nuclear Policy) sent a staff member to work on Harkin's campaign. Harkin defeated Jepsen.

Of some 1,250 anti-nuclear organizations around the country, the groups most active and visible on Capitol Hill and in political campaigns included Freeze Voter '84 (the Nuclear Weapons Freeze Campaign's PAC, headed by Randall Forsberg), SANE, the Council for a Livable World, Peace-PAC and Friends of the Earth. Traditionally liberal lobby groups, such as Common Cause, also joined the battle to halt the arms race.

Freeze backers contended that Reagan publicly addressed the issue of arms control only in the face of mounting international political pressure to moderate his anti-Soviet rhetoric and to make serious, concrete arms limitation proposals.

Although Reagan temporarily defused criticism with his zero option and START proposals, the freeze movement had gathered enough momentum to persevere. The movement's goal was to shift the focus of the nuclear arms debate from the size of the Soviet arms buildup and military threat to the dangers of nuclear war.

1982 House Freeze Resolution

Both in 1982 and 1983 freeze advocates in Congress rallied behind resolutions calling for "a mutual [and] verifiable" freeze to be followed by arms reductions.

The White House strongly opposed resolutions to freeze nuclear arms at existing levels on the ground that to do so would perpetuate a nuclear balance favoring the U.S.S.R. The 1982 version (H J Res 521) was sponsored by House Foreign Affairs Committee Chairman Clement J. Zablocki, D-Wis.

To counter sizable congressional support for H J Res 521, the Reagan administration lobbied vigorously for a competing measure more attuned to its position. The substitute, sponsored by William S. Broomfield, Mich., ranking Republican on Foreign Affairs, called for a freeze at "equal and substantially reduced levels" of nuclear arms. The administration succeeded in deflating support for the Zablocki version when the House Aug. 5 **on a key vote of 204-202 (R 151-27; D 53-175)** adopted the substitute language. The resolution, somewhat innocuous by this time, then passed, 273-125. *(1982 key votes, p. 895)*

By all accounts the administration's most effective argument in winning the last few votes for the substitute was that an immediate across-the-board freeze would jeopardize arms reduction talks then under way in Geneva. From that perspective the administration's two-vote victory was an unenthusiastic endorsement of its position.

Reagan supporters underscored the president's commitment to substantial arms reductions, as outlined in his START proposal. "I think everyone here is for a nuclear freeze," William L. Dickinson, R-Ala., told the House late in the 1982 debate. "They are for an end to the arms race. The only question is, on what terms?"

Zablocki's freeze language would end the arms race on the wrong terms, Dickinson warned, "lock[ing] ourselves into a position of inferiority vis-á-vis the Soviet Union."

But skepticism about the administration's commitment persuaded a number of members to vote for the Zablocki amendment. Les Aspin, D-Wis., who said he preferred resuscitation of the SALT II treaty, was one of several members who supported the Zablocki amendment to nudge the administration toward faster progress in arms control talks with Moscow.

The Republican-controlled Senate did not act on the 1982 measure.

1983 House Freeze Resolution

A new version of the Zablocki resolution was introduced early in the 98th Congress. The House Foreign Affairs Committee on March 8, 1983, approved a freeze resolution (H J Res 13) calling on the United States and the Soviet Union to pursue a mutual and verifiable freeze and to include negotiations on intermediate-range weapons in the START process. The measure, drafted by Stephen J. Solarz, D-N.Y., did not endorse an "immediate" freeze but said one should be "negotiated."

As the committee was voting, about 4,000 freeze advo-

cates from 43 states rallied outside the Capitol on behalf of the National Nuclear Freeze Campaign, while a smaller group organized by the National Coalition for Peace Through Strength gathered to protest a freeze.

Taking note of these events, Reagan repeated his opposition in his speech that day to the National Association of Evangelicals. Saying that "simple-minded appeasement or wishful thinking about our adversaries is folly," the president added that "a freeze would reward the Soviet Union for its enormous and unparalleled military buildup."

The president's warning appeared to have some effect. The resolution narrowly missed being amended by the House March 16 to endorse Reagan's arms control approach. After 42 hours of debate the resolution was finally passed May 4 by a hefty margin of 278-149, but only after an amendment was adopted that could require lifting the freeze if it were not followed by mutual arms reductions within a specified period. *(Details, p. 230)*

Senate Rejection of Freeze

The Senate Oct. 31 rejected, 58-40, an immediate nuclear weapons freeze. Earlier, the Senate Foreign Relations Committee had rejected a freeze proposal (S J Res 2) as well as a proposal for a weapons build-down agreement requiring the United States and the Soviet Union to retire an average of two nuclear weapons for each new one deployed.

Administration backing for a U.S.-Soviet nuclear arms build down was a key demand of a group of Senate moderates led by Foreign Relations Chairman Charles H. Percy, R-Ill., William S. Cohen, R-Maine, and Sam Nunn, D-Ga. The three, claiming support from many Senate Republicans, had sought a bargain of sorts: They would support MX procurement if the administration altered its negotiating position at the START talks in ways the senators thought would improve prospects for an agreement.

Although the president had committed himself in general terms to the build-down approach, he had not provided a specific proposal. Claiborne Pell, R.I., a freeze supporter and ranking Democrat on Foreign Relations, complained that senators were being asked to support a build-down without a clear idea of its form or any assurance that it would not set the stage for even more destabilizing weapons.

The build-down proposals, which had more than 40 Senate sponsors, would have allowed deployment of some new weapons, such as Pershing II and MX missiles, which leading freeze backers strongly opposed.

Percy insisted the build-down was less sketchy than the freeze proposal. Joseph R. Biden Jr., D-Del., a committee member, said the freeze should be viewed as a symbol. He saw the movement as "a reflection of the fact that we lack confidence in this administration's . . . desire and ability to reach an arms control agreement."

Although Percy and other build-down backers insisted there was no conflict between their proposal and the freeze, an aide to committee member Alan Cranston, D-Calif., reflected the view of many freeze backers that the build-down was a political threat — a false but "cosmetically attractive alternative," he said.

The fundamental issue dividing the senators, who aligned themselves either with the freeze or the build-down approach, was whether the U.S. and Soviet nuclear forces were essentially equivalent or the U.S. forces were in need of substantial modernization. The merit of the build-down approach, Cohen said, was that it would harness the incentive for modernization.

The defeat in the Senate came as no surprise. Freeze proponents had discounted any prospect of winning in the GOP-controlled chamber. Their goal, they had said, was simply to force all senators to take a public stand on the freeze before the 1984 elections.

1984 Campaign Issue

Democratic presidential candidate Walter F. Mondale made arms control an issue in the 1984 campaign, saying that Reagan had "failed to master what a president must know" to guard against nuclear war. As evidence, Mondale quoted from *Deadly Gambits*, a behind-the-scenes look at arms control under Reagan, by *Time* magazine diplomatic correspondent Strobe Talbott. The book described several gaffes Reagan had committed, including the president's statement that missiles launched from submarines could be recalled and that he was unaware when he made his first arms control proposal that land-based missiles made up the bulk of the Soviet Union's strategic forces. When Mondale raised these incidents during a debate with Reagan, the president countered by labeling Mondale as soft on defense.

Reagan scared some voters by talking about a nuclear "Armageddon," but Mondale could not persuade the electorate that Reagan was a warmonger.

Reagan-Gromyko Meeting

When Mondale chided Reagan for being the only U.S. president in recent years not to meet with his Soviet counterpart, Reagan explained that the deaths of Soviet leaders had given him three counterparts since he took office.

Late in September, however, Reagan met with Soviet Foreign Minister Andrei Gromyko. Moscow had begun hinting that it might be ready to resume discussions on reducing strategic arms. The Soviets undoubtedly realized that a Reagan-Gromyko meeting would enhance Reagan's chances for re-election. Apparently believing that he would win in any event, the Soviets chose to meet with Reagan before the election, when he had a greater stake in a favorable outcome. Although the meeting produced no substantive changes in the two countries' positions, it laid the groundwork for resumed arms control talks during Reagan's second term.

Resumption of Talks

Early in January 1985, Gromyko met with Secretary of State George P. Shultz. Afterwards they announced that the two superpowers would negotiate over three kinds of weapons: strategic nuclear missiles and bombers; intermediate-range nuclear forces in Europe; and space weaponry.

U.S. and Soviet negotiators resumed arms control talks in Geneva on March 12.

5

Commerce and Communications

Introduction   *261*
1981 Chronology   *263*
1982 Chronology   *269*
1983 Chronology   *274*
1984 Chronology   *278*

Commerce and Communications

Efforts to rewrite communications law occupied much time and energy during the 97th and 98th Congresses. Members were faced with the task of revising a technologically outdated body of law to meet sweeping change in the communications field.

Deregulation of the telecommunications industry and the reorganization of the American Telephone & Telegraph Co. (AT&T) were at the top of the legislative agenda. The Senate in 1981 passed a broad telecommunications bill — the first bill to reach the floor in the five years that Congress had been considering revisions to the 1934 Communications Act. But the legislation was superseded by the settlement of a Justice Department antitrust suit against AT&T that set the terms for deregulation and the breakup of the corporation. Congressional pressure subsequently forced the postponement of hikes in local telephone rates that were to result from AT&T's breakup.

Attempts to deregulate the broadcasting industry failed in both the 97th and 98th Congresses. Some revisions were made, but the broad changes sought by Senate deregulation advocates were blocked in the House. However, many of the changes were accomplished administratively by the pro-deregulation Federal Communications Commission (FCC).

Congressional efforts to deregulate the booming cable television industry proved more fruitful. Passage of legislation defining national policy for the cable television industry capped a four-year effort to balance the rights of the industry against those of cities granting franchises.

AT&T Deregulation

Congress and the administration moved on separate tracks to deregulate the telecommunications industry and restructure AT&T. The landmark bill passed by the Senate would have freed AT&T to enter previously closed unregulated and computer-oriented markets, such as data processing, by creating a separate subsidiary.

But in 1982, before the House could take up its version, considered by its sponsors to be more restrictive than the Senate-passed version, the administration through the Justice Department reached a proposed agreement with AT&T giving the corporation access to the lucrative unregulated markets but requiring it to divest itself of its 22 local telephone companies, or two-thirds of its assets. AT&T would retain its long-distance service.

Key members in the House and some senators still believed legislation was needed to supplement the settle-ment and to prevent undue increases in telephone rates. The House Energy and Commerce Committee and its Telecommunications Subcommittee worked to modify the settlement, but the bill was opposed by AT&T, which called on its stockholders and employees to write to their representatives.

Telecommunications Subcommittee Chairman Timothy E. Wirth, D-Colo., withdrew his bill in July 1982 because of what he charged was AT&T's campaign of "fear and distortion" against the measure and dilatory tactics that made it impossible to finish a bill.

The 98th Congress was left with the task of dealing with the aftermath of AT&T's Jan. 1, 1984, breakup — the anticipated rise in telephone rates. The FCC proposed to shift costs that had been paid by long-distance users to local telephone users, in effect increasing local rates.

Both chambers took steps to head off the rate increases and to establish a safety net for low-income persons who might be unable to afford service if rates should rise. The House in 1983 approved legislation banning the new charges. A Senate bill establishing a two-year moratorium on the charges was shelved in 1984 after the FCC bowed to members' pressure and delayed the new charges for residential and small-business customers. AT&T, which had billions of dollars riding on whether the costs were shifted to local customers, spent an estimated $4 million lobbying against the legislation.

Broadcasting Deregulation

Repeated attempts to deregulate the broadcasting industry fell victim to House opponents who contended there was too little competition to warrant lifting federal regulation.

Congress in 1981 increased broadcasting license terms.

References

Discussion of commerce and communications for the years 1945-64 may be found in *Congress and the Nation Vol. I*, pp. 517-562, 1159-1185; for the years 1965-68, *Congress and the Nation Vol. II*, pp. 227-251, 779-823; for the years 1969-72, *Congress and the Nation Vol. III*, pp. 147-176, 659-700; for the years 1973-76, *Congress and the Nation Vol. IV*, pp. 433-451, 505-555; for the years 1977-80, *Congress and the Nation Vol. V*, pp. 291-362.

Commerce and Communications

But Senate provisions that would have codified FCC actions to eliminate programming rules for radio were dropped during a House-Senate conference.

The next year the Senate passed a bill that would have significantly reduced regulation of radio and television, but there was no House action. Both chambers did approve legislation ordering the FCC to establish rules for granting broadcast licenses by lottery.

The Senate again in 1983 approved a bill ratifying a number of FCC rulings deregulating the industry, only to see it die in the House, where some members were demanding public interest guidelines for programming that the broadcasting industry found unacceptable. Legislation sponsored by 232 members of the House never got out of subcommittee.

Cable TV Deregulation

Congress fared better with its efforts to deregulate cable television — but just barely. After four years of controversy members managed to clear a deregulation bill one day before the 98th Congress adjourned.

Cities and other interest groups had blocked cable legislation during the 97th Congress, arguing that it would intrude into local affairs and restrict local government's authority.

Cable firms and the cities fought bitterly over the issue during the 98th Congress. The Senate passed a bill in 1983, but it was abandoned in the House because some cities complained it favored the industry over the cities.

As Congress neared adjournment, the industry and cities agreed to another compromise — their third in two years — which, with one further change, eventually cleared. The final bill clarified cities' rights to grant franchises for local cable operators, while limiting city authority over rates and programs. It outlined national procedures for franchise renewals, replacing a confusing hodgepodge of local processes.

Other Communications Issues

The future of public broadcasting remained cloudy during much of the 97th and 98th Congresses. President Reagan wanted to phase out federal subsidies on the grounds that public broadcasting catered to a cultural and intellectual elite and should be supported by its audience rather than, in part, by federal funds. Congress in 1981 agreed to make deep cuts in public broadcasting subsidies but restored some of the funding the next year. Two attempts to increase public broadcasting funding fell to presidential vetoes in 1984.

Hollywood won a battle with the television networks over the $800 million-a-year market in reruns of television shows. When the FCC proposed to repeal rules prohibiting ABC, NBC and CBS from having a share in shows they aired, independent producers, who depended on syndication rights for their profits, asked Congress to stop the agency. The House in 1983 passed a bill to delay the FCC rule, and in 1984 the FCC agreed to a two-year moratorium at the request of Reagan and a group of senators.

Consumer Legislation

Consumer advocates had a mixed record of success during the 97th and 98th Congresses. They found support on Capitol Hill to head off administration attacks they felt might devastate the Consumer Product Safety Commission (CPSC), but significant cutbacks in the agency were enacted and CPSC rules were made subject to a veto by Congress. Confusion over the validity of legislative vetoes — which the Supreme Court declared unconstitutional in mid-1983 — contributed to the 98th Congress' failure to enact a CPSC reauthorization.

Congress rejected Reagan's request for an immediate cutoff of funds for the National Consumer Cooperative Bank but did agree to make the bank a private financial institution much sooner than originally planned.

Prior to the Supreme Court's decision invalidating legislative vetoes, consumer groups had failed to block Congress' veto of a Federal Trade Commission (FTC) proposed rule on the sale of used cars. But efforts in Congress to bar the FTC from regulating doctors and other professionals and from promulgating a rule on funeral home directors' practices proved unsuccessful. Controversy over the legislative veto and FTC attempts to regulate professionals were major factors in the failure of the 97th and 98th Congresses to pass bills reauthorizing the agency.

In other action, consumer groups joined with business associations in pushing a bill to help businesses obtain product liability insurance. Consumer and other interest groups successfully opposed legislation limiting manufacturers' liability for unsafe products.

The 98th Congress failed to extend a decade-long ban on credit card surcharges, an issue on which consumer groups were divided. Women and civil rights groups lost out to the insurance industry in a battle over unisex insurance legislation that would have barred insurance companies from considering gender in computing premiums and benefits.

Small Business

Congress in 1981 approved legislation setting higher interest rates on most Small Business Administration (SBA) loans and reducing coverage on disaster loans. Interest rates on disaster loans were lowered by legislation approved in 1984. A separate bill to reauthorize SBA programs failed to clear that year.

Small businesses were guaranteed a share of the federal research and development budget by legislation enacted in 1982. The final bill, however, was watered down to meet the concerns of major universities and other groups that feared the loss of federal research dollars. Small businesses also received a boost from the passage of legislation designed to help them win federal procurement contracts.

Two SBA pilot programs aimed at assisting minority-owned businesses in acquiring government contracts were extended in 1983. A reauthorization attempt had failed in the previous Congress.

Corporate Practices

With the increase in corporate mergers and takeovers in recent years, "insider trading" — the illegal use of confidential information to profit in the stock market — was on the rise. Congress voted to strengthen the power of the Securities and Exchange Commission (SEC) to crack down on the practice.

Legislation to restrain controversial business tactics that had become increasingly common in corporate takeover fights got no further than House committee approval. The bill was opposed by the White House and the SEC.

Chronology
Of Action
On Commerce
And Communications

1981

Congress grappled with several important communications issues in 1981. The Senate approved legislation to deregulate the telecommunications industry and reorganize the American Telephone & Telegraph Co., and hearings were slated on the House version in 1982. Congress approved legislation increasing broadcasting license terms for radio and television, but Senate provisions that would have substantially deregulated radio broadcasting were dropped in conference. And the fate of public broadcasting funds was in question during much of the 97th Congress.

Consumer legislation was marked more by what was avoided than what was gained. The Consumer Product Safety Commission managed to escape an administration attempt either to abolish it or to put it under the Commerce Department, but budget cuts forced the agency to lay off many employees and Congress set new requirements for rulemaking. Another target of the administration — the National Consumer Cooperative Bank — also survived but had to give up its government-backed status and become a private institution sooner than originally planned. Action was postponed on a controversial Federal Trade Commission rule requiring used-car dealers to disclose information about known major defects in cars.

Broadcast Licenses

Commercial broadcasters won a partial victory in 1981 when Congress approved legislation to permit longer radio and television license terms, but the final bill did not go as far toward federal deregulation as the industry had wanted. Broadcasters had lobbied hard for Senate-passed provisions to substantially deregulate radio broadcasting, only to see the controversial Senate plan dropped in conference.

The broadcasting changes were attached to the omnibus budget reconciliation bill (HR 3982 — PL 97-35) cleared July 31. The measure established seven-year licenses for radio stations and five-year licenses for television stations, lengthening both from three years under previous law. Critics, including consumer, religious and labor groups, charged the extension would make it more difficult to protest inadequate broadcasting. The bill also gave the Federal Communications Commission (FCC) the option of allocating new licenses by lottery as an alternative to the existing practice of comparative hearings on applications. *(1982 lottery law, p. 272)*

But beyond these changes, House and Senate conferees agreed to continue the general regulation of broadcasting. Dropped in conference were such Senate provisions as

proposals to license radio stations for an indefinite period and to free radio stations from FCC requirements that they provide news and public affairs programming and that they survey the public regularly to determine audience concerns.

Conferees also dropped a plan, approved by both the House and Senate, to charge fees for FCC services to broadcasters. Senate conferees refused to accept fees without substantial deregulation.

Senate advocates of deregulation did not give up the fight, however. Shortly before adjournment the Senate Commerce Committee approved new legislation (S 1629) to reduce federal controls on broadcasters. The bill was approved by the Senate in 1982. *(1981-82 details, p. 273)*

PL 97-35 also repealed the FCC's permanent authorization and provided for a two-year authorization period. Conferees said the change was designed to give Congress the opportunity for regular oversight of FCC actions. The bill authorized $76.9 million annually in fiscal 1982-83.

Legislative History

The Senate version of the budget-cutting reconciliation bill (S 1377 — S Rept 97-139), passed June 25, incorporated broadcasting provisions previously approved by the Senate Commerce Committee. They included provisions of a bill (S 821 — S Rept 97-73) authorizing $76.9 million annually for fiscal 1982-84 and establishing fees for FCC services, plus deregulation provisions of other measures.

The House June 9 had passed separate legislation (HR 3239 — H Rept 97-84) authorizing $77.4 million for the FCC in fiscal 1982 and allowing the agency to impose fees for services.

Reconciliation conferees accepted the Senate's authorization figure but dropped its deregulation proposals. Congress approved the conference report (H Rept 97-208) on the measure July 31. *(Reconciliation action, p. 40)*

Provisions

As signed into law Aug. 13, Title XII of HR 3982 (PL 97-35):

● Increased television license terms, both for new licenses and renewals, to five years from three years.

● Increased radio license terms, both for new licenses and renewals, to seven years from three years.

● Allowed the FCC to grant new broadcast licenses either through a system of random selection, or lottery, from applicants deemed to be qualified, or through the existing system of comparative hearings on applications.

● Directed the FCC to give "significant preference" to groups under-represented in broadcasting when it used a lottery system for granting new licenses.

● Made it unlawful for a license applicant, without FCC approval, to withdraw his application in exchange for payment from another applicant.

● Changed the FCC's permanent authorization to a two-year period and authorized $76.9 million annually in fiscal 1982-83.

● Required the FCC to appoint a managing director for overall commission management and to report its goals and priorities to Congress annually.

● Required the FCC to complete as soon as possible a pending rulemaking proceeding on revising the uniform system of accounts for telephone companies. The legislation said the system must ensure proper allocation of all of

the telephone carriers' costs for telecommunications services, facilities and products.

Public Broadcasting

The 97th Congress went back and forth on the fate of funding for public broadcasting.

Pressed by the Reagan administration to reduce overall spending, Congress in 1981 slashed previously appropriated fiscal 1983 broadcasting funds to $137 million from $172 million.

But lawmakers rejected President Reagan's plans to cut public broadcast subsidies for fiscal 1984-86. The Corporation for Public Broadcasting (CPB), which disbursed federal aid to public stations, received authorizations in the budget-cutting reconciliation bill (HR 3982 — PL 97-35) of $130 million annually for fiscal 1984-86, $80 million more than Reagan requested for the three-year period.

Later in the year Congress appropriated only $105.6 million for public broadcasting in fiscal 1984. But it reversed itself in 1982 and voted to give the CPB the full $130 million for fiscal 1984, as well as for fiscal 1985.

Unlike most federal programs, public broadcasting received advance funding, a procedure intended to protect the system from political pressure. Congress violated this intent when it agreed to cut previously appropriated funds for fiscal 1983.

1981 Action

President Reagan sought $110 million for public broadcasting in fiscal 1984 and $100 million annually in 1985 and 1986. He also asked Congress to rescind $95 million previously appropriated for fiscal 1982-83.

Congress did not alter the $172 million fiscal 1982 appropriation, but it approved a $35 million fiscal 1983 rescission as part of a supplemental appropriations bill cleared June 4 (PL 97-12).

In calling for cuts in CPB funding, Reagan argued that taxpayers should not be required to subsidize the entertainment of others. CPB backers countered that public broadcasting deserved government support because it provided a special cultural service to the nation.

Legislative History. The Senate accepted the Reagan administration fiscal 1984-86 funding levels in an authorization bill reported by the Commerce Committee May 15 (S 720 — S Rept 97-98) and incorporated in the Senate reconciliation measure (S 1377 — S Rept 97-139), passed June 25.

The House June 24 passed separate legislation (HR 3238 — H Rept 97-82) authorizing $160 million for fiscal 1984, $145 million for 1985 and $130 million for 1986.

The reconciliation conference agreement (H Rept 97-208), approved by Congress July 31, authorized $130 million annually. Otherwise, the bill generally followed the more generous House provisions. It allowed public broadcasters for the first time to show sponsors' logos in an effort to secure more underwriting funds and permitted stations to lease out their facilities to earn money. Congress also permitted several public television and radio stations to experiment with advertisements to find out if stations could raise revenue through advertising without reducing the quality of public broadcasting.

The bill also set a mandatory formula for allocating subsidies in a move to end the traditional fighting between

CPB and the stations over who would control the federal funds.

Provisions. As signed into law Aug. 13, Title XII of HR 3982 (PL 97-35):

● Authorized $130 million annually for public broadcasting in fiscal 1984-86.

● Reduced the size of the CPB board to 11 members from 15, with membership to include 10 presidential appointees and the CPB president. No more than six members could belong to the same political party. One member must represent public television stations and one must represent public radio stations. Members' terms were reduced to five years from six years.

● Established a mandatory formula to allocate federal funds: 10 percent would go to CPB administration, program royalties, interconnection services, debt payment and other costs; 75 percent of the remainder would go to public television and 25 percent to public radio. Of the television funds, 75 percent would go directly to the stations, and the remainder would be for national programming. The radio funds would be split equally between grants to stations and funds for national programming.

The television and radio stations would pick up some of CPB's costs if certain expenses amounted to more than 60 percent of the corporation's allocated funds.

● Directed CPB and the stations to split equally the cost of interconnection facilities and operations, which link the stations in a type of "network" to share programs.

● Allowed only non-commercial stations that received no CPB grants to editorialize. But the stations would not be allowed to support or oppose candidates.

● Allowed public television and radio stations to air business logos of program sponsors as long as the announcements did not interrupt regular programming.

● Permitted an 18-month experiment during which several public television and radio licensees could air advertisements under limited conditions.

● Allowed public broadcasting stations to lease their facilities but barred the broadcast of advertisements.

● Required that the use of public broadcasting facilities for other purposes not interfere with public broadcasting services.

● Authorized $47 million over fiscal 1982-84 for public telecommunications facilities development under the Commerce Department's National Telecommunications and Information Administration, the agency with chief responsibility for developing national telecommunications policy.

1982 Action

Supporters of public broadcasting succeeded in 1982 in obtaining the full $130 million in federal subsidies for fiscal 1984 and 1985.

Although Congress had authorized $130 million for fiscal 1984, the corporation was to receive only $105.6 million under stopgap funding measures passed in 1981 and 1982 (PL 97-92, PL 97-161).

Congressional action to restore the funds came after CPB launched a lobbying campaign to try to reverse the budget cuts. CPB spokesmen predicted that less than the full $130 million would result in a loss of quality programming and could put some stations out of business.

An additional $24.4 million for fiscal 1984 was contained in two fiscal 1982 supplemental appropriations bills vetoed by Reagan (HR 5922, HR 6682). The funds remained in a third supplemental appropriations measure

(PL 97-216), which the president signed July 18.

CPB received the full $130 million for fiscal 1985 in a continuing appropriations resolution cleared by the lame-duck Congress and signed into law Dec. 21 (PL 97-377).

AT&T Deregulation

Legislation to deregulate much of the telecommunications industry and restructure the American Telephone & Telegraph Co. (AT&T) was passed by the Senate in October 1981. The House Energy and Commerce Committee planned to consider related legislation in 1982.

The Senate measure (S 898) was the first such bill to reach the floor of either chamber in the five years Congress had been considering revisions of the 1934 Communications Act.

However, the early 1982 settlement by the Justice Department of an antitrust suit against AT&T undercut congressional efforts at deregulation. *(Details of 1981-82 action, p. 270)*

New Western Union Service

Congress in 1981 cleared legislation (S 271 — PL 97-130) allowing Western Union to provide international telegraph and telex service and allowing international telegraph and telex carriers to compete against Western Union in the United States.

Western Union had been prevented from entering the international trade market by the 1934 Communications Act. In that act, Congress had created an antitrust exemption allowing Western Union and the Postal Telegraph and Cable Corp. to merge. The resulting company was then barred from international service on the grounds that the firm might use its domestic monopoly status to establish a monopoly abroad.

However, supporters of S 271 argued that some international carriers had begun limited operations in the United States, and Western Union should be allowed access to the international market. They also contended that international carriers were able to charge high prices because of the lack of competition.

Legislative History. The Senate passed S 271 (S Rept 97-25) June 22 by voice vote and without debate. The House Dec. 8 passed its version of the bill (HR 4927 — H Rept 97-356), also by voice vote.

A compromise version, worked out informally, was approved by both houses Dec. 16.

Provisions. As signed into law Dec. 29, S 271 (PL 97-130):

● Directed the Federal Communications Commission (FCC) to promote the development of competitive domestic and international telex and telegraph markets. The FCC was directed to reduce regulation as competition developed among carriers.

● Directed the FCC to require each carrier to provide facility interconnections to any other carrier upon reasonable request.

● Provided for a formula for sharing interconnecting service by domestic and foreign international carriers.

● Required that if any major carrier engaged in both domestic and international service, the firm had to be treated separately by the FCC as a domestic carrier and an international carrier for interconnection requirements.

If the separated domestic and international services provided interconnections to each other, the interconnections had to be made available at the same rates, conditions and quality to other carriers.

● Gave the FCC for three years the authority to order an agreement establishing conditions and rates for interconnections, if carriers failed to reach agreement within a 45-day period.

● Barred the FCC from approving a Western Union application to provide international service within four months after the company entered into an agreement with other carriers for interconnections.

● Released carriers seeking to provide domestic service from a requirement to submit an application to the FCC. The commission would have limited authority to require an application, however.

Small Business Loans

Congress in 1981 raised interest rates substantially on most Small Business Administration (SBA) loans and cut the amount of loss covered by disaster loans.

The provisions were included in the omnibus reconciliation legislation (HR 3982 — PL 97-35) cleared July 31. The bill was the vehicle for budget cuts sought by President Reagan and endorsed by Congress through its budget process. *(Reconciliation action, p. 40)*

The rate for direct business loans was increased to match the cost of money to the government plus up to 1 percent. At the time of enactment, the change produced a rate of 15.3 percent. Previously, borrowers had paid between 3 percent and about 12 percent.

House and Senate conferees also agreed (H Rept 97-208) to raise the rate for SBA disaster loans and reduced the amount of the loss covered from 100 percent to 85 percent. Businesses that were unable to obtain credit elsewhere would pay an 8 percent rate; the rate had been 5 percent. Credit-worthy businesses would pay the prevailing market rate; under previous law their rate had equaled the government's cost of money plus up to 1 percent.

Authorization Levels

PL 97-35 authorized $230 million annually for fiscal 1982-84 for SBA direct business loans. The House originally had authorized $260 million, matching President Reagan's request, while the Senate had approved $180 million. The bill set an annual limit of $3.3 billion for fiscal 1982-84 on the amount of guaranteed loans to businesses, somewhat more than the House had voted but substantially below the $4 billion Senate figure. The previous authorization (PL 96-302) was for $594 million for direct loans and $4.9 billion for guaranteed loans. PL 97-35 continued an open-ended authorization for disaster loans. *(Congress and the Nation Vol. V, p. 344)*

Provisions

As signed into law Aug. 13, Title XIX of HR 3982 (PL 97-35):

Disaster Loans. Authorized SBA to make direct or guaranteed loans to repair, rehabilitate or replace real or personal property damaged or destroyed by flood, riot, civil disorder or other catastrophe, if the damage or destruction

was not covered by insurance.

● Allowed SBA to refinance a mortgage or lien against a destroyed or damaged business or home.

● Allowed the loans to be made in an area declared a disaster by the president, agriculture secretary or SBA.

● Allowed loans to be made if the governor of a state certified to SBA that concerns suffered economic injury because of a disaster or if they were in need of assistance not otherwise available in the area, provided they could not obtain credit elsewhere.

Economic injury loans were made to small businesses that had suffered damage such as the loss of business because they were located in an area struck by a physical disaster.

● Extended the existing "credit elsewhere test," establishing whether a disaster loan applicant could qualify for privately financed loans, to include homeowner as well as business applicants. The test was used to determine the interest rate on the federal loan.

● Set the interest rate for homeowners unable to obtain credit elsewhere at one-half the cost of money to the government, plus up to 1 percent at SBA's discretion, but not to exceed 8 percent. Homeowners previously paid 3 percent on the first $55,000 of the loan.

● Set the interest rate for homeowners able to obtain credit from a bank or other lender at the full cost of money to the government, plus up to 1 percent.

● Set the interest rate for businesses unable to obtain credit elsewhere at no more than 8 percent. The interest rate had been 5 percent.

● Authorized the SBA administrator to set the interest rate for businesses able to obtain credit elsewhere, but at a level no higher than the prevailing market rate or the guaranteed business loan rate, whichever was lower. The rate previously had been based on the government's cost of money, plus up to 1 percent.

● Set the maximum term of a loan for businesses able to obtain credit elsewhere at three years; the previous law had provided an initial three-year term.

● Limited business disaster loans to 85 percent of the uninsured loss, down from 100 percent.

● Set homeowner loans at 100 percent of the uninsured loss, as provided by existing law. SBA had been lowering the percentage administratively.

● Placed a $500,000 limit on loans.

● Continued an open-ended authorization for the disaster loan program.

● Consolidated seven non-physical disaster loan programs, such as regulatory compliance, product disaster and economic dislocation loans, into a new program but provided no funds for fiscal 1982-84.

Business Loans. Provided direct and guaranteed business loans to small-business owners to construct, expand or convert facilities, including the acquisition of land and purchase of buildings, equipment or materials; to obtain working capital; or to finance residential or commercial construction or rehabilitation for sale.

● Provided that small-business owners able to obtain credit elsewhere could not receive SBA business loans.

● Consolidated previously separate business loan programs, such as economic opportunity and solar and energy conservation loans, into a single program.

● Set the maximum term for business loans at 25 years, except that any portion of the loan used to acquire land or to construct, convert or expand facilities could be extended.

● Authorized SBA to set the direct loan interest rate at the cost of money to the government plus 1 percent, or 15.3 percent at the time of enactment, except that loans to handicapped individuals would continue at 3 percent.

● Provided that SBA guarantee 90 percent of loans of $100,000 or less; 70-90 percent of loans between $100,000 and $714,285; less than 70 percent of loans over $714,285. SBA previously had guaranteed up to 90 percent of a loan.

● Authorized $230 million annually for fiscal 1982-84 for SBA direct business loans.

● Provided an annual limit of $3.3 billion for fiscal 1982-84 on the amount of guaranteed loans to businesses.

Small Business Research Funds

The Senate in December approved legislation (S 881) giving small businesses a share of the federal research and development dollar. The House Small Business Committee had reported a similar bill (HR 4326) in November.

Proponents of the legislation maintained that small businesses were among the most innovative firms, yet received only 3.5 percent to 4 percent of the estimated $40 billion federal research budget. But others, including major universities, feared the loss of federal research funds and lobbied against the measure.

A watered-down version was signed into law in 1982. *(Details of 1981-82 action, p. 273)*

Minority Businesses

The full House and the Senate Small Business Committee approved bills in 1981 to give a second chance to a pilot program designed to help minority businesses win government contracts. There was no further action, however, and the legislation died at the end of the 97th Congress. An extension was approved in 1983. *(Details, p. 276)*

As passed by voice vote Nov. 17, the House bill (HR 4500 — H Rept 97-304) would have extended for two years, through fiscal 1983, the so-called 8(a) minority small business pilot program. A similar Senate bill, reported Sept. 28 (S 1620 — S Rept 97-195), would have extended the pilot effort for 18 months, until March 31, 1983.

Under the regular 8(a) minority program, selected minority businesses received government contracts and special assistance to improve management or other practices so they could compete eventually for contracts without government help. Federal agencies offered contracts to the Small Business Administration (SBA), which then subcontracted the work to firms controlled by economically and socially disadvantaged individuals.

Under the pilot program, the president designated one federal agency to offer contracts, and SBA actually selected which of the agency's contracts would be awarded to the minority firms.

Critics charged that SBA had mismanaged the program, which was established under legislation enacted in 1978 (PL 95-507). *(Congress and the Nation Vol. V, p. 316)*

Tourism Promotion

Congress in 1981 approved legislation to beef up the federal role in promoting foreign tourism to the United States (S 304 — PL 97-63).

The measure replaced the Commerce Department's U.S. Travel Service (USTS) with an upgraded agency called the U.S. Travel and Tourism Administration (USTTA), to be headed by a new under secretary of commerce for travel and tourism.

Many members of Congress had contended that the USTS had not done an adequate job of funneling tourist dollars into the U.S. economy. But critics of the legislation objected that the government should not be involved in promoting a private industry.

Legislative History

The Reagan administration gave its approval only after the Senate-passed plan to create an independent tourism agency was dropped. Legislation similar to the Senate measure had been pocket-vetoed in 1980 by President Carter, who objected to creating a separate agency beyond presidential review. *(Congress and the Nation Vol. V, p. 346)*

The Senate had caught the administration by surprise when it bypassed the Commerce Committee and passed S 304 Jan. 27, the day it was introduced. The House July 28, by a 321-98 vote, passed a bill (HR 1311 — H Rept 97-107) to create an upgraded agency within the Commerce Department. The Senate adopted the conference report on S 304 (H Rept 97-252) Sept. 29 and the House approved it Oct. 1, 288-112.

Consumer Product Safety

The Consumer Product Safety Commission (CPSC) escaped dismantlement in 1981 when Congress ignored the Reagan administration's request to abolish it and reauthorized the independent regulatory agency for two years. Congress did cut the agency's budget, however, and set new requirements for rulemaking.

Business critics had complained that the CPSC did not understand manufacturing and product use and that it over-regulated in its efforts to protect consumers. The administration had wanted to shift the CPSC's duties to other agencies, or, in lieu of that, to slash the commission's budget.

There had been strong support on Capitol Hill for placing the commission under the Commerce Department. But consumer advocates successfully argued that folding the agency into Commerce, which was responsible primarily for business promotion, would blunt the CPSC's effectiveness.

The budget-cutting reconciliation legislation (HR 3982 — PL 97-35) approved by Congress July 31 included the administration's proposed funding levels of $33 million for fiscal 1982 and $35 million for 1983. While the reconciliation conference agreement (H Rept 97-208) maintained the CPSC's independence, the budget cuts were expected to result in layoffs of 25-30 percent of the staff. *(Budget reconciliation bill, p. 40)*

In addition, new requirements were set for developing product safety rules, including cost-benefit analyses, and restrictions were placed on the release of information businesses considered confidential. Also, one chamber of Congress was allowed to veto CPSC regulations if the other chamber did not object. This provision was nullified in 1983 when the Supreme Court ruled that the legislative veto device was unconstitutional. *(Legislative veto, p. 833)*

Legislative History

The CPSC, established in May 1973, had been under attack from the beginning by consumers, businesses and Congress. In 1976 the agency had been accused of mismanagement. In 1978 a White House panel had recommended a short authorization and abolishing or substantially reorganizing it in the future. President Carter rejected that recommendation. *(Background, Congress and the Nation Vol. III, p. 685; Congress and the Nation Vol. V, p. 358)*

By 1981 some of the agency's critics were saying it had significantly improved its operations. And CPSC supporters contended that it had prevented thousands of injuries and hundreds of deaths annually. For example, its regulations and standards had resulted in banning hair dryers that contained asbestos and barring toys with small parts that could be swallowed by children.

Disregarding Reagan's proposal to dismantle the agency, a House Energy and Commerce subcommittee approved legislation authorizing $33 million in fiscal 1982, $35 million in 1983 and $37 million in 1984, but the measure was withheld from full committee action in May because of fears that there were enough votes to transfer the CPSC to the Commerce Department. Rather than risk that, supporters slipped the subcommittee plan into the budget reconciliation bill.

The Senate Commerce Committee had reported a bill (S 1155 — S Rept 97-102) authorizing $33 million annually for fiscal 1982 and 1983.

Provisions

As signed into law Aug. 13, Title XII of HR 3982 (PL 97-35):

Safety Standards. Directed the CPSC to rely on voluntary safety standards developed by industry groups or individuals, rather than mandatory standards, when compliance would eliminate or adequately reduce risk of injury and when substantial compliance with the voluntary standards was likely.

● Eliminated CPSC authority to issue safety standards containing product design requirements and required the agency to express standards in terms of performance requirements.

Rulemaking Analysis. Provided detailed guidelines for rulemaking proceedings, which required cost-benefit analyses of proposed mandatory standards and advance notice of proceedings.

The agency was required to invite proposals for voluntary standards and to end a proceeding if a satisfactory voluntary standard was developed.

The legislation also required three findings before the CPSC could issue mandatory safety rules. First, when industry had adopted a voluntary rule dealing with a risk of injury, the commission must find that compliance with the voluntary standard was not likely to result in adequate reduction of the risk or that it was unlikely that there would be substantial compliance. Second, the benefits of the rule must bear a reasonable relationship to the costs. Third, the rule must impose the least burdensome requirement in preventing or adequately reducing the risk of injury.

Information Disclosure. Prohibited the agency from disclosing business information marked confidential by the manufacturer that would cause him substantial competitive market damage if released. Prior to the release of information considered confidential, the agency must

notify the manufacturer, thereby giving him the opportunity to seek a temporary restraining order in U.S. district court to stop the release.

The agency could expedite the release of certain information in cases of emergency and other situations, such as imminent health hazards.

● Prohibited the agency from disclosing confidential commercial information through a request made under the Freedom of Information Act. Previously the agency was not compelled to release the information.

● Barred disclosure of a manufacturer's information indicating that a new product might be hazardous unless: the CPSC had issued a complaint alleging that the product presented a substantial hazard; the commission had accepted a settlement agreement from the manufacturer; or the manufacturer agreed to disclosure.

Advisory Panels. Directed the CPSC to appoint Chronic Hazard Advisory Panels to advise on cancer, birth defects and gene mutations associated with substances in consumer products. The CPSC could not issue a notice of advance proposed rulemaking relating to chronic hazards unless a panel reported on the substance of concern.

Legislative Veto. Allowed one chamber of Congress to veto safety standards and regulations if the other chamber did not object.

Information Gathering. Limited the gathering of information to that necessary to carry out a specific regulatory or enforcement function of the agency.

Lawn Mowers. Directed the CPSC to amend its lawn mower safety standard, which required mowers to stop when the user took his hand off the handle and to restart automatically. The CPSC was required to provide an alternative that would allow the engine to be started manually.

Amusement Rides. Eliminated CPSC jurisdiction over amusement rides that were operated by a fixed-location amusement park. *(1984 legislation, p. 285)*

Authorizations. Authorized $33 million for the commission in fiscal 1982 and $35 million in fiscal 1983.

Consumer Cooperative Bank

Congress in 1981 advanced the timetable for severing government ties with the National Consumer Cooperative Bank, but it refused to cut off federal support immediately as President Reagan had requested.

Lawmakers authorized fiscal 1982 funding for the Co-op Bank, which had been targeted for extinction by the Reagan administration, in the budget-cutting reconciliation bill (HR 3982 — PL 97-35) cleared July 31. The bill stipulated that the bank was to become a private financial institution by Dec. 31, 1981. Under its originating legislation (PL 95-351), the bank would not have been required to move toward private status until 1990.

The Co-op Bank had been created in 1978 to promote the cooperative movement. Co-ops provide housing, food, health care and marketing services at lower costs to members than if they individually sought services on the private market. The bank actually opened in 1980. *(Background, Congress and the Nation Vol. V, p. 357)*

Co-ops had sought help from the federal government because they had trouble securing loans from private sources. Supporters said commercial banks did not want to lend funds to co-ops because they did not understand co-op management. The Reagan administration contended that

sound co-ops could secure private financing and should not be subsidized by taxpayers.

Legislative History

The Co-op Bank found an unlikely source of support in the House, where 18 Republicans threatened to vote against the GOP alternative to the Budget Committee's reconciliation bill unless the plan included funds for the bank. Because the president needed every GOP vote to win approval of the plan — later adopted 217-211 — the Republican House leadership included an authorization for the bank. *(Reconciliation action, p. 40)*

As passed by the House June 26, the bill authorized $61 million for fiscal 1982, as well as funds for fiscal 1983-84. The Senate version (S 1377 — S Rept 97-139), passed a day earlier, denied further funding for bank loans and provided for elimination of the bank. The conference agreement (H Rept 97-208) provided a fiscal 1982 authorization of $47 million for the bank's market-rate loans to co-ops and $14 million for low-interest loans. A continuing appropriations resolution (H J Res 370 — PL 97-92) cleared Dec. 1 reduced those amounts to $41 million and $4.8 million.

Provisions

As signed into law Aug. 13, Title III of HR 3982 (PL 97-35):

● Required the Treasury to convert its Co-op Bank stock to notes by Dec. 31, 1981, or 10 days after enactment of fiscal 1982 appropriations for the bank, whichever was later. The bank was to repay the notes by Dec. 31, 2020.

● Continued the bank's exemption from state and local taxes, except for real estate taxes.

● Provided that the president appoint three of the bank board's 15 members. The presidential appointees must include a representative of small business, a representative of low-income co-ops and a federal official. The other members would be elected by bank stockholders.

● Directed the Farm Credit Administration and the General Accounting Office to audit the bank's records.

● Directed the bank to spin off the Office of Self-Help Development and Technical Assistance, which provided low-interest loans and technical aid to low-income co-ops. The office was to become a non-profit corporation, whose directors would be named by the bank board.

● Provided fiscal 1982 authorizations of $14 million for the bank's low-interest loans and technical assistance and $47 million for the bank's basic market-rate loans.

FTC Used-Car Rule Veto

A congressional attempt to overturn a Federal Trade Commission (FTC) regulation on used cars was blocked in 1981 by parliamentary maneuvering in the Senate.

The FTC rule demanded that dealers disclose to potential buyers known defects in cars and whether a car carried a warranty. Resolutions to disapprove the rule were adopted by the Senate Commerce Committee Dec. 10 and its House counterpart Dec. 11 (H Con Res 178 — H Rept 97-417).

Congress approved a veto resolution in 1982, but its action was invalidated by the Supreme Court the following year. *(1982 action, p. 273; legislative veto ruling, p. 833)*

Cash Discount Ban

Congress completed action in 1981 on legislation that permitted merchants to offer unlimited discounts on cash purchases while prohibiting them from imposing surcharges on credit card sales.

The bill (HR 31 — PL 97-25) repealed the existing 5 percent ceiling on discounts merchants were permitted to offer customers for cash purchases. It also extended until Feb. 27, 1984, a prohibition on surcharges for purchases by credit card or under open-end credit plans. This ban had lapsed Feb. 27 while Congress considered the legislation.

A short-term extension of the credit card surcharge ban failed to clear Congress in 1984. *(1984 action, p. 284)*

The House originally passed HR 31 Feb. 24 by a 372-4 vote. The Senate approved its version (S 414 — S Rept 97-23) March 12 by voice vote after rejecting, 41-56, an amendment to delete the credit card surcharge provisions.

Subsequently, however, Senate and House conferees deadlocked over an unrelated Senate amendment, and the conference report was not filed until June 23 (H Rept 97-159). The House adopted the conference report June 24, and the Senate cleared the measure July 14.

Product Liability Insurance

Congress in 1981 approved legislation (HR 2120 — PL 97-45) to help businesses obtain insurance against damage claims involving their products.

The new law generally pre-empted state laws that restricted the formation of business "risk retention groups" for self-insurance or "purchasing groups" to buy product liability insurance jointly at favorable rates.

Both business associations and consumer groups had pushed for the legislation. Businesses had complained that product liability insurance was either prohibitively expensive or simply not available. A company could go bankrupt if it were subject to a large court judgment and did not have insurance, or if it had a high deductible charge, they argued.

Consumer advocates backed the proposal because they feared consumers would not be able to collect in court if businesses were not covered.

The insurance industry had fought similar legislation in 1980, partly because those proposals had required Commerce Department approval of risk retention groups, which the industry argued would be an unwarranted federal intrusion into a state-regulated area. The 1981 measure did not provide for federal regulation and the insurance industry dropped its active opposition.

The legislation (H Rept 97-190) was approved by the House by voice vote July 28. The Senate accepted the House bill by voice vote Sept. 11 after indefinitely postponing action on its own similar measure (S 1096 — S Rept 97-172).

Provisions

As signed into law Sept. 25, HR 2120 (PL 97-45):
● Allowed businesses to form risk retention groups to assume and share the liability risk for either products or completed operations. Completed operations were those that involved product installation or repairs by a firm outside its own premises. A group could not exclude anyone from membership to obtain a competitive advantage over that person.

● Allowed an offshore risk retention group licensed in Bermuda or the Cayman Islands before Jan. 1, 1985, to continue operating if it certified to the insurance commissioner of at least one state that the group satisfied that state's capitalization requirements.

This provision was designed to encourage states to reform laws restricting operations of risk retention groups and thus encourage the formation of groups in those states. Offshore groups had been established because of favorable operating conditions and tax benefits.

● Exempted risk retention groups and persons who provided services to those groups from restrictive state laws and orders except under certain circumstances. For example, a state might require a group to pay premium taxes, submit reports required of licensed insurers relating to product liability insurance losses and expenses, and submit to a state examination if there was reason to believe that the group was in a "financially impaired condition."

● Exempted purchasing groups generally from restrictive state laws and orders.

Daylight-Saving Time

The House passed legislation (HR 4437) in 1981 to extend daylight-saving time (DST) to eight months a year, but the Senate never acted on the bill.

Under existing law DST ran for six months, from the last Sunday of April to the last Sunday of October. Clocks were set ahead one hour in April and back again in October. HR 4437 would have started DST on the first Sunday in March. *(DST background, Congress and the Nation Vol. IV, p. 804)*

Supporters of HR 4437 said the change would result in more daylight hours for work and recreation, as well as significant energy savings because of the reduced need for electricity.

Opponents argued that energy savings would be minimal and the change could cause traffic dangers for schoolchildren in rural areas in the Western time zones. The sun rises later in those areas, so children would be traveling to school in the dark. Critics also said the bill would cause difficulties for farmers, who would have to tend their animals in morning darkness.

The House passed HR 4437 (H Rept 97-243) Oct. 28 by a 243-165 vote. In the Senate, however, opponents blocked Commerce Committee action on a companion bill.

1982

Several years' efforts to update telecommunications policy came to an abrupt halt in 1982. A 1981 Senate bill to restructure the American Telephone & Telegraph Co. (AT&T) and deregulate much of the telecommunications industry was undercut in January 1982 when the Justice Department and AT&T announced a settlement to an antitrust case. A House subcommittee bill to modify the settlement plan was withdrawn from consideration in midyear.

Congress directed the Federal Communications Commission to establish rules for granting broadcast licenses by

lottery, but the House again thwarted Senate efforts to deregulate the broadcast industry.

A watered-down measure guaranteeing small businesses a specific share of the federal research budget was signed into law in 1982.

Consumer advocates had mixed success during the session. Congress overturned a Federal Trade Commission (FTC) regulation requiring used-car dealers to disclose information about known major defects in cars they sold — an action that was to be invalidated by the Supreme Court the following year. But consumers won against the American Medical Association, which unsuccessfully sought legislation exempting doctors and other professionals from FTC antitrust jurisdiction.

AT&T Deregulation

Congressional efforts to deregulate much of the telecommunications industry and restructure the American Telephone & Telegraph Co. (AT&T) were sidetracked by the announcement early in 1982 of a proposed settlement of a Justice Department antitrust suit against AT&T.

In October 1981 the Senate had passed a far-reaching telecommunications measure (S 898), the first bill to reach the floor in the five years that Congress had been considering revisions to the 1934 Communications Act.

A substantially different bill (HR 5158), which critics of AT&T said would provide more safeguards against the possibility of AT&T unfairly overwhelming its competition, was introduced in late 1981 in the House. The bill, revised in 1982 to deal with what sponsor Timothy E. Wirth, D-Colo., saw as gaps left by the proposed antitrust settlement, was abruptly withdrawn from consideration in July 1982. Wirth charged that AT&T supporters had used dilatory tactics that made it impossible to finish the bill before the end of the 97th Congress.

The settlement agreement, announced Jan. 8, 1982, had gone beyond the pending House and Senate bills. The agreement permitted AT&T to enter unregulated and computer-oriented fields, such as data processing, if it divested itself of its 22 local telephone operating companies.

Furthermore, it gave AT&T relatively free rein to use its research and manufacturing arms — Bell Laboratories and Western Electric — to enter the new market and allowed AT&T to retain its long-distance operations.

AT&T initially had opposed divestiture but acquiesced because the plan contained fewer restrictions on non-regulated activities than the pending legislation, according to AT&T Chairman Charles Brown. Both bills, as well as a deregulation plan put forward in 1980 by the Federal Communications Commission (FCC), would have required AT&T to establish a separate subsidiary to enter unregulated markets but did not call for divestiture.

The proposed agreement raised some concerns on Capitol Hill. Among those was the fear that the plan to split up the AT&T network could result in substantial hikes in local telephone rates because the local rates would no longer be subsidized by AT&T's long-distance service. Congress went to work on this problem in the 98th Congress. (Details, pp. 275, 278)

Other questions were raised about future state regulation of the divested telephone companies and the quality of local service. There also were concerns about the degree of competition within the telecommunications industry and the possible funneling of funds from AT&T's regulated long-distance telephone service into the new unregulated businesses AT&T would be allowed to enter.

To meet some of these concerns, modifications of the proposed settlement were announced in August 1982.

Antitrust Agreement

The Justice Department-AT&T plan modified a 1956 consent decree that settled a 1949 antitrust suit and barred AT&T from unregulated activities, in effect restricting the firm to providing regulated telephone service. The agreement also called for the dismissal of the Justice Department's antitrust suit, which had been filed in 1974.

The modification permitted AT&T, in addition to retaining Bell Labs and Western Electric, to continue to provide long-distance service under government economic regulation through its Long Lines Department. AT&T, rather than the local companies, would provide telephones.

The agreement did not specify how AT&T would divest itself of the 22 local telephone operating companies. There could be one new giant company to provide local service, a prospect critics said would not promote competition. Or there could be many separate firms.

The local companies would provide regulated local telephone service and would allow access to long-distance carriers, such as AT&T or MCI.

The local companies would not be allowed to favor AT&T in granting access to the local telephone network, in providing service quality, or in purchasing products and services. They would charge a fee to connect long-distance carriers with the network.

Until Sept. 1, 1987, however, the local company could require AT&T to provide any service needed to allow the company to fulfill the requirements of the agreement.

Responding to concerns raised by Rep. Wirth and others, U.S. District Judge Harold H. Greene of Washington, D.C., Aug. 11 called for changes in the settlement. Greene had presided over the yearlong trial of the Justice Department antitrust suit against AT&T.

Greene said the settlement was in the public interest, but modifications would be necessary to ensure the financial strength of the local operating companies and to limit telephone rate increases.

One of the proposed modifications gave Greene the authority to approve AT&T's reorganization plan under the settlement.

Greene said he would resume the antitrust trial if AT&T and the Justice Department did not agree to the modifications. The two parties accepted the changes Aug. 19, and the new agreement was approved by Greene Aug. 24.

The modifications approved by the court:

● Allowed the local operating companies to produce the *Yellow Pages* advertising directories. The original settlement would have transferred *Yellow Pages* to AT&T. HR 5158 and S 898 would have allowed the local companies to retain the *Yellow Pages* revenue, estimated at more than $2 billion a year.

Greene said production of *Yellow Pages* by the local operating companies would generate a substantial subsidy for local telephone rates.

● Allowed the local operating companies to market customer premises equipment, such as ordinary telephones. The original settlement would have transferred the equipment to AT&T.

Permitting the local companies to market the equipment would "provide needed competition for AT&T," Greene said.

● Barred AT&T from engaging in electronic publishing over its own transmission facilities, although it would be allowed to offer limited electronic directory and weather services. The court could lift the restriction after seven years unless it found that competitive conditions required an extension.

Greene said the electronic publishing industry was still in its infancy, and if AT&T were allowed into the industry now "there would be a substantial risk not only that it would stifle the efforts of other electronic publishers but that it would acquire a substantial monopoly over the generation of news. . . . Such a development would strike at a principle which lies at the heart of the First Amendment: that the American people are entitled to a diversity of sources of information."

Newspaper publishers succeeded in including restrictions in HR 5158 and S 898 generally barring AT&T's entry into electronic publishing over its own lines.

Background

The Communications Act of 1934 was enacted at a time when one out of every three homes had a telephone, and policy makers believed a monopoly was the key to creating a nationwide network.

Without competitive pressures during the early years, AT&T grew to become the largest corporation in the world. Eventually virtually every home and business became wired into an interlocking network that spanned the country.

But the nature of telephones began to change; telephone lines could be used to transmit high-speed data as well as human conversation, and telephone calls could be transmitted by microwave and satellite. Other firms entered the scene and chipped at the monopoly.

The FCC's Carterfone decision in 1956, upheld by the U.S. Supreme Court in 1968, allowed another firm to hook up its car radio phones to the Bell System, breaking the equipment monopoly. Later, specialized carriers providing long-distance service by microwave were allowed to connect to the AT&T local lines.

Some of those firms, however, complained that AT&T unfairly restricted their access to the network and the equipment sales field. AT&T still made most of the telephone equipment, bought most of the equipment and provided most of the telephone service.

AT&T argued that the network would be damaged by improper equipment and complained of the restrictions on its use of new technologies. Among its chief targets was the 1956 consent decree barring AT&T from entering unregulated, but highly lucrative, telecommunications fields.

The consent decree, AT&T officials said, had no place in a competitive environment. AT&T argued that since it already employed the new technology, it should be allowed to compete with other firms. The company's telephone switching equipment was basically a computer operation that could be used to manage the transmissions that currently were sent along unchanged.

The increased opportunities of telecommunications led to mounting pressure to revise the 1934 law and resulting regulations and to clarify who could provide the new services and under what circumstances.

Prior to 1981, however, congressional efforts to rewrite

the telecommunications law progressed no further than committees, with most of the action on the House side. *(Congress and the Nation Vol. V, p. 347)*

FCC Deregulation Move

Since Congress had not come up with a solution to the problem, the FCC in April 1980 moved administratively to deregulate telecommunications.

The FCC held that only basic telephone service was subject to regulation. If AT&T wanted to sell unregulated products and services, it would be required to create a separate subsidiary.

The FCC order also restricted the information flow between the parent company and the subsidiary to prevent the subsidiary from having an unfair advantage over its competitors. In addition, the subsidiary would be barred from owning transmission facilities.

The FCC deregulation did not halt legislative efforts. Some industry and congressional observers questioned whether the FCC had the authority to deregulate on its own. Their position was that Congress should set such far-reaching policy.

1981 Senate Action

The Senate passed S 898 Oct. 7, 1981, by a 90-4 vote.

S 898 would have allowed AT&T to enter new unregulated and computer-oriented markets, such as data processing, which were forbidden to it under the 1956 consent decree. However, the monopoly would have had to set up a separate subsidiary to handle the new services.

The sale of telephone and other customer-premises equipment was to be deregulated, but regulation of basic telephone service was to continue.

Committee Action. S 898 was reported (S Rept 97-170) by the Senate Commerce Committee July 27 by a 16-1 vote. The lone dissenter was Ernest F. Hollings, D-S.C., ranking minority member and former chairman of the Communications Subcommittee, who contended the bill would not adequately prevent AT&T from overwhelming its competition.

During markup, the committee added restrictions on AT&T's entry into electronic publishing and on AT&T's providing of an electronic "Yellow Pages," two chief concerns of the American Newspaper Publishers Association. Also added were restrictions on AT&T's entry into the home alarm industry and restraints on local regulation of cable television rates.

Support, Opposition. The Reagan administration, like its predecessor, found it difficult to secure Justice Department endorsement of the legislation. Although S 898 disavowed any intent of affecting pending antitrust suits, the Justice Department was still concerned that the legislation would somehow interfere. The administration eventually endorsed the thrust of S 898.

An AT&T spokesman said Bell still had reservations about parts of S 898, but it was pleased that the committee moved the bill along.

Many of AT&T's existing and potential competitors, however, continued to oppose S 898 because of what they termed a lack of safeguards concerning the separate subsidiary. Critics claimed the subsidiary — dubbed "Baby Bell" — would not really be separate but would be a "giant clone" of AT&T.

Floor Action. A major issue during three days of

debate Oct. 5, 6 and 7 was whether S 898 sufficiently protected AT&T competitors.

The Judiciary and Commerce committees and Assistant Attorney General William F. Baxter worked out a number of amendments to help ensure adequate separation between AT&T and the subsidiary and to foster competition. They included a guarantee that AT&T competitors have adequate access to the local networks. The package was approved by voice vote Oct. 6.

Several other amendments were adopted Oct. 6, including one deleting language restricting local governments' authority to regulate basic cable television rates. The National League of Cities had lobbied strenuously for the amendment, which was adopted by a 59-34 vote.

1982 House Action

In a surprise announcement July 20, 1982, House Telecommunications Subcommittee Chairman Wirth withdrew HR 5158, his bill to modify the proposed antitrust settlement between AT&T and the Justice Department. In announcing the withdrawal, Wirth charged that AT&T had used a campaign of "fear and distortion" against HR 5158 and that AT&T supporters had used dilatory tactics that made it impossible to finish the bill.

HR 5158, introduced Dec. 10, 1981, had been rewritten in 1982 to address what Wirth considered gaps left by the antitrust agreement.

The bill would have barred AT&T from using revenue from regulated long-distance service to subsidize unregulated, competitive businesses. It also would have prevented AT&T from transmitting its own electronic publishing services and would have allowed the divested companies to sell new telephone equipment.

Supporters said the bill was needed to prevent undue increases in local telephone rates, to protect the viability of local telephone companies after they were separated from AT&T and to guard against potential anti-competitive actions by a restructured AT&T.

AT&T Opposition. AT&T attacked the new version of HR 5158, contending that it unfairly and severely restricted the firm while making it easier for other telecommunications companies to compete.

James E. Olson, vice chairman of the AT&T board, contended that HR 5158 could disrupt the nation's telephone system by placing substantial burdens on AT&T's long-distance operations. He said the bill's requirement that AT&T form a separate subsidiary for long-distance operations would restrict business dealings between the subsidiary and the parent company, including AT&T's research and manufacturing arms, Bell Laboratories and Western Electric.

AT&T said Congress should delay legislation until the agreement was approved and urged its one million employees, three million stockholders and 190,000 retirees to object to Wirth's bill. Thousands of letters protesting the legislation poured into House offices.

Procedural Delays. HR 5158 had been unanimously approved by Wirth's Telecommunications Subcommittee March 25. After seven days of markup by the full committee, Wirth July 20 still claimed he had the votes to report the bill.

But Wirth said the procedural delays used by committee members sympathetic to AT&T — such as forcing a formal reading of the 130-page bill and conducting extensive debate on each amendment — were likely to continue

on the House floor and, if the bill passed, in conference with the Senate. He also said AT&T tried to have the bill referred to House committees ranging from Agriculture to Ways and Means.

Noting that only 27 legislative days remained before Congress' targeted adjournment date, Wirth said, "The only way to pass legislation now would be to accept an agreement dictated by AT&T."

FCC Lottery Rules

The Federal Communications Commission (FCC) was ordered to establish rules for granting broadcast licenses by random selection under legislation approved by Congress in 1982.

Although the bill (HR 3239 — PL 97-259) did not require use of a lottery instead of the existing method of comparative hearings on applications, Congress insisted that regulations for a lottery be established. The 1981 budget reconciliation law (PL 97-35) had directed the FCC to establish a lottery, but the commission had not done so, contending that the requirements were unworkable. *(1981 legislation, p. 263)*

The 1982 measure was a collection of various communications bills (S 929, S 2181, HR 5008, HR 6162) that the Senate Aug. 18 substituted for the language of HR 3239, a bill passed by the House in 1981. The original version of HR 3239 had been incorporated in the 1981 reconciliation act.

The new legislation cleared Congress Aug. 19 when both chambers adopted the conference report on the bill (H Rept 97-765).

Provisions. As signed into law Sept. 12, HR 3239 (PL 97-259):

● Directed the FCC within 180 days of enactment to adopt rules for a random selection system for granting broadcast licenses and required that "significant preference" be given to minority groups to help increase diversification of ownership of mass media outlets. (The conference report provided guidelines for establishing a lottery.)

● Authorized the FCC to eliminate the individual licensing of citizens band (CB) radio operators.

● Allowed the FCC to use amateur radio operators on a voluntary basis to administer and update amateur radio license examinations. The bill also permitted the FCC to accept the volunteer services of amateur radio and CB operators to monitor radio frequencies for violation of FCC rules.

● Repealed a provision of a 1978 law (PL 95-234) that would have terminated the existing formula used by the FCC for determining the reasonableness of rates charged for cable television attachments to utility poles. *(Congress and the Nation Vol. V, p. 320)*

● Made clear that the FCC had jurisdiction over intrastate radio communications. This provision was necessary to ensure that the FCC could charge CB radio operators with violation of commission rules.

● Required the FCC to establish minimum standards for televisions and other home electronic equipment to reduce their susceptibility to radio interference.

● Allowed the FCC to grant radio operator licenses to aliens eligible for employment in the United States.

● Relaxed the existing bar against FCC employees having an interest in a firm involved in wire or radio communications. The new standard would prohibit ownership only

when there was a significant interest in communications, manufacturing or sales activities subject to FCC regulation.

● Established rules for FCC regulation of private land mobile services and eased the process for granting private land mobile licenses. Private land mobile services include emergency and business vehicle radios.

Broadcast Deregulation

The Senate in 1982 approved legislation (S 1629) to significantly reduce federal regulation of radio and television. But some key House members contended there was not enough competition in broadcasting to warrant lifting federal regulation and the bill died when the House failed to act.

S 1629 would have codified steps taken by the Federal Communications Commission (FCC) to deregulate radio broadcasting, such as barring the agency from imposing public affairs programming requirements.

The bill also would have eliminated the radio and TV license renewal procedure of comparing the existing licensee with competing applicants. Licenses generally would be renewed unless there had been serious legal violations. Legislation instructing the FCC to prepare for license lotteries was enacted in 1982. *(Details, p. 272)*

In addition, an amendment accepted by the Senate would have required fees for certain FCC services.

S 1629 (S Rept 97-292) was passed March 31 by voice vote. The Senate had passed similar legislation as part of its 1981 budget reconciliation measure but had lost much of it in conference negotiations. *(1981 action, p. 263)*

Public Broadcasting

Under pressure from the Corporation for Public Broadcasting (CPB) and its backers, Congress reversed a 1981 decision and agreed to fund public broadcasting at its authorized level for fiscal 1984. Congress had authorized $130 million but had appropriated only $105.6 million as part of late-year budget cuts. Public broadcasting received advance funding as a means of insulating it from political pressure. *(1981-82 action, p. 264)*

Small Business Research Funds

Legislation (S 881 — PL 97-219) guaranteeing small businesses a share of the federal research budget was enacted in 1982, but only after it had been diluted substantially because of strong opposition.

The measure required all federal agencies with research and development (R&D) budgets exceeding $100 million annually to set aside for small business concerns 1.25 percent of the agency's research budget that was contracted out. The set-aside would amount to about $375 million of the government's estimated $40 billion annual research budget.

The measure was designed to reverse a perceived decline in technological innovation by funneling more research money to small, inventive entrepreneurs. It had the support of the Reagan administration and met with little opposition in 1981 when the Senate unanimously passed it and the House Small Business Committee unanimously reported a similar measure.

But by spring 1982 a late lobbying drive against the bill was taking effect. The proposal faced strenuous criticism from major universities and the American Electronics Association. They argued that the program would siphon federal research dollars away from universities and that mandatory set-asides were wasteful because they required agencies to spend their annual quotas of grants regardless of the need for such spending.

In addition, six House committees took exception to the plan and wanted to remove agencies from the bill.

Legislative Action

The Senate approved S 881 Dec. 8, 1981, by a 90-0 vote. The Senate bill (S Rept 97-194) called for a 1 percent set-aside.

The House Small Business Committee reported its version Nov. 20 by a 40-0 vote (HR 4326 — H Rept 97-349, Part I). The six committees seeking exemptions for various agencies filed their reports in March 1982 (H Rept 97-349, Parts II-VII).

Before taking HR 4326 to the floor, the Small Business panel sought to defuse opposition by lowering the set-aside from the original 3 percent to 1.25 percent and exempting certain intelligence agencies from the set-aside provision.

During floor debate the House agreed to exempt all intelligence research and atomic energy defense programs from the set-aside program, but it rejected several additional exemption proposals.

The House approved HR 4326 June 23 by a 353-57 vote and substituted its language for the text of S 881. The Senate accepted the House version by voice vote June 29.

Provisions

As signed into law July 22, S 881 (PL 97-219):

● Created Small Business Innovation Research (SBIR) programs, under which a portion of a federal agency's R&D budget was to be reserved for awards to small businesses.

● Required federal agencies with R&D budgets of more than $100 million — not including in-house research — to earmark specific percentages of that budget for small businesses. The percentage would increase from 0.2 percent in the first fiscal year of the program's operation to 0.6 percent in the second, 1.0 percent in the third and 1.25 percent in the fourth and each subsequent year.

● Allowed a five-year phase-in for agencies with extramural R&D budgets of more than $10 billion, a provision that applied at that time only to the Defense Department. Such agencies had to spend 0.1 percent in the first year, 0.3 percent in the second, 0.5 percent in the third, 1.0 percent in the fourth and 1.25 percent in the fifth and subsequent years.

● Exempted from the SBIR requirements all intelligence agency research programs, atomic energy defense programs and the Agency for International Development's support of international research centers or grants to foreign countries.

FTC Used-Car Rule Veto

Congress in 1982 for the first time used its Federal Trade Commission (FTC) veto authority to kill the FTC's proposed rule requiring used-car dealers to disclose information about auto defects.

The rule was blocked May 26 — the last day allowed by law for congressional action — when the House adopted by a 286-133 vote a resolution of disapproval reported by its Energy and Commerce Committee May 25 (S Con Res 60 — H Rept 97-586). The Senate had adopted S Con Res 60 May 18, 69-27.

However, the Supreme Court invalidated the congressional action in 1983. *(Legislative veto, p. 833)*

The FTC in July 1984 issued a new rule that would require used-car dealers to disclose whether a car was still under warranty and what repairs would be covered.

Congressional Veto Authority

The 1980 FTC authorization act (PL 96-252) allowed Congress to overturn an FTC rule without the president's signature if both chambers passed a resolution of disapproval within 90 calendar days of continuous session after the rule had been submitted. It represented the first time Congress had given itself the right to disapprove actions of an independent regulatory agency. *(Congress and the Nation Vol. V, p. 362)*

The Consumers Union of the United States challenged the constitutionality of the veto of the used-car rule in the U.S. Court of Appeals for the District of Columbia. It argued that the veto process was invalid because the president's signature was not required and noted that the Constitution required approval by both houses and review by the president to enact a law.

The appeals court Oct. 22, 1982, overturned the used-car rule veto, and the Senate appealed the decision to the Supreme Court. In a June 1983 decision the Supreme Court declared the legislative veto to be unconstitutional, and in July the court reiterated its position by affirming the lower court's decision in the FTC case.

FTC Rule

The rule Congress vetoed had been issued in 1981 after almost 10 years of investigations, hearings and deliberations. It was tougher than the one eventually adopted in 1984 in that it required used-car dealers to disclose not only the extent of warranty coverage but also major known defects in automobiles.

Dealers contended that expensive inspections would be required to protect them from possible litigation, thereby adding to the cars' cost. Others argued that the rule was an unnecessary federal intrusion in an area best left to state regulation.

Consumer advocates and other supporters of the rule said it was a modest consumer protection measure and did not require inspections.

Both the Senate and House Commerce committees approved resolutions of disapproval in December 1981, but neither measure reached the floor before Congress adjourned for the year. *(1981 action, p. 268)*

FTC Regulation of Doctors

Efforts to bar the Federal Trade Commission (FTC) from regulating doctors and other professionals failed during the 1982 lame-duck session.

The American Medical Association (AMA), which lobbied for an exemption for professionals from FTC authority, argued that the FTC had no mandate from Congress to regulate professionals already licensed by states and that the agency was interfering in quality of care issues.

Agency spokesmen and their supporters countered that the FTC authority was needed to prevent professionals and their associations from conducting boycotts, price-fixing and other activities that limited competition, led to higher consumer costs and reduced the choice of services.

The battle over new restrictions was fought on several fronts: the FTC reauthorization bill, the commission's annual appropriations measure and a continuing resolution providing funding for government agencies whose regular fiscal 1983 appropriations had not been enacted.

The House Dec. 1 passed a bill reauthorizing the agency (HR 6995 — H Rept 97-809, Parts I and II) after adopting, by a 245-155 vote, an amendment exempting professionals from FTC jurisdiction. The bill also limited FTC regulation of unfair or deceptive business practices or false advertising and allowed Congress to continue to veto agency rules. *(FTC veto, p. 273)*

But Senate opponents blocked floor action on a bill containing the exemption (S 2499 — S Rept 97-451), and Congress never completed action on the reauthorization measure. The 1980 authorization (PL 96-252) for the agency expired Sept. 30.

A bitter House fight over FTC restrictions was averted Dec. 9 during debate on the State, Justice, Commerce appropriations bill (HR 6957) when James J. Florio, D-N.J., a supporter of the agency, raised a point of order against including the FTC's fiscal 1983 appropriation because no authorization had been approved. The funds were eliminated, and no FTC amendments were allowed.

Funds for the FTC then were added to a continuing appropriations resolution (H J Res 631 — PL 97-377). During consideration of the resolution, the Senate Dec. 17 tabled, **on a 59-37 key vote (R 31-21; D 28-16),** an amendment that would have barred use of funds by the FTC to regulate professionals already regulated by states. H J Res 631, cleared Dec. 20, appropriated $63.61 million for the FTC in fiscal 1983 and extended the legislative veto provision and other restrictions in the agency's 1980 authorization. *(1982 key votes, p. 895)*

1983

Telephone and broadcasting controversies placed heavy demands on Congress in 1983, with the House and Senate in several cases unable to agree on legislation.

The Jan. 1, 1984, breakup of the American Telephone & Telegraph Co. raised the specter of rapidly rising local telephone rates. Both chambers took steps to head off increased rates proposed by the Federal Communications Commission (FCC), but only the House completed floor action in 1983.

House and Senate members were sharply divided over broadcast deregulation. The Senate approved a bill ratifying a number of FCC deregulation moves, but legislation on the House side remained blocked in a subcommittee. The Senate also passed legislation meeting some of the requests of cable television operators who wanted freedom from what they called a bewildering array of local restrictions.

The House approved legislation to delay for six months a controversial FCC proposal to allow the major television networks to profit from TV reruns. The Senate was ready to take similar action when the FCC agreed to hold off on a final decision until 1984.

The House approved legislation to delay for six months a controversial FCC proposal to allow the major television networks to profit from TV reruns. The Senate was ready to take similar action when the FCC agreed to hold off on a final decision until 1984.

Increased funding for the public broadcasting system was approved as part of an FCC authorization bill. Congress failed to complete action on authorizations for the Federal Trade Commission and the Consumer Product Safety Commission.

Phone Rate Hike

Foes of a Federal Communications Commission (FCC) plan to raise local telephone rates scored a major victory in 1983 when the House passed legislation to reject the FCC proposal.

The bill (HR 4102) prohibited the FCC from imposing a new monthly fee on residential and single-line business phone users but permitted the charge to be levied on multiline businesses. The action marked a bitter defeat for the FCC and the American Telephone & Telegraph Co.

A milder bill (S 1660) imposing a two-year moratorium on the charges was reported in October by the Senate Commerce Committee, but in early 1984 the Senate voted not to take up the measure after the FCC agreed to postpone any price hike until mid-1985. *(1983-84 action, p. 278)*

Broadcast Deregulation

As in 1982, the Senate in 1983 saw legislation it had passed to deregulate the broadcasting industry blocked by opposition in the House.

Although the Senate Feb. 17 passed the deregulation bill (S 55), the House Energy and Commerce Subcommittee on Telecommunications did not reach a consensus before adjournment in November. The stalemate continued in 1984, and the legislation died at the end of the 98th Congress. *(1983-84 action, p. 281)*

Cable Television Deregulation

Efforts to reduce the power of cities to regulate cable television systems moved forward in 1983, with measures passed by the Senate (S 66) and approved by a key House subcommittee (HR 4103).

Cities and other interest groups had succeeded in blocking similar legislation in 1981 and 1982, contending that the bills would intrude into local affairs and would restrict local governments' authority. The coalition, however, split over the legislation proposed in 1983.

Negotiations continued in 1984, and Congress finally cleared a deregulation bill (S 66 — PL 98-549) Oct. 11, one day before the 98th Congress adjourned. *(1983-84 action, p. 279)*

Television Rerun Rights

A controversial Federal Communications Commission (FCC) proposal to allow the television networks to tap into the lucrative rerun syndication market sent the networks'

foes rushing to Congress in 1983 for legislation to stop the FCC.

The House in 1983 passed a bill (HR 2250) to delay the FCC proposal until mid-1984. Senate committee markup of the bill was suspended after the FCC temporarily postponed its rules changes. In 1984 the FCC agreed to a two-year moratorium on its plan. *(1983-84 action, p. 282)*

Public Broadcasting

The public broadcasting system got a boost in its funding for fiscal 1984-86 under a Federal Communications Commission (FCC) authorization passed in 1983.

The legislation (HR 2755 — PL 98-214) authorized funding for the Corporation for Public Broadcasting (CPB) at $145 million in fiscal 1984, $153 million in fiscal 1985 and $162 million in fiscal 1986. The increases recouped a portion of CPB funding cut in 1981, when Congress approved authorizations of $130 million annually for fiscal 1984-86 as part of its budget-cutting reconciliation bill (PL 97-35). *(Details, p. 264)*

The bill also imposed a series of financial controls on National Public Radio (NPR), which had been forced to borrow money and negotiate other aid from the CPB to overcome a financial mismanagement crisis.

NPR, which provided programming and a satellite link for 280 member public radio stations, sharply curtailed its operations and dismissed more than 140 employees in 1983 after it was revealed that the network faced a $9.1 million deficit. The financial crisis, resolved only after the CPB agreed to a bailout plan, led to the resignations of NPR President Frank Mankiewicz and other top executives.

HR 2755 was passed in both chambers Nov. 18. During a brief debate on the bill (H Rept 98-356) Nov. 17, the House rejected 141-277 an amendment to reduce the public broadcasting authorizations.

Two CPB authorization bills were vetoed in 1984. *(Details, p. 282)*

Provisions

As signed into law Dec. 8, HR 2755 (PL 98-214):

● Authorized $91.2 million for the Federal Communications Commission in each of fiscal years 1984-85.

● Authorized $145 million in fiscal 1984, $153 million in fiscal 1985 and $162 million in fiscal 1986 for CPB.

● Prohibited the CPB from distributing federal funds to NPR unless NPR had implemented financial procedures recommended by a certified public accountant and deemed prudent by the comptroller general; adopted a balanced budget; and provided the CPB with continuous access to all NPR financial records.

● Provided that the financial supervision and controls on NPR imposed by the bill would be lifted when NPR had covered debts accumulated before Oct. 1, 1983, when fiscal 1984 began.

● Reversed a 1981 law that would have permitted the CPB president to serve as chairman of the board and allowed the board to elect one of its members as chairman.

● Made it a crime to provide obscene telephone messages, such as so-called "dial it" services, whether made directly or by recording and without regard to whether the sender of the message initiated the call, in the District of Columbia or across state lines or U.S. borders that could be received by a person under the age of 18.

● Provided for violators of the ban on obscene messages to be subject to criminal penalties of up to $50,000 in fines and up to six months in prison and a civil fine of up to $50,000 a day for each day during which a violation occurred for commercial purposes.

● Provided that a defendant could escape conviction if he met regulations to be prescribed by the FCC to prevent persons under the age of 18 from receiving the obscene messages.

Insider Trading Curbs

Legislation to strengthen the power of the Securities and Exchange Commission to prosecute a war on insider trading was approved by the House in 1983.

The measure (HR 559) was passed by the Senate and signed into law in 1984. *(Details, p. 283)*

"Insider trading" referred to the use of non-public "material" information to buy and sell securities. It included advance tips on such things as corporate earnings reports, lucrative contracts, oil strikes, mergers, news reports or product failures. Abuses had multiplied in recent years with the increase in corporate mergers and takeovers — news of which caused stock prices to rise and fall dramatically.

Small Business Contract Aid

Congress in 1983 enacted legislation designed to increase competition for government procurement contracts and make it easier for small businesses to receive these contracts, primarily by requiring advance notice. *(1984 procurement legislation, p. 790)*

The measure (S 272 — PL 98-72) required federal agencies and departments to publish notice, with certain exceptions, of upcoming federal contracts worth $10,000 or more in the *Commerce Business Daily* at least 15 days prior to soliciting contract bids. In addition, federal agencies had to allow at least 30 days for receipt of bids or proposals.

Federal departments also were required to publish notice in the *Commerce Business Daily* of prime contract awards exceeding $25,000 in which subcontracting was likely, unless the procurement was classified because of security reasons.

The measure also made it more difficult for federal departments to negotiate a sole-source contract with a single company by requiring, in most circumstances, the approval of the head of the procurement division or his deputy. The sole source provision of the bill applied to procurement contracts valued at $1 million in fiscal year 1984, $500,000 in fiscal 1985 and $300,000 in fiscal 1986 and subsequent years.

The Senate approved S 272 Feb. 3 and the House passed an amended version March 8. The conference report on the bill (H Rept 98-263) was adopted by the Senate June 27 and by the House Aug. 1.

Minority Businesses

Congress in 1983 cleared legislation (S 273 — PL 98-47) reauthorizing two pilot programs of the Small Business Administration (SBA) aimed at assisting minority-owned and other disadvantaged small businesses.

Section 8(a) of the Small Business Act of 1953 gave the SBA authority to enter into procurement contracts with federal agencies and then subcontract the work to socially and economically disadvantaged small businesses.

A 1978 law (PL 95-507) set up a pilot program requiring one federal agency, designated by the president, to allow the SBA to select which of the agency's contracts would be awarded to minority firms. The Department of the Army was chosen as the pilot agency. *(Congress and the Nation Vol. V, p. 316)*

The 1978 law set up another pilot program authorizing SBA to waive, under certain conditions, the federal bonding requirements that otherwise would be in force for government contracts awarded through the 8(a) program.

Both programs had been extended for one year in 1980 (PL 96-481) but had expired Sept. 30, 1981. A reauthorization attempt had failed in 1981. *(Details, p. 266)*

PL 98-47 revived the pilot programs, effective Oct. 1, 1983, and required the president to select a new federal agency to participate in the programs. During the first three years of the program only 14 contracts worth approximately $100 million had been awarded.

The Senate passed S 273 Feb. 3. The House passed the bill Feb. 15, after substituting the language of HR 861 (H Rept 98-2). The Senate June 27 adopted the conference report on S 273 (H Rept 98-262); the House, June 30.

FTC Authorization

The 98th Congress failed to enact legislation to reauthorize the Federal Trade Commission (FTC). The agency had been operating without an authorization since Sept. 30, 1982.

Senate and House committees in 1983 reported authorization bills (S 1714, HR 2970, HR 2974) but neither chamber completed action. Congress' power to veto agency rules and FTC attempts to regulate doctors and other professionals were major issues.

The bill reported by the Senate Commerce Committee Sept. 1 (S 1714 — S Rept 98-215) was silent on the legislative veto, a mechanism that the Supreme Court had ruled unconstitutional June 23. However, a veto alternative had been expected to be offered on the floor. *(Legislative veto, p. 833)*

HR 2970, as reported (H Rept 98-156, Part I) by the House Commerce Committee May 16, prior to the court's action, made permanent the power of Congress to veto FTC rules. The authority was provided by the 1980 FTC act (PL 96-252). *(Congress and the Nation Vol. V, p. 847)*

However, both the Rules and Judiciary committees ordered the bill reported without recommendation (H Rept 98-156, Parts II and III). On May 16 Rules reported an authorization bill (HR 2974 — H Rept 98-157) to continue the veto authority only through fiscal 1984, pending a decision by the Supreme Court, and to authorize funding for one year.

On the regulation of professionals, the Senate bill included a compromise forged by the American Medical Association and FTC staffs. It provided that the agency could not challenge anti-competitive activity by professionals if the activity was required and supervised by the states. HR 2970 contained a similar provision, but it also allowed the FTC to challenge a state law or rule that purported to relate to training and educational require-

ments but in fact dealt with business practices. HR 2974 did not address the regulation of professionals.

An attempt to exempt professionals from FTC jurisdiction had blocked passage of an authorization in 1982. *(Details, p. 274)*

Congress appropriated $63.5 million for the FTC in fiscal 1984 (HR 3222 — PL 98-166) and $64.3 million in fiscal 1985 (HR 5712 — PL 98-411) but only after battles in the House over appropriating funds for the agency without an authorization.

HR 5712 barred the FTC from bringing antitrust suits against local governments unless the FTC oversight committees specifically allowed such suits in the FTC's authorization.

FTC Funeral Rule

An effort to block a Federal Trade Commission (FTC) rule concerning funeral home directors' practices was unsuccessful in 1983.

The rule, in the making since 1975, required funeral directors to disclose the prices of individual services and goods included in a package, and barred a director from making misrepresentations. The rule was opposed by the industry, which contended it was unnecessary and too costly for the majority of funeral directors, who were honorable. Supporters argued that the rule was necessary so that vulnerable bereaved customers would have full information.

A resolution of disapproval (H Con Res 70) was reported unfavorably May 9 by a House Energy and Commerce subcommittee, but the full committee did not act before the June 23 Supreme Court ruling holding legislative vetoes unconstitutional. *(Ruling, p. 833)*

Congressional aides said that the pending court decision may have been a factor in the lack of enthusiasm for vetoing the rule. Another factor may have been concern about bad publicity surrounding the 1982 congressional veto of an FTC rule requiring disclosure of certain information by used car dealers. *(Details, p. 273)*

The FTC funeral rule was upheld in January 1984 by the 4th Circuit Court of Appeals in Richmond, Va., clearing the way for full implementation.

Consumer Product Safety

Legislation (S 861) reauthorizing funding for the Consumer Product Safety Commission (CPSC) was caught up in the confusion over the validity of legislative vetoes, and House-Senate differences were not resolved in 1983.

The Senate passed its CPSC reauthorization (S Rept 98-57) by voice vote June 16, before the Supreme Court ruled that a legislative veto not presented to the president was unconstitutional. The Senate in effect extended the existing veto, which permitted one chamber to veto a CPSC rule if the other chamber did not object (PL 97-35). *(Legislative veto, p. 833; PL 97-35, p. 40)*

The House passed an amended version of S 861 by voice vote June 29, after the court decision. The bill included two floor amendments that presented alternatives to the existing legislative veto. One barred the spending of funds to implement a major rule unless a joint resolution approving it had been passed by Congress and sent to the president for his signature. The other provided that a rule

would not go into effect for 90 days, allowing time for Congress to enact a resolution of disapproval, which would be sent to the president.

In addition, there were differences over funding. The Senate bill authorized $35 million in fiscal 1984 and fiscal 1985, the amounts reported by the Commerce Committee April 12. The House measure authorized $35.7 million in fiscal 1984, $37.5 million in fiscal 1985 and $39.4 million in fiscal 1986. President Reagan requested $32 million for fiscal 1984.

The House-approved authorization levels represented a significant reduction from those reported by the House Energy and Commerce Committee May 12 (HR 2668 — H Rept 98-114). During floor action June 29, the House voted 238-177 to slash the funding and reduce the authorization period recommended by the committee. Henry A. Waxman, D-Calif., chairman of the Subcommittee on Health, said the cuts were due partly to fears that Congress would lose control over regulatory agencies as a result of the court ruling.

In 1983 Congress appropriated $35 million in fiscal 1984 for the CPSC (HR 3133 — PL 98-45) and in 1984 appropriated $36 million in fiscal 1985 (HR 5713 — PL 98-371).

Credit Card Surcharges, Fraud

The House Nov. 16 approved two bills on the use of credit cards.

Surcharges. By a vote of 349-73, the House passed HR 4278 to extend until July 31, 1984, a 1981 ban on surcharges for purchases by credit card or under open-end credit plans. The existing surcharge ban was scheduled to expire Feb. 27, 1984. No further action was taken on the bill in 1983, and attempts to enact compromise legislation temporarily extending the surcharge ban proved futile in 1984. *(Details, p. 284)*

Fraud. By a vote of 422-0, the House passed HR 3622 (H Rept 98-426) to broaden laws protecting customers against fraudulent use of their credit cards. HR 3622 would have made it a federal crime to possess more than five counterfeit credit cards or other payment devices and to steal more than $1,000 in a single year through credit card fraud regardless of how many cards were used (thus closing a loophole in existing law that limited it to the use of a single card).

The bill also would have restricted disclosure of credit card numbers.

In 1984 the House tacked HR 3622 onto legislation extending the ban on credit card surcharges; the Senate then refused to take up the surcharge bill.

Daylight-Saving Time

Reversing action it had taken two years earlier, the House in 1983 defeated legislation to extend daylight-saving time (DST) by two months.

HR 1398 (H Rept 98-80) provided for the start of DST on the first Sunday in March instead of the last Sunday in April. It would have run to the last Sunday in October, as under existing law.

The House rejected the bill 199-211, after adopting 221-187 an amendment allowing states to exempt themselves from the additional two months.

In 1981 the House passed similar legislation 243-165, but the Senate took no action. *(Details, p. 269)*

1984

Several controversial communications issues were on the congressional agenda in 1984.

Under pressure from Congress, the Federal Communications Commission (FCC) postponed until June 1985 an order that residential and single-line business phone customers pay a charge for the right of access to long-distance service. The FCC also backed off — at least temporarily — from its proposal to allow networks to profit from television reruns. Bills to mandate delays were shelved.

After repeated setbacks, a bill defining national policy for the cable television industry was passed just before adjournment. The broadcasting industry once again lost its battle for deregulation legislation, and bills to increase the public broadcasting system's funding triggered two presidential vetoes.

Penalties for using confidential information to profit in the stock market were increased by legislation enacted in 1984.

The insurance industry triumphed over women's groups when a House committee gutted a bill mandating equal insurance benefits and rates for men and women. But a formidable business alliance got no further than a Senate committee in its push for a law limiting manufacturers' liability for unsafe products.

Phone Rate Hike

Legislation to block increases in telephone rates for residential and small business users was shelved in 1984, when the Federal Communications Commission (FCC), under pressure from Congress, postponed the proposed charges for the right of access to long-distance service.

The House in 1983 passed a bill (HR 4102) that would have banned altogether the rate increases for residential and small business phone users. In 1984, after the FCC postponed the charges, the Senate voted not to take up a milder bill (S 1660) that would have delayed the new charges for two years, through 1985.

The FCC had proposed a flat charge on residential and business phone users for the right of access to long-distance service, whether they used long-distance service or not. The fees originally were to start at $2 per month for residential customers and $6 per month for businesses, rising yearly until 1990.

The fees were designed to eventually recover $6.5 billion that was being paid by long-distance users to help maintain wires, poles and other equipment shared by all users. The $6.5 billion amounted to a subsidy that helped keep local rates low.

The FCC and American Telephone & Telegraph Co. (AT&T) said that shifting the charges from long-distance to local users was essential to the success of the Jan. 1, 1984, court-ordered breakup of AT&T. Local companies would separate from AT&T on Jan. 1 and would no longer get that subsidy from AT&T. AT&T would become one of several long-distance companies. *(Background, p. 270)*

However, because AT&T accounted for more than 90 percent of long-distance billings, it had billions of dollars riding on whether long-distance or local customers covered the costs. AT&T and the FCC argued that continuing to make long-distance users pay would drive up long-distance prices and encourage the development of private systems bypassing the local network. They said the FCC plan recognized the new competitive environment of telecommunications and reflected a proper shift to cost-based pricing. AT&T spent an estimated $4 million lobbying against the legislation.

Backers of the legislation said the FCC proposal would mean an increase of $7 to $8 per month in the average monthly phone bill of American consumers by 1990, undermining a policy dating to 1934 that called for universal telephone service. Telephone service would become too expensive for the poor, they said.

The access fees for residential and business telephone users originally were set to begin Jan. 1, 1984. The FCC subsequently delayed the charges until April 3, 1984. On Jan. 25, 1984, the FCC reaffirmed a Jan. 16 decision to put off the charges for residential and single-line business users until at least June 1985 and to cap the charge at $4 per month until 1990.

The FCC voted Dec. 19 for a $1 per month charge for residential and single-line businesses, effective June 1985. The charges would increase to $2 per month in 1986 and would be capped at that, pending FCC hearings in 1986.

Multi-line businesses began paying access charges on May 25, 1984.

House Bill

Under HR 4102 as passed by the House by voice vote Nov. 10, 1983, residential and single-line business customers would have paid no access charge, but businesses with more than one telephone line would have paid $6 per month. The multi-line businesses would have provided $1.3 billion of the $6.5 billion at issue.

The bill would have required long-distance companies, including AT&T and its competitors, to put up $3.9 billion of the cost of jointly used facilities, with the remaining $1.3 billion recovered through charges on private phone systems that indirectly interconnected with the local phone system.

Two funds to help keep phone rates affordable for high-cost rural areas and low-income customers were to be established by the bill. The money would have come from a small surcharge added to long distance calls.

Committee Action. The Energy and Commerce Committee, after sometimes contentious debate spanning seven meetings, approved HR 4102 on a 27-15 party-line vote. The bill was reported Nov. 3, 1983 (H Rept 98-479).

The committee had begun its markup in a charged atmosphere because a bill (HR 5158) opposed by AT&T died in an unusually bitter fight in 1982. Opponents had employed dilatory tactics that halted committee action. *(Details, p. 270)*

Opponents of HR 4102 had indicated in 1983 that delay again would be their chosen weapon. However, Commerce Chairman John D. Dingell, D-Mich., wielding his gavel, used his power as chairman to prevent delays.

During the committee debate, panel members rejected several key amendments supported by AT&T, thus paving the way for approval of HR 4102.

Floor Action. The House approved HR 4102 by voice

vote Nov. 10, 1983. Passage of the bill had been forecast by the rejection on a **key vote of 142-264 (R 134-19; D 8-245)** of a substitute offered by Tom Tauke, R-Iowa, that would have phased in the FCC access charge on residential and small business telephone users beginning in 1985 and limited the charge to $1 per month the first year, rising to $4 per month by 1988. *(1983 key votes, p. 911)*

About five of the seven hours of debate on HR 4102 were spent on Tauke's plan. Tauke cast his amendment as a compromise between HR 4102 and the FCC's plan, which he and other Republicans argued was essential to preserve the long-distance system after the breakup of AT&T. Tauke said his bill would provide more money to subsidize low-income users and to defray the high costs of rural service.

Telecommunications Subcommittee Chairman Timothy E. Wirth, D-Colo., and other backers of HR 4102 argued that banning the access charge was necessary to keep local phone rates from rising too much. They said Tauke's plan would destroy HR 4102 and that Tauke's provisions favoring rural phone users were intended to "Balkanize" the House. Much of the debate centered on whether the Tauke substitute or HR 4102 would better protect rural phone service.

Senate Bill

S 1660, as introduced, would have banned the FCC fees for residential and small business phone users. However, the bill was amended in committee to provide for a two-year moratorium on the access charges. S 1660 also provided for funds to subsidize service in high-cost rural areas and to assure service for low-income users.

Committee Action. A divided Senate Commerce Committee refused to endorse the bill and accepted 9-6 an amendment by Frank R. Lautenberg, D-N.J., wiping out the provisions of S 1660 and substituting a one-year moratorium on the access charges for residential customers.

The panel later agreed to a compromise that extended the moratorium to two years and exempted small businesses with only one telephone line from the FCC's access fees.

S 1660 was reported Oct. 7, 1983 (S Rept 98-270).

Floor Action. After four days of debate, the Senate Jan. 26, 1984, by a 44-40 vote blocked a motion to take up S 1660. The Senate vote came one day after the FCC reaffirmed its decision to delay the fees. The FCC acted after 32 senators wrote requesting the delay.

While some members expressed satisfaction that the FCC had responded to congressional pressure, Commerce Committee Chairman Bob Packwood, R-Ore., chief sponsor of S 1660, did not claim victory. Packwood urged Congress to settle the matter by statute rather than leaving it up to the FCC.

Cable Television Deregulation

One day before adjournment, the 98th Congress approved legislation defining national policy for the cable television industry. Passage of the deregulation measure (S 66 — PL 98-549) culminated a four-year effort to balance the rights of the cable television industry against those of the cities that granted franchises.

Cable companies had pushed for a national policy to protect them from what they considered to be a hodge-podge of local regulations that restricted the growth of the industry. Cities wanted to retain some control through the franchising process and in 1984 sought to counter rulings by the Federal Communications Commission (FCC) and U.S. Supreme Court that permitted federal regulation to supersede local or state actions.

The legislation that cleared Congress Oct. 11, 1984, was considerably different from the original S 66, passed by the Senate in 1983. That version was abandoned in the House because some cities complained its terms were too favorable to the industry.

Finding a compromise acceptable to the industry and cities, however, was not easy. The cable television bill (HR 4103) approved by the House in 1984 was the third version of the measure proposed in two years. Further compromise with the Senate was necessary before cable legislation finally cleared.

The final bill recognized cities' power to grant and renew franchises but outlined standard procedures to be followed so that cable companies would be less vulnerable to arbitrary and uncertain local decisions. S 66 limited cities' control over cable programming, allowed cities to regulate rates for only two years except under limited circumstances and capped the franchise fees cities could charge companies at 5 percent of local revenues. The bill also contained provisions to protect the privacy of subscribers.

Background

A cable system picked up programming signals from antennas, microwave or satellite relays, and sent the signals by cable to subscribers' television sets. Cable re-transmitted over-the-air television signals and provided special programming, such as movies, sports and 24-hour news shows.

By 1983 there were more than 4,800 cable systems in the United States, serving 31.1 million households, or 37 percent of the households that had television.

The industry began to boom in the 1970s when the FCC started relaxing its controls and cable operators were able to offer more than distant over-the-air television programs.

But cable operators contended that as federal regulation decreased, local and state governments stepped up their controls. The operators argued that burdensome and uncertain local regulation impeded their development. They said local regulatory schemes put them at a competitive disadvantage with other types of telecommunications companies that were not regulated.

Cities and other interest groups had succeeded in 1981 in blocking efforts to reduce local regulation of cable television systems, as part of a telecommunications bill. *(AT&T bill, p. 270)*

Senate Action

After two days of debate, the Senate approved S 66 June 14, 1983, by a 87-9 vote. The bill had been reported by the Senate Commerce, Science and Transportation Committee April 27 (S Rept 98-67).

The bill encompassed a compromise reached by the National League of Cities and the National Cable Television Association (NCTA). Two of the major areas of compromise had involved franchise fees and local regulation of rates.

However, the U.S. Conference of Mayors and a group

of cities, including New York City and Dallas, the American Civil Liberties Union and others continued to oppose the bill. They objected that it allowed automatic rate increases by cable firms and virtually required cities to renew franchises.

During floor consideration, S 66 became enmeshed in two issues regarding telephone service: the expected increases in residential and rural telephone rates and the regulation of certain telecommunications services such as data processing. The Senate adopted 97-0 an amendment supporting efforts to hold rates down. *(Phone rate legislation, p. 278)*

The Senate rejected 44-55 an amendment that would have required cable firms to be subject to the same state regulatory restrictions as local phone companies when offering telecommunications services that could be provided by the phone companies. American Telephone & Telegraph Company (AT&T) waged a hard-fought battle against S 66 because the bill allowed cable firms to offer data services without regulation. The final bill provided for state regulation of two-way services such as data and voice transmission.

House Action

The House Oct. 1, 1984, passed a compromise version of HR 4103 by voice vote and amended the text to S 66. Two earlier versions failed to reach the House floor because of differences between NCTA and groups representing cities, such as the U.S. Conference of Mayors and the National League of Cities.

The House Energy and Commerce Subcommittee on Telecommunications in November 1983 approved a version of HR 4103 that sharply reduced local power to regulate cable and contained restrictions cable operators opposed.

In May 1984 the NCTA and the cities groups announced a new compromise. A revised bill was reported by the House Commerce Committee Aug. 1 (H Rept 98-934).

But the industry almost immediately called for revisions in the wake of a June 18 Supreme Court decision striking down Oklahoma's ban on cable transmission of wine ads and reaffirming the authority of the FCC to preempt state and local regulation of cable TV *(Capital Cities Cable Inc. et al. v. Crisp)*. Some cable TV operators were anxious to put aside HR 4103, with its limited decontrol, and rush to the FCC for full deregulation. *(Supreme Court decision, p. 758)*

Members in both chambers prodded the industry and cities to resolve their differences. The two sides Sept. 26 announced they had reached another compromise, which included agreement to end cities' control over cable rates after two years, instead of four years as the committee bill had provided and immediately as cable operators had wanted. The compromise also created a standard process for franchise renewals. These changes and others were amended to the bill before final House passage.

Final Action

The appointment of Senate conferees was blocked by several members who objected to a House affirmative action provision. The guidelines in the provision were similar to existing FCC regulations, but some Senate Republicans objected to what they regarded as "quotas."

Key members privately pronounced the measure dead, but when Congress continued in session past the expected adjournment date of Oct. 4, negotiations resumed. On Oct. 5 the bill's sponsors in the Senate agreed to strike the affirmative action section, but that prompted Howard M. Metzenbaum, D-Ohio, a supporter of the provision, to block floor action.

On Oct. 11, key House members agreed to drop all references to the percentages of cable TV jobs to be filled by women and minorities, and the Senate adopted an amendment strengthening the FCC's power to enforce its existing regulations. Several other amendments were adopted, and House language prohibiting a newspaper from owning a cable system in its city was deleted before both chambers cleared S 66 by voice votes Oct. 11.

Provisions

As signed into law Oct. 30, the Cable Telecommunications Act (S 66 — PL 98-549):

• Stipulated that cities could regulate cable rates only for basic service — the transmission of signals from local broadcast stations — and only for two years after enactment. After that, rates would not be regulated.

• Permitted cable companies to raise subscription rates by up to 5 percent a year, without prior approval, during the two years that rates were locally regulated.

• Stated that cities had the power to grant and renew franchises for local cable systems.

• Replaced state and local renewal procedures with national standards, which included optional hearings, criteria for local officials' decisions, a court appeals process and compensation for firms forced to sell property when franchises were revoked.

• Required that all parts of a city be served, to guard against bypassing low-income areas.

• Capped the franchise fees that a city could charge a cable TV company at 5 percent of the company's local gross revenues.

• Exempted from regulation one-way cable services such as videotex, teletext, computer software and dial-a-movie, but provided that two-way services such as data and voice transmission would continue to be regulated by state utility commissions, as telephone companies were.

• Permitted cities to require that cable companies reserve channels for public, educational and government use.

• Precluded cities from demanding specific video or information programs, although broad categories — such as news or children's shows — could be requested.

• Allowed cities to ban programs they judged to be obscene and required companies to provide "lock box" devices to subscribers who wanted to prevent their children from watching objectionable shows.

• Provided that cable operators could drop or change promised services but only after negotiations with local officials.

• Required channels to be available for lease by commercial interests with programs to air, free of editorial control of the cable company.

• Prohibited local television or telephone companies from also owning an area's cable franchise, unless the purchase was made before July 1, 1984, or unless the FCC permitted a telephone company to provide cable service to a rural area that otherwise might not attract other cable companies.

• Protected subscribers' privacy by requiring their prior approval before cable companies could disclose any "personally identifiable information," such as their program

choices or viewing habits.

● Set civil and criminal penalties for the theft of cable services, such as tapping neighbors' wires or using converters, satellite dishes or other devices to receive cable signals without paying the company.

● Strengthened FCC power to enforce anti-discrimination regulations.

● Lengthened the time allowed for public comment on cable licensing matters, giving interested parties a better chance to participate.

● Established a congressional commission to study telecommunications policies.

Broadcast Deregulation

Congressional efforts to deregulate the broadcasting industry failed in the 98th Congress, as they had in the previous Congress.

Legislation (HR 2382), sponsored by 232 members of the House, never got out of the House Energy and Commerce Subcommittee on Telecommunications in 1984 because some members demanded public-interest guidelines for programming that the industry would not accept. After nearly a year of on-and-off negotiations, subcommittee members gave up their efforts to reach agreement on a deregulation bill.

The Senate in 1983 approved legislation (S 55) that would have made license renewals for radio and television station owners automatic unless there had been serious legal violations.

A similar Senate-passed bill died in 1982 when the House failed to act on it, and Senate deregulation provisions attached to a 1981 budget reconciliation bill were dropped at the insistence of House members. *(1981 bill, p. 263; 1982 bill, p. 273)*

Nevertheless, many of the changes sought by the broadcasting industry were accomplished administratively through rules changes approved by the pro-deregulation Federal Communications Commission (FCC).

Philosophical Differences

Behind the battle over deregulation was a basic philosophical difference about the federal role in setting standards governing the content of what could be broadcast.

Proponents of deregulation contended the industry had reached the point where government controls over program content were no longer necessary because competition in the open market would see that most viewers' needs were met. They argued that radio stations were so diverse and competitive that listeners were assured a full choice of programming and that cable technology was providing much the same choice in television.

But critics did not believe the broadcasting business had become all that diverse, especially in rural areas where there were few over-the-air broadcast stations or cable TV systems.

Even though FCC regulations seldom had been used to deny a broadcaster's license, the critics said the government should retain its regulatory power to make sure broadcasters paid attention to their audience. Their view was that the industry's deregulation proposals would have allowed broadcasters to save a lot of money, enjoy permanent licensing and escape responsibility for local coverage.

Broadcast Freedom Bill

An effort to repeal several sections of the 1934 Communications Act, including the so-called Fairness Doctrine that required stations to air all sides of public issues, failed in 1984. Legislation (S 1917) sponsored by Bob Packwood, R-Ore., was rejected by the Senate Commerce, Science and Transportation Committee, which Packwood chaired.

As originally filed, Packwood's bill also would have repealed the equal time rule, which held that if any political candidate received air time, rivals could claim the same; the "reasonable access rule," which held that federal candidates could demand that stations accept their political advertising at any time; and the "lowest unit rate" rule, which allowed candidates to pay for their ads at the cheapest rate available.

To win committee support for his bill, Packwood revised the bill to apply only to radio and only for a five-year experimental period. He also dropped the provisions repealing the reasonable access and low-rate rules. Nonetheless, the committee June 13 rejected S 1917 by a 6-11 vote.

The major umbrella organization fighting deregulation was the Telecommunications Research and Action Council, which included 120 labor, civil rights, church and consumer groups.

Senate Action

S 55 was passed by voice vote with little debate Feb. 17, 1983, two days after it was reported by the Senate Commerce Committee.

The legislation codified FCC radio deregulation efforts, such as barring the FCC from requiring radio broadcasters to provide news and public affairs programming, and limiting the number of commercials.

In addition, S 55 eliminated the existing license renewal requirement that the performance and qualifications of radio and TV stations be compared with the service promised by a new applicant (called "comparative renewal"). The bill also required broadcasters to pay fees to help cover the cost of remaining FCC regulation.

House Action

The Senate bill ran into opposition in the House. Timothy E. Wirth, D-Colo., chairman of the Subcommittee on Telecommunications, said the bill was too lenient.

HR 2382, the principal House deregulation bill, went even further than S 55. It not only codified the FCC's deregulation of radio and TV, but also eliminated any fee broadcasters would pay.

In the spring of 1983, broadcasters charged that

Wirth's subcommittee had bottled up the deregulation legislation and sought the support of Commerce Committee Chairman John D. Dingell, D-Mich., and other panel members for a move to circumvent Wirth's panel. During ensuing negotiations, Wirth promised to submit legislation to the full committee by Oct. 15, 1983.

But that promise fell by the wayside when no consensus emerged from a lengthy series of meetings between opposing sides on the issue.

Negotiations continued in the next session. Wirth had dropped his insistence on two issues that had doomed past deregulation efforts — comparative license renewal and spectrum fees for broadcasters' use of public airwaves. But he insisted that any deregulation bill have public-interest safeguards, such as requirements that TV broadcasters air minimum amounts of news, public affairs and educational children's programming.

The National Association of Broadcasters, the radio and TV trade organization, would not accept Wirth's demands and broke with the subcommittee in March 1984. The broadcasters again tried to persuade Dingell to take the matter out of Wirth's grip but Dingell refused. The talks between Wirth and the chief sponsors of HR 2382, Tom Tauke, R-Iowa, and W. J. "Billy" Tauzin, D-La., broke down the next month.

Television Rerun Rights

Congressional efforts to delay proposed rules allowing television networks to profit from TV reruns became unnecessary in 1984 when the Federal Communications Commission (FCC) agreed to a two-year moratorium on its controversial proposal.

The House in 1983 passed a bill (HR 2250) to delay the FCC rules' effect until June 1, 1984. Then, in March 1984, the FCC agreed to put off its proposal at the request of President Reagan and a group of senators.

The FCC had sparked a storm in 1983 when it proposed to repeal 1970 rules that had prohibited the major networks — ABC, NBC and CBS — from controlling or selling reruns of programs they originally aired. Opponents of the changes — Hollywood studios, independent producers, actors and others — rushed to Congress for legislation to stop the FCC.

The networks had ardently supported the FCC's proposed change, arguing that it would mean greater diversity and competition. They said they needed to share in the $800 million-a-year rerun syndication market to contend with emerging competition from cable and satellite networks.

Independent producers had argued the opposite. They said independent television stations and program producers had made major gains under the FCC rules and would be at a competitive disadvantage without them. They said the networks would dominate TV if the rules were lifted.

Legislative History

There were a number of efforts to block the FCC plans. The main legislative vehicle was HR 2250.

The House Nov. 8, 1983, passed by voice vote, under suspension of the rules, HR 2250 to delay at least until June 1, 1984, the FCC plan to modify its rules on TV rerun syndication rights. The House Energy and Commerce Committee's report on the bill (H Rept 98-483), filed Nov.

4, stated that a six-month moratorium on the proposed rules changes would give Congress a chance to study the issues and might induce the networks and their foes to compromise.

Senate action on HR 2250 had been expected in 1983. In October the Senate had adopted a six-month ban on the rule change in an amendment to a fiscal 1984 supplemental appropriations bill (HR 3959). The provision was dropped in conference.

But in November the Senate Commerce Committee suspended its markup of HR 2250 until at least March 15, 1984. That action was taken after the FCC decided to delay any rules changes at least until May 10 to give the networks and their opponents time to compromise.

Talks between the two sides broke down in January 1984. Meanwhile, President Reagan intervened, entreating the FCC to wait two years. The FCC agreed after 15 key senators echoed the same request in a March letter.

Public Broadcasting

Bipartisan efforts to restore administration budget cuts for public broadcasting failed twice in 1984, when President Reagan vetoed bills that would have authorized more than three times his funding request.

In both cases the president said the increases could not be justified in light of the need to exercise spending restraint to lower the federal budget deficit.

Since 1981 Reagan had tried to phase out the federal subsidy to the Corporation for Public Broadcasting (CPB). CPB, a non-profit corporation that administered funding for public television and radio stations and for special, non-commercial programming, depended on federal funds for about 20 percent of its budget.

The administration contended that the corporation catered to a cultural and intellectual elite and should be privately supported by its audience. Congress had agreed to some earlier cuts, but in 1984 members were determined to restore funding. *(Previous authorizations, pp. 264, 275)*

The bills vetoed in 1984 were:

● S 2436, which authorized $761 million for fiscal 1987-89 for CPB and $159 million for fiscal 1985-87 for the Public Telecommunications Facilities Program, which provided grants for broadcast equipment. The Senate passed S 2436 (S Rept 98-432) June 15 and the House approved, 302-91, a companion measure (HR 5541 — H Rept 98-772) July 24. Final passage by the House was delayed until Aug. 8, because a member objected to a routine motion to attach the text of HR 5541 to the Senate-passed bill. The Senate Aug. 9 cleared S 2436 for the president. President Reagan vetoed the bill Aug. 29.

● S 607, which authorized $675 million over three years for CPB and $100 million over three years for the facilities program. S 607 was passed by the Senate Sept. 20 and by the House, 308-86, Oct. 5. Reagan pocket-vetoed the measure on Oct. 19, after Congress had adjourned *sine die*. (When Congress is in session, a bill becomes law without the president's signature if he does not act upon it within 10 days, excluding Sundays. When Congress has adjourned within the 10-day period, the president may pocket-veto the bill by not acting upon it.)

The administration had proposed a total of $255 million for CPB and sought no funds for the facilities program.

Failure to enact the reauthorization bills did not immediately affect funding for the two programs.

Congress had included $200 million for fiscal 1987 for CPB in the Labor, Health and Human Services, Education appropriations bill (HR 6028 — PL 98-619). CPB funds were appropriated two years in advance in an effort to insulate the corporation from political pressures.

Earlier, $24 million for fiscal 1985 for the facilities program was included in the Commerce, Justice, State and the Judiciary appropriations bill (HR 5712 — PL 98-411).

Insider Trading Curbs

Penalties for using confidential information to profit in the stock market were increased by legislation enacted in 1984.

The measure (HR 559 — PL 98-376) required a person convicted of insider trading to forfeit any gains made (or losses avoided) and to pay civil fines of up to three times the amount of profit. Previously, the penalty was limited to forfeiture of profits gained or losses avoided.

The new law also raised the maximum criminal penalty for defrauding the market to $100,000, from the $10,000 ceiling set 50 years earlier.

The Securities and Exchange Commission (SEC) had asked for the new powers as part of a campaign to crack down on insider trading, which had become widespread in recent years as corporate mergers and acquisitions and trading in stock options increased in frequency.

"Insider trading" referred to the illegal practice of exploiting non-public information to buy or sell a security on the expectation that its price would move dramatically up or down once the information became public.

The final version of HR 559 included Senate amendments clarifying that the bill also applied to trading in stock options and allowing the SEC to bar or suspend dealers who had been disciplined by the Commodity Futures Trading Commission for violating the Commodity Exchange Act.

The House passed HR 559 (H Rept 98-355) Sept. 19, 1983. The Senate approved its version (S 910) June 29, 1984. The House July 25 accepted the Senate's minor changes, thus clearing the bill for the president.

Corporate Takeover Reforms

Amid bipartisan concern about corporate takeover battles, the House Energy and Commerce Committee Sept. 17 reported legislation to halt some of the more controversial business tactics used. The measure, which was opposed by the Reagan administration and the Securities and Exchange Commission (SEC), was not taken up by the full House.

The bill (HR 5693 — H Rept 98-1028) would have limited moves by a bidder and the defenses of its target company. Restrictions would have been placed on two widely questioned practices: "golden parachutes," the lucrative severance packages given to executives whose jobs were jeopardized by possible takeovers, and "greenmail," the premium price that a company paid a would-be raider to buy back its stock.

Both Republican and Democratic supporters said the changes would have benefited stockholders, whose shares often lost value in the skirmishing. The Reagan administration opposed the bill as unnecessary and an intrusion on states' rights to regulate commerce. The SEC, which pro-

posed the legislation initially, objected to a provision doubling from 20 days to 40 days the amount of time that a tender offer — a public invitation to buy stockholders' shares — must be open for stockholders to consider.

The Senate did not have a companion bill, but restrictions on golden parachutes and greenmail were included in a Senate-passed banking bill (S 2851). *(Banking bill, p. 92)*

Small Business Programs

Congress failed in 1984 to reauthorize Small Business Administration (SBA) programs, although both houses passed bills to do so.

A separate bill to increase the fiscal 1984 authorization for three SBA loan programs passed both houses in slightly different form, but it also failed to clear.

Congress did approve several SBA disaster loan provisions as part of the fiscal 1984 budget reconciliation bill.

SBA Reauthorization

The Senate Oct. 7, 1983, by voice vote approved a fiscal 1984-85 authorization for the SBA (S 1323 — S Rept 98-129). S 1323, which had the support of the Reagan administration, would have eliminated direct federal loans to small businesses, except for those that were minority-owned.

The House March 15, 1984, by a 386-11 vote, passed HR 3020 (H Rept 98-182), authorizing SBA funds for fiscal 1984-86.

The House-passed bill continued the direct loan program and resurrected a provision, repealed in 1981 (PL 97-35), allowing loan assistance to firms harmed by the devaluation of the Mexican peso. Attempts on the House floor to eliminate the direct-loan program for all but minority-owned firms and to delete the Mexican peso provision were defeated.

HR 3020 required the SBA to guarantee loans for purchase of pollution control equipment, when part of the construction money came from tax-exempt bonds. The SBA had refused to guarantee such loans since 1982, and the administration opposed the provision.

The House adopted amendments providing for the extension of disaster loan assistance to fishing and agricultural businesses harmed by "El Niño," an unusual and severe pattern of ocean currents off the West Coast in 1982 and 1983.

Conferees on the bill were appointed, but they never met because of the administration's threat to veto any legislation with the El Niño provision, and other disagreements.

Fiscal 1984 Loan Programs

A bill (HR 6013) raising the fiscal 1984 authorizations for three SBA programs to levels provided in the agency's fiscal 1984 appropriations bill (HR 3222 — PL 98-166) also did not reach conference.

HR 6013 would have raised authorizations for the handicapped loan program, the Small Business Investment Corporations, and the Minority Enterprise Small Business Investment Corporations.

As passed by the House July 30 by voice vote, HR 6013 (H Rept 98-914) also included language, similar to that in

HR 3020, requiring the SBA to guarantee loans for purchase of pollution control equipment, when money from tax-exempt bonds was involved.

The Senate passed the bill by voice vote Sept. 17, after agreeing to drop the provision on pollution control equipment.

The House insisted on its provision and the Senate failed to respond to the House request for a conference.

Disaster Loan Provisions

The fiscal 1984 budget reconciliation bill (HR 4169 — PL 98-270), cleared by Congress April 5, included several provisions on SBA disaster loans. *(Story, p. 60)*

HR 4169 extended, until Sept. 30, 1986, a requirement that farmers seek disaster loans from the Farmers Home Administration before seeking more favorable SBA loans.

The bill reduced interest rates on SBA disaster loans, imposing ceilings of 4 percent on loans to homeowners and businesses that could not find credit elsewhere, 8 percent on loans to those that could. The interest rates had been raised in 1981. *(Details, p. 265)*

The reconciliation measure made eligible for SBA disaster assistance businesses adversely affected by the payment-in-kind farm acreage reduction program and by the devaluation of the Mexican peso. Direct loans for physical disasters were limited to $500 million annually in fiscal 1984-86, non-physical disasters to $100 million annually.

Unisex Insurance

Legislation barring insurance companies from considering gender in computing insurance premiums and benefits never reached the floor during the 98th Congress.

Supporters of a House bill (HR 100) mandating equal insurance rates for men and women abandoned it in 1984 after the House Energy and Commerce Committee drastically revised the measure. The Senate Commerce Committee in 1983 had postponed action on the Senate's version (S 372) until the General Accounting Office studied the effects of the bill. The Senate panel had reported a unisex insurance bill in 1982 (S 2204 — S Rept 97-161).

As introduced, HR 100 applied to both individual and group insurance plans, required all health plans to provide maternity and abortion coverage, and called for equal pension benefits even if contributions to the plan had been made under sex-based rates.

The substitute approved by the House Commerce panel March 28, 1984, applied only to group programs and not to individual plans — thus exempting most auto and many life and health insurance plans. As amended, HR 100 also would have made maternity coverage optional for individual health insurance and required health plans with abortion coverage to be higher priced. Equal pension payments would not have been required unless contributions had been made on a unisex basis.

The committee action was a defeat for a coalition of women's and civil rights groups. Victory went to the insurance industry, which had mounted a multi-million-dollar effort against the legislation.

There was no further action on HR 100, and no report was filed.

Sponsors of the substitute claimed the original bill would have cost the industry billions of dollars and added more than $1 billion to women's auto and life insurance

premiums. The industry contended that sex characteristics were legitimate factors for risk calculations since women generally lived longer, had fewer accidents and were healthier.

Supporters of the original version said women received pension and annuity payments up to 15 percent lower than men's because of the assumption that women lived longer to collect. Conversely, they claimed that men who were health-conscious and who drove safely were penalized on the basis of their sex. They said insurance rates should be based instead on such factors as life-style, smoking and drinking habits, and driving records.

Credit Card Surcharges

Due to an impasse in the Senate, Congress did not renew a ban on credit card surcharges that expired Feb. 27, 1984.

The House passed a bill (HR 5026) to extend until May 31, 1985, a decade-long prohibition against merchants adding fees to cover costs of processing credit card transactions, but the Senate took no action. HR 5026 was a compromise between the Senate, which had voted to allow surcharges, and the House, which had voted in 1983 and 1984 to extend the ban.

Groups supporting surcharges, including the Consumer Federation of America, argued that cash customers were paying higher prices to make up for credit-card paperwork costs. A Federal Reserve Board study issued in 1983 found that retailers' costs of processing credit card transactions added an average 3.1 percent to prices, forcing cash customers to subsidize credit customers' purchases.

Consumer groups opposing the surcharges contended merchants would not lower prices if extra fees were permitted. Credit card companies battled the surcharges out of concern that, if enacted, customers would use their cards less.

The surcharge ban was last enacted in 1981. Despite Congress' inaction in 1984, most merchants did not begin imposing surcharges for fear of violating federal truth-in-lending or state usury laws. *(1981 extension, p. 269)*

Legislative History

The House Nov. 16, 1983, passed 349-73 a bill (HR 4278) to extend until July 31, 1984, a ban on surcharges for purchases by credit card or under open-end credit plans. The Reagan administration viewed the surcharge ban as unwarranted government intervention in the private sector.

On Feb. 28, 1984 — the day after the surcharge ban expired — the Senate passed 84-0 a bill (S 2335) to continue the ban until May 15, 1984, giving the House and Senate time to settle their differences. The Senate also approved by voice vote S 2336 to allow the extra fees.

The House Feb. 29 passed by voice vote S 2335 but added to the bill the text of HR 3622, passed by the House in 1983, providing penalties for credit card fraud. The tactic riled senators pursuing their own anti-fraud legislation and further tangled the knot over credit card surcharges. *(Fraud bill, p. 277)*

The Senate took no action on the House-amended S 2335. A compromise then was worked out allowing a temporary extension of the ban, until May 31, 1985.

The House April 3 passed 355-34 the compromise bill

(HR 5026), but the Senate took no action because of threats of amendments both from senators backing the fees and from those opposed to them.

Recall of Dangerous Toys

A loophole in federal law that prevented products hazardous to children from being recalled as quickly as other dangerous goods was closed by Congress in 1984.

Congress Oct. 3 cleared legislation (HR 5818 — PL 98-491) allowing the Consumer Product Safety Commission (CPSC) to order toys, furniture or clothes for children to be pulled from the market immediately — just as other faulty products were — if the commission found "substantial risk of injury." The CPSC could publish notice of the defect, order a recall and require a retailer to repair, replace or refund a purchase.

Previously, children's products were regulated under the Federal Hazardous Substances Act, rather than the later Consumer Product Safety Act that created the commission. The earlier law required the CPSC to go through a time-consuming administrative process before it could order a recall of children's goods.

The House passed HR 5818 (H Rept 98-895) Aug. 6 by voice vote. A companion measure (S 2650 — S Rept 98-591) was passed by the Senate Sept. 12 by voice vote. The Senate Oct. 3 approved HR 5818 with minor amendments, which the House accepted later that day.

Product Liability

A coalition of businesses failed to win passage of a national law that would pre-empt state laws regarding victims' lawsuits against defective products.

As in two previous Congresses, the industry-backed product liability bill (S 44) got no further than the Senate Commerce, Science and Transportation Committee, which reported the measure May 23 (S Rept 98-476). *(1981 bill, p. 269)*

S 44, which was endorsed by the Reagan administration, would have replaced in many cases the existing legal standard holding firms to "strict liability" for injuries caused by their products with one demanding proof of a manufacturer's negligence.

Opponents said the bill would make it difficult — perhaps impossible — for victims to recover damages. State officials said the bill, which would have prohibited access to federal courts if a plaintiff and defendant were from the same state, was an unprecedented intrusion on states' rights.

Dalkon Shield Link

One of the most controversial provisions would have allowed only one victim to receive punitive damages from a firm facing multiple claims for punitive and compensatory damages. This provision was included at the request of Paul S. Trible Jr., R-Va., and Richmond-based A. H. Robins Co. The pharmaceutical maker had been the target of more than 11,000 lawsuits by women alleging injuries from its Dalkon Shield intrauterine contraceptive device. A Senate source called the bill's link with the company "our biggest problem."

Other Legislation

'Fire-Safe' Cigarettes

Congress Oct. 4 cleared legislation (HR 1880 — PL 98-567) authorizing a study of the feasibility of developing "fire-safe" cigarettes that would be less likely to ignite household furnishings.

The legislation, developed in cooperation with the Tobacco Institute, created a 15-member group, including four members from the institute, to advise Congress within two and a half years whether a fire-safe cigarette could be produced. The final version delegated the lead role in the study to the Consumer Product Safety Commission with prominent roles for the U.S. Fire Administration and the Department of Health and Human Services.

The House passed HR 1880 (H Rept 98-917) Aug. 6. The Senate passed the bill, amended, Sept. 21. Minor amendments were added by the House Oct. 1; the Senate, accepting the House changes, cleared the measure for the president Oct. 4.

Park Ride Inspections

The House Oct. 2, by a vote of 300-119, passed a bill (HR 5790 — H Rept 98-1072) to restore some federal oversight of amusement rides at fixed park sites. There was no further action on the bill before adjournment.

In 1981 Congress rescinded the Consumer Product Safety Commission's authority over rides at permanent sites, leaving the commission the authority only to inspect rides or order repairs for traveling carnivals. *(1981 legislation, p. 267)*

HR 5790 would have reinstated the commission's power to inspect fixed rides, but only in states — 20 at the time of consideration — that had no inspection laws or in cases where a ride had caused injury or death. The bill also would have required park operators to report dangerous rides to the commission, so it could act as a national clearinghouse for such information.

Odometer Fraud Bill

The Senate Oct. 10 passed legislation to assure used-car buyers of the accuracy of a vehicle's mileage meter. The House did not act on the measure.

The odometer anti-fraud bill (S 1407 — S Rept 98-504) was intended to close a gap in existing law, which banned rolling back mileage, but lacked record-keeping requirements, according to backers.

The bill, which had the support of the National Automobile Dealers Association, would have required states to print a car's mileage on both the title and the owner's annual registration card. The owner's most recent registration card would have to be included with any application to transfer a title to a new owner.

One out of seven of the 20 million used cars sold annually had had its odometer rolled back, the National Highway Traffic Safety Administration estimated.

Election Projections

Congress approved a non-binding resolution (H Con Res 321) calling on the news media to refrain from characterizing or predicting the outcome of an election until the

polls had closed.

However, the major networks ignored the request during the 1984 presidential election and, before the polls had closed on the West Coast, projected that President Reagan had won re-election.

The resolution, adopted by a 352-65 vote in the House June 26 and by voice vote in the Senate (S Rept 98-600) Sept. 21, was spawned by complaints about early network projections of the outcome of the 1980 presidential election.

Members complained that early projections discouraged late voter turnout. Many Democrats blamed the networks for the hair-thin losses in 1980 of two members of Congress (Al Ullman, D-Ore., 1957-81; and James C. Corman, D-Calif., 1961-81) and uncounted local elections in the West.

Network representatives said the resolution infringed on their First Amendment rights and argued there was little evidence that voter turnout was impaired by their projections.

6

Transportation Policy

Introduction   *289*
1981 Chronology   *291*
1982 Chronology   *301*
1983 Chronology   *317*
1984 Chronology   *321*

Transportation Policy

With the ink barely dry on legislation that deregulated much of the transportation industry, Ronald Reagan came into office determined to transform the industry even more.

The new president wanted to reshape national transportation policy. In keeping with his "New Federalism" plan, Reagan sought to cut federal spending for transportation programs and to shift responsibilities to states, local governments and transportation users.

Reagan called for an end to federal subsidies for the Conrail freight railroad and advocated its quick sale. He proposed major cuts in federal subsidies for Amtrak passenger service. He wanted to phase out mass transit subsidies and to return responsibility for most roads, excluding the Interstate system, to state and local governments.

The president espoused a pay-as-you-go concept under which those who benefited from federal transportation programs would help defray their cost through user fees. He wanted to reduce the federal financial role by imposing or increasing fees for owners of airlines, private planes, boats and barge lines.

Many of Reagan's proposals were resisted on Capitol Hill. Congressional critics argued that federally aided programs — such as Amtrak, Conrail, highway construction and mass transit — were important to the nation's economy and would be crippled by some of the administration's proposals. Rather than agreeing to end or restructure programs, Congress in many cases compromised by reducing funding and sometimes imposing more restrictions. Thus, while the administration did not obtain all the cuts it wanted, it did win some curtailment.

Other proposals made little headway on Capitol Hill. Such was the case with several of Reagan's user fee proposals. And a New Federalism plan to return to the states responsibility for mass transit and for urban and secondary roads aroused such opposition in the 97th Congress that it was quietly shelved without being offered as specific legislation. A proposal in 1983 to fold several highway programs into a "megablock" grant to the states went nowhere.

Conrail, Amtrak

Conrail and Amtrak evaded administration proposals in 1981 that some critics predicted would have destroyed the federally subsidized freight and passenger railroads.

To prevent Conrail from continuing to be a drain on the federal budget, the administration wanted Congress to end federal subsidies and give the transportation secretary

flexibility to dispose of unprofitable Conrail lines. With a number of members fearful that the breakup of Conrail would mean the loss of vital service, a compromise was crafted to assure them that the secretary would make a good-faith effort to sell the railroad as one system. Conrail experienced a remarkable turnaround: It began to turn a profit in 1981 and attracted several prospective buyers by 1984. The administration in early 1985 proposed the sale of Conrail to Norfolk Southern Corp.

Congress refused to make major cuts in Amtrak's federal subsidies but did enact an authorization bill requiring the railroad to take steps necessary to stay within its available funding. Concern over Amtrak's government debts contributed to the 98th Congress' failure to pass an Amtrak authorization. The debt issue was resolved administratively.

Highways, Mass Transit

Enactment of major highway/mass transit legislation in 1982 required significant compromises by both the administration and Congress.

The legislation had become stalled during the regular session of Congress, in part because of the president's opposition to raising taxes on gasoline — the first such hike since 1959. But after the November 1982 election, when unemployment reached 10.7 percent, the measure was wrapped in the aura of a "jobs bill" that would provide some 300,000 jobs. It also was touted as a beginning in the repair of the nation's crumbling transportation infrastructure — cratered highways, inadequate bridges, broken down buses and poor subway tracks. It quickly won bipartisan support. Reagan soon jumped on the bandwagon, labeling the increased taxes as "user fees" and endorsing the bill as a vitally needed effort to repair the transportation infrastructure.

References

Discussion of transportation policy for the years 1945-64 may be found in *Congress and the Nation Vol. I*, pp. 517-561; for the years 1965-68, *Congress and the Nation Vol. II*, pp. 227-251; for the years 1969-72, *Congress and the Nation Vol. III*, pp. 147-176; for the years 1973-76, *Congress and the Nation Vol. IV*, pp. 505-555; for the years 1977-80, *Congress and the Nation Vol. V*, pp. 291-349.

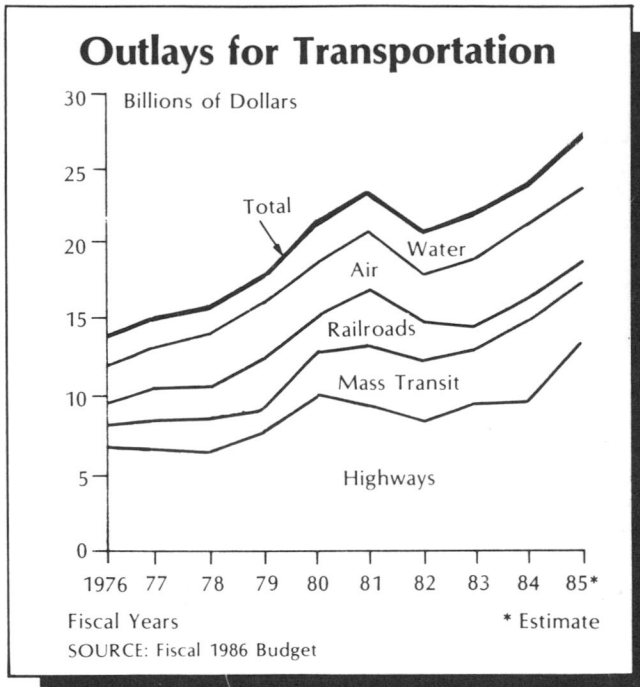

Outlays for Transportation

Billions of Dollars

Total

Water

Air

Railroads

Mass Transit

Highways

1976 77 78 79 80 81 82 83 84 85*

Fiscal Years   * Estimate

SOURCE: Fiscal 1986 Budget

Another major trade-off concerned mass transit operating subsidies. The administration dropped its earlier threats to veto subsidies beyond fiscal 1984 and Congress in turn agreed to deep cuts in the subsidies. The final bill also provided for the first major diversion of gas tax monies — 1 cent a gallon — for public transportation.

The administration dropped its New Federalism proposal to turn back urban and rural road programs to the states, largely in a move to win support for the bill from some key members who opposed the turnback.

Highway legislation did not fare as well in the 98th Congress. Bills allocating to the states money for Interstate highway construction became stalled in both 1983 and 1984, thus leaving most states out of cash for Interstate construction and raising the possibility that the Interstate system might not be completed by its 1990 target date.

Airlines

Congress in 1982 revived the airport development program after resolving longstanding disputes over the direction and scope of the program and over aviation taxes. Congress met the president part way in his request for aviation user fees. Aviation taxes were raised, although not as high as Reagan had requested, and formulas were established for increased use of the Airport and Airway Trust Fund for operation of the air traffic control system. Congress historically had resisted using the trust fund for operations, but Reagan contended that aviation users, not the general taxpayer, should bear the major portion of the costs of federal aviation programs.

Other Legislation

Bus Deregulation. The inter-city bus industry in 1982 became the fourth transportation industry to undergo

significant deregulation in as many years when Congress, with the approval of the administration, passed legislation to relax federal and state regulation of buses. The bus bill followed on the heels of previously enacted laws that eased regulation of airlines, railroads and trucks.

Maritime Legislation. An administration proposal to eliminate subsidies for new U.S. ship construction was approved by Congress in 1981. In a move to ease the impact of the bill, Congress temporarily allowed owners of U.S.-flag ships under limited circumstances to buy or to build foreign vessels and still be eligible for federal operating subsidies. Legislation that would have extended the foreign-built provision was blocked in 1982 in the Senate. A House attempt in 1984 to revive ship construction subsidies failed.

The U.S. international shipping industry won a long-sought victory in 1984 when Congress cleared a bill expanding the industry's antitrust immunity for setting prices and dividing routes. The legislation marked the first major change in shipping regulation in more than 20 years.

Safety Issues. The Department of Transportation (DOT) in 1984 issued a regulation requiring mandatory crash protection in cars by 1989, unless states representing two-thirds of the U.S. population passed mandatory seatbelt-use laws. The regulation represented a significant reversal of course for the Reagan administration, which had opposed government interference in auto manufacturing.

In another reversal, President Reagan lobbied for and signed into law in 1984 a bill to pressure states to raise their minimum drinking age to 21. The president initially opposed the legislation as an infringement on states' rights.

Strikes

President Reagan took a hard line on several strikes within the transportation industry. When the Professional Air Traffic Controllers Organization (PATCO) went on strike Aug. 3, 1981, Reagan fired 11,400 of its members and had the union's bargaining rights revoked for violating a no-strike commitment. PATCO subsequently disbanded and filed for bankruptcy.

A four-day national railroad strike was ended Sept. 22, 1982, when Congress passed legislation, requested by Reagan, ordering the 26,000 striking members of the Brotherhood of Locomotive Engineers back on the job.

The 30,000-member Independent Truckers Association staged a violence-marred strike Jan. 31 through Feb. 10, 1983, to protest the scheduled sixfold increase in heavy-truck user fees mandated by the 1982 Surface Transportation Assistance Act. The strike ended after 35 members of Congress promised to review the fees.

DOT Leadership

Drew Lewis served as Reagan's first transportation secretary. Considered one of Reagan's most capable Cabinet members, Lewis resigned in early 1983 to become chief executive officer of Warner Amex Cable Communications Inc. *(Cabinet profiles, p. 1024)*

Reagan tapped Elizabeth Hanford Dole, his assistant for public liaison and a former member of the Federal Trade Commission, to succeed Lewis. Dole was married to Senate Finance Committee Chairman Robert Dole, R-Kan.

Chronology
Of Action
On Transportation

1981

President Reagan's efforts to sharply reduce federal support for transportation programs and to shift many federal costs to states, local governments and transportation users ran into heavy resistance in Congress in 1981. Instead of accepting the full scope of Reagan's plans, Congress fashioned compromises providing for reduced funding and in some cases more restrictions.

In keeping with its view that general taxpayers should not have to subsidize freight and passenger railroads, the Reagan administration made several proposals aimed at getting the government out of the railroad business. The administration proposed to phase out funding for Conrail by the end of 1982 and sell or transfer its lines to other railroads. But Congress voted to give the federally subsidized freight railroad more time and money to become successful and thereby more attractive for sale as a single entity. While rebuffing proposed cuts in federal subsidies for Amtrak passenger service, Congress did require Amtrak to do whatever was necessary to operate within its available resources.

Congress passed a limited Interstate highway bill, putting off more comprehensive legislation until 1982, when members would have a better estimate of available revenue.

Several changes in national maritime policy were approved, and the Maritime Administration was shifted from the Commerce Department to Transportation in a move that some hoped would focus more government attention on the problems of the financially ailing maritime industry.

The House continued efforts to ease government regulation of transportation when it passed an inter-city bus deregulation bill.

Conrail

Congress rejected an administration plan for the quick sale of segments of Conrail, the federally subsidized freight railroad, and gave the troubled rail system a second chance to be returned to the private sector as a single entity.

The reprieve, contained in the budget-cutting reconciliation legislation (HR 3982 — PL 97-35) cleared July 31, established a timetable for ending federal subsidies and set out conditions governing the sale of Conrail, either in segments or as a single system. *(Proposed sale, p. 326)*

Conrail had been created by Congress in the early 1970s out of the Penn Central Railroad and six other bankrupt lines in an attempt to preserve freight rail service in the Northeast and Midwest. The original projections of financial independence in 1979 were dashed by management problems, expensive labor agreements and other difficulties. *(Background, box, p. 292)*

By 1981, Conrail had received about $6 billion in federal aid, and its administrators believed that under certain conditions and with additional limited federal aid, it could become profitable.

But the Reagan administration called for an end to federal subsidies by fiscal 1983 and wanted to give the transportation secretary a free hand in selling portions of the system to private enterprise.

The timing of the sale was important to many members of Congress, particularly those from the Northeast and Midwest who were afraid that quick, piecemeal sale would result in the loss of vital freight rail service. Their concern eventually led to revisions that protected the Conrail system from what some members considered abrupt sale.

PL 97-35 stated that if Conrail's banker and monitor, the U.S. Railway Association (USRA), determined June 1, 1983, that Conrail would not be profitable, then Conrail could be sold piecemeal. But if it were deemed profitable, Conrail could be sold only as a single system until Oct. 31, 1983.

There would be a second profitability test then, and if Conrail were deemed profitable, it could be sold only as a single system until June 1, 1984. If it were deemed not profitable, needed additional subsidies or buyers could not be found for an intact system by that date, the transportation secretary would be allowed to sell Conrail piecemeal after Oct. 31, 1983.

The reconciliation agreement authorized $262 million for operating subsidies through Aug. 1, 1983, and $400 million for labor protection benefits, such as severance pay.

Congress also tried to help Conrail become profitable and more attractive to potential buyers. For example, the new legislation allowed the passenger commuter operations that Conrail inherited in the Northeast to be spun off to a new Amtrak commuter subsidiary. Also, Conrail's expensive labor protection benefits program was repealed and new scaled-down benefits were established.

Background

The administration in its March budget announced that it wanted to end federal aid to Conrail by fiscal 1983. It proposed to sell Conrail lines to private railroads and substantially scale back expensive employee benefits, a plan that some union leaders warned could lead to a nationwide strike.

Existing employee benefits, mandated under 1973 legislation (PL 97-236), were designed to compensate workers for wages, benefits or jobs lost when Conrail was created. They covered about 11,000 Conrail employees until age 65. Some employees had been receiving $50 to $1,800 a month under the program. *(Congress and the Nation Vol. IV, p. 513)*

Transportation Secretary Drew Lewis said the administration proposal would preserve 95 percent of the existing Conrail freight service. The railroad at the time operated about 17,000 miles of track in 17 states and had about 80,000 employees. Under the administration plan, local transit authorities would take over Conrail's commuter operations.

USRA and Conrail proposed alternative plans aimed at enabling the railroad to turn a profit. They said Conrail had to be relieved of responsibility for the labor benefits, whose costs negated the economies obtained by job reductions. USRA also suggested that Congress consider reducing the amount of benefits.

Conrail, Amtrak Plagued by Problems at Outset...

Conrail and Amtrak were born out of a desperate desire to maintain a Northeast freight system and nationwide passenger service.

But maintenance of these systems did not come cheaply. By 1981 Conrail had received about $6 billion in federal aid, Amtrak more than $3 billion.

The financial picture for both railroads began to improve in 1981, but spokesmen for the passenger and freight systems said they still needed more federal help, setting off a debate on Capitol Hill over the railroads' futures.

Subsidy supporters maintained that Conrail and Amtrak had not progressed further largely because they inherited far more serious problems than originally detected by federal and rail planners. And in Conrail's case, no one in authority foresaw the seriousness of the Northeast's economic problems and the decline in rail traffic.

Some supporters believed the two railroads still could become financially independent with proper planning, prudent pruning of routes, improved labor agreements, good management and adequate subsidies in the interim.

Critics, in addition to citing the need to restrain federal expenditures, also pointed to what they called poor management, bad planning and excessive labor agreements.

The railroads' supporters prevailed in 1981 against administration plans to cut subsidies and sell off segments of Conrail. But Congress mandated changes aimed at making the railroads more viable enterprises. *(Conrail, p. 291; Amtrak, p. 295)*

Conrail

Conrail had its beginnings in a series of Penn Central Railroad crises. Penn Central was formed in 1968 by the merger of the Pennsylvania and New York Central railroads in an effort to improve efficiency. *(Congress and the Nation Vol. II, p. 249)*

That effort, however, failed. The Penn Central continued to suffer financial and labor difficulties, which Congress could not ignore. The railroad delivered 20 percent of the nation's freight and operated 70 percent of the passenger service over a system covering 16 states and connecting 72 cities. Lawmakers stepped in to avert strikes, and after the Penn Central filed for reorganization on June 22, 1970, provided loan guarantees of up to $125 million (PL 91-663).

But the emergency loans were not enough. In 1973 Penn Central trustees called for $600 million in federal aid over four years.

The Nixon administration rejected the request on Feb. 7, and the next day, when the railroad was

scheduled to begin eliminating one of every two brakemen carried on most trains, 28,000 employees walked off the job. The same day Congress passed a law (PL 93-5) ending the strike and directing the transportation secretary to develop a proposal to save Northeastern rail service. The plan called for establishing a government corporation to run the system. *(Congress and the Nation Vol. IV, p. 516)*

Late in 1973 Congress approved legislation (PL 93-236) consolidating Penn Central and six other Northeast and Midwest bankrupt lines into one giant railroad — the Consolidated Rail Corp., or Conrail. Conrail also inherited some passenger commuter service. By 1981 Conrail operated over about 17,000 miles of track in 17 states.

The 1973 legislation also created the U.S. Railway Association (USRA), a non-profit government corporation, to be Conrail's banker and monitor. The USRA funneled federal subsidies to Conrail and reviewed its operations and progress. Congress directed the USRA to develop a restructuring plan, called the "final system plan," which was to produce a profit, preserve existing patterns of rail service, promote competition and reduce job losses.

By not objecting, Congress in November 1975 gave its consent to the USRA railroad reorganization plan. That plan envisioned a profitable Conrail by 1979. *(Congress and the Nation Vol. IV, p. 536)*

The 1973 act had given Conrail $2.5 billion in federal aid to cover start-up costs. In early 1976 another law passed (PL 94-210) authorizing $2.1 billion for Conrail. In 1978 Congress authorized (PL 95-565) an additional $1.2 billion. *(Congress and the Nation Vol. IV, pp. 513, 536; Congress and the Nation Vol. V, p. 311)*

Problems

By the early 1980s Conrail had not fulfilled the promises and expectations of 1975.

Although the reasons were complex, a number of factors were usually cited. These included the changing and declining economy of the Northeast, high operating costs resulting from inherited bankrupt lines and expensive labor agreements, and the political difficulty of cutting service, according to rail experts, shippers and congressional staffers. The situation, they said, was compounded by unrealistic forecasts of traffic and subsidy needs.

Conrail and USRA forecasts were off the mark. The 1975 final system plan estimated that Conrail would accumulate net losses of $200 million from 1976 through 1980. Projections available in early 1981 showed accumulated net losses of $1.4 billion.

A December 1980 USRA report said those losses, combined with the money needed for rehabilitation

... But Supporters See Improvements in 1980s

and maintenance, drove Conrail's federal funding needs to $3.1 billion as of December, more than $1 billion above the forecast. Conrail estimated early in 1981 that it would need from $900 million to $3.7 billion more through 1985.

Congress in 1981 authorized $262 million for operations through Aug. 1, 1983, and $400 million for labor protection benefits.

Promises

Although the 1980 railroad deregulation act was not going to be Conrail's savior as originally predicted by Conrail, it was expected to help improve revenue.

For example, Conrail was able to take advantage of the new freedom to collect surcharges on rates for traffic handled jointly with other railroads. That, Conrail argued, would give it a more equitable share of joint route revenue and eliminate carrying some traffic at a loss. The USRA estimated that deregulation might increase Conrail revenues, in 1979 dollars, to $3.3 billion from $2.8 billion by 1985.

In addition, legislation approved in 1981 allowed Conrail to spin off costly commuter operations, which were draining about $100 million a year from Conrail, to a new Amtrak subsidiary. The measure also scaled down Conrail's expensive labor protection benefits program.

Amtrak

By the late 1920s America's romance with passenger trains was cooling off. Although there were 20,000 trains carrying 77 percent of all passengers traveling by common carrier, the automobile had captured 79.8 percent of inter-city passenger miles. The decline increased after World War II, pressured by the spread of highways and the newcomer airlines.

The railroads' financial pinch was severe, but federal rules made it difficult for them to drop passenger service. In 1958 Congress made it easier (PL 85-625) to end unprofitable service and passenger trains declined further. By 1970 there were fewer than 400 trains a day.

In 1969 the Transportation Department and Penn Central began a demonstration project on the route between New York and Washington to determine if improved passenger rail service in a densely populated area would be popular. The collapse of the Penn Central in 1970 was a key factor in building congressional support for a rail passenger corporation.

Congress in 1970 approved legislation (PL 91-518) setting up a government, for-profit corporation, first known as Railpax and then as Amtrak, to take over the most unprofitable part of the nation's passenger rail business. Amtrak began service in 1971. *(Congress and the Nation Vol. III, p. 161)*

Railroads could transfer their passenger service to Amtrak and pay Amtrak to run it. Railroads continuing passenger trains had to operate them for at least five years. By 1981 there was only one private passenger railroad left, an Amtrak official said.

In 1976 Congress authorized subsidies (PL 94-555) for Amtrak operations in the Northeast Corridor, connecting Boston, New York and Washington, and Amtrak bought the high-speed corridor from Conrail. By early 1981 $2.5 billion had been authorized to repair the badly deteriorated tracks and facilities.

Improvements in System

Amtrak was under almost constant attack from the beginning. Passengers complained about delays, inadequate air conditioning and heating, and generally poor or infrequent service. Administrations consistently tried to cut lightly used routes to save money.

However, pressure from members of Congress to keep service in their districts prevented significant reductions until 1979. At that time Congress approved a 16 percent reduction in routes (PL 96-73), leaving about 22,000 miles, and established criteria for retaining routes. *(Congress and the Nation Vol. V, p. 323)*

Although Amtrak continued to lose money, much of the critical clamor had quieted down by early 1981. Improvements in the system, thanks to new and renovated cars, included a jump in on-time performance to 69 percent in 1980 from 57 percent in 1979 and a 23 percent hike in revenue in 1980. The railroad was recovering 41.1 percent of its costs, up from 38.5 percent in 1979.

Passenger complaints were down 40 percent in 1980. Ridership had increased, to 21.4 million passengers in 1979, up from 18.9 million in 1978.

Cost control was so improved, Amtrak's 1979 annual report said, it cost the railroad only $4 million to earn the $34.2 million increase in revenue above projections for the year.

While Amtrak supporters contended that service had vastly improved, they did not believe Amtrak ever would be able to do more than recover its operating costs on some routes. Some believed the future for Amtrak would lie in rail service along densely populated corridors between major cities. The Northeast Corridor, still under repair in 1981, was the model or test track for such service, Amtrak supporters said.

According to law, once the $485 million federal subsidy authorized for labor protection benefits was exhausted, Conrail would be responsible for making the payments itself. About $305 million already had been spent, even though the fund was supposed to last past the year 2000.

Conrail and USRA proposed changes in work rules and other concessions from employees to help reduce operating costs. USRA also was critical of management costs.

USRA said Conrail could operate profitably by 1985 if the recommended changes were made and if the system received an additional $400 million to $600 million in federal aid, including aid authorized in the 1980 railroad deregulation act (PL 96-448). *(Congress and the Nation Vol. V, p. 336)*

Legislative History

The House and Senate Commerce committees initially reported separate Conrail reauthorization bills (S 1100, HR 3559), but those measures had to be revised to achieve spending cuts required under the budget reconciliation process. *(Reconciliation, p. 40)*

Senate Action. The Senate Commerce Committee reported S 1100 May 15 (S Rept 97-101). Key members objected to the bill's provision for the immediate sale of Conrail if the railroad were determined to be unprofitable, however, and a compromise version putting off Conrail's sale was announced June 9. The compromise was offered June 25 as a floor amendment to the Senate reconciliation bill (S 1377) and accepted by voice vote.

As passed, the bill allowed the sale of a profitable Conrail as a single entity until Aug. 1, 1983; an unprofitable Conrail could be sold in pieces after Dec. 1, 1982. It authorized $400 million for labor protection benefits and $150 million in fiscal 1982 and 1983 for operating subsidies.

House Action. The House Commerce Committee June 18 reported HR 3559 (H Rept 97-153), authorizing $375 million in new money, continuing an existing $100 million authorization for operating subsidies and authorizing $315 million in fiscal 1982 and 1983 for labor protection benefits. The bill also prevented the sale of parcels of Conrail until 1984.

During action on its reconciliation cuts, the Commerce Committee deadlocked 21-21 over a package put together by Committee Chairman John D. Dingell, D-Mich., and a GOP alternative sponsored by James T. Broyhill, R-N.C. In assembling its reconciliation bill, the Budget Committee incorporated the Dingell plan, which was endorsed by a majority of the Commerce panel's Democrats.

Although the full House adopted a comprehensive Republican alternative for the Budget Committee bill, the Broyhill provisions on Conrail, Amtrak and other issues were troublesome to many Republicans from the Northeast, and GOP leaders pulled them from their budget package. Thus the Dingell provisions remained in the reconciliation bill passed by the House June 26.

Conference, Final Action. Senate-House conferees filed their report on the bill July 29 (H Rept 97-208).

The final agreement in some respects went beyond the House bill, which generally gave Conrail more time to become profitable than the Senate and administration proposed. The administration argued that the House did not give the transportation secretary enough flexibility.

Conferees settled on $262 million for Conrail operations and $400 million for labor protection benefits.

Both chambers approved the final version July 31.

Provisions

As signed into law Aug. 13, the Conrail provisions of HR 3982 (Title XI of PL 97-35):

● Set goals designed to help Conrail become profitable, including reducing non-union wages and benefits and making layoffs comparable to the reductions and layoffs for union workers contained in a new collective bargaining agreement. The collective bargaining agreement was to save $200 million a year, beginning April 1, 1981, through reduced wage increases, benefits or other labor costs.

Commuter Service. Ended on Jan. 1, 1983, Conrail's obligation to operate short-haul passenger commuter service, which it inherited when Congress established Conrail.

● Directed Amtrak to establish by Nov. 1, 1981, a subsidiary called the Amtrak Commuter Services Corp. to operate commuter service for authorities that previously contracted with Conrail.

Commuter authorities involved included those in the New York City area, Connecticut, Maryland, southeastern Pennsylvania, New Jersey and Massachusetts.

● Established a six-member board for the commuter subsidiary, with membership drawn from Amtrak and commuter authorities.

● Authorized the commuter subsidiary to own, manage or contract for the operation of commuter service. The subsidiary was authorized to operate commuter service only for full reimbursement.

● Directed the subsidiary to provide access to rail tracks to a commuter authority that operated its own service or contracted from someone else.

● Prohibited the use by the commuter subsidiary of federal subsidies authorized for Amtrak's inter-city operations.

● Authorized $50 million in fiscal 1982 for the Amtrak subsidiary and for commuter authorities that operated service. The funds would be available until Oct. 1, 1986.

Conrail Sale. Authorized $262 million through Aug. 1, 1983, for Conrail operating subsidies.

● Exempted Conrail from state taxes until Conrail's property was sold.

● Allowed the transportation secretary any time after enactment to submit to Congress a plan for the sale of federal stock in Conrail. The plan could be vetoed by both chambers of Congress. Sale of the stock rather than Conrail properties would maintain the railroad as a single system.

In 1983 the Supreme Court outlawed the legislative veto device, which Congress had included in many laws. *(Story, p. 833)*

● Established conditions for the sale of Conrail. On June 1, 1983, the U.S. Railway Association board was to determine whether Conrail would be a profitable railroad. If it were determined that Conrail would not be profitable, the secretary could sell Conrail piecemeal.

If Conrail were deemed profitable, the secretary could sell it only as a single entity until Oct. 31, 1983, when there would be a second profitability test.

If determined to be profitable, the railroad could be sold only as a system until June 1, 1984. If unprofitable, the railroad could be sold in pieces. The secretary also could sell Conrail piecemeal if the railroad required more subsidies than authorized in the legislation.

After June 1, 1984, the secretary could notify the USRA that he had been unable to sell Conrail as a single entity. If USRA concurred, Conrail employees would have 90 days to submit a purchase plan. If the secretary disap-

proved the plan. he could begin to sell off Conrail in pieces. If USRA did not concur with the secretary on the piece-meal sale, he must try to sell Conrail as a system.

● Required that 75 percent of the total rail service operated by Conrail be maintained if the railroad were sold piecemeal.

● Allowed either chamber of Congress to veto the piece-meal sale of Conrail.

● Directed Conrail by Jan. 1, 1982, to determine which of its subsidiaries were not profitable the previous year and to try to sell any that were unprofitable, unless the USRA determined that the benefits of ownership outweighed the financial loss.

Labor Protection Benefits. Required the secretary of labor and labor union representatives within 90 days of enactment to work out a new labor protection agreement for employees who had been covered by the statutory "Title V" Conrail labor protection program.

If no agreement were reached, the secretary was required to prescribe a benefit program within 30 days. *(Congress and the Nation Vol. V, p. 336; Congress and the Nation Vol. IV, p. 547)*

The agreement might provide for the use of funds for severance, moving expenses, retraining expenses, insurance and other costs. No more than $20,000 might be paid to any individual employee. Eligibility for benefits would terminate two years after enactment.

● Repealed Conrail's existing Title V labor protection benefits program as of Oct. 1, 1981.

● Authorized up to $25 million to pay Title V benefits that accrued before repeal of the program.

● Allowed Conrail to pay brakemen and firemen up to $25,000 in severance to reduce the railroad's work force by 4,600.

● Gave laid-off employees right of first hire by other railroads under certain conditions.

● Allowed Conrail to contract for work that could not be done by existing or furloughed employees.

● Barred new collective bargaining agreements from including additional labor protection benefits before April 1, 1984.

● Barred state laws or regulations from requiring Conrail, Amtrak or Amtrak Commuter to employ a certain number of persons.

● Directed Conrail to enter into collective bargaining agreements that provided for the creation of a fact-finding panel to recommend changes in operating practices that would result in greater productivity.

● Authorized $400 million for labor protection benefits to remain available until expended.

● Provided for the transfer of some Conrail employees to Amtrak Commuter, commuter authorities and railroads that acquired Conrail properties.

Other Provisions. Reconstituted the USRA board so that its members included the USRA chairman, the transportation secretary, the U.S. comptroller general, the Interstate Commerce Commission chairman and the Conrail chairman.

The legislation eliminated representation of cities, states, labor, railroads and shippers.

● Provided for a presidentially appointed emergency board to investigate and settle disputes between a publicly funded and operated carrier providing commuter service and its employees.

● Barred strikes by Amtrak Commuter or commuter authority employees against Conrail or vice versa.

Amtrak

Congress in 1981 spared Amtrak from having to make major cuts in its routes during the next year, but put the federally subsidized passenger railroad on notice that it must keep a tight watch on its budget.

The budget reconciliation legislation (HR 3982 — PL 97-35) authorized $735 million for Amtrak in fiscal 1982 and $788 million in fiscal 1983. The bill, the vehicle for sweeping budget cuts proposed by President Reagan, exceeded Reagan's request for Amtrak funding. The administration had sought to limit the fiscal 1982 authorization to $613 million. The final $735 million figure cut $313 million from projected fiscal 1982 spending for existing programs, according to Congressional Budget Office estimates.

Amtrak said Reagan's proposal would allow trains to run only in the Northeast Corridor, which linked Washington, New York and Boston. The railroad found support among members from outside the Northeast who were concerned that their states would lose service and from Northeastern members who feared Amtrak would lose congressional support if it served only their area.

But lawmakers also required Amtrak to recover at least 50 percent of its operating costs from the fare box or other non-federal source in fiscal 1982, which raised the prospect of higher fares. The bill mandated some cost-saving steps that might help Amtrak hold down fare increases, such as deferring interest on Amtrak's federal debt and exempting it from certain state taxes.

Under HR 3982 Amtrak could operate only trains that met performance criteria established by Congress in 1979 (PL 96-73). The 1979 law's intent was to stop uneconomical "political" trains that ran through the districts of important members. *(Box, p. 296)*

Senate conferees had sought to repeal the criteria and let Amtrak decide how best to operate the system. They argued that the standards could be interpreted in different ways and thus require cutting some Western trains, even though they were performing well.

As a compromise, Amtrak was allowed to modify some routes so that they could meet the performance standards.

The legislation also shortcut an administration plan to leave the Northeast Corridor improvement project unfinished. The bill directed the transportation secretary to complete the project as outlined by law. *(Congress and the Nation Vol. V, p. 339)*

Legislative Action

Both the Senate and House included Amtrak authorizations in their budget-cutting reconciliation bills. *(Reconciliation, p. 40)*

Senate Action. The Senate Commerce Committee initially went along with the administration cuts. The committee May 15 reported a bill with a $613 million subsidy for fiscal 1982 (S 1199 — S Rept 97-96).

The administration argued that taxpayers should not subsidize rail service and disputed Amtrak's claim that the cuts would limit passenger service to the Northeast Corridor.

As hometown newspapers churned out editorials protesting the threat to local service and hundreds of letters from constituents supporting Amtrak started pouring into members' offices, lawmakers began to get uneasy. Many senators, including Republicans, lobbied for more money.

In the face of this pressure, Commerce Chairman Bob

The *Cardinal* Runs Again

From Amtrak's beginning in 1971, White House economizers regularly attempted to truncate the federally subsidized passenger railroad network. But friends of the railroad rode to the rescue, aided by popular and nostalgic support for passenger trains and the loyalty of individual lawmakers for their home-state routes.

The continuing saga of the *Cardinal* — a Washington-to-Chicago train running through the home state of Senate Minority Leader Robert C. Byrd, D-W.Va. — was a case in point.

Performance Criteria. In 1979 Congress established criteria to determine which trains would continue to operate (PL 96-73). The *Cardinal* and the *Shenandoah* — another train running through West Virginia and a favorite of House Commerce Committee Chairman Harley O. Staggers, D-W.Va. — were unable to meet the criteria. However, they were kept running on a temporary basis and given two years to meet the criteria. *(Background, Congress and the Nation Vol. V, p. 323)*

In 1981 Amtrak officials let it be known that the *Cardinal* and the *Shenandoah* were big money-losers and would not be continued. Staggers had retired from Congress in January 1981 and the *Shenandoah* followed him into retirement later that year. But the *Cardinal* survived.

1981 Action. The conference report on the budget reconciliation act (PL 97-35), cleared July 31, 1981, directed Amtrak to try to retain the *Cardinal* train service. Amtrak nonetheless canceled the *Cardinal* on Oct. 1, 1981, because of inadequate ridership.

The train was canceled on the same day Congress cleared a temporary appropriations resolution (H J Res 325 — PL 97-51) that directed Amtrak not to terminate the *Cardinal* route.

The Senate Appropriations Committee thereupon included in the fiscal 1982 transportation appropriations bill (HR 4209) a provision directing Amtrak to restore the *Cardinal* service. The committee contended that ridership was steadily improving and actually met the criteria in June and July 1981.

When HR 4209 came to the floor, Minority Leader Byrd led the fight to retain the *Cardinal* provision. An amendment to delete the *Cardinal* requirement, offered by Commerce Committee Chairman Bob Packwood, R-Ore., failed 34-53.

Despite some House objections, the *Cardinal* provision remained in the final version of HR 4209 (PL 97-102), which was signed into law Dec. 15. The *Cardinal* service was resumed in January 1982 as a triweekly, rather than the previously daily, service.

Packwood, R-Ore., asked Reagan budget director David A. Stockman just how serious the administration was about the Amtrak cuts. Packwood aides said the senator did not want to ask his colleagues to support the Reagan budget request — cutting their own trains and incurring the political consequences — if the administration intended to give in during an eventual House-Senate conference.

Packwood was told the administration was not firm about the cuts, as long as the panel met its total budget targets.

The Commerce Committee then agreed to raise the fiscal 1982 funding to $735 million, with another $735 million for fiscal 1983. The increase was included in the savings package recommended to the Budget Committee and incorporated in the Senate reconciliation measure (S 1377), passed June 25.

House Action. The Senate's fiscal 1982 authorization matched the $735 million reported May 19 by the House Energy and Commerce Committee (HR 3568 — H Rept 97-81). The House bill also authorized $842 million for fiscal 1983. The Commerce panel rejected an attempt by some Republican members to revert to Reagan's request.

The authorizations were folded into a budget-cutting package supported by a majority of committee Democrats and wound up in the reconciliation bill passed by the House June 26. Controversy over Amtrak, Conrail and other issues caused alternative provisions to be dropped from a comprehensive Republican reconciliation plan that was narrowly adopted on the House floor.

Final Action. The conference report on HR 3982 (H Rept 97-208) was cleared by Congress July 31. Conferees roughly split the difference between the Senate and House Amtrak authorizations for fiscal 1983.

Provisions

As signed into law Aug. 13, Title XI of HR 3982 (PL 97-35):

Amtrak Board. Reconstituted the Amtrak board of directors to include nine members: the transportation secretary or a representative, the Amtrak president and seven members appointed by the president.

The presidential appointees would include two federal officials representing the government's preferred stockholdings in Amtrak, two persons representing commuter authorities and three representing rail labor, governors of states with an interest in rail transportation, and businesses with an interest in rail. The existing board included the Amtrak president, transportation secretary, three representatives of railroads and eight members appointed by the president, including three consumer representatives.

Performance Standards. Required Amtrak to submit proposed changes in performance criteria to Congress. The changes were to become effective unless either chamber disapproved them.

This legislative veto mechanism was ruled unconstitutional by the Supreme Court in 1983. *(Story, p. 833)*

● Required Amtrak beginning Oct. 1, 1981, to continue existing service if it met the performance criteria after the railroad took into account projected fare increases and any state or local contributions.

Costs. Required Amtrak to reduce the deficit from its on-board food and beverage operations by 50 percent in fiscal 1982 and to eliminate the deficit by Sept. 30, 1982.

● Required Amtrak to recover at least 50 percent of its operating costs from non-federal sources.

• Required Amtrak to take whatever actions necessary to stay within its available funding. Such actions might include changes in service frequency, fare hikes, reduction in on-board service costs such as sleeper and dining cars, and restructuring or discontinuing routes.

• Required Amtrak by Oct. 1, 1983, to reduce management costs by at least 10 percent of the administrative costs incurred during the year prior to June 1, 1981.

Northeast Corridor. Required the transportation secretary to complete the Northeast Corridor improvement project in accordance with the goals set out in existing law.

The conferees said it was their intent that all funds authorized for the project be used to complete improvements. Reagan had planned to cut $310 million from the $2.5 billion total project authorization previously approved by Congress.

As part of the $2.5 billion total project authorization, the bill authorized $200 million in fiscal 1982 and $185 million in fiscal 1983, the amounts proposed by Reagan.

Other Provisions. Authorized $735 million for Amtrak in fiscal 1982 and $788 million in fiscal 1983.

• Increased Amtrak's loan guarantee level to $930 million from $900 million to cover the final payment on the purchase of the Northeast Corridor.

• Converted Amtrak's federal debt to preferred stock to be held by the government beginning Oct. 1, 1981.

• Deferred Amtrak's interest payment to the federal government until Sept. 30, 1983. The interest deferral would amount to $82 million in fiscal 1982 and $100 million in fiscal 1983.

• Exempted Amtrak from state or local requirements that set minimum crew numbers.

• Exempted Amtrak from certain property taxes.

• Allowed Amtrak to run special state train routes if the state paid at least 45 percent of the operating costs in the first year and 65 percent in each year thereafter. The state was required to pay 50 percent of the capital costs each year. Under existing law, the program provided an 80 percent federal share of operating costs in the first year, decreasing to 50 percent by the third year.

• Authorized $40 million in fiscal 1982, $44 million in 1983 and $48 million in 1984 for local rail assistance. The federal share of the local rail assistance program was reduced to 70 percent from 80 percent.

Highway Authorizations

A compromise highway bill approved in the waning days of the 1981 session gave the Reagan administration some of the Interstate cost-savings and repair program revisions it requested. But the legislation (HR 3210 — PL 97-134) was not as comprehensive as the administration had proposed nor did it grant key requests such as phasing out federal funding for urban and rural road systems.

The bill, designed to complete the Interstate Highway System at a $15 billion savings, resolved an impasse between the House and Senate over the scope of the legislation that had prevented states from obligating Interstate construction funds.

The measure affected only Interstate programs, tightening eligibility for construction funds and expanding a major repair program, as President Reagan requested. It also reduced previously authorized construction funds (PL 95-599) for fiscal 1983 to $3.1 billion from $3.2 billion. *(Congress and the Nation Vol. V, p. 304)*

Congress in 1982 approved a $71.3 billion highway/ mass transit program, to be financed by increasing the federal gasoline tax. *(Story, p. 301)*

House-Senate Dispute. HR 3210 represented a victory for the House because of its narrow scope. The president and the Senate wanted comprehensive multi-year legislation dealing with both Interstate and non-Interstate highway programs that reduced federal spending over a period of years and allowed states to target scarce funds.

The House, while agreeing to some of the Interstate program changes, wanted only a one-year bill, with comprehensive legislation postponed until 1982 when more would be known about potential revenue. Also, some members wanted to tie the popular highway program to mass transit legislation in an effort to protect transit from expected administration-backed cuts.

States had been affected by the dispute between the House and Senate because, even though Interstate construction funds had been authorized through fiscal 1990 by previous law, new legislation was needed to direct the transportation secretary to apportion fiscal 1983 funds. States normally obligated funds a year in advance. HR 3210 did provide for the fiscal 1983 apportionment.

Completing the Interstate. About 95 percent of the 42,500-mile Interstate System had been completed at a cost of more than $70 billion since the program began in 1956. The federal government paid 90 percent of the construction costs, and the states paid the rest.

Without changes in the law, completing the remaining segments would have required $53.8 billion in federal and state funds, largely because of escalating construction costs.

In limiting eligibility for construction funds, HR 3210 reduced the estimated total cost of completing the system to $38.9 billion. Projects no longer eligible for construction money — such as providing extra lanes — could be financed under the expanded repair program.

Administration Proposals

The Reagan administration adopted the general course set by the 1978 highway act (PL 95-599) and the Carter administration: Finish the 42,500-mile Interstate Highway System and repair the deteriorating highways. But some of Reagan's methods differed significantly from those of the past. *(Congress and the Nation Vol. V, p. 304)*

He proposed realigning the financial partnership of the federal, state and local governments for many major road and safety programs. Reagan wanted to shift more responsibility to states and localities, a change that congressional and other critics said could drain local finances and delay needed projects and repairs.

The 1978 act authorized highway aid through fiscal 1982 and the Highway Trust Fund through fiscal 1984. Reagan sought major changes that would:

• End funds in fiscal 1984 for many urban and rural road and safety programs and drop funds in fiscal 1982 to enforce the 55 mph speed limit. *(Background, Congress and the Nation Vol. IV, pp. 231, 211; 55 mph speed limit, p. 300)*

• Allow the transportation secretary to drop some proposed Interstate segments, leaving gaps to be financed by non-federal sources or left undone.

• Encourage timely completion of the Interstate by tightening eligibility for construction money, and require some work, such as noise control features and landscaping,

to compete for funding under other programs.

● Increase federal funds for Interstate repairs from $275 million in fiscal 1982 to $2.7 billion in fiscal 1987 and increase the federal share from 75 percent to 90 percent.

● Limit obligations for Highway Trust Fund spending to $8.15 billion in fiscal 1982 and $8.675 billion in 1983. The fiscal 1981 cap was $8.75 billion. (Highway Trust Fund, box, p. 304)

House Action

The House rebuffed much of Reagan's request, although it did agree to a modified plan to reduce the cost of completing the Interstate System.

HR 3210, reported by the House Public Works Committee May 19 (H Rept 97-92) and passed by the House Sept. 24 on a 377-25 vote, limited eligibility for Interstate construction funds to unstarted segments that would be built to a new minimum standard. By not allowing funds for some special features and for already-opened Interstate segments, the House bill was expected to reduce the federal-state cost of completing the system to $37 billion. Reagan's plan would have tightened eligibility further, resulting in an estimated cost of about $31.5 billion.

HR 3210 authorized $3.1 billion in fiscal 1983 for Interstate construction, expanded a major repair program, set an $8.2 billion ceiling on fiscal 1982 trust fund spending, excluding emergency projects, and included authorizations for repair programs and Primary System roads.

Senate Action

The Senate Nov. 16 passed highway legislation (S 1024) that met Reagan part way.

S 1024 accepted the concepts of tightening eligibility for Interstate construction funds, expanding repair programs for deteriorating Interstate highways and a multi-year approach, all major points in Reagan's program. But it continued funding for urban and rural highways and excluded a proposal to allow the transportation secretary to drop proposed Interstate segments under certain conditions without previous recommendation from state and local officials.

Before reporting S 1024 Oct. 7 (S Rept 97-202), the Senate Environment and Public Works Committee answered Reagan's call for a 12 percent cut in federal spending and sliced $1 billion from the bill's fiscal 1982 authorizations, reducing them to a total of $7.6 billion. But when the bill reached the floor, the committee offered an amendment — which was accepted by voice vote — to restore $500 million because Congress had not cut other programs similarly. The amendment also raised the limit on obligations from the Highway Trust Fund to $7.7 billion, excluding emergency relief, from the committee bill's $7.2 billion. Unchanged by the floor amendment was the $3.1 billion fiscal 1983 authorization for Interstate construction.

As passed by voice vote, S 1024 authorized about $28 billion for Interstate construction for fiscal 1982-90. The cost of completing the Interstate System was estimated at $35.8 billion, as compared to the House estimate of $37 billion and the administration's estimate of $31.5 billion.

Final Action

A compromise on the highway bill was reached informally by key members without a conference. The House

approved it Dec. 15 by voice vote and the Senate concurred by voice vote Dec. 16.

Provisions

As signed into law Dec. 29, HR 3210 (PL 97-134):

● Authorized $800 million annually for fiscal 1983 and 1984 for an expanded Interstate repair program. The fiscal 1983 level was previously $275 million.

● Directed the transportation secretary to apportion the fiscal 1983 Interstate construction funds based on an estimated cost to complete the system of $38.9 billion.

● Reduced the fiscal 1983 Interstate construction authorization to $3.1 billion from $3.2 billion.

● Limited eligibility for Interstate highway construction funds. The bill generally allowed funding for no more than six lanes in rural areas or in urban areas under 400,000 population, and no more than eight lanes in urban areas over 400,000. Some special lanes for high occupancy vehicles also would be eligible.

Generally ineligible for funding would be weigh stations, pedestrian and bikeway facilities and features not essential to meet safety or environmental requirements.

● Expanded the "3R" repair program — resurfacing, restoration and rehabilitation — to a "4R" program that would include reconstruction. The federal match for 4R projects was increased to 90 percent from 75 percent, with the state paying the rest. Projects no longer eligible for Interstate construction money could be financed with 4R funds.

● Reduced the limit on obligations for Highway Trust Fund spending to $8 billion in fiscal 1982, excluding emergency relief.

The budget reconciliation law enacted earlier in the year (HR 3982 — PL 97-35) had imposed ceilings of $8.2 billion in fiscal 1982 and $8.8 billion in fiscal 1983.

Airport Development

Congress in 1981 granted a temporary funding reprieve to the federally supported airport development program that had expired in 1980, but a stalemate continued over the scope and direction of the program.

In 1982 the House and Senate resolved their differences and passed a multi-year reauthorization bill (HR 4961 — PL 97-248). (1981-82 action, p. 308)

The omnibus budget reconciliation bill (HR 3982 — PL 97-35) approved by Congress July 31 authorized $450 million in fiscal 1981 for airport development, including new and expanded runways. A fiscal 1981 supplemental appropriations act (PL 97-12), cleared June 4, had provided $450 million for airport development, but no money had been spent because the authorization for the program had expired Sept. 30, 1980, due to disputes over its direction. (Congress and the Nation Vol. V, p. 341)

The disputes continued in 1981. The Senate Commerce Committee and the House Science and Technology and Public Works and Transportation committees reported multi-year authorizations (S 508 — S Rept 97-97; HR 2643 — H Rept 97-24, Parts I and II) for the airport program, but the measures were radically different and were not brought to the floor in either chamber in 1981.

The House July 27 passed a $450 million fiscal 1981 authorization (HR 4182 — H Rept 97-198) for the program. House and Senate budget conferees agreed to include the

measure in HR 3982. The original House reconciliation bill had not contained a fiscal 1981 authorization, and the Senate version simply set a ceiling on Airport and Airway Trust Fund spending. *(Reconciliation, p. 40)*

The final version of HR 3982 (PL 97-35, Title XI) authorized $450 million in fiscal 1981 for airport development, planning and noise compatibility projects. The funds would come from the Airport and Airway Trust Fund. At least $25 million of the funds would be used for noise compatibility projects. The bill also limited fiscal 1982 spending from the trust fund to $600 million.

Maritime Subsidy Programs

Congress accepted President Reagan's decision to eliminate new U.S. ship construction subsidies for fiscal 1982, but it attempted to ease the impact by broadening eligibility for ship operating subsidies.

The omnibus budget reconciliation bill (HR 3982 — PL 97-35) cleared July 31 allowed owners of U.S.-flag ships under limited circumstances to buy or build foreign vessels in fiscal 1982 and 1983 and still be eligible for operating subsidies for their ships. The bill authorized $417.1 million for operating subsidies in fiscal 1982.

Previously, ships had to be built in American yards to qualify for the subsidies, and an American operator accepting subsidies could own only U.S.-built ships. The subsidies were intended to help make U.S. ships competitive with foreign vessels.

U.S. shipbuilders feared that the provision, included in the House reconciliation bill but not the Senate version, would lead to the further deterioration of the financially ailing maritime industry. Supporters sought to protect the industry while Congress and the administration worked out a plan to revitalize it.

Conferees (H Rept 97-208) agreed to allow the purchase of foreign ships in fiscal 1982 if no funds were available to subsidize the construction in American yards and in fiscal 1983 if the president requested at least $100 million for construction subsidies or an equivalent alternative shipbuilding program. *(1982 action, p. 316; 1983-84 action, p. 324)*

The reconciliation bill also allowed an ocean freight forwarder, who arranged for shipments, to ship property that he or a business associate owned as long as he did not receive compensation from the vessel selected for the job. The change, which removed an existing legal prohibition, was to expire Dec. 31, 1983.

Some smaller freight forwarders contended the change could lead to illegal rebates for shipments, which would give competitors an advantage. The House included the provision in its bill to help diversified transportation companies whose operations included freight forwarding.

The House provisions were similar to those contained in a bill reported May 19 (HR 2526 — H Rept 97-63) by the House Merchant Marine and Fisheries Committee. An authorization bill had been reported by the Senate Commerce Committee May 14 (S 1017 — S Rept 97-64).

The Senate approved its reconciliation bill June 25 and the House passed its version June 26. HR 3982 cleared Congress July 31. *(Reconciliation action, p. 40)*

Provisions. As signed into law Aug. 13, major maritime provisions of HR 3982 (Title XVI of PL 97-35):

● Authorized $417,148,000 for ship operating subsidies and $85.4 million for other programs in fiscal 1982.

● Imposed ceilings of $1.65 billion on loan guarantees for the commercial demonstration ocean thermal energy conversion program and $850 million on loan guarantees for fishing vessels and fishery facilities.

● Allowed an operator receiving or applying for operating subsidies to build or acquire vessels in a foreign shipyard until Sept. 30, 1983, if the administration determined that the application for subsidy could not be approved due to the unavailability of construction subsidies.

The provision was effective for fiscal 1983 only if the president requested at least $100 million in construction subsidies or proposed an alternative program that would create equivalent merchant shipbuilding activity in privately owned domestic shipyards. ˙

● Allowed a freight forwarder to arrange a shipment in which he or a related company or official had an interest as long as the forwarder did not receive compensation. The provision would expire Dec. 31, 1983.

Maritime Transfer

Congress approved legislation in 1981 to move the Maritime Administration from the jurisdiction of the Commerce Department to the Transportation Department (DOT).

Enactment of the bill (HR 4074 — PL 97-31) meant that a single department, Transportation, would be responsible for coordinating all transportation programs.

That was the intent of President Johnson when he proposed creating DOT in 1966, but opposition from the maritime industry, which wanted maritime programs to have more prominence, led to legislation (PL 89-670) excluding the Maritime Administration from the new department. Industry officials accepted the proposal when it was renewed by President Reagan in 1981 because they believed maritime issues would receive strong support from Transportation Secretary Drew Lewis. *(Congress and the Nation Vol. II, p. 232)*

The Maritime Administration was responsible for programs aiding the development and operation of the Merchant Marine and included the administration of vessel construction and operating subsidy programs.

The House passed HR 4074 (H Rept 97-199) July 27 by voice vote. The Senate approved it July 29, also by voice vote.

Mass Transit Programs

Congress in 1981 acceded to President Reagan's request for deep reductions in federal mass transit spending.

The Omnibus Reconciliation Act (HR 3982 — PL 97-35) cleared July 31 limited fiscal 1982 authorizations for the programs to $3.8 billion — a $1.3 billion reduction from projected spending under existing programs, according to Congressional Budget Office estimates. *(Reconciliation, p. 40)*

Title XI of the reconciliation measure reduced capital subsidies to $1.5 billion from the existing $1.6 billion; formula grants, which included operating and some capital subsidies, to $1.5 billion from $1.8 billion; and rural transit aid to $75 million from $120 million. *(Congress and the Nation Vol. V, p. 304)*

The conference agreement (H Rept 97-208) generally followed the House bill. It did not address Reagan's plan to

phase out mass transit operating subsidies by 1985. Congress extended operating subsidies in 1982 as part of legislation that raised the federal gasoline tax to finance highway and mass transit projects. *(Story, p. 301)*

Bus Deregulation

The House in 1981 overwhelmingly passed legislation (HR 3663) to relax government regulation of the inter-city bus industry and give companies more freedom to determine their own routes and rates.

The Senate approved bus deregulation in 1982, making the bus industry the fourth transportation industry to undergo significant deregulation since 1978. *(1981-82 action, p. 310)*

Transportation Safety

Congress Oct. 21 approved legislation (S 1000 — PL 97-74) authorizing $60.5 million for the National Transportation Safety Board (NTSB) in fiscal 1981-83 and giving the board's accident investigations priority over those conducted by other federal agencies. Members of Congress said they wanted to ensure that one agency was responsible for coordinating transportation accident investigations.

Fiscal 1982-84 funding of $100 million annually for highway safety programs of the National Highway Traffic Safety Administration (NHTSA) had been authorized separately in the budget reconciliation bill (HR 3982 — PL 97-35) cleared July 31.

In action on the reconciliation bill, Congress rejected Reagan's plan to eliminate specific funding for state enforcement of the controversial national 55 mph speed limit, although it did reduce the authorization level. *(Details, below; reconciliation action, p. 40)*

NTSB Authorization. The National Transportation Safety Board was established by the Independent Safety Board Act of 1974 (PL 93-633) to investigate and help prevent transportation accidents, especially those involving shipments of potentially hazardous materials. *(Background, Congress and the Nation Vol. IV, p. 527)*

The board's authorization lapsed in 1980 when it was tied to hazardous materials legislation that died because of a House dispute over an unrelated provision. However, NTSB received an appropriation through the fiscal 1981 appropriations act (PL 96-400) for the Transportation Department and related agencies.

S 1000 was reported by the Senate Commerce Committee April 23 (S Rept 97-41) and passed by the Senate by voice vote May 4. The House Energy and Commerce Committee and the Public Works Committee May 19 reported similar legislation (HR 3404 — H Rept 97-108, Parts I and II). The House passed the bill by voice vote Oct. 13 and substituted its text for the Senate-passed bill. The Senate accepted the House version Oct. 21.

55 MPH Speed Limit. The highway provisions of the reconciliation bill (Title XI) required that at least $20 million be spent annually on enforcing the 55 mph speed limit, down from $67.5 million annually in existing law (PL 95-599). *(Congress and the Nation Vol. V, p. 304)*

The legislation continued funding penalties for states that failed to meet minimum compliance standards for enforcement of the speed limit. The compliance level for fiscal 1982 and 1983 was dropped back to 50 percent of the motorists driving 55 mph, from 60 percent and 70 percent, respectively.

Hazardous Transport

The House Oct. 20 overwhelmingly passed legislation to improve the safety of transporting hazardous materials, after deleting language banning large shipments of radioactive substances through New York City.

Similar legislation was reported by a Senate committee in 1981 but did not come up for floor consideration during the 97th Congress. *(1984 action, p. 328)*

Approved by a 410-2 vote, the House bill (HR 3403 — H Rept 97-87, Parts I and II) authorized $8.3 million annually for fiscal 1982 and 1983 for federal programs related to the safe shipment of hazardous materials and for new regional centers to improve the training of state and local personnel.

A similar bill died in 1980 because of a dispute over delaying a federal rule establishing a routing system for transporting radioactive material on highways. *(Congress and the Nation Vol. V, p. 334)*

The Transportation Department (DOT) rule was opposed by New York City officials concerned about shipments from Long Island nuclear facilities. They said that when the rule went into effect Feb. 1, 1982, it would override cities that wanted to prohibit the movement of nuclear waste through their boundaries.

As reported by the House Public Works Committee May 19, HR 3403 prohibited transporting large quantities of radioactive materials by motor vehicle or railroad through New York City, except under limited conditions.

Geraldine A. Ferraro, D-N.Y., who represented part of New York City, pushed the committee language, but because of the strong opposition by the administration and others, she agreed to a floor compromise offered by Chairman James J. Howard, D-N.J. Howard's amendment, accepted by voice vote, directed the transportation secretary to devise a method for analyzing risks and costs associated with transporting radioactive materials by highway, railroad, and barge or other vessel.

The Ferraro provision had been criticized for possibly exposing smaller communities to potentially greater risks because of inadequate roads. Norman F. Lent, R-N.Y., who represented part of Long Island, said it "prematurely and arbitrarily" rejected the rule that "seeks to balance national and local interests by providing a uniform national highway routing plan."

The bill, without the Ferraro provision, was reported by a second committee, House Energy and Commerce, May 19. Similar legislation (S 960 — S Rept 97-99) was reported May 15 by the Senate Commerce Committee.

Other Legislation

Coast Guard Authorizations

Congress in 1981 approved legislation (S 831 — PL 97-136) authorizing $1.99 billion for the Coast Guard in fiscal 1982. The final measure exceeded the authorizations contained in earlier versions passed by the House and Senate, reflecting the concern of some members that the Coast Guard was inadequately funded.

As passed by the Senate May 4, S 831 (S Rept 97-45) authorized $1.83 billion. The House Dec. 14 approved a $1.9 billion version (HR 2559 — H Rept 97-62). The $1.99 billion figure was worked out informally and was accepted by both the House and Senate Dec. 16.

Pipeline Safety

Legislation authorizing funds for federal and state safety programs for gas pipelines became stalled in 1981 over the issue of truck-width limitations.

The House June 1 passed by voice vote a bill (HR 3420 — H Rept 97-89, Parts I and II) authorizing more than $8 million for the programs in fiscal 1982. The Senate June 2 passed by voice vote a similar bill (S 1099 — S Rept 97-74), which would have authorized more than $8 million in both fiscal 1982 and 1983, but the Senate then invalidated the action in an effort to reach a compromise with the House.

In acting on a compromise version of HR 3420 July 17, the Senate added a provision allowing states to issue permits for trucks 102 inches wide to use Interstate highways under limited conditions. Truck widths had been limited to 96 inches. *(1982, 1984 action, pp. 307, 324)*

There was no further action on HR 3420 until the closing days of the 1982 session, when Congress dropped the pipeline safety authorizations and substituted unrelated provisions involving the Alaska Railroad. *(Story, p. 314)*

The pipeline safety programs were funded in fiscal 1982 84 by Department of Transportation appropriations bills. A fiscal 1985 authorization cleared Congress in 1984. *(Story, p. 328)*

Congress in 1979 toughened pipeline safety regulations because of accidents involving exploding liquefied natural gas (LNG) and liquefied petroleum gas (LPG). The gases were used for home heating, cooking, industrial activities and other purposes. *(Congress and the Nation Vol. V, p. 327)*

Rock Island Railroad

Congress included in Western Union legislation (S 271 — PL 97-130) cleared Dec. 16 an unrelated provision to ensure continued rail service on the bankrupt Rock Island Railroad until May 15, 1982. The provision was designed to clarify a 1980 law (PL 96-254) to maintain service during disposition of the rail lines. It had been in a Senate bill (S 1879 — S Rept 97-299) reported by the Commerce Committee Dec. 14. *(1980 law, Congress and the Nation Vol. V, p. 339; Western Union bill, p. 265)*

1982

The most important transportation initiative in 1982 — legislation to finish the Interstate Highway System and make needed highway, bridge and transit repairs — became stalled during the regular session for several reasons, including President Reagan's initial rejection of an increase in the federal gasoline tax. But recession-induced increases in unemployment spurred the lame-duck Congress to approve a comprehensive highway and mass transit bill that included the first hike in the gas tax since 1959 and the first diversion of gas tax revenues — 1 cent a gallon — for public transportation. Reagan opposed job creation legislation, but he ultimately endorsed the tax increase bill as a vitally needed effort to repair the transportation system.

Congress revived the federal airport development program, which had expired in 1980, partly because of disputes over the program's direction. Aviation taxes were raised, but not as high as the administration had proposed, and lawmakers partly met Reagan's demand for increased use of the aviation trust fund for operating the air traffic control system.

Congress continued its efforts to relax federal and state regulation of transportation, and inter-city buses became the fourth transportation industry to undergo significant deregulation in as many years.

With unemployment on the rise and the economy worsening, the Senate and House acted quickly to end a four-day national railroad strike.

Maritime bills did not do well in 1982. Measures to broaden antitrust immunity for ocean-liner cartels and to continue a "buy foreign" program begun in 1981 were blocked in the Senate.

Coal slurry pipeline legislation was approved by House and Senate committees, but then went nowhere. President Reagan's proposals for user fees to recover federal costs for port operations and improvements suffered the same fate.

Gas Tax, Highway/Transit Aid

Legislation increasing the gasoline tax for the first time since 1959 and authorizing record funding for highway construction, road repairs and mass transit was cleared in the closing hours of the 97th Congress.

Passage of the comprehensive bill (HR 6211 — PL 97-424) did not come easily. The legislation bogged down during the regular session, due to President Reagan's initial opposition to a gas tax increase, a jurisdictional dispute in the House and disagreement over mass transit changes in the Senate.

The measure began moving again after the November elections, when the unemployment rate soared to 10.7 percent and pressure mounted for action to create new jobs. Both Congress and the White House made significant compromises, including Reagan's decision to support the gas tax hike. A series of filibusters in the Senate, however, prevented the bill from clearing until Dec. 23.

HR 6211 authorized a record $71 billion for fiscal 1983-86 — $53.6 billion for highways and $17.76 billion for mass transit systems. The previous high had been the 1978 authorization of $54 billion (PL 95-599). *(Congress and the Nation Vol. V, p. 304; 1981 legislation, p. 297)*

The bill, the Transportation Assistance Act of 1982, raised the gasoline tax 5 cents, to 9 cents a gallon, beginning April 1, 1983. The fuel tax change was expected to raise an additional $5.5 billion a year to repair deteriorating roads and transit systems, finish the Interstate Highway System and provide jobs for some of the 12 million Americans who were unemployed. Although Reagan insisted the measure was not a jobs bill, supporters maintained it would create more than 300,000 jobs. *(Other 1981 jobs action, p. 648)*

Truck taxes also were increased substantially, despite intense lobbying by trucking industry officials who contended the tax burden would force some companies out of business. As a trade-off, states were required to allow big-

Infrastructure Repairs: Trillion-Dollar Job

The crumbling infrastructure — the foundation of roads, bridges, transit and other facilities upon which the nation depended to deliver essential services — took the congressional spotlight immediately after the November 1982 elections.

Spurred by rising unemployment and Democratic election gains, Congress Dec. 23 cleared a transportation aid bill (HR 6211 — PL 97-424) affecting a substantial portion of the infrastructure: highways and mass transit.

The bill authorized more than $71 billion to finish the Interstate Highway System and to pay for road, bridge and mass transit improvements. It raised an additional $5.5 billion a year to help pay for the programs through a 5-cent increase in the gas tax. *(Story, p. 301)*

Varied Needs

Estimates of the costs of making all needed repairs to public facilities ranged from several hundred billion dollars to $3 trillion.

The types of infrastructure needs were varied. Transportation Secretary Drew Lewis, the Associated General Contractors of America and others cited examples such as these:

● One out of five bridges in the nation needed immediate major repairs. The life of a bridge was about 50 years, and 40 percent already were more than 40 years old.

● More than 4,000 miles, or 10 percent, of the Interstate Highway System needed replacement or major repairs. More than 26,000 miles would require major repairs through 1995.

● If highway conditions continued to decline at their current rate, the average motorist's costs could increase by up to 25 percent in 1995 because of the wear and tear on automobiles and increased gasoline use.

● Twenty percent of all subway cars were more than 25 years old, while the design life generally was about 20 years. Sixty-seven percent of all track needed upgrading.

● Capital needs for transit replacement and repairs would total $50 billion over the next 10 years.

● A 1982 study for the House Wednesday Group, made up of Republican members, said more than one-half of the nation's communities had wastewater treatment systems at full capacity and could not support further economic development.

Maintenance Deferred

Federal officials and others blamed age and deferred maintenance for the deterioration of the roads, bridges and other facilities.

For example, Interstate highways built when the program began in the late 1950s and many bridges built earlier had outlived their design. Also, unanticipated increases in traffic added to wear and tear. Some bridges were structurally sound but could not sustain modern traffic loads, requiring big trucks to detour.

The economic straits of all levels of government confronted with competing needs had led to the postponement of much of the necessary maintenance. A 1982 Urban Institute study noted that the most distressed older cities had the slowest growing tax bases and were under financial pressure to defer capital spending on their facilities.

Developing cities faced problems that were more associated with their growth. Their roads and water systems were not built to sustain the growth they had experienced, and they were under pressure to emphasize new construction rather than maintenance.

High Costs

The Office of Management and Budget could not supply an overall estimate of total needs. But various groups provided figures involving some segments of the nation's infrastructure.

The Transportation Department and the Federal Highway Administration reported in 1981 that from $275 billion to $363 billion in federal and state funds was needed to maintain federally aided roads in their 1978 condition.

Transportation officials said $60 billion was needed to rebuild and repair bridges on and off federally aided systems.

A 1980 survey by the Environmental Protection Agency said the states needed $119.9 billion through the year 2000 to upgrade and repair sewage treatment plants, interceptor sewers and other lines. Of that total, $91.2 billion was for backlog projects.

Pat Choate, who prepared the House Wednesday Group's 1982 report, estimated total needs at $2.5 trillion to $3 trillion just to maintain existing levels of service. He said national public works investments shrank from 3.6 percent of gross national product in 1965 to less than 1.7 percent in 1980.

All levels of government spent about $80 billion in 1980 on public works, he said, with the federal government spending 10 percent of the funds directly and providing 40 percent to state and local governments.

The contractors' group, representing an industry in which unemployment exceeded 20 percent, said $909.9 billion was required for established infrastructure improvements, not including the needs of private health facilities, police stations, firehouses, libraries and prisons.

ger and heavier trucks on the highways.

HR 6211 set a $12.1 billion ceiling on obligations from the Highway Trust Fund for highway construction and related programs for fiscal 1983, increasing to $14.45 billion in fiscal 1986. *(Highway Trust Fund, box, p. 304)*

Although primarily described as a highway and transit repair measure, the bill authorized $4 billion annually for new Interstate highway construction in fiscal 1984-87.

The legislation made a number of changes in transportation policy.

One significant change was a provision that earmarked 1 cent of the increased gas tax for mass transit, the first substantial diversion of the Highway Trust Fund for public transportation purposes.

Congress also established a new block grant program for mass transit and, over the objections of the Reagan administration, continued transit operating subsidies beyond fiscal 1984.

In addition, lawmakers agreed to allocate more mass transit funds by formulas based on service factors rather than population. Northern cities heavily dependent on mass transit despite declining populations sought formulas that would favor cities with existing service.

States were guaranteed that their highway aid apportionments would equal at least 85 percent of the highway taxes paid by their motorists. The law also allowed states to defer a portion of their local share of federally funded projects in fiscal 1983 and 1984.

Stopgap Bill

Congressional committees reported multi-year highway authorization bills in May (HR 6211 — H Rept 97-555, HR 7092 — H Rept 97-838, S 2574 — S Rept 97-421) but later scrapped them because of uncertainties over revenues that followed Reagan's initial refusal to endorse the gas tax hike on which the proposals were predicated. Instead, lawmakers Oct. 1 approved a scaled-down version of S 2574 that authorized about $5 billion for highway programs in fiscal 1984. The funds would carry states for three to six months, supporters said.

Provisions. As signed into law Oct. 15, S 2574 (PL 97-327):

• Authorized $3.225 billion in fiscal 1984 for Interstate construction, down from the existing authorization of $3.625 billion for fiscal 1984.

• Directed the transportation secretary to apportion the 1984 Interstate funds to the states.

• Provided that other highway authorizations be reduced according to a formula based on the length of time covered by a temporary appropriations resolution (PL 97-276), or a reduction of less than one-fourth.

• Authorized the following amounts, to be reduced by the formula: $1.5 billion for primary highways; $400 million, rural roads; $800 million, urban roads; $900 million, bridge repairs and replacement; $200 million for elimination of highway hazards; and $190 million for rail-highway crossings.

Lame-Duck Action

Comprehensive highway/gas tax proposals were revived after the November elections. The legislation was wrapped in the aura of a "jobs bill" that would provide some 300,000 jobs and begin the repair of the crumbling physical infrastructure of the nation. *(Box, p. 302)*

House Speaker Thomas P. O'Neill Jr., D-Mass., and Senate Majority Leader Howard H. Baker Jr., R-Tenn., announced Nov. 22 that they would work together in the lame-duck session for enactment of gas tax legislation to help counter unemployment.

Reagan jumped on the bandwagon Nov. 23, endorsing a gas tax increase as a vitally needed effort to repair the transportation infrastructure.

"There's no question but obviously there will be some employment with it, but it is not a jobs bill as such. It is a necessity. It's a problem that we have to meet, and we'd be doing this if there were no recession at all," Reagan said.

Administration Plan. The administration's tax plan called for the entire $5.5 billion to come from a hike in the gas and diesel fuel tax, although there would be changes in other highway taxes. The plan also funneled 1 cent per gallon of the tax to mass transit for capital projects, providing an estimated $1.1 billion a year.

The administration asked Congress to authorize about $100 billion over six years to complete the Interstate System, repair highways and bridges, shore up mass transit systems and related projects. Of that total, almost $20 billion would go to transit.

Earlier threats of a presidential veto of subsidies for mass transit operations beyond fiscal 1984 dissolved. However, members in turn agreed to make deeper cuts in operating subsidies than many had wanted.

The administration also dropped its proposal to turn back urban and rural road programs to the states, largely in an effort to reduce opposition to the overall bill. Some key members representing both rural and urban interests opposed the turnback.

Tenuous Coalition. Transportation Secretary Drew Lewis had been working all year developing a coalition to support the gas tax legislation. He had won mass transit support by promising the first major diversion of gas tax monies — 1 cent a gallon — for public transportation. And he brought along highway builders, who previously opposed gas tax revenues for non-highway uses, by pushing for increased road funding.

Trucking interests fiercely fought increased highway-use taxes, but the tenuous remaining coalition of supporters succeeded in passing the bill.

House. House Public Works Committee members drafted a substitute for HR 6211, the multi-year bill they had reported May 17, when they returned from the election recess Nov. 29. The Ways and Means Committee Dec. 3 approved gas and truck tax changes to be offered as a tax title to HR 6211 on the floor.

The House began consideration of the bill Dec. 6 and finally passed it by a 262-143 vote in the early hours of Dec. 7. As passed, the bill authorized $71.3 billion over four years. It provided for a 5-cent increase in the gas tax, 1 cent of which would be funneled to mass transit projects.

In earlier action, the House narrowly adopted the rule governing floor consideration of the measure by a **197-194 key vote (R 59-114; D 138-80).** Members opposing the fuel or truck taxes fought the rule, which barred amendments to the bill's tax provisions. The bill's supporters argued that significant tax changes would jeopardize passage. *(1982 key votes, p. 895)*

Before passing the bill, the House adopted two amendments designed to head off opposition from states concerned about losing funds. One required that each state receive at least 85 cents in highway apportionments for each $1 that its motorists paid into the Highway Trust

Highway Trust Fund

Building and repairing the federal highway systems had been accomplished primarily through the Highway Trust Fund, created by the Highway Act of 1956 (PL 84-627) and financed by highway user taxes. The major revenue source was the gasoline tax, first set at 3 cents per gallon, later at 4 cents, and raised in 1983 to 9 cents, 1 cent of which would go into a mass transit account. There also had been taxes on trucks, tires, heavy truck use and other items.

Before the trust fund was established, federal funding for highways came from the general Treasury, which received the highway user taxes.

Federal Role

The trust fund was designed to construct high priority roads, with states paying for routine maintenance. Interstate funding was on a 90-10 sharing basis between the federal and state governments. Primary, secondary and urban roads were on a 70-30 basis, but the federal share was later raised to 75 percent.

States and local governments owned the highways within their jurisdictions. To receive federal aid, however, states had to build highways according to federal standards.

Federal highway user taxes provided almost 20 percent of all revenue in 1979 for all highway programs; state user taxes provided more than 42 percent. The remainder came from state and local general tax funds, bonds and other monies.

Apportionment of Funds

Under the Highway Trust Fund method, Congress enacted legislation authorizing a total amount for eligible highway programs. The Federal Highway Administration (FHWA) apportioned sums to states according to various formulas based on population, land area, mileage and road needs. The 1982 highway bill (PL 97-424) revised the primary-highways formula and guaranteed states their highway aid apportionments would equal at least 85 percent of the highway taxes paid by their motorists. *(Story, p. 301)*

The FHWA did not actually apportion cash but designated the amount states could commit on behalf of the federal government.

Once a road project had federal approval, states could incur obligations before Congress actually appropriated the funds. The states were reimbursed for the federal share of the cost later when Congress approved an appropriation.

The rate of trust fund spending was controlled by annual ceilings set by Congress.

Fund. The second allowed states to defer their matching share of road projects funded by the revenues from the gas tax increase in fiscal 1983. The states would have to repay the money or have their future aid cut.

The House defeated three attempts to waive or weaken a provision clarifying that the Davis-Bacon Act, which required that an area's prevailing wage rate be paid on federally funded highway projects, applied not only to new construction but to major highway repairs as well. Sponsors of the amendments said the requirements resulted in inflated wages and that more jobs could be created by the bill without Davis-Bacon.

Senate. When the Senate returned for the lame-duck session, the Environment and Public Works Committee Dec. 9 reported a new highway bill (S 3043 — S Rept 97-676). The Finance Committee Dec. 9 approved its own tax package and substituted it for all of the House language in HR 6211. A compromise mass transit bill (S 3072) was discharged Dec. 3 from the Banking, Housing and Urban Affairs Committee. And the Commerce Committee Dec. 6 approved a highway safety title to the administration bill (S 3044).

The Senate leadership plan was to call up the Finance Committee's version of HR 6211 as the main bill and then to combine all the committees' measures as a substitute, to be offered by Senate Majority Leader Baker.

However, Senate action was held up by a handful of conservative Republicans, led by Jesse Helms, R-N.C., who objected to the tax increases. Their delaying tactics forced weekend and early-morning sessions, leaving tempers badly frayed. The delaying tactics, which began when the Senate took up the bill Dec. 10 and continued until passage 11 days later, resulted in five Senate votes on motions to invoke cloture to cut off debate. They at one point imperiled action on a stopgap funding resolution needed to prevent federal offices from shutting down. Action also was slowed by numerous amendments, including some offered by Republican and Democratic supporters of the bill.

The Senate finally passed its bill by a **56-34 key vote (R 35-15; D 21-19)**, in a session that extended into the early hours of Dec. 21, after adopting the Baker substitute, as amended, 71-24. The Senate version of HR 6211 authorized $70.4 billion over five years for highways and $12.3 billion over three years for transit. It provided for a 5-cent increase in the gas tax and transferred 1 cent of the tax on each gallon to mass transit programs, as did the House version. *(1982 key votes, p. 895)*

During consideration of the bill, the Senate rejected a $5.3 billion Democratic job creation proposal on a 44-53 party-line vote. The amendment would have eliminated the 5-cent fuel tax increase and financed the highway repair program by trimming the scheduled July 1983 tax cut for upper-income taxpayers. The core of the Democrats' proposal was a $2 billion "light" public works program funding small-scale projects such as bridge painting and public housing repair. *(1983 action, p. 663)*

The Senate approved a compromise version of a Democratic plan to extend unemployment benefits by two to five weeks. It also adopted a number of unrelated tax amendments and voted to reduce the bill's tax on heavy trucks. An amendment aimed at limiting increases in natural gas heating bills failed.

Conference, Final Action. With members increasingly impatient to go home for the Christmas holidays, Senate-House conferees reached agreement on a compromise measure Dec. 21 (H Rept 97-987).

The compromise followed the four-year structure of the House bill, generally authorizing funds through fiscal 1986 for highways and mass transit.

Under the compromise, states were allowed to defer for two years payment of their matching share of highway projects funded by the tax increase.

Conferees bogged down over the insistence by House members that the formula for allocating funds for primary highways — major urban and rural roads — be based on population. The House formula would have favored the urbanized Eastern states and California, at the expense of the large but sparsely populated Western states.

The conferees agreed to allow a state to receive the higher amount from either the existing formula, which included land area and highway mileage factors, or a new one based only on urban and rural population. The amount would be reduced to keep the apportionments within the authorized level.

The conferees did not accept the House changes in the formula for allocating major repair monies for the Interstates. The House had wanted to focus on car and truck fuel use, which would have benefited the urbanized states. The existing formula was based on traffic and lane miles.

Mass transit subsidies were cut along the lines of the Senate bill, up to 20 percent of the fiscal 1982 amount for the largest cities. But a provision was included to allow communities to spend up to their fiscal 1982 level in exchange for some of their capital funds.

A protectionist "Buy America" provision in the House bill was moderated in the compromise.

Conferees also accepted the unemployment benefits extension and some unrelated tax provisions included in the Senate bill. *(Unemployment benefits, p. 654)*

The House adopted the conference report by a 180-87 vote Dec. 21, then adjourned for the year. Senate action, however, continued to be delayed by filibusters. After invoking cloture for a sixth and final time, the Senate adopted the conference report Dec. 23, 54-33, clearing the way for adjournment.

Provisions

As signed into law Jan. 6, 1983, HR 6211 (PL 97-424):

Highways

● Authorized $4 billion for Interstate construction each year for fiscal 1984-90. A one-year authorization (PL 97-327) cleared before the November recess provided for $3.225 billion in 1984.

Earlier law (PL 94-280) authorized $3.625 billion a year for 1985-1990.

Under this program, states could obligate their apportionment of Interstate federal aid one year before the authorization.

● Provided that no state receive less than one-half of 1 percent of the total Interstate apportionment.

● Set a ceiling on obligations from the Highway Trust Fund of $12.1 billion for fiscal 1983; $12.75 billion, 1984; $13.55 billion, 1985; and $14.45 billion, 1986.

● Authorized funding for primary highways of $1.85 billion in fiscal 1983, $2.1 billion in 1984, $2.3 billion in 1985 and $2.45 billion in 1986; for rural highways, $650 million each year for fiscal 1983-86; and for urban highways, $800 million each year for fiscal 1983-86. The fiscal 1983 totals included funds previously authorized by PL 97-327.

● Required states beginning in fiscal 1984 to spend at least 40 percent of the funds for primary, rural and urban highways on major repair work, except under certain circumstances.

● Authorized $1.95 billion in fiscal 1984 for Interstate reconstruction, repairs, resurfacing and rehabilitation — known as the "4-R" program — up from $800 million previously authorized; $2.4 billion, 1985; $2.8 billion, 1986; and $3.15 billion, 1987.

● Authorized out of the Highway Trust Fund $257 million in fiscal 1983 for highway projects that communities and states substituted for planned Interstate highway segments, $700 million annually for 1984 and 1985, and $725 million for 1986. The 1983 funds would be added to $518 million previously appropriated from general revenues.

● Changed the formula for apportioning funds for primary highways, which were major urban and rural roads. The existing formula included factors on population, land area and miles of primary routes. Under the change, a state would receive the higher amount from either the existing formula or a new one based only on urban and rural population. The amount would be reduced to keep the apportionments within the authorized level.

● Authorized $300 million in fiscal 1983 specifically for discretionary funds for special high-cost Interstate segments. Under existing law, about $200 million a year in Interstate monies unused by states reverted to this fund.

● Apportioned bridge repair and replacement funds by a formula based on the latest inventory of bridge needs and state costs of completing the work.

Truck Size, Weight. Set standards for truck size and weight. States were required to allow trucks up to 80,000 pounds on Interstate highways, up from 73,280 pounds, or lose federal highway funds.

Vehicle lengths were set at 48 feet for a single truck trailer or 28 feet for each semitrailer in a double combination. States could not regulate overall length or bar twin-trailer trucks. The limits applied to Interstate and qualified primary routes.

● Increased federal assistance by 5 percent for highway and bridge surfacing or restoration projects done with recycled materials. The federal share could be 80 to 85 percent of the cost, depending on the type of project.

● Provided, beginning in fiscal 1985, that a state require proof of payment of the federal truck highway use tax before registering the vehicle or face the loss of up to 25 percent of its federal highway funds.

● Allowed a state to defer payment of its share of projects funded by increased highway monies for fiscal 1983 and 1984. If it did not "repay" that share, half of the balance would be deducted from its apportionment for 1985 and half for 1986.

● Clarified that Davis-Bacon Act requirements applied to major repair projects on federally aided highways, as well as to new construction. The Davis-Bacon Act required wages for federally funded projects be paid at the prevailing rates of the area.

● Required that each state's highway apportionment be equal to at least 85 percent of the highway taxes its motorists paid into the Highway Trust Fund. The 1-cent-per-gallon fuel tax revenue slated for mass transit would not be included. The bill authorized such sums as necessary out of the trust fund to provide the 85 percent floor.

● Authorized $50 million annually in fiscal 1983-86 for demonstration railroad relocation projects.

● Authorized $100 million a year from the Highway Trust Fund for emergency highway projects.

Buy America. Required that cement, steel and manufactured products used in federally funded highway and certain transit projects, such as rail tracks and bus garages, be American-made if they cost no more than 25 percent more than foreign products. The differential was set at 10 percent for mass transit buses and rail cars. The requirement could be waived if the transportation secretary determined that it was inconsistent with the public interest or that the product was not reasonably available.

● Authorized $1.6 billion in fiscal 1983 for bridge repairs and replacement, including an earlier authorization (PL 97-327); $1.65 billion, 1984; $1.75 billion, 1985; and $2.05 billion, 1986.

● Authorized $200 million annually for fiscal 1983-86 to eliminate highway hazards.

NHTSA. Authorized $100 million annually for fiscal 1985 and 1986 for National Highway Traffic Safety Administration (NHTSA) highway safety programs.

● Authorized $20 million out of the total NHTSA authorization annually for fiscal 1985 and 1986 for enforcing the national 55-miles-per-hour speed limit. The bill directed the transportation secretary to arrange with the National Academy of Sciences for a study on the benefits of the speed limit and whether state laws provided a substantial deterrent to violations of the limit.

● Set a ceiling of $100 million annually for fiscal 1985 and 1986 on Highway Trust Fund obligations for NHTSA highway safety programs and a limit of $10 million a year for 1985 and 1986 for Federal Highway Administration safety programs.

● Authorized $190 million annually for fiscal 1983-86 for railroad-highway crossing projects.

● Encouraged each state to prohibit the sale of alcoholic beverages to people under 21 years of age.

Mass Transit

● Authorized a total of $4.098 billion in fiscal 1983 for mass transit; $4.471 billion, 1984; $4.54 billion, 1985; and $4.65 billion, 1986.

● Provided that of the total authorized for transit, $1.6 billion be for discretionary capital grants in fiscal 1983; $1.25 billion, 1984; $1.1 billion, 1985; and $1.1 billion, 1986. Those monies would be available for major capital projects, such as new bus facilities.

● Authorized $68 million for rural formula grants in fiscal 1983. The program would be folded into the urban formula block grant program in fiscal 1984.

● Authorized $365 million in fiscal 1983 for transit projects substituted for planned Interstate highway segments; $380 million, 1984; $390 million, 1985; and $400 million, 1986.

Block Grants. Created a block grant program for transit funds allocated by formula. The monies would be available on an annual grant basis for capital and operating expenses, rather than on a project-by-project basis.

Of the total, the bill authorized $779 million for block grants in fiscal 1983; $2.75 billion, 1984; $2.95 billion, 1985; and $3.05 billion, 1986. The existing formula program was authorized at $1.2 billion in fiscal 1983, and then folded into the block grant program.

● Restricted the use of block grant funds for mass transit operating expenses. Cities over one million population could use funds amounting to 80 percent of their 1982 operating subsidy level for transit operating costs. Cities from 200,000 to one million could use up to 90 percent of

the 1982 level; and cities under 200,000 could use up to 95 percent.

In fiscal 1983 and 1984, communities could use up to 100 percent of their 1982 operating subsidy level for operating costs, but they would lose some of their capital funds as a penalty.

● Apportioned most rail funds by a formula based 60 percent on miles of revenue-producing service and 40 percent on the total miles of routes.

Also, an "incentive tier" was included, starting in fiscal 1984, to provide additional monies based on the number of miles of passenger service and the cost of moving passengers.

● Apportioned bus monies to cities over 200,000 by a formula based 50 percent on population and 50 percent on bus vehicle miles in service. The bill provided an "incentive tier" like that for rail funding.

Bus funds would be apportioned to cities under 200,000 by formula based on population.

Taxes

● Increased the federal 4-cent-a-gallon fuel tax to 9 cents a gallon for gas, diesel fuel and motorboat fuel.

The tax would be effective April 1, 1983, through Sept. 30, 1988.

● Exempted methanol and ethanol from the fuel tax if they were not produced from petroleum or natural gas.

● Exempted gasohol, a mixture of alcohol and gasoline, from 5 cents a gallon of the tax.

● Exempted from the fuel tax state and local governments; inter-city, school and local buses; farm vehicles; and off-highway business vehicles.

● Continued the 4-cent-a-gallon tax exemption for taxicabs.

● Repealed taxes on lubricating oil, truck parts and tread rubber.

● Set a 12 percent tax on the retail sale price of trucks over 33,000 pounds and truck trailers over 26,000 pounds, effective April 1, 1983. The tax was 10 percent of manufacturer's sale price for trucks and trailers over 10,000 pounds.

● Set new graduated highway use taxes for trucks, generally effective July 1, 1984, through June 30, 1988. The maximum tax for 80,000-pound trucks was increased from $240 to $1,600, July 1, 1984; $1,700, July 1, 1986; $1,800, July 1, 1987; and $1,900, July 1, 1988.

● Set new graduated taxes for tires over 40 pounds, exempting most passenger car tires. The bill charged 15 cents for each pound between 40 and 70; 30 cents for each pound between 70 and 90; 50 cents for each pound over 90. The tax would be effective Jan. 1, 1984. The tax had been 9.75 cents per pound for all tires.

● Extended the authority for the Highway Trust Fund through Sept. 30, 1988.

● Increased the cap from $20 million to $45 million on motorboat fuel tax revenues transferred annually from the Highway Trust Fund to the National Recreational Boating Safety and Facilities Improvement Fund. The boating fund's balance could not exceed $45 million. The boating fund monies were intended for state boating safety programs and boating facilities.

● Provided that if unfunded authorizations exceeded two years of Highway Trust Fund receipts, state apportionments would be reduced proportionately.

● Created an account in the trust fund for monies from 1 cent of the fuel tax hike for transit capital projects.

State-by-State Highway Aid

Following are the amounts the states received in actual highway aid in fiscal year 1982, the amounts they would be eligible for in fiscal 1983 as a result of the increased taxes contained in the 1983 highway-gas tax legislation, and an estimate of fiscal 1984 aid *(in thousands of dollars)*.

State	1982	1983	1984 (estimate)
Alabama	$ 156,800	$ 217,298	$ 230,013
Alaska	107,639	141,043	150,741
Arizona	105,466	145,082	161,796
Arkansas	75,770	113,009	123,540
California	671,676	907,299	1,009,593
Colorado	118,393	164,909	204,417
Connecticut	137,053	185,382	256,408
Delaware	35,273	48,723	52,114
Florida	312,060	405,032	451,607
Georgia	251,562	329,630	351,745
Hawaii	81,206	98,860	102,251
Idaho	55,300	72,038	77,165
Illinois	256,532	389,834	488,444
Indiana	109,539	237,871	265,769
Iowa	94,734	142,687	209,552
Kansas	98,755	147,676	157,373
Kentucky	171,896	214,524	228,629
Louisiana	249,646	290,598	302,525
Maine	43,213	57,958	61,614
Maryland	268,817	335,146	363,617
Massachusetts	170,525	221,341	235,119
Michigan	188,959	339,330	378,377
Minnesota	158,686	197,623	223,541
Mississippi	71,171	128,245	137,580
Missouri	131,699	236,947	255,716
Montana	66,738	99,948	109,084
Nebraska	68,255	100,781	113,266

State	1982	1983	1984 (estimate)
Nevada	$ 47,667	$ 66,089	$ 71,243
New Hampshire	41,067	53,775	57,292
New Jersey	180,107	267,003	287,668
New Mexico	63,489	91,022	100,295
New York	396,545	590,797	645,029
North Carolina	148,492	249,304	278,699
North Dakota	53,070	73,439	78,927
Ohio	214,526	411,881	459,483
Oklahoma	89,932	163,314	182,547
Oregon	97,630	132,475	158,870
Pennsylvania	341,122	470,283	513,286
Rhode Island	80,167	96,970	150,031
South Carolina	106,693	141,564	152,374
South Dakota	52,816	75,629	81,887
Tennessee	141,186	213,273	268,026
Texas	438,686	755,403	843,737
Utah	81,143	108,975	116,849
Vermont	41,518	52,118	55,667
Virginia	208,728	268,229	285,170
Washington	221,215	280,354	294,140
West Virginia	113,236	158,774	165,759
Wisconsin	110,211	176,703	196,653
Wyoming	51,855	75,452	82,632
Dist. of Columbia	51,991	63,229	68,021
Puerto Rico	29,479	42,782	47,176
TOTAL	$7,659,934	$11,047,607	$12,343,057

SOURCE: Federal Highway Administration

Miscellaneous

● Authorized $10 million in fiscal 1984 for state development of programs to enforce federal commercial vehicle safety regulations; $20 million, 1985; $30 million, 1986; $40 million, 1987; and $50 million, 1988. The federal share of the costs of such programs was set at 80 percent.

● Protected trucking employees from dismissal or discipline for filing a complaint regarding the violation of a commercial motor vehicle safety rule.

● Provided $401 million over fiscal 1983-85 from the Reforestation Trust Fund, the boating trust fund and the Saltonstall-Kennedy Fund. The funds would be used for forest redevelopment, state boating safety programs and boating facilities, and fisheries development.

Truck Size

Congress approved legislation in 1982 to bring some uniformity to conflicting state regulations regarding commercial truck size.

The 1956 highway act (PL 84-627) generally had prohibited trucks wider than 96 inches from using Interstate highways. Rhode Island, Connecticut and Hawaii had allowed wider trucks on Interstates because of laws predating the federal act. Some states had allowed 102-inch-wide trucks with special permits.

In its massive 1982 highway-gas tax legislation (HR 6211 — PL 97-424), Congress set vehicle lengths at 48 feet for a single truck trailer or 28 feet for each semitrailer in a double combination. States were not permitted to regulate overall length or bar twin-trailer trucks. The limits applied to Interstate and qualified primary routes.

PL 97-424 also required states to allow trucks up to 80,000 pounds on Interstate highways, up from 73,280 pounds, or lose federal highway funds. *(Details, highway bill action, p. 301)*

The fiscal 1983 appropriations bill for the Department of Transportation and related agencies (PL 97-369), approved in 1982, denied highway funds to states that did not permit trucks 102 inches wide on primary and Interstate highways. In 1983 Congress passed legislation (S 926 — PL 98-17) raising the nationwide maximum width to 102 inches. *(1984 exemptions, p. 324)*

1981 Action. Several unsuccessful attempts had been made in 1981 to enact legislation setting standards for truck length and width.

A truck-width provision had been included in the Senate version of the 1981 budget reconciliation legislation but was taken out before floor consideration because of concerns about including issues not directly related to the budget.

It also had been attached to a bill (HR 3420) authorizing funds for pipeline safety programs. That legislation became stalled in the House because of the truck-size provision. *(Story, p. 301)*

And the Senate Commerce Committee Dec. 14, 1981, had reported a bill (S 1402 — S Rept 97-298) barring a state from imposing length limitations of less than 48 feet for certain trailers and from regulating the overall length of the entire truck. The bill also permitted 102-inch-wide trucks on Interstate highways.

The timber industry, which was important to the economies of Oregon and other states, contended that it needed the wider trucks for more efficient shipping.

Airport Development Aid

Congressional disputes over the direction and scope of the airport development program and aviation taxes were resolved in 1982, and the program was reauthorized by a general tax increase bill (HR 4961 — PL 97-248). The airport development act (PL 91-258) had expired two years before, although it was reprieved briefly in 1981. *(1981 action, p. 298)*

The tax bill authorized $4.8 billion for airport development projects in fiscal 1982-87 and about $7.4 billion from the Airport and Airway Trust Fund for Federal Aviation Administration (FAA) operation of the air traffic control system.

The measure also increased the airline passenger ticket tax to 8 percent, from 5 percent; increased the general aviation fuel tax to 12 cents a gallon, from 4 cents; and imposed a jet fuel tax of 14 cents a gallon. The 7-cent-a-gallon jet fuel tax had expired.

After the airport legislation expired in 1980, taxes had been reduced or dropped entirely. The expiration meant that no new monies were going into the Airport and Airways Trust Fund, which financed the development program. The remaining taxes were deposited into other accounts.

The Senate Commerce and House Public Works and Science and Technology committees had reported authorizing bills (S 508 — S Rept 97-97, HR 2643 — H Rept 97-24, Parts I and II) in 1981 but were unable to bring them to the floor. The stalemate was caused partly by disagreement over the direction of the program. HR 2643 would have maintained the existing structure of the program, while S 508 would have "defederalized," or dropped, the 69 largest airports from the development funding program. S 508 was designed to remove the government as middleman and to allow the airports to negotiate with the airlines for development funds.

Compromises

The final 1982 measure involved trade-offs between the two chambers and between Congress and the administration over the development program's structure, tax levels and the amount of aviation tax revenues that should be spent on operating the air traffic control system.

The Senate dropped its plan, which had had the support of the administration, to defederalize major airports, and the basic structure of the program was left intact.

The tax increases were not as steep as those sought by the administration. President Reagan had proposed general aviation gas tax levels of 12 cents a gallon in fiscal 1982, rising to 20 cents in fiscal 1987; and jet fuel taxes of 14 cents a gallon, rising to 22 cents in the same period. Conferees accepted the Senate-passed levels, which were higher than the ticket and jet fuel taxes in a bill (HR 4800 — H Rept 97-510) approved by the Ways and Means Committee May 12.

The tax proposals had resulted in conflicting pressures on Congress. The active general aviation lobby resisted the proposed taxes. At the same time, Reagan said funds for airport development and the modernization of the air traffic control system, which Congress wanted, were contingent on the tax increases.

Congress and the White House compromised on the final bill's tax levels and funds were authorized for development and airway system improvements.

Congress partly met Reagan's demand for increased use of the Airport and Airway Trust Fund for operating the air traffic control system. Reagan contended that aviation users, not the general taxpayer, should bear the major portion of the costs of federal aviation programs. However, Congress historically had resisted using the trust fund for operations, and contended that the taxes were passed with the intention of being used for airport development, not operations.

The final bill established formulas for authorizing operations funding, amounting to $1.462 billion in fiscal 1983, up from the 1982 level of $800 million. Reagan had sought a $2 billion share from the trust fund for a proposed $2.55 billion program to operate the air traffic control system.

HR 4961 put strings on the authorizations to help ensure that monies for airport development projects would be spent. Some members were concerned that the administration might hold up funds to reduce budget deficits.

Legislative Action

The stalemate over the airport program had been broken when the Senate Finance Committee, in its search for revenues to reduce the federal deficit, decided to include increased and new aviation taxes in the 1982 omnibus tax bill. *(Tax bill story, p. 72)*

Sen. Bob Packwood, R-Ore., a member of the Finance panel and chairman of the Commerce Committee, obtained the support of the Commerce Committee majority to add authorizations for the airport program to the tax bill. One of his goals was to ensure that the aviation taxes were not spent on non-airport projects. Packwood and others feared that a fragile industry coalition supporting the airport package would be split if the authorizations were not tied to the taxes in the same bill, specifying how they would be spent.

But the tactic drew harsh criticism on the floor from senators such as Howard W. Cannon, D-Nev., who charged that it was a backdoor effort to enact proposals that had not been approved by the entire Commerce Committee.

Packwood's proposal was adopted by a 93-5 vote during floor debate July 20, but only after a challenge to its germaneness and a motion to delete Packwood's proposal from the bill were defeated.

FAA Unveils $9 Billion Modernization Plan

The Federal Aviation Administration (FAA) made public Jan. 28, 1982, its proposal for a $9 billion modernization program involving high-capability computers and greatly increased automation to handle the heavier air traffic expected in the future. It would improve communications, save fuel, reduce accident risks and eventually result in a $25 billion savings in operating and maintenance costs, the FAA said.

A key element of the plan was criticized by the Rand Corp., a consultant hired by the FAA to analyze the plan. Rand said the proposal shifted too much decision making from human controllers to computers, raising potential safety problems. However, FAA officials and other consultants maintained that the program was safe.

President Reagan's fiscal 1983 authorization requests included $725 million for equipment to begin the modernization plan, $300 million of which was contingent on enactment of his proposed increase in aviation taxes. *(Aviation taxes, p. 308)*

Congested Airways

Although members of Congress and aviation industry officials greeted the complex, 450-page FAA plan cautiously, there was general agreement that the airway system needed substantial modernization.

The existing air traffic control system was a mixture of different types of equipment, techniques and procedures developed over 40 years, and it was labor intensive.

"It is the safest, most efficient system in the world, but it is very expensive to operate and maintain; expansion capability is limited; and adaptability is difficult," the FAA said in its modernization proposal.

There were then more than 225,000 aircraft sharing the skies over the United States. The FAA said the number of aircraft operations was expected to grow 116 percent from 1980 to the year 2000.

FAA officials said the modernization plan was not the result of the 1981 Professional Air Traffic Controllers Organization (PATCO) strike, but the walkout highlighted the need for a major overhaul of the system. *(Strike, p. 290)*

By early 1982 there were about 9,500 air traffic controllers. There had been 17,500 controllers before the strike.

The FAA Proposal

If the airway system was not updated, 28,000 controllers probably would be needed through the year 2000 to handle expected traffic demands, an FAA official said. With the plan's new computers, the

FAA said, it would need no more than 9,500 to 12,000 controllers.

The FAA plan, the result of a 10-month review within the agency, would provide an integrated approach to overhaul the entire air traffic control system, officials said. Highlights of the proposal included:

New Computers. Replace the existing air traffic control computers developed in the 1960s to allow higher levels of automation, greater computer capacity and increased productivity. The new computers would be more adaptable to future needs.

A new computer program, known as "automated en route air traffic control" (AERA), would be phased in to take over some duties being performed by controllers. This was the subject of the Rand Corp. report.

Around the year 2000, AERA was expected to automatically probe for potential route conflicts and to provide solutions directly to the airplane pilots in the cockpit. AERA would keep track of flight plans, plan direct routes, clear pilots for altitude, direction and radio frequency changes, and provide weather information.

A controller would monitor the system and intervene only in case of computer error, in emergencies, in situations that the computer could not handle as well or upon pilot request, FAA officials said.

Facility Consolidation. Because the new equipment would be more versatile than existing machines, the FAA would be able to consolidate more than 200 en route and terminal control facilities into 60 by the year 2000.

En route centers controlled aircraft between airports, and terminal facilities handled traffic in the vicinity of airports.

Flight Service Stations. These facilities, aimed at serving general (non-airline) aviation, would be automated and consolidated to improve weather and flight services.

Ground-to-Air. Radar systems were slated for upgrading, with a major new surveillance-data link, known as Mode S. Mode S would link the ground computers with the aircraft, acting like existing transponders in aircraft that allowed ground control centers to automatically identify the craft's location.

In addition, Mode S would serve as a link between aircraft for a new system to alert pilots when other planes were near.

Weather Services. The plan also called for a major upgrading of weather information services for pilots.

Microwave Landing System (MLS). The FAA would begin installing the new MLS at airports in 1984 to provide more precise landing guidance than the existing system.

The Senate passed the tax bill July 23 and the House July 28 sent the bill to conference without debate. Both chambers accepted the conference report (H Rept 97-760) Aug. 19.

Provisions

As signed into law Sept. 3, the aviation-related provisions of HR 4961 (PL 97-248):

Taxes. Raised $2.8 billion in various taxes for the Airport and Airway Trust Fund by making changes that included: increasing the passenger ticket tax from 5 percent to 8 percent; raising the general aviation gasoline tax from 4 cents a gallon to 12 cents a gallon; imposing a 14-cent-a-gallon tax on jet fuel; and reinstating the 5 percent air freight waybill and $3 international departure ticket taxes.

The taxes would expire after four years unless extended by Congress. The new taxes would go into effect Sept. 1, 1982.

Airport Program: Authorized for airport development and noise abatement projects $450 million in fiscal 1982; $600 million, 1983; $793.5 million, 1984; $912 million, 1985; $1.017 billion, 1986; and $1.017 billion, 1987. Unused authorizations could be carried over.

Congress provided an additional $475 million for airport development projects over fiscal 1983-85 as part of the gas tax/highway authorization bill cleared Dec. 23 (HR 6211). *(Highway bill, p. 301)*

● Authorized $261 million in fiscal 1982 for facilities and equipment; $725 million, in 1983; $1.393 billion, 1984; $1.407 billion, 1985; $1.377 billion, 1986; and $1.164 billion, 1987. Unused authorizations could be carried over. The funds would help finance the administration's multibillion-dollar program to modernize the air traffic control system.

● Authorized $72 million for research, engineering and development in fiscal 1982; $134 million, 1983; $286 million, 1984; $269 million, 1985; $215 million, 1986; and $193 million, 1987.

● Authorized $800 million in fiscal 1982 from the Airport and Airway Trust Fund for FAA operations and maintenance of the air traffic control system.

● Established formulas for authorizing funds from the Airport and Airway Trust Fund for FAA operations and maintenance of the air traffic control system. The formulas based the operation funds on the level of funding made available each year for airport development.

A House staffer said the formulas amounted to $1.462 billion in fiscal 1983 for operations if the full airport development authorization was spent; $1.245 billion, 1984; $1.271 billion, 1985; $1.306 billion, 1986; and $1.362 billion, 1987.

The bill provided for the reduction in trust fund monies for operations if facilities and equipment monies were not spent.

● Provided for apportionment of development funds to primary airports based on a passenger enplanement formula that was the same as in existing law. The amount apportioned to each primary airport would be increased by 10 percent in fiscal 1984, 20 percent in 1985, 25 percent in 1986 and 30 percent in 1987.

● Provided that a primary airport receive not less than $200,000 nor more than $12.5 million in development apportionments in any fiscal year. The total amount of all apportionments based on enplanements could not exceed 50 percent of the amount authorized in a fiscal year.

● Allocated an apportionment to states of 12 percent of airport development funds to pay for projects at general aviation and reliever airports, which were general aviation airports designed to relieve congestion at major airports.

● Allowed a primary airport to use the larger of $200,000 or 60 percent of its apportionment for terminal facilities. The funds could be used for terminals only after all necessary safety, security and passenger enplaning-deplaning facilities had been provided.

● Allocated out of total airport development authorizations 10 percent for the development and improvement of reliever airports; 8 percent for noise abatement projects; and 5.5 percent for commuter airports.

Airline Pact

A routine aviation insurance bill (HR 5930 — PL 97-309) became the focus of a battle between the airline industry and pilots when a labor protection requirement was tacked on during conference.

The provision, which was dropped during a second conference, would have required the payment of benefits under certain circumstances to airline employees affected by mergers, acquisitions and other transactions. Airlines had opposed the provision because of its potential cost.

The first conference report (H Rept 97-722) was recommitted Aug. 12 by the Senate by a vote of 59-38 on the grounds that the provision exceeded the scope of the conference. A second conference report (H Rept 97-864) dropped that provision and kept a Senate provision allowing the Civil Aeronautics Board (CAB) to continue its discretionary authority to impose such benefits through Jan. 1, 1985.

The 1978 airline deregulation act (PL 95-504) had slated the CAB to transfer its authority over domestic mergers and other transactions to the Justice Department at the beginning of 1983, but PL 97-309 extended the authority for two years. *(Congress and the Nation Vol. V, p. 311)*

HR 5930 was passed by the House (H Rept 97-519) June 2 and the Senate June 21. The bill cleared Sept. 30, when both the House and Senate approved the second conference report.

PL 97-309 extended the aviation war risk insurance program through Sept. 30, 1987, and set certain requirements for National Transportation Safety Board (NTSB) membership and for NTSB disclosure of cockpit recordings associated with accidents.

Bus Deregulation

Legislation to relax federal and state regulation of the inter-city bus industry was approved by Congress Aug. 20.

The measure (HR 3663 — PL 97-261) was designed to promote competition within the bus industry, and between buses and private cars and airlines. Supporters said the bill would allow bus carriers to respond quickly to changing marketplace conditions with less interference from government, particularly by the states.

The bill made it easier for new companies to start service and for existing carriers to expand operations. Unprofitable routes could be dropped more easily, and companies could change their rates with less government interference.

At the same time, however, the measure narrowed the industry's antitrust immunity and set the stage for the elimination of immunity from antitrust laws for collective rate making.

The legislation pre-empted some state rules, such as ones barring buses from picking up or dropping off passengers on intermediate points along routes.

The final version of the bill eased House-approved restrictions on Canadian and Mexican truck and bus carriers. The House originally passed the bill in 1981. Senate passage occurred June 30, 1982.

With enactment of HR 3663, the bus industry became the fourth transportation industry to undergo significant deregulation in as many years. Regulatory reform laws affecting railroads (PL 96-448) and trucks (PL 96-296) were passed in 1980. An airline deregulation measure (PL 95-504) was approved in 1978. (Congress and the Nation Vol. V, pp. 336, 331, 311)

In contrast to the sometimes sharp disputes over these earlier deregulation laws, the bus bill was relatively non-controversial and had the backing of the industry. The greatest concern expressed by members of Congress was whether relaxing government regulation would result in a reduction in service to small towns. The bill's supporters, however, pointed out that its statement of national policy called for maintaining service to small communities and that it contained safeguards for rural travelers and shippers.

Background

Inter-city bus industry officials said federal and state regulations were unnecessarily restrictive and needed to be loosened to allow companies to operate more efficiently and compete more vigorously — both with each other and with airlines and private cars.

They cited as an example regulations that had forbidden buses to pick up or drop off passengers at intermediate points along routes. And, some industry officials contended, state regulators had kept rates for service within states unduly low.

Industry ridership and profits had declined during the 1970s because of competition from automobiles and airlines. But both measures of the industry's health — ridership and revenues — had improved during 1979 and 1980. (Box, this page)

1981 House Action

HR 3663 moved quickly through the House Public Works Committee, which reported it without debate Nov. 17, 1981 (H Rept 97-334). Two days later the House passed the bill by a 305-83 vote, after less than an hour of debate and without substantive amendments. The measure had been worked out with various segments of the industry, labor, consumer advocates and others.

The final bill was "something the industry can live with," American Bus Association President Arthur D. Lewis said. The association, which represented small and large bus companies, supported the bill.

Some of the small bus companies had been concerned about deregulation, fearing they would be swamped by Greyhound Lines Inc. or Trailways Inc., which dominated the industry. Greyhound, particularly, would have preferred full deregulation.

Labor was concerned that jobs would be lost when

Inter-City Bus Industry

At the time Congress took up bus deregulation legislation in 1981, the bus industry had been regulated by the Interstate Commerce Commission (ICC) for 45 years under the same act that had governed the trucking industry, the 1935 Motor Carrier Act.

There were about 750 ICC-certified inter-city bus companies. But unlike the trucking industry, the bus industry was noted for the high level of control by a small number of companies. The 46 Class I, or largest, firms received 74 percent of all inter-city bus operating revenue. The two largest firms accounted for about 85 percent of the Class I revenues in 1978.

Greyhound Lines Inc. and its controlled affiliates dominated the industry and generated 60.4 percent of the Class I operating revenues in 1978. Trailways Inc. and its affiliates, the second largest entity, generated 24.5 percent of the Class I operating revenue.

The bus industry also faced tough competition from automobiles and airlines. According to the American Bus Association, there was a substantial decline in traffic and decrease in profits from 1969 to 1978. The number of passenger trips fell about 14.6 percent, from 396 million in 1969 to 332 million in 1977. Net operating revenues fell about 42.5 percent, from $94 million in 1969 to $54 million in 1978.

But industry ridership and profits showed improvement in 1979 and 1980. The bus group reported an increase in passengers to 360 million in 1979 and 375 million to 380 million in 1980. This was largely "due to the growing uncertainty over fuel supplies and prices, and possibly a greater public awareness of the inter-city bus as an alternative means of transportation," the ICC said. Net operating revenue increased to $90.2 million in 1979 and $133.5 million in 1980.

Airlines had surpassed the bus industry in the number of "passenger miles," but more people actually traveled by bus for inter-city trips, the ICC pointed out. (Passenger miles, box, p. 313)

The ICC noted that most of the large companies and many of the smaller regional carriers belonged to the only industry rate bureau, the National Bus Traffic Association, which had been set up to help determine regular route rates, other charges and general industry increases. The bureau's committees were dominated by Greyhound and Trailways, the ICC said.

The 1982 bus deregulation law eliminated antitrust immunity for certain rates and required a study commission to report to Congress as to whether there was a need for continued antitrust immunity for collective rate making.

companies left markets. The bill included provisions to give laid-off employees priority for new bus jobs.

The Reagan administration did not take a formal position, although Transportation Secretary Drew Lewis told the Public Works Committee during hearings in the spring that the administration supported bus deregulation.

1982 Senate, Final Action

The Senate approved its version of HR 3663 June 30, 1982, by an 85-10 vote. The bill had been reported by the Commerce Committee May 20 (S Rept 97-411).

The Senate bill provided for more deregulation than the House-passed version. Senate provisions permitting a bus company to operate were considered more liberal than the House entry provisions. While both bills allowed carriers to raise or decrease rates within a "zone of rate freedom," the Senate bill generally eliminated regulation of rates after three years.

The Senate version won the overall support of the administration when the Senate accepted a Commerce Committee amendment to soften restrictions on Canadian and Mexican truck and bus carriers operating in the United States. U.S. truckers had complained that Mexican laws prevented them from doing business in Mexico and laws in Canada unfairly limited them. Administration officials feared the original provision was too harsh and warned of a veto.

Conference, Final Action. The conference report on HR 3663 (H Rept 97-780) reflected a compromise worked out by key members of Congress, bus industry representatives and administration officials. The House adopted the conference report Aug. 19 by voice vote, and the Senate approved it the following day, 84-8, clearing the measure for the president.

Provisions

As signed into law Sept. 20, the Bus Regulatory Reform Act of 1981 (HR 3663 — PL 97-261):

National Policy. Directed the Interstate Commerce Commission (ICC) to reduce regulation and promote competition.

● Called for national policy guidelines requiring the ICC to cooperate with states on transportation matters and requiring the commission to ensure that federal reform initiatives were not nullified by state actions. The measure also provided guidelines for the regulation of motor carriers — trucks and buses — to include maintaining service to small towns and shippers, and maintaining a sound and competitive privately owned motor carrier system.

Entry. Directed the ICC to permit a bus company to operate if it was "fit, willing and able" to provide the service, unless the ICC found, on the basis of evidence presented by an objector, that the service would not be consistent with the public interest.

● Directed the ICC to authorize a company to provide regular-route service entirely in one state over an existing interstate route unless the intrastate service would have a significant adverse effect on a competing commuter bus operation. The ICC also must allow intrastate service to points along a new interstate route unless it found that the service was not consistent with the public interest. The burden of proof would be on the objector.

● Provided that the ICC, in making findings relating to the public interest, consider national transportation policy, the value of competition, the impact on service to small communities and whether issuance of the permit would impair the ability of any other carrier to provide a substantial portion of its regular-route service.

● Required that determinations on fitness and public interest be made on a case-by-case basis rather than by an industrywide rulemaking proceeding.

● Barred the ICC for two years following enactment from granting operating authority to Canadian or Mexican truck and bus carriers. The president could extend the moratorium for either country if that country was substantially prohibiting U.S. carriers from receiving authority to provide service within its boundaries. The president could lift or modify the moratorium if he found it was in the national interest and if he first notified Congress.

Restrictions Removed. Provided that an ICC certificate to provide interstate transportation was deemed to authorize round-trip operations where only one-way authority currently existed, and special and charter transportation from all points in a state in any instance in which the transportation authority was limited.

● Required the ICC within 90 days upon a carrier's request to remove any restriction on transportation to intermediate points on the carrier's interstate route, unless the ICC found, on the basis of evidence presented by an objector, that the service would adversely affect a competing commuter bus operation.

● Allowed a carrier to transport special or charter passengers in the same vehicle with regular-route passengers.

Rates. Established a rule of rate making that must be considered by the ICC in determining whether rates were reasonable. The rule would authorize revenue levels adequate to allow a well-managed carrier to cover costs and earn a fair return.

Antitrust. Prohibited carriers belonging to a rate bureau from discussing or voting on any single-line rate as of Jan. 1, 1983, and barred carriers as of Jan. 1, 1984, from discussing or voting on any joint rate. Single-line rates were charges for service handled by one carrier, while joint rates were charges for service handled by more than one.

The ban would not apply to general industry rate changes. Antitrust immunity would remain for broad changes in tariff structure, changes in promotional and innovative fares, and support services for members. A study of the need for continued antitrust immunity was required.

Zone of Rate Freedom. Allowed carriers to raise or decrease rates within a "zone of rate freedom" without ICC approval.

The ICC would not be allowed to suspend, revise or revoke the rate because it was unreasonably high or low if the change was not more than 10 percent above or 20 percent below the rate in effect one year prior to the proposed charge. One year later, the zone would change to 15 percent above to 25 percent below the effective rate. Two years later the zone would be 20 percent above to 30 percent below the effective rate. By the third year, regulation of independent rates generally would be eliminated except when a rate was predatory or discriminatory.

A carrier would have to notify the ICC that it wanted its rate considered under this provision. Antitrust laws would apply to proposals for using the zone. Use of general rate increases would count against the upward zone.

Special, Charter Rates. Prohibited the ICC from suspending, revising or revoking a rate for special or charter service except on the basis that the rates were preda-

Auto, Bus, Air and Rail Passenger Miles

The following table compares inter-city travel by auto, bus, air and rail by billions of passenger miles and the percentage of travel assigned to each. Totals may not add up to 100 percent because of rounding.

Year	Auto	Percent	Bus	Percent	Air *	Percent	Rail **	Percent
1950	438.3	87.2	22.7	4.5	9.3	1.8	32.5	6.5
1955	637.4	89.9	21.9	3.1	21.3	3.0	28.7	4.0
1960	706.1	90.7	19.3	2.5	31.7	4.1	21.6	2.8
1965	817.7	89.6	23.8	2.6	53.7	5.9	17.6	1.9
1970	1,026.0	87.6	25.3	2.2	109.5	9.3	10.9	0.9
1971	1,071.0	88.1	25.5	2.1	110.7	9.1	8.9	0.7
1972	1,129.0	87.8	25.6	2.0	123.0	9.6	8.7	0.7
1973	1,162.8	87.4	26.4	2.0	132.4	9.9	9.3	0.7
1974	1,121.9	86.6	27.7	2.1	135.4	10.5	10.5	0.8
1975	1,170.7	87.2	25.4	1.9	136.9	10.2	10.1	0.8
1976	1,259.6	87.0	25.1	1.7	152.3	10.5	10.5	0.7
1977	1,316.0	86.8	26.0	1.7	164.2	10.8	10.4	0.7
1978	1,362.3	85.8	25.6	1.6	189.1	11.9	10.5	0.7
1979	1,322.4	84.0	27.7	1.8	212.7	13.5	11.6	0.7
1980	1,300.4	84.3	27.4	1.8	204.4	13.2	11.0	0.7
1981	1,319.3	84.6	26.8	1.7	201.4	12.9	11.4	0.7
1982	1,344.9	84.3	26.9	1.7	213.6	13.4	10.9	0.7
1983	1,392.6	83.8	26.4	1.6	231.7	13.9	11.1	0.7

* Commercial scheduled and non-scheduled airlines.
** Rail data includes commuter trips.

SOURCE: *Transportation Policy Associates,* Transportation in America

tory. Collective consideration of special operations or charter service would be eliminated.

● Provided that entry for contract bus carriers would be based on a "fit, willing and able" entry test, defined as a carrier meeting safety and insurance requirements.

● Exempted brokers for bus service from ICC regulation except for requirements for bonds or insurance. A broker was someone other than a bus carrier who arranged bus transportation for compensation.

Service Reductions. Lessened restrictions on a bus company's ability to reduce or abandon service.

A carrier would have to meet certain conditions before the ICC could approve its proposal to reduce service, such as the carrier must be requesting to reduce or abandon both intrastate and interstate service along a route, the carrier must show that a state had denied or not acted finally on its request, and the carrier must have notified the governor, appropriate state agency and affected communities that it intended to petition the ICC for action.

The ICC would have to approve the request unless an objector showed that discontinuing the service was inconsistent with the public interest or that continuing the service was not an unreasonable burden on commerce. In making that determination, the ICC would have to consider national policy; whether the carrier was receiving or had received an offer of financial assistance; whether there was reasonable alternative service; whether interstate and

intrastate revenues for the service to be stopped were less than the variable costs of providing the transportation; and whether granting the request would adversely affect commuter buses. The carrier would bear the burden of proving that continuing the service was a financial hardship.

The ICC could order the carrier to continue service for up to 165 days. The legislation also pre-empted state laws relating to discontinuance or reduction in certain intrastate service unless the laws required notice of up to 30 days.

State Regulation. Required the ICC to establish rates, rules or practices applicable to intrastate service if the carrier had a request denied or not acted upon finally by a state agency, and if the ICC determined that the rate, rule or practice in effect caused unreasonable discrimination against or imposed an unreasonable burden on interstate commerce. The carrier must notify the state and interested parties.

State rate-making authority over intrastate rates of solely intrastate carriers would not be affected.

● Barred a state from enacting or enforcing any law or rule relating to scheduling of bus service except to the extent of requiring up to 30 days' notice of changes.

Miscellaneous. Permitted the ICC to suspend a carrier's operating permit in an expedited manner if the carrier was operating in a way that was an imminent hazard to public health or property.

● Allowed the ICC to provide administrative aid to local

governments and small carriers that wanted to participate in proceedings dealing with pre-emption of state authority.

● Required a bus carrier to give priority for jobs to employees laid off for other than cause within 10 years of enactment of the legislation. The ICC was directed to keep a list of available bus jobs.

Rail Strike

A four-day national railroad strike ended when Congress Sept. 22 passed legislation (S J Res 250 — PL 97-262) requested by President Reagan. The measure ordered the 26,000 striking members of the Brotherhood of Locomotive Engineers back to work and imposed the settlement recommended earlier by a presidential Emergency Board. The settlement barred the union from striking through June 30, 1984.

Some members of Congress had misgivings about passing legislation that imposed a settlement containing a no-strike provision. But those misgivings were outweighed by concerns that the strike eventually might throw a million people out of work and cost the economy $1 billion a day.

The strike, which began at 12:01 a.m. Sept. 19, affected 117 railroads outside the Northeast and was quickly felt by coal mines and the auto industry. General Motors closed its truck assembly plant in St. Louis Sept. 20. Eight coal mines in West Virginia were closed.

The administration estimated that 300,000 to 500,000 workers had been idled. Also, 150,000 commuters, primarily in Chicago, were sent scurrying for other transportation.

Conrail, the federally subsidized freight railroad in the Northeast, had reached its own labor agreement in 1981 and was not affected by the strike. Amtrak passenger lines in the Northeast also were not affected.

While members were concerned about alienating organized labor, they had received signals from other unions that there would be no retaliation on the issue at the polls.

Rex Hardesty, spokesman for the AFL-CIO, said the organization was "bothered on principle" by the proposal. But, he added, "In this deep a recession, the shutdown of America's railroads was more harm than the public could take."

The last time Congress had intervened in a rail labor dispute was in 1971 when Congress cleared a bill (PL 92-17) to end a two-day strike. (*Congress and the Nation Vol. III, p. 168*)

The Senate passed S J Res 250 by voice vote Sept. 21.

The House approved the Senate resolution by a 383-17 vote Sept. 22, after rejecting 37-361 an amendment that would have suspended the strike for 140 days while negotiations resumed.

An identical measure had been reported by the House Energy and Commerce Committee (H J Res 600 — H Rept 97-853).

Alaska Railroad

Congress approved legislation Dec. 21 providing for the transfer of the Alaska Railroad to the State of Alaska, thereby ending a bitter dispute between two senators.

The compromise (HR 3420 — PL 97-468), worked out by Senate Majority Whip Ted Stevens, R-Alaska, and Sen. Howard M. Metzenbaum, D-Ohio, provided for the U.S. Railway Association (USRA) to determine the fair market value of the railroad. That appraisal would then be used in negotiations for the sale of the federally owned railroad. The state would not have to buy the railroad if it did not like the price.

The House Aug. 12 had passed an omnibus railroad bill (HR 6308 — H Rept 97-571, Parts I and II) providing for Alaska's purchase of the Alaska Railroad. A bill (S 1500 — S Rept 97-479) that would have transferred the railroad to the state for no payment had been reported in the Senate, but Metzenbaum branded it a federal giveaway and blocked floor action on the measure. He maintained that the railroad and its properties might be worth more than $500 million.

The state, while willing to take over the railroad, did not want to pay for it. Alaska officials contended the state would be responsible for more than $100 million in necessary improvements, and the transfer would be subject to costly employee protection conditions and probably to existing claims to some railroad lands. Stevens also pointed out that there had been no offers to purchase the railroad since it went on the market in 1970.

In the waning days of the lame-duck session, the House Dec. 20 attached Alaska rail transfer language to HR 3420, an unrelated pipeline safety bill that both chambers had passed in different forms in 1981. The pipeline provisions were stripped from the measure and other railroad provisions added, as well as a shipping antitrust measure that Metzenbaum also was blocking. (*Antitrust p. 316*)

The Senate approved HR 3420 Dec. 21, after substituting the Stevens-Metzenbaum compromise and deleting the shipping provisions. The House accepted the Senate version that same day.

Other Provisions. As signed into law Jan. 14, 1983, HR 3420 (PL 97-468) also:

● Authorized a $35 million grant for labor protection benefits for former Rock Island Railroad employees. Earlier legislation (PL 96-254) had required that $75 million be paid in benefits to former employees of the bankrupt railroad. But the Supreme Court March 2 struck down the provision, saying it was unconstitutional for Congress to pass a bankruptcy law applying to only one bankrupt organization. (*Congress and the Nation Vol. V, p. 339*)

● Authorized $75 million for the transition costs of the transfer of Conrail commuter lines to an Amtrak subsidiary and other commuter agencies. The funds would be in addition to $50 million previously authorized to help in the transfer of commuter lines inherited by Conrail, the federally subsidized freight railroad. (*Conrail, p. 291*)

● Required the eventual appropriation of the entire $2.5 billion authorized for the Northeast Corridor improvement project and identified specific improvements to be accomplished. The corridor linked Washington, D.C., New York City and Boston. The administration in 1981 announced it would reduce the scope of the project and spend only $2.19 billion. (*Background, p. 295*)

● Authorized $52 million in fiscal 1983 and $55.3 million in fiscal 1984 for Federal Railroad Administration safety programs.

● Required the transportation secretary within one year after enactment to issue rules to require that the construction, maintenance and operation of rail equipment be done in a manner to increase the safety of passengers.

● Authorized $55 million for fiscal 1983-85 for a loan program that helped railroads repair and rebuild facilities and equipment.

Coal Slurry Pipelines

Legislation to promote the construction of coal slurry pipelines as an alternative to shipping Western coal by rail was reported in both the House and Senate in 1982. But rail interests and other opponents succeeded in blocking floor action on either bill during the 97th Congress.

The measures (HR 4230, S 1844) would have allowed federally approved firms to use the power of eminent domain to obtain rights of way across private lands in order to build coal slurry pipelines.

Coal slurry is pulverized coal mixed with water and shipped by underground pipe. The water is later reclaimed and the coal burned to generate electricity.

The only operating pipeline in 1982 was the Black Mesa Pipeline, which connected the Black Mesa coal mine in northeastern Arizona with a power plant in southern Nevada. Others were planned but had been blocked by the refusal of railroads to grant rights of way.

Similar legislation had gone down to a stunning defeat in the House in 1978. Legislation had been reported again during the 96th Congress, but opponents had kept it from reaching the House floor or moving out of a Senate committee. *(Congress and the Nation Vol. V, p. 489)*

Proponents took up the battle again in the 98th Congress. A coal slurry pipeline bill was soundly defeated by the House in 1983. *(Details, p. 319)*

Opposition, Support

Railroads and rail unions argued that giving pipeline companies the right of federal eminent domain to condemn land, including railroad rights of way, would be unfair and would cost them business and jobs. Railroads were the major haulers of coal.

"We have a right to protest the government fostering a competitor," Daniel L. Lang, a spokesman for the Association of American Railroads, said.

Also, some Western states fought the legislation, contending it would pre-empt their rights to allocate scarce water.

In addition, President Reagan became the first president to come out against federal eminent domain for slurry lines since it was proposed by President Kennedy in 1962. Reagan said it would encroach on states' rights.

"We were dealt a severe blow by the administration. I can't believe a Republican administration that believes in competition would be against this," House Interior Committee Chairman Morris K. Udall, D-Ariz., said.

Slurry supporters — electric utilities, pipeline companies, non-rail unions, coal interests and some consumer advocates — had contended that railroads had blocked pipelines from crossing their properties in an attempt to prevent competition. They said competition would help reduce the cost of coal, and thus lower electricity costs.

A new coalition called the Alliance for Coal and Competitive Transportation lobbied members from the Northeast and Midwest who had traditionally opposed coal slurry bills.

Committee Action

Committee action on the bills highlighted the deep divisions over the legislation.

HR 4230 (H Rept 97-423, Part I) was reported Jan. 29 by the House Interior and Insular Affairs Committee. The committee had approved the bill by a 21-20 vote.

The House Public Works and Transportation Committee, by a 24-21 vote, reported HR 4230 Aug. 10 (H Rept 97-423, Part II). The Public Works bill was reported with only one amendment — a "Buy America" provision — although critics, spearheaded by Bob Edgar, D-Pa., and Bud Shuster, R-Pa., had offered more than a dozen other amendments, many of which effectively would have gutted the bill. They held off a final vote for nearly two days with roll-call votes, quorum calls and full use of the time allowed for debate.

The Senate Energy and Natural Resources Committee reported a similar bill (S 1844 — S Rept 97-528) Aug. 17 after several days of contentious markup. Opponents delayed action by offering a flurry of amendments before the committee voted 14-6 to approve the bill.

The pattern of support and opposition was similar in both the House and Senate panels: Members from the South and West tended to support the proposal, and members from Midwestern and Eastern coal-producing states tended to oppose it.

Port User Fees

House and Senate committees in the 97th Congress reported legislation that for the first time would have required commercial vessels to pay a share of the cost of federal port dredging projects. Neither bill, however, reached the floor before the end of the Congress.

President Reagan had proposed that local port authorities pay 100 percent of both new port construction and maintenance rather than having the federal government continue to foot the bill. His plan called for local authorities to recover their costs through user fees.

Many members of Congress as well as special interests said Reagan's proposal went too far. They argued that the fees would be excessive and that the plan did not properly account for public benefits, such as an improved economy resulting from deeper ports that could handle the large vessels necessary for coal trade.

The Senate bill (S 1692 — S Rept 97-301), reported Dec. 15, 1981, by the Environment and Public Works Committee, went further than the House bill (HR 4627) toward meeting Reagan's proposals. It would have required local authorities to pay the full cost of new port improvements and up to 25 percent of routine port dredging costs.

HR 4627, reported March 9, 1982, by the House Merchant Marine and Fisheries Committee (H Rept 97-454), required local authorities to pay a share of the costs of maintenance and improvements for depths beyond 45 feet.

Both bills allowed port authorities to levy fees on port users to recover their share of the costs.

Representatives of ports were split on the cost-sharing legislation. Smaller ports feared they would be unable to raise the necessary funds. Some larger ports believed they could manage the financing, but they wanted to reduce the time required to complete projects.

Both bills contained provisions designed to reduce the completion time for projects from the existing estimate of 26 years, partly by speeding approval of federal permits for projects.

HR 4627 also contained a cargo preference provision that would require that U.S.-flag ships carry a portion of American exports and imports of dry-bulk commodities, such as coal and grain. The last significant attempt to pass

a cargo preference bill was in 1977, but it was defeated in the House. *(Congress and the Nation Vol. V, p. 297)*

Maritime Subsidy Programs

Legislation that would have allowed U.S.-flag ship operators to continue to buy foreign vessels without losing their federal operating subsidies died in 1982 because Congress was unable to clear it before the lame-duck session ended.

Sen. Howard M. Metzenbaum, D-Ohio, blocked consideration of the conference report on a compromise fiscal 1983 maritime authorization bill (S 2336 — H Rept 97-961) because he opposed providing operating subsidies to companies that bought foreign-built ships.

The provision for buying abroad was an extension of a temporary change in law approved in 1981 in the budget reconciliation act (PL 97-35). *(Details, pp. 40, 299)*

The 1981 law also had eliminated domestic construction subsidies at the request of President Reagan. In 1982 the House Merchant Marine and Fisheries Committee attempted to reinstate the subsidies by reporting a maritime authorization bill (HR 5723 — H Rept 97-539) that included $100 million for construction subsidies. But the House bowed to administration pressure and the subsidies were dropped before the measure was brought to the floor. The House passed HR 5723 Sept. 28.

The Senate June 24 had passed S 2336 (S Rept 97-408), which included the buy-foreign program extension for fiscal 1983.

The conference version of S 2336 would have authorized $572.4 million in fiscal 1983 for maritime programs, including about $454 million for operating subsidies. Despite Congress' failure to enact S 2336, operating subsidies were continued at that level by a continuing appropriations resolution (PL 97-377).

Maritime Antitrust Immunity

Legislation sought by maritime interests and the Reagan administration to grant broad antitrust immunity to international ocean liner cartels was among the casualties of the 1982 post-election session.

Although the House overwhelmingly approved an antitrust bill (HR 4374), supporters were unable to obtain a Senate vote before adjournment. Sen. Howard M. Metzenbaum, D-Ohio, objected to bringing up what he called "atrocious" legislation. At one point late in the lame-duck session, compromise language worked out by key members was attached to another bill (HR 3420), but Metzenbaum blocked that, too.

A maritime antitrust measure finally cleared in 1984. *(Story, p. 317)*

Supporters contended that the legislation would clarify congressional intent in the 1916 Shipping Act by specifying that liner cartels, or conferences, could collectively fix rates, pool revenues and conduct other international shipping activities with immunity from antitrust laws. They said judicial interpretations and regulatory actions impeded the financially troubled American merchant marine from competing in a worldwide industry that accepted joint activities as routine.

Opponents argued that the bill was a bailout for an inefficient industry. They contended that by greatly expanding immunity, the bill would allow companies acting in concert to raise shipping rates for exports and imports, resulting in higher costs to consumers.

The House Sept. 15 passed HR 4374 (H Rept 97-611, Parts I and II) by a 350-33 vote under suspension of the rules, a procedure that prevented opponents from offering amendments and required a two-thirds majority vote for passage. Modifications had been made in HR 4374 by the Merchant Marine and Judiciary committees before it was brought to the floor.

The Senate version (S 1593 — S Rept 97-414) had been reported by the Commerce Committee May 25, but it was not brought up for consideration because of Metzenbaum's opposition. The Senate in 1980 had passed legislation to broaden the antitrust immunity of ocean carrier conferences. *(Congress and the Nation Vol. V, p. 343)*

Other Legislation

Coast Guard Authorizations

Members of Congress, critical of President Reagan's plan to trim Coast Guard funding while increasing other defense spending, approved legislation in 1982 authorizing more than the president requested.

The measure (S 2252 — PL 97-322) authorized $2.38 billion for Coast Guard activities in fiscal 1983 and $2.68 billion in fiscal 1984. The president had requested $1.99 billion in new budget authority in fiscal 1983 compared to about $2 billion in fiscal 1982. The bill was $800 million over the first fiscal 1983 budget resolution.

Rep. Walter B. Jones, D-N.C., chairman of the Merchant Marine Committee, said the funding hike was needed to cover military pay and benefits increases, higher fuel costs, a program to interrupt boats carrying Haitians trying to illegally enter the United States, and to prevent closings or reduced operations at Coast Guard facilities.

Besides the specific authorizations listed, the final measure assumed the authorization of "such sums as may be necessary" for retired pay in fiscal 1983 and 1984.

The Senate approved S 2252 (S Rept 97-361) May 5 and the House passed its version (HR 5617 — H Rept 97-563, Parts I and II) July 15 by a 348-25 vote. The House version exceeded both the Senate and administration levels.

In an effort to avoid a conference, the Senate Sept. 27 agreed to increase its fiscal 1983 authorization for operations by $100 million and to drop its specific amounts for retirement pay. The House accepted the amended Senate version Sept. 29, clearing the bill.

Drunken Driving

States that cracked down on drunken driving were made eligible for extra highway safety funds under legislation approved by Congress in 1982.

The bill (HR 6170 — PL 97-364) authorized $25 million in fiscal 1983 and $50 million annually in fiscal 1984 and 1985 for states that enacted stricter drunken-driving laws.

The legislation also authorized $9.1 million for fiscal 1983-87 to computerize and maintain the National Driver Register, which was intended to help states identify drivers with a history of serious traffic offenses. The Reagan ad-

ministration had proposed eliminating funding for the register in fiscal 1982 but later supported it.

HR 6170 (H Rept 97-867) was passed by the House Sept. 29. The Senate had passed more restrictive legislation (S 2158 — S Rept 97-360) May 11 but agreed to the compromise House bill Oct. 1.

In 1984 Congress moved to combat drunken driving by young people by pressuring states to raise their minimum drinking age to 21. *(Story, p. 322)*

Highway Safety Agency

Congress Oct. 1 cleared legislation (HR 6273 — PL 97-331) that prohibited the National Highway Traffic Safety Administration (NHTSA) from requiring independent tire dealers and distributors to complete tire registration forms.

Instead, the dealers were required to give purchasers a registration form with the tire identification numbers, which they could then return directly to tire manufacturers. Tire registration was used to notify owners of defective tires that could cause accidents.

The legislation also authorized $51.4 million in fiscal 1983 for NHTSA activities; $55 million, fiscal 1984; and $58.7 million, fiscal 1985. This was consistent with the administration's budget request for fiscal 1983.

HR 6273 was approved by the House (H Rept 97-576) June 14 and the Senate (S Rept 97-505) Oct. 1.

1983

The U.S. international shipping industry won important victories in 1983 when both the Senate and House approved bills to expand the industry's antitrust immunity and revise federal regulation. Differences between the bills were resolved in 1984. Enactment of the shipping act marked the first major change in shipping regulation in more than 20 years.

Railroads also scored big in 1983 when the House decisively rejected legislation granting the right of federal eminent domain to coal slurry pipeline companies. The pipeline industry had sought such legislation for years and believed it had enough support to make the vote close. But railroads, whose virtual monopoly over coal transportation was threatened, conducted a heavy lobbying effort and the measure was defeated by 53 votes.

Congressional inaction in 1983 on a highway bill jeopardized new Interstate highway construction and left a number of emergency highway repair projects without funds. Both chambers passed a bill authorizing emergency highway repair funds and permitting the allocation of Interstate construction funds from the Highway Trust Fund, but a controversial provision added by the House blocked a conference.

Differences between the House and Senate also prevented final passage of a maritime authorization measure.

Maritime Antitrust Immunity

The U.S. international shipping industry neared a long-sought goal in 1983 with Senate and House passage of legislation broadening antitrust immunity and revising federal regulation. In 1984 Congress completed action on the bill (S 47 — PL 98-237), the first major change in shipping regulation in more than 20 years.

The final measure, the Shipping Act of 1984, relaxed restrictions on international cartels, known as conferences, among U.S. ocean liner companies that made agreements limiting and controlling competition in international shipping, such as setting prices, and dividing routes and cargoes. Pacts that met the standards set by S 47 would be approved automatically by the Federal Maritime Commission (FMC) and exempt from antitrust laws.

Previously, conference agreements had been granted limited antitrust immunity if the FMC judged them to be in the public interest. The burden of proof had been on the conferences to show that their agreements were just. FMC review had often taken years as interested parties intervened in the deliberations.

The legislation expedited FMC procedures so that, if an agreement met specific criteria listed in the law, it would become effective within a specified time period. The FMC could intervene if an agreement violated the listed prohibitions, would reduce competition and result in an unreasonable reduction in services or unreasonable increase in cost.

S 47 also permitted a conference member to take independent action and allowed establishment of shippers' associations.

Background

The Senate had passed a bill in 1980 granting broad immunity, but a more complex measure was held up in the House. In 1982 the House overwhelmingly passed legislation, only to see a similar Senate bill tied up in the lame-duck session because of objections by Howard M. Metzenbaum, D-Ohio. *(Congress and the Nation Vol. V, p. 343; 1982 legislation, p. 316)*

Opponents of changes in the antitrust law included consumer groups, which claimed shipping costs would increase, and free market advocates, who contended that the legislation provided too broad a grant of antitrust immunity for practices that would be illegal in other businesses.

But supporters of S 47 argued that changes were needed because of the special nature of international shipping. The 1916 Shipping Act had granted the cartels some immunity from prosecution under antitrust laws for their collective agreements. But court interpretations of the law and of federal regulations had created uncertainty over what was acceptable and what was not. There had been confusion, for example, over the guidelines that FMC followed in approving agreements reached by a conference. That delayed implementation of agreements and placed U.S. ships in an untenable competitive position, sponsors said.

In addition, U.S. shipping companies were at a disadvantage because foreign companies generally did not have to answer to a counterpart to the FMC in their own nations, and they escaped the restrictions placed on U.S. vessels. Supporters said the proposed legislation would put the ailing U.S.-flag ship liner industry on an equal footing with foreign liners by clarifying the 1916 law.

1983 Senate Action

The Senate Commerce Committee Feb. 17 reported S 47. The committee also reported an identical bill (S 504 —

S Rept 98-3) and referred it to the Judiciary Committee. Two bills were reported in the hopes that if one were blocked, the other would reach the floor.

The Judiciary Committee reported S 504 Feb. 22 with amendments to moderate what members said were anti-competitive effects of the bill.

The Senate passed S 47 March 1 by a vote of 64-33, after opponents dropped their filibuster against it. Metzenbaum, the leading opponent, said he believed the public had been alerted to the substance of the bill over five days of debate and nothing would be gained by further delay. Two Metzenbaum amendments were rejected during floor action.

An amendment providing for independent action by a cartel liner under certain circumstances was adopted by voice vote. Several Judiciary Committee amendments also were adopted. However, one controversial committee amendment, which would have eliminated the requirement that tariffs be filed with and enforced by the FMC, was effectively killed when the Senate accepted 61-31 an amendment maintaining FMC enforcement. Supporters of the amendment, including the Reagan administration and the Federal Trade Commission, contended the government should not enforce price-fixing agreements.

1983 House Action

The House Merchant Marine and Fisheries Committee April 12 reported HR 1878 (H Rept 98-53, Part I), a bill similar to the Senate-passed S 47. The Judiciary Committee July 1 reported the bill (H Rept 98-53, Part II) with changes that weakened the power of cartels to take collective actions.

Some ocean liner industry officials said no bill would be better than the Judiciary version.

The two committees agreed to eliminate two Judiciary provisions that were troublesome to the ocean liner industry. One would have terminated the antitrust exemption for the industry on Dec. 31, 1988; the other would have deleted the requirement that tariffs be filed with and enforced by the FMC.

The House Oct. 17 agreed by voice vote to suspend the rules and pass the companion bill, a procedure that barred amendments. The House then passed S 47 by voice vote, after substituting the language of HR 1878.

1984 Conference, Final Action

A major difference between the Senate- and House-passed bills was the House provision authorizing FMC intervention against anti-competitive agreements even if they did not violate specific prohibitions of the bill. The Senate bill permitted intervention only if an agreement violated one of the prohibitions.

Conferees agreed on specific prohibitions as well as language giving the FMC discretion to seek an injunction under certain circumstances.

Other differences resolved by conferees included questions as to whether shippers could form councils to negotiate with the shipowners, when a member of a conference could take independent action and whether a special commission or the General Accounting Office should conduct a study of the industry.

The Senate Feb. 23, 1984, adopted the conference report (H Rept 98-600) on a 74-12 vote, and the House March 6, 1984, approved it by voice vote.

Provisions

As signed into law March 20, 1984, the Shipping Act of 1984 (S 47 — PL 98-237):

● Made the act effective 90 days after it was enacted into law.

● Specified that all joint agreements among ocean common carriers to fix rates; pool or apportion traffic revenues, earnings or losses; regulate sailings and cargo volume; engage in exclusive or cooperative working arrangements; and control, regulate or prevent competition in international ocean transportation were covered by the act. Common carriers transported packaged goods between U.S. and foreign ports; bulk carriers, which transported grain and oil, were not covered.

● Stipulated that agreements involving international transportation by U.S. marine terminal operators, which furnished dock or other facilities, were covered by the act.

● Defined "shippers association" as a group of shippers that consolidated or distributed freight on a non-profit basis for the members of the group to secure carload, truckload or other volume rates or contracts. The association could negotiate rates on behalf of its members, and shipowners were prohibited from refusing to negotiate with the association.

● Required that all joint agreements be filed with the FMC.

● Mandated that all agreements conform to detailed requirements, including allowing free entry or exit from conference membership to any carrier and permitting carriers after 10 days' notice to independently offer a different rate or service other than agreed on by the conference. In addition, each agreement must at the request of any conference member require an independent neutral body to police the obligations of the conference and its members.

● Directed the FMC to reject any agreement that did not meet the requirements enumerated in the law and to give the reasons for the rejection.

● Specified that, unless rejected by the FMC, agreements became effective 45 days after filing or 30 days after being published in the *Federal Register*, whichever was later.

● Authorized the FMC to request additional information and justification for the agreement. Unless rejected by the FMC, the agreement would become effective 45 days after receipt of the additional information or a statement explaining why the request was not heeded.

● Allowed the FMC to honor a request to act on an agreement in an expedited period of time of no less than 14 days.

● Authorized the FMC to seek a federal court injunction barring the implementation of an agreement, even if the agreement did not violate prohibited acts listed in the law. An injunction could be sought if the FMC determined that the agreement violated a general standard stating that "the agreement is likely, by a reduction in competition, to produce an unreasonable reduction in transportation service or an unreasonable increase in transportation cost." The burden of proof would be on the FMC, and third parties would not be allowed to intervene in court.

Antitrust Exemption. Exempted from antitrust laws all agreements filed and approved by the FMC under the provisions of the act, and activities undertaken by carriers "with a reasonable basis to conclude" that the activity was pursuant to an agreement that would be acceptable to the FMC.

● Authorized the FMC to exempt any class of agree-

ments or activities from the requirements of the act and from antitrust laws if it determined they would not be discriminatory, substantially reduce competition or be detrimental to commerce.

● Exempted from antitrust laws certain agreements involving foreign inland shipments (intermodal agreements) and foreign storage and handling. This allowed liner conferences to set rates on a shipment from its origin to its destination, even if non-waterborne modes were to be used.

● Eliminated existing law that permitted private antitrust suits for treble damages when the alleged violation involved an infraction of the shipping act.

Tariffs. Required that each common carrier and conference subject to the act file all tariffs, or schedules, showing rates, charges, classifications, rules and practices, with the FMC. Tariffs covering bulk cargo, forest products, recycled metal scrap and wastepaper were exempted.

● Permitted different rates for shipments of a specified volume of goods over a specified period of time.

● Authorized common carriers or conferences to enter into service contracts with shippers or shippers' associations in which the carrier agreed to provide a certain amount of space and shippers agreed to ship a certain amount of cargo over a period of time.

● Prohibited rate increases from becoming effective earlier than 30 days after filing with the FMC, unless the FMC approved. Rate decreases would be effective upon filing.

Government-Owned Carriers. Continued existing law governing carriers owned or controlled by foreign governments, including prohibiting "unjust or unreasonable" low rates or other conditions of service.

● Exempted carriers of nations with most-favored-nation treaties with the United States, and exempted rates of foreign carriers for shipments between their home country and the United States.

● Authorized the FMC to suspend the rates of foreign government-owned carriers, on 60 days' notice, if it believed they were unjust and unreasonable, and limited the suspension to no more than 180 days while the FMC investigated the issue.

● Required the FMC to notify the president of a suspension or disapproval order within 10 days.

● Authorized the president to request the FMC to delay its order if he found that it was in the interests of foreign policy or national defense.

Prohibited Acts. In addition to specific acts barred by previous laws, the 1984 act:

● Prohibited false billing, classification, weighing or measurement in order to obtain lower rates.

● Prohibited common carriers from discriminating against shippers in rates or service, or rebates or refunds.

● Barred carriers from refusing to negotiate with a shippers' association or retaliating against a shipper by refusing cargo space because the shipper had patronized another carrier or filed a complaint.

● Prohibited a conference or group of two or more common carriers from boycotting shippers, restricting use of intermodal services or technological innovations, allocating shippers among specific carriers or engaging in any predatory practice aimed at denying entry or eliminating participation in a particular route to a common carrier not a member of the conference.

● Barred loyalty contracts, except when they met antitrust laws for exclusive contracts that governed other industries. Loyalty contracts were agreements by which a shipper received a lower rate by committing all or a portion

of its cargo to a carrier or conference.

Complaints. Authorized any person to file a complaint with the FMC and seek reparations. However, only the FMC could allege that agreements were substantially anti-competitive.

● Authorized the FMC to investigate any matter that might involve a violation of the act and impose sanctions, including fines of up to twice the amount of injury shown, within three years of the alleged violation. The FMC or the complainant could seek a federal court injunction against a continuation of the activity in question.

Penalties. Authorized the FMC to levy a civil penalty of up to $25,000 for each knowing violation of the act and a penalty of up to $5,000 for other violations.

● Authorized the FMC to suspend for up to 12 months any and all tariffs of a common carrier violating the act.

● Permitted the FMC to levy a penalty of up to $50,000 for each shipment made by a common carrier under a tariff that had been suspended.

● Required the FMC to notify the president of any punitive action within 10 days.

● Required the FMC to notify the president of any order under this section and authorized him to overturn that action within 10 days if it were determined to be in the interest of national defense or foreign policy.

● Permitted alleged violators to appeal through the courts and authorized the attorney general at the request of the FMC to obtain court-ordered payment of penalties.

Study and Advisory Commission. Established, five and a half years after enactment, a 17-member Advisory Commission on Conferences in Ocean Shipping to include a Cabinet-level officer and eight members of the private sector appointed by the president, four members of the Senate and four members of the House.

● Authorized $500,000 to carry out the commission's activities.

● Required the commission to conduct a comprehensive study of conferences in ocean shipping and recommend whether the national interest would be best served by prohibiting conferences, or by permitting conferences with open or closed membership, with a report to be submitted to the president and Congress within a year of the establishment of the commission.

● Required the FMC, during the five years after enactment, to collect and analyze information on the impact of the act on international shipping, including changes in price and service, time involved in regulatory proceedings and the general status of independent carriers.

Within six months after the end of the five-year period, the FMC must report to the Departments of Justice and Transportation, the Federal Trade Commission and the newly created Advisory Commission on Conferences in Ocean Shipping.

Coal Slurry Pipelines

The House Sept. 27 decisively rejected a bill that would have granted the right of federal eminent domain to coal slurry pipeline companies.

The margin of defeat — by a **key vote of 182-235 (R 85-75; D 97-160)** — surprised supporters of the measure (HR 1010), who had expected a close vote. A companion bill (S 267) was not considered on the Senate floor in the 98th Congress. *(1983 key votes, p. 911)*

The vote was a victory for railroads, whose virtual

monopoly in coal transportation in many areas would have been threatened by the pipelines. The bill would have made it easier for pipeline companies to obtain railroad and other rights of way needed for construction; eminent domain authority permitted them to acquire rights of way through the courts.

Another factor in the vote was the concern of some members over the allocation to pipelines of scarce water in arid Western states. Slurry is crushed coal mixed with water shipped by pipe.

It was the first time in five years that such legislation had reached the House floor. A similar bill was defeated in the House in 1978 by a 161-246 vote. Coal slurry pipeline bills were reported in the House during the 96th Congress and in both chambers during the 97th Congress, but opponents blocked floor action. *(Congress and the Nation Vol. V, p. 489; 1982 action, p. 315)*

Background

Several pipelines had been proposed to carry coal from Western states, southern Illinois and the Appalachian Mountains to power plants as much as 1,500 miles away. The 273-mile Black Mesa Pipeline, the only line in operation, carried about four million tons of coal a year from a mine in northeastern Arizona to a power plant in Nevada.

Slurry proponents said they needed the ability to invoke federal eminent domain to secure the rights of way needed to build the other pipelines.

For years railroads and rail-worker unions vigorously fought coal slurry bills on the grounds that pipelines would reduce the amount of coal hauled by trains and lead to a loss of railroad jobs. They were joined in opposing the legislation by some environmental groups, which feared potential damage caused by pipelines, and an array of agricultural organizations worried about water supplies and higher rail rates.

Pipeline proponents maintained that transporting the coal by pipeline would be cheaper than by railroad. They said it would foster competition and would result in lower electricity costs to consumers. Backers of the legislation included such groups as the Consumer Federation of America and the American Association of Retired Persons.

Legislative Action

The House bill was a compromise between the versions reported by the Interior Committee April 15 and by the Public Works and Transportation Committee June 14 (H Rept 98-64, Parts I and II). The chief difference involved which agency would certify pipeline companies as eligible for eminent domain; the compromise gave certification authority to both the Interior Department and the Interstate Commerce Commission.

Water rights would have to be obtained from affected states before eminent domain authority could be exercised.

The Interior Committee ordered the legislation reported by a 27-13 vote, the Public Works Committee by a 32-10 vote. Both panels had rejected attempts by slurry opponents to scuttle the bill during committee consideration.

Potential problems with HR 1010 were forecast when the Rules Committee approved a rule for consideration of the bill by a close 7-5 vote. Because at least 91 amendments had been prepared for introduction, the quick floor vote killing the bill came as a surprise to many observers, in-

cluding supporters of the bill and lobbyists.

Slurry opponents, however, had decided secretly the week before to scrap the amendments and to vote quickly on the bill. They believed they could win and that any amendment might have made the measure more palatable to critics, leading to its enactment.

After the first amendment — a proposal for an interstate compact to allocate water rights — was rejected 162-257, the chair called for additional amendments. When no one responded, the House proceeded to the vote on final passage.

Senate Bill. S 267 was reported (S Rept 98-61) by the Energy and Natural Resources Committee April 19. The panel accepted several amendments, including a package to ensure that the bill would not erode state control over water supplies, before approving S 267 by a 13-7 vote.

Highway Aid

The House and Senate in 1983 were unable to agree on a bill (HR 3103) to provide an additional $150 million for emergency highway repair and to permit the allocation of $4 billion in Interstate construction funds from the Highway Trust Fund.

Although both chambers passed HR 3103, House provisions adding $140 million for what critics termed "pork barrel" projects dragged the legislation down. The House also added a controversial trucking antitrust exemption that prompted angry senators to block a conference.

Congress failed again in 1984 to reach agreement on highway legislation. Only an emergency bill releasing six months' worth of funds was cleared. *(1983-84 action, p. 321)*

Maritime Authorization

Both the Senate and House approved maritime authorization bills in 1983, but unresolved differences over repayment of federal construction subsidies kept the legislation from clearing before adjournment.

The House bill (HR 2114) drastically curtailed a proposed Transportation Department regulation that would have allowed vessels built with the aid of federal subsidies to enter domestic trade if the subsidy were repaid. The Senate bill (S 1037) did not mention subsidies. No action to resolve the difference was taken.

Congress enacted a non-controversial maritime authorization bill in 1984. *(1983-84 action, p. 324)*

Amtrak

Legislation authorizing a fiscal 1984 operating subsidy for Amtrak was not enacted in 1983, partly because of concerns about government debts owed by the federally subsidized passenger railroad.

At issue was the scheduled default of Amtrak on Oct. 1, 1983, on about $1 billion in federal loan guarantees. Administrative steps subsequently were taken to deal with that problem.

Congress again in 1984 failed to complete action on an Amtrak authorization. The House passed a bill (HR 3648), but the Senate bill (S 2537) did not reach the floor. *(1983-84 action, p. 326)*

Transportation Safety Board

Congress in 1983 cleared legislation (S 967 — PL 98-37) authorizing a total of $73.2 million for the National Transportation Safety Board (NTSB) for fiscal 1984-86.

The board investigated transportation and pipeline accidents and made special studies relating to transportation safety. Reduced funding in fiscal 1982 had resulted in a NTSB staff reduction of 27 percent. *(Previous authorization, p. 300)*

The Senate by voice vote approved the bill (S Rept 98-43) April 7. The House May 24 approved 372-43 a similar bill (HR 1707 — H Rept 98-154, Parts I and II) before clearing the Senate bill for the president.

1984

For the second consecutive year, Congress failed to clear legislation releasing to the states money for Interstate highway construction. The breakup of a conference on the highway legislation left a majority of the states out of cash for Interstate construction and raised the possibility of a delay in completion of the Interstate Highway System.

In a significant reversal of course for the Reagan administration, the Department of Transportation in 1984 issued a regulation supporting mandatory crash protection. Congressional efforts to require air bags in some automobiles were largely superseded by the rule.

The administration also reversed itself on legislation designed to combat drunken driving by young people. Despite initial misgivings, President Reagan lobbied for and signed into law a measure to pressure states to raise their minimum drinking age to 21.

The ocean-liner industry won a long-sought goal with the completion of conference action on legislation expanding the industry's antitrust immunity. Congress also completed action on a maritime authorization bill, something it had been unable to do in 1982 and 1983.

Congress again failed to enact an Amtrak authorization. The House passed an Amtrak bill with a controversial provision allowing Congress to veto any sale of Conrail, but there was no Senate floor action. The Conrail provision proved unnecessary in 1984, but early the next year the administration recommended that Conrail be sold to Norfolk Southern Corp.

Highway Aid

The 98th Congress failed to clear comprehensive legislation to release to the states money for Interstate highway construction projects.

The House and Senate passed measures in both 1983 and 1984 but were unable to resolve their differences.

In 1983 both chambers approved legislation (HR 3103) to allocate some $4 billion in fiscal 1984 for Interstate projects. But the House added $140 million for what critics termed "pork barrel" projects, as well as a controversial trucking antitrust exemption that prompted angry senators to block a conference.

An emergency bill releasing six months' worth of fiscal 1984 funds (HR 4957 — PL 98-229) was cleared in March

1984. Distribution of the remainder of fiscal 1984 funds was to have come with enactment of fiscal 1985 legislation.

But highway funding was stalled again in 1984. Both chambers passed measures to permit the allocation of about $7.2 billion from the Highway Trust Fund for fiscal 1984 and 1985. House insistence that the bill cover both mass transit and highways delayed a conference until shortly before adjournment. The conference broke up when House members refused to accept a Senate proposal to limit funding for special highway and bridge projects.

Because a comprehensive bill was not enacted, states received only about a quarter of the money they should have gotten over the two years, leaving most states virtually out of cash for Interstate construction and raising the possibility that the Interstate Highway System might not be completed by the 1990 target date. *(Background, p. 297)*

Under the Interstate highway program, money raised from gas and diesel taxes and other road-related fees that made up the Highway Trust Fund was distributed to the states according to formula, but the money could not be allocated without congressional approval. Congress was to approve by Oct. 1 the state allocations for the next fiscal year, based on cost estimates approved by the Transportation Department. Then the states were able to obligate the funds set aside for them.

The approval process had, in recent years, become controversial as members sought to alter the formulas or to add extra highway projects for their districts, beyond the projects covered by their states' formula allocations.

1983 Legislation

As passed by the House by voice vote June 13, HR 3103 (H Rept 98-240) provided an additional $150 million from the Highway Trust Fund for emergency road repairs and made a number of changes in the Surface Transportation Assistance Act of 1982 (PL 97-424). *(1982 legislation, p. 301)*

When the Senate Oct. 25 passed the bill 91-2, it added the Interstate fund allocations to the states and made a number of other changes, sending the measure back to the House.

The House then added amendments extending antitrust exemptions for trucking companies that engaged in certain rate-setting practices and earmarking an additional $140 million for a number of highway projects.

The House additions quickly brought complaints from senators and administration officials.

Senate Commerce Committee Chairman Bob Packwood, R-Ore., objected to the antitrust exemption, which his committee had been working on for months. He was angered by what he regarded as the House's unilateral extension of antitrust immunity, which the industry wanted, without industry concessions in return.

Most of the complaints from senators focused on the antitrust issue, as pork barrel was not an exclusive province of the House. But administration officials objected to both House additions.

Efforts to salvage the critical portions of the bill during the waning days of the session were unsuccessful.

Emergency Legislation

To provide time to settle controversies surrounding the allocation of Interstate highway funds, Congress early in 1984 cleared legislation (HR 4957 — PL 98-229) releas-

ing about half of the money for a one-year period to the states. HR 4957 was basically a stripped-down version of HR 3103.

The bill released about half of the $4 billion earmarked for fiscal 1985 Interstate construction. Construction funds are allocated a year in advance. It also provided half of the $700 million earmarked for fiscal 1984 projects approved by local authorities as substitutes for once-planned Interstate highways.

HR 4957 also authorized an additional $150 million from the Highway Trust Fund for road repairs of damage caused by unusually bad weather in 1983. It removed a $30 million limit for emergency repair funds for each state.

The bill authorized the use of 4R (resurfacing, restoring, rehabilitating and reconstructing) funds to upgrade highways newly designated as part of the Interstate system and removed cement from road construction materials required by law to be made in the United States.

The House by voice vote Feb. 29 passed the bill, and the Senate by voice vote March 2 cleared the measure for the president. There was no committee action in either chamber.

1984 Legislation

The House passed HR 5504 (H Rept 98-768) June 7 by a vote of 297-73. In addition to allocating funds for Interstate construction, the bill contained 52 special projects with an estimated price tag of $2.45 billion. The demonstration projects were attractive because they were 100 percent federally financed, while regular federal Interstate construction funds allocated by formula paid for only 90 percent.

The House-passed bill changed the formula for allocating highway repair funds to the states. An attempt to block the change was defeated, 93-315. HR 5504 also increased funding for mass transit capital projects.

A key floor amendment, approved by voice vote, blocked distribution of certain highway funds to states unless they enacted a minimum drinking age. A similar provision, aimed at reducing drunken driving among teenagers, was subsequently enacted into law as an amendment to HR 4616 (PL 98-363). *(Details, this page)*

Two highway bills (S 2527, S 3024) were considered in the Senate.

Floor action on S 2527 (S Rept 98-524) was stalled when an attempt was made to attach a controversial civil rights measure to the bill.

When S 2527 was brought up Sept. 20, it was filibustered by the two Illinois senators, Republican Charles H. Percy and Democrat Alan J. Dixon, who objected to changing the method for calculating the distribution of funds to the states. The only state to be seriously hurt under the change was Illinois, which would lose $30 million the first year.

The Senate Sept. 24 voted 70-12 to shut off debate, but Dixon persisted in his delaying tactics. In an effort to free the fund allocations from procedural and other controversies, the Senate took up a substitute bill, S 3024. The bill included provisions to satisfy the Illinois senators.

The Senate Oct. 4 approved S 3024 by voice vote, after voting 75-21 to table a controversial amendment to change the formula for distributing highway repair money to the states. The Senate-passed bill contained 16 special projects with an estimated cost of $178.6 million.

A House-Senate conference on the highway legislation

was delayed until Oct. 11, one day before adjournment, by House insistence that the bill also cover mass transit.

House members finally agreed to go to conference without discussing the mass transit issue, but the conference broke up because Senate conferees were determined to maintain language to cap funding for special highway and bridge projects.

The final Senate proposal would have required states to pick up one-third of the cost of the demonstration projects, which were currently 100 percent federally funded, and placed a $30 million cap on each project. In addition, the Senate proposal would have allowed only preliminary planning on a major Boston project supported by House Speaker Thomas P. O'Neill Jr., D-Mass.

Air Bag Rule

Congressional attempts to require automakers to put air bags in some automobiles were largely superseded by a Transportation Department (DOT) regulation, issued July 11, 1984, supporting mandatory crash protection.

The new rule required automakers to phase in crash protection — air bags, automatically closing seat belts or "crashproof" interiors — between 1986 and 1989. It left a loophole for manufacturers, however. If states representing two-thirds of the U.S. population passed laws by April 1, 1989, making seat belt use mandatory, the regulation would not apply.

New York enacted the first such law in June 1984, and automakers were expected to press other states to follow. They said consumers would object to the extra cost of safety devices, which DOT estimated at $320 per vehicle for air bags and $45 for passive safety belts.

The air bag issue had bounced between Congress, DOT and the courts since 1969, when the government first tried to require them. *(Congress and the Nation Vol. V, p. 296)*

The Senate Commerce, Science and Transportation Committee Oct. 27, 1983, reported a bill (S 1108 — S Rept 98-283) that would have applied only to one line of cars from each major manufacturer; however, it did not reach the floor.

The DOT rule reflected a significant switch for the Reagan administration, which in 1981 rescinded a Carter administration rule that would have required passive restraints on all cars by 1984. The Supreme Court termed the rescission "arbitrary and capricious" in June 1983 in a suit brought by insurance companies, and required DOT to reconsider. *(Court decision, p. 746)*

Consumer groups were not pleased by the new regulation. Joan Claybrook, who as administrator of the National Highway Traffic Safety Administration had formulated the Carter administration air bag rule, criticized the "long delay" before the public could purchase air bags.

Drunken Driving

In response to growing pressure to curb drunken driving, Congress in 1984 approved a bill to encourage states to raise the minimum drinking age to 21.

The legislation (HR 4616 — PL 98-363) took a "carrot and stick" approach. For the "stick," it required withholding a portion of federal highway funds from states that by 1987 had not enacted laws prohibiting the purchase or possession of alcohol by persons under the age of 21. The

"carrot" provided financial incentives for states to institute mandatory minimum sentences for drunken drivers.

In the past, federal action had focused only on establishing financial incentives to encourage states to crack down on drunken driving. A 1982 law (HR 6170 — PL 97-364) authorized an extra $125 million in highway safety funds in fiscal 1983-85 for states that established tough drunken-driving laws. A 21-year-old drinking age was one of several suggested remedies. *(Details, p. 316)*

As of 1984, 22 states had a minimum drinking age of 21, and Arizona was to join them Jan. 1, 1985. Nine states permitted people younger than 21 to drink beer or wine.

Support, Opposition

Impetus for a stronger approach came from a number of groups, including Mothers Against Drunk Drivers (MADD), a grass-roots group claiming a half-million members in 44 states. Largely composed of victims of drunken drivers, and victims' relatives, MADD campaigned in state after state using their own tragic stories to dramatize the problem.

MADD said federal action was needed to establish a uniform drinking age because states with a minimum drinking age of 21 found that their teenagers drove to neighboring states where it was legal to drink at a younger age. That created what MADD called "blood borders" as teenagers drove home drunk.

Supporters of national legislation argued that 50 percent of the 45,000 annual traffic deaths were caused by drunken drivers, with between 5,000 and 10,000 of the fatalities being under 21. Alcohol-related accidents were the leading cause of death among youths 15-24 years old, they said.

Opposition to a national minimum drinking age came from student groups, restaurant owners, retail sellers of alcohol and the Distilled Spirits Council of the United States. Conservatives argued that requiring a national minimum age was an infringement of states' rights and constituted age discrimination.

While President Reagan supported a 21-year drinking age, he initially opposed the legislation on the grounds it violated states' rights, but later supported it.

Legislative Action

The House Energy and Commerce Committee Feb. 29 reported HR 3870 (H Rept 98-606) making it a federal crime under certain circumstances to sell alcoholic beverages to anyone under 21.

The legislation never reached the floor, and on June 7 the House by voice vote added to a controversial highway funding bill (HR 5504) an amendment withholding certain highway aid from states that failed to raise the drinking age to 21. *(Highway funding, p. 321)*

The Senate's highway aid bill (S 2527) was mired in controversy of its own, and advocates of tougher drunken-driving laws chose as the vehicle for their efforts HR 4616 (H Rept 98-641), a non-controversial child safety restraint bill passed by the House April 30.

Several key senators held up action, however, until a compromise was reached that permitted them to add amendments providing incentives to states to strengthen penalties for drunken drivers of any age.

The Senate rejected, 35-62, an amendment to HR 4616 providing financial incentives to encourage, but not re-

quire, states to raise their legal drinking age to 21. Opponents of the amendment pointed to the 1982 law that offered extra funds to states that enacted 21-year-old drinking ages. They said only four states had done so.

A compromise amendment combining both punishments and incentives was offered by Frank R. Lautenberg, D-N.J., and was adopted June 26 by a **key vote of 81-16 (R 45-10; D 36-6)**. The Senate then passed HR 4616 by voice vote. *(1984 key votes, p. 927)*

With the pre-July 4 recess jam of legislation, it appeared the House might not act on the Senate amendment. But Rep. James J. Howard, D-N.J., chairman of the Public Works and Transportation Committee and chief sponsor of the House drinking-age amendment, squeezed the bill onto the calendar.

Early in the morning of June 28, with only a score of members left on the floor, the House agreed to the measure by voice vote, clearing it for the president.

Provisions

As signed into law July 17, HR 4616 (PL 98-363):

● Authorized $126.5 million in fiscal 1985 and $132 million in fiscal 1986 for grants to the states for highway safety programs.

● Required states to spend at least 8 percent of their highway safety funds for programs to promote the use of child safety restraints in automobiles.

● Added state-sponsored programs to combat driving under the influence of drugs to the criteria under which states could receive incentive grants under PL 97-364 to combat drunken driving.

● Authorized a total of $23.5 million in fiscal 1985 and 1986 to help states computerize their traffic records to pinpoint places where traffic accidents occurred most frequently.

● Penalized states with a drinking age under 21 by withholding 5 percent of their federal highway funds (not including highway safety funds) in fiscal 1987 and 10 percent in 1988; those funds could be restored if a state subsequently raised its drinking age to 21.

● Provided incentive grants, up to 5 percent of current highway safety funds, for states that enacted mandatory minimum sentences for those convicted of drunken driving.

Auto Theft Bill

Congress in 1984 approved legislation to blunt the illegal market in stolen auto parts by requiring identification marks on major auto components, such as doors and fenders.

Impetus for the legislation (HR 6257 — PL 98-547) came from reports that auto theft had risen dramatically — one car was stolen every 31 seconds — and that thieves were more likely to be members of organized crime than individual "joy riders."

Crime rings, through so-called "chop shops," dismantled stolen autos and resold parts. Loss of property and higher insurance costs drove the price of auto theft as high as $5 billion a year nationwide, according to bill supporters.

Similar proposals had failed in the past because automakers objected to the added cost of marking parts. To soften the opposition of the auto industry, the final version of HR 6257 required fewer auto lines to be marked than originally proposed and provided for exemptions to the

auto parts marking requirement.

As signed into law, HR 6257 required domestic and foreign auto manufacturers to mark a vehicle identification number (VIN) on 14 parts, to be chosen by the secretary of transportation. Only car lines with higher-than-average theft rates would have to be marked, but no firm would have to mark more than 14 lines. (A "line" was defined as a group of automobiles distributed by a manufacturer; for example, Ford's Mustang and Thunderbird would be "lines.")

The law also established criminal penalties for trafficking in stolen parts and for removing VINs. It allowed car makers to avoid VIN requirements if car models included anti-theft devices known as "black boxes." General Motors was the only automaker to have the black boxes under development, congressional staff aides said.

Legislative Action

The House approved HR 6257 by voice vote Oct. 1. The House Energy and Commerce Committee had reported the bill Sept. 26 (H Rept 98-1087, Part I) after shelving a more restrictive measure sponsored by Timothy E. Wirth, D-Colo. The new version was the product of long negotiations between Wirth and Chairman John D. Dingell, D-Mich., whose state was home to the auto manufacturers.

A companion Senate bill (S 1400 — S Rept 98-478) was reported May 23 by the Senate Commerce, Science and Transportation Committee, but never came up for a floor vote because of a controversy involving auto bumper standards. The Senate accepted the House version Oct. 4 by voice vote, thus clearing the bill for the president.

Provisions

As signed into law Oct. 25, major provisions of the Motor Vehicle Theft Law Enforcement Act of 1984 (HR 6257 — PL 98-547):

● Required auto manufacturers to place identification numbers on the 14 major parts of vehicle lines that had a higher than average rate of theft.

● Defined "major part" to include the engine; transmission; doors; hood; grille; bumpers; fenders; deck lid, tailgate or hatchback; rear quarter panels; trunk floor plan; and frame or supporting structure.

● Limited to 14 the number of car lines any single manufacturer would be required to mark.

● Stipulated that if the manufacturer and secretary disagreed on which lines or parts to mark, the secretary would make the selection after proper notice to the manufacturer.

● Required the selection of lines and parts to be made at least six months prior to the beginning of a model year.

● Allowed a manufacturer to petition the secretary for an exemption if a line of vehicles was equipped with an anti-theft device that was standard equipment and that was determined by the secretary to be effective.

● Stipulated that the cost of identification not exceed $15 per vehicle.

● Established civil penalties for violation by manufacturers of $1,000 for each violation, up to a maximum of $250,000.

● Established penalties for trafficking in, importing or exporting stolen motor vehicles and their parts. Persons convicted of removing or altering an identification number would be subject to a fine of up to $5,000 and/or a maxi-

mum of five years in prison. Persons convicted of trafficking in stolen motor vehicles would be subject to a $25,000 fine and/or a maximum 10-year prison sentence. Those who knowingly imported or exported stolen vehicles and parts would be subject to a $10,000 fine and/or up to five years in prison.

Truck Size

States were given the right to ask the Department of Transportation (DOT) to ban large tandem trucks from unsafe portions of the Interstate Highway System under legislation (S 2217 — PL 98-554) enacted in 1984.

The bill also improved the uniformity of truck safety laws and broadened the power of DOT to enforce truck safety regulations.

Some older portions of the Interstate system did not meet standards for lane width, but in 1982 and 1983, states lost the power to ban from Interstate highways single-trailer trucks 48 feet long, tandem rigs with 28-foot trailers and trucks less than 102 inches wide. (*Truck size story, p. 307*)

But state officials and auto safety groups continued to complain that the big rigs were a hazard on many older Interstate segments. Some states tried to ban tandem trailers from certain highways, but the U.S. Supreme Court held that the action infringed on the federal right to regulate interstate commerce.

As approved by the Senate by voice vote Oct. 2, S 2217 (S Rept 98-505) incorporated provisions of a motor carrier safety bill (S 2174 — S Rept 98-424). The House, which had passed a more limited bill (HR 5568 — H Rept 98-926) Aug. 6, approved S 2217 with minor amendments by voice vote Oct. 11. The Senate concurred in the House amendments later that day.

Maritime Antitrust Immunity

After years of frustration, the ocean-liner industry persuaded Congress in 1984 to expand its antitrust immunity for setting prices and dividing routes.

The Shipping Act of 1984 (S 47 — PL 98-237), which updated federal regulation of the maritime industry, passed both the Senate and House in 1983, but differences were not resolved by conferees until 1984. (*1983-84 action, p. 317*)

The final measure gave shipowners virtual antitrust immunity to meet in cartels — or conferences — to take collective action to limit competition in international shipping. While opponents argued that the grant of immunity was too broad, supporters said it was needed to allow U.S. firms to compete with foreign companies.

Maritime Authorization

Congress in 1984 approved a $468.6 million fiscal 1985 authorization for the Maritime Administration in the Department of Transportation (DOT). In addition, $12.3 million for the Federal Maritime Commission was authorized.

The legislation (S 2499 — PL 98-556) was the first maritime authorization to clear Congress since 1981. (*1981 bill, p. 299*)

In 1982 the conference report on a maritime authoriza-

tion bill had been blocked in the Senate because of opposition to a provision allowing U.S.-flag ship operators to buy foreign vessels without losing their federal operating subsidies. *(1982 bill, p. 316)*

In 1983, differences over repayment of federal construction subsidies kept a maritime authorization bill from clearing before adjournment. *(1983 bill, details below)*

Congress avoided controversial policy changes in passing S 2499. The House, however, made a separate attempt to revive subsidies for commercial shipbuilding, but the effort failed because of Senate and administration opposition.

1983 Maritime Authorization

Both the House and Senate in 1983 approved maritime authorization bills with similar funding levels. The Senate measure (S 1037), passed by voice vote April 28, provided $498.1 million in fiscal 1984. The version (HR 2114 — H Rept 98-131) passed 281-35 by the House Nov. 4 authorized $486.8 million.

The bills, however, differed on ship construction subsidies. At issue was a proposed DOT regulation that would allow U.S.-flag vessels that had been built with federal construction subsidies to automatically enter the lucrative domestic trade, if the subsidies were repaid. Such vessels had not been permitted to engage in domestic trade, although the law permitted the transportation secretary to grant temporary entry if the vessel owner reimbursed the government for some of the subsidy.

The House bill drastically curtailed the proposed regulation; the Senate bill did not address the issue. No action was taken to resolve the difference.

DOT was barred from putting the rule into effect until June 15, 1984, by a provision in the appropriations bill for the Commerce, Justice and State departments (PL 98-166). The appropriations bill also provided fiscal 1984 funding for maritime programs.

1984 Maritime Authorization

After two years of controversies, Congress in 1984 succeeded in passing legislation to reauthorize Maritime Administration programs.

As cleared, S 2499 authorized $377.8 million to subsidize operations of a fleet of about 142 U.S.-flag ships in foreign trade; $10 million for research and development; and $80.8 million for operations and training, including a House provision authorizing $5 million to convert the *Santa Mercedes* to a training vessel for delivery to the state of Massachusetts. The bill also included a Senate provision to authorize $12.3 million for the Federal Maritime Commission, which regulated foreign and domestic shipping in U.S. commerce. The final bill authorized about $8 million more than President Reagan requested.

The House passed its version (HR 4706 — H Rept 98-635) by voice vote April 3. The Senate Oct. 11 by voice vote passed S 2499 (S Rept 98-445) after amending it to include provisions accepted by the House in HR 4706. Later that day the House by voice vote agreed to the Senate-passed version, clearing S 2499 for the president.

Subsidy Revival Attempt

House proponents of subsidies for commercial shipbuilding attempted in 1984 to revive the program, which had been unfunded since 1980.

The House Sept. 5 by voice vote passed HR 5220 (H Rept 98-757), which would have authorized $50 million in fiscal 1985 for a longstanding government program to buy used vessels for the National Defense Reserve Fleet and $200 million for the first year of a new Shipyard Incentive Program to provide shipbuilding subsidies.

Proponents, particularly members of the House Merchant Marine and Fisheries Committee, argued that idle U.S. shipyards had deteriorated or closed as a result of subsidy cuts during the Reagan administration. They contended the yards would be hard pressed to mobilize for production in case of war.

The Reagan administration, with Congress' backing, had not funded shipbuilding programs and had bought out many existing federal contracts. Administration officials said private yards were adequately subsidized by Navy contracts.

Senate and administration opposition prevented further action on the bill.

CAB Consumer Powers Transfer

Congress in 1984 enacted legislation (HR 5297 — PL 98-443) to transfer consumer protection powers of the Civil Aeronautics Board (CAB) to the Department of Transportation (DOT) when the CAB went out of business Jan. 1, 1985.

The 1978 airline deregulation law (PL 95-504) required the CAB to go out of existence, but made no provision to transfer to another agency such consumer and regulatory activities as controlling smoking on flights and bumping passengers to other flights. HR 5297 did not affect the deregulation of routes and fares established by the 1978 legislation. *(Congress and the Nation Vol. V, p. 311)*

HR 5297 also transferred to DOT the power to approve antitrust matters such as approval of airline mergers and granting of antitrust exemptions. Antitrust waivers had been required for some key industry practices, including the system that allowed airlines to use standardized tickets and to check baggage through to a final destination.

The Reagan administration had wanted the Federal Trade Commission to take over the CAB's consumer-related functions and the Justice Department to absorb the antitrust matters.

Legislative History

The House passed HR 5297 (H Rept 98-793) by voice vote June 5. The measure was reported May 21 by the Public Works and Transportation Committee.

The Senate Commerce, Science and Transportation Committee July 25 reported a similar bill (S 2796 — S Rept 98-565), but with a controversial amendment to give individuals and communities the right to petition DOT to redress grievances. Transportation Secretary Elizabeth Hanford Dole said the provision might lead to re-regulation of the airline industry and warned it could trigger a veto of the bill.

During floor action, the Senate amended the bill to give the Justice Department authority over certain antitrust matters. The Senate passed an amended version of HR 5297 by voice vote Aug. 8.

Senate-House conferees accepted the House position

on transferring antitrust authority to DOT and dropped the Senate provision permitting DOT to hear grievances against airlines. The House adopted the conference report (H Rept 98-1025) Sept. 19 and the Senate accepted it Sept. 20.

Provisions

As signed into law Oct. 4, the Civil Aeronautics Board Sunset Act of 1984 (HR 5297 — PL 98-443):

● Transferred from the CAB to DOT authority to continue consumer protection rules such as those regulating smoking on flights, baggage damage and bumping of passengers to other flights.

● Transferred from the CAB to DOT the authority to approve consolidations, mergers and antitrust exemptions for airlines.

● Transferred from the CAB to DOT authority to deal with competitive abuses, preserving a controversial ruling by the CAB governing computer reservation systems.

● Gave DOT authority to certify an air carrier's fitness.

● Required DOT to consider the question of access for the handicapped to airports in issuing rules or orders.

Amtrak

Congress failed to enact an Amtrak authorization during the 98th Congress.

In 1983 authorization bills were reported in both chambers but neither was passed, partly because of concerns about government debts owed by the federally subsidized passenger railroad.

In 1984 the House passed an Amtrak bill (HR 3648), but the Senate did not consider Amtrak authorization legislation on the floor.

Fiscal 1984 funding for the railroad was provided by a Transportation appropriations bill (PL 98-78) and fiscal 1985 funding by a continuing appropriations resolution (PL 98-473).

Amtrak's Debt

Prior to 1976, Amtrak had received federal loans made by the Federal Financing Bank (FFB) and guaranteed by the Department of Transportation (DOT). It was thought that Amtrak would become profitable and be able to repay the loans.

It soon became clear, however, that Amtrak would require continued federal aid, and Congress began appropriating direct grants for both operating and capital costs.

In 1981 Congress deferred the interest on the FFB loans until Sept. 30, 1983, to help the railroad hold down fare increases and asked DOT for recommendations for ways of relieving the debt.

On Oct. 1, 1983, Amtrak was technically in default on about $880 million in principal and $200 million in interest, but the railroad was relieved of having to pay its debt to the FFB under an administrative agreement reached with DOT. The department took title to the FFB notes that it had guaranteed and assumed liability for the FFB obligation.

House Action

The House March 6 by voice vote passed HR 3648 authorizing $730 million for Amtrak in fiscal 1984 and $724 million in 1985. The bill had been reported Sept. 21, 1983, by the House Energy and Commerce Committee (H Rept 98-371).

HR 3648 came to the floor in 1983 but the issue of Amtrak's debt blocked action on the bill. The House Oct. 6, 1983, rejected 151-198 a proposal to discharge Amtrak of its debt by allowing it to issue preferred stock to DOT.

The section of the bill on Amtrak's debt was dropped in 1984 because of the administrative steps taken to repay the debt.

But a new controversy came to the forefront: the future of Conrail. Efforts to delete language allowing Congress to veto any sale of the freight railroad proved unsuccessful. *(Details, below)*

Amendments adopted by the House included fiscal 1985 authorizations for the U.S. Railway Association and the Federal Railroad Administration Office of Administrator.

Senate Action

In 1983 and 1984 Amtrak authorization bills were reported in the Senate, but neither reached the floor.

The Senate Commerce, Science and Transportation Committee May 9, 1983, reported S 1117 (S Rept 98-79), but the bill, along with a proposed amendment dealing with Amtrak's debt, was held up partly because of questions about its impact on the budget.

The Commerce Committee May 17, 1984, reported S 2537 (S Rept 98-457), which omitted provisions pertaining to the debt repayment and to Conrail. The bill contained authorizations for Amtrak, the Federal Railroad Administration (FRA) and the Railroad Accounting Principles Board. The House passed separate authorizations for the FRA and the board. *(Details, p. 329)*

Conrail

Under the watchful eye of Congress, the Department of Transportation (DOT) in 1984 began sifting through the bids of potential buyers of Conrail. Early in 1985 Transportation Secretary Elizabeth Hanford Dole recommended to Congress that the government-owned freight railroad be sold to the Norfolk Southern Corp.

Immediately after the Feb. 8, 1985, announcement that Norfolk Southern had been selected from among three bidders, opposition surfaced on Capitol Hill from members representing the Northeast and the Midwest, the areas Conrail served. Other members of Congress, which had to pass implementing legislation for any sale of Conrail, warned that they would scrutinize the plan closely and would consider options rejected by DOT.

The Purchase Offer

Norfolk Southern offered the government $1.2 billion in cash for its 85 percent share of Conrail, plus any cash in excess of the $800 million Conrail had on hand in early 1985. Norfolk Southern also agreed to forgo almost $2.4 billion in potential tax advantages and agreed to a series of covenants designed to keep Conrail intact. It offered Conrail employees, who owned the remaining 15 percent, $375 million.

Dole said she chose Norfolk Southern over offers from the two other leading bidders, Alleghany Corp. and a group

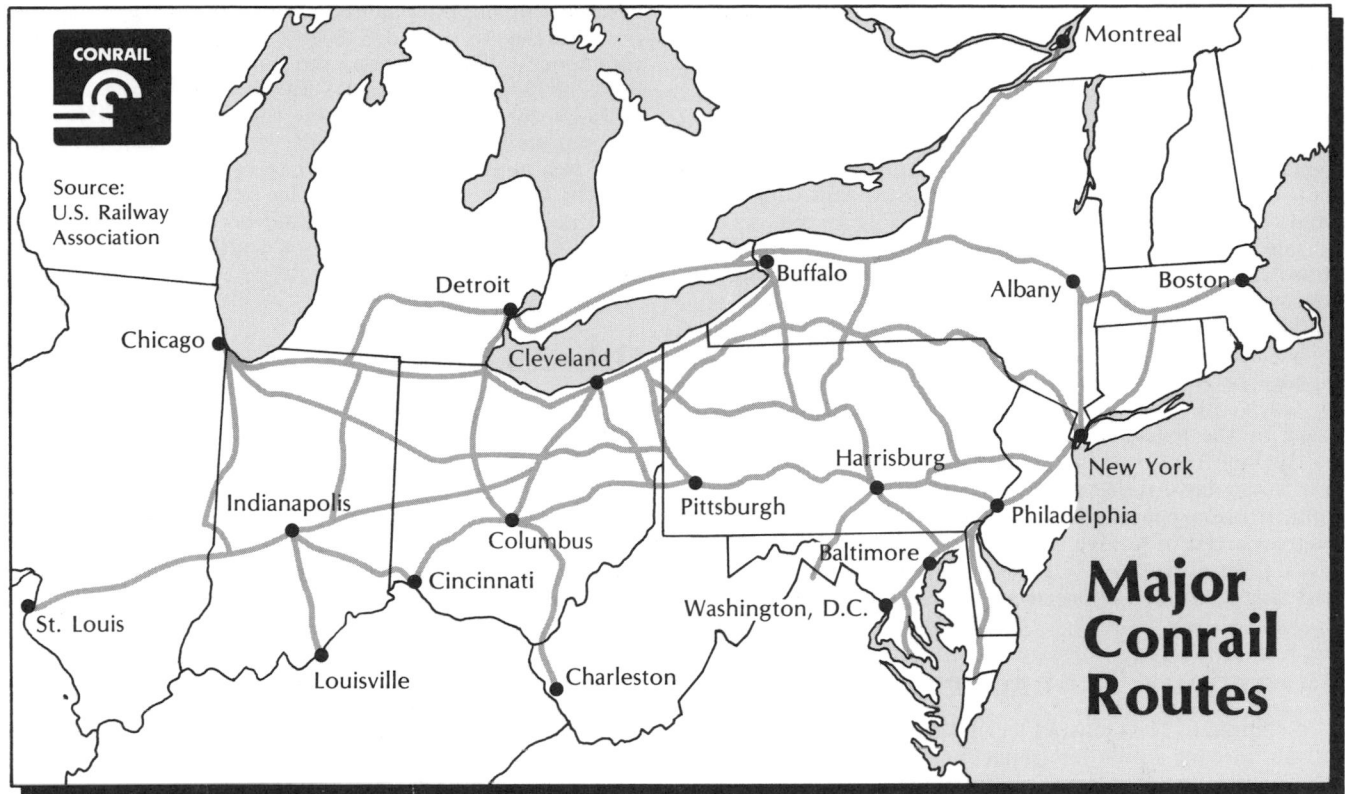

CONRAIL

Source:
U.S. Railway
Association

Montreal

Buffalo · Albany · Boston

Detroit

Chicago · Cleveland

Harrisburg · New York

Indianapolis · Pittsburgh · Philadelphia

Columbus · Baltimore

Cincinnati

St. Louis · Washington, D.C.

Louisville · Charleston

Major Conrail Routes

of investors led by J. Willard Marriott Jr., because of its railroad experience.

If approved, the sale would create the nation's largest rail network, stretching from New Orleans and Jacksonville, Fla., to Boston, Montreal and Kansas City. Norfolk Southern in early 1985 operated two railroads, the Southern, and the Norfolk and Western, covering 18,000 miles in 20 states. Conrail's service area included 13,500 miles in 14 states and Canada.

Opposition to DOT's proposal was expected to come from labor, competing railroads, shippers and the management of Conrail, all of which had considerable influence on Capitol Hill. Critics said the sale would reduce competition, increase shipping prices, curtail service and eliminate jobs.

Background

When the Reagan administration took office, it quickly determined that the government's involvement in Conrail, created by Congress in 1975, threatened the budget and also violated Reagan's principles opposing government interference in the private sector. *(Conrail background box, p. 292)*

In April 1981 Transportation Secretary Drew Lewis, saying that Conrail would soak up another $4 billion in subsidies by 1985, proposed that the government sell Conrail piecemeal.

Congressional opposition blocked the administration's plan but an alternative proposal was developed. Omnibus budget reconciliation legislation (PL 97-35) enacted in

1981 allowed Conrail to divest itself of money-losing commuter railroads and made it easier to eliminate little-used routes and lay off employees. The law stated that Conrail could eventually be sold to private enterprise, but it forbade DOT to sell it piece by piece if Conrail became profitable. *(1981 legislation, p. 291)*

Conrail, which had been a sinkhole for federal funds, experienced a remarkable turnaround starting in 1981. Conrail's balance sheet turned from red ink to black. In 1980 it suffered a net loss of $244 million, but it took its last federal subsidies in June 1981. It made profits of $39 million in 1981, $174 million in 1982 and $313 million in 1983. Its 1984 profit of $500 million was among the best in the industry.

1984 Legislative Action

Congress had been skeptical of the negotiations between DOT and potential buyers of the newly profitable railroad. As adjournment approached in 1984 and DOT failed to recommend a preferred buyer, Congress ignored DOT's draft of the legislation required to ease any sale.

Earlier in 1984 there had been concern by lawmakers that the administration might be able to sell Conrail without consulting Congress.

Included in PL 97-35, the 1981 statute permitting Conrail's sale, was a provision allowing Congress, without presidential review, to veto any DOT plan to sell Conrail. But Supreme Court actions in June and July 1983 invalidated legislative vetoes not presented to the president for his signature. *(Legislative veto, p. 833)*

Because of the court actions, the House Energy and Commerce Committee in 1983 added to an Amtrak authorization bill (HR 3648) a provision requiring the passage of a law before allowing the sale of Conrail to go through. *(Amtrak bill, p. 326)*

Before passing HR 3648, the House March 6, 1984, rejected 147-254 an amendment to eliminate the requirement. Opponents of the amendment argued that congressional review was needed to prevent DOT from making a bad sale. But James T. Broyhill, R-N.C., the amendment's sponsor, said the prospect of congressional rejection of a proposed sale would have a chilling effect on negotiations, a position shared by DOT.

S 2537, an Amtrak authorization bill, did not contain language pertaining to the Conrail sale. The measure did not reach the floor, and no Amtrak authorization was passed by the Senate during the 98th Congress.

By June 1984, however, it had become clear that Congress would have a decisive role in any Conrail sale. The administration conceded that no sale could occur unless Congress acted to forgive Conrail's $3.2 billion debt to the federal government and to remove constraints on management that had been imposed when Conrail was created.

Hazardous Transport

Congress in 1984 cleared legislation (S 2706 — PL 98-559) authorizing funds for Department of Transportation (DOT) programs regulating shipments of hazardous materials.

Disputes over the transporting of radioactive materials had blocked legislation during the 96th and 97th Congresses. *(1979-80 action, Congress and the Nation Vol. V, pp. 330, 334; 1981 action, p. 300)*

S 2706 authorized $7.5 million for fiscal 1985 and $8 million for 1986 for the DOT programs. The legislation also authorized the transportation secretary to contract with private entities to participate in a central system to report hazardous material transportation accidents. In addition, S 2706 required the secretary and the Federal Emergency Management Agency to jointly study emergency response planning.

The Senate passed S 2706 (S Rept 98-479) June 15. On Oct. 11 the House amended and passed the bill; the Senate accepted the House amendment, clearing S 2706 for the president. One-year authorization bills (HR 5530 — H Rept 98-774, Part I; HR 5642 — H Rept 98-794, Part I) had been reported in the House in May.

Pipeline Safety

Legislation authorizing $8.6 million in fiscal 1985 for pipeline safety programs supervised by the Department of Transportation (DOT) was enacted in 1984.

The final compromise (S 2688 — PL 98-464) accepted the House-passed one-year authorization period instead of the two-year period approved by the Senate and requested by the Reagan administration. The shorter time period was to provide impetus for DOT to make improvements in the pipeline inspection program in 1985 before the one-year authorization expired. The improvements were recommended by the General Accounting Office.

The bill also provided for a one-time survey of interstate pipeline facilities built before 1940 and a study of the feasibility of shipping methanol through existing pipelines.

The Senate passed S 2688 (S Rept 98-456) by voice vote June 21. The House passed its version (HR 5313 — H Rept 98-780, Parts I and II) by voice vote June 25, then passed S 2688 after substituting the language of HR 5313. A compromise bill, worked out without a formal conference, was approved by the Senate by voice vote Sept. 21, and the House cleared it by voice vote Sept. 26.

Pipeline safety legislation had become stalled in 1981 over the unrelated issue of truck width limitations. *(1981 action, p. 301)*

Other Legislation

Coast Guard Authorizations

Congress in 1984 approved legislation (S 2526 — PL 98-557) authorizing Coast Guard funding of about $2.4 billion for fiscal 1985 and $2.6 billion for fiscal 1986.

The 1985 funding was about 10 percent more than the president sought but only about 1 percent more than fiscal 1984 spending. *(Previous authorization, p. 316)*

S 2526 authorized a penalty of a $5,000 fine and/or a year in jail for operating a boat while intoxicated. Existing law had set penalties for operating a boat in a negligent manner that endangered safety. The measure also set minimum Coast Guard personnel levels, updated the language of Coast Guard administrative statutes that referred only to one sex, and prohibited the sale of recreational boats with known safety defects.

The Senate passed S 2526 (S Rept 98-454) by voice vote Oct. 5, and the House gave its approval by voice vote Oct. 9. The House had passed a slightly different authorization bill (HR 4841 — H Rept 98-631) March 29 by a vote of 348-38.

Boating, Fishing Taxes

Legislation was enacted in 1984 expanding a tax on sport fishing equipment and redirecting a tax on motorboat fuels to set aside more funds for fish restoration and boating safety programs.

The provisions were included in the deficit reduction package (HR 4170 — PL 98-369), cleared by Congress June 27. *(Deficit reduction bill, p. 56)*

HR 4170 created an Aquatic Resources Trust Fund within the Treasury to receive and reallocate the revenues from Oct. 1, 1984, through March 31, 1989. Revenues from motorboat fuel taxes, up to $45 million per year, were to go into a Boating Safety Account. Two-thirds of the money was to be allocated for state boating safety projects and one-third for Coast Guard recreational boating safety service.

Revenues from expanding the number of articles subject to the existing 10 percent excise tax on sport fishing equipment, as well as additional funds from the motorboat fuel tax and certain import duties, were to go into a Sport Fish Restoration Account. The money was slated for sport fisheries, improved access for recreational boaters and aquatic resource education.

The House passed its version of the boating and fishing tax legislation (HR 2163 — H Rept 98-133, Parts I and II) July 12, 1983. The Senate subsequently used HR 2163 as the vehicle for floor action on its deficit reduction package.

Puerto Rico Cruises

In 1984 Congress sent to the president legislation (HR 89 — PL 98-563) to permit foreign-flag ships to transport passengers between Puerto Rico and the U.S. mainland when no U.S.-flag ship was available. Previously, foreign-flag vessels had been permitted to dock in Puerto Rico, but customs regulations had barred passengers from disembarking for more than 24 hours.

Supporters of HR 89 said that no U.S.-qualified ship had transported passengers between Puerto Rico and other U.S. ports for 30 years and that the existing law restricted vacation and business travel. But opponents, including maritime unions and U.S. shipping companies, said HR 89 would discourage U.S. ship operators from trying to revive coastal service.

The House, 390-25, passed HR 89 (H Rept 98-733) May 15. The Senate passed the bill with minor changes (S Rept 98-658) Oct. 11, and the House agreed to the changes later that day.

In 1982 similar legislation had been passed 387-0 by the House but had been blocked in the Senate.

Railroad Issues

The House in 1984 passed bills to authorize the Federal Railroad Administration (FRA) and the Railroad Accounting Principles Board.

The House Sept. 20 passed legislation (HR 5585 — H Rept 98-795) authorizing $55.4 million in fiscal 1985 and $57.7 million in 1986 for the safety programs of the FRA. The bill also gave the Department of Transportation (DOT) 60 days to issue rules on drug and alcohol abuse among railroad workers and, over Reagan administration objections, gave railroad employees the right to sue DOT for enforcement of safety standards.

The House Feb. 7 passed HR 4439 (H Rept 98-594) authorizing $1 million each year for fiscal 1984-86 for the accounting board, an independent group that was to develop accounting methods to help the Interstate Commerce Commission evaluate the financial condition of railroads.

In the Senate, authorizations for the FRA and the accounting board were included in an Amtrak authorization bill (S 2537 — S Rept 98-457), which did not reach the floor. *(Amtrak provisions, p. 326)*

7

Energy Policy

Introduction   333
Mineral Leasing   339
Nuclear Power   361
Oil and Gas Regulation   375
Research and Development   393

Energy Policy

Congress in 1981-84 all but forgot the national energy problems that it had spent the previous decade trying to solve.

Energy policy had preoccupied Congress through most of the 1970s as Americans suffered through serious fuel shortages and rapidly escalating energy costs. In the years following the 1973 Arab oil embargo, the federal government struggled to cope with an energy "crisis" that President Carter in 1977 declared "the moral equivalent of war."

But in the early 1980s Congress and the federal government stepped aside while world market forces granted the nation a reprieve, at least temporarily, from its energy nightmares of 1974-80. President Reagan in 1981 abandoned Carter's call for energy-conserving sacrifices to curb U.S. dependence on foreign oil imports. Instead, he promised that the nation could produce its way out of energy problems by spurring development of its own domestic fuels, if only the U.S. government let market incentives operate.

In the following years energy demand fell off dramatically as the crude oil price increases during the late 1970s contributed to a worldwide economic recession and forced the United States and other nations to curtail their use of fuel. World crude prices, once expected to top $50 a barrel in 1982, instead dropped from $35 a barrel to $28 a barrel; economists talked of an international oil glut. U.S. oil imports fell significantly, and the Organization of Petroleum Exporting Countries (OPEC) lost its power to keep world crude prices rising.

By 1985 the stormy political debates over energy policy of the 1970s had lost their thunder. With gasoline plentiful — in some regions selling for less than $1 a gallon for the first time in five years — energy no longer ranked among the American public's central worries. With no crisis to raise an alarm, members of Congress who were still concerned about the adequacy of the nation's long-term fuel supplies could generate little political momentum for challenging Reagan's determination to scale back federal control over U.S. energy markets.

1970s Energy Strategy

Throughout the 1970s Congress and three presidents had searched, at times in near-desperation, for actions the federal government could take to control or at least soften the blow from the nation's severe energy problems.

The American way of life suffered major dislocations following the "oil shock" of 1973. The price of oil climbed from $3 to $11.65 per barrel in three months in 1973, and it zoomed to more than $30 per barrel following the cutoff of Iranian oil in 1979. Natural gas shortages closed factories and schools during the winters of 1972-73 and 1976-77.

Speed limits, thermostats and industrial output were lowered, while inflation and international debt soared.

Congress responded between 1974 and 1980 by trying to boost production, to reduce demand, to stockpile reserves and to find new fuels. The government tried to soften the economic impact by price and allocation controls.

The United States depended on imported foreign crude for nearly half of its critical oil supplies in 1977, so the government could do little to insulate the U.S. economy from the OPEC cartel's successful campaign for tenfold increases in the prices that industrial nations paid for crude oil. The nation's own oil production had peaked in 1970, and the U.S. energy industry could pump only part of the oil and natural gas the nation needed to fill an ever-growing appetite for liquid fuels for industry, residential use and transportation.

The government's efforts to regulate how those domestic supplies were used — while holding their prices below accelerating world market levels — seemed only to discourage new production and encourage fuel-wasting uses. So Congress in 1978 set in motion gradual deregulation of natural gas prices, and Carter the following year began phasing out federal price ceilings on domestic oil.

During Carter's four-year term, between 1977 and 1981, Congress also created a separate Cabinet-level Department of Energy (DOE), regulated industrial fuel consumption, provided federal tax and subsidy incentives for energy conservation investments, imposed a "windfall profits" tax on rising oil prices and launched what members

References

Discussion of energy policy for the years 1945-64 may be found in *Congress and the Nation Vol. I*, pp. 800-907; for the years 1965-68, *Congress and the Nation Vol. II*, pp. 495-528; for the years 1969-72, *Congress and the Nation Vol. III*, pp. 841-849; for the years 1973-76, *Congress and the Nation Vol. IV*, pp. 201-286; for the years 1977-80, *Congress and the Nation Vol. V*, pp. 451-530.

expected to be a crash program to develop synthetic liquid fuels from coal, oil shale and other resources.

Reagan Energy Strategy

Just days after replacing Carter in the White House, Reagan in January 1981 lifted remaining federal oil price controls that President Nixon had first imposed a decade earlier. Although Carter already had scheduled complete oil decontrol within another nine months, the new president's step signaled that Reagan meant what he said during the 1980 presidential campaign about cutting back the government's efforts to manage U.S. energy markets.

During the campaign Reagan had contended that federal actions had caused, rather than helped, the nation's energy problems. Declaring that "America must get to work producing more energy," he pledged to keep the government from interfering with marketplace supply-and-demand incentives that would encourage domestic fuel development. Reagan vowed to abolish the Department of Energy (DOE), an agency that conservatives viewed as an unneeded instrument for federal meddling in energy matters.

With two notable exceptions Reagan's conservative-dominated administration followed a free market philosophy that assigned the federal government a minimal role in dealing with energy supplies and prices. Congress refused to dismantle DOE, but Reagan's first-term energy secretaries — former South Carolina Gov. James B. Edwards, an oral surgeon, and Donald P. Hodel, former deputy secretary of the interior — de-emphasized the department's programs to promote conservation, encourage solar and other alternative technologies, and develop new ways to burn fossil fuels. While Edwards and Hodel gave DOE a low profile, Secretary of the Interior James G. Watt took the lead as chairman of Reagan's Cabinet Council on Natural Resources and the Environment in shaping the administration's agenda for easing federal regulatory restraints on the U.S. energy industry.

In two policy areas the administration stepped up federal action to promote nuclear power and to open the government's own federally owned lands and waters for fossil fuel development. Warning that the nation in the 1990s faced a "capacity crunch" in electrical power generation, DOE officials tried to bolster the nation's faltering nuclear power industry by seeking solutions to safety concerns, construction delays and financial troubles that were forcing utilities to mothball ambitious plans to build new reactors. Before resigning under congressional fire in 1983, Watt moved aggressively with controversial plans to accelerate federal coal and oil and gas leasing on public lands, while opening pristine wilderness areas and vast Outer Continental Shelf tracts for exploratory drilling. *(Watt background, p. 406)*

Through those DOE and Interior programs — and through Environmental Protection Agency stands on federal clean air regulations — the administration pursued a policy of spurring domestic energy production by easing environmental restraints on the nation's petroleum, coal and electric power industries.

Congress resisted Watt's leasing program, and members remained skeptical about the safety of nuclear power. But in addition to political opposition, the administration's pro-growth strategy ran into trouble from market conditions created by ample supplies and falling energy consumption. With electric power demand lagging far below previous projections, electric utilities mothballed partly built nuclear plants and canceled expensive plans to expand generating capacity. And with coal markets depressed, Congress halted Watt's ambitious coal leasing plans after critics charged that the Interior Department was selling federally owned reserves at prices below fair market value.

In most energy and environmental policy areas administration officials pursued their agenda through budget decisions and administrative changes. The White House sent Congress only limited legislative proposals, backing efforts to speed nuclear plant licensing, provide for nuclear waste disposal and tighten accounting procedures applied to oil and gas production from federal lands. But with deep divisions within Congress dimming prospects for tackling controversial matters, the administration backed away from expected efforts to speed up natural gas deregulation and overhaul federal clean air standards.

Congressional Reconsideration

Given administration hostility to active federal intervention, Congress spent most of 1981-84 reconsidering old energy policy decisions instead of launching new programs.

Not sharing the administration's enthusiasm for free market policies, members of Congress by and large still were oriented toward federal efforts to conserve energy and prepare for future emergencies. Many members, especially Democrats who held key energy policy-making posts in the House leadership and committees, doubted that U.S. oil and gas reserves could be expanded significantly by drilling previously unexplored federal lands and coastal waters. Concerned by safety and environmental problems, members no longer looked to nuclear power to meet the nation's long-term electrical energy needs. In alliance with politically influential environmental groups, House Democrats stood guard against what they considered administration plans to sacrifice the environmental safeguards enacted

Outlays for Energy

Billions of Dollars

(Line chart showing Total, Other, Conservation, Energy Supply, and Emergency Preparedness outlays for Fiscal Years 1976 through 1985*)

Fiscal Years

* Estimate

SOURCE: Fiscal 1986 Budget

during the 1970s to promote domestic fuel supplies.

Yet in balancing energy concerns with environmental and economic goals, Congress concluded that some decisions the government made during the 1970s had been mistaken. After several years of debate, for instance, lawmakers in 1983 halted federal financial support for building the Clinch River breeder reactor at Oak Ridge, Tenn. Bowing to similar second thoughts, Congress in 1984 cut in half federal funding for promoting a synthetic fuels industry.

World Oil Market Turnaround

In putting those programs in place, federal energy planners during the 1970s had expected world oil prices to keep escalating. But nobody, either in the White House or Congress, could have predicted the dramatic turnaround in world oil markets during the early 1980s.

From 1973 on it appeared that the OPEC cartel of oil-producing nations held power to keep world crude prices rising indefinitely. But during the late 1970s a worldwide recession cut energy demand; industrial nations meanwhile found new sources of fuel

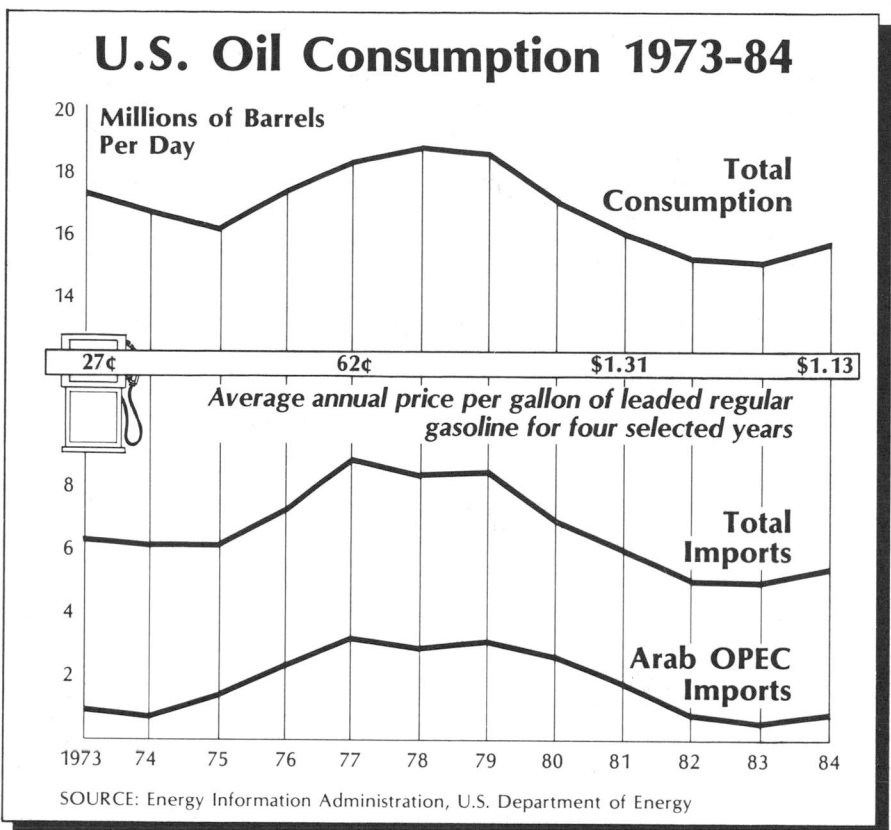

U.S. Oil Consumption 1973-84

Millions of Barrels Per Day

Total Consumption

27¢ 62¢ $1.31 $1.13

Average annual price per gallon of leaded regular gasoline for four selected years

Total Imports

Arab OPEC Imports

1973 74 75 76 77 78 79 80 81 82 83 84

SOURCE: Energy Information Administration, U.S. Department of Energy

to replace imports from the politically unstable Persian Gulf region. Throughout the industrial world consumers adopted fuel-saving practices as higher energy costs increased incentives for conservation.

The resulting slump in world oil demand left a large glut of oil and international markets that put downward pressure on prices. A week before Christmas in 1982, oil ministers from the 13 OPEC nations met in Vienna, Austria, but adjourned in disarray, unable to reach agreement on production quotas for OPEC member countries. Two years later, with member nations unilaterally discounting their oil, OPEC cut its official price below $30 a barrel. Unable to agree on production cutbacks to defend its official price, the organization, for the time being at least, had lost its ability to control world energy markets.

While European nations and Japan still relied heavily on Middle East oil, the United States began buying most of its imported oil from Mexico and Venezuela. As total oil demand fell, the nation depended less on foreign crude suppliers. U.S. oil imports had peaked at 47 percent of national consumption in 1977, but by 1983 the nation imported only 28 percent of its needs.

Falling world energy demand badly hurt Third World nations, notably Mexico, that had counted on rising oil revenues to pay off heavy debts to international banks. In the United States petroleum industry profits plunged, and exploratory drilling for new reserves fell off with the drop in oil prices. Carter's 1979 decontrol decision helped spark a drilling boom in 1980-81 as major oil companies and independent "wildcat" drillers stepped up their search for domestic oil and natural gas that could be sold at world price levels. But many independent firms, drilling rig suppliers and other oilfield firms went bankrupt in the follow-

ing years after borrowing heavily in anticipation of rising prices.

Even major international oil companies went through a period of consolidation. In a series of mergers, giant energy companies eager to expand their dwindling oil reserves acquired other major oil companies. Members of Congress expressed alarm that the mergers increased industry concentration and consumed financial resources that otherwise could be spent to discover new petroleum resources. But the administration refused to intervene, and Congress sidetracked proposals for a temporary moratorium on major oil company mergers.

Natural Gas Prices

Reagan's decision to lift all oil price controls encouraged natural gas producers to expect that the administration would follow up by asking Congress to speed deregulation of natural gas as well. But although Reagan's Cabinet in 1981 recommended prompt deregulation, congressional protests over rising prices allowed by the Natural Gas Policy Act of 1978 foreclosed chances for ending federal ceilings on natural gas prices ahead of schedule.

Like oil, gas was in surplus. But while oil prices fell, natural gas prices rose as the 1978 law gradually raised federal price ceilings. Natural gas warmed about 55 million households and supplied 25 percent of U.S. energy needs, including those of important industries. Business and consumer groups howled as higher cost gas flowed through interstate pipelines, sending gas bills soaring through most of the nation.

Members of Congress, responding to those complaints, introduced dozens of bills for dealing with the problem.

Some members suggested the solution to rising prices was the reimposition of price controls, which were being removed gradually according to the schedule established by the Natural Gas Policy Act of 1978. The Reagan administration, on the other hand, attributed the problems to the controls themselves.

Neither the 97th nor the 98th Congress could resolve the difficult technical and economic questions posed by natural gas deregulation. A natural gas bill did reach the Senate floor late in the 1983 session, but members soundly rejected competing proposals to phase out all remaining federal price controls on natural gas or, alternatively, to retain existing controls and roll back prices to August 1982 levels. The House in 1984 scrapped Energy and Commerce Committee legislation that attempted to iron out problems in natural gas markets but threatened a bitter regional fight on the floor that would divide both Democrats and Republicans.

Congressional inaction allowed price controls to expire on roughly half of all U.S. gas supplies on Jan. 1, 1985, as Congress had scheduled in the 1978 law. Despite warnings that continued deregulation would produce a sudden price "fly-up," gas prices seemed to level off during the first months of 1985.

Nuclear Industry Troubles

Reagan gave the nuclear industry a boost in 1981 with a policy statement that overturned his predecessor's ban on the reprocessing of burned nuclear fuel into more fuel, waste and plutonium. He also promised to cut government red tape and increased the nuclear energy budget while cutting all other energy programs.

But Reagan's support was insufficient to rescue the industry from its troubles. Still on the defensive after the 1979 Three Mile Island nuclear reactor accident in Pennsylvania, nuclear power companies lost public confidence in the ability of nuclear reactors to generate electric power without risking public health and safety.

The congressional decision to cancel the Clinch River breeder project symbolized the nation's growing disillusionment with nuclear technologies that once had promised nearly limitless supplies of electric power. Environmental group challenges, financial woes and growing anti-nuclear political sentiment combined to make the industry's prospects for future expansion doubtful.

With electricity demand lagging below projections made a decade earlier, U.S. electric utilities had placed no new reactor orders for seven years. While some new plants were brought on line, utilities canceled or delayed construction of other planned units that had been plagued by faulty designs, construction problems, legal challenges, labor disputes or rising interest rates that made them too costly to finish.

In the Pacific Northwest souring prospects for nuclear power were magnified by the largest municipal bond default in U.S. history. The Washington Public Power Supply System (WPPSS), nicknamed "Whoops" by its critics, in 1983 defaulted on $2.25 billion in bonds it had issued to build two canceled nuclear plants.

Congress took some steps to deal with the industry's problems. In 1982 it authorized the Nuclear Regulatory Commission (NRC) to issue temporary licenses to permit utilities to start operating newly built reactors before full-scale NRC hearings had been completed. NRC never used that authority, however, and Congress refused to renew it.

Also in 1982, after four years of bickering, Congress completed work on a plan to provide both temporary and permanent repositories, operated by the federal government, to dispose of spent nuclear fuel that had been piling up at civilian power plants throughout the country. But the disposal of highly radioactive nuclear waste remained an inflammatory political issue, and congressional delegations and local residents quickly protested at the end of 1984 when Energy Department officials identified three regions they were considering for a permanent disposal facility.

Conservation Program Cutbacks

Following up on his campaign pledge, Reagan asked Congress to abolish the Energy Department and turn most of its programs over to the Department of Commerce. But influential Republican senators resisted the plan, and Congress took no action.

Through budget reductions, however, the administration significantly shifted DOE's focus. During Carter's term Congress substantially bolstered federal funding for DOE conservation programs and for research on solar energy and other renewable energy technologies that promised to curb the nation's appetite for fossil fuels.

But the Reagan administration contended that rising energy prices should offer sufficient incentives for business and individuals to invest in conservation and renewable energy technologies. The administration curtailed funding for conservation efforts, trying to eliminate some federal assistance programs that were popular in Congress. The administration drastically cut funds for solar research, arguing that it was time to turn the task of demonstrating commercial solar equipment to private industry. It also curtailed DOE research on fossil fuel technologies to develop cleaner, more efficient ways to burn coal and petroleum.

Congress restored some of Reagan's cuts, but funding fell well below the levels during Carter's administration. Congressional critics complained that by shifting limited funds toward nuclear programs, the administration was cutting short conservation and alternative energy programs that could yield long-term benefits by reducing demand for imported oil.

Before Reagan took office, "we had a very balanced energy budget — spending was spread reasonably among all energy technologies," Rep. Richard L. Ottinger, D-N.Y., chairman of the House Subcommittee on Energy Conservation and Power, argued during 1984 debate on DOE's conservation budget. But during Reagan's term "this balance was destroyed," Ottinger claimed. "Since 1981 solar energy programs have been cut by 70 percent. Conservation programs have been cut by 50 percent. Fossil energy was cut by over 80 percent. Meanwhile, nuclear fission (including waste) and nuclear fusion have remained about the same."

"The net result," he maintained, was a "shift toward an all-nuclear budget."

Preparing for Future Shortages

Congress offered only token protests when Reagan in 1981 ended federal oil price controls, along with the mechanism for allocating petroleum products that the government used during the 1970s' shortages. But the administration and Congress differed over whether the government should keep presidential authority to control oil markets in place, ready for use in future emergencies.

Reagan's Energy Secretaries: Edwards, Hodel

Two men served as secretary of the Department of Energy (DOE) during President Reagan's first term. With the administration curtailing federal government regulation of energy markets, neither secretary took a prominent role in dealing with U.S. energy concerns.

Reagan's first energy secretary, former South Carolina Gov. James B. Edwards, frequently spoke about abolishing the department he headed in 1981-82. His successor, former Under Secretary of the Interior Donald P. Hodel, proved an effective manager for the department but followed the administration's policy of de-emphasizing most DOE functions except for those promoting nuclear power.

Before replacing Edwards Nov. 5, 1982, Hodel served as chief deputy to Interior Secretary James G. Watt (1981-83), who dominated the administration's natural resource policies as chairman of the Cabinet Council on Natural Resources and Environment.

Reagan in January 1985 nominated Hodel to replace William P. Clark, Watt's successor, as interior secretary. Reagan nominated John S. Herrington, assistant to the president for personnel, to replace Hodel as energy secretary.

Congress had created the Department of Energy in 1977 at President Carter's request. Carter's secretaries of energy, James R. Schlesinger and Charles W. Duncan Jr., had played leading roles in government attempts to counter rising energy prices and develop long-term supplies of fuel.

James B. Edwards

Reagan defeated Carter in the 1980 presidential election after campaigning on a pledge to reduce government interference in energy markets and abolish the separate Energy Department.

In selecting Edwards, an oral surgeon, as his first energy secretary, Reagan found someone who shared his basic philosophy: Get government out of the way so private industry could produce more energy.

Shortly before Reagan appointed him to the DOE post, Edwards had declared that "I'd like to go to Washington and close the Energy Department and work myself out of a job."

Edwards had little experience in dealing with energy issues. But as South Carolina governor, he had been an unabashed advocate of developing nuclear power. Environmental groups were dismayed by Edwards' strong backing for commercial reprocessing of spent nuclear fuel into fresh fuel, plutonium and liquid wastes.

The Senate confirmed Edwards' appointment by a 93-3 vote on Jan. 22, 1981.

As energy secretary, Edwards continued to back nuclear research and development as offering the best long-term solution to U.S. energy needs. On most energy matters, however, Edwards kept a low profile as Watt took the lead in pushing more rapid development of domestic fuels, especially coal, oil and natural gas from federally owned lands and Outer Continental Shelf waters that were leased by the Interior Department.

During Edwards' tenure the administration drew up plans to dismantle DOE and transfer most government energy programs to the Commerce Department. But Congress took no action on the reorganization plan. Edwards, who had made it clear he would leave the government before the expiration of Reagan's first term, resigned Nov. 5, 1982, to become president of the Medical University of South Carolina. *(DOE reorganization, p. 397)*

Donald P. Hodel

In selecting Hodel to replace Edwards, the administration ignored environmental group critics of his close ties to Watt and his record of supporting nuclear power.

Before being named interior under secretary, Hodel was administrator from 1972 to 1977 of the Bonneville Power Administration (BPA), a federally owned agency that marketed hydroelectric power from 30 federal dams to states in the Pacific Northwest. During Hodel's tenure, BPA joined many U.S. utility companies in predicting that demand for power would far outstrip supply by the early 1980s. The agency stopped selling cheap federal power to investor-owned utilities in 1973, and put public utilities on notice in 1976 that it would not be able to meet their additional power demands after July 1983.

That warning, according to critics, led to an explosion of high-cost power plant construction. The Washington Public Power Supply Service (WPPSS) — nicknamed "Whoops" by critics — embarked on an ambitious program to build five new plants. Two nuclear plants were later canceled, leading to the default of $2.25 billion in WPPSS bonds in July 1983.

The Senate confirmed Hodel as energy secretary by an 86-8 vote on Dec. 8, 1982.

Hodel improved DOE employee morale by playing down talk of abolishing the department. He also won praise from some members of Congress, even Democrats who opposed his policies.

After Hodel was nominated to be interior secretary in 1985, House Energy Committee Chairman John D. Dingell, D-Mich., said that he and Hodel "enjoyed a pretty good relationship." House Interior Committee Chairman Morris K. Udall, D-Ariz., criticized the Hodel and Herrington appointments in 1985 but said that he had worked effectively with Hodel on 1982 nuclear waste legislation.

Energy Policy

Administration officials and many congressional Republicans maintained that oil price and allocation programs during the 1970s had exacerbated, if not actually created, the shortages the nation endured. While defending the price and allocation controls as a necessary if unsatisfactory response to critical problems, congressional Democrats acknowledged that the previous decade's battles over routine federal regulation of the day-to-day marketplace in petroleum and natural gas had been settled in favor of deregulation. But many members, including conservative Republican senators, contended that public clamor in the event of another oil shortage would force Congress and the government again to step in to regulate petroleum markets.

Senate Energy and Natural Resources Committee Chairman James A. McClure, R-Idaho, for one, tried unsuccessfully to persuade the White House to accept some standby emergency planning that would head off more intrusive congressional action after a shortage had developed. But the Senate in 1982 unexpectedly upheld the president's veto of legislation granting him standby authority to control oil markets. Congress thereafter gave up efforts to force the administration to draft plans for dealing with energy emergencies. But it continued to prod the administration to fill the Strategic Petroleum Reserve (SPR), created in 1976 as a backup national oil supply during market shortages, more rapidly than White House budget makers wanted.

Long-Term Energy Worries

Although the U.S. energy situation undeniably brightened in 1983-84, skeptics still warned that the nation remained vulnerable to future oil supply disruptions. Critics of Reagan administration policies maintained that most cutbacks in national energy consumption were produced by declining industrial activity, not by true conservation. That conclusion suggested that the U.S. economy would have a hard time recovering from the oil shocks of the 1970s, since industries that had depended on cheap oil probably would never revive. Even if the economy rebounded, growing energy demand would quickly make the nation dependent on foreign oil, restoring OPEC's stranglehold on the U.S. economic future.

Although the United States had curtailed its reliance on imports in the early 1980s, experts warned that several factors kept the nation's energy security in doubt:

● Oil prices were set in the international marketplace, over which the United States had little direct control. Excess capacity in the Western world helped keep OPEC from raising prices, but there was not a lot of breathing space. Some major reserves, such as Great Britain's North Sea and Alaska's Prudhoe Bay fields, would soon begin to decline. World demand was growing, particularly in communist and developing countries. If things reached the point where the rest of the world was producing petroleum at capacity without meeting demand, the Middle East again would control the price of oil.

● The long-term outlook was not good. The Middle East had 55 percent of the world's proven oil reserves, the United States only 4 percent.

● The federal Strategic Petroleum Reserve held 434 million barrels of oil in early 1985, enough to make up for the loss of all imports for 90 days at existing rates of consumption. But the practical value of the SPR was unknown. Its existence may have helped forestall panic buying in 1984, during the Iran-Iraq war, but the United States had no concrete plan for how or when to use it. Debates continued over whether to tap the reserves in the event of a shortage to keep prices from rising, or to save them for a clearly major catastrophe.

● While the United States had shifted its import patterns, its allies remained heavily dependent on Persian Gulf oil. Japan imported 60 percent of its supplies from the gulf, Western Europe 20 to 40 percent. In the event of a shortage, would the United States use its reserves to bail out these countries, possibly subjecting U.S. consumers to gas lines and price rises, or would it stand by while other nations bid up the price?

● U.S. consumption of petroleum had begun to rise again, and production, which had remained essentially flat in recent years, had not met that new demand. Production was still 8 percent below the peak year 1970.

A 1984 report by the congressional Office of Technology Assessment concluded that the nation was in far better shape than in 1973, but "a large and enduring shortfall and oil price increase would have severe economic consequences on the United States, even with full drawdown of the Strategic Petroleum Reserve and available private stocks."

Chronology
Of Action
On Mineral Leasing

1981-82

Congress in 1981-82 resisted Reagan administration plans to expand energy production from federal lands and offshore waters.

Secretary of the Interior James G. Watt took office in 1981 determined to step up Interior Department efforts to lease federally owned coal, oil and gas, and other minerals for development by private industry. But in a series of politically charged confrontations, the 97th Congress whittled back Watt's ambitious leasing plans by declaring federal wilderness areas and some pristine coastal waters off limits to oil and gas exploration.

Watt proposed no changes in the basic federal laws that authorized the Interior Department to lease minerals beneath public lands and the federally controlled Outer Continental Shelf (OCS) for drilling and mining by private companies. As a result, Congress shaped the administration's energy leasing plans only by reacting against Watt's policies for managing federal lands and resources. As Watt's intentions became clear, Congress acted to overrule Interior plans to let oil and gas companies explore untouched public lands for new petroleum deposits.

In 1981 and again in 1982 Congress ruled out oil and gas leasing in federal wilderness areas, thwarting Watt's efforts to encourage exploration in those lands before a 1984 deadline that Congress had set 20 years earlier. In both years Congress also prohibited Interior from leasing rights to explore off the central and northern California coasts for federally owned oil and gas resources.

Under vigorous lobbying by environmental groups, members concluded that Watt's leasing plans risked damage to wildlife and pristine ecosystems in federal wilderness and ocean basins. They also heeded charges by conservation professionals and economists that Interior would be selling valuable public resources at bargain prices by leasing them while world energy demand was depressed.

By the end of 1982 members also were growing concerned about Watt's plans for leasing huge quantities of federally owned coal while energy demand was lagging.

Even as it questioned Watt's leasing goals, Congress in 1982 approved the administration's request to tighten management of federal oil and gas resources. To prevent outright oil theft and to improve collection of federal oil and gas royalties, Congress approved legislation that strengthened Interior Department procedures for enforcing lease terms and accounting for royalty payments.

Wilderness Leasing

Congress in 1981-82 blocked Interior Secretary James G. Watt from opening federal wilderness lands to oil and gas exploration.

The House Interior and Insular Affairs Committee in 1981 forced Watt to delay Interior Department decisions on leasing rights to explore wilderness areas within the U.S. national forests for oil and gas deposits. Congress followed up in 1982 by passing a fiscal 1983 Interior appropriations bill that barred leasing in those primitive federal lands through Sept. 30, 1983.

Three months later, on Jan. 1, 1984, a provision in the Wilderness Act of 1964 permanently closed federal lands within the national wilderness system to further mineral leasing. Congress meanwhile resisted Watt's demand that it act quickly to release for development additional national forest lands that were being considered as possible wilderness areas.

In creating the federal wilderness system in 1964, Congress kept wilderness areas within national forests — but not national parks — open to mineral leasing for 20 years. After the Reagan administration took office in 1981, Watt began prodding U.S. Bureau of Land Management (BLM) officials to grant pending oil company requests for rights to explore wilderness regions lying above promising formations. But Congress, led by the House Interior and Appropriations committees, took legislative steps that stalled BLM approval of those leases as the Jan. 1, 1984, deadline for leasing approached.

In addition to designated wilderness preserves, Congress forbade leasing in lands that the U.S. Forest Service had recommended for protection or for further study of their wild character. Suspicious of Watt's motives, members and their environmental group allies ignored the secretary's 1982 offer to bar mining and drilling in wilderness areas until the year 2000 while the government surveyed them for valuable mineral deposits.

By heading off Watt's wilderness leasing plans, the 97th Congress heeded environmentalist leaders and sportsmen's groups who were fighting the Reagan administration's plans to accelerate petroleum, coal and other resource development on federal forests and rangelands in Western states. In the Democratic House, opposition to Watt's pro-development policies was led by Interior Committee Chairman Morris K. Udall, D-Ariz.; John F. Seiberling, D-Ohio, chairman of the Interior Subcommittee on Public Lands and National Parks; and Sidney R. Yates, D-Ill., chairman of the Appropriations Subcommittee on Interior.

The outcome frustrated oil company officials and Western businessmen who contended that the government should permit the industry to study promising public lands — especially hot prospects near recent Rocky Mountain Overthrust Belt discoveries — before "locking them up" in protected wilderness areas off limits to drilling rigs and seismic exploration. Starting in the late 1970s "wildcat" drilling in Wyoming and Utah discovered huge natural gas reserves along the Overthrust Belt, a geologic formation that followed the Rocky Mountain chain. The discoveries whetted industry interest in leasing rights to explore national forests and range lands, including some wild lands that lay above or close to promising formations.

As the controversy mounted, however, even Western Republicans who backed Watt's philosophy turned against wilderness leasing plans. Manuel Lujan Jr., N.M., the Interior Committee's top-ranking Republican, supported efforts to ban wilderness leasing after Interior in September 1981 granted three leases allowing exploratory drilling beneath the Capitan Wilderness in New Mexico. Senate Energy and Natural Resources Committee Chairman James

Mineral Leasing

A. McClure, R-Idaho, who also chaired the Senate Appropriations Subcommittee on Interior, bottled up initial House anti-leasing bills but eventually accepted the 1982 appropriations bill rider.

Watt bowed to congressional sentiment after the fiscal 1983 prohibition was approved. On the day President Reagan signed the bill, Watt promised that the department would not "try to slip things through" by granting leases in wilderness areas during the 90 days between Sept. 30, 1983, when the fiscal 1983 ban expired, and Jan. 1, 1984, when the permanent prohibition that Congress scheduled in 1964 went into effect. As events turned out, Watt resigned the Interior post on Oct. 9, 1983. *(Watt and Congress, box, p. 406)*

Background

In the Mineral Leasing Act of 1920, Congress gave the interior secretary the authority to lease at his discretion the rights to find and produce oil and gas beneath federally owned public lands. That authority applied to all public domain lands, largely in Western states, that were managed by the Interior Department and by the U.S. Forest Service as part of the national forests. But through legislative and administrative actions, the government in subsequent years restricted oil and gas exploration on millions of acres to protect scenic views, natural ecosystems, archeological sites and other non-consumptive values.

In creating most national parks from the public lands, Congress prohibited mineral leasing within their boundaries. Interior and Forest Service officials barred exploration on other lands through administrative "withdrawals" from availability under leasing programs. Starting in the 1920s, Forest Service officials designated large roadless regions within the national forests for protection in their wild state.

1964 Wilderness Act. In the 1964 wilderness law, Congress gave those still-wild lands protection by statute. Since the mid-1950s conservation groups had been pressing the House and Senate to sanction the wilderness system by law, which would be more difficult to revoke than administrative decisions by Forest Service officials. Timber companies, mining firms, ranchers and other commercial interests in Western states with large expanses of national forest objected that a permanent wilderness system would deny access to commercial resources that might be needed in the future. *(Background, Congress and the Nation Vol. I, p. 1061)*

The Wilderness Act declared that the government should preserve its wild lands as "an area where the earth and its community of life are untrammeled by man, where man himself is a visitor who does not remain." To keep wilderness that way, the law prohibited logging, commercial ventures, construction of roads or buildings, and use of motor transportation within wilderness boundaries.

But at the insistence of Rep. Wayne N. Aspinall, D-Colo. (1949-73), then-House Interior Committee chairman, Congress accepted compromise provisions that protected some commercial interests in wilderness areas. The law permitted ranchers to continue grazing livestock on wilderness forests, and it honored previously filed mining claims on those lands. For 20 years, until midnight Dec. 31, 1983, the law allowed prospectors to stake mining claims to hardrock minerals in wilderness areas under the Mining Law of 1872. For the same 20-year period, the law also continued the interior secretary's authority to lease coal, oil and gas,

and other resources beneath those lands under the Mineral Leasing Act of 1920.

Congress initially set aside 9.1 million acres in wilderness areas established by the 1964 law. By 1983 it had expanded the national forest wilderness system to 25 million acres through subsequent legislation. Congress also created 35 million acres of wilderness in national parks, where mining and leasing were prohibited, and another 19 million acres in national wildlife refuges. In the early 1980s Congress was reviewing, through state-by-state bills, Forest Service proposals drawn up during the Carter administration to expand the national forest wilderness system to 33 million acres. Meanwhile, BLM was studying 24 million acres that it had identified on Interior Department lands for possible wilderness status. *(Wilderness legislation, p. 470)*

While wilderness remained technically open for leasing, the government in practice permitted little actual activity in those areas. Concentrating their drilling programs in areas with proven potential, oil and gas companies indicated little interest in exploring rugged mountain wilderness terrain where drilling would be costly. In managing its wilderness, the Forest Service also discouraged mineral development by severely restricting activity that might alter natural landscapes.

BLM, an Interior agency, issued oil and gas leases on national forests as well as its own lands. But the bureau in practice required exploration crews to obtain Forest Service consent to operate on forest lands. Between 1964 and 1982 the government granted only 50 oil and gas leases on existing Forest Service wilderness or candidate wilderness areas.

New Leasing Demands. Starting in the late 1970s deep wildcat wells discovered huge new petroleum fields, chiefly producing natural gas, along the Rocky Mountain Overthrust Belt formation in Wyoming, Utah and Idaho. Oil and gas companies eagerly sought leases to explore national forests and Interior lands that made up most of the region, including several designated wilderness areas, proposed additions, candidate wilderness study areas and lands surrounding national parks. Company officials contended that advances in seismic exploration technology, using helicopters and lightweight equipment to monitor underground formations, made it practical to study rugged mountains and forests with no permanent environmental damage. Slant drilling techniques also made it possible to extract oil or gas from beneath a wilderness area with wells drilled from outside its boundaries.

During the same period, both the Forest Service and BLM were studying millions of acres for possible wilderness protection. After identifying roadless areas for possible designation, the agencies restricted access until Congress decided whether or not to include them in the wilderness system. Some regions that the agencies proposed for preservation or for further study lay over promising formations near recent Overthrust Belt discoveries. In Wyoming alone, a 1981 General Accounting Office (GAO) study for Congress estimated that 483,000 acres of BLM wilderness study areas and 1.3 million acres of recommended national forest wilderness had oil and gas potential.

As of early 1982 BLM had granted about 5,000 oil and gas leases covering 26 percent of the 24 million acres it was studying for possible wilderness recommendation. The government had issued at least 337 leases on 19.5 million acres in national forests that were being reviewed by Congress or

Watt Contempt Citation: Showdown Avoided

The House Energy and Commerce Committee in 1982 dropped a request that Congress hold Secretary of the Interior James G. Watt in contempt.

In a 23-19 party-line vote, the panel Feb. 25 recommended a contempt citation against Watt for refusing to turn over Cabinet documents to subcommittee investigators. But President Reagan settled the dispute in March by sending a batch of closely held presidential papers to the Capitol so committee members could read them.

The panel's Subcommittee on Oversight and Investigations in 1981 had subpoenaed Interior Department documents that dealt with the leasing of minerals from federally owned lands to Canadian companies. The subcommittee was investigating charges that some Canadian firms were using unfair advantages conferred by that nation's laws in efforts to acquire U.S. energy firms, including St. Joe Minerals Corp. and Cities Service Co.

Federal law prohibited the Interior Department from leasing federal mineral rights to firms based in countries that denied similar rights to U.S. companies. In February 1982 Watt decided that Canada was entitled to such reciprocal status, which permitted Canadian firms to produce minerals that they leased on federally owned lands in the United States.

The subcommittee issued its subpoena for the documents in September 1981 after Watt refused to provide them. Claiming executive privilege for the first time, Reagan in October refused to let Watt comply. The documents in question included material prepared for Cabinet sessions and State Department cables from Canada.

The Energy and Commerce Committee voted to cite Watt for contempt in February 1982 after negotiations between Chairman John D. Dingell, D-Mich., and White House counsel Fred F. Fielding failed to produce agreement on the papers. If the full House had approved the contempt resolution, Watt could have faced trial and, if convicted, imprisonment for up to a year.

To avoid the confrontation with Watt, Dingell proposed that committee members and staff be allowed to review the papers in question for eight hours. The White House offered a compromise, which was accepted: four hours' review, for members only.

Six of the Oversight Subcommittee's 17 members, four Democrats and two Republicans, showed up to read the papers March 18. Some, including Dingell, took detailed notes; they were not allowed to make photocopies. A White House aide and a Capitol policeman made sure no one else read the papers. Dingell aides said the arrangement sustained the right of Congress to see presidential documents.

The House had never voted a Cabinet officer in contempt, although in December 1982 it voted a contempt citation against Anne M. Gorsuch, administrator of the Environmental Protection Agency. Gorsuch was cited for refusing to comply, on Reagan's orders, with a House subpoena for documents on enforcement of a 1980 law on cleanup of hazardous wastes. *(Gorsuch contempt citation, p. 449)*

Watt resigned under fire in 1983. *(Story, p. 406)*

---

studied by the Forest Service for preservation. A backlog of 891 lease applications was pending on Forest Service wilderness and wilderness candidate areas, with another 745 applications pending for leases on Forest Service wilderness study areas.

After taking charge of the Interior Department in 1981, Watt backed the industry's demand for a chance to explore both designated and potential wilderness areas to assess their oil and gas potential before the Wilderness Act barred leasing. "If we are to put much of this area off limits to exploration and potential development, it should be done so consciously and with full recognition of the values to be forgone," Watt maintained in a 1982 letter to Sen. Malcolm Wallop, R-Wyo., chairman of the Senate Energy and Natural Resources Subcommittee on Public Lands and Reserved Water.

But environmentalists contested industry assessments of wilderness areas' oil and gas potential. A 1982 Wilderness Society study, updated in 1983, calculated that wilderness regions might hold 3.9 percent of the nation's undiscovered oil reserves and 3.4 percent of its undiscovered gas, not counting offshore petroleum deposits. Conservation groups contended that oil companies should first explore less fragile lands, keeping wilderness areas as a last resort for development only in event of a severe energy emergency. "What we're talking about are supplies that can be measured in a few days of national petroleum consumption," Brant Calkin, the Sierra Club's Southwest representative, argued in 1981. "That's not adequate promise to put in roads [into wilderness areas] that are going to last a lot longer than the oil will."

1981 Interior Committee Stance

Twice in 1981 the House Interior Committee challenged Watt's leasing plans in response to industry plans for exploratory activity in Montana and New Mexico wildernesses. Watt complied with the committee's stand reluctantly, agreeing to shelve wilderness leasing actions until mid-1982.

Montana Wilderness Test. In the first test of congressional opposition to wilderness leasing, the Interior panel May 21 voted 23-18 to order Watt to close three national forest wilderness areas, located south of Glacier National Park in Montana, to oil and gas leasing.

Invoking a little-used provision of a 1976 public land

law, the committee directed the secretary to withdraw the land from leasing to head off Forest Service approval of seismic testing in important grizzly bear habitat. Watt complied a month later, but the Justice Department subsequently refused to defend the committee's action against legal challenges.

In its May 21 vote, the panel approved a resolution offered by Pat Williams, D-Mont., ordering Watt to withdraw the entire 1.5 million acres of the Bob Marshall, Scapegoat and Great Bear wilderness areas on Montana national forest lands.

The committee's resolution was based on a little-used provision of the Federal Land Policy and Management Act of 1976 (FLPMA, PL 94-579). The act allowed the secretary to order the immediate withdrawal of specific land if either the secretary or the House Interior or Senate Energy committees determined that an emergency existed requiring the land to be protected from development. At the time the 1976 law was being considered, the attorney general said the provision might be unconstitutional. *(FLPMA, Congress and the Nation Vol. IV, p. 314)*

The provision had been used by the committee once before, when it voted in 1979 to protect water wells in Ventura, Calif., from uranium mine tailings. In addition, Carter administration Interior Secretary Cecil D. Andrus used it Nov. 16, 1978, to withdraw 110 million acres of Alaskan land after the 95th Congress failed to pass legislation to protect them. *(Alaska withdrawals, Congress and the Nation Vol. V, p. 556)*

The Montana wilderness areas, which formed the headwaters of the Missouri and Columbia rivers, lay along the Overthrust Belt. When the committee acted, 343 lease applications from oil companies seeking to explore the region were pending before the Forest Service. The resolution's backers said they proposed that the committee intervene because they feared the Forest Service would grant a request by a Denver-based geophysical exploration firm that wanted permission to detonate 5,400 separate seismic charges in and around the wilderness to test the oil and gas potential of underlying rock formations.

The committee resolution left the three areas off-limits for leasing until the 1984 cutoff imposed by the 1964 Wilderness Act went into effect. Although Watt bowed to the panel's wishes, the Reagan administration joined in a court challenge to the resolution. Mountain States Legal Foundation, a conservative public interest law group that Watt had headed before taking the Interior post, filed a lawsuit contending that the FLPMA provision under which the committee acted was unconstitutional. In an Aug. 6 letter to House Speaker Thomas P. O'Neill Jr., D-Mass., Attorney General William French Smith announced that the Justice Department, instead of defending the land withdrawal, would side with the plaintiffs in the case. Smith contended that the FLPMA provision amounted to a one-house veto of the sort that the Justice Department consistently opposed as a congressional intrusion on executive branch powers. In a subsequent decision on a separate dispute, the U.S. Supreme Court ruled that one-house veto provisions were unconstitutional. *(Legislative veto, special report, p. 833)*

Six-Month Moratorium. In a second 1981 showdown the Interior panel voted 41-1 Nov. 20 to ask the administration to hold up action on any oil and gas leases in wilderness areas until June 1, 1982. Watt agreed to go along with the moratorium under pressure from committee Republicans.

The committee acted after Interior officials leased 700 acres in the Capitan Mountain Wilderness Area, in Lujan's state, without conducting environmental studies or notifying Congress. Lujan responded by introducing a resolution that would have prevented the department from issuing oil and gas leases on the 23.4 million acres of wilderness in the lower 48 states. After a Nov. 19 meeting with Lujan and Interior Committee Republicans Dick Cheney, Wyo., and Don Young, Alaska, Watt promised that the department would complete environmental studies and notify Congress and the public before granting wilderness leases. The next day, however, the panel requested the six-month moratorium to give Congress time to consider legislation to protect wilderness from leasing.

1982 Appropriations Rider

With congressional displeasure more evident, Watt agreed to hold off oil and gas leasing in all wilderness areas and proposed preserves until the 97th Congress adjourned at the end of 1982. That still left a one-year "window" for leasing until the permanent ban went into effect, however, and the entire Congress moved to close it in 1982.

As the controversy continued, Watt threw Congress and environmentalists off balance by proposing a plan that appeared to reverse his 1981 stance on wilderness. In a Feb. 21 network television interview, Watt suggested legislation to close wilderness areas to oil and gas leasing until the year 2000.

Environmental group leaders initially hailed Watt's announcement but attacked it after Interior officials leaked draft legislation.

Watt proposed closing wilderness areas while the government surveyed them and reported to Congress every five years on what minerals it was finding. After the year 2000 Congress could vote to open some areas to development if it determined such a step was needed.

Because the measure was silent on what would become of all wilderness acreage after the year 2000, it caused consternation among some in Congress and the environmental community who feared it would lift wilderness protections after that date. Another provision raising some hackles set deadlines for Congress to act on pending wilderness proposals or they would be "released" for non-wilderness uses such as logging.

The proposal gave Congress until Jan. 1, 1985, to act on 1979 recommendations for wilderness designation by the Carter administration as part of its wilderness review of roadless forest service areas (RARE II). If Congress failed to act, the areas would be released for other uses, such as logging and mining.

Such "release" language — favored by timber and mining interests — had been proposed for national forest wilderness areas by Sens. S. I. Hayakawa, R-Calif., and Jesse Helms, R-N.C., but their measure never emerged from the Senate Energy Committee.

Under Watt's plan, no drilling or mining would be allowed in the wilderness areas unless ordered by the president because of an urgent national need — such as an energy or strategic-mineral shortage. Congress would have 60 days in which to pass legislation blocking such presidential action, but that bill would have to be signed by the president.

Seiberling, the House Public Lands Subcommittee chairman, dismissed Watt's plan as "the most sweeping and devastating *anti*-wilderness bill I have ever seen."

Federal Oil and Gas Production 1980-84

Year	Offshore	Onshore	Indian	Total	Percent of U.S. Production
		OIL *(in barrels)*			
1980	277,388,975	149,699,287	21,991,788	449,080,050	14.3
1981	289,765,405	155,573,698	21,944,904	467,284,007	14.9
1982	321,211,457	149,612,769	19,809,921	490,634,147	15.6
1983	340,703,336	150,636,957	20,106,903	511,447,196	16.2
1984	370,239,014	152,339,422	21,801,347	544,379,783	17
		NATURAL GAS *(in thousand cubic feet)*			
1980	4,641,456,983	1,030,801,880	115,338,224	5,787,597,088	28.7
1981	4,849,536,728	1,083,063,410	119,482,985	6,052,083,123	30.3
1982	4,679,511,272	1,161,244,656	132,996,448	5,973,752,376	32.2
1983	3,939,826,470	986,555,606	117,720,541	5,044,102,617	30.6
1984	4,537,641,051	1,112,769,625	100,116,825	5,750,527,501	31.8

SOURCE: U.S. Minerals Management Service

Seiberling's subcommittee responded in June by drafting legislation to ban wilderness leasing that the full House approved overwhelmingly. But the Senate Energy panel bottled up the measure, forcing leasing opponents to make their case through the annual appropriations process.

Interior Committee Bill. The Public Lands Subcommittee bill, approved by the full Interior panel on a 34-7 vote June 24 (HR 6542 — H Rept 97-638), covered 33 million acres in the lower 48 states that were already designated as wilderness, recommended for protection by the Forest Service or under study for wilderness status. The bill excluded wilderness land in Alaska, where separate 1980 Alaska lands legislation had resolved the status of wilderness areas. *(Congress and the Nation Vol. V, p. 577)*

The measure allowed energy and mineral prospecting and inventories that were "compatible with the preservation of the wilderness environment," but it barred seismic surveys conducted with explosives. It gave the president authority to ask Congress to approve mineral development on a specific tract of withdrawn land in cases of "urgent national need." On a point of order raised by Seiberling, the committee fended off an amendment by Bill Hendon, R-N.C., to add language that would release proposed wilderness areas for development if Congress failed to act promptly to resolve their status. Seiberling contended that release language should be considered as part of comprehensive wilderness legislation, not a "narrowly drawn" measure dealing only with mineral leasing.

The House passed HR 6542 by a 340-58 vote Aug. 12, turning down amendments offered by Young to open wilderness study areas to leasing and permit surface blasting with explosives during seismic studies in wilderness areas. In urging the House to act, leasing opponents said Watt

had been completing paperwork on pending lease applications so the department could grant them quickly when the previous moratorium expired.

But McClure and other senators wanted to trade off an extended leasing ban for "release" language that would force Congress to resolve quickly the status of proposed additions to the wilderness system. The Senate panel bottled up the House-passed bill, along with a companion measure sponsored by Henry M. Jackson, D-Wash., the committee's second-ranking Democrat and former chairman.

Appropriations Riders. Fearful that the Interior legislation would be held up too long for action by the 97th Congress, backers of the leasing ban shifted tactics in September. Over the following months Congress amended legislation funding Interior operations to block the department from processing and granting wilderness lease applications.

Congress first wrote an amendment barring the department from spending money to process wilderness lease applications into a continuing resolution (H J Res 599 — PL 97-276) appropriating funds for government operations after fiscal 1983 began Oct. 1. Yates offered the amendment in the House Appropriations Committee, and McClure and Jackson cosponsored the amendment during Senate action on the resolution. McClure supported the processing freeze to reaffirm and clarify the existing leasing moratorium. Watt himself, in a letter to Senate Appropriations Committee Chairman Mark O. Hatfield, R-Ore., urged the panel to approve the freeze to relieve congressional doubts about whether he was observing the moratorium.

Congress subsequently extended the moratorium

through fiscal 1983 with an amendment to the regular Interior appropriations measure cleared in December. In reporting the bill (HR 7356 — H Rept 97-942) Dec. 2, the House Appropriations panel approved language that banned oil and gas leasing, and mineral surveys, in all designated wilderness areas, in all congressionally designated wilderness study areas and in all Forest Service RARE II areas recommended for wilderness designation or for further planning. The ban extended until Congress had made a final determination of the status of lands not already formally designated as wilderness.

The committee noted its prohibition did not extend to BLM lands under study for possible wilderness designation, but it said the Interior Department "should take whatever action is necessary to ensure the Congress' prerogative to designate BLM wilderness study areas as wilderness is not foreclosed by leasing or mineral survey activities."

The full House passed HR 7356 Dec. 3 without discussing the leasing ban. In considering the bill, the Senate Appropriations Committee turned down McClure's proposals to allow leasing in wilderness study areas, approve seismic testing in wilderness areas and declare by law that the environmental impact statements that the Forest Service drafted on its RARE II recommendations were sufficient, thus blocking further legal challenges by environmentalists who objected to the agency's decisions. Before passing the bill Dec. 14, the Senate approved a substitute amendment, offered by John Melcher, D-Mont., to a similar proposal by McClure, that contained the key points sought by leasing opponents. Melcher's proposal barred leasing in designated wilderness, areas recommended for wilderness and areas under study for wilderness. It also banned seismic studies using explosives.

The conference version (H Rept 97-978), cleared Dec. 19, included the Senate wilderness language. President Reagan signed the bill on Dec. 30 (PL 97-394).

Oil and Gas Royalties

Congress in 1982 tightened Interior Department procedures for collecting royalties on oil and gas produced from federal lands. Responding to charges of chronic mismanagement, lawmakers Dec. 21 cleared legislation (HR 5121 — PL 97-451) giving the secretary of the interior stronger authority to make sure that companies leasing the right to extract oil and gas from public lands paid the government all the royalties they owed.

In January a special commission appointed by Interior Secretary James G. Watt had charged that the federal government was losing $200 million to $500 million in revenues a year from underpaid royalties and outright theft of oil from wells on public lands. Watt had ordered the study after Western state governments and Indian tribes had complained that lax Interior Department enforcement was costing them millions of dollars in lost revenues from oil and gas production within their borders.

Watt responded by setting up a new Interior agency, the U.S. Minerals Management Service (MMS), to handle revenues from federal energy leasing programs. In PL 97-451 Congress followed up by approving the commission's recommendations for improving lease operator record-keeping, tightening well-site security and toughening Interior enforcement of the financial terms of federal oil and gas leases.

Background

In the Mineral Leasing Act of 1920, Congress set up a system for leasing oil and gas beneath federally owned lands for discovery and production by private companies. The law charged leaseholders annual rentals for access to public lands and required them to pay the federal government a royalty of 12.5 percent of the value of the oil and gas they extracted.

The 1920 law required competitive bidding for leases on lands known to hold oil and gas but allowed the Interior Department to grant leases without competition to companies that wanted to explore for unknown deposits. To win competitive leases companies offered the government a bonus payment through sealed bidding with competitors. Annual rentals, revised by amendments to the 1920 law over the years, by 1982 still were set at only $2 an acre for most non-competitive exploratory leases. Competitive leases ran for five years and non-competitive leases for 10 years, or as long as production continued.

But royalty payments produced the most revenue from federal energy leasing programs. In 1982 royalties on most federal land leases remained at 12.5 percent, although the department charged 16 2/3 percent royalties for leasing oil and gas reserves in the federally owned Outer Continental Shelf (OCS) and in the National Petroleum Reserve on Alaska's North Slope.

Federal leasing revenues surged in the 1970s with the rise in oil and gas prices. Before 1973 a 12.5 percent royalty brought the government around 25 cents per barrel of oil, but the federal share jumped to the neighborhood of $3 per barrel with decontrol of U.S. crude oil prices. In 1982 the government collected $874 million in royalties and other revenues from oil and gas leases on federal lands, along with another $146 million in oil and gas revenues from leases on Indian reservations, according to U.S. Minerals Management Service figures. In the same year the government took in $3.8 billion in royalties and rents from offshore oil and gas production. Oil and gas companies also paid nearly $4 billion in bonus bids for offshore leases that year and another $95.3 million in bonuses for competitive onshore leases.

With the growth in royalties, federal oil and gas leases became an important source of revenues for the U.S. Treasury. Indian tribes and state governments with oil-producing federal lands within their borders also reaped financial benefits. Interior passed along all mineral leasing revenues from Indian lands to tribal governments or individual Native American landowners. And under the Mineral Leasing Act the federal government shared half of its royalties from onshore mineral production with state governments. In a 1976 law revising Interior coal-leasing procedures, Congress increased the state share of all mineral leasing revenues to 50 percent from 37.5 percent. In Alaska, state and local governments received more than 75 percent of federal oil and gas royalties. *(1976 coal leasing amendments, Congress and the Nation Vol. IV, p. 275)*

Three Interior Department agencies shared authority over federal oil and gas leases. The Bureau of Land Management (BLM) issued both competitive and non-competitive leases to drill on public lands, including national forests, federal rangelands and offshore OCS waters. The U.S. Geological Survey's (USGS) Conservation Division made technical evaluations of petroleum resources that drilling discovered, supervised drilling rig operations and collected royalties. In addition, the U.S. Bureau of Indian Affairs

Federal Oil and Gas Revenues
1980-84

(Calendar years)

	1980	1981	1982	1983	1984
OFFSHORE					
Royalties, rents	$2,132,528,739	$3,287,279,402	$3,814,871,635	$3,375,688,165	$4,002,850,048
Bonus payments on new leases	4,204,640,257	6,602,665,712	3,987,490,009	5,749,016,369	4,037,050,308
ONSHORE					
Royalties, rents	$ 628,685,267	$ 879,514,201	$ 873,969,795	$ 871,277,978	$1,134,450,076
Bonus payments on new leases	22,048,947	103,314,389	95,304,216	31,150,106	50,068,801

SOURCE: U.S. Minerals Management Service

(BIA), as trustee of Indian tribal resources, issued leases for drilling on Indian reservations.

Mismanagement Charges. Those agencies supervised drilling and production from federal oil and gas leases that were scattered over vast expanses of public mountains and deserts. Despite longstanding complaints of thefts and underpaid royalties, Interior officials had never come up with procedures to keep track of how much oil and gas was being produced from federal leases and how much well operators owed in royalties. USGS collected royalties on an honor system without independently verifying the production that leaseholders reported to the government.

Since 1979, studies by Congress, state governments, tribal leaders, the General Accounting Office and the Interior Department itself had found federal lease supervision too lax to detect and prevent irregularities. Concern increased in the early 1980s after oil prices rose and Watt announced plans to expand oil and gas exploration on public lands.

In Wyoming, Watt's native state, Arapahoe and Shoshone tribal leaders on the Wind River Reservation urged Interior to cancel existing oil and gas leases after allegations of theft and underpaid royalties. California and 10 other states filed suit against the federal government to demand that Interior account for royalties back to 1920.

In response to those pressures, Watt in July 1981 appointed a Commission on Fiscal Accountability of the Nation's Energy Resources, chaired by David F. Linowes, a University of Illinois professor, to investigate such charges. In a scathing report issued Jan. 21, 1982, the commission charged that the federal government was losing $200 million to $500 million annually due to oil thefts and royalty underpayments by oil companies.

The commission found that accounting and collection procedures were outmoded, enforcement was weak, penalties were insufficient and security on well sites was lax.

The report said oil company royalties, which should reach $14 billion a year by 1990, were collected almost totally on the honor system.

"The government has no way of verifying independently how much oil and gas are taken from leases on federal and Indian lands," said Linowes. "Site security is deficient. Theft of oil common."

MMS Established. After the Linowes commission issued its report, Watt overhauled the Interior Department's royalty collection system. Under a department reorganization completed in 1983, Watt shifted the Conservation Division out of the scientifically oriented USGS to form a new agency, the Minerals Management Service. The new service continued to hold the Conservation Division's responsibility for collecting federal mineral royalties. It also took over the authority to lease offshore oil and gas reserves, a function previously performed by BLM. BLM retained authority to lease onshore minerals beneath public lands, and it also took on some of the former USGS division's responsibility to regulate drilling operations under federal leases.

In the process, Watt announced that the department would impose tighter internal controls on the leasing process and hire and train new field inspectors to supervise drilling and pumping. He also called for new legislation to tighten royalty collection and management procedures.

1982 Legislative Action

Congress responded by passing HR 5121 to implement procedures proposed by the commission. Before clearing the bill, however, the House and Senate three times sent it back and forth between the chambers in a dispute over House provisions giving the interior secretary power to boost onshore oil and gas royalties to 16 2/3 percent.

The House included that proposal when it passed HR 5121 by voice vote on Sept. 29. The House Interior Committee wrote the royalty raise provision, originated by Rep. George Miller, D-Calif., into the bill when it reported the measure Sept. 23 (H Rept 97-859).

But the Senate left the royalty provision out of a substitute version that House and Senate committee staff members drafted on orders from Senate Energy and Natural Resources Committee Chairman James A. McClure, R-

Idaho, and House Interior Chairman Morris K. Udall, D-Ariz. The Senate passed its version on Dec. 6 after accepting the compromise measure as a substitute for separate legislation (S 2305 — S Rept 97-512) drafted by McClure's committee in July.

The Senate Energy panel's bill had allowed the interior secretary to delegate to state governments the authority to collect oil and gas revenues due the federal government. The compromise dropped that provision, which was vigorously opposed by Sen. John Melcher, D-Mont. The compromise did allow the secretary to permit state and tribal governments to carry out audits, inspections and investigations on federal oil and gas leases to improve state or tribal severance tax collections — and possibly increase federal royalties as well.

Miller and House managers of the legislation balked at leaving out the royalty raise provision. But the House Dec. 21 gave in, dropping the provision and sending HR 5121 to the president.

Major Provisions. As signed into law Jan. 12, 1983, major provisions of HR 5121 (PL 97-451):

● Required thorough record-keeping and reporting by operators, leaseholders and holders of interests in leases.

● Required lease operators to set up and carry out site security plans to prevent theft.

● Required transporters of oil from leases to document where it came from and where it was going.

● Required royalty payments on lost or wasted oil and gas.

● Directed the interior secretary to conduct annual inspections of every lease site producing significant quantities of oil or gas.

● Required the federal government to pay proceeds from royalties promptly on a monthly schedule, and to provide a complete statement accounting for the payment, to states and Indian tribes owed such royalty payments.

● Set criminal penalties of up to $50,000 or two years' imprisonment or both for the most serious violation of the act.

● Set civil penalties for stealing oil and gas from federal leases, failing to pay royalties or refusing to comply with reporting and audit requirements.

● Authorized the secretary to delegate to states and Indian tribes the power to conduct inspections, audits and investigations at federal oil and gas leases.

Naval Petroleum Reserves

Congress in 1981 refused to overrule President Reagan's proposal to continue pumping oil from the federal government's naval petroleum reserves in California and Wyoming.

The House Armed Services Committee in December tried to block further production, contending that the government instead should save the naval oil reserves for military use during future emergencies. But neither the full House nor the Senate took action to reject Reagan's plan during the 90-day period allowed for congressional disapproval.

As a result, the government maintained maximum oil production that Congress authorized in 1976 from the naval petroleum reserves at Elk Hills, Calif., and Teapot Dome, Wyo.

The president told Congress Oct. 6 that maximum production from the reserves for another three years would serve the national interest. The Department of Energy (DOE) office that managed the reserves had recommended that Elk Hills be "shut in" to produce only a minimum level of oil required to sustain the field. But DOE officials acknowledged that the president decided to maintain all-out production to preserve the $2 billion a year in revenues that the U.S. Treasury received by selling oil from the reserves.

In addition, petroleum refiners in California, Reagan's home state, since 1976 had relied heavily on high-quality Elk Hills crude in operating their refineries.

Background

In the early 1900s, when U.S. petroleum consumption was starting to rise, President Theodore Roosevelt began withdrawing federal lands that might hold petroleum reserves to keep private parties from claiming them under homesteading and mining laws. President Taft, Roosevelt's successor, followed up in 1909 by withdrawing three million acres in California and Wyoming to keep those lands in federal ownership. The U.S. Navy at the time was converting from coal to fuel oil to power its ships, and a 1909 U.S. Geological Survey report warned the Interior Department that the Navy might soon be forced to buy back oil from public lands that were being claimed by private owners.

By 1924 the government had formally established four naval petroleum reserves and three oil shale reserves from some of those lands to conserve their oil for future use. Taft designated the Elk Hills reserve in 1912 on 46,000 acres in Kern County, Calif., and President Wilson established the Teapot Dome reserve in 1916 on 46,000 acres north of Casper, Wyo. The other naval reserves were at Buena Vista, Calif., adjacent to Elk Hills, and on the North Slope of Alaska.

In 1922, during the Harding administration, leases that Interior Secretary Albert B. Fall granted without competitive bidding for oil production from the Teapot Dome and Elk Hills reserves led to the Teapot Dome scandal. *(Background, Congress and the Nation Vol. I, p. 973; Congress and the Nation Vol. IV, p. 216)*

By the early 1970s the Teapot Dome and Buena Vista reserves had been largely depleted. But Elk Hills still contained more than one billion barrels, while the Alaskan reserve holding an estimated 10 to 30 billion barrels remained undeveloped. President Nixon in late 1973 asked Congress to authorize production of 160,000 barrels of oil a day from Elk Hills to assure sufficient supplies of military fuel, but Congress took no action.

In 1976 Congress approved President Ford's request to permit the Navy to sell oil from the California and Wyoming reserves for a six-year period. The legislation (PL 94-258) gave the president authority to extend maximum production for three years after notifying Congress. The law allowed either the House or the Senate to veto the extension by acting within a 90-day period. PL 94-258 also transferred the Alaska reserve from the Navy to the Interior Department. It gave Interior authority to explore the Alaska reserve but prohibited oil production. *(1976 law, Congress and the Nation Vol. IV, p. 274)*

Teapot Dome was producing only about 3,000 barrels of oil a day in 1981, but Elk Hills, in an emergency, could pump nearly 250,000 barrels daily. (The daily peacetime requirement of the Defense Department was about 450,000 barrels a day.)

Standard Oil Co. of California (Chevron) owned 20

percent of the Elk Hills reserve, although the Navy controlled production.

Elk Hills oil was a light crude that was exceptionally high in quality and low in sulfur content. About 100,000 barrels a day were being sold to California refiners, who mixed it with heavier, lower-quality oil in a blend that was piped to West Coast refineries. According to a staff report prepared for the House Energy and Commerce Committee, which studied the issue but did not act on it, "a number of California small refiners have become very dependent on Elk Hills crude oil over the past six years."

Part of the remaining oil went to Chevron, as its share, and part was sold to the Defense Department.

1981 Extension

Using authority granted by the 1976 law, Reagan Oct. 6 certified that continuing maximum production from the reserves would be in the national interest. But the House Armed Services Committee voted 19-13 on Dec. 9 to approve a resolution (H Res 287 — H Rept 97-392) to disapprove the president's decision.

Although the Armed Services Committee traditionally operated in a bipartisan manner, Democratic members voted 15-4 for the resolution of disapproval, while the Republicans opposed it 4-9.

One argument made by Armed Services for shutting in Elk Hills was that a West Coast supply of crude oil was needed in case of a national emergency. Although there were more than 200 million barrels of oil in the Strategic Petroleum Reserve on the U.S. Gulf Coast, that oil could get to the West Coast only by ship through the Panama Canal.

The full House never took up the disapproval resolution, and the Senate took no action.

Outer Continental Shelf

Congress in 1981-82 balked at Interior Secretary James G. Watt's plan to open virtually all federally controlled offshore waters for oil and gas exploration.

Three months after taking office, Watt in 1981 announced plans to accelerate the Carter administration's program for leasing oil and gas drilling rights on the federal Outer Continental Shelf (OCS). A year later, Watt approved a five-year OCS leasing schedule that aimed to offer more than one billion acres of the coastal sea floor by 1987 for exploration by oil and gas companies.

Watt made accelerated offshore oil and gas leasing the centerpiece of the Reagan administration's efforts to expand the nation's production of its own energy supplies. In the short run, "America's greatest hope for reducing our dependency on foreign sources [of oil] is the Outer Continental Shelf," the secretary told the Senate Energy and Natural Resources Subcommittee on Energy Conservation and Supply in Sept. 8, 1982, testimony.

The Interior Department had been leasing offshore oil and gas since 1954, but exploration and discoveries had been confined to the Gulf of Mexico and the Southern California coastlines. By speeding up lease sales and condensing environmental reviews, Watt maintained, the government could give the industry a chance to select and explore other promising regions, especially off the Alaska coast, to inventory their oil and gas potential.

In the process, the Reagan administration hoped that

the Interior Department would take in between $40 billion and $80 billion for the U.S. Treasury in 1982-87 from OCS leasing bonus bids, rents and oil and gas royalties.

But the 97th Congress stepped in with legislation that ruled out leasing in environmentally sensitive waters off the northern California and New Jersey coastlines. Environmental groups and coastal state governors meanwhile mounted legal and political challenges that forced the Interior Department to postpone planned lease sales in unexplored California and Alaska offshore basins.

With a 1969 offshore well blowout off the Santa Barbara, Calif., coast still much on members' minds, Congress responded to environmentalists' protests that accelerated leasing would raise the risk of destructive oil spills that would threaten pristine waters and important fishing grounds. Watt's critics also charged that the government would sacrifice potentially larger revenues by leasing offshore oil and gas reserves while world energy demand was depressed. *(1983-84 leasing bans, p. 357)*

Background

In 1953 Congress asserted federal government control over mineral development on about 1.1 billion acres of submerged sea floor three miles or more off the nation's coastlines. Settling rival state and federal claims, Congress in the Submerged Lands Act of 1953 (PL 83-31) recognized coastal state governments' authority to manage the sea bed and its resources within three miles of their coasts. In the Outer Continental Shelf Lands Act (PL 83-212) passed the same year, Congress established federal authority over the OCS beyond the three-mile limit and gave the interior secretary authority to lease its oil and gas resources for exploration and development by private companies.

In the following 25 years the Interior Department's Bureau of Land Management (BLM) offered 12 million acres, roughly 1 percent of the OCS, for oil and gas development. BLM actually sold leases for 5.3 million acres off the Texas and Louisiana coasts in the Gulf of Mexico and another 1.3 million acres along the Pacific Coast in Southern California. Between 1953 and 1983 industry produced 6.3 billion barrels of oil and 62.1 trillion cubic feet of natural gas from federal OCS leases. During that 30-year period the industry paid the federal government $47.1 billion in bonus bidding for leases and $20.7 billion in rents and royalties on oil and gas production at a rate of 16-2/3 percent. *(1953 laws, Congress and the Nation Vol. I, p. 1401; oil and gas revenues, box, p. 345)*

By the early 1980s federal OCS leases produced roughly 10 percent of U.S. domestic oil output and 25 percent of its natural gas. Geologists generally agreed that unexplored OCS regions held the nation's best prospects for discovering new oil and gas resources. Since world oil prices began climbing in the mid-1970s, the industry had been eager to explore promising offshore frontiers off the Pacific Coast of northern California, the Atlantic Coast of New England and the Mid-Atlantic states, and along Alaska's deeply indented bays and peninsulas. *(Map, p. 348)*

The Nixon and Ford administrations drew up plans in the 1970s for expanding OCS leasing into frontier regions. But since the 1969 oil well blowout in the Santa Barbara Channel blackened beaches north of Los Angeles, killing thousands of fish and waterfowl, opposition had been mounting to offshore drilling as too dangerous to the environment. And plans for leasing in frontier waters drew intense opposition from state governors, local officials, the

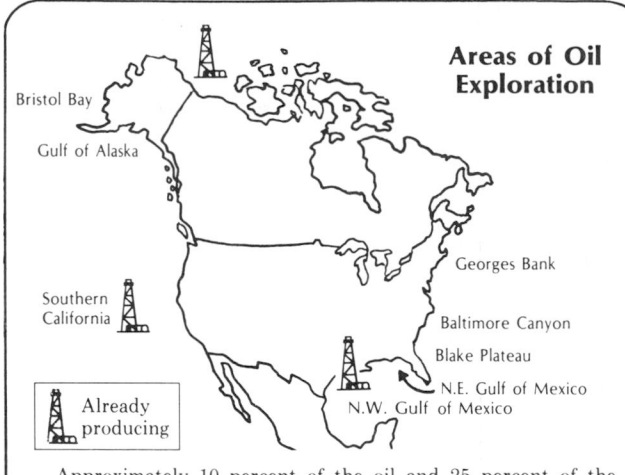

Areas of Oil Exploration

Bristol Bay

Gulf of Alaska

Southern California

Georges Bank

Baltimore Canyon

Blake Plateau

N.E. Gulf of Mexico

N.W. Gulf of Mexico

Already producing

Approximately 10 percent of the oil and 25 percent of the natural gas produced in the United States come from wells drilled beneath offshore waters.

fishing and tourist industries and environmental activists in coastal states who feared that scenic beaches and productive marine resources could be ruined.

Congress in 1978 revised the 1953 OCS law in an effort to meet environmental concerns while encouraging offshore petroleum development. In Outer Continental Shelf Lands Act Amendments (PL 95-372) enacted with President Carter's support, Congress tightened environmental controls on drilling operations, directed Interior to consider recommendations from state governors in scheduling lease sales, and specified procedures to foster competition among oil companies in bidding for OCS leases.

The law directed the interior secretary to draw up a five-year schedule for planned OCS lease sales, taking into account the relative environmental sensitivity and marine productivity of areas under consideration for exploration. In scheduling sales, the secretary also was directed to assure that the government received "fair market value" for its OCS resources. *(1978 OCS amendments, Congress and the Nation Vol. V, p. 485)*

Operating under the new standards, Cecil D. Andrus, Carter's secretary of the interior, in 1980 scheduled 36 OCS sales to offer about 27.5 million acres to the industry by 1985. The Andrus program envisioned an average of seven lease sales a year, double the leasing pace in the 1970s. It targeted the Gulf of Mexico as the primary leasing area but included 10 sales in Alaskan waters. It excluded four areas — the Florida Straits, the Washington and Oregon coasts, Alaska's Bristol Bay and southern Aleutian Shelf — that had once been considered for leasing.

The Andrus program encountered stiff resistance from state officials and environmental groups. Massachusetts filed suit against leasing in the Georges Bank fishing grounds off the North Atlantic coast, and Alaska urged Interior to delay three of the 10 planned sales near its shores. California Gov. Edmund G. Brown Jr., D, urged the department to exclude 33 tracts in the northern reaches of the Santa Maria Basin off his state from a proposed 1981 sale, arguing that oil spills could threaten migrating gray whales and the endangered California sea otter. A week before the 1980 presidential election, Andrus deleted four untouched offshore basins off northern California from the 1981 lease offering.

Watt Leasing Plan

After replacing Andrus, Watt determined that Interior should open as much OCS acreage as possible for exploration, giving industry a chance to assess the oil and gas potential of all remaining untapped offshore regions within 10 to 15 years.

In February 1981 Watt stunned California officials and angered the state's congressional delegation by announcing that he was reconsidering Andrus' decision the previous year to bar leasing in the four Pacific basins. Controversy over OCS leasing grew in the following two years as Interior put together a five-year plan that was much more ambitious than the Carter administration's schedule.

Watt outlined his goals in April 1981, announcing an accelerated program that scheduled 41 sales, an average of more than eight a year, over 1982-86. Watt also revised Interior leasing procedures to expedite environmental and economic reviews — and let the industry identify for leasing the offshore regions it considered most promising.

In the past Interior officials had put limited OCS areas up for bidding after studying their geologic and environmental characteristics. Before offering to lease drilling rights, the department estimated a fair bonus bid for each price as a standard for judging whether the bids oil companies made would pay the government fair market value.

Watt's program, put into final form in July 1982, essentially offered vast areas of the federal OCS for leasing to the oil and gas industry. After companies had selected promising regions where they wanted to drill through competitive bids, Interior officials would conduct site-specific environmental studies on the tracts that industry wanted. The department also determined the fair market value of OCS leases only after taking bids to gauge demand for tracts.

"The market will select lease tracts instead of the government," Watt said in defending the five-year program. "Fair market value will be set by competition, not solely on government economic models." Interior officials contended that the program would speed up the leasing process by eliminating extensive environmental and economic studies on tracts that drew no interest. Except for the Santa Barbara spill, Watt maintained, offshore drilling had been conducted with little environmental damage. Drilling rig operations were much less risky, administration spokesmen argued, than the threat of spills from tankers carrying imported oil to U.S. refineries. While the government would open virtually the entire OCS for bidding, they pointed out, whether the amount of acreage leased would actually rise above previous levels depended on market demand for offshore oil.

Critics' Challenges

State officials, environmental groups and some economists challenged Watt's reasoning. They argued that drilling posed unacceptable risks to fishing and marine life in pristine offshore waters. Friends of the Earth, an environmental organization, in 1981 called Watt's accelerated leasing program "overly ambitious" and worried that "environmental concerns will be downplayed or disregarded."

Watt's critics also challenged the proposed sales on economic grounds. With world oil demand lagging, they contended, the government was likely to receive bids far below long-term value if Watt insisted on leasing so much OCS acreage in five years. While Watt maintained that his

program would promote competition within the oil industry, critics said that intense bidding for OCS tracts was unlikely. In 13 previous sales, Interior received two or fewer bids on 58 percent of the tracts it leased, and only a single bid on 38 percent of the tracts, according to department figures.

Critics also charged that the industry had neither the interest, nor enough drilling rigs, to explore so much acreage in five years. Even some oil executives worried that Watt, by moving so fast, would stir political opposition and invite legal challenges that would stall leasing for years.

Throughout 1981-82, state and local governments in coastal states joined with environmental groups to press lawsuits to block specific OCS lease sales. In July 1981 U.S. District Court Judge Mariana Pfaelzer blocked Interior from accepting bids for 29 tracts in the northern reaches of the Santa Maria Basin off central California. California Gov. Brown had urged Watt to withhold the tracts from bidding to protect migrating whales and otters. By offering the tracts anyway, the judge ruled, Watt violated the federal Coastal Zone Management Act of 1972, a law that provided federal financial assistance to help states develop plans for controlling development along their coastlines. California contended that leasing the Santa Maria tracts would be inconsistent with the state's coastal management plan. *(Background, Congress and the Nation Vol. III, p. 799)*

In the following years legal challenges held up planned sales off Alaska and Massachusetts. After negotiations with Alaska Gov. Jay Hammond, R, and his successor Bill Sheffield, D, in 1981-82, Watt dropped plans to open two sensitive Alaskan basins. Watt also delayed controversial California lease sales while the government appealed the district judge's decision.

Exploratory drilling in the OCS off Alaska and the Atlantic coastline during the late 1970s and early 1980s produced no major discoveries. But oil industry executives and geologists remained convinced that federal offshore waters offered the best prospects for finding new domestic oil and gas reserves. During 1981-82 expanded OCS leasing paid off with successful drilling that suggested major reserves beneath the Santa Maria Basin, just 40 miles from the Santa Barbara well that blew in 1969 and south of the disputed tracts where Congress and California state officials held up leasing plans.

Congressional Response

From the start, Watt's plans for all-out OCS leasing drew heated opposition from Congress. Neither the House nor the Senate tried to thwart the entire five-year plan. But Congress blocked leasing in untouched California and New Jersey waters through funding cutoff amendments that the House Appropriations Committee wrote into Interior Department appropriations bills for fiscal 1982 and 1983.

The administration underestimated fears among environmentalists and coastal state residents that oil spills would damage pristine waters and beaches. Watt's announcement that he would consider leasing in the four California offshore basins that Andrus decided to keep off-limits turned into a political blunder. "I don't think any of us recognized the emotional fervor that surrounded that [leasing] issue," Stanley H. Hulett, Watt's director of congressional and legislative affairs, acknowledged in 1981.

Watt was personally convinced that the national inter-

Pauley Group Leases

An Arkansas senator's protests in 1981-82 thwarted oil companies' request that Congress restore potentially lucrative oil leases off the California coast that had expired in 1973.

The House Aug. 4, 1981, passed, without much debate, legislation (HR 1946 — H Rept 97-173) to reinstate two leases to drill for oil on the federally controlled Outer Continental Shelf in the Santa Barbara Channel northwest of Los Angeles. The U.S. Interior Department granted the leases in 1968 to the Pauley Group, a consortium of 11 independent oil companies led by Pauley Petroleum Inc. But the five-year leases ran out while the companies were engaged in a legal dispute over liability standards that Interior imposed after a 1969 oil spill from a nearby well blackened Santa Barbara beaches.

Two years after the Pauley leases expired, Standard Oil Co. of California (Chevron) discovered oil on an adjacent Santa Barbara Channel tract, making the two leases potentially much more valuable. By 1981 Standard Oil Co. of Indiana (Amoco), Gulf Oil Corp. and other major oil companies had joined the independent firms as members of the Pauley Group consortium.

The Pauley Group lobbied heavily, starting in 1980, for congressional action to restore the leases. But Sen. Dale Bumpers, D-Ark., a high-ranking Democrat on the Senate Energy and Natural Resources Committee, blocked Senate approval of the request in 1980 and again in 1981 by threatening to filibuster if the measure came up on the floor.

As a result, the Senate panel never reached agreement on the House-passed 1981 legislation. Sen. Malcolm Wallop, R-Wyo., led the fight to reinstate the leases during Energy Committee deliberations, contending that Congress should encourage independents to enter costly offshore exploration efforts in competition with major oil companies. But Bumpers objected that giving the leases back could cost the Treasury $1 billion in revenues that the Interior Department might win by auctioning the Pauley Group tracts a second time to the highest bidder.

est required exploring the California basins, one House member later recalled, and was surprised when California Republicans refused to rally behind opening them for leasing. But with political sentiment in the state running strongly against leasing, most of the state's Republican and Democratic members joined to oppose reconsideration of Andrus' ruling. The delegation held stormy meetings with Watt, wrote angry letters to President Reagan and maneuvered for House Appropriations Committee action to deny

funding for opening the disputed basins. Rep. Don H. Clausen, R-Calif., whose district fronted three of the four offshore basins along the state's central and northern coastline, lobbied heavily for blocking the leases through the appropriations process.

1981 Legislation. The House committee complied in June 1981 when it drafted a fiscal 1982 Interior appropriations bill (HR 4035 — H Rept 97-163). Through an amendment by Les AuCoin, D-Ore., the panel prohibited any leasing, exploration or development in four offshore California basins — the Santa Cruz, Bodega, Point Arena, and Eel River basins — along the state's coastline from just south of San Francisco to the Oregon border. The Eel River Basin lay closest to AuCoin's state. Watt personally lobbied Appropriations Committee members, but the administration was unable to persuade even the panel's Republicans to oppose AuCoin's proposal.

The full House accepted the leasing cutoff amendment when it passed HR 4035 on July 22. The Senate Appropriations Committee dropped the provision when it reported the bill July 23 (S Rept 97-166). But House and Senate conferees Nov. 4 restored AuCoin's amendment in the final version (H Rept 97-315). Congress cleared the Interior appropriations measure on Dec. 10, and Reagan signed it on Dec. 23 (PL 97-100).

1982 Amendment. Congress in 1982 expanded the offshore leasing prohibition through provisions in the fiscal 1983 Interior appropriations measure (HR 7356 — PL 97-394). In its final form, the bill barred leasing along the entire central and northern California coast, including the four basins protected by the 1981 appropriations rider, and areas off the New Jersey coast as well.

In reporting HR 7356 Dec. 2 (H Rept 97-942), the House Appropriations Committee renewed the California offshore leasing ban and extended it to cover the state's entire coastline from the Santa Maria area to the Oregon border. Before passing the bill Dec. 3, the House adopted an amendment by Jim Courter, R-N.J., that banned leasing in environmentally sensitive fish and shellfish breeding grounds in the Atlantic off New Jersey. Courter said his proposal removed 1.5 percent of Atlantic tracts that Interior planned to offer for leasing in 1983.

The Senate Appropriations Committee, in reporting HR 7356 Dec. 8, narrowed the House language to limit the leasing ban to the New Jersey coastal area and the four California basins that Congress protected in 1981. The Senate passed its version Dec. 14. In a compromise version (H Rept 97-978), House and Senate conferees banned leasing off the California coast north of Morro Bay, farther north than the point where the House-approved provision would have barred exploration. Congress cleared the compromise bill on Dec. 19.

Offshore Revenue Sharing

Congress in 1982 considered but eventually sidetracked a request to share federal offshore oil and gas leasing revenues to help coastal state governments manage development along their shorelines.

The House Sept. 29 passed legislation (HR 5543) to contribute up to $300 million a year in federal offshore oil and gas revenues to federal marine research and to state coastal zone management programs. The bill made 34 states, territories and possessions that bordered oceans and the Great Lakes eligible to share funds generated by the

bonus bids, rents and royalties that the oil industry paid to lease the right to drill for oil and gas on the federally controlled Outer Continental Shelf (OCS).

The House approved the measure by a 260-134 vote. But the Reagan administration, counting on rising offshore oil and gas revenues to reduce the federal budget deficit, opposed the legislation. The House-passed measure died in the Senate. *(1983-84 efforts, p. 359)*

In April 1981 Secretary of the Interior James G. Watt unveiled an ambitious five-year plan to open virtually the entire federal OCS — the seabed floor three miles or more offshore — for oil and gas leasing. Many coastal state governments joined environmentalists to challenge leasing in unexplored basins off their coasts, arguing that drilling activity and potential oil spills could damage marine life and threaten their fishing and tourist industries. *(Background, p. 347)*

At the same time, coastal states were demanding that the federal government turn over some of its OCS leasing revenues to upgrade their efforts to protect shorelines against damaging development, cope with the side effects of OCS drilling, and manage fisheries and marine life. In proposing the House legislation, members from coastal states pointed out that the federal government since 1920 had been sharing its mineral leasing revenues from onshore public lands with the states, mostly with the West, where federally owned lands were located. Under the Mineral Leasing Act of 1920, subsequently amended in 1976, Congress directed the U.S. Interior Department to turn over 50 percent of revenues from leasing coal, oil and gas, and other minerals on public lands to state governments. In fiscal 1981 public land states received $781 million in federal mineral revenues.

Under the House legislation, "coastal states will finally have a small share of revenues attributable to extraction of oil and gas from federal offshore lands," said Walter B. Jones, D-N.C., chairman of the Merchant Marine and Fisheries Committee. The House measure (H Rept 97-628) allocated 10 to 20 percent of the $300 million annual total to the National Sea Grant College Program, a marine research and technical assistance program. It divided the remainder, as block grants, among the coastal and Great Lakes states.

By granting the states a share of its OCS revenues, the federal government could give them more incentive to cooperate with OCS development, some members argued. "If the states cannot act as partners in this process, they are going to act to obstruct the process through litigious means," said Norman E. D'Amours, D-N.H., chairman of the Merchant Marine Subcommittee on Oceanography. If that happened, he went on, the federal Treasury could lose billions of dollars in offshore revenues if state challenges delayed OCS leasing.

Watershed Leasing

Congress in 1982 ruled out federal oil and gas leasing on national forest lands that supplied drinking water to Seattle and Tacoma, Wash.

Over U.S. Forest Service objections, the Interior Department early in the year granted leases for oil and gas exploration on a national forest in Washington mountains that serve as a watershed for the two cities. The city governments protested, and the state's entire congressional delegation — including Sen. Henry M. Jackson, D, former

Senate Energy and Natural Resources Committee chairman — joined to force officials to cancel the leases.

Joined by Washington Sen. Slade Gorton, a Republican, Jackson attached an amendment barring leasing in the watershed region to legislation (S 1210 — PL 97-350) authorizing spending by the President's Council on Environmental Quality (CEQ). Jackson and Gorton contended the leases demonstrated that the Reagan administration was opening federal lands throughout the West without taking sufficient account of their value for other purposes.

The Washington delegation's response demonstrated growing concern, even in some Western states, about Interior Secretary James G. Watt's efforts to step up federal energy leasing. The issue also illustrated conflicting demands on national forests and federal rangelands that held potential energy reserves but also provided water and recreation opportunities for the residents of large Western cities.

In early April the Interior Department's Bureau of Land Management (BLM) announced it had granted five oil and gas exploration leases on the lands in the Mount Baker-Snoqualmie National Forest. The controversial action was taken despite objections from the Forest Service and the existence of a cooperative agreement between the service and the cities calling for management practices designed to protect the watershed.

BLM eventually canceled the leases under pressure from the Washington congressional delegation. But Gorton and Jackson decided to make sure Interior could not reinstate them, and the Senate June 14 approved an amendment they offered to the CEQ authorization legislation. The House accepted the amendment, and President Reagan signed the measure Oct. 18. (CEQ debate, Environment chapter, p. 451)

The Jackson-Gorton amendment barred mineral leasing on national forest lands that lay within the Seattle and Tacoma drinking-water watershed. During Senate floor debate, the sponsors suggested that the administration's failure to recognize the natural values that public lands provide was undermining public support for developing federal energy resources.

In floor remarks June 14, Gorton charged that the administration's environmental policy "is that oil and gas exploration, even where there is no known oil and gas reserves, outweighs the protection of the natural forested areas in which the population of two large American cities draws its drinking water. I do not believe that this is a good policy."

Jackson criticized the Interior Department's "helter-skelter approach" to oil and gas leasing on public lands. The Washington Democrat said the department's "act first and think later" policy "is bound to stimulate widespread opposition to development, even in circumstances where development would be appropriate."

Coal Leasing

Congress grew uneasy during 1982 over Interior Secretary James G. Watt's plans for rapidly leasing federally owned coal reserves in the West.

At Watt's direction, the Interior Department in 1981-82 began to accelerate a federal coal leasing program that the Carter administration had set in motion. Congress, in debating the department's fiscal 1983 appropriations, narrowly defeated proposals by Watt's critics to curtail funding to slow the department's ambitious leasing schedule.

In clearing the fiscal 1983 Interior appropriations bill (HR 7356 — PL 97-394) Dec. 19, Congress granted the Reagan administration's full $15.79 million request for coal leasing efforts by Interior's Bureau of Land Management (BLM). But the Republican-controlled Senate took note of a growing coal leasing controversy when it defeated, by a one-vote margin, a proposal by Sen. Dale Bumpers, D-Ark., to cut BLM's budget by $2.13 million. (Coal leasing controversy details, 1983-84 chronology, p. 352)

In passing HR 7356 on Dec. 3, the House accepted its Appropriations Committee's recommendation (H Rept 97-942) to trim the BLM coal leasing budget to $13.66 million. The Senate Appropriations Subcommittee on Interior, chaired by James A. McClure, R-Idaho, restored the full $15.79 million request. During full committee debate, Bumpers attempted to cut that back to the House-approved amount to head off BLM plans for leasing an additional 3.7 billion tons of coal in two scheduled sales.

Bumpers and other critics of administration coal policy said the Treasury was not receiving fair market value for coal lands Watts leased, because BLM had set minimum bids too low and was quickly selling large amounts of coal at a time when coal company reserves were high. McClure, however, said that some of those reserves had to be dedicated through long-term contracts to mine-head power plants to make construction of the plants economically feasible.

Bumpers, admitting he lacked the votes to approve his amendment in committee, withdrew it, saying he would offer it on the floor.

In Dec. 14 floor debate, the Senate defeated Bumpers' amendment by a 47-48 margin. In a conference agreement reached on Dec. 16 (H Rept 97-978), House and Senate conferees agreed to fully fund the coal leasing program but voted to delay two sales planned during fiscal 1983 for at least three months, deferring one of them until fiscal 1984. The dispute foreshadowed a controversy that erupted in 1983, prodding the 98th Congress to clamp a moratorium on coal lease sales while Interior reassessed BLM's program.

1983-84

The 98th Congress slowed the Reagan administration's drive to open federal lands and waters for energy development.

In another bitter confrontation with Secretary of the Interior James G. Watt, Congress in 1983 halted the federal coal leasing program. Watt had rapidly accelerated the Carter administration's coal leasing schedule despite sagging coal demand. Congress stepped in to impose a temporary moratorium and set up a special commission to study whether Interior Department officials were offering too much coal on already depressed markets.

The dispute led to Watt's resignation. Interior Secretary William P. Clark, Watt's successor, overhauled coal leasing procedures and scaled back the department's ambitious plans for oil and gas leasing in federal offshore waters. Clark's conciliatory approach tempered congressional, environmental group and state government protests against the administration's plans to bolster U.S. energy

supplies by expanding federal mineral leasing.

Congress nonetheless extended legislative bans on leasing in sensitive coastal waters. The administration's last-minute opposition sidetracked legislation to share federal offshore leasing revenues with coastal state governments. And Congress made no effort to overturn a 1984 Supreme Court decision that strengthened Interior Department authority to offer federal offshore waters for oil and gas exploration despite state government objections.

Coal Leasing Moratorium

Congress in 1983 halted the Reagan administration's plans to speed up leasing of federally owned coal reserves.

Although national energy demand was slumping, Interior Secretary James G. Watt in 1981-82 accelerated the Carter administration's schedule for federal coal lease sales. But Congress in October 1983 stepped in to order a temporary leasing moratorium that eventually extended to 1985.

Lawmakers imposed the moratorium, through an amendment to the fiscal 1984 Interior Department appropriations bill (HR 3363 — PL 98-146), while a blue-ribbon commission studied the department's coal leasing program. Congress earlier in the year had ordered Watt to set up the commission to investigate charges that Interior in 1982 had sold rights to mine federal coal at "firesale prices" in the coal-rich Powder River Basin of Wyoming and Montana.

Interior Secretary William P. Clark, who replaced Watt in the midst of the coal leasing controversy, subsequently suspended further lease sales while the department overhauled its coal leasing procedures. By mid-1985 Interior still had no timetable for resuming large-scale leasing.

But the moratorium frustrated the administration's plans to open billions of tons of federal low-sulfur coal in six Western states for development by private mining companies. The furor deepened divisions among Western state governors, environmental groups and the U.S. energy industry over whether the government should resume large-scale leasing of its Western coal reserves to supply future U.S. demand for fuel.

By offering large coal reserves, while at the same time curtailing federal strip-mining controls, Watt undermined political support for an Interior coal leasing program revived by the Carter administration after a previous 10-year moratorium that lasted through the 1970s. In the process "Watt introduced a lot of uncertainty into a [coal leasing] system that was nearing a point of stability," Frank Gregg, who directed Interior's Bureau of Land Management (BLM) during the Carter administration, contended in 1983.

Shifting Interior coal leasing policies revealed the difficult judgments that Congress and executive branch officials must make in managing the government's vast mineral resources. The U.S. government owned 60 percent of the West's low-sulfur coal reserves, resources that the nation eventually would need to develop synthetic liquid fuels and generate electric power throughout the country. But the spectacular swings in U.S. energy markets from the early 1970s to the early 1980s made it difficult to predict how soon those reserves should be developed.

It took coal companies an average of seven years to put new mines into operation. As a result, federal coal leased in the early 1980s could be available for production only in the following decade. If Interior officials leased more coal

than mining companies demanded, they risked falling short of the "fair market value" that Congress demanded for federal coal resources. But if the department leased too little coal, the government risked future shortages that could drive fuel prices upward and leave the nation dependent on foreign oil imports.

Under Cecil D. Andrus, Carter's interior secretary, the department fashioned a comprehensive coal management program that tried to match leasing levels to predicted electric power and synthetic fuel demand.

Watt and Garrey E. Carruthers, the assistant interior secretary for land and water resources, substantially boosted Andrus' preliminary targets for the tonnage of federally owned coal that Interior planned to put up for bidding. In line with the Reagan administration's free market philosophy, Watt and Carruthers contended that the government should bolster private mining companies' coal reserves, then let energy demand determine how quickly federal coal would be mined.

Just as Interior expanded its leasing goals, however, a worldwide oil glut and lagging electric power demand curtailed expected markets for coal. In the 1982 Powder River sale Interior offered 1.6 billion tons for lease, double the Carter administration target. By early 1982 House Appropriations Committee and congressional General Accounting Office (GAO) investigators were questioning whether the procedures that Interior followed in offering the Powder River coal violated the department's obligation to obtain fair prices for public resources.

Congress responded in July 1983 by amending a fiscal 1983 supplemental appropriations bill (HR 3069 — PL 98-63) to order Watt to appoint a five-member commission to review Interior coal leasing procedures. Congress followed up in September by approving the temporary moratorium after the department defied a House Interior and Insular Affairs Committee demand that it cancel a scheduled lease auction for federal coal in the Fort Union Basin of Montana and North Dakota. At the height of the controversy Watt resigned under congressional fire after publicly joking that he had appointed "a black, . . . a woman, two Jews and a cripple" to the coal leasing commission. *(Watt career, p. 406)*

That commission, led by University of Illinois professor David F. Linowes, in February 1984 proposed significant changes in the way Interior conducted its coal leasing program. Clark accepted most of the group's recommendations, but Interior was still revising its program when Clark resigned as secretary in 1985. In the meantime members of Congress, Western state governments, environmental groups, economists and the coal industry continued to debate how rapidly the government should offer its vast Western coal reserves for development.

Background

The U.S. government assumed ownership of vast coal and other mineral deposits beneath Western lands it acquired on behalf of the nation through 19th century territorial expansion. As settlement pushed west, the government sold or granted some of its coal-bearing lands to state governments, homesteaders and railroads. In the early decades of the 20th century the government began holding onto increasingly valuable mineral resources. Even when the government turned surface title over to ranchers and other private owners, it reserved title to minerals beneath the ground for the public benefit.

In the Mineral Leasing Act of 1920 Congress gave the secretary of the interior discretionary power to lease federally owned coal, oil and gas and other minerals for development by private companies. The 1920 law directed the department to collect royalties from the leaseholders based on the value of resources they extracted. It required Interior officials to auction rights to mine known federal coal deposits to companies that bid the highest bonus payment to win leases. But it granted companies a "preference right" to lease previously unknown coal reserves that they discovered on public lands without bidding.

The federal government owned roughly 200 billion tons of coal, including some Southern coal fields. But most federal coal lay in six Western states — Montana, Wyoming, North Dakota, Colorado, Utah and New Mexico — in thick seams lying close to the surface. Before the 1960s there was little demand for Western coal deposits that were

far from the nation's population and industrial centers. As national electric power demand grew, however, mining companies began eyeing the West's largely untapped coal reserves that could be extracted cheaply through strip-mining methods.

The federal Clean Air Act of 1970 also increased interest in Western coal deposits that were generally low in sulfur content. By burning low-sulfur fuel, power plants and factories could meet federal sulfur emission standards without installing expensive equipment to cleanse the smokestack gases. During the 1960s and early 1970s electric utilities built huge coal-fired power plants at Rock Springs, Wyo.; Colstrip, Mont.; Craig, Colo.; and the Four Corners region of New Mexico to generate power for fast-growing Western cities. Utilities in Texas, the Midwest and other distant regions began shipping coal from Western fields to fuel their power plants.

1970s Leasing Moratorium. The federal government owned 60 percent of the West's coal, including deposits beneath federal lands and reserved rights to coal beneath "split-estate" private surface holdings. The federal government also effectively controlled another 20 percent of the region's reserves under adjacent state or private lands that could be mined only in combination with federally owned deposits. Yet even as demand for Western coal rose, legal and political pressures forced the Interior Department to halt all new federal coal leasing for a decade.

By 1970 Interior had issued more than 500 leases for federal coal, and mining companies had filed more than 170 preference right lease applications for coal they had discovered on federal lands. Yet BLM, the agency that handled the mineral leasing system, in 1970 reported that federal coal production in the six Western coal states actually had fallen since World War II, suggesting that leaseholders were keeping federal deposits in the ground — speculating that its value would rise — in the knowledge that Interior had never enforced stipulations that the coal be mined in timely fashion.

Interior Secretary Rogers C. B. Morton responded in 1971 by halting most new leasing while officials drafted a new leasing program. The moratorium eventually was extended for 10 years, until 1981, while Congress and successive administrations debated how the government should handle its valuable coal resources. The Ford administration in 1975 proposed a leasing program that relied on the mining industry to nominate federal tracts that companies were interested in leasing. Western governors, environmentalists and farmers and ranchers living near federal coal deposits objected to that system, and the U.S. District Court for the District of Columbia ruled in 1977 that the department's environmental impact statement on the overall coal leasing program was inadequate.

Revised Coal Leasing System

Congress meanwhile replaced 1920 Mineral Leasing Act provisions with an updated leasing law for federal coal deposits. In the Federal Coal Leasing Amendments Act of 1976 (PL 94-377), enacted over President Ford's veto, Congress abolished future preference right leasing and instead directed that all federal coal be leased through competitive bidding. The 1976 law also required that all accepted bonus bids for coal leases provide the government with "fair market value." It raised federal coal royalties, previously assessed at 5 cents per ton of production, to at least 12½ percent of the value of surface-mined coal at the mine. It

---

Coal Leasing System

Under the Federal Coal Leasing Amendments Act of 1976 (PL 94-377) the government was authorized to lease certain public lands to companies or individuals for the purpose of mining coal. *(Congress and the Nation Vol. I, p. 1000; Congress and the Nation Vol. IV, p. 275)*

Under the 1976 law the interior secretary had to award the leases by competitive bidding but could accept no bid that he determined to be less than the fair market value of the lease. Leaseholders paid in a number of ways for the privilege of mining publicly owned coal and putting the proceeds in their own pockets.

First, they paid "bonus bids," one-time, upfront payments to the government, to win award of the lease. This was the main area where competition worked to maximize revenue for the federal Treasury.

Second, they paid rents each year the lease was in effect, usually a nominal amount of a few dollars per acre.

Third, they paid royalties, an amount set by the interior secretary at 12½ percent of the value of surface-mined coal (8 percent for underground coal) at the mine.

Fourth, like other corporations, they paid taxes to the state and federal governments. Coal mining firms paid "severance taxes" to states, often amounting to an even higher percentage of the value of coal extracted than that paid for royalties.

Fifth, they paid certain mandatory expenses, such as that for reclamation of strip-mined land, that were required by federal law.

All these items were on top of the basic costs of doing business, such as mining and transporting the coal itself. The ultimate cost of coal delivered to the customer's door was thus likely to be many times its value in the ground.

gave the interior secretary authority to charge a lower royalty rate — 8 percent in 1983 — for deep federal coal veins that had to be extracted through underground mining tunnels.

To combat speculation, the 1976 law imposed a "diligent development" provision that required companies to start mining federal coal within 10 years or forfeit their leases. It set the term of federal coal leases at 20 years, with extensions for so long as coal could be mined in commercial quantities. Another provision increased, to 50 percent from 37½ percent, the portion of revenues from leasing federal minerals that the Interior Department shared with state governments where the resources were extracted. The U.S. coal industry opposed the revised system, and Ford in vetoing the measure objected to "rigidities, complications and burdensome regulations" that he contended would inhibit federal coal production. But a strongly Democratic House and Senate overrode the veto by substantial margins. *(Congress and the Nation Vol. IV, p. 275)*

Congress the same year cleared the Federal Land Policy and Management Act of 1976 (FLPMA, PL 94-579), giving Interior's Bureau of Land Management specific authority to regulate coal leasing as well as other uses of public lands it administered. In 1977, after President Carter took office, Congress also cleared the Surface Mining Control and Reclamation Act (SMCRA, PL 95-87) imposing federal regulation of coal strip-mining operations on both private and federally owned lands.

In combination with the 1976 coal leasing amendments, those measures substantially expanded Interior Department control over the way mining companies managed and extracted the coal they leased on federal lands. *(FLPMA, Congress and the Nation Vol. IV, p. 314; SMCRA, Congress and the Nation Vol. V, p. 544)*

Carter Coal Program. After taking office in 1977, the Carter administration spent two years redrafting Interior's coal leasing program. Unveiled in 1979, the Carter program attempted to set Interior coal leasing levels to match Department of Energy (DOE) computer forecasts of expected coal demand. After DOE determined coal production goals and calculated expected output from existing mines, Interior officials would set targets for leasing additional federal coal to make up anticipated shortfalls in national production. BLM in the meantime began studying federal coal tracts to screen out lands where low coal energy content, critical wildlife habitat or other conflicting values made strip mining undesirable. Andrus formed regional coal teams, composed of BLM state office directors and governors from states within the six Western coal regions, to review Interior's leasing goals, rank which tracts should be made available for leasing first and draw up lease sale schedules for the interior secretary to consider.

Andrus in 1979 scheduled sales to offer nearly 1.5 billion tons of coal, half of that in the Powder River Basin, for leasing during 1981-82. BLM continued to process pending preference right lease applications, filed before Congress revised the leasing system in 1976, for as much as 5.8 billion tons of federal coal. In setting its preliminary leasing targets BLM allowed a 25 percent "fudge factor" to match unexpectedly high demand. Under the Carter program "we could lease and produce far more coal than the market could possibly absorb," Gregg, Carter's BLM director, maintained in 1983.

Western coal-state governors, environmental groups and the coal industry by and large backed the Andrus program as a way to meet national energy needs while protecting the region's interests. But critics argued that the government's efforts to plan its leasing goals on the basis of computer forecasts of energy demand could not keep up with shifting market conditions. DOE in fact sharply revised its regional coal production goals as 1979 foreign oil price increases, Carter's plan to promote a synthetic fuels industry, reduced electric power demand and rising natural gas prices altered the nation's energy supply and demand outlook.

Watt Leasing Speedup. After a 10-year moratorium the Interior Department resumed coal leasing in January 1981 with a sale in the Green River-Ham's Fork region of Wyoming and Colorado that had been scheduled under the Andrus program. Watt took office the same month and began revising the coal program to fit the administration's free market philosophy. At Watt's direction Interior accelerated its lease sale schedule and streamlined the Andrus leasing regulations. Scrapping DOE's formal production goals, Interior adopted a policy of setting leasing goals to meet the mining industry's demand for coal reserves. The Reagan administration's goal was to increase coal market competition by providing many companies with ample reserves of federal coal, then let market supply and demand determine where and how fast those resources would be produced. *(1981-82 developments, p. 339)*

1982 Powder River Sale

Although leasing had resumed in 1981, Interior officials viewed the 1982 Powder River sale as an opportunity to prove that the government could offer large amounts of coal for lease without the disruptions that caused the 1970s moratorium. The Powder River Basin was the West's richest coal region, with 146 billion tons of recoverable reserves, and the federal government owned about 80 percent of that total. In scheduling the sale in 1979, Andrus had set a preliminary target of 776 million tons. With the regional coal team's consent, BLM in 1981 doubled the final target to a range of 1.4 billion to 1.5 billion tons. In February 1982, two months before the sale, Watt himself raised the Powder River leasing goal again, to 2.2 billion tons. During the intervening three years, however, world oil prices had started to fall and demand for Western coal reserves plunged far below expectations in the late 1970s. Although those trends became evident during the winter of 1981-82, Interior officials went ahead with what they termed the largest coal lease sale in U.S. history.

In the April 1982 Powder River sale, Interior received bids totaling $54.7 million on 11 tracts holding 1.6 billion tons of coal. No bids were received on some tracts and others were dropped from the offering because Interior officials were unable to obtain consent from private owners of surface lands above federal coal deposits. Although the sale received little national attention at the time, during the following year controversy broke out in Congress over whether the administration had driven bonus bids below fair market value by offering so much coal on depressed markets.

1983 Congressional Investigations. A year after the Powder River sale was held, the House Appropriations Committee and the General Accounting Office issued reports that criticized the way Interior had handled the bidding.

In a report released April 20 the House committee investigations staff contended that Watt's leasing policies had reduced the federal government's dollar return for

public resources. "Such large-scale leasing under poor economic conditions distorts the market by flooding it with leased coal," the Appropriations staff report said. "It temporarily reduces fair market value and allows the industry to acquire coal at firesale prices." In a May 11 report GAO found that Interior received far less than fair market value for the Powder River leases and recommended that Congress revise coal leasing law to prevent such underpayment.

Charges of mismanagement and even possible impropriety in the sale centered on a last-minute change in the system for making bonus bids. Until a few weeks before the Powder River sale, the system called for Interior officials to calculate "minimum acceptable bids" representing "fair market value" before the sale. But shortly after field officials sent their calculations to Washington, D.C., top headquarters officials decided to change the bidding system.

The new system replaced minimum acceptable bids with what were called "entry level bids." These were intended to be the point, well below fair market value, at which bidding could open, with an assumption that auction-like competition would bid up the price.

Critics of Watt's coal leasing program also charged that Interior officials had leaked the minimum acceptable bids for the Powder River sale to coal companies before the sale was announced.

Powder River Bids. Bidding for the Powder River coal demonstrated flaws in the government's competitive leasing procedures. Of 11 tracts that Interior actually leased in the April 1982 sale, only eight received more than one bid and the other three received only two bids. The results failed to bear out the administration's belief that competitive bidding would produce a fair price for federal coal reserves.

Legislative Action

Watt's coal leasing plans had drawn congressional fire long before the critical reports on the Powder River sale were issued. Efforts to slow or block the coal program began in 1982, when the House Appropriations Subcommittee on Interior wrote into its version of a fiscal 1982 Interior appropriations bill (HR 7356) a provision to cut BLM funding for coal leasing activities by $2.1 million. Although the House accepted the cutback, the Senate Appropriations Committee restored the funds. The full Senate rejected, by a 47-48 vote, an amendment offered by Dale Bumpers, D-Ark., to go along with the House cutback. *(1982 developments, p. 351)*

The coal leasing controversy heated up in 1983. House Interior and Insular Affairs Committee Chairman Morris K. Udall, D-Ariz., in May introduced legislation (HR 3018) to impose a leasing moratorium for at least one year while Interior developed new leasing procedures. There was no action on Udall's bill, but House coal leasing critics, led by Sidney R. Yates, D-Ill., again attacked the program through riders to appropriations bills.

Linowes Commission. The House May 25 passed a fiscal 1983 supplemental appropriations bill (HR 3069 — H Rept 98-207) that barred further coal leasing through Sept. 30, the end of fiscal 1983. But the Senate, after heavy administration and coal industry lobbying, June 14 defeated by a 48-51 margin a Bumpers amendment to go along with the moratorium.

Although conferees July 20 dropped the House moratorium, they wrote into the final version a provision ordering Watt to set up a commission to study coal pricing

issues. The House had approved the provision as part of a regular fiscal 1984 appropriations bill (HR 3363) that it passed June 28.

Watt Aug. 4 appointed Linowes to head the Commission on Fair Market Policy for Federal Coal Leasing. Linowes previously chaired a separate commission appointed by Watt to study the government's oil and gas royalty program. That panel's report served as the basis for a law enacted in 1982 tightening the system for collecting royalties from oil and gas production on federal and Indian lands. *(Story, p. 344)*

Moratorium Proposal. Even as the Linowes commission was being formed, House critics pressed efforts to halt Watt's coal program. On June 7 Yates' subcommittee had approved the fiscal 1984 Interior appropriations measure with another coal leasing moratorium attached. The provision, accepted by the full Appropriations Committee when it reported HR 3363 on June 21 (H Rept 98-253) kept the moratorium in effect while Interior's coal leasing program was studied by the independent commission. The coal leasing moratorium was one of several restrictions the bill imposed on Watt's mineral and energy leasing policies. *(Offshore oil leasing provisions, p. 357)*

The full House passed HR 3363, with its leasing bans intact, on June 28. The Senate Appropriations Subcommittee on Interior again stripped coal leasing restrictions from the measure before sending it to the full committee, which reported HR 3363 without the moratorium provision on July 19 (S Rept 98-184). Debate on other issues stalled the Interior appropriations measure on the Senate floor as Congress recessed in August. By the time the Senate took up the coal leasing issue on Sept. 20, Watt had angered congressional leaders by ordering Interior to conduct a Sept. 14 coal lease sale in the Fort Union region of North Dakota and Montana despite a House Interior Committee resolution directing that the sale be postponed. *(Box, p. 356)*

With the Fort Union dispute fresh in senators' minds, Bumpers offered a leasing moratorium amendment on Sept. 20. This time the Senate approved it on a **63-33 key vote (R 23-29; D 40-4)**, with 16 members who had opposed Bumpers' moratorium proposal in June switching to support the amendment to HR 3363. Bumpers said the moratorium was needed to keep Watt from "trying to give away our national heritage to whoever happens to show up." *(1983 key votes, p. 911)*

Bumpers' amendment barred spending for new coal leasing, with certain exceptions, until 90 days after the Linowes commission reported to Congress on the Interior Department's coal leasing policies. The House-passed moratorium set no deadline for Congress to act after the Linowes report.

Watt Resignation. Stung by the Senate's stand, Watt accused Congress of ignoring U.S. energy needs that he contended were threatened by conflicts in the Middle East and Central America. "The world is ready to ignite and your secretary of the interior has to deal with 535 members of Congress that don't seem to be concerned about the future supply of energy in America," Watt complained in a Sept. 21 breakfast speech to the U.S. Chamber of Commerce.

In that same speech Watt touched off a new round of criticism on Capitol Hill and elsewhere with a remark about the composition of the Linowes commission. "We have every kind of mix you can have. I have a black, I have a woman, two Jews and a cripple. And we have talent," said

Fort Union Lease Sale Stalled

As Congress debated a federal coal leasing moratorium, the House of Representatives and environmental groups went to court to bar the Interior Department from issuing leases to mine coal in the Fort Union region of North Dakota and Montana.

Defying a House Interior and Insular Affairs Committee resolution, Secretary of the Interior James G. Watt had ordered U.S. Bureau of Land Management (BLM) officials to go ahead with the Fort Union sale in September 1983. But Louis F. Oberdorfer, a U.S. district court judge in Washington, D.C., later that month directed Interior to postpone actually issuing leases for the coal. The ruling remained in effect in the spring of 1985, and BLM had yet to grant the leases while it reviewed federal coal leasing procedures.

Some congressional critics initially objected to the Fort Union sale on environmental grounds. But the issue took on symbolic importance as a test of whether Congress would allow Watt's coal leasing plans to continue unchecked. After Interior ignored the House committee's demand to postpone the Fort Union sale, the Senate reversed its previous backing for Watt's coal program by accepting a House-passed moratorium on further lease sales as part of a 1984 Interior appropriations bill (HR 3363 — PL 98-146).

Committee Action. By a party-line vote of 27-14, the House panel Aug. 3 approved a resolution that directed Watt to withdraw federally owned lands in the Fort Union area from the coal leasing program. The committee invoked a little-used provision of the 1976 Federal Land Policy and Management Act (PL 94-579) that required the secretary to withdraw public lands from development temporarily if the appropriate committee of either the House or Senate notified him that emergency measures had to be taken "to preserve values that would otherwise be lost." *(Congress and the Nation Vol. IV, p. 314)*

Environmental groups Sept. 8 filed a lawsuit in an attempt to stop final award of the Fort Union leases. Oberdorfer Sept. 9 denied their request for a temporary restraining order, and the department Sept. 14 opened bids for eight Fort Union coal tracts. The sale drew little interest from coal companies.

The day after the sale Interior lawyers notified environmental groups that the department might award the leases within 15 days, before the lawsuit was settled. House and environmental group lawyers argued that awarding the leases could grant coal companies a property right to the leases, making it hard to overturn the sale without compensating them for the coal. But Oberdorfer Sept. 16 issued an order temporarily blocking Watt from making the sale final. On Sept. 28 the judge issued another order that barred Interior from issuing the leases in defiance of the House committee resolution.

Watt. He later described his comments as "unfortunate" and apologized for them, but the political uproar continued. On Oct. 9 Watt resigned.

Moratorium Approved. As demands for Watt's dismissal mounted, House and Senate conferees had adopted the Bumpers moratorium in approving HR 3363 Sept. 29 (H Rept 98-399).

Before approving the conference version on Oct. 20, the Senate adopted an amendment that exempted specified coal tracts in Colorado and Montana from the moratorium, permitting Interior to lease additional coal to coal companies that claimed they needed it to maintain existing mine operations. The House accepted the Senate amendment the same day, clearing HR 3363 for the president.

Linowes Commission Report

In a report submitted to Clark in February 1984, the Linowes commission urged Interior to establish a predictable and stable coal leasing schedule to supply fuel for U.S. consumption. But the commission, faulting the department for offering so much Powder River coal on depressed markets, also proposed that the government maintain "the flexibility to change the timing of lease sales and the quantity of coal offered based on its assessment of market conditions."

Since the federal government held potential monopoly power in Western coal markets, the commission suggested that Interior's inability to respond quickly to shifting demand could exaggerate coal price fluctuations. "Indeed, in the 1979-80 boom period, the unavailability of new federal coal leases due to the moratorium [during the 1970s] probably drove coal reserve prices higher in an already inflated market for Western coal reserves," the report noted. "In 1982 the leasing of more coal, planned in response to 1979-80 circumstances, may have further lowered prices in a new depressed market for coal reserves."

Reviewing the 1982 Powder River sale, the commission concluded "that the Interior Department probably offered excessive amounts of federal coal in a declining market and that this, in turn, probably lessened the prospect of receiving fair market value. At the very least, the Interior Department made serious errors in judgment in its procedures for conducting the 1982 Powder River lease sale and failed to provide a sound rationale for many of its actions."

Commission Recommendations. For future lease sales the commission recommended that the government continue to rely on competitive bonus bidding to obtain fair market value for most federal coal deposits. But it offered 36 proposals, including six requiring legislation by Congress, to improve the department's coal management program.

Among its major recommendations the commission urged Interior rapidly to finish processing pending prefer-

ence right lease applications (PRLAs) for non-competitive federal coal tracts, then take those reserves into account before leasing additional reserves. In selecting tracts for future sales, the commission maintained, Interior should first offer reserves that were likely to attract bids from more than one company. In leasing tracts where no competition was expected — such as reserves that could be developed only as part of an existing adjacent mine — the commission suggested that Interior officials have authority to negotiate a fair price directly with existing mine operators without going through the bidding process.

The report urged Interior to restore public support for the coal leasing program in Western states by giving Regional Coal Teams composed of BLM officials and state governors a significant role "both in establishing leasing levels and in setting leasing schedules."

The commission took no stand on whether state severance taxes on coal — including a controversial 30 percent tax levied by Montana — placed an unreasonable financial burden on energy consumers in other states and regions. The Supreme Court, in a 1981 decision, found the Montana severance tax was valid under the Constitution; but Midwestern and Southern congressional delegations introduced legislation in Congress to set a 12½ percent cap on state severance taxes on coal from federally owned lands.

Diligent Development Law. The commission proposed congressional action to deal with other coal leasing problems, including the effect of the 10-year diligent development requirement and surface owner rights on the value of federally owned coal. By forcing companies to start mining federally owned coal within 10 years or lose their leases, the report noted, the diligent development standard in the 1976 coal leasing law might stimulate excessive production even if market conditions provided an incentive to keep the coal in the ground. In addition, coal market economists told the commission that mining companies reduced the prices they bid for federal coal leases to take account of the risk that unexpected problems could keep them from beginning production in time to meet the 10-year deadline.

The commission recommended retaining the 10-year diligent development requirement to prevent speculation in federal coal leases. But it suggested that Congress should revise the law to allow companies to hold onto leases for another 10 years without starting production if they paid the government advance royalties, on an escalating schedule, for the coal they expected eventually to mine and sell.

The commission also suggested that Congress consider setting limits on payments that coal companies could make to obtain permission for mining from landowners who held title to the surface above government-owned coal deposits.

Clark Response

The congressionally imposed coal leasing moratorium expired on May 17, 1984, 90 days after the Linowes commission filed its report. But Clark successfully steered clear of renewed controversy over the program by voluntarily suspending further leasing until 1985.

After receiving the Linowes report, Clark told the Senate Energy and Natural Resources Committee in April that he would adopt all but one of the group's 30 administrative recommendations. An Interior spokesman said Clark also supported the commission's proposals for congressional legislation revising coal leasing laws. The secretary refused to agree to the commission's proposal that Interior require coal companies to turn over information on private coal transactions for officials to use in analyzing market pricing.

At least initially Clark's promise to revamp the coal leasing procedures failed to satisfy House Democratic critics of Watt's policies. Yates' Appropriations Subcommittee on Interior at first recommended extending the leasing moratorium through fiscal 1984. But after the subcommittee grilled Clark about coal leasing revisions during June 13-14 hearings, Yates withdrew the moratorium extension before the subcommittee approved a fiscal 1985 Interior appropriations measure.

Interior coal leasing plans remained on hold after Donald P. Hodel, former secretary of energy, replaced Clark in the Interior post in 1985. The department continued to draft an environmental impact statement on a revised coal leasing program. Except for occasional emergency sales to keep existing mines in operation, Interior officials predicted it would be late 1986 before the department was ready to resume large-scale leasing.

Offshore Leasing Bans

Congress in 1983 and 1984 extended temporary bans on federal oil and gas leasing off the California, Florida and Massachusetts coastlines.

Through amendments to fiscal 1984-85 Interior Department appropriations bills, Congress renewed 1981 and 1982 riders that prohibited the department from issuing drilling leases in specified Outer Continental Shelf (OCS) regions. State officials, environmental groups and congressional delegations from coastal states had vigorously protested Interior Secretary James G. Watt's plans to open previously untouched waters for oil and gas development. *(Previous action, p. 347)*

Federal offshore leasing remained controversial after Watt's 1983 resignation. After renewing OCS leasing bans for the fourth year in a row, House and Senate conferees on the fiscal 1985 Interior funding measure expressed hope that Congress no longer would need to impose leasing moratoriums if Interior officials took steps to protect marine resources in future offshore leasing decisions.

Fiscal 1984 Legislation

In drafting fiscal 1984 Interior appropriations legislation (HR 3363 — PL 87-146), the House Appropriations Committee in 1983 accepted proposals by Interior Subcommittee Chairman Sidney R. Yates, D-Ill., to protect California, Florida and Massachusetts coastal waters (H Rept 98-253).

The California and Florida offshore leasing bans proposed by Yates prompted intense committee debate before they were approved, in modified form, by voice vote. The panel softened the bans slightly to allow preparation for lease sales but not the sales themselves.

The California ban applied to waters off Southern California, from the U.S.-Mexico border north through San Diego County and some of Orange County, starting three miles out at the limit of state-controlled waters and reaching to about 20 miles offshore. It also included buffer zones around the Channel Islands and in the Santa Barbara Channel.

The one-year ban was requested in a June 6 letter to Yates signed by 23 of the 45 House members from California. That division within the state delegation, heightened by the pressure to develop a reportedly rich new petroleum

find in the area, made the ban hotly controversial.

The bill also renewed less controversial existing leasing bans for most of the northern California coastline and part of the central coastline that were included in the 1983 appropriation. The Florida rider applied to almost the entire Gulf of Mexico coastline of that state. The bill also prohibited the sale of leases in the Georges Bank area off the coast of New England.

The Senate (S Rept 98-184) stripped the offshore leasing bans from HR 3363 at the urging of James A. McClure, R-Idaho, chairman of the Senate Appropriations Subcommittee on Interior. In conference (H Rept 98-399) House and Senate negotiators restored the OCS provisions but scaled back the House prohibitions. Conferees reduced the number of Gulf of Mexico tracts off Florida where leasing was barred and substituted more complex provisions to cover Southern California coastal tracts up to 12 miles offshore.

Fiscal 1985 Legislation

In 1984 Congress renewed leasing prohibitions off California and in the Georges Bank fishing grounds off New England. Unable to finish work on regular Interior appropriations, the House and Senate wrote those riders into a yearlong fiscal 1985 omnibus continuing appropriations resolution (H J Res 648 — PL 98-473) that funded Interior programs.

In drafting a proposed Interior funding bill (HR 5973 — H Rept 98-886), the House Appropriations Committee had narrowly preserved the leasing prohibition in the Georges Bank region and in the three California areas. By a 20-21 vote, the committee rejected a proposal by Joseph M. McDade, R-Pa., ranking minority member of Yates' subcommittee, to strip those bans from the legislation.

Yates originally had proposed banning lease sales in the Atlantic Ocean off eastern Florida and in Bristol Bay and the St. George Basin off Alaska. But the subcommittee dropped the Florida and St. George Basin provisions, and the full committee deleted the Bristol Bay prohibition after Yates reported that Interior Secretary William P. Clark had agreed to seek further environmental data before proceeding with leasing in that area.

The Senate Appropriations panel again dropped the OCS leasing bans from its version of the bill (S Rept 98-578). The full Senate in October rolled the committee's proposals into the continuing resolution and House-Senate conferees attached the House-passed offshore leasing prohibitions to the final continuing measure.

Offshore Leasing: State Powers

Congress in 1984 sidetracked legislation to overturn a U.S. Supreme Court ruling that removed obstacles to the Reagan administration's offshore oil and gas leasing program.

In a Jan. 11 decision the court ruled against California's legal challenge to former Secretary of the Interior James G. Watt's 1981 decision to lease 115 federal tracts in the Santa Maria Basin off that state's coast for oil and gas exploration. By a 5-4 vote, the high court ruled in the case of *Secretary of the Interior v. California* that states could not block federal offshore lease sales by arguing that the sales were inconsistent with state plans for protecting their coastal areas. *(Court ruling, p. 754)*

California and other coastal states filed legal challenges after the administration drew up Interior Department plans to offer to lease virtually the entire federally controlled Outer Continental Shelf (OCS) for oil and gas exploration. Although the Supreme Court ruled against California's stand, Interior Secretary William P. Clark, who had replaced Watt in 1983, backed off from the administration's ambitious offshore leasing plans, slowing the pace of lease sales and smoothing relations with state officials.

Even so, the Senate Commerce, Science and Transportation Committee in May reported legislation (S 2324 — S Rept 98-512) to enlarge state government control over federal OCS leasing off their shorelines. The House Merchant Marine and Fisheries Subcommittee on Oceanography approved a similar bill (HR 4589) the same month. Both measures required that federal agencies manage offshore water resources in ways that were consistent with state coastal zone management plans drawn up under a 1972 federal law. But neither received further consideration.

Federal-State Conflicts

In its Jan. 11 ruling, the Supreme Court rejected California's contention that Interior Department decisions to lease OCS tracts for exploration could be blocked if development were inconsistent with state coastal zone management plans.

The decision sharply limited potential state government control over federal government decisions on managing its extensive offshore oil and gas deposits. Major petroleum-producing states such as Texas and Louisiana, and to some extent Alaska, generally welcomed drilling off their shores, both in federal waters and in state waters less than three miles from the coastline. But some heavily populated coastal states — including California, Oregon, Florida and Massachusetts — resisted federal offshore development. Environmentalist sentiment generally was stronger in those states and OCS development was viewed as threatening economically important fishing and recreation industries.

The court case involved a clash between two federal laws. The 1972 Coastal Zone Management Act (CZMA, PL 92-583) assured states that once they won federal approval for plans for managing and protecting their coastal areas, any federal action "directly affecting" those coastal zones would have to be consistent with the state plans insofar as possible. *(Congress and the Nation Vol. III, p. 799)*

Six years later Congress amended the Outer Continental Shelf Lands Act to overhaul federal programs for leasing OCS lands for development of oil and gas resources. *(Congress and the Nation Vol. V, p. 485)*

But the 1978 amendments (PL 95-372) did not end the frequent conflict between the federal interest in producing more energy and the state interest in protecting fishing and recreation industries along local shores.

While he did not start the conflict, Watt fueled the flames by proposing in April 1981 a five-year plan to offer up to one billion offshore acres, nearly the entire OCS, for oil and gas leasing. Watt submitted that plan to Congress for a 60-day review on May 11, 1982, and when Congress took no action to block it, put it into effect on July 21, 1982. *(Story, p. 347)*

When the administration moved in 1981 to sell leases on 115 tracts in the Santa Maria Basin off California, the state invoked the provision of CZMA requiring federal actions to be consistent with an adopted state management

plan. Both a federal district court and a federal appeals court sided with the state, blocking the lease sale.

Six other states filed separate court challenges to leasing off their coasts — Alaska, Maine, Massachusetts, New Jersey, New York and North Carolina.

Supreme Court Decision. The Supreme Court, however, ruled that the Interior Department did not have to make any "consistency" finding under the Coastal Zone Management Act before selling offshore oil and gas leases. Such determinations were required only at later stages of the development process, when exploration drilling and production began, the court said.

Justice Sandra Day O'Connor wrote the opinion, joined by Justices Lewis F. Powell Jr., William H. Rehnquist, Byron R. White and Chief Justice Warren E. Burger.

O'Connor said OCS lease sales were not actions "directly affecting" a state's coastal zone, adding that states did retain "considerable authority to veto inconsistent exploration or development and production plans."

Offshore Revenue Sharing

The Reagan administration's last-minute opposition in 1984 thwarted congressional proposals to share up to $300 million a year in federal offshore oil and gas revenues with coastal and Great Lakes state governments.

Interior Department leases for oil and gas exploration and production from the federally controlled Outer Continental Shelf (OCS) were expected to produce $6 billion in fiscal 1985 revenues for the deficit-ridden U.S. Treasury. Administration officials, led by White House Office of Management and Budget Director David A. Stockman, strongly opposed coastal state demands that the national government turn over part of those revenues to help them cope with the burdens of offshore drilling.

Under the Mineral Leasing Act of 1920, Congress granted states 50 percent of Interior mineral leasing revenues from onshore federal lands within their borders. But in laws that authorized oil and gas leasing in federal waters, lying three miles or more offshore, Congress made no provision for sharing the financial returns with states along the nation's coastlines.

In the early 1980s the Reagan administration's plans to open vast OCS tracts for petroleum exploration both promised even larger offshore revenues and threatened more extensive environmental damage and population growth for coastal states near promising OCS formations. *(OCS program, p. 347)*

The House responded in 1983 by approving legislation (HR 5), backed by coastal state members, that granted 31 states and five territories up to $300 million in OCS funds for their own ocean and coastal resource programs. Senate conferees in 1984 accepted a compromise revenue sharing plan as an amendment to unrelated fisheries legislation (S 2463). But the White House denounced the bill and a Senate filibuster threat blocked final action before Congress adjourned for the 1984 elections.

Coastal state governments and congressional delegations contended that offshore oil and gas drilling imposed substantial economic and social burdens on shoreline communities and that the federal government should help pay those costs. They argued that it was unfair for the government to give states half of its oil and gas revenues from onshore leasing without providing similar assistance to coastal states.

But the administration, straining to reduce federal budget deficits, resisted the revenue sharing plan as an unwarranted drain on the Treasury. Administration officials also maintained that the House formula for allocating shared revenues would provide "windfall payments" to states without oil and gas development off their coasts, including some that were opposing OCS leasing.

The House had passed offshore revenue sharing legislation in 1982, but the measure died in the Senate. *(Story, p. 350)*

1983 Action

The House Merchant Marine and Fisheries Committee, a panel dominated by members from coastal states, drew up the House legislation in 1983. Formally reported May 16 (H Rept 98-206), HR 5 required the Treasury to set aside in a special fund each year either $300 million or 10 percent of new offshore leasing revenue, whichever was less.

The bill gave states leeway on spending most of the funds but required that at least 25 percent be committed to state coastal management programs under the federal Coastal Zone Management Act of 1972, a program the administration wanted to phase out.

The House passed HR 5 by a 301-93 vote on Sept. 14. Before approving the bill, the House rejected amendments by Jack Fields, R-Texas, to limit eligibility to states with actual offshore energy development and exclude Great Lakes states from the program.

The Senate Commerce Committee in 1983 approved its own coastal revenue sharing bill (S 800 — S Rept 98-112). But the measure never reached the Senate floor.

1984 Conference Agreement

With the Senate refusing to act, the House in 1984 maneuvered its revenue sharing plan to conference by tacking it onto separate Senate-passed fisheries legislation (S 2463 — S Rept 98-391). The House passed its version of S 2463 on June 26 and House-Senate conferees reached agreement on compromise revenue sharing provisions on Aug. 8 (H Rept 98-1006).

Under the conference plan 4 percent of revenues from federal drilling leases, up to a maximum of $300 million the first year, was to be distributed to the states as block grants. Small increases were allowed in future years, based on a three-year average of revenues.

Funds were to be allocated according to a five-part formula based on shoreline mileage, population and energy activities. The largest recipients would have been Louisiana, Alaska and California. States bordering the Great Lakes were made eligible as well as those along the coasts.

House-Senate conferees agreed to delay filing their report until September in hope that the White House would support the compromise. But no sooner had conferees reached agreement than the administration released a letter denouncing the bill and threatening a veto.

Although the House easily approved the conference report Sept. 13, by a 312-94 margin, the administration marshaled enough Senate support to block its consideration there. When the report was brought to the Senate floor Oct. 9, John C. Danforth, R-Mo., and Dave Durenberger, R-Minn., indicated they were prepared to block it, by filibuster, if necessary. With Congress in a hurry to adjourn, there was no time to overcome their opposition.

Chronology
Of Action
On Nuclear Power

1981-82

Congress took major steps in 1981-82 to clear away obstacles facing the U.S. commercial nuclear power industry.

After deliberating through most of its two yearly sessions, the 97th Congress dealt with two of the industry's most troublesome problems: long delays in nuclear plant construction and the lack of safe methods for permanently disposing of radioactive reactor wastes. But members' lingering doubts about the economic health and fundamental safety of nuclear power generation technology were revealed in eroding House and Senate support for the costly Clinch River breeder reactor project.

Near the end of its 1982 post-election session, Congress cleared Nuclear Regulatory Commission authorization legislation that permitted the commission to grant electric utilities temporary licenses to start up newly built reactors before all licensing hearings had been completed. The lame-duck Congress also wrapped up a long-debated plan directing the federal government to develop and operate nuclear waste storage facilities to keep reactor byproducts isolated from the human environment.

Radioactive Wastes

Congress approved a national plan for disposing of the radioactive wastes produced by U.S. nuclear power plants.

As the 1982 post-election session drew to a close, lawmakers forged an agreement on comprehensive nuclear-waste legislation (HR 3809) that the House and Senate had been weighing for four years. President Reagan and the nuclear power industry had pushed hard for a congressional decision on what to do with spent reactor fuel that had been piling up at the nation's commercial nuclear plants.

The measure, signed into law by Reagan Jan. 7, 1983 (PL 97-425), spelled out timetables for the federal government to open an underground facility for storing spent fuel rods and other commercial wastes in perpetual isolation from the human environment. But to win the bill's passage, Congress exempted radioactive wastes from nuclear weapons production from most of the law's regulations.

The law directed the president to select an underground site by 1987 for a permanent waste repository that probably would be ready by the mid-1990s. For the meantime, the legislation authorized the Department of Energy (DOE) to provide temporary storage for spent civilian reactor fuel from power plants that ran out of space to hold it.

In addition to a permanent repository, Congress ordered DOE to draft experimental plans for storing nuclear wastes in man-made vaults where they could be monitored and eventually removed. The government could keep wastes there for 50 to 100 years, then retrieve them for permanent disposal or for reprocessing to remove plutonium.

Before the mid-1970s the nuclear industry generally had assumed that spent commercial power plant fuel would be reprocessed to yield plutonium that could be recycled into more reactor fuel. President Carter, concerned that recycled plutonium could be diverted instead to make nuclear bombs, in 1977 withdrew federal support for a commercial reprocessing plant then being built at Barnwell, S.C. Since then the government and industry had stepped up their search for alternative ways to store reactor wastes as spent fuel without further reprocessing.

The Reagan administration favored reprocessing as the ultimate solution to nuclear waste disposal. No commercial reprocessing industry operated in the United States during the early 1980s. But Congress kept that option open for future years by directing that government repositories store spent fuel in ways that would permit its later removal for reprocessing. *(Box, p. 363)*

Congress had been trying to put together a comprehensive nuclear waste measure since 1978. But action was slowed by debate over whether military and civilian wastes should be stored together and subjected to the same regulatory restrictions. And various members delayed consideration as they tried to make sure that DOE would not put a nuclear-waste dump within their states or districts. After four years of maneuvering, Congress exempted military wastes and gave a state's governor or legislature power to veto a federal disposal site within its borders. But Congress retained authority to overturn the state's stand through action by both the House and Senate.

Environmental groups opposed the final bill, arguing that tight deadlines could force the government to make hasty choices in evaluating repository sites and designing storage arrangements. They objected that temporary storage for spent reactor fuel would bail out nuclear utilities that had failed to develop safe methods for handling dangerous wastes created by their own plants. And they warned that shipping spent fuel around the country to federal waste repositories would risk thefts, sabotage and accidents that could threaten public health and safety.

Background

The U.S. government and electric utility corporations had been generating dangerous nuclear waste since the atomic bomb was developed during World War II. But nearly 40 years later the nation had yet to come up with a national policy for disposing of spent reactor fuel and other nuclear fission byproducts that would remain highly radioactive for thousands of years.

U.S. government reactors at Hanford, Wash., and Savannah River, S.C., that manufactured plutonium for nuclear weapons also produced intensely radioactive liquid wastes. Since 1957, when the nation's first commercial nuclear power plant began operations at Shippingsport, Pa., private utility reactors had been generating electricity from heat produced by chain reactions in fuel rods holding enriched uranium. Once the fuel was used up, the spent rods still held radioactive "high-level" wastes after they were removed from reactor cores. Both military and commercial nuclear operations, along with radiopharmaceutical manufacturing plants, medical and research centers, also produced large volumes of slightly contaminated "low-level" radioactive wastes.

Since the 1940s federal government military weapons plants and research facilities had produced more than 77 million gallons of liquid high-level wastes. The government had stored the military program wastes temporarily in steel tanks at the Washington and South Carolina plants and at the government's nuclear research center at Idaho Falls, Idaho. Between 1956 and 1976, about 500,000 gallons leaked into the ground at the Hanford plant from tanks that corroded faster than expected.

In the private sector, 82 nuclear power plants were in operation in 1982 in the United States. By 1980 the commercial industry had accumulated about 25,000 spent fuel assemblies that had been removed when reactors were refueled with fresh enriched uranium. In the absence of permanent disposal arrangements, nuclear plant operators had been storing spent fuel rods in pools of water at plant sites. But many utility operators said their plants were running out of storage space, and DOE in 1981 estimated that capacity at reactor sites would no longer be adequate by 1986.

For several years, federal officials had been studying underground formations as possible waste-storage sites. The government in 1972 abandoned the first site examined — a salt dome at Lyons, Kan. — after experts concluded that water might leak into the formation from old mining boreholes. In the mid-1970s the Energy Research and Development Administration, DOE's predecessor agency, developed plans to build a Waste Isolation Pilot Plant (WIPP) in underground salt beds near Carlsbad, N.M. Congress authorized WIPP as a demonstration project for disposing of both high-level and low-level military wastes. DOE in 1979 proposed expanding the plant to include an experimental facility for storing spent commercial fuel rods, subject to Nuclear Regulatory Commission (NRC) licensing. But Congress, through an amendment to fiscal 1980 nuclear weapons authorization legislation, restricted the project to its original purpose of storing wastes from weapons production. President Carter in 1980 attempted to cancel the WIPP program, proposing instead that the government build depositories, subject to NRC regulation, to handle military as well as high-level commercial wastes. But Congress continued to fund construction of a separate unlicensed WIPP project for handling military wastes. *(WIPP legislation, Congress and the Nation Vol. V, pp. 501, 525)*

DOE meanwhile surveyed other potential sites for storing nuclear wastes below ground in mined-out geologic formations. The NRC had ruled that, before selecting a permanent repository site, the government must consider at least three different sites in at least two different kinds of geologic formations.

The sites considered the leading contenders for a permanent repository were basalt formations at the government's Hanford, Wash., Nuclear Reservation; volcanic tuff formations at its Nevada nuclear test site; and several salt formations in Utah, Texas, Louisiana and Mississippi. Salt and granite formations in other states also had been surveyed, but not explored in great detail. In December 1984 the Energy Department listed three sites that officials wanted to consider for the permanent underground repository. They included the Hanford facility, near Richland in southeastern Washington state; Yucca Mountain, on the Nevada nuclear testing reservation 100 miles northwest of Las Vegas; and Deaf Smith County, in the Texas Panhandle 30 miles west of Amarillo. In announcing the three candidate sites, Secretary of Energy Donald P. Hodel con-

ceded, "It's fair to say that none of the states are supportive" of locating a repository within their borders.

In the same period, nuclear utilities pressed the government to provide some kind of interim "away-from-reactor" (AFR) storage for the spent fuel rods that the companies were keeping at power plants.

The most likely sites for away-from-reactor storage of spent fuel were considered to be defunct or never-used privately owned reprocessing facilities at Morris, Ill., Barnwell, S.C., and West Valley, N.Y.

Congress in 1980 established a national policy for handling low-level radioactive wastes — including slightly contaminated gloves, clothing, equipment and other materials — generated by commercial uses of nuclear energy. Through legislation passed that year, Congress gave state governments the responsibility to establish dumps where private low-level wastes could be buried. The law authorized states to form regional compacts among neighboring state governments to set up a regional facility to handle low-level wastes from a wider area. *(Low-level wastes, Congress and the Nation Vol. V, p. 524)*

The Senate in 1980 approved a bill directing the government to build above-ground storage vaults to temporarily store high-level wastes from defense as well as civilian facilities. But the House substituted a different measure setting a timetable for opening a permanent underground repository. Efforts to draft compromise legislation were blocked by Senate Energy Committee Chairman Henry M. Jackson's, D-Wash., objection to provisions allowing states to veto plans to store military wastes within their borders.

1981-82 Issues

The 97th Congress still faced some formidable technical and political questions when it took up nuclear-waste legislation in 1981. Nuclear industry spokesmen maintained that the nation possessed the technology to safely dispose of nuclear wastes in sealed containers that would keep radioactive materials isolated for as long as they remained dangerous. Joined by the Reagan administration, the industry urged Congress to move ahead with waste disposal plans to help restore sagging public confidence in nuclear power's safety.

Environmentalists and anti-nuclear activists, on the other hand, claimed that many unresolved technical questions left it doubtful that nuclear waste could be safely buried. They contended that no government plan could assure that buried waste would remain undisturbed for centuries in the future. They warned that earthquakes, groundwater intrusion, other geologic processes or even inadvertent drilling by men could pierce underground storage chambers and bring contaminated wastes into contact with human air and water supplies. Industry critics cautioned that transporting reactor byproducts to temporary and permanent storage sites would increase the risk of accident, theft or sabotage. And they opposed any legislation that would set tight deadlines for selecting depository locations, accelerate environmental impact reviews or short-circuit NRC procedures for licensing nuclear-waste storage facilities.

With those fears in mind, state governments and Indian tribal leaders were reluctant to accept nuclear-storage facilities. Thirty states had potential depository sites, but none was happy about the possibility that the federal government might build a nuclear dump within its borders. As a result, senators and representatives from those 30 states

Weapons Use Barred for Spent Civilian Fuel

Congress in 1982 barred the U.S. government from making nuclear weapons with spent fuel produced by commercial nuclear-power plants.

The Reagan administration, joined by congressional military committee leaders, in 1981 floated proposals to convert the plutonium produced in civilian reactor wastes into components for atomic weapons. But Congress, through an amendment to a Nuclear Regulatory Commission (NRC) authorization bill, blocked a step that opponents contended would end the nation's traditional commitment to keep military and civilian nuclear programs separate.

Converting spent civilian power plant fuel to weapons "would, in effect, turn commercial nuclear-power plants into bomb-making factories," Sen. Gary Hart, D-Colo., told the Senate in leading the fight to head off the idea's consideration. "It would seriously undermine U.S. efforts to halt the spread of nuclear weapons to countries that do not now have them."

Secretary of Energy James B. Edwards on Oct. 8, 1981, said that his department was considering the proposal. In Congress, House and Senate Armed Services Committee leaders favored consideration of refining spent civilian fuel to supply plutonium for the government's nuclear arsenal buildup. Defense experts predicted that plans to step up nuclear warhead production would require more plutonium than existing government reactors could produce.

What to do with the spent fuel produced by the nation's commercial nuclear reactors was an issue that Congress debated in considering nuclear-waste legislation. Utilities were not anxious to bury spent fuel, since it still held millions of dollars worth of uranium and plutonium, the key ingredient in making nuclear weapons. Some government officials, and some members of Congress, suggested that the government could save money by extracting plutonium from civilian wastes instead of building costly reactors to supply weapons components.

Because of the way it was burned in civilian reactors, plutonium that came from reprocessing of spent fuel generally was not pure enough to make

weapons. But government scientists were working on a laser process that they believed would be sufficiently developed in two or three years to make a decision to turn spent civilian fuel into the makings of nuclear weapons. Proponents said that would make sense because by the mid-1980s the government would not have enough plutonium to make all the weapons it had planned; unless civilian spent fuel was used, new facilities would have to be built to make plutonium, at a cost of $8 billion to $12 billion.

But Congress moved quickly to reinforce the distinction between civilian and military nuclear programs. Members who supported nuclear-power expansion warned that using spent fuel for weapons would only increase growing public concern about nuclear safety. "This could be the death knell for commercial nuclear power in the United States," Sen. Alan K. Simpson, R-Wyo., chairman of the Senate Energy and Public Works Subcommittee on Nuclear Regulation, contended in backing Hart's proposal to bar its consideration.

The Senate in 1981 attached Hart's amendment blocking military use of civilian fuel to fiscal 1982 energy and water appropriations legislation. Conferees dropped that amendment. But ignoring objections by Armed Services Committee Chairman John Tower, R-Texas, the Senate in 1982 revived the prohibition by voting 88-9 to add an amendment offered by Hart and Simpson to legislation (HR 2330) authorizing fiscal 1982-83 funding for NRC operations. The House accepted the amendment in conference, then defeated by a 107-281 vote a motion by Samuel S. Stratton, D-N.Y., chairman of the Armed Services Subcommittee on Procurement and Military Nuclear Systems, to strip the provision from the conference report. *(NRC legislation, p. 366)*

President Reagan signed HR 2330 into law Jan. 4, 1983 (PL 97-415). During 1981 debates on the issue, a senior member of the House Science Committee staff termed any plans to use spent civilian reactor fuel for bombs a "pipe dream that Congress will never allow to happen."

maneuvered throughout 1981-82 to write the nuclear-waste legislation in ways that would preclude selection of disposal sites within the regions they represented.

The choices that Congress was forced to make in setting nuclear-waste policy included:

● Permanent Disposal Facility. The Carter administration and environmental groups proposed that the government move ahead to place high-level wastes in deep underground formations, where they could be permanently removed from the surface environment. But some members of Congress, notably from the Gulf Coast states, proposed that the government first build experimental man-made

vaults, where waste could be held and monitored for a long period. They contended that man-made "monitored, retrievable storage" (MRS) would prove safer than underground disposal, thus making below-ground facilities unnecessary. Some members also wanted the government to build a pilot waste facility, not subject to NRC licensing, to test disposal technology and perhaps be converted into a permanent depository.

● AFR Disposal. The Carter administration had proposed building a federal "away-from-reactor" facility to store spent fuel rods from commercial power plants until a permanent repository was ready. Several bills proposed a

federal facility that would be funded by nuclear utilities. But the Reagan administration maintained that private industry, not the government, should provide AFR storage. And environmental groups opposed a temporary facility as an industry bailout. They also warned that the AFR plan would risk dangerous accidents as utilities began shipping spent fuel rods from around the country to the temporary federal facility.

● State Role. State officials and nuclear critics urged Congress to allow state governments and Indian tribes to veto a depository site within their borders. At the least, they argued, state and tribal leaders should be able to object early in the process, when a site was selected for study. Most proposed legislation allowed state or tribal governments to object to the federal government's decision to proceed with a repository, then let the veto stand if either the House or the Senate passed a resolution to uphold it. The industry preferred an alternative "two-house" procedure that required that both the House and the Senate, not just one chamber, uphold a state veto to let it stand.

● Military Waste. Carter proposed canceling WIPP and burying military waste along with spent commercial fuel rods in a permanent underground facility licensed by NRC. Environmental groups, citing leaks from high-level military wastes at Hanford, contended that the NRC should regulate disposal of military as well as commercial wastes. But some members of Congress, including House and Senate Armed Services Committee leaders, argued that NRC regulation could interfere with weapons production. They also said it would be a bad precedent to allow states to object to the siting of defense facilities — including nuclear storage facilities — within their borders. The 1980 nuclear waste bill died when some members refused to agree to let states object to storage within their borders of waste from the production of nuclear weapons.

● Funding. Most nuclear-waste proposals required that nuclear power consumers, not the federal government, pay for storing commercial wastes. Most bills imposed a mandatory surcharge on electricity generated by nuclear plants to cover the government's waste management costs.

Senate, House Action

In both the House and Senate, the leaders of the principal environment and energy committees maneuvered throughout 1981 and 1982 to put together comprehensive nuclear-waste legislation. In the fall of 1981 Senate Energy and Natural Resources Committee Chairman James A. McClure, R-Idaho, began pushing efforts to work out compromise legislation with other Senate panels. A year later, House Interior and Insular Affairs Committee Chairman Morris K. Udall, D-Ariz., spurred backstage negotiations with other House committee chairmen that finally produced a nuclear-waste measure that could win House approval.

Since Congress had abolished its once powerful Joint Atomic Energy Committee in 1977, three Senate committees and seven House panels shared jurisdiction over nuclear-waste legislation. While the joint committee had been protective toward nuclear industry interests, the fragmentation of responsibility among other standing House and Senate committees gave industry critics more opportunities to influence subcommittee and full committee deliberations. During the nuclear-waste debate, the shared jurisdiction slowed and complicated the process of drafting

disposal plans that both the House and Senate could support. It also produced a number of compromise bills that committee chairmen and staff members devised behind the scenes to reconcile conflicting committee positions. (*Joint committee abolished, Congress and the Nation Vol. V, p. 462*)

Through months of such negotiations, congressional leaders finally settled on a nuclear-waste plan directing the government to move ahead to build a permanent below-ground waste repository. Congress also authorized temporary away-from-reactor storage for spent fuel rods and experimental plans for a retrievable storage facility. But the House and Senate Armed Services committees intervened to preserve the option of developing a separate disposal system for nuclear waste from weapons production. And in a last-minute compromise, demanded by Sen. William Proxmire, D-Wis., Congress agreed to strengthen state government authority to refuse to bury nuclear wastes within its borders.

Senate Action. The Republican-led Senate acted first, passing a nuclear-waste measure (S 1662) by a 69-9 vote April 29, 1982. In general, the bill followed revisions the Senate Environment and Public Works Committee had proposed to a version drafted by the Energy and Natural Resources Committee in the fall of 1981.

S 1662 had been introduced in September 1981 by Energy Committee Chairman McClure; Environment Committee Chairman Robert T. Stafford, Vt.; and other Republican members of the two panels. McClure rammed the legislation through the Energy panel by an 11-4 vote Oct. 21. Under a procedure worked out when S 1662 was introduced, the Environment panel then had 30 days to act on the measure.

In its version, the Energy panel proposed both a permanent high-level waste repository and at least one temporary AFR facility for spent commercial fuel rods. At the behest of J. Bennett Johnston, D-La., who was seeking to block nuclear-waste disposal in Gulf Coast salt domes in his state, the panel's bill gave development of long-term retrievable storage technology equal emphasis with below-ground disposal. Johnston contended that man-made storage technology existed and would prove safer than underground disposal.

The Energy panel, eager to move a bill through Congress, exempted military wastes from its measure. The committee staff added a provision after markup sessions were finished that prohibited the commingling of civilian and military wastes. Senate Armed Services Committee Chairman John Tower, R-Texas, had warned McClure that his panel would demand that the bill be referred to it if the measure dealt with military wastes. Both the House and Senate Armed Services panels traditionally opposed any civilian agency control over military programs.

Stafford's Environment Committee Nov. 16 approved a revised version of S 1662 by an 11-0 vote. The Environment panel recommended that the government build a single repository for both military and civilian wastes, unless the president ruled that the national security dictated a separate defense-only facility. In addition, Stafford's committee proposed that the government begin building a retrievable storage facility only after it had selected and started developing a permanent underground disposal site. Environment Committee members wanted to give permanent disposal priority over a man-made facility, which future generations would be forced to maintain and monitor.

The Energy and Environment panels filed a joint re-

port (S Rept 97-282) on S 1662 on Nov. 30, 1981, but the Senate put off floor consideration until its 1982 session. The following March, the two committees agreed to take to the floor a compromise version, consisting mostly of the Environment panel's provisions, then work out their differences during Senate debate. The Armed Services Committee then claimed the bill, voting 9-2 on March 25 (S Rept 97-327) to strip out provisions dealing with military wastes.

During floor action, the Senate turned down efforts by senators to keep waste facilities out of their states. By a 47-43 vote, it tabled an amendment by Strom Thurmond, R-S.C., to delete provisions for building an away-from-reactor storage facility. Senators from South Carolina, New York and Illinois — the states where AFR storage was likely to be located — contended that utilities could find sufficient room in power plant storage pools until a permanent repository was available. The Senate also rejected amendments by Mississippi Sens. John C. Stennis, D, and Thad Cochran, R, to slow the timetable for selecting permanent repository sites. Stennis and Cochran wanted to provide more time for the government to survey alternative sites, thus easing pressure to select Mississippi salt domes that already had been identified for consideration.

The Senate tabled Proxmire's proposal to give state governments the right to veto any nuclear-waste facility. It also turned down an amendment by Howard W. Cannon, D-Nev., to require action by both the House and Senate to overturn a state veto.

But ignoring the Armed Services Committee's objection, the Senate voted to open the permanent depository to military as well as civilian wastes. By voice vote, it adopted an amendment by Gary Hart, D-Colo., and Alan K. Simpson, R-Wyo., chairman of the Environment Committee's Subcommittee on Nuclear Regulation, directing the government to plan to bury military wastes in the same facility unless the president determined that a separate defense-waste repository was needed.

House Action. The House Dec. 2, 1982, approved separate nuclear-waste legislation (HR 3809) during the post-election congressional session. Leaders from three House committees that shared primary jurisdiction on nuclear legislation had drafted a compromise measure in September that provided for a permanent repository, limited AFR storage and designing an MRS facility. As passed by the House, HR 3809 exempted military waste from most of its regulations and allowed either the House or the Senate to override a state veto of a permanent repository location.

The three committees — Science and Technology, Interior, and Energy and Commerce — had approved separate nuclear-waste measures in 1981 and earlier in 1982. The Science panel in December 1981 reported legislation (HR 5016 — H Rept 97-411, Part I) directing the government quickly to pick potential repository sites and build a test facility to gain public confidence in its ability safely to dispose of nuclear waste. In March the Interior Committee approved HR 3809 (H Rept 97-491, Part I), a more comprehensive bill that set a slower schedule for picking repository sites and allowed the government to provide away-from-reactor storage for spent fuel rods only as a last resort. Interior refused to exempt military waste, but the House Armed Services Committee claimed the bill and approved a separate version (H Rept 97-491, Part II) that stipulated the measure would not apply to weapons production wastes.

In the Energy and Commerce Committee, differences between two senior members delayed action until August.

Richard L. Ottinger, D-N.Y., chairman of the Energy Conservation and Power Subcommittee, and James T. Broyhill, R-N.C., the committee's senior Republican, remained at odds for months. Ottinger opposed interim federal storage of spent fuel rods and favored applying the same state participation and environmental review requirements to military as well as civilian waste. Broyhill, whose district included several power plants that were said to be running out of storage space, supported a large federal AFR and wanted to exempt military waste. Ottinger's own subcommittee adopted Broyhill's legislation in June. The full Energy and Commerce Committee Aug. 4 approved the measure (HR 6598 — H Rept 97-785, Part I) after Republicans and Southern Democrats defeated most efforts to revise it.

Trying to complete House action before Congress recessed for the 1982 congressional election campaign, Udall prodded leaders from the three committees to draft a 142-page compromise bill (HR 7187), introduced in September, that the House considered as a substitute for the text of HR 3809. The House began floor debate late that month, but put off final action until its post-election session. In late November and early December the House defeated several amendments that members had designed to keep waste facilities out of their districts. It rejected, by a 105-281 vote, a proposal by Edward J. Markey, D-Mass., to apply all of the bill's provisions to military waste. By a 190-184 vote Nov. 29, the House accepted Broyhill's amendment to weaken state authority to veto a waste repository by requiring that either the House or Senate back a state veto for it to stand. The compromise legislation allowed a veto to stand unless both chambers voted to overturn it; Broyhill's amendment was similar to the Senate measure.

Final Compromise

Udall had hoped that the Senate would simply accept HR 3809 as he had shepherded it through the House. But the Senate instead adopted, by voice vote on Dec. 20, yet another compromise version of HR 3809 that McClure's Energy Committee staff had drafted in consultation with key House and Senate members. Before approving the measure, the Senate approved several amendments, including three by Thurmond that gave states a larger role in decisions on where to store spent fuel rods temporarily. One Thurmond amendment also ordered that the spent fuel be removed from temporary storage within three years after a permanent repository was opened.

At Proxmire's insistence, the bill's sponsors accepted an amendment to make it easier for a state government to block a federal government decision to build a nuclear-waste repository within its boundaries. Proxmire, who earlier had proposed giving states an absolute power to veto a waste site without review by Congress, threatened to filibuster the measure unless the veto procedure that both the House and Senate had approved was strengthened. Under both the House and Senate bills a state veto would stand if state officials persuaded either the House or the Senate to uphold it. But Proxmire's amendment, adopted on the Senate floor Dec. 20, let a state veto take effect unless U.S. officials convinced both the House and Senate to pass a resolution overturning the state objection.

The House approved the final Senate bill a few hours later, by a 256-32 vote, despite some members' objections to the Senate reversal on state veto procedures. To make sure that the measure could be passed intact, the House took it up under a rule that allowed no amendments and

provided that the vote on adopting the rule was also the vote on passing the bill.

Provisions

As signed into law Jan. 7, 1983, major provisions of HR 3809 (PL 97-425):

Permanent Repositories. Required the president to submit to Congress by March 31, 1987, his recommendation of one site for a permanent federal repository for nuclear waste. The law directed the president to send Congress a recommendation for a second repository site by March 31, 1990.

● Permitted the government to store in the repositories both spent reactor fuel rods from nuclear power plants and high-level radioactive wastes produced by reprocessing spent fuel to extract plutonium. The law ordered that spent fuel rods be stored in ways that would permit their subsequent retrieval.

● Required the secretary of energy to apply for Nuclear Regulatory Commission (NRC) authorization to build a repository within 90 days after a site was selected. The law required the NRC to act on the application for a first repository by Jan. 1, 1989, and for a second by Jan. 1, 1992.

Spent Fuel Storage. Gave the Department of Energy (DOE) authority to develop temporary storage facilities for up to 1,900 metric tons of spent nuclear fuel from civilian reactors. The law allowed the government to transport spent fuel to existing federal facilities, build new storage facilities at reactor sites, or hold it in casks or other mobile equipment either at reactors or at federal facilities.

● Stipulated that the government would store only waste from utilities that had filled existing power plant storage tanks and were unable to reasonably expand reactor-site storage.

● Directed the government to collect fees from utilities whose wastes it handled to pay for interim storage.

● Ordered the government to take title of spent fuel at the reactor site and transport it to temporary storage.

Retrievable Storage Facility. Directed the energy secretary to report to Congress by June 1, 1985, on the potential for monitored, retrievable storage for nuclear wastes.

● Required that the NRC license a retrievable storage facility if Congress decided to authorize its construction.

State Veto. Allowed a state governor or legislature, or an Indian tribe, to veto a federal government decision to place a permanent repository or an interim spent fuel storage facility within its borders.

● Allowed the veto to stand unless both the House and Senate voted to overrule it within 90 days.

Nuclear Waste Fund. Created a fund, financed by fees paid by nuclear utilities, to pay the costs of building and operating permanent waste repositories. The law set the fee at one mill per kilowatt-hour of electricity generated by nuclear reactors.

Test and Evaluation Facility. Directed DOE to identify within one year three potential sites for a facility to test the feasibility of underground nuclear-waste storage. The law directed that the three sites lie within at least two different types of rock formation.

Military Exemption. Exempted nuclear waste produced from defense programs from most of the bill's provisions. The law required the government, if it decided to store military wastes in a civilian repository, to pay a pro rata share of the facility's costs.

NRC Authorization

Congress in 1982 agreed to accelerated federal licensing procedures to permit new nuclear power plants to begin generating electricity.

After two years of controversy, the House and Senate approved a measure that enabled the federal Nuclear Regulatory Commission (NRC) to allow electric utility companies to start up newly built nuclear plants before the commission completed public hearings on licensing the facilities. Congress wrote that provision into long-delayed legislation (HR 2330 — PL 97-415) authorizing NRC funding for fiscal 1982 and 1983.

The Reagan administration backed NRC authority to grant temporary operating licenses as part of its campaign to streamline federal regulation of the troubled nuclear power industry. President Reagan himself, in an Oct. 8, 1981, policy statement, maintained that hopes to expand electric power production by nuclear reactors had been "strangled in a morass of regulations that do not enhance safety, but that do cause extensive licensing delays and economic uncertainties."

To help correct that problem, HR 2330 gave the NRC power through the end of 1983 to issue temporary licenses to operate new nuclear reactors until public hearings were completed. When Congress began debating the interim licensing proposal in 1981, NRC licensing delays were expected to hold up power production from 13 nuclear plants scheduled to be completed in the following two years. Electric utilities that were building nuclear units complained bitterly that lengthy NRC hearings on granting operating licenses raised electricity rates for consumers by keeping new plants out of service for months after construction had been finished.

Environmental groups opposed interim licensing, contending that full-scale NRC hearings should be completed to assure that public safety would be protected before reactors began producing power. Congressional critics of the nuclear industry cited the 1979 accident at the Three Mile Island (TMI) nuclear plant in Pennsylvania in opposing any shortcuts in NRC procedures for determining whether reactors could be operated safely.

By the time Congress cleared HR 2330, concern about long delays in licensing nuclear plants was ebbing. NRC received no applications for temporary licenses in 1983, and Congress let the commission's authority to issue them expire on schedule at the end of the year. But NRC officials warned again in 1983 that temporary licenses might be necessary to prevent startup delays in five plants nearing completion. *(1983-84 NRC authorization bills, p. 373)*

As cleared, the NRC legislation carried provisions that suspended commission regulations ordering uranium mills to cover up radioactive tailings, the waste produced by processing uranium ore. Sen. Pete V. Domenici, R-N.M., proposed the amendments to stall NRC tailing cleanup rules that uranium industry officials and state officials in New Mexico contended were too costly.

In passing HR 2330, Congress also accepted a Senate amendment that prohibited the U.S. government from making nuclear weapons from the plutonium in the spent fuel produced by civilian reactors. The administration, along with House and Senate Armed Services Committee leaders, had suggested that the government consider reprocessing nuclear power plant waste as a cost-saving way to produce plutonium for military use. *(Box, p. 363)*

The measure authorized $485 million in fiscal 1982 and

$51 million in fiscal 1983 for NRC operations. But maneuvering over the mill tailings and spent fuel issues delayed final action until the last days of the lame-duck 1982 session. President Reagan signed HR 2330 on Jan. 3, 1983, well after fiscal 1982 was over and three months into fiscal 1983.

Background

Congress established the five-member NRC in 1974. As part of a general reorganization of federal energy research and regulation functions, Congress that year enacted legislation (PL 93-438) that abolished the federal Atomic Energy Commission (AEC), an agency created in 1946 to promote nuclear power development and regulate civilian nuclear plants. The 1974 law transferred the AEC's research programs to a new Energy Research and Development Administration, which was absorbed by the Department of Energy (DOE) in 1977. It also created NRC, composed of five members appointed by the president, to take over AEC responsibility to regulate the construction and operation of nuclear reactors for generating electricity. Ever since, NRC had been caught in the middle of continuing disputes over the safety of nuclear power plants. *(NRC creation, Congress and the Nation Vol. IV, p. 219)*

NRC procedure followed a two-step system for giving private utilities approval to build and then operate reactors. NRC granted a construction permit approving plans to build a nuclear plant. When the facility was ready, the commission subsequently granted an operating license allowing the utility to start the reactor and generate electricity. Before approving both steps, NRC officials conducted public hearings and drawn-out investigations. NRC officials reviewed license applications to determine whether proposed plants could be built and operated without unduly risking public health and safety or damaging the environment. They also investigated whether utilities planning to operate nuclear plants were properly insured against accidents.

After a utility decided to build a nuclear plant, it usually took 10 to 12 years to obtain an NRC construction permit, build the facility and obtain an NRC operating license. Utilities and reactor manufacturing companies contended that time-consuming NRC procedures and hearings were the primary cause of construction delays and cost overruns that vastly inflated the cost of bringing nuclear plants into operation. By the late 1970s lagging electric power demand and rising construction costs forced U.S. utilities to cancel more than 30 planned reactors and defer construction of dozens more.

In 1978, at the urging of Secretary of Energy James R. Schlesinger, the Carter administration proposed that Congress revise the nuclear licensing system to reduce construction time. The Carter plan would have authorized the NRC to approve joint construction permits and operating licenses, eliminating the need for two separate hearings. It also would have empowered the commission to approve nuclear plant sites and standard reactor designs before construction permits were filed. Schlesinger contended that the changes would cut the time required to design, build and license a new plant to 6.5 years. *(Licensing reform, Congress and the Nation Vol. V, p. 490)*

Congress paid little attention to Carter's 1978 licensing plan. Environmental groups and other nuclear industry critics continued to challenge existing NRC regulation as too lax to assure that nuclear plants could operate safely.

After the 1979 Three Mile Island mishap, Congress focused attention on tightening NRC controls instead of speeding plant licensing. A commission appointed by President Carter to investigate the accident recommended that the NRC be abolished and replaced by an executive branch agency headed by a single administrator. Carter instead reorganized the NRC in 1980 to give its chairman more authority. *(NRC reorganization, Congress and the Nation Vol. V, p. 521)*

In 1979 and again in 1980 congressional debates over how to respond to the nuclear power problems delayed action on NRC funding authorizations. Congress did not pass a fiscal 1980 NRC authorization until that year was more than half over, and it never approved an authorization bill at all for fiscal 1981. *(NRC authorizations, Congress and the Nation Vol. V, pp. 499, 521)*

1981 NRC Debates

The Reagan administration, committed to speeding nuclear power development, renewed efforts in 1981 to streamline federal regulation of the industry. But congressional action on NRC funds again bogged down, for nearly two years, in controversies over nuclear plant licensing, uranium mill tailings and the possibility of reprocessing spent nuclear fuel.

In April 1981 the NRC asked Congress for authority to grant interim licenses that would allow utilities to test reactors at low power before the commission completed two-year licensing hearings. House and Senate committees drafted NRC authorization bills approving interim licensing, but maneuvering over that issue and other controversial amendments delayed final action until the last days of the 1982 session.

The House in 1981 approved an Energy and Commerce Committee proposal to authorize temporary reactor licenses, overriding arguments that public safety would be jeopardized. But the threat of prolonged debate over an amendment blocking spent fuel reprocessing stalled Senate action on a similar measure in the last hours of the 1981 session.

The Senate delay disappointed utilities and reactor manufacturers, who had lobbied hard for NRC authority to grant interim licenses. The utilities said the delay between completion of construction and eventual operation resulted in higher costs for consumers because the utilities had to continue to pay the bills for the unused reactors while also providing power from other, usually more expensive, sources.

Congressional committees and individual members had received a large volume of mail from utility customers complaining of the licensing delays. Among the utilities facing delays were companies in California, North Carolina, Texas, New Jersey and Pennsylvania.

Environmental groups worked against the interim licensing provision. Mike Faden, a lobbyist for the Union of Concerned Scientists, which opposed nuclear power in general, said the hearing process was needed to protect the public safety. He attributed the licensing delays to diversion of NRC staff to examine safety problems at existing reactors as a result of the 1979 accident at the Three Mile Island nuclear reactor.

House Approval. The House Nov. 5, 1981, ignored nuclear power opponents' objections by passing a two-year NRC authorization bill (HR 2330) that included a compromise interim licensing provision. House Interior and En-

ergy and Commerce committee leaders, who shared jurisdiction over NRC legislation, worked out the compromise before the House took up HR 2330 to mute environmentalists' opposition.

The Interior panel in April reported HR 2330 (H Rept 97-22, Part I) in a relatively bland version that did not address controversial issues. The Energy and Commerce Committee June 4 approved its own version (H Rept 97-22, Part II) including interim licensing provisions. In May, Richard L. Ottinger, D-N.Y., chairman of the Subcommittee on Energy Conservation and Power, had surprised environmental lobbyists by working out a compromise on the issue with subcommittee Republicans. Ottinger explained that his subcommittee had acted to head off a House Appropriations Committee move to attach a temporary licensing rider to a supplemental fiscal 1981 appropriations bill.

The subcommittee proposal, accepted by the full Energy and Commerce panel, permitted the NRC to issue temporary operating licenses for fuel loading, low-power testing or full-scale power generation at new atomic plants before public hearings on permanent licensing were completed. Carlos J. Moorhead, Calif., the top-ranking subcommittee Republican, argued that the licensing provisions could save consumers more than $12 billion in additional electricity charges that could result from licensing delays. But Edward J. Markey, D-Mass., warned that granting temporary full-power licenses for new nuclear plants "would be to unlearn the lessons of Three Mile Island."

Before the House took up HR 2330 in November, Ottinger and Interior Committee Chairman Morris K. Udall, D-Ariz., neither known as a nuclear industry supporter, put together a second compromise temporary licensing provision. Ottinger and Udall said the provision was carefully written and would not be used if start-up delays were unlikely. Several environmental groups said they did not like the provision but accepted it as a reasonable compromise on the issue.

The administration and nuclear industry lobbyists strongly backed the Udall-Ottinger proposal. James T. Broyhill, R-N.C., predicted it would "save electric consumers over $1 billion in replacement power costs and 63 months of licensing delays at 11 completed power plants by the end of 1983."

The House passed HR 2330 with the compromise provision by voice vote Nov. 5. By a 90-304 margin, the House defeated Markey's amendment to strip the temporary licensing provision from the bill. House debate revealed disagreement over how many plants would encounter start-up delays unless temporary licenses were granted. Markey said the NRC had determined that there would be only 13 months of delays, nearly all at a controversial plant under construction at Diablo Canyon, Calif. "Diablo Canyon," Markey noted, "is the power plant that this past month was revealed to have been built using the wrong blueprints in the designing of the support system for the cooling of the core of the reactor."

Markey's amendment was supported by Toby Moffett, D-Conn., whose Government Operations Subcommittee on Environment, Energy and Natural Resources had issued a report concluding that there would be few delays in licensing nuclear plants. The report also found that public hearings would not cause the delays that took place.

Senate Stalemate. In the Senate, the Environment and Public Works Committee May 13 unanimously approved a two-year NRC authorization bill (S 1207 — S Rept 97-113) that contained interim licensing provisions. But Senate floor consideration was postponed over the summer and fall while Alan K. Simpson, R-Wyo., chairman of the panel's Subcommittee on Nuclear Regulation, tried to work out a compromise with Domenici on amendments protecting the U.S. uranium mining industry. Then, in the last hours of the 1981 session on Dec. 16, Henry M. Jackson, D-Wash., blocked action on the NRC bill by threatening to prolong debate on a proposed amendment that would prohibit the government to use spent fuel from civilian nuclear power plants to make atomic weapons. *(Spent fuel for weapons, box, p. 363)*

1982 Action

Congress took another full year to finish work on NRC authorization legislation. By 1982 it appeared only one utility would face NRC licensing delays — for just two months — and Congress approved interim licensing authority without much further debate. But Senate negotiations on military use of spent fuel, uranium mill tailings and uranium import curbs delayed final action until the 97th Congress' lame-duck session after the 1982 congressional elections.

In the end Congress accepted a Senate amendment, proposed by Simpson and Gary Hart, D-Colo., that barred the government from processing plutonium produced by fuel burned in civilian nuclear reactors to produce nuclear weapons. It also agreed to Domenici's proposal to delay the NRC's uranium tailing cleanup regulations. But after veto threats from the White House, the House refused to accept a companion amendment to impose a moratorium on uranium imports if they threatened the U.S. mining industry.

Senate Uranium Industry Amendments. The Senate in March passed the two-year NRC authorization bill drawn up by the Environment and Public Works Committee the previous May. The bill's provisions for interim licensing of new reactors were not an issue during floor debate, which focused mainly on the Simpson-Hart amendment barring military use of spent civilian power plant fuel.

The Senate approved the amendment, 88-9, before passing its version of HR 2330 by a 97-0 vote March 30.

By voice vote March 30, the Senate adopted a Domenici amendment that would bolster the sagging domestic uranium industry in two ways:

● It would delay the implementation of NRC regulations requiring the cleanup of radioactive uranium mill tailings. The industry said the regulations were too harsh and expensive.

● It also required that at least 80 percent of uranium used by U.S. utilities must be produced in the United States.

Domenici held up Senate floor action on NRC authorizations in 1981 in an effort to delay regulations that the commission issued in 1980 to require mining companies to clean up radioactive tailing piles at active uranium mines. The mining and processing of uranium ore produced sand-like radioactive wastes that were deposited on the surface near mills. Tons of tailings had been piled up near many mills, allowing radioactive particles to spread with the wind and water runoff. In some cases, local contractors had used tailings to build schools and houses.

Congress had passed a law (PL 95-604) in 1978 requiring the cleanup of abandoned mines and the establishment of regulations for controlling tailings at active mines. The

Environmental Protection Agency (EPA) was supposed to set health standards for tailings but it failed to act, so the NRC in 1980 issued its own regulations requiring mill operators to cover tailing piles with dirt to keep radioactive material from spreading. Implementation of the regulations had been delayed once by an amendment to the fiscal 1982 energy-water appropriations bill (PL 97-88), but Domenici wanted to delay them again through an amendment to the NRC authorization measure.

Domenici designed the second proposal to shield U.S. uranium mining companies against a surge of imported nuclear fuel from Canada and Australia. New Mexico, Domenici's state, was the nation's largest uranium producer. But since the late 1970s, a slowdown in the growth of nuclear power generation had forced the mining industry to cut production and close down some uranium operations. Although imported fuel supplied only about 12 percent of U.S. uranium demand in 1982, newly opened Canadian and Australian surface mines were producing low-cost ore that threatened to prolong the American industry's slump even if uranium demand eventually recovered.

Before passing HR 2330, the Senate approved an amendment by Wendell H. Ford, D-Ky., directing the NRC to beef up its quality assurance program by assigning at least one inspector to every nuclear plant construction site. Ford proposed the amendment because two plants being built along Kentucky's borders, one in Ohio and one in Indiana, had run into serious construction problems.

Final Action. Conferees negotiated sporadically for six months before agreeing in September on a compromise NRC bill (H Rept 97-884). The Senate approved the conference report Oct. 1, but two House committees held up final action until the post-election session by objecting to the Senate's prohibition on using civilian fuel for weapons and to modified uranium import restrictions. The House eventually upheld the weapons provision, but its stand against import curbs forced Domenici to accept a separate congressional resolution ordering the government to study the economic condition of the domestic uranium industry.

The conference agreement allowed the NRC to issue interim licenses through the end of 1983 if environmental and safety reviews of the new reactor had been completed. It also allowed the commission to make minor changes in license requirements for nuclear reactors without holding public hearings.

Without discussion, conferees retained the Senate amendment prohibiting the use of burned fuel from civilian nuclear reactors for the production of nuclear weapons. They also retained Senate language that would expand the NRC's program of checking the quality of construction at new plants.

On the mill tailings issue, conferees required EPA to issue standards for the cleanup of tailings by October 1983. The NRC then would have to issue new regulations, which would have to take economic costs into consideration.

In place of Domenici's amendment requiring U.S. utilities to use at least 80 percent domestic uranium, the conference agreement called for a two-year moratorium on new contracts for uranium imports if imports rose above 37.5 percent of U.S. consumption. The conferees said imports above this level could endanger national security.

However, U.S. Trade Representative William E. Brock III indicated that the provision could lead to a veto of the bill. In a Sept. 15 letter, Brock said the administration could not accept such an automatic trigger for a moratorium on uranium imports.

In its lame-duck session, the House Dec. 2 voted 241-148 to drop the uranium import provision from the conference report. Ways and Means Committee leaders objected that their panel should have considered the issue before Congress acted. Bill Frenzel, R-Minn., offered the motion to delete the provision, arguing that import restrictions would impose an "unfair trade barrier" and provoke Canada and Australia to retaliate.

Armed Services Committee leaders protested the Senate's ban on using plutonium from spent fuel for weapons. But the House defeated, by a 107-281 vote, a motion by Samuel S. Stratton, D-N.Y., also to drop that provision.

Domenici and Udall subsequently worked out an agreement that cleared the way for final action on NRC authorizations. Domenici consented to Senate approval Dec. 17 of the House-amended conference report on HR 2330. The Senate at the same time adopted a concurrent resolution (S Con Res 135) "correcting" HR 2330 by adding a revised uranium import section. The resolution, approved by the House Dec. 20, directed the president to conduct a study of the U.S. uranium and mining industry. It also ordered the Energy Department to consider restrictions if uranium imports grew to more than 37.5 percent of U.S. demand during the next 10 years.

Provisions

As signed into law Jan. 4, 1983, major provisions of HR 2330 (PL 97-415):

● Authorized appropriations of $485 million in fiscal 1982 and $513 million in fiscal 1983 for NRC operations.

● Gave NRC authority, through Dec. 31, 1983, to grant utilities temporary licenses to operate new nuclear reactors before the commission had concluded public hearings. If it determined there would be no threat to public health or the environment, NRC initially could permit a company to operate a reactor at only 5 percent of total power under a temporary license. Eventually, NRC could grant temporary licenses allowing full-power operation.

● Ordered the commission to assign at least one resident inspector to every nuclear plant project where construction was at least 15 percent complete.

● Suspended NRC regulations on cleaning up uranium mill tailings until the Environmental Protection Agency issued environmental standards. The provision directed EPA to issue those standards by October 1983.

● Barred the government from using plutonium from fuel burned in civilian nuclear reactors to make nuclear weapons.

Three Mile Island

Congress in 1982 sidetracked Pennsylvania members' plan to force nuclear utilities throughout the nation to share the cost of cleaning up the damaged Three Mile Island power plant reactor in their state.

General Public Utilities Corp. (GPU), the Three Mile Island (TMI) plant's owner, was seeking financial help with the estimated $1 billion cost of decontaminating the reactor and building that were damaged in a 1979 accident. The TMI mishap, the nuclear industry's worst accident, had reinforced doubts throughout the nation about whether nuclear power plants could be operated safely. (TMI accident, Congress and the Nation Vol. V, p. 500)

Financially troubled GPU had slowed its TMI cleanup

operations as it exhausted $300 million in insurance payments. Pennsylvania officials, fearing that the plant might leak radioactivity as time went by, drew up cost-sharing plans in an effort to decontaminate the TMI plant as soon as possible. The Senate Energy and Natural Resources Committee in March approved one cost-sharing measure, but Congress took no action.

Background

The accident at Three Mile Island occurred March 28, 1979. A valve stuck open on TMI-2, one of two reactors at the island in the Susquehanna River near Harrisburg, Pa., causing a loss of cooling water. The nuclear fuel core overheated and, at least partially, melted. Area residents were evacuated when it was feared a hydrogen explosion might rip the reactor building apart.

Most of the radioactive water was removed from the reactor building and the building adjoining it. But the toughest part of the cleanup remained: decontaminating the reactor building and then dealing with the reactor core.

State officials and congressional delegations from Pennsylvania and New Jersey, the regions served by GPU, contended that completing the cleanup was a national responsibility that would benefit all utilities. Gov. Richard L. Thornburgh, R-Pa., proposed a cost-sharing plan under which the federal government, the nation's utilities and nuclear manufacturers would pay about half the cost of the cleanup, with the other half coming from payments by GPU, its customers and the states of Pennsylvania and New Jersey.

Rep. Allen E. Ertel, D-Pa., who represented the district where the TMI plant lay, and Sen. John Heinz, R-Pa., pushed different plans to set up a quasi-public insurance corporation to insure nuclear plants and make a retroactive payment to cover three-fourths of the TMI cleanup costs. In September 1982 the Edison Electric Institute (EEI), an association of stockholder-owned utilities, proposed raising $192 million over six years for the TMI cleanup by imposing an annual fee on all electric utilities, plus a surcharge on those that operated nuclear-power plants.

Congressional Inaction

Those proposals foundered because of opposition to requiring ratepayers and shareholders of all nuclear utilities to share in the cost, and because of fears that such action would set a precedent for future federal "bailouts" for financially troubled utilities.

The American Public Power Association (APPA) opposed efforts to spread TMI cleanup costs to the nation's electricity users, saying it would set a bad precedent. APPA officials said GPU could raise its rates enough to finance the entire cleanup and still not have the highest electric rates in the region.

The Union of Concerned Scientists also opposed legislation that would allow utilities to pass their share of cleanup costs through to electricity consumers, in effect creating a "national tax" on electricity to help clean up Three Mile Island. Electricity rates already had risen more than 80 percent over the past year in some areas of the country, a spokesman for the group noted.

The Senate Energy Committee March 31 voted 12-8 to report one cleanup measure (S 1606) drafted by Heinz and Bill Bradley, D-N.J. The bill charged nuclear utilities a fee of 28 cents per kilowatt hour on nuclear generating capac-

ity, up to a maximum of $1.6 million a year for each company, over a six-year period. But the Senate Environment and Public Works Committee, sharply divided over TMI cleanup plans, July 27 voted 10-6 to report S 1606 without recommendation. The two committees filed a joint report Aug. 13 (S Rept 97-524), but they never took the bill to the floor.

The House Interior and Energy and Commerce committees held 1982 hearings on TMI cleanup proposals but reported no legislation.

Clinch River Reactor

Congressional support eroded in 1981-82 for building the costly Clinch River breeder reactor.

Congress appropriated $195 million in fiscal 1982 and $181 million in fiscal 1983 for U.S. Department of Energy (DOE) work on the breeder demonstration project. But for the first time the House voted in 1982 to kill the government's plan to build a demonstration breeder reactor on the Clinch River near Oak Ridge, Tenn.

The Clinch River project survived by a one-vote Senate margin, thanks to backing from President Reagan and Majority Leader Howard H. Baker Jr., a Tennessee Republican. But slipping House and Senate support foreshadowed a congressional decision in 1983 to cancel the 12-year-old program to demonstrate nuclear breeder technology. *(Clinch River debate, p. 371)*

First authorized in 1970, the Clinch River plant was intended to prove that breeder reactors, which ran on plutonium and produced more plutonium as a byproduct than they consumed, could generate electricity while also producing additional nuclear fuel. Environmentalists had opposed the project from the start, contending that breeder technology would increase the world's supply of dangerous plutonium, a key ingredient in nuclear weapons. Criticism mounted throughout the 1970s as the project's estimated cost soared from $700 million to more than $3.2 billion by 1981. President Carter in 1977 renounced plans to use plutonium as nuclear fuel in the United States and tried unsuccessfully to persuade Congress to scrap the Clinch River plant. *(Background, Congress and the Nation Vol. V, p. 522)*

After President Reagan took office in 1981, Baker persuaded the administration to budget funds to continue the project over objections by David A. Stockman, director of the White House Office of Management and Budget (OMB). But congressional doubts about the Clinch River program grew in the newly elected 97th Congress as fiscal conservatives worried about rising federal costs joined environmentalists to back efforts to eliminate the project.

In 1981 the House Science and Technology Committee, which previously had strongly backed breeder development, voted to delete Clinch River funds from legislation authorizing fiscal 1982 DOE appropriations. But with the White House maneuvering for Southern support for Reagan's budget-cutting plans, the Senate restored $228 million for Clinch River as part of a substitute budget reconciliation package (HR 3982 — PL 97-35) that the House eventually accepted.

Later that year, Congress cleared an energy-water appropriations bill for fiscal 1983 (HR 4144 — PL 97-88) providing $181 million to continue Clinch River plant engineering and site preparation. During debate on the bill, the House defeated an amendment to strip out Clinch River

funds by a **key 186-206 vote: R 70-104; D 116-102 (ND 107-38, SD 9-64)**, the closest House opponents had ever come to killing the project. The Senate later tabled, by a **key 48-46 vote: R 36-14; D 12-32 (ND 4-26, SD 8-6)**, an amendment to cut appropriations for federal contributions to the project in half. *(1981 key votes, p. 879)*

Congress in 1982 never completed work on fiscal 1983 energy-water appropriations, in part because of the continuing Clinch River debate. Instead, Congress funded those programs through continuing appropriations resolutions that provided $181 million for the breeder project even though the House voted to cancel it.

By a **key 217-196 vote: R 80-102; D 137-94 (ND 121-33, SD 16-61)**, the House in December approved a floor amendment to delete Clinch River appropriations from a second fiscal 1983 continuing resolution (H J Res 631 — PL 97-377). But the Senate, by a **key 49-48 vote: R 38-14; D 11-34 (ND 4-26, SD 7-8)**, rejected a similar amendment to the resolution; and House-Senate conferees ignored the House stand by including Clinch River funds in the final version (H Rept 97-980). Conferees did provide $1 million for DOE to explore alternative methods for financing the breeder project and report to Congress on its findings in 1983. *(1982 key votes, p. 895)*

1983-84

The 98th Congress offered the U.S. nuclear power industry little help with its financial and environmental troubles.

Lawmakers in fact abandoned the federal government's previous support for promoting nuclear breeder technologies. Concerned by rising costs and safety doubts, both the House and Senate in 1983 voted decisively to scrap the controversial Clinch River breeder reactor, a joint government-industry project that experts once had hailed as a solution to U.S. energy problems.

With members growing more skeptical about nuclear power prospects, Congress resisted the Reagan administration's plans to expedite nuclear power plant construction. It refused to renew Nuclear Regulatory Commission authority to grant utilities temporary licenses to operate new reactors before formal safety hearings had been completed.

Electric power industry plans for building new nuclear plants continued to be plagued by cost overruns, high interest rates and construction problems. In the Pacific Northwest, the Washington Public Power Supply System, nicknamed "Whoops" by nuclear critics, in 1983 defaulted on $2.25 billion in bonds for nuclear plant construction, but Congress showed little interest in stepping in to solve the industry's fiscal difficulties.

Clinch River Reactor

Congress in 1983 ended federal government support for building the Clinch River breeder reactor, a project that once promised the nation an almost limitless source of electrical power.

Both the House and Senate voted decisively to deny more funds for the decade-old breeder project. That action scrapped joint government-industry plans to demonstrate "fast breeder" nuclear technology that would produce more

fuel than it burned. In the process of generating electric power, a breeder would convert uranium into plutonium that could be removed to provide abundant nuclear fuel.

Congress first authorized the Clinch River project in 1970 and funded the breeder program throughout the following decade as a solution to the nation's long-term energy problems. By the 1980s, however, congressional support was being eroded by long delays, sharply rising costs, flattening electric power demand and concern about the safety of nuclear technology. Although the government had spent $1.5 billion on planning the project, construction never got under way at the site near Oak Ridge, Tenn.

In the late 1970s President Carter had tried to cancel the Clinch River program, arguing that breeder reactors producing plutonium, a key ingredient in atomic bombs, would encourage the spread of nuclear weapons. Congress nearly killed the project in 1981-82, despite President Reagan's support and powerful backing from Senate Majority Leader Howard H. Baker Jr., R-Tenn., in whose state the plant would have been built. By 1983, after the 98th Congress convened, most members concluded that the potential energy yield no longer justified the project's escalating costs or the technology's risks.

Both the House and Senate voted to scrap the Clinch River project by decisive margins. The House in May voted 388-1 to repeal existing law authorizing funds for the program. The Senate in October refused more money for the project 56-40.

Congress included no money for the Clinch River breeder in its fiscal 1984 energy and water development appropriations bill (HR 3132 — PL 98-50). The House and Senate ignored the Reagan administration's plea to salvage the project through a new plan for sharing the cost with private industry.

Background

Congress approved the breeder project as the nation entered a decade of uncertainty about how to develop and produce reliable supplies of energy. Because the technology could produce more fuel than it burned — hence the name "breeder" — the program showed promise of providing a nearly inexhaustible source of power for generating electricity for industrial and residential use. "The breeder could extend the life of our natural uranium fuel supply from decades to centuries," President Nixon told the nation in 1971.

By building the Clinch River plant, the government intended to demonstrate that breeder reactors could generate electricity on a commercial scale even as they produced plutonium for additional nuclear fuel. The government also hoped that the plant's construction would spur private companies to develop an industrial base for building additional privately financed breeders. As initially authorized, the Clinch River breeder was expected to cost $700 million, and private industry agreed to pay $250 million of that, slightly more than one-third of the total.

From the start environmental groups and anti-nuclear activists opposed the breeder program. Environmentalists feared the possibility of a horrendous accident — a meltdown of the reactor core, which, if secondary safety measures did not go as planned, could release clouds of lethal radioactive gases into the air.

Others said the breeder would promote the spread of nuclear weapons. Unlike normal "light water" nuclear reac-

tors, breeder reactors used and bred plutonium, a key ingredient of atomic bombs.

Congress insisted on funding the Clinch River program throughout the 1970s despite environmental and anti-nuclear groups' opposition. Concerned about potential nuclear weapons proliferation, Carter renounced plans for burning plutonium as nuclear fuel in the United States and asked Congress to terminate the demonstration breeder. But Congress repeatedly overrode Carter's policy, refusing in a series of 1977-79 votes to end Clinch River funding. *(Congress and the Nation Vol. IV, p. 262; Congress and the Nation Vol. V, p. 522)*

Research, development and design of the Clinch River reactor continued throughout the 1970s, incorporating innovations into the project. Breeder engineers dismissed press reports that Clinch River was technologically obsolete; they said the design of the reactor core was unique and far more efficient than the core design being used overseas.

Licensing procedures for the plant proceeded as planned. The NRC issued a final environmental statement in October 1982, and the major court challenges had been dealt with.

Economics

But as work proceeded, the initial $700 million projected cost of the project soared to $4 billion. Meanwhile energy conservation efforts and slowing economic growth held electric power demand well below levels that U.S. energy planners predicted when the Clinch River project was conceived. With national energy independence no longer the obsession that it was in the early 1970s, the economic justification for the breeder program was called into question. Even the Tennessee Valley Authority (TVA), which had promised to purchase the power from the Clinch River breeder, had no real need for it.

Clinch River designers originally planned to complete the plant by 1980, but that target had slipped by a decade. Congress by 1983 had appropriated $1.5 billion for the project as its total cost rose to $4 billion. Private industry, however, still was committed to pay only $250 million, by then only one-sixteenth of the total.

Not until September 1982 was any work done on the Clinch River site near Oak Ridge. Then, however, site clearing began, and a year later a 100-foot-deep hole the size of a football field was almost ready for concrete pouring.

Half of the $1.5 billion spent on the project had been used for research, development and design, all complete by 1983. In addition, some $749 million in component parts had been ordered.

Eroding Congressional Support

As costs shot up and the construction date slipped, fiscal conservatives in Congress turned against the Clinch River program.

These members supported nuclear power in general and gave little weight to traditional arguments that the breeder was environmentally unsafe or a threat to world peace. Their concern was money. Given the current budget squeeze, they said, funneling $200 million to $300 million a year into a research and development project that would not pay off for decades — or possibly ever — was unconscionable.

Among the most active of these conservative Clinch

'Whoops' Rescue Fails

A Senate filibuster threat in 1983 headed off a proposal to help rescue a financially troubled nuclear power project in the Pacific Northwest.

Beset by cost overruns and heavy debt, the Washington Public Power Supply System (WPPSS) July 25 defaulted on repaying $2.25 billion in bonds it had issued for building nuclear power plants. The system, a combination of public utilities that was labeled "Whoops" by critics, earlier had canceled two of five nuclear plants it had begun during the 1970s to supply predicted electric power demand that failed to develop.

The WPPSS default, the largest municipal bond default in U.S. history, left the system unable to borrow more funds from private lenders to complete its ambitious power generation plans. The system's widely publicized troubles underscored the financial problems and lagging electricity demand that were forcing utilities throughout the nation to scale back previous plans for expanding nuclear generating capacity.

Three days after WPPSS defaulted, Senate Energy and Natural Resources Committee Chairman James A. McClure, R-Idaho, proposed legislation (S 1701) to help the system finish construction of as many as three of the five planned nuclear plants. McClure's measure allowed WPPSS participants to set up a new lending authority under state law to finance completion of at least two of the plants sponsors hoped to salvage.

Not burdened by WPPSS' bad credit rating, the new entity in theory could borrow about $1 billion by selling bonds secured by a contract with the Bonneville Power Administration (BPA), a federally created power distribution network that had backed WPPSS' earlier bond issues. The new contract would commit BPA to pay the principal and interest on the new bonds directly to the new entity, its obligees or their trustees.

McClure's committee in August held hearings on S 1701. Even if passed by the Senate, however, the measure inevitably would have been referred to the House Energy Committee, chaired by John D. Dingell, D-Mich., an outspoken opponent of WPPSS aid. So McClure, who also chaired the Senate Appropriations Subcommittee on Interior, attached S 1701 to House-passed Interior appropriations legislation (HR 3363 — S Rept 98-184).

But when HR 3363 reached the Senate floor, Howard M. Metzenbaum, D-Ohio, and William Proxmire, D-Wis., stalled debate by threatening to filibuster against the amendment. The two called McClure's plan a bailout that would be paid by federal taxpayers. After a six-week impasse McClure gave up the effort to win approval of the WPPSS financing plan.

River opponents were Sen. Gordon J. Humphrey, R-N.H., and Rep. Vin Weber, R-Minn. Both helped lead the campaign against the breeder in Congress. Their opposition swayed other key conservatives who previously had supported the breeder, such as Reps. Trent Lott, R-Miss., and Phil Gramm, R-Texas.

Backing the efforts of these members was a group of conservative lobbying organizations, including the National Taxpayers Union and the Heritage Foundation.

In 1981-82 Baker and the rest of the Tennessee congressional delegation fought hard to keep the Clinch River project going. Baker helped convince the Reagan administration to support funding for the program over the objections of Office of Management and Budget (OMB) Director David A. Stockman. In lobbying fellow members, the Tennessee delegation pointed out that the project employed more than 3,500 workers, with preliminary work spread throughout the country, giving members in 32 states political incentive to support continued funding.

1981-82 Debates. During the Carter administration, the House Science and Technology Committee had provided key support for the program. But the panel reversed its stand in 1981, after the Reagan administration came to power and backed Clinch River. The committee in 1981 voted 22-18 to kill the project, but its action was overturned in the budget reconciliation bill (PL 97-35).

In 1982 the full House voted to kill Clinch River, but the Senate upheld the project by one vote. Conferees on a continuing appropriations resolution (PL 97-377) finally provided $181 million to keep work going through Sept. 30, 1983, but they prohibited any permanent construction work at the site and directed the Department of Energy (DOE) to study alternative financing. *(Details, p. 370)*

Reagan Cost-Sharing Plan. Responding to that directive, the administration in 1983 sent Congress a plan for raising additional private funds to build the Clinch River plant. The plan proposed raising $1 billion from private sources, $150 million through the sale of stock and the rest from the sale of bonds in 1990 and from funds already committed by utilities and other investors. But opponents pointed out that private industry would assume no more risk under the plan than under previous financing arrangements. By the time the administration sent the plan to Capitol Hill on Aug. 1, moreover, the House already had voted to kill the project and Senate support was dwindling.

1983 Congressional Action

House. In the House the Science and Technology panel led the effort to scuttle the Clinch River program. The committee voted 24-16 in April 1983 to halt all work on the project by Sept. 30 unless the government approved a new plan for sharing costs with private industry by that date.

It attached that provision to legislation (HR 2587 — H Rept 98-81) authorizing funds for Department of Energy civilian research and development programs for fiscal 1984.

Congress in its 1981 budget reconciliation bill already had authorized DOE research and development programs through fiscal 1984, and the House panel drafted HR 2587 primarily as a vehicle for House protests against administration energy policies.

During May 12 floor debate on the measure, the House approved by a 388-1 vote a separate committee-drafted amendment, offered by George E. Brown Jr., D-Calif., and Claudine Schneider, R-R.I., that simply repealed the 1981 reconciliation measure provision authorizing Clinch River funds. The House then passed HR 2587, but the Senate took no action.

Senate. The Senate, which kept the project alive by a single vote in 1982, sealed its fate in October by refusing to provide $1.5 billion to complete the plant.

The Senate Appropriations Committee Oct. 19 had approved an amendment, offered by Energy and Natural Resources Committee Chairman James A. McClure, R-Idaho, to appropriate $1.5 billion for Clinch River as part of a fiscal 1984 supplemental appropriations bill (HR 3959). But the full Senate Oct. 26 killed the McClure amendment by a **56-40 key vote (R 23-30; D 33-10)**. *(1983 key votes, p. 911)*

The margin of defeat was wider than either side of the Clinch River debate had expected.

NRC Authorization

Congress in 1984 reauthorized Nuclear Regulatory Commission (NRC) programs, but only after allowing the agency's power to grant temporary nuclear power plant operating licenses to expire.

In 1982 NRC authorization legislation, Congress had granted the agency authority to issue temporary licenses that would permit utilities to begin operating completed nuclear plants before NRC officials concluded the lengthy formal licensing process. But NRC granted no temporary licenses, despite warnings that at least five plants would be kept out of operation after construction was finished, and the authority expired on schedule at the end of 1983. *(1981-82 action, p. 366)*

During 1983, differences over whether to extend temporary licensing powers kept the House and Senate from reaching agreement on NRC authorization measures. In October 1984 Congress finally cleared a fiscal 1984-85 NRC authorization bill (S 1291 — PL 98-553) without renewed authority for temporary licenses.

Before approving that measure, the House and Senate had to compromise yet another dispute over planning to evacuate residents from areas near nuclear plants in the event of reactor accidents. In its final form the measure allowed NRC to approve utility evacuation plans even if state and local governments refused to take part in drafting them.

Senate Environment and Public Works Committee action on NRC reauthorizations had been stalled for several months in 1984 by differences over evacuation planning requirements.

The issue of emergency evacuation planning was of particular concern to New York, where the Long Island Lighting Company had been prevented from opening its Shoreham nuclear power plant in part because Suffolk County authorities refused to draw up an emergency evacuation plan. Such plans were required for the NRC to issue an operating license after the Three Mile Island, Pa., nuclear power plant accident in 1979. Suffolk County argued that population density on Long Island made evacuation impossible.

1983 Licensing Debate

The NRC and the nuclear power industry in 1983 asked Congress to extend the agency's interim licensing

authority as part of legislation reauthorizing NRC programs for fiscal 1984 and 1985. The House Energy and Commerce Committee approved the extension, but other House and Senate panels with jurisdiction over NRC authorizations refused to go along.

In the House the Interior and Insular Affairs Committee May 11 reported NRC authorization legislation (HR 2510 — H Rept 98-103, Part I) without provision for extending interim licensing powers. But the Energy and Commerce Committee, which reported the bill June 24 (H Rept 98-103, Part II), amended HR 2510 to continue NRC's temporary licensing authority beyond Dec. 31.

In the Senate the Environment and Public Works Committee May 16 reported a "shell" bill (S 1291 — S Rept 98-118) containing an extension of interim licensing authority. But the panel never intended S 1291 for floor debate, and it subsequently began hearings on various nuclear power issues. On Nov. 9 panel members voted 8-7 to delete the interim licensing provision.

Differences over licensing kept NRC legislation from reaching either the House or Senate floor in 1983. Congress continued funding NRC through the fiscal 1984 energy and water appropriations bill (HR 3132 — PL 98-50). But the agency's power to grant temporary operating licenses ended on Jan. 1, 1984, before officials had put it to use.

1984 Emergency Planning Compromise

After temporary licensing authority expired at the end of 1983, congressional debate on NRC authorizations shifted toward the controversy over emergency evacuation planning.

NRC policy adopted after the Three Mile Island accident accepted emergency evacuation plans drafted by utility companies only if planning by state and local officials was under way but had been delayed. In June 1983 planning problems nearly led to the shutdown of the already-operating Indian Point nuclear plant in New York. The planning dispute delayed Senate Environment Committee action on NRC legislation in 1984 while Alan K. Simpson, R-Wyo., chairman of the panel's Nuclear Regulation Subcommittee, and Daniel Patrick Moynihan, D-N.Y., tried to resolve New York officials' concerns.

Simpson and Moynihan finally reached a compromise that specified that even if state or local officials refused to take part in developing an emergency preparedness plan, the NRC could issue an operating license for a nuclear power plant if it determined that the utility itself had prepared an acceptable emergency preparedness plan. The

NRC was required to evaluate whether a plan submitted by a utility would work.

Previously the NRC had accepted utility emergency plans only when state or local officials were working on an emergency plan but it was delayed.

After Simpson and Moynihan reached agreement on emergency planning, the Senate Environment Committee June 19 voted 13-0 to report S 2846 (S Rept 98-546), which reflected the decisions made by the committee during the previous 13 months.

The Senate on Oct. 10 passed S 1291, after amending it to incorporate the text of S 2846. The House passed S 1291 without amendment on Oct. 11 (PL 98-553).

Power Plant Construction Costs

The Senate in 1984 scuttled a House proposal to limit federally regulated electric utilities' ability to charge customers for the cost of building new power plants that still were under construction.

The House Feb. 8 passed legislation (HR 555 — H Rept 98-350) that its Energy and Commerce Committee drafted in response to a 1983 Federal Energy Regulatory Commission (FERC) ruling. The Senate did not act on the measure, which the House passed by a 288-113 vote.

The commission, which regulated about 10 percent of the nation's electric power sales, permitted utilities to recover through immediate rate increases up to 50 percent of the interest they paid to borrow funds for ongoing plant construction.

The FERC rule, which went into effect July 1, 1983, followed similar decisions by many state regulatory agencies to permit interest costs for construction work in progress (CWIP) to be included in utility rate bases. Under standard rate-setting procedures, utilities could recover the direct costs of building power plants through a depreciation component in utility rates after the facilities went into service.

HR 555 would have restricted the use of CWIP charges to financially pressed utilities unable to borrow construction funds except at above-average rates. Its advocates maintained that restricting CWIP charges would hold consumer electricity rates lower and encourage utilities to consider alternatives to building costly plants. But the measure's opponents, mostly Republicans, replied that the restrictions would discourage needed investments in future generating capacity — and expose consumers to future "rate shocks" once charges were increased when new plants were completed.

Chronology
Of Action
On Oil and Gas
Regulation

1981-82

Congress went along in 1981-82 as President Reagan curtailed federal government control over petroleum supplies and prices.

Bowing to Reagan's free-market philosophy, the 97th Congress accepted the president's determination to end the government's efforts to regulate oil prices and allocate petroleum supplies during shortages. In the process, Congress repealed or allowed to expire several laws enacted during the 1970s to give the government power to manage energy problems.

Those decisions continued the process, launched by President Carter, of freeing U.S. oil production from federal regulations. The House and Senate offered few objections when Reagan lifted all remaining oil price controls eight months ahead of schedule. After months of maneuvering, Congress gave up attempts to extend standby presidential authority to control oil prices and supplies that Reagan vowed never to use.

To augment U.S. petroleum supplies, Congress pushed to fill the U.S. Strategic Petroleum Reserve and encourage construction of a natural gas pipeline from Alaska.

With natural gas prices escalating through 1981-82, congressional concern forced Reagan to put off his Cabinet's proposal to speed the previously scheduled deregulation of natural gas prices. But members also were unable to forge agreement on counter-proposals to reimpose federal gas price controls that were being phased out by 1985 under the Natural Gas Policy Act of 1978.

Oil Price Decontrol

Congress in 1981 accepted with few protests the end of federal price controls on U.S. crude oil production.

President Reagan, in one of his first acts in office, Jan. 28 terminated remaining federal regulations on domestic oil prices and supplies. That action freed U.S. oil prices for the first time since 1971 to rise and fall with world petroleum market levels.

Reagan's decision completed, eight months ahead of schedule, a gradual decontrol process that his Democratic predecessor, Jimmy Carter, had started in 1979. While final decontrol had little economic impact, Reagan's action demonstrated a conservative administration's determination to rely on free market forces to regulate the nation's energy supply and demand.

Through most of the 1970s a Democratic-controlled Congress had insisted that the federal government maintain controls over the price of oil produced in the United States while foreign oil prices climbed dramatically. But by 1981 most members evidently agreed that holding domestic oil prices below foreign levels discouraged exploration for new U.S. reserves and reduced incentives for Americans to cut oil consumption.

A Decade of Controls

President Nixon first imposed oil price controls on Aug. 16, 1971, as part of a general freeze on wages and prices throughout the U.S. economy. As federal energy policy debates dragged on over the following years, Congress refused to allow Nixon and President Ford to lift federal controls. Democratic members contended the controls were protecting American consumers against the full brunt of rapid oil price increases determined by the Organization of Petroleum Exporting Countries (OPEC) cartel.

The Nixon administration's Cost of Living Council in 1973 devised a two-tier oil pricing system that removed controls from oil produced from newly drilled wells but limited prices for "old" oil from wells drilled before that year. Less than a month after Arab oil-producing nations imposed an embargo on shipments to the United States, Congress wrote similar controls into law as part of the Emergency Petroleum Allocation Act of 1973. That measure was temporary, scheduled to expire in 1975. But Congress kept oil price controls in effect for another six years through subsequent laws.

Contending that higher oil prices would encourage energy conservation, President Ford in 1975 proposed to lift price controls while imposing a "windfall profits" tax on the resulting revenues unless oil companies reinvested them in exploring for new reserves. But the Democratic-dominated Congress protested, arguing that decontrol would benefit the oil companies at the expense of the already pressed consumer. The result was the extension, in the 1975 Energy Policy and Conservation Act, of mandatory price controls on oil until June 1, 1979. After that date, the act gave the president power to continue, modify or remove the controls. *(Congress and the Nation Vol. IV, pp. 209, 235)*

Movement for Decontrol

But energy prices rose despite controls, and supplies diminished in the four years between 1975 and 1979. Support for continued controls ebbed during Carter's term, as a Democratic White House and Congress struggled to fashion an energy conservation strategy. Congress in 1977 turned down Carter's plan to impose new taxes on U.S. oil production to bring its cost up to world levels. And Congress continued to find politically unacceptable strict government regulations to force Americans to curb energy consumption.

At the same time taxes and rules were going down in defeat, there was a growing acceptance of the idea that higher prices could spur conservation. By the late 1970s articulate defenses of that position were coming from academicians with liberal credentials and from some interest groups, such as environmentalists. They contended that conservation and alternative energy sources, such as solar power, would be more competitive economically if oil and gas prices were decontrolled. So long as oil and gas remained relatively inexpensive, they argued, people had no reason to adapt to the new energy era. The oil companies

and Republicans who had fought for years against controls suddenly had company.

In 1979 revolution in Iran slowed that country's oil production and set off another round of price increases, which broadened the gap between world market levels and prices that federal controls set on a portion of U.S. oil production. Carter went on television April 5, 1979, to announce he would use presidential authority that Congress had granted in the 1975 Energy Policy and Conservation Act to wind down domestic oil price controls. The Carter administration began the decontrol process on June 1, 1979, and scheduled the lifting of all controls by Oct. 1, 1981, when the 1975 law's price control provisions were due to expire. Carter's decontrol program meant that domestically produced oil then selling for $6 to $13 a barrel would be freed to climb to world market levels that were in the process of doubling, to more than $30 a barrel, as the Iranian crisis squeezed supplies from Middle East nations.

Carter proposed a "windfall" profits tax to accompany decontrol. The tax, approved by Congress in 1980, satisfied most remaining concerns for a majority of members by preventing the oil industry from getting an undeserved windfall from sharply rising prices. It also provided revenues to finance federal assistance to help low-income families cope with energy costs and to subsidize development of synthetic fuels and other alternative energy sources. *(Background, Congress and the Nation Vol. V, pp. 451, 495)*

Reaction to Reagan Decontrol

Reagan defeated Carter in the 1980 presidential election after pledging to promote production of additional domestic energy. The new president's decision to move up complete decontrol confirmed the oil industry's hopes that the conservative administration would back all-out exploration while scaling back federal energy regulation. Consumer groups opposed immediate decontrol, predicting that Reagan's action would prompt large price increases for gasoline and fuel oil. Senate liberals mounted one unsuccessful legislative challenge, but Congress took no action to keep oil price controls in effect.

In March Sen. Howard M. Metzenbaum, D-Ohio, offered provisions reimposing price controls on oil and gasoline as an amendment to legislation extending an antitrust law exemption for U.S. oil companies that participated in the International Energy Agency (IEA). Metzenbaum called the decontrol action "hasty and ill-advised," and he contended it would cost U.S. consumers $10 billion while adding an extra 1.1 percent to 1.4 percent to the U.S. inflation rate. James A. McClure, R-Idaho, the Senate Energy Committee chairman, retorted that recontrolling oil would be a "monumental mistake." McClure maintained that decontrol would ease U.S. dependence on foreign oil imports and increase domestic production.

The Senate defeated the Metzenbaum amendment, **on a key vote of 24-68: R 3-47; D 21-21 (ND 18-10, SD 3-11),** during March 10 debate on the IEA extension (S 573). Most of the 24 senators who voted for the amendment were from the Midwest and Northeast, regions that had been hit hard by rising fuel prices. *(1981 key votes, p. 879)*

The House never considered legislation to extend oil price controls. Metzenbaum, along with several other members of Congress, labor unions and consumer groups, filed a lawsuit to block Reagan's decontrol order. But a federal court in Washington, D.C., rejected their challenge to Reagan's order on March 4.

Standby Oil Allocation Authority

Congress in 1982 gave up a two-year effort to force President Reagan to accept standby power to control oil prices and supplies in the event of an energy emergency.

The president had sparred with Congress throughout 1981 over whether the federal government or private energy markets should allocate oil and set its price during future petroleum shortages. Both the House and Senate passed legislation directing the president to draw up contingency government plans for managing petroleum supplies despite Reagan's insistence that he did not want that authority.

The Republican-led Senate, in a surprising turnaround from its earlier stance, in March upheld Reagan's veto of standby allocation authority (S 1503). The 97th Congress later settled for compromise legislation that instead ordered the president to buy oil more rapidly than the administration had planned to fill the U.S. government's Strategic Petroleum Reserve in the Gulf Coast salt caverns of Texas and Louisiana. *(Story, p. 379)*

In signing that measure (S 2332 — PL 97-229), Reagan agreed to some House-drafted provisions that ordered the president to send Congress a plan for drawing from the strategic reserve to tide the nation through shortages. The bill also required the administration to keep collecting data on petroleum supplies and to submit various plans and reports on how it would respond to future supply curtailments. But the law essentially left Reagan free to let marketplace forces determine how oil would be shared if future production cutbacks confronted the nation with severe energy shortages.

The compromise also granted U.S. oil companies extended antitrust immunity that allowed them to share petroleum data with the International Energy Agency (IEA). Reagan had requested the extension. *(Story, p. 378)*

Through the veto Reagan successfully resisted bipartisan congressional proposals to extend the president's authority, first provided during the 1973 Arab oil embargo, to set oil prices and ration supplies among competing regions and industries. Administration officials maintained that the federal government's efforts to manage petroleum shortages in 1973 and again in 1979 actually had made them worse. In any future shortage, they contended, the government should let market adjustments run their course as prices rose to levels that would shrink energy demand to match reduced oil supplies.

Some congressional Democrats, notably Sen. Bill Bradley, D-N.J., shared the administration's skepticism about government allocation programs. But most congressional leaders, in the Republican-controlled Senate as well as the Democratic House, contended that the president still should have standby power to deal with supply disruptions. The government should draw up its plans now, they maintained, before a crisis like the 1973 embargo forced officials to make hasty decisions under intense political pressure from competing economic sectors to protect them against loss of vital energy supplies.

After the Senate veto vote, Energy Committee Chairman James A. McClure, R-Idaho, warned Reagan that "he had better pray, as he has never prayed before, that

there be no interruption of petroleum supplies during his term in office." Although U.S. oil imports had been falling, Western industrial nations remained heavily dependent on foreign oil production from politically unstable Middle East nations. A continuing war between Iran and Iraq from time to time threatened oil tanker shipments through the Persian Gulf from Saudi Arabia and other oil exporters. Through 1984, at least, no crisis had developed.

Background

In defeating President Carter in the 1980 presidential election, Reagan made a campaign pledge to rely on free-market competition to balance energy supplies and prices. Reagan brought to the White House a conservative's trust in private market incentives, along with a distrust of the government's ability to manage energy supplies fairly and efficiently. In winning the presidency, Reagan had pledged to dismantle most of the federal bureaucracy and regulations that Congress and previous presidents had put in place to handle the nation's energy policy during the shortage-plagued 1970s.

Reagan backed away from his campaign pledge to dismantle a separate Department of Energy (DOE) that Congress created in 1977. But the new administration, insisting that the market could do a better job of allocating oil during shortages than the government could, in 1981 opposed extension or replacement of the mandatory price and allocation regulations that Congress had required since the 1973 Arab oil embargo on oil shipments to the United States. *(Energy Department debate, p. 397)*

1973 Act. In the midst of that embargo, Congress passed the Emergency Petroleum Allocation Act of 1973 (EPAA, PL 93-159). That law, passed despite President Nixon's initial objections, directed the president to issue mandatory regulations for allocating and pricing crude oil and oil products. Nixon previously had set up a voluntary allocation program, and he had used discretionary authority previously provided by Congress to impose mandatory allocation systems for propane, heating oil, jet fuel and diesel fuel. But the voluntary program failed to distribute supplies evenly. By the time Congress cleared EPAA in mid-November, long lines of cars at gasoline stations were making the nation's energy problems plain to the American people.

PL 93-159 required the president to set up a comprehensive program to allocate oil and oil products among different regions and sectors of the petroleum industry. It also directed the president to set prices — or set out a formula for determining them — for crude oil, residual fuel oil and refined petroleum products. The law protected some oil users by requiring that independent refiners and retailers receive the same proportion of total crude or petroleum product supplies as they had in 1972. Major oil companies opposed mandatory allocations, but independent oil marketers favored a mandatory system that they contended would keep suppliers from driving them out of business by cutting off all their oil deliveries.

Congress extended the law in 1975 but modified the mandatory control provisions to make them discretionary starting in 1979. Congress at the same time provided for those standby authorities to expire altogether on Sept. 30, 1981. *(Congress and the Nation Vol. IV, pp. 209, 235)*

President Carter in 1979 used that discretionary power to begin gradually phasing out remaining oil price controls. Reagan, in one of his first acts as president, lifted the controls completely on Jan. 28, eight months before allocation authority expired. *(Oil price controls, p. 375)*

Administration Position. The administration took several months, however, to develop a position on extending the president's standby authority beyond Sept. 30. Congressional committees held hearings in May and June, and witnesses generally agreed that the president should have the power to intervene in the market during severe petroleum shortages. But there was no agreement on how to define how scarce oil should become before the president stepped in.

Tired of waiting for the administration to take a stand, Senate Energy Committee Chairman McClure and Rep. Philip R. Sharp, D-Ind., chairman of the House Energy and Commerce Subcommittee on Fossil and Synthetic Fuels, introduced their own legislation to extend the 1973 law. But at later hearings on July 28, Deputy Energy Secretary W. Kenneth Davis came out in opposition to any extension.

Davis contended that government management of past petroleum shortages had "seriously hampered the ability of the marketplace to respond to short-term problems and actually contributed to the supply shortage." He said other laws gave the administration sufficient authority to allocate fuel for national security needs. He said the nation was in a better position to weather future oil import curtailments because the Strategic Petroleum Reserve was being filled and privately held stocks were high.

But the congressional General Accounting Office (GAO), in a report released the day before the 1973 law expired, found that the United States remained "grossly unprepared" to cope with a major shortage. The report criticized the administration's plan to let market adjustments manage shortages as "inappropriate."

Vetoed 1981 Legislation

The president's authority to allocate oil expired on schedule on Sept. 30, 1981. In the months that followed, both the House and Senate ignored Reagan's objections by overwhelmingly approving bills to renew his standby allocation powers.

Senate. The Republican-led Senate moved first. The Senate Energy Committee approved a standby allocation measure (S 1503 — S Rept 97-199) by a 13-4 vote on Sept. 30, only hours before the 1973 authority expired. McClure drafted S 1503 as a simple measure giving the president broad discretionary powers. But the panel, during five voting sessions, produced a bill full of detailed provisions that McClure had hoped to avoid.

The bill directed Reagan to write within 90 days a plan to allocate oil during a "severe shortage" (undefined). It gave priority to the same list of users that were protected under EPAA, including farmers and refiners. It would override state oil allocation laws and would give Congress 15 days to veto any plan before the president could implement it. Presidential powers under the bill would expire Jan. 1, 1985, just before the end of Reagan's term.

A junior Democrat, Bradley, and a freshman Republican, Don Nickles of Oklahoma, provided the only strong support during committee deliberations for Reagan's free-market stance. The committee rejected an amendment by Nickles to gut the bill of price controls. It was defeated on a voice vote, supported only by Nickles and Bradley, after senior committee Democrats Henry M. Jackson, Wash., and J. Bennett Johnston, La., insisted that oil allocation authority would not work without strong price controls.

The full Senate passed S 1503 by an 85-7 vote on Oct. 29. The White House did not lobby actively against the bill. McClure took pains during floor debate to emphasize that the bill would not extend the mandatory allocation programs of the 1973 law but would replace them with discretionary authority for the president. But Bradley maintained that the measure would extend the "very authorities that have twice in this country caused gasoline lines."

House. The House drew up separate standby allocation legislation that encountered stronger opposition than the Senate measure. The House tied its bill with provisions that Reagan backed extending limited antitrust immunity for oil companies participating in IEA's energy management programs.

The House Energy and Commerce Committee Nov. 18 voted 28-14 to report the bill (HR 4700 — H Rept 97-363), drafted by Sharp's subcommittee. The measure required the president to write standby plans within six months for allocating oil during a "severe petroleum supply interruption." Congress would have to approve before any allocation plan went into effect.

Sharp said the measure would give the president "great flexibility" to handle any emergency. But opponents on the committee called it simply a "re-creation of EPAA." In dissenting views to the committee report, nine Republicans called the 1973 law "one of the worst energy statutes ever enacted. It created gasoline lines. It shut down factories. It subsidized imported oil. And it bailed out the inefficient oil refiners — all at an enormous cost to the average American consumer."

Several committee Democrats, on the other hand, felt HR 4700 gave the president too much discretion. The subcommittee rejected an amendment by Timothy E. Wirth, D-Colo., to write in more specific allocation procedures and give farmers and small refiners greater protection. The subcommittee also turned down a proposal by Phil Gramm, D-Texas, to specify that oil imports drop 20 percent for 20 days before the president could start allocating oil.

The full House passed HR 4700 by a 244-136 vote Dec. 14. Once again, the White House made little effort to persuade members to vote against the bill. Liberal Democrats objected that the measure left the president too much flexibility and made no provisions for gasoline rationing. But they voted for it anyway.

Reagan Veto. During the 1981 debates, the Democratic House gave more support to Reagan's free-market approach than the Republican Senate. But in an unexpected turnaround, the Senate in 1982 upheld Reagan's veto of a compromise version of the allocation legislation.

House and Senate conferees, unable to reach agreement before Congress adjourned its 1981 session, met early in 1982 to meld the two bills into a compromise version of S 1503 that they reported Feb. 17 (S Rept 97-313).

Like the House-passed bill, the compromise carried provisions extending IEA antitrust immunity.

The Senate approved the conference report March 2 by an 86-7 vote, with the same seven senators in opposition. Administration lobbyists again did not oppose the conference report in the Senate, but they worked against final passage in the House. The House nonetheless cleared S 1503 March 3, 246-144, with only eight more opposing votes than in the previous December.

In the days after Congress cleared S 1503, supporters and opponents bombarded the White House with calls and visits as Reagan decided whether to sign or veto the measure. McClure and four other influential Senate Republicans (Majority Leader Howard H. Baker Jr., Tenn.; Finance Committee Chairman Robert Dole, Kan.; Budget Committee Chairman Pete V. Domenici, N.M.; and Dave Durenberger, Minn.) pleaded with Reagan during a March 18 White House meeting to let S 1503 become law. Eight major oil companies, petroleum marketers and refiners, the nation's utilities, the AFL-CIO and other labor organizations, consumer groups, agricultural organizations and the National Governors' Association all called for renewed standby allocation powers.

But during the House debate on the conference report, opponents of the bill circulated a paper noting that Secretary of Energy James B. Edwards and senior White House advisers were urging Reagan to veto the bill. Just after the Senate leaders left, House Republicans James T. Broyhill, N.C., Trent Lott, Miss., and Tom Corcoran, Ill., were ushered into his office to back a veto. A few smaller oil companies, several airlines, the Holiday Inns motel chain and large industrial petroleum users — including General Motors, Bethlehem Steel and Goodyear — also lobbied the White House against S 1503.

Senate Reversal. Reagan cast the veto, the third of his presidency, on March 20. In his veto message, Reagan contended that the bill could be counterproductive to preparedness if businesses and individuals believed that the government would come to their rescue during shortages.

The Senate scheduled a vote on overriding the veto on March 24. It was the first time Congress attempted to overturn a Reagan veto. Confident that the Senate's overwhelming support for S 1503 would hold up, McClure and his allies already were devising strategy for what they expected would be a closer override fight in the House, where Reagan had more support. But the Senate, under intense White House pressure throughout the day of the vote, fell five votes shy of the two-thirds majority required to override the veto.

The Senate voted 58-36 to override, but 24 Republicans and three Democrats reversed their earlier position to provide the votes to sustain Reagan's action. Baker and Dole, who six days earlier had urged Reagan to sign S 1503, were among those who switched. After the vote McClure said that some administration officials had pressured organizations lobbying for S 1503 to back off. McClure said he guessed that several major oil companies' decisions to stop pushing the bill after Reagan vetoed it caused both Texas senators to reverse their votes to support the president.

During the override debate, Henry M. Jackson, Wash., top-ranking Energy Committee Democrat, warned that the administration had no contingency plans for dealing with an oil shortage, while political turmoil in the Middle East made import disruptions more likely. Howard M. Metzenbaum, D-Ohio, said the veto meant that "if there is another supply cutoff from the Middle East, the oil companies will decide who will get the scarce supplies of crude oil, gasoline and heating oil. And the oil companies, not the federal government, will decide what the price will be for the fuels that make this country run."

Antitrust Exemption

Six times in 1981-82 Congress approved legislation extending an antitrust law exemption that the federal government had granted since 1975 to oil companies that took part in International Energy Agency (IEA) programs for

managing international petroleum supplies.

Located in Paris, IEA coordinated a 21-nation effort to reduce world oil demand, build up stockpiles and prepare for sharing available supplies in an energy emergency. Because U.S. antitrust laws prohibited competing companies in the same industry from sharing information and allocating markets, oil companies demanded that Congress provide them with limited immunity from antitrust prosecution for participation in IEA programs.

Congress in 1981 approved two six-month extensions of the antitrust exemption, but the Senate Energy Committee bowed to Sen. Howard M. Metzenbaum's, D-Ohio, demand for hearings on U.S. participation before Congress agreed to a longer extension. In 1982 Congress granted four more short-term extensions after President Reagan vetoed standby oil allocation legislation (S 1503) that carried provisions extending the IEA exemption to mid-1983.

Background

Twenty-one U.S. oil companies participated in IEA programs in 1982. Major oil-consuming nations set up the agency in 1974 to manage oil supply and demand and draft plans for sharing petroleum stocks during shortages. The agreement called for sharing oil if a 7 percent shortage developed among all participating countries or within a single nation. As of 1984, the sharing arrangements had never been triggered.

Because its oil-sharing plans were so complex, the IEA left the mechanics of operating them to oil companies. U.S. companies that volunteered to take part shared oil supply information with IEA officials. If a shortage cropped up, IEA had authority to reroute international oil shipments.

Congress first granted participating oil companies antitrust protection in the Energy Policy and Conservation Act of 1975 (PL 94-163). Congress extended the exemption three times between 1973 and 1981. *(Previous extension, Congress and the Nation Vol. V, p. 502)*

1981 Extensions

The Reagan administration in 1981 requested a four-year extension of the IEA antitrust exemption. But Congress instead continued the immunity for a single year, through two six-month measures, while Metzenbaum questioned the value of U.S. participation in IEA planning.

With the last previous extension due to expire March 15, Congress on March 10 cleared legislation (HR 2166 — PL 97-5) keeping it in effect until Sept. 30. Sponsors contended that a shorter extension would give the administration time to decide whether to seek changes in the IEA program. The Senate and House Energy committees drew up similar six-month bills, and the House passed its version (HR 2166 — H Rept 97-9) unanimously. The Senate approved the House measure the same day after turning down a Metzenbaum amendment to reimpose domestic oil price controls. *(Oil decontrol, p. 375)*

In September the Senate panel drew up another six-month extension (S 1475 — PL 97-50) to sidestep committee member Metzenbaum's objections to IEA participation. In return for Metzenbaum's agreement not to oppose the bill, Chairman James A. McClure, R-Idaho, agreed to limit the second 1981 extension to six months, through March 1982, and to hold hearings on U.S. involvement with IEA. McClure also agreed that future antitrust extensions would be referred to the Senate Judiciary Committee, of which

Metzenbaum was also a member.

During Senate debate, Metzenbaum expressed doubt that "IEA can effectively allocate world oil supplies during a severe shortage." Citing a General Accounting Office (GAO) report, the Ohio senator contended that IEA plans probably would require the United States to export some of its oil to other nations during a worldwide shortage. He termed that arrangement a "one-sided deal." The Senate nonetheless adopted the measure by voice vote on Sept. 22, and the House cleared it Sept. 29.

1982 Extensions

Between March and July 1982 Congress was forced to approve three stopgap antitrust exemption extensions before finally clearing energy preparedness legislation that continued the exemption through Dec. 31, 1983.

Congress in March wrote an extension until July 1, 1983, into legislation granting the president standby petroleum allocation power. But Reagan vetoed that bill (S 1503), and the Senate upheld the veto. *(Story, p. 376)*

In the following months Congress approved three separate extensions that kept immunity in force until Aug. 1. On July 30 Congress approved an extension through the end of 1983 after tying it to compromise energy preparedness measures (S 2332 — PL 97-229) that directed Reagan to fill the government's Strategic Petroleum Reserve more rapidly and to draft plans for dealing with energy supply disruptions for review on Capitol Hill. *(Story, p. 379)*

Strategic Petroleum Reserve

Congress pressed the Reagan administration in 1981-82 to fill the federal government's Strategic Petroleum Reserve (SPR) more rapidly. *(1983 cutback, p. 390)*

In both years Congress approved legislation that urged President Reagan to pump at least 300,000 barrels of oil a day into storage as insurance against future energy shortages. But Congress in 1982 settled for a less costly compromise that allowed the administration to fill the reserve at a rate of 220,000 barrels a day until it held 500 million barrels, two-thirds of its authorized capacity.

Congress established the strategic reserve in 1975 to give the nation a backup supply if it lost access to foreign oil markets. Since 1977 the government had been stockpiling oil in salt caverns along the Gulf of Mexico coastline in Texas and Louisiana. *(Map, p. 380)*

After taking office in 1981, the Reagan administration stepped up oil purchases for the reserve to take advantage of falling prices and ample supplies on international markets. But Congress, led by Senate Energy Committee Chairman James A. McClure, R-Idaho, demanded that the Department of Energy (DOE) buy oil even faster to build up a larger stockpile.

Through its massive budget reconciliation measure enacted in Reagan's first year in office, Congress also tried to disguise the SPR's cost by establishing a special off-budget account so its funding would not count against the federal deficit.

The strategic reserve enjoyed as much bipartisan support in Congress as any government energy program. Members pushed hard to accelerate filling the reserve in the early 1980s, especially after Reagan vetoed a separate energy preparedness bill that would have given the president renewed authority to allocate oil during an energy shortage.

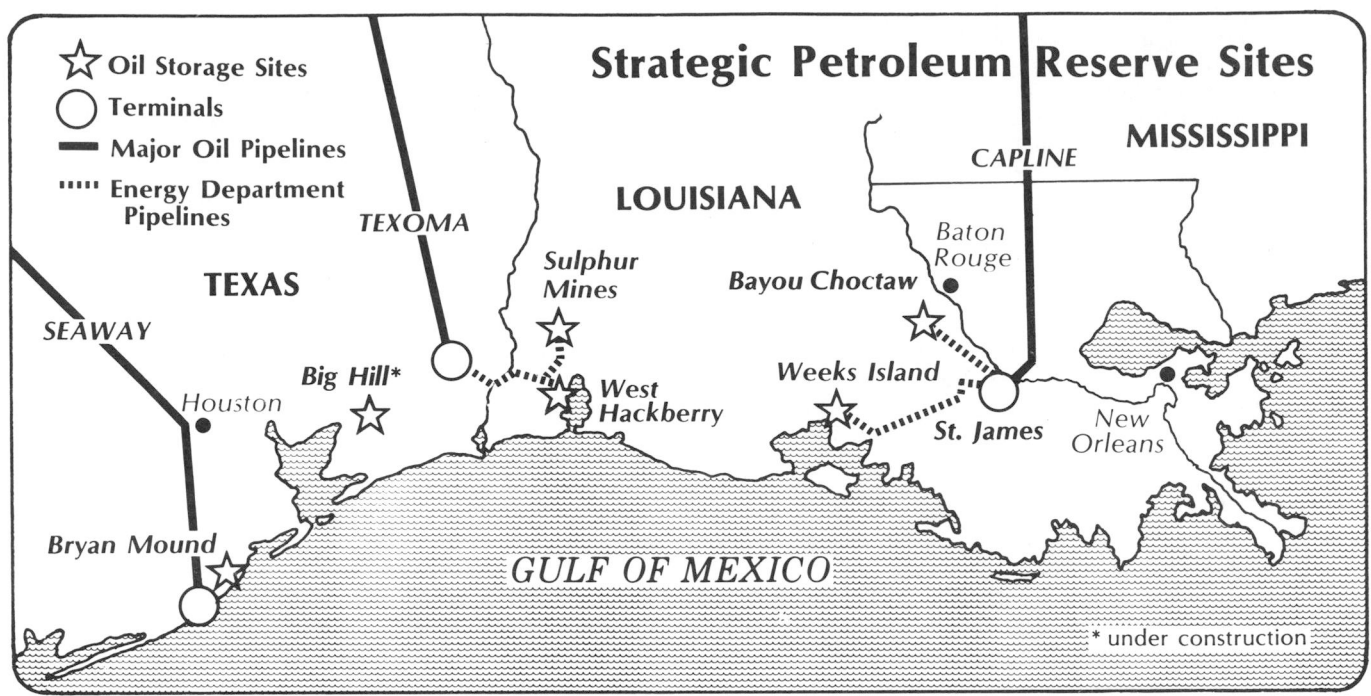

But concerned about soaring budget deficits, Congress ultimately accepted a compromise that allowed Reagan to buy oil at a slower rate than the 300,000-barrel-a-day target.

Congress had authorized storage of 750 million barrels of oil in the reserve. Late in 1983 the reserve held more than 365 million barrels, close to half the authorized capacity. A barrel holds 42 gallons of liquid petroleum.

Background

At President Ford's request, Congress created the strategic reserve as part of the Energy Policy and Conservation Act of 1975 (PL 94-163), a law that extended presidential powers to control oil prices and allocation. Congress approved government proposals to stockpile as much as one billion barrels within seven years as a hedge against import disruptions. *(Congress and the Nation Vol. IV, p. 235)*

Federal energy officials selected five abandoned salt mines in Texas and Louisiana for storing oil underground near existing Gulf Coast oil fields and distribution pipelines. They also planned eventually to place additional storage sites in other regions closer to where oil would be needed in emergencies. But in the late 1970s sharp world oil price increases, Middle East politics and technical problems in preparing the salt caverns as storage tanks combined to slow the filling of the reserve and boost its expected cost.

President Carter took office in 1977 and moved to buy 500 million barrels of oil for the reserve by the end of 1980, two years ahead of the Ford administration's schedule. The government pumped the first oil into the reserve in July 1977. But DOE officials admitted that the program was initially plagued by overambitious goals. By early 1979 the government had stored 91 million barrels in the SPR; but pumps had yet to be installed to withdraw the oil for use.

In that year revolution in Iran curtailed that country's oil production and disrupted world petroleum markets. The price of oil escalated from $13 a barrel in late 1978 to

$30 or more a barrel in early 1980, sharply increasing the cost of purchasing oil for storage. The Carter administration stopped buying oil for the reserve altogether between March 1979 and September 1980.

Yielding to pressure from Saudi Arabia, the administration held off on filling the reserve even after world supply restrictions eased later in 1979. Saudi Arabia, the largest oil producer belonging to the Organization of Petroleum Exporting Countries (OPEC), stepped up its production to stabilize the international market after the Iranian revolution and resisted higher prices sought by other OPEC nations. Saudi officials had long opposed the U.S. stockpile and worried that new SPR purchases would tighten world supplies and heighten pressure from some Saudi political groups that wanted to cut back production. So the Saudi government quietly threatened to cut back its output if the United States resumed filling its reserve.

But Congress stepped in to order stockpiling to resume in 1980. Sen. Bill Bradley, D-N.J., a freshman Senate Energy Committee member, in 1979 traveled to Saudi Arabia to confer with officials but came back convinced that benefits from filling the reserve far outweighed the risk of Saudi cutbacks. In approving Carter's request to set up a federal synthetic fuels corporation, Congress in 1980 adopted an amendment by Bradley and Sen. Robert Dole, R-Kan., ordering the president to start putting 100,000 barrels a day into storage on Oct. 1, 1980. To make sure that the administration complied, conferees on the bill followed a tactic suggested by veteran House legislator John D. Dingell, D-Mich., writing in a provision that would halt sale of oil from the government's Elk Hills, Calif., petroleum reserve if DOE failed to resume filling the SPR at the rate specified. *(Congress and the Nation Vol. V, p. 517)*

1981 Energy Reconciliation

Following congressional orders, the Carter administration again started filling the reserve on Sept. 23, 1980. The

Reagan administration, in 1981 revisions to the fiscal 1982 budget, planned to pump 230,000 barrels a day into the SPR. But Congress, through the 1981 budget reconciliation package, directed that the SPR be filled at a rate of 300,000 barrels a day.

Even as Congress pushed to stockpile more oil, however, members were looking for alternative ways for the government to finance the growing cost of the reserve. The government had spent nearly $7 billion on the SPR since the mid-1970s, and it was estimated that another $40 billion would be required during the 1980s. Concerned by the potential impact on its budget-balancing efforts, Congress in the 1981 reconciliation package (HR 3982 — PL 97-35) voted not to count SPR spending in the government's annual budget. *(Reconciliation action, p. 40)*

In what members freely admitted was "creative accounting," the reconciliation bill authorized $3.9 billion to buy and store crude oil in the Strategic Petroleum Reserve but established a special off-budget account for it.

Another $260 million was included on-budget to administer the program and to expand the storage facilities, located in Louisiana and Texas. The administration had requested all on-budget funding for the reserve.

Some members, principally on the Budget committees, believed that private funding, such as oil bonds, could be found to pay for the oil, so the funds were knocked out of the budget. But the financial community and the administration opposed private financing, and with no alternative in sight, Congress was faced with either increasing the budget by $3.9 billion or leaving funding for the SPR off-budget. It decided to authorize the spending but simply not count it.

1982 Preparedness Bill

Congress repeated its instructions for filling the strategic reserve in a 1982 compromise on energy preparedness policy. The Senate, unable to override Reagan's veto of an earlier measure granting the president standby oil allocation powers, joined the House to prod the president again to build up oil stockpiles more rapidly than the administration had planned. *(Standby allocation veto, p. 376)*

The compromise measure (S 2332 — PL 97-229) directed the president to fill the SPR at a rate of at least 220,000 barrels a day. It also ordered the administration to submit plans for distributing oil from the reserve in times of shortage. The measure repeated the previous goal of adding 300,000 barrels a day to SPR storage. Congress empowered the president to waive that target, however, and instead set a minimum fill rate of 220,000 barrels a day until the stockpile reached 500 million barrels. Congress tacked those provisions onto administration-backed legislation that kept in effect the antitrust immunity that Congress previously had granted to allow U.S. oil companies to share data with the International Energy Agency (IEA).

The measure also carried several provisions ordering the administration to submit various reports on its plans for coping with emergency energy shortages. *(IEA extensions, p. 378)*

In its fiscal 1983 budget proposal, the administration planned to fill the reserve at a rate of 208,000 barrels per day. But the Senate Energy Committee, in reporting S 2332 (S Rept 97-393) on May 13, coupled a routine IEA immunity extension with provisions ordering the president to boost the rate to 300,000 barrels a day and to draw up contingency plans for an oil shortage.

Chairman McClure, who had led the fight for the vetoed allocation bill, said the government lacked the capacity to respond to an oil emergency and therefore should fill the reserve as fast as possible.

Reagan protested that the rate set by the committee bill would cost the government an extra $3.6 billion over two years. But the full Senate, before passing S 2332 on May 26, defeated by a 44-51 margin a White House-backed amendment to hold the minimum fill rate at the 208,000 barrels a day contemplated by the budget. Budget Committee Chairman Pete V. Domenici, R-N.M., offered the amendment, urging the Senate to stand firm against spending increases. Domenici said that Reagan had more than doubled the oil stockpile since taking office. But McClure and others countered that it would be cheaper in the long run to buy more oil while supplies were plentiful and prices relatively low.

McClure said that although Reagan called for a fill rate of 208,000 barrels a day in his fiscal 1983 budget, he actually planned to put only about 180,000 barrels a day into the reserve. The constraint was the slowly expanding capacity of the Gulf Coast salt domes to hold more oil.

S 2332 allowed temporary storage of SPR oil in leased facilities, such as above-ground tanks or in tanker ships, until more salt dome space was ready.

Henry M. Jackson, Wash., ranking Democrat on the Energy Committee, said it was absolutely vital for national security reasons to fill the reserve as quickly as possible. Jackson accused the administration of "fiddling while Rome burns when it comes to energy."

In the House the Energy and Commerce Committee May 24 reported a separate bill (HR 6337 — H Rept 97-585, Part I) that the administration found more acceptable. The House panel directed the president to fill the SPR at a minimum rate of 200,000 barrels a day while urging that the rate be increased to 300,000 barrels a day if he found it "fiscally prudent to do so." HR 6337 also extended the IEA antitrust exemption and ordered the administration to submit a series of reports on potential economic effects of an oil shortage and steps the government could take to reduce them. The bill also directed the administration to continue collecting data from the states on petroleum product pricing and consumption.

At a 200,000-barrel-a-day fill rate, the SPR would contain 500 million barrels by the end of 1985, according to Philip R. Sharp, D-Ind., chairman of the House Energy Subcommittee on Fossil and Synthetic Fuels. That would last more than 250 days in the event of a Middle East oil cutoff, Sharp said. The reserve held about 145 days' worth of oil in mid-1982, he said.

The House passed the bill June 23 with only minor amendments. A House-Senate conference committee July 21 agreed on a compromise version of S 2332 (S Rept 97-663) that set the SPR fill rate at 300,000 barrels a day unless the president certified that to meet that goal would not be in the national interest. Conferees agreed on an absolute minimum rate of 220,000 barrels a day, and they accepted a compromise Dec. 31, 1983, expiration date for the IEA antitrust immunity extension.

The House approved the conference report on July 29 and the Senate on July 30.

Major Provisions. As signed into law Aug. 3, major provisions of S 2332 (PL 97-229):

● Required the president to fill the Strategic Petroleum Reserve at a rate of at least 300,000 barrels a day unless he certified that to do so would not be in the national interest.

• Set an absolute minimum fill rate of 220,000 barrels of oil per day, or higher if funds were available.

• Required the government to maintain that minimum rate until the reserve contained at least 500 million barrels and urged the president to seek to maintain the rate until the stockpile reached its authorized level of 750 million barrels.

• Authorized the government to store oil for the reserve in "interim storage facilities" such as above-ground steel tanks or tanker ships.

• Required the president to send Congress by Dec. 1, 1982, a plan for distributing oil from the reserve in times of shortage. Subsequent changes to the plan would require congressional approval.

• Directed the president to submit several reports describing the administration's authority and plans for dealing with energy shortages.

• Extended through Dec. 31, 1983, the antitrust defense for companies that shared information with the International Energy Agency.

Oil Company Mergers

The House in 1981 expressed concern about major oil companies' attempts to enlarge their domestic oil reserves by taking over smaller oil firms.

On the last night of its 1981 session the House Dec. 16 passed a bill (HR 5274) imposing a seven-month moratorium on oil company mergers. But the Senate never considered the legislation, as sponsors were unable to overcome parliamentary obstacles. *(1983-84 action, p. 390)*

Influential House members from Midwestern states proposed the moratorium in an effort to block Mobil Oil Corp. from acquiring Ohio-based Marathon Oil Co. At the time the House acted, Mobil and U.S. Steel Corp. were locked in a multibillion-dollar bidding war for Marathon, the nation's 14th-ranked domestic oil producer. Sponsors also hoped to prod the Reagan administration to oppose takeovers that members contended would diminish competition among oil companies, particularly in some regions.

House Energy and Commerce Committee Chairman John D. Dingell, D-Mich., and Clarence J. Brown, R-Ohio, top-ranking Republican on the panel's Fossil and Synthetic Fuels Subcommittee, combined to ram the bill through the House by a 233-107 margin just minutes before it closed its doors for the year. Philip R. Sharp, D-Ind., the subcommittee chairman, said he hoped the measure would "shake up the administration," which he said had been indifferent toward large company mergers. The bill also put the energy industry on notice of congressional unhappiness over such takeovers before more such efforts were launched, Sharp said.

As passed by the House, HR 5274 imposed a seven-month moratorium, retroactive to Dec. 1, 1981, barring any of the nation's nine largest oil-producing companies from acquiring another firm ranked in the top 40 producers. Mobil, ranked ninth in domestic crude production, had been trying for months to take over Marathon. When it appeared U.S. Steel would acquire Marathon instead, Mobil threatened to acquire both companies. But the U.S. Supreme Court on Jan. 6, 1982, rejected Mobil's last-ditch appeal to halt U.S. Steel's bid, clearing the way for Marathon to merge with the steelmaking company.

Despite the House stand, the trend toward consolidation in the U.S. oil industry continued during the early 1980s. Some major companies, eager to expand their oil reserves, found it cheaper to buy up other firms with substantial reserves than to drill costly and risky exploratory wells. Mobil tried twice in 1981 to "drill for oil on the floor of the New York Stock Exchange," in the words of several members of Congress. Before trying to acquire Marathon, Mobil had lost a bidding war for Conoco Inc. to E. I. du Pont de Nemours & Co. In subsequent years Mobil took over Superior Oil, Texaco acquired Getty Oil, and Occidental Petroleum bought Cities Service after lengthy takeover battles. In 1984 Standard Oil of California (Chevron) acquired Gulf Oil Corp., the fifth-largest U.S. oil company.

Natural Gas Deregulation

Congress took no action in 1981-82 to deal with escalating natural gas prices. *(1983-84 action, p. 387)*

With homeowners and industry protesting rising gas costs, Congress in 1982 came under election-year pressure to revise a 1978 law on natural gas pricing. But neither the House nor the Senate developed a consensus for wrestling with market distortions that pushed prices upward even as gas consumption was falling.

Members remained badly divided over whether the federal government should roll back gas prices or lift its remaining controls on the prices that producers charged at the wellhead. President Reagan as a result backed away from a 1980 campaign pledge to deregulate natural gas prices completely. And congressional leaders sidetracked consumer groups' demand that Congress legislate stricter controls that would reduce prices to lower levels.

Escalating Gas Prices

U.S. oil prices fell in 1982 with a glut on world petroleum markets. Natural gas was also in plentiful supply, as economic recession and rising prices combined to cut demand 3 percent below 1981 levels. Yet gas, unlike oil, continued to climb in price despite an ample surplus. The price of gas for heating homes rose nearly 18 percent above year-earlier levels, according to Department of Energy (DOE) estimates.

Most experts blamed the workings of the Natural Gas Policy Act of 1978 (PL 95-621), passed by Congress as part of the Carter administration's responses to gas shortages in the mid-1970s. To encourage gas producers to find and develop new supplies, the law scheduled periodic large increases in the wellhead prices that federal regulations set for various categories of gas production. It allowed prices to rise until 1985, then freed roughly half of all gas supplies from all federal price limits.

The 1978 law set up a complex scheme that allowed higher prices for newer gas reserves discovered in 1977 and thereafter. It also ended controls altogether on high-cost gas that was difficult to find and produce, such as from deposits more than 15,000 feet beneath the surface. Eager to assure themselves adequate supplies, pipeline companies that bought and transported gas for resale signed long-term contracts in the following years that committed them to purchasing large amounts of higher priced gas. Many contracts included "take-or-pay" clauses that required pipelines to take delivery on, or at least pay for, as much as 90 percent of the contracted amount, whether or not there was demand for that much gas. *(Background, Congress and the Nation Vol. V, p. 468)*

As a result of those contracts, pipeline companies were forced to buy more expensive gas even when cheaper supplies were available. Passed through to consumers at the end of the pipelines, those costs produced rapid increases in natural gas bills for heating homes and firing industrial furnaces. The resulting outcry sparked new debate in Washington over federal natural gas policy.

Reagan Proposal Abandoned

Reagan's Cabinet in 1981 recommended that the administration push for full natural gas deregulation. Arguing that price controls distorted market operations, officials suggested that removing controls could actually bring about a fall in prices. By 1982, however, congressional opposition and industry divisions forced Reagan to abandon the proposal.

Some gas-producing company officials lobbied hard for quick action on deregulation. But other producers who sold high-priced gas from deep wells feared that lifting controls on lower-cost gas would drive their own earnings down. And gas pipeline companies and distributors shied away from deregulation proposals that might allow gas prices to rise so high that their customers would switch to other fuels.

With consumer groups calling for even tougher controls, senior congressional Republicans warned Reagan against pushing for 1982 legislation. On March 1 the president announced that he no longer intended to submit the issue to Congress. In April the Federal Energy Regulatory Commission (FERC), the agency that administered gas price controls, issued a "notice of inquiry" indicating that it was studying administrative action to partially deregulate old gas prices. But congressional critics challenged the commission's authority to make major changes in pricing regulations.

Congressional Response

As consumers' protests against gas prices rolled in, members of Congress introduced more than 100 bills dealing with natural gas. Through the summer months of 1982, the House Energy and Commerce Subcommittee on Fossil and Synthetic Fuels held extensive hearings on natural gas issues. But the 97th Congress never attempted to thresh out gas pricing problems fully through debate on legislation.

When Congress returned after the 1982 elections for a lame-duck session, several members offered gas-pricing amendments during debate on legislation raising gasoline taxes to pay for highway and other infrastructure repairs. During Dec. 14 debate, the Senate rejected an amendment, proposed by Nancy Landon Kassebaum, R-Kan., aimed at limiting increases in natural gas heating bills.

The amendment would have allowed FERC to annul or modify "take-or-pay" provisions for natural gas a buyer had contracted for whether it took that gas or not. The amendment also would have frozen wellhead prices at the Oct. 1 level until Jan. 1, 1985.

Opposing the amendment, J. Bennett Johnston, D-La., a member of the Energy and Natural Resources Committee, said the situation was too complicated to be dealt with in such a short time.

By a 56-38 vote, the Senate tabled the first portion of the amendment, dealing with take-or-pay contracts. It tabled the second, price freeze, portion, 62-33.

Subsequently, the Senate adopted a resolution (S Res 515) directing the FERC to consider ways to correct the contract problems. The resolution, proposed by Energy Committee Chairman James A. McClure, R-Idaho, was adopted 90-3.

The measure also said that pipeline companies and producers should enter into negotiations to eliminate the contract problems, and that available federal aid should be provided to low-income natural gas consumers.

Power Plant Conversion

Congress in 1981 scrapped a three-year-old law that ordered U.S. electric utilities to convert natural gas-burning power plants to coal or other fuels by 1990.

Through partisan political logrolling in the House Energy and Commerce Committee, Congress wrote the repeal into its massive 1981 budget reconciliation package (HR 3982 — PL 97-35). That action responded to utilities' complaint that the 1978 law would force them to scrap perfectly good gas-fired generating stations after 1989 even though natural gas supplies probably would be plentiful.

The reversal illustrated the difficulties that Congress and federal energy agencies were to face in trying to develop national plans for managing U.S. fuel supplies in the future. When Congress approved the 1978 Fuel Use Act, the Carter administration was predicting that the nation would start to exhaust its natural gas reserves in the 1990s. But in the following three years most energy experts concluded that newly discovered gas deposits and lagging energy demand would give the country ample natural gas supplies well into the 21st century.

The House committee added provisions changing federal gas policy to attract key Southern Democrats' backing for a spending reduction package. By tacking them onto the reconciliation bill, the panel also headed off expected attempts to amend any separate legislation to lift all remaining federal controls on natural gas prices.

Background

Congress enacted the 1978 coal conversion law (PL 95-620) as part of President Carter's plan to cut U.S. consumption of imported oil and then-scarce natural gas supplies. Its provisions barred industry from building new factories or power plants burning oil or gas and required that existing gas-fired power plants be closed or converted to other fuels by Jan. 1, 1990. Another provision prohibited the burning of natural gas in outdoor decorative lights. Congress passed the Fuel Use Act as part of a five-measure legislative package that also granted tax incentives for conservation; promoted energy saving in homes, schools and hospitals; encouraged utility rate reform; and began gradually deregulating natural gas prices. *(1978 legislation, Congress and the Nation Vol. V, p. 468)*

Carter took office in January 1977, in the midst of severe natural gas shortages in the Northeast and Midwest. Gas producers in Texas, Louisiana and other producing states had been withholding supplies from interstate pipeline markets, subject to federal price controls, preferring to sell gas at higher prices to users within their states. During the winter of 1976-77, unusually cold weather throughout the East inflated gas demand for heating and rapidly depleted interstate supplies. By Feb. 1, 11 states had declared emergencies and closed schools and factories.

Three months after taking office, Carter sent Congress a national energy plan built around the assumption that U.S. natural gas reserves were starting to run out. Carter proposed extending federal price controls to intrastate gas markets, ending incentives to hold supplies off interstate pipelines. His program also envisioned discouraging industrial use of natural gas, reserving most supplies for residential heating and cooking. Congress, through an energy legislation package cleared on Oct. 15, 1978, approved those parts of Carter's plan. (1977 gas shortages, Congress and the Nation Vol. V, p. 458)

Through the Fuel Use Act, Congress directed industry to switch from gas to oil or coal. At the same time, it regulated intrastate gas and set up a complicated system for phasing out federal price controls on most gas by 1985. It freed from price controls gas produced from deep wells drilled 15,000 feet into the earth.

But by the time Congress acted, Carter administration officials later acknowledged, new evidence indicated that the United States actually possessed plenty of natural gas. In the following years, deregulation brought additional gas onto interstate markets and encouraged a drilling boom that discovered large gas reserves in deep formations in Oklahoma's Anadarko Basin and the Rocky Mountain Overthrust Belt formation in southwestern Wyoming and northeastern Utah. When the Iranian revolution curtailed foreign oil supplies in 1979, the Department of Energy began granting exemptions from the 1978 fuel use law to allow industries that had shifted to oil to switch back to burning gas. By 1982, when the U.S. economic recession cut energy demand, the nation actually had a natural gas glut on its hands.

Yet in the same period gas prices paid by business and homeowners escalated despite ample supplies. Expecting continued shortages, pipelines during the late 1970s signed contracts committing them to pay producers higher prices for gas as federal price ceilings were raised. As those prices were passed along to consumers, debate resumed in Congress over whether the government should extend gas price controls or lift them before 1985. The deregulation debate dragged on through 1984. But congressional leaders in 1981 were reluctant to take up legislation revising the 1978 fuel use law because deregulation proponents were likely to offer amendments on the House and Senate floors to end gas price controls. (Deregulation proposals, p. 382)

Reconciliation Action

Although the Reagan administration had not yet developed a natural gas policy, Congress went ahead to repeal parts of the 1978 fuel use law through amendments to the budget reconciliation measure it approved to implement President Reagan's federal spending cuts.

The House Energy Committee drew up parts of the reconciliation measure for full House consideration. Committee Democrats and Republicans drew up separate budget-cutting proposals, then included provisions repealing part of the 1978 fuel use law in efforts to build a committee majority behind their bills. Seeking support from three Southern Democrats, whose states would be most affected by the law barring utilities from burning gas after 1989, both sides wrote provisions repealing that "off-gas" requirement into their reconciliation packages.

Neither side could muster a committee majority on reconciliation. But the full House subsequently added the Democratic proposals — including the "off-gas" repeal and other provisions to force utilities to save gas through conservation — to its version of the reconciliation bill. Although the Senate Energy and Natural Resources Committee had not included the repeal, House and Senate conferees kept the House provision in the final reconciliation bill that Congress cleared July 31. (Reconciliation action, p. 40)

Conferees (H Rept 97-208) watered down the House conservation provision, requiring utilities to draw up a single five-year plan for saving natural gas. The bill also revised the 1978 law to make it easier for utilities to voluntarily convert from gas to coal while still complying with federal air pollution standards. The measure also repealed the 1978 prohibition on burning natural gas in outdoor lighting fixtures.

Alaska Gas Pipeline

Congress in 1981 agreed to let natural gas suppliers bill their customers in advance for the cost of building a 4,800-mile pipeline from Alaska to the continental United States.

With the $40 billion project's estimated cost rising dramatically, Congress Dec. 10 approved (S J Res 115 — PL 97-93) President Reagan's request to clear the way for natural gas consumers in 47 states to share the financial risk in completing the pipeline. That decision overturned former President Carter's 1977 ruling forbidding pipeline builders to charge potential consumers of Alaskan gas for construction costs until the entire pipeline was finished.

Congress also consented to Reagan's decision to waive Carter's ruling that barred oil companies that owned Alaskan gas reserves from owning any part of the pipeline.

In 1977, when federal energy planners believed the nation was running out of natural gas, Carter approved plans to build a pipeline to carry gas from Alaska's Prudhoe Bay fields south across that state and Canada to serve Midwest and Pacific Coast markets. Four years later, however, pipeline sponsors had yet to persuade banks to lend them funds to build the $27 billion segment across Alaska.

Even after Congress in 1981 waived Carter's financing restrictions, high interest rates and technical problems combined with lagging energy demand to stall Alaskan pipeline construction. The project's uncertain prospects left in doubt how soon the nation could tap Alaska's huge natural gas reserves to meet energy demand in faraway industrial and population centers. Debate over Reagan's waiver package demonstrated continued congressional divisions over how the government, consumers and industry should share the soaring costs of energy development efforts.

Background

In 1968 oil companies exploring Prudhoe Bay on Alaska's northern Arctic Coast discovered huge oil and natural gas deposits. The companies in 1977 finished building a controversial $9 billion pipeline that shipped 1.7 million barrels of oil a day 800 miles across the state to be loaded on tankers at Valdez on Alaska's southern coastline. For years industry and government planners had studied proposals for piping Prudhoe Bay's extensive gas reserves across Alaska and Canada to reach Lower 48 energy markets.

Prudhoe Bay discoveries held 9 billion barrels of recoverable oil and roughly 26 trillion cubic feet of natural

gas, an estimated 13 percent of known U.S. gas reserves. In the mid-1970s most U.S. energy experts concluded that the nation was starting to exhaust its natural gas supplies. Congress and Carter, alarmed by temporary gas shortages that closed schools and factories during bitter winter weather, moved to expedite a decision on several competing proposals for transporting Alaskan gas to the continental United States.

In 1976 Congress passed the Alaska Natural Gas Transportation Act (PL 94-586), which directed the president to decide whether such an Alaskan gas transportation system should be built and to pick one of the competing proposals. *(Congress and the Nation Vol. IV, p. 284)*

Once a decision was made, and approved by Congress, the act authorized federal officials to waive normal procedures to expedite construction. It also restricted review of the project by the courts. The act provided that the president's decision and subsequent modifications to it be approved by Congress within 60 days of submission. Proposed waivers to the decision could be rejected but not modified.

In 1977 Carter decided the Alaska project should go forward. He selected a proposal to build a pipeline that followed the route of the oil pipeline south from Prudhoe Bay past Fairbanks, and then followed the Alaska Highway through Canada to Calgary, Alberta. From there, the line would split, with one section going to the West Coast of the United States, the other to the Midwest. The pipeline would deliver about 2.5 billion cubic feet of Alaskan natural gas a day to the United States.

The president negotiated a treaty with Canada providing that neither country would discriminate in its tax treatment of the pipeline. The Senate ratified the treaty in November 1977.

Carter's decision stipulated that the pipeline was to be financed by the private sector, not the government. It also specified that gas consumers could not be charged for construction costs until the entire system was finished. And to satisfy Justice Department antitrust concerns, the oil companies that owned the Prudhoe Bay gas were prohibited from owning any part of the pipeline.

Despite reservations by some members, Congress by joint resolution (PL 95-158) in November 1977 approved Carter's decision with all its specifications. *(Congress and the Nation Vol. V, p. 466)*

Soaring Cost Problems

But by 1981 the estimated costs of building the entire pipeline system had soared to $40 billion from the $10 billion projection in 1977. Technical problems involved in installing a 48-inch pipe in frozen tundra and cooling the gas to keep it from thawing the ground helped push the projected cost of the 745-mile Alaska portion from $3.3 billion to $27 billion. The lower legs from Canada to the Pacific Coast and Midwest were nearing completion. Northwest Energy Co. of Salt Lake City, Utah, the firm heading the consortium of gas companies planning the Alaska segment, had obtained most needed construction permits. But the banks that were considering financing the pipeline — Chase Manhattan, Citibank, Morgan Guaranty Trust and Bank of America — balked at lending the consortium $22.5 billion for construction unless the terms that Carter had set were altered.

Northwest responded by negotiating an agreement with Exxon, Standard Oil of Ohio (Sohio), and Atlantic Richfield (ARCO), the oil companies that owned Prudhoe

Bay gas reserves, under which those corporations would put up 30 percent of the financing in return for a 30 percent share of pipeline ownership. The banks also insisted that natural gas suppliers be allowed to "pre-bill" current consumers for pipeline costs as construction proceeded, not just after Alaskan gas began to flow.

Pipeline Waiver Proposal

In June the consortium asked the Reagan administration to seek congressional approval of a package of waivers to Carter's 1977 decision, removing some of the barriers to financing the project. It took six months of negotiations, parliamentary maneuvering, and intense lobbying by the companies and by consumer organization opponents before Congress approved a modified waiver agreement.

Proponents of the waivers contended that allowing oil company ownership and pre-billing of consumers would spread the financial risks of opening Alaska's natural gas reserves to help meet the country's energy needs. Opponents called the proposal "the greatest consumer rip-off in U.S. history" and warned that it might ultimately lead to the federal government's assuming the cost of building the pipeline. Edwin Rothschild, director of Energy Action, a consumer group, called the proposed waivers "a complete betrayal" of pipeline sponsors' earlier promise to build the project with private financing.

But pipeline sponsors put on a heavy lobbying campaign that overmatched consumer advocates. Labor unions whose members could expect jobs on pipeline construction worked with the sponsoring companies. "This has been one of the finest lobbying jobs Congress has ever seen," Sen. Howard M. Metzenbaum, D-Ohio, said as he led Senate opposition to the waivers.

Modified Package. Even with that backing for the waivers, the Reagan administration hesitated while officials tried to negotiate agreement among key House and Senate leaders before submitting a waiver package. In July four senators drafted a more modest set of waivers that would only allow customers to be billed as large portions of the pipeline were completed. The four — James A. Mc-Clure, R-Idaho, chairman of the Senate Energy Committee; Henry M. Jackson, D-Wash., the committee's ranking minority member; and Alaska's two Republican senators, Frank H. Murkowski and Ted Stevens — asked Reagan to send their package to Congress right away.

But leaders of two House committees — Energy and Commerce, and Interior — balked. They said the waivers probably would be rejected by the House because they shifted the risk of the pipeline to consumers.

In August the administration gave up efforts to reconcile the two groups. At the urging of the four senators, pipeline sponsors and the Canadian government, Reagan Oct. 15 sent Congress a waiver package similar to what the senators had proposed.

The Senate Energy Committee endorsed the modified waiver package (S J Res 115 — S Rept 97-272) Nov. 10, with Metzenbaum casting the lone dissent. The full Senate approved the resolution by a 75-19 margin on Nov. 19.

Metzenbaum said the waivers were "unfair, inequitable and unjust" because they put too much burden on consumers. "This is a bailout bill for the oil companies, who sure don't need any bailout," he said.

But Jackson argued that consumers would be hurt more by the failure to bring the gas to market than by the risk put on them by the waivers. Even a year's delay,

Jackson said, would cost consumers $3 billion to $6 billion.

Stevens brushed aside charges by a public interest group, Congress Watch, that companies involved in the pipeline had given more than $82,000 in 1981 in campaign contributions to members of Congress and campaign committees. He said the contributions would have been made anyway and were not tied to the waivers.

House Maneuvering. In the House, members from the Midwest and East, regions where residents relied most heavily on natural gas for heating and cooking, led opposition to the waivers. The Interior and the Energy and Commerce committees shared jurisdiction over the waivers, and pipeline backers initially were not sure that the Energy panel would approve the package.

The Interior Committee acted first, voting 32-7 on Nov. 12 for a resolution (H J Res 341 — H Rept 97-350, Part I) identical to the Senate measure. Chairman Morris K. Udall, D-Ariz., supported the waivers despite some misgivings, particularly about allowing early billing. Udall contended there was a good chance that the pipeline could not be financed even with the waivers, but concluded that rejecting them would give "a kick in the teeth" to Canada. At U.S. urging, Udall noted, Canada already had completed one part of the pipeline that had begun delivering Canadian gas to U.S. customers. Several Interior opponents, including John F. Seiberling, D-Ohio, contended that the waivers would place too great a burden on consumers. Seiberling maintained that the initial price of Alaskan gas would be $18 to $20 per thousand cubic feet, five times the prevailing 1981 level.

The top-ranking Energy and Commerce Committee Republicans — James T. Broyhill, N.C., and Clarence J. Brown, Ohio — strongly opposed the waivers over the summer months while the administration considered the proposal. But the panel finally went along with the package, approving H J Res 341 (H Rept 97-350, Part II) by a 27-14 margin on Nov. 19.

Broyhill and Brown voted against the waivers, but neither led the committee opposition. That task fell to Richard L. Ottinger, D-N.Y., and Tom Corcoran, R-Ill. Corcoran proposed that the government instead remove price controls on Alaskan gas and let oil companies finance the pipeline from profits on higher-priced gas.

During House floor debate Dec. 8-10, opponents warned that the waivers could be the first step toward federal financing for the pipeline. They argued that other methods for transporting gas from Alaska, such as shipping it in liquid form in tankers, would prove cheaper than building the pipeline. But supporters, including Majority Leader Jim Wright, D-Texas, argued that delaying the pipeline would cost consumers more in the long run.

Philip R. Sharp, D-Ind., chairman of the Energy Subcommittee on Fossil Fuels, maintained that failure to go forward with pipeline construction would put consumers in danger of lacking adequate gas supplies. Even in the worst case if the pipeline were delayed, Sharp argued, the pre-billing provision would add no more than $1.75 a month to the average consumer's natural gas bill.

The House passed H J Res 341 by a 233-173 vote Dec. 9. Members split along regional lines, with the six-state New England delegation casting only one vote for the waivers. Representatives from the 12 Midwest states opposed the resolution by a 42-73 margin. Members from the gas-producing states of Texas, Oklahoma and Louisiana, on the other hand, voted 23-1 for the package.

Corcoran delayed final action another day through an unusual parliamentary tactic. After the House approved H J Res 341, Corcoran objected to a routine unanimous consent request that the House then pass the identical Senate resolution. Metzenbaum joined in the stalling tactics by vowing to filibuster any Senate attempts to accept the House-passed resolution.

Aided by consumer advocate Ralph Nader, Corcoran tried to generate new opposition during the delay. But sponsors got clearance from the House Rules Committee to bring S J Res 115 to the floor on Dec. 10. Opponents managed to narrow the previous day's margin by 18 votes, but the full House still passed the Senate resolution, 230-188, giving final congressional consent to the waivers.

Provisions. As signed into law Dec. 15, major provisions of S J Res 115 (PL 97-93):

● Allowed three major oil companies that owned Prudhoe Bay, Alaska, natural gas reserves to own part of the proposed pipeline to transport the gas from Alaska.

● Allowed consumers to be billed for costs of building the pipeline before gas was actually transported. If completion were delayed beyond the date that the Federal Energy Regulatory Commission determined it should be finished, consumers could be billed for part of construction costs if at least one of three segments — the Alaskan pipeline, a connecting pipeline through Canada or a gas conditioning plant at Prudhoe Bay — were ready for operation.

● Allowed pipeline sponsors to treat a $6 billion conditioning plant at Prudhoe Bay, for preparing natural gas for shipping through the pipeline, as part of the project that could eventually be charged to gas consumers.

1983-84

Congress in 1983-84 continued to accept relaxed federal government controls on the U.S. oil and gas industry.

Despite spurting natural gas rates, members were unable to agree on revising a 1978 law that gradually was lifting federal gas price ceilings. Consumer protests and industry divisions forced President Reagan to shelve a proposal to remove federal gas price controls completely. Although the House and Senate spent months working on natural gas issues, deep regional splits between gas-producing and gas-consuming states' delegations forced congressional leaders to scrap proposals to roll back gas prices or force producers to renegotiate long-term contracts.

With oil prices falling and gasoline in ample supply, Congress faced no urgent problems in the world and national oil markets. Congressional leaders worried that the nation was ill-prepared for future oil shortages, but neither the House nor the Senate attempted to revive standby oil price and allocation authority. Mergers by some of the nation's largest oil companies alarmed some members, but the administration and Congress made no move to block further industry consolidation.

Unable to persuade Reagan to accept emergency planning, Congress continued to prod the administration to rapidly fill the government's Strategic Petroleum Reserve. In a compromise with the White House, Congress accepted administration plans to slow oil purchases for the reserve as a money-saving measure.

Natural Gas Deregulation

Congress in 1984 gave up attempts to revise federal controls on rapidly escalating natural gas prices.

As natural gas rates skyrocketed in 1982 and 1983, industrial and residential consumers put Congress under intense pressure to tighten a 1978 law that was gradually lifting federal gas price regulations. Energy experts on both sides of Capitol Hill worked on the controversial issue for months, but neither the House nor the Senate could develop a consensus approach for ironing out troubles in the nation's natural gas markets. *(1981-82 developments, p. 382)*

Members remained bitterly split over whether Congress should roll back natural gas prices or lift federal controls completely. With gas producers and pipeline operators themselves divided, President Reagan in 1982 had backed away from a campaign pledge to speed full natural gas deregulation. And congressional leaders called off floor debate on compromise gas pricing bills that threatened to divide both Republicans and Democrats in bitter regional fights between delegations from gas-producing states in the Southwest and gas-consuming states in the Midwest and Northeast.

"It's just too controversial," House Speaker Thomas P. O'Neill Jr., D-Mass., told a Sept. 26, 1984, press conference in declaring natural gas pricing legislation dead for the 98th Congress.

By virtually identical margins the Senate in late 1983 had rejected two diametrically opposed plans: one to roll back prices to 1982 levels and the other to phase out all remaining controls in 44 months. The House Energy and Commerce Committee subsequently fashioned a shaky compromise behind legislation (HR 4277) to freeze some gas prices temporarily while forcing gas producers to renegotiate contracts for high-priced gas. But with 1984 elections approaching, neither House nor Senate leaders were willing to take the gas-pricing debate to the floor.

Congressional inaction left in place a schedule for partially lifting federal natural gas price controls that Congress had approved in the Natural Gas Policy Act of 1978 (PL 95-621). The 1978 law put a permanent but periodically adjusted ceiling on prices for "old" gas, produced from wells that had been drilled before April 20, 1977. Effective on Jan. 1, 1985, however, the law terminated price controls on "new" gas from wells drilled after the 1977 cutoff.

With Congress unable to agree on a new pricing scheme, federal ceilings on "new" gas amounting to about half of U.S. production expired on schedule at the end of 1984.

Background

The 1978 law had ended four decades of comprehensive federal regulation of natural gas prices. Federal controls, in combination with local utility commission authority over retail gas rates, imposed "wellhead to burner-tip" regulation that created a tremendously complex industry, fraught with problems.

The natural gas industries operated in three segments: major oil companies and independent producers who drilled wells and sold gas to pipelines; pipeline companies who transported the gas from oil fields to distant markets; and local gas utilities who bought gas from the pipelines and resold it to industrial and residential users.

FPC Regulation. In the Natural Gas Act of 1938, Congress gave the Federal Power Commission (FPC) the power to regulate wholesale gas rates that pipelines charged for gas shipped in interstate commerce. The Supreme Court, ruling on the *Phillips Petroleum* case (347 US 674), extended FPC regulation to the wellhead prices that producers charged for gas they sold to those pipelines. Until 1978 the federal government imposed no controls on gas that was sold in intrastate markets without crossing state lines. *(Background, Congress and the Nation Vol. I, p. 980)*

Natural Gas Policy Act

The Federal Energy Regulatory Commission (FERC), set up in 1977 to replace the Federal Power Commission, was responsible for administering the Natural Gas Policy Act of 1978.

The law, the second major gas pricing act passed by Congress, extended federal jurisdiction for the first time to sales of gas within the producing state. Such intrastate sales accounted for 40 to 45 percent of total nationwide sales.

Also set out by the 1978 law was a scheme for gradually ending price controls on new discoveries and on certain intrastate gas. For wells in production before 1977, controls were to continue indefinitely, until the wells had been depleted. More than 20 different categories of gas were defined by the complex pricing law.

The first categories of gas to be deregulated were high-cost gas produced from below 15,000 feet from wells drilled after Feb. 19, 1977; from geopressurized brine; from coal seams; and from Devonian shale. The deregulation date was Nov. 1, 1979.

Gas sold under intrastate contracts existing as of April 1977 was to be decontrolled on Jan. 1, 1985, if the price exceeded $1 per million Btus (per thousand cubic feet) as of Dec. 31, 1984. If the price was lower, the gas was not to be deregulated.

New natural gas was defined as that tapped after April 20, 1977. The price of gas from new reservoirs, from new onshore wells either 2.5 miles from or 1,000 feet deeper than the nearest pre-1977 well, and from new Outer Continental Shelf leases was to be decontrolled on Jan. 1, 1985. Also to be decontrolled then was gas from wells closer to producing wells, but still from below 5,000 feet. On July 1, 1987, gas from new onshore wells above 5,000 feet was to be decontrolled.

Gas already under production in 1977 was to continue under FERC regulation, and prices could not exceed price ceilings set by the commission. The ceilings were to be adjusted to reflect inflation.

Oil and Gas Regulation

Congress in 1956 passed legislation to exempt gas producers again from federal regulation, but President Eisenhower vetoed the bill because an oil company lawyer lobbying on its behalf had offered Sen. Francis Case, R-S.D., a $2,500 campaign contribution. The scandal caused Congress to shy away from deregulation proposals over the following decades, but the U.S. petroleum industry continued to protest what it regarded as troublesome federal interference in natural gas markets.

With the nation facing difficult energy shortages, Presidents Nixon and Ford between 1973 and 1976 asked Congress to end federal price controls to let interstate prices rise to the level of intrastate markets. In 1975 natural gas sold within the state where it was produced brought prices three or four times the top regulated interstate price of 52 cents per thousand cubic feet. Deregulation proponents argued that higher interstate prices would encourage producers to channel more gas into interstate markets and step up exploration for new gas reserves.

The Senate in 1975 approved legislation to gradually remove federal price ceilings from natural gas. But the House in 1976 approved much different legislation to lift controls over small gas producers but extend federal regulation to the gas that major companies sold on intrastate markets. Senate deregulation supporters chose not to go to conference, and the FPC reduced the pressure for legislative action with a 1976 administrative decision that raised the top nationwide price ceiling from 52 cents per thousand cubic feet (mcf) to $1.42. *(Deregulation debates, Congress and the Nation Vol. IV, pp. 214, 225, 249, 270)*

1978 Deregulation Law. Alarmed by severe natural gas shortages in the Northeast and Midwest during the winter of 1976-77, President Carter in his 1977 energy program proposed extending federal price ceilings to intrastate markets in gas-producing states. The House accepted Carter's plan, which allowed gas prices to rise to slightly higher levels. But the Senate, after overcoming a lengthy filibuster by deregulation foes, again approved a gradual deregulation measure. After long negotiations that carried nine months into 1978, House-Senate conferees fashioned a compromise bill that Congress cleared as the 1978 Natural Gas Policy Act. *(Congress and the Nation Vol. V, p. 468)*

In the 1978 law Congress tried to combat natural gas shortages by increasing incentives to search for new gas supplies. Extending federal controls to intrastate gas markets, the law divided gas production into various categories, subject to price ceilings set by the Federal Energy Regulatory Commission (FERC), a body that Congress had set up to replace the FPC in 1977. While holding "old" gas prices at lower levels, the law allowed large periodic increases in the producer price of newly discovered gas, defined as production from wells drilled after April 20, 1977, the date of Carter's energy message to Congress. It allowed regulated gas prices to rise steadily through 1984, then freed all "new" gas from federal price ceilings on Jan. 1, 1985. *(Details, box, p. 387)*

New Problems

The legislation solved the supply problem. With the higher prices, gas shortages ended immediately, as gas companies rerouted high-cost gas from the intrastate markets in Texas and Louisiana, where prices had always been free from federal regulation, to the interstate market. Exploration for new supplies increased and in 1981, according to some producers, newly discovered supplies equaled de-

pleted reserves for the first time since 1967.

But the 1978 law also heralded a new set of problems, nearly as vexing as those it solved. The legislation established a complex scheme for pricing gas reserves, based on their age and the difficulty of tapping them. Old gas — gas reserves discovered before 1977 — was priced the lowest; new gas was priced at a higher level; and certain kinds of high-cost gas, such as gas from wells deeper than 15,000 feet, were freed from price regulation altogether.

Price Distortions. In the years following passage of the measure, pipeline companies, which act as wholesalers for the gas industry, bid eagerly to contract for new supplies of gas. They were anxious to prevent shortages from recurring. And because FERC, which regulated pipeline prices, guaranteed pipeline companies a certain rate of return on their fixed assets, those companies had little incentive to keep gas costs down.

As a result pipeline companies agreed to long-term contracts requiring them to purchase large amounts of gas at the highest legal price. In some cases they agreed to buy deregulated gas at rates that far exceeded the price the market was willing to pay. But FERC allowed them to "roll in" this expensive gas with cheap, regulated gas and charge an average price. That average price climbed rapidly and steadily.

The upward pressure on gas prices was compounded by "take or pay" contracts that some pipelines signed. Those contract provisions obligated pipelines to pay for as much as 90 or 95 percent of the volume of gas they had agreed to purchase, whether or not there was demand for it when the time came for delivery.

Natural Gas Glut. As producers delivered more expensive gas, average prices throughout the nation rose rapidly. The average residential price per thousand cubic feet of gas jumped from $2.63 in 1978 to $4.90 in September 1981, then to $5.82 a year later. For consumers the price surge was all the more galling because it occurred at a time when gas was in ample supply.

Even as gradual deregulation expanded gas supplies on interstate markets, demand for gas fell off in the early 1980s as an economic recession cut industrial use, homeowners conserved more expensive energy, and businesses switched to alternative fuels. By 1982 gas prices in most parts of the country had caught up with the price of No. 6 residual fuel oil, a competing fuel that could be burned by factories and electricity-generating plants. In perfectly functioning markets, declining demand would have forced gas producers to cut the prices they charged pipeline operators. But with the deregulation format and contract provisions insulating producers from market forces, prices kept rising beyond the theoretical "market clearing price" that would balance supply with demand.

Pressures for Congressional Action

Reagan had called for full deregulation during his 1980 presidential campaign, arguing that ceilings on gas prices caused severe distortions in the U.S. economy. By 1983, however, the White House and congressional Republican leaders recognized that there was insufficient support in the House and Senate for immediately lifting remaining federal price controls, especially as protests against skyrocketing gas rates poured into Capitol Hill.

Under pressure from constituents, some Republican senators and representatives who usually opposed price controls began to call for steps to curb the price surge. The

Citizen/Labor Energy coalition (CLEC), an amalgam of 300 labor unions, farm groups, senior citizens' organizations and consumer advocates, generated grass-roots pressure by sending volunteers out to knock on doors in key members' districts, urging residents to demand action to ease gas bills. Local utility companies, which usually fought consumer organizations over rate increases, aided the lobbying campaign.

Industry Split. Divisions within the industry complicated the debate. Not all gas producers, for instance, were enthusiastic about decontrolling old gas that was subject to lower price ceilings. Producers holding large reserves of old gas vigorously supported decontrol, but producers specializing in more expensive new gas or deep gas feared declining revenues as the price of their gas fell to a new, overall market level.

The same split existed among pipeline companies. Those carrying large amounts of old gas would have to pay more for their supplies under deregulation, as would their customers. The opposite was true for interstate and intrastate pipelines delivering new gas.

Producers and pipelines also took opposite stands on "take or pay" contract provisions. Pipelines wanted legal authority to break those costly contracts, but producers objected to federal action that would force them to renegotiate with buyers.

Revised Administration Proposal. Reagan in February 1983 sent Congress a revised natural gas proposal that called for eventual, not immediate, deregulation. The administration proposed to end price controls on any gas for which a new contract was signed or an old contract was renegotiated.

Although gas sold under existing contracts would remain under price controls, the administration plan allowed producers or pipelines to break any contract that had not been renegotiated, starting in 1985. The administration also proposed to let pipelines reduce their obligations under "take or pay" contracts and to allow utilities and gas users to buy gas supplies directly from producers, then pay pipelines "contract carriage" fees for transporting the gas they acquired.

CLEC Alternative. In March 1983 a group of House members, mostly Democrats, proposed an alternative to Reagan's plan that had been drafted in consultation with CLEC. Nancy Landon Kassebaum, R-Kan., introduced the CLEC alternative in slightly different form in the Senate.

The consumer group's measure maintained controls on old gas indefinitely, rolled back new gas prices to 1982 levels and delayed until 1987 the scheduled 1985 expiration of price ceilings on new gas. Like the administration plan, it permitted pipelines to break "take or pay" contracts and set limits on price increases that pipelines could pass through to customers.

As Congress debated those proposals during 1983, many pipelines that were obligated to buy high-priced gas found ways to break those contracts, without congressional help, in order to buy cheaper gas from other producers.

1983 Senate Indecision

The Senate in 1983 was unable to choose between alternative gas-pricing proposals.

After working from April through July, the Senate Energy and Natural Resources Committee July 26 voted 11-9 to report legislation (S 1715 — S Rept 98-205) to decontrol all natural gas within 44 months, by Jan. 1, 1986.

The panel put together that two-vote margin only by sending the bill to the floor without a favorable recommendation that the full Senate accept its provisions.

The Senate took up S 1715 three months later but made little progress during two weeks of off-and-on debate. Then, in two Nov. 15 votes, senators made it clear that neither the committee bill nor the consumer group alternative could command a floor majority.

By a 26-71 vote the Senate rejected the Kassebaum proposal (S 996) as an amendment to S 1715. Minutes later the Senate voted 28-67 to reject the committee bill itself. In the following days Energy Committee Chairman James A. McClure, R-Idaho, met with about a dozen senators representing both sides of the debate, but they were unable to agree on a compromise approach before the Senate adjourned Nov. 18.

McClure and 11 other senators met informally during the spring of 1984, but they were unable to develop a consensus gas-pricing bill for further floor consideration.

1983 House Subcommittee Bill

In the House the Energy and Commerce Subcommittee on Fossil and Synthetic Fuels July 29 voted 10-9 to approve a bill (HR 4277) that made few changes in existing natural gas regulations.

Before the full committee began considering the bill, Subcommittee Chairman Philip R. Sharp, D-Ind., and Energy and Commerce Chairman John D. Dingell, D-Mich., unveiled a new consumer-oriented measure that not only retained price controls on old gas but rolled back new gas prices to September 1982 levels. The Dingell-Sharp substitute kept federal controls on existing new gas production beyond Jan. 1, 1985, permitting deregulation only for gas that was put on the market after that date for the first time.

Dingell, who had vowed that deregulation of oil and gas prices would take place "over my dead body," in November suspended Energy and Commerce markups on HR 4277 after losing a 23-19 test vote on the consumer-oriented Dingell-Sharp alternative.

1984 House Committee Bill

In April 1984 the Energy and Commerce Committee approved HR 4277 (H Rept 98-814) by a narrow two-vote margin. Before approving the bill, however, the panel substituted a compromise measure, engineered by Sharp with Dingell's support, that attempted to force pipelines and producers to renegotiate contracts that were forcing gas prices upward. As part of the compromise Sharp agreed to drop price rollbacks and extend federal controls in return for support from several Republicans for provisions to bring about adjustments in contracts that governed the natural gas market.

The panel reported HR 4277 by a 22-20 vote, fending off efforts by producer-state Democrats and most of its Republicans to break apart a coalition Sharp had put together behind the compromise. But few members were enthusiastic about the revised bill, and the Reagan administration strenuously opposed it. Shortly before the House recessed in August, Speaker O'Neill asked the Rules Committee to consider clearing the gas bill for floor debate. But HR 4277 vanished from the Rules Committee agenda in September after members complained during a Democratic caucus meeting that the bill would force them to vote on a

no-win issue that would hurt the Democratic presidential ticket in gas-producing states. On Sept. 26 O'Neill formally declared the measure dead.

Energy Preparedness

Congress in 1983-84 again took no major action to strengthen federal government preparations for future energy shortages.

Despite efforts by Senate Energy and Natural Resources Committee Chairman James A. McClure, R-Idaho, to prod the administration to plan for potential supply disruptions, neither the House nor the Senate approved comprehensive energy preparedness legislation.

President Reagan in 1982 had vetoed legislation granting the president standby authority to allocate oil and control its price during emergency energy shortages. *(Story, p. 376)*

Reagan continued to insist that the marketplace, not the government, should allocate oil among competing uses during future emergencies. McClure and other members of Congress, worried that the oil shortages the nation experienced in 1973 and 1979 could be repeated, urged the administration to accept some form of standby authority to deal with unexpected disruptions. But with energy in ample supply and gasoline prices falling, there was no public clamor for congressional action to prepare for emergency situations.

In 1983 the Senate Energy panel adopted a proposal by Howard M. Metzenbaum, D-Ohio, that would have terminated an existing antitrust exemption for oil companies participating in the International Energy Agency (IEA) unless Reagan signed legislation conferring standby oil control powers. Although the Senate approved the amendment as part of legislation extending the IEA exemption, the House refused to accept it. *(IEA bill, this page)*

SPR Test Sale Proposal

Acting on the only preparedness measure that received much congressional attention, the House Sept. 18, 1984, approved a bill (HR 3880 — H Rept 98-1033) that directed the government to conduct a test sale of 1.1 million barrels of oil from the Strategic Petroleum Reserve (SPR). But the Senate did not consider the proposal.

Supporters of the bill argued that a test sale was needed to boost public confidence in the reserve and to work out technical problems in the paperwork and actual transfer of the oil from underground storage in Louisiana and Texas to refineries.

The administration did not oppose the bill but said a test sale in times of an oil surplus would be of little help in indicating problems that could arise in using SPR oil in times of an energy crisis.

Strategic Petroleum Reserve

Congress and the White House compromised in 1983 on the rate at which the nation should fill the Strategic Petroleum Reserve (SPR), its storehouse of fuel for an emergency.

Congress approved a reduction from 220,000 barrels per day to 186,000 barrels per day as the minimum rate at which the reserve was to be filled. The administration had wanted to slow the fill rate to 145,000 barrels a day.

In proposing the slowdown, primarily as a money-saving measure, administration officials maintained that because oil imports had decreased and the possibility of an oil embargo was less likely, it was no longer imperative that the nation move quickly to build its reserve.

Congress in 1982 (PL 97-229) required the president to fill the reserve at a rate of 300,000 barrels per day unless he certified that to do so was not in the national interest. An absolute minimum rate of 220,000 barrels per day was set. *(Details, p. 379)*

In clearing a fiscal 1984 Interior Department appropriations bill (HR 3363 — PL 98-146), Congress in 1983 accepted provisions reducing the minimum fill rate for the reserve to 186,000 barrels per day. The measure provided $650 million to buy oil for the reserve, permitting the Department of Energy to purchase about 15 million gallons for fiscal 1985.

Oil Company Mergers

Alarmed by three major oil company mergers, Congress in early 1984 discussed but eventually abandoned proposals to bar such combinations until their impact could be studied.

In February Texaco Inc., the nation's third-largest oil company, offered $10.1 billion for Getty Oil Co., the No. 13 company. Within weeks two other mergers were announced: Standard Oil of California (SoCal), the No. 5 oil company, bid $13.2 billion for No. 4 Gulf Oil Corp.; and Mobil Corp., the second-largest U.S. oil company, offered $5.7 billion for Superior Oil Co.

After the Texaco-Getty merger was announced, Sens. J. Bennett Johnston, D-La., Howard M. Metzenbaum, D-Ohio, and Warren B. Rudman, R-N.H., launched a move for legislation to impose a temporary moratorium on further mergers. Concerned that major oil companies were "drilling for oil in Wall Street" instead of searching for new deposits, the senators argued that costly mergers left surviving companies deeply in debt and unable to spend much money on exploring for new oil and gas reserves that would expand the nation's energy supplies.

But President Reagan offered no opposition to the mergers, and Secretary of Energy Donald P. Hodel said the oil industry's growing concentration would not hurt future energy supplies. Several congressional committees held hearings on merger moratorium proposals, but none reported a bill. And the Senate twice turned aside moratorium amendments that Johnston offered on the floor. *(Previous action, p. 382)*

Antitrust Exemption Extension

Congress in 1984 once more extended an antitrust exemption to allow U.S. oil companies to participate in international oil-sharing arrangements during times of crisis.

In November 1983 both the House and Senate approved legislation extending the exemption for companies that took part in the International Energy Agency (IEA), a mechanism that industrial nations formed in 1974 to allocate oil among the United States and its allies in the event of a worldwide petroleum shortage. But final action was delayed until March 1984 by House refusal to accept a

Senate amendment that would have terminated the exemption unless President Reagan went along with legislation giving the White House power to control oil supplies and prices during shortages. *(Previous action, p. 378)*

Reagan in 1982 vetoed a standby oil allocation measure, arguing that the market should allocate prices and supplies. *(Allocation power debate, p. 376)*

The House Nov. 7, 1983, passed legislation (HR 4194 — H Rept 98-472) that simply extended the antitrust exemption, which was due to expire at the end of the year, through June 30, 1985. But the Senate, before passing the measure on Nov. 17, attached an amendment by Howard M. Metzenbaum, D-Ohio, designed to force Reagan to accept standby allocation powers. Metzenbaum's proposal ended the antitrust exemption on June 30, 1984, unless a law conferring standby allocation powers on the president had been enacted by that date.

The House refused to accept the Senate version, and the exemption expired. In March Metzenbaum agreed to give up his amendment, since it was clear that the proposal did not have strong support from Senate leaders. The House and Senate finally cleared the conference report on HR 4194 (H Rept 98-620) on March 15, and Reagan signed it five days later (PL 98-239).

Chronology
Of Action
On Energy Research
And Development

1981-82

Congress in 1981-82 fought, with only partial success, President Reagan's plans to scale back federal government programs to promote conservation and develop alternative energy sources.

By the end of 1982 the 97th Congress had shouldered aside Reagan's request to abolish the U.S. Department of Energy (DOE) altogether. But with congressional consent, the administration sharply curtailed DOE research and development spending on solar energy, alternative fossil fuel technologies and conservation programs.

DOE support for those programs had soared during the Carter administration. But the Reagan administration maintained that the government should concentrate its research on building a technical base and leave commercial development to private industry.

Most members of Congress, however, responded skeptically to the administration's premise that rising oil and gas prices offered sufficient incentive for consumers to cut fuel use and for industry to perfect alternative energy sources. Through action on various DOE authorization and appropriation bills, Congress ordered the department to spend more than the president had requested to develop and test new energy technologies. Congress also insisted on funding some politically popular conservation programs — such as federal assistance for insulating homes occupied by the poor and elderly — that the administration wanted to terminate or fund through block grants to state governments.

Reagan spared nuclear power development from his budget-cutting proposals. Committed to restoring the nuclear industry's growth, the administration called for stepped-up spending on DOE research and testing on advanced nuclear fission, fusion and other experimental programs. Congress generally went along, although House and Senate support eroded during 1981-82 for DOE plans to build an experimental breeder reactor at Clinch River, Tenn. *(Nuclear power developments, p. 361)*

1981 Energy Reconciliation

Congress in 1981 pared funding authorizations for federal energy programs as part of its budget-cutting drive.

In drawing up far-reaching budget reconciliation legislation (HR 3982 — PL 97-35), however, the House and Senate nevertheless provided more funds than President Reagan proposed for Department of Energy (DOE) conservation and alternative energy research. Congress also overruled the administration's plans to scrap a federal

bank created during the last year of the Carter administration to channel subsidized loans to promote conservation and solar energy investments. *(Reconciliation action, p. 40)*

As cleared July 31, the reconciliation bill included six major energy sections that:

● Provided a three-year authorization for the Energy Department, the first DOE authorization to clear Congress since the department was established in 1977.

● Authorized fiscal 1982-84 appropriations for the federal solar and conservation bank.

● Reduced previously authorized funds to subsidize production of alcohol fuels.

● Eased a 1976 law to make federal energy efficiency standards for new buildings voluntary instead of mandatory.

● Set up a new off-budget account for funding the purchase of oil to fill the government's Strategic Petroleum Reserve (SPR). *(SPR debates, p. 379)*

● Repealed a 1978 law that would have forced utilities to close generating stations that burned natural gas after 1989 or convert them to coal or other fuels. *(Gas policy, p. 383)*

Three-Year DOE Authorizations

Congress authorized spending on DOE programs for three years, fiscal 1982-84, as part of the budget-cutting reconciliation package.

The measure authorized $5.65 billion for the department's civilian energy programs in fiscal 1982, according to Congressional Budget Office (CBO) figures, about $544 million more than President Reagan's revised budget had requested. The bill also authorized $6.78 billion in fiscal 1983 and $7.03 billion in fiscal 1984, although the administration had not submitted budgets for those years.

After taking office in January, Reagan had revised President Carter's fiscal 1982 budget to step up nuclear research funding while cutting DOE spending for solar, conservation and synthetic fuel programs. The funds that Congress added to DOE authorizations were mostly for solar and conservation programs. Congress also managed to preserve several programs the administration had sought to cut or eliminate that remained popular among House and Senate members.

Even with congressional additions, the reconciliation measure authorized $656 million less in fiscal 1982 than Congress had provided for DOE civilian programs in fiscal 1981 and $2.4 billion less than Carter had requested for the same programs in fiscal 1982 before he left the White House in January.

The fiscal 1982 totals did not reflect the $3.9 billion for the Strategic Petroleum Reserve that was included in the bill but not counted in the final figure. They also did not include about $5 billion for nuclear weapons produced and developed by DOE.

It was the first DOE authorization legislation that Congress had ever passed. Although Congress had created the department in 1977, previous bills to authorize funds for its programs had been stalled by controversies over the direction of federal energy programs, principally research on breeder reactors. But in 1981 congressional leaders finally pushed a three-year DOE authorization through the House and Senate by adding it to the urgently debated budget-cutting package.

Conservation. HR 3982 authorized $376 million in fiscal 1982 for energy conservation programs run by state

and local governments, including $175 million to weatherize the homes of poor families.

The administration had requested only $195 million for these programs and nothing for weatherization, which it said could be funded through a block grant to states from the Housing and Urban Development Department (HUD).

The House reconciliation bill would have killed the weatherization program, but the Senate continued it and the conference committee agreed with the Senate.

States could get additional money for weatherization from a $1.9 billion block grant for low-income energy assistance that also was included in the reconciliation bill. Up to 15 percent of the amount states received for energy aid could be spend on weatherization. *(Block grant, p. 588)*

The reconciliation package authorized funding for several other conservation programs that the administration wanted to drop altogether. They included programs to promote efficient use of energy by consumer products, industrial processes and community energy systems.

Solar and Fossil Energy. The reconciliation bill authorized $303 million in fiscal 1982 for solar energy programs, $110 million more than was requested by Reagan but $249 million less than the Carter administration asked.

Within the solar accounts, Congress added $38 million to the $56 million request for research on solar cells that turned sunlight directly into electricity; $29 million to the $19 million requested for windmill programs; $17 million to the $43 million requested for solar heating research; and $18 million to create electricity from temperature differences in the oceans, a program the administration wanted killed.

Congress added $44 million to the president's fiscal 1982 request of $435 million for fossil energy programs. The extra money included additions of $8 million to the $106 million requested for producing liquid fuels from coal; $7 million to the $29 million requested for electrical fuel cells; $29 million for a new method of generating electricity from coal, for which the administration had not requested funding; and $6 million to the $16 million requested for oil shale research. Congress cut $6 million from the $60 million requested for advanced coal research.

Other DOE Programs. Through House maneuvering on the reconciliation bill, Congress authorized $228 million in fiscal 1982 to continue the controversial Clinch River breeder project. In other provisions authorizing DOE nuclear programs, the reconciliation package cut the administration's proposal for nuclear fission research, added funds for nuclear fusion research and restored funding Reagan wanted to terminate for research on gas-cooled reactors that would be practical in arid regions of the West, which lacked water for cooling reactors.

In other major revisions of the president's DOE budget proposal, Congress added $55 million to the $28 million requested for regulatory programs, including emergency planning and the department's efforts to recover $10 billion in oil company overcharges for the period when oil was subject to federal price controls. Congress also expanded authorized funding levels for research on batteries and experimental electric energy systems.

Solar Bank Funding

Lawmakers balked at Reagan's proposal to terminate a federally funded bank established in 1980 to promote solar energy and conservation.

Congress instead provided a three-year funding au-

thorization for the Solar Energy and Conservation Bank, a Department of Housing and Urban Development agency set up by 1980 synthetic fuels legislation. A coalition of city governments and interest groups subsequently took HUD to court to force the administration to put the solar bank into operation.

Reagan proposed eliminating the bank in March 1981, contending that rising oil prices and existing federal tax credits provided sufficient incentive for conservation and solar technology without federally subsidized loans. Although Congress insisted on funding the bank's operations, conservation and solar power advocates contended that restrictive HUD regulations and the administration's continued efforts to eliminate federal financial support were limiting its effectiveness.

Congress established HUD's solar bank as part of 1980 legislation that created the federal Synthetic Fuels Corp. (PL 96-294). Modeled on the Government National Mortgage Association, the solar bank was empowered to make subsidized loans to businessmen or homeowners to buy solar equipment or make energy-saving improvements in residential or commercial buildings. *(Background, Congress and the Nation Vol. V, p. 516)*

When Reagan took office in January 1981, the solar bank had not yet begun operations. The new administration fired the bank's planning staff, refused to issue regulations for its operations and proposed terminating the program. But Congress, in a rebuke to the president, wrote provisions authorizing solar bank lending into the budget reconciliation measure.

The reconciliation bill authorized appropriations of $50 million to the bank each year in fiscal 1982-84. A coalition of interest groups and cities sued HUD for impounding congressionally appropriated money, and a federal district court in June 1982 ordered the government to put the bank into operation. HUD subsequently issued regulations and allocated $30.4 million to states for distribution as they completed agreements with the department.

Administration critics maintained that HUD's management of the solar bank was reducing the availability of federally subsidized solar and conservation loans. HUD proposed distributing the funds through existing state programs, but the bank's backers contended that more borrowers could take advantage of the program if loans were channeled through financial institutions, city governments and credit unions. Proposed HUD regulations limited use of bank funds to conservation measures and passive solar building construction, thus denying loans for purchasing active solar equipment such as water heaters.

Alcohol Fuels Subsidy

The reconciliation measure cut $280 million from previously authorized funds that the 1980 synthetic fuels law provided for alcohol fuels subsidies.

In creating the federal synthetic fuels corporation, Congress also set up a $1.2 billion program jointly administered by DOE and the U.S. Department of Agriculture (USDA) to promote alcohol fuel production from crops and crop residues, timber and timber wastes, and from animal wastes. The law set a goal of at least 60,000 barrels a day of alcohol production by the end of 1982. It authorized $600 million each for DOE and the Agriculture Department for loans, loan guarantees, price guarantees and purchase agreements designed to provide incentives for private companies to build and operate plants for processing agricul-

tural and forestry resources into fuels.

Through the reconciliation measure, Congress reduced the $1.2 billion authorization to $920 million, with $460 million each for the DOE and USDA programs. With gasoline prices leveling off in the early 1980s, ambitious hopes for encouraging American drivers to switch to "gasohol" fuels using less petroleum had yet to be realized.

Building Efficiency Standards

In action on the reconciliation bill, Congress backed away from a 1976 law that directed the federal government to enforce mandatory energy efficiency standards for all new houses, apartments and commercial buildings.

The 1981 bill made federal building standards voluntary instead of mandatory, but it left in place the 1976 law's directive that all new federal government buildings meet the government's own efficiency standards.

In 1976 Congress had approved mandatory standards as part of legislation (PL 93-275) extending the Federal Energy Administration, a temporary agency that managed federal energy policy under the Nixon and Ford administrations. The Senate wrote the standards into the measure through a floor amendment proposed by Ernest F. Hollings, D-S.C., and Edward M. Kennedy, D-Mass. That amendment, later accepted by the House in conference, directed the Department of Housing and Urban Development to draw up performance standards for energy efficiency in all new commercial and residential buildings.

The 1976 law ordered the government to force compliance with those standards by cutting off federal financial assistance — including mortgage loans from federally regulated banks and thrift institutions — for residential and commercial construction in states that failed to adopt and enforce the federal standards. The Ford administration had backed those stringent sanctions, but House conferees had stalled similar legislation by objecting that the provision would cut off most mortgage credit for new home construction in areas that failed to meet federal insulation standards. The House accepted the Hollings-Kennedy amendment but insisted that the final version require congressional consent, after HUD had drafted the standards, before the government began imposing sanctions.

But Congress, through a House amendment to the reconciliation bill, struck mandatory efficiency standards for all but federal buildings from the 1976 law. Instead, the measure converted HUD regulations to "voluntary performance standards ... solely as guidelines for the purpose of providing technical assistance for the design and construction of energy efficient buildings."

Fiscal 1982 Appropriations

Congress in 1981 rearranged administration priorities for Department of Energy (DOE) programs in action on two fiscal 1982 appropriations bills. While both chambers made some last-minute cuts in the measures to heed President Reagan's September call for further spending reductions, the final DOE appropriations beefed up administration proposals for funding the government's solar, conservation and fossil fuel research programs.

Energy-Water Funds

Congress Nov. 21 cleared a fiscal 1982 energy and water development appropriations bill (HR 4144 — PL 97-88) that provided $8.1 billion for DOE. That amount included $4.7 billion for the nuclear weapons research, development and manufacturing that DOE performed for the Department of Defense. The bill appropriated $3.4 billion for DOE civilian programs, about $3.1 million more than the administration's request.

In both the House and Senate, debate on the DOE budget centered on the Clinch River breeder project. Opponents fell short — by 20 votes in the House and two in the Senate — of deleting Clinch River funds from the bill. As cleared, HR 4144 appropriated $2.3 billion for energy research and development, including $195 million for the breeder project. *(Details of action on Clinch River project, pp. 370, 371)*

Both the House and Senate Appropriations committees recommended that Congress substantially boost Reagan's plans for solar energy spending. Reagan initially requested $193 million for solar development, less than half the $500 million Congress appropriated for fiscal 1981. In passing HR 4144 July 24, the House accepted its Appropriations Committee's decision to raise that to $304 million. The committee had reported a $13.2 billion version of the bill July 14 (H Rept 97-177).

The committee also added $24 million to the amount requested for turning sunlight directly into electricity and increased funds for advanced windmills by $20 million. It included $29 million for converting the ocean's temperature differences into electric power, a program the administration wanted to cancel, and set up a $24 million solar account, which the administration could spend, with the committee's permission, on a variety of solar projects.

The panel provided $972 million for non-military nuclear fission programs, about $7 million more than the budget request and $52 million more than the 1981 appropriation.

In addition to the funds for the breeder reactor, the committee provided $35 million for research on a gascooled nuclear reactor, a program the administration had not sought to fund. The program was supported by Western members of Congress because it could be used in arid regions that did not have enough water to operate watercooled reactors.

Reagan revised his DOE budget request in September, slashing proposed solar development appropriations to $183 million. The Senate Appropriations Committee reported (S Rept 97-256) a $12.4 billion version of the House-passed bill on Oct. 28, recommending $244 million for solar programs. The Senate accepted that figure in passing HR 4144 Nov. 5.

In a conference agreement reached Nov. 18 (H Rept 97-345), House and Senate negotiators provided about $83 million more than Reagan requested for solar energy programs and about $23 million less than the president wanted for nuclear fission research. Congress cleared the final bill Nov. 21.

Conservation, Fossil Fuels

A few weeks later Congress cleared a separate appropriations bill that provided another $1.1 billion for DOE's conservation, regulation and fossil energy programs. Congress appropriated funds for those programs, once part of the Interior Department, through a bill (HR 4035 — PL 97-100) providing $7.2 billion in fiscal 1982 for Interior, DOE, the U.S. Forest Service, Indian health and education, and various federal arts and humanities programs.

Research and Development

Through action on the measure, Congress increased Reagan's $992.9 million proposal for DOE programs by $74.2 million. Congress also wrote in language barring the Interior Department from conducting four controversial offshore oil and gas lease sales off the California coastline. *(Offshore leasing, p. 357)*

The bill appropriated $191.4 million to DOE for managing the U.S. Strategic Petroleum Reserve. Following instructions that Congress had approved in its earlier budget reconciliation law (PL 97-35), the measure appropriated another $3.4 billion for filling the reserve in a special off-budget account that was not counted in the bill's total appropriations or in federal budget outlays. *(Strategic reserve, p. 379)*

Accepting their Appropriations committees' proposals, both the House and Senate rebuffed administration plans to end some popular DOE programs and substantially increased proposed funds for conservation and alternative fuels research. The administration had proposed the largest cuts for energy conservation programs, but the House committee added $177 million to the $195 million request. The House panel also added $33 million to Reagan's $12 million request for a DOE compliance program to force major oil companies to refund overcharges to consumers. It provided $150 million for home weatherization and $15 million for the energy extension services, ignoring administration plans to fold the programs into block grants.

As passed by the House July 22, HR 4035 (H Rept 97-163) included the committee's proposal to appropriate $463 million for fossil fuel research and development, $46 million more than the budget request.

In the Senate, the Appropriations Committee July 23 recommended appropriating $1.09 billion for DOE fossil fuel programs, not counting the funds for filling the petroleum reserve. The Senate panel also rejected administration plans to eliminate funds for several conservation programs, providing $112.5 million to weatherize low-income homes, $18.6 million for building and community services, $23.6 million for industrial conservation, $21 million for transportation efficiency programs and $39 million for conservation grants and extension services.

Before passing HR 4035 (S Rept 97-166) Oct. 7, the full Senate adopted an amendment by James A. McClure, R-Idaho, chairman of the Appropriations Subcommittee on Interior and Related Agencies, that trimmed $163 million from fiscal 1982 appropriations, including $23 million from DOE fossil fuel research. Even so, in the first test of the Republican-controlled Senate's support for Reagan's Sept. 24 demand for additional budget cutbacks, senators demonstrated continued backing for DOE programs by voting 87-8 to pass a bill that still exceeded Reagan's revised request by $1 billion.

But before approving the conference version (H Rept 97-315) of HR 4035 Dec. 10, the Senate cut another $56.9 billion from DOE fossil fuel program appropriations to meet Reagan's demand to trim 4 percent from the bill's final appropriations. The House Nov. 12 had adopted the conference report, which appropriated $7.54 billion for DOE, Interior and other programs, $1.1 billion more than the administration's September budget revision. To avert a showdown with the White House, the Senate approved amendments reducing fiscal 1982 appropriations under the compromise version by $314.3 million and also deleting $5.4 million from deferred fiscal 1981 funds that were earmarked for a synthetic fuels demonstration plant. The House approved the Senate's revisions, clearing the bill.

Fiscal 1983 Appropriations

The struggle over the Department of Energy (DOE) budget resumed in 1982. Congress again moved to increase administration budget requests for DOE research and development programs. Neither the House nor the Senate finished work on fiscal 1983 energy and water program appropriations, however. And controversies over Interior Department programs delayed final action on related DOE program funds until well after the fiscal year had started.

Energy-Water Funds

Neither the House nor the Senate brought a regular appropriations bill for DOE's research and development programs to the floor. Congress instead funded those programs at their fiscal 1982 levels through a fiscal 1983 continuing appropriations resolution (H J Res 631 — PL 97-377).

Both the House and Senate Appropriations committees made it clear they opposed the administration's attempts to curtail DOE research programs. In reporting a regular appropriations bill in September, the House panel provided substantial increases over administration requests for solar programs, geothermal energy, electric energy systems, nuclear fission and fusion research, environmental programs and basic energy research.

Conservation, Fossil Fuels

In its 1982 post-election session, Congress Dec. 19 cleared a $7.5 billion fiscal 1983 appropriations bill (HR 7356 — PL 97-394) for Interior, DOE and other agencies. The measure increased the president's budget requests by $923 million, including additional funds for DOE conservation, synfuels research and alternative energy technology programs.

During debate on the Interior appropriations bill, both the House and Senate voted to give the administration far more for the Energy Department than the $443.06 million it requested. The House approved $926.76 million in new budget authority, while the Senate voted $826.15 million.

Much of that increase came in fossil energy research and development — mostly "synfuels" projects. While the administration requested $106.90 million for fossil research, the House approved $297.06 million and the Senate $247.51 million.

Much of the remaining Energy Department add-on came in energy conservation programs. The administration had asked $21.8 million — which would have ended most energy conservation programs run by the department. But the House refused to go along, giving conservation programs $317.79 million in new budget authority. The Senate voted $264.53 million for the programs. Both bills allotted additional funds for conservation programs through transfers.

Approved in the Interior appropriations bill — but not included in its totals — was a $2.07 billion expenditure for buying oil to put in the Strategic Petroleum Reserve, the funding requested by the administration. That amount compared with $3.68 billion for fiscal 1982 and $2.69 billion for fiscal 1981.

Formerly counted in budget totals, the Strategic Petroleum Reserve went "off-budget" in fiscal 1982, when pressure to cut the budget and fill the reserve mounted simultaneously. *(Strategic reserve, p. 379)*

The House passed HR 7356 (H Rept 97-942) Dec. 3, and the Senate passed its bill Dec. 14. In compromising the House and Senate versions, the conference report on HR 7356 (H Rept 97-978) appropriated $808 million for DOE, $365 million more than Reagan had requested.

Department of Energy

Congress in 1982 sidetracked President Reagan's plan to abolish the five-year-old Department of Energy (DOE).

During his 1980 presidential campaign, Reagan had pledged to dismantle DOE and rely on the marketplace, not federal government intervention, to solve the nation's energy problems. But neither the Democratic House nor the Republican Senate took up the president's 1982 proposal to transfer most DOE authorities to the Commerce Department and other government agencies.

Key members of Congress, such as Senate Energy and Natural Resources Committee Chairman James A. McClure, R-Idaho, were concerned that dropping energy as a Cabinet-level department would signal the nation and the world that the federal government was not serious about dealing with energy supply problems. Numerous groups opposed revising a federal energy program structure that they felt protected their interests, while key senators objected to plans that might cost their committees jurisdiction over DOE programs that Reagan wanted to transfer to other departments.

By the end of 1982, Donald P. Hodel, Reagan's newly appointed secretary of energy, told the Senate Energy panel that he recognized there was little support in Congress for abolishing DOE. Hodel said the plan no longer was a top department priority.

Administration Infighting

Reagan first outlined his plan to abolish DOE and send most of its programs to the Commerce Department when he submitted his fiscal 1983 budget Feb. 6, 1982. However, the legislation introduced in May differed substantially from the original proposal.

The original plan had been delayed for months because of infighting among administration officials over how DOE would be divided up. Much of the struggle reportedly was between Interior Secretary James G. Watt and Commerce Secretary Malcolm Baldrige, both of whom wanted some of DOE's programs.

There also was controversy over where to put DOE's defense activities — the research and production of nuclear weapons, which accounted for nearly half the department's budget; 13 senators wrote Reagan, asking him not to put those activities under either Commerce or Interior.

Baldrige emerged the big winner when the original plan was announced Feb. 6. Reagan said he would ask Congress to transfer about 70 percent of DOE's programs to a new Energy Research and Technology Administration in the Commerce Department. The remaining energy programs would go to Interior.

However, key senators still had objections to the plan, many of them having to do with loss of committee jurisdiction over programs that would be transferred to other departments. After months of negotiations, the administration scrapped its original proposal and called instead for two new deputy secretaries of commerce — one for nuclear weapons programs and one for all other energy programs. A

few other energy functions would be transferred to the Justice, Interior and Agriculture departments.

Chilly Reception

In both the House and Senate, leading members from each party gave Reagan's plan a chilly reception. Both chambers in 1977 had supported President Carter's decision to set up a separate Energy Department by wide margins, and Baldrige acknowledged that there was no real constituency for abolishing it. Although the administration claimed that reorganizing the federal energy policy structure would save the government money, the Congressional Budget Office found no significant spending reductions under the administration proposal.

Legislation to dismantle DOE was introduced in the Senate in May. No sponsors could even be found to introduce a bill in the House until August. The measures were referred to the Senate Governmental Affairs Committee and to the House Government Operations and Energy and Commerce committees. But the panels took no further action.

1983-84

Congress in 1983-84 continued to approve cutbacks in federal energy development and conservation programs, including subsidies for development of a U.S. synthetic fuels industry.

Reconsidering a commitment Congress had made just four years earlier, the House and Senate in 1984 rescinded $7.4 billion in previously approved funding for the U.S. Synthetic Fuels Corporation. Congress had set up the federally funded corporation in 1980, hoping to spur private industry to perfect technologies for converting coal, oil shale, tar sands and biomass resources to commercial liquid fuels.

But with oil prices falling instead of rising, industry in the early 1980s abandoned synfuels projects. Members had second thoughts about the environmental and economic obstacles that a synfuels industry would face, and Congress went along with the Reagan administration's demand for cutbacks in the synfuels corporation's funding.

Congress continued to insist on spending more than the administration sought for federal conservation, solar and fossil fuel development programs. Department of Energy (DOE) funding for those efforts nonetheless stayed below previous levels as the administration channeled a larger proportion of the DOE budget into nuclear power programs.

Synfuels Funding Cutback

Just four years after it launched the program, Congress in 1984 cut federal synthetic fuels development funding in half.

In two deficit-cutting steps, Congress rescinded $7.375 billion in funds previously appropriated for the U.S. Synthetic Fuels Corporation (SFC). Congress set up the federal corporation in 1980 to funnel subsidies to help private business develop a commercial industry to convert coal, oil

shale, tar sands and other raw materials into synthetic fuels.

President Reagan in May had asked Congress for a $9 billion rescission for the troubled synfuels corporation. With falling world oil prices undercutting synthetic fuel prospects, some members of Congress had demanded that the government scale back SFC funding or scrap the program altogether.

Congress had created the corporation at President Carter's request in 1980, after a decade of energy disruptions. With experts predicting that world oil prices would keep soaring to $42.50 a barrel and beyond, the Carter administration and congressional backers envisioned that federal subsidies would give private ventures the incentive they needed to perfect ways of extracting alternative fuels from the nation's own ample supplies of potential synthetic fuels.

Instead oil prices fell below $30 a barrel, far less than the level at which proposed synfuel processes could compete. The Reagan administration, which preferred to let energy markets provide the incentives for new forms of fuel, meanwhile gave the SFC program little priority in its energy strategy.

Background

For at least half a century synthetic fuels had held out the promise of expanding U.S. supplies of critical liquid forms of energy that could be easily transported or burned in internal combustion engines. Despite decades of research, however, industry had yet to demonstrate technologies for making synthetic liquid fuels at a cost that could compete with petroleum or natural gas. As a result U.S. energy firms rapidly produced the nation's naturally occurring oil and gas deposits while synthetic fuel conversion projects remained at the experimental stage.

Synthetic fuel projects envisioned creating liquid fuels from coal, oil shale or biomass. The nation possessed ample coal reserves, including huge low-sulfur deposits beneath federally owned lands in the West. Colorado, Utah and Wyoming also held vast oil shale deposits, mostly federally owned, containing an estimated 400 billion to 700 billion barrels of oil that could be recovered by heating the rock to high temperatures. The nation also had available about 600 million tons of biomass — including farm and forest products and residues as well as municipal solid wastes — that could be converted to fuel oil and alcohol for blending with gasoline to make gasohol fuels for automobiles.

Sporadic Congressional Interest. Congress began subsidizing synthetic fuels development in World War II, when experts were saying domestic oil reserves would last only another dozen years. The Synthetic Liquids Fuel Act passed in 1944 provided $30 million over the next five years for research and demonstration plants that converted coal, oil shale, trees and vegetative matter into liquid fuels. A three-year, $30 million extension was approved in 1948, with another $27.6 million voted in 1950, when the authorization was extended through 1955. (*Congress and the Nation Vol. I, p. 994*)

In the years following expiration of the act the Bureau of Mines, under its basic research authorization, continued its experiments with oil shale and liquefaction and gasification of coal. A special coal research bill was approved in 1960, setting up a new office of Coal Research in the Interior Department.

The oil embargo and price increases by the Organization of Petroleum Exporting Countries (OPEC) in 1973-74 renewed interest in synthetic fuels, which still had not been developed commercially in the United States. President Ford in his 1975 State of the Union message called on Congress to provide new incentives to spur production by 1985 of the equivalent of one million barrels a day of synthetic fuels. Although the market was not ready for synfuels, Ford thought the government should help along a new industry that might be crucial during future embargoes. Ford in 1975 endorsed Vice President Nelson A. Rockefeller's proposal to set up an Energy Independence Authority to provide private and federal backing for loans to develop synthetic fuels technologies and other energy projects.

The AFL-CIO and industry groups backed federal synfuels loan guarantees. But environmental groups, concerned by potential air and groundwater pollution from coal and oil shale conversion, lobbied against federal financial support for the industry. Western state governments also were alarmed by potential pollution, boomtown growth and demand for scarce water if a synthetic fuels industry suddenly took hold in their region.

President Carter in April 1979 called for massive federal financial support to spur synthetic fuel development as Iranian oil production cutbacks sent world oil prices soaring beyond $30 a barrel and created gasoline shortages in the United States. Carter asked Congress to create a synfuels corporation to manage $88 billion in federal financial incentives to spur synthetic fuels production reaching 2.5 million barrels a day by 1990.

1980 Law. Finally cleared in June 1980, the Energy Security Act (PL 96-294) set a goal of producing the equivalent of at least 500,000 barrels of crude oil a day by 1987, increasing to two million barrels a day by 1992.

The law established the quasi-governmental Synthetic Fuels Corporation and directed its seven-member board to offer loans, loan guarantees, purchase agreements or price guarantees to nudge private industry to design and build a synthetic fuels conversion industry. In setting up the program, Congress provided for federal funding that ultimately could reach $88 billion over the following decade.

The law authorized an initial $14.9 billion for the corporation through fiscal 1984. At that point SFC was to submit a detailed report to Congress on its future strategy. Thereafter Congress could make additional authorizations, subject to annual appropriations, up to another $68 billion by 1990.

Carter in September 1980 named John C. Sawhill, a deputy secretary of energy and former energy adviser to President Ford, as SFC board chairman and chief operating officer. (*Congress and the Nation Vol. V, p. 512*)

Ebbing Synfuels Prospects

From the start the federal synthetic fuels program disappointed its congressional backers. Reagan in 1981 fired Carter's synfuels corporation directors, and political maneuvering slowed the process of selecting their replacements. And, as the corporation geared up to go into operation, the turnaround in world oil markets cut short previous enthusiasm for developing synthetic fuel technologies. Many potential synfuel sponsors backed off.

In January 1982 SFC accepted 11 synfuel projects for possible federal support. But in May, with synthetic fuel prospects ebbing, Exxon Corp. abruptly abandoned its huge Colony oil shale project in western Colorado. Con-

struction continued on a Union Oil Co. oil shale plant in Colorado and on a Great Plains coal gasification project in North Dakota, but private backers of other projects lost interest. By early 1984 SFC had found only one small project to support and had committed just $120 million of the nearly $15 billion Congress made available four years before. House Majority Leader Jim Wright, D-Texas, a prime backer of the 1980 legislation, and other supporters complained that the SFC board was moving too slowly.

SFC Internal Problems. A series of embarrassing revelations of internal problems at the SFC fueled congressional doubts and left the board for a time without a quorum to make decisions. In August 1983 SFC President Victor A. Schroeder resigned amid conflict-of-interest charges. On April 26, 1984, his successor to the $135,000-a-year post, Victor M. Thompson, also resigned under fire for failing to disclose when he was appointed that his actions as head of a Tulsa, Okla., bank were being investigated by the Securities and Exchange Commission.

Just before Thompson quit, the board approved $1.4 billion in subsidies for two controversial projects. His departure, followed by another 1984 resignation, left the board with just two members.

By year's end Reagan had made three recess appointments to the board — thus allowing it to resume operations.

Reagan Cutback Request. As the White House in May 1984 announced that Reagan would fill the SFC board vacancies, the president proposed substantially scaling back the corporation's spending authority. The administration asked Congress to cancel $9 billion in SFC spending authority and restrict the remaining funds to projects that met a "market test." By limiting SFC support to projects that could produce fuels at costs not significantly higher than competing fuels, the White House plan would have ruled out most proposed facilities then under SFC consideration.

Reagan's proposal effectively pre-empted congressional attempts to scale back or even kill the SFC. Even so, his plan did not go far enough for some congressional critics of the synfuels program. Sen. William Proxmire, D-Wis., complained that Reagan "should have gone all the way and shut it down."

First Rescission

Just two days after Reagan asked for a $9 billion cutback, the Senate voted to rescind $2 billion in SFC funding as part of a deficit-cutting package that the House previously had passed. Senate Republican leaders persuaded five moderate Republicans to go along with the spending cut measure by agreeing to channel the $2 billion from synfuels program savings to non-defense discretionary programs. Although the House had provided for no SFC rescission, conferees accepted the $2 billion cut in the final budget-cutting legislation (HR 4170 — PL 98-369) that Congress cleared June 27.

Second Rescission

Despite strong opposition from House Majority Leader Wright, one of the SFC's stoutest congressional defenders, Congress in October continuing appropriations legislation (H J Res 648 — PL 98-473) cut another $5.375 billion from previously approved synfuels funding.

House. In July Wright had fought hard to keep any SFC cutbacks from reaching the House floor. As part of annual Interior Department appropriations legislation (HR 5973), the House Rules Committee obliged the majority leader, voting 7-4 on July 24 to approve a rule for floor debate on the interior appropriations bill that would bar anticipated SFC rescission amendments. But the House rejected the rule on a **148-261 key vote (R 21-135; D 127-126)**, after Office of Management and Budget Director David A. Stockman personally called some members to lobby for an opportunity to bring amendments curtailing synfuels funding to the floor. *(1984 key votes, p. 927)*

The Reagan administration backed an amendment, offered by Silvio O. Conte, R-Mass., to rescind $10 billion, most of the corporation's remaining funds. But the House Aug. 2 approved by a 236-177 vote an amendment by William R. Ratchford, D-Conn., that replaced Conte's amendment with a $5 billion rescission.

SFC critics argued during House debate that the nation could ill afford to spend billions promoting synthetic fuels projects that could damage the environment while cutting domestic programs. SFC backers contended that the government should push ahead, despite falling oil prices, with technologies that ultimately would reduce U.S. dependence on foreign energy supplies from volatile regions such as the Persian Gulf nations. "How shall we expect the United States ever really to be taken seriously in the world," Wright asked during debate, "if, only five years after the second Arab oil embargo brought our nation to its economic knees for the second time in a decade, we abandon the goal of energy independence by doing away with the one long-term program . . . to achieve that goal?"

Senate. The Senate never acted on its Appropriations Committee's version of the Interior funding bill, which contained no SFC rescission. After working out a compromise with the administration, however, the Senate panel approved a $5.2 billion synfuels funding reduction as part of H J Res 648. The compromise set $750 million of that rescission aside in a special account, not returned to the U.S. Treasury, for projects to demonstrate cleaner ways to burn coal.

Conference. In the conference agreement on H J Res 648 (H Rept 98-1159), cleared Oct. 11, House-Senate conferees agreed to strip $5.375 billion from the synfuels program, with $750 million of that amount assigned to the Senate's coal program.

The rescission left the SFC with about $8 billion to spend. Of that, $5.7 billion was earmarked for projects that already had received letters of intent from the SFC. Half of any money not spent on those projects was to revert to the Treasury.

Fiscal 1984-85 Appropriations

Congress in 1983-84 continued to resist Reagan administration budget cutbacks for Department of Energy (DOE) research and conservation programs.

Through action on fiscal 1984 and fiscal 1985 appropriations bills, Congress again sharply increased the president's budget requests for solar energy research, energy conservation assistance, fossil fuels development and other DOE programs that remained popular among members. Even so, spending for those efforts remained well below the fiscal 1981 levels that Congress had provided before Reagan took office.

With congressional agreement early in 1983 to scrap

the Clinch River breeder reactor project, House and Senate debates on DOE appropriations during the 98th Congress were relatively free of controversy. Considering the department's budget in two separate annual appropriations measures, Congress provided $11.2 billion in fiscal 1984 and $11.8 billion in fiscal 1985 for DOE operations. Those funds included $6.5 billion in fiscal 1984 and $7.3 billion in fiscal 1985 for the department's nuclear weapons programs. *(Clinch River, p. 371)*

In action on DOE's civilian energy programs, Congress generally accepted or slightly cut administration requests for nuclear fission and fusion research, uranium enrichment and other energy programs that the administration treated favorably. For both fiscal 1984 and 1985, however, Congress approved substantial increases above administration requests for solar, conservation, fossil fuels research and other programs that members wanted to preserve.

Energy-Water

With the Clinch River debate settled, Congress in both 1983 and 1984 cleared energy and water appropriations bills that provided the bulk of DOE funds with little debate on energy programs. Congressional deliberations instead focused on federal water projects funded by the bill and on DOE's nuclear weapons development programs.

In considering DOE's research budget, however, Congress continued to refuse Reagan's request for deep slashes in solar energy funding. As before, the administration contended that solar technologies were nearing the point where private business could bring them into commercial production. For fiscal 1984 DOE proposed cutting the solar energy development spending to $87 million, far below the $202 million level of fiscal 1983. But Congress in 1983 insisted on spending $185 million in fiscal 1984 through action on energy-water appropriations legislation (HR 3132 — PL 98-50).

The Senate Appropriations Committee, in reporting its version of the energy-water measure (S Rept 98-153), stated the congressional case for continued federal support for research on solar and other renewable sources of energy: "The committee agrees that the marketplace must ultimately decide the future role of the solar technologies. The committee does not agree, however, that most solar and renewables research has been developed to the point where the private sector alone can be expected to carry forward with its development."

In its fiscal 1985 budget the administration bowed to congressional support for solar in proposing nearly $164 million for the program. In the fiscal 1985 energy-water appropriations bill (HR 5653 — PL 98-360) Congress maintained funding at roughly the fiscal 1984 level. Before passing HR 5653, however, the House defeated, 171-229, an amendment by Richard L. Ottinger, D-N.Y., chairman of the House Energy Subcommittee on Energy Conservation and Power, to shift $43.1 million from DOE's breeder reactor research budget into solar research and other programs.

Conservation, Fossil Fuels

Congress also protected various DOE conservation and fossil fuel research programs, funded as part of annual Interior Department appropriations bills, that the administration had been trying for four years to curtail sharply or eliminate altogether.

In the fiscal 1984 Interior appropriations bill (HR 3363 — PL 98-146) Congress appropriated nearly $1.2 billion for DOE programs, roughly double the $666.6 million that the White House sought. The president requested $74.4 million for DOE conservation assistance programs, down from $429.1 million in fiscal 1983, with no funds for low-income home weatherization assistance and school and hospital grants. Those programs were popular in the Northeast, where heating bills were high, and the House Appropriations Committee approved $243.5 million for weatherization aid and $98 million for school and hospital grants as it boosted total conservation appropriations to $528 million. The House committee also recommended $265.9 million for fossil energy research, well above the administration's $94 million request.

Although the Senate Appropriations Committee trimmed the House-passed figures, the full Senate adopted an amendment by Paul E. Tsongas, D-Mass., and John Heinz, R-Pa., that added $27 million for energy conservation. In its final form the fiscal 1984 Interior appropriations measure included $431.1 million for conservation programs and $259.2 million for fossil fuel research and development. Congress subsequently appropriated another $1 million for fossil fuel programs.

Congress in 1984 funded Interior and DOE conservation and fossil fuel programs through an omnibus continuing appropriations resolution (H J Res 648 — PL 98-473).

In the continuing measure Congress approved $275 million for fossil energy research and development, well above Reagan's $200 million request. Congress provided $459 million for energy conservation programs, although Reagan requested only $390 million. Much of that money went to state and local grant programs that were especially popular with members from the Northeast and Midwest, including the home weatherization program, funded at $191 million. *(Weatherization, p. 603)*

Energy Audits

House-Senate differences in 1984 stalled efforts to revamp a popular federal program requiring U.S. utilities to offer to conduct "energy audits" of customers' homes.

Failing to agree on a single approach to reform, the House and Senate allowed the Residential Conservation Service (RCS) program established in 1978 to lapse at the end of the year.

In a compromise supported by both the electric power industry and conservationists, the House July 30 passed legislation (HR 5946 — H Rept 98-903) extending the RCS for five years but allowing utilities to improve conservation through alternative programs instead of residential audits. The House measure also killed a separate program, the Commercial and Apartment Conservation Service (CACS), that had been established in 1980 but had yet to go into operation. Utilities opposed the CACS program.

The Senate balked at the comprehensive approach, however, revising the House bill to provide a one-year extension for the RCS and a delay in starting up the other program (S Rept 98-625). The House and Senate were unable to resolve their differences before adjournment.

The RCS program was established in 1978 (PL 95-619). It was under fire because it reached a tiny proportion of homes, most of them affluent, and because most of the cost of energy audits was passed along to consumers by utilities. *(Background, Congress and the Nation Vol. V, p. 468)*

8

Environmental Policy

Introduction	*403*
Clean Air	*411*
Federal Water Policy	*425*
EPA Pollution Control Programs	*449*
Federal Land Management	*463*
Wildlife Protection	*477*

Environmental Policy

Congress in 1981-84 defended federal environmental protection programs against the Reagan administration's conservative challenge.

President Reagan took office in 1981 pledging to cut the costs that federal environmental regulations imposed on U.S. business and communities. But Congress, alarmed by administration stands on controlling pollution and managing natural resources, kept in force the major laws and policies that the federal government had adopted in the 1970s to protect the nation's air, water, soil, wild lands and other natural resources.

Through budget cuts and administrative decisions, however, Secretary of the Interior James G. Watt and other Reagan appointees shifted federal agencies away from protecting environmental values and toward promoting economic growth. Even with a Republican Senate majority, House Democrats and their environmental group allies fought back to preserve the environmental programs that Congress had launched under previous Republican and Democratic administrations.

Congress checkmated many administration policies for managing federally owned lands and resources and enforcing Environmental Protection Agency (EPA) pollution control regulations. In defending the status quo, however, members shied away from tackling tough technical and political questions about whether existing statutes and regulations could effectively control pollution and preserve natural values without taking an unjustified toll on the U.S. economy through lost jobs and profits and continued reliance on foreign supplies of energy.

As a result, 10 major environmental laws expired or were left up for renewal when Reagan began his second term in the White House in 1985. Congress in 1984 did dramatically tighten federal controls on handling and disposing of toxic wastes, taking away EPA administrative discretion that members contended the agency had abused in enforcing previous law.

After bitter wrangling, Congress and the administration made at least one other lasting contribution to environmental preservation. Under a compromise worked out by Senate Republicans and House Democrats, Congress in 1984 passed and Reagan signed a series of laws that began settling the long-raging debate over how much of the lands in the U.S. national forests should be preserved as permanent wilderness and how much should be kept open for logging and other development.

Yet White House resistance and regional divisions within Congress prevented revision of federal clean air and clean water laws. Concerned by potential economic costs, the administration and Congress took a go-slow approach toward environmentalists' demand that the federal government curb Midwestern power plant emissions, which studies found produced "acid rain" that damaged Eastern lakes and forests.

Swings of the Pendulum

Watt's combative attitude and a scandal over EPA's handling of toxic waste dump cleanups left House Democrats and environmental groups distrustful of Reagan's commitment to environmental protection. The administration's stance and environmentalists' angry response all but shattered the bipartisan tradition that united Republicans and Democrats, in the White House and on Capitol Hill, behind efforts during the 1970s to control pollution and conserve the nation's natural wealth.

Reagan himself concentrated his attention on tax, budget and foreign policy matters, sending Congress few specific proposals for revising environmental policies. But the men and women Reagan appointed to key environmental posts lost little time in interpreting his 1980 presidential election landslide over Jimmy Carter as a mandate to reverse the natural resource and pollution control policies that Carter's Democratic administration had pursued.

Vowing to "swing the pendulum back to center" from Carter's preservationist stance, Watt slowed the expansion of national parks and wildlife refuges while speeding up the development of federally owned lands and offshore waters for oil and gas, coal and other mineral wealth.

EPA Administrator Anne M. Burford, like Watt a conservative Colorado lawyer, at the same time shifted that

References

Discussion of environmental action for the years 1945-64 may be found in *Congress and the Nation Vol. I*, pp. 769-1095; for the years 1965-68, *Congress and the Nation Vol. II*, pp. 461-528; for the years 1969-72, *Congress and the Nation Vol. III*, pp. 743-849; for the years 1973-76, *Congress and the Nation Vol. IV*, pp. 287-320; for the years 1977-80, *Congress and the Nation Vol. V*, pp. 533-597.

Interior Department's Diverse, Sensitive Role

The furor over Secretary of the Interior James G. Watt demonstrated the diverse and sensitive role the Interior Department played in carrying out federal natural resource policies.

Congress created the department in 1849 and assigned it the task of managing the vast public lands that the national government acquired with the nation's western territories. Throughout the 19th century the department's principal goal was to transfer federally owned lands to homesteaders, ranchers, newly formed state governments, railroads and other owners to encourage settlement of the West. Over the years, however, Congress complicated the department's missions by assigning it responsibility for developing water resources, leasing federal minerals, preserving national parks, protecting wildlife habitat and supervising American Indian reservations.

Conflicting Responsibilities. As Watt himself put it in a 1982 television interview, "The secretary of the interior is sitting on a department filled with conflict." The department's National Park Service struggles to preserve scenic vistas in national parks while hosting millions of visitors each year who come to view them. Its U.S. Fish and Wildlife Service designates endangered species for protection and manages national wildlife refuges for waterfowl and animals, but it also traps and hunts coyotes and other predators to keep them from damaging farmers' crops and ranchers' livestock. The Bureau of Land Management (BLM) manages more than 300 million acres of public lands, largely in Western states, for multiple uses that include mining, oil and gas drilling, livestock grazing, hiking, hunting, archeological digs and other, often irreconcilable, activities.

In addition, Interior's Bureau of Reclamation has built and operates dams, reservoirs and irrigation systems throughout 17 predominantly arid Western states. Its U.S. Geological Survey studies the nation's geologic characteristics and maps the extent of valuable mineral deposits beneath federal lands and forests. Its Bureau of Mines studies mining techniques, while its Office of Surface Mining enforces a 1977 federal law limiting damage from strip-mining coal on private as well as public lands. Its Bureau of Indian Affairs acts as trustee for Native American tribes in managing reservation lands and resources. Its Minerals Management Service, an agency that Watt set up in 1982, collects royalties from federal mineral leases and also manages the government's Outer Continental Shelf oil and gas leasing program in federally controlled coastal waters.

In addition to valuable coal, oil and gas, oil shale and other minerals, BLM administers some productive federal timber stands in Washington and Oregon. But the U.S. Forest Service, a separate agency within the Agriculture Department, manages most federal timberlands as part of the 187-million-acre national forest system.

Resource Management Shift. For years Congress generally was content to set broad goals for federal resource management, leaving the interior secretary discretion to administer the lands and resources the department controlled. Most interior secretaries came from Western states, and the department staff was largely drawn from Westerners. Politically powerful public land users, notably ranchers, loggers, miners and farmers who relied on federal irrigation water, wielded strong influence over decision making by Interior officials who viewed the department's primary task as making federal resources available for economic production.

During the 1970s, however, new environmental protection laws forced Interior agencies to pay increasing attention to preserving wilderness, protecting wildlife and correcting environmental damage from resource production. Meanwhile national energy problems increased pressure on the department to step up production of federally owned coal, onshore oil and gas and offshore petroleum deposits.

During the late 1960s and 1970s the National Environmental Protection Act, Endangered Species Act and other new laws forced Interior agencies to consider how public land resource development affected wildlife, air and water quality, and undisturbed wild country. In 1976 Congress through the Federal Land Policy and Management Act gave BLM a permanent mandate for managing remaining public lands for multiple uses, including natural values as well as resource production. Conservation groups also began questioning the way Interior managed BLM lands, planned Bureau of Reclamation water projects and handled its mineral leasing efforts.

It fell to President Carter, a Democrat elected in 1976 with strong environmentalist backing, to implement the more balanced resource management policies that Congress mandated in the early 1970s.

While initially viewed as acceptable to Western interests, Carter's interior secretary, former Idaho Gov. Cecil D. Andrus, angered advocates of resource development by appointing environmental activists to key Interior posts and by expanding funding and manpower for BLM's conservation efforts. In its first weeks in office the administration also offended Western congressional delegations by releasing a "hit list" of authorized water projects that officials planned to cancel. Carter's resource policies sparked a "Sagebrush Rebellion" in Western states among miners, ranchers, state legislators and other interests that previously had dominated Interior policy making. In selecting Watt as his interior secretary in 1981, President Reagan signaled his intention to overhaul Carter's preservationist approach.

agency's adversarial approach to the industries it regulated toward one of mutual cooperation, while granting states more responsibility to enforce federal pollution standards. (Burford was known as Anne M. Gorsuch until her 1983 marriage to Robert Burford, a former Colorado rancher who served as director of Interior's Bureau of Land Management.)

John B. Crowell Jr., a timber company counsel whom Reagan named assistant secretary of agriculture in charge of the U.S. Forest Service, pushed plans to step up timber harvest from national forests to fill the logging industry's needs. In other federal resource agencies, within both Interior and other departments, administration officials also turned sympathetic ears to industry demands for cutting back on environmental restraints when they conflicted with the president's goal of spurring U.S. economic growth.

As some environmentalist leaders acknowledged, the Reagan administration's policies addressed legitimate concerns about the economic and social consequences of federal environmental policies. Business and community leaders complained throughout the 1970s about arbitrary EPA standards that were forcing the steel, automobile, electric utility and other U.S. industries to invest heavily in pollution control equipment, making their products more costly and less competitive with foreign imports. In the West, the core of Reagan's conservative political support, governors, miners, ranchers and recreation business leaders in the late 1970s led a "Sagebrush Rebellion" against Carter administration land and water policies that Westerners contended limited the region's economic prospects.

Congressional Backlash

When Reagan took office in 1981, along with a new Republican majority in the Senate, environmental group lobbyists feared that the administration could muster the strength to push Congress into relaxing numerous regulatory statutes and going along with its pro-development approach to federally controlled resources.

That appeared feasible early in 1981, when the president commanded a working majority in Congress — at least on economic issues — of Republicans and conservative Sun Belt Democrats. By March 1981 Reagan had proposed drastic cutbacks in the politically popular federal program of grants for construction of local sewage systems. By the end of the year Congress had voted those reductions, along with cuts in the EPA budget that were part of broader domestic spending cuts.

But environmentalists and their legislative allies dug in their heels on other issues before the 97th Congress. With surprising ease they managed to stave off administration proposals to relax both the Clean Air Act and the regulatory provisions of the Clean Water Act.

With environmentalists raising an alarm over Watt's plans for developing federal lands, Congress also stepped in to block some controversial decisions. Western senators, led by Senate Energy and Natural Resources Committee Chairman James A. McClure, R-Idaho, welcomed Watt's efforts to reverse public land policies adopted by Cecil D. Andrus, Carter's interior secretary. But House Democratic leaders on environmental legislation — notably Interior and Insular Affairs Committee Chairman Morris K. Udall, D-Ariz.; Appropriations Subcommittee on Interior Chairman Sidney R. Yates, D-Ill.; and Henry A. Waxman, D-Calif., chairman of the Energy and Commerce Subcommittee on Health and Environment — led a series of fights to

preserve Interior and EPA programs that they had helped launch during the previous decade.

On many issues Watt and Burford stirred angry congressional resistance by taking hard-line stands without consulting members or listening to environmental groups' positions. Congress responded, through legislative riders, oversight hearings and angry exchanges in the press that forced the administration to back off from some controversial initiatives.

In the 1982 elections environmental groups gained new strength on Capitol Hill as Democrats picked up 26 seats in the House and held their own in the Senate.

Emboldened by such success at the polls, they went on the offensive in the 98th Congress, seeking to beef up laws on air and water pollution and toxic waste disposal and cleanup.

But the environmentalists soon discovered the same time-honored truth the Reagan administration had learned the hard way: It is easier to hold the high ground than to capture it, to defend the status quo than to change it.

In 1983 both Watt and Burford resigned under congressional fire as members launched investigations into Interior's coal leasing program and EPA's handling of the superfund program. Their successors — Interior Secretary William P. Clark and EPA Administrator William P. Ruckelshaus — improved environmental enforcement, opened communications with environmental groups and shifted controversial agendas to the back burner as the 1984 presidential election approached. During the campaign Reagan proclaimed the administration's environmental record the "best-kept secret" of his first White House term.

But environmental groups remained skeptical at best, and they continued to attack Interior's mineral leasing goals and EPA's reluctance to propose strict controls on acid rain drifting over the Northeast from Midwestern coal-fired power plant smokestacks. Taking unprecedented stands, the Sierra Club and Friends of the Earth, two major environmental groups, endorsed Walter F. Mondale, Carter's vice president, in his unsuccessful 1984 Democratic campaign to defeat Reagan.

Watt Controversies

For nearly three years Watt took the lead in trying to reshape the government's environmental objectives. In the process he quickly emerged as the most visible and controversial secretary of the interior in half a century.

Watt announced early on that he wanted to shift national public lands policy away from preservation and toward resource exploration and development. "I will err on the side of public use vs. preservation," he declared.

Most of his efforts to change the thrust of federal land policy were made out of the congressional limelight. Using budgetary recommendations, administrative and regulatory actions, the secretary shifted money and personnel away from protecting the environmental, wilderness and scenic values of federal lands and put them into developing oil, gas, minerals and timber.

Watt's ambitious agenda and abrasive manner quickly stirred stiff opposition from Congress, environmental groups and state governments. He clashed frequently with the Democratic leaders of House committees that authorized and appropriated funds for Interior programs. Watt barred Interior officials from consulting leading environmental groups in developing plans for managing public

Watt's Last Gaffe: Quip Forces Resignation . . .

For nearly three years, Congress fought with Secretary of the Interior James G. Watt to control the course of federal policy for managing natural resources.

After taking over the Interior Department in 1981, Watt moved forcefully to promote development of the vast coal, oil, gas and other natural riches the department controlled on public lands owned by the U.S. government. Congress resisted most of Watt's plans, led by House Democrats who were determined to protect the safeguards that the government developed in the 1970s to preserve federally owned lands and resources for the benefit of future generations.

From the start Watt emerged as the most combative and controversial proponent of the Reagan administration's strategy for encouraging natural resource production to fuel U.S. economic recovery. Through budget cutbacks and widespread staff changes, Watt steered Interior's resource-managing agencies away from the conservationist goals that congressional environmental laws and former Secretary Cecil D. Andrus had set during the Carter administration.

In keeping with the administration's faith in free market economic forces, Watt prodded the department back toward its once traditional mission of promoting rapid development of federally owned energy, timber, water projects and other resources by private business for consumption by the American public. As chairman of Reagan's Cabinet Council on Natural Resources and the Environment, Watt influenced energy, timber, water and pollution control policies followed by the Energy Department, Environmental Protection Agency (EPA), U.S. Forest Service and other federal agencies. *(Interior Department role, box, p. 404)*

In the Senate, with a Republican majority elected in 1980 congressional elections, Western senators who assumed leadership positions backed Watt's efforts to spur resource development on federally owned lands that made up the bulk of the 11-state region. Through his rhetoric as well as his politics Watt soothed Western interests that in the late 1970s mounted a "Sagebrush Rebellion" against President Carter's land and water policies.

Yet Watt's aggressive leadership style, combined with a penchant for jokes and ideological statements that offended many groups, embroiled the secretary in a series of political controversies that eventually forced him to resign in October 1983.

Watt Background

Born in Wyoming, Watt brought a Westerner's pro-development perspective to the Interior post. But through extensive service in Washington, D.C., both on the Senate staff and in various natural resource agencies, Watt also developed an insider's knowledge and political skills for dealing with the Interior bureaucracy.

Watt worked on the staff of Sen. Milward L. Simpson, R-Wyo. (1962-67), in the 1960s, then held several posts during the Nixon and Ford administrations.

After serving as deputy assistant secretary of the interior for water and power resources, Watt in 1972 was named head of the department's Bureau of Outdoor Recreation.

President Ford in 1975 appointed Watt to the Federal Power Commission, an energy regulatory agency that the Carter administration in 1977 merged into the newly formed Department of Energy.

After leaving the commission, Watt moved to Denver, Colo., as president of the Mountain States Legal Foundation, a conservative public interest legal group founded by Joseph Coors, a Colorado brewing heir, and other businessmen. In that position, Watt challenged many of the environmental protection policies that Interior adopted under Andrus, in the process developing a reputation among Western interests as archenemy of environmental groups. In the foundation's 1979-80 report, Watt vowed to "check the power of the federal government wherever possible in issues pertaining to the use of federal lands and the development of the West."

Despite environmentalists' misgivings about Watt's views, the Senate confirmed his appointment by an 83-12 margin on Jan. 22, 1981. Reagan later named Watt chairman of the President's Cabinet Council on Natural Resources and the Environment, putting the interior secretary in a position to influence administration policies adopted by the U.S. Forest Service, Army Corps of Engineers and other agencies outside his department.

In addition, the administration named a number of other officials with similar views and past ties to Watt to fill key environmental posts. They included Anne M. Gorsuch, a former Colorado state legislator, as administrator of EPA; her future husband, Robert F. Burford, a Colorado rancher, as director of Interior's BLM; Garrey E. Carruthers, former New Mexico State University professor and New Mexico Republican Party chairman, as assistant interior secretary for land and water resources; and John B. Crowell Jr., former general counsel to Louisiana-Pacific Corp., the nation's second-largest timber company, as assistant secretary of agriculture for natural resources and the environment, the official who supervised the Forest Service. All replaced Carter administration officials who had been considered sympathetic to environmental concerns.

... Ending Long Resource Development Battle

Controversial Watt Programs

After taking over the Interior Department, Watt moved forcefully to "swing the pendulum back to center" from the preservationist tack that Carter administration officials had taken in managing federal resources. Watt sought no major legislation from Congress but instead shifted the department's priorities through budget cuts and personnel changes. Watt fired or demoted career Interior employees and relied heavily on advisers he brought into the department. Through budget decisions he strengthened Interior programs for promoting resource development while curtailing conservation efforts.

The secretary deeply angered environmentalist leaders by refusing to meet them personally and by reducing their access, both in Washington and at the local level, to Interior decision-making procedures. Only a few months after Watt took office, the Sierra Club, Wilderness Society, National Audubon Society and other environmental groups demanded his ouster. Even the National Wildlife Federation, considered the most conservative of major conservation organizations, joined in calling for Watt's resignation.

Watt maintained that the government could protect its scenic wild lands and manage other public lands for resource production. In speeches and public pronouncements, the secretary invoked the once-traditional definition of conservation as requiring wise *use* of public resources for public benefits. "The key to conservation is management," he told the North American Wildlife and Natural Resources Conference in 1981. "Conservation is not the blind locking away of huge areas and their resources because of emotional appeals."

Following up on that philosophy, Watt accelerated Interior plans for leasing coal, offshore oil and gas, and onshore petroleum deposits beneath federal lands. He also tried to open national forest wilderness lands, especially along the petroleum-rich Overthrust Belt region in Wyoming, Utah and Idaho, for mineral exploration. He slowed national park land purchases, although Congress rejected his plan to divert Land and Water Conservation Fund money from park expansion to repairing existing park facilities. As part of the Reagan administration plan to reduce the national debt, Watt also drew up proposals to sell off small, hard-to-manage federal tracts to private owners.

Watt's admirers contended that the secretary's controversial methods were essential to push his programs through a reluctant Interior bureaucracy and overcome resistance from members of Congress, congressional committee staffs and environmental groups who had supported the Carter policies. Sen. Malcolm Wallop, R-Wyo., chairman of the Senate Energy and Natural Resources Subcommittee on Public Lands, in 1981 called Watt "hands-down the first real secretary of the interior that the country has had in a couple of decades."

But environmentalists, economists and some resource professionals contended that Watt's campaign to promote rapid federal resource production went far beyond wise stewardship of public lands. In leasing vast coal and oil reserves to private companies while world energy markets were slack, they argued, the secretary violated his obligation as trustee of public lands to obtain fair market value for them. Critics suggested that Watt's ambitious leasing plans stemmed more from his philosophical distaste for federal government control over valuable land and resources. "The secretary's feeling is that the federal government should not be the owner of land and resources," Frank Gregg, BLM director during the Carter administration, commented in 1983.

1983 Resignation

Watt's policies embroiled Interior in a series of heated political controversies. For most of his tenure, however, Watt enjoyed strong support from conservative political and business leaders, especially in Western states, who had been an important part of Reagan's 1980 presidential campaign constituency. Despite growing clamor for his dismissal, the White House through 1981-82 continued to back Watt's performance.

After Republican losses in the 1982 congressional elections, Watt's political standing eroded. During his term in office Watt's combative speeches and sometimes inflammatory phrases offended important national political interests. Watt for instance angered American Indian leaders by calling reservations a dramatic example of the "failures of socialism." Watt frequently went out of his way to dismiss environmental group leaders as elitists who pursued selfish interests at the expense of other Americans.

By mid-1983 Watt's backers among Western congressional delegations were growing worried that the increasingly unpopular secretary would hurt Republican chances in 1984 presidential and congressional elections. Influential members called for his resignation after Watt publicly joked that he had appointed "a black ... a woman, two Jews and a cripple" to an Interior Department commission that was reviewing the controversial coal leasing program.

Watt submitted his resignation to the president on Oct. 9, 1983, insisting that his campaign to speed federal resource development had left behind "a legacy that will aid Americans in the decades ahead."

Reagan named William P. Clark, his national security adviser, to succeed Watt. *(Clark, box, p. 474)*

lands. Although he had vowed to make the Interior Department a "good neighbor" to the West, Watt alienated some Western governors with his plans to accelerate energy development on public lands in their states.

As protests mounted, Congress bottled up Interior legislative proposals that were part of Reagan's budget-cutting program. Through action on the department's appropriations requests, Congress stalled or slowed Watt's plans to halt federal land purchases for national parks, open wilderness for oil and gas exploration, accelerate offshore oil and gas leasing, and rapidly lease federal coal deposits. It also opposed but ultimately went along with administration efforts to revamp federal water policies machinery and to reorganize Interior's Office of Surface Mining, the agency that enforced federal strip-mining standards.

Watt's Downfall

Watt met his downfall in 1983. A series of public relations disasters and controversy over Interior's coal leasing program forced Republican senators to give up their previous backing for the secretary. Facing a Senate "no confidence" vote, Watt finally resigned Oct. 9.

Reagan named Clark, his trusted national security adviser, to replace Watt. Although Clark never disavowed the pro-development thrust of Watt's tenure, he put off until 1985 many decisions on controversial public land issues, such as revising and reviving the troubled coal leasing program. Clark himself left the Interior post in 1985, and Reagan selected Donald P. Hodel, Watt's former under secretary who had served as secretary of energy in 1982-84, to take over as interior secretary.

Struggle Over EPA

Like Watt, EPA Administrator Burford was considered more sympathetic than her predecessors to the industries the agency dealt with. Although Congress refused to ease pollution control standards by revising environmental laws, EPA during Burford's tenure took steps to grant regulatory relief through budget and administrative decisions.

Under Burford's leadership EPA took a less adversarial approach toward industry. Burford gleaned most of her top administrators from the ranks of major corporations. In the regulatory area, she abolished the agency's office of enforcement, preferring to rely on negotiating agreements for voluntary industry compliance with federal pollution standards. She cut back the number of enforcement cases that EPA took to court and reviewed pollution regulations to ease industry burdens. The administration simultaneously slashed the EPA budget, from $1.3 billion in fiscal 1981 to $1.09 billion in fiscal 1982, including deep cuts in the agency's research and development programs.

From the start House members questioned whether EPA relations with industry were growing too friendly. In 1981 Rep. Toby Moffett, D-Conn., chairman of the Government Operations Subcommittee on the Environment, criticized Gorsuch and other top agency officials during oversight hearings to investigate meetings EPA had held with chemical industry representatives to discuss proposed regulatory actions affecting that industry.

Three other congressional panels joined Moffett's in holding oversight hearings to determine whether EPA was using deep budget cuts and regulatory "reforms" to retreat from its congressionally mandated pollution control duties.

Using leaked EPA budget documents, a group comprised largely of former EPA officials formed the "Save EPA Committee." The group kept Congress and the press up to date on the administration's 1983 budget proposals, which it claimed would "demolish" the agency.

"Unable to repeal the country's environmental laws because the public would never stand for it," said William Drayton, former EPA assistant administrator for planning and management and a member of Save EPA, "Reagan is gutting them through the personnel and budgetary back doors."

When it disagreed with agency actions, Congress could rarely do much more than raise a fuss. But in some cases that was enough. After noisy congressional protests, for example, EPA backed off from a decision to suspend an existing ban on dumping toxic liquid wastes into unlined landfills, and from plans to consider relaxing or repealing restrictions on lead in gasoline.

EPA Scandals

The struggle over EPA came to a head in 1983, when Burford resigned in the midst of a series of congressional investigations into the agency's conduct under Reagan.

The firestorm broke out around Burford on Dec. 16, 1982, when the House cited her for contempt of Congress. She had refused, on written orders from Reagan and legal advice from the Justice Department, to turn over documents subpoenaed by a House subcommittee.

In the following three months House subcommittees aired charges, in hearing rooms crowded with television cameras, that EPA officials under Burford had been lax in enforcing hazardous waste laws, made "sweetheart deals" with polluters, stood to profit from conflicts of interest, manipulated toxic cleanup grants to influence elections, shredded papers subpoenaed by Congress and used political "hit lists" to terminate science advisers and civil service employees who disagreed with the Reagan philosophy of rapid deregulation.

After Burford resigned March 9, Reagan quickly named EPA's first administrator, Ruckelshaus, to succeed her. Ruckelshaus, highly regarded for both policy judgment and personal integrity, was unanimously confirmed by the Senate May 17.

But environmentalists remained unconvinced that the White House gave Ruckelshaus the leeway to pursue environmental goals over objections by the Office of Management and Budget (OMB), which exercised final control over many EPA decisions. They contended that Reagan needed a strong environmental advocate within the White House staff to counter OMB Director David A. Stockman's pressure for budget cutbacks in environmental programs. Those doubts increased after Ruckelshaus abruptly resigned the EPA post Nov. 28, 1984. Reagan named Lee M. Thomas, the EPA assistant administrator who headed the agency's toxic waste programs, to replace Ruckelshaus.

Clean Air Act Stalemate

While Congress forced EPA to move more aggressively to control pollution, the House and Senate were unable to forge legislative agreements on revising existing environmental laws. House and Senate committees spent four years, covering both the 97th and the 98th Congress, trying without success to rewrite the federal Clean Air Act of

1970, the nation's flagship environmental protection measure.

After Reagan's election industry leaders had hoped — and environmental groups had feared — that his administration would push a major relaxation of the law through the 97th Congress. Industry complained that the law saddled it — and ultimately consumers — with billions of dollars in cleanup costs. Environmentalists countered that air pollution, left unchecked, cost as much or more in damage to human health, crops and property. After weighing air pollution issues for four years, neither House nor Senate committees came up with Clean Air Act revisions that congressional leaders were willing to take to the floor.

Toxic Waste Measures

Environmental advocates were more successful in pressing legislation to tighten federal controls on toxic wastes. The EPA superfund scandal and widespread publicity about dangerous waste dumps across the nation spurred congressional action.

Taking the most significant pollution control action during Reagan's first term, Congress in 1984 reauthorized the Resource Conservation and Recovery Act (RCRA) of 1976, the law ordering EPA to regulate how business handled, stored and disposed of hazardous waste chemicals. In the 1984 revisions Congress banned disposal of hazardous liquids in landfills, from which they might seep into groundwater supplies, and extended EPA regulations for disposing of hazardous materials to tens of thousands of small businesses, from dry cleaners to gasoline filling stations.

The bill's enactment demonstrated how potent toxic wastes had become as a political issue. The House passed the measure in November 1983, but the Senate acted only after Democrats made clear at their July 1984 convention that they intended to use Reagan's record on the control and cleanup of such wastes against him. The logjam of objections that had stalled the bill short of the Senate floor finally broke after the Democratic convention, when the administration signaled it wanted an environmental bill to sign. The Senate refused to go along, however, with 1984 legislation to renew the trouble-plagued superfund program a year ahead of schedule.

Federal Water Policy

Congress struggled for four years, with few results, to reconcile costly federal water pollution and development programs with Reagan's budget-cutting demands.

Prodded by Reagan's refusal to request new funding for EPA sewer construction grants unless spiraling costs were curtailed, lawmakers in 1981 cut annual authorizations for the program from $5 billion to $2.5 billion. But Congress made little progress in revising federal water pollution control laws that gave EPA power to regulate industrial and municipal wastewater discharges. The House in 1984 passed legislation revamping the Clean Water Act and the Safe Drinking Water Act, but the Senate took no action.

Budget problems and regional rivalries thwarted congressional efforts to fund new water development projects by the Army Corps of Engineers and Interior's Bureau of Reclamation. Watt came into office pledging to back water projects that Carter's environment-minded administration tried to kill, but internal administration debate over "cost-

Environmental Spending

The following table lists budget authority and outlays for federal natural resources and environment programs for fiscal 1981-85 *(in millions of dollars)*:

	Budget Authority	Outlays
Water resources		
1981	$ 4,079	$ 4,132
1982	3,913	3,948
1983	4,608	3,904
1984	3,779	4,068
1985*	3,916	4,293
Conservation and land management		
1981	1,364	1,191
1982	902	1,084
1983	1,883	1,503
1984	1,389	1,302
1985*	793	979
Recreational resources		
1981	1,252	1,597
1982	1,220	1,435
1983	1,581	1,454
1984	1,453	1,581
1985*	1,480	1,622
Pollution control and abatement		
1981	2,982	5,170
1982	3,645	5,012
1983	3,677	4,263
1984	4,037	4,044
1985*	4,257	4,387
Other natural resources		
1981	1,494	1,478
1982	1,583	1,519
1983	1,547	1,548
1984	1,622	1,595
1985*	1,761	1,744
Totals, Fiscal 1981-85		
1981	$11,171	$13,568
1982	11,263	12,998
1983	13,297	12,672
1984	12,280	12,591
1985*	12,207	13,024

* Estimated figures.

SOURCE: Fiscal 1986 Budget, Historical Tables

sharing" arrangements requiring state and local governments to pay part of construction costs delayed agreement on launching new projects. Meanwhile congressional delegations from Eastern states jockeyed for more funding for sewer repairs in their region as the price of supporting Western reclamation and flood control projects.

Just before the Democratic convention, the House in 1984 approved an omnibus $18 billion water development bill authorizing more than 300 projects, mainly in the East. But the Senate never took up its own $11 billion version, in part because Western senators objected to proposals to create a national water policy board, replacing one that Congress abolished at Reagan's request in 1982. The board could have put the Reclamation Bureau, which served the West, and the Corps of Engineers under one policy-making mechanism.

Western water interests got more done in Congress than Eastern ones. The Reclamation Bureau once again increased its share of the total available water appropriations at the expense of the Corps of Engineers. Westerners also got a $650 million dam safety bill, a reaffirmation of below-market pricing for federal hydroelectric power from the Hoover Dam, new projects for controlling salinity in the Colorado River and a demonstration of ways to recharge an aquifer that was slowly being pumped dry beneath the High Plains states.

National Forest Policy

During Reagan's first three years in office Congress resisted administration attempts to accelerate logging in national forests and to resolve the status of roadless lands that the Forest Service had identified as potential wilderness.

Assistant Secretary of Agriculture Crowell, formerly general counsel to Louisiana-Pacific Corp., the nation's second-largest timber company, prodded Forest Service planners to abandon conservative timber harvest schedules that restricted logging in "old-growth" Pacific Northwest forests that industry was eager to cut. Backed by McClure and other Republican senators from Western states, the administration urged Congress to move quickly to designate wilderness areas and open other forest lands for timber production.

The wilderness debate had been building since President Carter in 1977 sent Congress his recommendations for expanding wilderness areas in the national forest system, based on the Forest Service's RARE II survey of remaining roadless regions. Congress ever since had been slowly working its way through those proposals in state-by-state bills, usually offered by congressional delegations from the state involved. The state-by-state process meant that in most cases loggers, miners and environmentalists had to reach consensus on which lands deserved protection, then win support from most members of a state's delegation.

As the designation process dragged on, McClure and other senators demanded that Congress "release" roadless lands for multiple-use development that the Forest Service had left out of its RARE II proposals. But environmentalists opposed the release procedure, preferring to keep the lands undeveloped for possible inclusion in an expanded wilderness system. McClure finally negotiated a compromise in 1984 with Rep. John F. Seiberling, D-Ohio, chairman of the House Interior Subcommittee on Public Lands, clearing the way for an outpouring of wilderness legislation. The bills set aside for protection more than 8.3 million acres in 20 states while releasing more than 14.6 million acres for possible development.

Chronology
Of Action
On Clean Air

1981-82

President Reagan took office in 1981 committed to scaling back clean air regulations that he maintained were curtailing U.S. industrial expansion. Throughout 1981-82 industry and some labor union leaders pressed Congress to revise the 1970 law and its 1977 amendments to defer deadlines and ease Environmental Protection Agency (EPA) regulations for complying with national air quality standards.

Congress granted some relief to the hard-pressed steel industry. But after two years of intensive review and often bitter debate, neither the House Energy and Commerce Committee nor the Senate Environment and Public Works Committee came up with legislation revising clean air laws that could win full congressional approval.

The stalemate left the 1970 Clean Air Act intact, assuring continuing debate over the economic costs of removing pollutants from the nation's air. The congressional stalemate stemmed from members' reluctance to rewrite the law, first enacted at the start of the nation's environmental era, when Americans gave broad support to tough federal government action to clean up the air they breathed.

Clean Air Act Revisions

Congress in 1981-82 backed away from controversial proposals to ease federal clean air regulations.

Elected by a 1980 landslide, President Reagan took office in 1981 committed to make major changes in the federal Clean Air Act of 1970. American industry meanwhile mounted intense pressure to persuade Congress to cut back on costly pollution control rules for factories and motor vehicles.

When the 97th Congress convened, the Reagan administration expected to make Clean Air Act revisions the first order of business in its plans to promote economic expansion by freeing U.S. industry from federal regulations. But environmental groups viewed the clean air law as an indispensable tool for the government's commitment to protect the environment. With key congressional allies, both in the Democratic House and Republican Senate, they fought a successful holding action throughout 1981 and 1982 against relaxing air quality goals. House and Senate environment committees grappled for months with complicated clean air issues, but neither sent a bill to the floor.

Throughout the 1970s steelmakers, automobile manufacturers, electric utilities and other major industries had protested federal Environmental Protection Agency (EPA) rules for curbing factory and motor vehicle emissions into the nation's air. Congress revised the law several times, adopting major amendments in 1977; but business and labor leaders nonetheless still maintained that EPA regulations were costing the United States far more in lost jobs and profits than was necessary to improve air quality.

To protect public health and preserve scenic vistas, the Clean Air Act gave EPA power to regulate discharges into the air from factory smokestacks and vehicle tailpipes in every corner of the United States. The law called for national standards for common and poisonous pollutants, and it forced American industry to spend billions of dollars to install costly emission control equipment on aging factories, in new plants and on most cars and trucks it sold to American drivers. It ordered state governments to clean up polluted air over large cities and industrial centers. Through 1977 amendments it also ordered states to impose strict controls on industrial growth in rural and small-town regions to keep their pure air from deteriorating to more polluted levels.

In setting federal air standards, Congress and EPA made technical judgments that in effect dictated how American industry operated factories, how it designed its products and where it could build new plants or install modern facilities. The clean air law and EPA regulations also attempted delicate economic and political trade-offs, protecting Eastern and Midwestern "Frost Belt" industrial centers and coal fields against competition from Southern and Western "Sun Belt" states with cleaner air and clean-burning coal deposits.

Less than a month before the 1982 congressional elections, the president listed Clean Air Act revisions as one of five economic policy priorities, contending that a less stringent law, "while protecting the environment, will make it possible for industry to rebuild its productive base and create more jobs." EPA officials meanwhile prepared to ban new industrial construction and cut federal clean air assistance to hundreds of counties that were unable to meet national air quality standards by a deadline that Congress had set for the end of 1982.

But by then both the House and Senate had given up efforts to draft legislation to extend deadlines and adjust existing clean air standards. In the Republican Senate, Environment and Public Works Committee Chairman Robert T. Stafford, a moderate from environment-conscious Vermont, in August had fashioned a modest bill to "fine-tune" the law without gutting national air standards. In the Democratic House, however, the Energy and Commerce Committee had deadlocked in often bitter maneuvering between two key leaders over how drastically to ease clean air regulations.

Committee Chairman John D. Dingell, a Michigan Democrat from the leading auto-producing state, pushed hard from the start for industry-backed legislation to ease federal auto emission standards, relax industrial cleanup goals, allow more pollution in pristine regions' air and extend nationwide EPA deadlines. But Henry A. Waxman, a Democrat from smog-ridden Southern California who chaired the panel's Subcommittee on Health and Environment, fought a steady delaying action against Dingell's goals, in alliance with environmental lobbyists. The panel split badly between Dingell and Waxman factions and eventually broke off markup sessions.

Neither the House nor the Senate committee could reconcile demands by industry, environmental and regional interests that wanted to rewrite the landmark law along lines to their own liking. Clean Air Act authorizations expired at the end of fiscal 1981, but EPA regulations remained on the books. Congress appropriated funds for

the agency to enforce the law through annual appropriations bills for the Department of Housing and Urban Development and certain independent agencies.

The 1982 deadline for states to comply with national air quality standards passed as scheduled on Dec. 31. EPA in 1983 began procedures for imposing sanctions on 218 communities that violated those limits, but Congress stepped in by approving a one-year moratorium on those penalties. *(Sanctions moratorium, p. 422)*

Background

In the Clean Air Act of 1970 (PL 91-604), Congress directed the federal government to protect the American public's health by cleaning up polluted air. Taken together, the 1970 act and amendments that Congress approved in 1977 (PL 95-95) formed the nation's most complex and far-reaching environmental protection law.

Enforced by the Environmental Protection Agency, the Clean Air Act regulated virtually all air-polluting activity by U.S. industry, transportation, real estate development and the production and use of energy. The 1970 law had forced industry and electric utilities to spend billions of dollars on emission control equipment and automobile manufacturers to equip cars with costly anti-pollution devices. The law imposed controversial duties on state and local governments, and its restrictions on building new plants that would degrade air quality may have altered the pace and distribution of economic growth among different cities and regions across the country.

Environmental groups considered the Clean Air Act the foundation of the federal government's commitment to environmental protection. By vast majorities the American people generally backed government efforts to clean up polluted air and make sure that pristine airsheds remained unspoiled. But as EPA imposed the law's requirements, corporation and labor group leaders heatedly objected that the government was forcing entire industries to install expensive pollution control equipment at the cost of jobs and profits. State and city government officials also protested the agency's sometimes halting efforts to mandate Clean Air Act compliance.

Since the early 1970s the law's requirements in fact had reduced some types of air pollution and kept others from growing worse as the nation grew, built new factories and drove more cars and trucks. But progress was uneven and many industries resisted complying with EPA standards by challenging them in court or persuading Congress to extend the law's deadlines.

1970 Law. Congress began taking note of air pollution problems just after the Korean War. By 1970, a landmark year for environmental action, public concern about declining air quality prompted President Nixon to request a stronger federal clean air program. In his 1970 environmental message, Nixon proposed that the federal government set national standards to limit specific air pollutants, regulate smokestack emissions from stationary sources such as factories and utility power plants and test emission control devices on motor vehicles. Congress complied later that year, passing the Clean Air Act of 1970 by a unanimous vote in the Senate and only a single dissenting vote in the House.

The 1970 law directed EPA, the independent pollution control agency that Nixon had created earlier that year, to set national standards for major air pollutants, without regard to economic costs. Even while calling for nationwide air quality goals, the law left to the states the responsibility to draft plans for meeting those standards within 247 air quality control regions across the country. State governments and EPA shared responsibility for enforcing the standards.

As a first step, the law directed EPA to determine the maximum permissible concentrations for at least seven common air pollutants that the agency found harmful to human health or the environment. It required EPA to set two types of "national ambient air quality standards," without considering compliance costs: primary standards to protect human health, with a margin of safety for the elderly, infants and other vulnerable persons; and secondary standards to keep pollutants from impairing visibility or damaging crops, buildings and water supplies. Congress set a 1977 deadline for the entire nation to meet the primary health standards.

The law also ordered EPA to set maximum emission standards, on an industry-by-industry basis, for newly built plants and factories (new source performance standards). It required state governments to draw up state implementation plans, subject to EPA approval, for meeting federal air quality standards. The law required states to order factories in "non-attainment regions" that failed to meet the standards to retrofit their plants with pollution control equipment, without regard to cost. To expand plants or build new plants, companies had to install equipment that limited pollutants to the lowest level emitted by any similar facility in the country.

In a separate title the law set a detailed timetable for reducing hydrocarbon, carbon monoxide and nitrogen oxide emissions by trucks and automobiles. The law gave the EPA administrator authority to waive the deadlines for meeting those standards for about one year. *(1970 law, Congress and the Nation Vol. III, p. 763)*

1977 Amendments. In the early 1970s Congress backed away somewhat from its ambitious air quality goals by revising the 1970 law. Congress and EPA waived auto emission compliance deadlines in 1973, 1974 and again in 1975. In 1977, with the deadline for meeting primary standards approaching but many regions still out of compliance, Congress approved major Clean Air Act amendments (PL 95-95).

Under pressure from President Carter and the automobile industry, Congress in the 1977 amendments extended auto emission standards for 1977 models for two additional years, then set tighter limits for 1980, 1981 and 1982 models. In other major revisions of the 1970 law, Congress delayed the deadline for meeting national air standards until 1982 and gave cities with especially severe oxidant and carbon monoxide pollution an additional five years, through 1987, to meet EPA goals.

In addition to extending the deadline, Congress allowed states to issue permits for new stationary sources in non-attainment regions after mid-1979 only if pollution from existing plants or factories had been reduced enough to offset the new facility's emissions. To put a new plant into operation in an area that failed to meet national standards, a company thereafter had to purchase emission offsets from previously operating factories, either by buying and closing down an old plant or by buying equipment to reduce its emissions.

Congress in 1977 also approved a system to prevent development from spoiling the pristine air above national parks, wilderness areas and other regions where lack of industry had left the air much purer than national stan-

Major Air Pollutants and Their Health Effects

Pollutant	Major Sources	Characteristics and Effects
Carbon Monoxide (CO)	Vehicle exhausts	Colorless, odorless poisonous gas. Replaces oxygen in red blood cells, causing dizziness, unconsciousness or death.
Hydrocarbons (HC)	Incomplete combustion of gasoline; evaporation of petroleum fuels, solvents and paints	Although some are poisonous, most are not. React with NO_2 to form ozone, or smog.
Lead (Pb)	Anti-knock agents in gasoline	Accumulates in the bone and soft tissues. Affects blood-forming organs, kidneys and nervous system. Suspected of causing learning disabilities in young children.
Nitrogen Dioxide (NO_2)	Industrial processes, vehicle exhausts	Causes structural and chemical changes in the lungs. Lowers resistance to respiratory infections. Reacts in sunlight with hydrocarbons to produce smog. Contributes to acid rain.
Ozone (O_3)	Formed when HC and NO_2 react	Principal constituent of smog. Irritates mucous membranes, causing coughing, choking, impaired lung function. Aggravates chronic asthma and bronchitis.
Total Suspended Particulates (TSP)	Industrial plants, heating boilers, auto engines, dust	Larger visible types (soot, smoke or dust) can clog the lung sacs. Smaller invisible particles can pass into the bloodstream. Often carry carcinogens and toxic metals; impair visibility.
Sulfur Dioxide (SO_2)	Burning coal and oil, industrial processes	Corrosive, poisonous gas. Associated with coughs, colds and bronchitis. Contributes to acid rain.

SOURCE: Environmental Protection Agency

dards. A 1973 Supreme Court decision, on a case brought by environmental groups, had interpreted the 1970 Clean Air Act as requiring EPA to prevent significant deterioration in air quality in areas without major pollution. EPA in 1974 drew up regulations to implement that requirement. Congress largely wrote those regulations into the 1977 amendments, over objections by some Western senators who contended that stricter air quality standards would discourage economic growth in the region.

As approved by Congress, the prevention of significant deterioration (PSD) standards established three categories for regions where air quality was better than national EPA standards. The 1977 law classified most large national parks and wilderness areas in the strictest Class I category, allowing only small increments over brief periods in sulfur dioxide and particulate emissions that might obscure their scenic vistas. The law assigned all other clean air regions to a less restrictive Class II category, and it allowed states to petition EPA to designate some as Class III regions, where even more pollution could be tolerated to accommodate economic growth. In no case could pollution in Class III areas exceed national ambient standards, however, and the law required companies building plants in PSD regions to install the best available control technology, regardless of how expensive that equipment was. *(1977 amendments, Congress and the Nation Vol. IV, p. 303; Congress and the Nation Vol. V, p. 535)*

Clean Air Act Controversies

The 1977 Clean Air Act amendments were 180 pages long, three times the length of the 1970 law. The revised act set forth an immensely complicated scheme for cleaning up polluted air in urban and industrial centers and preserving air quality throughout the rest of the country. But in the early 1980s the nation remained sharply divided over whether EPA was enforcing the law fairly and whether the resulting air quality improvement justified the economic cost to U.S. industries and regions. *(Clean air act requirements, box, p. 415)*

Ten years after passage of the 1970 law, the process of implementing federal clean air standards was still proceeding slowly. EPA moved cautiously in enforcing the law, yet it was forced to base acceptable pollutant standards on scientific data and technical conclusions that environmentalists and business groups often challenged. Major indus-

tries — notably automobile manufacturers, steelmakers, metal smelters and electric utilities — complained that EPA requirements forced them to spend billions of dollars on non-productive emission control equipment that raised consumer prices and made their products less competitive. State government agencies objected that EPA officials delayed approving state air quality programs while meddling in local enforcement issues. Environmental groups, on the other hand, maintained that EPA's delays in setting standards and congressional deadline extensions had needlessly allowed companies to continue polluting the air with substances that endangered human health.

National Air Standards. The national ambient air quality standards set by EPA formed the heart of the Clean Air Act. The rest of the law was designed to force states to meet those EPA goals within deadlines set by Congress. By 1981, however, industrial groups were calling for changes in the way EPA arrived at those standards, which they viewed as unnecessarily strict and costly.

In the existing Clean Air Act Congress gave EPA authority to set the standards at levels providing "an adequate margin of safety," not just for the general population, but for infants, the elderly and other persons with health problems that made them especially susceptible to damage from air pollution. The law also directed EPA to determine the standards without taking costs into account, although it allowed states to consider costs when imposing emission limits on specific plants.

Critics of EPA standards within business and industry argued that the government should set clean air goals to protect the general population against major risks, instead of trying to prevent any danger to vulnerable groups.

Many business groups had argued that the benefits of environmental control should outweigh or balance the costs of pollution control equipment.

Environmentalists feared that changing EPA standards would alter the law's basic thrust. They argued that proposals for cost-benefit analysis of the standards were smokescreens for gutting the 1970 act. Opponents of the cost-benefit approach charged that it would be nearly impossible to put accurate price tags on intangible benefits from cleaner air.

Mobile Sources. The act set limits for automobile emissions of hydrocarbons (HC), carbon monoxide (CO) and oxides of nitrogen (NOx) and required a 90 percent reduction from uncontrolled levels for HC and CO by 1982. NOx was to be reduced by 75 percent. The EPA could waive certain standards if public health did not require the statutory standards or if the technology to meet them did not exist.

The major auto manufacturers wanted the 1981 CO standard of 3.4 grams per mile to be relaxed to 7.0 grams per mile and the 1.0 gram per mile NOx standard reduced to 2.0 grams per mile.

The proposal was tough to sell to Congress because it would mean removing equipment already on most cars and rolling back standards that already could be met.

One reason industry wanted a weaker NOx standard was to allow production of more diesels. But environmentalists were concerned about the proliferation of diesels because their emissions were suspected of causing cancer.

Industrial Growth. Along with automobiles, factories, electric power plants and other industrial plants were the major contributors to air pollution over U.S. cities. Industrial smokestacks produced nearly all sulfur dioxide emissions, more than 80 percent of particulates and

more than half of nitrogen oxides that were spewed into the air. As a result, EPA efforts to curb pollution strictly regulated emissions from both existing and newly built plants.

In regulating those emissions, EPA indirectly influenced where new plants were built, how much they cost to operate and how long older factories were kept running. Some business and labor leaders protested that the government, in setting air quality standards, in effect was setting limits to economic growth in both long-time industrial centers and in fast-growing Sun Belt states.

To meet EPA ambient air standards, the Clean Air Act required state governments to order existing factories in polluted regions to retrofit furnaces, power plants and other equipment with devices to reduce emissions. The law also gave EPA and the states power to review all plans to build new plants or improve existing facilities to make sure that their owners installed the best possible pollution control technology.

Throughout the 1970s business officials complained that the expensive equipment they installed to reduce emissions from existing plants was often balky, was costly to run and consumed a great deal of energy. Industry also said that EPA and state procedures for granting permits for new or expanded facilities were time-consuming and duplicative.

Before building a new plant in a clean air area, a company had to obtain a permit from the state air pollution board requiring the best possible pollution control equipment for every emission source at that plant.

In certain dirtier areas the requirements were even tougher. Owners of new factories had to promise to install the best control equipment and clean up emissions at existing plants.

Non-Attainment Areas. In polluted urban areas, Congress and EPA set up a complicated regulatory system to allow companies to build new plants or modernize existing facilities without making air quality worse.

In the 1977 amendments Congress devised an "offset" system to encourage economic growth in industrial centers even while already contaminated air was cleaned up. To build a new plant that would emit a pollutant for which the area already exceeded national standards, a company could in effect buy a right to pollute the air by cutting back similar emissions from an existing facility previously in operation.

The offset system sought to reduce total emissions by requiring that the resulting reductions more than offset the sulfur dioxide a new plant produced. A company could obtain offsets by buying new pollution control equipment for an existing plant, or it could buy an old factory and close it down if its emissions would be too expensive to correct. A firm wanting to build or modernize a plant also could buy "pollution reduction credits" from another company that earned them by installing cleanup equipment.

Congress hoped that the offset system would give companies market incentives to develop new ways to control air pollution. But industry complained that offsets in practice were often unavailable in areas where companies wanted to expand. Opponents of the system also charged that existing industries that controlled offset rights could keep competitors from moving into an area and control the region's economic growth.

Industry wanted to eliminate the offset system and extend the 1982 deadline for achieving national standards in a non-attainment area that was showing improvement

The Clean Air Act in a Nutshell

The primary goal of the Clean Air Act was to control the seven most common air pollutants.

It also sought to limit toxic pollutants that caused death or serious illness, but the Environmental Protection Agency (EPA) had moved slowly in regulating such dangerous emissions.

To control the seven pollutants, the act directed EPA to determine maximum concentrations of each that should be allowed nationwide. EPA set those limits — called **national ambient air quality standards (NAAQS)** — for the seven pollutants: carbon monoxide, hydrocarbons, lead, nitrogen dioxide, ozone, particulates and sulfur dioxide.

The act directed EPA to set two types of these standards — primary and secondary — without considering the cost of compliance. **Primary standards** were to protect human health with an added margin of safety for vulnerable segments of the population like the elderly and infants. **Secondary standards** were to prevent damage to such things as crops, visibility, buildings, water and materials. The act set Dec. 31, 1982, as the deadline for the nation to meet the primary standards. Five-year extensions were available for regions with severe automobile-related pollution. No specific deadline was set for meeting the secondary standards.

EPA Responsibilities

Besides issuing national air quality standards for the seven basic pollutants, EPA was to set maximum emission limits for plants and factories, called **new source performance standards (NSPS)**. These standards were to be set on an industry-by-industry basis for states to use as guidelines in setting more specific emission restrictions for individual factories. For existing factories, EPA was to issue **control technique guidelines (CTG)**, which told states what types of pollution control equipment could be economically retrofitted on existing plants.

EPA was also to monitor compliance by motor vehicle manufacturers with the act's deadlines for new vehicles to meet tailpipe emission standards. The standards were designed to clean up 90 percent of the hydrocarbons and carbon monoxide, and 75 percent of the nitrogen oxides emitted from vehicles.

State Responsibilities

Taking into account the federally set emission standards for new factories and vehicles, states were directed to develop **state implementation plans (SIPs)** outlining how they intended to clean up the air within their borders by the 1982 deadline.

EPA could ban construction of large new polluting industries in areas that violated the federal standards, if the state did not have an approved SIP.

Under the act the country was divided into 247 regional air basins, called **air quality control regions (AQCRs)**. Regions were classified into two categories.

Regions that violated standards for one or more of the seven pollutants were designated **non-attainment areas** for those pollutants. States had to limit new construction of pollution sources until the air in these "dirty" areas was brought up to federal standards.

Regions that met the standards for specific pollutants were called **attainment areas** for those pollutants. States could not allow the air in these areas to deteriorate beyond certain levels, and were to enforce a complex set of **prevention of significant deterioration (PSD)** rules. A region could be a non-attainment area for one pollutant and a PSD area for others.

Existing factories in non-attainment areas were required by states to retrofit their plants with pollution control equipment representing **reasonably available control technology (RACT)**.

Companies wanting to expand or build new plants in these dirty-air areas were required to install equipment that limited pollution to the least amount emitted by any similar factory anywhere in the country. These **lowest achievable emission rate (LAER)** requirements were to be set by the states without regard to cost.

New plants could not be built in dirty-air areas unless pollution from existing factories or plants was reduced enough to *more than compensate* for the pollution expected from the new plant.

Thus a company wanting to build in a non-attainment area not only had to install the best possible pollution control equipment, but also had to purchase **emission offsets** from existing companies. Companies could obtain offsets by buying new pollution control equipment for an existing polluter or buying and closing down an old plant.

States in non-attainment areas could have until 1987 to meet the carbon monoxide and ozone standards if they required annual inspection and maintenance of catalytic converters on cars. Federal sewer and highway construction funds could be withheld from states that did not initiate such inspection and maintenance programs. The act mandated that new plants in PSD areas, the act mandated that new plants install **best available control technology (BACT)**, defined by states on a factory-by-factory basis. Companies also had to conduct one-year computer modeling and monitoring tests to show that the proposed plant would not degrade the air quality beyond the specific levels, or **increments,** outlined in the act.

over the long term. Some industry groups also proposed that Congress terminate EPA authority to ban plant construction in non-attainment areas that lacked state plans showing they could meet the 1982 deadline. Business leaders complained that EPA often applied the bans to new factories when automobile pollution was the major cause of poor air quality.

PSD System. The Clean Air Act imposed its most widely felt restrictions through the 1977 amendments to prevent air pollution from growing worse in areas that already met federal standards.

Those provisions, known as the prevention of significant deterioration program, were designed to keep the air in regions that met standards for specific pollutants from deteriorating beyond pre-set ceilings, or "increments," that would keep it cleaner than national standards. Since nearly every U.S. city and county already met federal standards for at least one pollutant, the PSD system applied virtually across the nation. But its economic impact was potentially heaviest in fast-growing regions in the West and South that were attractive to industries seeking to build new plants and expand into new markets.

Environmental groups maintained that the PSD system would keep growth from degrading the pure air above less-developed regions to the extent that industrialization had polluted older cities. But some critics charged that Congress designed the PSD system to limit economic growth in the Southern and Western Sun Belt states, thus protecting the economic base of the industrial Frost Belt states in the Northeast and Midwest.

The act established three classes of PSD areas ranging from Class I, having the cleanest air, to Class III, where the air was allowed to become the dirtiest.

Besides installing the best pollution control equipment and showing its pollution would not violate the increments, companies wanting to build near PSD areas had to show that their emissions would not impair visibility in nearby Class I national parks or wilderness areas. But since most of the West's oil, coal and oil shale reserves were located right next to such Class I areas, a major conflict was anticipated between the clean air law and the nation's goals of energy independence.

However, the National Commission on Air Quality in 1981 found that the PSD program would not hamper energy development in the Southwest through 1995.

But the commission, following its final report, concluded that only the Class I PSD program had been successful in maintaining air quality. Class II and Class III programs, according to the commission, were causing delays in permitting new industries and red tape involved in the process held up industrial progress to some extent. Business representatives joined the commission in maintaining that the location of industries in the West would be adversely affected if the standard was retained.

Coal-Burning Utilities. Coal-fired power plants that U.S. utility companies operated to generate electricity in the early 1980s discharged more than half of the dangerous sulfur dioxide emissions into the nation's air. EPA's efforts to reduce those discharges, both from existing and newly built power plants, produced continuing controversy over whether clean air regulations impeded development of the nation's abundant coal reserves as dependable energy supplies.

The Clean Air Act controlled sulfur dioxide, along with nitrogen oxide and particulate emissions, from coal-fired power plant smokestacks. Sulfur dioxide gas caused respiratory difficulties, mixing with other air pollutants to cause coughs, bronchitis, asthma and emphysema. Sulfur dioxide emissions from coal-burning boilers in Ohio Valley and other Midwest plants were also prime suspects as the source of acid rain precipitation as they drifted over New York, New England and eastern Canada lakes and forests. *(Acid rain debate, below)*

Utility plant operators identified several alternative ways to reduce sulfur dioxide emissions by burning coal with low natural sulfur content, by chemically cleaning coal to reduce its sulfur components before burning, or by installing flue gas "scrubbers" to remove sulfur dioxide as a liquid or solid precipitant from the gases given off by coal combustion before it was released to the air through plant smokestacks.

EPA, with backing from Congress and environmental groups, prescribed installation of flue-gas scrubbers throughout the electric power industry as the preferred way to curb sulfur dioxide pollution. Throughout the 1970s the agency pressed state air pollution officials to force utilities to retrofit previously built power plants with costly scrubbers in order to meet sulfur dioxide standards. As mandated by Congress in the 1977 amendments, EPA in 1979 set uniform new source performance standards that required that all coal-fired plants built after 1978 be equipped with scrubbers.

In the 1977 amendments Congress protected markets for high-sulfur Eastern and Midwest coal by in effect requiring utilities to install scrubbers on new plants even if the facility could meet sulfur-dioxide standards without them by burning low-sulfur Western coal. In a compromise between coal-producing regions, the "percentage reduction" standards required utilities to remove between 70 and 90 percent of sulfur dioxide from flue gases, depending on coal sulfur contents. But utility executives, Western mining firms and economists objected that EPA's scrubber policy arbitrarily saddled power plants with costly and cranky emission control methods and restricted development of the nation's ample and easily mined Western coal reserves.

EPA maintained that scrubbers had worked well in Japan and for U.S. utilities that bought and maintained high-quality equipment. Environmental groups insisted that sulfur dioxide was so dangerous that the government should force utilities to remove as much of it as possible from the air. Clean air proponents also said officials could more easily enforce emission reductions by technological controls such as scrubbers rather than through content of the fuel power plants consumed.

With a scrubber for a 500-megawatt power plant costing $50 million, according to the Edison Electric Institute, utilities resisted installing them on existing plants through lawsuits, deliberate delay, lobbying state agencies and other strategies. In the Ohio Valley, where 21 aging plants produced the most concentrated source of sulfur pollution in the country, utilities fought hard for exemptions. State pollution control plans in many Midwestern states allowed utilities to bring coal-fired plants into compliance with local ambient air standards by building tall stacks that discharged pollutants high in the air, where prevailing winds blew sulfur dioxide over the eastern United States and Canada.

To avoid building costly scrubber-equipped plants, some utilities kept older power plants in operation longer than previously planned, prolonging pollution from their smokestacks.

Environmentalists' Agenda

National environmental groups, in addition to opposing major weakening in existing clean air rules, in the early 1980s pushed for the federal government to crack down harder on some forms of air pollution that EPA had yet to regulate. In particular, conservationists demanded faster action to control airborne toxics and fine particulates in the air. And they urged Congress to force even stricter limits on sulfur dioxide emissions from coal-fired plants in response to growing concern about the destructive effect of acid rain on forests, lakes and even buildings.

Acid Rain. As evidence accumulated, acid rain emerged in the early 1980s as a major clean air issue. Some scientists concluded that sulfur dioxide from power plant stacks and nitrogen oxide from automobile exhausts combined in the air with snow, rain or sleet, then fell back to earth in acidic concentrations that contaminated soils and water. Biologists maintained that acid rain was destroying forests and disrupting natural ecosystems in lakes, particularly in the Northeastern United States and Canada. They identified power plants burning high-sulfur coal in Ohio, Indiana, Illinois and Kentucky as likely sources of acid precipitation.

Environmental groups, Northeastern state governors and the Canadian government demanded that the U.S. government move to cut sulfur dioxide emissions in half. But Midwestern utilities and coal mining firms maintained that the acid rain evidence was insufficient to justify the cost of reducing emissions. The Reagan administration called for further study of the problem, and Congress was reluctant to tackle complicated proposals that might raise consumers' electric bills or cost miners' jobs in West Virginia, Ohio, Indiana and Illinois coal fields. *(1983-84 acid rain debate, p. 420)*

Airborne Toxics. Environmentalists also wanted Congress to put EPA on a "fast track" in controlling cancer-causing pollutants. From 1970, when it was first directed to start regulating hazardous pollutants, to early 1981 EPA had issued regulations for only four, although dozens had been found to cause such diseases as leukemia and lung cancer.

Fine Particulates. Environmentalists were urging Congress to direct EPA to start controlling fine particulates within one year.

Although larger particulates were controlled by EPA, the agency had not yet issued emissions standards for fine particles — those less than 1/1000 of an inch in diameter — which were easily inhaled deep into the lungs. They hampered breathing, caused respiratory disease and aggravated heart and lung disease. EPA had promised since 1973 to control these pollutants, but only recently had set up a 100-station monitoring network to study the problem.

Reagan Position

In his 1980 campaign for the presidency Reagan pledged to revise federal clean air laws as part of a policy of reducing government regulation of U.S. industry. Critics of EPA clean air rules viewed Reagan's landslide victory over President Carter as a mandate for major changes in the law.

Before Reagan's inauguration, David A. Stockman, a Republican member of Congress from Michigan whom Reagan nominated as Office of Management and Budget (OMB) director, released a planning document that identified the Clean Air Act as the incoming administration's

---

Steel Cleanup Delay

Congress in 1981 gave the U.S. steel industry three more years to meet federal air pollution cleanup deadlines.

Following up on a federal advisory board's 1980 recommendation, Congress June 26 cleared legislation (HR 3520 — PL 97-23) that allowed steel companies to negotiate three-year extensions of a 1982 deadline the government previously had set for curtailing plant emissions.

The extension measure grew out of an agreement reached in the fall of 1980 by the advisory board composed of federal government, steel industry and United Steel Workers of America representatives. Company and labor officials in the financially strapped industry sought relief from 1977 Clean Air Act deadlines forcing it to make expensive investments in pollution control equipment.

The measure, signed by President Reagan on July 17, allowed the Environmental Protection Agency and steel companies to reach agreements on a case-by-case basis to defer pollution control measures until Dec. 31, 1985. It required the industry to use money saved by postponing installation of emission control equipment to modernize older plants.

Both the House and Senate passed the legislation and conference agreement by overwhelming margins. Rep. James T. Broyhill, R-N.C., the only House member who spoke against the bill during floor debate, objected that the extension granted special treatment to steel companies. He noted that many other industries were seeking relief from various Clean Air Act requirements.

---

prime target for deregulating industry. Stockman termed the 1977 amendments to the law "staggering excess built upon dubious scientific and economic premises." EPA funding authorizations for enforcing the Clean Air Act were due to expire on Sept. 30, 1981, and administration officials expected to push for far-reaching changes in the law during the 1981 congressional session.

On Capitol Hill the mood in favor of clean air laws appeared to have shifted since 1977. Some of the architects of the 1977 law were no longer in Congress to defend their handiwork. Republicans had captured control of the Senate in the 1980 elections, giving the president's party a majority on the Environment Committee, the panel that held jurisdiction over the clean air law. In the Democratic House, moreover, Energy Committee Chairman John Dingell, D-Mich., who represented a Detroit district that encompassed Ford Motor Co. headquarters and more than a dozen automobile manufacturing plants, was backing the troubled industry's requests that Congress ease auto emission standards to make U.S. cars more competitive with foreign imports.

1981 Air Quality Proposals

Concluding that the nation's air had grown "measurably better," a congressionally chartered commission in 1981 found that the Clean Air Act of 1970 generally was working well, without undue costs to the U.S. economy.

The National Commission on Air Quality, in a report released on March 2, maintained that federal clean air standards had neither significantly inhibited economic growth nor obstructed development of domestic energy resources. The commission nonetheless recommended that Congress streamline some provisions of the 1970 law and expand the act to control acid rain and reduce indoor pollution.

The commission, for instance, suggested that Congress scrap nationwide deadlines in 1982 and 1987 for states to comply with federal air quality standards. But it endorsed continuing the 1970 law's requirements that the Environmental Protection Agency (EPA) set national standards to protect the health of vulnerable persons, with an added margin of safety. The 13-member commission also specifically rejected proposals by some industry groups that EPA base air quality standards on cost-benefit analyses that took account of their economic as well as health impact.

In addition to repealing the 1982 and 1987 deadlines, the commission proposed that Congress simplify 1977 Clean Air Act Amendments procedures to prevent significant air quality deterioration (PSD) in Western regions where the air was cleaner than the national standards.

Recommendations Challenged

Those two revisions would represent a "serious weakening of the Clean Air Act," charged David Hawkins, an attorney for the National Clean Air Coalition, an environmental group.

The business community objected just as strenuously to other recommendations, including those to require that national standards continue to be set without considering cost, to control acid rain by reducing sulfur dioxide and to speed up the control of cancer-causing air pollutants and fine particles.

Sen. Gary Hart, D-Colo., the commission chairman, said the recommendations represented a "general consensus" on most clean air issues. Congress ordered the 643-page report in the 1977 amendments (PL 95-95) to the 1970 act (PL 91-604) in an effort to dispel some of the controversies over imposing national standards to clean up air. But the report touched off its own controversy, since its recommendations offended both environmentalists and industry.

Administration Delay. But the administration and industry evidently had misread public opinion on environmental protection and congressional willingness to tackle a major revision of clean air standards. In March 1981 the bipartisan National Commission on Air Quality set up by Congress in 1977 released a report contending that the Clean Air Act was sound and needed only some refinements. In mid-June pollster Louis Harris released a nationwide survey that found only 12 percent of respondents backed weakening the law.

As environmental groups mounted opposition to clean air revisions, the administration eventually switched strategy. Officials initially had promised to send Congress a legislative package by June 30, but Henry A. Waxman, D-Calif., the chairman of the House Energy Subcommittee on Environment, denounced an early draft that leaked to Capitol Hill. By August the administration backed away from committing itself to specific proposals.

Instead, Reagan Aug. 5 submitted a set of broadly worded principles for Congress to consider in revising the clean air laws. The shift in strategy was seen by many on Capitol Hill as a shrewd decision by the president not to stake his prestige on a bid for major revisions in the antipollution law in the face of polls showing massive public support for the act.

The administration's 11 principles would continue the nation's progress toward cleaner air, but "at a more reasoned pace," said EPA Administrator Anne M. Gorsuch. The principles — which called for relaxing pollution standards and delaying some cleanup deadlines — were adopted Aug. 4 by Reagan and the Cabinet. They were met with enthusiasm by industry groups, but with suspicion by environmental organizations.

1981 Congressional Deliberations

The administration, unable to come up with its own draft bill, lost the initiative on Clean Air Act deregulation. Without its own bill as a starting point, the White House had less opportunity to negotiate with House and Senate committees and to call on Republicans to back a presidential proposal. The administration's waffling also called into question the urgency of Reagan's demand for action to ease clean air standards.

As a result neither the House nor the Senate committees acted before Sept. 30, and Congress simply kept funding EPA clean air programs after fiscal 1982 began on Oct. 1. Waxman's subcommittee conducted hearings during the fall, and the full Senate committee began some tentative markup efforts. But neither panel came close to settling on a legislative package before the 1981 session ended.

Senate Committee Action. In November and early December the Senate Environment and Public Works Committee reviewed the existing Clean Air Act section by section and voted on members' proposals for revisions. In the process the panel ignored or turned down administration and industry proposals to relax automobile emission controls and national air standards.

House Subcommittee Delays. In the House Dingell pressed Waxman's subcommittee all year to act on clean air law revisions. Waxman conducted extensive hearings but balked at marking up legislation, delaying action until 1982.

Dingell pushed for a meeting Oct. 22 of the principal congressional players with Vice President George Bush. At the meeting Dingell reportedly threatened to yank the bill

out of Waxman's subcommittee if he did not move soon. Waxman, however, stood pat. Republicans on the House committee, who were mostly interested in getting changes in the act to help electric utilities and manufacturers, did not jump to Dingell's aid. If Congress eased up on auto emissions, it would have to clamp down on the manufacturers and utilities if clean air standards were to be met.

Some House Democrats, convinced clean air would be a good campaign issue in 1982, were upset at Dingell's push for action in 1981. Environmentalists also favored waiting, believing the closer it got to Election Day, the less willing Congress would be to weaken the law — an opinion shared by some industry spokesmen.

1982 Stalemate

Despite threatened EPA sanctions against hundreds of counties throughout the nation, Congress failed again in 1982 to draft clean air law revisions that either the House or the Senate found acceptable.

The Senate Environment Committee in August finally approved a clean air law reauthorization bill (S 3041) after nine months of markup sessions. But a bitter split between factions led by Dingell and Waxman forced the House Energy Committee to break off efforts to write its own clean air bill when Congress adjourned for its Labor Day recess.

As the Nov. 2 congressional elections approached, Reagan listed reauthorization of the Clean Air Act as one of his five top economic priorities. After the election, EPA officials warned that the agency would ban new plant construction and cut off federal grants to up to 472 counties unless Congress during its lame-duck session extended the law's Dec. 31 deadline for complying with national air quality standards. But the House panel never resumed markups on HR 5252, a comprehensive measure introduced on the last day of the 1981 session that Reagan and industry groups favored. And Senate leaders made no effort to schedule floor action on the Environment Committee's legislation.

Senate Committee Bill. The Senate committee completed its work on Aug. 19, approving S 3041 by a 15-1 vote. Formally reported Nov. 15 (S Rept 97-666), the measure modified the 1977 Clean Air Act in a number of ways without significantly relaxing federal clean air regulations. Steven D. Symms, R-Idaho, a proponent of loosening existing air quality standards, was the lone committee dissenter.

Throughout the Senate markups Stafford and other supporters of the existing clean air law remained in clear control of the committee.

To broaden support for a reauthorization bill, the Senate panel March 23 voted 15-1 to revise the PSD section of the law. The committee in May also approved amendments to slightly relax automobile and truck emission standards in high-altitude states, and it voted to ease sanctions against communities that failed to comply with federal standards. After a two-month break in markups, the panel approved 15-0 an amendment by George J. Mitchell, D-Maine, to combat acid rain by forcing industry and electric utilities in a 31-state region to cut sulfur dioxide emissions by eight million tons a year over a 12-year period.

Energy and Commerce Deadlock. In the House Waxman's subcommittee began marking up clean air revisions on Feb. 25. The chairman offered his own package (HR 5555) as a "moderate and constructive" alternative to the industry-backed HR 5252. But over the following month Dingell guided the industry bill through Waxman's own subcommittee largely untouched, backed by consistent support from eight Republicans and three other Democrats who favored relaxing clean air standards. The subcommittee twice refused to attach acid rain control provisions to the bill and it three times defeated proposals to remove industry-backed provisions to ease existing requirements that cities set up programs to inspect auto emission control devices to make sure they were working properly.

Full Committee Action. The tables turned, however, when the full Energy and Commerce Committee took up HR 5252 March 30. Chairman Dingell found the full committee hard to control, while Waxman and his environmental group allies mounted successful challenges to industry positions. In May Dingell halted markup sessions for three months, then called them off altogether after losing some critical votes in August.

Dingell had hoped to hold together a fragile coalition behind legislation that would relax both auto emission standards and industrial air quality regulations. To bolster support among members from Midwestern and Appalachian coal-producing states, moreover, Dingell proposed retaining the controversial "percentage reduction" requirement in existing law that protected markets for those regions' high-sulfur coal producers. But Dingell's coalition cracked as the panel maneuvered over proposals to repeal the percentage reduction requirement, curb power plant emissions in the Midwest to control acid rain, retain the PSD system to limit pollution in pristine Western regions and prod EPA to move more rapidly to control toxic air pollutants.

The House committee never resumed clean air markups after the Labor Day recess. Although committee members continued backstage negotiations, House and Senate leaders insisted on stripped-down legislative agendas that left no time for considering complex clean air issues. Environmentalists concluded that the next Congress would be more receptive to retaining tough clean air regulations, while industry and its allies opposed a simple extension of existing law that might reduce pressure on Congress to consider major revisions.

Reagan EPA Policies

Congress failed to act, but during the first two years of the Reagan administration EPA moved administratively to ease federal clean air regulations.

At the urging of the administration's Task Force on Regulatory Relief, chaired by Vice President Bush, EPA in 1981 began reconsidering regulations adopted during the Carter administration to tighten controls on motor vehicle exhausts. Under EPA Administrator Gorsuch, a conservative former Colorado legislator appointed by Reagan, the agency also slowed the process of developing hazardous air pollutant standards and prescribing specific standards for different categories of pollutants that newly built factories could emit.

Motor Vehicles. In April 1981 EPA listed 18 administrative actions that officials intended to take "to reduce the regulatory burden on the motor vehicle industry." The agency maintained that those actions would save automakers $800 million and cut auto prices $4 billion through 1986 without increasing air pollution. Under President Carter EPA had turned down industry appeals to consider most of the changes that the new administration proposed.

In August 1981 the vice president's task force asked

EPA to consider relaxing a regulation that was scheduled to force gasoline refiners to cut back on the amount of lead they added to boost octane ratings. The administration contended that new evidence on lead's health effects ·and falling demand for leaded gasoline made the tighter standard too stringent. The task force also urged EPA to extend an exemption that Congress had granted for small refineries, giving them until 1982 to reduce lead additives.

Congress stepped in to question EPA's objectivity on the lead issue. Rep. Toby Moffett, D-Conn., chairman of the House Government Operations Subcommittee on Environment, called oversight hearings to disclose that Gorsuch had met with representatives from Thriftway Co., a small New Mexico refinery, and allegedly given assurances that EPA would not enforce scheduled lead restrictions. After medical experts opposed relaxed lead standards during agency hearings, EPA in 1982 withdrew the proposed rules and imposed tighter lead standards. In early 1983 the agency started enforcement actions against Thriftway for violating lead-in-gasoline rules in 1981 and 1982.

Bubble Concept. EPA in 1981 revised its regulations, at the Bush task force's urging, to let industries modernize old plants in polluted areas without first obtaining government approval to install new equipment.

In its new rule, formally adopted in October 1981, EPA gave states authority to regulate industrial facilities in non-attainment areas under the so-called "bubble concept." Under its initial interpretation of the 1970 Clean Air Act, EPA had directed states to regulate emissions from each boiler, furnace or other installation that was a source of emissions to the air. In the 1977 Clean Air Act amendments Congress required states to conduct strict reviews of plans to build new sources in an area with unhealthy air before construction could proceed. Before building a new source a company had to demonstrate that the facility would reduce emissions to the lowest possible rate and that those levels would be offset by reduced emissions from other sources.

Under the bubble concept EPA allowed states to treat an entire plant, or every unit within a plant, as a single emission source, as if it were enclosed in a bubble that released emissions at a single point. Under that approach a company planning to modernize or replace a unit within a plant was no longer required to undergo review prior to construction so long as reduced emissions from another part of the plant offset the increased emissions from the new unit.

Administration officials and industry leaders contended that the bubble concept was consistent with the intent of Congress, which did not define emission "sources" in the 1970 law. By freeing industry plans to revamp facilities from detailed and costly EPA and state reviews, they added, the concept encouraged companies to replace old polluting equipment with cleaner-burning units.

EPA had considered adopting the bubble concept under specified circumstances during the Carter administration but eventually dropped the proposal. The Reagan administration revived it as part of its drive to reduce federal regulations on business and industry. By 1984, 31 states had opted for the bubble concept in enforcing clean air standards within their boundaries.

Environmentalists feared the policy would slow progress in cleaning up the air. In 1982 the U.S. Court of Appeals for the District of Columbia, acting on a suit brought by the Natural Resources Defense Council, blocked EPA's revised clean air rules, finding the bubble concept inconsistent with the Clean Air Act's purpose. But the U.S. Supreme Court, in a 1984 ruling on the administration's appeal, upheld the bubble concept and reinstated the EPA rule. *(Supreme Court decision, p. 755)*

1983-84

Still badly divided by regional and economic concerns, Congress in 1983-84 made no progress in resolving doubts about the federal government's commitment to cleaning up air pollution.

Worried about potential economic costs, the Reagan administration hesitated to propose federal action to control acid rain that was damaging forests, lakes and streams in the Northeast and eastern Canada. In Congress, Northeastern state delegations and environmental groups pressed legislation to curb power plant emissions in the Midwest that were blamed for acid rain pollution. But strong opposition from Ohio and nearby state delegations blocked House and Senate action on acid rain proposals.

The dispute stalled congressional deliberations on revising the Clean Air Act of 1970. Congress in early 1983 reduced pressure for revising the 1970 law by forbidding the Environmental Protection Agency to impose economic penalties on communities that had missed a 1982 deadline for complying with national air quality standards.

Clean Air/Acid Rain

Divided over how to combat acid rain, Congress in 1983-84 again put off revising the Clean Air Act of 1970.

As in 1981-82, committees in both the House and Senate worked for two years without results on proposals to overhaul the 1970 act, the nation's most complex and far-reaching environmental protection law. The act's existing clean air standards were controversial by themselves, and pressure to expand the law to control acid rain only compounded regional and philosophical differences over how to pay for improving the nation's air quality.

During the early 1980s scientific evidence continued to accumulate indicating that power plant and automobile emissions from the industrial Midwest produced acid rain — a weak solution of sulfuric or nitric acid — that damaged forests and lakes hundreds of miles downwind in the Northeast and eastern Canada. Environmental groups, Northeastern congressional delegations and the Canadian government demanded federal action to combat that pollution. But electric utilities and government officials from the Midwest and from Appalachian coal-producing states objected to proposals that would saddle those regions with heavy economic costs.

The Reagan administration itself was sharply split on acid rain issues and offered Congress little guidance. Environmental Protection Agency (EPA) Administrator William D. Ruckelshaus in 1983 recommended that the White House propose modest reductions in power plant emissions, but opponents led by Secretary of Energy Donald P. Hodel and Office of Management and Budget (OMB) Director David A. Stockman persuaded President Reagan to call for further acid rain studies. With the administration still divided, neither the House nor the Senate took clean air bills to the floor.

In early 1984 the Senate Environment and Public Works Committee drafted Clean Air Act revisions (S 768) imposing new controls on acid rain, but stiff opposition blocked further action. In the House Rep. Henry A. Waxman, D-Calif., a leading proponent of tough clean air standards, shelved a separate clean air bill after his Energy and Commerce Subcommittee on Health and the Environment voted 10-9 to strip acid rain controls from the measure.

As a result the original Clean Air Act, previously amended in 1977, remained on the books, even though funding authorizations under the law had expired in 1981. Congress continued to provide money in annual appropriations for EPA to enforce clean air standards. And industry, labor unions, state and local governments and economists continued to complain as the law forced them to make costly investments to cut industrial pollution and curtail emissions from automobile tailpipes. *(Background, 1981-82 clean air debates, p. 411)*

In mid-1983 Congress eased pressure on its members for quick action to revise the 1970 law. Through an amendment to EPA's annual appropriations bill, the House and Senate barred the agency from enforcing economic penalties on communities that had failed to meet a 1982 deadline for achieving national air quality standards. By imposing a one-year moratorium, Congress headed off EPA sanctions against more than 200 cities and towns throughout the country that might have prodded members to support industry and administration demands to relax existing clean air regulations. *(Story, p. 422)*

Acid Rain Debate

Demands to curb acid rain pollution complicated economic and political debates over federal clean air regulations. Reagan had been elected in 1980 after pledging to curtail government regulation of U.S. business and industry, and members were questioning whether EPA's efforts to force business to make expensive pollution control investments were costing the nation more than was justified in lost jobs and industrial production. But even as Congress began re-evaluating the economic costs of enforcing the Clean Air Act's requirements, environmental groups and state and local officials from the Northeast were urging tough action against acid rain that could cost electric utilities and their ratepayers billions of dollars.

Acid rain formed chiefly from sulfur dioxide spewed into the air by coal-burning electric power plants or from nitrogen oxide from automobile exhausts. Once aloft, those pollutants traveled hundreds of miles downwind, crossing state, regional and even international boundaries. Falling to the ground as rain or snow, the weak acid solutions were blamed for damaging trees and killing off fish in streams and lakes that lay beneath the path followed by prevailing wind currents.

Acid rain damage was most prominent in New England, upstate New York and eastern Canada. Most observers attributed acid rain in that region to a complex of coal-fired power plants along the Ohio River Valley in Ohio, Indiana, Illinois and Kentucky that burned high-sulfur coal from surrounding Appalachian coal fields. Some studies suggested that acid rain produced by coal-fired power plants and copper smelters in the Southwest and Mexico also threatened forests and lakes in the Rocky Mountain region.

Total U.S. sulfur dioxide emissions from man-made sources amounted to about 24.1 million metric tons per year, according to an Interagency Task Force on Acid Precipitation formed by 12 federal agencies. To combat acid rain, U.S. environmental groups and the Canadian government urged the federal government to cut those emissions in half, by about 12 million metric tons. With existing technologies, sulfur dioxide emissions could be curtailed by installing scrubbers to remove sulfur dioxide from smokestack gas or by switching to burning coal with lower sulfur content.

Political Complications. Choosing a strategy for controlling acid rain involved difficult political problems. Some approaches placed the burden of cleanup costs on the utilities emitting the most pollution — and ultimately on their ratepayers. Others spread the cost by charging utility customers nationwide, raising protests in Western areas, where utilities said they were not causing problems.

Utility industry groups said control costs would be huge, and they warned that electric bills in some places could rise by 50 percent. But environmentalists said government studies put costs far lower, involving rate increases of 2.5 percent to 10 percent.

One of the cheaper ways to reduce emissions of sulfur dioxide would be to burn low-sulfur Western coal. But West Virginia, Ohio, Indiana and Illinois, states that produced high-sulfur coal, feared this could cost miners' jobs and hurt their economies. Consequently, many bills required use of one of the most expensive control technologies: scrubbers that remove sulfur dioxide from smokestack gas.

1983 Cabinet Clash

EPA Administrator Ruckelshaus in 1983 began efforts to build a consensus within the administration behind a legislative initiative on acid rain. Reagan himself had listed acid rain as a top priority for quick action in a speech at the May 18 ceremony when Ruckelshaus was sworn in to replace Anne M. Burford, who had resigned under congressional fire for EPA's handling of toxic waste programs. *(Story, p. 454)*

Ruckelshaus in September outlined a range of options to Reagan's Cabinet Council on Natural Resources and Environment, recommending a plan for modest reductions in coal-fired power plant emissions. Ruckelshaus' proposal was more limited than most acid rain bills before Congress. Stockman, Hodel and other administration opponents contended that it would be too costly to electric power companies and their ratepayers. Reportedly, only Secretary of State George P. Shultz backed the EPA administrator's plan for an experimental reduction of three million to 4.4 million tons in sulfur dioxide emissions in a handful of Ohio Valley states.

Turning down Ruckelshaus' plan, Reagan instead urged more research, arguing that not enough was known about acid rain to justify an expensive control program. Democratic contenders for their party's 1984 presidential nomination condemned the administration's stand, making it an issue during early primary campaigns in New England, a region where concern about acid rain was growing.

Clean Air Legislative Debates

Environmental groups and their allies in Congress had spent 1981-82 fending off administration and industry pressure to ease existing clean air regulations. Bolstered by Democratic gains in the 1982 congressional elections, they

hoped to take the offensive during the 98th Congress to extend the Clean Air Act with existing EPA authority largely intact, while expanding the law to address acid rain pollution.

In the Senate, Environment and Public Works Committee Chairman Robert T. Stafford, a Republican from Vermont, in 1983 grew impatient with administration waffling on an issue that was a prime concern among environment-minded New England voters. In the House, the Democratic Caucus had increased the Energy and Commerce Committee's Democratic majority and appointed seven new members, most of whom were expected to back Waxman on clean air issues.

Stafford's panel in 1982 had drafted a clean air bill preserving most of the existing law and adding new acid rain controls. The House committee's efforts to draft a bill had broken down as Health and Environment Subcommittee Chairman Waxman clashed repeatedly with committee Chairman John D. Dingell, D-Mich., a representative from an automobile manufacturing state who pressed an industry-backed bill to relax existing standards. *(1981-82 committee action, p. 418)*

1984 Senate Committee Measure

Early in 1983 Stafford introduced a bill (S 768) identical to the measure the committee approved in 1982. The Senate panel took no action in 1983. The committee approved a few changes in early 1984, then agreed to report S 768 by a 16-2 vote on March 13.

Senators from the Northeastern and Western states dominated the Environment panel, and the committee's proposal for acid rain controls reflected their regional interests. Strengthening its 1982 measure, the panel raised the reductions that the bill required in utility sulfur dioxide emissions from eight million tons to 10 million tons a year. That goal would force utilities to cut emissions well below the levels that met EPA's health-based standards under the existing law. Following a "polluter pays" formula, the bill would have forced Midwestern and Ohio Valley states to bear the major costs of controlling acid rain.

The committee proposed allowing utilities to achieve those further reductions without installing expensive smokestack scrubbers by burning low-sulfur coal. To protect markets for Appalachian and Midwest high-sulfur coal fields, Congress in the existing Clean Air Act required all utilities to remove sulfur dioxide gas from smokestack gas, no matter how clean it was to start with. Members from Appalachian and Midwestern states stoutly defended that "percentage reduction requirement," which neutralized cost advantages for Western low-sulfur coal producers by forcing all coal-burning power plants to install expensive stack gas scrubbers. While the Senate panel agreed to abandon percentage reduction for meeting acid rain goals, it headed off an amendment by Max Baucus, D-Mont., to repeal the scrubber requirement in existing law for complying with EPA health standards.

Auto Pollution Controls. The Senate committee measure retained existing automobile pollution standards that most new cars already met. But the committee approved an amendment, offered by Dave Durenberger, R-Minn., with Stafford's support, that for the first time would have made it illegal for individual car owners to disconnect auto pollution control devices or burn leaded gasoline in engines equipped with catalytic converters requiring unleaded fuel. Existing law made it illegal for manufacturers or dealers to remove pollution devices, but EPA reported that misfueling and tampering with equipment still contributed seriously to air pollution from cars.

Bill Stalled. The Environment Committee formally reported S 768 on May 3 (S Rept 98-426), but the measure went no further. Despite the comfortable 16-2 committee margin, the bill faced widespread opposition in the Senate. Jennings Randolph, D-W.Va., the committee's ranking minority member, had cast one of the two votes against reporting S 768. Randolph, who represented a coal-producing state in the Ohio Valley, based his opposition on the acid rain provision. Senators from Midwestern states had called for delaying acid rain controls or spreading costs throughout the nation, and their numbers were stronger in the full Senate than in the Environment committee.

House Subcommittee Efforts

As the Senate panel prepared its report on S 786 in 1984, Waxman gave up efforts to draft clean air legislation after his House Energy and Commerce subcommittee May 2 scrapped his acid rain proposal.

Waxman had authored a clean air bill (HR 5314) to force the nation's 50 dirtiest utility plants to install expensive scrubbers but to spread the cost beyond their ratepayers by imposing a nationwide tax on electric bills. But Waxman was unable to overcome objections by Democrats from Midwestern states where the 50 plants were concentrated and by Western members who opposed forcing their region to pay for correcting pollution that it neither created nor suffered from.

Four Democrats — Dingell; Richard C. Shelby, Ala.; and Thomas A. Luken and Dennis E. Eckart, both from Ohio — joined the subcommittee's six Republicans in the 10-9 vote to strip the acid rain provisions from Waxman's legislation. Before the vote the subcommittee had accepted several amendments offered by Waxman in an effort to make the bill more acceptable to Eckart. The Ohio Democrat normally sided with environmentalists but represented a district that held two of the 50 plants the chairman had targeted. "We have done all we could for Ohio and that's not enough," Waxman said after Eckart provided the one-vote margin against the acid rain proposal.

Waxman called off further markups, terming the acid rain vote "a likely death knell" for clean air legislation in the 98th Congress, as indeed it proved to be.

EPA Sanctions Moratorium

Congress in 1983 barred the Environmental Protection Agency (EPA) from cutting off federal highway funds to communities that had failed to meet a federal clean air deadline.

In February the Reagan administration had notified 218 cities and towns around the nation that they faced the threat of economic sanctions for violating the Clean Air Act of 1970. The threatened sanctions put pressure on Congress to extend or relax EPA standards for meeting national air quality goals.

Congress instead imposed a one-year moratorium that banned sanctions on as many as 110 areas, through an amendment to a fiscal 1984 appropriations bill for the Department of Housing and Urban Development and independent agencies, including EPA (HR 3133 — PL 98-45).

Many supporters and critics of EPA clean air standards joined to grant a reprieve to communities that had missed a Dec. 31, 1982, deadline for complying with the agency's goal for the general quality of their air.

But some proponents of revising the 1970 law objected that extending the deadline would also let members of Congress off the hook by reducing incentives for action. With the moratorium on sanctions in place, "you can forget about having clean air legislation" even reported out of committee "during this Congress," Rep. David O'B. Martin, R-N.Y., predicted during House deliberations.

Threatened EPA Sanctions

As amended in 1977, the Clean Air Act set a Dec. 31, 1982, deadline for meeting EPA's "national ambient air quality standards" — goals for the quality of air in general circulation, rather than for the gas coming out of smokestacks. In certain areas with severe auto-related pollution, an extension to 1987 was allowed.

On Feb. 3, 1983, EPA put approximately 218 communities around the nation — including a number of big cities — on notice that they faced the threat of sanctions as a result of various air act violations.

EPA Administrator Anne M. Burford had put the sanctions machinery into motion in January, claiming existing law gave her no choice. She said communities that missed the Dec. 31, 1982, deadline would face bans on new construction and a cutoff of federal grants for highways and clean air programs.

Environmentalists charged that the administration was using the threat of sanctions as a way of pressuring Congress to act quickly on a clean air reauthorization bill. The Reagan administration, like automobile manufacturers

and many other industries, had been seeking a relaxation of the existing law.

Legislative Moratorium

With members under political pressure to keep sanctions from taking effect, the House June 2 attached a one-year moratorium to the EPA appropriations measure. William E. Dannemeyer, R-Calif., a critic of existing clean air standards, offered the amendment. But Health and Environment Subcommittee Chairman Henry A. Waxman, D-Calif., a leading defender of clean air goals, rose in support of the moratorium after last-minute negotiations produced agreement to narrow its scope.

Majority Leader Jim Wright, D-Texas, and Minority Leader Robert H. Michel, R-Ill., both supported the amendment. Energy and Commerce Committee Chairman John D. Dingell, D-Mich., opposed the moratorium. Dingell, who represented the nation's leading auto-producing state, had been urging the administration to impose the sanctions to prod Congress to act on a clean air bill that would ease auto pollution controls.

As approved by a **key vote of 227-136 (R 89-50; D 138-86)**, the Dannemeyer amendment prohibited EPA from imposing sanctions simply because an area had failed to meet the ambient air quality goal. In effect, that barred penalties against 75 to 111 of the 218 communities that EPA had notified. The remaining communities, cited for failing to draft or implement EPA-approved plans for meeting clean air goals, still faced possible sanctions. The Senate Appropriations Committee accepted the moratorium in its version of HR 3133 (S Rept 98-152) and the provision was not at issue in conference on the bill. *(1983 key votes, p. 911)*

Chronology
Of Action
On Federal Water Policy

1981-82

The 97th Congress took steps to re-evaluate federal government programs for developing water supplies and preventing water pollution.

Responding to President Reagan's demand for budget restraint, Congress in 1981 sharply curtailed Environmental Protection Agency grants for building municipal sewage treatment plants. It took no action, however, on Reagan's proposals for overhauling Clean Water Act regulations to force industry to install equipment to clean up water discharges.

The House and Senate meanwhile struggled with Interior Secretary James G. Watt for control over federal water development projects. Congress resisted the administration's plans to consolidate federal water development planning within the Interior Department, but it also refused to adopt proposals to create a national water board to coordinate federal and state water policies.

The maneuvering continued a stalemate that had developed during the Carter administration, slowing approval of new U.S. Army Corps of Engineers and U.S. Bureau of Reclamation water projects. Congress nonetheless completed one water policy reform by revising the Reclamation Act of 1902 to lift a 160-acre limit on farms eligible for federal irrigation water. While the administration debated policy for future water programs, Congress continued to fund previously authorized projects despite members' protests against their costs and environmental impacts.

The 97th Congress also extended several laws regulating use of ocean waters by protecting marine sanctuaries, controlling deep seabed mining and limiting ocean dumping.

Sewer Grants

Lawmakers in 1981 sharply curtailed federal grants for building municipal sewage treatment systems.

Prodded by President Reagan, Congress on Dec. 16 cleared legislation (HR 4503 — PL 97-117) that cut in half authorizations for the $5 billion-a-year program. To curb fast-rising federal costs, Congress also overhauled the system by which the government distributed financial assistance to force local governments to correct water pollution from municipal sewage wastes.

Environmentalists credited the federal grants with encouraging cities and towns throughout the nation to install or upgrade systems to collect and treat human wastes before dumping them into streams, lakes or oceans. Since authorizing the grants in 1972, however, Congress continually had expanded authorized spending to finance proposed projects in members' states and districts.

In its 1981 measure Congress authorized $2.4 billion a

year in fiscal 1982-85 for Environmental Protection Agency (EPA) grants for sewage treatment construction. But it revised the formula for distributing those grants in ways that reduced the federal government's obligation to finance projects that local officials wanted to build. Starting with fiscal 1985, the legislation cut federal contributions to 55 percent of construction costs. It also denied, starting in fiscal 1985, new EPA grants for expanding sewage treatment capacity to prepare booming regions for future population growth.

Congress created the construction grant program as part of the Federal Water Pollution Control Act of 1972 (PL 92-500). That law ordered municipal governments throughout the nation to clean up sewage discharges into rivers and lakes by building sophisticated "secondary" treatment plants. To finance those facilities Congress authorized EPA to provide federal grants to cover up to 75 percent of construction costs.

But federal costs soared far beyond early estimates in the 1970s, as communities drafted plans for expensive sewage treatment projects. State governments, local officials, construction firms, real estate developers and other business interests eagerly sought federal grants, both to improve aging municipal treatment systems and to expand capacity in anticipation of population growth. Congress had committed more than $30 billion to the grant program by the early 1980s, but EPA in 1980 estimated the cost of completing the job at $120 billion, requiring $90 billion more in federal grants.

Reagan drew the line after taking office in 1981, vowing to oppose continued funding for sewage treatment grants unless Congress cut back on federal obligations. Critics charged that the construction program encouraged local governments to buy expensive technical equipment that they were unable to maintain at full capacity. Critics also complained that the program provided federal subsidies for fast-growing communities that designed sewage treatment plants with generous "reserve capacity" to accommodate and even attract industrial and residential development.

Congress complied with Reagan's demand, although members were reluctant to scale back federal commitments on which state and local governments had counted. Despite regional feuding, the House and Senate eventually settled on compromise legislation that cut back federal grants to 55 percent of construction costs and focused them on cleaning up existing sewage problems. In the process Congress shifted federal grants away from Southern and Western states with fast-growing communities toward older cities in the Northeast and Midwest with inadequate sewer systems.

To win support from Sun Belt state delegations, however, Congress continued the existing formula through fiscal 1982, keeping many planned projects eligible. The bill revised the formula for fiscal 1983-85, but it also assured that no state would receive less than 90 percent of the sewage construction grants that the 1982 formula would have provided.

Background

Congress launched the ambitious sewage plant construction program in 1972. The Federal Water Pollution Control Act (PL 92-500), enacted over President Nixon's veto that year, authorized the federal government to make construction grants for up to 75 percent of the cost of upgrading municipal sewage treatment plants throughout

the nation to remove most pollutants from municipal wastes before discharging them into lakes, rivers or oceans.

The 1972 law replaced federal water pollution laws dating back to 1899. It set two goals — making all waters fishable and swimmable by 1983, and eliminating all polluted discharges into navigable waters by 1985 — and required both industry and municipal governments to install modern treatment facilities to meet those objectives. For industry, Congress set deadlines for installing improved pollution control equipment by 1977, then cutting discharges even more by using more sophisticated technology by 1984. *(1983-84 action, p. 439)*

To improve public sewage treatment, the law directed local governments to begin "secondary treatment" of sewage wastes, removing 85 percent of pollutants with bacteria that consumed organic wastes, by 1977. The law also required municipal governments to install the "best practicable" technology by mid-1983. To finance those improvements Congress gave EPA authority to pick up 75 percent of the cost through grants to state and local governments.

Congress amended the 1972 law when it passed the Clean Water Act of 1977 (PL 95-217). With the 1977 deadline for secondary treatment arriving, Congress gave municipalities that had yet to receive federal assistance an additional six years, until 1983, to clean up sewage discharges. Recognizing the need for more flexibility in effluent treatment methods, the 1977 law allowed cities to adopt "innovative and alternative technologies," such as recycling treated water or using it for irrigation, to comply with federal standards. The 1977 law authorized $5 billion a year through fiscal 1982 for EPA construction grants for municipal treatment facilities. *(1972 law, Congress and the Nation Vol. III, p. 792; 1977 amendments, Congress and the Nation Vol. V, p. 550)*

Congress amended the law again in 1980 (PL 96-483) to revise a requirement that industries discharging wastes into city-owned plants pay part of construction costs for those facilities. The 1980 measure also allowed states and cities to pick up more than their traditional 25 percent share of construction costs if their governors chose to do so. *(1980 amendments, Congress and the Nation Vol. V, p. 590)*

Construction Grant Criticisms

In the 1970s the sewage treatment plant construction grants grew rapidly into a multibillion-dollar program. Between 1972 and 1981 Congress authorized $38.98 billion and appropriated $33.3 billion for construction grants. EPA awarded 13,000 grants by 1981, and 3,200 plants were in operation.

Yet nearly every interest involved in the program — state governments that disbursed federal construction grants, engineers who built sewage treatment plants, congressional investigators, the congressional General Accounting Office (GAO) and EPA officials who administered the grants — criticized how it operated. Escalating costs were a major problem. Initial estimates were that the program would require a total investment of $63 billion in 1972 dollars. But because of inflation, bureaucratic delays and population growth, EPA estimated that by the year 2000 it could cost $120 billion to reach the cleanup goals, with the federal share approaching $90 billion.

Critics contended that state governments, in allocating funds for sewage facility construction, had given low priority to municipalities that contributed the most to water pollution. Readily available federal construction grants encouraged city governments to build costly and sophisticated plants. But Congress provided no federal subsidy to operate and maintain the equipment. Without adequate funds and technically qualified operators, some local governments operated new plants well below their design capacity.

Reagan Demand for Overhaul

Two months after taking office in January 1981, Reagan announced that he did not want to spend another penny on federal sewage construction grants until Congress overhauled the program. Reagan demanded and got a $1.7 billion rescission in fiscal 1981 grant appropriations but announced he would seek $2.4 billion for fiscal 1982 grants if Congress made the program more cost-effective.

In proposals sent to Congress in April, Reagan sought to reduce the federal government's future potential obligation from a projected $90 billion to $23 billion. The administration wanted to eliminate federal funding for new collection systems, for "reserve" treatment capacity to serve future population growth, for replacing or repairing existing sewers or leaking pipes and for storing overflows from combined storm and sanitary sewer systems.

The administration requested a one-year authorization, through fiscal 1982, to make the timing of construction grants consistent with the rest of the Clean Water Act, which came up for review in 1982. State water program administrators sought a six-year reauthorization to make funding for the grant program more predictable. Environmentalists also favored extending the construction program for more than one year, giving Congress a chance to review national water standards, clean water deadlines, and other controversial provisions of the existing law without the threat of changes in the construction grant formula hanging over its deliberations.

Congressional Action

Reagan's plan in effect called for shifting federal sewage construction grants from rural and high-growth regions in the South and West to older cities in the Northeast. It set off a bitter regional struggle in Congress between Sun Belt and Frost Belt state delegations.

Congress set the stage for overhauling the construction grant program in the budget-cutting reconciliation package it cleared in July 1981. By the end of the year Congress and the administration reached agreement on a four-year reauthorization bill that cut funding for construction grants in half and narrowed the scope of federally funded sewage treatment projects.

In the budget reconciliation measure (HR 3982 — PL 97-35), signed by the president Aug. 13, Congress limited fiscal 1981 construction grant authorizations to $2.5 billion. Yielding to Reagan's demand to revise the program, the House and Senate Public Works committees also agreed to language providing no fiscal 1982 funds unless legislation trimming federal grant commitments were enacted.

The panels followed up by drafting separate construction grant measures in September. The existing formula for distributing grants expired Sept. 30, but floor debate and a threatened presidential veto delayed final action until the end of the 1981 session.

Senate Action. With minimal debate the Senate Oct. 27 passed a four-year sewer grant authorization bill drafted

by its Environment and Public Works Committee (S 1716 — S Rept 97-204). Before approving the bill on Sept. 23, the panel revised Reagan's proposal for allocating sewer grants in ways that preserved more funds for fast-growing Sun Belt cities.

In the process the Senate committee bill cut potential federal obligations from $90 billion to $24 billion, according to EPA figures. The measure reduced the federal contribution to construction costs from 75 percent to 55 percent, starting in fiscal 1985, while authorizing $2.4 billion for grants in fiscal 1982 and $2.6 billion in each of the following three fiscal years.

During subcommittee and full committee markup sessions, the panel revised its formula for distributing sewer grants to assure that Sun Belt state senators would support the measure's passage. Sen. John H. Chafee, R-R.I., chairman of the panel's Subcommittee on Environmental Pollution, initially introduced legislation that prohibited federal grants from being used to finance either reserve treatment plant capacity to serve future populations or collection lines that reached into residential neighborhoods. Thus most of the money would have gone to older cities in the Northeast, where secondary sewage treatment plants — which still would be eligible for federal funds — were the top priority.

To broaden regional support for the measure, Chafee's subcommittee in July amended the bill to assure each state that it would receive at least 90 percent of the total grants that the old formula would have provided for municipal systems within its borders.

In September markup sessions the full Environment Committee made further concessions to Sun Belt senators, accepting proposals by Pete V. Domenici, R-N.M., that continued to fund some reserve treatment plants and collection lines for which EPA had previously approved grants. As Senate Budget Committee chairman, Domenici had spent most of 1981 browbeating colleagues to restrain federal spending. But Domenici also represented a fast-growing Southwestern state where federal sewage treatment grants provided a crucial catalyst for community expansion.

In another revision, the Senate panel accepted a compromise provision, offered by Daniel Patrick Moynihan, D-N.Y., to revise the industrial cost exclusion (ICE) provision that Congress had enacted in 1980. The 1980 amendment, sponsored by Robert T. Stafford, R-Vt., now the full committee chairman, banned use of federal grants to build treatment plant capacity to handle discharges by industry exceeding 50,000 gallons a day. Moynihan's amendment replaced that provision with a requirement that barred construction grants after Nov. 15, 1981, for treating industrial discharges "in excess of existing flows."

In addition to $2.6 billion in authorizations for fiscal 1983-85, the Senate panel provided $200 million annually in those years for grants to build facilities to store sewage overflows during storms to prevent contamination of marine bays and estuaries. The amendment aimed at controlling storm overflows from coastal cities near Chesapeake, San Francisco, Galveston and other bays, including Narragansett Bay off Chafee's state, Rhode Island.

House Action. On the same day that the Senate passed its bill, the House approved much different legislation drafted by its Public Works Committee (HR 4503 — H Rept 97-270). Defying Reagan's demand to overhaul the program, the House committee proposed extending the existing distribution formula and continuing federal grants

Reagan Plan: No Action

The 97th Congress took no action on 1982 Reagan administration proposals to extend federal deadlines for cleaning up water pollution by industry and municipal sewage treatment plants.

After months of delay the administration May 25 unveiled proposed legislation to revise the Federal Water Pollution Control Act of 1972 (PL 92-500). The proposal would have granted industry four additional years to comply with federal requirements for removing toxic wastes and other pollutants from wastes that factories and other facilities dumped into rivers and streams.

The administration also sought a five-year extension for municipal sewage treatment plants to comply with minimum ("secondary") treatment levels that the Environmental Protection Agency (EPA) set under the 1972 law. As amended by the 1977 Clean Water Act (PL 95-217), the law set a 1983 deadline for municipal waste treatment plants and a 1984 deadline for industrial plants to install equipment that met EPA standards for removing pollutants from discharges. *(Background, p. 425; 1983-84 action, p. 439)*

The amendments sought by the administration did not make as many changes in the act as a set of EPA proposals leaked earlier in the year. But they still promised to be controversial, and committees preoccupied with other business found no time to tackle them.

The Senate Environment and Public Works Committee May 27 reported a one-year reauthorization (S 2590 — S Rept 97-443) of the clean water law at a funding level of $299.3 million, but the Senate never acted on it.

for building new reserve capacity in anticipation of future population growth.

As drafted by the Subcommittee on Water Resources, the bill included sweeping "grandfather" provisions to protect sewage treatment projects already under way.

The subcommittee bill reduced potential federal obligations to make sewage treatment grants to about $53 billion. Before approving the measure on Sept. 30, the full Public Works Committee trimmed several billion dollars from that figure by approving an amendment to discontinue federal planning grants for preliminary work on treatment capacity to accommodate 20 years of growth. That change, proposed by subcommittee Chairman Robert A. Roe, D-N.J., limited planning grants to projects that provided only 10 years of future capacity.

Before the House took up HR 4503, the White House announced that Reagan opposed the committee's less stringent proposals for revising the sewer grant program. The House nonetheless passed the bill Oct. 27 by a 382-18 vote, with 163 Republicans joining 219 Democrats in supporting the legislation.

Conference Agreement. Reagan's opposition to the House bill cast the shadow of a veto threat over conference deliberations on sewer grant reauthorizations. House conferees contended that Congress should grandfather in most plants already under construction to give cities a transition period to adjust sewage treatment plans to federal budget cutbacks. But Chafee warned that the president might veto the bill unless more generous House provisions were cut back significantly.

During conference negotiations that lasted several weeks, House conferees resisted the Senate's provision for a multi-year authorization, preferring to consider future authorizations with other clean water issues in 1982. They also pressed their case for giving cities the flexibility to use federal grants for conservation measures, installing storm overflow facilities, and fixing leaky pipes in existing municipal sewer systems. Another sticking point was the Senate's $200 million yearly fund for catching runoff that might overload combined storm and sanitary sewer systems and dump sewage into marine bays.

Conferees Dec. 10 settled on a four-year authorization bill (H Rept 97-408) that continued the existing distribution formula for fiscal 1982 but revamped it for fiscal 1983-85. The final version kept all treatment plants and equipment eligible for construction grants until fiscal 1985. Starting in fiscal 1985, conferees agreed to cut the federal share of construction costs to 55 percent and to deny grants for reserve capacity in excess of existing population levels. The final bill made federal funds available starting in fiscal 1985 only for sewage treatment plants, large sewer lines and repairs to leaky pipes. It gave each state's governor discretion, however, to allocate 20 percent of the state's grants for sewer rehabilitation, collector system construction, combined storm and sanitary sewer overflows, and other new projects that otherwise would be ineligible. Conferees retained the $200 million authorization for correcting storm and sanitary sewer overflows into marine bays.

The final version incorporated a provision repealing the 1980 industrial cost exclusion. In May the House had passed separate legislation (HR 2957 — H Rept 97-90) repealing the exclusion.

The House and Senate both adopted the conference report by voice votes on Dec. 16.

Major Provisions

As signed into law Dec. 29, major provisions of HR 4503 (PL 97-117):

● Reduced the annual authorization ceiling for federal sewer grants from $5 billion to $2.4 billion for fiscal 1982-85, and established a $200 million fund, beginning in fiscal 1983, to correct storm and sanitary sewer overflows into marine bays and estuaries.

● Extended the existing grant allotment formula through fiscal 1982; used a combination of the existing formula and a new Senate allotment formula in fiscal 1983-85, ensuring that no state would receive less than 90 percent of what it would have received under the 1982 formula.

● Retained the 75 percent federal share until Oct. 1, 1984, after which the federal share was to be reduced to 55 percent, except that if a construction grant was awarded prior to that date for a primary, secondary or advanced treatment plant and related interceptors, or for correcting leaks, all subsequent segments and phases of that facility related to interceptors and leak repairs were to be funded

at the 75 percent level.

● Repealed the industrial cost exclusion provision of the Clean Water Act.

● Retained existing reserve capacity rules until Oct. 1, 1984, except that reserve capacity for any construction grant approved prior to Oct. 1, 1984, for a phase or segment of a treatment plant or interceptor, could be eligible for federal funding.

● Provided that beginning Oct. 1, 1984, no grant could be made for reserve treatment plant capacity in excess of population needs existing as of the date the construction grant was awarded, and in no event for needs in excess of those as of Oct. 1, 1990.

● Retained assistance for all projects currently eligible for federal funds until Oct. 1, 1984; for new projects, allowed up to 20 percent of a state's yearly allotment to be used, at the discretion of the governor, for categories such as correction of combined storm and sanitary sewer overflows, sewer rehabilitation and construction of collector systems; retained eligibility for correcting underground leaks.

● Deleted "grandfather" restrictions allowing only certain communities to discharge wastes that had not received full secondary treatment into deep ocean water, provided that the cities met environmental safeguards in the act, and provided that applications were received within one year from date of enactment. No waivers could be granted for the discharge of sewage sludge.

● Extended for five years, until July 1, 1988, a deadline for cities acting in good faith to begin secondary treatment of sewage wastes for five years.

Water Policy Planning

Congress in 1981 shelved a proposal to create an independent federal board to set national water policies.

House and Senate committees that authorized federal water projects drafted legislation to set up the board to coordinate water planning by federal and state government agencies. But four Western senators thwarted the panels' attempt to write the measure into 1981 budget reconciliation legislation.

The committees proposed the board in part to prevent Interior Secretary James G. Watt from taking control over federal water policy-making programs. In fiscal 1982 budget revisions President Reagan proposed abolishing the existing Water Resources Council (WRC) and consolidating federal water planning duties under Watt's direction.

Congress in the late 1970s had fiercely resisted President Carter's efforts to tighten executive branch control over costly water development projects. Still eager to preserve congressional freedom to fund new irrigation, flood control, inland waterway and other water projects, members feared that Reagan's reorganization plans would put Watt in position to dominate water resource program decisions.

As interior secretary, Watt directly supervised Bureau of Reclamation irrigation and electric power generation projects. As chairman of Reagan's Cabinet Council on Natural Resources and Environment, Watt also could influence water development programs run by the Army Corps of Engineers, a Defense Department agency, and by the Agriculture Department's Soil Conservation Service. Reagan's budget proposed assigning water planning functions to the Cabinet Council, which established a "working group on

water resources" to advise the president on water policy and draw up guidelines for determining which water projects the federal government should build.

Many senators and representatives strongly protested that the Cabinet Council would freeze Congress out of water policy deliberations until after key decisions had been made. As an alternative, House and Senate committees approved separate bills to set up an independent board, outside Interior Department control, that would report policy recommendations directly to Congress as well as to the president. In creating the new board, Congress also would make a long-overdue start toward developing a "strong, comprehensive water policy for this nation," Sen. James Abdnor, R-S.D., chairman of the Senate panel's Subcommittee on Water Resources, declared.

Background

The federal government began developing the nation's water resources for economic purposes in 1824. Over the following 150 years Congress gave three Cabinet departments, one semi-autonomous regional authority and an executive branch agency major responsibilities for managing the flow of rivers, streams and harbors, and for improving water quality.

Interior's Bureau of Reclamation, the Army Corps of Engineers, the Soil Conservation Service (SCS) and the Tennessee Valley Authority (TVA) conducted separate programs to build, maintain and operate dams and other structures that stored water for irrigation, controlled floods, generated electric power, controlled soil erosion and created lakes for recreation. Since 1972, moreover, the Environmental Protection Agency (EPA) had regulated industrial effluents and municipal sewage discharges to control water pollution throughout the nation.

In establishing water development programs, Congress used its broad constitutional power to regulate navigation on navigable streams. Despite its massive spending on water projects, the federal government generally conceded to state governments the power to regulate water use within their borders and allocate scarce supplies among competing users. But with authority thus fragmented among 50 state governments and several federal agencies, the nation never developed comprehensive plans for managing water resources.

Pork Barrel Politics. Over the years Congress expanded federal water development efforts into classic "pork barrel" programs. In drafting water project authorization bills, the House and Senate took care to ensure support by distributing government-financed construction among members' states and districts. State and local community leaders, eager to share in the federal largesse, formed regional alliances to support federal dam-building projects to promote economic growth by developing rivers and streams that flowed through their regions. Seven Western states along the Colorado River system, for instance, reached an interstate compact in 1921 allocating its waters for use within their borders. Then, led by powerful congressional leaders such as Rep. Wayne N. Aspinall, D-Colo. (1949-73), and Sen. Carl Hayden, D-Ariz. (House, 1912-27; Senate, 1927-69), the Colorado River states persuaded Congress to finance a system of massive dams along the river and its tributaries.

In cutting such political deals Congress often approved construction of water developments that had little economic justification, environmentalists and economists

charged. After Congress authorized federal construction grants to help local governments upgrade sewage treatment plants, members began practicing similar distributive politics to assure that their constituents benefited from the program. As a consequence Congress reacted suspiciously when presidents or executive branch officials proposed that the government coordinate its water development programs with national resource policy objectives. *(Sewer grants, p. 425)*

Research, Planning Programs. In the mid-1960s Congress attempted to develop federal machinery to coordinate water policy and promote research on conservation and technology for expanding water supplies.

Since 1908 dozens of commissions, studies and reports had called for a unified national water policy. In 1961 the Senate Select Committee on Water Resources recommended that the federal government expand water planning programs, periodically assess regional water supplies and draw up comprehensive management plans for all the nation's river basins. Congress incorporated most of the select committee's suggestions into two laws — the Water Resources Research Act of 1964 (PL 88-379) and the Water Resources Planning Act of 1965 (PL 89-80). *(Background, Congress and the Nation Vol. I, p. 897; Congress and the Nation Vol. II, p. 498)*

The laws were touted as the long-sought answer to the coordination problem. Sponsors said they would put an end to the fragmented, project-oriented approach to water planning. But the acts failed to achieve that goal. Environmentalists continued to criticize the nation's water program as riddled with economically unjustifiable projects built at the behest of politically powerful constituents or members of Congress.

The 1964 law set up an Office of Water Research and Technology, which provided grants to universities to develop better water conservation methods.

The 1965 act established the Water Resources Council, which was to be the focal point for national water planning. It was to encourage conservation and coordinate water quantity and quality programs. The law also established six river basin commissions to manage rivers on a regional basis.

But the council and the river basin commissions proved ineffective largely because neither had authority to enforce planning efforts. The WRC was unable to coordinate quantity and quality programs, mostly because it could not control two powerful water agencies — the Army Corps of Engineers and the Environmental Protection Agency. In addition, the council was chaired by the secretary of the interior, whose agency concentrated on Western water issues. That led states and other federal agencies to distrust the council's objectivity.

Carter Water Policy Review. In the late 1970s mounting environmental concerns combined with persistent federal budget deficits to slow federal construction of new water projects. Carter, a former Georgia governor, attempted a thorough overhaul of federal water policy between 1977 and 1981. But Carter's administration, heavily staffed with former environmental activists, got off on the wrong foot with Congress when the Interior Department announced in February 1977 a "hit list" of 19 partly built projects that the president wanted to cancel. Carter's plan infuriated members from states where the planned projects would be located. Although Congress eventually terminated funding for nine of the projects and modified plans for four others, the "hit list" contributed to a lasting im-

pression that Carter's administration would ignore legitimate proposals to develop water resources.

In 1978 Carter unveiled plans for national water policies that would tighten executive branch control over federal spending on dams and other projects. The administration proposal stressed water conservation measures as an alternative to costly construction projects to augment regional supplies. Carter proposed to impose tough criteria to make sure that future federally financed projects protected the environment, promoted water conservation and produced economic benefits that exceeded costs.

The administration sought to subject those projects to uniform procedures to assess their costs and benefits. In its major legislative request the administration proposed a cost-sharing plan to require states to pay 10 percent of the costs of projects that produced water, power and other resources for sale. For flood control projects and other facilities that produced no salable resources, the administration proposed requiring states to pay 5 percent of construction costs.

To implement those goals Carter announced that the Water Resources Council Congress had established in 1965 would review all projects proposed by federal water development agencies before they were submitted to Congress.

Carter's proposal for comprehensive water policies stirred opposition in Congress. Five days after he disclosed his plan, the House passed legislation to abolish the council and transfer its duties to the Interior Department. Congress eventually reauthorized the council but slashed its budget. In 1980, however, the House passed an omnibus water projects authorization bill that ignored Carter's reform proposals. *(Carter policies, Congress and the Nation Vol. V, pp. 566, 567, 587)*

Watt Water Policies

Taking over as interior secretary in 1981, Watt promised Western water interests that the Reagan administration would resume funding for new water construction. But the new administration, struggling to close the federal budget deficit, was reluctant to devote funds to dam-building projects until Congress and the states agreed on a cost-sharing formula. The administration's internal debate on cost-sharing proposals lasted throughout Reagan's first term, stalling congressional deliberations on water project authorizations. *(Cost-sharing plans, p. 440)*

The administration in the meantime proposed consolidating under Watt's control the water planning and research programs the government had launched in the 1960s. Reagan's budget proposed saving $111.5 million in fiscal 1981 and 1982 by eliminating the Water Resources Council, Interior's Office of Water Research and Technology and the six regional river basin commissions. Congress, reluctant to give Interior sole power over national water policy, resisted Reagan's plan to abolish those programs.

Water Board Legislation

House and Senate committees responded to Watt's consolidation plan by proposing a new national water policy board to replace the council. The panels also sought to continue funding for the river basin commissions and for state water planning programs.

In the Senate the Environment and Public Works Committee May 15 reported legislation (S 1095 — S Rept 97-120) creating a five-member board. The House Public

Dam Repair Funds

The Senate in 1982 sidetracked legislation to provide additional funds to repair aging federal dams in the West.

The House, in approving dam repair funds in April, adopted the Reagan administration's proposal to require farmers, industry and cities that used water and power from the dams to share in the cost of repairing them. But the Senate Energy and Natural Resources Committee left the cost-sharing provision out of its own dam repair bill, and both measures died when the 97th Congress adjourned.

Both the House and Senate committee bills increased to $650 million from $100 million funds that Congress authorized in 1978 for Bureau of Reclamation repairs on 56 dams. In the 1978 Reclamation Safety of Dams Act (PL 95-578), enacted after the federally built Teton Dam collapsed in Idaho, Congress provided the funds to detect and correct flows and damage to dams that the bureau began building early in the 20th century. *(1978 law, Congress and the Nation Vol. V, p. 571)*

The Reagan administration estimated the cost of completing the task at $650 million. To force federal water project beneficiaries to pick up part of the repair costs, administration officials urged both the Senate panel and the House Interior and Insular Affairs Committee to include cost-sharing amendments requiring them to repay the government within 50 years for part of the cost of repairs. *(Cost-sharing debate, 1983-84 action, p. 440)*

The House Interior Committee reported legislation (HR 3208 — H Rept 97-478) without cost-sharing language. But the full House, before passing the bill April 29, approved by a 212-140 margin an amendment by Rep. Gerald B. H. Solomon, R-N.Y., imposing a cost-sharing formula. The Senate panel reported its own bill (S 956 — S Rept 97-533) on Aug. 19 without cost-sharing requirements. Neither measure reached the Senate floor.

Works and Transportation Committee proposed a seven-member board (HR 3432 — H Rept 97-104, Part I). Reviewing the measure in July, the House Interior and Insular Affairs Committee added (HR 3432 — H Rept 97-104, Part II) a proposal to create a 21-member blue-ribbon commission — to include 12 members of Congress — to provide advice on what kind of water policy the country should have.

Both the House and Senate measures continued state planning grants and river basin commission funding. The Senate measure also continued federal water research grants to universities, although it accepted Reagan's plan

to abolish the Office of Water Research and Technology. Neither measure reached the floor.

Reconciliation Bill. In reviewing Reagan's requests to slash federal spending, both the House and Senate included provisions to create a new water policy board in their versions of budget-cutting reconciliation legislation. Unable to reach agreement on the board, conferees dropped the provisions from the final reconciliation measure (HR 3982 — PL 97-35).

Four senators objected to attaching S 1095 to the reconciliation measure. They were Energy Committee Chairman James A. McClure, R-Idaho; William L. Armstrong, R-Colo.; Alan K. Simpson, R-Wyo.; and Malcolm Wallop, R-Wyo.

The Senate bill provided $36 million for the new board and for water planning and research grants. The House bill provided $12.5 million for the board and planning grants. The conferees finally agreed to provide up to $12.5 million annually in fiscal 1982-84 for the board and water planning grants, if the authorizing legislation passed. In addition, $23.65 million would be provided annually in fiscal 1982-84 for water research activities administered by the Interior Department.

Water Policy Funding

Congress in 1981 insisted on funding the existing Water Resources Council and the Office of Water Research and Technology.

In a fiscal 1982 energy-water appropriations bill (HR 4144 — PL 97-88), Congress appropriated $3.8 million to keep the existing water council operating. That appropriation, however, was far below the $19.8 million the council received in fiscal 1981.

In appropriating fiscal 1982 funds for the Interior Department and related agencies (HR 4035 — PL 97-100), Congress also ignored Reagan's proposal to abolish the water research program by providing $10.6 million for the Office of Water Research and Technology. In its fiscal 1983 Interior appropriations bill (HR 7356 — PL 97-394), however, Congress accepted the water research office's demise and provided no further funding.

The House Appropriations Committee in 1982 recommended that Congress appropriate $500,000 in fiscal 1983 to continue the Water Resources Council. Neither the House nor the Senate acted on fiscal 1983 energy-water program appropriations, however, and Congress in 1983 accepted the council's elimination.

Reclamation Law Revision

Congress in 1982 revised the Reclamation Act of 1902 to provide federally subsidized water to irrigate private farms up to 960 acres in size.

Legislation cleared Sept. 29 (S 1409 — PL 97-293) raised a 160-acre limit set by the 1902 law on the amount of farmland irrigated by Interior Department reclamation projects that a single farmer could own. The measure also repealed the 1902 law's requirement that farmers who received federal project water live on or near their fields.

By revising the law, Congress recognized that the Bureau of Reclamation, the Interior Department's dam-building agency, had never enforced the 160-acre limit. In the process Congress headed off a long-running campaign by environmentalists and California land reform advocates to force Interior to deny low-cost water to wealthy individuals and corporations who irrigated thousands of acres, including some of the nation's richest farmlands, from federal reclamation projects.

Interior Secretary James G. Watt had warned that he had no choice but to start enforcing the 160-acre limit unless Congress changed the 1902 law. Backed by a 1976 federal court ruling, critics of federal reclamation programs pressed for strict enforcement of the acreage restriction to break up large agricultural operations and redistribute their land to small farmers. Environmental groups also charged that existing reclamation programs, by pricing water far below its market value, subsidized giant corporate farms and encouraged wasteful irrigation practices.

In lifting the limit to 960 acres, Congress agreed with Western farming interests who contended that a 160-acre farm was too small for modern agricultural operations. The revised law made individuals and small corporations eligible for federal project water to irrigate another 960 acres leased from other owners. But it required them to pay the government for the full cost of building projects and delivering water to the leased land.

Background

Congress passed the Reclamation Act of 1902 to promote economic development in the arid Western states. With President Theodore Roosevelt's enthusiastic backing, Congress in the 1902 law gave the Interior Department authority to build dams to store water and canals to distribute it to irrigate deserts and plains where rainfall was too sparse for farming. Congress expanded the law's objectives in subsequent decades to permit the Bureau of Reclamation to build massive multipurpose dams — including Hoover and Glen Canyon Dams on the Colorado River, Grand Coulee Dam on the Columbia River, the Central Valley Project in California and other projects — that generated electric power, supplied water for cities and industry and created lakes for recreation, in addition to irrigating farmlands. *(Reclamation program, Congress and the Nation Vol. I, p. 771)*

When Congress passed the 1902 law, federal officials envisioned that the West should be settled by families living on small farming operations. Throughout the 19th century the government had been selling or giving away the lands it acquired in Western territories in 640-acre sections, each one mile square. In the famous Homestead Act of 1862, Congress granted free title to 160 acres, a quarter section, of public lands to any citizen who settled the land and cultivated it for five years.

To focus benefits from federal reclamation projects on family-size farms, Congress in 1902 limited the amount of land an individual could water to 160 acres, the conventional homestead unit. The 1902 law allowed a farmer and spouse to receive federal project water for up to 320 acres, a half section of land. The law permitted a farmer to receive federal project water to irrigate more than 160 acres only if the owner signed a "recordable contract" with the Interior Department, promising to sell excess acreage within a specified period, usually 10 years, at the "dryland" price the acreage was worth before it could be irrigated.

Congress financed initial reclamation projects from receipts from public land sales, but the 1902 law required farmers to reimburse the government for the cost of irrigation water, without interest, over a 10-year period. Congress subsequently extended the repayment period for dif-

ferent projects to up to 60 years. In 1939 Congress limited farmers' obligation to repay the government for water project construction costs to their ability to pay, further expanding the below-cost irrigation water subsidy.

Acreage Limit Dispute. In the 80 years after Congress passed the 1902 Reclamation Act, the bureau built hundreds of projects in the 17 Western states where it operated. Bureau reclamation projects supplied water to irrigate about 10 million acres that produced more than 10 percent of the nation's total crop value. Federal projects supplied water to the West's richest agricultural regions, including the productive Central Valley in California, the leading agricultural state.

The 160-acre limit remained on the books, although it had been evaded on many water projects. Some of the nation's largest federally irrigated farms, particularly in California, covered thousands of acres, although much of the acreage was operated under lease. The question of whether lease arrangements violated the spirit of the 1902 law was at the heart of the dispute.

The old acreage limit had been poorly enforced for generations because of federal laxity, confusion created by later statutes and contradictory interpretations by courts and federal officials.

In 1976 a California group, Land is for People, won a federal court ruling that the group interpreted as an affirmation of the 160-acre limit.

President Carter's interior secretary, Cecil D. Andrus, set about enforcing the limit with a vigor that alarmed much of the farm community and the large corporations with interests in massive farms, particularly in California.

Congress had grappled periodically with the issue since then. The Senate passed a reclamation rewrite in 1979, and the House committee reported a bill in 1980. *(Congress and the Nation Vol. V, pp. 574, 594)*

Legislative Action

Congress in 1982 lifted the acreage limitation to 960 acres after bitter debate in both the House and Senate. To win its approval, Western members pushing to revise the 1902 limit had to overcome environmentalists' opposition and delaying tactics by Sen. Howard M. Metzenbaum, D-Ohio, a critic of reclamation subsidies.

House. The House May 6 passed, by a 228-117 vote, an Interior and Insular Affairs Committee bill (HR 5539 — H Rept 97-458) expanding the acreage limit to 960 acres. The bill made no changes in the price the government charged landowners for water to irrigate that much acreage. It set no limit on the number of leased acres a farmer could irrigate with federal project water, but it required a beneficiary to pay a higher rate for the additional water to recoup reclamation project costs.

Because the House had resisted earlier attempts to revise the reclamation law, passage of HR 5539 was a major victory for proponents of lifting the 160-acre limit. The House floor debate occasionally turned bitter. Opponents charged that the legislation continued billion-dollar subsidies to wealthy Western agribusinesses. They succeeded in tightening certain provisions through amendments, though they did not change the basic thrust of the legislation. They lost by voice vote on an amendment offered by David F. Emery, R-Maine, to shrink the size of farms receiving subsidized water to 640 acres.

Senate. The Senate passed a separate version July 16 that enlarged the acreage limit to 1,280 acres. Key members fashioned the measure as a compromise between environmentalist and farm critics of legislation that had been drafted by the Energy and Natural Resources Committee (S 1867 — S Rept 97-373) in April.

The committee proposed a 1,280-acre limit on irrigated acreage that an individual farmer could own, with additional leasing permitted up to a total farm size of 2,080 acres, to be eligible for subsidized rates. For farms exceeding that limit, a new "full cost" rate designed to recoup government expenses would apply to all leased acreage. Full-cost water under S 1867 would be more expensive than under the House bill because the Senate formula used interest rates reflecting current costs to the government of financing a project.

The Senate late July 16 approved the bill after an agreement by key members ended a day of delaying actions by Metzenbaum. The bill passed on a **key vote of 49-13 (R 30-3; D 19-10).** *(1982 key votes, p. 895)*

Some of the major changes made by the agreement were similar to amendments sought by environmentalists and farm critics of the legislation that were voted down during earlier debate July 14 and July 15.

The compromise reduced the acreage allowance from 2,080 acres to 1,280 acres. It allowed farms of that size to continue to receive reclamation water under existing subsidized rates. As in the original bill, farmers could receive water on additional acreage, but at a higher cost. Also changed was a complex formula for the price larger farms would have to pay for the additional water.

Conference Maneuvers. It took further maneuvering before the House and Senate settled on compromise legislation. House Interior Committee Chairman Morris K. Udall, D-Ariz., refused to go to conference on the reclamation bill until Congress settled an unrelated water rights dispute between the Papago Indian tribe and Tucson water users in his district. Once agreement was reached on the Papago dispute, Congress incorporated a compromise reclamation law revision along with the Indian water settlement into S 1409, a bill that authorized the Bureau of Reclamation to enlarge the Buffalo Bill Dam and Reservoir in Wyoming. *(Papago dispute, p. 435)*

Conference negotiations on the acreage limit were stormy. Metzenbaum repeatedly told conferees that farmers should pay more for water than either the House or the Senate bill required. Conferees settled on a 960-acre ownership limit for an individual or small corporation, with a separate 640-acre limit applied to corporations with more than 25 stockholders. The compromise permitted farm operators to receive irrigation water for an unlimited amount of leased land but required the government to charge them a full-cost rate based on unpaid construction costs and a minimum interest rate of 7.5 percent.

The Senate accepted the conference agreement (H Rept 97-855) on Sept. 24, and the House approved it Sept. 29.

Major Provisions

As signed into law Oct. 12, major reclamation law provisions of S 1409 (PL 97-293):

● Increased the acreage an individual or corporation of 25 persons or fewer could own to be eligible to receive subsidized water from 160 acres to 960 acres. A larger corporation or other legal entity of more than 25 persons could own up to 640 acres. The measure permitted farms to lease unlimited additional acreage but required payment of

the new full-cost rate for reclamation water used on the extra land.

- Required owners of land exceeding the new ownership limits to put such land under "recordable contract" with the secretary of the interior, to be sold. The sale must take place within 10 years, as under existing law, for excess land owned at the time of enactment. For contracts completed after enactment, the sale must take place within five years.

- Established new full-cost payment rates for water service to leased acreage exceeding the new owned acreage limits.

For individuals and small corporations in existing reclamation projects, the new rate would apply to leased acreage in excess of 960 acres; the existing subsidized rate would apply on owned or leased land up to 960 acres. For larger corporations receiving water before Oct. 1, 1981, the new rate would apply to land in excess of 320 acres.

The new rate would reflect unpaid project construction costs, plus interest, as determined by an average of all Treasury obligations at the time expenditures for a project were made. The interest rate formula followed the House proposal, except conferees specified that the interest rate could not drop below 7.5 percent.

Individuals in new projects and larger legal entities receiving water after Oct. 1, 1981, also would pay a new rate reflecting unpaid construction costs but with a different interest rate formula as passed by the Senate, and also with a 7.5 percent minimum.

Individuals and small corporations in new projects would pay the new rate for acreage in excess of 960 acres; larger corporations would pay it on all their land.

- Permitted water districts to choose whether to comply with the new law or to stay under the old law with its 160-acre ownership limit.

- Required farms in districts governed by existing law to pay "full cost" for water for acreage in excess of 160 acres, with the cost calculated under a new formula beginning four and one-half years after enactment. "Full cost" referred to the amount required to recover federal expenses for construction and operation of the water projects.

- Permitted individual farms in districts choosing the old law to elect instead to comply with the new law.

Water Project Appropriations

Congress in 1981-82 approved appropriations bills that continued to fund construction of controversial federal water projects.

In 1981 the House and Senate cleared a $12.5 billion appropriations measure for energy and water programs (HR 4144 — PL 97-88), including nearly $3.7 billion for Army Corps of Engineers and Bureau of Reclamation planning, construction and operations. Congress in 1982 failed to complete action on regular energy and water appropriations, but it maintained funding for water programs at fiscal 1982 levels through a fiscal 1983 continuing appropriations resolution (H J Res 631 — PL 97-377).

Despite heated opposition from environmentalists and fiscal conservatives, Congress in both years appropriated funds to continue construction of the Tennessee-Tombigbee Waterway, a partly built 232-mile barge canal to connect the Tennessee River to the Gulf of Mexico at Mobile, Ala. Congress also included funds to continue work on the Garrison Diversion project in North Dakota, even though a federal court had temporarily blocked construction on the

$1 billion project. *(1983-84 action on water project appropriations, p. 442)*

For fiscal 1982 Congress in 1981 appropriated $2.9 billion for Corps of Engineers water programs and $760 million for the Bureau of Reclamation, an Interior Department agency. Those amounts were $161.7 million more for the corps and $18.4 million more for the bureau than the Reagan administration sought.

In 1982 the House Appropriations Committee approved fiscal 1983 appropriations for the Corps of Engineers of nearly $3 billion, $236 million more than the administration requested. The panel also proposed $947 million for the Bureau of Reclamation, $13 million more than the budget request. Neither the House nor the Senate took regular water project appropriations to the floor.

Tenn-Tom Project

Critics in both the House and Senate came close during 1981 and 1982 to denying further appropriations to complete the $3 billion Tennessee-Tombigbee (Tenn-Tom) Waterway. But powerful congressional delegations from Alabama and Mississippi, the states where the canal was being built, fought off proposals to terminate funding.

First authorized in the 1940s, Tenn-Tom would be the largest water project in U.S. history. Sen. John C. Stennis, D-Miss., and other supporters had pushed the project to develop an inland waterway as a shortcut that barges could take from the Tennessee River along the Tombigbee River through Mississippi and Alabama to the Gulf port at Mobile. Proponents maintained that the canal, being built by the Army Corps of Engineers, would promote U.S. coal exports by providing a route for barge traffic from Appalachian coal fields to the sea.

Environmental groups had been fighting the Tenn-Tom project for years, contending that the economic benefits fell far short of the project's cost and the damage it would cause to the environment. The Association of American Railroads also lobbied against continued funding. If completed, the Tenn-Tom canal would compete for coal traffic with an existing rail system.

By 1982 the Corps of Engineers had spent about $1.3 billion building the Tenn-Tom project, the House Appropriations Committee noted. In supporting completion of the waterway, the panel estimated its total cost at $1.8 billion. Opponents said the cost could reach $3 billion because the lower part of the waterway would have to be straightened to accommodate expected barge traffic, but Congress had yet to authorize that work.

1981 Debate. By narrow margins, the House and Senate in 1981 defeated attempts to strip Tenn-Tom funds from fiscal 1982 energy and water program appropriations.

The Reagan administration requested $201 million for the project in its fiscal 1982 budget, but it made no major lobbying effort to defend its funding. The House Appropriations Committee cut $11 million from the Tenn-Tom proposals in reporting HR 4144 (H Rept 97-177). But Rep. Tom Bevill, D-Ala., chairman of the Appropriations Subcommittee on Energy and Water Development, led the fight for the project on the floor.

During floor debate the full House defeated, by a **198-208 key vote (R 108-70; D 90-138)**, an amendment to delete the $189 million Tenn-Tom appropriation that was offered by Joel Pritchard, R-Wash., and Bob Edgar, D-Pa. *(1981 key votes, p. 879)*

Freshman House members voted 42-30 for the amend-

Administration Power Rate Study Blocked

Congress in 1982 blocked a Reagan administration study of ways to raise low-cost rates for electric power generated by federal dam projects.

Since the New Deal days of the 1930s, federal government agencies had been selling cheap hydroelectric power from dams the government built in the South and West to promote regional economic growth. After taking office in 1981, Reagan administration officials began considering lifting rates to market levels to promote energy conservation and raise additional federal revenues.

But powerful members of Congress opposed the study, fearing that the administration would push for higher prices for federal power consumers in the Southeast and Northwest. Led by delegations from the big public power states of Washington, Oregon, Idaho and Tennessee, Congress in 1982 stepped in to bar spending for the study through amendments to fiscal 1983 continuing appropriations resolutions.

Cheap Public Power

The study would have considered ways to raise rates on power sold by the Tennessee Valley Authority (TVA), the Bonneville Power Administration and other federal power marketing agencies, to a level more in line with other electric rates.

The TVA was established in 1933 to provide electricity for residents of the Appalachian region. The Bonneville Power Administration followed soon afterwards, to market power produced by federal dams along the Columbia River. Four other federal power marketing authorities subsequently were established. Together, the agencies sold electricity in more than 30 states. *(Federal power programs, Congress and the Nation Vol. I, p. 771)*

Prices charged by federal power agencies were based on historical costs — the costs of a facility at the time of its completion. As a result, hydropower from dams completed decades ago was much less costly than electricity generated by coal and nuclear plants, built when construction costs were higher.

Cheap federal hydropower was a major reason

for the wide variation in electricity rates across the United States. A 1980 study by the Midwest Research Institute found that average rates ranged from 1.48 cents per kilowatt hour in Seattle to 11.8 cents in Connecticut — a variance of 800 percent.

The head of the administration study group, William A. Niskanen, contended that artificially low federal power rates distorted the distribution of the nation's resources and could lead to excessive energy consumption in some regions.

The Office of Management and Budget saw in the study a chance to raise revenues and cut the federal budget deficit. An analysis by the American Public Power Association suggested that a power price increase could bring in more than $1 billion a year in additional federal revenue.

Congressional Response

But House and Senate members denounced administration officials for launching the study in secrecy, without consulting Congress. They maintained that raising rates to reduce federal budget deficits would ignore the government's original goal in building hydroelectric projects to lift the standard of living in economically depressed parts of the nation.

Sen. Henry M. Jackson, D-Wash., said such a change might triple rates for some consumers in the Northwest, and Sen. Jim Sasser, D-Tenn., claimed it would raise rates by 25 percent for households in the Tennessee Valley.

An amendment barring the use of federal funds to conduct a study of federal power pricing was attached to the first fiscal 1983 continuing appropriations resolution (H J Res 599 — PL 97-276) Sept. 29. It was sponsored by Senate Energy Committee Chairman James A. McClure, R-Idaho, and other senators from public power states.

The amendment was retained in the final conference version of that bill, and later also was included in the second continuing resolution (H J Res 631 — PL 97-377), which funded the Department of Energy through fiscal 1983.

ment, suggesting that support for costly water projects would continue to decline. During debate, both sides aimed their arguments at the new members. Tenn-Tom supporters contended that Congress should complete a project in which the government already had made a large investment, but opponents maintained that it was time to rectify Congress' past mistake in authorizing the project in the first place.

After the House passed HR 4144 with the Tenn-Tom funds, the Senate rejected, by a **46-48 key vote (R 27-21; D 19-27)**, a floor amendment to delete the project's appropriation that was offered by Charles H. Percy, R-Ill.

In contrast to new House members, freshman senators elected in 1980 voted 7-11 against Percy's amendment.

Calling the waterway an "economic dinosaur," Percy said the coal companies were not seeking it and that the eventual traffic would not be enough to pay for operating it. Daniel Patrick Moynihan, D-N.Y., called it a perfect example of "pork barrel" abuse. If Congress did not start "acting responsibly" by killing it, the country would never support any more public works projects, he warned.

While J. Bennett Johnston, D-La., led the floor defense for Tenn-Tom funds, Stennis patroled the lobbies off the Senate floor, cornering undecided colleagues to per-

suade them to support the project. On the floor Johnston contended that the basic issue was "an age-old fight" between railroads and barge transportation. The railroads "have a monopoly, and they want to keep it," Johnston said. Jeremiah Denton, R-Ala., a first-term Republican, successfully persuaded most newly elected senators to support the canal.

1982 Action. Congress in 1982 continued to appropriate funds for the Tenn-Tom project through the fiscal 1983 continuing resolution. As cleared, however, the resolution carried a Senate amendment, sponsored by John H. Chafee, R-R.I., that prohibited use of funds either to study or to build improvements in the Tombigbee south of Demopolis, Ala., the portion that critics maintained would have to be straightened to allow barges to navigate.

Garrison Diversion Project

Congress kept the Garrison Diversion project for North Dakota alive in 1981-82 even though House opponents mustered the votes to strip funding from the fiscal 1983 continuing resolution.

Congress had authorized the Garrison project nearly 40 years earlier as part of the Pick-Sloan Plan for developing the Missouri River system in 10 states under the Flood Control Act of 1944. The Garrison project was designed to carry water from a Missouri River reservoir across North Dakota to irrigate about one million acres of farm land in the state. Its purpose was to compensate North Dakota for 500,000 acres of farm land flooded by Missouri River mainstream dams that the Corps of Engineers built to control floods in downstream states.

Although many Pick-Sloan projects had been completed, construction on the Garrison Diversion was only about 15 percent finished in the early 1980s. Congress regularly appropriated money for the project in the 1960s and 1970s, but a 1979 lawsuit and environmental group lobbying slowed work. Environmental groups objected that the project would destroy wetland habitat for waterfowl, and the National Taxpayers Union contended that the costs far exceeded benefits to North Dakota farmers. Canadians also opposed the project, maintaining that water draining north across the border from irrigated farm lands to the Souris River would alter the Hudson Bay region ecosystem. *(Pick-Sloan Plan, Congress and the Nation Vol. I, p. 802)*

In 1981 Congress appropriated $4 million for the Garrison Diversion as part of the fiscal 1982 energy-water appropriations bill. By a 188-206 vote, the House defeated an attempt by Rep. Silvio Conte, R-Mass., to strip out the funds. The Senate attached an amendment renewing congressional authorization for the Garrison project to the appropriations bill. Although conferees retained the Senate reauthorization language, the House refused by a 67-314 vote to accept the provision on an appropriation bill.

Opponents came closer to killing the Garrison project in 1982. Before passing the fiscal 1983 continuing resolution, the House approved Conte's attempt to delete Garrison funding by a 252-152 margin. The Senate restored the funds, however, and the conferees kept them in the final measure. The conference agreement did add provisions barring use of the money to build facilities that would affect water draining north into Canada.

The House also deleted funding for the O'Neill irrigation unit in Nebraska. But conferees restored funding for the O'Neill project as well.

Central Arizona Project

Congress in 1981 authorized an additional $350 million to $500 million to build Central Arizona Project distribution systems to deliver water to Phoenix and Tucson residents.

To take account of rising costs, Congress Dec. 9 cleared legislation (S 2177 — PL 97-373) under which authorizations for Bureau of Reclamation spending on the systems were indexed to offset inflation since the project was approved in 1968. In approving the indexing bill, however, Congress attached an amendment to force state and local governments in the region to pay 20 percent of the distribution system's cost.

The House wrote the cost-sharing provision, proposed by Bruce F. Vento, D-Minn., into the bill with the support of Republican fiscal conservatives and Democratic environmentalist members who had long complained that expensive federal water projects financed by federal taxpayers in effect subsidized wasteful water uses by residents in the arid Southwest without requiring them to pay part of construction costs.

Background. Congress authorized the $2.8 billion Central Arizona Project (CAP) in 1968 to enable Arizona to develop its share of Colorado River water. The Bureau of Reclamation designed the CAP as a 400-mile-long system of dams, aqueducts and other facilities to pump water from the Colorado on the state's western border to serve Phoenix and Tucson. Those fast-growing cities depended on groundwater supplies that were being depleted by rapid population growth. The CAP system also included facilities to deliver water to Arizona Indian tribes that had won a share of Colorado River water under a 1963 Supreme Court decision.

The 1968 law authorized $100 million for building non-Indian distribution systems. The bureau had yet to begin construction on those facilities, however, because CAP water was not expected to be available for irrigation until fiscal 1985. In the meantime inflation since 1968 had driven estimated construction costs up to $300 million-$500 million. Congress in 1968 had indexed costs for other parts of CAP, but not for distribution and drainage canals.

Legislative Action. The Senate approved indexing for non-Indian delivery systems by passing S 2177 (S Rept 97-389) May 19. The House passed the bill Sept. 30 (H Rept 97-776) after adopting Vento's amendment. The Vento amendment required state and local governments to pay their 20 percent share "up front," as construction proceeded. Under previous laws the beneficiaries of federal reclamation projects repaid the government, at artificially low interest rates, after water deliveries started. The Senate accepted the House-passed version with technical amendments Dec. 8, and the House cleared the measure by agreeing to the Senate changes Dec. 9.

Papago Indian Water Rights

Lawmakers in 1982 approved legislation to settle an Arizona water rights dispute between Tucson water users and the Papago Indian tribe.

House Interior and Insular Affairs Committee Chairman Morris K. Udall, D-Ariz., maneuvered through Congress a revised settlement (S 1409 — PL 97-293) to resolve Papago claims to groundwater reserves from which the Tucson area drew its water supplies. By settling the seven-

year-old legal challenge out of court, the measure cleared the way for further construction of the $1.7 billion Central Arizona Project (CAP).

President Reagan June 1 had vetoed an earlier bill (HR 5118), contending that it provided a federal bailout for Tucson residents, local governments and commercial interests that were fighting the Papago claims. Udall, whose district included Tucson and surrounding areas, took the lead in negotiating a compromise settlement that Congress accepted as part of major reclamation law reform legislation.

Under the settlement the Papago tribe relinquished all further claims to water in the basins underlying the Tucson area and agreed to cooperate in regional water management plans. In return Congress through S 1409 authorized nearly $40 million in federal appropriations to build irrigation facilities and provide the tribe with adequate annual water supplies.

Reagan Veto. Congress on May 13 cleared HR 5118, which had been drawn up by Udall's committee (H Rept 97-422) to implement a settlement that tribal and city leaders had negotiated.

HR 5118 reflected an agreement among the Indian tribe, miners, farmers and the city of Tucson aimed at ensuring an adequate yearly water supply to two Papago Indian reservations.

In vetoing HR 5118, Reagan complained that the U.S. government had not been party to negotiations that produced an agreement asking federal taxpayers to pay an initial $112 million and another $5 million annually.

Compromise Bill. Udall protested Reagan's veto, arguing that the federal government should help Western states resolve water rights disputes just as it helped settle Indian claims to land in Eastern states. Concluding that the House would refuse to override the veto, Udall supported a compromise settlement negotiated by a new bargaining team that included administration and congressional representatives. To win its approval Udall refused to go to conference on a separate measure (S 539) raising acreage limits on farms irrigated with federal project water until he got a resolution of the Papago dispute. The Reagan administration and Western state congressional delegations were pushing for action on the reclamation law reform measure. *(Reclamation, p. 431)*

Congress finally incorporated the compromise Papago settlement, along with reclamation acreage limit changes, into a third bill (S 1409) authorizing funds to enlarge the Buffalo Bill Dam and Reservoir in Wyoming. Cleared on Sept. 29, the final version of S 1409 (H Rept 97-855) authorized a total of $39.8 million for the Papago settlement, although much of that amount would be held in a special Treasury trust fund. Net outlays for the first year after enactment would be $9.75 million.

Ocean Dumping

Congress in 1982 imposed a two-year moratorium on Navy plans to dump low-level radioactive wastes in ocean waters.

The Senate, however, never took up broader House-passed legislation (HR 6113) to strengthen Environmental Protection Agency (EPA) control over the disposal of any waste materials off the nation's coastlines.

In 1981 Congress did grant the Reagan administration's request to double authorized fiscal 1982 spending for EPA efforts to identify potential sites where dredged materials, sewage sludge and industrial wastes could be safely dumped without disrupting marine environments.

Background. Congress in 1972 banned unregulated ocean dumping when it passed the Marine Protection, Research and Sanctuaries Act (PL 92-532). In 1977 Congress amended the law to prohibit municipal sewage treatment plants from dumping leftover sludge in ocean waters, a practice followed by large cities including New York City, Philadelphia and Camden, N.J. The 1977 measure set a Dec. 31, 1981, deadline for ending ocean disposal of sludge that environmentalists contended contaminated waters with potentially lethal cadmium, mercury and other metals. Congress renewed the deadline in 1980 and extended it to prohibit industrial waste dumping as well. *(Congress and the Nation Vol. III, p. 798; Congress and the Nation Vol. V, pp. 541, 594)*

The 1972 law authorized EPA to issue permits for the ocean dumping of waste materials, but only if it determined that dumping would not harm the marine environment or endanger public health. The permit must specify the type and quantity of material to be dumped, how long it could be dumped and where it was to be dumped. The law allowed, but did not require, EPA to designate sites for such dumping.

In January 1977 EPA designated 140 historically used dump sites for interim use while it conducted the required studies. The studies dragged on, and in 1980 the National Wildlife Federation sued EPA to challenge the continued authorization of dumping at unstudied or interim sites. The suit was settled in September 1980 with an agreement that required EPA to finish its studies and act on 48 of the most heavily used sites by March 1983.

1981 Action. To meet the court-approved schedule EPA in 1981 asked Congress to double its fiscal 1982 authorization for identifying possible ocean dumping sites. Congress granted the request in June by passing legislation (S 1213 — PL 97-16) that increased the authorization for the program to $4.2 million from the $2 million provided by the 1980 measure.

1982 House Legislation. The House followed up in 1982 by passing a bill (HR 6113) prodding EPA to move ahead with dump site selections. As passed by the House Sept. 20, HR 6113 made the site designation mandatory, not discretionary. It gave the agency six months to draw up a schedule for site designations and gave citizens the right to sue to force EPA to stick to its schedule.

The House ocean dumping bill reflected a compromise between the Merchant Marine and Fisheries Committee and the Public Works and Transportation Committee designed to balance environmental concerns against the need for ocean disposal sites for dredge spoil from coastal harbors and waterways. Merchant Marine reported the measure May 17; Public Works followed suit July 29 (H Rept 97-562, Parts I and II).

Radioactive Wastes. The Senate never approved HR 6113. But in the last days of the 1982 session Congress split off provisions from the House bill that barred radioactive waste dumping in oceans and passed them as part of highway/gasoline tax legislation (HR 6211 — PL 97-424) cleared Dec. 23. *(Story, p. 301)*

Those provisions imposed a two-year moratorium on ocean dumping of low-level radioactive wastes to give Congress time to review Navy proposals to scuttle decommissioned nuclear submarines, sinking them to the seabed floor. Navy officials also proposed dumping contaminated

soils produced by the Manhattan Project, the World War II program that developed the first nuclear bomb.

Opposed by environmentalists, the sub-scuttling proposal heated up in 1982 as Glen Sjoblom, who advocated the program for the Navy, was appointed head of EPA's radiation office.

The only exception to the moratorium allowed was for research-related dumping, and even that would have to meet elaborate safeguards against environmental risks and receive approval of both House and Senate in a joint resolution.

Seabed Mining

Congress in 1982 extended temporary federal regulation of deep seabed mining operations by U.S. industry.

In 1980 Congress had opened the way for U.S. mining companies to explore the ocean floor under federal government supervision while an international seabed mining treaty was being negotiated. The United Nations approved the resulting Law of the Sea Treaty on April 30, 1982, but the Reagan administration refused to sign it.

U.S. mining companies feared the treaty would deprive them of returns from the lead American industry held in technology for extracting minerals from the seabed floor. The treaty, signed by 117 nations in Jamaica Dec. 10, 1982, declared seabed resources to be the "common heritage of mankind." It established a global authority to regulate seabed mining and a global enterprise to which private mining companies would be required to sell their technology.

Background

At stake were rights to develop an estimated 1.5 trillion tons of potato-sized nodules containing manganese, copper, cobalt and nickel. The rocks lay beneath the high seas, far from any nation's territorial waters. The technology for recovering them was expensive and complicated, but feasible enough to arouse commercial interest.

In 1978 the United States had imported $2.4 billion worth of those metals, much of it from politically unstable nations. Those minerals, especially cobalt, manganese and nickel, were considered strategic or critical minerals for the United States because industry used them to make alloys that were essential in building advanced military aircraft and weapons, as well as in other manufacturing technologies.

Mining industry leaders maintained that the nation could develop seabed nodules as a substitute for undependable and costly foreign imports. But the Law of the Sea Conference, which began negotiating the treaty in 1973, cast doubt on whether U.S. industry could expect to reap financial benefits from expensive exploration efforts to find seabed deposits. A 1970 United Nations resolution, agreed to by the U.S. government, guided the conference by declaring that seabed resources were the "common heritage of mankind." Developing countries insisted during conference negotiations that the "common heritage" principle entitled them to a share of seabed riches.

To guarantee the security of exploration investments, mining companies in the 1970s asked Congress to pass legislation that would put the federal government's stamp of approval on their exploratory programs. Despite Carter administration misgivings, Congress in 1980 finally ap-

proved a measure (PL 96-283) that authorized exploration but barred commercial development of seabed minerals before 1988.

The law gave the National Oceanic and Atmospheric Administration (NOAA), a Commerce Department agency, authority to grant licenses for seabed exploration, subject to regulations to protect the ocean environment and recognize freedom of the seas for other nations. The law delayed commercial development so U.S. companies could comply with subsequent international rules if a treaty were completed by 1988. If no treaty were signed, the law provided for federal regulation of mineral extraction starting that year. *(Congress and the Nation Vol. V, p. 588)*

1982 Legislation

Although the Law of the Sea Conference had produced a treaty, Congress in 1982 reauthorized NOAA regulation for fiscal 1983 and 1984 after the U.S. government found the international agreement unacceptable.

The Senate Dec. 19 approved without amendment a House-passed measure (HR 6120 — PL 97-416) that authorized $1.5 million in fiscal 1983 and $2.2 million in fiscal 1984 to carry out NOAA's seabed mining program. Under the 1980 law and its reauthorization, NOAA held responsibility to develop regulations and issue licenses for seabed mineral exploration and commercial recovery. The agency was also responsible for protecting the environment, conserving seabed resources and assuring the safety of life and property in relation to seabed mining.

NOAA was to participate in negotiations with other countries that had seabed minerals programs, seeking to win recognition of U.S. licenses in return for U.S. recognition of their licenses.

Other Legislation

Oil Spill Liability

Congress in 1982 considered placing a $75 million limit on oil company liability stemming from spills from offshore drilling operations.

The House Dec. 13 passed by voice vote legislation (HR 5906) to clarify financial responsibility for damages and cleanup costs caused by offshore drilling accidents. The Senate never acted on the measure.

In a 1978 law revising Interior Department procedures for leasing federal Outer Continental Shelf (OCS) oil and gas reserves (PL 95-372), Congress set up a fund financed by a tax on offshore oil to compensate persons who were economically damaged by oil spills into coastal waters. The fund in turn could sue offshore drilling firms responsible for the spill. The 1978 law set a $35 million limit on personal damages, but it left offshore rig operators with unlimited liability for the costs of cleaning up the oil spilled into coastal waters and beaches.

To give the industry more certainty about the upper limit of costs a company could incur from a spill, the House bill set a total limit of $75 million for both damages and cleanup costs. The measure also sought to spell out clearly whether companies holding offshore leases, drilling contractors, pipeline owners and vessel operators could be held responsible for spills. The Coast Guard had interpreted the 1978 law as holding drilling contractors responsible but leaving leaseholders free from liability.

Federal Water Policy

The House-passed bill imposed a general liability on the leaseholder but spelled out conditions under which other companies involved in an offshore operation could be held accountable. The House Merchant Marine Committee reported the measure Sept. 23 (H Rept 97-861). There was no comparable Senate bill.

Marine Sanctuaries

Congress in 1981 reauthorized federal protection for marine sanctuaries off the nation's coastlines.

On Dec. 14 Congress cleared a bill (S 1003 — PL 97-109) continuing a Commerce Department program, launched in 1972, that designated environmentally sensitive offshore areas as sanctuaries to be preserved for conservation, recreation and esthetic values. The measure authorized $2.2 million in both fiscal 1982 and fiscal 1983 for the program, which was established by the Marine Protection, Research and Sanctuaries Act of 1972. The law also provided federal controls on waste dumping in ocean waters. *(Congress and the Nation Vol. III, p. 798; ocean dumping legislation, p. 436)*

The marine sanctuary program was similar to such on-land programs as the National Park System and the National Forest System. To date, six areas had been designated as marine sanctuaries — two off the Florida coast, two off the California coast and one each off the North Carolina and Georgia coasts.

Project Deauthorizations

Taking an unusual step, Congress Dec. 16 cleared legislation (S 1493 — PL 97-128) that rescinded about $2 billion in previously approved authorizations for 13 federal water projects. The deauthorization measure killed funding for half of the Dickey-Lincoln project, a controversial dam in northern Maine.

In deauthorizing the projects, Congress pared back only a modest portion of the $58.6 billion backlog of water development projects that previous Congresses had approved.

The Senate cleared the bill when it accepted amendments, added by the House during Nov. 23 debate, to allow persons to keep houseboats, cabins and docks on Army Corps of Engineers lake-front property until Dec. 31, 1989. The corps had been trying to force the owners to remove them. The Senate initially had passed S 1493, reported by its Environment and Public Works Committee (S Rept 97-270), on Nov. 18.

Urgent Reclamation Repairs

Congress in 1982 gave the Bureau of Reclamation authority to use emergency dam repair funds for municipal and industrial water supply projects.

The House Sept. 20 cleared legislation (S 1628 — PL 97-275) that made a bureau emergency repair fund set up in 1948 available to correct problems on any bureau project. In addition, the measure authorized use of the fund for facilities built under the Small Reclamation Projects Act of 1956 and the Distribution Systems Loan Act of 1956.

Congress set up the emergency fund in 1948 to finance emergency repairs on irrigation or electric power generating facilities that were built as part of Bureau of Reclamation water projects. While many federal reclamation dams were built primarily to store irrigation water and generate electric power, those projects also provided important water supplies for Western cities and industries.

The Senate passed S 1628, making the emergency fund available for municipal and industrial water projects, on May 10 (S Rept 97-363). The House approved the bill on Sept. 20 (H Rept 97-769).

WEB Pipeline

Congress in 1982 approved a pipeline and several water project studies to compensate South Dakota for farmland flooded by federal water developments along the Missouri River.

Agreeing to Senate amendments, the House Sept. 23 cleared legislation (HR 4347 — PL 97-273) that authorized construction of the proposed WEB pipeline. The project was designed to pipe water to 30,000 residents in rural South Dakota, in partial compensation for 540,000 acres that the federally funded Pick-Sloan flood control and power project had flooded in the state since 1944.

The bill authorized several studies of potential water developments to provide additional compensation. They included alternative uses for the Oahe irrigation project, a partially completed federal project that local opposition halted in 1977 after the government had spent $41 million on construction.

Under an agreement with the Carter administration, authorization of the WEB project depended on deauthorization of the Oahe project, estimated to cost as much as $900 million, by Sept. 30, 1981. Congress did not deauthorize Oahe, but the Reagan administration no longer insisted on this linkage. HR 4347 was expected to have the effect of blocking further construction on Oahe, but it did not formally deauthorize the project.

1983-84

Despite continued concern about the costs, Congress in 1983-84 made few changes in federal water development and pollution control programs.

Neither Congress nor the Reagan administration pushed hard for fundamental changes in federal water programs. The Democratic House in 1984 did pass a flurry of water legislation, but the Republican Senate sidetracked measures that the White House objected would make unacceptable commitments for future federal spending.

As a result, Congress failed to clear proposals to revise the Clean Water Act of 1977 or to toughen federal drinking water standards. With members and the administration split over forcing beneficiaries to share part of the cost, Congress again was unable to agree on launching expensive new projects for flood control, navigation, irrigation or electric power generation.

Setting a possible precedent for cost sharing on future development, the House and Senate in 1984 agreed to charge Westerners for part of the cost of repairing old or decaying federally built dams that were in danger of collapsing. But despite environmental group objections, Congress continued to fund previously approved water development projects. The House and Senate also insisted, over Reagan's veto, on continuing federal financial support for state water research programs.

Clean Water

Congress in 1983-84 again put off revising the federal water pollution control program.

The Clean Water Act of 1977 gave the Environmental Protection Agency (EPA) broad powers to regulate polluted discharges into the nation's lakes and rivers. Industry and environmentalists generally recognized that the law could stand some improvement, but neither the Reagan administration nor Congress gave clean water legislation much priority in the 1983 and 1984 sessions.

The House in 1984 did pass a compromise bill that offered concessions to environmental groups, industry and municipal sewage treatment program officials. But the administration objected to its potential cost, and the Senate never took up its own less expensive version.

Congressional deliberations on water pollution issues were relatively low key, in contrast to frequently angry clashes on proposals to combat acid rain and strengthen the Clean Air Act of 1970.

Some U.S. lakes and rivers had been dramatically cleaned up since the Water Pollution Control Act of 1972 went into effect, although there was little evidence that overall national water quality was improving. Congress revised and renamed the law in the Clean Water Act of 1977. But industry protested the law's "technology based standards," while municipal governments and local developers wanted increased federal assistance for sewage system construction. Although some environmentalists acknowledged that parts of the law were working poorly, they resisted major changes in the existing Clean Water Act that might endorse the Reagan administration's drive to reduce EPA authority to regulate pollution by industry.

Congress in 1981 had yielded to President Reagan's demand for major cutbacks in EPA grants under the 1972 law for municipal sewage treatment facilities. But to environmentalists' relief, the White House never followed up by challenging the basic strategy that the Clean Water Act set for cleaning up polluted waters. EPA in 1982 sent Congress a "wish list" for extending deadlines and easing requirements that industry, particularly chemical manufacturers, found burdensome. But Anne M. Gorsuch, then EPA administrator, signaled Congress that clean water legislation ranked low on the administration's environmental agenda by declaring the existing law "fundamentally sound as it stands without need for major or extensive revision at this time." *(1981-82 action on sewage treatment grants, p. 425)*

With little administration pressure for action, Congress moved slowly in debating clean water issues. Authorizations for spending to carry out part of the Clean Water Act expired in 1982, but Congress continued to fund enforcement through annual appropriations bills.

1983 Senate Committee Bills

In 1983 the Senate Environment and Public Works Committee drafted two measures extending the Clean Water Act and adjusting some provisions. Although the measures made few changes in existing law, neither reached the Senate floor in 1983 or 1984.

The Senate panel Sept. 21 reported a clean water reauthorization bill (S 431 — S Rept 98-233), drafted by John H. Chafee, chairman of its Subcommittee on Environmental Pollution, that amounted to a minor tuneup instead of a major overhaul of the 1972 law. The committee fol-

lowed up Oct. 26 by reporting a second bill (S 2006 — S Rept 98-282) that dealt with one controversial area by attempting to prod quicker action to control pollution produced by water running off farm lands, streets and other "non-point" sources. Both measures were reported by unanimous votes.

S 431 reauthorized Clean Water Act enforcement for four years, at slightly higher spending levels, and extended various deadlines for complying with EPA standards. It granted a Reagan administration proposal to extend the term of EPA pollution discharge permits for industry from five years to 10 years.

During markups on S 431 Dave Durenberger, R-Minn., withdrew a proposal to strengthen federal controls on "non-point" water pollution carried into lakes and streams by water running off farms, mines, construction sites and city streets. Although the Clean Water Act directed states to draw up land use plans to control polluted runoff, EPA had given the program low priority.

In reporting S 2006, however, the Senate committee recommended legislation authorizing $300 million over fiscal 1985-87 in grants for state planning to control non-point pollution.

House Legislation

The legislation the House passed in 1984 would have more than doubled authorized spending levels for EPA water pollution programs to more than $24 billion for fiscal 1985-88. For fiscal 1985 the measure (HR 3282) set a total spending ceiling of $6.2 billion, up from $2.6 billion under existing law. Responding to Reagan's demand for budget restraints, Congress in 1981 had cut annual authorizations for sewage treatment construction grants from $5 billion to $2.4 billion. In HR 3282, however, the House approved incremental increases in sewage grants that, in combination with a new $1.6 billion state-run revolving loan program, would restore total support for sewage construction to $5 billion a year by fiscal 1986-88.

While welcoming expanded funding, environmental groups opposed the legislation as reported by the House Public Works and Transportation Committee on June 6 (H Rept 98-827). Ed Hopkins, a lobbyist for the Clean Water Action Project, an environmental group, said the committee in effect was trying to reverse a number of reforms that Congress made in the construction grants program in 1981. Among other things, the panel made new "collector" sewer lines under residential streets eligible for grants, conferring what environmentalists regarded as a subsidy for new housing developments that could further overload municipal sewage treatment capacity.

The House passed HR 3282 by a 405-11 vote on June 26. Before passing the bill, however, the House adopted a substitute to the committee measure offered by Robert A. Roe, D-N.J., chairman of the Public Works Subcommittee on Water Resources, with support from committee leaders. Roe's amendment embodied a compromise, concluded June 20, that defused most of the environmental groups' objections to the committee legislation. Although some opponents remained dissatisfied, the final House bill offered concessions to most groups with interests at stake in the water pollution program.

The House rejected an attempt to remove a committee-approved deadline for New York City to limit the discharge of raw sewage into the Hudson River. Members from neighboring New Jersey had sought the deadline.

Safe Drinking Water

Congress in 1984 was unsuccessful in late-session efforts to impose tougher federal standards for drinking water purity.

In the last weeks of the session the House Sept. 18 approved legislation to spur the Environmental Protection Agency (EPA) into more aggressive enforcement of the Safe Drinking Water Act of 1974. The House-passed bill (HR 5959), a compromise among industry and environmental groups, also set up a $50-million-a-year program to force state governments to prevent contamination of groundwater formations that supplied half of the nation's drinking water supplies.

But the White House Office of Management and Budget (OMB) opposed the bill, objecting both to the cost of expanding EPA regulation and to the precedent of federal control over state groundwater management programs. The Senate Environment and Public Works Committee drafted a less ambitious bill (S 2649) as the session drew to a close, but House and Senate negotiators were unable to agree on compromise legislation that all sides could accept before the 98th Congress adjourned.

Background

The Safe Drinking Water Act (PL 93-523) empowered EPA to set national purity standards for drinking water systems, to be enforced by the states or directly by the agency if states did not do so. The national standards were to be based on recommendations by the National Academy of Sciences about what levels of pollution were acceptable if human health were the only consideration. EPA was to adjust these ideal levels to take feasibility and cost into account.

Implementation of this ambitious scheme lagged for several reasons. The academy, in 1977, declined to say how much of any given contaminant could be considered safe. The modestly funded water program was not always a top EPA priority, and agency efforts during the Carter administration to move ahead aggressively on several fronts were battered in court actions.

Rep. Dennis E. Eckart, D-Ohio, a cosponsor of the 1984 legislation, said he had learned that "you can lead the EPA to water but you can't make them regulate it." The bill, he added, "will make them do it."

House Legislation

Key members of the House Energy and Commerce Subcommittee on Health and the Environment drafted HR 5959 in private sessions with environmentalists and water industry officials. Subcommittee Chairman Henry A. Waxman, D-Calif., said EPA officials consulted on technical questions during negotiations had been "quite sympathetic to our position" on tighter drinking water standards.

Reported by the full Energy and Commerce Committee by voice vote on Sept. 18 (H Rept 98-1034), HR 5959 imposed specific deadlines for EPA to set drinking water quality standards. The measure gave EPA expanded power to order compliance with the standards and required the agency to monitor water quality more frequently. Another major section barred injection of toxic wastes above or into underground aquifers holding drinking water supplies. HR 5959 directed states to adopt EPA-approved plans for preventing contamination in underground drinking water sup-

plies. It authorized $35 million in matching grants for state and local programs to protect aquifers that served as the sole source of drinking water for entire towns or regions.

The House Sept. 18 passed HR 5959, by a 366-27 vote, as members shrugged off administration opposition to the bill.

Senate Compromise Negotiations

Senate Environment and Public Works Committee members drafted their own version in an effort to skirt OMB objections to the House bill. Reported on Sept. 28 (S Rept 98-641), S 2649 also set deadlines for EPA standards, strengthened enforcement powers, expanded monitoring and barred injection of hazardous wastes near drinking water supplies.

But the Senate committee dropped House provisions requiring states to launch groundwater protection programs and settled for a $15 million-a-year demonstration program for keeping sole-source aquifers pure. It also reworded language in several provisions that House sponsors had drafted to limit EPA's discretion or make it easier for the agency to take action against pollution. Environmental groups disliked the Senate proposal and Waxman declared that "I'd rather have no bill at all."

Through informal negotiations House and Senate sponsors worked out most differences by Oct. 4. But Waxman refused to agree to a Senate amendment, backed by Alan K. Simpson, R-Wyo., that allowed a court decision on drinking water regulations to be appealed to the U.S. appeals court in the region where the dispute arose. Existing law required that such appeals be heard by the federal appeals court in Washington, D.C. Waxman and Sen. Max Baucus, D-Mont., also rejected a demand by Sen. Steven D. Symms, R-Idaho, to retain existing law by dropping stronger health-related language for setting water purity standards that appeared in both the House bill and the compromise proposal.

Lobbyists for environmentalists expressed regret at losing the legislation but claimed that both the judicial review amendment and existing health standards would cause lengthy delays in setting national drinking water standards. Such delays, they said, would defeat the basic purpose of the legislation, which was to force quick standard setting by EPA.

Water Projects/Cost Sharing

Congress in 1983-84 again fell short in its drive to launch new federal water development projects.

Constrained by economic and environmental concerns, Congress had failed to pass an omnibus water projects authorization bill since 1976. It came close in 1984, but an $18 billion House-passed measure died in the closing days of the session.

Ever since President Carter in 1977 tried to cancel a "hit list" of previously approved projects, Congress had been struggling to justify funding to start new irrigation, flood control, navigation and other water project construction. Environmentalists challenged federal dam building programs that they contended wasted scarce water while ruining fish and wildlife habitat. Economists meanwhile questioned whether economic benefits from costly projects justified the expense to the federal taxpayers.

For four years the Reagan administration had tried to

come up with a "cost-sharing" formula acceptable to Congress that would weed out the most wasteful projects by requiring local governments or water users to pick up more of the construction costs. Protests by powerful Republican senators from the water-short West in 1983 headed off President Reagan's approval of a uniform government cost-sharing policy.

The House in 1984 approved tougher cost-sharing requirements when it passed an $18 billion omnibus bill authorizing the Army Corps of Engineers and the Interior Department's Bureau of Reclamation to start building more than 300 dams, locks, levees, harbor improvements and other water development and conservation projects (HR 3678 — H Rept 98-616, Parts I-IV). In the Senate, however, differences among three committees on cost sharing and other issues thwarted a time agreement allowing floor action on an $11 billion water projects authorization.

After waiting nearly four years for an authorization bill to settle on a cost-sharing plan, the House late in the 1984 session tried to tack funding for new projects onto a fiscal 1985 continuing appropriations measure. Despite last-minute negotiations, the Senate abandoned the effort after David A. Stockman, director of the White House Office of Management and Budget, opposed legislation funding any water projects until Congress approved basic cost-sharing reforms.

Background

The Army Corps of Engineers, the Bureau of Reclamation and the U.S. Soil Conservation Service (SCS), an Agriculture Department agency, built or maintained water projects in nearly every congressional district. The corps and SCS operated throughout the nation, but the bureau served only 17 Western states. The SCS primarily helped farmers and ranchers build small dams and other facilities to curb soil erosion, but the corps and bureau built and operated huge projects that often served multiple purposes, including irrigation, flood control, recreation and electric power generation.

These projects provided tangible economic benefits: municipal and industrial water supply, hydroelectric power, ports and waterways for shipping, irrigation water for farmers, recreational lakes, flood protection — and, in some cases, fish and wildlife habitat.

No less tangible were the political benefits available to members of Congress who could deliver such projects to their districts.

Since the early 1970s, however, funding for new projects had slowed to a fraction of what it was in the 1950s and 1960s and Congress had not approved an omnibus water projects authorization bill since 1976. President Ford signed that law authorizing $742 million worth of planning, design and construction in 36 states only weeks before the 1976 election. *(Congress and the Nation Vol. IV, p. 316)*

Even without new projects, however, the backlog of unfinished water projects, plus those authorized but not yet funded, approached $50 billion in value. Appropriations for the corps, reclamation bureau and SCS actually rose in nominal dollars during the 1970s, but most funds were going to finish projects already under construction and to maintain and operate existing facilities.

By the early 1980s members of Congress, state and local officials, farmers, barge operators, shipping companies and numerous other interests, especially in the South and West, were eager for approval of new project "starts."

The East and the Midwest were demanding federal assistance to replace or repair crumbling municipal water systems in older cities and other water facilities.

Cost-Sharing Debate

Reagan was expected to push for new starts after defeating Carter in 1980 with solid support in Western states. But Reagan's administration was slow to develop a clear policy for selecting and financing new projects. Administration officials were determined to force state and local beneficiaries to assume a far greater share of the costs, but the White House also worried about the political fallout in Reagan's Western stronghold.

The administration in May 1982 proposed fiscal 1983 funding to start nine new projects where state and local sponsors had agreed voluntarily to pay a greater share of costs than had historically been the case. But members of Congress saw the projects as a stalking horse for a controversial cost-sharing policy and the House and Senate Appropriations committees refused to approve the funds.

In June 1982 Reagan's Cabinet Council on Natural Resources and the Environment began considering a comprehensive proposal to drastically increase state and local funding requirements on all federal water projects. The policy at issue called for a 100 percent non-federal share in financing of hydropower and both municipal and industrial water supply, a 50 percent non-federal share for recreation and a 35 percent non-federal share for flood control and irrigation. Under existing laws cost-sharing rates differed from project to project and agency to agency.

The new policy would have required beneficiaries to pay a major share of project costs — and pay "up front," while projects were being built. Up-front local payment would have cut out the hefty hidden subsidy that resulted from the artificially low interest rates the federal government used to calculate local paybacks.

Joined by the White House Office of Management and Budget (OMB), Corps of Engineers officials pushed throughout 1983 for administration approval of a uniform cost-sharing formula that would apply both to the corps projects throughout the nation and to Bureau of Reclamation projects in the West. But Interior officials balked at a uniform policy, maintaining that the government should negotiate cost-sharing agreements separately for each project, taking into account the beneficiaries' ability to pay. Led by Sen. Paul Laxalt, R-Nev., a close Reagan friend, senators from Western states wrote the president in 1983 to warn against "an up-front financing scheme even more Draconian" than one proposed by the Carter administration. Reagan in January 1984 finally rejected any fixed cost-sharing formula in a letter that Secretary of the Interior William P. Clark personally delivered to Laxalt.

House Authorization Measure

The House in 1984 passed an $18 billion omnibus water projects bill that Robert A. Roe, D-N.J., chairman of the Public Works Subcommittee on Water Resources, had carefully put together a year earlier.

In Roe's bill, "omnibus" translated roughly as "something for everybody." HR 3678 contained provisions that offered cherished objectives to environmentalists, OMB budget-cutters and advocates of water policy reforms. Bringing the urban Northeast into a fraternity controlled by committee chairmen from Sun Belt states, the measure

set up a new $800 million yearly loan program for rehabilitating aging municipal water supply systems.

At its core, however, HR 3678 tried to revive the old-fashioned pork barrel politics by which Congress had always distributed water project benefits among its members' states and districts. As drafted by Roe's subcommittee, the bill ran close to 300 pages and authorized more than 280 specific projects, including at least 60 that modified previously approved plans. Roe's proposal caused some qualms in the Reagan administration. Not only did it authorize new spending not contained in the president's budget, but it also required state and local governments to pay a far smaller share of project costs than the administration had sought. In addition, the bill set up a seven-member national water policy board, independent from existing agencies, to coordinate water development goals. The administration had abolished the Water Resources Council, an earlier coordinating body and opposed congressional demands for a board that would include members appointed by Congress. *(Water board dispute, 1981-82 chronology, p. 428)*

Committee Action. Roe's subcommittee approved HR 3678 by voice vote on July 29, 1983, two days after the chairman introduced it, and the full Public Works panel accepted it by a 49-0 vote on Aug. 3. The Public Works Committee formally reported HR 3678 March 8, 1984, and four other House committees approved the measure during the week of April 9 (H Rept 98-616, Parts I-IV).

The House Merchant Marine and Fisheries Committee made the most significant changes in Roe's measure. It approved an amendment to set up a "fast track" permit process and federal loan guarantees for local costs in port development projects.

House Floor Action. The House passed HR 3678 by a 259-33 vote on June 29, 1984. After an intense debate that divided the Florida delegation, the House defeated by a 201-204 vote a proposal by E. Clay Shaw Jr., R-Fla., to deauthorize the partially completed Cross-Florida Barge Canal. The canal was one-third finished, but Congress had stopped providing construction funds nearly a decade earlier.

The administration and environmental groups both backed an amendment by Thomas E. Petri, R-Wis., to toughen Roe's cost-sharing proposals. But the House rejected, by an 85-213 margin, Petri's proposal to require local beneficiaries to pay part of their share "up front" during construction.

Senate Committee Differences

Three Senate committees in 1983-84 reported an $11 billion water projects authorization bill (S 1739). Unable to resolve their differences, committee leaders never took the measure to the floor.

The Senate Environment and Public Works Committee and the Senate Energy and Natural Resources Committee took fundamentally different stands on water policy reforms. The Environment panel held jurisdiction over the Corps of Engineers water development projects, most of which were built in the East; the Energy Committee dealt with authorizations for the Bureau of Reclamation, which operated only in the West. Reflecting differences between the corps and bureau over cost-sharing policy, the Environment Committee sought uniform repayment guidelines for most federal projects while Energy in effect insisted on a separate policy for bureau projects in arid Western states.

The Environment Committee reported S 1739 (S Rept 98-340) by a 14-2 vote on Nov. 17, 1983. The measure, approved by the panel's Water Resources Subcommittee on Sept. 20, hewed more closely than the House measure did to the administration's tentative cost-sharing approach. But it eased the administration's proposal to require local beneficiaries to pay their entire cash shares up front. The Environment bill also set up a National Board on Water Resources Policy.

But the Energy panel exempted the Bureau of Reclamation from those policies in reporting S 1739 on April 26, 1984 (S Rept 98-418). By a 10-8 vote the Energy Committee removed bureau projects from the proposed board's jurisdiction. And by voice vote the committee exempted bureau projects from the bill's cost-sharing requirements. The Senate Finance Committee also considered S 1739 and reported the measure on June 8 (S Rept 98-509).

Appropriations Committee Maneuvers

The House and Senate Appropriations committees meanwhile grew impatient waiting for the administration and authorizing committees to settle the cost-sharing debate. As they had for several years, the Appropriations committees took a stand of "no new starts" through regular appropriations measures until Congress had approved corps and bureau authorizations. In its fiscal 1985 budget the Reagan administration in 1984 proposed $50 million for 19 new projects where beneficiaries stood ready to share costs, but congressional panels objected to ranking on that basis.

In 1983 and again in 1984, however, the House and Senate Appropriations panels did recommend funding for some new starts in supplemental and continuing funding measures. While waiting for action on an authorization bill, the Appropriations committees in 1983 packaged some proposed new starts into a supplemental funding bill. The House passed its version (HR 3958), providing $119 million for 43 new projects, and the Senate Appropriations Committee approved a $78 million version for 27 projects, but action was never completed.

In September 1984 the House committee finally added the House-passed package of new starts, by then expanded to $139 million, to a fiscal 1985 continuing resolution (H J Res 648). In passing the resolution on Sept. 25, the full House not only approved appropriations for the new starts but also tacked on HR 3678, the omnibus authorization bill. On the same day, the Senate Appropriations Committee approved a continuing resolution providing $82.9 million for new starts but no authorization package.

But the Senate Oct. 4 rejected a compromise authorization amendment as non-germane to the continuing resolution. Senate Appropriations Committee Chairman Mark O. Hatfield, R-Ore., then tried to negotiate an agreement with the White House on a compromise providing funds for some new starts. But conferees reluctantly dropped all authorizations and new start appropriations after OMB Director Stockman wrote Hatfield to oppose funding any new projects before Congress voted cost-sharing reforms.

Water Project Appropriations

Congress in 1983-84 continued to appropriate funds for federal water projects, already under construction, that environmental groups wanted to halt.

Joined by fiscal conservatives, environmentalist members in the House challenged continued funding for controversial water projects in North Dakota and West Virginia. But influential senators from those states restored appropriations to allow federal water development agencies to keep construction under way.

In drawing up fiscal 1984 and fiscal 1985 energy and water development appropriations bills, Congress provided no funding for "new starts" to launch construction of planned water projects. The House and Senate Appropriations committees instead waited for the Reagan administration and congressional authorizing committees to settle a continuing dispute over "cost-sharing" arrangements to require regions that would benefit from new projects to pay part of "up-front" construction costs. *(Water projects debate, p. 440)*

Congress nonetheless appropriated $3.6 billion in fiscal 1984 and $3.8 billion in fiscal 1985 for the Army Corps of Engineers and the Bureau of Reclamation to continue construction and maintain previously authorized hydropower, flood control, irrigation and inland waterway projects. Those measures provided no additional appropriations for the Tennessee-Tombigbee Waterway, a controversial project designed to carry barge traffic from the Tennessee River to the Gulf of Mexico through Mississippi and Alabama. But $180 million in unspent funds carried over from the fiscal 1983 appropriation provided sufficient financing to essentially complete construction of the project's navigation features. *(Background, 1981-82 water appropriations, p. 433)*

In both 1983 and 1984 the Senate forced the House to accept appropriations to continue construction of the Garrison Diversion, a $1.1 billion system of aqueducts and irrigation canals in North Dakota. To keep the project going, however, the North Dakota delegation in 1984 had to negotiate a compromise with environmentalists that set up a special commission to study redesigning the project to reduce threats to wetlands, waterfowl and fish both in the state and in Canada.

Despite an unusual split within the West Virginia delegation, Congress in 1983 also maintained funding for the Stonewall Jackson Dam in that state. Breaking with congressional "pork barrel" traditions, Rep. Bob Wise, D-W.Va., persuaded the House to delete $26 million that the House Appropriations Committee had recommended for a project that was being built in his own district. Led by Senate Minority Leader Robert C. Byrd, D-W.Va., however, the rest of the state's delegation convinced House-Senate conferees to restore the funds in the final water projects appropriations.

Fiscal 1984 Energy/Water Appropriations

Congress in 1983 cleared a fiscal 1984 energy and water appropriations bill providing $2.6 billion for the Corps of Engineers and $961.7 million for the Bureau of Reclamation, an Interior Department agency.

In previous years controversies over funding the Tennessee-Tombigbee project and the Department of Energy's Clinch River breeder reactor had slowed debate on the energy/water measure. But the 1983 bill provided no money for those programs, and Congress completed action by June 29 (HR 3132 — PL 98-50).

In drafting HR 3132, the House Appropriations Committee rejected the Reagan administration's request for $22.3 million in Garrison Diversion construction funds.

The Senate Appropriations Committee restored the Garrison project request, but it specified that none of those funds could be used to build parts of the project that would affect Canadian waters.

Garrison Diversion Debate. For years environmental groups and the Canadian government had opposed the Garrison Diversion. Rep. Silvio O. Conte, R-Mass., a critic of "pork barrel" water projects, in 1982 persuaded the House to kill funding for the projects; but the Senate restored the appropriations.

In drafting the fiscal 1984 energy/water appropriations bill (H Rept 98-217), the House Appropriations Committee dropped the Reagan administration's request for $22.3 million in Garrison Diversion construction funds. After the House passed HR 3132 on June 7, the Senate Appropriations Committee restored the Garrison request, although it specified that none of the funds could be used to build parts that would affect drainage into Canadian waters (S Rept 98-153). Before passing HR 3132 on June 22, the full Senate voted 62-35 to table an amendment by Gordon J. Humphrey, R-N.H., to strip out the Garrison funds.

The following day Conte attempted to "give the House conferees some backbone" by offering a motion to instruct them to insist on zero funding for the Garrison project. But anticipating Conte's tactic, Byron L. Dorgan, D-N.D., the state's single House member, had been lobbying colleagues to back funding for a project that he contended was important to the North Dakota economy. House leaders backed Dorgan's position, and the House defeated Conte's instruction motion 150-215. That vote dramatically reversed a 100-vote margin against the project in a December 1982 vote seven months earlier. Conferees retained the Garrison funds in the conference report filed June 28 (H Rept 98-272).

Stonewall Jackson Dam. As drafted by the House committee, HR 3132 appropriated $26 million for the Stonewall Jackson Dam. But Wise, a first-term Democrat with populist leanings, broke with members' customary pursuit of federal water projects for their constituents. First authorized in 1965, the project's initial cost estimate of $34 million had risen to $205 million, and Wise argued there were cheaper methods of flood control that should be considered before the dam was finished. Although every other West Virginia member backed the project, the House by a 213-161 vote on June 7 accepted Wise's proposal to delete the funds.

The Senate Appropriations panel restored the Stonewall Jackson request. With Wise in the audience during House-Senate negotiations, conferees accepted the Senate funds after Byrd extolled the project's virtues. Despite his assault on the dam, Wise won re-election in 1984 with 69 percent of the vote in a safely Democratic district.

Fiscal 1985 Appropriations

Congress in 1984 again moved relatively speedily in approving a regular fiscal 1985 energy/water bill. Cleared by June 28, that bill (HR 5653 — PL 98-360) appropriated $2.8 billion for the corps and nearly $1.1 billion for the bureau.

The corps built, operated and maintained water projects throughout the nation, but mainly in the East. The bureau operated only in 17 Western states. The Senate, with more representation for sparsely populated Western states than in the House, generally shifted funds from the corps to the bureau in considering annual appropriations.

Garrison Controversy. The House Appropriations Committee again omitted Garrison funds from its fiscal 1985 recommendations (HR 5653 — H Rept 98-755), passed by the House on May 22, but proponents counted on the Senate to keep the project alive. As expected, the Senate panel approved the administration's full $53.6 million request for Garrison construction (S Rept 98-502).

Before the Senate committee marked up HR 5653, Mark Andrews, R-N.D., a member of the panel, negotiated a compromise with environmental groups that defused the perennial Garrison project controversy, at least for 1984. The compromise, adopted by voice vote on the Senate floor on June 21, directed the secretary of the interior to appoint a 12-member commission to study alternative ways to supply North Dakota's water needs with less damage to wildlife. If eight members agreed on a redesigned project, the compromise would fund that version. House conferees accepted the compromise as part of the final measure (H Rept 98-866).

Western Dam Repairs

Congress in 1984 agreed to charge local beneficiaries for 15 percent of the cost of repairing aging and faulty federal dams in the West.

Settling a four-year controversy over cost-sharing arrangements, Congress Aug. 10 cleared legislation (HR 1652 — PL 98-404) that authorized $650 million in new spending on repairs by the Interior Department's Bureau of Reclamation. The House completed action on the bill by accepting a Senate compromise that required recipients of water and other benefits from the dams to repay the government for 15 percent of the costs, some at market rates of interest.

Critics of federal water project subsidies hailed the decision as an important precedent for sharing the costs of building new dams and other structures. The Reagan administration and Congress had been deliberating since 1981 over proposals to force state and local beneficiaries to pay much larger shares of water projects that the Bureau of Reclamation and U.S. Army Corps of Engineers built to promote navigation, control floods, generate electric power or supply water to farmers and cities in their regions. *(Water project bill, p. 442)*

By requiring cost sharing for dam repairs, "I believe we establish the principle that virtually no federal water investment shall be immune from cost sharing," Sen. Howard M. Metzenbaum, D-Ohio, declared.

Reversing a 1982 stand, the House in passing HR 1652 had accepted its Interior and Insular Affairs Committee's proposal that the federal government assume the full costs of repairing dams built by the Bureau of Reclamation. Chairman Morris K. Udall, D-Ariz., led Western delegations in insisting that the Treasury should be responsible for repairing safety defects in dams that had been mostly built and designed by the government.

But Metzenbaum, a critic of federal subsidies for water development projects in the West, forced Senate Energy and Natural Resources Committee Chairman James A. McClure, R-Idaho, to agree to a compromise cost-sharing plan to assure Senate approval of the dam repair funding voted by the House.

In clearing HR 1652, Congress provided the bureau with funding authority to repair about 40 dams, some built as long ago as 1911, that had been found unsafe. Well over

half of the funds could be required to repair or replace six Salt River dams upstream from Phoenix, Ariz.

Background

Concern about the safety of federally built dams in the West had grown since 1976. The Bureau of Reclamation's Teton Dam in Idaho broke that year, and the resulting floods killed 11 people and caused about $400 million in damages. By 1984 the federal government had paid out $350 million in damage claims from the Teton Dam disaster.

Congress in 1978 authorized $100 million for safety repairs on federal dams (PL 98-578). But the bureau in the following years identified additional dams needing repairs that would be more costly. The bureau had been building dams in the 17 Western states since Congress passed the Reclamation Act of 1902. Bureau officials judged 40 of the dams unsafe because of faulty or obsolete engineering designs, new forecasts that upgraded flooding or earthquake risks, or structures that had simply rusted or crumbled with age.

The House in 1982 passed a bill (HR 3108) authorizing $550 million for dam repairs after adopting an amendment imposing a cost-sharing requirement. But the Senate Energy Committee rejected the cost-sharing amendment, and the proposal died at the end of the 97th Congress. *(Box, p. 430)*

The Reagan administration meanwhile continued to debate whether to apply uniform cost-sharing policies to Bureau of Reclamation projects. In 1982 the administration had urged Congress to require beneficiaries to share the costs of dam repairs. But influential Republican senators from Western states resisted cost-sharing formulas that would apply to bureau projects in the West as well as Army Corps of Engineers projects in other regions. President Reagan reversed direction from the administration's 1982 stand by declaring that the federal government should bear the entire costs of repairing faulty dams.

House Cost-Sharing Switch

As it had in 1982, Udall's Interior Committee May 16 reported legislation authorizing dam repair funds (HR 1652 — H Rept 98-168) without any cost-sharing requirements. Environmentalists and taxpayer groups again joined in backing a floor amendment to require water users to contribute to repairs. This time, however, the House followed the administration's reversal by rejecting the proposal.

Existing law required beneficiaries to pay for routine maintenance costs on federal projects, but the Interior bill required the government to pay for any additional repairs to correct safety problems. On the House floor two members from the Northeast — Gerald B. H. Solomon, R-N.Y., a fiscal conservative, and Bob Edgar, D-Pa., an environmentalist — teamed up to offer a proposal to force beneficiaries to repay some repair costs over a 50-year period. But by a **key vote of 194-192 (R 75-73; D 119-119)**, the House March 20 instead chose a substitute offered by Abraham Kazen Jr., D-Texas, chairman of the Interior Subcommittee on Water and Power Resources, that required cost sharing only if repairing a dam produced new economic benefits. Contending that very few repair projects would provide additional economic benefits, Solomon argued that Kazen's amendment would recoup little, if any, of the government's $650-million repair bill. *(1984 key votes, p. 927)*

Senate Cost-Sharing Provision

At Metzenbaum's insistence, however, the Senate tacked on compromise cost-sharing requirements before passing HR 1652. With Metzenbaum's objections to the House bill jeopardizing Senate passage, McClure and other Western senators negotiated an agreement with the Ohio senator for sharing part of repair costs.

The compromise allocated 15 percent of the costs of repairing a dam to various users of the water and power it supplied. Existing laws generally allowed beneficiaries to pay back dam construction costs at artificially low interest rates, conferring a substantial subsidy. But the Senate compromise required most users to repay repair costs at market rates — with an exception for irrigation farmers, who could pay their share back without interest, depending on their ability to bear the cost.

Without further committee action, the Senate Aug. 9 passed HR 1652 by voice vote after adopting Metzenbaum's amendment to implement the compromise. The House Aug. 10 agreed to the Senate revisions, clearing HR 1652 for President Reagan to sign into law on Aug. 28.

Hoover Dam Power Pricing

Lawmakers in 1984 shrugged off conservationists' objections and approved a 30-year extension in low-cost rates for electric power from Hoover Dam on the Colorado River.

In a crucial test for federal power and water policy, Congress July 31 cleared legislation (S 268 — PL 98-381) that kept expiring contracts for Hoover Dam power in effect until 2017. Those contracts sold electricity to Arizona, Nevada and Southern California at bargain rates that had been computed when the federal government finished building the dam in 1937.

Before passing S 268 on May 3, the House defeated a proposal backed by conservationists that would have canceled the Hoover Dam contracts and auctioned power to the highest bidders, at current market rates. Conservationists contended that higher rates would encourage energy conservation and reduce federal deficits by producing $3.5 billion during the first 10 years in additional power revenues. But senators and representatives from Western states that benefited from low-cost federal electricity maintained that it would be unfair to boost rates that had been based on what it cost the government to build the dam that generated the power.

To complete action on S 268, the Senate was forced to invoke cloture to cut off a one-man stand by Howard M. Metzenbaum, D-Ohio, against extending existing power prices.

Background

In the Boulder Canyon Project Act of 1928, Congress authorized the U.S. Bureau of Reclamation, an Interior Department agency, to build Hoover Dam where the Colorado flowed through Boulder Canyon, on the Arizona-Nevada border near Las Vegas, Nev. The government's first massive multiple-purpose water project, the dam controlled floods, stored water for farmers and cities in the Southwest, and generated hydroelectric power for Los Angeles and other fast-growing Southern California communities. It set a precedent for other huge dams that the bureau, Army Corps of Engineers and Tennessee Valley Authority built in the following decades to spur economic growth along the Columbia, Missouri, Tennessee, upper Colorado and other major U.S. rivers.

The Boulder Canyon Project Act, like other laws authorizing subsequent dam-building projects, required farmers, municipalities, industries and electric utilities that received water or power from a dam to repay the government for construction costs attributed to those functions. Those laws all set generous terms for repayment, usually over a 50-year period, setting interest rates by methods that usually conferred substantial subsidies at taxpayer expense. The 1937 contracts accordingly set prices for power from Hoover Dam at a low level — four-tenths of 1 percent per kilowatt hour — based on construction costs and prevailing interest rates during the 1930s. By the 1980s, when the Congressional Research Service calculated the average national price for electricity at 6.5 cents per kilowatt hour, Hoover Dam electric power was one of the greatest energy bargains in the world.

Hoover Dam Precedent. Hoover Dam was one of the first major federal power projects to near the end of its 50-year payback period. Contracts allocating and setting prices for the dam's power were due to expire on May 31, 1987, and a congressional decision on whether to extend or overhaul the existing price formula set a precedent that could heavily influence future economic conditions in regions, especially the West, that depended heavily on federally built dams for water and cheap electric power.

The Reagan administration in 1981 had begun studying ways to raise power rates on federal dam projects. But the Senate, through amendments to appropriations legislation, blocked a review that delegations from big public power states in the Southeast and West feared would produce a recommendation to close federal budget deficits by raising federal power prices. *(1981-82 action, p. 434)*

House Debate

As originally passed by the Senate in 1983, S 268 (S Rept 98-137) ratified the agreement on reallocating Hoover Dam power but preserved existing prices. The House passed its own version (HR 4275 — H Rept 98-648) on May 3, 1984, by a 279-95 vote, after turning down a floor amendment to make Hoover Dam power available to the highest bidder.

Barbara Boxer, D-Calif., from the San Francisco area, led the challenge to existing power pricing. Hoover Dam contracts supplied power to Los Angeles but not to San Francisco or San Diego, California's other major cities. Boxer offered an amendment to auction power to any utility willing to bid for it at current market rates, contending that S 268 would set "Depression-era prices for a 21st-century resource." Boxer also said Congress should break up "the exclusive Hoover club" by giving utilities a chance to bid on the power for Utah, Colorado, New Mexico and the rest of California.

House Interior and Insular Affairs Committee Chairman Morris K. Udall, D-Ariz., opposed Boxer's amendment. Not only would the amendment raise prices for 11 million ratepayers who now consumed Hoover Dam power, Udall maintained, but it also would disrupt pricing arrangements for other federal projects around the country. The House defeated Boxer's amendment by a 176-214 vote.

Senate Cloture

After approving HR 4275, the House substituted its provisions for S 268 and sent that bill back to the Senate.

But Metzenbaum and other critics prepared to fight final action on the measure. They argued that low Hoover power rates discouraged energy conservation, induced industry to relocate to the Southwest from other regions, and could cost the federal Treasury $6 billion in the following 10 years.

Metzenbaum drafted amendments to shorten the contract extension period to give Congress time to study and debate the issue, but the amendments were either tabled or ruled out of order. Metzenbaum had barely begun his fight before Senate leaders, after four hours of debate, moved to invoke cloture to end the debate. The July 30 vote went down to the wire as the leadership rounded up 60 votes, the minimum required to invoke cloture. The final tally was 60-28.

Metzenbaum gave up the following day after taking a bitter parting shot at his opponents' tactics. The Senate then voted 64-34 to concur in House amendments to S 268, clearing the bill for President Reagan to sign.

In addition to extending price contracts and approving the allocation of Hoover Dam power, the measure authorized the Interior Department to expand the dam's generating capacity by 500 megawatts, more than a third of its existing capacity. The legislation required power customers to pay for improvements to the dam, estimated to cost $77 million.

Water Research Veto Override

Congress in 1984 overrode President Reagan's veto to continue federal funding for state university water research institutes.

By overriding the veto, Congress March 22 enacted legislation (S 684 — PL 98-242) authorizing $36 million a year in fiscal 1985-89 for U.S. Interior Department support for water research at land grant colleges in 50 states and some U.S. territories.

Congress first authorized federal water research support in 1964 (PL 88-379). Operating with a mix of federal and state funding, many university institutes focused their research on state or regional water problems. Massachusetts researchers had studied acid rain, Pennsylvania studied mine drainage, and New Mexico specialized in desalinization technologies for making briny groundwater in arid regions usable for irrigation.

Arguing that states should finance those programs, Reagan had proposed ending federal financial support in his budget proposals for fiscal 1982 through 1985. But Congress kept the program alive through year-to-year appropriations, then reauthorized the program over the president's veto. *(Background, 1981-82 action, p. 431)*

In a concession to the administration, the House and Senate revised the final authorization measure in 1983 to require states to contribute a rising share of financial support for water research institutes. Interior Department officials then dropped their objections to the bill, but Reagan nonetheless followed an Office of Management and Budget recommendation by vetoing S 684 on Feb. 21, 1984.

Legislative Action

The Senate May 25, 1983, passed an original version of S 684 (S Rept 98-91) authorizing $21.1 million a year for water research. The House Oct. 31 passed its own version (HR 2911 — H Rept 98-416) boosting annual authoriza-

tions to $60 million. House and Senate managers then worked out a compromise version of S 684 authorizing $36 million a year.

The compromise authorized $10 million a year for matching grants to state university institutes and $20 million for matching grants for specific research projects selected by the interior secretary. The compromise raised the state matching requirement for the water institutes in stages, from one state dollar for each federal dollar in fiscal 1985-86 to two state dollars for every federal dollar by fiscal 1989.

The Senate approved the compromise version on Nov. 18, 1983, and the House agreed to the revisions by unanimous consent on Feb. 7, 1984. Reagan vetoed S 684 on Feb. 21, contending that state research institutes had reached a point where "they can stand and succeed on their own."

Hill strategists supporting S 684 took their time before mounting an override attempt, giving state university officials an opportunity to contact their House and Senate delegations and slowly building support on an issue that they admitted excited little political passion. The Republican-controlled Senate acted first, on March 21, and its 86-12 vote gave the House impetus to override by a 309-81 vote the following day.

Other Legislation

Ocean Dumping

The Senate in 1983-84 took no action on House legislation to tighten federal controls on dumping wastes in the ocean.

In both 1983 and 1984 the House passed bills to strengthen Environmental Protection Agency (EPA) control over ocean dumping while prodding the agency to move more quickly to designate seabed sites where wastes could be disposed of safely.

Title I of the Marine Protection, Research and Sanctuaries Act of 1972 (PL 92-532), known as the Ocean Dumping Act, gave EPA authority to issue permits allowing waste materials to be dumped in the ocean where they posed no threat to public health or the marine environment. The House-passed measures tightened standards for choosing dumping sites and set schedules to speed up EPA selections.

In 1983 the House Oct. 31 passed a bill reported by the Merchant Marine Committee and the Public Works and Transportation Committee (HR 1761 — H Rept 98-200, Parts I and II) dealing with the ocean dumping program. The House had passed similar legislation in 1982, but the Senate took no action. *(1981-82 action, p. 436)*

In 1984 the House Oct. 1 passed an ocean dumping bill (HR 4829 — H Rept 98-766, Parts I and II) for the third year in a row. The 1984 bill reauthorized the ocean dumping law for four years, at spending levels of $4.25 million annually, and tightened the EPA permit program. It carried a controversial provision that outlawed, after 18 months, dumping of municipal sewage sludge on a blighted sea-bottom region 12 miles off the New York-New Jersey coastline. EPA was in the process of designating a new dumping site 106 miles offshore to receive solids removed from the sewage of New York City and other cities. Some municipal officials resisted opposing the new site because of the cost of barging sludge that far offshore. Because it carried the provision, New York's senators put a "hold" on

HR 4829 when it reached the Senate, and the bill died at the end of the 1984 session.

Colorado River Salinity

Congress in 1984 authorized new federal projects to control salinity in the Colorado River.

The United States had a treaty obligation with Mexico to reduce dissolved salts and minerals in the Colorado, which flowed through Southwestern states and into Mexico before emptying into the Gulf of California. In a 1974 law (PL 93-320) Congress authorized a desalting plant near the Mexican border and four upstream control units. *(Congress and the Nation Vol. IV, p. 298)*

Through legislation cleared Oct. 9 (HR 2790 — PL 98-569), Congress amended the 1974 law to authorize one new salinity control unit and part of a second. The House passed the bill Oct. 2 (H Rept 98-1018) and the Senate approved it Oct. 5. The House cleared HR 2790 by accepting minor Senate amendments Oct. 9.

In addition to the new units, the bill authorized an upgraded U.S. Department of Agriculture program to reduce salinity by helping farmers irrigate more efficiently. Irrigation increased salinity along the Colorado and its tributaries by washing minerals from the soil and reducing water flows.

Increased salinity levels harmed crops on downstream farms that diverted water to fields.

High Plains Groundwater

Congress in 1984 approved a federal project to study potential ways to replenish falling groundwater reserves beneath High Plains farming states.

Since World War II farmers had been pumping water from the Ogallala Aquifer, a groundwater formation sprawling from Nebraska south to Texas, as they irrigated fields to expand production. As heavy pumping depleted the aquifer, a falling water table and rising pumping costs threatened the agriculture-based economies of Nebraska, Kansas, Oklahoma, West Texas and eastern Colorado and New Mexico.

Through legislation cleared Sept. 14 (HR 71 — PL 98-434) Congress authorized a $500,000 study of the Ogallala problem and $20 million to demonstrate technologies for recharging groundwater reserves by high-pressure injection of surface waters or other methods. The bill required $5 million in local matching funds for demonstration programs. The House passed HR 71 June 20, 1983 (H Rept 98-167). The Senate approved it Aug. 10, 1984 (S Rept 98-372), and the House cleared it Sept. 14 by accepting minor Senate amendments.

Chronology
Of Action
On EPA Pollution
Control Programs

1981-82

Congress in 1981-82 grew uneasy about how the Reagan administration was enforcing federal pollution laws.

Controversy built over the two years as the administration cut the Environmental Protection Agency (EPA) budget and revised the agency's regulations for curbing air and water pollution and cleaning up toxic wastes. *(Clean Air Act debate, p. 411; water pollution legislation, p. 425)*

As the 97th Congress prepared to adjourn, a brewing scandal over EPA's management of a 1980 "superfund" program for cleaning up abandoned hazardous wastes neared a climax with a House vote to cite EPA Administrator Anne M. Gorsuch for contempt of Congress. The dispute slowed congressional debate on legislation to tighten existing law regulating how companies handled potentially dangerous chemical wastes.

Despite congressional dismay over deep EPA budget cuts, Congress made no effort to override President Reagan's 1982 veto of legislation authorizing funds for EPA's research programs.

Congress also went along with the administration's decision to curtail drastically the Council on Environmental Quality (CEQ), a White House agency that advised the president on environmental issues.

But growing congressional opposition, especially in the Democratic House, forced the administration to abandon some plans to reduce environmental regulation of U.S. industry. EPA backed off from proposals to suspend key hazardous waste regulations, and Congress refused to abolish the agency's noise control program.

Gorsuch Contempt/Superfund

The House in late 1982 held Environmental Protection Agency (EPA) Administrator Anne M. Gorsuch in contempt of Congress.

On President Reagan's orders, Gorsuch had refused to turn over EPA documents to two House committees that were investigating the agency's enforcement of a 1980 "superfund" law for cleaning up hazardous wastes. By a **259-105 key vote (R 55-101; D 204-4)**, the House Dec. 16 responded by citing Gorsuch for contempt. She was the highest-ranking executive branch official to be cited for contempt of Congress. *(1982 key votes, p. 895)*

The House took that step as part of a continuing clash with the Reagan administration over the limits of the president's "executive privilege." But the dispute grew out of a fast-spreading controversy over how well administration officials, including Gorsuch, were enforcing federal environmental laws.

Members of Congress, especially in the Democratic House, contended that the Reagan administration was moving too slowly to clean up abandoned hazardous waste dumps and prosecute those responsible for damages. The House Public Works Committee and the House Energy and Commerce Oversight Subcommittee subpoenaed EPA documents on 160 hazardous waste sites that had been slated for early cleanup under the 1980 superfund law. But Gorsuch, backed by the Justice Department, withheld 74 documents, contending that premature disclosure by Congress might jeopardize the agency's enforcement decisions.

Three months after the House contempt vote, Gorsuch — known as Anne M. Burford following her marriage in February 1983 — resigned her post amid a bitter constitutional battle and six congressional investigations into the agency's handling of the $1.6 billion superfund program.

In the aftermath President Reagan named William D. Ruckelshaus, EPA's first administrator, to replace Gorsuch, and the 98th Congress increased the agency's budget and overhauled federal hazardous waste regulations. White House officials and House leaders negotiated a compromise agreement that permitted congressional investigators to study the disputed documents, and the House subsequently canceled the Gorsuch contempt citation. *(1983-84 developments, p. 454)*

Developing Confrontation

The confrontation began building in the spring of 1982, when members started questioning EPA's commitment to enforcing federal hazardous waste laws, including the emergency superfund program that Congress had created shortly before Reagan took office.

Congress cleared the superfund law on Dec. 3, 1980, a month after Reagan had defeated former President Carter in that years's presidential election. It fell to the Reagan administration to begin implementing the program that Carter had proposed to speed emergency cleanups of toxic contaminants that had been dumped or accidentally spilled into the environment.

In the Resource Conservation and Recovery Act of 1976 (PL 94-580) Congress directed EPA to regulate how business handled and disposed of dangerous liquid and solid waste materials. But in 1977 officials discovered that chemicals leaking from an abandoned dump were poisoning residents in the Love Canal subdivision, near Niagara Falls, N.Y. As more abandoned chemical wastelands were found in states throughout the nation, Congress drew up the superfund law to give EPA authority to clean them up to protect public health and the environment.

In the 1980 law, known as the Comprehensive Environmental Response, Liability and Compensation Act (PL 96-510), Congress created a $1.6 billion "superfund" to pay for immediate cleanup costs, avoiding time-consuming lawsuits to establish which persons or companies should be held responsible. The law contained liability provisions for government action to recover the cleanup costs and collect damages from dumpers who were responsible for hazardous waste contamination. It financed about 86 percent of the fund through a tax on the chemical and oil industries, with the remainder provided through congressional appropriations.

The law required EPA to draw up a list of priority cleanup sites by July 1981, then update that list at least every year. But the agency took nearly two years, until the end of 1982, to compile a list of 418 dump sites that

officials considered most dangerous to public health. Those sites received top priority, making them eligible to be cleaned up with superfund money as soon as EPA completed a two-month comment period.

In the meantime, however, congressional critics charged that EPA had been dragging its feet on cleaning up dangerous wastes while officials compiled the list. In addition, they questioned settlements that EPA had negotiated with chemical companies to recover costs of cleaning up wastes for which those firms were responsible. Two House subcommittees — the Public Works and Transportation Subcommittee on Investigations and Oversight and the Energy and Commerce Subcommittee on Oversight and Investigations — began investigating the superfund program.

The committees sought EPA superfund program documents as part of those investigations. On Nov. 22 Gorsuch was served with a subpoena that sought virtually every EPA document on 160 priority waste sites. Gorsuch said the subpoena covered 787,000 pages, and she refused to turn over 74 documents. Gorsuch said she acted on written orders from President Reagan, dated Nov. 30, in which he instructed her to withhold certain documents because their dissemination outside the executive branch "would impair my solemn responsibility to enforce the law." The White House contended some of the documents subpoenaed by the House Public Works Oversight Subcommittee concerned potential litigation and could jeopardize enforcement of the superfund law.

House Contempt Action

Voting along party lines, the House Public Works Committee Dec. 10 recommended that the House cite Gorsuch for contempt for refusing to turn over the documents. In a report supporting the contempt action (H Rept 97-968), the panel argued that Gorsuch's refusal had denied the subcommittee information it needed for its superfund investigation. The panel's "preliminary finding suggests that many hazardous waste sites are not being fully cleaned up, that chemical companies responsible for cleanup costs are not being held liable for their full share of the cleanup costs in every instance," Rep. Elliott H. Levitas, D-Ga., the subcommittee chairman, said. "We have got to find out whether sweetheart deals are being made in the settlement of cases," Levitas said.

The full House approved the contempt citation Dec. 16 after a brief but heated debate. Public Works Committee Chairman James J. Howard, D-N.J., said the panel had tried to negotiate a settlement that would have sidestepped the confrontation. Those efforts continued until moments before the 259-105 House vote.

With the House vote to hold Gorsuch in contempt, the superfund controversy escalated into a test of constitutional powers between the executive and legislative branches.

Executive Privilege

The dispute posed the first major confrontation over executive privilege since President Nixon tried to withhold White House tapes from Watergate prosecutors. (Watergate scandal, Congress and the Nation Vol. IV, p. 931)

Nixon was unsuccessful, as a unanimous Supreme Court in July 1974 ruled that his claim of executive privilege must yield to the ongoing criminal prosecution of Watergate defendants. The Gorsuch case involved the same sort of legal issue that existed in the Nixon case — defining the limits of executive privilege when that doctrine collided with the interests of another branch of government.

There were some important differences between the cases, however. In the Nixon matter the dispute was between a president protecting his own private communications and the judicial system. In the Gorsuch case the clash did not involve personal, presidential communications but rather an agency within the executive branch trying to keep certain documents from the legislative branch. Congressional staffers working on the case resisted the notion that executive privilege was involved at all.

In addition to helping refine the limits of executive privilege, the Gorsuch case offered a new opportunity for defining the scope of congressional contempt authority. The case marked the first time a person was held in contempt of Congress for refusing to produce information because of executive privilege. Most prior contempt cases involved private persons who refused to testify or produce documents based on other reasons, such as the Constitution's Fifth Amendment privilege against self-incrimination.

Justice Department Challenge. Although the House transmitted its contempt citation to the Justice Department for prosecution, the department immediately said it would not prosecute. Instead, it filed a lawsuit Dec. 16 challenging the constitutionality of the subpoena. A major element of the department's case rested on the Nixon tapes decision. While the Supreme Court ordered Nixon to turn over the White House tapes, the justices did find a constitutional underpinning for the concept of "presidential" privilege. But the privilege, they indicated, is not absolute.

Writing for the court, Chief Justice Warren E. Burger said, "Nowhere in the Constitution . . . is there any explicit reference to a privilege of confidentiality, yet to the extent this interest relates to the effective discharge of a president's powers, it is constitutionally based."

Nixon lost his case because the court determined that the interests of the ongoing Watergate trial outweighed the president's "generalized interest in confidentiality" of his communications.

In the Gorsuch case the Justice Department based Reagan's arguments on a claim that the Constitution implied a privilege of the executive to ensure the confidentiality of law enforcement files and of the process of policy deliberation.

The Justice Department claimed that the withheld documents included "sensitive memoranda or notes by EPA attorneys and investigators reflecting enforcement strategy, legal analysis, lists of potential witnesses, settlement considerations and similar materials the disclosure of which might adversely affect a pending enforcement action, overall enforcement policy or the rights of individuals."

Lawyers for the House Dec. 30 asked the U.S. District Court in Washington, D.C., to dismiss the Justice Department suit. Under the Constitution, they asserted, members of Congress could not be sued for legislative actions. The House motion called the Justice Department civil suit an "impermissible usurpation of the legislative function."

Disclosure Issue. Another separation of powers issue that arose in the dispute concerned the question of who had ultimate authority to declare specific documents sensi-

tive and off-limits to public disclosure.

What really sparked the whole dispute, according to the House committee report, was an EPA decision in September that committee investigators could not have access to EPA enforcement files unless those files had been "prescreened" by EPA officials. Taking the position that disclosure to Congress could be tantamount to public disclosure, the agency asserted that its duty was to make a decision on each document before disclosing it to Congress.

The Justice Department argued it had a duty to protect the confidentiality of open law enforcement files. Such files could contain unsubstantiated allegations of wrongdoing against individuals, and their disclosure could harm the reputations of those individuals and jeopardize government sources of information, the department said.

Moreover, the department said, disclosure before allegations were substantiated could jeopardize the success of any eventual prosecution — by warning a wrongdoer of any investigation under way or by subjecting investigators to congressional pressure.

In an Oct. 25 letter to Rep. John D. Dingell, D-Mich., chairman of the House Energy and Commerce Committee, EPA went even further, noting that some of the companies accused of hazardous waste dumping were located in the districts of members of the Energy subcommittee that was also looking into enforcement of the superfund law.

"Potential defendants could gain access to sensitive prosecutorial documents through their elected representatives," the EPA letter to Dingell said.

Rep. Albert Gore Jr., D-Tenn., called that statement "an insult to the Congress." Rep. Norman Y. Mineta, D-Calif., said Congress had for years kept secret Central Intelligence Agency documents that it needed to see.

House lawyers, while admitting some need for confidentiality, said it was up to Congress to provide such protection.

"It is our responsibility to discipline our members if they act improperly," said Rep. Bill Green, R-N.Y., referring to the possibility of leaks. "I do not think the executive branch can deny us documents on the assumption that our members will act improperly."

Previous Tests. The claim of executive privilege dated back to 1792, when President George Washington said he had the authority to decide what documents should be given to Congress concerning an army defeat in the Northwest Territory.

As it turned out, none of the papers concerning the army's devastating loss was deemed confidential, but most researchers nonetheless considered the clash to mark the first claim of executive privilege.

According to a Justice Department memo released after the Gorsuch contempt proceedings, presidents had relied on executive privilege 64 times.

Between the Nixon tapes case and Gorsuch contempt citation, there had been only two instances of presidents seeking to withhold documents from Congress. During the Carter administration, a House subcommittee sought documents concerning executive branch deliberations on President Carter's decision to impose a conservation fee on imports of crude oil and gasoline. Ultimately some — but not all — of the documents were given to the subcommittee, and the panel did not pursue documents that directly involved deliberations with the president.

In 1981 Reagan ordered Interior Secretary James G. Watt to withhold documents sought by a subcommittee concerning Canadian reciprocity under a mineral leasing

Council's Funding Cut

Congress in 1981-82 cut back funding for the president's Council on Environmental Quality (CEQ).

After taking office in 1981 President Reagan significantly curtailed the council's influence within the White House. Congress, through legislation (S 1210 — PL 97-350) cleared in 1982, accepted the administration's request to slash CEQ funding to $1,044,000 a year, 72 percent below the council's fiscal 1981 budget.

Congress created the CEQ as part of the National Environmental Policy Act of 1969 (PL 91-190), or NEPA. The landmark law assigned the council the tasks of assessing environmental quality, reviewing federal government programs that dealt with natural resources and proposing national environmental policies for the president's consideration. In addition to publishing extensive annual reports on environmental conditions, the CEQ supervised the process by which other federal agencies wrote and reviewed environmental impact statements to assess the potential environmental damage from government projects.

As part of the White House staff the council served as a visible symbol of federal commitment to protecting the environment. Under President Carter the CEQ enjoyed broad influence in setting federal policies.

The Reagan administration in 1981 considered abolishing CEQ altogether. Although the administration retained the council, Reagan fired all its professional employees and reduced the CEQ staff from 49 to 15 members. At Reagan's request Congress also drastically trimmed the CEQ budget, which in fiscal 1981 amounted to $3.6 million. Under A. Alan Hill, Reagan's CEQ chairman, the council cut back on published studies and focused its annual reports on environmental quality on the effectiveness and economic costs of existing environmental regulations.

Funding Bills. As enacted in 1969, NEPA provided a permanent $1 million annual authorization for CEQ operations. Congress authorized additional funds for the council through annual authorization bills under the Water and Environmental Quality Improvement Act of 1970 (PL 91-224). The administration in 1981 asked Congress to authorize only $44,000 in fiscal 1982 for CEQ staff under the 1970 law, bringing total council authorizations to $1,044,000. Congress eventually went along with Reagan's request, authorizing an additional $44,000 for CEQ in fiscal 1982-84 by clearing S 1210 on Oct. 1, 1982. The bill carried a Senate amendment barring oil and gas leasing on national forest lands within the Seattle and Tacoma, Wash., watersheds. *(Leasing ban, p. 350)*

law. After months of negotiations — which included a recommended contempt citation against Watt — the matter was resolved March 18, 1982, when members were allowed access to certain documents for one day. *(Watt confrontation, p. 341)*

Congressional Contempt Power

The congressional contempt power had almost as long a history as the doctrine of executive privilege. *(CQ Guide to Congress Third Edition, p. 163)*

In 1821 the Supreme Court held that the power of contempt was inherent under the Constitution. Without it, the court said, Congress was "exposed to every indignity and interruption that rudeness, caprice or even conspiracy may meditate against it." In decisions since then, however, the court had imposed certain limits on the contempt power, basically to protect witnesses from unwarranted punishment at the hands of Congress.

Hazardous Waste Disposal

Congress in 1981-82 began debating proposals to tighten the nation's principal law regulating the handling of hazardous wastes.

The House in 1982 passed legislation (HR 6307) to prod the Environmental Protection Agency (EPA) toward tougher enforcement of "cradle-to-grave" controls over dangerous materials. The Senate never acted, however, on a more modest bill (S 2432 — S Rept 97-445) drafted by its Environment and Public Works Committee that simply would have extended the Resource Conservation and Recovery Act of 1976.

In considering those measures, members raised an alarm about how vigorously the Reagan administration was cracking down on hazardous waste disposal. Influential House members joined with environmental groups to force EPA to retreat from suspending key regulations for assuring that industry was disposing of those wastes safely. In a related controversy, the House at the end of 1982 cited EPA Administrator Anne M. Gorsuch for contempt for refusing to turn over agency documents that two House committees sought for their investigation of EPA's efforts to clean up 160 abandoned hazardous waste sites with a $1.6 billion "superfund" that Congress had created in 1980. *(Superfund controversy, p. 449)*

The EPA superfund scandal eventually forced Gorsuch to resign her post in 1983. The 98th Congress continued to prod the administration to move more quickly to clean up abandoned waste dumps. In 1984 Congress finally cleared legislation extending and strengthening hazardous waste regulations under the 1976 law. *(Story, p. 457)*

In its 1982 legislation the House approved deadlines for EPA to license landfills to handle hazardous wastes or shut them down. The House bill also extended EPA regulation to cover small businesses such as gas stations and dry cleaners that generate such wastes in smaller quantities.

Background

The Resource Conservation and Recovery Act (PL 94-580), or RCRA, was enacted as an amendment to the 1965 Solid Waste Disposal Act. It was the basis for management of the nation's hazardous waste and for encouraging conservation and recovery of valuable materials and energy from solid wastes. *(Congress and the Nation Vol. IV, p. 309)*

Although the law sailed through Congress with little opposition in 1976, there had been growing controversy since then over EPA's efforts to enforce sections of the legislation designed to provide cradle-to-grave regulation of the generation, transportation, treatment, storage and disposal of hazardous wastes.

The agency did not issue its first major package of hazardous waste regulations until May 1980, and it had barely begun to implement them before the Reagan administration took office. After that EPA was hit with severe budget reductions and progress on several programs slowed accordingly.

According to the House Energy Committee report on HR 6307 (H Rept 97-570), final permits had been issued for only two of the nation's 9,980 waste treatment, storage or disposal facilities that were in existence prior to Nov. 19, 1980.

1982 House Legislation

The House Energy and Commerce Committee drafted HR 6307 in May to force EPA to move more quickly to issue or deny permits for waste disposal facilities and to set tougher standards for handling hazardous materials. The committee measure closed several "loopholes" in the 1976 law's coverage, notably an exemption for businesses that generated or handled only small quantities of wastes.

The House passed HR 6307 by a 317-32 vote on Sept. 8. It turned down, by a 148-182 margin, an amendment by Phil Gramm, D-Texas, to retain the existing law's exemption for small-quantity generators of hazardous wastes. Gramm contended that extending EPA regulations to small businesses would burden them with "mountains of paperwork" for little demonstrable environmental benefit.

EPA Regulations Reinstated

The administration in 1982 backed off from plans to suspend key EPA hazardous waste regulations.

After vehement protests by members of Congress and environmental groups, EPA reinstated a 1981 standard that banned the disposal of containers holding liquid wastes in unlined landfills. But state officials and environmental groups continued to fight an EPA proposal to allow landfills to devote 25 percent of the storage capacity to hazardous waste disposal.

In the past, barrels of dangerous chemicals were buried at conventional landfills. But after several years the drums could disintegrate, and unless the landfills were lined with an impermeable material, the chemicals could leak into nearby water supplies, as occurred in 1977 at the Love Canal neighborhood in Niagara Falls, N.Y.

Disposal Ban Reinstated. The disposal ban, which went into effect in November 1981, was part of the "interim" standards for toxic waste disposal set under RCRA while EPA developed permanent standards. EPA announced Feb. 25 that it was suspending the ban for 90 days, while comments were received on a new proposal — developed with the help of the Chemical Manufacturers Association — to allow up to 25 percent of a landfill's capacity to be used for hazardous liquids.

The Hazardous Waste Treatment Council and the Environmental Defense Fund promptly asked the U.S. Dis-

trict Court in Washington, D.C., to order EPA to restore the ban.

Several members of the House also denounced the proposal. Rep. Elliott H. Levitas, D-Ga., chairman of the House Public Works Committee's Oversight and Investigations Subcommittee, convened an oversight hearing March 10 to grill EPA on why the ban was lifted. "It would appear that the very type of control that would preclude the occurrence of future 'Love Canals' has been abandoned by the agency that is supposed to protect our waters," Levitas said.

At a public hearing March 11, Rep. Guy V. Molinari, R-N.Y., called the action "the equivalent of opening all jails for a period of 90 days, to determine if the criminals within could possibly pose a threat to the public on the outside."

In the face of such negative reaction, EPA retreated, announcing March 17 that it was reinstating the ban on disposal of containers with "free-standing" liquid visible inside.

EPA Research Veto

Congress in 1982 bowed to President Reagan's veto of legislation authorizing funds for Environmental Protection Agency (EPA) research programs.

In vetoing the measure (S 2577) on Oct. 22, Reagan objected that the bill threatened the objectivity of EPA's Scientific Advisory Board. The president also complained that the bill authorized substantially more than the administration requested for the agency's research and development efforts.

In clearing S 2577 on Oct. 1, Congress authorized $282 million in fiscal 1983 and $298 million in fiscal 1984 for EPA research and development, well above Reagan's fiscal 1983 budget request of $215.88 million. The measure also directed the EPA administrator to include representatives from industry, consumers, academic institutions, state governments and the general public in naming the agency's Science Advisory Board. Congress established the board in 1978 EPA research authorization legislation (PL 95-477) to advise the agency on the scientific merits of research data and conclusions.

EPA Research Program

EPA administered most of the nation's environmental laws, setting standards and issuing regulations to limit air and water pollution, purify drinking water, clean up hazardous wastes and control the disposal of toxic chemicals. The agency conducted extensive research programs to determine safe levels for pollutants and contaminants and to assess technologies for controlling them. During the 1970s critics contended that EPA had imposed strict regulatory controls despite inadequate scientific evidence to justify them.

Throughout 1981 and 1982 concern grew in Congress that Reagan's deep reductions in EPA research spending were undercutting the agency's ability to assess environmental problems. Administration officials insisted that EPA could absorb the savings through more efficient management. But during 1982 House debate on EPA research authorizations, Rep. James H. Scheuer, D-N.Y., chairman of the Science and Technology Subcommittee on Natural Resources, Agriculture Research and Environment, maintained that the administration's budget request, adjusted for inflation, represented a 50 percent reduction in EPA research funds since Reagan took office.

A cut of that magnitude, Scheuer said, "goes far beyond what can be offset by management improvements and cuts into the very heart of EPA's research function."

As cleared, S 2577 earmarked 20 percent of EPA research authorizations for long-term "basic" research on pollution problems. The bill also mandated EPA studies of indoor air pollution, a national environmental monitoring program and a program to assess the health and environmental effects of energy production.

Science Advisory Board

Congress created the EPA Science Advisory Board in 1978 to help assure the quality of the scientific data that the agency used in developing environmental regulations. The board was created under a 1978 law (PL 95-477) that required only that members be qualified by education or experience to evaluate scientific and technical information. *(PL 95-477, Congress and the Nation Vol. V, p. 571)*

In 1981-82 members of Congress protested that Anne M. Gorsuch, Reagan's EPA administrator, had filled key posts in the agency with officials who had close ties to industries that the agency regulated. Neither environmentalists nor members contended that Gorsuch had stacked the advisory board with industry allies, but they maintained that Congress should direct EPA to make sure that other interests were represented to keep an imbalance from developing.

In drafting S 2577, Congress incorporated provisions requiring the administrator to appoint board members from specified groups to assure balanced consideration of issues. But Reagan, in vetoing the bill, argued that the requirement "runs counter to the basic premise of modern scientific thought as an objective undertaking in which the views of special interests have no role."

House leaders thought they could muster a two-thirds majority to override Reagan's veto of EPA research authorizations. But the Senate was required to act first on the veto, and it made no attempt to override. Environment and Public Works Committee Chairman Robert T. Stafford, R-Vt., and Slade Gorton, R-Wash., chairman of the panel's Subcommittee on Toxic Substances and Environmental Oversight, concluded that the votes were lacking.

Toxic Substances Control

Congress in 1981 approved a two-year extension of the Toxic Substances Control Act of 1976 (PL 94-469).

In the 1976 law Congress gave the Environmental Protection Agency (EPA) responsibility for studying potential risks from chemical compounds and protecting the public from them. The Toxic Substances Control Act expanded EPA regulation of industrial and commercial chemicals and for the first time required chemical manufacturers to test potentially dangerous products before putting them on the market. Effective in 1979, the law banned the manufacture of PCBs (polychlorinated biphenyls), a class of chemical compounds used as insulators in electric transformers and capacitors that posed serious health hazards. *(Background, Congress and the Nation Vol. IV, p. 311)*

Through legislation cleared Dec. 16 (S 1211 — PL 97-129), Congress extended the 1976 law without substantial

changes. The measure authorized $60.1 million in fiscal 1982 and $63.5 million in fiscal 1983 for toxic substance regulation. It earmarked $1.5 million from the total each year for grants to state government toxic substances control programs.

Noise Control

The 97th Congress refused President Reagan's request to abolish a federal noise control program.

In his March 1981 budget message Reagan proposed phasing out Environmental Protection Agency (EPA) funds for enforcing federal noise level standards. Although federal noise control regulations would stay on the books, Reagan's plans would have left enforcement to state and local governments.

Reagan offered the proposal as part of the administration's plan to reduce federal regulation of U.S. business. But truck, motorcycle and railroad equipment manufacturers lobbied hard to retain noise controls as preferable to state and local standards that could vary widely.

Both the House and Senate in 1981 passed legislation extending federal authority to regulate noise produced by certain types of equipment. Their versions differed, however, and Congress made no effort to resolve them.

In the Noise Control Act of 1972 (PL 92-574) Congress gave EPA power to set noise emission standards for major noise-making products distributed in interstate commerce, including construction and transportation equipment, motors and engines, and electrical and electronic equipment. Although the law had been in effect nearly a decade, EPA had regulated noise from only a few sources: railroads, motor carriers, truck-mounted garbage compactors, air compressors and motorcycles. *(1972 law, Congress and the Nation Vol. III, p. 817)*

Reagan proposed leaving EPA noise regulations in effect but phasing out the agency's noise control enforcement program by 1982. The Reagan proposal produced a flurry of opposition from manufacturers of railroad and trucking equipment, who lobbied Republicans in Congress to retain federal standards for their products. Harley-Davidson Motorcycle Co., America's last remaining motorcycle manufacturer, also lobbied to preserve a 1980 EPA national noise standard.

House Action. The House Dec. 16, 1981, passed Energy and Commerce Committee legislation (HR 3071 — H Rept 97-85) that retained federal regulations for motorcycles, railroads and trucks. Giving Reagan what he asked for — and then some — the panel's Subcommittee on Commerce, Transportation and Tourism had drafted a measure that repealed EPA noise regulations along with the agency's enforcement funding. Subcommittee Chairman James J. Florio, D-N.J., and fellow Democrats subsequently offered no opposition after industry lobbyists persuaded the full committee to support continued federal standards.

Senate Action. In the Republican Senate, the Environment and Public Works Committee drafted a bill (S 1204 — S Rept 97-110) that eliminated mandatory federal noise standards but gave EPA authority to retain and even strengthen railroad and interstate motor carrier regulations. Before Senate passage July 14, William Proxmire, D, and Robert W. Kasten Jr., R, Wisconsin senators who represented the state where Harley-Davidson was located, offered an amendment to retain motorcycle noise controls as well. The Senate rejected the amendment, 40-55.

Risk Analysis

The Senate in 1982 sidetracked proposals for federal research on how to quantify health, safety and environmental risks in developing government regulations.

The House Aug. 2 passed a Science and Technology Committee bill (HR 6159 — H Rept 97-625) to set up a research and demonstration program to assess possible use of "risk analysis" by federal regulatory agencies. The Senate Commerce Committee in December approved similar legislation (S 3006), but the full Senate took no action.

The legislation defined risk analysis as the process of "quantifying a risk and determining an acceptable level of that risk for an individual, group, society or environment." Its proponents maintained that federal agencies often issued regulations to restrict or ban substances or activities without fully understanding how much of a threat they posed to the public.

The House-passed legislation directed the Office of Management and Budget and White House Office of Science and Technology Policy jointly to manage a research program covering nine federal agencies. Those agencies included the Food and Drug Administration, Environmental Protection Agency, Occupational Safety and Health Administration, Food Safety and Inspection Service, Nuclear Regulatory Commission, Department of Energy, Consumer Product Safety Commission, Federal Aviation Administration and Department of Transportation.

1983-84

Alarmed by Environmental Protection Agency (EPA) scandals, Congress in 1983-84 attempted to tighten federal controls over dangerous chemical wastes.

Early in 1983 EPA Administrator Anne M. Burford resigned, as congressional investigators probed the agency's enforcement of a 1980 "superfund" law for cleaning up abandoned dumps holding hazardous waste materials. Over the following two years Congress responded with legislation to force EPA to move more forcefully to correct past abuses and prevent them from recurring in the future.

In 1984 Congress renewed and expanded the federal Resource Conservation and Recovery Act, which directed EPA to impose "cradle-to-grave" regulation on how industry handled and disposed of hazardous waste materials.

As the presidential election approached, the Democratic House passed legislation to renew the superfund program a year ahead of schedule and boost EPA funds for the cleanup program. But the Reagan administration and Republican Senate delayed action until 1985.

While environmentalists remained dissatisfied with the administration's policies, William D. Ruckelshaus, who replaced Burford as EPA administrator, restored public confidence in the agency's ability to deal with hazardous wastes and other pollution problems.

Burford/Superfund Controversy

Congressional investigations into the Reagan administration's handling of toxic waste cleanups forced Environmental Protection Agency (EPA) Administrator Anne M. Burford to resign her post in 1983.

Burford quit on March 9 after months of controversy and a bitter constitutional clash with Congress. For more than a year six congressional panels had been investigating charges of mismanagement and improper conduct by EPA officials in running a $1.6 billion "superfund" program for cleaning up abandoned hazardous waste dumps.

The highly publicized scandals threw EPA into its worst turmoil since Congress created the agency in 1970. In addition to Burford, more than a dozen top EPA aides either resigned or were fired as Congress probed allegations of political manipulation, "sweetheart" deals, conflicts of interest, perjury and destruction of documents by agency officials.

The resulting disclosures fed congressional misgivings about administration policies that stressed voluntary industry compliance with environmental laws in place of vigorous EPA legal action against abuses.

Trying to repair political damage from the revelations, President Reagan March 21 picked William D. Ruckelshaus, who had been EPA's first director in 1970-73, as Burford's replacement. Before resigning at the end of 1984, Ruckelshaus restored public and congressional confidence in an agency that held responsibility for implementing key federal air, water and toxic pollution control programs. *(Ruckelshaus record as administrator of EPA in 1983-84, box, p. 456)*

The superfund fracas focused congressional attention on the administration's deep cutbacks in EPA's operating budget. Public alarm over the scandals and environmental group pressure for tougher EPA enforcement contributed to congressional approval of sharply increased agency budgets for fiscal 1984 and 1985.

On the day Burford resigned the White House agreed to meet House subcommittee demands for access to EPA superfund documents. In return, the House later dropped a 1982 contempt citation against Burford for refusing — on Reagan's orders — to turn the papers over to a House oversight committee. (Formerly Anne M. Gorsuch, the EPA administrator married Robert F. Burford, director of the Interior Department's Bureau of Land Management, on Feb. 20, 1983.)

Former EPA Assistant Administrator Rita M. Lavelle, director of the superfund program, was the only agency official who faced criminal charges as a result of the controversy. Lavelle, who was fired by Reagan on Feb. 7, was sentenced to six months in prison and a $10,000 fine in 1984 after being convicted on charges that she lied under oath during congressional testimony. Lavelle served her sentence in 1985.

Congressional Investigations

The investigations and hearings probing EPA actions grew out of earlier, more routine congressional oversight on how hazardous waste laws were being carried out by the executive branch.

The House Energy and Commerce Subcommittee on Oversight and Investigations, chaired by John D. Dingell, D-Mich., who also chaired the full committee, had begun looking into implementation of the 1980 "superfund" hazardous waste cleanup law as early as September 1980. Concerned about "the deliberate illegal dumping of hazardous substances and the involvement of organized crime in segments of the toxic waste industry," the subcommittee in a Dec. 16, 1982, report urged "a strong, effective federal deterrent" to illegal disposal.

What the subcommittee found, however, was a "dramatic decline" in hazardous waste enforcement litigation by EPA and the Justice Department since 1981, when the Reagan administration came into office.

As a Senate committee and four more House subcommittees joined in with their own investigations, the scope of inquiry widened to include additional charges:

● Possible conflict of interest, as in the case of superfund director Lavelle, who eventually legally removed herself from a California dumping case that involved her former employer, Aerojet-General Corp.

● Alleged political manipulation of superfund cleanup grants. Lavelle and Burford, for example, were accused of withholding a grant for the Stringfellow Acid Pits in California to avoid boosting the re-election campaign of Gov. Edmund G. Brown Jr., a Democrat.

● Possible destruction of evidence and obstruction of the congressional inquiry. One concern was raised by the installation of paper shredders at EPA's hazardous waste office after Burford refused to turn over subpoenaed documents.

● Alleged use of political "hit lists" to mark for termination EPA science advisers and civil service employees, as well as political appointees, who disagreed with the administration's policy of easing environmental regulation over industry.

White House Stand

The White House initially took a hard-line stand on the congressional probes in 1982, resisting subcommittee demands for internal EPA documents on grounds of executive privilege. After the controversy mushroomed in early 1983, however, the administration backed down and nudged Burford into resignation.

The dispute over congressional access to EPA documents meanwhile escalated a dispute over environmental policy into a confrontation over the constitutional powers of Congress and the president. On Reagan's written orders Burford in 1982 had refused to comply with a subpoena for EPA documents by the House Public Works Subcommittee on Investigations and Oversight. Following Justice Department advice, Reagan claimed the documents were protected by executive privilege because they discussed sensitive enforcement strategy for pending legal cases on hazardous waste dumping. In response, the House voted 259-105 on Dec. 16, 1982, to hold Burford in contempt of Congress. *(1982 dispute, p. 449)*

But the Justice Department refused to prosecute Burford. Instead, it filed suit on the day the House voted, seeking to block action on the contempt citation. The department claimed that the Constitution implied a privilege for the executive to ensure that law enforcement files and the policy deliberation process remained confidential. On Feb. 3, 1983, however, the U.S. District Court in Washington, D.C., granted a motion filed by lawyers for the House of Representatives to dismiss the Justice lawsuit.

Compromise on Documents

In the month after the Justice Department suit was dismissed, the administration and congressional subcommittees worked out compromise arrangements that gave members access to most EPA documents they had been seeking.

White House officials contacted Rep. Elliott H. Levi-

Ruckelshaus Restores EPA Image

In his second turn at the post, Environmental Protection Agency (EPA) Administrator William D. Ruckelshaus in 1983-84 restored the agency's reputation for effective and independent enforcement of the nation's environmental laws.

As EPA's first administrator under President Nixon in 1970-73, Ruckelshaus founded the agency that Congress created to regulate pollution in the nation's air, water and soil.

A decade later President Reagan brought Ruckelshaus back to the EPA after the agency had been tarnished by scandals over its handling of a "superfund" program to clean up hazardous wastes. He replaced Anne M. Burford, who resigned on March 9, 1983, under a barrage of congressional investigations into the superfund program. *(Story, p. 454)*

Background. By selecting Ruckelshaus, the White House quelled a political storm over environmental issues that superfund scandals had touched off. During his previous tenure at EPA, Ruckelshaus had earned a reputation for aggressively protecting the environment. A Republican from Indiana, he had taken a bipartisan approach to environmental issues.

But Ruckelshaus earned his greatest asset, a reputation for integrity on matters of conscience, after he left the EPA post to serve as deputy attorney general. Nixon dismissed him from that post in October 1973 for his refusal to fire Archibald Cox, the Watergate special prosecutor who was pressing the White House for tape recordings of Nixon's conversations. *(Congress and the Nation Vol. IV, p. 934)*

Ruckelshaus in 1975 joined Weyerhaeuser Company, a timber products firm headquartered in Tacoma, Wash., as senior vice president. In private life, he backed changes in environmental laws to reduce excessive costs and paperwork burdens on industry.

EPA Role. The Senate confirmed Ruckelshaus as EPA chief for the second time by a 97-0 vote on May 17, 1983. He took over an agency that had been badly shaken by budget cuts, staff reductions and the departure of key officials. Ruckelshaus brought in a new management team, persuaded the administration to increase EPA budgets, improved staff morale and dealt amiably with Congress, environmental groups and the news media.

Environmentalist critics questioned whether Ruckelshaus carried sufficient influence within an administration dominated by conservatives opposed to government regulation of business. On some issues, they noted, Ruckelshaus lost battles with Office of Management and Budget Director David A. Stockman, who frequently questioned whether the benefits of environmental protection programs were justified by economic costs. Stockman and Secretary of Energy Donald P. Hodel opposed Ruckelshaus' proposal for curbs on coal-fired power plant emissions that caused acid rain, for instance, and Reagan instead called for further study of the issue. *(Acid rain debate, p. 420)*

During his year-and-a-half tenure, Ruckelshaus did develop tougher EPA restrictions on lead in gasoline and impose mandatory controls on use of the pesticide ethylene dibromide (EDB).

Ruckelshaus announced his resignation on Nov. 28, 1984.

Successor. Reagan nominated Lee M. Thomas, the assistant EPA administrator who headed the agency's hazardous waste programs, as Ruckelshaus' replacement.

Thomas had been at EPA since early 1983, when he was named to succeed Rita M. Lavelle, fired Feb. 7 of that year in the midst of the controversy over management of the superfund program.

As associate director of the Federal Emergency Management Agency in 1981-83, Thomas had headed a task force to deal with dioxin contamination at Times Beach, Mo.

---

tas, D-Ga., chairman of the House Public Works Subcommittee on Investigations, and they reached agreement on Feb. 18 to permit panel members and staff to see the disputed documents under conditions to make sure that they were kept confidential. At a news conference two days earlier, Reagan said he no longer would insist on executive privilege in the matter. The president also announced that the Justice Department would mount its own investigations into alleged wrongdoing in EPA's hazardous waste program.

In return, Levitas agreed to try to persuade the House to cancel the contempt citation against Burford. The documents dispute dragged on until March 9, when Burford resigned and the White House finally satisfied demands by four other House subcommittees for agency documents.

Contempt Charge Dropped. The House Aug. 3 by voice vote approved a resolution dropping the Burford contempt citation. Levitas' subcommittee approved the resolution (H Res 180) on June 7, and the full Public Works and Transportation Committee reported it June 23 (H Rept 98-323). The resolution asserted the House position that executive branch officers must comply with congressional subpoenas and that federal prosecutors had a duty to proceed against anyone formally cited for contempt after defying such a subpoena.

Outcome of EPA Investigations

Twenty major EPA officials ultimately resigned in the wake of Burford's departure. Barely half a dozen actually had been accused of wrongdoing, and only Lavelle faced criminal charges. The Justice Department Aug. 11 said its

investigation had produced insufficient evidence to warrant criminal prosecution of Burford and five of her top aides.

Charges varied for each official. Most of the charges that Justice investigated involved conflicts of interest, destruction of subpoenaed documents and false testimony. Levitas used the term "whitewash" to describe the department's report.

Lavelle. The charges against Lavelle, the former EPA assistant administrator, stemmed from agency decisions on the Stringfellow Acid Pits dump site in California. Lavelle's former employer, Aerojet-General Corp., was listed as a dumper at the site. On June 18, 1982, Lavelle recused (legally removed) herself from decisions on the Stringfellow case. She testified under oath at three congressional hearings that she learned of Aerojet's involvement only the day before.

But on Aug. 4, 1982, Lavelle was indicted on charges of perjury and obstructing a congressional investigation. The indictment charged that Lavelle had lied under oath about when she first knew about Aerojet's involvement, and trial witnesses testified that she had been told as early as May 28, 1982. The indictment also charged that Lavelle had lied when she denied that superfund cleanup grants had been used for political purposes. A federal jury in Washington, D.C., found Lavelle guilty on Dec. 1 of four of the five counts. Lavelle began serving a six-month sentence on April 19, 1985.

Congressional Probes. Congressional panels slowed their EPA investigations after Ruckelshaus replaced Burford. Dingell's Energy and Commerce subcommittee issued a report on Aug. 30, 1984, revealing that Lavelle had repeated contacts with White House officials as she allegedly targeted superfund grants to help Republican and hurt Democratic candidates prior to 1982 congressional elections. The report also detailed charges that Lavelle removed or concealed documents from her office after Reagan fired her.

All four Republicans on the 13-member subcommittee disputed the report's conclusions and charged that the timing of its release during the 1984 presidential campaign was politically motivated. Dingell acknowledged in transmitting the report to the full Energy and Commerce Committee that Ruckelshaus had improved EPA's performance. Dingell also noted that Reagan was opposing pending legislation to expand the superfund program while "only six of the 546 sites on the national priority list of the most hazardous sites in the nation have been cleaned up." *(Superfund bill, p. 459)*

Reagan in 1984 named Burford chairman of the National Advisory Committee on Oceans and Administration. But she resigned that post after both the House and Senate adopted resolutions urging Reagan to withdraw her appointment.

Hazardous Waste Controls

Responding to Environmental Protection Agency (EPA) scandals, Congress in 1984 tightened federal controls over how business and industry handled hazardous chemical wastes.

Completing action that the House had started in 1982, Congress Oct. 5 cleared a measure (HR 2867 — PL 98-616) that strengthened EPA power to regulate "cradle-to-grave" storage and disposal of toxic, flammable, corrosive and explosive waste materials.

In passing HR 2867, Congress was prodded by growing public concern about environmental contamination by hazardous waste products that leaked or were dumped into the nation's soil and water. The legislation ordered EPA to enforce more aggressively the Resource Conservation and Recovery Act of 1976 (RCRA, PL 94-580), the federal government's chief law regulating the handling of dangerous wastes that were generated by industrial and business activity.

In extending the 1976 law for four years, Congress tried to close loopholes that Rep. James J. Florio, D-N.J., the chief House sponsor of the 1984 measure, said had freed roughly half of the nation's hazardous wastes from EPA rules requiring safe disposal. In the most controversial crackdown, Congress directed EPA to begin regulating small business operations such as gasoline stations and dry cleaners that produced smaller quantities of dangerous materials. Other provisions regulated underground tanks for storing petroleum and other substances and imposed sharp restrictions on disposing of wastes in landfills, ponds, underground mines, caves and salt formations.

Through those and other provisions Congress took its most concrete legislative steps to correct what members viewed as EPA's mismanagement of the government's campaign to clean up hazardous wastes that threatened public health and safety throughout the country. During a series of highly publicized congressional investigations in 1981-82, environmental groups and other critics had charged that the Reagan administration had weakened enforcement of the 1976 law to prevent hazardous pollution and moved too slowly to clean up existing waste dumps under a 1980 "superfund" law. Those controversies forced EPA Administrator Anne M. Burford to resign her post in March 1983. *(Story, p. 454)*

With the scandals in mind, Congress set tight deadlines for EPA to enforce rules for handling and disposing of hazardous materials that previously had escaped federal regulation. In drafting the legislation, House and Senate committees spelled out requirements in extensive detail, banning some practices by law unless EPA issued regulations finding them to be safe. The U.S. chemical industry and other critics of the legislation maintained that the authors were trying to write detailed regulations instead of law, going into areas where members of Congress lacked technical competence to make scientific judgments.

Background

While the 1980 superfund law was designed to finance the cleanup of past hazardous waste pollution, Congress enacted RCRA in 1976 to keep hazardous wastes from threatening the human environment. From the outset, however, EPA had trouble implementing a regulatory program that covered thousands of types of business wastes throughout the nation.

The 1976 law established more stringent standards for transporting, storing, treating and disposing of hazardous wastes than for ordinary household and municipal waste. EPA defined hazardous wastes generally as those that were toxic, flammable, corrosive or explosive.

Facilities handling hazardous waste had to have federal permits, or state permits issued under a federally approved program, showing that they met safety standards. Bringing existing facilities up to the standards and issuing all the final permits was expected to take years; in the

meantime existing facilities could get "interim status," largely just by applying for a permit.

RCRA also established a system for "cradle-to-grave" tracking of hazardous wastes. A standard EPA manifest form had to accompany such wastes on each stage of shipment, storage, treatment, recycling or final disposal, leaving a paper trail that enforcement officials could use in fixing responsibility for illegal disposal.

Although the law was passed in 1976, EPA did not finish issuing the main regulations for the hazardous waste program until 1982. Environmentalists criticized the Carter administration for foot-dragging in writing the complex regulations needed to actually control landfills and other hazardous waste facilities.

Meanwhile, a series of disclosures of hazardous waste contamination in several parts of the nation fueled demand for congressional action. In February 1983 EPA officials decided to spend about $33 million to buy out homeowners in Times Beach, Mo., a small community contaminated by dioxin. Florio, chairman of the House Energy and Commerce subcommittee that drafted HR 2867, noted that neither the type of toxic chemical wastes — dioxins — nor the practice that put them in Times Beach — the spraying of chemical-laced oil — was regulated under existing law.

The Reagan administration claimed credit for ending EPA delays. But environmental groups and congressional critics charged that the agency's 1982 regulations were too lax and their protests forced EPA officials to back off from proposals to ease reporting requirements and permit containers holding hazardous liquids to be deposited in landfills that lacked impermeable linings.

Although the House in 1982 passed legislation to tighten RCRA, the Senate never acted on a more modest proposal by its Environment and Public Works Committee. *(1981-82 debate, p. 452)*

1983 Action

Spurred by the EPA controversies, the House Energy and Commerce Committee and the Senate panel in 1983 drafted similar legislation to reauthorize and strengthen RCRA enforcement. The House passed its measure in November, but the Senate waited a full year before acting on its committee's proposals.

Both the House and Senate committees recommended that Congress expand EPA enforcement powers and strengthen the right of private citizens to sue violators of the 1976 law. Both bills placed tighter restrictions on landfill or pond disposal and set ambitious timetables for EPA to complete regulatory steps that had dragged on for years.

Despite objections by small business groups, the House and Senate measures also ordered EPA to start regulating firms and institutions that produced smaller quantities of hazardous wastes. Existing EPA regulations exempted generators of less than 1,000 kilograms per month of hazardous waste — or 2,200 pounds. At least 20 states already regulated small-quantity generators more stringently than the federal government.

However, trade associations for dry cleaners, auto repair shops and other small businesses objected to proposals for bringing small-quantity generators under the regulatory umbrella. To do so would mean unjustified costs and paperwork for their members, they said.

House Action. Florio's Energy and Commerce Subcommittee on Commerce, Transportation and Tourism drafted HR 2867 in April, but House action on the complex measure lasted through most of the 1983 session. The full Energy and Commerce Committee reported the measure May 17 (H Rept 98-198, Part I), then filed a supplemental report on June 9 (Part II). Because the measure strengthened EPA enforcement powers, it was then referred to the House Judiciary Committee. That panel reported it June 17 with amendments (Part III).

The House took up HR 2867 on Aug. 4 but finished its work nearly three months later. The House considered the bill intermittently during that period, but debate at times was intensive as members approved several floor amendments.

One significant amendment, adopted by voice vote on Oct. 6, eased the schedule for EPA to decide which hazardous wastes should be banned from land disposal. Another Oct. 6 amendment banned most disposal of liquid wastes in salt domes or underground injection wells without specific EPA or congressional approval.

During the final days of debate the House accepted two Judiciary Committee amendments to weaken Energy and Commerce provisions beefing up EPA's legal powers to enforce hazardous waste regulations. The Energy and Commerce Committee, contending that the Justice Department had failed to vigorously prosecute illegal hazardous waste dumping, proposed giving the EPA administrator power to press a civil action in court if the attorney general failed to file a case within 150 days after EPA turned it over to Justice. The Energy and Commerce bill also gave EPA's criminal investigators certain police powers.

But the Judiciary Committee objected that the Justice Department and the FBI should remain responsible for legal action against RCRA violations. By a 215-165 vote the House agreed to strike the provision allowing EPA to pursue cases if Justice delayed.

Judiciary members then pressed a second amendment to strike provisions giving EPA criminal investigators certain police powers. But the House instead adopted by a 292-125 vote a compromise amendment that directed the attorney general to deputize qualified EPA employees as special deputy U.S. marshals at the EPA administrator's request.

Before passing the bill by voice vote Nov. 3, the House defeated a proposal by Elliott H. Levitas, D-Ga., to require congressional consent before EPA could enforce regulations on small generators of hazardous wastes.

Senate Committee Bill. Moving at the same time as the House panels, the Senate Environment and Public Works Committee approved its bill (S 757) on July 28 and reported it Oct. 28 (S Rept 98-284). The thrust of the House and Senate committee measures was similar, although they differed on many details. But several senators objected to particular aspects of the bill, delaying floor consideration until the 1984 session.

1984 Compromise Legislation

Senate Majority Leader Howard H. Baker Jr., R-Tenn., finally brought the Environment committee bill to the floor in July 1984 after 52 senators signed a letter urging its consideration. The full Senate promptly passed HR 2867, by a 93-0 vote on July 25, after substituting the provisions of S 757 for the House version.

After some difficult negotiations, House and Senate conferees Oct. 3 filed a conference report (H Rept 98-1133) on a compromise four-year RCRA reauthorization. Most provisions of the House and Senate bills aimed at closing

loopholes in existing law and their differences were minor. Conferees blended House and Senate provisions for regulating small quantity generators, giving EPA until March 31, 1986, to issue rules for businesses and institutions that produced between 100 and 1,000 kilograms (220 to 2,200 pounds) of hazardous wastes per month.

To limit disposal of hazardous wastes on land, the conference bill immediately banned depositing them in underground mines and salt formations until EPA took certain regulatory actions. It also set a statutory prohibition, effective six months after enactment, on placing bulk or non-containerized liquid wastes in any landfill. It banned land disposal of specified wastes entirely, although the measure allowed extension of the effective date if no alternative disposal means were immediately available.

Avoiding a last-minute snarl, Senate conferees agreed to drop Senate provisions revising the 1980 superfund law that House negotiators insisted be considered in separate legislation extending the superfund program. The House accepted Senate provisions to regulate underground storage tanks, a problem that the House had dealt with through a separate superfund bill it passed in August. *(House superfund bill, this page)*

The House adopted the conference report on Oct. 3 and the Senate cleared the measure on Oct. 5.

Provisions

As signed into law Nov. 8, HR 2867 (PL 98-616) reauthorized RCRA for fiscal 1985-88. Major provisions of the law:

● Banned disposal of bulk or non-containerized liquid hazardous wastes in any landfill, effective six months after enactment.

● Directed EPA to issue regulations within 15 months to reduce as much as technologically feasible the disposal of containers holding liquid hazardous wastes in landfills.

● Banned land disposal of certain highly hazardous wastes, solvents and dioxins unless EPA issued regulations within specified periods determining that specific practices were safe.

● Required EPA to publish, within 24 months, a schedule for determining whether to ban land disposal of all other hazardous wastes listed under RCRA, considering first those presenting the greatest hazard. EPA had to issue those decisions for one-third of the remaining wastes within 45 months, two-thirds within 55 months and for all within 66 months.

● Banned land disposal of any of those wastes for which EPA failed to meet the 66-month deadline, but allowed for variances if EPA failed to meet the earlier deadlines.

● Banned disposal of liquid and other hazardous wastes in any salt dome, salt-bed formation, underground mine or cave. The ban began with enactment, but such disposal could be allowed if EPA later issued standards and, for a specific facility, found no environmental threat and issued a permit.

● Required EPA to issue by March 31, 1986, standards for handling hazardous wastes from generators of between 100 kilograms and 1,000 kilograms (200 to 2,200 pounds) per month. The standards could be less stringent than those for wastes from larger generators but had to protect human health and the environment. EPA could regulate generators of less than 100 kilograms per month if necessary to protect human health and the environment.

● Directed EPA to issue regulations setting safety standards for underground tanks used to store hazardous substances and petroleum products such as gasoline. The law allowed state governments to regulate underground tanks if their programs were as stringent as federal standards.

● Required EPA to issue technical standards for firms that produced, sold or burned fuels made from hazardous wastes.

● Made the RCRA ban on open dumping of hazardous wastes enforceable by lawsuits brought by private citizens.

● Required the attorney general, at EPA's request, to deputize qualified EPA employees as special marshals in RCRA criminal investigations.

● Banned the use of dioxin-contaminated wastes or any other hazardous waste as a dust suppressant, unless the waste was hazardous solely because of its ignitability.

● Required EPA to decide within one year whether to list used motor oil as a hazardous waste under RCRA and to issue standards for recycling it within two years.

● Banned underground injection of hazardous wastes into or above any formation that contained, within one-quarter mile of the well, an underground source of drinking water.

Superfund Renewal

The Senate in 1984 blocked a House election-year drive to expand the federal "superfund" program to clean up abandoned hazardous waste dumps.

Amid partisan bickering the House passed legislation (HR 5640) to renew the superfund for five years and boost its funding to $10.2 billion. The program, financed by congressional appropriations and a tax on crude oil and raw chemicals, gave the Environmental Protection Agency (EPA) power to clean up dangerous wastes that business and industry had left unattended at sites scattered across the country.

President Reagan opposed renewing the program until 1985, when taxes that Congress imposed to pay for the cleanup were due to expire. After maneuvering HR 5640 through the House as the presidential election campaign heated up, Democrats pushing for an expanded cleanup effort excoriated the president and charged that the Republican-controlled Senate had "caved in" to administration pressure to bottle up the superfund legislation.

The House passed its superfund renewal bill by a 323-33 vote on Aug. 10, after the Democratic National Convention in San Francisco. Led by Rep. Geraldine A. Ferraro, D-N.Y., the party's vice presidential nominee, House Democrats took the occasion to attack the administration's record in managing EPA pollution control programs.

Under political heat from environmental groups, the Senate Environment and Public Works Committee in September drafted a separate $7.5 billion superfund reauthorization. The full Senate never voted on the measure.

Background

Congressional maneuvering on the superfund renewal reflected the political potency of American voters' concern about environmental contamination by hazardous wastes discarded by business and industry. Throughout Reagan's first term environmental groups and key House subcommittee leaders had charged that EPA moved too slowly to get waste dump cleanups under way. Congressional investigations into the superfund program shook EPA to its foun-

dations, forcing agency Administrator Anne M. Burford to resign in 1983 and producing criminal charges against Rita M. Lavelle, the superfund director. *(Superfund controversy, p. 449)*

Congress created the superfund program in 1980 at President Carter's urging. Before 1976 toxic, corrosive, flammable and explosive materials could be legally dumped just about anywhere. Congress imposed federal regulation on hazardous wastes in the Resource Conservation and Recovery Act of 1976. By then, however, decades of abuse had left hazardous wastes scattered at thousands of neglected sites across the nation. In many dumps the hazardous materials had begun leaking into surrounding soil and underlying groundwater aquifers.

1980 Law. In the Comprehensive Environmental Responses, Compensation and Liability Act of 1980 (PL 96-510), Congress set up a $1.6 billion fund to cover the costs of cleaning up wastes that had been abandoned by those responsible for dumping. The law gave EPA power to go after whoever had caused the problem — including companies that generated or hauled the wastes or that owned or operated dump sites. If dump owners had disappeared, EPA could hold companies whose wastes had ended up in the dumps completely responsible for cleaning them up. If those responsible refused to act, EPA could clean up wastes itself, then sue them for up to three times the actual cost of the cleanup.

To finance cleanups if EPA was unable to recover costs, Congress set up a Hazardous Substance Response Trust Fund — dubbed the "superfund" — with 12.5 percent of the funds from general Treasury revenues and the rest from a tax on petroleum and on raw chemical "feedstocks" used to manufacture chemical products. EPA estimated that 71 percent of the nation's hazardous wastes came from the chemical industry.

Superfund Problems. It fell to the Reagan administration to launch the cleanup program. But environmentalists and congressional backers of the program suspected that EPA officials whom Burford appointed were less than enthusiastic about forcing industry to pay for correcting hazardous waste problems.

Among the problems congressional investigators found was that EPA was slow in setting up procedures needed to get the program started and slow in spending the money in the fund. Another finding was that EPA preferred to negotiate rather than litigate against dumpers to collect costs, a preference that was delaying cleanup, recovering less than full costs and settling for inadequate cleanups at many sites. EPA was charged with making "sweetheart deals" with industry.

As EPA officials meanwhile found more and more abandoned waste sites, it became clear that the $1.6 billion that Congress provided for a four-year period fell far short of what was needed to correct threats to health and safety. By 1984 EPA estimated that the nation held at least 22,000 dangerous waste dumps, with as many as 2,200 requiring urgent cleanups at a cost of between $8.4 billion and $16 billion. In 1985 the congressional Office of Technology Assessment estimated that the superfund program would require $100 billion over 50 years to complete its task.

In his January 1984 State of the Union message, Reagan said he would support extension of the superfund program beyond 1985. EPA Administrator William D. Ruckelshaus, Burford's successor, said in March that the administration would wait until 1985 to propose a reauthorization measure. The administration in 1985 proposed spending $5.3 billion on the superfund cleanup effort under a five-year extension.

1984 Action

With House Democrats eager to move ahead, Rep. James J. Florio, D-N.J., chairman of the House Energy and Commerce Subcommittee on Commerce, Transportation and Tourism, led a 1984 drive to renew and expand the superfund a year ahead of schedule. After the subcommittee in April rejected his initial proposal, Florio negotiated a compromise reauthorization measure that won backing from key Democratic committee chairmen and influential House Republicans, who often championed chemical industry positions on toxic waste issues.

House Committee Action. The compromise measure (HR 5640 — H Rept 98-890, Part I), approved by the full Energy and Commerce Committee June 20 by a 38-3 vote, provided for a cleanup fund of approximately $9 billion for fiscal 1986-90. Florio initially had sought provisions to compensate toxic dump victims, but the compromise dropped them. It did authorize health studies and measures to mitigate victims' exposure to hazardous wastes, and it kept provisions to authorize private lawsuits in federal courts to seek compensation for injuries caused by toxic dumping. Victims could sue for damages under existing liability laws in most states, but standards of proof and other legal obstacles made it hard for them to win their cases.

Two other House committees considered HR 5640 before it went to the floor. The Public Works and Transportation Committee July 31 accepted Florio's bill virtually unchanged. But the Ways and Means Committee, with jurisdiction over the bill's tax provisions, Aug. 2 approved by a 27-5 vote a package of amendments (H Rept 98-890, Part II) that shifted superfund tax burdens to oil companies from the chemical industry and other hazardous waste generators while boosting general Treasury revenue contributions. The Ways and Means amendments raised total funding for the five-year extension to $10.2 billion.

House Passage. The House approved HR 5640 on Aug. 10 after Democrats abandoned a planned maneuver to pressure the Senate to move its own reauthorization by linking the superfund measure to separate legislation extending federal hazardous waste control programs under the Resource Conservation and Recovery Act of 1976. *(RCRA reauthorization, p. 457)*

Before sending HR 5640 to the floor, the House Rules Committee Aug. 2 in effect upheld the Ways and Means tax package by approving ground rules for floor debate that blocked consideration of the Energy and Commerce revenue provisions. The full House settled a second major issue Aug. 9 by adopting, on a **208-200 key vote (R 135-22; D 73-178)**, an amendment by Harold S. Sawyer, R-Mich., that deleted the Energy committee provision giving private citizens the right to sue in federal court for damages from toxic waste dumps. By a 159-200 vote, the House defeated a proposal by Elliott H. Levitas, D-Ga., to set 12 percent of the superfund aside to compensate individuals who had been harmed by exposure to hazardous wastes. *(1984 key votes, p. 927)*

Partisan Sniping. In the 323-33 vote passing HR 5640, the superfund reauthorization drew overwhelming support from House Republicans as well as Democrats. Yet partisan sniping broke out during floor debate as Republicans objected to hasty legislative action while Democrats

countered that the bill was needed to prod the administration into cleaning up more waste sites. "I don't know the genesis of this measure," Barber B. Conable, R-N.Y., complained Aug. 9, "but I suspect it was the San Francisco Democratic convention."

Ferraro's debate comments on "the sorry performance of the EPA" underscored the political emphasis that Democrats placed on superfund reauthorization. The vice presidential candidate repeated her remarks before television cameras on the Capitol lawn, flanked by Florio and environmental group leaders.

Senate Inaction. After the August congressional recess for the Republican national convention, the Senate Environment panel Sept. 13 approved a "bare-bones" $7.5 billion superfund reauthorization bill (S 2892 — S Rept 98-631) introduced by Chairman Robert T. Stafford, R-Vt., and Jennings Randolph, D-W.Va., the panel's ranking minority member. The Senate committee proposed to basically renew the existing superfund law with few changes. The Senate Finance Committee held mid-September hearings on extending superfund taxes, but it took no action on the legislation.

Research Authorizations

The Senate in 1984 sidetracked House legislation boosting authorizations for Environmental Protection Agency (EPA) research programs for fiscal 1984-85.

The House Feb. 9 passed the bill (HR 2899 — H Rept 98-212) by a 362-9 vote amid confusion over the Reagan administration's position. The House Science and Technology Committee reported the measure in 1983 and later altered it after negotiations with EPA officials. But the Office of Management and Budget (OMB) Feb. 2 objected to funding levels and legislative restrictions set by the measure.

EPA officials were surprised by OMB's opposition, and the confusion fueled congressional charges that the budget office was setting the Reagan administration's environmental policy through spending restrictions that limited EPA's capability to enforce federal environmental laws. Rep. James H. Scheuer, D-N.Y., chairman of the subcommittee that handled the bill, contended that "EPA had the rug pulled out from under them by the real environmental policy makers in this administration — OMB."

House members had protested administration cuts in EPA spending on research programs. Reagan in 1982 vetoed an EPA authorization bill for fiscal 1983-84. *(1981-82 chronology, p. 457)*

Reagan had requested $205.5 million for EPA research in fiscal 1984 and $278 million for fiscal 1985. As passed by the House, HR 2899 woud have authorized $283.5 million for fiscal 1984 and $297.7 million for fiscal 1985, still well below the $355.6 million fiscal 1981 EPA research appropriation that Congress approved during the Carter administration.

Although the authorization bill died in the Senate, Congress funded EPA research and other programs through the fiscal 1985 appropriations bill (HR 5713 — PL 98-371) for the Department of Housing and Urban Development and various independent agencies.

Chronology Of Action On Federal Land Management

1981-82

The 97th Congress was frequently at odds with Secretary of the Interior James G. Watt over policy for managing federally owned lands.

In a series of budget battles, Congress rejected Watt's plan to halt federal land purchases for expansion of the national park system and divert funds to improving existing park facilities. Under Watt's direction the National Park Service slowed the pace of land acquisition. In contrast to the late 1970s, moreover, Congress made no major additions to the park system.

Sharp differences between the Republican Senate and the Democratic House also slowed congressional action on the Carter administration's 1979 proposals for expanding the national wilderness system within U.S. national forests. Congress and the administration meanwhile skirmished over curtailing federal strip-mining regulations.

In one of its few new environmental initiatives, Congress with Watt's endorsement approved legislation that established an Interior Department program to restrict commercial development on offshore barrier islands along the nation's coastlines.

National Park Expansion

Congress in 1981-82 overruled the Reagan administration's plan to stop buying land for the national park system.

Interior Secretary James G. Watt in 1981 proposed an indefinite moratorium on federal government land purchases to expand national parks and other public land holdings. At the same time Watt asked Congress for authority to spend the government's Land and Water Conservation Fund to repair and improve the country's 48 existing national parks, 78 national monuments, historic sites and other lands that already were part of the 73.6-million-acre national park system.

Watt reasoned that the National Park Service, an Interior Department agency, should first restore its existing parks before acquiring additional lands. But environmental groups charged that halting new park expansion would only force the government to pay more in the future for lands that should be protected by Park Service management. In the meantime, they went on, the government might forfeit the chance to keep those lands unspoiled by logging, mining or residential development by private owners.

Congress concurred, and both the Democratic House and Republican Senate substantially boosted the administration's fiscal 1981 and 1982 requests for land acquisition appropriations. Congress provided additional funds for Park Service maintenance, but it turned down Watt's proposal to divert the money from the Land and Water Conservation Fund, which had been set up in 1965 to finance federal land acquisitions from offshore oil and gas revenues.

Congress went along, for one year only, with Watt's proposal to halt fiscal 1982 grants from the fund for state government park purchases. But it refused the administration's request to abolish federal grants for urban parks and preserving historic buildings.

Background

Congress vastly expanded the national park system during the 1970s. The park system grew from 24.4 million acres in 1971 to more than 70 million acres as the government established new parks, monuments, historic sites and urban parks near or within major cities. Congress added most of those parks, notably in Alaska, by transferring public lands from other federal agencies to Park Service control. But lawmakers throughout the decade also created new parks and expanded existing areas, particularly in the East and around urban areas, by authorizing the Park Service to buy up privately owned lands with money from the Land and Water Conservation Fund.

Congress first began protecting national parks when it established Yellowstone National Park in 1872. Over the following century it expanded the system by designating other federally owned lands and accepting private land donations to form extensive parks, monuments, historic sites, recreation areas, seashore and lakeshore areas under Park Service management. Before the 1960s, however, the Park Service had only limited authority and funds to purchase lands for the system.

In authorizing the Cape Cod National Seashore in 1961, Congress for the first time gave the Park Service authority to acquire a large area primarily by buying the lands. Following a 1962 report by an Outdoor Recreation Resources Review Commission, President Kennedy set up a Bureau of Outdoor Recreation in the Interior Department to provide central planning for recreation area development. At the Kennedy and Johnson administration's request, Congress passed the Land and Water Conservation Fund Act of 1964 to earmark federal receipts from various sources, including federal recreation user fees, for land purchases by federal and state agencies.

The 1964 law provided 50 percent matching grants to the states for acquiring and developing recreation areas. It also provided funds for the Park Service, U.S. Fish and Wildlife Service, U.S. Forest Service and U.S. Bureau of Land Management to buy lands for parks, wildlife preservation areas and national forests.

As land costs rose in subsequent years, Congress expanded the fund and provided new sources of revenue. With user fees providing less revenue than expected, Congress in 1968 authorized direct appropriations to bring the fund up to $200 million a year. As an alternative, the 1968 law also assigned federal revenues from Outer Continental Shelf (OCS) oil and gas leasing to the fund to bring the total up to authorized levels. *(OCS leasing, p. 347)*

Funding for Park System Expansion. Several times during the 1970s, Congress authorized substantial increases in Land and Water Conservation Fund spending for federal land acquisition, state park purchase grants, and historic preservation projects. Rapidly rising OCS receipts provided additional funds, and Congress through

legislation passed in 1976 and 1977 increased annual authorizations for the fund to $900 million for fiscal 1978-1989. *(Congress and the Nation Vol. V, p. 555)*

With the fund expanded, Congress and the Nixon and Ford administrations began steadily enlarging the park system by expanding existing parks and creating new areas. In the 1970s the Park Service developed new types of recreation areas, including urban parks, national seashores, lakeshores and other units that often lay close to heavily populated metropolitan regions. Members of Congress were eager to expand the system, both to preserve unspoiled wild lands and to develop recreation areas for their constituents. In a 1978 omnibus parks bill, Congress authorized $1.2 billion for more than 100 parks and preservation projects in 44 states, the largest parks legislation in history. Pushed through by Rep. Phillip Burton, D-Calif. (1964-83), that measure approved so many projects in so many states that members referred to it as the "park barrel," a play on the congressional "pork barrel" practice of spreading spending on federal public works projects among dozens of congressional districts.

Congress in 1980 added another 43.6 million acres to the national park system by creating new parks in Alaska, as part of legislation that settled the status of federal lands making up most of that state. *(Congress and the Nation Vol. V, pp. 570, 577)*

Land Acquisition Debate. Conservationists applauded the rapid expansion of the national park system in the 1970s. But the Park Service struggled during the decade to come up with the funds and manpower to manage its fast-growing holdings. Some observers suggested that the designation of parks and recreation areas in crowded urbanized areas was eroding the park system's original purpose in preserving scenic wonders and unspoiled regions. Conservative critics and private landowners, especially those with homes and other property near or inside national parks, questioned whether the federal government ought to be adding to its already extensive public lands. Those groups were especially vocal in Western states, where the largest national parks were located.

Many national parks encompassed scattered private lands within the boundaries set by Congress. The Park Service followed a policy of buying up such privately owned "inholdings" within park boundaries to consolidate its lands and protect against development that would ruin natural values. Private owners often resisted selling to the government, and they protested what they regarded as Park Service pressure to sell. Such owners organized the National Inholders Association to lobby against Park Service land acquisition policies.

Watt, a Wyoming native, was receptive to criticisms of federal land acquisitions. During the Nixon and Ford administrations, Watt had been director of the Interior Department's Bureau of Outdoor Recreation, the agency that managed the Land and Water Conservation Fund and drafted plans for expanding national parks and other recreation areas. The Carter administration had renamed the bureau the Heritage Conservation and Recreation Service. Watt, after taking over as interior secretary, abolished the agency and transferred its functions to the Park Service. Ric Davidge, a former lobbyist for the National Inholders Association, was appointed aide to Ray Arnett, the assistant interior secretary for parks and wildlife, who supervised the Park Service.

Watt in 1981 proposed to slow the pace of federal land acquisitions for parks and other areas. In 1980 the congres-

sional General Accounting Office (GAO) released a report that found that sewers, roads and buildings within existing national parks were deteriorating or inadequate to serve growing numbers of visitors. The report identified 172 facilities in 12 national parks that failed to meet the federal government's own health and safety standards. Seizing on the GAO report, Watt proposed spending $105 million from the Land and Water Conservation Fund for repairs and improvements in existing parks instead of for park expansion.

Congressional Action

But Congress, through 1981-82 action on President Reagan's budget requests, refused Watt's plans to halt federal land expansion and to use the Land and Water Conservation Fund for upgrading the existing national park system.

Watt's proposal to divert funds for park repairs required congressional action to amend the 1964 law that established the Land and Water Conservation Fund. Congress was unwilling to revise the law, although it appropriated additional funds for park repairs as part of the regular Park Service budget.

Reconciliation Package. In drafting a 1981 budget reconciliation package (HR 3982 — PL 97-35) the House and Senate wrote in a statement declaring the "sense of Congress" that the government should continue acquiring land to expand national parks, forests and wildlife refuges, using money from the Land and Water Conservation Fund.

The reconciliation law recommended that at least $105 million be spent each year for upgrading parks, but the money would come from the National Park Service's operation and maintenance accounts, not from the land and water fund. The measure also recommended the continuation of federal grants to the states for historic preservation and acquisition of urban parks. The administration wanted them eliminated. *(Reconciliation action, p. 40)*

In addition to $105 million to restore and rehabilitate national park system units, the reconciliation measure recommended that annual appropriations targets for fiscal 1981-84 should be at least $275 million for the Land and Water Conservation Fund, $30 million for historic preservation grants and $10 million for urban park grants.

Fiscal 1982 Appropriations. Congress followed up in December 1981 by clearing a fiscal 1982 Interior Department appropriations bill (HR 4035 — PL 97-100) that appropriated $155.6 million for the Land and Water Conservation Fund. The measure appropriated an additional $105 million for Park Service maintenance to fund Watt's campaign for repairs and improvements. The administration had sought $45 million from the fund for land purchases along with the $105 million for existing park improvements.

The bill also provided $8 million for urban park grants and $26.5 million for historic preservation grants, programs that the administration wanted to terminate. But House and Senate conferees dropped an amendment, added by the Senate, that would have provided $102.3 million for grants for state park land purchases. Although Congress provided no funds for state park grants, the conference report (H Rept 97-315) insisted that the cuts would be effective for only one year.

In drafting HR 4035 in June (H Rept 97-163), the House Appropriations Committee had recommended appropriating $155.6 million from the Land and Water Con-

servation Fund and earmarked $100.5 million of that amount for buying private lands to complete park units. In the Republican Senate the Appropriations Committee voted 15-14 to increase authorized spending from the fund to $210.5 million and provide $102.3 million for state park grants. The House legislation provided no funds for state grants. In conference the House and Senate settled on the House figure for the fund and dropped the Senate's amendment funding the state grant program.

Fiscal 1983 Appropriations. Again in 1982 Congress insisted on substantially boosting the administration's requests for the national park system. Although Watt did not press the plan to divert Land and Water Conservation Fund money for park repairs, the administration proposed spending only $69.4 million in fiscal 1983 for federal land purchases and sought to eliminate state grants entirely. In approving fiscal 1983 Interior Department appropriations (HR 7356 — PL 97-394), however, both the House and Senate voted more than $200 million for federal land purchases. For fiscal 1983 Congress provided $206.5 million from the fund for national park purchases and $75 million for state assistance.

1981-82 Wilderness Legislation

The 97th Congress enacted bills to give federal wilderness protection to national forest lands in the following states. *(1983-84 designations, box, p. 471)*

State	Acres Designated (Public Law Number)
Alabama	6,780 (PL 97-411)
Indiana	12,953 (PL 97-384)
Missouri	6,888 (PL 97-407)
West Virginia	47,800 (PL 97-466)

Forest Wilderness System

Congress progressed slowly during 1981-82 in expanding the federal wilderness system.

By the end of its second session, the 97th Congress had enacted legislation to designate 74,421 acres in four Southern and Midwestern states as protected wilderness within U.S. national forests. But environmental groups continued to spar with the Reagan administration, timber companies and other commodity interests over how much of the 187-million-acre national forest system should be set aside for preservation.

As a result, separate legislation to protect much larger forest lands in California, Montana, Wyoming and Oregon died when the 97th Congress adjourned. And President Reagan on Jan. 14, 1983, vetoed a 1982 bill that designated wilderness in Florida, objecting to provisions to buy out pending phosphate mining leases in Osceola National Forest.

The stalemate thus carried over to the 98th Congress as the House and Senate tried to settle the status of 62 million acres, roughly a third of the national forests, that the U.S. Forest Service had studied in the late 1970s for possible wilderness designation. Western economic interests, joined by the Reagan administration, were pressing Congress to clear the way for timber harvesting and other uses on 36 million acres that the Forest Service recommended be kept open for multiple-use management. Even as Congress debated those proposals, a 1982 federal court decision blocked development of those lands. *(1983-84 action, p. 470)*

Background

In the Wilderness Act of 1964 (PL 88-577), Congress established the national wilderness system to preserve, by law, federally owned lands that still were largely untouched by man. *(Congress and the Nation Vol. I, p. 1061)*

The Interior Department and the Forest Service, part of the Department of Agriculture, managed most federal lands under "multiple-use" policies that tried to balance commercial development, recreation, wildlife habitat and other values. But the 1964 law put lands within the wilderness system off-limits to logging, mining, drilling, road building, motorized travel and other activities that would disrupt their natural silence and permanently mar their primeval qualities. Once added to the system, most wilderness lands could be used only for hiking, horseback riding, hunting, fishing, canoeing, nature study and other adventures that left no lasting evidence that men had been there.

It took an act of Congress to designate public lands as part of the federal wilderness system. By preserving wild lands through law, wilderness advocates argued, Congress would prevent federal management agencies from later reopening them for development without congressional consent. While Congress had created most wilderness areas in the lower 48 states from the 187 million-acre national forest system, it also had designated large tracts within the national parks and federal wildlife refuges for preservation by statute. Through a 1976 law Congress also ordered the U.S. Bureau of Land Management (BLM), an agency that controlled nearly 249 million acres in Alaska and Western states, to study 28 million acres of those public lands for possible wilderness status. *(Federal Land Policy and Management Act, Congress and the Nation Vol. IV, p. 314)*

Most of the wilderness areas designated by the 1964 law itself tended to be high mountain peaks and remote forests in Western states that held sparse timber and few mineral resources. But conservationists, in nominating other unspoiled lands for protection, urged the agencies and Congress to enlarge the wilderness system to preserve other types of ecosystems, at lower elevations in the West and in Southern and Eastern forests.

The Forest Service itself took a purist point of view, arguing that past timber harvests, cattle grazing, vehicle travel and other historic uses had eliminated many lands as candidates for preservation. Industry officals, joined by state and local officials in regions with large federal land holdings, often argued that the government had protected enough wild lands for hiking and other forms of recreation that only a relatively affluent minority of Americans could enjoy. They maintained that wilderness status would "lock up" valuable timber, exclude snowmobiles and other popular forms of recreation and deny the U.S. mineral industry

a chance to explore lands for potential oil and gas and other resources. Once Congress created a wilderness, they pointed out, it might be impossible to persuade the House and Senate to pass another law reopening lands for development.

RARE Survey. Caught in the middle of the debate, the Forest Service twice during the 1970s surveyed unspoiled lands within the national forests in an effort to settle, once and for all, on final boundaries for the wilderness system. During the Ford administration the Forest Service conducted a study of 56 million acres of land where no roads had yet been built. That Roadless Area Review and Evaluation (RARE I), completed in 1976, recommended that Congress classify about 12 million acres as wilderness. But the Sierra Club challenged the RARE I study in court, and the Forest Service settled out of court by agreeing to complete a land use plan and environmental impact statement before allowing any use that would alter the wild characteristics of any roadless area.

After the Carter administration took office in 1977, M. Rupert Cutler, a former Wilderness Society official who was appointed assistant secretary of agriculture for natural resources and environment, directed the Forest Service to conduct a second roadless area study (RARE II). With the U.S. timber industry eager to harvest more federal forests, the Carter administration wanted to settle the status of 62 million acres and draft an environmental impact statement that could hold up under court challenges. Following the agency's recommendations, President Carter in 1979 proposed that Congress designate 15.6 million acres as wilderness while the Forest Service conducted further studies on another 10.6 million acres of roadless areas. Before sending the RARE II results to Congress, Cutler directed the agency to prepare for managing the 36 million acres it had found unsuitable for wilderness for multiple uses, including timber harvests.

But wilderness groups, not satisfied with Carter's proposed additions, challenged the 1979 RARE II impact statement and filed lawsuits to block development on roadless lands that the Forest Service proposed to reopen for multiple use management. Congress, meanwhile, moved slowly on wilderness designations, considering the RARE II proposals through state-by-state bills that usually were drafted in close consultation with each state's House and Senate delegations.

In 1979-80 the 96th Congress designated 4.2 million acres in seven states as wilderness. Action slowed in 1981-82 after President Reagan defeated Carter and Western conservatives such as James A. McClure, R-Idaho, took over key congressional posts when Republicans won control of the Senate. During the 98th Congress John B. Crowell Jr., former general counsel to Louisiana-Pacific Corp., a leading timber company, replaced Cutler and urged Congress to move more quickly to free RARE II areas for development.

Allied with Crowell, McClure and other Western conservatives proposed that Congress combine new wilderness designations with "hard release" language that would prohibit executive branch agencies from ever again considering wilderness protection for RARE II lands that Congress left out as it expanded wilderness system boundaries. Conservation groups, on the other hand, would accept only "soft release" provisions that would allow the Forest Service to review roadless regions once more in 1992-94, when management plans for national forests were due to be rewritten.

Even as Congress debated RARE II, the results were questioned by court decisions. In October 1982 the 9th U.S. Circuit Court of Appeals upheld a lower court decision, in a lawsuit brought by the California state government and environmental groups, to bar development in 46 roadless areas within that state that the Forest Service proposed for multiple-use management. The court found that the agency's environmental impact statement failed to assess adequately the environmental consequences of non-wilderness designation. The administration responded in February 1983 by announcing that the Forest Service would throw out its RARE II results and start a new study.

Completed Wilderness Legislation

During its 1982 post-election session, Congress cleared five wilderness bills that stirred relatively less controversy. Those measures, all sent to the president between Dec. 13 and 20, enlarged the national forest wilderness system by designating wilderness areas in Hoosier National Forest in Indiana (S 2710 — PL 97-384); Talladega National Forest in Alabama (S 2955 — PL 97-411); Mark Twain National Forest in Missouri (S 1965 — PL 97-407); Monongahela National Forest in West Virginia (HR 5161 — PL 97-466); and Apalachicola, Ocala and Osceola national forests in Florida. The president pocket-vetoed the 49,150-acre Florida wilderness bill (HR 9) on Jan. 14, 1983.

California Wilderness Debate

McClure's Senate Committee sidetracked legislation that the House passed in 1981 to designate as wilderness 2.1 million acres of national forest in California, along with 1.4 million acres in national parks within that state.

The House passed the legislation, drafted by the Interior Committee (HR 4083 — H Rept 97-181), on July 17. Through maneuvering by Phillip Burton, D-Calif. (1964-83), who shepherded the California bill through committee, the House attached provisions on the floor that released 2.2 million acres in California from wilderness consideration until the Forest Service began its next round of roadless area reviews in the 1990s. The release provision, a compromise that environmentalists and the timber industry had negotiated in 1980, prohibited further wilderness lawsuits on California national forests and removed a court injunction against developing 590,000 acres of disputed lands.

But with the election of a Republican-controlled Senate in 1980, the industry refused to support the California compromise. Instead, it backed national release legislation (S 842), offered by California Sen. S. I. "Sam" Hayakawa, R, to set a 1985 deadline for Congress to act on RARE II recommendations, then bar future wilderness designations within national forests. Opponents of the California wilderness bill made no effort to defeat it during House committee and floor action, hoping to find the Senate more receptive to amendments. The Senate Energy panel held hearings in 1981 but took no action on the measure.

The Carter administration had proposed 1.3 million acres of national forest wilderness in California; the Reagan administration proposed protecting 1.2 million acres.

Other Stalled Bills

Congress never completed action in 1982 on other wilderness bills, including measures for Wyoming, Oregon, Montana and Missouri.

The Senate in December passed a Wyoming wilderness bill (S 2118 — S Rept 97-574) designating 678,449 acres and including a release provision. Malcolm Wallop, R-Wyo., steered the bill through the Senate Energy Committee, but Wyoming Gov. Ed Herschler, D, and the environmentalists opposed both the amount of land protected and the release language. The House took no action.

In the House the Interior and Insular Affairs Committee in December reported Oregon wilderness legislation (HR 7340 — H Rept 97-951) designating more than one million acres and setting 112,500 acres aside for further study. The Reagan administration opposed the bill, contending it designated roughly three times the acreage that the Forest Service had recommended for wilderness status. The full House Dec. 15 failed by a 247-141 vote to muster a two-thirds majority (259 in this case) needed to suspend the rules and pass the Oregon legislation.

The Senate in October passed an Energy Committee bill (S 1964 — S Rept 97-553) to create a 17,562-acre Irish Wilderness in Missouri. The House Interior Committee approved the measure, but it died when the full House defeated by a 186-191 vote the rule providing for floor debate. Opponents complained that Congress had conducted no field hearings to give local residents near the proposed wilderness a chance to express their views. In addition, the administration opposed the designation because lead deposits could lie beneath the area.

National Parks Protection

The House in 1982 approved legislation (HR 5162) to protect national parks from development, both within and outside their boundaries, that threatened their natural character.

Despite Interior Secretary James G. Watt's opposition, the House Sept. 29 passed the measure by a 319-84 vote. In the Republican-controlled Senate, however, the Energy and Natural Resources Committee took no action on the bill. The House passed a similar bill in 1983. *(Story, p. 475)*

As passed by the House, HR 5162 required the National Park Service, the Interior Department agency that managed the national parks, to identify and deal with threats to the national park system. Rep. John F. Seiberling, D-Ohio, chairman of the House Interior Subcommittee on Public Lands and National Parks, cited a 1980 Park Service report to Congress that detailed 4,345 specific threats to the quality of the parks.

Reported by the full Interior and Insular Affairs Committee on Sept. 28 (H Rept 97-881), the bill directed the Park Service to submit a "State of the Parks Report" to Congress every two years, detailing park problems and ways to solve them. The bill also required creation of a resource management plan for each park. It set up a consultation and review process to ensure that the parks were not harmed either by Interior Department actions or by actions taken by other federal agencies.

In a letter read by Rep. Dick Cheney, R-Wyo., during the House debate, Watt objected that HR 5162 duplicated existing laws and Park Service programs and imposed inflexible requirements on park management.

Seiberling countered that nearly all national parks "are being degraded or threatened with degradation in significant ways from activities both within and outside of their boundaries, and the trend is worsening." He noted that the 1980 Park Service report concluded that the leading internal threat to the parks was overuse by rising numbers of visitors.

The number of park visitors had jumped from 33 million in 1950 to 327 million in 1981. Some national parks also were threatened by commercial developments outside their boundaries, often on adjacent lands controlled by other federal land agencies. In Feb. 3 testimony before Seiberling's subcommittee, witnesses had noted that energy developers had applied for geothermal steam leases within a mile of some Yellowstone Park thermal features. They also noted an Energy Department proposal to establish a nuclear waste disposal facility within one-half mile of Canyonlands National Park in Utah and efforts by southern Florida fishing interests to reverse a Park Service decision to phase out commercial fishing in Everglades National Park.

National Park Repairs

Congress in 1982 set up a special fund to finance repairs to decaying visitor facilities in the national parks.

Through legislation cleared Dec. 21 (HR 7316 — PL 97-433), Congress set aside concession fees paid by private businesses to operate facilities in the parks to repair or replace government-owned cabins, restaurants, lodges and other buildings. In addition, the measure authorized annual appropriations to the fund of up to $1 million, to be spent only to the extent that it was matched by cash or in-kind contributions from the private sector.

HR 7316 applied to more than 1,000 buildings owned by the federal government in national parks, including cabins, small motels, lodges, restaurants, utility buildings and employee dormitories used to support these facilities.

Barrier Islands Development

Congress in 1981-82 ended federal government support for developing barrier islands along the nation's Atlantic and Gulf of Mexico coastlines.

As part of 1981 budget reconciliation legislation, Congress cut off federal flood insurance for new homes and other structures on undeveloped barrier islands. It followed up with separate 1982 legislation that curtailed federal spending to build roads, bridges and other structures on coastal islands that the Interior Department designated for preservation.

Those steps were among the few new environmental initiatives launched by the 97th Congress. The Reagan administration and environmental groups both backed the barrier island legislation, uniting to deny federal support for building homes and tourist facilities that threatened fragile dunes and wetlands, already vulnerable to flooding and erosion.

Barrier islands stretch along the Atlantic and Gulf coasts from Maine to Mexico. They act as buffers protecting the coastline, delicate wetlands and estuaries from the full force of hurricanes and ocean storms.

These islands and other coastal landforms were unstable as a result of erosion, flooding and other natural forces. Consequently, they could be very poor places to build houses, roads and other structures. Not only were the houses likely to wash away, but human activity could damage dunes and wetlands.

The government often paid twice for barrier island development: once to subsidize the original construction and again to bail out property owners hit by disaster.

By cutting off federal flood insurance and development assistance, Congress both protected the islands against damaging use and saved the government money.

1981 Flood Insurance Ban

Through the 1981 budget reconciliation bill (HR 3982 — Pl 97-35), Congress cut off federal flood insurance for new construction or major improvements in existing structures on coastal barriers that remained largely undeveloped.

Congress in 1968 had set up a federally backed flood insurance program as part of the Housing and Urban Development Act enacted that year (PL 90-448). In that law, Congress authorized the Department of Housing and Urban Development (HUD) to subsidize premiums paid by homeowners and small businesses in flood-prone regions to private insurance companies that formed a pool to sell insurance against flood damages. Private insurance companies had been reluctant to sell flood insurance because the market was limited, but potential losses from disastrous floods were great. *(Flood insurance law, Congress and the Nation Vol. II, p. 967)*

Environmentalists contended that the federal flood insurance program, however well-intentioned, encouraged developers to build homes, businesses and resorts in ecologically sensitive river flood plains and coastal islands that easily could be ruined by development.

During debate on the 1981 reconciliation bill, the House attached a proposal by its Banking, Finance and Urban Affairs Committee to halt federal flood insurance on undeveloped barrier islands after Oct. 1, 1983. The Senate reconciliation bill carried no similar provisions, but House-Senate conferees agreed to retain the House language. *(Reconciliation, p. 40)*

1982 Legislation

In the 1982 legislation (HR 1018 — PL 97-348), Congress established a Coastal Barrier Resources System under Interior Department supervision. After mapping out barrier landforms to be protected within that system, the law barred most spending for financial aid for building roads, airports, boat landings, bridges, causeways or other structures that would serve residential and business use of the islands. It also prohibited federal spending to stabilize barrier landforms or prevent erosion along inlets, shorelines or inshore lands within the system, except to protect life and property on adjacent areas.

The legislation moved smoothly through the House and Senate with backing from the administration and a diverse coalition of environmental, disaster relief and conservative groups.

The measure sparked controversy only when the House and Senate mapped out precisely which lands would be included in the coastal barrier system. Developers and landowners in several states lobbied during House deliberations to keep their properties outside the system boundaries, and the map lines in the House version (HR 3252 — H Rept 97-841) differed somewhat from the system laid out by the Senate bill (S 1018 — S Rept 97-419). In a conference agreement (H Rept 97-928), House and Senate negotiators adjusted the system boundaries to add land in Rhode Island, Delaware, North Carolina, Florida and Mississippi while deleting lands in Maine, New York, South Carolina and Alabama.

Major Provisions. As signed into law Oct. 18, major provisions of S 1018 (PL 97-348):

● Established a Coastal Barrier Resources System consisting of those barrier landforms listed in a series of maps accompanying the bill.

● Required the interior secretary to review the maps every five years and revise them to reflect changes caused by natural forces.

● Prohibited, with certain exceptions, new expenditures or financial aid for construction or purchase of roads, airports, boat landings, bridges, causeways and other structures on lands within the system.

● Barred federal spending to stabilize or prevent erosion of inlets, shorelines or inshore areas of the system, except where an emergency threatened life, land, or property adjacent to a unit of the system.

● Allowed federal spending to continue on lands within the system for fish and wildlife management projects, energy development, existing channel improvements, essential existing public roads, Coast Guard facilities and other specified purposes.

Strip-Mining Regulation

The House in 1981 protested but failed to block Secretary of the Interior James G. Watt's plan to scale back federal strip-mining regulation.

Watt in May announced plans to reorganize the Interior Department's Office of Surface Mining (OSM). Congress created the agency in 1977 strip-mining control legislation to regulate surface-mining operations and require land reclamation by U.S. coal-mining companies. *(1977 law, Congress and the Nation Vol. V, p. 544)*

In drafting a fiscal 1982 Interior Department appropriations bill, the House Appropriations Subcommittee on the Interior voted June 11 to prohibit the department from spending funds provided by the measure to carry out the OSM reorganization. Watt immediately ordered Interior officials to speed up the reorganization to put it into effect before fiscal 1982 began on Oct. 1.

The full Appropriations Committee retained the prohibition in Interior appropriations legislation that the House passed on July 22 (HR 4035 — H Rept 97-163). But the Senate Appropriations Committee dropped the provision, and House-Senate conferees left the House prohibition out of final Interior appropriations legislation.

In administering the Surface Mining Control and Reclamation Act of 1977, OSM officials approved mining plans and conducted inspections of coal surface-mining operations on private as well as federal lands. The law provided for OSM to turn over strip-mining regulation to state governments that adopted regulations at least as stringent as the federal agency's standards. As the Carter administration began implementing the law in the late 1970s, coal company executives and some Western state officials complained that OSM moved too slowly in approving state regulatory plans and imposed burdensome and duplicative regulations on strip-mining operations. "Embodied in this one office we find every abuse of government centered in one agency, directed at one industry," Watt himself told the National Coal Association convention in 1981.

The Reagan administration made no proposals for

amending the 1977 strip-mining law. But the administration appointed James Harris, a former Indiana state legislator who had led that state's legal challenge to the 1977 law, as OSM director. The administration cut the OSM budget and reduced the agency's staff from 1,001 to 628 employees. Through the controversial reorganization plan, Watt closed down the agency's field enforcement offices. Interior in 1981 also revised OSM regulations to eliminate specific federal mine design standards and give states primary enforcement authority.

The National Wildlife Federation filed legal challenges to the revised strip-mining regulations. In a 1984 decision a U.S. District Court judge in Washington, D.C., ruled that the regulations violated the 1977 law by delegating to state governments the authority to approve plans to mine coal from federal lands leased to private companies.

Payments in Lieu of Taxes

Congress in 1981 refused to cancel federal payments to county governments with tax-exempt public lands within their borders.

In a fiscal 1982 budget submitted before he left office, President Carter proposed ending those payments, known as payments in lieu of taxes (PILT). Congress first authorized the payments in 1976 to compensate local governments that were unable to levy property taxes on federally owned lands that in places made up most of their jurisdictions. *(Congress and the Nation Vol. IV, p. 318)*

Background. The 1976 law provided annual payments to counties, or other local governments with taxing powers, that encompassed national parks, national forests, U.S. Army Corps of Engineers or U.S. Bureau of Reclamation reservoirs or Interior Department public lands managed by the Bureau of Land Management. County officials had complained that their inability to tax federal government lands severely restricted local government revenues. Such resentment was especially strong in the West, where national forests and Interior Department lands took up large percentages of the land base.

Congress based those payments on a formula taking account of population, federal land acreage and county government revenues from mineral leasing, timber sale and other receipts from federal lands that the federal government shared with state and local governments. It limited each county's PILT payments to $1 million a year, and it excluded Indian reservations, military bases, wildlife refuges and General Services Administration office buildings and other facilities from the computation.

The PILT program directed most of its revenues to county governments with large expanses of federal lands that produced little or no revenue from timber, oil and gas, coal or other minerals. Annual appropriations for the payments in the early 1980s were about $100 million. Although Carter recommended abolishing the PILT program, President Reagan in his March 1981 budget revisions proposed to continue it with a $45 million fiscal 1982 appropriation.

Congressional Action. But Congress preserved most of the program's funding through action on the president's budget requests. In its 1981 budget-cutting reconciliation package (HR 3982 — PL 97-35), Congress recommended continuing PILT payments with a $100 million annual appropriation.

During 1981 action on fiscal 1982 Interior Department appropriations, the House Appropriations Committee voted to end the program. In its report on the measure (HR 4035 — H Rept 97-163), the panel argued that many counties received more from the payments than they would collect if federal lands were subject to local taxes. Before passing the bill July 22, the full House defeated, by a 96-320 vote, a floor amendment by Manuel Lujan Jr., R-N.M., to appropriate $100 million for the program.

In revising the House legislation, however, the Senate Appropriations Committee proposed (S Rept 97-166) $105 million for PILT in fiscal 1982. The Senate passed the bill Oct. 27 after approving an amendment by Thad Cochran, R-Miss., adding another $7 million to compensate states for tax-exempt national wildlife refuges within their borders. In conference, House and Senate negotiatiors agreed (H Rept 97-315) to continue the PILT program with a $105.5 million appropriation, of which $6 million was earmarked for states with wildlife refuges.

Mount St. Helens Monument

Congress in 1982 created a national monument on U.S. Forest Service lands in Washington that were devastated by the Mount St. Helens volcano when it erupted in 1980.

Through legislation cleared Aug. 17 (HR 6530 — PL 97-243), Congress established a 110,000-acre Mount St. Helens National Volcanic Monument within Gifford Pinchot National Forest. The measure set those lands aside, under U.S. Forest Service management, for resource preservation and scientific research. It allowed logging, recreation, hunting, fishing and other uses only to the extent they were compatible with those primary purposes.

In addition to existing national forest lands, the measure incorporated within the monument 30,000 acres of lands owned mainly by the Weyerhaeuser Co., Burlington Northern Inc., and the state of Washington. The law provided for exchanging nearby federally owned lands for those state and private tracts.

National Trails Legislation

The House in 1982 passed a bill (HR 861 — H Rept 97-267) to designate three new national scenic trails. The measure died in the Senate.

Passed by the House on May 11, HR 861 designated the Potomac Heritage, Natchez Trace and Florida trails as part of the National Trails System created by Congress in 1968 (PL 90-543). The bill authorized studies for six additional trail routes.

Sponsored by Rep. Phillip Burton, D-Calif. (1964-83), HR 861 was a scaled-down version of legislation that had passed both House and Senate in 1980 but never reached final action. Reported by the House Interior and Insular Affairs Committee in 1981, the bill eliminated most designations under the 1980 legislation that required future federal expenditures.

The House-passed measure carried a provision, opposed by the Reagan administration, that would have barred the government from charging entrance fees for the trails system, wild and scenic river areas, or national recreation areas. It also prohibited entrance fees at national parks where the cost of collecting them would exceed the resulting revenues.

President Reagan, in his fiscal 1983 budget, had proposed increasing federal revenues by $63 million a year by

raising national park entrance fees and by imposing fees for persons to enter recreation and wilderness areas, where access had previously been free of charge. *(1980 legislation, Congress and the Nation Vol. V, p. 596)*

The Senate Energy and Natural Resources Committee reported HR 861 Sept. 23, 1982 (S Rept 97-577), but the full Senate never passed it.

1983-84

With the resignation of Secretary of the Interior James G. Watt in 1983, the congressional spotlight shifted away from environmental protection on public lands managed by the federal government.

William P. Clark, President Reagan's close adviser, took over from Watt and quieted the angry protests that Watt's policies had stirred among House Democrats and environmental group leaders. Congress nonetheless debated major policy choices between developing federally owned resources and preserving the environmental quality of national parks, forests and range lands.

In what could prove one of its most lasting environmental decisions, Congress in 1984 settled some long-running disputes over preserving wilderness within the national forest system. Through 20 separate bills the House and Senate added more than 8.3 million acres to the federal wilderness system. In a compromise that environmentalists and timber companies negotiated as the 1984 presidential election approached, Congress at the same time released another 13.5 million acres of undeveloped national forest lands for logging, mining, oil and gas exploration and other commercial uses.

Clark defused another often bitter dispute by resuming federal land purchases, which Watt had proposed halting, to expand national parks and wildlife refuges. The Senate again killed House legislation to impose tougher controls on development near national park boundaries, however, and the House and Senate both sidestepped a controversial proposal to reopen national parks in Alaska for sport hunting. Congress did clear measures that expanded the federal Wild and Scenic Rivers System.

While Clark scaled back Watt's ambitious mineral leasing plans, Senate Republicans from Western states in general remained pleased with the Reagan administration's emphasis on developing federal lands that were managed by the Interior Department's Bureau of Land Management and the U.S. Forest Service, an Agriculture Department agency. House Democrats, on the other hand, still objected that the administration's budget and personnel decisions favored resource development over environmental protection programs. Members of Congress, for instance, resisted the administration's proposals to increase national forest timber harvests even though lumber demand was slumping. Congress in 1984 cleared legislation that allowed timber companies to buy out from high-cost contracts to cut national forest timber, signed in the late 1970s.

Forest Wilderness System

Congress in 1984 settled the status of more than 20 million acres of undeveloped land in U.S. national forests.

Ending years of uncertainty, the Senate and House cleared bills setting aside more than 8.3 million acres of forest lands in 20 states as federally protected wilderness. Those laws vastly expanded the national system for preserving pristine lands that Congress created in the Wilderness Act of 1964.

In the same measures Congress freed huge tracts in the national forests for possible logging, mining, oil and gas exploration and other commercial ventures. Under a compromise accepted by environmental groups and timber companies, the bills released 13.5 million acres of roadless lands that had been studied — but not yet selected — as wilderness preserves for "multiple-use management" by the U.S. Forest Service over the following 15 years.

President Reagan signed all of the 1984 wilderness bills, although his administration generally objected to keeping federal lands off-limits to development. After two decades of debate, however, the president's conservative Republican allies in the Senate were eager to wrap up a prolonged wilderness review that had tied up millions of acres in studies, planning, lawsuits and legislative maneuvering.

Since the mid-1970s the Forest Service had barred commercial development on about 62 million acres in the lower 48 states until Congress decided whether to protect them as federal wilderness. Environmental groups campaigned to protect as much land as possible, while the logging industry and other business interests grew impatient for access to millions of acres that held valuable timber and potential mineral resources. Congress finally broke the impasse after key House and Senate foes negotiated a compromise on how the government should manage unspoiled lands that Congress left out of an expanded national wilderness system.

Congress debated wilderness designations in state-by-state legislation. In drafting most wilderness bills, House and Senate delegations from each state united behind expanded wilderness boundaries drawn up through arduous negotiations among environmentalists and commercial interests. But the process bitterly divided members from some Western states, notably California and Oregon, where strong environmental movements and important timber industries had been fighting for years over millions of acres that the Forest Service had identified as roadless lands that still could be preserved in wild condition.

The Democratic House, generally sympathetic to environmentalist causes, in 1983 passed California and Oregon wilderness bills substantially boosting the acreage that the Reagan administration and the Forest Service wanted to preserve. In the Senate influential Western conservatives favored smaller wilderness designations and held out for language that would permanently "release" remaining roadless lands for commercial use, ruling them out for future wilderness expansions. Since environmentalists hoped they could persuade the Forest Service to recommend some of those lands for wilderness during the 1990s, the debate over releasing non-wilderness lands stalled final action between 1979 and 1983 on major wilderness system additions.

By 1984, however, both sides stood ready to resolve the impasse that tied up millions of acres in uncertain status. Senate Energy and Natural Resources Committee Chairman James A. McClure, R-Idaho, and Rep. John H. Seiberling, D-Ohio, chairman of the House Interior and Insular Affairs Subcommittee on Public Lands, May 2 agreed to set release terms that required wilderness reviews of forest

Interior Department range lands. Major wilderness additions in the East included 77,000 acres in New Hampshire, 68,750 acres in North Carolina and 55,984 acres in Virginia. *(1983-84 wilderness designations, box, this page; 1981-82 action, p. 465)*

The year's action brought to about 88.6 million acres the total amount of federally designated wilderness. Most of that, some 56.4 million acres, was in Alaska, with only 32.2 million acres in the lower 48 states. Alaska's wilderness was designated in a 1980 law after years of bitter arguments. *(Alaska lands, Congress and the Nation Vol. V, p. 577)*

1983 Wilderness Bills

The House in 1983 cranked out wilderness legislation for 10 states as members tried to head off the administration's plan for another roadless area study. But the Senate passed only two wilderness bills, and only the Montana bill cleared Congress.

The single measure (S 96 — PL 98-140) created a 259,000-acre wilderness, named for the late Sen. Lee Metcalf, D-Mont. (1962-78), in Beaverhead and Gallatin national forests. The Senate passed the measure April 13 (S Rept 98-16) and the House approved it Oct. 6 (H Rept 98-405) after adding more acreage. The Senate cleared the legislation Oct. 19 by accepting House amendments.

Other House-passed legislation in 1983 included controversial California and Oregon bills that expanded the Reagan administration's wilderness proposals. Rep. Phillip Burton, D-Calif., personally crafted the California bill (HR 1437 — H Rept 98-40) adding 58 national forest areas including 2.3 million within national parks as protected wilderness. The House passed the bill on April 12, two days after Burton died, by a 297-96 vote.

HR 1437 released 4.3 million acres of California forests for development. But the House by voice vote accepted Seiberling's amendment adding a package of "soft release" provisions permitting reassessment of their wilderness potential during the next Forest Service planning cycle.

Earlier in the year, the House March 21 had passed an Oregon bill (HR 1149 — H Rept 98-13) designating 1.1 million acres in 30 wilderness areas for protection. Oregon Democrats James Weaver, Les AuCoin and Ron Wyden backed the bill, while the Forest Service and the state's two Republican representatives opposed it. The House passed HR 1149 by a 252-93 vote after defeating floor challenges by Oregon Republicans Denny Smith and Robert F. Smith, who contended that it would cost forest industry jobs in the districts they represented.

The House in 1983 also passed wilderness bills for Missouri, New Hampshire, North Carolina, Vermont, Wisconsin, Alabama and Florida. The House Interior Committee revived the vetoed Florida bill after removing provisions to compensate four companies that had pending phosphate mining applications (HR 9 — H Rept 98-102, Parts I and II).

Senate Wyoming Bill. In addition to the Montana bill, the Senate April 13 passed by voice vote a bill (S 543 — S Rept 98-54) designating 635,729 acres in Wyoming national forests as wilderness. The Senate measure protected fewer lands than the RARE II proposal or the 2.4 million acres of additional wilderness that conservationists wanted for Wyoming.

It carried a provision releasing all non-wilderness forest lands in the state until the year 2000.

1983-84 Wilderness Legislation

The 98th Congress cleared bills to give federal wilderness protection to national forest lands in the following states. *(1981-82 designations, box, p. 465)*

State	Acres Designated (Public Law Number)
Arizona	1,054,000 (PL 98-406)* †
Arkansas	91,100 (PL 98-508)
California	3,210,560 (PL 98-425)† ‡
Florida	49,150 (PL 98-430)†
Georgia	14,439 (PL 98-514)
Mississippi	5,500 (PL 98-515)
Missouri	16,500 (PL 98-289)
Montana	259,000 (PL 98-140)
New Hampshire	77,000 (PL 98-323)
New Mexico	
San Juan Basin	27,840 (PL 98-603)*
North Carolina	68,750 (PL 98-324)†
Oregon	859,300 (PL 98-328)
Pennsylvania	9,705 (PL 98-585)†
Tennessee	24,942 (PL 98-578)
Texas	34,346 (PL 98-574)
Utah	750,000 (PL 98-428)
Vermont	41,260 (PL 98-322)†
Virginia	55,984 (PL 98-586)†
Washington	1,038,878 (PL 98-339)* †
Wisconsin	24,339 (PL 98-321)
Wyoming	884,049 (PL 98-550)†

* Includes acreage managed by Interior Department's Bureau of Land Management.
† Excludes additional protective designations, such as Wilderness Study Area or National Recreation Area, made in bill.
‡ Includes 1,418,230 acres of land already in national parks.

---

lands every 15 years. The accord broke the logjam of wilderness bills, and Congress wrote the compromise language into most of the 20 state-by-state measures it cleared before adjourning its 1984 session.

In all, Congress in 1984 added an area larger than the state of Maryland to the national wilderness system. In 1983 Congress had cleared a single bill that created a 259,000-acre wilderness area in Montana. In addition to California and Oregon, the 1984 legislation expanded the wilderness system in Arizona, Arkansas, Florida, Georgia, Mississippi, Missouri, New Hampshire, New Mexico, North Carolina, Pennsylvania, Tennessee, Texas, Utah, Vermont, Virginia, Washington, Wisconsin and Wyoming. The largest designations were 3.2 million acres in California, one million acres in Arizona, 859,300 acres in Oregon, one million acres in Washington, 750,000 acres in Utah and 884,000 acres in Wyoming — all Western states with huge expanses of federally owned national parks, forests and

1984 Compromise on Release

Through 1981-83 McClure had kept major House-passed wilderness bills bottled up in Senate committees. McClure's Energy Committee held jurisdiction over wilderness designations in Western national forests, while the Senate Agriculture Committee considered wilderness bills for national forests in Eastern states.

But during the spring of 1984 strategists for both sides of the wilderness dispute concluded that quickly resolving the impasse would be to their advantage. Timber companies, while still opposing extensive wilderness additions, chafed even more at congressional indecision that was keeping larger forest tracts on indefinite hold even though those lands had been tentatively ruled out for immediate wilderness status. Environmental groups meanwhile recognized that the 1984 election year offered a "window of opportunity" because Reagan, whose record on environment issues had been under fire, would be reluctant to veto wilderness legislation. Sources in some congressional delegations, such as Washington's, said the White House had provided assurances that the president would sign any wilderness bill Congress sent him in 1984 — but not necessarily in 1985, after Reagan had been re-elected.

Seiberling and McClure cleared the way for wilderness bill agreements with their May 2 compromise on release language. Congress made the release provision, which required wilderness reviews every 15 years, part of most of the wilderness measures it cleared in rapid succession in following months. "It was in everybody's interest to end the uncertainty," Seiberling observed. "That fact finally dawned on most of the hard-liners on the industry side as well as the environmentalists' side."

Bills Cleared

Once the logjam had been broken, both the House and Senate moved wilderness bills with relatively little controversy. California's two senators, Alan Cranston, D, and Pete Wilson, R, June 29 announced a compromise version of Burton's 1983 House bill, and 32 members of the state's 45-member House delegation endorsed it. The Senate passed the California bill on Aug. 9, and the House accepted the Senate revisions by a 368-41 vote on Sept. 12, although 11 California Republicans opposed it. President Reagan signed HR 1437 (PL 98-425) Sept. 28.

The Senate May 24 had passed a compromise Oregon bill drawn up by Mark O. Hatfield, R-Ore. House Democrats from Oregon accepted Hatfield's revisions, and the House June 6 concurred in the Senate amendments by a 281-99 vote despite continued objections by Robert F. Smith and Denny Smith, the state's two Republican representatives. Robert F. Smith complained that the final Oregon "compromise is being settled between the environmentalists — the environmentalists here and the environmentalists there," at the expense of jobs for Oregon loggers. HR 1149 was signed into law June 26 (PL 98-328).

The Senate also passed 1983 House bills for Florida, Missouri, New Hampshire, North Carolina, Vermont and Wisconsin. Congress in addition cleared wilderness bills that the House drafted in 1984 for Arizona, New Mexico, Pennsylvania, Tennessee, Texas and Virginia. The House cleared the Senate's 1983 Wyoming bill, and Congress approved wilderness bills drafted by Senate committees for Arkansas, Georgia, Mississippi, Utah and Washington. That brought to 20 the number of bills cleared in 1984.

Wild and Scenic Rivers

Congress in 1984 protected five rivers by adding them to the federal Wild and Scenic Rivers System.

Through various measures Congress expanded the system to take in parts of rivers in California, Arizona, Michigan and Oregon. It also temporarily protected New Hampshire, North Carolina and another Oregon river from proposed dams, roadbuilding and other destructive development while the government studied whether they should be permanently preserved.

In the Wild and Scenic Rivers Act of 1968 (PL 90-542), Congress set up a federal-state system for preserving wild rivers for rafting, fishing and other recreation. Similar in some ways to the national park and wilderness systems, the program protected the natural, free-flowing quality of rivers by barring federal dam projects and restricting roads and other developments that would step up human activity along their courses. *(Congress and the Nation Vol. II, p. 472)*

Many wild rivers ran through national parks, forests and other federal lands, giving the government direct control over riverbank development. The 1968 law also gave the government authority to acquire private lands along their banks, in some cases by condemnation, and to buy "scenic easements" from landowners who agreed not to develop their holdings in ways that would spoil the river.

Objections from private landowners had made many proposals for designating wild and scenic rivers controversial.

With energy costs rising, electric utilities and Western irrigation districts opposed protection for streams that were being considered as potential sites for dams generating hydroelectric power.

Such disputes had forced Congress to move slowly in expanding the original eight-river system protected by the 1968 law. In addition to protection by act of Congress, the law gave the secretary of interior power to designate a wild or scenic river by approving a state request for its preservation. Just before the Carter administration left office, Interior Secretary Cecil D. Andrus on Jan. 19, 1981, added five northern California rivers totaling 1,235 miles to the system. Timber and water interests in California took a legal challenge to the designations to the U.S. Supreme Court.

Conservation groups faulted the Reagan administration for downgrading the river protection program through budget cuts and reorganizations. Interior Secretary James G. Watt in 1981 abolished the department's Heritage Conservation and Recreation Service, which had managed the wild and scenic rivers program, and transferred its remnants to the National Park Service. The administration in 1982 unveiled a proposal to add eight new river segments to the system, but environmentalists contended that the administration's plan also would have made it more difficult to protect additional rivers and easier to develop them.

The Park Service had inventoried about 1,500 river segments totaling about 61,000 miles that the agency considered eligible for wild and scenic status. Through its 1984 additions, the first since Andrus' designations in 1981, Congress expanded the existing system to take in about 7,200 miles in 65 rivers or river segments.

In its most controversial 1984 step, Congress protected 83 miles of the Tuolumne River in California as a wild and scenic river through a provision that the Senate Energy and Natural Resources Committee attached to legislation expanding the federal wilderness system in that state (HR

1437 — PL 98-425). Interior and the U.S. Forest Service in 1978 had proposed the Tuolumne for wild and scenic status, but in 1982 two California irrigation districts were granted a Federal Energy Regulatory Commission (FERC) permit to study building a massive hydroelectric project on the river's main stem. About two-thirds of the state's 45-member House delegation sponsored legislation to protect the Tuolumne, but the administration and Rep. Tony Coelho, D-Calif., who represented Modesto, opposed designating the river until dam studies were finished.

Coelho was chairman of the Democratic Congressional Campaign Committee, which funneled funds and other support for fellow Democratic members needing help in re-election campaigns. He also served on the House Interior and Insular Affairs Committee, which considered wild and scenic rivers designations. But wild river advocates bypassed the influential Coelho's opposition by adding the designation to the California wilderness bill in the Senate. *(Wilderness bills, p. 470)*

As part of separate Arizona wilderness legislation (HR 4707 — PL 98-406), Congress conferred wild and scenic status on 39.5 miles of that state's Verde River. In other legislation, Congress also designated 23 miles of the Au Sable River in Michigan (S 2732 — PL 98-444), 112 miles of the Owyhee River and 50 miles of the Illinois River in Oregon (S 416 — PL 98-494). Congress also gave protected study status to the North Umpqua River in Oregon (PL 98-494), the Wildcat River in New Hampshire (HR 3921 — PL 98-323) and the Horsepasture River in North Carolina (HR 3601 — PL 98-484).

Forest Timber Contract Relief

Congress in 1984 granted logging companies in the Pacific Northwest relief from high-cost contracts to cut timber from national forests.

The industry had bid up prices for federal timber during the late 1970s, expecting a housing boom that would keep lumber prices rising. But as inflation fell off, some small logging companies faced possible bankruptcy if those contracts forced them to buy timber at prices well above what they could sell it for after cutting down trees and sawing them into lumber.

After resisting pleas for relief for several years, Congress Oct. 1 relented by passing legislation (HR 2838 — PL 98-478) that allowed the timber industry to "buy out" from contracts for up to 200 million board feet of federal timber. President Reagan somewhat reluctantly signed the measure, which Republicans in the Pacific Northwest maintained was essential to restore the region's important logging industry to economic health.

The so-called timber "bailout" issue had dominated congressional debates in 1982-84 on national forest policy. The dispute highlighted a U.S. Forest Service backlog of an estimated 40 billion board feet of standing timber that the agency had sold to timber companies but still remained uncut. It gave members of Congress ammunition to oppose the Reagan administration's campaign to accelerate future harvests from national forests to supply timber industry demand.

Background

The national forests held half of the nation's softwood sawtimber inventory, the bulk in Douglas fir, pine, spruce and other species growing in the Pacific Northwest region. The U.S. timber industry relied heavily on national forests in Washington, Oregon, Northern California and Idaho to meet national demand for lumber and other forest products. The Forest Service, a Department of Agriculture agency, managed most forests in the region. But the Bureau of Land Management (BLM), an Interior Department agency, also controlled rich productive timberlands in Oregon and Washington.

In the Southeast, the nation's other major timber region, logging companies grew most of their own trees on privately owned lands. Although major timber producers held extensive private forests in the Pacific Northwest, they bought most of the timber they harvested from the Forest Service and BLM. As the industry exhausted its own private forests, it began pressuring the agencies to accelerate harvests from mature "old-growth" stands of Douglas fir and other species to keep sawmills running until reforested trees planted on private lands were ready for harvest in the 21st century.

Alarmed by rapidly escalating new housing costs, the Carter administration in the late 1970s had prodded the Forest Service to step up timber harvests, particularly from the towering "old-growth" national forests of Washington, Oregon and Northern California. President Reagan in 1981 named John B. Crowell Jr., general counsel to Louisiana-Pacific Corp., a major purchaser of national forest timber, as assistant secretary of agriculture for environment and natural resources, the official who oversaw the Forest Service. Crowell directed the agency to plan for accelerated harvests that would as much as double national forest timber sales.

But environmental groups and congressional critics — led by Rep. James Weaver, D-Ore., the chairman of the House Interior Subcommittee on Forest Management, who also served on the Agriculture Committee — challenged the need for increasing harvests at a time when timber companies could not afford to cut a growing backlog of trees they already had signed contracts to buy.

Under existing law timber companies contracted with the federal government to buy and cut timber on publicly owned land. Contracts usually were awarded to the highest bidder, with proceeds going to the Treasury.

In the late 1970s inflation and heavy demand led companies to bid up contract prices for timber. But a subsequent collapse of the housing market coupled with sharp reductions in inflation left many firms stuck with contracts to buy timber at prices well above its current market value. A number of small companies faced possible bankruptcy unless relief was granted.

Sagging lumber markets already had forced the industry to lay off workers and close down sawmills that formed the economic base of many small Pacific Northwest towns. To keep the overbidding fiasco from further damaging the regional economy, Sen. Mark O. Hatfield, R-Ore., and other members backed legislation to allow timber purchasers to cancel up to 40 percent of their contract commitments to buy and harvest trees.

But the bailout proposal split the forest products industry. Southern timber operators opposed contract relief proposals that they contended would give their Pacific Northwest competitors an unfair advantage. Senate Agriculture Committee Chairman Jesse Helms, R-N.C., blocked Hatfield's legislation in 1982 and 1983. The administration also raised philosophical objections to a "bailout" and Crowell testified against Hatfield's bill in 1982.

Clark Disarms Watt Foes

In barely more than a year in the post, Secretary of the Interior William P. Clark quieted a stormy debate that his predecessor had sparked over managing federal lands and resources.

President Reagan in October 1983 picked Clark, a longtime Reagan adviser and troubleshooter, to succeed James G. Watt as head of the Interior Department. Clark never disowned Watt's policies, but his low-key management style and political skills disarmed House Democrats' and environmental groups' previously angry attacks on Watt's efforts to promote rapid development of federal coal, oil and gas, and other resources. *(Clark profile, p. 1023; Watt dispute, p. 406)*

In the process the president's former national security adviser returned Interior to "the humdrum agency it used to be," in the words of one longtime department staffer. Defusing bitter controversies over Watt's policies, Clark resumed buying lands for national parks, slowed plans for leasing federal offshore oil and gas, and halted federal coal lease sales while Interior officials overhauled leasing procedures. Softening Watt's hard-line rhetoric, Clark opened ties to House Democrats whom Watt had defied and consulted environmental group leaders whom Watt had excluded from the Interior policy-making process.

The Senate confirmed Clark's appointment by a 71-18 vote on Nov. 18, 1983. Before the vote the Senate tabled, 48-42, a non-binding "sense of the Senate" resolution urging Clark to reverse Watt policies that had angered many members of Congress.

Although environmental groups welcomed Clark's conciliatory style, they found little change in the administration's basic pro-development goals during his brief Interior tenure. Clark on Jan. 1, 1985, announced that he was resigning the Interior post to return to his ranch in California. Reagan named Secretary of Energy Donald P. Hodel, who previously had served as interior under secretary under Watt, to replace Clark.

The Senate Energy and Natural Resources Committee, which held jurisdiction over national forests in the West, nonetheless in 1982 approved a contract relief bill after Hatfield and J. Bennett Johnston, D-La., proposed revisions to defuse Southeastern timber interests' concerns about the competitive effects of Forest Service resale of timber at lower prices. But Howard M. Metzenbaum, D-Ohio, objected to granting relief for major timber companies as well as small sawmill operations and questioned the bill's impact on housing prices. His filibuster threat blocked Senate floor action on the 1982 bill.

Relief legislation remained stalled in 1983, but the Forest Service took administrative steps to allow companies to extend the term of their contracts by five years without paying interest. That took some pressure off the industry, but many firms kept pressing Congress for longer-term contract relief.

1984 Congressional Approval

The Senate Energy Committee revived the bill in 1984, attaching contract relief provisions to HR 2838, a House-passed measure authorizing government assistance to groups that volunteered to plant tree seedlings on federal lands. The revised measure allowed logging companies to buy out of contract obligations for up to 55 percent of the timber they had bought before 1982. It set forth a formula for calculating how much a company had to pay the government for contract relief, based on its potential loss and the amount of timber under contract. It set a ceiling of 200 million board feet on the total amount of timber under contract that the government could agree to take back. To protect Southeastern logging companies, the measure set limits on national forest timber sales in Washington and Oregon through fiscal 1991.

The committee reported HR 2838 (S Rept 98-596) on Aug. 27, and the full Senate passed it by a 94-2 vote on Sept. 26 after adopting four amendments that Metzenbaum offered to tighten contract buy-out terms. One Metzenbaum proposal set stiffer terms for larger companies to buy out from contracts than for smaller loggers that had bought less timber from national forests.

Office of Management and Budget Director David A. Stockman Oct. 1 urged the House to defeat a Senate proposal that he contended would "provide a small number of corporations with $400 million worth of special relief." But the House the same day cleared the legislation by voice vote, and Reagan signed it on Oct. 16.

Provisions

As signed into law Oct. 16, major provisions of HR 2838 (PL 98-478):

● Allowed logging companies to "buy out" of their purchase obligations for up to 55 percent of timber contracted for prior to Jan. 1, 1982, if they still held the contract.

● Set a maximum of 200 million board feet on the amount of timber subject to buy-out.

● Established a formula for determining how much companies had to pay to buy out of existing contracts.

● Limited to no more than 5.2 billion board feet the net amount of "merchantable sawtimber" that could be sold annually in Oregon and Washington through fiscal 1991.

Alaska Parks Hunting Debate

Congress in 1983-84 sidestepped a potentially divisive fight over reopening national parks in Alaska to sport hunting for big-game animals.

The Senate Energy and Natural Resources Committee Oct. 26, 1983, reported a bill (S 49 — S Rept 98-281) to permit sport hunting on about five million acres in Alaskan national parks. But the panel sent the bill to the floor without recommending that it be passed, and the Senate took no further action.

Congress had closed those lands for hunting in 1980,

when it passed the Alaska National Interest Lands Conservation Act (ANILCA, PL 96-487) settling the status of federally owned lands that make up most of that state.

Congress by law prohibited hunting in most U.S. national parks. In the 1980 Alaska land law, Congress created 43.6 million acres of new national parks from federally owned lands in the state. The law designated about 19 million acres of those lands as national park preserves, a rarely used category that differed from park status only by allowing sport hunting.

As drafted by the Senate committee, S 49 would have opened another five million acres in Alaska parks for hunting by reclassifying them as national park preserves. Alaska state officials, hunting guides, the National Rifle Association and hunters' groups backed the bill. The National Wildlife Federation and the Izaak Walton League, conservation groups representing mostly sportsmen, also endorsed the measure in concept. But the Wilderness Society, National Parks and Conservation Association and other preservation-oriented environmental groups opposed S 49 as a precedent for opening all national parks for hunting.

Parks Protection Bill

The House in 1983 tried to revive legislation, opposed by the Reagan administration, to strengthen controls over mining and other development that threatened national parks.

By a 321-82 vote, the House Oct. 4 passed a measure (HR 2379 — H Rept 98-170) similar to a bill it had approved in 1982. But the Senate Energy and Natural Resources Committee took no action on either the 1982 or 1983 House measures. *(1982 action, p. 467)*

Developed by John F. Seiberling, D-Ohio, chairman of the Interior and Insular Affairs Subcommittee on Public Lands and National Parks, the legislation laid out detailed planning and notification procedures to head off federal government actions that threatened to intrude on national parks. Those requirements applied to Interior's mineral leasing program and other federal agency decisions.

Western Republicans led opposition to HR 2379, particularly a provision that required the secretary of the interior to review federal agency decisions on lands "adjacent to" park boundaries. Westerners argued that Congress or the National Park Service could use that requirement to stymie resource development on national forests, other Interior Department lands or other federal holdings lying far from the parks themselves.

Before reporting the bill, the full Interior Committee rejected, by an 18-20 margin, an amendment by James V. Hansen, R-Utah, to let state legislatures define which lands lay "adjacent" to park boundaries. Hansen and other critics feared the bill would give the federal government veto power over local government decisions involving lands near national parks. Hansen tried again on the floor, but the full House defeated the amendment by a 160-245 vote after Seiberling maintained that it would effectively gut the bill.

Critical Materials Council

Congress in 1984 approved legislation creating a three-member National Critical Materials Council to advise the White House and recommend legislation to Congress to improve U.S. supplies of key defense and industrial materi-

als. The measure (S 373 — PL 98-373) also created two federal panels to oversee federal research programs in Arctic regions.

After taking office in 1981, President Reagan called for aggressive federal programs to develop new domestic sources of so-called "strategic minerals" that U.S. industry used to build high-performance jet fighters, other military equipment and various high-technology products. The United States relied heavily on foreign imports — some from nations of questionable political stability — for most of its supplies of critical materials like cobalt, chromium and manganese. Zaire provided about 40 percent of U.S. imports of cobalt, a metal not mined in the United States that was used to make strong and durable jet engine parts. South Africa and Gabon also were key suppliers of vital minerals for U.S. industry.

Reagan in 1981 announced plans to decrease America's minerals vulnerability by stockpiling critical metals, expanding federal research on mining technology and opening federal lands for more mineral exploration. Mining companies had been pushing the Interior Department to review federal land "withdrawals" that barred them from staking mining claims, suggesting that exploration might discover new domestic reserves of strategic minerals. Environmentalists and some resource experts, skeptical that federal lands held significant new resources, viewed the industry arguments as an attempt to persuade the government to lift restrictions on mining sensitive public lands.

As passed by the Senate on June 27, 1983, S 373 set up just the two Arctic research panels. But the House, before passing the bill on April 24, 1984, accepted a substitute text drafted by the House Science and Technology and Merchant Marine and Fisheries committees (H Rept 98-593, Parts I and II) adding provisions to create the critical materials council.

Reagan opposed the sweeping authority the House bill granted the materials council, preferring to keep control over materials policy in his Cabinet Council on Natural Resources and the Environment. When S 373 went back to the Senate, that chamber adopted amendments to dilute the new council's power, making it almost exclusively an advisory body. The House June 26 agreed to the Senate amendments, clearing the measure.

National Trails Legislation

Congress in 1983 established three additional national scenic trails and authorized studies of six proposed additions to the national trails system established in 1968 (PL 90-543). *(Congress and the Nation Vol. II, p. 472)*

The measure (S 271 — PL 98-11), passed by the Senate Feb. 3 and the House March 15, was generally similar to one passed in 1982 by the House but not the Senate. Unlike that bill, however, S 271 contained no language aimed at blocking imposition of entrance fees at national recreation areas, scenic trails or rivers. The House had supported such language, while the Republican-controlled Senate opposed it. *(1982 action, p. 469)*

As cleared, S 271 established three new national trails: Potomac Heritage National Scenic Trail, extending along the Potomac River for about 700 miles through Virginia, Maryland, the District of Columbia and Pennsylvania; Florida National Scenic Trail, extending about 1,300 miles in the state of Florida; and Natchez Trace National Scenic Trail, extending 694 miles from Nashville, Tenn., to Natchez, Miss.

Other Legislation

Truman Home Site

Congress in 1983 cleared legislation (S 287 — PL 98-32) that designated President Harry S Truman's home in Independence, Mo., as a national historic site.

The measure authorized the secretary of the interior to acquire and maintain the white frame house where Truman and his wife, Bess, lived from the time of their marriage until their deaths. As a national historic site the house became part of the National Park System.

Truman, the nation's 33rd president (1945-53), died in 1972. His wife lived in the Independence house until her death in 1982.

Oregon Land Tracts

Overriding President Reagan's veto, Congress in 1983 granted nine small tracts of public land in Oregon to individuals who had bought the parcels from a private developer 42 years before.

With no objections, the House Oct. 3 and the Senate Oct. 4 passed legislation (HR 1062) authorizing the secretary of the interior to give the tracts, amounting to 3.11 acres, to six elderly couples and two corporations. Due to a private surveyor's error, a developer in 1941 mistakenly sold the lots as part of a privately owned subdivision adjacent to federal lands in Lane County, Ore.

The landowners had been seeking to straighten out the title confusion since the early 1960s, but the Interior Department's Bureau of Land Management (BLM) contended it had no legal power to give them the land to correct the 1941 error. Staffers for Rep. James Weaver, D-Ore., the sponsor of HR 1062 who represented the district where the disputed tracts were located, said the BLM land was not being used for any public purpose. The Interior Department had found the land "uneconomical to manage as part of the public lands."

Reagan vetoed HR 1062 on Oct. 19, contending that the owners should pay the government fair market value for the land because the surveying error was not the government's fault. Members of both parties denounced the veto as an act of pettiness and insensitivity.

The House Oct. 25 voted to override the veto by a 297-125 margin, 15 more than the two-thirds majority required. Two hours later, the Senate voted 95-0 to override, enacting the bill into law (PL 98-137). It was the only time in 1983 that Congress overrode a presidential veto. *(Reagan vetoes, p. 1031)*

Chronology
Of Action
On Wildlife Protection

1981-82

Congress in 1981-82 kept federal wildlife laws intact despite Reagan administration cutbacks in environmental programs.

In one of its most significant environmental accomplishments, the 97th Congress extended the federal Endangered Species Act for three years. The measure streamlined procedures for listing and protecting wild plants and animals that were threatened with extinction. But it did not substantially relax the law's provisions that prohibited trade in those species and guarded their habitat against disruption.

In dealing with other wildlife issues, Congress continued a federal marine mammal protection program, toughened federal authority to crack down on illegal trade in wild fish and animals, and clarified federal and state cooperative powers to manage wildlife on federally owned lands. Despite opposition from animal protection groups, the Senate ratified a four-year extension of a treaty controlling North Pacific fur seal harvests.

Endangered Species Act

Congress in 1982 preserved the federal Endangered Species Act without major changes in its protection for threatened wildlife.

Early in the year environmental groups feared that the 1973 law itself was endangered by the Reagan administration's campaign to reduce the economic costs of environmental protection programs. But in reauthorizing the endangered species program for three years (HR 6133 — PL 97-304), Congress specifically ruled out the consideration of economic consequences when the Interior Department determined whether to protect rare fish, animal and plant species against threats to their survival.

Since Congress toughened federal protection for threatened wildlife, business and regional development groups had complained that designation of a species as endangered could block federal construction projects and private land developments that would disrupt remaining habitat. In the late 1970s, for instance, opponents of the Tennessee Valley Authority's (TVA) Tellico Dam in Tennessee forced the government temporarily to halt construction after a biologist found that the project would flood streams inhabited by the snail darter, an endangered three-inch fish. Congress in 1979 exempted the Tellico project from the endangered species law, permitting construction to resume.

Under James G. Watt, President Reagan's secretary of the interior, the department slowed down the process of listing additional species as endangered or threatened plants or animals whose existence should be protected.

Watt concentrated the department's resources on developing plans for managing species that already had been designated. Interior officials also adopted a policy of weighing the economic costs of preserving wild species before the department added them to the protected list.

Congress, in authorizing $39 million annually for the endangered species program for fiscal 1983-85, ordered the department to make listing decisions solely on biological grounds. The reauthorization measure also prodded the administration to move more quickly to protect additional species by setting a one-year deadline for decisions on petitions to list them for preservation. The 1982 law continued existing provisions that allowed Interior to consider economic costs when it designated lands as critical habitat for threatened wildlife to prevent its disruption.

Congress did streamline Interior Department procedures for assessing whether a planned project threatened endangered wildlife. The measure allowed federal agencies or private companies applying for federal permits to consult with Interior officials in advance to determine whether their plans might jeopardize a protected species. It also lifted the threat of criminal penalties and project shutdowns for industries that accidentally took an endangered plant or animal despite Interior-approved plans to protect the species.

Background

Congress began protecting endangered species in a 1966 law (PL 89-669) that directed the interior secretary to compile a list of fish and wildlife that were in immediate danger of extinction. The law gave the Interior Department expanded power to acquire lands to preserve such species' habitat, and it directed Interior, the Agriculture Department and the Defense Department — the federal government's largest land-owning agencies — to protect endangered species' habitat under their control. *(1966 law, Congress and the Nation Vol. II, p. 484)*

In 1973 Congress extended protection to species that were considered threatened, although not in immediate danger of becoming extinct. The 1973 law (PL 93-205) ordered the interior secretary to consider citizen petitions to add or delete a species from the endangered and threatened lists. Congress also made it a federal offense to buy, sell, possess, export or import any listed species, or a product made from such an animal. The taking of plants was not prohibited.

Through a provision that received little attention at the time, Congress in the 1973 law required federal agencies to ensure that their projects did not jeopardize a listed species or adversely affect its habitat. Agencies must obtain a permit by consulting with the Interior Department for land-based species or the Commerce Department for marine species. *(1973 law, Congress and the Nation Vol. IV, p. 289)*

In instances where no feasible alternative could be found, a proposed federal project could be exempted from provisions of the act. However, industry critics claimed the process was cumbersome and time-consuming.

Congress in 1978 also extended protection to endangered plants as well as animals. By then the Tellico controversy had produced an uproar over whether Congress had intended the law to rule out entire projects simply to protect little-known species. In another instance, the law was used to block construction of the proposed Dickey-Lincoln dam in northern Maine in order to protect a vari-

ety of snapdragon known as the furbish lousewort. This project eventually was modified to change the area that would be flooded.

Mostly in response to the Tellico controversy, Congress in 1978 set up a Cabinet-level board, usually referred to as the "God committee," that could permit construction of federal projects even if they might kill off species protected by the endangered species law. And in 1979 Congress exempted the Tellico Dam from protection of the law, through a provision attached to the fiscal 1980 energy and water appropriations bill. *(1978, 1979 revisions, Congress and the Nation Vol. V, pp. 573, 575)*

Before enactment of HR 6133, the Reagan administration had added only two new species to the endangered list, although more than a hundred candidates for listing were under consideration. The two additions, both made in 1982, were a tiny crustacean that lived in only one known place, the waters of the Washington, D.C., National Zoo, and an orchid found at two sites in Brazos County, Texas.

Environmental groups complained about the slow pace of the listing process. They also protested the administration's policy of weighing potential economic costs in deciding whether to add a species to the endangered list.

On the other hand, industries that needed federal permits for their projects complained that the existing law did not permit them to learn soon enough whether a project would jeopardize an endangered species or its critical habitat.

Congressional Action

Despite environmentalists' misgivings about Watt's wildlife policies, Congress extended the endangered species law with little of the controversy that accompanied its 1978 and 1979 debates on the snail darter issue.

Both House and Senate committees reported reauthorization legislation after staff members negotiated for months with industry representatives, state wildlife managers and environmental group lobbyists to craft changes that would streamline procedures without weakening the law's protections. Although Watt favored a one-year extension, the panels recommended a three-year reauthorization.

The House Merchant Marine and Fisheries Committee May 5 reported HR 6133 (H Rept 97-567), and the Senate Environment and Public Works Committee May 11 approved a separate bill (S 2309 — S Rept 97-418). The House passed its bill on June 8, and the Senate approved its measure the following day. After conferees resolved minor differences (H Rept 97-835), the Senate adopted the conference report on Sept. 20, and the House cleared the final version on Sept. 30.

Major Provisions

As signed into law Oct. 13, major provisions of HR 6133 (PL 97-304):

● Set a one-year deadline for the Interior Department to decide whether to list or delist a species after it received a petition containing substantial evidence on such questions. The current deadline was two years.

● Set a similar one-year deadline for decisions on petitions to revise a designation of critical habitat.

● Required listing decisions to be made solely on the biological question of whether the species was endangered or threatened.

● Continued to permit consideration of economic factors

in decisions on designating critical habitats.

● Provided that a decision by the interior secretary to reject petitions should be subject to judicial review.

● Allowed federal agencies (or, through them, applicants for federal permits) to enter into early, informal consultations with the Interior Department on whether a project would jeopardize any endangered species. Current rules did not allow consultation before a formal permit application, which left less leeway for the applicant to change his plans.

● Eliminated the threat of criminal penalties or project shutdown for industries that took threatened species incidentally in the course of other activities. This change applied only if the industry filed a plan with Interior in advance and had taken measures to minimize such "incidental takings," and if the taking would not jeopardize the existence of the species.

● Streamlined the current exemption mechanism in a way meant to reduce processing time from 360 days to 190 days. Without changing the standards for granting exemptions from the act's provisions, the bill substituted a secretarial report on whether they should be granted for a report by a review board.

● Authorized appropriations for each of the fiscal years 1983, 1984 and 1985 of up to $27 million for the Interior Department, $3.5 million for the Commerce Department, $1.85 million for the Agriculture Department, $6 million for grants to states, and $600,000 for the interior secretary and the Endangered Species Committee to be used in administering the exemptions process.

● Increased the maximum share of costs for which states could receive grants under the act from 66.6 percent to 75 percent for single-state projects and from 75 percent to 90 percent for multi-state projects.

Sikes Act Extension

Congress in 1982 clarified federal and state responsibilities for managing wildlife on federally owned lands.

On Dec. 17 Congress cleared legislation (HR 1952 — PL 97-396) that reauthorized funding to develop comprehensive plans for managing wildlife on more than 600 million acres of national forests, rangelands, military bases and other government lands. Congress ordered federal land management agencies to draft wildlife conservation plans, in consultation with state game and fish departments, in a 1960 law known as the Sikes Act.

Following the English common law tradition that wild game belonged to the sovereign king, state governments in the United States have generally held responsibility for managing fish and game animals even on federally owned lands. But in the 20th century the federal government stepped in with laws protecting migratory birds, endangered species and other wildlife with national significance. In many states, especially in the West, the federal government also controlled prime wildlife habitat on public lands managed by the Interior Department, the Agriculture Department's U.S. Forest Service, and the Department of Defense.

The 1960 Sikes Act provided for cooperative federal-state management of fish and wildlife on military bases, test facilities and other installations. Congress modified the law in 1968 and 1974, extending Sikes Act planning to other federal lands, notably 190 million acres in national forests and 310 million acres administered by the Interior Department's Bureau of Land Management (BLM). Al-

though the government managed most of those holdings for multiple uses, including mining and logging, Congress through the Sikes Act ordered Interior and Forest Service officials to develop plans for conserving wildlife on federal lands. Using those plans, federal and state officials drew up cooperative agreements for more specific wildlife programs.

In authorizing fiscal 1983-85 spending for the Sikes Act programs, HR 1952 clarified federal-state duties for protecting endangered and threatened species, improving wildlife habitat and other conservation efforts.

The measure authorized expenditures of $28.5 million annually in fiscal 1983 and 1984 and $26.5 million in fiscal 1985. Included in the total was an authorization of $2 million annually in fiscal 1983 and 1984 to complete a study of the decline of the striped bass population in Atlantic coastal waters. The study, ordered by Congress in 1979, was to determine why striped bass populations had been declining since 1970. The fish was popular among both commercial and recreational fishermen, and was of considerable economic significance to Atlantic coastal states.

Marine Mammal Protection

Congress in 1981 extended federal marine mammal protection programs for three years. In the process, it spelled out U.S. fishermen's legal obligation to reduce accidental killing of porpoises that were entangled in tuna nets.

Legislation cleared Sept. 29 (HR 4084 — PL 97-58) reauthorized the Marine Mammal Protection Act of 1972 for three years, through Sept. 30, 1984. The bill cleared when the Senate passed without change the version approved by the House Sept. 21 (H Rept 97-228).

The 1972 law (PL 92-522) prohibited the killing of most mammals that inhabited the oceans but were steadily declining in population. It directed the Interior Department and Commerce Department to conserve and manage whales, porpoises, dolphins, seals, sea lions, polar bears, walruses, manatees and sea otters. (Congress and the Nation Vol. III, p. 812)

The 1972 law granted exceptions to the ban on sea mammal hunting — for instance, for Aleut Indian seal harvests in Alaska's Pribiloff Islands. It also granted an exemption to the commercial tuna fishing industry for porpoises that drowned when they were accidentally caught in tuna nets. The law authorized a federal research program to devise fishing gear that would reduce porpoise deaths.

Since enactment of the law the number of porpoises taken in tuna fishing operations had dropped from an estimated 386,000 in 1972 to 15,303 in 1980.

The 1984 legislation retained the 1972 act's goal of reducing accidental porpoise deaths to "insignificant levels approaching a zero mortality and serious injury rate." However, it specified that yellowfin tuna fishermen could satisfy this objective through the use of the best equipment and techniques "that are economically and technologically practicable," a clarification designed to spare fishermen from continuing entanglement in litigation as a result of accidental porpoise kills.

The measure allowed other commercial fishermen, deep seabed mining groups, oceanographic researchers and oil and gas drillers accidentally to kill small numbers of marine mammals as long as there was a "negligible" impact on the species.

Fur Seal Treaty Extension

The Senate in 1981 ratified a four-year extension of a 1957 treaty limiting fur seal harvests from islands off Alaska and the Soviet Union.

Despite persistent public outcry against the annual seal slaughter, the Senate voted 94-0 to approve a 1980 Protocol (Exec S, 96th Cong, 2nd Sess) amending the 1957 treaty. The treaty divided annual sealskin harvests on North Pacific islands among the United States, the Soviet Union, Canada and Japan. The federal government paid the Aleut Indian tribe to harvest the U.S. share from Alaska's Pribiloff Islands for sale at a government auction.

Wildlife protection groups protested that the U.S. government should not subsidize the slaughter. The Senate Foreign Relations Committee, before recommending that the 1980 agreement be ratified, rejected a reservation to prohibit the United States from taking its share of the North Pacific seal harvest.

In the 1957 treaty, the Interim Convention on Conservation of North Pacific Fur Seals, the four nations agreed to halt harvesting seals for their skins on the high seas in the North Pacific Ocean. The practice of hunting on the open seas, called "pelagic sealing," had been decimating the North Pacific seal population.

In return for halting pelagic sealing, the United States and the Soviet Union agreed to share onshore sealskin harvests from islands off their coasts with Japan and Canada. The treaty assured the United States 70 percent, about 17,000 skins, from seals harvested each year on Alaska's Pribiloff Islands. It also assured the Soviet Union 70 percent of the harvest off its northeast coast. Japan and Canada shared the remaining 30 percent of both U.S. and Soviet harvests.

The Department of Commerce paid 80 Aleut Indians in Alaska $250,000 to harvest the skins for sale at government auction, and about $4 million was paid each year to support the tribe under the Fur Seal Act of 1966 (PL 89-72).

During Senate debate Claiborne Pell, D-R.I., maintained that the treaty no longer was needed to protect seals on the high seas because U.S. adoption of a 200-mile fishing zone off its coasts brought most of their migration routes under the protective provisions of the Marine Mammal Protection Act of 1972 (PL 92-522).

The bill also made it easier for states to take over the management of marine mammals within their waters, a provision sought by Alaska, where the greatest numbers of marine mammals are found.

It included a provision requiring federal support for

research aimed at developing new methods of locating and catching yellowfin tuna that could reduce the porpoise kills still further.

Illegal Wildlife Trade

Congress in 1981 strengthened the federal government's power to crack down on illegal fish and wildlife trade.

The House Nov. 4 cleared legislation (S 736 — PL 97-79) that imposed tougher penalties for importing or interstate trafficking in wildlife that was protected by federal, state or foreign law. The bill aimed at a lucrative illegal trade in fish, wild animals and plants that netted violators as much as $100 million in yearly profits while exposing domestic livestock, fish and pets to deadly exotic diseases.

The measure consolidated the nation's two wildlife smuggling laws, the Lacey Act of 1900 and the Black Bass Act of 1926. Those laws made it illegal to import or possess fish, wildlife or animal products that were taken, transported or sold in violation of a foreign, state or federal law. In addition, the 1981 law extended protection to plants that were illegally imported or taken across state lines.

1983-84

Congress in 1983-84 extended several federal wildlife protection programs, including financial support for buying threatened wetlands.

Both the House and Senate drafted legislation to step up federal wetlands purchases, using funds from federal offshore oil and gas leasing revenues. But final congressional approval was blocked by environmentalists' opposition to an unrelated House provision involving jetty projects on barrier islands off the North Carolina coast.

Wetlands Protection Program

Unable to agree on a more ambitious program, Congress in 1984 approved a 10-year extension of federal funding to preserve wildlife habitat on the nation's dwindling wetlands.

The House Sept. 20 passed legislation (HR 3082) to use $75 million a year from federal offshore oil and gas revenues to buy up wetlands to save them from development. Although the Senate was drafting a similar bill, controversy over building jetties between barrier islands off the North Carolina coast helped block final congressional action.

As a fallback, Congress Oct. 4 cleared a separate measure (HR 5271 — PL 98-548) extending to 1994 an existing program that channeled federal "duck stamp" revenues paid by hunters into conserving wetlands that provided breeding and feeding grounds for migratory waterfowl.

Wetlands are swamps, bogs or other lands with moist soils that offer productive habitat for wildlife. Environmental groups and federal and state wildlife agencies had grown increasingly alarmed as wetlands were rapidly drained, filled in and converted to farm land or urban developments.

For more than two decades Congress had been financing federal wetlands purchases through the Wetlands Loan Act of 1961 (PL 87-383). That law, as later amended, authorized $200 million in appropriations for the federal government to buy wetlands. The money was to be repaid eventually from duck stamp receipts. In the meantime, federal receipts from selling the stamps, which hunters were required to buy, went directly for wetlands conservation.

To accelerate wetlands purchases the House and Senate in 1984 considered legislation to set up a new $75 million-a-year fund, financed by offshore petroleum leasing revenues, to expand the national wildlife refuge system and help state governments buy up and preserve wetlands within their borders. The measures also forgave the 1961 program's entire $200 million "loan," thus freeing future duck stamp receipts for continued land purchases instead of repaying the funds to the Treasury.

When time ran out for clearing those bills, however, Congress settled for renewing the 1961 program, due to expire on Sept. 30, 1984, for another 10 years. That step in effect extended the Treasury loan until 1994, keeping all duck stamp revenues available for wetlands conservation.

Background

Even excluding Alaska and Hawaii, the lower 48 states originally contained 215 million acres of wetlands. By the 1980s, however, those wetlands had shrunk to fewer than 100 million acres; and the loss had accelerated in the post-World War II decades. Between the mid-1950s and mid-1970s, nine million acres of wetlands vanished, according to a 1985 report on a National Wetlands Inventory Project by the U.S. Fish and Wildlife Service. Texas, Louisiana and Florida were the states suffering the largest losses in coastal wetlands habitat.

Beginning in 1903, the federal government created national wildlife refuges by setting aside suitable government-owned lands. In the Migratory Bird Conservation Act of 1929, Congress gave the government authority to purchase new lands for wildlife refuges. The Migratory Bird Hunting Stamp Act of 1934 required hunters to buy federal waterfowl stamps — the duck stamp program — with proceeds devoted to purchases authorized by the 1929 law.

The Kennedy administration proposed the 1961 wetlands loan program to advance the U.S. Fish and Wildlife Service funds to speed up wetlands purchases while lands were still available. By 1984, Congress had appropriated $154 million of the total $200 million that had been authorized for the 1961 program, last extended in 1976. Once the loan expired, the law required the Fish and Wildlife Service to start repaying those funds to the Treasury by diverting 75 percent of duck stamp receipts. The agency collected an estimated $16 million a year from selling the stamps at a price of $7.50 each in 1984. *(Background, Congress and the Nation Vol. I, p. 1064)*

1983-84 Wetlands Legislation

1983 Extension. The House and Senate began considering proposals to beef up the wetlands conservation program in 1983. But with the Wetlands Loan Act due to expire on Sept. 30, Congress cleared a simple one-year extension (HR 2395 — PL 98-200) to give committees time to refine more ambitious measures.

1984 House Bill. The House in 1984 approved the

expanded wetlands program, but the Senate never acted. By a 351-45 vote on Sept. 20, the House passed the measure (HR 3082), drafted by the Merchant Marine and Fisheries Committee in 1983, to set up a new Wetlands Conservation Fund financed by offshore oil revenues.

As passed by the House, HR 3082 transferred $75 million a year to the new wetlands fund in fiscal 1985-94 from the Land and Water Conservation Fund, an existing program funding federal park and refuge purchases chiefly from offshore mineral leasing revenues. The bill also forgave the 1961 loan repayment obligation while raising duck stamp prices in steps from $7.50 to $15 each by fiscal 1988. The Merchant Marine Committee had reported HR 3082 in 1983, but the measure was then referred to two other House panels. The Interior and Insular Affairs and the Public Works and Transportation committees completed work on the bill March 6, and the Merchant Marine panel filed a supplemental report Sept. 11 (H Rept 98-440, Parts I-IV).

As sent to the floor, HR 3082 carried a rider to clear the way for a long-delayed project to protect Oregon Inlet off North Carolina that was backed by Merchant Marine Committee Chairman Walter B. Jones, D-N.C., and other members from that state. Congress in 1970 authorized construction of jetties to keep the inlet, which ran between two barrier islands, from filling up with sand that would block fishermen's year-round access to the open sea. But environmentalists argued that the jetties would disrupt natural currents along the coast, destroying parts of other barrier islands. And the Interior Department had blocked use of lands in Cape Hatteras National Seashore and the Pea Island National Wildlife Refuge for the jetty project.

HR 3082 ordered the department to make lands available for the jetties. The House, by a 194-203 vote, rejected an amendment to delete that provision offered by John F. Seiberling, D-Ohio, chairman of the Interior Subcommittee on Public Lands and National Parks. But environmentalists' objections to the Oregon Inlet project helped block Senate action on the bill in the waning days of the 1984 session.

The jetty project was expected to cost at least $94.5 million to build and another $4 million annually to maintain.

1984 Senate Measures. Earlier in 1984 two Senate committees had approved similar wetlands legislation (S 1329). The Senate Environment and Public Works Committee reported the bill Jan. 26 (S Rept 98-349), approving an approach that would automatically transfer $75 million a year from the Land and Water Conservation Fund to the existing migratory bird conservation program. The Senate Energy and Natural Resources Committee, before reporting S 1329 on April 6 (S Rept 98-383), adopted an amendment by Malcolm Wallop, R-Wyo., to authorize $75 million a year for wetlands acquisition but requiring Congress to provide the funds through annual appropriations. The Senate versions also forgave the existing $200 million loan entirely.

Ten-Year Extension. With the Oregon Inlet dispute stalling chances for clearing HR 3082, Congress Oct. 4 cleared separate legislation extending the 1961 wetlands loan program for 10 years, to Sept. 30, 1994. The House passed HR 5271 on Sept. 24, and the Senate approved an amended version on Oct. 4. The House cleared it Oct. 4 by agreeing to Senate amendments, including provisions that established new wildlife refuges in Connecticut and Louisiana.

Other Legislation

Marine Mammal Protection

Congress in 1984 renewed the federal Marine Mammal Protection Act of 1972 for another four years.

The 1972 law (PL 92-522) set up a management, research and regulatory program to preserve saltwater mammals. It gave the Commerce Department responsibility for protecting whales, dolphins, porpoises, sea lions and seals. The Interior Department was responsible for polar bears, walruses, sea otters, manatees and dugongs. Congress had previously reauthorized the law in 1981. *(Story, p. 479)*

The 1984 extension (HR 4997 — PL 98-364), cleared June 27, froze the existing 20,500-animal limit on porpoises that U.S. tuna fishermen could accidentally catch in the eastern Pacific. Improved fishing gear and techniques had reduced accidental killing of porpoises in tuna nets from an estimated 386,000 animals in 1972 to 8,258 in 1983, well below the law's requirement.

Striped Bass Conservation

Congress in 1984 approved legislation to prod Atlantic Coast states to conserve dwindling stocks of Atlantic striped bass, a popular game fish.

Cleared on Oct. 11, the measure (HR 5492 — PL 98-613) gave the secretary of commerce authority to declare a moratorium on striped bass fishing in any state that failed to reduce its annual catch of the species by 55 percent. That threat, applied to coastal states north of South Carolina, was intended to encourage state game officials to adopt an Atlantic States Marine Fisheries Commission plan to set a 24-inch minimum size for striped bass caught in the ocean and a 14-inch limit for fish caught in state waters. Striped bass landings had dropped dramatically since 1960, and environmentalists blamed overfishing and water pollution.

As passed by the House Oct. 4, HR 5492 (H Rept 98-1029) included a House Merchant Marine and Fisheries Committee proposal directing the government to study whether acid rain in Northeastern forests that supplied water to rivers flowing to the Atlantic was contributing to the striped bass decline. The Senate Oct. 11 approved an amendment dropping the acid rain study to meet objections by Minority Leader Robert C. Byrd, D-W.Va. Most experts blamed acid rain on Ohio Valley power plants that burned high-sulfur coal, and West Virginia was a major producer of that fuel.

Pribilof Seal Harvest

Congress in 1983 overhauled federal government support for fur seal harvesting by Aleut Indians on the Pribilof Islands off Alaska.

Through legislation (HR 2840 — PL 98-129) cleared Sept. 28, Congress set up a $20 million trust fund to help the Aleut tribe develop a self-sustaining economy no longer dependent on federally subsidized seal harvests.

Under a 1957 treaty, extended in 1981, the United States, Soviet Union, Japan and Canada divided annual sealskin harvests from North Pacific islands. Under the Fur Seal Act of 1966 (PL 89-702), the U.S. Commerce Department paid Aleuts to harvest the U.S. share on the Pribilof Islands for sale at government auction. The gov-

ernment also provided about $4 million a year to support the tribe. *(Treaty background, p. 479)*

Wildlife protection groups had protested against federal subsidies for seal hunting, and senators proposed phasing out the 1966 fur seal program during 1981 debate on ratifying a four-year treaty extension.

In revising the 1966 Fur Seal Act, HR 2840 authorized transfer of federal property on the islands to native and state government entities and provided for a one-time appropriation of $20 million to a Pribilof Island trust fund to help in the transition from an economy dependent on sealing and federal income support to one that was self-sustaining.

In fiscal 1983 $6.3 million was appropriated to carry out federal responsibilities on the islands, with 95 percent going to social welfare programs. The new trust fund was intended to assume the major share of those programs.

Matagorda Island Accord

A federal-state agreement for managing the Aransas National Wildlife Refuge was ratified by Congress in a bill (HR 1935 — PL 98-66) cleared July 22, 1983.

The refuge, on Matagorda Island, a 50,500-acre island on the Gulf of Mexico coastline, provided habitat for the endangered whooping crane and brown pelican. The federal and Texas state governments split ownership of the island, but the Reagan administration stirred opposition from conservation groups with a 1981 proposal to remove its lands from the national wildlife refuge system and turn them over to the state.

Under an agreement that settled the dispute, Texas made its state-owned lands part of the Aransas refuge. Texas took over responsibility for managing the refuge on the island, but subject to strict and enforceable guidelines set by the federal government.

9

Agricultural Policy

Introduction	*485*
1981 Chronology	*487*
1982 Chronology	*496*
1983 Chronology	*503*
1984 Chronology	*511*

Agricultural Policy

Fifty years after the federal government first paid farmers to plow under crops and slaughter surplus livestock, the Reagan administration launched a drive to end many Depression-era farm programs and eliminate the assumption that the federal government was directly responsible for farmers' well-being.

In 1934 Agriculture Secretary Henry A. Wallace had written that federal efforts to manage the farm economy were "but a temporary method for dealing with an emergency." Such interventions, Wallace warned, "seriously disturb . . . the farm economy." But since then the notion that Washington would guarantee minimum prices for commodities, supplement farmers' incomes and compensate farmers for efforts to cut back on surpluses had become embedded in the rural economy. Over time Congress had changed many of the specifics of the federal farm programs but left their basic shape intact.

By late 1984, however, Agriculture Secretary John R. Block, Senate Agriculture Committee Chairman Jesse Helms, R-N.C., and portions of the farm community were saying that the programs had, in fact, destabilized American agriculture and had to be changed radically.

Block, acknowledging that much of U.S. agriculture was sunk in a multi-year recession, told a farm policy conference that farms had been failing for nearly 50 years "with almost the same intensity, regardless of farm policies pursued. It's time to start something different."

Joining the assault were business and environmental leaders alarmed at the chronic economic and environmental problems of American agriculture and convinced that federal programs were making those problems worse.

A 1984 report by the Congressional Budget Office (CBO) reflected much of current thinking when it observed that the programs' twin goals — enhancing farm incomes during periods of surplus and stabilizing farm prices and incomes — were in conflict. And, the report observed, "Current farm programs have been progressively less able to achieve these conflicting objectives" left over from the 1930s.

When the programs began, nearly a fourth of the nation's population lived on farms and depended heavily on farm income; but by 1984, CBO reported, only 3 percent lived on farms and only "300,000 farms, or 12 percent of all farms, produce nearly 70 percent of farm output." Moreover, incomes of families living on these farms were, on an average, "well above average non-farm levels."

Probably the most significant change from the 1930s was the integration of farms into the domestic and international economies. By 1984 two of every five acres was grown for export, and exports accounted for about a quarter of gross farm income. Farm prices had become highly sensitive to a number of factors beyond the reach of domestic farm programs: currency exchange rates, changes in weather and crop production, trade and farm policies of foreign governments.

Trouble Signs

When Congress wrote a multi-year omnibus agriculture bill in 1981, the estimated four-year cost of price support, loan, subsidy and other aid programs for farmers was about $11 billion.

But the programs swiftly soaked up a billion dollars more than that amount in 1982 alone, and costs soared to $18.9 billion in 1983, when the administration also dispensed an additional $9 billion worth of surplus commodities to farmers through the PIK (payment-in-kind) program, which paid farmers for idling crop land. By 1984 U.S. Department of Agriculture (USDA) officials were putting four-year costs of the programs above $50 billion, a figure considered untenable by the Office of Management and Budget. The high program costs clearly signaled financial stress in American agriculture, particularly the mid-sized commercial farms of such heartland states as Iowa, Illinois and Kansas.

Banking experts reported that 15 percent of these commercial farms — those with annual sales of more than $40,000 — had precarious debt-to-asset ratios of 70 percent. Farms with that level of debt were thought unable to survive in current market conditions.

Yet the economic status of individual farmers was far from uniform, meaning that help desperately needed by

References

Discussion of agricultural policy for the years 1945-64 may be found in *Congress and the Nation Vol. I*, pp. 665-767; for the years 1965-68, *Congress and the Nation Vol. II*, pp. 555-597; for the years 1969-72, *Congress and the Nation Vol. III*, pp. 331-352; for the years 1973-76, *Congress and the Nation Vol. IV*, pp. 717-740; for the years 1977-80, *Congress and the Nation Vol. V*, pp. 365-395.

some was a windfall for others. Farms that managed to stay free of expensive debt were likely to be quietly holding their own. A tiny minority of highly capitalized, high-tech spreads dominated markets while scooping in million-dollar subsidies from Washington.

The problem to be solved — surplus production — was as old as the Depression that spawned the programs. USDA reckoned that the overall productive capacity exceeded agricultural markets by about 10 percent.

The surplus reflected agriculture's painful downward adjustment from the export boom of the 1970s, a decade of dizzying growth in farm exports, farm productivity, farm land values — and farmers' debt. In that period, exports had grown at what CBO called "the extraordinary rate of 20 percent per year, from about $7 billion in 1970 to nearly $41 billion in 1980."

By 1984 farm exports, instead of growing, were entering their fourth year of decline, with USDA predicting that export levels for the year would register a 15 percent drop from 1980. U.S. commodities were being crowded in global markets by expanding agricultural production of other nations, which was often buttressed with hefty subsidies.

The situation left those farmers who had borrowed heavily to expand in the 1970s, and to keep going in the early 1980s, unable to keep up loan payments. Their problems, by 1984, were beginning to sink the country bankers who had kept them going through two or three or four profitless years. In the first half of 1984, three agricultural banks failed; in the second six months, 22 went under, according to the Independent Bankers Association of America. Some analysts estimated that as much as 20 percent of the nation's $215 billion farm debt would have to be written off. The Federal Deposit Insurance Corp.'s June 30 list of banks with more problem loans than capital included more than 200 farm banks — twice the number reported a year earlier.

What made the debt problem acute was a dramatic deflation in the value of land, farmers' prime asset. In Iowa, for instance, farm land values had plummeted 37 percent since 1981.

Drastic Remedies

As 1984 drew to a close, the administration and its supporters, including Helms and much of the agribusiness community, were saying that such drastic problems called for drastic remedies.

The administration's stark solution was to ask Con-

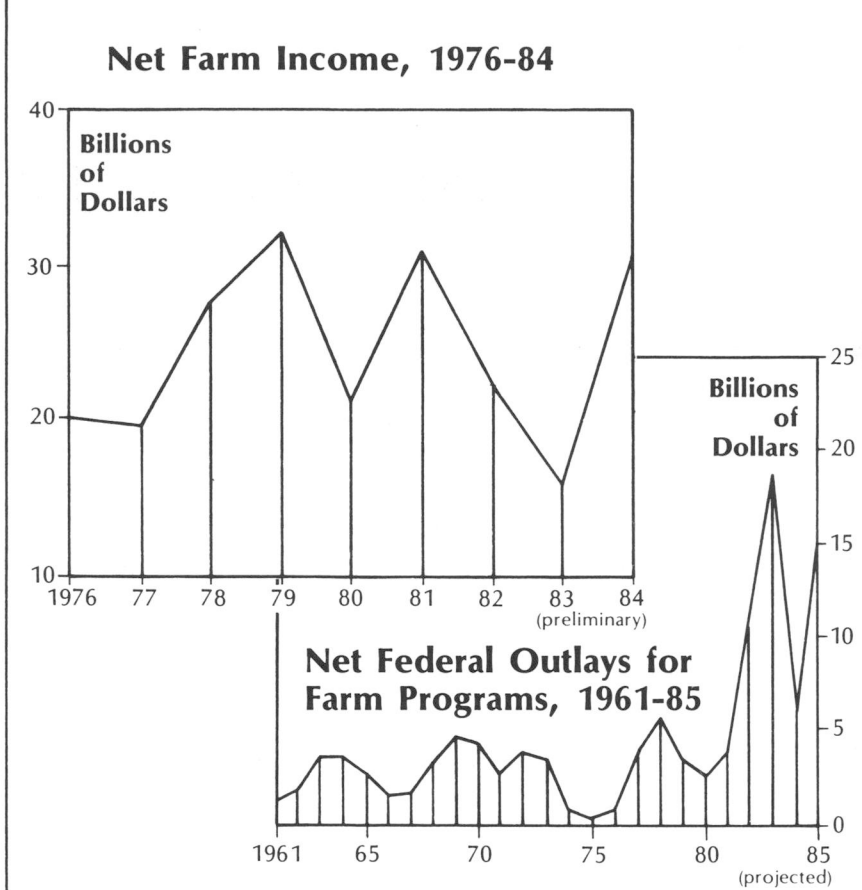

Large crop yields and soft global markets combined in 1982 to push to unprecedented levels federal expenditures on farm price-support loans, "deficiency" payments, storage for large surplus stock, dairy purchases and other farm support programs administered by the Commodity Credit Corporation of the Agriculture Department. This trend continued through 1983, when USDA initiated its "Payment-in-Kind" (PIK) program, paying farmers with surplus crops to idle about a third of the nation's crop land. Program costs dropped in 1984, thanks to the combined impact of PIK and a major drought, which reduced crop size. But expenditures were expected to climb back upward in 1985 as farmers sought to offset low market prices by growing more.

SOURCE: U.S. Department of Agriculture

gress to cut farm program spending in half and radically revise the policies underlying the programs. Such changes would, Block argued, put agriculture in fighting trim to compete in tight world markets.

Much of what the administration wanted could have been predicted from nearly four years' worth of speeches by Block and other USDA officials, who consistently argued that government programs had destabilized agriculture. Their anti-government stance, however, had been tempered by decisions during President Reagan's first term to run the enormous PIK program, the largest acreage reduction program in the history of such federal efforts, to launch the first payments ever to dairymen for cutting back on production, and to otherwise employ the very programs at which Block scoffed.

Chronology
Of Action
On Agriculture

1981

Ronald Reagan's first year as president brought stormy debates in Congress over his insistence on paring back farm programs and enacting major reductions in loans for farmers and rural communities. In the end, the president generally got what he wanted.

Reagan won a strategically important victory over the well-financed dairy lobby in March when Congress canceled a scheduled increase in dairy price supports. The president painted the victory as an important first step on the road to a balanced budget. The fight divided the dairy lobby internally and also helped set up stresses among commodity groups that later aided the administration's drive for a low-cost omnibus farm bill.

The Senate reluctantly complied with Reagan's demands for less-generous price support increases than commodity groups wanted. But House farm interests shepherded a far more costly bill all the way to conference before bowing to administration pressures. The final version continued major crop price supports with moderate increases and pruned existing support rates for dairy products. It also kept sugar and peanut programs, despite earlier House votes to eliminate them.

In other actions, Congress passed legislation raising interest rates for a number of federal farm loans and reinstated interest charges on loans to farmers hurt by the embargo of grain sales to the Soviet Union. The bill ended a mandatory waiver established in December 1980 on loans for 1980 and 1981 grain crops stored in the farmer-held reserves. The waiver was intended to aid farmers adversely affected by President Carter's Jan. 4, 1980, decision to impose the embargo. Reagan ended the embargo April 24, honoring a campaign pledge to farmers and eliminating a major irritant for Agriculture Committee members who had begun drafting the four-year farm legislation.

Meanwhile, farm income continued to decline, due partly to high equipment costs and bumper crops, which depressed prices for a number of commodities.

Farmers' cash expenses and total production costs increased about 9 percent in 1981, compared with a 5 percent increase in cash receipts. Interest rates reached record highs in August — 20 percent for commercial loans in some regions of the country.

Omnibus Farm Bill

Just before adjournment Dec. 16, a reluctant House by a two-vote margin cleared the four-year farm bill (S 884 — PL 97-98) the administration wanted.

Conflicting demands from a divided farm community, the Reagan administration, consumer advocates and food processors had kept the outcome in doubt until the final **key vote of 205-203 (R 125-59; D 80-144)** adopting the $11 billion conference agreement. *(1981 key votes, p. 879)*

President Reagan signed the measure Dec. 22. The Senate had approved it by a 68-31 vote Dec. 10.

The bill renewed basic food and farm programs for four years, replacing the 1977 law (PL 95-113) that had expired Sept. 30. *(Congress and the Nation Vol. V, p. 368)*

Coalition Shattered. The House action on the Agriculture and Food Act of 1981 capped a long and painful process. It was the first year that legislators had to craft farm programs to fit within a total dollar amount specified by the budget. That constraint forced commodity groups to compete directly for shares of a smaller federal pie and shattered their vote-trading relationships.

At critical points during the year, many farm-state members abandoned their log-rolling habits and voted against programs — such as dairy or sugar or peanuts — that were of minimal interest to their own constituents.

The resentment spawned by those votes meant that there was rarely a smoothly functioning coalition to move the farm bill along. Nor was there a united farm front against administration pressures to keep spending levels down.

Stirring up the longstanding rivalries within the farm coalition was a deliberate administration tactic, according to administration budget director David A. Stockman. It enabled Reagan to block what he viewed as budget-busting farm demands.

Other sources of pressure on farm groups during the year were record high interest rates and sagging commodity prices caused by bumper crops and rumors of renewed economic sanctions against the Soviet Union.

Compromises. The Republican Senate reluctantly complied with Reagan's demands for price support increases that were less generous than the commodity groups wanted. House farm interests shepherded a far more costly bill all the way to conference, and the conference itself dragged on for six weeks until House members bowed to administration pressures for cost reductions.

The House and Senate positions reversed the well-established pattern of senators being more generous to farmers than their urban and suburban colleagues in the House.

Total outlays for farm programs in the final version of S 884 were estimated at about $11 billion for the life of the bill, according to Agriculture Department (USDA) officials. That compared with a $16.6 billion estimate for the version passed by the House and $10.6 billion for the Senate bill. The $8.65 billion conference subtotal for commodity programs was about $400 million more than the Senate-passed level.

The final agreement generally continued the price support, research, Food for Peace and other farm programs. It included an $11.3 billion one-year extension of the food stamp program. *(Farm income, price support programs, box, p. 491; food stamps, p. 583)*

Except for the dairy program, whose minimum support level was significantly reduced from existing law, the bill increased major crop price supports, but it did not permit those supports to rise as rapidly in future years as many farmers wanted. Substantial changes were made in the tightly regulated peanut program and a new sugar price support program was created.

The bill set minimum support levels for dairymen in

dollars instead of linking them to a parity index as in the past. (Parity referred to the index comparing prices farmers paid and received; it was meant to reflect farmers' purchasing power during the prosperous 1910-1914 period.) The controversial new inflation index was to come into play only if government purchases of dairy products, as required by law, exceeded certain levels.

Reagan Request

As Congress began deliberating the renewal of farm programs that had survived since the 1930s, the situation resembled that of four years earlier: Farm interest groups clamored for financial relief in a troubled economy, and the new administration signaled that it wanted to lower farm program spending. In 1977 Congress had demanded substantially higher price support levels than the new Democratic president, Jimmy Carter, wanted. Congress won after a difficult struggle that permanently soured relations between farm-state members and Carter and his agriculture secretary, Bob Bergland.

Reagan's economic message to Congress urged hefty cuts in such deeply entrenched programs as the Farmers Home Administration (FmHA) and the Rural Electrification Administration (REA). The reductions were in line with the belief of Reagan's economic advisers that federal lending, including federal guarantees of private loans, distorted free-market forces.

Jesse Helms, R-N.C., new chairman of the Senate Agriculture Committee, and House Agriculture Committee Chairman E. "Kika" de la Garza, D-Texas, at first predicted that committee members and their constituencies would be willing to make do with less. "Farmers understand that unless this inflation is cured, they don't stand a chance no matter what kind of farm bill we pass," Helms said.

However, as the extent of the revisions the president had in mind became clear, both committees rebelled. Senate Democrats and Republicans — including Helms — introduced competing bills departing markedly from key administration proposals.

Reagan had asked Congress to eliminate target prices, a major form of price support, and to drop a number of production control programs. For basic price support loans, whose minimum levels were traditionally fixed in law, the president asked for broad, discretionary authority to set loan rates as supply and demand dictated. He also requested substantial changes in the farmer-held grain reserve.

The versions brought to the floor by the House and Senate Agriculture committees largely ignored those requests.

Divisions in the Farm Alliance

As Agriculture Secretary John R. Block was sounding the threat in August of a presidential veto of the developing farm bill because of budget constraints and objections to dairy and certain grain provisions, there were signs that the farm alliances were so shaky that the president's cost-cutting drive might prevail.

The pressures of the budget sent farm interests scrambling to protect their shrinking shares of the federal pie. An every-man-for-himself attitude threatened years of mutual accommodation in which lobbyists and members were inclined to look after each other's interests.

"It used to be that everybody could get their piece of

the pie, and if the pie was too small, they [Congress] could just make it bigger," one lobbyist explained. In 1981, he added, "There's not enough to go around." Sen. Robert Dole, R-Kan., remarked that farm coalitions always had been unstable but that in 1981, "It's worse. It's sort of dog-eat-dog."

The well-financed dairy lobby was isolated early in the year when Reagan persuaded Congress to cancel a scheduled price support increase. *(Story, p. 493)*

The peanut and tobacco programs were in particular trouble in both chambers, and the sugar price support program drew strong opposition in the House. Part of the opposition to the tightly controlled peanut and tobacco programs was attributed to an anti-regulation mood. Both programs operated under rigid allotments and quotas that limited growing rights to a select few. Critics called the system "feudalistic."

Part of the opposition, however, was traced to anti-Helms sentiment. Tobacco and peanuts were critical to the economy of North Carolina. Helms had alienated many members of Congress with his outspoken views on social issues, including abortion, mandatory school busing for desegregation and what he called excessive spending on food stamps and other social programs.

All three programs survived, but the tobacco program narrowly missed extinction in the Senate, the peanut program was modified against the wishes of peanut producers, and the sugar program came through with somewhat lower support prices than those approved in committee.

One potentially explosive issue was defused April 24 when Reagan ended the embargo of sales of U.S. grain to Russia. Farmers had chafed under the embargo ever since it was instituted by Carter in January 1980 to express disapproval of the Soviet invasion of Afghanistan. *(Story, p. 495)*

Even without the embargo, the 1981 crops were so large that farm prices fell far short of predicted highs, and pressures built quickly for higher price supports. In a move to strengthen prices, Block announced in September that the government would ask wheat farmers to cut back their acreage. The authority that Block proposed to use was one of the production controls that Reagan had asked Congress to cancel six months earlier.

Senate Action

Committee. The Senate Agriculture Committee disregarded most of the Reagan requests in its first week of voting and instead tentatively added several billion dollars for programs over the next four years.

Few members of either party spoke of the budget strictures they were breaching. But after the Senate panel agreed by a 10-5 vote April 27 to include a dairy price support plan favored by the industry and opposed by the administration, Dole warned, "The president won't stand for it."

The committee had chosen a 75 percent of parity minimum, not the 70 percent floor that the administration requested.

The following day, the panel by a vote of 5-11 rejected an administration plan for discretion to set wheat loan rates. It then endorsed a wheat and feed grain program offered by Dole that was, as he noted, "not supported" by the president.

More than once, Chairman Helms warned members that they would have to "march back down the hill" — that

is, reduce the cost of programs — before reporting a bill. "We've already broken the bank," Helms said after one session. Then, acknowledging to committee members that he, too, had his "special interests," Helms sat quietly while the committee endorsed his proposal to retain the peanut program without the changes that Reagan requested.

After a round of private caucuses, the committee scrapped its budget-breaking draft and on May 27 reported a version of S 884 (S Rept 97-126) that merely bent the upper spending limits imposed on it. According to chief Agriculture Department economist William G. Lesher, the committee bill would cost an estimated $2 billion to $2.5 billion in fiscal 1982, compared with $1.9 billion for Reagan's plan.

Floor. The bill passed by the Senate Sept. 18 by a vote of 49-32 conformed more to Reagan administration demands than the committee bill and gave many farmers less than they wanted for price support programs.

Floor action had been delayed while Congress completed Reagan's budget and tax bills. In the vote-bargaining over those measures, the administration reversed its opposition to the sugar program and to the existing peanut program, thus winning votes from conservative Southern House Democrats but angering Northern Democrats.

Bowing to the threat of a presidential veto, the Senate twice reduced committee-approved spending levels. Helms said the final numbers were worked out by key members of the administration and committee prior to floor action in an effort to trim costs.

Earlier in the evening of Sept. 18, the Senate adopted, 46-39, an amendment sponsored by Dole that substituted the target price levels sought by the administration for those that had been approved previously by the Agriculture panel in its compromise effort and revised by a series of floor amendments Sept. 14. Dole, who in 1978 had spearheaded a drive to raise grain price supports sharply, said his amendment cutting the target price levels for wheat, rice and feed grains reduced the outlays by an estimated $360 million through fiscal 1986.

In other action, the Senate trimmed rates for target prices for cotton and cut back dairy price supports. But it rejected attempts to kill or reduce a new price support program for sugar and to crack the peanut and tobacco programs open so that any farmer could grow the lucrative crops.

Tobacco's opponents thought they had enough votes to kill or substantially change the program, but their margin of victory vanished with defeats on a series of votes. In the last of them, the Senate Sept. 18 narrowly rejected, by a **key 41-40 vote (R 28-17; D 13-23)**, an amendment that would have scrapped the fixed tobacco support price and given the secretary of agriculture authority to lower support prices. *(1981 key votes, p. 879)*

House Action

Committee. The House Agriculture Committee began markup April 30 and on May 19 reported a budget-busting farm bill (HR 3603 — H Rept 97-106) that it said it intended to rewrite before seeking House approval.

The committee clearly felt the pressure to make reductions. But exasperated with confusing information about the budget process itself, the panel put off cost-cutting decisions until after the Memorial Day recess.

The basic programs renewed for four years by the committee bill would cost approximately $3.5 billion in fiscal 1982, while the congressional budget resolution (H Con Res 115), cleared May 21, set a $2.135 billion limit. *(Budget resolution, p. 38)*

Floor. After seven days of often-acrid debate beginning Oct. 2, the House Oct. 22 passed a bill that left none of the interested parties unscathed. The heavily amended committee bill passed by voice vote after members rejected, 180-193, a Republican amendment to convert the four-year reauthorization to a two-year measure.

When floor action was over, the self-styled "tobacco boys" — members from North Carolina and other tobacco-growing Southern states — had blocked a strong drive to end their highly regulated program.

Most other commodity groups suffered losses, either real or in their expectations. The bill raised grain loan rates and other financial programs for farmers but not as high as many of them wanted.

Dairymen had hoped to keep the 80 percent of parity price support level they had had for four years. But the House fixed the fiscal 1982 dairy support at the existing dollar level of $13.10 per hundredweight, which worked out to about 73 percent of parity. That could rise to a 75 percent minimum in later years.

In addition, the House canceled its committee's sugar program and voted to end the peanut program.

The Reagan administration was displeased with the House action. "It is unacceptable," Deputy Agriculture Secretary Richard E. Lyng said. The bill was within Reagan budget limits for fiscal 1982 but not for the next three years. The Congressional Budget Office estimated that the four-year costs of the bill would total $53.4 billion. Of that, $44.9 billion would be for food stamps, with $8.5 billion for farm programs. The four-year total for the administration-backed Senate bill, which did not include food stamps, was $6.732 billion.

Conference Action

While the administration did not directly threaten a veto, spokesmen warned that Reagan considered the more expensive House bill unacceptable, and Block urged conferees to adopt the Senate plan. Reagan himself had invited key conferees to the Oval Office just before the first conference session Nov. 4 and also sent a letter urging conferees to stick to the Senate bill.

But by Nov. 5 conferees had begun crafting a bill that risked rejection by both the House and the administration. By agreeing to include a new sugar price support program that the House had rejected, conferees risked House rebellion. And, because the bill appeared certain to cost hundreds of millions of dollars more during the next four years than Reagan wanted to spend, the legislation also risked a veto.

Conferees agreed 15-1 on Nov. 5 to keep the Senate's sugar price support program maintaining sugar prices at 18 cents per pound for the 1982 crop, with annual half-cent per pound increases thereafter.

On Nov. 6 a new dairy program was adopted. The House bill had allotted about $400 million more to dairy price supports over four years than the Senate. Dole produced a compromise that would put the four-year cost of the bill about $150 million above the Senate level.

A key point of disagreement continued to be the grain supports, with the Reagan administration urging thrift and a group of House conferees, led by former Agriculture Committee Chairman Thomas S. Foley, D-Wash., insisting they could compromise no more. "We've done 100 percent of the adjusting," Foley told conferees. "Nothing seems to

satisfy this administration except an absolute capitulation" by the House.

Wheat and feed grains price supports passed by the House would have cost some $4 billion more in the next four years than those approved by the Senate. But Foley and his allies Nov. 11 made an offer that would have cost about $100 million more than the Senate version Reagan favored. Conferees finally accepted a Dole compromise on wheat and feed grains that established a dual system of price supports — loans for which farmers put up their crops as collateral — and target prices, which provided direct cash payments to farmers.

Senate conferees Dec. 3 accepted a package of changes drafted under strong pressure from the administration. With that compromise, the bill would cost $428 million more over four years than the version passed by the Senate and backed by Reagan. That was $253 million less than the version tentatively accepted by conferees Nov. 19, when negotiations had stalled over spending levels for farm programs and a special exemption from bankruptcy laws for farmers (which later was dropped).

The new plan was negotiated privately by de la Garza and Helms with certain other conferees and Agriculture Secretary Block. It won the first explicit administration approval of the bill.

But the compromise so angered prominent House conferees who already had retreated from their more expensive version of the bill that seven of them, including Foley and Ed Jones, D-Tenn., refused to sign it. Jones said the bill ignored the worsening financial problems of farmers. USDA had forecast net farm income for 1982 at between $16 billion and $19 billion, a 42 percent drop from the 1979 total of $27.4 billion.

Although Senate conferees Dec. 3 took steps to ease potential House objections to the bill, House conferees did not accept it until Dec. 8 (H Rept 97-377).

Foley objected to the grain provisions and withheld his support from the bill until two days before the final House vote. His late decision to canvass for votes for the bill was essential to the narrow administration victory, according to Block.

Block said that another important element was the realization that the alternatives to S 884 would be much worse for farmers. Administration lobbyists argued that if Congress failed in 1981 to replace the expired 1977 act, farmers would get even less in 1982 because tighter budget constraints were sure to be in force. The other alternative, allowing the permanent farm statutes dating from 1938 and 1949 to take effect, would be too costly for the government and too confusing for farmers, according to the administration.

House Agriculture Committee Chairman de la Garza, in an emotional speech before the final vote, said, "This [bill] is nothing but a blood transfusion." But he added that nothing more for farmers could be wrung from the administration.

Not all farm groups objected to the bill. Representatives for cotton, corn and soybean growers endorsed Reagan's position after a Dec. 2 meeting between the president and representatives of 16 farm groups.

Major Provisions

As signed into law Dec. 22, the Agriculture and Food Act of 1981 (S 884 — PL 97-98) contained the following major agriculture provisions *(Food stamp provisions, p. 583)*:

Dairy

● Set dairy price supports at these minimums: for fiscal 1982, the existing level of $13.10 per hundredweight; for the following three fiscal years, $13.25, $14.00 and $14.60 respectively.

However, beginning in 1983, the minimum support would be 70 percent of parity in any year in which anticipated federal purchases of dairy products, as required by the program, would be less than $1 billion. (According to USDA estimates at the time of passage, 70 percent of parity would be $13.97 per hundredweight in fiscal 1983, $15.53 in 1984 and $17.40 in 1985.)

Or, the minimum would be 75 percent of parity if net purchases were estimated to be less than four billion pounds in fiscal 1983, 3.5 billion pounds in 1984 or 2.69 billion pounds in 1985.

● Continued milk marketing authority and the indemnity program that reimbursed dairymen for milk that could not be sold because of contamination by pesticides, toxic chemicals or nuclear fallout.

● Directed the secretary, using existing authority, to reduce the volume of dairy products owned by the Commodity Credit Corp. (CCC) so that outlays for the program did not exceed dairy spending levels assumed in budget legislation.

Wool and Mohair

● Set the wool support level at 77.5 percent of a statutory formula. (The 1981 rate was 85 percent.)

Wheat, Feed Grains, Cotton, Rice

● **Wheat.** Set commodity loans for wheat at no less than $3.55 a bushel. (The 1981 rate was $3.20.)

When the previous year's market price averaged not more than 105 percent of the loan rate, the secretary could lower the loan rate by no more than 10 percent and not below $3 per bushel.

● Set the wheat target price program minimum rate at $4.05 per bushel for the 1982 crop and $4.30, $4.45 and $4.65 respectively for the following three crop years. (The 1981 rate was $3.81.)

● **Feed Grains.** Established commodity loans for feed grains at no less than $2.55 a bushel for corn. (The 1981 rate was $2.40.) Rates for barley, oats, rye and grain sorghum would be pegged to the corn rate.

In a year when the previous year's market price averaged not more than 105 percent of the loan rate, the secretary could lower the loan rate by no more than 10 percent and not below $2 per bushel.

● Established feed grain target prices at no less than $2.70 per bushel for the 1982 corn crop and $2.86, $3.03 and $3.18 respectively for the following three crop years, with rates for other grains pegged to corn. (The 1981 corn rate was $2.40.)

● **Cotton.** Set commodity loans for cotton by formulas based on market prices, with a minimum of 55 cents a pound.

● Set cotton target prices at whichever of the following was the higher price for a given year: 120 percent of the cotton loan level, or 71 cents a pound for the 1982 crop, 76 cents for 1983, 81 cents for 1984 and 86 cents for 1985.

● Reduced the loan level for extra long staple ("pima") cotton to 75 to 125 percent of upland cotton, from 85 to 135 percent, and eliminated direct payments to producers.

● **Rice.** Repealed authority for rice acreage allotments

Farm Income, Price Support Programs

Permanent farm law, including major statutes passed in 1938 and 1949 and the charter of the Commodity Credit Corp. (CCC), gave the government broad authority to increase farm income, including establishing price supports at 100 percent of parity.

Parity referred to an index that related farm income to the purchasing power of farmers during 1910-14, a time when farm earnings were unusually high. Many economists criticized the parity index because it did not accurately reflect the dramatic increases in agricultural productivity.

Beginning in the 1960s, Congress reworked many of the more complex and costly provisions of the permanent agriculture statutes, substituting an assortment of devices to bolster farm income, some optional, some mandatory, known collectively as "price supports."

Both Republicans and Democrats backed the general proposition that farm policy should expose American agriculture to market forces, while preventing massive bankruptcies. That meant relatively low price supports.

For the most part, Congress also abandoned parity as an index for the price supports, choosing instead to link them to market prices, costs of production and similar factors.

Major forms of price supports included:

Commodity Loans

The basic mechanism to stabilize farm income was the commodity loan, whose level acted as a floor for market prices. The loans, administered by the CCC, permitted farmers to borrow from the government at a level pegged to a statutory per-bushel price of whatever crop the farmer offered as collateral. Farmers generally did not market their crops if prices fell below the loan levels; instead, they held them, or defaulted on their loans and let the government keep the crops. A variation on the basic price support loan was the "farmer-held reserve" program under which farmers borrowed against crops while retaining ownership and managing storage of them.

In 1980 Congress voted to give participants in the farmer-held reserve higher loan rates than those for basic commodity loans. Farmers in the reserve could not sell the stored crops for three years unless certain market conditions occurred. If a predetermined "release" market price was reached, farmers could sell their grain and repay their loans; if a higher "call" price was reached, they had to sell. *(Congress and the Nation Vol. V, p. 388)*

Target Prices

To provide a supplement for farm income in years when market prices were low, Congress in 1973 added target prices to the basic loan system. Target prices, calculated on the national average cost of producing a crop, were set above the loan levels for major commodities. If market prices failed to reach the target price level, farmers could collect "deficiency payments." *(Congress and the Nation Vol. IV, p. 719)*

Set-Asides, Disaster Payments

The government could limit production by requiring farmers to set aside — not plant — a portion of their customary acreage. In the years when the secretary announced a set-aside, only the farmers participating became eligible for other farm aid programs, including commodity loans.

There also were special grants — disaster payments — for such physical problems as drought, and a newly expanded, subsidized crop insurance plan to protect against damage from natural causes.

Miscellaneous

In addition to the price support loans, there were loans to cover damage from physical disasters and so-called "economic emergencies." The Farmers Home Administration (FmHA) lent money for a variety of projects broadly construed as rural development. The agency also provided start-up financing and loans covering operating costs for farmers unable to qualify for credit elsewhere. There also was an independent system of farm lending institutions that competed successfully with private banks.

In 1983 the administration initiated a temporary payment-in-kind (PIK) program that paid participating farmers in commodities they pledged not to plant. *(PIK program, p. 508)*

Dairy

The dairy program still was based on the parity index. Existing legislation set dairy price supports at 80 percent of parity with an adjustment every six months to reflect changes in costs.

Under the program, the government was required to purchase, in the form of butter, dried milk and cheese, all the milk that dairy farmers could not sell at a market price equivalent to the price support level. The government paid storage costs.

The dairy program was singled out for special legislation in 1981. President Reagan pushed through Congress a bill canceling a scheduled April 1 adjustment in the price support level. He argued that the scheduled hike would be too costly. *(Dairy legislation, p. 493)*

A bill enacted in 1982 froze dairy support prices at existing levels, and in 1983 Congress further revised the program. *(Stories, pp. 496, 504)*

and marketing quotas, thereby making loans and other program benefits available to all rice growers.

- Established commodity loans for rice at 75 percent of the target price but no lower than $8 per hundredweight.
- Continued the rice target price program at no less than $10.85 per hundredweight for 1982, $11.40, $11.90 and $12.40 respectively for the following three crop years.

Disaster Payments

- Continued disaster payments for damage to wheat, feed grains, cotton and rice, but only for producers for whom federal crop insurance was not available; however, authorized such payments, at the discretion of the secretary, if a disaster created an economic emergency too serious to be relieved by crop insurance or other federal aid.

Production Controls

- Continued authority for wheat and feed grain set-aside and for acreage reduction programs for those crops and cotton and rice. Permitted the secretary, in years of anticipated surplus, to require participation in those programs as a condition of eligibility for price supports.
- Also continued authority for wheat, feed grain, cotton and rice paid acreage diversion but without authority to require participation.
- Canceled authority for normal crop acreage planting requirements for cotton, which restricted a producer's acreage to what he had planted in previous years.
- Barred "cross-compliance" — compliance with other commodity program restrictions — as a condition for rice price supports.

Grain Reserves

- Continued the farmer-owned reserve program for wheat and feed grains, with loan rates at not less than those for commodity loans.
- Authorized the secretary to determine the terms under which farmers could sell grain from the reserve without penalty and the terms under which the secretary could encourage such withdrawals by ending storage payments or increasing interest rates.

    For the 1981 crop year, loan rates for crops in the reserve were higher than basic price support loans, and the terms under which grain could be withdrawn or forced out of the reserve were tied to market prices and were explicitly stated by law.
- Permitted the secretary to restrict the size of the reserve but specified that a wheat reserve could not be less than 700 million bushels and feed grains not less than one billion bushels.
- Barred Agriculture Department sales of federally owned grain, when a reserve was in effect, for less than 110 percent of the "release" price (the market price selected by the secretary at which farmers could sell their grain out of the reserve).
- Set interest rates for reserve loans at not less than the USDA cost of borrowing money from the Treasury, except that the secretary could adjust rates or waive interest.

Peanuts

- Repealed the peanut acreage allotment system, thus allowing farmers without the allotments to grow so-called "additional" peanuts. Additional peanuts, grown in excess of the national peanut poundage quota, could be sold abroad and could be sold for domestic use in years when domestic demand exceeded a national quota. They qualified for the lower of two federal price support loans.
- Continued the poundage quota system, setting the national quota at 1.2 million tons in 1982, down from the 1981 level of 1.4 million tons, and reducing the quota by steps to 1.1 million tons in 1985. Reductions in the quota were, to the extent feasible, to be applied to quota holders who did not themselves produce peanuts.

    (Individual farm quotas, as before, would be held only by those who had had acreage allotments; peanuts grown within the quota would be sold for domestic use and could qualify for the higher of two federal price support loans. These peanuts were referred to as "quota" or "edible" peanuts.)
- Set quota peanut price support loans at $550 a ton for the 1982 crop and additional peanut price support loans at a rate set by the secretary to recognize market conditions and to avoid net cost to the federal government. (The 1981 quota peanut loan rate was $455 a ton.)

Soybeans

- Set commodity loans at 75 percent of the national five-year average market price (omitting high and low years) but at no less than $5.02 a bushel. In a year when the previous year's market price averaged not more than 105 percent of the loan rate, the secretary could lower the loan rate by no more than 10 percent and not below $4.05 per bushel.
- Barred the secretary from making participation in any production control program a condition of eligibility for soybean loans.
- Barred storage reserve programs and payments to producers for storage of 1982-85 crops.

Sugar

- Required the secretary to support the price of sugar through duties and fees on imported sugar or other means, at 17 cents a pound for the 1982 crop and for the following three crop years, at 17.5 cents, 17.75 cents and 18 cents a pound. Also established a sugar purchase price of 16.75 cents a pound from the date of enactment to Oct. 1, 1982, when the loans would become available.

    Establishing the purchase price had the effect of permitting the government to set duties and fees, thereby raising domestic sugar prices and making purchases unnecessary, according to USDA officials.

Miscellaneous

- Expressed the sense of Congress that the tobacco program should operate at no net cost to taxpayers other than administrative expenses. Directed the secretary to determine if new authority was needed to do so and to request such authority from Congress.
- Authorized the secretary to seize, quarantine and treat crops, as well as physical premises, to eliminate infestations of plant pests, such as the Medfly, in emergencies but only if state or other efforts were inadequate.
- Continued existing limits on total payments so that individual farmers could receive no more than $50,000 in any year for all programs except disaster payments and no more than $100,000 in disaster payments.
- Continued the grazing and hay, and emergency feed programs, changing them from mandatory for the secretary

to discretionary, and made poultry producers eligible for the feed program.

● Authorized donation to local food banks for the needy and to nutrition programs for the elderly and children, of surplus food, such as dairy products, that had been bought by federal price support programs. Only commodities not committed to sales or other programs could be donated.

Export, Embargo, PL 480

● Required compensation to farmers affected by an embargo of U.S. commodity sales abroad for national security or foreign policy reasons but only if the embargo was limited to agricultural commodities and only if the affected nation bought more than 3 percent of U.S. exports of the affected commodity. Farmers would receive either or both: direct payments, based on the difference between 100 percent of parity and the average post-embargo market price of the affected commodity; commodity loans at 100 percent of parity. This was a permanent addition to farm law.

● Authorized set-aside or acreage limitation programs for 1982-85 crops, regardless of prior policy announcements, in the event of an embargo.

● Established a CCC revolving loan fund through Sept. 30, 1985, to promote export sales of commodities, with funds appropriated as needed.

● Authorized commodity export subsidies, at the discretion of the president, to offset subsidies used by other nations.

● Continued the Food for Peace (PL 480) program through Dec. 31, 1985, and raised to $1 billion, from $750 million, the annual ceiling for food donations to foreign nations.

● Permitted the domestic distilled spirits industry to participate in the PL 480 foreign market development program on the same basis as the beer and wine industries.

Credit and Rural Development

● Continued economic emergency loans through Sept. 30, 1982, but restricted new lending in fiscal 1982 to a total of $600 million. (Conference report language stipulated that the program was discretionary for the secretary.)

● Required the secretary to make farm storage facility loans in areas with facility shortages.

● Continued for 10 years the $30 million-per-year authorization for federal purchases of capital stock in the Rural Telephone Bank.

● Made small farm production cooperatives eligible for Farmers Home Administration (FmHA) operating and ownership loans and dropped restrictions on FmHA loans to unmarried persons.

Conservation

● Authorized a new soil conservation program for areas found by the secretary to have significant erosion problems. Farmers contracting to establish approved conservation projects could qualify for technical aid, payments for part of the cost of such projects.

● Authorized matching federal grants to local governments for conservation projects and authorized loans, to the extent provided by appropriations bills, to individual producers for conservation projects.

● Permitted local soil and water conservation boards to disapprove individual farmers' choices of acreage to use to comply with set-aside or paid land diversion programs.

● Authorized compensation for taking land out of pro-

duction and converting it to conservation use, also for promoting conservation tillage.

Dairy Price Supports

An administration bill (S 509 — PL 97-6) to cancel a scheduled April 1 increase in dairy price supports cleared Congress March 27. Congress approved further changes in the program July 31. *(Story, p. 494; 1982 changes, p. 496)*

Two years later Congress enacted legislation that overhauled federal dairy policy and further reduced federal price supports. That bill, however, met with strong administration objections because it contained provisions paying dairymen for not producing. *(Story, p. 504)*

S 509 was the first piece of Reagan's ambitious economic program to go before Congress. The president's allies and tacticians managed to blunt strong efforts by the dairy industry and some Democrats to make changes that were unacceptable to the White House.

The 90-cent per hundredweight increase in the federal price support for dairy products had been required by a provision in the 1977 farm law (PL 95-113), which was extended for two years in 1979 (PL 96-127). *(Congress and the Nation Vol. V, pp. 368, 387)*

Administration officials contended that the increase would cost consumers an additional 8 cents a gallon for milk. They also maintained that the dairy program stimulated overproduction and that eliminating the April 1 increase would save the federal government $147 million in 1981 in purchase and storage costs for dairy products. The program required the government to buy, in the form of butter, dried milk and cheese, all the milk that dairy farmers could not sell at the price support level. If the April 1 adjustment had not been blocked, the price support would have risen to $14.00 from the existing level of $13.10 per hundredweight.

Dairy spokesmen countered that inflation had so increased the expenses of dairymen that they needed the April 1 adjustment badly. They contended that low feed grain prices and relatively low beef prices — not the federal support program — had prompted high dairy production. Without the adjustment, they warned, small- to moderate-sized dairy operations would simply fold. Industry officials were divided on tactics, however, and generally did not attack the basic bill. Instead, they pressed for changes that could have delayed passage beyond the April 1 deadline.

Legislative History

Senate. The president won the first skirmish March 4 when the Senate Agriculture Committee voted 14-2 to cancel the scheduled increase. The administration pushed hard for the legislation in a lobbying effort that one congressional aide called a "full-court press." Reagan personally telephoned some panel members prior to the vote.

Members of the Senate committee clearly were uncomfortable with the choice of opposing dairy interests or of appearing to thwart the president's economic recovery package. Rudy Boschwitz, R-Minn., whose state was the nation's fourth largest dairy producer, said, "I told the people of Minnesota to hang in there with President Reagan — and I hope they hang in with me." The committee reported the bill (S Rept 97-24) March 10, with only two members voting against it and one voting "present."

After four days of debate, the Senate passed the mea-

sure March 25 by a vote of 88-5. Passage came after the chamber defeated on March 24, by a **key 38-60 vote (R 7-45; D 31-15)**, a controversial industry-backed amendment offered by John Melcher, D-Mont., to restrict imports of casein, an inexpensive milk protein used in manufacturing synthetic cheese, non-dairy "creamer" and certain other foods. The administration objected that the limitation would invite trade retaliation from other nations and that casein imports had not been shown to damage the American dairy industry. Adoption of the restriction could have caused serious jurisdictional complications and delays in the House. *(1981 key votes, p. 879)*

The Senate also adopted two non-binding amendments expressing objections to the continuing embargo on sales of U.S. grain to the Soviet Union. Reagan lifted the embargo April 24. *(Story, p. 495)*

House. At a March 18 meeting of the House Agriculture Livestock, Dairy and Poultry Subcommittee, Tony Coelho, D-Calif., and James M. Jeffords, R-Vt., said the panel gave Reagan a "victory" by approving a bill that would save only $20 million less than the president wanted.

In fact, the winner was the dairy industry, because the panel approved a four-year plan that appeared to lock in higher price supports, with less flexibility than Reagan wanted. A modified version of a proposal drafted by the milk producers, the subcommittee bill set the dairy price support at 75 to 80 percent of parity through 1985, with semiannual adjustments, depending on how much surplus milk, cheese and butter the government owned. But nothing in the measure prevented the support level from going higher than 80 percent. (Parity is the index comparing prices farmers pay and receive; it is meant to reflect farmers' purchasing power during the prosperous 1910-1914 period.)

The full Agriculture Committee reversed its subcommittee's decision one day later (March 19), partly at the urging of the House leadership not to be obstructionist and to allow the president "a clear shot at his bill." The measure was reported March 24 (HR 2594 — H Rept 97-12), and the House substituted its text for that of the Senate bill by voice vote March 26.

Final Action. The Senate accepted the House version without the embargo language and cleared S 509 for the president by voice vote March 27. Reagan signed it March 31.

Reconciliation Changes

The 1981 budget reconciliation bill brought higher interest rates for many federal farm loans and new charges for grading and inspecting cotton, tobacco and grain.

The massive budget-cutting bill (HR 3982 — PL 97-35), cleared by Congress July 31, also gave dairymen price supports at least 5 percentage points above the 70 percent parity level the Reagan administration wanted. *(Reconciliation action, p. 40)*

The legislation explicitly stated that the dairy program would be reconsidered during deliberations on the farm bill reauthorizing agricultural programs for four years. But controversy delayed enactment of the farm bill, and separate measures were passed to prevent dairymen from reaping a bonus throughout the year. *(Farm bill, p. 487)*

The reconciliation cuts were felt through much of the Agriculture Department (USDA). E. "Kika" de la Garza, D-Texas, chairman of the House Agriculture Committee,

noted that USDA programs were cut by $8.8 billion in fiscal 1982-84, some $3 billion more than was required.

Conferees completed work on the legislation July 24 after four days of negotiations. Key bargaining revolved around the Senate's refusal to accept the House provision for more liberal dairy price supports, while House conferees resisted Senate interest rate increases and other changes in farm lending programs.

The conference report (H Rept 97-208) included both the dairy program and lending revisions.

The Dairy Program

The House-passed dairy program that the reconciliation conferees retained was strongly opposed by the administration. Because Reagan believed that the statutory support price of 80 percent of parity encouraged farmers to produce more milk than Americans could consume, he already had persuaded Congress to cancel a scheduled April 1 adjustment in the support price for dairy products. *(Story, p. 493)*

That action left payments at $13.10 per hundredweight — a figure that was about 75 percent of parity in the spring but dropped to about 72 percent of parity by the end of the year. (Parity, an index of prices farmers pay and receive, was meant to approximate the earning power of farmers in 1910-14. The periodic adjustments were meant to reflect inflationary pressures.)

Under the dairy program, if a farmer was not able to sell his dairy products at a price equivalent to the percentage of parity set by law, the government had to buy the excess stocks at that price and store them. In 1980 the government bought 579 million pounds of butter, cheese and non-fat dry milk at a cost of $1.2 billion, excluding interest and storage charges.

Lowering the stipulated percentage of parity would decrease the government's costs. Reagan wanted Congress to give the agriculture secretary broad discretion to set the support level at 70 percent of parity, or even less, to discourage production.

The dairy provisions of the reconciliation measure set a 75 percent minimum price support but postponed semiannual adjustments until fiscal 1983. Legislators intended that the dairy program be reappraised during consideration of the four-year reauthorization of farm programs.

But the House and Senate became embroiled in controversy over the farm bill, and the 1977 law (PL 95-113) setting the existing level of supports expired Sept. 30. With that expiration, the reconciliation provision came into play, raising the price support from the existing $13.10 per hundredweight to $13.49. *(1977 law, Congress and the Nation Vol. V, p. 368)*

The missed deadline set off a legislative scramble to block the price support hike. On Oct. 1, by a 328-58 vote, the House approved legislation (HR 4612) delaying the increase until Nov. 15, by which time the new farm bill with lower price supports was to have been enacted. The Senate by voice vote Oct. 19 cleared the bill for the president, who signed it into law Oct. 20 (PL 97-67). When it became clear that farm bill conferees would not reach agreement by Nov. 15, an unrelated bill was amended to postpone the increase until the end of 1981. The bill (S 1322 — PL 97-77) was cleared for the president when it was passed by the House Nov. 12. The Senate had passed it Nov. 9.

In 1982 Congress passed a budget reconciliation bill that froze, and even provided for cutting, dairy price sup-

ports. The supports were further reduced in 1983. *(Stories, pp. 48, 504)*

Provisions

As signed into law Aug. 13, Title I of HR 3982 (PL 97-35) contained the following provisions:

● **Dairy Programs.** Set dairy price supports for fiscal years 1982-85 at a minimum of 75 percent of parity, an index based on farmers' costs and prices.

● Stipulated that the support level could rise to a maximum of 90 percent of parity and established a formula, based on government dairy stocks and anticipated purchases of dairy products under the program, for determining the actual parity support level each year.

● Required adjustments to reflect any increases in dairy imports.

● Provided also for semiannual adjustments in the actual payments, beginning in fiscal 1983, to offset changes in the parity index and thus keep the payments at the minimum 75 percent.

● **Commodity Credit Programs.** Gave the secretary of agriculture discretion to make loans for farm storage facilities, eliminating the existing requirement that the loans must be made available. This permitted the administration to cease offering the loans, as it had requested.

● Authorized federal collection of fees, with penalties for non-payment, for costs of official grading and/or inspections of grain, tobacco, cotton, "naval stores" (turpentine and resin) and inspecting warehouses in which agricultural commodities were stored. The effect was to shift the cost from the federal budget to purchasers of the commodities or other sources in the private sector.

The bill limited the total amounts that could be collected.

● **FmHA Loans.** Raised the interest for Farmers Home Administration (FmHA) loans for water and waste disposal and community facility projects to a level comparable to rates for municipal bonds. Retained the existing 5 percent rate for hardship cases.

● Increased interest by 2 percent on certain FmHA loans for projects that would convert prime farm land to non-farm uses, unless alternative sites were unavailable.

● Raised the interest for FmHA farm ownership loans to no more than half the cost of money to the government, and no less than 5 percent.

● Raised the interest for farm operating loans to 3 percentage points below the cost of money to the government.

● Earmarked 20 percent of the operating loans for low-income, limited-resource borrowers, down from the existing 25 percent.

● Stipulated that FmHA emergency loans for physical disasters be made only to farmers who had lost 30 percent or more of their crop, and for up to 80 percent of their losses. This affirmed an administrative action that had changed previous figures of 20 and 90 percent respectively.

● Raised interest rates on disaster loans from 5 percent to no more than 8 percent for borrowers without other sources of credit and to commercial rates for others.

● **Rural Electrification Administration (REA).** Fixed interest rates at 5 percent for REA-insured loans for telephone and electric systems instead of permitting the loan rates to range between 2 percent and 5 percent.

● Allowed loans at less than 5 percent, but no less than 2 percent, for hardship cases.

● Required the REA administrator, at the request of the borrower, to secure REA-guaranteed loans from the Federal Financing Bank at interest rates comparable to similar loans in that bank.

● **Gasohol.** Reduced to $460 million, from $600 million, funds administered by USDA for loans, loan guarantees, price guarantees and purchase agreements to promote production of alcohol and other fuels from biomass, such as crops and crop residues. The conference agreement included an identical reduction for the separate biomass fuels promotion program in the Department of Energy.

Grain Embargo, Loans

Less than a year after approving certain interest-free loans for farmers to compensate for the embargo of grain sales to Russia, Congress reinstated the charges. President Reagan signed the bill (S 1395 — PL 97-24) July 23.

The Senate approved S 1395 by voice vote June 25, and the House followed suit July 9.

The bill ended a mandatory interest waiver established in December 1980 (PL 96-494) on loans for 1980 and 1981 grain crops stored in the farmer-held reserve. The 1980 legislation was intended to aid farmers adversely affected by President Carter's Jan. 4, 1980, announcement establishing the embargo. Under PL 96-494, farmers borrowed from the government, using their crops as collateral, and could not sell them to repay the loan until certain market prices were reached. The program was intended to stabilize grain prices by keeping potential surpluses off the market. *(Background, Congress and the Nation Vol. V, p. 388)*

Carter had imposed the grain embargo as one of several measures to protest the Soviet Union's invasion of Afghanistan in December 1979. The embargo, which had been extremely unpopular among farmers, had cut off 17 million of the 25 million metric tons of grain that had been approved for sale to the Soviets. *(Congress and the Nation Vol. V, p. 82)*

Reagan lifted the embargo April 24. The administration then asked Congress to end the interest waiver, and the Agriculture Department refused to admit 1981 grain into the reserve program and make loans until the request was approved. The cancellation was expected to save the government $165 million in fiscal 1982.

The grain reserve was opened the same day the president signed the bill.

Crop Insurance

President Reagan May 22 signed an uncontroversial bill (S 730 — PL 97-11) to provide emergency financing to expand the subsidized crop insurance program mandated by Congress in 1980. *(Congress and the Nation Vol. V, p. 391)*

The measure passed the Senate by voice vote May 5 and the House by a vote of 384-5 May 19. It allowed the Federal Crop Insurance Corp. to spend up to $14 million for administrative expenses from funds normally reserved for indemnity payments to insured farmers.

The bill was reported by the Senate Agriculture Committee April 10 (S Rept 97-38). The House Agriculture Committee May 1 had reported a bill without the spending limit (HR 3020 — H Rept 97-27).

1982

Faced with massive surpluses, chronically depressed farm prices and mounting price support expenditures, Agriculture Secretary John R. Block asked Congress Dec. 9 to clear the way for a major reversal of administration farm policy. Congress, however, failed to ratify Block's "payment-in-kind" (PIK) plan, despite general acceptance of the concept.

Block proposed to retire up to half the nation's farm land in 1983, paying farmers in surplus crops, as well as cash, for not planting. When Congress failed to complete action, the administration Jan. 11, 1983, announced it would implement the program administratively.

As occurred in 1981, the dairy lobby was thwarted when Congress passed legislation freezing price supports at the existing level of $13.10 per hundred pounds for fiscal 1983 and 1984 in an effort to reduce program costs. Congress also cleared a bill requiring tobacco growers to repay the government for any losses in their price support loan program.

Conflicting demands of environmental, labor and state government groups, the American Farm Bureau Federation and manufacturers stalemated a revision of federal pesticide law in 1981.

Congress, however, defied State Department objections and sent to the president a sweeping ban on presidential embargoes on farm exports. The "contract sanctity" guarantee appeared in a four-year reauthorization of the Commodity Futures Trading Commission.

Farm Program Cuts

Two farm policy changes aimed at reducing grain and dairy surpluses were included in the budget-cutting reconciliation measure (HR 6955 — PL 97-253) approved by Congress Aug. 18. President Reagan signed the bill Sept. 8.

One provided new advance payments to farmers who agreed not to grow major crops. The theory was that the reduced production would lead to higher market prices and subsequently decrease the amounts the government would have to pay in the future for price supports to bolster farm income.

The second change had the effect of cutting up to $1 from the existing dairy price support of $13.10 per hundred pounds, unless dairymen reduced milk production sharply. That change, however, was dropped in 1983. *(Box, p. 505)*

The final bill did not include controversial House-passed dairy provisions establishing an industry-dominated board that in some cases could have set the level of price supports and could have levied assessments on farmers to pay for promotional programs.

The measure reduced projected increases in major farm and food stamp programs by $6.6 billion over fiscal 1983-85, according to Congressional Budget Office (CBO) estimates. The reduction was nearly twice the $3.3 billion amount required by the budget resolution (S Con Res 92) that had cleared June 23. *(Reconciliation bill, p. 48)*

House Action

Committee. The House Agriculture Committee reported its reconciliation measure, which ultimately was folded into the omnibus reconciliation bill, on Aug. 2 (HR 6892 — H Rept 97-687). Cuts in the farm programs exceeded the committee's reconciliation savings obligations, established in the budget resolution, by a projected $1.3 billion. The changes in the dairy, grains, cotton and rice programs, when added to revisions in food stamps, reduced federal spending by $4.6 billion in fiscal 1983-85, according to CBO.

The CBO estimates were challenged by administration officials, who contended that, instead of saving money, the bill would add at least $1 billion in new costs. Committee member Paul Findley, R-Ill., also complained that the savings were "ephemeral" and damaging to farmers in the long run.

Members of the agriculture panel were under strong pressure not only to meet budget reconciliation goals but also to put some cash into the hands of farmers to help them through a third year of high interest rates and depressed market prices. For major crops, the committee authorized payments to farmers who took land out of production.

The Reagan administration objected to the cash outlays required by the plan and also disapproved of federal intervention in farmers' production decisions. The deteriorating farm economy, however, had prompted the administration in July to adopt modest production controls for both the 1982 wheat and feed grains crops and for the 1983 wheat crop. Agriculture Secretary John R. Block asked wheat farmers to retire 20 percent of their land in 1983. Those doing so would qualify for advance payment of half their estimated deficiency payments — one type of price support. *(Price supports, box, p. 491)*

Findley objected that a strategy to boost U.S. grain prices while shrinking supplies would invite foreign competitors like Brazil and Canada to increase their own production. The United States would lose more of the world market to competitors, and price-depressing surpluses at home would continue, he predicted.

Floor. The House passed HR 6892 Aug. 10 by a 268-121 vote under special rules that limited amendments. According to Delbert L. Latta, R-Ohio, ranking minority member of the House Budget Committee, a major objection to the bill voiced by Republicans was that neither the farm nor the food stamp provisions saved the required amounts, despite CBO estimates.

The House bill's proposed dairy industry board, empowered to set some dairy price supports, assess dairymen for promotional activities and dispose of some dairy surpluses, was criticized as unconstitutional and monopolistic.

Latta also warned that the dairy plan would not discourage overproduction as promised, asserting that it would hike price supports to $16 per hundredweight by 1985, compared with the existing $13.10 level. But defenders of the bill insisted that the dairy plan would save money by reducing production and that the bill's payments to farmers for retiring crop land were essential. "I know members have heard time after time about the problems of our farmers. Let me tell them, this time our farmers really have problems," said Berkley Bedell, D-Iowa.

Senate Action

Committee. Like its House counterpart, the Senate Agriculture Committee focused on food stamps and the dairy program to reach its reconciliation savings goals.

Meeting in June and July, the committee approved

legislative changes providing an estimated $4.1 billion in savings from the two programs over fiscal 1983-85. Because the food stamp and dairy program savings together were more than enough to meet the reconciliation goal, the committee decided to try to help the ailing farm economy by authorizing additional funds for two agricultural programs. The panel called for advance payment to eligible farmers under the deficiency payment program of price supports for major crops. The committee also approved spending of up to $190 million for subsidies to promote agricultural exports.

The Agriculture Committee recommendations were incorporated in the omnibus reconciliation bill reported by the Budget Committee July 26 (S 2774 — H Rept 97-504).

Floor. The Senate passed the omnibus bill on a 72-24 vote Aug. 5. One of the few areas of controversy involved farm programs. Several attempts were made to increase the agriculture savings, but only one succeeded.

The largest cuts would have resulted from an amendment offered by Paula Hawkins, R-Fla., to lower dairy price supports from the existing level of $13.10 per hundredweight to $12.60 on the date of enactment and to $12.00 on Jan. 1, 1983. Hawkins' amendment was tabled 65-33. Another amendment to limit dairy price supports, offered by S. I. "Sam" Hayakawa, R-Calif., also failed, 48-49.

In other action, the Senate adopted an amendment by David L. Boren, D-Okla., setting up a program to pay farmers for not growing wheat, corn and feed grains. While costing the government money in the first year, the program would save $400 million over three years. Boren said farmers would receive $120 per acre for the 10 percent additional wheat acreage they set aside and $150 per acre for corn and feed grains set aside.

The House had adopted a similar program in its reconciliation bill.

Conference Compromise

Final action on the legislation came Aug. 18 when both houses adopted a conference report on the bill (H Rept 97-759).

Conferees on the agriculture section had reached agreement on a dairy plan during their third and final meeting Aug. 16. The dairy program, whose costs were estimated at nearly $2 billion in fiscal 1982, was the most difficult point to resolve; in earlier meetings, the conferees agreed to wheat and grain provisions.

Under the final legislation, the government still was required to buy all surplus products at the price of $13.10 per hundred pounds. But the secretary could withhold up to $1 of each $13.10 from payments to dairymen, unless surplus production fell below specified amounts. The withholding was expected to "return" more than $1 billion each year to the Treasury that otherwise would have been paid out in price supports. (The withholding provision was repealed in 1983. *(Story, p. 504)*)

In all, the dairy changes were expected to lower projected spending for the program by $4.2 billion in fiscal years 1983-85, according to the CBO. Three-year savings in program changes for wheat, feed grain and rice were estimated at $274 million.

Provisions

As enacted into law, the agriculture section of the fiscal 1983 budget reconciliation bill (HR 6955 — PL 97-

253) contained the following major provisions *(Food stamp story, provisions, p. 594):*

● **Dairy Program.** Froze price supports at the existing level of $13.10 per hundred pounds for fiscal years 1983 and 1984. For fiscal 1985, the price support would be whatever level of parity $13.10 translated into as of Oct. 1, 1983 — estimated in 1982 at about 61.2 percent, which would convert to about $14.05 per hundred pounds for fiscal 1985.

● Authorized the agriculture secretary to deduct 50 cents per hundred pounds from milk price support payments from Oct. 1, 1982, through fiscal 1985, unless federal purchases of surplus dairy products dropped below five billion pounds of milk equivalent annually.

● Authorized the secretary to deduct a second 50 cents per hundred pounds from milk price support payments from April 1, 1983, through fiscal 1985, unless purchases of surplus dairy products dropped below 7.5 billion pounds annually. The secretary could not make the second deduction until he had implemented a program rebating the deduction to farmers who reduced their production.

● Expanded authority of the Commodity Credit Corp. (CCC) to dispose of federally owned surplus dairy products by donations abroad and to needy households in the United States, with donations overseas coordinated with other aid programs.

● **Farm Programs.** Required early payments to farmers of one type of price supports known as deficiency payments for fiscal 1982 and 1983. Deficiency payments were paid by the government to farmers when the market price of a commodity failed to reach a higher target price set by law.

● Increased commodity loan rates to $3.65 a bushel for wheat and $2.65 a bushel for corn, 10 cents a bushel more than existing law provided. The rate determined how much a farmer could borrow against his crops.

● Required the secretary of agriculture to offer a 20 percent diversion for wheat, 15 percent for corn and 20 percent for rice.

In each case, a producer had to retire the specified acreage to qualify for price supports and other farm programs, and for special diversion payments on 5 percent of his land. The special payment rates were set at $3 a bushel for wheat, $3 per hundredweight for rice and $1.50 a bushel for corn, with the secretary having the authority to lower the rates by 10 percent.

● Mandated that each fiscal year through 1985, from $175 million to $190 million in CCC funds be devoted to export promotion.

Tobacco Bill

Congress July 15 approved legislation (HR 6590 — PL 97-218) aimed at eliminating costs to taxpayers of the federal tobacco program. Passage of the bill represented a critical victory for tobacco interests, who hoped that it would defuse criticism of the controversial program. The legislation, sponsored by Rep. Charlie Rose, D-N.C., was in response to a mandate contained in the 1981 omnibus farm bill (PL 97-98) that the tobacco program be run at no net cost to taxpayers, other than administrative expenses. *(1981 bill, p. 487)*

The 1982 tobacco act obligated growers who used the program to reimburse the federal government for losses resulting from the price support loans that were provided

to farmers. They were required to make new "contributions" for this purpose to special funds run by their cooperative marketing associations. The provision was repealed in 1983 as part of legislation making major revisions in the tobacco program. *(Story, p. 504)*

The measure also directed institutional owners of acreage allotments and marketing quotas for flue-cured tobacco to sell these federal "licenses to grow" to farmers who would use them. The bill did not disturb allotment and quota leasing arrangements among individuals.

The industry-backed package of changes in the tobacco program was criticized by an anti-smoking coalition of health groups because it continued federal involvement with a product that endangered human health. Other opponents, including Rep. Paul Findley, R-Ill., said the measure did not go far enough in charging tobacco farmers for the cost of their program. The bill did not require farmers to pay for administrative costs, estimated at $15.9 million in fiscal 1983.

Congressional Action

HR 6590 moved quickly through the House, pushed by Rose's desire to have it become law before July 15, the beginning of the 1982 tobacco marketing year. Rose's House Agriculture Subcommittee on Tobacco and Peanuts marked up the bill June 15, and the full Agriculture Committee reported it June 18 (H Rept 97-613). The bill passed the House by voice vote June 21. Rose fended off delaying objections by promising hearings in 1983 to foes of the program, led by Bob Shamansky, D-Ohio.

The Senate Agriculture Committee reported an amended version of the measure June 24 (no written report). The amendments required farmers of flue-cured and burley tobacco to contribute to the costs of the program.

However, efforts to move the legislation quickly through the Senate were blocked by the leading critic of the tobacco program, Thomas F. Eagleton, D-Mo. After Eagleton delayed action, Agriculture Secretary John R. Block postponed the beginning of the marketing year until July 22.

Prior to passing HR 6590 on July 14 by a 77-17 vote, the Senate killed by a **key vote of 49-47 (R 29-23; D 20-24)** an Eagleton amendment that would have authorized tobacco price support loans only through 1985, thus ending permanent authorization for these loans. The effect would have been to subject the controversial program to the periodic congressional review that other major farm programs were required to endure through the reauthorization process. *(1982 key votes, p. 895)*

Final action came July 15 when the House by voice vote accepted minor amendments added by the Senate.

Final Provisions

As signed into law July 20, the Tobacco Program Act of 1982 (HR 6590 — PL 97-218):

● Required tobacco producers, as a condition for holding allotments and quotas, to make payments into special funds operated by cooperative tobacco marketing associations. Also required payments, but beginning with the 1983 crop, by owners who leased their quotas. Required the funds to repay the federal government for losses of principal and interest from tobacco price support loans, which were administered through the associations.

● Authorized the secretary of agriculture to reduce the support rate for any grade of tobacco determined to be in surplus. Such reductions could not bring the weighted average support rate for all types of tobacco below 65 percent of what the rate would have been without the reduction. In a year when there would have been no increase, the overall average could not be less than that of the previous year. (The support rates were determined by a formula based on 1959 tobacco prices.)

● Permitted an individual producer of flue-cured tobacco in a surplus year to sell up to 10 percent of his crop in a special auction. Such tobacco would not be eligible for price support loans.

● Permitted an owner of a flue-cured tobacco quota to sell the quota to any "active" tobacco farmer within his county and defined an "active grower" as one who "shared the risk" of producing a crop in at least one out of three years preceding the sale. "Sharing the risk" could include investing in at least 20 percent of crop costs or leasing the allotment or quota.

A buyer who failed to "share the risk" of a tobacco crop within 18 months of purchase would be required to sell the allotment or quota. A buyer could not so reduce his acreage, after purchase of the quota, that the quota covered more than 50 percent of his land; to comply with this requirement, he must either buy more land or forfeit a portion of the quota. This provision was intended to encourage farmers to diversify their crops and not have the bulk of their land in tobacco.

● Required that allotments and quotas sold to comply with other provisions of the bill should be available to farmers who certified that they intended to become tobacco producers.

● Prohibited leasing of quotas and allotments in the fall, except during natural disaster conditions.

● Required that any corporate or institutional owner of an allotment or quota that was not "significantly involved" in managing or using the land for farming, must sell the allotment or quota by Dec. 1, 1983, or forfeit it. Forfeited quotas would be redistributed by county Agricultural Conservation and Stabilization committees.

PIK Bills

The Reagan administration failed to win congressional endorsement in 1982 of a major change in farm policy involving payments of federally owned commodities to farmers who reduced acreage. However, the administration announced early in January 1983 that it would proceed without legislation.

Bypassing its Agriculture Committee, the Democratic House approved a bill (HR 7439) Dec. 18 involving the so-called payment-in-kind (PIK) program. However, a more elaborate Senate version (S 3074), approved by the Agriculture Committee Dec. 13, became bogged down by deadline pressures. *(PIK program, box, p. 508)*

Senators testily objected to considering the bill, citing the gas tax filibuster of Agriculture Committee Chairman Jesse Helms, R-N.C. Shortly after midnight Dec. 20, when Helms told the Senate that PIK legislation was "vital," Paul E. Tsongas, D-Mass., said he would oppose action on the bill even though he supported it. "I will not participate in anything that rewards" obstructionists, Tsongas declared. *(Gas tax, p. 301)*

Both the House and Senate bills were intended to address what Agriculture Secretary John R. Block called

relatively minor changes in the law needed to protect the program from potential lawsuits. Block said the changes would clarify authority he already had.

One change would have exempted commodity payments in kind from a $50,000 limit on federal farm program payments to an individual farmer. The second would have exempted the PIK payments from a requirement that commodities owned by the Commodity Credit Corp. (CCC) could not be sold for less than 110 percent of the price at which grain could be sold out of the farmer-held reserve.

The CCC was the Agriculture Department agency that operated price support programs. It became the owner of wheat, corn and other farm commodities when farmers defaulted on federal loans. The reserve program permitted farmers to borrow from the federal government if they agreed to keep their crops in storage and not sell them until market prices reached a fixed "release" level.

A General Accounting Office (GAO) report criticizing the multimillion-dollar PIK payments to individual farmers — and the congressional reaction it provoked — prompted the Agriculture Department to announce Dec. 21, however, that it would impose a $50,000 limit on payments to individuals participating in the 1984 program. Only wheat farmers could qualify for PIK payments on 1984 crops.

Commodity Futures

President Reagan Jan. 12, 1983, signed into law a bill (HR 5447 — PL 97-444) reauthorizing the Commodity Futures Trading Commission (CFTC) through Sept. 30, 1986. The bill contained a controversial "contract sanctity" amendment requiring the president to guarantee the delivery of American farm exports for up to nine months even if he subsequently decided to impose a trade embargo.

Contract Sanctity Issue. Sponsored by Sen. Dave Durenberger, R-Minn., the contract sanctity provision had been adopted by voice vote before the Senate passed its version of the bill Oct. 1. The House-passed bill had no similar language. The amendment barred imposition of restrictions on the export of any agricultural commodity under contract at the time an embargo was imposed if delivery was scheduled within 270 days. Supporters said the guarantee was needed because the United States' reputation as a reliable supplier of food had been damaged severely by the 1980 embargo on grain sales to the Soviet Union and by previous trade restraints. Despite an earlier threat of a veto, conferees on the bill agreed Dec. 9 to retain the provision. *(Soviet grain embargo, Congress and the Nation Vol. V, pp. 82, 388; embargo lifted, p. 495)*

The rider drew objections from the State Department because it restricted the president's freedom to act in the future. But because the trade guarantee had wide support within the financially troubled farm community, administration officials had avoided making public objections to it.

Sen. Robert Dole, R-Kan., told conferees Dec. 9 that he and other supporters of the provision had offered to soften the language in conference if the State Department would agree to negotiate a long-term grain sale agreement with the Soviet Union. Although department officials did not respond to his offer, Dole said, "Now, at the last minute, they're calling frantically and saying, 'you've got to change this.'"

Administration officials sought, without success, to convince farm lobbyists and their congressional allies that they did not need the statutory guarantee because Reagan repeatedly had pledged to avoid trade embargoes, except in extreme circumstances. But supporters insisted a statutory guarantee was needed to assure foreign purchasers that U.S. export commitments would be honored despite an embargo or other foreign policy action.

Other Provisions. Other provisions of HR 5447 were intended to strengthen the hand of state law enforcement officials and individuals against fraudulent commodity operators. The bill also ratified an important jurisdictional agreement between the CFTC and the Securities and Exchange Commission (SEC).

In addition, under a compromise worked out between the commodities industry and the Office of Management and Budget, the final legislation affirmed CFTC authority to charge the industry fees for such services as approval of contracts. Both the House and Senate had rejected attempts to include administration-backed fees on individual commodities transactions, but conferees added the "service fee" language to avert another veto threat to the bill.

The fees would return about $3 million a year to the Treasury, according to Richard G. Lugar, R-Ind., chairman of the Senate Agriculture subcommittee with jurisdiction over the CFTC.

The administration originally had wanted Congress to authorize transaction fees to raise enough revenue to cover most of the CFTC's annual $23 million budget. But the industry objected that the fees would drain financial support from its new, self-regulatory group, the National Futures Association (NFA), and neither the House nor the Senate included the transaction fees in their CFTC bills.

The bill set a deadline by which the NFA must actively share regulatory responsibilities with the CFTC.

Background

Congressional committees struggled throughout 1982 to revise the regulation of an industry whose rapid growth in new directions made some members uneasy. At issue was how to treat the fast-growing trade in new hybrid financial instruments. The new instruments based so-called "forward" or future contracts on conventional stocks or bonds that were used by corporations and units of government to raise capital. Future contracts typically set a price for a given commodity on a specified date in the future. An option permitted an owner to buy or sell at a certain price in the future but imposed no obligation to do so. *(Terms, box, p. 500)*

Those types of contracts had been used for decades by speculators as well as buyers and sellers of agricultural commodities as a form of insurance against price changes. Inflation made the contracts attractive to dealers in non-farm goods, and the market responded with ingenious new variations. Futures or options were available, for example, on foreign currency, Treasury bonds, housing bonds and stock indexes.

Congress fueled the trend in 1974 when it wrote an unusually inclusive definition of "commodity" into the statute (PL 93-463) creating the CFTC. But fierce competition over new products between securities and futures industries continued to inspire occasional congressional plans for dismembering the CFTC. *(1974 action, Congress and the Nation Vol. IV, p. 723)*

The commission almost went out of business in 1978, when it came under fire for alleged ineffectiveness at screening firms and individuals for registration, slowness in

---

Futures Industry Terms

Following are definitions of terms used in the futures trading industry:

Commodity Futures Trading Commission (CFTC): A five-member federal board authorized by Congress in 1974 and charged with ensuring proper execution of customer orders and preventing unlawful manipulation, price distortion, fraud, cheating, fictitious trades and misuse of customer funds. Among its duties are licensing exchanges, registering brokers and certain other professionals, auditing records and bank accounts, monitoring trading, and prosecuting violators.

Futures Contract: A firm commitment to deliver or to receive a specified quantity and grade of a commodity during a designated month, with the price being determined by public auction among exchange members.

Leverage Contract: A standardized agreement calling for delivery of a commodity with payments against the total cost spread out over a period of time.

Option: A unilateral contract that gives the buyer the right to buy or sell a specified quantity of a commodity at a specific price within a specified period of time, regardless of the market price of that commodity.

SOURCES: Senate Agriculture Committee; Leuthold, Raymond M. and van Blokland, P. Jon, *Using the Futures Market in Financial Planning*, University of Illinois at Urbana-Champaign, College of Agriculture, Cooperative Extension Service.

---

moving against manipulations of the market and its lack of internal structure. In the end, however, Congress granted the CFTC a four-year reauthorization. *(Congress and the Nation Vol. V, p. 380)*

In December 1981 the CFTC and SEC voluntarily divided up much of the disputed turf, deciding which types of transactions would be regulated by each agency. The major features of the agreement were incorporated in the CFTC reauthorization legislation.

House Action

Committee. The bill reported by the Agriculture Committee May 17 (H Rept 97-565, Part I) ratified the CFTC-SEC agreement.

Although the CFTC was under the Agriculture Committee's jurisdiction, the House Energy and Commerce Committee, which had jurisdiction over the SEC, requested referral of the legislation.

Energy and Commerce Chairman John D. Dingell, D-Mich., disapproved strongly of the accord. He complained in an April 23 hearing held by the Commerce Subcommittee on Telecommunications, Consumer Protection and Finance that the CFTC was positioned to claim jurisdiction over securities and "eliminate competition from securities exchanges, much like PAC-men moving across a video screen."

"This trend must be stopped," he added.

The subcommittee hearing signaled deep skepticism in and out of Congress about the wisdom of the CFTC-SEC agreement. Although witnesses generally advised prompt congressional approval of the accord to eliminate uncertainties affecting markets, many also said it was time for Congress to rework regulation of financial markets. Some suggested merging the commodities and securities agencies.

Another concern was whether trading in the financial hybrids diverted capital from more productive, long-term investments. Those who defended such new instruments as options on stock indexes said that by acting as insurance against inflation, the instruments actually could encourage capital formation.

Before reporting the funding reauthorization June 21 (H Rept 97-565, Part II), the Energy and Commerce Committee agreed to changes expressing Chairman Dingell's misgivings. The first change gave the SEC power to veto CFTC approval of contracts on futures on an index or group of securities. This change disturbed one portion of the CFTC-SEC agreement ratified by the bill as reported by the House Agriculture Committee. The Commerce Committee's provision, however, was dropped from the final version of the bill, which retained the CFTC's exclusive jurisdiction but gave the SEC authority to review applications for contracts on securities indexes.

The second change broadened the scope of a study of the futures industry mandated by the Agriculture panel and shifted lead responsibility for the study from the CFTC to the Federal Reserve Board.

Floor. The House approved a four-year CFTC reauthorization by a 319-59 vote on Sept. 23, after rejecting an amendment that would have levied fees on individual futures transactions.

The bill strengthened the federal and state regulators in several respects and authorized the CFTC to delegate to the NFA key regulatory functions, such as registration of persons active in the futures markets.

The House Sept. 23 also passed by voice vote a related bill (HR 6156) making changes in federal securities statutes to make them conform to the CFTC-SEC agreement. HR 6156 had been reported June 24 by the House Energy and Commerce Committee and July 30 by the Agriculture Committee (H Rept 97-626, Parts I and II).

Senate, Final Action

The Senate Agriculture Committee reported its CFTC bill May 6 (S 2109 — S Rept 97-384). A companion measure conforming security laws to the CFTC-SEC agreement was reported May 12 by the Banking, Housing and Urban Affairs Committee (S 2260 — S Rept 97-390).

In floor debate, the Senate rejected a transaction fee amendment by a 27-66 vote before passing its CFTC bill Oct. 1 and attaching the language to the House bill.

In separate action, the Senate by a 91-0 vote passed the companion HR 6156, clearing the bill for the president (PL 97-303).

The Senate agreed to the conference report on the CFTC measure (H Rept 97-964) Dec. 15, and the House followed suit the next day, completing congressional action on HR 5447.

Provisions

As signed into law Jan. 12, 1983, the Futures Trading Act of 1982 (HR 5447 — PL 97-444) contained the following major provisions:

● Authorized funding as needed for activities of the CFTC through Sept. 30, 1986.

● **CFTC-SEC Accord.** Affirmed exclusive CFTC jurisdiction over commodity futures contracts and options on futures, including futures and options on so-called exempted securities, such as instruments of the Government National Mortgage Association and Treasury bills, but not on municipal securities.

● Barred CFTC jurisdiction over options on securities, including groups or indexes of securities, in effect affirming the jurisdiction of the Securities and Exchange Commission (SEC).

● Prohibited futures or options on futures on individual corporate bonds and securities or on municipal securities.

● Stated that nothing in the Commodity Exchange Act, the basic CFTC legislation, applied to options on foreign currency traded on a national securities exchange. The effect of the provision was to permit trading on such options on both commodity and stock exchanges.

● Affirmed CFTC jurisdiction over futures and options on futures on a group or index of securities, and spelled out standards for approval of contracts on such indexes. Barred CFTC approval of an application for this type of trading if the SEC found within 45 days, or 90 days in some circumstances, that the contract did not meet specified criteria.

● Affirmed CFTC jurisdiction over commodity pools except where pool transactions were subject to securities law, as in securities issued by pools.

● Broadened existing disclosure authority to permit the CFTC to give information on potentially disruptive transactions or market operations to a registered futures association or self-regulatory securities association.

● **Other Provisions.** Expanded categories of individuals subject to various commodity law provisions; made officials of commodity firms responsible for acts of their employees and agents under specified conditions.

● Affirmed that U.S. residents who sold foreign futures were subject to federal registration requirements and other regulations. (Federal regulations required individuals involved in futures and related transactions to register with the CFTC.)

● Explicitly barred the CFTC from regulating foreign markets.

● Expanded CFTC authority to set speculative limits, and affirmed the authority of contract markets and other licensed exchanges to set such limits for futures or option transactions; made violation of a market limit a violation of federal law, if the CFTC had approved the market limit.

● Affirmed CFTC authority to set temporary emergency margin levels and to fix position limits retroactively. (A margin was the amount of money or collateral that must be deposited by a client or broker to insure against loss on futures contracts; a position limit was the maximum interest an individual could hold on a commodity future or on all futures in one commodity.)

● Authorized states to enforce relevant state or federal laws against illegal commodity transactions occurring outside regulated exchanges and outside the regulatory structure of the CFTC.

● Authorized states to enforce anti-fraud sections of the Commodity Exchange Act in state courts, against persons registered as required by the federal law. Exempted floor brokers and registered futures associations from such state enforcement and authorized the CFTC to intervene in these proceedings.

● Required the commodity industry's self-regulatory group, the National Futures Association (NFA), to put into operation a specific regulatory program, as directed by the CFTC, by Sept. 30, 1985. Authorized the CFTC to require the NFA or similar self-regulatory groups to take over certain CFTC responsibilities, such as registration of commodity brokers and others involved in futures transactions.

● Authorized the CFTC to regulate leverage transactions as soon as practicable. (A leverage contract was an agreement calling for delivery of a commodity with payments made in installments.)

● Authorized private lawsuits, with certain limitations, against commodity dealers, trading advisers or contract markets by individuals who had been harmed by violation of the Commodity Exchange Act occurring on or off regulated markets.

● Required the Federal Reserve Board, with the assistance of the CFTC, the SEC and the Treasury, to conduct a study and report to Congress by Sept. 30, 1984, on the effect of futures and options trading on the economy, including the effect on capital investment in industry and business; also required that the study examine the impact of stock index futures on the securities on which they were based and on capital formation, with recommendations for legislation if needed.

● Restated existing authority for the CFTC to charge fees for such services as rule enforcement reviews of commodity exchanges; barred imposition of "user" fees or fees on individual commodities or options transactions.

● **Trade Guarantee.** Barred the president from prohibiting or restricting the export of any agricultural commodity that was under contract at the time the president imposed an embargo or other restriction on trade, if the contract provided for delivery of the commodity within 270 days of the imposition of such a restriction. However, the bill permitted restrictions on contracted agricultural sales abroad in time of war or national emergency.

Pesticide Law Revisions

Congress was unable in 1982 to reconcile conflicts surrounding a rewrite of federal pesticide law, despite nearly a year of negotiations among interested groups.

Although the House passed a two-year reauthorization (HR 5203) of the Federal Insecticide, Fungicide and Rodenticide Act (FIFRA) Aug. 11, sharp conflicts among environmentalists, pesticide makers and farmers kept the measure from reaching the Senate floor before the 97th Congress adjourned. Meanwhile, the Environmental Protection Agency (EPA), which administered federal pesticide programs, was able to continue its activities with appropriated funds. Congress finally cleared a one-year authorization Nov. 18, 1983. Further action was stalemated in 1984. *(1983 authorization, p. 509)*

The programs involved the registration with the federal government of chemicals used to kill insects, rodents, fungi and plants. To obtain registration — in effect a license to sell a product — manufacturers had to submit data to EPA. The last major rewrite of the law was in 1978. *(Congress and the Nation Vol. V, p. 568)*

Key controversies in 1982 were whether stricter state registration laws could pre-empt federal statutes, whether individuals would be able to sue to stop violations of pesticide laws and the confidentiality of industry information filed with state and federal governments.

House Action

In passing the bill Aug. 11, the House endorsed several proposals advanced by the pesticide industry. But it rejected a provision setting new limits on state authority to regulate pesticides more strictly than the federal government. Pesticide makers argued the provision was necessary to avoid having to comply with many varied state laws. The House also eliminated a section the industry wanted restricting public access to information about the health and safety of pesticides. Industry spokesmen contended that the information would infringe on trade secrets and that they needed to protect their costly research from competitors. Opponents of the limit, among them the American Association for the Advancement of Science, said the restrictions would prevent independent scientists from scrutinizing the industry research on which regulatory decisions were made.

During floor consideration, the House reinstated the right of individuals — farm workers, pesticide factory workers or others who might have been injured by violations of pesticide laws — to sue for relief in federal courts. That provision had been dropped by the Agriculture Committee in reporting the bill May 17 (H Rept 97-566). The AFL-CIO, migrant farm groups and environmentalists lobbied for the provision, while the American Farm Bureau Federation objected that it could be used to harass farmers.

The House version did honor some major industry objectives, and Luther W. Shaw, vice president for public affairs of the National Agricultural Chemicals Association, said he generally was pleased. The bill extended by five years the period of time in which a company could sell a new pesticide or a pesticide approved for a new use, without competition from other manufacturers.

Senate Action

The version of the bill reported by the Senate Agriculture Committee Sept. 20 (S Rept 97-551) pleased the industry but sparked swift and bitter complaints from state government officials, national environmental and labor groups, and a grass-roots organization known as the National Coalition Against the Misuse of Pesticides. Opponents objected to new restrictions on state regulation and the omission of the right of individuals to sue for violations of pesticide laws.

Like the House measure, the Senate committee's bill added five years to manufacturers' patentlike right to market a product without competition, and it beefed up penalties for violations of the confidentiality of trade-secret data submitted to EPA as part of the process of obtaining federal approval to market a pesticide.

The Senate committee bill reinstated a provision that had been dropped on the House floor setting special conditions on requests from state regulators for more health and safety data from manufacturers than the federal program required. Like the House-passed measure, the Senate committee bill also set deadlines for state action and required registration — permission to market a product — if states failed to act in time on applications. The only major change

from the House version was that federal courts, not EPA, would arbitrate disputes over state data requests.

J. B. Grant, executive secretary of the National Association of State Departments of Agriculture, said any restriction on state authority was unacceptable. His organization had played a major role in persuading House members to drop the state restrictions.

FmHA Authorization

Bills reauthorizing funding for the Farmers Home Administration (FmHA) died when the Senate failed to act before adjournment.

A measure approved Sept. 9 by the House, in addition to setting overall lending limits for fiscal 1983-85, also would have allowed financially pressed farmers to put off repaying certain federal loans. The bill (HR 5831 — H Rept 97-553, Parts I and II) was passed by a 372-39 vote.

The Senate, however, did not act on its companion measure, reported May 26 by the Agriculture Committee (S 2314 — S Rept 97-422). The Senate bill did not contain a loan deferral provision.

The administration objected strongly to authorizing postponement of FmHA loan repayments. The House bill required deferral to be granted if a farmer could show that his financial problems were not caused by bad management but by circumstances beyond his control, such as national economic conditions.

Advocates said that the depressed farm economy justified deferrals. But Rep. Tom Hagedorn, R-Minn., objected that deferral was an unwarranted "gift" of forgone interest to certain farmers. Hagedorn suggested that all FmHA farm borrowers, whether they had financial problems or not, would try to avoid loan payments in 1983.

The House bill exceeded lending ceilings requested in the president's budget and did not include the administration request to limit spending for emergency loans for physical disasters, which also had been ignored by the Senate committee.

In 1983 the House again approved a loan deferral program. A less ambitious Senate version did not reach the floor. *(Story, p. 509)*

Pressure for action to relieve the burdens of debt-ridden farmers continued, and in September 1984 the administration reversed course. Before leaving on a campaign tour of farm states, President Reagan announced a new, billion-dollar program of debt forgiveness and loan guarantees for farmers. *(Administration plan, box, p. 512)*

Migrant Farm Worker Relief

Congress Dec. 20 approved a major revision of federal laws governing the treatment of migrant farm workers.

The bill (HR 7102 — PL 97-470) replaced the existing Farm Labor Contractor Registration Act (FLCRA) with a new set of federal protections for migrant and seasonal workers.

Final action came when the House by voice vote accepted the version of the bill passed by the Senate Dec. 19. The House had passed its version (H Rept 97-885) Sept. 29.

The measure was a compromise that enjoyed support from the Reagan administration, unions and agricultural employers. The only serious obstacle it encountered came in the Senate, where Sam Nunn, D-Ga., temporarily

blocked action in hopes of using the bill as a vehicle for anti-racketeering legislation (S 1785) that was stalled in the House. *(Story, p. 657)*

Registration of Contractors

Agricultural groups had pushed for the legislation because farmers resented the burdens imposed on them by FLCRA (PL 88-582), which was passed by Congress in 1963 to prevent abuses by "crew leaders" — independent contractors who recruit and transport migrant workers from farm to farm. Its most important provision required contractors to register with the Labor Department. Congress in 1974 enacted amendments (PL 93-518) that broadened the coverage of the 1963 act and toughened its penalties. *(1963 law, Congress and the Nation Vol. I, p. 760; 1974 amendments, Congress and the Nation Vol. IV, p. 728)*

The Labor Department in recent years had required many farmers to register under the law as farm labor contractors. HR 7102 would prevent that by exempting "fixed-site" farm employers from the registration requirements imposed on farm labor contractors.

However, farm employers as well as farm labor contractors would have to satisfy other requirements in the bill involving treatment of workers. The bill required that workers receive adequate housing, safe transportation and correct information about their pay.

Provisions

As signed into law Jan. 14, 1983, the Migrant and Seasonal Agricultural Worker Protection Act (HR 7102 — PL 97-470):

● Made clear that fixed-site farm employers were not farm labor contractors, and thus were not required to register as such with the Labor Department.

● Defined farm labor contractors as persons who recruited, hired and transported migrant farm workers.

● Required farm labor contractors to register with the Labor Department; allowed the department to refuse to provide registration certificates to persons convicted of certain crimes.

● Prohibited farm labor contractors from knowingly hiring illegal aliens.

● Established protections for migrant farm workers by requiring farm employers as well as farm labor contractors to meet a series of standards involving payroll records, health, safety and housing.

● Created a separate legal category for seasonal farm workers, who performed temporary farm labor while returning to their homes each night; also established standards governing treatment of such workers.

● Provided for regulations governing the safe transportation of migrant and seasonal farm workers.

● Established criminal and civil penalties for violation of the law.

● Provided exemptions from the provisions of the bill for small and family businesses.

Other Legislation

Western Water Reclamation

Legislation cleared Sept. 29 (S 1409 — PL 97-293) settled for a time a long-running battle between environ-mentalists and Western farmers over the use of subsidized water from federal reclamation projects.

The bill substantially rewrote a 1902 law that imposed a 160-acre limit on the amount of federally irrigated acreage available to an individual. S 1409 increased the limit to 960 acres, raised prices for some water used by Western farmers and repealed a requirement that farmers live on or near their federally irrigated farms. Environmentalists had sought strict enforcement of the 160-acre limit to force the breakup of large agricultural operations and to redistribute the irrigated land to small farmers. *(Story, p. 431)*

Firearms for Border Patrols

Congress completed action Sept. 30 on a bill (HR 2035 — PL 97-312) permitting Agriculture Department "tick inspectors" to carry firearms when they patroled the U.S.-Mexico border to prevent livestock smuggling. The inspectors often encountered drug smugglers or illegal aliens.

The bill was reported (H Rept 97-515) by the House Agriculture Committee May 13 and passed the House by voice vote May 18.

The Senate Agriculture Committee reported the bill (S Rept 97-569) Sept. 22. The Senate passed it by voice vote Sept. 29 after adopting an amendment requiring imported grapes to meet quality standards of domestic federal marketing orders.

The House accepted the amended bill, clearing it for the president Sept. 30. It was signed into law Oct. 14.

Government Gasohol

Mountains of federally owned surplus grain could be converted to alcohol fuel for use by government agencies or for sale in commercial markets under a bill cleared by Congress Oct. 1.

The measure (HR 6142 — PL 97-358) authorized the Commodity Credit Corp. (CCC), the financial arm of the Agriculture Department that operated price support programs, to convert to fuel the grain it had accumulated as a result of price support loan defaults.

Rep. E. "Kika" de la Garza, D-Texas, chairman of the Agriculture Committee, said the bill could help alleviate pressure resulting from the record grain production predicted by the Agriculture Department.

The bill had been reported by his panel Sept. 26 (H Rept 97-874) and was passed by the House by voice vote Sept. 28. After discharging the Senate Agriculture Committee Oct. 1, the Senate approved the bill by voice vote.

1983

Despite President Reagan's distaste for government intervention in the farm economy, the president reluctantly signed legislation in 1983 authorizing a new program of payments to dairy farmers to cut milk production.

The measure also included major revisions in the tobacco program, as well as relief for livestock producers to help them cope with a severe summer drought. The tobacco provisions were important to an early Southern supporter of Reagan, Sen. Jesse Helms, R-N.C. Helms faced a tough re-election contest in 1984.

As federal spending for price supports and other farm subsidy programs reached record highs in 1983, the president tried unsuccessfully to persuade Congress to block scheduled increases in target prices, a major price support program for wheat and other crops.

Federal expenditures for farm price and income support programs totaled $18.9 billion in fiscal 1983, an increase of $12.3 billion in two years, the Council of Economic Advisers reported early in 1984. The total did not include the value of the surplus commodities — about $9.4 billion — used to pay farmers for reducing their crop acreage under the administration's payment-in-kind (PIK) program.

Blocking a scheduled increase in target prices was one way the administration sought to restrain the escalating costs of the subsidy programs. The administration strategy was to promise support for the dairy legislation if Congress would agree to the freeze on target prices.

Two days before adjournment the House passed a bill that trimmed the target price increases. The measure did not come to a vote in the Senate in 1983, but it was enacted in the spring of 1984.

Congressional approval was not required for the administration to begin a PIK program in January that encouraged additional acreage reduction, but Congress did enact special tax legislation when it appeared PIK participants could lose tax benefits normally enjoyed by farmers.

Dairy, Tobacco Programs

On Nov. 18, the last day of the 1983 session, Congress cleared legislation (HR 3385 — PL 98-180) authorizing payments to dairymen, partly financed by dairy farmers themselves, for producing less milk. The bill, which also lowered federal dairy price supports, was meant to reduce surplus dairy production.

Other provisions of the legislation temporarily froze tobacco price supports, ended double payments by growers to special tobacco support funds and phased out the renting of tobacco quotas to land away from the farms to which they were assigned.

For much of the year Agriculture Secretary John R. Block had supported the so-called "paid diversion" dairy plan as part of a larger strategy to win congressional approval of a freeze on target prices for wheat and other crops. The agriculture secretary, however, had withdrawn his support for the bill in the final weeks of the 1983 session.

Legislation to block increases in the target price program finally was cleared by Congress in 1984. *(Target price freeze, p. 511)*

Background

The dairy price support program guaranteed that the government would buy dairy products at a set price — at $13.10 per hundred pounds (hundredweight) of milk equivalent in mid-1983 — if producers could not sell the milk elsewhere.

With dairy production running about 10 percent greater than demand, the government was spending nearly $3 billion annually to buy the surplus. *(1981 action, p. 493)*

Industry representatives differed on how to reduce the surplus. On one side were those who wanted strict production limits for individual dairy farms. Other organizations argued for across-the-board cuts in federal price support levels instead of production controls.

House Committee Action

The House Agriculture Committee June 9 reported its dairy bill (HR 1875 — H Rept 98-237). On June 29 the panel approved separate legislation making extensive changes in the tobacco program (HR 1440), but that bill was never reported out of committee.

Under the committee's dairy bill, price support payments could drop by as much as $1.50 over two years, unless production fell below certain limits. However, dairymen who contracted to reduce production would be paid $10 for each 100 pounds they did not produce, up to certain limits. The new payments would last through part of fiscal 1985. The bill continued a controversial assessment paid by dairy producers, which partially financed the new payment program. *(Dairy assessments, box, p. 505)*

The administration had proposed the new plan to combine temporary production controls with the overall price support cuts in an effort to resolve industry divisions.

But then the administration told members of Congress that its support was contingent on simultaneous congressional approval of a freeze on target prices, a major type of price support for wheat, corn, cotton and rice.

J. Dawson Ahalt, the Agriculture Department's deputy assistant secretary for economics, said the target price freeze was needed to offset the cost of the new dairy plan, estimated initially at about $300 million-$400 million a year more than the existing program. Savings would amount to $370 million in fiscal 1984, Ahalt said.

In mid-June sponsors of HR 1875 dropped plans to bring the bill to the floor after House Minority Leader Robert H. Michel, R-Ill., Minority Whip Trent Lott, R-Miss., and Barber B. Conable Jr., R-N.Y., and three Democrats objected to the bill in a "dear colleague" letter. Conable introduced an alternative bill (HR 3292), backed by the conservative American Farm Bureau Federation, that omitted a central feature of HR 1875 — payments to dairymen for cutting production.

Senate Committee Action

The Senate Agriculture Committee June 23 reported a combined dairy-tobacco bill (S 1529 — S Rept 98-163). The dairy provisions basically followed HR 1875, with minor amendments. The tobacco provisions included a multi-year freeze of tobacco price supports and changes in the complex system of allotments and quotas.

Attempts were made by administration supporters at the June 16 meeting to combine the dairy legislation with the freeze on target prices the administration sought. But opponents blocked votes on the proposal. The dairy bill later came to the Senate floor under an agreement that barred amendments related to target prices.

Senate Floor Action

The Senate passed the legislation Oct. 7 by voice vote after inserting the provisions of S 1529 into HR 3385, a House-passed cotton bill. *(PIK cotton program, p. 508)*

Opponents of the dairy bill, including Daniel Patrick Moynihan, D-N.Y., argued that a simple reduction in the dairy price support level would reduce surplus production,

as it had in the past. But repeated attempts to substitute a price support cut for the diversion program, or to exempt certain groups of dairy farmers, failed.

The closest the bill's opponents came to success was a 44-40 vote on Oct. 6 to kill an amendment by Warren B. Rudman, R-N.H., that would have exempted dairymen who processed and sold the milk they produced. Rudman said these farmers were "not interested in some socialistic form of farming." They were, he added, "just asking to be left alone."

Sponsors of the legislation insisted that the paid diversion program was the only politically viable solution to industry problems. Senate Agriculture Committee Chairman Jesse Helms, R-N.C., repeatedly reminded senators that the dairy legislation was supported by a "fragile coalition" that would crack if any changes were made.

There was little controversy over the tobacco sections of the bill. The Senate adopted several amendments by tobacco state senators and on Oct. 6 killed, 57-33, an amendment by Howard M. Metzenbaum, D-Ohio, and Jake Garn, R-Utah, to repeal the federal tobacco price support program.

In other action, the Senate adopted an amendment by Lloyd Bentsen, D-Texas, to provide drought aid to livestock producers. *(Drought aid, box, p. 507)*

House Floor Action

The House Nov. 9 passed HR 4196, a bill with the same provisions as HR 1875 but with different effective dates.

Before passing HR 4196 by a 325-91 vote, the House rejected, **on a 174-250 key vote (R 97-65; D 77-185),** an alternative plan offered by Conable. The Conable plan simply would have reduced the dairy price support price by $1.50 and eliminated the unpopular federal assessment collected from dairy producers. *(1983 key votes, p. 911)*

In an Oct. 28 letter to Minority Leader Michel, Agriculture Secretary Block said that because the target price freeze was not imposed, he was switching support to the Conable bill.

During floor debate the House added two amendments to soften objections from livestock producers and dairymen in states with dairy promotion programs similar to a new national program authorized by the bill.

After approving the bill, the House substituted its language for that of HR 3385. Although the House dairy provisions were nearly identical to the Senate-passed version, the House bill did not include provisions to revise the tobacco program.

Conference, Final Action

Conferees completed work on HR 3385 (H Rept 98-556) on Nov. 15. The Senate approved the bill just before midnight on Nov. 17 and the House cleared it on Nov. 18, the last day of the session.

During the conference Agriculture Secretary Block urged conferees to cap total payments to individual dairymen under the diversion program, lower the rate at which payments were calculated and make other major changes.

House conferees said they could not accept the cap or the lower rate because there was not enough time to get the needed clearances from the House Rules Committee.

Other conference actions honored Block's requests — at least in part:

Dairy Assessments

The 1983 dairy-tobacco bill (HR 3385 — PL 98-180) repealed the second of two controversial assessments that Congress had approved in 1982 (PL 97-253) in an attempt to discourage overproduction in the dairy industry while offsetting costs of the federal dairy program. The 1982 law had provided for two 50-cent assessments on every hundred pounds of milk equivalent (as measured in butter, cheese and dry milk) produced by dairy farmers above certain levels.

The fee enraged dairymen and generated several lawsuits, one of which blocked the Agriculture Department in December 1982 from collecting the assessment. The department began collecting the first assessment in April 1983 and announced its intentions to collect the second 50-cent assessment if Congress provided no acceptable alternative.

When the legislation overhauling the federal dairy program and replacing the two assessments with a single assessment became entangled in disputes over other farm issues, Congress Aug. 4 abruptly passed a measure (S J Res 149) postponing the second assessment from Sept. 1 to Oct. 1.

President Reagan vetoed S J Res 149 on Aug. 23. His veto message said the $60 million the assessment would yield during September would help offset the $2.4 billion it was estimated the federal dairy program would cost in 1983.

● Conferees eliminated a Senate amendment that would have required tobacco importers to certify that tobacco brought into the United States had not been grown with pesticides banned here.

They retained, in weakened form, a direction that imported tobacco meet the same grade standards as American tobacco.

● Conferees weakened a House provision meant to mitigate the impact of dumping slaughtered dairy cows on the beef market. They retained a general instruction that the secretary of agriculture take all feasible steps to avoid the problem but dropped a "trigger" requiring action if beef prices declined a specified amount.

● Conferees tightened the base for calculating dairymen's production cuts although not as much as the administration had wanted. They also kept Senate-passed provisions ordering the secretary to let drought-stricken farmers buy poor-condition, surplus feed corn owned by the federal government.

Provisions

As signed into law Nov. 29, HR 3385 (PL 98-180):

Dairy. Reduced the federal dairy price support to $12.60 per hundredweight, from $13.10. Authorized two

Quota Costs, Tobacco Levies Growing

Unless a farmer in 1983 had what amounted to a federal "license" to sell all but three of the nearly 20 types of tobacco grown in America, he faced heavy financial penalties if he tried to sell tobacco.

And because of legislation passed in 1982, he had to help pay the storage and other costs for any excess tobacco left unsold at the end of the season.

But record surpluses had distorted the federal tobacco program, making per-farmer costs rise to uncomfortably high levels for many growers. It was those increases and the certainty that they would continue that were behind the drive for legislation to change the government tobacco program in 1983.

Licensing System

The "licensing" system consisted of federal allotments that specified the number of acres that could be planted in tobacco, together with quotas that limited the number of pounds a farmer could sell. A farmer selling tobacco at auction had to show a card obtained from a county Agricultural Stabilization and Conservation Service office listing his quota.

There was a fixed number of allotments, originally assigned to the land on which farmers were growing tobacco decades earlier. Active growers without such land had been able to rent the use of the allotments and quotas from their owners. However, under the 1983 tobacco bill (HR 3385 — PL 98-180) "off-farm" leasing of quotas would end after 1986 for flue-cured tobacco and was greatly reduced for burley tobacco. (Story, p. 504)

For the two major types of American tobacco — flue-cured and burley — the number of allotment owners dramatically outnumbered the number of growers. Burley was grown largely in Kentucky and Tennessee; flue-cured, primarily in the Carolinas.

The Agriculture Department (USDA) estimated in 1983 there were 40,000 to 50,000 actual producers of flue-cured tobacco and about 200,000 owners of allotments and quotas. For burley the proportion of active farmers who owned their allotments and quotas was higher — about 150,000 active growers to 300,000 owners.

Farmers within the system were eligible for federal price support loans set by law at a specific per-pound rate, which increased automatically every year unless Congress legislated otherwise, as it did in 1983. Whatever tobacco they could not sell on the market for a price that equaled or exceeded the loan rate, they could use as collateral for loans from the government. In 1982 the loan rates were $1.70 per pound for flue-cured tobacco, $1.75 for burley.

Cooperative growers' groups administered the loan program and held the surplus tobacco put up as collateral for later sale. Once farmers consigned their surplus to a cooperative, they could keep the loan money, and the cooperative was responsible for reselling the crop and repaying the government loan.

The assessment against tobacco farmers enacted in 1982 was meant to pay for any losses that occurred if the cooperative sold the surplus for less than the loan rate, and for interest and other costs. Previously such losses were borne by the federal government. (1982 legislation, p. 497)

To cover anticipated losses from the 1982 crop, the government collected $29.5 million from flue-cured growers and quota owners, and $7.7 million from burley growers and quota owners.

That did not prove to be enough, so in 1984, to cover "catch-up" 1982 costs and anticipated losses from the 1983 crop, the department expected to collect at least $32.5 million from burley growers and $85 million from flue-cured growers.

Increasing Costs

According to USDA economists, a grower of burley tobacco in 1982 paid, on an average, 53 cents per pound for combined quota and land, $1.35 per pound for such variable costs as seed and fertilizer, and a 1-cent-per-pound assessment for the new surplus-financing program. The $1.35 figure included a non-cash allowance of 49 cents for labor and management contributed by a farmer and his family.

The cash and non-cash outlays added up to $1.89 per pound — 8 cents more than the average price of $1.81 for which burley sold in 1982.

For flue-cured tobacco 1982 costs totaled $1.59: 46 cents for land and quota, $1.10 for variable and other costs (the non-cash allowance for labor and management was much smaller because there was more mechanization) and 3 cents for the assessment. Market prices averaged about $1.78 per pound.

Several program-related factors were driving up the cost of growing tobacco. One was that the assessments would jump for the 1983 crop to 7 cents per pound for flue-cured and to as much as 5 cents or 7 cents per pound for burley.

Prior to enactment of HR 3385, many producers who rented their allotments and quotas had been forced to pay the assessments twice: The law had required payments from both farmers and non-growing quota owners, who often simply increased the rental rate of their quotas by the amount of the assessment. HR 3385 did away with this practice.

Because the allotments and quotas were being reduced administratively by the government in an effort to cut the surplus, fierce competition for renting them had driven up their costs. Rental fees ranged from 25 cents per pound to 80 cents per pound.

further reductions of 50 cents each on April 1, 1985, and July 1, 1985, if federal purchases of milk in 1985 were estimated to exceed six billion pounds (as of April 1) or five billion pounds (as of July 1). However, the bill authorized an increase of at least 50 cents on July 1, 1985, if federal purchases were estimated at below five billion pounds and more milk was needed.

• Authorized a 15-month paid diversion program, from Jan. 1, 1984, until March 31, 1985. Producers who participated would cut production by 5 percent to 30 percent from their previous yields and would be paid at a rate of $10 per hundredweight.

• Retained an existing 50-cents-per-hundredweight assessment paid by dairy producers and earmarked it to help finance the paid diversion program; repealed a second 50-cent assessment.

• Directed the secretary of agriculture to take all feasible steps to minimize the impact on meat markets from the slaughter of dairy cows.

• Required each dairyman in the paid diversion program to submit a plan showing how much of his production cut would be achieved by selling cows for slaughter, and authorized revisions in diversion contracts to avoid a sudden dumping of dairy cows on the beef market. Directed the secretary to increase federal purchases of meat for food assistance programs.

Tobacco. Froze the 1984 price support level for flue-cured tobacco at the 1982 level. Retained the customary differential between the flue-cured level and that of burley, effectively permitting the secretary to freeze the burley level for the year. For the 1985 crop, continued the freeze for flue-cured only, but the price support could be raised to reflect a large increase in production costs, if such an increase occurred.

(The federal price support established minimum market prices for tobacco. Flue-cured tobacco was grown largely in the Carolinas and Georgia; burley was concentrated in Kentucky and Tennessee.)

• Authorized the secretary to reduce the support price for certain grades of flue-cured tobacco if the reductions were needed to improve the marketability of poor-quality grades. Set certain restrictions on the reductions that could be made and specified that the reductions should not be counted in computing future price support levels.

• Ended the leasing of quotas for flue-cured tobacco for use on other farms after the 1986 crop. For the 1985 and 1986 crops, required that such leasing agreements could not require payment for the lease until after the crop had been sold. For such "off-farm" leasing of burley quotas, reduced by half the total that could be leased and ended the fall leasing of burley quotas.

(Federal quotas determined how many pounds of tobacco a grower could market; they were assigned to specific farms but existing law permitted them to be leased for use on other farms.)

• Ended so-called "double" assessment payments to "no net cost" funds by eliminating a requirement that lessees make the payments.

The assessment-financed funds were established to pay for financial losses in the tobacco price support program, such as interest or losses in sales of surplus tobacco. Some growers renting quotas said they had been paying "twice" — once for themselves, and again because quota owners raised lease prices to cover their assessment payments.

• Postponed for one year, to Dec. 1, 1984, the deadline

Drought Aid for Farmers

The spell of hot, rainless weather during the summer of 1983 prompted members from farm states to search for ways to provide emergency drought aid to farmers. However, attempts to augment existing federal aid programs with wide-ranging relief were thwarted by the Reagan administration's opposition to additional federal farm aid. Farm supporters met with some success at the end of the session, adding a modest drought relief measure to dairy-tobacco legislation (HR 3385 — PL 98-180) cleared Nov. 18. *(Story, p. 504)*

The drought was exceptional in its breadth, affecting more than 28 states and devastating corn, soybean and other major crops. In testimony before the House Agriculture Committee on Sept. 21, Agriculture Secretary John R. Block acknowledged that "it probably is the most severe [drought] that we've had in the past 50 years."

But unlike earlier droughts, he said, many farmers could rely in 1983 on hefty payments from the crop insurance and payment-in-kind (PIK) programs. The PIK program provided payments in the form of surplus commodities to farmers who took crop land out of production in 1983. *(PIK, p. 508)*

The same day that Block testified, the House Appropriations Committee added a drought aid amendment to a fiscal 1984 continuing appropriations resolution (H J Res 367). However, H J Res 367 was loaded with so many controversial proposals that Congress put it aside and enacted a stripped-down measure (H J Res 368 — PL 98-107) free of unrelated amendments.

The House Agriculture Committee Nov. 4 reported a bill (HR 4052 — H Rept 98-488) broadening federal aid to farmers and ranchers harmed by the drought, but there was no further action on the legislation.

HR 3385, the dairy-tobacco bill cleared two weeks later, included Senate-passed provisions directing the agriculture secretary to permit drought-stricken farmers and ranchers to buy, at 75 percent of the current price support loan rate (about $2 per bushel), federally owned surplus feed corn that was in poor condition.

by which non-farmer owners of flue-cured and burley tobacco quotas had to sell those quotas. Also exempted from the mandatory sale partnerships, estates or family farm corporations if the proceeds from leasing went to individuals, and educational institutions that used their allotments for instruction or demonstration.

Egg Promotion. Authorized egg producers, subject to approval of the secretary, to adopt marketing orders

placing certain limits on the marketing of eggs and providing for disposal of surplus eggs. Also authorized a marketing order for research and promotion of eggs.

Drought Relief. Directed the agriculture secretary to let farmers and ranchers in drought areas buy, at 75 percent of the current price support loan rate (about $2 per bushel), federally owned surplus feed corn that was in poor condition. *(Box, p. 507)*

PIK Plan

President Reagan announced Jan. 11 that the federal government would pay farmers in surplus wheat, corn, cotton and rice if they would agree not to plant those crops in 1983. The administration said the program, called "payment-in-kind," or PIK, was based on existing statutory authority and did not require congressional approval. *(1982 PIK legislation, p. 498)*

But when it became clear that the program could expose participants to a potentially serious tax burden, the administration pressed for changes in tax law for program participants. The tax changes received swift congressional approval in a bill (HR 1296 — PL 98-4) that the president signed March 11.

The administration was unable later in the year, however, to extend the tax changes to cover a 1984 wheat PIK program unveiled by the Agriculture Department in August. By that time PIK had drawn strong criticism from several quarters as reports circulated of farmers reaping large payments for not planting.

Background

Under the PIK program, wheat, corn, grain sorghum, cotton and rice farmers who joined previously announced acreage reduction programs could also receive PIK payments for retiring an additional 10 to 30 percent of their land. Sign-up for the program began Jan. 24.

Payment rates were 95 percent of yield per acre in wheat and 80 percent of yield per acre for other crops. PIK payments would be made with crops that farmers had used as collateral for federal price support and farmer-held reserve loans, or from stocks that had become federal property because of default by farmers on the loans. In many cases farmers could simply reassume full ownership of crops on which they had borrowed.

PIK payments were made at harvest times; to avert dumping the crops on the market, the federal government paid storage costs for five months or, for reserve crops, 12 months.

Individual farmers could bid to take entire farms out of production in return for PIK payments; whole-farm bids were accepted if participation in the basic PIK program lagged. In no county could more than half the acreage base in eligible crops be retired.

Questions arose concerning whether farmers had to pay taxes on the commodities in the year in which they received them, or could defer tax payments until the commodities were sold. Farmers were not taxed on their crops until they sold them, even if that occurred several years after the harvest.

However, the Internal Revenue Service viewed the PIK commodities as the equivalent of income, liable to taxes in the year in which the commodities were received. Without the change, farmers could have faced tax pay-

ments on two crops in the same year — crops they raised and sold and PIK commodities. They also would be shoved into higher tax brackets.

It was unclear whether land idled in return for commodity payments would still be eligible for special treatment under federal estate tax law.

Legislative Action

Committee. As reported by the House Ways and Means Committee March 2, HR 1296 (H Rept 98-14) made one-year alterations in tax law. The bill permitted farmers to defer income tax payments on PIK commodities until they were sold. It also stipulated that land taken out of production could continue to qualify for special treatment accorded farm land by estate tax law.

The Senate version (S 690), reported by the Finance Committee March 4, made the changes in tax law permanent.

Floor. The day before the deadline for farmers to join the PIK program, Congress completed action on the tax legislation.

The House passed HR 1296 by a 401-1 vote on March 8. The Senate passed its version the same day by voice vote. HR 1296 cleared March 10 when the Senate accepted final House changes in the measure.

The PIK tax legislation was not controversial. But Rep. Fortney H. "Pete" Stark, D-Calif., chairman of the Ways and Means subcommittee that crafted the bill, and members of his subcommittee had strong reservations about its impact. They forced the Senate to accept the tax modifications for one year only.

Provisions

As signed into law March 11, HR 1296 (PL 98-4):

● Permitted participants in the 1983 PIK program to defer income tax payments on the commodities they received in the program until the commodities sold.

● Permitted crop land idled by 1983 PIK participants to continue to be valued as farm land for estate tax purposes, thereby retaining eligibility for lower tax rates and installment payments of taxes.

PIK Cotton Program

Congress July 29 enacted legislation modifying the terms of cotton farmers' participation in the government's complex payment-in-kind (PIK) program after the cotton growers complained they were being treated unfairly.

The PIK provision — reopening cotton bidding on the same terms offered producers of feed grains — was included in a fiscal 1983 supplemental appropriations bill (HR 3069 — PL 98-63). Administration objections to the additional costs generated by the cotton program — estimated at $75 million-$100 million — were not strong enough to threaten enactment of the supplemental. President Reagan signed the measure July 30.

The PIK section of HR 3069 was meant to rectify a problem that arose when the administration found it did not own enough surplus cotton, wheat and corn to make promised payments to PIK farmers. Under PIK, producers were paid with surplus crops to take farm land out of production in an effort to reduce the unsold surpluses that were depressing market prices. The Agriculture Depart-

ment did not own enough of the surplus to meet its commitments to farmers because much of it was being used as collateral for federal price support loans and thus was still owned by individual farmers. *(PIK, p. 508)*

To resolve the problem the department in May asked farmers what they would accept to supply stocks for PIK needs. But because the department, in an attempt to save money, offered less favorable terms for cotton than for other commodities, it failed to acquire enough cotton.

The Agriculture Department then invoked a clause in the farmers' PIK contracts requiring them to take out price support loans on their 1983 crop. The plan was to foreclose on the loans, so the farmers would keep the loan money and the government would take possession of the cotton.

But changing market conditions made such forced "sales" extremely costly to producers. The cotton language in HR 3069 permitted farmers to offer again to sell their cotton to the government, but on more attractive terms than in the first round of bidding.

Legislative Action. The House Agriculture Committee July 12 reported legislation (HR 3385 — H Rept 98-289) making cotton PIK changes; the Senate Agriculture Committee had approved provisions similar to the House's on June 23 in a target price measure (HR 2733 — S Rept 98-164). *(Target price freeze, p. 511)*

The cotton-PIK language eventually made its way into several different bills as cotton lobbyists sought to ensure its consideration. Before winding up in the supplemental, it also appeared in the Senate version of a dairy-tobacco bill (S 1529) and in the Senate's Agriculture appropriations bill (HR 3223).

Farm 'Recession Relief'

Despite objections from the Reagan administration, the House May 3 overwhelmingly approved legislation to provide "recession relief" to farmers.

The House bill (HR 1190 — H Rept 98-48), passed by a 378-35 vote, permitted hard-pressed farmers who met certain criteria to delay loan repayments to the Farmers Home Administration (FmHA). The bill also made it easier for farmers hit by drought or other physical disasters to qualify for FmHA disaster loans, and required the secretary of agriculture to offer "economic emergency" loans.

The administration claimed these provisions would give a few farmers tremendous windfall aid and open the Treasury to enormous expense. Officials said FmHA already was easing terms and deferring payments on a case-by-case basis.

A similar FmHA authorization bill was reported by the Senate Agriculture Committee March 18 (S 24 — S Rept 98-28), but no further action was taken on the bill. Legislation enacted in 1984 (PL 98-258), however, liberalized terms for federal loans to farmers. *(Target price freeze, p. 511; 1984 Reagan aid plan, p. 512; 1982 action, p. 502)*

Provisions. Major provisions of HR 1190:

● Barred the agriculture secretary from foreclosing on FmHA loans and required him to consolidate or reschedule a loan, or defer repayment, at the request of a borrower who could demonstrate to the secretary's satisfaction that he was a good manager, that he could not repay because of circumstances beyond his control and that he had a good chance of repaying after the deferral.

● Continued economic emergency loans until Sept. 30, 1984, and required the secretary to make the loans avail-

able. Authorized $300 million annually in fiscal 1983 and 1984. As reported, the bill had authorized $1.2 billion in fiscal 1983.

● Authorized an extra $200 million for farm operating loans in fiscal 1983, for a total of $1.7 billion, and earmarked the money for new borrowers.

● Extended to 15 years, from seven, the maximum time for repayment of a consolidated or rescheduled FmHA loan.

● Specified that a farmer could qualify for emergency disaster loans on the basis of damage to his farm, though the county in which the farm was located had not been designated a disaster area.

● Conferred eligibility to borrowers for additional disaster-related loans for three or four years after the original emergency loan (depending on the date of the original loan).

● Established an overall $250 million limit on insured or guaranteed loans for business and industrial development.

● Set annual FmHA authorization ceilings for fiscal years 1984-86: $1 billion for real estate loans; $500 million for insured water and sewer facility loans; $1 billion for industrial development loans; $300 million for insured community facility loans. Also authorized funds as needed for emergency (physical disaster) loans.

Pesticide Reauthorization

A simple one-year reauthorization (HR 2785 — PL 98-201) of the federal government's controversial pesticide control programs cleared Congress Nov. 18.

HR 2785, extending the Federal Insecticide, Fungicide and Rodenticide Act (FIFRA), was signed by the president Dec. 2.

The bill authorized $64.2 million in fiscal 1984 for the pesticide regulation program of the Environmental Protection Agency (EPA), about $8 million more than the presidential budget request. HR 2785 also extended through September 1987 the authority for a scientific advisory panel on pesticides.

The bill's sponsors decided to pass a simple funding measure and put aside, for the time being, controversial policy issues surrounding the federal regulation of pesticides. Disputes among pesticide makers, environmentalists, labor, farm and health groups had kept Congress from enacting a pesticide bill in 1982. *(Story, p. 501)*

Pesticide makers and the Reagan administration pushed for a two-year bill, but environmental groups objected that the longer reauthorization would delay action on urgent issues, including the release of manufacturers' information on the safety of certain chemicals.

The House Agriculture Committee reported a one-year authorization (H Rept 98-104) May 11, and the House passed the bill May 17 by voice vote. It won Senate approval Nov. 18, also by voice vote.

The authorization was not extended in 1984.

Tobacco Price Support Lid

Facing a late July deadline for the opening of tobacco markets, Congress July 14 approved a one-year freeze on tobacco price supports (HR 3392 — PL 98-59).

A major component of the federal tobacco program, price support loans determined the prices at which the crop

U.S.-U.S.S.R. Grain Pact

Agriculture Secretary John R. Block and U.S. Trade Representative William E. Brock III announced July 28, 1983, that the United States and the Soviet Union had concluded a new, five-year grain sales agreement.

The pact, which took effect Oct. 1, committed the United States to sell — and the Soviet Union to buy — at least nine million metric tons and up to 12 million metric tons of wheat and corn each year. It also permitted the Soviet Union to substitute a purchase of 500,000 metric tons of soybeans or soy meal for one million tons of wheat or corn; in a year when that occurred, the minimum combined sale of wheat and corn would be eight million tons. The expiring U.S.-U.S.S.R. grain pact called for annual sales of six million to eight million metric tons, with no provision for soybean sales.

Block said the new pact generally followed the terms of the U.S.-U.S.S.R. agreement that expired in 1983. That pact guaranteed delivery of the specified minimums and permitted either side to opt out of its commitment under certain conditions, such as a short supply in the United States. It was the guarantee that continued some grain shipments to the U.S.S.R. during the grain embargo imposed by President Carter in 1980 after the Soviet invasion of Afghanistan.

President Reagan ended the unpopular Carter embargo April 24, 1981, but to protest the establishment of martial law in Poland he refused until 1983 to negotiate a new long-term pact. Instead the existing agreement was continued on a year-to-year basis. Farm state critics said that practice encouraged the Soviet Union to find other, apparently more reliable sources of grain. *(Embargo, Congress and the Nation Vol. V, pp. 82, 388; 1981 action, p. 495)*

was sold. Advocates hoped that holding the price support loans at 1982 levels instead of letting them rise in 1983 as scheduled would promote more sales — and less surplus.

The House passed HR 3392 (H Rept 98-288) July 11 by voice vote. Sponsor Charlie Rose, D-N.C., held off attacks by an anti-smoking coalition of health groups only by promising floor votes later in 1983 on HR 1440, a more extensive revision of the tobacco program. HR 1440, however, never was reported out of committee and decisions on major changes in the tobacco program were reached in conference on HR 3385, the Senate's combined dairy-to-bacco bill. *(Dairy-tobacco bill, p. 504)*

The Senate approved HR 3392 July 13 with an amendment allowing the agriculture secretary to lower the annual burley tobacco marketing quota by 15 percent and requiring a study of imported burley tobacco to determine whether an import quota on the commodity was warranted

to protect U.S. producers. Under existing law the secretary could reduce quotas by 5 percent when it appeared that supply would exceed demand. A lowered quota would cut into farmers' profits because it meant they could sell less tobacco.

Both chambers subsequently agreed to a compromise amendment authorizing the secretary to decrease quotas by 10 percent.

Other Legislation

Target Price Freeze

The administration spent much of the year trying, without success, to persuade Congress to block scheduled increases in target prices, a major price support program for wheat and other crops.

On Nov. 16, two days before Congress adjourned, the House by voice vote passed a bill (HR 4072) to which the administration objected. Congress completed action on target price freeze legislation in 1984. *(Details, 1984 action, p. 511)*

Specialty Cotton Program

A bill to change the terms of federal aid for growers of a special long-fiber cotton ("extra-long staple") was signed by President Reagan Aug. 26 (HR 3190 — PL 98-88). Reported by the House Agriculture Committee (H Rept 98-256) on June 22, the bill passed the House June 27 and the Senate Aug. 4.

HR 3190 was intended to reduce surplus stocks of the cotton by lowering the federal commodity loan rate and allowing the agriculture secretary to sell surplus stocks at prices he determined to be appropriate.

The loan rate effectively set minimum market prices; under the new formula authorized in the bill, the 1984 rate would drop to 82.5 cents a pound, instead of 96.25 cents. The bill also made the cotton eligible, for the first time, for "deficiency payments" if market prices dropped below a target price; authorized paid acreage reduction programs for the crop; and permitted the agriculture secretary to require participation in an acreage reduction program as a condition for price support loans and deficiency payments in years when stocks were excessive. Extra-long staple cotton, grown in three Southwestern states, comprised a very small part of total U.S. cotton production.

Wheat Program Announcements

Twice in 1983 Congress approved legislation requiring the Agriculture Department to meet early deadlines for announcing the terms of federal wheat and feed grain programs, such as acreage reduction. President Reagan vetoed the original bill (HR 3564) on Aug. 12, arguing that the federal government needed more leeway to cope with unexpected developments, such as drought or early frost.

The bill eventually enacted (HR 3914 — PL 98-100) differed from the vetoed version only in allowing the secretary of agriculture to change a program within 30 days after it was announced if there was a change during that period in the supply of the commodity in question.

HR 3914, approved by voice vote in the House Sept. 20 and in the Senate Sept. 21, provided that for the 1984 and 1985 feed grain crops, the government's announcement had

to be made by Sept. 30 (instead of Nov. 15) of the year before that in which the crop was harvested. For the 1985 wheat crop the deadline was July 1, 1984 (instead of Aug. 15, 1984).

'Sodbuster' Conservation Bill

The Senate passed a notable change in federal land conservation policy just hours before adjournment of its 1983 session. The so-called "sodbuster" bill (S 663), passed by voice vote Nov. 18, made crops grown on easily erodible land ineligible for federal price supports, loans, federally subsidized crop insurance and disaster payments.

The House acted on the measure in 1984, but the legislation stalled in conference over penalties for plowing up erosion-prone land. *(Story, p. 515)*

Export Subsidy Program

The Senate Agriculture Committee March 16 reported legislation (S 822 — S Rept 98-27) to establish an aggressive export subsidy program for U.S.-produced food and fiber.

The Senate Foreign Relations Committee subsequently considered the bill and reported it (S Rept 98-37) March 24, but there was no further action on the measure.

The committee members almost unanimously put a large share of the blame for sagging U.S. farm exports on what they viewed as predatory trade practices by the European Community and a handful of other nations. They contended that American farmers had been unfairly undersold in foreign markets and that U.S. agriculture had to retaliate in kind to regain those markets.

1984

The Reagan administration in 1984 finally succeeded in persuading Congress to block increases in the target price program, a goal it had been seeking since late 1982. The target price program made cash payments to farmers when market prices for crops fell below specified levels.

The price the administration had to pay for the freeze, however, was earlier cash payments to farmers in 1984 for not growing certain crops in 1985 and liberalized terms for federal loans to farmers.

With American agriculture sunk in a multi-year recession, and farm debt at a record high of $215 billion in 1984, the administration took other actions to expand farm credit and relax loan repayment terms for farmers that it had opposed for two years.

Additional funds for federal guarantees for private farm loans were included in a fiscal 1984 supplemental appropriations bill, and the president unveiled a plan allowing deferral of principal repayments with interest forgiveness on troubled Farmers Home Administration loans to farmers.

Although both the House and the Senate passed landmark legislation to discourage farming on easily erodible land, conferees were unable to resolve disagreements between the two versions of the bill. Popular legislation to shore up the federal fund that lent money to rural electric

and telephone systems also failed to clear Congress when Senate critics blocked debate on the measure.

Target Price Freeze

Congress April 3 approved legislation imposing a "freeze" on scheduled increases in the "targets" used to determine payment levels for corn, cotton and rice. The legislation also cut the target price for wheat.

Enactment of the bill culminated a two-year effort by the Reagan administration to block the target price increases. But to win passage of the measure (HR 4072 — PL 98-258) the administration had to give ground on other farm issues.

In return for the freeze, the administration agreed to give farmers early cash payments in 1984 for not growing wheat, corn, cotton and rice in 1985. The bill also liberalized terms for federal loans to farmers and spelled out administration commitments to boost farm exports and food donations abroad.

What began as an administration-backed thrift measure appeared to many members an election-year wish list by the time Congress cleared it.

The freeze on target price increases was nevertheless a notable achievement for the administration because it meant that bidding on future levels for the price support began at much lower levels in 1985, when Congress was scheduled to reauthorize farm programs in an omnibus agriculture bill.

In 1981, the last time Congress considered omnibus farm legislation, the Reagan administration had proposed to do away with the target price program altogether. *(Omnibus farm bill, p. 487)*

Background

The target price program made "deficiency payments" to eligible producers of wheat, corn, cotton and rice whenever the market prices for crops dropped below targets set by law. Secretary of Agriculture John R. Block unsuccessfully sought to end the program in 1981.

Creation of the 1984 bill began in November 1982 when the Reagan administration proposed to offer its huge 1983 acreage reduction (payment-in-kind, or PIK) program in exchange for congressional approval of a freeze on target prices at 1983 levels. PIK used surplus commodities to pay farmers who agreed to scale back on the crops they raised. *(PIK, p. 498)*

In 1983 the Reagan administration again urged Congress to hold target prices at the 1983 levels, instead of allowing them to rise automatically over the next two years.

Administration officials said the scheduled increases were expensive and not needed because of low inflation rates. And Block believed that the increases perversely encouraged farmers to overplant at a time of massive surpluses.

Opponents contended that the increases were critical to draw farmers into acreage reduction programs, which were meant to reduce surpluses. To qualify for the payments, farmers had to participate in such programs.

The administration promised support for new dairy legislation if Congress enacted the freeze in 1983. President Reagan ultimately signed the dairy bill even though Congress did not approve the freeze. *(Dairy-tobacco bill, p. 504)*

Reagan Shifts Gears, Endorses Aid to Farmers

After two years of opposing legislation to relax repayment terms on loans to financially strapped farmers, the Reagan administration reversed course Sept. 18 and offered farmers a new, billion-dollar program of debt forgiveness and loan guarantees.

A total of $650 million for federal guarantees for private farm loans, one part of the administration plan, was included in a fiscal 1984 supplemental appropriations bill (HR 6040 — PL 98-396) cleared Aug. 10. The president had not requested this money; legislators had added it earlier in 1984 after the Independent Bankers Association lobbied for a billion-dollar farm loan guarantee plan.

As much as $700 million from a fund set up by the Farmers Home Administration (FmHA) could be spent on another part of the plan, deferral of principal repayments with interest forgiveness, on troubled FmHA loans to farmers.

The House had passed broader credit plans in 1982 and 1983, but a version approved by the Senate Agriculture Committee never came to the floor for a vote. Agriculture Department officials had insisted then that such measures were unneeded because they already were working with individual farmers experiencing credit problems. The department repeatedly had been sued for not using existing authority to defer loan repayments for debt-ridden farmers. *(1982 FmHA authorization, p. 502; 1983 farm 'recession relief,' p. 509)*

The credit plan was unveiled by President Reagan the day before he left on a re-election campaign tour through financially troubled Midwestern farm states. Farm debt, probably the most painful political issue in the farm community, stood at a record high of $215 billion, up from $166 billion in 1980.

Reagan Plan

The administration plan:

● Authorized FmHA to defer interest payments on 25 percent of the principal of a loan, up to $100,000, for up to five years. The interest that would have been charged on that portion of the principal, for that period, would never have to be paid. Agriculture Secretary John R. Block said the outer limit for the program was $700 million.

● Authorized FmHA to guarantee repayment of private and farm credit system loans to farmers under special terms, applying only to so-called "non-performing" or "classified" loans (which borrowers could not pay). These guarantees were available if the private lender agreed to lower by at least 10 percent the principal owed by a farm borrower; the guarantee covered 90 percent of the reduced loan.

● Established two-person county teams, with expertise in farm management and lending, to work out financial plans with farmers and their creditors.

● Authorized the Agriculture Department to pay private lending institutions to process FmHA loan applications.

Other Farm Aid

The credit plan was the last of a series of administration actions taken in 1984 to aid farmers. On Sept. 14 the Agriculture Department announced its 1985 price support programs for feed grains, cotton and rice, authorizing cash payments to growers of upland cotton and rice for cutting back harvests.

Growers of feed grains, cotton, rice and wheat also were offered an estimated $2 billion worth of "advance deficiency payments" when they signed up for participation in 1985 federal crop programs. Deficiency payments were made when market prices for a crop fell below a legally established "target" figure; the amount paid to a farmer was the difference between the target price and a lower market price.

The administration sought, without success, to end the target price program in 1981. In 1984 it persuaded Congress to freeze scheduled increases in the crop target prices. *(Story, p. 511)*

The administration also requested an International Trade Commission investigation of tobacco imports, and it announced new U.S. grain sales to the Soviet Union, together with a presidential pledge to sell the Russians even more.

1983 Action

House. Congress took little action on the target price freeze proposal until the closing days of the 1983 session, when the House passed HR 4072. That version, however, modified only wheat target prices and added incentives to draw wheat farmers into the stringent 1984 wheat acreage reduction program. Reacting to fears of a massive wheat crop in the spring of 1984, the House hoped to attract more farmers to the government progam to reduce wheat production.

There was no committee report on the bill, which the House passed Nov. 16 by voice vote. Earlier in the year the administration had tried and failed to prod the House Agriculture Committee into a quick vote to stop increases in target prices.

Senate. The administration had more luck with the Senate Agriculture Committee, which reported target price freeze legislation (HR 2733 — H Rept 98-164) June 23. By a 10-7 vote the committee approved the administration plan to let the secretary of agriculture keep target prices at fiscal 1983 levels for fiscal 1984 and 1985.

But opponents of the bill won a tactical victory when

they forced the committee to report the freeze as a separate bill instead of combining it with tobacco and dairy program revisions approved June 16. (The target price language was added by the committee to HR 2733, a House-passed bill promoting development of a domestic rubber plant, guayule.)

Without the protective shield of the tobacco and dairy provisions, the freeze was left open to threats of a filibuster and other delaying tactics. Such threats prompted Majority Leader Howard H. Baker Jr., R-Tenn., on July 28 to halt Senate work on HR 2733. Opponents had begun what they called "a really thorough debate of American agricultural policies." Opponents prevented formal floor debate during the remainder of the session.

1984 Action

Faced with a meager sign-up for the wheat program, administration officials renewed negotiations in early March. These stretched out over weeks as farm state members sought concessions from the administration.

Senate Committee Action. The Senate Agriculture Committee, rushing to beat spring plantings, approved an expanded version of HR 4072 March 8.

The committee bill partly met the goal of the administration, which sought the target price freeze. And it partly met demands of farm groups that said they needed more aid to recover from the 1983 drought.

The bill was negotiated in private sessions by Sen. Robert Dole, R-Kan., budget director David A. Stockman and other senators with strong interests in the affected crops — wheat, corn and feed grains, cotton and rice. As part of the bargain, the administration offered to boost funding for the Food for Peace program, which sent surplus food overseas to needy nations, and for guaranteed loans for farm exports.

The Agriculture Department estimated that the target price cut, and improved participation in acreage reduction programs, would lower farm program spending by about $3 billion in 1984-87. But members were skeptical about the savings. When Sen. Roger W. Jepsen, R-Iowa, asked whether the amount was $3 billion, Dole shot back, "I wouldn't want to bet on it."

Senate Floor Action. The Senate passed HR 4072 March 22 following lengthy discussions with farm state senators and further concessions by the administration. Passage came on a **78-10 key vote (R 50-2; D 28-8).** *(1984 key votes, p. 927)*

Howell Heflin, D-Ala., negotiated an amendment to sweeten the terms for cotton by making a paid diversion program more likely in 1985. David Pryor, D-Ark., won approval of an amendment that improved payments to rice farmers if surplus commodities triggered an acreage reduction program in 1985. Other amendments adopted by the Senate included a proposal by John Melcher, D-Mont., to establish a program to channel surplus dairy products and wheat to needy nations.

Conference. The conference on HR 4072 was marked by attempts by House members to leave their imprint on a rewrite of farm programs that had been crafted by the Senate and the Reagan administration.

House conferees won modest changes in the bill's cotton and rice provisions and authority for new loans for farmers based on corn raised to feed livestock. But Senate conferees — backed by Agriculture Department officials — rejected more costly cotton and rice plans.

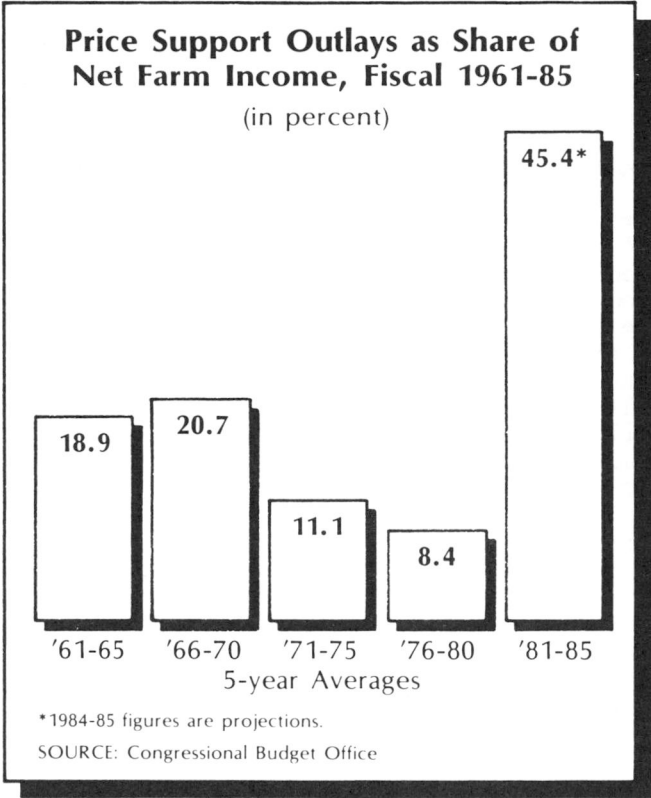

Price Support Outlays as Share of Net Farm Income, Fiscal 1961-85

(in percent)

18.9	20.7	11.1	8.4	45.4*
'61-65	'66-70	'71-75	'76-80	'81-85

5-year Averages

*1984-85 figures are projections.

SOURCE: Congressional Budget Office

In major decisions conferees:

● Eliminated House-approved early target price "deficiency payments" to wheat farmers. The bill, however, did provide early payments to farmers for reducing their crops.

● Added to the new rice program an additional, intermediate level of surplus that would trigger a paid acreage reduction program in 1985.

● Revised the new cotton program to expand the paid acreage reduction program under certain circumstances.

● Authorized, but did not require, federal loans to farmers that would be based, indirectly, on the corn they harvested before maturity to use as silage to feed livestock.

● Rejected a conservation package proposed by Rep. Ed Jones, D-Tenn. Most of the conferees appeared to back the package, which combined "sodbuster" language with financial incentives for conservation. It was the financial incentives that drew opposition from GOP senators and administration representatives. *(Sodbuster bill, p. 515)*

The Senate approved the conference report (H Rept 98-646) on HR 4072 April 2 by voice vote. The House cleared the measure the following day on a 379-11 vote.

Provisions

As signed into law April 10, HR 4072 (PL 98-258):

Target Prices. Set the wheat target price at $4.38 per bushel for 1984 and 1985 crops (instead of $4.45 and $4.65, respectively, as in existing law). The bill also authorized 1984 and 1985 wheat acreage reduction programs in which farmers who reduced their wheat harvest by 30 percent qualified for basic farm program benefits such as price supports. For a third of that amount — 10 percent of his base — a farmer would be paid $2.70 a bushel.

The administration's 1984 wheat program had called for a 30 percent reduction in a farmer's total acreage devoted to wheat as a condition for receiving farm program benefits, with no payments. It also permitted farmers to set aside up to 20 percent more land and receive a payment-in-kind of surplus wheat for doing so. HR 4072 raised the PIK payment rate to 85 percent of expected yield from the administration's 75 percent.

● Permitted farmers to graze livestock or harvest hay on idled wheat acreage in states where this practice had been approved by the state committees of farmers that helped administer federal price supports and other programs.

● Kept 1985 target prices at 1984 levels of $3.03 a bushel for corn, 81 cents per pound for cotton and $11.90 per hundred pounds (hundredweight) for rice. If current law had not been modified, target prices for these commodities would have risen in 1985 to $3.18 for corn, 86 cents for cotton and $12.40 for rice. Also required the Agriculture Department to offer 1985 crop reduction programs if the "carryovers" of surplus commodities at the end of the year exceeded specified levels.

For each crop the bill spelled out various combinations of paid and unpaid participation levels and set payment rates at $1.50 a bushel for corn and 35 cents a pound for cotton and a minimum rate of $3.50 per hundredweight for rice. The rice payment increased with the size of the surplus.

● Authorized loans to farmers who harvested 1984 or 1985 corn before it matured, for silage. The collateral was not the silage, however, but corn a producer would buy for purposes of securing the loan.

● Permitted farmers to sign up in 1984 for 1985 programs and receive half the set-aside payment when they enlisted; farmers in the 1984 wheat program also received early payments.

Export Aid. Stated the sense of Congress that the administration should make the following increases, above current spending levels, to expand farm exports: in fiscal 1984, $150 million for the Food for Peace (PL 480) program, in addition to the $90 million PL 480 supplemental appropriation for African food aid, and $500 million in guaranteed export loans from the Commodity Credit Corp. (CCC); in fiscal 1985, $175 million for PL 480; $1.1 billion in CCC funds for export credit guarantees and $100 million in direct export loans from the CCC. Also provided in 1985 another $50 million either for PL 480 or for the CCC export credits.

● Authorized a two-year pilot project in which the CCC acquired through barter or exchange 40,000 tons of milk processed by the ultra-high temperature method for donation to needy nations. Milk sterilized by ultra-high temperature treatment needed no refrigeration and had a shelf life of five months.

● Permitted donation overseas of CCC-owned surplus wheat through a program that currently donated CCC dairy goods.

Domestic Credit. Mandated that applications for disaster loans be filed within eight months after a disaster. Previously deadlines were set administratively and ranged from six months to a year after a county was designated a disaster area.

● Stipulated that farm assets used as collateral for emergency disaster loans would carry the value they had a year before a disaster declaration rather than the value they had at the time the loan was negotiated.

● Required that $250 million in economic emergency direct loans be made available in fiscal 1984 and mandated that $310 million be available for insured loans in the program; authorized additional insured loans.

● Required the secretary of agriculture to make emergency disaster loans available to farmers in counties contiguous to those designated eligible for disaster assistance, with these loans based on individual losses.

● Raised the ceiling on Farmers Home Administration (FmHA) farm operating loans to individuals to $200,000 and on guaranteed operating loans to $400,000. Existing limits were $100,000 and $200,000, respectively.

● Required that the interest rate for FmHA loans that had been rescheduled — renegotiated because farmers could not make payments — be the lower of either the rate of the original loan or the rate prevailing at the time of the rescheduling. Also extended to 15 years, from seven years, the maximum repayment period for rescheduled loans.

● Required at least 20 percent of farm ownership and operating direct loans in fiscal 1984 to be reserved for low-income farmers with limited resources. These borrowers qualified for lower interest rates on the loans.

● Authorized rescheduling of FmHA loans for borrowers who agreed to plant timber on crop or pasture land and use proceeds from timber sales to repay the loan.

● Prohibited FmHA personnel from buying farm land for which an FmHA loan had been denied for three years after a loan refusal.

REA Loan Repayments

Popular legislation to shore up the federal fund that lent money to rural electric and telephone systems failed to clear Congress in 1984. Last-minute attempts to win a Senate vote were blocked Oct. 10 when Howard M. Metzenbaum, D-Ohio, and Alan K. Simpson, R-Wyo., objected to Senate debate on the bill.

The measure would have revised loan repayment terms both for utilities borrowing from the Rural Electrification Administration (REA) and for REA's substantial debts to the U.S. Treasury. REA supporters claimed the agency's major lending fund would run out of money in the next decade, and that a rescue was essential to preserve rural electric and telephone systems. The fund had been lending money to rural utilities at 5 percent interest or lower, while paying much higher interest rates to borrow it.

The legislation (HR 3050 — H Rept 98-588, Part I) passed the House March 1 by a 283-111 vote. It had been approved by the House Agriculture Committee in October 1983.

The measure ran into trouble in May when Simpson objected to its costs, to sales of REA-subsidized power to wealthy corporations, and to REA involvement in the financially troubled nuclear power industry.

Until Simpson announced his objections in a blunt letter sent May 3 to his Senate colleagues, the legislation had been moving easily through Congress, helped by skillful lobbying by the electric and telephone cooperatives and independent telephone systems that relied on REA. The bill had rolled through the House despite isolated warnings the plan was neither as cheap nor as effective as advocates said. Some 46 senators had signed on as sponsors.

Despite Simpson's misgivings, the Senate Agriculture Committee approved its companion bill (S 1300 — S Rept 98-545) June 7. The Senate panel changed a formula for setting interest rates on REA loans to electric and tele-

phone utilities to ensure that utilities' interest payments would cover REA's interest payments on the money it borrowed. A second amendment required approval by the Federal Financing Bank for refinancing of one type of REA debt. Another would have required special low-interest loans to utilities facing financial problems, an amendment that greatly reduced the number of utilities eligible for loans.

Had the bill cleared Congress, President Reagan likely would have vetoed it. The administration objected to the plan's cost but was unable to find a member to introduce a stringent, alternative REA bill that Reagan sent to Congress in early April.

The intricacies of S 1300 confused debate, masking an underlying conflict between the administration and the utilities. S 1300 would have effectively locked in the size of the agency — and some of its key policies that the Reagan administration sought to change. Administration officials wanted to reduce the amount of money lent by REA, raise loan rates to what it cost the government to get the money, and target the loans to utilities with intractable financial problems.

'Sodbuster' Conservation Bill

The 98th Congress failed to complete action on landmark legislation to discourage farming on easily erodible land.

The Senate in 1983 passed a "sodbuster" bill to deny federal farm program benefits to crops grown on fragile land, and the House approved the sodbuster plan in 1984 as part of a broader soil conservation bill. However, the legislation stalled when conferees were unable to agree on penalties for plowing up erosion-prone land.

The Senate in 1984 added sodbuster language to the fiscal 1985 agriculture appropriations bill (HR 5743), but the provision was dropped in conference.

1983 Action

The Senate passed its version of the sodbuster bill (S 663) by voice vote Nov. 18, 1983. The bill made crops grown on easily erodible land ineligible for federal price supports, loans, federally subsidized crop insurance and disaster payments.

Before passing the bill, the Senate adopted an amendment by sponsor William L. Armstrong, R-Colo., to narrow the scope of the version reported Nov. 2 by the Senate Agriculture Committee (S Rept 98-296). The committee bill would have barred the farm benefits for an entire crop if any part of it were grown on highly erodible land. Armstrong's amendment restored the bill to the form in which he had introduced it.

The bill for the first time would have linked eligibility for federal farm program benefits directly to a farmer's conservation practices. Other federal conservation efforts generally relied on financial incentives. Armstrong pointed out that the bill did not dictate land use decisions to farmers but simply ended federal subsidies for cultivation of fragile land.

The measure was not retroactive. Benefits would be denied only to specified types of land brought into cultivation after enactment. Although some 40 million acres of extremely fragile lands already were cultivated — about 10 percent of the total crop land base — Armstrong claimed

another 250 million vulnerable acres could be plowed unless the government made it financially unattractive to do so.

1984 Action

The House May 8 passed by voice vote a more restrictive bill: While S 663 barred farm benefits only for the crop or crops planted on erodible land, the House bill (HR 3457 — H Rept 98-696) denied benefits for all of a farmer's crops if any part were grown on fragile land. HR 3457 combined sodbuster penalties with payments to farmers who instituted long-term conservation practices on fragile crop land.

Both the House and Senate bills made farmers who plowed fragile land ineligible for farm aid — federal price support programs, federally subsidized crop insurance, Farmers Home Administration loans and disaster payments. With certain exceptions, the prohibition applied to the year in which the erodible land was plowed.

But conferees were unable to resolve a major disagreement over cutting the aid just for crops planted on erodible land or for all a farmer's crop.

Senate conferees also refused to accept an additional conservation "reserve" program in the House bill that would pay farmers for retiring over-used crop land for extended periods of time. As in the "soil bank" program begun in the 1950s, the land would have been planted with crops that prevented erosion, such as hay or timber, for several years.

The Reagan administration supported a sodbuster provision halfway between the Senate and House versions — one that would have barred program benefits to all of a specific crop if a part of it were produced on erodible land. But the administration objected strongly to the long-term conservation plan in the House bill.

Other Legislation

Grain, Cotton Inspection

Congress in 1984 cleared two bills to continue programs requiring grain and cotton producers to pay for the federal services that established the quality of their crops.

One measure (HR 5221 — PL 98-469) extended, through Sept. 30, 1988, so-called user fees that financed the Department of Agriculture's Federal Grain Inspection Service. The service was responsible for inspecting and weighing grain and supervised comparable state agencies that carried out these functions.

The House passed HR 5221 (H Rept 98-756) May 21 by voice vote, and the Senate cleared the bill by voice vote Sept. 28.

The second bill (S 2085 — PL 98-403) continued, through the same date, authorization for fees paid by cotton producers for Agriculture Department classification and grading. The measure won voice vote approval in the Senate (S Rept 98-395) on May 2. The House passed a slightly different version May 21. The Senate accepted the House version Aug. 10.

The user fees were authorized in 1981 in response to the Reagan administration's broad policy of shifting the cost of certain federal agricultural services to those who used them. Authority for both fees expired in September. The grain measure made non-controversial changes related

Agriculture

to short-term investment of producers' fees by the federal government and the cap on the portion of fees that could be used for administrative costs. The cotton bill also revised certain terms of the fee program.

Farm Disaster Loans

Congress April 5 cleared legislation (HR 4169 — PL 98-270) that extended for three years, until Sept. 30, 1986, a requirement that farmers seek disaster loans from the Farmers Home Administration before seeking more favorable loans from the Small Business Administration (SBA). The bill, a budget reconciliation measure carried over from 1983, also made other changes in the SBA disaster loan program. *(Reconciliation bill, p. 60)*

Honey Promotion

A bill (HR 5358 — PL 98-590) empowering honey producers and importers to establish a self-financed program to advertise and otherwise promote the consumption of honey was signed by President Reagan Oct. 30.

The House approved its version of the bill (H Rept 98-892) by voice vote July 24. The Senate passed the measure by voice vote Oct. 4.

The program, subject to a vote of approval by a majority of the industry, was to be financed by assessments levied against producers and importers. Participation was voluntary.

Central Kitchen Inspections

President Reagan Oct. 17 signed a non-controversial bill (HR 5223 — PL 98-487) that exempted certain central restaurant kitchens from inspection requirements of federal meat and poultry laws. The bill passed the House (H Rept 98-885) July 24 by voice vote. The Senate approved its version of the bill Oct. 2 by voice vote after adding an amendment requiring central kitchens to continue to keep records mandated by the meat and poultry laws and permitting the Agriculture Department to examine central kitchens' facilities, inventories and records. The House accepted the Senate amendment by voice vote the next day.

The legislation put central kitchens on the same footing as individual restaurants, which already were exempt from those requirements. Central kitchens, which prepared ready-to-eat food served in branch restaurants, were still subject to health and safety inspections by state and local authorities. Meat prepared in those kitchens was subject to federal inspection elsewhere.

10

Health, Education and Welfare

Introduction	*519*
Health	*521*
Education	*555*
Welfare	*581*
Veterans	*613*

Health, Education and Welfare

Ronald Reagan came to the presidency in 1981 determined to change the direction of federal social policy in America.

After two decades of explosive growth in federal spending for health, education, welfare and other social programs, Reagan wanted to reverse the trend. He espoused a "New Federalism" under which the federal role in social programs would be reduced and greater responsibility shifted to state and local governments. He wanted less — less spending, less federal involvement, less regulation, less paperwork.

His attacks on federal programs — and spending — struck a responsive chord in voters in 1980. Conservatives won a sweeping electoral victory, installing Reagan in the White House, a Republican majority in the Senate and more Republican members in the House.

With his electoral mandate, Reagan wasted no time once in office. A month after his inauguration, he went before Congress to outline his budget-cutting proposals, including major reductions in social programs. Six months later Congress enacted the largest spending and tax cuts in its history, slashing fiscal 1982 spending $35 billion below projected levels and reducing personal and corporate income taxes by $37.7 billion. About $25 billion in cuts — some 70 percent of the budget savings — were made in social programs.

The Reagan administration saw this as just the first step toward a more profound revision of social policy. But, while some further reductions were approved by the 97th and 98th Congresses, they had neither the scope nor the impact of the cutbacks and changes approved in 1981. Moreover, Reagan's plans for a New Federalism fell short of the president's goals, as Congress either modified or ignored many of his proposals to fold existing programs into block grants and to shift responsibility for other programs. *(Details, pp. 773, 777; federal spending for income security, graph, p. 520)*

'Social Safety Net'

Reagan appealed to Congress Feb. 18, 1981, to give America a new economic beginning by adopting his ambitious plan to scale back the growth of government and return billions of dollars of taxes to workers and businesses.

The president maintained that his program was "even-handed" and could be accomplished "without harm to government's legitimate purpose or to our responsibility to all who need our benevolence."

He promised to retain a "social safety net" of programs for the truly needy. "We will continue to fulfill the obligations that spring from our national conscience," the president said. "Those who through no fault of their own must depend on the rest of us, the poverty stricken, the disabled, the elderly, all those with true need, can rest assured that the social safety net of programs they depend on are exempt from any cuts." *(Text of Reagan economic address to Congress, p. 1038)*

The programs Reagan included in the social safety net were Social Security, Supplemental Security Income (SSI), Medicare, veterans' pensions, school breakfast and lunch programs for low-income students, summer jobs for low-income youth and the Head Start program for preschool children.

Although cuts eventually were made in some of these programs, the Reagan administration continued to insist that the truly needy had been protected and the safety net was intact — points disputed by administration critics.

In a 1984 analysis of Reagan's first-term record, the Urban Institute concluded that people completely dependent on the government for support still had a safety net of federal support, but those partially dependent had suffered severe setbacks. The Reagan spending cuts had hit mainly the working poor, the study said, while the Reagan tax cuts had not helped the poor at all.

The study reported that in the four years since 1980, disposable income of the poorest one-fifth of all American families had declined by 7.6 percent after inflation, while the income of the top one-fifth had risen by 8.7 percent.

"Some widening of the income distribution would have taken place from 1980 to 1984 irrespective of who had been president," the report observed. "But the particular policy mix of tax and benefit reductions that President Reagan chose exacerbated the trend."

1981 Spending Cuts

Almost all the sweeping budget cuts Congress approved in 1981 were made in one package, an omnibus reconciliation measure designed to carry out cuts proposed by Reagan and endorsed by Congress through its budget process. That one piece of legislation touched on virtually every federal activity except defense.

Federal social programs — in health, education and welfare — were targeted for the greatest cuts. The social safety net programs generally escaped the deep budget cuts other programs suffered. Similarly, other social program

Outlays for Income Security

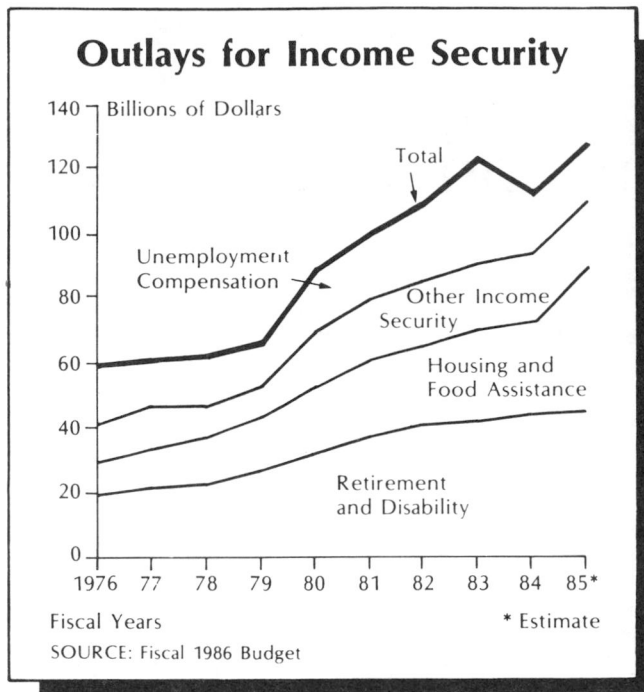

Billions of Dollars

Total

Unemployment Compensation

Other Income Security

Housing and Food Assistance

Retirement and Disability

Fiscal Years   * Estimate

1976 77 78 79 80 81 82 83 84 85*

SOURCE: Fiscal 1986 Budget

benefits for the extremely poor — those with little or no income who were totally dependent on government help — in most cases were not reduced severely. However, the working poor — families that had some job income but still were near the poverty level — suffered serious losses.

Major cuts or changes made in social programs by the budget reconciliation bill included:

Health. Medicaid payments to the states were cut; Medicare recipients were required to pay a greater share of the cost of their care; funding for a number of categorical health programs was reduced and many of the programs were folded into new block grants; substantial cuts were made in aid to health professionals, as well as in the health planning system and the Professional Standards Review Organization program; funding for Public Health Service hospitals was ended.

Education. Spending levels for a number of elementary and secondary education programs were cut, a variety of small programs were combined in one block grant, and part of the impact aid program, for school districts educating children of federally connected parents, was slated for termination; at the higher education level, a "needs test" to limit eligibility for guaranteed student loans was established and funding for Pell grants for college students was limited to amounts well below the estimated cost of full operation of the program.

Welfare. Major cuts were made in Aid to Families with Dependent Children (AFDC) benefits to working parents and states were permitted to require AFDC recipients to work in exchange for benefits; the food stamp program was scaled back substantially by tightening eligibility, curtailing inflation-based adjustments in benefit levels and cutting benefits during a recipient's first month in the program; child nutrition programs were cut substantially by reducing subsidies for school meals and tightening eligi-

bility for free and reduced-price meals; the Community Services Administration was abolished and a community services block grant established.

Subsequent Legislative Action

A deepening recession and the results of the 1981 cuts kept the 97th Congress from approving many major changes in social programs in 1982. As the unemployment rate soared, nearing 11 percent by year's end, Congress became less interested in cutting social programs.

While they generally escaped deep spending cuts at the hands of Congress in 1982, however, health, education and welfare programs and the people who relied on them came under increasing stress. Programs such as AFDC, Medicaid and guaranteed loans for college students experienced for the first time the full effects of the 1981 spending cuts. Important changes resulting from the budget cuts, combined with the economic recession, included:

• A shift of welfare funds from the working poor to the non-working poor.

• An increased health cost burden on private health insurers and patients, combined with a cut in services.

• Reductions in enrollment at many private colleges and universities and layoffs of public school teachers.

The 98th Congress was less on the defensive than its predecessor had been. It ignored administration requests for changes and cuts in social programs and took steps, albeit cautious and limited ones, to reverse some earlier Reagan policies.

In the health field, Congress ignored the administration's pro-competition proposals to reduce health care costs, but it worked with the administration in formulating legislation to stem Medicare costs by setting fixed prices for hospital care, by temporarily freezing physician fees and by raising out-of-pocket expenses for Medicare recipients. A new child health plan was added to the Medicaid program, but Congress lost its earlier interest in providing health insurance for the unemployed.

After 1981 the administration made little headway in seeking further cuts in the growth of college student aid programs. Congress, after blocking in 1981 administration attempts to rewrite the rules for college assistance programs, mandated its own rules in subsequent years. Congress shied away from establishing major new education programs and, when it did approve a new program, such as the science-math education program enacted in 1984, appropriated far less money than it had authorized. But increased spending for a variety of existing education programs was authorized in 1984, a record-high appropriation for the Education Department was passed, and several programs slated to be terminated, such as part of the impact aid program, were extended. President Reagan's plan to abolish the Education Department was ignored by Congress, and his tuition tax credit plan was rejected.

After bearing the brunt of the 1981 budget cuts, social welfare programs were spared further deep cuts. Alarmed at recession-spawned unemployment, Congress early in 1983 pressured the administration to drop its opposition to jobs and humanitarian relief legislation. As part of that bill, Congress ordered the government to step up giveaways of surplus federally owned food. In other social welfare action, efforts to restore some of the Reagan-era cuts in food stamps and child nutrition programs were unsuccessful.

Health Policy

President Reagan's goals for the health care system in America were similar to those in other social fields: to lower costs and to reduce the federal role. And, as in those other fields, he had a mixed record of success.

For years health care costs had been rising faster than the nation's inflation rate. In 1981, Reagan's first year in office, the rate of spending for medical services in the United States grew by 12.5 percent, compared with an overall inflation rate of 8.9 percent, as measured by the Labor Department. The 1981 medical care inflation rate was the largest, up to the time, since the department began tracking those costs in 1935.

Early in his administration Reagan outlined his health legislation agenda. In keeping with his "New Federalism" plan, he proposed dismantling the array of categorical grant programs built up over the years to attack specific health problems, and replacing them with unrestricted block grants to states.

His plan called for abolition of the nation's health planning system and professional standards review organizations (PSROs) — the two regulatory mechanisms by which the government had attempted to hold down health care costs and ensure proper distribution of services. The plan also recommended capping the federal contribution to Medicaid, the federal-state health care program for the poor; ending subsidies to health maintenance organizations (HMOs); shutting down Public Health Service (PHS) hospitals; and eliminating subsidies for training physicians and other health professionals.

Statistical Backdrop

Reagan proposed his legislative agenda against a backdrop of spiraling health costs.

In 1966 per capita spending for health — including such items as research and construction of facilities — was $212.32. By 1981 that figure had risen to $1,216.

A different statistical series of the Health Care Financing Administration, excluding research and construction, showed the nation's personal health care expenditures rising from $39.6 billion in 1966 to $217 billion in 1980.

America also was spending more for health insurance. In 1980 employers and individuals collectively paid $77.7 billion in premiums for commercial health insurance and Blue Cross-Blue Shield coverage. That compared with a national total of $12.8 billion in 1966, according to statistics gathered by the Health Insurance Institute.

Not only had health care spending increased, but its rate of growth was also accelerating. Between 1966 and 1967 personal health care expenditures grew 10.6 percent; between 1979 and 1980 the increase was 15.2 percent. Much of the increase appeared to be "real" inflation — that is, rising prices. In 1980 higher prices accounted for 75 percent of the growth in personal health care expenditures, while population changes accounted for 8 percent and "intensity," or changes in the use or kinds of services, for 17 percent, according to the Department of Health and Human Services (HHS).

Hospital rates galloped upward at almost double the inflation rate during the year ending in March 1981, according to HHS figures. Total health spending took 9.4 percent of the gross national product, as compared with 6.2 percent in 1965. Nearly 11 percent of the federal budget was being devoted to health spending each year.

Medicare

Health care for the aged accounted for an ever larger share of the escalating health care costs for the nation. Federal, state and local governments, which picked up about three-fifths of the health care tab for the aged, primarily through Medicare and Medicaid, were finding they no longer could absorb such large, uncontrollable costs without impairing other programs.

And the prospect was that the problems would only get worse. Not only were per capita health care costs higher for the aged, but there was a growing number of persons over age 65. The elderly population rose from 9.7 percent of the population in 1970 to 11.1 percent in 1980. It was projected that by the year 2030, when the post-World War II "baby-boom" generation had aged, persons over 65 would comprise an unprecedented 20.4 percent of the total population.

Medicare insured about 27 million elderly and three

References

Discussion of health policy for the years 1945-64 may be found in *Congress and the Nation Vol. I*, pp. 1122-1194; for the years 1965-68, *Congress and the Nation Vol. II*, pp. 665-707; for the years 1969-72, *Congress and the Nation Vol. III*, pp. 551-580; for the years 1973-76, *Congress and the Nation Vol. IV*, pp. 323-375; for the years 1977-80, *Congress and the Nation Vol. V*, pp. 601-653.

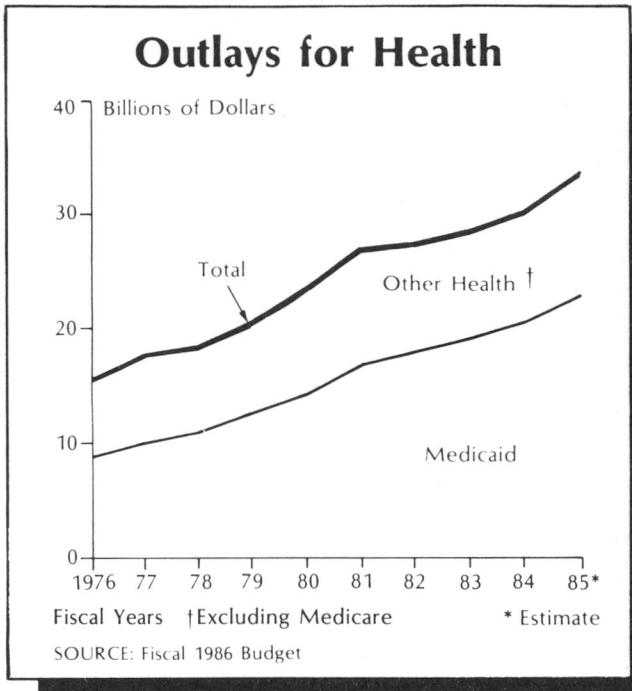

Outlays for Health

Billions of Dollars

Total

Other Health †

Medicaid

1976 77 78 79 80 81 82 83 84 85*

Fiscal Years   †Excluding Medicare   * Estimate

SOURCE: Fiscal 1986 Budget

million disabled persons against hospital, physician and related medical expenses by the mid-1980s. It paid out about $32 billion in fiscal 1980. The price tag had jumped to nearly $58 billion by fiscal 1984 and it was estimated that it would approach $96 billion by 1990.

The 97th and 98th Congresses took steps to put the brakes on Medicare spending by legislating spending cuts, a fundamental change in the hospital payment system, a freeze on doctors' fees and increases in out-of-pocket costs for Medicare recipients. But members shied away from actions — such as deep benefit cuts, large tax increases or both — needed to resolve Medicare's long-range problems.

Reports varied as to what effect the dramatically rising health care costs would have on the Hospital Insurance (HI) Trust Fund, which financed most of Medicare. In the early 1980s Social Security trustees of the HI fund projected that even with scheduled increases in the Social Security tax, which financed the fund, the HI trust fund might go broke shortly after 1990. In 1983 HI's prospects looked even more bleak, when the Congressional Budget Office predicted the fund would run out of money as early as 1987.

But in early 1985 the Social Security trustees projected in their annual report that financing for Medicare would be sufficient until 1998. HHS Secretary Margaret M. Heckler said the new hospital payment system enacted in 1983, which set Medicare fees in advance, was a prime factor in the improved outlook. The report also assumed enactment of a one-year freeze on hospital reimbursements proposed by Reagan in 1985.

However, the trustees' report noted that for the system to remain solvent over the next 25 years benefits would have to be cut by 19 percent or payroll taxes used to finance the program raised 24 percent. The report also warned that the system could go broke as early as 1992 if

economic conditions proved worse than expected. *(Medicare spending, graph, p. 644)*

Medicaid

Federal Medicaid funding totaled $21 billion in fiscal 1984, subsidizing health care for some 20 million people — welfare recipients plus many elderly and disabled who relied on Medicaid to pay for long-term care. The federal government paid about 55 percent of Medicaid costs, the states the rest. *(Medicaid spending, graph, this page)*

As with Medicare, demographic trends were also beginning to take their toll on the federal-state program in the 1980s. While the majority of recipients of Medicaid were welfare families, their medical bill consumed only about one-quarter of the program's expenditures.

A much larger — and growing — share of Medicaid funding was going to care for the elderly and disabled, many of whom were middle-income until they exhausted their savings on nursing home bills. The share of Medicaid's budget eaten up by those expenditures grew from 34 percent in 1973 to 43 percent in 1982, even though nursing home residents comprised only 7.3 percent of Medicaid recipients in 1982. Demand for long-term health care would burgeon in the decades ahead as the baby-boom generation aged.

Reagan's proposal in 1981 to place a rigid cap on federal contributions to Medicaid provoked one of the most bitter battles in Congress, with the administration losing badly. Lawmakers did agree to save $3 billion in fiscal 1982-84, reducing by a set percentage each year the amount to which states would otherwise be entitled. States could avoid the full reduction by instituting various cost-saving measures. A second round of cuts was approved in 1982. Congress voted in 1984 to expand the Medicaid program to provide for a Child Health Assurance Program.

Other Health Programs

In other major legislative action, Reagan's 1981 block grant proposal triggered a battle that ended with Congress agreeing to funding cuts but folding fewer programs than the administration had proposed into block grants and imposing a number of conditions on how the money was to be spent.

Also during Reagan's first term, Congress voted to replace the PSRO program with physician review boards but continued in much-reduced form the health planning system, partly because even foes saw it as one of the few sources of cost control. Congress in 1981 reduced spending for the training of health care professionals but refused to end the subsidies. Extension of the subsidy programs in 1984 triggered a presidential veto. The vetoed bill also would have ended most aid to HMO programs, as requested by the administration. Congress agreed to end federal funding of PHS hospitals.

Landmark legislation aimed at making many more inexpensive "generic" versions of brand-name drugs available to consumers was enacted. Congress also cleared bills to promote development of more drugs for rare diseases, to require sharp new warnings for cigarette packages and to ensure that severely handicapped infants were not denied medical treatment.

Chronology
Of Action
On Health

1981

Congress put its own stamp on President Reagan's proposals to curtail federal health programs, part of the new president's broader campaign to slow the growth of federal spending.

While the legislators gave Reagan much of what he asked for, they balked at some health proposals and significantly altered others. The main vehicle for health program changes was the Omnibus Reconciliation Act of 1981, a massive package of budget-cutting measures sought by the president and approved by Congress through its budget process.

Reagan's proposal to consolidate 25 separate health programs into two block grants to the states — with a 25 percent cut in funding — met with only partial success. Congress went along with the reduction in funding, for savings averaging about $1 billion a year in fiscal 1982-84. But it approved four block grants, encompassing only 19 programs, and kept a number of restrictions on the states' use of block grant funds.

In a move to hold down soaring federal health care costs, the Senate and House agreed after a bitter battle to cut $1 billion annually from projected federal spending for Medicaid, the federal-state health care program for the poor. But they refused to put a rigid "cap" on federal Medicaid payments to the states, as Reagan had requested.

Congress also approved savings of more than $1 billion annually in the Medicare program for the elderly and disabled, including provisions that required beneficiaries to pay more of their health care costs. The president originally had said Medicare would be exempt from cuts as part of his "social safety net, protecting programs for the elderly and others who rely on government for their very existence." He later asked for about $1 billion in savings, and Congress cut even deeper than that.

In further major reconciliation action, lawmakers ended per-student grants to medical schools and substantially reduced spending for other programs of aid to health professionals. They agreed to cut spending for two controversial types of medical regulation — the health planning system and Professional Standards Review Organizations — but declined to go along with administration requests to kill the programs. They also cut off federal funding of Public Health Service hospitals and repealed the right of merchant seamen to free medical care — an entitlement dating from 1798.

Health Block Grants, Funding Cut

Congress substantially revised President Reagan's proposal to fold 25 health programs into two block grants to the states, but the administration still won major reduc-

tions in funding under the 1981 budget reconciliation bill, cleared July 31 (HR 3982 — PL 97-35).

That measure incorporated budget cuts sought by Reagan and endorsed by Congress in the first fiscal 1982 budget resolution (H Con Res 115). *(Reconciliation action, p. 40)*

The reconciliation bill set up four health block grants, which shifted to the states responsibility for 19 health programs formerly run by the federal government. But Congress refused to remove from federal control several other programs that Reagan had wanted to fold into the block grants, including family planning, health centers for migrant workers and venereal disease prevention programs. It also imposed a number of conditions on the states' use of block grant funds, rather than giving them total control over how the money would be spent, as Reagan had proposed. *(Details, box, p. 524)*

Overall spending on the programs was cut by about 25 percent, for savings averaging about $1 billion a year in fiscal 1982-84.

Block Grant Controversy

In his March 10 budget Reagan asked Congress to lump 25 separate, or "categorical," health programs into two block grants and to cut their funding by 25 percent. The largest block grant, for general health services, would be funded at $1.1 billion in 1982; the second, for preventive health services, would get $260 million.

The erosion of Reagan's plan began in the Senate Labor and Human Resources Committee, where a coalition of Democrats and two Republicans kept Chairman Orrin G. Hatch, R-Utah, from pushing through the proposal. The panel eventually worked out a compromise that set up two health block grants but retained substantial federal authority over spending.

In the House, the Democratic version of health block grants prevailed when Republicans decided not to put their plan to a vote. That meant continuation under federal control of several programs that Reagan wanted to shift to state responsibility.

After protracted negotiations, conferees agreed to put 19 programs together in four block grants but to leave others under federal control. The block grants were for preventive health and health services; alcohol/drug abuse and mental health services; primary health care; and maternal and child health.

The conferees kept a number of restrictions on the states' use of block grant funds. Most restrictive was the primary care block grant, which consisted solely of aid to community health centers.

Funding of the block grants was based on the fiscal 1981 appropriation for each of the separate programs, which was adjusted for inflation and then reduced by 25 percent.

Senate Action

The Senate Labor and Human Resources Committee June 10 approved a watered-down version of Reagan's block grant proposal. The move ended a weeks-long deadlock during which two Republican members sided with the Democratic minority to tie up committee action.

The committee approved two health block grants but refused to include a number of the programs Reagan wanted included. It approved cuts in funding but insisted

Reconciliation's Health Block Grants...

Following is a description of the health block grants established by Congress in PL 97-35:

Preventive Health Services

Congress authorized $95 million for fiscal 1982, $96.5 million for 1983 and $98.5 million for 1984.

Emergency Medical Services. Designed to encourage establishment of regional emergency medical systems, this program was responsible for such visible and popular health care improvements as emergency helicopters and ambulances, the 911 emergency telephone number and CPR (cardiopulmonary resuscitation) programs that trained citizens to give emergency aid to heart attack victims.

Set up in 1973 (PL 93-154) and reauthorized in 1976 (PL 94-573) and 1979 (PL 96-142), the program received $30 million in 1981 appropriations. The reconciliation bill (HR 3982 — PL 97-35) required states to continue funding grantees for one year; after that, states could decide whether to continue the program and at what level.

Health Incentive Grants. Established in 1966 and revised in 1978 (PL 95-626), this program provided grants to states for preventive health services. For fiscal 1981, $60 million was authorized. Congress originally appropriated $36 million for fiscal 1981 but later reduced that to $9 million.

Hypertension Control. In 1975 (PL 94-63) and again in 1978 (PL 95-626), Congress authorized grants to state health authorities for screening, detection, diagnosis and prevention of hypertension, particularly among high-risk and hard-to-reach populations. An estimated 60 million persons in the United States had elevated blood pressure, 35 million of them having a problem severe enough to increase their chances of death or illness from heart attack, heart failure, stroke or kidney failure. In fiscal 1981 $29 million was authorized, $20 million appropriated.

PL 97-35 required states in fiscal 1982 to spend on hypertension an amount equal to 75 percent of 1981 federal spending in the state for hypertension control; in fiscal 1983, 70 percent; 1984, 60 percent.

Rodent Control. Concerned about control of disease spread by rats and other rodents in urban areas, Congress authorized this program in 1967 (PL 90-174) at the request of President Johnson. It was reauthorized in 1978 (PL 95-626). In fiscal 1981 $17 million was authorized, $13.5 million appropriated.

Fluoridation. Authorized in 1978, this program helped communities fluoridate their water and aided fluoridation treatment provided in schools. In 1981 $5 million was authorized and appropriated.

Health Education, Risk Reduction. These programs were established in 1978 (PL 95-626). In fiscal 1981 Congress authorized $8 million for dem-onstration projects to evaluate methods of organizing and delivering comprehensive preventive health services, and $15 million to help states and localities deter smoking and the use of alcoholic beverages among children and adolescents.

Home Health Services. In 1978 (PL 95-626), Congress authorized demonstration grants to help set up new home health agencies or expand those in areas with inadequate medical services. For fiscal 1981 $15.5 million was authorized, but no funds were appropriated.

Rape Crisis Centers. The Mental Health Systems Act of 1980 (PL 96-398) set up grants for services to victims of rape, but no funds were authorized until fiscal 1982. For that year $9 million was authorized, with $12 million in both 1983 and 1984. The reconciliation bill earmarked $3 million annually for the program in fiscal 1982-84, to be distributed among the states on the basis of population.

Alcohol and Drug Abuse, Mental Health

Congress authorized $491 million in fiscal 1982, $511 million in 1983 and $532 million in 1984.

Mental Health. As part of the nationwide trend away from institutional care of the mentally ill, Congress in 1963 first provided funding to community centers designed to treat mental illness primarily on an outpatient basis. Since the program's inception, the number of institutionalized persons had dropped from 500,000 to 148,000. In contrast, more than 2.4 million persons received some type of service from mental health centers in 1980. Under the program, more than 750 local mental health centers were established; as of 1980 about 20 percent of these were no longer receiving federal support.

In 1980 Congress extended the program through fiscal 1981 (PL 96-398) but revamped it starting in fiscal 1982, when grants were to be targeted toward certain populations, such as the chronically mentally ill and the elderly. In addition, states were given more responsibility for distributing grant funds.

The reconciliation bill required states in fiscal 1982-84 to continue funding each community mental health center that received federal funds in fiscal 1981, as long as it met certain qualifications and had received federal funding for less than eight years. The same percentage of funds would have to be spent on mental health as was spent when the funds were under federal control. In fiscal 1982 this restriction would apply to 100 percent of the block grant; in fiscal 1983 to 95 percent; in fiscal 1984 to 85 percent.

Alcohol, Drug Abuse. Congress in 1970 began funding programs to help prevent and treat alcohol and drug abuse. The programs were reauthorized in 1979 (PL 96-180, PL 96-181) after Congress rejected

...Ease Federal Control of 19 Programs

President Carter's proposal to fold them into block grants along with mental health programs. In 1981 $180 million was authorized and $101 million appropriated for alcohol abuse grants. For drug abuse, $230 million was authorized, $178 million appropriated.

Of the amount allotted for the two programs, a state would have to spend 35 percent on alcoholism and 35 percent on drug abuse, with use of the remaining 30 percent up to the state. Twenty percent of a state's funds would have to be used for early intervention programs designed to discourage alcohol and drug abuse.

Primary Care Block Grants

Congress authorized $280 million for fiscal 1982, $302.5 million for fiscal 1983 and $327 million for fiscal 1984. Only one program, community health centers, was included in the block grant.

Community Health Centers. Congress first authorized grants for community health centers in 1966 (PL 89-749). In 1978 (PL 95-626) the program was extended through fiscal 1981.

The program provided grants to state and local governments and to non-profit private groups for delivery of primary health care services to medically underserved populations. In 1981 about 571 rural and 291 urban grantees participated, serving 5.2 million people. The fiscal 1981 authorization was $472 million; the appropriation was $325 million.

The reconciliation bill ensured continued federal spending for community health care by giving the program its own block grant. The transition to state control was carefully spelled out. In fiscal 1982 the federal government would continue to distribute grants and operate the program. States could ask to take over the program, but the secretary of health and human services (HHS) would have to approve the requests. If a state took over the program in fiscal 1983, it would be required to fund all of those who received grants in the previous year. The federal government would continue running the program through fiscal 1984 if a state did not request control.

Maternal and Child Health

Congress authorized $373 million in each of fiscal years 1982, 1983 and 1984. Fifteen percent of that funding in fiscal 1982 and 10 to 15 percent in fiscal 1983 and 1984 would be retained by the HHS secretary for special projects of regional and national significance, for genetic disease testing and counseling, and for hemophilia diagnostic and treatment centers.

Maternal and Child Health and Crippled Children's Services. Under Title V of the Social Security Act, Congress since 1935 had been providing funds to states to reduce infant mortality, to promote maternal and child health and to treat crippled children. To receive funds, states had to have approved allocation plans. The most recent changes were enacted in 1967 (PL 90-24). The program had a permanent $399.8 million authorization; $357.4 million was appropriated in fiscal 1981.

SSI Disabled Children. Under the Social Security Act, $30 million was authorized annually to provide services to disabled children receiving Supplemental Security Income (SSI) benefits. The fiscal 1981 appropriation was $30 million.

Lead-Based Paint Poisoning Prevention. Administered by the Centers for Disease Control, this program screened children for exposure to lead poisoning, which usually occurred when children in older homes ate chips of paint made with lead. Consumption of lead can cause blindness, seizures, mental retardation, behavioral disorders and death. The program also sought to prevent poisoning through education and identification of hazards. In 1980 about 490,000 children were screened; about 35,900 were found to have excessive amounts of lead in their systems. In fiscal 1981 $15 million was authorized; $10.8 million was appropriated.

Sudden Infant Death Syndrome. Established in 1974 (PL 93-270) as part of the Public Health Service Act, this program required the HHS secretary to develop and disseminate information related to Sudden Infant Death Syndrome — the sudden death of an apparently healthy infant. The program, authorized at $7 million and funded at $2.8 million in fiscal 1981, also provided counseling for parents. In 1980 42 projects received grants.

Hemophilia. In 1975 (PL 94-63), Congress established this program to provide grants to set up hemophilia diagnosis and treatment centers. It was reauthorized in 1978 (PL 95-626). Hemophilia is a genetic deficiency in blood clotting that is transmitted from mothers to sons. Under the Public Health Service Act, $6 million was authorized in fiscal 1981; $3.3 million was appropriated.

Genetic Diseases. Sickle cell anemia, Cooley's anemia, Tay-Sachs, cystic fibrosis and other genetic diseases were the target when Congress in 1972 (PL 92-294, PL 92-414) first authorized funding for genetic testing and counseling centers. The most recent reauthorization was in 1978 (PL 95-626). In fiscal 1981 $26 million was authorized, $16.4 million appropriated.

Adolescent Pregnancy. Though authorized as a categorical program, aid to pregnant teenagers also was made an eligible use of funds in the maternal and child health block grant. Congress established the program in 1978 (PL 95-626). In fiscal 1981 $75 million was authorized, $10 million appropriated.

on keeping some federal strings on the money. The compromise, required to win the votes of Lowell P. Weicker Jr., R-Conn., and Robert T. Stafford, R-Vt., did not please the panel's most conservative Republicans because it strayed too far from Reagan's plan.

The principal issue in the committee dispute had been over who should administer health programs. Under existing law, some programs, such as the community health center program, were run almost entirely by the Health and Human Services Department (HHS). Others were administered by state agencies, but under strict HHS regulations.

The administration wanted to give the states complete control of the programs and let them allocate funds among them as they saw fit. The only requirement would be that funds in a block grant be spent on programs within that block. But committee Democrats, joined by Weicker and Stafford, insisted the federal government had a responsibility for providing "quality health care for all Americans," as ranking Democrat Edward M. Kennedy, Mass., put it. The compromise plan provided that federal funds would be disbursed and administered by the states under contracts stipulating certain conditions.

In earlier action, the Senate Finance Committee approved May 5 a separate maternal and child health block grant as part of its reconciliation package. The Finance Committee was unwilling to lump maternal and child health programs in its jurisdiction into a block grant with programs under the jurisdiction of Labor and Human Resources.

The Senate approved both the Finance Committee block grant and the two Human Resources Committee block grants as part of its reconciliation bill (S 1377 — S Rept 97-139), passed June 25.

House Action

The House committee with jurisdiction over most health programs, Energy and Commerce, was unable to agree on a reconciliation package. So its chairman, John D. Dingell, D-Mich., forwarded a proposal backed by a majority of committee Democrats to the House Budget Committee for inclusion in the reconciliation bill.

The Energy and Commerce provisions remained in the House-passed version of HR 3982 despite House adoption June 26 of a Republican substitute for the reconciliation provisions reported by the Budget Committee June 19 (H Rept 97-158). Republicans decided not to offer Reagan's health program on the floor when they came up short of votes to win its approval.

The House bill differed sharply from the Senate measure. It consolidated 15 programs into three block grants (maternal and child health, preventive health services, alcohol and drug abuse), although it attached federal strings to the grants. It left intact separate funding for such programs as community, migrant and mental health centers, the controversial family planning program and venereal disease control.

The House cut spending for health programs, but by less than 25 percent in most cases. Mental health spending was cut 30 percent, however.

Conference Action

The conference on the huge reconciliation bill involved more than 250 members of Congress, who split up into 58 subgroups to consider various sections of the legislation.

After what Hatch called "the toughest reconciliation conference of all," conferees reached final agreement on the health block grant provisions July 28.

Although the Senate Labor and Human Resources Committee had included a number of federal strings on the administration of certain programs placed within its two block grants, conferees — at the insistence of the House — placed further restrictions on the states and set up a third program containing only the community health centers program.

(A separate set of conferees had approved the fourth health block grant, maternal and child health, July 23.)

After a lengthy and bitter dispute, the conferees decided to keep family planning as a separate categorical program run by the federal government.

As part of the compromise on family planning, Hatch won inclusion in the final reconciliation bill of a teenage sexuality program that had been reported by his committee July 21 (S 1090 — S Rept 97-161). The program, funded at $30 million a year for three years, continued an existing program, authorized in 1978 (PL 95-626), that provided pregnant teenagers with prenatal care and counseling.

But it also would fund "prevention services" to discourage sexual activity among teenagers. It contained controversial restrictions on abortion counseling and required parental consent before teenagers could participate.

Reconciliation conferees modified S 1090 to prohibit any references to abortion during counseling sessions funded under the program, unless such information was requested by the teenager and her parents. Counseling about adoption and contraception was allowed, but contraceptives could not be provided under the program unless they were not available elsewhere in a community.

The final bill also reauthorized several health programs and included radiation protection legislation that had been pushed for years by Sen. Jennings Randolph, D-W.Va.

Provisions

As signed into law Aug. 13, Title IX of HR 3982 (PL 97-35) included the following provisions:

Block Grants

Preventive Health and Health Services. Combined eight existing categorical programs into a preventive health and health services block grant. The combined programs were emergency medical services; health incentive grants; hypertension control; rodent control; fluoridation; health education and risk reduction; home health services, and rape crisis centers.

● Required that in fiscal 1982 states spend an amount equal to 75 percent of fiscal 1981 federal spending on the hypertension program. In fiscal 1983, the figure would be 70 percent, and in fiscal 1984, 60 percent.

● Earmarked $3 million a year for rape crisis centers, to be distributed among the states on the basis of population.

Alcohol/Drug Abuse, Mental Health. Combined existing alcohol abuse, drug abuse and mental health programs into a block grant.

● Required states to continue funding each community mental health center that received federal funds in fiscal 1981 as long as the center was eligible.

● Required a state to divide spending between alcohol

and drug abuse and mental health according to the same percentages used by the federal government in the state in fiscal 1980. In fiscal 1982 the restriction applied to 100 percent of funds; in fiscal 1983, 95 percent; and in fiscal 1984, 85 percent.

● Set out a formula for allocation of the share of a state's funds directed toward alcohol and drug abuse, with 35 percent required to be spent on alcohol abuse programs, 35 percent on drug abuse and the remaining 30 percent as the state chose.

Primary Care. Set up a primary care block grant consisting solely of a program to fund community health centers. The program would provide grants to government and private non-profit entities providing health care services to medically underserved populations. State responsibility was to be increased gradually.

● Provided that, starting in fiscal 1983, a state could request to take over administration of its share of the funding, subject to approval by the secretary of health and human services. Otherwise, the federal government would continue to administer the program.

● Required that states in fiscal 1983 fund all centers that received federal grants in fiscal 1982.

● Required that states provide matching funds or in-kind services in fiscal 1983 and 1984 in order to receive federal funds. The match was set at 20 percent in 1983 and 33.33 percent in 1984. No federal funds could be used for administrative expenses.

Maternal and Child Health Services. Combined seven categorical programs into a maternal and child health block grant. Eligible services under the block grant were those dealing with maternal and child health and services for crippled children, disabled children receiving Supplemental Security Income, prevention of lead-based paint poisoning, Sudden Infant Death Syndrome, hemophilia, genetic diseases and adolescent pregnancy.

● Required the HHS secretary to retain 15 percent of available funding in fiscal 1982 (and 10 to 15 percent in 1983 and 1984) for special projects of regional and national significance, genetic disease testing and counseling programs, and for hemophilia diagnostic and treatment centers.

Categorical Programs

● Reauthorized as categorical programs the childhood immunization, venereal disease control, tuberculosis prevention and control, migrant health centers, family planning and adolescent pregnancy programs.

● Added to the list of services to be provided under the adolescent pregnancy program the counseling of teenagers to discourage premarital sexual activity.

● Stipulated that of the $30 million authorized for the adolescent pregnancy program in each of fiscal years 1982-84, $10 million would be used for research and $20 million for services. No more than one-third of the latter could be used for the new sexual counseling program.

● Also reauthorized the following health programs: developmental disabilities, which provided services to handicapped persons; the National Centers for Health Services Research, Health Statistics and Health Care Technology; assistance to medical libraries; the National Research Service Awards, which provided training in biomedical research; health planning; assistance to HMOs; health manpower; and alcohol and drug abuse prevention, treatment and rehabilitation.

Radiation Safety

● Required the secretary of HHS to establish minimum accreditation standards for programs training individuals to perform radiological procedures and for certification of such persons (other than physicians, dentists and certain other practitioners). The secretary also was directed to draft a model statute setting out safe radiological procedures. States were given three years to adopt the standards and safety rules.

● Required the secretary to establish guidelines for safe radiological procedures and directed each department of the federal government to comply with the guidelines.

Medicaid, Medicare Cuts

Congress in 1981 agreed to cut projected federal spending for Medicaid by about $1 billion a year, but it rejected a Reagan administration proposal to set a rigid ceiling on the federal contribution to the state-run health care program for the poor.

The Medicaid cut and a reduction of more than $1 billion in projected spending for Medicare, the health care program for the elderly and disabled, were included in the budget reconciliation bill, cleared July 31 (HR 3982 — PL 97-35). That bill incorporated budget cuts sought by President Reagan and endorsed by Congress through its budget process. *(Reconciliation, p. 40)*

Among other changes, the bill's Medicaid and Medicare provisions modified the guarantee that Medicaid recipients be free to choose their health care providers; increased the deductibles that must be paid by Medicare beneficiaries for hospital costs and for supplementary health insurance; and continued the Professional Standards Review Organizations (PSRO) program, which Reagan wanted to abolish. Congress did eliminate the PSRO program in 1982. *(Story, p. 532)*

Despite the cuts in HR 3982, federal spending for Medicare and Medicaid continued to increase because of rising health care costs. Net Medicare costs to the federal government totaled nearly $46.6 billion in fiscal 1982, up from $39.1 billion in 1981; Medicaid costs rose to $17.4 billion from $16.9 billion.

Congress voted further cuts in 1982, 1983, and 1984. *(Stories, pp. 532, 538, 544)*

Medicaid Controversy

The ceiling on Medicaid spending was one of the most controversial and bitterly fought proposals in Reagan's fiscal 1982 budget. The administration wanted to halt continued increases in the federal government's Medicaid bill by placing a cap on the federal share of the program's funding. The federal government paid about 55 percent of Medicaid costs, the states 45 percent. Reagan proposed that in fiscal 1982 the federal government limit its spending on Medicaid to 5 percent more than it spent in 1981.

The Senate agreed to the concept, but set the cap at 9 percent. The House rejected Reagan's approach, voting instead simply to reduce the federal spending level by a given percentage each year; it reduced the amount states would otherwise be entitled to receive by 3 percent in fiscal 1982, 2 percent in 1983 and 1 percent in 1984.

The conference compromise rejected the cap but required higher percentage reductions than voted by the

House — 3 percent in 1982, 4 percent in 1983 and 4.5 percent in 1984. States could avoid the full reduction by instituting effective cost-saving measures. Also, states suffering from high unemployment could get additional federal dollars to cover persons newly eligible for Medicaid.

Legislative History

Reagan Budget. President Reagan's March 10 budget estimated federal outlays in fiscal 1982 of $47.1 billion for Medicare and $18 billion for Medicaid.

The administration originally said Medicare would be exempt from cuts because the program was part of its "social safety net." However, Reagan later proposed about $1 billion in Medicare spending reductions, to be achieved mainly by repealing new benefits enacted in 1980, which had not yet gone into effect, and by changes in hospital reimbursement policies. *(Congress and the Nation Vol. V, p. 643)*

The administration proposed to cut about $1 billion from Medicaid spending by limiting federal outlays to 5 percent more than the 1981 level — even though health care costs were expected to rise by more than 15 percent.

Senate Action. The Senate Finance Committee made significant changes in the administration's proposals May 5, when it approved a legislative savings package required under the budget reconciliation process. The new package was proposed by Chairman Robert Dole, R-Kan., and adopted with only minor changes.

The committee nearly doubled Reagan's proposed Medicare savings, cutting an estimated $1.98 billion. Among other things, it voted to raise premiums and deductibles for the optional "Part B" Medicare insurance plan (covering physicians' services), authorize civil money penalties for Medicare fraud, make Medicare the secondary payor for renal disease if an individual also had a private insurance plan covering the disease, and make changes in hospital reimbursement policies.

The biggest single "saving" was achieved by a budgetary maneuver — shifting back to the fiscal 1981 budget several weeks of Medicare payments to hospitals that Congress in 1980 had shifted to the 1982 budget.

The Finance Committee boosted Reagan's proposed cap on Medicaid spending to 9 percent from 5 percent. Then, to save money, it adopted a provision reducing the minimum federal match for state Medicaid programs to 40 percent.

Before passing its reconciliation bill (S 1377 — S Rept 97-139) June 25, the Senate adopted an amendment to keep Medicare as the primary health insurance provider for federal employees with dual coverage. The amendment was first rejected, 47-50, but later adopted, 51-47.

In an action that surprised and angered federal employee unions, the Finance Committee had voted to transfer primary responsibility for the health insurance coverage of certain federal employees and retirees from Medicare to the Federal Employee Health Benefits program. The House bill included a similar transfer provision.

House Action. The House Ways and Means Committee, which had jurisdiction over the "Part A" Medicare insurance system (covering hospital cost reimbursement), agreed May 19 to cut spending by more than $1.7 billion — about $500 million more than Reagan recommended. It adopted the larger cut so that fewer reductions would have to be made in public assistance programs to meet its reconciliation savings requirement.

Like the Senate committee, the panel made its largest "saving" by budgetary maneuvering on hospital reimbursements that, in effect, would cut spending in fiscal 1982 by pushing the expenditure back into fiscal 1981.

The House Energy and Commerce Committee, which had jurisdiction over Medicare Part B and Medicaid, was unable to agree on a reconciliation plan. Consequently, a package approved by a majority of the panel's Democratic members was included in the House reconciliation bill (HR 3982 — H Rept 97-158). The Democratic package did not include a Medicaid cap; it achieved identical savings by reducing the federal contribution to the program by 3 percent in fiscal 1982, 2 percent in 1983 and 1 percent in 1984.

Although the House June 26 adopted an administration-supported alternative to its budget reconciliation bill, the Republican measure did not include health and energy provisions. Thus the savings package drawn up by Democratic members of the Energy and Commerce Committee remained in the bill.

Conference Action. After bitter disagreement over what to do about Medicaid, reconciliation conferees finally agreed to reject a cap but to cut spending for the program by 3 percent in fiscal 1982, for an estimated saving of $920 million; 4 percent in 1983, saving $944 million; and 4.5 percent in 1984, saving $1 billion.

In other actions the conferees:

● Dropped a Senate proposal to reduce the federal Medicaid contribution to states with above-average per capita income.

● Gave states greater flexibility in applying the "freedom of choice" guarantee for selection of health care providers by Medicaid patients, but stopped short of repealing it, as the Senate bill did.

● Dropped a Senate requirement indexing premiums for the optional Part B Medicare insurance to inflation. The annual deductible was raised to $75, as in the Senate bill, however.

● Allowed the secretary of health and human services (HHS) to terminate up to 30 percent of existing PSROs by the end of fiscal 1982, but did not end the entire program, as the House bill did. Conferees also cut the federal share of the cost of operating PSROs to 75 percent, from 100 percent.

● Dropped a House provision making Medicare the secondary payor for certain federal employees and retirees covered by the Federal Employee Health Benefits Program.

● Accepted a House provision prohibiting Medicare Part B and Medicaid payments for drugs found to be ineffective or not medically necessary.

The compromise health provisions were included in the conference report on HR 3982, filed July 29 (H Rept 97-208).

Provisions

As signed into law Aug. 13, the Medicaid and Medicare provisions of HR 3982 (Title XXI of PL 97-35):

Medicaid. Reduced the Medicaid payments the states otherwise would be entitled to receive from the federal government by 3 percent in fiscal 1982, 4 percent in 1983 and 4.5 percent in 1984.

● Provided that the cut in the federal payment be reduced by one percentage point if a state had a qualified

cost review program; by one percentage point if it had an unemployment rate equal to 150 percent of the national average, and by one percentage point if the total amount of the state's recoveries for fraud and abuse was equal to 1 percent of the federal contribution to that state.

● Provided that a state could win an increase in its federal payment by holding down costs. The supplemental federal payment would be equal to the difference between actual costs and a target figure, but could not exceed the amount by which that year's federal payment had been reduced under the percentage cuts.

The target for fiscal 1982 would be to hold costs to no more than 9 percent above the fiscal 1981 level; fiscal 1983 and 1984 targets would be set by the secretary of health and human services based on the medical care expenditure category of the Consumer Price Index.

● Directed the comptroller general to report to Congress by Oct. 1, 1982, on the existing formula for determining the federal contribution to each state's Medicaid program.

● Loosened federal requirements that states opting to cover the medically needy make eligible for the coverage all medically needy persons.

Under existing law that category included individuals who were aged, blind, disabled or members of families with dependent children, who had too much income to qualify for cash assistance programs but not enough to afford medical care.

The revised rule required that coverage apply to pregnant women and that it not discriminate against home health care, but otherwise gave states more flexibility in defining "medically needy."

● Repealed the requirement that hospital reimbursement under Medicaid be based on the determination of "reasonable cost" used by the Medicare program. States still would be required to have reimbursement schedules sufficient to ensure that Medicaid patients had "reasonable access to services of adequate quality."

● Modified the provision of existing law guaranteeing freedom of choice for Medicaid recipients. The new provision allowed states to arrange through competitive bidding for laboratory services or medical devices for Medicaid patients; restrict the physicians or facilities available to recipients who overutilized services; limit participation in Medicaid by a provider who performed services not considered medically necessary or of poor quality; and implement a case-management system that could require recipients to use only certain providers.

States would have to apply to the secretary of HHS for a waiver from the freedom of choice provision in order to impose the above restrictions. A waiver would be considered granted if the secretary had not responded within 90 days with either a denial or a request for additional information.

● Authorized states, subject to approval by the secretary of HHS, to provide Medicaid coverage for certain home or community-based services.

● Repealed a requirement that states not contract with health maintenance organizations (HMOs) in which Medicaid and Medicare enrollees made up more than 50 percent of the membership. The limit was raised to 75 percent of the membership.

● Repealed a penalty of 1 percent in federal matching payments for Aid to Families with Dependent Children for states that did not meet certain performance standards for Early and Periodic Screening, Diagnosis and Treatment Services under Medicaid.

Medicare. Repealed a provision making eligible for Medicare reimbursement treatment given at alcohol detoxification facilities not connected with hospitals or clinics. The provision took effect April 1, 1981.

● Required Part A Medicare beneficiaries to pay for the first $256 of hospital costs in fiscal 1982, instead of $228 as under existing law. The deductible would be increased to $292 in fiscal 1983 and $328 in 1984. The changes were accomplished by changing from $40 to $45 the base figure used in a formula.

● Increased to $75, from $60, the deductible for participants in the optional Part B Medicare coverage of physician services, beginning in calendar year 1982.

● Repealed a provision that allowed Medicare beneficiaries to count expenses incurred in the last quarter of the previous calendar year when determining whether they had met the annual Part B deductible for the new year.

● Reduced to 5 percent, from 8.5 percent, the differential added to average routine nursing costs to cover what hospitals claimed were the higher costs of caring for elderly Medicare patients.

● Directed the secretary of HHS to issue regulations setting limits on charges for outpatient services for which hospitals could be reimbursed under Medicare and Medicaid.

● Directed the secretary to reimburse hospitals for inpatient services only to the extent that costs did not exceed 108 percent of the mean cost of providing similar services at a comparable group of hospitals.

● Set as the limit on reimbursement for home health agencies the 75th percentile, instead of the 80th, of average per-visit costs.

● Required that private health insurance held by renal dialysis patients provide primary reimbursement for the first year of dialysis services, with Medicare covering any remaining costs.

● Eliminated open enrollment for Medicare and instead allowed enrollment only between Jan. 1 and March 31.

Both Programs. Allowed federal reimbursement of costs related to the closing or conversion of under-utilized hospital facilities.

● Prohibited payment for drugs determined by the secretary of HHS to be medically ineffective.

● Required that payments be withheld from physicians or other health care providers who had refused to return earlier overpayments or cooperate in investigations.

● Authorized penalties of up to $2,000 for fraudulent claims under Medicare or Medicaid; also authorized the secretary of HHS to assess a recipient for up to twice the amount of a fraudulent claim and to bar from participation in the programs anyone found to have filed a fraudulent claim. The government would have to provide opportunity for a hearing on the matter; a determination of fraud could be appealed to the U.S. Court of Appeals in the appropriate circuit.

PSROs. Directed the secretary to assess the performance of Professional Standards Review Organizations — groups of physicians that monitored federally provided health care to determine whether the treatment was necessary and of high quality. Upon finding that a PSRO had been ineffective or inefficient, the secretary could refuse to renew the agreement providing federal funding. However, no more than 30 percent of PSROs could be terminated in fiscal 1982.

● Gave states the option of contracting with PSROs for review of Medicaid services.

Health Manpower Programs

Continuing a trend of the past several years, Congress in 1981 substantially reduced federal spending for the education of doctors, nurses and other health professionals.

It made the cuts as part of the budget reconciliation bill, cleared July 31 (HR 3982 — PL 97-35). That measure consolidated in a single package budget cuts sought by President Reagan and endorsed by Congress in the first fiscal 1982 budget resolution (H Con Res 115). *(Reconciliation, p. 40)*

Although Congress reauthorized loans and other aid for health manpower training, it provided less than half the amount spent in fiscal 1980. Total funding for the programs was set at $218.8 million for fiscal 1982, compared with more than $478 million in 1980. That amount still was almost $100 million more than Reagan had wanted to spend; he requested $125 million for the programs in 1982.

Congress went along with the administration request to end the program of "capitation grants," which had provided per-student payments to medical and nursing schools since 1971. But the president was less successful in his effort to wind down the National Health Service Corps (NHSC). Established in 1972 (PL 92-585), the program provided scholarships for the education of doctors and other health professionals who then served a year in a medically underserved area in return for each year of aid. *(Background, Congress and the Nation Vol. V, p. 652)*

Legislative History

Both the House- and Senate-passed versions of the reconciliation bill (HR 3982, S 1377) trimmed funding for health manpower training, the Senate making much deeper cuts than the House. The Senate agreed not to award new NHSC scholarships, but the House bill continued the program. The conference compromise (H Rept 97-208) authorized 550 new scholarships for each of fiscal years 1982-84.

Although the changes ended up as part of reconciliation, the Senate Labor and Human Resources Committee had reported legislation May 15 dealing with health manpower programs (S 799 — S Rept 97-124) and the NHSC (S 801 — S Rept 97-125).

As introduced by committee Chairman Orrin G. Hatch, R-Utah, S 799 would have made even deeper cuts in federal aid for medical students. But two moderate Republican members of the panel, Lowell P. Weicker Jr., Conn., and Robert T. Stafford, Vt., joined with the Democratic minority on a number of liberalizing amendments sponsored by Edward M. Kennedy, D-Mass. The final bill still reflected the bulk of Hatch's budget cuts, however.

The administration argued that health professions students could use general student aid programs just as other students did. However, the reconciliation bill also made deep cutbacks in those programs.

Provisions

As signed into law Aug. 13, Title XXVII of HR 3982 (PL 97-35):

NHSC. Reauthorized the National Health Service Corps, providing for continuation of scholarships already awarded for the education of health professionals and for 550 new awards in each of fiscal years 1982-84.

● Directed the secretary of health and human services (HHS) to re-evaluate the method used for defining areas short of health professionals. Members of the NHSC served in these "health manpower shortage areas."

● Revised rules dealing with private practice to make it more attractive for NHSC recipients to serve their required time as private practitioners rather than as members of the corps. In addition, the bill authorized subsidies to those choosing this option, such as payment of the individual's malpractice insurance or a partial income supplement.

Health Manpower. Authorized $218.8 million for health manpower programs in fiscal 1982, $238.55 million in 1983 and $249.3 million in 1984.

● Extended the Health Professions Student Loans program, which contributed to school loan funds administered by medical school financial aid officers. The ceiling on the interest rate charged was increased to 9 percent, from 7 percent.

● Extended the Health Education Assistance Loan (HEAL) program, which guaranteed loans made by private lenders to health professions students. The bill increased to $20,000 the maximum loan guaranteed in each academic year for students enrolled in schools of medicine, osteopathy, dentistry, veterinary medicine, optometry and podiatry, and increased to $12,500 the maximum available to students enrolled in schools of pharmacy, chiropractic or public health, or graduate programs in health administration or clinical psychology.

● Extended the program providing full first-year scholarships in health professions schools to students with exceptional financial need.

● Extended the program aiding medical schools in financial distress, which was directed at four schools with high enrollments of minority-group students.

● Extended funding of area health education centers (AHECs) — training programs located away from schools' major campuses and in a medically underserved area.

● Repealed the authorization for capitation grants for medical and nursing schools, but continued the program for schools of public health, with authorizations of $6.5 million in fiscal 1982, $7 million in 1983 and $7.5 million in 1984.

● Directed the HHS secretary to arrange for a study of physician supply and distribution, with the cost not to exceed $2 million.

Saccharin Ban Deferral

President Reagan Aug. 14 signed legislation (S 1278 — PL 97-42) that extended for two years, through Aug. 14, 1983, a prohibition against banning use of saccharin, the artificial sweetener that had been linked to cancer in laboratory animals. Congress approved a further two-year extension in 1983. *(Story, p. 541)*

The previous moratorium law (PL 96-273) expired June 30, but the Food and Drug Administration (FDA) had made no move to remove saccharin from the food supply, pending congressional action. *(Congress and the Nation Vol. V, p. 650)*

Both the Reagan administration and key members of Congress supported the two-year extension. Under the law, products still had to be labeled with warnings about possible risks to health from saccharin, and studies on the health effects of the substance would continue.

Drafted by Senate Labor and Human Resources Committee Chairman Orrin G. Hatch, R-Utah, S 1278 had the support of ranking minority member Edward M. Kennedy,

D-Mass. It was endorsed June 8 by Health and Human Services Secretary Richard S. Schweiker.

In the House, Henry A. Waxman, D-Calif., chairman of the Energy and Commerce Subcommittee on Health, agreed to expedite the legislation despite his reservations about the continued use of saccharin. His panel planned to undertake a thorough review of all existing food safety laws, he said.

The Labor and Human Resources Committee reported S 1278 June 19 (S Rept 97-140), and the Senate passed it by voice vote June 25. The House agreed to the Senate bill by voice vote July 31.

PHS Hospital Funding

Congress in 1981 ended federal funding of the eight hospitals and 27 clinics operated by the U.S. Public Health Service (PHS) and repealed the right of merchant seamen to free medical care — an entitlement that dated back to 1798.

The changes were made as part of the budget-cutting reconciliation bill, cleared July 31 (HR 3982 — PL 97-35). *(Reconciliation, p. 40)*

The PHS facilities originally were established to treat merchant seamen, free of charge, because of fears that they might bring communicable diseases into the country from overseas. Some 400,000 fishermen, oil rig workers, Coast Guardsmen, marine engineers, waterway operators and others also had been made eligible for free care at the facilities. In addition, the hospitals had been used to treat U.S. military personnel, Cuban and Indochinese refugees and victims of hurricanes and other natural disasters.

Many residents of communities in which the hospitals were located also relied on them for health care. Twenty-five to 30 percent of the patients at three of the hospitals — in Staten Island, N.Y., Seattle and Baltimore — were local citizens, and they and those communities vigorously fought the cutoff of federal funding. The other PHS hospitals were in Norfolk, Va.; New Orleans; San Francisco; Boston; and Nassau Bay, Texas.

At one time the PHS operated 28 hospitals in addition to its clinics. Twenty had closed over the years. Presidents since Dwight D. Eisenhower had tried to shut down all or part of the system as an economy move. Like other administrations before it, the Reagan administration argued that the free health care was unnecessary and unwarranted.

The reconciliation bill permitted transfer of the PHS hospitals to state, local or private control and authorized funding to aid in the transition or to pay the costs of shutting down the hospitals. The funding had not been requested by the administration but was added by Congress.

The bill also authorized funding to continue hospital care through fiscal 1982 for merchant seamen already under treatment.

Koop Nomination

Dr. C. Everett Koop, President Reagan's choice to be surgeon general and director of the U.S. Public Health Service (PHS), was confirmed by the Senate Nov. 16 after months of controversy. The vote was 68-24.

The Labor and Human Resources Committee had approved the nomination by an 11-5 vote Oct. 28.

As surgeon general, Koop was to head the PHS commissioned corps, an elite, quasi-military group of about 7,000 medical service personnel who staffed Indian Health Service facilities and other federal health posts, including the eight PHS hospitals until federal funding for those institutions was cut off by the 1981 budget reconciliation bill. *(Story, this page)*

Koop, a prominent Philadelphia pediatric surgeon noted for a 1977 operation to separate Siamese twins and for his outspoken anti-abortion views, had to overcome a number of obstacles in his appointment to the nation's top public health position.

Koop's nomination was delayed for months because by law the surgeon general had to be a member of the PHS commissioned corps and under the age of 64. Koop was 64 and not in the corps. *(Background, Congress and the Nation Vol. I, p. 1129)*

Congress eventually changed the requirements, through amendments to an unrelated banking bill (HR 31 — PL 97-25) and the budget reconciliation bill (HR 3982 — PL 97-35), but Koop still had to undergo close scrutiny of his views and experience.

Although his critics focused their attack on his alleged lack of experience in the public health field, it was Koop's views on abortion and other women-related issues that underlay much of the opposition to his nomination.

In speeches and writings, Koop had expressed the view that abortion could lead to a cheapening of moral standards, resulting in government persecution of religion, the killing of defective babies and euthanasia for the elderly and the ill. He also had come out against the intrauterine device (IUD), a popular birth control method, and decried the use of amniocentesis, a surgical procedure used to determine whether a fetus was defective. He blamed Planned Parenthood for increased sexual activity among teenagers and opposed test-tube conceptions.

The American Public Health Association, which represented PHS professionals, opposed Koop, as did feminist groups such as the National Organization for Women.

Koop promised at his confirmation hearings that he would not use the surgeon general's post as a "pulpit" for his anti-abortion beliefs.

Health Planning System

Although the Reagan administration called for a phase-out of the federal health planning system, Congress in 1981 decided to continue it for one year at a substantially reduced level of funding.

The reauthorization was included in the budget-cutting reconciliation bill, cleared July 31 (HR 3982 — PL 97-35). In 1982, 1983 and 1984 Congress extended the health planning program through the appropriations process, despite continuing administration efforts to abolish it. *(Reconciliation, p. 40; 1982-84 action, pp. 537, 543)*

Authorized in 1974 (PL 93-641) and last extended in 1979 (PL 96-79), the health planning program was intended to curb unneeded hospital expansions and duplication in the provision of services and purchase of major medical equipment. A hospital was required to obtain a "certificate of need" from the state before proceeding with major changes. *(Previous extension, Congress and the Nation Vol. V, p. 628)*

The program funded local planning groups, known as health systems agencies (HSAs), which were controlled by

locally selected boards made up of consumers and providers of health care. The HSAs, of which there were more than 200 in 1980, were to review any proposed expansion of health services and facilities in their areas and monitor local spending on health by the federal government. Supporters of the program contended that it helped hold down health care costs; opponents called it unnecessary federal interference.

In putting together its reconciliation package (S 1377), the Senate went along with Reagan, voting to terminate funding of the local boards in fiscal 1983. The House bill continued funding in fiscal 1982 but did not extend the program beyond that. Conferees (H Rept 97-208) authorized fiscal 1982 funding of $102 million, but did not address the question of future federal aid.

The authorization represented a substantial reduction from the fiscal 1980 funding level of $157.7 million. Total fiscal 1982 funding was $117.4 million, following an $18 million rescission of previous appropriations (HR 3512 — PL 97-12), cleared June 4.

Provisions

As signed into law Aug. 13, the health planning provisions of HR 3982 (PL 97-35, Title IX):

● Authorized $102 million for the health planning program in fiscal 1982; provided that no more than $65 million could be spent on HSAs.

● Raised the threshold of expenditures subject to review by planning agencies to $600,000 for capital outlays, from $150,000; to $400,000 for major medical equipment, from $150,000; and to $250,000 for the annual operating costs of new services, from $75,000.

● Authorized governors to ask the health and human services secretary to eliminate federal funding of HSAs in their states if they certified that state-level health planning agencies, which also received funding under the program, would take over the functions of the HSAs.

● Reduced the minimum grant for HSAs to $100,000, from $245,000, and allowed HSAs to accept contributions from health insurance companies.

● Extended for one year the deadline by which states must comply with federal planning requirements or face penalties.

Federal Aid to HMOs

Rejecting an administration proposal, Congress continued federal aid to health maintenance organizations (HMOs), which provide health service to members for fixed fees.

The budget reconciliation bill (HR 3982 — PL 97-35), cleared July 31, authorized $21 million annually in fiscal 1982-84 for grants, loans and loan guarantees to HMOs. That was less than half the amount spent in fiscal 1980. Congress had provided $43.8 million for fiscal 1981, but a rescission approved June 4 (HR 3512 — PL 97-12) reduced that to $8.8 million. *(Reconciliation, p. 40)*

HMOs had been eligible for federal subsidies since 1973. With the subsidies went federal regulation, guaranteeing members certain basic health services; there were 120 federally qualified HMOs at the end of 1980. Grants, loans and loan guarantees, last reauthorized in 1978 (PL 95-559), were to expire Sept. 30, 1981. *(Congress and the Nation Vol. V, p. 621; 1984 action, p. 551)*

Although the reauthorization was included in the reconciliation bill, committees in both houses had approved HMO bills earlier in the year.

The House Energy and Commerce Committee reported its bill May 19 (HR 3398 — H Rept 97-88). The text later was included in the House-passed reconciliation measure. The Senate Labor and Human Resources Committee reported its version May 15 (S 1029 — S Rept 97-127), but the bill never reached the Senate floor.

In addition to the $21 million annual authorization for HMOs over fiscal 1982-84, the reconciliation bill provided for funding as needed to maintain $5 million in the loan fund at the end of each fiscal year.

It also modified the requirement that HMOs base their premiums on communitywide, rather than individual, health care costs. The change would permit use of classes of individuals in rate-setting, so that higher-cost groups, such as the elderly, would have to pay higher premiums. Conferees said (H Rept 97-208) that the revised system would give HMOs "substantial new flexibility" in setting their rates.

1982

Confronted with spiraling budget deficits, an election-year Congress reluctantly agreed to a second round of cuts in the Medicare and Medicaid programs, which already had sustained substantial cuts in 1981.

As part of its 1982 deficit reduction legislation, Congress voted three-year savings of $13.3 billion in Medicare, the federal health care program for the elderly and disabled, and $1.14 billion in Medicaid, the federal-state health care program for the poor. By Reagan administration estimates, the two programs together were expected to aid nearly one out of every five Americans in 1983.

The principal 1982 cost-cutting changes established new ceilings on Medicare payments to doctors and hospitals. The bill also included several benefit expansions, which advocates said would save money over the long run by encouraging the use of less expensive forms of care.

Critics of the cost-cutting changes warned that reducing federal spending for the programs would simply shift costs onto others — hospitals, state and local governments, private insurers and the poor and elderly beneficiaries of the programs themselves. But Congress had adopted a budget resolution that required spending reductions in the programs of $13.7 billion in fiscal 1983-85, so members generally felt they had little choice but to agree to the cuts.

In other action, Congress approved administration-opposed legislation to promote the development of "orphan drugs" — drugs for diseases affecting so few people that costs of development appeared to exceed potential profits. But heavy lobbying efforts failed to win passage of a measure to establish a new research institute on arthritis within the National Institutes of Health. While reauthorizations for several health programs failed to clear before adjournment, the programs were kept alive by appropriations.

Medicaid, Medicare Cuts

Congress made numerous changes in Medicare and Medicaid in 1982, cutting projected federal spending for the programs by about $14.4 billion over fiscal 1983-85.

The cuts were included in budget reconciliation legislation cleared Aug. 19. The bill (HR 4961 — PL 97-248) cut spending and increased taxes to meet deficit reduction requirements of the fiscal 1983 budget resolution (H Con Res 115). *(Reconciliation action, p. 48)*

Medicare, the federal health care program for the elderly and disabled, accounted for $13.3 billion of the spending reductions made by the bill. Savings were estimated at $2.9 billion in fiscal 1983, $4.4 billion in 1984 and $6 billion in 1985.

Another $1.14 billion was cut from projected spending for Medicaid, the federal-state health care program for the poor. Savings in that program were estimated at $275 million in fiscal 1983, $364 million in 1984 and $502 million in 1985.

The principal cost-cutting changes made by the bill were new ceilings on Medicare payments to hospitals and doctors. The legislation also required employers to offer Medicare-eligible workers comparable coverage under their company health plans and required federal employees to pay a 1.3 percent payroll tax for Medicare coverage, a move designed to raise $2.5 billion over three years.

The bill also provided several benefit expansions, including Medicare coverage for hospice care of terminally ill patients, a new payment system to promote Medicare enrollments in the prepaid health plans known as health maintenance organizations (HMOs), and Medicaid coverage for certain disabled children kept at home rather than in a hospital.

Congress rejected several proposals to require elderly Medicare patients to pay more out of their own pockets for their care, but it did permit states to require Medicaid beneficiaries to pay nominal fees for health care services.

HR 4961 also eliminated the Professional Standards Review Organization (PSRO) program, which had survived administration repeal efforts in 1981. Instead, the bill provided for peer review of Medicare and Medicaid claims by physician review boards under contract with the Department of Health and Human Services (HHS). *(1981 action, p. 527)*

Congress already had made a number of cost-cutting changes in Medicare and Medicaid as part of the 1981 budget reconciliation bill (PL 97-35). But the fiscal 1983 budget resolution required $13.7 billion in additional cuts in the programs over fiscal 1983-85. *(1981 budget cuts, p. 527)*

Legislative History

Reagan Budget. In his Feb. 8 budget message, President Reagan asked Congress to cut nearly $3.6 billion from projected spending for Medicare and Medicaid in fiscal 1983. His legislative proposals ranged from bringing federal employees under Medicare to requiring children of institutionalized Medicaid beneficiaries to pay part of the cost of their parents' care. Another $1 billion would be cut through administrative changes not requiring legislative action, he said.

The Reagan budget, with its projected deficit of $91.5 billion, found little support in Congress. But the Senate and House took months to settle on an alternative budget strategy. Not until June 23 did Congress clear a budget resolution (S Con Res 92) establishing spending limits for the 1983 fiscal year and calling for about $125.5 billion in deficit reduction measures for fiscal 1983-85. *(Budget resolution, p. 46)*

Senate Action. Moving quickly to comply with these "reconciliation" instructions, the Senate Finance Committee voted June 24 to cut $15.2 billion from Medicare and Medicaid spending over fiscal 1983-85 — $1.5 billion more than it was required to cut. Its savings proposals became part of a reconciliation tax increase measure that the panel attached to HR 4961, a minor House-passed revenue bill. Finance reported the bill July 12 (S Rept 97-494). *(Reconciliation tax action, p. 72)*

The committee called for a major restructuring of the way the government reimbursed hospitals for Medicare patients, which would increase out-of-pocket costs for both Medicare and Medicaid recipients. The biggest new money-savers were two limits on what Medicare paid hospitals and a requirement that employers include workers over the age of 65 in company health plans, thus making Medicare the secondary payer for individuals working past the age of 65. Another major Medicare change restricted increases in physician fee payments.

The Senate passed HR 4961 early July 23 by a largely party-line vote of 50-47.

In its only major change to the spending side of the bill, the Senate unanimously adopted an amendment by Dave Durenberger, R-Minn., to restore approximately $400 million in Medicare spending over the three-year period.

House Action. The House Ways and Means Committee, which had jurisdiction over the "Part A" Medicare insurance system (covering hospital cost reimbursement), July 15 endorsed a package of reductions in the projected growth of the program in fiscal 1983-85.

The committee bill (HR 6877), approved in an unusual closed-door meeting, aimed to reduce Medicare spending by about $12 billion in fiscal 1983-85.

New restraints on payments to hospitals, similar to those in the Senate bill, were the major source of savings. The panel also called on the secretary of HHS to develop a prospective reimbursement plan for hospitals by Dec. 31, 1982, and put it into effect by July 1, 1983, unless Congress disapproved it. *(1983 action, p. 274)*

The House Energy and Commerce Committee, which had jurisdiction over Medicaid and optional "Part B" Medicare insurance (covering physicians' services), approved a short list of changes in those programs July 28 and reported the legislation Aug. 17 (HR 6877 — H Rept 97-757).

Although the budget resolution directed the Energy and Commerce Committee to reduce projected spending for Medicaid by $2.2 billion in fiscal 1983-85, the panel recommended only $683 million in Medicaid savings. The remainder of its $2.059 billion savings total came from revisions in Medicare, including two new restraints on payments to doctors.

The committee also included in its budget package a plan it had approved in 1981 (HR 3399 — H Rept 97-119) to promote enrollment of Medicare beneficiaries in HMOs.

Final Action. In an unusual procedure, the House decided July 28 to skip floor votes on the tax increase/spending cut package and go directly to conference with the Senate on HR 4961.

Senate-House conferees agreed on the least controversial Medicare-Medicaid provisions during sessions Aug. 3, 4 and 5. They accepted proposals to extend Medicare coverage to hospice care for terminally ill patients and to authorize a new payment method for Medicare beneficiaries who wanted to enroll in prepaid health plans. They also agreed to let states impose nominal co-payments on Medicaid

beneficiaries, with certain exemptions, and liens against the homes of certain institutionalized Medicaid recipients.

However, three days of deadlock over other health and welfare cuts were not broken until Aug. 12. The hang-up occurred because House Democrats wanted to restore some of the cuts made in Medicaid and welfare programs by the 1981 reconciliation bill. House conferees finally yielded after senators agreed to go along with several welfare and unemployment provisions the House supported.

In addition, the conferees inserted in the bill a provision, not included in either the Senate or House committee bills, barring HHS from implementing certain proposed changes in nursing home certification requirements for a period of six months after enactment of the bill. The conferees said the moratorium was intended to allow time for further review of the controversial regulations.

Among proposals rejected by conferees were provisions that would cap physician-fee increases, require co-payments for home health care services and increase the deductible for Medicare Part B.

The conference report (H Rept 97-760), filed Aug. 17, was approved by the House Aug. 19 by a vote of 226-207. The Senate approved it the same day, 52-47.

Provisions

As signed into law Sept. 3, HR 4961 (PL 97-248) made the following changes in the Medicare and Medicaid programs:

Medicare

Hospital Reimbursement. Established two new limits on reimbursement rates for hospitals:

1) The first change expanded an existing limit that restricted payments to a hospital for routine operating costs (bed, board and routine nursing) to no more than 108 percent of the average of such costs of similar hospitals. The new limit would apply to both routine and ancillary services, such as laboratory work or drugs, and to average costs-per-case. It would limit payment to an individual hospital to no more than 120 percent of the average for similar hospitals in fiscal 1983, 115 percent in 1984 and 110 percent in 1985 and following years.

Rural hospitals with fewer than 50 beds were exempted from the limit, and adjustments were allowed for psychiatric hospitals, those with large numbers of Medicaid, uninsured low-income and/or Medicare patients, and certain other hospitals.

2) The second limit, effective for up to three years beginning in fiscal 1983, restricted the overall annual rate of increase in a hospital's payments for operating costs, calculated on a per-case basis. Payments would be the previous year's amount, increased by the same percentage that an index of hospital wages and prices went up, plus 1 percent.

A hospital whose costs rose less in a year than the amount calculated by this formula could keep part of the difference; one whose costs rose more than the formula permitted could get one-fourth of its "excess" costs reimbursed in the first two years of the program, but none thereafter. The secretary of HHS was authorized to adjust an individual hospital's target rate up or down, for case mix or other factors.

● Permitted the secretary to calculate Medicare payments under state standards instead of the new federal limits, in states with cost control programs that met certain criteria.

● Required the HHS secretary to implement existing law to end a private-room subsidy for hospitals, create a single payment limit for nursing facilities and home health services, and end duplicate payments for outpatient services.

● Required the secretary to implement existing law on payments to hospital-based doctors, such as pathologists. The law restricted payments under Part B (physician services) to services provided directly by doctors, and required Part A (hospitalization) rates for related services, such as laboratory work, not performed directly by the doctors.

● Barred payments for services calculated on a percentage basis, as when a laboratory received a percentage of total payments to a hospital, but exempted services where percentage arrangements were customary or provided incentives for efficiency.

● Suspended payments to hospitals for the last six weeks of fiscal years 1983 and 1984, so that the payments would be made after the beginning of the following fiscal year.

● Canceled the 5 percent "differential" added to routine nursing costs to cover what hospitals and nursing facilities claimed were higher costs of caring for the elderly.

● Barred reimbursement of hospitals and skilled nursing facilities for charity care given to fulfill requirements of the Hill-Burton Act, which provided hospital construction funds.

● Prohibited Medicare reimbursement to hospitals for costs of actions taken directly to influence employees' views of unionization.

Other Reimbursement Provisions. Canceled a special reimbursement rate that paid hospital-based radiologists and pathologists 100 percent of their charges. The effect would be to treat them the same as other doctors, who received 80 percent of "reasonable" charges from Medicare (adjusted to reflect the beneficiary's annual deductible).

● Prohibited reimbursements for surgical assistants in teaching hospitals, except in unusual medical circumstances.

● Required health-care providers to pay interest on Medicare overpayments when they delayed returning these funds to the government; also required the government to pay interest on money it delayed sending to hospitals to make up for underpayments.

Federal Employee Coverage. Made federal employees eligible for Medicare coverage, and required them to pay the 1.3 percent Federal Insurance Contributions Act (FICA) tax for their coverage.

Under existing law, federal employees did not pay the tax, but about 80 percent of retired federal employees over age 65 received Medicare coverage anyway because of previous non-government employment or through their spouses.

Employer Health Plans. Required employers to offer the same health insurance coverage to 65-to-69-year-old workers and their dependents that they provided for younger workers, and made Medicare the secondary payer for those covered by a company plan. In effect, Medicare would become a supplementary insurance plan for those individuals choosing private coverage, the reverse of what existing law provided. Employees who chose not to join their employer's health plan would continue to receive their primary coverage from Medicare.

Employers with fewer than 20 employees were exempted from the provision.

HMO Enrollment. Authorized prospective payments to HMOs that enrolled Medicare beneficiaries, at rates that could be adjusted for such factors as age, sex and health status of beneficiaries; set certain conditions for plans that enrolled these beneficiaries.

Hospice Care. Authorized payments for hospice services for terminally ill patients, through Sept. 30, 1986, with some limitations, such as a 5 percent co-payment for covered drugs.

Extended Care. Authorized the HHS secretary to end a requirement that a patient must be hospitalized for at least three days to qualify for coverage of treatment in a skilled nursing facility, if the secretary determined that such a change would not increase program costs.

Ineffective Drugs. Reaffirmed a provision of the 1981 reconciliation bill that barred Medicare and Medicaid payments for drugs that had not met Food and Drug Administration standards for effectiveness.

Premiums. Stipulated that premium rates for Medicare Part B coverage should be set to ensure that premiums would cover 25 percent of program costs. Existing law provided for gradual premium rate increases, but since 1974 the proportion of program costs paid by beneficiaries, through premiums, had declined from 47 percent to about 24 percent. As of July 1, 1982, the monthly premium was $12.20; with the change made by HR 4961, premiums would be $13.70 (instead of $13.10) beginning July 1, 1983, and $15.30 (instead of $14), beginning July 1, 1984.

The existing method of calculating Part B premium rates was to resume July 1, 1985. Congress in 1984 extended the 25 percent requirement for two years. *(1984 action, p. 544)*

Merchant Seamen. Authorized eligible merchant seamen to enroll in Medicare Part B without a late-enrollment penalty, through Dec. 31, 1982. Seamen lost access to Public Health Service care in 1981, and normally would be subject to a late enrollment penalty. *(1981 action, p. 531)*

Worker Standards. Extended through Sept. 30, 1983, the HHS secretary's authority to determine the proficiency of health care workers, including those in clinical laboratories, who did not meet certain educational standards.

Audit, Medical Review. Increased by $45 million a year funding for audit and medical review activities by the fiscal intermediaries that administered Medicare.

Medicaid

● Permitted states to require Medicaid beneficiaries to pay nominal fees for medical services; exempted children, services for medical emergencies, pregnancy and family planning, patients in nursing homes, and welfare recipients enrolled in HMOs.

● Permitted states to put liens on the property of permanently institutionalized beneficiaries, to recover costs of medical services to the beneficiary, but only if the home was not needed by the patient, his dependents or certain others. Also permitted states, in certain circumstances, to deny Medicaid for a period of time to individuals who sold their homes below market prices.

● Repealed existing error rate reduction targets and instead required states to lower program error rates to 3 percent, beginning in fiscal 1983. Also delayed for six months, until mid-1983, penalties for failure to comply with error rate reduction targets.

● Stipulated that the value of an individual's burial policy would not be included in his financial assets when determining Medicaid or Supplemental Security Income (SSI) eligibility; also permitted states to exclude such assets from individual eligibility calculations for Medicaid.

● Permitted states to provide Medicaid coverage on an outpatient basis for disabled children who under existing law qualified for SSI and Medicaid only while they were in a hospital or other institution.

● Delayed for six months after enactment HHS regulations loosening survey and certification requirements for nursing homes.

● Authorized Medicaid funding for American Samoa.

Peer Review Organizations

● Repealed the existing Professional Standards Review Organization program and instead required the secretary of HHS to provide for peer review of Medicare and Medicaid claims by contracting for such reviews with organizations composed largely of practicing physicians, to be known as Provider Reimbursement Review Boards.

● Barred review contracts with organizations owned by or affiliated with providers. The intent was to prevent hospitals or other providers from reviewing their own claims.

● Exempted the peer-review organizations from the

Medicare Means Test

Congress in 1982 expressed its opposition to "any proposal to impose a 'means test' on eligibility for the Medicare program or benefits provided by the Medicare program."

The non-binding language was included in a fiscal 1983 stopgap funding resolution (H J Res 599 — PL 97-276), cleared Oct. 1. It had been added to the resolution by the Senate Sept. 29, on a 70-29 vote, and accepted by House-Senate conferees.

The action followed news reports that the Reagan administration was considering such a proposal as a way of saving money in the fiscal 1984 budget, to be submitted early in 1983.

Congressional Democrats reacted angrily to the reports, and sense-of-Congress resolutions opposing a means test were introduced in both chambers. Sponsors said limiting Medicare coverage only to persons who demonstrated financial need would profoundly alter the character of the Medicare program and would be a breach of faith with the American people.

Medicare was established in 1965 as part of the Social Security system, to provide health insurance to people over 65 and to the disabled, regardless of income. About 27 million elderly and three million disabled persons were enrolled by the mid-1980s. *(Background, Congress and the Nation Vol. II, p. 751)*

Freedom of Information Act (requiring disclosure to the public upon request). Required disclosure to an appropriate state agency, with enough information to identify a particular practitioner or institutional provider, in cases where there appeared to be a risk to the public health. Also required disclosure of specific information, on request, to federal or state agencies concerned with program fraud and abuse, and to state licensure or certification agencies.

• Barred the secretary of HHS from terminating an existing PSRO until he had contracted with a review organization to take over its functions.

• Directed the secretary to create statewide review areas by consolidating existing PSRO areas, but permitted a locality or region with a high volume of services to be treated as a separate review area.

• Empowered peer-review organizations, through fiscal intermediaries, to deny payment for services they found to be part of a pattern of "inappropriate" use, but only if the provider had been given a chance to correct the problem and had failed to do so.

• Permitted states or other entities, such as private insurers, to use the peer review organizations; authorized federal matching payments of 75 percent for reviewing Medicaid claims.

'Orphan Drugs'

Legislation to promote the development of more drugs for rare, disabling diseases cleared Congress in the closing days of the session.

The House approved the final compromise bill (HR 5238) Dec. 14, and the Senate cleared it Dec. 17, both by voice vote. Despite objections to the measure within his own administration, President Reagan signed it into law Jan. 4, 1983 (PL 97-414).

The bill was intended to encourage drug companies to invest in developing drugs for diseases such as Huntington's disease, myoclonus and others that afflicted so few people that development costs exceeded likely profits.

Sales of such "orphan drugs" could be expected to bring in $3 million to $5 million a year, compared with costs of as much as $70 million for testing a drug and bringing it through the Food and Drug Administration (FDA) approval process, according to industry spokesmen.

HR 5238 authorized tax credits and grants to promote the development of these rare-disease drugs. It also authorized seven years of exclusive marketing rights for rare-disease drugs that were not patentable. Other sections of the measure were designed to ease regulatory barriers for orphan drug approval by directing the FDA to tell a manufacturer precisely what tests it would require before granting approval to market a drug.

Treasury officials had objected to sections of the bill that would allow drug makers to claim tax credits for what they spent to test new drugs on human patients, required before a drug could be approved by the FDA.

Legislative History

The House originally passed the bill (H Rept 97-840) by voice vote Sept. 28. The Senate dropped the House-approved tax credits and substituted loans for drug development costs before approving the measure Oct. 1. The Senate also added a number of unrelated amendments, including an authorization for start-up funds for home health services and a provision requiring the Department of Health and Human Services (HHS) to develop the statistics on exposure to nuclear tests and cancer in humans exposed to fallout from the tests.

The final version of the bill retained these and other Senate-passed amendments and authorized both grants for orphan drug development and a modified version of the tax credit. The compromise was worked out informally, without a conference.

Provisions

As signed into law Jan. 4, 1983, HR 5238 (PL 97-414):

Drug Development. Authorized the secretary of health and human services, at the request of a manufacturer or sponsor, to designate drugs for treatment of a rare disease or condition — that is, one that occurred so infrequently in the United States that costs of developing the drug appeared to exceed potential profits.

• Required the secretary, at the request of the sponsor of a drug for a rare illness, to specify required clinical and non-clinical tests the drug must undergo for approval, if the secretary found the drug qualified as a rare-disease drug.

• Provided that a company winning approval to market a designated drug that was not patentable could have exclusive marketing rights for seven years after approval. However, other companies could be allowed to sell such a drug within the first seven years if the original marketer was unable to produce enough of the drug for all individuals with the disease or if the original marketer consented to sales by another company.

• Directed the secretary to encourage developers of orphan drugs to design clinical trials that would permit persons afflicted with a disease who needed the drug to join the experimental group, if there was no other drug to treat their condition.

• Established a federal Orphan Products Board, with representatives of the FDA, the National Institutes of Health (NIH) and other agencies, to promote development of drugs, biologicals and devices for rare illnesses by evaluating approval procedures, coordinating research and other activities.

• Authorized tax credits for half of a drug developer's costs in clinical (human) trials of drugs meeting the bill's criteria for designation.

• Authorized the tax credit for testing expenses paid or obligated after Dec. 31, 1982, and before Jan. 1, 1988; allowed the credit for testing done outside the United States in certain circumstances; barred the credit for investigators eligible for grants authorized by the bill.

• Permitted, in addition to the tax credit, a partial tax deduction on the expenses for which the credit could be claimed.

Home Health Care. Authorized $5 million a year in fiscal 1983-84 for grants and loans to public and non-profit private groups, and loans to for-profit groups, to pay start-up costs of establishing and operating home health programs.

• Stipulated that grants and loans should go to entities in areas without adequate home health care services, particularly areas where transportation to existing health care services was inadequate or areas with a large percentage of old, poor or disabled residents.

• Specified that, to qualify for loans, for-profit entities must be fiscally sound, must be unable to obtain a loan from non-federal lenders and must pay interest comparable

to what it cost the federal government to raise the money. Public and private non-profit groups must meet standards set by HHS to qualify for grants.

● Authorized $2 million a year in fiscal 1983-84 for grants and contracts to establish training programs for homemaker health aides; specified standards for such programs; provided that programs to train persons aged 50 or older would have high priority.

● Authorized demonstration projects to identify patients suitable for home health services.

Radiation and Cancer. Required the secretary of HHS to conduct research and develop analyses that would lead to "credible" estimates of: the risk of thyroid cancer associated with exposure to Iodine 131; individuals' exposure to Iodine 131 by fallout from nuclear bombs; and Americans' exposure to Iodine 131 by fallout from above-ground nuclear bomb tests in Nevada during the 1950s. Required a report to Congress on these activities within a year of enactment.

● Required the secretary to develop and publish, within a year of enactment, statistical tables showing the risk of cancer associated with exposure to radiation, with such variables as size of radiation dose, age at time of exposure, time elapsed between exposure and development of cancer, and other factors. Required simultaneous publication of assessments of the accuracy of the tables and formulas used to devise them.

Other Provisions. Required HHS to fund at least 10 comprehensive sickle cell disease research centers at medical schools.

● Authorized $400,000 in fiscal 1983 and $800,000 in fiscal 1984 for nurse-anesthetist training programs.

● Revised the allocation formula for alcohol, drug abuse and mental health block grants.

● Provided an extended period of patent protection for a product cleared for interstate sales by the FDA and then subjected to a stay of the regulation permitting sales, if such a stay was in effect Jan. 1, 1981. The provision was designed for Aspartame, a low-calorie sweetener.

National Institutes of Health

Congress failed to complete action in 1982 on bills to reauthorize funding for National Institutes of Health (NIH) devoted to research on cancer and heart, lung and blood diseases and to create a new national research institute on arthritis.

Arthritis sufferers and organizations representing them had mounted a strenuous lobbying campaign for a separate institute. Under the existing NIH structure, arthritis research was financed through the National Institute of Arthritis, Diabetes and Digestive and Kidney Diseases.

Advocates of a separate institute argued that arthritis research was "lost in the shuffle." Opponents, including the Reagan administration and several medical organizations, said a separate institute would be a questionable use of scarce federal health dollars.

The proposal initially met resistance from key Republicans in both the House and Senate, but as the lobbying effort grew, some skeptics either backed off or joined as cosponsors. Several decided that it would be fruitless to fight the idea.

A provision creating the new institute passed the House Sept. 30 as part of a three-year, $6.6 billion authori-

zation bill (HR 6457 — H Rept 97-791) for the National Cancer Institute and the National Heart, Lung and Blood Institute. HR 6457 also provided explicit statutory authorizations for 11 of the National Institutes of Health, which had permanent authorizations. Efforts to require the health institutes to go through the normal authorization process required of almost all other federal agencies had been a matter of controversy for several years. *(Congress and the Nation Vol. V, p. 651)*

The Senate never took up the House bill or a less costly Senate measure (S 2311 — S Rept 97-461) reauthorizing the cancer and heart-lung-blood institutes. Key senators were reluctant to debate a controversial House-passed amendment, sponsored by Rep. William E. Dannemeyer, R-Calif., that would have banned most medical research on living human fetuses.

In a last-minute effort to salvage the arthritis institute, a separate authorization (S 1939) was discharged from the Labor and Human Resources Committee and passed by the Senate Dec. 20. However, Dannemeyer objected to bringing the bill to the House floor, and the measure died.

Despite the lack of authorizations, full-year funding for the existing institutes was included in a fiscal 1983 continuing appropriations resolution (H J Res 631 — PL 97-377).

Authorizing legislation was cleared in 1984 but was vetoed by President Reagan. *(Story, p. 543)*

Alcohol, Drug Abuse Research

The 97th Congress failed to complete action on legislation reauthorizing the National Institute on Alcohol Abuse and Alcoholism and the National Institute on Drug Abuse. Both were components of the Alcohol, Drug Abuse and Mental Health Administration, itself an arm of the Department of Health and Human Services.

The House Sept. 20 passed a three-year reauthorization for the two federal research institutes (HR 6458 — H Rept 97-768). The Senate passed a two-year bill (S 2365 — S Rept 97-468) Oct. 1. A compromise version of HR 6458 was approved by the House Dec. 16, but the Senate did not take up the bill before adjournment, and the measure died.

Although the bill did not clear, funding for the institutes was included in a fiscal 1983 continuing appropriations resolution, cleared Dec. 20 (H J Res 631 — PL 97-377).

Health Planning System

As in 1981, the Reagan administration failed to end or severely limit funding for the embattled federal health planning system in 1982. The controversial program was kept alive by a fiscal 1983 continuing appropriations resolution (H J Res 631 — PL 97-377) following the failure of efforts to reauthorize it as optional block grants to the states.

The controversy over health planning continued without resolution in the next Congress. *(1981 action, p. 531; 1983-84 developments, p. 543)*

Supporters of planning, recognizing that they did not have the votes to keep the system alive in its existing form, had agreed to support the block grants idea, which was put forward by Republicans, principally Rep. Edward R. Madigan, Ill. The Republicans had no particular fondness for

the program but felt one was needed to help hold down medical cost increases, at least until the administration came up with its long-promised "pro-competition" legislation to deregulate the health care delivery system.

The House Sept. 24 passed a bill (HR 6173 — H Rept 97-784) that would have converted the health planning system into an optional block grant program with much reduced funding and powers. It also included a modified version of the program in another bill (HR 6458), approved Dec. 16, reauthorizing the federal research institutes on alcoholism and drug abuse. The Senate did not act on either bill.

The continuing resolution funded the program at the fiscal 1982 level of $64.4 million. The president had requested only $2 million.

Health Promotion

A two-year reauthorization of health information and health promotion programs (HR 6384) passed the House Sept. 13, but the Senate did not act on the measure.

The House passed the bill by voice vote under suspension of the rules, a procedure that barred floor amendments and required a two-thirds vote for passage. The Energy and Commerce Committee had reported it Aug. 19 (H Rept 97-767).

The existing authorization for the programs, included in a 1979 nurse training bill (PL 96-76), expired Sept. 30. *(Congress and the Nation Vol. V, p. 635)*

HR 6384 authorized $8 million in fiscal 1983 and $9 million in 1984 for grants and contracts to foster research and programs dealing with health information and health promotion, preventive health services and "education in the appropriate use of health care." The funds would be in addition to money appropriated under the preventive health and health services block grant to the states, approved by Congress as part of the 1981 budget reconciliation bill (PL 97-35). *(Story, p. 523)*

In the Senate, an omnibus health programs extension bill (S 2311 — S Rept 97-461) was reported by the Labor and Human Resources Committee May 28 but was never brought to the floor.

Despite the failure of the authorization bills to clear, the various health programs were funded by a fiscal 1983 continuing appropriations resolution cleared by Congress Dec. 20 (H J Res 631 — PL 97-377).

FTC Regulation of Doctors

Despite an intense lobbying campaign by the American Medical Association (AMA), legislation exempting doctors and other professionals from regulation by the Federal Trade Commission (FTC) did not clear Congress in 1982. The House approved an exemption as part of an FTC authorization measure, but opponents succeeded in blocking Senate action on that measure and stalling action on funding for the agency.

The issue was resolved, temporarily at least, in the early hours of Dec. 17 when the Senate staved off efforts to add an exemption for professionals from a continuing appropriations resolution (H J Res 631). The Senate acted on a **59-37 key vote (R 31-21; D 28-16)**. *(1982 key votes, p. 895; details of action on FTC authorization, p. 274)*

1983

Congress moved quickly in 1983 to significantly change the way the Medicare program paid for hospital care for elderly and disabled patients. Legislation cleared March 25 established a policy of paying "fixed prices" for specific treatments, replacing the existing system of generally paying whatever the hospital said patient care cost. The largely untested new method, put forward by the Reagan administration, was intended to help stem inflation of health care costs by forcing hospitals to carefully budget the use of their resources.

However, the change did not address the larger question of the threat of bankruptcy of the Hospital Insurance Trust Fund. In early 1983 the Congressional Budget Office estimated that the fund, which paid for the hospitalization of Medicare beneficiaries, could run out of money as early as 1987. At the end of the year Congress had discussed the issue in broad terms but had not developed an answer to the question of how much the nation should pay for the medical care of the elderly and disabled. *(Bankruptcy issue, p. 521)*

In addition to the new Medicare payment plan, the president's fiscal 1984 budget included a long-promised initiative to stem increases in the cost of health care by promoting more competition. There were no surprises: Academic economists had, for years, been recommending the concepts that showed up in the budget.

Reagan's overall goal was to increase the amount that citizens paid out-of-pocket for medical care. Advocates argued that if Americans were more conscious of the high costs of medical care, they more frequently would use organized medical services, which were said to be thrifty in their use of expensive procedures. None of the proposals received much attention from Congress in 1983.

Early in the year, when the unemployment rate stood at double-digit highs, the notion of providing health insurance for the unemployed gained impressive support from both Democrats and prominent Republicans. Reagan administration officials agreed to go along, although they stipulated that Congress had to provide a way to pay for it. That stipulation became one of several major stumbling blocks to enactment. The House approved a bill but the proposal never reached the Senate floor.

Medicare Cuts

Congress enacted a fundamental change in Medicare, the federal health care program for the elderly and disabled, as part of a major Social Security bill cleared March 25.

The 1983 law (HR 1900 — PL 98-21) authorized a largely untested new method of calculating Medicare payments to hospitals. When Congress acted, the program was paying, within certain limits, what each hospital said it cost to treat Medicare patients. The new method instead fixed payment rates for treatment of each of more than 400 medical conditions.

Faced with a forecast that the Medicare program could go bankrupt within four years, Congress moved with exceptional speed. The administration first sent the new Medicare plan to Congress in late December 1982 and produced

a detailed legislative proposal in February 1983. The plan was rushed through Congress on a fast track, coupled with the "must" Social Security bill, and was signed into law April 20.

The Medicare payment reform did not, in itself, end the threat of bankruptcy for Medicare's Hospital Insurance (HI) Trust Fund, but it was expected to give hospitals time and incentives to improve their management before Congress overhauled the entire program.

In ordering a "prospective" reimbursement system, Congress was asking for a method that would let the government determine, in advance, how much the program would pay each year to hospitals for treating Medicare patients.

Advocates of the change said the old system, which paid hospitals for their costs after services were rendered, inflated medical costs because its financial incentives fostered the wasteful overuse of treatments and procedures, instead of discouraging their use. They also claimed that Medicare inflation played a major role in driving up the costs of health care nationally.

Skeptics warned that the new system could create powerful financial incentives for hospitals to withhold needed medical treatment from patients, or to extract more money from Medicare by deceptive billing or unnecessary hospitalizations.

In addition to the new payment plan, other attempts were made in 1983 to cut Medicare costs. To meet budget reconciliation requirements House and Senate committees also readied a series of relatively modest money-saving changes in Medicare — including a temporary freeze on physician fees with controversial restrictions to keep doctors from passing on more costs to patients. Neither chamber completed action on its reconciliation bill in 1983 but the fee freeze and other changes in Medicare were enacted in 1984 as part of a deficit reduction package (HR 4170 — PL 98-369). (Details, p. 56)

Congress also enacted legislation cutting Medicare costs in 1981 and 1982. (Previous action, pp. 527, 532)

Background

The Congressional Budget Office (CBO) estimated in February 1983 that the HI trust fund, which financed hospitalization of Medicare beneficiaries, would run out of money as early as 1987. The basic problem, CBO said, was that the cost of hospital care was rising faster than the federal taxes that replenished the fund. (Latest estimates, pp. 521, 544)

Health experts blamed health care cost increases on a number of factors, including simple price inflation and the aging of the population. But many thought the most important cause of rising health costs was the ever-increasing number and sophistication of treatments — surgical and medical — that ailing Americans, including Medicare beneficiaries, were receiving.

In 1982 the cost of health care rose by 11 percent, nearly three times the 3.9 percent general increase in consumer prices for the year.

Congress had laid the tracks for the Medicare payment change in August 1982 when it passed a major tax bill (PL 97-248) that included two stringent new limits on Medicare payment rates for hospitals. Sponsors assumed that the limits, together with the existing system of calculating Medicare payments to hospitals, would be promptly replaced by a new payment method. The tax bill also ordered

the Health and Human Services Department (HHS) to design and send Congress a new "prospective" payment system for Medicare within five months.

The 1982 limits were intended to save the federal government money, but they had clear political impact as well. Hospital groups said the harsh new limits were insensitive to legitimate differences among hospitals in operating costs. The limits made the payment-by-diagnosis plan appear to be a comparatively attractive alternative.

The new plan thus had the support of major segments of the hospital industry, including the American Hospital Association and the Federation of American Hospitals, as well as of the administration and such key members of Congress as House Ways and Means Committee Chairman Dan Rostenkowski, D-Ill., and Senate Finance Committee Chairman Robert Dole, R-Kan. Other groups, such as the American Medical Association and the Blue Cross and Blue Shield Associations, were critical of the plan but did not actively oppose it.

Opposition from hospital groups had defeated a major Carter administration hospital cost control bill in 1979. (Congress and the Nation Vol. V, p. 630)

Legislative History

On Dec. 28, 1982, HHS sent Congress its "prospective" plan that called for standard prices for treating medical conditions in Medicare patients.

The HHS report outlined a method of using hospital medical and financial data to assign an average cost, or price, for treating each of 467 "diagnosis related groups" (DRGs). It did not say what the prices would be, but the goal of the plan was to hold overall Medicare expenditures to the same level as that resulting from the 1982 tax law limits. The plan allowed only a few adjustments in the national "prices" to be paid by Medicare.

The administration produced its detailed legislative proposal (HR 1705) on Feb. 22, 1983. Just two days later the House Ways and Means Health Subcommittee amended and approved the plan. The full committee approved it on March 2.

The committee reported its Medicare plan March 4 (H Rept 98-25) and sent it to the House floor as part of the Social Security bill (HR 1900), under a rule permitting no amendments to the Medicare section. The House passed HR 1900 March 9, 282-148.

The House version included changes that gave hospitals more grounds to claim special treatment in the new system, and states more latitude to depart from the DRG methodology.

The Senate Finance Committee reported a similar measure March 11 (S 1 — S Rept 98-23). S 1's Medicare provisions were generally the same as those in the House bill.

The Senate passed its version March 23 by a vote of 88-9, after adopting an amendment that expanded exceptions from the Medicare payment plan to include certain rural hospitals and large regional and national referral centers.

Both the House and Senate versions followed the administration's plan of set prices for inpatient treatment of different illnesses, and prohibited charging individual patients more than the set price. The two bills substituted a four-year phase-in of the new payment method for the Oct. 1 effective date suggested by the administration. Both required separate rates for urban and rural hospitals, and for

Efforts to Ban or Limit Abortion Continue

Abortion remained a divisive issue in the 97th and 98th Congresses, as it had in every Congress since the Supreme Court in 1973 handed down its decision legalizing abortion.

Although foes of abortion made several attempts to overturn the Supreme Court ruling, all such efforts failed, as they had in previous years. However, Congress continued to include in various appropriations bills restrictions on the use of federal funds for abortions. Two programs particularly caught up in the abortion controversy in the 1981-84 period were Medicaid, the federal-state health insurance program for the poor, and federal employee health insurance. *(Anti-abortion legislation, p. 690)*

President Reagan supported the efforts of abortion foes by championing a constitutional amendment and bills to outlaw abortion. But Reagan gave little encouragement to federal programs to deter unwanted pregnancies or provide pregnant women alternatives to abortion.

As soon as he took office in 1981, the president sought cuts in the government's three main programs related to pregnancy prevention and assistance for pregnant women.

Aside from a desire to reduce the budget, part of the reason, according to administration officials, was profound discomfort with government involvement in family planning programs. Some of Reagan's staunchest supporters believed the government should have no role in providing services or information on sex education or contraception.

Congress refused to go along with Reagan's cuts in two of the three programs that provided alternatives to abortion. But the president in 1981 was successful in cutting by almost one-fourth the money available for the government's major family planning program, Title X of the Public Health Service Act of 1970.

While funding for Title X increased after that 1981 cut, it had not yet reached the level in 1984 that it was at in President Carter's last year in office.

Two new federal initiatives related to abortion alternatives were proposed, neither by the administration. One was the Adolescent Family Life Program. Established in 1981, the program was spending nearly $15 million in fiscal 1985 on 59 demonstration projects to discourage teenagers from engaging in sexual activity, while encouraging those who did become pregnant to carry their pregnancies to term.

No abortion counseling was allowed. But this provision, along with another that encouraged religious organizations to apply for grants, resulted in a lawsuit challenging the constitutionality of the entire program.

The other initiative, enacted in 1984, was a modification of Medicaid to require state coverage for first-time pregnant women. Known as the Child Health Assurance Program (CHAP), it was the result of a compromise between congressional opponents and supporters of abortion. *(CHAP, p. 546)*

---

different regions. And both departed from the administration proposal by mandating that hospital admission patterns and other factors be reviewed to guard against costly manipulations of the new system, or poor care for patients.

House and Senate conferees agreed to the final shape of HR 1900 during a 12-hour session March 24, as colleagues waited impatiently to leave for the Easter recess. The primary points of disagreement were over Social Security issues, not the Medicare plan.

The House adopted the conference report (H Rept 98-47) March 24 by a 243-102 vote. The Senate gave its final approval, 58-14, in the early morning hours of March 25, clearing the bill for the president.

Provisions

As signed into law April 20, the Medicare provisions of HR 1900 (PL 98-21):

● Replaced the existing Medicare hospitalization ("Part A") cost reimbursement system with one in which inpatient hospital operating costs were determined in advance and paid on a per-case basis, according to rates established for specific medical conditions or combinations of conditions (known as "diagnosis related groups," or DRGs).

The rates were to be derived from existing Medicare data, updated to reflect hospital cost increases in fiscal 1983, and updated again in fiscal 1984 and 1985, to reflect cost increases plus 1 percent. The bill specified that for those two years the system would be "budget neutral" — that is, total expenditures under it would be the same as they would have been under the existing reimbursement system with the spending limits enacted as part of the 1982 Tax Equity and Fiscal Responsibility Act.

● Required the secretary of HHS, in consultation with an advisory group of experts established by the bill, to decide annually, beginning in fiscal 1986, whether rate adjustments were needed; also required the secretary, with the advice of the group, to readjust the basic DRG classifications in fiscal 1986 and at least every four years thereafter to reflect changing treatment patterns and other factors.

● Generally barred hospitals from billing patients for more than the Medicare DRG payment, except for co-payments required by existing law.

● Authorized the secretary, for the first three years after enactment, to let a hospital continue billing the non-hospitalization Medicare plan ("Part B") for inpatient services, but only if the hospital had used such billing so

extensively that immediate compliance with the new law would be disruptive, and if the payments were deducted from the hospital's DRG payments.

● Required DRG adjustments to reflect a hospital's additional costs from being required to join the Social Security system; also, repealed a reduction in Medicare payment rates for a hospital leaving Social Security.

● Excluded from DRG calculations hospital capital costs (for financing construction, major equipment purchases and similar expenses); also excluded a special Medicare payment for interest ("net return on equity") to investor-owned (for-profit) hospitals.

Both exclusions were to continue until Oct. 1, 1986. Until then these costs were to be paid under the existing reimbursement system except that the equity payment rate was reduced from 150 percent of the investment return of the Medicare Health Insurance fund to 100 percent of that return. (At the time the bill cleared, this meant a reduction to 12 percent, from 18 percent.)

● Excluded from the DRG a hospital's direct teaching expenses, such as interns' salaries, meaning that these expenses continued to be reimbursed under the existing cost-based system. The bill also provided for DRG payment for indirect educational expenses, at double the rate of the existing system.

● Provided for adjustments in the basic DRG rates to reflect regional differences in labor costs; also provided for separate DRG payment rates for urban and rural hospitals and, for the first three years after enactment, separate DRG rates in each of the nation's nine census divisions.

● Provided for a three-year phase-in of the program, with an increasing portion of-hospital costs paid under the new system until DRGs covered 100 percent of hospital costs in the fourth year.

● Required the secretary of HHS to continue the existing hospital cost-reporting system until at least the end of fiscal 1988.

● Required payments in addition to the DRG rate for atypical cases with higher costs because of exceptionally long hospital stays or other reasons.

● Exempted from the DRG system psychiatric, long-term care and children's hospitals and psychiatric and rehabilitation units of acute-care hospitals.

● Required the secretary to provide exceptions or adjustments for: hospitals serving as sole sources of care in a community; public or other hospitals serving a disproportionately large number of low-income or Medicare patients; hospitals serving as regional or national referral centers; hospitals involved in cancer treatment and research; and hospitals in Hawaii and Alaska.

● Required hospitals, as a condition for receiving Medicare payments, to contract by Oct. 1, 1984, with federally designated peer review organizations for reviews of quality of care, appropriateness of admissions, validity of diagnostic information provided by the hospital and other factors. It authorized payment for review activities, as needed, from Medicare Part A funds.

● Authorized certain payment options, if requested, for prepaid health plans such as health maintenance organizations (HMOs).

● Continued authority for Medicare demonstration projects and for different Medicare payments in state hospital cost control programs that met certain criteria; barred the secretary from requiring that the state programs be based on DRGs or that they produce a rate of cost increase lower than national rates; required the secretary to permit state programs to continue as long as they met specified criteria and to make a decision within 60 days on whether to approve new state programs, which would have to meet certain new standards; permitted the secretary to reduce payments to hospitals in a state with a cost control system if the secretary determined that amounts paid for three years for Medicare hospitalizations were higher than they would have been under the national DRG system.

● Continued most existing authority for administrative and judicial review of Medicare payment decisions, but excluded DRG payment rates and classifications from review.

● Required the secretary to study and report to Congress on: inclusion of capital and equity costs in the DRG system; the impact of hospital prospective payment systems on skilled nursing facilities and on other providers, and the feasibility of applying DRGs to nursing facilities; the impact of the DRG system — to be reported each year from 1984 through 1987 — on individual hospitals, classes of hospitals, beneficiaries and other entities, such as private insurers, that paid hospitals; physician fees for inpatient care and the feasibility of including them in the DRG system; the feasibility of including exempted hospitals in the DRG system; the impact of different state systems.

● Barred Medicare payments after three years for new capital projects unless approved by state "1122" review programs.

Saccharin Ban Deferral

Congress in 1983 extended for two years a qualified ban on government action against saccharin, the artificial sweetener linked in controversial research to cancer in laboratory animals.

It was the third extension of the prohibition since Congress in 1977 blocked the Food and Drug Administration (FDA) from barring the use of the non-caloric sweetener in the nation's food supply. *(Congress and the Nation Vol. V, pp. 612, 650)*

The bill (S 89 — PL 98-22) simply changed the expiration date of the moratorium on FDA action against saccharin, extending it for two years from the date of enactment. The existing law (PL 97-42) was due to expire Aug. 14, 1983. *(1981 extension, p. 530)*

S 89 left intact requirements that saccharin-sweetened products, and stores selling them, display health warnings. It also continued authority for studies of the health effects of the substance.

Senate Labor and Human Resources Chairman Orrin G. Hatch, R-Utah, sponsor of the legislation, pointed out that the measure did not bar the FDA from acting "should information become available demonstrating a public health risk from continued use of saccharin." He noted that new information could be produced from two large-scale animal studies that were in progress at that time.

Hatch's committee reported S 89 March 23 (S Rept 98-32), and the Senate passed it April 5 by voice vote without debate. The House approved it by voice vote April 13.

Alcohol, Drug Abuse Research

Congress in 1983 approved a two-year authorization for the federal research and information programs on alcoholism and drug abuse.

The legislation (S 126 — PL 98-24) authorized $33.5 million in fiscal 1983 and $45.8 million in fiscal 1984 for research and other activities of the National Institute on Alcohol Abuse and Alcoholism, plus $47.4 million in 1983 and $56.2 million in 1984 for activities of the National Institute on Drug Abuse.

The Senate passed S 126 (S Rept 98-29) April 5 and the House passed it April 13, both by voice vote.

S 126 was similar to a bill that failed to win final approval during the 97th Congress. *(Details, p. 537)*

Health Emergency Fund

A new $30 million fund to help federal agencies deal quickly with health emergencies was enacted in 1983.

The measure (HR 2713 — PL 98-49) established a revolving fund and authorized $30 million for fiscal 1984 and such sums as necessary each year thereafter to bring the fund back to that level.

The money was intended to let such agencies as the Centers for Disease Control and the National Institutes of Health respond to public health emergencies without diverting funds from their other programs. The legislation was a response particularly to the outbreak of acquired immune deficiency syndrome (AIDS) and the 1982 cyanide contamination of Tylenol.

The bill was enacted despite the objections of Health and Human Services Secretary Margaret M. Heckler, who had said that, in the case of AIDS, the extra funds were unneeded. But her predecessor, Richard S. Schweiker, had proposed a $20 million fund.

The House passed HR 2713 (H Rept 98-143) by voice vote June 13 and the Senate approved it by voice vote June 28.

Hospice Payments

Congress in 1983 approved legislation (HR 3677 — PL 98-90) permitting hospices, which provided home health care and related services for terminally ill patients, to receive up to $6,500 per Medicare patient for such care.

Medicare payments for hospice care had been authorized in 1982 legislation (PL 97-248), but sponsors said that because of a technical error in that bill, the payments would be capped at a much lower rate — about $4,200 per case — than Congress had intended. The low payment rate would not cover costs of care and terminally ill Medicare patients were likely to use more expensive hospital or nursing home care instead, they said. *(1982 legislation, p. 532)*

The House passed HR 3677 (H Rept 98-333) Aug. 1 by voice vote. The Senate cleared it by voice vote Aug. 3.

Jobless Health Insurance

Despite early support from prominent Republicans and Democrats in both houses, legislation creating new publicly financed health insurance programs for unemployed Americans did not become law in 1983.

The House Aug. 3 approved a $4 billion plan (HR 3021), and the Senate Finance and Labor and Human Resources committees each reported more limited versions (S 951 — S Rept 98-193; S 242 — S Rept 98-181), but the legislation did not come to the Senate floor.

Reagan administration officials reluctantly had agreed to accept the new health insurance program, but only if Congress also explicitly provided a way to pay for it.

That stipulation became one of the major stumbling blocks to enactment. By mid-summer, momentum for the bill slowed as sponsors disagreed sharply among themselves about how to finance the new program.

Other conflicts were less visible but equally important in the failure of the bill. Some liberals privately worried about creating a new program at the same time that impoverished Americans were being excluded from Medicaid because of budget reductions. Conservative opponents argued that the deficit did not permit any new programs. And, although the program in the House bill was meant only to last through fiscal 1985, critics predicted that it would be difficult or impossible to keep it from continuing indefinitely.

Many of the objections surfaced in the House debate on the bill in August. By fall, the tide had turned against enactment. Unemployment statistics had improved and Congress was struggling unsuccessfully to pass omnibus budget-cutting legislation that some sponsors had hoped would include the insurance plan. There were strong objections in the Senate to a tax provision meant to provide funds for the insurance program, and sponsors repeatedly failed to persuade the Senate to include start-up funds for the program in all-purpose appropriations bills.

Background

At the time Congress began considering the legislation, most American workers with health insurance were covered by employment-based group policies, financed partially or entirely by the employer. Such coverage often continued for a short period after a worker left a job, but experts estimated that about 60 percent of group-insured workers lost coverage within 30 days after their jobs ended.

Congressional hearings began in January 1983, when unemployment stood at a 41-year high of 10.7 percent and affected both goods-producing and service industries.

Of the 12 million unemployed, 2.6 million had been out of work for 27 weeks or longer. The Congressional Budget Office (CBO) estimated that by December 1982 approximately 10.7 million Americans had lost employer-based group health coverage because of unemployment. By June CBO was estimating that in fiscal 1984, 9.6 million persons would be without job-related health benefits. When their dependents were included in the count, some 19.1 million Americans would be uninsured, according to CBO.

Witnesses reported that hospitals and physicians in some regions of the country were turning away uninsured patients or requiring cash deposits before they would treat them.

The last time health insurance for the unemployed came before Congress was in 1975, when unemployment reached 8.5 percent. That year House and Senate committees approved legislation but became embroiled in disputes over jurisdiction and other matters. Those disputes reflected underlying concerns about setting precedents for national health insurance. *(Congress and the Nation Vol. IV, p. 353)*

Legislative History

The House Energy and Commerce Committee June 7 reported HR 3021 (H Rept 98-236, Part I) authorizing

through fiscal 1985 a state-administered entitlement program, guaranteeing a specified package of medical benefits to all eligible laid-off workers. The measure also included new permanent standards for private employer-based group health insurance plans and authorized grants to hospitals in areas of high unemployment and many non-paying patients.

HR 3021 did not include a funding mechanism. Sponsors maintained that preliminary congressional decisions to allot funds for the program in the fiscal 1984 budget resolution (H Con Res 91) meant that Congress had decided to fund the plan out of general revenues. H Con Res 91, which cleared June 23, assumed spending of $4 billion in fiscal 1983-85 for the insurance program, with the funding contingent upon enactment of authorizing legislation. *(Budget resolution, p. 51)*

The House Ways and Means Committee June 30 reported its version of HR 3021 (H Rept 98-236, Part II), which replaced the entitlement program with a block grant insurance plan. It was the Ways and Means version that came to the floor and was passed with minor change by the House Aug. 3 by a 252-174 vote. The bill authorized $3.757 million for fiscal 1983-85 block grants to the states and $233 million for fiscal 1984-86 grants to hospitals.

The Senate Labor and Human Resources Committee July 14 reported a jobless health insurance plan as part of a bill to aid dislocated workers (S 242 — S Rept 98-181). The insurance plan called for a program of block grants to states and required changes in private, group-based health insurance. The bill, which authorized a total of $1.8 billion for fiscal 1983-85 block grants, made availability of the money contingent on enactment of a separate revenue-raising bill to fund the program. There was no further action on the bill.

The Senate Finance Committee July 25 reported another $1.8 billion block grant insurance plan (S 951 — S Rept 98-193). S 951, however, unlike the other bills, provided a source of funds for the program: two money-saving changes in Medicare, the federal medical program for the elderly.

Because of strong disputes over the proposed Medicare cuts, the Finance Committee agreed to substitute a change in income-averaging rules for federal taxes. But that plan drew filibuster threats from conservatives and the legislation did not come to the Senate floor.

Medicaid Child Health Plan

Both the House Energy and Commerce Committee and the Senate Finance Committee in 1983 approved proposals to establish a Child Health Assurance Program (CHAP).

However, neither chamber passed the legislation, which would open Medicaid to more impoverished women during pregnancy, and to young children.

A CHAP proposal was enacted in 1984 as part of a tax increase/spending cut measure (HR 4170 — PL 98-369). *(1983-84 action, p. 546)*

National Institutes of Health

The House in 1983 passed a compromise three-year reauthorization (HR 2350) for biomedical research programs, including authority for new institutes devoted to

arthritis and related diseases, and nursing. Opponents in a bitter fight over setting National Institutes of Health (NIH) research priorities had resolved their differences and crafted the compromise that the House approved Nov. 17. A four-year bill (S 773) with lower authorization levels was reported in the Senate but did not come to the floor.

Congress in 1984 cleared an NIH authorization bill (S 540), but the legislation was vetoed by President Reagan, who was opposed to new institutes on arthritis and nursing. *(1983-84 details, p. 550)*

Cigarette Warning Labels

Foes of smoking made some headway in 1983 when the Senate Labor and Human Resources Committee reported a bill (S 772) mandating a tough new health warning label for cigarettes.

The House Energy and Commerce Subcommittee on Health endorsed a different version requiring a series of stiff new warnings, to be rotated on cigarette packages and advertisements so as to catch smokers' attention.

Legislation requiring four rotating warnings for cigarette packages and advertisements was enacted in 1984. *(1983-84 action, p. 548)*

Health Planning System

A multi-year struggle over whether to continue a much-criticized health regulatory system continued in 1983, but with little overt activity and with no resolution.

A bill reauthorizing the federal health planning program for three years, with substantial changes in policy, was reported May 24 by the House Energy and Commerce Committee (HR 2934 — H Rept 98-218). But no further action occurred, and the planning program was simply continued for a year at the existing funding level by the fiscal 1984 continuing appropriations resolution (PL 98-151).

Since 1981 the Reagan administration had sought to end health planning altogether. But even conservative supporters of the administration became reluctant to scrap planning without some alternative to control costs, such as competition among medical providers.

In 1981 Congress declined to end health planning, but it substantially reduced funding as part of the budget-cutting reconciliation legislation (PL 97-35). In 1982 the House twice passed planning reauthorizations, with policy changes, but the Senate did not act. The program was given a second one-year extension by the fiscal 1983 continuing resolution (PL 97-377). *(Previous action, pp. 531, 537)*

In 1984 $79 million for health planning was included in the fiscal 1985 continuing appropriations resolution (PL 98-473) since the program still had not been reauthorized.

1984

Medicare, the federal health program for the elderly and disabled, continued to be at the top of the health legislation agenda. After enacting new controls on hospital payments by Medicare in 1983, Congress in 1984 approved

a second major Reagan-era control, a temporary freeze on Medicare payment rates to doctors. Congress amended the freeze proposal to prevent doctors from raising their fees during the freeze and passing higher costs on directly to their patients. Congress also approved an increase in out-of-pocket costs for Medicare recipients and a limit on the rate of increase in Medicare payments to hospitals.

But neither the 1984 changes nor Medicare savings measures enacted in previous years were considered adequate to stave off bankruptcy in Medicare's Hospital Insurance (HI) Trust Fund. Most members considered the actions required to save the program — deep benefit cuts, large tax increases or both — too difficult to address during an election year. When questioned as to whether election-year politics accounted for its relatively mild attack on Medicare costs, the administration responded that HI bankruptcy did not appear as imminent as previously feared. *(Bankruptcy issue, p. 521)*

In other 1984 action, Congress approved a new health initiative, the Child Health Assurance Program (CHAP). The new program, requiring that more low-income pregnant women and more young children be covered by Medicaid, had the support of both liberal and conservative members, who considered it prudent spending that would avoid far greater costs later.

Landmark legislation aimed at making many more inexpensive "generic" versions of brand-name drugs available to consumers also was enacted. Passage came after a year of difficult negotiations among brand-name drug manufacturers, "generic" drug companies and consumer groups.

Other health legislation passed in 1984 included a measure requiring sharp new health warnings for cigarette packages and advertisements and a bill meant to ease logistical problems associated with organ transplant surgery.

Two major health bills were vetoed by President Reagan. One would have created new research institutes on arthritis and nursing, and reauthorized selected medical research programs. The second would have continued community health programs and subsidies for training health professionals.

Although the president cited cost in his veto messages, he stressed policy disagreements with Congress.

Medicare Cuts

Having imposed new out-of-pocket costs on Medicare beneficiaries and clamped new spending controls on hospitals in previous years, Congress in 1984 ordered a temporary halt to increases in Medicare payment rates for doctors.

The fee freeze and other changes in Medicare, the nation's health program for the elderly and disabled, made up the largest spending reductions included in a multi-part deficit reduction package (HR 4170 — PL 98-369) cleared by Congress in June. *(Deficit reduction, p. 56)*

The fee freeze extended to October 1985. In addition, the bill established a controversial "assignment" program intended to keep doctors from simply passing on cost increases to patients during the freeze. Participation in the program was to be voluntary, but Congress enacted financial penalties for doctors who stayed out of the program. Those two provisions were estimated to make savings of $2.2 billion.

Another $1.2 billion in savings was expected from the bill's provisions increasing out-of-pocket costs for beneficiaries of Medicare.

The legislation also limited the rate of increase in Medicare payments to hospitals for fiscal 1985 and 1986. The provision applied both to the limits passed by Congress in 1982 to increase payments to hospitals for overall costs of caring for beneficiaries and to the 1983 system that established flat rates of payment per illness. The estimated savings were $1.1 billion. *(Previous action, pp. 532, 538)*

1983 Action

House and Senate committees in 1983 included in their budget reconciliation proposals several changes in Medicare costs, including a temporary freeze on doctors' fees. But the reconciliation bills were not passed in 1983.

Reagan Budget. President Reagan in his fiscal 1984 budget proposed a new Medicare payment plan, which Congress enacted in 1983.

In addition to this fundamental change in Medicare, Reagan proposed that Medicare beneficiaries pay substantially more out of their own pockets for short-term hospital stays, while at the same time a ceiling would be placed on out-of-pocket expenditures for "catastrophic" costs of lengthy hospitalizations. He also proposed that beneficiaries pay higher premiums for non-hospital (Part B) coverage; doctors accept a one-year freeze on increases in Medicare fees but not be barred from collecting more from patients during the freeze; Medicare give vouchers to beneficiaries who chose to leave the public program and buy private health coverage instead.

Much of what Reagan proposed appeared to be barred by the fiscal 1984 congressional budget resolution (H Con Res 91), which stipulated that any Medicare savings should not raise out-of-pocket costs for beneficiaries or restrict their access to medical services.

Senate Action. The Senate Finance Committee approved provisions temporarily raising premiums for non-hospital services and imposing a freeze on doctors' fees as part of a bill (S 951 — S Rept 98-193) setting up health insurance for the unemployed. S 951, which was reported July 25, did not come to the floor. *(Health insurance for the unemployed, p. 542)*

Similar Medicare provisions subsequently were included in the Senate's budget reconciliation plan (S 2062 — S Rept 98-300), which was reported Nov. 4 by the Budget Committee, but the Senate did not complete action on the bill.

House Action. The Ways and Means Committee included Medicare savings provisions in its reconciliation tax plan (HR 4170 — H Rept 98-432, Part I), reported Oct. 21. The committee, however, decided to offer as a floor amendment a temporary freeze on doctors' fees and related "assignment" sections meant to force doctors to accept Medicare fees as payment in full for their hospital services. These "assignment" sections, vehemently opposed by the American Medical Association (AMA), were intended to protect beneficiaries from higher costs if doctors decided to elude the freeze by charging patients themselves more. Many members feared that including these controversial sections in the bill could lead to the defeat of the entire tax package.

The House Nov. 17 declined to consider the tax bill, thus foreclosing consideration of the Ways and Means Medicare plan and similar provisions reported Oct. 26 by

the Energy and Commerce Committee (HR 4136 — H Rept 98-442, Part I). *(Tax bill, p. 79)*

1984 Action

The doctor's fee freeze, with new restraints to keep doctors from evading the freeze, was enacted in 1984 as part of HR 4170, the deficit reduction bill.

Reagan Budget. President Reagan in his fiscal 1985 budget renewed his proposals for a one-year freeze on physicians' fees, a postponement of eligibility for Medicare until a month after a person's 65th birthday, and an increase in premium payments by beneficiaries. But he omitted his proposal to increase out-of-pocket payments by Medicare recipients for short-term hospital stays, while providing coverage for "catastrophic" illness.

When reporters asked whether election-year politics accounted for the relatively mild attack on Medicare costs, Margaret M. Heckler, secretary of the Department of Health and Human Services (HHS), said that bankruptcy of the Medicare Hospital Insurance (HI) Trust Fund did not appear as imminent as previously feared. In 1983 the Congressional Budget Office (CBO) predicted the HI fund could be out of money as early as 1987. But HHS in 1984 said that the solvency of the fund was projected through the five-year budget period (1985-89). *(1985 estimate, p. 521)*

House Action. The Ways and Means Committee's Medicare provisions, split off from HR 4170 in a move to blunt floor opposition to the tax bill, were added to the House budget reconciliation bill (HR 5394).

During floor consideration of HR 5394, the House bowed to AMA pressure and rejected an amendment to impose a one-year freeze on physicians' fees paid by Medicare and to require doctors to accept set fees for their hospital services. This eliminated about $1 billion of Ways and Means' proposed $1.8 billion in Medicare savings. Although most members supported the fee freeze, Republicans and rural Democrats balked at the related "assignment" provisions.

Knowing the votes against the amendment were overwhelming, the Democratic leadership did not force a roll call on the Medicare amendment. A Republican motion to send HR 5394 back to committee with instructions to include provisions for a one-year physician fee freeze, without mandatory assignment, and eliminate all spending increases in the bill was defeated in a **key vote of 172-242 (R 157-2; D 15-240)**. *(1984 key votes, p. 927)*

As passed by the House April 12, HR 5394 included changes in Medicare fee schedules covering reimbursement for laboratory services. HR 5394's spending cut provisions subsequently were incorporated in HR 4170.

Senate Action. The Senate Finance Committee's Medicare proposals went much further than the Ways and Means proposals. The Senate panel approved a hike in out-of-pocket costs paid by Medicare beneficiaries, as well as a freeze on doctors' fees in Medicare cases and penalties for physicians who refused to accept "assignment" of Medicare fees. The Senate package also restricted Medicare reimbursements to hospitals and rounded off premium payments to the next lower dollar.

The Senate April 13 by a 76-5 vote approved a tax increase package that included cuts in Medicare costs totaling about $9 billion over four years. The package was attached to a minor House-passed tariff bill (HR 2163).

Consideration of HR 2163 continued as the Senate debated various deficit reduction plans. During the floor debate the Senate rejected several amendments to restore cuts in the Medicare program. On May 17 the Senate substituted the provisions of HR 2163 and passed HR 4170 by a 74-23 vote.

Conference, Final Action. The Senate-passed physician fee freeze and mandatory "assignment" provisions were among the biggest stumbling blocks in the conference on HR 4170. Conferees agreed on a 15-month fee freeze that was to be voluntary but set financial penalties for those not participating in the program.

Conferees also agreed to increase the premiums paid by Medicare beneficiaries, although they did not accept the high levels the Senate had approved for later years.

The final bill limited Medicare reimbursement of hospital costs, set a schedule of rates for reimbursement for outpatient laboratory tests, and made employers provide health care coverage for certain non-working spouses of employees. Conferees rejected Senate provisions to delay Medicare eligibility one month, to round down Medicare benefits to the next lower dollar and to allow the non-hospital (Part B) deductible paid by beneficiaries to rise automatically with inflation.

The House June 27 approved the conference report on HR 4170 (H Rept 98-861) by a 268-155 vote. The Senate accepted it later that day by an 83-15 vote.

Provisions

As signed into law July 18, 1984, the Medicare provisions of HR 4170 (PL 98-369):

Physician Fee Freeze. Barred for 15 months, beginning July 1, 1984, increases in the amounts the Medicare system reimbursed doctors for services performed for Medicare patients.

Doctors were not required to accept Medicare "assignment," that is, agree to accept Medicare reimbursement as full payment for services, except for required beneficiary deductibles and co-payments. But those who did accept assignment for all their Medicare patients would have an advantage when new Medicare reimbursement fees were calculated after the freeze was lifted.

Doctors who accepted Medicare patients, but did not abide by the freeze, were subject to stiff penalties.

Assignment. Established a voluntary assignment program in which doctors committed themselves in advance, for a year, to accept assignment for all their Medicare patients. Participation was encouraged by publishing lists and otherwise informing the elderly about which doctors took assignment, and by offering expedited payment procedures for physicians in the voluntary program.

Premiums. Extended through 1987 a requirement that beneficiaries' premium payments for coverage of non-hospital services (Part B Medicare coverage) be calculated so that altogether, these payments yielded 25 percent of Part B program costs. The provision increased the 1986 monthly premium from an estimated $17.70 to $19.10 and from $18.60 to $21.30 in 1987.

Working Aged. Permitted non-working wives and husbands, aged 65 to 69, to make the employment-based health coverage of their spouses their primary medical plan, rendering Medicare a supplementary, "secondary payer." The choice could be made even if the working spouse had not yet reached 65. Also, required employers to offer to these older spouses the same medical coverage they provided to spouses of younger employees.

Hospital Reimbursement. Limited for fiscal 1985 and 1986 the rate of increase in Medicare payments to hospitals. The provision applied both to the limits, passed by Congress in 1982, for increases in Medicare payments to hospitals for overall costs of caring for beneficiaries and to a new system, passed in 1983, of flat rates of payment per illness. The latter system, based on "diagnosis related groups," was being phased in to replace the older, "cost-based" payment system.

Laboratory Fees. Established a schedule of fixed fees for Medicare payments for tests conducted by independent laboratories for outpatients. The schedule set fees at 60 percent of the charges (or 62 percent for hospital laboratory work on outpatients) prevailing in the year beginning July 1, 1984.

Medicare would pay 100 percent of the scheduled fee to laboratories or doctors accepting assignment for laboratory tests. (This meant waiver of required out-of-pocket payments by patients for coinsurance or deductibles.) Those not accepting assignment would, as under existing law, receive 80 percent of the scheduled fee, with no waiver of patients' payments. Laboratories were required to bill Medicare directly.

Hospital Assets. Revised rules for revaluing, for purposes of calculating certain Medicare payments, a hospital's capital-related costs, such as depreciation and interest. The revised rules were meant to limit increases in the value of such capital costs when hospital ownership changed.

Skilled Nursing Facilities. Restored the use of separate limits on Medicare payments to hospital-based and free-standing nursing facilities, with a somewhat higher rate for hospital-based units in recognition of their higher costs.

Inpatient/Outpatient Costs. Required the secretary of health and human services to issue regulations barring hospitals from including, in certain claims for outpatient services, costly expenses related to inpatient services.

Medicare Coverage. Authorized Medicare to pay for immunization against viral hepatitis for Medicare-covered kidney disease patients on dialysis and to pay for supplies needed by hemophiliacs for treating themselves with a substance that promoted blood clotting.

Durable Medical Equipment. Authorized 20 percent co-payments by beneficiaries for durable medical equipment provided by home health care services.

Medicaid Child Health Plan

Congress in 1984 enacted legislation requiring states to broaden their Medicaid coverage to include more low-income women during pregnancy and more young children.

The Child Health Assurance Program (CHAP) was included in the deficit reduction bill (HR 4170 — PL 98-369) cleared by Congress in late June. *(Deficit reduction, p. 56)*

Enactment of the new program, estimated to cost about $270 million over a three-year period, ended a five-year, on-again-off-again effort to require states to expand prenatal and pediatric care under Medicaid, the federal-state health care program for the poor. Previously, states could cover first-time pregnant women, but Congress did not require it.

The new program covered certain first-time pregnant women and pregnant women in two-parent families in which the principal wage earner was unemployed, as well as certain poor children up through age 5. Passage of the plan was largely the result of an agreement between liberal and conservative members who felt it was both fiscally and morally desirable to assure prenatal and infant care. They argued that early care would prevent more expensive medical and social problems later in life.

Several other Medicaid provisions were included in HR 4170, but House-Senate conferees rejected a Senate-approved provision to extend for three years a cutback in federal matching funds to states. The cutback had been imposed in 1981 and was to expire in 1984. *(1981 bill, p. 527)*

Also included in HR 4170 were provisions to raise the annual authorization level for the maternal and child health block grant program and to provide Medicaid benefits to those who could no longer collect Aid to Families with Dependent Children (AFDC) because of limits on earnings enacted in 1981. *(Maternal and child health block grants, p. 523; 1981 AFDC law, p. 586)*

Background

The case for the CHAP proposal was based on statistics showing that despite improvements, U.S. infant mortality rates still were worse than those of some other developed nations. Infant mortality rates indicated the number of deaths in the first 12 months of life. The U.S. rate in 1980 was 11.8 deaths per 1,000 live births. Countries with lower rates included Canada, 10.9; Denmark, 8.5; France, 10.0; Japan, 7.4; Norway, 8.8; Spain, 11.1; and Sweden, 6.7. Developed nations with rates comparable to or higher than those of the United States included Austria, East Germany, Italy and West Germany.

For black infants the infant mortality rate was twice that of whites, and comparable to infant death rates in some impoverished, Third World nations.

Factors associated with infant mortality included absence of or poor medical care during pregnancy, poor nutrition, the youth of the mother, substance abuse and smoking during pregnancy, and poverty. Supporters of the legislation were particularly concerned with low-birthweight babies — weighing 5.5 pounds or less — who carried a high risk of death within the first year, or of lasting illness or disability.

The Washington-based Children's Defense Fund led the drive for CHAP. Supporters also included the American Academy of Pediatrics, the American Public Health Association and the United States Catholic Conference.

The focus on problem pregnancies and infancies reflected a pragmatic decision to attack a specific well-documented problem — infant mortality — that would respond to a modest investment. In the Carter administration the children's fund pushed a more ambitious CHAP bill only to see it fail. *(Congress and the Nation Vol. V, p. 636)*

Legislative History

1983. The House Energy and Commerce Committee Oct. 26, 1983, reported a broad Medicaid CHAP plan that was incorporated in the committee's Medicare budget reconciliation proposals (HR 4136 — H Rept 98-442, Part I). There was no further action on that bill.

Sponsors decided to offer the child health plan as a floor amendment to HR 4170 in the final days of the session, but the House Nov. 17 rejected a rule providing for

floor consideration of the bill. *(Tax bill, p. 79)*

The Senate Finance Committee attached a much more modest child health plan to two different bills (S 951 — S Rept 98-193, S 2062 — S Rept 98-300) but neither was passed by the Senate.

1984. In 1984 the House included the CHAP proposal in its budget reconciliation bill (HR 5394), which passed April 12. The House plan called for $560 million to aid impoverished pregnant women and children. The provisions subsequently were incorporated in HR 4170, which had passed April 11.

The Senate version of HR 4170, which passed May 17, called for about $36 million over the next three years to assist low-income women during first pregnancies.

Conferees settled on a $270 million child health program. On June 27 the House approved the conference report on HR 4170 (H Rept 98-861) by a 268-155 vote, and the Senate approved it by an 83-15 vote.

Provisions

As signed into law July 18, 1984, the child health and Medicaid-related provisions of HR 4170 (PL 98-369):

Children and Pregnant Women. Required states to provide Medicaid assistance to certain needy women and children not receiving coverage in some states.

The Child Health Assurance Program would assist poor, first-time pregnant women once their pregnancy had been verified, pregnant women in two-parent families in which the principal breadwinner was unemployed and poor children born on or after Oct. 1, 1983, up to age 5 in two-parent families.

Federal Matching. Increased annual limits on Medicaid matching payments to Puerto Rico, the Virgin Islands, Guam, the Northern Mariana Islands and American Samoa.

Assignment of Rights. Mandated that states require Medicaid beneficiaries to assign to the states any right they had to other health benefits programs (so that states could collect from such programs any available payments for medical care of the covered beneficiaries). Existing law permitted, but did not require, states to do this.

Nursing Care. Relaxed certain requirements, on which Medicaid payments were contingent, for periodic certification by doctors that a beneficiary still needed care in a nursing facility.

Maternal and Child Health. Raised the annual authorization for the maternal and child health block grant program from $373 million to a permanent level of $478 million, the level appropriated in 1983, beginning in fiscal year 1984.

Aid to Families With Dependent Children (AFDC). Made several changes in the AFDC program to help families who were thrown off the rolls, or were subject to removal from the rolls, as a result of changes made to the program in 1981. These included allowing up to 15 months of additional Medicaid coverage to those who lost AFDC benefits because they had taken low-paying jobs.

The bill also expanded AFDC eligibility to families with higher incomes than existing law allowed.

Generic Drugs

Congress in 1984 approved a landmark drug bill intended to make cheaper versions of many widely prescribed drugs available to consumers while giving manufacturers extra-long patents for new brand-name pharmaceuticals.

The last time Congress passed a drug law of such magnitude was in 1962, when it adopted the requirement that manufacturers demonstrate efficacy — as well as safety — of new drugs. *(Congress and the Nation Vol. I, p. 1181)*

The Food and Drug Administration (FDA) estimated that under the bill (S 1538 — PL 98-417) more than 150 drugs could be offered in cheaper generic forms — saving consumers $1 billion over the next 12 years. Publicly funded programs such as Medicaid and veterans' health services also were expected to save substantial amounts on drug purchases.

Passage of the bill concluded nearly a year of intense and difficult negotiations among the research-based companies that created new, brand-name drugs, generic-drug makers and representatives of consumers, the elderly and organized labor.

Throughout the legislative process nearly a dozen research-based firms doggedly insisted on further concessions. Until just before final passage the "dissident" firms, as they were termed, fought against their trade association, the Pharmaceutical Manufacturers Association (PMA), which had led compromise negotiations. The fight was so bitter that top PMA officials resigned abruptly.

Background

The 1984 dispute was the tail-end of exceptionally long-running battles over public policy and drugs, dating back to the early 1960s when Sen. Estes Kefauver, D-Tenn. (House, 1939-49; Senate, 1949-63), had pressed unsuccessfully for cheaper drugs. *(Congress and the Nation Vol. I, p. 1754)*

The Carter administration had proposed major revisions in drug regulation in 1978; the Senate passed a somewhat different version in 1979, but that legislation died without further action. *(Congress and the Nation Vol. V, p. 641)*

In 1982 a broad patent term restoration measure had died after failing to pass the House, in large part because of objections that it made too many concessions to drug makers without any offsetting benefits in the form of more inexpensive drugs for consumers. *(Details, p. 693)*

In the 1984 measure, one key section directed the FDA to expand its use of a special fast-track procedure for approving generic drugs. Those duplicates of expensive brand-name drugs, sold by their chemical names, retailed for 50 percent to 80 percent less.

The agency had been using the expedited procedure only for drugs it had approved before 1962. That meant that so-called "post-1962" drugs still enjoyed exclusive marketing, free of competition, even after their patents expired. The expense of going through the regular FDA approval procedures generally discouraged generic versions of post-1962 drugs.

A second section, intended to create more financial incentives for the development of new drugs, gave drug companies up to five more years of patent protection for new drugs, as well as certain other exclusive marketing rights. Companies had complained that a significant part of the standard 17-year patent was lost to regulatory reviews. A patent for a new drug usually was obtained shortly after discovery, but subsequent testing and FDA approval took up to $70 million and 10 years, according to the firms.

Legislative History

Passage of the drug legislation marked a successful alliance between Rep. Henry A. Waxman, D-Calif., a liberal, and Sen. Orrin G. Hatch, R-Utah, a conservative. The two sponsored compromise legislation in June.

A revised version of their bill was reported (HR 3605 — H Rept 98-857, Part I) June 21 by the Energy and Commerce Committee. The Judiciary Committee reported (H Rept 98-857, Part II) the bill Aug. 1, after rejecting amendments that appeared to address the interests of the dissenting companies. The Judiciary panel agreed to an amendment knocking out of the bill a new, patent-like exclusive marketing right for drugs that were not eligible for patents.

A new, somewhat different version (S 2926) of the bill reflecting further negotiations went directly to the Senate floor Aug. 10, bypassing committee consideration and winning Senate approval that day by voice vote. The new version reflected relatively modest additional concessions by Hatch and Waxman to the dissenting companies.

The non-patent marketing rights excised in the House Judiciary Committee and put back in the new Senate version continued to be controversial enough to threaten survival of the bill up to the last minute. Opponents complained that the bill gave too much monopoly power to well-heeled drug companies. Sen. Howard M. Metzenbaum, D-Ohio, the only senator to vote against passage of S 2926, was particularly concerned that a provision dealing with exclusive marketing rights and delay for litigation was too much protection from competition.

When HR 3605 came to the House floor Sept. 6, a series of amendments were adopted to bring it into line with the Senate-passed bill. The House approved one substantive change from the Senate bill, reflecting a concession to Metzenbaum and others in his camp. It shortened the time a drug would be protected by the provision relating to marketing rights and delay for litigation.

The House rejected, by huge margins, several amendments that would have upset the bill's delicate balance between consumer and generic drug interests and those of companies making brand-name products. The House added an unrelated textile labeling section to gain some political advantage during technical procedural maneuvers.

House passage Sept. 6 came on an overwhelming 362-0 vote. The House then substituted its amended bill for the text of an unrelated Senate-passed patent measure (S 1538) and returned it to the Senate for approval.

Final action came Sept. 12 when the Senate by voice vote accepted the House amendments.

Provisions

As signed into law Sept. 24, S 1538 (PL 98-417):

Drug Approval. Directed the FDA to make broader use of its expedited approval procedure for generic copies of patented drugs, upon expiration of the patent. The procedure waived requirements for testing to show that a drug was safe and effective; it required only that a generic drug be shown to be the chemical duplicate of the original (which had undergone safety and effectiveness tests). Existing FDA practice was to allow the expedited procedure, known as an abbreviated new drug application (ANDA), only for generic copies of drugs that received FDA marketing approval prior to 1962.

Generic copies of drugs that had been approved by the FDA between 1962 and 1982 would qualify for ANDA approval upon expiration of the patents. Copies of drugs approved between 1982 and the date of enactment of S 1538 would qualify for ANDA approval only after a 10-year period of exclusive marketing, authorized by the bill. Generic versions of drugs approved after enactment would be eligible for the ANDA procedure after the expiration of the patents, including any extension of the patents authorized by the bill.

● Directed the FDA to withhold ANDA approval of a generic drug in cases in which a generic maker had legally challenged the validity of the patent for the drug to be copied. In such cases the FDA must withhold approval of a generic drug until a court decision on the challenge, but no longer than 30 months.

● Provided an additional exclusive marketing right, apart from a patent extension, for new drugs approved by the FDA after enactment of the bill. The exclusive marketing would be available only for drugs that did not have active patents.

For drugs that were new chemical entities, no generic copies could be marketed for five years after FDA approval of the original. For drugs that were not new chemical entities but required extensive clinical testing — generally over-the-counter versions of prescription drugs — no generic versions could be marketed for three years after approval. In both cases, a generic company could begin the required testing in anticipation of expiration of the exclusive marketing date.

For drugs approved between 1982 and the date of enactment, no generic versions could be marketed for two years after approval.

No legal challenges to a patent could be filed until the end of the exclusive marketing period, except for drugs protected for five years. For them a challenge could be filed at the end of the fourth year, meaning that the 30-month delay for litigation would begin at that time.

Patents. Authorized a single extension of a patent on a new drug for humans, a medical device, or a food or color additive, subject to FDA approval. The extension would add up to two years of patent protection for drugs awaiting FDA approval at the time of enactment, or up to five years for drugs submitted for approval after enactment.

● Permitted an applicant for an extension of a product with several patents to select the patent on which to seek the extension.

● Provided that the total time of patent protection left to a product after FDA approval, plus any extension, could not exceed 14 years. (Previously drug patents could have had only eight or 10 years remaining after FDA marketing approval.)

● Permitted testing of a patented drug, prior to expiration of the patent, for purposes of securing FDA approval to market a generic version of the drug after the expiration of its patent.

Textiles. Required that clothing sold in the United States be conspicuously labeled to show country of origin and that mail-order and other catalogues indicate whether clothing was manufactured in this country or imported.

Cigarette Warning Labels

Legislation (HR 3979 — PL 98-474) requiring sharp new warnings for cigarette packages and advertisements was cleared by Congress in 1984.

Four new labels, to be rotated periodically, warned of cancer, heart disease and other health problems, and ad-

vised smokers that cigarette smoke contained carbon monoxide. Health groups sought the new labels after the Federal Trade Commission (FTC) in 1981 reported that the existing general health warning had lost impact. That warning read: "Warning: The Surgeon General Has Determined That Cigarette Smoking Is Dangerous To Your Health."

The four new warning statements to be required on the packages and advertising of all cigarette brands sold in the United States one year after enactment of HR 3979 were:

SURGEON GENERAL'S WARNING: Smoking Causes Lung Cancer, Heart Disease, Emphysema, and May Complicate Pregnancy.

SURGEON GENERAL'S WARNING: Quitting Smoking Now Greatly Reduces Serious Risks to Your Health.

SURGEON GENERAL'S WARNING: Smoking by Pregnant Women May Result in Fetal Injury, Premature Birth and Low Birth Weight.

SURGEON GENERAL'S WARNING: Cigarette Smoke Contains Carbon Monoxide.

Texts for outdoor billboard ads were to be slightly shorter.

Until 1984 tobacco interests had fiercely fought any change in the existing general warning label. But growing pressure in Congress, including strong support for higher cigarette taxes, prompted industry officials to negotiate a labeling compromise, according to members working on the bill. Tobacco officials refused publicly to acknowledge their participation, reportedly because of their belief that any industry statement linking smoking to cancer or other illnesses might invite liability suits.

HR 3979 also required cigarette makers and importers to inform the Department of Health and Human Services (HHS) of all chemicals added to tobacco in cigarettes. HHS would transmit to Congress information on the additives and any health hazards without identifying either a manufacturer or a brand name. Previously manufacturers had voluntarily informed HHS of the most commonly used additives.

In other cigarette-related action, Congress in 1984 decided to let the existing 16-cent-a-pack federal tax on cigarettes drop to 8 cents on Oct. 1, 1985 (HR 4170 — PL 98-369). Congress also mandated a study on the feasibility of developing "fire-safe" cigarettes (HR 1880 — PL 98-567). (*Tax, p. 79; study, p. 285*)

Legislative History

The House approved HR 3979 by voice vote Sept. 10. The bill had been reported by the Energy and Commerce Committee May 23 (H Rept 98-805), after months-long negotiations to reach a compromise acceptable to health groups and tobacco interests. An early version of the labeling bill (HR 1824) had won subcommittee approval in 1983 but had been stalled by controversy.

The Senate Sept. 26 approved HR 3979 with minor amendments. A series of very negative findings on cigarettes and health were dropped from the bill text and language was added to make clear cigarette distributors or retailers could not be held responsible for the rotation system. HR 3979 bypassed committee consideration, but the Senate Labor and Human Resources Committee had reported a bill (S 772 — S Rept 98-177) July 13, 1983.

The House Sept. 26 by voice vote cleared the amended version of HR 3979 for the president.

Organ Transplant System

Congress in 1984 approved legislation meant to ease logistical problems associated with organ transplant surgery.

The measure (S 2048 — PL 98-507) established a national computerized network to match transplant patients with organs, and it provided funds to upgrade and coordinate local and regional agencies that procured human organs for transplantation. It made selling organs for transplantation a federal crime.

The bill also created a task force to evaluate the ethical, legal, economic and other difficult issues raised by the expensive lifesaving surgery.

Transplant Problems

Those steps were designed to ease the problems that had driven families of some transplant patients to enlist the aid of the White House, prominent politicians and the media in appeals for organs and for funds to finance the operations.

Medical developments, especially the approval of a powerful new immunosuppressive drug called cyclosporine, made organ transplant surgery more feasible. Immunosuppressive drugs helped prevent the rejection by a patient of a transplanted organ.

But the operations and especially the post-surgical care cost tens of thousands of dollars. The federal government and private insurers generally had resisted paying for the transplant procedures except under pressure from the press and politicians. Moreover, there were shortages of organs and uneven success in matching patients with those that were available.

The final bill omitted a controversial House-passed provision that would have financed cyclosporine for low-income transplant patients. The drug cost about $5,000 per year per patient.

Legislative History

The House Energy and Commerce Committee reported an organ transplant bill (HR 4080 — H Rept 98-575, Part I), Nov. 18, 1983, but the legislation went through several revisions before reaching the floor.

The most far-reaching change proposed by the committee bill — and one vehemently opposed by the American Medical Association and the Reagan administration — was a provision allowing Medicare to limit payments for transplants or other sophisticated procedures to medical centers with proven records of success and, possibly, to patients who had been diagnosed as suffering certain ailments.

Existing Medicare practice was an "all-or-nothing" policy of financing difficult, expensive procedures everywhere, or nowhere. Except for kidneys, Medicare generally had designated organ transplants as "experimental" and refused to pay for them. Because Medicaid, the federal-state medical program for the poor, and private insurers patterned their coverage on Medicare, the proposed change might have had a wide impact. The private insurance industry, which faced enormous pressure to pay for the operations, urged even more restrictions than those proposed by the bill.

HR 4080 also contained another controversial provision, one providing for federal funding of cyclosporine.

A second organ transplant bill (HR 5580 — H Rept 98-769) was reported by the Energy and Commerce Committee May 15, 1984. The new bill continued to authorize federal financing of immunosuppressive drugs but omitted Medicare and Medicaid provisions. Removing the Medicare and Medicaid references meant the legislation would not go to the Ways and Means Committee, where there was a real possibility that much of the bill would have been rejected.

The House approved HR 5580 June 21 by a vote of 396-6, after rejecting 25-379 an amendment to reduce the bill's authorizations and drop the authorization for immunosuppressive drugs.

The rejected amendment would have brought the House measure in line with a leaner transplant bill (S 2048) approved April 11 by the Senate by voice vote. S 2048 had been reported (S Rept 98-382) April 6 by the Labor and Human Resources Committee.

The conference report on the bill (H Rept 98-1127) was not filed until Oct. 2. The drug funding issue held up agreement for months because House sponsor Albert Gore Jr., D-Tenn., was reluctant to yield on the funding. However, a September *New England Journal of Medicine* article reported two deaths resulting from cyclosporine and highlighted continuing discussions within the medical community about the relative benefits and risks of the drug. Gore agreed to drop the drug funding and instead made medical and policy questions raised by the immunosuppressive therapy the top priority for the new task force.

Conferees also reduced the authorization for grants for organ procurement agencies from the House-passed six years, to three years, and reduced the authorized funding from $40 million to $25 million.

The House Oct. 3 and the Senate Oct. 4 by voice votes adopted the conference report (H Rept 98-1127).

Provisions

As signed into law Oct. 19, S 2048 (PL 98-507):

● Created a task force to study and report on ethical, legal, financial and other questions associated with organ transplant surgery. Among the issues before the task force would be the allocation of the surgery and the limited supply of human organs, extent of insurance coverage, establishment of a national voluntary registry of volunteer organ donors and, as the first priority, the medical value of immunosuppressive therapy and payments for such therapy.

● Authorized $2 million annually to support a national computerized system for matching patients with scarce organs.

● Authorized $5 million in fiscal year 1985, $8 million in 1986 and $12 million in 1987 for grants to create or upgrade local and regional agencies that procured human organs for transplantation and that participated in the national matching network. Specified that task force recommendations should be taken into account but that agency funding was not contingent on the recommendations.

● Prohibited the purchase or sale of human organs for transplantation and authorized fines of up to $50,000 and/or imprisonment for up to five years for knowingly violating the prohibition.

● Directed the secretary of health and human services (HHS) to assign responsibility for administering organ transplant programs to the Public Health Service or to some other unit.

● Provided for a national registry of transplant patients to facilitate scientific evaluations of procedures.

NIH Bill Veto

President Reagan Oct. 30 vetoed legislation (S 540) creating new research institutes on arthritis and nursing and reauthorizing selected medical research programs.

Reagan termed the new institutes authorized by S 540 "unnecessary" and "premature." He noted a study of the organizational structure of the National Institutes of Health (NIH) was to be released by the Institute of Medicine, part of the National Academy of Sciences.

He also objected to "overly specific requirements for the management of research that place undue constraints on executive branch authorities and functions."

Congress had cleared the $4.7 billion authorization bill Oct. 9 in the final days of the 98th Congress, after resolving a longstanding dispute over limits on federally funded fetal research that had blocked an NIH authorization bill in 1982. S 540 affirmed most of the rules on fetal research then in use, but suspended temporarily the waiver for one type of research until a new congressionally appointed bioethics commission established by S 540 studied questions raised by the research and other issues. *(1982 legislation, p. 537)*

S 540 included fiscal 1985 and 1986 authorizations for the federal cancer and heart-lung-blood research institutes and provided explicit statutory authority for the other 11 existing institutes that had had permanent authorizations and, therefore, had not undergone periodic authorizations. The bill also authorized fiscal 1985-86 funding for the medical library and research award programs; authorized several special research programs on certain diseases; authorized a study of the health effects of nuclear energy and a cancer screening center for persons exposed to radioactive fallout from nuclear bomb tests in Nevada; and spelled out procedures for investigations of scientific misconduct in NIH-funded research and for the care of research animals.

In his veto message Reagan said "adequate authority" to continue the vetoed health programs was provided by the fiscal 1985 continuing appropriations resolution (PL 98-473).

Legislative History

The House Nov. 17, 1983, approved by voice vote legislation (HR 2350) authorizing $7.6 billion through fiscal 1986 for the national institutes and other research functions, and for the establishment of new research institutes on arthritis and nursing.

HR 2350 had been reported May 16 by the House Energy and Commerce Committee (H Rept 98-191) but floor action had been blocked in July by opposition to the bill's directives to set up committees or otherwise highlight research on specific diseases. Opponents charged the directives inappropriately exposed NIH research priorities to political considerations and could squander money on less promising work while underfunding research that was ripe for development. After months of negotiations, a compromise version of HR 2350 was crafted that still highlighted certain areas for research but omitted much of what previously had drawn opposition.

The Senate did not take up HR 2350 or a less costly

version (S 773 — S Rept 98-110) reported May 16, 1983, by the Senate Labor and Human Resources Committee. S 540, a bill establishing an arthritis institute, was discharged from the Senate panel May 22, 1984, and passed by the Senate by voice vote May 24. The bill also broadened the mandate of the Office of Technology Assessment to include work on biomedical ethics.

The Senate-passed bill acquired authorizations of other major NIH programs and a new nursing institute when the House June 5 passed S 540 after substituting the text of HR 2350.

Conferees compromised on a $4.7 billion authorization compared with a $3.9 billion budget request for the cancer and heart-lung-blood institutes. They also agreed on fetal research guidelines that generally followed those of the House version, with one exception. The bill barred NIH for three years from permitting rarely used waivers of a standard requiring that research present only minimal risk to fetuses in the womb.

The Senate by voice vote Oct. 9 adopted the conference report (H Rept 98-1155), and the House by voice vote later that day cleared it for the president.

Health Professions Aid Veto

President Reagan Oct. 30 vetoed legislation (S 2574) that would have continued community health programs and subsidies for training health professionals.

In vetoing S 2574, Reagan noted that the bill authorized 41 percent more in spending than he had requested.

He said the legislation took "the wrong approach" by continuing "obsolete federal subsidies" at a time of anticipated surpluses of doctors and nurses, and by maintaining "a static and rigid categorical framework" for health professions aid.

Reagan objected to continuing National Health Service Corps scholarships, which required recipients to practice in health shortage areas, contending that new scholarships were no longer needed.

He also protested the bill's repeal of "a key reform" proposed by his administration and approved by Congress in 1981 — a little-used block grant program for community health centers serving indigent populations in areas with few medical resources. States had virtually ignored the optional grant program, which would have saddled them with new spending and administrative responsibilities. S 2574 would have created a smaller block grant to support primary care programs run by states. *(1981 legislation, p. 523)*

As cleared by Congress, S 2574 would have authorized in fiscal 1985-87 $487.3 million for aid to medical and other schools and their students; $226.2 million for aid to nursing schools and their students; and National Health Service Corps scholarship funds as needed. The bill also would have authorized for fiscal 1985-88 $1.7 billion for community health centers and $213 million for migrant health centers; $76 million for the new primary care block grant to states and a new technical assistance program; and $400,000 annually for certain Health Maintenance Organization (HMO) programs, while ending other HMO programs. *(1981 HMO bill, p. 532)*

In his veto message, Reagan said "adequate authority" to continue the vetoed health programs in fiscal 1985 was provided by the continuing appropriations resolution (PL 98-473).

Legislative History

The Senate June 28 passed S 2574 (S Rept 98-492), authorizing aid to nursing schools and their students, as well as three other bills whose provisions later were incorporated in the final health professions bill. They were: S 2308 (S Rept 98-490), authorizing aid for community and migrant health care programs; S 2311 (S Rept 98-401), authorizing HMO aid; S 2559 (S Rept 98-491), authorizing aid to students pursuing health careers, and funds for two health research centers. Together the bills authorized nearly $2.7 billion for the various programs.

The House Sept. 6 passed by voice vote a $2.9 billion authorization (HR 5602), after agreeing to trim $218.6 million from the $3.1 billion committee version (H Rept 98-817). The bill included authorizations for funding aid to medical and other schools; aid to nursing schools and their students; the National Health Service Corps; HMOs; and community and migrant health centers.

The Senate adopted the conference report (H Rept 98-1143) by voice vote Oct. 4 and the House cleared it Oct. 9 by a vote of 363-13.

Alcohol, Drug Abuse Research

Congress in 1984 approved a multi-year reauthorization of federal research, prevention and treatment programs for alcohol, drug abuse and mental health problems.

The measure (S 2303 — PL 98-509) authorized $1.95 billion for the programs in fiscal 1985-87. *(Previous authoriziation, p. 541)*

The Senate authorized block grants for state programs and research funds in separate bills. S 2303 (S Rept 98-381), authorizing nearly $1.6 billion in block grants for fiscal 1985-87, was passed by voice vote April 26. The Senate June 28 approved by voice vote S 2615 (S Rept 98-477) authorizing a total of $419.5 million in fiscal 1985-87 for research programs.

The House June 11 by a vote of 360-33 passed HR 5603 authorizing nearly $1.7 billion for state grants in fiscal 1985-87 and a total of $239 million for research in fiscal 1985-86. The bill also authorized funds for programs dealing with individuals with developmental disabilities. On June 28 the House passed S 2303 by voice vote after substituting the text of HR 5603.

The developmental disabilities sections were dropped in conference, and Congress subsequently enacted HR 5603 authorizing funds for those programs. *(Story, p. 609)*

The conference version of S 2303 (H Rept 98-1123) was approved by both the Senate and House Oct. 4.

Provisions

As signed into law Oct. 19, S 2303 (PL 98-509):

● Authorized $515 million in fiscal 1985, $545 million in 1986 and $576 million in 1987 for block grants to states for alcohol, drug abuse and mental health services.

● Authorized $52 million in fiscal 1985 and $61 million in 1986 for research by the National Institute on Alcohol Abuse and Alcoholism.

● Authorized $68 million in fiscal 1985 and $74 million in 1986 for research by the National Institute on Drug Abuse.

● Authorized $20 million annually in fiscal years 1985-87 for mental health community services grants administered by the National Institute of Mental Health.

• Required states to allocate not less than 5 percent of their block grants to initiate and expand treatment of substance abuse among women, and 10 percent of the grants for mental health services for disturbed children and adolescents.

Preventive Health

Congress Oct. 9 cleared a three-year, $707 million reauthorization (S 2301 — PL 98-555) of funding for childhood immunization, tuberculosis control and other preventive health programs.

The final measure was a compromise version of bills passed by the Senate Sept. 28 (S 2301 — S Rept 98-393) and the House Oct. 1 (HR 5538 — H Rept 98-1063).

Provisions. As signed into law Oct. 30, S 2301 (PL 98-555):

• Authorized $98.5 million each year for fiscal 1985-87 for block grants for such programs as rape prevention, hypertension, fluoridation and urban rat control.

• Authorized for childhood immunization programs, $52 million in fiscal 1985, $59 million in 1986 and $65 million in 1987.

• Authorized for tuberculosis control, $8 million in fiscal 1985, $9 million in 1986 and $10 million in 1987.

• Authorized venereal disease programs, including programs designed to prevent acquired immune deficiency syndrome, at $57 million in fiscal 1985, $62.5 million in 1986 and $68 million in 1987.

• Authorized $5 million per year for state planning and $2 million per year for new demonstration projects on emergency medical services for children.

Health Promotion

Congress in 1984 cleared a three-year, $269 million reauthorization (S 771 — PL 98-551) of two federal centers that collected health statistics and studied health care services, and a third office that coordinated health promotion and disease prevention research and other projects.

The bill also authorized new research centers at universities, expanded the mission of the health care services office within the Department of Health and Human Services, and created a new federal advisory council on health care technology. The bill also provided federal funds for a second health technology panel associated with the National Academy of Sciences.

The measure included a clarification of the definition of an orphan drug. Those drugs, developed for rare diseases, qualified for special regulatory and tax treatment. *(Orphan drugs, p. 536)*

S 771 first passed the Senate in 1983. Portions of the final version had passed the House and Senate in 1983 and 1984 as sections of other bills (HR 2350, HR 5496, S 540). The House passed S 771 Oct. 9 and the Senate cleared the measure Oct. 11.

Family Life Programs

Congress Oct. 9 cleared a one-year reauthorization of federal grant programs for family planning and adolescent family life projects to aid pregnant teenagers.

The bill (S 2616 — PL 98-512) authorized $162.6 mil-

Health Leadership

Richard S. Schweiker served as secretary of health and human services during the first two years of President Reagan's first term. Schweiker had been a U.S. senator from Pennsylvania, 1969-81, and a U.S. representative from Pennsylvania's 13th District, 1961-69.

Leadership of the massive Department of Health and Human Services was passed to another congressional veteran in March 1983, when former Rep. Margaret M. Heckler succeeded Schweiker, who had resigned. After eight terms in the House, Heckler had lost her redrawn Massachusetts district in 1982.

Schweiker's departure unsettled the health community because he had expertise in the field and adeptness in political fights within the administration. Heckler brought no notable expertise in the programs she would administer, nor was she known as a legislative leader in Congress.

After months of controversy, Dr. C. Everett Koop was confirmed in November 1981 as surgeon general and director of the U.S. Public Health Service (PHS). PHS professionals and feminist groups had opposed the prominent Philadelphia pediatric surgeon's nomination. Koop's outspoken anti-abortion views underlay much of the opposition. *(Details, p. 531)*

Health leadership on Capitol Hill also underwent some changes. At the beginning of the 97th Congress, the new chairman of the Senate Labor and Human Resources Committee, Orrin G. Hatch, R-Utah, abolished the Health Subcommittee that Sen. Edward M. Kennedy, D-Mass., had used as his pulpit to promote the virtues of national health insurance. Hatch wanted to have health issues in his domain, but under Senate rules he could not chair the subcommittee without giving up his chairmanship of the Judiciary Subcommittee on the Constitution. So he eliminated the health panel and announced that health legislation would be handled at the full committee level. David Durenberger, R-Minn., became chairman of the Senate Finance Health Subcommittee, which had responsibility for Medicaid and Medicare.

On the House side, Rep. Henry A. Waxman, D-Calif., continued as chairman of the House Energy and Commerce Subcommittee on Health and the Environment. Andrew Jacobs Jr., D-Ind., took over the chairmanship of the House Ways and Means Health Subcommittee, which had jurisdiction over Medicare.

Sen. Hatch, a conservative, and Rep. Waxman, a liberal, forged successful alliances on some important pieces of health legislation, including generic drug and cigarette labeling bills.

lion for family planning grants and $30 million for family life projects for fiscal 1985. The family life projects provided teenagers with job and adoption services, counseling and other alternatives to abortion, and discouraged teen sexual activity.

Both chambers had passed multi-year reauthorizations, but reconciling differences was delayed by disagreement on whether to require federally funded family planning services to notify parents of teenagers seeking contraceptives.

In January 1983 the Department of Health and Human Services (HHS) had issued regulations requiring birth control clinics that received federal funds to notify parents before prescribing contraceptives for unmarried teenagers. The so-called "squeal" rule was condemned by medical groups. It was struck down in District of Columbia and New York courts on the grounds that HHS had misread congressional intent on parental notification. The department lost several appeals and, at the end of November, decided that it would not appeal to the Supreme Court.

The Reagan administration unsuccessfully sought to require the notification, while the House Energy and Commerce Committee report (HR 5600 — H Rept 98-804) pointedly restated existing law, which directed agencies to encourage parent-child communication about teenagers' use of the agency's services, to the extent practicable.

The final bill made no major policy changes in either the family planning or family life program. Conferees agreed to limit the authorization to one year with the intention of dealing with the issue in 1985.

Legislative History. The House June 11 passed HR 5600 by a 290-102 vote, reauthorizing for three years funding for family planning services, the adolescent family life program and preventive health services block grants. The bill made no changes in the family planning or adolescent life programs, despite a Reagan administration request to fold them into a block grant. The administration also objected to the bill's earmarking of funds for rape crisis programs and to the total funding level.

The Senate June 29 by voice vote passed S 2616 (S Rept 98-496), a three-year reauthorization for the family life program.

The House passed S 2616 on Aug. 10 after substituting the text of HR 5600.

House and Senate negotiators agreed to retain the family planning and adolescent family life provisions, but the other House provisions were dropped. Those issues were addressed later in S 2301 (PL 98-555). (Details, p. 552)

The Senate adopted the conference report (H Rept 98-1154) by voice vote Oct. 9, and the House by voice vote cleared it for the president later in the day.

'Baby Doe' Bill

Legislation designed to ensure that severely handicapped infants were not denied the medical treatment they needed to live was approved by Congress Sept. 28, after months of negotiations over the emotional issue.

The so-called "Baby Doe" provisions were included in a bill (HR 1904 — PL 98-457) authorizing funds for federal programs to prevent and treat child abuse.

The bill required states, in order to receive federal child protection aid, to have procedures for responding to reports of medical neglect of handicapped infants. But it made clear that doctors would not have to take heroic steps to save the life of an infant if treatment would be futile. (Details, p. 606)

Hospice Payments

Congress in 1984 cleared legislation designed to encourage hospices to participate in the Medicare program.

Hospices offered terminal patients a less expensive form of treatment than hospitals and provided social support for the patients and their families.

The measure (HR 5386 — PL 98-617) raised the Medicare payment rate for routine home patient care by hospices from $46.25 per day to $53.17, subject to annual review by the secretary of health and human services. The final bill also extended certain federal aid to states for foster care.

The bill (H Rept 98-1100) was passed by the House Oct. 1 by voice vote. The Senate approved it Oct. 11 after adding an amendment extending for one year certain provisions of the Adoption Assistance and Child Welfare Act of 1980 (PL 96-272). The amendment allowed states to use certain federal foster care funds for child welfare services and to claim federal matching payments for children whose parents voluntarily placed them in foster care. The House Oct. 1 had passed a bill (HR 6266 — H Rept 98-1048) containing the two foster care provisions. (Congress and the Nation Vol. V, p. 710)

The House accepted the Senate changes Oct. 11, clearing HR 5386 for the president.

Heroin for Cancer Patients

Emotional pleas for cancer patients dying in terrible pain did not convince the House to let doctors use heroin, under controlled circumstances, to relieve the suffering.

After an unusually impassioned debate, the House Sept. 19 rejected, by a 55-355 vote, a bill (HR 5290 — H Rept 98-689) that would have permitted the federal government to provide hospital and hospice pharmacies with diacetylmorphine, commonly known as heroin.

Heroin was banned from medical use in the United States in the 1920s because of concern about its addictive properties. The temporary program would have let doctors use the drug in treating dying patients whose severe pain did not respond to other medications.

A group representing families of cancer patients, the National Committee on the Treatment of Intractable Pain, had sought the legislation since the 1970s. Heroin had been used as a painkiller in England for a number of years and in this country in research programs sponsored by the National Cancer Institute.

But the Reagan administration and the American Medical Association lobbied strongly against it, arguing that it set a bad precedent and that supplies of the drug might be diverted to illegal use.

Sponsors countered that the amount of heroin that would be used in the program — perhaps 15 pounds a year — was minuscule compared with the tons of illegal heroin flooding the nation.

Before rejecting the bill, the House also turned down, by a 178-232 vote, an amendment to increase penalties for illegal diversion of the drug, and strengthen controls on its medical use.

Computer Tampering

A bill to impose sizable fines and jail sentences on computer "hackers" if, for the fun of it, they tapped into or changed computerized medical records was passed Sept. 17 by the House. The Senate did not act on the measure.

The bill (HR 5831 — H Rept 98-918) authorized fines of up to $5,000 or prison sentences of up to a year for unauthorized access to computerized medical records. For unauthorized altering of the records, the fine was up to $25,000, the prison term up to five years.

Penalties for computer tampering were included in an omnibus crime bill enacted in 1984. *(Story, p. 698)*

The bill responded to a well-publicized incident in 1983 in which teenage computer enthusiasts, using a home computer, broke into the computerized records of cancer patients at Memorial Sloan-Kettering Cancer Center in New York.

Education Policy

President Reagan was committed to restructuring federal involvement in education. He wanted to reduce federal spending for education, abolish the Education Department, and redirect money and authority to state and local levels.

In his first two years in office, his budgets called for significant reductions in education spending — including proposals to eliminate some programs and consolidate others into block grants.

The sweeping budget reconciliation law approved by Congress in 1981 included tighter eligibility restrictions on college student loans, a new education block grant that replaced 29 relatively small programs and limits on education spending through fiscal 1984.

None of those changes went as far as Reagan wanted, and the administration made little headway in reducing education spending in subsequent years. But Congress did put the brakes on the growth of education spending, after two decades of rapid expansion.

By 1984, however, Congress had begun to reverse some of the policy changes and budget cuts in education that the administration had won earlier. Members of the 98th Congress moved on a course independent of the administration — unlike the 97th Congress, which had adopted a defensive posture, reacting to Reagan's budget cuts and his proposals to restructure the federal role in education.

Lawmakers' steps in 1984 were halting and cautious. But they did take education programs out of the holding pattern that had stalled virtually all initiatives since the 96th Congress, when major bills expanding aid to needy college students and creating the Department of Education were passed.

Declining Quality of Schools

Part of the backdrop for education initiatives in the 98th Congress was the nationwide concern over the declining quality of American public schools.

In April 1983 the federally appointed National Commission on Excellence in Education issued a report spotlighting problems in the schools. The commission's report, *A Nation at Risk*, concluded that the country had been "committing an act of unthinking, unilateral educational disarmament" in allowing academic standards to decline. "If an unfriendly foreign power had attempted to impose on America the mediocre educational performance that exists today, we might well have viewed it as an act of war," it said.

Among the ills cited by the commission were high illiteracy rates, declining standardized test scores, poor teacher training and increasing need for colleges and businesses to provide remedial education. It laid out a long agenda of needed changes, including stiffer graduation requirements, longer school days and higher teachers' salaries.

The panel's dismal diagnosis was considered by some educators to be overstated. But its basic concerns subsequently were echoed by other organizations, including the Education Commission of the States, the Twentieth Century Fund, the National Science Board and the Carnegie Foundation for the Advancement of Teaching.

The wide publicity given to the excellence commission's report gave new impetus to reform efforts under way in state capitals and local school districts. With many states moving to raise academic standards and upgrade teaching, observers claimed the education system was undergoing its most comprehensive reassessment since the late 1950s.

When the Soviet Union in 1957 launched the sputnik satellite, it set off a paroxysm of anxiety about science and technical training in the United States. In 1958, less than a year after sputnik went into space, Congress enacted a landmark crash program of federal aid to education — the National Defense Education Act (NDEA).

By contrast, the 98th Congress responded cautiously to the perceived education crisis of the 1980s. Democrats advocated but could not pass an ambitious, broad-based new program of school aid reminiscent of NDEA. Facing a tight budget and a public seen as not supportive of government initiatives, what new programs the 98th Congress did enact were modest, low-cost and carefully targeted.

Even those modest new programs, coupled with a significant increase Congress approved in the Education Department's budget, were seen by many education lobbyists as an important reaffirmation of the federal role in education.

That role, traditionally, had been very limited and

References

Discussion of education policy for the years 1945-64 may be found in *Congress and the Nation Vol. I*, pp. 1195-1215; for the years 1965-68, *Congress and the Nation Vol. II*, pp. 709-733; for the years 1969-72, *Congress and the Nation Vol. III*, pp. 581-604; for the years 1973-76, *Congress and the Nation Vol. IV*, pp. 377-402; for the years 1977-80, *Congress and the Nation Vol. V*, pp. 655-677.

narrowly defined. States and localities had borne the primary responsibility for financing education and governing its substance. Of the $226 billion spent on schools and colleges in 1983-84, only about $19 billion, or 8.4 percent, came from the federal government, according to the National Center for Education Statistics.

1981 Reconciliation Cuts

The 1981 budget reconciliation bill became the vehicle for major changes and cutbacks in federal educational programs. The bill, however, still did not go as far as the administration had wanted.

In 1981 the president proposed consolidating 44 elementary and secondary education programs into two block grants and reducing their funding by 25 percent. Congress feared that would undermine the two core federal programs — aid for compensatory education of the disadvantaged and education of handicapped children — and instead compromised on a plan to keep these two programs separate while consolidating 29 smaller programs.

The reconciliation bill also provided for the eventual elimination of part of the impact aid program of assistance to school districts educating the children of federally connected parents. Every president since Eisenhower had tried — and failed — to eliminate the program, which in 1981 gave money to 3,900 school systems sprinkled among nearly all congressional districts. Even the most die-hard conservatives would show up each year to testify in support of the program. But in 1981 fiscal austerity won out and many longtime supporters of impact aid felt bound to support the president's budget cuts. In 1984, however, Congress reversed itself and voted to continue the program.

Federal aid to college students also was cut sharply by the 1981 reconciliation bill. According to an Urban Institute study, by fiscal 1981 federal spending on student aid (excluding GI Bill and Social Security payments) accounted for nearly 80 percent of the tuition and fee income of all colleges and universities in the United States, as compared with 39 percent in fiscal 1976. The 1981 reconciliation bill established a "needs test" to limit eligibility for Guaranteed Student Loans (GSL) and set spending limits for Pell grants for college students that were far below estimated future costs.

Reagan also pressed successfully for the elimination of Social Security benefits for college students, on the grounds that such aid was not provided on the basis of financial need. The program provided about $2 billion a year in aid before Congress voted as part of the reconciliation bill to phase it out.

Resistance to Reagan Proposals

After 1981 Reagan made little progress in his efforts to reduce spending and restructure federal involvement.

Congress rejected administration proposals to make further cuts in college student loan and grant programs, and approved legislation setting the rules for college assistance programs.

In 1982 Congress blocked Education Department regulations limiting federal controls over certain elementary and secondary education programs, including compensatory education for the disadvantaged. It also pressured the department to withdraw regulations governing handicapped education.

Tuition tax credits for parents sending their children to private schools — one of the cornerstones of Reagan's education policy — were rejected by the Senate in 1983.

Congressional Initiatives

Congress in 1984 passed a record high, $17.7 billion appropriation for the Education Department in fiscal 1985 — up from the $15.4 billion provided the previous year and considerably more than the administration had sought. While much of the growth was in mandatory, entitlement spending, the increase in discretionary spending alone amounted to almost 12 percent. The administration's budget request of $15.4 billion marked the first time since taking office that Reagan had not recommended cutting Education Department funding.

Congress' move to restore education spending did not compensate for losses in many areas. The Education Department would spend less in fiscal 1985 than it had in 1980 for programs such as vocational and adult education, impact aid and activities covered by the education block grant. *(Education spending, box, p. 580)*

But in other areas, including big-ticket items such as aid for the disadvantaged and handicapped, fiscal 1985 spending would exceed pre-Reagan levels.

Other efforts to undo, at least partially, some of the austerity measures that were imposed in 1981 included:

● An omnibus education bill that extended 10 education programs and raised spending ceilings to $1.2 billion in fiscal 1985, about 30 percent more than was allowed under the fiscal 1984 limits set by the reconciliation bill.

● A new program of aid to magnet schools in districts undergoing desegregation, capping a two-year effort to resurrect a desegregation aid program that was abolished when Congress created the education block grant in 1981.

● Extension of two education programs — impact aid to certain school districts and the Follow Through program for disadvantaged schoolchildren — that were slated to be eliminated under the reconciliation bill.

The 98th Congress also authorized several programs to promote school improvement. Among these was legislation authorizing almost $1 billion over two years to help train more math and science teachers.

Very little money, however, actually was appropriated for the new programs. Congress appropriated no funds for the math-science program in its first year and only $100 million for the second year. Nonetheless, some saw the measure as carrying important symbolism as the first significant step the federal government had taken to raise the quality of U.S. education.

Education Department

President Reagan's 1982 proposal to abolish the Education Department — in fulfillment of a 1980 campaign pledge — gradually faded from view.

Reagan had opposed the Cabinet-level agency as a symbol and tool of an overly intrusive federal role in education. But his plan to transform the department into a stripped-down agency with limited regulatory powers was ignored by Congress.

Chronology
Of Action
On Education

1981

President Reagan's ambitious plan to scale back the federal role in education met with mixed success in 1981. While Congress agreed to major funding cuts, it sharply curtailed the president's proposal to transfer authority over education programs to state and local governments.

The changes were included in the 1981 reconciliation bill, which incorporated budget cuts sought by Reagan and endorsed by Congress through its budget process. In his first budget message to Congress March 10, the president proposed consolidating 44 elementary and secondary education programs into two block grants and reducing their funding by 25 percent. States could use the funds as they wished to help children with special educational needs and to improve school programs.

The proposal ran into heavy opposition in Congress, largely because of fears that it would undermine the two core federal programs: aid for the education of disadvantaged and handicapped children. A lengthy deadlock in the Republican-controlled Senate Labor and Human Resources Committee finally produced a compromise plan that maintained the separate status of those programs, while establishing one block grant out of a variety of small programs. The House ultimately went along with the plan, overruling the recommendations of its Democratic-controlled Education and Labor Committee.

The reconciliation bill also cut the rapidly growing college student aid programs, but not as much as Reagan requested. Congress approved a modified version of the "needs test" proposed by Reagan to limit eligibility for the Guaranteed Student Loan (GSL) program. The test would apply only to students from families with incomes of more than $30,000 annually; Reagan had proposed a needs test for all loan applicants. The bill also limited funding for Pell grants for college students to amounts well below the estimated cost of full operation of the program, reducing aid for several million low- and middle-income students.

Finally, Congress took a step toward a goal sought for decades by half a dozen presidents: eliminating the impact aid program of assistance to school districts educating children of federally connected parents. The reconciliation bill provided for a phase-out of payments to school districts with children whose parents either lived or worked on federal property. Payments for children whose parents both lived and worked on federal property would continue.

College Student Aid

Despite heavy lobbying by education interests, federal aid to college students was cut sharply by the budget reconciliation bill cleared July 31 (HR 3982 — PL 97-35).

The massive bill consolidated in a single package budget cuts sought by President Reagan and endorsed by Congress in the first fiscal 1982 budget resolution (H Con Res 115). *(Reconciliation, p. 40)*

As requested by Reagan, the reconciliation bill established a "needs test" to limit Guaranteed Student Loans (GSLs) for students to the amounts needed to cover educational costs. However, the test was applicable only to students from families with incomes over $30,000; the administration wanted to apply the test to all students.

The bill also set spending limits for the Pell grant program that were far below the estimated operational cost of the program in future years. As a result, millions of low- and middle-income students faced grant reductions.

The reconciliation bill also required students to pay an "origination fee" of 5 percent of the value of the loan to be applied against the interest subsidy the government paid to banks.

Pell grants, formerly known as basic educational opportunity grants (BEOGs), were the cornerstone of federal aid to college students. They had covered up to one-half of a student's educational costs. Approximately 2.6 million students had received the grants in the 1980-81 school year.

The $2-billion-a-year GSL program had come under fire because large numbers of middle- and upper-income students were said to have taken out the low-interest loans even though they did not need help in paying for school, while their families used their resources for investments paying a higher return.

Since 1978, when GSL eligibility was extended to all students, regardless of income, the program had become the fastest growing federal entitlement program — one that guarantees benefits to everyone who meets requirements set by law. Students could borrow up to $2,500 a year at interest of 9 percent; the government paid all of the interest while a student was in school and any interest over 9 percent after he left school.

In 1982 and 1983 Congress blocked administration efforts to tighten eligibility rules for the two college student aid programs. *(Background, Congress and the Nation Vol. V, p. 672; 1982 action, p. 562; 1983 action, p. 566)*

Other provisions of the 1981 reconciliation bill eliminated Social Security benefits for post-secondary students. The bill also substantially reduced federal spending for the education of doctors and other health professionals. *(Stories, pp. 645, 564)*

Legislative History

Budget Request. In his first budget to Congress, Reagan called for deep cuts in federal aid to higher education, which accounted for nearly half of all federal education spending. With special emphasis on cutting Pell grants and the GSL program, he requested outlays of $12.4 billion for higher education in fiscal 1982, $1.2 billion less than the amount appropriated in 1981.

Reagan proposed to require students and their parents to pay a greater share of college costs before becoming eligible for a loan and to restrict loan eligibility through the establishment of a needs test for all student applicants.

The administration's other chief cost-saving proposal was to end the federal interest subsidy of loans to student borrowers while they were in school.

Severe cuts in Pell grant spending limits also were called for in the budget proposal.

College Student Aid Rules

Congress Dec. 10 blocked proposed Education Department regulations governing the distribution of Pell grant assistance to college students.

The rules were overturned by a resolution (S Res 256) approved by the Senate by voice vote. They would have barred most students from families with incomes over $15,000 a year from receiving grants.

Congress also inserted a provision in the fiscal 1982 continuing appropriations resolution (H J Res 370 — PL 97-92) setting guidelines for the Education Department to follow in drawing up new regulations.

The original regulations came about because Congress provided only $2.28 billion for Pell grants in fiscal 1982, far less than the nearly $4 billion required for full operation of the program. Pell grants had provided up to half of school attendance costs for lower- and middle-income students.

To cut costs, the Education Department proposed that parents of students seeking Pell grants be required to contribute a high proportion of their income — 40 to 55 percent of their "discretionary" income after living expenses — to their child's education. A family contribution of 10.5 percent was expected for the 1981-82 school year.

Part of the reason for the rigorous new standard was to achieve savings to make up for the additional cost of provisions in the 1980 higher education act. That law (PL 96-374) required the liberalization of rules affecting independent students and the computation of home value and taxes in determining benefit amounts. *(Congress and the Nation Vol. V, p. 672)*

H J Res 370 and S Res 256 sought to avoid the high family contribution requirements by putting off the scheduled liberalizations of benefit rules. But even with those savings, S Res 256 still had to recommend family contribution levels ranging from 11 percent to 25 percent of discretionary income in order to keep the program within its appropriated level.

The rules were extended in 1983 and 1984. *(Details, pp. 562, 575)*

Saying the proposed cuts could be "devastating," state and local school officials, teachers' unions, higher education institutions, college students, their parents and a wide range of special education groups vigorously opposed them.

Education Secretary T. H. Bell admitted the reductions would cause "pain" for many, but he said they were a "necessity" if inflation was to be brought under control.

House Action. Despite their opposition to cuts in social programs, House Education and Labor Committee Democrats pushed through a reconciliation package that basically met their target of $12.1 billion in spending reductions for fiscal 1982, including $1.4 billion in cuts in college student aid.

The major cost-cutting provision agreed to by the panel restricted eligibility for guaranteed loans to students from families with incomes below $25,000.

The committee sent its reconciliation package to the Budget Committee by a 24-4 vote June 10, along with a statement of strong disapproval. It took Democratic members almost a week to work out the proposal.

Their hopes for separate floor votes on the most controversial cuts were dashed when the House June 26 adopted the administration's budget package as a substitute for the reconciliation measure reported by the Budget Committee (H Rept 97-158).

As passed by the House, the bill included Reagan's proposal to make all students subject to the needs test. It also required student borrowers to pay an origination fee amounting to 4 percent of the value of their loan, and increased the interest rate on parental loans to 14 percent, from 9 percent.

Senate Action. The Senate Labor and Human Resources Committee approved a reconciliation package June 10 that ignored the administration's higher education requests. It voted to continue the interest-free loan program while students were in school and set an eligibility ceiling of $25,000; students whose family income exceeded that figure would have to pass the financial need test to qualify.

The committee imposed a 5 percent fee on student loans, raised interest rates on loans to parents by the same amount as the House and increased the interest rate on National Direct Student Loans to 7 percent, from 4 percent.

The Senate passed its version of the reconciliation bill June 25 (S 1377 — S Rept 97-139) with no changes in the higher education provisions approved by the committee.

Conference Action. Conferees on the higher education section generally settled on GSL provisions that were more generous to students than either the House or Senate bills.

Under the conference agreement (H Rept 97-208) approved July 31, students from families with incomes below $30,000 a year could continue to borrow up to $2,500 a year in federally guaranteed loans. Students from families with higher incomes were eligible for loans only after passing the needs test.

Conferees decided to leave with the Education Department the authority to set the portion of income that parents were expected to contribute to their child's education, which would determine the actual effects of the new needs test. However, the conference agreement gave either house of Congress veto power over the department's GSL needs analysis, a provision the Senate used Dec. 10. *(Box, this page)*

(The Supreme Court ruled in 1983 that such legislative veto provisions were unconstitutional. *(Story, p. 833)*)

Accepted in modified form was a House provision setting a $1,000 minimum loan to students requiring between $500 and $1,000, and allowing students whose need was less than $500 to borrow only the amount needed to cover educational costs.

Also in accordance with the House action, the conferees agreed to raise to 14 percent from 9 percent the interest on loans to parents, but provided that the rate would fall to 12 percent if the interest on 91-day Treasury bills was below 14 percent.

The 5 percent origination fee in the Senate bill was adopted, rather than the 4 percent agreed to in the House bill.

Spending limits for Pell grants were set between the House and Senate levels, substantially reducing grants to individual students.

Provisions

As signed into law Aug. 13, the student assistance provisions of the Omnibus Reconciliation Act (Title V of HR 3982 — PL 97-35):

Student Loans. Established a "needs test" limiting the amount of individual guaranteed student loans to a student's "remaining need" — the difference between his educational costs (tuition, room and board and other expenses) and his educational resources, including the expected contribution from his family and other forms of financial assistance.

● Applied the needs test only to students from families with incomes over $30,000 a year. Students from families with incomes below $30,000 could continue to borrow up to the $2,500 annual maximum.

● Gave the secretary of education authority to determine the assessment rate applied to discretionary income in determining the expected contribution from the family; made the regulations setting the assessment rate subject to a veto by either House or Senate.

● Allowed students to borrow $1,000 if their remaining need was between $500 and $1,000; those with remaining need of less than $500 could borrow only the amount of need.

● Required ex-students who had received loan repayment deferments while in military or volunteer service to begin repayment immediately at the end of their period of service. However, ex-students would continue to get a six-month grace period from loan repayment requirements after they left school.

● Allowed banks to charge a 5 percent origination fee, to be deducted from the amount of each loan at the time it was made; reduced the federal subsidies paid to banks by the amount of the origination fee; made the fee effective 10 days after enactment of the bill.

● Required student borrowers to repay at least $600 a year on their GSL debt after they left school. The previous minimum repayment was $360.

● Gave the Education Department authority to collect defaulted loans that had been guaranteed by the states.

● Increased the interest rate on loans to parents to 14 percent, from 9 percent, effective Oct. 1, 1981; provided that if the 12-month average interest rate on 91-day Treasury bills was 14 percent or less, the interest rate would be 12 percent.

● Allowed independent students to borrow under the parental loan program.

● Reduced the annual ceiling on guaranteed loans to independent students to $2,500, from $3,000, with an aggregate loan limit of $12,500.

● Expanded the authority of the Student Loan Marketing Association (Sallie Mae) to engage in loan activities in cases where GSL loans were not sufficiently available.

● Eliminated the $10 "institutional allowance" paid to schools for each student participating in the GSL program and reduced the allowance for each Pell grant recipient to $5, from $10.

● Increased to 5 percent, from 4 percent, the interest rate on National Direct Student Loans processed on or after Oct. 1, 1981.

Pell Grants. Established the following limits on spending for the Pell grant program of basic educational opportunity grants to college students: $2.65 billion in fiscal 1982, $2.8 billion in 1983 and $3 billion in 1984.

● Authorized the Education Department to modify Pell grant regulations to restrict individual grants, so that annual spending would not exceed the cap; made the proposed rules changes subject to congressional approval.

Elementary, Secondary Aid

President Reagan's proposal to convert existing elementary and secondary education programs into block grants met with only limited success in 1981.

In the Education Consolidation and Improvement Act (ECIA), cleared July 31, Congress established one education block grant to states, replacing a variety of small categorical education programs. But it maintained as separate programs the two main mechanisms of federal education aid — the $3.5 billion-a-year program of compensatory education for economically disadvantaged children, known as Title I, and the $1 billion-a-year program of aid for education of the handicapped.

President Reagan had sought to lump a variety of education programs — including Title I and handicapped education — into block grants and cut their combined funding by 25 percent.

ECIA was part of the massive 1981 reconciliation bill (HR 3982 — PL 97-35), which consolidated in a single package budget cuts sought by President Reagan and endorsed by Congress in the first fiscal 1982 budget resolution (H Con Res 115). *(Reconciliation, p. 40)*

The 1981 reconciliation bill did make changes in the Title I program aimed at reducing federal regulation requirements imposed on local schools. Congress attempted to amend these changes in 1982, but the proposal was vetoed. Another bill to "correct drafting errors" in the reconciliation bill passed in 1983. *(Education bill vetoes, p. 564; ECIA amendments, p. 568)*

The 1981 bill also provided for the eventual elimination of the "B" part of the impact aid program. "B" payments, which went to school districts that educated children whose parents either lived or worked on federal property (but not both), would be ended after fiscal year 1984. *(Impact aid, p. 560)*

Title I was the heart of the Elementary and Secondary Education Act (ESEA), the nation's first broad general program of federal aid to education. Originally enacted in 1965 (PL 89-10), the law was last extended in 1978. *(Congress and the Nation Vol. V, p. 659)*

Education for the handicapped had been ensured by the landmark Education for All Handicapped Children Act which became law in 1975 (PL 94-142). The act required states for the first time to provide "free and adequate" public education for the nation's eight million handicapped children. *(Congress and the Nation Vol. IV, p. 389)*

Legislative History

Block Grant Proposal. Espousing his proposal, Reagan said state and local officials knew best what children in their communities needed, and that block grants

Impact Aid Cut

Congress in 1981 finally took a step toward a goal sought by every president since Dwight D. Eisenhower: eliminating the impact aid program of assistance to school districts educating the children of federally connected parents.

Threats that school districts might begin to charge tuition to children from military bases kept the program from being cut even more deeply.

Because some schools in nearly every congressional district got a share of impact aid funds, Congress routinely had rebuffed presidential requests to kill the program, which was started in 1950 (PL 81-874). *(Congress and the Nation Vol. II, p. 714)*

In 1981, however, under pressure to cut federal spending, Congress provided for a phase-out over three years of category "B" payments, which went to school districts with children whose parents either lived or worked on tax-exempt federal property. The phase-out was included in the budget reconciliation bill cleared July 31 (HR 3982 — PL 97-35). Payments for children whose parents both lived and worked on federal property would continue.

Because of a drafting error, the bill eliminated category "B" payments as of the end of fiscal 1983, even though the conference report on the bill stated that the payments should continue through 1984. The payment extension finally was included in the fiscal 1984 defense authorization bill (S 675 — PL 98-94). *(Story, p. 225)*

The reconciliation bill cut impact aid funding to $475 million in fiscal 1982, from $757 million in 1981. President Reagan had sought an even deeper cut, to $353 million.

The House originally was sympathetic to cutting the program. In an effort to protect funding for other programs, particularly compensatory education for disadvantaged children, the House Education and Labor Committee voted to eliminate impact aid funding altogether. It reversed the action later, however, and the final House bill included $401 million for impact aid.

In the Senate, the Labor and Human Resources Committee included only $200 million for impact aid in its reconciliation bill. But Armed Services Chairman John Tower, R-Texas, worried that the cut would hurt school districts near military bases, successfully pressed a floor amendment raising the amount to $500 million. Conferees compromised on $475 million (H Rept 97-208).

In 1984 the controversial program won a reprieve. Congress authorized fiscal 1985-88 impact aid, including category B payments, as part of an omnibus school aid bill (S 2496 — PL 98-511). *(Details, p. 573)*

would give them more control over how federal education funds were spent. Block grants also would end burdensome federal regulations and paperwork, which educators had long complained about, he added.

Requesting $4.4 billion for the block grants in fiscal 1982, $1.1 billion less than fiscal 1981 funding for the programs, Reagan said the funding cuts would be offset by administrative savings. The Congressional Budget Office, however, warned that savings would fall far short of the cuts, and in some cases, program administration could actually cost more under the block grants. *(Block grant controversy, p. 773)*

As submitted to Congress, the block grant proposal called for the consolidation of 44 programs into block grants to state and local educational agencies for two general purposes: meeting special educational needs and improving school programs. Within those general purposes the agencies could distribute the money as they saw fit; they would not be required to fund any particular program or serve any particular group of children. Most sections of ESEA, including Title I, the Education for All Handicapped Children Act and several other education laws, would be repealed.

The proposal did not require any matching of funds by states or localities, nor did it bar them from using the federal funds to supplant their own education spending.

The plan ran into stiff opposition both in and out of Congress. Aligned against educational block grants were civil rights groups, parents of handicapped children, groups representing children and the poor, and key members of Congress. Many of these groups had fought for years to get existing education programs enacted and adequately funded. They said the reason federal programs were created in the first place was that states and localities were unable or unwilling to provide the needed services. *(School lunch program cuts, p. 591)*

Educators and state officials hailed the block grant proposal, but protested the 25 funding percent cut.

Senate, House Action. Reagan's proposal was met with reservations or downright hostility by key members of both the House Education and Labor and the Senate Labor and Human Resources committees, the panels with jurisdiction over education programs. However, to meet budget reconciliation requirements, members eventually were forced to agree to funding cuts, and they adopted a scaled-down block grant.

The Senate committee deadlocked for weeks over Reagan's block grant proposals before agreeing to a compromise that left Title I and handicapped education out of the education block grant.

Its proposals were forwarded to the Budget Committee for inclusion in the reconciliation bill (S 1377 — S Rept 97-139) reported by the Budget panel June 17. The measure passed the Senate June 25.

The House Education and Labor Committee rejected the block grant proposal entirely. But the House, in adopting the Republican substitute for the reconciliation measure reported by the Budget Committee June 26 (HR 3982 — H Rept 97-158), agreed to a small education block grant similar to the one approved by the Senate.

Conference Action. With similar block grants in both the House and Senate bills, the biggest problem that had to be resolved in conference was the relative funding levels for Title I and impact aid.

The conferees finally compromised on funding for the two programs that appeased both the House and Senate.

Title I was provided funding levels similar to the House request, and impact aid received funding in line with the Senate bill.

Funding for category "B" payments for fiscal 1984, however, was inadvertently dropped in the reconciliation bill. Congress restored the payments in 1983 action by including the funding in the 1984 defense authorization (S 675 — PL 98-94).

The Women's Educational Equity Act (WEEA), a program intended to help women overcome sexual discrimination in education, proved to be the last major dispute in conference. Although the Senate wanted to turn the program over to the states, House conferees and a group of WEEA supporters at the conference meeting, including Sen. Edward M. Kennedy, D-Mass., prevailed; the federal program was maintained with a separate categorical authorization.

The conference report on HR 3982 was filed July 29 (H Rept 97-208) and approved by both chambers July 31.

Provisions

As signed into law Aug. 13, the Education Consolidation and Improvement Act (Title V of HR 3982 — PL 97-35):

● Revised the compensatory education program for disadvantaged children, authorized by Title I of the Elementary and Secondary Education Act (ESEA), to simplify administration and reduce federal requirements and reporting. The program was extended through Sept. 30, 1987.

● Required that compensatory education funds continue to be provided for low-income children enrolled in private schools.

● Continued the requirements of existing law that local education agencies provide services for students enrolled in Title I schools that were comparable to the services provided to students in other schools; use Title I funds to supplement, not replace, their own funds, and not reduce substantially their aggregate educational spending.

● Provided for a gradual phase-out, over three years, of the "B" part of the impact aid program; left the amounts going to the different impact aid categories up to the appropriations process, as under existing law.

● Established a consolidated program of assistance for the education of refugee children.

Education Block Grant. Consolidated, for fiscal years 1982 through 1987, a variety of smaller education programs into a single block grant to state and local education agencies; made the new program effective July 1, 1982.

The programs included in the block grant were basic skills, special projects, educational improvement, state leadership, emergency school aid, community schools and additional programs authorized by Titles II-VI, VIII and IX (except women's educational equity) of ESEA; alcohol and drug abuse education; Teacher Corps and Teacher Centers; Follow Through; pre-college science teacher training and career education.

● Provided that block grant funds would be distributed according to school-age population in each state; guaranteed small states at least .5 percent of the total.

● Required states to distribute at least 80 percent of their block grant funds to local education agencies.

● Divided the programs funded under the block grant into three parts: basic skills (reading, writing and computation instruction), educational improvement and support services (libraries, instructional equipment, guidance and counseling, and programs addressing problems of the concentration or isolation of children from minority groups), and special projects (metric, arts, consumer and environmental education, programs for gifted and talented children, ethnic heritage studies, Follow Through and teacher training).

● Provided for a phased-in transition to the block grant for the Follow Through program, an adjunct to the Head Start preschool program. The transition was to be completed by Oct. 1, 1984. *(Head Start, p. 590)*

● Reserved 6 percent of block grant funds for discretionary programs of the secretary of education; required that the funds first be used for the inexpensive book distribution, arts in education and alcohol and drug abuse education programs.

● Continued existing ESEA requirements that education authorities maintain their levels of spending, use block grant funds to supplement their own activities and provide assistance to children enrolled in private schools as well as public.

● Allowed the Education Department to provide technical assistance and guidelines, but not binding regulations, governing local implementation of programs funded by the block grants.

● Gave the department authority to withhold funds from a state if it failed to meet federal requirements under the block grant.

● Repealed the separate statutory authority for the categorical programs being consolidated into the block grant.

1982

Congress in 1982 held firm against administration proposals for further curtailment of federal education programs. Meanwhile, the 1981 budget cuts combined with a deepening recession to lower enrollment at many private colleges and sharply reduce federally subsidized student loans.

Aided by heavy lobbying pressure from colleges, students and their parents, Congress refused to go along with proposed cutbacks in the Guaranteed Student Loan program and the Pell grant program for low- and middle-income college students.

Congress also blocked proposed Education Department regulations that would have limited federal controls over compensatory education for disadvantaged children and other elementary and secondary education programs. It successfully pressured the administration to withdraw regulations governing handicapped education.

In other legislative action, President Reagan's tuition tax credit proposal was approved by a Senate committee but went no further. The bill would have provided parents with an income tax credit of up to $300 a year for each child in private elementary and secondary schools.

There was no action in 1982 on Reagan's proposal to replace the Education Department with an independent government foundation. Opposition was so strong that the administration did not even send Congress formal legislation to implement the plan, which was outlined in the fiscal 1983 budget.

Education

College Student Aid

Determined to head off administration efforts to cut back higher education aid and frustrated by Education Department delays in issuing aid regulations, Congress Sept. 29 cleared legislation (S 2852 — PL 97-301) setting the rules for college assistance programs for the 1983-84 school year.

The bill also restored eligibility for student aid to some 50,000 veterans who had lost it as a result of legislation passed in 1981. Another provision made it possible for the Student Loan Marketing Association (Sallie Mae), the federally chartered corporation that provided capital for student loan programs, to continue borrowing funds on the private money markets.

The legislation, which mandated extension of student aid regulations already in place for the 1982-83 school year into the following year, primarily affected Pell grants and Guaranteed Student Loans (GSLs). The regulations set the amounts a student's family was expected to contribute to his education, depending on family income. That in turn determined how much assistance the student could receive, when compared with his educational costs.

The Education Department had issued proposed regulations Aug. 2 — four months after they were due — that could have resulted in a $1.2 billion reduction in student aid funding.

In effect, S 2852 barred the department from increasing the share of college costs that a student's family was expected to provide. It would ensure that about the same number of students would be eligible for aid in 1983-84 as in 1982-83.

The maximum Pell grant was raised by the legislation to $1,800, or 50 percent of the cost of attendance, for the 1983-84 school year. The administration had wanted to cut

---

Draft Registration Rule

Congress in 1982 voted to bar federal aid to male college students who failed to register with the Selective Service System. It did so through an amendment attached to the fiscal 1983 defense authorization (S 2248 — PL 97-252).

The amendment originally was adopted by the House on a 303-95 vote. An amendment requiring the Department of Education to transmit to the Selective Service System the information needed to enforce the provision was adopted by voice vote. *(Authorization, p. 217)*

In 1984 the Supreme Court reversed a lower court ruling that the 1982 law was unconstitutional. The requirement that all college students seeking federal financial aid had to certify that they were in compliance with the draft registration law had taken effect Oct. 1, 1983. *(Box, p. 574)*

---

the maximum grant to $1,600, from the existing level of $1,670.

Congress had blocked the Education Department's attempt to set regulations in 1981. Those rules would have barred grants to most students from families with incomes of $15,000 or more a year. *(1981 aid cuts, p. 557; regulations, p. 558)*

The 1982 legislation was part of a continuing battle between the Reagan administration and Congress over federal spending for college student assistance. Congress Sept. 10 overrode Reagan's veto of a fiscal 1982 supplemental appropriations bill (HR 6863 — PL 97-257) that contained less money for defense and more for social programs — including $217 million for Pell grants — than Reagan wanted. *(1983 action, p. 566; 1984 action, p. 575)*

Legislative Action

Reagan Budget. In his Feb. 6 budget, President Reagan proposed deep cuts in aid to higher education, particularly in the Guaranteed Student Loan program. Reagan proposed to save $762 million in fiscal 1983 by making graduate and professional students ineligible for GSLs, doubling the 5 percent "origination" fee charged when a loan was taken out, applying a financial "need" test to all students seeking loans and raising the expected family contribution to a student's educational costs.

Recommended spending for Pell grants, the principal government aid program for low-income students, was slashed from $2.2 billion in fiscal 1982 to $1.4 billion in 1983 and $1 billion in 1984 and 1985. The administration estimated that would cut about 700,000 students from the program.

Senate Action. The Senate Labor and Human Resources Committee reported S 2852 Sept. 9 (S Rept 97-538), and the Senate passed it by voice vote Sept. 16.

The main focus of the Senate bill was on Sallie Mae borrowing. The goal of the Sallie Mae provision was to reassure private lenders that they would have a chance at getting their money back in the unlikely event that the corporation went bankrupt. However, the provision would remain in effect for only two years, giving Congress further opportunity to review the whole issue of Sallie Mae's purpose and operations.

Another provision of the Senate bill authorized state agencies to consolidate student loans. States could buy up multiple loans owed by individual students to banks, and convert them into a single loan with an easier repayment schedule. Estimating costs of up to $200 million a year, the administration threatened a veto if the final version contained this provision.

The bill also restored eligibility for Pell grants for veterans who had lost it in 1981.

House Action. The House Education and Labor Committee reported its version of the bill Sept. 16 (HR 7048 — H Rept 97-814). The measure passed the House Sept. 22.

Much of the House debate concentrated on the Education Department's unsuccessful efforts to formulate student aid regulations within congressional deadlines.

Besides restoring the eligibility of veterans who had lost their Pell grants in 1981, the House also set aside $30 million from the 1982 Pell grant supplemental appropriation to be used for veterans.

Conference Action. Conferees approved a compromise version of the bill Sept. 23. They agreed to drop the

Senate provision allowing consolidation of student loans, clearing the way for administration approval. They accepted a House provision setting aside $30 million for Pell grants for veterans, with an amendment requiring that one-third of GI Bill benefits be counted as direct student aid.

The Senate approved the conference report (S Rept 97-589) Sept. 27, the House Sept. 29, both by voice vote.

Provisions

As signed into law Oct. 13, S 2852 (PL 97-301):

● Required the Education Department (ED) to use the same rules for calculating the expected family contribution to a student's educational costs in the 1983-84 school year that it used in 1982-83, with certain adjustments.

● Also required ED to use the adjusted 1982-83 rules in 1984-85, if it failed to publish new rules by May 15, 1983.

● Provided that 1984-85 regulations issued by ED could be overturned by a vote of one house of Congress. Such so-called legislative vetoes were declared unconstitutional by the Supreme Court in 1983. *(Legislative veto, p. 833)*

● Continued through the 1983-84 school year the existing maximum on individual Pell grants of $1,800 or 50 percent of a student's cost of attending school.

● Reserved $30 million of the fiscal 1982 supplemental appropriation (PL 97-257) for Pell grants for the purpose of restoring Pell grant aid to those veterans who lost it when a 1981 law (PL 97-92) required that all GI Bill payments to veterans be considered as student aid in computing Pell grant eligibility; required instead that one-third of GI Bill benefits be considered as aid.

● Established a formula for reduction of Pell grants in case appropriations were insufficient to fund all awards, so that low-income students whose families were expected to contribute $200 or less would receive their full awards.

● Provided that if funding for supplemental educational opportunity grants, the college work-study program or national direct student loans in fiscal 1983-85 was less than the fiscal 1981 funding level, the available funds would be allocated to the states in the same ratio as the 1981 funds.

● Extended for two years, through Sept. 30, 1984, the waiver of the presumption that the federal government had the first claim on assets if the Student Loan Marketing Association were to declare bankruptcy.

● Terminated on Aug. 1, 1983, Sallie Mae's authority to consolidate loans held by students. *(Extension attempt, p. 566)*

Education Regulations

Congress in 1982 vetoed regulations proposed by the Education Department dealing with compensatory education for disadvantaged children and other elementary and secondary education programs. Further regulations, dealing with the education of handicapped children, were withdrawn in the face of congressional opposition.

The regulations would have loosened federal controls over the programs. The administration contended they would give more flexibility to program administrators, while retaining basic protections for those affected by the regulations.

Opposition came from interest groups and members of Congress who feared that the regulations would lead to inadequate services.

Also at issue was the traditional institutional conflict over Congress' right to control executive departments. The regulations drew bipartisan opposition as attempts to undermine Congress' authority.

Handicapped Education

The Education Department sought through the proposed rules to remove many of the requirements placed on local schools under the 1975 Education for All Handicapped Children Act (PL 94-142). The changes were viewed by critics as an effort by the department to scuttle the 1975 law in the face of Congress' refusal to do so. *(1975 law, Congress and the Nation Vol. IV, p. 389)*

Issued Aug. 4, the regulations would have allowed states and local schools to set their own guidelines, standards and timetables in meeting the mandate of providing an "appropriate" education to the handicapped. These included reducing the list of health-related services schools had to provide to handicapped students, and weakening the role of parents in determining the types of services offered to their children.

The Education Department also proposed to loosen a key provision of the law — the "mainstreaming" requirement. The law required that, if possible, schools teach handicapped children in the same classrooms with non-handicapped students. The new regulations would allow schools to keep handicapped students out of regular classrooms if their presence caused serious disruptions.

Although Education Secretary T. H. Bell insisted the proposal would maintain the basic protections of the 1975 law, the plan ran into heavy criticism from the well-organized handicapped education lobby and its congressional allies.

Opposition was strong enough that a resolution to overturn the regulations could have passed. But the regulations had been proposed only in draft form, so Congress could not take formal action to block them. They were scheduled to be issued in final form in early November, when Congress would not be in session.

To forestall that action, Sen. Lowell P. Weicker Jr., R-Conn., chairman of the Senate Subcommittee on the Handicapped, offered an amendment to the fiscal 1982 supplemental appropriations bill (HR 6863) on Aug. 10, expressing the sense of Congress that the department should not put handicapped education regulations into effect before Congress had a chance to vote on them. The Senate adopted the amendment on a 93-4 vote, and the provision was retained in the final version of the bill.

Although the provision had no legal force, it showed the depth of opposition to the regulations. On Sept. 29 Bell announced that he was withdrawing six of the controversial changes, including those relaxing the mainstreaming requirements.

Bell's refusal to withdraw the entire set of regulations prompted the House Education and Labor Committee to report a resolution Sept. 30 (H Res 558 — H Rept 97-906) stating the sense of the House in opposition to the regulations as a whole. No further congressional action was taken in 1982 as the regulations never were put into effect.

Other Education Programs

The Education Department July 29 issued regulations to implement provisions of the 1981 budget reconciliation bill (PL 97-35) involving the compensatory education pro-

gram for disadvantaged children (Title I) and the new education block grant. *(1981 bill, p. 559)*

Controversy centered on an administration contention that most provisions of the General Education Provisions Act (GEPA) did not apply to the programs. GEPA, enacted in 1968, established a host of procedural and funding guidelines for federal elementary and secondary education programs. It also allowed Congress to block education regulations by a two-house veto, a mechanism that was ruled unconstitutional by the Supreme Court in 1983. *(Story, p. 833)*

From the congressional point of view, the key effect of eliminating GEPA jurisdiction was that it would deprive Congress of the power to block future regulations for the programs. Educators also lobbied against the proposal, fearing funding delays prevented by GEPA provisions.

Congressional reaction to the proposal was heated because the authors of the block grant legislation in 1981 had explicitly stated that they intended GEPA to apply to it. ED insisted the legislative history was ambiguous.

Faced with the possible loss of its ability to veto regulations and angered by the apparent flouting of its intentions, Congress moved quickly to block the administration's proposed changes. The House Education and Labor Committee Aug. 5 reported a resolution to overturn the rules (H Con Res 388 — H Rept 97-701). The House approved it unanimously on Aug. 10, and the Senate approved it by voice vote the same day.

In the wake of the congressional veto, ED officials said they would rewrite the regulations and make GEPA applicable.

Tuition Tax Credit

The Senate Finance Committee Sept. 23 reported a modified version of President Reagan's tuition tax credit proposal (HR 1635 — S Rept 97-576). There was no further action, however, and the legislation died when Congress adjourned.

The Senate killed a similar proposal in 1983. *(Story, p. 567)*

As reported, HR 1635 would have provided tax credits equal to half of private school tuition costs, up to a maximum of $300 per child by 1985. The credits would have been available only for tuition at private elementary and secondary schools, not for college tuition. The committee reduced the benefit levels proposed by the administration and added additional anti-discrimination protections.

Most of the aid under the plan would have gone to parents of students in Catholic parochial schools, which enrolled the bulk of the nation's five million private school students.

Although Reagan had supported tuition tax credits during his 1980 campaign, the administration did not submit its legislative proposal to Congress until mid-1982. Catholic groups had put considerable pressure on the administration to offer the plan. Public education groups and civil libertarians opposed it.

Congress had come close to approving tuition tax credits in 1978, the last time it seriously considered the issue. A bruising lobbying battle over credits for elementary and secondary students effectively killed a bill that would have provided tax credits for college tuition. *(Congress and the Nation Vol. V, p. 244)*

Education Bill Vetoes

President Reagan in January 1983 pocket-vetoed two education bills cleared by Congress in the last week of the post-election session, which adjourned Dec. 23.

One bill (S 2623) authorized federal assistance to the nation's 18 tribally controlled community colleges. The other (HR 7336) made numerous amendments to the 1981 Education Consolidation and Improvement Act (ECIA).

When Congress is in session, a bill becomes law without the president's signature if he does not act upon it within 10 days, excluding Sundays, from the time he receives it. But if Congress adjourns within that 10-day period, the bill is killed, or pocket-vetoed, even if the president does not formally veto it.

Indian Colleges. Reagan Jan. 3, 1983, pocket-vetoed the Tribally Controlled Community Colleges Act (S 2623), which cleared Congress Dec. 20. The bill authorized funds for construction of new facilities at the Indian schools, plus $5 million a year to fund endowments.

The House Education and Labor Committee had reported a companion bill Aug. 12 (HR 6485 — H Rept 97-736). The Senate Indian Affairs Committee reported S 2623 Dec. 13 (S Rept 97-681), and the Senate passed it Dec. 16. House passage followed a day later. The Senate adopted the conference report on the bill (H Rept 97-979) Dec. 19, the House Dec. 20, both by voice vote.

Reagan rejected the bill's contention that support of the colleges was part of the federal government's trust responsibility toward Indian tribes. He also opposed spending money on a new building program.

A similar bill, which omitted reference to trust responsibility and included a revised building program, was signed by the president in 1983. *(Story, p. 569)*

ECIA Amendments. On Jan. 12, 1983, Reagan pocket-vetoed HR 7336, which amended the 1981 Education Consolidation and Improvement Act (ECIA). ECIA, passed as part of the 1981 budget reconciliation act (PL 97-35), made changes in the Title I program of aid to disadvantaged children and combined 28 education programs into a block grant to the states. *(Story, p. 559)*

The bill was reported Dec. 17 by the Education and Labor Committee (H Rept 97-977) and passed the House the same day. The Senate passed it Dec. 20, completing congressional action.

The bill would have increased school districts' flexibility in targeting aid to disadvantaged children; made clear that Title I aid could be provided to private school pupils, preschool children of migrant workers and Indian children; and made clear that Education Department regulations on ECIA programs were subject to congressional review.

Reagan rejected the assertion that it was the government's trust responsibility to Indians to provide aid to Indian children, the same argument he made in vetoing the Indian colleges bill.

He also said the bill would hamper administration efforts to help children of migrant workers, and called the congressional veto provision an "unwarranted intrusion" on executive branch authority.

Congress earlier in the year had overturned a set of Education Department regulations in a battle over the legislative veto. The device was ruled unconstitutional by the Supreme Court in 1983. Legislation containing several other provisions of HR 7336 became law that year. *(Regulations, p. 563; legislative veto, p. 833; 1983 legislative action, p. 568)*

Anti-Busing Efforts

A sweeping amendment that virtually would have ended court-ordered school busing for racial balance was adopted by the Senate in 1982, after an on-again-off-again eight-month fight. The amendment, attached to a fiscal 1982 Justice Department authorization bill (S 951), was the toughest anti-busing rider ever approved by either chamber.

But when the bill was sent to the House, it was quickly buried in the Judiciary Committee. Although House proponents of the anti-busing legislation circulated a petition to discharge the committee and bring the measure directly to the House floor, they were unable to gather the necessary 218 signatures. *(Summary of 1981-84 action on busing legislation, p. 705)*

Science Education

Legislation to expand the federal role in science education was reported by two House committees in 1982, but no further action was taken.

The Engineering and Science Manpower Act (HR 7130) was reported by the Science and Technology Committee Oct. 5 (H Rept 97-933, Part I). The Education and Labor Committee approved major amendments to the bill Nov. 30 (Part II).

HR 7130 and dozens of related bills introduced during the 97th Congress reflected the growing national concern over the quality and lack of federal policy in science education. The U.S. science sector had warned that the deteriorating quality of science instruction could leave the United States without the trained people needed to compete in the world economy.

High on the list of deficiencies was the shortage of qualified mathematics, science and engineering teachers on all levels, mainly because industry offered much higher salaries to trained personnel than did the teaching profession.

Major Controversies

The major controversies between the House panels was over who would administer a new science education program and how the funds would be distributed. The Science Committee bill emphasized applied science grants to universities, with funds distributed through the National Science Foundation according to evaluations of projects by panels of scientists. The Education and Labor Committee wanted to distribute funds through the Education Department, largely by formula to states and local schools.

Congress in 1984 approved legislation authorizing $1 billion over two years for math and science education. *(Story, p. 570)*

ED Dismantlement

In keeping with his 1980 presidential campaign pledge, President Reagan in 1982 proposed legislation to dismantle the Education Department. But congressional reaction to the plan was so cool that the administration decided not to push legislation to demote the department from a Cabinet agency to an independent foundation.

The Education Department, created by a 1979 law (PL 96-88), had been in operation since 1980. To many conservatives, it was a symbol of federal government intrusion into areas of purely local concern. *(Congress and the Nation Vol. V, p. 667)*

Although the department was not universally popular in the education community when it was created, virtually all education groups mobilized in support of it when it was threatened with dismantlement. Educators feared its abolition was part of a broader administration effort to cut federal aid to education.

Reagan's plan was to convert much of the department into an independent Foundation for Educational Assistance that would retain control of major grant programs, including financial aid to college students and the education of disadvantaged and handicapped children. But the proposal also called for the termination of many programs and the transfer of others.

In addition, the administration recommended that the foundation have reduced authority over civil rights laws, transferring the litigation of civil rights cases to the Justice Department. Critics of the plan said the proposed change in authority would cripple federal efforts to ensure equal access to educational opportunities.

1983

Reports of the declining quality of public education triggered debate in 1983 over education reform. Wide publicity was given to a report of the federally appointed National Commission on Excellence in Education, which spotlighted high illiteracy rates, falling standardized test scores and poor teacher training as among the signs that public education was in trouble. Similar conclusions were reached by other national panels.

President Reagan, while embracing some of the findings, maintained that more money and an expanded federal role were not the answer. The president, however, did retreat from his administration's previous efforts to make deep cuts in the Education Department's budget. Reagan requested $13.2 billion for the agency for fiscal 1984 — still about $2.1 billion less than was appropriated the previous year but a healthy increase over the $9.95 billion Reagan requested in fiscal 1983.

Congress for its part held hearings and laid the groundwork for an examination of the federal role in education. The House in 1983 approved a bill to fund a national summit conference on education to address the issue raised by the various reports.

But faced with a soaring deficit, members were hesitant to start costly new programs. One exception was a new program requested by Reagan to improve science and mathematics education. Legislation to upgrade instruction in these fields was approved by the House in 1983.

In other legislative action, Congress passed a bill requiring the Department of Education to continue using existing eligibility rules for the college Pell grant and Guaranteed Student Loan programs, but it approved only a short-term extension of a program allowing the consolidation of student loans.

After months of controversy Congress cleared legislation extending the Rehabilitation Act, as well as a number of education programs for the handicapped.

Tuition tax credit legislation — one of President Reagan's top priorities in education — was rejected by the Senate in 1983. Its defeat in the Senate was a major setback for tax credit proponents, who had seen no action on comparable legislation in the House.

College Student Aid

Moving to block Reagan administration efforts to rewrite eligibility standards for college student aid, Congress cleared legislation requiring the Department of Education to continue using existing eligibility rules for Pell grants and Guaranteed Student Loans (HR 3394 — PL 98-79).

However, the principal controversy during debate on HR 3394 involved provisions extending a program that allowed people to consolidate their student loans and take longer to repay them. Faced with administration opposition to a three-year extension of the program, Congress reauthorized loan consolidation only until Nov. 1, 1983. Legislation (HR 4350) to revive the program after it died Nov. 1 was approved by the House Nov. 16, but the Senate took no action on the bill before Congress adjourned.

Background

Each year since the Reagan administration had taken office, Congress had blocked the student aid eligibility rules proposed by the Education Department — either through a resolution of disapproval or legislation setting more liberal rules. *(1981 action, p. 557; 1982 action, p. 562)*

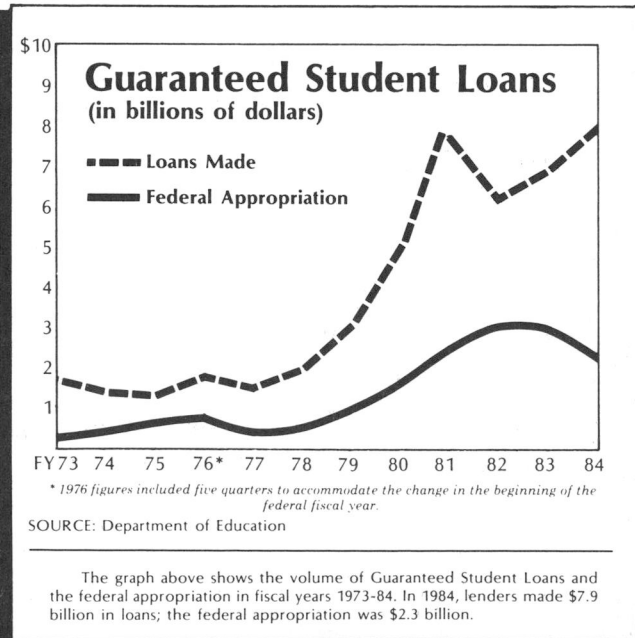

Guaranteed Student Loans
(in billions of dollars)

▪▪▪ Loans Made
▬▬ Federal Appropriation

FY 73 74 75 76* 77 78 79 80 81 82 83 84

* *1976 figures included five quarters to accommodate the change in the beginning of the federal fiscal year.*

SOURCE: Department of Education

The graph above shows the volume of Guaranteed Student Loans and the federal appropriation in fiscal years 1973-84. In 1984, lenders made $7.9 billion in loans; the federal appropriation was $2.3 billion.

In the wake of a 1983 Supreme Court decision striking down the legislative veto, Congress' authority to disapprove education regulations was thrown into question. *(Story, p. 833)*

The student aid rules for 1984-85 and 1985-86 were set as part of HR 3394, which was needed to extend the Student Loan Marketing Association's (Sallie Mae) loan consolidation authority past Aug. 1. The program had been established in an effort to reduce student loan defaults by allowing borrowers with large debts (more than $5,000 from more than one lender or more than $7,500 from a single lender) to consolidate their loans and stretch repayments over longer periods of time.

Only Sallie Mae, the federally chartered corporation that provided capital for student loans, was given the authority to consolidate loans. But Congress was under pressure to allow state loan guarantee agencies and banks to offer similar repayment plans. Private lenders and state agencies argued that if only Sallie Mae had consolidation authority, it could take away their larger loans and leave them with smaller loans, more costly to administer.

Legislative History

The House Education and Labor Committee reported HR 3394 July 27 (H Rept 98-324), and the House passed an amended version Aug. 1.

HR 3394 mandated the use of existing income eligibility requirements for Pell grants and Guaranteed Student Loans through the 1985-86 school year.

The committee bill also increased the commuter allowance for Pell grant applicants from $1,100 to $1,600 for the 1984-85 school year and to $2,100 for 1985-86. The allowance, for students who did not live at home or in approved university housing, was part of a formula used to determine students' cost of attending college. In 1983, Pell grant recipients were eligible for about $1,800 or half of their cost of attendance, whichever was less.

As approved by the committee, HR 3394 would have extended Sallie Mae's loan consolidation authority to Sept. 30, 1986, and allowed private lenders and state loan guarantee agencies to consolidate loans as well.

However, because of the administration's last-minute objections to the cost of consolidating the loans, the bill was amended before floor action Aug. 1 — the day the Sallie Mae authority expired — to extend authority only until Nov. 1, 1983. Provisions allowing state guarantee agencies and private lenders to consolidate loans were dropped.

The House approved the amended bill Aug. 1, and the Senate passed it the next day, both by voice vote. A minor Senate amendment, dropping the provision increasing the commuter allowance for 1985-86, was accepted by the House Aug. 3, clearing the bill.

Provisions

As signed into law Aug. 15, HR 3394 (PL 98-79):

● Wrote into law existing income eligibility requirements for Pell grants and Guaranteed Student Loans and extended them through the 1985-86 school year. Pell grants were the principal government aid program for low-income students. *(1986-87 extension, p. 573)*

● Increased from $1,100 to $1,600 the living allowance for commuting students who applied for Pell grants in 1984-85.

● Extended until Nov. 1 the authority of the Student Loan Marketing Association to consolidate student loans.

Handicapped, Rehabilitation Aid

Legislation reauthorizing major federal programs supporting education and vocational training for the handicapped cleared Congress Nov. 18, the final day of the session.

Passage of the measure (S 1341 — PL 98-199) came after several months of controversy over provisions added by the House to a reauthorization of the billion-dollar Rehabilitation Act, the basic federal aid program for vocational rehabilitation of handicapped persons. *(Rehabilitation Act background, Congress and the Nation Vol. V, p. 696; handicapped education background, Congress and the Nation Vol. IV, p. 389; 1982 regulations dispute, p. 563)*

The final bill combined elements of bills that had dealt separately with vocational rehabilitation programs (S 1340, HR 3520) and education for the handicapped (S 1341, HR 3435).

When the Senate passed its two bills, they were relatively straightforward reauthorizations of programs with broad bipartisan support. But problems arose when the House approved a vocational rehabilitation bill (HR 3520) that added $1.6 billion in fiscal 1984 spending authority for 11 unrelated education and social services programs.

The Senate, objecting to the House additions, refused to participate in a conference on the Rehabilitation Act. The logjam was broken when members agreed to postpone until 1984 any attempt to reconcile differences on the non-rehabilitation provisions. A compromise bill cleared Congress after the basic reauthorization of the Rehabilitation Act was attached as an amendment to the bill reauthorizing handicapped education programs (S 1341). *(1984 action on Rehabilitation Act, p. 608)*

Legislative History

Rehabilitation Act. The House Education and Labor Committee May 16 reported (HR 2461 — H Rept 98-137) a five-year reauthorization of the Rehabilitation Act, along with a controversial Democratic-backed rider to raise spending limits for a number of education and social service programs, including education of the poor, impact aid and child nutrition. Democrats viewed the increases as necessary to reverse budget cuts required by the 1981 budget reconciliation law (PL 97-35). The higher authorizations would allow the House to increase appropriations above PL 97-35's ceilings, to the targets set by the fiscal 1984 budget resolution (H Con Res 91). *(H Con Res 91, p. 51)*

HR 2461, however, failed to get a rule allowing floor action after the Education Committee's Republicans complained that the increased authorizations were "non-germane." The Education panel July 19 reported a new measure (HR 3520 — H Rept 98-298) that was virtually identical to the original. This time, however, the section in question was germane because it was included in the bill as introduced.

HR 3520 was passed Sept. 13 by a vote of 324-79 after a GOP-backed amendment to drop the non-rehabilitation programs failed on a party-line vote of 124-283.

In contrast to the partisan squabbling in the House,

the Senate July 26 by voice vote passed with little controversy a three-year reauthorization of the rehabilitation programs (S 1340 — S Rept 98-168).

Although the rehabilitation authorizations in the House and Senate versions were relatively close, Sen. Orrin G. Hatch, R-Utah, chairman of the Labor and Human Resources Committee, objected to the House's addition of the non-rehabilitation programs and refused to agree to a conference.

The deadlock was broken in the last week of the session. Key House and Senate members agreed to enact the non-controversial aspects of the bills, while postponing bargaining over the other provisions.

The vehicle chosen for enacting the key parts of the rehabilitation bill was pending legislation that extended education programs for the handicapped.

Handicapped Education. Legislation (S 1341 — S Rept 98-191) extending for three years several discretionary programs that assisted states in providing education for the handicapped was passed by the Senate June 27 by voice vote.

A similar bill (HR 3435 — H Rept 98-410) was reported in the House. When the bill came to the floor Nov. 17, the House accepted amendments adding the non-controversial portions of its vocational rehabilitation bill and bringing the authorizations in its handicapped bill in line with the Senate's.

After passing HR 3435 by a 415-1 vote, the House substituted its language for that of S 1341. The Senate accepted the amendments by voice vote Nov. 18, clearing the measure.

Provisions

As signed into law Dec. 2, S 1341 (PL 98-199) authorized:

Rehabilitation Act. $1.038 billion for fiscal 1984 and additional amounts for fiscal 1985 and 1986 for the state grant program of the Rehabilitation Act of 1973 (PL 93-112).

● $117.1 million for nine discretionary programs and "such sums as needed" for a 10th program (probably about $1 million) for fiscal 1984.

Education of the Handicapped. $163.8 million for fiscal 1984, $171.6 million for fiscal 1985 and $179.6 million for fiscal 1986 for 11 discretionary programs that supported research and training activities that aided the states in administering the $1 billion state block grant program of the Education of All Handicapped Children Act (PL 94-142).

● $200,000 for each of fiscal years 1984 through 1986 to re-establish a National Advisory Committee on the Education of Handicapped Children to review programs and laws affecting handicapped children. An earlier committee existed from 1966-77.

Tuition Tax Credit

One of the top items on President Reagan's education agenda failed a key test Nov. 16 when the Senate by a vote of 59-38 killed a proposal to provide income tax credits for tuition payments to private elementary and secondary schools.

The action came months after the Senate Finance Committee approved a tax credit bill (S 528). Under heavy

pressure from the administration to bring the issue to a vote during the waning days of the session, Finance Committee Chairman Robert Dole, R-Kan., introduced the tax credit plan as an amendment to a House-passed tariff bill (H J Res 290).

The amendment provided credits of up to $300 a year for each child attending private school. Its defeat in the Senate was a major setback for tax credit proponents.

Most of the aid under the president's tax credit plan would have gone to parents of students in schools operated by the Roman Catholic Church, which enrolled the bulk of the nation's five million private school students. Many Catholic-run schools had closed as attendance declined, and Catholic educators pressed for tuition tax credits for parents to help keep their school system from going under completely.

Legislative History

The Senate tax credit proposal originally was reported June 20 by the Finance Committee (S 528 — S Rept 98-154). A similar House proposal (HR 1730) languished in the Ways and Means Committee, whose chairman, Dan Rostenkowski, D-Ill., opposed the idea. To avoid the Rostenkowski roadblock, Senate supporters planned all along to attach the tuition tax credit as an amendment to another measure, preferably one already passed by the House. H J Res 290 had been passed by the House June 28.

The amendment rejected by the Senate called for a tax credit — to be subtracted from taxes owed — of 50 percent of the tuition paid to a qualified private school that met standards prohibiting racial discrimination. During the first year, the maximum credit would be $100 per student. The maximum would rise to $200 the second year and $300 in subsequent years. Parents with incomes above $40,000 would receive a smaller credit and, in the case of incomes above $50,000, none at all.

Opposition. Opponents argued that the proposal would hurt public education, while not appreciably helping low- and middle-income parents who wished to send their children to private schools. They objected to the administration's proposal of an expensive new program at the same time it was invoking the need to reduce budget deficits as a reason not to increase federal aid to public schools. They also complained that such an important proposal should not be taken up in the final days of the session.

Furthermore, opponents rejected suggestions that the tuition tax credit plan met the requirements of a June 29 Supreme Court decision upholding, 5-4, a Minnesota state income tax deduction for public and private school tuition, textbooks and transportation. They argued that the federal proposal was not sufficiently similar to the Minnesota law to pass Supreme Court review.

The Senate Finance Committee legislation differed from the Minnesota law in several important respects. First, it benefited only parents of private and parochial school students. Second, it provided tax credits rather than deductions. And finally, it covered only tuition outlays. *(Mueller v. Allen, p. 739)*

Previous Attempts. The Senate Finance Committee had approved a tuition tax credit proposal in 1982, but there had been no further action. *(Details, p. 564)*

In 1978 both the House and Senate passed bills providing tax credits for college tuition. But the House version also provided credits for elementary and secondary school tuition expenses. When a House-Senate conference committee dropped this provision, the House refused to accept

tax credits only for college tuition, and the bill died. *(Congress and the Nation Vol. V, p. 244)*

There were a number of tuition tax credit proposals prior to 1978. The Senate passed college tuition tax credit amendments in 1976 and 1977, but they were dropped in conference with the House, which was more interested in credits for elementary and secondary school students.

Elementary, Secondary Aid

Congress Nov. 18 cleared legislation (HR 1035 — PL 98-211) amending the Education Consolidation and Improvement Act (ECIA) of 1981, which included the major programs of federal aid to elementary and secondary schools.

The measure made changes designed to clarify language, resolve questions of legislative intent and eliminate drafting errors in ECIA, which was enacted as part of the 1981 budget reconciliation bill (PL 97-35). *(Story, p. 559)*

As passed by the House by voice vote April 12, HR 1035 (H Rept 98-51) not only clarified and corrected ECIA but also restored through fiscal 1984 "category B" impact aid payments to school districts that educated children whose parents either lived or worked on federal property.

Congress had agreed in 1981 to phase out the impact aid program over three years. But due to a drafting error in the reconciliation bill, the payments were eliminated as of the end of fiscal 1983, even though the conference report on the bill stated that the payments should continue through 1984.

The category B funds were dropped from a similar bill (S 1008 — S Rept 98-166) approved by the Senate by voice vote Aug. 4 because the fiscal 1984 defense authorization bill (S 675 — PL 98-94) had authorized $565 million for the program. The controversial program got a four-year reprieve in 1984 when impact aid authorizations were included in an omnibus education bill. *(Impact aid background, box, p. 560; omnibus education bill, p. 573)*

Education Spending Hike

An effort to boost fiscal 1984 spending for federal education programs failed in the Senate Oct. 4. During consideration of the fiscal 1984 Labor, Health and Human Services, Education appropriations bill (HR 3913), the Senate sidetracked an amendment to add $559 million to the bill's $13.5 billion for Education Department programs.

Amendment sponsors argued that the increase was in line with Congress' fiscal 1984 budget, but opponents used the threat of a presidential veto to kill the proposal by a **50-45 key vote (R 49-5; D 1-40)** on a procedural question. *(1983 key votes, p. 911)*

On Oct. 7 the Senate by voice vote substituted the text of its bill for HR 1035. The conference report (H Rept 98-574) was approved by both chambers Nov. 18 by voice vote.

Provisions

As signed into law Dec. 8, HR 1035 (PL 98-211):

• Clarified ECIA language that unintentionally excluded preschool children of migratory workers from services covered by the act.

• Blocked Education Department efforts to limit eligibility for the migrant program by changing the definition of a "currently migratory child" and making other regulatory changes.

• Allowed local school districts more flexibility in administering education aid to the disadvantaged.

• Clarified an ambiguity in the 1981 education law by unequivocally extending the bilingual education program through fiscal 1984.

Endowment Aid

Congress Sept. 26 cleared legislation (S 1872 — PL 98-95) designed to increase funding to help small developing colleges build their endowment funds.

Black colleges were the prime beneficiaries of the extra $4.8 million authorized in fiscal 1984 for challenge grants, which had to be matched dollar for dollar in non-federal funds. The bill raised the authorization for Title III of the Higher Education Act from the $129.6 million set by the 1981 budget reconciliation law (PL 97-35) to $134.4 million; challenge grants, originally authorized at $9.6 million, received all of the increase.

Twenty percent of the funds for grants in fiscal 1984 were for endowments and 80 percent funded college programs. For fiscal 1985 the grants were authorized at $50 million, all to be used for endowments.

The bill also raised the fiscal 1984 authorization for Howard University in Washington, D.C., by $14.5 million, to $159.7 million.

S 1872 was approved by the Senate Sept. 22, and the House Sept. 26. A different version (HR 2144 — H Rept 98-76) had been reported earlier in the House.

Technical changes in PL 98-95 were made in 1984 to prevent the inadvertent cutoff of federal funds (HR 5287 — PL 98-312).

Tribal Colleges

Congress Nov. 17 cleared a measure (S 726 — PL 98-192) authorizing operating, endowment and construction funds for fiscal 1985-87 for 18 colleges controlled by Indian tribes.

The bill was an altered version of a 97th Congress measure (S 2623) that President Reagan had pocket-vetoed in January after objecting to new construction funds and to language referring to the federal government's trust responsibility toward Indians. *(Veto, p. 564)*

S 726 did not include the trust responsibility language and authorized "such sums as may be necessary" for new construction or renovation only after the General Services Administration found need for the work. The colleges had to pay 20 percent of the building costs.

The bill authorized for each of the three years $30 million for program grants, $3.2 million for technical assistance and $5 million for a new endowment program.

The House Education and Labor Committee April 28 reported a tribal college bill (HR 2307 — H Rept 98-77). On May 3, the bill failed in the House, after the Reagan administration expressed opposition to provisions authorizing new endowment and construction expenditures.

The bill, brought to the floor under suspension of the rules, won a majority of votes, 255-148, but fell 14 short of the two-thirds required for passage under the suspension procedure.

The Senate Select Committee on Indian Affairs reported S 726 April 26 (S Rept 98-64). The Senate May 25 passed by voice vote a three-year extension of the federal program.

The House Oct. 20 by voice vote amended the Senate bill to delete the sections that had drawn administration objections. Both chambers approved the conference report (H Rept 98-505) by voice vote Nov. 17.

Desegregation Aid

The House June 7 approved legislation to revive a program of aid to school systems experiencing problems as a result of school desegregation. A compromise version was enacted in 1984.

The 1983 bill (HR 2207) would have established a new version of the 1972 Emergency School Aid Act (ESAA). ESAA was one of the few major education programs to be folded into an education block grant set up by the 1981 budget reconciliation law (PL 97-35). *(Story, p. 559)*

No action was taken on a companion Senate bill (S 1256). But in 1984 a compromise version targeting aid more narrowly than the ESAA program was enacted as part of a mathematics and science education measure (HR 1310 — PL 98-377). That bill provided $75 million a year through fiscal 1986 for magnet schools that were part of a desegregation plan. Magnet schools provided programs in such subjects as music or science to attract students of diverse racial, social and ethnic backgrounds. *(1984 legislation, p. 571)*

HR 2207 would have authorized a three-year program of grants at $100 million a year to be used for a variety of projects, such as setting up magnet schools or giving special training to teachers, to help them carry out desegregation plans.

Supporters of HR 2207 argued that many school systems needed extra funds, separate from the block grant, to help them implement desegregation. They said the consolidation of ESAA with a number of smaller programs had resulted in reduced funds, while many more districts had become eligible for the aid under the new block grant formula for distributing funds. They cited the example of Buffalo, N.Y., which received $6.6 million in ESAA funds in 1981 but had only $1 million available for desegregation programs in 1982.

Opponents feared that the re-establishment of ESAA might result in the dismantling of the block grant. They also argued that, instead of providing short-term help for schools undergoing desegregation, the ESAA program had become just another form of ongoing aid to schools.

HR 2207 was reported by the House Education and Labor Committee May 16 (H Rept 98-136) and passed by the House June 7 by a vote of 299-120.

Math-Science Education

Despite widespread concern about the declining quality of mathematics and science education, Congress failed in 1983 to finish work on legislation designed to address the problem.

The House March 2 easily passed HR 1310, which authorized new grants for teacher training and other programs to upgrade instruction in science, math and foreign language. A similar bill (S 1285) was reported in the Senate but was stalled by efforts to use the politically popular measure as a vehicle for extraneous amendments.

Congress cleared a math-science bill in 1984 that included a controversial Senate amendment allowing student religious groups equal access to school facilities offered to other extracurricular groups, as well as a compromise Senate amendment authorizing new aid for certain schools undergoing desegregation. *(1983-84 action, p. 571)*

Educational Summit

Responding to a spate of reports calling for major reforms in the public schools, the House Oct. 3 passed legislation (HR 3245 — H Rept 98-396) to finance a national summit conference on education.

The bill authorized $500,000 for a conference of education leaders to develop recommendations for federal and state legislation to improve the public schools.

The recommendations would address issues raised by the National Commission on Excellence in Education, the Carnegie Foundation for the Advancement of Teaching, the National Science Foundation and other organizations that had issued reports critical of public education.

There was no action in the Senate on HR 3245.

In 1984, however, the Senate added a similar provision, authorizing $500,000 for a national summit on school improvement, to vocational education legislation (HR 4164 — PL 98-1129). *(1984 action, p. 576)*

Other Legislation

Peace Academy

A bill to establish a U.S. Academy of Peace was reported Sept. 27 by the Senate Labor and Human Resources Committee but never reached the floor.

The measure (S 564 — S Rept 98-244) would have authorized $23.5 million for the acquisition of an academy site and for the first two years of operation.

In 1984 Congress approved legislation (HR 5167 — PL 98-525) authorizing funds for a U.S. Institute of Peace. *(Details, p. 579)*

Close Up, Law Programs

The House Oct. 21 passed a bill extending a program that provided high school students a glimpse of the workings of the federal government. No action was taken by the Senate.

The bill (HR 3324 — H Rept 98-286), which was passed 233-78, authorized $1.5 million a year in fiscal years 1983-85 for the Allen J. Ellender Fellowship program, honoring the late Democratic senator from Louisiana (1937-

72). The fellowships helped low-income students and their teachers participate in a weeklong program in Washington, D.C., conducted by the Close Up Foundation. HR 3324 also authorized certain law-related education programs.

Legislation (HR 2943 — H Rept 98-138) reauthorizing the Close Up program and another program, the Washington Workshops Foundation, failed June 7, on a 230-190 vote, to receive the necessary two-thirds vote for passage under suspension of the rules. Opponents objected to linking the two programs. Congress in 1984 cleared legislation (HR 5287 — PL 98-312) with similar law-related education and Ellender fellowship provisions. *(Story, p. 578)*

Sex Discrimination

In a symbolic action, the House Nov. 16 adopted, by a 414-8 vote, a resolution (H Res 190 — H Rept 98-418) opposing any effort to narrow the interpretation of Title IX of the 1972 Education Amendments. That title barred discrimination based on sex in education programs receiving federal funds.

In a case before the Supreme Court, *Grove City College v. Bell*, the administration argued that the ban applied only to the specific programs in a school that received federal aid, not to all programs at a recipient institution. *(1984 Grove City legislation, p. 708)*

1984

After more than a year of highly publicized pronouncements about the need to bolster the quality of U.S. schools, legislation responding to those concerns met a mixed record of success.

A record high, $17.7 billion appropriation for the Education Department in fiscal 1985 was approved. The administration had requested $15.4 billion, the amount provided the previous year.

Congress cleared a measure authorizing $1 billion over two years to improve mathematics and science education, a politically popular bill that had become a lightning rod for controversial amendments. Before the bill was enacted, the new education program was overshadowed by debate over religion in public schools. The final version included a much-disputed proposal requiring schools to allow voluntary student religious groups to meet in school facilities on the same terms as other extracurricular groups.

Congress also approved a scholarship program to attract bright students into teaching and to keep good teachers in the profession, as part of an omnibus social services bill.

But a bill that would have set up a broad new program of school improvement aid, heavily lobbied by the National Education Association, died on the House floor without having been brought to a vote. Republican plans to introduce amendments on school prayer and other controversial social issues spoiled Democrats' appetite for further action.

A number of education programs were extended. An omnibus education bill reauthorized 10 expiring programs, including bilingual education and aid for the education of adults, Indians, women and immigrants. Vocational education and library aid programs also were extended.

Math-Science Education

A new two-year program to bolster the quality of mathematics and science education was authorized by Congress in 1984.

The measure (HR 1310 — PL 98-377) authorized $965 million over fiscal 1984-85 for new programs in the Education Department and National Science Foundation (NSF) to upgrade math and science instruction, primarily through teacher training and retraining.

Because of widespread concern about the deteriorating quality of science and math education, HR 1310 was a politically popular measure, so much so that it became a lightning rod for controversial amendments.

Before the bill was enacted, the new education program was overshadowed by debate over religion in public schools. Added to the math-science bill was a much-disputed proposal requiring schools to allow voluntary student religious groups to meet in school facilities before and after school hours on the same terms as other extracurricular groups. *(Details, p. 572)*

The final bill also included a rider to aid magnet schools in communities undergoing desegregation — a compromise drafted by proponents and opponents of reviving a desegregation aid program that had been abolished.

As a result of miscellaneous amendments tacked on along the way, HR 1310 also authorized $857 million for unrelated education programs — the aid to magnet schools, grants for education reform projects and funds for removing hazardous asbestos from schools.

Background

The principal impetus behind the math-science education proposal was congressional concern over the shortage of qualified math and science teachers and evidence of declining science knowledge among students.

The growing concern was fueled in 1983 by a spate of highly publicized reports decrying the state of American education, particularly in the areas of math, science and foreign languages.

The Reagan administration, in one of its few proposals to establish a new federal education program, requested $75 million in fiscal 1984 to bolster science education. That request included a new $50 million block grant to states to increase the number of high school math and science teachers.

As cleared, HR 1310 far exceeded the president's request. However, actual appropriations fell short of HR 1310's spending ceilings. No funds were appropriated for fiscal 1984 and $100 million was provided in fiscal 1985.

Some education advocates nonetheless believed HR 1310 was important symbolically as the first significant step taken by the federal government to shore up the quality of U.S. schools. Some critics, however, argued that the bill failed to deal with the root of the teacher shortage problem — higher salaries elsewhere.

Legislative Action

House Action. The House overwhelmingly passed HR 1310 March 2, 1983. The House bill authorized $425 million in fiscal 1984 to improve math, science and foreign language programs, of which $295 million was to be administered by the Department of Education and $130 million by the NSF.

HR 1310 had been reported by the Education and Labor Committee Feb. 17 (H Rept 98-6, Part I) and Science and Technology Committee Feb. 25 (Part II). The bill was a compromise that melded provisions of bills introduced earlier by the chairmen of the two committees. A similar bill had failed to reach the House floor in 1982 because the two panels could not agree on how funds would be distributed. *(Story, p. 565)*

The House approved HR 1310 by a 348-54 vote, after rejecting a barrage of amendments from disgruntled Republicans who protested that the bill cost too much and did not adequately address the nation's fundamental short-term need for more math and science teachers.

Senate Action. The Senate June 27, 1984, passed HR 1310 after substituting its version, which authorized $965 million in fiscal 1984-85 for math-science education and $857 million for unrelated education programs.

The Senate Labor and Human Resources Committee reported a math-science bill (S 1285 — S Rept 98-151) May 16, 1983. But the measure was not brought to the floor in 1983, to prevent the politically popular measure from being used as a vehicle for extraneous amendments — especially a planned amendment to set up a new $100 million program of aid to schools undergoing desegregation. The amendment was drafted to succeed the Emergency School Aid Act (ESAA), a desegregation aid program that had been folded into an education block grant in 1981. The House had approved a similar proposal (HR 2207) in 1983. *(Background, p. 569)*

When S 1285 came to the floor in June 1984, key members agreed on a compromise amendment that targeted aid more narrowly than the ESAA program. The amendment was approved 86-3.

The Senate also approved by voice votes an amendment revamping and extending a program of aid to schools for removal of hazardous asbestos and an amendment authorizing grants for education reform projects.

Another roadblock to final action on S 1285 came June 6 with introduction of an amendment to allow student religious groups to meet in public schools. Debate on the controversial amendment was cut short and the bill was laid aside. When the bill was brought back to the floor June 27, a compromise school access amendment was approved 88-11.

The Senate managed to avoid another flare-up over S 1285 when the White House and its Senate allies dropped plans to push a contested amendment to lower the minimum wage for teenagers during the summer months.

An amendment authorizing funds for after-school day-care centers was rejected 51-42. A compromise proposal was included in an omnibus social services bill (S 2565 — PL 98-558). *(Story, p. 603)*

Final Action. The House July 25 eliminated the need for a conference by accepting the Senate version.

It considered the Senate bill under unusual procedures that allowed separate up-or-down votes on the school access amendment, which was approved 337-77, and on the remaining provisions of the math-science bill. The measure was cleared for the president after the House voted 393-15 to accept the education provisions of the Senate bill.

Provisions

As signed into law Aug. 11, the education provisions of HR 1310 (PL 98-377):

● **Math and Science Education.** Authorized $350 million in fiscal 1984 and $400 million in 1985 for Education Department grants to states for training and retraining of math and science teachers. However, 10 percent of the funds were earmarked for grants to be distributed at the discretion of the secretary of education.

● Required states to use 70 percent of their allocations for improving instruction at the elementary and secondary level and 30 percent for higher education.

● Allowed states to approve the use of funds for improving foreign language and computer instruction in cases where a school district had no need to bolster its math and science programs.

● Authorized $45 million in fiscal 1984 and $80 million in 1985 for additional programs to be administered by the NSF, including grants for teacher training institutes and for the development of instructional materials, awards to recognize outstanding teachers and merit scholarships for college students who planned to become math or science teachers.

● Authorized $30 million in fiscal 1984 and $60 million in 1985 to support joint projects involving educational institutions and the private sector in improving math, science and engineering education.

● **Magnet Schools.** Authorized $75 million a year in fiscal years 1984-86 for magnet schools, which provided special programs in such subjects as music or science to attract students of diverse racial, social and ethnic backgrounds.

School Prayer

Despite pressure from President Reagan and conservative religious groups, neither the 97th nor 98th Congress cleared proposals allowing prayer in public schools.

The Senate in 1984 rejected a proposed constitutional amendment allowing organized, recited prayer in public schools (S J Res 73) — as well as an alternative that would have permitted silent prayer. The school prayer issue had triggered filibusters in the Senate in 1981 and 1982.

The House in 1984 attached to an omnibus school aid bill (S 2496) language barring schools from denying individuals the opportunity to engage in moments of silent prayer. Faced with the threat of a Senate filibuster, a House-Senate conference dropped the provision. *(School aid bill, p. 573)*

Also in 1984, the House insisted on continuing a ban on the use of appropriations for the Departments of Labor, Health and Human Services and Education to prevent voluntary school prayer programs (HR 6028). The Senate had approved a watered-down version of the ban, which had been part of the law since 1980. *(Details of action on school prayer issue, p. 703)*

● Specified that a school district would be eligible for aid if it was carrying out a voluntary or court-ordered desegregation plan or if it lost at least $1 million as a result of the elimination of the ESAA program in 1981.

● **School Asbestos.** Authorized aid for removing asbestos from school buildings, to be administered by the Environmental Protection Agency (EPA). A similar program had been authorized in 1980 to be run by the Education Department, but Congress never appropriated money for it.

● Authorized funding for the EPA program at $50 million a year in fiscal 1984 and 1985 and $100 million in each of the next five years for grants or 20-year interest-free loans to remove asbestos from schools.

● **Educational Excellence.** Authorized $16 million in fiscal 1984 and 1985 for awards to school districts to carry out education improvement projects.

Access for Religious Groups

Congress in 1984 approved legislation allowing student religious organizations to meet in public high schools on the same terms as other student groups. The measure (HR 1310 — PL 98-377) cleared after months of elaborate parliamentary maneuvering and controversy over religion in public schools.

The final version required federally funded high schools to allow all voluntary student groups — including religious ones — to meet in school facilities before and after class hours, if other extracurricular groups were given such access.

The so-called "equal access" proposal was cleared as an amendment to a popular education bill designed to improve science and mathematics instruction. The House had passed its version of the math-science bill in 1983. *(Details, p. 571)*

The school access proposals were prompted by concern among religious organizations that student religious groups had been barred from using school facilities while other student organizations were permitted to meet there. The legislation was strongly supported by President Reagan, whose 1984 re-election campaign emphasized support for religious and other "traditional" values.

The issue gathered momentum after the Senate March 20 handily rejected a proposed constitutional amendment (S J Res 73) to permit organized, recited prayer in the public schools. The vote was 56-44, 11 short of the required two-thirds majority. *(Box, this page)*

The access bill was viewed by many in Congress as a political safety net that might protect them from the ire of constituents angered by the defeat of the school prayer amendment.

While critics charged that the legislation represented a "backdoor" effort to bring religion into public schools, access bills drew support from many members who had opposed the school prayer amendment.

The House May 15 narrowly defeated an access bill (HR 5345) that protected only religious groups rather than all student groups.

Opponents hoped the school access issue was dead after HR 5345's defeat, but the issue was revived when a companion school access measure was introduced in the Senate as an amendment to the math-science education bill (S 1285). A revised version of the amendment subsequently was accepted by both chambers.

Legislative Action

House Action. Equal access legislation was put on a fast track in the House by Education and Labor Committee Chairman Carl D. Perkins, D-Ky., a cosponsor of HR 5345.

As reported (H Rept 98-710) by the Education panel April 26, HR 5345 would have required public secondary schools to permit students to meet in school facilities for religious purposes during non-instructional hours if they had a general policy of letting other student groups meet in the building. The penalty for failing to provide equal access would have been the loss of federal education aid.

Sponsors of HR 5345 included the funding cutoff rather than judicial remedies to keep the measure from being reviewed by the House Judiciary Committee, where key opponents were likely to bury it.

Critics charged that the bill was an unconstitutional effort to bring religion into the public schools and would interject the federal government into the decisions of local school districts.

But supporters said HR 5345 was designed only to protect the free speech rights of student religious groups. They also said HR 5345 was intended to extend to high schools the principle of a 1981 Supreme Court decision that permitted religious groups to meet on college campuses. *(Supreme Court decisions, p. 715)*

Proponents of the access bill sought quick House floor action, while critics tried to stall and drum up enough opposition to block HR 5345.

After several delays, the bill was brought to the House floor May 15 under suspension of the rules, a procedure that barred amendments and required a two-thirds majority for passage. The motion to suspend the rules and pass HR 5345 failed on a **key vote of 270-151 (R 147-17; D 123-134)**, 11 short of the two-thirds majority needed. *(1984 key votes, p. 927)*

Senate Action. The Senate Judiciary Committee in 1983 had approved legislation (S 1059) authorizing student religious groups in elementary and secondary schools to meet in public school buildings during non-class hours, if the school had a general policy of allowing other student groups to use school facilities. S 1059 would have provided legal remedies for those whose rights were violated. The bill was reported (S Rept 98-357) Feb. 22, 1984.

In the wake of the House's failure to approve HR 5345, it was considered unlikely that the Senate would act on its companion bill. Nonetheless, the issue resurfaced June 6 when an equal access amendment to a math-science education bill (S 1285) was introduced.

The amendment took many by surprise, including Senate Majority Leader Howard H. Baker Jr., R-Tenn., who cut short the debate on the proposal.

Before S 1285 was brought back to the floor June 27, the school access amendment was revised to answer criticisms raised to the original amendment and earlier equal access proposals, thereby avoiding a filibuster.

The compromise amendment extended the equal access principle to all student groups, not just religious student groups. The revised version strengthened protections against student meetings being controlled by outsiders and required meetings to be held before or after school. The amendment defined more narrowly which schools had to comply — only those that received federal funds and allowed their facilities to be used by groups whose activities were not related to an educational curriculum. The Senate measure did not include specific sanctions but made clear that schools would not be penalized by cutting off federal education funds.

Despite the changes, the amendment drew harsh words during Senate floor debate from critics who saw it as a last-ditch effort to allow prayer in schools. The Senate accepted the compromise amendment June 27, 88-11. It went on to pass HR 1310 after substituting the text of its own bill.

Final Action. HR 1310 was cleared for the president without going to conference. After another round of legislative maneuvering by proponents and opponents of the school access bill, the House July 25, in an unusual two-part vote under suspension of the rules, accepted the Senate-passed version. The equal access amendment was adopted 337-77 and the math-science education provisions were approved 393-15.

Provisions

As signed into law Aug. 11, the school access provisions of HR 1310 (PL 98-377):

● Made it unlawful for a secondary school receiving federal funds to deny use of its buildings to religious, political and other student groups before and after school while granting such access to other "non-curriculum related" groups. Schools that allowed only curriculum-related groups to meet did not have to comply with the equal access requirements.

● Specified that the meetings be voluntary and student-initiated, with no sponsorship by the school or government, and that they not be controlled or regularly attended by outsiders.

● Stipulated that school officials could be present at religious meetings only as monitors, not as participants.

● Barred states and school districts from requiring any person to participate in religious activity or from expending public funds beyond the cost of providing space for student meetings.

● Specified that the measure did not permit states and school districts to discriminate against small student groups.

● Stipulated that schools found in violation of the law not be penalized by the cutoff of federal funds.

● Specified that the law did not restrict the right of schools to maintain order and discipline and protect the well-being of students and faculty.

Omnibus Education Bill

Congress in 1984 approved a major overhaul of federal aid to bilingual education as part of an omnibus bill (S 2496 — PL 98-511) to extend 10 expiring education programs.

In addition to bilingual education grants, the measure also reauthorized for four years or more: "impact aid" for school districts that educated the children of federal employees; aid for the education of adults, Indians and immigrants; the Women's Educational Equity Act; the National Center for Education Statistics; the National Assessment of Educational Progress; aid for education in the Virgin Islands; and teacher training in U.S. territories.

A conference committee paved the way for final action when negotiators agreed to drop a controversial rider to the House version of S 2496 that required schools to allow moments of silent prayer.

As passed by the Senate, S 2496 had included only a five-year reauthorization of aid to adult education. But the House version (HR 11) was an omnibus bill extending a number of education programs. The Senate had dealt with some of the programs in separate bills.

The most significant changes made by S 2496 were in federal aid to bilingual education, even though the Senate had considered no legislation on the politically sensitive subject. The final bill retained the major elements of a House-passed compromise that had been crafted amid controversy over the effectiveness of bilingual methods, which provided non-English-speaking students with academic instruction in their native languages while they were learning English.

The compromise attempted to strike a middle ground between bilingual advocates who wanted to continue focusing federal aid on dual language instruction and others who wanted to provide support for alternatives to bilingual methods, such as "immersing" students in a structured English program that did not include separate instruction in their mother tongues. The changes did not go as far as the Reagan administration and some members wanted, but they were enough to avert a major confrontation with critics of bilingual education when the bill went to the House floor.

However, floor consideration of the omnibus bill was marked by controversy over another hotly contested election-year issue — prayer in public schools. After rejecting a stronger proposal, the House approved the watered-down silent prayer amendment that later was dropped in conference.

Legislative History

Senate Action. The Senate June 28 by voice vote approved S 2496, extending federal aid to adult education. The bill had been reported (S Rept 98-503) by the Labor and Human Resources Committee May 23.

Draft Registration Ruling

The Supreme Court July 5 overturned a 1983 decision by a U.S. district court judge who had ruled that a law (PL 97-252) linking federal student aid to draft registration was unconstitutional. *(Selective Service System v. Minnesota Public Interest Research Group, p. 762)*

The law required students applying for federal financial aid to sign a form certifying that they had registered for the draft or were not required to do so — because, for example, they were female. Originally, the law was to apply to all college students who received loans and grants after July 1, 1983. But, because many colleges could not implement it that quickly, the Education Department did not require strict enforcement until Oct. 1, 1983. *(Box on law, p. 562)*

The bill had been considered amid growing concern about adult illiteracy. Backing down from earlier efforts to merge vocational and adult education into a state block grant, the administration in 1984 endorsed keeping a separate adult education program to help combat the illiteracy problem.

House Action. The House approved HR 11 July 26 by a 307-85 vote. The bill had been reported (H Rept 98-748) by the Education and Labor Committee May 15.

Bilingual education had been a key issue during committee consideration. To satisfy critics of bilingual education, the committee came up with a compromise under which a portion of the money appropriated for bilingual grants would be earmarked for alternative methods.

Floor debate, which began July 25, was dominated largely by the issue of prayer in public schools. The initial impetus behind bringing up the prayer issue came from conservative Republicans who had relentlessly criticized House Democrats for refusing to allow debate on school prayer legislation.

The House July 26 approved an amendment to require schools receiving federal money to permit students to participate in moments of silent prayer.

Before agreeing to the proposal, the House rejected a stronger amendment pushed by conservatives that would have allowed spoken prayer in schools. The conservatives' plan, rejected by a 194-215 vote, would have cut off federal funds to schools that prohibited silent or spoken prayer.

Then, in two roll-call votes of 378-29 and 356-50, members adopted the silent prayer language.

At year's end a case challenging the silent prayer issue was pending before the Supreme Court, which was expected to rule in 1985 on the constitutionality of an Alabama law authorizing public schools to begin each day with a moment of silent prayer or meditation.

After the school prayer controversy was settled, the House turned back to the basic provisions of HR 11.

Debate over the spending levels proposed in the bill sparked another round of partisan controversy, with Republicans and Democrats jockeying for position over the election-year issues of fiscal responsibility and support for education.

Republicans characterized the bill as a "budget buster" that would have exceeded by $1.7 billion the amount that had been envisioned under the House-passed budget resolution.

About $1 billion of the excess was the result of a technicality unintended by the bill's sponsors and was corrected by an amendment adopted July 25.

An amendment by Bill Goodling, R-Pa., to cut the bill's fiscal 1985 authorization to about $974 million was rejected by a **key vote of 169-233 (R 133-20; D 36-213)**. The House then adopted 397-0 an amendment to trim the overall authorization from about $1.7 billion to $1.32 billion. (In conference, the fiscal 1985 price tag was reduced to about $1.2 billion.) *(1984 key votes, p. 927)*

The House substituted the text of HR 11 for S 2496, the Senate's adult education bill.

Although the Senate version of S 2496 did not include most of the programs covered by the House version, the Senate had taken action on several education programs in other legislation:

● A five-year extension of the Women's Educational Equity Act was approved by the Senate under an amendment to a vocational education bill (HR 4164). *(Story, p. 576)*

● The Senate-passed version of a library aid bill (HR

2878) included amendments to reauthorize the National Center for Education Statistics and the National Assessment of Educational Progress. *(Story, p. 578)*

● The Senate voted to extend impact aid as an amendment to the fiscal 1985 defense authorization bill (HR 5167). *(Story, p. 235)*

Conference Action. After House negotiators agreed to drop the silent prayer provision, other elements of the bill fell into place relatively quickly.

The final measure's adult education provisions came, with only minor revisions, from the Senate-passed bill. For other programs, conferees accepted the major elements of the House-passed bill. The concessions on both sides had to do principally with funding levels and the duration of each program's authorization.

House negotiators granted concessions considered important to blunting Reagan administration opposition to the bill. Conferees modified a House provision requiring the Education Department to undo a controversial 1983 reorganization and dropped a provision overhauling the department's audit procedures.

A House provision extending aid for school asbestos removal was dropped. The program already had been covered in another education bill (HR 1310 — PL 98-377). *(Story, p. 572)*

Final Action. The conference report (H Rept 98-1128) was adopted by voice vote by the Senate Oct. 3 and by the House Oct. 4.

President Reagan signed the measure Oct. 19, although he said he still objected to portions of the bill, including the extension of impact aid "B" payments. The president also said that he would continue to seek broader reforms in the bilingual education program. *(Impact aid, box, p. 560)*

Provisions

The programs reauthorized under the bill were extended for either four or five years. Authorizations for fiscal 1985 totaled some $1.2 billion. Except where noted, the conference report set no specific spending ceilings for fiscal years after 1985.

As signed into law Oct. 19, S 2496 (PL 98-511):

Adult Education. Extended through fiscal 1988 grants to states for adult education programs to teach individuals basic literacy skills, authorizing $140 million in fiscal 1985.

● Earmarked 5 percent of adult education funds for the secretary of education to use for research and other special projects, stipulating that the discretionary fund not be established unless total appropriations exceeded $112 million.

● Allowed states to use funds at for-profit institutions if they could provide services not available at public schools or could provide equivalent training for less cost. Profit-making organizations also were made eligible for grants from the secretary's discretionary fund.

Bilingual Education. Authorized a revised program of aid to bilingual education through fiscal 1988, setting a $176 million spending ceiling for 1985.

● Earmarked 60 percent of funds for grants to local programs. Of that, 75 percent was earmarked for "transitional" bilingual programs, which provided some academic instruction in students' native languages while they learned English.

● Earmarked up to 10 percent of total funding for alter-

College Student Aid

In 1984 the Reagan administration for the second year in a row proposed revamping college student aid to put increased emphasis on student "self help" in paying tuition bills. Congress again turned a cold shoulder to the administration's idea.

Instead, Congress voted to maintain existing eligibility standards for Pell grants, as well as Guaranteed Student Loans, through academic year 1986-87, under an amendment to an omnibus education bill (S 2496 — PL 98-511). *(Provision, p. 573)*

Congress allowed the maximum Pell grant to increase from $1,900 to $2,100 in fiscal 1985. The fiscal 1985 appropriations bill for the Education Department (HR 6028 — PL 98-619) included $3.6 billion for Pell grants.

---

natives to transitional bilingual instruction, such as English-as-a-second-language classes. Alternative programs would get 4 percent of appropriations up to $140 million and half of any additional funds, but no more than 10 percent of the total.

● Set aside 25 percent of total appropriations for teacher training.

● Required "transitional" bilingual programs receiving aid to provide structured English-language instruction and classes in the students' native language "to the extent necessary" for a child to learn English.

● Mandated that programs receiving aid, whether they used bilingual or alternative methods, be designed so that students could meet promotion and graduation standards.

● Authorized new grants to school districts for bilingual classes comprised of both English-speaking and limited-English-speaking students; programs of proven academic excellence; English instruction for students' families; preschool and other special bilingual programs; and development of teaching materials.

● Authorized grants to state education agencies, universities and other groups for bilingual education data collection, evaluation and research.

Impact Aid. Authorized $740 million in fiscal 1985, rising $20 million a year to $800 million in 1988, for impact aid, including category B payments that continued to be limited, as they were in 1984, to no more than one-third the amount to which districts were entitled under the formula set in law.

● Extended through fiscal 1988 other forms of impact aid, including school building funds and disaster aid.

● Eliminated the requirement that a school district enroll at least 10 eligible children in order to receive impact aid payments.

● Limited the amount of money the Education Department could collect in one fiscal year from school districts that received overpayments under the impact aid program

that reimbursed districts for revenues lost from federally owned, non-taxable property.

Women's Education. Authorized $10 million in fiscal 1985, $12 million in 1986, $14 million in 1987, $16 million in 1988 and $20 million in 1989 for the Women's Educational Equity Act, which supported projects to promote equitable treatment of women in education.

● Dropped from $15 million to $6 million the amount of money that must be appropriated before local projects could be funded. Below that "trigger," only projects of national significance could be financed.

● Clarified the purposes of small grants for innovative sex equity projects and increased the limit on awards from $25,000 to $40,000.

● Specified that the National Advisory Council on Women's Educational Programs should include men as well as women, and members with expertise in education and in student financial assistance.

Indian Education. Required the Bureau of Indian Affairs, before closing any schools it operated, to notify and consult with affected Indian tribes and school boards, and to make a study to ensure that adequate alternative services were available for each child.

● Provided for consultation with Indian tribes and communities when boundaries were drawn for attendance at schools operated by the Bureau of Indian Affairs.

● Permitted funds to be distributed in advance of the fiscal year for which they were appropriated for schools operated or financed by the Bureau of Indian Affairs.

● Authorized Education Department aid to school districts that educated Indian children through fiscal 1986, setting a $100 million spending ceiling in 1985, and provided for three automatic one-year extensions of the program after fiscal 1986.

● Eliminated the ceiling on the number of fellowships awarded to Indians for graduate study, which were limited to 200 a year.

Immigrant Education. Authorized $30 million in fiscal 1985 and $40 million a year in 1986-89 for aid to school districts that educated large numbers of immigrant children.

● Specified that a school district was eligible for aid if it enrolled at least 500 immigrant children or if such children made up at least 3 percent of total enrollment.

General Provisions. Required the Education Department to establish within the Office of Elementary and Secondary Education an office to administer aid for the education of migrant workers.

● Authorized $8 million in fiscal 1985 and $10.8 million a year in 1986-89 for the National Assessment of Educational Progress, a project to evaluate children's academic achievement, and provided for the project to make data available on a state-by-state basis.

● Authorized $10 million in fiscal 1985, rising $2 million a year to $18 million in 1989 for grants and contracts by the National Center for Education Statistics.

● Barred state and local education agencies from using Education Department funds to buy equipment when the purchase would result in financial gain to a professional organization that represented the interest of the purchaser or its employees.

● Authorized $5 million in fiscal 1985 and $7 million a year in 1986-89 in education aid to the Virgin Islands and for teacher training in U.S. territories.

College Student Aid. Required the Education Department to continue using existing eligibility rules for Pell grants and for Guaranteed Student Loans through academic year 1986-87. *(College student aid, box, p. 558; previous extensions, pp. 562, 566; 1984 legislative action, box, p. 575)*

Vocational Education

Congress in 1984 approved a five-year extension of federal aid to vocational education that put more emphasis on improving and modernizing vocational training.

The measure (HR 4164 — PL 98-524) was the first overhaul of vocational education programs since 1976. Key issues during Congress' reassessment of vocational education included the treatment of handicapped, disadvantaged and other "under-served" groups; the need to modernize vocational education programs; how much discretion to give the states in using federal money to meet local needs; what role the business community should have in planning and evaluating programs.

Congress rejected the Reagan administration's proposal to simplify the program and increase states' discretion. For three years the administration had proposed turning federal aid to vocational education into a simplified block grant to states.

But the bill cleared by Congress continued to funnel funds through the states and expanded existing requirements that states set aside proportions of their grants to improve access to vocational programs for groups that traditionally had been poorly served, such as the handicapped. The rest would be used to upgrade vocational programs and initiate new ones.

In an effort to bring vocational programs more in line with changing times, the bill provided for increased coordination with the private sector and for special attention to the training needs of women and workers looking for new job skills.

The final bill authorized $950 million in fiscal 1985 — 28 percent more than the president requested — and set no specific spending caps for 1986-89.

As cleared, HR 4164 also included a Senate amendment authorizing $500,000 for a national summit conference on ways to improve education. The House in 1983 had passed a similar bill (HR 3245) but the Senate had not acted on it. *(Story, p. 570)*

Background

The Vocational Education Act of 1963 (PL 88-210) was due to expire at the end of fiscal 1984. The congressional review came on the heels of deep funding cuts for vocational education, which dropped from $779 million in fiscal 1980 to $656 million in fiscal 1982. Spending since then had been restored but only to $739 million in fiscal 1984.

The budget squeeze spurred some members to recommend narrowing the focus of vocational aid and sent interest groups scrambling to ensure that their constituents were not given short shrift in the overhaul.

Vocational education programs — where students learned job skills in areas ranging from agriculture to business, from upholstering to tool and die making — had been primarily financed with state and local money. The federal program provided only about 10 percent of the $7.3 billion spent on vocational programs in fiscal 1981, the most recent year for which figures were available.

Although federal aid accounted for only a small share

of the total spent, support for vocational training was one of the oldest forms of federal aid to education. Long before the Great Society programs of the 1960s to promote equal educational opportunity, the federal government was helping states finance occupational training.

The Smith-Hughes Act of 1917 (PL 64-347) authorized matching grants to states for secondary school programs in agriculture, home economics, trade and industrial subjects.

With the enactment of the Vocational Education Act of 1963, Congress moved away from funding programs in specific occupations and expanded the goal of federal aid to include helping those with "special educational handicaps." *(Congress and the Nation Vol. I, p. 1220)*

Although most federal aid continued to be used for basic maintenance of vocational programs, Congress put more emphasis on meeting the special needs of the disadvantaged and handicapped in later revisions of the act.

As amended in 1976, the act required states to use 20 percent of their basic grants to serve disadvantaged students — including those with limited proficiency in English — and 10 percent for the handicapped. The 1976 law also required states to take steps to eliminate sex-role stereotyping in vocational education. *(Congress and the Nation Vol. IV, p. 393)*

Legislative History

House Action. The House passed HR 4164 March 8 by an overwhelming 373-4 vote, despite some Republicans' criticism that it made only "cosmetic" changes in existing law. The bill had been reported (H Rept 98-612) by the Education and Labor Committee March 5.

The House-passed bill extended vocational education programs through fiscal 1989 at funding levels to be determined by Congress. Committee language permanently authorizing the programs had been dropped and the five-year authorization substituted in an amendment adopted by voice vote.

The House rejected 60-313 an amendment limiting funding to new or upgraded programs and allowing support for basic maintenance of existing programs only in exceptional cases. Opponents argued that many programs in economically depressed areas could not continue without federal maintenance funds.

The House adopted 205-173 an amendment prohibiting federal vocational funds from being used to buy equipment if the purchase would result in financial gain to a professional organization that represented the purchaser or its employees. The amendment was prompted by controversy over a new catalog of educational computer software endorsed by the National Education Association (NEA), based on evaluations by teachers. Part of the profits from the sale of the software was to go to a foundation established by the NEA, leading some members to question whether the union would benefit.

Senate Action. The Senate Aug. 8 passed HR 4164 by voice vote after substituting the text of the Senate's vocational education bill (S 2341). No major changes were made in the bill as reported (S Rept 98-507) May 23 by the Senate Labor and Human Resources Committee.

The Senate-passed bill authorized $923.7 million for vocational education in fiscal 1985 and such sums as Congress considered necessary in fiscal 1986-89. The measure dropped existing provisions in law allowing states to use grants for the basic maintenance of vocational programs.

Instead, it required that about half of each state's

grants be used for expanding training opportunities for groups that had had limited access to vocational education. The remaining half of state grants was to be used for improving and modernizing vocational programs.

The bill also authorized $500,000 for a national summit conference on school improvement and authorized a five-year extension of the Women's Educational Equity Act.

Conference Action. Conferees were able to decide quickly how much money to authorize, but questions as to how it would be spent proved more difficult.

One thorny issue for conferees was whether to continue to allow federal funds to be used for basic maintenance of existing vocational programs — a provision of law maintained in modified form in the House bill but omitted in the Senate version. Conferees agreed to allow only part of the basic state grant — those funds earmarked for special groups — to be used for basic maintenance.

They compromised on a set-aside of 32 percent of state grant funds earmarked for serving handicapped and disadvantaged students. The House version had set aside 30 percent, the Senate 35 percent.

Conferees locked horns over improving vocational training for women. The House had allotted 5 percent for eliminating sex stereotyping in vocational training, while the Senate set aside twice as much for women's programs and targeted it on single parents and homemakers. Conferees agreed to earmark 3.5 percent for eliminating sex stereotyping and 8.5 percent for single parents and homemakers.

Conferees accepted a House provision on equipment purchases and a Senate provision authorizing an education summit meeting. Conferees dropped a Senate provision extending the Women's Educational Equity Act, which was subsequently extended by an omnibus school aid bill (S 2496 — PL 98-511). *(Omnibus aid bill, p. 573)*

Final Action. The Senate agreed to the conference report (H Rept 98-1129) Oct. 3 and the House Oct. 4 by voice votes.

Provisions

As signed into law Oct. 19, HR 4164 (PL 98-524):

Authorizations. Set funding at $950 million in fiscal 1985, and such sums as Congress considered necessary in 1986-89. The authorizations included:

● $835.3 million for basic grants to states. Of the total, 2 percent was held in reserve by the Education Department for national programs, including research and data collection, and an additional 1.5 percent was earmarked for programs serving Indians and native Hawaiians.

● $15 million for training projects run jointly by schools and community organizations.

● $32 million for consumer and homemaking education.

● $35 million for adult training, coordinating with programs for retraining dislocated workers under the Job Training Partnership Act (JTPA). *(Story, p. 655)*

● $1 million for guidance and counseling services.

● $20 million for joint projects with industry for high-technology training, limiting federal aid to no more than half the cost of such projects.

● $8 million for state councils on vocational education.

● $3.7 million for bilingual vocational education.

State Grants. Allocated funds to states under a formula based on the population in various age groups and per capita income.

● Stipulated that states spend 43 percent of their federal funds for upgrading and modernizing training programs or starting new ones.

The remaining 57 percent was earmarked for expanding access to training for members of specified groups that had been poorly served by vocational programs. Of those funds, states were required to spend: 10 percent (as in existing law) for the handicapped; 22 percent (up from 20 percent) for the disadvantaged and for students with limited proficiency in English; 3.5 percent for eliminating sex stereotyping in vocational education; 12 percent for training and retraining adults; 8.5 percent for single parents and homemakers; and 1 percent for prison inmates.

● Specified that states could use only part of their grants — funds earmarked for special populations — for basic maintenance of existing programs.

● **Miscellaneous.** Barred states from spending more than 7 percent of their federal money for administrative expenses.

● Required states to assign at least one employee full time to administer programs to serve women.

● Directed state boards of vocational education to establish technical committees of representatives of industry, trade groups and labor to provide advice on tailoring programs to meet labor market needs.

● Required states to submit an initial three-year plan, to be updated every two years, assessing how to meet the needs of the job market and students. The plans had to be reviewed by state councils that oversaw JTPA programs.

● Required states to allocate at least 80 percent of their funds to local programs, including all of the money earmarked for the handicapped and disadvantaged.

● Mandated that federal funds for disadvantaged and handicapped students cover no more than 50 percent of the extra cost of serving them.

● Required funds both for the disadvantaged and the handicapped to be allocated to localities based not only on the number of such students served in the previous year, but also on the number of economically disadvantaged students enrolled. The new formula was designed to channel more money into low-income areas.

● Barred the use of funds for the purchase of equipment if the purchase would result in financial gain to a professional organization representing the interests of the purchaser or its employees.

National Programs. Established a 17-member National Council on Vocational Education to advise the president and Congress on vocational education needs, with particular emphasis on cooperating with private industry to ensure that job training corresponded with job openings.

● Earmarked national program funds in the following manner: 35 percent to support research, with at least $6 million a year for a National Center for Research in Vocational Education; 35 percent for demonstration projects, including projects for dislocated and older workers; and 30 percent for data collection.

Education Summit. Retained a Senate amendment authorizing $500,000 for a national summit conference on ways to improve education.

Library Aid

Congress in 1984 reauthorized the Library Services and Construction Act (PL 84-597) through 1989.

The Reagan administration had tried for nearly three years to eliminate federal aid to libraries on the grounds that the 1956 library act had accomplished its purpose of improving access to public libraries. But the continuation of the popular programs faced little opposition on Capitol Hill.

The final measure (HR 2878 — PL 98-480) authorized a total of $839 million for grants to improve and build libraries: $151 million in fiscal 1985, $161 million in 1986, $171 million in 1987, $181 million in 1988 and $175 million in 1989.

It included new grants for libraries to buy foreign-language materials and to coordinate literacy programs and authorized $2 million for an endowment fund at Howard University in Washington, D.C.

The bill also included riders authorizing $22 million for projects at four universities: the University of Hartford, University of Kansas, University of Georgia and University of Massachusetts at Boston.

Legislative History

The House Jan. 31 approved HR 2878 by a vote of 357-39. The bill had been reported (H Rept 98-165) by the Education and Labor Committee May 16, 1983. During floor action the House rejected 144-248 an amendment to allow a presidential line-item veto over money authorized by the bill. *(Line-item veto issue, p. 52)*

The Senate June 21 by voice vote passed HR 2878 after substituting the text of a companion version (S 2490). The Senate bill, reported (S Rept 98-486) by the Labor and Human Resources Committee May 23, also reauthorized funding for the National Center for Education Statistics and the National Assessment of Educational Progress and authorized funds to establish an endowment at Howard University. The Senate adopted a floor amendment authorizing funds for three university construction projects.

Before sending the bill on to conference, the House Aug. 8 amended HR 2878 to add a pet project of its own: funding for a John W. McCormack Institute of Public Affairs at the University of Massachusetts, honoring the late Democratic representative from Massachusetts (1928-71) and Speaker of the House (1962-71). The authorization had been the subject of a separate bill (HR 4066 — H Rept 98-963).

Conferees accepted the Senate's five-year authorization but tilted slightly toward the House-passed funding totals. Conferees retained the four special university construction grants and the endowment fund for Howard University.

Authorization for the National Center for Education Statistics and the National Assessment of Educational Progress was dropped and subsequently included in an omnibus education bill (S 2496 — PL 98-511). *(Omnibus education bill, p. 573)*

The House adopted the conference report (H Rept 98-1075) Oct. 2 and the Senate Oct. 3, both by voice vote.

Close Up, Law Programs

Congress May 23 cleared legislation (HR 5287 — PL 98-312) that kept alive several small education programs the Reagan administration had wanted to eliminate, including the Department of Education's law school clinical experience program and the Allen J. Ellender Fellowship program, which helped low-income students participate in

a weeklong program in Washington, D.C., sponsored by the Close Up Foundation. Ellender, a Democratic senator from Louisiana (1937-72), was president pro tempore of the Senate when he died in 1972.

The bill also prevented the inadvertent cutoff of aid to certain colleges that would have resulted from small-college endowment legislation passed in 1983. *(Story, p. 569)*

As originally passed by the House May 1 by voice vote, HR 5287 simply made technical changes in the 1983 endowment law. The Senate added the other education provisions before passing the bill by voice vote May 16. The House accepted the Senate amendments May 23. The House in 1983 had passed a bill (HR 3324) with similar law-related education and Ellender fellowship provisions. *(Story, p. 570)*

Provisions. As signed into law June 12, HR 5287 (PL 98-312):

● Extended the Department of Education's law school clinical experience program, authorizing $1.5 million in fiscal 1985, $2 million in 1986, $2 million in 1987, $2.5 million in 1988 and $3 million in 1989.

● Authorized $1.5 million annually in fiscal 1984 and 1985, $2 million each year in fiscal 1986 and 1987, and $2.5 million in both fiscal 1988 and 1989 for the Allen J. Ellender Fellowship program.

● Earmarked $1 million in the education secretary's discretionary fund for a law-related education program. That program had been folded into an education block grant created in 1981.

● Authorized $3.4 million for grants to the Urban Education Foundation of Pennsylvania Inc., to renovate facilities at its urban research park in Philadelphia.

● Made technical changes in a law (PL 98-95) passed in 1983 to prevent the inadvertent cutoff of federal funds to an endowment assistance program for small colleges.

Other Legislation

Peace Institute

Congress in 1984 authorized the establishment of a U.S. Institute for Peace to be dedicated to the study of peace and conflict resolution.

The fiscal 1985 defense authorization bill (HR 5167 — PL 98-525), which cleared Congress Sept. 27, authorized some $6 million in fiscal 1985 and $10 million in 1986 to establish the institute. *(Defense authorization, p. 235)*

The Senate June 20 had adopted by voice vote an amendment to HR 5167 to authorize $23.5 million over two years to acquire and operate a peace academy in Washington, D.C. A similar proposal had been reported (S 564 — S Rept 98-244) by the Senate Labor and Human Resources Committee Sept. 27, 1983.

Conferees on HR 5167 dropped the Senate-passed $7.5 million capitalization fund and made the "academy" a research institute that would neither acquire property nor operate as a school. An institute grants program was named after retiring Sen. Jennings Randolph, D-W.Va., who had been pushing for a federal "peace" entity for decades.

Teacher Scholarships

Scholarships to draw bright students into teaching — and to keep good teachers in the profession — were autho-

rized by a bill passed by the House Aug. 8.

Although there was no Senate action on the measure, the House bill was similar to a scholarship program that later was included in an omnibus social services bill (S 2565) cleared by Congress. *(Story, p. 603)*

The House bill (HR 4477 — H Rept 98-964), approved by voice vote, would have authorized in fiscal 1986-90 four-year college scholarships named in honor of Carl D. Perkins, D-Ky. (1949-84), who died Aug. 3. Perkins had been chairman of the Education and Labor Committee since 1967.

To help retain good teachers, the bill also authorized one-year fellowships or sabbaticals for two teachers in each congressional district.

School Improvement Aid

A bill (HR 5609 — H Rept 98-754) that would have set up a broad new program of school improvement aid died on the House floor without having been brought to a vote.

Republican plans to introduce amendments on school prayer and other controversial issues spoiled Democrats' appetite for further action on the measure. Although heavily lobbied by the National Education Association (NEA), HR 5609 was not brought back to the floor after general debate was completed Sept. 13.

Republicans charged that the bill, which would have authorized an estimated $8.6 billion over three years for school improvement projects, was an election-year ploy by Democrats.

The measure, cosponsored by more than half the members of the House, was a top legislative priority of the NEA, the nation's largest teachers' union and a prominent backer of Democrat Walter F. Mondale's bid for the presidency.

Education Leadership

T. H. Bell served as secretary of education during the first Reagan term. He had been U.S. commissioner of education, 1974-76, and Utah commissioner of higher education since 1976. Bell, who had fought within the administration to moderate proposals to curb education spending, resigned as secretary at the end of 1984 and was succeeded in 1985 by William J. Bennett, former chairman of the National Endowment for the Humanities. *(Cabinet profiles, p. 1017)*

Orrin G. Hatch, R-Utah, became chairman of the Senate Labor and Human Resources Committee in 1981. The chairmanship of the House Education and Labor Committee changed hands in 1984 for the first time since 1967, after the Aug. 3 death of Carl D. Perkins, D-Ky. An 18-term congressional veteran, Perkins played a key role in creating major federal education and job training programs. He was succeeded as chairman by another vetaran of the War on Poverty, Augustus F. Hawkins, D-Calif.

Appropriations for Major Federal Education Programs

(Fiscal years, in millions of dollars)

	1980	1981	1982	1983	1984	1985*
Department of Education, All Programs	$14,115	$14,805	$14,743	$15,422	$15,379	$17,716
Compensatory Education for the Disadvantaged	3,215	3,104	3,034	3,200	3,480	3,688
Education Block Grant (and predecessor programs)	743	523	470	479	479	532
Impact Aid	755	682	456	540	585	695
Education of the Handicapped	1,049	1,025	1,069	1,199	1,239	1,321
Vocational Education	779	682	656	729	738	738
College Student Aid	3,455	3,802	3,569	3,618	3,987	4,621†
Guaranteed Student Loans	1,609	2,535	3,074	3,101	2,257	3,079

* *Appropriated through adjournment of 98th Congress.*

† *Does not include $250 million appropriated for Pell grants in fiscal 1985 to cover a funding shortfall in the previous year.*

SOURCE: Department of Education

Foreign Language Aid

The House Feb. 23 passed, by a 265-120 vote, legislation aimed at improving foreign language education.

The measure (HR 2708 — H Rept 98-162) would have authorized $50 million each year in fiscal 1984-86 for support of model school programs and for grants to colleges based on the number of students enrolled in foreign language courses.

During House debate supporters of the bill noted that only 15 percent of all high school students were enrolled in foreign language courses and argued that the measure would provide incentives to expand and improve programs.

There was no Senate action on the bill.

New GI Bill

Congress in 1984 approved a new three-year, voluntary test program of college-level education benefits for military recruits. The new GI Bill was included in a defense authorization bill (HR 5167 — PL 98-525).

The armed services had been successful in recruiting for the all-volunteer U.S. military in recent years, but Pentagon officials acknowledged that a civilian job shortage was at least partly responsible. Sponsors argued that the new program was needed to attract talented recruits into the military once the economy improved and more civilian job opportunities were available. *(New GI Bill details, p. 621)*

Sex Discrimination

The House passed but the Senate refused to act on legislation (HR 5490) to overturn a 1984 Supreme Court decision restricting enforcement of Title IX of the 1972 Education Amendments. That law barred discrimination based on sex in any education "program or activity" receiving federal aid. The court held that the ban did not apply to all activities of a recipient institution, but only to the particular program or activity receiving federal funds *(Grove City College v. Bell)*.

HR 5490 would have amended the 1972 act and three other civil rights laws to make clear that any "recipient" of aid, not simply any "program or activity," would be required to conform to anti-bias laws. *(Details, p. 708)*

Welfare Policy

President Reagan came to office in 1981 determined to stem the growth of federal social programs and to shift more responsibility to the states for welfare and other forms of aid to the poor.

Congress put up some barricades against a complete "Reagan revolution" in social welfare policy by refusing to give Reagan all he wanted. But major changes were made.

The greatest reductions in social programs came in 1981, when programs for poor and lower middle-income persons were cut by about $25 billion. Additional cuts were ordered in 1982, but the deepening recession and the effects of the 1981 budget cuts kept the 97th Congress from approving further deep cuts in social programs. There were no major social welfare reductions in the 98th Congress.

The effect of the budget cuts and program changes was debated throughout the president's first term and became an issue in the 1984 presidential campaign.

Reagan insisted that his social welfare policies were designed to provide benefits to the "truly needy" and provide a more equitable distribution of aid among those who qualified. Soon after he took office, he pledged that the "social safety net" of programs for the truly needy would be left intact. *(Social safety net, p. 519)*

Reagan's critics claimed that his economic recovery program was built on the backs of the poor, that federal programs to help low-income individuals and families were cut to finance an unnecessarily large defense program and to compensate for massive income tax cuts of benefit primarily to the wealthy.

Reagan and his supporters countered that the welfare program reductions were needed to curb the excessive federal spending that was fueling double-digit inflation and creating a dependency on the federal government.

The growth of social welfare programs had been a central issue of U.S. domestic policy since the mid-1960s when President Johnson declared "unconditional war on poverty in America." Pursuing Johnson's goal of a "Great Society," Congress had expanded the means-tested entitlement programs for the poor. The experimental food stamp program begun in 1961 was made permanent in 1964. Medicaid was founded in 1965 to provide medical care to the poor. Enrollment in Aid to Families with Dependent Children (AFDC) was expanded in 1967 to include families with working parents. Subsequent efforts by Presidents Nixon, Ford and Carter to revamp the welfare system were unsuccessful. And Congress created new programs or vastly expanded others.

Between 1960 and 1980 participation in AFDC rose from 803,000 to 3.8 million families and from 3.1 million to

11.1 million individuals; the federal share of AFDC payments rose from $2 billion to $6 billion. Federal outlays for food stamps, at just $30 million in 1964, soared to $9.1 billion in 1980. Spending for other programs targeted on the poor and near-poor reached tens of billions of dollars.

Poverty Statistics

In the debate over Reagan's policies, poverty statistics became a political football, with analysts disagreeing over who should be counted as poor.

The debate over how to measure poverty had taken on new importance since 1979 when the Census Bureau began to report yearly increases in the poverty rate. From 11.4 percent of the population in 1978, the rate moved up to 11.7 percent in 1979, 13.2 percent in 1980, 14.0 percent in 1981, 15.0 percent in 1982. The number of people in poverty increased to 35.3 million in 1983, bringing the poverty rate to 15.2 percent. The bureau attributed the rise to inflation and the recessions of 1980 and 1981-82.

Administration officials said the incidence of poverty was overstated by the way the Census Bureau set the poverty rate, because it did not count as income the value of "in-kind" benefits such as food stamps and medical care subsidies for the poor.

Budget director David A. Stockman had said in late 1983 that the poverty rate would drop by one-third if the measurement of income included in-kind benefits — a prediction that was borne out when the Census Bureau in February 1984 issued an analysis taking account of in-kind benefits. But however poverty was measured, the bureau found the poverty rate increased from 1979 to 1982.

In the 1984 presidential campaign the administration's critics tried to pin part of the blame for the increase in poverty on cuts in aid to the needy under Reagan. They cited, for example, a study by the Congressional Research Service that showed some 560,000 people had fallen below

References

Discussion of welfare policy for the years 1945-64 may be found in *Congress and the Nation Vol. I*, pp. 1225-1331; for the years 1965-68, *Congress and the Nation Vol. II*, pp. 745-778; for the years 1969-72, *Congress and the Nation Vol. III*, pp. 605-633; for the years 1973-76, *Congress and the Nation Vol. IV*, pp. 403-432; for the years 1977-80, *Congress and the Nation Vol. V*, pp. 679-712.

the poverty line in 1982 because of changes in federal social programs for the poor.

But Reagan and his supporters insisted that the social safety net remained intact, and that the poor were better off because of economic improvements and lower inflation.

Program Cuts, Changes

The major cuts in social welfare programs occurred early in Reagan's first term. By August 1981 Congress had enacted the largest spending and tax cuts in its history; some 70 percent of the budget savings came in programs affecting the poor and lower middle-income persons. Perhaps the biggest change was to reduce benefits for the working poor and focus federal welfare assistance primarily on the non-working poor.

Congress was less receptive to Reagan's budget-cutting requests in subsequent years, although some cuts in poverty programs were enacted.

AFDC. Congress in 1981 approved major cuts in AFDC, the core government welfare program. Reflecting the administration's philosophy that welfare payments should go only to people who had no other source of income, the legislation sharply curtailed the "work incentives" in existing law that permitted families with substantial earned income to receive AFDC benefits. Congress also allowed states to set up "workfare" programs, under which able-bodied adult recipients would have to work a certain number of hours each month. Half the states did set up workfare programs, mostly on a small-scale, demonstration basis. But both the 97th and 98th Congresses resisted the president's proposal to make workfare plans mandatory.

Further cuts in the AFDC program were approved in 1982, but they were far smaller than those enacted in 1981 and far short of the president's proposal. Congress in 1984 voted to expand eligibility to families with higher incomes.

Estimates of the number of families who lost eligibility because of the 1981-82 changes ranged from 400,000 to 500,000. Another 300,000 had their benefit levels reduced on average between $150 and $200 per month, according to an Urban Institute study published in 1984.

Critics had predicted that the changes would undermine the incentive for welfare recipients to find work, by penalizing people as their job earnings increased. But the General Accounting Office reported in April 1984 that its investigators found no evidence that former welfare recipients were quitting their jobs to requalify for assistance.

Food Stamps. The food stamp program, whose costs had doubled in the previous three years, was a prime target for administration and congressional budget cutters. The program was scaled back substantially. Legislation approved in 1981 tightened eligibility standards, held down inflation adjustments in benefit levels and cut benefits to people during their first month on the program, among other changes. Smaller cuts were voted in 1982.

As a result of the changes, more than one million people were dropped from the food stamp rolls and nearly all other recipients had their real benefit levels reduced.

Efforts in Congress in 1983 and 1984 to restore some of the Reagan-era cuts generally proved unsuccessful.

Child Nutrition. Child nutrition programs also suffered major cuts in 1981 as Congress reduced subsidies for school meals and tightened eligibility for free and reduced-price meals.

According to the 1984 Urban Institute study, participation in the school lunch program by fiscal 1985 would be reduced by about three million children, including one million eligible for free or reduced-price meals. However, Congress increased funding for the popular women, infants and children (WIC) program, despite Reagan's request to fold it into a block grant at reduced funding levels.

Supplemental Income. The 97th Congress approved few cuts in the Supplemental Security Income (SSI) program for low-income aged, blind and disabled persons.

SSI benefits were increased by the 98th Congress as part of Social Security legislation approved in 1983, and 1984 deficit reduction legislation raised the assets a person could have and still qualify for SSI benefits.

Anti-Poverty Programs. The last major bastions of the 1960s' War on Poverty met sharply different fates.

Congress in 1981 abolished the principal anti-poverty agency, the Community Services Administration, replacing it with a block grant to the states, with reduced funding.

Another holdover, Volunteers in Service to America (VISTA), was severely cut in 1981. Congress in subsequent years resisted administration attempts to dismantle it.

In contrast, the ever-popular Head Start preschool program for low-income children had its funding level raised in 1981, one of the few social programs to do so. Modest spending increases were approved again in 1984.

Other Programs. Congress in 1981 rejected Reagan's proposal for two new block grants in the areas of social services and energy assistance, and instead extended the existing programs, with some changes. Cuts in the social services program, already a block grant, were estimated at 22 percent by the Congressional Budget Office.

Other programs cut back included Medicaid, the state-federal program to pay for the medical care for low-income persons, and housing aid, which provided rent subsidies for low-income families and aid to public housing projects to help cover construction and operating expenses.

Expanded Programs

Congress seized the initiative in 1983 and ordered the administration to step up giveaways of surplus federally owned food. The congressional action came amid increasing reports that needy Americans were going hungry because of the recession and budget cuts in federal food programs. The administration had attempted to play down the reports, but in August 1983, with the poverty rate at a 19-year high, Reagan ordered a task force to study the issue.

Responding to reports of increasing incidence of child abuse, Congress in 1984 reauthorized at significantly higher spending levels federal programs to prevent and treat child abuse. That bill also included so-called "Baby Doe" provisions aimed at ensuring that severely handicapped infants received necessary medical treatment. In separate legislation Congress authorized additional funds for child abuse prevention.

A key element of a legislative package designed to remedy economic discrimination against women was enacted in 1984 when the president signed a bill to strengthen the collection of delinquent child support payments.

Also enacted in 1984 was a new Child Health Assurance Program (CHAP), requiring states to broaden their Medicaid coverage to include more low-income women during pregnancy, and more young children.

Chronology
Of Action
On Welfare

1981

The federal government's social programs bore the brunt of President Reagan's campaign to cut the federal budget in 1981. The year saw a radical departure from the expansion of social programs that took place during the 1960s and 1970s.

Congress acted to cut programs for the poor and lower middle-income persons by about $25 billion.

For the Reagan administration, the changes were regarded as only the first step in a more profound revision of national social policy. A key part of Reagan's program, only partially successful in Congress, was to transfer much of the federal role in social programs to state and local governments.

Another element of the Reagan plan was his promise to protect the "truly needy" through a "social safety net" of programs that would be spared from major cuts. However, the working poor — families that had some job income but still were near the poverty level — suffered serious losses. Cutbacks in food stamps, welfare, school lunches and other programs fell most heavily on working families. Critics said the cuts would discourage many poor people from holding jobs.

While cutting benefits to the working poor, the administration also sought to require welfare recipients to work in exchange for their benefits. Congress eventually approved provisions allowing states to set up "workfare" programs for Aid to Families with Dependent Children (AFDC) and food stamp recipients.

The most important legislation affecting social programs passed during 1981 was the budget-cutting reconciliation bill, which made hundreds of changes in important social programs. Some 70 percent of the reconciliation bill's $35.2 billion fiscal 1982 savings came in programs earmarked for poor and lower middle-income persons.

The Congressional Budget Office, various Cabinet departments and outside interest groups attempted to calculate the effects of the reconciliation changes. Their best estimates showed that as a result of that measure alone, not counting further spending cuts achieved through the appropriations process:

● 687,000 households lost all or part of their AFDC benefits. The loss of benefits fell most heavily on households with earnings, and those in states with relatively low benefit levels.

According to some studies, the changes meant that welfare mothers who worked would have little or no more income than those who did not.

● 1.1 million people lost their food stamps. The largest group thrown off the program was people with incomes over 130 percent of the federal poverty level. Residents of boardinghouses and strikers also lost their food stamp benefits.

In addition, changes in inflation adjustments of benefit and deduction levels caused a reduction of $27.50 in the average monthly benefit of a family of four.

● School lunch prices were higher and portion sizes were smaller. About 500,000 students who had been getting free meals now had to pay the new reduced-price rate of 40 cents; 450,000 who had been paying the old reduced price of 20 cents now had to pay the new full-price rate, averaging 75 cents. The average full-price meal in the 1980-81 school year had been 60 cents.

Children from low-income families continued to receive free meals. However, the American School Food Service Association warned that cuts in federal subsidies would force some school districts to close their lunch programs, leaving children without a hot meal in spite of their eligibility.

Food Stamp Legislation

Long a target of attack by congressional conservatives because of alleged waste, fraud and abuse, the food stamp program experienced major reductions during the budget-cutting surge of 1981.

The most important changes were contained in the massive budget reconciliation bill (HR 3982 — PL 97-35), which was expected to eliminate more than one million people from the food stamp rolls and reduce benefits to most of the rest. About 22.4 million persons received food stamps, which they could exchange for food at grocery stores, in 1981.

The reconciliation measure, cleared July 31, cut food stamp spending even more sharply than the Reagan administration had requested, for savings of $6 billion over a three-year period. The burden of the reconciliation legislation fell most heavily on the working poor and recipients who were in their first month of the program.

Congress rejected an administration proposal to reduce food stamp benefits to families whose children received federally subsidized free lunches at school. Also rejected was a proposal by Senate Agriculture Committee Chairman Jesse Helms, R-N.C., to restore the purchase requirement for food stamps. That longstanding provision, ended by Congress in 1977, had required recipients to put up some of their own money in order to get a larger value in food stamps.

Further changes in the food stamp program were contained in the omnibus farm bill (S 884 — PL 97-98) that cleared Dec. 16. The bill authorized $11.3 billion for the program in fiscal 1982, a ceiling that was expected to be adequate to fund the program fully for the entire year.

In the past several years the program had run short of money before the year's end, and Congress had had to provide emergency supplemental funding. To assure full funding in fiscal 1981, Congress June 30 cleared legislation (HR 3991 — PL 97-18) providing an additional $1.8 billion for the program through Sept. 30, bringing the fiscal 1981 ceiling to $11.5 billion.

Background

Begun as a pilot project in 1961, the food stamp program originally was aimed as much at removing surplus agricultural commodities from the market as at improving the diet of low-income families. The program grew rapidly, however. By the 1970s increasing enrollments, spiraling

costs and allegations of fraud and mismanagement spurred congressional efforts to overhaul the program.

Because food stamps were an entitlement, spending for the program was uncontrollable and open-ended; the government had to pay out whatever was needed to give food stamps to every eligible family that applied for them. Benefits were adjusted twice a year according to changes in food prices, so costs escalated rapidly.

In 1977, as part of a four-year reauthorization of the program (PL 95-113), Congress attempted to bring costs under control by imposing ceilings on annual food stamp spending. But food prices and unemployment rose at a much greater rate than economists had predicted, and the ceilings had to be raised to keep benefits from being cut. *(Congress and the Nation Vol. V, pp. 681, 699, 701)*

The fiscal 1981 ceiling, set by the 1980 food stamp amendments (PL 96-249), was $9.7 billion. Early in 1981, however, it became clear that the cost of the program — pushed up by unexpectedly high unemployment and inflation — would far exceed that amount. With administration support, Congress approved legislation (HR 3991 — PL 97-18) raising the ceiling to $11.5 billion. The bill was passed by the House June 23 and the Senate early June 26.

Reconciliation Cuts

Congress cut $1.7 billion from projected fiscal 1982 food stamp costs in HR 3982, the omnibus reconciliation bill cleared July 31. The bill carried out budget cuts sought by President Reagan and endorsed by Congress through its budget process. *(Reconciliation, p. 40)*

In assembling their reconciliation packages, the Senate and House Budget committees incorporated cost-saving provisions of separate food stamp measures approved by the Senate and House Agriculture committees May 12.

Food Stamp Bills. The Agriculture committees had included the cost-saving provisions in bills reauthorizing the food stamp program through fiscal 1985. The House bill (HR 3109) provided estimated fiscal 1982 savings of $1.23 billion, compared with $1.85 billion in the Senate bill (S 1007 — S Rept 97-128). The Senate panel estimated the administration's proposed cuts at $1.5 billion.

Both committees agreed to exclude from the program all households with incomes in excess of 130 percent of the federal poverty level, provide less generous inflation adjustments in benefits and reduce benefits to most recipients during their first month in the program. But they rejected the administration's biggest single savings proposal, which would have cut about $500 million by reducing food stamp benefits to families whose children received federally subsidized free lunches at school.

After resisting the proposal for years, the House Agriculture Committee joined the Senate panel in supporting a ban on food stamps for households involved in labor strikes. Congress had adopted some restrictions on benefits to striking families in both 1979 and 1980.

The Senate passed S 1007 by a 77-17 vote June 10 after rejecting even sharper reductions proposed by the program's critics. An amendment that would have restored the pre-1977 purchase requirement for food stamps was defeated 33-66.

There was no further action on the separate reauthorization bills. Their cost-cutting provisions subsequently were folded into the reconciliation bill, while a one-year spending authorization and certain other provisions were included in the farm bill passed later in the year.

Reconciliation Action. The Senate passed its version of the reconciliation bill (S 1377 — S Rept 97-139), including the food stamp cuts, June 25 without substantial change. The following day the House substituted a Republican-designed alternative for the reconciliation measure drafted by its Democratic-controlled committees (H Rept 97-158), thus narrowing the differences between the Senate and House food stamp provisions.

There still were some differences, however, that led to a difficult conference. In three days of sometimes acrimonious meetings, the conferees approved cuts totaling $1.657 billion in fiscal 1982 — $199 million more than the $1.458 billion the reconciliation instructions required them to cut. Conferees resisted pressure from Helms for still deeper slashes in the program.

Most of the new savings were achieved by a decision to freeze the income deduction for excess shelter costs through June 1983, as the Senate bill provided. The House bill had permitted annual inflation adjustments to reflect changes in the shelter, fuel and utilities components in the Consumer Price Index.

Both reconciliation bills restricted eligibility to households with gross monthly incomes at or below 130 percent of the poverty level ($8,450 for a non-farm family of four in 1981), but the conferees accepted a Senate provision exempting households with elderly or disabled members from the new income test.

Conferees also softened the effect of two provisions that opponents said would encourage food stamp recipients working at low-paying jobs to quit and go on welfare instead. They agreed to lower the earned-income deduction (the amount subtracted from a household's gross income for purposes of computing its benefit levels) to 18 percent of a household's earnings from the existing level of 20 percent. The Senate bill reduced the figure to 15 percent, while the House bill made no change.

Both chambers agreed to the conference report (H Rept 97-208) July 31.

Farm Bill Action

Fiscal 1982 funding for the food stamp program was authorized in the omnibus farm bill (S 884 — PL 97-98), which cleared Dec. 16. *(Farm bill details, p. 487)*

Unlike the Senate, which had passed a separate food stamp bill in June, the House included the food stamp reauthorization in its version of the farm bill (HR 3603 — H Rept 97-106), passed Oct. 22.

Before HR 3603 came to the floor, food program advocates reached a compromise with administration officials on the funding level for fiscal 1982. The $11.3 billion authorization ceiling provided by the bill was $700 million more than the $10.6 billion favored by the administration. The Senate had approved a $10.9 billion ceiling for the year as part of S 1007.

The compromise was adopted by voice vote on the House floor. It set the authorization levels at $11.3 billion in fiscal 1982, $11.2 billion in 1983, $11.1 billion in 1984 and $11.3 billion in 1985.

The farm bill conference, which included food stamp provisions from the House farm bill and the Senate food stamp bill, was a difficult one stretching over several months.

While conferees were principally concerned with agricultural issues such as price supports, they also deadlocked over food stamps. They never were able to resolve a House-Senate dispute over the method of making future inflation

adjustments in food stamp benefits.

Because of their intractable differences over the inflation adjustments, conferees decided to settle for a one-year reauthorization of the program, at $11.3 billion. That meant Congress would have to act again on the program in 1982, thus reopening the inflation adjustment issue. *(1982 action, p. 594)*

Final Provisions

Reconciliation Bill. As signed into law Aug. 13, the food stamp provisions of HR 3982 (Title I of PL 97-35):

● Limited eligibility for the program to households with total incomes below 130 percent of the federally defined poverty level. The bill maintained the "net" eligibility limit for households containing elderly or disabled members at 100 percent of poverty, with various income deductions that in most cases pushed the effective income limit to 130 percent of poverty.

● Required that parents and children living together be treated as one household in determining food stamp eligibility and benefits, but allowed them to be treated as separate households if at least one parent was 60 or older.

● Required that all residents of a house with paying boarders be treated as a single household for benefit calculations.

● Postponed the annual inflation adjustment of the "thrifty food plan" — the government's list of low-cost foods used in calculating benefits. The adjustments would be delayed from the Jan. 1 date in existing law until April 1, 1982, July 1, 1983, and Oct. 1 in each succeeding year.

The adjustment date was further pushed back in the 1981 farm bill and again in 1982. *(Farm bill, below; 1982 action, p. 594)*

● Required that inflation adjustments in the standard deduction and in the excess shelter and day-care cost deduction be based on a version of the Consumer Price Index that excluded home ownership costs.

● Froze until July 1, 1983, the existing levels for the standard and excess shelter deductions; beginning in 1984, deduction levels would be adjusted on Oct. 1 of each year.

● Reduced to 18 percent, from 20 percent, the portion of earned income to be disregarded in computing income for the purpose of determining benefits.

● Required states to use a system of "periodic retrospective income accounting" to calculate recipients' income. Under the system, benefits would be based on a household's actual income in a preceding period of time, rather than on an estimate of its expected income in the future, as under existing law. In addition, recipients would be required to file periodic reports of their income, instead of having to report only when there had been some change in their circumstances.

● Excluded from the program households in which a member was participating in a strike, unless the household was eligible for the program before the strike. Households that were eligible would not receive increased benefits as a result of the loss of the striking worker's income.

● Determined benefit levels for households during their first month on the program according to the day of the month on which they applied. Under existing law, households received a full month's benefits, regardless of when they applied. The new law would provide half-a-month's benefits to recipients who applied on the 15th of the month, for example, and one-thirtieth of a month's benefits for those who applied on the last day of the month.

● Prohibited federal funding of outreach programs aimed at informing eligible persons of their rights to receive food stamps.

● Increased penalties for persons found to have engaged in fraud or misrepresentation in applying for or receiving benefits.

● Repealed increases in deductions established by a 1980 law and scheduled to go into effect in fiscal 1982. The provisions would have created a separate dependent care deduction of up to $90 a month and lowered to $25 a month, from $35, the level above which elderly and disabled persons could deduct their medical expenses. *(Congress and the Nation Vol. V, p. 701)*

● Established, beginning July 1, 1982, a nutritional block grant program for Puerto Rico (as proposed by Reagan), replacing existing federal nutrition programs. The block grant would allow food stamps to be distributed in the form of cash; it would provide 100 percent of the nutritional assistance given to needy persons on the island, and 50 percent of the related administrative costs, up to a maximum of $825 million a year.

In 1982 Congress voted to terminate the program Oct. 1, 1983, but that deadline was postponed the following year. *(Stories, pp. 594, 602)*

● Extended a provision in existing law that allowed certain states to provide cash payments in lieu of food stamps to aged, blind and disabled Supplemental Security Income (SSI) recipients.

Farm Bill. As signed into law Dec. 22, the food stamp provisions of the farm bill (S 884 — PL 97-98):

● Authorized a spending ceiling of $11.3 billion for the food stamp program in fiscal 1982.

● Required the secretary of agriculture to permit towns and other jurisdictions to require food stamp participants to work at public- or private-sector jobs, with payment in stamps at the minimum wage rate.

● Permitted Alaska to use a separate thrifty food plan to determine benefits for its rural areas.

● Barred deductions for household expenses paid by a third party in calculating income for eligibility.

● Required that income and resources of sponsors of certain aliens be included in eligibility and benefit determinations.

● Permitted the agriculture secretary to change standards for estimating the value of vehicles for determining eligibility and benefits.

● Made households receiving food stamps ineligible for the program if the wage earner voluntarily quit a job.

● Made participants who did not comply with either Aid to Families with Dependent Children (AFDC) or unemployment compensation work requirements subject to sanctions if they did not comply with the annual food stamp work registration requirement.

● Made states financially liable for losses of food stamps.

● Repealed the 60-day transfer provision that permitted uninterrupted benefits for a household moving from one political entity to another.

● Permitted states, in certain circumstances, to avoid a requirement that recipients be notified of pending loss of eligibility 30 days before such loss.

● Repealed a requirement that the Agriculture Department restore food stamps to households wrongfully denied, if a year had expired before the household applied for restoration.

● Required state agencies to use Social Security and state unemployment wage and benefit information in certifying recipients.

● Required the agriculture secretary to permit political

entities to issue food stamps by certified mail.

• Repealed program staffing standards for states.

• Required states to meet federal standards for denials and terminations or lose 55 percent of their federal funds for administrative costs; also required states with error rates exceeding 5 percent to develop corrective plans.

• Required that a participating household provide a Social Security number.

• Continued "cash out" pilot projects, which provided cash instead of stamps, and made AFDC families eligible for such projects.

• Authorized grants and contracts for developing methods of monitoring the nutritional status of high-risk populations.

• Set penalties for fraudulent misuse of commodities.

• Authorized pilot projects, for two years, to provide commodities to poor, elderly people, and extended through fiscal 1985 commodity distribution programs for poor pregnant women, new mothers and young children.

• Postponed until Oct. 1, 1982, adjustments for inflation in the thrifty food plan, which was used to determine benefit levels for recipients, and set future annual adjustments for Oct. 1. *(Reconciliation provision, above)*

In 1982 Congress again delayed, and reduced, scheduled adjustments in the thrifty food plan. The changes were included in that year's budget reconciliation legislation (HR 6955 — PL 97-253). *(Food stamp changes, p. 594; 1982 reconciliation action, p. 48)*

• Authorized designated investigators in the Agriculture Department inspector general's office to carry firearms and, in connection with investigations of probable violations of food stamp or other laws under the department's jurisdiction, to execute warrants for searches or seizures of evidence and for arrests, and to arrest without warrants when a criminal violation had occurred in the presence of the investigator or he had probable cause to believe such a violation had occurred.

• Made banks and other so-called "first endorsers" (distributors of food stamps) liable for paying for food stamp losses if they ignored certain procedures for identifying recipients.

• Specified that federal, state or local low-income energy aid could not be counted as income in determining eligibility for food stamps if it was specifically designated as energy aid and if it was provided on a seasonal basis for no more than six months each year.

• Permitted parents living with children to qualify separately for food stamps if one of the parents received disability or certain other forms of aid, and if parents and children bought and prepared food separately.

• Permitted members of federally recognized Indian tribes not living on reservations to qualify for food stamps.

• Authorized pilot projects in which recipients of SSI, Medicaid or AFDC who met food stamp income eligibility requirements would not have to make separate, duplicate applications for stamps.

• Required retail stores accepting food stamps to display instructions for reporting food stamp fraud; also required that program applications state that incorrect information could result in denial of stamps and criminal prosecution.

• Permitted local, state and federal law enforcement officials investigating alleged food stamp violations to inspect information from food stamp applications.

• Required prison sentences for persons convicted of food stamp violations more than once, and authorized courts to suspend such violators for up to 18 months, in addition to any other disqualification period.

Welfare Benefits

The omnibus budget reconciliation bill cleared by Congress July 31 (HR 3982 — PL 97-35) made substantial reductions in assistance to working mothers who received benefits under the core government welfare program, Aid to Families with Dependent Children (AFDC).

The reconciliation bill incorporated budget-cutting measures ordered by Congress in the first fiscal 1982 budget resolution (H Con Res 115). The AFDC reductions were in line with the Reagan administration's policy of making welfare programs a "safety net" for the extremely poor, rather than an income supplement for those with marginal incomes. In 1982 Congress reduced funding for welfare programs still further, although not as much as the administration wanted. *(Reconciliation bill, p. 40; 1982 action, p. 596)*

The Department of Health and Human Services (HHS) estimated that about 687,000 of the 3.9 million households on the AFDC rolls would lose all or some of their benefits as a result of the 1981 legislation. Some 408,000 families would be dropped from the program altogether, while 279,000 would receive reduced benefits.

The Congressional Budget Office estimated the program changes mandated by the bill would save $1.2 billion in fiscal 1982, $1.4 billion in 1983 and $1.4 billion in 1984.

Critics said the changes would discourage many welfare mothers from working. In many states, recipients would have little or no more net income from working than from staying home, they said.

However, the legislation emphasized work by allowing states to set up "workfare" programs under which recipients would do community service work in exchange for their benefits. States were not required to establish such programs, although President Reagan had favored mandatory workfare plans.

Other provisions of HR 3982 attempted to strengthen child support enforcement, a proposal endorsed by the administration. That program sought to reduce AFDC costs by collecting child support payments from the absent fathers of low-income children. Congress enacted major child support legislation in 1984. *(Story, p. 605)*

Legislative History

President Reagan, in his March 10 budget proposal, called for major changes in AFDC. Without changes, federal spending for the program would be about $7.7 billion in 1982, with state governments spending an approximately equal amount on it, according to HHS.

Reagan proposed a mandatory workfare requirement (which he had instituted in California when he was governor of that state) and other major changes in AFDC aimed at saving about $1 billion in fiscal 1982. Among the changes were revisions in accounting procedures that would reduce benefit eligibility substantially.

In approving its reconciliation package May 5, the Senate Finance Committee decided to let the states determine whether to operate workfare programs. The administration's major savings proposals were left intact, however.

The House Ways and Means Committee approved a similar package May 19. It also made workfare programs optional.

The committees' recommendations were included in omnibus reconciliation measures reported to the House and Senate in June (HR 3982 — H Rept 97-158, S 1377 — S Rept 97-139).

The Senate passed S 1377 June 25. Before passing HR 3982 the following day, the House adopted a Republican-sponsored substitute, known as Gramm-Latta II, that made the AFDC provisions of the House and Senate bills virtually identical.

Gramm-Latta II added $450 million to the $720 million in savings approved by the Ways and Means Committee, largely by further reducing benefits to AFDC recipients who had job income. It barred an "income disregard" — a part of earned income that is not counted in determining eligibility and benefits — after a recipient had worked for four months, required that the earned-income tax credit for the working poor be considered as monthly income, and adopted most of the other cost-saving provisions of the Senate reconciliation bill.

The only significant difference resolved by conferees (H Rept 97-208) was acceptance of a House provision limiting AFDC benefits provided to recent immigrants. Congress completed action on the measure July 31.

Provisions

As signed into law Aug. 13, the welfare provisions of HR 3982 (Title XXIII of PL 97-35):

AFDC Benefit Reductions. Reduced benefits to working AFDC recipients by limiting the disregards subtracted from their earnings in calculating eligibility and benefits. Eligibility and benefit calculations would include a standard income disregard of $75 a month, in place of the disregards for itemized work expenses and a disregard for care of dependent children or incapacitated adults of up to $160 a month allowed under existing law. In addition, benefit calculations would use a disregard of $30 a month plus one-third of the remaining earned income, as under existing law; however, the disregard would be used only during the first four months of the recipient's employment.

● Excluded from the program families with property resources (excluding the home and one automobile) whose equity value exceeded $1,000, or a lower amount set by states.

● Allowed states to reduce AFDC payments to families who also received food stamps or housing subsidies by counting those benefits as income.

● Excluded from the program families with total incomes in excess of 150 percent of a state's "standard of need."

● Required that money received by a family in a lump-sum payment (such as a retroactive Social Security payment) be counted as income over a number of months, rather than just during the month it was received, as under existing law.

● Required that benefits to families eligible for earned-income tax credits be based on the assumption that the family received the payments in the form of monthly advance payments, even if they did not.

● Required states to consider a portion of the income of a stepparent living with a child in determining AFDC eligibility and benefits.

AFDC Workfare. Allowed states to establish "community work experience" programs for AFDC recipients. Under the programs, recipients could be required to perform work in such areas as health, social services, education and public safety. The number of hours of work each month could not exceed the number produced by dividing the family's AFDC benefit by the greater of the federal or state minimum wage.

● Allowed states to establish "work supplementation

Who Defines Poverty?

The 1981 reconciliation bill (HR 3982 — PL 97-35) prompted a brief but bitter debate over who should define poverty. The final bill provided that the official "poverty line," used to determine eligibility for food stamps, free school lunches and other federal assistance, would be established by the Office of Management and Budget (OMB) and would be revised at least once a year by the secretary of health and human services (HHS) to reflect changes in the Consumer Price Index.

The debate began when a provision was inserted in the House-passed bill — the administration-backed Gramm-Latta II substitute — declaring that "the Office of Management and Budget is authorized to define poverty and to revise the definition of poverty for each year."

Although backers insisted the provision simply restated law that had been in effect for years, it set off a bitter partisan fight in the House. Majority Leader Jim Wright, D-Texas, and other Democrats said the provision would give extraordinary power to OMB, and perhaps signal a sweeping change in how the government decided who was poor enough to qualify for food stamps and other assistance programs.

Donald W. Moran, OMB associate director, said OMB already had the authority outlined in the provision and denied that it contemplated any changes of the sort predicted by the Democrats.

The Senate bill had no comparable provision. The final version was an apparent compromise.

The poverty income figure was used by government agencies for several purposes, such as counting the number of poor people living in an area to determine how funding for programs targeted on low-income populations should be distributed, and determining who qualified for certain federal benefits.

In 1981 the official poverty-level income for a non-farm family of four was $8,450 a year. That figure reflected only cash income. Democratic critics feared the Reagan administration would use the reconciliation bill provision to begin counting the dollar value of food stamps, Medicaid and other benefits as "income," as some administration officials wanted to do.

The original poverty index was developed in 1963. In 1969 the Budget Bureau (OMB's predecessor) established a revised version as "the standard data series on poverty for the statistical use of all executive agencies." In 1972 and 1974 legislation (PL 92-424, PL 93-643), Congress directed federal agencies using the poverty line to adjust the figure at least once a year, based on Consumer Price Index changes and taking account of such factors as family size.

programs." Under the programs, states would be allowed to reduce their regular AFDC grants in order to generate funds for jobs that would be available to recipients on a voluntary basis. The jobs would be with the government, public or private non-profit agencies, or private day-care centers.

● Provided that states operating work supplementation programs could not receive more federal matching funds than they would have if they had continued to operate their AFDC programs in the previous fashion.

● Allowed states to participate in a work incentive demonstration project, aimed at testing alternatives to the existing AFDC work requirements.

AFDC Eligibility Restrictions. Prohibited payment of AFDC benefits to families in which the mother or father was participating in a labor strike.

● Limited children's eligibility for AFDC to those 18 or under; allowed states to provide benefits to 18-year-olds who still were enrolled in high school or technical school.

● Allowed states to provide AFDC benefits to pregnant women who had no other children, but only during the final four months of their pregnancy.

● Provided that states that chose to provide AFDC benefits to two-parent families in which one parent was unemployed could do so only if the "principal wage earner" — the parent who had earned more in the preceding two years — was unemployed.

● Continued an existing exemption from the program's work requirements for parents with children under age 6 only if the parent was providing full-time care for the child, with only brief and infrequent absences.

Monthly Retrospective Income Accounting. Required states to establish a system for determining benefit levels known as "monthly retrospective income accounting." Under the system, benefit levels would be determined according to actual recipient income and circumstances in the preceding month; under existing law, most states used a prospective system that estimated client circumstances for the next month. In addition, recipients would be required to file monthly reports on their income; existing practice in most states required only that recipients report changes in their circumstances.

● Barred states from making AFDC payments to families eligible for less than $10 in monthly assistance; however, such families would continue to be eligible for programs, such as Medicaid, that were tied to AFDC.

● Expanded states' ability to provide benefits in the form of "vendor payments" to businesses, such as landlords and utility companies, on behalf of AFDC recipients.

● Required that states take action to recover benefit payments made to recipients in excess of the amounts to which they were entitled, and to restore funds to recipients who received less than they were entitled.

● Reduced to 50 percent, from 75 percent, the federal share of state and local costs of training AFDC personnel.

● Limited AFDC eligibility only to persons who were U.S. citizens or legal aliens.

● Required that a portion of the income of the sponsor of an alien applying for AFDC be considered as income and resources of the alien, in determining eligibility and benefits, for three years following the alien's entry into the country.

Child Support Enforcement. Expanded the states' ability to use the Internal Revenue Service (IRS) to collect overdue child support payments by allowing the IRS to withhold money from a tax refund due to a delinquent parent.

● Allowed state agencies to collect support payments for a parent, as well as for a child.

● Required states to levy a 10 percent fee, to be charged against the absent parent, for collecting child support payments for non-AFDC families. (This provision was repealed in 1982 reconciliation legislation. *(Story, p. 596))*

● Provided that a child support obligation for an AFDC family not be discharged because of the bankruptcy of the absent parent.

● Required state agencies to withhold a portion of unemployment benefits due to persons who owed past-due child support payments and forward that money to the state child support agency.

Supplemental Security Income. Required states to use a retrospective income accounting system for determining Supplemental Security Income (SSI) benefits, paid to needy aged, blind and disabled persons.

● Limited the existing authority of the Department of Health and Human Services to pay state vocational rehabilitation agencies for services provided to blind or disabled SSI recipients.

Social Services, Energy Aid

Congress balked at the Reagan administration's proposals for two new block grant programs in the areas of social services and energy assistance.

Instead, the budget reconciliation bill approved July 31 (HR 3982 — PL 97-35) extended the existing social service block grant and low-income energy assistance programs, with some changes. *(Reconciliation, p. 40)*

The social services program, authorized by Title XX of the Social Security Act, was slightly expanded by consolidation with programs for U.S. territories and for training of social service workers. Funding for the program was reduced, however, and states no longer were required to match their share of federal money with their own funds.

The social services program, already a block grant under existing law, provided funds to states for a variety of programs such as day care, family planning, counseling and aid to the mentally retarded.

Congress refused to include legal services, community services and child welfare programs in the block grant as the administration proposed. Legal services and child welfare programs were continued as categorical programs, and community services programs were put into their own block grant. Block grants are federal payments to state or local governments for generally specified purposes. The money must be spent on programs in the general area, but state and local governments make the decisions on specifically how the money is used. Categorical grants can be used only for specific programs as directed by Congress. *(Adoption aid, child welfare, Congress and the Nation Vol. V, p. 710; community services, p. 590; block grants, p. 773)*

Other provisions of the reconciliation bill simplified the existing program of aid for the heating and cooling needs of the poor. Congress did not approve the transfer of short-term aid to welfare families in emergencies, which the administration had requested. *(Background, Congress and the Nation Vol. V, p. 707; 1984 action, p. 603)*

Legislative Action

Senate. The Senate Finance Committee, in its reconciliation package approved May 5, adopted a hybrid form of block grant for social service programs in its jurisdiction.

Chairman Robert Dole, R-Kan., referred to the proposal as a "targeted block grant."

It lumped seven programs together in a block grant (social services, day care, state and local social services training, child welfare services, child welfare services training, foster care and adoption assistance), but required states to maintain spending for three of them (child welfare, foster care, adoption assistance) at a minimum of 75 percent of the existing level.

The committee cut 25 percent from the funding of the programs, as requested by the president, for a saving of $1.07 billion.

The Senate approved its reconciliation bill June 25.

House. The House Ways and Means Committee May 19 rejected the administration's social services and emergency assistance block grant proposals, but agreed to cut spending for low-income energy assistance by almost 40 percent ($850 million).

However, in adopting the administration-backed Gramm-Latta II reconciliation substitute, the House June 26 agreed to a block grant combining social services, community services and some other small programs. The block grant did not include the child welfare, foster care or adoption assistance programs.

Conference Action. Conferees had two major differences to resolve on the social services program: funding levels and the fate of the child welfare, foster care and adoption assistance programs.

They dropped the three child welfare programs from the block grant, as well as some smaller programs for abused children and runaway youth the House had included. The House provision including community services programs in the block grant was deleted by a different set of reconciliation conferees, who established the community services block grant.

The funding level accepted by conferees for social services was $2.4 billion in fiscal 1982, rising to $2.7 billion by fiscal 1986. Those amounts did not include funding for the community services or child welfare programs, which would have separate funding authorities. Fiscal 1981 funding was $3 billion.

Both chambers approved the conference report (II Rept 97-208) July 31.

Provisions

As signed into law Aug. 13, the social services and energy assistance provisions of HR 3982 (PL 97-35, Titles XXIII and XXVI):

Social Services. Continued the existing block grant program providing funds to states for a variety of social services to individuals and families authorized by Title XX of the Social Security Act.

● Authorized states to use their funds for programs such as child care, foster care, meal delivery, legal aid, training of social service workers and delinquency prevention, but placed no specific requirements on the types of programs.

● Required states to develop and make public a report on how their Title XX funds would be used, including information about activities to be supported and characteristics of individuals to be served.

● Authorized $2.4 billion in fiscal 1982, $2.45 billion in 1983, $2.5 billion in 1984, $2.6 billion in 1985 and $2.7 billion in 1986 and succeeding years; made the program an appropriated entitlement. Entitlement programs guarantee a certain level of benefits to all who meet the eligibility requirements.

Social Program Spending

Congress approved most of the budget cuts President Reagan proposed shortly after he took office in 1981, but it balked when he sought a second round of cuts later in the year.

Only weeks after enactment of the omnibus reconciliation bill (HR 3982 — PL 97-35), which slashed $35.2 billion from projected fiscal 1982 spending, Reagan asked Congress Sept. 24 to cut a further $13 billion by paring appropriations measures and cutting back non-discretionary entitlement programs such as Medicaid and food stamps. He also called for $3 billion in new revenues.

In the first test of congressional support for the president's new plan, the House Oct. 6 rejected, by an 81-vote margin, efforts to force Reagan-backed cuts in popular social programs funded by the fiscal 1982 appropriations bill for the departments of Labor, Health and Human Services and Education (HR 4560).

The defection of 39 Republicans, mostly from the Northeast and Midwest, killed a Republican leadership motion to recommit the $87.2 billion bill to the Appropriations Committee for additional cuts. The motion to recommit the bill was rejected by a **key 168-249 vote (R 140-39; D 28-210)**. *(1981 key votes, p. 879)*

"I don't think we can make the [budget] balancing act by just touching this bill," protested Carl D. Pursell, R-Mich. "If we send this bill back to committee, to cut only it, without looking at the defense budget and the water projects, it's unfair."

"This bill is America's investment in humanity and we cannot afford to reduce funding," said the ranking Republican on the Appropriations Committee, Silvio O. Conte, Mass.

Given the negative congressional response to his plan, especially among Republicans, Reagan ultimately agreed to settle for $4 billion in cuts and to postpone his entitlement and tax proposals. Meanwhile, the appropriations process ground to a halt, and most of the government was funded under a series of short-term continuing appropriations resolutions. *(1981 budget action, p. 37)*

● Repealed a requirement that states match a portion of their federal Title XX allocation with their own funds.

● Gave each state a share of the funds based on its share of the national population; allotted part of the total funds, under a separate formula, to social service programs in the territories.

● Allowed a state to transfer up to 10 percent of its allocation to other block grant programs.

● Repealed existing requirements that states use at least 50 percent of their social service funds to provide services to welfare recipients, and that they provide services only to persons with incomes below 115 percent of the state's median income.

● Prohibited states from using the funds for purchase of buildings, room and board costs, wage payments other than for hiring welfare recipients to work in day-care centers, medical care, institutional or educational services, or for cash payments.

Home Energy Assistance. Authorized $1.875 billion for each of fiscal years 1982-84 to help low-income families meet home energy costs.

● Allowed states to transfer up to 10 percent of their funds under this program to community services, social services and certain health block grants.

● Allowed states to use federal funds to provide benefits only to recipients of welfare, food stamps or veterans' pensions, or to households with incomes below either 150 percent of the poverty level or 60 percent of the state's median income.

● Gave states the option of having the federal government make energy assistance payments directly to qualified Supplemental Security Income recipients.

● Imposed on states requirements for public participation, an appeals process, coordination with other federal programs, outreach to eligible households and financial controls.

● Allowed states to spend up to 15 percent of their funds on "weatherization" — home improvements aimed at reducing energy consumption — for low-income households.

● Provided that assistance supplied under the program should not be considered as income in determining eligibility and benefits under other federal and state programs.

● Allowed states to make payments directly to energy suppliers; also allowed use of funds to provide state tax credits to companies that supplied energy to low-income households at reduced rates.

● Prohibited use of grants for the purchase or improvement of land, or for construction or improvement of buildings except for low-cost residential weatherization and other energy-related home repairs.

Anti-Poverty Programs

Some federal anti-poverty programs came up losers and others winners in the sweeping budget-cutting reconciliation bill cleared by Congress July 31 (HR 3982 — PL 97-35).

The principal anti-poverty agency, the Community Services Administration (CSA), was abolished and replaced by a new community services block grant to the states, with reduced funding. *(Reconciliation bill, p. 40)*

Funding of $389.4 million was authorized for the block grant in each of fiscal years 1982-86. CSA's fiscal 1981 appropriation was $537.8 million.

CSA, successor to the 1960s' Office of Economic Opportunity, financed local community action agencies and community economic development programs. The Reagan administration had proposed to include community services as part of a much larger social services block grant, but Congress rejected that plan. *(Story, p. 588)*

Another holdover from President Johnson's War on Poverty — VISTA (Volunteers in Service to America) — retained its separate identity but was severely cut back. President Reagan proposed to cut VISTA's 1982 funding to $20.7 million, from $42.8 million in President Carter's budget. Congress earmarked only $16 million for the program in fiscal 1982, dropping to $8 million in 1983. VISTA volunteers worked in poverty areas; they were paid a fed-

eral stipend. *(1983 action, p. 602; 1984 action, p. 610)*

Volunteer programs for the elderly, including Foster Grandparents, a favorite of first lady Nancy Reagan, were funded at much higher levels.

In contrast to the other programs, the Head Start preschool program for children from low-income families — probably the most popular legacy of the War on Poverty — emerged from the reconciliation process with an increase in its funding level, one of the few social programs to do so. The reconciliation bill authorized the administration's request of $950 million for it in fiscal 1982, up from the 1981 funding level of $820 million. President Reagan had included Head Start in his "social safety net" of seven programs he said were immune from budget cuts. The program provided education, health and social services to low-income and handicapped children aged 3-5. About 375,000 children were enrolled in 1,262 local Head Start programs in 1981. *(1984 action, p. 603)*

Legislative History

The Senate version of the reconciliation bill (S 1377 — S Rept 97-139), passed June 25, authorized only $820 million for Head Start in 1982. But on July 14 the Senate instructed its conferees on the bill to support a $950 million authorization, the amount the Democratic-controlled House Education and Labor Committee had recommended in its reconciliation proposal.

Through a staff error, the Head Start authorization was dropped from the Republican reconciliation substitute passed by the House June 26, causing momentary concern about the program's fate. But there was no opposition in the conference committee to the higher funding levels.

The other main issue in the conference was the fate of community services programs. The Senate, while abolishing CSA, had at least preserved the separate status of community services programs as part of a new block grant. The House-passed bill, by contrast, lumped community services programs into the social services block grant, ending their separate status.

House Democrats on the conference committee had little enthusiasm for including the community services programs in the social services block grant, and readily agreed to the Senate's separate block grant proposal. The only remaining dispute concerned protections for existing community action agencies (CAAs) previously funded by CSA. Conferees adopted a provision requiring states to turn over at least 90 percent of their fiscal 1982 community services block grant funds to the local anti-poverty groups.

The conference report on the bill (H Rept 97-208) was approved by both houses July 31.

Provisions

As signed into law Aug. 13, the anti-poverty provisions of HR 3982 (Title VI of PL 97-35):

Community Services Block Grant. Established a community services block grant, replacing programs formerly administered by the Community Services Administration.

● Terminated the CSA and created instead an Office of Community Services within the Department of Health and Human Services (HHS).

● Authorized $389.4 million for the block grants in each of fiscal years 1982-86.

● Distributed funds to states in the same ratio as funds

were distributed in 1981 under the existing CSA programs; guaranteed each state at least .25 percent of the total distributed to states; set aside .5 percent of funds for the territories.

● Required states to use the block grant funds for programs with a measurable effect on the causes of poverty, and to help people with problems such as jobs, education and housing.

● Provided for annual revisions by the secretary of HHS of the "poverty line" established by the Office of Management and Budget to reflect changes in the Consumer Price Index. *(Background, box, p. 587)*

● Required states in fiscal 1982 to provide at least 90 percent of their allotments to community action agencies and migrant farm worker organizations. Beginning in fiscal 1983, states would have to provide at least 90 percent of their allotments to local governments, which would either use the funds directly or give them to CAAs.

● Established procedures for planning, public participation, applications and coordination that states would have to meet in order to qualify for block grant assistance.

● Required that existing CAAs be given special consideration as grant recipients.

● Allowed states to transfer up to 5 percent of their allotments to Older Americans, Head Start or energy crisis intervention programs.

● Authorized HHS to withhold funds from states found to have misused funds.

● Prohibited the use of block grant funds for political activities or construction.

● Set aside 9 percent of the funds for discretionary programs of HHS; allowed funding of existing community economic development programs as part of the HHS discretionary programs.

● Established transition provisions allowing HHS to operate the existing programs in fiscal 1982, at state option.

Head Start. Authorized funds for Head Start at the following levels: $950 million in fiscal 1982, $1.007 billion in 1983 and $1.058 billion in 1984.

● Revised the formula for distribution of Head Start funds to states and territories.

● Set aside 13 percent of the funds for Head Start programs for Indians, migrants and children in the territories.

● Required that at least 10 percent of children served by the program in each state be handicapped children.

● Set fiscal, planning and administrative standards for Head Start agencies; authorized HHS to establish regulations concerning eligibility and hearing procedures, and to provide training, technical and research assistance to local agencies.

● Required Head Start agencies to provide for parental participation in decision-making.

● Limited participation in Head Start programs to children from families with incomes below the poverty level, but allowed for participation by other children in certain circumstances.

Other Programs. Authorized funds for domestic volunteer anti-poverty programs at the following levels: $25.8 million in fiscal 1982 and $15.4 million in 1983.

● Reserved for the Volunteers in Service to America program $16 million in fiscal 1982 and $8 million in 1983.

● Authorized $125.1 million in fiscal 1982 and $130 million in fiscal 1983 for senior volunteer programs — retired senior volunteers, foster grandparents and senior companions — and for administrative costs.

● Authorized $715 million in fiscal 1982 and $793.3 million in 1983 for Older Americans programs.

● Provided a separate authorization for community service employment for the aged, at $277.1 million in fiscal 1982 and $293.7 million in 1983; provided for additional funding in case the authorized levels were insufficient to maintain 54,000 job slots of 20 hours per week.

● Authorized $1.009 billion in fiscal 1982 and $1.054 billion in 1983 for vocational rehabilitation programs.

● Authorized $7 million in each of fiscal years 1982-84 for child abuse prevention and treatment programs.

● Authorized the use of community services block grant funds for community economic development grants and loans in urban and rural low-income areas, formerly authorized under Title VII of the Economic Opportunity Act.

Child Nutrition Programs

Child nutrition programs suffered major cuts in the budget reconciliation bill cleared by Congress July 31 (HR 3982 — PL 97-35).

The massive bill carried out budget cuts sought by President Reagan and endorsed by Congress through its budget process. *(Reconciliation, p. 40)*

The legislation made reductions of up to 40 percent in subsidies for meals served to school children from middle- and upper-income families. Cuts in subsidies for the poor were smaller, but eligibility for free and reduced-price meals for children from low-income families was tightened.

Critics predicted that many "paying" children would drop out of the program because of the higher prices they would have to pay for their school meals; as they did, some schools would be forced to close their lunch and breakfast programs, leaving many poor children without meals even though they were eligible for them, the critics said.

Before enactment of the reconciliation bill, the federal government provided subsidies totaling 37 cents (20.25 cents cash, 16.75 cents in commodities) for each school lunch served, with additional cash subsidies of 91.5 cents for each free lunch and 71.5 cents for each reduced-price lunch.

HR 3982 cut the basic subsidy to 21.5 cents (10.5 cents in cash, 11 cents in commodities), plus an additional 2 cents a lunch in so-called "safety net" schools, where 60 percent or more of the students received free or reduced-price lunches. The special subsidy for free lunches was set at 98.75 cents; for reduced-price lunches, 58.75 cents.

Under the new law, children from families making less than 130 percent of the official poverty level (those with an income up to $11,375 for a family of four) were eligible for free lunches. Reduced-price lunches were available to children from families with incomes up to 185 percent of the poverty level (up to $15,630 for a family of four). The reconciliation bill doubled the lunch price for those children, from 20 cents to 40 cents.

The bill also sought to cut federal costs by ensuring that ineligible children did not receive free or reduced-price meals. It called for stepped-up efforts to verify the true incomes of parents applying for the low-cost school meals.

Another provision required the Agriculture Department to review and revise existing school lunch regulations with an eye to reducing the cost of meals. The department subsequently issued new rules, allowing a reduction in the nutritional content of the meals; they proved so controversial that they had to be withdrawn. *(Box, p. 592)*

The reconciliation bill eliminated the special milk program, which subsidized milk distribution to school chil-

School Lunch Regulations

After a barrage of criticism, the Reagan administration backed away from its plans to allow smaller meals in the school lunch program.

The Sept. 4 draft regulations would have allowed schools and day-care centers to reduce the size of the portions they served to children whose meals were subsidized by the school lunch, school breakfast and day-care center meal programs. They also would have given schools new ways to meet requirements for serving meat, vegetables and fruits, bread and milk — substituting the soybean curd tofu for meat, for example, or ketchup or relish for a vegetable.

The proposed regulations caused acute political embarrassment to the administration and were withdrawn Sept. 25. Agriculture Secretary John R. Block said he and the president still believed the intent of the proposed revisions was sound, but he said the regulations would be reconsidered because of the adverse public reaction.

Food and Nutrition Service (FNS) officials said the regulations were intended to help schools cope with cuts in subsidies ordered by the budget reconciliation bill (PL 97-35). *(Story, p. 591)*

But nutrition groups such as the Food Research and Action Center said the changes would violate the longstanding goal of the school lunch program, to provide children with one-third of their minimum daily nutritional requirements. The new meal patterns would provide less than one-third of an elementary schoolchild's need for magnesium, iron, thiamin and vitamin B, according to FNS estimates.

Democratic critics of the Reagan administration jumped on the regulations, which attracted a wave of negative publicity. Senate Democrats, in a well-covered media event Sept. 24, sat down to what they said would be a typical school lunch under the new regulations: a meat-and-soybean patty, a few french fries, ketchup, one slice of white bread and three-fourths of a glass of milk.

Sen. John Melcher, D-Mont., introduced an amendment to a pending debt limit bill (H J Res 265) to bar the FNS from implementing any regulations to change the program's goal of supplying one-third of a child's nutritional requirements. He eventually withdrew his amendment when the leadership promised to bring to the floor a nonbinding resolution to that effect instead.

The Senate adopted such a resolution (S Res 218) Dec. 9 by a 92-0 vote.

Sen. Gary Hart, D-Colo., also offered an amendment to the debt limit bill to provide more money for school lunches by cutting tax deductions for business meals. That amendment was tabled (killed) Sept. 28 by a 58-30 vote.

dren, except in schools that had no federal feeding programs. It also placed spending ceilings on the supplemental feeding program for women, infants and children (WIC). The administration had sought both actions.

The summer feeding program, which had been troubled by allegations of waste and fraud, was sharply restricted under the bill, but Congress did not eliminate it as the administration requested.

Legislative History

In his March budget, President Reagan proposed to cut federal spending for child nutrition programs by $1.8 billion. The biggest savings would come from eliminating federal subsidies for lunches served to some 14.5 million children from middle- and upper-income families.

That would cut federal costs by more than $9 billion by 1986 and enable the administration to target benefits to the neediest children, according to the budget. As part of Reagan's social "safety net," about 10 million poor children would continue to receive free school lunches and breakfasts, the administration said.

Neither the House nor the Senate reconciliation bill went as far as the administration requested in cutting the programs. The Senate Agriculture Committee approved reductions of about $1.5 billion; the House Education and Labor Committee reluctantly agreed to $1.1 billion in cuts. However, the Education and Labor Committee provisions were dropped when the House June 26 adopted the Republican-backed Gramm-Latta II substitute for the committee version of HR 3982 (H Rept 97-158), removing many of the potential conflicts between the House and Senate bills. The Senate had passed its version (S 1377 — S Rept 97-139) June 25.

Conferees reached agreement on the child nutrition provisions July 21, making cuts totaling $1.5 billion for fiscal 1982. The conference report on the bill (H Rept 97-208) was approved by both houses July 31.

Provisions

As signed into law Aug. 13, the child nutrition provisions of HR 3982 (Title VIII of PL 97-35):

- Reduced federal subsidies, in both cash and commodities, for school meals.
- Provided the following reimbursement rates for each school lunch served during the 1981-82 school year: 10.5 cents in cash and 11 cents' worth of commodities.
- Set the additional subsidies to schools at 98.75 cents for each free lunch served and 58.75 cents for each lunch served at a reduced price, during the 1981-82 school year.
- Established a special "safety net" provision to increase by 2 cents the basic cash reimbursement rate for each lunch served in schools in which 60 percent or more of the students received free or reduced-price meals.
- Provided annual, rather than semiannual, inflation adjustments in reimbursement rates.
- Set the following reimbursement rates for each school breakfast served during the 1981-82 school year: paid, 8.25 cents; reduced-price, 28.5 cents; free, 57 cents.
- Prohibited schools from charging more than 30 cents for a reduced-price breakfast.
- Tightened eligibility standards under which schools could receive extra "severe need" assistance for the breakfast programs.
- Lowered the income eligibility limits for students receiving federally subsidized free and reduced-price school

meals. The income limit for free meals (under existing law, 125 percent of the federal poverty limit, plus an $80 standard monthly income deduction) would be 130 percent of poverty, without a standard deduction; beginning July 1, 1983, the income limits for free meals would be the same as those applied to the food stamp program. For reduced-price meals, the limit would be 185 percent of poverty, without a standard deduction, in place of the existing law's 195 percent, with a standard deduction.

● Provided for increased efforts to verify the income information supplied by parents in applying for free and reduced-price school meals.

● Provided that the application forms for free and reduced-price meals could not indicate the actual income limit for receipt of free meals.

● Required applicants for free and reduced-price meals to provide the Social Security numbers of all adult members of the household.

● Eliminated federal assistance for school purchase of food service equipment.

● Eliminated the special milk program, which subsidized milk distribution to children in addition to the milk served under other school feeding programs; allowed the program to continue in schools that participated in no other federal feeding program.

● Excluded private schools with annual tuitions above $1,500 from participation in the school lunch or breakfast programs.

● Required states to provide their own funds for school lunches in an amount equal to at least 30 percent of the amount received by schools in the state under the basic federal program of lunch reimbursement during the 1980-81 school year.

● Specified that a state in which the education agency was prohibited by law from disbursing state funds to private schools was not required to match the federal funds made available for meals served in such private schools.

● Limited the summer food service program to areas in which at least 50 percent of the children met the income eligibility standards for free and reduced-price school meals; limited local sponsorship of the program to public or private non-profit schools, local governments and non-profit residential camps.

● Reduced federal subsidies for meals served in child-care centers, and determined the amount of subsidy according to the income needs of each child, rather than according to the percentage of low-income children in each center. Under the legislation, child-care subsidies for breakfasts, lunches and dinners would be set in accordance with the subsidies provided for meals served in schools; reimbursements for snacks served in centers would be 2.75 cents for paid snacks, 15 cents for reduced-price snacks and 30 cents for free snacks.

● Restricted participation in the child-care food program to children aged 12 or younger, handicapped children or the children of migrant workers up to age 16.

● Required the secretary of agriculture to review existing regulations, including those pertaining to nutritional requirements, to determine ways to reduce the costs of school meals. Within 90 days, the secretary must promulgate new regulations based on this review. These could entail changes in the "meal patterns" that set the minimum amounts of certain types of food required to be included in a school meal.

● Prohibited states in the future from turning over administration of school feeding programs to the department; allowed the department to administer additional programs

only when necessary to provide funds to private schools in states that were prohibited by law from providing funds or services to private schools.

● Gave school districts the option to extend to elementary school students the right to refuse to accept food they did not intend to eat.

● Expanded federal assistance to "commodity only" schools, which received commodity support for meal service but did not participate in the regular school lunch program; in return for the increased support, the schools would have to provide meals that met the standards for the regular program.

● Set authorization ceilings for the following programs: for the supplemental feeding program for women, infants and children, $1.017 billion in fiscal 1982, $1.06 billion in 1983, $1.126 billion in 1984; for nutrition education and training, $5 million in fiscal 1982 and each succeeding year.

Older Americans Act

Congress Dec. 16 cleared legislation (S 1086 — PL 97-115) extending Older Americans Act programs for three years, through fiscal 1984.

The measure made few major changes in the politically popular programs, which funded local centers providing nutritional and social service assistance, such as legal aid and counseling, to 9.3 million elderly in 1980.

The bill did not include the Reagan administration's proposal to merge home-delivered and group meal programs into a single authorization providing grants to states.

However, it did provide increased flexibility for state and local aging centers. It allowed them to transfer up to 20 percent of their funds between their nutrition and social service programs, and removed an existing requirement that agencies spend at least half of their social service funds on "priority services" such as transportation and legal aid.

Congress had last extended the programs, originally authorized by the 1965 Older Americans Act, in 1978 (PL 95-478). The act was extended again in 1984. *(1978 action, Congress and the Nation Vol. V, p. 694; 1984 action, p. 609)*

Legislative History

The Senate passed S 1086 Nov. 2 by a 75-0 vote after attaching a resolution reaffirming its unanimous opposition to taxation of Social Security benefits. *(Social Security, p. 645)*

Other than tacking on the non-binding statement, the Senate made relatively few changes in S 1086 as reported by the Labor and Human Resources Committee July 20 (S Rept 97-159).

The House passed its version of the bill (HR 3046) Nov. 20 by a 379-4 vote. No one spoke in opposition to extension of the Older Americans programs.

The biggest change in the House bill, reported by the Education and Labor Committee May 19 (H Rept 97-70), was forced by the budget reconciliation measure (HR 3982 — PL 97-35), which limited total spending for Older Americans programs to $992 million in fiscal 1982. *(Reconciliation bill, p. 40)*

The committee bill, reported with a total authorization estimated by the Congressional Budget Office at $1.8 billion, was amended on the floor to conform to the reconciliation limits.

Like the Senate bill, HR 3046 retained separate authorizations for the social services, home-delivered meals and group meals programs.

Conferees filed their report on the bill Dec. 10 (H Rept 97-386). The Senate adopted the conference report Dec. 11 by a 90-0 vote, and the House approved it by voice vote Dec. 16, clearing the bill.

Provisions

As signed into law Dec. 29, S 1086 (PL 97-115):

● Extended the authorizations for Older Americans Act programs for fiscal years 1982-84.

● Preserved the existing separate authorizations for the congregate and home-delivered meal programs.

● Allowed states to transfer up to 20 percent of federal funds between their nutrition and social service programs.

● Abolished the provision in existing law that required agencies serving the aged to spend at least 50 percent of their social services funds on access, in-home and legal services; however, agencies still were required to spend an "adequate portion" of their funds on these services.

● Allowed congregate meal programs to provide food to handicapped or disabled persons who were under age 60 but who lived in housing facilities occupied primarily by the elderly.

● Allowed state agencies to fund other services, such as crime prevention, employment services and education.

● Required the Labor Department to develop training and placement programs to find private employment for older workers.

● Authorized $1.08 billion in fiscal 1982, $1.16 billion in 1983 and $1.24 billion in 1984 for programs in the bill.

● Within those totals, authorized $277.1 million in fiscal 1982, $296.5 million in 1983 and $317.3 million in 1984 for community service employment of the elderly; allowed higher spending levels if necessary to maintain 54,200 part-time employment positions of at least 20 hours a week.

● Limited the value of federal commodity contributions to nutrition programs for the elderly to $93.2 million in fiscal 1982, $100 million in 1983 and $105 million in 1984; allowed additional funds if needed to maintain the program at its 1981 level.

● Eliminated the authorization for the National Information and Resource Clearing House for the Aging.

1982

A deepening recession and the impact of the 1981 budget cuts kept Congress from approving many of the deep reductions in welfare programs requested by President Reagan in 1982.

In authorizing fiscal 1983-85 spending ceilings for the food stamp program, Congress agreed to cut projected spending by $1.9 billion over the three-year period. But the $12.87 billion fiscal 1983 ceiling provided by the bill was still nearly $3.3 billion more than the president sought and $1.5 billion more than Congress had voted for fiscal 1982. The measure held down inflation adjustments in benefit levels, tightened eligibility standards and strengthened work requirements for food stamp recipients. Other provisions penalized states that poorly administered the program.

Congress also approved legislation providing fiscal 1983-85 savings of $1.1 billion — far short of the $7.7 billion Reagan requested — in the core federal welfare program, Aid to Families with Dependent Children (AFDC), in child support enforcement and in the Supplemental Security Income (SSI) program for the aged, blind and disabled. Major provisions of the bill allowed states to require AFDC applicants and recipients to participate in job search programs, increased penalties for states with high error rates in the administration of benefits and reduced welfare payments through a variety of administrative provisions. The bill did not include a mandatory "workfare" program for welfare recipients or new block grant proposals for child welfare and emergency assistance, as Reagan had urged in 1981 and 1982.

The welfare cuts approved by Congress in 1982 fell most heavily on the working poor, who received federal benefits to supplement their small earned incomes. By sharply reducing food stamps and other benefits to those with earned income, the cuts were a disincentive to work, anti-poverty groups argued. They predicted many poor workers would quit their jobs and go completely on welfare.

Meanwhile, the budget-slashing 1981 reconciliation law was increasing the emphasis on work requirements for welfare recipients. Some two dozen states established workfare programs, under which recipients performed public service work for their communities in exchange for benefits.

The number of poor people in the United States increased significantly during the year, although budget cuts held down the number receiving welfare and other forms of assistance to the poor.

Food Stamp Program

For the second year, Congress in 1982 revised the food stamp program in an effort to hold down soaring costs. The revisions, included in a budget-cutting reconciliation bill cleared Aug. 18 (HR 6955 — PL 97-253), were expected to save $1.9 billion in fiscal 1983-85; they would not reduce federal spending for the program, but simply slow its rate of growth. *(Reconciliation, p. 48)*

Congress had made numerous changes in the food stamp law in 1981, but could not agree on the timing of inflation-related increases in benefits. So the program was reauthorized for only one year, forcing further action in 1982. *(1981 action, p. 583)*

HR 6955 cut an estimated $548 million from projected fiscal 1983 spending for food stamps, which recipients could exchange for food at grocery stores. It limited food stamp spending to $12.87 billion in fiscal 1983, $13.14 billion in 1984 and $13.93 billion in 1985. Congress repeatedly had imposed spending ceilings on food stamps in recent years, only to raise them when the program needed more money to continue full operation.

The federal government spent $11.3 billion to provide about 20.5 million persons with food stamps in fiscal 1982.

For recipients, the revisions made in the program by HR 6955 meant less generous adjustments in benefits to account for rising food prices, and tighter eligibility standards. The bill also strengthened work requirements and authorized pilot projects in which recipients would lose their food stamps if they did not work at least 20 hours a week. States were required to reduce their error rates in awarding food stamp benefits or lose some of the federal funds they received for administering the program.

Congress rejected proposals by the Reagan administra-

tion and by several conservative Republican senators to make deeper cuts in the program and to put a greater share of the burden of the cuts on recipients.

Administration Proposal

The Reagan administration, in its Feb. 6 budget, proposed to cut food stamp spending by nearly 20 percent in fiscal 1983. The administration asked Congress to hold spending to $9.6 billion, down from the $11.3 billion fiscal 1982 level. Some of its proposed changes would have sharply reduced benefits to recipients with earned income.

The working poor would have been most severely affected by a proposal to eliminate the "earned-income disregard." That provision allowed recipients with jobs to exclude 18 percent of their work income from the calculations that determined benefits. The 1981 reconciliation law already had reduced it to 18 percent from 20 percent.

A further cut in benefits to recipients with relatively higher incomes would have been achieved by increasing the "benefit reduction rate." Under existing law, benefits were reduced by 30 cents for each dollar of income (after various deductions were taken into account). President Reagan sought to raise that to 35 cents. Thus, for each $100 of income, a food stamp recipient would lose $35 in food stamp benefits.

The administration also proposed to count energy assistance as income in determining benefits, require food stamp applicants to look for a job, eliminate benefits to persons eligible for less than $10 a month in food stamps, round benefits down to the next lower dollar and require states to lower their error rates in determining eligibility and benefits or lose administrative funds.

Senate Action

The Senate Agriculture Committee worked on food stamp legislation in May and June. Its proposals were folded into the omnibus reconciliation bill reported by the Senate Budget Committee July 26 (S 2774 — S Rept 97-504).

The committee-approved revisions were designed to provide savings of $815 million in fiscal 1983, $846 million in 1984 and $908 million in 1985.

Despite the cuts, the legislation approved by the committee was something of a victory for food stamp advocates, especially Nutrition Subcommittee Chairman Robert Dole, R-Kan. The savings were achieved by provisions — such as delaying inflation adjustments of benefits or penalizing states with poorly administered programs — that were expected to have less impact on recipients than those sought by committee Chairman Jesse Helms, R-N.C.

Dole also was successful in adding to the reconciliation bill a three-year reauthorization for the food stamp program, which he said would give it a respite from the repeated changes made in it by Congress in recent years.

In passing the reconciliation bill by a 72-24 vote Aug. 5, the Senate approved the Agriculture Committee's food stamp provisions without amendment.

House Action

The House Agriculture Committee July 28 approved cuts totaling $1.3 billion in reauthorizing the food stamp program through fiscal 1985. The cuts were included in a separate food and agriculture reconciliation bill the panel reported Aug. 2 (HR 6892 — H Rept 97-687).

The committee was closely divided over food stamp issues. Several key amendments were decided by one- and two-vote margins.

The reductions approved by the committee were substantially less than those made by the Senate bill. Most of the savings were achieved by imposing penalties on states with poorly run food stamp programs and by a variety of relatively small changes in accounting procedures used to determine benefit levels. The panel rejected efforts to impose more stringent penalties on states that made frequent errors in distributing food stamps and to slow the inflation updating of food stamp benefit levels in future years.

The House passed HR 6892 without amendments Aug. 10 by a 268-121 vote. A Republican substitute, which would have made some additional cuts in food stamps, failed 181-210.

Later that day the provisions of HR 6892 were folded into the omnibus reconciliation bill, HR 6955.

Conference, Final Action

Conferees on the reconciliation bill agreed Aug. 13 on food stamp savings provisions that generally split the difference between the $2.1 billion worth of cuts approved by the Senate and the $1.3 billion approved by the House.

Because of House objections, they rejected a Senate-passed plan to let states substitute cash payments for food stamps. They also followed the House in canceling a program, enacted in 1981, that had allowed the substitution of cash for food stamps in Puerto Rico.

The conferees accepted a modified version of a Senate plan to slow inflation adjustments in the "thrifty food plan," the government's list of low-cost foods whose price determined the value of stamps given to beneficiaries, and approved four pilot projects requiring food stamp recipients to work 20 hours a week or participate in a workfare program.

The conference report on the bill was filed Aug. 16 (H Rept 97-759), and the House and Senate approved it Aug. 18.

Provisions

As signed into law Sept. 8, the food stamp provisions of the budget reconciliation bill (HR 6955 — PL 97-253):

Spending Levels. Reauthorized the food stamp program for three years, through Sept. 30, 1985. Set authorization levels, or spending caps, of $12.874 billion for fiscal 1983, $13.145 billion for 1984 and $13.933 billion for 1985, including $825 million a year for Puerto Rico.

The authorizations included a 5 percent "cushion" on top of a basic estimate of projected costs, to allow appropriations to rise if poor economic conditions brought more people into the program than anticipated.

Benefits. Delayed scheduled adjustments in the thrifty food plan. The bill called for the plan to be updated on Oct. 1, 1982, to reflect food price changes for the 21 months ending June 30, 1982, minus 1 percent. The Oct. 1, 1983, and Oct. 1, 1984, adjustments would reflect food price changes for the 12 months ending the preceding June, also minus 1 percent. The Oct. 1, 1985, adjustment would reflect food price changes for the 12 months ending in the preceding June, but without the 1 percent reduction.

● Delayed the next inflation adjustment of the standard deduction, used in determining benefits, until Oct. 1, 1983. The deduction, which was $85 a month in 1982, would be adjusted July 1, 1983.

• Required that food stamp benefits be rounded down to the nearest dollar. Previously, benefits had been rounded up or down to the nearest dollar.

• Barred payments of prorated benefits of less than $10 a month and revised certain dates for prorating.

• Barred benefit increases to a household whose income dropped because of a penalty for non-compliance with welfare laws.

Eligibility. Provided that a permanently disabled individual aged 60 or older, who was unable to prepare his or her own food and who lived with others, could, along with his or her spouse, qualify for food stamps as a separate household if the gross income of the people with whom the disabled person lived was no more than 65 percent above the official poverty line.

• Made disabled veterans and their survivors eligible for food stamps under certain circumstances.

• Disqualified from the program households with net monthly incomes (after various expense disregards and deductions) above 100 percent of the federal poverty level, unless the household contained an elderly or disabled member. In addition, to be eligible for food stamps, a household's gross monthly income must not exceed 130 percent of the poverty level. In 1982 the poverty level as used in the food stamp program was $9,300 a year in net income for a non-farm family of four.

• Allowed states to use a standard utility allowance in calculating a household's expenses to determine eligibility.

• Required that accessible pension funds and savings or retirement accounts be counted in determining eligibility for food stamps, except in certain circumstances.

• Permitted households to qualify for food stamps if all members received Aid to Families with Dependent Children (AFDC) and if the household's gross income did not exceed 130 percent of the federal poverty level.

• Permitted states to allow certain types of households to report their incomes less frequently than every month; also permitted states to revise periodic reporting rules to conform with AFDC reporting requirements.

• Specified that college or other postsecondary students could qualify for food stamps only if they had a child under age 6 (or under age 12 if no satisfactory child care was available) and received AFDC benefits.

• Allowed the secretary of agriculture to determine the beginning of the disqualification period for food stamp participants who voluntarily quit their jobs without good cause. Lengthened the period of ineligibility to 90 days, from 60 days. Specified that federal, state or local government employees who lost their jobs because they participated in a strike would be considered as having quit voluntarily.

Work Requirements. Permitted states to require that unemployed food stamp applicants — as well as recipients — actively look for work.

• Applied work registration requirements to parents or caretakers of young children when there was another able-bodied parent or caretaker in the household. Under existing law, persons responsible for the care of children under 6 were exempt from work registration requirements. The effect of the change was to require the second parent or caretaker to look for work when the youngest child in a household became 6 years old.

• Authorized four pilot projects to determine the effect of disqualifying individuals who did not work at least 20 hours a week or participate in a workfare program.

• Ended an automatic exemption from the workfare requirement for food stamp recipients who spent at least 20 hours a week in a work incentive program, but permitted states to continue the exemption if they wished. Also revised the maximum number of workfare hours required of a recipient, and provided for some reimbursements to states for workfare administrative expenses.

Administration. Authorized the agriculture secretary to limit the use of food stamps for purchases from house-to-house tradesmen to cases where access to grocery stores was limited.

• Permitted the secretary to limit the number of households for which one individual could serve as an authorized representative and to establish verification standards for such households and representatives.

• Required that food stamps be supplied within five days of application to destitute migrant or seasonal farm workers with liquid assets of less than $100, or to households with gross incomes lower than $150 a month.

• Required states to establish a system for determining periodically that no individual was receiving food stamps in more than one jurisdiction in the state.

• Permitted states to require food stamp applications to be included in applications for AFDC or general assistance; also permitted states to make food stamp eligibility determinations on the basis of AFDC or general assistance files. Affirmed that food stamp eligibility could continue after disqualification from AFDC, and that food stamp disqualification decisions must be made separately.

• Required states to determine, at least every year, that people who had been "cashed out" of the program were not still receiving food stamps in addition to cash payments.

• Permitted the agriculture secretary to require states to issue food stamp cards, for use in an automatic data processing system, instead of stamps, if he determined that such a system was necessary to control fraud and abuse.

• Doubled, to $10,000, the maximum civil penalty for each violation of food stamp law by stores. Established disqualification periods for violators, with permanent disqualification for a third violation for trafficking in food stamps or related documents. Also authorized the secretary to require bonds from disqualified stores that wished to re-enter the program.

• Permitted states to keep part of the funds they recovered from fraudulent issues of food stamps, unless the state made a mistake in issuing them.

• Required states to reduce payment error rates to 9 percent for fiscal year 1983, 7 percent for fiscal 1984 and 5 percent for fiscal 1985 and thereafter. Those failing to meet the goals would lose some of their administrative funds.

Puerto Rico. Barred Puerto Rico from distributing its share of federal food stamp funds in the form of cash after Oct. 1, 1983, thus ending the nutritional assistance block grant program for the commonwealth that was established by the 1981 budget reconciliation act (PL 97-35). *(Story, p. 583)*

In 1983 (HR 4252 — PL 98-204) Congress postponed the deadline for terminating the cash assistance program until Oct. 1, 1985.

Welfare Benefits

Congress in 1982 approved changes in federal welfare programs designed to cut an estimated $1.1 billion from anticipated spending for those programs in fiscal 1983-85. The total was far short of the $7.7 billion reduction sought by the Reagan administration.

The changes were incorporated in the massive tax increase/spending cut bill cleared by Congress Aug. 19 (HR 4961 — PL 97-248). The bill was one of two deficit reduction measures enacted in 1982 as part of the budget reconciliation process. *(Reconciliation, p. 48)*

Changes were made in the core federal welfare program, Aid to Families with Dependent Children (AFDC), in child support enforcement and in the Supplemental Security Income (SSI) program for the aged, blind and disabled. Savings over the three-year period were estimated at $343 million in AFDC, $384 million in child support enforcement and $386 million in SSI.

Among other things, the bill allowed states to require AFDC applicants and recipients to participate in job search programs, increased penalties for states with high error rates in the administration of benefits and reduced welfare payments through a variety of administrative provisions. It did not include a mandatory "workfare" program for welfare recipients or new block grant proposals for child welfare and emergency assistance, as President Reagan had urged in 1981 and 1982.

Legislative Action

Senate. The Senate Finance Committee approved reconciliation changes designed to pare $2.1 billion from federal spending for welfare programs in fiscal 1983-85 — only about one-fourth of the cut sought by the administration. The changes were included in the committee's tax increase/spending cut package, which was attached to a minor House-passed revenue bill and reported July 12 (HR 4961 — S Rept 97-494).

The committee agreed to $1.6 billion in cuts in AFDC, child support enforcement and SSI. It accepted Reagan proposals to end AFDC parent benefits when the youngest child turned 16; include all children, even those earning income, in determining a family's AFDC benefit; and count the income of an unrelated adult in the AFDC household as part of the family income. It also agreed to round SSI and AFDC benefit payments down to the next lower dollar and to prorate benefits according to the day of the month the application was made or eligibility requirements were met.

The committee rejected the administration proposal to require welfare recipients to participate in workfare programs, although it did include a provision requiring applicants for AFDC to undertake efforts to find employment.

The committee also rejected proposed cuts in the social services block grant program and consolidation of child welfare services into block grants.

A major savings measure proposed by the administration and accepted by the committee was the imposition of penalties on states that had high error rates in administering AFDC. The committee also agreed to repeal the AFDC emergency assistance program, as proposed by Reagan.

The Senate passed HR 4961 by a 50-47 vote in the session that began July 22. It made no changes in the welfare spending provisions.

House Action. The House Ways and Means Committee, in an unusual closed-door meeting July 15, approved limited savings in welfare programs as part of a $20.9 billion health and welfare reconciliation package. Among the welfare provisions agreed to was one that would allow states to insist that individuals look for jobs before they began receiving AFDC payments.

The committee had been directed to cut $2.2 billion from projected fiscal 1983-85 spending for AFDC, SSI and child support enforcement. It had been expected to vote

down many of the required reconciliation cuts, thus forcing Republicans to offer amendments on the House floor making reductions in the politically sensitive health and welfare programs. Instead, the committee held its meeting in private, took no recorded votes and came out with savings close to what it was instructed to achieve.

The committee was unable to agree on the revenue-raising provisions of its reconciliation package, however. To avoid painful floor votes on tax increases in an election year, Ways and Means persuaded the House to go directly to conference on the Senate-passed tax/spending bill.

Conference, Final Action. In conference on HR 4961, House Democrats attempted unsuccessfully to restore some of the cuts made in Medicaid and AFDC in 1981. By some estimates, the changes would have added $1 billion to the cost of the programs in fiscal 1983-85.

Sen. Russell B. Long, D-La., ranking Senate Democrat on the conference committee, adamantly opposed the move, arguing that conferees should be "trying to get the genie back in the bottle as far as spending is concerned."

The conferees eventually agreed to a spending package that cut income security programs such as AFDC and SSI by $1.1 billion over the three-year period. The conference agreement on the spending cuts and tax increases was filed Aug. 17 (H Rept 97-760).

The House adopted the conference report Aug. 19, 226-207, despite attacks by liberal Democrats on the cuts in social programs. The Senate then approved the measure, 52-47, clearing it for the president.

Provisions

As signed into law Sept. 3, the welfare provisions of HR 4961 (PL 97-248):

AFDC. Required states to round their need standards and monthly benefit amounts in the AFDC program to the next lower dollar.

● Provided for prorating of AFDC benefits during a recipient's first month on the program according to the date on which the application was filed.

● Excluded from the program families in which the father was absent because of military service.

● Permitted states to require AFDC applicants and recipients to participate in a program of employment search beginning at the time of application.

● Required that a portion of the income of unrelated adults who shared living quarters with an AFDC family be included in calculating the family's AFDC benefits.

● Increased penalties paid by states whose error rates in awarding AFDC benefits exceeded 4 percent in fiscal 1983 and 3 percent in 1984 and 1985.

● Allowed states the option, for two additional years, of operating a Work Incentive (WIN) demonstration program authorized by the 1981 reconciliation law.

Child Support Enforcement. Repealed a provision of the 1981 reconciliation law that required states to charge a 10 percent fee for child support payments collected on behalf of non-AFDC families; permitted the states to charge a reasonable fee.

● Allowed collection of child support payments from the pay of a member of the armed forces if the absent parent was two months behind in his payments.

● Allowed states to retain a portion of child support payments collected for an AFDC family if the state already had paid benefits to the family for the month during which the child support funds were collected.

● Reduced the federal matching rate for state costs of

Medicaid Cuts

Medicaid, the federal-state health program for the poor, suffered substantial reductions in the budget-cutting efforts launched by the Reagan administration in 1981.

Moving to hold down soaring federal health care costs, Congress agreed after a bitter battle to cut Medicaid payments to the states in fiscal 1982-84. But it refused to put a rigid "cap" on federal payments as President Reagan had requested. The federal government paid about 55 percent of Medicaid costs, the states 45 percent. The 1981 changes were expected to cut federal costs for the program by about $1 billion annually. *(1981 cuts, p. 527)*

Congress approved a second round of Medicaid cuts in 1982, paring another $1.4 billion from the program over fiscal 1983-85. But further administration efforts to scale back the program made little headway. *(1982 cuts, p. 532)*

And in 1984 Congress approved a new child health plan requiring states to broaden their Medicaid coverage to include more low-income women during pregnancy and more young children. *(Details, p. 546)*

operating the child support enforcement program.

Supplemental Security Income. Established a prorating procedure under which SSI benefit levels for recipients during their first month on the program would be determined according to the day of the month on which they applied or met eligibility requirements. Under existing law, recipients received a full month's benefits regardless of what day of the month they applied.

● Provided for rounding of a recipient's benefit amounts to the next lower dollar.

● Required that SSI benefits be reduced in the first month in which a recipient received a cost-of-living increase in Social Security payments.

● Excluded from countable resources, for eligibility purposes, burial spaces for an individual or members of his immediate family. Burial funds of up to $1,500 each for the individual and his or her spouse also would be excluded if specifically set aside for this purpose.

1983

Record unemployment and reports of hunger in America captured headlines and the attention of Congress in 1983. With these issues as a backdrop, Reagan administration efforts to push a third round of social spending cuts proved unsuccessful.

The president's fiscal 1984 budget contained a number of requests for cutbacks in programs for the poor, including Aid to Families with Dependent Children, food stamps, child nutrition programs and energy aid to the poor.

But, unlike 1981 and 1982, Congress in 1983 did not acquiesce to any major social welfare reductions or program changes.

In fact, early in the session, Congress told the Agriculture Department to step up giveaways of surplus federally owned food and provided funds for distribution costs. The food assistance program and other social programs were included in a $4.6 billion jobs and humanitarian relief package enacted in March. Despite administration objections, Congress later in the year approved a two-year extension of the food aid program.

But at the same time, while there was much talk among Democrats of reversing social spending cutbacks enacted in 1981 and 1982, little headway was made. Action on the second fiscal 1984 continuing appropriations resolution provided a good example. Under the threat of a presidential veto, a House Democratic initiative to add about $955 million for education and social programs was trimmed down in conference to about $99 million.

Congress did not complete action in 1983 on several other Democratic-sponsored measures to increase spending for social programs. Although the House in October voted to restore some funding cut from child nutrition programs, the bill was not acted on by the Senate.

The modest increases in food stamps that the fiscal 1984 budget resolution permitted were not enacted. And because the House and Senate did not agree on reauthorizing a number of volunteer and anti-poverty programs, including Volunteers in Service to America, fiscal 1984 funding for the programs was set lower than envisioned by either chamber.

Relief, Food Aid Bills

Alarmed at recession-spawned unemployment and reports that Americans were going hungry, Congress in 1983 took steps to provide broad humanitarian relief.

Early in the session Congress overwhelmingly approved and President Reagan signed into law a $4.6 billion jobs and humanitarian relief package (HR 1718 — PL 98-8).

As part of HR 1718, Congress told the Agriculture Department to step up giveaways of surplus federally owned food and provided funds for distribution costs. An August unemployment compensation bill (HR 3409 — PL 98-92) continued the mandate for the food distribution program and funding for distribution for two years.

Unemployment had hit 10.7 percent in December 1982. As unemployment peaked, soup kitchens and other emergency feeding centers began reporting massive increases in the number of people turning to them for food, and their reports received wide media coverage.

Local charities and elected officials, and Washington-based anti-poverty groups blamed the increases on the combined impact of the recession and Reagan-era cutbacks in the growth of food stamps and other aid programs for the poor.

Reagan administration officials responded that the federal government was spending more than ever on food aid — $18.6 billion in fiscal 1983. They maintained that the hunger reports were exaggerated. But in August, when the nation's poverty rate was reported at a 19-year high, the president ordered a study of the reports. *(Box, p. 600)*

The House in October voted to restore some funding cut from school lunch and other child nutrition programs and to make this aid available to more children of the "working poor." But that bill (HR 4091) was not acted on by the Senate.

Nor did Congress go ahead with the modest increases in food stamps that the fiscal 1984 budget resolution permitted. Advocates of expanded food aid feared that any move to liberalize food stamps would provoke strong counterattacks from members who thought the program should be cut further.

Congress also failed in 1984 to complete action on legislation restoring some Reagan-era cuts in food stamps, school lunch and other federal food aid programs. *(1984 action, p. 611)*

Jobs, Relief Bill

Congress approved a $4.6 billion jobs and humanitarian relief package March 24 as part of a $15.6 billion supplemental appropriations bill for the fiscal year ending Sept. 30, 1983. The president signed HR 1718 into law that same day.

The legislation marked the first major effort by the 98th Congress to address the severe economic problems that had left nearly 12 million people without jobs.

The jobs portion of HR 1718 represented a House-Senate compromise fashioned to fall within a $5 billion limit the president had set. Reagan Feb. 16, under congressional pressure, had dropped his opposition to jobs legislation and proposed his own $4.3 billion plan for recession relief — $4 billion for jobs and $300 million "in additional humanitarian relief for those in serious distress."

Two-thirds of the final $4.6 billion package was allotted to public works, general construction and water projects. The remaining funds were allocated to social services, health and humanitarian aid.

As cleared, HR 1718 included funds to expand the Agriculture Department's food distribution program. The bill appropriated $75 million for surplus food distribution and, in a separate title, appropriated $50 million to cover administrative, storage and delivery costs associated with food distribution programs.

The final bill also included $105 million for maternal and child health care; $100 million for the Women, Infants and Children (WIC) feeding program; $70 million for community and migrant health centers; $225 million for social service block grants directed at maintaining family health, preventing child abuse and providing day care and adoption services; $50 million for a college work-study program; $100 million for the emergency food and shelter program; and $25 million for community service block grants.

The House approved HR 1718 March 3 by a 324-95 vote. The relief package had grown on the floor to $4.9 billion from the $4.6 billion version reported March 1 by the House Appropriations Committee (H Rept 98-11).

The Senate approved its version March 17 by an 82-16 vote. During Senate floor action, $1.3 billion was added to the $3.9 billion relief package reported by the Senate Appropriations Committee March 7 (S Rept 98-17).

But a Democratic initiative to add nearly $1.7 billion to the package was rejected, 34-53.

The conference report (H Rept 98-44) on the measure was accepted March 22 by the House, 329-86, and by the Senate, 82-15. But final passage remained provisional for two days while the two chambers sought agreement on a complex targeting formula for distributing funds among states and economically distressed areas. HR 1718 — with a formula compromise — was cleared by the House March 24 by voice vote. *(Details on jobs program, p. 663)*

Food Assistance

Congress approved a two-year extension of the surplus food distribution program and authorized $50 million annually for distribution costs as part of an unemployment compensation bill (HR 3409 — PL 98-92) that cleared Aug. 4.

The food program had been authorized only through fiscal 1983 by HR 1718, the jobs and humanitarian relief bill. As soon as that measure had passed, sponsors focused on similar House and Senate bills (HR 1590, S 17) to continue the donations program through fiscal 1985.

The food donation legislation was meant to respond to problems of emergency soup kitchens and other charitable organizations that were providing hot meals (and, often, shelter) or groceries for the needy. A number of volunteer-staffed groups said their budgets were so limited that they could not afford to take the free surplus cheese that the administration had begun handing out late in 1981. They said they lacked money for storage, transportation and similar expenses, and that it was difficult to accept the commodities in bulk, without repackaging or processing into more usable forms.

Until early August the Reagan administration objected to extending the donations program past the Sept. 30 expiration date. But the hunger issue continued to receive attention in the media and Congress.

On Aug. 2 the Census Bureau reported that 15 percent of Americans were living below the poverty level. That same day President Reagan ordered a "no holds barred" study of the hunger reports. *(Box, p. 600)*

Two days later Congress cleared HR 3409, which included the food program expansion.

Legislative History. The Senate Agriculture Committee March 9 reported legislation (S 17 — S Rept 98-21) extending the food distribution program for two years. It differed from the final bill in several respects; most conspicuously, it did not have the $50 million-a-year authorization for distribution costs. There also were limits on processing expenditures and other program costs — $100 million a year, plus an amount equal to the projected costs of commodity storage or spoilage. Those limits did not include the value of the donated commodities, however.

Two House committees reported similar, stronger versions of the legislation. First, the House Education and Labor Committee, which had jurisdiction over child nutrition programs, reported a bill (HR 1513 — H Rept 98-39) on March 18. That measure ordered the distribution of all unobligated surplus Commodity Credit Corp. (CCC) stocks within 60 days of enactment. It also required the federal government to bear the full costs of processing the commodities. The bill was referred to the House Agriculture Committee, which then reported a similar version on May 16 (HR 1590 — H Rept 98-148).

Neither House bill directly authorized funds for distribution costs, but instead specified other funds to be used for that purpose. Their intent was to bypass the appropriations process — and thereby assure that money would be available even if the president refused to request it.

When the Agriculture Committee bill came to the House floor June 16, there was little debate, and it passed

Reports of Hunger in America Mount in 1983

By the beginning of 1983 a steady stream of news stories depicted hunger and hard times in cities and suburban neighborhoods.

The main sources for the stories were churches and other charitable organizations running food programs for the needy, and mayors and advocacy groups, such as the Food Research and Action Center (FRAC) based in Washington.

FRAC produced a widely publicized report in January that showed worsening infant mortality rates in seven states and 34 rural and urban areas between 1980 and 1981. Health experts considered poor nutrition during pregnancy to be a contributing factor to infant mortality. The FRAC report, based on a telephone survey by the organization, was criticized by administration officials who said that the data was not statistically reliable.

The news stories were followed by congressional hearings, including a series outside Washington by the House Agriculture Subcommittee on Domestic Marketing, Consumer Relations and Nutrition.

Subcommittee Chairman Leon E. Panetta, D-Calif., said he had begun the year with some skepticism about the hunger reports. By June, when the House debated its commodity distribution bill (HR 1590), he was telling his colleagues, "This country faces a very serious problem with regard to hunger."

As the House debated the bill, the U.S. Conference of Mayors presented a report on hunger in eight cities to the Senate Agriculture Subcommittee on Rural Development, Oversight and Investigations chaired by Mark Andrews, R-N.D. That report said, "Although there are several emergency problems of concern to the mayors at this time, hunger is probably the most prevalent and the most insidious."

City officials agreed, the report said, that unemployment was the primary cause of increased hunger, but contributing factors included cuts in federal funds, high shelter and energy costs, and increased numbers of transients failing to find work.

Administration Response

Reagan administration officials and their congressional allies maintained throughout the year that the reports of hunger were greatly overstated and that federal food programs were adequate. In a strongly worded speech in February, budget director David A. Stockman called the FRAC report "absolutely, totally and completely untrue."

The administration's basic argument was that the federal government was spending significantly more on food aid for the needy than ever before and the people excluded from aid programs because of budget cuts were not truly needy.

When queried about the apparent upturn in the use of emergency food centers, officials usually suggested that the centers' new clients were taking advantage of giveaways that they did not really need.

In May, concerned by complaints from the cheese industry that the federal giveaways had cut into commercial sales, the Agriculture Department sharply reduced its cheese distribution, a decision that later was reversed. The administration had initiated the cheese distribution in December 1981, partially to reduce the dairy surplus and partially in response to stories of need.

On Aug. 2 the Census Bureau reported that 15 percent of Americans were living below the poverty level — the highest percentage since 1965 when President Johnson launched his "war on poverty." The poverty level was defined as cash income of less than $9,862 for a family of four.

That same day Reagan, in a White House memorandum, said he was "perplexed" and "deeply concerned" about the hunger reports. Reagan called for establishment of a study group — subsequently known as the President's Task Force on Food Assistance — to look into the allegations. "If certain aspects of our food assistance programs require more funding, I want to know that too," Reagan wrote.

Task Force Report

The presidential task force Jan. 9, 1984, reported that "allegations of rampant hunger simply cannot be documented." It said that based on testimony it heard, "We cannot doubt that there is hunger in America." However, it maintained that there was "no evidence that widespread undernutrition is a major health problem in the United States."

Its major recommendations included allowing states to drop out of the food stamp and other federal food programs and to receive a block grant instead. States choosing block grant funding would decide how to distribute assistance to individuals and institutions. That would have meant an end to uniform national eligibility and benefit standards. The proposal drew immediate fire from the National Governors' Association, the U.S. Conference of Mayors, the National Association of Counties and advocates of the poor. They insisted that food aid was a national responsibility and that the proposed grants would be the first step in dumping that responsibility onto state and local governments.

Other recommendations included stiffening the penalties against states that failed to bring their food stamp error rates down to the level mandated by law. The task force also suggested modest increases in the assets a food stamp recipient could own and in the maximum food stamp allotment, and called for more timely collection of nutrition data.

by a vote of 389-18. The House approved an amendment to assure that a special wheat reserve for international emergencies would be replenished if it were used for the domestic donations. The House also adopted an amendment, sought by the Education and Labor panel, specifying that once money and food needs of emergency feeding centers had been met, the rest of a state's money and food generally could be distributed to other, non-emergency organizations that were eligible, such as schools.

Senate action on S 17 was delayed by Agriculture Committee Chairman Jesse Helms, R-N.C., who, like the administration, questioned the wisdom of making the food donation program more than a temporary entity.

But on Aug. 4 Congress unexpectedly cleared a compromise version that closely resembled the language in the jobs bill. The compromise had been negotiated with Helms, Senate sponsor Robert Dole, R-Kan., budget director David A. Stockman, and Rep. Leon E. Panetta, D-Calif., chairman of the House Agriculture Subcommittee on Domestic Marketing, Consumer Relations and Nutrition, and sponsor of the House bill. It was included in HR 3409, the unemployment compensation bill. *(Unemployment compensation details, p. 665)*

Provisions. As signed into law Sept. 2, HR 3409 (PL 98-92) included the following provisions relating to commodity distribution:

● Established a two-year program in which the secretary of agriculture was required to make available for distribution commodities acquired by Commodity Credit Corp. that the secretary determined were not obligated for other programs. Repealed the donations program, except for criminal penalties for misuse, on Sept. 30, 1985.

(The CCC was the Agriculture Department agency that managed farm price support programs and held the commodities acquired through these programs.)

● Specified that eligible recipients, if approved by states and/or the secretary, were: public and non-profit organizations that provided emergency food aid to the poor, including unemployed individuals; school lunch, summer camp and other child nutrition programs providing food service; nutrition projects for the elderly; projects of charitable institutions serving the needy; and disaster relief programs.

● Authorized the CCC to pay for initial processing or packaging of the commodities for institutional or home use before distribution.

● Authorized use in the program of up to 300,000 metric tons of wheat from the international emergency food reserve and required that the reserve be replenished before Oct. 1, 1985. Permitted CCC stocks to be used to replenish the reserve but, if purchases were needed to replenish, required that the purchases be made with appropriated funds.

● Directed the secretary to arrange for private companies to process donated commodities into forms suitable for home or institutional use, with processing expenses to be paid by agencies receiving the commodities.

● Required prompt distribution of commodities by the secretary to designated state agencies or directly to eligible recipient organizations, and prompt redistribution by states; provided that if recipient organizations' requests to a state for a specific commodity exceeded supplies, the state must give priority to organizations providing emergency food aid.

● Required states to determine which individuals were needy enough to qualify for free commodities for household use.

● Directed the secretary to act as needed to assure that organizations receiving the commodities not reduce their other expenditures for food, and to assure that the commodity donations not disrupt commercial sales.

● Prohibited agencies from receiving more commodities than they could use, with use determined by such factors as inventory records and storage capacity.

● Authorized $50 million annually, through fiscal 1985, for distribution to states for storage and distribution costs associated with the commodity donations; earmarked at least 20 percent of that amount each year for redistribution to local soup kitchens and other organizations providing emergency food aid to the needy and unemployed, to help defray their costs.

● Specified that the value of donated commodities and expenditures for processing not be deducted from appropriations made under this authorization.

● Suspended, for the donated commodities, a prohibition against the use of surplus commodities in jurisdictions where food stamps were available.

● Generally prohibited the sale of donated commodities.

● Stipulated that commodities distributed in the program not be counted as income or assets under federal, state or local laws.

● Authorized criminal penalties for fraudulent misuse of program commodities.

Child Nutrition Programs

The House in 1983 voted to let more children qualify for federally subsidized meals and to cut the prices that needy children paid for the food, but the Senate did not act on the legislation before adjournment.

Critics warned that President Reagan would veto the bill (HR 4091), but the House Oct. 25 voted 306-114 to pass it. The bill altered the eligibility levels and authorized funding for school lunch and other child nutrition programs, restoring about one-tenth of the $1.5 billion that Congress had cut from the programs in 1981. *(1981 action, p. 591)*

The Congressional Budget Office (CBO) estimated that HR 4091 would add $105.5 million to program spending in fiscal 1984 for 10 months, and $160 million in fiscal 1985. The total program costs under existing law were $3.4 billion annually.

Much of the bill, sponsors said, was meant to restore food aid to children of the "working poor." Many in this category had been dropped because of restrictions enacted in 1981.

The Reagan administration argued that new spending was unwarranted and that the 1981 budget cuts had not hurt impoverished children. Budget director Stockman wrote to House members that the administration had promised "that no needy child would be deprived of nutrition benefits" and "that promise has been kept."

But cosponsor Bill Goodling, R-Pa., in debate Oct. 24 called Stockman's claim "sheer hogwash." Goodling and Carl D. Perkins, D-Ky., chairman of the House Education and Labor Committee, said that many of the nation's most needy children had lost federally subsidized meals as an indirect result of the 1981 cuts.

A major goal of the cuts was sharp reductions in the number of middle-class children in the programs; but a growing number of schools found that without middle-class students making partial payments for the food, they could not afford to run food programs at all. So, Goodling argued,

Social Program Spending

Additional funds for education and social welfare were contained in a $316 billion fiscal 1984 continuing appropriations resolution that cleared Nov. 12. Final passage of the resolution (H J Res 413 — PL 98-151) came after a weeklong confrontation between House Democrats and President Reagan over the extra domestic spending the House had attached to the bill. Reagan's veto threat dissipated, however, when House and Senate conferees Nov. 11 whittled down the extra education and social welfare spending to $98.7 million, one-tenth of the $997.7 million that House Majority Leader Jim Wright, D-Texas, first proposed.

Democratic supporters of the Wright amendment argued that it would restore some of the domestic spending cuts that Reagan won from Congress in 1981. During House floor action on the resolution, Republicans demanded separate votes on the various components of the Wright amendment. In these votes the House adopted extra money for vocational education, schooling for immigrant children, community health centers, job training, child nutrition and several other services. After deleting funds for science centers at three universities, the House approved the remaining $954.4 million in the Wright amendment as a package, by a **254-155 key vote (R 22-134; D 232-21)**. The bill then passed Nov. 10 by a 224-189 vote. *(1983 key votes, p. 911)*

When the bill reached the Senate, the Senate adopted, by a vote of 53-36, an amendment striking the additional funds the House had added for domestic spending. The Senate approved H J Res 413 by voice vote early Nov. 11.

After days of White House warnings that Reagan would veto the bill because of the nearly $1 billion in education and social service spending, House and Senate conferees finally settled on a compromise that cut the domestic money to $98.7 million. Conferees filed their report late Nov. 11 (H Rept 98-540). In unusual Saturday sessions Nov. 12, the House adopted the report by a 173-136 vote, and the Senate approved the measure by voice vote.

The final bill divided the $98.7 million education-social welfare package among the following programs: education for the handicapped, $25 million; vocational rehabilitation, $10 million; schooling for immigrant children, $30 million; college work-study, $5 million; supplemental educational opportunity grants, $5 million; community health centers, $10 million; National Technical Institute for the Deaf, $1.7 million; Gallaudet College, $2 million; and food distribution and emergency shelter for the needy, $10 million.

poor children had remained eligible for food programs that often had gone out of existence.

Moreover, of those children disqualified from the school lunch program as a result of the 1981 changes, close to one million were poor, Goodling said.

Efforts to pass child nutrition bills in 1984 also failed. *(Details, p. 611)*

Food Stamps

Congress included $450 million for modest food stamp expansions in the fiscal 1984 budget resolution (H Con Res 91). That allotment was in a contingency fund, to be made available if Congress passed legislation authorizing the changes.

However, Congress passed neither the expansions nor any of the $1.1 billion worth of money-saving cuts in food stamps that the president's fiscal 1984 budget had requested. (The budget estimated that the food stamp program would cost $10.9 billion in fiscal 1984, assuming those changes were made.)

Members who wanted more food aid for the needy decided not to press for the food stamp expansions because they did not want to provoke counter-moves by Helms and like-minded members to push the president's budget cuts. *(1981-82 food stamp cuts, pp. 583, 594)*

At the end of the session Congress cleared a bill (HR 4252 — PL 98-204) postponing a deadline for termination of Puerto Rico's cash nutrition assistance program and giving states more flexibility in coping with new food stamp reporting requirements.

Other Legislation

SSI Benefits

Congress in 1983 enacted a six-month delay in cost-of-living adjustments (COLAs) for recipients of Supplemental Security Income (SSI), a federal assistance program for needy aged, blind and disabled persons. The change was included in Social Security legislation (HR 1900 — PL 98-21) cleared by Congress March 25.

To reduce the impact of the COLA delay, Congress increased the monthly SSI benefits $20 for individuals and $30 for couples, effective July 1, 1983. *(SSI provisions, p. 659)*

VISTA Authorization

Both the Senate and House passed bills in 1983 rebuffing the Reagan administration's effort to eliminate Volunteers in Service to America (VISTA). Congress, however, adjourned before a conference committee met to reconcile substantial differences between the two bills.

The Senate Sept. 14 passed S 1129 extending through fiscal 1986 a number of volunteer and anti-poverty programs administered by ACTION, including VISTA. The House passed its version (HR 2655) Oct. 28.

A compromise version was cleared in 1984. *(1983-84 action, p. 610)*

Vocational Rehabilitation

Congress in 1983 approved a simple fiscal 1984 funding authorization of federal vocational training programs for

the handicapped (S 1341 — PL 98-199).

Enactment of a more detailed rehabilitation reauthorization measure (S 1340) was blocked by controversy over a package of House amendments authorizing additional spending for unrelated education and social programs. When the Senate refused to go to conference on S 1340 because of the House amendments, the basic reauthorization was attached to S 1341, a bill authorizing education programs for the handicapped. *(Handicapped bill, p. 567)*

The logjam was broken and S 1340 cleared early in 1984 when the House agreed to drop its controversial rider. *(1984 action, p. 608)*

Child Support Enforcement

The House Nov. 16 overwhelmingly approved a measure (HR 4325) designed to encourage payment of child support. The key feature of the bill was the mandatory withholding of payments from the paychecks of those in arrears in court-ordered child support.

The Senate did not act on the legislation before adjournment in 1983, but a compromise bill was cleared in 1984. *(1983-84 action, p. 605)*

Older Americans Act

The House May 24 approved a bill (HR 2807 — H Rept 98-164) to provide additional funding for the popular Older Americans Act meals program. There was no Senate action.

HR 2807, passed by a 386-31 vote, would have authorized an additional $6.8 million in fiscal 1982 and $16 million in 1983 for the program of distribution of cash and commodities to senior nutrition programs. Sponsors said spending limits set in 1981 were too low to reimburse states for all the meals they served. *(1981 action, p. 593)*

The most controversial part of the bill would have removed the spending ceiling on the program for fiscal 1984, authorizing "such sums as are necessary." Opponents warned that the open-ended funding would restore the program to entitlement status, which it had before 1981. The Reagan administration opposed the bill.

Congress in 1984 reauthorized Older Americans Act programs through fiscal 1987. *(1984 action, p. 609)*

1984

With the Census Bureau continuing to report increases in the number of people living in poverty, the debate over social spending heated up in the election year. Administration critics tried to pin part of the blame for the increase in poverty on cuts in aid to the needy under President Reagan. But Reagan and his supporters insisted that the social safety net remained intact, and that the poor were better off because of economic improvements and lower inflation.

Democrats accused the administration of making election-year policy shifts in its fiscal 1985 budget. One example cited was the low-income energy assistance program. After failing to cut the aid for the previous two years, the administration called for budget authority for the program at its fiscal 1984 level of $1.87 billion and proposed that it be financed by revenues collected in settlements of lawsuits against oil companies for overcharging. Congress ignored the proposal for the new funding mechanism and authorized $2.14 billion in fiscal 1985, as part of an omnibus social services bill.

The administration recycled an earlier proposal for reforming Aid to Families with Dependent Children. But Congress took no action on the plan, which included a proposal for states to set up mandatory work programs for welfare recipients.

The White House and Congress did agree on the need to strengthen child support enforcement. Legislation requiring states to set up certain procedures for collecting delinquent child support payments was signed into law.

Other child-related legislation enacted in 1984 included laws providing for medical treatment for severely handicapped infants, child abuse prevention and treatment programs, extra funds for training child care workers, the popular Head Start program and expanded child care services.

Congress in 1984 also reauthorized vocational rehabilitation, developmental disabilities, Older Americans Act and ACTION programs.

Efforts to restore some Reagan-era cuts in food stamps, school lunch and other federal food programs failed in 1984.

Social Services, Energy Aid

Congress Oct. 9 approved an omnibus social services bill reauthorizing the popular Head Start program, as well as energy aid for the poor, community services block grants and other social services.

Pressure to clear the bill (S 2565 — PL 98-558) before adjournment provided an opportunity for members to make a last-minute push for their favorite legislative proposals. As a result, the final bill also incorporated several new education and social programs, including block grants to expand child care services, teacher scholarships and research grants for universities in the home states of key members — add-ons that led one critic to dub the measure a social services "Christmas tree."

Final action on S 2565 came after Senate and House negotiators worked out a compromise to break a logjam over the politically divisive formula for allocating energy aid for the poor. The formula was revised to respond to complaints of members from warm-weather regions that their constituents were being shortchanged, while protecting cold-weather states from drastic and sudden losses of energy aid.

The divisiveness over energy aid contrasted sharply with sentiments toward Head Start, which provided educational, health, nutrition and other social services for disadvantaged preschool children. The program had been widely hailed by both Republicans and Democrats and was one of the few major anti-poverty programs that had escaped the budget-cutting rigors of the Reagan administration. *(Previous authorization, p. 590)*

House Action

The House June 26 overwhelmingly approved a two-year extension of Head Start as part of legislation (HR 5885) that also reauthorized community services block grants and other social services.

An earlier version (HR 5145) had been defeated June 7

after Republicans bitterly objected to considering the bill under suspension of the rules — a procedure, often used for non-controversial bills, that limited debate, barred amendments and required a two-thirds vote for passage.

The 261-156 vote was 17 short of the two-thirds needed, handing a victory to Republicans who said the bill was too costly and complex to be considered under the procedure.

To meet Republican objections, the original version, reported by the Education and Labor Committee May 10 (H Rept 98-740), was scaled back from a five-year authorization to two years, thus cutting the total cost from about $8 billion to about $2.5 billion.

Republicans also objected to the reauthorization of the community services block grant, an anti-poverty program that the Reagan administration repeatedly proposed abolishing, and pointed out that it did not expire until 1986.

The administration had argued that the community services block grant, created by the 1981 budget reconciliation act, duplicated activities of the social services block grant. *(1981 authorizations, pp. 590, 588)*

But defenders of the block grant said it was the only federal program expressly directed at combating the causes of poverty at the community level. Supporters feared that the president would veto separate block grant legislation.

To defuse the issue, the revised version did not extend the block grant beyond its expiration date of 1986, although it did let spending increase by 5 percent in fiscal 1985 and 1986.

The House June 26 by a vote of 409-10 agreed to suspend the rules and passed the revised bill.

Senate, Final Action

The Senate Oct. 4 approved a compromise version of the omnibus social services bill (S 2565) that had been worked out by Senate and House negotiators.

Action had stalled in the Senate after the Labor and Human Resources Committee May 24 reported S 2565 to extend Head Start, community services grants and the low-income energy aid program (S Rept 98-484). A key obstacle was the formula for allocating energy assistance.

But with time for consideration of the bill running short, Senate and House negotiators worked out a compromise on the energy aid formula and other elements of S 2565 that they thought could be approved by the Senate without a floor fight and by the House without a formal conference.

Energy Aid Formula. The Senate Labor Committee extended the low-income energy assistance program as part of S 2565 but left the formula for allocating the assistance unchanged. *(Previous authorization, p. 588)*

Members from warm-weather regions complained that the existing allocation formula shortchanged their constituents because it did not take account of the cost of cooling as well as heating the homes of poor families.

Sen. J. Bennett Johnston, D-La., had planned to introduce an amendment during floor debate changing the formula to channel more money to Southern states.

The revised energy aid formula — which did not go as far as Johnston and other critics had wanted — based state allocations on total energy expenditures, including both heating and cooling, by low-income families. But it guaranteed that no state would receive less in fiscal 1985 than it did in 1984, and it protected states from sharp reductions in funds in fiscal 1986.

Weatherization Program. The Senate bill modified an Energy Department program to help low-income families pay for home weatherization work.

The weatherization program was established in 1976 (PL 94-385) to help low-income families pay for work such as insulation, weather-stripping and repairs that could cut their energy costs. An estimated one million homes had benefited from the weatherization program by 1984. *(Weatherization background, Congress and the Nation Vol. IV, p. 257)*

An effort to greatly increase authorized funding for the program had been rejected by the House early in the year. On Jan. 24 the House had slashed to $200 million a $500 million fiscal 1985 authorization reported by the House Energy Committee (HR 2615 — H Rept 98-108). The Senate took no action on the bill.

Energy Funding. Congress ignored President Reagan's proposal to shift funding for the weatherization and low-income energy assistance programs from the Treasury to a proposed new Petroleum Overcharge Restitution Fund. The fund was to be supported by fines paid by oil companies for overcharging their customers.

A continuing appropriations resolution cleared Oct. 11 (PL 98-473) provided $2.1 billion for low-income energy assistance in fiscal 1985. The program initially had been funded at $1.87 billion for fiscal 1984, but Congress March 27 approved (PL 98-248) an additional $200 million to help the poor pay fuel bills resulting from an unusually cold winter. *(Energy appropriations, p. 399)*

The main weatherization program received $191 million for fiscal 1985 in the continuing resolution. Fiscal 1984 funds totaled some $190 million.

Child Care Compromise. The Senate social services bill also resolved differences over new programs to expand child care services. The House May 14 had approved legislation (HR 4193 — H Rept 98-745) authorizing federal aid to help communities set up child care programs in school facilities before and after school hours. *(Story, p. 608)*

A similar measure reported by the Senate Labor and Human Resources Committee May 25 (S 1531 — S Rept 98-494) was opposed by committee Chairman Orrin G. Hatch, R-Utah, who argued that the federal government should not be directly involved in the funding of child care.

The compromise incorporated in S 2565 provided state block grants to help set up child care programs in school facilities and disseminate information about the availability of care for children, the elderly and the handicapped — an approach favored by Hatch. A similar information referral program had been included in the House Head Start bill.

Education Add-Ons. Most of the education add-ons had been introduced in response to a series of 1983 reports recommending improvements in U.S. schools. The teacher and merit scholarship programs were scaled-down versions of programs included in a measure (HR 4477) that had been approved by the House Aug. 8. *(Scholarship bill, p. 579)*

Many House members were pleased that the omnibus bill, when it came over from the Senate, included education initiatives they had backed, but other members were dismayed that the bill carried proposals that had not been formally considered by education committees in either the House or Senate — including funds for two university research centers.

House Approval. The House Oct. 9 approved the

Senate-passed compromise bill by a vote of 376-6, thus clearing S 2565 for the president's signature.

Provisions

As signed into law Oct. 30, S 2565 (PL 98-558):

Head Start. Authorized $1.09 billion in fiscal 1985 and $1.22 billion in 1986.

● Required the Department of Health and Human Services (HHS) to spend at least as much on Head Start training and technical assistance as was spent in fiscal 1982 — about $25 million.

● Barred HHS from changing the method for measuring income to prescribe eligibility for Head Start for two years, unless expressly approved by Congress.

Child Care. Authorized $20 million a year in fiscal 1985-86 for state block grants to help expand the availability of dependent care services.

● Specified that states use 40 percent of their allotments for grants to organizations to provide information about services for the care of children, the elderly and the handicapped.

● Specified that the remaining 60 percent of states' funds be used to help establish before- and after-school child care programs in community centers and unused school facilities.

Community Services Block Grant. Authorized $400 million in fiscal 1985 and $415 million in 1986 for the block grants, which supported community anti-poverty programs.

● Reduced from 90 percent to 83 percent the proportion of block grant funds states were required to give to community agencies that were receiving aid under anti-poverty programs that were abolished when the block grant was created in 1981.

● Authorized $2.5 million each year for fiscal 1985 and 1986 for community food and nutrition programs.

Follow Through. Authorized $10 million in fiscal 1985 and $7.5 million in 1986 for the Follow Through program, which provided services for disadvantaged children after they left preschool programs like Head Start.

Special Projects. Authorized $6 million to build a Center for Excellence in Education at Indiana University, which would conduct research and training for people who wanted to be schoolteachers and administrators.

● Authorized $4 million for the construction of a research center at the University of Utah to conduct research on the health effects of nuclear energy and other new energy technologies, and $6 million for cancer screening and research in a city in Utah that was affected by fallout from nuclear-weapons testing.

Low-Income Energy Assistance. Authorized $2.14 billion in fiscal 1985 and $2.28 billion in 1986.

● Required states to reserve a portion of their funds at least until March 15 each year to handle energy crises.

● Specified that states' allocations be based on total energy expenditures by low-income households, including heating and cooling costs.

● Specified that, under the revised allocation formula, no state would receive less in fiscal 1985 than it did in 1984. Other protections were included for small states and to limit the reductions that could be imposed on states in fiscal 1986.

● Dropped from 25 percent to 15 percent the proportion of energy aid that states were allowed to carry over to the next fiscal year.

Weatherization Aid. Liberalized weatherization eligibility requirements to conform with standards for eligibility in the low-income energy assistance program.

● Authorized use of weatherization funds to pay for furnace modifications.

● Struck down a requirement that the Energy Department follow a time-consuming rulemaking process before making new energy-saving measures eligible for weatherization funds.

● Changed an existing $1,600 per house maximum expenditure cap to allow individual expenditures of more than that as long as the average statewide expenditure was no more than $1,600 per house.

● Authorized homes that participated in pre-1979 weatherization programs to receive further weatherization assistance to meet new program guidelines.

● Authorized the energy secretary, beginning in fiscal 1986, to earmark between 5 percent and 15 percent of each year's funds for allocation to states that had done the best job providing weatherization assistance during the previous year.

Teacher Scholarships. Authorized $20 million in fiscal 1986, $21 million in 1987, $22 million in 1988 and $23 million in 1989 for scholarships of up to $5,000 a year for students who planned to become schoolteachers.

● Authorized $1 million in 1986, $2 million in 1987, $3 million in 1988 and $4 million in 1989 in one-year fellowships for outstanding teachers to take sabbaticals or pursue other projects.

Merit Scholarships. Authorized $8 million a year in fiscal 1986-88 for merit scholarships of up to $1,500 for outstanding college students.

Educational Administrators. Authorized $20 million a year in fiscal 1985-89 to establish training centers for elementary and secondary school administrators.

Native Americans. Extended through fiscal 1986 a program designed to promote economic and social self-sufficiency among Native Americans, authorizing the appropriation of such sums as Congress considered necessary.

Child Support Enforcement

Legislation to strengthen the collection of delinquent child support payments was enacted in 1984.

The measure (HR 4325 — PL 98-378) required states to set up procedures for the withholding of money from the paychecks of parents delinquent in court-ordered support payments. It also required states to pass laws allowing liens to be placed against a parent's property and to intercept federal and state income tax refunds on behalf of a child. Financial incentives were provided to reward states with effective enforcement programs.

HR 4325 made state assistance available to all those who requested help in collecting child support payments. Previously, such assistance had been provided only to recipients of Aid to Families with Dependent Children (AFDC).

The bill was designed to help up to two million children who were entitled to an estimated $4 billion in support payments.

It was an important piece of the Economic Equity Act, a package of legislative proposals aimed at improving the treatment of women in such areas as tax law, insurance and pensions. *(Details, p. 697)*

Legislative History

The federal-state child support program was established in 1975 to help families, most of them headed by women, locate absent parents, establish paternity and collect support payments. Legislation to strengthen the program was fueled by congressional concern about the growing number of parents who failed to make good on their child support promises. *(Background, Congress and the Nation Vol. IV, p. 426; 1981-82 changes, pp. 586, 596)*

Efforts to reduce such delinquencies drew support from both sides of the aisle and from the Reagan administration.

The House passed HR 4325 Nov. 16, 1983, by a 422-0 vote. The bill had been reported Nov. 10 by the Ways and Means Committee (H Rept 98-527).

The Senate passed its version of HR 4325 April 25, 1984, by a 94-0 vote. The bill had been reported by the Finance Committee April 9 (S Rept 98-387).

Although the House and Senate versions were substantially similar, there were some differences. Conferees accepted a House provision liberalizing Medicaid coverage for families who dropped off the welfare rolls as a result of receiving more child support. They also included in the final bill a Senate provision extending to non-welfare families a program that intercepted federal income tax refunds for parents behind on payments.

A compromise was reached on federal contributions to help cover state administrative costs. The House bill would have continued the existing contribution of 70 percent of the costs, while the Senate bill would have cut that to 65 percent over a five-year period, beginning in fiscal 1987. Conferees agreed to a drop from the 70 percent level to 66 percent by 1990.

The conference report (H Rept 98-925) was adopted by the Senate Aug. 1 by a 99-0 vote and by the House Aug. 8 by a 413-0 vote.

Provisions

As signed into law Aug. 16, the Child Support Enforcement Amendments of 1984 (HR 4325 — PL 98-378) stated that aid in obtaining court-ordered child support payments must be extended to all families.

Procedures. The bill required states to enact laws by Oct. 1, 1985, establishing the following:

● Employer withholding of wages, if support payments were delinquent, in an amount equal to one month's support or if the parent owing support requested withholding earlier.

● Imposition of liens against real and personal property for amounts of overdue support.

● Requiring parents who had a record of non-payment to post bonds or other financial guarantees to secure payment of overdue child support.

● Establishing expedited court or administrative procedures to obtain and enforce child support orders.

● Notifying individual AFDC recipients at least once a year of the amount of child support collected for them by the state.

● Permitting the establishment of paternity anytime before a child's 18th birthday.

● Making information available to credit agencies if the arrearage was $1,000 or more, and permitting states to provide information involving smaller amounts.

Withholding. The bill also:

● Limited the amount that could be withheld from a parent's paycheck to 55 percent of disposable income in the case of an absent parent — one who did not have custody of the child — with a second family, and 65 percent for an absent parent without a second family.

● Required states to follow legal procedures before withholding income, including notifying persons of withholding and of procedures to contest the withholding.

● Required employers of absent parents, upon proper notice, to withhold the stipulated amount from the parent's wages, to be forwarded to the proper state agency, and permitted states to reimburse employers for their costs of withholding.

● Directed states to levy fines against employers who fired, refused to employ or otherwise disciplined a parent whose wages must be withheld.

● Permitted states to extend withholding to income other than wages, such as pensions, bonuses and commissions, or dividends.

● Required states to withhold child support payments from state tax refunds and, through the Internal Revenue Service, to tap federal tax refunds.

Federal Funds. Required the federal government to pay 70 percent of state and local administrative costs for child support enforcement for fiscal years 1984-87, 68 percent in 1988-89 and 66 percent in 1990.

● Established a new system of incentive grants to reward states with good child support collection programs. Each state received as an incentive at least 6 percent of the amount it collected in child support. States with good records of child support assistance received up to 10 percent.

● Authorized special grants to promote improvements in interstate enforcement at $7 million in fiscal 1985, $12 million in 1986 and $15 million in 1987.

● Required the secretary of health and human services to issue regulations mandating states to petition courts to include medical support as part of a child support order whenever health care coverage was available to the parent without custody at reasonable cost.

● Stipulated that if a family lost AFDC benefits as a result of its income increasing from child support payments, the state must continue Medicaid health care coverage for four calendar months, effective upon the date of enactment.

● Required state child support agencies to undertake support collections on behalf of certain children receiving foster care effective Oct. 1, 1984. Those children were not specifically covered by previous law.

Child Abuse, 'Baby Doe'

Legislation designed to ensure that severely handicapped infants were not denied the medical treatment they needed to live cleared Congress in 1984, after months of negotiations over the emotional issue.

These "Baby Doe" provisions were included in a bill (HR 1904 — PL 98-457) that reauthorized at significantly higher spending levels federal programs to prevent and treat child abuse. *(Child abuse appropriations, p. 608)*

The bill required states, in order to receive federal child protection aid, to have procedures for responding to reports of medical neglect of handicapped infants. But it made clear that doctors would not have to take heroic steps to save the life of an infant if treatment would be futile.

The bill also authorized a new program to help states

provide shelter for battered wives and other victims of domestic violence.

The measure authorized $158.1 million in fiscal years 1984-87 to aid child abuse prevention programs. It also included $5 million a year for promoting the adoption of hard-to-place children, including severely handicapped infants. It authorized $63 million over three years for the new program to prevent family violence and aid state efforts to provide shelter to victims of domestic abuse.

The Reagan administration strongly supported HR 1904's Baby Doe provisions. However, it objected to the bill's increased funding authorizations and to the new family violence program.

Background

The bill's provisions to protect severely handicapped infants were sparked largely by the so-called Baby Doe case, in which a Bloomington, Ind., infant born with Down's syndrome and an incomplete esophagus was allowed to die.

The Department of Health and Human Services (HHS) had responded in 1983 by issuing regulations requiring hospitals to post notices saying it was illegal to withhold care from infants because of their disabilities, and providing a toll-free "hot line" for reporting cases of neglect. The regulations were struck down by a federal judge in April 1983 and reissued in modified form Jan. 12, 1984.

Legislative History

House Action. The House passed HR 1904 Feb. 2 by a vote of 396-4, despite appeals from opponents who argued that the federal government should not get involved in sensitive medical decisions about whether or not a severely handicapped infant should be allowed to die.

The bill, which reauthorized the Child Abuse Prevention and Treatment Act (PL 95-266), had been reported (H Rept 98-159) by the Education and Labor Committee May 16, 1983, amid controversy over the HHS regulations. *(Background, Congress and the Nation Vol. V, p. 692)*

The House rejected, by a **key vote of 182-231 (R 31-131; D 151-100)**, an amendment backed by the American Medical Association (AMA) and several other medical groups that would have dropped the infant protection provisions. The amendment, introduced by Rod Chandler, R-Wash., would have established a national commission to study the issue and required HHS to issue guidelines for hospitals that wanted to establish advisory panels on the treatment of handicapped babies. *(1984 key votes, p. 927)*

Echoing arguments made against the HHS Baby Doe regulations, critics of HR 1904 contended that the bill constituted an unwarranted federal intrusion in the decisions of doctors and families. Others said that the bill's infant care provisions were unnecessary because new rules established by HHS provided adequate protection.

Before passing the bill, the House approved, 367-31, an amendment authorizing $65 million over three years for projects to prevent family violence.

Senate Action. The Senate July 26 by a vote of 89-0 approved HR 1904 after substituting the text of its child protection bill (S 1003).

Floor action came after lawmakers of widely divergent political views endorsed a compromise amendment to S 1003 to ensure that handicapped babies received adequate

medical care for life-threatening conditions.

Controversy over how the Baby Doe issue should be handled had prevented S 1003 from coming to the Senate floor ever since it was approved by the Labor and Human Resources Committee May 16, 1983 (S Rept 98-246).

The compromise, accepted easily by voice vote, made clear that doctors would not be required to take extraordinary steps to keep handicapped babies alive under certain circumstances — if, for example, the treatment would only prolong the process of dying.

The exceptions were "painstakingly negotiated in an attempt to meet some of the concerns of the medical community," said one Senate aide. But the changes were not enough to win the support of the AMA.

An AMA spokesman said that the bill's infant care guidelines left no room for consideration of the "quality of life" severely handicapped infants would face if they could be kept alive indefinitely.

The compromise, however, was backed by a coalition of medical, disability and right-to-life groups.

Conference, Final Action. The conference bill drew heavily on the Senate version. Conferees were concerned that the House version of HR 1904 would have required doctors to make heroic efforts to keep handicapped babies alive, even when treatment was futile.

The compromise language specified that withholding care did not constitute medical neglect in certain circumstances, such as when an infant was "irreversibly comatose."

The conference report (H Rept 98-1038) was adopted by the House Sept. 26 and by the Senate Sept. 28.

Provisions

As signed into law Oct. 9, the Child Abuse Amendments of 1984 (HR 1904 — PL 98-457):

Child Abuse. Authorized $33.5 million in fiscal 1984, $40 million in 1985, $41.5 million in 1986 and $43.1 million in 1987 for the prevention and treatment of child abuse. If total appropriations in any year exceeded $30 million, the bill specified that $5 million be used for the prevention of sexual abuse and $5 million for grants to help states meet the Baby Doe requirements of the bill.

● Specified that at least $9 million of the total appropriated each year be used for grants to states and $11 million for research, demonstration projects, training and technical aid.

Handicapped Infants. Required states, to qualify for federal child protection grants, to establish procedures for responding to cases of medical neglect, including the withholding of treatment from disabled infants with life-threatening conditions. States must provide for coordination and consultation with hospital officials.

● Specified that withholding life-saving treatment from disabled infants would not constitute medical neglect in certain circumstances, such as when treatment would be futile, simply prolong dying or fail to correct all the life-threatening conditions.

● Authorized grants to help states set up procedures for preventing medical neglect of severely handicapped infants, education and training programs for parents and hospital officials who dealt with such babies, and services to promote their adoption.

Adoption Opportunities. Authorized $5 million a year through fiscal 1987 for grants to encourage adoption of handicapped or other hard-to-place children.

Family Violence. Authorized $11 million in fiscal 1985, $26 million in 1986 and $26 million in 1987 for matching grants to states to provide shelter and other services for the victims of domestic violence and for programs to prevent such abuse.

● Specified that at least 60 percent of funds distributed in the grant program be used for emergency shelters and other services.

● Authorized HHS to transfer up to $2 million each year to the attorney general for grants to train police to handle cases of domestic violence.

Child Abuse Funds

Faced with a rash of shocking reports of child abuse in day-care centers, Congress in 1984 moved to encourage states to step up training and screening of child care workers.

An omnibus appropriations bill for fiscal 1985 (H J Res 648 — PL 98-473) provided an additional $25 million for states for training child care workers. But states would get their full share of the extra money only if they established procedures for checking the employment history and criminal records of people who took care of children.

The measure also authorized a new program of matching grants for states that set up special funds for the prevention of child abuse.

Congress in September 1984 had cleared legislation (HR 1904 — PL 98-457) reauthorizing established programs for child abuse prevention and treatment. But Sen. Christopher J. Dodd, D-Conn., who proposed the matching grant program, said most of the limited funds available under programs authorized by PL 98-457 were used by states for treatment of victims of abuse, leaving little for prevention efforts. *(PL 98-457, p. 606)*

Although the matching grants were authorized for five years under H J Res 648, no funds were appropriated for them.

Legislative History

The House Sept. 25 by a vote of 369-37 adopted an amendment to H J Res 648 providing $50 million for training child care workers.

The Senate Oct. 2 adopted its version of the amendment setting spending at $25 million and authorizing the new matching grants for child abuse prevention.

Conferees accepted the Senate version. The House adopted the conference report (H Rept 98-1159) Oct. 10 on a 252-60 standing vote and the Senate adopted it Oct. 11 by a vote of 78-11.

Provisions

As signed into law Oct. 12, the child care provisions of H J Res 648 (PL 98-473):

Training. Appropriated an additional $25 million for the social services block grant in fiscal 1985.

● Specified that the extra money be allotted to states for training child care providers, licensing and enforcement officials and parents, particularly in the area of preventing abuse in child care programs.

● Required states to use the extra money to supplement, not supplant, the funds they otherwise would spend on training.

● Required the secretary of health and human services (HHS) to draft model standards for day-care centers, to provide guidance in such areas as staff training and evaluation, staff-child ratios, probation periods and background checks for new employees and visitation by parents. The guidelines, which were to be drafted by HHS within three months, would be distributed to states, but their adoption would not be mandatory.

● Required states receiving the child care training funds to establish, by Sept. 30, 1985, state laws requiring a nationwide check of criminal records and procedures for checking the employment history of child care personnel and employees of juvenile correctional and detention facilities. States that failed to comply would, in effect, have to repay half the training money they received by having future allotments under the social services block grant reduced.

Matching Grants. Authorized grants to states that established a trust fund or other special financing mechanism for child abuse prevention programs, such as public information campaigns and support for community prevention programs.

● Authorized Congress to appropriate such funding as it considered necessary for the new grants in fiscal years 1985-89.

● Limited federal grants to 25 percent of the money a state spent in the previous year for child abuse prevention — or an amount equaling 50 cents per child in the state, whichever was less.

'Latch-Key' Children Aid

The House May 14 approved legislation designed to address the needs of so-called "latch-key" children who had to fend for themselves because their working parents could not find affordable day care.

The bill (HR 4193 — H Rept 98-745) encouraged communities to set up before- and after-school child care programs in unused public school facilities or community centers. While the Senate did not act on a similar bill awaiting floor action, block grants to help set up programs in school facilities were authorized in an omnibus social services bill (S 2565 — PL 98-558) in 1984. *(Legislation, p. 603)*

HR 4193, reported May 14 by the Education and Labor Committee, would have authorized $30 million a year for fiscal 1985-87 for the program. The measure was opposed by the Reagan administration as unnecessary because the federal government already subsidized child care through other programs — such as the tax credit allowed for child care expenses.

The bill reported by the Senate Labor and Human Resources Committee May 25 (S 1531 — S Rept 98-494) would have authorized $15 million a year for fiscal 1984-86.

Vocational Rehabilitation

A three-year reauthorization of federal vocational training programs for the handicapped cleared Congress early in 1984, putting an end to months of controversy.

The measure (S 1340 — PL 98-221) authorized $1.038 billion for state grants in fiscal 1984, with the spending ceiling rising 7.7 percent in 1985 and in 1986. It also extended through fiscal 1986 several smaller vocational re-

habilitation programs, including research and training.

Both chambers in 1983 had passed legislation extending the Rehabilitation Act of 1973 (PL 93-112), but the House had added to its version a controversial package of amendments authorizing funds for unrelated education and social programs. Because of the amendments the Senate refused to go to conference, and only a simple fiscal 1984 authorization for the rehabilitation program (S 1341 — PL 98-199) was cleared. *(Story, p. 567)*

When conferees on S 1340 finally met in February 1984, House negotiators agreed to drop the disputed amendments, thus clearing the way for final passage.

Legislative History

The House Sept. 13, 1983, passed by a 324-79 vote a five-year reauthorization (HR 3520) of the popular vocational rehabilitation program. The bill, reported by the Education and Labor Committee July 19 (H Rept 98-298), also included a controversial Democratic-backed rider adding $1.6 billion in fiscal 1984 spending authority for 11 unrelated education and social services programs. During floor debate an attempt to drop the non-rehabilitation authorizations failed on a party-line vote.

The partisan House squabbling over HR 3520 contrasted with Senate passage July 26 by voice vote of a three-year reauthorization of the rehabilitation program (S 1340). S 1340 had been reported by the Labor and Human Resources Committee May 23 (S Rept 98-168).

Although the rehabilitation authorizations in HR 3520 and S 1340 were relatively close, the Senate refused to go to conference because of the non-rehabilitation programs in the House version. The deadlock was broken in the last week of the session when key House and Senate members agreed to clear a basic fiscal 1984 reauthorization of the Rehabilitation Act and postpone any attempt to reconcile differences over the controversial House additions. The rehabilitation provisions were attached to S 1341, a measure reauthorizing education programs for the handicapped, which cleared Nov. 18, 1983.

Conference agreement on S 1340 was reached early in 1984 after the House dropped its controversial package of amendments, as well as amendments providing aid to school districts with a large influx of immigrants and revising the allocation of low-income energy assistance.

Both chambers adopted the conference report on S 1340 (H Rept 98-595) Feb. 9.

Provisions

As signed into law Feb. 22, S 1340 (PL 98-221):

● Authorized $1.038 billion for state grants in fiscal 1984, $1.118 billion in 1985 and $1.203 billion in 1986.

● Authorized $121 million for discretionary programs in fiscal 1984, $134 million in 1985 and $145 million in 1986.

● Required states to set up programs to advise and protect the rights of the disabled. Many states had such programs, but they were not mandated.

Developmental Disabilities

Congress in 1984 cleared legislation authorizing significant spending increases for developmental disabilities programs. *(Background, Congress and the Nation Vol. IV, p. 354)*

The bill (HR 5603 — PL 98-527) authorized $75.7 million in fiscal 1985, $80.4 million in 1986 and $85.2 million in 1987 for the programs. Some $62 million had been appropriated for the programs in fiscal 1984.

Most of the money was for grants to states to provide and coordinate services for the disabled. Increased emphasis was placed on states' providing job-related services for the disabled.

Legislative History

The House June 11, by a vote of 360-33, approved HR 5603, a four-year authorization that included not only the developmental disabilities programs but also alcohol and drug abuse and mental health programs. The bill had been reported June 6 by the Energy and Commerce Committee (H Rept 98-826). The alcohol and drug abuse and mental health programs subsequently were addressed during conference on another bill (S 2303). *(Details, p. 551)*

The Senate June 26 by voice vote approved a three-year developmental disability authorization (S 2573). Two days later the Senate passed HR 5603 after substituting the text of S 2573. S 2573 had been reported May 25 by the Labor and Human Resources Committee (S Rept 98-493).

Conferees accepted the Senate-passed three-year authorization and generally split the difference between authorization totals, although they approved almost exactly the lower levels authorized by the House for special programs.

Under the compromise bill states were required to provide employment-related services after fiscal 1986 only if annual appropriations for state grants reached $50.25 million. The Senate version would have required states to provide such services but House members had feared the requirement would have forced states to discontinue other programs.

The conference report (H Rept 98-1074) was adopted by voice vote by the House Oct. 3 and by the Senate Oct. 4.

Older Americans Act

Congress in 1984 cleared legislation authorizing about $4 billion over three years for popular nutrition and social programs for the elderly.

The measure (S 2603 — PL 98-459) established a new program to promote health education for the elderly and extended, without major changes, existing programs under the Older Americans Act (PL 89-73).

Under the Older Americans Act, aid was distributed to state and regional agencies to provide meals, transportation and other services for the elderly.

Most of the programs, for which about $1.1 billion was appropriated in fiscal 1984, were run by the Department of Health and Human Services. The bill also reauthorized food aid administered by the Agriculture Department and a Labor Department community jobs program for the elderly.

Neither the House nor Senate versions of S 2603 had incorporated the Reagan administration's proposal to consolidate aid to the elderly into a block grant to the states. The bill, however, liberalized existing provisions that allowed states to transfer federal funds between their social service and nutrition programs.

S 2603 also included changes in the Age Discrimination in Employment Act (PL 95-256) affecting high-level

business executives and Americans working abroad.

The Older Americans Act was last extended in 1981. Legislation (HR 2807) to increase the authorizations approved in 1981 and to provide open-ended fiscal 1984 funding was approved by the House in 1983, but there was no Senate action. *(1981 action, p. 593; 1983 action, p. 603)*

Legislative History

The Senate May 24 passed S 2603 by voice vote. The bill had been reported by the Labor and Human Resources Committee May 18 (S Rept 98-467).

The House Aug. 8 approved, by a vote of 406-12, its version (HR 4785) and then substituted its text for S 2603. HR 4785 had been reported May 9 by the Education and Labor Committee (H Rept 98-737).

Final action on S 2603 came after congressional negotiators resolved the relatively minor differences between the two versions. The conference report (H Rept 98-1037) was accepted Sept. 26 by the Senate by voice vote and by the House by a vote of 393-2.

Provisions

As signed into law Oct. 9, S 2603 (PL 98-459):

● Authorized $1.26 billion in fiscal 1985, $1.3 billion in 1986 and $1.37 billion in 1987 for Older Americans Act programs. The total included $8.55 million in fiscal 1985 for new grants to universities to develop health education programs for the elderly. No spending ceiling was set for the new program in 1986 and 1987.

● Modified the manner in which the members of the Federal Council on the Aging were appointed. The president, the Senate and the House each would appoint five members; previously, the entire membership was appointed by the president.

● Put new emphasis on meeting the needs of minorities, aiding elderly victims of violence and abuse, and serving victims of Alzheimer's disease and their families.

● Increased the proportion of funds states could transfer between nutrition and social service programs from the existing 20 percent limit to 27 percent in fiscal 1985, 29 percent in 1986 and 30 percent in 1987.

● Modified the Community Service Employment program, which subsidized part-time jobs for low-income elderly people, to lower the cap on administrative expenses to 13.5 percent in fiscal 1986 and 12 percent in 1987. Labor Department regulations previously barred project sponsors from using more than 15 percent of their funds for administration.

● Modified a provision of the age discrimination act that allowed firms to force executives and other high-level professionals to retire after age 65 if they were entitled to retirement benefits of at least $27,000. The threshold was raised to $44,000. *(Congress and the Nation Vol. V, p. 414)*

● Extended coverage of the age law to American citizens who were working for U.S. companies abroad.

VISTA Authorization

Congress in 1984 extended the life of Volunteers in Service to America (VISTA), a remnant of President Johnson's War on Poverty that the Reagan administration had proposed for three years in a row to abolish.

The VISTA authorization was included in legislation (S 1129 — PL 98-288) extending through fiscal 1986 federally sponsored volunteer programs run by ACTION.

The Reagan administration had requested only $196,000 for VISTA in fiscal 1984 — to pay costs associated with the phase-out of the agency. The administration argued that VISTA had a controversial history of political advocacy and that volunteers ought to be just that, rather than being paid about $7,000 a year as VISTA volunteers were.

But congressional supporters argued that the program was cost-effective. They maintained that each VISTA volunteer generated about $24,000 in public- and private-sector resources each year.

Both the Senate and House in 1983 approved bills reauthorizing VISTA. As cleared in 1984, S 1129 included provisions designed to ensure that a minimum number of VISTA volunteers be hired before other programs were financed.

The final bill authorized $158.4 million in fiscal 1984, rising to $175.2 million in 1986, for ACTION programs, with most of the money earmarked for Older American Volunteer programs.

Legislative History

The Senate approved S 1129 Sept. 14, 1983, by voice vote. The bill had been reported by the Labor and Human Resources Committee July 14 (S Rept 98-182).

The House, after rejecting a Republican attempt to limit VISTA funding, approved its version (HR 2655) Oct. 28, 1983, by a 312-30 vote and substituted its text for that of the Senate bill. The House Education and Labor Committee had reported the bill May 16 (H Rept 98-161).

The Senate and House bills differed sharply on the funding mechanism for VISTA. The Senate version set spending ceilings for VISTA beginning with $15 million in fiscal 1984. But the House bill had set a "funding floor" of $25 million in 1984 — and more in subsequent years — to prevent funds from being diverted to other programs.

As a compromise the conference bill set spending ceilings for VISTA of $17 million in fiscal 1984, $20 million in fiscal 1985 and $25 million in fiscal 1986. But the measure specified minimum levels of VISTA service that had to be provided — a "floor" measured in volunteer service time rather than dollars. Congressional aides said about $14 million would have to be spent to support the required levels of service.

In its heyday, VISTA funding was considerably higher. In 1981, for example, the funding level was $34 million, but by fiscal 1983, it had dropped to $11.8 million. *(1981 authorization, p. 590)*

The conference report on S 1129 (H Rept 98-679) was approved by the Senate by voice vote April 11, 1984, and by the House by a vote of 369-25 May 8.

Provisions

As signed into law May 21, S 1129 (PL 98-288):

Anti-Poverty Programs. Required at least 20 percent of all VISTA volunteers to be older than 55.

● Expanded the list of possible assignments for VISTA volunteers to include addressing the problems of the homeless, unemployed, illiterate, hungry, and people with drug and alcohol problems.

● Provided for VISTA volunteers to be given training before and during their participation in a project.

• Prohibited the use of VISTA funds for projects that were not directed toward anti-poverty goals.

• Authorized $1.8 million a year through fiscal 1986 for Service Learning Programs, in which high school and college students worked in anti-poverty projects, and $1.984 million a year for Special Volunteer Programs for encouraging participation in volunteer services.

Older American Volunteers. Authorized $111.8 million in fiscal 1984, $115.3 million in 1985 and $118.4 million in 1986 for Retired Senior Volunteer, Senior Companion and Foster Grandparent programs.

• Increased the stipend for Senior Companions and Foster Grandparents from $2 to $2.20 an hour.

• Authorized a $12 million increase in the Senior Companion program for training volunteers to provide home-care services for the elderly.

• Stated that localities could not be required to contribute more than 30 percent of the cost of Retired Senior Volunteer projects, although larger contributions could be encouraged.

General Provisions. Authorized $25.8 million in fiscal 1984, $27 million in 1985 and $28 million in 1986 for administration of ACTION programs.

• Limited the number of consultants, outside experts and employees in certain non-civil-service positions that could be hired by ACTION.

• Required ACTION to give grant recipients at least 75 days' notice that their renewal might be denied.

SSI, AFDC Benefits

The deficit reduction package (HR 4170 — PL 98-369) cleared by Congress June 27 made several changes in the Supplemental Security Income (SSI) and Aid to Families with Dependent Children (AFDC) programs. *(Deficit reduction bill, p. 56)*

The bill raised the assets a needy aged, blind or disabled person could have and still qualify for SSI benefits. The existing $1,500 limit ($2,250 for couples) was gradually increased to $2,000 ($3,000 for couples) by 1989. The legislation also limited, in some cases substantially, the amount an individual's SSI payments could be reduced by the government in an attempt to recoup past overpayments.

HR 4170 made several changes in the AFDC program to help families who were thrown off the rolls, or were subject to removal from the rolls, as a result of changes made to the program in 1981. These included allowing up to 15 months of additional Medicaid coverage to those who lost AFDC benefits because they had taken low-paying jobs. The bill also expanded AFDC eligibility to families with higher incomes than existing law allowed. *(1981 changes, p. 586)*

Food Aid Bills

Because of a stalemate between advocates of more food aid to the poor and those seeking program reductions, Congress did not complete action on legislation partially restoring some Reagan-era cuts in food stamps, school lunch and other federal food aid programs.

Two House-passed bills to liberalize child nutrition programs (HR 7) and food stamps (HR 5151) died at the end of the session, as did a Senate Agriculture Committee bill (S 2722) that would have continued certain child nutri-

---

Social Welfare Leadership

Two congressional veterans headed the Department of Health and Human Services during Reagan's first term. Richard S. Schweiker served as secretary from 1981 until early 1983, when he resigned to head a trade and lobbying organization of life insurance companies. Schweiker had been a U.S. senator from Pennsylvania, 1969-81, and a U.S. representative from Pennsylvania's 13th District, 1961-69.

Former Rep. Margaret M. Heckler succeeded Schweiker in March 1983. Heckler had represented the 10th District of Massachusetts. She lost her bid for re-election in 1982 in a newly redrawn district. *(Cabinet profiles, p. 1017)*

The Republican takeover of the Senate in the 97th Congress meant major changes in panels handling social welfare issues. Conservative Orrin G. Hatch, R-Utah, took over as chairman of the Labor and Human Resources Committee and Jesse Helms, R-N.C., a frequent critic of the food stamp program, took over the panel that handled that issue, Agriculture. Robert Dole, R-Kan., became chairman of the Finance Committee.

On the House side, the House Education and Labor Committee remained in the hands of Carl D. Perkins, D-Ky., until his death in August 1984. Perkins was succeeded as chairman by Augustus F. Hawkins, D-Calif., another veteran of the War on Poverty. E. "Kika" de la Garza, D-Texas, became chairman of the House Agriculture Committee and Dan Rostenkowski, D-Ill., became chairman of the Ways and Means Committee in 1981.

---

tion programs at existing funding levels.

The expiring child nutrition programs were extended by a continuing appropriations resolution (PL 98-473), which also made one change in food stamps. The change restored food stamp benefit levels to 100 percent, from 99 percent, of the thrifty food plan. The government used the plan to measure the cost of an inexpensive diet and, in turn, to calculate food stamp benefit levels.

The House also created a new, non-legislating committee to call attention to hunger in America and abroad. But it rejected a proposal to provide more timely statistics on the nutritional status of Americans (HR 4684).

The House bills and the new committee were the House response to reports from emergency food services and the press, beginning in late 1981, that the recession and food program spending restraints had made it increasingly difficult for the poorest of Americans, and those who had lost their jobs, to eat properly.

The Reagan administration and its allies such as Sen. Jesse Helms, R-N.C., tended to discount the hunger reports and said that the food programs needed further tightening to prevent their abuse by those who could buy their

own food. Helms chaired the Senate Agriculture Committee, which had jurisdiction over food programs.

Advocates of program increases pointed out that a special commission appointed by President Reagan in 1983 to investigate the hunger reports had declared, early in 1984, that indeed there were hungry Americans — although it could not say how many, or how bad the problem was. There was, according to the commission, no overall monitoring of the nutritional status of Americans that could show whether the status of the poor had worsened. *(Hunger reports, box, p. 600)*

Child Nutrition

House Action. The House by a 343-72 vote May 1 passed a bill (HR 7) that would have liberalized eligibility standards for subsidized school meals and boosted government contributions for school breakfasts.

It also would have lowered the prices paid by students for reduced-price school lunches and breakfasts, and funded extra meals and snacks for children in home-based child care facilities.

The changes partly reversed cuts enacted in the 1981 reconciliation bill (PL 97-35); children of the working poor had been particularly hard hit by the cuts, according to advocates of HR 7. *(1981 action, p. 591)*

The changes already had passed the House as another bill (HR 4091) by a 306-114 vote in 1983. Backers sought a second vote because the Senate had ignored the bill. *(1983 action, p. 601)*

When the child nutrition measure returned to the House floor in 1984, it was as part of a four-year $9 billion reauthorization of expiring child nutrition programs. For one program, serving pregnant women, infants and children (WIC), the bill nearly doubled authorized spending levels in the next four years, to $2 billion.

Other expiring programs provided funds for nutrition education and training, summer food service for children, state administration expenses and food service equipment purchases.

Floor action on amendments reflected the major themes of debate that had begun in the Education and Labor Committee between liberal Democrats who wanted more aid for the poor and moderate Republicans who wanted to support the bill but in a less expensive form. The committee reported HR 7 March 23 (H Rept 98-633).

Before voting to pass an amended version of HR 7, the House by a 136-270 vote rejected a substitute that would have reauthorized the expiring programs for three years at existing spending levels and with no changes in existing policy.

Senate Action. The Senate Agriculture Committee on May 25 reported legislation (S 2722 — S Rept 98-489) continuing for two years expiring child nutrition programs, including WIC, which would be maintained at the existing caseload level of about three million persons.

The committee had agreed informally May 16 to report the bill and to continue private negotiations on whether to expand the bill on the Senate floor to include some restorations in food stamps, school lunch and other food aid programs.

No further action was taken, however. Committee Chairman Helms insisted that any program expansions be coupled with equivalent spending reductions. Although a bipartisan majority of the committee reportedly supported some liberalizations in the programs, similar to those going

through the House, Republican committee members did not want to force the issue in public.

Food Stamps

With the virtual certainty that it would not become law in 1984, the House Aug. 1 approved a hunger relief bill by a 9-to-1 margin. The billion-dollar food stamp bill (HR 5151) was passed by a 364-39 vote after members agreed to several changes in the version reported (H Rept 98-782) May 15 by the House Agriculture Committee.

Key sections of the bill made modest increases in food stamp eligibility and benefit levels, while beefing up federal penalties for states that failed to lower their program errors to specified levels. Other sections raised federal funding for state-run job search programs for the poor and explicitly specified that "street people" without fixed addresses could qualify for food stamps if they met other program eligibility standards.

There was little outright opposition to the bill, which had strong, bipartisan support. However, members also knew there was little likelihood of Senate action because of the stalemate between Helms and Agriculture Committee members backing more food aid. Moreover, budget director David A. Stockman, in a June 24 letter to Republican members, had warned of a presidential veto.

Many of the bill's provisions, such as those relating to homeless persons and assets and eligibility tests, had been recommended in January by the presidential task force on hunger. The bill was silent on that panel's major and most controversial recommendation, for an optional food aid block grant for states. And the House rejected by voice vote an amendment to authorize such block grants. *(Task force report, box, p. 600)*

New Hunger Committee

A new 17-member Select Committee on Hunger, chaired by Rep. Mickey Leland, D-Texas, was authorized by a 309-78 vote on Feb. 22 on a resolution (H Res 15 — H Rept 98-568) sketching out its duties.

A similar Senate select committee, chaired by George S. McGovern, D-S.D. (House, 1957-61; Senate, 1963-81), created in 1968, had effectively focused national attention on hunger problems and was credited with building political support for major expansions of the federal food programs during the 1970s.

Nutrition Update

The House on Oct. 2 by a 265-157 vote rejected a bill (HR 4684 — H Rept 98-1076) that would have created a coordinated 10-year program to track the nutritional status of Americans and set priorities for research on food and health. Because the bill was brought up under suspension of the rules, a two-thirds majority — 282 in this case — was required to pass the measure.

The bill would have authorized $5 million in fiscal 1985 and $3 million thereafter. It reflected six years of committee hearings on poor coordination and time lags in federal research on nutrition by the Agriculture Department and the Department of Health and Human Services.

Sponsors said that the results from existing programs were poorly coordinated and obsolete by the time they were analyzed and published. Opponents argued that the measure would duplicate existing efforts and was not needed.

Veterans' Programs

Congress has had a habit of enacting veterans' programs over the objections of presidents, who often have cited costs for their opposition. As one House Veterans' Affairs Committee staffer put it: "If we waited for an administration to act, we would have no veterans' laws."

Action during the 97th and 98th Congresses proved no exception. Veterans lost little ground during the budget-cutting first term of the Reagan administration. In fact, veterans made some impressive gains, many of them opposed by the White House.

Vietnam Vets Health Care

Among the most notable gains were those in health care for veterans of the Vietnam War.

The controversy over the long-term effects of exposure to the herbicide Agent Orange that had begun in the 1970s continued to rage in the 1980s. The herbicide, which contained the highly toxic chemical dioxin, had been used during the Vietnam War by the U.S. Army to destroy food crops and to defoliate the dense jungles that provided cover for the enemy.

A few years after the war ended, Vietnam veterans had begun to contact the Veterans Administration (VA) about a wide range of health problems they believed were caused by their exposure to Agent Orange, but the VA had refused the claims on the grounds that there was not sufficient proof that Agent Orange was the cause.

Congress in 1979 ordered a study of the health effects of the herbicide, but veterans continued to push for more. Temporary benefits for veterans were subsequently mandated pending the outcome of the study. In 1981 Congress approved legislation directing the VA to set up guidelines for providing medical care for veterans with problems linked to Agent Orange. In 1984 legislation was enacted requiring the VA to set up guidelines for compensating Vietnam veterans suffering from diseases believed to be caused by Agent Orange and to provide temporary disability payments for veterans suffering from two specific diseases. Both the 1981 and 1984 bills also covered veterans exposed to radiation from nuclear weapons testing or during occupation of Hiroshima and Nagasaki after the World War II bombing of those Japanese cities.

Vietnam veterans scored a victory on the Agent Orange issue in the courtroom as well. In September 1984 a U.S. district court judge in New York gave formal approval to an agreement reached in May between lawyers for Vietnam veterans and lawyers for seven major chemical companies that produced the defoliant. The agreement established a fund of $180 million, which was expected to reach $250 million by 1986 to 1990, when veterans would be able to draw on it. The chemical companies were to pay into the fund to compensate those exposed to Agent Orange. Details of who would be eligible to receive money from the fund and the amount of payments were unresolved in late 1984.

One party not named in the suit was the federal government, which contracted with the chemical companies to produce the herbicide during the Vietnam War. Veterans were prohibited by law from suing the government for actions committed during wartime, but spouses and children of Vietnam veterans had a suit pending against the federal government. The chemical companies also sued the federal government to reimburse them for the $180 million. Those suits remained unresolved in late 1984.

Other legislative victories for Vietnam veterans included the 1981 and 1983 extensions of the "storefront" readjustment counseling program, which the administration had wanted to end. The popular program helped Vietnam veterans experiencing war-related emotional problems to readjust to everyday life. The outreach program operated out of storefront centers. They were so called because many were located in business districts, away from VA facilities, which many Vietnam veterans did not trust.

Also authorized by Congress in 1984 — and opposed by the administration — were special programs for the treatment of veterans suffering from post-traumatic stress disorder, a condition affecting many Vietnam veterans.

WW II Vets Health Care

Health care for veterans of World War II also captured the attention of Congress, as members began to look to the future when the demand and costs for health care were expected to skyrocket.

References

Discussion of veterans' programs for the years 1945-64 may be found in *Congress and the Nation Vol. I*, pp. 1333-1373; for the years 1965-68, *Congress and the Nation Vol. II*, pp. 453-460; for the years 1969-72, *Congress and the Nation Vol. III*, pp. 537-548; for the years 1973-76, *Congress and the Nation Vol. IV*, pp. 158-181; for the years 1977-80, *Congress and the Nation Vol. V*, pp. 177-191.

Veterans' Spending

The following table shows the growth in federal funding for veterans' programs during fiscal 1981-85 (in millions of dollars):

	Budget Authority	Outlays
1981	$ 23,170	$ 22,991
1982	24,985	23,958
1983	25,364	24,846
1984	26,528	25,614
1985*	27,340	26,850

*Estimated figures.

SOURCE: Fiscal 1986 Budget, Historical Tables

During World War II some 16.5 million Americans served in the military; about 11.3 million of them were still living as of 1984 and most of them soon would turn 65. The number of veterans aged 65 and older — about four million — was expected to double by 1990 and triple by 2000, as veterans of the Korean War also turned 65. By the year 2000 two-thirds of all American men over 65 would be veterans.

For the Veterans Administration 65 was a key age because veterans then became entitled to health care regardless of income, if space was available. And aging would increase the need for health care.

As a result of this potential increase in demand, the cost of the VA health care system, $8.8 billion in 1984, was expected to shoot up to $9.85 billion by 1990 and $12.6 billion by 2000, according to the Congressional Budget Office.

Veterans' groups, as well as members of Congress charged with overseeing veterans' benefits, began to brace for the potential crunch and plan ways to deal with it.

Legislation enacted in 1983 included provisions designed to reduce the long-term costs to the federal government of veterans' health care by encouraging less expensive means of care.

Education Benefits

Advocates of a new GI Bill scored a victory in 1984 when Congress voted to authorize a three-year test program that would revive large-scale educational benefits to any military recruit. But members attached the condition that applicants help pay for the program through monthly contributions.

After eligibility for the last such program had lapsed in 1976, the armed services had done well in their recruiting, but Pentagon officials acknowledged that a civilian job shortage was at least partly responsible. Subsequently, a shrinking pool of potential recruits and an improving economy led to predictions on Capitol Hill that there would be future manpower shortages in the all-volunteer armed forces. Congress hoped to avert that situation with the enactment of the new GI Bill program.

In other 1984 action, Congress authorized a 10 percent increase in the Vietnam-era GI Bill and other veterans' education and rehabilitation benefits. The increase was the first since 1981.

Disabled Veterans' Payments

Congress approved four cost-of-living increases in benefits for veterans with service-connected disabilities and their families, as well as suvivors of veterans who had died of service-connected causes. An 11.2 percent cost-of-living adjustment (COLA) was approved in 1981 and a 7.4 percent COLA in 1982. Two increases were cleared in 1984: first a 3.5 percent increase, followed by a 3.2 percent increase.

Job Training Programs

Despite White House opposition, Congress in 1983 cleared an emergency job training measure for Korean War and Vietnam-era veterans facing long-term unemployment. The bill authorized a two-year, $300 million program to assist the veterans, whose unemployment rate stood at 12.3 percent in July. The administration had insisted that the improving economy would provide more jobs for veterans.

Chronology
Of Action
On Veterans' Affairs

1981

Veterans' Health Care

Vietnam veterans finally won their long fight to get medical treatment for veterans suffering from ailments attributed to Agent Orange, the toxic herbicide used to defoliate jungles in Vietnam. Legislation directing the Veterans Administration (VA) to provide the care cleared Congress Oct. 16 (HR 3499 — PL 97-72).

In addition to providing health care for veterans exposed to Agent Orange, the bill extended the "storefront" readjustment counseling program for Vietnam veterans, which the Reagan administration wanted to end, through Sept. 30, 1984. Congress again extended the counseling program in 1983. *(1983 action, p. 618)*

HR 3499 also required the VA to maintain a specified number of hospital and nursing home beds, at a higher level than the administration wanted, extended the period in which veterans could use certain education benefits and established a new small-business loan program for veterans.

In signing the bill Nov. 3, President Reagan expressed concern about its budgetary impact and said he would "weigh carefully any efforts to fund" the new small-business loan program. The administration opposed the legislation but did not lobby to defeat it.

Background

Veterans' groups had been trying for several years to get medical care for veterans exposed to Agent Orange in Vietnam, where an estimated 52 million pounds of the herbicide had been sprayed between 1961 and 1971. They claimed Agent Orange caused a wide range of maladies including cancer, liver damage, depression, sleeplessness, tingling or loss of sensation in limbs, malfunctioning of the body's disease-fighting system, miscarriages, stillbirths and birth defects in their children.

The VA had refused to allow the claims of veterans suffering from exposure to the chemical except to provide care for chloracne, a skin disease. VA officials said there was not sufficient proof that Agent Orange was the cause of the veterans' problems. Congress ordered a study in 1979 to produce data to make a determination about the herbicide. But veterans continued to lobby Congress for medical care. *(Congress and the Nation Vol. V, p. 184)*

The storefront readjustment counseling program for Vietnam veterans was established in 1979 after years of effort. The authorization expired Sept. 30, 1981. Although the program generally was regarded as a success, the administration did not seek to renew it, arguing that veterans could be treated in VA facilities at reduced cost. *(Congress and the Nation Vol. V, p. 186)*

Legislative History

The final version of HR 3499 combined two bills passed by the House June 2. HR 3499 (H Rept 97-79), containing the health care provisions, passed by a 388-0 vote. HR 3423 (H Rept 97-78), the educational training and business loan act, was approved 352-41.

The Senate passed its version of the veterans' health care legislation (S 921 — S Rept 97-89) June 16, 99-0.

The compromise version of the bill was worked out informally by senior members of the Veterans' Affairs committees. It was approved by the House Oct. 2 and by the Senate Oct. 16, both by voice votes.

The final bill included a Senate provision that charged the VA with determining what disabilities might have been caused by exposure to Agent Orange and thus be eligible for treatment. As passed by the House, HR 3499 would have provided care to Vietnam veterans for any condition that "may be associated with exposure" to Agent Orange. The compromise also followed S 921 by expanding coverage to include exposure to radiation and to other toxic herbicides or defoliants.

Provisions

As signed into law Nov. 3, HR 3499 (PL 97-72):

● Made veterans who served in Vietnam eligible for VA medical, hospital or nursing home care for problems linked to exposure to Agent Orange or other toxic herbicides or defoliants. Any veteran who served in Vietnam would be presumed to have been exposed. The VA would develop guidelines to determine what disabilities might have been caused by exposure and thus be eligible for treatment.

● Also made eligible for VA care veterans exposed to radiation from nuclear weapons testing or during occupation of the Japanese cities of Hiroshima and Nagasaki after World War II. Authority for care for both groups would expire one year after the completion of a study on the effects of exposure to Agent Orange.

● Expanded the scope of the study mandated by Congress in 1979 (PL 96-151) on the effects of Agent Orange to include other herbicides and defoliants and other factors of Vietnam service, including medications and environmental conditions.

● Extended the readjustment counseling program for Vietnam veterans through Sept. 30, 1984. The VA was directed to prepare to provide similar counseling services at its own medical facilities after that date.

● Allowed the VA to recover the costs of medical treatment for non-service-connected disabilities for which a veteran had insurance coverage.

● Extended through Dec. 31, 1983, the period during which Vietnam-era veterans could use remaining GI Bill eligibility to pursue on-the-job-training programs, vocational courses or a high school diploma.

● Extended through Sept. 30, 1984, the authority for government agencies to hire and train Vietnam-era veterans outside of normal civil service hiring rules.

● Established a small-business loan program to be run by the VA. Loans would be made to disabled and Vietnam-era veterans from a revolving fund authorized at $25 million. Veterans who had received loans from the Small Business Administration (SBA) would be ineligible for the new program. The program would expire Sept. 30, 1986.

● Required the VA to maintain a minimum of 90,000 hospital and nursing home beds, although up to 125,000 beds could be maintained if necessary.

Veterans' Benefit Cuts

In its budget-cutting reconciliation package (HR 3982 — PL 97-35), cleared July 31, Congress reduced certain educational, dental and burial benefits for veterans.

Major provisions ended GI Bill education benefits for veterans taking flight training courses, limited benefits for those taking correspondence courses and trimmed an education loan program designed to supplement GI Bill benefits.

Senate-House conferees estimated the changes would cut projected fiscal 1982 spending by $116.2 million, roughly the savings required of the Veterans' Affairs committees by the first fiscal 1982 budget resolution. The overall reconciliation bill revised federal programs to slash nearly $35.2 billion from a projected fiscal 1982 spending level of about $740 billion. *(Reconciliation, p. 40)*

Provisions

As signed into law Aug. 13, the veterans' provisions of the Omnibus Reconciliation Act (Title XX of HR 3982 — PL 97-35):

● Eliminated VA flight training benefits effective Oct. 31, 1981; allowed persons enrolled on Aug. 31, 1981, to continue to receive benefits.

● Reduced to 55 percent, from 70 percent, the portion of the fees the federal government paid for veterans taking education correspondence courses.

● Eliminated education loans supplementing GI Bill education benefits, effective Oct. 1, 1981; continued loan eligibility for certain Vietnam-era veterans.

● Reduced to three months, from one year, the period of time after discharge within which veterans must apply for dental treatment of conditions that were service-connected but not disabling; limited benefits to those who had served at least 180 days.

● Limited, in fiscal 1982-84, the $300 VA benefit for funeral and burial expenses to veterans entitled to receive VA disability or retirement benefits. Eligibility for the $150 burial plot benefit was not changed. Under previous law burial benefits totaling $450 were available to any veteran with wartime service.

Congress in 1982 reinstated funeral benefits for indigent veterans with non-service-related injuries. *(Story, p. 617)*

Disability Benefit Increase

Congress Oct. 2 cleared legislation (S 917 — PL 97-66) providing an 11.2 percent cost-of-living increase in benefits for veterans with service-connected disabilities.

The Senate passed S 917 (S Rept 97-153) by voice vote July 24; the House by voice vote passed a companion measure (HR 3995 — H Rept 97-179) Sept. 21. The House and Senate Veterans' Affairs committees worked out minor differences without a formal conference, and the compromise bill was approved by the Senate Oct. 1 and the House Oct. 2.

Congress cleared a further 7.4 percent cost-of-living adjustment (COLA) in disability benefits in 1982. Two further increases were approved in 1984. *(Stories, pp. 617, 622, 623)*

Provisions. As signed into law Oct. 17, S 917 (PL 97-66):

● Provided an average 11.2 percent increase in disability compensation for veterans with service-connected disabilities, effective Oct. 1, 1981.

● Provided an 11.2 percent benefit increase for families of severely disabled veterans and families of veterans who died from service-connected causes.

● Increased the maximum grant for disabled veterans who needed automobile adaptations to $4,400 from $3,800 and increased the grant for housing adaptations to $32,500 from $30,000.

● Increased maximum coverage under the servicemen's and veterans' life insurance policy to $35,000 from $20,000.

● Established a graduated payment mortgage program within the Veterans Administration.

● Extended payment of non-service-connected disability pensions to certain hospitalized veterans undergoing rehabilitation.

POW Benefits

Congress enacted legislation (HR 1100 — PL 97-37) making it easier for former prisoners of war (POWs) to receive compensation and health benefits from the Veterans Administration (VA).

The House passed HR 1100 (H Rept 97-28) June 2 by a vote of 394-2. A scaled-down version of the measure (S 468 — S Rept 97-88) passed the Senate by voice vote June 4. Members of the Veterans' Affairs committees informally worked out a compromise that was approved by the House and Senate July 30. Although the administration had expressed opposition to the legislation on budgetary grounds, it did not actively lobby against the bill.

Provisions. As signed into law Aug. 14, HR 1100 (PL 97-37):

● Required the VA administrator to appoint an Advisory Committee on Former Prisoners of War and to seek its advice on the needs of former POWs for compensation, health care and rehabilitation.

● Provided that certain disabilities of veterans who had been prisoners of war for at least 30 days would be presumed to be service-connected, for purposes of receiving VA compensation.

● Allowed VA treatment for psychoses and other mental conditions; eliminated the requirement in existing law that symptoms of such conditions must appear within two years of release for active duty.

● Made former POWs eligible for all types of VA health care; gave them priority over veterans with non-service-connected disabilities.

● Required the VA to maintain records for three years of all POW claims for compensation, and the disposition of such claims.

New GI Bill

The House Veterans' Affairs Committee May 19 reported legislation establishing a new program of educational assistance for veterans (HR 1400 — H Rept 97-80, Part I). The Armed Services Committee, which shared jurisdiction, reported a modified version of HR 1400 in 1982, but the measure did not reach the floor before adjournment. Congress approved a new "GI Bill" education program in 1984. *(Stories, pp. 618, 620, 621)*

1982

Veterans' Benefits Increase

Congress Sept. 29 cleared legislation (HR 6782 — PL 97-306) that granted disabled veterans a 7.4 percent cost-of-living raise and made a number of changes in veterans' education and employment programs. Congress in 1981 had approved an 11.2 percent veterans' cost-of-living adjustment (COLA). Lawmakers voted further increases in 1984. *(Stories, pp. 616, 622, 623)*

In addition to the COLA increase, HR 6782 consolidated Labor Department veterans' employment programs, established a new employment and training program directed toward Vietnam-era veterans and extended for one year the deadline for veterans to use education benefits for vocational and secondary education programs.

Legislative History

The provisions in the final bill originally were contained in two separate House bills (HR 6782, HR 6794). The House passed HR 6782 (H Rept 97-660), containing the 7.4 percent COLA increase, July 27 by a 400-0 vote. On Sept. 20, the House by voice vote passed HR 6794 (H Rept 97-799), dealing with veterans' education and employment programs.

The Senate approved its version of the bill Sept. 24 by voice vote. The Senate measure (S 2913 — S Rept 97-550) combined compensation, employment and education provisions.

The final compromise, worked out by staff members from the Veterans' Affairs committees, was approved by voice vote in the House Sept. 28 and the Senate Sept. 29.

Major Provisions

As signed into law Oct. 14, HR 6782 (PL 97-306):

• **Disability Benefits.** Authorized a 7.4 percent cost-of-living increase in compensation for veterans with service-connected disabilities and for survivors of service members or veterans who died from service-connected injuries.

• Increased compensation for dependents of disabled veterans and for certain blinded veterans.

• Made members of the Senior Reserve Officers' Training Corps (SROTC) eligible for disability compensation.

Education Programs. Made voluntary, instead of mandatory, the veterans' representatives ("vet reps") program, which provided educational benefits counseling to veterans returning to college.

• Eliminated a requirement that schools providing Veterans Administration (VA)-approved vocational courses must show that at least half their graduates had found jobs in the career field for which training was provided.

• Eased restrictions on the payment of vocational rehabilitation subsistence allowances to veterans jailed as the result of a felony to allow payment to those living in a halfway house or participating in a work release program.

• Barred VA educational payments to jailed veterans convicted of a felony if tuition and fees for the course were paid by another federal, state or local program or if no fees were charged for the course.

• Limited the VA's authority to deny eligibility for edu-

cation benefits to Vietnam-era veterans enrolled in vocational education, on-the-job training, apprenticeship or secondary education programs. Veterans could be denied eligibility only after a case-by-case review. Extended the eligibility period for one year, to Dec. 31, 1984.

Employment. Clarified the responsibilities of and made administrative improvements in the operation of the Labor Department's veterans' employment office.

• Expanded the responsibilities of the directors of state veterans' employment programs to include such duties as ensuring that discrimination complaints were resolved in a timely manner.

• Established a national employment and training program for veterans; authorized grants to local, state and non-profit organizations to operate the programs.

• Required federal contractors to report annually to the secretary of labor on veteran hiring activity.

Other Provisions. Reinstated the $300 burial benefit for indigent veterans. The 1981 Budget Reconciliation Act (PL 97-35) had ended the benefit for veterans with non-service-connected injuries whose deaths occurred after Oct. 1, 1981. *(1981 action, p. 616)*

• Provided that contracting out for services would be permitted within the VA health care system, but only where patient care would not suffer and where savings of at least 15 percent would result.

• Authorized the VA to guarantee loans made to veterans to refinance a manufactured (mobile) home or to purchase a lot for the unit.

• Provided that a minimum of two years of military service was required for eligibility for all federal veterans' rights and benefits.

Veterans' Health Care

Congress Aug. 20 cleared legislation (HR 6350 — PL 97-251) designed to deal with a severe shortage of nurses in Veterans' Administration (VA) hospitals. The VA had reported many vacancies on its hospital nursing staffs. As a result, some wards had to be closed, nursing staffs were overworked and many nurses were leaving. HR 6350 gave the VA new flexibility to offer pay and educational incentives to help attract and retain nurses, and contained several other provisions affecting veterans' programs.

The House passed HR 6350 (H Rept 97-543) June 15 by a 390-0 vote. The Senate passed its version of the bill (S 2385 — S Rept 97-467) June 21 by voice vote. Veterans' committee leaders worked out the differences without a formal conference. Their compromise version was approved by voice vote of the House Aug. 19 and the Senate Aug. 20.

Provisions

As signed into law Sept. 8, HR 6350 (PL 97-251):

• Provided that nurses who worked two 12-hour regularly scheduled tours of duty over a weekend in a VA health care facility would be considered to have worked a full basic workweek, if the VA administrator decided that was necessary to obtain or retain adequate nursing services.

• Allowed payment at the "weekend" rate for VA nurses working on Saturdays, at the administrator's discretion. Previously, only Sunday work qualified for the higher rate.

• Allowed full-time VA employees to participate in the VA health professional scholarship program on a part-time basis, rather than full-time, if they wished.

- Extended for one year, through Sept. 30, 1983, the VA's authority to contract for hospital and medical care for eligible veterans in Puerto Rico and the Virgin Islands.
- Allowed survivors and dependents of severely disabled veterans to become eligible again for the civilian health and medical program (CHAMPVA) if they had lost eligibility by becoming eligible for Medicare but then had exhausted their Medicare benefits.
- Extended for one year a VA alcohol and drug treatment and rehabilitation pilot program and the deadline for a report on the program. The program was extended through Sept. 30, 1983, the report date to March 31, 1984.
- Extended for four years, through fiscal 1986, a program for matching-fund grants to states for the construction of state veterans' homes and nursing homes.

New GI Bill Proposals

The House Armed Services Committee in 1982 joined the Veterans' Affairs Committee in calling for a new GI Bill program of education benefits for veterans, but legislation to establish the program never made it to the House floor. Armed Services reported the bill May 17 (HR 1400 — H Rept 97-80, Parts II and III) — a full year after the Veterans' Affairs Committee acted on it. Legislation finally cleared in 1984. *(1981 action, p. 616; 1984 bill, p. 621)*

The Veterans' Affairs bill would have provided a basic education benefit of $300 a month for 36 months, with increases to attract recruits for certain hard-to-fill jobs. The Armed Services bill would have provided a basic education benefit of $200 a month for 36 months, with increases for persons with critical skills or lengthy service. Service members who re-enlisted would be permitted to give up their education benefits in exchange for 25 percent of the value in cash. Both bills would have permitted personnel with more than 10 years' service to transfer the education benefits to their dependents.

Pentagon officials had said they needed the program to attract more qualified young people into the armed forces. In 1979, for the first time since the all-volunteer military began in 1973, all four branches of the service failed to reach their recruiting goals, and recruiting fell short again in 1980. In addition, some military commanders complained that the quality of the personnel they were getting was poor and hoped the prospect of new educational benefits would attract more middle-class youths of college aptitude to the service.

Eligibility for the previous GI Bill had expired in 1976. Although prospects for enactment of a new GI Bill were considered good when the 97th Congress opened in 1981, interest waned for several reasons. As the recession continued and jobs became scarcer, more young people were joining the armed forces anyway; in 1981 and 1982 the services met their recruiting quotas and reported an increase in "quality" of recruits as well. In addition, the growing federal deficit put a damper on the creation of any costly new programs. *(Background, Congress and the Nation Vol. I, p. 1335; Congress and the Nation Vol. II, p. 456; Congress and the Nation Vol. IV, p. 179)*

There was little support for a new GI Bill outside the House. Although President Reagan had pledged during the 1980 campaign to back a new GI Bill, the administration withdrew its endorsement as budget pressures mounted. The chairman of the Senate Veterans' Affairs Committee, Alan K. Simpson, R-Wyo., said he could not support new educational benefits during lean economic times while recruiting was good. Veterans' organizations, such as the American Legion and the Veterans of Foreign Wars, were on record as favoring a new GI Bill, but they gave it a low priority and did not lobby for it.

Other Legislation

Pell Grant Eligibility

Legislation cleared Sept. 29 (S 2852 — PL 97-301) included provisions that restored eligibility for college aid to some 50,000 veterans who had lost it as a result of legislation passed in 1981. *(1982 bill, p. 562)*

In a continuing appropriations measure approved in December 1981 (PL 97-92), Congress had stipulated that all GI benefits be considered as direct student aid. This eliminated up to 50,000 veterans from eligibility for Pell grants for college students. Previously, veterans who got GI Bill assistance often were able to get Pell grants as well, since only half of their veterans' benefits were counted as income in determining eligibility for the grants. S 2852 reinstated these benefits.

Reconciliation Changes

Congress made modest changes in veterans' programs as part of budget-cutting reconciliation legislation (HR 6955 — PL 97-253) cleared Aug. 18. Among other changes, pension rates and cost-of-living increases were rounded to the next lower dollar and a .5 percent user fee was imposed on VA-backed home loans. *(Story, p. 48)*

1983

Veterans' Health Care

Congress Nov. 3 cleared legislation (HR 2920 — PL 98-160) extending Vietnam veteran readjustment counseling centers for four more years until Sept. 30, 1988, and making other changes in veterans' health care services.

The popular "storefront" readjustment counseling centers first were authorized in 1979 (PL 96-22) and reauthorized in 1981 (PL 97-72) to help Vietnam veterans experiencing war-related emotional problems return to everyday life. During fiscal 1983 the 136 centers in operation had about 80,000 visits from Vietnam-era veterans. *(1981 action, p. 615)*

The Reagan administration had urged Congress not to pass a new authorization for the centers until a task force reported on how readjustment services best could be provided. Despite his objections to several provisions of the bill, President Reagan signed the measure into law Nov. 21, citing his "strong commitment to the welfare of America's veterans."

The wide-ranging bill also required studies on the effects of post-traumatic stress disorder, a condition affecting many Vietnam veterans and one reason for the counsel-

ing centers, and on the health effects of radiation testing on veterans who participated in nuclear weapons tests and in the cleanup of Hiroshima and Nagasaki, Japan, following the 1945 atomic bomb blasts there.

In addition, HR 2920 contained provisions aimed at reducing the long-term cost of Veterans Administration (VA) health care services by promoting preventive health care and alternatives to institutionalization, such as adult day care and community health care services. The bill also established within the VA a new advisory committee for women veterans, and required the VA administrator to take steps to ensure that the gender-specific health care needs of female veterans were met.

Legislative History

The House passed HR 2920 (H Rept 98-117) May 23 by voice vote. The Senate passed its version June 28, substituting the text of its own bill (S 578 — S Rept 98-145) for the language of HR 2920. The House-passed bill would have extended the centers for three years, the Senate bill for one year. Members of the Veterans' Affairs committees worked out a compromise measure that included the four-year extension. The compromise was approved by the House Nov. 2 and by the Senate Nov. 3, both by voice vote.

Provisions

As signed into law Nov. 21, HR 2920 (PL 98-160):

• Extended for four years, through Sept. 30, 1988, readjustment counseling centers for Vietnam-era veterans, and gave Vietnam veterans permanent eligibility for readjustment counseling.

• Required a study, with a report to Congress by Oct. 1, 1986, on the incidence, prevalence and effects of post-traumatic stress disorder and other psychological problems of Vietnam-era veterans.

• Increased per diem payments by the VA to state veterans' hospitals to approximately 30 percent of costs. The new rates were: for domiciliary care, $7.30; for nursing care, $17.05; for hospital care, $15.25.

• Established within the VA an Advisory Committee on Women Veterans to advise the administrator; also required the administrator to take steps to ensure that the VA was able to meet the gender-specific health care needs of women veterans.

• Required the VA administrator to justify any disposal of real property, and submit any proposal to Congress.

• Authorized, until Sept. 30, 1988, in-house adult day health care programs for veterans eligible for nursing home care; also clarified the VA's authority to place veterans in private VA-approved community residential care facilities.

• Authorized eligible veterans receiving health care in VA hospitals to receive certain preventive health care services. Also allowed veterans receiving care for service-connected disabilities or veterans rated 50 percent or more disabled to receive at least one preventive health care service as part of their treatment.

• Allowed the VA administrator to set pay rates and qualification standards for three groups of VA health care personnel: licensed physical therapists, licensed practical or vocational nurses and respiratory therapists. The authority had rested with the Office of Personnel Management.

• Required the administrator, unless he deemed it scientifically unfeasible, to provide for the conduct of an epidemiological study on the long-term adverse health effects of exposure of ionizing radiation from detonations of nuclear devices.

Emergency Job Training

Over administration objections, Congress Aug. 3 cleared an "emergency" veterans' job training bill (HR 2355 — PL 98-77) authorizing a two-year, $300 million program to pay employers to hire and train long-term unemployed Vietnam-era and Korean War veterans. *(1984 sign-up extension, p. 623)*

The measure was prompted by congressional concern over unemployment rates that remained high among veterans despite a drop in the national jobless rate as the economy recovered from the recession. Unemployment among veterans hit its highest level since World War II in February 1983, and although it declined after that, the unemployment rate for veterans between 25 and 29 was still at 12.3 percent in July.

While acknowledging that Vietnam-era veterans faced serious unemployment problems, the administration strongly opposed the legislation throughout its consideration in Congress on grounds that the economy was improving and would yield additional job opportunities for veterans. Nevertheless, President Reagan signed the bill into law Aug. 15.

A supplemental appropriations bill cleared by Congress just before the end of the session (PL 98-181) provided $75 million for the program. Another $75 million was provided in a fiscal 1984 continuing appropriations resolution (PL 98-151).

Legislative History

The House passed HR 2355 (H Rept 98-116) June 7 by a vote of 407-10. The Senate version of the bill (S 1033 — S Rept 98-132) passed by voice vote on June 15. House and Senate bills differed on eligibility requirements, funding levels and forms of aid. The final compromise, worked out informally by the House and Senate Veterans' Affairs committees, authorized $150 million a year for two years for the program. It limited eligibility to Vietnam-era and Korean War veterans who served at least 180 days or had a service-connected disability. The House provision authorizing benefits for vocational education was dropped, but employers were allowed to conduct their job training programs at vocational schools if they wished. The House approved the final version of the bill Aug. 2, the Senate the following day, both by voice vote.

Provisions

As signed into law Aug. 15, HR 2355 (PL 98-77):

• Established a new emergency veterans' job training program providing subsidies to employers to hire and train eligible unemployed veterans.

• Authorized $150 million in each of fiscal years 1984 and 1985 for the program. Appropriations would remain available through fiscal 1986.

• Limited eligibility for the program to veterans who served in the active military, naval or air service for at least 180 days during the Korean conflict or the Vietnam era or suffered a service-connected disability during those years. To receive the aid, a veteran had to be jobless and have

been unemployed for at least 15 of the 20 weeks immediately preceding his application for the program.

• Limited payments to employers who hired and trained eligible veterans to 50 percent of the veteran's starting salary, up to a maximum of $10,000. The training could last up to nine months for most veterans. The subsidy for disabled veterans could continue for 15 months.

• Provided that the training program in most cases had to last for at least six months for occupations in growth industries, for jobs requiring new technological skills or in fields for which jobs outnumbered the labor supply.

• Required employers to certify that after completion of the job training program, the veteran would be hired in a permanent, stable job for which he was trained; also required employers to certify that training would not be offered to a veteran who was already qualified for the job.

• Stipulated that employers could not lay off or fire other workers in order to participate in the new program.

• Allowed employers to contract with an educational institution to provide job training.

• Expanded GI Bill eligibility for Vietnam-era veterans to enable them to pursue associate degree programs that were predominantly vocational; barred veterans from receiving job training benefits under both the new program and other federal programs.

• Authorized the Veterans Administration (VA) and the Labor Department to jointly administer the program, but designated the VA as the lead agency.

Disability Benefit Increase

Both the Senate and House approved cost-of-living adjustments (COLAs) in disabled veterans' compensation benefits, but none was enacted into law in 1983. The Senate passed a bill (S 1388 — S Rept 98-249) Nov. 18 increasing by 3.5 percent the rate of compensation to disabled veterans, their dependents and survivors, and making changes in other veterans' programs.

The House Oct. 25 passed a budget reconciliation measure (HR 4169) that included a bill (HR 2937 — H Rept 98-228) authorizing a 4.1 percent cost-of-living (COLA) increase in disability payments and postponing the increase from Oct. 1, 1983, to April 1, 1984, as requested by the administration. HR 4169 did not clear in 1983.

A compromise version of S 1388 authorizing a 3.5 percent COLA was enacted in 1984, as was a second COLA increase of 3.2 percent. The COLA increase was dropped from HR 4169 following enactment of S 1388. *(1984 action, pp. 622, 623)*

Increases of 11.2 and 7.4 percent in service-connected disability had been approved by Congress in 1981 and 1982 respectively. *(1981 action, p. 616; 1982 action, p. 617)*

Mortgage Aid

Financial assistance for veterans facing foreclosure on home mortgages guaranteed by the Veterans Administration (VA) was approved by the House but was not considered in the Senate in 1983.

The House May 24 approved by a 394-23 vote a bill (HR 2948 — H Rept 98-118) providing aid to any veteran or surviving spouse who was unemployed or who suffered a substantial reduction in income. HR 2948 allowed the VA to use up to $150 million from its revolving fund for mort-

gage aid to prevent foreclosure.

The House also included $150 million for mortgage assistance for unemployed veterans in a fiscal 1984 appropriations bill (HR 3133 — PL 98-45), but the provision was dropped in conference with the Senate.

Some other provisions of HR 2948 were included in a veterans' benefits bill (S 1388) that cleared in 1984. *(Story, p. 622)*

New GI Bill

The House Veterans' Affairs Committee approved a package of education benefits designed to entice qualified young people to join the armed forces and stay in.

The bill, reported May 16 (HR 1400 — H Rept 98-185, Part I), was similar to legislation that stalled in the House during the 97th Congress. It represented a compromise worked out between the Veterans' Affairs Committee and the House Armed Services Committee, which shared jurisdiction. The measure was never brought to the House floor. *(1981-82 action, pp. 616, 618)*

A less sweeping test program was enacted in 1984 as part of a defense authorization bill (HR 5167). *(1984 action, p. 621)*

1984

Agent Orange Compensation

Congress in 1984 cleared legislation (HR 1961 — PL 98-542) that for the first time mandated compensation payments to some veterans who were exposed to Agent Orange, a defoliant used in Vietnam that was contaminated with a highly toxic chemical.

The new law, which required the Veterans Administration (VA) to establish a system for review of compensation claims by the VA, based on advice from a panel of scientific experts, acknowledged for the first time that exposure of Vietnam veterans to Agent Orange resulted in their contracting disease.

HR 1961 also required the VA to establish a second review system, with its own scientific panel, for compensation claims by veterans who participated in atmospheric atomic weapons tests or served in occupied Hiroshima and Nagasaki, Japan. Some of these veterans said they suffered from diseases resulting from exposure to low-level ionizing radiation.

Creation of the scientific advisory panels was designed to aid in determining which claims of Agent Orange- or radiation-induced death or disability had merit, and particularly to review the results of several major studies of the adverse health effects of exposure to Agent Orange and low-level radiation.

The temporary benefits mandated under the law were set to expire just before a major scientific review by the federal Centers for Disease Control (CDC) was due to be completed. The temporary payments would be extended or terminated, depending on the results of the study, which was expected to be completed by 1987 or 1988.

Background

Passage of the new law capped a decade-long effort to obtain health care and compensation for veterans exposed to Agent Orange. In 1979 Congress first ordered a study by the VA of the health effects of Agent Orange on veterans (PL 96-151). *(Congress and the Nation Vol. V, p. 184)*

And in 1981 veterans won a long fight to get the VA to provide medical treatment for ailments attributed to Agent Orange exposure, with passage of a law (PL 97-72) that also granted medical care to veterans who were exposed to low-level radiation. The law also expanded the study of Agent Orange health effects that was ordered in 1979. Conduct of that study was eventually transferred from the VA to the CDC. *(1981 action, p. 615)*

Just before adjourning in November 1983, Congress in a major veterans' health care bill (PL 98-160) asked the VA to conduct a study of the long-term health effects of exposure to low-level radiation, and agreed in a supplemental appropriations bill (PL 98-181) to spend $54 million on the CDC Agent Orange study. *(1983 action, p. 618)*

But, until enactment of HR 1961, Congress had set no policy on disability payments to veterans who claimed injury in the line of duty from radiation or Agent Orange exposure, and the VA had handled claims brought by veterans one by one.

An estimated 52 million pounds of the herbicide — code-named Agent Orange because of the color of the drums in which it was stored — were sprayed in South Vietnam between 1961 and 1971 to defoliate trees and destroy crops. The herbicide contained varying quantities of dioxin, one of the most toxic substances known.

Vietnam veterans blamed a variety of diseases, as well as birth defects in their children, on Agent Orange exposure. Specifically, such exposure was believed by some to cause chloracne, a skin rash; porphyria cutanea tarda, a liver condition that could affect up to 150,000 Vietnam veterans; and a cancer known as soft-tissue sarcoma, an often fatal disease that could affect about 30 Vietnam veterans a year.

Some veterans exposed to low-level ionizing radiation claimed the exposure caused cancer of the thyroid; polycythemia vera, a rare disease of the bone marrow; and leukemia.

At the time of final passage of HR 1961, Sen. Alan Cranston, D-Calif., ranking member of the Senate Committee on Veterans' Affairs, said that about 200,000 veterans had been exposed to radiation during atmospheric tests and another 110,000 had been exposed in Hiroshima and Nagasaki, according to figures from the Defense Nuclear Agency.

Cranston said the VA had received 2,566 claims relating to radiation exposure, including 985 involving malignancies, and 21,693 claims relating to Agent Orange exposure. Only 30 veterans had received compensation for diseases believed to be caused by exposure to radiation and 25 had been compensated for exposure to Agent Orange, Cranston said.

Legislative History

The House approved HR 1961 (H Rept 98-592) by voice vote Jan. 30. The bill represented a compromise between members who wanted to compensate veterans for a number of diseases they blamed on their exposure to Agent Orange and radiation, and those who wanted to delay action until the CDC study was finished. The com-

promise authorized payments to veterans until one year after completion of the study, at which time payments could be continued, if deemed warranted by the study results.

The Senate approved its version (S 1651) by a vote of 95-0 May 22 and then substituted the language of S 1651 for that of HR 1961. The Senate bill was a compromise worked out by Cranston, who wanted to require the VA to set compensation guidelines, and Veterans' Affairs Chairman Alan K. Simpson, R-Wyo., who had sponsored a nonbinding resolution simply urging the VA to set guidelines for reviewing scientific studies and resolving claims. The Cranston-Simpson compromise had the support of the administration and major veterans' groups.

House and Senate negotiators informally worked out a compromise, which generally reflected the Senate version of the bill. The compromise, which accepted the Senate approach of requiring the VA to write guidelines, also allowed temporary disability payments to veterans who suffered from two diseases believed to be caused by Agent Orange. The House bill had presumed that three specific diseases were caused by exposure to Agent Orange and three by radiation. The Senate had been reluctant to put such a presumption into law, without conclusive scientific evidence. The compromise dropped a Senate provision allowing judicial review of VA guidelines and claims decisions.

The House accepted the compromise Oct. 3, the Senate Oct. 4.

Provisions

As signed into law Oct. 24, HR 1961 (PL 98-542):

● Required the administrator of the Veterans Administration to set guidelines for deciding claims for compensation due to disability or death brought by veterans exposed to Agent Orange, a herbicide known to be contaminated with dioxin, a highly toxic chemical. The exposure must have occurred in Vietnam between Aug. 5, 1964, and May 7, 1975.

● Provided disability payments from Oct. 1, 1984, until Sept. 30, 1986, for veterans suffering from chloracne, a skin disease, or porphyria cutanea tarda (PCT), a liver disorder, two diseases believed to be caused by exposure to Agent Orange.

● Required the VA to set guidelines for deciding compensation claims brought by veterans exposed to low-level ionizing radiation during atmospheric atomic tests or the U.S. occupation of Hiroshima and Nagasaki, Japan, prior to July 1, 1946.

● Required the VA to create and consult with two eight-member scientific advisory committees, whose specialties were to be the adverse health effects of dioxin exposure and low-level radiation exposure.

● Directed the VA administrator, when writing guidelines or settling claims, to give veterans the benefit of the doubt where "there is an approximate balance of positive and negative evidence regarding the merits of an issue."

New GI Bill

Congress in 1984 authorized a large-scale program of college-level education benefits for military recruits as part of the defense authorization bill (HR 5167 — PL 98-525).

HR 5167 established a three-year, voluntary test pro-

gram which, unlike earlier GI Bill programs, would require contributions by participants to help pay for the program.

The first such program, enacted during World War II as part of a "GI Bill of Rights," was intended to help people who had served in the military at very low pay re-enter civilian life. It was reinstated during the Korean and Vietnam wars. *(Background, Congress and the Nation Vol. I, p. 1335; Congress and the Nation Vol. II, p. 456; Congress and the Nation Vol. IV, p. 180)*

The program was repealed in 1976, because men no longer were being drafted and because military pay had gone up substantially. Economic recession helped propel many job seekers into the military, easing serious recruitment problems.

But proponents of the existing all-volunteer U.S. military argued for years that a program of educational benefits would be needed to entice academically talented teenagers into the services once the economy began providing more civilian job opportunities. In addition, military personnel who qualified for benefits under the Vietnam-era program faced a Dec. 31, 1989, deadline for using those benefits.

Legislative History

House Action. In an effort to ease the recruiting crunch, House proponents tried to revive a wide-scale GI Bill in 1983. A bill (HR 1400 — H Rept 98-185) to establish a package of education benefits was reported in the House but was never brought to the floor. Nor was there any Senate action on the proposal. *(1983 action, p. 620)*

In 1984 a similar proposal was incorporated into HR 5167 (H Rept 98-691), the defense authorization bill passed by the House June 1, 298-98. *(Defense authorization, p. 235)*

The House-passed bill provided for military personnel a basic monthly educational stipend of $300 for up to 36 months, to be paid for through the budget of the Veterans Administration (VA). It also repealed the limiting date for the Vietnam-era GI Bill benefits.

The proposal was not debated on the House floor but the issue was the focus of intense procedural wrangling in the Senate.

Senate Action. The Senate's companion bill (S 2723 — S Rept 98-500), as reported from committee, also lifted the deadline for Vietnam-era GI Bill benefits. When S 2723 reached the floor, there appeared to be support for a broad revival of the GI Bill, similar to the House legislation. But the Senate subsequently reversed itself and approved a less sweeping package.

By a 47-45 vote June 13, the Senate killed an amendment that would have created a program fully funded by the government for everyone completing three years of active military duty, regardless of education or job. Backers of the amendment defended the plan as cost-effective and as a boon for educational opportunity, but critics portrayed it as a costly entitlement program that would lock the government into paying large educational benefits to veterans indefinitely.

The Senate then adopted, 72-20, an amendment offered by John Glenn, D-Ohio, to establish a four-year test program offering $500 a month in educational benefits for three years to high school graduates recruited for certain hard-to-fill jobs. The recruit would have to serve two years of active duty and contribute $250 a month. The plan was amended to make the benefits available for up to 12,500

persons entering military service between Sept. 30, 1984, and Sept. 30, 1988.

The Senate passed HR 5167, the defense authorization bill, June 21 by an 82-6 vote, after substituting the provisions of S 2723 for the House-passed GI Bill language.

Conference, Final Action. House-Senate conferees agreed to a three-year test program that was to be voluntary. Their report (H Rept 98-1080) incorporated the Senate concept of participants helping to pay for the program.

Veterans eligible for the Vietnam-era GI bill program could choose to accrue a new entitlement to $300 a month for 36 months after three additional years of active duty service with no reduction in basic pay. They would also be eligible to receive one-half of their educational entitlement under the Vietnam-era assistance program. Authority for persons to elect to participate in the existing Veterans' Educational Assistance Program (VEAP) was to be suspended during the three-year program. *(Congress and the Nation Vol. V, p. 190)*

The House approved the conference version of HR 5167 by voice vote Sept. 26. The Senate followed suit Sept. 27.

Provisions

As signed into law Oct. 19, the new GI Bill provisions of HR 5167 (PL 98-525):

● Set up a test program under which any recruit entering the service between June 1985 and July 1988 could contribute $100 per month for the first 12 months of service. That would guarantee payment by the Defense Department of at least $300 per month toward tuition and expenses for 36 months, for a total of $10,800.

● Gave the secretary of defense discretion to increase benefit levels for recruits in selected job specialties, to encourage enlistments or re-enlistments.

● Set up a separate program to pay $140 per month for educational expenses for 36 months to enlistees in the National Guard or reserve forces who met certain criteria and enlisted for six years.

Disability Benefits Increase

Congress Feb. 9 cleared legislation (S 1388 — PL 98-223) authorizing a 3.5 percent cost-of-living adjustment (COLA) in disabled veterans' compensation benefits.

The increase, effective April 1, 1984, affected benefits paid to some 2.25 million disabled veterans and their families, as well as to about 300,000 survivors of veterans who died of service-connected causes.

S 1388, which also made a number of other changes in veterans' programs, was the first of two veterans' COLA bills approved by Congress in 1984. HR 5688 (PL 98-543), cleared Oct. 9, provided another 3.2 percent increase, effective Dec. 1, 1984. That bill also increased GI Bill and other veterans' educational benefits. *(Story, p. 623)*

In passing S 1388, Congress endorsed one of President Reagan's fiscal 1985 budget recommendations — a 3.5 percent COLA for disabled veterans, their families and survivors, effective April 1, 1984. However, it also expressed the sense of Congress that the next COLA should take effect Dec. 1, 1984 — not April 1, 1985, as Reagan had requested.

Congress had approved an 11.2 percent COLA in 1981 and 7.4 percent in 1982. *(Previous congressional action, pp. 616, 617)*

Legislative History

As cleared, S 1388 was a compromise containing provisions from several bills passed by the House and Senate.

The Senate had passed its version of the bill (S Rept 98-249) Nov. 18, 1983. It authorized a 3.5 percent COLA and contained provisions from two House-passed veterans' bills (HR 2936, HR 2948), which expanded the Board of Veterans Appeals and made changes in the Veterans Administration (VA) home loan guaranty program. The House passed HR 2936 (H Rept 98-111) May 17, 1983, and the Senate passed an amended version June 15, 1983. HR 2948 (H Rept 98-118) was approved by the House May 24, 1983. *(HR 2948, p. 620)*

Also in 1983, the House Veterans' Affairs Committee reported a bill (HR 2937 — H Rept 98-228) authorizing a 4.1 percent COLA for disabled veterans. That bill became part of the budget reconciliation measure (HR 4169) passed by the House Oct. 25, 1983.

Staffs of the House and Senate Veterans' Affairs committees worked out a compromise version of S 1388, which the House accepted by voice vote Feb. 8 and the Senate Feb. 9, 1984. The COLA provision was dropped from the reconciliation bill following enactment of S 1388. *(Reconciliation bill, p. 60)*

Provisions

As signed into law March 2, S 1388 (PL 98-223):

● Increased disability benefits for veterans, dependents and survivors, and increased clothing allowances for certain disabled veterans, by 3.5 percent, effective April 1, 1984.

● Expressed the sense of Congress that future increases for veterans, dependents and survivors take effect on Dec. 1 of the fiscal year involved.

● Provided service-connected disability payments for former prisoners of war suffering from dysthymic disorder, or depressive neurosis.

● Increased benefits for blinded veterans who also suffered hearing loss from service-connected injuries.

● Provided that when a veteran received hospital care in excess of 21 days in one month for a service-connected disability, the period for payment of increased compensation on account of such care would begin the first day of that month.

● Permitted an adopted child to receive benefits even though the child was 18 or over at the time of adoption, if the child was incapable of self-support at age 18 and was a member of the veteran's household.

● Extended through fiscal 1989 authority to provide matching-fund grants to states for establishing, expanding or improving state veterans' cemeteries.

● Permitted certain Vietnam-era veterans ineligible for the Post-Vietnam Era Educational Assistance Program (VEAP), to elect to participate in VEAP in lieu of GI Bill benefits. *(VEAP suspension, GI Bill story, p. 621)*

● Conformed the level of survivors' educational assistance benefits for high school training to the level of Vietnam-era veterans' GI Bill benefits for such training.

● Barred concurrent receipt of benefits under more than one educational assistance program administered by the VA for pursuit of one program of education.

● Allowed restoration of VA home loan guaranty entitlement when a property was sold by a veteran-purchaser to a non-veteran and subsequently resold to an eligible veteran, if the new veteran-purchaser substituted his entitlement.

● Provided for the guaranty of a loan to a veteran for the purchase of a manufactured home if the lot on which the home was permanently affixed was owned or being purchased by the veteran, and the home, as affixed, was regarded as real property by the state.

● Expanded eligibility for veterans' employment and training programs to veterans with 10 or 20 percent disability, if the veteran was determined to have a serious employment handicap.

● Authorized the VA to permit VA-appointed fiduciaries to deduct from beneficiaries' estates certain limited commissions for services at the administrator's discretion.

● Authorized benefits for Senior Reserve Officers Training Corps members who incurred disabilities before Oct. 1, 1982.

Veterans' Leadership

Two Reagan appointees served as administrator of the Veterans Administration during President Reagan's first term. Robert P. Nimmo was confirmed by the Senate in July 1981 to head the agency. Nimmo was a former member of the California state Senate, 1976-81, and the state Assembly, 1973-76. Nimmo was succeeded as VA administrator by Harry N. Walters, who was confirmed by the Senate in December 1982. Walters had been assistant secretary of the Army for manpower and reserve affairs, 1981-82.

Both the Senate and House Veterans' Affairs committees had new chairmen at the beginning of the 97th Congress. Alan K. Simpson, R-Wyo., became chairman of the Senate panel and G. V. "Sonny" Montgomery, D-Miss., took over the House committee.

Disability, Education Benefits

Congress Oct. 9 cleared a bill (HR 5688 — PL 98-543) authorizing a 3.2 percent increase in disabled veterans' compensation benefits, effective Dec. 1, 1984.

The bill also provided a 10 percent increase in GI Bill and other veterans' education and rehabilitation benefits, effective Oct. 1, 1984. The increase was the first since 1981. *(PL 96-466, Congress and the Nation Vol. V, p. 189)*

President Reagan had requested a 4.3 percent cost-of-living adjustment (COLA) for disabled veterans, their families and survivors, to take effect April 1, 1985. Both the Senate and the House approved COLAs exceeding that level, but on the basis of lower inflation projections by the Congressional Budget Office, in October Congress agreed to the 3.2 percent figure. It refused to delay the increase to April, however.

HR 5688 was the second veterans' COLA bill enacted in 1984. An earlier bill (S 1388 — PL 98-223), cleared in February, authorized a 3.5 percent increase effective April 1, 1984, and stated that the next COLA should take effect on Dec. 1, 1984. *(Story, p. 622)*

Veterans

Legislative History

The final version of HR 5688 contained provisions from three different House bills. As passed by the House by voice vote June 18, HR 5688 (H Rept 98-828) provided for a 4.3 percent COLA effective Dec. 1, 1984, and made other changes affecting veterans' health, vocational training and benefit programs.

The House Aug. 6 approved legislation (HR 5398 — H Rept 98-775) authorizing a 15 percent increase in veterans' education benefits, and extending the veterans' readjustment appointment (VRA) program and certain provisions of the 1983 emergency veterans' job training act.

The House May 21 passed a bill (HR 5617 — H Rept 98-776) that increased grants for specially adapted housing for disabled veterans.

The Senate approved its version (S 2736 — S Rept 98-604) Oct. 2 by voice vote. The Senate bill provided for a 4.7 percent COLA and a 10 percent increase in veterans' educational and vocational rehabilitation benefits. The bill also extended the VRA program and sign-up period for the emergency job training program, and provided other assistance to disabled veterans.

The House Oct. 5 accepted the Senate version of HR 5688 with amendments reflecting bill sponsors' agreement on a 3.2 percent COLA and compromises between the two versions of the legislation. The Senate agreed to the compromise version Oct. 9.

Provisions

As signed into law Oct. 24, HR 5688 (PL 98-543):

● Authorized a 3.2 percent cost-of-living increase in compensation benefits for disabled veterans, their dependents and survivors, effective Dec. 1, 1984.

● Authorized a 10 percent increase in veterans' education assistance benefits, including the GI Bill and vocational rehabilitation benefits, effective Oct. 1, 1984.

● Extended for two years, until Sept. 30, 1986, the veterans' readjustment appointment program, which helped handicapped veterans get non-competitive appointments to federal jobs.

● Established a four-year pilot program providing education and vocational training for veterans under age 50 who were eligible for disability pensions.

● Established a four-year trial work period for 100 percent service-connected disabled veterans who might, with additional education and training, be able to work. Veterans would not lose their disabled rating while in the program.

● Extended certain provisions of the emergency veterans' job training program enacted in 1983 (PL 98-77). The bill gave veterans an additional three months (to Feb. 28, 1985) to sign up for the program and an extra six months (to Sept. 1, 1985) to begin their training. It also extended the availability of appropriated funds under the program for one year. *(1983 action, p. 619)*

● Increased the limit on grants to severely disabled veterans for specially adapted housing to $35,500, from $32,500, and for automotive adaptive equipment to $5,000, from $4,400, effective Jan. 1, 1985.

Veterans' Health Care

Congress Oct. 3 cleared a bill (HR 5618 — PL 98-528) authorizing special programs for the treatment of veterans suffering from post-traumatic stress disorder, a condition affecting many Vietnam veterans.

The measure also directed the Veterans Administration (VA) to set up guidelines for treatment of veterans for drug and alcohol abuse and dependency, and made other changes in veterans' health care programs.

Although the administration had opposed the provision calling for the establishment of treatment units for veterans suffering from post-traumatic stress disorder, President Reagan signed the bill into law.

The administration also opposed a House-passed provision that would have allowed the VA to fill prescriptions written by private physicians for treatment of veterans' service-connected disabilities. That provision was dropped from the final version of the bill.

Legislative History

The House passed HR 5618 (H Rept 98-779) May 21 by voice vote. The Senate passed HR 5618 Aug. 8 after substituting the text of a similar bill (S 2514 — S Rept 98-487).

The House and Senate Veterans' Affairs committees subsequently worked out a compromise between the two versions. The Senate panel objected to the prescription provision, and it was dropped from the bill. Also dropped was a Senate provision extending the VA's authority to contract with non-VA halfway houses and other community-based programs to provide drug and alcohol abuse treatment for veterans.

The House accepted the compromise version Oct. 2; the Senate Oct. 3.

Provisions

As signed into law Oct. 19, HR 5618 (PL 98-528):

● Authorized the VA to establish special programs for the treatment of veterans suffering from post-traumatic stress disorder.

● Authorized special programs for training health care personnel in the treatment of post-traumatic stress disorder.

● Directed the VA, after consulting with the attorney general, to issue regulations for security in VA facilities, including rules for conduct on VA property and penalties for violations of the rules. The VA could also set rules for enforcement and arrest authority of VA police officers.

● Directed the VA to provide guidelines for treatment of veterans for drug and alcohol abuse and dependency.

● Provided permanent authorization for the research and education activities of VA Geriatric Research, Education and Clinical Centers, which were to expire Sept. 30, 1984, and authorized "such sums as may be necessary" for the programs.

● Authorized grants to states for acquiring existing buildings to be used as health care facilities. Existing law had allowed grants only for new buildings.

● Required the VA to coordinate its health care programs with state, local and private programs, and to place special emphasis on veterans 65 or older.

● Authorized the VA to provide devices, including telecaptioning television decoders, to deaf disabled veterans.

● Required the VA to report by Sept. 30, 1985, on its programs for terminally ill veterans; required a study of health care services for veterans far from VA facilities.

Veterans' Job Preference

The House July 30 passed by voice vote a bill (HR 5799 — H Rept 98-915) providing job security for veterans employed by the federal government as guards, custodians, elevator operators and messengers. The Senate took no action on the measure.

Under existing law the four positions were reserved for veterans, unless no veterans were available. HR 5799 would have prohibited agencies from contracting out those positions if the contract would result in the veterans losing their jobs; it would have allowed agencies to reassign or transfer the veterans, if certain conditions were met.

The Reagan administration opposed the bill, arguing that it tied the government's hands in trying to contract out services, which the administration said saved money.

Veterans' Group Charter

Despite opposition from the Veterans of Foreign Wars (VFW), the House approved legislation (HR 4772 — H Rept 98-822) by a vote of 295-96 June 11 to grant a federal charter to the Vietnam Veterans of America Inc. (VVA). The Senate did not act on the bill.

The VFW objected to granting a federal charter for the 16,000-member organization because of differences it had with VVA President Robert E. Muller. In a letter to VFW officials, Cooper T. Holt, executive director of the VFW's Washington office, called Muller "a propaganda conduit for the Communist government of Vietnam."

Muller had visited Hanoi, and on one occasion laid a wreath on the tomb of North Vietnam's late president, Ho Chi Minh.

11

Housing and Urban Aid

Introduction   629
1981 Chronology   631
1982 Chronology   633
1983 Chronology   635
1984 Chronology   638

Housing and Urban Aid

The Reagan administration proposed a fundamental shift in federal housing and urban policies in the early 1980s.

Blight, housing shortages and economic decline, President Reagan said, represented the failure of past federal social programs. He consistently sought to reduce the federal role in solving urban problems, while increasing incentives for private sector initiatives.

Reagan persuaded Congress to accept substantial reductions in federal housing programs, but lawmakers resisted the president's attempts to eliminate or sharply curtail community development and other programs that aided cities.

Housing Programs

When Reagan took office in 1981, about one out of every three poor families who were renting lived in subsidized housing. Programs of the Department of Housing and Urban Development (HUD) supported more than three million rental units — about 11 percent of all the occupied apartments in the country. About 1.2 million units were public housing; the rest came under various federal subsidized housing programs.

In his first budget and in most years thereafter, Reagan proposed severe cuts in housing subsidies, particularly for programs to construct housing for the poor. Federal spending for subsidized housing dropped from $30 billion to $10 billion in four years.

Immediately upon taking office, Reagan sought to reduce the number of additional subsidized units to 210,000 for fiscal 1981, from the 254,500 recommended by President Jimmy Carter, and to 175,000 from 260,000 for fiscal 1982. Congress not only accepted the 1981 reductions but lowered the number authorized in the fiscal 1982 budget to 153,000. By the fiscal 1984 budget, the number of housing units authorized was down to 100,000.

Reagan wanted to take the federal government out of the business of building housing for the poor, and by and large he succeeded. In place of traditional construction programs Reagan supported the use of vouchers, which poor families could use like cash toward rent for housing they found on their own. Under existing housing subsidy programs, the subsidy went to the landlord or developer to encourage the provision of low-income housing. The subsidy was the difference between the market price of the rental unit and what the poor family could afford to pay.

With the housing supply supplemented by an administration-backed program to rehabilitate decaying dwellings, poor families could use vouchers to find existing housing on the free market, Reagan contended. Congress agreed to test the idea on a limited basis.

In justifying cutbacks in housing programs, the administration consistently rejected claims of a housing shortage in the United States. A controversial report by HUD in 1984 found evidence of 250,000 to 350,000 homeless persons nationwide, far short of the number private social welfare groups had estimated.

Private Housing Market

Confronted with the worst housing industry depression since World War II, Congress in 1982 approved legislation intended to stimulate single-family home construction by subsidizing interest rates for buyers of new homes. But Reagan vetoed the bill, which he labeled a "budget-busting bailout."

As interest rates dropped in late 1982, the private housing industry experienced a dramatic recovery, easing pressure for legislative action. Private housing starts, which had fallen below 1.1 billion annually in 1981 and 1982, surged to 1.7 billion annually in 1983-84.

Congress in 1984 approved legislation designed to increase the supply of mortgage money for homebuyers.

Urban Aid

From the outset of his administration Reagan sought to reduce the federal role in solving urban problems while increasing incentives for private sector initiatives.

Initially the administration wanted to save only those community development grants that would be matched with private or local funds. Unable to persuade Congress to accept that concept, the administration sought to loosen

References

Discussion of housing and urban aid action for the years 1945-64 may be found in *Congress and the Nation Vol. I*, pp. 459-515; for the years 1965-68, *Congress and the Nation Vol. II*, pp. 183-226; for the years 1969-72, *Congress and the Nation Vol. III*, pp. 635-657; for the years 1973-76, *Congress and the Nation Vol. IV*, pp. 471-502; for the years 1977-80, *Congress and the Nation Vol. V*, pp. 429-448.

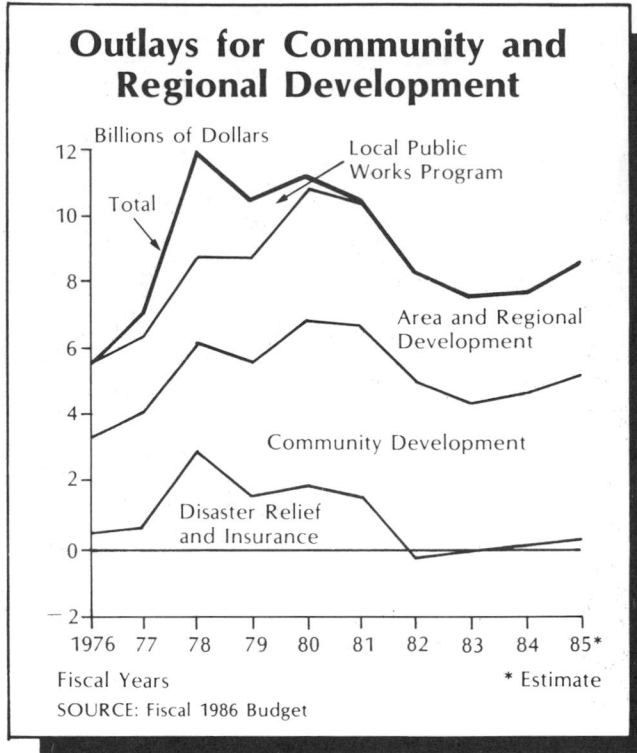

Outlays for Community and Regional Development

Billions of Dollars

Local Public Works Program

Total

Area and Regional Development

Community Development

Disaster Relief and Insurance

Fiscal Years   * Estimate

SOURCE: Fiscal 1986 Budget

the federal strings attached to the grants. Several federal requirements were eliminated in 1981 only to be restored in 1983 as Democrats argued that the government needed to be assured the money was being spent as Congress intended.

In his first budget Reagan proposed folding the Urban Development Action Grant (UDAG) program, which provided matching funds for private development in distressed urban areas, into the Community Development Block Grant (CDBG) program. The CDBG program gave cities a lump sum to use for activities such as housing rehabilitation, slum clearance or the construction of public buildings. Administration officials predicted that UDAGs would be phased out, but following a rebuff by Congress in 1981 the president recommended full funding for the program.

Fiscal Assistance

Reagan made little headway with his proposal to create "enterprise zones" to revive decaying urban areas, an idea he had promoted in the 1980 presidential campaign. The plan involved providing federal tax and regulatory relief to encourage businesses to locate or remain in designated zones in economically depressed neighborhoods. Congress — including some members of the president's own party in the Senate — was skeptical about the idea, and the proposal never became law.

The 1981-82 recession stiffened congressional opposition to Reagan's plans to abolish existing fiscal assistance programs. But lawmakers resisted the temptation to turn the programs into anti-recession measures to combat joblessness, as they had done in past recessions.

Reagan wanted to eliminate the Economic Development Administration (EDA), a relic of the "Great Society" of the 1960s that provided money for job-creating public works improvements. Congress insisted on continued funding for EDA, although at sharply reduced levels. EDA had been the vehicle for a separate $6 billion local public works program pushed by Democrats to combat the 1974-75 recession, but the bulk of the spending came after the recession ended. *(Graph, this page)*

Congress also won Reagan's agreement to a three-year extension of the general revenue sharing program of grants to local governments — but without the anti-recession aid that had been attached to the program in the 1970s. Reagan initially had recommended creation of a block grant that would combine revenue sharing and CDBGs. *(1981-84 action on fiscal assistance measures, p. 113)*

Chronology
Of Action
On Housing, Urban Aid

1981

Housing Authorization

President Reagan won much of what he requested for Department of Housing and Urban Development (HUD) programs in the budget-cutting reconciliation bill (HR 3982 — PL 97-35) cleared by Congress July 31.

For subsidized housing, Congress cut even more from the fiscal 1982 budget than the president requested. In March, Reagan proposed funds for 175,000 additional units of subsidized housing in fiscal 1982, a substantial cut from the 260,000 units proposed by the outgoing Carter administration. Subsidized housing included the Section 8 rental assistance program and public housing, which was owned and operated by public housing authorities.

The reconciliation bill authorized $18.09 billion for assisted housing, which would cover about 153,000 additional units in fiscal 1982. That was down from the House version of 158,000 units but a hike from the Senate proposal of 150,000 units. *(1983 authorization, p. 635)*

Congress also met Reagan's request to ease federal controls over Community Development Block Grants (CDBGs), which cities and counties used for a variety of urban projects. The amount authorized for the grants for fiscal 1982 was $4.17 billion, with $500 million set aside for the popular Urban Development Action Grant (UDAG) program. UDAG funds were intended to help local governments stimulate private development.

Reagan at one time proposed combining UDAG with the block grants, but Congress did not go along with that suggestion. In addition, Reagan wanted states, rather than the federal government, to administer the community development grants to small cities — those with populations under 50,000. Congress instead gave states the option to administer the small-cities program.

The 1974 Emergency Home Purchase Assistance Act (PL 93-449) failed to be reauthorized when conferees did not include House language extending the law through 1982. The Senate bill had no similar provision. The act was designed to aid the housing industry by allowing the government to buy conventional mortgages that were not government insured.

Congress also decided to phase out the Section 235 low-income homeownership assistance program.

The fiscal 1982 HUD appropriations bill (HR 4034 — PL 97-101), cleared Dec. 10, provided $17.37 billion for assisted housing, an amount expected to support 142,231 additional units. The bill also provided $3.46 billion for the CDBG program and $439.68 million for UDAG.

Legislative History

Funding authorizations for the Housing and Urban Development Department (HUD) became entangled in the reconciliation process in June, when House Banking Committee Democrats tried to thwart Senate efforts to cut back drastically on HUD programs. Hoping to avoid a direct conference with a housing authorization bill passed by the Senate June 3 (S 1197 — S Rept 97-87), the House committee attached its more generous housing measure to HR 3982, the budget-cutting reconciliation bill required by the first fiscal 1982 budget resolution. *(Reconciliation, p. 40)*

Senate Republicans, led by Banking Committee Chairman Jake Garn, R-Utah, thereupon added their HUD authorization to the Senate reconciliation package (S 2774), thus ensuring a conference on housing programs as part of the reconciliation process.

By the time the reconciliation bill got to conference, however, few controversies remained. Most House-Senate differences had been eliminated June 26 when the House adopted a Republican substitute for the reconciliation measure brought to the floor by Democratic leaders. The Republican substitute, known as "Gramm-Latta II," trimmed new housing units from 176,000 to 158,000 and revised the CDBG program, bringing the House much closer to the Senate position on housing issues.

The reconciliation conference report (H Rept 97-208), filed July 29, included the following agreements reached by conferees on the bill's housing provisions:

● **Rent Control.** Conferees agreed to drop a Senate provision that would have prohibited cities with rent control laws from receiving Section 8 money for new units or for substantial rehabilitation.

In exchange, House conferees agreed to drop a provision requiring state insurance plans for high-risk areas to charge policyholders in those areas the same rate as charged in the private market.

● **Income Eligibility.** The Senate had lowered the income eligibility requirement for new tenants in assisted housing to 50 percent of an area's median income, down from the existing 80 percent. The House did not include that provision.

Conferees came up with a three-part compromise that basically left the eligibility standard at 80 percent.

● **Public Housing Operating Subsidies.** Conferees agreed to $1.5 billion for operating subsidies. The House had proposed $1.6 billion; the Senate, $1.2 billion.

● **Government National Mortgage Association (GNMA).** The Senate agreed to a House provision that set the GNMA's authority to purchase mortgages at $1.97 billion. The Senate figure was $3.2 billion.

● **UDAG.** The House accepted a Senate provision that left UDAG as a separate entity, authorized at $500 million for fiscal 1982 and 1983. The House had made UDAG a separate item in the discretionary fund of the HUD secretary, authorized at $500 million for fiscal 1982.

● **Block Grants**. While both the House and Senate had eased federal controls over CDBGs, the House accepted Senate provisions that required a more detailed application process.

Major Provisions

As signed into law Aug. 13, the Housing and Community Development Amendments of 1981 (Title III of HR 3982 — PL 97-35):

Community Development

● Authorized $4.17 billion annually for fiscal 1982 and 1983, including $500 million each year for the UDAG program.

● **Public Participation.** Required that citizens be told the amount of funds available to a grantee and the proposed use of the money.

● Required an opportunity for citizens to comment on the applicant's performance in community development.

● Required a grantee to hold at least one public hearing.

● Required a grantee to certify to HUD that it had complied with requirements concerning publication of its statement of goals and citizen participation.

● **Housing Assistance Plans.** Deleted an existing requirement that small, so-called "non-entitlement" communities competing for discretionary funds prepare housing assistance plans as a part of their community development grant applications.

● Modified the housing assistance plan requirement for a large (over 50,000 population) "entitlement" community — which received funds by a formula — to include an estimate of housing needs based on low-income persons residing or expected to reside in the community as a result of existing or projected employment opportunities and population.

● **Performance Review.** Required the HUD secretary annually to review communities' performances under their grants to determine if primary objectives were being met.

● **Planning.** Made community planning activities eligible for CDBG funds to replace the "Section 701" planning program that was eliminated.

● **State Option.** Gave states the option to administer the small-cities' CDBG program. If a state decided not to administer the program, HUD would continue to do so.

● Required any state that decided to administer a small-cities' program to certify to HUD that: the state engaged or would engage in community development planning; provided or would provide local governments with technical assistance for community development; would provide state community development funds that were at least 10 percent of the community development funds allocated to the state; and consulted with local elected officials in non-entitlement communities concerning distribution of the federal funds.

● **UDAG.** Retained the UDAG program as a separate entity, authorized at $500 million for each of fiscal 1982 and 1983.

● Provided that if no funds were set aside for UDAG after fiscal 1983, any amount that might later become available would be added to the CDBG account.

● **Rehabilitation Loans.** Extended Section 312 rehabilitation loans through fiscal 1982 but repealed the authorization of $129 million for fiscal 1982. Loans were to be available only from an existing revolving loan fund.

● **Urban Homesteading.** Authorized $13.47 million annually for fiscal 1982 and 1983 for the urban homesteading program.

● **Neighborhood Reinvestment.** Authorized the Neighborhood Reinvestment Corp. at $13.43 million for fiscal 1981 and $14.95 million for fiscal 1982.

Housing Programs

● **Assisted Housing.** Authorized $18.09 billion in fiscal 1982 for subsidized housing, for 153,000 additional units.

● Authorized $906.96 million in annual contract authority for the additional units.

● Set aside $75 million from the annual contract authority funds for comprehensive improvement assistance.

● **Housing Mix.** Provided that, nationally, the HUD secretary should enter into contracts that resulted in 55 percent of the subsidies being used for new units, while the remaining 45 percent would be used for rehabilitated housing.

● Required the HUD secretary to alter the housing mix in particular communities to accommodate the preferences of local officials. Such alteration would take place after HUD allocated funds to the communities and after HUD consulted with local housing agencies.

● **Set-Asides.** Set aside 17,000 units under the Section 8 rental assistance program for use by state housing finance agencies; not more than 4,000 Section 8 units for the Farmers Home Administration (FmHA); and 2,500 units under the Indian housing program.

● **Public Housing Subsidies.** Authorized $1.5 billion for fiscal 1982 for public housing operating subsidies.

● **Discretionary Funds.** Allowed the HUD secretary to keep up to 15 percent of the available contract authority for all assisted housing for specified purposes, including unforeseeable housing needs and services for the handicapped or for minority enterprises.

● **Troubled Projects.** Provided $4 million for fiscal 1982 to assist multifamily projects experiencing financial difficulties.

● **Income, Rent.** Set the rent for Section 8 and public housing tenants at the highest of three figures — 30 percent of the family's monthly adjusted income, 10 percent of the family's monthly gross income or that part of a family's welfare payments specifically designated to meet housing costs in states that adjusted welfare to cover housing. Existing law set rent at 25 percent of a family's monthly adjusted income or 5 percent of gross monthly income.

● Defined income to mean income from all sources of each member of the household, as determined by criteria established by HUD.

● Left the income eligibility standard for tenants in assisted housing generally at 80 percent of the area median income. However, some of the HUD secretary's discretion was restricted to allow persons who made more than 80 percent of the median income to live in subsidized housing.

In addition, nationally, only 10 percent of the occupants in existing housing as of Oct. 1, 1981, could have incomes between 50 and 80 percent of the median income. The remaining tenants must earn less than 50 percent of the median income.

Finally, as additional units became available, only 5 percent nationally could be occupied by persons whose incomes fell between 50 and 80 percent of the median income.

The conferees said they did not intend that every low-income housing project or individual program meet the specified percentages.

● **Rent Increases.** Limited rent increases in new or substantially rehabilitated Section 8 housing to the amount of operating cost increases incurred by owners of comparable projects in the area suitable for families eligible for the assistance. Where no comparable units existed, the secretary could approve the rent increase using "the best available data" regarding operating cost increases in rental units.

● **Fraud, Abuse.** Allowed public housing agencies to retain part of the funds they recovered from money wrongfully paid as a result of fraud and abuse.

● **Income Mix.** Directed the HUD secretary to rescind a regulation that required an owner of assisted housing projects, during the initial renting of units, to rent 30

percent of the units to very-low-income families and to try to maintain 30 percent occupancy by such families. After the initial renting, the owner was to use his "best efforts" to keep 30 percent occupancy of such members.

● **Section 235 Homeownership.** Extended the authorization for the program through fiscal 1982 but set March 31, 1982, as the deadline for making any new HUD financial commitments.

● **Mobile Homes.** Allowed Section 8 subsidies to be used for units in mobile home parks under specified conditions.

● **FHA Interest.** Extended through Sept. 30, 1982, the HUD secretary's authority to set the Federal Housing Administration (FHA) interest rate above the statutory maximum of 6 percent to meet the market rate.

● **Emergency Assistance.** Ended the authorization for the 1974 Emergency Home Purchase Assistance Act (PL 93-449). *(Congress and the Nation Vol. IV, p. 483)*

● **GNMA.** Set the authority of the association to purchase mortgages in fiscal 1982 at $1.97 billion.

● **FHA Insurance.** Set the limit for FHA insurance authority at $41 billion for fiscal 1982.

● **Elderly, Handicapped.** Set HUD's borrowing limit for elderly and handicapped housing at $6.1 billion in fiscal 1982, some $830 million more than the fiscal 1981 level.

● **Loan Limits.** Increased HUD loan limits for a variety of housing programs, including home improvements for single-family residences, general improvements for apartments, loans for manufactured homes and for lots on which manufactured homes could be placed.

● **Counseling.** Authorized up to $6 million for housing counseling assistance in fiscal 1982 and up to $4 million in fiscal 1983.

● **New Communities.** Authorized up to $33.25 million for new communities in fiscal 1982.

● **Congregate Services.** Authorized $40 million for fiscal 1982 for the congregate services programs, which provided aid, including meals and some medical services, to low-income elderly and handicapped persons at home.

Flood, Crime and Riot Insurance

● Extended authorizations for flood, crime and riot insurance through Sept. 30, 1982; extended the urban riot reinsurance program through Sept. 30, 1985.

● Deleted a provision in the urban riot reinsurance program that required state insurance plans for high-risk areas to charge policyholders in those areas the same rate as charged in the private market.

Rural Housing

● Reauthorized for fiscal 1982 the following Farmers Home Administration loan and grant programs for rural housing: $50 million for loans and grants for repairing rural homes of very-low-income persons; $25 million for grants for housing for domestic farm workers; $2 million for rural housing technical assistance grants, with half earmarked for counseling buyers and delinquent borrowers; and $2 million for the program that reimbursed owners of FmHA-financed housing for construction defects.

● Extended through fiscal 1982 the $5 million authorization for the mutual and self-help housing assistance program, under which non-profit groups of low-income persons built their own homes with professional advice.

● Continued the rental assistance payment contracting authority, which provided rent subsidies for low-income individuals in rural areas.

● Authorized up to $3 million for capital for the land development fund and placed a new ceiling of $5 million on total site and acquisition loans in fiscal 1982.

Multi-Family Mortgage Foreclosure

● Provided a uniform, non-judicial procedure to cover HUD foreclosures on FHA-insured or HUD-assisted multi-family properties held by HUD and in default. The procedure replaced state laws. Conferees said the new owners — either HUD or another party — must continue the project as a subsidized residence, except in certain circumstances.

1982

Emergency Mortgage Aid

In the midst of the worst housing industry depression since World War II, Congress in 1982 approved an emergency mortgage subsidy program designed to revive the housing market. But President Reagan refused to sign the measure, and Congress failed to override his veto.

The $3 billion measure was inserted into an urgent fiscal 1982 supplemental appropriations bill (HR 5922), which was vetoed by the president June 24. The proposal was designed to stimulate single-family home construction and create jobs in the building trades by subsidizing interest rates for buyers of new homes. It was crafted by the home building and lumber industries, which were battered by the recession and high interest rates.

The president called the legislation a "budget-busting bailout." Noting that farmers, small businesses, the savings industry and automobile manufacturers also were suffering from the recession and high interest rates, Reagan said, "We cannot justify singling out one industry for special relief."

Legislative History

Senate Bill. The subsidy had its genesis in various other bills, notably a measure proposed by Sen. Richard G. Lugar, R-Ind. The measure, unanimously approved by the Senate Banking Committee April 21 (S 2226 — S Rept 97-362), was a $5.1 billion program that would have lowered the mortgage interest rate on new homes by as much as 4 percentage points. Subsidies would have been available to families with an annual income of $30,000 or less who were buying newly constructed homes. Lugar said the bill could put 700,000 persons back to work in construction-related jobs and spur up to 450,000 new housing starts in 1982.

House Democrats' Counterproposal. The House Banking Committee included a similar program, with a $3.5 billion price tag, in its fiscal 1983 housing authorization bill (HR 6296), but that measure never reached the House floor. *(Story, p. 634)*

Under pressure to help the recession-hit housing industry, House Democratic leaders agreed early in May to back a $1 billion mortgage subsidy bill (HR 6294). The bill was a cornerstone of a $2 billion jobs program to combat an unemployment rate that hit 9.4 percent in April. Other funds were to be funneled into public works projects to create jobs in the construction trades, where unemploy-

ment was 19.4 percent.

Appropriations Amendment. On May 11 the House passed HR 6294, authorizing $1 billion in 1982 to subsidize mortgage rates by as much as 6 percentage points. The next day it attached the $1 billion program to the supplemental appropriations bill by a **key vote of 343-67 (R 128-52; D 215-15).**

The Senate went along with the idea of including the mortgage subsidy in the supplemental appropriations bill. On May 27, it attached the full $5.1 billion Lugar plan to the funding bill by a **69-23 key vote (R 29-20; D 40-3).** *(1982 key votes, p. 895)*

Compromise Vetoed

Despite the threat of a presidential veto, House and Senate conferees on HR 5922 reached agreement in June on a $3 billion compromise for the mortgage subsidy program — halfway between the $5.1 billion approved by the Senate and the $1 billion backed by the House.

Of the $3 billion total for the program, $2.5 billion would have gone for mortgage subsidies for newly built homes. Families with incomes up to $30,000 a year would have been eligible for mortgages 4 percentage points below the market rate, down to an 11 percent rate.

Another $400 million would have been provided for mortgages on homes that had been built but not sold; the remaining funds were for subsidies on homes in "high cost" areas.

Reagan fulfilled his promise and vetoed the bill June 24. Later that day the House failed by 17 votes to obtain the two-thirds majority needed to override Reagan's veto. The vote was 253-151.

Housing Authorization

Congress adjourned without enacting a fiscal 1983 housing authorization bill, partly because of the reluctance of House Democrats to tailor their legislation to fit spending constraints set by President Reagan and the congressional budget resolution.

The House Banking Committee rejected Reagan's proposal to slash federal housing programs, and the panel's legislation far exceeded spending ceilings recommended by the president and the budget. It was not until December — too late for adequate floor consideration — that committee Democrats agreed to lower their sights and settle for a smaller housing program.

Subsidized housing funds were included in a continuing funding resolution (PL 97-377) cleared Dec. 20. The bill provided $8.65 billion for assisted housing and $2.5 billion for public housing modernization.

Congress enacted housing legislation in 1983. *(Story, p. 635; 1981 bill, p. 631)*

The authorization bills were reported by the House and Senate Banking committees in May (HR 6296 — H Rept 97-532, S 2607 — S Rept 97-463). The bills differed widely, but each included new housing production and rehabilitation initiatives to replace the troubled Section 8 rental assistance program, which had been criticized for its high costs and other shortcomings.

In a fundamental shift in federal housing policies, the administration wanted to end construction aid for low-income housing and instead to provide vouchers that poor families could apply toward rental housing. The House Banking Committee bill rejected the voucher plan, but the

Senate Banking Committee included a modified program in its bill.

Both bills exceeded the administration's funding request. Nearly all of the money in Reagan's fiscal 1983 housing budget would have come from rescissions, or cancellations, of funds previously obligated — including a rescission of $5 billion for subsidized housing — so virtually no new budget authority had been requested.

Both bills authorized $4.2 billion, the existing level, for Community Development Block Grants and Urban Development Action Grants.

A key point against the House committee bill was its $29.1 billion estimated cost for fiscal 1983. Controversy over the $14 billion Senate bill surrounded a proposal to convert Farmers Home Administration rural housing programs into block grants to the states.

Mortgage Assumption Plan

Provisions overriding state laws and judicial decisions banning enforcement of due-on-sale clauses in mortgage contracts were cleared on Oct. 1 as part of a savings and loan/banking bill (HR 6267 — PL 97-320). The provisions amplified a Supreme Court ruling restricting mortgage assumptions, while giving homeowners in certain states a three-year reprieve from the bill's tightened regulations.

The provisions, a compromise worked out with the real estate and savings industries, originally were included in the Senate Banking Committee's version of the bill. The Senate included them in HR 6267, passed Sept. 24, and House conferees accepted the Senate plan with minor changes. *(Savings and loan/banking bill, p. 87)*

Due-on-sale clauses required homeowners to pay off a mortgage when they sold their homes, denying new buyers the right to take over an old, low-cost loan. About 18 states had prohibited financial institutions from enforcing due-on-sale in an effort to help promote home sales through mortgage assumptions during a period of high interest rates.

By preventing mortgage assumptions without a lender's approval, due-on-sale provisions gave banks and savings institutions more flexibility during a period of volatile interest rates. With the skyrocketing rates of the past few years, lenders said they needed the tool so they could unload old, fixed-rate mortages and replace them with higher-yielding loans.

The Supreme Court June 28, in a victory for the savings industry, had overturned state laws barring due-on-sale enforcement by federally chartered savings and loan associations.

The bill took the court decision a step further by extending it to mortgages issued by commercial banks, mortgage banks and state-chartered savings institutions.

To appease beleaguered home sellers, however, the bill excluded from the new rules mortgages originated or assumed during a "window period." The period began on the date a state restricted due-on-sale enforcement and ended on the bill's enactment date, Oct. 15.

Federal savings and loan associations and federal savings banks were exempt from the "window period" provision because they fell under a 1976 Federal Home Loan Bank Board rule allowing due-on-sale clauses. The June 28 Supreme Court ruling upheld the bank board regulation.

In another concession to the real estate industry, the bill included non-binding language encouraging lenders to

negotiate blended rates when mortgages were assumed. With blended rates, lenders would meet borrowers halfway by providing loans at a level between the original interest rate and the current market rate.

The bill also delayed until July 1, 1983, a ban on mortgage assumptions proposed by the Federal Home Loan Mortgage Corp.

Other Legislation

FHA Insurance Premiums

Congress approved legislation requiring home buyers to pay a lump-sum premium for Federal Housing Administration (FHA) mortgage insurance, instead of spreading payments over the life of a mortgage. The change, expected to yield three-year budget savings of about $2 billion, was included in a budget reconciliation bill (HR 6955 — PL 97-253) cleared Aug. 18. *(Story, p. 48)*

Enterprise Zones

President Reagan March 23 sent to Congress his enterprise zone proposal, urging tax breaks and regulatory relief for businesses that provided new jobs in blighted areas. The enterprise zone plan did not reach a floor vote in 1982. It also failed in the 98th Congress. *(Stories, pp. 117, 119)*

1983

Housing Authorization

Congress and the White House put aside some of the sharp divisions that for two years had stymied an overhaul of housing programs and agreed in November on a compromise $15.6 billion housing reauthorization.

Although President Reagan objected to several provisions, he signed the bill Nov. 30 (HR 3959 — PL 98-181) because it was attached to legislation that he wanted badly — an $8.4 billion increase in the U.S. contribution to the International Monetary Fund (IMF). Both were added to a supplemental fiscal 1984 funding bill. *(IMF increase, p. 104)*

The maneuver of linking the housing and IMF provisions was engineered by House Banking Committee Chairman Fernand J. St Germain, D-R.I., to force enactment of a housing authorization in 1983.

The tactic broke a months-long logjam over the legislation. The House passed its version of the bill July 13, after cutting its $24.3 billion funding by one-third and making other changes. But the $17.6 billion Senate bill ran into serious trouble and was pulled from the floor June 21. Negotiations between congressional leaders and the administration produced the compromise measure that was cleared on the final day of the session, Nov. 18.

The Housing and Rural Recovery Act authorized a new program of grants for the rehabilitation and construction of rental housing, expected to produce 31,000 new units and 30,000 rehabilitated units. While some adminis-

tration proposals were rejected, the legislation included a Reagan initiative to replace a subsidy system with housing vouchers that low-income persons would apply toward rental housing, although at a reduced level.

The legislation reflected a drive by House Democrats to reverse policies set by the 1981 budget reconciliation bill, in which committee-approved recommendations on housing policy had been supplanted by Reagan administration proposals. *(1981 action, p. 631)*

Background

Reagan's fiscal 1984 budget recycled many of his earlier housing proposals, once again calling for a sharp cut in subsidized housing funds and a program of cash vouchers to provide housing for the poor.

The administration proposed cutting new budget authority for subsidized housing programs run by the Department of Housing and Urban Development (HUD) and the Agriculture Department from an estimated level of $5.7 billion in 1983 to approximately $400 million in 1984, after the rescission of previously obligated funds. Despite the steep decline, outlays for housing assistance were to rise from $9.6 billion in 1983 to $10.8 billion in 1984 because of commitments made in earlier years.

The cornerstone of the administration's HUD budget was the replacement of most low-income housing construction with a less costly voucher plan. Under the $1.36 billion program, 80,000 families and individuals would receive cash value certificates to apply toward the rent in existing housing they would find themselves. Each voucher would be worth about $2,000 a year.

All new subsidized households for 1984, except for 10,000 units for the elderly and handicapped, would come under the administration's proposed voucher program. Families would be expected to pay up to 30 percent of their income for rent. The federal subsidy would be the difference between the tenant contribution and a "reasonable rent level," which would be based on local market prices.

Senate Action

The Senate Banking Committee April 13 unanimously approved a $17.6 billion housing authorization bill (S 1338 — S Rept 98-142) that ignored Reagan administration proposals for sharp cuts in federal housing programs.

S 1338 reauthorized Community Development Block Grants for three years, created a modified new rental rehabilitation program and provided $7.65 billion in low-income housing subsidies in fiscal 1984.

The committee rejected several policy changes requested by the administration, including a proposal to count food stamps as income when calculating the amount tenants paid for government-assisted housing and a recommendation to convert rural housing programs into a new block grant.

The full Senate considered and substantially revised the bill June 21, but the threat of an extended and acrimonious debate forced the leadership to pull it from the floor.

Before putting aside the bill, the Senate adopted by voice vote an amendment offered by Banking Committee Chairman Jake Garn, R-Utah, and Housing Subcommittee Chairman John Tower, R-Texas. The amendment, designed to gain support for the bill, added some $351 million to the authorization, bringing the total close to $17.9 billion.

House Action

The House Banking Subcommittee on Housing April 26 approved HR 1, providing an estimated $24.6 billion in new budget authority. Subcommittee Democrats unanimously supported the bill; Republican members uniformly opposed it.

The subcommittee ignored the administration's request to disband low-income housing construction programs. Instead, it included a new $1.3 billion multi-family housing production program aimed at areas with critical rental housing shortages. The subcommittee also voted down a voucher demonstration project based on Reagan's proposal.

The full Banking Committee approved the bill May 10 by voice vote (H Rept 98-123). Although the Banking panel attached more than 20 amendments to HR 1, the committee essentially ratified the work of the subcommittee.

The House passed the bill July 13, 263-158, after slashing the housing funding by about one-third, to $15.6 billion.

Final Action

Although negotiations continued in an effort to bring the Senate bill back to the floor, by late summer supporters were pessimistic. The bill was "almost impossible to pass," Garn said.

Meanwhile, St Germain continued to insist that the Senate move on the housing bill as a condition of support for the IMF bill. That legislation was pending before a conference committee, which St Germain would chair.

"If the Senate doesn't act on a housing bill," St Germain said, "then the Senate will have killed the IMF."

Recognizing that St Germain was adamant, key administration officials in late September began negotiating with Garn and St Germain on a compromise housing bill linked with the IMF. Weeks of intense negotiations produced the package that Garn offered Nov. 17 as a floor amendment to the conference report on the fiscal 1984 supplemental appropriations bill. The Senate adopted the amendment, and the House cleared the measure Nov. 18.

Provisions

As signed into law Nov. 30, the housing provisions of HR 3959 (PL 98-181):

Community Development

● **Community Development Block Grants.** Authorized $3.468 billion in each of fiscal 1984, 1985 and 1986 for Community Development Block Grants, and required that $68.2 million, at most, be set aside each year for the secretary's discretionary fund.

Congress had appropriated $4.456 billion for fiscal 1983, including $1 billion provided in a jobs and anti-recession relief measure (PL 98-8) cleared March 22.

● Required cities and communities to spend at least 51 percent of their aid to benefit low- and moderate-income persons.

● Raised the percentage of public service activities eligible for funding from 10 percent to 15 percent.

● Allowed entitlement cities and urban counties that would be ineligible because of lost population to continue to receive entitlement grants through fiscal 1985.

● Required that, after fiscal 1984, a decision by a state to

administer the grant program for small cities would be permanent and final, allowing HUD to administer the program if states elected not to, and required that the governor of each state administering the program certify that each unit of local government be required to identify its community and housing needs, including the needs of low- and moderate-income persons.

● Restricted loan guarantees to certain grant recipients who could not complete the financing of an activity on time without the loan, and limited the total amount of guaranteed loans to $225 million in fiscal 1984.

● **Urban Development Action Grants.** Authorized $440 million in each of fiscal 1984, 1985 and 1986 for Urban Development Action Grants, including up to $2.5 million in each year for technical assistance to small cities.

● Clarified that cities of 50,000 or more that were eligible for assistance in fiscal 1983 would continue to be eligible until the secretary revised the standards for eligibility.

● Permitted cities of less than 50,000 that were near one another to apply for assistance as consortia.

● **Urban Homesteading.** Authorized $12 million in fiscal 1984 and $8 million in fiscal 1985 to transfer property to local governments with homesteading programs.

● Extended the required occupancy of a homesteaded property from three to five years prior to the homesteader's receipt of fee simple title, and extended time limits for completion of required repair work.

● Established a demonstration multi-family homesteading program, and required at least 75 percent of the occupants of multi-family homestead properties to be lower-income families.

● Earmarked $1 million for a demonstration project providing assistance to state and local governments for the purchase of real property.

● **Neighborhood Development.** Authorized $2 million in each of fiscal 1984 and 1985 for a demonstration neighborhood development program to create jobs, expand businesses, develop housing or deliver necessary services. The grants would match funds neighborhood development organizations raised privately. Individual grants were limited to $50,000 per year.

● **Section 312 Rehabilitation Loans.** Extended the rehabilitation loan program through fiscal 1984 with no additional authorization.

● **Neighborhood Investment Corporation.** Authorized $16.5 million in fiscal 1984 and such sums as necessary in fiscal 1985 for the independent corporation to stimulate private sector neighborhood revitalization.

Housing Aid

● Authorized $9.9 billion in budget authority in fiscal 1984 for housing assistance programs. That was expected to support 100,000 units.

● Granted priority for assisted housing to persons and families paying more than 50 percent of income for rent.

● Retained the requirement that tenants in assisted housing pay 30 percent of their income in rent, but established statutory deductions from income that would substantially reduce rents, including $480 per child, $400 for any elderly or handicapped family, medical expenses above 3 percent of income for elderly and handicapped, and child care expenses.

● **Housing Vouchers.** Authorized $242 million for a demonstration housing voucher program, providing certificates to low-income families to be used toward rent. This

was expected to support 15,000 units.

● Set a contract term with public housing agencies for an initial period of five years, and permitted up to two rent adjustments.

● **Public Housing.** Authorized $1.29 billion for fiscal 1984 for public housing, of which $390 million was available for Indian housing. This was expected to support 7,500 units of public housing and 2,500 units of Indian housing.

● Repealed the Section 8 rental assistance new construction program.

● Increased the limitation on single-person occupancy in public housing to 30 percent, if units were not expected to be occupied by families.

● Authorized the use of rental assistance funds for people living in single-room occupancy housing.

● Authorized a demonstration child care program using Community Development Block Grant funds.

● **Elderly, Handicapped.** Authorized $666.4 million in fiscal 1984 for Section 202 units for the elderly and handicapped, expected to fund 14,000 units.

● Authorized funds from existing housing and moderate rehabilitation programs to be used to assist elderly families who elected to live in shared housing arrangements.

● Set the interest rate for Section 202 loans for the elderly and handicapped at 9.25 percent.

● Eliminated the requirement for competitive bidding in construction contracts when the project development cost was less than $2 million, if the project rents would be less than 110 percent of the fair market rents for elderly and handicapped, or if the sponsor was a labor organization.

● Limited the number of efficiency units in a project to 25 percent, unless more was requested by the sponsor.

● Barred owners or managers of federally assisted rental housing from prohibiting elderly or handicapped tenants from owning common pets.

● **Joint HUD/HHS Program.** Authorized $10 million in fiscal 1984 and $15 million in fiscal 1985 to provide a workable linkage between HUD housing assistance and Health and Human Services housing and welfare aid.

● **Section 235 Homeownership Assistance.** Authorized payments to subsidize mortgage payments for a 10-year period but authorized no new budget authority.

● **Homeless Assistance.** Authorized $60 million in fiscal 1984 for grants to states, local governments, Indian tribes and non-profit groups to shelter the homeless.

● **Congregate Services.** Authorized $4 million in fiscal 1984 for the Congregate Housing Services Program and required a report on changes in the administration of the program by March 15, 1984.

New Rental Program

● Authorized $615 million in fiscal 1984 and 1985, including $150 million in fiscal 1984 for rehabilitation and $200 million for new construction, and $150 million in fiscal 1985 for rehabilitation and $115 million for new construction.

● Required rehabilitation grants to be based on a formula, and required construction grants to be available only to communities with a severe rental housing shortage.

● Required 100 percent of grants to benefit lower-income families. This requirement could be reduced to 70 percent if the recipient certified the reduction was necessary, and could be reduced to not less than 50 percent based on the secretary's determination.

● Allowed a structure to be assisted only if rehabilitation

or development would not cause involuntary displacement of very-low-income families by families who were not very-low-income.

● Limited grant assistance to 50 percent of the total costs associated with rehabilitation and development.

● Prohibited the conversion to condominiums or cooperative ownership for 10 years in the case of rehabilitation grants and 20 years in the case of development grants.

● **Rehabilitation.** Restricted grants to neighborhoods where the median income did not exceed 80 percent of the area median income.

● Required the secretary to assure an equitable distribution of funds for families, including large families with children, and required priority for projects containing units in substandard conditions occupied by very-low-income families.

● **Development.** Required at least 20 percent of the units, during a 20-year period, to be occupied by persons whose income did not exceed 80 percent of the area median income.

● Established criteria for selection, including the severity of rental shortages, non-federal public and private funds, maximum utilization of units for the least cost and the extent to which housing for lower-income persons and families was being met.

● Required the secretary to give priority for selection to those projects that exceeded the minimum requirement of at least 20 percent occupancy by persons whose income did not exceed 80 percent of the area median, projects in areas with long waiting lists for rental housing, and where there were fewer housing units available under other assisted housing programs.

● Limited rents for lower-income families to 30 percent of the adjusted income for families whose income equaled 50 percent of the area median income.

● Permitted states to administer funds for cities of less than 50,000, and permitted a state to administer its own rehabilitation or development program or distribute grants to units of local government.

● Exempted Davis-Bacon prevailing wage requirements for structures containing fewer than 12 units.

● Barred assistance to structures if the state or local government enacted a rent control statute after enactment.

Rural Housing

● **Farmers Home Administration (FmHA).** Required that not less than 40 percent of the units financed by Section 502 loans be available for very-low-income families or persons, and that 30 percent of the units in each state financed by Section 502 be available for very-low-income occupants.

● Permitted Section 502 loans to finance manufactured homes, providing that the home met requirements for any other home.

● Permitted loans under Section 504 to very-low-income families to improve or modernize rural homes.

● Directed FmHA to target rental aid to very-low-income families.

● Limited to 10 percent the amount of farm labor housing grants that could be used for grants to non-profit organizations for farm-worker housing outreach.

● Raised the tenant rent contribution for Section 515 rental assistance to 30 percent of income, and the definition of income was changed to conform to HUD programs.

● **Rural Housing Preservation Grants.** Authorized

$100 million in each of fiscal 1984 and 1985 for a new program of grants to communities for rehabilitation of single-family or rental housing owned or occupied by low- and very-low-income persons or families.

● Required the secretary, in making grants, to give priority to families whose income did not exceed 50 percent of the area median income, to areas with populations below 10,000, and to repair and rehabilitation activities that would produce the greatest improvement at the least cost.

Mortgage Aid

A widespread belief that the recession was ending helped to block renewed efforts in 1983 to provide emergency mortgage assistance for the unemployed.

The House May 11 narrowly approved a bill (HR 1983 — H Rept 98-32) authorizing $760 million in direct loans in fiscal 1983. The bill called for a revolving loan fund to aid some 100,000 homeowners threatened with foreclosure.

The administration strongly opposed the measure, which was a key part of the Democrats' anti-recession program. Critics forced Democrats to tighten the eligibility requirements during floor consideration.

Debate began April 19, but the measure repeatedly was pulled from the floor because the Democrats lacked sufficient votes to pass it. The bill finally passed on a **216-196 key vote (R 6-155; D 210-41)**. *(1983 key votes, p. 911)*

The Senate did not consider the House measure, and a plan pushed by some members to provide up to $750 million in loan guarantees was dropped from the fiscal 1984 housing authorization bill (S 1338 — S Rept 98-142) during floor debate June 21. An effort to add the mortgage guarantee plan to a fiscal 1984 appropriations bill (HR 3133) failed the same day.

Veterans' Aid. In related action, the House May 24 passed a bill (HR 2948 — H Rept 98-118) to help unemployed veterans avoid losing their homes. Passed by a 394-23, the bill would have allowed the Veterans Administration to use up to $150 million from its revolving fund for mortgage aid. The Senate did not consider the measure.

Mortgage Revenue Bonds

A popular program allowing states to increase the supply of mortgage money by issuing tax-exempt bonds expired Dec. 31 after Congress failed to extend the program.

The reauthorization was included in a tax measure (HR 4170 — H Rept 98-432) reported by the Ways and Means Committee Oct. 21. Congress completed action on the bill in 1984, extending the mortgage revenue bond program through 1987. *(Story, this page)*

1984

Housing Funds

Congress did not enact a housing authorization bill in 1984, but in approving a $12.1 billion appropriations bill

for the Department of Housing and Urban Development (HUD) and other agencies, lawmakers put their own stamp on the administration's housing policy. The bill (HR 5713 — PL 98-371), cleared June 27, provided 100,000 additional units of subsidized housing as the president had requested, but Congress rejected administration proposals on what type of housing should be funded.

Balking at an administration plan to provide cash vouchers — which could be used much like food stamps to apply toward rent — for 91,000 units, Congress limited the new voucher program to 38,500 units. But it also provided funding for 37,500 Section 8 rental units and 5,000 public housing apartments, both traditional assisted housing programs.

The administration wanted to substitute vouchers for the existing subsidy system in which payments were made to owners of private housing to make up the difference between what the tenant could pay and the market rent. The voucher system had been authorized in 1983 housing legislation. *(Story, p. 635)*

Mortgage Revenue Bonds

The 1984 deficit reduction bill (HR 4170 — PL 98-369) reinstated a popular program allowing states to increase the supply of mortgage money by issuing tax-exempt bonds. The bill, cleared June 27, reauthorized the program through 1987. The authority had expired Dec. 31, 1983. *(Background, Congress and the Nation Vol. V, p. 249)*

Under the program state or local housing finance agencies sold bonds to investors, who accepted lower interest rates on the bonds in return for federal tax exemption on the interest income. Proceeds from the sale were funneled into mortgage funds. Because the state paid a lower interest rate to the bondholder, it could charge the home buyer an interest rate below market levels.

State and local governments and housing industry officials strongly backed the program as a way of making low-cost mortgage money available. States had been using the program since 1970, cities since 1978.

The Reagan administration opposed extension of the tax exemption because of the loss of revenue to the Treasury. In 1981 and 1982 tax-exempt mortgage revenue bonds cost the federal government a total of more than $2.6 billion in lost revenue, according to the General Accounting Office. *(Deficit reduction bill, p. 79)*

Mortgage-Backed Securities

Despite some objections from the banking industry, the Congress Sept. 26 cleared a bill (S 2040 — PL 98-440) to make it easier for private companies to buy mortgages from banks and to sell securities backed by them.

The purpose of S 2040 was to increase the amount of money available for mortgages by removing impediments private companies had faced in dealing with mortgage-backed securities.

The bill removed some regulatory hurdles firms had encountered in entering the secondary mortgage market and maintained some protections for investors. It also expanded the authority of two federally backed mortgage corporations, allowing them to purchase loans on mobile homes and second mortgages.

The bill had been reported (S Rept 98-293) Nov. 2,

1983, by the Senate Banking Committee. The Senate passed the bill Nov. 17, 1983, followed by passage of a corrected version Feb. 9, 1984. The House passed an amended version Sept. 11, and the Senate approved the House changes Sept. 26.

Other Legislation

Enterprise Zones

President Reagan's enterprise zone plan to promote the development of inner cities failed to win congressional approval for the third year in a row.

The Senate included the enterprise zone proposal in its version of 1984 deficit reduction legislation (HR 4170 — PL 98-369), but the plan was dropped in conference with the House. The proposal was intended to bring jobs and development to decaying areas by providing tax breaks for businesses that located in them. *(Details, p. 119)*

Community Development Funds

In appropriating fiscal 1985 funds for the Department of Housing and Urban Development (HR 5713 — PL 98-371), Congress provided the full $3.47 billion for Community Development Block Grants that Congress had authorized in 1983. Those grants gave cities a lump sum to use for activities such as housing rehabilitation, slum clearance or the construction of public buildings. Urban Development Action Grants, which provided matching grants to distressed urban areas to stimulate economic activity, were funded at $440 million, also the amount authorized.

In addition, local governments received $4.6 billion under the general revenue sharing program. *(Fiscal assistance programs, p. 113)*

Labor and Pension Policy

Introduction　　　　　*643*
1981 Chronology　　　*645*
1982 Chronology　　　*651*
1983 Chronology　　　*658*
1984 Chronology　　　*667*

Labor and Pension Policy

The first Reagan administration was a period of great stress for American workers. The nation experienced its worst recession in half a century, driving the unemployment rate to a post-World War II peak of 10.7 percent at the end of 1982. Factories shut down across the country, amid fears that many jobs would never return. Import competition took a severe toll.

President Reagan opposed "make-work" jobs programs and other efforts to cushion the recession's impact. The new Republican president counted on restored economic growth to create jobs. He believed the government's role in job creation should be limited principally to providing incentives for private sector hiring and training of the hard-to-employ.

Congressional Democrats, who had responded to the recessions of the 1970s with massive job creation programs, were unable to use the same stimulants again. As the federal deficit mounted, costly Democratic jobs proposals fell before the budget-cutting pressures of the 1980s. A $71 billion highway and mass transit repair program was enacted at the end of 1982, but the program was to be financed through an increase in the federal gasoline tax. Reagan backed that measure, while denying that it was a jobs program. In addition, Congress and the president reached agreement early in 1983 on $4.6 billion in short-term funding for jobs and recession relief.

Legislation with long-term significance for American workers also was enacted early in 1983, as Congress and Reagan reached agreement on a measure to rescue the Social Security system from impending insolvency. The legislation followed the recommendations of a bipartisan commission that was appointed to depoliticize the highly emotional retirement issue.

The influence of organized labor continued to decline during the first Reagan term. Union leaders no longer had the clout they had enjoyed under Democratic administrations — with the notable exception of the Teamsters Union, which had backed Reagan in 1980. Reagan had won election in 1980 with the votes of more than 40 percent of union families, despite their leaders' endorsement of President Jimmy Carter. Union leaders had little contact with Reagan's labor secretary, Raymond J. Donovan, who resigned early in 1985 after he was indicted on larceny and fraud charges. Donovan had spent a good part of his four years in the Cabinet defending himself against charges that he had engaged in corrupt dealings as an officer of a New Jersey construction firm.

Labor Programs

The nation's jobless rate stood at 7.5 percent when Ronald Reagan took office in 1981; eight million people were unemployed, a figure that had fluctuated only slightly over the past year and a half. When Reagan called for sharp cuts in the federal budget, major labor programs were among the casualties.

Responding to Reagan's budget-cutting demands, Congress in 1981 cut the federal-state employment compensation program by more than $3.1 billion over fiscal 1982-84. Another $2.6 billion was slashed from the trade adjustment assistance program for workers who lost jobs as a result of competition from imports. As unemployment mounted in 1982, however, Congress voted to expand both programs.

At Reagan's behest Congress abolished the public service jobs program under the Comprehensive Employment and Training Act (CETA). CETA was a relatively easy target for Reagan because congressional support for the public service jobs program was already on the wane. He met with firm opposition, however, when he proposed eliminating smaller, more popular programs such as community service jobs for the elderly.

The administration backed an overhaul of training programs that eventually gave rise to the much smaller Job Training Partnership Act of 1982. The role of business and industry in running job training programs was greatly expanded under the 1982 act, which was funded at about $3.6 billion a year. In its heyday CETA distributed some $10 billion annually.

Rising unemployment in late 1982 made Congress increasingly sympathetic to direct federal jobs programs. As the unemployment rate reached its 10.7 percent peak in November and December 1982, and nearly 12 million peo-

References

Discussion of labor and pension policy for the years 1945-64 may be found in *Congress and the Nation Vol. I*, pp. 563-657, 1220-1224; for the years 1965-68, *Congress and the Nation Vol. II*, pp. 601-622, 734-743; for the years 1969-72, *Congress and the Nation Vol. III*, pp. 703-742; for the years 1973-76, *Congress and the Nation Vol. IV*, pp. 681-713; for the years 1977-80, *Congress and the Nation Vol. V*, pp. 399-425.

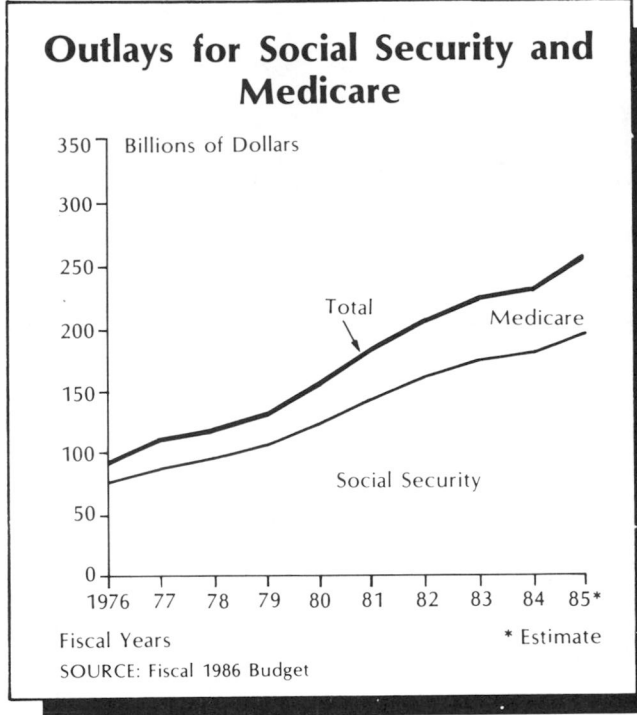

Outlays for Social Security and Medicare

Billions of Dollars

Total

Medicare

Social Security

1976 77 78 79 80 81 82 83 84 85*

Fiscal Years

* Estimate

SOURCE: Fiscal 1986 Budget

ple were out of work, Congress in its post-election session enacted legislation providing a 5-cents-a-gallon increase in the federal gasoline tax to pay for repairs to the nation's deteriorating roads and mass transit systems. President Reagan, who backed the bill, insisted it was not a jobs measure; supporters maintained it would create 300,000 jobs.

The president refused to accept direct funding for public works and other job-creating projects that both chambers included in a fiscal 1983 emergency spending measure during the 1982 lame-duck session. Facing a likely veto of the funding bill, Congress dropped the proposals.

In February 1983, under congressional pressure, Reagan abandoned his opposition to jobs legislation and proposed his own $4.3 billion recession relief plan. Congress in March approved $4.6 billion in jobs and recession relief spending for fiscal 1983; the package was tailored to win Reagan's acceptance.

House Democrats attempted to push further measures during 1983, including new jobs programs and measures to provide mortgage foreclosure relief and temporary health insurance for the unemployed. But their efforts were sidetracked as an unexpectedly robust economic recovery lowered the unemployment rate to 9.4 percent by July and 8.2 percent at year's end.

By May 1984 the jobless rate had fallen to 7.5 percent, the same rate Reagan had inherited when he took office in 1981, and Republicans in their 1984 party campaign platform could hail the administration for presiding over "the most rapid decline in unemployment of any post-World War II recovery."

However, major problems remained unresolved. No satisfactory solution had been found for unemployment problems stemming from the decline of basic industries and the displacement of workers whose job skills had become outmoded. And mounting demands for legislation to protect American workers from foreign competition posed an increasing threat to the administration's commitment to a free trade policy.

Pensions

In its most significant action on pension issues, Congress in 1983 approved major changes in the Social Security retirement program. Passage of the bill followed a two-year partisan fight over the future of the program that was provoked in 1981 by abortive administration attempts to cut benefits to keep the retirement system from insolvency.

Congressional Democrats and the administration found themselves at an impasse in 1981 over whether to cut benefits or raise taxes to keep retirement checks going to 36 million beneficiaries of the Old Age and Survivors Insurance Trust Fund. The political sensitivity of the issue threatened to prevent any solution acceptable to members of both parties.

The dilemma was resolved by the appointment of a 15-member National Commission on Social Security Reform on whose recommendations Congress was able quickly to fashion a compromise rescue package in early 1983. The key elements of the package included increased payroll taxes, a gradual rise in the retirement age and the inclusion of new federal employees under the system.

With elections just over the horizon, Congress in 1984 ended more than two years of legislative bickering and agreed to revamp a controversial Social Security disability review program. The bill was designed to make it more difficult for the administration to remove individuals from the disability benefit rolls. Congress acted in response to widespread complaints that the administration had been unduly zealous in carrying out a congressional mandate to cut down on waste in the disability program. Almost half of those reviewed had been disqualified from the program; many had their benefits restored on appeal.

With legislators eager to demonstrate their commitment to women in an election year, Congress in 1984 also approved legislation designed to make it easier for women to earn retirement benefits under private pension plans.

Chronology
Of Action
On Labor
And Pension Policy

1981

For labor the first session of the 97th Congress was marked by sagging legislative support, flourishing opposition from business and conservative groups and losing battles against Republican economic initiatives.

The tone was set by the Republican sweep in the 1980 elections, which expelled many union friends from Congress and inspired the fear of Reaganism in others. Perhaps worst of all, the elections undermined the credibility of union leaders by showing substantial rank-and-file backing for President Reagan and his programs. Election Day polls indicated members of union families had voted more than 40 percent for Reagan, ignoring their leaders' halfhearted endorsement of incumbent Democrat Jimmy Carter.

Labor's defeats were most stunning in the broad sphere of economic policy. Labor was on the losing side of virtually every major tax and spending test during Reagan's first year in office. For the first time in at least a decade the AFL-CIO in 1981 lost a majority of the roll-call votes it picked as "key issues" in both houses, and most of those defeats were on economic issues. Equally significant, the Democratic alternatives that lost bore little resemblance to a labor wish list; the debate was not whether to move to the right, but how far.

Responding to Reagan's call for wide-ranging budget cuts, Congress sharply curtailed priority labor programs. On the eve of the worst recession since the 1930s, lawmakers cut the federal-state unemployment compensation program by more than $3.1 billion over fiscal 1982-84. They pared another $2.6 billion from the trade adjustment assistance program, designed to help workers who lost their jobs as a result of competition from imports. Congress also finished off the remnants of the public service jobs program authorized by the Comprehensive Employment and Training Act (CETA).

Given this unfavorable climate, labor concentrated on damage control. While unions generally did not press for new labor protection laws in 1981, they had some success in resisting attacks on existing measures, such as proposals to curtail Davis-Bacon Act wage floors on federal contracts and to establish a subminimum wage for teenagers. Congress rejected a controversial administration plan to require jobless individuals to accept minimum wage jobs after 13 weeks of unemployment benefits.

Unions representing workers in sagging industries did try to muster support for measures to limit foreign competition. The United Steelworkers of America lined up with employers to generate pressure for limits on steel imports. The United Auto Workers rounded up cosponsors on a bill that would require all autos sold in the United States to contain a quota of American-made parts. The House passed this "domestic content" measure both in 1982 and 1983, but the Senate never acted.

At year's end AFL-CIO President Lane Kirkland was named a member of the National Commission on Social Security Reform, assuring labor a strong voice in efforts to fashion a rescue plan for the financially shaky retirement system. Creation of the commission followed a botched administration attempt earlier in the year to slash future Social Security benefits. Congress initially went along with an administration proposal to eliminate the minimum benefit, paid to those with low earnings under the system, but the public uproar that ensued persuaded both Congress and the White House to restore the minimum payment for current beneficiaries. The payment was reinstated as part of stopgap legislation to keep the retirement system from going broke in 1982.

Social Security Financing

As it had done in the past, Congress put off the politically sensitive task of overhauling the financially troubled Social Security system.

A highly charged partisan atmosphere hampered all substantive action in 1981. Democrats, burned by Republicans on tax and budget cuts, seized on the issue to illustrate their claims that the administration was attempting to balance the budget on the backs of the needy. Congressional Republicans, unnerved by the public furor that greeted Social Security cuts proposed by President Reagan May 12, were reluctant to go out on a limb alone.

Instead, Congress at year's end approved a stopgap measure (HR 4331 — PL 97-123) that would keep the system's largest trust fund, the Old Age and Survivors Insurance (OASI) fund, from going broke in the fall of 1982. HR 4331 allowed OASI to borrow money from the healthier Hospital Insurance and Disability Insurance trust funds — but only through the end of 1982.

The bill also restored the $122 minimum monthly benefit for current Social Security recipients. Congress had eliminated the minimum benefit at Reagan's request in its budget-cutting reconciliation bill (HR 3982 — PL 97-35) cleared July 31. Both the president and Congress retreated in the face of adverse public reaction.

Reagan also retreated on his other proposals, calling Sept. 24 for formation of a bipartisan commission to come up with recommendations for solving Social Security's funding problems. The 15-member panel, appointed Dec. 16, was given a Dec. 31, 1982, reporting deadline, effectively putting off any further debate until after the 1982 elections. Early in 1983 Congress approved legislation based on the commission's recommendations. *(Story, p. 659)*

Financing Crisis

Faced with sharply rising costs, Congress in 1977 had approved large payroll tax increases aimed at keeping the Social Security system solvent well into the next century. *(Congress and the Nation Vol. V, p. 235)*

It soon became apparent, however, that bad economic conditions were rapidly eroding OASI trust fund reserves. In 1980 Congress temporarily reallocated funds from the disability fund to the retirement fund (PL 96-403). But it was understood even then that further action was needed. Not only did the system confront a short-term cash flow

problem caused by recent inflation and high unemployment; it also faced a major funding crisis after the turn of the century. By that time, it was projected, there would be too few workers contributing to the system to support the millions of retirees from the so-called baby-boom generation.

Because of the imminent bankruptcy of OASI, many members of Congress and other observers thought 1981 might be the year to resolve the vexing, and politically touchy, problem of Social Security financing.

But what mood for action there may have been at the start of the year rapidly dissolved when the administration May 12 proposed sharp cuts in the Social Security program, including a reduction in benefits for early retirement at age 62; a one-time, three-month delay in the annual cost-of-living adjustment (COLA); tougher eligibility requirements for disability payments; and an altered benefit formula that would reduce initial benefits for future retirees.

Reagan earlier had proposed eliminating the minimum benefit, a floor on monthly payments intended to provide some protection for those with low earnings under the system. Without it, retirees received benefits based solely on prior earnings.

The president's proposals set off a tempest in Congress, where members of both parties were besieged by calls from angry constituents who feared drastic reductions in their benefits. Democrats charged that the administration was cutting the program not to save it, but to help balance the budget.

The Senate Democratic Conference approved a resolution that called the proposed reductions "a breach of faith with those aging Americans who have contributed to the Social Security system. . . ." The resolution went on to vow opposition to any changes that would "precipitously and unfairly deny those men and women approaching retirement age Social Security benefits on which they have planned. . . ."

The text of the resolution was offered as an amendment to a fiscal 1981 supplemental appropriations bill (HR 3512 — PL 97-12) by Daniel Patrick Moynihan, D-N.Y. After a lengthy debate it was killed on a **key 49-48 vote (R 48-2; D 1-46)** May 20. The Senate then unanimously adopted an amendment promising that Congress would not approve immediate or inequitable reductions in early retirees' benefits or cut more than necessary to save the system's finances. *(1981 key votes, p. 879)*

Following a week of attacks on his proposals, the president began to backpedal. "This administration is not wedded to any single solution," Reagan wrote congressional leaders May 21. "We recognize that members have alternative answers."

Reconciliation Cuts

Congress agreed to eliminate the minimum benefit, and approved some other Social Security cutbacks sought by the president, as part of HR 3982, the omnibus budget reconciliation bill cleared July 31. But it rejected Reagan's proposals to reduce benefits for early retirees and to delay the July 1982 COLA increase.

The massive reconciliation measure, passed by the Senate June 25 and the House June 26, carried out budget cuts sought by Reagan and endorsed by Congress through its budget process. The Social Security provisions were drafted by the Senate Finance and House Ways and Means committees and incorporated in the reconciliation savings measures reported by the House Budget Committee (H

Rept 97-158) and its Senate counterpart (S 1377 — S Rept 97-139). *(Reconciliation action, p. 40)*

Achieving a compromise on the Social Security provisions was one of the most difficult tasks that faced the conferees on the reconciliation bill. Differences between the two chambers involved disability requirements, vocational rehabilitation, the earnings limitation for retirees and timing for elimination of the minimum benefit. The House already had dropped a Ways and Means Committee recommendation to retain the minimum payment for current recipients when it adopted a Republican substitute for the measure reported by the Budget Committee.

Although both chambers had agreed to eliminate the minimum benefit, House and Senate votes July 21 demonstrated members' misgivings:

● The Republican-controlled Senate narrowly thwarted, on a 52-46 vote, an effort to save the minimum benefit through an amendment to pending tax cut legislation. *(Tax cut bill, p. 65)*

● The House adopted, 405-13, a resolution (H Res 181) urging reconciliation conferees to take steps "to ensure that Social Security benefits are not reduced for those currently receiving them."

Conferees nonetheless agreed July 23 to halt the minimum benefit at the end of February 1982 for all current recipients.

No one, including the Democratic sponsors of the House resolution, really had expected the conferees to reverse the previously adopted House position on the minimum benefit. But the Democrats, with thousands of senior citizens marching on the Capitol to protest Social Security changes, wanted to force Republicans to be counted on the issue.

After the conference report on the reconciliation bill was filed July 29 (H Rept 97-208), Democrats staged a last-ditch effort to restore the minimum benefit.

House Rules Committee Chairman Richard Bolling, D-Mo., threatened to refuse to convene his panel to clear the reconciliation bill for floor action unless the conference was reopened to restore the minimum benefit provisions.

But after House and Senate leaders of both parties met behind closed doors, the issue was resolved by allowing two separate House votes — one on the reconciliation conference report and one on HR 4331, the bill to reinstate the minimum benefit. The House accepted that arrangement July 31 by a **271-151 key vote (R 166-21; D 105-130)** on a procedural issue. Both chambers then went on to clear the reconciliation bill. *(1981 key votes, p. 879)*

Provisions. As signed into law Aug. 13, Title XXII of HR 3982 (PL 97-35) made the following major cutbacks in Social Security programs:

● Eliminated the $122 minimum monthly payment for all new recipients beginning with the December 1981 payment and for all current recipients for benefits paid after February 1982. Such recipients instead would receive benefits based on prior earnings.

● Changed age limitations on Supplemental Security Income (SSI) to allow individuals aged 60-64 who would be eligible for the minimum benefit before December to qualify for offsetting SSI payments if they met other eligibility requirements.

● Eliminated the $255 lump-sum death payment for deaths occurring after Aug. 31, 1981, in cases where there were no surviving spouses or dependent children.

● Required that those electing to retire at age 62, and their dependents, begin to receive Social Security benefits in the first full month of their entitlement. Under existing

law, if a worker retired in the middle of the month, he received benefits for the entire month. The provision was to take effect for September 1981 benefits.

• Extended for one year, until Jan. 1, 1983, existing limits on outside earnings for those under age 72. The age cap had been scheduled to drop to 70 in 1982.

• Eliminated payments for a parent caring for a child receiving benefits when the child reached age 16. Under existing law, these benefits ended when the child turned 18. The provision did not apply to parents caring for a disabled child. It was to take effect for existing recipients two years after the bill was signed into law; for all new recipients, two months after enactment.

• Eliminated benefits for new postsecondary students aged 18-22 after August 1982. Payments for current recipients and those eligible for such benefits before Sept. 1, 1981, who entered postsecondary school before May 1, 1982, were to be phased out gradually, 25 percent each year for the next four years through July 1985. Cost-of-living adjustments and payments for summer months were eliminated for all recipients.

• Reduced disability benefits by the amount received from other federal, state or local disability programs if combined benefits exceeded 80 percent of the worker's prior earnings. Existing law offset disability benefits only with workers' compensation payments.

• Made the offset provision applicable to workers aged 64 and under and their dependents, instead of those under 62 as current law required. The offsets would be made as soon as the non-Social Security payments began. The provision, which affected only new recipients, applied to those who became disabled no more than five months before the bill became law.

• Eliminated reimbursement of state vocational rehabilitation programs, except in cases where it could be shown that the program had resulted in removal of a disabled person from the Social Security rolls.

• Required rounding to the next lowest 10 cents at each stage of the benefit calculation except for the final benefit amount, which would be rounded to the next lowest dollar. Under existing law benefits were rounded to the next highest 10 cents.

Minimum Benefit Restoration

Congress Dec. 16 completed action on legislation reinstating for current beneficiaries the minimum benefit it had agreed to terminate less than five months earlier.

The House originally passed HR 4331 July 31, the same day it approved the reconciliation conference report. As passed by a 404-20 vote, the bill reinstated the minimum benefit for all current and future beneficiaries.

The Senate passed its version of HR 4331 by a 95-0 vote Oct. 15. The Senate bill restored the payment only for current beneficiaries who lived in the United States and did not have government pensions in excess of $300 a month. It also made stopgap arrangements to keep the OASI trust fund from going broke in 1982.

The Senate action followed President Reagan's Sept. 24 speech calling on Congress to restore the minimum benefit. "It was never our intention to take this support away from those who truly need it," Reagan said.

The major dispute of the six-week-long conference was whether the cost of restoring the benefit would be offset with other tax increases or benefit cuts. The deadlock was broken as adjournment neared and members faced the prospect of returning home without having resolved the emotional issue.

Conferees filed their report Dec. 14 (H Rept 97-409), only two days before the end of the session. The Senate approved the conference report by a 96-0 vote Dec. 15; the House approved it the following day, 412-10.

The final bill reinstated the minimum payment for all three million current recipients but eliminated the benefit for those who became eligible for Social Security after Dec. 31, 1981.

To pay for much of the $6.1 billion, five-year cost of restoring the benefit, Congress agreed to extend the 6.7 percent payroll tax to the first six months of sick pay, beginning Jan. 1, 1982. Under existing law, sick pay was taxed only in cases where employees were not covered by a specific company sick pay plan or system.

The bill also allowed the financially shaky OASI trust fund to borrow from the two other, healthier Social Security trust funds. That provision was to expire Dec. 31, 1982.

Provisions. As signed into law Dec. 29, HR 4331 (PL 97-123) made the following changes in the Social Security system:

• Continued the $122 minimum monthly benefit for all those eligible as of Jan. 1, 1982.

• Allowed members of religious orders to become eligible for the minimum until Dec. 31, 1991.

• Permitted borrowing among the Old Age and Survivors Insurance, Disability Insurance and Hospital Insurance trust funds until Dec. 31, 1982.

• Extended the payroll tax to the first six months of sick pay, with the exception of payments attributable to an employee's contribution to a third-party sick-pay plan.

• Made it a felony to alter or counterfeit a Social Security card.

• Required the Department of Health and Human Services (HHS) to contract by Jan. 1, 1982, to set up Aid to Families with Dependent Children home health aid experiments in at least seven states.

• Waived the Federal Privacy Act for prisoners so government agencies could give prisoners' Social Security numbers to HHS to prevent them from receiving illegal disability benefits. *(Background, Congress and the Nation Vol. IV, p. 585)*

• Required HHS to report to Congress in 90 days on its efforts to prevent Social Security payments from being sent to deceased individuals.

Unemployment Benefits

Congress July 31 approved sharp cuts in the federal-state unemployment compensation program as part of its sweeping budget reconciliation bill (HR 3982 — PL 97-35).

As requested by President Reagan, the bill terminated the nationwide extended benefits program, which provided benefits for up to 13 weeks — on top of 26 weeks of regular benefits — in all states during periods of high unemployment. The bill also stiffened requirements for payment of extended benefits within a state. Other provisions disqualified those who voluntarily quit military service from receiving any unemployment compensation and tightened rules governing federal loans to states that did not have sufficient unemployment tax revenues to cover benefit payments.

Legislators rejected a controversial administration proposal that would have required claimants to accept

minimum wage jobs after collecting 13 weeks of unemployment benefits.

The final legislation, cleared July 31, was a compromise (H Rept 97-208) of provisions drafted by the House Ways and Means and Senate Finance committees to achieve savings required by the first fiscal 1982 budget resolution (H Con Res 115). They were incorporated in the reconciliation savings measures reported by the House Budget Committee (H Rept 97-158) and its Senate counterpart (S 1377 — S Rept 97-139). *(Reconciliation action, p. 40)*

The reconciliation changes were expected to cut more than $3.1 billion from the program over fiscal 1982-84, but those savings proved illusory. By year's end the nation had slipped into the worst recession since the 1930s, and mounting unemployment caused Congress to expand jobless benefits in both 1982 and 1983. *(1982 action, p. 654; 1983 action, p. 665; background on unemployment programs, Congress and the Nation Vol. V, p. 422; Congress and the Nation Vol. IV, p. 709)*

Major Provisions. As signed into law Aug. 13, Title XXIV of HR 3982 (PL 97-35) made the following changes in unemployment compensation programs:

● Eliminated immediately the requirement that all states provide up to 13 weeks of extended unemployment benefits when the national insured unemployment rate (IUR) exceeded 4.5 percent.

● Excluded persons receiving extended unemployment benefits from the calculation of the IUR used to trigger extended benefits in states.

● Raised the triggers used to determine whether the extended benefits program would be available in a state, as follows:

1) The mandatory trigger, under which states had to provide extended benefits, would rise to 5 percent unemployment, from 4 percent under existing law; as under existing law, this trigger would apply only if the state IUR was at least 20 percent higher than the state average over the two previous years.

2) The optional trigger, under which states could choose to provide extended benefits, would rise to 6 percent, from 5 percent under existing law.

● Limited eligibility for extended benefits to claimants who had worked at least 20 weeks or had the "equivalent" in wages (defined as either 40 times the claimant's current weekly insurance payment or 1.5 times the claimant's wages over the quarter with the highest wages during a one-year base period prior to unemployment).

● Disqualified from any unemployment compensation those who voluntarily left military service at the end of their enlistment term and were eligible to re-enlist. The provision was effective for those who left the service on or after July 1, 1981.

● Required states to amend their unemployment compensation laws to allow for the above changes before employers in the state could be eligible for a 2.7 percent federal credit against taxes paid under the Federal Unemployment Tax Act (FUTA).

● Imposed an interest rate of up to 10 percent on loans made to states from the federal unemployment insurance trust fund between April 1, 1982, and Dec. 31, 1987.

● Set limits on the federal penalty imposed on states for failing to repay loans received from the federal unemployment insurance trust fund, if the states took certain steps to improve the solvency of their unemployment compensation programs.

CETA Jobs Programs

The budget-cutting reconciliation bill (HR 3982 — PL 97-35) finished off the troubled public service jobs programs authorized by the Comprehensive Employment and Training Act (CETA).

The two programs, which at one time had provided 725,000 jobs, were terminated at the end of fiscal 1981. The reconciliation bill authorized no funds for them in fiscal 1982.

The Reagan administration wanted to abolish the programs, which over the years had been plagued with reports of fraud, abuse and waste. One of the programs, authorized by CETA Title II-D, provided jobs to low-income persons with long-term employment problems. The other, CETA Title VI, was for people thrown out of work by short-term fluctuations in the economy. At the beginning of 1981, the two programs provided about 300,000 jobs. *(Background, Congress and the Nation Vol. V, p. 410)*

The reconciliation legislation also ordered reductions in other CETA job training programs and denied funding for the Youth Conservation Corps. Funding for other youth jobs programs had been authorized earlier in the year. *(Story, below)*

As cleared July 31, the reconciliation bill included provisions drafted by the Senate and House Labor committees, which were incorporated in the savings measures reported by the House Budget Committee (H Rept 97-158) and its Senate counterpart (S 1377 — S Rept 97-139). All told, the provisions cut 1982 CETA spending by $5.7 billion. *(Reconciliation, p. 40)*

Congress in 1982 replaced CETA with a new job training program. *(Story, p. 655)*

CETA Youth Jobs Programs

Legislation (S 1070 — PL 97-14) to extend through Sept. 30, 1982, the authorization for youth employment programs under the Comprehensive Employment and Training Act (CETA) cleared Congress June 2.

In his fiscal 1982 budget, President Reagan had proposed that the youth programs be joined with other parts of CETA in a single program of job training for the disadvantaged. But that proposal was sidetracked until 1982, when Congress replaced CETA with a new job training program. *(1982 action, p. 655)*

The Senate passed S 1070 by voice vote May 12. House passage followed June 2, 309-84.

The authorization for the CETA youth programs, established by Congress in 1977, expired at the end of fiscal 1980, but the programs continued to operate under the authority of temporary funding resolutions in fiscal 1981. The three programs — the Youth Incentive Entitlement Pilot Projects, the Youth Community Conservation and Improvement Projects, and the Youth Employment and Training Program — were intended to test various ways of improving the job prospects of disadvantaged youths aged 16-21. *(Congress and the Nation Vol. V, pp. 403, 424)*

Railroad Retirement System

Congress July 31 approved a major overhaul of the Railroad Retirement system in an effort to avert a threatened shortfall in the program as early as April 1982.

Changes made in the system — the only private pension plan run by the government — were part of a package agreed to by rail labor and management and incorporated in the budget reconciliation bill (HR 3982 — PL 97-35). The package also included a 2.25 percent increase in taxes for rail management and a 2 percent increase for rail employees.

The tax hike was adopted during the first week of August as part of President Reagan's Economic Recovery Tax Act of 1981 (HR 4242 — PL 97-34). *(Story, p. 65)*

The final legislation (H Rept 97-208) was a compromise of provisions drafted by the House Ways and Means and Senate Finance committees. The agreement was incorporated in the reconciliation savings measures reported by the House Budget Committee (H Rept 97-158) and its Senate counterpart (S 1377 — S Rept 97-139). *(Reconciliation, p. 40)*

Expected savings were approximately $620 million for fiscal 1982-84. But that amount was a net figure; many of the reconciliation changes involved benefit increases offered in exchange for the $1.7 billion increase in rail employee and employer taxes for fiscal 1982-84 adopted as part of HR 4242.

The major changes included a more generous benefit formula, authority for short-term borrowing from the Treasury and restrictions on "windfall" benefits — extra benefits given retirees as a result of 1974 legislation.

Those changes, combined with the tax increases, were expected to keep the system solvent for the next 10 years. But lower-than-expected railroad employment imposed further drains on the system, and Congress was forced to enact further changes in 1983. *(Story, p. 666)*

Background

The federal government assumed control over the Railroad Retirement system during the Depression when many private rail pension plans were going broke.

While rail employees were not covered under Social Security, they were guaranteed equivalent payments — called Tier I benefits. In addition, they received payments — Tier II benefits — that paralleled those they would have received under a private pension plan.

Beginning in 1951 a complex "interchange" was set up between Railroad Retirement and Social Security, under which the Railroad Retirement Account (RRA) paid Social Security an amount equal to what rail workers and employers would have paid in Social Security payroll taxes. In exchange, Social Security gave the RRA what it needed to pay benefits railroad retirees would have received had they been covered by Social Security.

A quirk in the retirement law before 1974 allowed workers who had been employed in both railroad- and Social Security-covered jobs to earn generous "windfall" benefits under each program. These payments drained the system over the years, leading to a major overhaul in 1974. As part of that reorganization, Congress agreed that the Treasury would assume the cost of these payments. *(1974 act, Congress and the Nation Vol. IV, p. 698)*

Despite the 1974 changes, the rail trust fund continued to face financial troubles. Outlays increased from $1.6 billion in 1970 to $5.3 billion in 1981, with projections put at about $7 billion by 1987. Receipts did not keep up with those increases, and trust fund reserves dropped from $2.7 billion to $1.9 billion in 1981.

At the end of 1981, 477,000 workers were covered by the system and an equal number were receiving benefits of $3.1 billion. In addition, nearly $2.3 billion was paid to about 559,000 dependents and survivors.

Major Provisions

As signed into law Aug. 13, Title XI of the budget reconciliation bill (HR 3982 — PL 97-35) included the following provisions affecting the Railroad Retirement system:

● Changed the method used for computing Tier II rail pension benefits to prevent the benefits from eroding with inflation.

● Provided for permanent annual cost-of-living increases of Tier II benefits.

● Ended the use of general retirement funds to pay for windfall benefits. This provision was expected to result in immediate payment reductions for some 400,000 recipients of windfall benefits.

● Eliminated pre-retirement cost-of-living indexing of windfall benefits.

● Eliminated new windfall benefits for non-dependent spouses who might be eligible for such benefits as a result of a court case. New windfall benefits also would be eliminated for all other spouses, widows or widowers of railroad employees.

● Adjusted the formula for reducing future benefit increases of early retirees to be consistent with the formula used for such benefits under Social Security.

● Lowered from 50 percent to 45 percent the amount of an employee's Tier II benefit granted a spouse, but removed existing caps on such spousal benefits.

● Revised the survivors' Tier II benefit formula to include a lower cost-of-living increase.

● Allowed for limited authority to borrow from Treasury funds to cover temporary funding shortfalls.

● Instituted an "early warning system" that required the Railroad Retirement Board to alert Congress to future funding problems. A report would be triggered whenever the board was required to borrow from the Treasury 50 percent or more of the money it needed to pay basic, Social Security-equivalent, benefits.

● Required that employees receive credit for actual months of service, rather than having months of service rounded up to the next highest year, for calculating benefits.

● Expanded the category of workers considered "currently connected" with the rail industry who qualified for more generous survivors' and supplemental benefits.

● Allowed divorced wives to collect basic benefits, equivalent to Social Security benefits, if they were married to the employee for at least 10 years, were no longer married and were at least 65 years old.

● Expanded basic benefit coverage to include surviving divorced wives and mothers and remarried widows.

● Eliminated, for workers hired on or after Oct. 1, 1981, supplemental benefits given to those with long-term rail service.

Black Lung Trust Fund

Congress in 1981 approved a labor-industry compromise plan to help bail out the financially troubled Black Lung Disability Trust Fund, which paid benefits to coal miners disabled by black lung disease.

The measure (HR 5159 — PL 97-119), cleared Dec. 16, doubled the excise tax on coal paid by producers and

tightened eligibility requirements for black lung benefits. It was based on an agreement worked out by mine operators, labor groups, insurance companies and the administration.

The package, enacted quickly during the last hectic days before Congress adjourned, also was the vehicle for several miscellaneous tax measures. *(Miscellaneous tax provisions, p. 71)*

The bill was reported by the House Ways and Means Committee Dec. 14 (H Rept 97-406, Part I). It passed the House by voice vote the next day. The Ways and Means version contained only the coal tax increase and other trust fund provisions. But the Senate amended it Dec. 16 to include the unrelated tax provisions and changes in black lung benefit requirements, then passed it, 63-30. Later that day the House agreed to the Senate version, 363-47, clearing it for the president.

Senate Finance Committee Chairman Robert Dole, R-Kan., warned Dec. 16 that passage of the bill was necessary to stop "the hemorrhaging" of the black lung program, which paid benefits to about 200,000 disabled coal miners and their survivors.

Background

Every year after its establishment in 1978, the trust fund had distributed more funds than it had taken in. The difference — about $1.5 billion by the end of fiscal 1981 — had come out of general revenues. Dole said the deficit could reach $9 billion by 1995 if no changes were made.

The fund was established in an attempt to shift most of the program's growing burden from the government to mine operators. Financed solely by the coal tax, it generally paid benefits for disabled workers who held mining jobs prior to 1970. The trust fund provided compensation when no responsible mine operator could be found and made temporary payments when operators challenged a claim. In most other cases, the "responsible" operator paid. Originally it was predicted that the excise taxes would cover most costs, but liberalized benefits and built-in incentives for operators to challenge claims had strained the fund's resources. *(Congress and the Nation Vol. V, pp. 408, 414)*

The Joint Committee on Taxation estimated that the new tax would raise $1.5 billion for the trust fund by fiscal 1986, although the increase in total federal revenues would be less because of lower income tax receipts. The Labor Department projected that with the tax increase, the fund would no longer have to borrow funds from the Treasury after 1985 and that its deficit would be wiped out as early as 1994.

While HR 5159 tightened eligibility requirements for benefits, it also transferred the responsibility for about 10,200 unresolved claims to the trust fund, more than offsetting savings from the benefit changes over the next five years. Some members objected to that; they also complained that the increased coal tax would be passed on to consumers and said the tightening of eligibility requirements did not go far enough.

Provisions

As signed into law Dec. 29, the black lung provisions of HR 5159 (PL 97-119):

● Doubled the manufacturers' excise tax on surface-mined coal to 50 cents a ton and the tax on underground coal to $1 a ton.

● Imposed a cap on the tax equal to 4 percent of the price for which the coal was sold. The existing cap was 2 percent.

● Made the higher tax effective from Jan. 1, 1982, to Jan. 1, 1996, or until the Black Lung Disability Trust Fund became solvent, whichever was earlier.

● Transferred responsibility from coal mine operators to the trust fund for 10,200 black lung claims rejected prior to 1978 changes in benefits, but later approved.

● Eliminated a provision in existing law requiring that the trust fund pay lump-sum back benefits when a claim was filed but was contested by the mine operator.

● Increased the interest rate due on trust fund advances to cover claims for which an operator was later found responsible. The rate was increased from 6 percent to the prevailing interest rate; in 1982 it was set at 15 percent.

● Revised the method for determining the interest rate used when the trust fund must repay funds lent by the Treasury so the rate would be closer to the fair market rate.

● Transferred provisions of the Black Lung Disability Trust Fund to the Internal Revenue Code.

Eligibility Standards. Allowed the Labor Department to seek a second physician's opinion in determining whether an applicant's X-rays indicated the presence of black lung disease (pneumoconiosis).

● Ended a provision of existing law that established the presumption, subject to rebuttal, that miners with 10 years' experience in the mines who died as a result of respiratory disease died because of black lung disease.

● Ended a provision that established the presumption that miners with 15 years in the mines who were totally disabled due to respiratory impairment were disabled due to black lung disease, even in the absence of a medical showing of black lung.

● Made both of the above changes applicable to claims filed after enactment of the bill.

● Ended a provision that established a presumption that survivors of miners who died before March 2, 1978, and who had spent 25 years in the mines before June 30, 1971, were entitled to survivors' benefits. This change would apply to claims filed more than six months after enactment of the bill.

● Ended a provision that allowed a miner's widow, in cases where there was no clear-cut medical evidence, to receive benefits by simply submitting an affidavit that the miner had had black lung before he died. Under the new law, only someone who did not stand to receive benefits in a case would be able to submit an affidavit.

Benefits. Limited payment of survivors' benefits to cases in which the miner died as a result of black lung disease; the change would apply to claims filed after enactment of the bill. Under existing law, survivors' benefits had been awarded in some cases where the miner's death was not due to black lung.

● Reduced black lung benefits for recipients who had earnings above the Social Security excess earnings limit.

● Provided for a study of the relationship between black lung benefits and other workers' compensation benefits.

Trade Adjustment Aid

The trade adjustment assistance program was scaled back substantially as part of the budget reconciliation package (HR 3982 — PL 97-35) cleared July 31.

Trade adjustment benefits went to workers who had been laid off from industries harmed by import competition. A small portion of the benefits also went to small-

and medium-sized firms suffering from imports.

Congress cut $2.6 billion from the program for fiscal 1982-84 by accepting administration requests to tighten eligibility and to require that claimants exhaust all unemployment compensation benefits before collecting trade adjustment assistance.

Some of the more liberal eligibility requirements were restored in 1982. The act was extended for two years in 1983. *(1982 action, p. 658; 1983 action, p. 665)*

The 1981 cutbacks were drafted by the House Ways and Means and Senate Finance committees and incorporated in the reconciliation savings measures reported by the House Budget Committee (H Rept 97-158) and its Senate counterpart (S 1377 — S Rept 97-139). *(Reconciliation, p. 40)*

The reductions were made in part because of criticisms that the program had not worked as originally intended. The Senate committee report cited a 1980 General Accounting Office study that found the weekly cash payments did little to help displaced workers adjust to their unemployment, were often received in lump sums after the claimant had found a job and might have been a disincentive for some to look for work.

The trade adjustment program was started in 1962 and expanded under the Trade Act of 1974. Bills to authorize additional aid failed to clear in 1978 and 1979. *(Background, Congress and the Nation Vol. V, p. 419; Congress and the Nation Vol. IV, p. 131)*

Major Provisions

As signed into law Aug. 13, Title XXV of HR 3982 (PL 97-35) included the following provisions:

● Extended for one year, to Sept. 30, 1983, the trade adjustment assistance program for workers and firms.

● Tightened the standard under which eligibility for trade adjustment assistance benefits were determined. Benefits would be provided to groups of workers only when it was found that foreign import competition was a "substantial cause" for the loss of their jobs. Existing law stipulated that import competition must have "contributed importantly" to the layoffs.

● Required workers to exhaust all unemployment compensation benefits before qualifying for trade adjustment assistance.

● Limited an individual's weekly payment under the adjustment assistance program to the amount received under unemployment insurance.

● Limited an individual's combined unemployment compensation and trade adjustment assistance payments to 52 weeks.

● Disqualified from benefits those workers who refused to seek or accept "suitable work" if prospects of returning to their line of work were not good.

● Authorized the secretary of labor to require workers to accept training or expand their job search, after the first eight weeks of eligibility.

● Required that job training be made available to workers, if certain other conditions were met.

● Increased job search and relocation allowances from a maximum of $500 for each worker to $600.

● Expanded the secretary of labor's responsibility to inform all workers about the program, its benefits and how to apply.

● Eliminated most retroactive lump-sum payments by limiting benefit payments to weeks of unemployment more than 60 days after workers filed a petition to qualify for assistance.

● Liberalized the requirement that workers be employed for 26 weeks during the year preceding unemployment by allowing certain leaves to be counted in the 26-week period.

● Authorized the secretary of commerce to provide each eligible industry with up to $2 million a year in technical assistance, including establishment of industrywide programs to develop new products.

1982

Recession gripped the nation in 1982. By year's end unemployment had risen to a post-World War II high of 10.7 percent, and 12 million people were out of work.

Democrats charged that high unemployment, one of the most apparent fallouts of the recession, was a clear sign that President Reagan's economic policies had failed. In part capitalizing on the issue before the November elections, they made several attempts to push large job creation programs.

The administration maintained that such plans involved massive government expenditures for "make-work, dead-end" jobs. Reagan's theory was that more jobs could be created by getting government spending under control and restoring economic growth.

Rising unemployment — and Democratic election gains — spurred enthusiasm for job creation programs in the post-election session. In December the Democratic-controlled House passed a $5.4 billion jobs program as part of a fiscal 1983 appropriations bill. The Republican Senate followed suit, approving a $1.2 billion public works program. However, both House and Senate plans eventually fell victim to White House opposition.

Instead, the administration proposed legislation to raise gasoline taxes and use the revenue for highway and mass transit improvements. Although Reagan denied the measure was a jobs program, it was expected to help create more than 300,000 new positions. Both houses went along with the plan, and the bill passed in the final days of the session, the only jobs initiative of the year.

In other anti-recession action, Congress established a temporary program of supplemental unemployment compensation to aid those who had exhausted benefits provided under existing law. The White House initially opposed the program on budgetary grounds but ultimately agreed to accept the extra-payment plan.

Lawmakers also approved a new job training program to replace the expiring Comprehensive Employment and Training Act (CETA). Unlike CETA, the new program did not provide public service jobs. Instead, it concentrated on providing skills instruction and other employment-related assistance to low-income people with severe problems in the job market.

Late in the year the United Auto Workers won a major victory when the House passed a bill to require foreign auto companies either to build more of their cars in the United States or to reduce their U.S. sales. The House vote was largely symbolic since there was little chance that the Republican Senate would act on the bill. But supporters said the House action would "send a signal to Japan" to reduce its trade barriers.

Apart from a spate of partisan rhetoric at election time, Congress managed to skirt the controversial Social Security issue throughout the year, while awaiting recommendations from the president's bipartisan National Commission on Social Security Reform.

Lawmakers approved a stopgap measure allowing individuals who were cut off the Social Security Disability Insurance rolls to collect benefits while they appealed their termination. Demands for corrective legislation followed a firestorm of complaints that many still-disabled individuals were being thrown off the rolls as the Reagan administration carried out a congressional mandate to rid the program of ineligible recipients.

Anti-Recession Jobs Plans

Despite mounting pressure for anti-recession jobs legislation, Congress adjourned Dec. 23 without approving any new direct federal job creation programs.

Prior to the Nov. 2 elections, in which the Democrats gained 26 House seats, demands for jobs measures came mostly from Democrats. But in the post-election session that began Nov. 29, when the unemployment rate was approaching its 10.7 percent postwar peak, GOP leaders joined in calling for jobs action.

President Reagan vigorously opposed what he described as "make-work job programs." But he did ultimately back, and Congress before adjournment approved, a 5-cents-a-gallon increase in the federal gasoline tax to finance repair of the nation's deteriorating roads and transit systems and to provide jobs for some of the 12 million unemployed Americans. Although Reagan insisted that the bipartisan measure (HR 6211 — PL 97-424) was not a jobs bill, others maintained it would create more than 300,000 jobs.

The gas tax was part of the Transportation Assistance Act of 1982 (HR 6211 — PL 97-424). The House passed HR 6211 Dec. 7, but Senate action was delayed by a series of filibusters by conservative Republicans who opposed the tax increase. As a result, Congress did not complete action on the bill until Dec. 23. *(Details of action, p. 301)*

Bowing to veto threats, Senate-House conferees earlier in the month had dropped jobs funding from an urgent appropriations measure (H J Res 631 — PL 97-377).

Congress, with Reagan's support, enacted a $4.6 billion emergency jobs package early in 1983. Other Democratic-sponsored jobs legislation made little headway. *(1983 action, pp. 663, 664; job creation history, box, p. 653)*

Appropriations Action

Both the House and Senate included funds for public works and other job-creating projects in H J Res 631, a continuing resolution to provide fiscal 1983 funding for agencies whose regular appropriations bills had not been enacted.

The House Appropriations Committee reported the resolution Dec. 10 (H Rept 97-959) after attaching a $5.4 billion Democratic jobs program to the bill. The job creation package increased funding for some three dozen existing federal programs ranging from rural waste disposal to government auto purchases. In addition, it provided money for two new efforts — $1 billion for an emergency jobs program run by the Labor Department and $50 million for emergency food and shelter programs, to be distributed by private groups.

During floor debate Dec. 14, Silvio O. Conte, R-Mass., the ranking Republican on the Appropriations Committee, warned that President Reagan had vowed not to sign the measure "with a jobs bill in it." Conte offered an amendment to delete the jobs program, but it failed on a **key 191-215 vote (R 171-7; D 20-208)**. The House then passed H J Res 631 Dec. 14 by a 204-200 vote.

The Senate version of the resolution, reported Dec. 15, provided $1.2 billion for a variety of public works projects to replace the $5.4 billion House plan. Committee Chairman Mark O. Hatfield, R-Ore., who advanced the proposal, called it a "reasonable, responsible approach in constructive activities."

The Senate passed H J Res 631 Dec. 19. Earlier it defeated an effort to delete the jobs program on a **46-50 key vote (R 39-12; D 7-38)**. *(1982 key votes, p. 895)*

Despite the House and Senate action, conferees agreed to drop any kind of jobs funding from the measure to forestall a presidential veto. "I think the time is so short, there is nothing to be gained by insisting on our position.... It's just a case of recognizing reality," said House Appropriations Committee Chairman Jamie L. Whitten, D-Miss.

Before approving the conference report (H Rept 97-980) Dec. 20, both Democratic and Republican leaders pledged to fight for jobs legislation when the 98th Congress convened in January.

Democratic Anti-Recession Package

Action on the gas tax bill and the continuing resolution capped a year of halting Democratic efforts to develop politically viable anti-recession legislation.

$1 Billion Jobs Plan. Democratic leaders, with an eye to the Nov. 2 elections, won House passage Sept. 16 of a $1 billion jobs plan (H J Res 562 — H Rept 97-764) that Republicans derided as "economic moonshine."

The bill, the centerpiece of a Democratic package aimed at creating jobs and stimulating the economy, would have provided $1 billion for the fiscal year ending Sept. 30 to create an estimated 200,000 temporary public works jobs.

The resolution had its genesis in a press conference held by Majority Leader Jim Wright, D-Texas, and Budget Committee Chairman James R. Jones, D-Okla., on May 7, the day the Labor Department announced a postwar-high unemployment rate of 9.4 percent. The jobs proposal was to be coupled with a $1 billion plan to provide lower mortgage interest rates for buyers of new homes, thus increasing jobs in the construction industry. The housing plan, subsequently increased to $3 billion in conference, was vetoed by Reagan as part of a supplemental appropriations bill (HR 5922). *(Emergency mortgage aid, p. 633)*

The Appropriations Committee reported H J Res 562 Aug. 18 (H Rept 97-764), both authorizing and appropriating funds for the jobs program. The House passed the measure Sept. 16 by a 223-169 vote, largely along party lines.

Republicans protested that the bill was a "callous election-year gimmick." But Democrats openly challenged the GOP to oppose such a program shortly before the Nov. 2 elections, as the unemployment rate was approaching double digits.

There was no further action on the House bill. An attempt by Sen. Edward M. Kennedy, D-Mass., to attach the measure to a fiscal 1983 funding resolution (H J Res 599) was blocked on a 60-37 Senate vote Sept. 29.

Fifty Years of U.S. Job Creation Efforts

Throughout their history, federal job creation programs have had conflicting goals of making permanent improvements in the economic backbone of the country, and immediately helping people who need jobs.

Carefully planned, longe-range capital improvements are a boon to future generations. But they are slow in helping hungry people in need.

Quick-starting repair and service projects ameliorate present suffering. But they do little lasting good, are open to fraud and waste, and are branded forever as "make-work, leaf-raking" jobs.

From the New Deal...

Two programs with similar initials, the Public Works Administration (PWA) and Works Progress Administrations (WPA), reflected the contrasting sides of job creation under the New Deal.

The PWA, established in 1933 with initial funding of $3.3 billion, focused on long-range projects. The program lasted for six years and spent a total of $6 billion.

PWA workers pushed the Skyline Drive through Virginia's Blue Ridge Mountains. They dug tunnels for subways in Chicago, built aircraft carriers and hundreds of schools and flood control projects. During the program's heyday, PWA workers helped build two-thirds of the new schools and sewage plants in the country.

Interior Secretary Harold L. Ickes ran PWA with a tight fist. He reviewed all projects, keeping the program free from any significant charges of waste or fraud. But Ickes' careful stewardship closed down the program. He was criticized by other members of the Roosevelt administration who argued that the PWA was failing to provide needed economic stimulus.

Better known than the PWA was the WPA, which stressed rapid employment for the jobless. It was set up by Congress in 1935 with a $5 billion appropriation. By 1943, when it ended, the WPA had cost $11 billion.

Under presidential adviser Harry Hopkins, the WPA provided a bewildering variety of jobs ranging from construction to the arts. Its participants worked on an estimated 600,000 miles of highways, 125,000 public buildings and 8,000 parks.

WPA workers also wrote a classic series of guides to the states, put on plays and circuses, performed symphonies and painted murals in post offices and other public buildings around the country.

All told, an estimated eight million workers received help from the program. During the height of the WPA, from 1935 to 1941, an average of 2.1 million people were on the rolls at any one time.

But the program was run poorly. Much of the money was spent on administration, and construction standards were low. To much of the public, WPA workers seemed forever to be resting on their shovels.

Other New Deal jobs programs included the Civilian Conservation Corps (CCC), which employed young men in environmental projects, and the Civil Works Administration (CWA), a short-lived program in the winter of 1933-34 that was plagued by waste and corruption charges.

...To the Eighties

After a hiatus of two decades, the government returned to direct job creation programs in the 1960s.

Congress in 1962 passed a $900 million accelerated public works bill (PL 87-658). It was a scaled-down version of President Kennedy's $2 billion proposal for pump-priming public works spending. *(Congress and the Nation Vol. I, p. 877)*

In the early 1970s, Congress and President Nixon clashed repeatedly over job creation programs. After two successful vetoes, bills establishing a $2.25 billion public service employment program (PL 92-54) and a $3.9 billion public works program (PL 92-65) were enacted in 1971. *(Congress and the Nation Vol. III, pp. 178, 740)*

The big program of the decade was the Local Public Works program (LPW) enacted in 1976-77. Acting against the mid-decade recession, Congress in 1976 passed a $2 billion program (PL 94-369) over President Ford's veto. It was followed in 1977 by a $4 billion addition (PL 95-28), proposed by President Carter as part of his economic stimulus package. *(Congress and the Nation Vol. IV, p. 708; Congress and the Nation Vol. V, p. 401)*

LPW funded a total of 10,616 projects. Most of the projects involved work on sewers, streets and bridges, and local government buildings. A related program, like LPW run by the Economic Development Administration (EDA), continued to fund public works projects in economically depressed areas. *(EDA, fiscal assistance, p. 115)*

The other main federal job creation programs were under the Comprehensive Employment and Training Act (CETA). Along with job training programs, CETA provided as many as 750,000 public jobs during the early years of the Carter administration.

There was a substantial amount of waste and fraud in CETA's public service employment programs, however, and the jobs generally were of little permanent benefit. Congress abolished public service employment in 1981, and even its most ardent supporters made only a token effort to re-establish it during 1982 congressional consideration of the job training legislation that replaced CETA. *(CETA, p. 648; job training, p. 655)*

Other Measures. Other components of the Democrats' anti-recession package included:

● A five-year Defense Production Act reauthorization (HR 5540) that called for $1 billion a year in new aid to industry, $250 million a year in new government grants for job training and $100 million a year in new aid for colleges — all in the name of industrial defense preparedness and all taken from the defense budget. The bill was pulled off the House floor Sept. 23 following adoption of a weakening amendment, and a simple six-month extension of the Defense Production Act (S 2375 — PL 97-336) was approved instead. *(Story, p. 116)*

● A bill (HR 5133), supported strongly by the United Auto Workers union, that would force reductions in sales of foreign cars unless foreign auto companies produced more of them inside the United States. The House passed the bill Dec. 15, but there was no Senate action on the measure. *(Story, p. 102)*

● Twin bills (HR 6967, S 2807) based on the theory that the Federal Reserve could and should reduce market interest rates and thus spur economic recovery. The bills were designed to force the Fed to target interest rates as well as the "money supply" in its control and regulation of the banking system. There was no action on the measures.

In addition to the central elements of the package, the Democrats sought extension of programs authorized by the Economic Development Administration (EDA), to which congressional Democrats had turned to provide jobs during previous recessions. The House passed a reauthorization bill (HR 6100) Aug. 12, but the extension ran up against a stone wall in the Senate. *(Story, p. 115)*

Unemployment Benefits

Faced with record unemployment and an election less than three months away, Congress agreed Aug. 19 to extend unemployment benefits by six to 10 weeks, for a maximum of 49 weeks in some states.

The new federal supplemental unemployment compensation program was adopted as part of a larger revenue increase/spending cut package (HR 4961 — PL 97-248) designed to reduce the federal budget deficit. *(Tax/spending bill, p. 72)*

The supplemental jobless benefits went into effect Sept. 12 and were expected to help approximately two million unemployed workers who had exhausted regular and extended benefits from the federal-state program. Before adjourning in December, Congress expanded the supplemental benefits, which were scheduled to run through March 31, 1983. The price tag for the combined package was expected to be about $2.7 billion. Congress voted a two-year extension of the program in 1983. *(Story, p. 665)*

The initial supplemental jobless aid was incorporated in the 1982 tax and spending bill in part because of widespread congressional concern over rising unemployment, which had reached a postwar high of 9.8 percent at the time of the vote. Members argued that with a lengthy recession more and more jobless workers were exhausting existing benefits but had little chance of finding work.

In addition, the bill's sponsors anticipated that the measure would attract election-year support for the controversial tax legislation.

Democrats had pushed for the additional benefits for much of the year, but met with little success until the Reagan administration — worried about rising joblessness — indicated it would back the plan.

"This is as large and as timely a benefit package as is going to come our way," House Ways and Means Committee Chairman Dan Rostenkowski, D-Ill., told his colleagues on the House floor Aug. 19. Ways and Means on May 25 had approved legislation (HR 6369 — H Rept 97-587) that called for 13 extra weeks of benefits, but targeted them to states with the highest unemployment. That measure never reached the floor.

The full Senate never voted on additional jobless benefits either, but it agreed Aug. 5 to a "sense of the Senate" resolution instructing conferees on the tax/spending bill to come up with the supplemental benefit program.

Supplemental Compensation Plan

Under HR 4961, jobless workers in every state were to receive the supplemental benefits, but the length of the extra payments was to be determined by the state's unemployment rate.

Most states had offered 26 weeks of regular benefits, with up to 13 weeks of extended benefits (EB) when state unemployment was high, for a maximum of 39 weeks.

The supplemental benefits program allowed an additional 10 weeks of payments in the 36 states (plus Puerto Rico and the Virgin Islands) that offered extended benefits on or after June 1, 1982. This meant a maximum of 49 weeks of benefits in states that still were providing extended benefits and up to 36 weeks of payments in those states that had gone, or would go, off the extended benefit program after June 1.

The remaining states, those with average insured unemployment rates of 3.5 percent or more, were allowed to pay eight more weeks of benefits, for a maximum of 34 weeks. Those with lower unemployment were able to provide six additional weeks, for a total of 32.

To cover the $2.1 billion cost of the new program, Congress agreed in the tax bill to lower the income level at which unemployment benefits would be taxed.

Previously, jobless benefits were not taxed unless an individual had an annual income over $20,000 ($25,000 for couples). The new law lowered these tax thresholds to $12,000 for individuals and $18,000 for married couples.

The provision, effective for benefits paid on or after Jan. 1, 1982, meant that funding for the supplemental program would come from general revenues and not from the financially strained trust funds of the unemployment program.

Impact of 1981 Changes

Ironically, the new supplemental benefits were scheduled to start at just about the same time cutbacks in unemployment compensation approved by Congress in 1981 went into effect.

Those changes, included in the 1981 reconciliation bill (PL 97-35), made it more difficult for states to qualify for extended unemployment benefits by raising from 4 percent to 5 percent the insured jobless rate (reflecting those collecting benefits) needed to offer the 13-week EB program. *(1981 action, p. 647)*

As a result, six to 12 of the 25 states offering 13 weeks of extended benefits triggered off the EB program Sept. 25, shortly after the additional 10 weeks became available. Other states were expected to trigger off EB later on.

So while the new change was an improvement over existing law, there was a net loss in benefits for many on the unemployment rolls.

Other Action

Additional Weeks. Congress Dec. 23 approved legislation (HR 6211 — PL 97-424) adding two to six more weeks of jobless payments to the supplemental benefits program, allowing up to 55 weeks of benefits for some unemployed workers. The extra benefits were approved as part of the highway authorization and gas tax bill cleared by Congress on the final day of the session. The gas tax was designed to finance highway repairs, creating an estimated 300,000 jobs. *(Jobs plans, p. 652; gas tax hike, p. 301)*

Under the new program, states would be eligible for six, four or two extra weeks of benefits depending on their insured jobless rate. About 30 states were expected to qualify for four more weeks. Like the benefits passed in the summer, the new supplemental payments were to expire on March 31, 1983.

Military Eligibility. Congress Oct. 1 cleared legislation that allowed 13 weeks of unemployment benefits for those who had been honorably discharged from military service and who generally had completed a full term of service. Under the 1981 reconciliation bill, only those who were not allowed to re-enlist could qualify for jobless payments. The provision, expected to cost $220 million over three years, was attached to a miscellaneous revenue measure (HR 4717 — PL 97-362).

Job Training Program

Congress completed action Oct. 1 on new job training legislation (S 2036 — PL 97-300) to replace the expiring Comprehensive Employment and Training Act (CETA).

The new program authorized by the bill provided training in job skills to the low-income unemployed. Unlike CETA, it did not pay for public service employment for the jobless. *(CETA background, p. 648)*

S 2036 gave more power to state governments in running job training programs. CETA had operated largely through city and county governments. In addition, the legislation provided for a greatly expanded role for private businesses in operating local training programs.

The bill did not set a specific funding level for the new program. But when S 2036 passed the Senate, sponsors estimated annual spending at $3.8 billion.

President Reagan repeatedly had prodded Congress to finish work on the bill, but there never was any real question that it would be enacted. Throughout its legislative history, S 2036 (S Rept 97-469) and its House companion (HR 5320 — H Rept 97-537) enjoyed overwhelming bipartisan support. The Senate passed S 2036 by a 95-0 vote July 1; the House approved HR 5320 by a 356-52 vote Aug. 4. Final action came when the House approved the conference report on the bill (H Rept 97-889) by a 339-12 vote Oct. 1. The Senate had approved the conference report Sept. 30.

Final Provisions

As signed into law Oct. 13, the Job Training Partnership Act (S 2036 — PL 97-300):

● Stated that the purpose of the bill was to aid youths and unskilled adults in entering the job market, and to provide job training to low-income individuals who faced serious problems in finding work.

● Authorized open-ended funding, for fiscal 1983 and thereafter, for the programs established by the bill, with specific requirements of $618 million for the Job Corps in fiscal 1983 and $2 million a year for the National Commission for Employment Policy; also set a maximum funding level for veterans', Indians', migrant farm workers' and other programs.

Structure of Programs. Gave the governor of each state the authority to designate, within certain limitations, the "service delivery areas," the units of government within which the job training programs would operate.

● Required a governor to approve a request to be a service delivery area from any unit of local government, or group of local government units, with a population of at least 200,000; the provision also applied to rural areas that had operated job programs under the expired CETA.

● Required each local service delivery area to establish a Private Industry Council (PIC), composed of business, labor, educational and community representatives; also required that a majority of the members and the chairman of each council be business representatives.

● Gave each PIC the responsibility, along with the local governments, for guiding the training programs. The PIC would provide for development of an overall plan of its training program, and would select either itself, the local government or a non-profit private group to administer the program.

● Established procedures for review and approval by the governor of the plans of each local training program.

● Authorized the Labor Department to develop "performance standards" measuring how successful programs were in increasing the earnings power and reducing the welfare dependency of program participants. A local program that failed to meet the standards after two years would be subject to reorganization or replacement by the governor.

● Limited spending by local programs on administrative and related costs to no more than 30 percent of their funds, thus ensuring that at least 70 percent was spent on direct training. The bill made clear that the 30 percent limitation would cover administration, supportive services and subsistence payments for participants.

● Allowed for waiver of the 30 percent limit on administrative funds in certain circumstances, such as unusually high unemployment in the area.

● Placed certain responsibilities on states, such as coordination of local job training and education programs, establishment of a state job training council, collection of information on labor markets in the state, and establishment of programs for job training of older workers.

● Established labor protections for participants in training programs, as well as protections for regular employees of businesses or agencies in which training participants might be placed.

● Gave the Labor Department and state governments authority to monitor use of funds by local programs and to impose sanctions in cases of misuse; also provided criminal penalties for persons found to have misused funds.

Training for the Disadvantaged. Authorized a program of grants to states and local areas for the training of low-income youths and adults.

● Distributed funds to states according to the following formula: one-third on the basis of each state's share of the total low-income population; one-third on the state's share of the total number of unemployed persons living in areas with unemployment rates over 6.5 percent; and one-third according to the ratio between the number of unemployed persons in the state in excess of 4.5 percent of the work force, and the total number of unemployed persons in excess of 4.5 percent of the work force.

Donovan Investigation

Concluding a nine-month investigation, federal special prosecutor Leon Silverman announced Sept. 13, 1982, that he had uncovered no evidence to warrant bringing charges against Secretary of Labor Raymond J. Donovan.

As he had in an earlier report, Silverman said there was "insufficient credible evidence" to support allegations that Donovan had engaged in illegal labor practices and was linked to organized crime.

Silverman's report did not end Donovan's troubles, however. In an indictment made public Oct. 2, 1984, a Bronx County, N.Y., grand jury charged Donovan with larceny and fraud concerning his financial dealings as vice president of a New Jersey construction firm. On March 15, 1985, Donovan resigned his Cabinet post after a New York Supreme Court judge refused to dismiss the charges. He had been on leave of absence while appealing the indictment.

Prosecutor's Reports. Silverman's initial report, released June 28, 1982, focused on a charge that Donovan had participated in an illegal payoff by his New Jersey firm, Schiavone Construction Co., to a corrupt labor union official.

The second report followed the Aug. 25 murder of the son of an underworld figure with alleged ties to Donovan. Silverman said he found no evidence to connect Donovan with the case.

The report left several loose threads hanging about other allegations involving Donovan and his construction firm. It said there were a "disturbing" number of allegations that Donovan was connected with organized crime figures. In addition, the special prosecutor turned over certain aspects of the case to other federal agencies for further investigation.

Background. A three-judge federal court panel in Washington, D.C., on Dec. 29, 1981, had appointed Silverman, a New York City attorney, to investigate allegations of corruption against the labor secretary. Donovan himself had requested the appointment of a special prosecutor.

Questions about Donovan's past had surfaced shortly after he was nominated for the labor post in 1981. The first round of allegations held up Donovan's confirmation for several weeks early in 1981. *(Cabinet profiles, p. 1023)*

Accepting the argument that nothing had been proven against Donovan, who heatedly denied wrongdoing, the Senate approved his nominations by an 80-17 vote. Subsequently it was disclosed that the FBI had damaging information that was provided to the White House but withheld from the Senate Labor Committee during hearings on Donovan's confirmation.

● Required states to distribute 78 percent of their allocation to local programs, according to the same formula used to distribute funds to states.

● Limited eligibility for the programs to economically disadvantaged persons, defined as those on welfare or food stamps, foster children or families with incomes below either the Office of Management and Budget poverty level, or 70 percent of the Bureau of Labor Statistics' lower living standard, whichever was higher.

● Stipulated that up to 10 percent of local program participants need not be economically disadvantaged, provided they had other employment problems such as a physical handicap, alcoholism or limited English proficiency.

● Required local programs to spend at least 40 percent of their funds on persons aged 16-21.

● Authorized use of funds for a wide variety of services, such as job counseling, skill training, remedial education or on-the-job training.

● Authorized funding of summer employment and training programs for youths.

Dislocated Workers. Established a program of training assistance for workers who had lost their jobs and were unlikely to get them back, for example because of the permanent closing of a factory.

● Distributed funds to states on the basis of the extent of unemployment, and the extent to which the unemployed had been out of work for 15 weeks or more.

● Required states to match federal funds for dislocated worker programs with an equal amount of their own money; allowed states with high unemployment to provide a reduced share.

National Programs. Authorized funds for national job training for native Americans and migrant and seasonal farm workers.

● Authorized the Job Corps as a national program of residential and non-residential centers for the training and education of disadvantaged young people; established rules and standards for participation, activities, allowances for participants and involvement by states.

● Authorized other national programs including training of veterans, research and demonstration, and labor market information.

● Authorized the National Commission for Employment Policy to review and evaluate national employment policy.

● Authorized training programs aimed at helping federal contractors meet federal affirmative action requirements.

● Extended the authorization of the federal Employment Service, to assist state employment offices.

Disability Benefits

After almost a year of legislative haggling, Congress in the final days of the session enacted a temporary measure to help thousands of individuals suddenly cut from the Social Security disability benefit rolls. Permanent legislation was enacted in 1984. *(Story, p. 667)*

The bill (HR 7093 — PL 97-455), cleared Dec. 21, allowed individuals dropped from the rolls before Oct. 1, 1983, to continue collecting payments while they appealed their termination. Benefits had to be repaid, however, if the appeal was lost.

Even though about two-thirds of those who appealed were eventually reinstated, they did not collect benefits during the appeals process, sometimes lasting longer than a year. As a result, many lost homes and savings — and a few died — while pursuing appeals.

"While this is only a temporary measure, it is a significant step in the right direction toward reform of a process in serious disarray," said Sen. John Heinz, R-Pa., chairman of the Senate Special Committee on Aging.

Besides allowing payments until an individual appealed to an administrative law judge, the measure allowed the secretary of health and human services to slow down the department's review of the disability rolls.

Congress mandated the review in 1980 after reports that as many as 20-30 percent of the approximately four million Disability Insurance recipients were no longer eligible. *(Congress and the Nation Vol. V, p. 705)*

The three-year review was to have started by 1982, but the Reagan administration began nine months early to weed out recipients with what some critics charged was excessive fervor. Some 265,000 recipients had been dropped from the program by the end of 1982, although the administration slowed its actions during the course of congressional debate on the legislation.

Legislative History

The disability bill's passage through Congress proved extremely difficult, despite general agreement among the House, the Senate and the administration that benefits should continue during appeals.

The House Ways and Means Committee May 26 reported a measure (HR 6181 — H Rept 97-588) that allowed payments through an initial appeal. It also provided for four additional months of "adjustment benefits" once it had been decided a recipient was no longer disabled.

However, groups representing the disabled balked at provisions making it more difficult for beneficiaries to introduce additional evidence before an administrative law judge, and the legislation was effectively killed by the time it reached the House Rules Committee.

In the Senate, several Republican and Democratic members worked behind the scenes to fashion a package similar to the one finally included in HR 7093. The Finance Committee approved the measure Sept. 28. To facilitate enactment, the committee attached its measure (S Rept 97-648) to a minor House-passed bill dealing with Virgin Islands taxation, but Sen. Russell B. Long, D-La., blocked a floor vote before the election recess.

Long objected to a provision that indicated Congress might be willing to accept changes making it more difficult for beneficiaries to be taken off the rolls. The language was modified before Senate passage by a 70-4 vote Dec. 3 and finally deleted in conference.

The Senate adopted the conference report (H Rept 97-985) by voice vote Dec. 21, and the House went on to clear the bill by a 259-0 vote the same day.

Provisions

As signed into law Jan. 12, 1983, HR 7093 (PL 97-455):
● Provided Disability Insurance payments and Medicare coverage to individuals appealing their termination from the disability rolls before Oct. 1, 1983. Benefits would have to be repaid should the appeal be lost.
● Required, as of Jan. 1, 1984, that face-to-face hearings be held when individuals initially appealed their termination from the rolls. Previously, some beneficiaries did not have such a meeting until they appeared before an administrative law judge, most often the final stage of appeal.
● Barred payments after June 1984 to an individual appealing a termination decision.

● Extended for seven months — until July 1, 1983 — an exemption from a law requiring that certain spousal Social Security benefits be reduced dollar-for-dollar by any public pension payments. However, the extension applied only to individuals who could prove that they were dependent on their spouse for more than half of their support.

American Conservation Corps

The House in 1982 passed a bill (HR 4861) to establish a new program to put unemployed young people to work on conservation and rehabilitation projects on federal and state lands.

The program, known as the American Conservation Corps (ACC), was to replace two similar programs — the Youth Conservation Corps and the Young Adult Conservation Corps — which the Reagan administration planned to terminate.

Ignoring administration opposition, the House June 9 voted 291-102 to establish the new program. However, the Senate never acted on the legislation, which had been reported by the Interior Committee May 4 and by the Education and Labor Committee May 17 (H Rept 97-500, Parts I and II).

A House effort to attach the provisions of HR 4861 to an unrelated Senate-passed bill (S 1501) failed in the closing days of the session.

A scaled-down version of HR 999 was pocket-vetoed in 1984. *(Story, p. 671)*

Racketeering, Longshore Bills

Two bills aimed at cracking down on alleged union corruption died at the end of the 97th Congress.

After passing the Senate easily, the Labor Racketeering Act (S 1785) and legislation revising the federal workers' compensation law for longshore workers (S 1182) ran into fatal opposition in the House, where Labor-Management Subcommittee Chairman Phillip Burton, D-Calif., declined to act on them. The Senate Dec. 19 added the text of S 1785 to an unrelated House bill (HR 1029), but there was no further action.

The Senate approved similar legislation in 1983. A longshore compensation bill was enacted in 1984. *(Stories, pp. 666, 671)*

Racketeering. S 1785 (S Rept 97-497) was passed by the Senate July 28 by voice vote. The bill would have increased the penalties for illegal practices by union and management officials and barred union officials who had been convicted of labor crimes from continuing to hold their union offices.

Sponsor Sam Nunn, D-Ga., whose investigations of waterfront corruption provided the impetus for the measure, called it "the most significant piece of anti-racketeering legislation that has come through the Congress since the Landrum-Griffin bill" of 1959. *(Background, Congress and the Nation Vol. I, p. 568)*

The bill had AFL-CIO support but was opposed by the Teamsters union.

Longshore. S 1182 (S Rept 97-498), passed by voice vote July 27, would have limited future increases in benefits paid to disabled dockworkers. Pushed by a coalition of shipping and insurance companies, the bill also would have limited the jurisdiction of the federal program, which provided disability insurance for dockworkers not covered by

state workers' compensation laws. *(Background, Congress and the Nation Vol. III, p. 730)*

The longshore bill also contained anti-fraud provisions designed to stop alleged abuse of the program by organized crime.

Social Security Financing

With the exception of some political rhetoric around election time, Congress managed to skirt the difficult issue of Social Security during most of 1982.

It waited instead for the report of President Reagan's bipartisan National Commission on Social Security Reform, which had been appointed at the end of 1981 to remove Social Security from the political arena.

The commission originally was scheduled to make its recommendations on saving the financially troubled retirement system by the end of the year but was granted an extension until Jan. 15, 1983. The commission met that deadline, with approval of a last-minute compromise plan that was enacted by Congress in March. *(Story, p. 659)*

Barring action, Social Security's largest trust fund, Old Age and Survivors Insurance (OASI), was set to run out of money by July 1983. Even if Congress allowed the OASI fund to continue to borrow from the system's healthier Disability and Hospital Insurance funds, all three would run out of money sometime in 1984.

In 1980 Congress had reallocated taxes temporarily from the Disability trust fund to OASI to avert a funding shortfall. In 1981, unable to reach agreement on a more comprehensive package, Congress agreed to allow OASI to borrow from the Disability and Hospital trust funds until the end of 1982. *(Story, p. 645)*

Jobs for Older Americans

Congress in 1982 expressed strong support for the community service employment program for older Americans, which the Reagan administration wanted to close down.

Legislation enacted over President Reagan's veto Sept. 10 (HR 6863 — PL 97-257) provided $211 million for the program in fiscal 1982. The president had vetoed the bill, a supplemental appropriations measure for the fiscal year ending Sept. 30, because he opposed funding for the jobs program and several education programs.

The Senate July 1 had adopted, by an 89-6 vote, a resolution (S Res 340) opposing the termination of the program. The action came two days after the Senate, at the administration's insistence, agreed to drop funding for the program from an earlier fiscal 1982 supplemental appropriations bill (HR 6685 — PL 97-216).

Congress in 1981 had reauthorized the jobs program for the elderly for three years. The program provided jobs in hospitals, libraries, day-care centers and senior-citizen programs for about 54,000 low-income elderly Americans. *(Story, p. 593)*

Trade Adjustment Aid

In clearing a miscellaneous tax measure Oct. 1 (HR 4717 — PL 97-362), Congress liberalized eligibility requirements for the trade adjustment assistance program by re-

pealing a tighter standard enacted in the the 1981 budget reconciliation law (PL 97-35).

Under the 1981 law, benefits were provided to groups of workers only when it was found that foreign import competition was a "substantial cause" for the loss of their jobs. HR 4717 restored previous language stipulating that import competition must have "contributed importantly" to the layoffs. *(1981 action, p. 650)*

The trade adjustment provisions had been atttached to the bill by the Senate Finance Committee before Senate passage Dec. 16, 1981. Both chambers adopted the conference report on the tax legislation (H Rept 97-929) by voice vote Oct. 1, 1982.

Congress extended the trade adjustment assistance program in 1983. *(Story, p. 665)*

Other Legislation

Domestic Content

The House Dec. 15 passed, **by a 215-188 key vote (R 44-130; D 171-58)**, a bill (HR 5133) to require all companies selling more than 100,000 cars a year in the United States to use set percentages of U.S. labor and parts. Stiff quotas would be applied to companies that failed to meet the bill's requirements. *(1982 key votes, p. 895)*

The measure was drafted by the United Auto Workers union, which thought it would help restore the more than one million jobs lost by workers in the automobile and related industries since 1978. The administration vigorously opposed the legislation.

The Senate did not act on either the 1982 bill or a similar measure passed by the House in 1983. *(Details, pp. 102, 108)*

Migrant Farm Workers

Congress in 1982 cleared legislation (HR 7102 — PL 97-470) establishing new protections for migrant farm workers. Among other provisions, the bill required farm employers as well as farm labor contractors to meet a series of standards involving payroll records, health, safety and housing. *(Details, p. 502)*

1983

Congress moved early in 1983 on two economic emergencies — a Social Security system that was rapidly running out of money and a deep recession that had left nearly 12 million people unemployed.

Acting on the recommendations of a bipartisan presidential commission, Congress March 25 approved one of the biggest overhauls of the Social Security system since the program began in 1937. The rescue of Social Security followed a two-year fight that was triggered in 1981 by Reagan administration proposals to cut benefits to keep the retirement system from insolvency.

Passage came shortly after Congress approved a $4.6 billion jobs and humanitarian relief package to reduce un-

employment that had reached 10.7 percent of the work force at the end of 1982.

Both the Social Security financing and job creation issues had become partisan battles before the year began. Disagreement about how to infuse the Social Security system with more money found Democrats arguing for tax increases rather than benefit cuts and Republicans taking the opposite position. Although there was no direct benefit cut in the final bill, the measure did include a provision raising the retirement age gradually to age 67 in the 21st century. Payroll taxes also were increased for both employers and employees, and new federal workers were brought into the program.

The Old-Age and Survivors Insurance Trust Fund would have run out of funds in July and faced serious financial troubles throughout the decade had Congress not acted. The Social Security financing package was expected to raise $165 billion over a seven-year period.

Responding to a second pressing issue, congressional Democrats early in 1983 renewed the battle they had waged unsuccessfully in 1982 for job creation legislation to combat high unemployment. The Democrats had been frustrated in their efforts to get a $5.4 billion jobs program through a Republican-controlled Senate in the face of White House opposition.

Bowing to the threat of continued political pressure, President Reagan in February proposed a $4.3 billion jobs plan, with the bulk of the money slated for accelerated spending for federal construction and repair projects. The proposal quickly grew to $4.9 billion in the House and $5.2 billion in the Senate. Conferees scaled down the final measure to $4.6 billion to gain presidential approval. Two-thirds of the package was allotted for public works, general construction and water projects, with the remaining funds for social services, health and humanitarian assistance.

House Democrats considered the measure "Phase I" of a campaign to aid the long-term unemployed. But "Phase II" proposals for public works and public service jobs programs had little success, as the unemployment rate began to decline and as the administration took a hard line on any further jobs legislation.

High unemployment rates did persuade Congress in 1983 to extend two other programs to assist people who had lost jobs: the federal supplemental unemployment compensation program that had gone into effect in 1982 and the trade adjustment assistance program for workers laid off from industries harmed by import competiton.

Social Security Rescue Plan

After almost two years of bitter political debate and inaction, Congress agreed in 1983 to make fundamental changes in the Social Security program intended to keep the system solvent into the 21st century.

The package adopted (HR 1900 — PL 98-21) raised the retirement age from 65 to 67 by the year 2027, delayed retirees' annual cost-of-living adjustments (COLAs) six months and increased payroll taxes for both employers and employees.

Other major changes included taxing benefits of high-income recipients and bringing into the system new federal employees, members of Congress, the president, vice president and federal judges.

If economic projections proved correct, the changes were expected not only to solve Social Security's immediate financial problems but also to generate enough money to cover the retirement of the so-called "baby boom" generation in the next century.

Partisan bickering about what to do to keep the retirement fund from going broke started in 1981 after the Reagan administration proposed cutting benefits. Democrats charged the administration with trying to balance the budget at the expense of the elderly, and called instead for higher payroll taxes to finance the system. *(Story, p. 645)*

Dealing with the politically sensitive issue of Social Security was made easier for Congress by having the recommendations of the National Commission on Social Security Reform on which to build consensus for legislation. The commission made its report in January 1983. *(Box, p. 662)*

Despite some last-minute hitches, legislation based on the commission report moved rapidly through Congress, largely because of congressional fears that any delay might cause the hard-won political consensus to unravel.

Also attached to the bill were a number of extraneous provisions, including a six-month extension of an emergency jobless benefits program to help more than two million unemployed workers. *(Jobless aid extension, p. 665)*

House Committee Action

The House Ways and Means Committee went quickly to work after the National Commission on Social Security Reform made its report Jan. 15. The Social Security Subcommittee agreed to HR 1900 on Feb. 23. The full committee reported the bill by a 32-3 vote on March 4 (H Rept 98-25).

Voting against the measure were Republicans Bill Archer, Texas (who was a member of the commission), Richard T. Schulze, Pa., and Philip M. Crane, Ill. Archer said the package did not make enough "substantive" changes in the system.

Setting the stage for a major House floor fight over raising the retirement age or increasing payroll taxes to keep Social Security solvent, the Ways and Means Committee agreed March 2 to ask the Rules Committee to allow floor votes on both issues.

In an effort to block a potentially divisive committee vote on raising the retirement age, Chairman Dan Rostenkowski, D-Ill., told members that the proposed rule allowing two separate floor votes on the issue had been agreed to informally by the House leadership, including Rules Committee Chairman Claude Pepper, D-Fla., a staunch defender of benefits for the elderly.

The proposed rule was expected to pit Pepper, who favored an increase in payroll taxes in the next century, against Social Security Subcommittee Chairman J. J. Pickle, D-Texas, and a large number of Republicans, who preferred an increase in the retirement age after the year 2000.

The Ways and Means Committee took the middle road by including the recommendations of its Social Security Subcommittee to combine both benefit cuts and payroll tax increases. The subcommittee had voted to reduce initial benefits approximately 5 percent for new beneficiaries beginning in the year 2000 and to raise the payroll tax on employers and employees from 7.65 percent to 7.89 percent in 2015.

Under the committee's proposed rule, that provision would be included in the final package if the other two amendments failed on the floor.

The committee revised a controversial subcommittee provision that would have allowed the Social Security sys-

Chronology of Social Security Rescue Efforts

1977. Social Security faced financial problems because high inflation was causing more benefits to be paid out than revenues taken in. Congress raised Social Security payroll taxes $227 billion over a 10-year period (PL 95-216). *(Congress and the Nation Vol. V, p. 235)*

1980. Economic conditions continued to worsen and so did the financial troubles of Social Security, despite scheduled tax increases. Congress reallocated, for two years, funds from the healthier Disability Insurance Trust Fund to the troubled Old Age and Survivors Insurance Trust Tund (PL 96-403).

May 12, 1981. The Reagan administration set off a firestorm of controversy by proposing drastic changes in the Social Security system to save it from possible financial insolvency. The plan included reduced benefits for early retirement, a delayed cost-of-living allowance and reduced benefit growth for future retirees. Critics charged the plan was unnecessary and a backdoor attempt at reducing the federal budget deficit.

May 23, 1981. After days of partisan rhetoric on both sides of the aisle, the Senate sent a clear message to the administration that its Social Security proposals were too hot to handle. It agreed 96-0 to a resolution against any "unfair" and "precipitous" cuts in Social Security benefits.

July 31, 1981. The House voted 404-20 to restore the $122 minimum monthly Social Security benefit eliminated in a budget reconciliation conference agreement. That move failed, but restoration of the benefit cut, proposed in the Reagan budget, became a battle cry for Democrats bent on making

political hay out of Reagan's unpopular Social Security proposals.

December 1981. Congress restored the minimum benefit and agreed to a stopgap funding plan to keep the Social Security system from going broke until 1983 (PL 97-123). As economic conditions became increasingly poor, so did the financial outlook for the retirement system. But the issue of Social Security had become so politicized during the year that major reform became impossible. Reagan appointed a 15-member commission to study the issue and report on Dec. 31, 1982, after the midterm elections. *(1981 action, p. 645)*

November 1982. The President's National Commission on Social Security Reform tried for three days to come up with some recommendations for saving the system. But all it could agree to was the size of the problem it faced — a $150 billion to $200 billion deficit over the next seven years. Democrats and Republicans on the panel differed over whether tax hikes or benefit cuts should form the bulk of the rescue plan.

December 1982. As the commission's reporting date drew near, it appeared unlikely that any specific set of recommendations would be adopted. Chairman Alan Greenspan asked the administration for, and received, a 15-day extension of the deadline.

Jan. 15, 1983. A core group of commission members met in a series of closed-door sessions, some with administration officials, to hammer out a last-ditch compromise plan to save Social Security. In the final hours of the commission's life, a bargain was struck.

---

tem to borrow from the Treasury in emergency situations. The change was adopted for the most part to win bipartisan support for the entire package. Republicans had charged that even limited general revenue borrowing could set a precedent for raiding the Treasury to keep Social Security afloat.

The committee agreed instead to an amendment by Bill Gradison, R-Ohio, that the Social Security trustees would be required to report to Congress if it appeared that any of the system's three trust funds — Old Age and Survivors Insurance (OASI), Hospital Insurance (HI) and Disability Insurance (DI) — were in danger. Congress could then approve an emergency plan, ranging from temporary benefit cuts or tax hikes to borrowing from the Treasury, to rebuild trust fund reserves.

The committee also adopted an amendment to replace a proposed deduction for increased payroll taxes for the self-employed with a new tax credit. The change was made largely to benefit low- and moderate-income taxpayers.

The committee accepted several subcommittee provisions to protect the system from unexpected fluctuations in the economy. These included a measure requiring the an-

nual COLA to reflect the lower of wage or price increases if trust fund reserves fell below a certain level, beginning in 1988. Existing law based the COLA on increases in the price level.

House Floor Action

The House March 9 passed HR 1900 by a 282-148 vote, following an emotional floor debate over the best way to solve the system's projected financial difficulties in the next century. Rules Committee Chairman Pepper proposed a .53 percentage point increase in the payroll taxes in the year 2010 to prevent a cut in benefits. Pepper's measure was rejected by a vote of 132-296, despite the backing of House Speaker Thomas P. O'Neill Jr., D-Mass.

"History is being written on this floor. We are changing the tradition of this country," O'Neill said when it became apparent that Pepper's attempts to prevent a retirement age increase would fail. "In America, each generation has always paid for the generation that has gone before them."

An amendment raising the retirement age, offered by

Social Security Subcommittee Chairman Pickle, was approved by a **228-202 key vote (R 152-14; D 76-188)**. *(1983 key votes, p. 911)*

The House agreed to raise the retirement age in two stages. The first would be a gradual increase from 65 to 66 over a six-year period ending in the year 2009. The second increase would be from 66 to 67 over another six-year period ending in the year 2027.

While individuals still would be able to take early retirement at age 62, their benefits would be reduced from the current 80 percent of full benefits to 70 percent in 2027.

Opponents seized on this last change and charged it would penalize millions of workers forced to retire early because of poor health or mandatory retirement.

But Pickle defended the age increase as necessary to keep up with changing demographics. He pointed out that life expectancy had increased more than 10 years since the 65-year retirement age was set in place over 40 years earlier.

Pickle's amendment also required the Department of Health and Human Services to make recommendations by Jan. 1, 1986, on how Congress should deal with individuals who could not retire later because of physically demanding jobs.

Those voting against passage of the bill included both liberals opposed to the higher retirement age and coverage of federal employees and conservatives opposed to additional taxes.

Senate Committee Action

The Senate Finance Committee March 11 reported its version (S 1 — S Rept 98-23) by a vote of 18-1. The dissenting vote was cast by Steven D. Symms, R-Idaho.

The Senate package included a one-year increase in the retirement age by the year 2015, but it also cut initial retirement benefits 5 percent after the turn of the century. The long-term financing proposal, offered by John Heinz, R-Pa., and adopted 13-4, called for a gradual increase in the retirement age from 65 to 66 over a 15-year period beginning in the year 2000. The Heinz amendment also eliminated over a five-year period a penalty imposed on beneficiaries who worked after they reached retirement age.

The committee rejected 15-2 a proposal by Daniel Patrick Moynihan, D-N.Y., to raise payroll taxes in the year 2010, in place of benefit cuts.

The panel also rejected 6-11 a motion by Russell B. Long, D-La., to delay the effective date of a provision calling for Social Security coverage of new federal employees until a supplemental civil service retirement plan could be established. *(Federal employees, p. 784)*

Besides agreeing to the package of long-term provisions, the committee made several other changes in the House-passed package. One of the major ones was a provision to cut beneficiaries' cost-of-living checks, as a last resort, if reserves in the Social Security trust funds fell below a certain level because of unexpectedly bad economic conditions. The provision was to go into effect in 1985, but was to be used only after all other emergency measures allowed in the bill — including borrowing among the system's three trust funds — had been exhausted.

Senate Floor Action

The Senate approved the Social Security package March 23, by a vote of 88-9, after brushing aside several attempts to unravel the compromise rescue plan.

"The strength of this package may be the weakness of its parts," Finance Committee Chairman Robert Dole, R-Kan., warned at the start of floor debate March 16. "If during the course of debate one of these should fall by the wayside . . . we probably [would] end up without a compromise and without a Social Security package this year."

Despite the warning, the Senate adopted by voice vote Long's amendment to delay coverage of federal employees under Social Security until a supplemental civil service retirement system could be established. That would cut the value of the rescue plan by $9.3 billion over the next decade, Dole said.

Conference, Final Action

House and Senate conferees agreed to the final shape of the bill (H Rept 98-47) during a 12-hour session March 24, as colleagues waited impatiently to leave for the Easter recess.

The primary stumbling block was over how to solve the system's long-range financial problems. The House measure called for a two-year increase in the retirement age while the Senate bill would have increased the age to 66, cut initial benefit payments 5 percent and eliminated a penalty for retirees earning outside income.

Another major difference was the provision in the Senate bill delaying coverage of new federal employees until a supplemental civil service retirement plan could be developed. House conferees charged that if the change were made, the entire Social Security bailout plan could be jeopardized by giving federal workers a chance to escape coverage altogether.

After hours of bargaining, mostly behind closed doors, conferees agreed to the House retirement age change, fearful that any tampering with the sensitive long-term provisions might doom the entire legislative package.

Senate conferees then agreed to recede on federal employee coverage.

The House adopted the conference report on March 24 by a 243-102 vote. The Senate gave its final approval in the early morning hours of March 25 by a 58-14 vote, completing congressional action.

Provisions

As signed into law April 20, HR 1900 (PL 98-21), the Social Security Amendments of 1983 (effective Jan. 1, 1984, unless otherwise noted):

Social Security. Required Social Security coverage of all new federal employees, current and future members of Congress, the president, the vice president, sitting federal judges, top political appointees and civil servants and legislative branch workers who did not choose to go under the Civil Service Retirement System by Dec. 31, 1983.

HR 1900 included language assuring current and retired federal workers that their civil service retirement benefits would not be reduced because of the bill.

● Required all employees of non-profit organizations to join Social Security as of Jan. 1, 1984, and prohibited any non-profit organization from withdrawing from the system on or after March 31, 1983.

● Prohibited state and local governments from withdrawing from Social Security coverage, as of the date of enactment. The bill allowed those state and local governments that previously had withdrawn from the system to return voluntarily.

Reform Commission Breaks Financing Impasse

The Reagan administration set off a two-year political battle in 1981 by recommending that Social Security benefits be cut to keep the retirement fund from going broke. Democrats charged the administration with trying to balance the budget at the expense of the elderly and called instead for higher payroll taxes to finance the system.

The solution to the impasse was the appointment in December 1981 of a 15-member National Commission on Social Security Reform. President Reagan, House Speaker Thomas P. O'Neill Jr., D-Mass., and Senate Majority Leader Howard H. Baker Jr., R-Tenn., each appointed five members. The commission originally was to issue its report by Dec. 31, 1982, but the deadline was extended until Jan. 15, 1983.

The commission reached final agreement after hectic negotiations only hours before its midnight reporting deadline. Until just a few days before the panel was to dissolve, it appeared the divided membership was unlikely to reach a compromise after almost a year of meetings.

But Republican economist Alan Greenspan, the commission's chairman, said members set aside differences in the end, with the knowledge that failure to reach a compromise could endanger the system. "All of us swallowed very hard and accepted individual notions that we personally could not actually support," he said.

The compromise brought together such diverse panel members as AFL-CIO President Lane Kirkland, National Association of Manufacturers President Alexander Trowbridge, House Rules Committee Chairman Claude Pepper, D-Fla., and Senate Finance Committee Chairman Robert Dole, R-Kan.

The White House had been reluctant to get too involved in the commission's politically sensitive negotiations. But it joined forces with panel members in the final days to avert a possibly embarrassing floor fight on Social Security if no agreement was reached.

The plan, approved by a 12-3 vote, called for both benefit cuts for retirees and tax hikes for employers and employees. The balance between the two had been the main sticking point among the commission's 15 members. Rep. Bill Archer, R-Texas, Sen. William L. Armstrong, R-Colo., and former Rep. Joe D. Waggonner Jr., D-La. (1961-79), voted against the plan.

Of the amount to be raised, about $40 billion was to come from a proposed six-month delay in the July 1983 cost-of-living adjustment (COLA) and a January payment date for all future COLAs. Another $40 billion was to be raised by increasing scheduled payroll tax hikes by 1990.

The panel could not agree on how to solve a projected Social Security shortfall in the 21st century when the post-World War II baby boom generation would begin to retire and there would be insufficient workers paying into the fund.

In a separate opinion eight of the panel's members — all Republican appointees — called for a gradual increase in the retirement age. A ninth member, Rep. Armstrong, added in his minority views that he also supported this plan.

But five Democratic appointees called instead for an additional .46 percentage point increase in the payroll tax in the year 2010, with a refundable income tax credit for employees.

● Taxed as regular income the Social Security benefits of individuals whose adjusted gross income (including tax-exempt interest income), combined with half of their Social Security benefits, exceeded $25,000. Benefits above a similar $32,000 threshold for a married couple filing a joint return were also to be taxed.

● Increased payroll taxes for self-employed individuals by 33 percent to equal the combined tax paid by employers and employees. To offset this increase, a tax credit was allowed of 2.7 percentage points in 1984, 2.3 percentage points in 1985 and 2.0 percentage points in 1986-89.

● Increased employer and employee payroll taxes from 6.7 percent to 7 percent of wages in 1984 and from 7.15 percent to 7.51 percent in 1988 and 1989.

● Delayed the annual July cost-of-living adjustment six months, until January, beginning with the July 1983 payment.

The COLA was to be provided in January 1984 even if the increase in the Consumer Price Index (CPI), on which the COLA was based, fell below 3 percent. Afterwards, as under prior law, the COLA would be forgone when the CPI fell that low.

● Allowed employees a .3 percentage point tax credit to offset the 1984 payroll tax increase. In effect, workers were required to pay only 6.7 percent in 1984, with the Treasury reimbursing the Social Security trust funds for the remaining .3 percentage point.

● Adjusted the annual COLA when reserves in the OASI and Disability Insurance trust funds were less than 15 percent of what would be needed for the year, for 1985 through 1988. In such cases the COLA would be based on the lower of the increase in the CPI or the increase in average wages.

After 1988 the lower of the two indexes was to be used whenever the trust funds contained less than 20 percent of what would be needed for the year. Whenever reserves reached 32 percent or more in later years, a "catch-up" benefit was to be paid to those who lost benefits when reserves were low.

● Required the Treasury to credit the Social Security trust funds at the beginning of each month with all of the payroll taxes that were expected to be received during that

month. Interest was to be paid by Social Security on any excess funds transferred. Previously payroll taxes were credited to the funds on a daily basis.

● Required the Social Security board of trustees to inform Congress in its annual report if the system was in danger of falling short of funds.

● Allowed the three Social Security trust funds — Old Age and Survivors Insurance, Disability Insurance and Hospital Insurance — to borrow from each other through 1987. However, OASI and DI would be unable to borrow from the ailing HI trust fund if its reserves fell below a certain level.

● Gradually increased the retirement age from 65 to 67 by the year 2027. The change was to be made in two steps. The age would be raised gradually to 66 over a six-year period ending in the year 2009. The second increase — from 66 to 67 — was to be made over another six-year period ending in the year 2027.

Early retirement still would be allowed at age 62, but benefits would be cut from 80 percent of full retirement benefits to 75 percent by the year 2009 and 70 percent by the year 2027.

● Required the secretary of health and human services (HHS) to study the effects of the retirement age change on those forced to retire early because of physically demanding work. The study, which also was to include recommendations on what if anything should be done to help such workers, was due by Jan. 1, 1986.

● Liberalized an existing penalty on retirees with outside earnings. Under prior law those under age 70 had their benefits reduced $1 for each $2 they earned above $6,600. The bill provided for a $1 reduction in benefits for each $3 earned, beginning in 1990.

● Increased the bonus individuals received for delaying retirement past the age of 65 from 3 percent of benefits a year to 8 percent a year. The bonus was to be phased in between 1990 and 2008, and was made available for those up to age 70.

● Removed the Social Security system from the "unified" federal budget, in which receipts and outlays from federal funds and trust funds were consolidated, beginning in fiscal year 1992. Until then Social Security was to be shown as a separate function within the federal budget.

● Reduced the so-called "windfall benefit" some retirees — most often former government employees — received when they worked for only a short time under the Social Security system. The bill cut the base retirement benefit of such workers.

● Permanently reallocated payroll taxes from the healthier DI trust fund to the OASI trust fund.

● Liberalized benefits designed especially to help widowed, divorced and disabled women. These included an increase in benefits for disabled widows and widowers aged 50-59.

● Included certain elective fringe benefits in the wage base subject to Social Security payroll taxes.

● Eliminated a credit previously allowed certain individuals under age 65, who collected government pensions, to compensate them for the fact that their pension income did not include tax-free Social Security benefits. It also liberalized a similar credit for certain individuals over age 65 who received few, if any, Social Security or Railroad Retirement benefits.

● Restricted benefits for convicted felons and for survivors and dependents of non-resident aliens.

Supplemental Security Income. Increased the monthly Supplemental Security Income (SSI) benefit $20 for individuals and $30 for couples, effective July 1, 1983.

● Delayed the July 1983 SSI cost-of-living increase for six months, until January 1984, and provided for payment of the annual COLA every January thereafter.

● Allowed payment of SSI benefits for the aged, blind and disabled poor who were housed for up to three months in public shelters. Previously, SSI benefits were allowed for those housed in private, but not public, shelters.

Jobs and Recession Relief

Reacting to unemployment that had reached post-World War II highs, Congress and President Reagan March 24 agreed on a $4.6 billion emergency jobs and recession relief program.

The package, which had been tailored to stay within limits acceptable to the president, was included in a $15.6 billion supplemental appropriations bill (HR 1718 — PL 98-8) for fiscal 1983.

Two-thirds of the final package was allotted for public works, general construction and water projects in the fiscal year ending Sept. 30. The remaining funds were allocated for social service, health and humanitarian assistance.

The largest single item in the package was $1 billion for Community Development Block Grants (CDBGs), spread fairly evenly between "bricks and mortar" projects and public service programs intended to create 80,000 jobs in the light construction industry. House-Senate conferees specified that $500 million of these funds could be used for public service jobs, such as home health and day care. The provision had been sought by women's groups who noted that few of the construction and public works jobs created by the bill would benefit women.

Additional funding also was provided for transportation, economic development, rural conservation, national park maintenance and other programs.

Democrats said the jobs funds were "Phase I" of a comprehensive program to lower unemployment, which had reached 10.7 percent of the civilian labor force at the end of 1982. Later in the year the House passed a Democratic "Phase II" jobs bill, aimed at reducing long-term unemployment. The Senate did not act on the measure. *(Phase II, p. 664)*

President Reagan signed HR 1718 March 24, only hours after it was cleared by Congress. The bill included $5 billion urgently needed to fund jobless payments in 27 states and the District of Columbia, as well as fiscal 1983 supplemental appropriations for several other programs.

Reagan Turnaround

President Reagan had blocked funding for jobs programs that both chambers had approved in December 1982. But, under pressure from Congress, he offered a plan of his own early in 1983. *(1982 action, p. 652)*

At a Feb. 16 press conference Reagan outlined a $4.3 billion plan to provide:

● $4 billion in accelerated spending for federal construction and repair projects. According to Reagan, "These projects directly and indirectly could provide as many as 470,000 jobs."

● $300 million "in additional humanitarian relief for those in serious distress."

The president also proposed $2.9 billion for a supple-

mentary unemployment insurance program, not included in the supplemental bill. *(Unemployment insurance, p. 665)*

"Contrary to previous plans, this is consistent with our basic long-term recovery program and my own personal principles," Reagan said. "It funds no make-work jobs."

House Action

Committee. The House Appropriations Committee Feb. 25 approved a $4.6 billion emergency employment and recession relief plan that reshuffled and expanded the Reagan administration jobs proposal by about $300 million.

As reported by the Appropriations Committee March 1 (H Rept 98-11), the bill also contained $5 billion requested by the administration to continue payment of jobless benefits under existing law.

Floor. The House March 3 approved HR 1718 by a 324-95 vote after boosting the program to $4.9 billion.

The bill drew sharp and fairly widespread criticism from members of both parties who complained that it did not go far enough in helping the needy and that it favored "pork barrel" projects in the home districts of Appropriations Committee members.

The House rejected, 158-256, a Republican proposal to shift some $675 million from public works and water projects to a variety of social programs and infrastructure projects that could be started immediately. The GOP effort would have cut $31.5 million from the overall plan.

Senate Action

Committee. As reported by the Senate Appropriations Committee March 7 (S Rept 98-17), the bill provided $3.9 billion in jobs and recession relief.

The biggest change the committee made in the House version of the package was to cut funding for Community Development Block Grants from $1.25 billion to $540 million. Of this amount, $250 million was reserved for urban areas with high unemployment, as provided by the House.

To offset the reduction in grants, the Senate provided $1 billion for off-budget loan guarantees under the CDBG program.

Floor. The Senate passed HR 1718 by an 82-16 vote March 17, after breaking a weeklong deadlock over an unrelated amendment to repeal withholding requirements for interest and dividend income. Sponsors of the withholding repealer finally agreed to attach it to other legislation, clearing the way for passage of HR 1718.

The Senate added $1.3 billion to the committee-approved anti-recession package, including $1.1 billion for accelerated revenue sharing payments to local governments.

A Democratic proposal to add $1.7 billion for various programs was rejected on a **34-53 key vote (R 2-46; D 32-7)**. Offered by Carl Levin, D-Mich., the amendment proposed an additional $1.3 billion for job creation and human services, including $1 billion for Community Development Block Grants and $390 million for health and humanitarian relief. Supporters claimed Levin's proposals would create 280,000 additional jobs. *(1983 key votes, p. 911)*

Conference, Final Action

The conference version of the bill, reported March 21 (H Rept 98-44), provided $4.6 billion for the jobs plan.

To bring the aid package within a $5 billion limit President Reagan had set, conferees deleted the $1.1 billion the Senate had provided for accelerated revenue sharing payments.

Conferees adopted sense of Congress language calling on the Federal Reserve, in combating inflation, to keep interest rates low enough to stimulate economic growth and reduce unemployment. They also directed the secretaries of the Treasury and commerce to "analyze the current trade crisis with the objective of keeping American exports competitive."

Both chambers adopted the conference report March 22, the House by a 329-86 vote and the Senate by an 82-15 tally.

But Congress did not complete action on the bill for another two days, when agreement finally was reached on a complex targeting formula for distributing funds among states and economically distressed areas.

'Phase II' Jobs Bills

House Democrats tried to move "Phase II" of their 1983 job creation program with a $3.5 billion public service jobs bill (HR 1036) and a $3.2 billion public works jobs proposal (HR 2544).

The Democrats hoped to gain political mileage from the jobs issue in the 1984 election campaign, but their Phase II plan lost momentum as unemployment dropped more rapidly than expected in 1983. Neither measure was enacted.

President Reagan had backed short-term "Phase I" jobs legislation enacted in March, but he opposed further jobs spending. *(Jobs and recession relief, p. 663)*

Public Service Jobs

The House passed HR 1036, its public service jobs measure, Sept. 21 by a party-line vote of 246-178. The Senate never considered the bill.

As passed by the House, HR 1036 authorized $3.5 billion in federal funds to create jobs for the long-term unemployed through projects to repair and renovate community facilities and public schools in areas of high unemployment.

HR 1036 authorized funds for grants to state and local governments with populations of 50,000 or more. Eighty percent of the funds were reserved for community improvement projects such as road and sewer projects, land and water reclamation and various health and social service activities. The remaining 20 percent was to be used for repair of public school facilities.

Funds were to be distributed on the basis of unemployment, with the money concentrated on areas with unemployment rates above the national average.

As reported by the House Education and Labor Committee May 16 (H Rept 98-199), the bill authorized $5 billion, but during floor action the House cut funding by $1.5 billion.

Public Works Plan

The House Public Works and Transportation Committee May 17 reported HR 2544, a $3.2 billion public works jobs proposal (H Rept 98-202). The measure sought to provide jobs by funding local road and public building projects, chiefly in areas with high unemployment. The bill

was approved by the Public Works Committee May 12, by a 31-19 party-line vote, after a sharp partisan fight.

As approved by the committee, HR 2544 would have channeled funds through the revenue sharing program. But the bulk of the funds, $2.4 billion, would have been distributed on the basis of state and local unemployment rates.

Related Measures

Other key parts of the Democratic anti-recession program in 1983 were a temporary health insurance program for the unemployed and an emergency veterans' job training bill.

Health insurance legislation passed the House Aug. 3 (HR 3021) but did not reach the floor in the Senate. *(Story, p. 542)*

Congress Aug. 3 cleared a veterans' job training bill (HR 2355 — PL 98-77). The measure authorized a two-year, $300 million program to pay employers to hire and train long-term unemployed veterans of the Vietnam and Korean wars. *(Story, p. 619)*

Jobless Aid Extension

Congress Oct. 21 approved legislation (HR 3929 — PL 98-135) extending a temporary program of federal supplemental unemployment compensation benefits through March 31, 1985.

The bill provided a minimum eight weeks and a maximum 14 weeks of federal supplemental benefits to persons who had used up all other state and federal jobless aid. It was the second extension of a program established in 1982 (PL 97-248). *(1982 action, p. 654)*

A previous extension had been approved in March as part of Social Security financing legislation (HR 1900 — PL 98-21).

The House passed HR 3929 (H Rept 98-377) Sept. 29 by a 327-92 vote. The measure won Senate approval the next day, 89-0. The conference report (H Rept 98-428) was adopted Oct. 21 — in the House by a vote of 300-5 and in the Senate by voice vote.

Because conferees failed to quickly agree on the bill, Congress Oct. 6 enacted a stopgap measure (HR 4101 — PL 98-118) to extend the unemployment program through Oct. 18. It had been slated to expire Sept. 30.

Major Provisions

As signed into law Oct. 24, HR 3929 (PL 98-135):

• Extended, from the week of Oct. 23, 1983, through the week of March 31, 1985, federal supplemental unemployment payments providing additional benefits to persons who had exhausted all other state and federal unemployment benefits.

• Provided that the maximum benefit weeks payable in a state would be no fewer than eight and no more than 14, determined by a formula based on a state's insured unemployment rate.

• Limited, beginning with the week of Oct. 23, 1983, the maximum number of weeks of benefits a state could gain or lose at any time under the program to two weeks, and provided that no state's maximum weeks of benefits could be adjusted up or down more often than each 13 weeks.

• Guaranteed individuals the same number of weeks of benefits they qualified for as of the time they became eligible for supplemental unemployment benefits, irrespective of adjustments to the maximum weeks payable in their state of residence.

• Provided that payments by employers to survivors or to the estates of deceased persons would be exempt from the Federal Unemployment Tax after the end of the calendar year in which the deceased died.

• Extended for two years, from Jan. 1, 1984, to Jan. 1, 1986, a law excluding wages paid to certain alien farm workers from the Federal Unemployment Tax.

• Increased, from $2.5 billion to $2.7 billion, in fiscal 1984 and subsequent fiscal years, the funds available for social services block grants to states authorized by Title XX of the Social Security Act.

Trade Adjustment Aid

A two-year extension of the trade adjustment assistance program (HR 3813 — PL 98-120) cleared Congress Sept. 30, just hours before the program was set to expire.

Trade adjustment benefits went to workers who had been laid off from industries harmed by import competition. A small portion of the benefits also went to small and medium-sized firms suffering from import competition.

The program was started in 1962 and expanded under the Trade Act of 1974. In 1981 Congress extended the program through Sept. 30, 1983, but drastically curtailed eligibility for benefits. Some of the more liberal eligibility requirements were restored in 1982. *(Previous action, pp. 650, 658)*

The Reagan administration sought the termination of trade adjustment assistance. High levels of unemployment, however, persuaded Congress to continue the benefits.

House Action

The House passed a bill (HR 3391 — H Rept 98-281) Sept. 15 that would have greatly expanded the program from its fiscal 1983 level. Workers laid off from firms supplying component parts or services to an industry affected by imports would have been eligible for benefits for the first time. And the government would have been required to approve training assistance under certain circumstances, regardless of whether funds were available. According to Congressional Budget Office estimates, the House bill would have cost $217 million in fiscal 1984. Four attempts by Bill Frenzel, R-Minn., to cut back the program failed by substantial margins.

Senate, Final Action

The Senate Finance Committee rejected the House changes and approved instead a simple two-year extension of the existing program, expected to cost $95 million in fiscal 1984. The only change made by the Senate was to give preference to firms that adopted employee stock ownership plans when granting trade adjustment assistance to companies.

The Senate Sept. 30 attached its trade adjustment assistance proposal to HR 3813, a House-passed measure extending the International Coffee Agreement for three years. The bill was then approved by voice vote.

The House gave its approval to the Senate's modest version of the bill later the same day, also by voice vote.

Railroad Retirement

Congress moved with rare dispatch to maintain the solvency of the federal railroad retirement and unemployment compensation programs through a combination of benefit reductions, tax increases and a federal contribution of $1.7 billion.

Legislation (HR 1646 — PL 98-76) cleared Aug. 2 contained benefit reductions for workers retiring before age 62, deferred cost-of-living increases for all retirees, and increased employer-worker taxes for fiscal 1984-86. The Congressional Budget Office estimated the changes would save $396 million in fiscal 1984, $1 billion in fiscal 1985, and $1.5 billion in fiscal 1986.

The railroad retirement system faced a deficit of $6 billion through fiscal 1988 and $13 billion by 1992 in the absence of remedial legislation.

The Railroad Retirement Board, which administered the rail retirement and unemployment compensation programs had said that if Congress failed to act before the start of its summer recess Aug. 5, the board would notify one million retirees on Sept. 1 that a major portion of their benefits would be cut 40 percent as of Oct. 1. The announcement was required under earlier rescue legislation, enacted in 1981. *(1981 action, p. 648)*

HR 1646 also bolstered the Railroad Unemployment Compensation fund through a 50 percent increase in the wage base on which rail employees paid unemployment taxes. A sharp drop in railroad employment in recent years had drained the fund, forcing it to borrow from the railroad retirement fund, thus exacerbating the retirement fund's problems.

Legislative History

The House passed HR 1646 Aug. 1 by a 398-5 vote. The bill as passed was an amalgam of measures approved by the House Energy and Commerce (H Rept 98-30, Part I) and Ways and Means committees (Part II).

The Reagan administration opposed the measure as written by the Energy and Commerce Committee but supported it as reported by the Ways and Means Committee and passed by the House and Senate.

The House adopted by voice vote an amendment by J. J. Pickle, D-Texas, to advance from July 1, 1984, to Jan. 1, 1984, the effective date of increases in employer and employee payroll taxes needed to finance Tier II benefits — the portion of railroad retirement benefits that were equivalent to a private pension plan. (Tier I benefits approximated Social Security.)

The Senate passed the bill Aug. 2 by a 95-2 vote, completing congressional action on the measure.

Major Provisions

As signed into law Aug. 12, HR 1646 (PL 98-76):

Taxes. Increased Tier II taxes for employers from 11.75 percent of a given employee's wages to 12.75 percent effective Jan. 1, 1984; to 13.75 percent effective Jan. 1, 1985; and to 14.75 percent effective Jan. 1, 1986.

● Increased Tier II taxes for employees from 2 percent of an employee's wages up to 2.75 percent effective Jan. 1, 1984; to 3.5 percent effective Jan. 1, 1985; and to 4.25 percent effective Jan. 1, 1986.

● Provided that, for the first time, Tier II benefits would be taxed as income, with revenue from the tax to be depos-ited in the Railroad Retirement Account until the end of fiscal year 1988 or until it totaled $877 million, whichever occurred earlier, and given to the Treasury afterward.

● Imposed on railroad employers a temporary tax, from July 1, 1986, to Sept. 30, 1990, equal to 2 percent of the first $7,000 in wages paid each employee. The tax would rise 0.3 percent each Jan. 1 until it reached 5 percent. The funds would be used to repay loans from the Railroad Retirement Account to the Railroad Unemployment Compensation fund.

● Increased Railroad Retirement Unemployment Compensation taxes 50 percent by raising the monthly wage base from $400 to $600, on which rail employers paid a tax of 8 percent.

● Provided for taxes on the so-called "windfall" benefits some retirees received by virtue of having worked under both the railroad retirement and Social Security pension plans.

● Changed the wage base upon which railroad retirement taxes were paid from a monthly to an annual basis as of Jan. 1, 1985, to conform with the wage base used by the Social Security system.

● Provided that sick pay received under railroad unemployment insurance would become subject to income tax beginning Jan. 1, 1984.

Cost of Living. Deferred a scheduled cost-of-living adjustment on Tier II benefits from July 1, 1984, to Jan. 1, 1985.

● Provided that future cost-of-living increases in Tier I benefits would be offset by reducing cost-of-living increases on Tier II benefits, up to a cumulative total of 5 percent.

Retirement. Provided that, until July 1, 1984, rail employees with 30 years of service could retire with full benefits at age 60 but that after July 1, 1984, individuals with 30 years of service who retired before they turned 62 would have their benefits permanently cut.

From July 1, 1984, until Dec. 31, 1985, employees with 30 years of service retiring between ages 60 and 62 would receive only 90 percent of Tier I benefits.

After Jan. 1, 1986, the reduction in Tier I benefits for such early retirees would be 20 percent.

Labor Reform Measures

Two labor reform measures that died in the House in 1982 failed there again in 1983. *(1982 story, p. 657)*

The bills — one to revamp federal workers' compensation for longshoremen, the other to curb union corruption — easily cleared the Senate for a second year in a row but neither received House consideration.

The longshoremen's bill (S 38) cleared Congress in 1984 (PL 98-426). *(1983-84 action, p. 671)*

The Senate passed the Labor Management Racketeering Act (S 336) 75-0 on June 20. It was reported by the Labor Committee May 11 (S Rept 98-83). The bill, which was identical to the 1982 legislation, increased penalties for union officials convicted of bribery or other corrupt practices under three core labor laws: the Labor-Management Relations Act of 1947, known as the Taft-Hartley Act (PL 80-101); the Employee Retirement Income Security Act of 1974, known as ERISA (PL 93-406); and the Labor-Management Reporting and Disclosure Act of 1959, known as the Landrum-Griffin Act (PL 86-257). *(Background, Taft-Hartley, Landrum-Griffin, Congress and the Nation Vol. I, p. 567; ERISA, Congress and the Nation Vol. IV, p. 690)*

The anti-racketeering bill grew out of an investigation into waterfront corruption that was conducted in 1981 by the Senate Governmental Affairs Permanent Subcommittee on Investigations.

Other Legislation

Social Security Disability

Congress was unable to reach agreement on changes in the troubled Social Security disability insurance program, despite more than a year of negotiations between legislators and special interest groups.

However, lawmakers Oct. 6 cleared a bill (HR 4101 — PL 98-118) extending provisions of existing law, thus giving Congress until early 1984 to come up with a plan to revise the process used for reviewing the disability rolls.

In 1984 Congress cleared a measure (PL 98-460) designed to protect the truly disabled from losing their benefits while removing ineligible recipients from the program. *(Story, p. 667)*

Since 1981 critics had charged that, in an effort to remove ineligible recipients from the disability rolls, the Reagan administration had also taken away benefits from thousands of still disabled persons. The administration had imposed a review of the rolls at the direction of Congress.

Congress approved stopgap legislation in 1982 to allow those thrown off the rolls to continue collecting benefits while their cases were under appeal, but more comprehensive legislation was postponed. *(1982 story, p. 656)*

Pension Equity

The Senate Nov. 18 passed a bill (HR 2769) making broad changes in pension law, two days after similar pension "equity" legislation was approved by the House Education and Labor Committee (HR 4280) and by the Senate Labor and Human Resources Committee (S 2110). HR 4280 cleared Congress in 1984. *(1983-84 action, p. 669)*

The bills liberalized pension coverage by strengthening the rights of spouses to pensions if a worker died before retirement age and by permitting workers to leave and subsequently return to a job without losing benefits for which they already had qualified.

Conservation Corps

The House March 1 passed a bill (HR 999) to establish an American Conservation Corps to provide jobs for unemployed and disadvantaged young people on public and Indian lands. The vote was 301-87.

The measure cleared Congress in 1984 but was pocket-vetoed by the president. The House had passed a similar bill in 1982. *(1983-84 action, p. 671; 1982 action, p. 657)*

1984

Congress spent little time on labor legislation in 1984, as unemployment dropped below 8 percent for the first time since 1981. But the November elections gave impetus to action on measures protecting the disabled, women and the elderly.

After three years of controversy over administration efforts to rid the Social Security disability rolls of ineligible recipients, lawmakers approved a measure making it more difficult for a person to be disqualified for benefits.

As part of an election-year effort to prove its commitment to women's issues, Congress passed a bill that attempted to free private pension law of sex discrimination. The Retirement Equity Act protected workers from losing pension credits if they left and subsequently returned to a job and ensured pension rights of homemakers whose working spouses died before reaching retirement age. Although the pension changes applied to both men and women, the bill was particularly helpful to women who interrupted careers to raise children or who depended on the pensions of their spouses.

Congress also assured Social Security recipients of a cost-of-living adjustment on Jan. 1, 1985, when it appeared the inflation rate might be too low to trigger the increase. Although the legislation turned out to be unnecessary by the time it was enacted, neither Congress nor the administration was willing to sacrifice the political credit associated with the measure.

The only major labor legislation to clear was a bill to revamp a special federal workers' compensation law for longshoremen. Critics charged that the existing program had been manipulated by organized crime and unscrupulous doctors.

Although Congress authorized a program to give thousands of young people conservation jobs on public and Indian lands, the bill was pocket-vetoed by President Reagan.

In October Labor Secretary Raymond J. Donovan was indicted by a Bronx County, N.Y., grand jury on larceny and fraud charges stemming from a 1982 investigation of his financial dealings as vice president of a New Jersey construction company. Donovan resigned his Cabinet post March 15, 1985, to stand trial on the charges. He had been on a leave of absence from the Labor Department while appealing the indictment. *(Donovan investigation, box, p. 656)*

Social Security Disability

A bill (HR 3755 — PL 98-460) to protect the disabled from being unfairly dropped from the Social Security disability rolls was cleared Sept. 19 by unanimous votes in both the House and the Senate.

Passage of the bill brought to a close a lengthy, convoluted and sometimes emotional legislative debate. The passions the issue sometimes evoked were not reflected in the overwhelming congressional support of the final package. *(Previous action, this page, p. 656)*

Background

In March 1981 the administration began a process of disability reviews in response to a 1980 congressional mandate to clean up an estimated $2 billion in program waste.

But disability groups and their allies in Congress complained that the administration undertook the reviews with unnecessary zeal. They charged the administration with attempting to trim the $18-billion-a-year program, which provided benefits to workers too disabled to hold a job, as

part of its overall effort to reduce the size of government.

Almost half of the 1.2 million individuals whose cases came under review were told they no longer qualified for benefits. But about 200,000 were reinstated after appealing their cases to independent administrative law judges.

Critics charged that many had been dropped from the rolls even though their medical condition had remained stable or worsened since they first were declared eligible for benefits. They charged the administration often based its decisions on flimsy and incomplete evidence, resulting in the loss of benefits for many individuals who were clearly unable to work.

Since the 1981 crackdown, congressional offices had been flooded with constituent complaints. News stories of thousands of disabled workers losing benefits, homes and, in some cases, their lives as a result of the reviews plagued politicians, many of whom were up for re-election in 1984.

Although there was broad support in Congress to do something about the program as early as 1983, there was tremendous conflict over just what should be done.

A number of senators, including Finance Committee Chairman Robert Dole, R-Kan., and Russell B. Long, D-La., the Finance panel's ranking minority member, were reluctant to make changes pushed by disability lobby groups that they said would counteract Congress' original directive to clean up the program.

The Social Security Administration also fought the legislation, claiming that it could correct most problems administratively.

But attempts by Health and Human Services (HHS) Secretary Richard S. Schweiker and his successor, Margaret M. Heckler, to address problems with the program failed to quell the criticism.

By early 1984 the disability reviews had all but collapsed, with half of the states either refusing or under court order not to administer the program. While the program was run by the federal government, the actual reviews were conducted by state agencies.

In addition, the administration routinely was losing disability cases in the federal courts, including a number of class action suits in which thousands of recipients were ordered back on the rolls. In an internal review of its litigation process, the Social Security Administration acknowledged that the "agency's credibility before the federal courts is at an all-time low."

In April, two weeks after the House had passed HR 3755, HHS Secretary Heckler did an about-face and announced a nationwide moratorium on the disability review program, pending the enactment of legislation.

House Action

Handing the Reagan administration one of its most resounding defeats, the House voted 410-1 March 27 to ease the administration's tough, new reviews of the Social Security disability rolls.

Philip M. Crane, R-Ill., cast the lone dissenting vote. The bill was reported (H Rept 98-618) by the House Ways and Means Committee March 14, although actual markup of the legislation had occurred in 1983.

The House bill required the administration to show that an individual's medical condition had improved before he or she could be taken off the rolls. It also made permanent a provision allowing individuals to collect benefits while appealing an adverse decision.

During an hour of debate on the House floor, member

after member spoke in favor of the legislation, many lambasting the administration's review process as "cruel" and "insensitive."

But some Republicans cautioned that the legislation would prove to be only a temporary solution and that other steps would have to be taken to keep a tight rein on the program. Barber B. Conable Jr., R-N.Y., noted a wide disparity in the estimated cost of the bill. The Congressional Budget Office said it would cost $1.5 billion over five years, compared with a $3.4 billion estimate by the Social Security Administration.

But Conable implored the administration to drop its opposition to the legislation and to work with Congress on fashioning an acceptable compromise.

Senate Action

The Senate Finance Committee May 16 approved S 476 (S Rept 98-466). Like HR 3755, the bill allowed individuals to continue collecting benefits if their medical condition had not improved since they had been placed on the rolls.

However, the Senate measure required the individual beneficiary to prove that his or her medical condition was the same or had worsened to continue collecting payments. The House measure shifted the burden of proof onto the Social Security Administration, requiring it to show an individual's condition had improved before benefits could be stopped.

Under S 476 the "medical improvement" provision would expire no later than three and a half years after enactment. The House version contained no expiration date.

The Senate bill also required lower cost-of-living increases in disability payments if the Social Security Disability Insurance trust fund — which financed the program — was expected to have less than 20 percent of the funds at the beginning of a year that it would need to pay the year's benefits, and if Congress took no corrective action.

According to Social Security actuaries, such a benefit cut could have come as early as 1988 under the most pessimistic economic assumptions.

While disability groups were not pleased with this and some of the other provisions of the Senate measure, spokesmen expressed satisfaction that the committee had finally acted, allowing the legislation to go to the Senate floor and be subject to revision in conference with the more favorable House measure.

Following the House's lead, the full Senate May 22 adopted the disability bill by a lopsided 96-0 vote. It passed the measure (HR 3755) after substituting the text of the Finance Committee bill (S 476) for the House version.

Conference Agreement

House and Senate conferees reached an informal agreement on the legislation Sept. 14 after lengthy behind-the-scenes negotiations.

Running through the discussions was the same conflict that had characterized much of the disability debate: discovering a way to protect the truly disabled from losing their benefits while trimming the program of ineligible recipients.

One of the biggest issues in disagreement was the medical improvement standard.

The final agreement more closely resembled the House

provision, which placed on the administration the burden of proving that an individual's medical condition had improved before benefits could be stopped. Language was added, however, to provide the administration with some flexibility in cases where an individual was clearly ineligible for disability payments.

Conferees also agreed to drop two of the most controversial items in disagreement, which could have threatened final passage.

They rejected a House provision that would have required the administration to apply a decision by a circuit court of appeals on a disability review case to all disability review cases within the circuit, or to appeal the case to the Supreme Court.

The administration routinely recognized such court decisions as applicable only to the individual case decided by the court. It had steadfastly opposed the kind of change mandated by the legislation.

However, conferees agreed to include language in their final report raising questions about the constitutionality of the administration's practice and urging the administration to have the issue resolved in the Supreme Court.

They also encouraged the administration to pursue its policy of "non-acquiescence" to court decisions only when it intended to appeal a decision all the way to the Supreme Court.

Also dropped from the final conference agreement was the Senate provision to reduce annual cost-of-living increases for disability recipients if reserves in the Disability Insurance trust fund fell too low, and if Congress failed to take action to correct the shortfall.

The Senate adopted the conference report (H Rept 98-1039) by a 99-0 vote Sept. 19. House approval came several hours later by a vote of 402-0.

Major Provisions

As signed into law Oct. 9, HR 3755 (PL 98-460):

Medical Improvement. Allowed the secretary of health and human services to terminate benefits only if there was substantial evidence that an individual's medical condition had improved since first being placed on the rolls and that the individual was able to work.

Benefits could also be cut if there was substantial evidence that:

● The individual had benefited from vocational therapy or advances in medical or vocational therapy or technology, and was able to work.

● An individual's impairment was not as disabling as originally thought, based on new or improved diagnostic techniques or evaluations.

● The original decision had been made in error or fraudulently obtained.

● The individual was unlawfully working, could not be located or failed to cooperate in the review process.

The new regulations were to go into effect within six months of enactment.

Eligibility. Applied the new medical improvement standard to all cases that came up for review after enactment, to cases still pending in the disability program's appeals process, to most cases pending in federal court and to cases in which a request for judicial review was made between March 15, 1984, and 60 days after enactment.

Congressional aides estimated that between 120,000 and 130,000 cases on appeal would be remanded to the secretary for reconsideration under this provision.

Benefits During Appeals. Allowed individuals who appealed their cases to continue collecting benefits until they had taken their appeal to an administrative law judge, one of the final steps of the appeals process. If the individual lost the case, the benefits had to be repaid.

Individuals whose cases were remanded to the secretary for reconsideration under the new medical improvement standard were allowed to collect benefits until a new decision was made.

The provision was effective through 1987 for Social Security disability recipients and was made permanent for disabled recipients of Supplemental Security Income.

Mental Impairments. Required, within 120 days of enactment, publication of new standards for evaluating mental disabilities. A moratorium on reviews of mentally impaired beneficiaries, in place since June 7, 1983, was to end with publication of the new standards.

The bill also required that efforts be made to have a qualified psychiatrist or psychologist participate in the determination of whether an individual was mentally disabled. Previously, only a physician and a state disability examiner had to review the case.

Review Standards. Made a number of changes in existing standards used to determine if an individual was disabled. Included in these changes was a requirement that the combined effects of an individual's multiple impairments be weighed in determining if there was a disability, even if each of the impairments alone would be insufficient for such a determination. Under prior law the combined effects of multiple impairments could not be considered.

The bill continued through 1986 the existing practice of rejecting as conclusive evidence of disability an individual's claim that he or she was in pain. It required, however, that the Department of Health and Human Services complete a study by Dec. 31, 1985, on the role of pain in determining disability.

State Compliance. Required the secretary of health and human services to take over disability operations in states that failed to comply with federal law.

Since the 1981 clampdown on the program, 10 states had refused to carry out the reviews under the new federal standards. But the federal government took no steps to take over administration of the program in those states.

Advisory Council. Required the appointment by June 1, 1985, of a 10-member panel of medical and vocational experts to advise the health and human services secretary on disability policies, standards and procedures.

Pension Equity

With an eye on the November elections, the House completed the process started by the Senate in 1983 of revising private pension law to improve retirement benefits of women. The final version of the Retirement Equity Act (HR 4280 — PL 98-397) was approved by the House and Senate in August.

The bill lowered the age at which young workers could start building up pension credits, allowed workers to leave their jobs for a longer period without losing pension rights if they returned to the job, and required that benefits earned by a person who died before retirement be paid to a surviving spouse. Since many women began working at an early age, but then left the work force temporarily to raise families, the changes made by HR 4280 were seen as having their greatest impact on women.

The Reagan administration, although it initially offered only lukewarm support for the measure, endorsed pension equity to combat charges that it was insensitive to women's rights issues.

Both the president and members of Congress hoped to reap political benefits from the measure. The bill, part of a legislative package designed to end economic bias toward women, had been championed by Democratic vice presidential nominee Geraldine A. Ferraro, D-N.Y.

Background

HR 4280 revised the 1974 Employee Retirement Income Security Act (ERISA), as well as provisions of the Internal Revenue Code that regulated pension plans, a key source of income for retired persons. *(Congress and the Nation Vol. IV, p. 690)*

Under ERISA employers were not required to offer pension plans, but those who did had to comply with certain minimum standards. ERISA, for example, mandated the maximum length of time employees could be required to work before they were "vested," or had a permanent right to employer-financed benefits even if they changed jobs before retirement.

Most employees had to work 10 years under a pension plan to become vested, and interruptions in a career could result in the loss of pension credits. Before enactment of HR 4280, employers were allowed to exclude workers from participating in a pension plan until they turned 25.

1983-84 Action

Senate. The Senate took the lead in pension equity legislation, passing a bill (HR 2769) Nov. 18, 1983, making broad changes in pension law. The measure provided survivors' benefits if an employee had worked at the same firm for 10 years and died after reaching age 45. HR 2769 also permitted up to a five-year break in service. The Finance Committee had attached the pension equity provisions to an unrelated House bill, which it reported Oct. 29 (S Rept 98-285). The Labor and Human Resources Committee had approved a similar measure Nov. 16.

House Committee. The House Ways and Means Committee approved HR 4280 March 27, 1984.

The Ways and Means Committee made some liberalizing changes in a version of HR 4280 that had been approved in November 1983 by the Education and Labor Committee, which also had jurisdiction over pension matters. A compromise version (H Rept 98-655, Part II) of the two committees' bills was reported by Ways and Means May 17.

As approved by Ways and Means, HR 4280 required most pension plans to provide benefits to a spouse if a vested employee died before reaching retirement age. The Education and Labor bill had provided automatic joint and survivor benefits only after an employee had worked for a company 10 years.

HR 4280 required pension plans to begin counting service toward vesting after employees turned 18 and lowered the minimum age for enrollment in pension plans from 25 to 21.

House Floor. The House May 22 unanimously approved HR 4280. The vote was 413-0.

The politically popular bill breezed through the House under expedited legislative procedures that permitted no amendments and required a two-thirds majority vote for passage. With time for debate limited by the procedure, floor managers were hard pressed to accommodate all the members who wanted to speak in support of the measure.

Final Action. After the House approved its version of the legislation, three committee staffs ironed out differences between the House and Senate versions of the bill — the House Education and Labor and Ways and Means committees and the Senate Finance Committee. The Senate Finance Committee July 31 approved the revised model.

The Senate passed the revised version of HR 4280 by voice vote on Aug. 6, and the House cleared the bill Aug. 9.

Provisions

As signed into law Aug. 23, HR 4280 (PL 98-397):

● Mandated that employees be permitted to participate in pension plans when they turned 21. Previously, employers did not have to enroll employees as plan participants until they reached 25.

● Required pension plans to count the years of employees' service from the time wage earners turned 18 in calculating when they had worked long enough to be vested. The minimum vesting age under existing pension law was 22.

● Permitted employees to leave a job and return without sacrificing the pension credit built up unless the break in service exceeded five consecutive years or the amount of time the employee worked at the job before leaving, whichever was greater. Under existing law unvested workers lost pension credits if their break in service exceeded the number of years they had worked under the pension plan.

● Barred pension plans from counting a one-year maternity or paternity leave as a break in service.

● Required pension plans to provide survivor benefits for the spouses of employees who died after they were vested regardless of the worker's age. Under existing law a spouse could be denied survivor benefits if the wage earner died before reaching minimum retirement age.

● Prohibited pension plan participants from waiving survivor coverage without the written consent of their spouses.

● Assured that employees who had accrued retirement benefits would not lose those benefits when an employer changed or terminated a pension plan.

● Increased from $1,750 to $3,500 the mandatory amount that an employer could provide as a lump sum when closing out a plan without the participant's request.

● Strengthened disclosure requirements for participants' pre-retirement survivor benefits and other pension rules. Generally, the provisions would apply to pension plans starting in 1985.

Social Security COLAs

Plagued by Democratic charges that he would cut Social Security benefits if re-elected, President Reagan took the offensive and proposed July 24 that the elderly receive a cost-of-living adjustment (COLA) in January 1985 even if inflation were too low to trigger one. Under existing law, enacted in 1981, no COLA was allowed if inflation for the previous year was below 3 percent, as it then was expected to be. *(1981 Social Security revisions, p. 645)*

The Senate responded quickly and two days later approved a one-year waiver of the trigger as an amendment to

a minor House-passed bill (HR 1428).

The Democratic-controlled House moved more slowly. Denying Reagan a chance to take full credit for the COLA increase at the Republican National Convention in August, the House passed its version of the COLA bill (HR 6299) Oct. 2.

By then it was apparent that the year's inflation would exceed the 3 percent threshold, and Democrats blasted the president for "needless meddling" with the program.

The Senate cleared HR 6299 Oct. 11 (PL 98-604).

Conservation Corps Veto

A proposal (HR 999) to set up an American Conservation Corps (ACC) was pocket-vetoed by President Reagan Oct. 30.

The measure would have authorized $225 million over three years to establish a program to give thousands of young people conservation jobs on public and Indian lands. The ACC was patterned on the Depression-era Civilian Conservation Corps (CCC).

In its first year the program would have provided about 18,500 jobs on conservation and rehabilitation projects, including both year-round and summer employment. Sponsors estimated that more than 37,000 jobs could be created if the program were fully funded at $100 million in 1987. Unemployed youths aged 16 to 25 would have been eligible for the year-round jobs program, while those aged 15 to 21 would have qualified for the summer jobs.

In his veto statement the president said the ACC proposal embodied "the discredited approach to youth unemployment that relies on artificial public sector employment."

The House originally passed HR 999 (H Rept 98-7, Parts I and II) March 1, 1983, by a 301-87 vote. The House version would have authorized $300 million a year over four years. The Senate passed a scaled-down version (S Rept 98-140) of the bill Oct. 3, 1984, by voice vote. The House accepted the Senate version by a 296-75 vote Oct. 9, completing congressional action on the bill.

The House had passed a similar measure in 1982. *(Story, p. 657)*

Longshore Compensation

Congress Sept. 20 cleared legislation (S 38 — PL 98-426) to revamp a special federal workers' compensation law for longshoremen.

The bill overhauled the Longshoremen's and Harbor Workers' Compensation Act to curb abuses and limit benefit increases under the program, which guaranteed compensation to dockworkers and other maritime employees for job-related injuries or death. It also scaled back coverage of the act to exclude certain kinds of employees who were not directly exposed to the hazards of maritime work, such as office clerical workers in maritime firms.

The bill broadened coverage for workers with occupational diseases by easing procedural requirements that had made it difficult for workers to get compensation for diseases with long latency periods.

Background

Congress established the federally regulated system to compensate disabled longshoremen in 1927, after the Su-

preme Court ruled that state compensation programs could not cover dockworkers working over navigable waters.

The cost of providing compensation was borne principally by employers, who generally took out insurance policies to cover the benefits. As under state workers' compensation laws, employees covered by the Longshoremen's Act were barred from suing their employers for damages.

In 1972 Congress boosted benefits and expanded the law's scope to include not only people who actually worked over water, but also a variety of onshore employees of maritime firms. Since then employers had complained about the cost of providing increased benefits and the difficulty of obtaining insurance to cover them.

Criticism of the act was further fueled in 1981, when a Senate investigation found the program had been manipulated by organized crime and unscrupulous doctors and workers. A bill intended to respond to those concerns, sponsored by Sen. Don Nickles, R-Okla., was passed by the Senate in 1982. It died in the House, but the legislation was revived by Nickles in the 98th Congress. *(1982 action, p. 657)*

Legislative History

S 38 was reported (S Rept 98-81) by the Senate Labor and Human Resources Committee May 10, 1983, and passed by the Senate by voice vote June 16, 1983.

The House Education and Labor Committee reported its version of S 38 (H Rept 98-570) Nov. 18, 1983, and the House passed the bill April 10, 1984. The House bill added provisions making it easier for workers to receive compensation for occupational disease.

The conference report on the bill (H Rept 98-1027) was approved by the House Sept. 18 and the Senate Sept. 20.

Major Provisions

As signed into law Sept. 28, S 38 (PL 98-426):

● Excluded from coverage under the Longshoremen's Act certain kinds of employees, such as office clerical workers, builders of small recreational boats and certain marina employees. Workers were excluded only if they were eligible for coverage by state workers' compensation programs.

● Repealed death benefits that currently were provided when workers receiving compensation died of causes unrelated to their occupational injuries.

● Limited death benefits, which had been unrestricted, to 200 percent of the national average weekly wage.

● Imposed a 5 percent limit on annual benefit increases. Increases were tied to increases in the national average weekly wage.

● Imposed new limits on workers' freedom to switch doctors, and required the Labor Department to compile a list of physicians not qualified to provide medical care under the act. Doctors would be placed on the list, and no reimbursement for their services would be paid for at least three years, if they had submitted false statements or charged excess fees.

● Extended the deadline for filing notice of a job-related injury to one year, from 30 days, for victims of occupational disease. The deadline for filing a claim was extended to two years, from one year.

● Authorized benefits for victims of occupational disease in cases where workers discovered their disability — or died — in retirement.

● Increased penalties for filing fraudulent claims.

Targeted Jobs Tax Credit

Congress June 27 approved a one-year extension, through Dec. 30, 1985, of a tax break designed to help the most disadvantaged workers find jobs.

Originally enacted in 1978, the targeted jobs tax credit permitted employers to claim tax credits over two years for part of the wages paid to people they hired from various "target" groups — including the handicapped, disadvantaged youths, Vietnam veterans, welfare recipients and former prison inmates. About 60 percent of the more than 400,000 workers hired with the subsidy in fiscal 1983 were disadvantaged youths. *(Background, Congress and the Nation Vol. V, p. 243)*

From 1978 to 1981 employers could receive tax breaks for workers already on the payroll who happened to be eligible, even though they had been hired without the inducement of the credit. In extending the program in 1981, as part of the year's sweeping tax cut legislation (PL 97-34), Congress stipulated that workers must be certified as eligible for the subsidy before they began employment.

Lawmakers voted a further extension of the program in 1982 tax increase legislation (PL 97-248). The Reagan administration backed an additional one-year extension in 1984, and Congress complied in the $63 billion deficit reduction package it cleared June 27 (HR 4170 — PL 98-369). *(Stories, pp. 65, 76, 79)*

Trade Adjustment Aid

Senators rebuffed a 1984 House effort to renew the trade adjustment assistance program, which aided workers who had been laid off from industries hurt by import competition. The program, which was not scheduled to expire until Sept. 30, 1985, had been criticized for failing to retrain workers adequately or to help them find new jobs.

The House passed a two-year extension June 28 as part of omnibus trade legislation (HR 3398), but Senate conferees Oct. 9 rejected the plan. *(Trade bill, p. 109)*

Congress had last extended the program in 1983. *(Previous action, pp. 665, 658, 650)*

13

Law and Justice

Law and Law Enforcement   *675*
Supreme Court   *711*

Law and Law Enforcement

Congress in the early 1980s approved some extensive changes in federal law enforcement statutes. In various pieces of legislation, Congress:

- Revised and rationalized the nation's criminal law;
- Placed the federal bankruptcy system back on a firm constitutional footing;
- Extended and strengthened the landmark Voting Rights Act;
- Restructured the U.S. Commission on Civil Rights;
- Enlarged the federal judiciary with the addition of 85 new judgeships.

Most of these accomplishments came without White House support or in spite of White House efforts. President Reagan's program included numerous legal and law enforcement proposals, but relatively few were realized in his first term.

The shock of the assassination attempt on the president in March 1981 spurred renewed efforts at gun control and later a push to revise the insanity defense used successfully by Reagan's assailant, John W. Hinckley Jr., to win acquittal.

For the most part, however, crime was little mentioned during Reagan's first year in office even though the nation appeared more concerned about this issue than it had been during the administration of Jimmy Carter. A Gallup Poll survey in 1981 showed that 54 percent of the Americans surveyed said there was more crime in their neighborhood than there had been the previous year. This was a dramatic increase over 1977 when only 43 percent of the citizens surveyed expressed such a view.

The FBI's Uniform Crime Reports showed a basis in fact for these feelings. The volume of crime in 1980 was up 18 percent over 1976.

During Reagan's term, however, crime leveled off; the FBI reported a 7 percent decline between 1982 and 1983, the largest drop in crime since 1960. The 1983 total was 1 percent below the 1979 figures.

Reagan reflected this concern in his 1982 State of the Union message, urging Congress to transform "our legal system, which overly protects the rights of criminals while it leaves society and the innocent victims of crime without justice."

A number of the specific anti-crime measures that the administration proposed later in 1982 were included in the omnibus crime legislation approved by Congress in 1984. This was legislation that President Reagan had consistently supported.

Because most crime was handled and prosecuted by state and local governments under their own laws, the changes in federal criminal law made by this massive legislation would have only an indirect effect on neighborhood crime. But the legislation did set up a new program of federal aid for state and local crime-fighting efforts.

The Reagan administration and its conservative supporters outside government strongly urged Congress to act on a number of controversial social issues, including ending the availability of abortions, restoring prayer in public schools and discarding busing as a means of desegregating public schools. But Congress, more concerned with pressing economic matters and loath to wade into such divisive thickets, did not approve any major measures in these areas during Reagan's first term.

The Republican takeover of the Senate in 1981 shifted the focus of debate on domestic legal issues from civil rights and crime to social issues, such as abortion and school prayers and prompted some observers to predict congressional action. The Senate Judiciary Committee, now a conservative mirror image of the staunchly liberal House Judiciary Committee, backed a number of these proposals, but the full Senate surprised observers and the White House by rejecting, in 1983, a constitutional amendment to ban abortion and, in 1984, a constitutional amendment to permit school prayer. The House Judiciary Committee simply enhanced its reputation as a burial ground for such conservative proposals during both the 97th and 98th Congresses.

Moreover, the Supreme Court in 1983 took more steam out of the anti-abortion push by reaffirming, 6-3, its 1973 decision that women had a constitutional right of privacy in deciding whether to have abortions. Reagan's nominee Sandra Day O'Connor was in dissent.

The court also temporarily defused the school prayer issue, agreeing early in 1984 to review its first school prayer case since the 1962-63 term when it declared state-pre-

References

Discussion of law enforcement policy for the years 1945-64 may be found in *Congress and the Nation Vol. I*, pp. 1671-1675; for the years 1965-68, *Congress and the Nation Vol. II*, pp. 309-334; for the years 1969-72, *Congress and the Nation Vol. III*, pp. 255-286; for the years 1973-76, *Congress and the Nation Vol. IV*, pp. 559-618; for the years 1977-80, *Congress and the Nation Vol. V*, pp. 715-753.

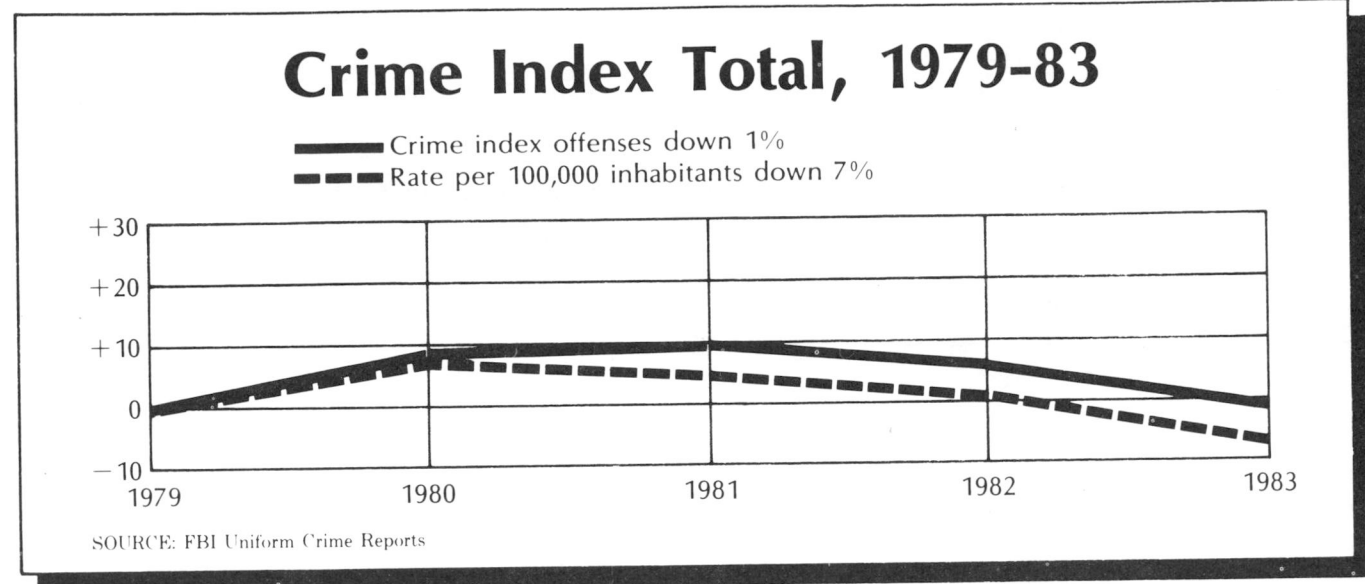

Crime Index Total, 1979-83

━━━━ Crime index offenses down 1%

■ ■ ■ ■ Rate per 100,000 inhabitants down 7%

SOURCE: FBI Uniform Crime Reports

scribed prayer in public schools unconstitutional. But in mid-1985, the court put Congress under renewed pressure to approve a school prayer amendment when it barred officially sanctioned silent prayer in classrooms. By 6-3, the justices struck down as unconstitutional an Alabama law authorizing a one-minute period of silence in all public schools for "meditation or voluntary prayers."

The administration itself made the push to limit busing through legislation unnecessary, moving in many parts of the country to reduce or end the use of this technique for desegregation.

The Reagan administration tried without success to kill the Legal Services Corporation established a decade earlier to provide legal services in civil matters to people too poor to pay a lawyer. But once again, Congress resisted, and at the end of Reagan's first term, the corporation was still alive although in questionable health.

Without much help from the White House, Congress approved a major extension of the landmark Voting Rights Act in 1982 and the following year an extension and restructuring of the Civil Rights Commission. The restructuring of that commission, one of the nation's oldest civil rights agencies, was the direct result of an unprecedented effort by Reagan to fire several of his critics on the commission and replace them with his nominees.

Unfinished Business

Left dead on the Capitol steps at the end of both the 97th and 98th Congresses was a wide-ranging immigration reform bill upon which both chambers had expended a great deal of time and effort.

Backed by the White House, the key provisions penalizing employers who hire illegal aliens and granting amnesty to illegal aliens in the country for a certain period of time sparked such varying reactions from different interest groups that its passage through Congress was like walking through a minefield.

Funding Justice

Although the mammoth federal law enforcement grant program of the 1970s, the Law Enforcement Assistance Administration (LEAA), officially went out of business in 1982, federal spending for the programs administered through the Justice Department rose from $2.2 billion in fiscal 1981 to $3.6 billion in fiscal 1985.

A new federal grant program was approved as part of the 1985 omnibus crime control bill, but it was not expected to mushroom after the fashion of the LEAA.

The FBI became a billion-dollar operation for the first time in fiscal 1984, spending more than the entire federal court system, whose funding rose from $631 million in fiscal 1981 to $977.9 million in fiscal 1985.

Judicial Impact

The Reagan administration came into office acutely aware that the federal judiciary — to which President Carter had named 262 new judges, most of them moderate to liberal — was firmly in the grip of men and women whose views of judicial power did not coincide with those of Reagan. The administration launched a concerted and systematic effort to appoint to all vacancies and new judicial posts men and women who believed in the limits of federal judicial power. By the end of Reagan's first term, this effort was having its effect.

In his first term, Reagan named the first woman to the Supreme Court, placing Sandra Day O'Connor on that bench in 1981. Her voting record and her well-articulated conservative views testified to the effective selection process employed by the administration in picking judicial nominees.

Reagan also named 166 other federal judges in his first term, most of them white Republican affluent men. Only 17 of his nominees, including O'Connor, were women; eight were Hispanic and two were black. These figures fell far below those of the Carter administration; Carter had appointed more women, black and Hispanic judges than any previous president.

Boosted by the creation of 85 more federal district and appeals court judgeships in 1984, Reagan looked forward to leaving his own conservative philosophy firmly imprinted upon the federal courts by the time he left the White House in 1989.

Chronology
Of Action
On Law Enforcement

1981

No major law enforcement legislation was enacted by the first session of the 97th Congress. At the end of the 1981 session, legislators could point only to a measure intended to improve the efficiency of the Immigration and Naturalization Service and a temporary authorization for the Justice Department. A third measure — making a single change in the Bankruptcy Act of 1978 — was vetoed by President Reagan.

Congress did rescue the Legal Services Corporation from death at the hands of the Reagan administration, providing funds for the continued operation of the agency through March 1982.

In addition to the perennial controversies over abortion, busing and school prayer — each of which drew its share of legislative attention during the term, Congress continued to wrestle with proposed revisions of the Voting Rights Act, federal immigration law and federal criminal law.

Legal Services Corporation

The 97th Congress kept the Legal Service Corporation (LSC) alive until March 31, 1982, with stopgap funding. The Reagan administration wished to abolish the seven-year-old corporation, which provided legal aid to the poor in civil cases. This plan was strongly opposed by LSC supporters in Congress, legal aid lawyers and the American Bar Association.

Both chambers voted to approve a two-year extension of the corporation's life, but such a reauthorization measure did not clear in 1981.

H J Res 370 (PL 97-92) contained $241 million for the Legal Services Corporation.

The House June 18 passed a two-year authorization bill (HR 3480 — H Rept 97-97) by a **key vote of 245-137 (R 59-116; D 186-21),** providing $241 million in fiscal 1982 and fiscal 1983. A bill (S 1533 — S Rept 97-171) providing $100 million for the corporation in fiscal 1982 was reported in the Senate but received no further action. *(1981 key votes, p. 879)*

The Senate included a two-year authorization for the Legal Services Corporation, at the level of $100 million per year, in the budget reconciliation bill (S 1377), but conferees removed it before approving the reconciliation package. *(Story, p. 40)*

Justice Authorization

For the second year in a row, Congress failed to complete action on a measure (S 951, HR 3462) authorizing the programs of the Justice Department.

The House passed its bill June 9 after adding an anti-busing rider to the measure. The Senate later in the year twice voted to break a filibuster against a similar rider to its version of the bill but did not complete action on the bill before the session ended. *(Busing measure, p. 705)*

However, Congress did approve a temporary authorization for the department's programs. A four-month extension, from Sept. 30, 1981, to Feb. 1, 1982, was approved by the House Oct. 27 and the Senate Oct. 30. The bill (HR 4608 — PL 97-76) was signed into law Nov. 5.

Immigration Law

Congress in 1981 cleared a measure (HR 4327 — PL 97-116) to improve the efficiency of the Immigration and Naturalization Service (INS), although more sweeping improvements in the nation's immigration system did not win the approval of both chambers. *(1982, 1984 action, pp. 692, 708)*

HR 4327 (H Rept 97-264) was approved by the House Oct. 13 and the Senate Dec. 16.

Provisions

As signed into law Dec. 29, major provisions of HR 4327 (PL 97-116):

● Eliminated the requirement that permanent resident aliens register each year with the INS.

● Eliminated certain requirements in naturalization proceedings, among them the requirement of two witnesses for a naturalization.

● Granted permanent resident status to foreign medical school graduates who had been practicing in the United States since Jan. 9, 1978, and extended the time an alien could reside in the United States to study medicine.

● Permitted aliens denied entry to the United States to be deported to a country other than that from which they came.

● Limited the current non-immigrant student visa to students in academic institutions and created a new classification for students in non-academic and vocational schools.

National Guard Torts

Congress in 1981 provided coverage for the National Guard under the Federal Tort Claims Act (PL 79-601), which generally governed claims against federal employees for injuries inflicted in the course of their duties.

The House approved the bill (HR 3799 — H Rept 97-384, Part I) Dec. 15; the Senate cleared the measure Dec. 16.

As signed into law, HR 3799 (PL 97-124) extended federal tort claims coverage to acts or omissions of members of the National Guard engaged in federally prescribed training activities. It also made federal tort claims procedures the exclusive remedy in medical malpractice actions involving National Guard members.

Bankruptcy Bill

Congress cleared — but President Reagan in 1981 vetoed — a bill (HR 4353) making a single change in the 1978 Bankruptcy Reform Act (PL 95-598).

Reagan Administration Immigration Proposals

President Reagan in 1981 proposed that Congress move to reform the nation's immigration system by:

● Stepping up efforts to halt the flow of illegal aliens into the country, including stopping and seizing U.S.-bound vessels carrying prospective illegal aliens.

● Imposing sanctions on employers who knowingly hired illegal aliens.

● Authorizing an experimental two-year program under which as many as 50,000 Mexican workers would be admitted to the United States, to work, for 9-12 months.

● Granting legal status to some of the three million to six million illegal aliens already in the United States.

● Empowering the president to declare an "immigration emergency" in which he could exercise broad powers, including the power to seal off any harbor, port, airport or road, to restrict Americans' travel to certain countries and to restrict the access of illegal aliens to federal courts.

The 97th Congress did not approve these proposals, but the immigration legislation that died at the end of the 98th Congress included certain aspects of the Reagan plan, among them the sanctions for employers and provision for the legalization of certain aliens. *(Story, p. 708)*

As approved by the House and Senate Dec. 16, HR 4353 (H Rept 97-414) placed a ceiling of $100,000 on the administrative fees to be paid in certain bankruptcy cases initiated before PL 95-598 took effect. PL 95-598 abolished administrative fees for all bankruptcy cases initiated after Sept. 30, 1979.

President Reagan vetoed the bill Dec. 29 because he said it would benefit creditors in one large bankruptcy case, a Chapter XI reorganization proceeding involving Fidelity Mortgage Investors in New York. That reorganization had begun before PL 95-598 took effect, and involved some $1.7 million in fees that would have been paid to a fund used to run the bankruptcy system.

Other Legislation

Voting Rights

The House in 1981 gave overwhelming approval to a bill extending the landmark 1965 Voting Rights Act, but the measure (HR 3112) did not win Senate approval until 1982. *(Story, p. 680)*

Criminal Code Revision

For the third time in four years, the Senate Judiciary Committee in 1981 approved a wide-ranging bill to revise and update federal criminal laws. But the measure (S 1630) went no further in 1981.

Civil Rights Commission

Both the House Judiciary Committee and a Senate Judiciary subcommittee in 1981 approved a fiscal 1982 authorization measure for the U.S. Civil Rights Commission, but neither measure reached the floor before the end of the session.

Patent Matters

A new federal appeals court primarily to handle patent cases was approved by both chambers in 1981, but the House and Senate could not agree until 1982 on the final version of the bill. *(Story, p. 686)*

The Senate July 9 passed a bill (S 255) to extend patent protection for drug manufacturers and others whose products are subject to federal regulatory review, providing additional years of protection to compensate the manufacturers for the time required for federal review. The House did not act on the issue in 1981.

Tris Reimbursement

The Senate, but not the House, in 1981 approved legislation (S 823) permitting companies that suffered losses because they produced Tris-treated sleepwear to seek federal reimbursement for those losses.

Congress completed action on the measure in 1982. *(Story, p. 688)*

Pretrial Services

The Senate in 1981 approved a bill (S 923) to expand 10 federal demonstration programs intended to help judges make decisions about granting pretrial bail. The House did not act on the measure until 1982. *(Story, p. 685)*

Foreign Antitrust Suits

The Senate approved legislation (S 816) in 1981 that would take away the right of foreign governments to recover treble damages through antitrust suits brought in U.S. courts. The House Judiciary Committee approved a similar bill (HR 5106) late in the year, but the full House did not act on it.

The bill approved by the Senate July 9 was designed to modify a 1978 Supreme Court ruling in the case of *Pfizer Inc. v. Government of India.*

The court held that foreign governments, like American corporations and consumers, could sue for triple damages in U.S. courts.

Aliens in Virgin Islands

The House in 1981 approved a bill (HR 3517) making 7,000 to 10,000 Virgin Islanders permanent residents of the United States.

The measure cleared Congress in 1982. *(Story, p. 688)*

Voting Rights Act in Action

The following chart shows the number of proposed changes in state election laws submitted to the Justice Department as required by the Voting Rights Act of 1965, and the number of changes to which the Justice Department has objected:

	Proposed election law changes				Justice Department objections
	1965-70*	1971-75	1976-80	Total	
Alabama	16	614	1,085	1,715	72
Alaska[1]	0	0	37	37	0
Arizona[2]	0	201	1,537	1,738	8
California[3]	—	12	683	695	5
Colorado[3]	—	0	233	233	0
Connecticut[4]	—	0	0	0	0
Florida[3]	—	1	167	168	0
Georgia	158	935	1,998	3,091	226
Hawaii[3]	0	0	9	9	0
Idaho[3]	0	0	1	1	0
Louisiana	5	882	1,709	2,596	136
Maine[3]	—	0	3	3	0
Massachusetts[4]	—	0	17	17	0
Michigan[4]	—	0	3	3	0
Mississippi	32	503	654	1,189	78
New Hampshire[4]	—	0	0	0	0
New Mexico[3]	—	0	65	65	0
New York[3]	—	166	326	492	5
Oklahoma[3]	—	0	1	1	0
North Carolina[3]	2	485	711	1,198	62
South Carolina	308	834	1,260	2,402	77
South Dakota	—	0	6	6	2
Texas	—	249	15,959	16,208	130
Virginia	57	1,093	1,780	2,930	14
Wyoming[3]	—	1	0	1	0
Total				34,798	815

* The pre-clearance requirement, requiring submissions of proposed election law changes to the Justice Department, was enacted in 1965. The provision was continued through the extensions of the act in 1970 and 1975.
[1] Entire state covered 1965-68; selected election districts covered 1970-72; entire state covered since 1975.
[2] Selected county or counties covered until 1975; entire state now covered.
[3] Selected county or counties covered rather than entire state.
[4] Selected town or towns covered rather than entire state.
— Not covered for years indicated.

SOURCE: U.S. Department of Justice

Constitutional Convention Procedures

The Senate Judiciary Committee was unable to complete action on a measure (S 817) establishing procedures for a constitutional convention after two members of the committee — Howell Heflin, D-Ala., and Joseph R. Biden Jr., D-Del. — staged a mini-filibuster to dramatize their concern that Congress retain for itself an active role in the convention process.

Article V of the Constitution provided that a constitutional convention must be called if two-thirds of the states (34) requested one. No procedures existed for running such a convention; S 817 would provide them.

As of the end of 1981, 30 states had called for a convention on an amendment to require a balanced federal budget. By the end of 1984, the number had risen to 32. (Balanced budget drive, box, p. 52)

Drug Programs

The House in 1981 approved a three-year extension for a federal drug abuse treatment program (HR 3963), but the Senate did not act on the matter.

Record, Tape, Film Piracy

The Senate in 1981 passed a bill (S 691) sharply increasing the penalties for record, tape and film piracy and counterfeiting, but the House took no action on the measure in 1981.

1982

Congress in 1982 strengthened and extended the landmark Voting Rights Act of 1965, and extended the special prosecutor law enacted in the wake of the Watergate scandal. Congress did not complete action on any other major piece of legislation in the law enforcement area during the year.

Voting Rights

Reaffirming its commitment to the ideal that every citizen should be able to vote, the 97th Congress extended for 25 years key provisions of the 1965 Voting Rights Act.

The 1982 measure (HR 3112 — PL 97-205) extended until 1997 the law's central enforcement mechanism, the requirement that affected areas obtain federal approval of any change in voting laws or practices before putting them into effect. PL 97-205 permitted affected jurisdictions to escape from this pre-clearance requirement by proving to a panel of three federal judges in the District of Columbia that they had engaged in no discrimination against voters for a decade.

The 1982 measure also made clear that a voting practice or law with the effect of discriminating against blacks or other minorities violated the Voting Rights Act, whatever its intent. This reversed a 1980 Supreme Court ruling in the case of *Mobile v. Bolden*, which held that a law was not in conflict with the Voting Rights Act unless it was intentionally discriminatory. *(Congress and the Nation Vol. V, p. 777)*

This was the third time that Congress had extended the Voting Rights Act (PL 89-110), widely considered the most effective civil rights measure enacted by Congress. Earlier extensions came in 1970 and 1975. *(Congress and the Nation Vol. II, p. 356; Congress and the Nation Vol. III, p. 498; Congress and the Nation Vol. IV, p. 668)*

Background

Enacted in the wake of the nationally televised violence in Selma, Ala., against civil rights workers attempting to register blacks to vote, the Voting Rights Act of 1965 was widely credited with the dramatic increase in the number of black and Hispanic voters taking part in state, local and federal elections across the United States in the 1970s and early 1980s.

Aimed squarely at discrimination in the South against blacks attempting to register or to vote, the law prohibited the use of literacy tests or any similar devices to disqualify voters. It also authorized the attorney general to send federal examiners into areas with low voter registration or participation to oversee voter registration and election procedures. These were permanent features of the law, requiring no extension.

The key enforcement section of the law required periodic extension. Section 5 required nine states and portions of more than a dozen others to obtain federal approval of any change in their election laws or procedures. That requirement was extended by PL 97-205 until 1997. Without extension it would have expired Aug. 6, 1982.

Section 5 applied to areas selected through a triggering formula based on use of a literacy test and voter registration statistics. In 1975 Congress amended the law to extend its protection to groups whose native language was not English. *(Voting rights in action, chart, p. 679)*

The nine affected states were: Alabama, Georgia, Louisiana, Mississippi, South Carolina, Virginia, Alaska, Texas and Arizona. The other areas covered under the law to a varying degree were counties in California, Colorado, Connecticut, Florida, Hawaii, Idaho, Maine, Massachusetts, Michigan, New Hampshire, New Mexico, New York, Oklahoma, North Carolina, South Dakota and Wyoming.

Legislative History

Passage of the measure was a victory for a coalition of civil rights groups that included black, Hispanic, labor, religious and civic organizations, cooperating under the umbrella of the Leadership Conference on Civil Rights. There was no major funded opposition to extending the law.

The bills extending the Voting Rights Act received widespread bipartisan support in both chambers, including strong backing from legislators representing the South, evidence of the growing political strength of that area's black voters.

Black Voter Registration

Percentage of eligible blacks registered to vote in 1964 and in 1976 in the six Southern states covered by the federal Voting Rights Act since 1965:

	1964	1976
Alabama	23.0%	58.1%
Georgia	44.0	56.3
Louisiana	32.0	63.9
Mississippi	6.7	67.4
South Carolina	38.8	60.6
Virginia	45.7	60.7

SOURCE: 1964 statistics, Voter Education Project of the Southern Regional Council; 1976 statistics, U.S. Census Bureau

Only 33 Southern Democrats in the House voted for the law when it was initially passed in 1965, and only 34 for the first extension in 1970. But by 1975, Southern Democratic support rose to 56. In 1981, when the House approved its version of PL 97-205, 71 Southern Democrats, more than twice as many as in 1965, voted to support the bill.

House Action

The House approved its version of HR 3112 during the first session of the 97th Congress. The vote of approval on Oct. 5, 1981, was overwhelming, 389-24, after fewer than 10 hours of debate. The House Judiciary Committee reported the bill (H Rept 97-227) Sept. 15.

The House extended the enforcement provisions until 1984, making them permanent after that time while instituting a new procedure through which covered areas could bail out of the pre-clearance requirement. HR 3112 also contained the language reversing *Mobile v. Bolden*. In a **key vote of 132-277 (R 102-75; D 30-202)** the House rejected a change in the forum for hearing certain voting discrimination cases. *(1982 key votes, p. 895)*

Senate Action

Senate supporters of HR 3112 had the measure placed directly on the Senate calendar Oct. 14, fearing that Senate Judiciary Committee Chairman Strom Thurmond, R-S.C., would delay committee action on the measure.

In December 1981, senators backing HR 3112 took still another precautionary step. They introduced an identical bill (S 1992) for which they had 61 cosponsors — one more than the number needed to choke off a filibuster.

But the Senate Judiciary Committee reported its version of S 1992 (S Rept 97-417) May 25, 1982. The committee bill, a compromise drafted by Sen. Robert Dole, R-Kan., extended the enforcement provisions for 25 years and contained language similar to that in the House bill concerning laws with discriminatory effect.

Senate consideration of the bill was delayed for a week by a desultory filibuster waged by the few senators who opposed it, led by Jesse Helms, R-N.C. Helms gave up the filibuster June 17 after Senate Majority Leader Howard H. Baker Jr., R-Tenn., announced that the Senate would not take up any other business until the voting rights bill was acted upon. The Senate June 18 approved the committee version of the bill by a vote of 85-8, after rejecting all amendments except a few technical changes.

Final Action

The House cleared the extension for the White House June 23, when it unanimously accepted the Senate version of the bill. Although he had urged a 10-year extension of Section 5 and opposed the provisions overturning the *Mobile* ruling, President Reagan signed the measure, calling the right to vote "the crown jewel of American liberties," and citing PL 97-205 as evidence of "our unbending commitment to voting rights."

Provisions

As signed into law June 29, HR 3112 (PL 97-205) amended the Voting Rights Act of 1965 to:

• Extend the pre-clearance requirements of Section 5, for 25 years, until 1997. This required all affected states and counties to obtain approval from the Justice Department before implementing any changes in election laws or procedures.

• Provide, beginning in 1984, a new method for affected states and counties to "bail out" of the coverage of Section 5. A jurisdiction could remove itself from the reach of this requirement by showing a three-judge panel in the District of Columbia that it had a clean voting rights record for the preceding decade.

• Require, as proof of a clean voting rights record, the following: evidence that there had not been any use of a voting test or device in a discriminatory way; that there had been no final judgment by a federal court finding a violation of the voting right law; that there had been no consent decree, settlement or agreement entered into during that period concerning voting rights violations; that there had been no need to send in federal examiners to register voters; that there had been full compliance by local officials with the pre-clearance requirement; that there had been a repeal of any changes objected to by the Justice Department; and evidence that the area had made constructive efforts to encourage minority group members to vote and to end any intimidation or harassment of prospective voters.

• Extend, until 1992, the requirement that certain areas of the country with large language minority populations provide bilingual election materials.

• Authorize blind, disabled or illiterate voters to receive aid in voting from a person of his or her choice, so long as that person was not the voter's employer or union officer.

• Declared that citizens bringing a voting rights lawsuit under Section 2 of the law could prove a violation of the law by showing that the challenged law or procedure had the effect of discriminating against certain voters. The court hearing such a case would look at the "totality of circumstances" to decide whether or not the law had been violated.

• Declared that there was no right to proportional representation for a minority group and that lack of such representation was only a single factor to be considered by a court in evaluating a voting rights suit.

Special Prosecutor Law

Congress in 1982 revised and extended for five years the special prosecutor law enacted in the wake of the Watergate scandal.

The legislation (S 2059) tightened the standards that trigger the appointment of a special prosecutor to investigate alleged wrongdoing by high government and campaign officials. It also limited the list of officials covered, reduced the number of years for which they were covered and renamed the special prosecutor, independent counsel.

The special prosecutor law, Title VI of the Ethics in Government Act of 1978 (PL 95-521), would have expired Oct. 1, 1983. *(Congress and the Nation Vol. V, p. 829)*

The Reagan administration opposed extension, contending that the attorney general was capable of handling any necessary investigation, regardless of its sensitivity.

Background

By the end of 1982 the special prosecutor law had been invoked only 11 times and in only three of those cases had a

Equal Rights Amendment Effort Fails

Just three states short of ratification, the proposed Equal Rights Amendment (ERA) to the Constitution died June 30, 1982. Thirty-five states had ratified the amendment; 38 were required.

The amendment was brief and to the point. The substantive language would have added to the Constitution the simple statement that: "Equality of rights under the law shall not be denied or abridged by the United States or by any state on account of sex."

However, the ERA stirred a national political and social debate out of all proportions to its apparent simplicity, and it was that debate that resulted in its death in 1982.

Congressional Approval

It took 49 years for Congress to approve the proposed amendment. First introduced in 1923, the amendment was approved by Congress March 22, 1972.

The House approved the amendment Oct. 12, 1971, by a vote of 354-24, substantially more than the two-thirds majority needed. The Senate approved the resolution six months later, March 22, 1972, by a vote of 84-8. *(Congress and the Nation Vol. III, p. 509)*

Ratification

Less than two hours after the Senate acted, Hawaii became the first state to ratify the amendment. It was followed by Alaska, California, Colorado, Connecticut, Delaware, Idaho, Indiana, Iowa, Kansas, Kentucky, Maine, Maryland, Massachusetts, Michigan, Minnesota, Montana, New Hampshire, New Jersey, New Mexico, Nebraska, New York, North Dakota, Ohio, Oregon, Pennsylvania, Rhode Island, South Dakota, Tennessee, Texas, Vermont, Washington, West Virginia, Wisconsin and Wyoming.

The original deadline for ratification was March 22, 1979. By early 1978, 35 states had ratified, but amendment supporters knew that extension of the ratification period was essential if they were to win the three additional states.

Congress in 1978 did extend the deadline by 39 months, until June 30, 1982. *(Extension, Congress and the Nation Vol. V, p. 798)*

But despite a massive fund-raising and lobbying effort by ERA supporters, not a single additional state ratified the ERA during the extension period. The defeat of the amendment was made certain in June 1982 when state legislatures in North Carolina, Florida and Illinois rejected it.

Most of the 15 states that rejected pressure to ratify were Southern states: Alabama, Arizona, Arkansas, Florida, Georgia, Illinois, Louisiana, Mississippi, Missouri, Nevada, North Carolina, Oklahoma, South Carolina, Utah and Virginia.

Three of the ratifying states, Idaho, Tennessee and Nebraska, raised further questions about ratification by rescinding their ratifying votes.

Outlook

On June 30, 1982, the day ERA officially died, Phyllis Schlafly, the head of Stop ERA and a leading opponent of the amendment, proclaimed that ERA was "not only dead now but forever in this century." It failed to win ratification, she said, because Americans understood that it would lead to erosion of family life and the draft of women for military service.

Pro-ERA leaders simultaneously vowed to continue their fight to add this language to the Constitution. They urged women to vote selectively in the future, looking closely at a candidate's stand on women's rights issues. Kathy Wilson, head of the National Women's Political Caucus, promised that work would continue "to change the political complexion of the [state] legislatures at large" by electing more women and more men receptive to women's rights and concerns.

Identical constitutional amendments were introduced in the 97th and 98th Congresses but were not approved.

On Nov. 15, 1983, the House by a **key vote of 278-147 (R 53-109; D 225-38)** fell six votes short of a required two-thirds majority needed to approve a new ERA resolution (H J Res 1). *(1983 key votes, p. 911)*

---

special prosecutor actually been appointed. None of the investigations produced evidence warranting prosecution.

The first two cases concerned allegations of drug use by Hamilton Jordan, then Jimmy Carter's White House chief of staff, and Timothy Kraft, then campaign manager for the Carter-Mondale Presidential Committee.

The third, involving charges of corruption against Labor Secretary Raymond J. Donovan was closed Sept. 13, 1982, with an announcement by special prosecutor Leon Silverman that there was insufficient evidence to support the charges. *(Subsequent Donovan developments, p. 656)*

Legislative History

The Senate approved S 2059 (S Rept 97-496) by voice vote on Aug. 12. The House approved it 347-37 on Dec. 13.

The Senate by voice vote accepted relatively minor House changes Dec. 16, clearing the bill for the White House.

Provisions

As signed into law Jan. 3, 1983, S 2059 (PL 97-409) included provisions that:

● Extended Title VI of the Ethics in Government Act until 1988.

● Renamed the special prosecutor as an independent counsel.

● Modified the standard by which a preliminary investigation was triggered to permit the attorney general to consider the credibility of the accuser and the specificity of the information received.

● Required appointment of independent counsel only when the attorney general "finds reasonable grounds to believe that further investigation or prosecution is warranted." (This was a significantly higher standard than that in effect from 1978 to 1983, which required appointment of a special prosecutor unless the charges were "so unsubstantiated that no further investigation is warranted.")

● Allowed the attorney general to name independent counsel to investigate any matter that he felt could not be investigated by him or another Justice Department officer without a possible conflict of interest.

● Restricted the list of persons to include only top-level officials close to the president or the attorney general.

Legal Services Corporation

The Legal Services Corporation (LSC) continued to cling to life through 1982, despite continued efforts by the Reagan administration to starve it of funds.

As in 1981, Congress appropriated $241 million for the organization for fiscal 1983, the same level of funds as in 1982 (H J Res 631 — PL 97-377). (1981 action, p. 677)

Supporters of the LSC argued that Reagan tried — by appointing members of the board of directors hostile to the work of the agency — to do by the back door what he could not accomplish directly: kill the agency.

Reagan nominated nine persons to the LSC board of directors, none were confirmed and all nominations were withdrawn at the year's end.

Given recess appointments to their posts in December 1981, seven of the board members served through 1982, amid growing controversy generated by disclosures that several of them had collected large consulting fees while serving on the board. As a result, Congress included language in the funding resolution restricting fees that could be paid to LSC board members.

Protecting Public Officials

Congress in 1982 approved three new laws providing expanded protection for government officials and persons entitled to Secret Service protection.

The first measure (S 907 — PL 97-285) made it a federal crime to kill, kidnap or assault Supreme Court justices, senior presidential and vice presidential aides, Cabinet officers and nominees, the second-ranking officials in each department and the director of the Central Intelligence Agency (CIA).

After the assassination of President John F. Kennedy, Congress in 1965 made it a crime to kill, kidnap or assault the president of the United States (PL 89-172). Until that time, such crimes were prosecuted under the laws of the states in which they occurred.

The March 30, 1981, shooting of President Reagan and three other men made clear the need for expanding the reach of federal law to protect these other officials. (Story, p. 847)

The maximum penalty provided by PL 97-285 was life imprisonment.

The Senate passed S 907 (S Rept 97-320) May 5; the House approved its version (H Rept 97-803) Sept. 14. The Senate Sept. 22 accepted the House amendments, clearing the bill for the White House.

Kidnap Threats

The second measure (HR 6168 — PL 97-297) made it a federal crime to threaten to kidnap the president, a former president, presidential candidates or any other person entitled to Secret Service protection. Until its passage there was no single federal law covering such threats; persons making such threats were usually prosecuted under state law.

HR 6168 passed the House by unanimous consent Aug. 16 (H Rept 97-725) and the Senate Sept. 28.

Secret Service Protection

The third measure (HR 4468 — PL 97-308) authorized the Secret Service to cordon off zones of protection around anyone entitled to Secret Service protection. PL 97-308 made it a crime to violate such a zone by unauthorized entry.

Such zones were customarily set up by the Secret Service, but there was no penalty for violating any zone except that around the president. PL 97-308 extended the penalties, up to a $1,000 fine and a year in prison, to cover violation of any such zone set up around any person protected by the Secret Service. This category included the vice president, presidential and vice presidential candidates, the president-elect, the vice president-elect, their families, and visiting heads of state.

HR 4468 was approved by the House March 18 (H Rept 97-451) and by the Senate Oct. 1.

Supreme Court Police

Congress in 1982 expanded the authority of the Supreme Court's 70-person police force, permitting officers to protect the Supreme Court justices and their official guests anywhere in the country.

The legislation (HR 6204 — PL 97-390) was requested by Chief Justice Warren E. Burger earlier, but took on added significance after Justice Byron R. White was attacked on July 15 by a man upset by court decisions on school busing and pornography. White, who was seated at the time, awaiting his turn to speak to a group in Salt Lake City, Utah, was pummeled but not seriously harmed.

PL 97-390 also authorized Supreme Court police to carry their firearms while performing their duties off the Supreme Court premises.

HR 6204 was approved by the House Aug. 16 (H Rept 97-704) and by the Senate Oct. 1. The House Dec. 13

Watergate Revisited: A Legislative Legacy

The Watergate scandal began on June 17, 1972, with the infamous break-in at the Democratic National Committee headquarters and culminated a little more than two years later, on Aug. 9, 1974, with the resignation of President Nixon.

The effects of the scandal did not end then, however. Throughout most of the ensuing decade, Congress considered and passed reform proposals that were born during the Watergate period.

Some sweeping new laws bearing on executive branch powers, such as the 1973 War Powers Act (PL 93-148) and the Congressional Budget and Impoundment Control Act of 1974 (PL 93-344), had nothing to do with Watergate but much to do with a related weakening of the Nixon presidency.

The roots of several public laws were traced directly to Watergate. This legislation included two landmark acts governing political campaigns and government ethics, as well as other laws more limited in scope.

Following is a description of the most significant laws rooted in Watergate:

Elections Campaign Amendments. Technically a package of amendments to the Federal Election Campaign Act of 1971 (PL 92-225), the Elections Campaign Amendments of 1974 (PL 93-443) legislation actually was a comprehensive rewrite of U.S. election law. *(Congress and the Nation Vol. IV, p. 991)*

The new law tightened financial disclosure requirements, set low contribution limits and expenditure ceilings for all federal election campaigns, established public financing for presidential primary and general election campaigns and created the Federal Election Commission (FEC) to enforce the law.

The campaign act was amended again in 1976 to partially restore and revise major parts of the 1974 law struck down by the Supreme Court. The 1976 campaign act amendments (PL 94-283) reconstituted the FEC and revised financial limits in the law.

Ethics in Government. The Ethics in Government Act of 1978 (PL 95-521) was the second piece of major reform legislation to grow out of the Watergate period. The broad law:

● Established a mechanism for appointing a special prosecutor to investigate allegations against high government officials;

● Set detailed financial disclosure requirements for the president, vice president, high executive branch officials, Supreme Court justices, federal judges, top judicial employees, members of Congress, key congressional aides and candidates for federal office;

● Placed new restrictions on business activities of federal workers who leave government;

● Established an Office of Government Ethics in the executive branch to regulate ethical conduct and monitor compliance with ethics laws.

Although the 1978 law could be traced directly to Watergate, by the time it finally was enacted it had been shaped by three major factors: the Watergate scandal itself; the reform movement inside Congress, which in 1977 produced Senate and House ethics codes that later were embodied in the law; and ethics proposals advanced by President Carter. *(Ethics, p. 785)*

Presidential Records. A 1978 law (PL 95-591), which grew out of Watergate-era controversy over Nixon's claim to ownership of his presidential papers and tape recordings made in the White House, declared that most records of future presidents, beginning in 1981, would be public property.

Congress first had applied that principle in 1974 by passing legislation (PL 93-526) specifically directed at Nixon's tapes and papers. The 1974 law, which nullified an agreement between Nixon and the General Services Administration (GSA), directed GSA to keep the Nixon materials and not destroy any of them without congressional permission. *(Congress and the Nation Vol. V, p. 830)*

Secret Service Spending. Angered over spending of more than $17 million by the Secret Service at Nixon's private homes, Congress in 1976 passed legislation (PL 94-524) to restrict such expenditures in the future. *(Congress and the Nation Vol. IV, p. 826)*

FBI Director's Term. Congress in 1976 limited to 10 years the term for the director of the Federal Bureau of Investigation. This limitation was attached to legislation extending the Law Enforcement Assistance Administration (PL 94-503).

The decision to limit the director's term reflected a reaction to the FBI's compromised independence during the Watergate cover-up, as well as concern over the agency's excessive independence before that period under the late FBI director, J. Edgar Hoover. *(Congress and the Nation Vol. IV, p. 604)*

Disclosure of Tax Returns. The Watergate investigation revealed that the Nixon White House had sought from the Internal Revenue Service the tax returns of people considered to be political enemies. As part of the Tax Reform Act of 1976 (PL 94-455), Congress put strict new limits on disclosure of tax return information to anyone outside the IRS. *(Congress and the Nation Vol. IV, p. 99)*

accepted two Senate amendments and cleared the legislation for the president.

Victims and Witnesses

Congress in 1982 passed a bill (S 2420 — PL 97-291) intended to make the federal courts more sensitive in dealing with the victims of crime and witnesses to crime.

PL 97-291 did not create a federal program to compensate victims of crime, but it did require judges to order restitution for victims in most cases involving violations of federal criminal laws.

The legislation was approved by the Senate (S Rept 97-532) Sept. 14 by voice vote; the House passed it Sept. 30, also by voice vote. Congress cleared the measure early on the morning of Oct. 2 before recessing for the 1982 elections.

As signed into law Oct. 12, S 2420 (PL 97-291):

● Made it a felony, punishable by a fine of up to $250,000 and a prison term of up to 10 years or both, to intimidate victims or witnesses of crime through physical force or threats of force.

● Allowed a prosecutor to seek a protective order to shield a witness, a victim, and their families from intimidation by a particular person.

● Provided that a defendant who tried to intimidate a victim or witness could have his bail revoked.

● Required that the sentencing report on a defendant include an impact statement outlining the financial, social, psychological and physical impact of the crime on the victim.

● Authorized a judge to order restitution to the victim in cases involving property loss or personal injury to cover uninsured medical expenses, property losses and funeral or burial costs.

Pretrial Services

Congress in 1982 expanded nationwide 10 demonstration pretrial services programs designed to help judges decide which defendants should be released on bail.

The programs were first authorized in 1974 as part of the Speedy Trial Act (PL 93-619), which set deadlines for trying persons charged with crimes. *(Congress and the Nation Vol. IV, p. 576)*

The 1982 measure (S 923 — PL 97-267) required creation of such programs in all 95 federal judicial districts.

The Senate passed the measure (S Rept 97-77) June 18, 1981. The House passed a similar bill (HR 3481 — H Rept 97-56) May 11, 1982. The Senate approved the conference report on S 923 (H Rept 97-792) Aug. 20. The House adopted the report, clearing the bill, Sept. 15.

Arson

Congress in 1982 upgraded the offense of arson to a major federal crime.

PL 97-298 (HR 6454) was designed to make clear that arson involving property in interstate or foreign commerce was a federal offense. Until its passage, arson could be prosecuted as a federal crime only if it could be shown that an explosion had occurred. That requirement was eliminated by the new law.

LEAA Shuts Down

After 14 years of dispensing federal aid to local law enforcement agencies, the Law Enforcement Assistance Administration (LEAA) went out of business on April 15, 1982.

Its demise was ordered on Dec. 30, 1981, by President Reagan's attorney general, William French Smith, but it had been foreshadowed by the agency's drastic restructuring in the final years of the Carter administration.

Over its lifetime, the agency had dispensed nearly $8 billion for programs such as upgraded police equipment, shelters for homeless youth, and special local task forces to prosecute "career criminals."

LEAA was created in 1968 amid nationwide concern over rising crime rates. Law enforcement in the United States had always been primarily a function of local and state governments, but Congress hoped that by providing federal grants to state and local law enforcement agencies it could improve their ability to combat crime. LEAA was enthusiastically adopted by the Nixon administration, under which its budget mushroomed from a first-year total of $63 million to nearly $1 billion by the mid-1970s.

HR 6454 was approved by the House Aug. 2 (H Rept 97-678) and the Senate Sept. 22. The House cleared the measure Sept. 28 by accepting the Senate amendments. President Reagan signed the bill Oct. 12.

Theft of Nuclear Materials

The 97th Congress approved a measure (HR 5228 — PL 97-351) making it a federal crime to obtain nuclear materials unlawfully and to use them to threaten or cause physical harm to individuals.

The maximum penalties for such theft and threats ranged from 20 years to life in prison, a $250,000 fine, or both for cases in which serious injury or death resulted.

PL 97-351 was intended to deter nuclear terrorism. It implemented a 1979 convention on protecting nuclear materials, which the United States signed with 33 other nations and which the Senate ratified July 30, 1981.

The law also authorized the attorney general to seek enforcement help from the military in certain emergencies resulting from nuclear thefts.

The House approved HR 5228 (H Rept 97-624) by a vote of 396-9 under suspension of the rules July 20. The Senate Judiciary Committee was discharged from consideration of HR 5228, and the bill was placed on the Senate calendar Aug. 5. The Senate amended and passed HR 5228 Sept. 14. The House agreed to some amendments, disagreed with others and returned the bill to the Senate Sept.

28. On Oct. 1 the Senate concurred in the House action, clearing the bill.

Missing Children

Congress in 1982 responded to increasing national concern about the large number of children reported missing each year by passing legislation (HR 6976 — PL 97-292) allowing the federal government to aid in the search for such children.

PL 97-292 authorized state and local officials and the Federal Bureau of Investigation (FBI) to enter into the FBI's central crime computer descriptive data about missing children. It also required officials to include in the FBI computer a clearinghouse file listing descriptions of unidentified bodies found anywhere in the country. Many of these were children.

The House approved HR 6976 (H Rept 97-820) Sept. 20 by voice vote under suspension of the rules. The Senate approved its version of the bill (S 1701 — S Rept 97-583) by voice vote Sept. 23. The House adopted the conference report (H Rept 97-911) Sept. 30; the Senate cleared the measure by approving it Oct. 1.

Record, Tape, Film Piracy

Congress in 1982 increased the penalties for record, tape and film piracy and counterfeiting. The piracy bill (S 691 — PL 97-180) was aimed at the mushrooming illegal industry that reproduced copyrighted records, tapes and films for sale.

PL 97-180 provided a maximum penalty of five years' imprisonment or a $250,000 fine, or both, for persons convicted of illegally reproducing and distributing as many as 1,000 records or 65 films in a 180-day period.

It provided for a one-year prison term, a $25,000 fine, or both, for copyright infringement of a lesser volume. Before passage of PL 97-180, the penalties were $10,000 or one year in prison, or both, for a first offense, and $25,000 or two years, or both, for a subsequent offense.

S 691 was approved by the Senate (S Rept 97-274) Dec. 1, 1981, by voice vote. The House approved a similar bill (HR 3530 — H Rept 97-495) May 10 and then passed the Senate bill, clearing it for the president.

Copyright Clause

Congress in 1982 overrode a presidential veto to enact a bill (HR 6198 — PL 97-215) extending federal copyright law to protect the American printing industry.

PL 97-215 extended until 1986 the so-called "manufacturing clause" in U.S. copyright law, which required most books and periodicals written in English by American authors to be printed and bound in the United States or Canada if they were to receive full copyright protection.

At the heart of the push for this bill was concern about more than 350,000 jobs in the domestic printing and related industries. A June 1981 Labor Department report warned that elimination of the clause would result in a massive loss of business to foreign printing companies and the loss of up to 367,000 jobs in the United States.

The bill (HR 6198 — H Rept 97-575) was approved by the House by voice vote June 15; the Senate approved the House version June 30.

President Reagan vetoed the bill July 8 as unnecessary to protect one of the most modern and efficient printing industries in the world. The veto was the seventh of Reagan's presidency, the first to be overridden.

Organized labor quickly mobilized to help supporters of the bill win enough votes to override the veto. The House voted July 13, 324-86, to override the veto. This provided 50 votes more than the two-thirds, 274, needed to override. The Senate quickly followed suit, 84-9, 22 votes more than the 62 required.

Patent Fees

Congress in 1982 approved a measure restructuring patent fees and authorizing operation of the U.S. Patent and Trademark office for fiscal years 1983-85.

The measure (HR 6260 — PL 97-247) established a two-tier system for payment of patent-user fees. Large firms were required to pay at a level that recouped 100 percent of the costs of patent application and maintenance; small firms, individual inventors and non-profit organizations paid at a rate intended to recoup only 50 percent of those costs.

The Reagan administration had proposed requiring all patent recipients to pay fees recovering 100 percent of the costs, but Congress refused to approve that approach.

PL 97-247 authorized appropriations of $76 million for the patent office in fiscal 1983 and as much as necessary for the other two years. Patent office operations also were funded by revenues from patents and trademark fees that were expected to provide the office a total operating budget in fiscal 1983 of $154.9 million.

The House approved HR 6260 (H Rept 97-542) June 8; the Senate cleared the bill Aug. 12.

Trademark Amendments

Congress in 1982 approved a bill (HR 5154 — PL 97-296) making clear that state and local governments could not require alteration of federally registered trademarks on signs, brochures, posters or stationery.

PL 97-296 amended the 1946 Lanham Trademark Act. It resulted from a decision by a three-judge federal court in Nevada that the 1946 law did not bar Nevada from requiring local real estate brokers to modify the trademarked logo of the Century 21 Real Estate Company.

The House passed HR 5154 (H Rept 97-778) Sept. 20. The Senate accepted the House bill the same day, clearing it for the president.

New Appeals Court

A new U.S. Court of Appeals for the Federal Circuit was created by Congress in 1982, primarily to handle patent cases.

President Reagan signed the measure (HR 4482 — PL 97-164) on April 2. The new court held its first session in Washington on Oct. 1.

The new court had exclusive jurisdiction over appeals from all decisions by federal district courts in patent cases and certain other specific types of cases, and over appeals from decisions of the Merit Systems Protection Board.

The new court consolidated within itself the functions of the old U.S. Court of Customs and Patent Appeals with

Law Enforcement Leaders, 1981-84

The nation's top law enforcement leadership was stable during President Reagan's first term in office.

Attorney General

William French Smith served as attorney general throughout the first term. Smith, formerly a partner in the large and prestigious Los Angeles firm of Gibson, Dunn and Crutcher, was Reagan's personal lawyer before being selected attorney general. He was confirmed in this position Jan. 22, 1981.

Three years and a day later, on Jan. 23, 1984, Smith announced that he was resigning to return to his law practice, effective upon confirmation of his successor. That same day, Reagan announced that he was nominating White House counselor Edwin Meese III, one of his closest advisers, as Smith's successor.

However, questions about Meese's personal finances set off a prolonged investigation that delayed Senate confirmation until 1985 and extended Smith's term as attorney general until the early weeks of Reagan's second term in the White House. *(Meese nomination, box, p. 707)*

Meese, who was confirmed by the Senate, 63-31, on Feb. 23, 1985, came to the post after a career spent mostly in politics, quite different from Smith's career in corporate law.

After eight years as a county deputy district attorney in California, Meese was part of Reagan's gubernatorial staff from 1967 until 1974, most of that time as chief of staff.

After three years of corporate law practice, he taught law at the University of San Diego until becoming a campaign adviser in 1980 and counselor to the president in 1981.

In the White House he was considered one of the president's inner circle, very influential in shaping administration policy, particularly on justice-related issues.

FBI Director

William Webster, chosen by President Carter in 1978 to lead the Federal Bureau of Investigation (FBI), continued to serve in that post during Reagan's first term.

Under his leadership, the FBI avoided the controversies and scandals that had beset it during the 1970s, and Webster himself was often mentioned as a possible Supreme Court nominee. Before becoming FBI director, he had served for several years as a judge on the 8th U.S. Circuit Court of Appeals. His term as FBI director would expire in 1988.

Congressional Committees

The gavel of the Senate Judiciary Committee passed from left to right in 1981, as Republicans took control of the Senate after the 1980 elections. Sen. Edward M. Kennedy, D-Mass., one of the Senate's most liberal members, surrendered the chairmanship of the Senate Judiciary Committee to Strom Thurmond, R-S.C., one of its staunchest conservatives.

For the 97th and 98th Congresses, the two Judiciary committees were ideological opposites. Thurmond, who had made his reputation as a states' rights activist who voted against every major civil rights bill before Congress, recruited several other noted conservatives to join the Senate Judiciary Committee. In general Thurmond and the committee were receptive to the Reagan administration's proposals in the area of law enforcement and individual rights.

The House Judiciary Committee, led by Rep. Peter W. Rodino Jr., D-N.J., remained solidly liberal as a result of Rodino's successful efforts to fill all vacancies on the panel with liberal members. Rodino spent most of his energies during the 97th and 98th Congresses bottling up conservative legislation in his committee.

Dismayed by many of the proposals endorsed by the administration, Rodino viewed his main mission during these years as defending individual civil and constitutional rights against such proposals as constitutional amendments to ban abortion or school busing or permit public school prayer, and legislation limiting the rights of criminal defendants and abolishing the Legal Services Corporation.

---

the appellate division of the U.S. Court of Claims. It was the only circuit court of appeals whose cases depended solely on their subject matter, not the area of the country within which they arose. All the other circuit courts of appeal had jurisdiction over cases arising in certain states.

PL 97-164 also created a new trial-level court, the U.S. Claims Court, to take over cases currently heard by the trial division of the U.S. Court of Claims. These were generally cases in which the government was a defendant, including many contract disputes.

HR 4482 (H Rept 97-312) was approved by the House Nov. 18, 1981. The Senate passed a companion measure (S 1700 — S Rept 97-275) Dec. 8, 1981, after attaching an unrelated provision concerning grain elevator bankruptcies. The House March 9 stripped that provision from the bill. The Senate March 22 concurred in that action, clearing the bill for the president.

Both chambers had passed similar bills in the 96th Congress but did not reach agreement on a final version of the bill before adjournment.

Federal Jurors

Congress in 1982 revised some of the laws concerning federal jurors.

The measure (S 2863 — PL 97-463) provided attorneys' fees for jurors for whom the court appointed a lawyer to challenge their employers' discrimination against workers who served on juries. Under current law, such fees were only available for privately retained attorneys.

PL 97-463 also provided that jury summonses would be sent through the regular mail, instead of registered or certified mail. It also provided that federal jurors were eligible for workers' compensation for jury-related injuries. Under current law, only federal employees were eligible for such compensation.

The Senate approved S 2863 Dec. 20; the House acted Dec. 21.

Foreign Antitrust Suits

Congress in 1982 cleared a bill (S 816 — PL 97-393) eliminating the right of foreign governments to recover treble damages in federal antitrust suits.

PL 97-393 modified a 1978 Supreme Court decision *(Pfizer Inc. v. Government of India)* in which the court held that foreign governments can sue for triple damages to recover financial losses resulting from violations of U.S. antitrust laws. *(Congress and the Nation Vol. V, p. 778)*

The 1982 law placed other nations on the same footing in such cases as the U.S. government, able to collect actual damages but no more in such cases. A truly commercial enterprise owned by a foreign government, however, still might collect treble damages in such a case if certain standards were met.

The Senate approved S 816 (S Rept 97-98) July 9, 1981; the House approved its version of the bill (HR 5106 — H Rept 97-476) April 27 by voice vote under suspension of the rules. On Dec. 13, the House modified S 816 to conform to HR 5106 and approved S 816. The Senate cleared the bill Dec. 15 by concurring in the House amendments.

Tris Reimbursement

For the second time in four years, Congress in 1982 approved legislation (S 823 — PL 97-395) allowing companies to seek federal reimbursement for losses resulting from the sale of Tris-treated children's sleepwear.

Congress cleared a similar bill in 1978, but President Carter vetoed it. *(Congress and the Nation Vol. V, p. 360)*

In the early 1970s a number of sleepwear manufacturers used the chemical Tris to ensure that the sleepwear was flame-resistant. In 1977, however, the Consumer Product Safety Commission banned Tris as a hazardous substance, a possible carcinogen. Manufacturers were required to repurchase all unsold or unwashed garments made from Tris-treated fabric.

The Senate approved S 823 (S Rept 97-130) June 18, 1981. Senate Judiciary Committee Chairman Strom Thurmond, R-S.C., had pushed for House action, attaching S 823 to two unrelated bills in the hope of obtaining House approval. Both efforts failed. *(Story, p. 678)*

The House finally approved the bill during the lame-duck session in December, after the Judiciary Subcommittee on Administrative Law and Governmental Relations bypassed the full committee and sent the measure directly to the floor. The House approved the bill by voice vote Dec. 13 under suspension of the rules. The Senate by voice vote accepted the House version of the bill Dec. 14.

Provisions

As signed into law Dec. 30, S 823 (PL 97-395):

● Allowed companies to file claims in the U.S. Claims Court to recover the cost of producing Tris-treated goods, transportation costs involved with returning the sleepwear, and costs associated with lawful disposal of Tris-treated products. No recovery was permitted for lost profits.

● Set standards for judges to use in determining whether compensation was due.

● Barred compensation unless a company produced proof that it had lawfully disposed of Tris-treated products.

● Barred recovery by a claimant who knowingly allowed the export of Tris-treated products after the CPSC ban was published June 14, 1978.

● Required successful claimants to repay the Small Business Administration if they had obtained any loans or loan guarantees because of Tris-related losses.

Service of Process

Congress in 1982 amended existing law to permit complaints in federal lawsuits to be served on parties by regular mail and to shift the cost of such service to the plaintiffs in the case.

Until this amendment, federal marshals personally served such complaints. Marshals would, under the new law, continue to serve complaints when ordered to do so by a federal judge, when the United States initiated a suit and when the case involved an indigent. The bill (HR 7154 — PL 97-462) also increased to $75,000 from $5,000 the penalty for failing to register with the State Department as a foreign agent.

HR 7154 was approved by the House Dec. 15 and the Senate Dec. 21.

Aliens in Virgin Islands

Congress in 1982 made some 7,000 to 10,000 aliens living in the U.S. Virgin Islands eligible to become permanent U.S. residents. The new law (HR 3517 — PL 97-271) granted permanent resident status to any alien who was admitted to the Virgin Islands as a temporary worker and had resided there continuously since June 30, 1975.

PL 97-271 abolished the temporary worker program as no longer needed. Under the law, an alien wishing to become a permanent resident had to make an application to the attorney general within one year of the law's enactment. *(1981 action, p. 678)*

PL 97-271 also gave the secretary of state discretionary authority to restrict the right of new permanent residents to employ the existing visa preference system to have relatives join them on the islands.

The House approved HR 3517 (H Rept 97-307) Nov. 4, 1981. The Senate approved it Aug. 20 by voice vote (S Rept 97-529). The House accepted the Senate amendments Sept. 8 by voice vote. President Reagan signed the bill Sept. 30.

'Amerasian' Immigration

Congress in 1982 cleared legislation (S 1698 — PL 97-359) intended to facilitate the immigration of 'Amerasian' children, Southeast Asians fathered by Americans, to the United States.

The Senate passed the bill Sept. 28 by voice vote; the House cleared the measure Oct. 1.

As signed into law Oct. 22, major provisions in S 1698 (PL 97-359):

● Allowed unmarried Amerasians to apply for admission to the United States under the "first preference" category.

● Authorized approval of these applications if there were reason to believe that the applicant was born after 1950 in Korea, Thailand, Vietnam, Laos or Kampuchea (Cambodia) and was fathered by a U.S. citizen.

● Required a guarantee of financial support for the immigrant from a sponsor who was a U.S. citizen or permanent resident and was at least 21 years old.

Refugee Resettlement

Congress in 1982 reauthorized for one more year, through fiscal 1983, refugee resettlement programs established in 1980 by the refugee reform law (PL 96-212). *(Congress and the Nation Vol. V, p. 740)*

The House approved the measure (HR 5879 — H Rept 97-541) June 22 by a vote of 357-58; the Senate cleared the bill (S Rept 97-638) Oct. 1.

HR 5879 (PL 97-363) set no funding limit overall for fiscal 1983 programs but specifically authorized $100 million for social services programs and $14 million for health programs for the refugees.

Other provisions made clear that the federal office administering the resettlement program should direct new refugees to areas other than ones where there were already large numbers of refugees and that there should be consultation with state and local governments about refugee placement. PL 97-363 required a refugee to participate in job or language training in order to receive cash assistance and provided that aid would be terminated if a refugee refused a suitable job offer.

PL 97-363 also required welfare agencies to notify voluntary agencies when a refugee had applied for welfare.

False Identification

Congress in 1982 moved to curb the spread of false identification documents such as drivers' licenses and birth certificates.

The new law (HR 6946 — PL 97-398) made it a federal offense to produce or transfer such false identification documents. It set a fine of up to $25,000 or a prison term of five years or both.

The House approved HR 6946 (H Rept 97-802) by voice vote Sept. 14; the Senate approved the bill Oct. 1. The conference report (H Rept 97-975) was filed Dec. 17; it was adopted by the House Dec. 17 and the Senate Dec. 19.

Employee Claims

Congress in 1982 approved a bill (HR 4688 — PL 97-226) that increased from $15,000 to $25,000 the amount that the United States can pay to settle claims brought by military and civilian government employees.

PL 97-226, which passed the House March 18 (H Rept 97-452) and the Senate July 14 (S Rept 97-482), amended the 1964 Military and Civilian Employees Claims Act (PL 88-558).

Crime Control Veto

Congress in 1982 cleared an anti-crime package whose main thrust was to combat drug trafficking, but President Reagan in January 1983 vetoed the measure (HR 3963), objecting to the creation of a new Cabinet-level drug enforcement office. *(1984 action, p. 698)*

HR 3963 began in 1981 as a three-year authorization of a program to monitor and treat drug abuse by convicted federal offenders released on parole or probation. The House approved that measure (H Rept 97-283) under suspension of the rules Oct. 26, 1981.

In the closing days of the 97th Congress, the drug treatment bill became the vehicle for six other anti-crime measures already approved by one chamber or the other.

The House Dec. 20 approved this conglomerate measure under suspension of the rules by a vote of 271-27. The Senate by voice vote the same day accepted the House package.

As sent to the president, HR 3963 contained the following major provisions:

Drug Monitoring and Treatment. Extended for three years a federal program under which all convicted federal offenders released on parole or probation were examined to determine if they abused drugs.

Further monitoring and treatment was provided for these offenders.

The measure authorized $4.5 million for fiscal 1983 and a $1 million increase in fiscal 1984 and again in fiscal 1985 for a total of $6.5 million in the last year.

Drug Offense Penalties. Increased substantially the penalties for producing and selling drugs and provided that all property in felony drug cases would be forfeited to the government. Both houses of Congress had approved these provisions as a separate measure (HR 7140 — H Rept 97-883), which passed the House Sept. 28 and the Senate Oct. 1.

Justice Assistance Act. Created a new grant program to aid states and local governments in combating crime, in place of the defunct Law Enforcement Assistance Administration (LEAA). Both the House and Senate had approved these provisions as a separate measure (HR 4481 — H Rept 97-293, S Rept 97-587) on Feb. 10 and Dec. 9, respectively.

Anti-Tampering. Made it a federal crime to tamper with food and drug products, a response to the seven deaths that occurred in October 1982 when consumers unknowingly ingested Extra-Strength Tylenol capsules laced with cyanide. These provisions had been approved by the Senate on Dec. 17 as S 3048.

Protecting Intelligence Officials. Made it a federal crime to assault or murder certain designated intelligence officials. The Senate had approved this measure as S 2552 (S Rept 97-575) on Oct. 1.

Career Criminals. Gave federal courts jurisdiction to try repeat offenders who used a firearm in burglaries or robberies and had at least two prior convictions for such crimes, and set mandatory minimum sentences for such

Congress and Supreme Court Thwarted . . .

Despite strong White House backing and the increasing political clout of Republicans on Capitol Hill, anti-abortion forces suffered major defeats during President Reagan's first term in office.

In 1982 the Senate Judiciary Committee for the first time approved a constitutional amendment to permit states to ban abortions. But in 1983 that advance ended in a double setback as the Supreme Court reaffirmed its 1973 decision barring state laws making abortion a crime and the Senate soundly rejected the constitutional amendment.

Congress continued to ban the use of federal funds to provide abortions for poor women, federal employees, Indians served by federal health programs, military personnel and Peace Corps volunteers unless the life of the mother was in danger. But no additional restrictions were enacted, and by 1984 advocates of choice in the area of childbearing were hopeful that they might be able to restore medical coverage for abortions for these groups.

With the exception of the funding restrictions, virtually all major efforts to curtail abortions came in the Senate, where a sympathetic Judiciary Committee provided leadership and support for such measures. The House Judiciary Committee, in contrast, had no interest in these proposals.

Background

On Jan. 22, 1973, the Supreme Court in the cases of *Roe v. Wade* and *Doe v. Bolton*, struck down state laws that made abortion a crime.

By a 7-2 vote the court declared that women had a constitutional right of privacy in deciding whether to bear a child. Early in pregnancy, the state had no business interfering in a woman's decision to have an abortion. As the pregnancy progressed, the state could impose some conditions upon abortion to protect the mother's health but not until the last trimester, the point at which the fetus might survive outside the mother's womb, could the state forbid abortions altogether.

Abortion opponents began work to overturn this decision through a constitutional amendment and to restrict the use of public funds for abortions.

Congress in 1973 prohibited the use of foreign aid funds for abortion, and in 1976 barred the use of Medicaid funds for abortions, except those required to save a mother's life. This Medicaid restriction was called the Hyde amendment after its sponsor, Rep. Henry J. Hyde, R-Ill. No constitutional amendment was approved in either a House or Senate committee until 1982. *(Congress and the Nation Vol. IV, pp. 365-366, 635)*

At the time, about $45 million in Medicaid funds were spent annually to pay for 250,000 to 300,000 abortions, 25-30 percent of all abortions performed in a year in the United States. When the Hyde amendment took effect in August 1977, Medicaid-funded abortions dropped to a few thousand each year.

In 1977 Congress slightly relaxed the Hyde amendment, permitting abortion funding when two doctors believed the procedure was necessary to prevent severe and long-lasting physical health damage to the mother or an abortion was necessary following a rape or episode of incest that had been promptly reported to police or public health authorities.

Two years later, in 1979, Congress dropped the physical health damage exception, tightening the Hyde amendment once again. In 1980, Congress further narrowed the exception by permitting Medicaid abortions to terminate a pregnancy resulting from a rape or incest only if the rape or incest was reported within 72 hours to proper authorities.

The Supreme Court in 1980, by a 5-4 vote, upheld the Hyde amendment. In *Harris v. McRae* the court declared that poor women had no constitutional right to abortions paid for by public revenues.

In 1978, Congress forbade the use of federal funds to pay for abortions for military personnel, their dependents and Peace Corps volunteers. *(Congress and the Nation Vol. V, pp. 811-813)*

Constitutional Amendments

Congress: 1981-82

The Senate Judiciary Subcommittee on the Constitution in December 1981 approved a proposed constitutional amendment declaring that the Constitution secured no right to an abortion. The proposed amendment gave states and Congress joint authority to restrict abortion.

Three months later, in March 1982, the full Judiciary Committee, by a 10-7 vote, approved the proposed amendment (S J Res 110), whose major sponsor was the Constitution Subcommittee's chairman, Orrin G. Hatch, R-Utah. This was the first time since *Roe v. Wade* in 1973 that a committee had approved an anti-abortion amendment.

The amendment was not brought to the Senate floor in 1982, in part because of divisions in the anti-abortion forces. The National Right to Life Committee and the National Conference of Catholic Bishops backed the Hatch amendment. Other anti-abortion groups, including the Washington-based March for Life, favored a measure sponsored by Sen. John P. East, R-N.C., declaring that life began at conception and states could legally protect life from that moment. The Senate Judiciary Subcommittee on Separation of Powers, chaired by East, approved that bill

... Anti-Abortion Efforts During 1981-84

in July 1981, but the Judiciary Committee did not act. Some groups preferred a proposal by Sen. Jesse Helms, R-N.C., providing a statutory, rather than a constitutional, ban on abortions by declaring *Roe v. Wade* to be erroneous and permitting state laws to protect unborn fetuses.

Late in 1982, a Senate filibuster prevented Helms from attaching his abortion proposal to an unrelated bill. A cloture vote fell 10 short.

By a **key vote of 47-46 (R 18-33; D 29-13)** on Sept. 15, 1982, the Senate tabled an anti-abortion amendment by Sen. Jesse Helms, R-N.C. *(1982 key votes, p. 895)*

Congress: 1983-84

In the 98th Congress, Sen. Thomas F. Eagleton, D-Mo., proposed a constitutional amendment stating: "A right to abortion is not secured by this Constitution." Those 10 words would overturn *Roe v. Wade* and permit each state to pass its own laws governing abortion, the situation that existed before the 1973 ruling. This language was the same as the first sentence of the Hatch amendment. The Constitution Subcommittee in March 1983, with Hatch's blessing, made Hatch's amendment identical to Eagleton's proposal. The measure, S J Res 3, was sent by a deadlocked Senate Judiciary Committee to the Senate floor in April without a recommendation.

Eagleton's language was not endorsed by advocates of abortion bans who backed a bill, by Sen. Roger W. Jepsen, R-Iowa, and Hyde in the House, that was similar to Helms' 1982 proposal. President Reagan endorsed this approach, which encouraged states to pass new anti-abortion laws and made permanent the ban on federal funding of abortions.

Although neither chamber voted on these proposals during the 98th Congress, the controversy they provoked in the Senate was in part responsible for that chamber's rejection of the Eagleton-Hatch constitutional amendment (S J Res 3) on June 28, 1983, by a **key vote of 49-50 (R 34-19; D 15-31)**, 18 votes short of the two-thirds required to approve a constitutional amendment. *(1983 key votes, p. 911)*

Funding Restrictions

The 97th and 98th Congresses continued to include the Hyde amendment in appropriations bills for the Department of Health and Human Services. Hyde's amendment barred the use of Medicaid funds for abortions unless the procedure was required to save the mother's life. The Senate May 21, 1981, by a **key vote of 52-43 (R 33-19; D 19-24)** included the Hyde amendment in a supplemental appropria-

tions bill (HR 3512). *(1981 key votes, p. 879)*

Congress also again barred funding of abortions through the foreign aid program in 1982 (PL 97-121), for military personnel (PL 97-114) and federal employees (PL 98-151). In 1981, controversy over the limitation on abortion funding in federal employee health programs killed the Treasury/Post Office appropriations bill. The House, 253-167, added an anti-abortion provision to this bill, but the Senate Appropriations Committee rejected the restriction. An attempt to insert the provision on the Senate floor caused so much confusion that the bill was pulled from debate and died at the end of the session.

This ban was included in the first (PL 97-276), but not the second, fiscal 1983 continuing resolution. After a concerted effort to defeat it was rejected in the House, the ban was included in the second fiscal 1984 continuing resolution (PL 98-151) and in the fiscal 1985 continuing resolution (PL 98-473).

Supreme Court Decision

The *Roe v. Wade* decision of 1973 was reaffirmed by the Supreme Court on June 15, 1983, a little more than a decade after the original ruling. Deciding five cases, the court held unconstitutional a variety of state and local restrictions on abortion.

In two Ohio cases, *Akron v. Akron Center for Reproductive Health, Akron Center for Reproductive Health v. Akron*, the court, 6-3, held invalid a number of provisions of a 1978 city ordinance considered a national model for anti-abortion regulation. Requirements struck down mandated that:

• all abortions after the first three months of pregnancy be performed in a hospital;

• physicians obtain parental or guardian consent for an abortion on a girl younger than 15;

• physicians give to women seeking abortions specific information about fetal development, abortion complications and alternatives to abortion; and

• at least 24 hours elapse between signing an abortion consent form and the abortion.

In the Missouri cases, *Planned Parenthood Association of Kansas City, Mo. v. Ashcroft, Ashcroft v. Planned Parenthood Association of Kansas City, Mo.*, the court 5-4 upheld several provisions of a challenged state law, including one that required unemancipated minors to obtain the consent of a parent or the court for an abortion.

In the Virginia case, *Simopoulos v. Virginia*, the court 8-1, upheld a state requirement that all second-trimester abortions be performed in hospitals, defined to include outpatient surgical clinics. Such clinics were not considered hospitals under the Akron ordinance the court held invalid the same day.

persons convicted under this law. Similar provisions had been approved by the Senate Sept. 30 as S 1688 (S Rept 97-585).

New Drug Office. Established a new Cabinet-level office to direct and coordinate national and international operations to combat drug traffic. The Senate approved similar provisions as part of S 2572 on Sept. 30. The director of this office would have had authority to direct other Cabinet officials, including the attorney general, to follow his directives.

Reagan vetoed HR 3963 on Jan. 14, 1983. A senior Justice Department official told reporters that the measure had been strongly opposed by the Justice, State and Treasury departments, all arguing that it would constitute a tremendous disruption of existing efforts to control drug traffic. He said that the Justice Department also opposed the "career criminals" provisions, which it saw as raising both constitutional and practical problems.

Criminal Code Reform

The Senate in 1982 passed a trimmed-down version of the perennial criminal code reform bill, but the House did not act on that measure in the 97th Congress.

The slimmed-down bill (S 2572) was approved by the Senate Sept. 30, 95-1. It included provisions for preventive detention, a new sentencing scheme that virtually abolished parole and provided for sentencing guidelines, increased drug trafficking penalties and new protections for top government officials and federal witnesses.

A proposed revision of the insanity defense was deleted from the bill before it came to the Senate floor. Interest in the insanity defense skyrocketed after a federal court jury June 21, 1982, found John W. Hinckley Jr. not guilty by reason of insanity in the March 30, 1981, shooting of President Reagan and three other men.

Some of the components of S 2572 were eventually included in the omnibus anti-crime bill (HR 3963) that President Reagan vetoed in January 1983. *(Story, p. 689)*

Earlier in the year efforts to win Senate approval of the comprehensive reform of the criminal code (S 1630 — S Rept 97-307) were blocked when the Senate in April failed to cut off debate on a motion to consider the bill. Not even a majority supported the move to invoke cloture and consider the bill.

The effort to revise the criminal code dated back to 1966, when a national commission was appointed to propose such reforms. S 1630 was the third complete criminal code overhaul measure to be approved by the Senate Judiciary Committee in five years. *(Background, Congress and the Nation Vol. V, pp. 728, 748)*

Immigration Reform

A wide-ranging immigration reform measure (HR 7357) died in the House late in the 97th Congress, a victim of opposition from organized labor, the Hispanic community, the business community and civil rights groups.

The bill — similar to one approved by the Senate, 80-19, Aug. 17 (S 2222 — S Rept 97-485) — was an ambitious package that provided sanctions for employers who knowingly hired illegal aliens, an amnesty program giving legal status to millions of undocumented workers already living in the United States, a temporary worker program for the agriculture industry, and new procedures for asylum, deportation and exclusion cases.

HR 7357 (H Rept 97-890, Parts I and II) and its Senate counterpart grew out of extensive hearings and study by the House and Senate Judiciary subcommittees overseeing immigration in 1981. They were the first proposals for comprehensive overhaul of the nation's immigration laws since 1952 and enactment of the McCarran-Walter Act (PL 82-414). *(Congress and the Nation Vol. I, p. 222)*

HR 7357 was approved by the Judiciary Committee and the Education and Labor Committee, but its doom was sealed when the Rules Committee Dec. 8 granted a rule permitting virtually unlimited amendments to be offered and debated.

By the time the House began work on the bill Dec. 16, some 300 amendments had been filed. The press of time and the lack of enthusiasm among House leaders for the bill made House approval impossible. The effort to win passage ended Dec. 18 when the leadership took the bill off the floor, but chief House sponsor Romano L. Mazzoli, D-Ky., promised to reintroduce the measure in the 98th Congress. *(Stories, pp. 697, 708)*

Extradition Revision

After moving through the Senate and two House committees, a bill to revise U.S. extradition procedures stalled and died in 1982 before reaching the House floor.

The bill (HR 6046 — H Rept 97-627, Parts I and II) was reported by the House Judiciary and Foreign Affairs committees in June and August. The Senate passed its version of the bill (S 1940 — S Repts 97-331, 97-475) after it had been considered by the Senate Judiciary and Foreign Relations committees.

But a coalition of religious and civil rights groups led by the American Civil Liberties Union were working against the bill, concerned about the protection of persons residing in the United States and sought by their own countries for "political crimes." The coalition had mustered sufficient opposition to the measure in the House to keep it off the floor in 1982.

Bankruptcy Impasse

After the Supreme Court June 28 held that Congress had overstepped constitutional boundaries in restructuring the bankruptcy court system in 1978, Congress failed twice to meet the court's deadlines for restructuring those courts.

Deciding the case of *Northern Pipeline Construction Co. v. Marathon Pipeline Co.*, the Supreme Court ruled 6-3 that Congress had given the new bankruptcy judges too much power and too little independence. The judges had basically the same authority over bankruptcy-related matters as a federal district judge, but they served only for 14-year terms, not for life, as federal district judges did. This compromised the independence of the judiciary too far, the court held. *(Decision, p. 744)*

The court set a deadline of Oct. 4 for Congress to remedy the situation. The House Judiciary Committee Sept. 15 reported a bill (HR 6978 — H Rept 97-807) to elevate the bankruptcy judges to the status of federal judges, but the full House did not act on the bill. House Democratic leaders opposed it because it would have given President Reagan 227 new judges to appoint.

In the final hours before the election recess began Oct. 2, Sen. Robert Dole, R-Kan., tried to win approval of a bill that covered many bankruptcy issues, including the court problem, but the threat of a filibuster prevented Senate action. *(1984 action, p. 702)*

When Congress failed to meet the Oct. 4 deadline, the court extended it to Dec. 24. After it became clear Dec. 22 that that deadline, too, would pass without action, the solicitor general requested still another extension, until March 25, 1983. The court Dec. 23 refused that request.

As of Dec. 27 an interim rule for handling bankruptcy cases went into effect, leaving the system in legal limbo.

A number of other measures concerning bankruptcy were approved by the Senate in 1982, but none won House approval. These included a bill (S 2297 — S Rept 97-527) designed to protect shopping center owners and tenants when tenants went bankrupt. The Senate approved that bill Oct. 1.

Also Oct. 1 the Senate approved a bill (S 3037) to expedite procedures for handling bankruptcies involving grain elevators.

The Senate Judiciary Committee reported a bill (S 2000 — S Rept 97-446) to make it more difficult for individuals to declare bankruptcy. These provisions were included in the bill that Dole was hoping to move through the Senate Oct. 2, but the filibuster blocked that plan.

Antitrust Damages

Proponents of a bill to allow companies charged with price-fixing to apportion among themselves the damages they were ordered to pay their victims gave up their fight for Senate approval early in December, frustrated by a Senate filibuster.

S 995 (S Rept 97-359) proposed to amend the 1914 Clayton Act, one of the nation's basic antitrust laws, to permit this practice of "contribution." Under existing law, the Supreme Court ruled in May 1981, there was no right of contribution: price-fixers were each liable for all damages involved in a price-fixing case, regardless of each defendant's level of participation. *(Supreme Court ruling, Texas Industries v. Radcliff Materials Inc., p. 741)*

This proposal was relatively non-controversial, but a second feature of S 995 that required a judge to reduce a plaintiff's claim against remaining defendants by the amount of any settling defendant's liability drew loud objections from plaintiffs in price-fixing cases. The claim reduction based on liability, not the amount for which the defendant actually settled, was viewed by plaintiffs as a bailout for defendant companies, depriving plaintiffs of their chance to collect adequate damages.

S 995 was reported in April, but did not come to the floor until December. The opposition, led by Max Baucus, D-Mont., Howard M. Metzenbaum, D-Ohio, and Warren B. Rudman, R-N.H., mounted a filibuster. Two votes to invoke cloture failed, the first by 22 votes, the second by 16. Senate Judiciary Chairman Strom Thurmond, R-S.C., chief sponsor of the bill, gave up the fight for passage after the second vote.

Justice Authorization

Congress in 1982 for the third year in a row did not pass an authorization bill for the Justice Department. Un-like other years, Congress made no attempt to pass even a stopgap authorization measure.

The Justice Department's last stopgap authorization (PL 97-76) expired Feb. 1, 1982. The department, with the blessing of the House and Senate Judiciary committees, simply continued to operate under various continuing appropriations resolutions.

The Senate approved an authorization measure (S 951) March 2, after adding the toughest anti-busing language ever approved by either chamber. The House Judiciary Committee had reported an authorization bill (HR 6297), but it never came to the House floor. *(Busing dispute, p. 705)*

Electronic Surveillance

The Senate in 1982 approved a bill (S 1640 — S Rept 97-319) clarifying procedures for obtaining a court order to authorize electronic surveillance, but the measure died in the House Judiciary Committee.

S 1640 would have required a federal agency requesting such an order to indicate whether or not a break-in was necessary to install the listening device. The Senate had approved similar legislation in 1980. *(Congress and the Nation Vol. V, p. 751)*

Court Jurisdiction

The House in 1982 approved a bill (HR 6872 — H Rept 97-824) that would give the Supreme Court greater discretion in deciding which cases it would hear argued. The Senate did not act on the measure.

Such a measure had been urged by all nine justices as a means of enabling the court better to control its growing workload. A similar bill passed the Senate in the 96th Congress but died in the House, primarily because the Senate added a school prayer provision.

The Senate in 1982 did approve another bill (S 675) establishing a commission to study the jurisdiction of federal and state courts and recommend changes, but the House did not act on that bill.

State Justice Institute

The Senate in 1982 approved a bill (S 537 — S Rept 97-175) to create a State Justice Institute to provide technical and financial aid to state courts, but the bill was not approved by the House. A similar bill was approved by the Senate in the 96th Congress and also died in the House.

Patent Extension

Legislation extending the patent term for up to seven years for drug manufacturers, chemical companies and others whose products are subject to pre-marketing federal review died with the 97th Congress. Under existing law a patent lasted for 17 years, a limit that was put into effect in 1861.

The House Sept. 15 refused by five votes to suspend the rules and pass the patent term extension bill (HR 6444 — H Rept 97-696). The Senate had passed a similar bill in 1981. *(Story, p. 678)*

Cable TV

A bill (HR 5949) to clarify the rights of cable television operators to retransmit copyrighted material died in the Senate at the end of the 97th Congress. The House passed the bill Sept. 28 by a vote of 347-53. The bill was reported by both the Judiciary and the Energy and Commerce committees (H Rept 97-559, Parts I and II).

The Reagan administration opposed the bill, which also restored certain protections for broadcast stations eliminated in 1981 by the Federal Communications Commission.

Surplus Property

The Senate in 1982 passed legislation (S 1422 — S Rept 97-322) authorizing the federal government to donate surplus property to any state for building or modernizing criminal justice facilities. The House did not act on the measure.

1983

The most important law enforcement measure approved by Congress in 1983 was the surprisingly controversial measure extending the life of the U.S. Civil Rights Commission. A tug of war between the White House and civil rights groups over the membership of the commission resulted in a restructuring of the agency.

Congress continued to work to reform the nation's criminal laws, its immigration policy and its bankruptcy system, but none of these tasks were completed in 1983.

Civil Rights Commission

Congress in 1983 extended the life of the U.S. Civil Rights Commission for six years, until Sept. 30, 1989. This legislation (HR 2230 — PL 98-183) provided a backdrop for an intense power struggle between President Reagan and civil rights groups over the membership of the commission. The commission was established in 1957 as an independent entity to investigate charges of civil rights violations. It had no enforcement authority; it could only report and make recommendations.

As originally established, the commission had six members appointed by the president and confirmed by the Senate with no more than three from the same political party. (Congress and the Nation Vol. I, p. 1622)

PL 98-183 restructured the commission into an eight-member panel, with four members appointed by the president and four by Congress.

The new structure was the direct result of President Reagan's unprecedented attempt to fire his critics on the commission and replace them with members of his own choice. Civil rights advocates contested such a move as undermining the independence of the commission.

Within days of the passage of HR 2230 on Nov. 16, the intricately negotiated agreement that had led to congressional approval of the bill unraveled into a bitter dispute between the White House, moderate Republican senators and civil rights activists.

Under the agreement, members of Congress understood that four of the administration critics were to be reappointed to the reconstituted commission: Blandina Cardenas Ramirez, a Democrat and an educator from San Antonio; Mary Frances Berry, an independent and a professor at Howard University Law School; and Mary Louise Smith and Jill Ruckelshaus, both Republicans. Ramirez and Berry were two of three members Reagan had attempted to fire. Smith, an Iowa GOP leader, was a former chairman of the Republican National Committee, while Ruckelshaus was the wife of William D. Ruckelshaus, head of the Environmental Protection Agency.

But early in December, after Congress had adjourned, the White House began to deny any agreement to reappoint the latter two.

Civil rights groups claimed that the administration was double-crossing them. They charged that the White House had reneged on its agreement because it feared it would lose control of the commission if Smith and Ruckelshaus were renamed.

When the dust settled, Reagan had appointed the incumbent Chairman Clarence M. Pendleton, a Republican; Morris Abram and John Bunzel, both Democrats; and Esther Gonzalez-Arroyo Buckley, a Republican teacher from Texas. Abram was the former president of Brandeis University and a well-known civil rights attorney. Bunzel was associated with the Hoover Institution at Stanford University, a conservative "think tank."

The congressional appointees were Berry; Ramirez; Robert Destro, a Democrat and professor of law at Catholic University; and Francis F. Guess, a black Republican who was Tennessee commissioner of labor.

Background

Except for President Dwight D. Eisenhower, who appointed all six members of the original commission, no president had ever appointed a majority of the commission or summarily dismissed a commissioner.

In 1974, President Richard M. Nixon asked Father Theodore M. Hesburgh to resign as chairman, which he did. All the other commissioners who had left their seats did so voluntarily or only at their death.

The law setting up the commission did not limit the commissioners' terms or address the question of their removal. In practice, most commissioners resigned after six or seven years.

Throughout its history, the commission was often critical of White House policies and was particularly critical of Reagan administration policies on busing and affirmative action during the first two years of Reagan's term.

The Reagan administration responded angrily. On May 26, a week after the House Judiciary Committee approved an extension of the commission's life, Reagan announced that he was replacing three of his most vocal critics on the commission — Ramirez, Berry and Rabbi Murray Saltzman, appointed to the commission in 1975 and its most senior member — with Abram, Destro and Bunzel.

Civil rights groups said they would fight the nominations, not because they opposed these particular individuals but because they felt that Reagan's move to replace his critics undermined the independence of the commission. They successfully held up confirmation of the three Reagan nominees while Congress acted on extending the life of the commission.

House Action

The House Judiciary Committee reported HR 2230 (H Rept 98-197) May 17, recommending an extension of the commission's life for 15 years.

After reducing the extension to five years by a vote of 400-24, the House Aug. 4 approved HR 2230 by voice vote. The House also approved an amendment stating that members of the commission could be removed from office only for "neglect of duty or malfeasance in office."

Senate, Final Action

The Senate Judiciary Committee held a hearing July 16 on the three Reagan nominations but was unable to muster the votes to confirm them before the August recess. During the recess and September, lobbyists led by Ralph G. Neas, executive director of the Leadership Conference on Civil Rights, an umbrella organization for 165 groups, kept a steady drumbeat of opposition to the appointments.

The White House remained adamant in its position. While this stalemate existed, the commission technically went out of business Sept. 30 but continued operating under the 60-day wind-down period provided in the law.

A compromise plan was drafted by Sens. Joseph R. Biden Jr., D-Del., Robert Dole, R-Kan., and Arlen Specter, R-Pa., under which the commission would become an eight-member body on which all current members could remain in office and Reagan could appoint two new members.

On Oct. 25, the day before the Senate Judiciary Committee was to vote on this plan, Reagan fired Berry, Ramirez and Saltzman.

The Senate began debating HR 2230 on Nov. 9. The same day, the House deleted funds for the commission from a fiscal 1984 appropriations bill then in conference, putting additional pressure on the Senate to work out an agreement or see the commission go out of business. Appropriation of funds for the commission could be considered de facto authorization.

After intense negotiations, the compromise plan developed by Biden, Dole and Specter was amended to White House satisfaction. The Senate Nov. 11 adopted this plan as an amendment to HR 2230, 79-5.

Biden and Specter spoke to the press immediately after the vote, explaining that an agreement had been reached over who would be named to the restructured commission.

The Senate approved the amended bill Nov. 14, 78-3. There was a brief delay when Sen. Roger Jepsen, R-Iowa, attempted to add anti-abortion language to HR 2230, but that amendment was killed 42-34 by a tabling motion.

The House Nov. 16 accepted the Senate version of the bill.

Fiscal 1984 funding of $11.89 million for the commission was restored to the Commerce, Justice, State appropriations bill (HR 3222 — PL 98-166), which also cleared Nov. 16.

Provisions

As signed into law Nov. 30, HR 2230 (PL 98-183):

● Reconstituted the Civil Rights Commission as an eight-member panel with four members appointed by the president, two by the Senate and two by the House.

● Provided that the commissioners would serve for six-year staggered terms and not more than four could belong to the same political party.

● Extended the life of the commission until Sept. 30, 1989, providing it the same powers that it had exercised in the past.

● Stated that the commissioners could be removed from office only for "neglect of duty or malfeasance in office."

● Provided that the president could designate the chairman, vice chairman and staff director, subject to approval by a majority of the commissioners.

Legal Services Corporation

The embattled Legal Services Corporation (LSC) survived 1983 despite continued efforts of the Reagan administration to abolish the agency.

Although no authorizing legislation was approved during the year, $275 million for the LSC was included in the fiscal 1984 appropriations bill for Commerce, Justice and State (HR 3222 — PL 98-166). PL 98-166 also included provisions severely limiting lobbying activities by LSC lawyers, barring the use of LSC funds for conducting training programs that deal with political advocacy, and limiting the compensation and benefits of LSC board members.

The amount provided in fiscal 1984 was $34 million above the fiscal 1983 amount, but significantly below the $321 million provided for the LSC in fiscal 1981, the last year of the Carter administration.

Authorization for the LSC expired in 1979, and efforts in both chambers over the next four years to reauthorize the agency were to no avail.

In May 1983 the House Judiciary Committee reported legislation (HR 2909 — H Rept 98-201) extending the life of the LSC for three years, but the bill remained in the House Rules Committee for the rest of the year. No LSC authorization bill emerged from the Senate Labor and Human Resources Committee, even though several were under consideration by the committee.

Unable to win Senate confirmation for his nominees to the LSC Board, President Reagan during congressional recesses appointed four members to that board, enough to conduct business. During the year, these four men led the agency: Robert E. McCarthy, a San Francisco lawyer who served as chairman; Milton Masson, a businessman; Donald E. Santarelli, an attorney who had served as a member of the Justice Department during the Nixon administration; and Ronald B. Frankum, a telecommunications consultant. As recess appointees they could serve through the 1984 session. (*LSC appointments, box, p. 1028*)

On Oct. 7, Reagan nominated 11 members to the LSC board. They were not confirmed by the Senate during 1983 and their nominations died at the end of the session.

Military Justice

Congress in 1983 revised and streamlined the Uniform Code of Military Justice, the body of law first enacted in 1950 (PL 81-506) and governing the military.

The most important provision of the measure (S 974 — PL 98-209) made it possible for either the government or the defendant in a military case to seek direct review by the Supreme Court of a decision by the Court of Military Appeals, the highest court in the military justice system. Cases would be appealed from this court just as they were from the federal and state civilian courts.

<table>
<tr><td>

Air Treaty Rejected

Responding to intense pressure from trial lawyers, the Senate in 1983 rejected a treaty that would have set new limits on damage awards to passengers in international air crashes. It was the first time in more than 20 years that the Senate had rejected a treaty.

In 1960, the Senate rejected an international law of the sea treaty. In 1978, it rejected a tax treaty with Great Britain but reversed itself within four days and ratified the treaty.

The March 8 vote on the air crash liability treaty, known as Montreal Protocols 3 and 4 (S Rept 98-1), was 50-42, 12 short of the two-thirds, 62 in this case, required for ratification of the agreement negotiated in 1975 by the Ford administration.

Opposition to the treaty was led by Ernest F. Hollings, D-S.C., who had successfully blocked consideration of the pact in the 97th Congress. Hollings called the treaty an "outrageous assault on public safety and a sweetheart deal" for foreign governments that own airlines. The Association of Trial Lawyers of America opposed the treaty as impinging upon a passenger's right to full compensation.

Proponents led by Nancy Landon Kassebaum, R-Kan., countered that air crash victims would benefit because the treaty would lead to higher, more swiftly resolved settlements than did current law. The Air Transport Association, the administration and the American Bar Association contended that the treaty would provide for fair and swift compensation.

The rejected treaty limited to $120,000 the amount that a passenger could recover to compensate for loss of future income. In addition, up to $200,000 could be recovered from a fund to be created by a surcharge on every ticket.

</td></tr>
</table>

Anti-Tampering Act

Responding to a rash of deaths in the Chicago area after the victims took Extra-Strength Tylenol capsules laced with cyanide, Congress in 1983 made it a federal crime to tamper with consumer products such as drugs, food and cosmetics.

The measure (S 216 — PL 98-127) made such tampering a felony, punishable by fines of up to $100,000 and prison terms including life. The severity of the possible sentence depended upon the degree of harm that resulted from the tampering; the heaviest penalties would be available in cases in which death resulted. An attempt to tamper was punishable by a fine of up to $25,000 and prison for as long as 10 years.

PL 98-127 replaced existing law that declared it a misdemeanor to adulterate a food, drug or cosmetic, unless there was intent to defraud, which elevated the crime to a felony.

The anti-tampering measure included an unrelated provision extending patent protection for an anesthetic called "Forane" during the time the drug was under review by federal regulators and could not be marketed. A wide-ranging patent extension bill including this drug died in 1982. *(Story, p. 693)*

An anti-tampering measure similar to S 216 was approved by Congress in 1982 as part of a larger anti-crime package vetoed by President Reagan. *(Story, p. 689)*

The Senate and House both approved their respective bills (S 216 — S Rept 98-69, HR 2174 — H Rept 98-93) May 9. Final action came when the House Sept. 29 and the Senate Sept. 30 approved a compromise version of S 216.

Constitutional Bicentennial

Congress in 1983 approved creation of a 23-member commission to plan and conduct a national celebration marking the 200th anniversary of the U.S. Constitution and Bill of Rights.

The presidentially appointed commission, whose members would be chosen from recommendations by all three branches of the government, was to report within two years with specific recommendations for observing this bicentennial in 1987.

The measure creating the commission (S 118 — PL 98-101) authorized the commission to spend up to $300,000 in fiscal 1983 and such sums as necessary in subsequent years. The commission would go out of existence Dec. 31, 1989.

The Senate approved the bill (S Rept 98-68) July 18; the House approved it Aug. 4; and the Senate cleared it Sept. 14.

Other Legislation

Equal Rights Amendment

A parliamentary power play to revive the proposed Equal Rights Amendment (ERA) to the Constitution failed in the House late in the 1983 session. *(Box, p. 682)*

When House Speaker Thomas P. O'Neill Jr., D-Mass, took the unusual step of bringing the ERA (H J Res 1) to the floor under suspension of the rules, a procedure generally reserved for noncontroversial legislation, the move backfired when the measure fell six votes short of winning the two-thirds approval required for a proposed constitu-

Until passage of PL 98-208 there was no authority for the court to review these decisions, unless an accused soldier used the indirect avenue of a collateral proceeding to win Supreme Court review.

The government had no avenue of appeal from the military system to the Supreme Court.

PL 98-208 also outlawed, as a matter of military law, various drug offenses already prohibited in civilian life, including the wrongful use, possession, manufacture, distribution, importation or exportation of all drugs illegal in civilian life, including heroin, cocaine and marijuana.

S 974 was approved by the Senate April 28 (S Rept 98-53); the House passed the measure under suspension of the rules on Nov. 16 (H Rept 98-549).

Final action came when the Senate Nov. 18 accepted the House version of the bill.

tional amendment. Measures considered by the House under suspension of the rules may be debated for no more than 40 minutes and may not be amended. The Nov. 15 **key vote was 278-147 (R 53-109; D 225-38),** six votes short of two-thirds of the members present and voting. *(1983 key votes, p. 911)*

H J Res 1 was identical to the proposed ERA that died June 30, 1982, three states short of the 38 needed to ratify it and add it to the Constitution. It stated: "Equality of rights under the law shall not be denied or abridged by the United States or by any state on account of sex."

The House Judiciary Committee, after a legalistic, arcane and sarcastic debate, approved H J Res 1 Nov. 9, 21-10. Twelve years earlier, in 1971, it had been approved, 32-3. Observers present at both the 1971 and 1983 committee sessions said they were quite different. Discussion at the first dealt primarily with large concerns such as the role of women in society. In 1983, the committee focused on more particular questions, such as the impact of the ERA on abortion policy, military matters, and public and parochial education, all issues that arose during state ratification debates in the 1970s.

Six days after the committee acted, Democratic leaders gambled and lost their push for House approval in 1983. O'Neill's decision to bring the proposal to the floor under suspension of rules angered most Republicans and some Democrats; 14 cosponsors of the ERA voted against it.

The decision to bring the ERA to the floor in this manner was prompted by concern among ERA advocates that under normal floor procedures, H J Res 1 would be amended to the point that it would be unacceptable to its own supporters. The Senate Judiciary Subcommittee on the Constitution held hearings on the ERA in 1983 but did not vote on the proposal. Orrin G. Hatch, R-Utah, the subcommittee chairman, opposed the ERA.

Women's Economic Equity Bills

Women's issues, apart from the Equal Rights Amendment, took on new prominence in 1983, as targeted legislation dealing with jobs, child care, individual retirement accounts, pension and insurance reform received attention from legislators in both chambers.

Among the most significant measures in this category were:

● Pension reform legislation expanding the rights of spouses to share in the pensions of workers who died before retirement age. The Senate approved such legislation in 1983; it was enacted in 1984. *(Story, p. 669)*

● Child support enforcement (HR 4325) requiring states to help parents in collecting child support payments through withholding funds from parents in arrears. The House approved this measure in 1983, and it was enacted in 1984. *(Story, p. 605)*

● Insurance reform bills (S 372, HR 100) outlawing sex-based discrimination in all forms of insurance remained in committee through 1983, kept from the floor by heavy opposition from the insurance industry.

● Tax equity proposals were under consideration by the Senate Finance and House Ways and Means committees, including suggestions that Congress increase the yearly amount that a nonworking spouse could contribute to an Individual Retirement Account, that Congress treat non-profit dependent care organizations for children and the elderly as tax-exempt organizations, and that it increase dependent-care tax credits.

Immigration

The Senate for the second year passed wide-ranging immigration reform legislation (S 529) in 1983, but the House again failed to take final action on a similar bill (HR 1510).

House Speaker Thomas P. O'Neill Jr., D-Mass., refused to permit the House bill to come to the floor in 1983, apparently because of the opposition of the Hispanic community to the measure. The House approved its bill in 1984, but the measure died in conference. *(Story, p. 708)*

Refugee Programs

The House, but not the Senate, approved legislation in 1983 (HR 3729) extending refugee resettlement programs for two more years. *(1984 action, p. 708)*

Anti-Crime Package

The Senate Judiciary Committee in 1983 approved its fifth omnibus anti-crime bill in a decade (S 1762), a slimmed-down version of past proposals including only relatively noncontroversial provisions. The full Senate did not consider the bill in 1983, but did approve it the following year. *(1984 action, p. 698)*

Anti-Crime Grants

The House in 1983 approved legislation (HR 2175) creating a new grant program to succeed the old Law Enforcement Assistance Administration (LEAA) in aiding states to combat crime, but the Senate did not act on the bill in 1983. Such a grant program was approved as part of the omnibus anti-crime bill (PL 98-473) enacted in 1984. *(Story, p. 698; LEAA, box, p. 685)*

Drug Treatment

The House in 1983 approved a measure (HR 2173) reauthorizing the federal program of drug abuse treatment and monitoring for federal offenders who were paroled or on probation. Congress cleared similar legislation in 1984. *(Story, p. 702)*

Child Pornography

Both the House and Senate passed bills toughening federal laws against child pornography, but Congress did not take final action on the measure (HR 3635, S 1469) until 1984. *(Story, p. 701)*

Bankruptcy Courts

The Senate, but not the House, approved legislation (S 1013) in 1983 to place the nation's bankruptcy courts on a sound constitutional footing. In 1984, Congress completed action on such a measure. *(Story, p. 702)*

Record Copyrights

The Senate in 1983 passed a bill (S 32) designed to provide record companies and songwriters a greater share of the profits earned by retail stores that rent record albums to customers. A revised version of the bill was enacted in 1984. *(Story, p. 707)*

Justice Authorization

For the fourth consecutive year, Congress did not complete action on a bill authorizing the programs of the Department of Justice, but the department was given authority and funds with which to operate as usual by the regular appropriations measure (HR 3222 — PL 98-166).

The Senate approved a fiscal 1984 authorization bill (S 1192) in 1983, but the House did not act.

1984

Congress in 1984 gave final approval to a comprehensive anti-crime bill and a measure restructuring the nation's bankruptcy courts and enlarging the federal judiciary by creating 85 new federal judgeships.

Both measures had been under consideration for some time. The anti-crime bill was the culmination of more than a decade of effort on Capitol Hill. The bankruptcy measure had been before Congress since 1982 when the Supreme Court invalidated a new bankruptcy court system set up in 1978.

The 98th Congress almost gave final approval to a massive immigration reform bill, but political considerations spelled death for that measure at the session's end.

Crime Control Package

Congress in 1984 completed work on the most comprehensive anti-crime measure since the Omnibus Crime Control and Safe Streets Act of 1968. *(Congress and the Nation Vol. II, p. 325)*

The crime control provisions rode to the White House on the back of the fiscal 1985 continuing appropriations resolution (H J Res 648 — PL 98-473) that cleared Oct. 11.

House Republicans, frustrated by the reluctance of the House Democratic leadership to act on the anti-crime package that the Senate had approved in February, decided to use the appropriations resolution, essential to keep the government running, to carry the anti-crime package.

On Sept. 25, by a **key vote of 243-166 (R 154-3; D 89-163)** the House sent H J Res 648 back to the Appropriations Committee with instructions to attach the crime legislation to the measure. *(1984 key votes, p. 927)*

The Appropriations Committee did so immediately. The House approved the measure Sept. 25 by a vote of 316-91. On Oct. 2, House Democrats countered by consolidating various separate anti-crime bills into a single measure that the House passed under suspension of the rules, 406-16.

The Senate agreed to retain the crime provisions as part of the continuing resolution; the measure was sent to the White House Oct. 11.

Reagan's Role

President Reagan could claim a large share of the credit for the enactment of this law, the culmination of more than a decade of effort to make major changes in the federal criminal code.

Beginning with a declaration of "all-out war on big-time organized crime and ... drug racketeers" in his Jan.

15, 1983, State of the Union message, Reagan made clear that these changes in the criminal laws were one of his top priorities. In March 1983, he sent Congress an anti-crime package containing a number of the proposals that became part of the 1984 law.

After the Senate passed its omnibus bill in February, Reagan repeatedly criticized the House for its failure to move on the matter. House Republicans took up the theme, criticizing the Democratic leadership in general and the House Judiciary Committee leaders in particular for failing to act.

The 1984 measure overhauled federal sentencing procedures, allowed pretrial detention of certain defendants, prohibited tampering with computers, banned unauthorized use of credit cards or bank-account access numbers and trafficking in counterfeit trademarked goods.

The new law also increased penalties for major drug offenses, set up a new program of federal grants for state anti-crime projects, and tightened the legal definition of insanity. The last change was the result of concern over the insanity acquittal of John W. Hinckley Jr., who shot President Reagan and three other people in a March 30, 1981, assassination attempt.

Although most lawmakers hailed passage of the new law, representatives of the American Civil Liberties Union (ACLU) expressed deep concern about the preventive detention, insanity and computer crime sections that, they warned, infringed too far on individual liberties.

Background

In 1966, a National Commission on Reform of Criminal Laws was created to consider a wholesale revision of the federal criminal code. The commission, led by Gov. Edmund G. Brown of California (1959-67), produced a report that led to the introduction in 1973 of the first omnibus criminal code reform measure, S 1.

Numerous hearings were conducted on the proposal, but neither the 93rd nor the 94th Congress acted on the bill. The Senate in 1978 approved a revised measure that omitted some of the more controversial provisions, but the House did not act during the 95th Congress.

The presidential bid of Sen. Edward M. Kennedy, D-Mass., one of the primary sponsors of this measure, sidetracked the bill during the 96th Congress, although the House Judiciary Committee did report a criminal code bill.

Work resumed in the 97th Congress, as the Senate Judiciary Committee reported still another criminal code bill early in 1982. The omnibus measure was too hot for the Senate to handle in an election year, but some of its less controversial provisions were passed separately by Congress late in the year. President Reagan pocket-vetoed that measure early in 1983, however, objecting to provisions creating a new centralized Cabinet-level office to combat drug trafficking. *(Story, p. 689)*

Senate Action

After several days of debate, the Senate approved its 1984 criminal code reform bill (S 1762) Feb. 2 by a vote of 91-1.

The Senate Judiciary Committee had reported the bill Aug. 4, 1983 (S Rept 98-225). To minimize the prospect that Senate passage of the crime package would be slowed by certain controversial issues, the committee split some of these off into separate bills.

Among these were measures proposing another Cabinet-level anti-drug-trafficking post, reinstituting the death penalty in federal law, restricting use of habeas corpus claims by state prisoners, and modifying the exclusionary rule. The drug post provisions were included in the omnibus bill; the other measures (S 1765, S 1763, S 1764) were passed by the Senate but not the House. *(Story, p. 708)*

The Senate then sought to facilitate House consideration of the most important sections of the bill by passing them as separate measures: a sentencing bill was passed 85-3 on Feb. 2; a pretrial detention bill was passed 84-0 on Feb. 3, and a bill expanding the government's authority to require forfeiture of property gained through criminal activity was approved by voice vote Feb. 3.

House Action

Until the end of the session, the House chose to deal with the many subjects contained in the crime control package as separate measures. During the year, the House approved 14 separate bills similar to provisions finally contained in the omnibus bill.

The House measures included bills:

● Increasing the hourly pay for court-appointed defense lawyers in federal criminal cases. This measure (HR 4307 — H Rept 98-764) was passed by voice vote May 21.

● Tightening controls on a federal program protecting federal witnesses in criminal cases (HR 4249 — H Rept 98-767). It was approved May 22 by a vote of 376-41.

● Creating a national clearinghouse to coordinate efforts to locate missing children. This bill (HR 4971 — H Rept 98-741) was approved June 4 by voice vote.

● Making it a crime to obtain unauthorized access to computers containing classified or protected information. The House passed this bill (HR 5616 — H Rept 98-894) July 24 by a vote of 395-0.

● Increasing criminal fines and improving collection efforts. The House approved this bill (HR 5846 — H Rept 98-906) by voice vote July 30.

● Making it easier to use foreign-kept business records at trials in the United States. The House approved this bill (HR 5919 — H Rept 98-907) by voice vote July 30.

● Closing loopholes in current laws prohibiting bribery and fraud involving financial institutions. The House also approved this bill (HR 5872 — H Rept 98-901) by voice vote July 30.

● Making it a federal crime to escape from federal custody or confinement that resulted from specified civil or criminal proceedings. The House approved this bill (HR 5526 — H Rept 98-902) July 30.

● Making it a federal crime to possess any contraband in prison. The House approved this measure (HR 5910 — H Rept 98-908) by voice vote July 30.

● Allowing forfeiture of assets of persons convicted of certain drug offenses and substantially increasing penalties for drug offenses. The House approved this bill (HR 4901 — H Rept 98-545, Parts I and II) Sept. 11 by voice vote.

● Increasing the authority of the Office of Drug Abuse Policy, created in 1972 (PL 92-255). The House passed this bill (HR 4028 — H Rept 98-1008) by voice vote Sept. 11.

● Creating new penalties for making and selling products with counterfeit trademarks. The House approved this bill (HR 6071 — H Rept 98-997) by a vote of 403-0 on Sept. 12.

● Increasing civil and criminal penalties for illicit financial transactions. This bill (HR 6031 — H Rept 98-984) was approved by the House Sept. 10 by voice vote.

● Increasing the authority of the Drug Enforcement Administration to control diversion of prescription drugs into the black market. The House approved this measure (HR 5656 — H Rept 98-835) Sept. 18 by voice vote.

After House Republicans engineered the linkage of the omnibus crime bill to the continuing resolution, House Democratic leaders Oct. 2 brought their own omnibus crime bill (HR 5690) to the floor. It was approved 406-16. Most of its provisions were parallel to those in the Senate bill.

Final Action

The House cleared H J Res 648 for the president Oct. 11, approving it by a vote of 252-60. The Senate had earlier that day approved the measure by a vote of 78-11.

Provisions

As signed into law Oct. 12, the major anti-crime provisions of H J Res 648 (PL 98-473):

Preventive Detention. Authorized federal judges to detain defendants before their trial if they determined that no conditions imposed upon the defendants' release would assure both their reappearance for trial and the safety of the community.

● Required detention after conviction pending sentencing or appeal unless a judge found clear and convincing evidence that the defendant was unlikely to flee or pose a danger to the community.

● Permitted appeal of release and detention orders by both the government and the defendant.

Sentencing Guidelines. Established a presidentially appointed commission of seven members to write guidelines for sentencing. The guidelines were to be completed within 18 months.

● Required judges to follow sentencing guidelines unless they stated in writing the reasons they did not apply them in a particular case.

● Authorized a defendant to appeal a sentence harsher than the guidelines prescribed and authorized the government to appeal a sentence more lenient than the guidelines.

● Eliminated parole for prisoners incarcerated after the guidelines took effect and phased out parole over a five-year period for prisoners incarcerated before the guidelines took effect.

Forfeiture: Seizure of Assets. Expanded the government's authority to require forfeiture of profits and proceeds from criminal enterprises.

● Permitted forfeiture of up to $100,000 in goods without a full-scale court proceeding.

Insanity Defense. Changed the definition of insanity to require a defendant, in order to use this claim as a defense, to prove that as a result of a severe mental disease or defect, he was unable to appreciate the nature and wrongfulness of his acts. Under the law before enactment of PL 98-473, a defendant was required to prove that he suffered from a mental disease or defect that left him unable to appreciate the criminality of his conduct or to obey the law.

● Placed the burden of proof of insanity on the defendant, who had to show by clear and convincing evidence that he met the new test. Under the law up until this change, the prosecutor had to show beyond a reasonable doubt that the defendant did not meet the insanity test.

● Provided for commitment to a mental hospital for

Balanced Budget Amendment

Popular concern about spending policies of the federal government was reflected in widespread efforts during President Reagan's first term for a constitutional amendment to require a balanced federal budget. Pressure to amend the Constitution developed in both state legislatures and Congress as the federal budget ran increasingly large deficits.

Between 1975 and 1984, 32 state legislatures had passed resolutions demanding that Congress convene a constitutional convention to consider such an amendment. In 1982 the Senate, but not the House, approved such an amendment. The House voted on the proposal but failed by 46 votes to give it the necessary two-thirds majority required for constitutional amendments.

In 1984 the Senate Judiciary Committee reported such an amendment (S J Res 5), but the full Senate did not vote on it. A companion House proposal remained bottled up in the Judiciary Committee, although the Democratic-controlled House in an election-year maneuver passed a bill requiring the president to submit a balanced budget. The Republican-controlled Senate ignored the bill. *(Details of action on balanced budget proposals, box, p. 52)*

---

anyone acquitted on insanity grounds until a court determined that his release would pose no danger to persons or property.

Drug Enforcement. Increased maximum fines for most serious drug offenses to $125,000 for individuals and $250,000 for trafficking in large quantities of certain drugs. Increased the maximum prison term from 15 to 20 years.

● Authorized judges to fine drug offenders up to twice their gross profits from their drug dealing.

● Increased first-offense penalties from a maximum of five to 15 years.

● Authorized the attorney general to impose, on an emergency basis, tight controls on new chemical substances when he found such controls necessary to avoid an imminent threat to public safety.

● Required anyone dispensing or producing controlled substances to register with the attorney general; authorized the suspension or revocation of that registration by the attorney general if he found it to pose a threat to the public health and safety.

Justice Assistance. Created a new block grant program to aid state and local governments and private nonprofit organizations in operating anti-crime programs of proven effectiveness.

● Set up a Bureau of Justice Assistance in the Justice Department to administer the grant program.

● Provided that each state was to receive at least $250,000 per year and that federal grant funds could pay no more than 50 percent of the program costs.

Violent Crime. Defined as federal crimes murder-for-hire involving interstate commerce, murder, kidnapping and assault in aid of racketeering activities, and willful damage of an energy facility when the damage exceeded $100,000.

● Revised and strengthened existing laws setting minimum mandatory sentences for use of a firearm in committing a federal crime.

● Prohibited carrying or using in a violent crime a handgun with armor-piercing ammunition; set a mandatory five-year prison term as the minimum penalty.

● Provided new penalties for kidnapping certain federal officials and for crimes against family members of certain federal officials.

Juvenile Justice. Reauthorized the Office of Juvenile Justice and Delinquency Prevention for fiscal 1985-88 to continue aiding states to develop programs to combat juvenile delinquency.

● Reauthorized the Runaway and Homeless Youth Act of 1974 (PL 93-415) for fiscal 1985-88 to continue aid to state and local facilities providing emergency shelter care for runaways.

● Provided for federal aid in locating missing children, establishing a national toll-free hotline for reporting information about missing children and a national clearinghouse to provide technical aid to agencies involved in locating those children.

Legal Procedure. Allowed federal prosecution, as adults, of certain juveniles charged with serious federal drug offenses or violent crimes.

● Authorized emergency wiretaps without a court order in situations involving immediate danger of death or serious physical injury, in child pornography cases, illegal currency transaction investigations and offenses against crime victims and witnesses.

Labor Racketeering. Increased penalties for labor bribery and payoffs in violation of the Taft-Hartley Act to a maximum of five years in prison and a $15,000 fine.

● Barred union officials from office for as much as 13 years after being convicted on corruption charges.

Foreign Currency. Increased penalties for violating record-keeping and reporting requirements concerning the transport of currency in and out of the country.

● Authorized customs officers to conduct warrantless searches of vehicles, vessels or persons entering or leaving the country if the officers suspected a violation of currency transaction laws.

Witness Protection. Substantially revised the witness protection program of the federal government under which witnesses can be relocated by the government, given new identities and federal protection from reprisals by the targets of their testimony.

● Gave the attorney general discretion to decide how long to protect a witness and to disclose or withhold information on his identity or location, except that he must disclose such information to state and local law enforcement officials when the person in question was sought for a serious crime.

● Required the attorney general to issue a written "memorandum of understanding" to the protected witness specifying the witness' responsibility under the program: to avoid criminal conduct, to pay all legal obligations, to testify and provide information to law enforcement officials and to take necessary steps to avoid detection.

● Authorized the attorney general to pay restitution or, in the case of death, compensation to any victim injured or

killed by a person protected under the federal program.

Foreign Business Records. Permitted use of foreign business records as evidence in criminal proceedings if certified information was provided about the production of the records.

● Transferred to the Justice Department responsibility for administering the Foreign Agents Registration Act.

● Clarified that the United States had jurisdiction over any offense committed by or against a national of the United States any place outside the jurisdiction of another country, such as in Antarctica, on ice floes, or on the moon.

Drug Policy Board. Created a National Drug Enforcement Policy Board to coordinate federal drug enforcement activities. The board was chaired by the attorney general and included the secretaries of state, Treasury, defense, health and human services, the director of the Office of Management and Budget, and the director of the Central Intelligence Agency.

Victim Compensation. Created a Crime Victims Fund in the Treasury Department financed through fines collected from persons convicted of federal offenses. The fund could not accumulate more than $100 million; deposits to the fund were barred after Sept. 30, 1988.

● Specified that half the amount in the fund each year would be available for grants to state victim compensation programs and half to states to provide victim assistance programs.

● Authorized a federal judge, upon request by a U.S. attorney, to order forfeiture of all or part of the proceeds the defendant or his designee received from a contract relating to depiction of the crime in a movie, book, newspaper, magazine, drama, radio or television production.

Trademark Counterfeiting. Prohibited trafficking in goods or services using a counterfeit trademark, and set a fine of up to $250,000, a prison term of up to five years, or both for a first offense by an individual. A corporation could be fined up to $1 million. A second offense by an individual would carry a fine of as much as $1 million and 15 years in prison, while an organization could be fined $5 million.

Credit Card Fraud. Set a maximum fine of $10,000 or twice the value obtained and a prison term of up to 10 years for using or trafficking in unauthorized credit cards or similar "access devices," such as bank card numbers, and obtaining at least $1,000 in that way in one year.

● Set a maximum fine of $50,000 or twice the value obtained and a maximum 15-year prison term for anyone using, producing or selling counterfeit access devices; provided a maximum $100,000 fine or twice the value obtained and a 20-year prison term for a second offense of either of these crimes.

Computer Fraud. Declared it a felony to gain or attempt to gain unauthorized access to a computer to obtain classified information to be used to the injury of the United States or advantage of another country.

● Provided first-offense penalties of up to $10,000 or twice the value obtained and a prison term of 10 years; permitted second-offense penalties of as much as a $100,000 fine or twice the value obtained and a 20-year prison term.

● Declared it a misdemeanor to enter a computer illegally and obtain legally protected financial and credit information, to enter a government computer illegally and affect its operations, or to use a government computer for purposes other than its authorized use.

● Set maximum first-offense penalties of $5,000 or twice

the value obtained and one year in prison; second offense could bring a $10,000 fine or twice the value obtained, and a maximum 10-year prison term.

Repeat Offenders. Allowed federal prosecution of specified repeat state offenders.

● Provided a mandatory 15-year prison term and $25,000 fine for any defendant with three previous state robbery or burglary convictions who possessed a firearm that had traveled in interstate commerce. The sentence could not be suspended or the defendant paroled.

Terrorism. Required that anyone found guilty of taking hostages inside the United States or outside the country to compel a third person or a government to act or cease to act should be imprisoned for life. (Specified that this provision was only to affect situations in which U.S. nationals were involved, the offender was found in the United States or the U.S. government was the target of the influence effort.)

● Set fines of up to $100,000 and 20 years in prison for persons destroying or damaging aircraft or aircraft facilities, or acting violently toward anyone on an aircraft.

● Increased to $10,000 and one year in prison the maximum penalty for carrying concealed weapons or explosives on an aircraft.

Attorneys' Fees and Salaries. Authorized an increase to $69,900 per year for U.S. attorneys.

● Increased the current rate for court-appointed defense counsel to $40 per hour for out-of-court work and $60 per hour for in-court work; increased the maximum payment for a felony case and for an appeal to $2,000 each and for a misdemeanor to $800.

Pharmacy Robberies

Congress in 1984 cleared legislation (S 422 — PL 98-305) declaring it a federal crime to steal controlled substances.

The measure was intended to deter thefts from pharmacies; pharmacists had been pressing for the legislation for years. They argued that because the street value of some of the drugs they dispensed was far greater than their actual cost, pharmacists were particularly vulnerable to attacks by those interested in diverting these drugs to the black market.

Although the Justice Department had general authority to prosecute such crimes, until late 1983, it had left such prosecutions to state authorities. Six months before Congress passed PL 98-305, the Justice Department said that it could live with such a measure.

The Senate approved the bill in February, both as separate legislation (S Rept 98-353) and as part of a larger anti-crime package (S 1762). The House passed its version of the bill (HR 5222 — H Rept 98-644) May 8. *(Anti-crime package, p. 698)*

Final action came May 17 when the Senate by voice vote accepted House amendments to S 422.

Child Pornography

Amid growing concern about sexual abuse of children, Congress in 1984 cleared a bill (HR 3635 — PL 98-292) strengthening federal laws against producing and distributing pornographic materials involving children.

PL 98-292 eliminated the requirement that such ma-

terials be found obscene before someone could be convicted for producing or distributing them. It also raised the age of children protected under the law from 16 to 18 years. It increased the fine for a first offense from $10,000 to as much as $100,000, and double that for a second offense.

The Senate approved its version of this bill (S 1469 — S Rept 98-169) July 16, 1983; the House approved HR 3635 (H Rept 98-536) Nov. 14, 1983.

The Senate approved a compromise version of HR 3635 March 30, 1984, and the House by voice vote approved that version May 8. As he signed the measure May 21, President Reagan announced that he was creating a national commission to study the effects of pornography on society.

Drug Treatment

Congress in 1984 extended for three years, through fiscal 1986, drug abuse programs directed at federal offenders.

The measure (HR 2173 — PL 98-236) was approved by the House May 9, 1983 (H Rept 98-87), but the Senate did not act until March 8, 1984, when it cleared the bill for the White House.

The programs involved were first authorized by Congress in 1966 (PL 89-793). They provided drug abuse testing and treatment to convicted federal offenders released on probation or parole.

Criminal Fine Collection

Congress in 1984 cleared legislation (HR 5846 — PL 98-596) designed to improve the collection of fines in federal criminal cases.

The House approved its bill July 30 by voice vote; the Senate endorsed a compromise version Oct. 11, which the House immediately sent on to the White House.

PL 98-596 gave federal judges the option of imposing as a fine either the amount set out in the applicable law, or twice the gain a defendant derived from his crime or the loss he inflicted on his victim or $100,000 for misdemeanors punishable by six months or more; $250,000 for misdemeanors resulting in any loss of life or for any felony, if the defendant was an individual or $500,000 if the defendant was an organization.

The law also imposed an interest rate of 1.5 percent per month on delinquent fines, increasing this rate to 25 percent when the fine was more than 90 days delinquent.

Airplanes and Drugs

Legislation designed to curb the use of airplanes to carry illegal drugs was sent to the White House by Congress in 1984.

The bill (S 1146 — PL 98-499) amended the Federal Aviation Act of 1958 to provide for revoking the airman and registration certificates of the pilots and owners of airplanes used in drug trafficking.

The Senate approved the measure (S Rept 98-228) Sept. 27, 1983. The House approved its companion bill (HR 1580 — H Rept 98-883) July 24, 1984. The Senate adopted the conference report (H Rept 98-1085) on Oct. 2, and the House followed suit Oct. 4.

Bankruptcy Courts

Two years after the Supreme Court voided the new bankruptcy court system approved by the 95th Congress, Congress in 1984 sent to the White House a measure putting these courts back on a sound legal footing.

The new bankruptcy law (HR 5174 — PL 98-353) also made significant changes in the substance of U.S. bankruptcy laws and authorized the creation of 85 new federal district and appeals court judgeships.

PL 98-353 was essentially remedial legislation, correcting a constitutional misstep by Congress in its 1978 overhaul of the nation's bankruptcy laws.

In the 1978 law (PL 95-598) Congress set up a new independent bankruptcy court system run by judges appointed by the president for 14-year terms. These bankruptcy judges had broad powers to resolve not just bankruptcy questions, but other legal disputes in which a bankrupt individual or company might be involved.

On June 28, 1982, the Supreme Court declared that Congress had acted unconstitutionally, giving the bankruptcy judges too much power and not enough independence from the other branches of the government.

The court gave Congress until Dec. 24, 1982, to remedy the situation. That deadline was not met and for a year and a half the nation's bankruptcy courts operated under interim rules set out by the U.S. Judicial Conference, the policy-making arm of the federal judiciary.

The House Judiciary Committee wrote legislation to increase the judges' independence by giving them life tenure, a move strongly opposed by the U.S. Judicial Conference. The Senate took a different approach by curtailing the power of the new judges.

The final version of PL 98-353 generally followed the Senate approach.

PL 98-353 also contained Congress' response to another Supreme Court decision. PL 98-353 declared that labor contracts could be rejected by debtor employers only after certain procedures were followed, thereby overturning the court's February 1984 decision permitting unilateral abrogation of these contracts by companies filing for reorganization under federal bankruptcy law.

This decision in *National Labor Relations Board v. Bildisco & Bildisco* set off a massive lobbying effort by organized labor that led to the labor contract provisions in PL 98-353. *(Decision, p. 744)*

Background

Overhauling a bankruptcy structure virtually unchanged since 1938, Congress in 1978 abolished the system of bankruptcy referees who operated as adjuncts to federal district judges. In their place, Congress set up an independent bankruptcy court system that was staffed by bankruptcy judges appointed by the president for 14-year terms.

Under the constitutional system of separated powers, the independence of federal judges was secured by the guarantee that they held their posts for life during good behavior and their salaries would not be reduced during their tenure. Because, under the revised law, the new bankruptcy court judges would serve for only 14 years they were not sufficiently independent to exercise the broad judicial powers they had been given, the Supreme Court held in the case of *Northern Pipeline Construction Co. v. Marathon Pipeline Co.*

School Prayer Advocates Made No Headway

Congress in 1984 rebuffed a constitutional amendment backed by the Reagan administration to permit organized recited prayers in public schools. The Supreme Court tacitly, in 1984, and explicitly, in 1985, affirmed its 1962-63 rulings that school prayer was in conflict with the First Amendment guarantees of religious freedom.

Also, in 1984, Congress approved an "equal access" bill ensuring student religious groups access to school meeting space.

Constitutional Amendment

The Senate March 20, 1984, rejected by a **key vote of 56-44 (R 37-18; D 19-26)** the administration-backed constitutional amendment to permit organized prayer in schools. The vote was 11 short of the two-thirds majority required to approve a proposed constitutional amendment. The Senate rejected school prayer constitutional amendments in 1966, by nine votes, and 1971, by 29 votes. Before the 1984 vote, the Senate tabled, 81-15, an alternative proposal to allow silent prayer or meditation in public schools. *(1984 key vote, p. 927)*

The proposed amendment (S J Res 73) declared: "Nothing in this Constitution shall be construed to prohibit individual or group prayer in public schools or other public institutions. No person shall be required by the United States or any state to participate in prayer. Neither the United States nor any state shall compose the words of any prayer to be said in public schools."

Moment of Silence Law

The court, in the *Wallace v. Jaffree* case, struck down an Alabama law authorizing a one-minute period of silence in all public schools for "meditation or voluntary prayer." This case, argued in 1984, was decided, by a 6-3 vote, June 4, 1985. The Reagan administration urged the court to approve the law.

The decision reaffirmed the court's 1962-63 rulings barring recited prayer and Bible readings in the schools. Justice John Paul Stevens said the state's "endorsement . . . of prayer activities at the beginning of each school day is not consistent with the established principle that the government must pursue a course of complete neutrality toward religion."

The decision was severely criticized by school prayer advocates, who predicted the ruling would give new momentum to their drive for a constitutional amendment. In another decision in 1984, on April 2, the court summarily affirmed an appeals court ruling that struck down as unconstitutional an Alabama law that permitted students to lead willing students in prayer at the beginning of class.

Equal Access Act

Congress in July 1984 approved the equal access bill (HR 1310 — PL 98-377). This legislation required public school officials to permit student religious groups in high schools to meet in the school buildings before or after school on the same terms as other student groups. The measure extended to high schools the same equal access principle that the Supreme Court had applied to public universities and colleges with its 1981 decision in the case of *Widmar v. Vincent. (Decision, p. 738; PL 98-377, p. 572)*

Separate legislation (HR 5345) on equal access for religious groups previously had failed to win House approval under procedures requiring a two-thirds majority for passage. HR 5345 required public secondary schools to permit students to meet in school facilities for religious purposes during non-instructional hours if other student groups were allowed to meet in the building. Although obtaining a majority, the bill fell 11 votes short of the required two-thirds majority on the **key vote of 270-151 (R 147-17; D 123-134)**. The provision later passed as part of HR 1310 did not single out only religious groups; it extended equal access to high school facilities to any group — political, religious or other — if other extracurricular groups could use the building. Critics of HR 5345 said that bill gave special legal protection to religious meetings while allowing schools to deny access to, for example, unpopular political groups. *(1984 key votes, p. 927)*

In separate action, the House approved language requiring schools receiving federal aid to permit students to participate in moments of silent prayer, but the prayer amendments died in conference.

Other Prayer Proposals

Unsuccessful on a constitutional amendment, school prayer advocates sought to put the issue beyond the reach of federal courts.

In 1976 the Senate rejected a broad proposal to eliminate federal court jurisdiction over all cases involving public schools, including prayer cases. In 1979, the Senate, 47-37, prohibited the Supreme Court from reviewing any state law related to voluntary prayers in public schools, but the proposal was not enacted.

School prayer advocates attempted during the four-year period to include language in the appropriations bills barring use of funds to prevent voluntary prayer in public schools.

They succeeded in some bills and not in others. However, these provisions needed annual renewal and did not provide the complete reversal of the court's decision that they sought.

Senate Action

The Senate April 27, 1983, passed its version of a new bankruptcy law (S 1013 — S Rept 98-55) by voice vote.

The House Judiciary Committee had reported its bill (HR 3) in February giving bankruptcy judges life tenure, but this bill stalled in the House Rules Committee, under pressure from the Judicial Conference and from House members hoping to amend existing bankruptcy law to make it more difficult to declare bankruptcy.

The Senate bill was more in line with the views of the Judicial Conference, retaining presidential appointment and 14-year terms for the new judges but curtailing their powers. At any time a district court judge could recall a bankruptcy case from a bankruptcy judge and district judges, not bankruptcy judges, were required to resolve non-bankruptcy questions arising in these cases.

S 1013 also created 61 new federal district judgeships and 24 new appeals court judgeships. It permitted a bankruptcy judge to dismiss a bankruptcy case when the judge determined that allowing a debtor to use this law to cancel debts would be an abuse of the law. It also contained provisions concerning shopping center, grain elevator and fish processor bankruptcies.

House Action

The House approved a compromise version (HR 5174) of its original bill (HR 3) March 21, 1984, by voice vote.

As introduced, HR 5174 created a system of independent bankruptcy judges with life tenure, authorized protection for labor contracts with bankrupt companies, and provided for 75 new federal judgeships.

The House discarded the life tenure plan for bankruptcy judges and voted, 250-161, to substitute a proposal under which bankruptcy judges, appointed by the federal appeals courts, were adjuncts to the district courts dealing only with bankruptcy questions. Other legal matters concerning bankrupts were to be resolved by the district courts.

Interim Action

The 1978 law had provided a transition period during which the new court system would be phased in. That period expired April 1, 1984.

In order to maintain a functioning bankruptcy court system until work was completed on the pending bankruptcy bill, Congress voted four times in 1984 to extend that transition period until HR 5174 was enacted (S 2507 — PL 98-249; S 2570 — PL 98-271; HR 2174 — PL 98-299; S 2776 — PL 98-325).

The additional time was needed while the House and Senate sponsors of the measures negotiated their differences. The Senate, prodded by business interests, objected to the House provisions overturning the Supreme Court's *Bildisco* decision. The House objected to the Senate bill's provisions providing special treatment for various types of bankruptcies.

Final Action

The Senate June 19 passed HR 5174 after amending it to reflect the provisions it had approved as part of S 1013. This step cleared the way for a conference on the legislation.

In conference, the House accepted the Senate provisions creating the new federal judgeships and the Senate accepted the House language undoing the effect of the Supreme Court's decision on abrogation of labor contracts.

On June 29 the House and then the Senate adopted the conference report, clearing the bill for the White House. The House vote was 394-0; the Senate approved the bill by voice vote.

Postscript Controversy

The nation's bankruptcy courts went out of business before Congress acted because the last extension of the transition period ended at midnight June 27, two days before Congress sent HR 5174 to the president.

To cover this gap, Congress included in HR 5174 a provision retroactively allowing all current bankruptcy judges to continue serving for up to 15 months without reappointment under the new system.

Because this amounted to congressional appointment of judges — something that the Constitution does not permit — both the Justice Department and the Administrative Office of the U.S. Courts opposed the measure as unconstitutional. In signing the legislation, President Reagan expressed his concern about this provision.

Three different federal district courts held later in 1984 that the provision was valid, and by the end of 1984, no appeal had been taken from any of these decisions.

Provisions

As signed into law July 10, the Bankruptcy Amendments and Federal Judgeship Act of 1984 (HR 5174 — PL 98-353):

• Authorized the regional federal courts of appeals to appoint bankruptcy judges for each of the 93 federal judicial districts, a total of 232 bankruptcy judges. The judges, adjuncts of the district courts, were to serve 14-year terms.

• Provided that district judges could refer to bankruptcy judges all proceedings arising under or related to cases arising under the federal bankruptcy law, Title 11 of the U.S. Code.

• Authorized bankruptcy judges to hear and determine all cases under Title 11, but provided that the bankruptcy judge's decision on matters that were not central to the bankruptcy claim would be submitted to the district judge who would make a final ruling based on the bankruptcy judge's findings.

• Authorized the district judge, with the consent of the parties, to refer a proceeding related to a bankruptcy case to a bankruptcy judge, and to withdraw any case or proceeding from the bankruptcy court.

• Specified that the salary of a bankruptcy judge would remain $66,100 per year until Congress changed it.

• Specified that the term of office of any bankruptcy judge serving on June 27, 1984, be extended until this bill was enacted.

• Authorized a total of 24 new appeals court judgeships, of which no more than 11 could be filled until after Jan. 21, 1985.

• Authorized a total of 61 new federal district court judgeships of which no more than 29 could be filled prior to Jan. 21, 1985.

• Allowed a judge to dismiss a consumer bankruptcy petition if the judge determined that the petition could result in abuse of the bankruptcy law.

● Barred a debtor from discharging debts owed to a single creditor of more than $500 for luxury goods, from discharging debts for services incurred within 40 days before an order for relief, or for cash advances of more than $1,000 that were extensions of consumer credit under an open-end plan obtained 20 days before an order for relief.

● Barred a private employer from discriminating against a bankrupt or a debtor or someone associated with a bankrupt or a debtor.

● Required bankruptcy judges in cases involving grain storage facilities to set up a timetable for disposing of the grain stored there and the proceeds from it; provided a similar expedited procedure for dealing with bankruptcies involving fish processors.

● Set a 60-day time limit for a trustee of a bankrupt shopping center tenant to assume or reject the shopping center lease.

● Barred the discharge in bankruptcy of debts incurred as the result of drunken driving.

● Established new procedures to protect those who deal in repurchase agreements, a principal means of financing U.S. government securities and money market instruments.

● Provided that a debtor company or the debtor's trustee could take over or break a collective bargaining agreement only in accordance with the procedures set out in PL 98-353.

● Set out those procedures that included: meeting with employee representatives to consider changes in the contract; bargaining in good faith to reach modifications in the contract; filing an application to reject the collective bargaining agreement and providing a judicial hearing on that application and a ruling within 30 days of the hearing's start.

● Permitted the company to terminate or alter any provisions of the collective bargaining agreement if the judge did not act within 30 days, pending the judge's ruling on the application.

● Authorized a judge to approve an application for rejecting a contract only if he found that the trustee had made a proposal that conformed to the law, the employee representative refused to accept it without good cause and the balance of equities clearly favored rejection.

Legal Services Corporation

The Legal Services Corporation (LSC) was still in existence at the end of President Reagan's first term and ended 1984 with increased funding and a full slate of directors. The corporation was established in 1974 to fund civil legal services for the poor.

Reagan attempted in the first years of his administration to abolish the LSC. Congress consistently refused, although it reduced LSC funds in fiscal 1982 and 1983 and imposed new restrictions on the corporation's activities.

However, in 1984 Congress increased funding for the LSC to $305 million in fiscal 1985, the highest level since $321 million in fiscal 1981. The LSC funds were contained in the Commerce, Justice, State appropriations bill (HR 5712 — PL 98-411). Between those peaks, LSC funding dropped to $241 million in fiscal 1982 and 1983 and $275 million in fiscal 1984.

In 1984 Reagan for the first time proposed to the Senate a full slate of directors for the LSC. None was confirmed. After Congress adjourned Reagan gave all 11 recess appointments, good through the end of the 1985

Busing: Disappearing Issue

Both Congress and the Reagan administration acted during 1981 through 1984 to prevent the use of busing to desegregate public schools.

In 1981 two Senate Judiciary subcommittees approved bills barring federal district courts from ordering busing to achieve racially balanced schools and authorizing them to dissolve existing busing orders. No further action was taken during the 97th or 98th Congresses.

The Senate on Sept. 16, 1981, by a **key vote of 61-36 (R 36-16; D 25-20)** invoked cloture and went on to approve a far-reaching anti-busing curb. However, the provision never became law. *(1981 key votes, p. 879)*

The language, approved by a vote of 58-38, barred the Justice Department from bringing any legal action that could lead directly or indirectly to court-ordered busing, prohibited federal courts from ordering busing except in narrowly defined circumstances, and allowed the attorney general to file suit on behalf of students who believed that they had been bused in violation of these standards. This last provision was designed to permit federal judges to overturn existing busing orders. But the rider died when the bill failed to clear.

The House approved anti-busing riders to the Justice Department authorization bill in 1981 and the State, Justice and Commerce appropriations bills in 1982, but they too were not enacted. The margin of approval in the House narrowed from 265-122 in 1981 to 243-153 in 1982.

The 98th Congress approved language, that had become routine, forbidding use of federal funds to bus schoolchildren to achieve desegregation. This language was added to the appropriations bills for the Departments of Education, Labor and Health and Human Services in fiscal 1984 and 1985 and had been part of the appropriations bill for federal education programs in one form or another since 1969. These riders were symbolic rather than practical because the Reagan administration did not approve of desegration busing in any event.

---

session of the 99th Congress. These appointments brought to a total of 30 the number of recess appointments Reagan had made to the LSC board from December 1981 through December 1984. Not a single LSC board member was confirmed during this period. *(Appointments, box, p. 1028)*

Cities and Antitrust

Congress in 1984 approved a measure (HR 6027 — PL 98-544) shielding local governments from monetary damage awards in antitrust suits.

Congress acted in response to concern aroused by a 1982 Supreme Court decision in *Community Communications Inc. v. City of Boulder, Colo.*, that held local governments liable to treble damage antitrust awards. Local government officials argued that cities and counties against which such awards were levied would face financial collapse.

PL 98-544 left courts free to order cities and counties to halt anti-competitive practices, but it forbade courts to penalize cities and counties for past anti-competitive actions by forcing them to pay large damage judgments to the complaining party.

The bill also restored the authority of the Federal Trade Commission to seek injunctions against local governments for anti-competitive practices. Congress had limited that authority in the fiscal 1985 Commerce, Justice, State appropriations bill (PL 98-411).

The House approved HR 6027 (H Rept 98-965) Aug. 8, 414-5; the Senate Oct. 4 amended its version of the bill (S 1578 — S Rept 98-593). Conferees reached agreement Oct. 9, and the House and Senate both approved their report (H Rept 98-1158) Oct. 11, clearing the bill for the White House.

Semiconductor Chips

Congress in 1984 gave the manufacturers of semiconductor chips, the brain of the microcomputer, 10 years of protection against illegal copying of their chips.

This copyright-style protection for the makers of the tiny silicon chips that set off the microcomputer revolution provided some shield from piracy by firms that could analyze and duplicate a chip from a photograph. Such pirates could sell the duplicated chip far more cheaply than the original manufacturer who had spent millions in research and development.

The most difficult part of drafting the chip protection legislation (HR 6163 — PL 98-620) was defining the chip in terms that would fit into existing law. A semiconductor chip is an intricate set of layers of material etched with unique designs. Those designs, known as "mask works," route electrical signals to perform specific tasks, such as running computers.

The "mask works" could not be copyrighted under existing law, but PL 98-620 created a new section of law for these chips and gave them a decade of protection almost identical to that provided by copyright law to other creations such as books or plays.

The omnibus bill (HR 6163 — PL 98-620) pasted together in the closing days of the 98th Congress also clarified certain trademark laws, modified patent law provisions, reduced the categories of civil cases entitled to speedy consideration in federal courts and created a new institute to help state courts.

Legislative History

The vehicle for all these varied provisions was a federal court housekeeping measure setting new sites for sessions of certain federal courts. The legislative history of the final version of HR 6163 was a crazy quilt.

The court housekeeping bill (HR 6163 — H Rept 98-1062) was approved by the House Sept. 24. The House had already approved its chip protection bill (HR 5525 — H Rept 98-781) June 11, the civil case schedule bill (HR 5645

— H Rept 98-985) Sept. 11, and the trademark provisions (HR 6285) Oct. 1.

The House had not acted on the patent provisions (HR 5003 — H Rept 98-983) and had failed to approve the State Justice Institute bill (HR 4145 — H Rept 98-685) when it was brought up under suspension of the rules in May.

The Senate Oct. 3 tacked all of those measures onto HR 6163. The Senate had approved a computer chip measure (S 1201 — S Rept 98-425) May 15 and a State Justice Institute bill (S 384 — S Rept 98-480) June 21.

Final action on the package came Oct. 9 when the House, without a dissenting vote, agreed to the Senate's amendments.

Provisions

As signed into law Nov. 8, HR 6163 (PL 98-620) contained the following major provisions:

● Revised the definition of a trademark to make clear that it did not lose trademark protection just because it also was used as a name of a unique product or service.

● Made clear that the only test for determining whether a registered trademark had become generic was whether the relevant public recognized it as identifying and distinguishing one specific product or service from others, regardless of who the maker was.

● Created a new part of the copyright title (Title 17 of the U.S. Code) to protect semiconductor chips from unauthorized copying for 10 years.

● Set up a private non-profit corporation, the State Justice Institute (SJI), to improve judicial administration in state courts; authorized the SJI to award grants and enter into contracts for research and demonstration projects; authorized $13 million for fiscal 1986, $15 million for each of fiscal 1987 and 1988.

● Deleted from federal law 80 provisions granting expedited treatment by federal courts for specific types of civil cases, retaining such treatment for cases involving personal liberty, requests for temporary restraining orders or preliminary injunctions or cases where "good cause" had been shown that a federal right would be maintained if federal courts acted speedily.

Joint Research Ventures

Congress in 1984 lowered antitrust obstacles to joint research and development ventures by separate companies. The measure (S 1841 — PL 98-462) enjoyed strong administration support and was intended to encourage technological innovation.

PL 98-462 made clear that such combined efforts did not automatically violate antitrust laws. If such a joint venture were challenged, courts were to apply a rule of reason in deciding whether or not there was a violation of antitrust laws producing an adverse effect on competition.

Under the law participants in such a joint research venture were required to register their joint research effort with the attorney general and the Federal Trade Commission. Such notice would be published in the *Federal Register*. Once the notice was filed the parties to the venture were protected against any but actual damages in an antitrust suit filed concerning the joint venture.

The House approved its bill (HR 5041 — H Rept 98-656) May 1; the Senate approved S 1841 (S Rept 98-427) July 31. The Senate approved the conference report (H

Meese Nomination Slowed by Finance Probe

White House counselor Edwin Meese III spent 1984 in a political limbo, nominated but not confirmed as the nation's attorney general.

The 13-month delay between nomination and confirmation was caused by concern about the propriety of Meese's personal financial dealings during his service in the White House.

Meese, one of President Reagan's closest advisers, was cleared of any criminal wrongdoing by a special prosecutor, appointed by Attorney General William French Smith at Meese's request. After a five-month investigation, the independent counsel, Jacob A. Stein, reported that he found no reason to prosecute Meese for any criminal act.

Meese was nominated Jan. 23, 1984, to succeed Smith, who wished to return to private life. Meese testified before the Senate Judiciary Committee March 1-2, answering questions about his civil rights views and his independence from the president. Meese then was asked about financial transactions surrounding the sale of his California home, in particular the appointment of Thomas J. Barrack as assistant secretary of Interior after Barrack had put together a deal to buy Meese's California home after it had been on the market for almost two years.

Meese also was questioned about a $60,000 loan he received from John R. McKean, a San Francisco accountant, subsequently named as a member and later chairman of the U.S. Postal Service Board of Governors. The loans were sought primarily to enable Meese to make payments on both his California house and his new home in Virginia near Washington. McKean was Meese's tax adviser. The loans were repaid in full with interest before the confirmation hearings began.

In addition, questions were raised about a loan of $15,000 to Meese's wife, Ursula, in December 1980, from Edwin Thomas, Meese's deputy in the White House and later a regional director of the General Services Administration in San Francisco. Meese did not include this loan on his financial disclosure statement to the Senate Judiciary Committee, an omission he described as inadvertent. The money was used to buy stock for the Meeses' children; the stock later was sold at a loss.

In addition, the committee inquired into Meese's knowledge of 1980 Democratic campaign strategy papers that ended up in the possession of the Reagan campaign.

With prospects for confirmation dimming, Meese on March 22 asked for appointment of a special prosecutor to examine the facts surrounding these matters. The post-Watergate Ethics in Government Act of 1978 created a mechanism for such an appointment; Congress amended the law in 1982 to change the investigator's name from special prosecutor to independent counsel. *(Story, p. 681)*

Stein, a Washington, D.C., trial lawyer, was named independent counsel April 2 by a special three-judge federal panel that authorized him to investigate and prosecute "any allegation or evidence of violation of any federal criminal law by Mr. Meese." Five months later, he reported Sept. 20 that he found no evidence of any criminal conduct by Meese.

But the Stein report did not lead to immediate confirmation. Opponents of Meese, led by Sen. Howard M. Metzenbaum, D-Ohio, and Common Cause, the self-styled public affairs lobby, argued that Meese was ethically insensitive, demonstrating a disregard for the appearance of probity.

Although Meese contended that he had always acted ethically, he agreed that his experience during the confirmation process had given him "a much higher level of sensitivity to matters" than he had brought to Washington. Now, he said, "I would take pains to avoid the appearance" of impropriety.

Meese was renominated for the post of attorney general, Jan. 3, 1985. He was confirmed by a vote of 63-31 on Feb. 23, a year and one month after his nomination, the longest confirmation wait for a Cabinet member in recent history.

Rept 98-1044) Sept. 26.

The House followed suit Oct. 1, clearing the bill for the White House.

Record Copyrights

Congress in 1984 approved a bill (S 32 — PL 98-450) barring commercial rentals of phonograph records unless the owner of the copyright on the record granted permission for the rental.

Exceptions were granted for non-profit libraries and educational institutions.

PL 98-450 modified the "first sale" doctrine that terminated certain rights of copyright owners at the point of the first sale of their product.

It provided that rentals, if authorized by the copyright owner, should generate special royalty fees for the copyright owner.

Only civil remedies were provided for violation of these provisions.

The Senate approved S 32 (S Rept 98-162) June 28, 1983; the House approved its version (HR 5938 — H Rept 98-987) Sept. 11, 1984.

Final action came Sept. 21 when the Senate accepted the House amendments.

Patent Law

Congress in 1984 approved several non-controversial changes in U.S. patent law (HR 6286 — PL 98-622).

PL 98-622 tightened existing law to prevent manufacturers from evading U.S. patent restrictions by making components of a patented product and shipping them abroad for assembly.

The measure also created an expedited new procedure through which inventors could obtain some limited defensive protection against infringement lawsuits by other persons claiming that they had invented some particular device first. The bill also created a new administrative board to handle disputes over who was the first inventor of a patentable invention.

The new board was combined with the existing board of appeals of the Patent and Trademark Office, which already had authority to decide whether a product or process was patentable.

PL 98-622 also created a National Commission on Innovation and Productivity to study the rights of inventors employed by government and private industry and to look into the reason for the decline in the number of patents issued to U.S. inventors and the rise in patents issued to foreign inventors.

The House approved HR 6286 by voice vote Oct. 1; the Senate approved its version of the bill (S 1535 — S Rept 98-663) Oct. 11. The House amended the bill the same day and the Senate approved the amended version later Oct. 11, clearing it for the White House.

Other Legislation

Immigration Reform

For the third consecutive year, Congress was unable to complete work on a sweeping immigration reform bill, the victim of swirling interest-group pressures and election-year qualms.

The bill that died in the final days of the 98th Congress had been approved by both chambers. It was designed to curb the growing flow of illegal aliens into the United States by penalizing employers who knowingly hired illegal aliens. It also authorized millions of illegal aliens who entered the country before 1981 to legalize their status and remain as legal residents.

It also expanded the program under which foreign workers may enter the country temporarily for agricultural work, and it overhauled exclusion, asylum and deportation procedures.

The measure drew fire from all sides. President Reagan generally supported it but had reservations about the cost of the legalization program. Hispanic lobbyists contended that the employer-sanction provisions would encourage employers to discriminate against persons who sounded or looked foreign.

Conservatives opposed the amnesty provisions, and neither labor nor big Western farmers were satisfied with the changes in the temporary worker program. Business groups were opposed to the employer sanction provisions.

The Senate had approved the measure (S 529) in May 1983 by a wide margin, 76-18. But the political liabilities that eventually doomed the bill caused House Speaker Thomas P. O'Neill Jr., D-Mass., to keep it off the House floor for the remainder of the 1983 session.

When the measure finally came before the full House in June 1984, the margin of approval in a **key vote** was extremely thin: **216-211 (R 91-73; D 125-138).** *(1984 key votes, p. 927)*

The summer's full political schedule delayed conference meetings until mid-September. Although supporters worked until the final days of the session hoping to achieve a compromise in time to win enactment, their effort failed on Oct. 11, one day before adjournment.

In 1982 the Senate had approved a similar bill that died on the House floor in the last days of the lame-duck session. *(Story, p. 692)*

Refugee Programs

Although the number of refugees admitted into the United States rose in 1984 to 71,000, Congress did not complete action on legislation reauthorizing the federal programs to assist in resettling refugees in the United States.

The programs were set up under PL 96-212, a 1980 law overhauling the process for admitting refugees to the United States. Admissions hit a peak in fiscal 1981 when 159,000 refugees were admitted to the country.

The House in November 1983 approved a bill (HR 3729 — H Rept 98-404) reauthorizing these programs for three years. The Senate Judiciary Committee reported its version of the bill (S Rept 98-564) in July 1984, but the full Senate did not act on the measure, which died at the end of the session.

Money for these programs was included in the fiscal 1985 continuing resolution (H J Res 648 — PL 98-473), which provided between $410 million and $460 million, the bulk of which would be used for cash and medical aid.

Civil Rights

The major civil rights measure of 1984 died Oct. 2 when the Senate voted 53-45 to table a bill that would have overturned a Supreme Court decision narrowing the reach of federal laws barring discrimination.

The Supreme Court Feb. 28, 1984, ruled in *Grove City College v. Bell* that Title IX of the 1972 Education Amendments did not ban sex discrimination in all programs at a school or college that received federal aid but only in the specific programs receiving the federal aid.

Because the language in Title IX was virtually identical to that in other federal laws forbidding recipients of federal aid to discriminate on the basis of race, color, national origin, handicaps or age, civil rights activists moved quickly to amend Title IX and the other laws to make clear the breadth of their coverage.

The House approved such a bill (HR 5490 — H Rept 98-829, Parts I and II) June 26 by a vote of 375-32, but the Senate version of the bill (S 2568) did not emerge from the Senate Labor and Human Resources Committee.

Supporters of the legislation in the Senate offered the House bill as an amendment to the continuing resolution (H J Res 648), but the amendment was tabled Oct. 2, 53-45, killing the bill for the 98th Congress.

On Sept. 27, the Senate by a **key vote of 51-48 (R 12-42; D 39-6)** decided that the civil rights language was germane to an appropriations measure before the Senate and therefore could be added as an amendment. However, the proposal became tied in a procedural knot and was tabled Oct. 2. *(1984 key votes, p. 927)*

Capital Punishment

The Senate, but not the House, in 1984 approved a measure re-establishing a federal death penalty for treason, espionage, federal crimes resulting in the death of another person and, in specific instances, attempts to kill the president.

The Senate approved this measure (S 1765 — S Rept 98-251) Feb. 22, but the House did not act on it.

Exclusionary Rule

The Senate moved in 1984 to relax the "exclusionary rule," which bars the use of illegally obtained evidence in criminal trials, but the House took no action on the matter.

The Senate approved the exclusionary rule bill (S 1764 — S Rept 98-350) Feb. 7 by a vote of 63-24. As approved, it would allow use of evidence obtained in violation of a suspect's constitutional rights if the police who seized it were acting in the good-faith reasonable belief that their conduct was legal.

The Supreme Court in July took much of the steam out of the push for final passage of S 1764 when it recognized a good-faith exception to the rule. In the case of *United States v. Leon*, the court acknowledged such an exception in the situation in which police obtained a search warrant only to discover later that it was technically defective. *(Decision, p. 717)*

Habeas Corpus

The Senate, but not the House, acted in 1984 to revise federal procedures for writs of habeas corpus. The Senate approved the measure (S 1763 — S Rept 98-226) Feb. 6 by a vote of 67-9. Its provisions would have made it more difficult for prisoners to invoke this writ as a means of obtaining their freedom.

Habeas corpus writs are used by prisoners who seek their release by arguing that their detention violated their constitutional rights. Such writs are usually a secondary avenue to relief, pursued only after prisoners have exhausted their direct appeals in state courts.

Supreme Court Jurisdiction

The House, but not the Senate, approved legislation in 1984 designed to lighten the workload of the Supreme Court.

The House Sept. 11 approved HR 5644 (H Rept 98-986) by voice vote. The measure eliminated the Supreme Court's "mandatory" jurisdiction — its responsibility to give special consideration to reviewing certain types of cases.

The bill was favored by all nine justices, who said it would give the court more control over its docket and

---

Attorneys' Fee Bill Vetoed

President Reagan in 1984 pocket-vetoed a bill approved by Congress to make permanent a law allowing the award of attorneys' fees to individuals and small businesses that successfully sued the government.

Congress cleared the bill (HR 5479) Oct. 11. It amended the Equal Access to Justice Act of 1980 (PL 96-481), which expired Oct. 1.

President Reagan pocket-vetoed the bill Nov. 8, objecting to two provisions that required the government to provide additional justification for agency action — in order to avoid having to pay these fees — and to pay interest on any awarded attorneys' fees not paid within 60 days.

Reagan said he approved making the law permanent and would work for such a measure in the 99th Congress.

---

would not keep any important questions of law from being resolved.

Justice Authorization

For the fifth consecutive year, Congress did not approve legislation giving the Justice Department formal authorization to operate its programs.

The Senate approved a fiscal 1985 authorization bill for the department (S 2606 — S Rept 98-498) June 15, but the House failed to act on its version of the measure (HR 5468 — H Rept 98-759) in 1984.

Constitutional Convention Procedures

As in the 97th Congress, the Senate Judiciary Committee approved a bill (S 119 — S Rept 98-594) establishing procedures for a constitutional convention. No further action was taken on the bill in 1984. *(1981 action, p. 679)*

Since 1975, 32 states had passed resolutions demanding that Congress convene a constitutional convention to consider amending the Constitution to require that the federal budget be balanced. If 34 states so request, Congress must call the convention. There had been no such convention since the Founding Fathers met in 1787 to draft the Constitution itself. *(Balanced budget amendment, p. 52)*

The Supreme Court

Ronald Reagan's first term in the White House was a time of change at the Supreme Court. By 1984, the Supreme Court seemed firmly committed to a conservative stance on important issues ranging from church and state to civil and criminal rights.

The new president significantly influenced this change through his power to fill court vacancies and — through the solicitor general — to argue cases that, if won, could direct national policy in new directions.

A New Justice

Less than six months after Reagan was inaugurated, he had the prized opportunity, which had eluded his predecessor, President Carter, to place a person of his choice on the Supreme Court. Justice Potter Stewart, 66, in an unexpected announcement on June 19, 1981, said he would retire at the end of the term in July. Stewart, who had been on the court for 23 years, said he wished to leave the demanding job of a justice while still in good health to enjoy more time with his family.

Reagan seized the opportunity. Distressed by polls showing low popularity among American women, Reagan fulfilled his campaign promise to name the first female member of the nation's highest court. On July 7, he introduced Sandra Day O'Connor, 51, a conservative Arizona judge, as his selection as Stewart's replacement. O'Connor's confirmation was never in doubt. The Senate Sept. 21 approved her nomination by a 99-0 roll call. She was sworn in Sept. 25, shortly before the October 1981 term of the court began.

O'Connor moved with apparent ease into her new role, joining the conservative wing of the court and providing an articulate new voice for that group of justices. By mid-1984, Democratic politicians, well into the presidential campaign, were warning that Reagan's re-election to a four-year term would allow him to appoint more justices and turn the court into a judicial copy of his administration's political philosophy. However, many court observers believed that the balance of power within the court had already shifted decisively with O'Connor's appointment. Later in the summer, the Democratic Party's platform virtually conceded this shift by emphasizing how far into the future the next president could, with several Supreme Court appointments, shape the Court. "Our next president will likely have the opportunity to shape that court, not just for his own term — or even for the rest of his own lifetime — but for the rest of ours and for our children's too," the platform declared.

The Justices

After Stewart's retirement and O'Connor's confirmation, the court's membership was unchanged for the rest of Reagan's first term. By 1984, it was one of the oldest courts in history. The average age of the justices was 70; at 54, O'Connor was the only justice under 60. There were five justices older than Reagan when he was re-elected as president at age 73. Although 70 was the average age at which death or serious illness has removed members from the court in the 20th century, none of the justices gave any sign that he was considering retirement.

The members of the court during this period were:

- Chief Justice Warren E. Burger, named to that post by President Nixon. Burger, born in 1907, marked his 15th anniversary as chief justice in June 1984.
- Justice William J. Brennan Jr., born in 1906, appointed by President Eisenhower in 1956.
- Justice Byron R. White, born in 1915, appointed by President Kennedy in 1962.
- Justice Thurgood Marshall, born in 1908, appointed by President Johnson in 1967.
- Justice Harry A. Blackmun, born in 1908, appointed by President Nixon in 1970.
- Justice Lewis F. Powell Jr., born in 1907, appointed by President Nixon in 1971.
- Justice William H. Rehnquist, born in 1924, appointed by President Nixon in 1971.
- Justice John Paul Stevens, born in 1920, appointed by President Ford in 1975.
- Justice Sandra Day O'Connor, born in 1930, appointed by President Reagan in 1981.

References

Discussion of the Supreme Court for the years 1945-64 may be found in *Congress and the Nation Vol. I*, pp. 1441-1454; for the years 1965-68, *Congress and the Nation Vol. II*, pp. 335-340; for the years 1969-72, *Congress and the Nation Vol. III*, pp. 287-327; for the years 1973-76, *Congress and the Nation Vol. IV*, pp. 619-659; for the years 1977-80, *Congress and the Nation Vol. V*, pp. 755-778.

Stewart to O'Connor: Moderate to Conservative

Justice Potter Stewart caught everyone off guard on the afternoon of June 19, 1981, when he announced that after 23 years on the Supreme Court, he had decided to retire as soon as the court completed its business for the current term.

"I've always believed that it is better to go too soon than to stay too long," said the typically plain-spoken justice, whose best-known judicial quotation was likely to be his comment in an obscenity case that even if the court could not develop a satisfactory definition of pornography: "I know it when I see it."

Stewart's Record

Stewart was named to the court in 1958 by President Eisenhower after he had served four years on the 6th U.S. Circuit Court of Appeals. At the time of his retirement on July 3, 1981, he was second only to Justice William J. Brennan Jr. in seniority. A moderate-to-conservative justice, Stewart disagreed with a number of the Warren Court's most controversial decisions, including its 1962 decision that New York violated the Constitution by prescribing a prayer for use in public school classrooms, and its 1966 Miranda decision ensuring the right of a suspect to be advised of his constitutional rights before being questioned by police.

After Chief Justice Warren E. Burger came to the court in 1969, Stewart found himself both more powerful and more comfortable. On a dozen major issues during the 1970s, he cast the deciding vote, determining the court's position on issues ranging from the death penalty to affirmative action. When the court in 1972 effectively struck down every death penalty law in the country, it was Stewart who most effectively summarized the reason. The offending laws permitted the ultimate sentence of death to be imposed "wantonly" and "freakishly," he said. "These death sentences are cruel and unusual in the same way that being struck down by lightning is cruel and unusual," he wrote.

O'Connor's Selection

Unlike her fellow justices, Sandra Day O'Connor brought to the bench solid political experience in all three branches of state government.

To a court that seemed generally lacking in charisma or cooperation, O'Connor brought political skills that would serve her well.

A native of southwestern Arizona, Sandra Day graduated from Stanford University in 1950 and Stanford Law School two years later. She married a fellow law student, John Jay O'Connor III; another fellow student — William H. Rehnquist — would later be a fellow justice.

After some time in private practice when her three sons were young, O'Connor served as an assistant state attorney general (1965-68), was appointed to the state senate in 1969 and then won two full terms, during which she was elected senate majority leader in 1973.

In 1974, O'Connor left the Legislature and ran for superior court judge, a post she won and in which she served until appointed to the Arizona Court of Appeals in 1979. It was from that post that Reagan elevated her to the Supreme Court.

Confirmation

Introduced as the nominee July 7, O'Connor was not formally nominated until Aug. 19. The Senate Judiciary Committee hearings were held Sept. 9-11. The committee voted 17-0 on Sept. 15 to recommend confirmation. The Senate voted 99-0 to confirm the nomination on Sept. 21. She was sworn in on Sept. 15 as the 102nd person — and the first woman — to serve as a member of the U.S. Supreme Court.

O'Connor's confirmation was never in doubt, despite noisy opposition to the nomination by anti-abortion groups who claimed she had voted in favor of abortion during her service in the Legislature.

The questions at the Senate Judiciary Committee hearings focused on her views on abortion and those votes she cast on the issue as a member of the Legislature. She parried demands that she state her views on the Supreme Court's landmark 1973 decision denying states the power to ban all abortions, although she said that she herself was personally opposed to abortion.

Her personal views, however, would not be a factor in deciding any case before her as a Supreme Court justice, she said: "Issues that come before the court should be resolved based on the facts ... and the law applicable to those facts." In response to other queries, O'Connor expressed a belief in judicial restraint and in the limited role of government generally and the courts in particular.

Before O'Connor replaced Stewart, the court seemed to be made up of two liberals, Brennan and Marshall; two conservatives, Burger and Rehnquist; and five men in the middle, Stewart, White, Blackmun, Powell and Stevens. During the early 1980s, however, the court realigned itself into a conservative wing in which O'Connor and Powell joined Burger and Rehnquist, a liberal wing in which Ste-

vens usually joined Brennan and Marshall, and two "swing men" — Blackmun and White — whose votes determined whether the liberals or the conservatives prevailed. Early in this period Blackmun seemed to ally himself more often with the liberals than the conservatives, but by mid-1984, he was once again back in the conservative camp. White too voted more and more with the conservatives, abandoning

them just often enough to retain his role as a swing vote in in the middle.

The Reagan Record

The federal government is always an active advocate before the Supreme Court. It is a party to many of the cases that are argued. The government's case is presented to the court by the solicitor general, the fourth-ranking official at the Justice Department, or one of the attorneys on his staff. The solicitor general's office argues more cases than any law firm in the country before the Supreme Court, and wins most of them.

Usually the solicitor general and his staff are urging the justices to uphold the status quo: to find constitutional an act of Congress or to uphold an executive regulation. However, the Reagan administration often used its opportunity, in arguing cases before the court, to urge the court to rethink its position on some significant national issue. In the 1982-83 term, the solicitor general asked the court to hold unconstitutional the legislative veto. The court agreed, voting 7-2, that this device could not constitutionally be used. *(Special report on legislative veto, p. 833)*

The administration also successfully urged the court to uphold a state income tax deduction for tuition and other school-related expenses, a deduction challenged because it primarily benefits parochial school patrons.

But the decisions were not all for the administration. The court in that same term rebuffed or sidestepped the administration's suggestion that it should:

● Give states and cities greater leeway to restrict abortions;

● Reconsider the government's policy of denying tax-exempt status to racially discriminatory private schools and colleges;

● Uphold rescission of the government's requirement that all American-made cars have air bags or automatic seat belts;

● Modify the controversial "exclusionary rule" that denies prosecutors the use of illegally obtained evidence;

● Limit the use of "affirmative action" to remedy past discrimination.

The next term, which began in October 1983 and ended midway through the election year of 1984, brought a significant improvement in the administration's fortunes before the court. In a series of major decisions, the court in 1984 adopted the administration's arguments and:

● Carved out a good faith exception to the exclusionary rule by permitting prosecutors to use evidence that police obtained acting in "good faith" that the search they were conducting was legal and was authorized by a search warrant;

● Permitted, for the first time, an exception to the rule that permits prosecutors to use a suspect's incriminating statements only if he is warned, before speaking, of his constitutional rights. The court held that in the interest of public safety police could question a suspect briefly — asking for example, "Where's your gun?" — before advising him of his rights;

● Emphasized the need to accommodate, rather than separate, the roles of church and state in American life, by permitting a city to use a nativity scene as part of its holiday display in the downtown area;

● Limited the reach of affirmative action by holding that Congress had denied federal judges the power to modify a valid seniority system in the interest of preserving affirma-

tive action hiring gains;

● Narrowed the reach of the federal law barring sex discrimination by schools and colleges receiving federal aid. The court reversed a decade of administrative interpretation of Title IX, the anti-discrimination law, and held that only the particular program receiving the federal aid at a school came within the ban;

● Upheld the Reagan administration's 1982 regulations severely curtailing travel to Cuba;

● Reinstated clean air regulations adopted by the Carter and Reagan administrations but challenged as too permissive by environmentalists.

The administration's new-found success was due in part to the choice of issues. Its earlier setbacks came on abortion, tax exemptions for discriminatory schools and rescission of auto safety regulations. In all three, the administration was seeking to change a settled area of law and policy, changes endorsed primarily by conservative activists or big business. In the 1983-84 term, however, the administration took stands on less explosive questions, adopting positions supported by a broad constituency in the nation at large. Furthermore, the administration did not argue that the court should overturn or disregard established precedent, but only that it should curtail activist federal judges who were extending those precedents too far. This argument was skillfully tailored to the belief of a majority of the justices that federal judges should apply the law, not set national policy. As the court itself said in one of its June 1984 decisions: "Federal judges — who have no constituency — have a duty to respect legitimate policy choices made by those who do."

Congress and the Court

Not since the New Deal collisions of the 1930s had Congress felt so keenly the power of the Supreme Court to curtail its actions as it did in June 1983. By denying Congress the use of the legislative veto, a device it had employed in more than 200 laws since 1932, the court seemed

---

U.S. Supreme Court Caseload

	1980-1981	1981-1982	1982-1983	1983-1984
Number of Cases on Docket	5,144	5,311	5,079	5,100
Cases Decided Summarily	122	126	119	81
Cases Argued and Decided	154	184	183	184
Number of Signed Opinions	123	141	151	151

SOURCE: U.S. Supreme Court

---

to alter the balance of power between Congress and the executive.

The court's ruling came by a 7-2 vote as it resolved a case that began as an immigration dispute, *Immigration and Naturalization Service v. Chadha.* In the court's entire history to the end of the previous term in July 1982, it had struck down all or portions of 110 federal laws. The decision was a major victory for the executive branch, which had traditionally opposed the legislative veto as intruding upon the executive branch responsibility to carry out the laws. It was a major defeat for Congress, whose attorneys had argued that the legislative veto was a useful and necessary modern invention that enabled Congress to delegate authority without abdicating responsibility.

The practical impact of the court's decision was unclear. Committees immediately moved to review existing laws that might be affected, and to explore alternatives for retaining some measure of congressional control over the implementation of the laws they approve.

During Reagan's first term, the court upheld a number of acts of Congress challenged as unconstitutional — among them the decision to continue a male-only draft, to impose a windfall profits tax on oil, to grant tax-exempt status to veterans' organizations no matter how much lobbying they did, and to deny federal student aid to men who failed to register for the draft.

But the court also struck down eight other federal laws or portions of the law as unconstitutional. Late in 1980, the court held that Congress had acted unconstitutionally in rescinding cost-of-living increases for federal judges in fiscal years 1977 and 1980 by passing the rescission after the fiscal years had begun. The result was a hefty pay increase, about 12 percent, for all sitting judges, including the justices themselves.

In 1982 the court first struck down the Rock Island Transition and Employee Assistance Act of 1980 (PL 96-254) as passed in violation of the constitutional provision that requires Congress to establish uniform laws on the subject of bankruptcy. PL 96-254 applied only to one railroad, giving its employees special protection.

Three months later, the court threw the nation's bankruptcy courts into confusion by ruling that Congress had acted unconstitutionally when it included provisions in the 1978 Bankruptcy Reform Act (PL 95-598) creating a new corps of bankruptcy judges with broad powers but limited terms. This violated Article III, which was designed to ensure that federal judicial power was exercised only by judges whose independence was assured by life tenure. The court gave Congress six months to come up with legislation curing this defect in the modernized bankruptcy system it had created in 1978. But not until two years after the court's decision did Congress finally complete action on the remedial legislation. *(Story, p. 702)*

First Amendment Cases

First Amendment issues proliferated on the Supreme Court's docket during this period. Four of the federal laws held unconstitutional during this period were found to conflict with First Amendment guarantees. The invalidated statutes:
- Barred all demonstrations on the public sidewalks adjacent to the Supreme Court;

Judicial Salaries

Although many federal judges still felt underpaid when they compared their income with that of their colleagues in private practice, judicial salaries took a quantum leap in the early 1980s, due primarily to a retroactive increase after the Supreme Court held that Congress improperly rescinded cost-of-living increases for federal judges in 1977 and 1980.

As the decade began the chief justice of the United States was being paid $75,000 a year; associate justices of the U.S. Supreme Court, $72,000; appeals court judges, $57,500; and district court judges, $54,500.

Five years later, as of Dec. 31, 1984, the chief justice received $104,700 a year; associate justices, $100,600; appeals court judges, $80,400; and district court judges, $76,000.

- Prohibited the mailing of any unsolicited advertisements of contraceptives;
- Prohibited editorials on public radio and television stations that accepted grants from the Corporation for Public Broadcasting;
- Banned all photographic reproductions of U.S. currency unless the photographs were for "philatelic, numismatic, newsworthy, historical and educational purposes."

Presidential Immunity

In the 1970s the court had greatly expanded the liability of Cabinet members, members of Congress and other federal officials to damage suits brought by persons who felt themselves injured by the actions of those officials. But in 1982, the court made clear that this trend had its limits. By a 5-4 vote in a case involving former President Richard M. Nixon, the court declared presidents absolutely immune from such suits for all official actions taken during their term in the White House.

The Caseload Controversy

The simmering debate over the workload of the Supreme Court — whether it was a problem and what might be the remedy — flared up again in 1982 after the court's caseload again passed the 5,000 mark for two consecutive years. Led by Chief Justice Burger, whose concern for the issue was of long duration, six other Supreme Court justices spoke out to express frustration with the press of cases before them. A variety of remedies were proposed, but none was acted upon. The caseload leveled off, at just over 5,000 in the next two terms, and the justices — having said their piece — went back to dealing with it, instead of talking about it.

Supreme Court Decisions
October 1980 — July 1984

Criminal Law

Fourth Amendment

Search and Seizure

United States v. Cortez (449 U.S. 411), decided by a 9-0 vote, Jan. 21, 1981. Burger wrote the opinion.

Facts that may seem insignificant to an untrained person can properly be used by law enforcement officers — in this case, border patrol officers in Arizona — to justify stopping a vehicle near the border and questioning its occupants.

Steagald v. United States (451 U.S. 204), decided by a 7-2 vote, April 21, 1981. Marshall wrote the opinion; Rehnquist and White dissented.

Police with a warrant for the arrest of a suspect may not enter and search the home of another person without obtaining a warrant for that search — even if they believe that the suspect may be at that home. "Warrantless searches of a home are impermissible absent consent or exigent circumstances," stated the majority.

Michigan v. Summers (452 U.S. 692), decided by a 6-3 vote, June 22, 1981. Stevens wrote the opinion; Stewart, Brennan and Marshall dissented.

Police did not act improperly when they detained a homeowner while searching his home for narcotics, even though they had a warrant only for the search — not for his arrest. Such a detention is a limited intrusion on personal security justified by substantial law enforcement interests in preventing flight, minimizing risk to police and facilitating the orderly completion of the search of the home.

New York v. Belton (453 U.S. 454), decided by a 6-3 vote, July 1, 1981. Stewart wrote the opinion; Brennan, Marshall and White dissented.

When the occupant of an automobile is lawfully arrested, police may, incident to his arrest and without a warrant, search the passenger compartment of the auto in which he was riding. Any evidence uncovered in that search, even in the closed pocket of clothing found within the passenger compartment, is admissible in court.

Robbins v. California (453 U.S. 420), decided by a 6-3 vote, July 1, 1981. Stewart wrote the opinion joined by three other justices; Powell and Burger concurred; Blackmun, Rehnquist and Stevens dissented.

Police may not, without a search warrant, open a closed piece of luggage or other container found in a lawfully searched car. If police open such a container without a warrant, its contents may not be used as evidence in court.

Washington v. Chrisman (455 U.S. 1), decided by a 6-3 vote, Jan. 13, 1982. Burger wrote the opinion; White, Brennan and Marshall dissented.

A policeman who arrested a student and accompanied him to the student's room could properly search that room without a warrant and seize evidence for use in court against the student and his roommate. The "plain view" exception to the warrant requirement of the Fourth Amendment permits a law enforcement officer to seize clearly incriminating evidence when it is discovered in a place where the officer has the right to be. Once an officer places someone under arrest he has the right to remain at that person's elbow at all times.

United States v. Ross (456 U.S. 798), decided by a 6-3 vote, June 1, 1982. Stevens wrote the opinion; White, Brennan and Marshall dissented.

Police officers who have stopped a vehicle and who have probable cause to suspect that drugs or other contraband are somewhere in it may search the entire vehicle as thoroughly as if they had a warrant, including all containers and packages found in the vehicle that might contain the object of the search. The contrary holding in *Robbins v. California* (1981) — requiring police to obtain a warrant to search such containers — is rejected. *(See above)*

United States v. Johnson (457 U.S. 537), decided by a 5-4 vote, June 21, 1982. Blackmun wrote the opinion; White, Burger, Rehnquist and O'Connor dissented.

The court's 1980 ruling in *Payton v. New York* that police may not, without a warrant or consent, enter a home to arrest its occupant applies to invalidate the 1977 arrest of a man whose case was still on appeal when the 1980 ruling was announced.

Taylor v. Alabama (457 U.S. 687), decided by a 5-4 vote, June 23, 1982. Marshall wrote the opinion; O'Connor, Burger, Powell and Rehnquist dissented.

A confession obtained, without physical coercion, from a suspect who was taken into custody without probable cause or a warrant and who was warned of his constitutional rights before confessing is inadmissible in court because it is the product of an illegal arrest.

United States v. Knotts (460 U.S. 276), decided by a 9-0 vote, March 2, 1983. Rehnquist wrote the opinion.

Minnesota law enforcement officers did not violate the Fourth Amendment guarantee against unreasonable search and seizure when they monitored signals from a beeper placed inside a container sold to a suspected drug manufacturer. The signals enabled police to follow the suspect's car to a cabin where police, armed with a search warrant, found a clandestine drug laboratory.

Monitoring the beeper signal did not violate the suspect's privacy and so was neither a "search" nor a "seizure" within the meaning of the Fourth Amendment.

Florida v. Royer (460 U.S. 491), decided by a 5-4 vote, March 23, 1983. White announced the judgment of the court in an opinion joined by three other justices; Brennan concurred; Rehnquist, Burger, O'Connor and Blackmun dissented.

Florida detectives acted illegally when they detained a man at the Miami International Airport because his appearance and manner fit a "drug courier profile." Therefore, the suspect's consent to a subsequent search of his luggage by the detectives was tainted by the illegality of his detention and was not valid. The profile alone does not constitute probable cause for the suspect's arrest.

Texas v. Brown (460 U.S. 730), decided by a 9-0 vote, April 19, 1983. Rehnquist announced the decision in

an opinion joined by three justices; the other justices concurred in separate opinions.

The court upheld the seizure of a party balloon of the type often used to store narcotics. It was taken from the seat of a car stopped by police at a routine driver's license checkpoint. The officer knew from experience of the use of these balloons to store drugs, and from observation of the balloon in plain view here thought that to be the situation.

Illinois v. Gates (462 U.S. 213), decided by a 6-3 vote, June 8, 1983. Rehnquist wrote the opinion; Brennan, Marshall and Stevens dissented.

Making it easier for police to obtain search warrants on the basis of anonymous tips, the court held that a magistrate asked to issue a warrant on this basis should make a common-sense decision based on the totality of the circumstances surrounding the tip and the efforts and success of police in verifying it. Among the factors to be considered are evidence of the veracity of the informant, the reliability of the report and the basis of the tipster's knowledge.

The court heard two rounds of arguments in this case. The second, at the court's request, had focused on the issue of a "good-faith" exception to the controversial exclusionary rule, which bars the use as evidence of illegally obtained items.

The question before the court was whether to permit the use of evidence taken by police who thought they were operating within constitutional bounds. The court finally decided not to resolve that issue in this case.

United States v. Villamonte-Marquez (462 U.S. 579), decided by a 6-3 vote, June 17, 1983. Rehnquist wrote the opinion; Brennan, Marshall and Stevens dissented.

Customs officers are authorized by Congress to board a vessel and inspect its documentation, even without a warrant or any suspicion of unlawful activity. A vessel on a waterway with ready access to the sea is subject to such boarding in order that customs officials may effectively police the waterways.

Florida v. Casal (462 U.S. 637), dismissed by a 9-0 vote, June 17, 1983. *Per curiam* (unsigned) opinion.

The court dismissed this case after hearing oral arguments, deciding that the lower court ruling under review rested on adequate and independent state grounds. The

case involved the suppression of 100 pounds of marijuana discovered on a fishing boat and used to convict two men of importing that drug. The Florida Supreme Court held the evidence could not be used against the men; the Supreme Court found that ruling to rest on sufficient grounds in state law, making federal review unnecessary.

Illinois v. Lafayette (462 U.S. 640), decided by a 9-0 vote, June 20, 1983. Burger wrote the opinion.

The court held reasonable and constitutional a police search and inventory of the possessions of a suspect who has been arrested and taken to the police station to be booked. No search warrant is required for this type of search.

United States v. Place (462 U.S. 696), decided by votes of 9-0 and 6-3, June 20, 1983. O'Connor wrote the opinion; Brennan, Blackmun and Marshall dissented in part.

The court held unanimously that federal narcotics agents acted unreasonably when they detained for 90 minutes the luggage of an airline passenger suspected of carrying drugs in order to have the luggage sniffed by a dog trained to detect drugs. Six members of the court went on to say, however, that this sort of "sniff" test was permissible, despite the Fourth Amendment's guarantee against unreasonable searches, so long as the detention of the luggage was brief.

Illinois v. Andreas (463 U.S. 765), decided by a 6-3 vote, July 5, 1983. Burger wrote the opinion; Brennan, Marshall and Stevens dissented.

Police officers do not need a search warrant to reopen a locked container that has already been lawfully opened by a customs agent who found it to contain narcotics, resealed it, and delivered it to its owner.

Michigan v. Long (463 U.S. 1032), decided by a 6-3 vote, July 6, 1983. O'Connor wrote the opinion; Brennan, Marshall and Stevens dissented.

Police may conduct a "protective search" of the interior of a car they have stopped, just as — under the 1968 decision in *Terry v. Ohio* — they may pat down or frisk a suspect they stop on the street.

This sort of warrantless search is reasonable and constitutional so long as it is limited to the areas of the passenger department in which a weapon might be hidden and is based upon a reasonable belief that the suspect is dangerous and may be able to seize a weapon from the area around him.

Michigan v. Clifford, decided by a 5-4 vote, Jan. 11, 1984. Powell announced the decision in an opinion joined by three other justices; Stevens concurred; Rehnquist, Burger, Blackmun and O'Connor dissented.

The warrantless entry and search of a burned residence five hours after the fire was extinguished, without notice to the absent residents of the dwelling, was a violation of the Fourth Amendment guarantee against unreasonable search and seizure.

Colorado v. Nunez, decided by a 9-0 vote, Feb. 21, 1984. *Per curiam* (unsigned) opinion.

The court dismissed this case after hearing arguments by state prosecutors challenging a state court's decision to suppress evidence because it had been obtained with a

---

Search and Seizure

The right of the people to be secure in their persons, houses, papers and effects, against unreasonable searches and seizures, shall not be violated, and no warrants shall issue, but upon probable cause, supported by oath or affirmation and particularly describing the place to be searched, and the persons or things to be seized.

Fourth Amendment, U.S. Constitution

search warrant issued on the basis of an informer's tip and the state would not disclose the identity of the informer. The justices decided that the state court's decision was based on state law, not federal law, and thus should be left intact.

United States v. Jacobsen, decided by a 7-2 vote, April 2, 1984. Stevens wrote the opinion; Brennan and Marshall dissented.

A federal narcotics agent is not required to obtain a warrant before conducting a chemical test on the contents of a damaged package handed over to the federal agent by a private company. A test that merely determines the identity of a substance does not compromise any legitimate privacy interest and thus need not be authorized by a warrant.

Oliver v. United States, Maine v. Thornton, decided by a 6-3 vote, April 17, 1984. Powell wrote the opinion; Marshall, Brennan and Stevens dissented.

Police need not obtain search warrants before searching privately owned open fields, even if the fields are marked by "no trespassing" signs and enclosed by gates and fences. One cannot legitimately expect that activities conducted outdoors in fields will remain private.

Immigration and Naturalization Service v. Delgado, decided by a 7-2 vote, April 17, 1984. Rehnquist wrote the opinion; Brennan and Marshall dissented.

Immigration agents need not obtain warrants, or have evidence that some workers at a particular factory are illegal aliens, before they move into a factory and "sweep" through it questioning workers about their citizenship. Such a "sweep" is not a seizure of the work force, since employees are free to move about and to leave as long as they answer questions about their citizenship to the satisfaction of the federal agents.

Welsh v. Wisconsin, decided by a 7-2 vote, May 15, 1984. Brennan wrote the opinion; White and Rehnquist dissented.

Police violated the Fourth Amendment's guarantee of privacy and security when they entered a home at night without a warrant in order to arrest the occupant for drunken driving. An immediate arrest was not justified by any special circumstances; the police should have obtained a warrant.

United States v. Karo, decided by a 6-3 vote, July 3, 1984. White wrote the opinion; Brennan, Marshall and Stevens dissented.

Federal agents did not violate the guarantee against unreasonable searches when they installed a beeper inside a can of ether purchased by suspected drug dealers and then followed the dealers by monitoring the beeper.

Warrantless use of the beeper to verify that the can was taken into a private home and use of that information as the basis for a search warrant for the home was a violation of the Fourth Amendment rights of the occupants of the house, but the warrant was justified on the basis of other untainted information.

Hudson v. Palmer, decided by votes of 9-0 and 5-4, July 3, 1984. Burger wrote the opinion; Stevens, Brennan, Blackmun and Marshall dissented.

The Fourth Amendment guarantee against unreason-

able search and seizure does not apply in prison cells. Prisoners have no reasonable expectation of privacy in their cells and are subject to random searches at any time.

As long as state law provides a remedy for a guard's intentional destruction of an inmate's personal property, such destruction does not deny the inmate due process of law.

United States v. Leon, decided by a 6-3 vote, July 5, 1984. White wrote the opinion; Brennan, Marshall and Stevens dissented.

Illegally obtained evidence may be used at a trial if the police who seized it had obtained a search warrant and thought they were acting legally. The court approved this "good faith" exception to the exclusionary rule it had adopted 70 years earlier forbidding the use of such evidence at a trial. Prosecutors had long been urging such an exception.

The court's decision in this case was limited to a situation in which police obtained a warrant and executed a search in accord with it, only to have the warrant later found to be defective. In such an instance, excluding valid evidence found in the search has no deterrent effect on police misconduct and exacts too high a price from society, the court held.

Massachusetts v. Sheppard, decided by a 7-2 vote, July 5, 1984. White wrote the opinion; Brennan and Marshall dissented.

The exclusionary rule need not be applied to exclude evidence obtained in a search authorized by a warrant that subsequently was held invalid because of a technical mistake on the part of the judge issuing it. This was the court's first application of the "good faith" exception to the rule adopted in *United States v. Leon* (above).

Segura v. United States, decided by a 5-4 vote, July 5, 1984. Burger wrote the opinion; Stevens, Brennan, Marshall and Blackmun dissented.

An illegal entry by police into an apartment, without a warrant, for the purpose of securing the premises does not require the exclusion of evidence taken later from that residence pursuant to a search authorized by a valid search warrant based upon information possessed by police before their illegal entry.

Fifth Amendment

Self-Incrimination

Carter v. Kentucky (450 U.S. 288), decided by an 8-1 vote, March 9, 1981. Stewart wrote the opinion; Rehnquist dissented.

Whenever a defendant does not wish to take the witness stand in his own defense — and requests the judge to instruct the jury that his failure to testify is not to be viewed as evidence of guilt — the judge is constitutionally obligated to give those instructions to protect the defendant's right to remain silent and not to be forced to incriminate himself.

Pillsbury Co. v. Conboy (459 U.S. 248), decided by a 7-2 vote, Jan. 11, 1983. Powell wrote the opinion; Stevens and O'Connor dissented.

Grand jury witnesses who are granted immunity from

use of their testimony against them may not be compelled, at a later time in civil proceedings, to verify their prior immunized testimony.

In such a situation, a witness is entitled to claim his Fifth Amendment privilege to remain silent rather than incriminate himself, and he may not be forced to testify over a valid assertion of that privilege.

South Dakota v. Neville (459 U.S. 553), decided by a 7-2 vote, Feb. 22, 1983. O'Connor wrote the opinion; Stevens and Marshall dissented.

An individual's privilege against self-incrimination is not violated when his refusal to submit to a blood-alcohol test is used as evidence against him when he is tried on charges of drunken driving.

United States v. Hasting (461 U.S. 499), decided by votes of 7-2 and 9-0, May 23, 1983. Burger wrote the opinion. Brennan and Marshall dissented.

A court of appeals impermissibly ignored the "harmless error" doctrine when it overturned the convictions of four men for kidnapping and rape, basing its action on the prosecutor's comments to the jury noting that the defendants did not attempt to rebut the government's evidence against them. The court of appeals found this to be a violation of the defendants' right to remain silent rather than be compelled to incriminate themselves.

The Supreme Court found these comments by the prosecutor amounted to harmless error in the face of the overwhelming evidence of guilt presented by the prosecutor and the weak defense mounted by the suspects.

Minnesota v. Murphy, decided by a 6-3 vote, Feb. 22, 1984. White wrote the opinion; Marshall, Stevens and Brennan dissented.

A probationer's statements to his probation officer are admissible in court. A probationer is not "in custody" when he is talking with his probation officer, and *Miranda v. Arizona* (1966) thus does not require that he be warned of his rights before being asked about crimes.

United States v. Doe, decided by votes of 9-0 and 6-3, Feb. 28, 1984. Powell wrote the opinion; Marshall, Brennan and Stevens dissented in part.

The Fifth Amendment guarantee against compelled

self-incrimination cannot be claimed by a businessman to avoid disclosure of voluntarily prepared business records of a sole proprietorship, the court held 6-3.

However, the court unanimously agreed that the government is required to grant at least a limited immunity from prosecution to a businessman producing such records under subpoena if it appears that his compliance — tacit admission that the records exist and are in his possession — may be incriminating.

New York v. Quarles, decided by votes of 5-4 and 6-3, June 12, 1984. Rehnquist wrote the opinion; O'Connor, Stevens, Marshall and Brennan dissented.

The court recognized a "public safety" exception to the rule set out in *Miranda v. Arizona* (1966), which denies prosecutors use of evidence obtained from a suspect not advised of his constitutional rights. This was the first exception the court had permitted to this rule.

In some situations, "concern for public safety" dictates that police ask a suspect a particular question immediately, such as "Where's the gun?" In these cases, the suspect's reply and any evidence it leads to may be used against him.

Berkemer v. McCarty, decided by a 9-0 vote, July 2, 1984. Marshall wrote the opinion.

Drivers stopped by police for questioning about traffic offenses do not have to be advised of their constitutional rights until they are taken into custody.

Anyone who has been arrested for any reason, however, must be warned of his right to remain silent and his right to have an attorney before he is questioned by police.

Double Jeopardy

United States v. DiFrancesco (449 U.S. 117), decided by a 5-4 vote, Dec. 9, 1980. Blackmun wrote the opinion; Brennan, White, Marshall and Stevens dissented.

The Fifth Amendment guarantee against double jeopardy is not violated by the provisions of the 1970 Organized Crime Control Act that permit federal prosecutors to appeal sentences that they consider too lenient for dangerous special offenders.

Hudson v. Louisiana (450 U.S. 40), decided by a 9-0 vote, Feb. 24, 1981. Powell wrote the opinion.

The double jeopardy clause forbids a state to retry a defendant for a crime if he has already been tried and convicted and the first verdict has been set aside for lack of evidence.

Albernaz v. United States (450 U.S. 333), decided by a 9-0 vote, March 9, 1981. Rehnquist wrote the opinion.

Congress did not violate the double jeopardy clause when it approved provisions of the Drug Abuse Prevention and Control Act of 1970 that allowed the imposition of consecutive prison sentences on persons found guilty of conspiring to import and to distribute marijuana, even if there was only a single conspiracy for the two purposes.

Bullington v. Missouri (451 U.S. 430), decided by a 5-4 vote, May 4, 1981. Blackmun wrote the opinion; Powell, Burger, White and Rehnquist dissented.

A state cannot have a second chance to try to convince a jury to impose the death sentence on a particular defendant. Once a jury has decided that a particular defendant should not be sentenced to die for his crime, that defen-

---

Double Jeopardy, Self-Incrimination

...Nor shall any person be subject for the same offense to be twice put in jeopardy of life or limb nor shall be compelled in any criminal case to be a witness against himself, nor be deprived of life, liberty, or property, without due process of law....

Fifth Amendment, U.S. Constitution

---

dant's right to be protected against double jeopardy forbids the state — even if a new trial is granted — to seek the death penalty.

Oregon v. Kennedy (456 U.S. 667), decided by a 9-0 vote, May 24, 1982. Rehnquist wrote the opinion.

A defendant is not deprived of his constitutional protection against double jeopardy when he is tried again on theft charges after a mistrial was declared in his first trial, at his request, because the prosecutor called him a "crook" during the trial.

Tibbs v. Florida (457 U.S. 31), decided by a 5-4 vote, June 7, 1982. O'Connor wrote the opinion; White, Brennan, Marshall and Blackmun dissented.

When a defendant's conviction has been reversed by a state appeals court that finds the guilty verdict contrary to the weight of the evidence presented at the trial, a retrial is not barred by the Fifth Amendment protection against double jeopardy. The reversal simply affords the defendant a second opportunity to seek an acquittal.

Missouri v. Hunter (459 U.S. 359), decided by a 7-2 vote, Jan. 19, 1983. Burger wrote the opinion; Marshall and Stevens dissented.

If a state legislature decides expressly to authorize multiple sentences for the same criminal action — for example, separate sentences for a person convicted both of first degree robbery and of an "armed criminal action" — imposition of such sentences does not violate the constitutional guarantee against double jeopardy.

Justices of Boston Municipal Court v. Lydon, decided by a 9-0 vote, April 18, 1984. White wrote the opinion.

Federal courts can entertain petitions for habeas corpus relief from persons who are free on personal recognizance. The guarantee against double jeopardy was not violated by Massachusetts' system, under which a defendant who elected a bench trial and was convicted was, upon appeal, entitled to a new trial before a jury.

Arizona v. Rumsey, decided by a 7-2 vote, May 29, 1984. O'Connor wrote the opinion; Rehnquist and White dissented.

Once a judge or jury has decided not to impose a death sentence on a convicted criminal, the double jeopardy guarantee forbids the state to argue for the death penalty in a second sentencing proceeding.

This applies even when the first sentence has been set aside by a higher court because it found that the sentencing judge misinterpreted the law.

Ohio v. Johnson, decided by votes of 7-2 and 6-3, June 11, 1984. Rehnquist wrote the opinion; Stevens and Marshall dissented; Brennan dissented in part.

A defendant who pleads guilty to the lesser two of four criminal charges, all related to the same criminal incident, cannot invoke the double jeopardy guarantee in order to avoid being tried on the two greater charges.

Richardson v. United States, decided by votes of 8-1 and 7-2, June 29, 1984. Rehnquist wrote the opinion; Brennan, Marshall and Stevens dissented.

When a jury deadlocks and a mistrial is declared, it is no violation of the double jeopardy guarantee for the de-

fendant to be retried on the unresolved charges. The double jeopardy guarantee applies only when some event, such as an acquittal, terminates the original jeopardy.

Sixth Amendment

Speedy Trial

United States v. MacDonald, decided by a 6-3 vote, March 31, 1982. Burger wrote the opinion; Marshall, Brennan and Blackmun dissented.

The Sixth Amendment guarantee of the right to a speedy trial applies to the period between arrest and indictment, not to the period after military charges have been dismissed against a suspect and before a civilian indictment has been obtained. Thus an Army doctor, initially charged by the military with the murder of his wife and daughters, was not denied his speedy trial right by the delay of several years between dismissal of the military charges and institution of the civilian charges.

The Sixth Amendment right to a speedy trial is not primarily intended to prevent prejudice to the defense caused by passage of time. That interest is protected by the due process clause and statutes of limitations. The speedy trial guarantee is intended to limit the impairment of liberty of an accused before trial and to shorten the disruption of life caused by unresolved criminal charges.

A Fair and Public Trial

Rosales-Lopez v. United States (451 U.S. 182), decided by a 6-3 vote, April 21, 1981. White wrote an opinion joined by three justices; Rehnquist and Burger concurred in the result; Stevens, Brennan and Marshall dissented.

A Mexican-American defendant was not denied his right to trial by an impartial jury when the trial judge refused to question prospective jurors about possible prejudice against Mexicans although he did question them about prejudice against aliens.

Smith v. Phillips (455 U.S. 209), decided by a 6-3 vote, Jan. 25, 1982. Rehnquist wrote the opinion; Marshall, Brennan and Stevens dissented.

A defendant's due process right to a fair trial was not violated simply because a juror in the case was applying for a job with the prosecutor's office as the murder trial was in process. The trial judge, in a hearing on the situation, found "beyond a reasonable doubt" that this situation did not result in any prejudice to the defendant.

"Due process does not require a new trial every time a juror has been placed in a potentially compromising situation. Were that the rule, few trials would be constitutionally acceptable. . . . Due process means a jury capable and willing to decide the case solely on the evidence before it, and a trial judge ever watchful to prevent prejudicial occurrences and to determine the effect of such occurrences when they happen," declared the majority.

Connecticut v. Johnson (460 U.S. 73), decided by a 5-4 vote, Feb. 23, 1983. Blackmun announced the court's judgment, joined in that opinion by three other justices; Justice Stevens concurred in that judgment; Powell, Burger, Rehnquist and O'Connor dissented.

The court upheld a decision by the Connecticut Su-

preme Court that a man on trial for attempted murder, kidnapping and sexual assault was denied a fair trial when the judge instructed jurors that "the law presumes that a person intends the ordinary consequences of his voluntary acts."

The state Supreme Court based its holding on a U.S. Supreme Court decision, *Sandstrom v. Montana*, that such an instruction denied a defendant due process of law by giving a juror the idea that whatever criminal action the defendant committed was committed with intent, instead of leaving it to the prosecutor to prove intent in that case.

The court did not resolve the primary question in the Johnson case — whether such an error in jury instructions could be considered harmless enough to permit the ensuing conviction to stand. Four justices felt that such a mistake could never be harmless and would always require reversal of a conviction. Justice Stevens felt the case should simply have been dismissed, but he joined the four other justices to form a majority to dispose of it.

Koehler v. Engle, affirmed by a 4-4 vote, March 26, 1984. *Per curiam* (unsigned) opinion; Marshall did not participate.

The court left intact an appeals court ruling that a trial judge improperly shifted the burden of proof to a defendant charged with murder when he instructed the jury that malice can be implied from any deliberate and cruel act, and that a person is presumed to intend the natural consequences of his actions.

James v. Kentucky, decided by a 7-1 vote, April 18, 1984. White wrote the opinion; Rehnquist dissented. Marshall did not participate in the decision.

A defendant whose lawyer asked the judge to admonish the jury not to draw any adverse inference from his failure to testify in his own behalf was, by the denial of that request, deprived of his right to have the jury so instructed to protect his right to remain silent.

Waller v. Georgia, Cole v. Georgia, decided by a 9-0 vote, May 21, 1984. Powell wrote the opinion.

A defendant's right to a public trial extends to pretrial hearings concerning the suppression of evidence. Such a hearing may be closed over a defendant's objection only if there is an overriding interest likely to be prejudiced by an open hearing. Even then, only as much of the hearing as is required to serve that interest may be closed, and the judge must consider reasonable alternatives to closure and make findings to support closure.

The court held that a Georgia judge erred in closing an entire seven-day hearing to protect evidence aired during several hours of the hearing.

Patton v. Yount, decided by a 6-2 vote, June 26, 1984. Powell wrote the opinion; Marshall did not participate; Brennan and Stevens dissented.

A murder defendant's second trial, four years after his first, was not prejudiced by excessive publicity. The record showed that publicity about the case diminished between the first and second trials and thus did not support his challenge to his conviction on these grounds.

Reed v. Ross, decided by a 5-4 vote, June 27, 1984. Powell wrote the opinion; Rehnquist, Brennan, Stevens and O'Connor dissented.

Where a constitutional claim is so novel that its legal basis is not reasonably available to an attorney, a defendant has cause for failing to raise that claim during his trial or appeal. Such claim may then serve as a basis for a request for a federal writ of habeas corpus.

A man convicted of murder in 1969 had valid cause not to challenge on appeal jury instructions requiring him to prove lack of malice in his actions. The Supreme Court did not rule such instructions improper until 1975.

Right to Counsel

United States v. Morrison (449 U.S. 361), decided by a 9-0 vote, Jan. 13, 1981. White wrote the opinion.

Without any showing that a defendant's right to the aid of counsel was infringed by the actions or remarks of federal agents, dismissal of the charges against her is too drastic a remedy for the misconduct of the federal agents.

Upjohn Co. v. United States (449 U.S. 383), decided by a 9-0 vote, Jan. 13, 1981. Rehnquist wrote the opinion.

The attorney-client privilege protects from disclosure virtually all communications involving legal matters between a corporation's counsel and its officers and employees. The court rebuffed the government's argument for a narrower privilege, protecting communications between only the attorney and a "control group" of officers and managers, the persons who in fact determine company policy.

Wood v. Georgia (450 U.S. 261), decided by a 5-4 vote, March 4, 1981. Powell wrote the opinion; White, Brennan, Marshall and Stewart dissented.

Because of a possible conflict of interest on the part of the lawyer who was paid by an employer to represent his employees who were charged with distributing obscene materials in an "adult" theater and bookstore, this case is not the appropriate one in which to decide the question it presents — whether it is constitutional, under the guarantee of equal protection, to imprison a probationer solely because he is unable to make the required installment payments on his fine. The state court that heard this case should reconsider it, looking at the conflict-of-interest situation.

Fair Trial

In all criminal prosecutions, the accused shall enjoy the right to a speedy and public trial, by an impartial jury of the state and district wherein the crime shall have been committed ... and to be informed of the nature and cause of the accusation; to be confronted with the witnesses against him; to have compulsory process for obtaining witnesses in his favor, and to have the assistance of counsel for his defense.

Sixth Amendment, U.S. Constitution

Estelle v. Smith (451 U.S. 454), decided by a 9-0 vote, May 18, 1981. Burger wrote the opinion.

It is unconstitutional for a state to impose a sentence of death on a defendant, basing that sentence in part on psychiatric testimony derived from an interview of the defendant by a state-appointed psychiatrist, when the defendant was not warned, prior to the interview, that he had the right to have his attorney present during the interview and to remain silent during the interview.

Edwards v. Arizona (451 U.S. 477), decided by a 9-0 vote, May 18, 1981. White wrote the opinion.

Once a defendant has invoked his right to have his attorney present during police questioning, all interrogation by police must cease and may not resume until the attorney is present or the defendant initiates a new conversation.

Morris v. Slappy (461 U.S. 1), decided by a 9-0 vote, April 20, 1983. Burger wrote the opinion.

A California trial judge did not deny a rape and burglary defendant his constitutional right to the aid of legal counsel when he refused to delay the trial after the defendant's first appointed defense counsel became ill and had to be replaced by another appointed attorney.

Oregon v. Bradshaw (462 U.S. 1039), decided by a 5-4 vote, June 23, 1983. Rehnquist wrote the opinion announcing the judgment of the court and joined by three other justices; Powell concurred; Marshall, Brennan, Blackmun and Stevens dissented.

A man arrested for drunken driving and informed of his right to remain silent and have the assistance of an attorney, who first says that he wishes to have his attorney present before any further questioning but later, before the attorney arrives, asks a policeman, "Well, what is going to happen to me now?" is not denied his constitutional rights by police who remind him of his request for counsel and then go on to converse with the suspect.

Jones v. Barnes (463 U.S. 745), decided by a 7-2 vote, July 5, 1983. Burger wrote the opinion; Brennan and Marshall dissented.

Court-appointed defense attorneys are not required to raise on appeal every non-frivolous claim suggested by their clients.

McKaskle v. Wiggins, decided by a 6-3 vote, Jan. 23, 1984. O'Connor wrote the opinion; White, Brennan and Marshall dissented.

So long as a defendant who wishes to act as his own attorney retains control over the organization and conduct of his defense and his role in that defense, some participation of standby appointed counsel does not deny him his right to act as his own attorney.

Flanagan v. United States, decided by a 9-0 vote, Feb. 21, 1984. O'Connor wrote the opinion.

A federal judge's decision to disqualify a single defense counsel who is representing all four defendants in a criminal case is not an immediately appealable order. Such an order may be reviewed by an appeals court only after trial.

Solem v. Stumes, decided by a 6-3 vote, Feb. 29, 1984. White wrote the opinion; Stevens, Brennan and Marshall dissented.

The Supreme Court's decision in *Edwards v. Arizona* (1981), which held that once a suspect has invoked his right to counsel, any subsequent conversation between him and police must be initiated by the suspect, should not be applied retroactively to events occurring before it was announced.

Strickland v. Washington, decided by an 8-1 vote, May 14, 1984. O'Connor wrote the opinion; Marshall dissented.

A defendant who claims his attorney was so ineffective that he was denied his constitutional right to the aid of counsel must show that the lawyer made errors at the trial so serious that they resulted in the defendant's being denied a fair trial. Without such a showing, this claim cannot succeed.

United States v. Cronic, decided by a 9-0 vote, May 14, 1984. Stevens wrote the opinion.

An appeals court erred when it inferred from an appointed attorney's lack of criminal law experience, and the brief period he was given to prepare for trial, that a defendant was denied the right to the effective aid of counsel. Such a conclusion must be supported by evidence of serious errors by counsel that so prejudiced the trial that the defendant was denied a fair trial.

United States v. Gouveia, decided by an 8-1 vote, May 29, 1984. Rehnquist wrote the decision; Marshall dissented.

Prison inmates, placed in administrative detention under suspicion of murdering a fellow inmate, are not entitled to have attorneys appointed to aid them until they are formally charged with a crime.

Nix v. Williams, decided by a 7-2 vote, June 11, 1984. Burger wrote the opinion; Brennan and Marshall dissented.

The court approved an "inevitable discovery" exception to the exclusionary rule, which bars the use at trial of evidence obtained in violation of a defendant's rights. Under this exception, such evidence may be used if the prosecution can prove by a preponderance of the evidence that it ultimately would have been discovered by lawful means.

The ruling came in the case of a man twice convicted of murder. In 1977, the justices reversed the first conviction because they found that the defendant had been denied his right to counsel by police who had persuaded him, by their conversation with each other during a long car trip without defendant's counsel, to lead them to the body of his victim *(Brewer v. Williams).*

In 1984, however, the court upheld the man's second conviction, rejecting arguments that any evidence related to the body of the victim was inadmissible as the "fruit" of police misconduct. The court held that because the body would inevitably have been discovered by a search then under way, the evidence could be used.

Eighth Amendment

Cruel and Unusual Punishment

Rhodes v. Chapman (452 U.S. 337), decided by an 8-1 vote, June 15, 1981. Powell wrote the opinion; Marshall dissented.

The constitutional ban on cruel and unusual punishment is not invariably offended by the practice, in a state maximum security prison, of placing two inmates in a cell for one.

Eddings v. Oklahoma (455 U.S. 104), decided by a 5-4 vote, Jan. 19, 1982. Powell wrote the opinion; Burger, White, Blackmun and Rehnquist dissented.

The death sentence imposed upon a defendant who was 16 when he killed a state patrolman must be set aside — and the sentence reconsidered by lower courts — because the sentencing judge refused to consider such potentially mitigating factors as the defendant's unhappy childhood and alleged emotional disturbance at the time of the crime. The Eighth Amendment requires that the sentencing authority in capital cases consider all relevant aspects of the individual offender's character and record and the circumstances of the particular crime.

Zant v. Stephens (456 U.S. 410), decided by a 6-3 vote, May 3, 1982. *Per curiam* (unsigned) opinion; Brennan, Marshall and Powell dissented.

The court returned this case to the Georgia Supreme Court, asking it to explain what basis there was in state law for holding a death sentence still valid after the state court had set aside one of the aggravating circumstances justifying the death penalty.

Hopper v. Evans (456 U.S. 605), decided by votes of 9-0 and 7-2, May 24, 1982. Burger wrote the opinion; Brennan and Marshall dissented in part.

The court reinstated the death sentence imposed on a convicted killer under an Alabama death penalty law subsequently held constitutionally defective. The court explained that the constitutional flaw in the statute was irrelevant to this individual's case.

Enmund v. Florida (458 U.S. 782), decided by a 5-4 vote, July 2, 1982. White wrote the opinion; O'Connor, Burger, Powell and Rehnquist dissented.

It is cruel and unusual punishment, disproportionate to the actions of the defendant, for the driver of a getaway car to be sentenced to death after he is convicted of first-degree murder and robbery when he did not himself witness the killings or kill the victims.

"Robbery is a serious crime deserving serious punishment. It is not, however ... 'so grievous an affront to

---

Due Process, Equal Protection

... Nor shall any state deprive any person of life, liberty, or property, without due process of law; nor deny to any person within its jurisdiction the equal protection of the laws.

14th Amendment, U.S. Constitution

---

humanity that the only adequate response may be the penalty of death,'" wrote the majority.

Zant v. Stephens (456 U.S. 410), decided by a 7-2 vote, June 22, 1983. Stevens wrote the opinion; Marshall and Brennan dissented.

The court upheld a death sentence imposed upon a man convicted of a murder committed after he had escaped from jail, even though one of the factors upon which the court relied in determining his sentence was later found to be unconstitutional. Because two other valid factors were properly considered by the sentencing jury, the sentence could stand.

Solem v. Helm (463 U.S. 277), decided by a 5-4 vote, June 28, 1983. Powell wrote the opinion; Burger, White, Rehnquist and O'Connor dissented.

South Dakota violated the constitutional guarantee against cruel and unusual punishment when it imposed a life sentence without possibility of parole on a man convicted on seven separate occasions of non-violent felonies.

For the first time, the court applied this constitutional provision to judge the relative severity of a prison sentence. The court said the Constitution prohibits not only barbaric punishments but also sentences that are disproportionate to the crime committed.

Barefoot v. Estelle (463 U.S. 880), decided by a 6-3 vote, July 6, 1983. White wrote the opinion; Brennan, Marshall and Blackmun dissented.

It is permissible, although not preferred procedure, for a federal appeals court to consider and decide simultaneously a death row inmate's request for a stay of execution and the merits of his appeal from a district court's denial of his petition for a writ of *habeas corpus*.

Such expedited procedures may only be used when an inmate is bringing a collateral challenge to his sentence after he has unsuccessfully appealed his state court conviction and sentence. Courts employing these procedures must give full consideration to the inmate's arguments.

On a separate point, the court held that the Constitution does not forbid the state to use at the sentencing proceedings the testimony of psychiatrists as to a defendant's future dangerousness to society, even if they have not interviewed or examined the inmate himself. Federal rules of evidence permit the use of such expert witnesses.

Barclay v. Florida (463 U.S. 939), decided by a 6-3 vote, July 6, 1983. Rehnquist announced the decision in an opinion joined by three justices; Marshall, Brennan and Blackmun dissented.

A death sentence imposed on a man convicted of a racially motivated murder need not be held invalid because the judge, in explaining his decision to impose a death sentence instead of the jury-recommended sentence of life in prison, cited his own Army experiences during World War II when he saw Nazi concentration camps and their victims. A judge in such a situation need not act as if he were in a vacuum, as if he had no experience, the court said. "It is entirely fitting for the moral, factual and legal judgment of judges and juries to play a meaningful role in sentencing."

The sentence need not be overturned just because one of the aggravating factors upon which it was based — the defendant's criminal record — is not a factor spelled out by state law for consideration during sentencing.

California v. Ramos (463 U.S. 992), decided by a 5-4 vote, July 6, 1983. O'Connor wrote the opinion; Brennan, Marshall, Blackmun and Stevens dissented.

Nothing in the Constitution prohibits a state from requiring judges to instruct juries in capital punishment cases that a sentence of life imprisonment without parole may be commuted by the governor to a sentence permitting parole.

Pulley v. Harris, decided by a 7-2 vote, Jan. 23, 1984. White wrote the opinion; Brennan and Marshall dissented.

The Constitution does not require state courts to review a death sentence to ensure that it is proportional to the punishment imposed on others convicted of similar crimes. Such proportionality review is permitted, but not required, by the constitutional guarantee of due process.

Spaziano v. Florida, decided by a 6-3 vote, July 2, 1984. Blackmun wrote the opinion; Stevens, Brennan and Marshall dissented.

A judge may disregard a jury's recommendation of a life sentence and impose a sentence of death instead.

Nothing in the Constitution requires that only juries decide to sentence someone to die. A judge may be given sole responsibility for imposing sentence and thus is free to override a jury's recommendation.

Excessive Bail

Murphy v. Hunt (455 U.S. 478), decided by an 8-1 vote, March 2, 1982. *Per curiam* (unsigned) opinion. White dissented.

The court dismissed a case challenging as unconstitutional a Nebraska law that precludes bail before trial for defendants charged with forcible sexual offenses when the proof or the presumption is great that they committed the crime charged. The court held this case moot because the pretrial period had passed; the defendant had been tried and could not benefit from a ruling on pretrial bail.

Due Process

Watkins v. Sowders, Summitt v. Sowders (449 U.S. 341), decided by a 7-2 vote, Jan. 13, 1981. Stewart wrote the opinion; Brennan and Marshall dissented.

The due process guarantee does not require a state judge to hold a hearing out of the jury's presence every time a defendant challenges a witness' identification of him as improperly obtained.

Chandler v. Florida (449 U.S. 560), decided by an 8-0 vote, Jan. 26, 1981. Burger wrote the opinion; Stevens did not participate in the decision.

Nothing in the Constitution — neither the guarantee of due process nor the promise of a fair trial — forbids states to experiment with television coverage of criminal trials.

Connecticut Board of Pardons v. Dumschat (452 U.S. 458), decided by a 7-2 vote, June 17, 1981. Burger wrote the opinion; Stevens and Marshall dissented.

Even though the Connecticut Board of Pardons grants about three of every four applications it receives for commutation of a life sentence, the due process guarantee does not require the board to provide a written statement of the reasons for its action to every inmate denied commutation.

United States v. Goodwin (457 U.S. 368), decided by a 7-2 vote, June 18, 1982. Stevens wrote the opinion; Brennan and Marshall dissented.

The court will not presume prosecutorial vindictiveness, in violation of the due process clause, in every case in which a lesser charge is changed to a greater one prior to trial. The court refused to reverse the felony conviction of a man who was charged with a felony only after he asserted his right to a jury trial on misdemeanor charges arising out of the same incident. Without proof of prosecutorial vindictiveness, the court refused to presume such misconduct on the part of the government.

United States v. Valenzuela-Bernal (458 U.S. 858), decided by a 7-2 vote, July 2, 1982. Rehnquist wrote the opinion; Brennan and Marshall dissented.

An individual charged for transporting an illegal alien failed to demonstrate that he was denied his Fifth Amendment right to due process and his Sixth Amendment right to compel the presence of witnesses by the government's deportation of two of his illegal alien passengers after the government concluded that they possessed no evidence material to his prosecution.

Marshall v. Lonberger (459 U.S. 422), decided by a 5-4 vote, Feb. 22, 1983. Rehnquist wrote the opinion; Stevens, Brennan, Marshall and Blackmun dissented.

A federal court erred when it threw out a state court murder conviction on grounds that the defendant was denied due process by the admission, at his trial, of the fact that four years before the murder he had pleaded guilty to attempted murder.

This was not admitted as evidence to prove his guilt of the pending charge but to serve as a factor upon which a death sentence could be based. He was sentenced to die. He challenged the use of the prior plea, arguing that it was not voluntarily made. The Supreme Court held that the federal court should not have disturbed the state court holding that the plea was voluntary and its use in this situation appropriate.

Jones v. United States (463 U.S. 354), decided by a 5-4 vote, June 29, 1983. Powell wrote the opinion; Brennan, Marshall, Blackmun and Stevens dissented.

A person found not guilty of a crime by reason of insanity may be confined in a mental institution for a longer period than he would have been imprisoned had he been convicted on the charge. The length of his hypothetical sentence is irrelevant to the purpose for which he was committed, and confinement beyond that term does not deprive him of liberty without due process of law.

Once it is established that a defendant is not guilty by reason of insanity, it is constitutional for the government to confine him until he has regained his mental health or is no longer a danger to himself or society.

Schall v. Martin, Abrams v. Martin, decided by a 6-3 vote, June 4, 1984. Rehnquist wrote the opinion; Brennan, Marshall and Stevens dissented.

For the first time, the court upheld a preventive detention law as constitutional. The justices ruled that New York's law permitting pretrial detention of juveniles when there is a serious risk that the juvenile may commit a serious crime before trial falls within the bounds set by the constitutional guarantee of due process.

Detention in such a case protects both the juvenile and

society, the court said, and the law contains sufficient procedural safeguards against violation of a juvenile's rights.

California v. Trombetta, decided by a 9-0 vote, June 11, 1984. Marshall wrote the opinion.

The due process guarantee does not require state police to preserve, for use by drunken driving defendants at trial, samples of a driver's breath at the time he or she was tested on an instrument measuring alcohol levels.

Thigpen v. Roberts, decided by a 7-2 vote, June 27, 1984. White wrote the opinion; O'Connor and Powell dissented.

Prosecutorial vindictiveness denied due process to a man who was charged with manslaughter while he was appealing his conviction on misdemeanor traffic offenses arising out of the fatal auto accident.

Hobby v. United States, decided by a 6-3 vote, July 2, 1984. Burger wrote the opinion; Marshall, Brennan and Stevens dissented.

Claims that blacks and women are discriminated against in the selection of federal grand jury foremen — who perform essentially ministerial functions — are not sufficient reason to conclude that a white male defendant indicted by a grand jury has been denied his due process right to fair treatment.

Wasman v. United States, decided by a 9-0 vote, July 3, 1984. Burger wrote the opinion.

When a defendant is retried on a charge after winning a reversal of his first conviction on appeal, the judge may impose a more severe sentence following a new conviction if he can cite conduct or events that occurred subsequent to the first sentencing that justify a harsher sentence the second time around.

Equal Protection

Bearden v. Georgia (461 U.S. 660), decided by a 9-0 vote, May 24, 1983. O'Connor wrote the opinion.

The guarantee of equal protection of the laws prohibits states from automatically revoking the probation of a defendant who fails to pay a fine or make some sort of financial restitution.

Such a revocation may be constitutional if an evaluation of the particular case in question shows the probationer has not made sufficient good faith efforts to pay the fine, and no alternative, such as community service or an extended payment schedule, is adequate to fulfill the state's interest in punishing him and deterring future crimes.

Organized Crime

United States v. Turkette (452 U.S. 576), decided by an 8-1 vote, June 17, 1981. White wrote the opinion; Stewart dissented.

Title IX of the Organized Crime Control Act of 1970 (PL 91-452) — Racketeer Influenced and Corrupt Organizations Act — was intended to reach both legitimate and illegitimate enterprises, allowing prosecution of persons who conduct the affairs of an enterprise in interstate commerce through a pattern of racketeering activities, whether that enterprise is completely illegitimate or was initially

legitimate and has been taken over by organized crime.

Russello v. United States, decided by a 9-0 vote, Nov. 1, 1983. Blackmun wrote the opinion.

Under the 1970 Racketeer Influenced and Corrupt Organizations Act, federal prosecutors may force organized crime figures to forfeit all profits and proceeds from racketeering activity, as well as their share in the business itself.

General

Ralston v. Robinson (454 U.S. 201), decided by a 6-3 vote, Dec. 2, 1981. Marshall wrote the opinion; Stevens, Brennan and O'Connor dissented.

A person sentenced initially under the rehabilitation-oriented Youth Corrections Act of 1950 who subsequently receives an adult sentence for crimes committed in prison may be treated thereafter as an adult if the judge imposing the adult term determines that the youth will not benefit from further treatment under the Youth Corrections Act.

McElroy v. United States (455 U.S. 642), decided by an 8-1 vote, March 23, 1982. O'Connor wrote the opinion; Stevens dissented.

Federal law barring the transportation of forged securities in interstate commerce does not require proof that the security was forged *before* traveling across state lines, but only that the security was forged at some point *and* was transported in interstate commerce.

Williams v. United States (458 U.S. 279), decided by a 5-4 vote, June 29, 1982. Blackmun wrote the opinion; White, Brennan, Marshall and Burger dissented.

Federal law making it a crime to make a false statement or to willfully overvalue an asset in order to influence the action of certain financial institutions does not apply to the deposit of "bad checks" in federally insured banks.

Dickerson v. New Banner Institute Inc. (460 U.S. 103), decided by a 5-4 vote, Feb. 23, 1983. Blackmun wrote the opinion; Brennan, Rehnquist, Stevens and O'Connnor dissented.

The federal law that makes it illegal for convicted felons to ship, transport or receive any firearm or ammunition in interstate commerce or to engage in the business of importing, manufacturing, or dealing in firearms applies to a man who pleaded guilty to a state crime of carrying a concealed handgun, was placed on probation for that crime, and subsequently had his record expunged of that judgment.

Tuten v. United States (460 U.S. 660), decided by a 9-0 vote, March 30, 1983. Marshall wrote the opinion.

In imposing sentence under a recidivist sentencing law, a trial court may consider the fact that the defendant was earlier placed on probation for two years under the Youth Corrections Act, and that this probationary sentence had not been set aside.

Bell v. United States (462 U.S. 356), decided by an 8-1 vote, June 13, 1983. Powell wrote the opinion; Stevens dissented.

The Federal Bank Robbery Act, which makes it a crime to steal money from a bank, proscribes the crime of obtaining money from a bank under false pretenses as well as the crime of actually robbing a bank.

Dixson v. United States, Hinton v. United States, decided by a 5-4 vote, Feb. 22, 1984. Marshall wrote the opinion; O'Connor, Brennan, Rehnquist and Stevens dissented.

Officials of a community-based private social service corporation that administers federal grant funds for a city are "public officials" subject to prosecution for bribery under the federal law barring bribery of public officials.

United States v. One Assortment of 89 Firearms, decided by a 9-0 vote, Feb. 22, 1984. Burger wrote the opinion.

The acquittal of a gun owner on charges of dealing in firearms without a license, in violation of federal law, does not bar a subsequent action by the government seeking forfeiture of his firearms.

United States v. Rodgers, decided by a 9-0 vote, April 30, 1984. Rehnquist wrote the opinion.

The law that prohibits knowing and willful false statements in any matter "within the jurisdiction of any department or agency of the United States" applies to statements made to Federal Bureau of Investigation and U.S. Secret Service concerning a fictitious plot to assassinate the president.

New York v. Uplinger, dismissed by a 5-4 vote as improvidently granted, May 29, 1984. *Per curiam* (unsigned) opinion; Burger, White, O'Connor and Rehnquist dissented.

After argument, the court dismissed New York's appeal of a state court decision holding unconstitutional a state law that prohibited loitering "in a public place for the purpose of engaging, or soliciting another person to engage, in deviate sexual intercourse or other sexual behavior of a deviate nature."

Mabry v. Johnson, decided by a 9-0 vote, June 11, 1984. Stevens wrote the opinion.

A defendant's acceptance of a plea bargain does not give him any constitutional right to have that bargain enforced. Withdrawal of the bargain by a prosecutor, before entry of plea, is no basis for challenging a later guilty plea entered in keeping with another less favorable plea bargain.

United States v. Yermian, decided by a 5-4 vote, June 27, 1984. Powell wrote the opinion; Rehnquist, Brennan, Stevens and O'Connor dissented.

An individual may be convicted of making false statements in a "matter within the jurisdiction of any department or agency of the United States" without the prosecution proving that he knew that the false statement came within federal jurisdiction.

Individual and Civil Rights

Abortion

H. L. v. Matheson (450 U.S. 398), decided by a 6-3 vote, March 23, 1981. Burger wrote the opinion; Marshall, Brennan and Blackmun dissented.

Utah law, which requires a doctor to notify the parents of a minor upon whom he is to perform an abortion, does not violate the minor's right of privacy in deciding whether to have the abortion, at least, when it is applied as in this case to an immature minor who is still dependent upon her parents. The law does not allow the parents to veto the abortion decision, but simply requires that they be notified beforehand.

City of Akron v. Akron Center for Reproductive Health Inc., Akron Center for Reproductive Health Inc. v. City of Akron (462 U.S. 416), decided by a 6-3 vote, June 15, 1983. Powell wrote the opinion; White, Rehnquist and O'Connor dissented.

The court held unconstitutional provisions of an Akron, Ohio, ordinance requiring that all abortions after the first trimester of pregnancy be performed in full-service hospitals; that physicians obtain the consent of a parent or legal guardian before performing an abortion on a minor under age 16; that physicians recite to women seeking abortions a litany of information about fetal development, alternatives to abortion and possible abortion complications; that the attending physician and no one else inform a patient of the particular risks associated with her own pregnancy or abortion; that there be a 24-hour waiting period between the time a woman signs a consent form authorizing an abortion and the time it is performed; and that fetal remains be given a "humane" disposal.

The court held all these requirements to be unreasonable infringements upon a woman's right to decide to have an abortion.

Planned Parenthood Association of Kansas City, Mo. v. Ashcroft, Ashcroft v. Planned Parenthood Association of Kansas City, Mo. (462 U.S. 476), decided by votes of 5-4 and 6-3, June 15, 1983. Powell wrote the opinion; Blackmun, Brennan, Marshall and Stevens dissented in part; O'Connor, White and Rehnquist dissented in part.

The court upheld provisions of a Missouri law requiring "unemancipated" minors to obtain parental or judicial consent for an abortion. This requirement was permissible, while a similar one in the Akron ordinance (above) was not, because Missouri's requirement spelled out an alternative means of obtaining consent for a minor who could not or would not obtain parental consent. The vote on this issue was 5-4.

The court also upheld requirements that tissue from an abortion be submitted to a pathologist for examination and that a second physician be present at late-pregnancy abortions. These rulings came by a 5-4 vote.

The court struck down, 6-3, a requirement that all abortions after the first trimester be performed in a general-care hospital.

Simopoulos v. Virginia (462 U.S. 506), decided by an 8-1 vote, June 15, 1983. Powell wrote the opinion; Stevens dissented.

The court upheld Virginia's law requiring that second-trimester abortions be performed in licensed hospitals. The court distinguished this hospitalization requirement from those struck down in the Akron and Missouri cases (above) because the Virginia law defined licensed outpatient surgical clinics as hospitals, and thus did not automatically increase the cost of an abortion.

Affirmative Action

Minnick v. California Department of Corrections (452 U.S. 105), decided by an 8-1 vote, June 1, 1981. Stevens wrote the opinion; Stewart dissented.

The court dismissed a challenge to California's corrections department's affirmative action plan, which allowed use of race or sex as an affirmative factor in job assignment and promotion decisions. The court dismissed the case because the record was ambiguous and required clarification by the state courts.

Boston Firefighters Union, Local 718 v. Boston Chapter, NAACP, Boston Police Patrolmen's Association v. Castro, Beecher v. Boston Chapter, NAACP (461 U.S. 477), decided by an 8-0 vote, May 16, 1983. *Per curiam* (unsigned) opinion; Marshall did not participate in the ruling.

After hearing oral arguments in this major affirmative action case, the court sent it back to lower courts for consideration of whether the matter was moot.

The Boston police and firemen's unions, backed by the Reagan administration, had argued that the principle of affirmative action had been extended too far by a federal judge. In order to preserve recent court-ordered minority hiring gains, the judge had ordered the city to ignore the usual seniority rule of "last hired, first fired" in making budget-dictated layoffs.

Subsequently, the Massachusetts Legislature ordered the police and fire departments to reinstate the laid-off workers and to guarantee them that they would not again be laid off for fiscal reasons.

Firefighters Local Union #1784 v. Stotts, decided by a 6-3 vote, June 11, 1984. White wrote the opinion; Brennan, Marshall and Stevens dissented.

Federal judges may not override a valid seniority system to preserve the jobs of black workers hired under an affirmative action plan.

The court overturned a federal court order directing the Memphis, Tenn., fire department to ignore its usual rule of "last hired, first fired" in carrying out budget-dictated layoffs.

The court held that the lower court lacked the authority to issue an order modifying the city's good-faith seniority system, the sort of system the Civil Rights Act of 1964 expressly immunized from challenge.

Aliens

Cabell v. Chavez-Salido (454 U.S. 432), decided by a 5-4 vote, Jan. 12, 1982. White wrote the opinion; Blackmun, Brennan, Marshall and Stevens dissented.

California may require that all peace officers be U.S. citizens, even when the category is a broad one, encompassing deputy probation officers. Such officers both exercise and symbolize the power of the political community and it is reasonable that they be required to be citizens.

Plyler v. Doe, Texas v. Certain Named and Unnamed Undocumented Alien Children (457 U.S. 202), decided by a 5-4 vote, June 15, 1982. Brennan wrote the opinion; Burger, Rehnquist, White and O'Connor dissented.

The 14th Amendment guarantees the equal protection of the laws to illegal aliens present in the United States. They are clearly persons within the jurisdiction of the state in which they reside, even if they have entered the country and that state illegally. Texas, therefore, may not deny illegal alien children a free public education; there is no national policy nor sufficient state interest presented to justify this action.

Toll v. Moreno (458 U.S. 1), decided by a 7-2 vote, June 28, 1982. Brennan wrote the opinion; Rehnquist and Burger dissented.

A state university policy of denying in-state status for purposes of tuition to non-immigrant aliens who live in the state because members of their families work nearby for international organizations is invalid under the supremacy clause because it conflicts with the national policy that encourages these aliens to establish a domicile in this country and provides them significant tax exemptions.

Landon v. Plasencia (459 U.S. 21), decided by votes of 9-0 and 8-1, Nov. 15, 1982. O'Connor wrote the opinion; Marshall dissented in part.

A permanent resident alien, charged upon return from temporary absence from the country with smuggling aliens, is not entitled to demand that the issues of 'entry' and possible exclusion be resolved in a deportation hearing instead of the exclusion hearing convened immediately, at the border, by the Immigration and Naturalization Service.

Immigration and Naturalization Service v. Phinpathya, decided by a 9-0 vote, Jan. 10, 1984. O'Connor wrote the opinion.

A deportable alien, absent from the United States for a three-month period during eight years of residence here, cannot avoid deportation by invoking a law authorizing suspension of deportation for an alien "who has been physically present in the United States for a continuous period of not less than seven years."

Bernal v. Fainter, decided by an 8-1 vote, May 30, 1984. Marshall wrote the opinion; Rehnquist dissented.

States may not deny resident aliens the right to become notaries public. The Constitution's guarantee of equal protection strictly limits the power of states to require that certain posts be held only by citizens.

In striking down a Texas law, the court ruled that the duties of a notary are not so closely bound up with self-government that the state is justified in reserving such jobs for U.S. citizens.

Immigration and Naturalization Service v. Stevic, decided by a 9-0 vote, June 5, 1984. Stevens wrote the opinion.

The Refugee Act of 1980 did not relax the standard of proof for persons who seek to avoid deportation by arguing that they will be subject to persecution in their homeland. Such persons still must prove that there is "a clear probability" of persecution in order to avoid deportation.

Sure-Tan v. National Labor Relations Board (NLRB), decided by votes of 7-2 and 5-4, June 25, 1984. O'Connor wrote the opinion; Rehnquist and Powell dissented in part; Brennan, Marshall, Stevens and Blackmun dissented in part.

Illegal aliens working in the United States are protected by federal labor law from reprisals for their efforts to organize a union, the court held, 7-2. The NLRB correctly held an employer guilty of an unfair labor practice

when he retaliated against employees organizing a union by reporting some of them to immigration authorities as illegal aliens.

But the court ruled, 5-4, that the appeals court reviewing the NLRB order exceeded its power when it ordered a minimum of six months' back pay for each of the alien workers. Such orders are properly tailored by the NLRB to each individual case.

Immigration and Naturalization Service v. Lopez-Mendoza, decided by a 5-4 vote, July 5, 1984. O'Connor wrote the opinion; Brennan, White, Marshall and Stevens dissented.

The exclusionary rule — which forbids the government to use evidence obtained in violation of a defendant's rights — cannot be invoked in civil deportation proceedings.

Attorneys' Fees

Blum v. Stenson, decided by a 9-0 vote, March 21, 1984. Powell wrote the opinion.

The court ruled that Congress, in passing the Civil Rights Attorneys' Fee Awards Act of 1976, did not intend judges to grant higher awards to attorneys in private law firms than to those in public-interest firms. The court rejected arguments that awards to public-interest firms should be based on costs, instead of on market rates charged by attorneys in private practice.

The court upheld an award of $79,000 to the Legal Aid Society of New York, which successfully represented a class of Medicaid recipients suing New York over an issue of eligibility. That fee was based on the market rate charged by New York attorneys for their services. The court reversed an additional fee award of almost $40,000, a bonus that it found unjustified by the facts of the situation.

Children

City of Mesquite v. Aladdin's Castle Inc. (455 U.S. 283), decided by votes of 9-0 and 7-2, Feb. 23, 1982. Stevens wrote the opinion; Powell and White dissented in part.

Sidestepping a ruling on whether or not children have a constitutional right to play coin-operated video games in shopping malls, the court sent this case back to a lower court for clarification of the appeals court ruling that an ordinance strictly limiting the use of such arcades by children was unconstitutional.

Mills v. Habluetzel (456 U.S. 91), decided by a 9-0 vote, April 5, 1982. Rehnquist wrote the opinion.

Once a state grants children the right to support from their natural fathers, the equal protection guarantee of the 14th Amendment prohibits the state from making it more difficult for illegitimate children than for legitimate children to exercise that right, unless the additional restrictions placed on the assertion of this right by illegitimate children are substantially related to a legitimate state interest. Texas unduly burdens this right by requiring that any suit brought to establish a child's paternity be brought within the first year of the child's life.

Pickett v. Brown (462 U.S. 1), decided by a 9-0 vote, June 6, 1983. Brennan wrote the opinion.

A Tennessee law requiring all paternity and support actions in behalf of illegitimate children to be filed by the

time the child is two years old is unconstitutional. Such a law denies illegitimate children the equal protection of the law because it imposes a time limit on their right to paternal support that is not imposed on legitimate children.

Lehr v. Robertson (463 U.S. 248), decided by a 6-3 vote, June 27, 1983. Stevens wrote the opinion; White Marshall and Blackmun dissented.

An unwed father who has developed no significant relationship with his child and does not seek to establish any legal tie with the child until after the child is two years old has no right to be notified by the state when the child is to be adopted by someone else.

The Constitution's guarantee of equal protection does not prevent a state from dealing differently with a parent who has established a relationship with his illegitimate child than it deals with one who has not.

Citizenship

Fedorenko v. United States (449 U.S. 490), decided by a 7-2 vote, Jan. 21, 1981. Marshall wrote the opinion; White and Stevens dissented.

A Russian native who concealed from immigration and naturalization officials the fact that he had served as a concentration camp guard must be stripped of his U.S. citizenship, acquired by naturalization in 1970. The concealment of his wartime activities more than 20 years earlier — when he obtained a visa to enter the United States under the Displaced Persons Act — rendered his eventual naturalization invalid because his admission to the United States was not lawful.

Zobel v. Williams (457 U.S. 55), decided by an 8-1 vote, June 14, 1982. Burger wrote the opinion; Rehnquist dissented.

Alaska violated the guarantee of equal protection when it provided for distribution of an oil and gas income dividend to each resident based on the number of years he or she had lived in Alaska since 1959, the year Alaska became a state. Alaska showed no valid state interest that was rationally served by distinguishing between individuals who were living in Alaska in 1959 and those who had come there to live since.

Kolender v. Lawson (461 U.S. 352), decided by a 7-2 vote, May 2, 1983. O'Conner wrote the opinion; White and Rehnquist dissented.

The court struck down as unconstitutionally vague a California law that permitted police to arrest anyone whom they stopped, suspecting of criminal activity, who failed to provide "credible and reliable" identification. By providing no standard by which police could judge the identification such a person might offer, the law left too much discretion in the hands of police. This encouraged arbitrary enforcement in violation of the constitutional guarantee of due process, the court said.

Civil Rights

City of Memphis v. Greene (451 U.S. 100), decided by a 6-3 vote, April 20, 1981. Stevens wrote the opinion; Marshall, Brennan and Blackmun dissented.

The decision by the City Council of Memphis, Tenn., to close off part of a street to reduce traffic and noise and to protect the safety of resident children — all of whom

were white — did not infringe on property rights of nearby black residents who were forced to use other streets through the now-closed area nor did this action constitute a "badge of slavery" forbidden by the 13th Amendment abolishing slavery.

The only "injury" that resulted from the action was too trivial to constitute a violation of the law or the Constitution. Without any evidence that the closing was racially motivated, it could not be successfully challenged as a "badge of slavery."

Consumers

Anderson Bros. Ford and Ford Motor Credit Co. v. Valencia (452 U.S. 205), decided by a 5-4 vote, June 8, 1981. White wrote the opinion; Stewart, Burger, Brennan and Marshall dissented.

The Truth in Lending Act does not require a creditor to disclose to a consumer who is borrowing money to buy a car that the consumer may forfeit certain insurance premiums to the creditor if the physical damage insurance on the car is canceled.

American Express Co. v. Koerner (452 U.S. 233), decided by a 9-0 vote, June 8, 1981. Blackmun wrote the opinion.

The procedures set out in the Truth in Lending Act for correcting credit card billing errors do not apply when the cardholder is a business rather than an individual.

Customs

United States v. $8,850 in U.S. Currency (461 U.S. 555), decided by an 8-1 vote, May 23, 1983. O'Connor wrote the opinion; Stevens dissented.

An 18-month delay between the seizure of currency for failure to declare it upon entering the country and the filing of a civil forfeiture action in federal court does not, without evidence of prejudice to the person from whom the currency was taken, violate that person's right to due process of law.

Damage Suits

Paratt v. Taylor (451 U.S. 527), decided by an 8-1 vote, May 18, 1981. Rehnquist wrote the opinion; Marshall dissented.

A prison inmate's right to due process was not violated when state prison officials lost a $23.50 hobby kit he ordered in the mail. State laws provide an adequate remedy for such a loss; a suit under the Civil Rights Act of 1871 — Section 1983 in modern form — is not justified by such a trivial "injury."

O'Dell v. Espinoza (456 U.S. 430), dismissed May 3, 1982. *Per curiam* (unsigned) opinion.

The court dismissed for want of jurisdiction a case from Colorado in which that state's Supreme Court had allowed the children of a man killed by Denver police to bring a civil rights damage suit against the police. Because the state Supreme Court had sent this case back for trial, the U.S. Supreme Court found that its decision was not a final judgment in the case subject to review by the nation's highest court.

Patsy v. Board of Regents of the State of Florida (457 U.S. 496), decided by a 7-2 vote, June 21, 1982. Marshall wrote the opinion; Powell and Burger dissented.

An individual need not exhaust all available state administrative remedies for a grievance before filing a civil rights damage suit in federal court against the individuals responsible for denying him his constitutional or other federal rights under color of state law.

Rendell-Baker v. Kohn (457 U.S. 830), decided by a 7-2 vote, June 25, 1982. Burger wrote the opinion; Brennan and Marshall dissented.

The receipt of substantial state funds by a private school does not make the actions of the school, in discharging teachers or other employees, state action. Such discharges are not action "under color of state law" and cannot form the basis for civil rights damage suits against the school. "Acts of such private contractors do not become acts of the government by reason of their significant or even total engagement in performing public contracts," stated the court.

Blum v. Yaretsky (457 U.S. 991), decided by a 7-2 vote, June 25, 1982. Rehnquist wrote the opinion; Brennan and Marshall dissented.

The fact that a business is regulated by the state does not convert the actions of the business into state action. A state will normally be held responsible for a private decision only when it has exercised coercive power or provided so much encouragement that the choice made must be considered the choice of the state.

The action of privately owned and operated nursing homes in transferring patients from nursing homes to less intensive care facilities is not "state action" even though the transferred patients are Medicaid recipients, for whose care the state reimburses the nursing home, and the transfers are in accord with federal Medicaid regulations. The decision to transfer a particular patient is made not by any state official, but by physicians and nursing home administrators.

Lugar v. Edmondson Oil Co. (457 U.S. 922), decided by a 5-4 vote, June 25, 1982. White wrote the opinion; Burger, Powell, Rehnquist and O'Connor dissented.

The action of a creditor in obtaining a writ of attachment against the property of his debtor, a writ obtained from and enforced with the aid of state officials, a county clerk and sheriff, is state action and action under color of state law. The creditor may thus be sued for damages if the debtor feels that the attachment denied him his constitutional right to due process.

General Building Contractors Association v. Pennsylvania (458 U.S. 375), decided by a 7-2 vote, June 29, 1982. Rehnquist wrote the opinion; Brennan and Marshall dissented.

An employer may not be held liable to a civil rights damage suit by persons alleging that the union hiring hall, which the employer is obligated to use as part of a collective bargaining agreement, engages in racial discrimination unless there is proof that the employers intended to discriminate.

Briscoe v. LaHue (460 U.S. 325), decided by a 6-3 vote, March 7, 1983. Stevens wrote the opinion; Brennan, Marshall and Blackmun dissented.

A police officer who allegedly commits perjury during a state criminal trial is immune from a suit for damages by the defendant against whom he testified. The law that permits damage suits against persons who violate another's rights while acting "under color of law" does not permit such suits based on testimony in judicial proceedings. Nor does it authorize such suits against judges, prosecutors and others who perform official roles in the judicial process.

Kush v. Rutledge (460 U.S. 719), decided by a 9-0 vote, April 4, 1983. Stevens wrote the opinion.

The provision of the Civil Rights Act of 1871 that prohibits conspiracies to interfere with the administration of justice in the federal courts may be invoked as the basis of a federal lawsuit by a white male football player against his former football coaches and the state university athletic director, whether or not his race or sex played any part in the matter under dispute.

Smith v. Wade (461 U.S. 30), decided by a 5-4 vote, April 20, 1983. Brennan wrote the opinion; Rehnquist, O'Connor, Burger and Powell dissented.

A prison inmate who was beaten and raped by his cellmates can recover punitive damages under the Civil Rights Act of 1871 against the guard on duty at the time of the assault if he can show the guard acted with reckless or callous indifference to the prisoner's rights.

Hensley v. Eckerhart (461 U.S. 424), decided by a 5-4 vote, May 16, 1983. Powell wrote the opinion; Brennan, Marshall, Blackmun and Stevens dissented.

The court set out guidelines for federal judges to follow under the Civil Rights Attorneys' Fee Awards Act of 1976 in awarding attorneys' fees to successful plaintiffs in civil rights cases.

The court held that fees for winners may be reduced if they did not prevail on all their claims. The court ordered a federal judge to reconsider an award of $133,000 to attorneys representing inmates of Missouri state prisons and hospitals who won a suit contending that the state was violating the constitutional rights of inmates.

Chappell v. Wallace (462 U.S. 296), decided by a 9-0 vote, June 13, 1983. Burger wrote the opinion.

Military servicemen may not sue for damages superior officers who have allegedly violated their constitutional rights in the course of their military service.

Haring v. Prosise (462 U.S. 306), decided by a 9-0 vote, June 13, 1983. Marshall wrote the opinion.

A defendant who pleads guilty to state drug charges — and does not challenge as illegal the police search uncovering the evidence against him — can still sue police for damages, claiming that their search violated his constitutional rights.

Chardon v. Soto (462 U.S. 650), decided by a 6-3 vote, June 20, 1983. Stevens wrote the opinion; Rehnquist, White and Powell dissented.

Until Congress approves a federal statute of limitations governing civil rights damage suits, federal courts must apply state statutes of limitations where applicable. Thus a federal court was correct in applying Puerto Rico's statute to a suit brought by several education officials who charged they were demoted because of their political views.

United Brotherhood of Carpenters & Joiners of America, Local #610 v. Scott (463 U.S. 825), decided by a 5-4 vote, July 5, 1983. White wrote the opinion; Blackmun, Brennan, Marshall and O'Connor dissented.

Without some state involvement, victims of a conspiracy by union members to attack non-union workers to deprive them of their First-Amendment right not to join a union may not use the Civil Rights Act of 1871 to sue their attackers.

Use of the provision of the 1871 law that permits federal damage suits by persons deprived of equal protection of the laws or equal privileges and immunities does not apply to conspiracies in which there is no evidence of racial or class-based motive. The law was originally known as the Ku Klux Klan Act and it was designed to protect blacks against mob violence; it does not reach conspiracies motivated by economic concerns.

McDonald v. City of West Branch, Mich., decided by a 9-0 vote, April 18, 1984. Brennan wrote the opinion.

A discharged city policeman may seek damages in federal court for violations of his First Amendment rights, even though an arbitrator declared his firing to be for just cause. Arbitration decisions made pursuant to a collective bargaining agreement do not foreclose federal civil rights damage suits.

Board of Education of Paris Union School District No. 95 v. Vail, affirmed by a 4-4 vote, April 23, 1984. Marshall did not take part in the decision.

By an equally divided vote, the court affirmed an appeals court ruling that a public school teacher whose contract was not renewed had a constitutionally protected interest in continued employment and could sue the school board for depriving him of that interest without due process of law. The school had assured the teacher that he would continue to be employed and gave no explanation for failing to renew the contract.

Tower v. Glover, decided by a 9-0 vote, June 25, 1984. O'Connor wrote the opinion.

Public defenders are not immune from damage suits brought by defendants who claim that they conspired with state officials to violate their clients' constitutional rights.

Any time a private individual conspires with state officials to deprive another of his federal constitutional rights, he acts "under color of" state law and comes within the reach of the civil rights law permitting damage suits protesting such violations.

Davis v. Scherer, decided by votes of 9-0 and 5-4, June 28, 1984. Powell wrote the opinion; Brennan, Marshall, Blackmun and Stevens dissented.

Although state officials violated administrative regulations in discharging a state employee, they retain qualified immunity from a civil rights damage suit brought by the employee, who argued that he was discharged in violation of his constitutional rights.

Equal Protection

United States Railroad Retirement Board v. Fritz (449 U.S. 166), decided by a 7-2 vote, Dec. 9, 1980. Rehnquist wrote the opinion; Brennan and Marshall dissented.

The Railroad Retirement Act of 1974 does not violate the guarantee of equal protection by allowing some retired railroad workers to receive both Social Security and railroad retirement benefits and allowing others to receive only the railroad retirement benefits. Congress had plausible reasons for making that distinction, and that is sufficient to justify it.

Schweiker v. Wilson (450 U.S. 221), decided by a 5-4 vote, March 4, 1981. Blackmun wrote the opinion; Powell, Brennan, Marshall and Stevens dissented.

Congress did not violate the guarantee of equal protection by granting a small supplemental security income allowance for the purchase of "comforts" to residents of public mental institutions whose care is funded by Medicaid, but not providing such an allowance to residents whose care is not paid for by Medicaid.

Jones v. Helms (452 U.S. 412), decided by a 9-0 vote, June 15, 1981. Stevens wrote the opinion.

A state does not act unconstitutionally when it provides a more severe punishment for parents who leave the state after abandoning their children than for those who remain in the state after the abandonment.

Palmore v. Sidoti, decided by a 9-0 vote, April 25, 1984. Burger wrote the opinion.

A state court offends the guarantee of equal protection when it takes custody of a child from the natural mother because of her remarriage to someone of a different race. "Private biases may be outside the reach of the law, but the law cannot, directly or indirectly, give them effect," the court ruled.

Handicapped Rights

University of Texas v. Camenisch (451 U.S. 390), decided by a 9-0 vote. Stewart wrote the opinion.

Before the Supreme Court resolves the issue, a lower court first must consider the contention of a deaf graduate student that he is entitled, under the Rehabilitation Act of 1973, to have a sign-language interpreter with him in class paid for by the university he was attending.

Board of Education of Hendrick Hudson Central School District v. Rowley (458 U.S. 176), decided by a 6-3 vote, June 28, 1982. Rehnquist wrote the opinion; White, Brennan and Marshall dissented.

The Education for All Handicapped Children Act of 1975 obliged school districts receiving funds under the act to provide each handicapped student a free appropriate public education. But it did not obligate the state to provide all the aid necessary to ensure that a student realizes his or her maximum potential. Instead, the law requires only the provision of personalized instruction accompanied by sufficient support services to permit the child to benefit educationally from that instruction.

Community Television of Southern California v. Gottfried, Federal Communications Commission (FCC) v. Gottfried (459 U.S. 498), decided by a 7-2 vote, Feb. 22, 1983. Stevens wrote the opinion; Brennan and Marshall dissented.

The FCC is not required to use its licensing procedures to enforce the 1973 Rehabilitation Act, which requires recipients of federal grants to make special provisions for the handicapped population. That law is to be enforced by the agencies that administer the grant programs.

Public television stations are under no greater obligation than commercial stations to provide captioned programming or otherwise accommodate the needs of hearing-impaired viewers.

Consolidated Rail Corp. v. Darrone, decided by a 9-0 vote, Feb. 28, 1984. Powell wrote the opinion.

Persons denied jobs because of a handicap may sue to enforce Section 504 of the Rehabilitation Act of 1973, which forbids discrimination against otherwise qualified individuals because of a handicap "under any program or activity receiving federal financial assistance."

Section 504 can be used to contest job bias against handicapped persons whether or not the primary purpose of the federal aid received by the employer was to create jobs.

Irving Independent School District v. Tatro, decided by votes of 9-0 and 6-3, July 5, 1984. Burger wrote the opinion; Brennan, Marshall and Stevens dissented.

Under the Education for All Handicapped Children Act (PL 94-142), a school district is obligated to provide catheterization to a child with spina bifida who requires the procedure every three or four hours to relieve her bladder. This is a "related supportive service" necessary to enable the child to remain in school and can be provided by an instructed lay person.

Nothing in the law, however, permits a court to award attorneys' fees to the parents of the child who won this case or to other parents who successfully sue to force schools to provide services to their children under PL 94-142.

Smith v. Robinson, decided by a 6-3 vote, July 5, 1984. Blackmun wrote the opinion; Brennan, Stevens and Marshall dissented.

Parents who sue to compel the state to provide their handicapped child with the free appropriate public education they are guaranteed by the Education for All Handicapped Children Act may not be awarded their attorneys' fees by a lower court, because that law does not provide for such awards. Related laws permitting fee awards may not be used as the basis for fee awards in PL 94-142 cases.

Housing

Havens Realty Corp. v. Coleman (455 U.S. 363), decided by a 9-0 vote, Feb. 24, 1982. Brennan wrote the opinion.

Under the Fair Housing Act of 1968, "testers" — persons who inquire about available housing primarily to collect evidence of alleged discrimination — have legal standing to sue landlords or Realtors when they uncover discriminatory practices. The law grants all persons a legal right to truthful information about available housing, and this right is violated when rental agents give false information to a black "tester."

Inmates

Cuyler v. Adams (449 U.S. 433), decided by a 6-3 vote, Jan. 21, 1981. Brennan wrote the opinion; Rehnquist, Burger and Stewart dissented.

A prisoner held in a state that had adopted the uniform extradition act is entitled to the protections of that

act, including the right to a hearing before he is transferred to another jurisdiction. Such a prisoner has the right, under the Interstate Agreement on Detainers, to a hearing in which he can contest the request of a state for his transfer to it.

Weaver v. Graham (450 U.S. 24), decided by a 9-0 vote, Feb. 24, 1981. Marshall wrote the opinion.

A state is forbidden by the Constitution's ban on *ex post facto* laws from changing the rules for computing a prisoner's time off for good behavior and applying those new rules to prisoners whose crime was committed before the law was changed, at least when the change slows the rate at which "time off" can be accumulated.

Howe v. Smith (452 U.S. 473), decided by an 8-1 vote, June 17, 1981. Burger wrote the opinion; Stewart dissented.

Under federal law, states may transfer prisoners to the federal prison system for a variety of reasons including, but not limited to, special treatment in programs that are not available in state prisons.

Hewitt v. Helms (459 U.S. 460), decided by a 5-4 vote, Feb. 22, 1983. Rehnquist wrote the opinion; Stevens, Brennan, Marshall and Blackmun dissented.

Prisoners retain only a narrow range of protected liberty interests. A prisoner suspected of a key role in a prison riot was not denied his rights to liberty or due process when he was confined to administrative, non-disciplinary segregation following the riot, while prison officials investigated his role in the disturbance. The prisoner received notice of the charges against him, hearings on the evidence and the opportunity to present a statement to the hearing.

Olim v. Wakinekona (461 U.S. 238), decided by votes of 6-3 and 7-2, April 26, 1983. Blackmun wrote the opinion; Marshall, Brennan and Stevens dissented.

A prisoner is not denied his right to due process when he is transferred from the state of his residence where he was convicted to an out-of-state prison. Once convicted, a person's constitutionally protected liberty is curtailed to the point that the state may confine him in any prison it selects.

Block v. Rutherford, decided by a 6-3 vote, July 3, 1984. Burger wrote the opinion; Marshall, Brennan and Stevens dissented.

Nothing in the Constitution grants prison inmates or pretrial detainees the right to "contact visits" with friends or family members. These are visits at which the inmate is permitted to embrace or touch the visitors.

Jobs

Equal Employment Opportunity Commission (EEOC) v. Associated Dry Goods Corp. (449 U.S. 590), decided by votes of 5-2 and 6-1, Jan. 26, 1981. Stewart wrote the opinion; Blackmun dissented in part; Stevens dissented. Powell and Rehnquist did not participate in the decision.

Federal law forbids the EEOC to disclose to the public information it obtains from a defendant employer in the course of investigating job bias charges, but that law does not prevent the EEOC from disclosing such information to the person who filed the complaint against the employer.

Texas Department of Community Affairs v. Burdine (450 U.S. 248), decided by a 9-0 vote, March 4, 1981. Powell wrote the opinion.

An employer charged with job discrimination must prove that he had legitimate non-discriminatory reasons for his challenged actions, but it is then up to the person bringing the charge to show that the explanation is only a pretext for discrimination. The court reversed a lower court's order requiring an employer charged with a discriminatory promotion to prove that the person promoted was better qualified than the one passed over.

Northwest Airlines v. Transport Workers Union of America (451 U.S. 77), decided by an 8-0 vote, April 20, 1981. Stevens wrote the opinion; Blackmun did not take part in the decision.

Neither statutory nor common law gives an employer, found guilty of discriminating against women employees in wage matters, the right to force the union — with whom the employer had agreed on the contested wage scale — to contribute to the monetary settlement that the employer must make with the discriminated-against employees.

Lehman v. Nakshian (453 U.S. 156), decided by a 5-4 vote, June 26, 1981. Stewart wrote the opinion; Brennan, Marshall, Blackmun and Stevens dissented.

A federal employee suing the United States government for violating the Age Discrimination in Employment Act of 1967 is not entitled to a jury trial on those charges. When Congress waives the government's immunity from suit, as it did in this law, the person bringing the suit has the right to trial by jury only if Congress affirmatively grants that right in such cases.

Logan v. Zimmerman Brush Co. (455 U.S. 422), decided by a 9-0 vote, Feb. 24, 1982. Blackmun wrote the opinion.

A handicapped man was denied his right to due process when his complaint of job discrimination was dismissed by a state fair employment practices commission because the commission had failed to act on the matter within the time set by law.

Zipes v. TWA Inc., Independent Federation of Flight Attendants v. TWA Inc. (455 U.S. 385), decided by an 8-0 vote, Feb. 24, 1982. White wrote the opinion; Stevens did not participate in the decision.

A federal court acted within its authority when it awarded retroactive seniority to stewardesses grounded by an airline because they became mothers, when no similar restriction was imposed on male flight attendants who became fathers. The award of retroactive seniority was appropriate even for stewardesses who filed their claims later than the legal deadline. It was not necessary that the stewardesses file charges with the Equal Employment Opportunity Commission before filing the lawsuit against their former employer.

American Tobacco Co. v. Patterson (456 U.S. 63), decided by a 5-4 vote, April 5, 1982. White wrote the opinion; Brennan, Marshall, Blackmun and Stevens dissented.

Workers challenging a seniority system as discriminatory under the 1964 Civil Rights Act must prove *both* that it had an adverse effect on women or minorities *and* that it was adopted with the intent to discriminate against them.

When Congress exempted *bona fide* seniority systems from challenge under the 1964 Act, unless they were adopted with the intent to discriminate, it included that exemption in both systems then in effect *and* those adopted after the act's passage, the court held.

Pullman-Standard v. Swint, United Steelworkers v. Swint (456 U.S. 273), decided by a 7-2 vote, April 27, 1982. White wrote the opinion; Marshall and Blackmun dissented.

A court of appeals erred when it overturned a trial court finding that a seniority system used by the Pullman-Standard Co., a manufacturer of railroad cars, was not intended to discriminate against black workers. Unless it found that the trial court's conclusion was clearly erroneous, the appeals court should have sent the matter back to the trial court for consideration of additional evidence relevant to the question of discriminatory intent.

Kremer v. Chemical Construction Co. (456 U.S. 461), decided by a 5-4 vote, May 17, 1982. White wrote the opinion; Blackmun, Brennan, Marshall and Stevens dissented.

Once a state court has upheld a state agency's finding that there is no basis for a charge of job discrimination, a federal court may not re-litigate that issue in a case brought under Title VII of the 1964 Civil Rights Act.

In 1790 Congress passed a law directing that all U.S. courts afford the same full-faith-and-credit to state court judgments that would apply in the state's own courts. That law, still in effect, was not superseded by Title VII.

General Telephone Company of the Southwest v. Falcon (457 U.S. 147), decided by votes of 9-0 and 8-1, June 14, 1982. Stevens wrote the opinion; Burger dissented in part.

An individual who alleges that he was denied a *promotion* because he is Mexican-American may not bring a class action on behalf of employees who were denied *employment* for that reason.

Sumitomo Shoji America v. Avagliano (457 U.S. 176), decided by a 9-0 vote, June 15, 1982. Burger wrote the opinion.

A company constituted under the laws of the United States or a single state is a company of the United States, subject to the laws of the United States, and not eligible for the exemption contained in certain treaties made by the United States that allows foreign corporations operating in the United States to hire as they wish, free of the fair employment requirements of U.S. law.

Connecticut v. Teal (457 U.S. 440), decided by a 5-4 vote, June 21, 1982. Brennan wrote the opinion; Powell, Burger, Rehnquist and O'Connor dissented.

An employer sued for violating the Civil Rights Act of 1964 by using a non-job-related test to select candidates for promotion when that test excludes more blacks than whites from consideration for promotion may not use as a complete defense the "bottom line" argument that in fact, more eligible blacks than whites are promoted.

Ford Motor Co. v. Equal Employment Opportunity Commission (458 U.S. 219), decided by a 6-3 vote, June 28, 1982. O'Connor wrote the opinion; Blackmun, Brennan and Marshall dissented.

An employer charged with discrimination in hiring can terminate the period for which he may be held liable to the claimant for back pay by unconditionally offering the claimant the job he had previously refused to offer — even if this offer does not include seniority retroactive to the date of the alleged discriminatory refusal.

U.S. Postal Service Board of Governors v. Aikens (460 U.S. 711), decided by a 9-0 vote, April 4, 1983. Rehnquist wrote the opinion.

A plaintiff in a job discrimination suit under Title VII of the 1964 Civil Rights Act is not required to produce direct proof of deliberate discrimination; indirect or circumstantial evidence is sufficient to move his case into the next stage, in which the employer must justify his decision to hire or promote someone else rather than the plaintiff.

Crown, Cork & Seal Co. v. Parker (462 U.S. 345), decided by a 9-0 vote, June 13, 1983. Blackmun wrote the opinion.

The pendency of a class action job discrimination suit halts the running of the 90-day statute of limitations on individual suits by persons who have been notified by the Equal Employment Opportunity Commission (EEOC) of their right to challenge their discharge as illegal.

Even if the class action case fails to win certification, a discharged worker can file an individual lawsuit against his employer under Title VII of the 1964 Civil Rights Act even though more than 90 days have passed since his receipt of the EEOC notice.

Guardians Association v. Civil Service Commission of City of New York (463 U.S. 582), decided by votes of 7-2 and 5-4, July 1, 1983. White announced the judgment of the court and wrote an opinion joined in part by Rehnquist; Marshall and White dissented in part; Burger, Powell, Rehnquist and O'Connor dissented in part; Brennan, Stevens and Blackmun dissented in part.

Without proof of intent to discriminate, private plaintiffs who sue their employer, a recipient of federal funds, for discriminating against them on the basis of race and national origin may not win compensatory relief such as back pay or retroactive seniority.

In the absence of a showing of intent, Title VI of the 1964 Civil Rights Act, which bars racial or ethnic discrimination by recipients of federal funds, entitles plaintiffs only to injunctions against such practices or judgments declaring them illegal. The vote on this point was 7-2.

However, five members of the court indicated that government agencies are free to adopt regulations to enforce Title VI by denying federal aid to recipients whose actions are discriminatory in effect, regardless of intent.

Equal Employment Opportunity Commission (EEOC) v. Shell Oil Co., decided by votes of 9-0 and 5-4, April 2, 1984. Marshall wrote the opinion; O'Connor, Burger, Powell and Rehnquist dissented in part.

The court ruled unanimously that a lower court should enforce a subpoena issued by the EEOC to Shell, seeking the company's records as an initial step in investigating charges that the company discriminated against black and female employees.

By 5-4, the court upheld the EEOC procedures in filing such a complaint, rejecting Shell's argument that such a complaint should include specific dates and other details of the allegedly discriminatory actions.

Westinghouse Electric Corp. v. Vaughn, April 30, 1984. *Per curiam* (unsigned) opinion.

The court dismissed without comment the company's appeal of a federal district court finding that a black employee, who admittedly had some work-related problems, was disqualified as a machine operator primarily because of her race.

Cooper v. Federal Reserve Bank of Richmond, decided by an 8-0 vote, June 25, 1984. Stevens wrote the opinion.

Individual workers who charge that they were the victims of illegal discrimination by their employer can pursue those claims in separate lawsuits even though a group of employees of which they were a part failed to prove that the employer systematically discriminated against them.

Burnett v. Grattan, decided by a 9-0 vote, June 27, 1984. Marshall wrote the opinion.

Federal courts may "borrow" statutes of limitations from state laws for actions under the Civil Rights Acts. However, a federal court erred in applying a strict limitation from a state law providing for administrative resolution of job bias claims to a job bias suit brought under the century-old civil rights acts permitting such suits. The longer period permitted by state law for filing civil suits would have been a more appropriate choice.

Mentally Ill

Pennhurst State School and Hospital v. Terri Lee Halderman, Mayor of City of Philadelphia v. Halderman, Pennsylvania Association for Retarded Citizens v. Pennhurst State School and Hospital, Commissioners and Mental Health/Mental Retardation Administrators for Bucks County v. Halderman, Pennhurst Parents-Staff Association v. Halderman (451 U.S. 1), decided by votes of 9-0 and 6-3, April 20, 1981. Rehnquist wrote the opinion; White, Brennan and Marshall dissented in part.

The Developmentally Disabled Assistance and Bill of Rights Act of 1975 (PL 94-103) did not grant to mentally retarded persons an enforceable right to be treated in the least restrictive situation. The statement in the law that persons have a right to receive treatment and housing in a setting "that is least restrictive of . . . personal liberty" was a general "finding" by Congress — not an obligation imposed upon states receiving federal funds for treatment of the mentally retarded.

Mills v. Rogers (457 U.S. 291), decided by a 9-0 vote, June 18, 1982. Powell wrote the opinion.

The court sent back to the appeals court, for reconsideration in light of an intervening decision by the Massachusetts Supreme Judicial Court, a case involving the successful claim by mental patients at a Massachusetts hospital that they had a constitutional right, under the due process guarantee, to refuse treatment with anit-psychotic drugs.

Mentally Retarded Persons

Youngberg v. Romeo (457 U.S. 307), decided by a 9-0 vote, June 18, 1982. Powell wrote the opinion.

Mentally retarded persons in state institutions have a constitutional right to safe conditions, freedom of movement and sufficient training to enable them to move safely and freely within that institution. The guarantee against deprivation of personal liberty without due process of law means that such persons will only be restrained or allowed to remain in less than completely safe conditions as a result of the decision of a qualified professional.

Mortgage Holders

Mennonite Board of Missions v. Adams (462 U.S. 791), decided by a 6-3 vote, June 22, 1983. Marshall wrote the opinion; O'Connor, Powell and Rehnquist dissented.

Mortgage holders have a constitutional right to be notified by mail or in person of the pending tax sale of property in which they have an interest. An Indiana law entitling a mortgage holder only to notice by publication was insufficient.

Parents

Little v. Streater (452 U.S. 1), decided by a 9-0 vote, June 1, 1981. Burger wrote the opinion.

Connecticut denies a putative father his due process rights when it compels a mother receiving public assistance to file a paternity proceeding against the putative father of her child, but denies the putative father requested blood tests, which could show that he is not the father, unless he can pay for them.

Lassiter v. Department of Social Services of Durham County (452 U.S. 18), decided by a 5-4 vote, June 1, 1981. Stewart wrote the opinion; Blackmun, Brennan, Marshall and Stevens dissented.

An indigent mother does not have a constitutional right to the aid of free legal counsel when the state moves to terminate her legal relationship with her child. The court has generally held that due process requires that counsel be appointed for an indigent only when he is threatened with the loss of his physical personal liberty. It is his interest in his personal freedom that triggers the right to appointed counsel.

Santosky v. Kramer (455 U.S. 745), decided by a 5-4 vote, March 24, 1982. Blackmun wrote the opinion; Rehnquist, Burger, White and O'Connor dissented.

Natural parents have a right to due process at state proceedings to terminate their parental rights over their children. Parents have a fundamental liberty interest in the care, custody and management of their children, which they do not lose simply because they are not model parents. The interests involved in such a proceeding require that the state's charge that parents are unfit be proved by more than just a fair preponderance of the evidence. The state's charge must be proved by at least clear and convincing evidence before a state may completely and irrevocably terminate the rights of parents in their child.

Schools

Washington v. Seattle School District No. 1 (458 U.S. 457), decided by a 5-4 vote, June 30, 1982. Blackmun wrote the opinion; Powell, Burger, Rehnquist and O'Connor dissented.

A 1978 voter-initiated state law prohibiting school boards from voluntarily using busing and pupil reassignment to desegregate public schools violates the equal pro-

tection clause. The law, Initiative 350, is clearly racially discriminatory in intent and operation and restructures the process deciding education policy in the state, removing decisions about the voluntary use of busing from local school boards to the state level.

Crawford v. Board of Education of City of Los Angeles (458 U.S. 527), decided by an 8-1 vote, June 30, 1982. Powell wrote the opinion; Marshall dissented.

Proposition 1, a 1979 voter-initiated amendment to the state constitution denying state courts the power to order busing unless it is needed to remedy a specific violation of the U.S. Constitution, is permissible under the equal protection clause. This change in the state constitution simply adopts for state courts the standard federal courts use in deciding when to order busing for school desegregation.

Sex Discrimination

Kirchberg v. Feenstra (450 U.S. 455), decided by a 9-0 vote, March 23, 1981. Marshall wrote the opinion.

Louisiana's law (no longer in effect) that gave a husband the right to dispose of community property without a wife's consent violated the constitutional guarantee of equal protection.

Michael M. v. Superior Court of Sonoma County, Calif. (450 U.S. 464), decided by a 5-4 vote, March 23, 1981. Rehnquist wrote an opinion joined by three other justices; Stewart and Blackmun concurred; Brennan, White, Marshall and Stevens dissented.

A state does not discriminate unconstitutionally against men by allowing a man to be prosecuted for having sexual relations with a girl under 18 to whom he is not married but exempting the girl involved from criminal liability. The court upheld California's statutory rape laws against a constitutional challenge, finding that the distinction between its treatment of men and women was justified as an appropriate means of preventing illegitimate teenage pregnancies.

County of Washington v. Gunther (452 U.S. 161), decided by a 5-4 vote, June 8, 1981. Brennan wrote the court's opinion; Rehnquist, Burger, Stewart and Powell dissented.

Women workers may sue their employers under the 1964 Civil Rights Act for discriminating against them on the basis of sex without first proving that they were denied "equal pay for equal work," a violation of the Equal Pay Act. A violation of the Civil Rights Act ban on sex discrimination in the workplace can be shown initially by simply demonstrating that a woman's sex was used against her in determining how much she was paid, the court held.

Rostker v. Goldberg (453 U.S. 57), decided by a 6-3 vote, June 25, 1981. Rehnquist wrote the opinion; White, Marshall and Brennan dissented.

Congress did not violate the Constitution when it decided to exclude women from the military draft. Because women are barred by law and policy from combat, they are not "similarly situated" with men for purposes of draft registration and thus Congress may properly treat the sexes differently.

North Haven Board of Education v. Bell (456 U.S. 512), decided by a 6-3 vote, May 17, 1982. Blackmun

wrote the opinion; Powell, Burger and Rehnquist dissented.

Title IX of the Education Amendments of 1972 — which provides that "no person . . . shall, on the basis of sex, be excluded from participation in, be denied the benefits of, or be subjected to discrimination under any education program or activity receiving federal financial assistance" — authorizes federal monitoring of the employment practices, as well as the treatment of students, of recipient school districts, colleges and universities.

The sanction for violating this prohibition — termination of federal funds — is program-specific; that is, funds are to be terminated only to programs in which discrimination has been found to exist.

Mississippi University for Women v. Hogan (458 U.S. 718), decided by a 5-4 vote, July 1, 1982. O'Connor wrote the opinion; Burger, Blackmun, Powell and Rehnquist dissented.

The policy of a state-supported university that has historically admitted only women to its school of nursing violates the constitutional guarantee of equal protection when applied to deny admission to a man merely because of his sex. To justify a law that classifies individuals on the basis of sex an "exceedingly persuasive justification" must be presented. The state did not meet that test in this case.

Newport News Shipbuilding & Dry Dock Co. v. Equal Employment Opportunity Commission (462 U.S. 669), decided by a 7-2 vote, June 20, 1983. Stevens wrote the opinion; Rehnquist and Powell dissented.

Employers violate Title VII of the 1964 Civil Rights Act and discriminate among their employees on the basis of sex when their health insurance plans provided less comprehensive pregnancy coverage for the wives of male employees than for the company's female employees. Such discrimination gives male employees a less inclusive package of health benefits for their dependents than female employees receive.

Arizona Governing Committee for Tax Deferred Annuity and Deferred Compensation Plans v. Norris (463 U.S. 1073), decided by two 5-4 votes, July 6, 1983. *Per curiam* (unsigned) opinion; Burger, Blackmun, Powell and Rehnquist dissented; Marshall, White, Brennan and Stevens dissented in part.

An employer's retirement plan may not include an annuity option under which women workers upon retirement receive smaller monthly payments than men who have contributed the same amounts during their working career.

Title VII of the 1964 Civil Rights Act requires that employees be treated by their employers as individuals, not members of groups, in determining pay and other conditions of employment.

The fact that women as a group live longer than men as a group is not a permissible basis for paying them different monthly retirement benefits. Marshall, White, Brennan, Stevens and O'Connor formed the majority on this point.

However, O'Connor, Burger, Blackmun, Powell and Rehnquist formed a majority to hold that this decision would not affect retirement benefits paid to women already retired and no longer contributing to a system, but instead would apply only to retirement benefits derived from contributions made after this decision. Those benefits must be

calculated without regard to the sex of the recipient.

Grove City College v. Bell, decided by votes of 6-3 and 9-0, Feb. 28, 1984. White wrote the opinion; Brennan, Marshall and Stevens dissented.

Title IX of the 1972 Education Amendments, which bars sex discrimination in any "program or activity" receiving federal aid, does not apply to all programs at an institution. By 6-3, the court said the ban on sex bias applies only to the particular program receiving the aid.

Title IX does apply to schools or colleges that receive federal aid only indirectly, through federal grants or loans to their students, the court ruled unanimously.

Hishon v. King & Spalding, decided by a 9-0 vote, May 22, 1984. Burger wrote the opinion.

Title VII of the 1964 Civil Rights Act applies to law firms, like other employers, forbidding them to discriminate among their employees on the basis of race or sex.

A woman who charged that she was denied fair consideration for partnership by a law firm because of her sex should have a chance to prove those charges in court.

Tax Exemptions

Bob Jones University v. United States, Goldsboro Christian Schools v. United States (461 U.S. 574), decided by an 8-1 vote, May 24, 1983. Burger wrote the opinion; Rehnquist dissented.

The Internal Revenue Service (IRS) did not exceed its authority when it denied tax-exempt status to private schools that discriminate against blacks. In light of the clear national policy against racial discrimination in education, the IRS was correct in declaring in 1970 that it would no longer grant tax-exempt status to discriminatory private schools.

Although the two schools in these cases contended their discriminatory policies were based upon sincerely held religious beliefs, the court held that the First Amendment did not preclude IRS denial of tax-favored status. The national interest in eradicating racial discrimination in education "substantially outweighs whatever burden denial of tax benefits places" on the exercise of the First Amendment freedom of religion.

Allen v. Wright, decided by a 5-3 vote, July 3, 1984. O'Connor wrote the opinion; Brennan, Stevens and Blackmun dissented; Marshall did not participate.

Parents of black public school students who had not suffered any specific, personal injury as a result of existing federal policy concerning tax-exempt status for private schools lack legal standing to sue the Internal Revenue Service for being too lenient in enforcing that policy.

Taxpayers

United States v. Rodgers (461 U.S. 677), decided by votes of 9-0 and 5-4, May 31, 1983. Brennan wrote the opinion; Blackmun, Rehnquist, Stevens and O'Connor dissented.

The Internal Revenue Service can force the sale of a couple's jointly owned home if one of the owners is delinquent in paying federal taxes. The existence of a state homestead law, which gives both husband and wife full legal interest in the property, does not protect such property from this tax sale.

Tenants

Greene v. Lindsey (456 U.S. 444), decided by a 6-3 vote, May 17, 1982. Brennan wrote the opinion; O'Connor, Burger and Rehnquist dissented.

A Kentucky law that permits service of process by posting summons on the door of tenant's apartment in public housing, where notices are "not infrequently" removed by children before being seen by occupants, does not comply with an essential requirement of due process that tenants be adequately notified of pending eviction proceedings.

Veterans

Monroe v. Standard Oil Co. (452 U.S. 549), decided by a 5-4 vote, June 17, 1981. Stewart wrote the opinion; Burger, Brennan, Blackmun and Powell dissented.

The Vietnam Era Veterans' Readjustment Assistance Act of 1974 (PL 93-508) does not require an employer to provide preferential scheduling of work hours for an employee who must be absent from work to fulfill his military reserve obligations.

First Amendment Rights

Freedom of Expression

Flynt v. Ohio (415 U.S. 619), decided by a 5-4 vote, May 18, 1981. *Per curiam* (unsigned) opinion; Stevens, Brennan, Stewart and Marshall dissented.

Because there is no final state court ruling in this case — in which the publisher of a "men's magazine," *Hustler*, argues that he was unfairly singled out for prosecution under a state obscenity law by politicians angered by his publication of a non-obscene political cartoon — it should not be considered at this time by the Supreme Court and is dismissed.

Schad v. Borough of Mount Ephraim (452 U.S. 61), decided by a 7-2 vote, June 1, 1981. White wrote the opinion; Burger and Rehnquist dissented.

A borough may not, without infringing upon the rights guaranteed by the First Amendment, enact a zoning ordinance forbidding all live entertainment from the borough. Such a ban prohibits a wide range of expression long held to be within the protection of the First Amendment.

United States Postal Service v. Council of Greenburgh Civic Association (453 U.S. 114), decided by a 7-2 vote, June 25, 1981. Rehnquist wrote the opinion; Marshall and Stevens dissented.

Congress did not violate the guarantees of the First Amendment when it passed a law forbidding persons or groups to place unstamped letters, notices and other "mailable matter" in post boxes used by the U.S. Postal Service for delivering mail to private homes.

California Medical Association v. Federal Election Commission (453 U.S. 182), decided by a 5-4 vote, June 26, 1981. Marshall wrote the opinion; Stewart, Burger, Powell and Rehnquist dissented.

The Federal Election Campaign Act (PL 96-187), which limits to $5,000 per year the amount that one individual or unincorporated association can contribute to one

political action committee, does not violate the guarantee of equal protection or the First Amendment rights of the contributor.

Haig v. Agee (453 U.S. 280), decided by a 7-2 vote, June 29, 1981. Burger wrote the opinion; Brennan and Marshall dissented.

Congress, in passing the Passport Act of 1926 authorizing the secretary of state to grant and issue passports, authorized the secretary also to revoke a citizen's passport. If the secretary may deny an application for a passport, he may revoke a passport for the same reasons.

Revocation of the passport in this case did not violate the freedom to travel outside the United States, the First Amendment freedom of expression of the individual who lost his passport or the guarantee of due process.

Metromedia Inc. v. City of San Diego (453 U.S. 490), decided by a 6-3 vote, July 2, 1981. White wrote an opinion joined by three other justices; Brennan and Blackmun concurred; Stevens dissented in part; Burger and Rehnquist dissented in part.

San Diego violated the First Amendment guarantee of freedom of expression when it enacted an ordinance banning most billboards within the city.

Citizens Against Rent Control/Coalition for Fair Housing v. City of Berkeley (454 U.S. 290), decided by an 8-1 vote, Dec. 14, 1981. Burger wrote the opinion; White dissented.

Citizens have a First Amendment right to contribute as much as they wish to groups opposing or supporting ballot issues, and that right is violated when a city limits such contributions to $250. Such a limit infringes upon the First Amendment guarantees of freedom of expression and the right of association. "Contributions by individuals to support concerted action by a committee advocating a position on a ballot measure is beyond question a very significant form of political expression," stated the court.

Princeton University v. Schmid (455 U.S. 100), decided by an 8-0 vote, Jan. 13, 1982. *Per curiam* (unsigned) opinion; Brennan did not take part in consideration of this case.

The court dismissed this case after hearing it argued, finding that Princeton University lacked the standing to challenge a ruling by the New Jersey Supreme Court that a

---

Religion, Speech and Press

Congress shall make no law respecting an establishment of religion, or prohibiting the free exercise thereof; or abridging the freedom of speech, or of the press; or the right of the people peaceably to assemble, and to petition the Government for a redress of grievances.

First Amendment, U.S. Constitution

---

non-student's First Amendment rights were violated when he was prosecuted for trespassing after he distributed political materials on the university campus without obtaining permission from university officials.

Common Cause v. Schmitt, Federal Election Commission v. Americans for Change (455 U.S. 129), decided by a 4-4 vote, Jan. 19, 1982. O'Connor did not participate.

The evenly divided court upheld, without opinion, a lower court's ruling that Congress violated the First Amendment's guarantee of free speech when it limited to $1,000 the amount an independent and unauthorized political action committee could spend in a presidential campaign.

In re R. M. J. (455 U.S. 191), decided by a 9-0 vote, Jan. 25, 1982. Powell wrote the opinion.

State rules governing advertising by attorneys may regulate such speech only to the extent necessary to prevent deceptive or misleading ads. Missouri infringed too far upon the First Amendment guarantee of freedom of expression when it restricted the categories of information that could be provided in lawyers' ads and specified the phrases to be used to describe areas of legal practice.

Brown v. Hartlage (456 U.S. 45), decided by a 9-0 vote, April 5, 1982. Brennan wrote the opinion.

Kentucky applied its campaign law too strictly when it voided a candidate's election as county commissioner because he had promised, if elected, to serve at a reduced salary. The state court held that this promise violated an anti-bribery election law forbidding candidates to promise anything of value to anyone in order to obtain that person's vote. The Supreme Court disagreed, declaring that in applying the law to this case, the state was impermissibly curtailing a candidate's First Amendment freedom of expression.

Board of Education, Island Trees Union Free School District #26 v. Pico (457 U.S. 853), decided by a 5-4 vote, June 25, 1982. Brennan announced the court's decision in an opinion joined by three other justices; White concurred in the decision; Burger, Powell, Rehnquist and O'Connor dissented.

The decision of a local school board to remove certain books from high school and junior high school libraries is subject to certain restrictions imposed by the First Amendment guarantee of freedom of ideas and expression. The court sent to trial a case in which several students challenged such school board action. The justices directed the lower court to ascertain whether the board had acted to remove unpopular ideas from the library, which would be impermissible under the First Amendment, or to remove vulgar and irrelevant material from the library, which would be permissible.

New York v. Ferber (458 U.S. 747), decided by a 9-0 vote, July 2, 1982. White wrote the opinion.

Pornographic depictions of children are outside the protection of the First Amendment. State laws prohibiting the promotion of sexual performances by children under 16 do not violate the First Amendment.

NAACP v. Claiborne Hardware Co. (458 U.S. 886), decided by an 8-0 vote, July 2, 1982. Stevens wrote

the opinion; Marshall did not participate in the decision.

A non-violent 1966 boycott by civil rights demonstrators of the shops of white merchants in Port Gibson, Miss., was speech and conduct protected by the First Amendment. Violence, however, is not protected by the First Amendment, and a state court may assess damages against those responsible for such violence. But such liability must be based on a record that reflects the individuals' participation in violent activity; it may not be lodged against individuals or a group simply on the basis of association.

Perry Education Association v. Perry Local Educators' Association (460 U.S. 37), decided by a 5-4 vote, Feb. 23, 1983. White wrote the opinion; Brennan, Marshall, Powell and Stevens dissented.

The First Amendment is not violated by a collective bargaining agreement between a school board and the local teachers' union that grants the union access to the interschool mail system and teacher mailboxes while denying such access to all rival unions.

The state may reserve the use of public property that is a forum for public communication for certain intended purposes, so long as the restriction thus imposed on speech is reasonable and is not an effort to suppress expression of particular views.

Connick v. Myers (461 U.S. 138), decided by a 5-4 vote, April 20, 1983. White wrote the opinion; Brennan, Marshall, Blackmun and Stevens dissented.

The First Amendment does not protect from dismissal public employees who complain about their working conditions or their supervisors. The First Amendment does not require a public employer to tolerate action that he reasonably believes will undermine his authority or the operation of his office.

United States v. Grace (461 U.S. 171), decided by votes of 9-0 and 7-2, April 20, 1983. White wrote the opinion; Marshall and Stevens dissented in part.

The First Amendment protects the freedom of individuals to use leaflets or picket signs to express their views while standing on the public sidewalks adjacent to the Supreme Court building. The court struck down as unconstitutional a federal law barring all demonstrations on those sidewalks.

Regan v. Taxation with Representation of Washington, Taxation with Representation of Washington v. Regan (461 U.S. 540), decided by a 9-0 vote, May 23, 1983. Rehnquist wrote the opinion.

Congress did not infringe upon the freedom of expression guaranteed by the First Amendment when it denied tax-exempt status to non-profit organizations who devote a substantial amount of their efforts to lobbying.

Congress did not violate the Fifth Amendment guarantee of equal protection when it exempted from this restriction all veterans' groups, permitting them to retain tax-exempt status no matter how much lobbying they did. This was a legitimate way of repaying veterans for the time they spent in military service to the country.

Bush v. Lucas (462 U.S. 367), decided by a 9-0 vote, June 13, 1983. Stevens wrote the opinion.

A federal employee demoted for criticizing his agency does not, in view of the statutory remedies for such alleg-

edly unconstitutional action, have the right to bring a damage suit against his employer for violating his First Amendment rights.

Bolger v. Youngs Drug Products Corp. (463 U.S. 60), decided by an 8-0 vote, June 24, 1983. Marshall wrote the opinion. Brennan did not take part in the decision.

The court held unconstitutional a federal law prohibiting the mailing of "any unsolicited advertisement of matter which is designed, adapted, or intended for preventing conception. . . ." This unduly infringed upon the freedom of speech protected by the First Amendment, a guarantee that provides some protection for commercial speech.

Minnesota State Board for Community Colleges v. Knight, decided by a 6-3 vote, Feb. 21, 1984. O'Connor wrote the opinion; Stevens, Brennan and Powell dissented.

Minnesota law did not deny state employees First Amendment rights of free speech and freedom of association by authorizing only selected employee representatives to confer with their employers on policy and employment matters outside the scope of mandatory bargaining.

"The Constitution does not grant to members of the public generally a right to be heard by public bodies making decisions of policy," declared the court. "To recognize a constitutional right to participate directly in government policymaking would work a revolution in existing government practices."

Los Angeles City Council v. Taxpayers for Vincent, decided by a 6-3 vote, May 15, 1984. Stevens wrote the opinion; Brennan, Marshall and Blackmun dissented.

Cities concerned about "visual clutter" may constitutionally ban the posting of signs on public property. A Los Angeles posting ban was an appropriate and constitutional means of minimizing such clutter. There was no hint of bias or censorship in passage or implementation of the ban, which applied to all posted signs, regardless of content. Also, there were alternative means of conveying the messages to be presented by posters.

Secretary of State of Maryland v. Munson, decided by a 5-4 vote, June 26, 1984. Blackmun wrote the opinion; Burger, Rehnquist, Powell and O'Connor dissented.

Charitable solicitations are "so intertwined with speech that they are entitled to the protections of the First Amendment," the court declared in striking down a Maryland law limiting to 25 percent of gross income the amount a charity could spend on fund-raising.

Clark v. Community for Creative Non-Violence, decided by a 7-2 vote, June 29, 1984. White wrote the opinion; Brennan and Marshall dissented.

The Reagan administration's ban on camping — defined to include sleeping — in certain national parks did not unconstitutionally burden freedom of expression.

Without deciding whether sleeping may in some situations constitute protected expression under the First Amendment, the court ruled that the ban in question was a reasonable restriction on the time, place and manner in which First Amendment rights may be exercised. The sleeping ban, applied in this case to Lafayette Park across from the White House, was a reasonable way for the gov-

ernment to try to maintain the good condition of the national parks for all visitors, the court ruled.

Federal Communications Commission v. League of Women Voters of California, decided by a 5-4 vote, July 2, 1984. Brennan wrote the opinion; Rehnquist, Burger, White and Stevens dissented.

Congress violated the First Amendment when it prohibited editorials on public radio and television stations that accepted grants from the Corporation for Public Broadcasting. The government presented no justification sufficient to support such a sweeping ban, which was aimed at "precisely that form of speech which the framers of the Bill of Rights were most anxious to protect — speech that is 'indispensable to the discovery and spread of political truth.' "

Right of Association

Democratic Party of the United States v. LaFollette (450 U.S. 107), decided by a 6-3 vote, Feb. 25, 1981. Stewart wrote the opinion; Powell, Blackmun and Rehnquist dissented.

Wisconsin may hold an "open primary" in which voters participate without declaring their allegiance to the party whose primary it is, but it cannot constitutionally compel the national party to recognize those primary results, when to do so would violate the party's rules and infringe upon its protected right of political association.

Brown v. Socialist Workers '74 Campaign Committee (Ohio) (459 U.S. 81), decided by a 6-3 vote, Dec. 8, 1982. Marshall wrote the opinion; O'Connor, Rehnquist and Stevens dissented.

The court held unconstitutional, as applied to minor-party candidates, an Ohio law requiring candidates for public office to disclose the name and address of each campaign contributor. The justices declared that such disclosure of contributors to minor parties might subject those persons to harassment, violating their First Amendment right to associate freely with persons of similar political views.

Anderson v. Celebrezze (460 U.S. 780), decided by a 5-4 vote, April 19, 1983. Stevens wrote the opinion; Rehnquist, White, Powell and O'Connor dissented.

Ohio law burdened the voting and First Amendment rights of independent candidates and voters by requiring independent candidates for president to file in March of an election year in order to appear on the ballot in November, while major party candidates were not compelled to meet such an early deadline. The issue was raised by John B. Anderson, who ran in 1980 as an independent candidate for president.

Roberts v. U.S. Jaycees, decided by a 7-0 vote, July 3, 1984. Brennan wrote the opinion; Burger and Blackmun did not participate.

Minnesota may invoke its public accommodations law to require the U.S. Jaycees, a large non-exclusive membership organization, to admit women as full members. A state's interest in ensuring equal treatment for its women citizens outweighs any First Amendment freedom of speech or association, the Jaycees asserted.

The First Amendment protects a freedom of intimate association in family and other personal relationships and a freedom of expressive association among larger groups. But the latter is not absolute, and in this case the state's compelling interest in ensuring women equal access to public accommodations outweighed that interest.

Church and State

Thomas v. Review Board of the Indiana Employment Security Division (450 U.S. 707), decided by an 8-1 vote, April 6, 1981. Burger wrote the opinion; Rehnquist dissented.

Indiana impermissibly burdened the right to free exercise of one's religion when it denied unemployment compensation benefits to a man who quit his job because his religious beliefs forbade his participation in the production of weapons.

St. Martin Evangelical Lutheran Church and Northwestern Lutheran Academy v. State of South Dakota (451 U.S. 772), decided by a 9-0 vote, May 26, 1981. Blackmun wrote the opinion.

Elementary and secondary schools that are controlled by a church and are not separate legal entities are exempt from the requirement that employers pay federal or state unemployment taxes.

Heffron v. International Society for Krishna Consciousness (452 U.S. 640), decided by votes of 5-4 and 9-0, June 22, 1981. White wrote the opinion; Brennan, Marshall, Stevens and Blackmun dissented in part.

Minnesota did not abridge the freedom of members of the Hare Krishna sect to exercise their religion when it made and enforced a rule that persons seeking to sell literature or solicit funds at the state fair must do so from a fixed booth. The state was also acting within constitutional limits when it restricted the free distribution of literature to a particular place on the fair grounds. Those rules were reasonable in light of the state's interest in maintaining order and avoiding congestion in a crowded public place.

Widmar v. Vincent (454 U.S. 263), decided by an 8-1 vote, Dec. 8, 1981. Powell wrote the opinion; White dissented.

A state university violates the First Amendment guarantee of freedom of expression when it denies use of its buildings and grounds to a recognized student group, while allowing other such groups use of those facilities, just because the excluded group wishes to hold religious meetings there. Once a university creates a forum generally open for use by student groups, it may not deny access to that forum to certain groups because of the subject of their meetings.

Valley Forge Christian College v. Americans United for Separation of Church and State (454 U.S. 464), decided by a 5-4 vote, Jan. 12, 1982. Rehnquist wrote the opinion; Brennan, Marshall, Blackmun and Stevens dissented.

A citizens' group that could not demonstrate a clear "injury" as a result of the transfer of surplus federal property to a church-related school lacks standing to bring a federal suit challenging that transfer as a violation of the First Amendment ban on state action "establishing" religion.

Larson v. Valente (456 U.S. 228), decided by a vote of 5-4, April 21, 1982. Brennan wrote the opinion; White, Rehnquist, Burger and O'Connor dissented.

Minnesota violated the Constitution's "establishment" clause and engaged in an official preference for certain denominations when it exempted from the registration and reporting requirements of state law those religious organizations that receive more than half their financial support from their members. The Supreme Court held the state law invalid in a case brought by the Unification Church of the Rev. Sun Myung Moon.

Larkin v. Grendel's Den (459 U.S. 116), decided by an 8-1 vote, Dec. 13, 1982. Burger wrote the opinion; Rehnquist dissented.

The First Amendment ban on state action establishing religion is violated by a Massachusetts law that gives schools and churches the power to block issuance of a liquor license to any establishment located within a 500-foot radius of the church or school.

Mueller v. Allen (463 U.S. 388), decided by a 5-4 vote, June 29, 1983. Rehnquist wrote the opinion; Marshall, Brennan, Blackmun and Stevens dissented.

A Minnesota law that gives parents a state income tax deduction for the cost of tuition, textbooks and transportation for their elementary and secondary school children up to a limit of $700 per older child and $500 per younger is permissible under the First Amendment.

Because the deduction is available to public school patrons as well as private school patrons, and because any aid to church schools is the result of individual choices, not state design, the court found that it met the test for such aid. The majority found that the deduction had a secular purpose, did not have the primary effect of advancing religion and did not entangle the state in religious affairs.

Marsh v. Chambers (463 U.S. 783), decided by a 6-3 vote, July 5, 1983. Burger wrote the opinion; Brennan, Marshall and Stevens dissented.

The First Amendment ban on establishment of religion is not offended by Nebraska's practice of opening daily sessions of the state Legislature with a prayer by a chaplain paid by the state. This practice has a long and unique history, dating back to the First Congress of the United States, which also adopted the First Amendment. "The practice of opening legislative sessions with prayer has become part of the fabric of our society," wrote the court.

Lynch v. Donnelly, decided by a 5-4 vote, March 5, 1984. Burger wrote the opinion; Brennan, Marshall, Blackmun and Stevens dissented.

The inclusion of a Nativity scene in a municipally sponsored Christmas holiday display in Pawtucket, R.I., did not violate the First Amendment ban on establishment of religion, the court ruled.

The Constitution "affirmatively mandates accommodation, not merely tolerance, of all religions, and forbids hostility toward any," the court majority declared. "There is an unbroken history of official acknowledgement by all three branches of government of the role of religion in American life from at least 1789," the justices noted.

Freedom of the Press

Minneapolis Star & Tribune Co. v. Minnesota Commissioner of Revenue (460 U.S. 575), decided by votes of 8-1 and 7-2, March 29, 1983. O'Connor wrote the opinion; White and Rehnquist dissented.

Minnesota violated the First Amendment's guarantee of freedom of the press when it taxed the use of paper and ink by newspapers that use those items in large volume.

Keeton v. Hustler Magazine Inc., decided by a 9-0 vote, March 20, 1984. Rehnquist wrote the opinion.

Nationally circulated newspapers and magazines can be sued in any state in which they have substantial circulation. The court held that a New York resident could sue Hustler, an Ohio corporation, for libel in a federal court in New Hampshire, because Hustler sold 10,000 to 15,000 copies of its magazine in that state each month.

Calder v. Jones, decided by a 9-0 vote, March 20, 1984. Rehnquist wrote the opinion.

California courts had jurisdiction over a libel case brought by actress Shirley Jones, a California resident, against an editor and writer of an article in the *National Enquirer*, which was published by a Florida corporation, even though the writer and editor live and work in Florida and had little or no contact with the state of California. The target of the article was California and a California resident; therefore California courts could exercise jurisdiction over those responsible for the article.

Bose Corp. v. Consumers Union of the United States, decided by a 6-3 vote, April 30, 1984. Stevens wrote the opinion; White, Rehnquist and O'Connor dissented.

Federal appeals courts reviewing libel damage awards won by public figures must independently review the evidence to determine whether it was sufficient to prove actual malice on the part of the press defendant. In such a review, appeals courts are not restricted by the federal rules of procedures, which permit appeals courts to overturn a trial court's finding of fact only if that finding was "clearly erroneous."

Seattle Times Co. v. Rhinehart, decided by a 9-0 vote, May 2, 1984. Powell wrote the opinion.

Freedom of the press is not violated by a court order restraining the publication of information about the members and supporters of a religious organization when that information was obtained through pretrial discovery compelled by the court.

Regan v. Time Inc., decided by votes of 5-4 and 8-1, July 3, 1984. White wrote the opinion; Brennan, Marshall, Blackmun, Powell and Stevens dissented.

Congress violated the First Amendment in 1958 when it amended a century-old law severely restricting the publication of photographs for "philatelic, numismatic, newsworthy, historical and educational purposes." This provision unconstitutionally distinguished among publications on the basis of content. Only Justice Stevens voted to uphold this aspect of the law.

The court upheld a portion of the law requiring that all illustrations be in black and white, be undersized or oversized, and that the negative and plates used be destroyed. Brennan, Marshall, Blackmun and Powell dissented.

Right of Access

Globe Newspaper Co. v. Superior Court (457 U.S. 596), decided by a 6-3 vote, June 23, 1982. Brennan

wrote the opinion; Burger, Rehnquist and Stevens dissented.

First Amendment rights of access to criminal trials are violated by a Massachusetts law mandating the closing of sex-crime trials to press and public during the testimony of a victim who is a minor.

Press-Enterprise Co. v. Superior Court of California, Riverside County, decided by a 9-0 vote, Jan. 18, 1984. Burger wrote the opinion.

Jury selection proceedings in criminal trials should be open to the press and public unless the judge finds an overriding interest requires that these proceedings be closed, the court ruled.

A California judge violated that right of access by excluding press and public from all but three days of a six-week jury selection process prior to a rape-murder trial. The judge presented no findings to support closure and did not consider alternatives.

Communications

Federal Communications Commission (FCC) v. WNCN Listeners Guild, Insilco Broadcasting Corp. v. WNCN Listeners Guild, American Broadcasting Cos. v. WNCN Listeners Guild, National Association of Broadcasters v. WNCN Listeners Guild (450 U.S. 582), decided by a 7-2 vote, March 24, 1981. White wrote the opinion; Marshall and Brennan dissented.

The Federal Communications Commission is not obligated to consider changes in the entertainment format of a radio station when it reviews an application for the renewal or transfer of the station's broadcast license.

CBS Inc. v. Federal Communications Commission (FCC), American Broadcasting Cos. Inc. v. FCC, National Broadcasting Co. Inc. v. FCC (453 U.S. 367), decided by a vote of 6-3, July 1, 1981. Burger wrote the opinion; White, Rehnquist and Stevens dissented.

Title I of the Federal Election Campaign Act of 1971 (PL 92-225) gives candidates for federal offices a right of access to the air waves once their campaigns are under way. Title I gives the Federal Communications Commission the authority to revoke a broadcaster's license for "willful or repeated failure to allow reasonable access to or to permit purchase of reasonable amounts of time for the use of a broadcasting station by a legally qualified candidate for federal elective office. . . ."

It is up to the FCC, not the networks, to decide when a campaign has begun and when a particular candidate may exercise this right in order to air political broadcasts on behalf of his candidacy.

Election Laws

Apportionment

Karcher v. Daggett (462 U.S. 725), decided by a 5-4 vote, June 22, 1983. Brennan wrote the opinion; White, Burger, Powell and Rehnquist dissented.

The court struck down the New Jersey congressional redistricting plan adopted following the 1980 Census, although there was less than a 1 percent variation between the most populous district and the least populous district.

The court reaffirmed that states must adhere as closely as possible to the "one person, one vote" standard of reapportionment. When precise equality is not achieved, the state must prove that the variations were necessary to achieve some important state goal. New Jersey had not proved that point in this case, the court held.

Brown v. Thomson (462 U.S. 835), decided by a 5-4 vote, June 22, 1983. Powell wrote the opinion; Brennan, White, Marshall and Blackmun dissented.

Wyoming law, which requires that each county have at least one representative in the state House of Representatives, is constitutional even though the population variance between the smallest county and the largest is 89 percent. The law is permissible in light of the state's legitimate interest in assuring each county its own representative, the court held.

Voting Rights

Ball v. James (451 U.S. 355), decided by a 5-4 vote, April 29, 1981. Stewart wrote the opinion; White, Brennan, Marshall and Blackmun dissented.

Arizona did not violate the constitutional guarantee of equal protection when it restricted the right to vote for directors of a water district to landowners in the district. The water district is not the sort of general governmental unit whose officials must be elected by the general populace under the "one person, one vote" rule. Instead, it had functions of a narrow special sort, more like a business than a government.

McDaniel v. Sanchez (452 U.S. 130), decided by a vote of 7-2, June 1, 1981. Stevens wrote the opinion; Stewart and Rehnquist dissented.

Even a reapportionment plan for a county's government developed by local officials under orders from a federal district court is subject to the federal pre-clearance requirements of the Voting Rights Act and must receive such federal approval before being put into effect.

Hathorn v. Lovorn (457 U.S. 255), decided by an 8-1 vote, June 15, 1982. O'Connor wrote the opinion; Rehnquist dissented.

State courts have both the power and the obligation to decide whether changes in election laws and procedures require pre-clearance with federal authorities under the Voting Rights Act of 1965. State courts must refrain from issuing any orders that conflict with the Voting Rights Act.

Rogers v. Lodge (458 U.S. 613), decided by a 6-3 vote, July 1, 1982. White wrote the opinion; Powell, Rehnquist and Stevens dissented.

In order to find an at-large system of electing county officials unconstitutional in violation of the 14th and 15th Amendments, courts must determine that the system is discriminatory in intent as well as effect.

A court may consider indirect as well as direct evidence of intent, however, wrote White, who explained that " 'an invidious discriminatory purpose may often be inferred from the totality of the relevant facts, including the fact, if it is true, that the law bears more heavily on one race than another.' "

Evidence permissible in such cases may include evidence of the exclusion of blacks from the political process, of official insensitivity to the needs of blacks, and the

socioeconomic status of an area's blacks.

City of Port Arthur, Texas v. United States (459 U.S. 159), decided by a 6-3 vote, Dec. 13, 1982. White wrote the opinion; Powell, Rehnquist, and O'Connor dissented.

A federal district court acted within its powers when it required the city of Port Arthur to elect certain members of its City Council by a plurality, rather than a majority vote, and conditioned its approval of a new plan for electing the City Council upon this change.

Federal approval of a change in the city's electoral system was required under the Voting Rights Act. The district court imposed the plurality requirement because it felt this would enhance the chances that black candidates would be elected to the council. The new electoral plan was adopted following the consolidation of Port Arthur and two nearby cities, a move that reduced the percentage of blacks in the city population from 45 to 40 percent.

City of Lockhart, Texas v. United States (460 U.S. 125), decided by votes of 8-1 and 6-3, Feb. 23, 1983. Powell wrote the opinion; White, Marshall and Blackmun dissented.

The city of Lockhart is entitled to federal approval of changes in the way in which members of its City Council are elected at-large to numbered posts on a staggered basis because although those changes may have some discriminatory effect, they have no retrogressive effect on minority voting strength.

McCain v. Lybrand, decided by a 9-0 vote, Feb. 21, 1984. Stevens wrote the opinion.

The attorney general's approval of 1971 changes in procedures for electing members of a county council, submitted for clearance as required by Section 5 of the Voting Rights Act, could not be interpreted as approval of 1966 election procedure changes that had not been submitted for such clearance.

Escambia County, Fla. v. McMillan, decided by an 8-1 vote, March 27, 1984. *Per curiam* (unsigned) opinion; Marshall dissented.

The court sent back to a federal appeals court a case in which an at-large system of electing county commissioners was challenged as unconstitutional, directing the appeals court to decide whether the Voting Rights Act provided a basis for upholding the district court decision that the at-large system violated the rights of black voters in the county.

Campaign Finance

Federal Election Commission v. Democratic Senatorial Campaign Committee, National Republican Senatorial Committee v. Democratic Senatorial Campaign Committee (454 U.S. 27), decided by a vote of 9-0, Nov. 10, 1981. White wrote the opinion.

The Federal Election Campaign Act of 1971 does not preclude national party committees from enlarging the amount they may legally spend in an election by assuming the spending authority granted by law to state party committees and making those expenditures as agents of the state committees.

Bread Political Action Committee v. Federal Election Commission (455 U.S. 577), decided by a 9-0 vote, March 8, 1982. O'Connor wrote the opinion.

Avoiding a decision on a challenge to federal election law provisions that limit solicitation by trade associations of political contributions from their members' stockholders and officers, the court held that under federal election law such trade associations and political action committees may not win expedited review of their challenges to such provisions. Expedited review of such challenges is available only to national committees of political parties, eligible voters and the Federal Election Commission.

Federal Election Commission v. National Right to Work Committee (459 U.S. 197), decided by a 9-0 vote, Dec. 13, 1982. Rehnquist wrote the opinion.

The Supreme Court refused to expand the target population from which certain political action committees (PACs) can solicit funds. Federal election law restricts nonstock corporate PACs, such as the Employee Rights Campaign Committee set up by the National Right to Work Committee, to soliciting funds from their members, executives and administrative staff. The National Right to Work Committee argued that its "members" were all persons who could be identified as sharing its philosophy and supporting its work. The court rejected this broad definition and ruled that because the PAC's charter, adopted under state law, declared that it had no members, it could only solicit funds from its executives and administrative staff.

General

Rivera-Rodriguez v. Popular Democratic Party (457 U.S. 1), decided by a 9-0 vote, June 7, 1982. Burger wrote the opinion.

Puerto Rico may, by law, vest in a political party the power to fill an interim vacancy in the Legislature resulting from the death of an incumbent member of that party. This does not violate the Constitution's guarantees of equal protection or freedom of political association.

Business Law

Agriculture: Milk Marketing

Block v. Community Nutrition Institute, decided by an 8-0 vote, June 4, 1984. O'Connor wrote the opinion; Stevens did not participate.

Congress did not give consumers any role in the development or enforcement of milk marketing orders under the Agricultural Marketing Agreement Act. Consumers thus have no authority to challenge those orders; the system providing for such orders is a closed one, limited to producers, handlers and the agriculture secretary.

Antitrust

Texas Industries v. Radcliff Materials Inc. (451 U.S. 630), decided by a 9-0 vote, May 26, 1981. Burger wrote the opinion.

Neither federal statute nor common law allows federal judges to permit companies charged with antitrust violations to force their co-conspirators to share in the financial penalties for their misdeeds. Congress, not the courts, must decide such a policy question.

H. A. Artists & Associates Inc. v. Actors' Equity Association (451 U.S. 704), decided by votes of 6-3 and

9-0, May 26, 1981. Stewart wrote the opinion; Brennan, Burger and Marshall dissented in part.

Actors' Equity, the union that represents most actors and actresses in the United States, operates a licensing system for the regulation of theatrical agents. In general the creation and maintenance of this system is exempt from the federal antitrust laws under their provisions exempting labor unions from challenge. The fees that Equity levies upon agents applying for licenses, however, are not justified and are not a permissible element of the exempt regulatory system.

National Gerimedical Hospital and Gerontology Center v. Blue Cross of Kansas City and Blue Cross Association (452 U.S. 378), decided by a 9-0 vote, June 15, 1981. Powell wrote the opinion.

Health insurance companies are not immune from antitrust charges brought by hospitals that were refused permission to participate in the insurance companies' insurance systems even though the insurance companies based their denial on the fact that the applicant hospital had not received approval for its construction from the local health systems agency as required by the National Health Care Planning and Resources Development Act (PL 93-641).

Community Communications Co. Inc. v. City of Boulder, Colo. (455 U.S. 40), decided by a 5-3 vote, Jan. 13, 1982. Brennan wrote the opinion; Rehnquist, Burger and O'Connor dissented; White did not participate in the decision.

Boulder's ordinance imposing a three-month moratorium on expansion of cable television systems within the city limits, a period within which the city invited competing systems to enter the market, is not immune from challenge under federal antitrust laws.

Such city action is not "state action" exempt from such challenge under *Parker v. Brown* (317 U.S. 341), because it is not taken to further a clearly expressed state policy.

Kaiser Steel Corp. v. Mullins (455 U.S. 72), decided by a 6-3 vote, Jan. 13, 1982. White wrote the opinion; Brennan, Marshall and Blackmun dissented.

A coal producer, party to a collective bargaining contract with the United Mine Workers that included provisions, not enforced for years, which the producer considered in violation of federal antitrust and labor laws, may raise the defense of their illegality when charged with failing to comply with the questionable provisions.

As a general rule, federal courts must defer to the National Labor Relations Board on such questions, but a federal court has a duty to determine whether or not a contract is in line with federal law before acting to enforce that contract.

American Society of Mechanical Engineers v. Hydrolevel Corp. (456 U.S. 556), decided by a 6-3 vote, May 17, 1982. Blackmun wrote the opinion; Powell, White and Rehnquist dissented.

Professional engineering societies and other non-profit membership organizations that issue standards and codes used in various areas of industry may be held liable under the antitrust laws for violations of those laws by their members. This liability, held the court, extends at least to actions of society members and "agents" taken with the apparent authority of the organization.

Arizona v. Maricopa County Medical Society (457 U.S. 332), decided by a 4-3 vote, June 18, 1982. Stevens wrote the opinion; Powell, Burger and Rehnquist dissented; Blackmun and O'Connor did not participate.

An agreement among competing physicians setting the maximum fees they would charge certain insurance companies for services to their policyholders amounts to price-fixing in violation of federal antitrust laws.

Blue Shield of Virginia v. McCready (457 U.S. 465), decided by a 5-4 vote, June 21, 1982. Brennan wrote the opinion; Rehnquist, Burger, O'Connor and Stevens dissented.

An individual whose insurance company refused to reimburse her for services provided by a psychologist, although it would have paid for those same services had they been provided by a psychiatrist, has standing to sue the insurance company and the state psychiatric association for triple damages under the Clayton Act. She has suffered injury as a result of their allegedly anti-competitive activity, even though she was not its primary target.

Union Labor Life Insurance v. Pireno (458 U.S. 119), decided by a 6-3 vote, June 28, 1982. Brennan wrote the opinion; Rehnquist, Burger and O'Connor dissented.

An insurance company's practice of obtaining advice from a peer review committee of the state chiropractic association on what fees charged by chiropractors to patients are reasonable and should be reimbursed by the company is not immune from scrutiny under the antitrust laws as part of the "business of insurance."

Associated General Contractors of California Inc. v. California State Council of Carpenters (459 U.S. 519), decided by an 8-1 vote, Feb. 22, 1983. Stevens wrote the opinion; Marshall dissented.

A union that charges that a contractors' association and its members have conspired to weaken the collective bargaining relationship between the union and the contractors is not a "person" injured by a potential antitrust violation within the meaning of the Clayton Act. It is therefore not eligible to sue for treble damages. Such suits may only be brought by persons who have been injured by the alleged conspiracy; the union did not show such injury.

Jefferson County Pharmaceutical Association Inc. v. Abbott Laboratories (460 U.S. 150), decided by a 5-4 vote, Feb. 23, 1983. Powell wrote the opinion; O'Connor, Brennan, Rehnquist and Stevens dissented.

Sales to state and local government agencies are not exempt from the price discrimination ban of the Robinson-Patman Act when those agencies are competing in the public marketplace with private business.

Falls City Industries Inc. v. Vanco Beverage Inc. (460 U.S. 428), decided by a 9-0 vote, March 22, 1983. Blackmun wrote the opinion.

A company charged with violating the Robinson-Patman Act's ban on price discrimination may successfully defend itself against those charges by arguing that it lowered its prices for all customers in a certain area in order to meet the prices of its competitors. This "meeting competition" defense is available even if the lower prices are set on an areawide, rather than a customer-by-customer, basis.

Illinois v. Abbott & Associates (460 U.S. 557), decided by a 9-0 vote, March 29, 1983. Stevens wrote the opinion.

In approving the Hart-Scott-Rodino Antitrust Improvements Act of 1976, Congress did not give state attorneys general any special right to see grand jury materials unless they can show a particularized need to gain access to such information.

BankAmerica Corp. v. United States (462 U.S. 122), decided by a 5-3 vote, June 8, 1983. Burger wrote the opinion; Powell did not participate in the decision; White, Brennan and Marshall dissented.

The Clayton Act, which prohibits persons from serving simultaneously as the director of two or more competing million-dollar corporations other than banks or common carriers, does not bar such interlocking directorates between a bank and a competing non-bank corporation such as an insurance company.

Monsanto Co. v. Spray-Rite Service Corp., decided by an 8-0 vote, March 20, 1984. Powell wrote the opinion; White did not participate in the decision.

The court upheld a $10.5 million antitrust judgment assessed against Monsanto after a jury found it had terminated Spray-Rite's distributorship of its products because the distributor consistently undercut the prices charged by other distributors.

Something more than evidence of complaints from other distributors about discount pricing must be presented to justify such a finding; there must be direct or circumstantial evidence that reasonably tends to prove that the manufacturer and others had a conscious intent to maintain resale price levels. Such evidence was presented in this case, and the judgment was upheld.

Jefferson Parish Hospital District No. 2 v. Hyde, decided by a 9-0 vote, March 27, 1984. Stevens wrote the opinion.

A hospital that is one of many in a large metropolitan area does not violate federal antitrust law by entering into an exclusive contract with one firm of anesthesiologists under which that firm provides all the anesthesia services for all surgery at that hospital. There is no evidence that this sort of arrangement, tying the provision of anesthesia by one firm to surgery at that hospital, is per se illegal or that it operates to restrain competition in the market.

Copperweld Corp. v. Independence Tube Corp., decided by a 5-3 vote, June 19, 1984. Burger wrote the opinion; White did not participate; Stevens, Brennan and Marshall dissented.

A corporation and its wholly owned subsidiary are not capable of conspiring to restrain trade in violation of Section 1 of the Sherman Antitrust Act.

The court overturned a $7.5 million damage award to Independence that had been based on a finding that Copperweld and its wholly owned subsidiary, Regal Tube, conspired together to urge suppliers not to deal with Independence, a new competitor.

National Collegiate Athletic Association (NCAA) v. Board of Regents of the University of Oklahoma, decided by a 7-2 vote, June 27, 1984. Stevens wrote the opinon; White and Rehnquist dissented.

An NCAA plan that limited the number of college football games that could be televised, limited the number of televised games in which any one school could appear, prohibited all members from selling television rights to football games except in accord with the NCAA plan, and fixed the minimum aggregate price to be paid for these rights by the networks violated federal antitrust laws.

This television package plan unreasonably restrained trade in violation of Section 1 of the Sherman Act.

Banking

Board of Governors of the Federal Reserve System v. Investment Company Institute (450 U.S. 46), decided by a 6-0 vote, Feb. 24, 1981. Stevens wrote the opinion; Stewart, Rehnquist and Powell did not participate in the decision.

The Federal Reserve Board acted within the authority granted it by the Bank Holding Company Act when it allowed bank holding companies and their non-banking subsidiaries to act as investment advisers to closed-end investment companies. Such investment advisory services are closely related to the kind of services long provided by bank trust departments.

Fidelity Federal Savings & Loan Association v. de la Cuesta (458 U.S. 141), decided by a 6-2 vote, June 28, 1982. Blackmun wrote the opinion; Powell did not participate; Rehnquist and Stevens dissented.

State efforts to prohibit enforcement of "due-on-sale" clauses in home loan instruments, which allow the mortgage lender to demand immediate payment in full whenever the mortgaged property is sold or transferred, are preempted by federal regulations issued by the Federal Home Loan Bank Board. The regulations grant federal savings and loan associations the right to include such clauses in their loan agreements. The Federal Home Loan Bank Board acted in accord with the authority granted it by Congress in the Home Owners' Loan Act of 1933 to regulate federal savings and loan associations.

First National City Bank v. Banco Para El Comercio Exterior de Cuba (462 U.S. 611), decided by votes of 9-0 and 6-3, June 17, 1983. O'Connor wrote the opinion; Stevens, Brennan and Blackmun dissented.

A U.S. bank whose assets in Cuba were nationalized in 1960 can make counterclaim for those losses against a Cuban bank that serves as an official autonomous credit institution for foreign trade and that sued the U.S. bank to collect a debt owed it by the U.S. bank.

Securities Industry Association v. Board of Governors of the Federal Reserve System, decided by a 6-3 vote, June 28, 1984. Blackmun wrote the opinion; O'Connor, Brennan and Stevens dissented.

Congress in 1933 drew a line separating commercial banking from investment banking; the Federal Reserve Board blurred that line when it approved a commercial bank's marketing of commercial paper for some of its corporate customers.

Section 16 of the Glass-Steagall Act forbids commercial banks to underwrite or market stocks, bonds, notes, or other securities. Commercial paper falls in this category and cannot be marketed under Section 16.

Securities Industry Association v. Board of Governors of the Federal Reserve System, decided

by a 9-0 vote, June 28, 1984. Powell wrote the opinion.

The Federal Reserve Board was within its authority when it permitted a bank holding company to acquire a discount securities brokerage firm.

Approving BankAmerica's acquisition of Charles Schwab & Co., the court held that the operation of a discount brokerage firm — basically the execution of buy and sell orders for customers, without investment advice — was similar to the business of many bank trust departments. Thus, the acquisition did not violate the Glass-Steagall Act of 1933, which forbids banks to underwrite or market securities.

Bankruptcy

Railway Labor Executives' Association v. Gibbons (455 U.S. 457), decided by a vote of 9-0, March 2, 1982. Rehnquist wrote the opinion.

Congress may not pass bankruptcy laws that apply to the affairs of only one bankrupt organization. The Constitution gives Congress the power to "establish . . . uniform Laws on the subject of bankruptcies throughout the United States."

The Rock Island Transition and Employee Assistance Act of 1980 (PL 96-254) applied only to the Rock Island Railroad, providing special protection to its employees not available to the employees of other bankrupt railroads. Thus that law violated the uniformity standard of the Constitution's bankruptcy clause. It was the first time that the court had held a federal bankruptcy act unconstitutional for this reason.

Northern Pipeline Construction Co. v. Marathon Pipe Line Co., United States v. Marathon Pipe Line Co. (458 U.S. 50), decided by a 6-3 vote, June 28, 1982. Brennan announced the decision in an opinion joined by three justices; Rehnquist and O'Connor concurred in the judgment; White, Burger and Powell dissented.

Congress acted in violation of Article III, which provides that federal judicial power should be exercised only by federal judges whose independence is assured by life tenure and fixed compensation, when it enacted provisions of the 1978 Bankruptcy Reform Act creating a new corps of bankruptcy judges who lack these guarantees of independence but have jurisdiction over all civil cases related to a bankrupt person or organization.

United States v. Security Industrial Bank (459 U.S. 70), decided by a 9-0 vote, Nov. 30, 1982. Rehnquist wrote the opinion.

The provisions of the Bankruptcy Reform Act of 1978 (PL 95-598) that exempt certain personal property from liens by creditors do not apply to consumer loans made before the law was enacted. With this holding, the court sidestepped a decision on whether such an exemption, had it applied retroactively, was unconstitutional.

United States v. Whiting Pools Inc. (462 U.S. 198), decided by a 9-0 vote, June 8, 1983. Blackmun wrote the opinion.

A bankruptcy court can compel the Internal Revenue Service (IRS) to return to a company in bankruptcy property that the IRS has seized to satisfy the company's tax bills.

National Labor Relations Board v. Bildisco &

Bildisco, decided by votes of 9-0 and 5-4, Feb. 22, 1984. Rehnquist wrote the opinion; Brennan, White, Marshall and Blackmun dissented in part.

A company attempting to reorganize its affairs under federal bankruptcy laws may, with a bankruptcy judge's permission, abrogate its collective bargaining contract upon a showing that the contract is burdensome and on balance, the best interests of the company, its creditors and its employees favor such a step. It is not necessary to show that the company will go out of business if it does not reject its contract.

By a 5-4 vote, the court also held that a failing company that has filed for bankruptcy is not guilty of an unfair labor practice if it unilaterally rejects or modifies certain provisions of its collective bargaining contract.

Copyright

Sony Corporation of America v. Universal Studios Inc., decided by a 5-4 vote, Jan. 17, 1984. Stevens wrote the opinion; Blackmun, Marshall, Powell and Rehnquist dissented.

Home taping of copyrighted television programs for personal, non-commercial use does not violate copyright laws. The court overturned a 1981 appeals court decision holding the Sony Corp., some of its retailers and its advertising agency liable for damages for contributing to copyright infringement by selling Sony's Betamax video recorders.

The primary use of these machines is "time-shift" recording, taping programs for later viewing at a more convenient time. This is a fair use of the machines, not a violation of copyright laws, the court held.

Air Cargo Liability Limits

Trans World Airlines Inc. v. Franklin Mint Corp., Franklin Mint Corp. v. Trans World Airlines Inc., decided by an 8-1 vote, April 17, 1984. O'Connor wrote the opinion; Stevens dissented.

Although Congress in 1978 repealed the official price for gold, the standard used under the Warsaw Convention to determine the limits of airline liability for lost cargo, the international limits set under that convention are still in effect for U.S. airlines.

Multi-Employer Pension Funds

Schneider Moving & Storage Co. v. Robbins, Prosser's Moving & Storage Co. v. Robbins, decided by a 9-0 vote, April 18, 1984. Powell wrote the opinion.

Trustees of a multi-employer trust fund may sue an employer directly for failing to make required contributions to the fund, without first submitting to arbitration a basic disagreement with that employer over the meaning of a term in the agreement setting up the fund.

Pension Benefit Guaranty Corp. v. R. A. Gray & Co., decided by a 9-0 vote, June 18, 1984. Brennan wrote the opinion.

Congress did not deny affected employers due process of law in making certain liability provisions of the Multi-employer Pension Plan Amendments Act of 1980 (PL 96-364) applicable to employers withdrawing from such plans in the five months prior to enactment. The contested provision required such employers to make a contribution to the

plan to cover future payments to employees.

This provision was a rational means of furthering a legitimate legislative purpose, the court held.

Patents

Diamond v. Diehr (450 U.S. 175), decided by a 5-4 vote, March 3, 1981. Rehnquist wrote the opinion; Stevens, Brennan, Blackmun and Marshall dissented.

Inventions and discoveries that involve computer programs may be patentable. Mathematical formulas are not patentable; computer programs are essentially mathematical formulas; but an industrial process does not become unpatentable just because it includes a formula or a program.

General Motors Corp. v. Devex Corp. (461 U.S. 648), decided by a 9-0 vote, May 24, 1983. Marshall wrote the opinion.

The court upheld an award of $11 million in interest, which had accrued before the judgment in a patent infringement case, to a company that had sued General Motors for infringing on its patent for making car bumpers. The court held that it was appropriate in some cases for courts to award interest dating back to the point at which the infringement began in order to adequately compensate the patent holder for his loss.

Price Discrimination

J. Truett Payne Co. v. Chrysler Motors Corp. (451 U.S. 557), decided by votes of 9-0 and 5-4, May 18, 1981. Rehnquist wrote the opinion; Powell, Brennan, Marshall and Blackmun dissented in part.

Businesses that prove that they faced price discrimination in violation of the ban of the Robinson-Patman Act must also prove that they were actually injured by that discrimination before they can be awarded damages.

Property Rights

Webb's Fabulous Pharmacies Inc. v. Beckwith (449 U.S. 155), decided by a 9-0 vote, Dec. 9, 1980. Blackmun wrote the opinion.

A county violates the constitutional ban on the taking of private property for public use without just compensation when it takes for itself interest earned on an interpleader fund, that is private, deposited in the county court registry, at least when there is a separate state law authorizing a fee — to the county — for services rendered with regard to the fund.

San Diego Gas & Electric Co. v. City of San Diego (450 U.S. 621), decided by a 5-4 vote, March 24, 1981. Blackmun wrote the opinion; Brennan, Stewart, Marshall and Powell dissented.

Utility's appeal of a state court ruling denying utility power to recover damages for the "taking" of its land for public use through its rezoning is dismissed because ruling by state court was not "final judgment" by that court on this case.

McCarty v. McCarty (453 U.S. 210), decided by a 6-3 vote, June 26, 1981. Blackmun wrote the opinion; Rehnquist, Brennan and Stewart dissented.

State courts, dividing a couple's property pursuant to a

divorce, may not consider the retirement pay of a retired military officer as community property. Thus the court effectively denied the divorced wife of a retired military officer any right to share in that retirement pay.

Kirby Forest Industries v. United States, decided by a 9-0 vote, May 21, 1984. Marshall wrote the opinion.

When government uses "straight-condemnation" proceedings to take privately owned timberland for a national preserve, the date of the taking of the land is the date that the government tenders payment to the landowner, not the date it institutes the proceedings. No interest is due for period between date of complaint and date of payment.

Ruckelshaus v. Monsanto Co., decided by votes of 8-0 and 7-1, June 26, 1984. Blackmun wrote the opinion; White did not participate; O'Connor dissented.

The court found "no constitutional infirmity" in two key provisions of the Federal Insecticide, Fungicide and Rodenticide Act as amended in 1978.

The two provisions permit the Environmental Protection Agency (EPA) to disclose to the public health and safety data submitted to it by a company applying to register a pesticide, and to use that data to evaluate a second company's application for a license for a similar pesticide.

Both provisions had been held unconstitutional by a lower court judge who upheld Monsanto's contention that they permitted the government to take trade secrets, private property, without just compensation. The court held that Monsanto knew that EPA could make such disclosure when it submitted the data, and thus could not claim that disclosure was a taking.

Railroads

Chicago and North Western Transportation Co. v. Kalo Brick & Tile Co. (450 U.S. 311), decided by a 9-0 vote, March 9, 1981. Marshall wrote the opinion.

A decision by the Interstate Commerce Commission to approve abandonment of certain railroad service may not be challenged in state courts.

Burlington Northern Inc. v. United States (459 U.S. 131), decided by a 9-0 vote, Dec. 13, 1982. Burger wrote the opinion.

A federal appeals court, reviewing a contested order from the Interstate Commerce Commission (ICC) concerning rail-freight rates, may order the ICC to reconsider those rates but may not itself decide what rates should be charged in the interim. It is the responsibility of the ICC to set such interim rates.

Regulation

American Medical Association v. Federal Trade Commission (455 U.S. 676), decided by a 4-4 vote, March 23, 1982. Blackmun did not take part in consideration of the case.

The evenly divided court affirmed an appeals court ruling that the Federal Trade Commission has jurisdiction to order a non-profit medical association to lift its restrictions on the dissemination of price information by doctors and its ban on advertising of physicians' services and alternative forms of medical care.

Southern Pacific Transportation Co. v. Commercial Metals Co. (456 U.S. 336), decided by a 9-0 vote, April 27, 1982. Blackmun wrote the opinion.

A railroad's violation of credit regulations issued by the Interstate Commerce Commission does not bar the railroad from collecting a lawful freight charge from a shipper who is in fact liable for that charge.

United States v. Generix Drug Corp. (460 U.S. 453), decided by a 9-0 vote, March 22, 1983. Stevens wrote the opinion.

Generic prescription drugs must receive pre-marketing approval from the Food and Drug Administration even if they contain exactly the same active ingredients as already approved brand name drugs.

Motor Vehicle Manufacturers Association of the United States v. State Farm Mutual Automobile Insurance Co., Consumer Alert v. State Farm, Department of Transportation v. State Farm (463 U.S. 29), decided by votes of 9-0 and 5-4, June 24, 1983. White wrote the opinion. Rehnquist, Burger, Powell and O'Connor dissented in part.

Federal agencies may not rescind existing regulations without a reasoned justification for the rescission. The National Highway Transportation Safety Administration acted arbitrarily and capriciously in 1981 when it rescinded a requirement that all cars be equipped with passive safety restraints — air bags or automatic seat belts — by September 1983. Four justices felt that although the rescission was unjustified on the issue of air bags and one type of seat belt, the agency did justify its rescission of the rule as to detachable seat belts.

Interstate Commerce Commission (ICC) v. American Trucking Associations Inc., decided by a 5-4 vote, June 5, 1984. Marshall wrote the opinion; O'Connor, Blackmun, Powell and Stevens dissented.

The ICC has inherent authority to reject a tariff setting trucking rates, even if the rates are already in effect, if it finds that the tariff violates motor-carrier rate-bureau agreements under the Motor Carrier Act of 1980. The ICC can order trucking companies to refund overcharges collected under the rate schedule while it was in effect.

Relocation Aid

Norfolk Redevelopment and Housing Authority v. C & P Telephone Company of Virginia, decided by an 8-0 vote, Nov. 1, 1983. Rehnquist wrote the opinion; Powell did not participate.

Public utilities are not eligible for relocation aid as "displaced persons" under the Uniform Relocation Act of 1970 when their transmission lines are displaced by federally funded projects. That law did not change the common law principle that a utility forced to relocate from a public right-of-way does so at its own expense.

Securities

Rubin v. United States (449 U.S. 424), decided by a 9-0 vote, Jan. 21, 1981. Burger wrote the opinion.

When an executive pledges corporate stock as collateral for a bank loan, his pledge is an "offer of sale" of that stock within the meaning of the anti-fraud provisions of federal securities law.

Steadman v. Securities and Exchange Commission (450 U.S. 91), decided by a 7-2 vote, Feb. 25, 1981. Brennan wrote the opinion; Powell and Stewart dissented.

The Securities and Exchange Commission (SEC) properly uses the standard of a preponderance of the evidence — rather than the stricter standard of clear and convincing evidence — in determining whether an individual or firm has violated the anti-fraud provisions of federal securities law.

Marine Bank v. Weaver (455 U.S. 551), decided by a 9-0 vote, March 8, 1982. Burger wrote the opinion.

Neither a certificate of deposit pledged to guarantee a loan nor a related agreement sharing a company's future profits with the guarantor of the loan is a "security" within the meaning of the Securities Exchange Act of 1934, and so these actions are not covered under the anti-fraud provisions of that law.

Merrill Lynch, Pierce, Fenner & Smith v. Curran, New York Mercantile Exchange v. Leist, Clayton Brokerage Co. v. Leist, Heinhold Commodities v. Leist (456 U.S. 353), decided by a 5-4 vote, May 3, 1982. Stevens wrote the opinion; Powell, Burger, Rehnquist and O'Connor dissented.

Private investors in commodity futures, as well as federal regulators, have the right to seek enforcement in court of federal laws governing trading in commodity futures. Investors may sue their brokers and the exchanges for damages in cases involving fraud or market manipulation. This private right to sue in such cases existed before enactment of the 1974 law creating the Commodity Futures Trading Commission and was left untouched by Congress in the passage of that law.

Herman & MacLean v. Huddleston, Huddleston v. Herman & MacLean (459 U.S. 375), decided by an 8-0 vote, Jan. 24, 1983. Marshall wrote the opinion; Powell did not participate in the court's consideration of the case.

Making it easier for individual victims of stock fraud to sue those who have defrauded them, the court held that such charges need only be proved by a preponderance of the evidence, rather than the stiffer standard of clear and convincing evidence. Such cases can be brought under both the Securities Exchange Act of 1934 and the Securities Act of 1933.

Dirks v. Securities and Exchange Commission (463 U.S. 646), decided by a 6-3 vote, July 1, 1983. Powell wrote the opinion; Blackmun, Brennan and Marshall dissented.

A securities analyst did not violate federal securities law that forbids the trading of stocks on the basis of inside information when he acted on the basis of a tip from a corporate insider and advised several of his clients to sell stock in a company that was about to collapse.

Individuals who receive such inside information are obligated to disclose it to the Securities and Exchange Commission or to abstain from trading on it altogether only if the person who gave them the information breached his duty to his stockholders by doing so and stands to gain personally as a result. No such breach occurred in this case.

Daily Income Fund Inc. v. Fox, decided by a 9-0 vote, Jan. 18, 1984. Brennan wrote the opinion.

Shareholders suing a mutual fund to recover allegedly excessive fees paid to fund advisers are not required by the federal rules of civil procedure to demand, before bringing suit, that the fund's directors recover the fees.

Securities and Exchange Commission v. O'Brien, decided by a 9-0 vote, June 18, 1984. Marshall wrote the opinion.

The Securities and Exchange Commission is not required to notify the persons who are the subject of non-public investigations when it issues subpoenas to third parties as part of such investigations.

Shipping

Scindia Steam Navigation Co. Ltd. v. De Los Santos (451 U.S. 156), decided by a 9-0 vote, April 21, 1981. White wrote the opinion.

A shipowner, within limits, is entitled to rely on the stevedore to detect problems in a ship and its equipment that may develop during the stevedore's use. The shipowner is not liable to longshoremen for injuries caused by dangers about which he did not know and about which he had no duty to inform himself. If a shipowner knows that a stevedore is continuing to use malfunctioning equipment at the risk of harm to longshoremen, the shipowner then has the duty to intervene and repair the equipment.

Rodriguez v. Compass Shipping Co. (451 U.S. 596), decided by a 9-0 vote, May 18, 1981. Stevens wrote the opinion.

A longshoreman may not prosecute a personal injury action against a negligent shipowner after his right to recover damages for his injury has been assigned to his employer through the provisions of the Longshoremen's and Harbor Workers' Compensation Act.

Griffin v. Oceanic Contractors Inc. (458 U.S. 564), decided by a 7-2 vote, June 30, 1982. Rehnquist wrote the opinion; Stevens and Blackmun dissented.

A federal district court has no discretion to limit the period for which a wage penalty is assessed under the Jones Act against a vessel owner for wages wrongly withheld from a seaman. This penalty must be assessed for each day that payment of the wages is withheld.

Taxation

Commissioner of Internal Revenue v. Portland Cement Company of Utah (450 U.S. 156), decided by a 9-0 vote, March 3, 1981. Powell wrote the opinion.

A cement miner and manufacturer must treat cement sold in bulk *and* in bags as his "first marketable product" for the purpose of determining his gross income from mining for figuring his depletion deduction.

United States v. Swank (451 U.S. 571), decided by a 7-2 vote, May 18, 1981. Stevens wrote the opinion; White and Stewart dissented.

A coal mine operator is entitled to claim a mineral depletion deduction on his federal income tax return, even if the person from whom he leases his mine can terminate the lease on short notice.

Rowan Cos. Inc. v. United States (452 U.S. 247), decided by a 6-3 vote, June 8, 1981. Powell wrote the opinion; White, Brennan and Marshall dissented.

The Internal Revenue Service may not require an employer to include certain fringe benefits — the value of meals and lodging provided to workers while on the job, for example — in the wage base upon which it pays Social Security and unemployment taxes. Those fringe benefits do not count as wages for the purposes of income tax withholding and thus should not be counted "wages" for these other purposes.

United States v. Vogel Fertilizer Co. (455 U.S. 16), decided by a 7-2 vote, Jan. 13, 1982. Brennan wrote the opinion; Blackmun and White dissented.

The court struck down as invalid a Treasury regulation concerning the definition of a controlled group of corporations described as a "brother-sister controlled group." The Treasury defined such a group as two or more corporations in which the same five or fewer persons own large percentages of stock "singly or in combination." The court said that under the Internal Revenue Code, such a group must be defined as two or more corporations in which the same five or fewer persons own large portions of stock in *each* of the "controlled" companies.

Merrion v. Jicarilla Apache Tribe, Amoco Production Co. v. Jicarilla Apache Tribe (455 U.S. 130), decided by a 6-3 vote, Jan. 25, 1982. Marshall wrote the opinion; Stevens, Rehnquist and Burger dissented.

Indian tribes may constitutionally impose severance taxes upon companies or individuals who develop mineral resources on Indian lands and remove them from those lands. Congress has the power to deny tribes that authority, but it has not done so, leaving with the tribes their inherent power to impose such taxes.

Jewett v. Commissioner of Internal Revenue (455 U.S. 305), decided by a 6-3 vote, Feb. 23, 1982. Stevens wrote the opinion; Blackmun, Rehnquist and O'Connor dissented.

A person who waits 33 years to disclaim a contingent interest in a testamentary trust waited too long for that disclaimer to exempt that interest from federal gift taxes.

Diedrich v. Commissioner of Internal Revenue (457 U.S. 191), decided by an 8-1 vote, June 15, 1982. Burger wrote the opinion; Rehnquist dissented.

Individuals who give property on the condition that the recipient pay the resulting gift tax receive taxable income to the extent that the gift tax exceeds the donor's investment in the gift.

Hillsboro National Bank v. Commissioner of Internal Revenue, United States v. Bliss Dairy (460 U.S. 370), decided by votes of 6-3 and 7-2, March 7, 1983. O'Connor wrote the opinion; Brennan, Stevens, Marshall and Blackmun dissented.

Physical recovery of funds, as in a tax refund, is not required to trigger the application of the so-called tax benefit rule. Under that rule, a taxpayer who deducts in one year an amount he expects to expend on some deductible item must report that amount as income in a subsequent year if the expected expense does not occur.

United States v. Rylander (460 U.S. 752), decided by an 8-1 vote, April 19, 1983. Rehnquist wrote the opinion; Marshall dissented.

A taxpayer held in civil contempt for refusing to produce certain corporate records sought by the Internal Revenue Service (IRS) cannot force the IRS to prove that he has those records simply by declaring that he does not and then invoking the Fifth Amendment privilege against compelled self-incrimination to avoid answering any further questions.

Commissioner of Internal Revenue v. Tufts (461 U.S. 300), decided by a 9-0 vote, May 2, 1983. Blackmun wrote the opinion.

The amount of gain realized on the sale of a property subject to a non-recourse mortgage that exceeded the fair market value of the property is not limited by the fair market value, but must be considered as the full value of the forgiven debt. (A non-recourse mortgage is one secured only by the value of the mortgaged property; the borrower assumes no personal liability for the loan.)

United States v. Ptasynski (462 U.S. 74), decided by a 9-0 vote, June 6, 1983. Powell wrote the opinion.

The windfall profits tax on domestic oil producers, enacted in 1980, is constitutional despite the fact that Congress exempted from the tax new oil produced on Alaska's North Slope. This exemption, even though framed in geographic terms, does not violate the constitutional requirement that taxes be uniform throughout the United States.

Aloha Airlines Inc. v. Director of Taxation of Hawaii, decided by a 9-0 vote, Nov. 1, 1983. Marshall wrote the opinion.

The Airport Development Acceleration Act of 1973 prohibited state taxes on air travel and pre-empted Hawaii law imposing a tax on the annual gross income of airlines operating entirely within that state.

Commissioner of Internal Revenue v. Engle, Farmar v. United States, decided by a 5-4 vote, Jan. 10, 1984. O'Connor wrote the opinion; Blackmun, Brennan, White and Marshall dissented.

Taxpayers who own oil and gas wells may take a depletion deduction on part of the income they receive from leaseholders, even in years when the wells do not produce oil or gas.

Badaracco v. Commissioner of Internal Revenue, Deleet Merchandising Corp. v. United States, decided by an 8-1 vote, Jan. 17, 1984. Blackmun wrote the opinion; Stevens dissented.

A taxpayer who files a false or fraudulent return and later files a correct amended return may still be assessed the appropriate tax and penalties from the first return at any time; the three-year limitation on assessment of federal income taxes does not apply in such circumstances.

Dickman v. Commissioner of Internal Revenue, decided by a 7-2 vote, Feb. 22, 1984. Burger wrote the opinion; Powell and Rehnquist dissented.

Intrafamily interest-free loans are subject to federal gift taxes. The tax is assessed against the donor on the value of the use of the money lent.

United States v. Arthur Young & Co., decided by a 9-0 vote, March 21, 1984. Burger wrote the opinion.

There is no immunity protecting the tax accrual workpapers of a company's independent auditor from a summons by the Internal Revenue Service.

Limbach v. The Hooven & Allison Co., decided by a 9-0 vote, April 18, 1984. Blackmun wrote the opinion.

Ohio's state tax commissioner may argue again, against the same company as earlier, in defense of a state property tax on certain imported goods held unconstitutional by the court in 1945, because in 1976 the court overruled the precedent upon which the 1945 decision was based (*Michelin Tire Corp. v. Wages* overruling *Low v. Austin,* 1872).

Westinghouse Electric Corp. v. Tully, decided by a 9-0 vote, April 24, 1984. Blackmun wrote the opinion.

New York discriminated against exports from other states in violation of the Commerce Clause when it permitted corporations to claim a tax credit on the accumulated income of their subsidiary Domestic International Sales Corporations only for gross receipts attributable to export shipments from New York.

Trademarks

Inwood Laboratories Inc. v. Ives Laboratories Inc. (456 U.S. 844), decided by a 9-0 vote, June 1, 1982. O'Connor wrote the opinion.

Manufacturers of a generic drug equivalent to a trademarked product are not guilty of trademark infringement because they marketed their drug in capsules that looked just like those of the trademarked product unless it is shown that they intentionally induced pharmacists to substitute the generic for the trademarked drug contrary to prescription specifications, or that they continued to supply the generic drug to pharmacists whom they knew were engaging in such mislabeling of drugs.

Labor Law

Barrentine v. Arkansas-Best Freight System (450 U.S. 728), decided by a 7-2 vote, April 6, 1981. Brennan wrote the opinion; Burger and Rehnquist dissented.

An employee may bring a federal suit charging his employer with violating the minimum wage provisions of the Fair Labor Standards Act even after he has successfully made the same claim to a joint grievance committee set up by his union's collective-bargaining agreement.

Universities Research Association Inc. v. Coutu (450 U.S. 754), decided by a 9-0 vote, April 6, 1981. Blackmun wrote the opinion.

The Davis-Bacon Act does not give an employee the right to sue for back wages under a contract that had been determined not to call for Davis-Bacon work and that does not contain any stipulation concerning the payment of the prevailing wage.

United Parcel Service v. Mitchell (451 U.S. 56), decided by an 8-1 vote, April 20, 1981. Rehnquist wrote the opinion; Stevens dissented in part.

A state statute of limitations for actions to vacate arbitration awards was properly applied to an employee's effort to sue in federal court his union and his former employer on the basis that he had been wrongfully discharged. This was the appropriate statute of limitations

because the employee had initially contested his firing through the grievance and arbitration procedures set up by the agreement between his union and his employer.

Complete Auto Transit v. Reis (451 U.S. 401), decided by a 7-2 vote, May 4, 1981. Brennan wrote the opinion; Burger and Rehnquist dissented.

Employers may not sue individual employees for damages after the employees strike in violation of a provision of their collective bargaining agreement. Congress deliberately limited the situations in which such a damages remedy might be used, allowing damage suits against unions, but not against individuals, for such violations of collective bargaining agreements.

Alessi v. Raybestos-Manhattan, Buczynski v. General Motors (451 U.S. 504), decided by an 8-0 vote, May 18, 1981. Marshall wrote the opinion; Brennan did not take part in the decision.

Employers are free, under the Employee Retirement Income Security Act of 1974, to reduce benefits to a retiree in an amount equal to the workers' compensation benefits he receives. Federal law permits such "offsets" and to that extent, pre-empts state laws forbidding them.

Clayton v. United Auto Workers (451 U.S. 679), decided by a 5-4 vote, May 26, 1981. Brennan wrote the opinon; Burger, Powell, Rehnquist and Stewart dissented.

A union member who lost his job for violating a rule set out by his employer did not have to exhaust the internal union appeals procedure (after the union withdrew its pursuit of his grievance) before filing suit against his union in federal court, charging it with breaching its duty to represent him fairly, and against the employer for dismissing him.

Plumbers and Pipefitters, AFL-CIO v. Local #334 (452 U.S. 615), decided by a 6-3 vote, June 22, 1981. Brennan wrote the opinion; Stevens, Rehnquist and Burger dissented.

Federal courts have jurisdiction to hear a suit brought by a local union against its parent international union, charging the parent union with violating its constitution by requiring the consolidation of certain locals.

First National Maintenance Corp. v. National Labor Relations Board (452 U.S. 666), decided by a 7-2 vote, June 22, 1981. Blackmun wrote the opinion; Brennan and Marshall dissented.

A company's management is not required by federal labor law to bargain with the union representing its employees over a decision to terminate a portion of its operations and put some workers out of a job.

National Labor Relations Board v. Amax Coal Co. (453 U.S. 322), decided by an 8-1 vote, June 29, 1981. Stewart wrote the opinion; Stevens dissented.

A trustee of an employee benefit trust, appointed by management, is not a representative of the employer for purposes of collective bargaining or grievance adjustment within the meaning of the National Labor Relations Act (NLRA). But the NLRA does not limit the freedom of a union to try to persuade an employer to choose a particular person as trustee. Nor does union pressure, such as a strike, to induce an employer to contribute to a multi-employer trust fund, amount to an unfair labor practice of dictating

to an employer who shall represent him in collective bargaining or grievance adjustments because employee benefit trustees do not engage in such activities.

National Labor Relations Board v. Hendricks County Rural Electric Membership Corp., Hendricks County Rural Electric Membership Corp. v. National Labor Relations Board (454 U.S. 170), decided by votes of 6-3 and 5-4, Dec. 2, 1981. Brennan wrote the opinion; Burger, Rehnquist, O'Connor and Powell dissented.

The only "confidential employees" exempt from the protection of federal labor law are those who enjoy the confidence of company officials involved in setting and carrying out labor relations policy. This exemption does not extend to secretaries and all employees who have access to some confidential information.

Charles D. Bonanno Linen Service Inc. v. National Labor Relations Board (454 U.S. 404), decided by a 5-4 vote, Jan. 12, 1982. White wrote the opinion; Burger, Rehnquist, O'Connor and Powell dissented.

An impasse in bargaining between a multi-employer group and a union does not justify the unilateral withdrawal of an employer from the bargaining unit.

United Mine Workers of America Health and Retirement Funds v. Robinson (455 U.S. 562), decided by a 9-0 vote, March 8, 1982. Stevens wrote the opinion.

The Labor Management Relations Act does not authorize federal courts to review the provisions of a collective-bargaining agreement for reasonableness including such provisions setting eligibility standards for health and welfare funds.

International Longshoremen's Association, AFL-CIO v. Allied International Inc. (456 U.S. 212), decided by a 9-0 vote. Powell wrote the opinion.

The refusal by an American longshoremen's union to unload cargo shipped from the Soviet Union, a step taken in protest of the Russian invasion of Afghanistan, is a secondary boycott, illegal under the National Labor Relations Act. The application of this ban on secondary boycotts to this boycott does not infringe on the First Amendment rights of the union and its members.

Finnegan v. Leu (456 U.S. 431), decided by a 9-0 vote, May 17, 1982. Burger wrote the opinion.

A union president who, after his election, removed from their union posts 15 individuals who under union constitution served at his pleasure and who had actively supported his opponent in the union election did not violate their First Amendment rights as guaranteed in federal labor law. That guarantees the free speech rights of members, not the tenure of union officers.

Woelke & Romero Framing Inc. v. National Labor Relations Board, Pacific Northwest Chapter of the Associated Builders & Contractors Inc. v. National Labor Relations Board, Oregon-Columbia Chapter, Associated General Contractors of America v. National Labor Relations Board (456 U.S. 645), decided by a 9-0 vote, May 24, 1982. Marshall wrote the opinion.

Federal labor law permits construction unions operating under collective bargaining agreements to demand that

contractors use subcontractors that recognize the union.

Summit Valley Industries Inc. v. Local 112, United Brotherhood of Carpenters and Joiners of America (456 U.S. 717), decided by a 9-0 vote, June 1, 1982. Marshall wrote the opinion.

A company or individual who successfully brings unfair labor practice charges against a union may, under the Labor Management Relations Act, seek damages to compensate him for injuries sustained as a result of the unfair labor practice, but attorneys' fees incurred by the complainant during the proceedings concerning the unfair labor practice charge before the National Labor Relations Board are not a proper element of those damages.

Jackson Transit Authority v. Local Div. 1285, Amalgamated Transit Union (457 U.S. 15), decided by a 9-0 vote, June 7, 1982. Blackmun wrote the opinion.

Labor disputes between the employees of a publicly owned transit system, which changed from private to public hands with aid provided through the Urban Mass Transportation Act of 1964, and the management of the transit system should be resolved in state courts, not federal courts. By providing for the preservation of transit systems' employees' bargaining rights, the 1964 Act did not create a federal cause of action allowing those rights to be enforced in federal court.

United Steelworkers of America v. Sadlowski (457 U.S. 102), decided by a 5-4 vote, June 14, 1982. Marshall wrote the opinion; White, Burger, Brennan and Blackmun dissented.

A United Steelworkers rule barring contributions by non-members to candidates for union office does not violate the provisions of the Labor Management Reporting and Disclosure Act of 1959, which guarantees union members freedom to sue and freedom of speech and assembly. The rule does affect those rights but it is justified by the union's interest in ensuring that non-members do not unduly influence union affairs.

Jacksonville Bulk Terminals Inc. v. International Longshoremen's Association (457 U.S. 702), decided by a 6-3 vote, June 24, 1982. Marshall wrote the opinion; Burger, Powell and Stevens dissented.

The Norris-LaGuardia Act, which bars federal courts from enjoining any strike involving or growing out of a labor dispute, denies a federal court the power to enjoin a politically motivated longshoremen's boycott of cargo coming from or going to the Soviet Union, even though that boycott was in violation of a no-strike clause and an arbitration clause in the union's collective bargaining contract.

Bowen v. United States Postal Service (459 U.S. 212), decided by a vote of 5-4, Jan. 11, 1983. Powell wrote the opinion; Rehnquist, White, Marshall and Blackmun dissented.

Labor unions that fail to provide fair representation to their members in cases of wrongful dismissal may be held jointly liable with the employer for wages the employee lost as a result of their misconduct or failure to act.

Shepard v. National Labor Relations Board (NLRB) (459 U.S. 344), decided by an 8-1 vote, Jan. 18, 1983. Rehnquist wrote the opinion; O'Connor dissented.

The NLRB acted within the area of discretion granted it by Congress when it decided not to order a union or contractors, who had illegally agreed not to deal with non-union dump truck drivers, to reimburse a dump truck operator who was compelled by this illegal agreement to join the union for the amount he paid in dues, initiation fees and fringe benefit contributions.

The NLRB issued an order directing the union and the contractors to cease this illegal boycott of independent truck drivers, but it refused to order the reimbursement, holding that it would not in any way carry out the remedial purposes of the National Labor Relations Act. Such a decision is within the authority granted the board by Congress.

Metropolitan Edison Co. v. National Labor Relations Board (460 U.S. 693), decided by a 9-0 vote, April 4, 1983. Powell wrote the opinion.

Union leaders cannot be punished by employers more severely than other workers for participating in illegal strikes, unless the labor contract specifically requires them to prevent such strikes.

This case involved a 1977 strike during construction of the Three Mile Island nuclear plant near Harrisburg, Pa. Metropolitan Edison, operator of the plant, disciplined leaders of the International Brotherhood of Electrical Workers when members of the union refused to cross a picket line set up by another union.

Jim McNeff Inc. v. Todd (461 U.S. 260), decided by a 9-0 vote, April 27, 1983. Burger wrote the opinion.

A construction union can sue a contractor to enforce a "pre-hire agreement," a contract between the contractor and union before the union had been selected to represent the contractor's employees. The agreement at issue required the contractor to contribute to a union health and pension fund.

Such agreements are generally prohibited under federal labor law but are allowed in the construction industry so that bidding contractors can estimate labor costs.

Bill Johnson's Restaurants Inc. v. National Labor Relations Board (NLRB) (461 U.S. 731), decided by a 9-0 vote, May 31, 1983. White wrote the opinion.

The NLRB may not halt proceedings in a state court lawsuit so long as the suit has a reasonable legal or factual basis, even if the suit is allegedly filed by an employer to retaliate against employees who are attempting to organize a union.

W. R. Grace & Co. v. Local #759, International Union of the United Rubber, Cork, Linoleum and Plastic Workers of America (461 U.S. 757), decided by a 9-0 vote, May 31, 1983. Blackmun wrote the opinion.

A company that furloughed white males in order to preserve the jobs of more recently hired women and black employees cannot escape damage claimed by the fired workers because of its layoff decision was the result of an anti-discrimination agreement. A discriminatory employer who signs conflicting labor agreements, one with a union and one with the Equal Employment Opportunity Commission, cannot use the latter as a shield against a suit charging it with violating the former agreement.

DelCostello v. International Brotherhood of Teamsters, United Steelworkers of America v.

Flowers (462 U.S. 151), decided by a 7-2 vote, June 8, 1983. Brennan wrote the opinion; Stevens and O'Connor dissented.

Federal labor law, not state laws limiting the period within which arbitration awards can be set aside, governs the right of employees to file suit against employers and unions alleging breach of a collective bargaining agreement and breach of the union's duty of fair representation in handling the resulting grievance or arbitration.

National Labor Relations Board (NLRB) v. Transportation Management Corp. (462 U.S. 393), decided by a 9-0 vote, June 15, 1983. White wrote the opinion.

The NLRB properly concluded that an employer violated federal labor law when it was shown, by a preponderance of the evidence, that hostility toward an employee's union organizing activities was a motivating factor in his dismissal and the employer had not proved by a preponderance of the evidence that the employee would have been discharged anyway for legitimate reasons.

Edward J. DeBartolo Corp. v. National Labor Relations Board (463 U.S. 147), decided by a 9-0 vote, June 24, 1983. Stevens wrote the opinion.

A union handbilling campaign urging a boycott of a shopping mall because the union has a dispute with the contractor building a store for one small tenant is a secondary boycott prohibited by the National Labor Relations Act. This campaign is not protected by the "publicity proviso," which permits a union to advise the public that one company sells the product of another company with which the union has a primary dispute.

Belknap Inc. v. Hale (463 U.S. 491), decided by a 6-3 vote, June 30, 1983. White wrote the opinion; Brennan, Marshall and Powell dissented.

Non-union workers, hired during a strike as permanent replacements for striking workers and then fired when the striking workers came back to work, may sue the employer in state courts for misrepresentation and breach of contract.

State court jurisdiction over such cases is not preempted by the National Labor Relations Act.

Bureau of Alcohol, Tobacco and Firearms v. Federal Labor Relations Authority, decided by a 9-0 vote, Nov. 29, 1983. Brennan wrote the opinion.

The Civil Service Reform Act of 1978 does not require federal agencies to pay a daily allowance and travel expenses to employees who must travel in order to act as negotiators for unions representing government employees. Employees receive their salary for days spent in such labor negotiations, but no additional allowances.

Donovan v. Lone Steer Inc., decided by a 9-0 vote, Jan. 17, 1984. Rehnquist wrote the opinion.

Federal wage and hour inspectors are not required to obtain a warrant before they issue administrative subpoenas ordering businesses to produce payroll records for inspection to check compliance with federal wage and hour laws.

Ellis v. Brotherhood of Railway, Airline and Steamship Clerks, decided by votes of 9-0 and 8-1, April 25, 1984. White wrote the opinion; Powell dissented in part.

Under a Railway Labor Act provision authorizing a union shop, a union may use dues collected from objecting employees to finance its conventions, social activities and publications, but not to pay for organization, litigation or death benefits. The union's use of dues for permissible purposes does not violate the First Amendment rights of objecting employees.

The union's plan to reimburse objecting employees a portion of the dues spent on impermissible purposes does not adequately remedy the improper use of these funds.

Local #82, Furniture & Piano Moving, Furniture Store Drivers, Helpers, Warehousemen & Packers v. Crowley, decided by an 8-1 vote, June 12, 1984. Brennan wrote the opinion; Stevens dissented.

A federal judge exceeded his authority under Title I of the Labor-Management Reporting and Disclosure Act when he declared a union election already under way to be in violation of members' rights and spelled out procedures for a new court-supervised election.

Occupational Safety

American Textile Manufacturers Institute v. Donovan, National Cotton Council v. Donovan (452 U.S. 490), decided by a 5-3 vote, June 17, 1981. Brennan wrote the opinion; Rehnquist, Burger and Stewart dissented; Powell did not participate in the decision.

Congress in passing the 1970 Occupational Safety and Health Act (PL 91-596) struck the balance between the costs and the benefits of new health and safety standards for American workers. That balance — in favor of the health benefits — is reflected in the language of the law that directs the Occupational Safety and Health Administration to set standards that assure "to the extent feasible" that no worker will suffer "material impairment of health" from exposure to a hazardous substance during his working life.

Therefore the court rebuffed the arguments of the business community, in particular the textile industry facing stringent new cotton dust standards, that the costs and benefits of those standards should be more carefully weighed. And the court upheld those new standards, in spite of arguments that the cost of implementing them could put some manufacturers out of business.

Donovan v. Dewey (452 U.S. 544), decided by an 8-1 vote, June 17, 1981. Marshall wrote the opinion; Stewart dissented.

Federal mine inspectors need not obtain search warrants before conducting routine inspection of mines, authorized by the Federal Mine Safety and Health Act of 1977 (PL 95-164).

The "notorious history" of mine accidents and unhealthy conditions and the regular schedule of federal inspections make a warrant unnecessary.

National Labor Relations Board v. City Disposal Systems Inc., decided by a 5-4 vote, March 21, 1984. Brennan wrote the opinion; O'Connor, Burger, Powell and Rehnquist dissented.

Under federal labor law, an employee covered by a collective bargaining agreement specifying that workers should not be required to drive unsafe vehicles is protected from reprisals if he refuses to drive a vehicle on grounds that he believes it to be unsafe.

Longshoremen and Harbor Workers

Potomac Electric Power Co. v. Director, Office of Workers' Compensation Programs, U.S. Department of Labor (449 U.S. 268), decided by an 8-1 vote, Dec. 15, 1980. Stevens wrote the opinion; Blackmun dissented.

Compensation for a permanent partial disability suffered by a worker covered by the Longshoremen's and Harbor Workers' Compensation Act must be determined in accord with a formula set out in that law if the injury is one of those specifically identified in the law. The alternative formula provided in the law for "all other cases" may not be used for injuries specifically identified in the law.

U.S. Industries/Federal Sheet Metal Inc. v. Director, Office of Workers' Compensation Programs, U.S. Department of Labor (455 U.S. 608), decided by a 6-2 vote, March 23, 1982. Stevens wrote the opinion; Brennan and Marshall dissented; O'Connor did not participate in the decision.

An appeals court erred when it presumed that an injury first noticed at home by a workman was in fact the result of an accident at work and thus made him eligible for disability benefits under the Longshoremen's and Harbor Workers' Compensation Act.

Director, Office of Workers' Compensation Programs v. Perini North River Associates (459 U.S. 297), decided by an 8-1 vote, Jan. 11, 1983. O'Connor wrote the opinion; Stevens dissented.

A construction worker injured while building a sewage disposal plant over a navigable waterway is engaged in "maritime employment" for the purposes of compensation under the Longshoremen's and Harbor Workers' Compensation Act.

Pallas Shipping Agency Ltd. v. Duris (461 U.S. 529), decided by a 9-0 vote, May 23, 1983. Marshall wrote the opinion.

Acceptance by an injured longshoreman of compensation voluntarily paid by his employer, but terminated after two years, does not trigger the provision of the Longshoremen's and Harbor Workers' Compensation Act that assigns to his employer after six months his right to sue any third party responsible for his injury.

Morrison-Knudsen Construction Co. v. Director, Office of Workers' Compensation Programs, U.S. Department of Labor (461 U.S. 624), decided by an 8-1 vote, May 24, 1983. Burger wrote the opinion; Marshall dissented.

In calculating the death benefits to be paid under the Longshoremen's and Harbor Workers' Compensation Act, the "wages" upon which those benefits are based do not include employer payments to union trust funds on behalf of the deceased employee.

Jones & Laughlin Steel Corp. v. Pfiefer (462 U.S. 523), decided by a 9-0 vote, June 15, 1983. Stevens wrote the opinion.

A longshoreman injured at work on a barge owned by his employer may sue the vessel owner, his employer, under the Longshoremen's and Harbor Workers' Compensation Act for causing his injury through negligence, even though he has already received compensation from his employer under the law.

Washington Metropolitan Area Transit Authority v. Johnson, decided by a 6-3 vote, June 26, 1984. Marshall wrote the opinion; Rehnquist, Brennan and Stevens dissented.

A general contractor subject to the provisions of the Longshoremen's and Harbor Workers' Compensation Act is immune from negligence damage suits by employees claiming they suffered respiratory ailments as a result of exposure to dust and other pollutants in the course of their work because the employer saw to it that those employees were covered by workmen's compensation insurance.

The immunity provisions of federal workmen's compensation law apply to general contractors as well a subcontractors who, in this case, were the actual employers of the plaintiff workmen.

Energy and Environment

Environmental Protection Agency (EPA) v. National Crushed Stone Association (449 U.S. 64), decided by an 8-0 vote, Dec. 2, 1980. White wrote the opinion; Powell did not participate in the decision.

Congress, in adopting 1977 standards for clean water, in the Federal Water Pollution Control Act Amendments of 1972, did not intend for the EPA to concern itself with the economic impact of compliance with those standards. The court rebuffed the argument that variances from such standards could be justified for plants for whom the cost of compliance might be so great as to force their closing.

Watt v. Alaska, Kenai Peninsula Borough v. Alaska (451 U.S. 259), decided by a 6-3 vote, April 21, 1981. Powell wrote the opinion; Stewart, Burger and Marshall dissented.

Revenues from oil and gas leases of federal land in the Kenai National Moose Range in Alaska, a wildlife refuge, should be distributed according to the formula set out in the Mineral Leasing Act of 1920 — 90 percent to the state and 10 percent to the U.S. Treasury, not the 25-75 percent split between county and federal government set out in the later Wildlife Refuge Revenue Sharing Act.

California v. Sierra Club, Kern County Water Agency v. Sierra Club (451 U.S. 287), decided by a 9-0 vote, April 28, 1981. White wrote the opinion.

Private citizens or groups are not authorized to bring suits to enforce the provisions of the Rivers and Harbors Act of 1899. Only the federal government may sue to enforce that law.

City of Milwaukee v. Illinois and Michigan (451 U.S. 304), decided by a vote of 6-3, April 28, 1981. Rehnquist wrote the opinion; Blackmun, Marshall and Stevens dissented.

A federal court lacks the power to impose more stringent water pollution control standards on a city than Congress has imposed under the Federal Water Pollution Control Act Amendments of 1972. That law set up a comprehensive system of standards and left no room for federal judges to set stricter ones.

Hodel v. Virginia Surface Mining and Reclamation Association, Virginia Surface Mining and Reclamation Association v. Hodel (452 U.S. 264), decided by a 9-0 vote, June 15, 1981. Marshall wrote the opinion.

Congress did not exceed its authority to regulate inter-state commerce when it enacted the Surface Mining Control and Reclamation Act of 1977 (PL 95-87). On its face, the strip-mining law, which imposes severe land use restrictions and strict reclamation requirements, does not violate the Constitution.

Hodel v. Indiana (452 U.S. 314), decided by a 9-0 vote, June 15, 1981. Marshall wrote the opinion.

Congress did not act unconstitutionally when it enacted the Surface Mining Control and Reclamation Act of 1977. On its face, the provisions of that law are not unconstitutional.

Middlesex County Sewerage Authority v. National Sea Clammers Association, Joint Meeting of Essex and Union Counties v. National Sea Clammers Association, City of New York v. National Sea Clammers Association, Environmental Protection Agency v. National Sea Clammers Association (457 U.S. 423), decided by votes of 9-0 and 7-2, June 25, 1981. Powell wrote the opinion; Stevens and Blackmun dissented in part.

Congress, in passing the Federal Water Pollution Control Act (PL 92-500) and the Marine Protection, Research and Sanctuaries Act (PL 92-532), did not authorize citizens to sue violators of those laws for money damages. Citizens may sue under those laws to halt pollution, but not to win damages compensating them for past pollution damage.

Arkansas Louisiana Gas Co v. Hall (453 U.S. 571), decided by a 5-3 vote, July 2, 1981. Marshall wrote the opinion; Powell, Stevens and Rehnquist dissented; Stewart did not participate in the decision.

Congress has granted the Federal Energy Regulatory Commission exclusive jurisdiction over the rate at which natural gas may be sold and a state court may not award damages to natural gas producers that are tantamount to a retroactive rate increase.

Weinberger v. Catholic Action of Hawaii/Peace Education Project (454 U.S. 139), decided by a 9-0 vote, Dec. 1, 1981. Rehnquist wrote the opinion.

The Department of Defense does not have to formulate and release a "hypothetical environmental impact statement" on the potential consequences of storing nuclear weapons at a naval base in Hawaii. Congress provided in the National Environmental Policy Act (PL 91-190) that public disclosure of required environmental impact statements was subject to provisions of the Freedom of Information Act.

Since information about the site of nuclear weapons is classified, any impact statement that would reveal such information is exempt from disclosure under the Freedom of Information Act.

Watt v. Energy Action Educational Foundation (454 U.S. 151), decided by a 9-0 vote, Dec. 1, 1981. O'Connor wrote the opinion.

The interior secretary has discretion to decide whether to experiment with non-cash-bonus bidding systems for offshore leasing. The 1978 Outer Continental Shelf Lands Act Amendments (PL 95-372) required a five-year period of experimentation with new bidding systems but did not demand experimentation with specific alternative systems.

Weinberger v. Romero-Barcelo (456 U.S. 305), decided by an 8-1 vote, April 27, 1982. White wrote the opinion; Stevens dissented.

Federal courts have some discretion in determining proper remedies for violations of the Federal Water Pollution Control Act. The justices held that a federal district court acted within permissible limits when it allowed the U.S. Navy to continue target practice on an island off Puerto Rico while it sought a permit for discharging ordnance into the coastal waters, as required under the law. An appeals court had ruled that the district court should have ordered a halt to the target practice until the permit was obtained.

Federal Energy Regulatory Commission v. Mississippi (456 U.S. 742), decided by votes of 9-0 and 5-4, June 1, 1982. Blackmun wrote the opinion; Powell, O'Connor, Burger and Rehnquist dissented in part.

Congress was within its power to regulate interstate commerce when it passed the Public Utility Regulatory Policies Act of 1978 (PL 95-617) directing state utility regulatory commissions to consider adopting certain rate-design and regulatory standards and to follow certain procedures when acting on those standards. (The majority held that PL 95-617 did not infringe upon powers reserved to the states under the 10th Amendment, but the four dissenters disagreed and said the law should be held unconstitutional.)

Energy Reserves Group Inc. v. Kansas Power & Light Co. Inc. (459 U.S. 400), decided by a 9-0 vote, Jan. 24, 1983. Blackmun wrote the opinion.

States retain the power to limit prices for the in-state sale of gas produced in the state even though Congress has moved to deregulate the price of natural gas sold interstate. The court upheld a 1979 Kansas law that permitted the state to continue regulating the intrastate price of gas produced under contracts already in effect when federal deregulation began in 1978.

North Dakota v. United States (460 U.S. 300), decided by a 7-2 vote, March 7, 1983. Blackmun wrote the opinion; O'Connor and Rehnquist dissented.

States that consent to the federal acquisition of waterfowl breeding and nesting grounds, authorized and funded under the Migratory Bird Hunting and Conservation Stamp Act and the Wetlands Act of 1961, cannot subsequently revoke that consent or impose new restrictions and conditions on those acquisitions.

Metropolitan Edison Co. v. People Against Nuclear Energy (PANE), United States Nuclear Regulatory Commission (NRC) v. PANE (460 U.S. 766), decided by a 9-0 vote, April 19, 1983. Rehnquist wrote the opinion.

The National Environmental Policy Act does not require the NRC to assess the risk of psychological harm to residents of communities near nuclear power plants before it approves a change in the operation of those plants.

Pacific Gas & Electric Co. v. State Energy Resources Conservation and Development Commission (461 U.S. 190), decided by a 9-0 vote, April 20, 1983. White wrote the opinion.

The Atomic Energy Act leaves the states sufficient

power to block construction of new nuclear power plants until an adequate federal plan for disposing of nuclear waste has been developed.

The court upheld a California law that imposed a moratorium on the construction of new plants until such a plan was adopted by the federal government. The court found the state law was not based on concern about the safety of nuclear power plants, an area in which state power is pre-empted by federal law, but on concern about the economic viability of nuclear power.

Block v. North Dakota (461 U.S. 273), decided by an 8-1 vote, May 2, 1983. White wrote the opinion; O'Connor dissented.

The Quiet Title Act of 1972 is the exclusive means by which states, or other adverse claimants, can challenge the U.S. title to real property. That law's 12-year statute of limitations applies to states just as it does to other parties suing under it.

Arkansas Electric Cooperative Corp. v. Arkansas Public Service Commission (461 U.S. 375), decided by a 7-2 vote, May 16, 1983. Brennan wrote the opinion; White and Burger dissented.

Neither the Constitution's grant of power to Congress to regulate interstate commerce, nor its clause stating that federal laws have supremacy over state laws when they conflict, is offended by a state commission's assertion of jurisdiction over the wholesale rates a rural power cooperative within the state charges to its members.

American Paper Institute Inc. v. American Electric Power Service Corp., Federal Energy Regulatory Commission (FERC) v. American Electric Power Service Corp. (461 U.S. 402), decided by an 8-0 vote, May 16, 1983. Marshall wrote the opinion; Powell did not participate in the decision.

The FERC acted properly in issuing two key regulations under the Public Utility Regulatory Policies Act of 1978. The first required utilities purchasing electricity from small firms that generate electricity as well as other forms of energy from the same source to pay these "cogenerators" the "full avoided cost" of producing that amount of power themselves or purchasing it elsewhere. The second regulation required these utilities to make the interconnections necessary to receive power from cogenerators.

Baltimore Gas & Electric Co. v. Natural Resources Defense Council Inc. (462 U.S. 87), decided by an 8-0 vote, June 6, 1983. O'Connor wrote the opinion; Powell did not participate in the decision.

The Nuclear Regulatory Commission does not have to consider the problem of the permanent storage of nuclear waste each time it licenses a new nuclear power plant. The court upheld an NRC rule that permits its licensing boards to assume, when licensing a new plant, that there will be a means of storing the wastes that plant generates without damaging the environment.

Watt v. Western Nuclear Inc. (462 U.S. 36), decided by a 5-4 vote, June 6, 1983. Marshall wrote the opinion; Powell, Rehnquist, Stevens and O'Connor dissented.

Gravel is a mineral within the meaning of the Stock-Raising Homestead Act of 1916, and thus gravel on land settled by homesteaders under that law remains the property of the U.S. government.

Nevada v. United States, Truckee-Carson Irrigation District v. United States, Pyramid Lake Paiute Tribe of Indians v. Truckee-Carson Irrigation District (463 U.S. 110), decided by a 9-0 vote, June 24, 1983. Rehnquist wrote the opinion.

The United States is barred by earlier federal court decisions from reopening water rights cases between Indians and state residents in order to seek additional allocations of water to Indians.

Public Service Commission of New York v. Mid-Louisiana Gas Co., Arizona Electric Power Cooperative v. Mid-Louisiana Gas Co., Michigan v. Mid-Louisiana Gas Co., Federal Energy Regulatory Commission v. Mid-Louisiana Gas Co. (463 U.S. 319), decided by a 5-4 vote, June 28, 1983. Stevens wrote the opinion; White, Brennan, Marshall and Blackmun dissented.

Natural gas pipeline companies that produce gas must be allowed to charge the same rate for their gas as independent producers are permitted under the Natural Gas Policy Act of 1978. The Federal Energy Regulatory Commission misinterpreted the 1978 law when it ruled to the contrary.

Ruckelshaus v. Sierra Club (463 U.S. 680), decided by a 5-4 vote, July 1, 1983. Rehnquist wrote the opinion; Stevens, Brennan, Marshall and Blackmun dissented.

Clean Air Act provisions that authorize federal judges in emissions-standards review cases to award attorneys' fees when appropriate authorize such fee awards only to parties who have succeeded in some measure on their claims.

Silkwood v. Kerr-McGee Corp., decided by a 5-4 vote, Jan. 11, 1984. White wrote the opinion; Powell, Burger, Marshall and Blackmun dissented.

The Atomic Energy Act, which asserts exclusive federal jurisdiction over nuclear safety, does not deny states the power to punish egregious violations of nuclear safety regulations through liability laws.

The court reinstated a $10 million punitive damages award made by an Oklahoma jury to the family of Karen Silkwood, a Kerr-McGee employee who died in an accident in 1974 after she was found to be contaminated with plutonium. Plutonium, a highly radioactive substance, was made into fuel pins for nuclear reactors at the Kerr-McGee plant at which Silkwood worked.

Secretary of the Interior v. California, Western Oil and Gas Association v. California, California v. Secretary of the Interior, decided by a 5-4 vote, Jan. 11, 1984. O'Connor wrote the opinion; Stevens, Brennan, Marshall and Blackmun dissented.

States may not block federal offshore lease sales by arguing that the sales are inconsistent with state plans for protecting coastal areas.

The 1972 Coastal Zone Management Act does not require the interior secretary to find lease sales on the Outer Continental Shelf consistent with the coastal management plans of adjacent states. Such consistency determinations are required by law only at later stages of oil and gas development.

Escondido Mutual Water Co. v. La Jolla, Rincon, San Pasqual, Pauma and Pala Bands of Mission Indians, decided by a 9-0 vote, May 15, 1984. White wrote the opinion.

The Federal Power Act requires the Federal Energy Regulatory Commission (FERC) to accept, as part of a license for a hydroelectric project on an Indian reservation, any conditions imposed by the interior secretary (who has jurisdiction over the reservation). This requirement applies only to reservations within which projects are located, not to nearby affected reservations.

The Mission Indian Relief Act of 1891 does not give Mission Indians veto power over FERC decisions to license hydroelectric projects.

Aluminum Company of America v. Central Lincoln Peoples' Utility District, decided by an 8-1 vote, June 5, 1984. Blackmun wrote the opinion; Stevens dissented.

The Bonneville Power Administration acted within its legal authority under the Pacific Northwest Electric Power Planning and Conservation Act of 1980 when it allocated power among its customers in a way challenged by public utilities as shortchanging them in favor of industrial and private utility companies.

Environmental Protection Agency v. Natural Resources Defense Council (NRDC), Chevron USA Inc. v. NRDC, American Iron and Steel Institute v. NRDC, decided by a 6-0 vote, June 25, 1984. Stevens wrote the opinion; Marshall, Rehnquist and O'Connor did not participate.

An Environmental Protection Agency decision to adopt the "bubble concept" for enforcing the Clean Air Act was a reasonable policy choice, well within the agency's authority under the law. Under that concept, an entire plant may be considered one source of air pollution, and changes in portions of the plant may be made without a full-scale environmental review if total emissions from the plant do not increase.

State Powers

Montana v. United States (450 U.S. 544), decided by a 6-3 vote, March 24, 1981. Stewart wrote the opinion; Blackmun, Brennan and Marshall dissented.

Title to the bed of the Big Horn River, which flows through an Indian reservation in Montana, passed to Montana when it was admitted to the Union; the tribe may regulate hunting and fishing by non-tribe members on tribal land, but not on land within the reservation that does not belong to the Indians.

G. D. Searle & Co. v. Cohn (455 U.S. 404), decided by votes of 8-1 and 7-2, Feb. 24, 1982. Blackmun wrote the opinion; Powell and Burger dissented in part; Stevens dissented.

A state law that bars the effect of the statute of limitations for suits against corporations based in other states that have no one in that state upon whom legal process may be served does not vacate the Constitution's promises of equal protection and due process. The effect of such a law in this case was to allow individuals to sue a corporation for the ill effects of a medication 11 years after the ill effects were evident, even though there is normally a two-year statute of limitation on such suits.

New England Power Co. v. New Hampshire, Massachusetts v. New Hampshire, Roberts v. New Hampshire (455 U.S. 331), decided by a 9-0 vote, Feb. 24, 1982. Burger wrote the opinion.

A ban imposed by New Hampshire on out-of-state sales of hydroelectric power produced at plants located on its rivers is unconstitutional, a clear violation of the intent behind the grant to Congress of the power to regulate interstate commerce. This ban was "precisely the sort of protectionist regulation that the commerce clause declares off-limits to the states."

Village of Hoffman Estates v. Flipside (455 U.S. 489), decided by an 8-0 vote, March 3, 1982. Marshall wrote the opinion; Stevens did not participate in the decision.

Cities are not barred by the Constitution from approving and enforcing ordinances regulating "head shops" that sell items designed or marketed for use with illegal drugs. If activities encouraging illegal drug use can be considered "speech" within the meaning of the First Amendment, then it is speech proposing an illegal transaction, which may — consistent with that amendment's guarantee — be regulated or banned entirely by the government.

United Transportation Union v. Long Island Rail Road Co. (455 U.S. 678), decided by a 9-0 vote, March 24, 1982. Burger wrote the opinion.

Applying the Railway Labor Act, which guarantees railroad workers the right to strike, to a state-owned railroad does not interfere so far into state affairs that it violates the 10th Amendment, even if the act displaces a state law forbidding strikes by state employees.

Congressional authority to regulate labor matters in the railroad industry has long been recognized. It is essential that this authority be extended in uniform fashion nationwide and not be displaced by state action. The 10th Amendment protects a state from federal interference that impairs its ability to carry out its essential functions, but operating a railroad is not one of those essential functions.

Cory v. White (457 U.S. 85), decided by a 6-3 vote, June 14, 1982. White wrote the opinion; Powell, Marshall and Stevens dissented.

The 11th Amendment forbids the federal courts to entertain suits brought by citizens against a state without the state's consent. This bars a suit in federal court, under the Federal Interpleader Act, initiated by the administrator of the estate of billionaire Howard Hughes in order to resolve conflicting claims by the states of California and Texas that Hughes was domiciled in their state at the time of his death.

Clements v. Fashing (457 U.S. 957), decided by a 5-4 vote, June 25, 1982. Rehnquist wrote the opinion; Brennan, Marshall, Blackmun and White dissented.

Texas does not violate the guarantee of equal protection by barring certain public officers from running for the state Legislature during the term for which they have been elected to another public office. Nor does the law, which creates a vacancy in an office whenever its holder announces his candidacy for some other state or federal office, violate the equal protection guarantee.

Alfred L. Snapp & Son Inc. v. Puerto Rico (458 U.S. 592), decided by an 8-0 vote, July 1, 1982. White wrote the opinion; Powell did not participate in the ruling.

Puerto Rico has standing to bring a *parens patriae* suit against Virginia apple growers, charging them with violating federal law concerning temporary migrant farm workers. Puerto Rico has a quasi-sovereign interest in the general well-being of its citizens, which this suit is brought to protect.

Florida Department of State v. Treasure Salvors Inc. (458 U.S. 670), decided by a 5-4 vote, July 1, 1982. Stevens announced the court's decision in an opinion joined by three justices; Brennan concurred; White, Powell, Rehnquist and O'Connor dissented.

The 11th Amendment does not bar a federal court from issuing a warrant of arrest directing federal seizure of artifacts taken from a sunken offshore vessel that are in the possession of state officials.

Bell v. New Jersey (461 U.S. 773), decided by a 9-0 vote, May 31, 1983. O'Connor wrote the opinion.

States that misspend federal education funds granted under Title I of the Elementary and Secondary Education Act of 1965 can be required to repay those misspent funds to the federal government. This repayment obligation can be enforced even if the funds were misused before 1978, when Congress specifically amended Title I to authorize repayment in such circumstances.

New Mexico v. Mescalero Apache Tribe (462 U.S. 324), decided by a 9-0 vote, June 13, 1983. Marshall wrote the opinion.

Federal law pre-empts the application of New Mexico hunting and fishing regulations to on-reservation hunting and fishing by non-members of an Indian tribe, once a tribe has with federal assistance set up a comprehensive plan for managing its wildlife resources.

City of Revere v. Massachusetts General Hospital (463 U.S. 239), decided by a 9-0 vote, June 27, 1983. Blackmun wrote the opinion.

The constitutional ban on cruel and unusual punishment obligated a city to see that persons injured while being arrested by police receive appropriate medical care, but it does not obligate the city to pay the medical bills which result. It is up to the state to decide who should pay the bill.

Migra v. Warren City School District Board of Education, decided by a 9-0 vote, Jan. 23, 1984. Blackmun wrote the decision.

The Constitution's "full faith and credit" clause applies to make final a state court judgment in a breach-of-contract case, and to preclude later federal civil rights damage suits based on the same situation and raising issues already resolved by state court.

Southland Corp. v. Keating, decided by votes of 7-2 and 6-3, Jan. 23, 1984. Burger wrote the opinion; O'Connor, Rehnquist and Stevens dissented.

The Federal Arbitration Act's guarantee of a right to arbitrate in commercial contracts containing arbitration clauses pre-empts California law that requires judicial consideration of claims brought under state franchise investment law and thereby renders unenforceable arbitration provisions in franchise contracts.

Michigan Canners & Freezers Association Inc.

v. Agricultural Marketing and Bargaining Board, decided by a 9-0 vote, June 11, 1984. Brennan wrote the opinion.

The Federal Agricultural Fair Practices Act, enacted to enable the development of voluntary agricultural cooperatives as counterparts to large agricultural processors, pre-empts the Michigan Agricultural Marketing and Bargaining Act insofar as the state law requires that all producers of a commodity abide by contracts negotiated by the association, which the state accredited as the bargaining unit for that commodity.

Hayfield Northern Railroad Co. Inc. v. Chicago & Northwestern Transportation Co., decided by a 9-0 vote, June 12, 1984. Marshall wrote the opinion.

The Staggers Rail Act of 1980, governing abandonment of certain rail lines and providing that shippers may obtain continued service by purchasing or subsidizing continued operation, did not pre-empt a state's use of its eminent domain powers to condemn abandoned rail property.

Brown v. Hotel & Restaurant Employees & Bartenders International Union Local #54, decided by a 4-3 vote, July 2, 1984. O'Connor wrote the opinion; Brennan and Marshall did not participate; White, Powell and Stevens dissented.

The National Labor Relations Act does not pre-empt New Jersey's law, which disqualifies persons who have been convicted of certain offenses or who associate with criminal offenders from holding offices in the union representing employees of the Atlantic City, N.J., casinos. Congress has recognized that some states find it necessary to impose such additional restrictions on the qualifications for union posts.

Privileges and Immunities

White v. Massachusetts Council of Construction Employers (460 U.S. 204), decided by votes of 9-0 and 7-2, Feb. 28, 1983. Rehnquist wrote the opinion; Blackmun and White dissented in part.

The power of a city to require that at least half the workers on each city-funded construction project be residents of the city is not pre-empted by the federal power to regulate interstate commerce.

Equal Employment Opportunity Commission v. Wyoming (460 U.S. 226), decided by a 5-4 vote, March 2, 1983. Brennan wrote the opinion; Burger, Powell, Rehnquist and O'Connor dissented.

The Age Discrimination in Employment Act, which forbids states to mandate retirement for certain employees at age 55, does not violate the 10th Amendment guarantee of state power and sovereignty.

Martinez v. Bynum (461 U.S. 321), decided by an 8-1 vote, May 2, 1983. Powell wrote the opinion; Marshall dissented.

States do not have to provide a free education to children who reside within their boundaries solely for the purpose of attending school. The court upheld a Texas law that allows school districts to require minors who live apart from their parents or legal guardians and within the district for the primary purpose of attending its schools to pay tuition.

United Building and Construction Trades Council of Camden County v. Mayor and Council of City of Camden, decided by an 8-1 vote, Feb. 21, 1984. Rehnquist wrote the opinion; Blackmun dissented.

A city ordinance requiring at least 40 percent of the employees on municipal public works projects to be city residents can be challenged as a violation of the constitutional requirement that each state extend to citizens of the other states all the privileges and immunities of its own citizens.

Hoover v. Ronwin, decided by a 4-3 vote, May 14, 1984. Powell wrote the opinion; Stevens, White and Blackmun dissented. Rehnquist and Powell did not participate.

The grading policies of the state bar examination committee, an agency of the Arizona Supreme Court, come within the category of "state action" immune from challenge under federal antitrust laws.

Pulliam v. Allen, decided by a 5-4 vote, May 14, 1984. Blackmun wrote the opinion; Powell, Burger, Rehnquist and O'Connor dissented.

Judges are not immune from prospective injunctions issued under the Civil Rights Act of 1971 forbidding them to act, in the future, in a way that infringes on the civil rights of individuals. Judges are not immune, under the 1976 Civil Rights Attorney's Fee Awards Act, from orders to pay the attorney's fees of persons who successfully sue them for such unconstitutional actions.

Property Rights

Texaco Inc. v. Short, Pond v. Walden (454 U.S. 516), decided by a 5-4 vote, Jan. 12, 1982. Stevens wrote the opinion; Brennan, White, Marshall and Powell dissented.

A state has the power to enact and enforce a law providing for the extinguishment of mineral rights that have been unused for 20 years; application of this law to extinguish such rights without any notice or hearing does not violate the constitutional guarantee of due process, the constitutional ban on impairment of contracts or the prohibition on the taking of property without just compensation.

Loretto v. Teleprompter Manhattan CATV Corp. (458 U.S. 419), decided by a 6-3 vote, June 30, 1982. Marshall wrote the opinion; Blackmun, Brennan and White dissented.

A New York law requiring a landlord to permit installation of cable television facilities upon his property in return for a nominal fee results in a "taking" of private property for public use without just compensation, a violation of the Fifth Amendment. This installation is a "permanent physical occupation of property," which the court has traditionally viewed as a taking of property.

Summa Corp. v. California, decided by an 8-0 vote, April 17, 1984. Rehnquist wrote the opinion; Marshall did not participate in the decision.

California, which did not claim any interest in Ballona Lagoon during 1852 proceedings that resulted in the issuance of a federal patent confirming the interest of private citizens, cannot more than a century later claim that it held an easement in the lagoon for commerce, navigation, fishing or other such public purposes.

Hawaii Housing Authority v. Midkiff, decided by an 8-0 vote, May 30, 1984. O'Connor wrote the opinion; Marshall did not participate in the decision.

The state government may use its power of eminent domain to take land from a few large landowners, through condemnation with compensation, in order to transfer ownership to many smaller landowners. This use of government power for a public purpose is well within the "policy power" government has traditionally exercised to promote the public welfare. The court upheld Hawaii's 1967 Land Reform Act, which had been challenged as an unconstitutional taking of private property for private purposes.

Regulation

State of Minnesota v. Clover Leaf Creamery Co. (449 U.S. 456), decided by a 7-1 vote, Jan. 21, 1981. Brennan wrote the opinion; Stevens dissented; Rehnquist did not take part in the decision.

The Minnesota Legislature did not violate the Constitution's guarantee of equal protection or infringe upon the values protected by the Commerce Clause, granting to the federal government the power to regulate commerce among the states, when it banned plastic non-returnable milk containers while allowing the use of other non-returnable milk containers such as paperboard cartons. The Legislature had a rational basis for making this distinction, and that is all the Constitution requires.

Kassel v. Consolidated Freightways Corp. (450 U.S. 662), decided by a 6-3 vote, March 24, 1981. Powell wrote an opinion joined by three justices; Brennan and Marshall concurred; Rehnquist, Burger and Stewart dissented.

Iowa impermissibly burdened interstate commerce when it banned the use of 65-foot double-trailer trucks within its borders, ostensibly for safety reasons.

Edgar v. MITE Corp. (457 U.S. 624), decided by a 6-3 vote, June 23, 1982. White wrote the opinion; Marshall, Brennan and Rehnquist dissented.

The Illinois Business Takeover Act, which imposes stricter requirements on companies bidding to take over other companies than does the federal Williams Act, is unconstitutional because it imposes burdens on interstate commerce that outweigh the local interests argued in justification of the state law.

Rice v. Norman Williams Co. (458 U.S. 654), decided by a 9-0 vote, July 1, 1982. Rehnquist wrote the opinion.

A California law that allows a liquor wholesaler to import only those brands of liquor for which he has been designated an "authorized agent" by the distiller is not invalid on its face as being in conflict with federal antitrust law, nor is it pre-empted by federal law governing the distribution of alcohol, nor is it in violation of the constitutional guarantees of equal protection or due process.

Sporhase v. Nebraska (458 U.S. 941), decided by a 7-2 vote, July 2, 1982. Stevens wrote the opinion; Rehnquist and O'Connor dissented.

Groundwater is an article of commerce subject to congressional regulation. Nebraska violated the commerce clause when it conditioned the export of its groundwater on the grant, by the recipient state, of reciprocal rights to take water from that state.

Philko Aviation Inc. v. Shacket (462 U.S. 406), decided by a 9-0 vote, June 15, 1983. White wrote the opinion.

Congress pre-empted state law when it approved part of the Federal Aviation Act that required that any transfer of title to an aircraft would not be valid against a third party until it was recorded with the Federal Aviation Administration (FAA). This provision of federal law pre-empts state laws that permit conveyance of title to aircraft by transfer of possession alone, without FAA recording.

Shaw v. Delta Air Lines Inc. (463 U.S. 85), decided by a 9-0 vote, June 24, 1983. Blackmun wrote the opinion.

New York's Human Rights Law, which forbids discrimination in employee benefit plans on the basis of pregnancy, is pre-empted with respect to plans subject to the federal Employee Retirement Income Security Act (ERISA) only insofar as it bars practices that are lawful under federal law. New York's Disability Benefits Law, which requires employers to pay sick leave benefits to employees unable to work because of pregnancy, is not preempted by ERISA.

Rice v. Rehner (463 U.S. 713), decided by a 6-3 vote, July 1, 1983. O'Connor wrote the opinion; Blackmun, Brennan and Marshall dissented.

California is not precluded by federal law from requiring a federally licensed Indian storekeeper who operates a store on an Indian reservation to obtain a state license to sell liquor for consumption off the premises.

South-Central Timber Development Inc. v. Wunnicke, decided by a 6-2 vote, May 22, 1984. White wrote the opinion; Rehnquist and O'Connor dissented; Marshall did not participate.

A state law specifying that timber from state lands may not be shipped out of state without partial processing in state unconstitutionally burdens interstate commerce and cannot be defended by the argument that Congress imposed a similar requirement on timber taken from federal land in the state. Such an argument can protect a similar state regulation only when congressional intent to sanction such regulations is unmistakable, which was not the case here.

Capital Cities Cable Inc. v. Crisp, decided by a 9-0 vote, June 18, 1984. Brennan wrote the opinion.

The court struck down Oklahoma's ban on the broadcasting of liquor ads, as applied to cable television systems operating within the state. This state regulation of the content of the cable programs, requiring deletion of such ads from out-of-state programs broadcast in-state, was in irreconcilable conflict with federal regulations governing cable television and requiring that cable operators carry broadcast signals "in full, without deletion or alteration."

Federal regulation of the entire array of signals carried by cable television systems pre-empts any state or local regulation of such signals, the court held.

State Courts

Allstate Insurance Co. v. Hague (449 U.S. 302), decided by a 5-3 vote, Jan. 13, 1981. Brennan wrote an opinion for himself and three justices; Stevens concurred in the judgment; Powell, Burger and Rehnquist dissented;

Stewart did not participate in the decision.

Minnesota is not constitutionally required to apply Wisconsin law in an insurance case involving benefits to be paid to a widow, currently residing in Minnesota, of a Wisconsin man who worked in Minnesota and was killed in an accident in Wisconsin.

Ridgway v. Ridgway (454 U.S. 46), decided by a 5-3 vote, Nov. 10, 1981. Blackmun wrote the opinion; Powell, Rehnquist and Stevens dissented; O'Connor did not participate.

A serviceman's designation of his beneficiary under the Servicemen's Group Life Insurance Act (PL 89-214) cannot be overridden by a state court, even if that designation is in direct conflict with the provisions of a divorce decree and settlement.

Underwriters National Assurance Co. v. North Carolina Life & Accident & Health Insurance Guaranty Association (455 U.S. 691), decided by a 9-0 vote, March 24, 1982. Marshall wrote the opinion.

The Constitution requires that "full faith and credit shall be given in each state to the public acts, records, and judicial proceedings of every other state." Under this provision, the judgment of an Indiana court on a matter was conclusive upon the merits of that matter in North Carolina courts and should be honored in those courts.

Gillette Co. v. Miner (459 U.S. 86), dismissed Dec. 6, 1982, without dissent.

After hearing oral arguments in the case, which involved state court jurisdiction over a class action suit in which many members of the class had no connection with the state, the court dismissed the case, stating there was no final judgment in it for the Supreme Court to review.

Local 926, International Union of Operating Engineers, AFL-CIO v. Jones (460 U.S. 669), decided by a 6-3 vote, April 4, 1983. White wrote the opinion; Rehnquist, Powell and O'Connor dissented.

The National Labor Relations Act pre-empts state court jurisdiction over a case in which a supervisory employee charges that a union had coerced his employer into firing him. This is a matter over which the National Labor Relations Board (NLRB) has exclusive jurisdiction. Although the NLRB official acting on this complaint in the first place dismissed it as based on insufficient evidence, the employee may not take this complaint to state courts, seeking damages from the union and the company.

Arizona v. San Carlos Apache Tribe of Arizona, Montana v. Northern Cheyenne Tribe of the Northern Cheyenne Indian Reservation (463 U.S. 545), decided by a 6-3 vote, July 1, 1983. Brennan wrote the opinion; Marshall, Stevens and Blackmun dissented.

State courts, as well as federal courts, have jurisdiction to hear water rights disputes involving Indian tribes.

Solem v. Bartlett, decided by a 9-0 vote, Feb. 22, 1984. Marshall wrote the opinion.

South Dakota has no criminal jurisdiction over an Indian who committed a crime on part of the Cheyenne River Sioux Reservation, which was opened to homesteading by non-Indians in 1908. The federal law opening this land to homesteading did not diminish the boundaries of the reservation.

Helicopteros Nacionales de Colombia, S. A. v. Hall, decided by an 8-1 vote, April 24, 1984. Blackmun wrote the opinion; Brennan dissented.

A Colombia corporation that contracted to provide transportation by helicopter for a joint venture headquartered in Houston during that company's construction of a pipeline in Peru has insufficient contact with Texas to permit a Texas court to assert jurisdiction over it in a lawsuit arising from a helicopter crash in Peru in which several U.S. citizens were killed.

Three Affiliated Tribes of the Fort Berthold Reservation v. Wold Engineering, P. C., decided by a 7-2 vote, May 29, 1984. Blackmun wrote the opinion; Rehnquist and Stevens dissented.

State trial courts may have jurisdiction over cases brought by Indian tribes against non-Indian defendants regarding matters arising within the reservation.

Taxation

Rosewell v. LaSalle National Bank (450 U.S. 503), decided by a 5-4 vote, March 24, 1981. Brennan wrote the opinion; Stevens, Stewart, Marshall and Powell dissented.

Federal courts should not intervene in property tax disputes in Illinois but should adhere to the Tax Injunction Act, which forbids such intervention as long as state law provides a "plain, speedy and efficient remedy" for the dispute. Illinois' property tax refund procedure, which requires the taxpayer to pay the protested tax before challenging it in state courts and which pays no interest on any amount refunded, is such a remedy for the purposes of the law.

Western and Southern Life Insurance Co. v. State Board of Equalization of California (451 U.S. 648), decided by a 7-2 vote, May 26, 1981. Brennan wrote the opinion; Stevens and Blackmun dissented.

Because Congress has given the states the freedom to regulate and to tax the insurance business, California does not act unconstitutionally when it imposes a "retaliatory" tax on some out-of-state insurance companies doing business in California. The contested tax is designed to ensure that such "foreign" insurance companies pay as much tax to California as California companies pay to the homestates of those companies.

Maryland v. Louisiana (452 U.S. 456), decided by a vote of 7-1, May 26, 1981. White wrote the opinion; Rehnquist dissented; Powell did not participate in the decision.

Louisiana acts unconstitutionally when it imposes a "first use" tax on gas from offshore wells that passes through the state on the way to out-of-state customers. Such a tax discriminates unfairly against out-of-state customers and thus violates the intent of the Constitution's grant to the federal government of the power to regulate interstate commerce.

Commonwealth Edison Co. v. Montana (453 U.S. 609), decided by a 6-3 vote, July 2, 1981. Marshall wrote the opinion; Blackmun, Powell and Stevens dissented.

Montana's severance tax on each ton of coal mined in the state, which varies up to as much as 30 percent of the sales price of the coal, does not violate the underlying principle of the Constitution's grant to the federal govern-

ment of the power to regulate interstate commerce or the Constitution's clause declaring federal law supreme over state law. The tax does not discriminate against out-of-state customers or consumers and it does not conflict with federal law or national energy policy.

United States v. New Mexico (455 U.S. 720), decided by a 9-0 vote, March 24, 1982. Blackmun wrote the opinion.

Corporations holding contracts with the federal government to manage government-owned facilities are not "instrumentalities of the United States" and are not exempt from state gross-receipts and compensating-use taxes imposed upon all persons doing business within the states. Immunity from state taxes is appropriate only when the tax falls on the U.S. government itself, or on an agency or instrumentality so closely connected to it that the two cannot realistically be viewed as separate.

ASARCO Inc. v. Idaho State Tax Commission (458 U.S. 307), decided by a 6-3 vote, June 29, 1982. Powell wrote the opinion; O'Connor, Blackmun and Rehnquist dissented.

The due process clause bars a state from levying a tax upon income outside the proper reach of the state's tax power. Idaho may not properly include within ASARCO's taxable income (for purposes of calculating ASARCO's state tax liability) part of the dividends and other payments that ASARCO received from its subsidiary corporations outside the state, because there is no showing that the parent and the subsidiaries form a "unitary business."

F. W. Woolworth Co. v. Taxation and Revenue Department of New Mexico (458 U.S. 354), decided by a 6-3 vote, June 29, 1982. Powell wrote the opinion; O'Connor, Blackmun and Rehnquist dissented.

New Mexico may not tax part of the dividends that a multinational corporation receives from its foreign subsidiaries unless it is shown that those foreign subsidiaries constitute a unitary business with the parent corporation.

Ramah Navajo School Board v. Bureau of Revenue of New Mexico (458 U.S. 832), decided by a 6-3 vote, July 2, 1982. Marshall wrote the opinion; Rehnquist, White and Stevens dissented.

Federal law denies New Mexico the power to tax the gross receipts of a non-Indian construction company paid by a tribal school board for the construction of a school on the reservation.

Xerox Corp. v. County of Harris, Texas (459 U.S. 145), decided by an 8-1 vote, Dec. 13, 1982. Burger wrote the opinion; Powell dissented.

State property taxes on goods held in a customs bonded warehouse after being assembled in a foreign country and prior to shipment to another foreign country conflict with the comprehensive customs system Congress has created, which permits duty-free storage in such warehouses.

Memphis Bank & Trust Co. v. Garner (459 U.S. 392), decided by a 9-0 vote, Jan. 24, 1983. Marshall wrote the opinion.

Tennessee's bank tax, which is imposed on the net earnings of banks doing business in the state, including interest the banks receive on U.S. bonds and on bonds

issued by other states, is a discriminatory tax in favor of Tennessee. It violates federal law exempting U.S. bonds from most state and local taxes.

Washington v. United States (460 U.S. 536), decided by a 5-4 vote, March 29, 1983. Rehnquist wrote the opinion; Blackmun, Marshall, Stevens and White dissented.

Federal contractors are not immune from state taxation. Washington state laws imposing a sales tax on contractors who build on federal land, but not on contractors building on non-federal land (because in those cases the tax is imposed on the landowner) is not unconstitutional. A tax is not invalid just because it treats those who deal with the federal government differently from others.

Exxon Corp. v. Eagerton, Exchange Oil and Gas Corp. v. Eagerton (462 U.S. 176), decided by a 9-0 vote, June 8, 1983. Marshall wrote the opinion.

Alabama may impose a severance tax on natural gas produced in-state, but it may not prohibit gas producers from passing on the cost of that gas to interstate customers. It can impose a ban on the pass-through of that cost to in-state customers, but federal law governs with regard to interstate sales.

Container Corporation of America v. Franchise Tax Board (463 U.S. 159), decided by 5-3 vote, June 27, 1983. Brennan wrote the opinion; Stevens did not participate; Powell, Burger and O'Connor dissented.

States may consider the worldwide income of U.S.-based multinational corporations in calculating the corporations' state tax liability. The income of foreign subsidiaries may be considered in the tax base for this assessment. This "worldwide unitary" method of taxation does not violate the due process guarantee or the Constitution's grant of power to the federal government to regulate interstate and foreign commerce.

American Bank & Trust Co. v. Dallas County (463 U.S. 855), decided by a 6-2 vote, July 5, 1983. Blackmun wrote the opinion; O'Connor did not participate; Rehnquist and Stevens dissented.

Texas, which imposes a property tax on the value of the stock of a commercial bank, cannot include the value of the U.S. securities held by the bank in the value of the bank stock. By including this value in the bank share value, Texas violates the federal law that exempts all U.S. obligations from state and local taxes.

South Carolina v. Regan, decided by votes of 9-0 and 8-1, Feb. 22, 1984. Brennan wrote the opinion; Stevens dissented in part.

The court agreed to exercise its original jurisdiction to consider fully this case between a state and the U.S. government. South Carolina challenged as unconstitutional provisions of the Tax Equity and Fiscal Responsibility Act of 1982 (PL 97-248) denying tax exemptions to interest paid on unregistered bonds. The state, backed by 23 other states, argued that forcing states to issue registered bonds burdened their powers to borrow money.

The court rejected the Reagan administration's argument that this case could not be brought in federal court because of the Anti-Injunction Act, which denied federal courts jurisdiction over cases to restrain the assessment of collection of taxes. The justices reasoned that Congress did not intend this ban to apply to cases such as this one, in which South Carolina had no alternative forum in which to pursue its claim.

Armco Inc. v. Harderty, decided by an 8-1 vote, June 12, 1984. Powell wrote the opinion; Rehnquist dissented.

West Virginia unconstitutionally discriminated against interstate commerce by imposing a gross receipts tax on businesses selling property at wholesale and exempting local manufacturers, who pay a higher manufacturing tax, from it.

Bacchus Imports Ltd. v. Dias, decided by a 5-3 vote, June 29, 1984. White wrote the opinion; Brennan did not participate; Stevens, Rehnquist and O'Connor dissented.

Hawaii's exemption of a local brandy and fruit wine from its 20 percent tax on wholesale liquor sales violated the Constitution by discriminating against interstate commerce in favor of local products.

Interstate Relations

Webb v. Webb (451 U.S. 493), decided by an 8-1 vote, May 18, 1981. White wrote the opinion; Marshall dissented.

The court dismissed a custody dispute case because no federal point of law had been raised during the proceedings in the state courts. The Supreme Court lacks jurisdiction over a case from state courts unless a federal question was raised and ruled upon by those courts.

United States v. Maine (452 U.S. 429), report of special master approved by an 8-0 vote, June 15, 1981. No opinion, simply issuance of a supplemental decree. Marshall did not participate in this case.

The decree specified the boundary line between the submerged lands belonging to the United States and those belonging to the state of Massachusetts.

California v. Arizona and the United States (452 U.S. 431), report of special master approved without dissent June 15, 1981. No opinion, simply a decree.

The decree described the ownership of certain parts of the bed of the former channel of the Colorado River.

United States v. Louisiana (452 U.S. 726), supplemental report of special master received and ordered filed without dissent, June 22, 1981. No opinion, simply entry of final decree. Marshall did not participate in this case.

The decree defined the boundary between the offshore submerged lands belonging to Louisiana and those belonging to the United States. It also required each government to make a full accounting of the revenues it derived from exploitation of the submerged lands belonging to the other.

Tennessee v. Arkansas (454 U.S. 351), decree issued Dec. 14, 1981.

The court approved a decree defining a disputed part of the boundary between Tennessee and Arkansas.

California ex rel. State Lands Commission v. United States (457 U.S. 273), decided by a 9-0 vote, June 18, 1982. White wrote the opinion.

The court ruled that the United States, not California, owned approximately 184 acres of land along the California coast that had been created through accretion to land already owned by the United States.

Colorado v. New Mexico (459 U.S. 176), decided by a 9-0 vote, Dec. 13, 1982. Marshall wrote the opinion.

This case concerned an effort by Colorado to divert water for the use of its residents from the Vermejo River, a non-navigable river that originates in southern Colorado and flows into New Mexico. The river's water is at present used entirely by New Mexicans.

A special master had been appointed by the Supreme Court in 1979 to resolve this water-rights dispute between Colorado and New Mexico. The special master recommended that Colorado be permitted to divert 4,000 acre-feet of water from the river each year; New Mexico objected, and the Supreme Court sent the matter back to the special master for more specific findings to support his recommendation.

Arizona v. California (460 U.S. 605), decided by votes of 8-0 and 5-3, March 30, 1983. White wrote the opinion; Marshall did not participate in the case; Brennan, Blackmun and Stevens dissented.

The court refused to grant five Indian tribes additional rights to water from the Colorado River. This case, an original one in the Supreme Court (that is, it had not been heard by any other court), was the oldest live case on the court's docket. It had been there since 1952, when Arizona sued California to limit its use of Colorado River water.

The government acknowledged that because of a mistake made in 1964, when water rights were allotted to the tribes and the states, the tribes had received less than they should have. But the court in this case refused to redistribute those rights, emphasizing the need for finality in such matters.

Texas v. New Mexico (462 U.S. 554), exceptions to the report of a special master sustained in part, overruled in part, by a 9-0 vote, June 17, 1983. Brennan wrote the opinion.

The court ordered further hearings in a dispute between Texas and New Mexico over the amount of water each state is entitled to from the Pecos River. The court rejected a plan to permit the U.S. representative on the Pecos River Commission to vote to resolve such disputes.

Idaho v. Oregon and Washington (444 U.S. 380), decided by a 6-3 vote, June 23, 1983. Blackmun wrote the opinion; O'Connor, Brennan and Stevens dissented.

The court dismissed an Idaho action against Oregon and Washington regarding the apportionment of certain fish that migrate between the Pacific Ocean and Idaho. The court found, on the basis of a special master's report, that Idaho had not shown that it had suffered sufficient injury under the present situation to justify a court order to remedy it.

Louisiana v. Mississippi, decided by a 9-0 vote, April 2, 1984. Blackmun wrote the opinion, confirming the report of the special master.

The bottom hole of an oil well in reach of the Mississippi River, which serves as the boundary between Louisiana and Mississippi, was throughout the disputed period west of the boundary line and within Louisiana.

Colorado v. New Mexico, decided by an 8-1 vote, June 4, 1984. O'Connor wrote the opinion; Stevens dissented.

Colorado failed to meet its burden of proving that water should be diverted for use in Colorado from the Vermejo River, which originates in Colorado, flows into New Mexico and historically has been used entirely by New Mexicans.

Powers of the President

Dames & Moore v. Regan (453 U.S. 654), decided by a 9-0 vote, July 2, 1981. Rehnquist wrote the opinion.

President Jimmy Carter acted within his statutory power to conduct foreign affairs when he reached the financial agreement with Iran that resulted in the release of 52 Americans held hostage in that country for more than 14 months. Carter was within his power when he agreed to nullify all federal court orders attaching the assets of Iranian businesses and the Iranian government in the United States and to transfer those assets back to Iran. It was also within the president's power to agree that all pending claims against Iran would be transferred to an international tribunal and would be heard and resolved there, not in U.S. courts. Congress, in the International Emergency Economic Powers Act of 1977 (PL 95-223) and a number of other earlier laws, gave the president powers broad enough to take these actions.

Weinberger v. Rossi (456 U.S. 25), decided by a 9-0 vote, March 31, 1982. Rehnquist wrote the opinion.

When Congress in 1971 banned job discrimination against U.S. citizens on military bases overseas unless such discrimination was permitted by a treaty, it used the word 'treaty' to include executive agreements with other nations as well as formal treaties ratified by the Senate. The court upheld executive agreements with other nations that give preferential treatment to citizens of nations where U.S. military bases are located.

Regan v. Wald, decided by a 5-4 vote, June 28, 1984. Rehnquist wrote the opinion; Brennan, Blackmun, Marshall and Powell dissented.

The court upheld the Reagan administration's 1982 restrictions on travel to Cuba, which a lower court had held unconstitutional because they had not been promulgated in keeping with procedures outlined by the 1977 International Emergency Economic Powers Act (PL 95-233).

A grandfather clause in that law, which limited executive power to impose economic sanctions on foreign countries in peacetime, preserved the president's authority to impose such restrictions on countries then subject to restrictions. That included travel to Cuba, because property transactions with Cuba were restricted in 1977.

Powers of Congress

United States v. Will (449 U.S. 200), decided by an 8-0 vote, Dec. 15, 1980. Burger wrote the opinion; Blackmun did not participate.

Congress may not rescind cost-of-living adjustments in the salaries of federal judges after those increases actually take effect; such an after-the-fact rescission violates the Constitution's guarantee that judicial salaries "shall not be

diminished during their Continuance in Office." Congress may rescind such adjustments if it acts before the beginning of the fiscal year in which they take effect.

The court thus held that Congress had properly rescinded cost-of-living increases for fiscal 1978 and 1979, acting before the first day of the new fiscal year, but had improperly tried to cancel those increases for fiscal 1977 and 1980, when the rescissions were not enacted until after Oct. 1. The effect of this ruling was an increase of about 12 percent in the salaries of all federal judges, including members of the Supreme Court.

Immigration and Naturalization Service v. Chadha, United States House of Representatives v. Chadha, United States Senate v. Chadha (462 U.S. 919), decided by a 7-2 vote, June 23, 1983. Burger wrote the opinion; White and Rehnquist dissented.

The one-house legislative veto, under which Congress claimed for itself the power to review and veto executive branch decisions implementing laws, is unconstitutional. It violates the separation of powers between the executive and legislative branches, and it runs counter to the "single, finely wrought and exhaustively considered procedure" the Constitution prescribes for the enactment of legislation: approval by both chambers and presentation to the president for his signature.

With this decision, invalidating a device included in one form or another in more than 200 laws enacted since 1932, the court struck down at one time more provisions in more federal laws than it had invalidated in its entire history. As of mid-1982, the court had struck down all or part of 110 federal laws as unconstitutional.

Selective Service System v. Minnesota Public Interest Research Group, decided by a 6-2 vote, July 5, 1984. Burger wrote the opinion; Brennan and Marshall dissented; Blackmun did not take part in the decision.

Congress did not violate the constitutional ban on bills of attainder when it approved a 1982 law (PL 97-252) denying federal student aid to male college students who fail to register for the military draft. A bill of attainder is a legislative measure imposing punishment upon an identifiable group without trial.

Congress acted not to punish non-registrants, but to encourage draft registration. Denial of a government benefit does not constitute punishment. Non-registrants are given a 30-day grace period within which to register after they are notified that they will otherwise be ineligible for federal student aid.

Federal Courts

Imperial County v. Munoz (449 U.S. 54), decided by a vote of 6-3, Dec. 2, 1980. Stewart wrote the opinion; Brennan, Stevens and Marshall dissented.

The Anti-Injunction Act forbids a federal district court from issuing an order restraining a county from enforcing a restriction, contained in a land-use permit, on the sale of water for use outside the county. The federal court should not issue such an order unless the persons seeking it were "strangers" not bound by state court orders concerning the water dispute.

Allen v. McCurry (449 U.S. 90), decided by a 6-3 vote, Dec. 9, 1980. Stewart wrote the opinion; Brennan, Blackmun and Marshall dissented.

Once a state court considers and rejects a defendant's claim that state police violated his constitutional rights in seizing evidence from him, that claim may not serve as the basis of a federal damage suit against those policemen.

Federal Trade Commission (FTC) v. Standard Oil Company of California (449 U.S. 232), decided by an 8-0 vote, Dec. 15, 1980. Powell wrote the opinion; Stewart did not participate in the decision.

Federal courts must await the completion of investigatory proceedings by the Federal Trade Commission before intervening in such matters. The ruling was a defeat for eight oil companies that had sought a federal court order halting an FTC investigation of charges of unfair competition and deceptive practices.

Delaware State College v. Ricks (449 U.S. 520), decided by a 5-4 vote, Dec. 15, 1980. Powell wrote the opinion; Stewart, Brennan, Marshall and Stevens dissented.

A faculty member who charges that he was denied academic tenure because of his national origin, a violation of the 1964 Civil Rights Act, has 180 days from that denial in which to file a complaint with the Equal Employment Opportunity Commission and three years from that date in which to file a federal lawsuit based on that charge. The court held that such complaints were filed too late by a man who believed that these time limits began to run only after he terminated his employment relationship with the school, a year after he was denied tenure.

Firestone Tire & Rubber Co. v. Risjord (449 U.S. 368), decided by a 9-0 vote, Jan. 13, 1981. Marshall wrote the opinion.

A federal district court order denying a motion by one party to disqualify counsel for the opposing party in a civil case is not a "final" decision that can be appealed to a higher court.

Sumner v. Mata (449 U.S. 539), decided by a vote of 6-3, Jan. 21, 1981. Rehnquist wrote the opinion; Brennan, Marshall and Stevens dissented.

Congress has made clear that federal courts considering the petitions of state prisoners for writs of *habeas corpus* must defer to state court decisions on matters of fact unless there is substantial reason to question the correctness of those decisions. If a federal court considering such a petition does decide that a state court erred on a matter of fact, it must set out its reasons for that decision in writing.

Carson v. American Brands Inc. (450 U.S. 79), decided by a 9-0 vote, Feb. 25, 1981. Brennan wrote the opinion.

The refusal of a federal district court to approve a consent decree agreed to by both sides in a job discrimination case is an action that can be appealed to a higher court.

Delta Air Lines Inc. v. August (450 U.S. 346), decided by a 6-3 vote, March 9, 1981. Stevens wrote the opinion; Rehnquist, Burger and Stewart dissented.

Under the Federal Rules of Civil Procedure, a plaintiff who refuses a defendant's offer to settle a job discrimination case and then loses the case cannot be required to pay the defendant's litigation costs.

Arizona v. Manypenny (451 U.S. 232), decided by a 7-2 vote, April 21, 1981. Blackmun wrote the opinion; Brennan and Marshall dissented.

The state of Arizona may appeal a federal court's acquittal of a federal border patrol agent on charges of assault. The assault occurred on federal land and in the course of the federal agent's duties so his trial, on state charges, took place in federal court. The state retained its right, under state law, to appeal the acquittal as if he had been tried in state court.

Gulf Oil Co. v. Bernard (452 U.S. 89), decided by a 9-0 vote, June 1, 1981. Powell wrote the opinion.

A federal judge lacks the power to bar parties and lawyers in a class action civil rights suit from communicating with other actual or potential members of the class without obtaining prior court approval.

Federated Department Stores v. Moitie (452 U.S. 394), decided by an 8-1 vote, June 15, 1981. Rehnquist wrote the opinion; Brennan dissented.

A group of customers seeking damages from two department store companies that allegedly engaged in price-fixing can no longer pursue their claims because they failed to appeal an earlier court decision dismissing their cases.

Gulf Offshore Co. v. Mobil Oil Corp. (453 U.S. 473), decided by an 8-0 vote, July 1, 1981. Powell wrote the opinion; Stewart did not take part in the decision.

Federal courts do not have exclusive jurisdiction over personal injury and indemnity cases arising under the Outer Continental Shelf Lands Act; state courts also may hear such cases.

Fair Assessment in Real Estate Association Inc. v. McNary (454 U.S. 100), decided by a 9-0 vote, Dec. 1, 1981. Rehnquist wrote the opinion.

The principle of comity restrains federal courts from hearing taxpayer damage suits brought to seek remedy for the operation of an allegedly unconstitutional state tax system.

Taxpayers with such complaints should seek a remedy in state courts; the decisions of those courts in their cases may ultimately be reviewed in federal courts.

Piper Aircraft Co. v. Reyno, Hartzell Propeller v. Reyno (454 U.S. 235), decided by a 4-3 vote, Dec. 8, 1981. Marshall wrote the opinion; White, Stevens and Brennan dissented; Powell and O'Connor did not participate in the decision.

A federal court may properly dismiss a lawsuit, finding that another court or another country provides a more convenient forum for resolution of the dispute, even if the law of the alternative forum is less favorable to the persons bringing the suit.

White v. New Hampshire Department of Employment Security (455 U.S. 445), decided by a 9-0 vote March 2, 1982. Powell wrote the opinion.

Individuals who successfully sue state and local governments for violating their constitutional rights are not bound by the 10-day limit set out in federal procedural rules in requesting that they be awarded their attorneys' fees under the Civil Rights Attorney's Fees Awards Act of 1976. They may make such a request more than 10 days after their victory.

Rose v. Lundy (455 U.S. 509), decided by an 8-1 vote, March 3, 1982. O'Connor wrote the opinion; Stevens dissented.

Federal courts presented with a petition from a state prisoner for a writ of *habeas corpus* that contains several constitutional claims, some of which have been pursued in state courts and some of which have not, should dismiss that petition. State inmates must give state courts the first opportunity to address such constitutional complaints. An inmate whose petition is dismissed for this reason may either delete from his petition the claims not presented to state courts and file it again in federal court, or he may return to the state courts to pursue his complaints there.

Lane v. Williams (455 U.S. 624), decided by a 6-3 vote, March 23, 1982. Stevens wrote the opinion; Marshall, Brennan and Blackmun dissented.

Two men who pleaded guilty to burglary in state court and later claimed they were denied due process because they were not informed that their negotiated sentences included mandatory three-year paroles may not obtain a writ of *habeas corpus* from federal courts eliminating the mandatory parole term because they have now served those terms and their cases are moot. Their cases would not be moot had they sought nullification of their plea bargains and the opportunity to plead anew.

Engle v. Isaac (456 U.S. 107), decided by votes of 6-3 and 7-2, April 5, 1982. O'Connor wrote the opinion; Stevens, Brennan and Marshall dissented.

State prisoners seeking collateral review of their convictions through a writ of *habeas corpus* from a federal court must show both cause for their failure to raise a constitutional objection at the time of their trial and actual prejudice as a result of the alleged constitutional violation before the writ can be granted.

United States v. Frady (456 U.S. 152), decided by a 6-1 vote, April 5, 1982. O'Connor wrote the opinion; Brennan dissented; Burger and Marshall did not participate.

A federal prisoner seeking collateral review of his conviction in an effort to vacate his sentence on the grounds of error occurring at his trial may not win relief unless he can prove cause for his failure to object to the error during his trial and actual prejudice as a result of the alleged error.

Insurance Corporation of Ireland Ltd. v. Compagnie des Bauxites de Guinea (456 U.S. 694), decided by a 9-0 vote, June 1, 1982. White wrote the opinion.

A federal district court did not deny due process to a corporation sued before it that was not a resident of the United States and that failed to comply with discovery orders seeking evidence relating to the existence of contacts with the United States when the district court simply assumed that such contacts existed and that jurisdiction was established.

Army and Air Force Exchange Service v. Sheehan (456 U.S. 728), decided by a 9-0 vote, June 1, 1982. Blackmun wrote the opinion.

The Tucker Act does not give federal courts jurisdiction over a suit against the U.S. government for money damages brought by a former government employee who alleges that he was discharged in violation of his right to due process.

California v. Grace Brethren Church, United States v. Grace Brethren Church, Grace Brethren Church v. United States (457 U.S. 393), decided by a 7-2 vote, June 18, 1982. O'Connor wrote the opinion; Stevens and Blackmun dissented.

The Tax Injunction Act deprives federal courts of jurisdiction to issue an injunction halting state collection of unemployment compensation tax when there is a speedy and efficient remedy, as in this case. That law also denies a federal court the power to declare the state law unconstitutional as an infringement on the First Amendment rights of certain religious schools not affiliated with churches.

Middlesex County Ethics Committee v. Garden State Bar Association (453 U.S. 1), decided by a 9-0 vote, June 21, 1982. Burger wrote the opinion.

A federal court should abstain from considering a challenge to the constitutionality of disciplinary rules and proceedings against an attorney charged with unethical conduct so long as that proceeding is under way within the jurisdiction of a state court and provides the attorney an opportunity to raise his constitutional claims before that body.

Foremost Insurance Co. v. Richardson (457 U.S. 668), decided by a 5-4 vote, June 23, 1982. Marshall wrote the opinion; Powell, Burger, Rehnquist and O'Connor dissented.

Federal admiralty jurisdiction extends to accidents occurring on navigable waters between two boats involved solely in recreational use.

Lehman v. Lycoming County Children's Services Agency (458 U.S. 502), decided by a 6-3 vote, June 30, 1982. Powell wrote the opinion; Blackmun, Brennan and Marshall dissented.

Federal courts do not have jurisdiction to consider petitions for *habeas corpus* relief brought by parents challenging state court action terminating their parental rights to their children.

Moses H. Cone Memorial Hospital v. Mercury Construction Corp. (460 U.S. 1), decided by a 6-3 vote, Feb. 23, 1983. Brennan wrote the opinion; Rehnquist, Burger and O'Connor dissented.

A federal district court abused its discretion in staying, and effectively dismissing, a lawsuit filed by a contractor against a hospital to compel the hospital to submit contract disputes between them to arbitration under federal arbitration law. The federal court cited as the reason for its action parallel state court litigation in the case. Only in exceptional circumstances should a federal district court decline to exercise its jurisdiction because of parallel state litigation. No such circumstances existed here.

District of Columbia Court of Appeals v. Feldman (460 U.S. 462), decided by an 8-1 vote, March 23, 1983. Brennan wrote the opinion; Stevens dissented.

Denial by the highest local court in the District of Columbia of petitions seeking waiver of a D.C. bar admission rule is a judicial action not subject to review by any federal court but the Supreme Court.

Federal district courts do have jurisdiction over general challenges to state bar rules, which are usually set out by state courts in non-judicial proceedings.

City of Los Angeles v. Lyons (461 U.S. 95), decided by a 5-4 vote, April 20, 1983. White wrote the opinion; Marshall, Brennan, Blackmun and Stevens dissented.

The court overturned a federal district judge's order barring Los Angeles police officers from using certain choke holds on suspects unless the officers were threatened with death or great bodily harm.

The Supreme Court held that a man subjected to this potentially fatal type of hold after being stopped by police for a traffic violation lacked standing to seek an injunction against its future use because he could not show that the choke hold would ever again be used against him.

Verlinden B. V. v. Central Bank of Nigeria (461 U.S. 480), decided by a 9-0 vote, May 23, 1983. Burger wrote the opinion.

Congress has the power to grant federal courts jurisdiction over cases brought by foreign corporations against foreign countries, even when the dispute is not a federal matter. Congress granted federal courts such jurisdiction in the Foreign Sovereign Immunities Act of 1976.

Franchise Tax Board of California v. Construction Laborers Vacation Trust for Southern California (463 U.S. 1), decided by a 9-0 vote, June 24, 1983. Brennan wrote the opinion.

A federal court lacks jurisdiction to hear a suit by a state to enforce state tax levies against funds held in trust for an employee benefit plan when the only federal issue is the defensive claim that the employee benefit plan is subject to the federal Employee Retirement Income Security Act.

United States v. Sells Engineering Inc. (463 U.S. 418), decided by a 5-4 vote, June 30, 1983. Brennan wrote the opinion; Burger, Powell, Rehnquist and O'Connor dissented.

Attorneys in the civil division of the Justice Department are not automatically entitled to access to transcripts or other records of federal grand jury investigations. To gain such access, these lawyers must obtain a federal court order by demonstrating a strong and particular need to see the records.

United States v. Baggot (463 U.S. 476), decided by an 8-1 vote, June 30, 1983. Brennan wrote the opinion; Burger dissented.

The Internal Revenue Service may not seek disclosure of otherwise secret grand jury materials for use in a civil tax audit. Disclosure is permitted by court order only if the materials will be used to prepare for particular litigation.

United States v. Mendoza, decided by a 9-0 vote, Jan. 10, 1984. Rehnquist wrote the opinion.

The United States is not foreclosed from litigating a constitutional question raised by a Filipino national seeking naturalization by the fact that the issue had been decided against the government in a similar earlier case.

In general, once a court has decided a matter of law or fact, that decision governs any later case arising out of a different situation but involving one of the parties to the earlier decision. The court held that this doctrine, called collateral estoppel, applied differently to the government than to private litigants, and would operate only when both parties were the same as those in the earlier case.

United States v. Stauffer Chemical Co., decided by a 9-0 vote, Jan. 10, 1984. Rehnquist wrote the opinion.

The government may not relitigate an issue in a case in which the parties are the same as a similar case in which the issue has already been decided. The court held that this doctrine of collateral estoppel prevented the United States from contesting a company's challenge to its use of private contractors as clean air inspectors because another federal court, acting in another case between the United States and the company, had forbidden the government to use private contractors for this purpose.

McDonough Power Equipment Inc. v. Greenwood, decided by a 9-0 vote, Jan. 18, 1984. Rehnquist wrote the opinion.

The failure of one juror to disclose relevant information during the jury selection process in a civil case is not sufficient reason for an appeals court to order a new trial unless there is evidence that the juror's dishonesty threatens the fairness of the trial.

Penhurst State School and Hospital v. Halderman, decided by a 5-4 vote, Jan. 23, 1984. Powell wrote the opinion; Stevens, Brennan, Marshall and Blackmun dissented.

Federal judges may not order state officials to comply with state laws. The 11th Amendment denies federal courts jurisdiction over cases brought by citizens against a state without its consent; federal courts therefore lack the power to hear cases in which citizens charge state officials with failing to carry out state law.

The court reversed a federal court order directing Pennsylvania officials to relocate mentally retarded residents of state schools in less restrictive environments. That order was based on a Pennsylvania law.

Heckler v. Edwards, decided by a 9-0 vote, March 21, 1984. Marshall wrote the opinion.

The law permitting a direct appeal to the Supreme Court from a U.S. district court ruling that a federal law is unconstitutional does not permit such a direct appeal when the constitutionality of the statute is not the issue on appeal.

Official Immunity

Dennis v. Sparks (449 U.S. 24), decided by a 9-0 vote, Nov. 17, 1980. White wrote the opinion.

A judge's immunity from a damage suit brought by someone injured by an improperly issued judicial order does not extend to protect from such a suit a private individual who bribed the judge to issue the protested order.

Kissinger v. Halperin (452 U.S. 713), decided by a 4-4 vote, June 22, 1981. No opinion. Rehnquist did not participate in the consideration of this case.

The court without opinion left standing the ruling of a lower court that former President Richard Nixon, former Secretary of State Henry A. Kissinger and former Attorney General John N. Mitchell were liable to a damage suit brought by an individual whose home they had illegally wiretapped.

City of Newport v. Fact Concerts Inc. (453 U.S. 247), decided by a 6-3 vote, June 26, 1981. Blackmun wrote the opinion; Brennan, Marshall and Stevens dissented.

A city may not be ordered to pay punitive damages as a result of a civil rights damage suit brought by persons who charge that the city violated their constitutional rights.

Polk County v. Dodson (454 U.S. 312), decided by an 8-1 vote, Dec. 14, 1981. Powell wrote the opinion; Blackmun dissented.

Public defenders, although paid by the state, owe their primary loyalty to the clients they represent and do not act "under color of state law" in that capacity. Therefore, they cannot be sued under the federal civil rights damage statute, Section 1983, for negligent representation. When performing certain other functions, public defenders may be acting under color of state law and thus be liable to such suits, but not when performing the traditional function of counsel to a criminal defendant.

Finley v. Murray (456 U.S. 604), dismissed May 17, 1982, without dissent.

In a *per curiam* (unsigned) statement, the court said that it should not have agreed to hear arguments in this case, which presented the question of the immunity of a circuit court clerk from a damage suit charging him with violating the civil rights of a woman arrested on the basis of an invalid warrant he issued.

Nixon v. Fitzgerald (457 U.S. 731), decided by a 5-4 vote, June 24, 1982. Powell wrote the opinion; White, Brennan, Marshall and Blackmun dissented.

Presidents are absolutely immune from civil damage suits for all official actions taken while in office. The court ruled in a case involving the claim of former Air Force cost analyst A. Ernest Fitzgerald that he lost his job, as punishment for his disclosure in congressional testimony of massive cost overruns on a defense transport plane, as a result of a White House conspiracy involving former President Richard M. Nixon. The majority said the electoral process and the impeachment mechanism provide sufficient remedy for presidential wrongdoing. The four dissenters said the ruling "places the president above the law" and was "a reversion to the old notion that the king can do no wrong."

Harlow v. Fitzgerald (457 U.S. 800), decided by an 8-1 vote, June 24, 1982. Powell wrote the opinion; Burger dissented.

Presidential aides do not have absolute immunity from civil rights damage suits by individuals who claim they have been denied their rights by those aides acting in their official capacity. A presidential aide can establish such immunity if he shows that the "responsibilities of his office embrace[d] a function so sensitive as to require a total shield from liability."

Presidential aides, like other executive officials, enjoy qualified immunity from such damage suits. The court set out a new standard for courts to use in weighing a qualified immunity defense. The court held that "government officials performing discretionary functions generally are shielded from liability for civil damages insofar as their conduct does not violate clearly established statutory or constitutional rights of which a reasonable person would have known." The court abandoned an earlier test that required inquiry into the motivation of the official in committing the challenged act.

Velde v. National Black Police Association (458 U.S. 591), decided by a 7-0 vote, June 30, 1982. Powell and Stevens did not participate. *Per curiam* (unsigned) opinion.

The court sent this case back to a lower court. It involved federal officials who were sued for failing to cut off federal aid to force recipient police departments to halt discrimination against women and blacks. The court said the lower court should consider this case in light of the ruling in *Harlow v. Fitzgerald* (above).

Government Employees

United States v. Clark (454 U.S. 555), decided by a 9-0 vote, Jan. 12, 1982. O'Connor wrote the opinion.

A federal employee who is promoted from the wage system pay scheme to the general schedule pay system is not entitled by law to an automatic two-step increase in pay; this automatic increase applies only to promotions and transfers within the general schedule pay system.

Wage Compensation, Garnishment

United States v. Lorenzetti, decided by a 9-0 vote, May 29, 1984. Blackmun wrote the opinion.

A federal employee compensated for medical expenses and lost wages incurred as a result of a work-related accident, as provided for under the Federal Employees' Compensation Act, is obligated by that law to reimburse the government if he receives "pain and suffering" compensation under state law from those who caused his injury.

Franchise Tax Board of California v. United States Postal Service, decided by a 9-0 vote, June 11, 1984. Stevens wrote the opinion.

Upon request, the U.S. Postal Service or other employer must garnish, or withhold from, a worker's wages to help a state collect overdue state income tax payments. No court order is needed for such action.

United States v. Morton, decided by a 9-0 vote, June 19, 1984. Stevens wrote the opinion.

The United States is not liable to a serviceman, whose wages it garnished subject to a state court order to collect alimony and child support from him, even though a reviewing court later held that the state court lacked jurisdiction over the serviceman necessary to issue the order.

Freedom of Information

McNichols v. Baldrige, Baldrige v. Shapiro (455 U.S. 345), decided by a 9-0 vote, Feb. 24, 1982. Burger wrote the opinion.

Congress explicitly provided that all raw census data reported by or on behalf of individuals should remain confidential, and neither the Freedom of Information Act nor the discovery provisions of federal court rules may be used to force disclosure of such information. The court thus blocked efforts of officials from Denver, Colo., and Essex Country, N.J., to obtain certain address lists used by 1980 census-takers in their areas. Both areas claimed their populations had been under-counted by census-takers who incorrectly described certain dwellings as vacant.

U.S. Department of State v. The Washington Post Co. (456 U.S. 595), decided by a 9-0 vote, May 17, 1982. Rehnquist wrote the opinion.

The exemption from disclosure under the Freedom of Information Act for "personnel and medical files and similar files the disclosure of which would constitute a clearly unwarranted invasion of personal privacy" encompasses information that may exist elsewhere in the public domain. The State Department could, under this exemption, refuse to disclose documents indicating whether two Iranian nationals held valid U.S. passports.

Federal Bureau of Investigation v. Abramson (456 U.S. 615), decided by a 5-4 vote, May 24, 1982. White wrote the opinion; Blackmun, Brennan, O'Connor and Marshall dissented.

The FBI may refuse, under an exemption provided by the Freedom of Information Act for law enforcement files, to disclose information contained in "name check" summaries prepared for the Nixon White House on certain public figures. This information had originally been collected for such files but was transmitted to the White House in summary form. The court held that it was still exempt.

Federal Trade Commission v. Grolier Inc. (462 U.S. 19), decided by a 9-0 vote, June 6, 1983. White wrote the opinion.

A Freedom of Information Act exemption that protects from disclosure under the law "interagency or intraagency memorandums or letters which would not be available by law to a party . . . in litigation with the agency" protects the documents used by government lawyers to prepare for litigation even after the litigation has ended.

United States v. Weber Aircraft Corp., decided by a 9-0 vote, March 20, 1984. Stevens wrote the opinion.

The Freedom of Information Act does not require disclosure of witness statements given in the course of a safety investigation of an Air Force plane crash. These statements are exempt as "inter-agency or intra-agency memorandums or letters, which would not be available by law to a party other than an agency in litigation with the agency."

Social Security, Health

Beltran v. Myers (451 U.S. 625), decided by a 9-0 vote, May 18, 1981. *Per curiam* (unsigned) opinion.

A federal appeals court should reconsider its decision backing California's denial of Medicaid benefits to persons who have recently disposed of their assets for less than full value. The appeals court should examine that ruling in light of a new law (PL 96-611) barring benefit payments for two years after a person transfers more than $12,000 in assets to family members or friends in order to become eligible for Medicaid or supplemental security income.

Schweiker v. Gray Panthers (453 U.S. 39), decided by a 6-3 vote, June 25, 1981. Powell wrote the opinion; Stevens, Brennan and Marshall dissented.

The Department of Health and Human Services was within its authority, under the Social Security Act, when it issued regulations for the Medicaid program that govern the extent to which states may consider the income of an applicant's spouse in determining eligibility for Medicaid.

Under those regulations states may assume that spousal income is always available to pay for the needs of an institutionalized spouse.

United States v. Lee (455 U.S. 252), decided by a 9-0 vote, Feb. 23, 1982. Burger wrote the decision.

Congress exempted from Social Security taxes only self-employed individuals whose religious beliefs forbid them to participate in the Social Security system. This does not allow an Amish farmer and carpenter who employs other members of his sect to refuse to pay Social Security taxes on their wages.

Although paying his workers' Social Security taxes may interfere with the right of the farmer to the free exercise of his religious beliefs, some such burdens may be justified if necessary to realize an overriding governmental interest. The government's interest in the fiscal vitality of the Social Security system is such an overriding interest.

Herweg v. Ray (455 U.S. 265), decided by an 8-1 vote, Feb. 23, 1982. Rehnquist wrote the opinion; Burger dissented.

A federal Medicaid regulation limiting the period during which a state may assume that the income of a non-institutionalized spouse is available to pay the expenses of an institutionalized spouse is a permissible exercise of federal authority under the Social Security Act.

United States v. Erika (456 U.S. 201), decided by a 9-0 vote, April 20, 1982. Powell wrote the opinion.

The Court of Claims lacks jurisdiction to review challenges to decisions by private insurance companies concerning the amount of benefits payable under part of the Medicare program.

Schweiker v. McClure (456 U.S. 188), decided by a 9-0 vote, April 20, 1982. Powell wrote the opinion.

The federal statutory scheme under which hearings on claims under the Medicare program are conducted by private insurance company employees does not deny Medicare claimants their due process rights, even though it is the insurance company that has already once denied the benefit claim.

Blum v. Bacon (457 U.S. 132), decided by a 9-0 vote, June 14, 1982. Marshall wrote the opinion.

A New York law that denies emergency cash assistance, a program set up with federal funding under the Social Security Act, to recipients of Aid to Families with Dependent Children, and denies this aid in any form to reimburse welfare recipients for lost or stolen welfare checks, is invalid because it conflicts with federal regulations forbidding inequitable treatment of individuals under the emergency assistance program.

Schweiker v. Hogan (457 U.S. 569), decided by a 9-0 vote, June 21, 1982. Stevens wrote the opinion.

Income requirements imposed by the Social Security Act for federal reimbursement of Medicaid benefits are not unconstitutional even when they result, under a state medicaid program, in lower benefits for some low-income, retired and disabled workers than for welfare recipients.

Heckler v. Campbell (461 U.S. 458), decided by votes of 9-0 and 8-1, May 16, 1983. Powell wrote the opinion; Marshall dissented.

The Social Security Administration may properly use standard medical-vocational guidelines to determine whether jobs exist that a claimant for disability benefits could perform despite his or her disability.

Heckler v. Mathews, decided by a 9-0 vote, March 5, 1984. Brennan wrote the opinion.

Congress acted within constitutional limits in 1977 when it decided, for a limited time and purpose, to reinstate the use of a provision of the Social Security Act that had been held unconstitutional by the Supreme Court.

The court approved continued use, for persons retiring before December 1982 and eligible for a government pension, of a dependency test that required husbands, but not wives, to prove dependence on their spouses before receiving spousal benefits under the law.

This provision was an exception to a pension offset provision approved in 1977 that required retired government workers receiving pensions to have their Social Security spousal benefits reduced by the amount of their pension. The exception was intended to protect those workers, mostly women, who planned for retirement expecting to receive both the full spousal benefits and their pensions.

Heckler v. Ringer, decided by a 6-3 vote, May 14, 1984. Rehnquist wrote the opinion; Stevens, Brennan and Marshall dissented.

Challenges to government rules denying Medicare reimbursement for certain surgical procedures may be brought in federal court only after all administrative remedies for such claims have been exhausted.

Heckler v. Community Health Services of Crawford County Inc., decided by a 9-0 vote, May 21, 1984. Stevens wrote the opinion.

A health care provider is obligated to reimburse the government for excess Medicare payments that the provider recieved as a result of an erroneous interpretation of government regulations by a government agent.

Heckler v. Day, decided by a 5-4 vote, May 22, 1984. Powell wrote the opinion; Marshall, Brennan, Blackmun and Stevens dissented.

Federal courts must not set deadlines for the government to meet in reviewing contested Social Security disability claims. In light of the awareness of Congress of the problem of delay in this process, and express rejection of mandatory deadlines it would be "an unwarranted judicial intrusion into this pervasively regulated area for federal courts to issue injunctions imposing deadlines."

Suits Against the United States

Lockheed Aircraft Corp. v. United States (460 U.S. 190), decided by a 7-2 vote, Feb. 23, 1983. Powell wrote the opinion; Rehnquist and Burger dissented.

The Federal Employees' Compensation Act does not bar a suit against the government by an aerospace company seeking contribution or indemnity to the company, which itself was sued for wrongful death by the estate of a government employee who died in the crash of an aircraft being used by the United States.

This case arose after the crash of an Air Force cargo plane during the Vietnam "baby lift" of 1975. One hundred forty-four people were killed. Relatives of some govern-

ment employees who were killed sued the airplane's manufacturer, Lockheed, for damages. Lockheed, in turn, sought to sue the government, contending the crash was caused by government negligence, which resulted in the failure of a rear loading door to close properly. The Supreme Court's decision permitted Lockheed to pursue its suit against the government.

Block v. Neal (460 U.S. 289), decided by a 9-0 vote, March 7, 1983. Marshall wrote the opinion.

Persons who receive Farmers Home Administration (FmHA) loans to build their homes can sue the federal government if FmHA inspectors fail adequately to inspect the construction of their homes, which are later found to be defective.

United States v. Mitchell (463 U.S. 206), decided by a 6-3 vote, June 27, 1983. Marshall wrote the opinion; Powell, Rehnquist and O'Connor dissented.

The United States can be sued for money damages by Indian tribes charging mismanagement of valuable timber lands on their reservations. The basis for these suits is the Tucker Act, which permits some suits against the government for grievances, and several other laws that give the federal government full responsibility to manage Indian resources for the benefit of Indians.

Kosak v. United States, decided by an 8-1 vote, March 21, 1984. Marshall wrote the opinion; Stevens dissented.

The U.S. government cannot be sued for alleged damage to private property that occurs while the property is in the custody of the U.S. Customs Service.

United States v. S.A. Empresa de Viacao Aerea Rio Grandense (VARIG Airlines), decided by a 9-0 vote, June 19, 1984. Burger wrote the opinion.

The U.S. government cannot be sued for damages by persons injured in an air crash involving an aircraft that the federal government certified as airworthy years earlier.

Federal inspections of this type fall within the dis-

cretionary-function exception to the Federal Tort Claims Act, which allows some damage suits against the government based on the negligence of its employees.

Miscellaneous

Bowsher v. Merck & Co., Merck & Co. v. Bowsher (460 U.S. 824), decided by votes of 5-4 and 7-2, April 19, 1983. O'Connor wrote the opinion; White, Marshall, Blackmun and Stevens dissented.

The authority of the comptroller general of the United States to examine the records of a contractor with whom the government has entered into a fixed-price negotiated contract for drugs extends only to the contractor's records of the direct costs of producing those drugs, and not to records concerning indirect costs such as research, marketing and promotion.

National Association of Greeting Card Publishers v. U.S. Postal Service, United Parcel Service of America v. U.S. Postal Service (462 U.S. 810), decided by a 9-0 vote, June 22, 1983. Blackmun wrote the opinion.

The Postal Rate Commission has broad discretion in setting rates for different classes of mail. It is not required by law to maximize its use of the "cost-of-service" principle, under which each class of mail pays the share of costs for the overall postal system directly attributable to it.

The Commission has the discretion to use whatever reliable way it chooses to attribute these costs to the various classes of mail.

Federal Communications Commission (FCC) v. ITT World Communications, decided by a 9-0 vote, April 30, 1984. Powell wrote the opinion.

The Government in the Sunshine Act does not require public access to informal consultations between members of the FCC and foreign communications officials. Such consultations are not "meetings" within the scope of the law's requirements.

14

General Government

Introduction	*771*
1981 Chronology	*773*
1982 Chronology	*777*
1983 Chronology	*784*
1984 Chronology	*788*

General Government

Ronald Reagan came to the presidency in 1981 promising to reverse the growth of the federal government. It was not his intention "to do away with government," Reagan said in his inaugural address, but "to make it work — work with us, not over us; to stand by our side, not ride our back."

One of the central elements of Reagan's policy was the redirection of power from the federal government to state and local governments through his "New Federalism" plan. Congress in 1981 agreed to consolidate a number of separate federal grant programs into block grants that states and localities could use for broadly specified purposes. But the sweeping transfer of powers proposed by Reagan in his 1982 New Federalism plan received virtually no congressional attention.

Another major Reagan policy effort — elimination of government "waste, fraud and abuse" — also fell short of the president's expectations. A presidential commission early in 1984 recommended changes in federal management and programs that it said would yield $424 billion in savings over three years. But few recommendations were implemented during the remainder of the year. Congress showed little inclination to act on commission proposals, many of which would require controversial changes of policy.

Block Grants

President Reagan saw block grants as the first step in the redirection of money and power to state and local governments. Reagan in 1981 proposed the conversion of 88 categorical programs into seven block grants, but Congress went only part way toward meeting his request.

The 1981 budget-cutting reconciliation bill consolidated 57 existing categorical federal programs, mainly in the areas of health, education and community services, into seven block grants. The programs were abolished as separate programs, and funding for the combined grants was cut by about 25 percent from the funding level for the separate programs.

Block grants are federal payments to state or local governments for generally specified purposes, such as health, education or law enforcement. The money must be spent on programs in the general area, but state or local officials make the decisions on specifically how the money was used. Categorical grants, on the other hand, can be used only for specific programs as directed by Congress and the federal agencies that wrote the regulations to implement the laws passed by Congress.

The concept of block grants had been pushed for years by Republicans and by state and local officials, who said programs could be run better at the local level than from Washington, D.C. However, supporters of many individual programs — Republicans as well as Democrats — fought to retain the separate identity of some programs, fearing they would be funded inadequately or would lose out altogether in competition with other programs.

Congress did not go nearly as far in consolidating programs as Reagan had requested. Yet administration officials from the president on down hailed creation of the block grants in 1981 as a significant step forward on the road to the "New Federalism."

Conservative critics called the watered-down final version "the worst of both worlds," putting the burden of responsibilities on state and local governments without giving them full authority. On the other side, a coalition of 100 groups involved with categorical programs labeled the block grants "a step toward abandonment of federal responsibility."

New Federalism

In 1982 Reagan attempted to take his "New Federalism" a step further. In his State of the Union address he called for a thorough restructuring of federal, state and local government responsibilities. He tentatively proposed the shift to states of some 40 social, transportation and community development programs — and revenues to help pay for them in the early phase. He also proposed a "swap" of the three principal welfare programs for the poor. The federal government would assume the full costs of Medicaid, the federal-state health program for the poor, while states took over food stamps and Aid to Families

References

Discussion of general government action for the years 1945-64 may be found in *Congress and the Nation Vol. I*, pp. 1455-1516; for the years 1965-68, *Congress and the Nation Vol. II*, pp. 655-660; for the years 1969-72, *Congress and the Nation Vol. III*, pp. 435-468; for the years 1973-76, *Congress and the Nation Vol. IV*, pp. 795-826; for the years 1977-80, *Congress and the Nation Vol. V*, pp. 817-870.

with Dependent Children (AFDC). The plan was revised later in 1982 to drop food stamps from the proposed swap and to reduce the number of programs to be turned back to the states.

But the "swap and turnback" plan got bogged down in negotiations with the National Governors' Association and similar groups, which were wary of receiving new responsibilities without adequate funds to pay for them, and no legislation was introduced.

In 1983 a new plan was sent to Congress under which 34 federal programs would be folded into four "megablock" grants to states and localities. The proposal to swap welfare programs had been dropped. None of the megablock grant proposals was enacted.

Grace Commission

In his 1980 campaign Reagan maintained that during his first year in office he could cut the federal budget by 2 percent simply by eliminating "waste, extravagance, abuse and outright fraud." As president, he said, he would "enlist the very best minds from business, labor and whatever quarter to conduct a detailed review of every department, bureau and agency that lived by federal appropriations."

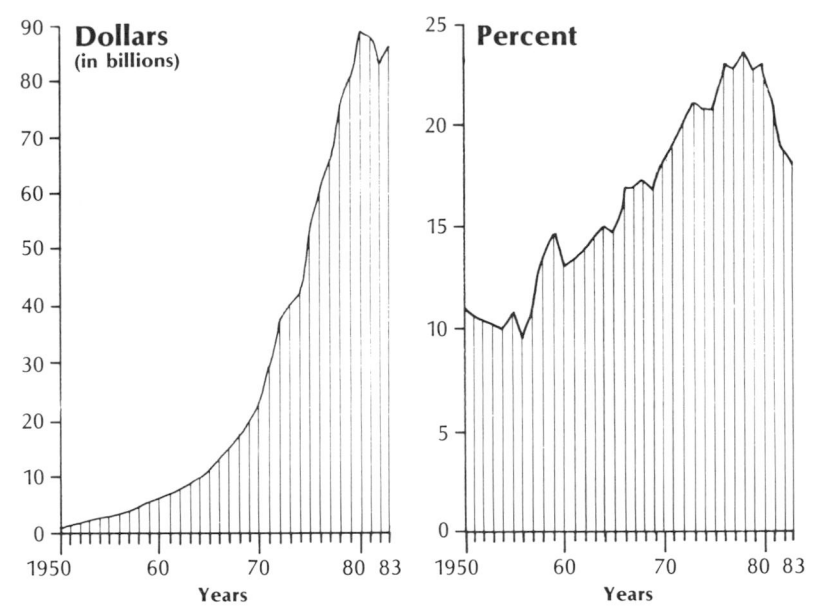

The graph on the left shows federal grants to state and local governments in billions of dollars. The graph on the right shows the percentage that those federal grants represented of state and local spending.

SOURCE: U.S. Treasury Department

The detailed review of the federal government that Reagan called for was undertaken by a commission he appointed, called the President's Private Sector Survey on Cost Control. It was more popularly known as the Grace commission, after its chairman, industrialist J. Peter Grace. The commission's 47-volume report, issued in January 1984, included 2,478 recommendations that the panel claimed would save $424 billion over three years.

Although the president cited the work of the commission regularly as validating his contention that fraud and waste existed in many areas of the federal government, the commission's work failed to have the impact the president sought. Critics charged that its claims of potential savings from administrative or management changes were overstated. The real savings from commission proposals, critics said, would have to come from program and policy changes, such as requiring a means test to determine if recipients of federal social welfare payments — Social Security, food stamps and Medicare, for example — really needed the benefits.

The commission, composed of 161 top business and organization executives, emphasized a shift to what it called sound business practices to eliminate waste. It predicted that the government's multibillion-dollar deficit could be virtually wiped out by the year 2000 "without raising taxes, without weakening America's needed defense buildup, and without harming in any way necessary social welfare programs."

Congress took little action to ratify commission recommendations that required congressional approval, with the result that only about $3 billion in savings could be cred-

ited to legislative changes. The administration claimed another $41 billion in savings from management changes.

Other Issues

Congress never approved administration-backed legislation that would have revamped federal rule-making procedures to give Congress, the White House and the courts more control over federal regulations. The administration wanted proposed rules subjected to cost-benefit analysis, with the least costly alternative to be chosen as the final rule. The Senate passed a regulatory reform bill in 1982, but the legislation died in the House.

And for three years Congress blocked Reagan's attempt to change the Freedom of Information Act to close off or delay the release of government records involved with national security or law enforcement. The administration proposed giving broad new powers to the attorney general to exempt all information relating to terrorism, organized crime and foreign counterintelligence investigations. The only change lawmakers were willing to accept was to allow the director of the Central Intelligence Agency to close the files relating to the identities of sources and methods used by the agency and records relating to the routine administration and management of intelligence activities.

Yielding to Congress, President Reagan in 1983 accepted legislation establishing a legal public holiday to honor the Rev. Dr. Martin Luther King Jr., the black civil rights leader who was assassinated in 1968. The administration initially had opposed the bill.

Chronology
Of Action
On General Government
Issues

1981

Reagan Block Grants

Block grants — President Reagan's first step in the redirection of money and power to the state and local levels — won only partial endorsement from Congress in 1981.

Legislation cleared July 31 consolidated 57 existing "categorical" federal programs, mainly in the areas of education, health and community services, into seven new block grants. The separate programs were abolished and funding for the combined grants was cut by about 25 percent.

The block grants were included in a massive budget reconciliation bill (HR 3982 — PL 97-35) that cut $35.2 billion from projected federal spending for fiscal 1982. *(Reconciliation, p. 40)*

Congress made substantial changes in the president's block grant proposals, setting federal standards and spending levels for some programs and refusing to include others in the block grants at all.

Block grants are federal payments to state or local governments for broadly specified purposes, such as health, education or law enforcement. The money must be spent on programs in the general area, but state or local officials make the decisions on specifically how the money is used. Categorical grants can be used only for specific programs as directed by Congress and the federal agencies that write the regulations to implement the laws passed by Congress.

The concept of block grants had been pushed for years by Republicans and by state and local officials, who said programs could be run better at the local level than from Washington, D.C. However, supporters of many individual programs — Republicans as well as Democrats — fought to retain their separate identity, fearing they would be funded inadequately or would lose out altogether in competition with other programs. *(Block grant history, box, p. 774)*

Reagan Proposals

In his Feb. 18 economic policy address to Congress, Reagan called for the conversion of 88 categorical programs into seven major block grants. That could save $23.9 billion over five years, the president said, by reducing wasteful administrative overhead and program duplication and by targeting programs more effectively through increased local control. The administration outlined specific block grants in its March 10 budget, which called for a cut of about 25 percent in funding for the consolidated programs, and generally eliminated requirements that states or localities match federal funding or maintain a certain level of expen-

ditures with their own funds. Since the consolidations would "allow for significant savings in administration and result in more efficient management, the reductions in funding need not cause a comparable reduction in services to the public," the budget said.

Reagan's major block grant proposals were:
● Two education block grants, one to states and one to local education agencies, replacing all or part of 44 separate elementary and secondary education programs.
● Two health block grants (health services and preventive health services) replacing 25 categorical programs.
● A social services block grant composed of 13 programs, including day care, child welfare, foster care and adoption assistance, developmental disabilities, rehabilitation services and community services programs operated by the Community Services Administration (CSA).
● A hardship assistance block grant, consolidating low-income energy assistance and several small emergency aid programs.
● A nutrition assistance block grant for Puerto Rico, replacing food stamps and other nutrition programs there.

The administration also proposed to combine the Urban Development Action Grant program with the existing Community Development Block Grant; to consolidate 10 programs operated by the Bureau of Indian Affairs as the first step toward an Indian block grant program, and to consolidate a number of employment and training programs and airport programs.

Legislative Action

Reagan's block grant proposals were thoroughly rewritten by Congress.

Even the Republican-controlled Senate refused to go along with the proposals as introduced. Key members of the Labor and Human Resources Committee strongly supported several existing education and health programs and feared they would lose funding, or even be eliminated, in the competition with other programs for funds in a block grant. They blocked committee action until Reagan's proposals were modified to protect those programs. The Senate Finance Committee also altered the president's plan.

The committee modifications were included in the Senate version of the reconciliation package (S 1377 — S Rept 97-139), passed June 25.

In the Democratic-controlled House, the block grant proposals were rejected outright by the Education and Labor and Ways and Means committees, and scaled down by the Energy and Commerce panel. Most of the block grants were added to the reconciliation bill on the floor June 26, when the House adopted a Republican alternative for the committee-reported version of HR 3982 (H Rept 97-158), but even then Republican members added protections for individual programs.

When the reconciliation bill went to conference, several Senate-approved block grants were restored to categorical grant status, including family planning, health centers for migrant workers and the Women's Educational Equity Act. Conferees also killed what remained of one of Reagan's biggest proposed consolidations, the social services block grant. In addition, they imposed restrictions and conditions not included in the Senate bill upon the states' administration of the block grants.

The conferees filed their report on HR 3982 July 29 (H Rept 97-208), and both chambers approved the measure July 31.

Block Grants: An Old Republican Idea

President Reagan's call for consolidation of scores of federal categorical grant programs into block grants echoed an old Republican theme.

GOP members of Congress had pushed the block grant approach since the 1960s as a way of turning federal decision-making back to state and local officials. While Congress rejected most of the proposals of Republican Presidents Nixon and Ford, the Reagan administration was more successful, benefiting from growing hostility to federal "strings" — the regulations and paperwork that generally accompany federal funds.

History of Block Grants

The block grant concept developed as a reaction against the long trend toward centralization of government authority in the federal government — a trend that accelerated enormously during the Depression and again during President Johnson's "Great Society" of the 1960s. *(Background, Congress and the Nation Vol. II, p. 164)*

Categorical grant programs had proliferated because the federal government could tap far more revenue sources than states and localities could, and because state and local officials often could not or would not provide funds to deal with certain problems.

The first major block grant was included in the Comprehensive Health Planning and Services Act of 1966 (PL 89-749), replacing a variety of grants to fight certain diseases with a broad comprehensive public health services grant. The only major requirement was that at least 15 percent of the funds had to be spent on mental health. *(Congress and the Nation Vol. II, p. 680)*

In 1967 Republicans almost succeeded in substituting block grants for the traditional categorical aid to education. Only an intensive lobbying campaign by the Johnson administration prevented adoption of the education block grant plan. *(Congress and the Nation Vol. II, p. 724)*

In 1968, over the opposition of President Johnson, congressional Republicans did succeed in incorporating block grants in two law enforcement measures — the Omnibus Crime Control and Safe Streets Act (PL 90-351) and the Juvenile Delinquency Prevention and Control Act (PL 90-445). *(Congress and the Nation Vol. II, pp. 323, 330)*

'New Federalism'

In 1969 President Nixon proposed a "New Federalism" in which power, funds and responsibility would be shifted from Washington back to the states. He called for general revenue sharing — a program of virtually unrestricted grants — followed in 1971 by "special revenue sharing" — $11 billion worth of block grants for six general purposes: education, urban development, rural development, transportation, job training and law enforcement. *(Congress and the Nation Vol. III, p. 98)*

General revenue sharing was enacted in 1972 (PL 92-512), but except for some law enforcement and manpower training block grants, the Democratic-controlled Congress generally ignored or rejected other block grant proposals from Nixon and his successor, Ford.

Ford proposed four major block grants in 1976, in the areas of health, education, child nutrition and social services. All were rejected.

Congressional Democrats accused the Republicans of using block grants to try to undo the social programs of Democratic administrations, and there was strong lobbying pressure against the grants by interest groups, many of which had lobbied for creation of the special categorical grants in the first place. They feared their programs would lose funds or be killed altogether if they were lumped in with other programs in a block grant. The same argument was made against Reagan's proposals, but with less success.

Provisions

As signed into law Aug. 13, the block grant provisions of HR 3982 (PL 97-35):

• Consolidated 19 existing categorical health programs into four health block grants: preventive health and health services; alcohol, drug abuse and mental health services; primary care; maternal and child health. *(Story, p. 523)*

• Consolidated 13 small education programs into a block grant. *(Story, p. 559)*

• Established a community services block grant, replacing programs administered by the CSA. *(Story, p. 590)*

• Established a nutritional assistance block grant for Puerto Rico, to replace food stamps and other federal nutrition programs in the commonwealth. *(Story, p. 583)*

• Provided that no state could receive block grant funds until it had prepared and made public a report on its planned use of the funds, allowed for comments on the report from interested parties and conducted a public hearing on it.

Federal Pay, Pensions

As part of its 1981 budget-cutting effort, Congress limited the annual Oct. 1 pay raise for federal white-collar employees and scaled back cost-of-living adjustments (COLAs) for federal retirees.

Top-level employees of the executive branch, whose salaries had been frozen in a long-running controversy over congressional pay, won substantial raises shortly before Congress adjourned in December. Many of the 49,000 employees affected had received only one modest increase since 1977. *(Action on congressional pay, p. 821)*

White-Collar Pay, Retirees' COLAs

The budget reconciliation bill (HR 3982 — PL 97-35), cleared July 31, set a 4.8 percent ceiling on the scheduled Oct. 1 pay raise for federal white-collar workers. Congress went along with President Reagan's proposal to impose the cap, even though a federal pay board set up to assure comparability between government and private sector pay had recommended salary increases of about 13.5 percent.

While accepting the 4.8 percent ceiling, lawmakers balked at Reagan's proposal to consider benefits as well as pay in determining future comparability adjustments.

Federal white-collar workers had received automatic salary adjustments annually since 1971 under the Federal Pay Comparability Act of 1970 (PL 91-656). The law permitted either house of Congress to overrule any presidential decision to alter the pay board recommendations. *(Congress and the Nation Vol. III, p. 454)*

In scaling back the 1981 increase, Congress reduced projected fiscal 1982 spending by $3.7 billion. Reconciliation instructions adopted in the fiscal 1982 budget resolution had called for savings in federal employee and postal programs totaling $5.2 billion.

Other provisions of the reconciliation bill substituted an annual cost-of-living adjustment for the twice-yearly COLA paid to federal retirees under existing law. Reagan had requested the change, which was expected to save $513 million in fiscal 1982.

The House approved the pay cap and COLA provisions June 26 when it adopted a Republican alternative for the reconciliation cuts approved by its Democratic-controlled authorizing committees (H Rept 97-158). The provisions had been passed by the Republican-controlled Senate June 26 in its version of the reconciliation measure (S 1377 — S Rept 97-139). *(Reconciliation, p. 40)*

Congress voted further COLA changes in 1982 and 1984. *(Stories, pp. 779, 792)*

Provisions. As signed into law Aug. 13, the federal pay provisions of HR 3982 (Title XVII of PL 97-35):

● Placed a 4.8 percent cap on the Oct. 1, 1981, salary increases for white-collar civilian employees.

● Cut back COLAs for civilian and military retirees from twice yearly to annually, with payments to be made March 1 based on the change in the Consumer Price Index during the preceding calendar year.

● Authorized awards of up to $20,000 each for the disclosure of fraud, waste or mismanagement by federal employees. The award program expired Sept. 30, 1984. *(Story, p. 792)*

● Established procedures by which federal agencies could remove members of the Senior Executive Service (SES) because of a reduction-in-force (RIF) required by reorganization, lack of funds or other reasons.

The SES, an elite cadre of federal bureaucrats who could receive bonuses and be transferred freely among agencies, was established under the 1978 Civil Service Reform Act (PL 95-454). *(Congress and the Nation Vol. V, p. 831)*

● Required cuts of $100 million from funds budgeted for

federal employees' travel and $500 million from funds budgeted for consultants' services in fiscal 1982.

Executive Pay Raise

Congress eased limitations on salaries paid to career government executives as part of a fiscal 1982 appropriations measure (H J Res 370 — PL 97-92) cleared Dec. 11.

The bill raised the Executive Level III pay ceiling, for personnel just below Cabinet officials and members of Congress, to $59,500 a year from $55,387.50. Pay caps for Level IV and V employees rose to $58,500 (from $52,750) and $57,500 (from $50,112.50) respectively. Level I and II officials, including members of Congress, were excluded from the increases.

Both career executives and members of Congress theoretically had been eligible for automatic salary adjustments each year since 1975, when they were brought under the Pay Comparability Act. Members of Congress usually declined to accept the pay adjustments, however, and in denying themselves a raise they often withheld it from other senior government officials as well. Top-level salaries had been capped since 1977, except for one 5.5 percent increase permitted in 1979.

Earlier in 1981 Congress had rejected a 16.8 percent pay raise recommended under separate procedures for itself, senior government executives, judges and others. President Carter had proposed the increase before leaving office in January in response to the quadrennial recommendations of the Commission on Executive, Legislative and Judicial Salaries. The commission had proposed hikes averaging 40 percent. Resolutions disapproving those increases were adopted March 12 by the House (H Res 109) and Senate (S Res 89, 90, 91, 92). *(Pay raise procedures, box, p. 824)*

Postal Service Reductions

Postal subsidies were cut and the start of the proposed nine-digit ZIP code delayed by the budget-cutting reconciliation legislation cleared July 31.

Title VII of the bill (HR 3982 — PL 97-35) sharply reduced authorizations for the independent U.S. Postal Service in fiscal 1982-84. The measure provided for a three-year phase-out of a public service subsidy that supported mail delivery to unprofitable areas. And authorizations for revenue forgone payments, which made up for income lost through subsidized postage rates for charities and other non-profit mailers, were cut by about one-third. Savings from the two provisions amounted to $956 million for fiscal 1982, $1.027 billion for fiscal 1983 and $1.087 billion for fiscal 1984.

The cuts fell about midway between the House and Senate figures. *(Background, Congress and the Nation Vol. V, pp. 318, 329; reconciliation action, p. 40)*

The bill also delayed the nine-digit ZIP code until Oct. 1, 1983, as the House had wanted. The Postal Service was permitted to advertise, train personnel, buy new sorting machines and take other preliminary steps necessary to start the system, but it was prohibited both from using the new sorting machines to process the expanded code and from offering discounts to businesses until Oct. 1, 1983.

Provisions. As signed into law Aug. 13, the postal provisions of HR 3982 (Title VII of PL 97-35):

● Authorized for the public service subsidy $250 million

in fiscal 1982, $100 million in fiscal 1983 and zero in fiscal 1984.

● Authorized for the revenue forgone subsidy $696 million in fiscal 1982, $708 million in fiscal 1983 and $760 million in fiscal 1984.

● Stipulated that if the full amount needed for the revenue forgone subsidy exceeded the authorization in any year, rates for third-class non-profit bulk mailers would be raised to make up the difference. All subsidized second-, third- and fourth-class mailers would face rate hikes if Congress failed to appropriate the full amount authorized in any year. Rates for materials for the blind and the handicapped were not affected.

● Deferred until fiscal 1985 the fiscal 1982-84 authorizations for transitional payments to help the Postal Service meet workmen's compensation and other unfunded liabilities of the old Post Office Department and required the Postal Service to meet the obligations from other sources.

● Provided that public service and other funds apportioned by the Treasury Department to the Postal Service be made quarterly, rather than annually.

● Barred the Postal Service during fiscal 1982-84 from taking any action to reduce or to plan to reduce the number of days for regular mail delivery.

● Barred the Postal Service from implementing the nine-digit ZIP code until Oct. 1, 1983, but allowed the agency to buy sorting machinery, advertise, train personnel and take other preliminary steps aimed at putting the code into effect on Oct. 1, 1983.

Regulatory Reform

Responding to complaints that the federal regulatory machinery had gotten out of hand, Senate and House committees in 1981 approved bills to rein in government rule-making agencies.

The Senate passed its bill (S 1080) early in 1982, but the House measure (HR 746) died in the Rules Committee when the 97th Congress adjourned. *(1981-82 legislative action, p. 777)*

Freedom of Information Act

Efforts of the Reagan administration and some members of Congress to restrict substantially the use of the Freedom of Information Act (FOIA) drew strong criticism from the press and made little headway in Congress in 1981.

Acting on a 3-2 vote Dec. 14, the Senate Judiciary Subcommittee on the Constitution approved a bill (S 1730) that borrowed heavily from the administration's sweeping proposals. These included giving broad new powers to the attorney general to exempt all information relating to terrorism, organized crime and foreign counterintelligence investigations. The measure also made it easier for the Central Intelligence Agency (CIA) to go to court to stop disclosure of information the agency considered to be sensitive, and increased protections for information businesses submitted to the government.

The full Judiciary Committee reported S 1730 in 1982, but there was no further action on that or similar House legislation. *(1982 action, p. 778)*

Congress passed legislation in 1984 closing certain CIA files from FOIA review. *(Story, p. 788)*

NASA Authorization

President Reagan Dec. 21 signed a bill (S 1098 — PL 97-96) authorizing $6.172 billion for the National Aeronautics and Space Administration in fiscal 1982. The conference report (H Rept 97-351) was adopted by the Senate Nov. 23 and by the House Dec. 8. The final dollar figure represented a compromise between the $6.222 billion approved by the Senate May 21 (S Rept 97-100) and the $6.122 billion approved by the House June 23 (HR 1257 — H Rept 97- 32).

The final measure included a $2.189 billion authorization for the space shuttle — $5 million less than the administration had requested — and authorized $215.3 million for a planetary exploration program that would include a mission to explore Jupiter.

Science Authorization

Congress failed to complete work on a fiscal 1982 authorization bill for the National Science Foundation. The House Sept. 23 passed a $1.08 billion authorization measure (HR 1520 — H Rept 97-34), but the Senate never acted on $1.04 billion versions reported by its Labor and Human Resources Committee (S 1200 — S Rept 97-131) and Commerce, Science and Transportation Committee (S 1194 — S Rept 97-72).

Although the authorization did not clear, Congress appropriated $993.8 million for the foundation in fiscal 1982 (PL 97-101). President Reagan had requested $909.5 million.

Arts, Humanities Funding

Congress restored about $60 million that President Reagan wanted to cut from the authorizations for the National Endowment for the Arts (NEA) and the National Endowment for the Humanities (NEH). The provisions were included in Title V of the budget-cutting reconciliation bill (HR 3982 — PL 97-35) cleared July 31. *(Reconciliation, p. 40)*

Reagan had sought $88 million for NEA and $85 million for NEH in fiscal 1982, a cut of 50 percent from President Carter's request for each of the endowments. The administration argued that the need to cut federal spending required cuts in funding for the two agencies and that the private sector should take more responsibility for supporting NEA and NEH.

But the bill reduced the authorization by only 25 percent, providing $119.3 million in fiscal 1982 for NEA and $113.7 million for NEH. These were the figures recommended by the Senate. The House had approved a $223 million lump sum for the two agencies for fiscal 1982. Previous authorizations for fiscal 1982 (PL 96-496) provided $190.5 million for NEA and $187.5 million for NEH.

Federal Debt Collection

Congress did not complete action in 1981 on legislation requested by the Reagan administration to speed up the collection of more than $25 billion in overdue federal loans. The legislation was aimed at making it easier for the government to enlist the aid of credit bureaus and collection

agencies in tracking down delinquent borrowers.

The House passed a limited version of the bill (HR 2811) May 18, but a broader Senate measure (S 1249) did not reach the floor in 1981. Congress completed action on the measure in 1982. *(1981-82 action, p. 780)*

Federal Building Policy

The Senate May 6 unanimously approved a bill (S 533) to revamp the way Congress approved new federal buildings. The House never acted on the measure, which would have established new standards for architectural design and energy efficiency and set planning requirements. S 533 was similar to a measure that died in 1980 when conferees deadlocked. *(Congress and the Nation Vol. V, p. 858)*

The Senate bill (S Rept 97-48) removed the exclusive power of the Senate Environment and House Public Works committees to authorize new construction and leases and required the GSA to prepare one- and five-year plans projecting space needs. The full House and Senate would vote on an annual authorization bill covering all proposed building projects for the year. No rental costs would be detailed because that would weaken GSA's bargaining position with landlords.

Other Legislation

Virgin Islands Constitution

A new constitution to be submitted to the voters of the U.S. Virgin Islands was approved by Congress June 16 (H J Res 238 — PL 97-21). The resolution had been passed by the House May 5 (H Rept 97-25) and the Senate June 3 (S Rept 97-66). The House accepted the Senate version June 16.

The constitution established a republican form of government with a unicameral legislature, an executive branch, an independent judiciary and a bill of rights. It also emphasized continued U.S. sovereignty over the islands. Congress gave the Virgin Islands the authority in 1976 (PL 94-584) to draw up a constitution, and a constitutional convention finished its work July 31, 1980.

Cost Estimates

The Senate Dec. 16 passed and cleared for the president a bill (HR 1465 — PL 97-108) to require the Congressional Budget Office (CBO) to estimate the cost of major legislation to state and local governments.

HR 1465 required CBO to prepare cost estimates on bills that would impose at least $200 million in annual costs on local governments. The bill, reported by the House Rules Committee Dec. 3 (H Rept 97-353), was passed by the House by voice vote Dec. 8. The Senate bypassed committee referral.

King Memorial

After sharp debate, the House Sept. 15 agreed to place in the Capitol a bust or statue of the Rev. Dr. Martin Luther King Jr. The resolution (H Con Res 153 — H Rept 97-217), adopted by a 386-16 vote, won Senate approval in 1982. *(Story, p. 784)*

Supporters of the legislation argued that the slain black leader deserved to be honored for his civil rights work and that black Americans should have a representative among the commemorative statues and busts that line the halls of the U.S. Capitol. But opponents objected that King's record did not justify the honor.

In 1983 Congress approved a national holiday to honor King. *(Story, p. 786)*

1982

'New Federalism'

In his first State of the Union address Jan. 26, President Reagan unveiled a sweeping proposal to transform the federal system, but his "New Federalism" got a cold shoulder from Congress and the states. In fact, administration attempts to translate the president's proposal into specific legislation bogged down completely during talks with state and local officials and interest groups. Reagan submitted no legislation, and Congress made no effort to initiate its own.

There were two parts to Reagan's federalism proposal. The first involved a dramatic shift of some 40 social, transportation and community development programs — and revenues to help pay for them in the early phase — to the states. The second called for a "swap" of the three principal welfare programs for the poor, with the federal government assuming the full cost of the Medicaid health program and the states taking over food stamps and Aid to Families with Dependent Children (AFDC).

Governors viewed the welfare swap as a mixed blessing. Although they welcomed the transfer of Medicaid costs to the federal government, the governors also wanted to shift all welfare costs as well in exchange for state assumption of costs in areas such as education. In addition, governors wanted the federalism plan to ensure federal support for states with limited capacities to raise more money through excise or other taxes.

Reaction among city and county officials was mixed as well. Some were optimistic that at last they would have some role in deciding how their funds would be spent. Many, however, were concerned that local interests could lose their share of funds after 1991, when federal support would be ended and states could provide money as they chose.

Regulatory Reform

Congress effectively killed regulatory reform legislation Dec. 9 when the House Rules Committee held a hearing on a regulatory reform bill (HR 746) but recessed without clearing the measure for floor action. The Senate had passed its version (S 1080) earlier in the year. Authorizing committees had approved the bills in 1981.

The regulatory reform legislation, which was supported by business lobbyists and the Reagan administration, would have revamped federal rule-making procedures to give Congress, the White House and the courts more control over the way regulations were promulgated and adopted. As the first overhaul of the Administrative Proce-

dure Act since it was written in 1946, the measure would have subjected major proposed rules to cost-benefit analysis, given Congress some form of legislative veto to override federal regulations and changed the way regulations were challenged in court.

Supporters said the legislation would streamline and reduce the cost of rule-making. But a coalition of public interest groups fought the legislation, arguing that it would hamper regulations needed to protect public health and safety.

Background

Regulatory reform efforts collapsed in controversy in the 96th Congress, although efforts to rein in the activist Federal Trade Commission succeeded to some degree. *(Background, Congress and the Nation Vol. V, p. 861)*

President Reagan moved early administratively to corral the rule-makers. On Jan. 22, 1981, he named Vice President George Bush to head a regulatory reform task force to review existing and proposed regulations and to oversee the development of legislative proposals. In addition, he placed a 60-day freeze on many new rules in order to review them.

Executive order 12291, issued Feb. 17, required executive branch agencies to examine the costs and benefits of all proposed and existing major rules and to pick the least costly alternative. Major rules were those that would cost businesses $100 million or more to comply with.

Regulators also were told to consider a rule's effect on particular industries and the economy as a whole. The Office of Management and Budget (OMB) was directed to oversee compliance.

Legislative Action

The Senate Judiciary Committee reported S 1080 (S Rept 97-284) July 17, 1981, and the Governmental Affairs Committee filed its report on the bill Sept. 18 (S Rept 97-305). A compromise version won unanimous Senate approval March 24, 1982.

The House Judiciary Committee approved HR 746 Dec. 8, 1981, and filed its report on the bill (H Rept 97-435) Feb. 25, 1982. Further action on the legislation was delayed by the resignation in March of its chief sponsor, George E. Danielson, D-Calif., who accepted a California judgeship.

The Rules Committee finally held a hearing on the measure in September and another in December following the election recess. Most of the members testifying, however, opposed the legislation.

With the session rapidly drawing to a close, the Rules Committee showed no appetite for wrestling with the complex and controversial legislation. The panel broke off hearings after nine House members had spoken against HR 746. Another 25 witnesses were awaiting an opportunity to testify.

Major Issues

Regulatory Analysis. The keystone of the proposed Regulatory Reform Act was the introduction of cost-benefit analysis into the federal rule-making process. Each agency would have to decide whether the benefits of a proposed rule outweighed its costs. The "regulatory analysis" would be conducted on major rules — those that generated $100 million a year in enforcement and compli-

ance costs. The president, through OMB or another designee, was given the power to make sure both independent and executive agencies complied with the cost-benefit requirement. However, time limits were added to ensure that OMB did not use its power to review agency compliance procedures as a means of stalling enactment of agency rules. And an amendment approved just before Senate passage required OMB to make public information about its role in a rule-making procedure.

Legislative Veto. One of the more controversial issues involved in the regulatory reform debate concerned the legislative veto. Both the House and Senate bills allowed a majority of both chambers to override federal regulations. But the House version of the legislative veto also required the president's signature and limited it to "major" rules, defined as those with an annual cost of $100 million or more. The more restrictive Senate provisions did not require presidential approval of a legislative veto and would apply to nearly all regulations proposed by executive and independent agencies.

While Congress debated the issue, a decision was pending by the U.S. Supreme Court on the constitutionality of the legislative veto. Critics argued that Congress should wait until the high court had ruled on the issue before writing legislation. The Senate adopted an amendment to S 1080 to sever the legislative veto provision if the Supreme Court found the veto unconstitutional. The court June 23, 1983, ruled the legislative veto unconstitutional. *(Story, p. 833)*

Court Role. As passed by the Senate, the legislation also made legal challenges to agency decisions easier by removing the benefit of the doubt often given to agencies under existing law. An amendment to the Senate bill instructed judges not to presume an agency's interpretation of law was necessarily correct, placing a greater burden on the agency to support its position. It was designed to eliminate a tradition of judicial deference to agency expertise. The House proposal also gave more direction to the courts on their role in reviewing agency decisions, but did not include Senate-adopted provisions that made it easier to challenge legally agency actions.

Freedom of Information Act

The 97th Congress did not complete action on legislative proposals backed by the Reagan administration to place new restrictions on the Freedom of Information Act (FOIA). Although the Senate Judiciary Committee reported a package of FOIA amendments May 20, the full Senate never took up the proposals. The House took no action at all on the issue.

The Senate Judiciary Committee approved a major revision of the FOIA in 1983, but the bill never made it to the floor. Congress in 1984 exempted certain CIA files from the act. *(Story, p. 788)*

Background

The FOIA was enacted in 1966 to make previously classified government files available to the public. Changes in the law enacted in 1974 over the veto of President Ford broadened access to certain information and were intended to remove bureaucratic obstacles erected to thwart implementation. *(Congress and the Nation Vol. IV, p. 805)*

President Reagan and various members of Congress,

including the chairman of the Senate Judiciary Committee's Constitution Subcommittee, Orrin G. Hatch, R-Utah, maintained that the FOIA had been misused. They sought certain changes in the law to ensure greater protection against disclosure of vital government records, particularly those having some relation to national security or law enforcement. They also were sympathetic to appeals by businessmen for changes that would shield more information corporations were required to submit to the federal government, including federal regulatory agencies.

Opposing any new restrictions were the news media, public interest organizations and academic groups. They contended that some of Hatch's proposals would give the government new powers to withhold information. Allowing the government more time to provide documents would encourage agencies to drag out response time, opponents argued. And public health and safety could be jeopardized if access to information supplied to the government by businesses — for example, on food and drugs, consumer goods, pollution hazards and employment practices — were restricted.

In 1981 Hatch proposed changes allowing the attorney general to protect information about federal investigations of organized crime and terrorism, giving agencies more time to release government files and making it more difficult for the public to see information supplied by businesses.

Many of the FOIA changes sought by Hatch and the administration were included in a bill (S 1730) approved by a 3-2 vote of Hatch's Constitution Subcommittee in December 1981.

1982 Compromise

The subcommittee measure met with intense opposition from critics in and out of Congress, and Hatch eventually was forced to give ground on proposals to protect business data submitted to the government, to let the government seal files on terrorism investigations and to charge service fees for processing information requests.

The Judiciary Committee approved the compromise package of amendments and ordered the bill reported May 20 by unanimous vote. The committee did not issue a written report before the session adjourned in December.

The compromise measure created new limits on public access to files dealing with organized crime, government informants and the Secret Service. It also allowed the withholding of information that "could reasonably be expected to cause a clearly unwarranted invasion" of personal privacy. The bill set new fees for processing FOIA requests but waived them for reporters, scholars and non-profit public interest groups. It also authorized the government to charge commercial users royalties for valuable technical information.

The compromise won praise from lobbyists and lawmakers on both sides of the issue, who agreed that the bill managed to limit public access to certain federal records without creating excess government secrecy.

Federal Pay, Pensions

Federal employees and pensioners felt the pinch of 1982 deficit reduction efforts as Congress scaled back retirees' benefits and agreed to hold pay raises for active employees to 4 percent.

Retirees' Benefits

In its budget-cutting reconciliation bill (HR 6955 — PL 97-253), cleared Aug. 18, Congress reduced cost-of-living hikes for federal retirees under age 62 and imposed one-month delays on all federal pension increases in 1983, 1984 and 1985. About 1.9 million civilian retirees and 2.2 million military retirees were affected by the pension changes, which were expected to reduce spending by about $3.3 billion through their three-year life.

Rejecting a proposed across-the-board cap of 4 percent on retirees' annual cost-of-living adjustments (COLAs), conferees (H Rept 97-759) instead agreed that all survivors, disabled retirees and retirees above age 62 would get a full COLA, but those under 62 would receive only 50 percent of the COLA. The bill also temporarily shifted the COLA award date from March 1 annually, as established in 1981 reconciliation legislation, to April 1 in 1983, May 1 in 1984 and June 1 in 1985. *(1982 reconciliation action, p. 48; 1981 COLA changes, p. 774; 1984 changes, p. 792)*

Related provisions eliminated "double-dipping" by military retirees who collected both military and civil service benefits and made technical changes in computing pay for federal workers and retirees, for total three-year savings of about $4.1 billion.

The fiscal 1983 budget resolution (S Con Res 92) had called for three-year cuts of more than $5 billion, mainly from a 4 percent ceiling on federal retirees' COLAs. In action on the reconciliation bill, the House Aug. 3 rejected the COLA limit and approved cuts of only $113 million. The Senate accepted the 4 percent cap Aug. 5. A day earlier it had rejected an amendment to remove the cap on a **48-51 key vote (R 10-44; D 38-7)**. *(1982 key votes, p. 895)*

Provisions. As signed into law Sept. 8, the federal pension provisions of HR 6955 (PL 97-253):

● Provided for 13-month intervals between retirees' cost-of-living adjustments in 1983-85, with COLAs to be awarded April 1, 1983, May 1, 1984, and June 1, 1985.

● Eliminated double-dipping by military retirees who obtained federal jobs, by reducing an individual's civilian pay by the amount of his military retirement COLA.

● Mandated that pension benefits be rounded down to the next lowest dollar, instead of to the nearest whole dollar.

● Delayed the date pensioners would receive their first payment from the day after they ended work to the first day of the month following retirement. This would not apply to individuals retiring involuntarily or on disability.

● Required that a significant reduction in force or a reduction in pay must occur before a worker could retire before age 55. The bill provided that a reasonable offer of a position would preclude an individual from eligibility for early retirement.

● Prohibited a retiree from receiving more in an annuity than the current salary of the position from which he or she retired.

White-Collar Pay Raise

A 4 percent pay raise for 1.4 million white-collar federal employees went into effect Oct. 1, when Congress accepted President Reagan's recommendation to hold the annual increase to that figure. No legislative action was necessary for the pay raise to take effect, but either house of Congress could have blocked the increase.

Reagan's proposal was far less than the 18.47 percent

raise a federal pay board found necessary to keep pace with private sector pay. Under the Federal Pay Comparability Act of 1970, federal white-collar wages must be annually adjusted to achieve comparability with similar private sector jobs. But Reagan noted that the act allowed him to propose an alternative "if such action is appropriate because of economic conditions." *(Congress and the Nation Vol. III, p. 454)*

Flexitime Extension

President Reagan July 23 signed a bill (S 2240 — PL 97-221) extending for three years an experiment that permitted flexible work hours for federal employees.

Legislation approved by Congress in 1978 (PL 95-390) originally allowed federal agencies to experiment with flexible scheduling. Agencies could choose to use flexitime, which staggered arrival and departure times within an eight-hour day, condensed schedules, which permitted employees to meet their 80-hour biweekly work requirement in less than 10 days, or a combination of the two. *(Congress and the Nation Vol. V, p. 839)*

S 2240, which was passed by the Senate June 30 and the House July 12, extended the program for three years from the date of enactment, or until July 23, 1985. Passage of the bill ended a dispute between the administration and employee unions that had led to House defeat of a permanent authorization bill (HR 5366) March 2.

The final compromise gave agency heads 90 days during which they could cancel existing flexitime if the programs increased costs, reduced productivity or diminished public service, but permitted unions to bargain for substitute plans to replace those discarded by management. The measure also allowed agencies and unions to negotiate decisions to begin or end new flexitime programs, with impasses to be resolved by the Federal Service Impasses Panel.

Debt Collection Act

President Reagan Oct. 25 signed a bill (HR 4613 — PL 97-365) designed to help the federal government collect more than $25 billion in unpaid federal debts.

HR 4613 authorized the government to enlist the aid of credit bureaus and collection agencies in tracking down delinquent borrowers. It required individuals to provide Social Security numbers when applying for a federal loan, permitted federal agencies to give collection firms the addresses of delinquent borrowers obtained from Internal Revenue Service (IRS) files, allowed wage deductions from federal employees who were delinquent in repaying government loans and imposed interest and penalty charges on overdue government debts.

Particularly important were provisions exempting credit bureaus from the requirements of the 1974 Privacy Act (PL 93-579) for purposes of listing any debts an individual might owe the federal government. Previously, if credit bureaus used federal debt information in compiling an individual's financial history, they became subject to the Privacy Act, which allowed individuals to inspect, challenge or amend their credit records. Credit bureaus, already subject to the 1970 Fair Credit Reporting Act disclosure and truth-in-reporting requirements, declined to list federal debts because they did not want to be subject to

two sets of rules. Thus, individuals who did not repay federal loans did not have to worry about blemishing their credit records. *(Congress and the Nation Vol. IV, p. 585)*

Legislative History

The Senate Governmental Affairs Committee reported its version of the debt collection bill (S 1249 — S Rept 97-378) July 17, 1981. It contained the Privacy Act exemption for credit bureaus and permitted addresses from IRS files to be given to collection agencies and credit bureaus.

The Senate Finance Committee Dec. 3, 1981, filed a report (S Rept 97-287) on the bill's tax-related provisions, including one providing IRS addresses to debt collectors only.

As reported April 29, 1982, by the House Ways and Means Committee, HR 4613 (H Rept 97-496) dealt only with IRS-related issues. For example, it would have allowed IRS addresses to go not only to debt collectors, but also to credit bureaus.

The House passed HR 4613 by a 402-3 vote May 5, and on May 18 it passed a separate bill (HR 2811 — H Rept 97-42) containing the Privacy Act exemption for credit bureaus.

The Senate passed an amended version of HR 4613 Sept. 28, and a compromise measure was approved by the House Sept. 30 and the Senate early Oct. 2. The final bill dropped the provision giving IRS addresses to credit bureaus and cut to 15 percent, from 25 percent, the amount that could be deducted from federal employees' wages to pay back a federal debt.

Provisions

As signed into law Oct. 25, HR 4613 (PL 97-365):
- Permitted federal agencies, except the IRS, to contract with private collection agencies for collection services.
- Exempted credit bureaus from Privacy Act restrictions.
- Allowed mailing addresses obtained from the IRS to be provided to private debt collectors.
- Required individuals to supply their Social Security numbers when applying for federal loans.
- Permitted deductions of up to 15 percent of a federal employee's salary, after taxes and retirement contributions, to pay off overdue debts owed the government.
- Authorized the IRS to tell other federal agencies whether an applicant for a government loan had an outstanding tax liability.
- Required agencies to charge interest and penalties on overdue debts.
- Made it a federal offense to assault federal employees collecting debts owed the federal government.

Mail Fraud

Both the Senate and House passed bills making it easier for the U.S. Postal Service to crack down on fraudulent mail-order schemes, but Congress did not complete action on the legislation in 1982.

The Senate approved its bill (S 1407 — S Rept 97-392) May 19, but the House did not pass its version (HR 7044 — H Rept 97-932) until Dec. 13. With time running out in the session, and significant differences separating the two chambers, no further action was taken.

Civil liberties groups and others expressed concern

over the legislation's potential infringement on constitutional rights. Before passing HR 7044, the House deleted a controversial proposal to give the Postal Service authority to issue civil investigative demands, similar to subpoenas, to examine books, records or other material related to a mail fraud investigation. The Senate bill gave the Postal Service more enforcement powers, including subpoena authority.

Congress enacted a compromise measure in 1983. *(Story, p. 787)*

Indian Claims

Congress Dec. 19 cleared legislation extending the time limit for American Indian tribes to bring lawsuits in certain damage cases. The extension was attached to a fiscal 1983 appropriations bill (HR 7356 — PL 97-394) after separate Indian claims legislation (H J Res 553 — H Rept 97-954) failed to win House approval Dec. 13.

Background. The legislation was designed to extend the deadline for legal action on about 17,000 Indian claims that arose before 1966. As trustee for Indian affairs, the federal government was responsible for filing lawsuits to press claims by Indians who said they were illegally stripped of land, money or fishing rights by private and government parties. Congress had renewed the statute of limitations three times, with the latest extension due to expire Dec. 31. If the statute of limitations had run out without government action on the cases, the United States would have been barred from starting lawsuits to recover money damages for Indian claims arising before July 18, 1966.

Backers of the extension warned that if the statute of limitations ran out before any disposition had been made of the old claims, the government could be held liable for not fulfilling its responsibility as trustee for the Indians. But opponents argued that Congress should end the litigation process and use private relief legislation to settle outstanding claims. *(Background, Congress and the Nation Vol. V, p. 856)*

Provisions. As signed into law Dec. 30, HR 7356 (PL 97-394) included the following Indian claims provisions:

● Required the secretary of interior, within 90 days of enactment, to publish in the *Federal Register* a list of all pending pre-1966 Indian claims, broken down tribe-by-tribe, reservation-by-reservation or state-by-state.

● Gave Indian tribes six months after publication of the list to submit to the Interior Department any additional pre-1966 claims they believed should be considered for litigation or legislative resolution.

● Gave the interior secretary 30 more days to publish a revised list of pending claims, incorporating any new ones submitted during the six-month comment period.

● Kept alive all Indian claims on the initial and revised lists pending action by the secretary of interior either rejecting a particular Indian claim or proposing legislation to settle it. The bill set no deadline for such action but required notice of any claim rejection to be published in the *Federal Register*.

● Set a one-year statute of limitations on the filing of lawsuits pursuing any claims the secretary of interior explicitly rejected in a notice published in the *Federal Register*.

● Set a three-year deadline for the filing of suits on any claim for which the interior secretary submitted a proposed legislative solution, or a report to Congress, with the time to begin running from the date of the legislative submission or report.

Contract Disputes Veto

President Reagan Oct. 15 vetoed a bill (HR 1371) designed to settle a dispute over federal interest payments to government contractors. Congress made no effort to override the veto.

The legislation, which would have amended the Contract Disputes Act of 1978, passed the House June 1, 1981, and the Senate Oct. 1, 1982. *(Background, Congress and the Nation Vol. V, p. 731)*

The bill made clear that interest the government was required to pay to contractors on claims in excess of $50,000 would accrue from the date such claims were submitted. Claims were submitted when contractors incurred unexpected expenses and a dispute arose over who should bear the cost. Interest was paid only to claimants who prevailed in such disputes. The vetoed bill also would have changed the 1978 act by requiring the Treasury secretary to set interest rates to be paid contractors.

In vetoing the bill, Reagan said he objected to Senate-added language requiring the government to pay interest from the time a claim was submitted. Existing law required interest payments from the date a claim was certified, or deemed to be accurate, Reagan maintained. Permitting interest to accrue from the date claims were submitted would result in an "increase in governmental obligations without any corresponding benefits to the claims resolution process," he said.

NASA Authorization

Congress Oct. 1 cleared legislation (HR 5890 — PL 97-324) authorizing $6.773 billion for the National Aeronautics and Space Administration (NASA) in fiscal 1983. The amount was $160 million more than the Reagan administration requested. The House passed HR 5890 (H Rept 97-502) May 13, and the Senate substituted its version (S 2604 — S Rept 97-449) June 9. The conference agreement (H Rept 97-897) provided $124.9 million more than the House recommended. The Senate bill matched the administration request.

Space Shuttle, Landsat

The final bill provided $1.8 billion for the space shuttle program and authorized NASA to begin production of a fifth orbiter for the space shuttle fleet. Although the Senate had wanted the Defense Department to reimburse NASA for the full cost of placing its cargo on the shuttle, the final bill allowed NASA to recover only a portion of the cost, directing the NASA administrator to set prices needed to recover the "fair value" of carrying Pentagon payloads into orbit on the shuttle.

In addition, the measure authorized the National Oceanic and Atmospheric Administration Landsat activities, which provided satellite scanning of the Earth's surface. The bill provided for satellite user fees and a plan to transfer future civil applications of such remote-sensing satellite systems to the private sector when Congress determined that a transfer would be in the national interest.

Science Authorization

For the second year, the Senate did not act on a House-passed funding authorization for the National Science Foundation (NSF).

The House May 19 passed a $1.089 billion fiscal 1983 authorization for NSF (HR 5842 — H Rept 97-485) after a floor fight over authorization levels for science and engineering education. Before passing the bill on a 282-111 vote, members accepted, 194-191, an amendment to cut $30 million for the education programs, thus bringing the authorization in line with the administration's $1.069 billion request. But the House subsequently approved, 203-188, an amendment restoring $20 million to the bill. HR 5842 also authorized $1.085 billion for NSF in fiscal 1982. A fiscal 1982 authorization had not cleared Congress in 1981. *(Story, p. 776)*

The Senate Commerce, Science and Technology Committee May 20 reported a $1.09 billion fiscal 1983 authorization (S 2551 — S Rept 97-407), and the Labor and Human Resources Committee May 28 reported a $1.084 billion authorization (S 2349 — S Rept 97-457), but the Senate never acted on either bill.

Despite the lack of authorization, Congress provided $1.092 billion for NSF in a fiscal 1983 appropriations bill (HR 6956 — PL 97-272) for various independent federal agencies.

NOAA Authorization

Congress failed to clear a two-year reauthorization bill (HR 6324 — H Rept 97-557) for the atmospheric, climatic and ocean pollution activities of the National Oceanic and Atmospheric Administration (NOAA).

As passed by the House Aug. 17, the bill would have authorized $544 million in fiscal 1983 and $576.5 million in fiscal 1984 for all NOAA research activities and selected operations. It would have increased President Reagan's funding requests for two polar-orbiting weather satellites and for research on atmospheric and ocean pollution, the Great Lakes, weather modification and solar flares.

The Senate passed an amended version in the session that began Dec. 16, but the House adjourned before considering the Senate changes. Although the authorization never cleared, Congress provided funding for the NOAA activities in the second continuing appropriations resolution (H J Res 631 — PL 97-377) for fiscal 1983.

Earthquake Hazards Reduction

In the closing days of the lame-duck session Congress cleared legislation authorizing $63.4 million in fiscal 1983 for a multi-agency effort to reduce the risks to life and property from future earthquakes. It also authorized "such funds as may be necessary" for the program in fiscal 1984.

Funds provided under the Earthquake Hazards Reduction Act (S 2273 — PL 97-464) were devoted to the first phase of an earthquake prediction network that would conduct research on the nature of earthquakes and analyze earthquake possibilities by developing seismic risk maps for the entire nation.

The Senate originally passed S 2273 (S Rept 97-336) April 29, and the House passed a companion measure (HR 6272 — H Rept 97-535) Sept. 14. The bill did not clear

until the session of Dec. 16 when the Senate accepted final House changes in the measure.

In 1983 the Senate passed a three-year reauthorization of the act, but similar legislation did not reach the floor in the House. *(Story, p. 788)*

Uniform Relocation Act

The Senate Aug. 5 passed legislation (S 2363 — S Rept 97-487) to revise a law governing the relocation of individuals and businesses displaced by federal projects. A companion measure (HR 6171) died in the House Public Works and Transportation Committee.

The Senate passed a similar bill in 1983, but again the House did not act. *(Story, p. 787)*

S 2363 would have expanded the scope of the Uniform Relocation Act of 1970 to cover persons displaced by rehabilitation and demolition projects by the Department of Housing and Urban Development (HUD), authorized up to $10,000 for displaced small businesses and non-profit organizations and raised the ceiling on moving payments to compensate for inflation. In addition, the bill would have changed the formula for subsidizing the rents of displaced persons to reflect a person's ability to pay, while lowering the total payment ceiling from $4,000 to $3,000. *(Background, Congress and the Nation Vol. III, p. 650)*

Roosevelt Memorial

Thirty-seven years after the death of Franklin Delano Roosevelt, Congress cleared a measure (S J Res 95 — PL 97-224) approving construction of a major memorial to the nation's longest-serving president.

The Senate passed S J Res 95 (S Rept 97-311) by voice vote March 8. The House approved an identical measure (H J Res 400 — H Rept 97-556) July 14.

S J Res 95 authorized appropriation of whatever funds were necessary for the construction, operation and maintenance of an FDR memorial on a 27-acre site in West Potomac Park in Washington, D.C., near the Tidal Basin and the Lincoln and Jefferson memorials. The new memorial would consist of a 14-foot-high garden wall winding past the cherry trees that edge the Tidal Basin and around waterfalls, pools, gardens and sculptures. It was designed by architect Lawrence Halperin and approved in 1979 by the Commission on Fine Arts and by the Franklin Delano Roosevelt Commission.

Background. A memorial to Roosevelt, whose four election victories made him president longer than any other chief executive, had been the subject of controversy for decades.

Before his death in 1945, Roosevelt reportedly told Supreme Court Justice Felix Frankfurter that he wanted no memorial bigger than a desk. The only existing memorial — a solid block of marble installed in 1965 opposite the National Archives building in Washington — was about desk size. It bore the simple inscription "In memory of Franklin Delano Roosevelt January 30, 1882 — April 12, 1945," and it was paid for through private donations.

Congress in 1955 passed legislation (PL 84-372) establishing the Franklin Delano Roosevelt Memorial Commission to plan a permanent Washington memorial to the nation's 32nd president. Four years later the site in West Potomac Park was set aside for that purpose (PL 86-214).

It was estimated that more than 500 attempts had been made to design an appropriate FDR memorial. Two formal design proposals were considered and rejected, and the one finally accepted was scaled back to reduce its cost.

Living Memorial. In a related action, the House March 23 passed HR 4750 (H Rept 97-460) authorizing a study on the possibility of making the Warm Springs, Ga., area a living memorial to Roosevelt. FDR died in Warm Springs.

The study was to address ways of preserving and using the property known as the Little White House, built by Roosevelt in 1931; surrounding pools and springs; the rehabilitation center and the 10,000-acre Franklin Delano Roosevelt State Park.

The Senate took no action on the bill.

Other Legislation

Prompt Pay Act

Legislation to encourage the federal government to pay its bills on time was signed into law (PL 97-177) by President Reagan May 21. The Senate passed the bill (S 1131 — S Rept 97-302) by voice vote Dec. 15, 1981, and the House substituted its version (HR 4709 — H Rept 97-461) March 23, 1982. The Senate accepted the House changes in S 1131 May 11.

The bill gave agencies 30 days to make payments, with a 15-day grace period before interest penalties began to accrue. Once the grace period expired, interest would accumulate from the 31st day at a rate to be set by the Treasury secretary.

Waste, Fraud Control

Congress Aug. 19 cleared a bill (HR 1526 — PL 97-255) to target fraud, waste and mismanagement in the federal government by requiring each federal agency to submit an annual report to the president on its internal accounting and administrative controls.

Final action came when the House accepted substitute provisions passed by the Senate Aug. 4 (S 864 — S Rept 97-312). The House passed its version of HR 1526 (H Rept 97-38) May 18, 1981.

Reports to Congress

Congress Dec. 8 cleared a bill (HR 6005 — PL 97-375) eliminating or modifying some 77 reports that executive branch agencies previously were required to submit to Congress on a regular basis. The legislation had been introduced at the request of the Office of Management and Budget, which had recommended the elimination or modification of 200 reports. The measure passed the House Sept. 20 and the Senate Dec. 8.

OMB Funds Study

The Senate Oct. 1 cleared a bill (S 2386 — PL 97-326) designed to ensure that the Office of Management and Budget (OMB) compiled and published data on the geographic distribution of federal funds. The bill required OMB to prepare a report detailing federal spending in each state, county, congressional district and municipality for fiscal 1983 through fiscal 1985. Existing data sources would be used for the OMB report, so no new funding was required.

The Community Services Administration (CSA), acting as agent for OMB, had produced these reports in the past, but when Congress abolished the CSA in 1981, OMB discontinued them. OMB proposed to replace the old reports with one that would provide data only on state-by-state distribution of federal funds, but Congress balked at the idea, insisting on the more detailed breakdowns.

As cleared, the bill incorporated the text of the House version (HR 7096 — H Rept 97-878), passed Sept. 28. The Senate passed S 2386 (S Rept 97-473) July 29.

Surplus Property Donation

The House Dec. 13 cleared for President Reagan a bill (S 1444 — PL 97-380) allowing the federal government to donate to state and local governments surplus military equipment loaned to them for civil defense purposes. Final action came when the House accepted without amendment the bill passed by the Senate Oct. 1. It was identical to a companion measure (HR 1856 — H Rept 97-910) that already had been reported by two House committees.

Tax-Exempt Aid for Brady

A bill allowing White House press secretary James S. Brady to accept contributions from tax-exempt charitable organizations to defray his medical expenses was cleared by Congress in 1982. Brady was seriously wounded in a March 30, 1981, assassination attempt on President Reagan. *(Story, p. 847)*

The legislation (S 2333 — PL 97-171), passed by both chambers April 1, exempted federal employees injured during an assassination or kidnapping attempt from a law forbidding federal workers from accepting any remuneration from sources outside the government.

Capitol Historical Society

The Senate Dec. 21 cleared a bill (HR 4491 — PL 97-447) exempting from District of Columbia sales taxes the U.S. Capitol Historical Society's sales on the Capitol grounds. The bill grew out of a dispute between the District of Columbia and the society, which had run a souvenir stand in the Capitol since 1964.

The House had approved HR 4491 Dec. 13 (H Rept 97-445). The bill provided that the non-profit society was not subject to the sales tax, and that the Capitol, the site of the sales, was not within the District's jurisdiction.

Olympic Coins

A bill allowing the federal government to market coins commemorating the 1984 Los Angeles Olympic Games was signed into law July 22 (S 1230 — PL 97-220).

As passed by the Senate Dec. 9, 1981, S 1230 had called for private marketing of the Olympic coins. But before passing S 1230 on May 20, 1982, the House substituted language giving the U.S. Treasury responsibility for marketing the coins. The Senate agreed to the House amendment July 1, clearing the bill.

As cleared, the bill required the government to mint 52 million coins in three designs, providing $600 million for the Olympic committees if all the coins were sold.

Smithsonian Museum

President Reagan June 24 signed into law a bill (HR 5659 — PL 97-203) authorizing a new museum for African art and a center for Eastern art in the Smithsonian Institution. The bill, passed by the House June 3 (H Rept 97-534) and the Senate June 9, authorized $36.5 million in federal funds and required a matching amount of private money for construction of the art showcases near the original Smithsonian building in Washington, D.C.

King Memorial

The Senate in the session of Dec. 20 cleared a resolution (H Con Res 153) calling for a bust or statue of the Rev. Dr. Martin Luther King Jr. to be placed in the U.S. Capitol. H Con Res 153, which did not require the president's signature, had been passed by the House Sept. 15, 1981. The civil rights leader, who was slain April 4, 1968, at the age of 39, thus became the first black person to be represented among the building's statues.

The resolution allowed expenditures of up to $25,000 for the memorial, which was to be chosen in a design competition sponsored by the Joint Committee on the Library.

After much controversy, Congress in 1983 approved a federal holiday to honor King. *(Story, p. 786)*

1983

Federal Workers' Social Security

Over the vehement protests of federal workers and their unions, Congress decided to require all new federal employees hired after Jan. 1, 1984, to join the Social Security system.

Current federal workers, who had their own retirement plan providing far more generous benefits than Social Security, were not affected by the move.

The change for new U.S. workers was made in a massive Social Security overhaul (HR 1900 — PL 98-21) that President Reagan signed into law on April 20. *(Social Security, p. 659)*

As cleared by Congress March 25, the bill extended Social Security coverage to new federal employees, current and future members of Congress, the president, the vice president, sitting federal judges, top political appointees and top civil servants. Legislative branch employees who did not choose to go under the Civil Service Retirement System by Dec. 31, 1983, also were covered.

Effective Jan. 1, 1984, all of these U.S. employees were subject to Social Security payroll taxes, which amounted to 7 percent of wages for 1984, rising to 7.51 percent in 1988 and 7.65 percent in 1990.

Federal employees already were contributing 7 percent of their pay to the Civil Service Retirement System. To avoid forcing new workers to pay 14 percent toward retirement, Congress Nov. 16 cleared a separate bill (HR 2077 — PL 98-168) that limited their contribution to the civil

service plan to 1.3 percent until a new supplemental retirement program was adopted or until January 1986, whichever was earlier.

Background

The proposal to bring new federal workers under the system was one recommendation of a sweeping financial rescue plan for Social Security proposed by a bipartisan commission that was appointed by Reagan in late 1981 and issued its recommendations Jan. 15.

This was not the first time Social Security coverage of federal employees had been seriously considered.

Most recently, Congress in 1977 rejected a plan to bring nearly seven million government workers and nonprofit corporation employees into the system, after federal unions and state and local governments lobbied hard

---

Civil Service/Social Security

Coverage: The Civil Service Retirement System covered more than 2.7 million civilian workers and paid benefits to approximately 1.7 million retirees and survivors in fiscal 1981. About 116 million workers participated in Social Security, and 36 million individuals drew benefits.

Contributions: Federal employees contributed 7 percent of their basic pay through payroll deductions to the civil service retirement fund, compared with a 6.7 percent payroll deduction for Social Security participants. In addition, federal workers as of Jan. 1, 1983, paid 1.3 percent of their basic pay for Medicare coverage, which was included in the 6.7 percent payroll deduction of workers covered by Social Security.

Federal agencies put in a matching amount for each employee, just as private employers matched their workers' Social Security contributions. The U.S. Treasury also contributed to the civil service fund from general revenues to help cover unfunded future liabilities caused by an anticipated gap between contributions received and benefits owed.

Benefits: In early 1983 the average monthly civil service benefit was $1,047, according to the Office of Personnel Management, compared with $406 a month for Social Security. Many Social Security recipients supplemented their retirement income with private pension benefits. Also, civil service benefits were taxable, whereas Social Security payments were tax-free.

Retirement Age: A federal worker could collect a full pension if he retired at age 55 with 30 years of service, age 60 with 20 years, or age 62 with five years in government. Under Social Security, a worker could retire at age 62 with partial benefits and age 65 with full benefits.

against compulsory participation. *(Congress and the Nation Vol. V, p. 235)*

Vincent Sombrotto, president of the National Association of Letter Carriers, warned that the existing Civil Service Retirement Fund would run out of money in about 20 years if new workers were pulled out. To cover the fund's existing liability at that point, Sombrotto said, would cost the government at least $185 billion from the general Treasury.

Federal employee groups mounted a $6 million lobbying effort against the commission's proposal. The Fund for Assuring an Independent Retirement (FAIR), a coalition of 25 organizations representing six million active and retired employees, took the lead role.

As the Social Security legislation began moving through Congress, the federal employee groups showered members with letters of protest and brought in workers from all over the nation, who roamed the corridors of Capitol Hill seeking to derail the provisions affecting them.

Legislative Action

The House passed HR 1900 on March 9 by a 282-148 vote. The Senate passed the measure March 23, 88-9, after approving an amendment by Russell B. Long, D-La., to delay coverage of federal employees under Social Security until a supplemental civil service retirement system could be established to provide them with an additional pension. The same amendment had been defeated in the Senate Finance Committee on a 6-11 vote.

Long's amendment was approved by voice vote, but only after several blocking attempts by the leadership.

Ted Stevens, R-Alaska, chairman of the Governmental Affairs Subcommittee on Civil Service, charged that the Long amendment would only give federal employees a chance to escape coverage altogether. That loss would cut the value of the rescue plan $9.3 billion over the next decade, said Finance Committee Chairman Robert Dole, R-Kan.

But Long argued it was unfair to expect federal employees to accept the new plan before they knew what supplemental benefits they would receive. "I do not think it's fair to ask these people to buy a pig in a poke," he said.

An alternative proposal by Stevens to cover new federal hires under Social Security, but not make them pay into the Civil Service Retirement System until a supplemental plan could be established, was rejected 45-50.

House-Senate conferees agreed to the final shape of the bill during a 12-hour session March 24 (H Rept 98-47). The Senate conferees agreed to recede on the federal employee provision by a vote of 4-3.

Federal Pay, Pensions

Some 1.4 million federal white-collar workers received a 3.5 percent pay increase effective Jan. 1, 1984, after 1983 Senate inaction on a fiscal 1984 reconciliation measure blocked them from receiving a 4 percent raise.

However, the Senate early in 1984 completed action on the reconciliation bill (HR 4169 — PL 98-270), which provided a 4 percent raise retroactive to Jan. 1.

Members of Congress also received the retroactive raise. *(Story, p. 832)*

The reconciliation bill was designed to achieve budget savings required by the fiscal 1984 budget resolution, but the retroactive pay increase added $249 million to federal spending for the year. *(Reconciliation, p. 60)*

Most of the bill's $8.2 billion in three-year savings came from provisions that delayed cost-of-living adjustments (COLAs) for federal retirees. COLA awards for civilian and military retirees were put off from May until December. Pension increases for retirees would be paid in January 1985.

1983 Action. President Reagan had recommended the 3.5 percent pay increase in an Aug. 31 executive order that also provided for a three-month delay in the annual federal pay raise scheduled for Oct. 1. By law, Reagan's proposal took effect when Congress did not overrule it.

The Senate did not complete floor action before adjournment on its version of the reconciliation bill (S 2062 — S Rept 98-300), reported Nov. 4. The bill provided for a 4 percent pay raise as of Jan. 1, 1984. It also sought to delay until January 1985 a scheduled May 1984 cost-of-living increase for federal retirees.

The House version of the reconciliation bill (HR 4169 — H Rept 98-425), passed Oct. 25, likewise called for a 4 percent increase in white-collar pay and a delay in retiree COLAs. By a 245-176 vote, the House agreed to delay the pay raise from Oct. 1, 1983 — the date recommended by the House Post Office and Civil Service Committee — until Jan. 1, 1984.

Under provisions of an omnibus continuing appropriations resolution (PL 98-151), pay raises for blue-collar ("wage scale") federal workers were limited to the same percentage and timetable as those for white-collar workers.

1984 Action. The Senate passed the House bill without change on April 5, 1984, completing congressional action on the reconciliation measure.

Government Ethics Office

Congress Oct. 27 completed action on a bill (S 461 — PL 98-150) that extended the Office of Government Ethics for five years, through Sept. 30, 1988, and closed some loopholes in federal conflict-of-interest laws.

The ethics office, created by the Ethics in Government Act of 1978 (PL 95-521), was an arm of the Office of Personnel Management (OPM). It was responsible for reviewing financial disclosure forms required of many executive branch officials, including the president and vice president, candidates for those offices, and presidential appointees requiring Senate confirmation.

It also advised officials on how to comply with various provisions of the federal ethics law, including those designed to avoid conflicts of interest. *(Background, Congress and the Nation Vol. V, p. 824)*

S 461 contained several provisions designed to strengthen the independence of the ethics office, including one that provided a five-year term for the ethics director and required a report to Congress if the president decided to remove him before his term expired.

Under previous law the director served at the pleasure of the president, and the Reagan administration opposed limitations on the president's removal authority.

Other provisions of the bill tightened financial disclosure rules for top presidential appointees and imposed new reporting rules on individuals who were required to divest themselves of conflicting interests or to place those interests in a blind trust. The bill also made top White House aides subject to the 15 percent limit on outside earned

income that applied to other high-level executive branch officials.

Legislative History. The Senate Governmental Affairs Committee reported S 461 March 24 (S Rept 98-59), and the Senate passed the bill April 6 by voice vote without debate.

The House Judiciary Committee reported its version of the bill May 5 (HR 2717 — H Rept 98-89, Part I), and the Post Office and Civil Service Committee, to which the measure also was referred, reported HR 2717 May 16 (Part II).

A compromise between the two committees' versions of the bill was passed by the House Sept. 19.

After being bounced back and forth between the two chambers to reconcile Senate-House differences, S 461 was cleared Oct. 27, when the Senate accepted final House changes in the bill.

Martin Luther King Holiday

Brushing aside earlier opposition, President Reagan Nov. 2 signed into law a bill (HR 3706 — PL 98-144) declaring the third Monday in January, beginning in 1986, a legal public holiday honoring the late civil rights leader, the Rev. Dr. Martin Luther King Jr.

Enactment of the legislation marked a major victory for civil rights groups, which had pushed for a holiday honoring King. *(Previous action, p. 784)*

It also marked a major defeat for Sen. Jesse Helms, R-N.C., who led the sometimes virulent opposition to the measure in the Senate. Helms questioned whether King was worthy of the recognition and objected to the cost of another public holiday.

King's birthday became the 10th legal holiday for federal employees.

The administration opposed the measure on grounds that King could be remembered more inexpensively without requiring another paid holiday for federal workers. Supporters of the bill, however, cited estimates of the government's cost as only about $18 million in 1986 and insisted that the symbolic value of honoring King was of greater importance.

On the day of Senate passage, Reagan told a nationally televised press conference: "Since they seem bent on making it a national holiday, I believe the symbolism of that day is important enough that I would — I'll sign that legislation when it reaches my desk."

Bills to honor King's Jan. 15 birthday had been introduced repeatedly since he was assassinated in Memphis, Tenn., on April 4, 1968. *(Congress and the Nation Vol. V, p. 846)*

Legislative History. The House Post Office and Civil Service Committee July 26 reported HR 3345 (H Rept 98-314) to designate the third Monday in January as a federal holiday honoring King.

The House passed HR 3706, an identical bill with 109 cosponsors, Aug. 2 by a 338-90 vote.

The Senate passed HR 3706 on Oct. 19 by a **key vote of 78-22 (R 37-18; D 41-4)**, following two days of often acrimonious and occasionally eloquent debate. There was no Senate committee action on the bill. *(1983 key votes, p. 911)*

Passage of the measure was a major setback for Helms, who tried in various ways to defeat the legislation. Before the vote on final passage, there were a number of attempts

to delay or change the bill. All but one were offered by opponents of the legislation.

NASA/Weather Satellites

Congress cleared a fiscal 1984 authorization (HR 2065 — PL 98-52) for the National Aeronautics and Space Administration (NASA) that included a provision barring the sale of the nation's land and weather satellites to private industry unless Congress passed a law approving any sale.

President Reagan March 8 had proposed that private firms be allowed to bid on the satellites separately or as a package. The government would then purchase needed weather information from the private owners, distributing some of the information free of charge and selling other data.

Congressional opposition centered on how much the sale would cost taxpayers, especially for specialized weather services. Critics also feared the sale could result in less accurate weather prediction, could be detrimental to national security, since the weather satellites served as backup to Pentagon satellites, and could lead to a monopoly of weather information. Only one firm, Communications Satellite Corp. (COMSAT), had proposed to purchase both the land and weather satellite systems.

The NASA measure, which authorized $7.3 billion for the agency, cleared June 29 when the House by voice vote accepted a compromise version of the bill. The Senate accepted the compromise June 28, also by voice vote. The House originally passed HR 2065 (H Rept 98-65) April 26, and the Senate passed its version (S 1096 — S Rept 98-108) June 15.

Science Authorization

For the third straight year authorizations for the National Science Foundation (NSF) failed to clear Congress in 1983. *(Previous action, pp. 776, 782)*

The House May 12 passed a bill (HR 2066 — H Rept 98-73) authorizing $1.34 billion for NSF programs in fiscal 1984. The Senate Labor and Human Resources Committee reported a similar bill May 16 (S 1087 — S Rept 98-195), but the full Senate did not act on the authorization. Congress nonetheless appropriated $1.32 billion for NSF programs in fiscal 1984 (PL 98-45).

NSF also was left without an authorization in 1984 when the Senate Labor and Commerce committees failed to resolve a jurisdictional dispute. Congress appropriated $1.5 billion for fiscal 1985 (PL 98-371).

Procurement Policy Office

Congress Nov. 17 cleared a bill (HR 2293 — PL 98-191) reauthorizing for four years the Office of Federal Procurement Policy (OFPP), a unit within the Office of Management and Budget.

The legislation strengthened the role of the OFPP in developing and guiding government procurement policies. HR 2293 also restored the office's authority — dropped by Congress in 1979 — to issue procurement policies and regulations. *(Background, Congress and the Nation Vol. V, p. 844)*

The House passed HR 2293 (H Rept 98-146) June 1,

and the Senate passed its version (S 1001 — S Rept 98-214) Nov. 15. The House agreed to the Senate amendments Nov. 17.

Mail Fraud

Congress Nov. 16 cleared a bill (S 450 — PL 98-186) giving the Postal Service new authority to deal with mail fraud. The bill was reported by the Senate Governmental Affairs Committee March 31 (S Rept 98-51) and passed the Senate Nov. 3. The House passed the measure Nov. 16.

The bill authorized the Postal Service, after a hearing before an administrative law judge, to issue orders requiring a person to cease and desist from engaging in false representation schemes, and provided a civil penalty of up to $10,000 a day for evading such orders.

Mail fraud legislation was passed by both the House and Senate in 1982, but Congress adjourned before a conference committee could work out minor differences in the two bills. *(1982 action, p. 780)*

Federal Debt Collection

Congress completed action Nov. 14 on a bill (S 376 — PL 98-167) to make it easier for federal agencies to contract with private debt collection firms for the collection of money owed to the federal government.

S 376 amended the Federal Debt Collection Act of 1982 (PL 97-365) to permit federal agencies to pay private debt collection services a percentage of the total amount of debt collected without having an advance appropriation. If a collection contract called for a fixed fee, an advance

OPM Personnel Rules

Congress in 1983 and 1984 barred the Office of Personnel Management (OPM) from implementing controversial regulations designed to link pay raises and job security for federal employees more closely to job performance. The ban ultimately was extended until July 1, 1985.

The rules, originally proposed in March 1983, would have eliminated automatic, within-grade pay raises and established instead a pay-for-performance system for 1.4 million white-collar federal employees. Federal employees' unions claimed the regulations were unfair to workers who had attained seniority and could lead to politicization of the work force.

Backing those claims, Congress included in fiscal 1984 and fiscal 1985 omnibus appropriations measures (PL 98-151, PL 98-461) provisions designed to keep the regulations from taking effect. An OPM attempt to circumvent the congressional prohibition was blocked in the courts.

appropriation would still be required. Contingent fee contracts had been barred under the 1982 act. *(1982 action, p. 780)*

The non-controversial measure was reported by the Senate Governmental Affairs Committee May 5 (S Rept 98-75) and passed by the Senate by voice vote May 20. The House passed it by a 397-3 vote Nov. 14, completing congressional action.

Indian Land Claim Veto

President Reagan April 5 vetoed a bill (S 366) to settle claims of the Mashantucket Pequot Indian Tribe to 800 acres of land in eastern Connecticut. Congress made no attempt to override the veto.

The measure — a compromise agreed to by the state, the Indian tribe and 14 eastern Connecticut landowners — had been passed by voice vote in the Senate Feb. 24 and the House March 22.

In his April 5 veto message, the president objected to a provision of S 366 that established a $900,000 federal claims settlement fund to compensate the Indians for their claims to the disputed land near Ledyard, Conn. The president said the state should pay at least half of the settlement costs.

School Tax Leasing Veto

President Reagan June 17 vetoed a bill (S 973) that would have allowed a North Carolina school to "lease" to outside investors tax benefits attributable to a building that had been rehabilitated with federal funds.

The amendment, sponsored by Sen. Jesse Helms, R-N.C., had been added on the Senate floor to a bill making minor and technical amendments to several laws affecting Indians. The bill had been passed by the Senate May 25 and the House June 1.

Reagan said he had no objection to the amendments, but he called the tax leasing arrangement "totally unjustifiable." The sale of tax benefits by tax-exempt entities through leasing transactions presented "tremendous potential for abuse and could result in billions of dollars of revenue loss to the federal government," Reagan said. *(Tax leasing, p. 79)*

Relocation Assistance

The Senate May 20 passed by voice vote a bill (S 531 — S Rept 98-71) to revise the Uniform Relocation Act, a 1970 law that required payments to individuals and businesses displaced by federally assisted projects such as highway construction and urban renewal.

The House did not act on the measure, which would have provided the first major overhaul of the 1970 relocation law (PL 91-646). *(Background, Congress and the Nation Vol. III, p. 650)*

As passed by the Senate, S 531 significantly broadened the class of individuals and businesses eligible for relocation aid and provided for payments of up to $10,000 to help small businesses and non-profit organizations re-establish at new locations. It also required the administration to develop a uniform set of federal regulations pertaining to the act.

The Senate passed a similar measure in 1982, but the House failed to act. *(1982 action, p. 782)*

Other Legislation

Federal Election Commission

The House passed and a Senate committee reported a $10.8 million fiscal 1984 authorization bill (HR 2621) for the Federal Election Commission (FEC), but there was no further action on the bill.

The House action came April 26 by voice vote, just four days after the bill was reported by the House Administration Committee (H Rept 98-71). The Senate Committee on Rules and Administration reported the bill May 16 (S Rept 98-102).

The commission had not been officially authorized since fiscal 1981.

Paperwork Reduction

The House Nov. 7 by voice vote passed a bill (HR 2718 — H Rept 98-147) aimed at decreasing the amount of government paperwork while improving the quality and availability of federally generated information.

The measure, a three-year reauthorization of the Paperwork Reduction Act of 1980 (PL 96-511), was referred to the Senate Governmental Affairs Committee. The bill went no further. *(Congress and the Nation Vol. V, p. 849)*

Bureau of Standards Funding

Congress did not complete action on a fiscal 1984 authorization for the National Bureau of Standards. Lawmakers nonetheless provided $115.7 million in fiscal 1984 appropriations (PL 98-166).

The Senate April 7 passed a $114.8 million authorization bill reported by the Commerce, Science and Transportation Committee March 31 (S 821 — S Rept 98-49), but the House did not act on a $130.1 million version reported by its Science and Technology Committee May 9 (HR 2513 — H Rept 98-95).

In 1984 President Reagan pocket-vetoed a fiscal 1985 authorization bill for the Bureau of Standards. *(1984 action, p. 789)*

Freedom of Information

The Senate Judiciary Committee Sept. 12 reported a bill (S 774 — S Rept 98-221) to overhaul the Freedom of Information Act (FOIA). The Senate passed the bill in 1984, but the measure died in the House.

The Senate Nov. 17, passed less sweeping legislation (S 1324 — S Rept 98-305) exempting the Central Intelligence Agency from some provisions of the FOIA. A similar bill cleared in 1984. *(1983-84 action, this page)*

Earthquake Hazards Reduction

The Senate April 7 by voice vote passed a bill (S 820) reauthorizing the Earthquake Hazards Reduction Act of 1982 (PL 97-464) for three years.

The measure cleared Congress in 1984. *(Details, p. 792)*

1984

Freedom of Information Act

Congress cleared legislation in 1984 granting the Central Intelligence Agency (CIA) an exemption from some provisions of the 18-year-old Freedom of Information Act (FOIA). But a major revision of the law that passed the Senate in February — the first such revision in a decade — was never reported out of House committee.

President Reagan signed HR 5164 (PL 98-477) on Oct. 15, authorizing the CIA director to close certain operational files from FOIA review. Although the files themselves were usually found to be exempt from disclosure, the CIA had requested, and under the new law received, a waiver from FOIA search and review requirements for those files.

A second, much more inclusive bill (S 774) passed the Senate by voice vote Feb. 27 after minimal debate. S 774 incorporated a number of administration-requested changes in FOIA to make it easier for agencies to close files from public view. The bill also incorporated changes sought by news organizations, including financial incentives for agencies to comply with the act's deadlines for responding to FOIA requests.

Although that bill, which was the result of three years of compromise and negotiations, passed the Senate with relative ease, it was quickly bottled up in the House Government Operations Committee, where it died. *(1981, 1982 action, pp. 776, 778)*

Background

The FOIA, originally enacted in 1966 (PL 89-487), required the federal government and its agencies to make available to citizens, upon request, all documents and records except those that fell into specified exempt categories.

In 1974, over President Ford's veto, Congress strengthened the law, imposing deadlines for agencies to respond to requests and permitting federal judges to review agency decisions to classify certain material. *(Congress and the Nation Vol. IV, p. 805)*

Upon taking office, President Reagan began an effort to curtail the availability of access to government information in several ways.

The proposed wholesale revision of FOIA and the proposal to tighten access to CIA files were part of that effort. The administration also proposed to expand the use of polygraphs and require lifetime pre-publication review of all material written by some 120,000 federal workers. A bill to prevent such action (HR 4681 — H Rept 98-961, Parts I and II) did not reach the House floor in 1984.

CIA Exemption

The Senate Sept. 28 by voice vote cleared and sent to the president HR 5164, authorizing the CIA director to close certain operational files from review under the FOIA.

The Senate accepted the House bill, which gave courts more latitude to review challenges to agency decisions than a similar measure (S 1324 — S Rept 98-305) the Senate had passed Nov. 17, 1983.

As cleared, the bill defined operational files to include records relating to the identities of sources and methods, and to the routine administration and management of intelligence activities.

HR 5164 continued to require the agency to search files in response to FOIA requests by individuals about themselves, or requests for information regarding covert actions or suspected CIA improprieties. And the bill reversed a ruling by the Justice Department and the Office of Management and Budget that invoked the 1974 Privacy Act to deny individuals FOIA access to information about themselves. Despite that provision, the Reagan administration supported the bill. *(Privacy Act, Congress and the Nation Vol. IV, p. 585)*

The measure also required the agency to report to Congress on its implementation of the bill.

HR 5164 was reported by the House Select Committee on Intelligence May 1 (H Rept 98-726, Part I) and the House Governmnent Operations Committee Sept. 10 (Part II). The House passed the bill Sept. 19 by a 369-36 vote.

FOIA Overhaul

As reported by the Senate Judiciary Committee Sept. 12, 1983, the more sweeping rewrite of the information act (S 774 — S Rept 98-221) was nearly identical to a bill reported by the panel in the 97th Congress. That bill never made it to the floor.

S 774 would have allowed the attorney general to withhold information about law enforcement and investigations of organized crime, given agencies more time to release records and made it more difficult to obtain information submitted by businesses to the government.

It also would have imposed uniform fees, based on the actual cost of processing FOIA requests, to search for, process and copy requested government information. It would have waived those fees automatically for journalists, scholars and non-profit groups.

NASA Authorization

A $7.5 billion fiscal 1985 authorization bill (HR 5154 — PL 98-361) for the National Aeronautics and Space Administration (NASA) cleared Congress June 28.

The measure authorized the agency to begin research and development on a permanent manned space station, which Reagan had proposed in his State of the Union message. HR 5154 also created a National Commission on Space to study space activities and formulate an agenda for the nation's civilian space program.

The House passed HR 5154 (H Rept 98-629) March 28 by a vote of 389-11, and the Senate passed its version (S Rept 98-455) by voice vote on June 21. The conference report on the bill (H Rept 98-873) was adopted by the Senate June 27 and the House the following day.

Landsat Sale

President Reagan July 17 signed into law a measure paving the way for the federal government to sell to the private sector satellites that took pictures of the Earth and the data from such satellites (HR 5155 — PL 98-365).

HR 5155 established guidelines for the gradual sale of the satellites, known as land-remote sensing satellites

(Landsat). The bill was reported by the House Science and Technology Committee April 3 (H Rept 98-647) and passed the House by voice vote April 9. The Senate passed its version (S Rept 98-458) by voice vote June 8. The bill cleared June 29 when the Senate accepted minor House changes to the Senate measure. *(Previous action, p. 781)*

Space Launch Licensing

Congress Oct. 9 completed action on a bill (HR 3942 — PL 98-575) designed to encourage and facilitate commercial space launches.

The bill prohibited anyone from launching satellites or other space objects from the United States without a license and gave the Department of Transportation (DOT) authority to issue such licenses.

The House passed HR 3942 (H Rept 98-816) June 5, and the Senate passed its version of the bill (S Rept 98-656) Oct. 9. The House agreed to the Senate version the same day, clearing it for the president.

Arts, Humanities Funding

Congress May 17 cleared legislation (HR 2751 — PL 98-306) that lifted spending ceilings set by the 1981 budget reconciliation act (PL 97-35) for cultural support agencies to bring the authorizations in line with actual appropriations for fiscal 1984 and 1985. *(1981 action, p. 776)*

HR 2751 authorized $166.5 million for the arts endowment, $158.8 million for the humanities and $20.2 million for the Institute of Museum Services in fiscal 1984. For fiscal 1985, the bill authorized such sums as Congress considered necessary. Appropriations for the three agencies for fiscal 1982-84 each year exceeded authorizations in the 1981 act.

The bill, reported by the House Education and Labor Committee May 16, 1983 (H Rept 98-163), was passed by the House Feb. 21 and the Senate April 5. It cleared May 17 after the House by voice vote accepted a minor Senate amendment.

Bureau of Standards Veto

President Reagan Oct. 30 pocket-vetoed the National Bureau of Standards fiscal 1985 authorization bill (HR 5172) because of provisions aimed at improving manufacturing technology in the United States, particularly in the area of robotics and automation.

The president said the robotics and automation provisions constituted an "unwarranted role" for the federal government in investment decisions that were best left to industry.

Although the authorization died with the veto, Congress appropriated almost $124 million for the agency in fiscal 1985 (PL 98-411).

HR 5172 was passed by the House (H Rept 98-650) May 2. The Senate passed its version (S 2458 — S Rept 98-423) June 26. On Sept. 21 the Senate by voice vote passed HR 5172, after adding provisions from a separate Senate-passed and House committee-reported bill (S 1286 — S Rept 98-431, H Rept 98-1078) designed to enhance manufacturing technology, especially through research into robotics and automation. The House Oct. 4 accepted the

Senate amendments to HR 5172 by voice vote, clearing the bill for the president.

NOAA Veto

President Reagan Oct. 19 pocket-vetoed a bill (S 1097) authorizing programs for the National Oceanic and Atmospheric Administration (NOAA) for fiscal 1984-86. Reagan said several provisions of the bill would have hampered the agency's management ability.

S 1097 authorized $2 billion over the three-year period for atmospheric, satellite and oceanic programs of the agency. The measure was passed by the Senate June 15, 1983 (S Rept 98-109), and the House Jan. 26, 1984. Both chambers adopted the conference report on S 1097 (H Rept 98-1093) Oct. 3. Congress previously had approved nearly $1.5 billion in fiscal 1985 appropriations for NOAA (PL 98-411).

The bill was the first comprehensive authorization for the agency since it was created by executive order in 1970. A two-year authorization failed to clear in 1982. *(1982 action, p. 782)*

National Archives

President Reagan signed on Oct. 19 a bill (S 905 — PL 98-497) making the National Archives and Records Administration a separate agency within the executive branch.

The National Archives had been independent from its creation in 1934 until 1949, when it was placed under the General Services Administration, which had just been created.

The Senate passed S 905 (S Rept 98-373) by voice vote June 21, and the House passed its version (HR 3987 — H Rept 98-707) Aug. 2. The conference report (H Rept 98-1124) cleared Oct. 4.

Government Reorganization

Two bills enacted in 1984 renewed the president's authority to make limited changes in the organization of Cabinet departments and federal agencies and ratified past government reorganizations.

Both bills were passed in response to a 1983 Supreme Court decision that declared unconstitutional the legislative veto, a provision by which one house of Congress could reject an action of the administration. *(Legislative veto, p. 833)*

The president's reorganization authority had expired April 7, 1981. *(Congress and the Nation Vol. V, p. 855)*

Previous laws authorizing the president to reorganize executive branch agencies contained legislative veto provisions. Concern that prior reorganizations might be declared illegal, because the laws under which they were effected might be declared unconstitutional, prompted Congress to ratify past reorganizations and to change the procedure by which Congress could object to a future reorganization plan.

The first 1984 reorganization bill (HR 6225 — PL 98-532) ratified all previous reorganizations of federal agencies and departments undertaken under previous laws. HR 6225 was passed by the House Oct. 1 (H Rept 98-1104) and the Senate Oct. 4. The president signed the bill Oct. 19.

The second reorganization bill (HR 1314 — PL 98-614) restored through Dec. 31, 1984, the president's authority to restructure government agencies without having to ask Congress to pass a law making the changes.

HR 1314 altered the procedure for congressional approval of proposed reorganizations, eliminating the one-house veto, which was ruled unconstitutional in the 1983 Supreme Court case.

In its place HR 1314 required that reorganization plans would take effect only if both House and Senate passed a joint resolution approving the plan, and the president signed the resolution. Congress had to act within 90 days of receiving the plan from the president, or the plan would be deemed disapproved.

HR 1314 was passed by the House April 10 (H Rept 98-128, Parts I and II) and the Senate Oct. 11. The president signed the bill Nov. 8.

Procurement Costs

President Reagan Oct. 30 signed a comprehensive bill (HR 4209 — PL 98-577) aimed at reducing the cost to all government agencies of buying spare parts and supplies. The bill sought to increase competition, limit overhead charges and special prices for commercially available goods, and boost small business participation in federal procurement.

Some provisions similar to those contained in HR 4209, as cleared, as well as provisions from two other procurement bills (HR 5084, HR 2133) were included in the Defense Authorization Act of 1984 (HR 5167 — PL 98-525). Those provisions primarily applied to Pentagon purchases. *(Defense authorization, p. 235)*

Congress included in the Deficit Reduction Act of 1984 (HR 4170 — PL 98-369) most provisions of a second bill (S 338) designed to increase competition primarily in non-defense contracting. The Senate had passed S 338 Nov. 11, 1983. *(Deficit reduction, p. 56)*

Enactment of the various procurement provisions culminated a two-year effort by six congressional committees to cut procurement costs. In 1983 Congress had cleared a bill (PL 98-191) reauthorizing and strengthening the Office of Federal Procurement Policy, an agency within the Office of Management and Budget. That bill restored the agency's responsibility for writing governmentwide regulations on procurement. *(Procurement policy office, p. 786)*

Congress also cleared in 1983 a bill (S 272 — PL 98-72) designed to increase competition for contracts, particularly by small businesses, by requiring advance notice of bidding.

HR 4209 was passed by the House May 21, 1984 (H Rept 98-528). The Senate passed a broader measure (S 2489 — S Rept 98-523) Aug. 7. A compromise version cleared Oct. 4.

Indian Legislation

President Reagan signed one bill for Indian economic development, but he pocket-vetoed two other measures affecting Indian health and reimbursement for two Indian tribes for irrigation construction.

The president Oct. 4 signed into law S 2614 (PL 98-449) extending grants and loan guarantees for Indian economic development. S 2614 authorized up to $5.5 million in

Grace Commission Savings Recommendations

The President's Private Sector Survey on Cost Control issued a 47-volume report in January 1984 with sweeping recommendations for changes in federal management and programs.

Headed by industrialist J. Peter Grace, the panel made more than 2,000 suggestions for changes that the report said would save $424 billion over three years. The commission, composed of 161 top business and organization executives, looked at 36 areas in the federal government, ranging from civil service pensions to data processing to entitlement programs.

By year's end, fewer than a fifth of the recommendations had been implemented, according to the White House. Congress showed little inclination to act on the commission proposals. The major objection was that many of the recommendations would require controversial changes of policy.

Claims Disputed

In February 1984 an analysis done jointly by the non-partisan Congressional Budget Office (CBO) and the General Accounting Office (GAO) disputed the claims of the Grace commission. CBO and GAO examined many of the commission's recommendations, representing 89 percent of the anticipated savings, and estimated they would save $98 billion over three years, a third of the amount estimated by Grace.

Noting that the biggest savings could come only from changes in federal programs enacted by Congress, not through administrative action, the CBO-GAO report said that most of the recommendations should be characterized as policy changes, not as improvements in efficiency or elimination of waste.

Among the anticipated three-year savings that would require major policy adjustments, the commission proposed:

● Requiring a means test to determine if recipients of federal social welfare payments, such as Social Security, food stamps and Medicare, really needed these benefits. Savings: $59 billion.

● Scaling down civil service and military retirement benefits, which the Grace panel claimed were three to six times higher than the best private plans. Savings: $61 billion.

● Repealing the Davis-Bacon Act, which required federal contractors to pay higher wages than they otherwise would in certain areas. Savings: $5 billion.

● "Privatizing" the agencies that sold federally generated electricity, an action that was predicted to approximately triple the price of hydroelectric power in the Northwest. Savings: $20 billion.

One key recommendation that Congress repeatedly refused to accept was that the president be given item veto power. That would have allowed him to knock out particular items to which he objected, without vetoing large bills — particularly appropriations bills — in their entirety. *(Story, p. 52)*

Some Savings Implemented

In a report issued July 18, the White House Office of Cabinet Affairs noted that $40.9 billion, or 9.6 percent of the total projected Grace commission savings, had been implemented.

Included in the total already saved was $2.4 billion from increasing contributions and reducing benefits under the railroad retirement system, as provided by legislation (PL 98-76) restoring the solvency of the system. *(Railroad retirement, p. 666)*

The total also included $2.7 billion saved from reducing the backlog in collecting delinquent taxes, $2.6 billion saved by paying bills on time, $2.1 billion saved by speeding up the deposit of funds received by the government, and $1.1 billion by adjusting the fill rate and construction schedule of the Strategic Petroleum Reserve.

Another $62.6 billion in savings was proposed in the administration's fiscal 1985 budget, the White House report said. Most of those proposals were ignored or rejected by Congress, including savings of $5.2 billion from reducing the grades of 31,000 federal employees, and $1.3 billion from charging user fees for deep port and inland navigation.

Several recommendations of the Grace commission, expected to save $3.2 billion, were included as provisions of 1984 deficit reduction legislation (HR 4170 — PL 98-369). *(Story, p. 56)*

One allowed the Treasury Department in limited cases to deduct from an individual's tax refund uncollected government debts, such as student loan repayments. Another accelerated the collection and deposit of non-tax receipts, such as custom duties.

Congress Criticized

One of the 47 volumes of the Grace commission report — "The Cost of Congressional Encroachment" — claimed that a large chunk of federal waste stemmed from members' efforts to bring water projects, military bases and federal offices to their districts, and to keep them there.

In addition to pork-barreling, it charged Congress with interfering in day-to-day executive agency decisions on pay scales, employee reorganizations and contracting.

The report pinned responsibility on Congress for approximately 100 examples of what the commission considered wasteful spending. An end to congressional interference in day-to-day agency management could save $7.8 billion in costs and snag $1.1 billion in new revenues over three years, the report said.

fiscal 1985 and thereafter for interest subsidies on guaranteed loans and up to $10 million in fiscal 1986 and thereafter for Indian business development grants. The Senate had passed the bill (S Rept 98-459) June 8, and the House passed its version (HR 5519 — H Rept 98-991) Sept. 11. A compromise version cleared Sept. 24.

Vetoed Bills. Citing a 22-year-old decision by the Indian Claims Commission, President Reagan Oct. 17 pocket-vetoed a bill (S 1967) that would have reimbursed the Gros Ventre and Assiniboine Tribes of the Fort Belknap Indian Community in Montana $457,000 for irrigation construction between 1895 and 1913. A claim for the same reimbursement had been dismissed by the Indian Claims Commission on Nov. 20, 1962. The bill (S Rept 98-406) was passed by the Senate June 26 and the House Oct. 2.

The other vetoed bill was S 2166, reauthorizing Indian health care programs for four years. In his Oct. 19 veto statement, Reagan criticized a new demonstration program authorized in the bill that would have made Indians in Montana who were eligible for state and local health services for the indigent also eligible for Indian Health Service programs. The Senate passed S 2166 (S Rept 98-471) Sept. 12, and the House passed its version (HR 4567 — H Rept 98-763) Sept. 24. The conference version (H Rept 98-1126) cleared Oct. 4.

Earthquake Hazards Reduction

President Reagan signed into law March 22 a bill (S 820 — PL 98-241) reauthorizing federal earthquake hazards reduction and fire prevention programs. The bill authorized $65.5 million in fiscal 1984 and $72.6 million in fiscal 1985.

The Senate passed S 820 (S Rept 98-42) April 7, 1983. The House passed S 820 Feb. 1, 1984, after substituting the language of its own bill (HR 2465 — H Rept 98-99, Parts I and II). The Senate accepted the House version March 8.

Federal Pay, COLAs

President Reagan Aug. 30 proposed a 3.5 percent pay raise for white-collar federal workers, effective Jan. 1, 1985. Members of Congress received an identical raise under a law that gave them the same salary increases as other white-collar federal employees. *(Story, p. 832)*

The raise was guaranteed to take effect — federal white-collar pay hikes were automatic — when Congress failed to vote otherwise before adjourning.

Early in the year Congress cleared legislation boosting to 4 percent from 3.5 percent the pay raise federal employees and members of Congress had received Jan. 1, 1984. The increase, which was retroactive to Jan. 1, was included in a reconciliation bill (HR 4169 — PL 98-270) cleared April 5. *(Reconciliation, p. 60; 1983 action, p. 785)*

The bill also delayed cost-of-living adjustments (COLAs) for federal retirees from May until December, with payments due in January 1985.

Whistleblower Awards

Administration objections blocked renewal of a program that authorized cash awards to federal employees who blew the whistle on waste, fraud and mismanagement in the government.

A bill (HR 5646) that would have extended the grants program for three years was passed by the House (H Rept 98-1053) Sept. 24 and the Senate Oct. 11. The bill died in the closing hours of the session when the House refused to accept a Senate amendment giving federal courts jurisdiction over complaints that whistleblowers had been harassed on the job for reporting waste or fraud. The administration opposed the amendment.

The whistleblower awards program was created by the Budget Reconciliation Act of 1981 (PL 97-35) as a trial program to expire Sept. 30, 1984. Over the three years of the program's existence, inspectors gave awards totaling $8,800, for cost savings estimated at more than $1 million. *(1981 federal pay action, p. 774)*

Former Spouse Benefits

Congress Oct. 10 cleared a bill (HR 2300 — PL 98-615) allowing former spouses of federal workers to receive survivor benefits.

HR 2300 permitted the Office of Personnel Management to recognize court orders granting survivor benefits to former spouses of federal employees and retirees.

The House Sept. 24 passed HR 2300 (H Rept 98-1054) by voice vote. Before passing HR 2300 Oct. 10, the Senate added provisions that made changes in the merit pay system affecting managers in civil service grades 13-15, and in the Senior Executive Service. The House accepted the Senate changes.

As cleared, the bill established a uniform five-tiered rating system, and provided for raises for employees who rated highly and for the denial of raises to those who rated poorly. The bill allowed cash awards for exceptional performers and established minimum and maximum levels for performance awards.

Other Legislation

National Party Conventions

President Reagan July 11 signed a bill authorizing increased federal payments to the Democratic and Republican parties for nominating convention costs. The bill (HR 5950 — PL 98-355) raised from $6 million to $8 million the ceiling on payments to each party out of the presidential election income tax checkoff fund.

The bill was reported by the House Ways and Means Committee June 28 (H Rept 98-877, Part I). By a 226-169 vote, the House passed the bill June 29. The Senate by voice vote passed the bill the same day, clearing it for the president.

Polling Place Accessibility

President Reagan signed a bill Sept. 28 (HR 1250 — PL 98-435) designed to make it easier for the elderly and handicapped to participate in federal elections by making polling places more accessible.

The House Administration Committee reported the bill June 21 (H Rept 98-852), and the House passed the bill June 25.

The Senate passed the bill Aug. 10 (S Rept 98-590),

with amendments clarifying that states had an option of accommodating handicapped or elderly voters whose home precincts were not accessible. The House accepted the Senate amendment Sept. 12.

D.C. Home Rule

Congress in 1984 approved a major revision to the District of Columbia Home Rule Act (PL 93-198) governing congressional review of laws enacted by the D.C. government.

The Home Rule Act and a provision in it that allowed Congress to reject laws passed by the District government became an issue after a June 1983 Supreme Court ruling declaring legislative veto provisions unconstitutional. *(Home Rule Act, Congress and the Nation Vol. IV, p. 797; legislative veto, p. 833)*

To remedy the confusion created by the ruling, Congress enacted legislation requiring passage of a joint resolution, which required the president's signature, to disapprove any law enacted by the District government. Existing law had allowed a simple resolution of either house to disapprove a District law.

The Home Rule Act change was included in an omnibus continuing appropriations resolution (H J Res 648 — PL 98-473) cleared Oct. 12. The House had passed a separate bill (HR 3932) in 1983, but the measure languished in the Senate because of administration objections.

Presidential Libraries

The House June 25 passed a bill (HR 5584 — H Rept 98-856) that would have required private donors to pay part of the cost of maintaining presidential libraries. The Senate never considered either that bill or a more far-reaching measure (S 563 — S Rept 98-637) that would have limited benefits to former presidents, including Secret Service protection, libraries and office staff.

Infrastructure Study

President Reagan Oct. 19 signed a bill (S 1330 — PL 98-501) requiring an annual study of the nation's infrastructure — roads, bridges, dams, water and sewer systems and the like — and requiring that the president's annual budget submission to Congress include a detailed summary of federal civilian and military construction projects. The bill was passed by the Senate Feb. 9 and the House May 15. The conference version (H Rept 98-1134) cleared Oct. 5.

15

Inside Congress

Introduction	*797*
Members and Procedures	*801*
Pay and Benefits	*821*
Legislative Veto	*833*

Inside Congress

"The most important thing we have done is rid ourselves of that subservient, timid mentality of the permanent minority. The Republican Party in the House is no longer content to go along. We want to go for broke." So said Minority Leader Robert H. Michel, R-Ill., at a House Republican Caucus in December 1984 in reflecting on the party's strategy during President Reagan's first term.

Michel's words bespoke more than GOP strategy. They described four years of turmoil and bitter confrontation between House Republicans and Democrats, four years of Republican frustration with minority status in the House (while the White House and the Senate were in GOP hands), and four years in which many of the party's "Young Turks," impatient with the Democrats' domination of the legislative process, decided to rely on "guerrilla" tactics to block the majority party's legislative agenda and embarrass the Democrats before a growing cable television audience.

The Senate, controlled by the Republicans for the first time in 26 years, was not immune to bitter partisanship. An inability to finish its work because of obstructionist tactics by some members gave credence to the charge by numerous political scientists and journalists that the Senate had been transformed from a closely knit body into a loose collection of individuals where the defense of one's views was equated with lawmaking.

Majority Leader Howard H. Baker Jr., R-Tenn., who retired at the close of the 98th Congress, had the onerous task of trying to persuade often obstinate senators to compromise their differences so the Senate could work its will on the president's legislative agenda. In his four years as majority leader, Baker had to contend with a Senate where courtesy, long a senatorial tradition, often was discarded in favor of confrontation and grandstanding.

Besides the increase in partisanship, Congress in 1981-84 was plagued with a continuing probe of the 1980 "Abscam" scandal as well as new scandals and ethical problems, an emotional dispute over televising House proceedings, pay and perquisite controversies, second thoughts about the efficacy of the congressional budget process, and the Supreme Court's sweeping decision in 1983 invalidating the legislative veto.

Budget Dominance

The federal budget and related issues dominated the legislative agenda during the 97th and 98th Congresses. Such concentration on a single subject in peacetime was a novel experience for lawmakers. Under the Reagan presidency, traditional procedures, institutions and customs were placed under great strain. Problems of the budget and the mounting federal deficit affected not only congressional consideration of authorization and appropriations bills, but the entire legislative record.

The attention given President Reagan's economic program — particularly budget cuts, military spending increases and taxes — left little time to draft, debate and pass the 13 annual appropriations bills that actually funded the budget decisions. More and more of the federal government had to be funded by massive stopgap funding bills, called continuing resolutions. This skewed the regular congressional budget process established by the 1974 Congressional Budget and Impoundment Control Act.

In 1981 Congress had to pass four continuing resolutions, with many government agencies operating for all of fiscal 1982 under such temporary funding measures. In 1982 Congress had cleared only three of the 13 regular appropriations bills by the start of the fiscal year, Oct. 1. Only four more were enacted during the lame-duck session requested by Reagan; six were left unfinished. Furthermore, because a continuing resolution was "must" legislation, it became a vehicle for all kinds of unrelated and nongermane issues, such as abortion and school prayer or more mundane special interest and "pork barrel" amendments.

The budget process was short-circuited in 1982 and 1983 when the leadership decided to drop a second budget resolution, as required by the 1974 budget act, because consideration of the first budget resolution was so lengthy and painful.

The budget "reconciliation" process, to bring existing tax and spending laws into conformity with the congressional budget resolutions, took up weeks of Congress' time

References

Discussion of congressional affairs for the years 1945-64 may be found in *Congress and the Nation Vol. I*, pp. 1407-1431; for the years 1965-68, *Congress and the Nation Vol. II*, pp. 893-924; for the years 1969-72, *Congress and the Nation Vol. III*, pp. 353-433; for the years 1973-76, *Congress and the Nation Vol. IV*, pp. 743-794; for the years 1977-80, *Congress and the Nation Vol. V*, pp. 873-953.

Congressional Pay

Lawmakers' pay rose from $60,662.50 in 1981 to $75,100 on Jan. 1, 1985. Members' expense accounts and other perquisites also increased in the 97th and 98th Congresses.

In 1982 Congress broke a 200-year tradition when it voted to pay a higher salary to representatives than to senators. While senators' pay remained at $60,662.50, representatives' salaries increased 15 percent, to $69,800. In return for freezing their salaries, senators removed a cap on their outside earnings.

In 1983 senators reconsidered their action and imposed a cap on honoraria of 30 percent of their congressional pay, effective Jan. 1, 1984. Congress also provided a 15 percent pay raise for senators, making their salary, effective July 1, 1983, the same as House members' once again.

in 1982. The conference committee appointed to draft a final version of that measure set a record for the number of House and Senate conferees, with more than 250 members working in 58 subconferences. The Appropriations committees, once considered the most powerful in Congress, were relegated to a secondary role.

The budget reconciliation process also affected regular Senate procedures by overshadowing Majority Leader Baker's use of unanimous consent agreements, the method by which the Senate considered most important bills. Reconciliation was used in part to avoid the need to obtain agreements on a bill-by-bill basis.

Another example of how the budgetary matters changed the normal routine was the treatment given the president's 1982 tax increase proposal. Although the Constitution requires the House to initiate all revenue-raising bills, the Senate drafted the massive tax increase legislation. The Constitution technically was complied with, since the Senate added the $98 billion measure to a minor House tax measure, but the House voted to go directly to conference with the Senate on the legislation. Thus no House hearings were held on the Senate-passed bill; no committee report was issued; and no House floor debate took place on the largest tax increase in U.S. history.

The emphasis on fiscal issues put a strain on members as well as the legislative process. Democrats felt humiliated in 1981 as the Reagan economic agenda sailed through Congress. Even in the Democrat-controlled House, the GOP was able to command an ideological majority on economic issues. Reagan was victorious because many conservative Democrats, who were labeled "Boll Weevils" by their party, abandoned the leadership and voted with the GOP.

Despite the legislative successes scored by Reagan, Congress was an unhappy institution, even for Republicans. It became increasingly hard for the president's own party loyalists to adapt to a legislative agenda dominated by budget issues. This was particularly so for Reagan's ideological conservatives, who wanted the administration to concentrate on enacting their social agenda.

House Partisanship

Although it had its roots in earlier years, partisanship in the House was particularly acute in Reagan's first term. House GOP members, emboldened by Reagan's victory over Jimmy Carter and their pickup of 33 seats in the 1980 elections, embarked upon a deliberate strategy of frontal assaults on the majority party. Rejecting business as usual, a group of junior members spearheaded attacks on Democratic-sponsored legislation and disrupted legislative proceedings. Long-dormant House rules adopted in earlier periods of rebellion and turmoil were resurrected and used to ridicule the Democrats and delay action on legislation. But beyond these goals was the broader objective of publicizing the GOP conservatives' legislative interests.

Speaker Thomas P. O'Neill Jr., D-Mass., was the lightning rod for the Republican attacks. He was seen by the GOP as inflexible, arbitrary and unwilling to share power. O'Neill was one of the most partisan Speakers in recent times. He actively fought Reagan's budget cuts in domestic programs and raised the issue of Reagan's fairness to minorities and the disadvantaged. Although the Speaker by tradition seldom voted except to break ties, O'Neill voted six times in 1981 alone.

Ironically, O'Neill was instrumental in Reagan's success in Congress on some of the president's biggest victories; for example, the 1982 income tax increase and Reagan's request for congressional authorization to station U.S. troops in Lebanon for 18 months. The Speaker also agreed in 1981 to place Reagan's economic program on a "fast track" to expedite the legislation.

House Rules. The Republican offensive began on the first day of the 97th Congress. The GOP was angry over several House rules changes instituted by the Democratic leadership that continued a trend begun in the 1970s of increasing and solidifying the power of the Speaker. But the issue that sparked the confrontation and set the tone for the next four years was the leadership's refusal to revise party ratios on four key committees to reflect the Republicans' 1980 election gains in the House. Once the GOP was convinced of the Speaker's intransigence, it decided to go public. Michel introduced amendments to change the committee ratios, but the Democrats ultimately prevailed. The seeds of bitterness had been sown.

Proposed rules changes introduced by House Democrats in January 1983 were even more controversial. While the leadership called the proposals a modest streamlining of House operations, Republicans accused the Democrats of trampling on the rights of the minority. The rules eventually were adopted by a party-line vote.

The most contentious change adopted made it harder for individual members to offer "limitation riders" to appropriations bills. These amendments had been used repeatedly by frustrated Republicans to get action on school prayer, abortion bans and other social issues they wanted addressed. Such riders were a way of getting around a House rule that barred legislative, or policy, amendments in appropriations bills. They are limitation amendments because they must be worded so as to prohibit the spending of funds in the bill for specific purposes.

Two other rules changes opposed by Republicans were designed to avoid what the leadership called "nuisance votes" on minor procedural matters.

Both Republican and Democratic opposition, however, forced the withdrawal of a controversial proposal that would have required a two-thirds majority, rather than a simple majority, to pull a proposed constitutional amendment out of the Judiciary Committee by means of a discharge petition.

Special Orders. Republican-Democratic acrimony reached a peak in 1984. For three years the GOP used "special orders" speeches — speeches given in the House after the close of regular legislative business — to attack the Democrats.

The main actors in this daily drama were junior Republicans calling themselves the Conservative Opportunity Society (COS), headed by Newt Gingrich, Ga. In May 1984 the COS used a special order to attack the foreign policy views of about 50 Democrats, some of whom later charged that the speech contained innuendoes that smacked of McCarthyism.

Speaker O'Neill retaliated by ordering the cable televison cameras to pan the chamber during special orders to show viewers that the House was virtually empty. Previously, the cameras had focused only on the member speaking.

After Gingrich appeared on the House floor and defended the foreign policy report, O'Neill lost his temper. The Speaker asserted that Gingrich had challenged "the Americanism" of Democrats named in the speech. He added: "It's the lowest thing I have ever seen in my 32 years in Congress." The outburst led to O'Neill's official chastisement; he became the first Speaker to be so reprimanded since 1797, according to congressional researchers.

In the aftermath of the shouting match there were Democratic calls for restrictions on use of the special orders speeches. Some members even called for an end to televised broadcasts of the House. Republicans, on the other hand, said that if the cameras were to pan the chamber it should be done throughout the daily sessions, not just during special orders. Despite the grumblings on both sides, none of several suggested remedies was adopted.

Other GOP Tactics. In addition to using the House TV cameras, the Republicans employed little-known House rules to tie up proceedings and dramatize their own legislative agenda. Their tactics were devised in response to the frustration they felt because efforts to block legislation in committee were more effective in the House than in the Senate. Senate floor procedures provided various ways to bypass committees if they refused to report legislation under their jurisdiction.

In the first successful use of the discharge petition in years, Republicans in 1982 brought to the floor a controversial constitutional amendment to balance the budget. The House Judiciary Committee had refused to take action on a balanced budget amendment for more than a year. (The proposed constitutional amendment subsequently was rejected by the House.) In addition, legislation to repeal an unpopular law requiring the withholding of taxes on dividends and interest income was forced from the Ways and Means Committee by discharge petition in 1983.

The difficulty of prying legislation from hostile committees led the COS to dust off a 1909 House rule, called Calendar Wednesday, in order to bring up its pet social issues. Though use of the procedure publicized these issues, Republicans were not successful in passing their legislation.

Nevertheless, the Republicans' skillful use of the amendment process during House debates forced the leadership to devise complicated "modified special rules" to

---

Court Rulings

The Supreme Court June 23, 1983, held in *Immigration and Naturalization Service v. Chadha* that the legislative veto was unconstitutional. Such vetoes, imposed by the House and Senate jointly, a single chamber or a committee, on government regulations and orders, without requiring the president's approval, were invalidated. The court said the legislative veto infringed on the balance of power between the three branches of government and on the constitutional requirement that all legislation passed by Congress must also be presented to the president for his signature or veto.

The decision affected some 200 laws enacted since 1932, including the War Powers Resolution of 1973, which was at issue in Reagan's 1983 request to keep U.S. troops in Lebanon, the 1976 Arms Export Control Act and the 1974 Congressional Budget and Impoundment Control Act.

Following the decision, Congress explored other ways to assert some control over executive branch rulemaking and regulations issued by independent agencies. The alternatives considered ranged from constitutional amendments to spending limitations. No sweeping substitute for the legislative veto was found, however.

President's Pocket-Veto Power. Congress fared better in a separate, lower court decision. In 1984 a federal appeals court ruled that President Reagan had acted unconstitutionally in 1983 when he pocket-vetoed legislation imposing conditions on aid to El Salvador. According to the court, a president did not have the authority to veto a bill by "pocketing" it — taking no action — between the first and second sessions of the same Congress. Only at the end of a two-year Congress was it permissible, constitutionally, the court said.

---

regulate House consideration of controversial bills.

Party Loyalty. House Democrats had their own internal troubles. In 1981 conservative party members who joined the GOP to help pass Reagan's economic plan demanded a larger say in setting party policy. One of these members, Phil Gramm, Texas, in January 1983 was stripped of his Budget Committee post because of his two-year collaboration with the White House on economic legislation and for supplying White House aides with the Democrats' budget strategy. In response Gramm resigned his seat, switched parties and was re-elected as a Republican.

Another Democrat, Eugene V. Atkinson, Pa., had switched parties in 1981 but retained his committee assignments because there were no clear-cut methods for removing disloyal members from committees. Also, Democrats doubted they had the votes on the House floor to oust Atkinson from his committee posts.

(As a result of the episodes, the Democrats' 1983 rules

changes included one in which continued assignment to House committees was made contingent upon representatives being members of their party caucus. And the Democratic Caucus further required a member to be thrown out of the caucus if he or she switched parties.)

Gramm and Atkinson were two of three conservative Democrats to switch parties within the 97th and 98th Congresses. Many other "Boll Weevil" Democrats organized as the Conservative Democratic Forum to demonstrate their discontent with O'Neill's leadership and to force changes in party policy. One result was that more conservatives were appointed to the Steering and Policy Committee and other key committees.

Senate Obstructionism

Because of its informality and rules allowing extended debate, the Senate has to operate on the basis of compromise, understanding and courtesy. But those ingredients were lacking during much of the 97th and 98th Congresses.

Majority Leader Baker had difficulty in obtaining approval from his colleagues for unanimous consent agreements governing debate on specific bills. Democrats were reluctant to give their consent to broad agreements restricting their flexibility. Conservative Republicans often were more concerned about advancing their own legislative concerns, even if they conflicted with the administration's and the Senate leadership's agenda.

The second session of the 97th Congress was particularly trying for Baker. From September to December 1982, the Senate took 15 cloture votes in attempts to end filibusters, a record for a four-month period. That span included a lame-duck session, which lasted from Nov. 29 until Dec. 23. Earlier, in February, a nine-month struggle by conservatives to enact anti-busing legislation was successful after a third filibuster against the legislation was stopped. In late summer, the Senate spent weeks in protracted debate over proposed anti-abortion and school prayer amendments offered by Jesse Helms, R-N.C., to an unrelated debt limit bill. Four times Helms tried to invoke cloture to stop the filibuster but did not succeed. After five weeks of debate,

Baker, supported by Barry Goldwater, R-Ariz., was able to derail Helms' amendments.

During the lame-duck session, conservatives organized to block passage of a gasoline tax increase. In this instance, Republicans battled among themselves, with Baker unable to control fellow Sens. Helms and John P. East, R-N.C., who refused to let the bill come to a vote. Sen. Alan K. Simpson, R-Wyo., remarked: "Seldom have I seen a more obdurate, more obnoxious performance."

Though that filibuster eventually was broken and the bill passed, the extent of the obstructionism in 1982 moved many senators to demand changes in the Senate's rules. Two separate studies of Senate rules and operations were made between 1981 and 1984, and many recommendations, some considered quite radical, were suggested. However, the majority leader decided not to push for their adoption, although more detailed consideration of one study's proposals was expected in the 99th Congress. Baker had already been disappointed by the Senate's failure under his leadership to approve his plan for gavel-to-gavel television coverage of Senate floor procedures.

Filibusters and filibuster threats continued throughout the 98th Congress. Drawn-out negotiations to devise agreements to avert filibusters, particularly in 1984, slowed work on most major legislation. And White House intransigence hindered Baker in his efforts to reach accommodations and unify Senate Republicans. Twelve cloture votes were taken that year, two of which dealt with Baker's attempt to bring his Senate television plan to a vote. *(Cloture votes, p. 977)*

Senate decorum was strained, too, by the need to decide the fate of Sen. Harrison A. Williams Jr., D-N.J., the only senator implicated in the FBI's Abscam operation in which undercover agents, posing as wealthy Arabs, offered bribes to elected officials. The Senate Ethics Committee had unanimously called for his expulsion in 1981 after he was convicted on nine counts, including bribery, conspiracy and receipt of an unlawful gratuity. Williams resigned in March 1982, when it became clear the Senate would vote to expel him.

Six House members also were convicted in the Abscam case and forced to leave the House.

Chronology
Of Action
On Congress:
Members and Procedures

1981

The first session of the 97th Congress, the first of Ronald Reagan's presidency, convened Jan. 5, 1981, and adjourned Dec. 16.

Republicans arrived in Washington optimistic about their chances of scoring key legislative victories. For the first time since January 1955, Republicans controlled the Senate. The change in the status of the two parties meant that the entire committee leadership shifted to the Republicans, with the Democrats relegated to minority status.

Although the Democrats narrowly retained a mathematical majority in the House after the November 1980 elections — the GOP had made a 33-seat gain — a conservative coalition of Republicans and Southern Democrats exerted ideological control on some issues, particularly economic matters. That coalition also threatened the Democratic leadership's grasp of House proceedings.

Although Democrats retained control of the committee structure in the House, election defeats and the increased number of Republicans forced several changes in committee chairmanships. But the Democratic leadership refused to revamp party ratios on four key committees to reflect the GOP gains.

House Republicans sought to dramatize their differences with the leadership. And they succeeded in dividing the Democratic rank-and-file in 1981 and winning votes of like-minded Democrats for the president's economic program. In the process the Democrats were made to appear disorganized and ineffective. Two Democrats — Reps. Eugene V. Atkinson, Pa., and Bob Stump, Ariz. — announced they would become Republicans. Stump deferred a formal switch until the 1982 election.

Organization

Senate

Most of the key Senate organizational decisions had been made at party caucuses held in December 1980. Republicans elected their leaders for the 97th Congress Dec. 2; Democrats chose theirs Dec. 4.

Majority Leadership. Howard H. Baker Jr., R-Tenn., was unopposed as the new Senate majority leader. Elected majority whip, also unopposed, was Ted Stevens, Alaska. Baker and Stevens served during the 96th Congress as the minority leader and minority whip, respectively.

In the sole contested GOP race, James A. McClure, Idaho, a conservative, defeated moderate John Heinz, Pa., 33-20, for chairmanship of the Senate Republican Confer-

ence, a GOP policy-making body. Heinz had chaired the National Republican Senatorial Committee during the highly successful 1980 campaign and was an early favorite. However, conservatives fought hard to elect McClure, maintaining that a conservative was needed to balance the party leadership.

Bob Packwood, Ore., succeeded Heinz as chairman of the GOP campaign committee.

GOP senators re-elected John Tower, Texas, as chairman of the Republican Policy Committee, and Jake Garn, Utah, as secretary of the Republican Conference.

Republican Strom Thurmond, S.C., became Senate president pro tempore. In recent times, the post has gone to the senator of the majority party with the longest Senate service. The president pro tempore is third in the line of presidential succession, after the vice president and the Speaker of the House.

Minority Leadership. The Democrats routinely elected former Majority Leader Robert C. Byrd, W.Va., as their minority leader and chairman of the Democratic Conference for the 97th Congress. Californian Alan Cranston, majority whip in the 96th Congress, was unopposed for minority whip, and Daniel K. Inouye, Hawaii, retained his post as Democratic Conference secretary.

Rules. The Republican leadership proposed no changes in the Senate's standing rules.

At a Dec. 1, 1980, meeting, Senate Democrats eliminated a party caucus rule giving new senators a leg up in obtaining choice committee assignments if their predecessors retired early. Freshman senators had been able to gain a few days' seniority by being appointed to fill vacancies created just before the end of a Congress. Senate Republicans had abolished a similar rule in August 1980.

Committee Realignment. New Senate committee assignments reinforced the assumption that the 97th Congress would take a sharp ideological turn to the right. Now controlled and headed by Republicans, the committees became more opposed to government regulation and significantly more conservative on fiscal matters than they were in the 96th Congress.

The composition of the new panels, especially Energy and Environment, also meant the Senate was likely to worry more about concerns of the West and less about concerns of the East and Midwest and was likely to be more sympathetic to the smaller, less developed states at the expense of the nation's older, industrial regions.

Republicans acted to increase the committees' ratios of Republicans to Democrats to reflect the GOP gains in the November elections.

House

Majority Leadership. The House re-elected Thomas P. O'Neill Jr., D-Mass., as Speaker for the 97th Congress over the Republican candidate, Robert H. Michel, Ill., by a 234-182 party-line vote.

At the Democrats' Dec. 8, 1980, party caucus, O'Neill and Majority Leader Jim Wright, Texas, had been unopposed. Wright announced he had named Thomas S. Foley, Wash., majority whip for the 97th Congress.

Reflecting conservative Democrats' increasing numbers in the House, a number of lesser posts were filled by moderates and conservatives, many of them Southerners. Gillis W. Long, La., a moderate, was elected chairman of the Democratic Caucus, succeeding Foley.

Minority Leadership. House Republicans selected

leaders known for their flexibility and willingness to negotiate with the Democrats rather than those who were strong partisans or rigid ideologues. For the post of minority leader, the Republicans chose Michel, a skilled legislative technician with a good working relationship with the Democratic leadership. Michel succeeded John J. Rhodes, Ariz., who voluntarily stepped down as GOP leader. Michel had been minority whip since 1974.

Committee Ratios. Final approval of committee assignments was delayed by a dispute over the party ratios on several committees. Although the ratio of House Democrats to Republicans was about 5-to-4 in the 97th Congress, O'Neill and the House Democratic Caucus insisted on retaining a 3-2 ratio on the Appropriations and Budget committees, a ratio of better than 2-to-1 on the Rules Committee and a ratio of slightly less than 2-to-1 on the Ways and Means Committee.

Democratic leaders argued that these larger margins were necessary to retain procedural control of the House, but Republicans charged the Democrats with attempting to alter the results of the November elections.

Barber B. Conable Jr., R-N.Y., incensed about the Ways and Means ratio in particular, attempted to press the issue. However, O'Neill refused to budge. Republican anger over the issue continued to fester throughout the 97th and 98th Congresses.

Abscam Scandal

In 1981 Sen. Harrison A. Williams, D-N.J., and Reps. Richard Kelly, R-Fla., and Raymond F. Lederer, D-Pa., were convicted for their involvement in the Abscam political corruption scandal. Their convictions brought the number of members caught in the FBI undercover operation to seven.

Senate Subpoena Power

A three-judge panel of the U.S. Court of Appeals for the District of Columbia Circuit on May 13, 1981, upheld a provision of the 1978 Ethics in Government Act (PL 95-521) giving the Senate a new mechanism to enforce its subpoenas.

That law allowed the jailing of recalcitrant witnesses until they provided the Senate or one of its committees with requested information. *(Ethics act, Congress and the Nation Vol. V, p. 824)*

Before 1978, Congress had two less effective ways to enforce subpoenas. Occasionally in congressional history, an individual found in contempt was held in the Capitol building until he agreed to supply requested information.

In 1857 Congress added a new enforcement weapon: the authority to seek criminal charges against an individual found in contempt. However, a criminal fine or imprisonment was only punitive in nature.

Williams, the only senator entangled in Abscam, was convicted May 1 on all nine counts for which he had been indicted. The Senate Ethics Committee recommended Aug. 24 that he be expelled. Williams resigned from Congress March 11, 1982, to stop expulsion proceedings initiated against him. *(Background, Abscam scandal, Congress and the Nation Vol. V, p. 931; Details, Williams case, p. 804)*

Lederer, the only House member implicated in Abscam to be re-elected in 1980, was convicted Jan. 9. He resigned from the House effective May 5. The House Committee on Standards of Official Conduct (ethics committee) April 28 had voted 10-2 in favor of expelling Lederer.

Kelly, who was defeated in a 1980 Florida primary, was convicted Jan. 26.

The House ethics committee announced July 28 it was ending its investigation of John P. Murtha, D-Pa., for misconduct in connection with the Abscam case. Murtha had been named an unindicted co-conspirator. *(Details, House members involved in Abscam, p. 806)*

Special-Interest Caucuses

The House Administration Committee decided Oct. 21 that special-interest caucuses and similar House legislative service organizations (LSOs) had to relinquish all outside funding or sever their official ties with Congress by 1983.

The committee ruling was agreed to by a unanimous vote, which constituted final action on the regulation; House concurrence was not required.

Under the new rule, congressional caucuses that wanted to continue accepting outside funds had to set up separate, non-profit foundations with private offices, staff and facilities. Beginning in 1982, LSOs were required to submit more frequent and more detailed financial reports to the House clerk than was previously necessary.

LSOs were groups of members of Congress who banded together to pursue a common legislative goal. In 1981 there were more than 50 such groups operating on Capitol Hill, including the House Democratic Caucus, the House Republican Study Committee, the Congressional Black Caucus, the Congressional Suburban Caucus, the Steel Caucus and the Environmental Study Conference.

At the time the new rule was implemented there were 26 such groups that had officially registered with the House, making them eligible to occupy space in House office buildings, have House telephone numbers and use House office supplies and equipment. These LSOs also were eligible to receive donations from members' official allowances to help pay for dues, staff salaries and subscriptions to LSO publications.

The House Administration Committee's action was prompted in part by a Sept. 18 report by the independent, Chicago-based Better Government Association (BGA), which charged that allowing private contributions to LSOs violated the spirit of House ethics rules because such contributions were forbidden to individual members. BGA said that eight of the 26 registered LSOs supplemented their budgets with direct contributions from outside sources.

Spellman Vacancy

For the first time in its history, the House in 1981 declared a vacancy because of a member's disability. The

Capitol Hill Area Development

The first master plan for development of the Capitol Hill area was submitted to Congress Sept. 25, 1981, by Capitol Architect George M. White. The 100-page report was intended to serve as a blueprint for Capitol Hill expansion and improvement over the next 50 to 75 years.

It laid out proposed sites for new House and Senate office buildings and suggested an underground expansion of the Capitol itself and numerous improvements in the layout and landscaping of the Capitol area grounds. The report did not advocate that Congress actually construct all the additional buildings. Instead, the plan instructed Congress where a new building should go if it were needed.

White first suggested a master plan in 1975 after unexpectedly strong neighborhood resistance foiled an attempt by House leaders to appropriate $22.5 million for the purchase of land adjacent to the Capitol grounds for another House office building. The final report provided that no homes would have to be destroyed to build any of the buildings suggested. (*Congress and the Nation Vol. IV, p. 777*)

The report recommended that Congress' first priority in putting the master plan into effect should be construction of another House office building, which would be the fourth. The report called the House side of Capitol Hill, to the south, "the most haphazardly built and unfinished section" of the Capitol grounds. The report set out sites for as many as nine new office buildings, which would be located in clusters behind the existing House offices.

For the area north of the Capitol, the plan suggested sites for three new Senate office buildings. Two would be on park land located behind the existing Russell and Dirksen Senate office buildings. The third would be next to Union Station, a few blocks from the Capitol.

New Supreme Court Building. The architect proposed that the Supreme Court remain in its present quarters on the east side of the Capitol for the next 50 to 75 years. Eventually, the report said, the court should be moved to "its own enclave in another appropriate location" to symbolize the separation of the judiciary from the legislative branch.

Transition District. To set the Capitol grounds off from the surrounding neighborhood, the report suggested setting up a "transition district" around Capitol Hill featuring new sidewalks and rows of trees. The report said the city should create a special district in the strip surrounding the area to protect the fronts of the existing town houses and to impose controls on the use of the adjoining land.

Capitol West Front. The architect's report suggested that the parking lot to the east of the Capitol be turned into a landscaped pedestrian plaza with two large fountains. Beneath the plaza, the architect suggested that Congress construct a three-level underground garage for 500 cars and an additional 86,000 square feet of office space.

The report took no position, however, on whether Congress should go ahead with White's controversial proposal, made in 1976, to expand the Capitol's crumbling west front. That decision was left to the five-member Commission on the West Central Front of the United States Capitol, which was formed in 1977. (*West front restoration, p. 815*)

GAO Faults Architect

The Capitol architect was taken to task Oct. 30, 1981, by the General Accounting Office (GAO), which found that inappropriate design and construction methods and inadequate controls had resulted in cost overruns, delays and management problems in the four major projects the architect had under way.

The four projects cited were construction of the Hart Senate Office Building and the James Madison Library of Congress building, and renovations of House Office Building Annex 2 and the Capitol power plant. All were running behind schedule and had experienced "significant cost overruns," according to the GAO report.

Hart Senate Office Building

The Hart Senate Office Building opened its doors Nov. 22, 1982, 10 years after the project was conceived. Plagued by cost overruns and considerable criticism, the building was named after the late Sen. Philip A. Hart, D-Mich. (1959-76). The third office building for senators, it had 50 office suites.

On Aug. 17, 1982, the Senate voted to stop construction of a $736,000 gymnasium in the new building. The 98-0 vote came on an amendment by Majority Leader Howard H. Baker Jr., R-Tenn., to an unrelated debt ceiling bill. "We're going to kill this snake once and for all," Baker told reporters. Baker's amendment did not save money earmarked for the new gym; it simply assured that the funds would be used for other items in the new building.

On Aug. 10 the Senate had killed a proposal by William Proxmire, D-Wis., to prohibit the spending of $736,400 to furnish the gymnasium. Proxmire complained the Senate already had two gymnasiums and did not need a third.

Despite the criticism, White said the one-million-square-foot building was built for "as little as possible." White, who acknowledged that structures built to house politicians were routinely criticized, said that if the building had cost $100 million, "we'd still get criticized. We might as well spend a little more and get it right."

Constitution gives the House the power to "be the Judge of the . . . Qualifications of its own members."

The House Feb. 24 adopted a resolution (H Res 80) declaring Maryland's 5th Congressional District seat vacant. The seat had been held by Democrat Gladys Noon Spellman, who had remained hospitalized in a semiconscious state since suffering a heart attack Oct. 31, 1980.

Spellman first entered the House in 1975. A week after suffering her heart attack, she was re-elected with more than 80 percent of the vote. However, her disability prevented her from being sworn in as a member of the 97th Congress.

In the only similar action, the House in late 1972 and early 1973 voted to declare two seats vacant after a court declared that the members elected to those seats were legally dead. The members — Reps. Thomas Hale Boggs Sr., D-La. (1941-43; 1947-73), and Nicholas J. Begich, D-Alaska (1971-72) — had been passengers in a plane that disappeared in October 1972.

Hinson Resignation

Rep. Jon C. Hinson, R-Miss., resigned from the House April 13 after being arrested on a morals charge in a Capitol Hill men's room. Under pressure from Mississippi and House Republican leaders, he announced his intention to resign March 13, slightly more than a month after his Feb. 4 arrest on a charge of attempted oral sodomy.

Hinson, who represented Mississippi's 4th District, was replaced by Democrat Wayne Dowdy, who won a run-off election July 7.

Hinson initially pleaded not guilty to the charge, a misdemeanor. But on May 28 he changed his plea to no contest and was sentenced to 30 days in jail. Judge David L. Norman of the District of Columbia Superior Court suspended the sentence and placed Hinson on a year's probation, subject to his continuing the medical treatment and counseling he began following his arrest.

Hinson was first elected to Congress in November 1978. In November 1980 he defeated two opponents to win re-election with 39 percent of the vote. During his re-election campaign, Hinson revealed that in 1976 he had been arrested for committing an obscene act in a homosexual trysting place in Arlington, Va.

He added that in 1977 he had been among the survivors of a fire at a Washington movie theater frequented by homosexuals. Hinson, however, denied that he was a homosexual.

1982

Congress was absorbed primarily in economic issues from the time President Reagan submitted his fiscal 1983 budget in February until the end of its lame-duck session in December. Many legislative decisions were collected into omnibus budget and reconciliation measures. Then, when Congress could not pass appropriations bills following these budget dictates, it wrapped most of its appropriations decisions into a series of massive continuing resolutions. The lame-duck session, which Reagan had called to

deal primarily with appropriations bills, produced far more anguish than legislation. *(Lame-duck sessions, p. 975)*

Filibusters became a regular occurrence in the Senate in 1982. The filibusters necessitated marathon sessions — at one point the Senate was in session for just shy of 38 straight hours. Senatorial courtesy was often discarded as senators shouted at one another, saying things they later regretted and had removed from the *Congressional Record*.

Both chambers faced ethics issues during the year. Senators had to debate the expulsion of one of their colleagues, Harrison A. Williams Jr., D-N.J., who resigned before a vote was taken to oust him over his conviction in the Abscam sting operation.

The House's image was damaged when Rep. Fred Richmond, D-N.Y., resigned his seat after pleading guilty to income tax evasion, possession of marijuana and making an illegal payment to a federal employee. His resignation came as the House ethics committee investigated published allegations of illicit sexual activity and cocaine use involving pages and members.

Williams Resignation

Harrison A. Williams, D-N.J., resigned from the Senate March 11, averting certain expulsion by his colleagues. With Williams' resignation, Congress closed its two-year investigation of members' wrongdoing that was uncovered by the FBI in its Abscam (a combination of the words Arab and scam) political corruption probe.

Press accounts first made public in February 1980, and subsequent court evidence, revealed the undercover FBI investigation, where agents disguised themselves as businessmen and Arab sheiks. The FBI eventually charged Williams and six House members in criminal wrongdoing, alleging that they accepted money from the phony sheiks, promising favors in return.

Some of the lawmakers were asked if they could use their Hill positions to help the Arabs obtain U.S. residency. Others were asked to use their influence in government to obtain federal grants and gambling licenses or to arrange real estate deals. Five of the seven legislators implicated in Abscam, including Williams, were videotaped accepting cash or stock. *(Details, Congress and the Nation Vol. V, p. 931)*

By leaving the Senate voluntarily, Williams avoided becoming the first senator to be expelled since the Civil War and the first in history to be ejected on grounds other than treason or disloyalty. However, Williams was the fourth senator convicted of a felony while in office. *(Convicted senators, box, p. 808)*

In 1984 the Senate Ethics Committee concluded a separate investigation into allegations that Williams had converted campaign contributions to his personal use. The committee found no evidence of wrongdoing. *(Story, p. 819)*

The Case Against Williams

Williams, a senator since 1959 and before that a U.S. representative from 1953 to 1957, resigned just hours before the Senate was ready to vote on expelling him — a vote that was virtually certain to go against the 23-year Senate veteran. He was the last member of Congress, and the only senator, to have been convicted on charges growing out of the Abscam scandal. All six House members had

No Voting Precedent in Williams Case

The May 1, 1981, conviction of Harrison A. Williams Jr., D-N.J., on charges brought as a result of the FBI's Abscam operation threw into question his right to vote on the Senate floor and in committee.

The rules of the House urged — but did not require — a convicted member to refrain from voting in committee and on the floor until the member either was cleared or re-elected. The Senate had no similar requirement.

Senate Ethics Committee Chairman Malcolm Wallop, R-Wyo., and Vice Chairman Howell Heflin, D-Ala., said at the time that they thought Williams would have to seek the Senate's permission to withhold his vote.

Mack Mattingly, R-Ga., a member of the committee, argued that until the committee had concluded its probe Williams "should not be afforded" the opportunity to vote. He called on Senate Democratic leaders to urge Williams not to vote. Williams, however, continued to do so.

Background

In the early 1900s it was the custom for a senator to voluntarily refrain from voting and from entering the Senate chamber after being indicted. The March 21, 1920, *New York Times*, for example, noted that Sen. Joseph R. Burton, R-Kan. (1901-06), convicted in November 1905 on charges of accepting a fee for services rendered before a U.S. department, chose to remain outside the Senate chamber because a colleague had threatened to offer a motion to exclude him from the Senate if he tried to enter.

"To draw his salary as a senator," the Times account continued, "Mr. Burton entered the Senate cloakroom and merely stuck his head into the Senate chamber, thus technically complying with the rule requiring the presence of senators on at least one day of the session before they can draw their salaries."

The custom was reversed, however, after the April 1924 indictment of Sen. Burton K. Wheeler, D-Mont. (1923-47), on a bribery charge.

Wheeler at the time headed a special committee investigating the failure of the Harding administration to prosecute federal officials suspected of influence-peddling in the Teapot Dome scandal. Wheeler maintained he had been framed by the very officials he was investigating.

Rather than stay off the floor, Wheeler demanded the right to speak to declare his innocence and to ask the Senate to investigate the charge. During the ensuing probe, he continued to vote.

Wheeler subsequently was cleared of any wrongdoing both by the Senate and by a federal jury. Since then, indicted senators have remained active in Senate affairs until they either were cleared or left the Senate and, like Williams, have continued to vote in committee and during Senate debates.

been convicted by January 1981. *(House members, box, p. 806)*

Williams had been convicted May 1, 1981, after a five-week trial, on nine counts including bribery, conspiracy, receipt of an unlawful gratuity, accepting outside compensation for the performance of official duties and interstate travel in aid of a racketeering enterprise. He had been indicted on Oct. 30, 1980.

Prosecutors were able to convince the federal court jury that Williams had accepted a hidden 18 percent interest in a titanium mine in Virginia in return for a promise to use his influence to obtain government contracts to buy the mine's output. As part of the deal, undercover FBI agents posing as wealthy Arabs and their associates promised to loan $100 million to the mining venture, owned by friends of Williams and Alexander Feinberg, a New Jersey lawyer. Prosecutors argued the loan would have been of direct benefit to Williams and that the senator was aware of this when he accepted the hidden interest in the mine.

Prosecutors further maintained that Williams had promised to use his influence to help an undercover agent posing as a wealthy Arab gain permanent U.S. residency.

Williams was sentenced Feb. 16, 1982, to three years in prison and fined $50,000. On Dec. 5, 1983, the Supreme Court refused to hear Williams' appeal, and on Jan. 19, 1984, he entered a federal prison camp in Allenwood, Pa.

Most Troubling Abscam Case. Of the charges against the seven legislators, the case against Williams was perhaps the most troubling to members. While the other Abscam defendants appeared in government-produced video and audio tapes to be eager participants in the government's bribery scheme, Williams actually turned down a cash bribe when undercover agents offered him one.

Williams was not convicted of accepting an offer of cash in exchange for promises of legislative favors but for his participation in an extremely complicated business scheme involving a hidden interest in a mining venture owned by several of Williams' friends.

Throughout his trial and, subsequently, during the Senate Ethics Committee hearings and the floor debate, Williams argued that he had committed no crime. Instead, he maintained that the government agents had "manufactured" the crimes of which he was accused after their other attempts to incriminate him had failed.

It was this possibility that most disturbed Williams' colleagues. And after Williams resigned, the Senate created an eight-member select committee to investigate whether there was Justice Department and FBI misconduct in Abscam. *(Details, below)*

Ultimately, however, most senators said they were convinced both that Williams' conduct was separate from the issue of possible government misconduct and that the senator actually had committed offenses serious enough to merit expulsion.

Six Members of the House ...

Six members of the House were convicted on charges stemming from Abscam, the FBI undercover probe of political corruption: John W. Jenrette, D-S.C., Richard Kelly, R-Fla., Raymond F. Lederer, D-Pa., John M. Murphy, D-N.Y., Michael "Ozzie" Myers, D-Pa., and Frank Thompson Jr., D-N.J. A seventh member, John P. Murtha, D-Pa., was named an unindicted co-conspirator. One senator, Harrison A. Williams Jr., D-N.J., also was convicted of wrongdoing in connection with the FBI operation. *(Williams, p. 804)*

The convicted House members and Williams were forced from Congress either by expulsion, resignation or electoral defeat.

Myers became the first House member to be expelled since 1861, the first to be expelled for misconduct other than treason and the fourth to be expelled in House history. *(House expulsion cases, Congress and the Nation Vol. V, p. 933)*

Lederer and Jenrette resigned from the House to stop expulsion proceedings against them. Lederer was the only House member convicted in Abscam to win re-election in November 1980.

Kelly, Murphy and Thompson were defeated in their re-election bids prior to their convictions and left Congress before disciplinary proceedings could be initiated against them. Kelly, the only Republican indicted in the Abscam scandal, lost in the September 1980 Florida primary. By the spring of 1985, he was the only member who had not begun his prison sentence.

Following is a summary of action taken in the cases against the House members involved in Abscam. *(Details, Congress and the Nation Vol. V, p. 931)*

Jenrette. Jenrette was convicted Oct. 7, 1980, on two counts of bribery and a single count of conspiracy. The House Standards of Official Conduct Committee (ethics committee) began its probe after Jenrette's conviction but was interrupted by a pre-election recess. On Dec. 3 the committee concluded that Jenrette had violated House rules and should be disciplined. He appeared before the committee Dec. 10, when it was considering a motion to expel him from the House. Jenrette that same day announced he would resign. He was sentenced Dec. 9, 1983, to two years in prison and five years' probation and fined $20,000. Jenrette reported to a federal prison camp in Atlanta on April 4, 1985.

Kelly. Kelly was convicted Jan. 26, 1981, of bribery and bribery conspiracy. Kelly was ordered acquitted May 13, 1982, by U.S. District Judge William B. Bryant of the District of Columbia in response to a defense motion for an acquittal judgment based on government violation of Kelly's due process. The government appealed the decision, and the U.S. District Court of Appeals for the District of Columbia reinstated Kelly's conviction May 10, 1983. On Oct. 11 the Supreme Court let the conviction stand. Kelly was sentenced Jan. 12, 1984, to six to 18 months in prison and three years' probation.

Lederer. Lederer was convicted Jan. 9, 1981, of bribery, conspiracy, accepting an illegal gratuity, and interstate travel to aid racketeering. Lederer announced April 29, 1981, his decision to resign from the House, one day after the ethics committee voted 10-2 in favor of expelling him. Lederer resigned effective May 5, 1981. On Aug. 13, 1981, he was sentenced to three years in federal prison, later reduced to one year, and fined $20,000. His conviction was upheld Sept. 3, 1982, by a federal appeals court in New York. The Supreme Court May 31, 1983, refused to hear

Senate Ethics Committee Probe. Although the Ethics Committee began looking at Williams in 1980 after press reports surfaced of his Abscam involvement, the panel delayed a full investigation until after the Justice Department had completed its investigation.

The formal probe began on May 5, 1981, after the committee decided there was "substantial credible evidence" that Williams was guilty of "improper conduct which may reflect upon the Senate" and violations of the Senate's rules on public financial disclosure and conflict of interest.

The committee hearings into misconduct charges against Williams opened July 14. Most of the evidence was in the form of video and audio tapes made by the FBI during its undercover investigation. The tapes had been made public during Williams' court trial.

Williams appeared before the panel July 28, arguing that he should not be punished by the Senate because he had not violated any Senate rules or broken any law. "I did

make mistakes, errors in judgment," Williams told the Ethics panel. "But I tell this committee under oath that . . . I never engaged in any illegal conduct, I never corrupted my office, and I never intended to do anything that would bring dishonor to the Senate."

Williams denied that he had agreed to accept a hidden interest in a Virginia titanium mine in return for a promise to use his influence to obtain government contracts to buy the mine's output. And he denied that he promised to use his influence to help an undercover agent posing as a wealthy Arab to gain permanent U.S. residency. He said he had intended only to help out some old friends who owned the mine to obtain a loan from a wealthy Arab businessman, who turned out to be an FBI agent.

He acknowledged that in his relations with his friends he had been "soft when I should have been strong. I am not a good judge of friends," he said. "I permitted my feelings of friendship to override my good judgment."

Williams also acknowledged that he had boasted of his

... Convicted in Abscam Probe

the case. Lederer was held in the Allenwood, Pa., federal prison camp and was released from a Philadelphia halfway house April 6, 1984.

Murphy and Thompson. Murphy, who was tried with Thompson, was convicted Dec. 3, 1980, of conspiracy, bribery and abetting receipt of an unlawful gratuity. He was found innocent of a charge that he accepted outside compensation for the performance of official duties. Murphy was sentenced Aug. 13, 1981, to three years in prison and fined $20,000. His conviction was upheld Sept. 3, 1982, by a federal appeals court in New York. On May 31, 1983, the Supreme Court rejected his appeal. Murphy served his term at a Danbury, Conn., prison camp and was released March 13, 1985, from a New York halfway house.

Thompson was convicted Dec. 3, 1980, of conspiracy, accepting outside compensation for the performance of outside duties, and receiving an unlawful gratuity. He was cleared of a bribery charge. Thompson was sentenced Aug. 13, 1981, to a maximum 15-year term and fined $40,000 pending medical tests for a heart condition. Federal Judge George C. Pratt emphasized that the maximum sentence was just a technicality. Thompson was resentenced on Oct. 25, 1983, to three years in prison and fined $20,000. A federal appeals court upheld his conviction on Sept. 3, 1982. The Supreme Court May 31, 1983, let that decision stand. In the spring of 1985 Thompson was serving his sentence at the federal penitentiary in Lexington, Ky.

On March 15, 1985, Murphy and Thompson were ordered to repay the government $47,500 — money they were convicted of taking from the undercover agents.

Myers. Myers was convicted Aug. 30, 1980, of bribery, conspiracy and interstate travel to aid racketeering. The House ethics committee voted 11-0 Sept. 16, 1980, that Myers had violated House rules and recommended on a 10-2 vote Sept. 24, 1980, that he be expelled from the House. Myers was expelled Oct. 2, 1980, by a vote of 376-30, well above the two-thirds required by the Constitution. Later that day Myers filed suit in U.S. District Court for the District of Columbia alleging that the House had deprived him of a fair trial before expelling him. The suit was dismissed Jan. 5, 1981. Myers had lost his bid for re-election in November 1980. He was sentenced Aug. 13, 1981, to three years in federal prison and fined $20,000. On Sept. 3, 1982, his conviction was upheld by a federal appeals court in New York; and on May 31, 1983, the Supreme Court refused to hear the case. Myers served his sentence in Allenwood, Pa., and, as of the spring of 1985, was in a Philadelphia halfway house.

Murtha. Murtha, named an unindicted co-conspirator, testified at the trial of Reps. Murphy and Thompson that Thompson had approached him on the House floor in October 1979 to tell him about a business deal with "Arab sheiks" involving $50,000 in "walking around money." An FBI videotape showed Murtha telling FBI agents that he was not interested in taking any cash "at this point." The House ethics committee announced July 28, 1981, that it was ending its investigation of Murtha because it "found on the basis of the evidence presented no reason to issue a statement of alleged violation." The attorney who had conducted the probe for the committee immediately resigned in protest. He had recommended that charges of wrongdoing be voted against Murtha. Murtha was re-elected in 1980, 1982 and 1984 to represent Pennsylvania's 12th District.

influence with high government officials "to an uncomfortable degree" in the presence of the bogus Arab and that he had accepted stock in the mine. But he said he believed the stock certificates to be worthless.

Williams dismissed each incriminating video- or audiotaped statement that had been presented at his trial. Undercover agents had "coached" him into making some of the statements, he said. Others, he maintained, were taken out of context or were merely "wacky" statements he made to impress the supposed Arab.

After a seven-hour, closed-door meeting Aug. 24, 1981, the Ethics Committee concluded that Williams' conduct had been "ethically repugnant" and recommended that he be expelled.

Related Court Action. On Nov. 23, 1981, Williams tried to stop Senate action on his expulsion by filing suit in U.S. District Court for the District of Columbia. He sought an injunction barring the Senate from taking up the expulsion resolution unless Senate leaders agreed to a rehearing of the case before the full Senate. The suit was dismissed Feb. 3, 1982, after U.S. District Judge Louis F. Oberdorfer of the District of Columbia ruled that Williams should have waited to file the suit until after the Senate had turned down his requests.

U.S. District Judge Gerhard A. Gesell Nov. 27, 1981, denied Williams' request for a temporary restraining order to bar the Senate from debating the expulsion resolution. Williams had filed the suit after Senate leaders Nov. 18 refused to allow him to turn the expulsion proceeding into a replay of his court trial and the Ethics Committee hearings. And the committee refused Williams an opportunity to present additional testimony, maintaining that the evidence was not new and did not justify reopening its hearings. But the panel said it had no objection to permitting Williams to present affidavits from witnesses or other written evidence directly to the Senate.

On Dec. 22, 1981, U.S. District Judge George C. Pratt rejected a series of post-trial motions filed by Williams' attorneys following his May conviction. Pratt delayed formally entering the verdict until he had considered those motions. Williams asked the judge to throw out the conviction, acquit him or grant him a new trial. He argued that the government had been overzealous in its pursuit of the Abscam investigation and had deprived him of his due process rights in order to obtain his conviction.

Senate Debate on Expulsion. Senate debate on the expulsion resolution (S Res 204) got underway March 3, 1982. (Debate had been postponed from an earlier date because Williams fell on the ice outside his New Jersey home, which aggravated a hernia condition and required emergency surgery.)

Joining Williams in his defense were Sen. Daniel K. Inouye, D-Hawaii, and Minority Whip Alan Cranston, D-Calif. Inouye had volunteered to act as Williams' counsel during the expulsion proceeding.

The committee's case against Williams was presented March 3 by Vice Chairman Howell Heflin, D-Ala. He argued that the evidence upheld the case against Williams, regardless of the government's conduct.

"At any point in this drawn out, sordid affair," Heflin said, "Sen. Williams could have said, 'Wait a minute. What you're proposing is wrong. This is not what I had in mind. I can't be involved in this.' But he didn't. He stayed; he discussed; he agreed; he promised; he pledged — to abuse his office, his public trust, for which now he must be expelled."

On March 4 Williams pleaded with his colleagues to reject the committee's expulsion recommendation. "I have not committed a crime, nor have I acted improperly," Williams said. He argued that it was government undercover investigators — not himself — who had behaved wrongly. His ensnarement in "the Abscam net," he said, resulted from an attempt by the government "to manufacture crime out of nothing."

Williams had asked the Senate to permit him to speak under oath — in order, he said, to waive "any constitutional protection I might have as a senator" against perjury charges. The Constitution protects members of Congress from prosecution for anything they say on the House or Senate floor.

However, the request was denied. Other senators suggested that an oath on this occasion might suggest that senators would be less truthful in the future if they did not first take an oath. And Majority Leader Howard H. Baker Jr., R-Tenn., told Williams that no oath could override the Constitution.

Williams said the committee's case against him consisted solely of "tainted" government evidence from the FBI investigation. In attempting to incriminate him, he said, the government itself had been guilty of perjury, conspiracy, obstruction of justice, forgery, fraud and impersonation of a foreign dignitary.

Until March 11 Williams stiffly resisted suggestions from several of his colleagues that he resign and save the Senate the anguish of going through an expulsion vote.

Beginning on March 9, senator after senator, among them some of Williams' closest associates, rose to announce that they had decided to vote for expulsion rather than censure. And Baker indicated that a poll of Senate Republicans had found near unanimous support for Williams' expulsion.

Perhaps the most dramatic speech of the entire pro-

Senators Convicted in Office

Sen. Harrison A. Williams Jr., D-N.J., was the fourth senator to have been convicted of criminal wrongdoing while in office.

The last sitting senator to be convicted before Williams was Truman H. Newberry, R-Mich. (1919-22), found guilty in March 1920 of election irregularities.

Newberry's conviction was reversed by the Supreme Court in May 1921. But he resigned his seat in November 1922 after realizing that despite the Supreme Court's finding,"his position could never be other than uncomfortable," according to "Senate Election, Expulsion and Censure Cases" (S Doc 92-7).

The other two sitting senators to have been convicted were:

● John H. Mitchell, R-Ore. (1873-79, 1885-97, 1901-05), convicted in July 1905 on charges of accepting compensation for services rendered before a U.S. department. He died in late 1905 while his conviction was on appeal.

● Joseph R. Burton, R-Kan. (1901-06), convicted in November 1905 for allegedly using the mails for fraudulent purposes and accepting compensation for services rendered before a U.S. department. Burton's conviction was upheld by the Supreme Court in May 1906, and in June he resigned from the Senate and served five months in prison.

---

ceeding occurred when Sen. Thomas F. Eagleton, D-Mo., the self-described "showcase liberal" on the Ethics panel and a longtime associate of Williams, took the floor to say he would vote for expulsion. "I ask 98 of my colleagues," Eagleton said. "Would any of you have engaged in this tawdry, greedy enterprise? . . . Sen. Williams has not had the good grace and good judgment to withdraw from this body. We should not perpetrate our own disgrace by asking him to stay."

Thus by March 11 it had become clear that the Senate would vote for expulsion.

Inouye delivered two lengthy speeches on Williams' behalf. The government's conduct in Abscam, Inouye said, "adds up to an encroachment on the legislative branch that we cannot tolerate if we are to be a separate but equal branch of government."

"None of us is safe. . . . This could have happened to any one of us," Inouye said. "It is only by a very tortured reading [of the evidence] that there is any wrongdoing at all," Inouye said, maintaining that Williams' worst crime might have been that he had behaved like "a fool. I do not feel that a senator should be expelled because he's a fool or did foolish things," Inouye said. "Maybe his most serious crime is that he embarrassed us."

After announcing that he would resign, Williams continued to argue that the Senate had erred in moving "pre-

maturely" toward expelling him before all the evidence was in on possible government misconduct in Abscam. "I did not wish to see the Senate bring dishonor to itself by expelling me," Williams said.

Congressional Criticism of FBI Role

Even though Congress felt it necessary to investigate seven of its members, the government's Abscam operation stirred congressional criticism of the FBI's role. There was wide agreement that the government had misbehaved in pursuing congressional targets of the undercover probe.

Much of the criticism was aimed at the premature leaking of allegations to the news media. Although the FBI probe had been conducted secretly for two years, law enforcement authorities learned in January 1980 that news organizations were preparing reports on the investigation. The authorities decided to abandon the undercover operation, notify the suspects and begin organizing the evidence.

Many members also expressed fear that the FBI had "entrapped" members into breaking the law by its undercover techniques. One House member involved in Abscam, Raymond F. Lederer, D-Pa., for example, used that argument in his defense. Others were concerned about the bureau's use of paid informants.

Senate Probe of FBI Role. Responding to those charges, the Senate March 25, 1982, set up a special committee to study the FBI's role. Composed of four Republicans and four Democrats and chaired by Charles McC. Mathias Jr., R-Md., the panel released its final report on Dec. 16. The report gave Abscam a "mixed review," with the good outweighing the bad.

During its nine-month investigation, the panel found that the Abscam operation had uncovered wrongdoing but that law enforcement agencies did not exert enough management control over the probe.

The report warned of the improper use of undercover techniques that "create risks to citizens' property, privacy and civil liberties, and may compromise law enforcement itself."

The committee found that the central responsibility of those involved with undercover techniques was to create a system that gave the public a balanced program of effective law enforcement and the preservation of civil liberties.

Specifically, the panel recommended a new federal law concerning entrapment and called for a new standard of "reasonable suspicion" before undercover agents offered someone the opportunity to commit a crime.

The panel called on Congress to pass legislation requiring the attorney general to create guidelines governing all undercover operations and to require the FBI, the Drug Enforcement Administration and the Immigration and Naturalization Service to conduct their undercover activities according to the attorney general's guidelines.

Legislation providing guidelines for conducting undercover operations was introduced in the Senate in 1983. In separate action, a House committee considered requiring the FBI to report to Congress on undercover activities. No further action was taken on the proposals during the 98th Congress.

Richmond Resignation

Rep. Fred W. Richmond, D-N.Y. (1975-82), pleaded guilty Aug. 25 in U.S. district court in Brooklyn, N.Y., to income tax evasion, possession of marijuana and making an illegal payment to a government employee. At the same time, he announced his resignation from the House, and, as part of an unusual plea bargain with federal prosecutors, agreed not to run for office again.

In a written statement Richmond said, "These acts to which I have pled guilty were irresponsible, unnecessary, foolish and wrong."

In return for his guilty plea and resignation, the government agreed not to prosecute him for other actions it had been investigating, including cocaine possession and his arranging for a prison escapee, using an alias, to be put on the House payroll.

The House Committee on Standards of Official Conduct, which had been investigating the allegations against Richmond, dropped its probe when he resigned.

The part of the plea bargain involving Richmond's resignation and promise not to run for re-election subsequently was voided by U.S. District Judge Jack B. Weinstein Nov. 10 on grounds that it was an "unconstitutional interference by the executive with the legislative branch of government" and that it "conflicted with the fundamental right of the people to elect their representatives."

Richmond was sentenced by Judge Weinstein to a year and a day in federal prison and fined $20,000. He began his prison sentence at the federal prison camp at Allenwood, Pa., on Dec. 6.

The only felony charge to which he pleaded guilty — tax evasion — involved Richmond's 1980 income, which he admitted in court was understated on his tax return. He did not report funds paid by his company, Walco National Corp., for his New York apartment. This reduced Richmond's tax liability by approximately $50,000.

Richmond had had an earlier brush with the law in 1978, when he was arrested on a morals charge. The charges were dropped after he completed a psychiatric treatment program.

Congressional Pages

Congress in 1982 reassessed its page system after reports were published alleging sexual activity involving pages and members.

A five-month investigation by the House Committee on Standards of Official Conduct (ethics committee) found no truth in the highly publicized allegations of illicit sexual relations, but a special House commission and a Senate management panel recommended changes in the page program, which brought young boys and girls to Washington to run errands for members.

The ethics committee investigation was headed by Joseph A. Califano Jr.

A separate Justice Department investigation into the allegations of homosexual activities between members of Congress and pages was closed Aug. 31 after officials were unable to corroborate charges made by Leroy Williams, a former page.

Williams, 18, claimed he had engaged in homosexual relations with three members of Congress and had arranged a liaison between a senator and a male prostitute. He later admitted he lied about the relationships.

Another page, Jeffrey Opp, 16, described several incidents of homosexual approaches by members of Congress. Opp later said he had exaggerated.

Califano also led an investigation into separate allegations of drug use and its distribution by members and staff. The allegations surfaced about the same time as the sexual misconduct charges. The investigation was concluded in 1983. *(House drug investigation, p. 815)*

Ethics Committee Investigation

The ethics committee investigation began after the House voted 407-1 on July 13 to adopt H Res 518, to authorize an investigation into allegations of:

● Improper or illegal sexual activity by members or congressional employees.

● Illicit use or distribution of drugs by members or employees.

● Preferential treatment by members or employees to those people, including pages, who may have provided either drugs or sexual favors.

In a 114-page preliminary report issued Dec. 14, Califano maintained that the charges were groundless, although he did learn of earlier misconduct. Investigation into this earlier misconduct eventually led to the censures of Reps. Gerry E. Studds, D-Mass., and Daniel B. Crane, R-Ill. *(Story, p. 813)*

Califano said most of the "allegations and rumors of misconduct were the product of teenage exaggeration, gossip, or even out-and-out fabrication that was often repeated mercilessly in a political capital that thrives on rumor."

Although the report dismissed the allegations, it said the lack of after-work supervision for pages was a serious problem.

The committee's final report (H Rept 98-297) was issued July 14, 1983.

The Page System

For most of its history, Congress had employed boys to run errands and do housekeeping chores. In the last decade female pages also had been employed.

During the academic year, there were 101 pages — 30 in the Senate and 71 in the House. Both chambers employed more in the summer. The Senate pages ranged in age from 14 to 18; House pages, from 16 to 18. They were appointed by individual members for periods of a few months to two years and were paid about $750 a month. They had to find their own housing, usually staying in boarding houses or shared apartments. Pages attended school early in the morning at classrooms in the Library of Congress. The school was operated by the District of Columbia public school system.

In 1976 House Doorkeeper James T. Molloy, overseer of the House pages, tried to warn Congress of the "potential time bomb" of unsupervised young pages. In hearings on the page school, Molloy told the House Education and Labor Committee that Congress had authorized construction of a page dormitory in 1970 but never appropriated the money to build it.

Page Program Revisions

The House in 1982 decided, for the third time in 20 years, to undertake an extensive examination of the page system. Speaker Thomas P. O'Neill Jr., D-Mass., in July set up a special Speaker's Commission on Pages, which recommended Aug. 16 that the system be retained but improved.

The Speaker's commission found that the page system was "essential to the efficient functioning of Congress." It rejected proposals to use college students and senior citizens as pages. It said pages should be 11th graders who were at least 16 years old and who would serve for only one semester. The panel also advised that the page school be improved.

The commission recommended that pages be housed in an old hotel that had been converted to House offices. The House in 1982 authorized making two floors of the building into a dormitory. House pages were required to live in the residence hall; Senate pages also could reside there if space was available. The residence hall was staffed by a director and five resident assistants. There was a nightly curfew.

To monitor the page system, the commission recommended the establishment of a Page Board. The board was created (H Res 611) Nov. 30.

A Senate group, the Senate Management Board, July 14 had made recommendations similar to those of the Speaker's commission. The board concluded that only 11th graders should be pages, that they should be housed in a single dormitory and get more supervision, and that their school should be improved. The Senate also established an advisory board.

Congress in 1983 considered, but did not clear, legislation proposing changes in the page system. *(Story, p. 813)*

Senate Television

Although Sen. Howard H. Baker Jr., R-Tenn., made television and radio coverage of Senate proceedings his first legislative priority when he assumed the post of majority leader in January 1981, he was unable to persuade his colleagues to go along.

Two measures to provide TV coverage of Senate debates were approved by the Senate Rules Committee during the 97th Congress, but neither was approved by the full Senate.

The first fell prey to a filibuster led by Russell B. Long, D-La.; the other never was debated by the Senate.

Attempts by Majority Leader Baker in the 98th Congress to win approval of Senate TV coverage also were unsuccessful. *(Story, p. 818)*

The House had had gavel-to-gavel television and radio coverage of its proceedings since 1979. Both chambers continued to prohibit the taking of still pictures by news photographers.

1981 Committee Action

The first broadcast resolution was reported (S Res 20 — S Rept 97-178) by the Senate Rules Committee Aug. 13, 1981. It was approved by voice vote.

The panel earlier had turned down a plan by the committee's ranking Democrat, Wendell H. Ford, Ky., that would have permitted only radio broadcasts. That plan was rejected 5-7 on a straight party-line vote.

S Res 20 called for continuous coverage of the Senate chamber by both television cameras and radio microphones. Broadcast details — such as when coverage would begin and who would own and control the cameras — would be regulated by the Rules Committee.

Committee members debated the cost of the system

and the impact television was likely to have on Senate proceedings. Baker argued that letting in the cameras was "neither radical nor novel" but merely "an extension electronically of the public gallery." Other members, however, suggested that televising floor proceedings might alter the historic character of Senate debate and cost too much.

Capitol Architect George M. White estimated the cost of the necessary broadcast equipment at $2.5 million to $3.5 million and the cost of operating and maintaining the system at $500,000 a year.

Baker announced Nov. 30 that Senate floor consideration of the measure would be put off until 1982 so senators could consider it "without the pressures of the clock."

1982 Senate Floor Action

The Senate Feb. 2, 1982, began preliminary debate on S Res 20. Sen. Long led the Democratic opposition to the plan. Democrats favored an alternative permitting only radio coverage, and perhaps television coverage on an ad hoc basis, of Senate deliberations.

Long argued that televising the Senate would be "a very great mistake and a net minus to the Senate." He said senators would give more frequent and longer speeches and that television would attract senators to the floor when they should be attending committee sessions.

Baker and Rules Committee Chairman Charles McC. Mathias Jr., R-Md., disputed Long's argument. "I do not think we are 100 moths fascinated by the candle of television," Mathias said.

"Whether we like it or not, we are what we are," Baker said. "We are elected by our constituents to serve them according to our talents, our disposition, our convictions. . . . We are a composite cross-section of this nation commissioned to debate the public's business in a public way."

Baker was unsuccessful in his efforts to cut off Long's filibuster. His first cloture motion against the filibuster failed by a 47-51 vote April 20, 13 shy of the 60 votes needed to cut off debate.

Before the Senate could vote on a second cloture motion, Baker reached a compromise with the Democrats that sent the proposal back to the Rules Committee for rewriting. By a 95-1 vote, the Senate April 21 adopted an amendment offered jointly by Baker and Minority Leader Robert C. Byrd, D-W.Va., that gave the committee 60 days to draft a complete plan for broadcast coverage of debates. It required the panel to seek the Senate's final approval of all aspects of the plan before it could be carried out. In addition, it struck from the resolution a requirement that Senate broadcasts provide gavel-to-gavel coverage of the chamber's actions.

Second Broadcast Resolution

The Rules Committee July 21 reported a new broadcast resolution (S Res 436 — S Rept 97-506). The vote was 7-5, divided along party lines. A Ford amendment to allow only radio coverage was rejected also on a party-line vote.

The committee said coverage would not require any changes in existing Senate rules, including those controlling voting and length of speeches.

Television and radio coverage would be gavel-to-gavel to provide a complete documentary, and would be free from editorial analysis. Only the senator actually speaking would be televised. The cameras would not pan the chamber or show the reactions of senators to what was said.

The report said Senate employees would operate the cameras by remote control. Pictures and sound would be provided free to news organizations. Tapes could not be used for political or commercial purposes.

Six cameras would be installed in the Senate chamber. To pay for coverage, the resolution authorized spending of $3.5 million.

In minority views appended to the report, the Democrats said their main reason for opposing television coverage was cost, which they said probably would be closer to $5 million.

The effect of television coverage on the operation of the Senate should be studied, they continued, while radio coverage, which would be relatively inexpensive ($54,000), should be implemented immediately. They argued that the presence of television could lead to more, longer and less relevant speeches, as well as more posturing by senators.

The legislation never came to a floor vote because of the strong opposition, and it died at the end of the 97th Congress.

House Chaplain Vote

By adopting H Res 413 on a 388-0 vote March 30, the House reaffirmed its right to appoint a chaplain and to open each day's session with a prayer.

The symbolic action was intended to signal members' concern over a March 9 decision by the U.S. Court of Appeals for the District of Columbia that could ultimately require both House and Senate to get rid of their chaplains or to stop paying them.

A three-judge panel of the appeals court ruled 2-1 that Congress' appointment of official chaplains was open to challenge on constitutional grounds by ordinary taxpayers.

The resolution said the court ruling "implied a lack of respect" for Congress and declared that the House considered its practice of employing a chaplain to be "an appropriate and constitutional exercise."

The decision came in a suit filed in June 1980 by Madalyn Murray O'Hair, Jon Garth Murray and the Society of Separationists, an atheist organization. The suit charged that using government money to support the chaplains' activities violated the First Amendment requirement that "Congress shall make no law respecting an establishment of religion."

The decision overturned a January 1981 ruling by U.S. District Judge Louis F. Oberdorfer that the suit should be dismissed without consideration of its merits. He ruled that the suit centered on a "political question" inappropriate for the court to judge, and that O'Hair and Murray lacked standing to sue.

The appeals court ruled that Congress could choose its officers and make its rules only so long as the Constitution was not violated. The effect of its ruling was to send the suit back to the district court for a decision of the case on its merits. The government took the case to the full appeals court, which heard arguments Oct. 27 but issued no decision in 1982.

The case was effectively disposed of when the Supreme Court July 5, 1983, upheld as constitutional the "deeply embedded" practice of opening sessions of Congress, the state legislatures and various court proceedings with a prayer. The court ruled 6-3 in *Marsh v. Chambers*, which challenged the Nebraska state Legislature's practice of

opening each session with a prayer by a chaplain paid for by the state. *(Supreme Court decision, p. 739)*

House Bicentennial Office

The House Dec. 17 adopted, 230-97, a resolution (H Res 621) establishing a House Office for the Bicentennial to be staffed by a professional historian appointed by the Speaker. Its purpose was to prepare for the celebration of the 200th anniversary of Congress in 1989.

Sponsors said the historian would be temporary — authority for the office would expire in 1989. A separate resolution (H Res 581) calling for a permanent House historian was defeated in September by a 132-180 vote.

The Senate has had a Historical Office since 1975, at a cost in 1982 of more than $155,000. Opponents of both House resolutions said the measures would cost too much. The expenses and salary of the historian under H Res 621 would come from the contingent fund of the House.

1983

The year opened with organizational rites for the 98th Congress. Benefiting from their 26-seat gain in the 1982 elections, House Democrats increased their majority on almost every House committee. Democratic leaders also forced through a series of changes in House rules, which they deemed necessary to streamline the legislative process.

In the Senate, Majority Leader Howard H. Baker Jr., R-Tenn., had more trouble getting the unruly Senate to work on legislation in a timely fashion. The Senate was repeatedly bogged down by filibusters and time-consuming amendments on major bills. Comprehensive rules changes recommended by two former senators received no action.

The House in July censured Reps. Daniel B. Crane, R-Ill., and Gerry E. Studds, D-Mass., for sexual misconduct with teenage congressional pages. By choosing to censure, the House rejected its ethics committee's recommendation to merely reprimand the two members, a less severe form of punishment.

The Supreme Court sent a tremor through Capitol Hill June 23 when it ruled that the legislative veto was unconstitutional. The veto device, included in some 200 laws over the past 50 years, allowed one or both houses to overturn an executive branch regulation or order. *(Legislative veto special report, p. 833)*

Organization

Senate

Senate Republicans and Democrats selected their leaders for the 98th Congress at party caucuses in December 1982.

Majority Leadership. The Senate Republican Conference unanimously re-elected Howard H. Baker Jr., Tenn., as majority leader; Ted Stevens, Alaska, as majority whip; James A. McClure, Idaho, as Republican Conference chairman; and Jake Garn, Utah, as Republican Conference secretary.

(Baker announced Jan. 21 that he would not seek re-election to the Senate when his term expired in 1985. He was first elected in 1966 and had been the leader of Senate Republicans since 1977, becoming majority leader when the Republicans took control of the Senate in 1981. Robert Dole, Kan., succeeded Baker as majority leader in the 99th Congress.)

The only Republican leader not re-elected was Bob Packwood, Ore., who was stripped of his chairmanship of the National Republican Senatorial Committee Dec. 1. Senate Republicans replaced him with Richard G. Lugar, Ind., by a 29-25 secret vote.

The campaign committee raised cash to help elect and re-elect Republican senators. Packwood headed the committee in 1977, 1978, 1981 and 1982 and was generally credited with turning it into a major fund-raising force. But Packwood had had some public differences with President Reagan.

Minority Leadership. Robert C. Byrd, W.Va., was re-elected minority leader and chairman of the Democratic Conference for the 98th Congress. Alan Cranston, Calif., retained his position as minority whip and Daniel K. Inouye, Hawaii, remained Democratic Conference secretary.

Senate Committees. There were no changes in Senate committee chairmen.

House

House Democrats re-elected all of their leaders for the 98th Congress, including Speaker Thomas P. O'Neill Jr., Mass., and Majority Leader Jim Wright, Texas, during a party caucus in December 1982.

As expected, the House Jan. 3, 1983, re-elected O'Neill as Speaker, a post he had held since 1977. O'Neill got 259 votes, all Democratic, compared with 155 votes, all Republican, for Minority Leader Robert H. Michel, Ill.

House Republicans also re-elected their leaders, including Minority Leader Michel and Minority Whip Trent Lott, Miss., during a party caucus in December.

House Committees. Democrats increased their voting majority on almost every House committee.

The changes resulted primarily from the 26-seat net gain Democrats made in elections to the 98th Congress in November 1982. The 269-166 lineup worked out to 62 percent Democrats and 38 percent Republicans. But on many panels, Democrats Jan. 6 gave themselves a better deal than that ratio would dictate.

In the only chairmanship change, Claude Pepper, D-Fla., was named chairman of the Rules Committee and confirmed by the caucus by a 211-5 vote Jan. 4.

In other action the Democratic Steering and Policy Committee Jan. 3 voted 26-4 to kick Phil Gramm, Texas, off the Budget Committee. Gramm had worked closely with the White House during the 97th Congress, even supplying presidential aides with Democratic budget strategy.

Gramm resigned from the House on Jan. 5, was re-elected as a Republican Feb. 12, and returned to Congress Feb. 22 — and to the Budget Committee as a minority member.

Bob Stump of Arizona, who switched in 1983 from the Democratic to the Republican Party, wound up losing his seat on the Veterans' Affairs Committee because the Democrats gave the GOP four fewer seats than in 1982.

House Rules Changes

After dropping the most controversial of several proposed changes in House rules, Democrats forced a package of changes through the House Jan. 3.

The Democratic leadership maintained the changes were necessary to streamline the legislative process and avoid unnecessary amendments and recorded votes. Republicans said the changes trampled on minority rights.

The most contentious of the new rules was one intended to make it harder for members to offer "limitation riders" to appropriations bills. Such amendments were worded to prohibit spending of funds for specific purposes, such as abortion. They had been used with increasing frequency by Republicans to evade a House ban on legislative amendments to appropriations bills.

The rules changes also gave the Democratic leadership the power to avoid what it viewed as "nuisance" votes on approving the previous day's *Journal* or on the normally routine procedure of resolving into the Committee of the Whole to consider a bill.

The rules package was approved by voice vote after a key procedural vote was won by Democrats, 249-156. Only two Democrats — Phil Gramm of Texas and Larry P. McDonald of Georgia — voted against the leadership.

Study of Senate Operations

Two former senators April 5 recommended sweeping changes in the way the Senate conducted its business. Their recommendations included placing more severe limits on debate, revising rules to ensure attendance, electing a permanent presiding officer, eliminating several standing committees and all staffed subcommittees and overhauling the congressional budget process.

The Committee on Rules and Administration held brief hearings on the recommendations in May, but no action was taken. Former Sens. James B. Pearson, R-Kan. (1962-78), and Abraham Ribicoff, D-Conn. (1963-81), conducted the study, which was ordered by the Senate in 1982.

While acknowledging that their proposals could be considered "quite radical," Pearson and Ribicoff said the basic nature of the Senate would not be changed, even though "these recommendations do represent a dramatic change in the daily life of the Senate and in how the Senate and its committee system work." The Senate in 1985 was expected to consider changes in its committee system, as recommended by a special Senate panel created in 1984 and headed by Dan Quayle, R-Ind.

House Sex Scandal

For the first time in the history of the House, two representatives in 1983 were censured for sexual misconduct. In separate votes July 20, the House censured Gerry E. Studds, D-Mass., and Daniel B. Crane, R-Ill., for sexual misconduct with teenage congressional pages. *(Previous House censures, Congress and the Nation Vol. V, p. 923)*

In voting to censure the two members, the House overturned a Committee on Standards of Official Conduct (ethics committee) recommendation that the two representatives be reprimanded. A reprimand was the least severe form of punishment the House could impose.

The penalty associated with either a reprimand or

Bomb Explosion in Capitol

On the evening of Nov. 7, 1983, a powerful bomb exploded in the second floor hallway of the Capitol near the office of Senate Minority Leader Robert C. Byrd, D-W.Va., about 30 feet from the Senate chamber.

The blast caused no injuries but brought the fear of terrorism home to employees at the Capitol.

A group called the Armed Resistance Unit claimed responsibility, saying the bombing was a protest against U.S. military "aggression" in Grenada and Lebanon.

Not long before the bombing, some members of Congress had warned of the possibility of a terrorist strike against the Capitol because of political violence overseas and at home. Capitol Police, armed with a new Secret Service study of security problems in the Capitol, had begun to implement extra security measures shortly before the explosion occurred. More elaborate and costly antiterrorist protective steps were taken after Congress adjourned for the year Nov. 18.

Political violence, and the increased security that followed it, were not new to Congress. The last time the Capitol was bombed, in 1971, lawmakers virtually doubled the size of the Capitol police force (the force stood at 1,222 in 1983) and spent over $4 million on new security equipment. *(1971 Capitol bombing, Congress and the Nation Vol. III, p. 372)*

The 1983 explosion blew out a wall partition and sent a shower of splintered wood, plaster and brick flying across the hall, shattering the windows of the Republican cloakroom. Furniture and walls in the cloakroom were peppered with the glass and rubble.

The doors to Byrd's office were blown off their hinges, nearby windows were blown out and surrounding walls were pockmarked with fist-sized holes. Major damage was done to arches, walls and the glazed-tile floor near the blast, but there was no structural damage to the building.

---

censure was public condemnation. But a censured member, in addition, was required to appear in the well of the House to hear the charges read against him or her.

Under the rules of the House Democratic Caucus, a censured Democrat also lost any chairmanship of a committee or subcommittee that the member held. As a result, Studds was removed as chairman of the Merchant Marine and Fisheries Committee's Coast Guard and Navigation Subcommittee.

The House's action capped a year-long investigation by the ethics panel into allegations of sexual misconduct and drug use by members and congressional pages. The

investigation was led by special counsel Joseph A. Califano Jr., who served as secretary of health, education and welfare in the Carter administration.

Reports on Studds, Crane

On July 14, 1983, the ethics committee issued its report (H Rept 98-297) on the investigation, along with separate reports on Studds (H Rept 98-295) and Crane (H Rept 98-296). The committee asserted that both Studds and Crane had had sexual relationships with teenage pages and thus had committed a "serious breach of duty owed by the House and its individual members to the young people who serve the House as its pages."

The panel reported that in 1973 Studds had a sexual relationship with a 17-year-old male page, who might have been 16 at the time the relationship began. In addition, the committee said Studds made sexual advances on two other male pages in 1973. Studds told his House colleagues July 14 that he was gay.

Crane, the panel said, had a sexual relationship with a 17-year-old female page in 1980. Since the legal age of consent in the District of Columbia was 16, the panel accused neither Studds nor Crane of a crime. Nevertheless, the panel felt that any sexual relationship, consensual or not, between a member and a page constituted improper sexual conduct.

Also on July 14, the panel voted to initiate disciplinary proceedings against James Howarth, former chief page in the House Doorkeeper's Office. According to the report, Howarth had a sexual relationship in 1980 with a female page under his direct supervision, and he gave her preferential treatment. The report also charged Howarth with purchasing cocaine in the House cloakroom from a former House employee. The committee Nov. 15 recommended that Howarth be dismissed; he subsequently resigned.

In choosing an appropriate penalty for Studds and Crane, Califano cited as precedents the two most recent cases of censure and expulsion, those of Charles H. Wilson, D-Calif. (1963-81), censured in 1980 for bribery, and Michael "Ozzie" Myers, D-Pa. (1976-80), convicted on Abscam bribery charges and expelled in 1980. Califano concluded, "Measured against the precedents, neither expulsion nor censure is warranted." He recommended a reprimand, and the committee agreed by an 11-1 vote. *(Wilson censure, Congress and the Nation Vol. V, p. 936; Myers expulsion, box, p. 806)*

A reprimand was not enough for some members. "I want to change the precedent," Newt Gingrich, R-Ga., said.

Studds announced July 19 that he had no intention of resigning. (Studds was re-elected in 1984; Crane lost his re-election bid.)

Censure Votes

In the House debate on the ethics committee's recommendation, Gingrich reiterated his charge that a reprimand was too mild. "With no malice toward any individual," he said, "I cannot see how a reprimand is in any way adequate." Gingrich wanted the two expelled.

Those who felt Studds and Crane deserved only a reprimand insisted that the punishment was indeed severe. "The member must live with this condemnation forever," said ethics committee Chairman Louis Stokes, D-Ohio.

Before the House could vote on the committee's recommendations, House Minority Leader Robert H. Michel, R-Ill., moved to change the recommendation from reprimand to censure. Michel said he sensed that members wanted a more severe punishment.

Michel's motion in Crane's case (H Res 266) was agreed to 289-136. The censure resolution then was adopted 421-3.

In Studds' case (H Res 265), Michel's motion was agreed to 338-87, and the House voted to censure Studds by a 420-3 vote.

Crane voted for his own censure. Studds voted "present" when the House voted on his censure.

Crane, who admitted to having a sexual relationship with a 17-year-old female page, approached the well of the House, then faced his silent colleagues as Speaker Thomas P. O'Neill Jr., D-Mass., read the resolution of censure to him. Studds, who the ethics committee found had a sexual relationship with a male page, faced the Speaker, hands clasped behind him, as O'Neill read his resolution of censure.

Congressional Pages

As an outgrowth of the ethics investigation, Congress in 1983 considered changes in the congressional page system. Under legislation (HR 3034) passed May 18 by the House and reported July 28 in the Senate (S Rept 98-201), pages would be appointed for up to one year, during their junior year in high school. *(Background, p. 809)*

The bill would permit Congress the flexibility to contract with the Washington, D.C., public school system or some other entity for schooling of congressional pages. It also would repeal permission for minor employees of members or committees to attend the page school.

The full Senate did not act on the legislation, and it died at the end of the 98th Congress.

Transcript Alterations

The House Committee on Standards of Official Conduct (ethics committee) in 1983 investigated charges of improper changes made in transcripts of committee proceedings.

In a report (H Rept 98-544) issued Nov. 9, the committee found "absolutely no evidence whatsoever of a pattern of improper alteration" of transcripts, but it recommended committees clarify how far they wanted to go in routine smoothing out of grammar and diction.

The ethics panel, however, did find improper changes made in the record of a bitterly partisan July 1982 joint hearing by four subcommittees on Environmental Protection Agency (EPA) actions. Those changes, it found, were made by Lester O. Brown, who resigned Sept. 2 from the staff of the House Government Operations Subcommittee on Energy, Environment and Natural Resources. Brown had been hired in May 1980 by subcommittee Chairman Toby Moffett, D-Conn.

Government Operations Committee Chairman Jack Brooks, D-Texas, said Brown told him "he personally had made unofficial changes in the record of a hearing conducted last year."

The ethics committee probe began after Republicans charged that their remarks in a hearing transcript entitled "EPA Oversight: One Year Review" had been changed in such a way as to make them look foolish. The hearing was held jointly July 21-22, 1982, by five subcommittees, one

from Government Operations and two each from Energy and Commerce and from Science and Technology.

When the record was published in May, an aide to Robert S. Walker, R-Pa., noticed one of Walker's comments had been changed from "Many members of the other party know that I am willing to take part in reasonable hearings," to "Many members of the other party know that I am *not* willing to take part in reasonable hearings."

Walker and others first asked the Science committee and then the full House to conduct an open investigation, but the House voted 409-0 June 30 to authorize an ethics committee investigation, which was done behind closed doors.

House Drug Investigation

The House Standards of Official Conduct Committee (ethics committee) ended a 16-month investigation into congressional drug use with a report, issued Nov. 17, that said there was insufficient evidence to conclude that allegations of drug use by two members of the House and by one former member were true.

The committee noted allegations against Reps. Ronald V. Dellums, D-Calif., and Charles Wilson, D-Texas, but found the evidence too skimpy to seek House action against them.

The Justice Department had announced July 27 that it had found insufficient evidence to prosecute Dellums, Wilson or former Rep. Barry M. Goldwater Jr., R-Calif. (1969-83), on cocaine charges.

All three men maintained their innocence of the allegations.

The ethics committee report (H Rept 98-559) said the panel had found "substantial evidence" that three former representatives either purchased or used cocaine or marijuana while they served in the House between 1978 and 1982. However, the committee did not name the three and, citing past House policy, did not pursue an investigation of former members.

Allegations of drug use by members and staff surfaced during the summer of 1982 at about the same time as the charges of sexual misconduct involving members and teenage pages. The ethics committee investigated both sets of allegations simultaneously. It hired Joseph A. Califano Jr. as its chief investigator. *(Page scandal, p. 809)*

The committee's findings on the page scandal led to the censure of Reps. Gerry E. Studds, D-Mass., and Daniel B. Crane, R-Ill. *(Studds, Crane censure, p. 813)*

The ethics committee recommended:

● The House leadership should assure that the capacity existed — either within the Capitol Police or another law enforcement agency — to carry out criminal investigations, including drug investigations, at the Capitol.

● The House should establish employee assistance programs to provide counseling and guidance to employees who had drug or alcohol problems.

● The House should establish fair and effective procedures for disciplining and discharging employees accused of misconduct.

West Front Restoration

A 20-year dispute between the House and Senate over the west front of the Capitol finally was resolved in 1983.

The House ended the two-decades-old stalemate by agreeing to provide $49 million to restore the deteriorating west central wall, the last exposed portion of the original building constructed between 1793 and 1829.

Maintenance on the wall, made of soft Aquia Creek sandstone on the exterior and brick and stone on the interior, had been put off repeatedly. It had been shored up twice with timbers.

For years, a majority of the House preferred a plan to extend the west front, providing additional offices for members and facilities for greeting tourists. A 32-foot extension of the east front was built between 1958 and 1962 at a cost of $11,383,000.

In 1972 the House approved $58 million for extension of the west front, but the Senate blocked the appropriation. The Senate opposed various extension plans, including a compromise providing 147,000 square feet of additional space that was drawn up in 1976 by George M. White, the architect of the Capitol.

In 1977 Congress established a Commission on the West Central Front of the United States Capitol, composed of the House and Senate Republican and Democratic leaderships, to resolve the controversy. The leadership of both parties favored some form of extension but never succeeded in winning over the Senate. *(Background, Congress and the Nation Vol. IV, p. 759)*

1983 Legislative Action

The House Appropriations Committee revived the controversy in May by approving $70.5 million to renovate and extend the west front. The money was added to a fiscal 1983 supplemental funding bill (HR 3069).

A committee amendment to reduce the bill's $70.5 million for an extension to $49 million — the amount estimated to be needed to repair the existing sandstone wall — was rejected.

However, the House on May 25 overturned the committee's action and overwhelmingly approved $49 million to be used only for repairing the wall. The House vote was 325-86.

Heavy lobbying by the American Institute of Architects and the National Trust for Historic Preservation convinced the House to reject the committee's extension plans.

The Senate June 16 accepted the House action without opposition. And it strengthened the restoration decision by adopting an amendment providing for a consulting architect to assist the Commission on the West Central Front of the Capitol in supervising the repair work.

The bill containing the restoration funds was enacted into law July 30 (PL 98-63).

Restoration work on the west front began in October 1983 and was expected to be completed by November 1987, according to the office of the Architect of the Capitol. *(Capitol Hill development plan, p. 803)*

Senate Day-Care Program

A day-care center for the children of Senate employees was authorized by the Senate Nov. 14, along with $20,000 in start-up costs for the program.

The Senate voted 50-31 to approve a resolution (S Res 269) establishing the child care center. The money came from Senate contingency funds.

The center, which was scheduled to open in January 1984 in a Senate annex, eventually would be self-supporting.

The House did not have a day care program of its own.

1984

The final session of the 98th Congress, which adjourned Oct. 12, was marred by election-year acrimony and repeated legislative stalemate. For the first time since 1978 lawmakers did not return to Washington for a post-election lame-duck session. *(Lame-duck sessions, p. 975)*

In the Senate, filibuster threats and drawn-out negotiations slowed work on almost every major piece of legislation considered during the year. Impending retirement limited the influence of Majority Leader Howard H. Baker Jr., R-Tenn., and White House intransigence hindered Republican solidarity on some major issues. In the House, the Democratic leadership faced challenges from junior members of its own party, as well as strident attacks from conservative Republicans.

Televising congressional proceedings was a volatile issue in both chambers in 1984. With his term about to run out, Baker made one last effort to convince his colleagues to allow television and radio coverage of the Senate. Such coverage was Baker's pet project, but he conceded defeat after a weeklong filibuster on the issue. In the House, where live broadcasts had begun in 1979, a group of Young Turk Republicans began using them to promote their conservative agenda. After months of needling, Democrats began to protest. An angry shouting match on the House floor May 15 between Speaker Thomas P. O'Neill Jr., D-Mass., and Rep. Newt Gingrich, R-Ga., led to the official chastisement of the Speaker for using derogatory words about another member. The clash symbolized the polarization between Democrats and Republicans that lasted all year.

Although there were no changes in the House and Senate power structure in 1984, the way was paved for several key leadership changes in succeeding years. In organizational meetings held late in the year for the 99th Congress, Senate Republicans selected a forceful new leader — Robert Dole, R-Kan. — who was expected to discipline Senate operations and stand up to the White House on divisive issues. Although he was challenged by Lawton Chiles, D-Fla., Robert C. Byrd, D-W.Va., was re-elected minority leader. The fact that there was a contest at all reflected the degree of discontent within the party.

Despite considerable ferment for change, Democrats in the House left their leadership and rules essentially intact, but internal Democratic maneuvering was intensified by O'Neill's decision to retire at the end of the 99th Congress. House Republicans likewise made no leadership changes.

House Television Dispute

Televised coverage of House proceedings, which began in 1979, created little controversy in its first five years in operation. But partisan skirmishes erupted in 1984 when conservative Republicans started delivering speeches, geared for the television audience, attacking and trying to embarrass House Democrats, particularly the leadership, and promoting their own political agenda.

Gavel-to-gavel coverage of the House was beamed to about 17 million homes nationwide by the Cable Satellite Public Affairs Network, or C-SPAN. According to estimates by Newt Gingrich, R-Ga., some 200,000 people might be watching the House on TV at any moment.

"That's not a bad crowd," boasted Gingrich, a leader of the self-styled Republican guerrillas. "This is the beginning of the ability to have a nationwide town meeting."

Almost every day the House was in session in 1984, Republicans, at the close of the day's legislative business when most members had left the chamber, attacked the Democrats in speeches called "special orders." The stated aim of Gingrich and about a dozen other junior Republicans was to bring before the House the conservatives' legislative agenda. But beyond that, their goal was to put the Democrats on the defensive on such volatile issues as school prayer and abortion.

Their strategy took its toll on the day-to-day operation of the House. No one expected the 1984 election year to be friendly, but few thought the House's veneer of courtesy would shatter so easily. Republicans called the Democrats "dictators" and "cheaters." Democrats retorted that the GOP agitators were "obnoxious" and "phony."

On May 8 Gingrich and Robert S. Walker, R-Pa., used a special order to read into the *Congressional Record* a study critical of Democrats' foreign policy statements over the past 15 years. The report by the conservative Republican Study Committee named about 50 House Democrats, some of whom later charged that it contained innuendos that smacked of McCarthyism.

Several Democrats complained to Speaker Thomas P. O'Neill Jr., D-Mass., that they had no chance to defend themselves during the special orders, which started at about 7:30 p.m. Gingrich later said he sent letters alerting each Democrat named in the report that it would be read, but several said they never received notice.

O'Neill, who under House rules controlled the television cameras, unilaterally decided May 10 to have the cameras pan the chamber during special orders to show that the room was often empty. Previously, the cameras had focused only on the member speaking.

Explaining his decision May 14, O'Neill said the GOP speechmaking was "a sham," and the public should know "when it's after hours, it's for home consumption."

When Gingrich appeared on the House floor the next day and defended the Republicans' foreign policy paper, O'Neill lost his temper. He charged that Gingrich had challenged "the Americanism" of Democrats named in the study, and he said, "It's the lowest thing I have ever seen in my 32 years in Congress."

O'Neill was officially chastised for using derogatory words about a member. Congressional researchers said he was the first Speaker since 1797 to be rebuked for his language.

Things became even more bitter on May 30, when the National Republican Congressional Committee began airing two 30-second television commercials that accused O'Neill of breaking House rules, falsifying records and bottling up legislation.

"Is this the way our Founding Fathers meant for things to be?" an announcer asked in one ad, as the camera focused on a portrait of George Washington, a tear welling up in his eye.

Guy Vander Jagt, R-Mich., chairman of the GOP cam-

President's Pocket-Veto Power

A federal appeals court ruled Aug. 29, 1984, that President Reagan acted unconstitutionally when he pocket-vetoed legislation in November 1983 that linked U.S. aid to El Salvador with progress in human rights there.

In a 2-1 decision, a panel of the U.S. Court of Appeals for the District of Columbia ruled that Reagan did not have the authority to veto the bill (HR 4042) by "pocketing" it — taking no action — between two sessions of the same Congress. *(El Salvador certification issue, p. 165)*

The Justice Department in early 1985 petitioned for a rehearing of the case before the full appeals court.

The decision came in a lawsuit filed by Rep. Michael D. Barnes, D-Md., and 32 other House Democrats. The full House and Senate later joined the case as plaintiffs.

Barnes, chairman of the Foreign Affairs Subcommittee on Western Hemisphere Affairs, had sponsored HR 4042.

The decision overturned a March 9 ruling by U.S. District Court Judge Thomas P. Jackson, who held that a president may exercise a pocket veto when Congress is between sessions, as Reagan did in 1983 when he refused to sign HR 4042 during the Thanksgiving-Christmas recess between the first and second sessions of the 98th Congress.

Constitution's Pocket-Veto Clause

At issue in the case was whether the president can pocket-veto a bill between the first and second session of a two-year term of Congress or during other intrasession recesses, or whether the pocket veto may be used only after Congress has adjourned at the end of a two-year congressional term.

The question involved a president's options after Congress had sent him a bill for his signature. When the legislature is in session, the president has 10 days, excluding Sundays, to sign a bill or veto it; a vetoed bill is returned to Congress with an explanation detailing the reasons for rejecting it. If the president neither signs nor vetoes a measure within the 10-day period while Congress is in session, it automatically becomes law.

However, Article I, Section 7, of the U.S. Constitution provides that a bill "shall not be a law" if "Congress by their adjournment prevent its return." With Congress not meeting, the president can, by declining to act, pocket-veto the bill because he does not have an opportunity to return it to Congress with his objections.

Attorneys for the members of Congress argued that Reagan should have used a normal veto procedure, which gives Congress a chance to override a veto by a two-thirds majority vote in both houses. They said a pocket veto may be used only if the return of a bill is "prevented" by Congress' final adjournment.

With HR 4042, congressional attorneys said, return was not prevented because both chambers appointed officers to receive presidential messages while Congress was away, and it was possible to reconvene members at the call of the leadership.

Background

From 1789 to 1980, presidents had vetoed 2,391 bills, 1,011 by pocket veto. President James Madison issued the first pocket veto in 1812.

Reagan, in his first term, had pocket-vetoed seven bills, but other than the El Salvador measure only one was between sessions of the same Congress. That veto was in December 1981 on a bankruptcy bill. *(Reagan vetoes, p. 1031)*

The precedent in law for the Constitution's pocket veto clause was set by a 1929 Supreme Court decision. In that case, based on President Calvin Coolidge's veto of an Indian claims bill during a four-month congressional recess, the court upheld the president's authority to pocket-veto a bill between sessions of the same Congress. The justices held that the term "adjournment" applied to any congressional break preventing the return of a bill within a 10-day period.

Questions arose in the early 1970s about what kind of a congressional adjournment "prevents" the return of a bill by the president. Court decisions in 1974 and 1976 specified that a president's power to use the pocket veto was restricted to final adjournments of Congresses.

The 1974 decision by the U.S. Court of Appeals for the District of Columbia stemmed from a lawsuit by Sen. Edward M. Kennedy, D-Mass., challenging President Nixon's use of a pocket veto during a six-day recess. The bill involved was a medical training measure. The appeals court upheld Kennedy's challenge and ruled that Nixon had improperly used his pocket-veto power.

Two years later, in another suit brought by Kennedy, the U.S. District Court for the District of Columbia broadened the first ruling. The court said pocket vetoes could not be used during adjournments between sessions of Congress or within a session if both chambers appointed agents to receive presidential messages. *(Congress and the Nation Vol. IV, p. 975)*

President Ford agreed not to use the pocket veto when Congress had appointed officials to receive veto messages. President Carter did not use any intersession pocket vetoes.

paign committee, said the $17,000 ad program was designed to show the public that "something is very wrong" in the House.

"It's not just the Speaker. It's the whole House that is out of order," Vander Jagt said.

The fight between O'Neill and Gingrich was the most venomous floor exchange observers had seen in years. And it signaled a polarization between Democrats and Republicans that lasted for the remainder of the year.

At year's end, Democrats debated but could not agree on a limit on special orders to prevent Republicans from using the free air time unchecked.

Senate TV Coverage

On Sept. 21 the Senate denied Majority Leader Howard H. Baker Jr., R-Tenn., his dream of bringing the chamber into the television age. By a 37-44 vote, senators rejected a cloture motion, drafted by Baker, to stop a weeklong filibuster against a resolution (S Res 66) to allow television and radio coverage of Senate debates — he retired from the Senate at the end of the year. Similar proposals died at the end of the 97th Congress. *(Earlier Baker TV efforts, p. 810)*

1983 Legislative Action

H Res 66 had been cleared for floor action by the Rules and Administration Committee June 15, 1983. By a 5-3 vote the committee sent S Res 66 to the Senate without a recommendation. The resolution was substantially the same as a measure it reported in July 1982.

S Res 66 allowed unedited, gavel-to-gavel television and radio coverage. The resolution required no Senate rules changes and permitted the camera to focus only on the senator who was recognized to speak. It prohibited the political or commercial use of tapes but would have provided them free to news organizations. (House rules prohibited members from using the tapes in their campaigns, but there were no restrictions on their use by non-incumbents.)

Senate opposition to the concept never waned, however. To ensure that the resolution would be cleared for floor debate by the committee, Baker omitted the word "favorably" in moving to report the measure. Mark O. Hatfield, R-Ore., who agreed to send the measure to the Senate, had indicated he would vote against it. Hatfield said television coverage might "reduce our stature."

Congressional Ethics Violations

Two representatives and one senator were investigated by congressional ethics committees in 1984. As a result of those probes:

● Rep. George Hansen, R-Idaho, was reprimanded by the House after he was convicted of violating the 1978 Ethics in Government Act.

● Rep. Geraldine A. Ferraro, D-N.Y., was found by the House Committee on Standards of Official Conduct (ethics committee) to have technically violated the same law.

● Sen. Mark O. Hatfield, R-Ore., was investigated by the Senate Ethics Committee staff because of questions arising

from his dealings with a Greek businessman. However, the committee found there was insufficient evidence of wrongdoing against Hatfield to justify a full-scale inquiry.

Hansen

The House July 31 reprimanded Hansen for failing to reveal various financial dealings as required to be disclosed under the 1978 Ethics in Government Act (PL 95-521). Hansen's conviction and reprimand stemmed from his failure to report nearly $334,000 in loans and profits between 1978 and 1981. A seven-term House member, Hansen was sentenced June 15 to between five and 15 months in prison and a $40,000 fine following his April 2 federal felony conviction on the disclosure charges. Hansen appealed his conviction, the first ever under the 1978 law. He was narrowly defeated in his re-election bid Nov. 6.

In reprimanding Hansen, the House handed down its mildest form of punishment. It also could have censured him or expelled him from office. The vote for a reprimand was 354-52 with six members voting present.

Leaders of the House ethics committee, which had recommended the reprimand by an 11-1 vote, used a parliamentary tactic to block a House vote to change the penalty to a censure or to include other House members.

During the debate, a defiant Hansen maintained his innocence, insisting that Reagan administration officials and other members of Congress had been caught in questionable financial reporting snags similar to his.

Hansen's 1984 conviction was not his first legal problem. In 1975 Hansen pleaded guilty to two misdemeanor charges of filing late and false campaign finance reports from his 1974 House primary. He received a two-month prison sentence that was suspended and instead paid a $2,000 fine.

Ferraro

The House ethics committee ruled Dec. 3 that Ferraro had technically violated government ethics laws about 10 times in failing to report or reporting incorrectly a number of items on her financial disclosure forms from 1978 through 1983.

The committee's vote, reportedly 8-2, was taken in secret.

No action was taken against Ferraro before her term expired Jan. 3, 1985. She had given up her House seat to run for vice president. The panel decided the House would not be able to act on the complaint against her while she was still a member.

Ferraro told reporters she felt "completely vindicated" by the ethics committee's report.

The 46-page report also concluded that Ferraro failed to meet the standards necessary for claiming to exempt her husband's financial interests from her financial disclosure forms. But the panel did not investigate that question.

Hatfield

The Senate ethics committee voted unanimously Sept. 25 that there was not enough evidence linking Hatfield to wrongdoing to warrant a full-scale investigation.

In July 1984 news reports linked the senator's assistance to Greek entrepreneur Basil A. Tsakos with Tsakos' $55,000 payment to Hatfield's wife, Antoinette. Hatfield,

chairman of the Senate Appropriations Committee, was subsequently investigated to determine whether there was any improper connection between his support of a trans-African oil pipeline promoted by Tsakos and the money Tsakos paid Mrs. Hatfield.

The senator insisted his wife legitimately earned the $55,000 for real estate work she did for Tsakos.

Hatfield later said it was a "mistake" for his wife to accept the money at a time when the senator was supporting Tsakos' trans-African pipeline in Congress.

But Hatfield maintained there was "nothing unethical or illegal" about his support for the pipeline and that his wife's real estate business was separate from his work as a senator.

Williams' Campaign Funds

On May 3 the Senate Ethics Committee announced it was ending an investigation into allegations that former Sen. Harrison A. Williams Jr., D-N.J., had converted campaign contributions to his personal use. Williams had resigned from the Senate in March 1982 after being convicted on charges stemming from Abscam, the FBI undercover probe into political corruption. *(Williams resignation, p. 804)*

Ted Stevens, R-Alaska, who took over the Ethics chairmanship at the start of the 98th Congress, said the committee found no evidence that Williams had "pocketed" campaign funds in violation of Senate rules.

Chronology
Of Action
On Congress:
Pay and Benefits

1981

Congressional Pay

Members of Congress shied away from voting themselves a direct salary increase in 1981, but they did take other action that increased their take-home pay.

Members sought to avoid taking a stand on raising their own salaries, knowing that such a move would be unpopular because of the fierce budget cutting the Reagan administration was exacting from virtually every government agency.

Members, however, used the fiscal 1982 legislative branch appropriations bill, which was included in a fiscal 1982 continuing appropriations resolution, as a vehicle for increasing their earnings above their 1981 salary of $60,622.50: a 30-year-old business tax deduction, which senators and representatives were allowed to take while working in Washington, D.C., as public officials, was expanded; a permanent funding mechanism for pay raises for members was established; and a $25,000 cap on Senate honoraria earnings was removed.

Provisions

As signed into law Oct. 1, the congressional pay benefits provisions of the continuing appropriations resolution (H J Res 325 — PL 97-51):

● Removed the existing $3,000 ceiling — in effect since 1952 — on the amount of business-related tax deductions members of Congress could claim for the period they spent working in Washington, D.C. *(Congress and the Nation Vol. I, p. 1429)*

The Joint Committee on Taxation estimated that the more liberal deduction provided a typical member in the 45 percent tax bracket with the equivalent of a $10,500 annual pay raise.

PL 97-51 made the change effective at the start of 1982. But on Dec. 11, 1981, Congress adopted an amendment to another emergency appropriations resolution (H J Res 370 — PL 97-92), making the deduction retroactive to cover calendar year 1981.

Because the new tax break was found to conflict with a provision of a 1976 tax law (PL 94-455), Congress attached language to a black lung benefits bill (HR 5159 — PL 97-119), broadening the effect of the tax deduction provision of PL 97-51, to allow taxpayers to deduct the cost of maintaining a second home for business purposes when it also was used as a residence. While applying to all taxpayers, the primary beneficiaries of this provision were members of Congress, who under existing law could not deduct such expenses if their families resided with them in Washington for more than 14 days. *(Black lung bill, p. 649)*

PL 97-119 also directed the Treasury secretary to determine the "appropriate" amount a member could deduct for business expenses while Congress was in session without having to substantiate them. The Treasury regulations were issued in 1982.

Reacting to strong public sentiment against the higher tax deductions, Congress in 1982 reinstated the $3,000 limit and made it effective Jan. 1, 1982. *(Story, p. 829)*

● Established a permanent mechanism for future pay hikes of members of Congress. Lawmakers returned to a previously used procedure whereby members received the annual governmentwide comparability pay increases without either chamber having to vote on the raise. In 1975 Congress had voted to include itself, other high-ranking federal officials and judges among government workers automatically receiving the comparability (now generally referred to as cost-of-living) raises. In 1977 Congress modified the procedure by requiring senators and representatives to vote on whether to accept the annual pay adjustments. (Four times, in 1977, 1978, 1980 and 1981, members had voted to block the raises.) PL 97-51, in effect, returned to the pay procedure that was in effect in 1975-76. Funds for congressional pay increases would automatically be appropriated. Members did not have to vote on approving the additional funds. Members, however, still could vote not to accept the automatic raises. The revised procedure took effect beginning with fiscal 1983.

● Removed the $25,000 limit on the amount senators could earn in honoraria — giving speeches, writing articles, making appearances — established in the 1976 Federal Election Campaign Act Amendments (PL 94-283). The restrictions on senators' earned income were lifted effective at the beginning of 1981.

Although PL 97-51 revoked the statutory limit on Senate earned income, it did not effect a Senate rule establishing an honoraria limit of 15 percent of a senator's salary that was scheduled to take effect in 1983. Congress in 1982 repealed the Senate rule. *(Story, p. 829)*

The provision also did not affect House members, who were restricted by a separate rule limiting their outside earnings to a maximum of 15 percent of their congressional salary, or $9,099.37. After failing in one attempt to loosen that restriction in 1981, members agreed at year's end to boost the limit to 30 percent. *(Story, p. 823)*

House Action

Committee. During House Appropriations Committee consideration of the fiscal 1982 legislative branch funding bill, Committee Chairman Jamie L. Whitten, D-Miss., attempted to push through repeal of the $3,000 ceiling on members' deductions for business-related expenses. The committee, however, refused to go along. Such a change, Whitten argued, would "put members on the same footing as private businessmen" in their ability to deduct living expenses while working away from home. It was backed by Silvio O. Conte, Mass., the ranking Republican on the Appropriations panel, and by Dan Rostenkowski, D-Ill., chairman of the House Ways and Means Committee.

In other action, the committee by voice vote reluctantly approved an amendment continuing a freeze on the salaries of all high-level federal employees — those earning $50,112.50 or more a year — including members of Congress. That freeze had been in effect since October 1979,

when Congress approved a 5.5 percent comparability increase. That action had raised members' salaries from $57,500 to $60,662.50 a year.

House committee members who chose to speak on the matter of pay generally supported the increase as well as the additional tax break. But when it came to a vote, the support dried up. Whitten did not even press for a vote, blaming the situation on media publicity.

The fiscal 1982 legislative funding bill was reported July 9 (HR 4120 — H Rept 97-170).

Floor. By mid-September, with the end of the fiscal year fast approaching, the money bill for the legislative branch still had not been considered by the House. So on Sept. 14 the Appropriations Committee tacked it onto the stopgap funding resolution (H J Res 325), which then was passed by the House Sept. 16 without further amendment.

Senate Action

Committee. The Senate Appropriations Committee adopted, 10-8, a Ted Stevens, R-Alaska, amendment removing the $25,000 annual ceiling on senators' honoraria earnings.

The panel tacked the legislative branch appropriations measure onto its continuing resolution before reporting it Sept. 23.

Floor. When the bill reached the full Senate, Majority Whip Stevens, who had tried unsuccessfully in 1980 to use a similar continuing resolution as a vehicle for a congressional pay raise, succeeded this time in eliminating the ceilings on members' allowable tax deductions and on outside earned income.

Eliminating the $3,000 limit on job-related tax deductions, Stevens said, would allow members of Congress to be treated "the same as all other citizens who are away from home on business." He argued that the $3,000 limit was not nearly enough to cover the high costs of living in or near the nation's capital. He said that repeal would help relieve the heavy burden on members of maintaining homes both in Washington and in their states or districts.

The amendment first was ruled out of order on grounds that it was legislation in an appropriations bill, a violation of congressional rules. Stevens, however, appealed, and the ruling was overturned by the Senate, 44-54.

The vote on the amendment itself was 48-48 at the end of the regulation time for a vote. But after a lengthy delay, Majority Leader Howard H. Baker Jr., R-Tenn., and Russell B. Long, D-La., cast their votes for the amendment, and it carried, 50-48.

William Proxmire, D-Wis., attempted to undo the committee's decision on senators' honoraria. He offered an amendment to delete the provision, but it was rejected 43-45.

Proxmire argued that it was wrong for the Senate to give itself a raise in a year when Congress was cutting many social programs. But Stevens responded that senators were allowed to have unlimited income from other sources such as book royalties or investments. If they went to the trouble of making a lot of speeches, he said, they had a right to the money.

The Senate also adopted, 50-45, a Stevens amendment to remove a "cap" on the pay of federal employees on the executive schedule and on upper-level Civil Service employees.

The Senate Sept. 25 passed H J Res 325 by a 47-44 vote.

Conference Action

When the bill went to a conference committee, House conferees offered a deal. They proposed an immediate 4.8 percent pay raise for members, which had not been in either House or Senate versions of H J Res 325, in return for House acceptance of the Senate provisions on honoraria, tax deductions and senior federal employee pay.

House conferees insisted that if high-ranking federal employees were to get a raise, they wanted one, too. Stevens was unable to round up enough votes among Senate conferees for a congressional pay raise. So both the lawmakers and senior federal officials lost their raises.

However, Stevens was able to get a majority of Senate conferees to accept the House proposal establishing a permanent appropriation for future congressional salaries, freeing members of the politically touchy issue of voting funds for their own raises.

The House adopted the conference report (H Rept 97-260) by voice vote and the Senate by a 64-28 vote on Sept 30. The Senate approved on a **key vote of 48-44 (R 37-13; D 11-31)** the changes instituting the permanent appropriation for congressional pay raises. *(1981 key votes, p. 879)*

And by an identical 48-44 vote, the Senate agreed to remove the $3,000 annual limit on members' business-related tax deductions.

Tax Deduction Clarification

A black lung benefits bill (HR 5159), which cleared Congress Dec. 16, the last day of the 1981 session, contained an unrelated amendment clarifying the types and extent of the tax deductions that were permissible under the newly enacted PL 97-51. It was discovered that the statute conflicted with a provision of a 1976 law limiting the amount of deductions that could be taken on second homes used in connection with a trade or business.

Under the combined effect of the 1976 and 1981 laws, a member of Congress who lived alone in Washington could depreciate the cost of a second home in the capital area as well as deduct his current housing expenses. But a member whose family resided with him in Washington more than 14 days a year was not eligible for the new tax break.

To remedy that situation, the House Dec. 15 attached a rider to a miscellaneous tax bill (HR 4961) enabling members living with their families in Washington to claim the same tax benefits as members living alone. The House passed the clarification by voice vote.

The Senate Dec. 16 opted for a broader approach. It not only included language in HR 5159 to enable a member living with his family in Washington to depreciate and claim a deduction on the costs of a second home but added a provision instructing the Treasury secretary to prescribe the appropriate business deduction a member could take for each day Congress was in session, without actually having to substantiate those expenses.

Senate Finance Committee Chairman Robert Dole, R-Kan., said the additional language was necessary to prevent members from taking excessive deductions. He said $75 a day had been suggested as an "appropriate amount for us to deduct," but he said colleagues had asked that the actual figure not be included in the bill "because the press will add up $75 times so many days in session and they will interpret it in some ways as looking like a tax credit or a pay raise."

Dole said members with higher daily expenses could

State Tax Exemption

The 4th U.S. Circuit Court of Appeals Jan. 5, 1981, upheld a lower court ruling that members of Congress who resided only part-time in Maryland were exempt from Maryland income taxes.

The decision confirmed a March 31, 1980, ruling by U.S. District Judge Frank A. Kaufman of Baltimore that the federal government was permitted to exempt members of Congress from such taxes.

The ruling resulted from a suit filed against Maryland by the Justice Department after the state continued to bill members for back taxes despite a 1977 law (PL 95-67) prohibiting the practice. Under the 1977 law, members were to be subject solely to the taxes levied by the states and localities they represented — where they had their official residence — even if they spent much less time in their home districts and states during their congressional careers than they did in Washington.

Though many out-of-state members resided in the District of Columbia and Virginia as well as in Maryland, only Maryland had attempted to collect income taxes from out-of-state representatives and senators.

---

claim the additional amount as long as they were able to substantiate it to the Internal Revenue Service. But because the daily deduction prescribed by the Treasury secretary would be deemed "appropriate" by law, members could claim that amount even if their actual expenses were lower.

The Senate version was passed by voice vote and returned to the House, which gave HR 5159 final approval.

Treasury regulations stipulating how members of Congress could calculate deductions were approved in January 1982.

16.8 Percent Pay Hike Rejected

While members had added substantially to their income indirectly, Congress early in 1981 refused to go along with a recommendation for a 16.8 percent pay raise for lawmakers and high-level government officials.

The House March 12 approved by voice vote H Res 109 stating that "it would be inappropriate at this time" to grant increases to legislators, senior government officials, judges and other federal employees.

The Senate subsequently adopted four resolutions disapproving federal salary hikes. The votes were: 93-0 denying a congressional pay raise (S Res 89); 91-3 disapproving raises for legislative branch staffers (S Res 90); 87-8 disapproving judicial branch raises (S Res 91); and 86-7 disapproving executive branch raises (S Res 92).

The House and Senate were acting on pay raises recommended by President Jimmy Carter just before he left

office Jan. 20, 1981. Carter Jan. 7 had proposed a $183.1 million plan that would have increased the salary of members of Congress to $70,853 (from $60,662) and a Cabinet secretary's salary to $81,328 (from $69,630).

Carter's initiative was the result of recommendations made Dec. 16, 1980, by the Commission on Executive, Legislative and Judicial Salaries, the so-called quadrennial review commission established to examine pay rates for members of Congress, federal judges, Cabinet officers and senior bureaucrats and make salary recommendations every four years. That nine-member body had proposed federal pay increases averaging 40 percent.

Since 1977 Congress was required to take separate roll-call votes in each house for each of the four categories of federal employees eligible for the pay recommendations submitted by the commission. That requirement did not affect the annual October comparability pay raises recommended by the president for most federal white-collar employees. *(Pay raise procedures, box, p. 824)*

President Ronald Reagan at first supported Carter's pay plan but later opposed it, citing his administration's budget-cutting policies.

House Earned Income Limit

In a skillfully executed surprise attack, a handful of House members Dec. 15 won approval of a change in House rules doubling the amount of outside income members were permitted to earn.

During a lull in House business, John P. Murtha, D-Pa., rose and asked for unanimous consent to approve a resolution (H Res 305) increasing the ceiling on House members' outside earnings from 15 percent of their official salary to 30 percent.

When no one objected, Murtha returned to his seat. The entire process took about 10 seconds.

About an hour later, a handful of members opposed to the rules changes demanded the floor to complain about the procedure. But when Robert S. Walker, R-Pa., requested that the rules change be reversed, several of his colleagues loudly voiced their objections, blocking any reconsideration.

The rules change meant that, beginning in 1981, House members would be able to earn up to $18,198.75 a year in outside income. That compared with $9,099.37 a year under the previous rule. But because the ceiling was lifted so late in the year, members had only about two weeks to earn the additional income permitted them in 1981.

The principal source of earned income for most members was honoraria payments for speeches, articles and appearances. The earned income ceiling, which went into effect in 1979, did not apply to unearned income such as dividends, interest or rent. Those types of income remained unlimited.

The Senate Oct. 1 had exempted itself from a $25,000 restriction on outside earned income contained in the 1976 Federal Election Campaign Act Amendments. *(Story, p. 821)*

Earlier House Rejection. The Dec. 15 action was in sharp contrast to an earlier House vote on a similar proposal. The House Oct. 28 on a **key vote of 147-271 (R 73-112; D 74-159)** rejected a proposal (H Res 251), drafted by House Rules Committee Chairman Richard Bolling, D-Mo., to raise the outside earned income ceiling from 15 percent to 40 percent of a member's salary for 1981

Congressional Pay Procedures Instituted . . .

Article I, Section 6, of the Constitution provides that "Senators and Representatives shall receive a Compensation for their Services, to be ascertained by Law, and paid out of the Treasury of the United States."

Members' salaries have been a political issue throughout the history of Congress. In trying to minimize the adverse political fallout from raising its own remuneration, Congress fell into the practice of incorporating pay increases in general legislation granting raises for most government workers, including at times the judiciary and the president. Even that tactic often failed to blunt critical reaction.

Although members of Congress are free to vote themselves a pay raise at any time under any legislative procedure used by the House and Senate, since the mid-1970s congressional salaries generally had been increased through one of two methods.

Quadrennial Pay Recommendations

Dissatisfaction in and out of Congress with the way congressional pay increases were being enacted led to the formation in 1967 of a nine-member Commission on Executive, Legislative and Judicial Salaries (quadrennial commission). Established by Congress (PL 90-206), the commission was authorized to review the salaries of lawmakers as well as federal judges and top officers of the executive branch every four years and to recommend changes in pay rates.

In reviewing top government officials' salaries, the commission, composed of private citizens, was mandated to propose pay scales at levels that were comparable to those for similar jobs in private industry. It was hoped that by making the salaries of federal officials competitive to those in the private

sector the government would be able to attract and keep the best qualified persons. The commission recommended pay scales only for judges and senior executive and legislative employees, not the majority of federal employees at the General Schedule (GS) levels.

The commission pay plan also was designed to relieve members of Congress of the politically sensitive task of having to approve their own pay increases.

Three members of the commission were appointed by the president, two by the president of the Senate, two by the Speaker of the House and two by the chief justice of the United States. Under the arrangement, first begun in 1968, the commission submitted pay recommendations to the president every four years. The president then included in his budget message submitted to Congress the following January the exact rates of pay "he deems advisable." His recommendations could be either higher or lower than those submitted by the commission, or he could propose that salaries not be altered.

Since 1977 the House and Senate had been required by law to act to accept or reject the president's recommendations within 60 days of receipt and to take separate roll-call votes on proposed pay raises for each of four categories of federal employees: members of Congress, congressional officials, Executive Schedule personnel and judges.

Comparability Adjustments

In 1975 Congress voted to make itself, judges and high-ranking executive branch officials eligible for the automatic comparability salary adjustments that had been given annually to GS and other statu-

---

through 1983, when the ceiling would revert to 15 percent. *(1981 key votes, p. 879)*

Bolling's proposal also would have increased the limit on each individual honorarium payment from $1,000 to $2,000.

The rule relaxation was supported by House leaders on both sides of the aisle. But the leaders did little in the way of lobbying, and opposition to the resolution crossed party lines.

Before defeating H Res 251, the House rejected by voice vote an amendment, offered by Tom Harkin, D-Iowa, that would have put off the increase until after the 1982 elections and would have limited it to one year.

House Expense Allowances

The House Administration Committee voted May 6 to increase House members' expense allowances, effective

May 1, 1981. The increase was approved by voice vote and did not require action by the full House to take effect.

According to the committee, the hike was necessary to cover increases in the cost of travel and office supplies, equipment and furnishings.

Both the House and Senate acted in 1982 to increase their members' expense allowances. *(Story, p. 829)*

Background

House members' expense allowances covered such costs as telephone, postage, office supplies and equipment, district office rental, constituent communications, computer services, travel and other official expenses.

The expense allowance made available to each member included a base sum plus an amount derived from a formula that took into account the cost of rental space in the member's district, the cost of travel between the member's home district and Washington, D.C., and the cost of the

... To Blunt Criticism of Salary Raises

tory federal white collar workers since 1971 under the Federal Pay Comparability Act of 1970 (HR 13000 — PL 91-656). Members of Congress no longer had to go on record every time they sought a pay raise. The procedure was revised in 1977 to require members of the House and Senate to vote to accept annual comparability raises. In 1982 Congress returned to the 1975 method whereby the annual raises automatically took effect unless the House and Senate voted to block the pay hike. *(1970 act, Congress and the Nation Vol. III, p. 454; 1975 amendments, Congress and the Nation Vol. IV, p. 813; 1977 amendment, Congress and the Nation Vol. V, p. 889)*

The 1970 act built upon the comparability adjustment provisions of the 1967 law that established the quadrennial commission. The comparability provisions of the 1967 act were temporary, having expired in 1969. The 1970 act was billed as a federal pay comparability measure — requiring a presidential pay agent to consider the salaries of similar positions in private industry before making pay recommendations.

The focus of government pay hikes in recent years had been on adjusting salaries to compensate for inflation rather than to achieve comparability with the private sector. Thus the government's annual pay adjustments often were referred to as cost-of-living (COLA) adjustments. Indeed, the 1975 law that made members of Congress and other high-ranking federal employees eligible for the automatic COLA pay hikes was labeled the Executive Salary Cost-of-Living Adjustment Act (PL 94-82). However, the new pay rates proposed by the president each year generally had not even kept pace with the inflation rate charted by the Labor Department's Consumer Price Index, much less satisfied the original goal of making them comparable to pay in private industry.

Under the federal comparability/cost-of-living pay procedure, the president issued governmentwide adjustments in pay rates each fall. If the president decided that his pay agent's recommended raise was too high — because of a national emergency or adverse economic conditions — he had to submit an alternative pay plan to Congress before Sept. 1. The president's alternative then took effect Oct. 1 unless either house rejected it. If that occurred, the original pay recommendation of the pay agent took effect. In 1983, in a budget-cutting move, the raises were postponed until Jan. 1, starting in 1984.

Although Congress received all documentation on each pay recommendation, no legislative action was required unless the lawmakers decided not to accept the president's adjusted rate.

When members of Congress declined to accept presidential pay adjustments, their action did not block the new rates from taking effect for other classes of federal employees. However, in denying a raise for themselves, members of Congress often had withheld it from other senior government officials as well. An unusual feature of the existing procedure allowed Congress to change its mind at any time and claim a raise it previously refused to accept. Legislators in 1982 became eligible for a hefty pay hike exceeding 27.2 percent because of accumulations of several annual pay adjustments that members did not take at the time they were implemented by the president.

In 1983 Congress eliminated all previous presidential pay hikes members had not already taken. That did not affect future presidential pay adjustments that Congress might decide not to accept.

---

member's telephone service.

Though particular sums of money were earmarked for these three major categories, all the money in a member's allowance could be used as each member saw fit, so long as it was spent on official expenses.

The last time a fundamental adjustment was made in members' expense allowances was in March 1977, at the time the House adopted a new ethics code. Until 1977 members had nine separate special allowances, and they had to adhere to specific limits on spending in each of the nine categories. The code consolidated the nine special allowances into two: the official expense allowance and a staff, or clerk-hire, allowance. It also banned unofficial office accounts and increased the expense allowance by $5,000 a year to compensate for the loss.

In September 1977 the House approved another increase to reflect rising district office rental costs. And in October 1979 the base allowance and funds allocated for transportation and office equipment were adjusted upward to meet higher inflation.

While increases in the base allowance generally required approval by the whole House, adjustments in any expense category to compensate for inflation required the approval of only the House Administration Committee.

Changes Approved

To cover the increasing cost of office supplies and equipment, the committee in 1981 increased each member's official expense account by $4,300 a year. But added to that amount were various supplementary allowances that differed with each member. Generally the farther away the member's district from Washington the higher his overall expense account.

To offset higher transportation costs, the committee approved mileage increases of 7 cents a mile for members whose districts were 3,000 or more miles from Washington, and 12 cents a mile for members whose districts were less

than 500 miles away. There were several categories in between these two.

The changes meant annual increases in the expense allowance ranging from at least $1,950 for members from districts close to Washington to about $24,600 a year for members whose districts were farthest away. The travel allowance worked out to about 32 round trips per year between Washington and a member's district. If a member chose to take more than 32 trips home, he could use other funds from his official expense account. In addition, members could draw upon other funds for travel on official business.

The committee raised from $27,000 to $35,000 the ceiling on district office furnishings that could be purchased from the General Services Administration during a member's tenure.

Franking Privilege

Legislation (S 1224) revising the congressional franking privilege and allowing senators to make franked statewide mass mailings was enacted into law in 1981.

The franking privilege allowed members of Congress to send letters and packages related to their official duties without charge under a reproduction of their signature in place of a stamp. Congress reimbursed the U.S. Postal Service quarterly from public funds for the cost of the franked mailings.

S 1224 both restricted and expanded the franking privilege. Some of the restrictions it wrote into law already were in effect as provisions of the House and Senate ethics codes. Others went further than existing limits.

The 1981 legislation was viewed by many as primarily a stopgap measure. Many senators maintained that the existing franking laws and regulations were archaic and that a comprehensive rewriting was necessary.

Related franking legislation was passed by the House in 1977 and 1979 but was never approved by the Senate. A bill was reported by the Senate Governmental Affairs Committee in 1978 but never came to a floor vote. *(Congress and the Nation Vol. V, pp. 910, 926)*

Congress established the franking privilege in 1789 — the first year it met. The free mailing privilege originally was established to make it easier for legislators to communicate with their constituents on matters of official business. *(History of the franking privilege, Guide to Congress Third Edition, p. 596)*

From the start, members recognized the possibility that the privilege might be abused, and Congress imposed controls on its use. Criticism that members used the privilege to promote their own re-election, however, persisted. Common Cause, a citizens' lobby, brought suit in 1973 charging that the frank was unconstitutional because the privilege promoted the re-election of incumbents. The Supreme Court in 1983 upheld the constitutionality of the frank. *(Story, p. 831)*

Legislative History

The Senate Governmental Affairs Committee reported S 1224 (S Rept 97-155) on July 17. Civil Service and General Services Subcommittee Chairman Ted Stevens, R-Alaska, had drafted the bill.

The panel said the legislation was intended to "again limit the opportunities for [the frank's] abuse, clarify the privilege and draw a line between what Congress considers primarily official/representative and primarily political."

A brief hearing on the measure was held June 16, at which Stevens said the measure was intended to strengthen, clarify and close loopholes in a 1973 law (PL 93-191) that established guidelines for use of the frank.

PL 93-191 gave House members the right to send out franked mass mailings to every address in their districts simply by addressing the required number of letters to "postal patron" and depositing them with the Postal Service. *(Congress and the Nation Vol. IV, p. 756)*

But the law did not extend that authority to senators, who continued to be governed by a regulation requiring their letters to bear a name and address.

S 1224 allowed senators to make statewide franked mass mailings if the envelopes bore a simplified form of address, such as the word "occupant" followed by a street address. In essence, this was the same as the House's postal patron mass mailings.

Stevens said it would save the Senate money by eliminating the need to return incorrectly addressed mail and by reducing the computer programming time needed to update senators' computerized mailing lists when constituents moved.

He noted that the Senate paid the Postal Service 25 cents for every piece of incorrectly addressed mail that was returned. A Senate Ethics Committee study found these returns cost the Senate $1.2 million in 1980, almost 6 percent of the $21 million total the Senate spent on mass mailings that year.

In its report, however, the committee acknowledged that the statewide mailing provision could result in "drastic increases" in the volume of franked congressional mail that might offset any cost savings.

The Senate sergeant-at-arms had estimated in 1981 that if every senator made four mass mailings a year the Senate would have to hire an additional 166 employees and would exceed its frank mail budget for the year by $57 million.

The panel called on the Senate Rules Committee and the House Commission on Congressional Mailing Standards (franking commission) to establish limits on such statewide mailings in the Senate and on districtwide mass mailings in the House. In order to give the Senate committee time to issue rules, language was added to the bill barring senators from making statewide postal patron mailings until 120 days after the bill's enactment. (The panel was unable to agree on regulations within this time period and had to further delay implementation of Senate postal patron mailings.)

The Senate passed the bill by voice vote July 20 without debate or amendments.

There was no House committee consideration of the bill. S 1224 was sent directly to the floor and was passed by the House by voice vote Oct. 13. House action accepting the Senate version completed congressional action.

Final Provisions

As signed into law Oct. 26, S 1224 (PL 97-69):

● Eliminated a member's authority to frank letters expressing solely the member's condolences or congratulations for a "personal" distinction such as a birthday. Franked letters expressing congratulations for a "public" distinction, such as becoming a citizen or being elected to public office, still were allowed.

● Permitted a member to frank otherwise frankable letters in which the member added a personal greeting to an individual's wife or family.

● Prohibited any franked mass mailing less than 60 days before any primary or general election in which the member making the mailing was a candidate. (In the Senate, this prohibition on mailings by candidates before a general election was broadened in 1983 to include all senators. *(Details, p. 831)*

● Prohibited a member who was a candidate for another public office — such as representative, senator, governor or president — from making mass mailings to any area served by the other office that was outside the member's existing district or state.

● Permitted the chairman of a congressional committee, if the chairman was a candidate in a primary or general election, to continue to make mass mailings at any time prior to that election if the mailings related to routine committee business.

● Granted to the Senate Select Ethics Committee and to the House Commission on Congressional Mailing Standards authority to enforce the franking rules and statutes and to further regulate use of the franking privilege.

● Defined a "mass mailing" as a mailing of more than 500 pieces of mail of which the content was "substantially identical." Exempted from the definition were letters sent out in response to incoming mail and mailings to the news media, to fellow members of Congress or to state, local or federal government officials.

● Extended to senators the postal patron mailing privilege enjoyed by the House; implementation of the provision was made dependent on regulations issued by the Senate Rules and Administration Committee. (The committee was not able to agree on a set of guidelines until Nov. 1, 1983. *(Story, p. 831)*)

● Authorized senators to make statewide mass mailings so long as the envelopes bore a simplified form of address, such as the word "occupant" and a street address, and provided such mailings were sent "by the most economical means practicable."

● Gave the Senate Rules Committee and the House Commission on Congressional Mailing Standards the authority to impose limitations on the number of pieces of mail that could be sent each year in districtwide or statewide mailings.

● Required House members to submit to the House Commission on Congressional Mailing Standards a sample of each postal patron mass mailing in advance, to determine whether it complied with the requirements of the franking law.

● Left it to the Senate Select Ethics Committee to decide whether senators, too, should be required to submit such samples in advance. But the committee opted for voluntary compliance; submission of newsletters in advance was never made a requirement.

● Authorized the entire cost of preparing and printing House and Senate mass mailings to be paid from federal funds, except that additional materials could be included in a mailing (even if printed and prepared at private expense) if they were of a "purely instructional or informational" nature.

● Permitted any designated surviving relative of a member who died in office to frank non-political correspondence that was related to the member's death.

● Ended the franking privilege for mailings of official business letters, public documents and agricultural materials 90 days after a member left Congress.

● Extended the House franking commission's jurisdiction to complaints against former members and House officials.

1982

House Members' Pay Hike

In a break with nearly two centuries of tradition, Congress decided in 1982 to pay larger salaries to representatives than to senators.

The unusual arrangement provided House members with a 15 percent pay raise, bringing their annual salaries to $69,800, effective Dec. 18. Senators' salaries remained at $60,662.50 per year. The pay hike was added as a rider to the second fiscal 1983 omnibus appropriations measure (H J Res 631 — PL 97-377).

The same legislation allowed senators to earn an unlimited amount of outside income, such as legal fees, business income and honoraria for speeches and articles. Outside earnings for representatives continued to be limited by House rules to 30 percent of members' salaries — $20,940 once the House pay raise took effect. *(Related action on senators' honoraria, p. 829)*

PL 97-377 also provided salary increases of up to 15 percent for about 32,000 senior government employees. The pay of Cabinet officers went from $69,630 a year to $80,100; senior bureaucrats went from $59,500 to a maximum of $68,400.

The raises also affected House and Senate staffers, although their precise pay levels were set by the members for whom they worked. Senate staffers were eligible for increases, although their bosses were not.

Legislative Action

The election-year pay raise proposal was brought up in Congress by Sen. Ted Stevens, R-Alaska. He inserted in two unrelated bills amendments that would have convened a special session of the Commission on Executive, Legislative and Judicial Salaries, the so-called quadrennial review commission.

The commission was not scheduled to meet again until 1984. Under Stevens' amendment, the panel would have made pay recommendations to President Reagan by Nov. 15, just after the 1982 congressional elections. Raises suggested by the commission were to become effective in 60 days unless both the House and Senate rejected them.

Nothing came of the Stevens strategy in those two bills. The House refused to accept the pay plan, in one case even after a conference committee had approved it as a rider to the 1982 omnibus budget reconciliation bill.

The next rounds of the pay fight occurred during congressional action on two emergency fiscal 1983 funding measures (H J Res 599, H J Res 631).

With the 1982 congressional elections facing them, members were reluctant to vote themselves a pay raise when they considered H J Res 599 in September. There

was no attempt through this bill to convene the quadrennial commission prematurely. Lawmakers, without any visible opposition, voted not to accept the comparability pay raise recommended by the president for most federal white-collar workers. The Oct. 1 recommended increase was 4 percent. Congress also barred senior government officials and judges from receiving that raise. Under the comparability pay procedure enacted in 1975, members of Congress received the annual raises automatically unless both houses chose not to accept them. *(1975 action, Congress and the Nation Vol. IV, p. 813)*

H J Res 599 (PL 97-276) expired Dec. 17, giving Congress another opportunity, after the November elections, to consider the pay issue. Before it did so, however, the General Accounting Office (GAO) reported that members were entitled to a pay raise totaling 27.2 percent, which would bring their pay to $77,300 per year. That was the percentage increase members would have received if they had taken the October comparability increases for four of the preceding five years. In those years, members had deferred the pay raises for themselves. The statutory salary rate for senior government employees — including members of Congress — went up each year at the time the president's annual October pay adjustment took effect, unless it was rejected outright by Congress. Although members had denied themselves the increases, the raises for those years

had never actually been rejected; thus Congress was able to claim them at any time.

When they considered legislation (H J Res 631) during their lame-duck session in December to replace the expired PL 97-276, members of Congress now felt they were able politically to vote themselves a 15 percent raise in pay. That amount ($9,100) was a little more than half the amount members were entitled to, according to the GAO calculations based on the annual comparability raises members had voted not to accept.

In an attempt to gain some bargaining leverage with the Senate, the House also added a provision limiting all members of Congress, including senators, to outside earned income of no more than 30 percent of their congressional salary.

The House version, passed Dec. 14, also contained a raise for Cabinet officers and senior bureaucrats, whose pay was affected by the freezes members of Congress had imposed on their own salaries.

Doubting that Congress would approve a salary hike of 27.2 percent, the House Legislative Appropriations Subcommittee agreed to limit the raise to 15 percent, which was about the aggregate increase in the Consumer Price Index duing the period.

Proponents of an increase argued that members had lost purchasing power in recent years as Congress rejected the October raises.

Pay proponents used a parliamentary tactic that made it easier for the House to approve the increase. The House voted first on the Appropriations Committee's 15 percent proposal, and many members who were opposed to a raise voted for it because it was smaller than the 27.2 percent increase cited by the GAO. The smaller increase was approved 303-109.

Then an amendment was offered to prohibit any raise. As the 15 minutes allotted for the vote ran out, the amendment seemingly had been defeated, 198-201. But after several other members were permitted to vote, the amendment went ahead 209-204. Then, amid considerable confusion on the House floor, more members were allowed to vote and others were allowed to switch their votes. Even Speaker Thomas P. O'Neill Jr., D-Mass., who customarily did not vote, cast a vote against the amendment. With the amendment opposing any raise ahead 208-207, lame-duck member Robert K. Dornan, R-Calif., voted no, and the amendment failed on a **208-208 key vote (R 121-65; D 87-143)**. It was the vote of Dornan and 70 other lame-duck members who sealed its fate. Lame-duck members opposed the amendment by a two-to-one margin: 24-47. *(1982 key votes, p. 895)*

The Senate Appropriations Committee deleted both the pay raise and the outside earnings limit when it considered H J Res 631 in December. That version then was passed by the Senate Dec. 19.

A conference committee compromise version (H Rept 97-980) incorporated the pay raise for House members, but not senators. Senior officials in the executive branch also received the raise. In exchange, the House conferees agreed to drop the 30 percent limit on senators' outside earned income.

Senators and representatives always had received the same salary except in 1795-96, when senators received $7 a day when they were in attendance and representatives $6 a day. *(Chart, this page)*

The House and Senate adopted the conference report Dec. 20, completing congressional action. The president signed the resolution Dec. 21.

Congressional Pay: $6 a Day to $75,100 a Year

Year	Salary
1789-1795	$6 per diem
1795-1796	$6 per diem (House)
	$7 per diem (Senate)
1796-1815	$6 per diem
1815-1817	$1,500 per year
1817-1855	$8 per diem
1855-1865	$3,000 per year
1865-1871	$5,000 per year
1871-1873	$7,500 per year
1873-1907	$5,000 per year
1907-1925	$7,500 per year
1925-1932	$10,000 per year
1932-1933	$9,000 per year
1933-1935	$8,500 per year
1935-1947	$10,000 per year
1947-1955	$12,500 per year
1955-1965	$22,500 per year
1965-1969	$30,000 per year
1969-1975	$42,500 per year
1975-1977	$44,600 per year
1977-1980	$57,500 per year
1980-1982	$60,662 per year
1982-1983	$69,800 per year (House)
1983	$69,800 per year (Senate)
1984	$72,600 per year
1985	$75,100 per year

Senate Earned Income Limit

The Senate Dec. 14 repealed a Senate rule that would have limited annual outside earned income to 15 percent of senators' congressional salary. Senators were free to earn as much as they wanted by giving speeches, writing articles, practicing law or by any other legal means. Had the Senate not acted, the cap, which amounted to about $9,100, would have gone into effect Jan. 1, 1983.

The Senate's 1977 ethics code had called for the 15 percent limit to take effect in 1979, but the Senate voted in March of that year to delay its implementation until 1983. *(Congress and the Nation Vol. V, p. 891)*

Congress in 1981 had repealed a provision of the 1976 Federal Election Campaign Act Amendments restricting senators to $25,000 annually in honoraria income. But the related limit in the ethics code was not affected by repeal of the honoraria provision in the campaign act. *(1981 action, p. 821)*

The Senate approved the legislation (S Res 512) abolishing the earned income limit on a **key vote of 54-38 (R 39-12; D 15-26)**. The House was not required to act on the Senate resolution. *(1982 key votes, p. 895)*

Senators agreed to forgo a salary increase in 1982 in exchange for repeal of the outside earned income limit. As part of the second fiscal 1983 continuing resolution (H J Res 631 — PL 97-377), House members received a 15 percent pay raise while senators got no raise but were freed of the earned income limit. *(Story, p. 827)*

Members' Expense Allowances

Expense allowances for members of the House and Senate were increased in 1982 in separate action.

House. The House Administration Committee Dec. 9 increased members' allowance for office expenses by 10 percent and the allowance for domestic travel by 15 percent, effective Jan. 3, 1983. The changes did not require House approval. *(Background, p. 824)*

The increase raised representatives' base expense allowance by $4,700, to $52,000 a year from $47,300.

For travel within the United States, each member received an allowance based on how far his district was from Washington, D.C. Before the increase, members who lived less than 500 miles away got 30 cents per mile. Those who lived more than 3,000 miles away got 18 cents per mile, with several categories in between. The new formula ranged from 21 to 35 cents a mile. The adjustments were needed because of higher air fares, according to the House committee.

The panel Dec. 9 also issued a ruling specifying that members could not be reimbursed for hotel stays in the same city or town as their legal residence. That action affected those members who did not maintain a home in their districts.

Members still could be reimbursed for stays in hotels in areas of their districts that were distant from their hometowns. Whether the distance was great enough to warrant reimbursement was left to the individual member's judgment.

Senate. Senators paid for travel expenses out of their official office expense account, which in 1982 ranged from $33,000 for a senator from Delaware to $143,000 for a senator from Hawaii. The amount received by individual senators for travel was based on a combination of state population and the distance of the state from Washington, D.C.

Effective Jan. 1, 1983, the amount allocated for senators' travel was increased by 10 percent. The change, the first adjustment since 1979, was included in an amendment to the first fiscal 1983 continuing appropriations resolution (H J Res 599 — PL 97-276), which was enacted Oct. 2.

Repeal of 1981 Tax Deduction

Under heavy pressure from constituents, Congress in 1982 reinstated the $3,000-a-year limit on business-related tax deductions that senators and representatives could take for living expenses while they were in Washington, D.C. The cap had been repealed in 1981. *(Story, p. 821)*

Upon removal of the $3,000 limit, taxpayers flooded Capitol Hill and the Internal Revenue Service with angry letters and phone calls protesting the new deductions. Common Cause, a citizens' lobby organization, criticized the tax deductions as unjustified and inequitable. It launched a nationwide "Give Taxpayers A Break" campaign to repeal the 1981 tax deduction. It pledged to get all representatives and senators to publicly disclose the amount of the tax deductions they took in 1981.

Responding to the public criticism, Congress in 1982 approved legislation repealing the 1981 deductions. The repeal, initiated by Sen. William Proxmire, D-Wis., was added as a rider to an emergency fiscal 1982 appropriations bill (HR 6685 — PL 97-216).

Although HR 6685 was enacted July 18, the repeal was made retroactive to Jan. 1. It nevertheless allowed members to keep the lucrative deductions they took on their 1981 tax returns.

Earlier in 1982, House members had threatened to delay action on the repeal unless senators agreed to limit their outside earned income to the maximum allowed representatives. That dispute stalled final action on HR 6685 and exacerbated a struggle between the House and Senate over the twin issues of members' tax breaks and honoraria. The House eventually backed down.

Later in the year, however, Congress voted to give House members — but not senators — a pay raise. And the Senate reaffirmed its 1981 decision repealing the ceiling on senators' outside earnings. *(House members' pay hike, p. 827; Senate earned income limit, this page)*

Legislative Action

The Senate first debated the repeal issue during consideration of H J Res 409, a fiscal 1982 emergency appropriations resolution. In this debate, senators went on record in favor of lower salaries, tougher tax deduction rules and public disclosure of tax returns for members of Congress. Sen. William L. Armstrong, R-Colo., offered the amendment to restore the $3,000 limit on business-related tax deductions. On four separate roll-call votes, the Senate affirmed its support for Armstrong's amendment.

Sen. Ted Stevens, R-Alaska, however, defended the liberalized deductions as compensation for the pain suffered by senators in having to live in the nation's capital. "I know of no town that has a worse crime standard, a worse set of schools, a worse circumstance to live and work in than the city of Washington," he said.

In response to the Armstrong amendment, Stevens offered an amendment to reduce salaries of members of

Congress by 10 percent, beginning April 1, 1982. The amendment, which would have cut pay to $54,596.25 a year from $60,662.50, was adopted 63-36.

An amendment by Paul E. Tsongas, D-Mass., to require printing of members' tax returns in the *Congressional Record* was approved 55-43. But the Senate rejected an amendment by Arlen Specter, R-Pa., to require members to provide substantiation for their business-related tax deductions.

Under heavy pressure from the Republican leadership, the three amendments eventually were eliminated on a parliamentary technicality.

Unwilling to reject the Armstrong amendment outright, the Senate instead ruled that the amendment, and the Stevens and Tsongas amendments attached to it, constituted legislation in an appropriations bill and therefore was out of order. The ruling of the chair against the Armstrong amendment was upheld by a 51-48 vote.

Ironically, the Senate in September 1981 had voted on exactly the same parliamentary question, in reverse fashion. At that time, the Senate overturned a ruling of the chair that the Stevens amendment to eliminate the $3,000 tax deduction limit was out of order.

The fate of the expanded tax deductions then became entangled in the urgent fiscal 1982 supplemental appropriations bill (HR 5922). On May 27 the Senate adopted an amendment by Proxmire to restore the $3,000 annual limit on members' business-related tax deductions. The Appropriations Committee had voted to end the automatic $75-a-day deduction, but it did not restore the $3,000 limit.

Many House members privately were reluctant to give up the increased tax deductions, which saved them several thousand dollars each in 1981 taxes. But they were unwilling to defend the tax breaks publicly, or to vote for them on the record.

So on June 9, when Patricia Schroeder, D-Colo., obtained a recorded vote on requiring House conferees to accept the Senate provision restoring the $3,000 limit, the outcome was assured. Her proposal was adopted, 356-43. And by a 176-218 vote, the House rejected a motion by John T. Myers, R-Ind., to instruct the conferees to eliminate the automatic $75-a-day deduction without restoring the $3,000 limit. That would have allowed members to claim whatever business-related deductions for Washington living expenses they could substantiate.

In the subsequent conference committee action on the bill, the House June 10, under heavy public pressure, accepted the provision repealing the 1981 tax break. But House conferees then retaliated by demanding that the Senate accept an $18,200 annual ceiling on outside income earned by senators.

That action unleashed a torrent of resentment and recriminations on all sides. House members verbally attacked Senate members, senators argued bitterly among themselves and just about every member jumped on the press.

While they were forced by Schroeder's amendment to accept the Senate provision, House conferees were furious with the Senate. They accused senators of hypocrisy for taking away the tax break while they continued to receive large honoraria from interest groups.

"You got a bunch of fat cats up there raking in the big bucks. They can be big statesmen because they can collect those big honoraria," said Silvio O. Conte, R-Mass.

Jake Garn, R-Utah, the most outspoken Senate opponent of restoring the $3,000 limit, responded that House members were "just as gutless" as senators on the issue. He attributed public attacks on the tax breaks to dishonest reporting by the press. Garn also lashed out at Proxmire. "You used this vehicle for political purposes because you're running this year," he shouted.

The motion to accept the Senate provision repealing the tax break — but also to limit senators' outside earnings to 30 percent of their congressional pay — was approved 10-8 by House conferees. The House already had that limit.

While they did not seriously consider the House proposal, Senate conferees narrowly rejected by a 10-11 vote a compromise plan offered by Stevens. That plan would have adjusted the $3,000 limit on deductions to the increase in consumer prices since 1952, when the limit was imposed. Under the amendment, the limit would have been about $10,800 in 1982.

The House approved the conference version of HR 5922 by voice vote; it then voted 381-29 to insist that the Senate accept the $18,200-a-year limit on honoraria and other outside earnings.

The Senate approved the conference report by voice vote. But senators refused to accept the amendment setting the $18,200 limit.

Faced with Senate opposition to the outside income limit, the House leadership adopted a new strategy. It brought up a new funding bill (HR 6645) stripped of the tax deduction and outside income limits provisions.

The House passed HR 6645 by voice vote June 23. But the Senate refused to go along with the stripped-down funding bill. The Senate voted to add the Proxmire amendment restoring the $3,000-a-year limit on members' deductions for Washington living expenses. Before action on that bill was completed, the House leadership agreed to accept HR 5922 without the amendment limiting senators' honoraria.

However, President Reagan vetoed HR 5922 because it contained an expensive housing appropriation.

Unable to muster the votes necessary to override the veto, Congress cleared a second supplemental (HR 6682), which Reagan also vetoed, complaining that it, too, was too expensive. A third bill (HR 6685), containing only the most urgently needed funding — plus the $3,000-a-year-tax-deduction limit — eventually was cleared by Congress July 15 and signed by the president July 18.

In January 1983 Sen. Russell B. Long, D-La., introduced legislation (S 70) to remove the $3,000 limit and allow senators and representatives to deduct whatever business expenses they incurred while living in Washington. The measure was never reported from committee and died at the end of the 98th Congress.

1983

Congressional Pay

Six months after House members took a 15 percent pay raise, Congress provided an identical raise for senators, making their salary $69,800 a year, effective July 1, 1983.

In return for the senators' pay hike, the Senate agreed

Social Security Coverage

For the first time, members of Congress in 1983 were brought into the Social Security program. Under the Social Security rescue plan (HR 1900 — PL 98-21), cleared in March, current and future members of Congress as well as all new federal employees, the president, the vice president, sitting federal judges, top political appointees, top civil servants and certain other legislative branch employees were covered, effective Jan. 1, 1984. On that date members began contributing 7 percent of their salaries to the Social Security Trust Fund. *(Social Security rescue, p. 659; federal workers coverage, p. 784)*

The fiscal 1984 legislative branch appropriations bill (HR 3135 — PL 98-51) contained a $1.1 million payment for the Social Security program. This was to cover the employer contribution for members of Congress, beginning Jan. 1, 1984.

to limit the amount of money senators could earn through honoraria — speeches, appearances and articles — to no more than 30 percent of their annual salaries. This limit went into effect Jan. 1, 1984.

Members of the House already had a 30 percent limit on their honoraria.

The Senate salary increase and earned income limit were contained in a fiscal 1983 supplemental appropriations bill (HR 3069 — PL 98-63).

During consideration of the supplemental, the House Appropriations Committee adopted an amendment offered by Silvio O. Conte, R-Mass., to limit senators' honoraria earnings to 30 percent of their salaries. This was seen as a direct slap at senators. Traditionally, neither chamber interfered with the internal workings of the other.

The issue was not contested on the House floor, and the bill was passed May 25.

The Senate spent a week in June trying to negotiate a satisfactory arrangement on pay and honoraria. It initially voted for a cap on honoraria but declined to accept a pay raise. Finally, it approved on a **key vote of 49-47 (R 29-25; D 20-22)** a Henry M. Jackson, D-Wash., amendment limiting honoraria to 30 percent of senators' salaries, which were increased 15 percent to $69,800. *(1983 key votes, p. 911)*

The Senate passed the bill June 16. A conference committee agreed to the pay/honoraria arrangement, and HR 3069 was cleared June 29.

Cost-of-Living Wage Hike

Congress in 1983 also let stand an additional cost-of-living pay raise that took effect Jan. 1, 1984. By not acting on the president's October pay raise recommendations, a 3.5 percent increase automatically went into effect at the start of 1984. The increase raised congressional salaries to $72,200.

Efforts to repeal the pay raise failed in early 1984.

Indeed, Congress voted to increase the 3.5 percent salary hike by one-half percentage point. *(Story, p. 832)*

Franking Privilege

The Supreme Court May 2 rejected a lawsuit challenging the constitutionality of the free mailing privilege of members of Congress.

In related congressional action, the House Commission on Congressional Mailing Standards (franking commission) issued additional franking restrictions, although the final revisions were mostly voluntary. And the Senate Rules and Administration Committee Nov. 1 finally agreed on guidelines for senators' franked statewide mass mailings. *(Background, p. 826)*

Supreme Court Ruling

Common Cause, a citizens' lobby, filed suit in October 1973 charging that the frank was unconstitutional because the free mailing privilege promoted the re-election of incumbents and therefore denied challengers equal protection of the law.

Common Cause argued that Congress should not have a franking privilege or, alternatively, that the free mailing privilege also should be granted to non-incumbent challengers. And it said that franked mail should not be allowed for mailings to groups of people whose selection identified the mailing as political.

After hearing arguments in 1981, a special three-judge panel of the U.S. District Court for the District of Columbia dismissed the lawsuit on Sept. 7, 1982. The court conceded that the franking privilege "confers a substantial advantage to incumbent congressional candidates over their challengers," but it found no constitutional violation.

Common Cause appealed the decision to the U.S. Supreme Court, but by a 6-3 vote May 2, 1983, the justices declined to consider the case of *Common Cause v. William F. Bolger.* That action left standing the lower court's ruling upholding the constitutionality of the franking privilege.

House Action

On June 7 the House franking commission watered down stricter rules it had proposed only two months earlier and issued a set of general, non-binding guidelines. The commission basically left responsibility for regulating the style and content of mass mailings to each member. Commission member William D. Ford, D-Mich., called this "the mature approach." Other members of the six-member panel disagreed, however. "They're as next to nothing as you can get," said Trent Lott, R-Miss., a commission member since 1977, who resigned from the panel June 15 in protest.

In response to criticism that the franking privilege continued to be used for political purposes, the House franking commission in April 1983 had proposed a new set of rules. The commission called for restricting the use of photos in newsletters, regulating the size of newsletters and the colors that could be displayed, and restricting the size of a member's name in a headline. In addition, the commission proposed that its staff issue advisory opinions on the frankability of all mass mailings of more than 1,000 pieces, not just postal patron mailing.

In recent years, mass mailings by House members had

de-emphasized the postal patron category. Instead, the trend was toward targeted groups of people who expressed strong interest in single issues such as abortion, school prayer, a balanced budget constitutional amendment and other controversial issues. Thus there was an increase in the volume of letters having names and addresses.

The commission's proposed changes provoked a sharply negative reaction from many members and their staffs. Some thought the content restrictions smacked of censorship. Others objected to a recommendation allowing members to send mail only in the capacity of a "federal-level representative" — prohibiting them from sending franked mail on purely local matters.

The negative feedback from House members, together with the Supreme Court's decision upholding the frank and a House vote favoring a $14 million increase in appropriations for franked mail in fiscal 1984, led the franking commission to issue revised guidelines.

"The primary responsibility for ensuring proper and cost-efficient use of the franking privilege," the House commission wrote, "lies with each individual member of the House who uses the privilege." Rather than the strict April limits, the June guidelines merely encouraged members to hold newsletters to four pages and limit the size and type of photographs in newsletters. The commission also suggested — but did not require — that members submit all mass mailings in advance to the commission for advisory opinions. A 1981 law (PL 97-69) did require postal patron mailings, a major category of congressional mass mailings, to be submitted in advance to the commission for advisory opinions.

Senate Action

After a two-year delay, the Senate Rules Committee Nov. 1 agreed on guidelines for postal patron mass mailings. After failing to meet the deadline for guidelines within 120 days of enactment of PL 97-69 — the 1981 law allowing senators to make franked statewide mass mailings — the panel met again in February 1982 but still was unable to reach a decision. It voted unanimously to delay implementation of the provision for the remainder of the 97th Congress.

As adopted Nov. 1, 1983, the committee-approved rules allowed postal patron mailings only for senators' announcements of forthcoming town meetings. The regulations, which took effect Dec. 1, also barred all franked mass mailings, except town meeting notices and opinion surveys, for 60 days immediately preceding any general election, even if the senator was not up for re-election. (The Standing Rules of the Senate already barred senators who were candidates for renomination and re-election from making mass mailings for the 60-day period prior to a state's senatorial primary and prior to the general election.)

1984

Congressional Pay

Members of Congress received a 3.5 percent cost-of-living pay raise, effective Jan. 1, 1985. The raise, under the automatic pay raise law for all federal workers, was guaranteed to take effect when Congress failed to vote otherwise before the 98th Congress adjourned Oct. 12. The increase, boosting lawmakers' salaries to $75,100, had been proposed by President Reagan Aug. 30.

The Senate earlier in 1984 had rejected an attempt to rescind a $2,400 cost-of-living increase, also 3.5 percent, that went into effect Jan. 1, 1984.

As part of the fiscal 1984 Budget Reconciliation Act (HR 4169 — PL 98-270), Congress in April 1984 increased the 3.5 percent salary hike by one-half percentage point, for a total 1984 pay raise of 4 percent. That action increased members' salaries to $72,600. *(Reconciliation act, p. 60)*

Pay Commission Proposal

The Senate Judiciary Committee March 22 reported a proposed constitutional amendment to establish an independent commission to set the salaries of members of Congress, but the Senate never considered the measure (S J Res 1 — S Rept 98-655) in 1984.

The committee sent the resolution to the Senate without a recommendation for or against passage.

Under existing law, Congress could raise or lower the pay of its members. Members automatically received the same annual pay raises the president awarded to white-collar federal employees.

Under S J Res 1, the president would have appointed a nine-member commission to set congressional salaries on July 1 of each even-numbered year. The salaries would take effect when the members of a newly elected Congress took office the following January and would stay in effect for that two-year Congress. *(Pay procedure, p. 824; background, Congress and the Nation Vol. V, p. 889)*

Special Report: Legislative Veto

In a dramatic demonstration of the complex relationships among the three branches of the federal system, the Supreme Court June 23, 1983, told Congress it could no longer use the legislative veto to ensure that the executive carried out the laws as Congress intended.

Adopting the presidents' traditional arguments against the legislative veto, the court held, 7-2, that the veto permitted Congress to intrude into the executive sphere. Use of the veto by Congress breached the separation of powers, in disregard of the "carefully crafted restraints" that the Constitution imposed on the federal system, the court held.

The response of the 98th Congress and the Reagan administration to the court's decision testified to the resilience and flexibility of the system of tripartite government. Despite the sweep of the court's ruling and the initial shockwaves it sent through Capitol Hill, the net practical effect was far less than anticipated.

There was no major shift of power away from Congress and into executive hands. Immediately after the decision, Congress moved to explore new ways of reasserting some measure of control over executive exercise of delegated power. The alternatives considered ranged from constitutional amendments to spending limitations.

By 1984 it was clear that Congress was not ready to adopt a single replacement for the legislative veto. Some laws containing veto provisions were revised, but there was no broad-brush response to the loss of this particular legislative tool.

Executive branch officials, the victors in this long-running constitutional debate, maintained the attitudes of conciliation and cooperation once mandated by the existence of the legislative veto.

Veto Background

The court's decision in the case of *Chadha v. Immigration and Naturalization Service*, with a single stroke, placed out of the reach of Congress a device that had been incorporated in more than 320 provisions of 210 laws over the half century since 1932.

The legislative veto permitted Congress to delegate authority to the executive branch or an administrative agency, while reserving to itself the right to veto the way the executive or the agency exercised that delegated power.

It was a particularly attractive oversight device. It was rarely used to reverse administrative action but highly effective as a means of keeping agency officials responsive to congressional concerns.

The veto came in various forms: one type permitted a single chamber to block an executive regulation or order; another required action by both chambers; another permitted particular committees to exercise the veto power.

Legislative veto provisions were part of landmark statutes in both foreign policy and domestic law, including the 1973 War Powers Resolution, the 1976 Arms Export Control act and the Congressional Budget and Impoundment Act of 1974. *(List of affected laws, p. 981)*

The legislative veto had been a source of controversy ever since 1932 when Congress wrote into the fiscal 1933 legislative branch appropriations act a provision giving either house of Congress a veto over President Hoover's forthcoming executive branch reorganization proposal. The House exercised that veto in 1933, blocking Hoover's reorganization order.

The legislative veto became an increasingly popular tool in the 1970s and early 1980s. This stemmed in part from members' distrust of the executive branch and public opposition to excessive government regulation and in part from the increasingly complex and technical subjects on which Congress was legislating. By 1983 there were approximately 110 laws in force containing veto provisions. Of that number, about one-third had been enacted since the mid-1970s. One law alone, the 1980 Energy Security Act, contained 21 separate veto provisions.

In the foreign policy area, the legislative veto was brandished more and more often in the early 1970s as Congress, stung by public outcry over President Nixon's handling of the Vietnam War, sought to reassert control over such military commitments abroad. *(Foreign policy legislative vetoes, box, p. 836)*

The Reagan View

Although presidents since Hoover had objected to the legislative veto, President Reagan nearly broke the mold. While campaigning for the presidency in 1980, he appeared to endorse the device.

In an Oct. 8, 1980, speech in Youngstown, Ohio, Reagan said, "To better control the growth of federal regulations we should . . . grant both Congress and the president greater authority to veto regulations approved by executive agencies."

After Reagan took office, though, institutional pressures modified his pro-veto stand.

On March 18, 1981, Attorney General William French Smith said the administration believed the legislative veto was unconstitutional if it "intrudes on the power of the

president to manage the executive branch."

James C. Miller III, then an official with the Office of Management and Budget (OMB) and later chairman of the Federal Trade Commission, said the administration opposed legislative vetoes of executive branch rules but would accept them for independent regulatory agency actions.

In November 1981, the administration modified its position further, saying it would back a two-house veto for all agencies provided it required the president's signature.

Finally, in December 1981, Christopher C. DeMuth, OMB director for information and regulatory affairs, said Reagan might veto a bill that would allow Congress to overturn executive agency rules without requiring the president's signature. In January 1982, Solicitor General Rex E. Lee, the administration's advocate before the court, was urging the court to declare the legislative veto unconstitutional.

The *Chadha* Case

The case in which the Supreme Court struck down the legislative veto began in 1974 when Jagdish Rai Chadha, a Kenyan East Indian who had overstayed his student visa, won a decision from the Immigration and Naturalization Service (INS) suspending his deportation.

In December 1975 the House of Representatives, exercising the one-house veto power granted it under a section of the 1952 Immigration and Naturalization Act, vetoed that suspension.

Chadha filed suit challenging the power of the House to overrule the INS. In 1980, the 9th U.S. Circuit Court of Appeals agreed and held the one-house veto of the INS action unconstitutional. The Supreme Court agreed in October 1981 to review that ruling.

The justices heard the case argued in February 1982, but on July 2, 1982, the last day of the 1981-82 term, the court ordered a second round of arguments in the case. Those arguments were held Oct. 7, 1982.

Chadha, meanwhile, had married an American citizen, become a father and settled down in this country.

The Arguments

The Constitution requires that laws be passed by both chambers of Congress and be presented to the president for his approval or disapproval. The legislative veto breaks this constitutional mold, argued the solicitor general in the *Chadha* case.

"The procedure established in that document for the exercise of legislative power was not a mere formality to be disregarded ... whenever Congress might believe it more convenient to exercise that power in some other way," continued the government's argument.

"By providing an opportunity for due deliberation by the two differently constituted Houses of Congress and a detached review of all proposed legislation by the President, the Framers intended to protect against improvident and ill-considered exercises of legislative power and encroachment upon the Executive," the government's attorneys declared.

Furthermore, their argument continued, the legislative veto violates the separation of powers by directly involving Congress in the execution of the laws, a function that the Constitution vests in the president and his subordinates.

If the legislative veto was held to be an appropriate device, the result would be the blending of legislative and

---

Varieties of Vetoes

Although many varieties of legislative veto were adopted over the years, they shared one common feature: they permitted all or part of Congress to block an executive action, with or without the president's approval.

One form of legislative veto permitted either house of Congress to block an agency plan or rule by passing a simple resolution of disapproval within a fixed period, usually 30 or 60 days, from the time of the agency's action. A variation permitted a one-house veto only if the second chamber did not overturn the first's action within a specified time.

Another common type of veto required passage of a concurrent resolution of disapproval by both houses.

A third form permitted one or more congressional committees to block an agency action. Yet another type required passage of a resolution approving a proposed rule or plan by one or both houses, or one or more congressional committees, before the plan or rule could be carried out.

Finally, some two-house veto plans required the president's signature, essentially making the congressional action equivalent to the passing of a whole new law.

---

executive power and "a wholesale departure from the constitutionally prescribed means for exercising legislative power," Solicitor General Lee warned.

In defense of the legislative veto, attorneys representing the House and Senate contended that it was an appropriate way of ensuring accountability. Furthermore, they emphasized, both the executive branch and Congress had found it "a realistic way of resolving practical issues in their relations."

"Its most important function has been to avoid or restrain broad delegations of authority to the President or agencies," they contended.

"It has not served to enact legislation outside the constitutional process," but rather has equipped Congress and the executive to respond effectively to unprecedented national problems.

Often in such situations, Congress has found it necessary to delegate broad authority to the executive branch, the congressional advocates continued.

Such delegation "risks unaccountable national policy-making" by unelected bureaucrats, rather than elected officials.

The legislative veto permitted Congress to retain control and ensure accountability.

The legislative veto does not "impair the system of checks and balances," the Senate's brief concluded. It is rather "a means of making that system work in the face of modern problems."

The Court's Decision

The legislative veto might be convenient, but it was not constitutional, the court ruled June 23, 1983, in the case of *Immigration and Naturalization Service v. Chadha*. It was the court's most important separation-of-powers ruling since the White House tapes case of the Watergate era, when the struggle was between President Nixon and the judicial branch of government.

The men who wrote the Constitution decided that "the legislative power of the federal government [should] be exercised in accord with a single, finely wrought and exhaustively considered procedure," the court declared. That procedure demands that a measure be approved by both houses of Congress and presented to the president for his signature or veto, the court said.

When Congress delegated to the executive branch the authority to issue regulations or make certain kinds of decisions, it "must abide by its delegation of authority until that delegation is legislatively altered or revoked," the court said. *(Text of majority and dissenting opinions, p. 981)*

Chief Justice Warren E. Burger spoke for six members of the majority in striking down the legislative veto. Joining him were Justices William J. Brennan Jr., Thurgood Marshall, Harry A. Blackmun, John Paul Stevens and Sandra Day O'Connor.

Justice Lewis F. Powell Jr. concurred in the court's judgment in the specific case at hand, but for different reasons.

Justice Byron R. White wrote a stinging dissent, decrying the "destructive scope" of the ruling. "Today's decision," said White, "strikes down in one fell swoop provisions in more laws enacted by Congress than the court has cumulatively invalidated in its history." (By the end of the 1981-82 term, the court had struck down as unconstitutional all or part of 110 federal laws.)

Justice William H. Rehnquist wrote his own dissent, which dealt only with the case before the court and did not discuss the legislative veto in general.

The Majority Opinion

Writing for the court, Chief Justice Burger vigorously endorsed the Constitution's scheme for separating and balancing the powers of the three branches of government — legislative, executive and judicial.

He acknowledged the practical and political difficulties this arrangement sometimes created but said: "Convenience and efficiency are not the primary objectives — or the hallmarks — of democratic government, and our inquiry is sharpened rather than blunted by the fact that congressional veto provisions are appearing with increasing frequency in statutes which delegate authority to executive and independent agencies."

"The hydraulic pressure inherent within each of the separate branches to exceed the outer limits of its power, even to accomplish desirable objectives, must be resisted," Burger said.

The Constitution sets out in "explicit and unambiguous provisions" the manner in which the legislative power is to be exercised, Burger noted. Article I states that bills shall be approved by both the House and the Senate and shall be presented to the president for his approval.

"It is beyond doubt that lawmaking was a power to be shared by both houses and the president," wrote Burger.

The one-house legislative veto runs afoul of these requirements, both of which have a clear purpose.

"The president's participation in the legislative process was to protect the executive branch from Congress and to protect the whole people from improvident laws," Burger said.

The majority's view that the legislative veto did not comport with this constitutional prescription was further reinforced, the chief justice explained, by the fact that the framers did set out four specific situations in which one house should act alone — the House to initiate impeachments, and the Senate to try impeachments, to confirm or reject presidential appointments, and to ratify or reject treaties.

The Dissent

In one of the longest dissenting opinions of his judicial career, one equaling the majority opinion in length, Justice White declared that the "prominence of the legislative veto mechanism in our contemporary political system and its importance to Congress can hardly be overstated."

By denying Congress the use of that mechanism, he said, the court presented Congress with "a Hobson's choice: either to refrain from delegating the necessary authority, leaving itself with a hopeless task of writing laws with the requisite specificity to cover endless special circumstances across the entire policy landscape, or in the alternative, to abdicate its lawmaking function to the executive branch and independent agencies.

"To choose the former leaves major national problems unresolved; to opt for the latter risks unaccountable policy-making by those not elected to fill that role," White wrote.

White said the legislative veto was "an important if not indispensable political invention that allows the president and Congress to resolve major constitutional and policy differences, assures the accountability of independent regulatory agencies and preserves Congress' control over lawmaking."

History showed, White wrote, that Congress had not used this veto as a "sword" with which it struck out to "aggrandize itself at the expense of the other branches." Instead, he said, it had used the veto as "a means of defense, a reservation of ultimate authority necessary if Congress is to fulfill its designated role under Article I as the nation's lawmaker."

"In my view, neither Article I of the Constitution nor the doctrine of separation of powers is violated by this mechanism by which our elected representatives preserve their voice in the governance of the nation," White concluded.

He said the power to exercise a legislative veto was not the same as the power to write new law without the approval of both chambers and the president.

The veto must in the first place be authorized by statute, he pointed out, and can only negate a proposal from the executive branch or an independent agency. "On its face," he wrote, "the legislative veto no more allows one house of Congress to make law than does the presidential veto confer such power upon the president."

The Follow-Up Rulings

Less than two weeks after its ruling in the *Chadha* case, the court made clear that it intended to invalidate not just one-house legislative vetoes, but virtually all existing

Congress Loses Major Foreign Policy Tool

By striking down the legislative veto, the Supreme Court stripped from Congress one of the major tools it had devised in its effort to exert more influence over foreign policy in the 1970s.

Congress had equipped itself with the legislative veto to curb presidential powers ranging from arms sales to declarations of national emergency. It enacted these laws in the early 1970s in response to President Nixon's conduct of the Vietnam War — and in spite of the bitter objections of Nixon's successor, Gerald R. Ford.

Although Congress had never actually used any of its foreign policy vetoes, its leaders frequently had threatened a veto to force the executive branch to consult more closely and accept compromises.

Following the court's decision, it was apparent that both Congress and the administration were hoping to avoid confrontations and that both appreciated the strength that developed from consultation on such matters. "From our point of view, nothing has changed," said one administration lawyer who dealt with foreign policy statutes. "We never conceded the constitutionality of the legislative veto in the first place. But as a practical matter, we would be fools to thumb our noses at Congress now."

The 98th Congress did not amend the affected laws to replace the legislative veto with any other similar device. Instead, the legislators effectively used alternative devices to limit the executive's discretion.

War Powers

The two most important veto provisions in this area were in the War Powers Resolution of 1973 (PL 93-148) and the Arms Export Control Act of 1976 (PL 94-329). Other major laws allowed Congress to veto exports of nuclear materials (the 1978 Nuclear Nonproliferation Act, PL 95-242), and to overturn the granting of most-favored-nation trading status to certain communist countries (the Jackson-Vanik amendment of 1974, PL 93-618). *(Favored nation trade, p. 107; nuclear non-proliferation, Congress and the Nation Vol. V, p. 147)*

The War Powers Resolution allowed Congress, by passing a concurrent resolution, to force the withdrawal of U.S. troops engaged in hostilities overseas without specific congressional authorization. That veto provision — which Congress had never exercised — appeared to be nullified by the court's decision. The Senate moved to replace that provision with a joint resolution provision late in 1983, but House conferees refused to approve that change. *(PL 93-148, Congress and the Nation Vol. IV, p. 849)*

However, another major section of the law remained intact. It prohibited the president from keeping U.S. forces in hostile situations overseas for more than 90 days unless Congress had declared war, had specifically authorized the president's action or had extended the time period. Although that provision had the effect of a legislative veto, it did not involve the simple or concurrent resolution vetoes that the Supreme Court challenged.

Congress invoked this section of the War Powers act for the first time in 1983 when it cleared a compromise measure (S J Res 159 — PL 98-119) authorizing U.S. Marines who were in Lebanon as part of a multinational peacekeeping force to remain there for up to 18 months. A key Senate aide pointed out that by specifying a fixed period of time in this law, Congress had less flexibility that it would have had under the current resolution veto provision that permitted it to force withdrawal at any time.

Although Reagan signed the bill Oct. 12, he expressed reservations about its constitutionality. *(Lebanon resolution, p. 156)*

Arms Export Law

The arms export law allowed Congress to veto major arms sales by concurrent resolution within 30 days of receiving a presidential notification of a planned sale. As amended in 1981, the veto applied to individual weapons or military equipment worth $14 million or more, and to package sales of $50 million or more. *(1981 amendment, p. 132)*

Congress never actually vetoed an arms sale, but it forced Presidents Carter and Reagan to make compromises during dramatic battles over sales to the Middle East. The closest fight was in 1981, when the Senate narrowly rejected a veto of the sale of AWACS radar planes to Saudi Arabia. *(Details, p. 129)*

The court's decision came down just as the Senate Foreign Relations and House Foreign Affairs committees were moving to place new restrictions on the president's powers. *(El Salvador, p. 165)*

Still effective after the loss of the legislative veto, however, was the provision of the arms export law requiring the president to report to Congress any arms sales exceeding $14 million for a single item or $50 million for a package of arms.

The usefulness of that requirement was highlighted in March 1984 when congressional opposition to the sale of Stinger anti-aircraft missiles to Jordan and Saudi Arabia forced President Reagan to withdraw the sale to Jordan and delay the sale to the Saudis. *(Mideast special report, p. 191)*

Reports of U.S. activity in Nicaragua made in compliance with this requirement served as the basis for congressional action in 1984 denying further funds for such activities unless both chambers approved. *(Story, p. 175)*

forms of the device.

Without opinion, the court July 6 affirmed two lower court decisions holding unconstitutional a one-house legislative veto provision in the 1978 Natural Gas Policy Act and a two-house legislative veto provision in the Federal Trade Commission Improvements Act of 1980.

In both cases, the U.S. Court of Appeals for the District of Columbia had ruled that the vetoes permitted Congress to intrude too far into the powers reserved by the Constitution to the other two branches of the federal government.

Justices Rehnquist and White, the dissenting justices in *Chadha*, voted to review the cases. White argued that the vetoes involved were different from the one struck down in *Chadha*, because *Chadha* involved a congressional veto of an executive branch decision, while in these cases, Congress was overturning decisions of independent regulatory commissions — the Federal Energy Regulatory Commission (FERC) and the Federal Trade Commission (FTC).

"To invalidate the device which allows Congress to maintain some control over the lawmaking process merely guarantees that the independent agencies, once created, for all practical purposes are a fourth branch of the government not subject to the direct control of either Congress or the executive branch. I cannot believe that the Constitution commands such a result," White wrote.

The FERC case involved the House's 1980 veto of the agency's so-called "Phase II" plan for deregulating natural gas prices.

The FTC case grew out of a 1982 congressional veto of a proposed rule requiring used-car dealers to disclose information on auto defects before a sale. *(Story, p. 273)*

Congress in 1980 included one of the broadest of all the legislative veto provisions in the Federal Trade Commission authorization (PL 96-252) allowing it to block any regulation of the independent regulatory agency if both houses passed a resolution of disapproval. *(Congress and the Nation Vol. V, p. 847)*

The used-car proposal was the only FTC rule vetoed prior to the court's ruling. A 1983 effort to block an FTC rule requiring funeral home directors to disclose detailed price information to customers failed.

Congressional Reaction

Initial congressional reaction to the court's decision was mixed. "It will mean some readjustment of a lot of laws," said Senate Majority Leader Howard H. Baker Jr., R-Tenn.

"We're going to be less willing to delegate in the future," said Charles E. Grassley, R-Iowa, a key Senate supporter of the veto.

"The unelected, unaccountable bureaucrats have gained too much power. They have become the fourth branch of government and we need to exert more authority over them," said Sen. Carl Levin, D-Mich., who along with Rep. Elliott H. Levitas, D-Ga. (1975-85), had been among the leading advocates of the legislative veto.

The veto's opponents, however, applauded the decision. "It's been a long time in coming," said Rep. Peter W. Rodino Jr., D-N.J., chairman of the House Judiciary Committee. "The legislative veto violates the orderly process of government. It's an invasion of the principle of separation of powers," Rodino said.

Sen. Patrick J. Leahy, D-Vt., said Congress would have to be more precise about its intent when it passed laws. "We pass such fuzzy legislation. Then we pass it on to administrative agencies and say: 'You work it out.' Then members and the president go out and campaign against those 'crazy bureaucrats,'" said Leahy.

And Rep. Joe Moakley, D-Mass., observed: "[B]y restraining Congress from immersing itself in every item of regulation and adjudication, the court has saved Congress from drowning in detail it lacks the institutional capacity to manage, and freed it to act within the scope of its legitimate role for shaping national policy."

Several members predicted that the ruling would dramatically change the relationship between the legislative and executive branches.

"Up to now, Congress and the president have shared power in hundreds of laws," said Levin. In those statutes, he said, "the Congress has permitted the president certain leeway subject to its saying no. If it is no longer permitted to veto such actions of the president, it is less likely to grant him the authority in the first place.

"The result," Levin said, "is that shared power is out the window and either a more costly legislative process or an imperial presidency will take its place."

The Aftermath

Discussion

In the weeks immediately after the Supreme Court's decision, major committees in both chambers convened hearings at which members, administration officials and legal experts assessed the impact of the *Chadha* ruling and explored alternatives.

The list of alternatives was long, including a constitutional amendment to legitimize the veto, the use of joint resolutions of disapproval or approval, "report and wait" provisions delaying implementation of a rule or decision by the executive for a specified period of time after Congress has been notified of it, and denying or limiting funds or budget authority for specific actions. *(Details, box, p. 838)*

The joint resolution seemed the most appealing alternative means of overturning executive decisions and regulations. Since it is approved by both chambers and presented to the president for his signature, it clearly avoided the court's constitutional objections to the veto.

Indeed, as Frederick M. Kaiser of the Congressional Research Service has written, "A joint resolution of approval, in fact, is the functional equivalent of a one-House veto," because if one house refuses to approve the joint resolution, the proposed action is blocked.

Practical considerations of legislative time and energy quickly sidetracked proposals for sweeping rewrites of all laws containing legislative vetoes. In most cases, the veto provisions were ignored, unless their presence cast such doubt over the validity of actions taken under the law that a rewrite was required. The inherent difficulty of winning approval of a constitutional amendment or other across-the-board alternative soon relegated those suggestions to the lower half of the congressional agenda as well.

Administration Position

Reagan administration officials downplayed the effect of the ruling on executive-legislative relations.

All the Alternatives...

To assist Congress in responding to the loss of the legislative veto, the Congressional Research Service (CRS) in December 1983 produced a study outlining the various "Alternatives to the Legislative Veto." The study was written by Frederick M. Kaiser, a CRS specialist in American national government. Kaiser described the following statutory alternatives through which Congress can control or influence executive branch action:

Committee Vetoes. These vetoes had been in use since the 1950s, and some two dozen were approved by Congress even after the Supreme Court held the legislative veto unconstitutional. These provisions, which allow a committee to approve or disapprove some agency action, are particularly useful in providing agencies flexibility in shifting — or re-programming — appropriated funds between budget categories within a departmental or agency budget.

Direct Override or Pre-emption. Congress can pass a law directly revoking or overruling executive branch action on some matter, or pre-empting that area by taking that action itself. For example, Congress itself wrote the language to be used to label saccharin products, instead of leaving the task to the Food and Drug Administration (FDA), Kaiser noted.

Modification of Agency Jurisdiction. Congress also can place certain matters beyond an agency's reach, either exempting them from regulation altogether or transferring them to another agency's jurisdiction. Once again, saccharin provides the example, Kaiser wrote, pointing out that Congress in 1983 again barred the FDA from banning saccharin.

Joint Resolution of Approval or Disapproval. By requiring both houses to approve or disapprove an agency action, and the president to sign such a joint resolution, Congress can meet the objections raised by the Supreme Court to the legislative veto and in many ways accomplish the same end. It is unlikely, however, Kaiser noted, that a president would sign a joint resolution disapproving an action of his administration. If he withheld his signature, the joint resolution would only become law if approved by a two-thirds vote of each chamber.

Limitations in Appropriations. By denying the use of funds for a specific activity, Congress can effectively nullify an executive branch decision to engage in that activity. But, wrote Kaiser, this way of overturning executive action is "a two-edged sword."

Such limitations are normally valid only for a fiscal year, and also are in conflict with the effort of the House and Senate leadership to curtail the addition of legislative provisions to appropriations bills.

As an example, Kaiser pointed to the disagreement between Interior Secretary James G. Watt and the Interior committees over the leasing of federal coal reserves, noting that language in the fiscal 1984 Interior appropriations bill placed a moratorium on such leasing until a special commission reported to Congress on current policies. *(Story, p. 352)*

Limitations in Authorizations. These are of particular usefulness in military construction and foreign affairs matters, wrote Kaiser. "The substantial and increasing number of program or agency budgets already under frequent authorizations (compared to the predominance of permanent or long-term authorizations until the 1970s) make these limitations more feasible now," he explained. "The shortened time period increases opportunities to review and influence agency behavior ... and adds congressional leverage over executive actions."

Kaiser pointed out the effort of some members of Congress to impose this type of limitation on MX procurement and deployment in the fiscal 1984 defense authorization bill, and a similar effort by the House to use this device in the Intelligence Authorization Act of fiscal 1983 to limit CIA covert operations in Nicaragua. *(Stories, pp. 225, 152)*

Prior Notification/Consultation. This is most often referred to as the "report and wait" provision, which does not usually permit a committee or Congress to reject a planned agency action without passing legislation. But, such provisions do ensure a committee the opportunity to block proposed action by legislation.

"One of the most comprehensive current examples of advance notification is found in the FY 1981 Intelligence Authorization Act," wrote Kaiser. That law directs that the House and Senate committees on intelligence be kept "fully and currently informed of all intelligence activities ... including any significant anticipated intelligence activity. ..." Other agencies subject to such requirements in certain areas include the Departments of Defense, Housing and Urban Development, Transportation, the Interstate Commerce Commission, the Nuclear Regulatory Commission and the Consumer Product Safety Commission.

Deputy Attorney General Edward C. Schmults said the administration would work with Congress in a "spirit of comity" to resolve the legislative and administrative problems resulting from the decision. He said the executive branch would continue to honor existing "report and wait" provisions.

Schmults also contended that only minor adjustments would be needed to fix laws that contained legislative veto provisions. In place of the veto, he said, "there are many effective and fully constitutional mechanisms whereby Congress can carry out its constitutional oversight functions."

House Rules Committee Action

Of immediate concern to the congressional leadership was what to do with pending legislation containing vetoes.

The House Rules Committee July 26 announced that it would not act on any bill containing a legislative veto if it had been reported from committee after the Supreme Court's decision on June 23.

The Rules Committee sent two such measures back to the Foreign Affairs Committee. That committee immediately amended a foreign aid authorization bill (HR 2992) to require a joint resolution — instead of a concurrent resolution which is not presented to the president for signature — to suspend military aid to El Salvador. The committee similarly amended an export administration measure (HR 3231). *(Stories, pp. 159, 107)*

Committee Vetoes

To the considerable surprise of observers, lawmakers approved 53 more legislative veto provisions in the 98th Congress, after the Supreme Court decision. Some of these laws were so far along in the legislative pipeline at the time of the ruling that Congress simply did not delete the veto provisions.

All but three of the 53 new provisions gave the veto power to a committee, not a chamber, and almost all these new provisions were contained in appropriations or authorization bills with fixed terms. Most expired by the end of fiscal 1985.

However, this particular type of veto — most often given to the Appropriations committees to ensure congressional approval of "reprogramming" of funds — that is, shifting of funds between accounts within an agency's budget — was the most likely to survive *Chadha*.

This arrangement was the product of the understanding between Congress and executive branch agencies that such cooperation on these matters was to mutual advantage. Since the 1950s, certain appropriations bills forbade such reprogramming unless it was approved by the Appropriations committees.

Although such restraints were now technically invalid under *Chadha*, the agency and Congress were likely to ignore that fact and continue to cooperate in this fashion, absent a specific legal challenge to the practice, congressional analysts predicted.

"The agencies are legally free to ignore the committees and spend the funds...," Louis Fisher of the Congressional Research Service told the Senate Judiciary Subcommittee on Administrative Practice in 1983. "They defer to the committees because they fear retribution in the form of budget cutbacks ... and other sanctions," he said.

Fisher predicted that "some matters that were open under the legislative veto will start to go underground." He said that he anticipated that committees might in the future delegate authority to an agency and say: "Before you do this, notify us."

"Notification will be the code word for the legislative veto," he concluded.

Joint Resolution

The week after *Chadha*, the House reflected the general state of congressional confusion on the issue by including two conflicting provisions — each intended to replace a legislative veto — in a bill authorizing the Consumer Product Safety Commission (CPSC).

One, written by veto advocate Rep. Levitas, required proposed commission actions to be approved by joint resolution before taking effect. A second, offered by Rep. Henry A. Waxman, D-Calif., permitted commission actions to take effect unless Congress passed a joint resolution of disapproval.

In part because of its inability to decide which of these provisions to endorse, the 98th Congress did not complete action on the CPSC authorization measure. *(Story, p. 277)*

Such irresolution was evident in November, when the House first adopted and then rejected, by cliff-hanger votes, a Levitas amendment requiring approval, by joint resolution, of certain hazardous waste rules promulgated by the Environmental Protection Agency. *(Story, p. 457)*

The Senate in October moved to amend a key provision of the War Powers act that had permitted Congress to use a concurrent resolution, basically a two-chamber veto not subject to presidential signature, to withdraw U.S. troops from hostilities abroad.

In place of that provision, the Senate substituted a joint resolution. This change was killed in conference. *(State Department authorization bill, story, p. 167)*

Reorganization Authority. By 1984, however, Congress seemed to agree that in certain circumstances the joint resolution provided the most effective mechanism for retaining a measure of control over matters previously subject to a legislative veto.

The first legislative veto had been approved in 1932 as part of a law permitting the president to reorganize executive branch agencies. Similar reorganization statutes had been in effect — with brief lapses — since 1932.

Congress in 1984 restored that presidential authority to restructure government agencies, which had expired in 1981, and replaced the one-house veto with a provision permitting reorganization plans to take effect only if approved by both the House and Senate through a joint resolution within 90 days of receiving the plan from the president. *(Story, p. 790)*

Congress also in 1984 settled another legal question raised by *Chadha* when it passed a law ratifying all previous reorganizations of the federal government under laws that had contained legislative veto provisions.

This action was made necessary by the filing of more than 100 lawsuits challenging as invalid a 1978 transfer of authority to enforce the Equal Pay Act and the Age Discrimination in Employment Act from the Labor Department to the Equal Employment Opportunity Commission.

These suits argued that because this transfer occurred under authority of a reorganization law containing a legislative veto provision, that entire statute was unconstitutional — and the reorganizations effected under it invalid. At least five federal courts had agreed that the transfer was invalid. The passage of the 1984 bill ratifying those reorganizations (PL 98-532) ended that litigation.

District of Columbia Laws. The 1973 law giving the District of Columbia a measure of home rule contained a provision permitting either the House or the Senate to veto laws passed by the D.C. government.

The Supreme Court's ruling that legislative vetoes were unconstitutional raised doubts about the validity of the entire District of Columbia Home Rule Act and the District's authority, as an independent government, to borrow money by issuing bonds.

To clear up such doubts, Congress in 1984 approved a measure, included in the continuing resolution for fiscal

The Veto Goes Underground

"With or without the legislative veto, Congress will remain a partner" in administering the laws, wrote Louis Fisher, one of the closest observers of the aftermath of *Chadha.*

In his book, "Constitutional Conflicts between Congress and the President" (1985), Fisher — a specialist in American government at the Congressional Research Service — predicted: "We should not be too surprised or disconcerted if, after the Court has closed the door to the legislative veto, we hear a number of windows being raised and perhaps new doors constructed, making the executive-legislative structure as accommodating as before for shared power."

Writing in a special issue of the *Public Administration Review,* 1985, Fisher recounted just such a "window-raising" episode.

In July 1984, a year after *Chadha,* Congress sent President Reagan the HUD-Independent Agencies appropriations bill that contained eight committee vetoes.

Reagan signed the bill (PL 98-371) but declared that "the time has come . . . to make clear that legislation containing legislative veto devices that comes to me for my approval or disapproval will be implemented in a manner consistent with the *Chadha* decision."

"The clear import" of Reagan's statement, Fisher writes, "was that the Administration did not feel bound by the statutory requirements" permitting committee vetoes.

In response, the House Appropriations Committee moved to repeal an agreement it had worked out four year earlier with the National Aeronautics and Space Administration (NASA), one of the independent agencies funded in PL 98-371.

Under this agreement, the appropriations bill for NASA set "caps" on various programs, usually at the level of the budget request. NASA was allowed to exceed those caps if the appropriations committees agreed.

Because of Reagan's threat to ignore such controls, the committee moved to repeal the agreement with NASA. "Both sides stood to lose," explains Fisher. "The Appropriations Committee would not be able to veto NASA proposals; NASA would not be able to exceed ceilings without enacting new legislation in a separate appropriations bill. Neither . . . wanted to enact a separate public law just to exceed a 'cap.' "

And so James M. Beggs, administrator of NASA, wrote the committees a letter that, Fisher comments, "reveals the pragmatic sense of give-and-take that is customary between executive agencies and congressional committees."

Beggs expressed concern about the rigid system that would result from repeal of the existing agreement with the committees. "Without some procedure for adjustment, other than a subsequent separate legislative enactment, these ceilings could seriously impact the ability of NASA to meet unforeseen technical changes or problems that are inherent in challenging R & D programs."

And so he proposed "that the present legislative procedure . . . be converted by this letter into an informal agreement by NASA not to exceed amounts for committee-designated programs without the approval of the committees on appropriations."

"This agreement would assume that both the statutory funding ceilings and the committee approval mechanisms would be deleted from the FY 1985 legislation, and that it would not be the normal practice to include either mechanism in future appropriations bills," Beggs continued.

"Further, the agreement would assume that future program ceiling amounts would be identified by the committees in the conference report accompanying NASA's annual appropriations act and confirmed by NASA. . . . NASA would not expend any funds over the ceilings identified in the conference report . . . without the prior approval of the committee."

"In short," Fisher concludes, NASA "would continue to honor legislative vetoes." Such non-statutory vetoes are, he wrote "not legal in effect. They are, however, in effect legal. Agencies are aware of the penalties that can be invoked by Congress if they decide to violate understandings and working relationships with their review committees."

1985 (PL 98-473), that required Congress to pass, and the president to sign, a joint resolution in order to disapprove any law passed by the D.C. government. *(Story, p. 793)*

Legislative Approval

In September 1983, the House Energy and Commerce Committee replaced one-house vetoes in an Amtrak authorization bill with "report and wait" provisions, requiring 120 days of legislative sessions to pass before any proposed route change could take effect.

The committee also replaced a provision permitting a legislative veto of any Department of Transportation plan to sell Conrail with a provision requiring Congress to approve a plan before a sale could occur. *(Story, p. 326)*

Earlier, the Senate Armed Services Committee replaced a one-house veto restriction on the president's control over military raises with a requirement that the president submit as legislation any pay raise differing from the recommendations of the secretary of defense.

16

The Reagan Presidency

First-Term Review   *843*
Reagan Profile   *844*
Assassination Attempt *847*
Bush Profile   *854*

The Reagan Presidency

Americans on Nov. 6, 1984, re-elected President Ronald Reagan by 59 percent of the popular vote — just shy of the 61 percent record established by President Lyndon B. Johnson in 1964. The Electoral College verdict broke the record, with 525 electoral votes. Reagan captured all but the District of Columbia and Minnesota, the home state of his Democratic opponent, former Vice President Walter F. Mondale.

As impressive as Reagan's victory was, a crucial question remained unanswered: Were the results a mandate to continue the "Reagan Revolution," which admirers had called the president's sharp departure from the policies of previous administrations — both Democratic and Republican? Or were they more an indication of the president's personal popularity, along with Mondale's persistent inability during the campaign to excite voters and rally broad support for the Democratic cause?

Countering any claim of a mandate was the relatively disappointing showing of Republican congressional candidates. Although GOP leaders once had held hopes of capturing as many as 25 to 30 House seats in the 99th Congress, they picked up only 15 seats in the House (after losing a disputed race decided in 1985) and lost two in the Senate. With such modest Republican House gains, Reagan clearly would not have the working majorities in 1985 and 1986 that he enjoyed in both the House and Senate when he first came into office in 1981.

One point was not debatable as President Reagan's first term ended: the remarkable recovery that the economy had staged in 1983 and 1984.

Although showing signs of slowing during the final months of 1984, the comeback had been unexpectedly strong. The recovery came after a deep recession that began the year Reagan entered the White House.

The prime lending rate in January 1981 was fluctuating between 20 and 20-1/2 percent, while the Consumer Price Index, the most widely used measure of inflation, was approaching 12 percent per year. Unemployment stood at 7.5 percent. By midterm, interest rates and the rate of inflation had dropped, but at the heavy price of a 10.7 percent unemployment rate — the highest since the end of World War II.

The economy began to recover in 1983. The Consumer Price Index held at a relatively low 3.8 percent during the year, and unemployment dipped to 8.2 percent in December. The prime interest rate, which had peaked at 21.5 percent in December 1980, had dropped back to 11 percent by the latter half of 1983. And the "real" gross national product (GNP) — the nation's total output of goods and services, adjusted for inflation — grew 3.3 percent during the first quarter of 1983, 9.4 percent in the second quarter, 6.8 percent in the third, and 5.9 percent in the fourth.

Continued high budget deficits throughout Reagan's first four years in office formed an uncertain backdrop for the economic expansion. While economists debated the theoretical effects of deficits, the budget gaps seemed to matter little in the day-to-day lives of most Americans, the vast majority of whom, polls showed, considered themselves substantially better off at the end than at the beginning of Reagan's first term.

A key calculation in the minds of many voters as the election neared, some observers believed, was the fact that they were sharing less of their income with the federal government. A personal income tax cut had formed the centerpiece of Reagan's economic program.

Reagan's predecessor, Jimmy Carter, believed that tax reductions would increase inflation, a principle reflected in the last budget Carter sent to Congress before leaving office on Jan. 20, 1981. But that document had only limited effect. Soon after he was sworn in, the new president sent to Congress his own budget, calling for the largest tax reduction in American history. Indeed, Reagan's first budget proposed massive, across-the-board spending cuts in all areas of domestic spending. The only budget category spared was defense. It was essentially this budget, complete with its dramatic tax cut, that was enacted in 1981.

Another fact apparently not lost on voters was that America was at peace. Despite anxiety over possible U.S. involvement in Central America and the deaths of American Marines on a peacekeeping mission in Lebanon, at the time of the 1984 election no U.S. servicemen were exposed to hostile fire in a foreign country.

Democrats as well as Republicans spoke of one dramatic difference between President Reagan's first term and the years preceding it back to the Vietnam War — an evident renewal of national pride. In the summer of 1979, President Carter had said in a speech that the country was suffering from a "crisis of confidence," and that the "erosion of our confidence in the future is threatening to destroy the social and political fabric of America." Just five years later, patriotism and confidence in the nation's future were basic themes on both sides of the 1984 presidential campaign.

How much Reagan had to do with the resurgence in the economy and in the national spirit could be argued. But the fact that it did happen during his first term in office resulted, deservedly or not, in his being awarded the credit at the polls. What was beyond dispute was that Reagan

Ronald Wilson Reagan of Tampico, Illinois ...

When he became president in 1981, Ronald Reagan already had lived a long and eventful life.

Movie star, television spokesman and governor of California, Reagan was a well-known figure to most Americans even before he began his pursuit of the presidency. Like Dwight D. Eisenhower and few other presidents, Reagan's national fame predated his political career.

Along with gaining him notoriety, Reagan's 30-year career in the entertainment business also shaped his abilities and outlook.

Years of experience as an actor and television host helped hone Reagan's talent for getting his message across. The consummate master of political television, he was unmatched in his ability to communicate directly to the people.

Reagan's approach to issues and the way he discussed them also reflected his time as an actor. He referred frequently to movies and their plots, and expressed a view of the world in which, as in Hollywood, the line between right and wrong was sharply drawn.

"We have been ... told there are no simple answers to complex problems," Reagan once said. "Well, the truth is there are simple answers, just not easy ones."

Reagan grew up in modest surroundings in several small towns in rural northern Illinois. Born Feb. 6, 1911, in Tampico, Ill., he was the younger of two sons of John and Nellie Wilson Reagan. His father was an alcoholic Irish Catholic who had trouble keeping a job; his mother was a Protestant of Scottish descent who loved the theater. When Reagan was nine, the family settled in Dixon, Ill.

After graduating from Eureka College, a small liberal arts institution near his home, Reagan began working as a sports announcer for a Davenport, Iowa, radio station. He developed a national reputation when the station joined the NBC network, which carried his football and baseball play-by-play throughout the Midwest.

Reagan was covering baseball spring training in California when an agent from Warner Brothers signed him to a film contract. In his 1937 movie debut, "Love Is On the Air," Reagan played a radio announcer who uncovered corruption in local government.

Over the next two decades, Reagan appeared in more than 50 movies. Although most of his films were not highly regarded by critics, he did have two notable roles — as George Gipp, a Notre Dame football player, in "Knute Rockne — All American," and as a small-town playboy who has his legs cut off in "Kings Row." But movies like "Bedtime for Bonzo," where he played opposite a chimpanzee, and "The Killers," in which he had his only villainous role, received less favorable responses from critics.

While in Hollywood, Reagan met and married another film star, Jane Wyman. Wed in 1940, the couple raised two children, Maureen and Michael. They were divorced in 1949. In 1952 Reagan married Nancy Davis, by whom he had two children, Patricia and Ronald. Reagan was the first divorced man ever elected president.

Reagan's career in politics began while he was still an actor. In 1947 he was elected president of the Screen Actors Guild, a major Hollywood labor union. He held that post for six years, working out several contract agreements with film studios. Reagan was the first former union chief ever to occupy the White House.

But Reagan's efforts in hunting down leftists in the film industry attracted more attention than his work as a labor negotiator. He was a strong supporter of the "blacklisting" of actors with alleged ties to the Communist Party, and in 1947 appeared before the

brought to Washington a philosophy that broke sharply with the past. The historic tax and spending cuts enacted in 1981 were clearly consequences of that philosophy. Although the economic effects of the cuts were debatable, they indisputably ushered in a period of sharp fiscal restraint. Also departing distinctly from the positions of previous administrations were Reagan's national security policies, two linchpins of which were his belief that the United States had fallen behind in the arms race with the Soviet Union and his insistence on substantial after-inflation increases in defense spending. Underlying Reagan's determination was his undisguised mistrust of the Soviet Union, which early in his term he labeled an "evil empire."

Assessing Reagan's first term shortly before he was reelected, Thomas E. Mann, executive director of the American Political Science Association, declared, "The agenda really has changed. In spite of the fact that the Democrats are now resisting budget cuts, the calls for continued and massive increases in federal programs are gone. Reagan has altered the terms on which politicians talk about government."

The Reagan Style

How much of this change in agenda came about because the historic pendulum had swung and Americans simply were ready for a change, and how much because of Reagan's political talents may be debated.

President Reagan was billed as the "great communicator" for his ability to project his ideas to audiences, both in person and via the electronic media. Some observers

... Sports Broadcaster, Movie Actor, Politician

House Un-American Activities Committee as a friendly witness in its investigation of communism in Hollywood.

During that period Reagan's political views underwent a profound transformation. A Democrat for much of his life, Reagan had been a "near-hopeless hemophiliac liberal," as he put it in his 1965 autobiography, "Where's the Rest of Me?" As he struggled to purge his union, however, he gradually became much more conservative. By 1952 he was working for Eisenhower's campaign, while still a Democrat. Two years after he supported Richard M. Nixon's 1960 presidential campaign, Reagan became a Republican.

By that time Reagan had all but abandoned his movie career in favor of television. His position as the host for the "GE Theatre" and corporate spokesman for General Electric from 1954 until 1962 gave him a political forum. It was an opportunity for Reagan to develop both his conservative political ideas and the set speech, with its anti-communist and anti-government themes, that he was to use so often during his rise to political prominence.

The turning point of Reagan's developing political career came in the fall of 1964, when he made a nationwide television speech seeking to revive Barry Goldwater's slumping presidential candidacy. In the speech, which marked his true arrival on the national political scene, Reagan spoke of the United States as "the only island of freedom that is left in the whole world."

Following that speech several California businessmen approached Reagan, then host of TV's "Death Valley Days," suggesting he run for governor. In a state where parties traditionally had held little influence, Reagan easily transformed his image from that of a television personality into a successful political figure.

Running for governor in 1966, Reagan easily defeated a GOP moderate, former San Francisco Mayor George Christopher, in the party primary. He went on to crush his general election opponent, incumbent Democratic Gov. Edmund G. Brown.

Reagan compiled a record as governor that was far more moderate that his conservative rhetoric. The highlights of his term generally fell into three areas: limiting government spending, cutting back on the welfare rolls and exercising more control over the massive state educational system. Reagan's supporters considered his efforts to overhaul the state welfare system to be his most successful endeavor as governor.

Almost immediately after his election as governor, Reagan took on national political importance. In 1968 he mounted a tentative campaign for president, switching from favorite son status to a full-fledged candidacy two days before the Republican National Convention. He received 186 convention votes for president that year.

Leaving the California governorship in 1974, Reagan waged a determined campaign for the 1976 GOP nomination against President Ford. After fighting through a long primary season, the two candidates were almost even in delegate support.

Reagan sought to expand his base by announcing in advance that moderate Pennsylvania Sen. Richard S. Schweiker would be his running mate. But he ended up losing to Ford by 60 votes at the convention.

After his 1976 defeat Reagan maintained a high profile. He started a political action committee to distribute money to Republican candidates. He continued his active schedule of paid speeches, radio commentaries and newspaper columns until Nov. 13, 1979, when he announced his presidential candidacy for 1980.

believed his skills could be attributed to his professional training as an actor. But few would doubt that his public relations success was undergirded by an infectious idealism about America. Many of the president's most affecting speeches expressed his optimistic conception of America's past and vision of her future.

"The guy has got four or five things he cares about deeply," according to Rep. Dick Cheney, R-Wyo., a member of the House GOP leadership. "He comes back to those themes repeatedly, and he's able to communicate them effectively to the country, and that's reflected in how Congress responds."

The good-natured persona that Reagan projected contributed to his personal popularity, and to his faculty for putting across political and economic ideas. The president would deflect criticism with a quick quip and a broad grin.

People who were present said he maintained his sense of humor even on his way to the operating room at a Washington, D.C., hospital in March 1981, after having been wounded in the chest by a would-be assassin. Reagan told his surgeons that he hoped they were Republicans.

Board Chairman

On another level of style, President Carter had been much more of a "hands-on" president than Reagan, who made a virtue of delegating authority. While Carter immersed himself in the details of government policy and administration, Reagan had made clear ever since his days as governor of California that he preferred to act in the role of a board chairman, overseeing the execution of his policies by his top assistants. (Reagan appointments, p. 1017)

Reagan's critics seized on this aspect of Reagan's style as evidence that the president lacked a personal interest in and grasp of important details of government. Mondale raised that point in both of his two campaign debates with President Reagan.

Age as Issue

Another factor raised by some of Reagan's critics during the 1984 campaign was his age. When he took his first oath of office, Reagan was 69 years old. He was the oldest first-term president in American history.

However, age did not seem to be a major problem for Reagan during his first term. Unlike some other presidents who seemed to tire and age visibly during their years in the White House, Reagan appeared to thrive. Americans were familiar with images of the president on horseback and chopping wood at his California ranch. Not long before the 1984 election a photograph on the cover of *Parade* magazine showed him working out on an exercise machine.

Reagan's faculty for walking away from criticism apparently unaffected was matched by an ability to escape serious blame for one disaster and a number of setbacks and embarrassments that occurred during his first four years in office.

The gravest foreign policy reversal of his first term was the collapse of his policy in Lebanon and the withdrawal of American forces from that country in February 1984. That action was preceded by the death of 241 Marines and other Americans in a catastrophic truck bombing by terrorists in Beirut the previous October. Other less disastrous setbacks involved some of the appointments Reagan had made to top government offices. James G. Watt resigned as interior secretary and Anne M. Burford resigned as director of the Environmental Protection Agency. Watt, who had been opposed by environmental groups from the beginning, quit after making politically damaging remarks. Burford resigned under fire after a long confrontation with Congress, largely over charges of mismanagement.

Reagan's nomination of White House Counselor Edwin Meese III to be attorney general was sidetracked after allegations of unethical and possibly criminal conduct were made during his confirmation hearings in March 1984. An independent counsel, Jacob Stein, reported in September 1984 that no basis existed for criminal charges against Meese.

Labor Secretary Raymond J. Donovan in the same year became the first incumbent Cabinet officer to be indicted on criminal charges. Donovan asserted that he was innocent of the charges of grand larceny, filing false instruments and falsifying business records in connection with a subway construction project, and declared that these allegations were politically motivated. Nevertheless, he took a leave of absence, resigning early in 1985.

But Reagan himself managed largely to stay aloof from many of the rough spots in his first term, leading Rep. Patricia Schroeder, D-Colo., to bestow on him the title of "the Teflon president." Blame, it seemed, would not stick to him.

Political Perspective

Reagan had begun his political career in 1964 by making a speech for the presidential candidacy of Barry Goldwater at the Republican National Convention. In that speech, Reagan denounced high taxes, government regulation and wasteful welfare programs. His election in 1980 was yet another victory in a long struggle by the conservative wing of the Republican Party to wrest control from the moderate Eastern wing.

The moderate side had controlled GOP presidential nominations from 1940 to Goldwater's nomination in 1964. The Easterners argued for an internationalist foreign policy and wanted to preserve most of Franklin D. Roosevelt's New Deal. Conservatives, centered in the Midwest, South and Southwest and in earlier years led by Robert A. Taft, took an essentially isolationist view of the world and scoffed at the moderates' accommodations to the social legislation of the New Deal as "me-tooism."

Pragmatic Streak

True to his philosophical moorings, Reagan during his first four years in office was one of the most doctrinaire presidents in modern times. But he also displayed a distinct streak of pragmatism at key turns, declining, for example, to fight as vigorously for such items on his conservative constituency's "social agenda" as anti-abortion and school prayer amendments to the Constitution as for his economic program. In fact the developments of Reagan's first four years as president can be seen in terms of a balancing of strong ideological beliefs and pressures from conservative backers with the practicalities of running the government.

For the first two years, the president was able virtually to ignore his outnumbered political opponents in Congress. Laurence I. Barrett, *Time* magazine White House correspondent, called the president's first year with Congress a "blitzkrieg" and a "fierce, rapid assault, not courtship."

Toward the end of 1982, House Speaker Thomas P. O'Neill Jr., D-Mass., complained, "The president doesn't know what compromise is. He thinks compromise is when we give him 80 percent of what he asks for and he gives us nothing. Cooperation is a two-way street. For two years, we have cooperated with the president and waited for him to cooperate with the congressional agenda. We are still waiting."

Reagan on occasion disappointed his supporters on the right of the political spectrum, who felt that he did not forcefully press Congress to enact legislation dealing with a range of issues on which they took strong moral stands. During the 1980 campaign and after the election, Reagan took decisively conservative stands on these matters. In 1982 he sent Congress a proposed constitutional amendment to allow organized voluntary prayer in public schools. The proposed amendment declared that "Nothing in this Constitution shall be construed to prohibit individual or group prayer in public schools or other public institutions. No person shall be required by the United States or any state to participate in prayer."

'Social Agenda'

However, the lobbying muscle that Reagan applied so effectively in behalf of his economic and defense programs during his first term was lacking in the case of the "social agenda." Facing determined opposition in the Democratic-controlled House, Reagan's school prayer amendment died at the end of the 97th Congress without even emerging from the Senate Judiciary Committee. Moreover, advocates were unsuccessful in trying to attach language to an appro-

Reagan Wounded in 1981 Assassination Attempt

President Reagan was wounded in the chest March 30, 1981, in an assassination attempt. The attack came as he walked toward his limousine after making a speech at a Washington, D.C., hotel.

A man standing with reporters, who were waiting for the president outside the hotel, fired six shots from a .22-caliber pistol. One of the bullets hit Reagan in the chest. White House press secretary James S. Brady, a Secret Service agent and a D.C. policeman also were wounded.

Reagan's assailant was later identified as John Warnock Hinckley Jr., 25. Hinckley was found not guilty by reason of insanity on June 21, 1982, and committed to St. Elizabeths Hospital in the District of Columbia.

Reagan recovered quickly from his injuries and was released from the hospital April 11.

Shooting Aftermath

After the shooting, Secret Service agents quickly hustled Reagan into the limousine, which sped first toward the White House but then went to the George Washington University Medical Center, about six blocks from the White House, when agents learned that Reagan had been hit.

Witnesses and doctors reported that Reagan collapsed after walking into the hospital emergency room, that he was coughing blood, having trouble breathing and required blood transfusions to stabilize his condition. He then was wheeled into surgery to remove the bullet from his left lung. The operation lasted more than two hours.

Meanwhile, law enforcement officers at the Washington Hilton Hotel had seized Hinckley immediately after the shots were fired. The son of a wealthy Colorado oil executive had neither job nor fixed address, and his parents said he had undergone psychiatric treatment. Letters found in his Washington hotel room indicated that Hinckley was in love with teenage movie actress Jodie Foster, and that he had planned the assassination attempt as a "historical act" to win her "respect and love."

Who Was in Charge?

One question raised by the shooting was who, really, was running the country in the hours immediately after the assassination attempt.

A decision by Secretary of State Alexander M. Haig Jr. to make a nationally televised statement that he was "in control" at the White House contributed to the muddle and reportedly prompted a behind-the-scenes squabble in the administration.

Meanwhile, however, Vice President George Bush stepped into the delicate role of substituting for the president without appearing to supplant him. Bush and members of the Cabinet decided not to invoke the 25th Amendment, the constitutional procedure for declaring the president disabled and transferring authority to the vice president. *(Amendment, Congress and the Nation Vol. II, p. 645)*

Some of the confusion may have been attributable to the fact that the president's top spokesman, Brady, had been critically wounded himself.

The word from James A. Baker III, White House chief of staff, and other sources was that high-ranking staff members had gathered quickly at the hospital while a number of Cabinet members collected in the White House "situation room," a communications center where National Security Council meetings took place.

A triangular chain of communication was established between the hospital, the situation room and the airplane carrying Bush back to Washington from Texas, where he had canceled a speaking engagement. This chain, Baker said, was meant to keep the government functioning and to ensure that the constitutional procedure for delegating presidential authority to Bush could be activated, if needed.

Legal opinions on the constitutional line of succession and provisions governing presidential disability were sought and delivered the same day by the Justice Department. *(Line of succession, Congress and the Nation Vol. I, p. 1435)*

Defense Secretary Caspar W. Weinberger "took charge of the national defense moves that were made, and we contacted leaders around the world," according to Sen. Alan Cranston, D-Calif., Senate minority whip, who was briefed with other congressional leaders on March 31 by White House counsel Edwin Meese III.

The next day, Reagan and his three top aides — Meese, Baker and Deputy Chief of Staff Michael K. Deaver — had their customary morning meeting, held in Reagan's hospital room instead of in the Oval Office. Contributing to the image of normalcy, Reagan signed legislation on his breakfast tray. And Reagan's schedule went unchanged, although Bush filled in for the president.

Eighth Sitting President

President Reagan was the eighth sitting American president to be the victim of an assassination attempt.

Of the five who were actually wounded, he was the only one to live. The four killed by assassins' bullets were Abraham Lincoln, James A. Garfield, William McKinley and John F. Kennedy. The three who escaped injury were Andrew Jackson, Harry S Truman and Gerald R. Ford.

priations bill that would have prevented the Justice Department from spending money to block implementation of voluntary school prayer programs.

Despite Reagan's efforts, conservatives suffered similar setbacks on the abortion issue. In 1983 the Supreme Court reaffirmed its landmark 1973 decision legalizing abortion. The Reagan administration had urged the court to step out of the abortion controversy and leave "further refinements" of the law to the state legislatures. Instead, the court told the legislatures to stop trying to influence a woman's choice whether or not to terminate a pregnancy. Her right to make that decision herself, in consultation only with a physician, was guaranteed by the Constitution along lines spelled out by the 1973 *Roe v. Wade* decision, the court said.

Anti-abortion groups vowed to redouble their efforts to win a constitutional amendment outlawing abortion. But less than two weeks after the 1983 decision, the Senate rejected a proposed amendment designed to overturn *Roe v. Wade*. Despite lobbying by Reagan, the vote was 49-50 (with Jesse Helms, R-N.C., voting "present"), 18 votes short of the two-thirds majority needed for a proposed amendment to be presented to the states. Efforts to eliminate court-ordered busing suffered similar setbacks.

Civil Rights Commission

Reagan's general handling of civil rights matters angered many black leaders and other civil rights advocates. The anger boiled over in 1983, when Reagan tried to fire his critics on the Civil Rights Commission and replace them with members of his own choice. Civil rights groups complained that the president was undermining the independence of the six-member commission, which had been created in 1957.

Following lengthy negotiations, Congress approved legislation restructuring the commission into an eight-member panel, with four members appointed by the president and four by Congress. However, controversy flared anew when Reagan abruptly fired three of the commissioners he had been trying to replace; two of the three were later renamed to the commission by Congress.

Economic Program

Congressional debates over items on the "social agenda," when they did take place, were often emotional and wearying. However, during most of Reagan's first term in office, these issues took a back seat to the president's main concern: the economy.

President Reagan's insistence on fulfilling what he perceived to be the mandate of his first election was nowhere more evident than in his push for the economic plan he initiated upon taking office. Less than seven months after Reagan was sworn in, Congress had approved the basic elements of that program, which called for the largest tax cut in U.S. history together with sweeping cuts in domestic spending programs.

Supply-Side Economics

Reagan's economic package was rooted in what had become known as supply-side economics, which basically held that all Americans would have greater incentive to work harder and save more if fewer tax dollars were taken from businesses and workers and if government growth were restricted. The supply-side theory postulated that such a program, in turn, would lead to increased investment, higher productivity and a decline in inflation.

Reagan's March 10, 1981, budget proposal rested on those supply-side calculations. It called for more than $40 billion in cuts from fiscal 1982 spending and a tax reduction of $53.9 billion.

When the program was enacted, the president had come closer than most observers expected to his goals, with $35.2 billion in budget cuts for fiscal 1982 and a $37.7 billion tax cut in the same fiscal year.

Among the wide variety of programs that were extensively cut were three key welfare programs: Aid to Families with Dependent Children, food stamps and child nutrition aid. And one of the last major components of the 1960s War on Poverty, the Community Services Administration, was abolished.

Reagan took the case for his unprecedented spending cuts to the people. He argued that the program was "even-handed" and would not do "harm to government's legitimate purpose or to our responsibility to all who need our benevolence."

Budget Deficits

Reagan linked his request for spending reductions to one of his key 1980 campaign themes; that is, the need to substantially reduce annual budget deficits. In his first inaugural, Reagan had said that decades of deficit spending, if continued, would "guarantee tremendous social, cultural, political and economic upheaval." However, as deficit forecasts began rising, the president began to back away from his commitment to balance the budget by 1984. Nevertheless, anxiety about continued high deficits formed a constant element in the economic debate throughout the four years of Reagan's first term providing a strong incentive in Congress to cut spending.

Spending and Tax Cuts

There was never any question that the conservative-leaning Senate would support the president. Moreover, although Democrats remained in nominal control of the House, a solid phalanx of Republican votes there combined with help from Southern conservative Democrats to deliver that chamber as well. The outcome was the approval by Congress of the fiscal 1982 package of spending cuts.

The law containing the tax cuts, the Economic Recovery Tax Act of 1981, was expected to save business and individual taxpayers $749 billion over the following five years. The loss in revenue to the Treasury, opponents argued, would increase inflation and lead to massive budget deficits. But the tax cut was an integral part of the Reagan economic program.

Before approving the tax package, Congress added a broad range of alterations aimed at easing passage of the plan. Reagan himself reshaped it several times. But on the essence of the plan, and its supply-side theoretical underpinnings, the president remained firm: across-the-board cuts in individual income taxes and more rapid write-offs for capital investment designed to accelerate productivity and the growth of the economy.

Sharp Departure

The measure represented a sharp departure from the tax policies that Congress, with its Democratic majorities, had pursued in the past. Democratic plans in previous years had tended to be more generous toward people at the low end of the income scale and to emphasize the restriction of "loopholes" — special treatment provided for certain kinds of income. The Reagan proposal, presumably energized by a middle-class "taxpayers' revolt," reversed some of the liberal "reforms" of the past. The personal tax cuts tended to benefit individuals with incomes toward the upper end of the scale.

Despite concessions Reagan granted in order to keep his coalition together, all sides recognized the final product as his own. On Aug. 1, after a conference agreement was reached on the differing versions of the package that had been passed by the House and Senate earlier in the week, Treasury Secretary Donald T. Regan told reporters, "This is President Reagan's economic tax recovery plan." He declared that the administration had received "95 percent" of what it had proposed.

Democrats did not argue that point. In fact, they were anxious to shift to the president the responsibility for the consequences of the untested supply-side approach. House Ways and Means Committee Chairman Dan Rostenkowski, D-Ill., told the House before the final vote, "This is the president's bill. It outlines a bold — and risky — economic strategy. Only time will tell whether the risks involved were worth taking."

1982 Recession Impact

By the end of 1982, one year after Congress passed the landmark Reagan spending and tax cut program, the recession had bottomed out. Interest rates and inflation had dropped during the year. After hovering around 16 percent for the first six months, the prime lending rate dropped to 11.5 percent in December. The Consumer Price Index rose only 3.9 percent in 1982, a dramatic drop from an 8.9 percent rise the previous year.

But the improvements were accompanied by the highest rate of unemployment since World War II. A 10.7 percent jobless rate translated into approximately 12 million Americans out of work; and with factories shutting down, many feared that substantial numbers of these jobs, especially in the old "smokestack" industries, might be lost forever.

At the same time, the international economic picture deteriorated. A strong U.S. dollar on international markets led to a record-high $31.6 billion trade deficit for 1982. Hundreds of loans by U.S. banks to Third World nations appeared shaky, spreading fears of harmful consequences to the U.S. economy.

A significant break in the remarkable string of congressional budget victories that had marked Reagan's first year in office came in his second year. With congressional elections looming in November, fewer members of Congress were willing to give the president more time to tune the economy.

Perhaps most frightening for many legislators was the fact that in at least one important way, the supply-side aspirations for the 1981 budget and tax cuts were not having the desired effects. Rather than shrinking deficits by stimulating the economy, the tax cuts were exacerbating the deficit projections. In Reagan's fiscal 1983 budget pro-

posal he estimated a $91.5 billion deficit. But by the end of 1982 it was expected that the actual figure would be closer to $180 billion. An annual deficit of $300 billion was seen as possible by fiscal 1988 unless something were done. Under these pressures, the president in the summer of 1982 reluctantly backed legislation to raise taxes by $98.3 billion over the following three years.

Congressional Initiative

But by that time another important shift had occurred: Reagan was no longer dominating the legislative process. Budget committees in both chambers — including the Republican-controlled Senate — rejected his fiscal 1983 budget request as unrealistic. The initiative for forging a federal tax and spending plan subsequently shifted away from the president and to Congress. The Senate and House began working on their own packages, which included higher taxes and more cuts in defense spending.

With Reagan taking a substantially less active role in the 1982 budget debate Congress finally agreed on a budget resolution that projected a $103.9 billion deficit in fiscal 1983. That plan, settled upon in June, called for congressional committees to produce $6.6 billion in spending cuts and $20.9 billion in revenue increases in fiscal 1983.

By the end of the year Congress had produced the spending reductions with surprising ease compared with previous years. But with only lukewarm White House support for the tax increases (euphemistically called "revenue enhancers") and with elections due in November, members of Congress achieved the increase in tax revenue only with political pain. The plan consisted largely of closing tax loopholes and increasing taxpayer compliance.

The loss by Reagan in September 1982 of a veto battle on an appropriations bill — his first significant budget defeat — symbolized the erosion of the dominance of Congress that he enjoyed during the first year of his administration.

1983 Erosion of Strength

Reagan's strength in Congress was eroded further in 1983 as a result of the 1982 elections, when 26 incumbent House Republicans were defeated and 57 new Democrats were elected.

The new alignment allowed House Speaker O'Neill to regain control of his chamber from the coalition of Republicans and "Boll Weevil" Democrats that had dictated the agenda for the earlier 97th Congress.

Although the Senate remained in the hands of the president's party, Republicans there took note of the fact that some GOP incumbents had found themselves in much closer contests than they had expected. The result was a Senate more inclined in 1983 toward independence from White House direction.

Unable to manipulate his legislative program as he had during his first and, to a lesser extent, second year in office, the president virtually sat on the congressional sidelines during 1983.

Congress struggled to work out important bipartisan agreements on Social Security, legislation on jobs, and appropriations. In a highly charged partisan atmosphere, Reagan's influence was limited to trying to shape legislation by threatening to veto any money bills that exceeded his budget targets. Congress did listen and produced spending bills that Reagan signed.

However, neither President Reagan nor Congress seemed able to do much more about soaring budget deficits than to publicly decry them. Early in the year, the president made a decision to stay out of Congress' struggles to find a way to dry up the red ink. In doing so, he apparently intended to avoid responsibility for any tax increases that, in his advisers' view, would be liabilities in his re-election campaign. Reagan's public position was that the only way to reduce the deficit was to reduce non-defense spending. He adamantly opposed any increases in taxes.

Reagan's refusal to provide strong leadership to reduce the deficit contributed to Congress's own pre-election jitters over the politically risky moves that would be required to ameliorate the problem. House Democratic leaders shrank from pushing tax increase legislation for fear of exposing their ranks to more Republican charges that they were the party of "tax and tax, spend and spend." Reflecting later on the year's events, House Budget Committee Chairman James R. Jones, D-Okla., observed, "The leadership, starting with the president, avoided all the tough problems and basically took the politically safe approach."

Democratic Counterattack

Once again in control of a 100-vote Democratic margin in the House, Speaker O'Neill kept up a steady drumfire of criticism against Reagan during 1983, striking the theme that Reagan's economic policies benefited mostly well-to-do Americans at the expense of those on the lower end of the income scale. Using the "fairness" issue as a banner, he pushed through the House a cap on the third year of Reagan's tax cut, as well as a series of bills to aid the unemployed.

None of the measures emerged from the Republican-controlled Senate, however, and the Democratic sniping lost much of its impact when the economy began showing signs of an unexpectedly strong recovery from the 1981-1982 recession. Inflation rose only 3.8 percent during 1983 and civilian unemployment dropped from a high of 10.7 percent in December 1982 to 8.2 percent the following year. Interest rates fell as well from the prime rate peak of 21.5 percent in December 1980 to 10.5 percent early in 1983.

1984 Deficit 'Down Payment'

Although the economic comeback continued into 1984, fears of continued high deficits and their possible consequences once again dominated Reagan's relations with Congress in the final year of his first term.

In his State of the Union address Jan. 25, Reagan asked Congress to join him in a bipartisan effort to make a "down payment" on reducing the federal deficit. He proposed a $100 billion reduction through fiscal 1987.

Both Republicans and Democrats immediately rejected the budget submitted by Reagan in early February 1984, saying it did not go far enough toward reducing the deficit. The administration estimated a $180.4 billion deficit under its plan for fiscal 1985, with deficits dropping in later years.

Members of both parties especially criticized the president's proposed 13 percent "real" increase for defense programs, which they said was not consistent with sharp constraints in other segments of the budget.

Congress approved the first installment of Reagan's deficit "down payment" in late June 1984 by adopting a package of spending cuts and tax increases to reduce the

deficit by $63 billion over four years. The president signed the bill, which formed the core of deficit-cutting legislation enacted in 1984, on July 18.

This measure was expected to generate about $50 billion in new taxes, mostly by eliminating a wide range of tax loopholes and shelters, and to cut government spending by about $13 billion through fiscal 1987. Although Reagan first had warned that he would not accept any tax increases until more spending restraints were increased, he notified members before the final vote that he would sign the bill.

Fiscal 1985 Budget Resolution

However, disagreements over the defense budget continued to hamstring the negotiations between the White House and the bipartisan leadership group throughout the summer and into the early fall. By that time there was tremendous pressure to adjourn the 98th Congress so members could return home to campaign for re-election, and leaders in the House and Senate were vowing that they would not return after November for a lame-duck session. It was under those circumstances that the House in October approved the long-delayed fiscal 1985 budget resolution.

The product of the yearlong, three-way tug of war among Reagan, the House and the Senate was an agreement to cut deficits by $149.2 billion through fiscal year 1987. Major elements of the plan included $50.8 billion in increased revenues, $58.3 billion from smaller increases in the defense budget, and $12.2 billion in savings from entitlements and other mandatory benefit programs.

Defense Policy

One of the most notable breaks President Reagan made with the rhetoric of his 1980 presidential campaign came in the area of national defense.

During the campaign and through several weeks following his victory, conservative defense analysts who had long supported Reagan predicted that the new administration would depart radically from the defense programs of the Nixon, Ford and Carter administrations.

But with the unveiling of Reagan's first defense budget in March 1981, it became apparent that the administration would largely disregard the recommendations that had been advanced by some of the president's most conservative allies.

One such supporter, William R. Van Cleave, had been Reagan's campaign adviser on defense and had been appointed to head the Reagan Pentagon transition team. For three years, Van Cleave had advocated a program of "quick fixes" aimed at rapidly strengthening the U.S. nuclear arsenal. This package was intended to close what Van Cleave and his associates called the "window of vulnerability," the period during which Soviet missiles theoretically would be able to destroy all but a handful of U.S. intercontinental ballistic missiles (ICBMs) in a surprise attack.

Van Cleave's views were supported by only a minority of strategic arms specialists. And even with Reagan's proposed defense spending increases Van Cleave's program would have required painful budget choices. Most senior military officers and hard-line defense analysts placed a higher priority on improving U.S. conventional forces than on new strategic forces. An exception was the B-1 bomber.

'Star Wars' Plan

Another course urged by some conservatives but regarded as dubious by many defense experts was an idea that, though first rejected by the new administration, would make a repeat appearance in the 1984 presidential campaign in the form of what critics referred to as the "star wars" proposal.

During the 1980 campaign this idea was embodied in a renewed emphasis on anti-missile defenses as a cornerstone of U.S. nuclear policy. In 1980 and continuing into 1981, a group of senators led by conservative Western Republicans began to contend that a nuclear attack could be deterred by U.S. defenses able to shoot down Soviet missiles and bombers — rather than by threatening a retaliatory attack.

Their argument rested on the premise that technical developments held out the possibility of a virtually leak-proof defense of U.S. territory. They maintained that new anti-missile missiles would be much more effective than a system briefly deployed and then scrapped in 1976. And they held that within a decade, laser-armed space satellites could destroy Soviet missiles soon after they were launched.

Most senior Pentagon scientists and military leaders were skeptical. They warned that new defensive arms would require years of development and were a long way from deployment.

Critics of these conservative initiatives prevailed for a time, and although the first Reagan defense budget contained some favorable references to new defense techniques, the administration did not request any radical increase in strategic defense funds.

Pentagon Appointments

Conservative Reagan supporters also were disappointed by the new president's appointments to senior Pentagon positions. Some criticized Reagan's choice of Caspar W. Weinberger, a longtime Reagan associate, as secretary of defense, because of Weinberger's lack of experience with defense issues. Then, nearly a month before the new administration took office, Weinberger abruptly dismissed Van Cleave and his defense transition team. The core issue was Van Cleave's commitment to the discredited "quick fix" program.

Conservatives also expressed unhappiness over the selection of Frank C. Carlucci as deputy secretary. Carlucci had served as Weinberger's deputy during the Nixon and Ford administrations when Weinberger was secretary of health, education and welfare.

Partly balancing those defeats for conservatives were some important appointment victories, including Reagan's choice of John F. Lehman Jr., a leading GOP critic of Carter's defense policy, as Navy secretary. Other key Pentagon appointments included conservatives — Fred C. Ikle as under secretary for policy and Richard N. Perle as assistant secretary in charge of policies involving U.S. relations with the Soviet Union and Europe.

Budgets as Symbols

Conservatives were pleased by the accelerated pace of military spending achieved under the Reagan administration. Actually, it continued a trend that was started by the Carter administration after the invasion of Afghanistan by the Soviet Union.

Reagan proposed bigger military budgets as symbols that, as *Time* magazine put it, "the United States was a practicing superpower again."

Although Congress trimmed his increases, it approved the general outlines of his defense program during his first four years as president. This support extended to almost all of his weapons requests, including production of the B-1 bomber and a stepped-up modernization program for the Navy. The exception was the recommendation for the MX missile, which ran into opposition partly because of widespread doubts about Reagan's commitment to nuclear arms control.

Although the final package was not quite as large as the program he had originally requested, the president had remarkable success in obtaining the defense program he wanted in 1981. The $200 billion fiscal 1982 defense appropriation was the largest peacetime appropriations bill ever approved up to that time.

However, a development later in 1981 foreshadowed a serious source of friction between Reagan and members of Congress, including legislators of his own party. Prominent members of the Republican leadership began warning that the defense budget would not be sacrosanct in future budget cutting.

Many of Reagan's GOP critics in Congress had accepted his original March budget proposal, which called for a 14.6 percent increase in defense spending over the Carter budget, while cutting virtually all controllable domestic programs. But by August and September 1981, complaints about the Defense Department began emerging within the president's congressional coalition when the prospect of a huge deficit triggered a reassessment of the fiscal 1982 budget by the administration.

Reagan did cut his original defense request, but by only about half the amount proposed by David A. Stockman, director of the Office of Management and Budget, and some other Republicans.

Victory for Reagan

Congress wound up approving slightly less than the revised budget request — still yielding Reagan a substantial victory in his quest to increase military spending dramatically. But influential Republican committee chairmen in the Senate warned that another round of domestic spending cuts could not be accompanied by continued rapid growth in the Pentagon budget.

Nervousness in Congress continued in 1982 over the administration's calls for continued rapid acceleration of defense spending at a time when deficits were reaching record-high levels and when Reagan was insisting on greater domestic restraints. Criticism came not only from liberals but prominent conservatives as well, who were alarmed at a prospective fiscal 1983 deficit that was expected to be far above a projected $91.5 billion. For their part, liberals were concerned that the Pentagon budget would grow by 13.1 percent in real terms, while many domestic programs were being severely cut.

Slowed Momentum

These widespread apprehensions accounted for the substantial checking in 1982 of the political momentum Reagan had generated for his defense buildup. Although the basic shape of his original $258 billion defense budget

was largely left intact, it was subjected to a sharp paring back: a reduction of nearly $19 billion in budget authority, representing a cut of more than 7 percent in the program.

Congress in 1982 also refused to approve initial production funds for the MX intercontinental missile, marking the first time the legislature had ever denied funds for a major nuclear weapon system requested by a president. However, the action was a deferral rather than an outright cancellation, and it was prompted as much by concerns over the nuclear arms race and a controversy over the basing mode for the weapon as by alarm over the state of the economy.

1983 Defense Spending

Despite the setback to Republican strength in Congress dealt by the 1982 elections, President Reagan held his own on defense issues in 1983.

Hard-line conservatives complained that the president had yielded on crucial points in the administration's planned military buildup and its nuclear arms policy. But the basic outlines of the policies he brought with him to the White House were intact: a continued overall defense buildup, although not at the pace Reagan wanted; and the advancement of major elements of his nuclear buildup: the B-1 bomber, the Pershing missile and several versions of the cruise missile. Although the margin of victory in the House was small, Congress also approved the initial production of the MX missile.

Reagan Request

Reagan requested a fiscal 1984 defense budget 10 percent larger, after inflation, than the FY 1983 amount. Congress trimmed that increase to 5 percent. And by the time it had finished action on appropriations bills, the actual increase amounted to about 4 percent — a reduction from the January budget request of about $18 billion.

But this pared-back increase still outstripped the rate at which President Carter had been willing to raise defense spending in all but 1980, his last full year in office, when he sought a real increase of 5 percent.

In fact, by 1983 the scope of the defense budget debate had narrowed considerably from only a few years earlier. Few members of Congress disputed the assumption that increases were needed beyond those required merely to keep pace with inflation. The question was how big the increases should be, in view of concerns about the arms race and about budget deficits and the resulting competition for dollars for domestic programs.

Thus, the basic question of not whether but by how much to increase defense spending permeated the 1984 defense spending debate. The final product — a $219 billion defense authorization — reflected the same pattern that had been set since the outset of the Reagan administration: Congress agreed to go along with the fundamental shape of the plan but insisted on lower costs.

Modest Reductions

The bill that cleared Congress on Sept. 27 made proportionately modest reductions, but very few of the cuts posed any substantial challenge to the president's defense policy.

The nearest Congress came to rejecting a major element was its action on the MX missile. In a late-session compromise, Congress essentially decided to postpone a decision on resuming production of the weapon until spring 1985 — well after the 1984 elections.

By that time the MX had become a central focus of growing criticism of Reagan's arms control policy.

Arms Control

An increasingly heard criticism of Reagan's first four years in office was the lack of progress toward an agreement with the Soviet Union on slowing down the arms race.

President Reagan entered office making no secret of his distrust of the Soviet Union or of his belief that the United States lagged behind the other superpower in the strength of its nuclear arsenal and should catch up before entering into any agreement to limit further buildups.

Yet the perception in Congress that Reagan was not really interested in furthering negotiations resulted in resistance to some elements of his proposed defense buildup, especially the MX missile program. By the end of the president's first term, production of the MX was being held virtual hostage by congressional critics who wanted some evidence of concrete progress toward meaningful negotiations.

Arms control was another area where Reagan could be seen as being pulled in two directions: by his own basic conservatism and that of the hard-line conservatives who backed his election and by congressional moderates whose support he needed and sometimes traded for.

Hard-line conservatives believed that the entire U.S.-Soviet arms control process that produced the SALT I and SALT II agreements had worked to Moscow's advantage. They believed those pacts favored the Russians to begin with and that the Soviets cheated on them to boot. Further, they feared that the existence of an arms control agreement gave the American public and policy makers a false sense of security, undercutting the American will to offset the Soviet arms buildup or even to challenge cheating by the Russians. Those conservatives, led on Capitol Hill by Sen. Helms, vigorously opposed any arms control agreements that did not essentially eliminate the large, multiple-warhead ballistic missiles that were the core of the Soviet strategic arsenal.

It was not until November 1981, toward the end of Reagan's first year in office, that he embarked on an arms control initiative. In a speech on Nov. 18 he proposed a "zero-option" that would abolish U.S. and Soviet medium-range missiles in Europe. He declared that if the Soviet Union would decommission its 250 SS-20 missiles, along with some older, shorter-range weapons, the United States would suspend its plans to deploy 108 Pershing II ballistic missiles and 464 ground-launched cruise missiles in Europe.

Soviet View

The Reagan plan did not take into account the long-held Soviet view that any limitation of nuclear weapons in Europe must take account of all arms capable of reaching Soviet territory, including those in British and French missile-launching submarines and in many warplanes of the NATO countries. Nevertheless, on Nov. 30, 1981, U.S. and Soviet negotiators met in Geneva, Switzerland, to discuss limitations on the deployment of intermediate-range nuclear weapons based in Europe.

Reagan also proposed on Nov. 18, 1981, that the two superpowers resume negotiations in 1982 on long-range strategic weapons. But Reagan argued against the essence of the unratified Strategic Arms Limitation Treaty (SALT II), which, he said, would have allowed both countries to continue expanding their nuclear forces. Instead, the president urged that the goal of the new talks should be substantial reductions in existing strategic arsenals. Reagan suggested that to symbolize this change in objectives, the new negotiations be called START: Strategic Arms Reduction Talks.

However, critics continued to express doubt that the president was committed to serious negotiations, misgivings that fed a growing nuclear freeze movement. That effort hit a zenith in an Aug. 5, 1982, showdown in the House in which the switch of one vote would have given victory to freeze backers. In the form nearly approved by the House, the resolution would have called on the United States and the Soviet Union to begin a freeze on the testing, production or deployment of nuclear weapons or nuclear delivery vehicles, such as long-range bombers or missiles.

Freeze Movement

As pressure from the freeze movement grew, Reagan on May 9 unveiled a negotiating offer for the Strategic Arms Reduction Talks with Moscow. He proposed sharply cutting both nations' arsenals of land-based ICBMs to equal levels, but the freeze movement already had gained too much momentum to be deflected. The administration avoided defeat in an August 1982 House vote on the freeze by offering moderate Republicans and conservative Democrats an alternative resolution that used the politically potent word "freeze," but redefined it to support the administration's insistence that a freeze would occur only after both superpowers' strategic arsenals had been reduced to lower and equal levels.

Although Reagan won a one-vote victory on the freeze resolution, some of his own supporters in Congress bluntly warned that they were looking for results from the president's arms control efforts.

With his re-election secure, and Congress poised to kill the missile system that Reagan billed as a bargaining chip at the negotiating table with the Soviet Union, the president in late 1984 pledged to make arms control a top priority of his second term.

Foreign Policy

Reagan's general views on foreign relations were well-known when he entered office. He tended to see the world's conflicts in the light of superpower rivalry and to see the interests of the United States as part of an ongoing struggle between Western democratic values and communism. As in the case of Grenada, Reagan clearly was willing to use U.S. force in defense of those values when to do so seemed feasible. Indeed, critics complained that he was too quick to resort to military pressure before diplomatic solutions to a problem had been thoroughly explored.

The legacy of Reagan's first administration in the area of foreign policy, however, probably would not be seen in terms of creative breakthroughs, as was the case with President Nixon's resumption of U.S. relations with China. Reagan did not bring to the White House a set of firm foreign

Presidential Support

President Reagan's support in Congress slipped nearly 17 percent during his first four years in office, according to Congressional Quarterly's annual study of presidential support. In 1981 Congress responded to Reagan's 1980 landslide election by backing Reagan on 82.4 percent of the votes on which the president took a clear-cut position. His support score fell to 72.4 percent in 1982, 67.1 percent in 1983 and 65.8 percent in 1984.

Only two of the last seven presidents had experienced a larger slippage. President Eisenhower suffered a 19-point drop in his first term and President Johnson had an 18-point loss over his term that began in 1965. Reagan's 1984 score was more than nine points below President Carter's rating in his final year in office.

Although CQ's study illustrates the political differences between presidents and Congress, it does not measure how much of a president's program is actually enacted. The study counts only issues that reach a roll-call vote on the House or Senate floor, and then only votes where the president's support or opposition is clear. All votes, whether major or minor, are weighted equally. And an issue that takes many roll calls to resolve may influence the study more than matters settled by a single vote.

CQ tries to determine what the president personally, as distinct from other administration officials, does and does not want in the way of legislative action by analyzing his messages to Congress, press conference remarks and other public statements and documents.

Each member's record on votes included in the study is tallied at year's end, and the member is rated according to the percentage of the time he voted the way the president preferred. The aggregate percentage for all members constitutes the president's support rating.

policy goals. Some observers believed his foreign policy decisions for the most part lacked the decisiveness and thorough preparation Reagan showed in formulating and promoting his economic program. They said his conservative economic views and anti-communist outlook did not provide him with a clear-cut guide for creating a foreign policy structure.

Asked about his foreign policy in July 1981, the president answered, "I just don't happen to believe it is necessary to spell out in detail and in advance a formula which will guide our every move in international relations. Basically good foreign policy is the use of good common sense in dealing with friends and potential adversaries."

Vice President George Bush: Reagan's Critic ...

The man who once called Ronald Reagan's program "voodoo economics" became the chief drumbeater for Reagan's administration.

Despite initial skepticism from Reagan himself, and the outspoken hostility of some conservatives, Vice President George Bush managed to establish himself as a trusted White House team player. Moreover, he was able to maintain at least some of the expansion of vice presidential authority achieved by his predecessor, former Vice President Walter F. Mondale.

Bush's impact on the administration was most significant in the area of foreign affairs, both in terms of developing policy and in dealing directly with other governments. He also was important in determining administration positions on issues such as regulatory reform and control of illegal drugs.

But it was Bush's tireless cheerleading for his boss that warmed the hearts of Reaganites. After traveling hundreds of thousands of miles making speeches for the administration's program, and gaining a close personal relationship with Reagan, Bush effectively squelched any idea that he would not be on the ticket in 1984.

Active Vice President

A key moment in Bush's vice presidential career came in March 1981, when Reagan, over the opposition of Secretary of State Alexander M. Haig Jr., appointed Bush to be chairman of the Special Situation Group, the administration's crisis management committee. Within a few days Bush faced a major crisis — the wounding of Reagan in an assassination attempt.

From that time on, Bush was deeply involved in working out the administration's position on key foreign policy issues. When the Soviet-backed government of Poland declared martial law in December 1981, for example, Bush pushed for sanctions against the Soviet and Polish governments. Bush also played a key role during the collapse of the Lebanese government in February 1984. With Reagan out of town and the U.S.-backed Lebanese army disintegrating, Bush took charge of deliberations that led to the withdrawal of U.S. forces from Beirut.

Reagan also used Bush as a sort of roving ambassador, sending him on missions that ranged from giving the government of El Salvador a warning on human rights abuses, to trying to mend relations with the Indian government.

Perhaps Bush's most significant mission came in February 1983, when he toured seven European countries. Bush's cogent presentation of Reagan's position on arms control helped quiet opposition to the installation of U.S. intermediate-range missiles on the continent. In February 1984 Reagan sent Bush to Moscow as head of the American delegation to the funeral of Soviet leader Yuri V. Andropov.

On domestic issues, Bush focused much of his energy on two task forces. One, on regulatory reform, completed its work in August 1983 with a report outlining proposals that it said would save government and business $150 billion over 10 years through changes in federal regulations. Another task force, on South Florida, sought to increase coordination among federal agencies trying to stem the illegal drug flow from South America.

Three times during his term, Bush made use of one of the few real powers granted to the vice president by the Constitution — the right to cast the deciding vote in case of a tie in the Senate. In 1983 he twice voted to save the administration's proposal to begin manufacturing lethal chemical weapons for the first time since 1969. In June 1984 he cast the deciding vote to preserve funding for the MX missile.

Although his career was based in Texas, Bush's roots were in New England, and in the moderate Eastern Republican faction that once held sway in the party. His father, Prescott Bush, represented Connecticut in the Senate from 1952 to 1963.

The product of a wealthy upbringing, Bush was born in Milton, Mass., June 12, 1924, and graduated from Phillips Academy, an elite prep school in Andover, Mass. As a Navy pilot in World War II, he was shot down over the Pacific. He was rescued by a U.S. submarine that had raced a Japanese ship to get to him.

Returning from the war, Bush entered Yale University. After graduation in 1948, he moved to Texas

Decisive Actions

There were times when Reagan enunciated clearly defined objectives and acted decisively. They tended to be the occasions when he used military force or concentrated on military and related policies: sending Marines into Lebanon in 1982 to stabilize the government there; invading Grenada in 1983 to prevent the island nation from becoming a Soviet or Cuban military base; and increasing military assistance to U.S. allies in the Middle East and Central America.

The most controversial of these actions were providing aid to the government of El Salvador and rebels fighting the leftist government of Nicaragua; successfully lobbying Congress in favor of the sale of five radar planes (AWACS) to Saudi Arabia in 1981; and insisting on the deployment of Pershing II and cruise missiles in Western Europe during 1983.

...Becomes Administration's Chief Cheerleader

to enter the oil business. His first jobs were as a warehouse sweeper and then salesman with an oil supply company of which his father was a director.

Backed by family money, Bush in 1951 helped start the Bush-Overby Development Co. Two years later, he co-founded Zapata Petroleum Corp., and in 1954 became president of Zapata Off-Shore Co. While living in Houston, Bush was active in local politics, becoming chairman of the Harris County Republican organization.

By 1964 Bush was ready to enter electoral politics. He won the Republican Senate nomination after a three-way primary and runoff, but lost to Democratic incumbent Ralph Yarborough in November.

Bush then lowered his sights, and in 1966 won election to the House from a newly created district in the affluent Houston suburbs. During his four-year House career, he voted a generally conservative line and defended oil industry interests on the Ways and Means Committee. But he also backed some civil rights and environmental protection legislation.

Bush tried again for the Senate in 1970. He had hoped to run again against the liberal Yarborough, but the senator was defeated in the Democratic primary by the more conservative Lloyd Bentsen. Despite help from President Nixon, Bush lost by nearly 160,000 votes.

Bush entered the second phase of his public career in December 1970, when Nixon appointed him ambassador to the United Nations, an appointment that drew criticism because of Bush's lack of experience in foreign affairs. As ambassador, Bush worked out an agreement to reduce the U.S. share of the organization's funding. He also defended the administration's policy of allowing "two Chinas" — Taiwan and the People's Republic — to be represented in the General Assembly.

Bush's next job was more controversial. In December 1972 Nixon picked Bush to head the Republican National Committee, replacing Kansas Sen. Robert Dole. That left Bush with the unenviable task of chairing the party during the Watergate investigation. Although he remained publicly loyal to the embattled president throughout the crisis, Bush later said he had privately urged Nixon to resign.

In August 1974, when Gerald R. Ford succeeded Nixon, Bush was mentioned as a possibility to fill the vacant vice presidency. Instead, Ford named Bush to be the U.S. envoy to Peking. Bush attracted little attention in that post. Slightly more than a year later, Ford fired William E. Colby as CIA director and named Bush to replace him.

Idaho Democrat Frank Church, chairman of the Senate Intelligence Committee, opposed the selection of Bush for the CIA because of his past political roles, particularly as Republican chairman. Church also was concerned that Bush might be chosen as Ford's 1976 running mate. After Ford promised not to pick Bush as his vice president, Bush was confirmed by the Senate.

Bush's next public role was as a candidate for the 1980 Republican presidential nomination. His selection by Reagan as his vice presidential choice marked the first time in 20 years that a presidential nominee had named a pre-convention rival as his ticket partner.

The independently wealthy Bush had spent almost two years in his quest for the presidency. Following the script that won Jimmy Carter the 1976 Democratic nomination, he assiduously worked states with primaries scheduled for early in the election season, in hopes of attracting attention to his candidacy.

The plan worked well in the fall of 1979, when Bush won several straw votes at state and local GOP meetings. The aim was to attract news media notice, and it worked. The plan also worked well in the important Iowa precinct caucuses in January 1980, when Bush defeated front-runner Reagan. Gaining on Reagan in the polls, Bush extolled his "Big Mo," or momentum.

The turning point in Bush's campaign came during a Feb. 23 debate with Reagan in Nashua, N.H. Bush, who wanted the debate to be limited to himself and Reagan, said nothing when the former California governor denounced banning other candidates from the debate. The incident deflated Bush's image. Although the Texan went on to win six primaries, he never could match Reagan's delegate totals. He withdrew from the race on May 26.

State Department Appointments

Reagan's first secretary of state was Alexander M. Haig Jr., a former Army general and NATO commander known for his loyal service as President Nixon's White House chief of staff during the Watergate scandals. Haig remained controversial during his year and a half in office, declaring himself Reagan's foreign policy "vicar" and engaging in jealous turf fights over policy formulation with other administration figures. Haig openly complained that "someone" in the White House — presumably Richard V. Allen, the president's assistant for national security affairs — was waging a political "guerrilla campaign" against him. In January 1982 Reagan replaced Allen with one of his most trusted deputies, William C. Clark, who had served as deputy secretary of state. Haig suddenly resigned in June, later saying that his departure was not entirely voluntary.

George P. Shultz, a former economics professor, corpo-

rate executive, and Nixon Cabinet officer whom Reagan named to replace Haig, changed both the style and substance of U.S. foreign policy.

The change in style was noticeable immediately: Haig's aggressive rhetoric was replaced by Shultz' somewhat bland utterances. The shifts of policy focus and tone were evident in a range of administration policies, ranging from Shultz' quiet work to negotiate an end to the economic sanctions Reagan had imposed against the Soviet Union in retaliation for its pressure on Poland, to the development of administration policy toward the Middle East. Haig had dealt with problems in the latter region in terms of the East-West conflict, but Shultz showed more interest in resolving the Arab-Israeli dispute.

Central America

Shultz insisted that he was merely carrying out the wishes of Ronald Reagan. And Reagan's Central America policies, especially in the cases of El Salvador and Nicaragua, were fueling criticism that the president was too quickly inclined to military solutions.

El Salvador. Early in his first year, Reagan set out to shore up the embattled centrist junta in El Salvador, where leftist guerrillas attempted a "final offensive" in an effort to topple the junta in the days before Reagan took office. Declaring that the United States would "draw the line" in El Salvador against communist interference in Central America, the administration decided to assist the government of José Napoleón Duarte by sending more arms aid and U.S. military advisers. This action, coupled with dissatisfaction in Congress over El Salvador's human rights record, touched off a debate that lasted throughout the first Reagan administration.

Nicaragua. The other focus of U.S. interest in Central America was Nicaragua. Reagan had been in office for only a few months in 1981 when he suspended a Carter administration program of U.S. economic aid to Nicaragua. Reagan charged that the leftist Sandinistas who had come to power in 1979 were seeking to establish a Marxist state under the influence of Cuba and the Soviet Union. Later in 1981 he authorized U.S. support, through the Central Intelligence Agency, for Nicaraguan exiles in Honduras who had taken up arms against the Sandinistas.

Few members of Congress openly sympathized with the Sandinista leadership, which had taken on many of the repressive characteristics of communist regimes. But Democrats in the House, especially members of the House Intelligence Committee, became increasingly alarmed that the administration was expanding the scope of the Nicaraguan operation beyond the limits of U.S. and international law, with the aim of ousting the government of a foreign country.

Along with the controversy over El Salvador, Nicaragua remained as a source of friction between Reagan and his foreign policy critics.

Human Rights

Reagan's handling of the problems in El Salvador and Nicaragua resurrected in many Americans fears of becoming involved in another Vietnam-style war, with the United States once again cast in the role of backing unpopular rulers with records of human rights violations.

The Reagan administration rejected Carter's dedication to holding anti-communist authoritarian governments publicly accountable for their human rights records by withholding aid to those with flagrant ones. Reagan and his aides said they would promote human rights through "quiet diplomacy" instead.

The president's representative to the United Nations, Jeane J. Kirkpatrick, postulated a controversial theory about human rights, drawing a distinction between totalitarian and authoritarian governments and asserting that the latter held out more hope of reform. Later, a new and stronger human rights policy adopted by the administration mollified some administration critics.

Soviet Union

Reagan changed the tone of U.S. relations with its chief adversary, the Soviet Union, as early as his first press conference as president. He unhesitatingly replied in answer to a reporter's question that he firmly believed that the goal of the Soviets was world domination. In a comment that seemed startling, Reagan added that the Soviets "reserve unto themselves the right to commit any crime, to lie, to cheat in order to attain that, and that is moral [in their view], not immoral, and we operate on a different set of standards."

The problems of dealing with the Soviet Union on a cohesive basis during Reagan's first term were compounded by the deaths of two successive Soviet leaders, Leonid I. Brezhnev and Yuri V. Andropov.

As with his economic and defense programs, Reagan showed little inclination to negotiate with Congress to reach compromises on controversial foreign issues. Perhaps the best evidence of that was his steadfast refusal, initially, to acknowledge any congressional role in the stationing of U.S. Marines in Lebanon.

In August 1983, after units of an international peace-keeping force came under fire in Beirut, resulting in the deaths of two American Marines, Congress sought to reassert its authority under the 1973 War Powers Resolution to participate in future decisions affecting the Marine contingent.

Only after prolonged negotiations was Reagan willing to give Congress a say. And in doing so, he insisted on congressional approval of his plan to keep the Marines in Lebanon for an additional 18 months — to mid-April 1985. The president opposed efforts to shorten that period, despite the Oct. 23, 1983, terrorist attack on U.S. forces in Beirut that killed 241 American servicemen, most of whom were Marines.

Pragmatism

One contrast to a somewhat militant foreign policy was Reagan's cautious reaction to the September 1983 shooting down of a South Korean airliner by the Soviet Union. All 269 passengers aboard were lost, including a member of Congress.

Reagan's restraint in the airline incident was an example of his ability to distance himself to a degree from his more militant conservative supporters, who after the downing of the airliner called for tough sanctions against the Soviet Union.

At the end of his first term, it appeared that the pragmatism Reagan could display would be put to a strong test as the president vowed to make an arms control agreement with the Soviet Union a top priority of his second term.

Other Questions

In addition to arms control, other key questions remained as President Reagan's first term drew to a close in 1984.

They included the direction of the economy, the performance of which had such a vital role in the perception of Reagan's competence and thus in his re-election; and the fate of further efforts to reduce federal budget deficits, in light of the president's continued resistance to tax increases and to pressures to reduce the rate of growth in defense spending.

Other difficult issues facing the second-term Reagan presidency included the nation's deteriorating competitiveness in international markets, reflected in skyrocketing trade deficits and continuing high unemployment, and unresolved conflicts over U.S. policy in Central America and the Middle East. Further disputes over emotional social issues such as abortion were in prospect as well.

But in the framework of one presidential term coming to a close, the sweeping re-election of Ronald Reagan seemed to be evidence that the great majority of Americans were satisfied with the way their country was being governed.

Appendix

Glossary of Terms	*861*
The Legislative Process	*873*
Key Votes, 1981-84	*877*
Membership Lists	*945*
Members of Congress	*953*
Congressional Committees	*963*
Post-Election Sessions	*975*
Senate Cloture Votes	*977*
Legislative Veto Opinions	*981*
Reapportionment	*993*
Reagan Appointments	*1017*
Presidential Vetoes	*1031*
Presidential Texts	*1033*
Political Charts	*1087*

APPENDIX

Glossary of Congressional Terms

Act—The term for legislation once it has passed both houses of Congress and has been signed by the president or passed over his veto, thus becoming law. *(See below.)* Also used in parliamentary terminology for a bill that has been passed by one house and engrossed. *(See Engrossed Bill.)*

Adjournment Sine Die—Adjournment without definitely fixing a day for reconvening; literally "adjournment without a day." Usually used to connote the final adjournment of a session of Congress. A session can continue until noon, Jan. 3, of the following year, when, under the 20th Amendment to the Constitution, it automatically terminates. Both houses must agree to a concurrent resolution for either house to adjourn for more than three days.

Adjournment to a Day Certain—Adjournment under a motion or resolution that fixes the next time of meeting. Under the Constitution, neither house can adjourn for more than three days without the concurrence of the other. A session of Congress is not ended by adjournment to a day certain.

Amendment—A proposal of a member of Congress to alter the language, provisions or stipulations in a bill or in another amendment. An amendment usually is printed, debated and voted upon in the same manner as a bill.

Amendment in the Nature of a Substitute—Usually an amendment that seeks to replace the entire text of a bill. Passage of this type of amendment strikes out everything after the enacting clause and inserts a new version of the bill. An amendment in the nature of a substitute also can refer to an amendment that replaces a large portion of the text of a bill.

Appeal—A member's challenge of a ruling or decision made by the presiding officer of the chamber. In the Senate, the senator appeals to members of the chamber to override the decision. If carried by a majority vote, the appeal nullifies the chair's ruling. In the House, the decision of the Speaker traditionally has been final; seldom are there appeals to the members to reverse the Speaker's stand. To appeal a ruling is considered an attack on the Speaker.

Appropriations Bill—A bill that gives legal authority to spend or obligate money from the Treasury. The Constitution disallows money to be drawn from the Treasury "but in Consequence of Appropriations made by Law."

It usually is the case that an appropriations bill provides the actual monies approved by authorization bills, but not necessarily the full amount permissible under the authorization measures. By congressional custom, an appropriations bill originates in the House, and it is not supposed to be considered by the full House or Senate until the related authorization measure is enacted. Under the 1974 Congressional Budget and Impoundment Control Act, general appropriations bills are supposed to be enacted by the seventh day after Labor Day before the start of the fiscal year to which they apply, but in recent years this deadline rarely has been met.

In addition to general appropriations bills, there are two specialized types. *(See Continuing Resolution, Supplemental Appropriations Bill.)*

Authorization—Basic, substantive legislation that establishes or continues the legal operation of a federal program or agency, either indefinitely or for a specific period of time, or which sanctions a particular type of obligation or expenditure. An authorization normally is a prerequisite for an appropriation or other kind of budget authority. Under the rules of both houses, the appropriation for a program or agency may not be considered until its authorization has been considered. An authorization also may limit the amount of budget authority to be provided or may authorize the appropriation of "such sums as may be necessary." *(See also Backdoor Spending.)*

Backdoor Spending—Budget authority provided in legislation outside the normal appropriations process. The most common forms of backdoor spending are borrowing authority, contract authority and entitlements. *(See below.)* In some cases, such as interest on the public debt, a permanent appropriation is provided that becomes available without further action by Congress. The 1974 budget act places limits on the use of backdoor spending.

Bills—Most legislative proposals before Congress are in the form of bills and are designated by HR in the House of Representatives or S in the Senate, according to the house in which they originate, and by a number assigned in the order in which they are introduced during the two-year period of a congressional term. "Public bills" deal with general questions and become public laws if approved by Congress and signed by the president. "Private bills" deal with individual matters such as claims against the government, immigration and naturalization cases, land titles, etc., and become private laws if approved and signed. *(See also Concurrent Resolution, Joint Resolution, Resolution.)*

Bills Introduced—In both the House and Senate, any number of members may join in introducing a single bill or resolution. The first member listed is the sponsor of the bill, and all members' names following his are the bill's cosponsors.

Many bills are committee bills and are introduced under the name of the chairman of the committee or subcommittee. All appropriations bills fall into this category. A committee frequently holds hearings on a number of related bills and may agree to one of them or to an entirely new bill. *(See also Report, Clean Bill, By Request.)*

Bills Referred—When introduced, a bill is referred to the committee or committees that have jurisdiction over the subject with which the bill is concerned. Under the standing rules of the House and Senate, bills are referred by the Speaker in the House and by the presiding officer in the Senate. In practice, the House and Senate parliamentarians act for these officials and refer the vast majority of bills.

Borrowing Authority—Statutory authority that permits a federal agency to incur obligations and make payments for specified purposes with borrowed money. The 1974 budget act sets limits on new borrowing authority, except in certain instances, to the extent or amount provided in appropriations acts.

Budget—The document sent to Congress by the president early each year estimating government revenue and expenditures for the ensuing fiscal year.

Budget Authority—Authority to enter into obligations that will result in immediate or future outlays involving federal funds. The basic forms of budget authority are appropriations, contract authority and borrowing authority. Budget authority may be classified by (1) the period of availability (one-year, multiple-year or without a time limitation), (2) the timing of congressional action (current or permanent), or (3) the manner of determining the amount available (definite or indefinite).

Budget Process—The congressional budget process is organized around two concurrent resolutions. The deadline for approval of the first resolution is May 15. The resolution must be passed before the House and Senate consider appropriations, revenue and entitlement legislation. The deadline for the second budget resolution is Sept. 15, two weeks before the Oct. 1 start of the next fiscal year. (Congress has failed to meet these deadlines in recent years.) The purpose of the budget resolutions is to guide and restrain Congress in its actions on appropriations, spending and revenue bills. A concurrent resolution does not have the force of law. Consequently, Congress cannot appropriate money, impose taxes or directly limit federal expenditures by means of a budget resolution. Unless it otherwise stipulates, Congress is not bound by the targets in the first budget resolution when it acts on appropriations and tax legislation. The second resolution sets a ceiling on new budget authority and outlays and a floor on revenues for the coming year. After its adoption a point of order can be raised against any legislation that would cause expenditures to exceed or revenues to drop below budgeted amounts. Congress can revise its budget decisions at any time during the fiscal year by adopting supplementary budget resolutions.

Budget Reconciliation—The 1974 budget act provides for a "reconciliation" procedure for bringing existing tax and spending laws into conformity with the congressional budget resolutions. Under the procedure, Congress instructs designated legislative committees to approve measures adjusting revenues and expenditures by a certain amount. The committees have a deadline by which they must report the legislation, but they have the discretion of deciding what changes are to be made. The recommendations of the various committees are consolidated without change by the Budget committees into an omnibus reconciliation bill, which then must be considered and approved by both houses of Congress.

By Request—A phrase used when a senator or representative introduces a bill at the request of an executive agency or private organization but does not necessarily endorse the legislation.

Calendar—An agenda or list of business awaiting possible action by each chamber. The House uses five legislative calendars. *(See Consent, Discharge, House, Private and Union Calendar.)*

In the Senate, all legislative matters reported from committee go on one calendar. They are listed there in the order in which committees report them or the Senate places them on the calendar, but may be called up out of order by the majority leader, either by obtaining unanimous consent of the Senate or by a motion to call up a bill. The Senate also uses one non-legislative calendar; this is used for treaties and nominations. *(See Executive Calendar.)*

Calendar Wednesday—In the House, committees, on Wednesdays, may be called in the order in which they appear in Rule X of the House, for the purpose of bringing up any of their bills from either the House or the Union Calendar, except bills that are privileged. General debate is limited to two hours. Bills called up from the Union Calendar are considered in Committee of the Whole. Calendar Wednesday is not observed during the last two weeks of a session and may be dispensed with at other times by a two-thirds vote. This procedure is rarely used and routinely is dispensed with by unanimous consent.

Call of the Calendar—Senate bills that are not brought up for debate by a motion, unanimous consent or a unanimous consent agreement are brought before the Senate for action when the calendar listing them is "called." Bills must be called in the order listed. Measures considered by this method usually are non-controversial, and debate is limited to a total of five minutes for each senator on the bill and any amendments proposed to it.

Chamber—The meeting place for the membership of either the House or the Senate; also the membership of the House or Senate meeting as such.

Clean Bill—Frequently after a committee has finished a major revision of a bill, one of the committee members, usually the chairman, will assemble the changes and what is left of the original bill into a new measure and introduce it as a "clean bill." The revised measure, which is given a new number, then is referred back to the committee, which reports it to the floor for consideration. This often is a timesaver, as committee-recommended changes in a clean bill do not have to be considered and voted on by the chamber. Reporting a clean bill also protects committee amendments that might be subject to points of order concerning germaneness.

Clerk of the House—Chief administrative officer of the House of Representatives, with duties corresponding to those of the secretary of the Senate. *(See also Secretary of the Senate.)*

Cloture—The process by which a filibuster can be ended in the Senate other than by unanimous consent. A motion for cloture can apply to any measure before the Senate, including a proposal to change the chamber's rules. A cloture motion requires the signatures of 16 senators to be introduced, and to end a filibuster the cloture motion must obtain the votes of three-fifths of the entire Senate membership (60 if there are no vacancies), except that to end a filibuster against a proposal to amend the standing rules of the Senate a two-thirds vote of senators present and voting is required. The cloture request is put to a roll-call vote one hour after the Senate meets on the second day following introduction of the motion. If approved, cloture limits each senator to one hour of debate. The bill or amendment in question comes to a final vote after 100 hours of consideration (including debate time and the time it takes to conduct roll calls, quorum calls and other procedural motions). *(See Filibuster.)*

Committee—A division of the House or Senate that prepares legislation for action by the parent chamber or makes investigations as directed by the parent chamber. There are several types of committees. *(See Standing and Select or Special Committees.)* Most standing committees are divided into subcommittees, which study legislation, hold hearings and report bills, with or without amendments, to the full committee. Only the full committee can report legislation for action by the House or Senate.

Committee of the Whole—The working title of what is formally "The Committee of the Whole House (of Representatives) on the State of the Union." The membership is comprised of all House members sitting as a committee. Any 100 members who are present on the floor of the chamber to consider legislation comprise a quorum of the committee. Any legislation, however, must first have passed through the regular legislative or Appropriations committee and have been placed on the calendar.

Technically, the Committee of the Whole considers only bills directly or indirectly appropriating money, authorizing appropriations or involving taxes or charges on the public. Because the Committee of the Whole need number only 100 representatives, a quorum is more readily attained, and legislative business is expedited. Before 1971, members' positions were not individually recorded on votes taken in Committee of the Whole. *(See Teller Vote.)*

When the full House resolves itself into the Committee of the Whole, it supplants the Speaker with a "chairman." A measure is debated and amendments may be proposed, with votes on amendments as needed. *(See Five-Minute Rule.)* When the committee completes its work on the measure, it dissolves itself by "rising." The Speaker returns, and the chairman of the Committee of the Whole reports to the House that the committee's work has been completed. At this time members may demand a roll-call vote on any amendment *adopted* in the Committee of the Whole. The final vote is on passage of the legislation.

Committee Veto—A requirement added to a few statutes directing that certain policy directives by an executive department or agency be reviewed by certain congressional committees before they are implemented. Under common practice, the government department or agency and the committees involved are expected to reach a consensus before the directives are carried out. *(See also Legislative.)*

Concurrent Resolution—A concurrent resolution, designated H Con Res or S Con Res, must be adopted by both houses, but it is not sent to the president for his signature and therefore does not have the force of law. A concurrent resolution, for example, is used to fix the time for adjournment of a Congress. It also is used as the vehicle for expressing the sense of Congress on various foreign policy and domestic issues, and it serves as the vehicle for coordinated decisions on the federal budget under the 1974 Congressional Budget and Impoundment Control Act. *(See also Bills, Joint Resolution, Resolution.)*

Conference—A meeting between the representatives of the House and the Senate to reconcile differences between the two houses on provisions of a bill passed by both chambers. Members of the conference committee are appointed by the Speaker and the presiding officer of the Senate and are called "managers" for their respective chambers. A majority of the managers for each house must reach agreement on the provisions of the bill (often a compromise between the versions of the two chambers) before it can be considered by either chamber in the form of a "conference report." When the conference report goes to the floor, it cannot be amended, and, if it is not approved by both chambers, the bill may go back to conference under certain situations, or a new conference must be convened. Many rules and informal practices govern the conduct of conference committees.

Bills that are passed by both houses with only minor differences need not be sent to conference. Either chamber may "concur" in the other's amendments, completing action on the legislation. Sometimes leaders of the committees of jurisdiction work out an informal compromise instead of having a formal conference. *(See Custody of the Papers.)*

Confirmations—*(See Nominations.)*

Congressional Record—The daily, printed account of proceedings in both the House and Senate chambers, showing substantially verbatim debate, statements and a record of floor action. Highlights of legislative and committee action are embodied in a Daily Digest section of the Record, and members are entitled to have their extraneous remarks printed in an appendix known as "Extension of Remarks." Members may edit and revise remarks made on the floor during debate, and quotations from debate reported by the press are not always found in the Record.

Beginning on March 1, 1978, the Record incorporated a procedure to distinguish remarks spoken on the floor of the House and Senate from undelivered speeches. Congress directed that all speeches, articles and other matter that members inserted in the Record without actually reading them on the floor were to be set off by large black dots, or bullets. However, a loophole allows a member to avoid the bulleting if he delivers any portion of the speech in person.

Congressional Terms of Office—Normally begin on Jan. 3 of the year following a general election and are two years for representatives and six years for senators.

Representatives elected in special elections are sworn in for the remainder of a term. A person may be appointed to fill a Senate vacancy and serves until a successor is elected; the successor serves until the end of the term applying to the vacant seat.

Consent Calendar—Members of the House may place on this calendar most bills on the Union or House Calendar that are considered to be non-controversial. Bills on the Consent Calendar normally are called on the first and third Mondays of each month. On the first occasion that a bill is called in this manner, consideration may be blocked by the objection of any member. The second time, if there are three objections, the bill is stricken from the Consent Calendar. If less than three members object, the bill is given immediate consideration.

A bill on the Consent Calendar may be postponed in another way. A member may ask that the measure be passed over "without prejudice." In that case, no objection is recorded against the bill, and its status on the Consent Calendar remains unchanged. A bill stricken from the Consent Calendar remains on the Union or House Calendar.

Cosponsor—*(See Bills Introduced.)*

Continuing Resolution—A joint resolution drafted by Congress "continuing appropriations" for specific ongoing activities of a government department or departments when a fiscal year begins and Congress has not yet enacted all of the regular appropriations bills for that year. The continuing resolution usually specifies a maximum rate at which the agency may incur obligations. This usually is based on the rate for the previous year, the president's budget request or an appropriation bill for that year passed by either or both houses of Congress, but not cleared.

Contract Authority—Budget authority contained in an authorization bill that permits the federal government to enter into contracts or other obligations for future payments from funds not yet appropriated by Congress. The assumption is that funds will be available for payment in a subsequent appropriation act.

Controllable Budget Items—In federal budgeting this refers to programs for which the budget authority or outlays during a fiscal year can be controlled without changing existing, substantive law. The concept "relatively uncontrollable under current law" includes outlays for open-ended programs and fixed costs such as interest on the public debt, Social Security benefits, veterans' benefits and outlays to liquidate prior-year obligations.

Correcting Recorded Votes—Rules prohibit members from changing their votes after the result has been announced. But, occasionally hours, days or months after a vote has been taken, a member may announce that he was "incorrectly recorded." In the Senate, a request to change one's vote almost always receives unanimous consent. In the House, members are prohibited from changing their votes if tallied by the electronic voting system installed in 1973. If taken by roll call, it is permissible if consent is granted.

Current Services Estimates—Estimated budget authority and outlays for federal programs and operations for the forthcoming fiscal year based on continuation of existing levels of service without policy changes. These estimates of budget authority and outlays, accompanied by the underlying economic and policy assumptions upon which they are based, are transmitted by the president to Congress when the budget is submitted.

Custody of the Papers—To reconcile differences between the House and Senate versions of a bill, a conference may be arranged. The chamber with "custody of the papers" — the engrossed bill, engrossed amendments, messages of transmittal — is the only body empowered to request the conference. By custom, the chamber that asks for a conference is the last to act on the conference report once agreement has been reached on the bill by the conferees. Custody of the papers sometimes is manipulated to ensure that a particular chamber acts either first or last on the conference report.

Deferrals of Budget Authority—Any action taken by U.S. government officials that withholds, delays or precludes the obligation or expenditure of budget authority. The 1974 budget act requires a special message from the president to Congress reporting a proposed deferral. Deferrals may not extend beyond the end of the fiscal year in which the message reporting the deferral is transmitted. *(See also Rescission Bill.)*

Dilatory Motion—A motion made for the purpose of killing time and preventing action on a bill or amendment. House rules outlaw dilatory motions, but enforcement is largely within the discretion of the Speaker or chairman of the Committee of the Whole. The Senate does not have a rule banning dilatory motions, except under cloture.

Discharge a Committee—Occasionally, attempts are made to relieve a committee from jurisdiction over a measure before it. This is attempted more often in the House than in the Senate, and the procedure rarely is successful.

In the House, if a committee does not report a bill within 30 days after the measure is referred to it, any member may file a discharge motion. Once offered the motion is treated as a petition needing the signatures of 218 members (a majority of the House). After the required signatures have been obtained, there is a delay of seven days. Thereafter, on the second and fourth Mondays of each month, except during the last six days of a session, any member who has signed the petition must be recognized, if he so desires, to move that the committee be discharged. Debate on the motion to discharge is limited to 20 minutes, and, if the motion is carried, consideration of the bill becomes a matter of high privilege.

If a resolution to consider a bill is held up in the Rules Committee for more than seven legislative days, any member may enter a motion to discharge the committee. The motion is handled like any other discharge petition in the House.

Occasionally, to expedite non-controversial legislative business, a committee is discharged by unanimous consent of the House, and a petition is not required. *(Senate procedure, see Discharge Resolution.)*

Discharge Calendar—The House calendar to which motions to discharge committees are referred when they have the required number of signatures (218) and are awaiting floor action.

Discharge Petition—*(See Discharge a Committee.)*

Discharge Resolution—In the Senate, a special motion that any senator may introduce to relieve a committee from consideration of a bill before it. The resolution can be called up for Senate approval or disapproval in the same manner as any other Senate business. *(House procedure, see Discharge a Committee.)*

Division of a Question for Voting—A practice that is more common in the Senate but also used in the House, a member may demand a division of an amendment or a motion for purposes of voting. Where an amendment or motion can be divided, the individual parts are voted on separately when a member demands a division. This procedure occurs most often during the consideration of conference reports.

Division Vote—*(See Standing Vote.)*

Enacting Clause—Key phrase in bills beginning, "Be it enacted by the Senate and House of Representatives...." A successful motion to strike it from legislation kills the measure.

Engrossed Bill—The final copy of a bill as passed by one chamber, with the text as amended by floor action and certified by the clerk of the House or the secretary of the Senate.

Enrolled Bill—The final copy of a bill that has been passed in identical form by both chambers. It is certified by an officer of the house of origin (clerk of the House or secretary of the Senate) and then sent on for the signatures of the House Speaker, the Senate president pro tempore and the president of the United States. An enrolled bill is printed on parchment.

Entitlement Program—A federal program that guarantees a certain level of benefits to persons or other entities who meet requirements set by law, such as Social Security or unemployment benefits. It thus leaves no discretion with Congress on how much money to appropriate.

Executive Calendar—This is a non-legislative calendar in the Senate on which presidential documents such as treaties and nominations are listed.

Executive Document—A document, usually a treaty, sent to the Senate by the president for consideration or approval. Executive documents are identified for each session of Congress as Executive A, 97th Congress, 1st Session; Executive B, etc. They are referred to committee in the same manner as other measures. Unlike legislative documents, however, treaties do not die at the end of a Congress but remain "live" proposals until acted on by the Senate or withdrawn by the president.

Executive Session—A meeting of a Senate or House committee (or occasionally of either chamber) that only its members may attend. Witnesses regularly appear at committee meetings in executive session — for example, Defense Department officials during presentations of classified defense information. Other members of Congress may be invited, but the public and press are not allowed to attend.

Expenditures—The actual spending of money as distinguished from the appropriation of funds. Expenditures are made by the disbursing officers of the administration; appropriations are made only by Congress. The two are rarely identical in any fiscal year. In addition to some current budget authority, expenditures may represent budget authority made available one, two or more years earlier.

Filibuster—A time-delaying tactic associated with the Senate and used by a minority in an effort to prevent a vote on a bill or amendment that probably would pass if voted upon directly. The most common method is to take advantage of the Senate's rules permitting unlimited debate, but other forms of parliamentary maneuvering may be used. The stricter rules used by the House make filibusters more difficult, but delaying tactics are employed occasionally through various procedural devices allowed by House rules. *(Senate filibusters, see Cloture.)*

Fiscal Year—Financial operations of the government are carried out in a 12-month fiscal year, beginning on Oct. 1 and ending on Sept. 30. The fiscal year carries the date of the calendar year in which it ends. (From fiscal year 1844 to fiscal year 1976, the fiscal year began July 1 and ended the following June 30.)

Five-Minute Rule—A debate-limiting rule of the House that is invoked when the House sits as the Committee of the Whole. Under the rule, a member offering an amendment is allowed to speak five minutes in its favor, and an opponent of the amendment is allowed to speak five minutes in opposition. Debate is then closed. In practice, amendments regularly are debated more than 10 minutes, with members gaining the floor by offering pro forma amendments or obtaining unanimous consent to speak longer than five minutes. *(See Strike Out the Last Word.)*

Floor Manager—A member who has the task of steering legislation through floor debate and the amendment process to a final vote in the House or the Senate. Floor managers are usually chairmen or ranking members of the committee that reported the bill. Managers are responsible for apportioning the debate time granted supporters of the bill. The ranking minority member of the committee normally apportions time for the minority party's participation in the debate.

Frank—A member's facsimile signature, which is used on envelopes in lieu of stamps, for the member's official outgoing mail. The "franking privilege" is the right to send mail postage-free.

Germane—Pertaining to the subject matter of the measure at hand. All House amendments must be germane to the bill being considered. The Senate requires that amendments be germane when they are proposed to general appropriation bills, bills being considered once cloture has been adopted, or, frequently, when proceeding under a unanimous consent agreement placing a time limit on consideration of a bill. The 1974 budget act also requires that amendments to concurrent budget resolutions be germane. In the House, floor debate must be germane, and the first three hours of debate each day in the Senate must be germane to the pending business.

Grandfather Clause—A provision exempting persons or other entities already engaged in an activity from rules or legislation affecting that activity. Grandfather clauses sometimes are added to legislation in order to avoid antagonizing groups with established interests in the activities affected.

Grants-in-Aid—Payments by the federal government to states, local governments or individuals in support of specified programs, services or activities.

Guaranteed Loans—Loans to third parties for which the federal government in the event of default guarantees, in whole or in part, the repayment of principal or interest to a lender or holder of a security.

Hearings—Committee sessions for taking testimony from witnesses. At hearings on legislation, witnesses usually include specialists, government officials and spokesmen for persons or entities affected by the bill or bills under study. Hearings related to special investigations bring forth a variety of witnesses. Committees sometimes use their subpoena power to summon reluctant witnesses. The public and press may attend open hearings, but are barred from closed, or "executive," hearings. The vast majority of hearings are open to the public. *(See Executive Session.)*

Hold-Harmless Clause—A provision added to legislation to ensure that recipients of federal funds do not receive less in a future year than they did in the current year if a new formula for allocating funds authorized in the legislation would result in a reduction to the recipients. This clause has been used most frequently to soften the impact of sudden reductions in federal grants.

Hopper—Box on House clerk's desk where members deposit bills and resolutions to introduce them. *(See also Bills Introduced.)*

Hour Rule—A provision in the rules of the House that permits one hour of debate time for each member on amendments debated in the House of Representatives sitting as the House. Therefore, the House normally amends bills while sitting as the Committee of the Whole, where the five-minute rule on amendments operates. *(See Committee of the Whole, Five-Minute Rule.)*

House—The House of Representatives, as distinct from the Senate, although each body is a "house" of Congress.

House as in Committee of the Whole—A procedure that can be used to expedite consideration of certain measures such as continuing resolutions and, when there is debate, private bills. The procedure only can be invoked with the unanimous consent of the House or a rule from the Rules Committee and has procedural elements of both the House sitting as the House of Representatives, such as the Speaker presiding and the previous question motion being in order, and the House sitting as the Committee of the Whole, such as the five-minute rule pertaining.

House Calendar—A listing for action by the House of public bills that do not directly or indirectly appropriate money or raise revenue.

Immunity—The constitutional privilege of members of Congress to make verbal statements on the floor and in committee for which they cannot be sued or arrested for slander or libel. Also, freedom from arrest while traveling to or from sessions of Congress or on official business. Members in this status may be arrested only for treason, felonies or a breach of the peace, as defined by congressional manuals.

Impoundments—Any action taken by the executive branch that delays or precludes the obligation or expenditure of budget authority previously approved by Congress. *(See also Deferrals of Budget Authority, Rescission Bill.)*

Joint Committee—A committee composed of a specified number of members of both the House and Senate. A joint committee may be investigative or research-oriented, an example of the latter being the Joint Economic Committee. Others have housekeeping duties such as the joint committees on Printing and on the Library of Congress.

Joint Resolution—A joint resolution, designated H J Res or S J Res, requires the approval of both houses and the signature of the president, just as a bill does, and has the force of law if approved. There is no practical difference between a bill and a joint resolution. A joint resolution generally is used to deal with a limited matter such as a single appropriation.

Joint resolutions also are used to propose amendments to the Constitution in Congress. They do not require a presidential signature, but become a part of the Constitution when three-fourths of the states have ratified them.

Journal—The official record of the proceedings of the House and Senate. The *Journal* records the actions taken in each chamber, but, unlike the *Congressional Record*, it does not include the substantially verbatim report of speeches, debates, etc.

Law—An act of Congress that has been signed by the president or passed over his veto by Congress. Public bills, when signed, become public laws, and are cited by the letters PL and a hyphenated number. The two digits before the number correspond to the Congress, and the one or more digits after the hyphen refer to the numerical sequence in which the bills were signed by the president during that Congress. Private bills, when signed, become private laws. *(See also Slip Laws, Statutes at Large, U.S. Code.)*

Legislative Day—The "day" extending from the time either house meets after an adjournment until the time it next adjourns. Because the House normally adjourns from day to day, legislative days and calendar days usually coincide. But in the Senate, a legislative day may, and frequently does, extend over several calendar days. *(See Recess.)*

Legislative Veto—A procedure permitting either the House or Senate, or both chambers, to review proposed executive branch regulations or actions and to block or modify those with which they disagree. The specifics of the procedure may vary, but Congress generally provides for a

legislative veto by including in a bill a provision that administrative rules or action taken to implement the law are to go into effect at the end of a designated period of time unless blocked by either or both houses of Congress. Another version of the veto provides for congressional reconsideration and rejection of regulations already in effect.

The Supreme Court ruling of June 23, 1983, restricted greatly the form and use of the legislative veto as an unconstitutional violation of the lawmaking procedure provided in the Constitution.

Lobby—A group seeking to influence the passage or defeat of legislation. Originally the term referred to persons frequenting the lobbies or corridors of legislative chambers in order to speak to lawmakers.

The definition of a lobby and the activity of lobbying is a matter of differing interpretation. By some definitions, lobbying is limited to direct attempts to influence lawmakers through personal interviews and persuasion. Under other definitions, lobbying includes attempts at indirect, or "grass-roots," influence, such as persuading members of a group to write or visit their district's representative and state's senators or attempting to create a climate of opinion favorable to a desired legislative goal.

The right to attempt to influence legislation is based on the First Amendment to the Constitution, which says Congress shall make no law abridging the right of the people "to petition the government for a redress of grievances."

Majority Leader—The majority leader is elected by his party colleagues. In the Senate, in consultation with the minority leader and his colleagues, the majority leader directs the legislative schedule for the chamber. He also is his party's spokesman and chief strategist. In the House, the majority leader is second to the Speaker in the majority party's leadership and serves as his party's legislative strategist.

Majority Whip—In effect, the assistant majority leader, in either the House or Senate. His job is to help marshal majority forces in support of party strategy and legislation.

Manual—The official handbook in each house prescribing in detail its organization, procedures and operations.

Marking Up a Bill—Going through the contents of a piece of legislation in committee or subcommittee, considering its provisions in large and small portions, acting on amendments to provisions and proposed revisions to the language, inserting new sections and phraseology, etc. If the bill is extensively amended, the committee's version may be introduced as a separate bill, with a new number, before being considered by the full House or Senate. *(See Clean Bill.)*

Minority Leader—Floor leader for the minority party in each chamber. *(See also Majority Leader.)*

Minority Whip—Performs duties of whip for the minority party. *(See also Majority Whip.)*

Morning Hour—The time set aside at the beginning of each legislative day for the consideration of regular, routine business. The "hour" is of indefinite duration in the House, where it is rarely used.

In the Senate it is the first two hours of a session following an adjournment, as distinguished from a recess. The morning hour can be terminated earlier if the morning business has been completed. Business includes such matters as messages from the president, communications from the heads of departments, messages from the House, the presentation of petitions, reports of standing and select committees and the introduction of bills and resolutions. During the first hour of the morning hour in the Senate, no motion to proceed to the consideration of any bill on the calendar is in order except by unanimous consent. During the second hour, motions can be made but must be decided without debate. Senate committees may meet while the Senate conducts morning hour.

Motion—In the House or Senate chamber, a request by a member to institute any one of a wide array of parliamentary actions. He "moves" for a certain procedure, the consideration of a measure, etc. The precedence of motions, and whether they are debatable, is set forth in the House and Senate manuals. *(See some specific motions above and below.)*

Nominations—Presidential appointments to office subject to Senate confirmation. Although most nominations win quick Senate approval, some are controversial and become the topic of hearings and debate. Sometimes senators object to appointees for patronage reasons — for example, when a nomination to a local federal job is made without consulting the senators of the state concerned. In some situations a senator may object that the nominee is "personally obnoxious" to him. Usually other senators join in blocking such appointments out of courtesy to their colleagues. *(See Senatorial Courtesy.)*

One-Minute Speeches—Addresses by House members at the beginning of a legislative day. The speeches may cover any subject but are limited to one minute's duration.

Override a Veto—If the president disapproves a bill and sends it back to Congress with his objections, Congress may try to override his veto and enact the bill into law. Neither house is required to attempt to override a veto. The override of a veto requires a recorded vote with a two-thirds majority in each chamber. The question put to each house is: "Shall the bill pass, the objections of the president to the contrary notwithstanding?" *(See also Pocket Veto, Veto.)*

Oversight Committee—A congressional committee, or designated subcommittee of a committee, that is charged with general oversight of one or more federal agencies' programs and activities. Usually, the oversight panel for a particular agency also is the authorizing committee for that agency's programs and operations.

Pair—An voluntary arrangement between two lawmakers, usually on opposite sides of an issue. If passage of the measure requires a two-thirds majority vote, a pair would require two members favoring the action to one opposed to it. Pairs can take one of three forms — specific, general and live. The names of lawmakers pairing on a given vote and their stands, if known, are printed in the *Congressional Record.*

The specific pair applies to one or more votes on the same subject. On special pairs, lawmakers usually specify how they would have voted.

A general pair in the Senate, now rarely used, applies to all votes on which the members pairing are on opposite sides. It usually does not specify the positions of the senators pairing. In a general pair in the House, no agreement is involved. A representative expecting to be absent may notify the House clerk he wishes to make a "general" pair. His name then is paired arbitrarily with that of another member desiring a pair, and the list is printed in the *Congressional Record.* He may or may not be paired with a member taking the opposite position. General pairs in the House give no indication of how a member would have voted.

A live pair involves two members, one present for the vote, the other absent. The member present casts his vote and then withdraws it and votes "present." He then announces that he has a live pair with a colleague, identifying how each would have voted on the question. A live pair subtracts the vote of the member in attendance from the final vote tabulation.

Petition—A request or plea sent to one or both chambers from an organization or private citizens' group asking support of particular legislation or favorable consideration of a matter not yet receiving congressional attention. Petitions are referred to appropriate committees.

Pocket Veto—The act of the president in withholding his approval of a bill after Congress has adjourned. When Congress is in session, a bill becomes law without the president's signature if he does not act upon it within 10 days, excluding Sundays, from the time he gets it. But if Congress adjourns sine die within that 10-day period, the bill will die even if the president does not formally veto it. *(See also Veto.)*

Point of Order—An objection raised by a member that the chamber is departing from rules governing its conduct of business. The objector cites the rule violated, the chair sustaining his objection if correctly made. Order is restored by the chair's suspending proceedings of the chamber until it conforms to the prescribed "order of business."

President of the Senate—Under the Constitution, the vice president of the United States presides over the Senate. In his absence, the president pro tempore, or a senator designated by the president pro tempore, presides over the chamber.

President Pro Tempore—The chief officer of the Senate in the absence of the vice president; literally, but loosely, the president for a time. The president pro tempore is elected by his fellow senators, and the recent practice has been to elect the senator of the majority party with the longest period of continuous service.

Previous Question—A motion for the previous question, when carried, has the effect of cutting off all debate, preventing the offering of further amendments, and forcing a vote on the pending matter. In the House, the previous question is not permitted in the Committee of the Whole. The motion for the previous question is a debate-limiting device and is not in order in the Senate.

Printed Amendment—A House rule guarantees five minutes of floor debate in support and five minutes in opposition, and no other debate time, on amendments printed in the *Congressional Record* at least one day prior to the amendment's consideration in the Committee of the Whole.

In the Senate, while amendments may be submitted for printing, they have no parliamentary standing or status. An amendment submitted for printing in the Senate, however, may be called up by any senator.

Private Calendar—In the House, private bills dealing with individual matters such as claims against the government, immigration, land titles, etc., are put on this calendar. The private calendar must be called on the first Tuesday of each month, and the Speaker may call it on the third Tuesday of each month as well.

When a private bill is before the chamber, two members may block its consideration, which recommits the bill to committee. Backers of a recommitted private bill have recourse. The measure can be put into an "omnibus claims bill" — several private bills rolled into one. As with any bill, no part of an omnibus claims bill may be deleted without a vote. When the private bill goes back to the House floor in this form, it can be deleted from the omnibus bill only by majority vote.

Privilege—Privilege relates to the rights of members of Congress and to the relative priority of the motions and actions they may make in their respective chambers. The two are distinct. "Privileged questions" deal with legislative business. "Questions of privilege" concern legislators themselves.

Privileged Questions—The order in which bills, motions and other legislative measures are considered by Congress is governed by strict priorities. A motion to table, for instance, is more privileged than a motion to recommit. Thus, a motion to recommit can be superseded by a motion to table, and a vote would be forced on the latter motion only. A motion to adjourn, however, takes precedence over a tabling motion and thus is considered of the "highest privilege." *(See also Questions of Privilege.)*

Pro Forma Amendment—*(See Strike Out the Last Word.)*

Public Laws—*(See Law.)*

Questions of Privilege—These are matters affecting members of Congress individually or collectively. Matters affecting the rights, safety, dignity and integrity of proceedings of the House or Senate as a whole are questions of privilege in both chambers.

Questions involving individual members are called questions of "personal privilege." A member rising to ask a question of personal privilege is given precedence over almost all other proceedings. An annotation in the House rules points out that the privilege rests primarily on the Constitution, which gives him a conditional immunity from arrest and an unconditional freedom to speak in the House. *(See also Privileged Questions.)*

Quorum—The number of members whose presence is necessary for the transaction of business. In the Senate and House, it is a majority of the membership. A quorum is 100

in the Committee of the Whole House. If a point of order is made that a quorum is not present, the only business that is in order is either a motion to adjourn or a motion to direct the sergeant-at-arms to request the attendance of absentees.

Readings of Bills—Traditional parliamentary procedure required bills to be read three times before they were passed. This custom is of little modern significance. Normally a bill is considered to have its first reading when it is introduced and printed, by title, in the *Congressional Record.* In the House, its second reading comes when floor consideration begins. (This is the most likely point at which there is an actual reading of the bill, if there is any.) The second reading in the Senate is supposed to occur on the legislative day after the measure is introduced, but before it is referred to committee. The third reading (again, usually by title) takes place when floor action has been completed on amendments.

Recess—Distinguished from adjournment *(see above)* in that a recess does not end a legislative day and therefore does not interrupt unfinished business. The rules in each house set forth certain matters to be taken up and disposed of at the beginning of each legislative day. The House usually adjourns from day to day. The Senate often recesses, thus meeting on the same legislative day for several calendar days or even weeks at a time.

Recognition—The power of recognition of a member is lodged in the Speaker of the House and the presiding officer of the Senate. The presiding officer names the member who will speak first when two or more members simultaneously request recognition.

Recommit to Committee—A motion, made on the floor after a bill has been debated, to return it to the committee that reported it. If approved, recommittal usually is considered a death blow to the bill. In the House, a motion to recommit can be made only by a member opposed to the bill, and, in recognizing a member to make the motion, the Speaker gives preference to members of the minority party over majority party members.

A motion to recommit may include instructions to the committee to report the bill again with specific amendments or by a certain date. Or, the instructions may direct that a particular study be made, with no definite deadline for further action. If the recommittal motion includes instructions to "report the bill back forthwith" and the motion is adopted, floor action on the bill continues; the committee does not actually reconsider the legislation.

Reconciliation—*(See Budget Reconciliation.)*

Reconsider a Vote—A motion to reconsider the vote by which an action was taken has, until it is disposed of, the effect of putting the action in abeyance. In the Senate, the motion can be made only by a member who voted on the prevailing side of the original question or by a member who did not vote at all. In the House, it can be made only by a member on the prevailing side.

A common practice in the Senate after close votes on an issue is a motion to reconsider, followed by a motion to table the motion to reconsider. On this motion to table, senators vote as they voted on the original question, which allows the motion to table to prevail, assuming there are no

switches. The matter then is finally closed and further motions to reconsider are not entertained. In the House, as a routine precaution, a motion to reconsider usually is made every time a measure is passed. Such a motion almost always is tabled immediately, thus shutting off the possibility of future reconsideration, except by unanimous consent.

Motions to reconsider must be entered in the Senate within the next two days of actual session after the original vote has been taken. In the House they must be entered either on the same day or on the next succeeding day the House is in session.

Recorded Vote—A vote upon which each member's stand is individually made known. In the Senate, this is accomplished through a roll call of the entire membership, to which each senator on the floor must answer "yea," "nay" or, if he does not wish to vote, "present." Since January 1973, the House has used an electronic voting system for recorded votes, including yea-and-nay votes formerly taken by roll calls.

When not required by the Constitution, a recorded vote can be obtained on questions in the House on the demand of one-fifth (44 members) of a quorum or one-fourth (25) of a quorum in the Committee of the Whole. *(See Yeas and Nays.)*

Report—Both a verb and a noun as a congressional term. A committee that has been examining a bill referred to it by the parent chamber "reports" its findings and recommendations to the chamber when it completes consideration and returns the measure. The process is called "reporting" a bill.

A "report" is the document setting forth the committee's explanation of its action. Senate and House reports are numbered separately and are designated S Rept or H Rept. When a committee report is not unanimous, the dissenting committee members may file a statement of their views, called minority views and referred to as a minority report. Members in disagreement with some provisions of a bill may file additional or supplementary views. Sometimes a bill is reported without a committee recommendation.

Adverse reports occasionally are submitted by legislative committees. However, when a committee is opposed to a bill, it usually fails to report the bill at all. Some laws require that committee reports — favorable or adverse — be made.

Rescission Bill—A bill rescinding or canceling budget authority previously made available by Congress. The president may request a rescission to reduce spending or because the budget authority no longer is needed. Under the 1974 budget act, however, unless Congress approves a rescission bill within 45 days of continuous session after receipt of the proposal, the funds must be made available for obligation. *(See also Deferrals of Budget Authority.)*

Resolution—A "simple" resolution, designated H Res or S Res, deals with matters entirely within the prerogatives of one house or the other. It requires neither passage by the other chamber nor approval by the president, and it does not have the force of law. Most resolutions deal with the rules or procedures of one house. They also are used to express the sentiments of a single house such as condolences to the family of a deceased member or to comment

on foreign policy or executive business. A simple resolution is the vehicle for a "rule" from the House Rules Committee. *(See also Concurrent and Joint Resolutions, Rules.)*

Rider—An amendment, usually not germane, that its sponsor hopes to get through more easily by including it in other legislation. Riders become law if the bills embodying them are enacted. Amendments providing legislative directives in appropriations bills are outstanding examples of riders, though technically legislation is banned from appropriations bills. The House, unlike the Senate, has a strict germaneness rule; thus, riders usually are Senate devices to get legislation enacted quickly or to bypass lengthy House consideration and, possibly, opposition.

Rules—The term has two specific congressional meanings. A rule may be a standing order governing the conduct of House or Senate business and listed among the permanent rules of either chamber. The rules deal with duties of officers, the order of business, admission to the floor, parliamentary procedures on handling amendments and voting, jurisdictions of committees, etc.

In the House, a rule also may be a resolution reported by its Rules Committee to govern the handling of a particular bill on the floor. The committee may report a "rule," also called a "special order," in the form of a simple resolution. If the resolution is adopted by the House, the temporary rule becomes as valid as any standing rule and lapses only after action has been completed on the measure to which it pertains. A rule sets the time limit on general debate. It also may waive points of order against provisions of the bill in question such as non-germane language or against certain amendments intended to be proposed to the bill from the floor. It may even forbid all amendments or all amendments except those proposed by the legislative committee that handled the bill. In this instance, it is known as a "closed" or "gag" rule as opposed to an "open" rule, which puts no limitation on floor amemdments, thus leaving the bill completely open to alteration by the adoption of germane amendments.

Secretary of the Senate—Chief administrative officer of the Senate, responsible for overseeing the duties of Senate employees, educating Senate pages, administering oaths, handling the registration of lobbyists, and handling other tasks necessary for the continuing operation of the Senate. *(See also Clerk of the House.)*

Select or Special Committee—A committee set up for a special purpose and, usually, for a limited time by resolution of either the House or Senate. Most special committees are investigative and lack legislative authority — legislation is not referred to them and they cannot report bills to their parent chamber. *(See also Standing Committees.)*

Senatorial Courtesy—Sometimes referred to as "the courtesy of the Senate," it is a general practice — with no written rule — applied to consideration of executive nominations. Generally, it means that nominations from a state are not to be confirmed unless they have been approved by the senators of the president's party of that state, with other senators following their colleagues' lead in the attitude they take toward consideration of such nominations. *(See Nominations.)*

Sine Die—*(See Adjournment Sine Die.)*

Slip Laws—The first official publication of a bill that has been enacted and signed into law. Each is published separately in unbound single-sheet or pamphlet form. *(See also Law, Statutes at Large, U.S. Code.)*

Speaker—The presiding officer of the House of Representatives, selected by the caucus of the party to which he belongs and formally elected by the whole House.

Special Session—A session of Congress after it has adjourned sine die, completing its regular session. Special sessions are convened by the president.

Spending Authority—The 1974 budget act defines spending authority as borrowing authority, contract authority and entitlement authority *(see above),* for which budget authority is not provided in advance by appropriation acts.

Sponsor—*(See Bills Introduced.)*

Standing Committees—Committees permanently established by House and Senate rules. The standing committees of the House were last reorganized by the committee reorganization act of 1974. The last major realignment of Senate committees was in the committee system reorganization of 1977. The standing committees are legislative committees — legislation may be referred to them and they may report bills and resolutions to their parent chambers. *(See also Select or Special Committees.)*

Standing Vote—A non-recorded vote used in both the House and Senate. (A standing vote also is called a division vote.) Members in favor of a proposal stand and are counted by the presiding officer. Then members opposed stand and are counted. There is no record of how individual members voted.

Statutes at Large—A chronological arrangement of the laws enacted in each session of Congress. Though indexed, the laws are not arranged by subject matter, and there is not an indication of how they changed previously enacted laws. *(See also Law, Slip Laws, U.S. Code.)*

Strike from the Record—Remarks made on the House floor may offend some member, who moves that the offending words be "taken down" for the Speaker's cognizance, and then expunged from the debate as published in the *Congressional Record.*

Strike Out the Last Word—A motion whereby a House member is entitled to speak for five minutes on an amendment then being debated by the chamber. A member gains recognition from the chair by moving to "strike out the last word" of the amendment or section of the bill under consideration. The motion is pro forma, requires no vote and does not change the amendment being debated.

Substitute—A motion, amendment or entire bill introduced in place of the pending legislative business. Passage of a substitute measure kills the original measure by supplanting it. The substitute also may be amended. *(See also Amendment in the Nature of a Substitute.)*

Supplemental Appropriation Bill—Legislation appropriating funds after the regular annual appropriation bill *(see above)* for a federal department or agency has been enacted. A supplemental appropriation provides additional budget authority beyond original estimates for programs or activities, including new programs authorized after the enactment of the regular appropriation act, for which the need for funds is too urgent to be postponed until enactment of the next year's regular appropriation bill.

Suspend the Rules—Often a time-saving procedure for passing bills in the House. The wording of the motion, which may be made by any member recognized by the Speaker, is: "I move to suspend the rules and pass the bill. . . ." A favorable vote by two-thirds of those present is required for passage. Debate is limited to 40 minutes and no amendments from the floor are permitted. If a two-thirds favorable vote is not attained, the bill may be considered later under regular procedures. The suspension procedure is in order every Monday and Tuesday and is intended to be reserved for non-controversial bills.

Table a Bill—A motion to "lay on the table" is not debatable in either house, and usually it is a method of making a final, adverse disposition of a matter. In the Senate, however, different language sometimes is used. The motion may be worded to let a bill "lie on the table," perhaps for subsequent "picking up." This motion is more flexible, keeping the bill pending for later action, if desired. Tabling motions on amendments are effective debate-ending devices in the Senate.

Teller Vote—This is a largely moribund House procedure in the Committee of the Whole. Members file past tellers and are counted as for, or against, a measure, but they are not recorded individually. In the House, tellers are ordered upon demand of one-fifth of a quorum. This is 44 in the House, 20 in the Committee of the Whole.

The House also has a recorded teller vote, now largely supplanted by the electronic voting procedure, under which the votes of each member are made public just as they would be on a recorded vote. *(See above.)*

Treaties—Executive proposals — in the form of resolutions of ratification — which must be submitted to the Senate for approval by two-thirds of the senators present. Treaties today are normally sent to the Foreign Relations Committee for scrutiny before the Senate takes action. Foreign Relations has jurisdiction over all treaties, regardless of the subject matter. Treaties are read three times and debated on the floor in much the same manner as legislative proposals. After approval by the Senate, treaties are formally ratified by the president.

Trust Funds—Funds collected and used by the federal government for carrying out specific purposes and programs according to terms of a trust agreement or statute such as the Social Security and unemployment compensation trust funds. Such funds are administered by the government in a fiduciary capacity and are not available for the general purposes of the government.

Unanimous Consent—Proceedings of the House or Senate and action on legislation often take place upon the unanimous consent of the chamber, whether or not a rule of the chamber is being violated. Unanimous consent is used to expedite floor action and frequently is used in a routine fashion such as by a senator requesting the unanimous consent of the Senate to have specified members of his staff present on the floor during debate on a specific amendment.

Unanimous Consent Agreement—A device used in the Senate to expedite legislation. Much of the Senate's legislative business, dealing with both minor and controversial issues, is conducted through unanimous consent or unanimous consent agreements. On major legislation, such agreements usually are printed and transmitted to all senators in advance of floor debate. Once agreed to, they are binding on all members unless the Senate, by unanimous consent, agrees to modify them. An agreement may list the order in which various bills are to be considered, specify the length of time bills and contested amendments are to be debated and when they are to be voted upon and, frequently, require that all amendments introduced be germane to the bill under consideration. In this regard, unanimous consent agreements are similar to the "rules" issued by the House Rules Committee for bills pending in the House. *(See above.)*

Union Calendar—Bills that directly or indirectly appropriate money or raise revenue are placed on this House calendar according to the date they are reported from committee.

U.S. Code—A consolidation and codification of the general and permanent laws of the United States arranged by subject under 50 titles, the first six dealing with general or political subjects, and the other 44 alphabetically arranged from agriculture to war. The code is revised every six years, and a supplement is published after each session of Congress. *(See also Law, Slip Laws, Statutes at Large.)*

Veto—Disapproval by the president of a bill or joint resolution (other than one proposing an amendment to the Constitution). When Congress is in session, the president must veto a bill within 10 days, excluding Sundays, after he has received it; otherwise, it becomes law without his signature. When the president vetoes a bill, he returns it to the house of origin along with a message stating his objections. *(See also Pocket Veto, Override a Veto.)*

Voice Vote—In either the House or Senate, members answer "aye" or "no" in chorus, and the presiding officer decides the result. The term also is used loosely to indicate action by unanimous consent or without objection.

Whip—*(See Majority and Minority Whip.)*

Without Objection—Used in lieu of a vote on non-controversial motions, amendments or bills that may be passed in either the House or Senate if no member voices an objection.

Yeas and Nays—The Constitution requires that yea-and-nay votes be taken and recorded when requested by one-fifth of the members present. In the House, the Speaker determines whether one-fifth of the members present requested a vote. In the Senate, practice requires only 11 members. The Constitution requires the yeas and nays on a veto override attempt. *(See Recorded Vote.)*

How a Bill Becomes Law

This graphic shows the most typical way in which proposed legislation is enacted into law. There are more complicated, as well as simpler, routes, and most bills never become law. The process is illustrated with two hypothetical bills, House bill No. 1 (HR 1) and

Senate bill No. 2 (S 2). Bills must be passed by both houses in identical form before they can be sent to the president. The path of HR 1 is traced by a solid line, that of S 2 by a broken line. In practice most bills begins as similar proposals in both houses.

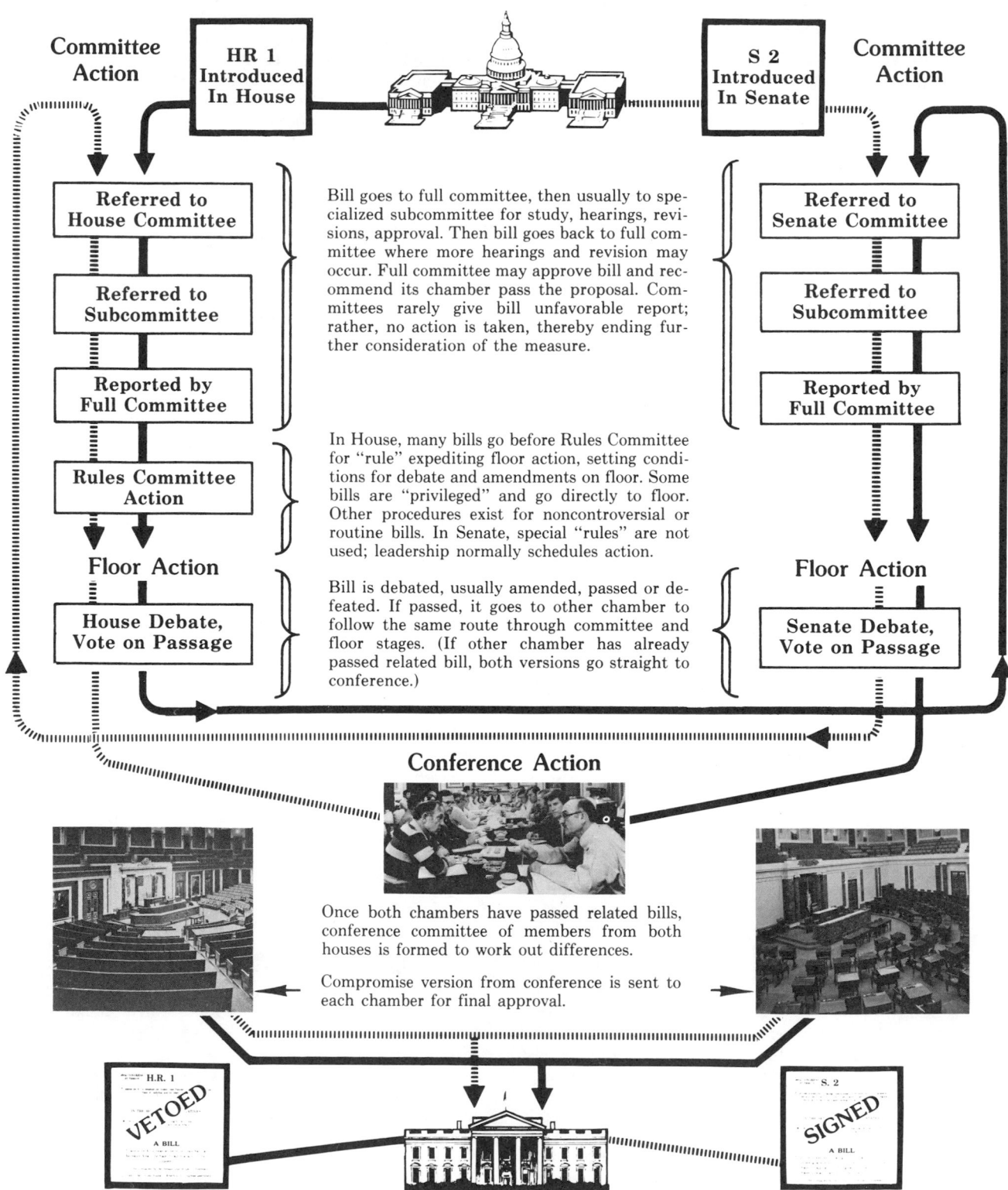

Committee Action

HR 1 Introduced In House

S 2 Introduced In Senate

Committee Action

Referred to House Committee

Referred to Subcommittee

Reported by Full Committee

Bill goes to full committee, then usually to specialized subcommittee for study, hearings, revisions, approval. Then bill goes back to full committee where more hearings and revision may occur. Full committee may approve bill and recommend its chamber pass the proposal. Committees rarely give bill unfavorable report; rather, no action is taken, thereby ending further consideration of the measure.

Referred to Senate Committee

Referred to Subcommittee

Reported by Full Committee

Rules Committee Action

In House, many bills go before Rules Committee for "rule" expediting floor action, setting conditions for debate and amendments on floor. Some bills are "privileged" and go directly to floor. Other procedures exist for noncontroversial or routine bills. In Senate, special "rules" are not used; leadership normally schedules action.

Floor Action

House Debate, Vote on Passage

Bill is debated, usually amended, passed or defeated. If passed, it goes to other chamber to follow the same route through committee and floor stages. (If other chamber has already passed related bill, both versions go straight to conference.)

Floor Action

Senate Debate, Vote on Passage

Conference Action

Once both chambers have passed related bills, conference committee of members from both houses is formed to work out differences.

Compromise version from conference is sent to each chamber for final approval.

H.R. 1 VETOED A BILL

S. 2 SIGNED A BILL

Compromise bill approved by both houses is sent to the president, who can sign it into law or veto it and return it to Congress. Congress may override veto by a two-thirds majority vote in both houses; bill then becomes law without president's signature.

The Legislative Process in Brief

Note: Parliamentary terms used below are defined in the glossary.

Introduction of Bills

A House member (including the resident commissioner of Puerto Rico and non-voting delegates of the District of Columbia, Guam, the Virgin Islands and American Samoa) may introduce any one of several types of bills and resolutions by handing it to the clerk of the House or placing it in a box called the hopper. A senator first gains recognition of the presiding officer to announce the introduction of a bill. If objection is offered by any senator, the introduction of the bill is postponed until the following day.

As the next step in either the House or Senate, the bill is numbered, referred to the appropriate committee, labeled with the sponsor's name, and sent to the Government Printing Office so that copies can be made for subsequent study and action. Senate bills may be jointly sponsored and carry several senators' names. Until 1978, the House limited the number of members who could cosponsor any one bill; the ceiling was eliminated at the beginning of the 96th Congress. A bill written in the executive branch and proposed as an administration measure usually is introduced by the chairman of the congressional committee that has jurisdiction.

Bills—Prefixed with "HR" in the House, "S" in the Senate, followed by a number. Used as the form for most legislation, whether general or special, public or private.

Joint Resolutions—Designated H J Res or S J Res. Subject to the same procedure as bills, with the exception of a joint resolution proposing an amendment to the Constitution. The latter must be approved by two-thirds of both houses and is thereupon sent directly to the administrator of general services for submission to the states for ratification rather than being presented to the president for his approval.

Concurrent Resolutions—Designated H Con Res or S Con Res. Used for matters affecting the operations of both houses. These resolutions do not become law.

Resolutions—Designated H Res or S Res. Used for a matter concerning the operation of either house alone and adopted only by the chamber in which it originates.

Committee Action

A bill is referred to the appropriate committee by a House parliamentarian in the Speaker's order, or by the Senate president. Sponsors may indicate their preferences for referral, although custom and chamber rule generally govern. An exception is the referral of private bills, which are sent to whatever group is designated by their sponsors. Bills are technically considered "read for the first time" when referred to House committees.

When a bill reaches a committee it is placed on the group's calendar. At that time it comes under the sharpest congressional focus. Its chances for passage are quickly determined — and the great majority of bills falls by the legislative roadside. Failure of a committee to act on a bill is equivalent to killing it; the measure can be withdrawn from the group's purview only by a discharge petition signed by a majority of the House membership on House bills, or by adoption of a special resolution in the Senate. Discharge attempts rarely succeed.

The first committee action taken on a bill usually is a request for comment on it by interested agencies of the government. The committee chairman may assign the bill to a subcommittee for study and hearings, or it may be considered by the full committee. Hearings may be public, closed (executive session), or both. A subcommittee, after considering a bill, reports to the full committee its recommendations for action and any proposed amendments.

The full committee then votes on its recommendation to the House or Senate. This procedure is called "ordering a bill reported." Occasionally a committee may order a bill reported unfavorably; most of the time a report, submitted by the chairman of the committee to the House or Senate, calls for favorable action on the measure since the committee can effectively "kill" a bill by simply failing to take any action.

When a committee sends a bill to the chamber floor, it explains its reasons in a written statement, called a report, which accompanies the bill. Often committee members opposing a measure issue dissenting minority statements that are included in the report.

Usually, the committee "marks up" or proposes amendments to the bill. If they are substantial and the measure is complicated, the committee may order a "clean bill" introduced, which will embody the proposed amendments. The original bill then is put aside and the "clean bill," with a new number, is reported to the floor.

The chamber must approve, alter, or reject the committee amendments before the bill itself can be put to a vote.

Floor Action

After a bill is reported back to the house where it originated, it is placed on the calendar.

There are five legislative calendars in the House, issued in one cumulative calendar titled *Calendars of the United States House of Representatives and History of Legislation.* The House calendars are:

The Union Calendar to which are referred bills raising revenues, general appropriations bills and any measures directly or indirectly appropriating money or property. It is the Calendar of the Committee of the Whole House on the State of the Union.

Progress of Legislation

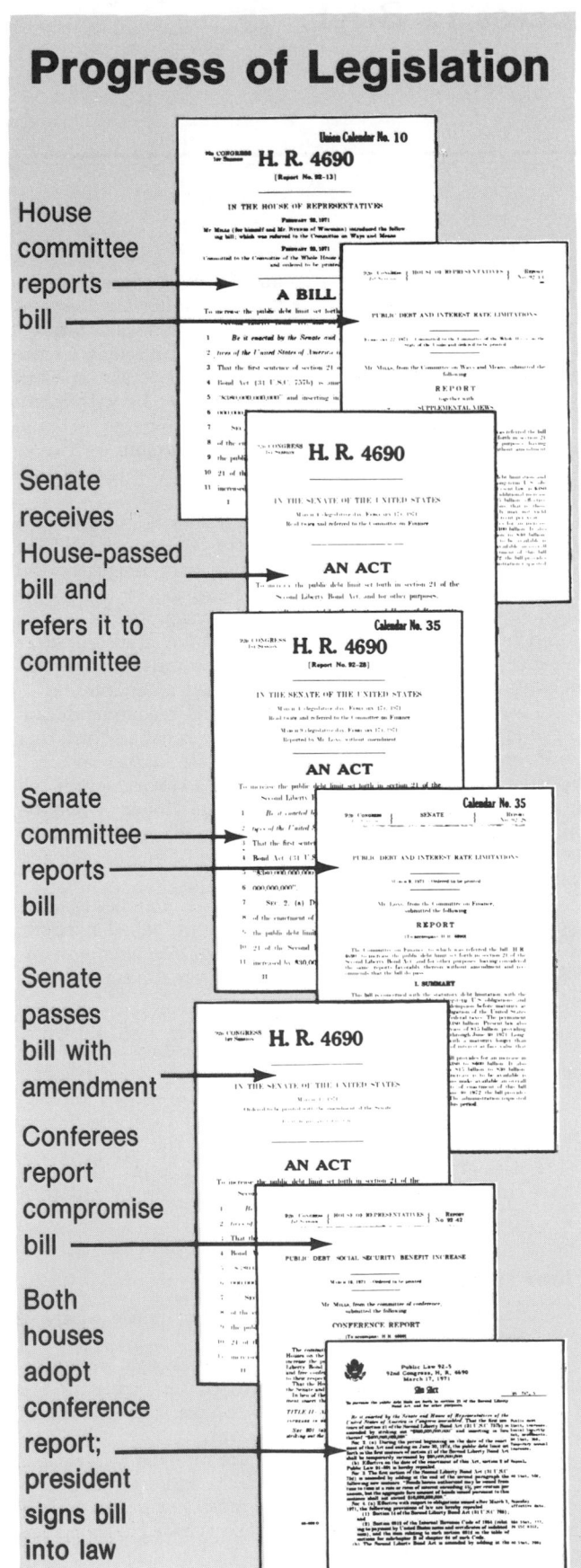

House committee reports bill

Senate receives House-passed bill and refers it to committee

Senate committee reports bill

Senate passes bill with amendment

Conferees report compromise bill

Both houses adopt conference report; president signs bill into law

The House Calendar to which are referred bills of public character not raising revenue or appropriating money or property.

The Consent Calendar to which are referred bills of a non-controversial nature that are passed without debate when the Consent Calendar is called on the first and third Mondays of each month.

The Private Calendar to which are referred bills for relief in the nature of claims against the United States or private immigration bills that are passed without debate when the Private Calendar is called the first and third Tuesdays of each month.

The Discharge Calendar to which are referred motions to discharge committees when the necessary signatures are signed to a discharge petition.

There is only one legislative calendar in the Senate and one "executive calendar" for treaties and nominations submitted to the Senate. When the Senate Calendar is called, each senator is limited to five minutes' debate on each bill.

Debate. A bill is brought to debate by varying procedures. If a routine measure, it may await the call of the calendar. If it is urgent or important, it can be taken up in the Senate either by unanimous consent or by a majority vote. The policy committee of the majority party in the Senate schedules the bills that it wants taken up for debate.

In the House, precedence is granted if a special rule is obtained from the Rules Committee. A request for a special rule is usually made by the chairman of the committee that favorably reported the bill, supported by the bill's sponsor and other committee members. The request, considered by the Rules Committee in the same fashion that other committees consider legislative measures, is in the form of a resolution providing for immediate consideration of the bill. The Rules Committee reports the resolution to the House where it is debated and voted upon in the same fashion as regular bills. If the Rules Committee should fail to report a rule requested by a committee, there are several ways to bring the bill to the House floor — under suspension of the rules, on Calendar Wednesday or by a discharge motion.

The resolutions providing special rules are important because they specify how long the bill may be debated and whether it may be amended from the floor. If floor amendments are banned, the bill is considered under a "closed rule," which permits only members of the committee that first reported the measure to the House to alter its language, subject to chamber acceptance.

When a bill is debated under an "open rule," amendments may be offered from the floor. Committee amendments are always taken up first, but may be changed, as may all amendments up to the second degree; i.e., an amendment to an amendment to an amendment is not in order.

Duration of debate in the House depends on whether the bill is under discussion by the House proper or before the House when it is sitting as the Committee of the Whole House on the State of the Union. In the former, the amount of time for debate is determined either by special rule or is allocated with an hour for each member if the measure is under consideration without a rule. In the Committee of the Whole the amount of time agreed on for general debate is equally divided between proponents and opponents. At the end of general discussion, the bill is read section by section for amendment. Debate on an amendment is lim-

ited to five minutes for each side.

Senate debate is usually unlimited. It can be halted only by unanimous consent by "cloture," which requires a three-fifths majority of the entire Senate except for proposed changes in the Senate rules. The latter requires a two-thirds vote.

The House sits as the Committee of the Whole when it considers any tax measure or bill dealing with public appropriations. It can also resolve itself into the Committee of the Whole if a member moves to do so and the motion is carried. The Speaker appoints a member to serve as the chairman. The rules of the House permit the Committee of the Whole to meet with any 100 members on the floor, and to amend and act on bills with a quorum of the 100, within the time limitations mentioned previously. When the Committee of the Whole has acted, it "rises," the Speaker returns as the presiding officer of the House and the member appointed chairman of the Committee of the Whole reports the action of the committee and its recommendations (amendments adopted).

Votes. Voting on bills may occur repeatedly before they are finally approved or rejected. The House votes on the rule for the bill and on various amendments to the bill. Voting on amendments often is a more illuminating test of a bill's support than is the final tally. Sometimes members approve final passage of bills after vigorously supporting amendments that, if adopted, would have scuttled the legislation.

The Senate has three different methods of voting: an untabulated voice, a standing vote (called a division) and a recorded roll call to which members answer "yea" or "nay" when their names are called. The House also employs voice and standing votes, but since January 1973 yeas and nays have been recorded by an electronic voting device, eliminating the need for time-consuming roll calls.

Another method of voting, used in the House only, is the teller vote. Traditionally, members filed up the center aisle past counters; only vote totals were announced. Since 1971, one-fifth of a quorum can demand that the votes of individual members be recorded, thereby forcing them to take a public position on amendments to key bills. Electronic voting now is commonly used for this purpose.

After amendments to a bill have been voted upon, a vote may be taken on a motion to recommit the bill to committee. If carried, this vote removes the bill from the chamber's calendar. If the motion is unsuccessful, the bill then is "read for the third time." An actual reading usually is dispensed with. Until 1965, an opponent of a bill could delay this move by objecting and asking for a full reading of an engrossed (certified in final form) copy of the bill. After the "third reading," the vote on final passage is taken.

The final vote may be followed by a motion to reconsider, and this motion itself may be followed by a move to lay the motion on the table. Usually, those voting for the bill's passage vote for the tabling motion, thus safeguarding the final passage action. With that, the bill has been formally passed by the chamber. While a motion to reconsider a Senate vote is pending on a bill, the measure cannot be sent to the House.

Action in Second House

After a bill is passed it is sent to the other chamber. This body may then take one of several steps. It may pass the bill as is — accepting the other chamber's language. It may send the bill to committee for scrutiny or alteration, or

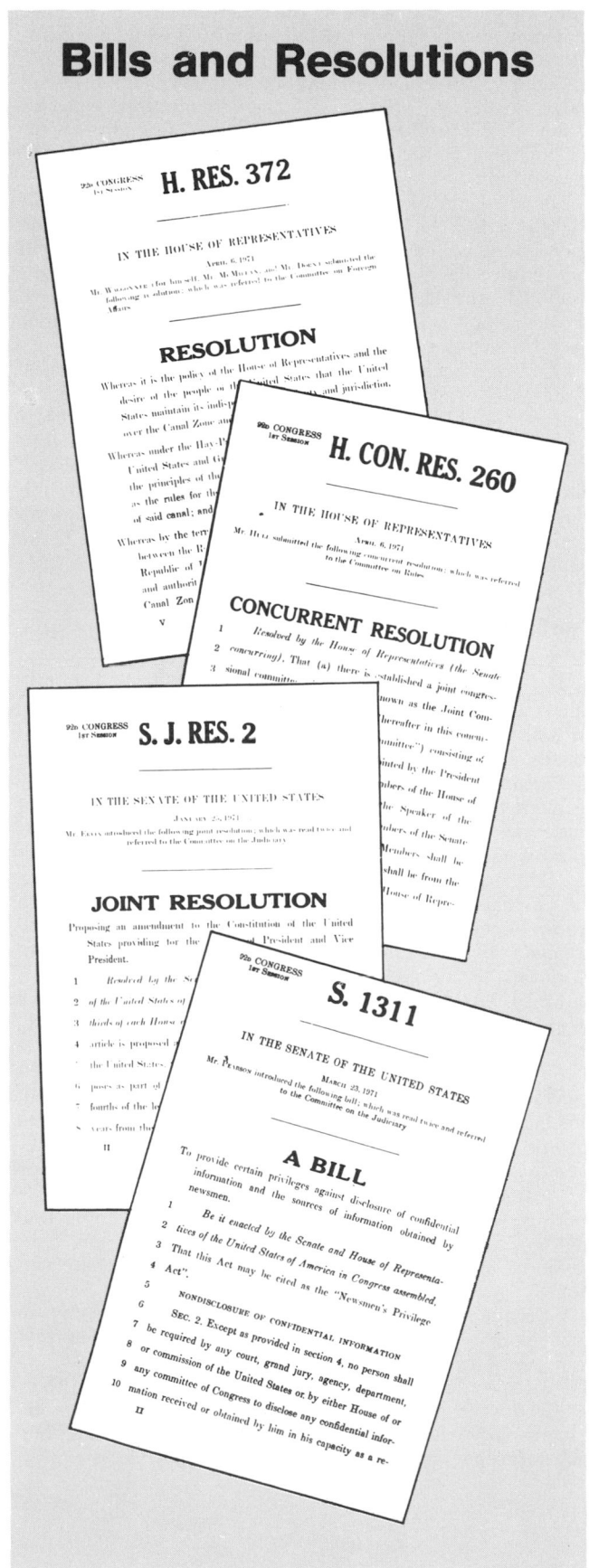

Bills and Resolutions

reject the entire bill, advising the other house of its actions. Or it may simply ignore the bill submitted while it continues work on its own version of the proposed legislation. Frequently, one chamber may approve a version of a bill that is greatly at variance with the version already passed by the other house, and then substitute its amendments for the language of the other, retaining only the latter's bill designation.

A provision of the Legislative Reorganization Act of 1970 permits a separate House vote on any non-germane amendment added by the Senate to a House-passed bill and requires a majority vote to retain the amendment. Previously the House was forced to act on the bill as a whole; the only way to defeat the non-germane amendment was to reject the entire bill.

Often the second chamber makes only minor changes. If these are readily agreed to by the other house, the bill then is routed to the White House for signing. However, if the opposite chamber basically alters the bill submitted to it, the measure usually is "sent to conference." The chamber that has possession of the "papers" (engrossed bill, engrossed amendments, messages of transmittal) requests a conference and the other chamber must agree to it. If the second house does not agree, the bill dies.

Conference, Final Action

Conference. A conference undertakes to harmonize conflicting House and Senate versions of a legislative bill. The conference is usually staffed by senior members (conferees), appointed by the presiding officers of the two houses, from the committees that managed the bills. Under this arrangement the conferees of one house have the duty of trying to maintain their chamber's position in the face of amending actions by the conferees (also referred to as "managers") of the other house.

The number of conferees from each chamber may vary, the range usually being from three to nine members in each group, depending upon the length or complexity of the bill involved. There may be five representatives and three senators on the conference committee, or the reverse. But a majority vote controls the action of each group so that a large representation does not give one chamber a voting advantage over the other chamber's conferees.

Theoretically, conferees are not allowed to write new legislation in reconciling the two versions before them, but this curb sometimes is bypassed. Many bills have been put into acceptable compromise form only after new language was provided by the conferees. The 1970 Reorganization Act attempted to tighten restrictions on conferees by forbidding them to introduce any language on a topic that neither chamber sent to conference or to modify any topic beyond the scope of the different House and Senate versions.

Frequently the ironing out of difficulties takes days or even weeks. Conferences on involved appropriations bills sometimes are particularly drawn out.

As a conference proceeds, conferees reconcile differences between the versions, but generally they grant concessions only insofar as they remain sure that the chamber they represent will accept the compromises. Occasionally,

uncertainty over how either house will react, or the positive refusal of a chamber to back down on a disputed amendment, results in an impasse, and the bills die in conference even though each was approved by its sponsoring chamber.

Conferees sometimes go back to their respective chambers for further instructions, when they report certain portions in disagreement. Then the chamber concerned can either "recede and concur" in the amendment of the other house, or "insist on its amendment."

When the conferees have reached agreement, they prepare a conference report embodying their recommendations (compromises). The reports, in document form, must be submitted to each house.

The conference report must be approved by each house. Consequently, approval of the report is approval of the compromise bill. In the order of voting on conference reports, the chamber which asked for a conference yields to the other chamber the opportunity to vote first.

Final Steps. After a bill has been passed by both the House and Senate in identical form, all of the original papers are sent to the enrolling clerk of the chamber in which the bill originated. He then prepares an enrolled bill, which is printed on parchment paper. When this bill has been certified as correct by the secretary of the Senate or the clerk of the House, depending on which chamber originated the bill, it is signed first (no matter whether it originated in the Senate or House) by the Speaker of the House and then by the president of the Senate. It is next sent to the White House to await action.

If the president approves the bill, he signs it, dates it and usually writes the word "approved" on the document. If he does not sign it within 10 days (Sundays excepted) and Congress is in session, the bill becomes law without his signature.

However, should Congress adjourn before the 10 days expire, and the president has failed to sign the measure, it does not become law. This procedure is called the pocket veto.

A president vetoes a bill by refusing to sign it and before the 10-day period expires, returning it to Congress with a message stating his reasons. The message is sent to the chamber that originated the bill. If no action is taken there on the message, the bill dies. Congress, however, can attempt to override the president's veto and enact the bill, "the objections of the president to the contrary notwithstanding." Overriding of a veto requires a two-thirds vote of those present, who must number a quorum and vote by roll call.

Debate can precede this vote, with motions permitted to lay the message on the table, postpone action on it, or refer it to committee. If the president's veto is overridden by a two-thirds vote in both houses, the bill becomes law. Otherwise it is dead.

When bills are passed finally and signed, or passed over a veto, they are given law numbers in numerical order as they become law. There are two series of numbers, one for public and one for private laws, starting at the number "1" for each two-year term of Congress. They are then identified by law number and by Congress — i.e., Private Law 21, 97th Congress; Public Law 250, 97th Congress (or PL 97-250).

Key Votes, 1981-84

Congressional Quarterly each year selects a series of key votes on major issues.

Selection of Issues. An issue is judged by the extent it represents one or more of the following:

- A matter of major controversy.
- A test of presidential or political power.
- A decision of potentially great impact on the nation and lives of Americans.

Selection of Votes. For each series of related votes on an issue, only one key vote is ordinarily chosen. This vote is the roll call in the House or Senate that in the opinion of Congressional Quarterly was the most important in determining the outcome.

In the description of the key votes, the designation ND denotes Northern Democrats, and the designation SD denotes Southern Democrats.

1981 Key Votes

Senate

1. Anti-Busing Rider

The Senate Sept. 16 invoked cloture and approved the most far-reaching anti-busing curb to date when it adopted an amendment to the Justice Department authorization bill (S 951).

The 61-36 cloture vote cut off a filibuster led by Lowell P. Weicker Jr., R-Conn. The vote was the first successful cloture effort out of five attempts since Weicker launched his filibuster in June, meeting the requirement of three-fifths of total Senate membership (60) needed to cut off debate. The breakdown on the vote was: R 36-16; D 25-20 (ND 11-19, SD 14-1).

The Senate then adopted the anti-busing amendment of J. Bennett Johnston, D-La., by a vote of 60-39.

The Johnston amendment would bar federal judges from ordering busing except in very narrow circumstances. It also would allow the attorney general to file lawsuits on behalf of students who believed they had been bused in violation of the standards set out in the Johnston proposal, opening the way for overturning existing busing orders.

The Johnston proposal was attached to another amendment to S 951, sponsored by Jesse Helms, R-N.C. This proposal would prevent the Justice Department from spending money to bring any legal action that could lead, directly or indirectly, to court-ordered busing.

With outnumbered opponents of the anti-busing proposals employing delaying tactics, the Senate did not pass S 951 before the first session of the 97th Congress ended.

2. Saudi AWACS

The Reagan administration based its Middle East policy on what it called a "strategic consensus" among nations there that the Soviet Union posed the primary threat to them, notwithstanding their regional disputes.

To improve U.S. relations with oil giant Saudi Arabia, in part to nurture the Middle East consensus it perceived, the administration decided in the spring of 1981 to sell Saudi Arabia five sophisticated Airborne Warning and Control System (AWACS) radar planes and other military equipment.

The decision posed the first major test in Congress of President Reagan's authority in foreign policy.

Israel strongly opposed the AWACS sale, viewing it as a threat to Israeli air superiority in the Middle East, and the American Jewish community began to campaign against it from the moment the administration acknowledged its plans.

Critics in Congress said it was unwise to entrust the secrets of the computer-assisted AWACS surveillance system to a nation that often had opposed U.S. policy in the Middle East and whose ruling royal family was seen as vulnerable to being overthrown.

Saudi Arabia cast the deal as a test of U.S.-Saudi relations. The administration argued that Saudi air defenses must be bolstered to protect Saudi oil fields along the eastern coast of the Arabian Peninsula — the source of much of the industrial West's oil supplies.

Reagan's problem was that Congress could veto the AWACS sale under a law giving it the right to block major arms deals by passing a concurrent resolution within 30 days of receiving formal notice.

Formal notice of the deal was delivered on Oct. 1, giving Congress until Oct. 30 to veto the sale.

The House passed a resolution of disapproval (H Con Res 194) on Oct. 14 by an overwhelming vote of 301-111. *(House key vote 4)*

But Reagan won on the issue after he put his personal prestige on the line. He argued that a congressional veto would undermine his authority to conduct foreign policy, and the Senate rejected H Con Res 194 on Oct. 28 by a dramatic vote of 48-52: R 12-41; D 36-11 (ND 28-4, SD 8-7).

3. MX Missile

In its first vote on the issue since 1979, the Senate April 7 tabled an amendment that would have made a symbolic reduction in funds for the MX mobile intercontinental missile.

At the time of the vote, the administration was reviewing alternative approaches to keeping the new missile hidden from Soviet observation.

Critics of the missile saw that review as the ideal time to force a reconsideration of the basic premise behind deploying the MX: that a new, more accurate U.S. missile was needed because existing land-based missiles were vulnerable to a Soviet first strike.

Most Armed Services Committee members and senior Air Force officers favored the mobile basing technique proposed by President Carter, under which each MX would be shuttled among nearly two dozen hidden launch sites.

During Senate consideration of a fiscal 1981 defense supplemental authorizations bill (S 694), Larry Pressler, R-S.D., offered an amendment that would have deleted $7 million for research related to MX.

Pressler said the amendment would be a "clear signal" to the Pentagon and the administration that Congress was concerned about the missile and wanted to know how it would be based before voting funds for it.

Opponents of the amendment said that it would, instead, send a signal to the Soviet Union that the United States was not serious about modernizing its nuclear forces.

The Senate tabled (killed) the Pressler amendment on a 79-15 vote: R 44-6; D 35-9 (ND 20-9, SD 15-0).

4. Tenn-Tom Waterway

Since the 1940s, powerful members of Congress had fought first to authorize and then to appropriate money for the Tennessee-Tombigbee Waterway.

By 1981 about $1 billion had already been spent on the 232-mile inland canal, designed to connect the Tennessee River with the Tombigbee River and enable barges to navigate from Appalachian coal fields to the seaport of Mobile, Ala.

Environmentalists opposed the project as damaging and taxpayer organizations said it was too costly. They warned that "Tenn-Tom," as it was called, would cost $3 billion by the time it was finished.

When the Senate considered the fiscal 1982 energy and water appropriations bill (HR 4144) Nov. 4, a bipartisan group of senators tried to delete the $189 million in the bill for the canal.

Led by Charles H. Percy, R-Ill., and Daniel Patrick Moynihan, D-N.Y., they argued that the project was consuming too much of the money available for water projects. They said supporters of the project were overstating the benefits, and called it an "economic dinosaur."

Supporters said the canal was too near finished to be abandoned. They said it was needed to get coal to the sea for export, and estimated that it would generate $145 million a year in commerce.

The supporters insisted the total cost of the project would be only $1.8 billion, and charged that opponents were misrepresenting it. They said the railroads were behind efforts to kill the waterway to stifle competition for coal transportation.

J. Bennett Johnston, D-La., led the floor debate against Percy's amendment while 80-year-old John C. Stennis, D-Miss., the waterway's principal supporter over the years, twisted arms for votes. Percy's amendment to delete the funding for the waterway was defeated 46-48: R 27-21; D 19-27 (ND 17-14, SD 2-13).

The vote was the closest opponents of the project had ever come to winning, although Johnston said the vote was not as close as it appeared because six senators who voted against Tenn-Tom had promised to switch their votes if necessary to save the project.

Senators said after the vote that backers of the project had suggested to uncommitted senators that they support Tenn-Tom if they wanted support for other projects in which they were interested. They also played on affection for Stennis, suggesting that saving Tenn-Tom would help his re-election chances.

While a majority of House freshmen voted to kill Tenn-Tom *(House key vote 7)*, senators first elected in 1980 opposed Percy's amendment 7-11. The new members' votes were crucial because seven senators who had supported the project in the past voted to kill it in 1981.

5. Clinch River Breeder Reactor

In the 1970s the proposed Clinch River (Tenn.) breeder reactor had become a symbol in the fight over the future of nuclear power.

Anti-nuclear groups had long fought the reactor, and President Carter tried for four years to kill the project, which was designed to generate electricity while producing more plutonium fuel than it used. Carter worried that the plutonium could be stolen and used to make nuclear weapons.

But Congress continued to fund the program. By 1981 more than $1 billion had been spent of a total cost now estimated to be at least $3.2 billion, and construction had not even begun.

President Reagan's budget director, David A. Stock-man, had strenuously opposed the project as uneconomical when he was a member of Congress, and left funding for Clinch River out of the president's fiscal 1982 budget. But Senate Majority Leader Howard H. Baker Jr., R-Tenn., persuaded Reagan to request $254 million for it.

The Senate Appropriations Committee included $180 million for the reactor in the fiscal 1982 energy and water appropriations bill (HR 4144).

When the measure came to the Senate floor Nov. 4, Dale Bumpers, D-Ark., and Gordon J. Humphrey, R-N.H., tried to kill the project. They called it an economic white elephant that would be technologically obsolete by the time it was completed.

But their amendment to delete the $180 million was first amended to cut only $90 million and then tabled (killed) by a vote of 48-46: R 36-14; D 12-32 (ND 4-26, SD 8-6). It was the closest Clinch River opponents had ever come to killing the project.

While budget-conscious freshmen House members voted 36-34 to kill the project *(House key vote 8)*, Baker managed to persuade 14 of the 18 new Senate members to vote with him to support it.

Opponents managed a second vote the next day, but lost again by a five-vote margin. That day Baker had Vice President George Bush standing by to vote to save the project in case of a tie.

6. Abortion

The long-running fight over government funding of abortions for poor women was effectively ended when the Senate voted to bar such abortions except when needed to save a mother's life.

The vote was crucial because the Senate, over the years, had been a bastion of support for abortion funding. The House long had backed the so-called Hyde amendment (named for its sponsor, Rep. Henry J. Hyde, R-Ill.) to bar Medicaid funding of abortions in non-life-threatening situations.

Past House-Senate disputes over the Hyde amendment had produced lengthy deadlocks in conference. Compromises between the two bodies had allowed payment for abortions when the pregnancy was caused by rape or incest.

The new Senate Republican majority, including many members who were elected on strong anti-abortion platforms, moved decisively against abortion funding.

Despite attempts by Republican leaders to keep a supplemental appropriations bill (HR 3512) free from controversial legislative provisions, the Senate restored the Hyde amendment May 21 by a 52-43 vote: R 33-19; D 19-24 (ND 12-18, SD 7-6).

Debate on the amendment opened old wounds within the Republican Party, which had been deeply divided over the abortion funding issue.

Bob Packwood, R-Ore., a leading spokesman for abortion funding, accused Hyde amendment supporters of seeking to impose a "Cotton Mather mentality" on the country. But Jesse Helms, R-N.C., said the anti-abortion movement would not forgive those who voted against the Hyde amendment.

7. Debt Limit Increase

An increase in the federal debt limit was an unlikely candidate for fiscally conservative President Reagan's first legislative victory. But on Feb. 6 the Senate approved a

measure (HR 1553) that raised the debt ceiling to $985 billion through Sept. 30, 1982, thus providing President Reagan with his maiden Capitol Hill success.

The Senate vote was 73-18: R 46-3; D 27-15 (ND 20-7, SD 7-8).

The vote cleared the bill for the president's signature since the House had approved it a day earlier by a 305-104 margin. *(House key vote 9)*

Had Congress failed to act, the outstanding debt would have hit the existing $935.1 billion ceiling by mid-February, leaving the government unable to meet its borrowing needs.

Just before the Senate vote on the measure, Finance Committee Chairman Robert Dole, R-Kan., joked that there had "been a lot of rapid conversion around here on this issue."

Republicans who in the past had opposed debt limit increases, charging that they were "fiscally irresponsible," acceded to the request of their president and voted for the bill. It was really leftover business from the Carter administration, they claimed.

8. Budget Cut Instructions

Budget reconciliation was the vehicle that moved President Reagan's philosophy of fiscal austerity from rhetoric to reality. And Senate action on April 2 to instruct Senate committees to cut $36.9 billion from fiscal 1982 spending was the first major step toward enactment of his budget-cutting proposals.

Under reconciliation, the spending cut instructions went to 14 authorizing and appropriations committees, where members were required to change existing programs to make the required savings.

Without waiting for action on the first fiscal 1982 budget resolution, the Senate adopted separate reconciliation instructions (S Con Res 9) by an 88-10 vote: R 51-1; D 37-9 (ND 22-9, SD 15-0).

Senate leaders — including Majority Leader Howard H. Baker Jr., R-Tenn., and Senate Budget Committee Chairman Pete V. Domenici, R-N.M. — and budget director David A. Stockman agreed that using reconciliation would put the administration's budget-cutting efforts on the fast track.

Together they were able to keep most Republicans united behind the spending reductions. On the final vote only one GOP senator — Lowell P. Weicker Jr., R-Conn., voted "no."

The Democrats, however, were deeply divided. Because many of the more conservative members of the party frequently voted with the Republicans, liberal Democrats did not come close to winning adoption of the more than 20 amendments they introduced.

9. Social Security

When President Reagan May 12 announced proposals to cut Social Security benefits, congressional Democrats saw a political opportunity they could not pass up.

Congress was in the midst of one of the biggest budget battles ever and the minority party, buoyed by public outrage at the proposed cuts in Social Security, repeatedly charged the administration with balancing its budget on the backs of the elderly.

For Republicans, the issue proved to be an embarrassing one.

The first major rebuff of the administration's plans came only a week after they were announced. On May 20 Sen. Daniel Patrick Moynihan, D-N.Y., offered a "sense of the Senate" amendment to a fiscal 1981 supplemental appropriations bill (HR 3512) condemning Reagan's plans as "a breach of faith" with the American elderly. It also stated that Congress would not "precipitously and unfairly" cut Social Security benefits.

The amendment was tabled (killed) by a vote of 49-48: R 48-2; D 1-46 (ND 0-32, SD 1-14).

Almost immediately after that vote, however, the Senate unanimously adopted a toned-down version of the amendment that promised Congress would not make any more cuts in the financially troubled program than were necessary to keep it solvent.

Reagan eventually withdrew his proposals and Congress passed a stopgap measure (HR 4331) to keep Social Security's largest trust fund, Old-Age and Survivors' Insurance, from going broke in 1982. At the end of the session, Senate Minority Leader Robert C. Byrd, D-W.Va., labeled the defeat of the administration's Social Security plans "a victory where victories, for Democrats, appear to be scarce."

10. Tax Indexing

During floor debate on President Reagan's individual and business tax cut package (H J Res 266), Senate Republicans added a provision intended to put an automatic cap on the growth of government spending for years to come.

The Finance Committee amendment, requiring that individual income taxes be indexed annually beginning in 1985 to offset the effects of inflation, was adopted July 16 by a vote of 57-40: R 43-8, D 14-32 (ND 11-20, SD 3-12).

The measure was vigorously opposed by Democrats and some Republicans who charged it would tie the hands of both the administration and Congress in making future budget and tax decisions.

But proponents argued that the government unfairly received a tax "bonus" each year as inflation pushed individuals into higher and higher tax brackets. They said such built-in revenue growth made it too easy for Congress to spend more taxpayers' money.

While lauded at the time as a major victory for fiscal conservatism, indexing soon appeared to be a possible victim of the government spending it was designed to contain. By the end of the year, projections of annual budget deficits approaching $200 billion made some economists and politicians skeptical that indexing would ever take effect.

11. Targeting Tax Cuts

One of the two major components of President Reagan's tax cut program — accelerated write-offs for capital investment — enjoyed fairly broad Senate support. But his proposed 23 percent across-the-board cut in individual income taxes became the primary target for Democratic opposition to the bill — and to the administration's entire economic philosophy.

Many Democrats charged that because income taxes were progressive the bulk of the reduction would be enjoyed by the wealthy, while the poor and middle class would hardly benefit at all. In addition, they said, the cut would mean a loss of $196 billion in tax revenues over the

following three years, seriously jeopardizing the goal of a balanced budget in 1984.

The administration and its Republican defenders said the tax cuts would spur enough economic growth to solve many of the country's fiscal problems.

Sen. Ernest F. Hollings, D-S.C., July 23 offered an amendment to the tax bill (H J Res 266) that included a one-year, 10 percent cut in individual income taxes, with much of the relief targeted to those earning under $50,000. He said his cut was more likely than the president's to result in a balanced 1984 budget.

However, public and congressional support was strong for giving the new administration and its revolutionary supply-side tax policies a chance. The amendment was rejected 26-71: R 0-51; D-26-20 (ND 20-12, SD 6-8).

12. Congressional Pay Raise

Seeking to avoid politically embarrassing votes in the future, the Senate approved a permanent funding mechanism for pay raises for members of Congress. The action made it much more likely, although not certain, that members will get future pay raises along with other federal employees.

Congressional salaries have risen very slowly in recent years because members of Congress have been extremely reluctant to go on record in favor of giving themselves more money. Amendments to annual legislative appropriations bills have frozen the pay at $60,622.50 a year since 1979.

During conference action on a continuing appropriations resolution (H J Res 325), the House proposed that members get a 4.8 percent pay raise. That was rejected by Senate conferees. However, conferees agreed to establish a permanent appropriation for congressional pay increases.

When the conference report came to the Senate Sept. 30, the permanent appropriation provision was approved by a 48-44 vote: R 37-13; D 11-31 (ND 7-22, SD 4-9).

As under existing law, the president in the future will propose annual cost-of-living increases for federal employees, including members of Congress. Congress still could reject those proposals.

If the presidential pay proposal is approved, however, the money for increased congressional salaries will automatically be spent from the Treasury. There will no longer be a need to include funds for the raise in the legislative appropriations measure.

13. Oil Decontrol

One of President Reagan's first actions after taking office was his Jan. 28 decontrol of oil prices. Under a plan proposed by his predecessor, President Carter, some controls would have remained in effect until Sept. 30, 1981.

Reagan said allowing the free market to determine oil prices would stimulate production and encourage conservation. The administration predicted only a moderate rise in oil and gasoline prices as a result of deregulation, but critics of the action were outraged.

Sen. Howard M. Metzenbaum, D-Ohio, other members of Congress, labor unions and consumer groups filed suit to block the decontrol order, but their effort was rejected by a federal court March 4.

Metzenbaum admitted he did not have the votes to overturn Reagan's order, but he insisted on a vote to force Republican senators to put a "stamp of approval" on the action. He said that would let the voters know which senators supported higher prices for gasoline and fuel oil.

When the Senate March 10 considered a bill (S 573) extending antitrust exemptions for oil companies participating in the International Energy Agency, Metzenbaum offered an amendment to nullify Reagan's decontrol order. Although floor debate was one-sided in support of the amendment (opponents knew they had the votes to kill it and did not bother to speak at length on the issue), the amendment was rejected 24-68: R 3-47; D 21-21 (ND 18-10, SD 3-11).

Senators supporting the amendment were mostly liberals from the Midwest and Northeast, areas that had been hit hard by rising fuel prices.

14. Tobacco Price Supports

For the first time in decades, Congress voted on whether tobacco price supports and strict marketing regulations should continue. The politically powerful program survived, but only by a few votes in the Senate.

President Reagan's budget-cutting and deregulation drives provided new arguments and new allies in Congress for the health groups and liberal members who had attacked the tobacco program before. A further embarrassment for the program was testimony, at an International Trade Commission hearing, that government-owned tobacco stocks were deteriorating in warehouses, at considerable cost to taxpayers.

Tobacco's opponents said that when the White House stressed a free-market approach, it was time to end what amounted to a federal monopoly for certain farmers to grow the crop.

Food stamp reductions and cost-cutting in farm and other programs prompted some members to say that tobacco also should bear its share of the budget cuts.

Tobacco's advocates declared the program was essential to the economy of the rural South. They suggested that without the program, cigarette smoking and its related health problems might grow because cheap tobacco would flood the market. The problem with deteriorating stocks could be cured, they said, by discouraging tobacco imports.

Tobacco's opponents thought they had just enough votes to kill or substantially change the program when the Senate considered the omnibus farm bill (S 884). But when tobacco votes were pushed into evening hours Sept. 17 during debate on the farm bill, their slender margins of victory vanished.

First the Senate refused to kill the program outright by 53-42. Then it narrowly rejected, by a 48-45 vote, an amendment by Sen. Thomas F. Eagleton, D-Mo., that would have replaced the fixed support price with discretionary authority for the agriculture secretary to lower support prices. The fixed price support was one of the program's most attractive features for growers.

On Sept. 18, Eagleton tried again with a similar amendment but lost when the amendment was tabled (killed) by a vote of 41-40: R 28-17; D 13-23 (ND 6-20, SD 7-3). The Senate then passed the farm bill.

The House later defeated an anti-tobacco amendment but added a recommendation to the farm bill that the program should be run without cost to taxpayers.

15. Dairy Price Supports

President Reagan prevailed in an early test of his policy proposals March 27 when Congress canceled a scheduled increase in dairy price supports.

Under the dairy program, the government is required to buy in the form of dry milk, butter and cheese, all the dairy products farmers are unable to sell at a price equal to the support price. The support price was due to be increased April 1 from its current level of $13.10 per hundredweight to $14.00.

The Reagan administration argued that the existing support price was so high that it stimulated dairymen to produce more milk, butter and cheese than Americans would buy. The scheduled increase would raise consumer prices and feed inflation, administration officials said.

Opponents insisted that low feed and livestock prices, not the federal program, had boosted production. They held that foregoing the April 1 price increase would mean small- to moderate-sized dairy operations would have to fold.

Dairy lobbyists disagreed on whether to fight the cancellation directly, but they coalesced around amendments that would have delayed congressional action.

A key amendment by Sen. John Melcher, D-Mont., to sharply curtail imports of a milk protein called casein would have caused serious jurisdictional problems and delays in the House. Melcher argued that imports of casein contributed to overproduction by disrupting the domestic market.

The administration objected that Melcher's amendment would invite trade retaliation from foreign purchasers of American farm products.

The Republican leadership initially lost a motion to table (kill) Melcher's amendment and kept the dairy bill (S 509) off the Senate floor for a week.

But by March 24, the administration had mustered enough support to defeat the amendment on a 38-60 vote: R 7-45; D 31-15 (ND 19-12, SD 12-3), and the bill later passed by 88-5.

16. B-1 Bomber

By a wider than expected margin, the Senate Dec. 3 turned down an amendment to the fiscal 1982 defense appropriations bill (HR 4995) that would have shifted funds from production of the B-1 bomber to a long list of conventional weapons and combat-readiness improvements.

Criticism of President Carter's 1977 decision to cancel the B-1 program long had been a staple of Republican political oratory. But by Oct. 2, when President Reagan announced his decision to buy 100 of the planes, some Republicans voiced second thoughts about the program because of its cost — estimated by some at $40 billion — and skyrocketing predictions of the fiscal 1982 deficit.

Some critics charged that existing B-52s could penetrate Soviet defenses for nearly as long as the B-1s and that a radical new kind of bomber called "stealth" could be in service by 1990 to replace the B-52. The stealth plane would be designed to avoid Soviet detection gear.

The administration won over Republican skeptics in mid-November by arguing that the cost of modernizing and operating the B-52s would almost equal the cost of buying and operating the B-1s.

Intertwined with the B-1 issue on this vote was an effort by Senate Democrats to forge a party alternative to Reagan's defense program. Defense specialists spanning a broad band of the party's political spectrum used the defense bill to attack the administration for funding exotic nuclear weapons by diverting funds from the combat readiness of conventional forces.

On a series of votes on amendments to the bill, the Senate split along nearly straight party lines, with most Democrats backing various "readiness" increases.

When several of those efforts were linked to an attack on the B-1, the consolidated amendment lost the support of many Democrats who supported the new bomber, and was rejected 28-66: R 5-43; D 23-23 (ND 18-13, SD 5-10).

House

1. Earned Income Limit

The House rejected by a wide margin Oct. 28 a proposal to relax a restriction in the House ethics code on the amount of outside income House members could earn in addition to their official salaries.

The proposal (H Res 251), drafted by House Rules Committee Chairman Richard Bolling, D-Mo., would have raised the ceiling on a member's outside earned income from 15 percent to 40 percent of the member's official salary. The increase would have applied to members' earnings for 1981 through 1983, after which the ceiling would have reverted to 15 percent.

The vote to reject the proposal meant that at their current annual salary of $60,662.50, members continued to be bound by a cap of $9,099.37 a year in outside earned income. Under the Bolling proposal, the ceiling would have risen to $24,265 a year.

The relaxation of the rule appeared to enjoy widespread support and was backed by House leaders on both sides of the aisle. Spurring supporters on was the Senate's total elimination of similar restrictions on senators' outside earned income.

But in an emotional debate, opponents cited the difficulty of voting for a "backdoor pay raise" during a time of widespread budget cutting and argued that the move would weaken the ethics code.

Finally, defeat of Bolling's proposal was assured when opponents forced a recorded vote on the matter. The resolution was rejected 147-271: R 73-112; D 74-159 (ND 49-107, SD 25-52).

But less than two months later, when a recorded vote was avoided, the House reversed itself and approved a similar relaxation of the outside income rule.

On Dec. 15, the day before the end of the first session, the House approved by unanimous consent a request by Rep. John P. Murtha, D-Pa., that the earned income ceiling be raised from 15 percent to 30 percent, beginning in 1981. That proposal (H Res 305) sailed through in about 10 seconds.

2. Legal Services Corporation

The House ignored a proposal by the Reagan administration to abolish the Legal Services Corporation and on June 18 voted 245-137 to reauthorize the agency for two years at $241 million annually.

HR 3480 passed with some Republican support, although GOP members voted overwhelmingly against reauthorization: R 59-116; D 186-21 (ND 137-3, SD 49-18).

President Reagan wanted to abolish the 7-year-old corporation and let states provide legal services to the poor through social services block grants.

That plan met with strong opposition from LSC supporters inside and outside Congress. They argued that states — even with help from the private bar — would be unable to provide meaningful legal representation to the poor.

The vote on final passage did not reflect the intensity of the three-day debate on the bill. A number of amendments were adopted restricting the activities of LSC lawyers. These included a ban on so-called "class action" lawsuits against local, state or federal government agencies, restrictions on the type of aliens who can be represented and a tougher ban on lobbying activities.

3. Voting Rights Act

Signaling its support for a strong bill (HR 3112) to extend the 1965 Voting Rights Act, the House Oct. 5 rejected an amendment that would have changed the forum for hearing certain voting discrimination cases.

The amendment sponsored by M. Caldwell Butler, R-Va., would have required that cases involving jurisdictions covered by key enforcement provisions of the act be heard by three-judge federal panels in those jurisdictions. The amendment specified that none of the judges could be from the jurisdiction involved in the suit.

Under current law, such suits are heard by a three-judge panel in the District of Columbia.

Proponents of the amendment contended that it was burdensome and unnecessary to hear voting cases in Washington, D.C. They argued that there are good federal judges all over the country who are capable of properly handling a voting discrimination case.

Opponents of the amendment contended that it was important to have uniformity in voting-rights decisions and that all cases should be heard by one court. They noted further that the D.C. court had developed expertise in this area of the law.

Supporters of a strong extension bill knew that HR 3112 was out of danger when the Butler amendment was defeated handily by a 132-277 vote: R 102-75; D 30-202 (ND 4-153, SD 26-49).

4. Saudi AWACS

The Reagan administration based its Middle East policy on what it called a "strategic consensus" among nations there that the Soviet Union posed the primary threat to them, notwithstanding their regional disputes.

To improve U.S. relations with oil giant Saudi Arabia, in part to nurture the Middle East consensus it perceived, the administration decided in the spring of 1981 to sell Saudi Arabia five sophisticated Airborne Warning and Control System (AWACS) radar planes and other military equipment.

The decision posed the first major test in Congress of President Reagan's authority in foreign policy.

Israel strongly opposed the AWACS sale, viewing it as a threat to Israeli air superiority in the Middle East, and the American Jewish community began to campaign against it from the moment the administration acknowledged its plans.

Critics in Congress said it was unwise to entrust the secrets of the computer-assisted AWACS surveillance system to a nation that often had opposed U.S. policy in the Middle East and whose ruling royal family was seen as vulnerable to being overthrown.

Saudi Arabia cast the deal as a test of U.S.-Saudi relations. The administration argued that Saudi air defenses must be bolstered to protect Saudi oil fields along the eastern coast of the Arabian Peninsula — the source of much of the industrial West's oil supplies.

Reagan's problem was that Congress could veto the AWACS sale under a law giving it the right to block major arms deals by passing a concurrent resolution within 30 days of receiving formal notice.

Formal notice of the deal was delivered on Oct. 1, giving Congress until Oct. 30 to veto the sale.

The House passed a resolution of disapproval (H Con Res 194) on Oct. 14 by an overwhelming vote of 301-111: R 108-78; D 193-33 (ND 149-5, SD 44-28).

But Reagan won on the issue after he put his personal prestige on the line. He argued that a congressional veto would undermine his authority to conduct foreign policy, and the Senate failed by a dramatic 48-52 vote on Oct. 28 to pass H Con Res 194. *(Senate key vote 2)*

5. B-1 Bomber

After a narrow victory in the Defense Appropriations Subcommittee, House critics of the B-1 bomber were swamped 3-1 on Nov. 18 when they tried to delete $1.8 billion in B-1 procurement funds from the defense appropriations bill (HR 4995).

B-1 critics argued that the plane would not long be able to penetrate Soviet air defenses and that it would drain funds from development of a new "stealth" bomber, designed to evade Soviet radar.

But supporters of the B-1 — which President Carter had canceled in June 1977 and President Reagan revived in October 1981 — cited much more optimistic assessments of the B-1's effectiveness against Soviet defenses. And they warned that the technical feasibility of a stealth bomber remained uncertain.

What likely would have been a victory for B-1 supporters in any case became a cinch when Reagan announced a nuclear arms-control proposal to Moscow a few hours before the B-1 vote. B-1 supporters insisted that a vote against the plane would undermine the U.S. bargaining position in arms control talks with the Russians.

The amendment to delete B-1 funds was rejected 142-263: R 21-157; D 121-106 (ND 111-42, SD 10-64).

6. MX Missile

What might have been a much closer fight became a 2-1 rout when House critics of the MX missile tried Nov. 18 to delete the program from the defense appropriations bill (HR 4995) hours after President Reagan made his nuclear arms reduction proposal to the Soviet Union.

Republicans and conservative House Democrats stampeded to support both the MX and the B-1 bomber as a symbol of their backing for the president's initiative and to ensure that he would have "bargaining chips" in dealing with Moscow.

MX opponents insisted that continued work on the missile should await selection of a final basing technique, which Reagan had deferred until 1984. The final design of the missile would be affected by whether it was launched from an airplane or from deep underground, they said, citing two possible basing techniques.

But the bargaining-chip argument pervaded the debate on an amendment to delete some $1.9 billion for the

MX from the defense bill, and the amendment was rejected 139-264: R 27-151; D 112-113 (ND 103-48, SD 9-65).

7. Tenn-Tom Waterway

Serving notice that they were less inclined than in the past to go along automatically with funding of costly water projects, House members came closer to killing funding for the 232-mile Tennessee-Tombigbee Waterway than ever before.

With budgetary concerns added to longstanding environmental objections, opponents of the canal managed to come within 20 votes of killing it.

Concentrating on fiscally conservative freshman members, lobbyists from environmental and taxpayer groups worked for several weeks lining up votes against "Tenn-Tom," the costliest water project in the nation's history.

When the fiscal 1982 energy and water appropriations bill (HR 4144) came to the House floor July 23, freshman members helped lead the move to delete the $189 million in funding for Tenn-Tom from the bill.

Although the freshmen voted 42-30 for the amendment, enough veteran members stuck with the project to save it, and the amendment failed, 198-208: R 108-70; D 90-138 (ND 82-70, SD 8-68).

As in the Senate (Senate key vote 4), opponents of Tenn-Tom argued that the waterway would cost $3 billion and produce few economic benefits. They said it would be better to kill the canal and have "half a white elephant" than a whole one. Supporters countered that the project would cost only $1.8 billion and claimed the benefits would be substantial.

8. Clinch River Breeder Reactor

Just as on the Tenn-Tom Waterway vote, economy-minded House freshmen came closer to killing the funding for the Clinch River (Tenn.) breeder reactor than ever before.

Freshman members had persuaded the House Science Committee to deauthorize the project in May, but that decision was overturned in the massive budget reconciliation bill (HR 3982) in June. The freshmen tried again July 24 when funding for Clinch River came to the House floor in the fiscal 1982 energy and water appropriations bill (HR 4144).

While proponents argued that the project would pay for itself through the sale of electricity and that the $1 billion already spent on it would be wasted if it were killed, opponents insisted the breeder reactor could not be justified on economic grounds.

Freshman members voted 36-34 for an amendment to delete the $228 million for the project from the bill, but the rest of the House was not persuaded and the amendment was rejected 186-206: R 70-104; D 116-102 (ND 107-38, SD 9-64).

Twenty-eight members, mostly conservative Republicans, who had voted for the project in 1979 voted against it July 24; however, 20 members (19 of them Democrats) who had voted to kill the project in 1979 voted July 24 to continue it.

9. Debt Limit Increase

For the first time in many of their careers, House Republicans joined Democrats on Feb. 5 to approve a measure (HR 1553) raising the public debt limit to $985 billion through Sept. 30, 1982. The vote was 305-104: R 150-36; D 155-68 (ND 112-37, SD 43-31).

The Senate passed the bill a day later, clearing the bill. (Senate key vote 7)

It was President Reagan's first legislative victory.

Without an increase in the debt ceiling, the outstanding debt would have hit the existing $935.1 billion limit by mid-February, thus preventing the government from meeting its borrowing needs.

GOP members, who often had called a vote to increase the debt limit "fiscally irresponsible," argued that this was merely leftover business from the Carter administration. Marjorie S. Holt, R-Md., justified fiscal conservatives' support for the debt limit increase by noting: "I see for the first time some glimmer of hope that we will bring federal spending under control."

10. Budget Cut Instructions

The May 7 House vote to accept the administration-backed Gramm-Latta budget-cutting plan was both a political and a budget milestone.

It was the first formal endorsement in the Democratic-controlled House of Reagan's campaign mandate to slash federal spending.

With the help of 63 Democrats, the House voted 253-176 — R 190-0; D 63-176 (ND 17-144, SD 46-32) — to order its authorizing committees to come up with $36.6 billion in spending cuts for fiscal 1982.

These reconciliation instructions were included in the first budget resolution (H Con Res 115) that set a fiscal 1982 spending target of $688.8 billion, contemplated a $31 billion deficit and provided room for the president's proposed $51.3 billion tax cut.

The cuts made under reconciliation would be permanent cuts in authorizations, and signaled a shift in power from the traditional purse-string stronghold — the Appropriations Committee — to the Budget and authorizing committees.

In accepting the Gramm-Latta substitute to the budget resolution, the House turned aside the product of its own Budget Committee, which had called for slightly higher spending but a smaller tax cut.

The chief difference between the two measures, however, was that the Budget Committee's reconciliation plan followed the more traditional use of reconciliation. It called for authorizing committees to cut $15.8 billion in fiscal 1982 spending and $23.6 billion in cuts from programs funded by appropriations, which could be changed in future years.

11. Reconciliation Budget Cuts

In a stunning victory for the Reagan administration, the House voted on June 26 to overturn the work of its authorizing and Budget committees and instead accept an administration-backed package of $37.3 billion in budget cuts known as Gramm-Latta II.

The narrow 217-211 victory on the GOP alternative to the budget reconciliation bill (HR 3982) was achieved with the help of 29 hard-core conservative Democrats, thus solidifying the coalition that would put into place the entire Reagan economic program. The complete vote breakdown: R 188-2; D 29-209 (ND 3-157, SD 26-52).

Before the vote to substitute the Gramm-Latta provi-

sions, Delbert L. Latta, R-Ohio, a cosponsor of the amendment and ranking GOP member of the House Budget Committee, framed the vote this way: "It is a question of whether we can turn the country around economically or not."

Members of both political parties, however, were upset with the almost complete lack of details about the Gramm-Latta proposal before the vote was taken. The package of cuts covered the entire spectrum of federal programs — save defense.

"This has been a terrible way to legislate, but we have no alternatives," lamented Barber B. Conable Jr., R-N.Y.

There were two reasons the administration felt it necessary to draft a substitute for the $37.6 billion package agreed to by the authorizing committees and compiled by the Budget Committee. First, the Republicans claimed, the committees had failed to cut back entitlement programs. In addition, they said, the authorizing panels had not gone far enough to fold many categorical social programs together into block grants.

12. Tax Cuts

The Democratic-controlled House proved the major battleground for the administration's controversial plans to reduce individual income and business investment taxes.

The Ways and Means Committee attempted to fashion an alternative to Reagan's tax-cut proposals that would appeal to both waivering conservative Democrats — who had defected to back the administration on an earlier budget vote — and party liberals.

Their package (HR 4242) called for a two-year, 15 percent cut in individual income taxes skewed to help those earning below $50,000 a year. An additional 10 percent cut during the third year would have been triggered if the economy performed well. The bill also would have cut corporate income tax rates, as well as provided for accelerated depreciation.

The administration proposed a 23 percent across-the-board cut in individual income taxes and accelerated depreciation for business.

But in a fierce bidding war for votes, special tax breaks were added to both packages, making it increasingly difficult to distinguish between the two. With a heavy, last-minute lobbying effort by the administration, a number of crucial Democratic votes were wooed to the Republican side.

The administration-backed substitute to the committee bill, offered by Barber B. Conable Jr., R-N.Y., and conservative Democrat Kent Hance, Texas, was adopted July 29 by a vote of 238-195: R 190-1; D 48-194 (ND 12-151, SD 36-43).

13. Social Security Minimum

After President Reagan told a joint session of Congress Feb. 18 that "the full retirement benefits" of 36 million Social Security recipients would "be continued," Democrats sought to hold him to his word. They condemned his proposal three weeks later to eliminate the $122 minimum monthly benefit for some 3 million Social Security recipients as a cruel reversal of policy.

Despite the public furor over the cut and growing Republican apprehension, both houses went ahead and separately agreed to cut the benefit as part of a budget reconciliation bill (HR 3982). But when it came time for final approval of the conference agreement, House members balked.

As a result of negotiations between House and Senate leaders eager to resolve the budget issue, House Rules Committee Chairman Richard Bolling, D-Mo., proposed a rule July 31 to allow consideration of both the reconciliation conference agreement and a bill (HR 4331) to restore the full minimum benefit.

By a vote of 271-151: R 166-21; D 105-130 (ND 56-101, SD 49-29), the House agreed to end debate and the possibility of further amendment on the rule, thus paving the way for passage of the rule, HR 4331, and the conference report.

Although most Democrats expressed support for the minimum benefit, many voted against ending debate because they opposed the entire reconciliation package.

The Senate voted Oct. 15 to restore the minimum payment for some current recipients, and after a lengthy conference Congress agreed to keep the benefit for all current recipients. However, it extended the Social Security payroll tax to the first six months of sick pay to cover most of the $6.1 billion cost for 1982-86 of restoring the benefit.

14. Social Program Spending

The House coalition that had passed President Reagan's economic program cracked on the issue of direct spending cuts in social programs.

More than three dozen Republicans deserted their party leadership to oppose a motion to cut spending in the $87.2 billion appropriations bill for the departments of Labor, Health and Human Services and Education (HR 4560). Reagan Sept. 24 had called for new cuts in fiscal 1982 spending.

On Oct. 6, Ralph Regula, R-Ohio, offered a motion to recommit the bill to the Appropriations Committee to make reductions in spending. His motion — the first test of congressional support for Reagan's revised budget — was rejected 168-249: R 140-39; D 28-210 (ND 3-157, SD 25-53).

The vote showed the potential power of the "Gypsy Moths," a group of moderate House GOP members, mostly from the Northeast and Midwest. These Frost Belt Republicans opposed cuts in programs, such as job training and fuel assistance to the poor, that were particularly helpful to their districts, many of which were facing economic hard times.

Gypsy Moth Carl D. Pursell, R-Mich., said the group did not want further social spending cuts without accompanying reductions in other areas. "I don't think we can make the [budget] balancing act by just touching this bill," he told the House. "We want to see a quid pro quo on cuts in [such programs as] defense, water projects and tobacco."

15. Foreign Aid Appropriations

Always an unpopular program, foreign aid was the subject of especially rancorous disputes in a year when domestic spending was being cut deeply.

Congress was hamstrung in trying to fashion a foreign aid program by a fundamental disagreement in the House between conservative Republicans and liberal Democrats over the ratio of military-to-development aid.

The Reagan administration asked Congress to substantially increase U.S. military aid while stringing out contributions to some international development banks to

reduce federal spending.

The House Appropriations Committee reported its aid appropriations bill (HR 4559) on Sept. 22. But the dispute over military *vs.* development aid made Democrats reluctant to bring the measure to the floor.

The stalemate was broken after a fight between President Reagan and Congress in late November over a stopgap funding measure for most of the federal government.

Reagan challenged Congress to accept its responsibility to pass the appropriations bills. House Speaker Thomas P. O'Neill Jr., D-Mass., responded that the House had passed all its appropriations bills except for HR 4559. O'Neill promised to get HR 4559 to the floor if Reagan would round up enough GOP votes to pass it.

Reagan and Secretary of State Alexander M. Haig Jr. then made personal appeals to House Republicans to get the aid bill through Congress.

The House finally took up HR 4559 on Dec. 11 and handled it in whirlwind fashion, with key Republicans leading the fight for it by stressing the national security role of foreign aid.

The House passed the bill by a vote of 199-166. GOP members voted 84-87 against it. But enough of them supported the measure to get it through the House with the help of a majority of Democrats, who voted for it 115-79 (ND 95-36, SD 20-43).

Both houses cleared the conference report on HR 4559 on Dec. 16, marking the first time Congress had cleared a foreign aid appropriations bill since 1978.

16. Omnibus Farm Bill

Fierce competition for a share of the federal pie shattered the historic coalition of farm groups and slowed work on the four-year renewal of farm programs (S 884). The Senate passed a bill meeting President Reagan's stringent budget specifications, but the House passed a far more costly version.

The conference dragged on for six weeks while the administration adamantly held out for revisions and unhappy House members choked down substantial cuts in their bill.

The final conference agreement was approved amid such bitterness that some key House members like Thomas S. Foley, D-Wash., Democraic whip and former Agriculture Committee chairman, withheld support until the last.

The Senate adopted the conference report Dec. 10 by a vote of 68-31.

But the painful process continued in the House until the last night of the session on Dec. 16, when the House narrowly cleared the bill for the president by a vote of 205-203: R 125-59; D 80-144 (ND 27-121, SD 53-23).

The two-vote margin reflected the strong pressures on members. Many wanted the bill to pass because the alternatives — having to revert to antiquated and expensive permanent farm laws or to face the 1982 elections with a farm bill rewrite — were worse. But they also wanted the record to show they opposed it because consumer groups, food processors and certain farm interests objected strenuously.

Dairymen opposed provisions that expressed their minimum supports in dollars instead of percentages of parity, the controversial farm inflation index. Wheat growers also were disturbed by support levels that some felt did not protect them from inflation.

Consumer groups objected that peanut and sugar provisions would cost American families billions of dollars. But sugar, peanut, corn, cotton, rice and soybean groups all backed the bill.

The administration had successfully followed a strategy, according to budget director David A. Stockman, of dividing the farm coalition to hold down program increases that farmers wanted.

KEY

Y Voted for (yea).
Paired for.
+ Announced for.
N Voted against (nay).
X Paired against.
- Announced against.
P Voted "present".
C Voted "present" to avoid possible conflict of interest.
? Did not vote or otherwise make a position known.

Democrats   Republicans

	1	2	3	4	5	6	7	8
ALABAMA								
Denton	Y	N	Y	N	Y	Y	Y	Y
Heflin	Y	Y	Y	N	Y	?	N	Y
ALASKA								
Murkowski	Y	N	Y	N	Y	Y	Y	Y
Stevens	N	N	Y	X	?	N	?	Y
ARIZONA								
Goldwater	Y	N	Y	?	?	Y	Y	Y
DeConcini	Y	Y	Y	N	N	Y	N	Y
ARKANSAS								
Bumpers	N	Y	Y	N	N	N	Y	Y
Pryor	Y	Y	Y	N	N	N	N	Y
CALIFORNIA								
Hayakawa	Y	N	Y	N	Y	N	Y	Y
Cranston	N	Y	Y	N	N	?	Y	N
COLORADO								
Armstrong	Y	N	Y	N	Y	N	Y	Y
Hart	N	Y	Y	Y	N	Y	Y	Y
CONNECTICUT								
Weicker	N	Y	N	?	?	N	Y	N
Dodd	N	Y	N	N	N	N	Y	N
DELAWARE								
Roth	Y	Y	?	Y	N	Y	Y	Y
Biden	Y	Y	?	Y	N	Y	Y	Y
FLORIDA								
Hawkins	Y	Y	Y	#	Y	Y	Y	Y
Chiles	Y	Y	Y	Y	N	Y	Y	Y
GEORGIA								
Mattingly	Y	N	Y	N	Y	Y	N	Y
Nunn	Y	N	Y	N	N	N	N	Y
HAWAII								
Inouye	N	Y	Y	N	N	X	Y	Y
Matsunaga	N	Y	N	N	N	N	Y	Y
IDAHO								
McClure	Y	N	Y	N	Y	N	Y	Y
Symms	Y	N	Y	N	Y	Y	Y	Y
ILLINOIS								
Percy	N	N	Y	N	N	N	Y	Y
Dixon	Y	Y	Y	Y	N	Y	N	Y
INDIANA								
Lugar	Y	N	Y	N	Y	Y	Y	Y
Quayle	Y	N	Y	Y	N	Y	Y	Y

	1	2	3	4	5	6	7	8
IOWA								
Grassley	Y	N	Y	Y	Y	Y	Y	Y
Jepsen	Y	N	Y	Y	N	Y	Y	Y
KANSAS								
Dole	Y	N	Y	N	Y	Y	Y	Y
Kassebaum	Y	N	N	Y	N	N	Y	Y
KENTUCKY								
Ford	Y	Y	Y	N	Y	N	Y	N
Huddleston	Y	N	Y	N	Y	Y	N	Y
LOUISIANA								
Johnston	Y	N	Y	N	Y	Y	Y	Y
Long	Y	N	Y	N	Y	#	Y	Y
MAINE								
Cohen	N	N	Y	Y	N	N	?	Y
Mitchell	N	Y	Y	N	N	Y	Y	Y
MARYLAND								
Mathias	N	N	?	Y	Y	?	?	+
Sarbanes	N	Y	Y	Y	N	N	Y	N
MASSACHUSETTS								
Kennedy	X	Y	N	Y	N	N	Y	N
Tsongas	N	Y	N	Y	N	N	?	N
MICHIGAN								
Levin	N	Y	Y	N	N	N	Y	N
Riegle	N	Y	N	Y	N	N	N	Y
MINNESOTA								
Boschwitz	N	Y	Y	N	Y	Y	Y	Y
Durenberger	N	Y	?	N	Y	Y	Y	Y
MISSISSIPPI								
Cochran	Y	N	Y	N	Y	N	Y	Y
Stennis	Y	N	Y	N	Y	N	Y	Y
MISSOURI								
Danforth	Y	Y	Y	Y	Y	Y	Y	Y
Eagleton	N	Y	N	Y	N	Y	Y	N
MONTANA								
Baucus	N	Y	Y	Y	N	N	N	Y
Melcher	Y	N	Y	N	N	Y	-	Y
NEBRASKA								
Exon	Y	N	Y	N	N	Y	N	Y
Zorinsky	Y	N	?	Y	Y	Y	N	Y
NEVADA								
Laxalt	Y	N	Y	?	Y	Y	Y	Y
Cannon	Y	Y	Y	?	+	Y	?	Y

	1	2	3	4	5	6	7	8
NEW HAMPSHIRE								
Humphrey	Y	N	Y	N	Y	Y	Y	Y
Rudman	N	N	Y	Y	Y	N	Y	Y
NEW JERSEY								
Bradley	N	Y	Y	Y	N	N	Y	Y
Williams	N	Y	?	Y	N	N	Y	?
NEW MEXICO								
Domenici	Y	N	Y	Y	Y	Y	Y	Y
Schmitt	Y	N	Y	N	Y	N	Y	Y
NEW YORK								
D'Amato	Y	Y	Y	N	Y	Y	Y	Y
Moynihan	N	Y	Y	Y	?	N	?	Y
NORTH CAROLINA								
East	Y	N	Y	N	Y	Y	Y	Y
Helms	Y	N	Y	Y	Y	Y	Y	Y
NORTH DAKOTA								
Andrews	N	N	Y	N	Y	Y	Y	Y
Burdick	N	Y	Y	N	Y	N	Y	Y
OHIO								
Glenn	N	Y	Y	N	N	N	?	Y
Metzenbaum	N	Y	N	Y	N	N	N	N
OKLAHOMA								
Nickles	Y	N	Y	N	N	Y	Y	Y
Boren	Y	N	Y	N	?	Y	N	Y
OREGON								
Hatfield	N	Y	N	N	N	N	Y	Y
Packwood	N	Y	N	Y	N	?	Y	Y
PENNSYLVANIA								
Heinz	N	Y	Y	Y	Y	Y	Y	Y
Specter	N	Y	Y	Y	Y	N	Y	Y
RHODE ISLAND								
Chafee	N	N	Y	N	N	N	Y	Y
Pell	#	Y	N	Y	N	N	Y	N
SOUTH CAROLINA								
Thurmond	Y	N	Y	N	Y	Y	Y	Y
Hollings	Y	Y	Y	N	N	N	Y	Y
SOUTH DAKOTA								
Abdnor	Y	N	Y	N	Y	Y	Y	Y
Pressler	N	N	N	Y	Y	Y	Y	Y
TENNESSEE								
Baker	Y	N	N	N	N	Y	N	Y
Sasser	Y	Y	Y	N	Y	Y	Y	N

	1	2	3	4	5	6	7	8
TEXAS								
Tower	Y	N	Y	N	Y	N	Y	Y
Bentsen	Y	Y	Y	N	Y	Y	Y	Y
UTAH								
Garn	Y	N	Y	Y	Y	Y	Y	Y
Hatch	Y	N	Y	N	Y	Y	Y	Y
VERMONT								
Stafford	?	N	Y	Y	Y	N	Y	Y
Leahy	N	Y	Y	Y	N	N	Y	Y
VIRGINIA								
Warner	Y	N	Y	N	Y	Y	Y	Y
Byrd*	Y	N	Y	N	N	N	Y	Y
WASHINGTON								
Gorton	N	N	Y	Y	Y	N	Y	Y
Jackson	Y	Y	Y	N	Y	N	Y	Y
WEST VIRGINIA								
Byrd	Y	Y	Y	N	Y	Y	Y	Y
Randolph	Y	N	Y	N	Y	Y	Y	Y
WISCONSIN								
Kasten	Y	Y	Y	N	Y	N	Y	Y
Proxmire	Y	Y	N	Y	N	Y	N	Y
WYOMING								
Simpson	Y	N	Y	N	Y	N	Y	Y
Wallop	Y	N	Y	Y	N	Y	N	Y

ND - Northern Democrats   SD - Southern Democrats (Southern states - Ala., Ark., Fla., Ga., Ky., La., Miss., N.C., Okla., S.C., Tenn., Texas, Va.)   *Byrd elected as an independent.*

1. S 951. Justice Department Authorization. Johnston, D-La., motion to invoke cloture (thus limiting debate) on the Helms, R-N.C.-Johnston amendment to prohibit federal courts in most instances from ordering school busing for racial balance. Motion agreed to 61-36: R 36-16; D 25-20 (ND 11-19, SD 14-1), Sept. 16, 1981. A three-fifths vote (60) of the full Senate is required to invoke cloture.

2. H Con Res 194. Saudi AWACS. Adoption of the concurrent resolution disapproving the proposal by President Reagan to sell Saudi Arabia an $8.5 billion package of military equipment consisting of five E-3A Airborne Warning and Control System (AWACS) radar planes, 1,177 AIM-9L Sidewinder air-to-air missiles, 101 sets of conformal fuel tanks for F-15 fighter planes and six to eight KC-707 tanker aircraft. Rejected 48-52: R 12-41; D 36-11 (ND 28-4, SD 8-7), Oct. 28, 1981. A "nay" was a vote supporting the president's position.

3. S 694. Fiscal 1981 Supplemental Defense Authorization. Tower, R-Texas, motion to table (kill) the Pressler, R-S.D., amendment to delete $7 million for research related to the MX missile. Motion agreed to 79-15: R 44-6; D 35-9 (ND 20-9, SD 15-0), April 7, 1981.

4. HR 4144. Energy and Water Development Appropriations, Fiscal 1982. Percy, R-Ill., amendment to delete $189 million for the continued construction of the Tennessee-Tombigbee Waterway. The effect would be to cancel the project. Rejected 46-48: R 27-21; D 19-27 (ND 17-14, SD 2-13), Nov. 4, 1981. A "nay" was a vote supporting the president's position.

5. HR 4144. Energy and Water Development Appropriations, Fiscal 1982. Johnston, D-La., motion to table (kill) the Bumpers, D-Ark., amendment as amended by the Tsongas, D-Mass., amendment, to reduce by half ($90 million) the appropriation for the Clinch River (Tenn.) nuclear breeder reactor. Motion agreed to 48-46: R 36-14; D 12-32 (ND 4-26, SD 8-6), Nov. 4, 1981. A "yea" was a vote supporting the president's position.

6. HR 3512. Fiscal 1981 Supplemental Appropriations. Helms, R-N.C., motion to table (kill) the Appropriations Committee amendment to delete House-passed language prohibiting Medicaid funding of abortions except when needed to save the mother's life. (The effect of the motion was to restore the House prohibition to the bill.) Motion agreed to 52-43: R 33-19; D 19-24 (ND 12-18, SD 7-6), May 21, 1981. A "yea" was a vote supporting the president's position.

7. HR 1553. Debt Limit Increase. Passage of the bill to increase the public debt limit to $985 billion through Sept. 30, 1981. Passed (thus cleared for the president) 73-18: R 46-3; D 27-15 (ND 20-7; SD 7-8), Feb. 6, 1981. A "yea" was a vote supporting the president's position.

8. S Con Res 9. Budget Reconciliation Instructions. Adoption of the concurrent resolution to instruct 14 Senate authorizing and appropriations committees to cut $36.9 billion from fiscal 1982 spending. Adopted 88-10: R 51-1; D 37-9 (ND 22-9, SD 15-0), April 2, 1981. A "yea" was a vote supporting the president's position.

Senator	9	10	11	12	13	14	15	16
ALABAMA								
Denton	Y	Y	N	Y	N	Y	N	?
Heflin	N	Y	N	N	N	Y	Y	N
ALASKA								
Murkowski	Y	Y	N	Y	N	?	N	N
Stevens	Y	Y	?	Y	N	Y	?	N
ARIZONA								
Goldwater	Y	Y	N	Y	N	Y	N	-
DeConcini	N	Y	N	N	N	N	Y	-
ARKANSAS								
Bumpers	N	N	Y	N	Y	?	Y	Y
Pryor	N	Y	N	N	N	N	Y	Y
CALIFORNIA								
Hayakawa	Y	?	N	Y	N	Y	N	?
Cranston	N	N	Y	Y	?	?	N	N
COLORADO								
Armstrong	Y	Y	N	N	N	Y	N	N
Hart	N	Y	Y	N	?	N	Y	Y
CONNECTICUT								
Weicker	N	N	N	?	N	?	N	N
Dodd	N	N	Y	Y	Y	?	?	Y
DELAWARE								
Roth	N	Y	N	Y	N	Y	N	N
Biden	N	N	Y	N	Y	N	N	Y
FLORIDA								
Hawkins	?	Y	N	Y	Y	Y	N	N
Chiles	N	N	Y	N	N	?	Y	N
GEORGIA								
Mattingly	Y	Y	N	N	N	Y	N	N
Nunn	N	N	Y	N	N	Y	N	Y
HAWAII								
Inouye	N	N	Y	Y	Y	?	N	N
Matsunaga	N	N	Y	?	Y	Y	N	Y
IDAHO								
McClure	Y	Y	N	Y	N	Y	N	N
Symms	Y	Y	N	Y	N	Y	N	N
ILLINOIS								
Percy	Y	Y	N	Y	N	N	N	N
Dixon	N	Y	N	N	N	N	N	N
INDIANA								
Lugar	Y	Y	N	Y	N	Y	N	N
Quayle	Y	Y	N	Y	N	N	N	N
IOWA								
Grassley	Y	Y	N	N	N	Y	Y	N
Jepsen	Y	Y	N	Y	N	Y	N	N
KANSAS								
Dole	Y	Y	N	Y	X	Y	N	N
Kassebaum	Y	Y	N	Y	N	N	N	Y
KENTUCKY								
Ford	N	N	Y	N	N	Y	Y	Y
Huddleston	N	N	Y	Y	Y	Y	Y	N
LOUISIANA								
Johnston	N	N	N	Y	N	?	Y	N
Long	N	N	N	?	N	Y	Y	N
MAINE								
Cohen	Y	Y	N	N	N	Y	N	N
Mitchell	N	N	N	N	Y	X	X	Y
MARYLAND								
Mathias	?	N	?	Y	N	N	N	Y
Sarbanes	N	N	N	N	Y	Y	Y	Y
MASSACHUSETTS								
Kennedy	N	N	Y	Y	?	N	N	Y
Tsongas	N	?	Y	Y	N	?	N	Y
MICHIGAN								
Levin	N	Y	Y	N	Y	N	Y	Y
Riegle	N	Y	N	N	Y	N	Y	Y
MINNESOTA								
Boschwitz	Y	Y	N	Y	N	Y	N	N
Durenberger	Y	Y	N	Y	N	N	Y	N
MISSISSIPPI								
Cochran	Y	N	Y	N	Y	Y	N	N
Stennis	N	N	N	Y	N	#	Y	N
MISSOURI								
Danforth	Y	Y	N	N	N	Y	N	N
Eagleton	N	N	Y	Y	Y	N	Y	Y
MONTANA								
Baucus	N	Y	N	N	N	N	Y	Y
Melcher	N	Y	N	N	N	Y	Y	N
NEBRASKA								
Exon	N	Y	N	N	N	N	Y	N
Zorinsky	N	Y	N	N	N	N	Y	N
NEVADA								
Laxalt	Y	Y	N	Y	N	?	N	N
Cannon	N	N	N	?	Y	N	Y	N
NEW HAMPSHIRE								
Humphrey	Y	Y	N	N	N	N	N	N
Rudman	Y	Y	N	?	N	Y	N	N
NEW JERSEY								
Bradley	N	N	Y	N	N	-	N	Y
Williams	N	N	Y	Y	Y	N	N	Y
NEW MEXICO								
Domenici	Y	?	N	Y	N	Y	N	N
Schmitt	Y	Y	N	N	N	Y	N	N
NEW YORK								
D'Amato	Y	Y	N	Y	-	+	N	N
Moynihan	N	Y	N	?	Y	N	N	N
NORTH CAROLINA								
East	Y	Y	N	?	N	Y	N	N
Helms	Y	Y	N	N	N	Y	N	N
NORTH DAKOTA								
Andrews	Y	Y	N	N	N	Y	Y	N
Burdick	N	N	N	N	N	Y	Y	N
OHIO								
Glenn	N	N	Y	N	N	N	N	N
Metzenbaum	N	N	Y	N	Y	N	Y	N
OKLAHOMA								
Nickles	Y	Y	N	N	N	N	N	N
Boren	N	Y	N	N	N	N	Y	N
OREGON								
Hatfield	Y	Y	N	Y	N	N	N	Y
Packwood	Y	Y	N	Y	N	N	N	N
PENNSYLVANIA								
Heinz	Y	N	Y	N	Y	N	?	-
Specter	Y	Y	N	Y	N	X	X	N
RHODE ISLAND								
Chafee	Y	Y	N	Y	N	Y	N	N
Pell	N	N	Y	N	Y	N	N	Y
SOUTH CAROLINA								
Thurmond	Y	Y	N	Y	N	Y	N	N
Hollings	N	N	Y	Y	Y	#	N	Y
SOUTH DAKOTA								
Abdnor	Y	Y	N	N	N	Y	N	N
Pressler	?	Y	Y	N	N	Y	Y	Y
TENNESSEE								
Baker	Y	N	N	Y	#	Y	N	N
Sasser	N	N	N	N	+	Y	Y	N
TEXAS								
Tower	Y	Y	N	Y	N	+	N	N
Bentsen	N	N	-	N	N	N	Y	N
UTAH								
Garn	Y	Y	N	N	N	N	N	N
Hatch	Y	Y	N	Y	N	N	N	N
VERMONT								
Stafford	Y	Y	N	N	N	?	Y	N
Leahy	N	N	Y	N	Y	N	Y	Y
VIRGINIA								
Warner	Y	Y	N	Y	N	Y	N	N
Byrd*	Y	N	N	?	N	Y	N	N
WASHINGTON								
Gorton	Y	Y	N	N	N	N	N	N
Jackson	N	N	Y	N	Y	N	Y	N
WEST VIRGINIA								
Byrd	N	N	Y	N	Y	Y	Y	Y
Randolph	N	N	Y	N	-	Y	Y	N
WISCONSIN								
Kasten	Y	Y	N	N	N	N	N	N
Proxmire	N	Y	N	N	Y	N	Y	N
WYOMING								
Simpson	Y	Y	N	Y	N	N	N	N
Wallop	Y	N	N	Y	N	Y	N	-

KEY

Y Voted for (yea).
\# Paired for.
\+ Announced for.
N Voted against (nay).
X Paired against.
\- Announced against.
P Voted "present".
C Voted "present" to avoid possible conflict of interest.
? Did not vote or otherwise make a position known.

Democrats   *Republicans*

ND - Northern Democrats   SD - Southern Democrats (Southern states - Ala., Ark., Fla., Ga., Ky., La., Miss., N.C., Okla., S.C., Tenn., Texas, Va.)   *Byrd elected as an independent.*

9. HR 3512. Fiscal 1981 Supplemental Appropriations. Hatfield, R-Ore., motion to table (kill) the Moynihan, D-N.Y., amendment stating the sense of the Senate in opposition to President Reagan's proposed reductions on Social Security benefits. Motion agreed to 49-48: R 48-2; D 1-46 (ND 0-32, SD 1-14), May 20, 1981. A "yea" was a vote supporting the president's position.

10. H J Res 266. Tax Cuts. Finance Committee amendment to require, beginning in 1985, that individual income taxes be adjusted, or indexed, annually to offset the effects of inflation. Adopted 57-40: R 43-8; D 14-32 (ND 11-20, SD 3-12), July 16, 1981.

11. H J Res 266. Tax Cuts. Hollings, D-S.C., amendment to the Finance Committee bill limiting the size of personal tax reductions and targeting them to middle-income taxpayers in order to achieve a balanced budget by 1984. Rejected 26-71: R 0-51; D 26-20 (ND 20-12, SD 6-8), July 22, 1981. A "nay" was a vote supporting the president's position.

12. H J Res 325. Fiscal 1982 Continuing Appropriations. Hatfield, R-Ore., motion to accept language proposed by House-Senate conferees to provide for a permanent appropriation of funds for congressional pay increases, when recommended by the president and upheld by Congress. Motion agreed to 48-44: R 37-13; D 11-31 (ND 7-22, SD 4-9), Sept. 30, 1981.

13. S 573. Oil Industry Antitrust Exemption. Metzenbaum, D-Ohio, amendment to nullify President Reagan's Jan. 28 order terminating immediately all remaining controls on oil and gasoline. Rejected 24-68: R 3-47; D 21-21 (ND 18-10; SD 3-11), March 10, 1981. A "nay" was a vote supporting the president's position. (The bill, to extend through Sept. 30, 1981, antitrust exemptions for oil companies participating in the programs of the International Energy Agency, subsequently was passed by voice vote.)

14. S 884. Agriculture and Food Act of 1981. Huddleston, D-Ky., motion to table (kill) the Eagleton, D-Mo., amendment to allow the agriculture secretary to establish price support levels for certain grades of tobacco deemed by the secretary to be in excessive supply and non-competitive, except that the level may not go below 75 percent of the level established for the 1982 crop of that kind of tobacco. Motion agreed to 41-40: R 28-17; D 13-23 (ND 6-20, SD 7-3), Sept. 18, 1981.

15. S 509. Milk Price Supports. Melcher, D-Mont., amendment to establish a quota on the importation of casein products into the United States. Rejected 38-60: R 7-45; D 31-15 (ND 19-12, SD 12-3), March 24, 1981. A "nay" was a vote supporting the president's position.

16. HR 4995. Defense Appropriations, Fiscal 1982. Hollings, D-S.C., amendment to delete from the bill $2.429 billion for research on and procurement of the B-1B bomber, and to distribute the money among other accounts. Rejected 28-66: R 5-43; D 23-23 (ND 18-13, SD 5-10), Dec. 3, 1981. A "nay" was a vote supporting the president's position.

1. H Res 251. House Earned Income Limit. Adoption of the resolution to increase the limitation on House members' outside earned income from 15 percent to 40 percent of their official salary, and to increase the limit on each individual honorarium payment for a speech, article or personal appearance from $1,000 to $2,000, for calendar years 1981 through 1983. Rejected 147-271: R 73-112; D 74-159 (ND 49-107, SD 25-52), Oct. 28, 1981.

2. HR 3480. Legal Services Corporation. Passage of the bill to reauthorize the Legal Services Corporation for fiscal 1982-83, at $241 million annually. Passed 245-137: R 59-116; D 186-21 (ND 137-3, SD 49-18), June 18, 1981. A "nay" was a vote supporting the president's position.

3. HR 3112. Voting Rights Act Extension. Butler, R-Va., amendment to allow three-judge federal district courts to hear petitions by jurisdictions seeking to bail out from coverage of the Voting Rights Act. Rejected 132-277: R 102-75; D 30-202 (ND 4-153, SD 26-49), Oct. 5, 1981.

4. H Con Res 194. Disapproving AWACS Sale. Adoption of the concurrent resolution disapproving the sale to Saudi Arabia of Airborne Warning and Control System (AWACS) radar planes, conformal fuel tanks for F-15 aircraft, AIM-9L Sidewinder missiles and KC-707 aerial refueling aircraft. Adopted 301-111: R 108-78; D 193-33 (ND 149-5, SD 44-28), Oct. 14, 1981. A "nay" was a vote supporting the president's position.

5. HR 4995. Defense Department Appropriations, Fiscal 1982. Addabbo, D-N.Y., amendment to delete $1.801 billion from Air Force procurement intended for the B-1 bomber. Rejected 142-263: R 21-157; D 121-106 (ND 111-42, SD 10-64), Nov. 18, 1981. A "nay" was a vote supporting the president's position.

6. HR 4995. Defense Department Appropriations, Fiscal 1982. Addabbo, D-N.Y., amendment to delete $1,913,200,000 in Air Force research, development, test and evaluation funds for the MX missile and basing system. Rejected 139-264: R 27-151; D 112-113 (ND 103-48, SD 9-65), Nov. 18, 1981. A "nay" was a vote supporting the president's position.

7. HR 4144. Energy and Water Development Appropriations, Fiscal 1982. Pritchard, R-Wash., amendment, to the Myers, R-Ind., amendment, to delete $189 million for the Tennessee-Tombigbee Waterway. Rejected 198-208: R 108-70; D 90-138 (ND 82-70, SD 8-68), July 23, 1981. A "nay" was a vote supporting the president's position.

8. HR 4144. Energy and Water Development Appropriations, Fiscal 1982. Coughlin, R-Pa., amendment to delete $228 million for the Clinch River (Tenn.) nuclear breeder reactor. Rejected 186-206: R 70-104; D 116-102 (ND 107-38, SD 9-64), July 24, 1981. A "nay" was a vote supporting the president's position.

---

1. Rep. William R. Cotter, D-Conn., died Sept. 9, 1981.
2. Rep. Thomas P. O'Neill Jr., D-Mass., as Speaker, votes at his own discretion.
3. Rep. Wayne Dowdy, D-Miss., sworn in July 9, 1981, to succeed Jon Hinson, R, who resigned April 13, 1981.
4. Rep. Michael G. Oxley, R-Ohio, sworn in July 21, 1981, to succeed Tennyson Guyer, R, who died April 12, 1981.
5. Rep. Joseph F. Smith, D-Pa., sworn in July 28, 1981, to succeed Raymond F. Lederer, D, who resigned May 5, 1981.
6. Rep. Eugene V. Atkinson, Pa. switched his party affiliation from Democrat to Republican on Oct. 14, 1981.
7. Rep. Marilyn Lloyd Bouquard, D-Tenn., was known as Marilyn Lloyd in the 98th Congress.

KEY

Y	Voted for (yea).
#	Paired for.
+	Announced for.
N	Voted against (nay).
X	Paired against.
-	Announced against.
P	Voted "present".
C	Voted "present" to avoid possible conflict of interest.
?	Did not vote or otherwise make a position known.

Democrats *Republicans*

Member	1	2	3	4	5	6	7	8
ALABAMA								
1 *Edwards*	Y	N	Y	Y	N	N	N	N
2 *Dickinson*	Y	X	Y	N	N	N	N	N
3 Nichols	N	N	Y	N	N	N	N	N
4 Bevill	N	N	Y	N	N	N	N	N
5 Flippo	N	N	Y	N	N	N	N	?
6 *Smith*	N	N	Y	N	N	N	N	N
7 Shelby	N	N	Y	N	N	N	N	N
ALASKA								
AL *Young*	Y	N	N	Y	N	N	N	N
ARIZONA								
1 *Rhodes*	Y	N	Y	N	?	X	N	N
2 Udall	Y	Y	N	Y	Y	N	N	Y
3 *Stump*	N	N	Y	N	N	N	N	N
4 *Rudd*	Y	X	Y	Y	N	N	N	N
ARKANSAS								
1 Alexander	Y	Y	N	N	N	N	N	N
2 *Bethune*	N	N	Y	N	N	N	N	Y
3 *Hammerschmidt*	N	N	N	N	N	N	N	N
4 Anthony	N	Y	N	N	N	N	N	N
CALIFORNIA								
1 *Chappie*	N	X	Y	Y	N	N	?	?
2 *Clausen*	N	Y	Y	Y	N	N	N	N
3 Matsui	Y	Y	N	Y	N	N	N	Y
4 Fazio	Y	Y	N	Y	N	N	N	Y
5 Burton, J.	?	P	?	?	Y	Y	Y	Y
6 Burton, P.	N	Y	N	?	Y	Y	#	Y
7 Miller	N	Y	N	Y	Y	Y	Y	Y
8 Dellums	Y	Y	N	Y	Y	Y	Y	Y
9 Stark	?	Y	N	Y	Y	Y	Y	Y
10 Edwards	N	Y	N	Y	Y	Y	Y	#
11 Lantos	N	+	N	Y	Y	Y	Y	Y
12 *McCloskey*	Y	Y	N	N	?	?	Y	Y
13 Mineta	N	Y	N	Y	Y	Y	Y	Y
14 Shumway	Y	N	Y	N	N	N	N	N
15 Coelho	Y	Y	N	Y	N	Y	N	N
16 Panetta	N	Y	N	Y	Y	Y	Y	Y
17 Pashayan	N	?	?	Y	N	N	N	N
18 Thomas	Y	X	#	N	N	N	N	N
19 Lagomarsino	N	N	Y	N	N	N	N	N
20 Goldwater	Y	N	Y	Y	?	?	N	N
21 Fiedler	N	N	?	Y	N	N	Y	N
22 Moorhead	N	N	Y	N	N	N	N	N
23 Beilenson	N	Y	N	Y	Y	Y	Y	Y
24 Waxman	Y	Y	N	Y	Y	Y	Y	Y
25 Roybal	Y	Y	N	Y	Y	Y	Y	Y
26 *Rousselot*	Y	N	Y	N	Y	N	Y	?
27 *Dornan*	Y	N	N	Y	?	?	#	Y
28 Dixon	N	Y	N	Y	X	#	N	Y
29 Hawkins	N	?	N	Y	N	N	N	N
30 Danielson	N	Y	N	Y	N	Y	Y	Y
31 Dymally	Y	Y	N	Y	N	?	?	?
32 Anderson	N	Y	N	Y	N	N	Y	N
33 Grisham	Y	N	Y	N	-	-	Y	N
34 Lungren	Y	N	Y	N	N	N	Y	N
35 Dreier	N	N	Y	N	N	N	Y	N
36 Brown	N	N	Y	N	N	Y	N	Y
37 *Lewis*	Y	N	?	Y	N	N	X	N
38 Patterson	Y	Y	N	Y	N	N	Y	Y
39 Dannemeyer	Y	N	#	N	N	N	Y	N
40 *Badham*	Y	X	X	?	N	N	N	N
41 *Lowery*	?	N	Y	Y	N	N	N	N
42 Hunter	N	Y	N	Y	N	N	N	Y
43 *Burgener*	Y	N	Y	?	N	N	X	X
COLORADO								
1 Schroeder	N	Y	N	Y	Y	Y	Y	Y
2 Wirth	N	Y	N	Y	Y	Y	Y	Y
3 Kogovsek	N	?	N	Y	Y	Y	Y	Y
4 *Brown*	N	N	Y	Y	Y	N	N	Y
5 *Kramer*	N	N	Y	N	N	N	N	N
CONNECTICUT								
1 Cotter [1]	?						?	?
2 Gejdenson	N	Y	N	Y	Y	Y	Y	Y
3 *DeNardis*	N	Y	N	Y	Y	Y	Y	Y
4 *McKinney*	Y	Y	N	Y	Y	Y	Y	Y
5 Ratchford	N	Y	N	Y	Y	Y	Y	Y
6 Moffett	N	#	X	Y	Y	Y	Y	Y
DELAWARE								
AL *Evans*	N	Y	Y	Y	N	N	Y	Y
FLORIDA								
1 Hutto	N	N	Y	N	N	N	N	N
2 Fuqua	N	Y	N	N	N	N	N	N
3 Bennett	N	Y	N	Y	N	N	N	N
4 Chappell	Y	N	Y	N	N	N	N	N
5 *McCollum*	N	Y	Y	N	N	N	N	N
6 *Young*	N	N	Y	N	Y	N	N	N
7 Gibbons	Y	?	N	Y	Y	N	N	?
8 Ireland	N	N	N	N	N	N	N	N
9 Nelson	N	N	N	N	N	N	N	N
10 *Bafalis*	N	N	Y	N	N	Y	N	N
11 Mica	N	Y	N	Y	Y	N	N	N
12 *Shaw*	Y	N	Y	N	N	N	Y	Y
13 Lehman	N	?	Y	Y	Y	Y	Y	Y
14 Pepper	#	Y	?	#	X	X	N	Y
15 Fascell	N	Y	N	Y	Y	X	N	Y
GEORGIA								
1 Ginn	N	Y	N	Y	N	N	N	N
2 Hatcher	N	Y	Y	N	N	N	Y	N
3 Brinkley	N	Y	Y	N	N	N	Y	N
4 Levitas	N	Y	Y	?	N	N	Y	N
5 Fowler	N	Y	N	#	Y	Y	Y	Y
6 *Gingrich*	Y	N	Y	N	N	N	Y	N
7 McDonald	Y	X	Y	N	X	X	Y	N
8 Evans	Y	Y	Y	N	N	N	N	N
9 Jenkins	N	Y	Y	N	N	N	N	?
10 Barnard	N	Y	Y	X	N	N	N	N
HAWAII								
1 Heftel	N	Y	N	Y	N	Y	N	Y
2 Akaka	Y	Y	N	Y	N	N	N	N
IDAHO								
1 *Craig*	Y	N	Y	N	N	N	N	N
2 *Hansen*	Y	N	Y	N	N	N	X	N
ILLINOIS								
1 Washington	N	Y	N	Y	Y	Y	Y	Y
2 Savage	Y	Y	N	?	Y	Y	?	Y
3 Russo	Y	Y	N	Y	N	Y	N	Y
4 *Derwinski*	N	N	N	Y	N	N	N	N
5 Fary	?	Y	N	Y	N	N	Y	N
6 *Hyde*	Y	N	N	N	N	N	Y	N
7 Collins	Y	Y	N	Y	Y	Y	Y	Y
8 Rostenkowski	Y	Y	N	Y	Y	N	N	N
9 Yates	N	Y	N	Y	Y	Y	Y	Y
10 *Porter*	Y	Y	N	Y	N	Y	Y	Y
11 Annunzio	Y	Y	N	Y	N	N	N	N
12 *Crane, P.*	Y	N	#	?	N	N	Y	
13 *McClory*	N	N	Y	N	N	N	Y	N
14 *Erlenborn*	Y	Y	N	N	N	N	N	N
15 *Corcoran*	X	N	N	Y	N	N	N	?
16 *Martin*	N	Y	N	Y	N	Y	N	?
17 *O'Brien*	N	Y	Y	N	N	N	N	N
18 *Michel*	Y	N	Y	N	N	N	N	N
19 *Railsback*	Y	Y	N	Y	Y	Y	Y	Y
20 *Findley*	Y	Y	N	Y	Y	Y	Y	Y
21 *Madigan*	Y	N	Y	?	?	Y	Y	N
22 *Crane, D.*	Y	N	Y	N	N	Y	Y	Y
23 Price	Y	?	N	N	N	N	N	N
24 Simon	Y	?	N	Y	Y	Y	N	Y
INDIANA								
1 Benjamin	N	Y	N	Y	Y	N	N	N
2 Fithian	N	Y	N	Y	Y	Y	Y	Y
3 *Hiler*	N	N	N	N	N	N	N	N
4 *Coats*	N	N	N	N	N	Y	N	N
5 *Hillis*	N	N	N	Y	N	N	N	Y
6 Evans	N	Y	N	Y	Y	Y	N	N
7 *Myers*	Y	N	Y	N	N	N	N	N
8 *Deckard*	N	N	Y	N	N	Y	N	Y
9 Hamilton	N	Y	N	N	N	Y	N	N
10 Sharp	N	Y	N	Y	N	Y	N	Y
11 Jacobs	N	Y	N	Y	Y	Y	Y	Y
IOWA								
1 *Leach*	N	Y	N	Y	Y	Y	Y	Y
2 *Tauke*	N	Y	N	N	Y	Y	Y	Y
3 *Evans*	N	Y	N	Y	N	N	N	N
4 Smith	N	Y	N	Y	Y	Y	Y	Y
5 Harkin	N	?	N	Y	Y	Y	Y	Y
6 Bedell	N	?	N	Y	?	?	Y	Y

ND - Northern Democrats   SD - Southern Democrats

	1	2	3	4	5	6	7	8
KANSAS								
1 ***Roberts***	N	N	Y	N	N	N	Y	N
2 ***Jeffries***	N	N	Y	N	N	N	Y	N
3 ***Winn***	N	N	Y	Y	N	N	N	N
4 Glickman	N	Y	N	Y	Y	Y	Y	Y
5 ***Whittaker***	N	N	Y	Y	N	N	Y	N
KENTUCKY								
1 Hubbard	N	Y	?	N	N	N	N	N
2 Natcher	N	Y	N	Y	N	N	N	N
3 Mazzoli	N	+	N	Y	Y	Y	+	N
4 ***Snyder***	Y	N	Y	N	N	N	N	Y
5 ***Rogers***	N	N	Y	N	N	N	N	N
6 ***Hopkins***	N	Y	N	N	N	N	Y	Y
7 Perkins	N	Y	N	Y	N	N	N	N
LOUISIANA								
1 ***Livingston***	Y	X	Y	Y	N	N	N	N
2 Boggs	Y	Y	N	Y	N	N	N	N
3 Tauzin	Y	Y	Y	Y	N	N	N	N
4 Roemer	N	Y	Y	Y	N	N	N	N
5 Huckaby	N	Y	Y	N	N	N	N	N
6 ***Moore***	Y	Y	Y	Y	N	N	Y	Y
7 Breaux	Y	?	Y	Y	X	X	N	N
8 Long	N	+	N	Y	N	N	N	N
MAINE								
1 ***Emery***	N	Y	N	Y	N	N	Y	Y
2 ***Snowe***	N	N	N	Y	N	N	Y	Y
MARYLAND								
1 Dyson	N	N	N	Y	N	N	N	N
2 Long	N	Y	N	Y	Y	Y	N	N
3 Mikulski	N	Y	N	Y	Y	Y	Y	Y
4 ***Holt***	N	N	N	N	N	N	N	N
5 Hoyer	Y	Y	N	Y	N	N	N	Y
6 Byron	N	Y	N	Y	N	N	N	N
7 Mitchell	Y	Y	N	Y	Y	Y	?	Y
8 Barnes	N	Y	N	Y	Y	Y	Y	Y
MASSACHUSETTS								
1 ***Conte***	Y	Y	N	Y	Y	Y	Y	Y
2 Boland	N	Y	N	Y	Y	Y	Y	Y
3 Early	Y	?	N	Y	Y	Y	Y	Y
4 Frank	N	Y	N	Y	Y	Y	Y	Y
5 Shannon	N	Y	N	Y	Y	Y	Y	Y
6 Mavroules	N	Y	N	Y	Y	Y	Y	N
7 Markey	N	Y	N	Y	Y	Y	Y	Y
8 O'Neill [2]								
9 Moakley	Y	?	N	Y	#	#	?	Y
10 ***Heckler***	N	Y	N	Y	Y	N	Y	Y
11 Donnelly	N	?	N	Y	#	?	N	Y
12 Studds	N	Y	N	Y	Y	Y	Y	Y
MICHIGAN								
1 Conyers	#	#	N	Y	Y	Y	N	Y
2 ***Pursell***	N	Y	N	Y	Y	Y	Y	Y
3 Wolpe	N	Y	N	Y	Y	Y	Y	Y
4 ***Siljander***	Y	N	Y	Y	N	N	Y	Y
5 ***Sawyer***	N	Y	Y	N	N	N	Y	Y
6 ***Dunn***	N	Y	N	Y	?	N	Y	Y
7 Kildee	N	Y	N	Y	Y	Y	Y	Y
8 Traxler	N	Y	N	Y	Y	Y	N	Y
9 ***Vander Jagt***	Y	N	Y	Y	N	N	Y	N
10 Albosta	N	?	N	Y	Y	N	N	Y
11 ***Davis***	N	Y	N	N	X	N	Y	N
12 Bonior	N	Y	N	Y	Y	Y	Y	Y
13 Crockett	N	Y	N	Y	N	Y	N	Y
14 Hertel	N	Y	N	Y	Y	Y	Y	Y
15 Ford	Y	Y	N	Y	Y	Y	N	N
16 Dingell	N	Y	X	Y	Y	Y	Y	Y
17 Brodhead	N	Y	N	Y	Y	Y	Y	Y
18 Blanchard	N	Y	N	Y	Y	Y	Y	Y
19 ***Broomfield***	N	N	N	Y	N	N	Y	Y
MINNESOTA								
1 ***Erdahl***	N	Y	N	Y	Y	Y	Y	Y
2 ***Hagedorn***	Y	Y	Y	N	?	?	N	N
3 ***Frenzel***	Y	#	Y	Y	N	N	Y	?
4 Vento	N	Y	N	Y	Y	N	Y	#
5 Sabo	N	Y	N	Y	Y	Y	N	Y
6 ***Weber***	N	N	N	Y	Y	Y	Y	Y
7 ***Stangeland***	N	N	Y	N	N	N	N	N
8 Oberstar	N	Y	N	Y	Y	Y	N	Y
MISSISSIPPI								
1 Whitten	N	Y	Y	N	N	N	N	N
2 Bowen	N	Y	Y	N	N	N	N	N
3 Montgomery	N	N	Y	N	N	N	N	N
4 Dowdy [3]	N		N	Y	N	N	N	N
5 ***Lott***	Y	N	Y	N	N	N	N	N
MISSOURI								
1 Clay	Y	Y	N	Y	Y	Y	Y	Y
2 Young	N	Y	N	Y	N	Y	N	N
3 Gephardt	N	Y	N	Y	N	N	Y	Y
4 Skelton	N	?	N	Y	N	N	N	N
5 Bolling	Y	Y	N	?	?	?	Y	?
6 ***Coleman***	N	Y	Y	N	N	N	N	N
7 ***Taylor***	Y	N	Y	N	N	N	N	N
8 ***Bailey***	N	N	N	N	N	N	?	N
9 Volkmer	N	Y	N	Y	N	N	N	N
10 ***Emerson***	N	N	Y	N	N	N	N	N
MONTANA								
1 Williams	N	Y	N	Y	Y	Y	N	Y
2 ***Marlenee***	N	Y	Y	N	N	?	Y	Y
NEBRASKA								
1 ***Bereuter***	N	N	Y	N	N	N	Y	N
2 ***Daub***	N	N	N	N	N	N	Y	N
3 ***Smith***	N	N	Y	N	N	Y	N	N
NEVADA								
AL Santini	N	N	Y	Y	N	N	Y	?
NEW HAMPSHIRE								
1 D'Amours	N	Y	N	Y	Y	N	?	Y
2 ***Gregg***	N	N	N	Y	N	Y	Y	Y
NEW JERSEY								
1 Florio	?	?	N	Y	#	?	Y	#
2 Hughes	N	Y	N	Y	Y	N	N	Y
3 Howard	Y	Y	N	Y	Y	Y	N	Y
4 ***Smith***	N	N	N	Y	N	Y	Y	Y
5 ***Fenwick***	N	Y	N	Y	Y	Y	Y	Y
6 ***Forsythe***	N	Y	N	Y	?	?	Y	N
7 ***Roukema***	N	N	N	Y	N	N	Y	N
8 Roe	Y	Y	N	Y	N	N	N	N
9 ***Hollenbeck***	N	Y	N	Y	Y	Y	Y	N
10 Rodino	Y	Y	N	Y	Y	Y	Y	Y
11 Minish	N	Y	N	Y	Y	Y	Y	Y
12 ***Rinaldo***	N	Y	N	Y	N	N	Y	N
13 ***Courter***	N	Y	N	Y	N	N	Y	N
14 Guarini	Y	Y	N	Y	Y	Y	N	Y
15 Dwyer	N	Y	N	Y	Y	Y	N	N
NEW MEXICO								
1 ***Lujan***	Y	Y	N	Y	N	N	N	N
2 ***Skeen***	N	Y	Y	N	N	N	N	N
NEW YORK								
1 ***Carney***	N	N	Y	Y	N	N	N	N
2 Downey	N	Y	N	Y	Y	Y	?	?
3 ***Carman***	Y	N	Y	Y	N	N	Y	Y
4 ***Lent***	Y	Y	N	Y	N	N	Y	N
5 ***McGrath***	N	N	N	Y	N	N	Y	Y
6 ***LeBoutillier***	N	N	N	Y	N	N	Y	N
7 Addabbo	Y	Y	N	Y	Y	Y	N	N
8 Rosenthal	N	Y	N	Y	Y	Y	?	?
9 Ferraro	Y	Y	N	Y	Y	Y	Y	Y
10 Biaggi	Y	Y	N	Y	Y	N	N	X
11 Scheuer	Y	Y	N	Y	Y	Y	N	Y
12 Chisholm	Y	Y	N	Y	#	#	N	Y
13 Solarz	N	Y	N	Y	Y	Y	Y	Y
14 Richmond	Y	Y	N	Y	Y	Y	Y	#
15 Zeferetti	Y	#	N	Y	N	Y	N	N
16 Schumer	N	Y	N	Y	Y	Y	Y	Y
17 ***Molinari***	Y	?	Y	Y	N	Y	Y	Y
18 ***Green***	Y	Y	N	Y	Y	Y	Y	Y
19 Rangel	Y	Y	N	Y	Y	Y	N	Y
20 Weiss	N	Y	N	Y	Y	Y	Y	Y
21 Garcia	N	Y	N	?	Y	?	N	?
22 Bingham	N	Y	N	Y	Y	Y	Y	Y
23 Peyser	Y	#	?	Y	Y	N	Y	Y
24 Ottinger	Y	Y	N	Y	Y	Y	Y	Y
25 ***Fish***	Y	Y	N	Y	N	N	Y	Y
26 ***Gilman***	N	Y	N	Y	N	N	-	Y
27 McHugh	N	Y	N	Y	Y	Y	Y	Y
28 Stratton	N	Y	N	X	N	N	N	N
29 ***Solomon***	N	N	Y	N	N	N	Y	N
30 ***Martin***	Y	N	Y	N	?	?	Y	?
31 ***Mitchell***	N	?	N	N	N	N	Y	Y
32 ***Wortley***	Y	N	N	Y	N	N	N	Y
33 ***Lee***	N	N	Y	Y	N	N	N	N
34 ***Horton***	N	Y	X	Y	Y	Y	N	?
35 ***Conable***	Y	N	Y	N	N	N	Y	N
36 LaFalce	N	?	N	Y	Y	Y	N	Y
37 Nowak	N	Y	N	Y	Y	Y	N	Y
38 ***Kemp***	Y	N	N	Y	N	N	?	?
39 Lundine	N	Y	N	Y	Y	Y	Y	Y
NORTH CAROLINA								
1 Jones	X	Y	X	?	?	?	N	N
2 Fountain	N	Y	N	N	N	N	Y	N
3 Whitley	N	Y	N	N	N	N	N	N
4 Andrews	N	Y	N	N	N	N	N	N
5 Neal	N	Y	N	Y	N	N	Y	Y
6 ***Johnston***	#	X	Y	N	?	?	Y	Y
7 Rose	Y	?	N	N	N	N	N	N
8 Hefner	N	Y	N	Y	N	N	N	N
9 ***Martin***	Y	Y	Y	Y	N	N	Y	?
10 ***Broyhill***	N	N	Y	N	N	N	Y	N
11 ***Hendon***	N	N	N	Y	N	N	N	?
NORTH DAKOTA								
AL Dorgan	N	Y	N	Y	+	+	N	Y
OHIO								
1 ***Gradison***	Y	Y	N	Y	N	N	Y	Y
2 Luken	Y	?	N	Y	N	N	N	Y
3 Hall	N	Y	N	Y	N	N	Y	Y
4 ***Oxley*** [4]	N		Y	N	N	N	N	N
5 ***Latta***	Y	N	Y	N	N	N	X	N
6 ***McEwen***	N	N	Y	N	N	N	N	N
7 ***Brown***	N	?	N	Y	N	N	N	?
8 ***Kindness***	N	N	Y	Y	N	N	N	N
9 ***Weber***	N	Y	N	Y	N	N	Y	Y
10 ***Miller***	N	N	Y	N	N	N	N	N
11 ***Stanton***	Y	Y	N	N	N	N	Y	Y
12 Shamansky	N	Y	N	Y	N	N	Y	Y
13 Pease	N	Y	N	Y	Y	Y	Y	Y
14 Seiberling	N	Y	N	Y	Y	Y	Y	Y
15 ***Wylie***	N	Y	N	N	N	N	?	Y
16 ***Regula***	N	Y	N	N	N	N	N	N
17 ***Ashbrook***	N	N	?	Y	N	N	N	N
18 Applegate	N	Y	Y	Y	N	N	Y	Y
19 ***Williams***	N	Y	X	Y	N	N	N	Y
20 Oakar	N	Y	?	Y	N	N	N	Y
21 Stokes	Y	Y	N	Y	Y	Y	N	N
22 Eckart	N	Y	N	Y	N	Y	Y	Y
23 Mottl	N	Y	Y	Y	N	N	Y	?
OKLAHOMA								
1 Jones	Y	Y	N	Y	N	N	N	N
2 Synar	N	Y	N	Y	N	Y	Y	Y
3 Watkins	N	Y	N	Y	N	N	N	N
4 McCurdy	N	Y	N	Y	N	N	N	Y
5 ***Edwards***	Y	N	Y	N	N	N	N	Y
6 English	Y	Y	N	Y	N	N	N	N
OREGON								
1 AuCoin	N	Y	N	Y	Y	Y	N	Y
2 ***Smith***	Y	N	Y	Y	N	N	Y	Y
3 Wyden	N	Y	N	Y	Y	Y	Y	Y
4 Weaver	N	Y	N	Y	Y	Y	Y	Y
PENNSYLVANIA								
1 Foglietta	Y	Y	N	Y	Y	Y	Y	Y
2 Gray	Y	?	N	Y	Y	Y	N	?
3 Smith [5]	Y		N	Y	N	N		
4 ***Dougherty***	?	N	N	Y	N	N	Y	N
5 ***Schulze***	Y	N	N	N	N	N	Y	N
6 Yatron	N	Y	N	Y	N	N	Y	Y
7 Edgar	N	Y	N	Y	Y	Y	Y	Y
8 ***Coyne, J.***	N	N	N	Y	N	N	Y	N
9 ***Shuster***	Y	N	Y	Y	N	N	N	N
10 ***McDade***	Y	#	N	?	N	N	N	Y
11 ***Nelligan***	N	N	N	Y	N	N	Y	N
12 Murtha	Y	Y	N	Y	Y	N	N	N
13 ***Coughlin***	?	Y	N	Y	N	Y	Y	Y
14 Coyne, W.	N	Y	N	Y	Y	Y	Y	N
15 ***Ritter***	N	N	N	Y	N	N	+	Y
16 ***Walker***	N	N	N	Y	N	N	Y	N
17 Ertel	N	Y	N	Y	Y	N	N	Y
18 Walgren	N	Y	N	Y	Y	Y	Y	Y
19 ***Goodling***	N	N	Y	N	N	Y	Y	Y
20 Gaydos	N	Y	N	Y	N	Y	?	?
21 Bailey	Y	Y	N	Y	N	N	N	N
22 Murphy	N	Y	N	Y	Y	Y	Y	N
23 ***Clinger***	N	Y	Y	N	N	N	Y	Y
24 ***Marks***	N	Y	N	Y	N	N	Y	N
25 ***Atkinson*** [6]	N	Y	N	?	N	N	Y	N
RHODE ISLAND								
1 St Germain	N	Y	N	Y	Y	Y	N	Y
2 ***Schneider***	N	Y	N	Y	Y	Y	Y	Y
SOUTH CAROLINA								
1 ***Hartnett***	Y	N	Y	N	N	N	Y	N
2 ***Spence***	N	N	Y	N	N	N	N	N
3 Derrick	Y	N	N	N	Y	N	Y	N
4 ***Campbell***	Y	N	Y	N	N	N	N	N
5 Holland	Y	N	N	?	N	N	N	N
6 ***Napier***	N	N	Y	N	N	N	N	N
SOUTH DAKOTA								
1 Daschle	N	Y	N	Y	N	N	N	Y
2 ***Roberts***	N	N	Y	Y	N	N	+	-
TENNESSEE								
1 ***Quillen***	Y	N	Y	N	N	N	N	X
2 ***Duncan***	N	Y	N	Y	X	?	N	N
3 Bouquard [7]	N	Y	N	Y	N	N	N	N
4 Gore	N	Y	N	Y	Y	N	N	N
5 Boner	N	?	N	Y	N	N	N	N
6 ***Beard***	X	Y	?	Y	N	N	N	N
7 Jones	N	Y	N	Y	N	N	N	N
8 Ford	Y	?	N	Y	Y	Y	N	N
TEXAS								
1 Hall, S.	N	N	Y	N	N	N	N	N
2 Wilson	Y	Y	N	N	N	N	N	N
3 ***Collins***	N	N	Y	Y	N	N	Y	Y
4 Hall, R.	N	Y	Y	Y	N	N	N	N
5 Mattox	Y	Y	N	Y	#	?	#	#
6 Gramm	Y	N	Y	N	N	N	N	N
7 ***Archer***	N	N	Y	Y	N	N	Y	N
8 ***Fields***	Y	N	Y	Y	N	N	N	N
9 Brooks	Y	#	?	?	Y	Y	N	N
10 Pickle	N	Y	N	Y	N	N	N	N
11 Leath	Y	N	Y	N	N	N	N	N
12 Wright	Y	#	N	Y	N	N	N	N
13 Hightower	N	Y	N	N	N	N	N	N
14 Patman	N	N	Y	N	N	N	N	N
15 de la Garza	N	Y	N	Y	N	N	N	N
16 White	Y	Y	N	N	N	N	N	N
17 Stenholm	N	N	Y	N	N	N	N	N
18 Leland	Y	Y	N	Y	Y	Y	Y	Y
19 Hance	Y	N	N	N	N	N	N	N
20 Gonzalez	Y	Y	N	Y	N	N	N	P
21 ***Loeffler***	N	N	Y	Y	N	N	N	N
22 ***Paul***	Y	N	#	Y	Y	?	Y	Y
23 Kazen	N	Y	N	N	N	N	N	N
24 Frost	N	Y	N	Y	N	N	?	?
UTAH								
1 ***Hansen***	N	X	Y	N	N	N	X	?
2 ***Marriott***	N	N	N	N	N	N	N	N
VERMONT								
AL ***Jeffords***	N	?	Y	Y	Y	Y	Y	Y
VIRGINIA								
1 ***Trible***	N	N	Y	Y	N	N	N	Y
2 ***Whitehurst***	N	Y	Y	?	N	N	Y	N
3 ***Bliley***	?	N	Y	Y	N	N	N	N
4 ***Daniel, R.***	Y	N	Y	N	N	N	Y	Y
5 Daniel, D.	Y	N	Y	N	N	N	N	N
6 ***Butler***	N	Y	Y	N	N	N	Y	N
7 ***Robinson***	Y	N	Y	N	N	N	N	N
8 ***Parris***	N	N	Y	N	N	N	N	N
9 ***Wampler***	Y	Y	Y	N	N	N	N	N
10 ***Wolf***	N	N	Y	Y	N	N	Y	N
WASHINGTON								
1 ***Pritchard***	N	Y	?	N	?	?	Y	?
2 Swift	N	Y	N	Y	Y	N	Y	Y
3 Bonker	N	Y	-	?	Y	Y	?	Y
4 ***Morrison***	N	N	Y	N	N	N	N	N
5 Foley	Y	Y	N	Y	N	N	N	N
6 Dicks	N	Y	N	Y	N	N	N	N
7 Lowry	N	Y	N	?	Y	Y	Y	Y
WEST VIRGINIA								
1 Mollohan	?	#	N	N	N	N	N	N
2 ***Benedict***	Y	N	#	Y	N	N	N	Y
3 ***Staton***	Y	N	Y	N	N	N	N	Y
4 Rahall	Y	Y	N	N	Y	Y	N	Y
WISCONSIN								
1 Aspin	N	Y	N	Y	Y	N	Y	Y
2 Kastenmeier	N	Y	N	Y	Y	Y	Y	Y
3 ***Gunderson***	N	N	N	N	Y	N	Y	Y
4 Zablocki	Y	Y	N	N	N	N	N	N
5 Reuss	Y	Y	N	Y	#	#	Y	?
6 ***Petri***	N	N	N	Y	Y	Y	Y	Y
7 Obey	N	Y	N	Y	Y	Y	Y	Y
8 ***Roth***	N	N	?	N	N	N	Y	N
9 ***Sensenbrenner***	N	N	N	Y	N	N	Y	Y
WYOMING								
AL ***Cheney***	Y	N	Y	N	N	N	N	X

Southern states - Ala., Ark., Fla., Ga., Ky., La., Miss., N.C., Okla., S.C., Tenn., Texas, Va.

9. HR 1553. Debt Limit Increase. Passage of the bill to increase the public debt limit to $985 billion through Sept. 30, 1981. Passed 305-104: R 150-36; D 155-68 (ND 112-37, SD 43-31), Feb. 5, 1981. A "yea" was a vote supporting the president's position.

10. H Con Res 115. Fiscal 1982 Budget Targets. Latta, R-Ohio, substitute, to the resolution as reported by the Budget Committee, to decrease budget authority by $23.1 billion, outlays by $25.7 billion and revenues by $31.1 billion, resulting in a $31 billion deficit for fiscal 1982. Adopted 253-176: R 190-0; D 63-176 (ND 17-144, SD 46-32), May 7, 1981. A "yea" was a vote supporting the president's position.

11. HR 3982. Budget Reconciliation. Latta, R-Ohio, amendments, considered *en bloc*, to strike parts of six titles of the bill recommended by the following committees — Agriculture; Banking, Finance and Urban Affairs; Education and Labor; Post Office and Civil Service; Science and Technology; and Ways and Means — and to substitute provisions endorsed by President Reagan. Adopted 217-211: R 188-2; D 29-209 (ND 3-157, SD 26-52), June 26, 1981. A "yea" was a vote supporting the president's position.

12. HR 4242. Tax Cuts. Conable, R-N.Y., substitute amendment to the bill to reduce individual income tax rates by 25 percent across-the-board over three years, to index tax rates beginning in 1985 and to provide business and investment tax incentives. Adopted 238-195: R 190-1; D 48-194 (ND 12-151, SD 36-43), July 29, 1981. A "yea" was a vote supporting the president's position.

13. HR 4331/HR 3982. Minimum Social Security Benefits/Budget Reconciliation. Bolling, D-Mo., motion to order the previous question (thus ending debate and the possibility of amendment) on the rule (H Res 203) providing for consideration of 1) the bill (HR 4331) to amend the Omnibus Budget Reconciliation Act of 1981 (HR 3982) to restore minimum Social Security benefits and 2) the reconciliation act conference report. Motion agreed to 271-151: R 166-21; D 105-130 (ND 56-101, SD 49-29), July 31, 1981.

14. HR 4560. Labor-HHS-Education Appropriations, Fiscal 1982. Regula, R-Ohio, motion to recommit the bill to the Appropriations Committee. Rejected 168-249: R 140-39; D 28-210 (ND 3-157; SD 25-53), Oct. 6, 1981. (The bill, appropriating $87,181,250,000 for the departments of Labor, Health and Human Services, and Education, and related agencies, subsequently was passed by voice vote.) A "yea" was a vote supporting the president's position.

15. HR 4559. Foreign Aid Appropriations, Fiscal 1982. Passage of the bill to appropriate $7,440,280,064 for foreign aid and related programs in fiscal 1982. Passed 199-166: R 84-87; D 115-79 (ND 95-36, SD 20-43), Dec. 11, 1981. (The president had requested $7,775,098,683.)

16. S 884. Agriculture and Food Act of 1981. Adoption of the conference report on the bill to reauthorize for four years price support and other farm programs and, for one year, food stamps. Adopted 205-203: R 125-59; D 80-144 (ND 27-121, SD 53-23), Dec. 16, 1981. A "yea" was a vote supporting the president's position.

1. Rep. William R. Cotter, D-Conn., died Sept. 8, 1981.
2. Rep. Steny Hoyer, D-Md., sworn in June 3, 1981, to succeed Gladys Noon Spellman, D, whose seat the House declared vacant on Feb. 24, 1981, due to her illness.
3. Rep. Thomas P. O'Neill Jr., D-Mass., as Speaker, votes at his own discretion.
4. Rep. Mark Siljander, R-Mich., sworn in April 28, 1981, to succeed David A. Stockman, R, who resigned Jan. 27, 1981.
5. Rep. Wayne Dowdy, D-Miss., sworn in July 9, 1981, to succeed Jon Hinson, R, who resigned April 13, 1981.
6. Rep. Michael G. Oxley, R-Ohio, sworn in July 21, 1981, to succeed Tennyson Guyer, R, who died April 12, 1981.
7. Rep. Joseph F. Smith, D-Pa., sworn in July 28, 1981, to succeed Raymond F. Lederer, D, who resigned May 5, 1981.
8. Rep. Eugene V. Atkinson, Pa., switched his party affiliation from Democrat to Republican on Oct. 14, 1981.
9. Rep. Marilyn Lloyd Bouquard, D-Tenn., was known as Marilyn Lloyd in the 98th Congress.

KEY

Y Voted for (yea).
Paired for.
+ Announced for.
N Voted against (nay).
X Paired against.
- Announced against.
P Voted "present".
C Voted "present" to avoid possible conflict of interest.
? Did not vote or otherwise make a position known.

Democrats   *Republicans*

	9	10	11	12	13	14	15	16
ALABAMA								
1 *Edwards*	Y	Y	Y	Y	Y	Y	Y	Y
2 *Dickinson*	Y	Y	Y	Y	Y	Y	?	Y
3 Nichols	N	Y	Y	N	Y	N	N	Y
4 Bevill	N	Y	N	N	N	N	N	Y
5 Flippo	N	Y	Y	N	N	N	?	Y
6 *Smith*	Y	Y	Y	Y	Y	Y	?	Y
7 Shelby	N	Y	Y	Y	Y	Y	N	Y
ALASKA								
AL *Young*	Y	Y	Y	Y	Y	N	N	Y
ARIZONA								
1 *Rhodes*	Y	Y	Y	Y	Y	Y	Y	Y
2 Udall	Y	N	N	N	Y	N	Y	Y
3 Stump	N	Y	Y	N	N	Y	N	Y
4 *Rudd*	Y	Y	Y	Y	Y	Y	N	Y
ARKANSAS								
1 Alexander	Y	N	N	N	N	N	?	Y
2 *Bethune*	Y	Y	Y	Y	?	?	N	Y
3 *Hammerschmidt*	Y	Y	Y	Y	Y	Y	N	Y
4 Anthony	Y	N	N	N	Y	N	?	Y
CALIFORNIA								
1 *Chappie*	N	Y	Y	Y	Y	Y	?	Y
2 *Clausen*	Y	Y	Y	Y	Y	Y	Y	Y
3 Matsui	Y	N	N	N	Y	N	Y	Y
4 Fazio	?	N	N	N	Y	N	Y	Y
5 Burton, J.	?	N	?	N	N	?	?	#
6 Burton, P.	Y	N	N	N	N	N	Y	N
7 Miller	N	N	N	N	N	N	Y	N
8 Dellums	N	N	N	N	N	N	N	N
9 Stark	Y	N	N	N	N	N	Y	N
10 Edwards	Y	N	N	N	N	N	Y	N
11 Lantos	N	N	N	N	N	N	Y	N
12 *McCloskey*	Y	Y	Y	Y	Y	Y	?	Y
13 Mineta	Y	N	N	N	Y	N	Y	Y
14 *Shumway*	Y	Y	Y	Y	Y	Y	N	Y
15 Coelho	Y	N	N	N	Y	N	Y	Y
16 Panetta	Y	N	N	N	Y	N	Y	Y
17 *Pashayan*	N	Y	Y	Y	?	N	Y	Y
18 Thomas	Y	Y	Y	Y	?	Y	Y	Y
19 *Lagomarsino*	Y	Y	Y	Y	Y	Y	Y	Y
20 *Goldwater*	?	Y	Y	Y	?	Y	X	Y
21 *Fiedler*	Y	Y	Y	Y	?	Y	Y	Y
22 *Moorhead*	N	Y	Y	Y	Y	N	Y	?
23 Beilenson	Y	N	N	N	Y	N	Y	Y
24 Waxman	Y	N	N	N	N	N	Y	N
25 Roybal	?	N	N	N	N	N	Y	N
26 *Rousselot*	N	Y	Y	Y	Y	Y	N	Y
27 *Dornan*	Y	Y	Y	Y	?	Y	?	Y
28 Dixon	Y	N	N	N	N	N	Y	N
29 Hawkins	N	N	N	N	N	N	Y	N
30 Danielson	Y	N	-	N	Y	N	Y	Y
31 Dymally	Y	N	?	N	N	N	Y	Y
32 Anderson	N	N	N	N	N	N	Y	Y
33 *Grisham*	Y	Y	Y	Y	Y	Y	N	Y
34 *Lungren*	Y	Y	Y	Y	Y	Y	N	Y
35 *Dreier*	N	Y	Y	Y	Y	Y	N	Y
36 Brown	Y	N	N	N	N	N	?	Y
37 *Lewis*	Y	Y	Y	Y	Y	Y	Y	Y
38 Patterson	Y	N	N	N	Y	N	Y	Y
39 *Dannemeyer*	N	Y	Y	Y	N	Y	?	Y
40 *Badham*	Y	Y	Y	Y	Y	Y	Y	Y
41 *Lowery*	Y	Y	Y	Y	Y	Y	N	Y
42 *Hunter*	Y	Y	Y	Y	Y	Y	N	Y
43 *Burgener*	Y	Y	Y	Y	Y	Y	Y	#
COLORADO								
1 Schroeder	N	N	N	N	N	N	N	N
2 Wirth	Y	N	N	N	N	N	Y	N
3 Kogovsek	Y	N	N	N	N	N	N	Y
4 *Brown*	Y	Y	Y	Y	Y	Y	N	Y

	9	10	11	12	13	14	15	16
5 *Kramer*	Y	Y	Y	Y	Y	Y	?	N
CONNECTICUT								
1 Cotter [1]	?	?	?	?	?			
2 Gejdenson	Y	N	N	N	Y	N	Y	N
3 *DeNardis*	N	Y	Y	Y	N	Y	N	Y
4 *McKinney*	Y	Y	Y	Y	N	Y	N	Y
5 Ratchford	Y	N	N	N	N	N	Y	N
6 Moffett	Y	N	N	N	N	N	Y	?
DELAWARE								
AL *Evans*	Y	Y	Y	Y	Y	Y	Y	Y
FLORIDA								
1 Hutto	Y	Y	Y	Y	Y	Y	?	Y
2 Fuqua	?	Y	N	N	Y	N	Y	Y
3 Bennett	N	N	N	N	N	N	N	Y
4 Chappell	N	Y	Y	Y	Y	Y	N	Y
5 *McCollum*	?	Y	Y	Y	Y	Y	N	Y
6 *Young*	Y	Y	Y	Y	Y	Y	N	#
7 Gibbons	Y	N	N	N	N	N	Y	Y
8 Ireland	Y	Y	Y	Y	Y	Y	Y	Y
9 Nelson	Y	Y	Y	N	Y	N	Y	Y
10 *Bafalis*	Y	Y	Y	Y	Y	Y	N	Y
11 Mica	Y	Y	Y	Y	N	N	Y	Y
12 *Shaw*	Y	Y	Y	Y	Y	Y	N	Y
13 Lehman	Y	N	N	N	N	N	Y	Y
14 Pepper	Y	N	N	N	N	Y	Y	Y
15 Fascell	Y	N	N	N	?	N	Y	N
GEORGIA								
1 Ginn	Y	Y	Y	N	N	N	N	Y
2 Hatcher	Y	Y	Y	Y	N	?	?	Y
3 Brinkley	Y	Y	Y	N	N	N	N	Y
4 Levitas	N	Y	N	N	N	N	N	Y
5 Fowler	Y	N	N	N	N	N	N	Y
6 *Gingrich*	Y	Y	Y	Y	?	Y	Y	Y
7 McDonald	N	Y	Y	Y	Y	Y	?	?
8 Evans	N	Y	Y	Y	Y	Y	?	?
9 Jenkins	Y	Y	N	N	Y	N	?	Y
10 Barnard	N	Y	Y	Y	Y	Y	?	Y
HAWAII								
1 Heftel	N	N	N	?	N	N	Y	Y
2 Akaka	N	N	N	N	N	N	Y	Y
IDAHO								
1 *Craig*	N	Y	Y	Y	Y	Y	N	Y
2 *Hansen*	N	Y	Y	Y	Y	Y	N	Y
ILLINOIS								
1 Washington	Y	N	N	N	N	N	Y	N
2 Savage	Y	N	N	N	?	N	N	N
3 Russo	Y	N	N	N	N	N	X	X
4 *Derwinski*	Y	Y	Y	Y	Y	Y	?	Y
5 Fary	Y	N	N	N	N	N	N	N
6 *Hyde*	Y	Y	Y	Y	Y	Y	Y	Y
7 Collins	Y	N	N	N	N	N	#	#
8 Rostenkowski	Y	N	N	N	?	N	Y	N
9 Yates	N	N	N	N	N	N	Y	N
10 *Porter*	Y	Y	Y	Y	Y	Y	N	Y
11 Annunzio	Y	N	N	N	N	N	Y	N
12 *Crane, P.*	N	Y	Y	Y	Y	Y	N	Y
13 *McClory*	Y	Y	Y	Y	Y	Y	N	Y
14 *Erlenborn*	Y	Y	Y	Y	Y	Y	N	Y
15 *Corcoran*	Y	Y	Y	Y	Y	Y	N	Y
16 *Martin*	Y	Y	Y	Y	Y	?	N	Y
17 *O'Brien*	Y	Y	Y	Y	Y	Y	N	Y
18 *Michel*	Y	Y	Y	Y	Y	Y	N	Y
19 *Railsback*	Y	Y	Y	Y	Y	?	Y	Y
20 *Findley*	Y	Y	Y	Y	Y	Y	N	Y
21 *Madigan*	Y	Y	Y	Y	Y	Y	Y	Y
22 *Crane, D.*	N	Y	Y	Y	Y	Y	N	Y
23 Price	Y	N	N	N	Y	N	Y	Y
24 Simon	Y	N	N	?	N	?	Y	Y
INDIANA								
1 Benjamin	Y	N	N	N	Y	N	Y	N
2 Fithian	X	N	N	N	N	N	N	N
3 *Hiler*	Y	Y	Y	Y	N	N	N	N
4 *Coats*	Y	Y	Y	Y	Y	Y	N	Y
5 *Hillis*	Y	Y	Y	Y	Y	Y	Y	Y
6 Evans	N	Y	N	N	N	N	?	N
7 *Myers*	N	Y	N	N	N	N	?	Y
8 *Deckard*	Y	Y	Y	Y	Y	Y	N	Y
9 Hamilton	Y	N	N	N	N	N	Y	N
10 Sharp	Y	N	N	N	N	N	Y	N
11 Jacobs	N	Y	N	N	N	N	N	N
IOWA								
1 *Leach*	Y	Y	Y	Y	Y	Y	Y	Y
2 *Tauke*	Y	Y	Y	Y	Y	Y	N	Y
3 *Evans*	N	Y	Y	Y	Y	Y	N	Y
4 Smith	Y	N	N	N	N	N	Y	Y
5 Harkin	N	N	N	N	N	N	N	Y
6 Bedell	N	N	N	N	N	?	N	Y

ND - Northern Democrats   SD - Southern Democrats

	9	10	11	12	13	14	15	16
KANSAS								
1 ***Roberts***	Y	Y	Y	Y	Y	Y	N	N
2 ***Jeffries***	N	Y	Y	Y	Y	Y	N	Y
3 ***Winn***	Y	Y	Y	Y	Y	Y	Y	Y
4 Glickman	Y	N	N	Y	N	N	Y	N
5 ***Whittaker***	Y	Y	Y	Y	Y	Y	N	Y
KENTUCKY								
1 Hubbard	N	N	N	Y	Y	N	N	N
2 Natcher	Y	Y	N	N	N	N	N	Y
3 Mazzoli	Y	Y	N	Y	Y	N	Y	Y
4 ***Snyder***	Y	Y	Y	Y	N	N	N	Y
5 ***Rogers***	Y	Y	Y	Y	N	N	N	Y
6 ***Hopkins***	Y	Y	Y	Y	N	N	N	Y
7 Perkins	Y	N	N	N	N	N	N	Y
LOUISIANA								
1 ***Livingston***	Y	Y	Y	Y	Y	N	Y	Y
2 Boggs	Y	N	N	N	Y	N	Y	Y
3 Tauzin	N	Y	Y	N	Y	Y	N	Y
4 Roemer	Y	Y	N	Y	Y	Y	N	Y
5 Huckaby	N	Y	Y	Y	Y	Y	N	Y
6 ***Moore***	N	Y	Y	Y	Y	Y	N	Y
7 Breaux	N	Y	Y	N	Y	Y	Y	Y
8 Long	Y	N	N	N	Y	N	Y	Y
MAINE								
1 ***Emery***	Y	Y	Y	Y	Y	Y	N	Y
2 ***Snowe***	Y	Y	Y	Y	Y	N	Y	Y
MARYLAND								
1 Dyson	N	Y	N	Y	N	N	N	Y
2 Long	Y	Y	N	N	N	N	Y	Y
3 Mikulski	N	N	N	N	N	N	Y	N
4 ***Holt***	Y	Y	Y	Y	Y	N	N	Y
5 Hoyer [2]			N	N	Y	N	Y	N
6 Byron	N	Y	Y	Y	Y	N	N	N
7 Mitchell	Y	N	N	N	N	N	Y	N
8 Barnes	Y	N	N	N	N	N	Y	N
MASSACHUSETTS								
1 ***Conte***	Y	Y	Y	Y	Y	N	Y	?
2 Boland	Y	N	N	N	Y	N	#	N
3 Early	N	N	N	N	N	N	?	N
4 Frank	Y	N	N	N	Y	N	Y	N
5 Shannon	Y	N	N	N	Y	N	?	N
6 Mavroules	Y	N	N	N	Y	N	Y	N
7 Markey	Y	N	N	N	Y	N	Y	N
8 O'Neill [3]			N	N				
9 Moakley	Y	N	N	N	Y	N	Y	N
10 ***Heckler***	Y	Y	Y	Y	N	N	Y	N
11 Donnelly	Y	N	N	N	Y	N	N	N
12 Studds	Y	N	N	N	N	N	Y	N
MICHIGAN								
1 Conyers	Y	N	N	N	N	N	N	N
2 ***Pursell***	Y	Y	Y	Y	Y	N	#	N
3 Wolpe	Y	N	N	N	N	N	Y	N
4 ***Siljander*** [4]		Y	Y	Y	Y	Y	Y	N
5 ***Sawyer***	Y	Y	Y	Y	Y	Y	Y	Y
6 ***Dunn***	N	Y	Y	Y	Y	Y	N	Y
7 Kildee	Y	N	N	N	N	N	Y	N
8 Traxler	Y	N	N	N	N	N	?	N
9 ***Vander Jagt***	Y	Y	Y	Y	Y	Y	Y	Y
10 Albosta	Y	Y	N	N	N	N	?	N
11 ***Davis***	Y	Y	Y	Y	N	N	N	N
12 Bonior	Y	N	N	N	N	N	Y	N
13 Crockett	Y	N	N	N	N	N	?	N
14 Hertel	N	N	N	N	N	N	Y	N
15 Ford	Y	N	N	N	N	N	N	?
16 Dingell	Y	N	N	N	Y	N	Y	Y
17 Brodhead	Y	N	N	N	Y	N	N	N
18 Blanchard	Y	N	N	N	N	N	N	?
19 ***Broomfield***	Y	Y	Y	Y	Y	Y	Y	X
MINNESOTA								
1 ***Erdahl***	Y	Y	Y	Y	Y	N	Y	Y
2 ***Hagedorn***	Y	Y	Y	Y	Y	Y	Y	Y
3 ***Frenzel***	Y	Y	Y	Y	Y	Y	Y	Y
4 Vento	Y	N	N	N	N	N	Y	?
5 Sabo	Y	N	N	N	Y	N	Y	N
6 ***Weber***	Y	Y	Y	Y	Y	Y	N	N
7 ***Stangeland***	Y	Y	Y	Y	Y	Y	Y	Y
8 Oberstar	Y	N	N	N	N	N	Y	N
MISSISSIPPI								
1 Whitten	Y	N	N	N	N	N	N	Y
2 Bowen	Y	Y	N	Y	N	N	Y	Y
3 Montgomery	Y	Y	Y	Y	Y	Y	N	Y
4 Dowdy [5]				N	N	Y	N	N
5 ***Lott***	Y	Y	Y	Y	Y	Y	N	Y
MISSOURI								
1 Clay	N	N	N	N	N	N	?	N
2 Young	N	Y	N	N	?	N	N	?
3 Gephardt	Y	N	N	N	Y	N	N	N
4 Skelton	Y	Y	N	N	Y	N	N	N
5 Bolling	Y	N	N	N	Y	N	?	?
6 ***Coleman***	Y	Y	Y	Y	Y	Y	N	Y
7 ***Taylor***	Y	Y	Y	Y	Y	Y	N	Y
8 ***Bailey***	Y	Y	Y	Y	Y	Y	N	Y
9 Volkmer	X	Y	N	N	N	N	N	N
10 ***Emerson***	Y	Y	Y	Y	Y	Y	N	Y
MONTANA								
1 Williams	Y	N	N	N	N	N	N	N
2 ***Marlenee***	Y	Y	Y	Y	Y	Y	N	N
NEBRASKA								
1 ***Bereuter***	Y	Y	Y	Y	Y	Y	Y	N
2 ***Daub***	Y	Y	Y	Y	Y	Y	N	N
3 ***Smith***	Y	Y	Y	Y	Y	Y	N	N
NEVADA								
AL Santini	N	Y	Y	Y	Y	N	N	X
NEW HAMPSHIRE								
1 D'Amours	N	N	N	N	N	N	N	N
2 ***Gregg***	#	Y	Y	Y	Y	Y	Y	N
NEW JERSEY								
1 Florio	Y	N	N	N	N	?	Y	N
2 Hughes	N	N	N	N	N	N	N	N
3 Howard	#	N	N	N	N	N	Y	N
4 ***Smith***	Y	Y	Y	Y	N	N	Y	Y
5 ***Fenwick***	Y	Y	Y	Y	Y	N	Y	N
6 ***Forsythe***	Y	Y	Y	Y	Y	Y	Y	Y
7 ***Roukema***	Y	Y	Y	Y	Y	N	Y	N
8 Roe	Y	N	N	N	N	N	Y	N
9 ***Hollenbeck***	Y	Y	Y	Y	N	N	Y	Y
10 Rodino	Y	N	N	N	N	N	N	N
11 Minish	Y	N	N	?	N	N	Y	N
12 ***Rinaldo***	Y	Y	Y	Y	N	N	Y	N
13 ***Courter***	Y	Y	Y	Y	Y	Y	Y	N
14 Guarini	Y	N	N	N	N	N	N	N
15 Dwyer	Y	N	N	N	N	N	Y	X
NEW MEXICO								
1 ***Lujan***	N	Y	Y	Y	Y	Y	N	N
2 ***Skeen***	Y	Y	Y	Y	Y	Y	N	Y
NEW YORK								
1 ***Carney***	N	Y	Y	Y	Y	N	Y	N
2 Downey	Y	N	N	N	N	N	Y	N
3 ***Carman***	N	Y	Y	Y	N	Y	Y	N
4 ***Lent***	Y	Y	Y	Y	N	Y	Y	N
5 ***McGrath***	N	Y	Y	Y	N	Y	Y	N
6 ***LeBoutillier***	Y	Y	Y	Y	Y	Y	Y	N
7 Addabbo	Y	N	N	N	Y	N	Y	N
8 Rosenthal	?	N	N	N	N	N	?	N
9 Ferraro	N	N	N	N	N	N	Y	N
10 Biaggi	Y	N	N	Y	N	N	?	N
11 Scheuer	Y	N	N	N	N	N	Y	N
12 Chisholm	Y	N	N	N	Y	?	?	N
13 Solarz	Y	N	N	N	N	N	Y	N
14 Richmond	Y	N	N	N	?	N	#	Y
15 Zeferetti	X	N	N	N	Y	N	Y	N
16 Schumer	Y	N	N	N	N	N	Y	N
17 ***Molinari***	N	Y	Y	Y	Y	Y	Y	N
18 ***Green***	Y	Y	Y	Y	Y	N	Y	Y
19 Rangel	#	N	N	N	N	N	Y	N
20 Weiss	Y	N	N	N	N	N	Y	N
21 Garcia	Y	N	N	N	N	N	?	N
22 Bingham	Y	N	N	N	N	N	Y	N
23 Peyser	Y	N	N	N	N	N	Y	N
24 Ottinger	N	N	N	N	N	N	Y	N
25 ***Fish***	Y	Y	Y	Y	N	N	#	N
26 ***Gilman***	Y	Y	Y	Y	N	N	Y	N
27 McHugh	Y	N	N	N	N	N	Y	N
28 Stratton	Y	N	N	N	N	N	Y	Y
29 ***Solomon***	X	Y	Y	Y	Y	Y	N	N
30 ***Martin***	Y	Y	Y	Y	Y	Y	N	N
31 ***Mitchell***	Y	Y	Y	Y	Y	N	Y	N
32 ***Wortley***	Y	Y	Y	Y	Y	Y	Y	N
33 ***Lee***	Y	Y	Y	Y	Y	Y	N	N
34 ***Horton***	Y	Y	Y	Y	Y	N	Y	N
35 ***Conable***	Y	Y	Y	Y	Y	Y	Y	Y
36 LaFalce	Y	N	N	N	N	N	Y	?
37 Nowak	Y	N	N	N	N	N	?	N
38 ***Kemp***	Y	Y	Y	Y	Y	Y	Y	Y
39 Lundine	?	N	N	Y	N	N	Y	N
NORTH CAROLINA								
1 Jones	Y	N	N	N	Y	?	N	Y
2 Fountain	N	Y	N	Y	Y	Y	N	Y
3 Whitley	Y	N	N	N	Y	Y	?	Y
4 Andrews	?	Y	N	N	Y	Y	N	Y
5 Neal	N	N	N	N	N	N	N	Y
6 ***Johnston***	N	Y	Y	Y	Y	?	Y	Y
7 Rose	?	N	N	N	Y	N	?	Y
8 Hefner	Y	N	N	N	Y	N	X	Y
9 ***Martin***	Y	Y	Y	Y	N	Y	N	Y
10 ***Broyhill***	Y	Y	Y	Y	Y	Y	N	Y
11 ***Hendon***	N	Y	Y	Y	Y	Y	N	Y
NORTH DAKOTA								
AL Dorgan	Y	N	N	N	Y	N	Y	N
OHIO								
1 ***Gradison***	Y	Y	Y	Y	Y	Y	Y	N
2 Luken	Y	Y	N	Y	N	N	Y	N
3 Hall	?	Y	N	N	Y	N	Y	N
4 ***Oxley*** [6]				Y	Y	Y	Y	Y
5 ***Latta***	Y	Y	Y	Y	Y	Y	N	Y
6 ***McEwen***	Y	Y	Y	Y	Y	Y	N	Y
7 ***Brown***	Y	Y	Y	Y	Y	?	?	Y
8 ***Kindness***	Y	Y	Y	Y	Y	Y	N	N
9 ***Weber***	Y	Y	Y	Y	Y	Y	Y	Y
10 ***Miller***	N	Y	Y	Y	Y	Y	N	N
11 ***Stanton***	Y	Y	Y	Y	Y	Y	Y	Y
12 Shamansky	Y	N	N	N	N	N	Y	N
13 Pease	Y	N	N	N	N	N	?	N
14 Seiberling	Y	N	N	N	N	N	Y	N
15 ***Wylie***	Y	Y	Y	Y	Y	Y	Y	Y
16 ***Regula***	Y	Y	Y	Y	Y	Y	Y	N
17 ***Ashbrook***	N	Y	Y	Y	Y	Y	N	Y
18 Applegate	N	N	N	N	N	N	N	N
19 ***Williams***	Y	Y	Y	Y	Y	N	?	N
20 Oakar	Y	N	N	N	N	N	?	N
21 Stokes	Y	N	N	N	N	N	Y	N
22 Eckart	N	N	N	N	N	N	Y	N
23 Mottl	N	Y	N	Y	N	Y	?	N
OKLAHOMA								
1 Jones	Y	N	N	N	Y	N	N	Y
2 Synar	Y	N	N	N	N	N	Y	N
3 Watkins	N	N	N	N	Y	N	N	N
4 McCurdy	N	N	N	Y	Y	N	N	N
5 ***Edwards***	Y	Y	Y	Y	Y	Y	N	Y
6 English	N	Y	N	Y	Y	N	N	N
OREGON								
1 AuCoin	N	N	N	N	N	N	?	?
2 ***Smith***	N	Y	Y	Y	Y	Y	N	Y
3 Wyden	N	N	N	N	N	N	Y	N
4 Weaver	N	N	N	N	N	N	N	N
PENNSYLVANIA								
1 Foglietta	Y	N	N	N	N	N	Y	N
2 Gray	Y	N	N	N	N	N	Y	N
3 Smith [7]				N	Y	N	Y	N
4 ***Dougherty***	Y	Y	N	Y	Y	N	Y	N
5 ***Schulze***	Y	Y	Y	Y	Y	Y	N	Y
6 Yatron	N	Y	N	Y	N	N	?	N
7 Edgar	N	N	N	N	N	N	Y	N
8 ***Coyne, J.***	Y	Y	Y	Y	Y	Y	Y	N
9 ***Shuster***	Y	Y	Y	Y	Y	Y	N	Y
10 ***McDade***	Y	Y	Y	Y	Y	N	N	?
11 ***Nelligan***	Y	Y	Y	Y	Y	N	N	Y
12 Murtha	Y	N	N	N	Y	N	Y	N
13 ***Coughlin***	Y	Y	Y	Y	Y	Y	Y	N
14 Coyne, W.	Y	N	N	N	N	N	Y	N
15 ***Ritter***	Y	Y	Y	Y	Y	Y	N	N
16 ***Walker***	Y	Y	Y	Y	Y	Y	N	N
17 Ertel	Y	N	N	N	N	N	?	N
18 Walgren	Y	N	N	N	N	N	?	N
19 ***Goodling***	Y	Y	Y	Y	Y	N	N	N
20 Gaydos	N	N	N	N	Y	N	N	?
21 Bailey	Y	N	N	N	Y	N	N	Y
22 Murphy	N	N	N	N	N	N	?	N
23 ***Clinger***	Y	Y	Y	Y	Y	N	Y	Y
24 ***Marks***	Y	Y	Y	Y	Y	Y	?	Y
25 ***Atkinson*** [8]	N	Y	N	Y	N	Y	N	Y
RHODE ISLAND								
1 St Germain	Y	N	N	N	N	N	?	N
2 ***Schneider***	Y	Y	N	Y	N	N	Y	N
SOUTH CAROLINA								
1 ***Hartnett***	Y	Y	Y	Y	Y	Y	#	Y
2 ***Spence***	N	Y	Y	Y	Y	Y	N	Y
3 Derrick	N	Y	N	N	Y	N	N	Y
4 ***Campbell***	Y	Y	Y	Y	Y	Y	Y	Y
5 Holland	Y	Y	Y	N	Y	N	?	?
6 ***Napier***	Y	Y	Y	Y	N	?	N	Y
SOUTH DAKOTA								
1 Daschle	N	N	N	N	N	N	N	N
2 ***Roberts***	N	Y	Y	Y	Y	?	N	N
TENNESSEE								
1 ***Quillen***	Y	Y	Y	Y	Y	Y	X	#
2 ***Duncan***	Y	Y	Y	Y	Y	Y	?	Y
3 Bouquard [9]	N	Y	N	Y	N	N	N	N
4 Gore	Y	N	N	N	N	N	Y	N
5 Boner	N	N	N	Y	Y	Y	N	N
6 ***Beard***	Y	Y	Y	Y	Y	?	?	Y
7 Jones	N	Y	N	Y	Y	N	X	N
8 Ford	Y	N	N	N	N	N	Y	P
TEXAS								
1 Hall, S.	N	Y	Y	Y	Y	Y	N	N
2 Wilson	Y	Y	Y	N	N	N	Y	N
3 ***Collins***	N	Y	Y	Y	Y	Y	N	Y
4 Hall, R.	N	Y	N	Y	N	Y	N	N
5 Mattox	N	N	N	N	N	N	Y	N
6 Gramm	Y	Y	Y	Y	Y	Y	N	Y
7 ***Archer***	Y	Y	Y	Y	Y	Y	N	N
8 ***Fields***	N	Y	Y	Y	Y	Y	N	Y
9 Brooks	N	N	N	N	N	N	?	Y
10 Pickle	Y	N	N	N	Y	Y	Y	Y
11 Leath	N	Y	Y	Y	Y	Y	N	N
12 Wright	Y	N	N	N	N	N	?	Y
13 Hightower	Y	Y	Y	Y	N	N	N	N
14 Patman	N	N	N	N	N	N	N	N
15 de la Garza	N	N	N	Y	Y	N	N	Y
16 White	Y	Y	Y	N	N	N	N	Y
17 Stenholm	Y	Y	Y	Y	Y	Y	N	N
18 Leland	?	N	N	N	N	N	Y	N
19 Hance	Y	Y	Y	Y	Y	Y	?	N
20 Gonzalez	Y	N	N	N	N	N	N	N
21 ***Loeffler***	Y	Y	Y	Y	Y	Y	Y	Y
22 ***Paul***	N	Y	Y	Y	Y	Y	N	N
23 Kazen	N	N	N	N	N	N	N	Y
24 Frost	Y	N	N	N	Y	N	Y	N
UTAH								
1 ***Hansen***	N	Y	Y	Y	Y	Y	N	Y
2 ***Marriott***	Y	Y	Y	Y	Y	?	N	Y
VERMONT								
AL ***Jeffords***	Y	Y	Y	N	N	N	Y	N
VIRGINIA								
1 ***Trible***	Y	Y	Y	Y	Y	Y	N	Y
2 ***Whitehurst***	Y	Y	Y	Y	Y	Y	?	?
3 ***Bliley***	Y	Y	Y	Y	Y	Y	Y	Y
4 ***Daniel, R.***	Y	Y	Y	Y	Y	Y	N	Y
5 Daniel, D.	Y	Y	Y	Y	Y	Y	N	Y
6 ***Butler***	Y	Y	Y	Y	Y	Y	Y	Y
7 ***Robinson***	Y	Y	Y	Y	Y	Y	N	Y
8 ***Parris***	Y	Y	Y	Y	Y	?	N	Y
9 ***Wampler***	Y	Y	Y	Y	Y	N	N	Y
10 ***Wolf***	Y	Y	Y	Y	N	Y	Y	Y
WASHINGTON								
1 ***Pritchard***	Y	Y	Y	Y	Y	N	Y	N
2 Swift	Y	N	N	N	Y	N	Y	N
3 Bonker	Y	N	N	N	Y	N	Y	Y
4 ***Morrison***	Y	Y	Y	Y	Y	Y	Y	Y
5 Foley	Y	N	N	N	Y	N	Y	Y
6 Dicks	Y	N	N	Y	Y	N	Y	Y
7 Lowry	Y	N	N	N	Y	N	Y	N
WEST VIRGINIA								
1 Mollohan	Y	N	N	N	Y	N	Y	N
2 ***Benedict***	Y	Y	Y	Y	Y	Y	N	Y
3 ***Staton***	N	Y	Y	Y	Y	Y	X	Y
4 Rahall	#	N	N	N	N	N	N	N
WISCONSIN								
1 Aspin	Y	N	N	N	N	N	?	N
2 Kastenmeier	N	N	N	N	N	N	N	N
3 ***Gunderson***	N	Y	Y	Y	Y	Y	N	N
4 Zablocki	Y	N	N	N	Y	N	Y	N
5 Reuss	Y	N	N	N	N	N	Y	N
6 ***Petri***	Y	Y	Y	Y	Y	Y	N	N
7 Obey	N	N	N	N	N	N	N	N
8 ***Roth***	N	Y	Y	Y	Y	Y	N	N
9 ***Sensenbrenner***	N	Y	Y	Y	Y	Y	N	N
WYOMING								
AL ***Cheney***	Y	Y	Y	Y	Y	Y	Y	Y

Southern states - Ala., Ark., Fla., Ga., Ky., La., Miss., N.C., Okla., S.C., Tenn., Texas, Va.

1982 Key Votes

Senate

1. Fiscal 1983 Budget

Congress gave short shrift to President Reagan's fiscal 1983 budget, in marked contrast to its ratification of Reagan's initial budget in 1981. But it took the lawmakers months to fashion their own substitute for the president's blueprint, which had called for further sweeping cuts in domestic spending combined with unprecedented increases in military programs.

Senate Republicans ultimately succeeded May 21 in pushing through their fiscal 1983 budget proposal (S Con Res 92) on a near party-line vote of 49-43: R 46-2; D 3-41 (ND 1-28, SD 2-13).

Senate action followed the collapse of prolonged efforts by White House and bipartisan congressional negotiators to draft a compromise plan. The White House agreed to some concessions only after the Republican-controlled Senate Budget Committee unanimously repudiated the president's budget and prepared to report a budget resolution the administration did not support.

Senate Republicans successfully fended off Democratic attempts to restore funding for many domestic programs and to repeal the third installment of the 1981 individual income tax cut. But in order to secure passage, GOP leaders acceded to pressure from moderate Republicans and partisan sniping from Democrats to eliminate from the resolution reported by the Budget Committee a proposal to reduce the cost of Social Security benefits by $40 billion over three years.

The Senate-passed resolution called for $784.3 billion in spending, $668.4 billion in revenues and a $115.9 billion deficit in fiscal 1983. The measure included reconciliation instructions that required Senate and House committees to recommend legislative savings to meet the resolution's deficit reduction targets.

The House June 10 adopted a Republican substitute for President Reagan's fiscal 1983 budget by a narrow 220-207 margin. *(House key vote 3)*

2. Emergency Housing Aid

Senate Republicans signaled their willingness to break with President Reagan over providing aid to the troubled economy when they voted May 27 for a $5.1 billion housing aid program. Despite Reagan's strong opposition to the housing industry "bailout," the Senate approved the amendment offered by Richard G. Lugar, R-Ind., by a vote of 69-23: R 29-20; D 40-3 (ND 27-1, SD 13-2).

The amendment to the fiscal 1982 "urgent" supplemental appropriations bill (HR 5922) would have provided mortgage interest rate assistance to buyers of new homes. It would have allowed families with incomes of up to $37,000 a year to get subsidies to lower their interest rate by up to 4 percentage points on mortgages of up to $77,600.

Under heavy political pressure to do something about high unemployment in an election year, Lugar and other Republican backers of the amendment argued that high interest rates were preventing all but the wealthiest families from being able to buy a new home. They said interest rate subsidies would spur new construction, create up to 700,000 new jobs and help lead the economy out of its deep recession.

Although the aid was reduced to $3 billion in conference with the House, which had passed a $1 billion housing measure, Reagan followed through on his threat to veto the bill, and the housing program never went into effect. *(House key vote 1)*

3. Tobacco Price Supports

The perils-of-Pauline existence of the tobacco price-support program was illustrated by a July 14 Senate vote of 49-47: R 29-23; D 20-24 (ND 7-23, SD 13-1) to preserve the program's permanent status in law.

The vote came the week before the Senate soundly overrode tobacco state efforts to kill a plan to double the excise taxes on cigarettes and then adopted a conciliatory compromise to repeal the increase on Sept. 30, 1985.

At issue July 14 was an industry-backed bill (HR 6590) designed to silence tobacco's critics by making new assessments on tobacco growers to help pay the costs of the price-support program. The vote killed an amendment by Sen. Thomas F. Eagleton, D-Mo., that would have ended tobacco's permanent authorization by continuing it just through 1985, when other major commodity programs were scheduled to expire.

Permanent status in the past helped tobacco allies evade debate and votes on the program. Nevertheless, foes had become more and more vocal, criticizing what they called a politically protected "feudal" system of federal allotments and quotas, which amounted to licenses to grow the lucrative crop.

In 1981, critics forced a series of votes on the program. At one point the Senate came within 11 votes of canceling the program altogether, and the 1981 farm bill (PL 97-98) required that the program be operated at no net cost to the Treasury.

4. Western Water Law

Moving to end a longstanding fight between environmentalists and Western farmers, Congress rewrote an 80-year-old law governing the use of federal irrigation water on private farm land. The bill cleared by Congress raised price farmers pay for some of the water and greatly increased the number of federally irrigated acres an individual could farm.

Advocates said the changes recognized modern farming practices in Western states that were served by federal water reclamation projects. They also claimed that the new

law would encourage water conservation and the development of smaller farms, as environmentalists wanted. But angry environmental groups were not satisfied and called the measure a sellout to large corporate farms, some of which controlled thousands of cheaply irrigated acres.

Acting on those objections, Sen. Howard M. Metzenbaum, D-Ohio, delayed floor action on the measure for several days, using quorum calls and other dilatory tactics. He broke off his mini-filibuster only when bill sponsors agreed to offer a compromise amendment raising prices for some of the water above those of the committee bill and reducing new farm acreage limits somewhat. On July 16, the Senate adopted the compromise by a 60-5 vote.

With the logjam broken, the Senate then passed the bill (HR 5539) by a 49-13 vote, clearing the way for a House-Senate conference and enactment of the law: R 30-3; D 19-10 (ND 12-10, SD 7-9).

5. Tax/Spending Reconciliation

One of the most difficult pieces of legislation to be enacted in the 97th Congress was a bill (HR 4961) to raise taxes $98.3 billion and to cut spending $17.5 billion over three years.

Not only did it come shortly before the midterm elections, but support of the measure meant an about-face for many members from the tax-cutting themes they had espoused the year before. In addition, provisions calling for higher tobacco taxes and the withholding of tax from interest and dividend income proved particularly troublesome to many members.

But in the end, Senate Finance Committee Chairman Robert Dole, R-Kan., was able to push a carefully crafted package through the reluctant Senate. He did so in part by threatening to take the bill back to committee and substitute even more unpopular tax hikes for any provisions defeated on the floor.

Members were caught in a bind since they already had voted to raise the $98.3 billion as a deficit-reducing measure in the fiscal 1983 budget resolution (S Con Res 92) adopted May 21. *(Senate key vote 1)*

The final vote on passage of the bill early July 23 was close — 50-47: R 49-3; D 1-44 (ND 0-30, SD 1-14). Democrats, with the exception of Independent Harry F. Byrd Jr., Va., who caucused with the minority party, did nothing to help Republicans out of their fiscal predicament.

That left the House with two choices: to come up with its own tax-increase package or go directly to conference with the Senate. By a 208-197 vote, the House July 28 opted to proceed to conference. *(House key vote 5)*

6. Balanced Budget Constitutional Amendment

Balanced-budget lobbying groups and Senate fiscal conservatives scored a victory Aug. 4 as the Senate approved a proposed constitutional amendment (S J Res 58) requiring a balanced federal budget except in times of declared war or when three-fifths of the Congress agreed to deficit spending. The vote was also a victory for President Reagan, who endorsed the amendment even as he presided over record deficits.

The vote was 69-31, two more than the two-thirds of those present and voting (67 in this case) required to pass a constitutional amendment: R 47-7; D 22-24 (ND 9-22, SD 13-2).

Despite election-year jitters and pressure from Rea-

gan, the House subsequently defeated the balanced budget amendment 236-187, 46 votes short of the two-thirds required. *(House key vote 9)*

S J Res 58 won the backing of Robert Dole, R-Kan., chairman of the Finance Committee, and Pete V. Domenici, R-N.M., chairman of the Budget Committee, although Domenici did not support the measure until he secured a package of amendments he said added more flexibility to the amendment. Appropriations Chairman Mark O. Hatfield, R-Ore., also voted for the measure.

Proponents contended that a constitutional amendment was needed to force fiscal discipline upon Congress. But opponents said the amendment was unworkable and complained that while Congress would have to adopt a balanced budget, the president could submit a document with deficit spending.

Opponents conceded at the outset, however, that their fight was a tough one. They said many senators were unwilling to oppose the amendment publicly because it would look like a vote against the concept of balanced budgets.

7. Cap on Federal COLAs

Efforts to limit automatic cost-of-living adjustments (COLAs) in federal retirement programs illustrated the difficulties confronting Congress as it set out to curb spending under government entitlement programs, which guarantee a certain level of benefits to all persons who meet the requirements set by law.

Although the fiscal 1983 budget resolution (S Con Res 92) had recommended a 4 percent cap on COLAs for federal and military retirees to meet its deficit reduction requirements, a more modest limit on COLA spending barely squeaked through Congress as part of the Omnibus Reconciliation Act of 1982.

The Senate Aug. 4 narrowly defeated by a 48-51 vote — R 10-44; D 38-7 (ND 30-1, SD 8-6) — an amendment to eliminate a 4 percent COLA cap for federal and military retirees from its version of the reconciliation bill (S 2774).

The Senate action came one day after the House snubbed its reconciliation instructions by refusing to impose the COLA cap. Senate-House conferees ultimately settled on a plan to delay federal COLA increases by one month in each of the next three years and to cut in half COLAs for federal retirees under age 62, for three-year budget savings of $4.1 billion.

Budget leaders applauded the move as a first step toward controlling automatic increases in Social Security and other federal benefit programs. "This is a historic change," said Senate Budget Committee Chairman Pete V. Domenici, R-N.M.

8. Veto Override

Smacking President Reagan with his first significant budget defeat, Congress Sept. 10 overrode his Aug. 28 veto of a $14.2 billion supplemental appropriations bill (HR 6863) that he called a "budget buster."

Reagan objected that the bill cut his request for defense spending while providing $918 million too much for social spending — money he had not requested and some of which he had previously vetoed.

Members of Congress denied the bill was a budget buster. They pointed out that it was nearly $2 billion under Reagan's total request for additional fiscal 1982 funding. Congress, they said, had simply put its own stamp on the

spending priorities, allowing less for the military and more for education and jobs for senior citizens.

Returning from its Labor Day recess, the House voted to override the veto Sept. 9 by a vote of 301-117. *(House key vote 7)*

Worried by the unexpectedly strong override vote in the House, the White House lobbied furiously to get senators to stick with the president. It even arranged to have several flown back to Washington for the vote. But despite Reagan's personal pleas to many senators and the presence of Vice President George Bush in the chamber, the Republican-controlled Senate Sept. 10 also voted to override. The margin was as close as it could get — 60-30, the exact two-thirds majority required: R 21-26; D 39-4 (ND 31-0, SD 8-4).

Appropriations Committee Chairman Mark O. Hatfield, R-Ore., who had caught a late-night flight from Oregon to lead the Senate fight for the override, said Reagan had acted on "very poor advice."

Of the 11 Republican senators up for re-election in 1982, seven voted against Reagan, two voted with him and two were absent.

9. Abortion

Efforts to pass anti-abortion legislation came to a halt in the Senate Sept. 15 after members grew weary of a filibuster and voted to lay aside a proposal designed to virtually ban abortion.

The vote marked the end of an 18-month drive by a handful of senators and interest groups who had hoped that the Republican takeover of the Senate in the 97th Congress would result in legislation sharply restricting a woman's right to an abortion.

The showdown came on an anti-abortion amendment by Sen. Jesse Helms, R-N.C., to unrelated debt limit legislation (H J Res 520). A week-long effort by President Reagan in support of the Helms proposal was to no avail, as one-third of the Senate's Republicans voted with a majority of its Democrats to kill the amendment.

The vote on the motion to table, and thus kill, the Helms anti-abortion amendment, which technically was an amendment to a separate Helms school prayer amendment to the debt bill, was 47-46: R 18-33; D 29-13 (ND 22-7, SD 7-6).

The underlying school prayer amendment was derailed Sept. 23 when the Senate by a 79-16 vote adopted a motion by Majority Leader Howard H. Baker Jr., R-Tenn., to recommit the debt ceiling measure to the Finance Committee with instructions to strip off all amendments.

Throughout the six-week Senate debate on abortion and school prayer, opponents labeled both Helms amendments "court-stripping" proposals, charging they would unwisely and unconstitutionally infringe upon the power of the federal courts to review laws enacted by the states and Congress.

10. Senators' Income Limits

In 1977, as a condition for taking a $12,900 pay raise, both House and Senate agreed to strict ethics codes for members. One provision in both codes limited the outside earnings of senators and representatives to 15 percent of their salaries.

This limit was to apply only to earned income, such as honoraria for speeches or legal work, not to unearned in-

come, such as dividend payments. A separate 1976 law (PL 94-283) had limited the net amount members could receive in honoraria for speeches, appearances or articles to $25,000 annually.

However, in 1979, when the 15 percent limit on outside income in the Senate was to take effect, members voted to delay the effective date until Jan. 1, 1983.

And in 1981, Congress repealed the $25,000 honoraria limit. Some senators earned as much as $48,000 during that year.

As the 1983 effective date for the 15 percent limit approached, the Senate Dec. 14, with little debate, approved a resolution (S Res 512) abolishing that restriction as well. The vote was 54-38: R 39-12; D 15-26 (ND 9-19, SD 6-7).

Fourteen senators who had voted for the 15 percent limit in 1977 switched in 1982 and voted to abolish it.

No House action was required. The change meant that senators could earn as much as they chose beyond their Senate salary by giving speeches, practicing law or any other legal means.

The Senate's decision also laid the groundwork for a salary deal with the House. As part of the second continuing resolution (H J Res 631), representatives, who retained a 30 percent limit on outside income, got a 15 percent pay raise. Senators got no raise but had no ceilings on outside income. *(House key vote 12)*

11. MX Missile

President Reagan won the Senate round of his battle to begin production of the MX missile, but only after he had substantially compromised with congressional critics of the so-called "dense pack" basing method.

On Nov. 22, Reagan proposed deployment of 100 MXs in heavily armored underground silos close together. He argued that attacking Soviet missile warheads would destroy each other while leaving most of the MXs unscathed.

He argued that the new, more powerful land-based MX missile was needed to offset Moscow's arsenal of ICBM warheads, which were more numerous and more powerful than current U.S. weapons. He also maintained that the Russians would agree to reduce their nuclear arsenals only if confronted by clear indications that the United States would match Soviet forces if no arms control agreement was reached.

The House voted Dec. 7 against appropriating money for procurement of the missile. *(House key vote 11)*

On Dec. 15, the Senate Appropriations Committee adopted 16-12 an amendment that left the MX procurement money in the second fiscal 1983 continuing resolution (H J Res 631) that contained appropriations for the Defense Department, but barred its expenditure until Congress approved an MX basing method by concurrent resolution.

The White House and senior senators of both parties who supported MX then drafted an amendment to the committee provision that would guarantee congressional action within 45 days of the time the president submitted a report to Congress on dense pack and various alternative basing methods.

This would preclude a filibuster against a resolution to approve a basing method.

On Dec. 17, the Senate adopted the administration-sanctioned amendment 56-42: R 41-12; D 15-30 (ND 6-24, SD 9-6).

12. Clinch River Breeder Reactor

Twice in 1982, the Senate by a one-vote margin chose to continue funding for the controversial Clinch River nuclear breeder reactor.

The votes were a test of strength for Senate Majority Leader Howard H. Baker Jr., R-Tenn., whose state was the home of the Clinch River site. Support for the project in both houses of Congress had been declining in recent years, and traditionally pro-nuclear conservative groups such as the Heritage Foundation had gone on record against it.

"If it were not for the majority leader, if it were not being built in his state, it would long ago have been terminated," Dale Bumpers, D-Ark., said Dec. 17, after the Senate upheld the project for the second time. Baker reportedly herded some of his Republican colleagues who were reluctant to take a stand on the issue onto the Senate floor during the final minutes of the vote.

That vote came just three days after the House had voted 217-196 to kill Clinch River. (*House key vote 13*)

A compromise agreement later was worked out in conference that continued funding at the 1982 level for engineering and site preparation but prohibited construction of any major facilities.

The Clinch River project, authorized in 1970, was designed to demonstrate the feasibility of breeder reactors — nuclear power reactors that run on plutonium and create, as a byproduct, more plutonium than they consume. The reactor originally was scheduled to be completed in 1983 but because of controversy and delays, ground was not broken until September 1982. Official cost estimates of the project soared from $700 million to $3.6 billion, while the need for the reactor became more difficult to demonstrate.

The Senate first took up the issue Sept. 29, when it defeated a Bumpers amendment to delete Clinch River funds from the first fiscal 1983 continuing appropriations resolution (H J Res 599). After losing by a single vote then, opponents hoped they could win the vote on the second continuing resolution (H J Res 631) in December. But the Appropriations Committee amendment reinstating the Clinch River funds, which had been deleted by the House, passed 49-48: R 38-14; D 11-34 (ND 4-26, SD 7-8).

13. Doctors, Federal Trade Commission

Congressional allies of the Federal Trade Commission (FTC) blocked an attempt to exempt doctors and other professionals from agency jurisdiction.

Their success came seven months after both the House and Senate overwhelmingly vetoed an FTC rule requiring used-car dealers to disclose information about auto defects.

The American Medical Association (AMA) had lobbied successfully to include the exemption for doctors and other state-regulated professionals in a House-passed authorization bill and a Senate committee bill. The AMA said that Congress had not given the FTC authority to regulate doctors and that the agency had interfered with quality of care issues.

Administration officials, the FTC and others argued that the FTC had authority to regulate anti-competitive business practices of professionals, such as price-setting and boycotts, and should be allowed to retain that power.

Opponents of the exemption blocked it on three fronts: an FTC authorization, a regular appropriations bill and the second fiscal 1983 continuing appropriations resolution.

They prevented Senate consideration of an FTC authorization bill that contained the exemption, thereby avoiding a House-Senate conference on the authorization.

Then because there was no authorization, the supporters succeeded in getting the House to delete FTC funds from the regular fiscal 1983 State, Justice, Commerce appropriations (HR 6957). That prevented new FTC restrictions, including the exemption for professionals, from being attached to the appropriations bill.

However, the second fiscal 1983 continuing appropriations resolution then before the Senate (H J Res 631) included FTC monies and continued some existing curbs, such as the congressional veto over agency rules. The measure also contained a provision by Warren B. Rudman, R-N.H., allowing the FTC to regulate doctors as long as it did not interfere with state laws governing professional training and experience requirements. Rudman, an opponent of the exemption for professionals, argued that no group should be above the law.

In a session that began Dec. 16, James A. McClure, R-Idaho, offered an amendment to bar the use of FTC funds to regulate professionals. The Senate by a vote of 59-37 adopted a Rudman motion to table, or kill, the McClure amendment: R 31-21; D 28-16 (ND 23-7, SD 5-9).

That allowed the Senate to go to conference with the House with only the less restrictive Rudman language under consideration. When the provision was dropped by the conferees, FTC supporters claimed victory, as did the AMA, which opposed the Rudman provision because even with its qualifications, it gave explicit congressional approval to FTC regulation of professionals.

14. Job Creation

Reacting to a mounting unemployment rate and Democratic election gains, the Senate Appropriations Committee added $1.2 billion for jobs under a variety of public works programs to its version of the second fiscal 1983 continuing appropriations resolution (H J Res 631).

Appropriations Committee Chairman Mark O. Hatfield, R-Ore., argued that "this was the only opportunity the Senate will have" in the lame-duck session to show its concern about jobs.

But Budget Committee Chairman Pete V. Domenici, R-N.M., called the jobs money "pork-barrel personified." He said the Senate should not engage in a bidding war with the House, which had included $5.4 billion for job creation in its version of the funding bill.

Domenici, along with Majority Leader Howard H. Baker Jr., R-Tenn., and Finance Committee Chairman Robert Dole, R-Kan., sought to delete the $1.2 billion for jobs during floor action early Dec. 17. Their amendment was defeated 46-50: R 39-12; D 7-38 (ND 3-27, SD 4-11).

In the House, a Republican motion to recommit the continuing resolution to the Appropriations Committee with instructions to delete the $5.4 billion for jobs programs was rejected 191-215. (*House key vote 14*)

Although both the Senate and House versions of the continuing resolution thus included money for jobs programs, conferees bowed to President Reagan's veto threats and dropped the jobs funding from the final measure.

15. Highway-Gas Tax Bill

A series of filibusters and a host of amendments threatened Senate passage of a bill to raise gasoline taxes for the first time since 1959. The legislation (HR 6211) increasing highway taxes to finance highway, bridge and

mass transit improvements had been wrapped in the aura of a jobs bill, winning both bipartisan congressional support and the backing of the president.

In contrast to the House, which had comfortably approved the package one day after a 197-194 vote Dec. 6 on adoption of a rule for its consideration, the Senate staggered through days and nights of marathon sessions punctuated by bitter debate before passing its version of the bill in a session that began Dec. 20. *(House key vote 10)*

The filibusters started as soon as the Senate began considering the bill Dec. 10. It was unclear whether there would be enough time in the lame-duck session for the Senate to pass the bill and go to conference with the House.

Supporters contended that the bill was necessary to complete the Interstate Highway System, repair the nation's deteriorating transportation infrastructure and help create more than 300,000 new jobs. Under the measure, the gas tax was increased a nickel, to a total of 9 cents a gallon, to raise an additional $5.5 billion a year to help pay for the improvements. Heavy trucks also had to pay higher taxes.

Four Republicans — Jesse Helms, N.C., John P. East, N.C., Gordon J. Humphrey, N.H., and Don Nickles, Okla. — objected to the tax increases, contending that a recession was a bad time to hike taxes.

Their tactics forced a series of time-consuming parliamentary manuevers that left tempers frayed and prompted intensified lobbying by the administration and highway interests. Finally, the Senate passed the bill 56-34: R 35-15; D 21-19 (ND 14-12, SD 7-7).

The Senate version authorized about $70 billion for highways through fiscal 1987 and about $12 billion for mass transit through fiscal 1985, and increased gas and other highway taxes.

A conference report authorizing more than $71 billion for highways and mass transit over four years was adopted by the House Dec. 21. Filbusters continued to delay Senate action until Dec. 23, when it adopted the report.

House

1. Emergency Housing Aid

Facing growing pressure to do something for the recession-hit housing industry, House Democratic leaders agreed to back a $1 billion mortgage interest rate subsidy program. The measure, added as an amendment to the fiscal 1982 "urgent" supplemental appropriations bill (HR 5922), was adopted May 12 by a vote of 343-67: R 128-52; D 215-15 (ND 149-6, SD 66-9).

The amendment was the first in a series of job-creation proposals pushed by House Democrats in 1982 in an effort to counter rapidly rising unemployment.

Actually, the Democratic leadership initially did not want to include the program in the supplemental funding bill, which contained a number of time-sensitive appropriations needed to keep government agencies in operation. President Reagan opposed the housing "bailout," and it seemed destined to lead to a veto of the whole bill.

But the amendment was needed to forestall House approval of a Republican-backed amendment that threatened one of the pet projects of Majority Leader Jim Wright, D-Texas: the synthetic fuels program. Thomas B. Evans Jr., R-Del., and Tom Corcoran, R-Ill., were proposing an amendment to take $1 billion from funds already appropriated for the synfuels program, to be used to create

low-interest housing loans.

When it appeared that the House would approve the Evans-Corcoran amendment, the Democrats came up with their own housing aid program that did not take money from synfuels. With strong lobbying support from the housing industry, the amendment carried easily.

The Senate subsequently passed a $5.1 billion housing aid program. *(Senate key vote 2)*

Conferees compromised on a $3 billion program, but Reagan carried out his veto threat and the program never became law.

2. Medicare Funding

In a clear-cut guns vs. butter vote that led to defeat of the first fiscal 1983 budget resolution (H Con Res 345), the House May 27 agreed to increase Medicare outlays by $4.85 billion while cutting defense spending by the same amount.

The 228-196 vote — R 64-125; D 164-71 (ND 136-20, SD 28-51) — came on an amendment offered by Mary Rose Oakar, D-Ohio, to the administration-backed substitute for the resolution.

Democrats saw in the Oakar amendment a chance to cast their Republican colleagues as people who would "choose a 40-year-old battleship over their 80-year-old mother," as one Democrat put it. Republicans who opposed defense cuts were nonetheless reluctant to be portrayed as voting against the elderly in an election year.

House Minority Leader Robert H. Michel, R-Ill., said adoption of the Oakar amendment was the "margin of difference" that meant defeat for the GOP budget plan. The Oakar amendment also was added to the other major budget alternatives the House was considering, all of which went down to defeat May 27-28.

3. Fiscal 1983 Budget

On its second attempt to pass a budget resolution, the House June 10 adopted a Republican substitute for President Reagan's fiscal 1983 budget, which had been sent to the floor by the House Budget Committee (H Con Res 352). This was the final repudiation of the Reagan budget.

The Senate May 21 had adopted its own version of a fiscal 1983 budget resolution by a vote of 49-43. *(Senate key vote 1)*

By squeezing the deficit below $100 billion and maintaining party discipline, House Republican leaders eked out a narrow 220-207 — R 174-15; D 46-192 (ND 9-151, SD 37-41) — victory for the substitute, named after the ranking Republican member of the Budget Committee, Delbert L. Latta, Ohio. The specter of continued stalemate and fiscal chaos helped assure approval of the resolution, which subsequently passed by a 219-206 margin.

The measure called for $765.17 billion in spending, $665.90 billion in revenues and a $99.27 billion deficit in fiscal 1983. The House resolution followed the same pattern as the Senate version — making further cuts in entitlement and discretionary domestic spending while allowing sizable increases for defense and maintaining the third installment of the 1981 individual income tax cut.

4. Chemical Weapons

The House July 22 rejected an administration move to begin production of a new type of lethal, chemical weapons called "binary munitions."

The administration maintained that the new weapons were needed to prod the Soviet Union to negotiate a chemical weapons ban and to deter use of the large Soviet chemical weapons arsenal. Current U.S. chemical weapons were inadequate for either purpose, the administration argued, because they were becoming unsafe to handle due to internal chemical reactions.

But opponents of production of binary weapons warned that production of the new arms would surrender the valuable propaganda leverage the United States had gained by abstaining from chemical weapons production for the past 13 years. Most of the opponents also maintained that the new weapons were militarily unnecessary. Existing chemical weapons stocks were sufficient to force enemy troops to don clumsy and tiring protective suits and masks, they said.

The showdown came during debate on the fiscal 1983 defense authorization bill (HR 6030) when the House in effect rejected the administration position 192-225: R 112-72; D 80-153 (ND 27-132, SD 53-21).

5. Tax Increases

With an election looming in November, House Democrats gladly let the Republican-controlled Senate take the lead in putting together a tax-increase bill to help reduce the federal budget deficit. *(Senate key vote 5)*

Even though the Constitution requires all tax legislation to originate in the House, Ways and Means Committee Chairman Dan Rostenkowski, D-Ill., made it clear early on that he saw the deficit as a Republican problem and raising taxes as a Republican responsibility.

When the Senate did produce its own package July 22, it was attached to a minor House-passed measure (HR 4961) to address the technical niceties of the Constitution.

That left the House with two choices: to come up with its own tax-increase package or to go directly to conference with the Senate. After a short-lived attempt to produce a tax-hike plan within Ways and Means, Rostenkowski decided it was hopeless. Even if one could pass the committee, floor passage looked doubtful.

The committee agreed to bypass the House and go directly to conference on the Senate bill. The House agreed July 28 by a vote of 208-197: R 44-137; D 164-60 (ND 116-35, SD 48-25).

Despite considerable rhetoric that the House was shirking its constitutional duties, many members were relieved that they would not have their fingerprints on the politically troublesome legislation.

6. Nuclear Freeze

The administration averted by the narrowest of margins a major symbolic rebuff to its nuclear arms policy when the House Aug. 5 rejected a call for a nuclear weapons "freeze."

The freeze proposal had its roots in a far-flung grass-roots movement that had swelled through the spring, fueled largely by doubts that the administration was seriously committed to seeking arms control agreements with Moscow.

As reported by the House Foreign Affairs Committee in late June, the freeze resolution (H J Res 521) called on the United States and Soviet Union to decide "when and how to achieve a mutual verifiable freeze" on the testing, production and deployment of nuclear arms.

This was a direct challenge to the administration's position that the U.S.-Soviet nuclear balance currently was tilted to Moscow's advantage.

The administration and congressional backers drafted an alternative that also called for a "freeze," but with the qualification that it be at "equal and substantially reduced levels," thus endorsing Reagan's position that the current U.S. nuclear weapons deficit would have to be erased in any arms control agreement.

Despite ferocious White House lobbying, Reagan's position prevailed in the House by a margin of only two votes. A switch by one member would have created a tie that would have defeated the administration's alternative.

The administration-backed substitute was approved 204-202: R 151-27; D 53-175 (ND 11-149, SD 42-26).

7. Veto Override

When President Reagan vetoed a $14.2 billion fiscal 1982 supplemental appropriations bill (HR 6863) Aug. 28, he called it a budget buster. While cutting his request for defense spending, he said, the measure contained $918 million for social spending that he had not requested and some of which had been in previously vetoed bills.

But members of Congress insisted the president was simply wrong in his accounting. They noted that the bill was nearly $2 billion under his total request for additional fiscal 1982 funding, and said they supported increased funding for education and for jobs for senior citizens.

When the House returned from its Labor Day recess, a sizable bloc of angry Republicans joined unified Democrats in supplying the two-thirds majority for the House to override the veto. They did it with 22 votes to spare. The Sept. 9 vote to override the president was 301-117: R 81-104; D 220-13 (ND 157-1, SD 63-12).

The Senate made the override stick the next day by a vote of 60-30. It was Reagan's first significant budget defeat. *(Senate key vote 8)*

The president tried to block the override in the House, promising members he would sign a subsequent bill containing employment money for the elderly and that he would not seek additional funds for defense. But the promises came too late for many members who had already committed themselves while in their districts to vote to override. Senior citizen groups and education organizations had lobbied hard for the override.

Helping to lead the House effort against Reagan was Rep. Silvio O. Conte, Mass., the senior Republican on the Appropriations Committee. Calling the veto an affront to Congress, Conte said, "You just don't have 435 robots up here in Congress that are going to vote in lockstep."

8. Pipeline Sanctions

A close vote in the House of Representatives helped prod President Reagan to drop his most visible effort to punish the Soviet Union for its interference in Poland. The vote may also have sparked a reassessment by Congress and the administration of the effectiveness of conducting economic war for political purposes.

The key vote was on Sept. 29, when the House voted 206-203 to weaken a bill (HR 6838) that would have forced Reagan to lift the most controversial of a series of economic sanctions he had imposed on the Soviet Union. A broad range of members in both parties complained that the sanctions hurt American workers and businesses more than

the Soviets. The breakdown on the vote was R 124-57; D 82-146 (ND 41-111, SD 41-35).

The closeness of the vote demonstrated the depth of congressional unhappiness with an important element of Reagan's foreign policy. Administration officials lobbied vigorously against the bill, arguing that passage of the measure would undercut negotiations then under way between the United States and its European allies on trade with the Soviets.

The sanctions prohibited American companies, their foreign subsidiaries and foreign companies using U.S. licenses from selling to the Soviet Union equipment or technology for the transmission or refining of oil and gas. One goal of the sanctions was to prevent the Soviets from using U.S. technology to build a 2,600-mile natural gas pipeline from Siberia to Western Europe.

Reagan himself lifted the pipeline-related sanctions on Nov. 13, saying they had accomplished the purpose of demonstrating U.S. concern with Soviet pressure on Poland. Reagan also said the United States and its Western allies had agreed to conduct a study of ways to limit future trade that bolstered the Soviet economy.

Administration critics, however, said Reagan was merely heeding the signal he had been given by the House vote: that there was little political support for the sanctions, which had failed to change Soviet behavior and had ruptured relations between the United States and its closest allies.

American business leaders said the failure of the sanctions on those counts should make the Reagan administration more hesitant in the future to use trade as a political weapon.

9. Balanced Budget Constitutional Amendment

Despite pressure from President Reagan and pre-election jitters, the House Oct. 1 rejected a proposed constitutional amendment to require a balanced federal budget (H J Res 350).

The vote on the measure was 236-187, 46 short of the two-thirds majority of those present and voting (282 in this case) required to pass a constitutional amendment: R 167-20; D 69-167 (ND 12-147, SD 57-20).

The vote ended a three-day struggle that featured some arm-twisting by Vice President George Bush and an appearance by President Reagan Sept. 30 to drum up support for the amendment.

The maneuvering had begun in earnest Sept. 29 when a group of Republicans led by Bush and Barber B. Conable Jr., R-N.Y., rounded up the last 16 signatures on a discharge petition that pried H J Res 350 from a hostile House Judiciary Committee that had kept the legislation buried for a year.

The Senate Aug. 4 had approved its own version of a balanced budget amendment by a 69-31 vote, two more than the two-thirds required. *(Senate key vote 6)*

Giving impetus to the drive for a balanced budget amendment was a seven-year-old effort by outside groups led by the National Taxpayers Union to force the calling of a constitutional convention to consider a balanced budget proposal.

Under Article V of the Constitution, a convention must be called if two-thirds of the states (34) request one. At the end of 1982, 31 states had made such a request, although there was no agreement on whether all 31 convention calls were valid.

10. Highway-Gas Tax Bill

The opposition of the trucking industry to substantial increases in highway-use taxes for heavy trucks posed a strong threat to House passage of legislation to raise funds for highway, bridge and mass transit improvements.

The bill raised fuel taxes a nickel, for a total of 9 cents a gallon, and increased the maximum highway use tax for an 80,000-pound truck to $2,000, up from $240.

Truckers, contending that the tax increases were too severe, lobbied intensely against the bill. Although there was general backing for the legislation (HR 6211), a fragile coalition of cities, road builders, public transit operators, Republicans, Democrats, administration officials and others was not sure that the House would be able to pass the measure.

Members opposing the truck or fuel taxes attacked the rule (H Res 620) because it allowed amendments to the highway and transit portions of the bill but not to the tax title. They almost succeeded in blocking floor consideration. The rule was adopted Dec. 6 by 197-194: R 59-114; D 138-80 (ND 112-34, SD 26-46).

The bill's supporters, who argued that significant changes in the taxes would jeopardize passage, breathed easier when the House accepted the tax title by a vote of 236-169 at 12:30 a.m., Dec. 7. The House later passed the bill by a 262-143 vote.

In the Senate, a filibuster by a handful of opponents led by Jesse Helms, R-N.C., delayed action on the gas tax bill until just before Christmas. But the measure finally passed Dec. 21 by a 56-34 vote. *(Senate key vote 15)*

11. MX Missile

The House vote Dec. 7 against initial procurement of MX missiles marked the first time that either house of Congress had voted against a major nuclear arms program requested by a president.

Despite strong White House objections, the House deleted from the fiscal 1983 defense appropriations bill (HR 7355) $988 million earmarked for procurement of the first five production line versions of the MX.

The large House majority included liberals who long had opposed MX in any form, for fear that it would elicit from Moscow a further escalation in the arms race. But they were joined by moderates and conservatives who were alarmed at the cost of Reagan's defense buildup and suspicious of the technical feasibility of the so-called "dense pack" basing method for the missile.

In this technique, announced by Reagan on Nov. 22, 100 MXs would be placed close together in heavily armored underground silos. The administration argued that explosions from attacking Soviet missile warheads would destroy other Soviet missiles while leaving most of the MXs unscathed.

Reagan argued that the new, more powerful land-based missile was needed to offset Moscow's arsenal of ICBM warheads, which are more numerous and more powerful than current U.S. weapons. And he said that the new missile was needed to give the Russians an incentive to agree to nuclear arms reductions.

The vote against MX procurement was 245-176: R 50-138; D 195-38 (ND 151-7, SD 44-31).

The Senate Dec. 17 returned MX procurement money to the second fiscal 1983 continuing appropriations resolution but barred its expenditure unless Congress approved a basing mode. *(Senate key vote 11)*

12. House Pay Raise

After more than three years without a pay raise, Congress in December 1982 gave House members a 15 percent increase, bringing salaries to $69,800 a year. Senators stayed at the old rate of $60,662.50.

In October, as part of the first fiscal 1983 continuing appropriations resolution (H J Res 599) Congress had voted to cap its pay, blocking what members then believed would be a 4 percent raise. The resolution, however, was to expire Dec. 17.

While Congress was in its post-election recess, confusion arose over the exact size of the raise members would get if the cap were lifted. The General Accounting Office ruled Dec. 10 that the increase actually would be 27.2 percent. The higher figure included several cost-of-living raises from previous years that Congress had voted not to take.

The issue came to a House vote Dec. 14 as part of the second fiscal 1983 continuing resolution (H J Res 631. Supporters of a raise offered an amendment limiting it to 15 percent — about $9,100. Faced with a raise of either 27.2 percent or 15 percent, the House supported the lower figure on a 303-109 vote.

But then Bob Traxler, D-Mich., offered an amendment to continue the freeze on congressional pay, keeping salaries at $60,662.50.

Only because of substantial help from lame-duck members, who no longer had to answer to the voters, the Traxler amendment failed on a tie, 208-208: R 121-65; D 87-143 (ND 46-109, SD 41-34).

The 71 lame ducks who voted on the Traxler amendment opposed it by 2-to-1, 24-47. While Republicans voted 121-65 for the amendment, 48 Republican lame ducks voted 21-27 against it.

The pay raise for House members but not senators was contained in the final version of the bill. The Senate agreed not to take a raise for itself, but senators retained their prerogative to earn unlimited amounts in outside income. *(Senate key vote 10)*

The result was the first time that representatives had made more than senators. Since the 1st Congress in 1789, members of both chambers had been paid the same, except for one year, 1795-96, when senators were paid $7 a day and representatives $6.

13. Clinch River Breeder Reactor

More than a decade of House support for the controversial Clinch River nuclear breeder reactor ended Dec. 14 when members voted 217-196 to deny funds for the project.

Environmentalists were jubilant. They had opposed the project since its inception, questioning its safety and arguing that it would increase supplies of plutonium that could be used to manufacture nuclear weapons.

But it was budget concerns that finally led the House to reverse its stance on the breeder. Expressing the sentiment of many members who had backed the project previously but voted against it in 1982, Phil Gramm, D-Texas, said, "I have supported Clinch River since I first came to Congress. But as we look at the budget deficit, we have got to set a new higher standard for spending."

The House action was reversed by the Senate three days later, by a one-vote margin, but it nevertheless marked a watershed in the history of the breeder reactor. *(Senate key vote 12)*

The Clinch River project, located near Oak Ridge, Tenn., was authorized in 1970. It was designed to demonstrate the feasibility of breeder reactors — nuclear power reactors that run on plutonium and create as a byproduct more plutonium than they consume. The reactor originally was scheduled for completion in 1983, but it was surrounded by controversy and plagued with delays. Ground was not broken until September 1982. In the meantime, official cost estimates soared from $700 million to $3.6 billion; more than $1.3 billion already had been spent.

The need for the project also had become more difficult to demonstrate. The growth in electricity demand, once expected to rise at a long-term average of 7 percent a year, was projected in 1982 to rise at an average pace of 3 percent a year. And new uranium deposits had been found, reducing fears of a fuel shortage for traditional — and less costly — light water reactors.

Faced with these circumstances, 19 Republicans and 16 Democrats who had supported funding for Clinch River in 1981 voted against it in 1982. The amendment by Lawrence Coughlin, R-Pa., to bar the use of funds for the project was attached to the second fiscal 1983 continuing appropriations resolution (H J Res 631) by a vote of 217-196: R 80-102; D 137-94 (ND 121-33, SD 16-61).

14. Job Creation

The House Appropriations Committee included $5.4 billion for jobs programs in its version of the second fiscal 1983 continuing appropriations resolution (H J Res 631).

In addition to adding funds for existing programs, the measure provided $1 billion for a new jobs program to be run by the Labor Department and $50 million for emergency food and shelter to be distributed by private voluntary agencies.

Many House Republicans opposed the jobs program on grounds that it was a scattershot approach, with a little money for projects in almost every congressional district. They also argued that President Reagan would veto the bill if the funds were included.

A Republican motion to recommit the bill to the Appropriations Committee with instructions to delete the $5.4 billion in jobs money failed Dec. 14 on a 191-215 vote: R 171-7; D 20-208 (ND 2-150, SD 18-58).

Although the Senate version of the resolution also included money for jobs programs, conferees dropped the jobs funding from the final measure to avert a presidential veto. *(Senate key vote 14)*

15. Auto Domestic Content Requirements

As unemployment rose during 1982, so did protectionist sentiment in Congress.

Most of the legislative proposals were directed toward Japan, whose exports to the United States during the year exceeded its imports from the United States by more than $20 billion. "While Japanese cars invade our highways, American workers pay for the defense of Japan," complained Rep. Don J. Pease, D-Ohio.

The most drastic piece of protectionist legislation considered during the year was the domestic content bill (HR 5133). Drafted by the United Auto Workers union (UAW), the measure would have required all companies selling more than 100,000 cars a year in the United States to use a certain proportion of U.S. labor and parts. Toyota and Nissan (Datsun), the major Japanese manufacturers, would

have been forced to use 70 to 75 percent domestic content in the cars they sell here. Toyo Kogyo (Mazda) and Honda would have had to achieve ratios of between 20 and 40 percent.

The bill came under heavy attack from the Reagan administration and from free-traders in Congress. U.S. Trade Representative William E. Brock III called it "the worst piece of economic legislation since the 1930s."

But the UAW lobbied fervently for the bill, and the opposition was much less intense. On Dec. 15, the measure passed the House by a vote of 215-188: R 44-130; D 171-58 (ND 132-20, SD 39-38).

The vote was largely a symbolic one. Even the bill's supporters admitted that it had little chance of passing the Senate in the closing days of the lame-duck session. But they argued that House passage would send a clear signal to Japan, encouraging that nation to change its trading practices.

The signal, however, was made considerably less clear by an amendment successfully sponsored by lame-duck Rep. Millicent Fenwick, R-N.J. Fenwick's amendment said the measure should not "supersede" any "treaty, international convention or agreement on tariffs and trade." The bill's opponents said the domestic content requirements clearly violated the General Agreement on Tariffs and Trade, and therefore Fenwick's amendment "gutted" the bill.

16. Gorsuch Contempt of Congress

Congress and the Reagan administration were at loggerheads on environmental issues for most of the 97th Congress. But a Dec. 16 House vote to cite Environmental Protection Agency (EPA) Administrator Anne M. Gorsuch for contempt of Congress escalated that underlying political conflict into a constitutional showdown. Gorsuch was the highest ranking executive branch official to be cited for contempt of Congress.

Especially in the Democratic-controlled House, members accused the Reagan administration of failing to enforce adequately major provisions of environmental laws that Congress had passed during the 1970s.

The contempt vote grew out of efforts by two House subcommittees to oversee EPA enforcement of the 1980 "superfund" law for cleanup of abandoned hazardous waste dumps. On written orders from President Reagan, Gorsuch withheld enforcement documents subpoenaed by the House Public Works and Transportation Subcommittee on Investigations and Oversight.

The disputed documents included enforcement strategies, legal analysis, witness lists and "settlement considerations." The administration claimed its pursuit of pending cases could be jeopardized if the documents were to become public or fall into the hands of defendants. Subcommittee Chairman Elliott H. Levitas, D-Ga., said that early evidence showed companies responsible for hazardous waste dumping were not being held liable for their full share of cleanup costs and that the documents were needed "to find out whether sweetheart deals are being made."

More than one-third of all House Republicans voting on the contempt resolution (H Res 632) joined most Democrats in the final vote of 259-105: R 55-101; D 204-4 (ND 145-2, SD 59-2). Some of those Republicans said protection of congressional prerogatives outweighed their loyalty to the party leadership or the administration.

Instead of referring the charge against Gorsuch to the U.S. attorney for the District of Columbia for presentation to a grand jury, the procedure called for under the criminal contempt statute, the Justice Department filed a civil suit seeking to block further action on the House citation. The House Dec. 30 filed a motion seeking dismissal of that suit, claiming all constitutional issues involved in the separation-of-powers clash could be resolved in the course of proceedings on the criminal contempt charge.

Appendix

KEY

Y	Voted for (yea).
#	Paired for.
+	Announced for.
N	Voted against (nay).
X	Paired against.
-	Announced against.
P	Voted "present".
C	Voted "present" to avoid possible conflict of interest.
?	Did not vote or otherwise make a position known.

Democrats   *Republicans*

	1	2	3	4	5	6	7	8
ALABAMA								
Denton	Y	?	Y	Y	Y	Y	N	N
Heflin	Y	Y	Y	?	N	Y	Y	N
ALASKA								
Murkowski	Y	N	?	?	Y	Y	N	N
Stevens	?	Y	Y	Y	Y	Y	N	N
ARIZONA								
Goldwater	Y	N	Y	Y	-	Y	N	N
DeConcini	-	Y	N	Y	N	Y	Y	Y
ARKANSAS								
Bumpers	N	Y	N	?	N	N	Y	Y
Pryor	N	Y	?	Y	N	Y	Y	Y
CALIFORNIA								
Hayakawa	Y	N	Y	+	Y	Y	N	N
Cranston	N	Y	Y	Y	N	N	Y	Y
COLORADO								
Armstrong	Y	N	Y	Y	Y	Y	N	N
Hart	N	N	N	Y	N	N	Y	Y
CONNECTICUT								
Weicker	N	Y	?	?	-	N	Y	Y
Dodd	N	Y	N	?	N	N	Y	Y
DELAWARE								
Roth	Y	N	N	N	Y	Y	N	Y
Biden	N	Y	N	N	N	N	Y	Y
FLORIDA								
Hawkins	Y	Y	Y	+	N	Y	N	N
Chiles	N	Y	Y	?	N	Y	Y	Y
GEORGIA								
Mattingly	Y	N	Y	Y	N	Y	N	N
Nunn	N	Y	Y	Y	N	Y	N	Y
HAWAII								
Inouye	N	?	Y	Y	-	N	Y	Y
Matsunaga	N	Y	Y	Y	N	Y	Y	Y
IDAHO								
McClure	Y	N	Y	Y	Y	Y	N	?
Symms	Y	N	Y	Y	Y	Y	N	N
ILLINOIS								
Percy	Y	?	N	+	Y	Y	N	N
Dixon	N	Y	N	N	N	Y	Y	Y
INDIANA								
Lugar	Y	Y	N	Y	Y	Y	N	?
Quayle	Y	Y	N	Y	Y	Y	N	?
IOWA								
Grassley	Y	Y	Y	Y	Y	Y	N	Y
Jepsen	Y	Y	N	?	Y	Y	N	Y
KANSAS								
Dole	Y	N	Y	Y	Y	Y	N	N
Kassebaum	Y	N	Y	?	Y	N	N	N
KENTUCKY								
Ford	N	Y	Y	Y	N	N	Y	Y
Huddleston	N	Y	Y	Y	N	Y	Y	Y
LOUISIANA								
Johnston	N	N	Y	N	Y	N	N	N
Long	N	Y	Y	Y	N	Y	N	N
MAINE								
Cohen	Y	N	N	X	Y	N	N	Y
Mitchell	N	Y	N	?	N	N	Y	Y
MARYLAND								
Mathias	Y	N	N	X	Y	N	Y	Y
Sarbanes	N	Y	Y	N	N	N	Y	Y
MASSACHUSETTS								
Kennedy	N	Y	N	+	N	N	Y	Y
Tsongas	N	Y	N	N	N	N	Y	Y
MICHIGAN								
Levin	N	Y	N	N	N	N	Y	Y
Riegle	N	Y	N	X	N	N	Y	Y
MINNESOTA								
Boschwitz	Y	Y	Y	?	Y	Y	N	N
Durenberger	?	+	N	+	Y	Y	Y	Y
MISSISSIPPI								
Cochran	Y	Y	Y	?	Y	Y	N	?
Stennis	Y	Y	Y	?	N	Y	?	#
MISSOURI								
Danforth	Y	Y	N	Y	Y	N	N	Y
Eagleton	N	Y	N	Y	N	N	Y	Y
MONTANA								
Baucus	N	Y	N	Y	N	N	N	Y
Melcher	-	Y	Y	#	N	Y	Y	Y
NEBRASKA								
Exon	N	Y	N	?	N	Y	Y	Y
Zorinsky	Y	Y	N	N	N	Y	Y	Y
NEVADA								
Laxalt	Y	Y	Y	Y	Y	Y	N	N
Cannon	N	+	N	#	N	Y	Y	Y
NEW HAMPSHIRE								
Humphrey	Y	N	N	Y	Y	Y	N	N
Rudman	Y	Y	Y	Y	Y	Y	N	Y
NEW JERSEY								
Brady	Y	N	Y	#	Y	Y	N	N
Bradley	N	Y	N	N	N	N	Y	Y
NEW MEXICO								
Domenici	Y	N	Y	Y	Y	Y	N	Y
Schmitt	+	?	Y	#	Y	Y	N	#
NEW YORK								
D'Amato	Y	Y	N	+	Y	Y	N	Y
Moynihan	N	Y	N	N	N	N	Y	Y
NORTH CAROLINA								
East	Y	N	Y	Y	Y	Y	N	N
Helms	N	Y	Y	Y	Y	Y	N	N
NORTH DAKOTA								
Andrews	Y	Y	Y	?	Y	Y	Y	Y
Burdick	N	Y	Y	?	N	Y	Y	Y
OHIO								
Glenn	N	Y	?	Y	N	Y	N	Y
Metzenbaum	N	Y	N	N	N	N	Y	Y
OKLAHOMA								
Nickles	Y	N	N	+	Y	Y	N	N
Boren	N	Y	Y	?	N	Y	N	Y
OREGON								
Hatfield	+	Y	N	Y	N	Y	N	Y
Packwood	Y	Y	N	Y	Y	Y	N	Y
PENNSYLVANIA								
Heinz	Y	Y	N	?	Y	N	Y	Y
Specter	Y	Y	N	N	Y	Y	Y	?
RHODE ISLAND								
Chafee	Y	Y	N	Y	Y	N	N	Y
Pell	N	+	N	Y	N	N	Y	Y
SOUTH CAROLINA								
Thurmond	Y	Y	Y	Y	Y	Y	N	N
Hollings	N	Y	Y	?	N	Y	N	+
SOUTH DAKOTA								
Abdnor	Y	Y	Y	?	Y	Y	N	Y
Pressler	?	+	Y	+	Y	Y	Y	Y
TENNESSEE								
Baker	Y	N	Y	Y	Y	Y	N	N
Sasser	N	Y	Y	+	N	Y	Y	Y
TEXAS								
Tower	Y	Y	Y	Y	Y	Y	N	X
Bentsen	N	Y	Y	Y	N	Y	Y	?
UTAH								
Garn	Y	Y	N	Y	Y	Y	N	N
Hatch	Y	Y	N	Y	Y	Y	N	N
VERMONT								
Stafford	+	Y	Y	?	Y	Y	Y	Y
Leahy	N	Y	N	X	N	N	Y	Y
VIRGINIA								
Warner	Y	N	Y	Y	Y	Y	Y	N
Byrd*	N	N	Y	?	Y	Y	N	N
WASHINGTON								
Gorton	Y	Y	N	Y	Y	N	N	Y
Jackson	N	Y	N	Y	N	N	Y	Y
WEST VIRGINIA								
Byrd	N	Y	Y	Y	N	Y	Y	Y
Randolph	N	Y	N	Y	N	N	Y	Y
WISCONSIN								
Kasten	Y	Y	N	N	N	N	N	N
Proxmire	N	Y	N	N	N	Y	N	Y
WYOMING								
Simpson	Y	N	N	Y	Y	Y	N	N
Wallop	Y	N	N	Y	Y	Y	N	N

ND - Northern Democrats   SD - Southern Democrats (Southern states - Ala., Ark., Fla., Ga., Ky., La., Miss., N.C., Okla., S.C., Tenn., Texas, Va.)   * Byrd elected as an independent.

1. S Con Res 92. First Budget Resolution, Fiscal 1983. Adoption of the concurrent resolution to set budget targets for the fiscal year ending Sept. 30, 1983, as follows: budget authority, $835.7 billion; outlays, $784.3 billion; revenues, $668.4 billion; and deficit, $115.9 billion. The resolution also set preliminary goals for fiscal 1984-85, revised binding budget levels for fiscal 1982 and included reconciliation instructions requiring Senate and House committees to recommend legislative savings to meet the budget targets. Adopted 49-43: R 46-2; D 3-41 (ND 1-28, SD 2-13), May 21, 1982.

2. HR 5922. Urgent Supplemental Appropriations, Fiscal 1982. Lugar, R-Ind., amendment to establish a new subsidy program to provide mortgages at below-market interest rates for buyers of new homes. The amendment contained a fiscal 1982 appropriation of $5.1 billion. Adopted 69-23: R 29-20; D 40-3 (ND 27-1, SD 13-2), May 27, 1982. A "nay" was a vote supporting the president's position.

3. HR 6590. Tobacco Program Revisions. Baker, R-Tenn., motion to table (kill) the Eagleton, D-Mo., amendment to authorize tobacco price support loans through 1985 (thus ending permanent authorization for these loans). Motion agreed to 49-47: R 29-23; D 20-24 (ND 7-23, SD 13-1), July 14, 1982.

4. HR 5539. Reclamation Law Amendments. Passage of the bill to increase acreage limitations for farms irrigated by water from reclamation projects, to raise the price for some of that water, and to make other changes in federal reclamation laws. Passed 49-13: R 30-3; D 19-10 (ND 12-10, SD 7-0), July 16, 1982.

5. HR 4961. Budget Reconciliation Tax Increases/Spending Cuts. Passage of the bill to increase taxes $99 billion for fiscal years 1983-85 and to cut welfare, Medicare and Medicaid spending $17 billion for the same three years, in compliance with reconciliation instructions in the fiscal 1983 budget resolution (S Con Res 92). Passed 50-47: R 49-3; D 1-44 (ND 0-30, SD 1-14), in the session which began July 22, 1982.

6. S J Res 58. Balanced Budget/Tax Limitation Amendment. Passage of the joint resolution to propose an amendment to the Constitution to require a balanced budget at the beginning of each fiscal year unless a three-fifths majority of Congress agreed to deficit spending. The amendment could be waived during the time of a declared war. Passed 69-31: R 47-7; D 22-24 (ND 9-22, SD 13-2), Aug. 4, 1982. A two-thirds majority of those present and voting (67 in this case) of both houses is required for passage of a joint resolution proposing an amendment to the Constitution. A "yea" was a vote supporting the president's position.

7. S 2774. Omnibus Reconciliation Act. Riegle, D-Mich., amendment to delete provisions that would impose a 4 percent cap on cost-of-living adjustments for federal and military retirees but retain the cap for members of Congress who retire after the date of the bill's enactment. Rejected 48-51: R 10-44; D 38-7 (ND 30-1, SD 8-6), Aug. 4, 1982.

8. HR 6863. Supplemental Appropriations, Fiscal 1982. Passage, over President Reagan's Aug. 28 veto, of the bill to appropriate $14,578,111,924 in new fiscal 1982 budget authority for federal military and civilian pay raises, commodity credit programs, defense and other programs, and to rescind $400,846,000 in previously appropriated funds. Passed (thus enacted into law) 60-30: R 21-26; D 39-4 (ND 31-0, SD 8-4), Sept. 10, 1982. A two-thirds majority of those present and voting (60 in this case) of both houses is required to override a veto. A "nay" was a vote supporting the president's position. (The House voted to override the veto the previous day (see vote 7, p. 906).)

	9	10	11	12	13	14	15
ALABAMA							
Denton	N	N	Y	Y	N	Y	N
Heflin	N	N	Y	Y	N	N	N
ALASKA							
Murkowski	N	Y	Y	Y	Y	Y	Y
Stevens	Y	Y	Y	Y	N	Y	Y
ARIZONA							
Goldwater	N	#	?	#	?	?	?
DeConcini	N	-	Y	N	N	N	Y
ARKANSAS							
Bumpers	Y	Y	N	N	Y	N	N
Pryor	Y	Y	N	N	Y	N	N
CALIFORNIA							
Hayakawa	Y	Y	Y	Y	Y	Y	Y
Cranston	Y	Y	N	N	Y	N	?
COLORADO							
Armstrong	N	Y	Y	N	N	Y	N
Hart	Y	Y	N	N	Y	N	Y
CONNECTICUT							
Weicker	Y	Y	N	Y	N	Y	N
Dodd	Y	Y	N	N	Y	N	Y
DELAWARE							
Roth	Y	Y	Y	N	N	Y	Y
Biden	N	N	N	N	Y	N	N
FLORIDA							
Hawkins	N	N	Y	Y	Y	Y	N
Chiles	N	N	Y	N	Y	Y	Y
GEORGIA							
Mattingly	N	N	Y	Y	Y	Y	N
Nunn	Y	N	Y	N	Y	Y	Y
HAWAII							
Inouye	Y	Y	N	N	N	N	N
Matsunaga	Y	X	N	N	N	N	Y
IDAHO							
McClure	N	Y	Y	Y	N	Y	Y
Symms	N	Y	Y	Y	N	Y	Y
ILLINOIS							
Percy	Y	Y	Y	N	Y	Y	Y
Dixon	Y	Y	N	N	Y	N	Y
INDIANA							
Lugar	N	Y	Y	N	Y	Y	Y
Quayle	N	Y	Y	N	Y	Y	Y

	9	10	11	12	13	14	15
IOWA							
Grassley	N	N	Y	Y	N	Y	Y
Jepsen	N	Y	Y	Y	N	Y	Y
KANSAS							
Dole	N	Y	Y	Y	Y	Y	Y
Kassebaum	Y	Y	N	N	Y	Y	Y
KENTUCKY							
Ford	N	N	N	N	N	N	N
Huddleston	N	N	N	Y	N	N	Y
LOUISIANA							
Johnston	-	#	Y	Y	N	N	N
Long	N	N	Y	Y	?	N	Y
MAINE							
Cohen	Y	N	Y	N	Y	N	N
Mitchell	Y	N	N	N	Y	N	N
MARYLAND							
Mathias	Y	#	N	Y	Y	?	Y
Sarbanes	Y	N	N	N	Y	N	N
MASSACHUSETTS							
Kennedy	Y	N	N	N	Y	N	-
Tsongas	Y	Y	N	N	Y	N	Y
MICHIGAN							
Levin	Y	N	N	N	Y	N	N
Riegle	Y	N	N	N	Y	N	N
MINNESOTA							
Boschwitz	N	Y	Y	N	Y	N	Y
Durenberger	N	Y	N	N	Y	Y	Y
MISSISSIPPI							
Cochran	N	Y	Y	N	N	N	N
Stennis	N	Y	Y	Y	N	N	Y
MISSOURI							
Danforth	N	Y	Y	N	Y	N	Y
Eagleton	N	N	N	N	Y	N	N
MONTANA							
Baucus	Y	N	N	N	Y	N	Y
Melcher	Y	N	N	N	N	N	Y
NEBRASKA							
Exon	N	N	Y	N	Y	N	Y
Zorinsky	N	N	Y	Y	N	Y	N
NEVADA							
Laxalt	N	Y	Y	Y	N	Y	Y
Cannon	?	N	Y	Y	Y	N	?

	9	10	11	12	13	14	15
NEW HAMPSHIRE							
Humphrey	N	Y	Y	N	Y	N	N
Rudman	Y	Y	Y	Y	Y	N	Y
NEW JERSEY							
Brady	Y	Y	Y	Y	Y	Y	Y
Bradley	Y	N	N	N	Y	N	N
NEW MEXICO							
Domenici	N	Y	Y	Y	N	Y	Y
Schmitt	Y	X	Y	Y	N	N	Y
NEW YORK							
D'Amato	N	Y	Y	Y	Y	N	Y
Moynihan	Y	?	N	N	Y	N	?
NORTH CAROLINA							
East	N	N	Y	Y	N	Y	N
Helms	N	N	Y	Y	N	Y	N
NORTH DAKOTA							
Andrews	N	N	N	Y	Y	N	Y
Burdick	Y	N	N	Y	Y	N	Y
OHIO							
Glenn	+	Y	?	-	?	?	Y
Metzenbaum	Y	N	N	N	Y	N	N
OKLAHOMA							
Nickles	N	N	N	N	N	N	N
Boren	?	N	Y	Y	N	Y	N
OREGON							
Hatfield	N	Y	N	X	Y	N	?
Packwood	Y	Y	N	N	Y	N	Y
PENNSYLVANIA							
Heinz	+	Y	N	Y	Y	N	?
Specter	Y	Y	N	Y	Y	N	Y
RHODE ISLAND							
Chafee	Y	Y	N	N	Y	N	N
Pell	Y	N	N	N	Y	N	Y
SOUTH CAROLINA							
Thurmond	N	Y	Y	Y	Y	Y	Y
Hollings	Y	Y	N	N	N	N	?
SOUTH DAKOTA							
Abdnor	N	N	N	Y	Y	Y	Y
Pressler	N	N	N	Y	N	Y	Y
TENNESSEE							
Baker	X	Y	Y	Y	Y	Y	Y
Sasser	Y	X	N	Y	N	N	N

KEY

Y	Voted for (yea).
#	Paired for.
+	Announced for.
N	Voted against (nay).
X	Paired against.
-	Announced against.
P	Voted "present".
C	Voted "present" to avoid possible conflict of interest.
?	Did not vote or otherwise make a position known.

Democrats *Republicans*

	9	10	11	12	13	14	15
TEXAS							
Tower	Y	Y	Y	Y	N	Y	N
Bentsen	Y	Y	Y	N	N	N	Y
UTAH							
Garn	N	Y	Y	Y	N	Y	N
Hatch	N	Y	Y	Y	-	Y	-
VERMONT							
Stafford	#	Y	N	N	Y	N	Y
Leahy	Y	Y	N	N	Y	N	Y
VIRGINIA							
Warner	N	Y	Y	Y	Y	Y	Y
Byrd*	Y	Y	Y	N	Y	Y	Y
WASHINGTON							
Gorton	Y	Y	Y	Y	Y	Y	Y
Jackson	Y	N	Y	Y	Y	N	+
WEST VIRGINIA							
Byrd	Y	N	Y	N	Y	N	N
Randolph	N	Y	N	N	N	N	Y
WISCONSIN							
Kasten	N	N	Y	N	Y	N	N
Proxmire	N	N	N	N	Y	N	N
WYOMING							
Simpson	Y	Y	Y	Y	N	Y	N
Wallop	Y	Y	Y	Y	N	?	N

ND - Northern Democrats   SD - Southern Democrats (Southern states - Ala., Ark., Fla., Ga., Ky., La., Miss., N.C., Okla., S.C., Tenn., Texas, Va.)   * Byrd elected as an independent.

9. H J Res 520. Temporary Debt Limit Increase. Hayakawa, R-Calif., motion to table (kill) the Helms, R-N.C., amendment designed to ban abortion, which was an amendment to the Helms amendment (stripping the Supreme Court of jurisdiction to review any case involving voluntary prayers in public schools) to the committee version of the bill. Motion agreed to 47-46: R 18-33; D 29-13 (ND 22-7, SD 7-6), Sept. 15, 1982.

10. S Res 512. Outside Income of Senators. Adoption of the resolution to abolish the limit in the Senate rules on the total income senators may receive from outside sources, including money for speeches and articles. Adopted 54-38: R 39-12; D 15-26 (ND 9-19, SD 6-7), Dec. 14, 1982.

11. H J Res 631. Continuing Appropriations, Fiscal 1983/MX Missile. Jackson, D-Wash., amendment to bar the use of funds in the bill for procurement of the MX missile until Congress by concurrent resolution had approved a basing mode for it; set out procedures for congressional consideration of the concurrent resolution, and required the president to submit a detailed report on basing mode options to Congress by March 1, 1983. Adopted 56-42: R 41-12; D 15-30 (ND 6-24, SD 9-6), in the session which began Dec. 16, 1982. A "yea" was a vote supporting the president's position.

12. H J Res 631. Continuing Appropriations, Fiscal 1983/Clinch River. Appropriations Committee amendment to drop the House-approved provision in the bill eliminating construction funds for the Clinch River (Tenn.) nuclear breeder reactor. Adopted 49-48: R 38-14; D 11-34 (ND 4-26, SD 7-8), in the session which began Dec. 16, 1982. A "yea" was a vote supporting the president's position.

13. H J Res 631. Continuing Appropriations, Fiscal 1983/Federal Trade Commission. Rudman, R-N.H., motion to table (kill) the McClure, R-Idaho, amendment to bar the use of funds by the Federal Trade Commission to investigate or make rules relating to the medical or other professions that were licensed and regulated by the states. Motion agreed to 59-37: R 31-21; D 28-16 (ND 23-7, SD 5-9), in the session which began Dec. 16, 1982. A "yea" was a vote supporting the president's position.

14. H J Res 631. Continuing Appropriations, Fiscal 1983. Domenici, R-N.M., amendment to delete the section of the joint resolution providing $1.2 billion for public works jobs. Rejected 46-50: R 39-12; D 7-38 (ND 3-27, SD 4-11), in the session which began Dec. 16, 1982. A "yea" was a vote supporting the president's position.

15. HR 6211. Transportation Assistance Act of 1982. Passage of the bill to authorize approximately $70 billion for highways through fiscal 1987 and approximately $12 billion for transit through fiscal 1985, and increase gasoline and other highway taxes. Passed 56-34: R 35-15; D 21-19 (ND 14-12, SD 7-7), in the session which began Dec. 20, 1982. A "yea" was a vote supporting the president's position.

Appendix

1. HR 5922. Urgent Supplemental Appropriations, Fiscal 1982. Boland, D-Mass., amendment to provide $1 billion to the Department of Housing and Urban Development for mortgage interest subsidy payments to home buyers with family income not exceeding 130 percent of the median income for their area. Adopted 343-67: R 128-52; D 215-15 (ND 149-6, SD 66-9), May 12, 1982.

2. H Con Res 345. First Budget Resolution, Fiscal 1983. Oakar, D-Ohio, amendment, to the Latta, R-Ohio, substitute, to increase budget authority by $400 million and outlays by $4.85 billion for health programs in fiscal 1983 to accommodate Medicare funding at current services levels, and to make corresponding reductions in defense programs. Adopted 228-196: R 64-125; D 164-71 (ND 136-20, SD 28-51), May 27, 1982.

3. H Con Res 352. First Budget Resolution, Fiscal 1983. Latta, R-Ohio, substitute for the president's fiscal 1983 budget submission, to set budget targets for the fiscal year ending Sept. 30, 1983, as follows: budget authority, $800.38 billion; outlays, $765.17 billion; revenues, $665.9 billion; and deficit, $99.27 billion. Adopted 220-207: R 174-15; D 46-192 (ND 9-151, SD 37-41), June 10, 1982.

4. HR 6030. Defense Department Authorizations, Fiscal 1983. Courter, R-N.J., substitute for the Zablocki, D-Wis., amendment, to ban the production of binary munitions unless one existing chemical weapon were destroyed for each new binary weapon built. Rejected 192-225: R 112-72; D 80-153 (ND 27-132, SD 53-21), July 22, 1982. A "yea" was a vote supporting the president's position. (The Zablocki amendment to delete $54 million earmarked for procurement of binary chemical munitions and barring the use of any authorized funds for that program subsequently was adopted.)

5. HR 4961. Budget Reconciliation Tax Increases/Spending Cuts. Rostenkowski, D-Ill., motion to disagree to the Senate amendments to the bill and to agree to a conference requested by the Senate. Motion agreed to 208-197: R 44-137; D 164-60 (ND 116-35, SD 48-25), July 28, 1982.

6. H J Res 521. Nuclear Arms Freeze. Broomfield, R-Mich., substitute to call for a nuclear weapons freeze by the United States and the Soviet Union at equal and substantially reduced levels. Adopted 204-202: R 151-27; D 53-175 (ND 11-149, SD 42-26), Aug. 5, 1982. A "yea" was a vote supporting the president's position. (As reported, the resolution had called for the United States and the Soviet Union to decide when and how to implement an immediate freeze on nuclear arms.)

7. HR 6863. Supplemental Appropriations, Fiscal 1982. Passage, over President Reagan's Aug. 28 veto, of the bill to appropriate $14,578,111,924 in new fiscal 1982 budget authority for federal military and civilian pay raises, commodity credit programs, defense and other programs, and to rescind $400,846,000 in previously appropriated funds. Passed 301-117: R 81-104; D 220-13 (ND 157-1, SD 63-12), Sept. 9, 1982. A two-thirds majority of those present and voting (279 in this case) of both houses is required to override a veto. A "nay" was a vote supporting the president's position. (The Senate also voted to override the veto *(see vote 8, p. 12-C)*, so the bill was enacted.)

8. HR 6838. Soviet Economic Sanctions. Broomfield, R-Mich., motion to recommit the bill to the Foreign Affairs Committee with instructions to insert an amendment repealing economic sanctions against the Soviet Union 90 days after enactment of the bill, provided that during that period the president certified to Congress that the Soviet Union was not using forced labor on certain construction projects. The original bill would have immediately repealed economic sanctions against the Soviet Union. Motion agreed to 206-203: R 124-57; D 82-146 (ND 41-111, SD 41-35), Sept. 29, 1982. A "yea" was a vote supporting the president's position.

KEY

Y	Voted for (yea).
#	Paired for.
+	Announced for.
N	Voted against (nay).
X	Paired against.
-	Announced against.
P	Voted "present".
C	Voted "present" to avoid possible conflict of interest.
?	Did not vote or otherwise make a position known.

Democrats *Republicans*

	1	2	3	4	5	6	7	8
ALABAMA								
1 *Edwards*	Y	N	Y	Y	Y	Y	Y	Y
2 *Dickinson*	Y	N	Y	N	Y	N	Y	N
3 Nichols	N	N	Y	Y	Y	Y	?	Y
4 Bevill	Y	Y	N	Y	N	Y	Y	Y
5 Flippo	Y	Y	N	Y	Y	Y	Y	Y
6 *Smith*	Y	N	Y	N	Y	N	Y	Y
7 Shelby	Y	N	Y	N	Y	N	Y	Y
ALASKA								
AL *Young*	N	N	Y	Y	Y	Y	#	Y
ARIZONA								
1 *Rhodes*	N	?	Y	?	Y	Y	Y	Y
2 Udall	Y	Y	N	Y	N	Y	N	Y
3 *Stump*	N	N	Y	N	Y	N	?	Y
4 *Rudd*	N	N	Y	Y	N	Y	?	Y
ARKANSAS								
1 Alexander	Y	N	N	Y	Y	N	Y	N
2 *Bethune*	N	N	Y	N	N	Y	N	Y
3 *Hammerschmidt*	Y	N	Y	N	Y	N	Y	Y
4 Anthony	Y	Y	N	Y	Y	N	Y	N
CALIFORNIA								
1 *Chappie*	N	N	Y	?	N	Y	Y	Y
2 *Clausen*	Y	N	Y	N	N	Y	Y	Y
3 Matsui	Y	Y	N	Y	N	Y	N	Y
4 Fazio	Y	Y	N	Y	N	Y	N	N
5 Burton, J.	?	?	X	?	?	N	Y	?
6 Burton, P.	Y	Y	N	Y	N	Y	N	N
7 Miller	Y	Y	N	Y	N	Y	N	N
8 Dellums	Y	Y	N	Y	N	Y	N	N
9 Stark	Y	Y	N	Y	N	Y	N	N
10 Edwards	Y	Y	N	Y	N	Y	N	N
11 Lantos	Y	Y	N	Y	N	Y	N	N
12 *McCloskey*	?	N	Y	N	?	N	N	N
13 Mineta	Y	N	N	N	Y	N	Y	N
14 *Shumway*	N	N	Y	N	Y	N	Y	N
15 Coelho	Y	Y	N	Y	N	Y	N	Y
16 Panetta	Y	N	N	N	Y	N	Y	N
17 *Pashayan*	Y	Y	Y	Y	N	Y	N	Y
18 *Thomas*	Y	N	Y	N	Y	N	Y	Y
19 *Lagomarsino*	Y	N	Y	N	Y	N	Y	Y
20 *Goldwater*	?	N	#	Y	N	?	N	Y
21 *Fiedler*	Y	N	Y	N	Y	Y	Y	Y
22 *Moorhead*	N	N	Y	N	Y	N	Y	N
23 Beilenson	N	N	N	N	Y	N	Y	N
24 Waxman	Y	Y	N	N	Y	N	Y	N
25 Roybal	Y	N	N	Y	N	Y	N	N
26 *Rousselot*	N	N	Y	N	Y	N	Y	N
27 *Dornan*	N	N	?	Y	?	N	Y	Y
28 Dixon	Y	Y	N	Y	N	Y	N	N
29 Hawkins	?	Y	Y	N	Y	N	Y	N
30 Martinez[1]				N	N	Y	N	Y	N
31 Dymally	?	Y	N	N	?	N	Y	N
32 Anderson	Y	Y	N	Y	N	N	N	Y
33 *Grisham*	?	N	Y	Y	N	Y	N	Y
34 *Lungren*	N	N	Y	Y	N	Y	N	Y
35 *Dreier*	?	N	Y	Y	N	Y	N	Y
36 Brown	Y	Y	N	Y	N	Y	N	Y
37 *Lewis*	Y	N	Y	N	Y	N	Y	Y
38 Patterson	Y	Y	N	Y	Y	N	Y	N
39 *Dannemeyer*	N	N	Y	N	Y	N	Y	N
40 *Badham*	N	N	Y	N	Y	N	Y	N
41 *Lowery*	Y	N	Y	N	Y	N	Y	N
42 *Hunter*	N	N	Y	Y	N	Y	N	Y
43 *Burgener*	Y	N	Y	?	Y	Y	Y	N
COLORADO								
1 Schroeder	Y	Y	N	N	Y	N	?	N
2 Wirth	Y	N	N	N	Y	N	Y	N
3 Kogovsek	Y	Y	N	N	Y	N	Y	N
4 *Brown*	N	Y	Y	N	N	Y	N	Y

	1	2	3	4	5	6	7	8
5 *Kramer*	N	N	Y	N	Y	N	Y	N
CONNECTICUT								
1 Kennelly	Y	Y	N	N	Y	N	Y	Y
2 Gejdenson	Y	Y	N	N	Y	N	Y	N
3 *DeNardis*	Y	Y	N	N	N	N	Y	N
4 *McKinney*	Y	Y	N	N	N	N	Y	N
5 Ratchford	Y	Y	N	N	N	N	Y	N
6 Moffett	Y	Y	N	N	?	N	Y	?
DELAWARE								
AL *Evans*	Y	Y	Y	N	N	N	Y	Y
FLORIDA								
1 Hutto	Y	N	Y	N	Y	Y	Y	Y
2 Fuqua	Y	N	Y	N	Y	?	Y	Y
3 Bennett	Y	N	N	Y	Y	Y	N	Y
4 Chappell	Y	N	Y	N	Y	Y	Y	?
5 *McCollum*	Y	N	Y	N	Y	Y	Y	?
6 *Young*	Y	N	Y	N	Y	N	Y	?
7 Gibbons	N	N	Y	Y	Y	N	N	Y
8 Ireland	Y	N	Y	N	Y	N	Y	N
9 Nelson	Y	N	Y	Y	Y	Y	Y	Y
10 *Bafalis*	Y	N	Y	?	?	?	?	?
11 Mica	Y	Y	N	N	Y	N	Y	N
12 *Shaw*	N	N	Y	N	Y	N	Y	N
13 Lehman	Y	Y	N	N	Y	N	Y	N
14 Pepper	Y	Y	N	-	?	N	Y	N
15 Fascell	N	Y	N	N	Y	N	Y	N
GEORGIA								
1 Ginn	?	N	Y	?	?	?	Y	Y
2 Hatcher	Y	N	Y	Y	Y	Y	Y	Y
3 Brinkley	Y	Y	Y	Y	Y	Y	Y	Y
4 Levitas	Y	N	Y	Y	N	Y	N	Y
5 Fowler	Y	N	Y	N	Y	N	Y	N
6 *Gingrich*	Y	N	Y	N	Y	N	Y	N
7 McDonald	N	N	Y	N	Y	N	Y	N
8 Evans	Y	N	Y	N	Y	?	?	Y
9 Jenkins	Y	N	Y	Y	Y	Y	Y	Y
10 Barnard	Y	N	Y	Y	Y	Y	Y	Y
HAWAII								
1 Heftel	?	Y	Y	Y	Y	N	Y	N
2 Akaka	Y	Y	N	Y	N	Y	N	Y
IDAHO								
1 *Craig*	Y	N	Y	N	N	Y	N	Y
2 *Hansen*	N	N	Y	N	Y	N	Y	N
ILLINOIS								
1 Washington	Y	Y	N	N	N	N	Y	N
2 Savage	Y	Y	N	N	Y	N	Y	N
3 Russo	Y	Y	N	N	Y	N	Y	N
4 *Derwinski*	Y	N	Y	Y	Y	Y	Y	N
5 Fary	Y	Y	N	Y	N	Y	N	N
6 *Hyde*	Y	N	Y	N	Y	N	Y	N
7 Collins	Y	N	N	N	N	N	Y	N
8 Rostenkowski	Y	Y	N	Y	N	Y	N	N
9 Yates	Y	Y	N	N	?	N	Y	N
10 *Porter*	Y	N	N	Y	N	Y	N	N
11 Annunzio	Y	Y	N	Y	N	Y	N	N
12 *Crane, P.*	N	N	Y	N	Y	N	Y	N
13 *McClory*	Y	N	Y	N	Y	?	Y	N
14 *Erlenborn*	N	N	Y	N	Y	N	Y	N
15 *Corcoran*	N	N	Y	N	Y	N	Y	N
16 *Martin*	N	N	Y	N	N	N	N	N
17 *O'Brien*	Y	N	Y	N	#	Y	Y	X
18 *Michel*	N	N	Y	N	Y	N	Y	N
19 *Railsback*	Y	Y	Y	N	Y	X	Y	N
20 *Findley*	Y	Y	N	N	Y	N	N	N
21 *Madigan*	Y	N	Y	Y	Y	N	Y	N
22 *Crane, D.*	N	N	Y	N	Y	N	Y	N
23 Price	Y	N	N	Y	Y	Y	Y	N
24 Simon	Y	Y	N	Y	N	Y	N	N
INDIANA								
1 Hall[2]								
2 Fithian	Y	Y	N	N	N	N	Y	N
3 *Hiler*	Y	N	Y	N	Y	N	Y	N
4 *Coats*	Y	N	Y	N	Y	N	Y	N
5 *Hillis*	Y	N	Y	N	Y	N	Y	N
6 Evans	Y	N	Y	N	?	Y	N	Y
7 *Myers*	Y	N	Y	N	Y	N	Y	N
8 *Deckard*	Y	Y	N	Y	N	N	Y	N
9 Hamilton	Y	Y	Y	N	Y	N	Y	N
10 Sharp	Y	Y	N	N	N	N	Y	N
11 Jacobs	Y	Y	N	N	Y	N	Y	N
IOWA								
1 *Leach*	Y	Y	Y	N	N	N	Y	N
2 *Tauke*	Y	Y	Y	N	N	N	Y	N
3 *Evans*	Y	Y	Y	N	N	N	Y	N
4 Smith	Y	Y	N	N	N	N	Y	N
5 Harkin	Y	Y	N	N	N	N	Y	N
6 Bedell	Y	Y	N	N	Y	N	Y	N

ND - Northern Democrats   SD - Southern Democrats

	1	2	3	4	5	6	7	8
KANSAS								
1 ***Roberts***	N	N	Y	N	N	Y	N	N
2 ***Jeffries***	N	N	Y	Y	N	Y	N	Y
3 ***Winn***	Y	N	Y	Y	N	Y	N	Y
4 Glickman	Y	N	N	N	Y	N	Y	N
5 ***Whittaker***	N	N	Y	N	N	Y	N	Y
KENTUCKY								
1 Hubbard	Y	N	N	Y	N	Y	N	Y
2 Natcher	Y	Y	N	N	N	N	Y	N
3 Mazzoli	Y	N	N	N	Y	N	Y	N
4 ***Snyder***	N	Y	Y	Y	N	Y	N	Y
5 ***Rogers***	Y	N	Y	Y	N	Y	Y	Y
6 ***Hopkins***	Y	Y	Y	N	N	Y	Y	Y
7 Perkins	Y	Y	N	N	N	N	Y	N
LOUISIANA								
1 ***Livingston***	?	N	Y	Y	N	Y	N	Y
2 Boggs	Y	Y	N	Y	Y	N	Y	N
3 Tauzin	Y	N	Y	Y	N	Y	N	N
4 Roemer	N	N	Y	Y	Y	Y	N	N
5 Huckaby	Y	N	Y	Y	Y	Y	Y	N
6 ***Moore***	Y	N	Y	Y	N	Y	N	N
7 Breaux	Y	N	Y	?	Y	Y	Y	N
8 Long	Y	Y	N	Y	Y	?	Y	Y
MAINE								
1 ***Emery***	Y	Y	Y	N	Y	Y	Y	Y
2 ***Snowe***	Y	Y	Y	N	Y	N	Y	N
MARYLAND								
1 Dyson	Y	Y	Y	Y	Y	Y	Y	Y
2 Long	N	N	N	N	Y	N	Y	Y
3 Mikulski	?	Y	N	N	Y	N	Y	Y
4 ***Holt***	N	Y	Y	Y	N	Y	Y	Y
5 Hoyer	Y	Y	N	N	Y	N	Y	N
6 Byron	Y	Y	Y	Y	Y	Y	Y	Y
7 Mitchell	Y	Y	N	N	?	N	Y	N
8 Barnes	Y	Y	N	-	N	N	Y	N
MASSACHUSETTS								
1 ***Conte***	Y	Y	Y	N	Y	N	Y	N
2 Boland	Y	Y	N	N	Y	N	Y	N
3 Early	N	Y	N	N	?	N	Y	Y
4 Frank	Y	Y	N	N	N	N	Y	Y
5 Shannon	Y	Y	N	N	N	N	Y	N
6 Mavroules	Y	Y	N	N	Y	N	Y	Y
7 Markey	Y	Y	N	N	Y	N	Y	N
8 O'Neill[3]						N	Y	
9 Moakley	Y	Y	N	N	Y	N	Y	N
10 ***Heckler***	Y	Y	N	N	N	N	Y	Y
11 Donnelly	N	N	N	N	Y	N	Y	Y
12 Studds	Y	Y	N	N	N	N	Y	N
MICHIGAN								
1 Conyers	Y	Y	N	N	Y	N	Y	Y
2 ***Pursell***	Y	Y	Y	N	Y	N	Y	N
3 Wolpe	Y	Y	N	N	Y	N	Y	N
4 ***Siljander***	Y	N	Y	Y	?	Y	N	Y
5 ***Sawyer***	Y	N	Y	N	N	Y	N	Y
6 ***Dunn***	Y	N	Y	N	N	Y	Y	N
7 Kildee	Y	Y	N	N	N	N	Y	N
8 Traxler	Y	Y	N	N	Y	N	Y	N
9 ***Vander Jagt***	Y	N	Y	N	Y	Y	Y	Y
10 Albosta	Y	Y	N	N	Y	N	Y	N
11 ***Davis***	Y	Y	Y	Y	N	Y	Y	Y
12 Bonior	Y	Y	N	N	?	N	Y	Y
13 Crockett	Y	?	N	N	Y	N	Y	N
14 Hertel	Y	Y	N	N	Y	N	Y	N
15 Ford	Y	Y	N	N	Y	N	Y	N
16 Dingell	Y	Y	N	Y	Y	N	Y	N
17 Brodhead	Y	Y	N	N	Y	N	Y	N
18 Blanchard	Y	Y	N	N	?	N	Y	?
19 ***Broomfield***	Y	N	Y	Y	N	Y	N	Y
MINNESOTA								
1 ***Erdahl***	Y	N	Y	N	N	N	Y	N
2 ***Hagedorn***	N	N	Y	Y	N	Y	N	Y
3 ***Frenzel***	N	N	Y	N	Y	Y	N	N
4 Vento	Y	Y	N	N	Y	N	Y	N
5 Sabo	Y	Y	N	N	Y	N	Y	N
6 ***Weber***	N	N	Y	N	N	Y	N	N
7 ***Stangeland***	Y	Y	Y	Y	N	Y	Y	N
8 Oberstar	Y	Y	N	N	Y	N	Y	N
MISSISSIPPI								
1 Whitten	Y	Y	N	N	N	?	Y	N
2 Bowen	Y	N	N	?	Y	N	?	N
3 Montgomery	Y	N	Y	Y	Y	Y	N	Y
4 Dowdy	Y	Y	N	Y	?	N	Y	N
5 ***Lott***	Y	N	Y	Y	Y	Y	N	Y
MISSOURI								
1 Clay	Y	Y	N	?	?	N	Y	?
2 Young	Y	N	Y	Y	Y	N	Y	N
3 Gephardt	N	N	Y	Y	Y	N	Y	N

	1	2	3	4	5	6	7	8
4 Skelton	Y	N	Y	Y	N	?	Y	?
5 Bolling	Y	Y	?	Y	Y	?	Y	N
6 ***Coleman***	Y	Y	Y	?	N	Y	Y	Y
7 ***Taylor***	N	N	Y	Y	N	Y	N	N
8 ***Bailey***	Y	N	Y	N	N	Y	N	N
9 Volkmer	Y	Y	Y	Y	N	N	Y	N
10 ***Emerson***	Y	N	Y	?	N	Y	Y	N
MONTANA								
1 Williams	Y	Y	N	N	N	N	Y	N
2 ***Marlenee***	Y	Y	Y	Y	N	Y	N	N
NEBRASKA								
1 ***Bereuter***	Y	Y	Y	N	N	Y	Y	Y
2 ***Daub***	Y	Y	Y	N	N	Y	N	Y
3 ***Smith***	Y	Y	Y	N	N	Y	Y	N
NEVADA								
AL Santini	Y	Y	N	?	N	Y	Y	?
NEW HAMPSHIRE								
1 D'Amours	Y	Y	N	N	N	N	Y	Y
2 ***Gregg***	N	N	Y	N	N	N	N	Y
NEW JERSEY								
1 Florio	Y	Y	N	N	N	N	Y	N
2 Hughes	Y	Y	N	N	N	N	Y	Y
3 Howard	Y	Y	N	N	Y	N	Y	N
4 ***Smith***	Y	Y	N	N	N	N	Y	Y
5 ***Fenwick***	?	Y	Y	N	N	N	Y	N
6 ***Forsythe***	Y	Y	Y	N	Y	Y	N	#
7 ***Roukema***	N	Y	Y	N	N	N	Y	N
8 Roe	Y	Y	N	N	N	N	Y	N
9 ***Hollenbeck***	Y	Y	N	N	N	N	Y	N
10 Rodino	Y	Y	N	N	Y	N	Y	N
11 Minish	Y	Y	N	N	Y	N	Y	Y
12 ***Rinaldo***	Y	Y	N	N	N	N	Y	Y
13 ***Courter***	Y	Y	Y	Y	N	Y	N	Y
14 Guarini	Y	Y	N	N	Y	N	Y	N
15 Dwyer	Y	Y	N	N	Y	N	Y	N
NEW MEXICO								
1 ***Lujan***	Y	Y	Y	Y	N	#	N	Y
2 ***Skeen***	N	N	Y	Y	N	Y	N	Y
NEW YORK								
1 ***Carney***	Y	N	Y	Y	N	Y	N	Y
2 Downey	Y	Y	N	N	Y	N	Y	N
3 ***Carman***	Y	N	Y	N	N	Y	N	Y
4 ***Lent***	Y	Y	Y	Y	N	Y	Y	Y
5 ***McGrath***	Y	Y	Y	N	N	-	Y	Y
6 ***LeBoutillier***	Y	Y	Y	Y	N	Y	Y	?
7 Addabbo	Y	Y	N	N	Y	N	Y	Y
8 Rosenthal	Y	?	N	N	Y	X	Y	N
9 Ferraro	Y	Y	N	N	Y	N	Y	N
10 Biaggi	Y	Y	N	N	Y	N	Y	Y
11 Scheuer	Y	Y	N	N	Y	N	Y	?
12 Chisholm	Y	?	N	N	Y	N	Y	N
13 Solarz	Y	Y	N	N	Y	N	Y	N
14 Richmond[4]	Y	Y	N	N	Y	N		
15 Zeferetti	Y	Y	N	N	Y	N	Y	Y
16 Schumer	Y	Y	N	N	Y	N	?	N
17 ***Molinari***	Y	Y	Y	N	N	Y	Y	Y
18 ***Green***	N	Y	N	N	N	N	Y	Y
19 Rangel	Y	Y	N	N	Y	N	Y	N
20 Weiss	Y	Y	N	N	Y	N	?	?
21 Garcia	Y	?	N	N	Y	N	Y	N
22 Bingham	Y	?	N	N	Y	N	Y	N
23 Peyser	Y	Y	N	N	Y	N	Y	Y
24 Ottinger	Y	Y	N	N	N	N	Y	Y
25 ***Fish***	Y	Y	Y	N	Y	Y	Y	N
26 ***Gilman***	Y	Y	N	Y	N	Y	Y	Y
27 McHugh	Y	Y	N	N	N	N	Y	N
28 Stratton	Y	N	N	Y	Y	Y	Y	N
29 ***Solomon***	Y	N	Y	?	N	Y	N	Y
30 ***Martin***	Y	N	Y	Y	N	Y	Y	Y
31 ***Mitchell***	Y	N	Y	Y	N	Y	Y	Y
32 ***Wortley***	Y	N	Y	Y	N	Y	Y	Y
33 ***Lee***	Y	Y	Y	N	-	Y	Y	Y
34 ***Horton***	Y	Y	Y	N	N	N	Y	N
35 ***Conable***	N	N	Y	Y	Y	Y	Y	N
36 LaFalce	Y	Y	N	N	N	N	Y	N
37 Nowak	Y	Y	N	N	N	N	Y	Y
38 ***Kemp***	N	N	N	Y	N	Y	N	Y
39 Lundine	Y	Y	N	N	Y	N	Y	N
NORTH CAROLINA								
1 Jones	Y	Y	N	Y	Y	Y	Y	N
2 Fountain	Y	N	Y	Y	N	Y	Y	Y
3 Whitley	Y	N	Y	Y	Y	Y	Y	Y
4 Andrews	Y	N	N	Y	N	?	Y	Y
5 Neal	?	N	N	Y	N	N	Y	Y
6 ***Johnston***	N	N	Y	Y	N	Y	N	Y
7 Rose	Y	N	N	N	Y	N	Y	N
8 Hefner	Y	N	N	Y	Y	Y	Y	Y

	1	2	3	4	5	6	7	8
9 ***Martin***	Y	N	Y	N	N	Y	N	Y
10 ***Broyhill***	N	N	Y	Y	Y	Y	N	Y
11 ***Hendon***	Y	N	Y	Y	N	Y	Y	Y
NORTH DAKOTA								
AL Dorgan	Y	Y	N	N	Y	N	Y	N
OHIO								
1 ***Gradison***	N	N	Y	Y	N	Y	N	N
2 Luken	Y	Y	N	N	Y	N	Y	N
3 Hall	Y	Y	N	N	N	N	N	N
4 ***Oxley***	Y	N	Y	N	N	Y	N	N
5 ***Latta***	N	N	Y	Y	Y	Y	N	Y
6 ***McEwen***	Y	N	Y	N	N	Y	N	Y
7 ***Brown***	?	Y	Y	?	?	?	?	?
8 ***Kindness***	Y	N	Y	Y	N	Y	N	Y
9 ***Weber***	Y	Y	Y	N	N	Y	Y	N
10 ***Miller***	N	N	Y	Y	Y	Y	N	Y
11 ***Stanton***	?	?	Y	Y	Y	Y	N	N
12 Shamansky	Y	Y	N	N	Y	N	Y	N
13 Pease	Y	Y	N	N	Y	N	Y	N
14 Seiberling	Y	Y	N	N	Y	N	Y	N
15 ***Wylie***	Y	Y	Y	Y	N	?	N	?
16 ***Regula***	Y	N	Y	N	Y	Y	Y	Y
17 ***Ashbrook***[5]				Y	N	Y	N	Y
18 Applegate	Y	Y	N	Y	Y	N	Y	Y
19 ***Williams***	Y	Y	Y	N	N	Y	Y	N
20 Oakar	Y	Y	N	N	?	N	Y	Y
21 Stokes	Y	Y	N	N	Y	N	Y	N
22 Eckart	Y	Y	N	N	N	N	Y	N
23 Mottl	Y	Y	N	Y	N	N	Y	Y
OKLAHOMA								
1 Jones	Y	N	N	N	Y	N	Y	N
2 Synar	Y	N	N	N	N	-	Y	N
3 Watkins	Y	N	N	Y	Y	N	Y	Y
4 McCurdy	Y	N	Y	N	N	Y	Y	N
5 ***Edwards***	Y	N	Y	N	Y	Y	N	Y
6 English	Y	N	N	Y	N	Y	Y	Y
OREGON								
1 AuCoin	Y	Y	N	N	Y	N	Y	N
2 ***Smith***	Y	N	Y	Y	N	Y	N	Y
3 Wyden	Y	Y	N	N	Y	N	Y	N
4 Weaver	Y	Y	N	N	Y	N	Y	N
PENNSYLVANIA								
1 Foglietta	?	Y	N	N	Y	N	Y	Y
2 Gray	Y	Y	N	N	Y	N	Y	N
3 Smith	?	Y	N	N	?	Y	Y	Y
4 ***Dougherty***	Y	Y	N	Y	Y	Y	Y	Y
5 ***Schulze***	Y	N	Y	Y	N	#	Y	?
6 Yatron	Y	Y	N	N	N	N	Y	Y
7 Edgar	Y	Y	N	N	N	N	Y	N
8 ***Coyne, J.***	Y	N	Y	Y	N	Y	Y	Y
9 ***Shuster***	Y	Y	Y	N	N	Y	Y	Y
10 ***McDade***	Y	Y	Y	N	Y	#	Y	N
11 ***Nelligan***	Y	Y	Y	Y	N	Y	Y	Y
12 Murtha	Y	N	N	Y	Y	Y	Y	Y
13 ***Coughlin***	Y	N	Y	N	Y	Y	Y	Y
14 Coyne, W.	Y	Y	N	N	Y	N	Y	N
15 ***Ritter***	Y	Y	Y	Y	N	Y	N	Y
16 ***Walker***	N	N	Y	N	N	Y	N	Y
17 Ertel	Y	Y	N	N	N	N	Y	?
18 Walgren	Y	Y	N	N	Y	N	Y	N
19 ***Goodling***	N	N	Y	N	N	P	Y	N
20 Gaydos	Y	Y	N	N	Y	Y	Y	Y
21 Bailey	Y	N	N	Y	Y	Y	Y	Y
22 Murphy	Y	Y	N	Y	Y	N	Y	Y
23 ***Clinger***	N	N	Y	Y	N	Y	Y	N
24 ***Marks***	Y	Y	N	?	?	Y	Y	?
25 ***Atkinson***	Y	Y	Y	Y	Y	Y	N	Y
RHODE ISLAND								
1 St Germain	Y	Y	N	N	N	N	Y	N
2 ***Schneider***	+	Y	N	N	Y	N	Y	N
SOUTH CAROLINA								
1 ***Hartnett***	N	N	Y	Y	Y	Y	N	Y
2 ***Spence***	Y	N	Y	Y	N	Y	N	Y
3 Derrick	Y	Y	N	N	Y	N	Y	N
4 ***Campbell***	?	N	Y	Y	N	Y	N	Y
5 Holland	Y	Y	?	Y	Y	?	Y	Y
6 ***Napier***	Y	N	Y	Y	N	Y	N	Y
SOUTH DAKOTA								
1 Daschle	Y	Y	N	N	N	N	Y	N
2 ***Roberts***	Y	N	Y	N	N	Y	Y	N
TENNESSEE								
1 ***Quillen***	Y	Y	Y	Y	Y	Y	N	Y
2 ***Duncan***	Y	Y	Y	Y	Y	Y	Y	Y
3 Bouquard[6]	Y	N	N	Y	N	?	Y	N
4 Gore	Y	Y	N	Y	Y	N	Y	N
5 Boner	Y	Y	N	Y	N	N	Y	Y
6 ***Beard***	Y	N	Y	Y	X	?	Y	?

	1	2	3	4	5	6	7	8
7 Jones	Y	Y	Y	?	?	?	Y	N
8 Ford	?	Y	N	N	?	X	Y	N
TEXAS								
1 Hall, S.	Y	N	Y	N	N	Y	N	Y
2 Wilson	Y	N	Y	Y	Y	Y	Y	Y
3 ***Collins***	N	N	Y	Y	?	?	X	?
4 Hall, R.	Y	N	Y	Y	N	Y	N	N
5 Mattox	?	Y	N	N	Y	?	#	?
6 Gramm	N	N	Y	Y	Y	Y	N	Y
7 ***Archer***	Y	N	Y	Y	Y	Y	N	N
8 ***Fields***	Y	N	Y	Y	N	Y	N	Y
9 Brooks	Y	N	N	Y	Y	N	Y	N
10 Pickle	Y	Y	Y	N	Y	Y	Y	N
11 Leath	N	N	Y	Y	?	Y	Y	Y
12 Wright	Y	N	N	Y	Y	N	Y	N
13 Hightower	Y	N	Y	N	Y	Y	Y	N
14 Patman	Y	N	Y	Y	Y	Y	N	Y
15 de la Garza	Y	Y	N	Y	Y	Y	Y	Y
16 White	Y	N	Y	Y	Y	Y	Y	Y
17 Stenholm	N	N	Y	Y	Y	Y	N	Y
18 Leland	Y	Y	N	N	Y	N	Y	N
19 Hance	N	N	Y	Y	Y	Y	Y	Y
20 Gonzalez	Y	Y	N	N	N	N	Y	Y
21 ***Loeffler***	Y	N	Y	Y	Y	Y	N	Y
22 ***Paul***	N	N	Y	N	N	Y	N	N
23 Kazen	Y	N	N	Y	N	Y	Y	Y
24 Frost	Y	Y	N	Y	Y	N	Y	N
UTAH								
1 ***Hansen***	?	N	Y	Y	?	Y	N	Y
2 ***Marriott***	Y	N	Y	Y	N	Y	?	Y
VERMONT								
AL ***Jeffords***	Y	Y	N	N	Y	N	Y	N
VIRGINIA								
1 ***Trible***	Y	N	Y	Y	N	Y	N	Y
2 ***Whitehurst***	Y	N	Y	Y	N	Y	N	Y
3 ***Bliley***	Y	N	Y	Y	N	Y	N	Y
4 ***Daniel, R.***	Y	N	Y	Y	N	Y	N	Y
5 Daniel, D.	Y	N	Y	Y	Y	Y	Y	?
6 ***Butler***	N	N	Y	Y	Y	Y	N	Y
7 ***Robinson***	Y	N	Y	Y	N	Y	Y	Y
8 ***Parris***	Y	Y	Y	N	N	Y	Y	Y
9 ***Wampler***	Y	Y	Y	Y	N	Y	Y	Y
10 ***Wolf***	Y	Y	Y	Y	N	Y	Y	Y
WASHINGTON								
1 ***Pritchard***	Y	N	Y	N	Y	N	Y	N
2 Swift	Y	N	N	N	Y	N	Y	N
3 Bonker	Y	N	N	N	Y	N	Y	N
4 ***Morrison***	Y	N	Y	Y	Y	Y	Y	Y
5 Foley	Y	N	N	N	Y	N	Y	N
6 Dicks	Y	N	N	Y	Y	N	Y	N
7 Lowry	Y	Y	N	N	Y	N	Y	N
WEST VIRGINIA								
1 Mollohan	Y	Y	N	Y	Y	Y	Y	Y
2 ***Benedict***	Y	N	Y	N	Y	Y	N	N
3 ***Staton***	Y	N	Y	Y	N	Y	N	Y
4 Rahall	Y	Y	N	N	?	N	Y	Y
WISCONSIN								
1 Aspin	Y	N	N	N	Y	N	Y	N
2 Kastenmeier	Y	Y	N	N	N	N	Y	N
3 ***Gunderson***	Y	Y	Y	N	N	N	Y	N
4 Zablocki	Y	Y	N	N	Y	N	Y	N
5 Reuss	Y	Y	N	N	Y	N	Y	N
6 ***Petri***	N	Y	Y	Y	N	Y	Y	Y
7 Obey	Y	Y	N	N	Y	N	Y	N
8 ***Roth***	Y	N	Y	N	N	Y	N	Y
9 ***Sensenbrenner***	Y	N	N	N	N	Y	N	Y
WYOMING								
AL ***Cheney***	N	N	Y	Y	Y	Y	N	Y

1. Rep. Matthew G. Martinez, D-Calif., sworn in July 15, 1982, to succeed George E. Danielson, D, who resigned March 9, 1982.

2. Rep. Katie Hall, D-Ind., sworn in Nov. 29, 1982, to succeed Adam Benjamin Jr., D, who died Sept. 7, 1982.

3. Rep. Thomas P. O'Neill Jr., D-Mass., as Speaker, votes at his own discretion.

4. Rep. Fred Richmond, D-N.Y., resigned, Aug. 25, 1982.

5. Rep. Jean S. Ashbrook, R-Ohio, sworn in July 12, 1982, to succeed her husband, John M. Ashbrook, R, who died April 24, 1982.

6. Rep. Marilyn Lloyd Bouquard, D-Tenn., was known as Marilyn Lloyd in the 98th Congress.

Southern states - Ala., Ark., Fla., Ga., Ky., La., Miss., N.C., Okla., S.C., Tenn., Texas, Va.

9. H J Res 350. Balanced Budget Constitutional Amendment. Passage of the joint resolution to propose an amendment to the Constitution to require Congress to adopt a balanced federal budget every year, except in time of war, unless a three-fifths majority of Congress agreed to deficit spending. Rejected 236-187: R 167-20; D 69-167 (ND 12-147, SD 57-20), Oct. 1, 1982. A two-thirds majority of those present and voting (282 in this case) of both houses is required for passage of a joint resolution proposing an amendment to the Constitution. A "yea" was a vote supporting the president's position.

10. HR 6211. Transportation Assistance Act of 1982. Adoption of the rule (H Res 620) providing for House floor consideration of the bill to authorize funds for highway and mass transit programs for fiscal 1983-1986 and to increase gasoline and other highway taxes. Adopted 197-194: R 59-114; D 138-80 (ND 112-34, SD 26-46), Dec. 6, 1982.

11. HR 7355. Department of Defense Appropriations, Fiscal 1983. Addabbo, D-N.Y., amendment to delete $988 million for procurement of five MX missiles. Adopted 245-176: R 50-138; D 195-38 (ND 151-7, SD 44-31), Dec. 7, 1982. A "nay" was a vote supporting the president's position.

12. H J Res 631. Continuing Appropriations, Fiscal 1983/Pay Raise. Traxler, D-Mich., amendment to retain the existing cap on salaries of members of Congress at $60,662.50 a year. Rejected 208-208: R 121-65; D 87-143 (ND 46-109, SD 41-34), Dec. 14, 1982.

13. H J Res 631. Continuing Appropriations, Fiscal 1983/Clinch River. Coughlin, R-Pa., amendment to bar use of funds provided by the joint resolution for research and development, design or construction of the Clinch River breeder reactor. Adopted 217-196: R 80-102; D 137-94 (ND 121-33, SD 16-61), Dec. 14, 1982. A "nay" was a vote supporting the president's position.

14. H J Res 631. Continuing Appropriations, Fiscal 1983/Jobs. Conte, R-Mass., motion to recommit the joint resolution to the Appropriations Committee with instructions to delete jobs program funding (Title II) and add $44 million in funding for Radio Liberty. Motion rejected 191-215: R 171-7; D 20-208 (ND 2-150, SD 18-58), Dec. 14, 1982. A "yea" was a vote supporting the president's position.

15. HR 5133. Automobile Domestic Content Requirements. Passage of the bill to require automakers to use set percentages of U.S. labor and parts in automobiles they sell in the United States. Passed 215-188: R 44-130; D 171-58 (ND 132-20, SD 39-38), Dec. 15, 1982. A "nay" was a vote supporting the president's position.

16. H Res 632. Contempt of Congress Proceedings Against Anne M. Gorsuch. Adoption of the resolution to cite Environmental Protection Agency Administrator Anne M. Gorsuch for contempt of Congress for refusing to furnish certain documents under subpoena to the House Public Works and Transportation Subcommittee on Investigations and Oversight. Adopted 259-105: R 55-101; D 204-4 (ND 145-2, SD 59-2), Dec. 16, 1982.

KEY	
Y	Voted for (yea).
#	Paired for.
+	Announced for.
N	Voted against (nay).
X	Paired against.
-	Announced against.
P	Voted "present".
C	Voted "present" to avoid possible conflict of interest.
?	Did not vote or otherwise make a position known.

Democrats *Republicans*

	9	10	11	12	13	14	15	16
ALABAMA								
1 *Edwards*	Y	Y	N	Y	N	Y	N	?
2 *Dickinson*	Y	N	N	Y	N	Y	N	N
3 Nichols	Y	N	N	Y	N	Y	Y	?
4 Bevill	Y	?	N	Y	N	Y	Y	Y
5 Flippo	Y	Y	N	Y	N	N	Y	#
6 *Smith*	Y	N	N	Y	N	Y	Y	N
7 Shelby	Y	N	N	Y	N	N	Y	Y
ALASKA								
AL *Young*	Y	N	N	N	Y	?	?	
ARIZONA								
1 *Rhodes*	N	Y	N	N	?	?	?	?
2 Udall	N	Y	Y	N	Y	N	Y	Y
3 *Stump*	Y	N	N	Y	N	Y	N	N
4 *Rudd*	Y	N	N	Y	N	Y	N	N
ARKANSAS								
1 Alexander	N	?	?	N	N	N	#	?
2 *Bethune*	N	N	N	Y	Y	Y	N	N
3 *Hammerschmidt*	Y	N	N	Y	N	Y	N	N
4 Anthony	Y	Y	Y	N	N	N	N	Y
CALIFORNIA								
1 *Chappie*	Y	N	N	?	?	#	N	N
2 *Clausen*	Y	Y	N	Y	N	Y	X	N
3 Matsui	N	Y	Y	N	Y	N	Y	Y
4 Fazio	N	Y	Y	N	Y	N	Y	Y
5 Burton, J.	N	Y	Y	?	?	X	#	Y
6 Burton, P.	N	Y	Y	N	Y	N	Y	Y
7 Miller	N	Y	N	N	Y	N	Y	Y
8 Dellums	N	Y	Y	N	Y	N	Y	Y
9 Stark	N	Y	Y	N	Y	N	Y	Y
10 Edwards	N	Y	Y	N	Y	N	Y	Y
11 Lantos	N	?	Y	Y	Y	N	Y	?
12 *McCloskey*	?	?	Y	N	Y	N	Y	Y
13 Mineta	N	Y	Y	N	N	N	Y	Y
14 *Shumway*	Y	N	N	Y	N	Y	N	N
15 Coelho	N	Y	Y	N	N	N	Y	Y
16 Panetta	N	Y	Y	Y	Y	N	N	Y
17 *Pashayan*	Y	Y	N	N	Y	N	N	N
18 *Thomas*	Y	Y	N	N	?	#	N	?
19 *Lagomarsino*	Y	Y	N	Y	N	Y	N	N
20 *Goldwater*	?	N	N	?	N	?	?	?
21 *Fiedler*	Y	N	N	Y	N	N	N	N
22 *Moorhead*	Y	N	Y	N	Y	N	N	N
23 Beilenson	N	Y	Y	?	?	?	N	Y
24 Waxman	N	Y	Y	N	Y	N	Y	Y
25 Roybal	N	Y	Y	N	Y	N	Y	Y
26 *Rousselot*	Y	Y	N	N	Y	N	Y	N
27 *Dornan*	Y	Y	N	N	N	N	N	?
28 Dixon	N	Y	Y	N	Y	N	Y	Y
29 Hawkins	N	Y	Y	N	Y	N	Y	?
30 Martinez	N	Y	?	?	Y	N	Y	?
31 Dymally	N	Y	Y	N	Y	N	Y	?
32 Anderson	Y	Y	Y	Y	N	N	N	Y
33 Grisham	Y	Y	N	N	N	N	N	N
34 *Lungren*	Y	N	N	Y	N	Y	N	N
35 *Dreier*	Y	N	N	Y	N	Y	N	N
36 Brown	N	Y	Y	N	Y	N	?	?
37 *Lewis*	Y	Y	N	N	N	Y	N	?
38 Patterson	N	?	Y	N	Y	N	Y	Y
39 *Dannemeyer*	Y	N	N	Y	N	N	X	X
40 *Badham*	#	N	N	N	Y	X	X	
41 *Lowery*	Y	Y	N	Y	N	Y	N	N
42 *Hunter*	Y	N	N	Y	N	Y	N	N
43 *Burgener*	Y	Y	N	N	N	Y	N	X
COLORADO								
1 Schroeder	N	N	Y	Y	Y	?	?	Y
2 Wirth	N	Y	Y	Y	Y	N	Y	Y
3 Kogovsek	N	Y	Y	N	Y	N	Y	N
4 *Brown*	Y	N	N	Y	Y	Y	N	N

	9	10	11	12	13	14	15	16
5 *Kramer*	Y	N	N	Y	Y	Y	N	N
CONNECTICUT								
1 Kennelly	N	Y	Y	N	Y	N	Y	Y
2 Gejdenson	N	N	Y	N	Y	N	Y	Y
3 *DeNardis*	N	?	Y	N	Y	?	N	Y
4 *McKinney*	N	N	Y	Y	Y	Y	Y	Y
5 Ratchford	N	Y	Y	Y	N	Y	N	Y
6 Moffett	N	Y	Y	N	?	Y	?	
DELAWARE								
AL *Evans*	Y	Y	N	N	Y	?	N	?
FLORIDA								
1 Hutto	Y	N	N	N	N	N	N	Y
2 Fuqua	Y	N	Y	Y	N	N	N	#
3 Bennett	Y	Y	Y	N	N	N	N	Y
4 Chappell	#	N	N	N	N	N	N	Y
5 *McCollum*	Y	N	N	Y	Y	Y	N	Y
6 *Young*	Y	N	N	Y	N	Y	N	Y
7 Gibbons	Y	Y	Y	N	N	N	N	Y
8 Ireland	Y	N	N	Y	N	Y	N	?
9 Nelson	Y	Y	N	N	N	N	N	Y
10 *Bafalis*	Y	?	?	N	N	N	N	N
11 Mica	Y	Y	Y	N	N	N	Y	Y
12 *Shaw*	Y	Y	N	Y	Y	Y	N	N
13 Lehman	N	?	Y	?	?	?	?	?
14 Pepper	N	Y	Y	N	N	N	N	Y
15 Fascell	N	?	Y	Y	Y	N	Y	Y
GEORGIA								
1 Ginn	Y	N	N	N	N	N	N	Y
2 Hatcher	Y	N	N	Y	N	Y	N	Y
3 Brinkley	Y	N	Y	N	N	N	N	Y
4 Levitas	Y	N	?	Y	Y	Y	Y	Y
5 Fowler	N	Y	Y	Y	Y	Y	Y	Y
6 *Gingrich*	Y	N	N	Y	N	Y	N	Y
7 McDonald	Y	N	N	Y	N	Y	N	N
8 Evans	Y	N	N	?	?	?	N	?
9 Jenkins	Y	Y	Y	N	Y	Y	Y	Y
10 Barnard	Y	N	N	N	N	N	N	Y
HAWAII								
1 Heftel	N	?	Y	N	Y	N	Y	Y
2 Akaka	N	Y	Y	N	N	N	Y	Y
IDAHO								
1 *Craig*	Y	N	N	Y	N	Y	N	X
2 *Hansen*	Y	N	N	Y	N	Y	N	N
ILLINOIS								
1 Washington	N	?	Y	?	Y	N	Y	Y
2 Savage	N	?	Y	N	Y	N	Y	Y
3 Russo	N	Y	Y	N	Y	N	Y	Y
4 *Derwinski*	Y	Y	N	N	N	N	N	N
5 Fary	N	Y	Y	?	?	X	Y	Y
6 *Hyde*	Y	N	N	N	N	Y	N	Y
7 Collins	N	Y	Y	N	Y	N	Y	Y
8 Rostenkowski	N	Y	Y	N	N	N	N	Y
9 Yates	N	Y	Y	N	Y	N	?	Y
10 *Porter*	Y	N	Y	N	Y	N	N	N
11 Annunzio	N	Y	Y	N	Y	N	N	Y
12 *Crane, P.*	Y	N	N	Y	Y	Y	N	Y
13 *McClory*	Y	Y	N	N	N	N	N	N
14 *Erlenborn*	Y	Y	N	N	N	Y	N	N
15 *Corcoran*	Y	Y	N	Y	N	Y	N	N
16 *Martin*	Y	Y	Y	N	Y	Y	N	Y
17 O'Brien	Y	Y	Y	Y	Y	Y	Y	?
18 *Michel*	Y	Y	N	N	N	N	N	N
19 *Railsback*	Y	Y	Y	?	?	?	Y	?
20 *Findley*	Y	N	Y	N	Y	Y	?	Y
21 *Madigan*	Y	N	N	Y	N	Y	Y	N
22 *Crane, D.*	Y	N	N	Y	N	Y	N	?
23 Price	N	Y	N	N	N	N	N	Y
24 Simon	N	Y	N	Y	N	Y	Y	Y
INDIANA								
1 Hall[1]		Y	Y	N	Y	N	Y	Y
2 Fithian	N	N	Y	N	?	N	Y	Y
3 *Hiler*	Y	N	N	Y	Y	Y	N	N
4 *Coats*	Y	N	Y	N	Y	Y	N	?
5 *Hillis*	Y	?	N	Y	Y	Y	Y	N
6 Evans	N	?	Y	N	N	N	Y	Y
7 *Myers*	Y	N	N	N	N	Y	N	N
8 *Deckard*	Y	?	Y	Y	Y	Y	N	Y
9 Hamilton	N	N	Y	Y	N	Y	Y	Y
10 Sharp	N	N	Y	Y	N	Y	N	Y
11 Jacobs	Y	N	Y	Y	Y	N	Y	?
IOWA								
1 *Leach*	Y	N	Y	Y	Y	Y	Y	Y
2 *Tauke*	Y	N	Y	Y	Y	Y	X	Y
3 *Evans*	Y	N	Y	N	Y	N	Y	Y
4 Smith	N	Y	N	N	N	N	N	Y
5 Harkin	N	N	Y	Y	N	Y	N	Y
6 Bedell	N	N	Y	Y	Y	N	N	Y

ND - Northern Democrats   SD - Southern Democrats

	9	10	11	12	13	14	15	16
KANSAS								
1 ***Roberts***	Y	N	Y	Y	N	Y	N	N
2 ***Jeffries***	Y	N	N	Y	Y	Y	N	X
3 ***Winn***	Y	?	N	N	N	Y	N	N
4 Glickman	N	N	Y	Y	Y	N	N	Y
5 ***Whittaker***	Y	N	Y	Y	Y	Y	N	Y
KENTUCKY								
1 Hubbard	Y	N	Y	Y	N	Y	Y	?
2 Natcher	Y	Y	Y	Y	N	N	Y	Y
3 Mazzoli	N	Y	Y	N	N	N	Y	Y
4 ***Snyder***	Y	Y	Y	Y	Y	Y	Y	?
5 ***Rogers***	Y	N	N	Y	Y	Y	Y	N
6 ***Hopkins***	Y	N	Y	Y	Y	Y	Y	Y
7 Perkins	N	N	Y	Y	N	N	Y	Y
LOUISIANA								
1 ***Livingston***	Y	N	N	N	N	Y	N	Y
2 Boggs	N	Y	Y	N	N	N	Y	Y
3 Tauzin	Y	N	N	Y	N	Y	Y	Y
4 Roemer	Y	N	Y	Y	Y	Y	Y	Y
5 Huckaby	Y	N	Y	Y	Y	Y	N	?
6 ***Moore***	Y	N	N	Y	Y	Y	N	Y
7 Breaux	Y	Y	N	N	N	N	N	Y
8 Long	N	Y	Y	N	N	N	Y	Y
MAINE								
1 ***Emery***	Y	?	N	Y	Y	Y	?	N
2 ***Snowe***	Y	N	Y	Y	Y	Y	N	Y
MARYLAND								
1 Dyson	Y	Y	Y	Y	N	N	Y	Y
2 Long	N	Y	Y	Y	Y	N	Y	?
3 Mikulski	N	Y	Y	Y	Y	N	Y	Y
4 ***Holt***	Y	N	N	N	N	Y	N	?
5 Hoyer	N	Y	Y	N	Y	N	Y	Y
6 Byron	Y	?	Y	Y	Y	N	N	Y
7 Mitchell	N	Y	Y	Y	Y	N	Y	Y
8 Barnes	N	?	Y	N	Y	N	Y	Y
MASSACHUSETTS								
1 ***Conte***	N	?	Y	N	Y	Y	Y	Y
2 Boland	N	Y	Y	Y	Y	N	Y	Y
3 Early	N	Y	Y	N	Y	N	Y	Y
4 Frank	N	Y	Y	Y	Y	N	Y	?
5 Shannon	N	Y	Y	N	Y	N	Y	Y
6 Mavroules	N	Y	Y	N	Y	N	Y	Y
7 Markey	N	Y	Y	N	Y	N	Y	Y
8 O'Neill[2]				N				
9 Moakley	N	Y	Y	N	Y	N	Y	Y
10 ***Heckler***	N	Y	?	N	Y	?	?	?
11 Donnelly	N	Y	Y	N	Y	N	N	Y
12 Studds	N	N	Y	N	Y	N	Y	Y
MICHIGAN								
1 Conyers	N	N	Y	N	Y	N	Y	Y
2 ***Pursell***	Y	N	Y	Y	Y	Y	?	?
3 Wolpe	N	Y	Y	Y	Y	N	Y	Y
4 ***Siljander***	Y	N	N	Y	N	Y	Y	N
5 ***Sawyer***	Y	N	N	Y	Y	Y	N	N
6 ***Dunn***	Y	?	N	Y	Y	Y	Y	N
7 Kildee	N	Y	Y	Y	Y	N	Y	Y
8 Traxler	N	Y	Y	Y	Y	N	Y	Y
9 ***Vander Jagt***	Y	N	N	Y	Y	Y	N	?
10 Albosta	N	N	Y	Y	Y	N	Y	Y
11 ***Davis***	Y	N	N	Y	N	N	Y	Y
12 Bonior	N	Y	Y	Y	Y	N	Y	Y
13 Crockett	N	Y	Y	N	Y	N	Y	Y
14 Hertel	N	Y	Y	Y	Y	N	Y	Y
15 Ford	N	Y	Y	N	Y	N	Y	Y
16 Dingell	N	Y	Y	N	Y	N	Y	Y
17 Brodhead	N	Y	Y	N	Y	N	Y	Y
18 Blanchard	?	?	?	?	?	?	#	?
19 ***Broomfield***	Y	N	N	N	Y	Y	Y	?
MINNESOTA								
1 ***Erdahl***	Y	N	Y	Y	?	Y	N	Y
2 ***Hagedorn***	Y	N	N	?	?	?	?	?
3 ***Frenzel***	Y	N	Y	N	Y	Y	N	Y
4 Vento	N	Y	Y	N	Y	N	Y	Y
5 Sabo	N	Y	Y	N	Y	N	Y	Y
6 ***Weber***	Y	N	Y	Y	Y	Y	N	Y
7 ***Stangeland***	Y	N	N	Y	N	Y	N	N
8 Oberstar	N	N	N	Y	N	Y	Y	Y
MISSISSIPPI								
1 Whitten	Y	Y	Y	N	N	N	Y	Y
2 Bowen	Y	Y	N	N	N	N	N	Y
3 Montgomery	Y	Y	N	?	N	Y	N	Y
4 Dowdy	Y	Y	Y	N	N	N	Y	Y
5 ***Lott***	Y	Y	N	N	Y	Y	N	N
MISSOURI								
1 Clay	N	Y	Y	N	Y	N	Y	Y
2 Young	N	Y	Y	N	N	N	Y	Y
3 Gephardt	N	Y	Y	Y	Y	N	Y	Y

	9	10	11	12	13	14	15	16
4 Skelton	Y	?	?	N	N	N	Y	Y
5 Bolling	N	Y	?	N	?	?	?	?
6 ***Coleman***	Y	N	N	N	N	Y	Y	Y
7 ***Taylor***	Y	?	N	Y	N	Y	N	N
8 ***Bailey***	Y	N	N	Y	Y	Y	N	N
9 Volkmer	Y	N	Y	Y	Y	N	Y	Y
10 ***Emerson***	Y	N	N	Y	N	Y	N	N
MONTANA								
1 Williams	N	N	Y	N	Y	N	Y	Y
2 ***Marlenee***	Y	?	N	N	N	Y	N	N
NEBRASKA								
1 ***Bereuter***	Y	N	N	Y	N	Y	N	Y
2 ***Daub***	Y	N	N	Y	N	Y	N	N
3 ***Smith***	Y	N	Y	Y	N	Y	N	N
NEVADA								
AL Santini	Y	?	?	Y	N	?	N	?
NEW HAMPSHIRE								
1 D'Amours	N	Y	Y	Y	Y	N	?	Y
2 ***Gregg***	Y	Y	Y	Y	Y	Y	N	N
NEW JERSEY								
1 Florio	N	?	Y	N	Y	N	Y	Y
2 Hughes	N	N	Y	Y	Y	N	Y	Y
3 Howard	N	Y	Y	N	Y	N	Y	Y
4 ***Smith***	Y	Y	Y	Y	Y	N	Y	N
5 ***Fenwick***	Y	Y	Y	N	Y	Y	N	Y
6 ***Forsythe***	?	Y	Y	N	N	Y	?	N
7 ***Roukema***	N	N	Y	Y	N	Y	N	Y
8 Roe	N	N	Y	N	N	N	Y	Y
9 ***Hollenbeck***	N	Y	Y	N	N	?	Y	N
10 Rodino	N	Y	Y	N	Y	N	Y	Y
11 Minish	N	Y	Y	N	Y	N	Y	Y
12 ***Rinaldo***	N	Y	Y	Y	N	N	Y	Y
13 ***Courter***	Y	N	N	Y	Y	Y	N	Y
14 Guarini	X	Y	Y	N	Y	N	Y	Y
15 Dwyer	N	Y	Y	N	N	N	Y	Y
NEW MEXICO								
1 ***Lujan***	Y	N	N	Y	N	Y	N	N
2 ***Skeen***	Y	N	N	Y	N	Y	N	N
NEW YORK								
1 ***Carney***	Y	?	N	N	N	Y	N	N
2 Downey	N	Y	Y	N	Y	N	Y	Y
3 ***Carman***	Y	Y	N	N	Y	Y	N	N
4 ***Lent***	Y	Y	Y	N	Y	Y	N	N
5 ***McGrath***	Y	Y	Y	N	Y	Y	N	N
6 ***LeBoutillier***	Y	?	N	Y	Y	Y	?	?
7 Addabbo	N	Y	Y	N	Y	N	Y	Y
8 Rosenthal	N	Y	Y	?	Y	N	Y	?
9 Ferraro	N	Y	Y	N	Y	N	Y	Y
10 Biaggi	N	Y	Y	N	N	N	Y	Y
11 Scheuer	N	Y	Y	N	Y	N	Y	Y
12 Chisholm	N	?	Y	N	Y	N	Y	Y
13 Solarz	N	Y	Y	N	Y	N	Y	Y
14 Richmond[3]								
15 Zeferetti	N	?	Y	N	N	N	?	Y
16 Schumer	N	Y	Y	N	Y	N	Y	Y
17 ***Molinari***	Y	?	N	N	Y	Y	N	Y
18 ***Green***	N	Y	Y	N	Y	Y	N	Y
19 Rangel	N	Y	Y	N	Y	N	Y	Y
20 Weiss	N	N	Y	N	Y	N	Y	Y
21 Garcia	N	Y	Y	N	Y	N	Y	?
22 Bingham	N	Y	Y	N	Y	?	N	Y
23 Peyser	N	Y	Y	N	Y	N	Y	Y
24 Ottinger	N	N	Y	N	Y	N	Y	Y
25 ***Fish***	Y	Y	N	N	Y	Y	Y	Y
26 ***Gilman***	N	N	N	Y	Y	Y	Y	Y
27 McHugh	N	Y	Y	N	Y	N	N	Y
28 Stratton	N	Y	N	N	N	N	Y	Y
29 ***Solomon***	Y	N	N	Y	N	Y	Y	N
30 ***Martin***	Y	N	N	Y	Y	Y	N	Y
31 ***Mitchell***	Y	N	N	Y	Y	Y	N	Y
32 ***Wortley***	Y	Y	N	Y	Y	Y	Y	N
33 ***Lee***	Y	N	N	Y	N	Y	Y	?
34 ***Horton***	N	N	Y	Y	N	Y	Y	?
35 ***Conable***	Y	Y	N	Y	N	Y	N	Y
36 LaFalce	N	N	Y	N	Y	N	Y	Y
37 Nowak	N	N	Y	N	Y	N	Y	Y
38 ***Kemp***	N	N	N	N	Y	Y	N	?
39 Lundine	N	N	Y	N	Y	N	Y	?
NORTH CAROLINA								
1 Jones	Y	Y	Y	N	N	N	Y	?
2 Fountain	Y	N	N	N	N	Y	N	Y
3 Whitley	Y	N	N	Y	N	N	N	Y
4 Andrews	Y	N	Y	N	N	N	N	Y
5 Neal	Y	N	Y	Y	Y	N	N	Y
6 ***Johnston***	Y	Y	N	N	?	Y	N	N
7 Rose	Y	Y	Y	Y	N	N	Y	?
8 Hefner	Y	N	?	Y	N	N	N	Y

	9	10	11	12	13	14	15	16
9 ***Martin***	Y	N	N	N	N	Y	N	N
10 ***Broyhill***	Y	N	N	Y	N	Y	N	N
11 ***Hendon***	Y	?	N	Y	N	Y	N	N
NORTH DAKOTA								
AL Dorgan	N	Y	Y	Y	N	N	Y	Y
OHIO								
1 ***Gradison***	Y	Y	Y	Y	Y	Y	N	Y
2 Luken	N	Y	Y	N	N	N	Y	Y
3 Hall	N	Y	Y	N	Y	N	Y	Y
4 ***Oxley***	Y	N	N	Y	N	Y	N	N
5 ***Latta***	Y	Y	N	Y	N	Y	Y	N
6 ***McEwen***	Y	N	N	Y	N	Y	Y	N
7 ***Brown***	Y	Y	N	Y	N	Y	?	N
8 ***Kindness***	Y	N	N	Y	N	?	Y	N
9 ***Weber***	Y	N	N	Y	Y	Y	N	N
10 ***Miller***	Y	N	N	Y	N	Y	Y	Y
11 ***Stanton***	Y	?	N	N	N	Y	N	?
12 Shamansky	N	Y	Y	Y	Y	N	Y	Y
13 Pease	N	Y	Y	Y	Y	N	Y	Y
14 Seiberling	N	N	Y	N	Y	N	Y	Y
15 ***Wylie***	Y	Y	N	Y	Y	Y	Y	N
16 ***Regula***	Y	N	N	Y	N	Y	Y	Y
17 ***Ashbrook***	Y	N	N	N	N	Y	N	?
18 Applegate	Y	Y	Y	Y	Y	N	Y	Y
19 ***Williams***	Y	N	Y	Y	N	N	Y	#
20 Oakar	N	Y	Y	Y	Y	N	Y	Y
21 Stokes	N	Y	Y	N	Y	N	#	Y
22 Eckart	Y	Y	Y	Y	Y	N	Y	Y
23 Mottl	Y	?	N	Y	N	N	Y	Y
OKLAHOMA								
1 Jones	N	N	Y	Y	N	N	N	Y
2 Synar	N	N	Y	Y	Y	Y	N	Y
3 Watkins	Y	Y	Y	Y	N	N	Y	Y
4 McCurdy	Y	N	Y	Y	Y	Y	Y	Y
5 ***Edwards***	?	N	N	Y	Y	Y	N	Y
6 English	Y	N	Y	Y	N	Y	Y	Y
OREGON								
1 AuCoin	N	Y	Y	Y	?	N	N	Y
2 ***Smith***	Y	N	Y	Y	N	Y	N	Y
3 Wyden	N	Y	Y	Y	Y	N	N	Y
4 Weaver	N	N	Y	?	Y	N	Y	Y
PENNSYLVANIA								
1 Foglietta	N	Y	Y	N	Y	N	Y	Y
2 Gray	N	Y	Y	N	Y	N	Y	Y
3 Smith	N	Y	Y	N	N	?	Y	?
4 ***Dougherty***	N	Y	?	N	?	N	Y	?
5 ***Schulze***	Y	Y	N	?	?	?	?	?
6 Yatron	N	N	Y	Y	N	N	Y	Y
7 Edgar	N	Y	Y	N	Y	N	Y	Y
8 ***Coyne, J.***	Y	?	N	Y	Y	Y	?	N
9 ***Shuster***	Y	Y	?	?	?	?	?	?
10 ***McDade***	N	Y	Y	N	Y	Y	N	Y
11 ***Nelligan***	N	Y	N	Y	N	Y	Y	Y
12 Murtha	N	Y	N	N	N	N	Y	Y
13 ***Coughlin***	Y	Y	Y	N	Y	Y	Y	N
14 Coyne, W.	N	Y	Y	N	N	N	Y	Y
15 ***Ritter***	Y	N	N	Y	Y	Y	Y	N
16 ***Walker***	Y	N	N	Y	Y	Y	N	N
17 Ertel	N	N	Y	N	Y	N	Y	Y
18 Walgren	N	Y	Y	Y	Y	N	Y	Y
19 ***Goodling***	Y	N	Y	N	Y	Y	Y	Y
20 Gaydos	N	Y	Y	Y	N	N	Y	Y
21 Bailey	N	Y	N	N	N	N	Y	Y
22 Murphy	N	N	Y	N	N	N	Y	Y
23 ***Clinger***	Y	Y	Y	Y	Y	Y	N	N
24 ***Marks***	N	?	Y	N	N	N	Y	Y
25 ***Atkinson***	Y	?	N	Y	N	Y	N	N
RHODE ISLAND								
1 St Germain	N	Y	Y	N	Y	N	Y	Y
2 ***Schneider***	N	N	Y	Y	Y	Y	Y	Y
SOUTH CAROLINA								
1 ***Hartnett***	Y	N	N	N	N	Y	N	N
2 ***Spence***	Y	N	N	Y	N	Y	N	N
3 Derrick	Y	Y	Y	N	Y	N	N	#
4 ***Campbell***	Y	N	N	N	N	Y	N	?
5 Holland	N	N	Y	N	N	N	N	?
6 ***Napier***	Y	N	N	N	N	Y	N	N
SOUTH DAKOTA								
1 Daschle	Y	N	Y	Y	Y	Y	?	Y
2 ***Roberts***	Y	N	N	Y	N	Y	N	N
TENNESSEE								
1 ***Quillen***	Y	N	N	Y	N	Y	N	N
2 ***Duncan***	Y	N	N	Y	N	Y	N	N
3 Bouquard[4]	Y	N	Y	Y	N	N	N	Y
4 Gore	N	N	Y	Y	N	N	N	Y
5 Boner	Y	N	Y	Y	N	N	Y	Y
6 ***Beard***	Y	N	N	Y	?	?	X	?

	9	10	11	12	13	14	15	16
7 Jones	Y	N	Y	Y	N	N	Y	Y
8 Ford	N	N	Y	N	N	N	Y	Y
TEXAS								
1 Hall, S.	Y	N	N	Y	N	N	Y	Y
2 Wilson	Y	N	N	?	N	?	Y	Y
3 ***Collins***	Y	N	N	Y	Y	Y	N	N
4 Hall, R.	Y	N	N	Y	N	N	Y	Y
5 Mattox	N	?	?	N	Y	N	Y	Y
6 Gramm	Y	N	N	Y	Y	Y	N	N
7 ***Archer***	Y	Y	N	Y	N	Y	N	?
8 ***Fields***	Y	Y	N	Y	N	Y	N	N
9 Brooks	N	Y	Y	N	N	N	Y	Y
10 Pickle	Y	Y	Y	Y	N	N	N	Y
11 Leath	Y	N	N	N	N	N	N	?
12 Wright	N	Y	Y	N	N	N	Y	Y
13 Hightower	Y	N	N	Y	N	N	N	Y
14 Patman	Y	N	N	Y	N	N	N	Y
15 de la Garza	Y	N	N	Y	Y	N	N	Y
16 White	Y	N	N	N	N	N	N	Y
17 Stenholm	Y	N	N	Y	N	Y	N	Y
18 Leland	N	?	Y	N	Y	N	Y	Y
19 Hance	Y	?	N	Y	N	N	N	Y
20 Gonzalez	N	N	Y	N	N	N	Y	Y
21 ***Loeffler***	Y	N	N	Y	N	Y	N	N
22 ***Paul***	Y	N	Y	Y	Y	Y	N	Y
23 Kazen	Y	N	N	Y	N	N	N	Y
24 Frost	N	Y	Y	N	Y	N	Y	Y
UTAH								
1 ***Hansen***	Y	N	N	Y	N	Y	N	N
2 ***Marriott***	Y	N	N	Y	N	Y	N	N
VERMONT								
AL ***Jeffords***	N	N	Y	N	Y	Y	N	Y
VIRGINIA								
1 ***Trible***	Y	N	N	N	Y	Y	N	N
2 ***Whitehurst***	Y	Y	N	Y	N	Y	N	N
3 ***Bliley***	Y	N	N	N	N	Y	N	N
4 ***Daniel, R.***	Y	Y	N	N	N	Y	N	N
5 Daniel, D.	?	N	N	N	N	Y	N	Y
6 ***Butler***	Y	N	N	N	N	Y	N	N
7 ***Robinson***	Y	N	N	N	N	Y	N	N
8 ***Parris***	Y	Y	N	Y	N	Y	N	Y
9 ***Wampler***	Y	N	N	N	N	Y	N	N
10 ***Wolf***	Y	N	N	N	Y	Y	N	N
WASHINGTON								
1 ***Pritchard***	N	Y	Y	N	Y	Y	N	Y
2 Swift	N	N	Y	N	Y	N	Y	Y
3 Bonker	N	-	Y	N	Y	N	N	Y
4 ***Morrison***	Y	N	N	Y	N	Y	N	N
5 Foley	N	Y	Y	N	N	N	N	Y
6 Dicks	N	Y	Y	N	Y	N	Y	Y
7 Lowry	N	Y	Y	N	Y	N	N	Y
WEST VIRGINIA								
1 Mollohan	N	Y	N	N	N	N	Y	Y
2 ***Benedict***	Y	N	N	Y	N	Y	N	N
3 ***Staton***	Y	Y	N	N	N	Y	N	N
4 Rahall	N	N	Y	N	Y	N	Y	Y
WISCONSIN								
1 Aspin	N	N	Y	Y	Y	N	Y	Y
2 Kastenmeier	N	N	Y	N	Y	N	Y	Y
3 ***Gunderson***	Y	N	Y	Y	Y	Y	N	Y
4 Zablocki	N	Y	Y	N	N	N	Y	Y
5 Reuss	N	Y	Y	N	Y	N	N	Y
6 ***Petri***	Y	N	Y	Y	Y	Y	N	Y
7 Obey	N	N	Y	N	Y	N	Y	Y
8 ***Roth***	Y	N	N	Y	N	Y	Y	N
9 ***Sensenbrenner***	Y	N	Y	Y	Y	Y	N	Y
WYOMING								
AL ***Cheney***	Y	N	N	Y	N	Y	N	N

1. Rep. Katie Hall, D-Ind., sworn in Nov. 29, 1982, to succeed Adam Benjamin Jr., D, who died Sept. 7, 1982.

2. Rep. Thomas P. O'Neill Jr., D-Mass., as Speaker, votes at his own discretion.

3. Rep. Fred Richmond, D-N.Y., resigned, August 25, 1982.

4. Rep. Marilyn Lloyd Bouquard, D-Tenn., was known as Marilyn Lloyd in the 98th Congress.

Southern states - Ala., Ark., Fla., Ga., Ky., La., Miss., N.C., Okla., S.C., Tenn., Texas, Va.

1983 Key Votes

Senate

1. Anti-Recession Assistance

Double-digit unemployment resulting from the worst recession since World War II stimulated a variety of emergency relief proposals early in the 1983 session. Attempting to capitalize on what they saw as a traditional Democratic issue, Democratic members of Congress tried to beef up a limited job stimulus and humanitarian aid package announced by President Reagan Feb. 16.

During floor debate March 11, Senate Democrats proposed a nearly $1.7 billion increase in a $3.7 billion emergency relief measure (HR 1718) reported by the Senate Appropriations Committee. Offered by Sen. Carl Levin, D-Mich., chairman of the Democratic Task Force on Emergency Human Needs, the amendment would have added $1.3 billion for job creation and human services, including $1 billion for community development block grants, and $390 million for health and humanitarian relief.

Supporters claimed Levin's proposals would create an additional 280,000 jobs. "We're trying to take care of the millions of people whose basic needs have not been met," said Alan J. Dixon, D-Ill.

But the Republican-controlled Senate rejected the plan on a near party-line vote of 34-53: R 2-46; D 32-7 (ND 25-4, SD 7-3).

A $4.6 billion jobs and relief package cleared Congress March 24 as part of a $15.6 billion supplemental appropriations bill for fiscal 1983. The final House-Senate compromise was scaled specifically to stay within limits acceptable to the Reagan administration.

2. Fiscal 1984 Budget

Defying President Reagan and the GOP leadership, moderate Republicans and Democrats won Senate passage May 19 of a fiscal 1984 budget blueprint that increased taxes and domestic spending while slowing the defense buildup sought by the president and cutting $14.5 billion from his revised deficit estimates.

The Senate approved its budget resolution (S Con Res 27) at the end of a grueling session during which members twice rejected a leadership plan that had the reluctant support of the president and initially turned down the budget they ultimately adopted. Final approval came after Budget Committee Chairman Pete V. Domenici, R-N.M., and other opponents of the plan switched their votes to keep the nine-year-old congressional budget process from collapsing. The final tally was 50-49: R 21-32; D 29-17 (ND 24-8, SD 5-9).

The House-passed budget resolution called on Congress to approve much higher tax increases, a lower rate of defense spending, and significantly higher domestic spending than the Senate budget plan. *(House key vote 2)*

3. Senators' Pay Raise

The Senate June 16 voted to give senators a 15 percent pay raise, increasing their annual salaries from $60,662.50 to $69,800. The $9,138 pay hike, which took effect July 1, 1983, put senators at the same salary level as House members. The House raised members' pay in December 1982.

At the same time, the Senate approved a 30 percent cap, effective Jan. 1, 1984, on the honoraria income senators may receive for speeches, articles and appearances. The $20,940 annual limit already applied to all outside income earned by House members.

The pay raise and honoraria cap were included in an amendment to a fiscal 1983 supplemental appropriations bill (HR 3069 — PL 98-63) that Congress cleared July 29. The Senate agreed to the pay raise by a vote of 49-47: R 29-25; D 20-22 (ND 16-13, SD 4-9).

Although senators did not take a pay raise when House members did in 1982, they had no cap on their honoraria earnings. After honoraria reports for 1982 were made public in May, showing that 19 senators received more than $40,000 each, the House attached an amendment to HR 3069 extending the 30 percent cap to senators. The Senate Appropriations Committee eliminated the honoraria limit, but the full Senate reversed that action June 9, imposing the cap while rejecting amendments to raise senators' pay. Finally, on June 16, Henry M. Jackson, D-Wash., offered the successful amendment that raised salaries and capped honoraria.

Despite frequent complaints that their salaries were insufficient to support homes in their states and in the Washington, D.C., area, members were reluctant to approve pay hikes. Of senators up for re-election in 1984, 24 voted against the pay raise and seven supported it.

4. Abortion

The Senate June 28 rejected a proposed constitutional amendment designed to overturn the Supreme Court's 1973 *Roe v. Wade* decision that made abortion legal.

The vote on the amendment (S J Res 3) was 49-50, with Jesse Helms, R-N.C., voting present. This was 18 votes short of the two-thirds majority needed to pass an amendment. Republicans voted almost 2-1 in favor of the proposal, while Democrats opposed it by almost the same ratio: R 34-19; D 15-31 (ND 7-25, SD 8-6).

The Senate action on S J Res 3 marked the first time either house of Congress had voted on a constitutional amendment aimed at overturning the Supreme Court's abortion ruling.

Sponsored by Orrin G. Hatch, R-Utah, the measure simply stated: "A right to abortion is not secured by this Constitution." By knocking out the constitutional underpinnings for abortion rights, it was designed to authorize Congress and the states to pass new laws to restrict or prohibit abortion.

The anti-abortion movement was split on the strategy behind S J Res 3. Some favored Hatch's approach, while others — led by Helms — thought Congress should pass a statute defining a fetus as a "person" with the same constitutionally guaranteed right to life as any other person. This would require only a simple majority vote in Congress, and no ratification by the states.

Neither the House nor its Judiciary Committee acted on any comparable abortion amendment or bill in 1983.

5. Chemical Weapons

The Senate July 13 approved Reagan administration plans to begin manufacturing lethal chemical weapons for the first time since 1969, but only by the narrowest of margins, with Vice President George Bush casting a tie-breaking vote. It was the first time since 1977 that the vice president had cast a Senate vote.

At stake were new types of nerve gas bombs and artillery shells, called "binary munitions." The administration insisted that binary production was needed to deter Moscow's use of its large arsenal of chemical weapons and to provide an incentive for Soviet agreement to a ban on chemical weapons. Existing U.S. chemical weapons were inadequate, they said, because they were dangerous for U.S. troops to handle and were losing some of their potency because of chemical deterioration.

Opponents countered that the new weapons were militarily superfluous since there was a large enough supply of usable U.S. chemical weapons to force enemy troops to don clumsy protective suits and masks. Moreover, they argued, production of new chemical weapons would surrender the propaganda advantage the United States had earned from 14 years' abstention from chemical weapons production.

The key Senate vote on the issue came on a motion to table (and thus kill) an amendment to delete binary weapons production funds from the fiscal 1984 defense authorization bill (S 675). The motion was agreed to 50-49: R 35-17; D 14-32 (ND 5-27, SD 9-5), with Vice President Bush casting the deciding "yea" vote to break a 49-49 tie.

The scenario was replayed Nov. 8, when an amendment adding the nerve gas funds to the fiscal 1984 defense appropriations bill (HR 4185) was agreed to 47-46. Again, Bush cast the deciding vote for binary production.

Although the nerve gas provision remained in the authorization bill, it was ultimately deleted — at the insistence of the House — from HR 4185, the defense appropriations measure. *(House key vote 15)*

6. Interest and Dividend Withholding

Months of pressure from the banking industry and the public persuaded Congress to undo a tax reform it had approved only a year earlier: a requirement for 10 percent withholding of taxes on interest and dividend income.

The banking industry stimulated a massive letter-writing campaign against the plan, arguing that the withholding requirement would impose an unfair financial burden on honest taxpayers, as well as banks.

Opponents of repeal countered that the banks were deceiving the American public by portraying withholding as a new tax, rather than as a means of enforcing tax laws already on the books, but the lobbying campaign paid off.

Sealing a major victory for the banks, the Senate July 28 cleared a withholding repeal measure (HR 2973) by a vote of 90-7: R 51-2; D 39-5 (ND 25-5, SD 14-0).

President Reagan, who initially vowed to veto a withholding repealer, yielded when it became clear that such a veto almost certainly would be overridden. The addition of stiffer withholding compliance requirements, plus inclusion of the trade and tax portions of his Caribbean Basin Initiative, helped ensure Reagan's approval of the bill.

7. Coal Leasing

A collapse of Senate support for the coal-leasing policies of Interior Secretary James G. Watt was evident in a Sept. 20 vote to impose a moratorium on federal coal leasing.

The vote came on an amendment offered by Dale Bumpers, D-Ark., to the fiscal 1984 Interior Department appropriations bill (HR 3363 — PL 98-146). That amendment barred the use of funds in the bill for any leasing of coal on federal lands until 90 days after a study commission created to review leasing policies reported its recommendations. It was adopted 63-33: R 23-29, D 40-4 (ND 29-1, SD 11-3).

Bumpers charged that Watt's leasing program was selling too much coal too fast, and bringing less than the fair market value of the coal as a return to the Treasury.

Twice in the preceding year, the Senate had narrowly rejected similar Bumpers amendments. The first vote came Dec. 14, 1982, when a leasing-ban rider to the fiscal 1983 Interior appropriations bill (PL 97-394) was rejected 47-48. On June 14, 1983, the Senate by 48-51 rejected a similar amendment to a fiscal 1983 supplemental appropriations measure (HR 3069 — PL 98-63).

Those two votes split along party lines, with most Republicans backing Watt and most Democrats opposing him. Thirteen of the 16 senators who switched to Bumpers' side between June 14 and Sept. 20 were Republicans.

The House had approved a slightly different version of the coal-leasing ban, but the variances were easily reconciled in conference.

On Sept. 21, the day after the Senate vote, Watt sparked an uproar by characterizing his appointees to the leasing study commission as "a black ... a woman, two Jews and a cripple."

That remark proved to be the last straw for many Republican senators, who feared Watt's penchant for politically damaging remarks was harming their own prospects as well as President Reagan's. With his Senate support eroding rapidly, Watt resigned Oct. 9.

8. Marines in Lebanon

In late August, the first combat casualties among U.S. Marines in Lebanon prompted members of Congress to question U.S. policies and goals in that troubled country. President Reagan had sent more than 1,200 Marines to Lebanon in 1982 to serve in a multinational peacekeeping force.

To calm growing fears on Capitol Hill, Reagan in early September conducted private negotiations with key congressional leaders. The result was an agreement among Reagan, House Speaker Thomas P. O'Neill Jr., D-Mass., and Senate Majority Leader Howard H. Baker Jr., R-Tenn. Reagan agreed to sign legislation specifically invoking for the first time the major provision of the 1973 War Powers Resolution (PL 93-148) that required congressional approval for U.S. troops to be stationed in combat situations for more than 60 to 90 days. In return, O'Neill and Baker

agreed to authorize the Marines to stay in Lebanon for an additional 18 months.

The compromise agreement was put into a joint resolution, which the House passed, 270-161, on Sept. 28. *(House key vote 9)*

When the Senate took up the measure (S J Res 159, as amended) the following day, the ultimate outcome was not seriously in doubt, but it was uncertain how many Republican senators would oppose the resolution. Senate Democrats, unable to reach an agreement with Reagan during separate negotiations, had refused to accept the Reagan-O'Neill-Baker compromise.

As it happened, the vote broke almost purely along party lines. After rejecting several amendments offered by Democrats to tighten limits on the mission of the Marines, the Senate passed the resolution 54-46: R 52-3; D 2-43 (ND 2-29, SD 0-14).

On Oct. 23, just 11 days after Reagan signed the resolution into law (PL 98-119), terrorist bombings in Beirut killed 239 Marines, sailors and soldiers and 58 French paratroopers. Efforts to revise or revoke the Lebanon resolution in the wake of the bombings fell short in both houses.

9. Education Spending

Senators supporting more money for federal education programs came up short Oct. 4 during debate over the fiscal 1984 Labor, Health and Human Services, Education appropriations bill (HR 3913 — PL 98-139). An amendment by Bill Bradley, D-N.J., Ernest F. Hollings, D-S.C., and Robert T. Stafford, R-Vt., that would have added $559 million to the bill's $13.5 billion total for Department of Education programs was killed on a procedural move.

House Democrats succeeded Sept. 22 in adding $300 million in education and job training programs to the House-passed version of HR 3913. But education supporters in the Senate met with less success.

Led by Bradley, the amendment's backers argued that the extra money would bring the bill's total up to spending levels contained in the fiscal 1984 budget approved by the Senate in May. They were beaten back, however, by the Republican manager of the bill, Lowell P. Weicker Jr., Conn., himself a longtime supporter of increased funding for education. Weicker used the threat of a presidential veto to win enough support to kill the Bradley amendment with a parliamentary maneuver.

The Bradley amendment was ruled out of order by the chair because it would have increased funding above authorized levels, a judgment immediately appealed by Bradley. His appeal was tabled (killed) by a 50-45 party-line vote: R 49-5; D 1-40 (ND 1-26, SD 0-14).

10. Martin Luther King Holiday

After a two-day debate that was alternately bitter and eloquent, the Senate Oct. 19 overcame a recalcitrant conservative minority led by Jesse Helms, R-N.C., and voted to declare the third Monday in January, beginning in 1986, a legal public holiday honoring the Rev. Dr. Martin Luther King Jr., the civil rights leader assassinated in 1968.

The bill (HR 3706) passed by a vote of 78-22: R 37-18; D 41-4 (ND 28-3, SD 13-1).

Setting aside earlier opposition to the legislation, President Reagan signed it into law (PL 98-144) at a ceremony in the Rose Garden. The ceremony, attended by leaders of the civil rights establishment, was indicative of the symbolism the measure had taken on. Supporters argued that creation of the holiday honored not only King, but the entire civil rights movement as well. Leaders of the Aug. 27 march on Washington commemorating the 20th anniversary of King's "I have a dream" speech, made creation of the holiday a priority.

The House passed the bill relatively quickly, by a 338-90 vote Aug. 2. The Senate leadership then placed it directly on the calendar, where it could be brought up at any time.

Majority Leader Howard H. Baker Jr., R-Tenn., tried to bring it up just before the August recess, but decided not to when Helms indicated he would begin a lengthy debate.

While some opponents argued against the cost of a 10th public holiday, others, especially Helms, suggested King was not worthy of the singular recognition a legal holiday would confer. When the measure came up after the recess, Helms began a brief filibuster, based on allegations that King had ties with the Communist Party. Along with several conservative groups, Helms sued demanding release of FBI documents on King, sealed until the year 2027 by a court order. However, a federal judge refused to break the seal.

Helms and his allies attempted to send HR 3706 to the Judiciary Committee for hearings and offered numerous amendments to the bill, but all their efforts fell by lopsided margins.

However, concern about the cost of additional federal holidays did lead the Senate to pass a separate measure limiting to 10 the number of legal public holidays.

11. Clinch River Breeder Reactor

Congress in 1983 voted not to provide any more funds for the construction of the controversial Clinch River Breeder Reactor project. The apparent death of the demonstration nuclear power plant came after a series of votes over the preceding three years showed steadily dwindling support for the plutonium-powered project near Oak Ridge, Tenn.

Before the decisive vote was cast by the Senate Oct. 26, both the House and Senate Appropriations committees had declined to recommend fiscal 1984 funding, and the House May 12 had voted overwhelmingly against the Clinch River project.

Thus, when the Senate voted on a proposal to provide $1.5 billion to complete the federal share of payments under a new funding scheme, Clinch River's demise was not completely unexpected.

Opponents were concerned that Majority Leader Howard H. Baker Jr., R-Tenn., the project's godfather, would once more be able to prevail on his colleagues to support the project. But Baker did not argue in its defense during floor debate — leaving that task to Energy and Natural Resources Committee Chairman James A. McClure, R-Idaho.

Unmoved by McClure's arguments, the Senate turned down the Clinch River funding, which was contained in an amendment to a fiscal 1984 supplemental appropriations bill (HR 3959). The vote, on a motion to table the amendment, was 56-40: R 23-30; D 33-10 (ND 26-4, SD 7-6).

Both sides said they believed concern over the ultimate cost of the project, which was authorized by Congress in 1970, was the deciding factor in its defeat. The federal government had already spent $1.6 billion on the project.

12. Nuclear Freeze

In its first vote on the issue, the Senate Oct. 31 turned aside a resolution calling for a mutual and verifiable freeze on the testing, production and deployment of U.S. and Soviet nuclear weapons.

The resolution had earned widespread, grass-roots backing since late 1981. A heavily amended version of it was passed by the House in May. *(House key vote 3)*

Freeze advocates argued that a rough balance currently existed between U.S. and Soviet nuclear forces, with each sufficient to deter an attack by the other. U.S. advantages in bombers and missile-firing submarines offset Soviet advantages in the number and size of land-based ICBMs, they maintained. By this logic, President Reagan's planned nuclear buildup was not only unnecessary but dangerous, because of its emphasis on missiles such as the MX, accurate enough to threaten a first strike on armored Soviet missile launchers.

Opponents warned that a freeze would block the replacement of older American weapons with modern ones. They also argued a freeze would bar the development of new weapons — such as the small, single-warhead ICBM dubbed "Midgetman" — that might make the nuclear balance more stable.

The fundamental objection to the freeze by many administration officials and others rested on the belief that ICBMs were unique among nuclear weapons because of the short time within which they could deliver a surprise attack. From that premise, it followed that the Soviet advantages in ICBMs could not be tolerated nor would Moscow agree to reduce its ICBM force unless threatened by similar U.S. weapons — particularly, the MX missile, which a freeze would prevent.

The freeze was offered as an amendment to the bill (H J Res 308) increasing the ceiling on the national debt. A motion to table (and thus kill) the amendment was agreed to 58-40: R 46-7; D 12-33 (ND 3-28, SD 9-5).

13. Debt Limit/Deficit Control

Senators anxious to press their case for deficit control measures succeeded Oct. 31 in defeating an urgent increase in the public debt limit sought by the Reagan administration. The vote was 39-56: R 28-25; D 11-31 (ND 10-19, SD 1-12).

Conservative Republicans led the attack on the legislation (H J Res 308), without which the government could not continue to borrow money to pay its bills. They hoped to force action on bold steps to reduce federal spending — including enhanced presidential authority to impound, or withhold from spending, funds appropriated by Congress.

The GOP conservatives were joined by members of both parties who hoped to pressure Congress in the waning days of the session to agree on a major package of spending cuts and administration-opposed tax increases. That deficit-reduction effort failed, however, and before adjourning for the year the Senate joined the House in approving a $1.49 trillion debt limit measure.

14. MX Missile

The Senate Nov. 7 decisively rejected an effort to bar funding for production of the MX missile, the centerpiece of the Reagan administration's nuclear arms buildup.

The vote came just six days after the House, by a much

tighter nine-vote margin, had likewise voted to keep $2.1 billion in MX money in the fiscal 1984 defense appropriations bill (HR 4185). The funds were earmarked to build the first 21 production-line versions of the big ICBM. *(House key vote 10)*

The missile, which was flight-tested for the first time in June, would carry 10 nuclear warheads, each with enough power and accuracy to destroy armored Soviet missile launchers and command posts.

The administration insisted the MX was needed to offset a Soviet force of more than 600 ICBMs of comparable power and accuracy. It argued that such land-based missiles cast a political influence far more powerful than other nuclear weapons and, accordingly, that continued Soviet advantages in the number and power of ICBMs could not be tolerated.

Members who shared this view were joined in supporting MX by others who were more skeptical about the importance of MX, but were willing to support it in return for a shift by the administration to arms control negotiating positions deemed more likely to win Soviet agreement.

MX opponents argued that the missile would destabilize the U.S.-Soviet nuclear balance. They said MX would threaten the ICBMs that comprised the bulk of the Soviet nuclear force while itself being vulnerable to Soviet attack, since it would be deployed in existing U.S. missile silos.

They also rejected claims that ICBMs enjoyed unique diplomatic potency compared with other nuclear weapons, and insisted that superior U.S. bombers and missile submarines offset any Soviet advantage in land-based missiles.

The key Senate vote on the missile came on a motion offered by Sen. Dale Bumpers, D-Ark., to delete from HR 4185 the $2.1 billion earmarked to begin MX production. That amendment was rejected 37-56: R 6-46; D 31-10 (ND 24-3, SD 7-7).

House

1. Social Security

Acting on one of the sensitive issues left unresolved by the National Commission on Social Security Reform, the House March 9 voted to raise the normal Social Security retirement age gradually from 65 to 67 between the year 2000 and 2027. It thus rejected a Ways and Means Committee plan to reduce initial benefit levels beginning in 2000 and raise payroll taxes beginning in 2015. The vote was 228-202: R 152-14; D 76-188 (ND 23-152, SD 53-36).

The choice between raising the retirement age and increasing taxes to help maintain long-term solvency of the Social Security system had been one of the main points of controversy surrounding the crisis over Social Security financing. The bipartisan reform commission had been unable to reach agreement on measures to deal with the system's long-range problems.

The Senate ultimately went along with the House in approving a two-year increase in the retirement age. In other respects, the Social Security financing bill (HR 1900) closely paralleled the Jan. 15 recommendations of the bipartisan reform commission.

2. Fiscal 1984 Budget

After two years as mere onlookers, House Democrats scored a major budget victory March 23, when the House

approved the first budget resolution for fiscal 1984 (H Con Res 91). The vote was 229-196: R 4-160; D 225-36 (ND 168-6, SD 57-30).

The budget plan adopted by the House was essentially a Democratic political manifesto. Conceived by the entire Democratic membership, it added approximately $33 billion in domestic spending to the president's fiscal 1984 requests. Much of that money was earmarked for human needs programs that were significantly cut in the fiscal 1982 and 1983 budgets.

To pay for these programs, the plan reduced the president's proposed rate of growth in defense spending from 10 percent to 4 percent. And it also called for $30 billion in additional revenues in fiscal 1984. Reagan opposed tax increases.

The Republicans charged that the plan was a return to the old policies of "tax and tax, spend and spend." But they were unable to contrive a plan of their own and unwilling to bring the president's original budget up for a vote. The vacuum left by the Republicans allowed conservative Democratic "Boll Weevils," who had voted with the Republicans in 1981-82, to return to the fold and vote with their party leadership.

The Republican-controlled Senate also reordered Reagan's budget priorities. *(Senate key vote 2)*

3. Nuclear Freeze

The House May 4 approved a resolution (H J Res 13) calling for negotiation of a mutual and verifiable freeze on the testing, production and deployment of U.S. and Soviet nuclear arms. But the measure passed only after days of debate spread over three months and the adoption of several amendments intended by freeze opponents to mute its impact on Reagan administration nuclear arms policy.

The Senate later rejected a slightly different version of the freeze resolution. *(Senate key vote 12)*

Freeze advocates insisted that U.S. and Soviet nuclear forces currently were in overall balance and that a freeze was the only way to prevent escalation of the race by both sides to deploy new or improved weapons. In addition, they warned that both military establishments planned new weapons, such as the MX missile, that would make the nuclear balance more unstable because they would be sufficiently fast and accurate to threaten a first strike.

The administration opposed a freeze, arguing it would block new U.S. programs that were needed both to replace obsolescent weapons and to give Moscow an incentive to agree to substantial mutual reductions in the U.S. and Soviet nuclear arsenals. To freeze the arsenals at this point merely would cement Soviet advantages, officials said.

Freeze critics succeeded in attaching some amendments, including one specifying that any freeze agreement would expire if it did not lead to substantial reductions in the U.S. and Soviet missile forces.

The amended resolution was passed by a 278-149 vote: R 60-106; D 218-43 (ND 168-4, SD 50-39).

4. Emergency Mortgage Aid

As part of an effort to provide federal anti-recession aid — and to distance itself from the Republican administration — the Democratic leadership in the House pushed for passage of a measure providing $760 million in fiscal 1983 for a temporary loan program to help unemployed homeowners meet mortgage payments. The bill also in-cluded $100 million in fiscal 1984 funding for emergency shelter for the homeless.

Debate on the bill (HR 1983) was bitter and partisan. The House considered it May 11, after weeks in which the leadership pulled the measure from the schedule because it lacked the votes needed for passage. Opponents argued the program was too expensive in a time of high deficits and would eventually lead to the creation of a new entitlement program.

To make it more palatable to doubting members, House Democrats agreed to tighten eligibility requirements for the temporary loan program.

The House narrowly rejected an attempt by Buddy Roemer, D-La., to gut the bill by stripping out the loan program and simply asking lenders to practice forbearance. It then voted 216-196 for the program: R 6-155; D 210-41 (ND 158-8, SD 52-33).

However, the mortgage assistance program never became law. The Senate Banking Committee agreed to a loan guarantee program and included it in its housing authorization bill (S 1338). But the final housing authorization, which cleared Congress Nov. 18, omitted mortgage assistance.

In addition, an appropriation for mortgage assistance loans, passed by the House, was dropped in conference with the Senate. Shelter for the homeless was authorized, however, at $60 million.

5. Clean Air Act Sanctions

The House defused a political time bomb June 2 when it voted to bar the Environmental Protection Agency (EPA) from imposing penalties on communities that had missed a Dec. 31, 1982, deadline for meeting national clean air standards.

The Reagan administration had threatened to impose the sanctions on some 218 communities around the nation. Environmentalists charged the administration was trying to pressure lawmakers into moving on a long-stalled reauthorization of the Clean Air Act in hopes that a new version would ease a range of existing anti-pollution requirements.

Congress had been deadlocked for more than two years on competing proposals to rewrite the law.

Neither side had been willing to allow a simple extension of the air quality deadlines without getting other concessions it wanted. But in a surprise move, the House June 2 voted a one-year moratorium on the penalties, 227-136: R 89-50; D 138-86 (ND 88-58, SD 50-28).

The vote was on an amendment prohibiting use of funds in the fiscal 1984 Housing and Urban Development appropriations bill (HR 3133) to impose the sanctions.

The vote fractured most existing coalitions on clean air issues, cutting across parties, regions and regulatory philosophies. The amendment was offered by William E. Dannemeyer, R-Calif., an advocate of Reagan administration environmental policies who usually was aligned with conservative and industry forces seeking relaxation of the Clean Air Act.

But it also won support from a number of House members who favored the existing law.

The moratorium on penalties was included in the version of the bill passed by the Senate and signed into law by President Reagan July 12. Its adoption put an end to efforts to move a Clean Air Act reauthorization in the first session of the 98th Congress.

6. Covert Action in Nicaragua

In their one symbolic challenge to President Reagan's foreign policy, House Democrats twice voted to end "covert" U.S. aid to some 10,000 guerrillas fighting to overthrow the leftist government of Nicaragua. Congress had not publicly questioned a secret CIA operation since 1976, when it forced the Ford administration to drop its support for a pro-Western faction fighting for control of Angola.

The Democrats insisted the covert aid in Nicaragua violated international law, undermined U.S. credibility as a peacemaker in Central America and actually strengthened the Nicaraguan government's support among its own people. Administration officials gave varying reasons for the aid. First, they said it was aimed at interdicting the flow of arms through Nicaragua to leftist guerrillas in El Salvador and elsewhere in Central America. Later, they said the covert aid was forcing the Sandinista government in Nicaragua to "turn inward" and thus reduce its support for the Salvadoran guerrillas.

The House first took a stand against the covert aid on July 28, when it passed a bill (HR 2760) terminating the aid at a secret date and substituting for it a program to openly help nations in Central America combat cross-border arms shipments. The vote was 228-195: R 18-145; D 210-50 (ND 163-9, SD 47-41).

The GOP-controlled Senate refused to follow suit, and Reagan and Congress ultimately reached a compromise on the issue. Congress provided $24 million to continue the covert aid in fiscal 1984, but Reagan was required to seek congressional approval for additional funds.

7. IMF Participation

President Reagan had to fight with his fellow Republicans and court House Democrats to win approval for an increase in the U.S. contribution to the International Monetary Fund (IMF). The effort nearly backfired, however, after Democrats who had sided with the president on a key amendment were attacked by Republicans.

The $8.4 billion U.S. share of a nearly $32 billion IMF increase finally cleared Congress as part of an unrelated measure.

The IMF increase was needed to provide short-term aid to debt-ridden developing countries, and proponents said failure to approve it could cause a drop in world trade and possibly a global financial collapse. Opponents, however, called the increase a "big-bank bailout," a rescue operation for banking institutions that had imprudently made huge loans to countries burdened with debt.

The House originally passed the IMF increase (HR 2957) Aug. 3 on a 217-211 vote: R 72-94; D 145-117 (ND 106-68, SD 39-49).

But some Democrats later threatened to withdraw their support for the bill to protest a Republican press release criticizing their votes against an amendment that was also opposed by the president. Reagan ultimately sent a thank-you letter to every Democrat who supported him on the amendment.

A second obstacle to the IMF increase was the refusal of House Democrats to go to conference on the bill until the Senate agreed to an unrelated housing authorization. A deal was struck late in the session that combined the IMF measure with the housing bill as a single amendment to the conference report on a supplemental fiscal 1984 appropriations bill (HR 3959).

8. Coal Slurry Pipeline

By a surprising margin, the House Sept. 27 rejected a bill (HR 1010) giving the right of federal eminent domain to qualified coal slurry pipeline companies.

It was the first time in five years that such legislation had reached the House floor. In 1978, a similar bill was defeated 161-246. Coal slurry backers believed support for the idea had increased substantially since then.

But the tally of 182-235: R 85-75; D 97-160 (ND 52-120, SD 45-40) showed the continued lobbying muscle of the railroads, which in many areas enjoyed a virtual monopoly on coal transportation. They were joined by a number of farmers' organizations in fighting the bill.

Sen. J. Bennett Johnston, D-La., chief sponsor of a similar Senate bill (S 267), assessed the margin of the House vote and declined to press for Senate consideration of his measure.

Several pipeline companies proposed to carry coal slurry, fine particles of pulverized coal mixed with water, from Western states, southern Illinois and the Appalachian Mountains to power plants as much as 1,500 miles away.

Federal eminent domain rights were viewed as crucial to the development of the slurry industry. Only one slurry line was currently in operation; other efforts to obtain the needed rights of way had been blocked, often by railroads.

Supporters argued that moving coal via pipelines would result in lower electricity costs to consumers. But the railroads contended that coal slurry pipelines would deprive them of much-needed revenue, and farmers' groups were concerned the railroads would recoup by charging higher costs for transporting farm goods.

9. Marines in Lebanon

The backing of Speaker Thomas P. O'Neill Jr., D-Mass., was the key that led to House passage Sept. 28 of a controversial resolution (H J Res 364) allowing President Reagan to keep U.S. Marines in Lebanon until early 1985.

Reagan had sent more than 1,200 Marines to Lebanon in 1982 to serve in a multinational peacekeeping force. Congress accepted that action without question until several Marines were killed by sniper and artillery fire in late August and early September 1983.

With congressional concern on the rise, Reagan in early September conducted private negotiations with O'Neill and Senate Majority Leader Howard H. Baker Jr., R-Tenn. As a result, Reagan agreed to sign legislation specifically invoking for the first time the major provision of the 1973 War Powers Resolution (PL 93-148), which required congressional approval for U.S. troops to be stationed in combat situations for more than 60-90 days. In return, O'Neill and Baker agreed to authorize the Marines to stay in Lebanon for an additional 18 months.

The House passed the compromise agreement Sept. 28 after rejecting an effort by some Democrats to force an earlier withdrawal of the Marines. Nearly half the Democrats in the House went along with O'Neill and supported the agreement. The vote was 270-161: R 140-27; D 130-134 (ND 70-105, SD 60-29).

The Senate passed its version of the resolution (S J Res 159, as amended) the next day, 54-46. The House accepted the Senate's slightly different version later that day, clearing it for the president. (Senate key vote 8)

Reagan signed the bill into law (PL 98-119) on Oct. 12. Just 11 days later, terrorist bombings in Beirut killed 241

Marines, sailors and soldiers and 58 French paratroopers. Efforts to revise or revoke the Lebanon resolution in the wake of the bombings fell short in both houses.

10. MX Missile

The House Nov. 1 approved production of the first 21 MX missiles by a margin of only nine votes.

The Senate followed suit by a far wider margin Nov. 7, assuring inclusion of $2.1 billion for MX in the fiscal 1984 defense appropriations bill. *(Senate key vote 14)*

The administration viewed the missile as the most significant element of its nuclear buildup. The planned deployment of 100 MXs, each with 10 very accurate warheads, would pose the same threat to armored Soviet missile silos that the Soviet Union's missile force currently posed to U.S. missiles. Only that kind of threat would give Moscow an incentive to negotiate substantial mutual reductions in such large, multi-warhead ICBMs, some MX supporters insisted.

They were joined by a small group of moderate Democrats who were less certain that MX was required in its own right, but who were willing to support it in return for a moderation of administration arms control policy.

MX opponents warned that the missile would make the U.S.-Soviet nuclear balance dangerously unstable because of the threat it posed to Soviet ICBMs. They argued the MX threat might tempt Moscow to launch its land-based missiles — which comprise the bulk of its nuclear arsenal — at the first, possibly erroneous sign of a U.S. attack.

If a new U.S. ICBM were needed, some MX foes argued, it should be a small missile that could be made relatively invulnerable to Soviet attack — unlike the large silo-based MXs — by being carried around in a mobile launcher. Such a smaller missile — dubbed Midgetman — would have to carry only a single warhead and thus would remove uncertainty introduced into the current nuclear balance by each ICBM's ability to destroy several enemy missiles, thus conferring a potential advantage to whichever side launched its missiles first.

The key House vote on the missile came on an amendment to delete from the fiscal 1984 defense appropriations bill (HR 4185) $2.1 billion for 21 MX missiles. The amendment was rejected 208-217: R 18-145; D 190-72 (ND 156-18, SD 34-54).

11. Social Programs Spending

Seeking to restore domestic spending cuts made in 1981, House Democratic leaders Nov. 8 produced an amendment to a stopgap spending bill adding $997.7 million for education, job training, low-income energy assistance and other social programs.

The amendment to the second fiscal 1984 continuing resolution (H J Res 403) was offered by Majority Leader Jim Wright, D-Texas. Supporters said the proposal would force Congress and Reagan to decide whether to back up with hard cash their expressed concern over the state of American education. Democratic leaders also wanted to force Reagan to choose between more domestic spending or a veto of politically popular programs.

Reagan adamantly opposed the extra money, and Republicans demanded separate votes on the various components of the Wright amendment. In those votes, the House adopted more money for vocational education, schooling for immigrant children, community health centers, job training, child nutrition and other services, rejecting only a section providing $43 million for science centers at three universities.

After deleting the money for science centers, the House approved the remaining $954.4 million in the Wright amendment as a package. The vote was 254-155: R 22-134; D 232-21 (ND 162-7, SD 70-14).

Although the Wright amendment was adopted, the entire continuing resolution was rejected later that night by a 203-206 vote. The defeat came when impatient freshman Democrats mounted a symbolic protest against the stalemate on deficit reduction legislation and joined Republicans to reject the stopgap money bill.

When the House considered a new continuing resolution (H J Res 413) Nov. 10, the Wright amendment again was accepted. But the Senate voted 53-36 against the extra domestic money.

With Reagan threatening to veto the continuing resolution because of the Wright money, House and Senate conferees Nov. 11 trimmed the $954.4 million down to $98.7 million. The money was divided among education for the handicapped, vocational rehabilitation, immigrant education, college student aid, community health centers, colleges for the deaf and emergency shelters for the homeless. Reagan signed H J Res 413 (PL 98-151) Nov. 14.

12. Dairy Program

Faced with an expensive, continuously growing dairy surplus, the House Nov. 9 had a clear choice between two alternative methods of dealing with the problem. It endorsed a plan, pushed by the dairy industry, to pay dairy farmers for the first time to cut back production. For years, the federal government had compensated crop farmers for holding down production, but there had been no payments on a national scale to dairymen for producing less milk.

The House rejected an alternative plan to authorize immediate, sharp cuts in federal dairy price supports. The support establishes the price paid by the federal dairy program for surplus milk. Advocates said price support cuts in past years had reduced surplus production and would do so again; they called the 15-month payment program an expensive mistake, and said dairy farmers would figure out ways to collect the payments without permanently reducing productive capacity.

But the House rejected these arguments, and the price support cut, proposed by Barber B. Conable Jr., R-N.Y., lost 174-250: R 97-65; D 77-185 (ND 52-122, SD 25-63).

The House subsequently passed the payment plan (HR 4196). Its supporters noted dairy farmers themselves would be financing part of the program, and they argued that family dairy farms should be protected from unreasonable economic shocks associated with production cuts.

The administration initially backed the payment plan, but Agriculture Secretary John R. Block later announced he preferred Conable's price support cut. The American Farm Bureau Federation, consumer representatives and livestock producers also lined up behind Conable.

The paid diversion plan was controversial enough that the House emphatically refused in mid-October to let sponsors scoot a Senate-passed version (HR 3385) straight through to conference, without amendments. But when the bill came up a second time Nov. 9, dairy lobbyists had mustered enough support from key Democratic leaders — and from commodity groups benefiting from other provi-

Appendix

sions dealing with tobacco program changes, egg production and drought relief — to soundly defeat Conable's amendment.

13. Universal Telephone Service

A $4 million lobbying campaign by the American Telephone & Telegraph Co. (AT&T) failed Nov. 10 when the House rejected by a party-line vote a Federal Communications Commission (FCC) plan to raise local phone rates.

The FCC had proposed levying a flat charge of $2 per month for residential users and $6 per month per line for small-business users, beginning Jan. 1, 1984, for the right of access to long-distance service. The fees would rise in the future.

The FCC and AT&T argued the access charges were essential to the success of the scheduled Jan. 1, 1984, court-ordered breakup of AT&T.

Under the existing system, local telephone companies received some $6.5 billion a year from interstate long-distance tolls to help cover the costs of wires, poles and other equipment. After Jan. 1, when the local companies separated from AT&T, they no longer would get that subsidy.

The FCC plan would shift the subsidy to local users. AT&T, the FCC and their Republican allies argued that unless long-distance users were relieved of the burden of paying the subsidy, allowing long-distance rates to fall, the large firms that make the bulk of long-distance calls would turn to new technologies to set up their own communications networks. The result, they said, would shrink the rate base, requiring local phone users to pay higher rates in the long run.

The bill under consideration (HR 4102) would prohibit the FCC from imposing the access charge on residential customers and business users that had only one line, and would require long-distance users to continue to pay part of the costs of the wires, poles and other facilities shared with local users.

The bill's sponsor, Timothy E. Wirth, D-Colo., chairman of the House Energy and Commerce Subcommittee on Telecommunications, and his allies argued that the FCC plan was unfair. They said it would shift a cost properly borne by long-distance callers to local users and would charge local users for the right to use long-distance even if they made no such calls. They contended phone service would become so expensive that the poor and some rural citizens could not afford it.

The key vote came when the House rejected by 142-264 a substitute bill offered by Tom Tauke, R-Iowa, that would have let the FCC phase in the access charges at lower levels than the $2 a month the FCC planned. The vote was 142-264: R 134-19; D 8-245 (ND 1-169, SD 7-76).

The House went on to pass the bill by voice vote, but final action on the issue awaited Senate action on a milder bill (S 1660) that would delay the FCC plan for two years.

14. Equal Rights Amendment

The House Democratic leadership tried to revive the Equal Rights Amendment (ERA) Nov. 15 by putting the proposal on a parliamentary fast track, but the tactic angered a number of House members and the ERA failed.

The vote on H J Res 1 was 278-147, six short of the two-thirds majority required to pass it. Democrats voted overwhelmingly for the ERA, while Republicans voted against the measure by a 2-1 margin: R 53-109; D 225-38 (ND 164-13, SD 61-25).

The wording of H J Res 1 was identical to that of an earlier ERA that died June 30, 1982, three states short of the three-fourths (38) needed to ratify it: "Equality of rights under the law shall not be denied or abridged by the United States or by any state on account of sex."

Speaker Thomas P. O'Neill Jr., D-Mass., took the unusual step of bringing the ERA to the floor under suspension of the rules, a procedure that allows only 40 minutes' debate and no amendments. Generally, it is reserved for non-controversial measures.

O'Neill and ERA sponsors feared that if H J Res 1 went to the floor under normal procedures, amendments would be adopted making it inapplicable to abortion policy, the military draft and military combat regulations, among other areas of existing law. Realizing that such amendments would make the ERA unacceptable to many of its supporters, they opted to send the proposal to the floor under a procedure barring amendments entirely.

The ERA was a priority issue for many women's groups, and Democrats hoped the sharp partisan divergence on the amendment would weigh heavily in the 1984 elections.

Although ERA hearings were held in a Senate Judiciary subcommittee, that panel took no action on the proposal in 1983.

15. Nerve Gas Production

For the third time in two years, the House Nov. 15 voted against resuming the production of lethal chemical weapons. It instructed conferees on the fiscal 1984 defense appropriations bill (HR 4185) to oppose adamantly $124.4 million for production of so-called "binary munitions." These are aerial bombs and artillery shells designed to dispense lethal nerve gas.

The administration insisted Moscow's use of its large stocks of chemical weapons could be deterred only if U.S. forces possessed comparable weapons. And officials also contended that only a viable U.S. chemical weapons threat would induce Moscow to negotiate a chemical weapons ban.

Binary weapons opponents insisted that existing U.S. chemical weapons would be adequate in case of a conflict. Critics also argued that, because of the widespread revulsion against chemical weapons, U.S. binary production would surrender a propaganda advantage that Washington reaped from its own 14-year abstention from chemical weapons production, while Soviet forces and allies were widely believed to have used such weapons in Afghanistan, Laos and Cambodia.

The key vote was on an amendment to a motion to instruct the House conferees that had the effect of insisting on the House position of denying production funding for the nerve gas weapons. The amendment was agreed to 258-166: R 60-103; D 198-63 (ND 162-12, SD 36-51).

16. Tax Increases

The House killed any chance for consideration of a limited $8 billion tax increase measure (HR 4170) during the 1983 session when it refused Nov. 17 to approve the rule governing floor consideration of the measure. The vote against the rule was 204-214: R 13-149; D 191-65 (ND 147-23, SD 44-42).

Many House Democrats believed that they could co-

opt the deficit-reduction issue by urging increases in taxes. President Reagan, however, was unequivocal in his opposition to tax increases of any size.

House leaders were lukewarm toward the measure. Although they ultimately backed the effort, they saw little to be gained by approving a controversial tax bill that the Senate was unlikely to approve and the president would certainly veto.

The chief controversy over the bill, which was drafted in part to meet fiscal 1984 deficit-reduction requirements, involved proposed limits on tax-exempt industrial development bonds (IDBs). Other provisions of the bill would extend the mortgage revenue bond program, revamp the taxation of life insurance companies, give statutory tax exemption to most existing fringe benefits, and restrict the use of sale/lease-back schemes by non-profit entities.

State / Senator	1	2	3	4	5	6	7
ALABAMA							
Denton	N	N	Y	Y	Y	Y	N
Heflin	N	N	N	Y	Y	Y	Y
ALASKA							
Murkowski	N	N	N	Y	+	Y	N
Stevens	N	Y	Y	N	Y	N	Y
ARIZONA							
Goldwater	N	?	Y	N	?	Y	N
DeConcini	N	N	Y	N	Y	N	Y
ARKANSAS							
Bumpers	Y	N	N	N	Y	Y	N
Pryor	Y	Y	N	N	N	Y	Y
CALIFORNIA							
Wilson	N	N	N	N	Y	Y	N
Cranston	#	N	?	N	N	N	Y
COLORADO							
Armstrong	?	N	N	Y	Y	Y	N
Hart	?	Y	?	N	N	?	Y
CONNECTICUT							
Weicker	?	Y	N	N	N	Y	N
Dodd	Y	Y	N	N	N	N	Y
DELAWARE							
Roth	N	N	N	Y	N	N	Y
Biden	Y	Y	N	N	N	Y	Y
FLORIDA							
Hawkins	N	N	Y	Y	Y	Y	Y
Chiles	Y	Y	Y	Y	N	Y	Y
GEORGIA							
Mattingly	N	N	N	Y	Y	Y	Y
Nunn	N	N	N	Y	Y	Y	Y
HAWAII							
Inouye	Y	Y	?	N	N	Y	?
Matsunaga	?	Y	Y	N	N	Y	Y
IDAHO							
McClure	N	N	N	Y	Y	Y	N
Symms	?	N	N	Y	Y	Y	N
ILLINOIS							
Percy	N	Y	Y	N	N	Y	Y
Dixon	Y	Y	N*	N	Y	Y	Y
INDIANA							
Lugar	N	N	Y	Y	Y	Y	Y
Quayle	N	N	Y	Y	Y	Y	Y

State / Senator	1	2	3	4	5	6	7
IOWA							
Grassley	N	N	N	Y	N	Y	Y
Jepsen	N	N	N	Y	Y	Y	Y
KANSAS							
Dole	?	N	Y	Y	Y	Y	N
Kassebaum	N	Y	Y	N	N	Y	N
KENTUCKY							
Ford	Y	N	N	Y	N	Y	Y
Huddleston	Y	Y	N	Y	N	Y	Y
LOUISIANA							
Johnston	?	N	N	Y	Y	Y	Y
Long	Y	N	Y	Y	Y	Y	Y
MAINE							
Cohen	N	Y	N	N	Y	N	Y
Mitchell	Y	Y	N	N	N	Y	Y
MARYLAND							
Mathias	Y	Y	Y	N	N	N	?
Sarbanes	Y	Y	Y	N	N	Y	Y
MASSACHUSETTS							
Kennedy	Y	Y	Y	N	N	Y	Y
Tsongas	Y	Y	Y	N	N	Y	Y
MICHIGAN							
Levin	Y	Y	N	N	N	Y	Y
Riegle	Y	Y	N	N	N	Y	Y
MINNESOTA							
Boschwitz	N	Y	N	Y	N	Y	Y
Durenberger	?	N	Y	Y	N	Y	N
MISSISSIPPI							
Cochran	N	Y	N	Y	N	Y	N
Stennis	N	Y	Y	Y	Y	Y	Y
MISSOURI							
Danforth	N	Y	N	Y	N	N	N
Eagleton	Y	Y	Y	Y	N	Y	Y
MONTANA							
Baucus	Y	N	N	N	N	Y	Y
Melcher	Y	N	Y	Y	N	Y	Y
NEBRASKA							
Exon	N	N	N	Y	N	Y	Y
Zorinsky	N	N	N	Y	Y	Y	Y
NEVADA							
Hecht	N	N	N	Y	Y	Y	N
Laxalt	N	N	N	Y	Y	Y	N

State / Senator	1	2	3	4	5	6	7
NEW HAMPSHIRE							
Humphrey	N	N	N	Y	Y	Y	Y
Rudman	N	Y	Y	N	Y	Y	Y
NEW JERSEY							
Bradley	Y	Y	N	N	N	Y	Y
Lautenberg	Y	Y	Y	N	N	N	Y
NEW MEXICO							
Domenici	N	Y	N	Y	Y	?	N
Bingaman	Y	Y	Y	N	N	Y	Y
NEW YORK							
D'Amato	N	Y	Y	Y	N	Y	Y
Moynihan	Y	Y	Y	N	N	Y	Y
NORTH CAROLINA							
East	N	N	N	Y	Y	Y	N
Helms	N	N	N	P	Y	Y	N
NORTH DAKOTA							
Andrews	N	Y	Y	N	Y	N	N
Burdick	Y	Y	Y	N	N	Y	N
OHIO							
Glenn	Y	Y	Y	N	Y	?	Y
Metzenbaum	Y	Y	Y	N	N	N	Y
OKLAHOMA							
Nickles	N	N	N	Y	Y	Y	N
Boren	X	N	N	N	N	Y	N
OREGON							
Hatfield	N	Y	Y	N	Y	Y	Y
Packwood	N	Y	Y	N	N	Y	Y
PENNSYLVANIA							
Heinz	N	Y	N	N	N	Y	N
Specter	Y	Y	N	N	N	Y	Y
RHODE ISLAND							
Chafee	N	Y	Y	N	N	Y	Y
Pell	Y	Y	N	N	N	Y	Y
SOUTH CAROLINA							
Thurmond	N	N	Y	Y	Y	Y	-
Hollings	?	N	N	N	Y	Y	Y
SOUTH DAKOTA							
Abdnor	N	N	N	Y	Y	Y	N
Pressler	N	N	N	Y	N	Y	N
TENNESSEE							
Baker	N	N	Y	Y	Y	Y	?
Sasser	Y	Y	-	N	N	Y	N

State / Senator	1	2	3	4	5	6	7
TEXAS							
Tower	?	N	Y	N	Y	Y	N
Bentsen	?	Y	Y	N	Y	Y	Y
UTAH							
Garn	N	N	N	Y	Y	Y	N
Hatch	N	N	Y	Y	Y	Y	N
VERMONT							
Stafford	N	Y	Y	N	Y	Y	Y
Leahy	Y	N	N	N	N	Y	Y
VIRGINIA							
Trible	N	N	Y	Y	Y	Y	N
Warner	N	N	N	Y	Y	Y	Y
WASHINGTON							
Gorton	N	Y	Y	N	N	Y	Y
Evans [1]							Y
WEST VIRGINIA							
Byrd	Y	Y	Y	N	N	Y	Y
Randolph	Y	Y	Y	Y	N	Y	Y
WISCONSIN							
Kasten	N	N	N	Y	Y	Y	Y
Proxmire	N	N	N	Y	N	Y	Y
WYOMING							
Simpson	N	Y	N	N	Y	N	N
Wallop	N	N	N	Y	Y	Y	N

KEY

Y	Voted for (yea).
#	Paired for.
+	Announced for.
N	Voted against (nay).
X	Paired against.
-	Announced against.
P	Voted "present".
C	Voted "present" to avoid possible conflict of interest.
?	Did not vote or otherwise make a position known.

Democrats   *Republicans*

ND - Northern Democrats   SD - Southern Democrats (Southern states - Ala., Ark., Fla., Ga., Ky., La., Miss., N.C., Okla., S.C., Tenn., Texas, Va.)

1. Sen. Daniel J. Evans, R-Wash., sworn in Sept. 12, 1983, to succeed Henry M. Jackson, D, who died Sept. 1, 1983.

1. HR 1718. Emergency Supplemental Appropriations, Fiscal 1983/Jobs. Levin, D-Mich., amendment to add $1.665 billion for job creation, emergency food and shelter assistance and emergency health assistance. Rejected 34-53: R 2-46; D 32-7 (ND 25-4, SD 7-3), March 11, 1983.

2. S Con Res 27. First Budget Resolution, Fiscal 1984. Adoption of the concurrent resolution to set fiscal 1984 budget targets as follows: budget authority, $914.7 billion; outlays, $849.7 billion; revenues, $671.1 billion; and deficit, $178.6 billion. Adopted 50-49: R 21-32; D 29-17 (ND 24-8, SD 5-9), May 19, 1983.

3. HR. 3069. Supplemental Appropriations, Fiscal 1983. Jackson, D-Wash., amendment to raise senators' salaries to $69,800 beginning July 1, 1983, and, beginning Jan. 1, 1984, to limit the acceptance of honoraria to 30 percent of pay. Adopted 49-47: R 29-25; D 20-22 (ND 16-13, SD 4-9), June 16, 1983.

4. S J Res 3. Human Life Federalism Amendment. Passage of the joint resolution to propose an amendment to the Constitution that would overturn the 1973 Supreme Court decision, *Roe v. Wade*, which made abortion legal. Rejected 49-50: R 34-19; D 15-31 (ND 7-25, SD 8-6), June 28, 1983. A two-thirds majority of those present and voting (67 in this case) of both houses is required for passage of a joint resolution proposing an amendment to the Constitution. A "yea" was a vote supporting the president's position.

5. S 675. Omnibus Defense Authorizations. Tower, R-Texas, motion to table (kill) the Pryor, D-Ark., amendment to prohibit the production of lethal binary chemical munitions and related production facilities. Motion agreed to 50-49: R 35-17; D 14-32 (ND 5-27, SD 9-5), July 13, 1983, with Vice President Bush casting a "yea" vote to break the 49-49 tie. A "yea" was a vote supporting the president's position.

6. HR 2973. Interest and Dividend Tax Withholding/Caribbean Basin Initiative. Adoption of the conference report on the bill to repeal interest and dividend withholding requirements due to take effect Aug. 5; to impose new tax compliance requirements and penalties; and to provide trade and tax incentives to certain Caribbean nations. Adopted (thus cleared for the president) 90-7: R 51-2; D 39-5 (ND 25-5, SD 14-0), July 28, 1983.

7. HR 3363. Interior Appropriations, Fiscal 1984. Bumpers, D-Ark., amendment to ban all further coal leasing on federal lands until 90 days after a special commission created to study the Interior Department's coal leasing policies has completed its report. Adopted 63-33: R 23-29; D 40-4 (ND 29-1, SD 11-3), Sept. 20, 1983.

	8	9	10	11	12	13	14
ALABAMA							
Denton	Y	Y	Y	N	Y	N	N
Heflin	N	N	Y	N	Y	N	N
ALASKA							
Murkowski	Y	Y	N	N	Y	N	N
Stevens	Y	Y	Y	N	Y	Y	Y
ARIZONA							
Goldwater	Y	Y	N	X	Y	N	N
DeConcini	N	N	Y	Y	Y	N	?
ARKANSAS							
Bumpers	N	N	Y	Y	N	N	Y
Pryor	N	N	Y	Y	N	N	Y
CALIFORNIA							
Wilson	Y	Y	Y	Y	Y	N	N
Cranston	N	?	Y	Y	N	?	Y
COLORADO							
Armstrong	Y	Y	Y	Y	Y	N	N
Hart	N	N	Y	Y	N	?	Y
CONNECTICUT							
Weicker	N	Y	Y	N	N	?	Y
Dodd	N	N	Y	Y	N	Y	Y
DELAWARE							
Roth	N	Y	Y	Y	Y	Y	N
Biden	N	N	Y	Y	N	N	Y
FLORIDA							
Hawkins	Y	Y	Y	Y	Y	N	N
Chiles	N	N	Y	Y	N	N	N
GEORGIA							
Mattingly	Y	Y	Y	Y	Y	N	N
Nunn	N	N	Y	Y	N	N	N
HAWAII							
Inouye	N	?	Y	Y	N	N	?
Matsunaga	N	N	Y	Y	N	Y	Y
IDAHO							
McClure	Y	Y	N	N	Y	N	N
Symms	Y	Y	N	N	Y	N	N
ILLINOIS							
Percy	Y	Y	Y	Y	Y	Y	N
Dixon	N	N	Y	Y	N	N	?
INDIANA							
Lugar	Y	Y	Y	Y	Y	Y	N
Quayle	Y	Y	Y	Y	Y	N	N
IOWA							
Grassley	Y	Y	N	N	Y	N	N
Jepsen	Y	Y	N	Y	Y	N	N
KANSAS							
Dole	Y	Y	Y	N	Y	Y	N
Kassebaum	Y	Y	Y	Y	Y	Y	N
KENTUCKY							
Ford	N	N	Y	Y	Y	Y	N
Huddleston	N	N	Y	N	N	N	Y
LOUISIANA							
Johnston	N	N	Y	N	Y	N	N
Long	N	N	Y	N	Y	N	N
MAINE							
Cohen	Y	N	Y	Y	Y	Y	N
Mitchell	Y	N	Y	Y	N	N	Y
MARYLAND							
Mathias	Y	?	Y	N	N	Y	N
Sarbanes	N	N	Y	Y	N	N	Y
MASSACHUSETTS							
Kennedy	N	N	Y	Y	N	N	Y
Tsongas	N	N	Y	Y	N	Y	Y
MICHIGAN							
Levin	N	N	Y	Y	N	Y	Y
Riegle	N	-	Y	+	N	N	Y
MINNESOTA							
Boschwitz	Y	Y	Y	Y	?	?	N
Durenberger	Y	Y	Y	Y	Y	Y	?
MISSISSIPPI							
Cochran	Y	N	Y	N	Y	Y	N
Stennis	N	N	N	N	Y	Y	N
MISSOURI							
Danforth	Y	Y	Y	N	Y	Y	N
Eagleton	N	N	Y	Y	N	Y	Y
MONTANA							
Baucus	N	N	Y	Y	N	N	Y
Melcher	N	N	Y	Y	N	N	Y
NEBRASKA							
Exon	N	N	N	Y	Y	N	Y
Zorinsky	Y	N	N	N	Y	N	N
NEVADA							
Hecht	Y	Y	N	N	Y	N	N
Laxalt	Y	Y	Y	N	?	Y	N
NEW HAMPSHIRE							
Humphrey	Y	Y	N	Y	Y	N	Y
Rudman	Y	Y	N	Y	Y	N	N
NEW JERSEY							
Bradley	N	N	Y	Y	N	Y	Y
Lautenberg	N	N	Y	Y	N	N	+
NEW MEXICO							
Domenici	Y	Y	Y	N	Y	Y	Y
Bingaman	N	N	Y	N	Y	Y	Y
NEW YORK							
D'Amato	Y	Y	Y	N	Y	N	N
Moynihan	N	N	Y	N	Y	N	Y
NORTH CAROLINA							
East	Y	Y	N	N	Y	N	N
Helms	Y	Y	N	N	Y	N	N
NORTH DAKOTA							
Andrews	Y	Y	Y	N	Y	Y	Y
Burdick	N	N	Y	N	N	N	Y
OHIO							
Glenn	N	?	Y	Y	N	Y	Y
Metzenbaum	N	N	Y	N	Y	N	N
OKLAHOMA							
Nickles	Y	Y	N	Y	Y	N	N
Boren	N	N	Y	Y	Y	N	Y
OREGON							
Hatfield	N	Y	Y	Y	N	Y	Y
Packwood	Y	Y	Y	Y	Y	Y	?
PENNSYLVANIA							
Heinz	Y	Y	Y	N	Y	Y	N
Specter	Y	N	Y	N	N	Y	N
RHODE ISLAND							
Chafee	Y	Y	Y	Y	N	Y	N
Pell	N	N	Y	Y	N	N	Y
SOUTH CAROLINA							
Thurmond	Y	Y	Y	N	Y	Y	N
Hollings	N	N	Y	+	N	?	Y
SOUTH DAKOTA							
Abdnor	Y	Y	N	Y	Y	N	N
Pressler	Y	N	N	Y	Y	N	N
TENNESSEE							
Baker	Y	Y	Y	N	Y	N	N
Sasser	N	N	Y	N	N	N	Y
TEXAS							
Tower	Y	Y	N	N	Y	N	N
Bentsen	N	N	Y	Y	Y	N	N
UTAH							
Garn	Y	Y	N	N	Y	Y	N
Hatch	Y	Y	N	N	Y	N	N
VERMONT							
Stafford	Y	N	Y	#	N	Y	Y
Leahy	N	N	Y	Y	N	N	Y
VIRGINIA							
Trible	Y	Y	Y	Y	Y	N	N
Warner	Y	Y	Y	Y	Y	N	N
WASHINGTON							
Gorton	Y	Y	Y	N	Y	Y	N
Evans	Y	Y	Y	N	Y	Y	?
WEST VIRGINIA							
Byrd	N	N	Y	N	N	N	N
Randolph	N	N	N	N	N	N	N
WISCONSIN							
Kasten	Y	Y	Y	N	Y	N	N
Proxmire	N	Y	Y	Y	N	N	Y
WYOMING							
Simpson	Y	Y	Y	Y	Y	Y	N
Wallop	Y	Y	N	N	Y	Y	N

KEY

Y Voted for (yea).
Paired for.
+ Announced for.
N Voted against (nay).
X Paired against.
- Announced against.
P Voted "present".
C Voted "present" to avoid possible conflict of interest.
? Did not vote or otherwise make a position known.

Democrats   *Republicans*

ND - Northern Democrats   SD - Southern Democrats (Southern states - Ala., Ark., Fla., Ga., Ky., La., Miss., N.C., Okla., S.C., Tenn., Texas, Va.)

8. S J Res 159. Multinational Force in Lebanon. Passage of the joint resolution to provide statutory authorization under the War Powers Resolution for continued U.S. participation in the multinational peacekeeping force in Lebanon for up to 18 months after the enactment of the resolution. Passed 54-46: R 52-3; D 2-43 (ND 2-29, SD 0-14), Sept. 29, 1983. A "yea" was a vote supporting the president's position.

9. HR 3913. Labor, Health and Human Services, Education Appropriations, Fiscal 1984. Weicker, R-Conn., motion to table (kill) the Bradley, D-N.J., appeal of the chair's ruling that a Bradley amendment to add $559 million for education programs was out of order because it would have increased funding above authorized levels. Motion agreed to 50-45: R 49-5; D 1-40 (ND 1-26, SD 0-14), Oct. 4, 1983. A "yea" was a vote supporting the president's position.

10. HR 3706. Martin Luther King Jr. Holiday. Passage of the bill to declare the third Monday in January a legal public holiday honoring Martin Luther King Jr. Passed 78-22: R 37-18; D 41-4 (ND 28-3, SD 13-1), Oct. 19, 1983.

11. HR 3959. Supplemental Appropriations, Fiscal 1984. Humphrey, R-N.H., motion to table (kill) the Senate Appropriations Committee amendment to add $1.5 billion to the bill to complete the Clinch River breeder reactor in Tennessee. Motion agreed to 56-40: R 23-30; D 33-10 (ND 26-4, SD 7-6), Oct. 26, 1983.

12. H J Res 308. Debt Limit Increase. Dole, R-Kan., motion to table (kill) the Kennedy, D-Mass., amendment to call for a mutual and verifiable freeze on and reduction in nuclear weapons. Motion agreed to 58-40: R 46-7; D 12-33 (ND 3-28, SD 9-5), Oct. 31, 1983. A "yea" was a vote supporting the president's position.

13. H J Res 308. Debt Limit Increase. Passage of the bill to increase the public debt limit to $1.45 trillion, from $1.389 trillion. Rejected 39-56: R 28-25; D 11-31 (ND 10-19, SD 1-12), Oct. 31, 1983.

14. HR 4185. Defense Department Appropriations, Fiscal 1984. Bumpers, D-Ark., amendment to delete $2.1 billion for 21 MX missiles. Rejected 37-56: R 6-46; D 31-10 (ND 24-3, SD 7-7), Nov. 7, 1983. A "nay" was a vote supporting the president's position.

1. HR 1900. Social Security Act Amendments. Pickle, D-Texas, amendment to gradually raise the normal Social Security retirement age from 65 to 67 after the year 2000, and to delete provisions of the Ways and Means Committee bill that would reduce initial benefit levels beginning in the year 2000 and raise payroll taxes beginning in the year 2015. Adopted 228-202: R 152-14; D 76-188 (ND 23-152, SD 53-36), March 9, 1983. A "yea" was a vote supporting the president's position.

2. H Con Res 91. First Budget Resolution, Fiscal 1984. Adoption of the first concurrent budget resolution to set spending and revenue targets for the fiscal year ending Sept. 30, 1984, as follows: budget authority, $936.55 billion; outlays, $863.55 billion; revenues, $689.1 billion; and deficit, $174.45 billion. The resolution also set preliminary goals for fiscal 1985-86, revised budget levels for fiscal 1983 and included reconciliation instructions requiring House committees to recommend legislative savings to meet the budget targets. Adopted 229-196: R 4-160; D 225-36 (ND 168-6, SD 57-30), March 23, 1983.

3. H J Res 13. Nuclear Freeze. Passage of the joint resolution calling for a mutual and verifiable freeze on and reduction in nuclear weapons. Passed 278-149: R 60-106; D 218-43 (ND 168-4, SD 50-39), May 4, 1983. A "nay" was a vote supporting the president's position.

4. HR 1983. Emergency Housing Assistance Act. Passage of the bill to authorize $760 million in fiscal 1983 for a temporary loan program to help unemployed homeowners make their mortgage payments, and $100 million in fiscal 1984 for emergency shelter for the homeless. Passed 216-196: R 6-155; D 210-41 (ND 158-8, SD 52-33), May 11, 1983. A "nay" was a vote supporting the president's position.

5. HR 3133. Department of Housing and Urban Development Appropriations, Fiscal 1984. Dannemeyer, R-Calif., amendment to prohibit the Environmental Protection Agency from using any funds provided by the bill to impose sanctions on any area for failing to attain any national ambient air quality standard established under the Clean Air Act. Adopted 227-136: R 89-50; D 138-86 (ND 88-58, SD 50-28), June 2, 1983.

6. HR 2760. Prohibition on Covert Action in Nicaragua. Passage of the bill to prohibit, at a classified date specified by the House Intelligence Committee, support by U.S. intelligence agencies for military or paramilitary operations in Nicaragua and to authorize $30 million in fiscal 1983 and $50 million in fiscal 1984 to help friendly countries in Central America interdict cross-border shipments of arms to anti-government forces in the region. The bill also directed the president to seek action by the Organization of American States to resolve the conflicts in Central America and to seek an agreement by the government of Nicaragua to halt its support for anti-government forces in the region. Passed 228-195: R 18-145; D 210-50 (ND 163-9, SD 47-41), July 28, 1983. A "nay" was a vote supporting the president's position.

7. HR 2957. International Recovery and Financial Stability Act. Passage of the bill to authorize an $8.4 billion increase in U.S. participation in the International Monetary Fund, extend for two years with some changes the authority for the Export-Import Bank, and provide multilateral development aid. Passed 217-211: R 72-94; D 145-117 (ND 106-68, SD 39-49), Aug. 3, 1983. A "yea" was a vote supporting the president's position.

8. HR 1010. Coal Pipeline Act. Passage of the bill to grant federal power of eminent domain to certified coal slurry pipeline companies. Rejected 182-235: R 85-75; D 97-160 (ND 52-120, SD 45-40), Sept. 27, 1983.

1. Rep. Sala Burton, D-Calif., sworn in June 28, 1983, to succeed her husband, Phillip Burton, D, who died April 10, 1983.

2. Rep. Daniel L. Schaefer, R-Colo., sworn in April 7, 1983, to succeed Rep.-elect Jack Swigert, R, who died Dec. 27, 1982.

3. Rep. George W. "Buddy" Darden, D-Ga., sworn in Nov. 10, 1983, to succeed Larry P. McDonald, D, who died Sept. 1, 1983.

4. Rep. Charles A. Hayes, D-Ill., sworn in Sept. 12, 1983, to succeed Harold Washington, D, who resigned April 30, 1983.

5. Rep. Thomas P. O'Neill Jr., D-Mass., as Speaker, votes at his own discretion.

6. Rep. Gary L. Ackerman, D-N.Y., sworn in March 2, 1983, to succeed Benjamin S. Rosenthal, D, who died Jan. 4, 1983.

7. Rep. Marilyn Lloyd, D-Tenn., was known as Marilyn Lloyd Bouquard in the 97th Congress.

8. Rep. Phil Gramm, D-Texas, resigned Jan. 5, 1983, and was re-elected Feb. 12 as a Republican and was sworn in Feb. 22, 1983.

KEY

Y	Voted for (yea).
#	Paired for.
+	Announced for.
N	Voted against (nay).
X	Paired against.
-	Announced against.
P	Voted "present".
C	Voted "present" to avoid possible conflict of interest.
?	Did not vote or otherwise make a position known.

Democrats   *Republicans*

	1	2	3	4	5	6	7	8
ALABAMA								
1 *Edwards*	Y	N	N	N	Y	N	Y	N
2 *Dickinson*	Y	N	X	?	N	Y	N	
3 Nichols	N	N	N	N	Y	N	N	N
4 Bevill	N	Y	N	Y	N	N	N	
5 Flippo	Y	Y	N	Y	Y	N	N	N
6 Erdreich	N	N	N	Y	Y	N	N	
7 Shelby	Y	N	N	Y	N	N	N	N
ALASKA								
AL *Young*	Y	N	Y	N	?	N	N	Y
ARIZONA								
1 *McCain*	Y	N	N	N	?	N	N	Y
2 Udall	Y	Y	Y	Y	Y	Y	Y	Y
3 *Stump*	Y	N	N	N	Y	N	N	N
4 *Rudd*	Y	N	N	N	Y	N	N	N
5 McNulty	Y	Y	Y	N	Y	Y	Y	Y
ARKANSAS								
1 Alexander	Y	Y	Y	Y	?	Y	Y	Y
2 *Bethune*	Y	N	N	N	Y	N	N	N
3 *Hammerschmidt*	Y	N	N	N	Y	N	N	N
4 Anthony	Y	Y	Y	N	Y	Y	Y	N
CALIFORNIA								
1 Bosco	N	Y	Y	Y	N	Y	N	Y
2 *Chappie*	Y	N	Y	N	?	?	N	Y
3 Matsui	Y	Y	Y	Y	Y	Y	Y	N
4 Fazio	N	Y	Y	Y	Y	N	Y	N
5 Burton [1]						Y	Y	N
6 Boxer	N	Y	Y	Y	Y	Y	Y	N
7 Miller	N	Y	Y	Y	Y	N	N	N
8 Dellums	N	Y	Y	Y	Y	Y	Y	N
9 Stark	Y	Y	Y	Y	N	Y	Y	N
10 Edwards	N	Y	Y	Y	Y	Y	Y	N
11 Lantos	N	Y	+	#	Y	Y	Y	N
12 *Zschau*	Y	N	Y	N	Y	Y	Y	Y
13 Mineta	N	Y	Y	Y	Y	Y	Y	Y
14 *Shumway*	Y	N	N	N	Y	N	N	Y
15 Coelho	N	Y	Y	Y	Y	Y	Y	N
16 Panetta	N	Y	Y	Y	+	Y	Y	Y
17 *Pashayan*	Y	N	N	N	?	N	N	?
18 Lehman	N	Y	Y	Y	Y	Y	Y	Y
19 *Lagomarsino*	Y	N	N	N	Y	N	Y	Y
20 *Thomas*	Y	N	Y	N	Y	N	N	Y
21 *Fiedler*	Y	N	Y	N	Y	N	N	Y
22 *Moorhead*	Y	N	N	N	Y	N	N	Y
23 Beilenson	Y	Y	Y	Y	N	Y	Y	Y
24 Waxman	N	Y	?	Y	Y	Y	Y	N
25 Roybal	N	Y	Y	Y	N	Y	Y	N
26 Berman	N	Y	Y	Y	?	Y	Y	N
27 Levine	N	Y	Y	Y	+	Y	Y	Y
28 Dixon	N	Y	Y	#	?	Y	Y	N
29 Hawkins	N	Y	Y	Y	?	Y	Y	Y
30 Martinez	N	Y	Y	?	?	Y	Y	Y
31 Dymally	N	Y	Y	Y	Y	Y	Y	Y
32 Anderson	N	Y	Y	Y	Y	Y	N	Y
33 *Dreier*	Y	N	N	N	Y	N	N	Y
34 Torres	N	Y	Y	Y	+	Y	Y	Y
35 *Lewis*	Y	N	N	N	Y	N	N	N
36 Brown	N	Y	Y	Y	Y	Y	Y	Y
37 *McCandless*	Y	N	N	N	Y	N	N	Y
38 Patterson	N	Y	Y	Y	Y	Y	Y	N
39 *Dannemeyer*	Y	N	N	X	N	N	N	Y
40 *Badham*	Y	N	N	N	?	N	Y	Y
41 *Lowery*	Y	N	N	N	Y	N	N	Y
42 *Lungren*	Y	N	N	N	Y	N	N	Y

	1	2	3	4	5	6	7	8
43 *Packard*	Y	N	N	N	Y	N	N	Y
44 Bates	Y	Y	Y	Y	Y	Y	N	Y
45 *Hunter*	Y	N	N	N	Y	N	N	Y
COLORADO								
1 Schroeder	N	Y	Y	N	Y	Y	N	N
2 Wirth	N	Y	Y	Y	Y	Y	Y	N
3 Kogovsek	N	Y	Y	Y	Y	Y	Y	Y
4 *Brown*	Y	N	N	N	N	N	N	Y
5 *Kramer*	Y	N	N	N	Y	N	N	Y
6 *Schaefer* [2]			N	N	Y	N	N	Y
CONNECTICUT								
1 Kennelly	N	Y	Y	Y	N	Y	Y	N
2 Gejdenson	N	Y	Y	Y	N	Y	Y	N
3 Morrison	N	Y	Y	Y	N	Y	Y	N
4 *McKinney*	Y	N	Y	N	Y	Y	Y	N
5 Ratchford	N	Y	Y	Y	N	Y	Y	N
6 *Johnson*	N	N	Y	N	N	N	N	Y
DELAWARE								
AL Carper	Y	Y	Y	Y	N	Y	Y	N
FLORIDA								
1 Hutto	Y	N	N	N	Y	N	N	Y
2 Fuqua	Y	Y	Y	N	N	N	N	Y
3 Bennett	Y	N	N	N	Y	N	N	N
4 Chappell	Y	N	N	N	N	N	N	N
5 *McCollum*	Y	N	N	N	Y	N	N	X
6 MacKay	Y	Y	N	Y	Y	N	Y	Y
7 Gibbons	Y	Y	Y	Y	Y	Y	Y	?
8 *Young*	Y	N	N	N	Y	N	N	Y
9 *Bilirakis*	Y	N	N	N	Y	N	N	Y
10 Ireland	Y	N	N	N	Y	N	Y	Y
11 Nelson	N	Y	N	N	N	N	N	Y
12 *Lewis*	N	N	N	N	Y	N	N	Y
13 *Mack*	Y	N	N	N	N	N	N	Y
14 Mica	N	Y	N	N	?	N	Y	Y
15 *Shaw*	Y	N	N	N	Y	N	N	Y
16 Smith	N	Y	Y	Y	?	Y	Y	Y
17 Lehman	N	Y	Y	Y	N	Y	Y	N
18 Pepper	N	Y	Y	Y	N	Y	Y	N
19 Fascell	N	Y	Y	Y	Y	Y	Y	N
GEORGIA								
1 Thomas	Y	N	N	Y	N	N	N	N
2 Hatcher	Y	N	?	Y	N	N	Y	N
3 Ray	Y	N	N	N	Y	N	N	N
4 Levitas	Y	N	N	N	N	N	N	N
5 Fowler	N	Y	Y	Y	Y	Y	Y	N
6 *Gingrich*	Y	N	N	N	Y	N	N	N
7 Darden [3]								
8 Rowland	Y	N	N	Y	?	N	N	N
9 Jenkins	Y	N	N	N	N	N	N	N
10 Barnard	Y	N	N	N	N	N	Y	N
HAWAII								
1 Heftel	Y	Y	Y	?	?	?	?	?
2 Akaka	N	Y	Y	Y	N	Y	Y	Y
IDAHO								
1 *Craig*	Y	N	N	N	?	N	N	N
2 *Hansen*	Y	N	N	N	Y	N	N	N
ILLINOIS								
1 Hayes [4]								Y
2 Savage	N	Y	Y	Y	Y	Y	N	N
3 Russo	N	N	Y	N	Y	N	N	N
4 *O'Brien*	Y	N	Y	N	Y	N	N	Y
5 Lipinski	Y	Y	N	N	N	N	N	Y
6 *Hyde*	Y	N	N	N	Y	N	Y	Y
7 Collins	N	Y	Y	Y	?	Y	Y	N
8 Rostenkowski	Y	Y	Y	Y	N	Y	Y	N
9 Yates	N	Y	Y	Y	Y	Y	Y	N
10 *Porter*	Y	N	N	N	N	N	Y	Y
11 Annunzio	Y	Y	Y	N	N	Y	N	Y
12 *Crane, P.*	Y	N	N	N	N	N	N	N
13 *Erlenborn*	Y	N	N	N	Y	N	N	Y
14 *Corcoran*	Y	N	N	N	N	N	N	X
15 *Madigan*	Y	N	N	N	Y	N	N	Y
16 *Martin*	Y	N	N	N	N	N	N	Y
17 Evans	N	Y	Y	Y	Y	Y	N	Y
18 *Michel*	Y	N	X	N	Y	N	Y	Y
19 *Crane, D.*	Y	N	N	N	N	N	N	N
20 Durbin	N	Y	Y	Y	Y	N	N	Y
21 Price	N	Y	Y	Y	?	Y	N	N
22 Simon	N	Y	Y	?	Y	Y	N	N
INDIANA								
1 Hall	N	Y	Y	Y	Y	Y	Y	N
2 Sharp	N	Y	Y	Y	Y	Y	Y	Y
3 *Hiler*	Y	N	N	N	N	N	N	Y
4 *Coats*	Y	N	N	N	N	N	N	Y
5 Hillis	Y	N	N	Y	N	Y	N	Y

ND - Northern Democrats   SD - Southern Democrats

	1	2	3	4	5	6	7	8
6 ***Burton***	Y	N	N	N	Y	N	N	Y
7 ***Myers***	Y	N	N	N	Y	N	N	?
8 McCloskey	N	Y	Y	Y	N	Y	N	N
9 Hamilton	Y	Y	Y	N	Y	Y	Y	N
10 Jacobs	N	Y	Y	Y	Y	Y	N	N
IOWA								
1 ***Leach***	Y	N	Y	N	?	Y	Y	N
2 ***Tauke***	Y	N	Y	N	N	N	Y	?
3 ***Evans***	Y	N	Y	N	N	Y	Y	N
4 Smith	N	N	Y	Y	N	Y	Y	Y
5 Harkin	N	Y	Y	Y	?	Y	N	N
6 Bedell	Y	Y	Y	Y	N	Y	Y	N
KANSAS								
1 ***Roberts***	Y	N	N	N	N	N	N	N
2 Slattery	Y	Y	Y	N	N	Y	N	N
3 ***Winn***	Y	N	N	N	N	N	N	N
4 Glickman	Y	Y	Y	N	N	Y	Y	N
5 ***Whittaker***	Y	N	Y	N	N	N	N	N
KENTUCKY								
1 Hubbard	N	Y	N	Y	Y	N	Y	N
2 Natcher	N	Y	Y	Y	N	Y	N	N
3 Mazzoli	Y	Y	Y	Y	N	Y	Y	N
4 ***Snyder***	N	N	N	N	Y	N	N	N
5 ***Rogers***	Y	N	N	N	Y	N	N	N
6 ***Hopkins***	Y	N	Y	N	N	N	N	#
7 Perkins	N	Y	Y	Y	N	Y	N	N
LOUISIANA								
1 ***Livingston***	Y	N	N	N	N	N	Y	Y
2 Boggs	N	Y	Y	Y	Y	Y	Y	Y
3 Tauzin	Y	N	N	N	N	N	N	Y
4 Roemer	Y	N	N	N	N	N	N	Y
5 Huckaby	N	N	N	N	N	N	Y	Y
6 ***Moore***	Y	N	N	N	N	N	N	Y
7 Breaux	Y	N	N	N	N	N	N	Y
8 Long	N	Y	Y	Y	Y	Y	Y	Y
MAINE								
1 ***McKernan***	Y	N	Y	N	N	Y	Y	Y
2 ***Snowe***	Y	N	Y	N	N	Y	Y	Y
MARYLAND								
1 Dyson	N	N	N	Y	Y	N	N	N
2 Long	N	Y	Y	Y	?	Y	N	N
3 Mikulski	N	Y	Y	Y	Y	Y	N	N
4 ***Holt***	Y	N	N	N	?	N	N	Y
5 Hoyer	N	Y	Y	Y	N	#	Y	N
6 Byron	Y	N	N	N	Y	N	N	N
7 Mitchell	N	Y	Y	Y	N	Y	N	N
8 Barnes	N	Y	Y	Y	Y	Y	Y	N
MASSACHUSETTS								
1 ***Conte***	N	N	Y	N	?	Y	Y	N
2 Boland	?	Y	Y	Y	N	Y	Y	Y
3 Early	N	Y	Y	?	N	Y	N	Y
4 Frank	N	Y	Y	Y	Y	Y	Y	Y
5 Shannon	N	Y	Y	Y	N	Y	Y	Y
6 Mavroules	N	Y	Y	Y	N	Y	Y	Y
7 Markey	N	Y	Y	Y	Y	Y	Y	N
8 O'Neill [5]								
9 Moakley	N	Y	Y	Y	N	Y	Y	N
10 Studds	Y	Y	Y	Y	N	Y	Y	N
11 Donnelly	N	Y	Y	Y	N	Y	N	Y
MICHIGAN								
1 Conyers	N	Y	Y	Y	?	Y	N	Y
2 ***Pursell***	Y	N	Y	N	?	N	Y	Y
3 Wolpe	N	Y	Y	Y	Y	Y	Y	?
4 ***Siljander***	Y	N	N	N	?	N	N	N
5 ***Sawyer***	Y	N	Y	N	N	N	Y	Y
6 Carr	N	Y	Y	Y	N	Y	N	N
7 Kildee	N	Y	Y	Y	N	Y	N	N
8 Traxler	N	Y	Y	Y	?	Y	N	N
9 ***Vander Jagt***	Y	N	Y	N	N	N	Y	Y
10 Albosta	N	Y	Y	Y	N	Y	N	Y
11 ***Davis***	N	N	Y	Y	N	N	N	Y
12 Bonior	N	Y	Y	Y	N	Y	Y	N
13 Crockett	N	Y	?	Y	?	N	N	N
14 Hertel	N	Y	Y	Y	N	Y	N	N
15 Ford	N	Y	Y	Y	N	Y	N	N
16 Dingell	N	Y	Y	Y	N	Y	Y	Y
17 Levin	N	Y	Y	Y	Y	Y	Y	N
18 ***Broomfield***	Y	N	N	N	N	N	Y	N
MINNESOTA								
1 Penny	Y	Y	Y	Y	Y	Y	N	N
2 ***Weber***	Y	N	N	N	N	N	N	N
3 ***Frenzel***	Y	N	Y	N	?	N	Y	?
4 Vento	N	Y	Y	Y	Y	Y	Y	N
5 Sabo	N	Y	Y	Y	?	Y	Y	N
6 Sikorski	N	Y	Y	Y	Y	Y	Y	N
7 ***Stangeland***	Y	N	Y	N	Y	?	Y	N
8 Oberstar	N	Y	Y	Y	Y	Y	N	N
MISSISSIPPI								
1 Whitten	N	Y	Y	Y	N	Y	N	N
2 ***Franklin***	Y	N	N	N	Y	N	N	Y
3 Montgomery	Y	N	N	N	Y	N	N	Y
4 Dowdy	N	Y	Y	Y	Y	?	N	N
5 ***Lott***	Y	N	N	N	Y	N	N	Y
MISSOURI								
1 Clay	N	Y	Y	Y	?	Y	Y	N
2 Young	N	Y	Y	Y	Y	Y	Y	Y
3 Gephardt	N	Y	Y	Y	Y	Y	N	N
4 Skelton	N	N	Y	Y	?	N	N	N
5 Wheat	N	Y	Y	Y	Y	Y	N	N
6 ***Coleman***	Y	N	N	N	N	N	N	N
7 ***Taylor***	Y	N	N	N	Y	N	N	N
8 ***Emerson***	Y	N	N	N	Y	N	N	N
9 Volkmer	N	Y	Y	Y	Y	Y	N	N
MONTANA								
1 Williams	N	Y	Y	Y	Y	Y	Y	N
2 ***Marlenee***	Y	N	N	X	?	N	N	N
NEBRASKA								
1 ***Bereuter***	Y	N	N	N	N	N	Y	N
2 ***Daub***	Y	N	N	N	Y	N	N	N
3 ***Smith***	Y	N	N	N	Y	N	N	N
NEVADA								
1 Reid	N	Y	Y	Y	Y	Y	N	N
2 ***Vucanovich***	Y	N	N	N	+	N	N	Y
NEW HAMPSHIRE								
1 D'Amours	N	Y	Y	Y	N	Y	N	N
2 ***Gregg***	Y	N	Y	N	Y	N	N	Y
NEW JERSEY								
1 Florio	N	Y	Y	Y	+	Y	N	N
2 Hughes	N	Y	Y	Y	N	Y	N	N
3 Howard	N	Y	Y	Y	?	Y	N	Y
4 ***Smith***	Y	N	Y	Y	N	N	Y	N
5 ***Roukema***	Y	N	Y	N	N	Y	Y	Y
6 Dwyer	N	Y	Y	#	N	Y	Y	Y
7 ***Rinaldo***	N	Y	Y	Y	N	N	N	N
8 Roe	N	Y	Y	Y	N	Y	Y	Y
9 Torricelli	N	Y	Y	Y	Y	Y	Y	N
10 Rodino	N	Y	Y	Y	N	Y	Y	Y
11 Minish	N	Y	Y	Y	N	Y	Y	N
12 ***Courter***	Y	N	N	N	N	N	N	Y
13 ***Forsythe***	Y	N	?	N	+	N	Y	Y
14 Guarini	N	Y	Y	Y	N	Y	Y	Y
NEW MEXICO								
1 ***Lujan***	Y	N	Y	N	Y	N	N	Y
2 ***Skeen***	Y	N	N	N	Y	N	Y	N
3 Richardson	N	Y	Y	Y	Y	Y	N	N
NEW YORK								
1 ***Carney***	Y	N	N	N	?	N	N	Y
2 Downey	Y	Y	Y	Y	N	Y	Y	N
3 Mrazek	N	Y	Y	N	N	Y	N	N
4 ***Lent***	Y	N	Y	N	N	N	Y	N
5 ***McGrath***	Y	N	Y	N	N	N	N	Y
6 Addabbo	N	Y	Y	Y	Y	#	N	N
7 Ackerman [6]	N	Y	Y	Y	N	Y	Y	Y
8 Scheuer	N	Y	Y	Y	Y	Y	Y	N
9 Ferraro	N	Y	Y	Y	N	Y	N	Y
10 Schumer	N	Y	Y	Y	Y	Y	Y	Y
11 Towns	N	Y	Y	Y	N	Y	Y	Y
12 Owens	N	Y	Y	?	N	Y	Y	N
13 Solarz	N	Y	Y	Y	Y	+	Y	Y
14 ***Molinari***	N	N	N	N	N	X	Y	N
15 ***Green***	Y	Y	Y	N	N	Y	Y	Y
16 Rangel	N	Y	Y	Y	Y	Y	Y	Y
17 Weiss	N	Y	Y	Y	+	Y	Y	Y
18 Garcia	N	Y	Y	Y	N	Y	Y	N
19 Biaggi	N	Y	Y	Y	Y	Y	N	?
20 Ottinger	N	Y	Y	Y	Y	Y	Y	N
21 ***Fish***	Y	N	Y	N	Y	Y	Y	Y
22 ***Gilman***	N	N	N	N	Y	N	Y	N
23 Stratton	Y	N	N	Y	?	N	Y	N
24 ***Solomon***	Y	N	N	N	N	N	N	N
25 ***Boehlert***	Y	N	Y	N	N	Y	Y	N
26 ***Martin***	Y	N	N	N	N	N	Y	Y
27 ***Wortley***	Y	N	N	N	Y	N	Y	Y
28 McHugh	N	Y	Y	Y	Y	Y	Y	N
29 ***Horton***	Y	N	Y	N	Y	Y	Y	N
30 ***Conable***	Y	N	N	N	Y	N	Y	Y
31 ***Kemp***	Y	N	N	N	Y	N	N	N
32 LaFalce	N	Y	Y	?	N	Y	Y	N
33 Nowak	N	Y	Y	Y	Y	Y	Y	N
34 Lundine	Y	Y	Y	Y	Y	Y	Y	Y
NORTH CAROLINA								
1 Jones	Y	Y	Y	Y	N	Y	N	Y
2 Valentine	Y	N	N	N	Y	Y	N	Y
3 Whitley	Y	N	N	Y	Y	Y	N	N
4 Andrews	N	Y	Y	N	Y	Y	Y	Y
5 Neal	?	#	Y	Y	Y	Y	Y	Y
6 Britt	N	Y	Y	Y	N	Y	Y	Y
7 Rose	N	Y	Y	Y	Y	Y	N	Y
8 Hefner	Y	Y	Y	#	Y	Y	N	N
9 ***Martin***	Y	N	Y	N	Y	N	Y	Y
10 ***Broyhill***	Y	N	Y	N	Y	N	N	Y
11 Clarke	N	Y	Y	N	N	Y	Y	Y
NORTH DAKOTA								
AL Dorgan	N	Y	Y	N	Y	Y	N	N
OHIO								
1 Luken	N	Y	Y	Y	N	Y	Y	?
2 ***Gradison***	Y	N	N	N	?	N	Y	Y
3 Hall	N	Y	Y	Y	Y	Y	Y	N
4 ***Oxley***	Y	N	N	N	Y	N	Y	N
5 ***Latta***	Y	N	N	N	Y	N	Y	N
6 ***McEwen***	Y	N	N	N	Y	N	Y	N
7 ***DeWine***	Y	N	N	N	N	N	Y	N
8 ***Kindness***	Y	N	N	N	N	N	Y	N
9 Kaptur	N	Y	Y	Y	N	Y	N	N
10 ***Miller***	N	N	N	N	Y	N	N	N
11 Eckart	N	Y	Y	Y	Y	Y	N	N
12 ***Kasich***	Y	N	N	N	Y	N	N	N
13 Pease	N	Y	Y	Y	Y	Y	Y	N
14 Seiberling	N	Y	Y	Y	Y	Y	Y	Y
15 ***Wylie***	Y	N	Y	N	N	N	Y	N
16 ***Regula***	N	N	Y	N	N	N	Y	N
17 ***Williams***	N	X	Y	Y	N	Y	Y	N
18 Applegate	N	Y	Y	Y	Y	N	N	N
19 Feighan	N	Y	Y	Y	Y	Y	N	N
20 Oakar	N	Y	Y	Y	Y	Y	Y	N
21 Stokes	N	Y	Y	Y	N	Y	#	N
OKLAHOMA								
1 Jones	Y	Y	Y	N	Y	Y	Y	Y
2 Synar	Y	Y	Y	Y	Y	Y	Y	Y
3 Watkins	Y	Y	Y	Y	Y	Y	N	Y
4 McCurdy	Y	Y	N	N	Y	Y	N	Y
5 ***Edwards***	Y	X	N	N	Y	N	N	Y
6 English	Y	N	N	N	Y	Y	N	Y
OREGON								
1 AuCoin	Y	Y	Y	Y	?	Y	Y	N
2 ***Smith, R.***	Y	N	Y	X	Y	N	N	Y
3 Wyden	N	Y	Y	Y	Y	Y	Y	N
4 Weaver	N	Y	Y	Y	Y	Y	N	N
5 ***Smith, D.***	Y	N	N	N	?	N	N	Y
PENNSYLVANIA								
1 Foglietta	N	Y	Y	Y	?	Y	Y	Y
2 Gray	N	Y	Y	Y	N	Y	Y	Y
3 Borski	N	Y	Y	Y	Y	Y	Y	Y
4 Kolter	N	Y	Y	Y	?	Y	N	N
5 ***Schulze***	Y	N	Y	N	?	N	N	Y
6 Yatron	N	?	Y	Y	Y	Y	N	N
7 Edgar	N	Y	Y	+	N	Y	Y	N
8 Kostmayer	N	Y	Y	Y	?	Y	Y	Y
9 ***Shuster***	Y	N	Y	N	?	N	N	N
10 ***McDade***	N	N	Y	?	N	?	Y	N
11 Harrison	N	Y	Y	Y	Y	Y	N	X
12 Murtha	N	Y	Y	Y	Y	N	Y	N
13 ***Coughlin***	Y	N	Y	N	N	Y	Y	N
14 Coyne	N	Y	Y	Y	N	Y	Y	N
15 ***Ritter***	Y	N	N	N	N	N	N	Y
16 ***Walker***	Y	N	N	N	Y	N	N	N
17 ***Gekas***	Y	N	N	N	Y	N	Y	N
18 Walgren	N	Y	Y	Y	Y	Y	N	Y
19 ***Goodling***	N	N	Y	N	Y	N	Y	N
20 Gaydos	N	?	Y	Y	Y	N	Y	N
21 ***Ridge***	Y	N	Y	Y	Y	Y	Y	N
22 Murphy	N	Y	Y	Y	Y	Y	N	N
23 ***Clinger***	Y	N	Y	N	N	N	Y	Y
RHODE ISLAND								
1 St Germain	N	Y	Y	Y	N	Y	Y	Y
2 ***Schneider***	N	Y	Y	Y	?	Y	Y	N
SOUTH CAROLINA								
1 ***Hartnett***	Y	N	N	N	Y	N	N	X
2 ***Spence***	Y	N	N	N	Y	N	N	N
3 Derrick	N	Y	Y	N	?	Y	Y	N
4 ***Campbell***	Y	N	N	N	Y	N	Y	N
5 Spratt	N	Y	Y	?	Y	Y	Y	N
6 Tallon	N	Y	Y	N	Y	N	N	N
SOUTH DAKOTA								
AL Daschle	Y	Y	Y	Y	Y	Y	N	Y
TENNESSEE								
1 ***Quillen***	Y	N	N	N	Y	N	Y	N
2 ***Duncan***	Y	N	N	N	?	N	N	N
3 Lloyd [7]	Y	Y	N	N	?	N	N	N
4 Cooper	Y	Y	N	N	N	Y	Y	N
5 Boner	N	Y	Y	Y	Y	N	Y	N
6 Gore	N	Y	Y	Y	Y	Y	Y	N
7 ***Sundquist***	Y	N	N	N	Y	N	N	Y
8 Jones	N	Y	Y	Y	?	X	N	N
9 Ford	N	Y	Y	#	Y	Y	Y	?
TEXAS								
1 Hall, S.	Y	N	N	Y	Y	N	N	Y
2 Wilson	Y	X	N	?	?	N	?	Y
3 ***Bartlett***	Y	N	N	N	Y	N	Y	Y
4 Hall, R.	Y	N	N	Y	Y	N	?	N
5 Bryant	N	Y	Y	Y	Y	Y	N	N
6 ***Gramm*** [8]	Y	N	N	N	Y	N	N	Y
7 ***Archer***	Y	N	N	N	Y	N	N	Y
8 ***Fields***	Y	N	N	N	Y	N	N	Y
9 Brooks	Y	#	Y	Y	Y	Y	N	#
10 Pickle	Y	Y	Y	N	N	Y	N	Y
11 Leath	Y	N	N	?	Y	N	N	Y
12 Wright	Y	Y	Y	Y	Y	Y	Y	Y
13 Hightower	Y	Y	N	Y	N	N	Y	Y
14 Patman	N	Y	N	Y	Y	N	N	Y
15 de la Garza	Y	Y	Y	Y	N	Y	N	Y
16 Coleman	Y	Y	Y	Y	Y	Y	Y	N
17 Stenholm	Y	N	N	N	Y	N	N	Y
18 Leland	N	Y	Y	Y	Y	Y	Y	Y
19 Hance	Y	N	N	Y	Y	N	N	Y
20 Gonzalez	N	Y	Y	Y	Y	Y	N	Y
21 ***Loeffler***	Y	N	N	N	Y	N	N	Y
22 ***Paul***	Y	N	N	N	Y	N	N	N
23 Kazen	Y	N	Y	Y	?	N	N	Y
24 Frost	N	Y	Y	Y	?	Y	Y	N
25 Andrews	Y	Y	N	Y	Y	Y	Y	Y
26 Vandergriff	Y	N	Y	N	Y	N	Y	#
27 Ortiz	Y	Y	N	Y	Y	Y	N	Y
UTAH								
1 ***Hansen***	Y	N	N	N	?	N	N	Y
2 ***Marriott***	Y	N	N	N	Y	N	Y	Y
3 ***Nielson***	Y	N	N	N	+	N	N	Y
VERMONT								
AL ***Jeffords***	Y	Y	Y	N	N	Y	Y	N
VIRGINIA								
1 ***Bateman***	Y	N	N	N	Y	N	Y	N
2 ***Whitehurst***	Y	N	N	N	Y	N	Y	N
3 ***Bliley***	Y	N	N	N	Y	N	N	N
4 Sisisky	N	Y	N	Y	?	N	N	N
5 Daniel	Y	N	N	N	Y	N	N	N
6 Olin	Y	Y	Y	N	N	Y	N	N
7 ***Robinson***	Y	N	N	N	Y	N	N	Y
8 ***Parris***	Y	N	N	N	N	N	N	Y
9 Boucher	N	Y	Y	Y	Y	Y	Y	N
10 ***Wolf***	Y	N	N	N	N	N	N	Y
WASHINGTON								
1 ***Pritchard***	Y	N	Y	N	?	Y	Y	Y
2 Swift	N	Y	Y	Y	Y	Y	Y	N
3 Bonker	N	Y	Y	Y	+	Y	Y	N
4 ***Morrison***	Y	N	Y	N	+	N	Y	N
5 Foley	N	Y	Y	Y	Y	Y	Y	N
6 Dicks	N	Y	Y	Y	Y	Y	Y	N
7 Lowry	N	Y	Y	Y	Y	Y	Y	N
8 ***Chandler***	Y	N	Y	N	Y	N	Y	Y
WEST VIRGINIA								
1 Mollohan	N	Y	Y	Y	Y	Y	N	N
2 Staggers	N	Y	Y	Y	Y	Y	N	N
3 Wise	N	Y	Y	Y	Y	Y	N	N
4 Rahall	N	Y	Y	Y	?	Y	N	N
WISCONSIN								
1 Aspin	N	Y	Y	Y	Y	Y	Y	N
2 Kastenmeier	N	Y	Y	Y	N	Y	N	N
3 ***Gunderson***	Y	N	Y	N	N	N	N	N
4 Zablocki	N	Y	Y	Y	Y	Y	Y	Y
5 Moody	N	Y	Y	Y	Y	Y	Y	Y
6 ***Petri***	Y	N	Y	N	N	N	N	Y
7 Obey	N	Y	Y	Y	Y	Y	Y	N
8 ***Roth***	Y	N	Y	N	Y	N	N	Y
9 ***Sensenbrenner***	Y	N	Y	N	Y	N	N	N
WYOMING								
AL ***Cheney***	Y	N	N	N	?	N	Y	Y

Southern states - Ala., Ark., Fla., Ga., Ky., La., Miss., N.C., Okla., S.C., Tenn., Texas, Va.

9. H J Res 364. Multinational Force in Lebanon. Passage of the joint resolution to provide statutory authorization under the War Powers Resolution for continued U.S. participation in the multinational peacekeeping force in Lebanon for up to 18 months after the enactment of the resolution. Passed 270-161: R 140-27; D 130-134 (ND 70-105, SD 60-29), Sept. 28, 1983. A "yea" was a vote supporting the president's position.

10. HR 4185. Defense Department Appropriations, Fiscal 1984. Addabbo, D-N.Y., amendment to delete $2.1 billion for procurement of 21 MX missiles. Rejected 208-217: R 18-145; D 190-72 (ND 156-18, SD 34-54), Nov. 1, 1983. A "nay" was a vote supporting the president's position.

11. H J Res 403. Continuing Appropriations, Fiscal 1984. Wright, D-Texas, amendment to increase funding in the bill by approximately $955 million for an assortment of programs, most of them concerning education. Adopted 254-155: R 22-134; D 232-21 (ND 162-7, SD 70-14), Nov. 8, 1983. A "nay" was a vote supporting the president's position.

12. HR 4196. Dairy Production Stabilization. Conable, R-N.Y., substitute to authorize the secretary of agriculture to reduce the existing $13.10 (per hundred pounds) federal dairy support by as much as $1.50, and to repeal two existing dairy assessments, each 50 cents per hundred pounds. Rejected 174-250: R 97-65; D 77-185 (ND 52-122, SD 25-63), Nov. 9, 1983. A "yea" was a vote supporting the president's position.

13. HR 4102. Universal Telephone Service. Tauke, R-Iowa, substitute to phase in, rather than ban, the Federal Communications Commission plan to impose an access charge on residential and small business telephone users for the right to long-distance service, but only as of Jan. 1, 1985, rather than April 3, 1984, and at levels of no more than $1 a month the first year, rather than $2, rising to $4 a month by 1988. Rejected 142-264: R 134-19; D 8-245 (ND 1-169, SD 7-76), Nov. 10, 1983.

14. H J Res 1. Equal Rights Amendment. Rodino, D-N.J., motion to suspend the rules and pass the joint resolution to propose an amendment to the Constitution declaring, "Equality of rights under the law shall not be denied or abridged by the United States or by any state on account of sex." Motion rejected 278-147: R 53-109; D 225-38 (ND 164-13, SD 61-25), Nov. 15, 1983. A two-thirds majority of those present and voting (284 in this case) is required for passage under suspension of the rules. A "nay" was a vote supporting the president's position.

15. HR 4185. Defense Department Appropriations, Fiscal 1984. Porter, R-Ill., amendment, to the Young, R-Fla., motion to instruct House conferees, to insist on the House position, namely opposition to $124.4 million for production facilities for and procurement of chemical munitions. Motion agreed to 258-166: R 60-103; D 198-63 (ND 162-12, SD 36-51), Nov. 15, 1983. A "nay" was a vote supporting the president's position.

16. HR 4170. Tax Reform Act. Adoption of the rule (H Res 376) providing for House floor consideration of the bill to raise $8 billion in revenues over fiscal 1984-86 through a variety of changes in tax law. The main elements of the bill dealt with mortgage revenue bonds, industrial development bonds, fringe benefits, tax simplification, curbs on sale/lease-back schemes by non-profit groups and the taxation of life insurance companies. The bill also made substantial savings in the Medicare program and revised administration of the Social Security Disability Insurance program. Rejected 204-214: R 13-149; D 191-65 (ND 147-23, SD 44-42), Nov. 17, 1983.

1. Rep. George W. "Buddy" Darden, D-Ga., sworn in Nov. 10, 1983, to succeed Larry P. McDonald, D, who died Sept. 1, 1983.
2. Rep. Thomas P. O'Neill Jr., D-Mass., as Speaker, votes at his own discretion.
3. Rep. Marilyn Lloyd, D-Tenn., was known as Marilyn Lloyd Bouquard in the 97th Congress.

KEY

Y Voted for (yea).
\# Paired for.
+ Announced for.
N Voted against (nay).
X Paired against.
- Announced against.
P Voted "present".
C Voted "present" to avoid possible conflict of interest.
? Did not vote or otherwise make a position known.

Democrats *Republicans*

	9	10	11	12	13	14	15	16
ALABAMA								
1 *Edwards*	Y	N	N	N	Y	N	N	N
2 *Dickinson*	Y	N	N	N	?	N	N	N
3 Nichols	N	N	N	N	N	N	N	N
4 Bevill	Y	N	Y	N	Y	N	Y	N
5 Flippo	N	N	N	N	N	Y	N	Y
6 Erdreich	Y	N	N	N	Y	Y	Y	N
7 Shelby	N	N	Y	N	N	N	N	N
ALASKA								
AL *Young*	Y	N	?	N	Y	N	Y	N
ARIZONA								
1 *McCain*	N	N	N	Y	Y	N	N	N
2 Udall	N	Y	Y	N	Y	Y	Y	Y
3 *Stump*	Y	N	N	Y	N	N	N	N
4 *Rudd*	Y	N	N	Y	N	N	N	N
5 McNulty	N	Y	Y	N	Y	Y	Y	Y
ARKANSAS								
1 Alexander	Y	N	Y	N	Y	N	Y	N
2 *Bethune*	Y	N	N	Y	N	Y	N	N
3 *Hammerschmidt*	Y	N	N	Y	N	Y	N	N
4 Anthony	Y	Y	Y	Y	N	+	N	Y
CALIFORNIA								
1 Bosco	N	Y	Y	N	N	Y	Y	Y
2 *Chappie*	Y	N	N	Y	Y	Y	N	N
3 Matsui	Y	Y	Y	N	Y	Y	Y	Y
4 Fazio	Y	N	Y	N	N	?	?	Y
5 Burton	Y	Y	Y	N	Y	Y	Y	Y
6 Boxer	N	Y	Y	N	Y	Y	Y	Y
7 Miller	N	Y	Y	N	Y	Y	Y	Y
8 Dellums	N	Y	Y	N	Y	Y	Y	Y
9 Stark	N	Y	Y	X	Y	Y	Y	Y
10 Edwards	N	Y	Y	N	Y	Y	Y	Y
11 Lantos	Y	Y	Y	N	Y	Y	Y	Y
12 *Zschau*	Y	N	Y	Y	Y	Y	N	N
13 Mineta	N	Y	Y	N	Y	Y	Y	Y
14 *Shumway*	Y	N	Y	Y	Y	N	N	N
15 Coelho	?	Y	Y	N	Y	Y	Y	Y
16 Panetta	Y	Y	Y	N	Y	Y	Y	Y
17 *Pashayan*	Y	N	N	Y	Y	N	N	N
18 Lehman	Y	?	Y	N	Y	Y	Y	Y
19 *Lagomarsino*	Y	N	N	Y	Y	N	N	N
20 *Thomas*	Y	N	N	Y	Y	Y	N	N
21 *Fiedler*	Y	N	Y	Y	Y	N	N	N
22 *Moorhead*	Y	N	N	Y	N	N	N	N
23 Beilenson	Y	Y	Y	N	N	Y	Y	Y
24 Waxman	N	Y	Y	Y	N	Y	Y	Y
25 Roybal	N	Y	Y	N	N	Y	?	Y
26 Berman	Y	Y	Y	N	Y	N	Y	Y
27 Levine	Y	Y	Y	N	Y	Y	Y	Y
28 Dixon	N	Y	Y	N	N	Y	Y	Y
29 Hawkins	Y	Y	Y	N	Y	Y	Y	\#
30 Martinez	N	Y	Y	N	Y	Y	Y	Y
31 Dymally	N	?	Y	Y	N	Y	Y	\#
32 Anderson	Y	N	Y	N	Y	Y	Y	Y
33 *Dreier*	Y	N	N	Y	N	N	N	N
34 Torres	Y	Y	Y	Y	?	Y	Y	Y
35 *Lewis*	Y	N	N	Y	Y	?	?	X
36 Brown	Y	Y	Y	?	Y	Y	Y	Y
37 *McCandless*	Y	N	N	Y	Y	N	N	N
38 Patterson	Y	Y	Y	N	Y	Y	Y	Y
39 *Dannemeyer*	N	N	N	Y	N	N	N	N
40 *Badham*	Y	N	N	Y	Y	N	N	N
41 *Lowery*	Y	N	N	Y	Y	N	N	N
42 *Lungren*	Y	N	N	Y	Y	N	N	N

	9	10	11	12	13	14	15	16
43 *Packard*	Y	N	N	Y	N	N	N	N
44 Bates	N	Y	Y	N	N	Y	Y	Y
45 *Hunter*	Y	N	N	Y	N	N	N	N
COLORADO								
1 Schroeder	N	Y	Y	N	Y	N	Y	N
2 Wirth	N	Y	Y	N	N	Y	Y	Y
3 Kogovsek	Y	Y	Y	N	Y	Y	Y	Y
4 *Brown*	N	N	N	Y	Y	Y	Y	N
5 *Kramer*	Y	N	N	N	?	N	N	N
6 *Schaefer*	Y	N	N	Y	N	Y	N	N
CONNECTICUT								
1 Kennelly	N	Y	Y	N	N	Y	Y	Y
2 Gejdenson	Y	Y	Y	N	Y	Y	Y	Y
3 Morrison	N	Y	Y	N	N	Y	Y	Y
4 *McKinney*	Y	Y	Y	Y	Y	Y	Y	Y
5 Ratchford	N	Y	Y	N	N	Y	Y	Y
6 *Johnson*	Y	Y	Y	N	Y	Y	Y	Y
DELAWARE								
AL Carper	N	Y	Y	Y	Y	Y	Y	N
FLORIDA								
1 Hutto	Y	N	N	N	N	N	N	N
2 Fuqua	Y	N	Y	N	N	Y	N	N
3 Bennett	N	Y	N	N	N	N	N	Y
4 Chappell	Y	N	Y	N	N	Y	N	Y
5 *McCollum*	Y	N	N	Y	N	N	N	N
6 MacKay	Y	Y	Y	N	Y	N	Y	Y
7 Gibbons	N	Y	Y	Y	Y	Y	Y	Y
8 *Young*	N	N	N	N	N	N	N	N
9 *Bilirakis*	Y	N	N	N	N	N	N	N
10 Ireland	Y	N	N	N	N	N	N	N
11 Nelson	Y	N	Y	N	Y	N	Y	Y
12 *Lewis*	Y	N	Y	N	\#	Y	Y	Y
13 *Mack*	Y	N	N	Y	N	N	N	N
14 Mica	Y	Y	N	N	Y	Y	X	Y
15 *Shaw*	Y	N	N	Y	N	N	N	N
16 Smith	Y	Y	Y	N	Y	Y	Y	Y
17 Lehman	Y	Y	N	Y	Y	Y	Y	Y
18 Pepper	Y	Y	Y	N	Y	Y	Y	Y
19 Fascell	Y	Y	Y	N	Y	Y	Y	Y
GEORGIA								
1 Thomas	Y	N	Y	N	Y	N	Y	N
2 Hatcher	N	Y	N	N	Y	N	Y	N
3 Ray	N	N	N	N	N	N	N	X
4 Levitas	N	N	Y	N	Y	N	Y	N
5 Fowler	Y	Y	Y	N	Y	Y	Y	Y
6 *Gingrich*	Y	N	N	N	N	Y	N	N
7 Darden [1]					N	Y	N	N
8 Rowland	Y	N	N	Y	N	Y	N	N
9 Jenkins	Y	N	?	N	?	?	?	?
10 Barnard	Y	?	N	N	Y	N	N	N
HAWAII								
1 Heftel	?	Y	Y	N	N	Y	Y	Y
2 Akaka	Y	Y	Y	N	N	Y	Y	Y
IDAHO								
1 *Craig*	Y	N	N	Y	Y	N	N	N
2 *Hansen*	Y	N	N	Y	Y	N	N	N
ILLINOIS								
1 Hayes	N	Y	Y	N	N	Y	Y	Y
2 Savage	N	Y	Y	N	N	Y	Y	Y
3 Russo	N	Y	Y	N	?	N	Y	Y
4 *O'Brien*	Y	N	?	Y	\#	Y	N	N
5 Lipinski	N	N	Y	N	N	Y	N	Y
6 *Hyde*	Y	N	N	N	N	N	N	N
7 Collins	N	Y	Y	N	Y	Y	Y	?
8 Rostenkowski	Y	Y	N	N	Y	N	Y	Y
9 Yates	N	Y	Y	N	Y	Y	Y	Y
10 *Porter*	Y	N	Y	Y	Y	Y	Y	N
11 Annunzio	Y	Y	Y	N	Y	N	Y	Y
12 *Crane, P.*	N	N	N	Y	N	N	N	N
13 *Erlenborn*	Y	N	N	Y	Y	N	N	N
14 *Corcoran*	Y	X	N	Y	N	N	N	N
15 *Madigan*	Y	N	N	Y	Y	Y	N	N
16 *Martin*	Y	N	N	Y	Y	Y	Y	Y
17 Evans	N	Y	Y	N	N	Y	N	N
18 *Michel*	Y	N	N	Y	Y	N	N	N
19 *Crane, D.*	N	N	N	Y	N	N	N	N
20 Durbin	N	Y	Y	N	N	Y	Y	Y
21 Price	Y	N	N	N	Y	N	N	Y
22 Simon	Y	\#	Y	N	X	Y	Y	?
INDIANA								
1 Hall	N	Y	Y	N	N	Y	Y	Y
2 Sharp	N	Y	Y	N	N	Y	Y	Y
3 *Hiler*	Y	N	N	N	N	Y	N	N
4 *Coats*	Y	N	N	Y	N	Y	N	N
5 *Hillis*	N	N	N	Y	N	N	N	N

ND - Northern Democrats   SD - Southern Democrats

	9	10	11	12	13	14	15	16
6 ***Burton***	Y	N	N	N	?	N	N	N
7 ***Myers***	N	N	N	N	Y	N	N	N
8 McCloskey	N	Y	Y	Y	N	Y	Y	Y
9 Hamilton	Y	Y	Y	N	N	Y	Y	Y
10 Jacobs	N	Y	Y	N	N	Y	Y	Y
IOWA								
1 ***Leach***	Y	Y	Y	Y	Y	Y	Y	?
2 ***Tauke***	N	Y	N	N	Y	N	Y	N
3 ***Evans***	Y	#	Y	Y	Y	Y	Y	N
4 Smith	N	Y	N	N	N	Y	Y	N
5 Harkin	N	Y	Y	N	N	Y	Y	N
6 Bedell	N	Y	Y	N	N	N	Y	N
KANSAS								
1 ***Roberts***	Y	N	N	Y	Y	N	Y	N
2 Slattery	Y	Y	N	N	N	Y	Y	Y
3 ***Winn***	Y	N	?	?	#	N	N	N
4 Glickman	Y	Y	N	Y	N	Y	Y	Y
5 ***Whittaker***	Y	N	N	Y	Y	N	Y	N
KENTUCKY								
1 Hubbard	N	N	Y	N	N	N	N	N
2 Natcher	N	Y	N	N	N	Y	Y	N
3 Mazzoli	N	Y	Y	Y	N	N	Y	Y
4 ***Snyder***	N	N	N	N	N	N	N	N
5 ***Rogers***	Y	N	N	N	Y	N	N	N
6 ***Hopkins***	N	N	N	N	Y	Y	Y	N
7 Perkins	N	Y	Y	N	N	Y	Y	N
LOUISIANA								
1 ***Livingston***	Y	N	N	Y	Y	N	N	N
2 Boggs	Y	N	Y	N	N	Y	Y	N
3 Tauzin	Y	N	N	N	N	Y	N	N
4 Roemer	N	N	N	Y	N	N	Y	N
5 Huckaby	Y	N	N	N	Y	Y	Y	N
6 ***Moore***	Y	N	N	Y	Y	N	N	Y
7 Breaux	Y	N	N	N	N	Y	N	N
8 Long	Y	Y	Y	Y	N	Y	Y	Y
MAINE								
1 ***McKernan***	Y	N	Y	N	N	Y	Y	N
2 ***Snowe***	Y	N	Y	N	N	Y	Y	N
MARYLAND								
1 Dyson	Y	Y	N	Y	N	Y	N	N
2 Long	N	Y	Y	N	N	Y	N	Y
3 Mikulski	Y	Y	Y	N	N	Y	Y	N
4 ***Holt***	Y	N	N	Y	Y	Y	N	N
5 Hoyer	Y	N	Y	N	N	Y	Y	Y
6 Byron	N	N	Y	N	N	Y	N	N
7 Mitchell	N	Y	Y	Y	N	Y	Y	Y
8 Barnes	Y	Y	Y	Y	N	Y	Y	Y
MASSACHUSETTS								
1 ***Conte***	N	Y	N	Y	Y	Y	Y	N
2 Boland	Y	Y	Y	Y	N	Y	Y	Y
3 Early	N	Y	?	?	?	Y	Y	N
4 Frank	N	Y	Y	Y	N	Y	Y	Y
5 Shannon	N	Y	Y	Y	N	Y	Y	Y
6 Mavroules	Y	Y	Y	Y	?	Y	Y	Y
7 Markey	Y	Y	Y	Y	N	Y	Y	Y
8 O'Neill [2]						Y		
9 Moakley	Y	Y	Y	Y	N	Y	Y	Y
10 Studds	N	Y	Y	Y	N	Y	Y	Y
11 Donnelly	N	Y	Y	Y	N	Y	N	Y
MICHIGAN								
1 Conyers	N	Y	Y	N	N	Y	Y	Y
2 ***Pursell***	Y	N	N	N	N	Y	Y	N
3 Wolpe	N	Y	Y	N	N	Y	Y	Y
4 ***Siljander***	Y	N	N	N	Y	N	N	N
5 ***Sawyer***	Y	?	N	N	N	?	?	N
6 Carr	Y	Y	Y	N	N	Y	Y	N
7 Kildee	N	Y	Y	N	N	Y	Y	Y
8 Traxler	N	Y	Y	N	N	Y	Y	Y
9 ***Vander Jagt***	Y	X	N	Y	Y	N	Y	Y
10 Albosta	N	Y	Y	N	N	Y	Y	N
11 ***Davis***	Y	N	Y	N	Y	N	N	N
12 Bonior	Y	Y	Y	N	N	Y	Y	Y
13 Crockett	N	Y	Y	N	N	Y	Y	Y
14 Hertel	N	Y	Y	N	N	Y	Y	Y
15 Ford	N	Y	Y	N	N	Y	Y	Y
16 Dingell	N	Y	Y	N	N	Y	Y	Y
17 Levin	Y	Y	Y	N	N	Y	Y	Y
18 ***Broomfield***	Y	N	N	Y	?	N	Y	N
MINNESOTA								
1 Penny	N	Y	Y	N	N	Y	Y	Y
2 ***Weber***	Y	N	N	N	N	N	Y	N
3 ***Frenzel***	Y	N	N	N	Y	Y	Y	Y
4 Vento	N	Y	Y	N	N	Y	Y	Y
5 Sabo	N	Y	Y	N	N	Y	Y	Y
6 Sikorski	N	Y	Y	N	N	Y	Y	Y

	9	10	11	12	13	14	15	16
7 ***Stangeland***	Y	N	N	N	N	N	N	N
8 Oberstar	N	Y	Y	N	N	Y	Y	N
MISSISSIPPI								
1 Whitten	Y	Y	Y	N	N	Y	Y	N
2 ***Franklin***	Y	N	N	Y	Y	N	N	N
3 Montgomery	Y	N	N	Y	?	N	N	N
4 Dowdy	N	Y	Y	N	N	Y	N	?
5 ***Lott***	Y	N	N	N	Y	N	N	N
MISSOURI								
1 Clay	N	Y	Y	N	N	Y	Y	?
2 Young	N	Y	Y	N	N	N	N	N
3 Gephardt	Y	Y	Y	N	N	Y	Y	Y
4 Skelton	N	N	Y	N	N	N	N	N
5 Wheat	N	Y	Y	N	N	Y	Y	Y
6 ***Coleman***	Y	N	N	N	N	N	N	N
7 ***Taylor***	Y	N	N	N	Y	N	N	N
8 ***Emerson***	Y	N	N	N	Y	N	N	N
9 Volkmer	N	Y	Y	N	N	Y	Y	Y
MONTANA								
1 Williams	Y	Y	Y	N	N	Y	Y	Y
2 ***Marlenee***	Y	N	N	N	N	N	N	N
NEBRASKA								
1 ***Bereuter***	N	Y	N	N	Y	Y	N	N
2 ***Daub***	Y	N	N	N	Y	Y	Y	N
3 ***Smith***	Y	Y	N	Y	#	Y	N	N
NEVADA								
1 Reid	Y	N	Y	N	N	N	Y	Y
2 ***Vucanovich***	Y	N	N	Y	Y	N	N	N
NEW HAMPSHIRE								
1 D'Amours	Y	Y	Y	Y	N	Y	Y	N
2 ***Gregg***	Y	N	N	Y	Y	Y	Y	N
NEW JERSEY								
1 Florio	N	Y	?	N	N	Y	Y	Y
2 Hughes	Y	Y	N	N	N	Y	N	Y
3 Howard	N	Y	?	Y	N	Y	Y	Y
4 ***Smith***	Y	Y	Y	Y	Y	N	Y	N
5 ***Roukema***	Y	Y	Y	Y	Y	Y	Y	Y
6 Dwyer	Y	Y	Y	Y	N	Y	Y	Y
7 ***Rinaldo***	Y	N	Y	N	Y	Y	Y	N
8 Roe	Y	Y	Y	Y	N	Y	Y	Y
9 Torricelli	Y	Y	Y	N	N	Y	Y	Y
10 Rodino	N	Y	Y	N	N	Y	Y	Y
11 Minish	Y	Y	Y	Y	N	Y	Y	Y
12 ***Courter***	Y	N	N	Y	Y	Y	N	N
13 ***Forsythe***	Y	Y	N	N	Y	N	Y	N
14 Guarini	N	Y	Y	N	N	Y	Y	Y
NEW MEXICO								
1 ***Lujan***	Y	N	N	Y	Y	Y	N	N
2 ***Skeen***	Y	N	N	Y	Y	N	N	N
3 Richardson	N	Y	Y	N	N	Y	Y	N
NEW YORK								
1 ***Carney***	Y	N	N	Y	Y	N	Y	N
2 Downey	N	Y	Y	Y	N	Y	Y	Y
3 Mrazek	Y	Y	Y	Y	N	Y	Y	Y
4 ***Lent***	Y	N	N	Y	Y	?	N	N
5 ***McGrath***	Y	N	N	Y	Y	N	Y	N
6 Addabbo	N	Y	Y	N	N	Y	Y	Y
7 Ackerman	Y	Y	Y	N	N	Y	Y	Y
8 Scheuer	Y	Y	Y	N	N	Y	Y	Y
9 Ferraro	N	Y	Y	N	N	Y	Y	Y
10 Schumer	Y	Y	Y	Y	N	Y	Y	Y
11 Towns	N	Y	Y	N	N	Y	Y	Y
12 Owens	N	Y	Y	N	N	Y	Y	Y
13 Solarz	Y	Y	Y	?	X	Y	Y	?
14 ***Molinari***	Y	N	?	?	?	?	?	N
15 ***Green***	Y	Y	Y	Y	Y	Y	Y	N
16 Rangel	N	Y	Y	Y	N	Y	Y	Y
17 Weiss	N	Y	Y	Y	N	Y	Y	Y
18 Garcia	N	N	?	N	N	#	Y	Y
19 Biaggi	Y	Y	Y	Y	N	Y	Y	N
20 Ottinger	N	Y	Y	Y	N	Y	Y	Y
21 ***Fish***	Y	N	N	N	Y	N	Y	N
22 ***Gilman***	Y	N	Y	N	Y	Y	N	N
23 Stratton	N	N	?	N	N	Y	N	Y
24 ***Solomon***	Y	N	N	N	Y	N	N	N
25 ***Boehlert***	Y	N	Y	N	Y	Y	Y	N
26 ***Martin***	Y	N	N	Y	#	N	N	N
27 ***Wortley***	Y	N	N	Y	Y	Y	Y	N
28 McHugh	N	Y	Y	N	N	Y	Y	Y
29 ***Horton***	N	N	N	Y	Y	Y	Y	N
30 ***Conable***	Y	N	N	Y	Y	Y	N	Y
31 ***Kemp***	Y	N	N	Y	Y	N	N	?
32 LaFalce	N	Y	Y	Y	N	Y	Y	Y
33 Nowak	N	Y	Y	Y	N	N	Y	Y
34 Lundine	N	Y	Y	N	N	Y	Y	N

	9	10	11	12	13	14	15	16
NORTH CAROLINA								
1 Jones	Y	N	Y	N	N	Y	Y	N
2 Valentine	Y	Y	Y	N	N	N	N	Y
3 Whitley	Y	N	Y	N	N	Y	N	Y
4 Andrews	N	Y	Y	N	N	Y	N	Y
5 Neal	N	N	Y	N	N	Y	Y	Y
6 Britt	Y	N	Y	Y	?	Y	Y	Y
7 Rose	Y	Y	Y	N	N	Y	N	Y
8 Hefner	Y	N	?	N	N	Y	N	Y
9 ***Martin***	Y	N	N	Y	Y	N	Y	N
10 ***Broyhill***	Y	N	N	Y	Y	N	Y	N
11 Clarke	Y	Y	Y	Y	N	Y	N	Y
NORTH DAKOTA								
AL Dorgan	N	Y	Y	N	N	Y	Y	#
OHIO								
1 Luken	N	Y	?	Y	N	N	Y	Y
2 ***Gradison***	N	Y	N	Y	Y	Y	Y	N
3 Hall	Y	Y	Y	Y	N	Y	Y	Y
4 ***Oxley***	Y	N	N	N	Y	N	Y	N
5 ***Latta***	Y	N	N	Y	Y	N	N	N
6 ***McEwen***	Y	N	N	N	Y	N	N	N
7 ***DeWine***	Y	N	?	N	Y	N	N	N
8 ***Kindness***	Y	N	N	N	Y	N	N	N
9 Kaptur	N	Y	Y	N	N	Y	Y	Y
10 ***Miller***	N	N	N	N	Y	N	Y	N
11 Eckart	N	Y	Y	N	N	Y	Y	Y
12 ***Kasich***	N	N	N	N	Y	N	N	N
13 Pease	N	Y	Y	N	N	Y	Y	Y
14 Seiberling	Y	Y	Y	N	N	Y	Y	Y
15 ***Wylie***	Y	N	N	N	Y	N	N	Y
16 ***Regula***	Y	N	N	N	Y	Y	Y	N
17 ***Williams***	Y	N	?	N	N	Y	Y	N
18 Applegate	N	Y	Y	N	N	Y	Y	Y
19 Feighan	Y	Y	Y	N	N	Y	Y	Y
20 Oakar	Y	Y	Y	N	N	Y	Y	Y
21 Stokes	N	Y	Y	Y	N	Y	Y	Y
OKLAHOMA								
1 Jones	N	N	Y	N	N	Y	N	Y
2 Synar	Y	Y	Y	N	N	Y	Y	N
3 Watkins	N	N	Y	Y	N	Y	Y	N
4 McCurdy	N	N	Y	N	N	Y	N	Y
5 ***Edwards***	Y	N	?	Y	Y	N	Y	N
6 English	N	N	Y	N	N	Y	Y	N
OREGON								
1 AuCoin	N	Y	N	N	N	Y	Y	N
2 ***Smith, R.***	Y	N	N	Y	N	N	Y	N
3 Wyden	N	Y	Y	N	N	Y	Y	N
4 Weaver	N	Y	Y	N	N	Y	Y	N
5 ***Smith, D.***	N	N	N	Y	?	N	N	N
PENNSYLVANIA								
1 Foglietta	Y	Y	Y	Y	N	Y	Y	Y
2 Gray	N	Y	Y	N	N	Y	Y	Y
3 Borski	Y	Y	Y	N	N	Y	Y	Y
4 Kolter	Y	Y	Y	N	N	Y	Y	Y
5 ***Schulze***	N	N	N	N	?	N	N	N
6 Yatron	Y	N	Y	N	N	N	Y	Y
7 Edgar	N	Y	+	N	N	Y	Y	Y
8 Kostmayer	Y	Y	Y	N	N	Y	Y	Y
9 ***Shuster***	Y	N	N	N	Y	N	N	N
10 ***McDade***	Y	N	N	N	N	N	N	N
11 Harrison	Y	Y	Y	N	N	Y	Y	Y
12 Murtha	Y	N	Y	N	N	N	N	Y
13 ***Coughlin***	Y	N	Y	Y	Y	Y	Y	N
14 Coyne	Y	Y	Y	Y	N	Y	Y	Y
15 ***Ritter***	Y	N	N	N	Y	N	N	N
16 ***Walker***	N	N	N	Y	Y	N	Y	N
17 ***Gekas***	Y	N	N	N	Y	Y	Y	N
18 Walgren	N	Y	Y	Y	N	Y	Y	Y
19 ***Goodling***	Y	Y	N	N	Y	Y	Y	N
20 Gaydos	N	N	Y	N	N	N	N	Y
21 ***Ridge***	Y	Y	Y	N	N	Y	N	N
22 Murphy	N	Y	Y	N	N	Y	Y	Y
23 ***Clinger***	Y	N	N	N	Y	Y	Y	N
RHODE ISLAND								
1 St Germain	N	Y	Y	Y	N	N	Y	Y
2 ***Schneider***	Y	Y	Y	Y	Y	Y	Y	N
SOUTH CAROLINA								
1 ***Hartnett***	Y	N	N	Y	Y	N	N	N
2 ***Spence***	Y	N	N	Y	Y	N	N	N
3 Derrick	N	Y	Y	Y	N	Y	Y	Y
4 ***Campbell***	Y	N	N	Y	Y	N	N	N
5 Spratt	Y	Y	Y	Y	N	Y	Y	Y
6 Tallon	Y	Y	Y	N	N	Y	Y	N
SOUTH DAKOTA								
AL Daschle	N	Y	Y	N	N	Y	Y	N

	9	10	11	12	13	14	15	16
TENNESSEE								
1 ***Quillen***	Y	N	N	N	Y	N	N	Y
2 ***Duncan***	Y	N	N	N	Y	N	Y	Y
3 Lloyd [3]	Y	N	Y	N	N	N	N	N
4 Cooper	Y	N	Y	N	N	N	Y	Y
5 Boner	Y	N	Y	N	N	Y	N	N
6 Gore	Y	N	Y	N	N	Y	Y	N
7 ***Sundquist***	Y	N	N	N	Y	N	N	Y
8 Jones	Y	N	Y	N	N	N	N	N
9 Ford	Y	Y	?	N	N	Y	Y	Y
TEXAS								
1 Hall, S.	N	N	N	N	N	N	N	Y
2 Wilson	Y	N	Y	N	N	Y	N	Y
3 ***Bartlett***	Y	N	N	Y	Y	N	N	N
4 Hall, R.	N	N	Y	N	Y	N	Y	N
5 Bryant	N	Y	Y	N	N	Y	Y	Y
6 ***Gramm***	Y	N	?	?	?	N	N	N
7 ***Archer***	N	N	N	Y	Y	N	N	N
8 ***Fields***	N	N	N	Y	Y	N	N	N
9 Brooks	N	Y	Y	Y	N	Y	N	N
10 Pickle	Y	N	Y	Y	N	Y	Y	Y
11 Leath	Y	N	?	N	N	N	N	N
12 Wright	Y	Y	Y	N	N	Y	N	Y
13 Hightower	Y	N	Y	Y	N	X	N	N
14 Patman	N	N	Y	Y	N	Y	N	N
15 de la Garza	Y	N	Y	N	?	Y	N	Y
16 Coleman	Y	Y	Y	Y	N	Y	N	Y
17 Stenholm	N	N	N	N	?	N	N	N
18 Leland	N	Y	?	N	N	Y	Y	Y
19 Hance	N	N	Y	?	X	#	?	?
20 Gonzalez	N	Y	Y	N	N	Y	Y	N
21 ***Loeffler***	Y	N	N	Y	Y	N	N	N
22 ***Paul***	N	Y	?	?	?	?	?	N
23 Kazen	Y	N	Y	Y	N	N	N	N
24 Frost	Y	N	Y	N	N	Y	Y	N
25 Andrews	Y	N	Y	N	N	Y	N	Y
26 Vandergriff	Y	N	Y	N	N	N	N	N
27 Ortiz	Y	N	Y	Y	N	Y	N	Y
UTAH								
1 ***Hansen***	Y	N	N	Y	Y	N	N	X
2 ***Marriott***	Y	N	N	Y	Y	N	N	N
3 ***Nielson***	Y	N	N	Y	Y	N	N	N
VERMONT								
AL ***Jeffords***	Y	Y	Y	N	N	Y	Y	N
VIRGINIA								
1 ***Bateman***	Y	N	N	Y	Y	N	N	N
2 ***Whitehurst***	Y	N	N	Y	Y	Y	N	N
3 ***Bliley***	Y	N	N	Y	Y	N	N	N
4 Sisisky	Y	Y	Y	N	N	Y	N	Y
5 Daniel	Y	N	N	Y	N	N	N	N
6 Olin	Y	Y	Y	Y	N	Y	Y	Y
7 ***Robinson***	Y	N	N	Y	Y	N	N	N
8 ***Parris***	Y	N	N	Y	Y	Y	Y	N
9 Boucher	Y	Y	Y	N	N	Y	?	N
10 ***Wolf***	Y	N	N	Y	Y	N	N	N
WASHINGTON								
1 ***Pritchard***	Y	N	?	?	Y	Y	Y	?
2 Swift	N	Y	Y	N	N	Y	Y	Y
3 Bonker	Y	Y	Y	N	N	Y	Y	Y
4 ***Morrison***	Y	N	Y	N	Y	Y	N	N
5 Foley	Y	N	Y	N	N	Y	Y	Y
6 Dicks	Y	N	Y	N	N	Y	Y	Y
7 Lowry	N	Y	?	?	N	Y	Y	Y
8 ***Chandler***	Y	N	Y	Y	Y	Y	N	N
WEST VIRGINIA								
1 Mollohan	Y	N	Y	N	N	N	N	Y
2 Staggers	Y	Y	Y	N	N	Y	Y	Y
3 Wise	N	Y	Y	N	N	Y	Y	Y
4 Rahall	Y	Y	Y	N	N	Y	Y	Y
WISCONSIN								
1 Aspin	Y	N	Y	N	N	Y	Y	Y
2 Kastenmeier	N	Y	Y	N	N	Y	Y	Y
3 ***Gunderson***	N	N	N	N	N	Y	Y	N
4 Zablocki	Y	N	Y	N	N	Y	Y	Y
5 Moody	N	Y	Y	Y	N	Y	?	Y
6 ***Petri***	N	Y	N	N	N	Y	N	Y
7 Obey	N	Y	Y	N	N	Y	Y	Y
8 ***Roth***	N	N	N	N	Y	N	N	N
9 ***Sensenbrenner***	N	N	N	N	Y	N	Y	N
WYOMING								
AL ***Cheney***	Y	N	?	Y	Y	N	N	N

Southern states - Ala., Ark., Fla., Ga., Ky., La., Miss., N.C., Okla., S.C., Tenn., Texas, Va.

1984 Key Votes

Senate

1. School Prayer

The Senate March 20 rejected a proposed constitutional amendment to permit organized, recited prayer in public schools and other public places. It was the first time since 1970 that the Senate had voted on a constitutional amendment on school prayer; then, a similar though not identical proposal was rejected.

The House did not consider any constitutional amendment on prayer in 1984.

The vote on the Senate proposal (S J Res 73) was 56-44, 11 shy of the two-thirds majority required. Republicans voted for the amendment 37-18, while Democrats opposed it, 19-26 (ND 6-25, SD 13-1).

The vote was a setback for President Reagan, who had lobbied for the amendment, and for fundamentalist Christian groups, which had pressed for a constitutional amendment to overturn a series of Supreme Court decisions since 1962 that barred prayers and Bible readings in the public schools.

Before voting on S J Res 73, the Senate defeated, 81-15, an alternative proposal that would have allowed group silent prayer in public schools.

The defeat of the prayer amendment resulted in a strategy shift by proponents of school prayer. Within weeks, they turned their attention to enacting a law to allow student religious groups to meet in public schools on the same terms as other student groups. *(House key vote 6)*

2. Farm Bill

The administration won a qualified victory after trying for more than a year to halt scheduled increases in a major type of crop price support, target prices. What began as a thrift measure became, for many members, an election-year cornucopia of concessions to farmers by the time it cleared the House April 3.

Still, the target price freeze (HR 4072 — PL 98-258) was an achievement for the administration because it meant that bidding on future levels for the important price support program would start at lower levels in 1985, when Congress was scheduled to reauthorize farm programs in an omnibus farm bill.

The target price program provided cash to farmers when market prices for major crops dropped below statutory "targets." In its 1981 farm bill the administration had sought, without success, to end the program. By 1983, administration officials were urging Congress to halt the expensive annual boosts in the targets, arguing that they encouraged farmers to overproduce for surplus-glutted markets.

Farm lobbyists told the administration they would give up the scheduled support increases if they got something in return.

The basic bill was negotiated in private sessions with the administration and farm-state senators; progress occasionally stalled as commodity groups voiced new requests. As the Senate was winding up debate on the bill, a final adjustment for rice producers was being completed off the floor. The freeze bill passed the Senate March 22 on a 78-10 vote, with Republicans voting 50-2, Democrats 28-8 (ND 20-4, SD 8-4). By that time, it had acquired paid acreage reductions for crops in 1985 (with early payments to participants in 1984), liberalized loan terms for Farmers Home Administration borrowers, and administration commitments to boost farm exports and food donations abroad.

The final version of the farm measure emerged from the House-Senate conference little changed from the Senate-passed bill.

3. El Salvador Aid

Nearly three years after the Reagan administration began providing substantial amounts of military aid to help the government of El Salvador fight leftist guerrillas, the Senate in March and April held its first major debate on U.S. policy in the region.

Pending before the Senate, as it acted on an "urgent" fiscal 1984 supplemental appropriations bill (H J Res 492 — PL 98-332) was a Reagan request for $92.7 million in military aid to the Salvadoran regime, on top of $64.8 million that Congress had approved previously for the year. Early during Senate consideration of the issue, the administration settled for a compromise figure of $61.75 million, negotiated by Daniel K. Inouye, D-Hawaii. But other Democrats, among them leading critics of Reagan's policies in Central America, pressed for a much lower figure of $21 million, which they said was enough to keep the Salvadoran army supplied through that country's presidential election in May.

On April 2, the Senate rejected an amendment by Edward M. Kennedy, D-Mass., that would have allowed only $21 million in additional Salvador aid. The vote was 25-63: R 2-48; D 23-15 (ND 21-5, SD 2-10).

Coupled with House approval on May 10 of a foreign aid authorizations bill (HR 5119) containing all of Reagan's requests for El Salvador, the Senate's April 2 vote helped end a longstanding debate in Congress about the wisdom of U.S. involvement in the civil war in that country.

Congress eventually approved the $61.75 million included in the urgent supplemental, plus another $70 million for El Salvador in a later supplemental (HR 6040 — PL 98-396), bringing the total for fiscal 1984 to $196.55 million. *(House key vote 5)*

4. Troops in El Salvador

During Senate debate on the "urgent" supplemental appropriations bill for fiscal 1984 (H J Res 492 — PL 98-332), a majority of Democrats decided to put that chamber

on record on the question of limiting the president's discretion to send combat troops to Central America. Reagan long had insisted that he had no intention of involving U.S. forces directly in Central America's civil wars. But some Democrats expressed a belief that Reagan would send troops to the region to avert the spread of communism, and they wanted Congress to play a direct role in any such decision.

The Senate on March 29 rejected, by wide margins, two proposals by Edward M. Kennedy, D-Mass., requiring congressional authorization for the introduction of combat troops in Central America.

Early in April, most Senate Democrats reached agreement on another proposal that would have required the president to seek congressional authorization before sending combat troops into or over El Salvador. An exception would be made if introduction of troops was needed immediately to evacuate U.S. citizens. On April 4, Patrick J. Leahy, D-Vt., offered that proposal as an amendment to H J Res 492, and it was tabled on a 59-36 vote: R 49-5; D 10-31 (ND 2-25, SD 8-6). Because the amendment had support from a broad range of Democrats, it was the clearest test in 1984 of congressional sentiment on the issue of direct U.S. involvement in Central America's wars.

5. Tax Indexing

Ever since Congress agreed in 1981 to index federal income taxes to offset the effects of inflation, Democrats and some moderate Republicans had been trying to repeal or delay the law, set to go into effect in 1985. They had argued that a country with annual budget deficits approaching $200 billion could ill afford to reduce taxes approximately $51 billion over the next three years.

But they had been defeated every time — in part because of Reagan's strong support of indexing. He repeatedly threatened to veto any change in indexing or the across-the-board income tax cuts in the Economic Recovery Tax Act of 1981.

In a last attempt to change indexing before it went into effect, Sen. John H. Chafee, R-R.I., proposed an amendment to the Deficit Reduction Act of 1984 (HR 2163) to delay the Jan. 1, 1985, effective date for three years. Critics argued that the delay would hit middle-income taxpayers the hardest. But Chafee replied that the best way to help "the taxpayers of this country is to reduce the deficit."

His arguments failed to convince most of his GOP colleagues and even some Democrats, whose standard-bearer Walter F. Mondale had made an indexing delay part of his economic program. A motion by Finance Committee Chairman Robert Dole, R-Kan., to table (kill) Chafee's amendment was agreed to April 10, 57-38: R 46-7; D 11-31 (ND 8-22, SD 3-9).

6. Real Estate Taxes

Congress tried again, as it had done for the past three years, to help reduce the federal deficit by raising revenues through a hodgepodge of tax measures, including some to close loopholes and improve taxpayer compliance. As before, legislators faced strong lobbying pressure from interest groups to back away from proposed tax hikes.

A key challenge to 1984 efforts came from the real estate industry, which objected to a Finance Committee proposal to increase from 15 to 20 years the minimum time period over which a building could be depreciated, or writ-

ten off against taxes. Proponents of the change argued that the shorter time period was overly generous and had spurred the growth of abusive real estate tax shelters. Opponents argued that a 20-year depreciation requirement would inhibit investment in real estate.

But the influence of the real estate industry was evident during the Senate floor debate on the Deficit Reduction Act of 1984 (HR 2163), which included provisions to raise $47.7 billion in taxes through fiscal year 1987. An amendment by Rudy Boschwitz, R-Minn., to set the real estate depreciation period at 20 years in 1984, 19 years in 1985 and 18 years thereafter was adopted early April 13, 62-19: R 37-8; D 25-11 (ND 17-10, SD 8-1). To help offset revenue losses, the Boschwitz amendment included a provision to reduce tax credits for the rehabilitation of old buildings.

Finance Committee Chairman Robert Dole, R-Kan., who had fought to keep the committee package intact, said: "You do around here what you have the votes to do. The point is [the real estate interests] have the votes."

In conference, the rehabilitation tax credit change was dropped and the real estate depreciation period was set at 18 years (PL 98-369).

7. Deficit-Reduction Plan

In the culmination of four weeks of bitter debate, the Senate on May 17 accepted a modified deficit-reduction package backed by Reagan and the Senate GOP leadership. The plan was adopted 65-32: R 53-0; D 12-32 (ND 6-24, SD 6-8). But the margin of approval belied the intensity of the chamber's struggle over budget-cutting proposals.

Acceptance of the "Rose Garden" plan, so called because Reagan endorsed it in the White House Rose Garden March 15, was guaranteed once Senate Majority Leader Howard H. Baker Jr., R-Tenn., and White House officials struck a deal with GOP dissidents who had been pressing for higher domestic spending.

Proposals aimed at trimming federal deficits were debated at length in both the House and Senate. The House approved a measure to slash deficits by $182 billion through 1987. The Rose Garden plan called for $140 billion in deficit cuts through the same period. *(House key vote 3)*

Key components of the Senate plan were three-year spending caps on defense and domestic spending. Under the caps, military spending authority would rise by 7 percent annually; the budget for other discretionary spending would be $139.8 billion in fiscal 1985, $144.3 billion in fiscal 1986 and $151.5 billion in fiscal 1987. Taxes would increase by $47.7 billion under the Senate plan, about the same as in the House budget. The House budget called for annual defense spending to rise at a 3.5 percent rate, adjusted for inflation.

Passage of the Rose Garden plan was preceded by close votes on several alternative spending cut/tax increase measures. In one plan, Senate Democrats sought to cut deficits by $204 billion; among the provisions were limiting defense growth to 4 percent and delaying tax indexing for two years. That plan failed May 8 on a 49-49 tie. On May 10 the Senate, 48-46, shelved a plan supported by GOP moderates that would have combined the defense and domestic spending caps and given appropriating committees some leeway in shifting money from defense to social programs.

The GOP leadership broke the logjam May 16 when it convinced five moderate Republicans to support a proposal

adding $2 billion to the non-defense appropriations cap. The Senate accepted the plan, 62-37.

The Rose Garden plan vote came the next day on an amendment to HR 2163, a miscellaneous trade bill. The tax provisions were added to HR 4170 (PL 98-369); the spending targets were incorporated in S Con Res 106.

House-Senate agreement on defense spending hung up resolution of spending questions until the closing days of the session.

8. Anti-Missile Defense

By a margin of two votes, the Senate on June 13 killed an amendment that would have trimmed $100 million from Reagan's proposal to develop a space-based defense against Soviet ballistic missiles. This was the first vote taken in either house on Reagan's "strategic defense initiative" — which critics had labeled "Star Wars."

The vote came on an amendment to the fiscal 1985 defense authorization bill (S 2723). Reagan requested $1.78 billion for development of the anti-missile project and the Senate Armed Services Committee had trimmed the amount to $1.63 billion. An amendment by Charles H. Percy, R-Ill., that would have further reduced the amount was tabled, and thus killed, 47-45: R 40-10; D 7-35 (ND 3-26, SD 4-9).

When Reagan called for the initiative in a televised address on March 23, 1983, he set the sweeping goal of making nuclear weapons "impotent and obsolete." Many observers took this statement to mean that the new program would substitute a "leak-proof" defense for the long-standing U.S. policy of deterring Soviet attack by threat of nuclear retaliation.

Critics of Reagan's Star Wars plan argued almost unanimously that a perfect defense would be impossible. At best, they warned, a U.S. effort to develop such weapons would extend the arms race to outer space and shatter the 1972 U.S.-Soviet treaty limiting anti-missile defenses.

There was no corresponding floor vote in the House, where opponents of Reagan's plans for new weapons in space concentrated on trying to block tests of the anti-satellite (ASAT) missile. The House version of the fiscal 1985 defense appropriations bill slashed funding for the anti-missile plan to $1.1 billion. The final appropriations compromise was $1.4 billion.

9. MX Missile

The Senate June 14 approved continued production of MX intercontinental missiles, but only by the vote of Vice President George Bush. Bush broke a 48-48 tie, to table, and thus kill, an amendment to the fiscal 1985 defense authorization bill (S 2723) that would have barred production of additional MXs in fiscal 1985.

In 1983, Congress had narrowly approved production of the first 21 MXs.

Though barring production of more missiles in fiscal 1985, the June 14 amendment would have approved several hundred million dollars in MX-related procurement funds so that the missile production line would be kept available to resume production if the missile were approved in fiscal 1986. The precise mechanics of the amendment were obscure, but its intent was clear: it gave senators a chance to register their unhappiness with Reagan's MX plan without taking political responsibility for voting to kill the program.

MX, which would be the first U.S. long-range ballistic missile with enough power and accuracy to attack armored Soviet missile launchers and command posts, had been the centerpiece of the administration's nuclear arms program. The administration argued that the rapidity with which they could hit their targets gave ICBMs much more symbolic "clout" than other nuclear weapons and that the current Soviet advantage in such weapons was intolerable.

Most MX opponents rejected the administration's focus on land-based missiles such as the MX, arguing that Soviet advantages in such weapons could be offset by U.S. advantages in other kinds of nuclear arms. Moreover, they said, since MX would be deployed in existing missile silos, which were vulnerable to Soviet attack, the new and more powerful missile would simply increase Moscow's incentive to launch a first strike in case of a severe superpower crisis.

The GOP-led Senate clearly was not prepared to vote to kill MX: Shortly before the key vote, it voted 55-41 to kill an amendment that would have denied MX production funds in fiscal 1985. But by abandoning in early 1983 the long search for an invulnerable way to deploy MX, Reagan paved the way for a weakening of support for the program reflected in the June 14 vote to table the anti-production amendment: R 43-10; D 5-38 (ND 2-28, SD 3-10) with Bush casting a "yea" vote to break the 48-48 tie.

The House had voted to block additional MX production unless Congress voted in 1985 to allow it. *(House key vote 9)*

The final compromise allowed production of a second batch of 21 MXs if Congress passed two resolutions approving that move in the spring of 1985.

10. Aid to Nicaraguan 'Contras'

For Congress and the Reagan administration, the most contentious foreign policy issue was the so-called "secret" war in Nicaragua. Since early 1982, thousands of U.S.-paid and equipped guerrillas, called "contras," were battling the leftist government of Nicaragua. The House Democratic leadership in 1983 staked out a clear position in opposition to the war. But until early 1984, the administration had backing for the war from key Democrats in the Senate, especially from members of the Intelligence Committee.

In April, Senate Intelligence Committee Chairman Barry Goldwater, R-Ariz., disclosed on the Senate floor that the CIA had helped the contras mine three Nicaraguan harbors. Goldwater and other committee members were outraged, not so much by the mining as by the fact that the CIA had not notified them in advance.

The immediate product of that outrage was the Senate's adoption on April 10 of a non-binding statement opposing the mining. Also as a result of the mining, several Democrats on the Senate Intelligence Committee — among them committee Vice Chairman Daniel Patrick Moynihan, N.Y., and former Chairman Daniel K. Inouye, Hawaii — decided to drop their support for the Nicaraguan war.

On June 18, as the Senate was debating the fiscal 1985 defense authorizations bill (S 2723), Edward M. Kennedy, D-Mass., offered an amendment stating that the bill did not authorize U.S. aid to the contras. To that amendment, Inouye offered a substitute authorizing $2 million to move the contras out of Nicaragua and $4 million for their "humanitarian support" once they left.

The Senate tabled the underlying Kennedy amendment, taking with it Inouye's substitute proposal, by a vote of 58-38: R 48-6; D 10-32 (ND 2-26, SD 8-6). Nevertheless,

the vote showed that support for the Nicaraguan war was fading in the Senate. Among the 38 who opposed the war were five Intelligence Committee members who previously had backed it: Moynihan; Inouye; Lloyd Bentsen, D-Texas; Walter D. Huddleston, D-Ky., and William S. Cohen, R-Maine.

A week later, on June 25, the Senate voted 88-1 to delete Reagan's pending request for $21 million to continue aid to the contras through fiscal 1984. In October, conferees on a fiscal 1985 continuing appropriations resolution (H J Res 648 — PL 98-473) decided to bar any aid to the contras until March 1985. *(House key vote 8)*

11. Drunken Driving

Faced with an intense lobbying effort by relatives of victims of drunken driving, Congress acted to pressure states into raising their minimum drinking age to 21. The law (HR 4616 — PL 98-363) would withhold a portion of federal highway funds if a state did not set its minimum drinking age at 21 by 1987.

When the proposal surfaced in a House committee early in 1984, it was opposed by the administration as an infringement on states' rights. The administration argued that establishing the legal drinking age had been a state prerogative, and 27 states allowed people younger than 21 to purchase or possess alcohol.

Nevertheless, in June the House added to a highway funding bill an amendment that would withhold certain funds from states that did not have a 21-year limit. As Congress raced toward the July 4 recess, prospects for enactment were clouded because floor action on the Senate's highway bill had been blocked by various disputes.

A group called Mothers Against Drunk Drivers (MADD) and a number of other organizations continued their crusade backing a national drinking age limit, maintaining that the varying laws created a patchwork quilt of "blood borders" that let young people drive across state lines to drink in states with low minimum ages, causing accidents on their way home.

The mothers buttonholed legislators like veteran campaigners, creating an atmosphere that Sen. Gordon J. Humphrey, R-N.H., called "a public relations effort over the last 10 days which has panicked half the town." The president switched position and supported the legislation.

The path for the legislation was cleared June 21 when senators reached a compromise that combined the withholding of funds if the 21-year limit was not established and providing incentive grants for states to establish other safety programs. When the compromise came up on the Senate floor June 26 in the form of an amendment offered by Frank R. Lautenberg, D-N.J., it was opposed by a handful of members who opposed the coercive approach of withholding funds, and by some who thought it unfairly discriminated against an age group.

But after rejecting an attempt to substitute a financial incentive program for the punitive approach, the Senate whisked the Lautenberg amendment through by a vote of 81-16: R 45-10; D 36-6 (ND 25-3, SD 11-3). Two days later the House agreed to the Senate amendment, clearing the measure for the president.

12. Appropriations Holdup

Upset with Senate unwillingness to resolve defense spending issues and angered at the chamber's virtual dis-

missal of the congressional budget process, Democrats led by Lawton Chiles, D-Fla., stopped the chamber's work for a week in early August. The first attempt to limit the Democratic filibuster failed, 54-31: R 46-3; D 8-28 (ND 4-20, SD 4-8). Although a second motion to cut off debate succeeded, the Democrats' ploy eventually forced the GOP leadership to agree to negotiations with the House leaders on Pentagon spending.

The Democratic filibuster began Aug. 1, when Chiles objected to a motion to waive provisions of the 1974 Congressional Budget and Impoundment Control Act (PL 93-344) and take up the fiscal 1985 agriculture appropriations bill (HR 5743). The act required Congress to adopt a budget resolution before considering appropriations bills. The Senate had previously agreed to waive the Budget Act to debate fiscal 1985 funding bills; the House May 22 approved a blanket waiver for all 1985 appropriations bills.

A House-Senate conference on the budget resolution (H Con Res 280) had stalled over setting a fiscal 1985 spending level for defense. The Senate plan envisioned a 7 percent increase; the House plan, 3.5 percent.

Chiles' crusade struck a chord among his colleagues, and Majority Leader Howard H. Baker Jr., R-Tenn., Aug. 6 fell six votes short of the necessary 60 to cut off the Chiles-led filibuster.

Cloture was invoked Aug. 8, 68-30, but Chiles immediately threatened to object to a Budget Act waiver when the GOP leadership put the District of Columbia appropriations bill on the schedule.

Chiles Aug. 9 suggested that the defense spending impasse could be broken at a "summit" meeting of the Republican and Democratic leadership and the chairmen of the Budget and defense authorizing committees and the Defense appropriations subcommittees. Baker, faced with Chiles' vow to continue objecting to budget waiver, endorsed the summit meeting proposal, and Chiles withdrew his filibuster threat.

13. Civil Rights

Civil rights advocates were stymied in an effort to pass legislation ensuring that no part of an institution receiving federal funds could discriminate on the basis of race, sex, age or handicap.

The bill (HR 5490, S 2568) would have overturned the Supreme Court's Feb. 28 ruling in *Grove City College v. Bell*, which narrowed the reach of Title IX of the 1972 Education Amendments. The court ruled that the law's ban on sex bias in any education "program or activity" receiving federal funds applied only to the program getting aid and not to the entire institution. Three other laws barring discrimination on race, age or handicap had similar wording, and civil rights lawyers warned that the court's ruling could restrict their enforcement as well. The *Grove City* bill would have amended all four laws to make clear that any "recipient" of aid, not just the program or activity involved, would have to conform to the anti-bias laws.

The House passed HR 5490 by a 375-32 margin June 26. But in the Senate, opponents led by Orrin G. Hatch, R-Utah, kept S 2568 bottled up in the Labor and Human Resources Committee. Majority Leader Howard H. Baker Jr., R-Tenn., refused to call up the House version for floor debate, so supporters of the measure sought to attach the measure to the fiscal 1985 continuing appropriations resolution (H J Res 648).

The key vote came Sept. 27 when Minority Leader

Robert C. Byrd, D-W.Va., offered the civil rights measure as an amendment to H J Res 648 and asked the Senate to determine whether the amendment, a legislative proposal, was "germane" to the funding bill. The Senate decided that it was germane, and therefore eligible for further action, by a vote of 51-48: R 12-42; D 39-6 (ND 30-1, SD 9-5).

However, Hatch had offered amendments to the funding bill on school busing, gun control and tuition tax credits. The Senate became tied in a procedural knot, with these issues obstructing movement on the funding bill. After four days, Sen. Bob Packwood, R-Ore., a chief sponsor of the civil rights bill, moved to table, and thus kill, the *Grove City* amendment. His motion was agreed to 53-45, ending the civil rights fight for the 98th Congress. The other amendments then fell.

House

1. Handicapped Infants

Entering a touchy area of medical and ethical controversy, the House Feb. 2 approved legislation (HR 1904 — PL 98-457) designed to protect severely handicapped infants from medical neglect.

Backed by the administration, right-to-life groups and advocates for the disabled, the legislation was drafted in response to widely publicized "Baby Doe" cases, in which doctors and families had withheld medical treatment and care that handicapped infants needed to stay alive.

HR 1904 required states, as a condition of receiving federal aid for child abuse prevention programs, to have procedures for reporting cases in which handicapped infants were denied treatment for life-threatening conditions. The American Medical Association (AMA) and other critics saw the bill as an unwarranted government intrusion in the decisions of families and physicians.

The key House vote came on an amendment by Rod Chandler, R-Wash., to strike the "Baby Doe" language and instead require the Department of Health and Human Services to issue guidelines for hospitals that wanted to set up advisory panels on the treatment of handicapped babies.

The Chandler amendment, supported by the AMA and other medical organizations, was rejected by the House 182-231: R 31-131; D 151-100 (ND 97-69, SD 54-31).

The opposition of many medical groups to the bill was later blunted, when the Senate adopted a revised version that made clear that doctors would not have to take heroic steps to save the life of an infant if treatment would be futile. But even the compromise language, which was largely incorporated by a conference committee into the final version of the bill, did not go far enough to win the support of the AMA.

2. Water Project Cost-Sharing

The administration and Western states triumphed March 20 when the House voted against asking local beneficiaries of federal dams in the West to help pay for safety repairs. The vote, which pitted region against region, came on an amendment that substituted a mostly federal payment formula for a beneficiary-pays formula sought by environmentalists and taxpayer groups.

The amendment was adopted 194-192: R 75-73; D 119-119 (ND 61-91, SD 58-28).

This was a crucial vote on the cost-sharing issue, which had split Congress for at least eight years and stopped the authorization of most new water projects. The bill in question (HR 1652) authorized $650 million in work to repair and rebuild unsafe, aging dams located largely in the West.

The vote represented a turnaround from April 29, 1982, when the House by 212-140 adopted a user-pays amendment to a similar dam repair bill. But the House was following the lead of Reagan, who had done his own about-face on cost-sharing for dam safety projects. The president's switch, outlined in a Jan. 24 policy statement, seemed a direct response to the pleas of Republicans from the West, a bastion of Reagan support in the 1980 election. Fifteen Western GOP senators had warned Reagan in 1983 that his re-election hopes, and their own, could be damaged by policies that appeared "anti-West" and "anti-water."

The House's vote was partly offset by the Senate, which approved a version with some cost-sharing requirements after filibuster threats by Howard M. Metzenbaum, D-Ohio. That version was enacted (PL 98-404).

3. Adoption of the Budget Resolution

House approval of a fiscal 1985 budget resolution capped an effort by House Democratic leaders to devise a deficit-cutting strategy that would be easy to explain to constituents and exhibit the party's commitment to fiscal discipline. The vote was 250-168: R 21-139; D 229-29 (ND 159-13, SD 70-16).

The resolution (H Con Res 280) did nothing to reduce federal deficits; rather, it set fiscal targets. Once adopted April 5, however, it led the way to House approval of a measure (HR 4170 — PL 98-369) raising $49.2 billion in taxes through fiscal 1987, and other deficit-cutting measures. H Con Res 280 envisioned deficit reductions totaling $182 billion through 1987. The Senate's "Rose Garden" plan called for cuts of $140 billion through the same period. *(Senate key vote 7)*

The plan's key feature was the "pay-as-you-go" concept, which barred spending boosts above inflation, except for defense and a small number of programs for the poor, for which there would have to be offsetting tax hikes. Republicans attacked pay-as-you-go as a "simple sham," but the scheme's apparent appeal as prudent budgeting and the Democratic leaders' backing ensured its approval.

The plan called for defense spending to grow at 3.5 percent a year, adjusted for inflation. Differences with the GOP-led Senate, whose package would have raised Pentagon spending 7 percent a year, blocked consideration of the budget resolution until the end of the session.

4. Physician Fee Freeze

Having previously clamped new Medicare spending limits on hospitals and raised beneficiaries' out-of-pocket costs, Congress in 1984 turned to doctors to cut costs of the financially troubled program.

The basic plan — a freeze on increases in Medicare payments to doctors — was backed by congressional leaders, the administration and the American Medical Association (AMA).

But the AMA objected vehemently to a related "mandatory assignment" plan that would force doctors to accept the "frozen" Medicare fees as full payment for their services. (Assignment, optional under existing law, meant that a doctor would bill Medicare directly and accept program payment as full reimbursement for his services. The law

also permitted doctors to bill Medicare beneficiaries directly, charging more than Medicare would pay and requiring the beneficiary to pay the difference.)

The House in April rejected freeze plans, both with mandatory assignment provisions and without. Yet by June, Congress had approved a Medicare fee freeze along with a "voluntary" assignment plan that levied substantial financial penalties on doctors who did not accept assignment. Both were included in a larger "deficit reduction" tax and spending-cut bill (HR 4170 — PL 98-369), cleared by the Senate June 27.

When the House debated an earlier version of the bill (HR 5394) on April 12, Rep. Andrew Jacobs Jr., D-Ind., proposed a yearlong freeze on Medicare physician fees for inpatient hospital care, with provisions that would have effectively deprived doctors of hospital admitting privileges if they refused assignment. Jacobs offered the amendment on the floor after failing to get majority support for it in the Ways and Means Committee.

Opponents argued that assignment would harm elderly Medicare beneficiaries by discouraging doctors from treating them. And, they said, assignment would not in itself save the government any money. (Government savings from the freeze had been estimated at nearly a billion dollars.)

Supporters said mandatory assignment was essential to keep doctors from raising their fees despite the freeze and passing along the extra cost to Medicare patients.

But the House rejected Jacobs' plan by voice vote. It then rejected by 172-242 a Republican motion to recommit the bill to committee with instructions to add a freeze on both inpatient and outpatient fees for Medicare, without mandatory assignment. The vote on recommittal reflected mixed motives. Some members were unwilling to freeze the doctor fees without an assignment plan to protect Medicare patients against higher costs.

The recommittal motion also forced a rare choice between competing health priorities because it also would have struck from the bill a new Medicaid child health initiative that was backed by the Democratic leadership.

And finally, a vote to recommit is generally viewed by the majority as an undesirable surrender to the minority. The 172-242 vote against the recommittal motion split along party lines: R 157-2; D 15-240 (ND 3-170, SD 12-70).

The Senate subsequently included in its deficit reduction plan a one-year Medicare fee freeze, with a new voluntary assignment program and a modified second-year freeze for doctors not participating in assignment.

That plan also disturbed the AMA, but the final bill coupled a "voluntary" plan with a 15-month Medicare freeze on both inpatient and outpatient services. Doctors staying out of the assignment plan were still subject to the freeze and faced penalties in future calculations of Medicare fees at the end of the freeze. The AMA subsequently filed a lawsuit challenging the constitutionality of the assignment provisions.

5. El Salvador Aid

On May 6, voters in El Salvador went to the polls and made José Napoleón Duarte, leader of the center-left Christian Democratic Party, their first freely elected president in some 50 years.

Four days later, members of the U.S. House of Representatives cast their first votes in three years on the issue of U.S. military aid to El Salvador. The result was a close, but decisive, victory for Reagan's program of increasing financial backing of the Salvadoran regime.

The key vote came as the House was considering a bill (HR 5119) authorizing foreign aid programs in fiscal 1984-85. The House adopted an amendment by William S. Broomfield, R-Mich., approving all the aid Reagan sought for El Salvador and other Central American countries. The vote was 212-208: R 156-8; D 56-200 (ND 7-167, SD 49-33).

The immediate effect of the vote was to break a political logjam on another piece of legislation — an "urgent" supplemental spending bill (H J Res 492) including $61.75 million for El Salvador. Over the longer term, the vote demonstrated that members of Congress were willing to give Duarte enough aid to keep his government afloat in its battle against leftist guerrillas. *(Senate key vote 3)*

6. Religious Groups in Schools

In the wake of the Senate's rejection of a constitutional amendment to allow prayer in public schools, controversy over religion in the schools shifted to another legislative battleground. *(Senate key vote 1)*

An administration-backed bill (HR 5345) to allow student religious groups to meet in public high schools was narrowly defeated by the House May 15. Another version of the so-called "equal access" proposal later cleared Congress (HR 1310 — PL 98-377), but only after supporters agreed to several key changes to address criticisms made during House debate on HR 5345.

HR 5345 would have cut off federal funds to high schools that refused to allow religious groups to meet on school premises if other student organizations were granted such access. Critics saw it as a "back door" effort to bring prayer into the schools. But supporters of HR 5345 included some members who opposed the prayer amendment; many in Congress saw the access bill as a way to show constituents that they were not hostile to religion.

HR 5345 garnered a majority of votes, but it fell short of the two-thirds margin needed to pass because it had been brought up under special procedures that barred amendments. The House vote was 270-151: R 147-17; D 123-134 (ND 47-122, SD 76-12).

In later Senate action, a companion school access proposal was redrawn to extend the bill's protections to political and other student groups — not just religious ones. That and other changes blunted the opposition of some critics who objected to singling out religious groups for special protection. The revised Senate proposal was cleared by Congress as an amendment to a popular education bill.

7. Anti-Satellite Test Ban

By a hefty margin, the House voted for a moratorium on tests of the anti-satellite (ASAT) missile against a target in space, so long as Moscow observed a similar restriction.

Pointing out that the Soviet Union had tested ASAT weapons about 20 times since the late 1960s, the administration argued that a similar U.S. weapon was needed to give the Russians an incentive to negotiate the mutual abolition of ASATs. But that argument was clouded by the administration's insistence that the U.S. ASAT was needed to neutralize some Soviet satellites that could guide Soviet weapons against U.S. units in case of war.

ASAT opponents argued that the current Soviet version was primitive and could not be used in any realistic military scenario to blind U.S. satellites. However, they

warned, U.S. deployment of its superior weapon would move Moscow to develop an equally capable ASAT. This would threaten communications satellites, on which the United States was more dependent than was Moscow. Accordingly, the critics argued, it would be worth allowing the Russians a symbolic monopoly on ASATs in hopes of averting development of effective anti-satellite arms.

The key House vote came May 23 on an amendment to the fiscal 1985 defense authorization bill that was adopted 238-181: R 39-122; D 199-59 (ND 162-10, SD 37-49).

The Senate voted to bar ASAT target tests unless the president certified his willingness to negotiate "the strictest possible limits" on the weapons. The final version of the defense authorization bill (HR 5167) allowed only two "successful" ASAT target tests in fiscal 1985. The final defense appropriations measure, included in an omnibus continuing resolution (H J Res 648 — PL 98-473) barred any target tests until March 1, 1985, and allowed only three tests in the remainder of the fiscal year.

8. Aid to Nicaraguan 'Contras'

Reaffirming its opposition to the U.S.-backed war in Nicaragua, the House on May 24 rejected Reagan's request for $21 million to continue aiding Nicaraguan rebels in fiscal 1984. The vote was 241-177: R 24-132; D 217-45 (ND 169-6, SD 48-39).

The Democratic-controlled House had voted twice in 1983 against CIA aid to several thousand guerrillas, called "contras," who were battling to overthrow the leftist government of Nicaragua. Coupled with diminishing support in the Senate for aiding the rebels, the May 24 vote on a 1984 supplemental funding bill (H J Res 492) forced Reagan to back down on his request. The vote also gave House leaders a strong hand in negotiations later on aid to the contras for fiscal 1985. With House leaders refusing to back down, the administration was forced to accept a prohibition on further aid until February, 1985. *(Senate key vote 10)*

9. MX Missile

A yearlong campaign against the MX missile finally eked out a two-vote margin of victory on the night of May 31. The House adopted an amendment to the defense authorization bill (HR 5167) barring production of additional MX missiles in fiscal 1985 unless Congress adopted a joint resolution after April 1, 1985, approving the move.

MX production had been the administration's highest political priority among many controversial nuclear arms issues. According to the administration, it was imperative to break the Soviets' monopoly on large, accurate, land-based missiles to persuade them to negotiate sharp reductions in their arsenal of more than 600 such weapons.

Opponents warned that since MX could attack Soviet missiles but would itself be vulnerable to Soviet attack, the nuclear balance would be much less stable if MX were deployed. In a series of votes in 1983, an intense, grassroots lobbying campaign closed in on the MX.

On May 15, 1984, an effort to kill outright MX procurement failed by six votes. But two weeks later, after the House Democratic leadership lent new horsepower to the anti-MX campaign, the amendment blocking MX production until after a vote in the spring of 1985 was adopted 199-197: R 17-141; D 182-56 (ND 149-15, SD 33-41).

The Senate had narrowly agreed to production of 21 of the 40 MXs Reagan had requested. In the end, Congress approved 21 missiles, but barred use of the funds unless it passed two joint resolutions of approval next March.

10. Immigration

In a dramatic June 20 roll call, the House passed a comprehensive immigration reform bill by a five-vote margin. The controversial measure (HR 1510) had been working its way through the legislative process since 1981, and had twice passed the Senate, but this was the first time the House had voted on the legislation.

The legislation was designed to stem the flood of illegal immigration into the United States, primarily by penalizing employers who knowingly hire illegal aliens. At the same time, it would have permitted millions of individuals already in the United States illegally to obtain legal status.

The vote was a cliffhanger, seesawing for most of the 15-minute roll call. Only in the final seconds did proponents edge ahead, 216-211: R 91-73; D 125-138 (ND 76-98, SD 49-40).

The vote produced an unusual coalition, with some liberal Democrats joining conservatives of both parties in opposing the bill. The liberal Democrats sided with Hispanic members, who charged that employer sanctions would make businesses reluctant to hire any worker who appeared foreign or spoke with an accent. Conservatives opposing the measure disliked its amnesty provisions.

The closeness of the vote on final passage was a surprise, because amendments considered during the debate had been adopted or rejected, as sponsors had wished, by comfortable margins. However, the narrow victory reflected the deep divisions among members of Congress over how to rewrite immigration laws. Despite a monthlong House-Senate conference in September, members of the two chambers could not reach an accord on a final compromise version. The measure died in the conference committee as the 98th Congress drew to a close.

11. Synfuels Corporation Cutback

In an unexpected defeat for House Majority Leader Jim Wright, D-Texas, and a victory for the Reagan administration, the House July 25 demanded a say on the fate of the trouble-plagued U.S. Synthetic Fuels Corporation (SFC). The House defeated a rule for consideration of the Interior appropriations bill (HR 5973) that would have barred any amendments to rescind SFC funds.

The vote was 148-261: R 21-135; D 127-126 (ND 66-101, SD 61-25).

The White House May 14 had asked Congress to rescind $9.5 billion in SFC funds, roughly two-thirds of its available money. A rash of resignations that came amid charges of mismanagement and conflict-of-interest had left the SFC without a quorum and virtually paralyzed.

Set up in 1980 after a decade of oil supply disruptions, the SFC was meant to encourage commercialization of fuels made from coal, shale, and tar sands by giving loans and price supports to private companies. But the corporation was slow to spend the $20 billion Congress gave it, and firms began withdrawing project proposals as oil prices dropped.

Wright, an SFC backer, made a speech supporting the rule and buttonholed members at the door during the vote. David A. Stockman, director of the Office of Management and Budget, called some members before the vote, asking

them to oppose the rule.

Defeat of a rule having House leadership backing was relatively uncommon. It was only the second time in the 98th Congress that such a rule had been rejected.

Congress stripped $2 billion from the corporation as part of its deficit-reduction package (HR 4170 — PL 98-369) and another $5.375 billion as part of the fiscal 1984 continuing resolution, H J Res 648 (PL 98-473).

12. Education Spending

House Republicans challenged Democrats to live up to their campaign promises of fiscal restraint when a five-year omnibus education bill (HR 11) came to the House floor July 26.

But with support for education looming as another election-year issue, the House rejected an amendment by Bill Goodling, R-Pa., to cut the amount authorized by the bill from about $1.7 billion to $974 million in fiscal 1985.

Republicans reminded Democrats of the "new realism" about federal spending that Walter F. Mondale had promised just one week earlier, when he accepted the Democratic presidential nomination.

Goodling said his proposal would have authorized $33.6 million more than was appropriated in 1984 for the 10 education programs included in the bill, but his amendment was rejected 169-233: R 133-20; D 36-213 (ND 13-154, SD 23-59).

After turning down that proposal, Democrats introduced their own amendment to scale back spending levels — although not as far as Goodling had proposed. As amended and approved by the House, the bill authorized $1.32 billion in fiscal 1985.

Before clearing Congress and being signed by the president, however, the bill's 1985 price tag was further trimmed in conference with the Senate to about $1.2 billion (PL 98-511).

13. Superfund Right to Sue

The House voted Aug. 9 against giving citizens the right to sue in federal court for damages caused by hazardous-waste dumping, yielding to opposition from the Reagan administration and chemical and insurance companies.

The issue came up during floor consideration of a bill (HR 5640) to renew the "superfund" hazardous-waste cleanup law. The citizen's right to sue had been included in the version of the bill reported by the House Energy Committee, but the House adopted an amendment by Harold S. Sawyer, R-Mich., to strike that provision, 208-200: R 135-22; D 73-178 (ND 23-146, SD 50-32).

The vote went to the heart of one of the most controversial aspects of the superfund renewal — whether and how to compensate victims of incidents such as the one at Love Canal in New York, where residents were faced with medical problems and houses they could not live in.

The Energy Committee language would have allowed citizens to sue dumpers in federal court for compensation in such cases. Currently, citizens could sue under liability laws in most states, but standards of proof and other legal obstacles made such suits very hard to win.

The House vote was uncluttered by the issue of whether the federal government could afford to compensate victims.

The superfund renewal bill was eventually passed by the House but died in the Senate.

14. Crime

In a move that capped a yearlong GOP drive to force a House vote on a comprehensive anti-crime package, the House Sept. 25 voted to send the fiscal 1985 continuing appropriations resolution (H J Res 648 — PL 98-473) back to committee with instructions to attach the crime legislation to it. The vote was 243-166: R 154-3; D 89-163 (ND 35-134, SD 54-29).

That vote effectively ensured that the crime legislation, which Reagan backed, would clear the 98th Congress. The Senate had passed the crime package by a 91-1 vote on Feb. 2. But advocates of the Senate measure had been frustrated by the House Judiciary Committee's bill-by-bill approach to crime, and by its failure to act on key elements of the package until late in the session. They decided the procedural move was the best way to guarantee action.

The Senate kept the crime provisions in its version of H J Res 648, and a compromise that actually expanded the package was cleared Oct. 11 as part of the final funding bill.

The crime package included provisions that overhauled federal sentencing procedures, requiring judges to stay within guidelines to be drawn up by a special commission; authorized pretrial detention of suspects deemed dangerous to the community; tightened the definition of insanity; stiffened penalties for drug trafficking; prohibited trafficking in goods bearing counterfeit trademarks; re-established a program of anti-crime grants for the states; authorized federal aid to victims of crime and set stiff new penalties for terrorist activities.

15. Duty-Free Exports

The House flirted with handing the Reagan administration a major trade defeat, before rejecting a proposal that would have dropped Taiwan, Hong Kong and South Korea from a program that gave special treatment to exports from developing nations. The Oct. 3 vote was 174-233: R 14-142; D 160-91 (ND 128-38, SD 32-53).

The amendment, offered by Richard A. Gephardt, D-Mo., to an omnibus trade package (HR 3398), would have made the three nations ineligible for the generalized system of preferences (GSP), which permitted some exports from Third World nations to enter the United States duty-free. The trio received more than half the GSP benefits offered by Washington.

Administration officials argued that the carrot of duty-free status was needed to entice beneficiaries to open their markets to U.S. goods, stop counterfeiting U.S. products and meet U.S. standards of worker rights. They also stressed GSP's importance to developing nations and industrialized countries with similar programs as a symbol of the U.S. commitment to free trade.

However, many lawmakers objected to "giving away" benefits to the three countries, which competed vigorously with the United States.

In the final version of HR 3398 benefits to the comparatively wealthier developing nations were phased out. The program was renewed for eight and one-half years, instead of the 10 years requested by the administration. And, for the first time, benefits were tied to recipients' steps to comply with U.S. requirements to lower trade barriers.

16. Export Administration Act/South Africa

Defying the Senate and White House, the House Oct. 11 insisted upon a ban on new commercial bank loans to

the South African government to protest the racial policy of apartheid. The vote was 269-62: R 96-50; D 173-12 (ND 121-2, SD 52-10). It effectively killed plans to renew the Export Administration Act.

The ban had been agreed to in a House-Senate conference on the original version of a bill (S 979). However, after the conference deadlocked, the Senate Oct. 10 approved a last-ditch compromise bill (HR 4230) that gave up one provision the Senate wanted — greater Pentagon review of

export licenses — and one proposal the House insisted on — the ban on bank loans.

However, the House members voted to restore the ban, knowing that it probably would kill the bill in the Senate.

The administration strongly opposed the ban, preferring inducements, rather than sanctions, to prod South Africa to overturn its policy of separating the races.

Seventeen members of the Black Caucus voted present to protest the ban as too mild.

Appendix

	1 2 3 4 5 6 7		1 2 3 4 5 6 7		1 2 3 4 5 6 7

	1 2 3 4 5 6 7
ALABAMA	
Denton	Y Y N Y Y + Y
Heflin	Y Y N Y Y Y Y
ALASKA	
Murkowski	Y Y N Y Y Y Y
Stevens	Y Y N Y Y ? Y
ARIZONA	
Goldwater	N N N Y Y ? Y
DeConcini	N ? ? ? Y ? N
ARKANSAS	
Bumpers	N N ? N N Y N
Pryor	Y N N N Y Y Y
CALIFORNIA	
Wilson	Y Y N Y Y Y Y
Cranston	N ? Y N N ? N
COLORADO	
Armstrong	Y Y N Y Y Y Y
Hart	N ? ? ? ? ? ?
CONNECTICUT	
Weicker	N ? Y N - ? Y
Dodd	N ? Y N N Y Y
DELAWARE	
Roth	Y N N Y Y Y Y
Biden	N Y N N Y Y Y
FLORIDA	
Hawkins	Y Y N Y Y Y Y
Chiles	Y Y N Y N Y N
GEORGIA	
Mattingly	Y Y N Y Y Y Y
Nunn	Y Y N Y N Y Y
HAWAII	
Inouye	N Y N N N Y N
Matsunaga	N Y N N N Y N
IDAHO	
McClure	Y Y N Y Y ? Y
Symms	Y Y N Y Y ? Y
ILLINOIS	
Percy	Y ? N Y Y Y Y
Dixon	N + N N N Y N
INDIANA	
Lugar	Y Y N Y N Y Y
Quayle	Y Y - Y Y Y Y

	1 2 3 4 5 6 7
IOWA	
Grassley	Y Y N Y Y Y Y
Jepsen	Y Y N Y Y Y ?
KANSAS	
Dole	Y Y N Y Y Y Y
Kassebaum	N + N Y Y N Y
KENTUCKY	
Ford	Y Y Y N N Y N
Huddleston	Y ? ? Y N ? Y
LOUISIANA	
Johnston	Y N N Y N ? N
Long	Y X N Y N N Y
MAINE	
Cohen	N Y N Y Y N Y
Mitchell	N Y Y N N N N
MARYLAND	
Mathias	N N Y N ? N ?
Sarbanes	N Y N N N N N
MASSACHUSETTS	
Kennedy	N Y N N N N N
Tsongas	N Y Y ? N Y N
MICHIGAN	
Levin	N Y N Y N Y N
Riegle	N Y N N N Y N
MINNESOTA	
Boschwitz	N Y N Y Y Y Y
Durenberger	N Y N Y Y ? Y
MISSISSIPPI	
Cochran	Y Y N Y Y Y Y
Stennis	Y Y N Y ? ? N
MISSOURI	
Danforth	N Y N Y Y N Y
Eagleton	N Y Y N N ? N
MONTANA	
Baucus	N Y N Y N Y Y
Melcher	Y Y Y N Y Y N
NEBRASKA	
Exon	Y N N Y Y Y Y
Zorinsky	Y N Y Y Y Y Y
NEVADA	
Hecht	Y Y N Y Y Y Y
Laxalt	Y Y N Y Y Y Y

	1 2 3 4 5 6 7
NEW HAMPSHIRE	
Humphrey	Y Y N Y Y N Y
Rudman	N Y N Y Y Y Y
NEW JERSEY	
Bradley	N Y N N Y N N
Lautenberg	N Y Y N N N N
NEW MEXICO	
Domenici	Y Y N Y Y Y Y
Bingaman	N Y Y N N Y N
NEW YORK	
D'Amato	Y Y ? Y Y Y Y
Moynihan	N # ? N N N N
NORTH CAROLINA	
East	Y Y N Y Y Y Y
Helms	Y Y N Y Y Y Y
NORTH DAKOTA	
Andrews	N Y N N N N Y
Burdick	N Y ? ? N Y N
OHIO	
Glenn	N Y N Y N N N
Metzenbaum	N N ? N N N N
OKLAHOMA	
Nickles	Y Y ? Y Y Y Y
Boren	Y Y N Y Y Y Y
OREGON	
Hatfield	N Y N Y N Y Y
Packwood	N Y ? Y Y ? Y
PENNSYLVANIA	
Heinz	N Y N Y N N Y
Specter	N Y N N Y N Y
RHODE ISLAND	
Chafee	N Y N Y N N Y
Pell	N N Y N N N N
SOUTH CAROLINA	
Thurmond	Y Y N Y Y Y Y
Hollings	Y N N N N ? N
SOUTH DAKOTA	
Abdnor	Y Y N Y Y Y Y
Pressler	Y Y N N N ? Y
TENNESSEE	
Baker	Y Y N Y Y Y Y
Sasser	Y Y Y N N Y N

	1 2 3 4 5 6 7
TEXAS	
Tower	Y Y N Y Y Y Y
Bentsen	Y Y N N ? ? N
UTAH	
Garn	Y Y N Y Y Y Y
Hatch	Y Y N Y Y Y Y
VERMONT	
Stafford	N Y ? ? N ? Y
Leahy	N Y Y N N N N
VIRGINIA	
Trible	Y Y N Y Y Y Y
Warner	Y Y N Y Y Y Y
WASHINGTON	
Evans	N Y N Y N N Y
Gorton	N Y N Y Y Y Y
WEST VIRGINIA	
Byrd	Y Y N N Y N Y
Randolph	Y + Y N N Y N
WISCONSIN	
Kasten	Y Y N Y Y Y Y
Proxmire	Y Y N N N N Y
WYOMING	
Simpson	Y Y N Y Y Y Y
Wallop	Y Y N Y Y Y Y

ND - Northern Democrats   SD - Southern Democrats (Southern states - Ala., Ark., Fla., Ga., Ky., La., Miss., N.C., Okla., S.C., Tenn., Texas, Va.)

---

1. S J Res 73. Constitutional Amendment on School Prayer. Passage of the joint resolution to propose an amendment to the Constitution to permit organized, recited prayer in public schools and other public places. Rejected 56-44: R 37-18; D 19-26 (ND 6-25, SD 13-1), March 20, 1984. A two-thirds majority of those present and voting (67 in this case) of both houses is required for passage of a joint resolution proposing an amendment to the Constitution. A "yea" was a vote supporting the president's position.

2. HR 4072. Agricultural Programs Adjustment Act. Passage of the bill to cut target prices for wheat in 1984 and 1985 and to freeze 1985 target prices for corn, cotton and rice at 1984 levels. It also set terms for a wheat acreage reduction program in 1984 and 1985, required acreage reduction programs in 1985 for corn, cotton and rice if certain levels of surpluses were reached, enlarged farm credit programs, authorized changes in disaster loan programs and expanded farm export programs. Passed 78-10: R 50-2; D 28-8 (ND 20-4, SD 8-4), March 22, 1984. A "yea" was a vote supporting the president's position.

3. H J Res 492. Department of Agriculture, Fiscal 1984 Urgent Supplemental Appropriations. Kennedy, D-Mass., amendment to cut funding for military assistance to El Salvador from $61.75 million to $21 million. Rejected 25-63: R 2-48; D 23-15 (ND 21-5, SD 2-10), April 2, 1984. A "nay" was a vote supporting the president's position.

4. H J Res 492. Department of Agriculture, Fiscal 1984 Urgent Supplemental Appropriations. Baker, R-Tenn., motion to table (kill) the Leahy, D-Vt., amendment to require congressional authorization for the introduction of combat troops in or over El Salvador. Motion agreed to 59-36: R 49-5; D 10-31 (ND 2-25, SD 8-6), April 4, 1984. A "yea" was a vote supporting the president's position.

5. HR 2163. Deficit Reduction. Dole, R-Kan., motion to table (kill) the Chafee, R-R.I., amendment to the Dole, R-Kan., amendment, to delay until Jan. 1, 1988, the effective date for indexing tax brackets to offset inflation. Motion agreed to 57-38: R 46-7; D 11-31 (ND 8-22, SD 3-9), April 10, 1984. A "yea" was a vote supporting the president's position. (The Dole amendment, to raise $48 billion in new tax revenues through fiscal 1987, subsequently was adopted 76-5.)

6. HR 2163. Deficit Reduction. Boschwitz, R-Minn., amendment to the Dole, R-Kan., amendment, to change the current 15-year depreciation life for real property to 20 years in 1984, 19 years in 1985 and 18 years thereafter, and to reduce the investment tax credits available for rehabilitation of old buildings. Adopted 62-19: R 37-8; D 25-11 (ND 17-10, SD 8-1), in the session that began April 12, 1984. (The Dole amendment, to raise $48 billion in new tax revenues through fiscal 1987, subsequently was adopted 76-5.)

7. HR 2163. Deficit Reduction. Baker, R-Tenn., amendment to reduce federal deficits by $140 billion through fiscal 1987 by increasing taxes, limiting the increases in military spending, cutting federal benefit and other non-defense programs. Adopted 65-32: R 53-0; D 12-32 (ND 6-24, SD 6-8), May 17, 1984. A "yea" was a vote supporting the president's position.

	8	9	10	11	12	13
ALABAMA						
Denton	Y	Y	Y	Y	Y	N
Heflin	Y	Y	Y	Y	Y	N
ALASKA						
Murkowski	Y	Y	Y	Y	Y	N
Stevens	Y	Y	Y	Y	Y	N
ARIZONA						
Goldwater	Y	Y	Y	N	Y	N
DeConcini	Y	#	Y	Y	#	Y
ARKANSAS						
Bumpers	?	N	N	Y	N	Y
Pryor	N	N	N	Y	Y	Y
CALIFORNIA						
Wilson	Y	Y	Y	Y	Y	N
Cranston	N	N	N	Y	X	Y
COLORADO						
Armstrong	Y	Y	Y	N	Y	N
Hart	N	N	?	?	N	Y
CONNECTICUT						
Weicker	N	N	N	Y	N	Y
Dodd	N	N	N	Y	N	Y
DELAWARE						
Roth	?	Y	Y	Y	Y	N
Biden	N	N	N	Y	N	Y
FLORIDA						
Hawkins	Y	Y	Y	Y	?	N
Chiles	N	N	Y	Y	N	Y
GEORGIA						
Mattingly	Y	Y	Y	Y	Y	N
Nunn	N	Y	Y	Y	N	N
HAWAII						
Inouye	N	N	N	Y	N	Y
Matsunaga	N	N	N	Y	N	Y
IDAHO						
McClure	Y	Y	Y	N	?	N
Symms	Y	Y	Y	N	Y	N
ILLINOIS						
Percy	N	?	?	Y	?	?
Dixon	N	N	Y	+	N	Y
INDIANA						
Lugar	Y	Y	Y	Y	Y	N
Quayle	Y	Y	Y	Y	Y	N

	8	9	10	11	12	13
IOWA						
Grassley	Y	N	Y	N	?	N
Jepsen	Y	Y	Y	Y	Y	N
KANSAS						
Dole	Y	Y	Y	Y	Y	N
Kassebaum	Y	Y	N	Y	Y	N
KENTUCKY						
Ford	N	N	N	Y	Y	Y
Huddleston	N	N	N	Y	Y	Y
LOUISIANA						
Johnston	N	N	Y	N	N	Y
Long	Y	N	Y	N	N	N
MAINE						
Cohen	N	Y	N	Y	?	Y
Mitchell	N	N	N	Y	N	Y
MARYLAND						
Mathias	N	N	Y	Y	Y	Y
Sarbanes	N	N	N	Y	N	Y
MASSACHUSETTS						
Kennedy	-	N	N	Y	N	Y
Tsongas	?	N	N	Y	X	Y
MICHIGAN						
Levin	N	N	N	Y	N	Y
Riegle	N	N	N	Y	N	Y
MINNESOTA						
Boschwitz	N	Y	Y	Y	N	Y
Durenberger	N	N	Y	Y	?	Y
MISSISSIPPI						
Cochran	Y	Y	Y	Y	Y	N
Stennis	N	Y	Y	N	N	N
MISSOURI						
Danforth	Y	Y	Y	Y	Y	N
Eagleton	N	N	N	Y	N	Y
MONTANA						
Baucus	N	N	N	N	-	Y
Melcher	N	N	N	N	N	Y
NEBRASKA						
Exon	N	N	?	Y	Y	Y
Zorinsky	Y	Y	N	Y	Y	N
NEVADA						
Hecht	Y	Y	Y	Y	Y	N
Laxalt	Y	Y	Y	Y	Y	N

	8	9	10	11	12	13
NEW HAMPSHIRE						
Humphrey	Y	N	Y	N	N	N
Rudman	Y	Y	Y	Y	Y	N
NEW JERSEY						
Bradley	N	N	N	Y	X	Y
Lautenberg	N	N	N	Y	N	Y
NEW MEXICO						
Domenici	Y	Y	Y	Y	Y	N
Bingaman	N	N	N	Y	N	Y
NEW YORK						
D'Amato	Y	Y	Y	Y	Y	Y
Moynihan	N	N	N	Y	N	Y
NORTH CAROLINA						
East	Y	Y	Y	Y	Y	N
Helms	Y	Y	Y	Y	Y	N
NORTH DAKOTA						
Andrews	?	?	Y	Y	Y	Y
Burdick	N	N	N	+	#	Y
OHIO						
Glenn	Y	N	Y	N	Y	N
Metzenbaum	N	N	N	Y	N	Y
OKLAHOMA						
Nickles	Y	Y	Y	Y	Y	N
Boren	Y	N	Y	Y	#	N
OREGON						
Hatfield	N	N	N	Y	N	Y
Packwood	Y	N	Y	Y	Y	Y
PENNSYLVANIA						
Heinz	N	Y	Y	Y	Y	Y
Specter	Y	N	Y	Y	Y	Y
RHODE ISLAND						
Chafee	N	Y	Y	Y	Y	Y
Pell	N	N	-	Y	Y	Y
SOUTH CAROLINA						
Thurmond	Y	Y	Y	N	Y	N
Hollings	Y	N	Y	Y	N	Y
SOUTH DAKOTA						
Abdnor	Y	Y	Y	Y	Y	N
Pressler	N	N	N	Y	Y	N
TENNESSEE						
Baker	#	Y	Y	Y	Y	N
Sasser	N	N	N	Y	N	Y

KEY

Y Voted for (yea).
Paired for.
+ Announced for.
N Voted against (nay).
X Paired against.
- Announced against.
P Voted "present".
C Voted "present" to avoid possible conflict of interest.
? Did not vote or otherwise make a position known.

Democrats *Republicans*

	8	9	10	11	12	13
TEXAS						
Tower	Y	Y	Y	Y	Y	N
Bentsen	N	X	N	Y	?	Y
UTAH						
Garn	Y	Y	Y	Y	Y	N
Hatch	Y	Y	Y	Y	Y	N
VERMONT						
Stafford	X	N	N	Y	Y	Y
Leahy	N	N	N	N	?	Y
VIRGINIA						
Trible	Y	Y	Y	Y	Y	N
Warner	Y	Y	Y	Y	Y	N
WASHINGTON						
Evans	Y	Y	Y	N	N	N
Gorton	Y	Y	Y	N	N	N
WEST VIRGINIA						
Byrd	N	Y	N	Y	N	Y
Randolph	N	N	N	Y	Y	Y
WISCONSIN						
Kasten	+	Y	Y	Y	Y	N
Proxmire	N	N	N	Y	N	Y
WYOMING						
Simpson	Y	Y	Y	N	Y	N
Wallop	Y	Y	Y	N	Y	N

ND - Northern Democrats   SD - Southern Democrats (Southern states - Ala., Ark., Fla., Ga., Ky., La., Miss., N.C., Okla., S.C., Tenn., Texas, Va.)

8. S 2723. Omnibus Defense Authorization. Tower, R-Texas, motion to table (kill) the Percy, R-Ill., amendment to reduce by $100 million the amount authorized for the strategic defense initiative. Motion agreed to 47-45: R 40-10; D 7-35 (ND 3-26, SD 4-9), June 13, 1984. A "yea" was a vote supporting the president's position.

9. S 2723. Omnibus Defense Authorization. Tower, R-Texas, motion to table (kill) the Moynihan, D-N.Y., amendment to produce no additional MX missiles in fiscal 1985 but to keep the MX production line ready for production pending completion of a new study of the mobile, single-warhead "Midgetman" missile. Motion agreed to 49-48: R 43-10; D 5-38 (ND 2-28, SD 3-10), June 14, 1984, with Vice President Bush casting a "yea" vote to break the 48-48 tie. A "yea" was a vote supporting the president's position.

10. S 2723. Omnibus Defense Authorization. Tower, R-Texas, motion to table (kill) the Kennedy, D-Mass., amendment to provide that nothing in the bill shall be construed as authorization for funds to assist insurgent military forces in Nicaragua (the so-called "contras"). Motion agreed to 58-38: R 48-6; D 10-32 (ND 2-26, SD 8-6), June 18, 1984. A "yea" was a vote supporting the president's position.

11. HR 4616. Motor Vehicle Safety/Minimum Drinking Age. Lautenberg, D-N.J., amendment to withhold a percentage of highway funds from states whose minimum drinking ages are under 21 and to provide incentives for other actions aimed at reducing drunken driving. Adopted 81-16: R 45-10; D 36-6 (ND 25-3, SD 11-3), June 26, 1984. A "yea" was a vote supporting the president's position.

12. HR 5743. Agriculture Appropriations, Fiscal 1985. Baker, R-Tenn., motion to invoke cloture (thus limiting debate) on the Baker motion to waive provisions of the Congressional Budget Act that would bar consideration of an appropriations bill prior to adoption of the conference report on the first budget resolution. Motion rejected 54-31: R 46-3; D 8-28 (ND 4-20, SD 4-8), Aug. 6, 1984. A three-fifths majority vote (60) of the total Senate is required to invoke cloture.

13. H J Res 648. Continuing Appropriations, Fiscal 1985. Judgment of the Senate whether the Byrd, D-W.Va., amendment to attach S 2568, civil rights legislation overturning the Supreme Court's ruling in *Grove City College v. Bell*, to the continuing appropriations resolution was germane. Ruled germane 51-48: R 12-42; D 39-6 (ND 30-1, SD 9-5), Sept. 27, 1984.

1. HR 1904. Child Abuse Amendments. Chandler, R-Wash., substitute to the Murphy, D-Pa., amendment, to strike language requiring states that receive federal child-protection grants to ensure that severely handicapped infants receive adequate medical treatment and nutrition, and instead to establish a study commission and require the Department of Health and Human Services to issue guidelines for hospitals that want to establish advisory panels on the treatment of the handicapped infants. Rejected 182-231: R 31-131; D 151-100 (ND 97-69, SD 54-31), Feb. 2, 1984. (The Murphy amendment, clarifying the intent of the infant-protection provisions, subsequently was adopted by voice vote.) A "nay" was a vote supporting the president's position.

2. HR 1652. Reclamation Dam Safety. Kazen, D-Texas, substitute to the Solomon, R-N.Y., amendment, to require reimbursement only for new project benefits by local users and beneficiaries of projects in the bill, which authorized an additional $650 million for safety-related repair of dams administered by the Bureau of Reclamation. Adopted 194-192: R 75-73; D 119-119 (ND 61-91, SD 58-28), March 20, 1984. A "yea" was a vote supporting the president's position.

3. H Con Res 280. First Budget Resolution, Fiscal 1985. Adoption of the first concurrent budget resolution for fiscal 1985 to set targets for the fiscal year ending Sept. 30, 1985, as follows: budget authority, $1,002.1 billion; outlays, $918.2 billion; revenues, $742.7 billion; and deficit, $174.5 billion. The resolution also set preliminary goals for fiscal 1986-87, revised budget levels for fiscal 1984 and included reconciliation instructions requiring House and Senate committees to recommend legislative savings to meet the budget targets. Adopted 250-168: R 21-139; D 229-29 (ND 159-13, SD 70-16), April 5, 1984.

4. HR 5394. Omnibus Budget Reconciliation Act. Moore, R-La., motion to recommit the bill to the House Ways and Means Committee with instructions to include provisions imposing a one-year physician fee freeze for Medicare services and to strike provisions in the measure that increased spending. Motion rejected 172-242: R 157-2; D 15-240 (ND 3-170, SD 12-70), April 12, 1984.

5. HR 5119. Foreign Assistance Authorization. Broomfield, R-Mich., amendment to authorize President Reagan's requests for military, economic and development aid for Central American countries in fiscal 1984-85, and to allow military aid for El Salvador in fiscal 1985 if the president certified to Congress that the government had made "demonstrated progress" on human rights and other issues. Adopted 212-208: R 156-8; D 56-200 (ND 7-167, SD 49-33), May 10, 1984. A "yea" was a vote supporting the president's position.

6. HR 5345. Equal Access Act. Perkins, D-Ky., motion to suspend the rules and pass the bill to allow student religious groups to meet in public secondary schools during non-class hours if other groups do so. Motion rejected 270-151: R 147-17; D 123-134 (ND 47-122, SD 76-12), May 15, 1984. A two-thirds majority of those present and voting (281 in this case) is required for passage under suspension of the rules. A "yea" was a vote supporting the president's position.

7. HR 5167. Department of Defense Authorization. Gore, D-Tenn., amendment to the Brown, D-Calif., amendment, to provide that no funds may be used to test the anti-satellite missile (ASAT) against a target in space unless the Soviet Union conducts a test of its ASAT after enactment of the bill. Adopted 238-181: R 39-122; D 199-59 (ND 162-10, SD 37-49), May 23, 1984. A "nay" was a vote supporting the president's position.

8. H J Res 492. Department of Agriculture, Fiscal 1984 Urgent Supplemental Appropriations. Boland, D-Mass., motion that the House recede from its disagreement to the Senate amendment providing $21 million in covert aid to Nicaraguan rebels, with an amendment providing no funds for Nicaraguan rebels. Motion agreed to 241-177: R 24-132; D 217-45 (ND 169-6, SD 48-39), May 24, 1984. A "nay" was a vote supporting the president's position.

1. Rep. Carl D. Perkins, D-Ky., died Aug. 3, 1984.
2. Rep. Thomas P. O'Neill Jr., D-Mass., as Speaker, votes at his own discretion.
3. Rep. Edwin B. Forsythe, R-N.J., died March 29, 1984.
4. Rep. Marilyn Lloyd, D-Tenn., was known as Marilyn Lloyd Bouquard in the 97th Congress.
5. Rep. Gerald D. Kleczka, D-Wis., was sworn in April 10, 1984, to succeed Clement J. Zablocki, D, who died Dec. 3, 1983.

KEY

Y Voted for (yea).
Paired for.
+ Announced for.
N Voted against (nay).
- Paired against.
- Announced against.
P Voted "present".
C Voted "present" to avoid possible conflict of interest.
? Did not vote or otherwise make a position known.

Democrats *Republicans*

	1	2	3	4	5	6	7	8
ALABAMA								
1 *Edwards*	N	Y	N	Y	Y	Y	N	N
2 *Dickinson*	N	Y	N	#	Y	Y	N	N
3 Nichols	?	Y	Y	Y	Y	Y	N	N
4 Bevill	N	Y	N	?	Y	Y	N	N
5 Flippo	Y	Y	Y	N	Y	Y	N	N
6 Erdreich	N	Y	N	Y	Y	Y	N	N
7 Shelby	N	Y	N	Y	Y	Y	N	N
ALASKA								
AL *Young*	N	Y	N	Y	Y	Y	N	N
ARIZONA								
1 *McCain*	N	Y	N	Y	Y	Y	N	N
2 Udall	Y	Y	Y	N	N	N	Y	Y
3 *Stump*	N	Y	N	Y	Y	Y	N	N
4 *Rudd*	N	Y	N	#	Y	Y	N	N
5 McNulty	N	Y	Y	N	N	N	Y	Y
ARKANSAS								
1 Alexander	Y	Y	Y	N	Y	Y	Y	Y
2 *Bethune*	N	Y	Y	Y	Y	Y	N	N
3 *Hammerschmidt*	N	Y	N	Y	Y	Y	N	N
4 Anthony	Y	N	Y	N	N	Y	N	Y
CALIFORNIA								
1 Bosco	Y	?	Y	N	N	N	Y	Y
2 *Chappie*	N	Y	N	Y	Y	Y	N	N
3 Matsui	Y	Y	Y	N	N	N	Y	Y
4 Fazio	Y	Y	Y	N	N	?	Y	Y
5 Burton	Y	Y	Y	N	N	N	Y	Y
6 Boxer	Y	?	Y	N	N	N	Y	Y
7 Miller	Y	Y	Y	N	N	N	Y	Y
8 Dellums	Y	N	N	N	N	N	Y	Y
9 Stark	Y	N	Y	N	N	N	Y	Y
10 Edwards	Y	N	N	N	N	N	Y	Y
11 Lantos	Y	Y	Y	X	N	N	Y	Y
12 *Zschau*	Y	N	N	Y	Y	N	Y	Y
13 Mineta	Y	Y	Y	N	N	N	Y	Y
14 *Shumway*	N	Y	N	Y	Y	Y	N	N
15 Coelho	Y	Y	Y	N	N	N	Y	Y
16 Panetta	Y	Y	Y	N	N	N	Y	Y
17 *Pashayan*	N	Y	N	Y	Y	Y	N	N
18 Lehman	Y	Y	Y	N	N	Y	Y	Y
19 *Lagomarsino*	N	Y	N	Y	Y	Y	N	N
20 *Thomas*	Y	?	N	Y	Y	Y	N	N
21 *Fiedler*	Y	Y	N	Y	Y	Y	N	N
22 *Moorhead*	N	Y	N	Y	Y	Y	N	N
23 Beilenson	Y	N	Y	N	N	N	Y	Y
24 Waxman	Y	Y	Y	N	N	N	Y	Y
25 Roybal	Y	Y	Y	N	N	N	Y	Y
26 Berman	Y	N	Y	N	N	N	Y	Y
27 Levine	Y	N	N	N	N	N	Y	Y
28 Dixon	Y	Y	Y	N	N	N	Y	Y
29 Hawkins	Y	Y	#	N	N	N	Y	Y
30 Martinez	Y	Y	Y	N	N	Y	Y	Y
31 Dymally	Y	N	N	N	N	Y	Y	Y
32 Anderson	Y	Y	Y	N	N	Y	Y	Y
33 *Dreier*	N	?	N	Y	Y	Y	N	N
34 Torres	Y	Y	Y	N	N	Y	Y	Y
35 *Lewis*	N	Y	N	Y	Y	Y	N	?
36 Brown	Y	Y	Y	N	N	N	Y	Y
37 *McCandless*	Y	Y	N	Y	Y	Y	N	N
38 Patterson	Y	Y	Y	N	Y	?	?	Y
39 *Dannemeyer*	N	Y	N	Y	Y	Y	N	N
40 *Badham*	N	Y	N	Y	Y	Y	N	N
41 *Lowery*	N	Y	N	Y	Y	Y	N	N
42 *Lungren*	N	Y	N	Y	Y	Y	N	N

	1	2	3	4	5	6	7	8
43 *Packard*	N	Y	N	Y	Y	Y	N	N
44 Bates	Y	Y	Y	N	N	?	Y	Y
45 *Hunter*	N	Y	N	Y	Y	Y	N	N
COLORADO								
1 Schroeder	Y	Y	Y	N	N	N	Y	Y
2 Wirth	Y	Y	Y	N	N	N	Y	Y
3 Kogovsek	Y	Y	Y	N	N	N	Y	Y
4 *Brown*	Y	N	Y	Y	Y	Y	N	Y
5 *Kramer*	N	Y	N	Y	Y	Y	N	N
6 *Schaefer*	N	Y	N	Y	Y	Y	N	N
CONNECTICUT								
1 Kennelly	Y	?	Y	N	N	N	Y	Y
2 Gejdenson	Y	Y	Y	N	N	N	Y	Y
3 Morrison	Y	N	Y	N	N	N	Y	Y
4 *McKinney*	Y	Y	Y	Y	N	N	Y	Y
5 Ratchford	Y	Y	Y	N	N	N	Y	Y
6 *Johnson*	Y	N	Y	Y	Y	N	Y	N
DELAWARE								
AL Carper	Y	N	N	N	N	Y	N	Y
FLORIDA								
1 Hutto	N	Y	Y	Y	Y	Y	N	N
2 Fuqua	N	Y	Y	N	Y	Y	N	N
3 Bennett	N	Y	Y	Y	Y	Y	N	Y
4 Chappell	Y	Y	Y	N	Y	Y	N	N
5 *McCollum*	N	N	N	Y	Y	Y	N	N
6 MacKay	Y	N	N	N	N	Y	N	Y
7 Gibbons	Y	N	N	N	N	N	Y	Y
8 *Young*	N	N	N	Y	Y	Y	N	N
9 *Bilirakis*	N	N	N	Y	Y	Y	N	N
10 *Ireland*	N	?	N	Y	Y	N	N	N
11 Nelson	N	N	Y	N	Y	Y	N	N
12 *Lewis*	N	N	N	Y	Y	Y	N	N
13 *Mack*	N	N	Y	Y	Y	Y	N	N
14 Mica	N	Y	Y	N	Y	Y	Y	N
15 *Shaw*	N	N	N	Y	Y	Y	N	N
16 Smith	Y	N	N	N	N	N	Y	Y
17 Lehman	Y	N	N	N	N	N	Y	Y
18 Pepper	#	Y	Y	N	N	N	Y	Y
19 Fascell	Y	N	Y	N	N	N	Y	Y
GEORGIA								
1 Thomas	Y	N	Y	N	Y	N	Y	Y
2 Hatcher	Y	N	Y	Y	Y	N	?	?
3 Ray	N	N	?	N	Y	Y	N	N
4 Levitas	Y	N	N	Y	Y	Y	Y	N
5 Fowler	Y	Y	Y	N	N	N	Y	Y
6 *Gingrich*	N	N	N	Y	Y	Y	N	N
7 Darden	Y	N	N	N	Y	N	N	N
8 Rowland	Y	N	Y	N	Y	N	Y	N
9 Jenkins	Y	N	Y	Y	Y	Y	N	N
10 Barnard	Y	N	N	N	Y	Y	?	N
HAWAII								
1 Heftel	?	?	?	?	N	Y	Y	Y
2 Akaka	Y	Y	Y	N	N	N	N	Y
IDAHO								
1 *Craig*	N	Y	N	#	Y	Y	N	N
2 *Hansen*	N	?	?	?	?	?	?	?
ILLINOIS								
1 Hayes	Y	?	Y	N	N	N	Y	Y
2 Savage	#	?	Y	N	N	N	Y	Y
3 Russo	N	N	Y	N	N	N	Y	Y
4 *O'Brien*	N	?	N	Y	Y	Y	N	N
5 Lipinski	N	?	Y	N	N	Y	N	Y
6 *Hyde*	N	?	X	Y	Y	N	N	N
7 Collins	Y	?	N	Y	N	N	Y	Y
8 Rostenkowski	N	?	Y	N	?	Y	Y	Y
9 Yates	Y	N	N	N	N	N	Y	Y
10 *Porter*	Y	Y	Y	Y	Y	N	Y	N
11 Annunzio	N	?	Y	N	N	N	Y	Y
12 *Crane, P.*	N	N	N	Y	N	N	N	N
13 *Erlenborn*	N	?	?	Y	Y	Y	N	N
14 *Corcoran*	X	?	N	Y	Y	Y	N	N
15 *Madigan*	N	N	N	Y	Y	Y	N	N
16 *Martin*	Y	?	N	Y	Y	Y	N	N
17 Evans	N	?	Y	N	N	Y	Y	Y
18 *Michel*	N	?	N	Y	Y	N	N	N
19 *Crane, D.*	N	?	N	Y	Y	Y	N	N
20 Durbin	Y	?	Y	N	N	N	Y	Y
21 Price	N	?	Y	N	Y	N	Y	Y
22 Simon	?	?	Y	X	N	N	Y	Y
INDIANA								
1 Hall	Y	?	Y	N	?	?	Y	Y
2 Sharp	N	N	Y	N	N	Y	-	Y
3 *Hiler*	N	N	N	Y	Y	Y	N	N
4 *Coats*	N	N	N	Y	Y	Y	N	N
5 *Hillis*	N	N	N	Y	Y	Y	N	N

ND - Northern Democrats   SD - Southern Democrats

	1	2	3	4	5	6	7	8
6 ***Burton***	N	N	N	Y	Y	Y	N	N
7 ***Myers***	N	Y	N	Y	Y	Y	N	N
8 McCloskey	N	?	Y	N	N	Y	Y	Y
9 Hamilton	N	N	Y	N	N	Y	Y	Y
10 Jacobs	Y	N	Y	N	N	Y	Y	Y
IOWA								
1 ***Leach***	N	N	N	Y	N	N	Y	Y
2 ***Tauke***	N	N	N	Y	Y	Y	Y	Y
3 ***Evans***	N	N	N	Y	Y	Y	Y	Y
4 Smith	?	Y	N	N	N	N	Y	Y
5 Harkin	N	?	N	N	N	Y	Y	Y
6 Bedell	N	N	Y	N	N	Y	Y	Y
KANSAS								
1 ***Roberts***	N	Y	N	Y	Y	Y	N	N
2 Slattery	N	N	N	N	N	N	Y	Y
3 ***Winn***	N	Y	N	Y	Y	Y	N	N
4 Glickman	N	N	Y	N	N	N	Y	Y
5 ***Whittaker***	Y	Y	N	Y	Y	Y	N	N
KENTUCKY								
1 Hubbard	Y	Y	?	Y	Y	Y	N	N
2 Natcher	N	Y	Y	N	N	Y	N	Y
3 Mazzoli	N	N	Y	N	N	Y	Y	Y
4 ***Snyder***	N	Y	N	Y	Y	Y	N	N
5 ***Rogers***	Y	Y	N	Y	Y	Y	N	?
6 ***Hopkins***	Y	Y	N	Y	Y	Y	Y	N
7 Perkins [1]	N	Y	Y	N	N	Y	N	Y
LOUISIANA								
1 ***Livingston***	N	Y	N	Y	Y	Y	N	N
2 Boggs	N	Y	Y	N	?	Y	Y	Y
3 Tauzin	X	Y	N	X	Y	Y	N	N
4 Roemer	N	N	N	N	Y	Y	Y	N
5 Huckaby	N	Y	Y	N	Y	Y	Y	N
6 ***Moore***	N	Y	N	Y	Y	Y	Y	N
7 Breaux	Y	Y	N	N	Y	Y	N	N
8 Long	N	Y	Y	N	N	Y	Y	Y
MAINE								
1 ***McKernan***	Y	N	Y	Y	Y	Y	Y	Y
2 ***Snowe***	Y	N	Y	Y	Y	Y	Y	Y
MARYLAND								
1 Dyson	N	N	Y	Y	Y	Y	N	N
2 Long	Y	N	Y	N	N	N	Y	Y
3 Mikulski	Y	N	Y	N	N	N	?	Y
4 ***Holt***	N	?	N	Y	Y	Y	N	N
5 Hoyer	N	Y	Y	N	N	N	Y	Y
6 Byron	N	N	N	N	Y	Y	N	N
7 Mitchell	Y	?	Y	N	N	N	Y	Y
8 Barnes	N	Y	Y	N	N	N	Y	Y
MASSACHUSETTS								
1 ***Conte***	N	N	Y	Y	N	N	Y	Y
2 Boland	X	N	Y	N	N	N	Y	Y
3 Early	?	N	Y	N	N	N	Y	Y
4 Frank	Y	N	Y	N	N	N	Y	Y
5 Shannon	?	?	Y	N	N	N	Y	Y
6 Mavroules	N	N	Y	N	N	N	Y	Y
7 Markey	Y	?	Y	N	N	N	+	Y
8 O'Neill [2]								
9 Moakley	N	N	Y	N	N	N	Y	Y
10 Studds	Y	N	Y	N	N	N	Y	Y
11 Donnelly	X	Y	Y	N	N	N	Y	Y
MICHIGAN								
1 Conyers	Y	N	Y	N	N	N	Y	Y
2 ***Pursell***	Y	?	N	Y	Y	Y	Y	Y
3 Wolpe	Y	N	Y	N	N	N	Y	Y
4 ***Siljander***	N	?	N	Y	Y	Y	N	N
5 ***Sawyer***	N	Y	N	Y	Y	Y	N	?
6 Carr	N	N	N	N	N	Y	Y	Y
7 Kildee	N	N	Y	N	N	N	Y	Y
8 Traxler	N	N	Y	N	N	Y	Y	?
9 ***Vander Jagt***	N	N	N	#	Y	Y	N	N
10 Albosta	N	N	Y	N	N	Y	Y	Y
11 ***Davis***	N	?	Y	Y	Y	Y	N	N
12 Bonior	N	N	Y	N	N	N	Y	Y
13 Crockett	Y	Y	N	N	N	N	Y	Y
14 Hertel	N	N	Y	N	N	N	Y	Y
15 Ford	#	Y	Y	N	N	N	Y	Y
16 Dingell	Y	N	Y	N	N	Y	Y	Y
17 Levin	Y	N	Y	N	N	N	Y	Y
18 ***Broomfield***	N	N	Y	Y	Y	Y	Y	N
MINNESOTA								
1 Penny	N	N	Y	N	N	Y	Y	Y
2 ***Weber***	N	N	N	Y	Y	Y	N	N
3 ***Frenzel***	Y	?	N	Y	Y	Y	Y	N
4 Vento	N	N	Y	N	N	N	Y	Y
5 Sabo	Y	Y	Y	N	N	N	Y	Y
6 Sikorski	N	N	Y	N	N	Y	Y	Y
7 ***Stangeland***	N	Y	N	Y	Y	Y	N	N
8 Oberstar	N	N	Y	N	N	N	Y	Y
MISSISSIPPI								
1 Whitten	N	Y	Y	N	N	Y	N	Y
2 ***Franklin***	Y	Y	N	Y	Y	Y	N	N
3 Montgomery	N	Y	Y	Y	Y	Y	N	N
4 Dowdy	Y	Y	Y	N	Y	Y	N	N
5 ***Lott***	N	Y	N	Y	Y	Y	N	N
MISSOURI								
1 Clay	Y	?	Y	N	N	N	Y	Y
2 Young	N	Y	Y	N	N	N	N	Y
3 Gephardt	N	N	Y	N	N	N	Y	Y
4 Skelton	N	Y	Y	N	Y	Y	N	N
5 Wheat	Y	N	Y	N	N	N	Y	Y
6 ***Coleman***	N	N	N	Y	Y	N	N	N
7 ***Taylor***	N	Y	N	Y	Y	Y	N	N
8 ***Emerson***	N	?	N	Y	Y	Y	N	N
9 Volkmer	N	N	Y	N	N	Y	Y	Y
MONTANA								
1 Williams	Y	N	Y	N	N	N	Y	Y
2 ***Marlenee***	N	Y	N	Y	Y	Y	N	N
NEBRASKA								
1 ***Bereuter***	N	Y	Y	Y	Y	Y	Y	N
2 ***Daub***	N	Y	N	Y	Y	Y	N	N
3 ***Smith***	N	Y	N	Y	Y	Y	N	N
NEVADA								
1 Reid	N	Y	Y	N	N	N	Y	Y
2 ***Vucanovich***	N	Y	N	Y	Y	Y	N	N
NEW HAMPSHIRE								
1 D'Amours	N	N	Y	N	N	Y	Y	Y
2 ***Gregg***	N	N	N	Y	Y	Y	N	N
NEW JERSEY								
1 Florio	N	N	Y	N	N	N	Y	Y
2 Hughes	Y	N	Y	N	N	Y	Y	Y
3 Howard	Y	Y	Y	N	N	N	Y	Y
4 ***Smith***	N	N	N	Y	Y	Y	Y	N
5 ***Roukema***	N	N	N	Y	N	Y	Y	?
6 Dwyer	Y	N	Y	N	N	N	Y	Y
7 ***Rinaldo***	N	N	N	N	Y	Y	Y	N
8 Roe	N	Y	Y	N	N	N	Y	Y
9 Torricelli	Y	N	Y	N	N	N	N	Y
10 Rodino	Y	N	Y	N	N	N	Y	Y
11 Minish	N	N	Y	N	Y	N	Y	Y
12 ***Courter***	N	Y	N	Y	Y	Y	?	N
13 ***Forsythe*** [3]	?	?						
14 Guarini	Y	N	Y	N	N	N	Y	Y
NEW MEXICO								
1 ***Lujan***	N	Y	N	Y	Y	Y	N	N
2 ***Skeen***	N	Y	N	Y	Y	Y	N	N
3 Richardson	Y	Y	Y	N	N	Y	Y	Y
NEW YORK								
1 ***Carney***	N	Y	N	Y	Y	Y	N	N
2 Downey	Y	N	Y	N	N	N	Y	Y
3 Mrazek	Y	N	Y	N	N	N	Y	Y
4 ***Lent***	N	N	X	Y	Y	N	N	N
5 ***McGrath***	N	N	N	Y	Y	N	N	N
6 Addabbo	N	N	Y	N	N	N	Y	Y
7 Ackerman	Y	N	Y	N	N	N	Y	Y
8 Scheuer	Y	N	Y	N	N	N	Y	Y
9 Ferraro	Y	N	Y	N	N	?	Y	Y
10 Schumer	Y	N	Y	N	N	N	Y	Y
11 Towns	Y	N	Y	N	N	N	Y	Y
12 Owens	Y	N	Y	N	N	N	Y	Y
13 Solarz	Y	N	Y	N	N	X	Y	Y
14 ***Molinari***	N	N	N	Y	Y	Y	N	N
15 ***Green***	Y	N	N	N	N	N	Y	Y
16 Rangel	Y	N	Y	N	N	N	Y	Y
17 Weiss	Y	N	Y	N	N	N	Y	Y
18 Garcia	Y	Y	Y	N	N	N	Y	Y
19 Biaggi	N	Y	Y	N	N	Y	Y	Y
20 Ottinger	Y	N	Y	N	N	N	Y	Y
21 ***Fish***	N	N	N	Y	Y	N	Y	Y
22 ***Gilman***	Y	N	N	Y	Y	N	Y	N
23 Stratton	N	N	Y	N	Y	Y	N	N
24 ***Solomon***	N	N	N	Y	Y	Y	N	N
25 ***Boehlert***	N	N	#	Y	Y	Y	Y	Y
26 ***Martin***	N	N	N	Y	Y	Y	N	N
27 ***Wortley***	N	N	N	Y	Y	Y	N	N
28 McHugh	N	N	Y	N	N	N	Y	Y
29 ***Horton***	Y	N	Y	Y	Y	Y	Y	Y
30 ***Conable***	Y	N	N	Y	Y	Y	N	N
31 ***Kemp***	N	N	N	Y	Y	Y	N	N
32 LaFalce	N	N	Y	N	N	Y	Y	#
33 Nowak	N	N	Y	N	N	Y	Y	Y
34 Lundine	N	N	Y	N	N	Y	?	Y
NORTH CAROLINA								
1 Jones	Y	Y	Y	?	N	Y	Y	Y
2 Valentine	Y	Y	Y	N	Y	Y	N	Y
3 Whitley	Y	Y	Y	N	Y	Y	N	Y
4 Andrews	Y	N	Y	N	?	Y	?	Y
5 Neal	Y	N	Y	N	N	Y	Y	Y
6 Britt	Y	N	Y	N	N	Y	Y	Y
7 Rose	Y	Y	Y	N	N	Y	Y	Y
8 Hefner	N	Y	Y	N	N	Y	Y	Y
9 ***Martin***	N	Y	N	Y	Y	Y	?	?
10 ***Broyhill***	N	N	Y	Y	Y	Y	N	N
11 Clarke	Y	Y	Y	N	N	Y	Y	Y
NORTH DAKOTA								
AL Dorgan	N	Y	N	N	N	N	Y	Y
OHIO								
1 Luken	N	Y	Y	N	N	Y	Y	Y
2 ***Gradison***	N	N	N	Y	Y	N	Y	Y
3 Hall	N	N	?	N	N	Y	Y	Y
4 ***Oxley***	N	N	N	Y	Y	Y	Y	N
5 ***Latta***	N	N	N	Y	Y	Y	N	N
6 ***McEwen***	N	Y	N	Y	Y	Y	N	N
7 ***DeWine***	N	N	N	Y	Y	Y	N	N
8 ***Kindness***	N	N	N	Y	Y	Y	N	N
9 Kaptur	Y	N	Y	N	N	Y	Y	Y
10 ***Miller***	N	N	N	Y	Y	Y	N	N
11 Eckart	Y	N	N	N	N	Y	Y	Y
12 ***Kasich***	N	N	N	Y	Y	Y	N	N
13 Pease	N	N	Y	N	N	Y	Y	Y
14 Seiberling	Y	Y	Y	N	N	N	Y	Y
15 ***Wylie***	N	Y	Y	Y	Y	Y	N	N
16 ***Regula***	N	Y	N	Y	Y	Y	Y	Y
17 ***Williams***	N	Y	Y	Y	Y	Y	Y	?
18 Applegate	N	N	N	N	N	Y	N	Y
19 Feighan	Y	N	N	N	N	N	Y	Y
20 Oakar	N	N	Y	N	N	N	Y	Y
21 Stokes	#	N	Y	N	N	N	Y	Y
OKLAHOMA								
1 Jones	N	Y	Y	N	N	Y	N	Y
2 Synar	Y	Y	Y	N	N	N	Y	Y
3 Watkins	Y	Y	Y	N	?	Y	N	?
4 McCurdy	Y	Y	Y	N	Y	Y	N	Y
5 ***Edwards***	N	Y	N	Y	Y	Y	N	N
6 English	N	Y	N	N	Y	Y	N	N
OREGON								
1 AuCoin	Y	Y	N	Y	N	N	Y	Y
2 ***Smith, R.***	N	Y	N	Y	Y	Y	N	N
3 Wyden	Y	Y	Y	N	N	N	Y	Y
4 Weaver	Y	?	Y	N	N	Y	Y	Y
5 ***Smith, D.***	N	Y	N	Y	Y	#	N	N
PENNSYLVANIA								
1 Foglietta	Y	?	#	N	N	N	Y	Y
2 Gray	Y	N	Y	N	N	N	Y	Y
3 Borski	N	N	Y	N	N	N	Y	Y
4 Kolter	N	Y	Y	N	N	Y	Y	Y
5 ***Schulze***	N	N	N	Y	Y	Y	N	N
6 Yatron	N	N	Y	N	N	Y	Y	Y
7 Edgar	Y	N	Y	N	N	N	Y	Y
8 Kostmayer	Y	N	Y	N	N	N	Y	Y
9 ***Shuster***	Y	N	N	Y	Y	Y	N	N
10 ***McDade***	N	N	N	Y	Y	Y	N	N
11 Harrison	N	?	Y	?	N	Y	Y	Y
12 Murtha	N	Y	Y	N	Y	?	Y	N
13 ***Coughlin***	N	N	N	Y	Y	N	Y	N
14 Coyne	N	N	Y	N	N	N	Y	Y
15 ***Ritter***	N	N	N	Y	Y	Y	Y	N
16 ***Walker***	N	N	N	Y	Y	Y	N	N
17 ***Gekas***	Y	N	N	Y	Y	Y	N	N
18 Walgren	Y	N	Y	N	N	N	Y	Y
19 ***Goodling***	X	Y	Y	Y	Y	Y	Y	Y
20 Gaydos	N	Y	N	N	N	Y	Y	N
21 ***Ridge***	N	N	Y	Y	Y	Y	Y	Y
22 Murphy	N	Y	N	Y	N	Y	Y	Y
23 ***Clinger***	N	N	Y	Y	Y	Y	Y	N
RHODE ISLAND								
1 St Germain	N	Y	Y	N	N	Y	Y	Y
2 ***Schneider***	Y	N	Y	Y	N	N	N	Y
SOUTH CAROLINA								
1 ***Hartnett***	N	N	N	Y	Y	Y	N	N
2 ***Spence***	N	N	N	Y	Y	Y	N	N
3 Derrick	Y	Y	Y	N	N	Y	Y	Y
4 ***Campbell***	N	N	N	Y	Y	Y	N	N
5 Spratt	Y	N	Y	N	N	Y	Y	Y
6 Tallon	Y	N	Y	N	Y	Y	Y	N
SOUTH DAKOTA								
AL Daschle	Y	Y	Y	N	N	Y	Y	Y
TENNESSEE								
1 ***Quillen***	Y	Y	N	Y	Y	Y	N	N
2 ***Duncan***	Y	Y	N	Y	Y	Y	N	N
3 Lloyd [4]	N	Y	N	N	Y	Y	N	N
4 Cooper	Y	N	Y	N	N	N	Y	Y
5 Boner	Y	Y	Y	X	Y	Y	Y	Y
6 Gore	N	Y	Y	N	N	Y	Y	Y
7 ***Sundquist***	N	Y	N	Y	Y	Y	N	N
8 Jones	Y	Y	Y	N	?	Y	Y	Y
9 Ford	Y	Y	Y	N	?	N	Y	Y
TEXAS								
1 Hall, S.	N	Y	Y	Y	Y	Y	N	N
2 Wilson	N	Y	Y	?	Y	Y	N	Y
3 ***Bartlett***	N	Y	N	Y	Y	Y	N	N
4 Hall, R.	N	Y	N	Y	Y	Y	N	N
5 Bryant	Y	?	Y	N	N	N	Y	Y
6 ***Gramm***	N	Y	N	Y	Y	Y	?	?
7 ***Archer***	N	N	N	Y	Y	Y	N	N
8 ***Fields***	N	N	N	Y	Y	Y	N	N
9 Brooks	Y	Y	Y	N	N	Y	?	Y
10 Pickle	Y	Y	Y	N	Y	Y	Y	Y
11 Leath	Y	Y	N	Y	Y	Y	N	N
12 Wright	Y	Y	Y	N	Y	Y	N	Y
13 Hightower	Y	Y	Y	Y	Y	Y	N	N
14 Patman	Y	Y	N	N	Y	Y	N	N
15 de la Garza	N	?	Y	N	Y	Y	N	Y
16 Coleman	Y	Y	Y	N	Y	Y	N	Y
17 Stenholm	N	Y	Y	Y	Y	Y	N	N
18 Leland	#	N	Y	N	N	N	Y	Y
19 Hance	?	?	X	X	?	#	?	X
20 Gonzalez	Y	Y	N	N	N	N	N	Y
21 ***Loeffler***	Y	Y	N	Y	Y	Y	N	N
22 ***Paul***	?	?	?	?	N	Y	N	Y
23 Kazen	Y	Y	?	?	?	Y	N	N
24 Frost	Y	Y	Y	?	N	N	N	Y
25 Andrews	Y	Y	Y	N	Y	Y	N	Y
26 Vandergriff	Y	Y	N	N	Y	P	N	N
27 Ortiz	N	Y	Y	N	Y	Y	N	Y
UTAH								
1 ***Hansen***	N	Y	N	Y	?	Y	N	N
2 ***Marriott***	N	Y	N	#	Y	Y	N	?
3 ***Nielson***	N	Y	N	Y	Y	Y	N	N
VERMONT								
AL ***Jeffords***	?	N	Y	Y	N	Y	Y	Y
VIRGINIA								
1 ***Bateman***	N	Y	N	Y	Y	Y	N	N
2 ***Whitehurst***	Y	Y	N	Y	Y	Y	N	N
3 ***Bliley***	N	N	N	Y	Y	Y	N	N
4 Sisisky	Y	N	Y	N	Y	Y	N	N
5 Daniel	N	N	N	Y	Y	Y	N	N
6 Olin	Y	N	Y	N	N	Y	Y	Y
7 ***Robinson***	N	N	N	Y	Y	Y	N	N
8 ***Parris***	N	N	N	Y	Y	Y	N	N
9 Boucher	Y	N	Y	N	N	Y	Y	Y
10 ***Wolf***	N	N	N	Y	Y	Y	N	N
WASHINGTON								
1 ***Pritchard***	Y	Y	Y	Y	Y	Y	Y	Y
2 Swift	Y	Y	Y	N	N	N	Y	Y
3 Bonker	N	Y	Y	N	N	Y	Y	Y
4 ***Morrison***	Y	Y	N	Y	Y	Y	N	N
5 Foley	Y	Y	Y	N	N	N	Y	Y
6 Dicks	Y	Y	Y	N	N	N	Y	Y
7 Lowry	Y	Y	Y	N	N	N	Y	Y
8 ***Chandler***	Y	Y	Y	Y	Y	Y	Y	Y
WEST VIRGINIA								
1 Mollohan	N	Y	Y	N	Y	Y	Y	Y
2 Staggers	N	N	Y	N	N	Y	Y	Y
3 Wise	N	Y	Y	N	N	Y	Y	Y
4 Rahall	N	Y	Y	N	N	?	Y	Y
WISCONSIN								
1 Aspin	N	N	Y	N	N	N	Y	Y
2 Kastenmeier	Y	N	Y	N	N	N	Y	Y
3 ***Gunderson***	N	N	N	Y	Y	Y	Y	Y
4 Kleczka [5]				N	N	N	Y	Y
5 Moody	Y	N	Y	N	?	N	Y	Y
6 ***Petri***	N	N	Y	Y	Y	Y	N	N
7 Obey	N	N	Y	N	N	N	Y	Y
8 ***Roth***	N	?	N	Y	Y	Y	N	N
9 ***Sensenbrenner***	N	N	N	Y	Y	Y	?	?
WYOMING								
AL ***Cheney***	N	Y	N	Y	Y	Y	N	N

Southern states - Ala., Ark., Fla., Ga., Ky., La., Miss., N.C., Okla., S.C., Tenn., Texas, Va.

Appendix

9. HR 5167. Department of Defense Authorization.
Bennett, D-Fla., amendment to the Dickinson, R-Ala., amendment, to prohibit the obligation of funds appropriated for production of MX missiles unless Congress had given its approval by passing a joint resolution after April 1, 1985. Adopted 199-197: R 17-141; D 182-56 (ND 149-15, SD 33-41), May 31, 1984. (The Dickinson amendment, as amended, subsequently was adopted 198-197.) A "nay" was a vote supporting the president's position.

10. HR 1510. Immigration Reform and Control Act.
Passage of the bill to revise immigration laws to impose sanctions on employers who knowingly hire illegal aliens, provide legal status for many illegal aliens already in the United States, expand an existing temporary foreign worker program, create a new guest-worker program and overhaul procedures for handling asylum, deportation and exclusion cases. Passed 216-211: R 91-73; D 125-138 (ND 76-98, SD 49-40), June 20, 1984. A "yea" was a vote supporting the president's position.

11. HR 5973. Interior Appropriations, Fiscal 1985.
Adoption of the rule (H Res 551) providing for House floor consideration of the bill to make fiscal 1985 appropriations for the Interior Department and related agencies. H Res 551 would not have waived points of order against amendments to rescind appropriated funds from the U.S. Synthetic Fuels Corporation. Rejected 148-261: R 21-135; D 127-126 (ND 66-101, SD 61-25), July 25, 1984. A "nay" was a vote supporting the president's position.

12. HR 11. Education Amendments/School Prayer.
Goodling, R-Pa., perfecting amendment to the Ford, D-Mich., substitute for the Goodling amendment to reduce fiscal 1985 authorizations for education programs in the bill from $1.7 billion to $974 million. The perfecting amendment was identical to the original Goodling proposal that the Ford substitute would have blocked from coming to a vote. Rejected 169-233: R 133-20; D 36-213 (ND 13-154, SD 23-59), July 26, 1984.

13. HR 5640. Superfund Expansion.
Sawyer, R-Mich., amendment to delete from the bill a section giving citizens the right to sue in federal court for damages caused by hazardous-waste dumping. Adopted 208-200: R 135-22; D 73-178 (ND 23-146, SD 50-32), Aug. 9, 1984.

14. H J Res 648. Continuing Appropriations, Fiscal 1985.
Lungren, R-Calif., motion to recommit the joint resolution to the Committee on Appropriations with instructions to attach the provisions of HR 5963, the Comprehensive Crime Control Act of 1984. Motion agreed to 243-166: R 154-3; D 89-163 (ND 35-134, SD 54-29), Sept. 25, 1984. A "yea" was a vote supporting the president's position.

15. HR 6023. Generalized System of Preferences Renewal Act.
Gephardt, D-Mo., amendment to remove Taiwan, Hong Kong and South Korea from the list of countries eligible for duty-free treatment under the generalized system of preferences. Rejected 174-233: R 14-142; D 160-91 (ND 128-38, SD 32-53), Oct. 3, 1984. (The bill subsequently was passed by voice vote.) A "nay" was a vote supporting the president's position.

16. HR 4230. Export Administration Act.
Fascell, D-Fla., motion to concur in the Senate amendment with an amendment to ban U.S. commercial bank loans to the government of South Africa. Motion agreed to 269-62: R 96-50; D 173-12 (ND 121-2, SD 52-10), Oct. 11, 1984.

1. Rep. Carl D. Perkins, D-Ky., died Aug. 3, 1984.
2. Rep. Thomas P. O'Neill Jr., D-Mass., as Speaker, votes at his own discretion.
3. Rep. Edwin B. Forsythe, R-N.J., died March 29, 1984.
4. Rep. Marilyn Lloyd, D-Tenn., was known as Marilyn Lloyd Bouquard in the 97th Congress.
5. Rep. Gerald D. Kleczka, D-Wis., was sworn in April 10, 1984, to succeed Clement J. Zablocki, D, who died Dec. 3, 1983.

KEY

Y Voted for (yea).
\# Paired for.
+ Announced for.
N Voted against (nay).
X Paired against.
- Announced against.
P Voted "present".
C Voted "present" to avoid possible conflict of interest.
? Did not vote or otherwise make a position known.

Democrats   *Republicans*

	9	10	11	12	13	14	15	16
ALABAMA								
1 *Edwards*	N	Y	?	Y	Y	Y	N	Y
2 *Dickinson*	N	N	N	Y	Y	Y	N	?
3 Nichols	N	N	Y	N	Y	N	N	N
4 Bevill	N	N	Y	N	Y	N	N	Y
5 Flippo	N	N	Y	?	Y	Y	Y	Y
6 Erdreich	-	N	N	N	Y	Y	Y	Y
7 Shelby	N	N	N	N	?	Y	Y	Y
ALASKA								
AL *Young*	N	N	N	N	Y	Y	?	Y
ARIZONA								
1 *McCain*	N	N	N	Y	Y	Y	N	Y
2 Udall	Y	N	N	N	N	N	?	?
3 *Stump*	N	N	?	?	Y	Y	N	N
4 *Rudd*	N	N	Y	Y	Y	Y	?	?
5 McNulty	Y	N	N	N	Y	N	?	?
ARKANSAS								
1 Alexander	?	Y	Y	?	N	X	Y	?
2 *Bethune*	N	N	N	Y	?	?	N	?
3 *Hammerschmidt*	N	Y	N	Y	Y	?	N	?
4 Anthony	?	Y	#	Y	?	N	N	Y
CALIFORNIA								
1 Bosco	Y	N	N	N	Y	N	Y	Y
2 *Chappie*	N	N	N	?	Y	Y	N	N
3 Matsui	Y	N	N	Y	N	N	N	Y
4 Fazio	N	N	Y	N	N	N	Y	Y
5 Burton	Y	N	N	N	?	?	Y	Y
6 Boxer	Y	N	N	?	N	N	Y	Y
7 Miller	Y	N	N	N	N	N	Y	Y
8 Dellums	Y	N	N	N	N	N	Y	P
9 Stark	Y	Y	N	N	N	Y	N	Y
10 Edwards	Y	N	N	N	N	N	N	Y
11 Lantos	Y	N	N	N	N	N	N	Y
12 *Zschau*	Y	N	N	Y	Y	Y	N	Y
13 Mineta	Y	N	N	N	N	N	N	Y
14 *Shumway*	N	N	N	Y	Y	Y	N	N
15 Coelho	Y	N	N	N	N	N	N	Y
16 Panetta	Y	Y	N	N	Y	N	N	Y
17 *Pashayan*	N	N	N	Y	Y	Y	N	Y
18 Lehman	Y	N	N	N	N	N	N	Y
19 *Lagomarsino*	N	N	N	Y	Y	Y	N	N
20 *Thomas*	N	Y	N	Y	?	Y	N	N
21 *Fiedler*	N	N	N	Y	Y	Y	N	N
22 *Moorhead*	N	Y	N	Y	Y	Y	N	N
23 Beilenson	Y	Y	Y	N	N	Y	N	Y
24 Waxman	Y	N	?	N	N	N	N	?
25 Roybal	Y	N	N	N	N	N	Y	?
26 Berman	Y	N	N	N	N	N	N	Y
27 Levine	Y	N	N	N	N	N	N	Y
28 Dixon	#	N	Y	N	N	N	N	P
29 Hawkins	?	N	Y	N	N	N	Y	P
30 Martinez	Y	N	N	N	N	N	N	Y
31 Dymally	?	N	N	N	N	N	N	Y
32 Anderson	N	N	N	N	N	N	N	Y
33 *Dreier*	N	N	Y	Y	Y	Y	N	N
34 Torres	Y	N	Y	N	N	N	Y	Y
35 *Lewis*	N	N	Y	Y	Y	Y	N	Y
36 Brown	Y	N	N	N	N	?	?	?
37 *McCandless*	N	Y	N	Y	Y	Y	N	N
38 Patterson	N	Y	N	N	Y	N	N	Y
39 *Dannemeyer*	N	Y	Y	+	Y	Y	N	N
40 *Badham*	N	Y	Y	Y	Y	Y	N	Y
41 *Lowery*	N	Y	N	Y	Y	Y	N	Y
42 *Lungren*	N	Y	N	Y	Y	Y	N	N

	9	10	11	12	13	14	15	16
43 *Packard*	N	Y	N	Y	Y	Y	N	?
44 Bates	Y	Y	N	N	N	Y	Y	?
45 *Hunter*	N	N	N	Y	Y	Y	N	N
COLORADO								
1 Schroeder	Y	N	N	N	N	N	N	?
2 Wirth	Y	N	Y	N	N	Y	N	Y
3 Kogovsek	Y	N	Y	?	N	N	N	Y
4 *Brown*	N	N	N	Y	Y	Y	N	Y
5 *Kramer*	N	N	Y	Y	Y	Y	N	Y
6 *Schaefer*	N	Y	N	Y	Y	Y	N	N
CONNECTICUT								
1 Kennelly	Y	N	N	Y	N	Y	N	Y
2 Gejdenson	Y	N	N	N	N	N	N	Y
3 Morrison	Y	N	N	Y	N	Y	N	?
4 *McKinney*	#	Y	Y	N	N	Y	N	Y
5 Ratchford	Y	N	N	N	N	Y	N	?
6 *Johnson*	Y	Y	N	Y	Y	Y	N	Y
DELAWARE								
AL Carper	Y	Y	Y	N	N	Y	Y	Y
FLORIDA								
1 Hutto	N	Y	Y	N	Y	Y	N	N
2 Fuqua	N	Y	Y	Y	Y	Y	N	?
3 Bennett	Y	Y	Y	Y	Y	N	Y	N
4 Chappell	N	Y	Y	Y	Y	Y	N	?
5 *McCollum*	N	Y	Y	Y	Y	Y	N	N
6 MacKay	Y	Y	N	Y	N	Y	N	?
7 Gibbons	?	Y	Y	Y	Y	N	Y	Y
8 *Young*	N	Y	Y	Y	Y	Y	N	N
9 *Bilirakis*	N	N	N	Y	Y	Y	N	N
10 *Ireland*	N	Y	Y	Y	Y	Y	N	N
11 Nelson	N	Y	Y	Y	Y	Y	N	Y
12 *Lewis*	N	Y	Y	Y	Y	Y	N	N
13 *Mack*	N	N	N	Y	Y	Y	N	N
14 Mica	Y	Y	Y	Y	Y	N	Y	Y
15 *Shaw*	N	Y	N	?	Y	Y	N	?
16 Smith	Y	Y	N	N	N	N	N	Y
17 Lehman	Y	Y	N	N	N	N	N	Y
18 Pepper	N	Y	Y	N	?	Y	Y	Y
19 Fascell	Y	Y	Y	N	N	N	N	Y
GEORGIA								
1 Thomas	N	N	N	N	N	N	N	Y
2 Hatcher	?	N	Y	?	?	?	Y	Y
3 Ray	N	N	Y	Y	Y	N	N	Y
4 Levitas	N	Y	Y	Y	Y	Y	N	Y
5 Fowler	Y	N	N	N	N	N	N	Y
6 *Gingrich*	N	Y	?	Y	Y	Y	N	N
7 Darden	N	N	Y	Y	Y	Y	N	Y
8 Rowland	N	N	Y	N	N	N	N	Y
9 Jenkins	?	N	Y	N	Y	N	Y	?
10 Barnard	?	N	N	N	N	Y	?	N
HAWAII								
1 Heftel	Y	Y	?	N	Y	Y	N	?
2 Akaka	Y	N	Y	N	N	N	N	Y
IDAHO								
1 *Craig*	N	N	N	Y	Y	Y	N	Y
2 *Hansen*	?	?	?	?	?	Y	?	?
ILLINOIS								
1 Hayes	Y	N	N	N	N	N	Y	P
2 Savage	Y	N	N	N	N	N	Y	P
3 Russo	Y	N	N	N	N	Y	N	Y
4 *O'Brien*	N	Y	X	N	Y	Y	N	Y
5 Lipinski	N	Y	N	N	N	N	Y	?
6 *Hyde*	N	Y	Y	Y	Y	Y	N	N
7 Collins	Y	N	N	N	N	N	N	P
8 Rostenkowski	Y	Y	?	?	N	N	Y	Y
9 Yates	Y	N	Y	N	Y	N	N	Y
10 *Porter*	N	N	N	Y	Y	Y	N	Y
11 Annunzio	Y	Y	N	N	N	Y	N	Y
12 *Crane, P.*	N	N	N	Y	Y	Y	N	N
13 *Erlenborn*	N	Y	N	Y	Y	Y	?	Y
14 *Corcoran*	N	Y	N	Y	Y	+	N	Y
15 *Madigan*	N	Y	N	Y	N	Y	N	Y
16 *Martin*	N	N	N	Y	Y	Y	N	Y
17 Evans	Y	N	N	N	N	N	N	Y
18 *Michel*	N	Y	N	Y	Y	Y	N	Y
19 *Crane, D.*	N	N	N	Y	Y	Y	N	N
20 Durbin	Y	Y	N	N	N	Y	N	Y
21 Price	N	Y	Y	N	N	N	N	Y
22 Simon	?	N	?	?	?	?	?	?
INDIANA								
1 Hall	Y	N	N	N	N	N	N	P
2 Sharp	Y	Y	N	N	N	Y	N	Y
3 *Hiler*	N	Y	N	Y	Y	Y	N	?
4 *Coats*	N	Y	N	Y	Y	Y	N	Y
5 Hillis	N	N	N	Y	Y	Y	N	Y

ND - Northern Democrats   SD - Southern Democrats

	9	10	11	12	13	14	15	16
6 ***Burton***	N	Y	N	Y	Y	Y	N	N
7 ***Myers***	N	Y	Y	Y	Y	N	N	Y
8 McCloskey	Y	Y	N	N	N	Y	Y	Y
9 Hamilton	Y	Y	N	N	N	Y	N	Y
10 Jacobs	Y	N	N	N	N	N	Y	Y
IOWA								
1 ***Leach***	Y	Y	N	N	Y	Y	N	Y
2 ***Tauke***	Y	Y	N	Y	Y	Y	?	Y
3 ***Evans***	Y	Y	N	Y	Y	Y	N	Y
4 Smith	Y	Y	Y	N	N	Y	Y	Y
5 Harkin	Y	Y	N	N	N	Y	N	?
6 Bedell	Y	Y	N	N	N	Y	P	Y
KANSAS								
1 ***Roberts***	N	N	N	Y	Y	Y	N	Y
2 Slattery	Y	Y	N	Y	Y	Y	Y	Y
3 ***Winn***	N	Y	Y	Y	Y	Y	N	Y
4 Glickman	Y	Y	N	N	Y	N	Y	Y
5 ***Whittaker***	N	Y	N	Y	Y	Y	N	Y
KENTUCKY								
1 Hubbard	Y	N	Y	?	Y	Y	N	N
2 Natcher	Y	Y	Y	N	Y	N	Y	Y
3 Mazzoli	Y	Y	Y	N	Y	Y	N	Y
4 ***Snyder***	N	N	N	Y	Y	Y	N	N
5 ***Rogers***	N	N	Y	Y	Y	Y	N	N
6 ***Hopkins***	N	N	N	Y	Y	Y	N	N
7 Perkins [1]	Y	N	Y	N				
LOUISIANA								
1 ***Livingston***	N	Y	N	Y	Y	Y	N	N
2 Boggs	Y	Y	Y	N	N	?	N	P
3 Tauzin	N	N	N	Y	Y	Y	Y	Y
4 Roemer	N	N	N	Y	Y	Y	N	Y
5 Huckaby	N	N	Y	Y	Y	Y	N	Y
6 ***Moore***	N	N	N	Y	Y	Y	N	Y
7 Breaux	N	Y	Y	Y	Y	Y	N	?
8 Long	Y	Y	Y	N	Y	N	Y	?
MAINE								
1 ***McKernan***	N	Y	N	Y	N	Y	Y	Y
2 ***Snowe***	N	Y	Y	Y	N	Y	Y	Y
MARYLAND								
1 Dyson	Y	N	N	N	Y	Y	Y	?
2 Long	Y	Y	Y	N	N	Y	N	Y
3 Mikulski	Y	?	N	N	N	N	Y	?
4 ***Holt***	N	Y	N	Y	Y	Y	N	Y
5 Hoyer	Y	Y	N	N	?	X	Y	Y
6 Byron	N	Y	Y	Y	Y	Y	N	Y
7 Mitchell	Y	N	N	N	N	N	Y	P
8 Barnes	Y	Y	N	N	N	N	Y	Y
MASSACHUSETTS								
1 ***Conte***	Y	Y	N	N	N	Y	Y	Y
2 Boland	Y	Y	Y	?	N	N	Y	Y
3 Early	Y	Y	Y	?	N	N	Y	?
4 Frank	Y	Y	N	N	N	N	Y	Y
5 Shannon	Y	?	?	N	N	N	?	?
6 Mavroules	Y	Y	Y	N	N	N	Y	Y
7 Markey	Y	N	N	N	N	N	Y	Y
8 O'Neill [2]	Y							
9 Moakley	Y	Y	Y	N	N	N	Y	Y
10 Studds	Y	Y	N	?	N	N	Y	Y
11 Donnelly	Y	Y	Y	N	N	N	Y	Y
MICHIGAN								
1 Conyers	Y	N	N	N	N	N	Y	P
2 ***Pursell***	N	N	N	Y	?	Y	?	?
3 Wolpe	Y	N	N	N	N	N	Y	Y
4 ***Siljander***	N	N	N	Y	Y	Y	N	?
5 ***Sawyer***	X	Y	N	Y	Y	Y	N	?
6 Carr	Y	N	Y	N	N	Y	Y	Y
7 Kildee	Y	N	N	N	N	N	Y	Y
8 Traxler	Y	Y	Y	N	N	N	Y	Y
9 ***Vander Jagt***	X	N	N	Y	Y	Y	N	?
10 Albosta	Y	N	Y	Y	N	Y	Y	?
11 ***Davis***	N	Y	N	N	N	Y	N	Y
12 Bonior	Y	Y	Y	N	?	N	Y	?
13 Crockett	?	N	Y	N	N	N	Y	?
14 Hertel	Y	N	N	N	N	Y	Y	Y
15 Ford	Y	N	N	N	N	N	Y	Y
16 Dingell	Y	Y	Y	N	N	N	Y	Y
17 Levin	Y	Y	N	N	N	N	Y	Y
18 ***Broomfield***	N	N	N	Y	Y	Y	N	Y
MINNESOTA								
1 Penny	Y	Y	N	Y	N	N	N	Y
2 ***Weber***	N	Y	N	Y	N	Y	N	Y
3 ***Frenzel***	N	Y	N	Y	Y	Y	N	Y
4 Vento	Y	N	N	?	N	N	Y	Y
5 Sabo	#	Y	Y	N	N	N	N	Y
6 Sikorski	Y	N	N	N	N	N	Y	Y

	9	10	11	12	13	14	15	16
7 ***Stangeland***	N	Y	N	Y	Y	Y	N	Y
8 Oberstar	Y	N	Y	N	N	N	Y	Y
MISSISSIPPI								
1 Whitten	Y	N	Y	N	Y	N	Y	Y
2 ***Franklin***	N	Y	N	Y	Y	#	N	Y
3 Montgomery	N	Y	Y	Y	Y	Y	Y	?
4 Dowdy	?	Y	N	N	N	Y	Y	?
5 ***Lott***	N	Y	N	Y	Y	Y	N	N
MISSOURI								
1 Clay	Y	N	?	N	N	N	Y	P
2 Young	Y	N	#	N	X	Y	Y	Y
3 Gephardt	Y	N	N	N	N	N	Y	?
4 Skelton	N	N	Y	N	N	N	Y	?
5 Wheat	Y	N	Y	N	N	N	Y	P
6 ***Coleman***	N	N	N	Y	Y	Y	N	Y
7 ***Taylor***	N	Y	N	?	Y	Y	N	N
8 ***Emerson***	N	N	N	Y	Y	Y	N	Y
9 Volkmer	Y	N	Y	N	N	Y	Y	Y
MONTANA								
1 Williams	Y	-	N	N	N	N	?	Y
2 ***Marlenee***	N	N	N	Y	Y	?	N	Y
NEBRASKA								
1 ***Bereuter***	Y	Y	N	Y	Y	Y	N	Y
2 ***Daub***	N	N	N	Y	Y	Y	N	Y
3 ***Smith***	Y	Y	N	Y	Y	Y	N	Y
NEVADA								
1 Reid	N	N	Y	N	N	N	Y	?
2 ***Vucanovich***	N	Y	N	Y	Y	Y	N	Y
NEW HAMPSHIRE								
1 D'Amours	Y	Y	N	Y	N	#	Y	?
2 ***Gregg***	N	Y	N	Y	N	Y	N	Y
NEW JERSEY								
1 Florio	Y	N	N	N	N	N	Y	Y
2 Hughes	N	N	N	Y	Y	N	N	Y
3 Howard	?	Y	N	N	N	N	Y	?
4 ***Smith***	N	Y	N	N	N	Y	Y	Y
5 ***Roukema***	Y	N	N	Y	Y	Y	N	Y
6 Dwyer	Y	Y	Y	N	N	Y	Y	Y
7 ***Rinaldo***	N	N	N	?	N	Y	Y	Y
8 Roe	?	Y	N	N	Y	N	Y	Y
9 Torricelli	Y	Y	N	N	N	N	Y	Y
10 Rodino	#	Y	Y	N	N	N	Y	Y
11 Minish	Y	N	N	N	N	Y	?	Y
12 ***Courter***	N	N	N	?	Y	Y	N	N
13 ***Forsythe*** [3]								
14 Guarini	?	N	Y	N	N	X	Y	Y
NEW MEXICO								
1 ***Lujan***	N	N	N	Y	Y	Y	N	N
2 ***Skeen***	N	N	N	Y	Y	Y	N	N
3 Richardson	Y	N	N	N	N	N	Y	Y
NEW YORK								
1 ***Carney***	N	N	N	Y	Y	Y	N	Y
2 Downey	Y	Y	N	N	N	N	N	Y
3 Mrazek	Y	Y	N	N	N	Y	Y	Y
4 ***Lent***	N	N	N	Y	N	Y	N	N
5 ***McGrath***	N	N	N	Y	N	#	?	Y
6 Addabbo	Y	N	Y	N	N	N	Y	Y
7 Ackerman	#	N	N	N	N	N	N	Y
8 Scheuer	Y	Y	N	N	N	N	N	Y
9 Ferraro	Y	N	?	?	N	?	?	?
10 Schumer	Y	Y	N	N	?	N	Y	Y
11 Towns	Y	N	N	N	N	N	Y	P
12 Owens	Y	N	N	N	N	N	Y	P
13 Solarz	Y	Y	N	N	N	N	N	Y
14 ***Molinari***	N	Y	N	Y	N	Y	N	Y
15 ***Green***	Y	Y	N	N	N	Y	N	Y
16 Rangel	Y	N	N	N	N	N	Y	P
17 Weiss	Y	N	N	N	N	N	N	Y
18 Garcia	Y	N	N	N	N	N	Y	Y
19 Biaggi	Y	N	?	N	N	N	N	Y
20 Ottinger	Y	Y	N	N	N	N	Y	?
21 ***Fish***	N	Y	N	Y	Y	Y	?	Y
22 ***Gilman***	N	Y	N	N	N	N	Y	Y
23 Stratton	N	N	?	N	Y	Y	N	N
24 ***Solomon***	N	N	N	Y	Y	Y	Y	N
25 ***Boehlert***	N	Y	N	N	N	N	Y	Y
26 ***Martin***	N	N	N	Y	Y	Y	N	Y
27 ***Wortley***	N	Y	N	Y	Y	Y	N	N
28 McHugh	Y	Y	N	N	N	N	N	Y
29 ***Horton***	N	N	X	N	N	Y	N	?
30 ***Conable***	N	Y	N	?	Y	Y	N	N
31 ***Kemp***	N	N	N	Y	Y	Y	N	Y
32 LaFalce	Y	Y	Y	N	N	N	?	Y
33 Nowak	Y	Y	Y	N	N	N	Y	Y
34 Lundine	?	Y	Y	Y	N	Y	Y	?

	9	10	11	12	13	14	15	16
NORTH CAROLINA								
1 Jones	Y	N	Y	N	Y	N	?	Y
2 Valentine	N	Y	Y	N	Y	Y	Y	Y
3 Whitley	N	Y	Y	N	Y	Y	N	?
4 Andrews	Y	Y	N	N	Y	Y	N	Y
5 Neal	Y	Y	N	?	N	Y	N	Y
6 Britt	N	Y	Y	N	Y	Y	Y	Y
7 Rose	Y	Y	Y	N	Y	Y	Y	Y
8 Hefner	N	Y	Y	N	Y	Y	N	?
9 ***Martin***	N	Y	N	Y	?	?	?	?
10 ***Broyhill***	N	Y	N	Y	Y	Y	Y	Y
11 Clarke	Y	Y	N	N	?	N	Y	?
NORTH DAKOTA								
AL Dorgan	Y	Y	Y	N	N	N	Y	Y
OHIO								
1 Luken	Y	Y	N	N	Y	Y	Y	Y
2 ***Gradison***	Y	Y	N	Y	Y	Y	N	Y
3 Hall	Y	N	N	N	N	N	Y	Y
4 ***Oxley***	N	Y	N	+	Y	Y	N	Y
5 ***Latta***	N	N	N	Y	Y	Y	N	N
6 ***McEwen***	N	Y	N	Y	#	Y	N	?
7 ***DeWine***	N	Y	N	Y	Y	Y	N	N
8 ***Kindness***	N	N	N	Y	Y	Y	N	N
9 Kaptur	Y	N	N	N	N	Y	N	?
10 ***Miller***	N	Y	N	Y	Y	Y	N	N
11 Eckart	Y	Y	N	N	N	Y	Y	Y
12 ***Kasich***	N	Y	N	Y	Y	Y	Y	N
13 Pease	Y	Y	N	N	Y	N	N	Y
14 Seiberling	Y	Y	N	N	N	N	Y	Y
15 ***Wylie***	N	Y	N	Y	Y	Y	N	Y
16 ***Regula***	N	N	Y	Y	Y	Y	Y	Y
17 ***Williams***	N	N	N	N	?	?	Y	?
18 Applegate	Y	N	Y	Y	Y	Y	Y	N
19 Feighan	Y	Y	N	N	N	N	Y	Y
20 Oakar	Y	N	N	N	N	N	Y	?
21 Stokes	Y	N	N	N	N	N	Y	P
OKLAHOMA								
1 Jones	Y	Y	N	N	Y	Y	N	Y
2 Synar	Y	Y	N	N	Y	N	N	Y
3 Watkins	N	N	Y	N	Y	Y	N	Y
4 McCurdy	?	Y	N	N	Y	Y	N	?
5 ***Edwards***	X	N	Y	Y	Y	Y	N	N
6 English	?	N	N	Y	Y	Y	N	Y
OREGON								
1 AuCoin	Y	N	Y	N	N	Y	N	Y
2 ***Smith, R.***	N	N	N	Y	Y	Y	N	Y
3 Wyden	Y	N	Y	N	N	N	N	Y
4 Weaver	Y	Y	N	N	N	N	Y	?
5 ***Smith, D.***	N	Y	N	Y	Y	Y	N	N
PENNSYLVANIA								
1 Foglietta	Y	N	N	N	N	N	Y	?
2 Gray	Y	N	Y	N	N	N	Y	?
3 Borski	Y	N	N	N	N	N	Y	Y
4 Kolter	?	N	Y	Y	N	N	Y	Y
5 ***Schulze***	N	Y	Y	Y	Y	Y	N	?
6 Yatron	N	N	Y	N	N	Y	?	Y
7 Edgar	Y	N	N	N	N	N	N	Y
8 Kostmayer	Y	Y	N	N	N	Y	Y	Y
9 ***Shuster***	N	N	Y	Y	Y	Y	N	N
10 ***McDade***	N	Y	Y	Y	N	Y	N	Y
11 Harrison	Y	Y	Y	N	?	?	Y	Y
12 Murtha	N	Y	Y	N	Y	N	Y	Y
13 ***Coughlin***	Y	Y	N	N	N	Y	N	Y
14 Coyne	Y	Y	Y	N	N	N	Y	Y
15 ***Ritter***	N	Y	N	Y	N	Y	Y	Y
16 ***Walker***	N	Y	N	Y	Y	Y	N	Y
17 ***Gekas***	N	Y	N	Y	Y	Y	N	N
18 Walgren	Y	Y	N	Y	N	N	Y	?
19 ***Goodling***	Y	N	N	Y	Y	Y	N	Y
20 Gaydos	Y	N	Y	N	N	N	N	Y
21 ***Ridge***	Y	Y	N	Y	Y	Y	Y	Y
22 Murphy	Y	N	Y	N	Y	N	Y	?
23 ***Clinger***	N	Y	Y	Y	Y	Y	N	Y
RHODE ISLAND								
1 St Germain	Y	Y	N	?	N	N	Y	Y
2 ***Schneider***	Y	Y	N	N	N	Y	Y	Y
SOUTH CAROLINA								
1 ***Hartnett***	N	N	N	Y	Y	Y	N	N
2 ***Spence***	N	N	N	Y	Y	Y	N	N
3 Derrick	Y	Y	Y	Y	Y	Y	N	?
4 ***Campbell***	N	Y	?	Y	Y	Y	N	Y
5 Spratt	Y	Y	N	N	Y	N	N	Y
6 Tallon	Y	Y	N	N	Y	Y	N	?
SOUTH DAKOTA								
AL Daschle	Y	Y	Y	Y	Y	N	N	Y

	9	10	11	12	13	14	15	16
TENNESSEE								
1 ***Quillen***	N	Y	Y	N	Y	N	N	N
2 ***Duncan***	N	N	Y	N	Y	Y	N	Y
3 Lloyd [4]	N	Y	Y	N	Y	Y	N	N
4 Cooper	N	Y	Y	N	N	N	N	?
5 Boner	N	Y	Y	N	N	N	Y	?
6 Gore	N	Y	N	N	N	N	Y	Y
7 ***Sundquist***	N	N	N	N	Y	Y	N	Y
8 Jones	N	Y	?	?	N	N	Y	Y
9 Ford	Y	Y	N	N	N	N	Y	P
TEXAS								
1 Hall, S.	N	N	Y	Y	?	Y	N	N
2 Wilson	X	Y	?	N	Y	Y	?	Y
3 ***Bartlett***	N	N	N	Y	Y	Y	N	Y
4 Hall, R.	N	N	Y	Y	N	Y	N	N
5 Bryant	#	N	Y	N	N	N	Y	Y
6 ***Gramm***	N	N	?	?	Y	?	?	?
7 ***Archer***	N	N	N	Y	Y	Y	N	Y
8 ***Fields***	N	N	N	Y	Y	Y	N	Y
9 Brooks	Y	N	Y	N	Y	N	Y	Y
10 Pickle	Y	Y	Y	N	Y	Y	N	?
11 Leath	X	N	Y	N	Y	Y	N	?
12 Wright	Y	Y	Y	N	N	N	N	Y
13 Hightower	N	N	Y	Y	Y	Y	N	Y
14 Patman	N	N	Y	Y	Y	Y	Y	N
15 de la Garza	N	N	Y	N	N	N	N	?
16 Coleman	Y	N	Y	N	N	Y	N	?
17 Stenholm	N	N	N	Y	Y	Y	N	?
18 Leland	#	?	Y	N	N	X	Y	P
19 Hance	X	N	Y	N	Y	Y	N	?
20 Gonzalez	Y	N	Y	N	N	N	Y	N
21 ***Loeffler***	N	N	Y	Y	Y	Y	N	Y
22 ***Paul***	Y	N	N	Y	Y	N	N	?
23 Kazen	N	N	Y	N	Y	N	N	Y
24 Frost	X	N	Y	?	N	N	Y	Y
25 Andrews	N	N	Y	N	N	Y	Y	Y
26 Vandergriff	N	N	Y	N	Y	Y	N	Y
27 Ortiz	N	N	N	N	N	N	N	Y
UTAH								
1 ***Hansen***	N	Y	N	Y	Y	Y	N	N
2 ***Marriott***	X	N	?	?	?	Y	N	?
3 ***Nielson***	N	Y	Y	Y	Y	Y	N	N
VERMONT								
AL ***Jeffords***	#	Y	N	Y	N	Y	N	Y
VIRGINIA								
1 ***Bateman***	N	Y	N	Y	?	Y	N	N
2 ***Whitehurst***	N	Y	N	Y	Y	Y	N	Y
3 ***Bliley***	N	N	N	Y	Y	Y	N	Y
4 Sisisky	Y	Y	N	N	Y	Y	N	Y
5 Daniel	N	N	Y	Y	Y	Y	N	N
6 Olin	Y	N	N	Y	?	Y	Y	Y
7 ***Robinson***	N	N	-	Y	Y	Y	N	N
8 ***Parris***	N	N	Y	Y	Y	Y	N	Y
9 Boucher	Y	Y	Y	N	N	N	N	Y
10 ***Wolf***	N	Y	N	Y	Y	Y	N	Y
WASHINGTON								
1 ***Pritchard***	N	Y	?	?	?	Y	N	Y
2 Swift	Y	N	N	N	N	N	N	Y
3 Bonker	?	Y	N	N	N	N	N	Y
4 ***Morrison***	N	Y	N	N	Y	Y	N	Y
5 Foley	Y	Y	Y	N	Y	N	N	Y
6 Dicks	N	Y	N	N	N	N	N	Y
7 Lowry	Y	N	N	N	N	N	N	Y
8 ***Chandler***	N	Y	N	N	Y	Y	N	Y
WEST VIRGINIA								
1 Mollohan	N	N	Y	N	Y	N	Y	Y
2 Staggers	Y	N	Y	N	N	N	Y	Y
3 Wise	Y	N	Y	N	N	Y	Y	Y
4 Rahall	Y	Y	Y	N	?	Y	Y	Y
WISCONSIN								
1 Aspin	N	Y	Y	N	N	N	Y	?
2 Kastenmeier	Y	Y	N	N	N	N	Y	Y
3 ***Gunderson***	N	Y	N	Y	Y	Y	N	Y
4 Kleczka [5]	Y	Y	N	N	Y	N	Y	Y
5 Moody	Y	Y	N	Y	N	?	Y	Y
6 ***Petri***	Y	Y	N	Y	Y	Y	N	Y
7 Obey	Y	Y	N	N	N	N	N	Y
8 ***Roth***	N	N	Y	Y	Y	Y	N	Y
9 ***Sensenbrenner***	?	?	N	Y	Y	Y	N	Y
WYOMING								
AL ***Cheney***	N	Y	N	Y	Y	#	?	N

Southern states - Ala., Ark., Fla., Ga., Ky., La., Miss., N.C., Okla., S.C., Tenn., Texas, Va.

Congress and Its Members

Membership Lists	*945*
Members of Congress	*953*
Congressional Committees	*963*
Post-Election Sessions	*975*
Senate Cloture Votes	*977*
Legislative Veto Opinions	*981*

Senate Membership in the 97th Congress

Lineup as of Jan. 3, 1981: Republicans 53, Democrats 47*

ALABAMA
Howell Heflin (D)
Jeremiah Denton (R)

ALASKA
Frank H. Murkowski (R)
Ted Stevens (R)

ARIZONA
Dennis DeConcini (D)
Barry Goldwater (R)

ARKANSAS
Dale Bumpers (D)
David Pryor (D)

CALIFORNIA
Alan Cranston (D)
S. I. "Sam" Hayakawa (R)

COLORADO
Gary Hart (D)
William L. Armstrong (R)

CONNECTICUT
Christopher J. Dodd (D)
Lowell P. Weicker Jr. (R)

DELAWARE
Joseph R. Biden Jr. (D)
William V. Roth Jr. (R)

FLORIDA
Lawton Chiles (D)
Paula Hawkins (R)

GEORGIA
Sam Nunn (D)
Mack Mattingly (R)

HAWAII
Daniel K. Inouye (D)
Spark M. Matsunaga (D)

IDAHO
James A. McClure (R)
Steven D. Symms (R)

ILLINOIS
Alan J. Dixon (D)
Charles H. Percy (R)

INDIANA
Richard G. Lugar (R)
Dan Quayle (R)

IOWA
Charles E. Grassley (R)
Roger W. Jepsen (R)

KANSAS
Robert Dole (R)
Nancy Landon Kassebaum (R)

KENTUCKY
Wendell H. Ford (D)
Walter "Dee" Huddleston (D)

LOUISIANA
J. Bennett Johnston (D)
Russell B. Long (D)

MAINE
George J. Mitchell (D)
William S. Cohen (R)

MARYLAND
Paul S. Sarbanes (D)
Charles McC. Mathias Jr. (R)

MASSACHUSETTS
Edward M. Kennedy (D)
Paul E. Tsongas (D)

MICHIGAN
Carl Levin (D)
Donald W. Riegle Jr. (D)

MINNESOTA
Rudy Boschwitz (R)
David Durenberger (R)

MISSISSIPPI
John C. Stennis (D)
Thad Cochran (R)

MISSOURI
Thomas F. Eagleton (D)
John C. Danforth (R)

MONTANA
Max Baucus (D)
John Melcher (D)

NEBRASKA
J. James Exon (D)
Edward Zorinsky (D)

NEVADA
Howard W. Cannon (D)
Paul Laxalt (R)

NEW HAMPSHIRE
Gordon J. Humphrey (R)
Warren Rudman (R)

NEW JERSEY
Bill Bradley (D)
Harrison A. Williams Jr. (D)
(resigned March 11, 1982)
Nicholas F. Brady (R)
*(sworn in April 20, 1982;
resigned Dec. 27, 1982)*
Frank Lautenberg (D)
(sworn in Dec. 27, 1982)

NEW MEXICO
Pete V. Domenici (R)
Harrison "Jack" Schmitt (R)

NEW YORK
Daniel Patrick Moynihan (D)
Alfonse M. D'Amato (R)

NORTH CAROLINA
John P. East (R)
Jesse Helms (R)

NORTH DAKOTA
Quentin N. Burdick (D)
Mark Andrews (R)

OHIO
John Glenn (D)
Howard M. Metzenbaum (D)

OKLAHOMA
David L. Boren (D)
Don Nickles (R)

OREGON
Mark O. Hatfield (R)
Bob Packwood (R)

PENNSYLVANIA
John Heinz (R)
Arlen Specter (R)

RHODE ISLAND
Claiborne Pell (D)
John H. Chafee (R)

SOUTH CAROLINA
Ernest F. Hollings (D)
Strom Thurmond (R)

SOUTH DAKOTA
James Abdnor (R)
Larry Pressler (R)

TENNESSEE
Jim Sasser (D)
Howard H. Baker Jr. (R)

TEXAS
Lloyd Bentsen (D)
John Tower (R)

UTAH
Jake Garn (R)
Orrin G. Hatch (R)

VERMONT
Patrick J. Leahy (D)
Robert T. Stafford (R)

VIRGINIA
Harry F. Byrd Jr. (I)
John W. Warner (R)

WASHINGTON
Henry M. Jackson (D)
Slade Gorton (R)

WEST VIRGINIA
Robert C. Byrd (D)
Jennings Randolph (D)

WISCONSIN
William Proxmire (D)
Robert W. Kasten Jr. (R)

WYOMING
Alan K. Simpson (R)
Malcolm Wallop (R)

* Includes Byrd, Va., elected as an independent.

Appendix

House Membership in the 97th Congress

Lineup as of Jan. 3, 1981: Republicans 192, Democrats 243*

ALABAMA
1. Jack Edwards (R)
2. William L. Dickinson (R)
3. Bill Nichols (D)
4. Tom Bevill (D)
5. Ronnie G. Flippo (D)
6. Albert Lee Smith Jr. (R)
7. Richard C. Shelby (D)

ALASKA
AL Don Young (R)

ARIZONA
1. John J. Rhodes (R)
2. Morris K. Udall (D)
3. Bob Stump (D)
4. Eldon Rudd (R)

ARKANSAS
1. Bill Alexander (D)
2. Ed Bethune (R)
3. John Paul Hammerschmidt (R)
4. Beryl Anthony Jr. (D)

CALIFORNIA
1. Eugene A. Chappie (R)
2. Don H. Clausen (R)
3. Robert T. Matsui (D)
4. Vic Fazio (D)
5. John L. Burton (D)
6. Phillip Burton (D)
7. George Miller (D)
8. Ronald V. Dellums (D)
9. Fortney H. "Pete" Stark (D)
10. Don Edwards (D)
11. Tom Lantos (D)
12. Paul N. McCloskey Jr. (R)
13. Norman Y. Mineta (D)
14. Norman D. Shumway (R)
15. Tony Coelho (D)
16. Leon E. Panetta (D)
17. Charles "Chip" Pashayan Jr. (R)
18. William M. Thomas (R)
19. Robert J. Lagomarsino (R)
20. Barry M. Goldwater Jr. (R)
21. Bobbi Fiedler (R)
22. Carlos J. Moorhead (R)
23. Anthony C. Beilenson (D)
24. Henry A. Waxman (D)
25. Edward R. Roybal (D)
26. John H. Rousselot (R)
27. Robert K. Dornan (R)
28. Julian C. Dixon (D)
29. Augustus F. Hawkins (D)
30. George E. Danielson (D)
    (resigned March 9, 1982)
    Matthew G. Martinez (D)
    (sworn in July 15, 1982)
31. Mervyn M. Dymally (D)
32. Glenn M. Anderson (D)
33. Wayne Grisham (R)
34. Dan Lungren (R)
35. David Dreier (R)
36. George E. Brown Jr. (D)
37. Jerry Lewis (R)
38. Jerry M. Patterson (D)
39. William E. Dannemeyer (R)
40. Robert E. Badham (R)
41. Bill Lowery (R)
42. Duncan L. Hunter (R)
43. Clair W. Burgener (R)

COLORADO
1. Patricia Schroeder (D)
2. Timothy E. Wirth (D)
3. Ray Kogovsek (D)
4. Hank Brown (R)
5. Ken Kramer (R)

CONNECTICUT
1. William R. Cotter (D)
    (died Sept. 8, 1981)
    Barbara B. Kennelly (D)
    (sworn in Jan. 25, 1982)
2. Samuel Gejdenson (D)
3. Lawrence J. DeNardis (R)
4. Stewart B. McKinney (R)
5. William R. Ratchford (D)
6. Toby Moffett (D)

DELAWARE
AL Thomas B. Evans Jr. (R)

FLORIDA
1. Earl Hutto (D)
2. Don Fuqua (D)
3. Charles E. Bennett (D)
4. Bill Chappell Jr. (D)
5. Bill McCollum (R)
6. C. W. Bill Young (R)
7. Sam Gibbons (D)
8. Andy Ireland (D)
9. Bill Nelson (D)
10. L. A. "Skip" Bafalis (R)
11. Dan Mica (D)
12. Clay Shaw (R)
13. William Lehman (D)
14. Claude Pepper (D)
15. Dante B. Fascell (D)

GEORGIA
1. Bo Ginn (D)
2. Charles F. Hatcher (D)
3. Jack Brinkley (D)
4. Elliott H. Levitas (D)
5. Wyche Fowler Jr. (D)
6. Newt Gingrich (R)
7. Larry P. McDonald (D)
8. Billy Lee Evans (D)
9. Ed Jenkins (D)
10. Doug Barnard (D)

HAWAII
1. Cecil Heftel (D)
2. Daniel K. Akaka (D)

IDAHO
1. Larry Craig (R)
2. George Hansen (R)

ILLINOIS
1. Harold Washington (D)
2. Gus Savage (D)
3. Marty Russo (D)
4. Edward J. Derwinski (R)
5. John G. Fary (D)
6. Henry J. Hyde (R)
7. Cardiss Collins (D)
8. Dan Rostenkowski (D)
9. Sidney R. Yates (D)
10. John E. Porter (R)
11. Frank Annunzio (D)
12. Philip M. Crane (R)
13. Robert McClory (R)
14. John N. Erlenborn (R)
15. Tom Corcoran (R)
16. Lynn M. Martin (R)
17. George M. O'Brien (R)
18. Robert H. Michel (R)
19. Tom Railsback (R)
20. Paul Findley (R)
21. Edward R. Madigan (R)
22. Daniel B. Crane (R)
23. Melvin Price (D)
24. Paul Simon (D)

INDIANA
1. Adam Benjamin Jr. (D)
    (died Sept. 7, 1982)
    Katie Hall (D)
    (sworn in Nov. 29, 1982)
2. Floyd Fithian (D)
3. John P. Hiler (R)
4. Daniel R. Coats (R)
5. Elwood Hillis (R)
6. David W. Evans (D)
7. John T. Myers (R)
8. H. Joel Deckard (R)
9. Lee H. Hamilton (D)
10. Phil Sharp (D)
11. Andy Jacobs Jr. (D)

IOWA
1. Jim Leach (R)
2. Tom Tauke (R)
3. Cooper Evans (R)
4. Neal Smith (D)
5. Tom Harkin (D)
6. Berkley Bedell (D)

KANSAS
1. Pat Roberts (R)
2. Jim Jeffries (R)
3. Larry Winn Jr. (R)
4. Dan Glickman (D)
5. Bob Whittaker (R)

KENTUCKY
1. Carroll Hubbard Jr. (D)
2. William H. Natcher (D)
3. Romano L. Mazzoli (D)
4. Gene Snyder (R)
5. Harold Rogers (R)
6. Larry J. Hopkins (R)
7. Carl D. Perkins (D)

LOUISIANA
1. Robert L. Livingston (R)
2. Lindy Boggs (D)
3. W. J. "Billy" Tauzin (D)
4. Buddy Roemer (D)
5. Jerry Huckaby (D)
6. W. Henson Moore (R)
7. John B. Breaux (D)
8. Gillis W. Long (D)

MAINE
1. David F. Emery (R)
2. Olympia J. Snowe (R)

MARYLAND
1. Roy Dyson (D)
2. Clarence D. Long (D)
3. Barbara A. Mikulski (D)
4. Marjorie S. Holt (R)
5. Gladys Noon Spellman (D)
    (seat declared vacant Feb. 24, 1981)
    Steny Hoyer (D)
    (sworn in June 3, 1981)
6. Beverly B. Byron (D)
7. Parren J. Mitchell (D)
8. Michael D. Barnes (D)

MASSACHUSETTS
1. Silvio O. Conte (R)
2. Edward P. Boland (D)
3. Joseph D. Early (D)
4. Barney Frank (D)
5. James M. Shannon (D)
6. Nicholas Mavroules (D)
7. Edward J. Markey (D)
8. Thomas P. O'Neill Jr. (D)
9. Joe Moakley (D)
10. Margaret M. Heckler (R)
11. Brian J. Donnelly (D)
12. Gerry E. Studds (D)

MICHIGAN
1. John Conyers Jr. (D)
2. Carl D. Pursell (R)
3. Howard Wolpe (D)
4. David A. Stockman (R)
    (resigned Jan. 27, 1981)
    Mark Siljander (R)
    (sworn in April 28, 1981)
5. Harold S. Sawyer (R)
6. Jim Dunn (R)
7. Dale E. Kildee (D)
8. Bob Traxler (D)
9. Guy Vander Jagt (R)
10. Don Albosta (D)
11. Robert W. Davis (R)
12. David E. Bonior (D)
13. George W. Crockett Jr. (D)
14. Dennis M. Hertel (D)
15. William D. Ford (D)
16. John D. Dingell (D)
17. William M. Brodhead (D)
18. James J. Blanchard (D)
19. William S. Broomfield (R)

MINNESOTA
1. Arlen Erdahl (R)
2. Tom Hagedorn (R)
3. Bill Frenzel (R)
4. Bruce F. Vento (D)
5. Martin Olav Sabo (D)
6. Vin Weber (R)
7. Arlan Stangeland (R)
8. James L. Oberstar (D)

MISSISSIPPI
1. Jamie L. Whitten (D)
2. David R. Bowen (D)
3. G. V. "Sonny" Montgomery (D)
4. Jon C. Hinson (R)
    (resigned April 13, 1981)
    Wayne Dowdy (D)
    (sworn in July 9, 1981)
5. Trent Lott (R)

MISSOURI
1. William Clay (D)

2. Robert A. Young (D)
3. Richard A. Gephardt (D)
4. Ike Skelton (D)
5. Richard Bolling (D)
6. E. Thomas Coleman (R)
7. Gene Taylor (R)
8. Wendell Bailey (R)
9. Harold L. Volkmer (D)
10. Bill Emerson (R)

MONTANA
1. Pat Williams (D)
2. Ron Marlenee (R)

NEBRASKA
1. Douglas K. Bereuter (R)
2. Hal Daub (R)
3. Virginia Smith (R)

NEVADA
AL Jim Santini (D)

NEW HAMPSHIRE
1. Norman E. D'Amours (D)
2. Judd Gregg (R)

NEW JERSEY
1. James J. Florio (D)
2. William J. Hughes (D)
3. James J. Howard (D)
4. Christopher H. Smith (R)
5. Millicent Fenwick (R)
6. Edwin B. Forsythe (R)
7. Marge Roukema (R)
8. Robert A. Roe (D)
9. Harold C. Hollenbeck (R)
10. Peter W. Rodino Jr. (D)
11. Joseph G. Minish (D)
12. Matthew J. Rinaldo (R)
13. Jim Courter (R)
14. Frank J. Guarini (D)
15. Bernard J. Dwyer (D)

NEW MEXICO
1. Manuel Lujan Jr. (R)
2. Joe Skeen (R)

NEW YORK
1. William Carney (R)
2. Thomas J. Downey (D)
3. Gregory W. Carman (R)
4. Norman F. Lent (R)
5. Raymond J. McGrath (R)
6. John LeBoutillier (R)
7. Joseph P. Addabbo (D)
8. Benjamin S. Rosenthal (D)
9. Geraldine A. Ferraro (D)
10. Mario Biaggi (D)
11. James H. Scheuer (D)
12. Shirley Chisholm (D)
13. Stephen J. Solarz (D)
14. Fred Richmond (D)
    (resigned Aug. 25, 1982)
15. Leo C. Zeferetti (D)
16. Charles E. Schumer (D)
17. Guy V. Molinari (R)
18. S. William Green (R)
19. Charles B. Rangel (D)
20. Ted Weiss (D)
21. Robert Garcia (D)

22. Jonathan B. Bingham (D)
23. Peter A. Peyser (D)
24. Richard L. Ottinger (D)
25. Hamilton Fish Jr. (R)
26. Benjamin A. Gilman (R)
27. Matthew F. McHugh (D)
28. Samuel S. Stratton (D)
29. Gerald B. Solomon (R)
30. David O'B. Martin (R)
31. Donald J. Mitchell (R)
32. George Wortley (R)
33. Gary A. Lee (R)
34. Frank Horton (R)
35. Barber B. Conable Jr. (R)
36. John J. LaFalce (D)
37. Henry J. Nowak (D)
38. Jack F. Kemp (R)
39. Stanley N. Lundine (D)

NORTH CAROLINA
1. Walter B. Jones (D)
2. L. H. Fountain (D)
3. Charles Whitley (D)
4. Ike F. Andrews (D)
5. Stephen L. Neal (D)
6. Eugene Johnston (R)
7. Charlie Rose (D)
8. W. G. "Bill" Hefner (D)
9. James G. Martin (R)
10. James T. Broyhill (R)
11. William M. Hendon (R)

NORTH DAKOTA
AL Byron L. Dorgan (D)

OHIO
1. Bill Gradison (R)
2. Thomas A. Luken (D)
3. Tony P. Hall (D)
4. Tennyson Guyer (R)
   (died April 12, 1981)
   Michael G. Oxley (R)
   (sworn in July 21, 1981)
5. Delbert L. Latta (R)
6. Bob McEwen (R)
7. Clarence J. Brown (R)
8. Thomas N. Kindness (R)
9. Ed Weber (R)
10. Clarence E. Miller (R)
11. J. William Stanton (R)
12. Robert N. Shamansky (D)
13. Don J. Pease (D)
14. John F. Seiberling (D)
15. Chalmers P. Wylie (R)
16. Ralph S. Regula (R)
17. John M. Ashbrook (R)
    (died April 24, 1982)
    Jean S. Ashbrook (R)
    (sworn in July 12, 1982)
18. Douglas Applegate (D)
19. Lyle Williams (R)
20. Mary Rose Oakar (D)
21. Louis Stokes (D)
22. Dennis E. Eckart (D)
23. Ronald M. Mottl (D)

OKLAHOMA
1. James R. Jones (D)
2. Mike Synar (D)
3. Wes Watkins (D)
4. Dave McCurdy (D)

5. Mickey Edwards (R)
6. Glenn English (D)

OREGON
1. Les AuCoin (D)
2. Denny Smith (R)
3. Ron Wyden (D)
4. James Weaver (D)

PENNSYLVANIA
1. Thomas M. Foglietta (I)
2. William H. Gray III (D)
3. Raymond F. Lederer (D)
   (resigned May 5, 1981)
   Joseph F. Smith (D)
   (sworn in July 28, 1981)
4. Charles F. Dougherty (R)
5. Richard T. Schulze (R)
6. Gus Yatron (D)
7. Robert W. Edgar (D)
8. James K. Coyne (R)
9. Bud Shuster (R) ·
10. Joseph M. McDade (R)
11. James L. Nelligan (R)
12. John P. Murtha (D)
13. Lawrence Coughlin (R)
14. William J. Coyne (D)
15. Don Ritter (R)
16. Robert S. Walker (R)
17. Allen E. Ertel (D)
18. Doug Walgren (D)
19. Bill Goodling (R)
20. Joseph M. Gaydos (D)
21. Don Bailey (D)
22. Austin J. Murphy (D)
23. William F. Clinger Jr. (R)
24. Marc L. Marks (R)
25. Eugene V. Atkinson (D)
    *(switched to Republican
    Party Oct. 14, 1981)*

RHODE ISLAND
1. Fernand J. St Germain (D)
2. Claudine Schneider (R)

SOUTH CAROLINA
1. Thomas F. Hartnett (R)
2. Floyd Spence (R)
3. Butler Derrick (D)
4. Carroll A. Campbell Jr. (R)
5. Ken Holland (D)
6. John L. Napier (R)

SOUTH DAKOTA
1. Thomas A. Daschle (D)
2. Clint Roberts (R)

TENNESSEE
1. James H. Quillen (R)
2. John J. Duncan (R)
3. Marilyn Lloyd Bouquard (D) †
4. Albert Gore Jr. (D)
5. Bill Boner (D)
6. Robin L. Beard Jr. (R)
7. Ed Jones (D)
8. Harold E. Ford (D)

TEXAS
1. Sam B. Hall Jr. (D)
2. Charles Wilson (D)

3. James M. Collins (R)
4. Ralph M. Hall (D)
5. Jim Mattox (D)
6. Phil Gramm (D)
7. Bill Archer (R)
8. Jack Fields (R)
9. Jack Brooks (D)
10. J. J. Pickle (D)
11. Marvin Leath (D)
12. Jim Wright (D)
13. Jack Hightower (D)
14. William N. Patman (D)
15. E. "Kika" de la Garza (D)
16. Richard C. White (D)
17. Charles W. Stenholm (D)
18. Mickey Leland (D)
19. Kent Hance (D)
20. Henry B. Gonzalez (D)
21. Tom Loeffler (R)
22. Ron Paul (R)
23. Abraham Kazen Jr. (D)
24. Martin Frost (D)

UTAH
1. James V. Hansen (R)
2. Dan Marriott (R)

VERMONT
AL James M. Jeffords (R)

VIRGINIA
1. Paul S. Trible Jr. (R)
2. G. William Whitehurst (R)
3. Thomas J. Bliley Jr. (R)
4. Robert W. Daniel Jr. (R)
5. Dan Daniel (D)
6. M. Caldwell Butler (R)
7. J. Kenneth Robinson (R)
8. Stanford E. Parris (R)
9. William C. Wampler (R)
10. Frank R. Wolf (R)

WASHINGTON
1. Joel Pritchard (R)
2. Al Swift (D)
3. Don Bonker (D)
4. Sid Morrison (R)
5. Thomas S. Foley (D)
6. Norman D. Dicks (D)
7. Mike Lowry (D)

WEST VIRGINIA
1. Robert H. Mollohan (D)
2. Cleve Benedict (R)
3. Mick Staton (R)
4. Nick J. Rahall (D)

WISCONSIN
1. Les Aspin (D)
2. Robert W. Kastenmeier (D)
3. Steven Gunderson (R)
4. Clement J. Zablocki (D)
5. Henry S. Reuss (D)
6. Thomas E. Petri (R)
7. David R. Obey (D)
8. Toby Roth (R)
9. F. James Sensenbrenner (R)

WYOMING
AL Richard B. Cheney (R)

* Includes Foglietta, Pa., elected as an independent.
† Also known as Marilyn Lloyd.

Membership Changes, 97th and 98th Congresses

97th Congress

Senate

Party	Member	Died	Resigned	Successor	Party	Appointed	Sworn In
D	Harrison A. Williams Jr., N.J.		3/11/82	Nicholas F. Brady	R	4/12/82	4/20/82
R	Nicholas F. Brady, N.J.		12/27/82	Frank Lautenberg	D	12/27/82	12/27/82

House

Party	Member	Died	Resigned	Successor	Party	Elected	Sworn In
R	David A. Stockman, Mich.		1/27/81	Mark Siljander	R	4/21/81	4/28/81
D	Gladys Noon Spellman, Md.		2/24/81 *	Steny Hoyer	D	5/19/81	6/3/81
R	Tennyson Guyer, Ohio	4/12/81		Michael G. Oxley	R	6/25/81	7/21/81
R	Jon C. Hinson, Miss.		4/13/81	Wayne Dowdy	D	7/7/81	7/9/81
D	Raymond F. Lederer, Pa.		5/5/81	Joseph F. Smith	D	7/21/81	7/28/81
D	William R. Cotter, Conn.	9/8/81		Barbara B. Kennelly	D	1/12/82	1/25/82
D	Eugene V. Atkinson, Pa.			Atkinson switched to the Republican Party on Oct. 14, 1981.			
D	George E. Danielson, Calif.		3/9/82	Matthew G. Martinez	D	7/13/82	7/15/82
R	John M. Ashbrook, Ohio	4/24/82		Jean S. Ashbrook	R	6/29/82	7/12/82
D	Fred Richmond, N.Y.		8/25/82				
D	Adam Benjamin Jr., Ind.	9/7/82		Katie Hall	D	11/2/82	11/29/82

98th Congress

Senate

Party	Member	Died	Resigned	Successor	Party	Appointed	Sworn In
D	Henry M. Jackson, Wash.	9/1/83		Daniel J. Evans	R	9/8/83 †	9/12/83

House

Party	Member	Died	Resigned	Successor	Party	Elected	Sworn In
R	Jack Swigert, Colo.	12/27/82		Daniel L. Schaefer	R	3/29/83	4/7/83
D	Benjamin S. Rosenthal, N.Y.	1/4/83		Gary L. Ackerman	D	3/1/83	3/2/83
D	Phil Gramm, Texas		1/5/83	Phil Gramm	R	2/12/83	2/22/83
D	Phillip Burton, Calif.	4/10/83		Sala Burton	D	6/21/83	6/28/83
D	Harold Washington, Ill.		4/30/83	Charles A. Hayes	D	8/23/83	9/12/83
D	Larry P. McDonald, Ga.	9/1/83		George W. "Buddy" Darden	D	11/8/83	11/10/83
D	Clement J. Zablocki, Wis.	12/3/83		Gerald D. Kleczka	D	4/3/84	4/10/84
R	Edwin B. Forsythe, N.J.	3/29/84		H. James Saxton	R	11/6/84	
D	Andy Ireland, Fla.			Ireland switched to the Republican Party on July 5, 1984.			
D	Carl D. Perkins, Ky.	8/3/84		Carl C. "Chris" Perkins	D	11/6/84	

* Spellman suffered cardiac arrest four days before the November general election and remained in a trance-like state of consciousness from that time. Although she was elected to the 97th Congress, she was never sworn in as a member. On Feb. 24, 1981, the House voted to declare her seat vacant.

† Evans subsequently was elected to fill the remaining five years of the term expiring Jan. 3, 1989.

Senate Membership in the 98th Congress

Lineup as of Jan. 3, 1983: Republicans 54, Democrats 46

ALABAMA
Howell Heflin (D)
Jeremiah Denton (R)

ALASKA
Frank H. Murkowski (R)
Ted Stevens (R)

ARIZONA
Dennis DeConcini (D)
Barry Goldwater (R)

ARKANSAS
Dale Bumpers (D)
David Pryor (D)

CALIFORNIA
Alan Cranston (D)
Pete Wilson (R)

COLORADO
Gary Hart (D)
William L. Armstrong (R)

CONNECTICUT
Christopher J. Dodd (D)
Lowell P. Weicker Jr. (R)

DELAWARE
Joseph R. Biden Jr. (D)
William V. Roth Jr. (R)

FLORIDA
Lawton Chiles (D)
Paula Hawkins (R)

GEORGIA
Sam Nunn (D)
Mack Mattingly (R)

HAWAII
Daniel K. Inouye (D)
Spark M. Matsunaga (D)

IDAHO
James A. McClure (R)
Steven D. Symms (R)

ILLINOIS
Alan J. Dixon (D)
Charles H. Percy (R)

INDIANA
Richard G. Lugar (R)
Dan Quayle (R)

IOWA
Charles E. Grassley (R)
Roger W. Jepsen (R)

KANSAS
Robert Dole (R)
Nancy Landon Kassebaum (R)

KENTUCKY
Wendell H. Ford (D)
Walter D. Huddleston (D)

LOUISIANA
J. Bennett Johnston (D)
Russell B. Long (D)

MAINE
George J. Mitchell (D)
William S. Cohen (R)

MARYLAND
Paul S. Sarbanes (D)
Charles McC. Mathias Jr. (R)

MASSACHUSETTS
Edward M. Kennedy (D)
Paul E. Tsongas (D)

MICHIGAN
Carl Levin (D)
Donald W. Riegle Jr. (D)

MINNESOTA
Rudy Boschwitz (R)
David Durenberger (R)

MISSISSIPPI
John C. Stennis (D)
Thad Cochran (R)

MISSOURI
Thomas F. Eagleton (D)
John C. Danforth (R)

MONTANA
Max Baucus (D)
John Melcher (D)

NEBRASKA
J. James Exon (D)
Edward Zorinsky (D)

NEVADA
Chic Hecht (R)
Paul Laxalt (R)

NEW HAMPSHIRE
Gordon J. Humphrey (R)
Warren B. Rudman (R)

NEW JERSEY
Bill Bradley (D)
Frank R. Lautenberg (D)

NEW MEXICO
Jeff Bingaman (D)
Pete V. Domenici (R)

NEW YORK
Daniel Patrick Moynihan (D)
Alfonse M. D'Amato (R)

NORTH CAROLINA
John P. East (R)
Jesse Helms (R)

NORTH DAKOTA
Quentin N. Burdick (D)
Mark Andrews (R)

OHIO
John Glenn (D)
Howard M. Metzenbaum (D)

OKLAHOMA
David L. Boren (D)
Don Nickles (R)

OREGON
Mark O. Hatfield (R)
Bob Packwood (R)

PENNSYLVANIA
John Heinz (R)
Arlen Specter (R)

RHODE ISLAND
Claiborne Pell (D)
John H. Chafee (R)

SOUTH CAROLINA
Ernest F. Hollings (D)
Strom Thurmond (R)

SOUTH DAKOTA
James Abdnor (R)
Larry Pressler (R)

TENNESSEE
Jim Sasser (D)
Howard H. Baker Jr. (R)

TEXAS
Lloyd Bentsen (D)
John Tower (R)

UTAH
Jake Garn (R)
Orrin G. Hatch (R)

VERMONT
Patrick J. Leahy (D)
Robert T. Stafford (R)

VIRGINIA
Paul S. Trible Jr. (R)
John W. Warner (R)

WASHINGTON
Henry M. Jackson (D)
(died Sept. 1, 1983)
Slade Gorton (R)
Daniel J. Evans (R)
(sworn in Sept. 12, 1983)

WEST VIRGINIA
Robert C. Byrd (D)
Jennings Randolph (D)

WISCONSIN
William Proxmire (D)
Robert W. Kasten Jr. (R)

WYOMING
Alan K. Simpson (R)
Malcolm Wallop (R)

Appendix

House Membership in the 98th Congress

Lineup as of Jan. 3, 1983: Republicans 165, Democrats 269, Vacancy 1

ALABAMA
1. Jack Edwards (R)
2. William L. Dickinson (R)
3. Bill Nichols (D)
4. Tom Bevill (D)
5. Ronnie G. Flippo (D)
6. Ben Erdreich (D)
7. Richard C. Shelby (D)

ALASKA
AL Don Young (R)

ARIZONA
1. John McCain (R)
2. Morris K. Udall (D)
3. Bob Stump (R)
4. Eldon Rudd (R)
5. Jim McNulty (D)

ARKANSAS
1. Bill Alexander (D)
2. Ed Bethune (R)
3. John Paul Hammerschmidt (R)
4. Beryl Anthony Jr. (D)

CALIFORNIA
1. Douglas H. Bosco (D)
2. Gene Chappie (R)
3. Robert T. Matsui (D)
4. Vic Fazio (D)
5. Phillip Burton (D)
   (died April 10, 1983)
   Sala Burton (D)
   (sworn in June 28, 1983)
6. Barbara Boxer (D)
7. George Miller (D)
8. Ronald V. Dellums (D)
9. Fortney H. "Pete" Stark (D)
10. Don Edwards (D)
11. Tom Lantos (D)
12. Ed Zschau (R)
13. Norman Y. Mineta (D)
14. Norman D. Shumway (R)
15. Tony Coelho (D)
16. Leon E. Panetta (D)
17. Charles Pashayan Jr. (R)
18. Richard Lehman (D)
19. Robert J. Lagomarsino (R)
20. William M. Thomas (R)
21. Bobbi Fiedler (R)
22. Carlos J. Moorhead (R)
23. Anthony C. Beilenson (D)
24. Henry A. Waxman (D)
25. Edward R. Roybal (D)
26. Howard L. Berman (D)
27. Mel Levine (D)
28. Julian C. Dixon (D)
29. Augustus F. Hawkins (D)
30. Matthew G. Martinez (D)
31. Mervyn M. Dymally (D)
32. Glenn M. Anderson (D)
33. David Dreier (R)
34. Esteban Torres (D)
35. Jerry Lewis (R)
36. George E. Brown Jr. (D)
37. Al McCandless (R)
38. Jerry M. Patterson (D)
39. William E. Dannemeyer (R)
40. Robert E. Badham (R)
41. Bill Lowery (R)
42. Dan Lungren (R)
43. Ron Packard (R)
44. Jim Bates (D)
45. Duncan L. Hunter (R)

COLORADO
1. Patricia Schroeder (D)
2. Timothy E. Wirth (D)
3. Ray Kogovsek (D)
4. Hank Brown (R)
5. Ken Kramer (R)
6. Jack Swigert (R)
   (died Dec. 27, 1982)
   Daniel L. Schaefer (R)
   (sworn in April 7, 1983)

CONNECTICUT
1. Barbara B. Kennelly (D)
2. Sam Gejdenson (D)
3. Bruce A. Morrison (D)
4. Stewart B. McKinney (R)
5. William R. Ratchford (D)
6. Nancy L. Johnson (R)

DELAWARE
AL Thomas R. Carper (D)

FLORIDA
1. Earl Hutto (D)
2. Don Fuqua (D)
3. Charles E. Bennett (D)
4. Bill Chappell Jr. (D)
5. Bill McCollum (R)
6. Kenneth H. MacKay (D)
7. Sam Gibbons (D)
8. C.W. Bill Young (R)
9. Michael Bilirakis (R)
10. Andy Ireland (D)
    (switched to Republican Party July 5, 1984)
11. Bill Nelson (D)
12. Tom Lewis (R)
13. Connie Mack III (R)
14. Daniel A. Mica (D)
15. E. Clay Shaw Jr. (R)
16. Larry Smith (D)
17. William Lehman (D)
18. Claude Pepper (D)
19. Dante B. Fascell (D)

GEORGIA
1. Lindsay Thomas (D)
2. Charles Hatcher (D)
3. Richard Ray (D)
4. Elliott H. Levitas (D)
5. Wyche Fowler Jr. (D)
6. Newt Gingrich (R)
7. Larry P. McDonald (D)
   (died Sept. 1, 1983)
   George W. "Buddy" Darden (D)
   (sworn in Nov. 10, 1983)
8. J. Roy Rowland (D)
9. Ed Jenkins (D)
10. Doug Barnard Jr. (D)

HAWAII
1. Cecil Heftel (D)
2. Daniel K. Akaka (D)

IDAHO
1. Larry E. Craig (R)
2. George Hansen (R)

ILLINOIS
1. Harold Washington (D)
   (resigned April 30, 1983)
   Charles A. Hayes (D)
   (sworn in Sept. 12, 1983)
2. Gus Savage (D)
3. Marty Russo (D)
4. George M. O'Brien (R)
5. William O. Lipinski (D)
6. Henry J. Hyde (R)
7. Cardiss Collins (D)
8. Dan Rostenkowski (D)
9. Sidney R. Yates (D)
10. John Edward Porter (R)
11. Frank Annunzio (D)
12. Philip M. Crane (R)
13. John N. Erlenborn (R)
14. Tom Corcoran (R)
15. Edward R. Madigan (R)
16. Lynn Martin (R)
17. Lane Evans (D)
18. Robert H. Michel (R)
19. Daniel B. Crane (R)
20. Richard J. Durbin (D)
21. Melvin Price (D)
22. Paul Simon (D)

INDIANA
1. Katie Hall (D)
2. Philip R. Sharp (D)
3. John Hiler (R)
4. Dan Coats (R)
5. Elwood Hillis (R)
6. Dan Burton (R)
7. John T. Myers (R)
8. Francis X. McCloskey (D)
9. Lee H. Hamilton (D)
10. Andrew Jacobs Jr. (D)

IOWA
1. Jim Leach (R)
2. Tom Tauke (R)
3. Cooper Evans (R)
4. Neal Smith (D)
5. Tom Harkin (D)
6. Berkley Bedell (D)

KANSAS
1. Pat Roberts (R)
2. Jim Slattery (D)
3. Larry Winn Jr. (R)
4. Dan Glickman (D)
5. Bob Whittaker (R)

KENTUCKY
1. Carroll Hubbard Jr. (D)
2. William H. Natcher (D)
3. Romano L. Mazzoli (D)
4. Gene Snyder (R)
5. Harold Rogers (R)
6. Larry J. Hopkins (R)
7. Carl D. Perkins (D) *
   (died Aug. 3, 1984)

LOUISIANA
1. Bob Livingston (R)
2. Lindy (Mrs. Hale) Boggs (D)
3. W.J. "Billy" Tauzin (D)
4. Buddy Roemer (D)
5. Jerry Huckaby (D)
6. Henson Moore (R)
7. John B. Breaux (D)
8. Gillis W. Long (D)

MAINE
1. John R. McKernan Jr. (R)
2. Olympia J. Snowe (R)

MARYLAND
1. Roy Dyson (D)
2. Clarence D. Long (D)
3. Barbara A. Mikulski (D)
4. Marjorie S. Holt (R)
5. Steny H. Hoyer (D)
6. Beverly B. Byron (D)
7. Parren J. Mitchell (D)
8. Michael D. Barnes (D)

MASSACHUSETTS
1. Silvio O. Conte (R)
2. Edward P. Boland (D)
3. Joseph D. Early (D)
4. Barney Frank (D)
5. James M. Shannon (D)
6. Nicholas Mavroules (D)
7. Edward J. Markey (D)
8. Thomas P. O'Neill Jr. (D)
9. Joe Moakley (D)
10. Gerry E. Studds (D)
11. Brian J. Donnelly (D)

MICHIGAN
1. John Conyers Jr. (D)
2. Carl D. Pursell (R)
3. Howard Wolpe (D)
4. Mark Siljander (R)
5. Harold S. Sawyer (R)
6. Bob Carr (D)
7. Dale E. Kildee (D)
8. Bob Traxler (D)
9. Guy Vander Jagt (R)
10. Don Albosta (D)
11. Robert W. Davis (R)
12. David E. Bonior (D)
13. George W. Crockett Jr. (D)
14. Dennis M. Hertel (D)
15. William D. Ford (D)
16. John D. Dingell (D)
17. Sander Levin (D)
18. William S. Broomfield (R)

MINNESOTA
1. Timothy J. Penny (D)
2. Vin Weber (R)
3. Bill Frenzel (R)
4. Bruce F. Vento (D)
5. Martin Olav Sabo (D)
6. Gerry Sikorski (D)
7. Arlan Stangeland (R)
8. James L. Oberstar (D)

MISSISSIPPI
1. Jamie L. Whitten (D)
2. Webb Franklin (R)
3. G. V. "Sonny" Montgomery (D)
4. Wayne Dowdy (D)
5. Trent Lott (R)

MISSOURI
1. William Clay (D)
2. Robert A. Young (D)

3. Richard A. Gephardt (D)
4. Ike Skelton (D)
5. Alan Wheat (D)
6. E. Thomas Coleman (R)
7. Gene Taylor (R)
8. Bill Emerson (R)
9. Harold L. Volkmer (D)

MONTANA
1. Pat Williams (D)
2. Ron Marlenee (R)

NEBRASKA
1. Douglas K. Bereuter (R)
2. Hal Daub (R)
3. Virginia Smith (R)

NEVADA
1. Harry Reid (D)
2. Barbara Vucanovich (R)

NEW HAMPSHIRE
1. Norman E. D'Amours (D)
2. Judd Gregg (R)

NEW JERSEY
1. James J. Florio (D)
2. William J. Hughes (D)
3. James J. Howard (D)
4. Christopher H. Smith (R)
5. Marge Roukema (R)
6. Bernard J. Dwyer (D)
7. Matthew J. Rinaldo (R)
8. Robert A. Roe (D)
9. Robert G. Torricelli (D)
10. Peter W. Rodino Jr. (D)
11. Joseph G. Minish (D)
12. Jim Courter (R)
13. Edwin B. Forsythe (R) †
    (died March 29, 1984)
14. Frank J. Guarini (D)

NEW MEXICO
1. Manuel Lujan Jr. (R)
2. Joe Skeen (R)
3. Bill Richardson (D)

NEW YORK
1. William Carney (R)
2. Thomas J. Downey (D)
3. Robert J. Mrazek (D)
4. Norman F. Lent (R)
5. Raymond J. McGrath (R)
6. Joseph P. Addabbo (D)
7. Benjamin S. Rosenthal (D)
   (died Jan. 4, 1983)
   Gary L. Ackerman (D)
   (sworn in March 2, 1983)
8. James H. Scheuer (D)
9. Geraldine A. Ferraro (D)
10. Charles E. Schumer (D)
11. Edolphus Towns (D)
12. Major R. Owens (D)
13. Stephen J. Solarz (D)
14. Guy V. Molinari (R)
15. Bill Green (R)
16. Charles B. Rangel (D)
17. Ted Weiss (D)
18. Robert Garcia (D)
19. Mario Biaggi (D)

20. Richard L. Ottinger (D)
21. Hamilton Fish Jr. (R)
22. Benjamin A. Gilman (R)
23. Samuel S. Stratton (D)
24. Gerald B. H. Solomon (R)
25. Sherwood L. Boehlert (R)
26. David O'B. Martin (R)
27. George C. Wortley (R)
28. Matthew F. McHugh (D)
29. Frank Horton (R)
30. Barber B. Conable Jr. (R)
31. Jack F. Kemp (R)
32. John J. LaFalce (D)
33. Henry J. Nowak (D)
34. Stanley N. Lundine (D)

NORTH CAROLINA
1. Walter B. Jones (D)
2. I. T. "Tim" Valentine Jr. (D)
3. Charles Whitley (D)
4. Ike Andrews (D)
5. Stephen L. Neal (D)
6. Charles Robin Britt (D)
7. Charlie Rose (D)
8. W. G. "Bill" Hefner (D)
9. James G. Martin (R)
10. James T. Broyhill (R)
11. James McClure Clarke (D)

NORTH DAKOTA
AL Byron L. Dorgan (D)

OHIO
1. Thomas A. Luken (D)
2. Bill Gradison (R)
3. Tony P. Hall (D)
4. Michael G. Oxley (R)
5. Delbert L. Latta (R)
6. Bob McEwen (R)
7. Michael Dewine (R)
8. Thomas N. Kindness (R)
9. Marcy Kaptur (D)
10. Clarence E. Miller (R)
11. Dennis E. Eckart (D)
12. John R. Kasich (R)
13. Don J. Pease (D)
14. John F. Seiberling (D)
15. Chalmers P. Wylie (R)
16. Ralph Regula (R)
17. Lyle Williams (R)
18. Douglas Applegate (D)
19. Edward F. Feighan (D)
20. Mary Rose Oakar (D)
21. Louis Stokes (D)

OKLAHOMA
1. James R. Jones (D)
2. Mike Synar (D)
3. Wes Watkins (D)
4. Dave McCurdy (D)
5. Mickey Edwards (R)
6. Glenn English (D)

OREGON
1. Les AuCoin (D)
2. Bob Smith (R)
3. Ron Wyden (D)
4. James Weaver (D)
5. Denny Smith (R)

PENNSYLVANIA
1. Thomas M. Foglietta (D)
2. William H. Gray III (D)
3. Robert A. Borski (D)
4. Joseph P. Kolter (D)
5. Richard T. Schulze (R)
6. Gus Yatron (D)
7. Robert W. Edgar (D)
8. Peter H. Kostmayer (D)
9. Bud Shuster (R)
10. Joseph M. McDade (R)
11. Frank Harrison (D)
12. John P. Murtha (D)
13. Lawrence Coughlin (R)
14. William J. Coyne (D)
15. Don Ritter (R)
16. Robert S. Walker (R)
17. George W. Gekas (R)
18. Doug Walgren (D)
19. Bill Goodling (R)
20. Joseph M. Gaydos (D)
21. Thomas J. Ridge (R)
22. Austin J. Murphy (D)
23. William F. Clinger Jr. (R)

RHODE ISLAND
1. Fernand J. St Germain (D)
2. Claudine Schneider (R)

SOUTH CAROLINA
1. Thomas F. Hartnett (R)
2. Floyd Spence (R)
3. Butler Derrick (D)
4. Carroll A. Campbell Jr. (R)
5. John Spratt (D)
6. Robert M. Tallon Jr. (D)

SOUTH DAKOTA
AL Thomas A. Daschle (D)

TENNESSEE
1. James H. Quillen (R)
2. John J. Duncan (R)
3. Marilyn Lloyd (D) ‡
4. Jim Cooper (D)
5. Bill Boner (D)
6. Albert Gore Jr. (D)
7. Don Sundquist (R)
8. Ed Jones (D)
9. Harold E. Ford (D)

TEXAS
1. Sam B. Hall Jr. (D)
2. Charles Wilson (D)
3. Steve Bartlett (R)
4. Ralph M. Hall (D)
5. John Bryant (D)
6. Phil Gramm (D)
   (resigned Jan. 5, 1983)
   Phil Gramm (R)
   (sworn in Feb. 22, 1983)
7. Bill Archer (R)
8. Jack Fields (R)
9. Jack Brooks (D)
10. J. J. Pickle (D)
11. Marvin Leath (D)
12. Jim Wright (D)
13. Jack Hightower (D)

14. Bill Patman (D)
15. E. "Kika" de la Garza (D)
16. Ronald Coleman (D)
17. Charles W. Stenholm (D)
18. Mickey Leland (D)
19. Kent Hance (D)
20. Henry B. Gonzalez (D)
21. Tom Loeffler (R)
22. Ron Paul (R)
23. Abraham Kazen Jr. (D)
24. Martin Frost (D)
25. Mike Andrews (D)
26. Tom Vandergriff (D)
27. Solomon P. Ortiz (D)

UTAH
1. James V. Hansen (R)
2. Dan Marriott (R)
3. Howard C. Nielson (R)

VERMONT
AL James M. Jeffords (R)

VIRGINIA
1. Herbert H. Bateman (R)
2. G. William Whitehurst (R)
3. Thomas J. Bliley Jr. (R)
4. Norman Sisisky (D)
5. Dan Daniel (D)
6. James R. Olin (D)
7. J. Kenneth Robinson (R)
8. Stan Parris (R)
9. Frederick C. Boucher (D)
10. Frank R. Wolf (R)

WASHINGTON
1. Joel Pritchard (R)
2. Al Swift (D)
3. Don Bonker (D)
4. Sid Morrison (R)
5. Thomas S. Foley (D)
6. Norman D. Dicks (D)
7. Mike Lowry (D)
8. Rodney Chandler (R)

WEST VIRGINIA
1. Alan B. Mollohan (D)
2. Harley O. Staggers Jr. (D)
3. Bob Wise (D)
4. Nick J. Rahall II (D)

WISCONSIN
1. Les Aspin (D)
2. Robert W. Kastenmeier (D)
3. Steve Gunderson (R)
4. Clement J. Zablocki (D)
   (died Dec. 3, 1983)
   Gerald D. Kleczka (D)
   (sworn in April 10, 1984)
5. Jim Moody (D)
6. Thomas E. Petri (R)
7. David R. Obey (D)
8. Toby Roth (R)
9. F. James Sensenbrenner Jr. (R)

WYOMING
AL Dick Cheney (R)

* Carl C. Perkins, D, was elected Nov. 6, 1984, to fill Perkins' remaining term and to the 99th Congress. He was sworn in Jan. 3, 1985.
† H. James Saxton, R, was elected Nov. 6, 1984, to fill Forsythe's remaining term and to the 99th Congress. He was sworn in Jan. 3, 1985.
‡ Marilyn Lloyd was known as Marilyn Lloyd Bouquard in the 97th Congress.

Members of Congress: 1981-85

The names in this index include, alphabetically, all senators, representatives, resident commissioners and territorial delegates who served in the 97th and 98th Congresses — from 1981 to 1985.

The material is organized as follows: name; relationship to other members and presidents and vice presidents; party; state (of service); date of birth; date of death (if applicable); congressional service; service as president, vice president, member of the Cabinet or Supreme Court, governor, Speaker of the House, president pro tempore of the Senate and chairman of the Democratic or Republican National Committee. If the member changed parties during his or her congressional service, party designation appearing after the member's name is that which applied at the end of such service and further breakdown is included after dates of congressional service. Party designation is multiple only if the member was elected by two or more parties at the same time. Where service date is left open, member was still serving in the 99th Congress.

Dates of service are inclusive, starting in year of service and ending when service ends. Under the Constitution, terms of service since 1934 have been from Jan. 3 to Jan. 3. In actual practice, members often have been sworn in on other dates at the beginning of a Congress. Exact date is shown (where available) if member began or ended his service in mid-term.

The major sources for the following list were the *Congressional Directory* and Congressional Quarterly's *Almanac, Guide to Congress, Guide to U.S. Elections* and *Weekly Report.*

In the list, D Stands for Democrat; I, Independent; L, Liberal; New Prog., New Progressive; and R, Republican.

A

ABDNOR, James (R S.D.) Feb. 13, 1923-—; House 1973-81; Senate 1981-—.

ACKERMAN, Gary L. (D N.Y.) Nov. 19, 1942-—; House March 2, 1983-—.

ADDABBO, Joseph P. (D N.Y.) March 17, 1925-—; House 1961-—.

AKAKA, Daniel K. (D Hawaii) Sept. 11, 1924-—; House 1977-—.

ALBOSTA, Donald Joseph (D Mich.) Dec. 5, 1925-—; House 1979-85.

ALEXANDER, William Vollie Jr. (D Ark.) Jan. 16, 1934-—; House 1969-—.

ANDERSON, Glenn M. (D Calif.) Feb. 21, 1913-—; House 1969-—.

ANDREWS, Ike Franklin (D N.C.) Sept. 2, 1925-—; House 1973-85.

ANDREWS, Mark (R N.D.) May 19, 1926-—; House Oct. 22, 1963-81; Senate 1981-—.

ANDREWS, Michael Allen (D Texas) Feb. 7, 1944-—; House 1983-—.

ANNUNZIO, Frank (D Ill.) Jan. 12, 1915-—; House 1965-—.

ANTHONY, Beryl Franklin Jr. (D Ark.) Feb. 21, 1938-—; House 1979-—.

APPLEGATE, Douglas (D Ohio) March 27, 1928-—; House 1977-—.

ARCHER, William Reynolds Jr. (R Texas) March 22, 1928-—; House 1971-—.

ARMSTRONG, William Lester (R Colo.) March 16, 1937-—; House 1973-79; Senate 1979-—.

ASHBROOK, Jean S. (widow of John Milan Ashbrook) (R Ohio) Sept. 21, 1934-—; House July 12, 1982-83.

ASHBROOK, John Milan (son of William Albert Ashbrook) (R Ohio) Sept. 21, 1928-April 24, 1982; House 1961-April 24, 1982.

ASPIN, Les (D Wis.) July 21, 1938-—; House 1971-—.

ATKINSON, Eugene Vincent (R Pa.) April 5, 1927-—; House 1979-83 (1979-Oct. 14, 1981 Democrat; Oct. 14, 1981-83 Republican.)

AuCOIN, Les (D Ore.) Oct. 21, 1942-—; House 1975-—.

B

BADHAM, Robert E. (R Calif.) June 9, 1929-—; House 1977-—.

BAFALIS, Louis Arthur (R Fla.) Sept. 28, 1929-—; House 1973-83.

BAILEY, Donald Allen (D Pa.) July 21, 1945-—; House 1979-83.

BAILEY, Wendell (R Mo.) July 31, 1940-—; House 1981-83.

BAKER, Howard Henry Jr. (son of Howard Henry Baker and Irene B. Baker, son-in-law of Everett McKinley Dirksen) (R Tenn.) Nov. 15, 1925-—; Senate 1967-85; Senate majority leader 1981-85.

BARNARD, D. Douglas Jr. (D Ga.) March 20, 1922-—; House 1977-—.

BARNES, Michael Darr (D Md.) Sept. 3, 1943-—; House 1979-—.

BARTLETT, Steve (R Texas) Sept. 19, 1947-—; House 1983-—.

BATEMAN, Herbert H. (R Va.) Aug. 7, 1928-—; House 1983-—.

BATES, Jim (D Calif.) July 21, 1941-—; House 1983-—.

BAUCUS, Max Sieben (D Mont.) Dec. 11, 1941-—; House 1975-Dec. 14, 1978; Senate Dec. 15, 1978-—.

BEARD, Robin Leo Jr. (R Tenn.) Aug. 21, 1939-—; House 1973-83.

BEDELL, Berkley Warren (D Iowa) March 5, 1921-—; House 1975-—.

BEILENSON, Anthony Charles (D Calif.) Oct. 26, 1932-—; House 1977-—.

BENEDICT, Cleve (R W. Va.) March 21, 1935-—; House 1981-83.

BENJAMIN, Adam Jr. (D Ind.) Aug. 6, 1935-Sept. 7, 1982; House 1977-Sept. 7, 1982.

BENNETT, Charles Edward (D Fla.) Dec. 2, 1910-—; House 1949-—.

BENTSEN, Lloyd Millard Jr. (D Texas) Feb. 11, 1921-—; House Dec. 4, 1948-55; Senate 1971-—.

BEREUTER, Douglas K. (R Neb.) Oct. 6, 1939- —; House 1979- —.

BERMAN, Howard L. (D Calif.) April 15, 1941- —; House 1983- —.

BETHUNE, Edwin Ruthvin (R Ark.) Dec. 19, 1934- —; House 1979-85.

BEVILL, Tom (D Ala.) March 27, 1921- —; House 1967- —.

BIAGGI, Mario (D N.Y.) Oct. 26, 1917- —; House 1969- —.

BIDEN, Joseph Robinette Jr. (D Del.) Nov. 20, 1942- —; Senate 1973- —.

BILIRAKIS, Michael (R Fla.) July 16, 1930- —; House 1983- —.

BINGAMAN, Jeff (D N.M.) Oct. 3, 1943- —; Senate 1983- —.

BINGHAM, Jonathan Brewster (son of Hiram Bingham) (D N.Y.) April 24, 1914- —; House 1965-83.

BLANCHARD, James Johnston (D Mich.) Aug. 8, 1942- —; House 1975-83; Gov. 1983- —.

BLILEY, Thomas J. Jr. (R Va.) Jan. 28, 1932- —; House 1981- —.

BOEHLERT, Sherwood L. (D N.Y.) June 28, 1936- —; House 1983- —.

BOGGS, Corinne Claiborne (widow of Thomas Hale Boggs Sr.) (D La.) March 13, 1916- —; House March 20, 1973- —.

BOLAND, Edward Patrick (D Mass.) Oct. 1, 1911- —; House 1953- —.

BOLLING, Richard Walker (D Mo.) May 17, 1916- —; House 1949-83.

BONER, William Hill (D Tenn.) Feb. 14, 1945- —; House 1979- —.

BONIOR, David Edward (D Mich.) June 6, 1945- —; House 1977- —.

BONKER, Don Leroy (D Wash.) March 7, 1937- —; House 1975- —.

BOREN, David Lyle (son of Lyle H. Boren) (D Okla.) April 21, 1941- —; Senate 1979- —; Gov. 1975-79.

BORSKI, Robert Anthony Jr. (D Pa.) Oct. 20, 1948- —; House 1983- —.

BOSCHWITZ, Rudolf Eli (R Minn.) Nov. 7, 1930- —; Senate Dec. 30, 1978- —.

BOSCO, Douglas H. (D Calif.) July 28, 1946- —; House 1983- —.

BOUCHER, Frederick C. (D Va.) Aug. 1, 1946- —; House 1983- —.

BOWEN, David Reece (D Miss.) Oct. 21, 1932- —; House 1973-83.

BOXER, Barbara (D Calif.) Nov. 11, 1940- —; House 1983- —.

BRADLEY, William Warren (D N.J.) July 28, 1943- —; Senate 1979- —.

BRADY, Nicholas (R N.J.) April 11, 1930- —; Senate April 20, 1982-Dec. 27, 1982.

BREAUX, John Berlinger (D La.) March 1, 1944- —; House Sept. 30, 1972- —.

BRINKLEY, Jack Thomas (D Ga.) Dec. 22, 1930- —; House 1967-83.

BRITT, Charles Robin (D N.C.) June 29, 1942- —; House 1983-85.

BRODHEAD, William McNulty (D Mich.) Sept. 12, 1941- —; House 1975-83.

BROOKS, Jack Bascom (D Texas) Dec. 18, 1922- —; House 1953- —.

BROOMFIELD, William S. (R Mich.) April 28, 1922- —; House 1957- —.

BROWN, Clarence J. Jr. (son of Clarence J. Brown) (R Ohio) June 18, 1927- —; House Nov. 2, 1965-83.

BROWN, George E. Jr. (D Calif.) March 6, 1920- —; House 1963-71, 1973- —.

BROWN, Hank (R Colo.) Feb. 12, 1940- —; House 1981- —.

BROYHILL, James T. (R N.C.) Aug. 19, 1927- —; House 1963- —.

BRYANT, John Wiley (D Texas) Feb. 22, 1947- —; House 1983- —.

BUMPERS, Dale (D Ark.) Aug. 12, 1925- —; Senate 1975- —; Gov. 1971-75.

BURDICK, Quentin Northrop (son of Usher Lloyd Burdick, brother-in-law of Robert Woodrow Levering) (D N.D.) June 19, 1908- —; House 1959-Aug. 8, 1960; Senate Aug. 8, 1960- —.

BURGENER, Clair Walter (R Calif.) Dec. 5, 1921- —; House 1973-83.

BURTON, Danny Lee (R Ind.) June 21, 1938- —; House 1983- —.

BURTON, John Lowell (brother of Phillip Burton) (D Calif.) Dec. 15, 1932- —; House June 25, 1974-83.

BURTON, Phillip (brother of John Lowell Burton) (D Calif.) June 1, 1926-April 10, 1983; House Feb. 18, 1964-April 10, 1983.

BURTON, Sala (widow of Phillip Burton) (D Calif.) April 1, 1925- —; House June 28, 1983- —.

BUTLER, Manley Caldwell (R Va.) June 2, 1925- —; House Nov. 7, 1972-83.

BYRD, Harry Flood Jr. (son of Harry Flood Byrd) (I Va.) Dec. 20, 1914- —; Senate Nov. 12, 1965-83; (1965-71 Democrat, 1971-83 Independent).

BYRD, Robert Carlyle (D W.Va.) Jan. 15, 1918- —; House 1953-59; Senate 1959- —; Senate majority leader 1977-81.

BYRON, Beverly Barton Butcher (widow of Goodloe Edgar Bryon) (D Md.) July 26, 1932- —; House 1979- —.

C

CAMPBELL, Carroll Ashmore Jr. (R S.C.) July 24, 1940- —; House 1979- —.

CANNON, Howard Walter (D Nev.) Jan. 26, 1912- —; Senate 1959-83.

CARMAN, Gregory W. (R N.Y.) Jan. 31, 1937- —; House 1981-83.

CARNEY, William (R N.Y.) July 1, 1942- —; House 1979- —.

CARPER, Thomas Richard (D Del.) Jan. 23, 1947- —; House 1983- —.

CARR, Milton Robert (D Mich.) March 27, 1943- —; House 1975-81, 1983- —.

CHAFEE, John Hubbard (R R.I.) Oct. 22, 1922- —; Senate Dec. 29, 1976- —; Gov. 1963-69.

CHANDLER, Rodney (R Wash.) July 13, 1942- —; House 1983- —.

CHAPPELL, William Venroe Jr. (D Fla.) Feb. 3, 1922- —; House 1969- —.

CHAPPIE, Eugene A. (R Calif.) March 21, 1920- —; House 1981- —.

CHENEY, Richard Bruce (R Wyo.) Jan. 30, 1941- —; House 1979- —.

CHILES, Lawton Mainor Jr. (D Fla.) April 3, 1930- —; Senate 1971- —.

CHISHOLM, Shirley Anita (D N.Y.) Nov. 30, 1924- —; House 1969-83.

CLARKE, James McClure (D N.C.) June 12, 1917- —; House 1983-85.

CLAUSEN, Don Holst (R Calif.) April 27, 1923- —; House Jan. 22, 1963-83.

CLAY, William Lacey (D Mo.) April 30, 1931- —; House 1969- —.

CLINGER, William Floyd Jr. (R Pa.) April 4, 1929- —; House 1979- —.

COATS, Daniel R. (R Ind.) May 16, 1943- —; House 1981- —.

COCHRAN, William Thad (R Miss.) Dec. 7, 1937- —; House 1973-Dec. 26, 1978; Senate Dec. 27, 1978- —.

COELHO, Anthony Lee (D Calif.) June 15, 1942- —; House 1979- —.

COHEN, William Sebastian (R Maine) Aug. 28, 1940- —; House 1973-79; Senate 1979- —.

COLEMAN, E. Thomas (R Mo.) May 29, 1943- —; House Nov. 2, 1976- —.

COLEMAN, Ronald D. (D Texas) Nov. 29, 1941- —; House 1983- —.

COLLINS, Cardiss (widow of George Washington Collins) (D Ill.) Sept. 24, 1931- —; House June 5, 1973- —.

COLLINS, James M. (R Texas) April 29, 1916- —; House Aug. 24, 1968-83.

CONABLE, Barber B. Jr. (R N.Y.) Nov. 2, 1922- —; House 1965-85.

CONTE, Silvio Otto (R Mass.) Nov. 9, 1921- —; House 1959- —.

CONYERS, John Jr. (D Mich.) May 16, 1929- —; House 1965- —.

COOPER, James Haynes Shofner (D Tenn.) June 19, 1954- —; House 1983- —.

CORCORAN, Thomas J. (R Ill.) May 23, 1939- —; House 1977-85.

CORRADA del RIO, Baltasar (New Prog. P.R.) April 10, 1935- —; House (Res. Comm.) 1977-85.

COTTER, William Ross (D Conn.) July 18, 1926-Sept. 8, 1981; House 1971-Sept. 8, 1981.

COUGHLIN, Robert Lawrence (nephew of Clarence Dennis Coughlin) (R Pa.) April 11, 1929- —; House 1969- —.

COURTER, James Andrew (R N.J.) Oct. 14, 1941- —; House 1979- —.

COYNE, James K. (R Pa.) Nov. 17, 1946- —; House 1981-83.

COYNE, William J. (D Pa.) Aug. 24, 1936- —; House 1981- —.

CRAIG, Larry E. (R Idaho) July 20, 1945- —; House 1981- —.

CRANE, Daniel Bever (brother of Philip Miller Crane) (R Ill.) Jan. 10, 1936- —; House 1979-85.

CRANE, Philip Miller (brother of Daniel Bever Crane) (R Ill.) Nov. 3, 1930- —; House Nov. 25, 1969- —.

CRANSTON, Alan (D Calif.) June 19, 1914- —; Senate 1969- —.

CROCKETT, George W. Jr. (D Mich.) Aug. 10, 1909- —; House Nov. 12, 1980- —.

D

D'AMATO, Alfonse M. (R N.Y.) Aug. 1, 1937- —; Senate 1981- —.

D'AMOURS, Norman Edward (D N.H.) Oct. 14, 1937- —; House 1975-85.

DANFORTH, John Claggett (R Mo.) Sept. 5, 1936- —; Senate Dec. 27, 1976- —.

DANIEL, Robert Williams Jr. (R Va.) March 17, 1936- —; House 1973-83.

DANIEL, W. C. (Dan) (D Va.) May 12, 1914- —; House 1969- —.

DANIELSON, George Elmore (D Calif.) Feb. 20, 1915- —; House 1971-March 9, 1982.

DANNEMEYER, William Edward (R Calif.) Sept. 22, 1929- —; House 1979- —.

DARDEN, George (Buddy) (D Ga.) Nov. 22, 1943- —; House Nov. 10, 1983- —.

DASCHLE, Thomas Andrew (D S.D.) Dec. 9, 1947- —; House 1979- —.

DAUB, Harold J. Jr. (R Neb.) April 23, 1941- —; House 1981- —.

DAVIS, Robert William (R Mich.) July 31, 1932- —; House 1979- —.

DECKARD, H. Joel (R Ind.) March 7, 1942- —; House 1979-83.

DeCONCINI, Dennis (D Ariz.) May 8, 1937- —; Senate 1977- —.

DE LA GARZA II, Eligio (D Texas) Sept. 22, 1927- —; House 1965- —.

DELLUMS, Ronald V. (D Calif.) Nov. 24, 1935- —; House 1971- —.

DE LUGO, Ron (D V.I.) Aug. 2, 1930- —; House (Terr. Del.) 1973-79, 1981- —.

DeNARDIS, Lawrence J. (R Conn.) March 18, 1938- —; House 1981-83.

DENTON, Jeremiah (R Ala.) July 15, 1924- —; Senate 1981- —.

DERRICK, Butler Carson Jr. (D S.C.) Sept. 30, 1936- —; House 1975- —.

DERWINSKI, Edward Joseph (R Ill.) Sept. 15, 1926- —; House 1959-83.

DeWINE, Michael (R Ohio) Jan. 5, 1947- —; House 1983- —.

DICKINSON, William Louis (R Ala.) June 5, 1925- —; House 1965- —.

DICKS, Norman Devalois (D Wash.) Dec. 16, 1940- —; House 1977- —.

DINGELL, John David Jr. (son of John David Dingell) (D Mich.) July 8, 1926- —; House Dec. 13, 1955- —.

DIXON, Alan J. (D Ill.) July 7, 1927- —; Senate 1981- —.

DIXON, Julian Carey (D Calif.) Aug. 8, 1934- —; House 1979- —.

DODD, Christopher John (son of Thomas Joseph Dodd) (D Conn.) May 27, 1944- —; House 1975-81; Senate 1981- —.

DOLE, Robert J. (R Kan.) July 22, 1923- —; House 1961-69; Senate 1969- —; Chrmn. Rep. Nat. Comm. 1971-73; Senate majority leader 1985- —.

DOMENICI, Pete Vichi (R N.M.) May 7, 1932- —; Senate 1973- —.

DONNELLY, Brian Joseph (D Mass.) March 2, 1947- —; House 1979- —.

DORGAN, Byron L. (D N.D.) May 14, 1942- —; House 1981- —.

DORNAN, Robert Kenneth (R Calif.) April 3, 1933- —; House 1977-83, 1985- —.

DOUGHERTY, Charles Francis (R Pa.) June 26, 1937- —; House 1979-83.

DOWDY, Wayne (D Miss.) July 27, 1943- —; House July 9, 1981- —.

DOWNEY, Thomas Joseph (D N.Y.) Jan. 28, 1949- —; House 1975- —.

DREIER, David T. (R Calif.) July 5, 1952- —; House 1981- —.

DUNCAN, John J. (R Tenn.) March 24, 1919- —; House 1965- —.

DUNN, Jim (R Mich.) July 21, 1943- —; House 1981-83.

DURBIN, Richard Joseph (D Ill.) Nov. 21, 1944- —; House 1983- —.

DURENBERGER, David Ferdinand (R Minn.) Aug. 19, 1934- —; Senate Nov. 8, 1978- —.

DWYER, Bernard J. (D N.J.) Jan. 24, 1921- —; House 1981- —.

DYMALLY, Mervyn M. (D Calif.) May 12, 1926- —; House 1981- —.

DYSON, Roy (D Md.) Nov. 15, 1948- —; House 1981- —.

E

EAGLETON, Thomas F. (D Mo.) Sept. 4, 1929- —; Senate Dec. 28, 1968- —.

EARLY, Joseph Daniel (D Mass.) Jan. 31, 1933- —; House 1975- —.

EAST, John P. (R N.C.) May 5, 1931- —; Senate 1981- —.

ECKART, Dennis E. (D Ohio) April 6, 1950- —; House 1981- —.

EDGAR, Robert William (D Pa.) May 29, 1943- —; House 1975- —.

EDWARDS, Don (D Calif.) Jan. 6, 1915- —; House 1963- —.

EDWARDS, Jack (William Jackson) (R Ala.) Sept. 20, 1928- —; House 1965-85.

EDWARDS, Marvin H. (R Okla.) July 12, 1937- —; House 1977- —.

EMERSON, William (R Mo.) Jan. 1, 1938- —; House 1981- —.

EMERY, David Farnham (R Maine) Sept. 1, 1948- —; House 1975-83.

ENGLISH, Glenn Lee Jr. (D Okla.) Nov. 30, 1940- —; House 1975- —.

ERDAHL, Arlen Ingolf (R Minn.) Feb 27, 1931- —; House 1979-83.

ERDREICH, Ben (D Ala.) Dec. 9, 1938- —; House 1983- —.

ERLENBORN, John Neal (R Ill.) Feb. 8, 1927- —; House 1965-85.

ERTEL, Allen Edward (D Pa.) Nov. 7, 1936- —; House 1977-83.

EVANS, Billy Lee (D Ga.) Nov. 10, 1941- —; House 1977-83.

EVANS, Cooper (R Iowa) May 26, 1924- —; House 1981- —.

EVANS, Daniel J. (R Wash.) Oct. 16, 1925- —; Senate Sept. 12, 1983- —.

EVANS, David Walter (D Ind.) Aug. 17, 1946- —; House 1975-83.

EVANS, Lane (D Ill.) Aug. 4, 1951- —; House 1983- —.

EVANS, Thomas Beverley Jr. (R Del.) Nov. 5, 1931- —; House 1977-83; Co-Chrmn. Rep. Nat. Comm. 1971-73.

EXON, John James (D Neb.) Aug. 9, 1921- —; Senate 1979- —; Gov. 1971-79.

Appendix

F

FARY, John George (D Ill.) April 11, 1911-June 7, 1984; House July 8, 1975-83.

FASCELL, Dante Bruno (D Fla.) March 9, 1917- –; House 1955- –.

FAUNTROY, Walter Edward (D D.C.) Feb. 6, 1933- –; House (Delegate) March 23, 1971- –.

FAZIO, Victor Herbert (D Calif.) Oct. 11, 1942- –; House 1979- –.

FEIGHAN, Edward Farrell (nephew of Michael Aloysius Feighan) (D Ohio) Oct. 22, 1947- –; House 1983- –.

FENWICK, Millicent Hammond (R N.J.) Feb. 25, 1910- –; House 1975-83.

FERRARO, Geraldine Anne (D N.Y.) Aug. 26, 1935- –; House 1979-85.

FIEDLER, Bobbi (R Calif.) April 22, 1937- –; House 1981- –.

FIELDS, Jack (R Texas) Feb. 3, 1952- –; House 1981- –.

FINDLEY, Paul (R Ill.) June 23, 1921- –; House 1961-83.

FISH, Hamilton Jr. (son of Hamilton Fish Jr. born in 1888; grandson of Hamilton Fish born in 1849, great-grandson of Hamilton Fish born in 1808) (R N.Y.) June 3, 1926- –; House 1969- –.

FITHIAN, Floyd James (D Ind.) Nov. 3, 1928- –; House 1975-83.

FLIPPO, Ronnie G. (D Ala.) Aug. 15, 1937- –; House 1977- –.

FLORIO, James Joseph (D N.J.) Aug. 29, 1937- –; House 1975- –.

FOGLIETTA, Thomas M. (I Pa.) Dec. 3, 1928- –; House 1981- –.

FOLEY, Thomas Stephen (D Wash.) March 6, 1929- –; House 1965- –.

FORD, Harold Eugene (D Tenn.) May 20, 1945- –; House 1975- –.

FORD, Wendell Hampton (D Ky.) Sept. 8, 1924- –; Senate Dec. 28, 1974- –; Gov. 1971-74.

FORD, William David (D Mich.) Aug. 6, 1927- –; House 1965- –.

FORSYTHE, Edwin Bell (R N.J.) Jan. 17, 1916-March 29, 1984; House Nov. 3, 1970-March 29, 1984.

FOUNTAIN, Lawrence H. (D N.C.) April 23, 1913- –; House 1953-83.

FOWLER, William Wyche Jr. (D Ga.) Oct. 6, 1940- –; House April 6, 1977- –.

FRANK, Barney (D Mass.) March 31, 1940- –; House 1981- –.

FRANKLIN, William Webster (R Miss.) Dec. 13, 1941- –; House 1983- –.

FRENZEL, William E. (R Minn.) July 31, 1928- –; House 1971- –.

FROST, Jonas Martin III (D Texas) Jan. 1, 1942- –; House 1979- –.

FUQUA, Don (D Fla.) Aug. 20, 1933- –; House 1963- –.

G

GARCIA, Robert (D N.Y.) Jan. 9, 1933- –; House Feb. 21, 1978- –.

GARN, Edwin Jacob (R Utah) Oct. 12, 1932- –; Senate Dec. 21, 1974- –.

GAYDOS, Joseph M. (D Pa.) July 3, 1926- –; House Nov. 5, 1968- –.

GEJDENSON, Samuel (D Conn.) May 20, 1948- –; House 1981- –.

GEKAS, George William (R Pa.) April 14, 1930- –; House 1983- –.

GEPHARDT, Richard Andrew (D Mo.) Jan. 31, 1941- –; House 1977- –.

GIBBONS, Sam M. (D Fla.) Jan. 20, 1920- –; House 1963- –.

GILMAN, Benjamin Arthur (R N.Y.) Dec. 6, 1922- –; House 1973- –.

GINGRICH, Newton Leroy (R Ga.) June 17, 1943- –; House 1979- –.

GINN, Ronald Bryan (D Ga.) May 31, 1934- –; House 1973-83.

GLENN, John Herschel Jr. (D Ohio) July 18, 1921- –; Senate Dec. 24, 1974- –.

GLICKMAN, Daniel Robert (D Kan.) Nov. 24, 1944- –; House 1977- –.

GOLDWATER, Barry Morris (father of Barry Morris Goldwater Jr.) (R Ariz.) Jan. 1, 1909- –; Senate 1953-65, 1969- –.

GOLDWATER, Barry Morris Jr. (son of Barry Morris Goldwater) (R Calif.) July 15, 1938- –; House April 29, 1969-83.

GONZALEZ, Henry B. (D Texas) May 3, 1916- –; House Nov. 4, 1961- –.

GOODLING, William Franklin (son of George Atlee Goodling) (R Pa.) Dec. 5, 1927- –; House 1975- –.

GORE, Albert Arnold Jr. (son of Albert Arnold Gore) (D Tenn.) March 31, 1948- –; House 1977-85; Senate 1985- –.

GORTON, Slade (R Wash.) Jan. 8, 1928- –; Senate 1981- –.

GRADISON, Willis David Jr. (R Ohio) Dec. 28, 1928- –; House 1975- –.

GRAMM, William Philip (R Texas) July 8, 1942- –; House 1979-85; Senate 1985- – (1979-Jan. 5, 1983, Democrat; Feb. 22, 1983- – Republican).

GRASSLEY, Charles Ernest (R Iowa) Sept. 17, 1933- –; House 1975-81; Senate 1981- –.

GRAY, William H. III (D Pa.) Aug. 20, 1941- –; House 1979- –.

GREEN, Sedgwick William (R N.Y.) Oct. 16, 1929- –; House Feb. 21, 1978- –.

GREGG, Judd (R N.H.) Feb. 14, 1947- –; House 1981- –.

GRISHAM, Wayne Richard (R Calif.) Jan. 10, 1923- –; House 1979-83.

GUARINI, Frank Joseph (D N.J.) Aug. 20, 1924- –; House 1979- –.

GUNDERSON, Steven (R Wis.) May 10, 1951- –; House 1981- –.

GUYER, Tennyson (R Ohio) Nov. 29, 1913-April 12, 1981; House 1973-April 12, 1981.

H

HAGEDORN, Thomas Michael (R Minn.) Nov. 27, 1943- –; House 1975-83.

HALL, Katie Beatrice Green (D Ind.) April 3, 1938- –; House Nov. 29, 1982- –.

HALL, Ralph M. (D Texas) May 3, 1923- –; House 1981- –.

HALL, Sam Blakeley Jr. (D Texas) Jan. 11, 1924- –; House June 19, 1976-May 27, 1985.

HALL, Tony Patrick (D Ohio) Jan. 16, 1942- –; House 1979- –.

HAMILTON, Lee Herbert (D Ind.) April 20, 1931- –; House 1965- –.

HAMMERSCHMIDT, John Paul (R Ark.) May 4, 1922- –; House 1967- –.

HANCE, Kent Ronald (D Texas) Nov. 14, 1942- –; House 1979-85.

HANSEN, George Vernon (R Idaho) Sept. 14, 1930- –; House 1965-69, 1975-85.

HANSEN, James V. (R Utah) Aug. 14, 1932- –; House 1981- –.

HARKIN, Thomas Richard (D Iowa) Nov. 19, 1939- –; House 1975-85; Senate 1985- –.

HARRISON, Frank (D Pa.) Feb. 2, 1940- –; House 1983-85.

HART, Gary Warren (D Colo.) Nov. 28, 1937- –; Senate 1975- –.

HARTNETT, Thomas F. (R S.C.) Aug. 7, 1941- –; House 1981- –.

HATCH, Orrin Grant (R Utah) March 22, 1934- –; Senate 1977- –.

HATCHER, Charles F. (D Ga.) July 1, 1939- –; House 1981- –.

HATFIELD, Mark Odom (R Ore.) July 12, 1922- –; Senate Jan. 10, 1967- –; Gov. 1959-67.

HAWKINS, Augustus F. (D Calif.) Aug. 31, 1907- –; House 1963- –.

HAWKINS, Paula (R Fla.) Jan. 24, 1927- –; Senate 1981- –.

HAYAKAWA, Samuel Ichiye (R Calif.) July 18, 1906- –; Senate Jan. 2, 1977-83.

HAYES, Charles Arthur (D Ill.) Feb. 17, 1918- –; House Sept. 12, 1983- –.

HECHT, Chic (R Nev.) Nov. 30, 1928- —; Senate 1983- —.

HECKLER, Margaret M. (R Mass.) June 21, 1931- —; House 1967-83; Secy. Health and Human Services 1983- —.

HEFLIN, Howell Thomas (D Ala.) June 19, 1921- —; Senate 1979- —.

HEFNER, Willie Gathrel (D N.C.) April 11, 1930- —; House 1975- —.

HEFTEL, Cecil (D Hawaii) Sept. 30, 1924- —; House 1977- —.

HEINZ, Henry John III (R Pa.) Oct. 23, 1938- —; House Nov. 2, 1971-77; Senate 1977- —.

HELMS, Jesse Alexander (R N.C.) Oct. 18, 1921- —; Senate 1973- —.

HENDON, William A. (R N.C.) Nov. 9, 1944- —; House 1981-83, 1985- —.

HERTEL, Dennis M. (D Mich.) Dec. 7, 1938- —; House 1981- —.

HIGHTOWER, Jack English (D Texas) Sept. 6, 1926- —; House 1975-85.

HILER, John P. (R Ind.) April 24, 1953- —; House 1981- —.

HILLIS, Elwood Haynes (R Ind.) March 6, 1926- —; House 1971- —.

HINSON, Jon C. (R Miss.) March 16, 1942- —; House 1979-April 13, 1981.

HOLLAND, Kenneth Lamar (D S.C.) Nov. 24, 1934- —; House 1975-83.

HOLLENBECK, Harold Capistran (R N.J.) Dec. 29, 1938- —; House 1977-83.

HOLLINGS, Ernest F. (D S.C.) Jan. 1, 1922- —; Senate Nov. 9, 1966- —; Gov. 1959-63.

HOLT, Marjorie Sewell (R Md.) Sept. 17, 1920- —; House 1973- —.

HOPKINS, Larry Jones (R Ky.) Oct. 25, 1933- —; House 1979- —.

HORTON, Frank Jefferson (R N.Y.) Dec. 12, 1919- —; House 1963- —.

HOWARD, James John (D N.J.) July 24, 1927- —; House 1965- —.

HOYER, Steny (D Md.) June 14, 1939- —; House June 3, 1981- —.

HUBBARD, Carroll Jr. (D Ky.) July 7, 1937- —; House 1975- —.

HUCKABY, Thomas Jerry (D La.) July 19, 1941- —; House 1977- —.

HUDDLESTON, Walter Darlington (D Ky.) April 15, 1926- —; Senate 1973-85.

HUGHES, William John (D N.J.) Oct. 17, 1932- —; House 1975- —.

HUMPHREY, Gordon J. (R N.H.) Oct. 7, 1940- —; Senate 1979- —.

HUNTER, Duncan L. (R Calif.) May 31, 1948- —; House 1981- —.

HUTTO, Earl Dewitt (D Fla.) May 12, 1926- —; House 1979- —.

HYDE, Henry John (R Ill.) April 18, 1924- —; House 1975- —.

I

INOUYE, Daniel Ken (D Hawaii) Sept. 7, 1924- —; House Aug. 21, 1959-63; Senate 1963- —.

IRELAND, Andrew P. (R Fla.) Aug. 23, 1930- —; House 1977- — (1977-July 5, 1984, Democrat; July 5, 1984- —, Republican).

J

JACKSON, Henry Martin (D Wash.) May 31, 1912-Sept. 1, 1983; House 1941-53; Senate 1953-Sept. 1, 1983; Chrmn. Dem. Nat. Comm. 1960-61.

JACOBS, Andrew Jr. (son of Andrew Jacobs Sr., husband of Martha Elizabeth Keys) (D Ind.) Feb. 24, 1932- —; House 1965-73, 1975- —.

JEFFORDS, James Merrill (R Vt.) May 11, 1934- —; House 1975- —.

JEFFRIES, James Edmund (R Kan.) June 1, 1925- —; House 1979-83.

JENKINS, Edgar Lanier (D Ga.) Jan. 4, 1933- —; House 1977- —.

JEPSEN, Roger William (R Iowa) Dec. 23, 1928- —; Senate 1979-85.

JOHNSON, Nancy Lee (R Conn.) Jan. 5, 1935- —; House 1983- —.

JOHNSTON, John Bennett Jr. (D La.) June 10, 1932- —; Senate Nov. 14, 1972- —.

JOHNSTON, W. Eugene (R N.C.) March 3, 1936- —; House 1981-83.

JONES, Ed (D Tenn.) April 20, 1912- —; House March 25, 1969- —.

JONES, James Robert (D Okla.) May 5, 1939- —; House 1973- —.

JONES, Walter B. (D N.C.) Aug. 19, 1913- —; House Feb. 5, 1966- —.

K

KAPTUR, Marcia Carolyn (D Ohio) June 17, 1946- —; House 1983- —.

KASICH, John R. (R Ohio) May 13, 1952- —; House 1983- —.

KASSEBAUM, Nancy Landon (R Kan.) July 29, 1932- —; Senate Dec. 23, 1978- —.

KASTEN, Robert Walter Jr. (R Wis.) June 19, 1942- —; House 1975-79; Senate 1981- —.

KASTENMEIER, Robert William (D Wis.) Jan. 24, 1924- —; House 1959- —.

KAZEN, Abraham Jr. (D Texas) Jan. 17, 1919- —; House 1967-85.

KEMP, Jack French (R N.Y.) July 13, 1935- —; House 1971- —.

KENNEDY, Edward Moore (brother of John Fitzgerald Kennedy and Robert Francis Kennedy, grandson of John Francis Fitzgerald) (D Mass.) Feb. 22, 1932- —; Senate Nov. 7, 1962- —.

KENNELLY, Barbara Bailey (D Conn.) July 10, 1936- —; House Jan. 25, 1982- —.

KILDEE, Dale Edward (D Mich.) Sept. 16, 1929- —; House 1977- —.

KINDNESS, Thomas Norman (R Ohio) Aug. 26, 1929- —; House 1975- —.

KLECZKA, Gerald (D Wis.) Nov. 26, 1943- —; House Apr. 10, 1984- —.

KOLTER, Joseph Paul (D Pa.) Sept. 3, 1926- —; House 1983- —.

KOGOVSEK, Raymond Peter (D Colo.) Aug. 19, 1941- —; House 1979-85.

KOSTMAYER, Peter Houston (D Pa.) Sept. 27, 1946- —; House 1977-81, 1983- —.

KRAMER, Kenneth Bentley (R Colo.) Feb. 19, 1942- —; House 1979- —.

L

LAFALCE, John Joseph (D N.Y.) Oct. 6, 1939- —; House 1975- —.

LAGOMARSINO, Robert John (R Calif.) Sept. 4, 1926- —; House March 5, 1974- —.

LANTOS, Tom (D Calif.) Feb. 1, 1928- —; House 1981- —.

LATTA, Delbert Leroy (R Ohio) March 5, 1920- —; House 1959- —.

LAUTENBERG, Frank R. (D N.J.) Jan. 23, 1924- —; Senate Dec. 27, 1982- —.

LAXALT, Paul Dominique (R Nev.) Aug. 2, 1922- —; Senate Dec. 18, 1974- —; Gov. 1967-71.

LEACH, James A. S. (R Iowa) Oct. 15, 1942- —; House 1977- —.

LEAHY, Patrick Joseph (D Vt.) March 31, 1940- —; Senate 1975- —.

LEATH, James Marvin (D Texas) May 6, 1931- —; House 1979- —.

LeBOUTILLIER, John (R N.Y.) May 26, 1953- —; House 1981-83.

LEDERER, Raymond Francis (D Pa.) May 19, 1938- —; House 1977-May 5, 1981.

LEE, Gary A. (R N.Y.) Aug. 18, 1933- —; House 1979-83.

LEHMAN, Richard Henry (D Calif.) July 20, 1948- —; House 1983- —.

LEHMAN, William (D Fla.) Oct. 4, 1913- —; House 1973- —.

LELAND, George Thomas (Mickey) (D Texas) Nov. 27, 1944- —; House 1979- —.

LENT, Norman Frederick (R N.Y.) March 23, 1931- —; House 1971- —.

Appendix

LEVIN, Carl Milton (brother of Sander Martin Levin) (D Mich.) June 28, 1934--; Senate 1979--.

LEVIN, Sander Martin (brother of Carl Milton Levin) (D Mich.) Sept. 6, 1931--; House 1983--.

LEVINE, Mel (D Calif.) June 7, 1943--; House 1983--.

LEVITAS, Elliott Harris (D Ga.) Dec. 26, 1930---; House 1975-85.

LEWIS, Jerry (R Calif.) Oct. 21, 1934--; House 1979--.

LEWIS, Thomas F. (R Fla.) Oct. 26, 1924--; House 1983--.

LIPINSKI, William Oliver (D Ill.) Dec. 22, 1937--; House 1983--.

LIVINGSTON, Robert (Bob) Linligthgow Jr. (R La.) April 30, 1943--; House Sept. 7, 1977--.

LLOYD, Marilyn Laird (known as Marilyn Lloyd Bouquard in the 97th Congress) (D Tenn.) Jan. 3, 1929--; House 1975--.

LOEFFLER, Thomas Gilbert (R Texas) Aug. 1, 1946--; House 1979--.

LONG, Clarence Dickinson (D Md.) Dec. 11, 1908--; House 1963-85.

LONG, Gillis William (cousin of Huey Pierce Long, Rose McConnell Long, Russell Billiu Long and George Shannon Long) (D La.) May 4, 1923-Jan. 20, 1985; House 1963-65, 1973-Jan. 20, 1985.

LONG, Russell Billiu (son of Huey Pierce Long and Rose McConnell Long, nephew of George Shannon Long) (D La.) Nov. 3, 1918---; Senate Dec. 31, 1948--.

LOTT, Chester Trent (R Miss.) Oct. 9, 1941--; House 1973--.

LOWERY, Bill (R Calif.) May 2, 1947--; House 1981--.

LOWRY, Michael E. (D Wash.) March 8, 1939---; House 1979--.

LUGAR, Richard Green (R Ind.) April 4, 1932---; Senate 1977--.

LUJAN, Manuel Jr. (R N.M.) May 12, 1928--; House 1969--.

LUKEN, Thomas Andrew (D Ohio) July 9, 1925--; House March 5, 1974-75, 1977--.

LUNDINE, Stanley N. (D N.Y.) Feb. 4, 1939--; House March 8, 1976--.

LUNGREN, Daniel Edward (R Calif.) Sept. 22, 1946--; House 1979--.

M

MACK, Connie III (R Fla.) Oct. 29, 1940--; House 1983--.

MacKAY, Kenneth Hood (D Fla.) March 22, 1933--; House 1983--.

MADIGAN, Edward Rell (R Ill.) Jan. 13, 1936---; House 1973--.

MARKEY, Edward John (D Mass.) July 11, 1946--; House Nov. 2, 1976-85.

MARKS, Marc Lincoln (R Pa.) Feb. 12, 1927--; House 1977-83.

MARLENEE, Ronald Charles (R Mont.) Aug. 8, 1935--; House 1977--.

MARRIOTT, David Daniel (R Utah) Nov. 2, 1939--; House 1977-85.

MARTIN, David O'B. (R N.Y.) April 26, 1944---; House 1981--.

MARTIN, James Grubbs (R N.C.) Dec. 11, 1935--; House 1973-85; Gov. 1985--.

MARTIN, Lynn Morley (R Ill.) Dec. 26, 1939---; House 1981--.

MARTINEZ, Matthew G. (D Calif.) Feb. 14, 1929--; House July 15, 1982--.

MATHIAS, Charles McC. Jr. (R Md.) July 24, 1922--; House 1961-69; Senate 1969--.

MATSUI, Robert Takeo (D Calif.) Sept. 17, 1941--; House 1979--.

MATSUNAGA, Spark Masayuki (D Hawaii) Oct. 8, 1916--; House 1963-77; Senate 1977--.

MATTINGLY, Mack (R Ga.) Jan. 7, 1931--; Senate 1981--.

MATTOX, James Albon (D Texas) Aug. 29, 1943--; House 1977-83.

MAVROULES, Nicholas (D Mass.) Nov. 1, 1929--; House 1979--.

MAZZOLI, Romano Louis (D Ky.) Nov. 2, 1932---; House 1971--.

McCAIN, John Sidney II (R Ariz.) Aug. 29, 1936--; House 1983--.

McCANDLESS, Alfred A. (R Calif.) July 23, 1927--; House 1983--.

McCLORY, Robert (R Ill.) Jan. 31, 1908--; House 1963-83.

McCLOSKEY, Francis X. (D Ind.) June 12, 1939--; House 1983--.

McCLOSKEY, Paul N. (Pete) Jr. (R Calif.) Sept. 29, 1927--; House Dec. 12, 1967-83.

McCLURE, James A. (R Idaho) Dec. 27, 1924---; House 1967-73; Senate 1973--.

McCOLLUM, Bill (R Fla.) July 12, 1944--; House 1981--.

McCURDY, David K. (D Okla.) March 30, 1950--; House 1981--.

McDADE, Joseph Michael (R Pa.) Sept. 29, 1931--; House 1963--.

McDONALD, Lawrence Patton (D Ga.) April 1, 1935-Sept. 1, 1983; House 1975-Sept. 1, 1983.

McEWEN, Robert D. (R Ohio) Jan. 12, 1950--; House 1981--.

McGRATH, Raymond J. (R N.Y.) March 27, 1941--; House 1981--.

McHUGH, Matthew Francis (D N.Y.) Dec. 6, 1938--; House 1975--.

McKERNAN, John R. Jr. (R Maine) May 20, 1948--; House 1983--.

McKINNEY, Stewart Brett (R Conn.) Jan. 30, 1931--; House 1971--.

McNULTY, James Francis Jr. (D Ariz.) Oct. 18, 1925--; House 1983-85.

MELCHER, John (D Mont.) Sept. 6, 1924--; House June 24, 1969-77; Senate 1977--.

METZENBAUM, Howard Morton (D Ohio) June 4, 1917--; Senate Jan. 4-Dec. 23, 1974, Dec. 29, 1976--.

MICA, Daniel Andrew (D Fla.) Feb. 4, 1944--; House 1979--.

MICHEL, Robert Henry (R Ill.) March 2, 1923---; House 1957--.

MIKULSKI, Barbara Ann (D Md.) July 20, 1936--; House 1977--.

MILLER, Clarence E. (R Ohio) Nov. 1, 1917--; House 1967--.

MILLER, George (D Calif.) May 17, 1945--; House 1975--.

MINETA, Norman Yoshio (D Calif.) Nov. 12, 1931--; House 1975--.

MINISH, Joseph George (D N.J.) Sept. 1, 1916---; House 1963-85.

MITCHELL, Donald Jerome (R N.Y.) May 8, 1923--; House 1973-83.

MITCHELL, George John (D Maine) Aug. 20, 1933--; Senate May 19, 1980--.

MITCHELL, Parren James (D Md.) April 29, 1922--; House 1971--.

MOAKLEY, John Joseph (D Mass.) April 27, 1927--; House 1973-- (1973-75 Independent Democrat, 1975-- Democrat).

MOFFETT, Anthony Joseph (D Conn.) Aug. 18, 1944--; House 1975-83.

MOLINARI, Guy V. (R N.Y.) Nov. 23, 1928--; House 1981--.

MOLLOHAN, Alan B. (son of Robert Homer Mollohan) (D W.Va.) May 14, 1943--; House 1983--.

MOLLOHAN, Robert Homer (father of Alan B. Mollohan) (D W.Va.) Sept. 18, 1909--; House 1953-57, 1969-83.

MONTGOMERY, Gillespie V. (D Miss.) Aug. 5, 1920--; House 1967--.

MOODY, Jim (D Wis.) Sept. 2, 1935--; House 1983--.

MOORE, William Henson (R La.) Oct. 4, 1939---; House Jan. 7, 1975--.

MOORHEAD, Carlos John (R Calif.) May 6, 1922--; House 1973--.

MORRISON, Bruce A. (D Conn.) Oct. 8, 1944---; House 1983--.

MORRISON, Sid (R Wash.) May 13, 1933- —; House 1981- —.

MOTTL, Ronald Milton (D Ohio) Feb. 6, 1934- —; House 1975-83.

MOYNIHAN, Daniel Patrick (D N.Y.) March 16, 1927- —; Senate 1977- —.

MRAZEK, Robert J. (D N.Y.) Nov. 5, 1945- —; House 1983- —.

MURKOWSKI, Frank H. (R Alaska) March 28, 1933- —; Senate 1981- —.

MURPHY, Austin J. (D Pa.) June 17, 1927- —; House 1977- —.

MURTHA, John Patrick Jr. (D Pa.) Jan. 17, 1932- —; House Feb. 5, 1974- —.

MYERS, John Thomas (R Ind.) Feb. 8, 1927- —; House 1967- —.

N

NAPIER, John L. (R S.C.) May 16, 1947- —; House 1981-83.

NATCHER, William Huston (D Ky.) Sept. 11, 1909- —; House Aug. 1, 1953- —.

NEAL, Stephen Lybrook (D N.C.) Nov. 7, 1934- —; House 1975- —.

NELLIGAN, James L. (R Pa.) Feb. 14, 1929- —; House 1981-83.

NELSON, Clarence William (Bill) (D Fla.) Sept. 29, 1942- —; House 1979- —.

NICHOLS, William (D Ala.) Oct. 16, 1918- —; House 1967- —.

NICKLES, Donald L. (R Okla.) Dec. 6, 1948- —; Senate 1981- —.

NIELSON, Howard Curtis (R Utah) Sept. 12, 1924- —; House 1983- —.

NOWAK, Henry James (D N.Y.) Feb. 21, 1935- —; House 1975- —.

NUNN, Samuel Augustus (D Ga.) Sept. 8, 1938- —; Senate Nov. 8, 1972- —.

O

OAKAR, Mary Rose (D Ohio) March 5, 1940- —; House 1977- —.

OBERSTAR, James Louis (D Minn.) Sept. 10, 1934- —; House 1975-85.

OBEY, David Ross (D Wis.) Oct. 3, 1938- —; House April 1, 1969- —.

O'BRIEN, George Miller (R Ill.) June 17, 1917- —; House 1973- —.

OLIN, James R. (D Va.) Feb. 28, 1920- —; House 1983- —.

O'NEILL, Thomas Phillip Jr. (D Mass.) Dec. 9, 1912- —; House 1953- —; House majority leader 1973-77; Speaker 1977- —.

ORTIZ, Solomon Porfirio (D Texas) June 3, 1937- —; House 1983- —.

OTTINGER, Richard Lawrence (D N.Y.) Jan. 27, 1929- —; House 1965-71, 1975-85.

OWENS, Major Robert Odell (D N.Y.) June 28, 1936- —; House 1983- —.

OXLEY, Michael Garver (R Ohio) Feb. 11, 1944- —; House July 21, 1981- —.

P

PACKARD, Ron (R Calif.) Jan. 19, 1931- —; House 1983- —.

PACKWOOD, Robert William (R Ore.) Sept. 11, 1932- —; Senate 1969- —.

PANETTA, Leon Edward (D Calif.) June 28, 1938- —; House 1977- —.

PARRIS, Stanford E. (R Va.) Sept. 9, 1929- —; House 1973-75; House 1981- —.

PASHAYAN, Charles Sahag (Chip) Jr. (R Calif.) March 27, 1941- —; House 1979- —.

PATMAN, William N. (D Texas) March 26, 1927- —; House 1981-85.

PATTERSON, Jerry Mumford (D Calif.) Oct. 25, 1934- —; House 1975-85.

PAUL, Ronald Ernest (R Texas) Aug. 20, 1935- —; House April 3, 1976-77, 1979-85.

PEASE, Donald James (D Ohio) Sept. 26, 1931- —; House 1977- —.

PELL, Claiborne de Borda (son of Herbert Claiborne Pell Jr.) (D R.I.) Nov. 22, 1918- —; Senate 1961- —.

PENNY, Timothy J. (D Minn.) Nov. 19, 1951- —; House 1983- —.

PEPPER, Claude Denson (D Fla.) Sept. 8, 1900- —; Senate Nov. 4, 1936-51; House 1963- —.

PERCY, Charles Harting (R Ill.) Sept. 27, 1919- —; Senate 1967-85.

PERKINS, Carl Dewey (D Ky.) Oct. 15, 1912-Aug. 3, 1984; House 1949-Aug. 3, 1984.

PERKINS, Carl C. "Chris" (son of Carl Dewey Perkins) (D Ky.) Aug. 6, 1954- —; House 1985- —.

PETRI, Thomas E. (R Wis.) May 28, 1940- —; House April 9, 1979- —.

PEYSER, Peter A. (D N.Y.) Sept. 7, 1921- —; House 1971-77, 1979-83.

PICKLE, J. J. (Jake) (D Texas) Oct. 11, 1913- —; House Dec. 21, 1963- —.

PORTER, John Edward (R Ill.) June 1, 1935- —; House Jan. 24, 1980- —.

PRESSLER, Larry Lee (R S.D.) March 29, 1942- —; House 1975-79; Senate 1979- —.

PRICE, Charles Melvin (D Ill.) Jan. 1, 1905- —; House 1945- —.

PRITCHARD, Joel McFee (R Wash.) May 5, 1925- —; House 1973-85.

PROXMIRE, William (D Wis.) Nov. 11, 1915- —; Senate Aug. 28, 1957- —.

PRYOR, David Hampton (D Ark.) Aug. 29, 1934- —; House Nov. 8, 1966-73; Senate 1979- —; Gov. 1975-79.

PURSELL, Carl Duane (R Mich.) Dec. 19, 1932- —; House 1977- —.

Q

QUAYLE, James Danforth (R Ind.) Feb. 4, 1947- —; House 1977-81; Senate 1981- —.

QUILLEN, James H. (Jimmy) (R Tenn.) Jan. 11, 1916- —; House 1963- —.

R

RAHALL, Nick Joe II (D W.Va.) May 20, 1949- —; House 1977- —.

RAILSBACK, Thomas F. (R Ill.) Jan. 22, 1932- —; House 1967-83.

RANDOLPH, Jennings (D W.Va.) March 8, 1902- —; House 1933-47; Senate Nov. 5, 1958-85.

RANGEL, Charles Bernard (D N.Y.) June 1, 1930- —; House 1971- —.

RATCHFORD, William Richard (D Conn.) May 24, 1934- —; House 1979-85.

RAY, Richard Belmont (D Ga.) Feb. 2, 1927- —; House 1983- —.

REGULA, Ralph Strauss (R Ohio) Dec. 3, 1924- —; House 1973- —.

REID, Harry (D Nev.) Dec. 2, 1939- —; House 1983- —.

REUSS, Henry Schoellkopf (D Wis.) Feb. 22, 1912- —; House 1955-83.

RHODES, John Jacob (R Ariz.) Sept. 18, 1916- —; House 1953-83.

RICHARDSON, William Blaine (D N.M.) Nov. 15, 1947- —; House 1983- —.

RICHMOND, Frederick William (D N.Y.) Nov. 15, 1923- —; House 1975-Aug. 25, 1982.

RIDGE, Thomas Joseph (R Pa.) Aug. 26, 1945- —; House 1983- —.

RIEGLE, Donald Wayne Jr. (D Mich.) Feb. 4, 1938- —; House 1967-Dec. 30, 1976; Senate Dec. 30, 1976- — (1967-Feb. 27, 1973 Republican; Feb. 27, 1973- — Democrat).

RINALDO, Matthew John (R N.J.) Sept. 1, 1931- —; House 1973- —.

RITTER, Donald Lawrence (R Pa.) Oct. 21, 1940- —; House 1979- —.

ROBERTS, Clint (R S.D.) Jan. 30, 1935- —; House 1981-83.

ROBERTS, Pat (R Kan.) April 20, 1936- —; House 1981- —.

ROBINSON, James Kenneth (R Va.) May 14, 1916- —; House 1971-85.

RODINO, Peter Wallace Jr. (D N.J.) June 7, 1909- —; House 1949- —.

Appendix

ROE, Robert A. (D N.J.) Feb. 28, 1924- —; House Nov. 4, 1969- —.

ROEMER, Buddy (D La.) Oct. 4, 1943- —; House 1981- —.

ROGERS, Harold (R Ky.) Dec. 31, 1937- —; House 1981- —.

ROSE, Charles Gradison III (D N.C.) Aug. 10, 1939- —; House 1973- —.

ROSENTHAL, Benjamin S. (D/L N.Y.) June 8, 1923-Jan. 4, 1983; House Feb. 20, 1962-Jan. 4, 1983.

ROSTENKOWSKI, Daniel David (Dan) (D Ill.) Jan. 2, 1928- —; House 1959- —.

ROTH, Tobias A. (R Wis.) Oct. 10, 1938- —; House 1979- —.

ROTH, William V. Jr. (R Del.) July 22, 1921- —; House 1967-Dec. 31, 1970; Senate Jan. 1, 1971- —.

ROUKEMA, Marge (R N.J.) Sept. 19, 1929- —; House 1981- —.

ROUSSELOT, John Harbin (R Calif.) Nov. 1, 1927- —; House 1961-63, June 30, 1970-83.

ROWLAND, James Roy Jr. (D Ga.) Feb. 3, 1926- —; House 1983- —.

ROYBAL, Edward R. (D Calif.) Feb. 10, 1916- —; House 1963- —.

RUDD, Eldon Dean (R Ariz.) July 15, 1920- —; House 1977- —.

RUDMAN, Warren (R N.H.) May 13, 1930- —; Senate Dec. 29, 1980- —.

RUSSO, Martin Anthony (D Ill.) Jan. 23, 1944- —; House 1975- —.

S

SABO, Martin Olav (D Minn.) Feb. 28, 1938- —; House 1979- —.

ST GERMAIN, Fernand Joseph (D R.I.) Jan. 9, 1928- —; House 1961- —.

SANTINI, James David (D Nev.) Aug. 13, 1937- —; House 1975-83.

SARBANES, Paul Spyros (D Md.) Feb. 3, 1933- —; House 1971-77; Senate 1977- —.

SASSER, James Ralph (D Tenn.) Sept. 30, 1931- —; Senate 1977- —.

SAVAGE, Gus (D Ill.) Oct. 30, 1925- —; House 1981- —.

SAWYER, Harold S. (R Mich.) March 21, 1920- —; House 1977-85.

SAXTON, H. James (R N.J.) Jan. 22, 1943- —; House 1985- —.

SCHAEFER, Daniel L. (R Colo.) Jan. 25, 1936- —; House April 7, 1983- —.

SCHEUER, James Haas (D N.Y.) Feb. 6, 1920- —; House 1965-73, 1975- —.

SCHMITT, Harrison Hagan (R N.M.) July 3, 1935- —; Senate 1977-83.

SCHNEIDER, Claudine (R R.I.) March 25, 1947- —; House 1981- —.

SCHROEDER, Patricia Scott (D Colo.) July 30, 1940- —; House 1973- —.

SCHULZE, Richard Taylor (R Pa.) Aug. 7, 1929- —; House 1975- —.

SCHUMER, Charles E. (D N.Y.) Nov. 23, 1951- —; House 1981- —.

SEIBERLING, John Frederick (D Ohio) Sept. 8, 1918- ; House 1971- —.

SENSENBRENNER, Frank James Jr. (R Wis.) June 14, 1943- —; House 1979- —.

SHAMANSKY, Robert N. (D Ohio) April 18, 1927- —; House 1981-83.

SHANNON, James Michael (D Mass.) April 4, 1952- —; House 1979-85.

SHARP, Philip Riley (D Ind.) July 15, 1942- —; House 1975- —.

SHAW, E. Clay (R Fla.) April 19, 1939- —; House 1981- —.

SHELBY, Richard Craig (D Ala.) May 6, 1934- —; House 1979- —.

SHUMWAY, Norman David (R Calif.) July 28, 1934- —; House 1979- —.

SHUSTER, E. G. (Bud) (R Pa.) Jan. 23, 1932- —; House 1973- —.

SIKORSKI, Gerry (D Minn.) April 26, 1948- —; House 1983- —.

SILJANDER, Mark Deli (R Mich.) June 11, 1951- —; House April 28, 1981- —.

SIMON, Paul Martin (D Ill.) Nov. 29, 1928- —; House 1975-85; Senate 1985- —.

SIMPSON, Alan Kooi (R Wyo.) Sept. 2, 1931- —; Senate Jan. 1, 1979- —.

SISISKY, Norman (D Va.) June 9, 1927- —; House 1983- —.

SKEEN, Joseph R. (R N.M.) June 30, 1927- —; House 1981- —.

SKELTON, Ike N. (D Mo.) Dec. 20, 1931- —; House 1977- —.

SLATTERY, James Charles (D Kan.) Aug. 4, 1948- —; House 1983- —.

SMITH, Albert Lee (R Ala.) Aug. 31, 1931- —; House 1981-83.

SMITH, Christopher H. (R N.J.) March 4, 1953- —; House 1981- —.

SMITH, Denny (R Ore.) Jan. 19, 1938- —; House 1981- —.

SMITH, Joseph F. (D Pa.) Jan. 24, 1920- —; House July 28, 1981- —.

SMITH, Lawrence Jack (D Fla.) April 25, 1941- —; House 1983- —.

SMITH, Neal Edward (D Iowa) March 23, 1920- —; House 1959- —.

SMITH, Robert Freeman (R Ore.) June 16, 1931- —; House 1983- —.

SMITH, Virginia Dodd (R Neb.) June 30, 1911- —; House 1975- —.

SNOWE, Olympia Jean Bouchles (R Maine) Feb. 21, 1947- —; House 1979- —.

SNYDER, Marion Gene (R Ky.) Jan. 26, 1928- —; House 1963-65, 1967- —.

SOLARZ, Stephen Joshua (D N.Y.) Sept. 12, 1940- —; House 1975- —.

SOLOMON, Gerald B. (R N.Y.) Aug. 14, 1930- —; House 1979- —.

SPECTER, Arlen (R Pa.) Feb. 12, 1930- —; Senate 1981- —.

SPELLMAN, Gladys Noon (D Md.) March 1, 1918- —; House 1975-Feb. 24, 1981.

SPENCE, Floyd Davidson (R S.C.) April 9, 1928- —; House 1971- —.

SPRATT, John M. Jr. (D S.C.) Nov. 1, 1942- —; House 1983- —.

STAFFORD, Robert Theodore (R Vt.) Aug. 8, 1913- —; House 1961-Sept. 16, 1971; Senate Sept. 16, 1971- —; Gov. 1959-61.

STAGGERS, Harley Orrin Jr. (son of Harley Orrin Staggers) (D W. Va.) Feb. 22, 1951- —; House 1983- —.

STANGELAND, Arlan Ingehart (R Minn.) Feb. 8, 1930- —; House March 1, 1977- —.

STANTON, John William (R Ohio) Feb. 20, 1924- —; House 1965-83.

STARK, Fortney Hillman (D Calif.) Nov. 11, 1931- —; House 1973- —.

STATON, David Mick (R W.Va.) Feb. 11, 1940- —; House 1981-83.

STENHOLM, Charles Walter (D Texas) Oct. 26, 1938- —; House 1979- —.

STENNIS, John Cornelius (D Miss.) Aug. 3, 1901- —; Senate Nov. 5, 1947- —.

STEVENS, Theodore F. (Ted) (R Alaska) Nov. 18, 1923- —; Senate Dec. 24, 1968- —.

STOCKMAN, David Alan (R Mich.) Nov. 10, 1946- —; House 1977-Jan. 27, 1981; Director, Office of Management and Budget 1981-July 31, 1985.

STOKES, Louis (D Ohio) Feb. 23, 1925- —; House 1969- —.

STRATTON, Samuel Studdiford (D N.Y.) Sept. 27, 1916- —; House 1959- —.

STUDDS, Gerry Eastman (D Mass.) May 12, 1937- —; House 1973- —.

STUMP, Robert (R Ariz.) April 4, 1927- —; House 1977- — (1977-83 Democrat; 1983- — Republican).

SUNDQUIST, Donald Kenneth (R Tenn.) March 15, 1936- —; House 1983- —.

SUNIA, Fofo I. F. (D American Samoa) March 13, 1937- —; House 1981- —.

SWIFT, Allen (D Wash.) Sept. 12, 1935- —; House 1979- —.

SWIGERT, John Leonard (R Col.) Aug. 30, 1931-Dec. 27, 1982; elected to House 1982, but did not serve.

SYMMS, Steven Douglas (R Idaho) April 23, 1938-—; House 1973-81; Senate 1981-—.

SYNAR, Michael Lynn (D Okla.) Oct. 17, 1950-—; House 1979-—.

T

TALLON, Robert M. (D S.C.) Aug. 8, 1946-—; House 1983-—.

TAUKE, Thomas Joseph (R Iowa) Oct. 11, 1950-—; House 1979-—.

TAUZIN, W. J. (Billy) (D La.) June 14, 1943-—; House May 22, 1980-—.

TAYLOR, Gene (R Mo.) Feb. 10, 1928-—; House 1973-—.

THOMAS, Robert Lindsay (D Ga.) Nov. 20, 1943-—; House 1983-—.

THOMAS, William Marshall (R Calif.) Dec. 6, 1941-—; House 1979-—.

THURMOND, James Strom (R S.C.) Dec. 5, 1902-—; Senate Dec. 24, 1954-April 4, 1956, Nov. 7, 1956-—; Pres. pro tempore 1981-—. Gov. 1947-51 (1947-51, 1954-56, 1956-Sept. 16, 1964 Democrat; Sept. 16, 1964-— Republican).

TORRES, Estaban Edward (D Calif.) Jan. 27, 1930-—; House 1983-—.

TORRICELLI, Robert G. (D N.J.) Aug. 26, 1951-—; House 1983-—.

TOWER, John Goodwin (R Texas) Sept. 29, 1925-—; Senate June 15, 1961-85.

TOWNS, Edolphus (D N.Y.) July 21, 1934-—; House 1983-—.

TRAXLER, Jerome Bob (D Mich.) July 21, 1931-—; House April 16, 1974-—.

TRIBLE, Paul Seward Jr. (R Va.) Dec. 29, 1946-—; House 1977-83; Senate 1983-—.

TSONGAS, Paul Efthemios (D Mass.) Feb. 14, 1941-—; House 1975-79; Senate 1979-85.

U

UDALL, Morris King (brother of Stewart Lee Udall) (D Ariz.) June 15, 1922-—; House May 2, 1961-—.

V

VALENTINE, Tim (D N.C.) March 15, 1926-—; House 1983-—.

VANDERGRIFF, Tom (D Texas) Jan. 29, 1926-—; House 1983-85.

VANDER JAGT, Guy Adrian (R Mich.) Aug. 26, 1931-—; House Nov. 8, 1966-—.

VENTO, Bruce Frank (D Minn.) Oct. 7, 1940-—; House 1977-—.

VOLKMER, Harold Lee (D Mo.) April 4, 1931-—; House 1977-—.

VUCANOVICH, Barbara Farrell (R Nev.) June 22, 1921-—; House 1983-—.

W

WALGREN, Douglas (D Pa.) Dec. 28, 1940-—; House 1977-—.

WALKER, Robert Smith (R Pa.) Dec. 23, 1942-—; House 1977-—.

WALLOP, Malcolm (R Wyo.) Feb. 27, 1933-—; Senate 1977-—.

WAMPLER, William Creed (R Va.) April 21, 1926-—; House 1953-55, 1967-83.

WARNER, John William (R Va.) Feb. 18, 1927-—; Senate Jan. 2, 1979-—.

WASHINGTON, Harold (D Ill.) April 15, 1922-—; House 1981-April 30, 1983.

WATKINS, Wesley Wade (D Okla.) Dec. 15, 1938-—; House 1977-—.

WAXMAN, Henry Arnold (D Calif.) Sept. 12, 1939-—; House 1975-—.

WEAVER, James Howard (D Ore.) Aug. 8, 1927-—; House 1975-—.

WEBER, Ed (R Ohio) July 26, 1931-—; House 1981-—.

WEBER, Vin (R Minn.) July 24, 1952-—; House 1981-83.

WEICKER, Lowell Palmer Jr. (R Conn.) May 16, 1931-—; House 1969-71; Senate 1971-—.

WEISS, Theodore S. (D N.Y.) Sept. 17, 1927-—; House 1977-—.

WHEAT, Alan D. (D Mo.) Oct. 16, 1951-—; House 1983-—.

WHITE, Richard Crawford (D Texas) April 29, 1923-—; House 1965-83.

WHITEHURST, George William (R Va.) March 12, 1925-—; House 1969-—.

WHITLEY, Charles Orville (D N.C.) Jan. 3, 1927-—; House 1977-—.

WHITTAKER, Robert (R Kan.) Sept. 18, 1939-—; House 1979-—.

WHITTEN, Jamie Lloyd (D Miss.) April 18, 1910-—; House Nov. 4, 1941-—.

WILLIAMS, Harrison Arlington Jr. (D N.J.) Dec. 10, 1919-—; House Nov. 3, 1953-57; Senate 1959-March 11, 1982.

WILLIAMS, Lyle (R Ohio) Aug. 23, 1942-—; House 1979-85.

WILLIAMS, Pat (D Mont.) Oct. 30, 1937-—; House 1979-—.

WILSON, Charles (D Texas) June 1, 1933-—; House 1973-—.

WILSON, Pete (R Calif.) Aug. 23, 1933-—; Senate 1983-—.

WINN, Larry Jr. (R Kan.) Aug. 22, 1919-—; House 1967-85.

WIRTH, Timothy Endicott (D Colo.) Sept. 22, 1939-—; House 1975-—.

WISE, Robert Ellsworth Jr. (D W.Va.) Jan. 6, 1948-—; House 1983-—.

WOLF, Frank R. (R Va.) Jan. 30, 1939-—; House 1981-—.

WOLPE, Howard Eliot (D Mich.) Nov. 2, 1939-—; House 1979-—.

WON PAT, Antonio Borja (D Guam) Dec. 10, 1908-—; House 1973-85.

WORTLEY, George (R N.Y.) Dec. 8, 1928-—; House 1981-—.

WRIGHT, James Claude Jr. (D Texas) Dec. 22, 1922-—; House 1955-—; House majority leader 1977-—.

WYDEN, Ron (D Ore.) May 3, 1949-—; House 1981-—.

WYLIE, Chalmers Pangburn (R Ohio) Nov. 23, 1920-—; House 1967-—.

Y

YATES, Sidney Richard (D Ill.) Aug. 27, 1909-—; House 1949-63, 1965-—.

YATRON, Gus (D Pa.) Oct. 16, 1927-—; House 1969-—.

YOUNG, Charles William (Bill) (R Fla.) Dec. 16, 1930-—; House 1971-—.

YOUNG, Donald Edwin (R Alaska) June 9, 1933-—; House March 6, 1973-—.

YOUNG, Robert A. (D Mo.) Nov. 27, 1923-—; House 1977-—.

Z

ZABLOCKI, Clement John (D Wis.) Nov. 18, 1912-Dec. 3, 1983; House 1949-Dec. 3, 1983.

ZEFERETTI, Leo C. (D N.Y.) July 15, 1927-—; House 1975-83.

ZORINSKY, Edward (D Neb.) Nov. 11, 1928-—; Senate Dec. 28, 1976-—.

ZSCHAU, Ed (R Calif.) Jan. 6, 1940-—; House 1983-—.

Congressional Committees, 97th and 98th Congresses

Following is a list of congressional committees and subcommittees in the 97th and 98th Congresses. Committee chairmen and the dates of their service in that capacity also are included. Ranking minority members, listed in italics, and subcommittee chairmen served during both Congresses unless otherwise noted.

Senate committee and subcommittee chairmen are Republicans and ranking minority members are Democrats. House chairmen are Democrats; ranking members, Republicans.

Senate Committees

Agriculture, Nutrition and Forestry

Agriculture in general; animal industry and diseases; crop insurance and soil conservation; farm credit and farm security; food from fresh waters; food stamp programs; forestry in general; home economics; human nutrition; inspection of livestock, meat and agricultural products; pests and pesticides; plant industry, soils and agricultural engineering; rural development, rural electrification and watersheds; school nutrition programs; matters relating to food, nutrition and rural affairs.

R 9 - D 8 *(97th Congress)*
R 10 - D 8 *(98th Congress)*

Jesse Helms, N.C. (1981-85)
Walter D. Huddleston, Ky.

Agricultural Credit and Rural Electrification — Paula Hawkins, Fla.
Agricultural Production, Marketing and Stabilization of Prices — Thad Cochran, Miss.
Agricultural Research and General Legislation — Richard G. Lugar, Ind.
Foreign Agricultural Policy — Rudy Boschwitz, Minn.
Forestry, Water Resources and Environment (97th Congress) — S. I. "Sam" Hayakawa, Calif.
Nutrition — Robert Dole, Kan.
Rural Development, Oversight and Investigations — Mark Andrews, N.D.
Soil and Water Conservation (97th Congress) — Roger W. Jepsen, Iowa
Soil and Water Conservation, Forestry and Environment (98th Congress) — Roger W. Jepsen, Iowa

Appropriations

Appropriation of revenue for support of the government; rescission of appropriations; new spending authority under the Congressional Budget Act.

R 15 - D 14
Mark O. Hatfield, Ore. (1981-85)
William Proxmire, Wis. (97th Congress)
John C. Stennis, Miss. (98th Congress)

Agriculture and Related Agencies (97th Congress) — Thad Cochran, Miss.
Agriculture, Rural Development and Related Agencies (98th Congress) — Thad Cochran, Miss.
Commerce, Justice, State and Judiciary and Related Agencies (98th Congress) — Paul Laxalt, Nev.
Defense — Ted Stevens, Alaska
District of Columbia — Alfonse M. D'Amato, N.Y. (97th Congress); Arlen Specter, Pa. (98th Congress)
Energy and Water Development — Mark O. Hatfield, Ore.
Foreign Operations — Bob Kasten, Wis.
HUD - Independent Agencies — Jake Garn, Utah
Interior (97th Congress) — James A. McClure, Idaho
Interior and Related Agencies (98th Congress) — James A. McClure, Idaho
Labor, Health and Human Services, Education and Related Agencies — Harrison "Jack" Schmitt, N.M. (97th Congress); Lowell P. Weicker Jr., Conn. (98th Congress)
Legislative Branch — Mack Mattingly, Ga. (97th Congress); Alfonse M. D'Amato, N.Y. (98th Congress)
Military Construction — Paul Laxalt, Nev. (97th Congress); Mack Mattingly, Ga. (98th Congress)
State, Justice, Commerce, the Judiciary (97th Congress) — Lowell P. Weicker Jr., Conn.
Transportation (97th Congress) — Mark Andrews, N.D.
Transportation and Related Agencies (98th Congress) — Mark Andrews, N.D.
Treasury, Postal Service, General Government — James Abdnor, S.D.

References

The names and dates of terms of chairmen of standing committees for the years 1947-65 may be found in *Congress and the Nation Vol. I*, pp. 32a-35a; for the years 1947-69, in *Congress and the Nation Vol. II*, pp. 46a-50a; for the years 1947-73, in *Congress and the Nation Vol. III*, pp. 52a-56a; for the years 1947-77, in *Congress and the Nation Vol. IV*, pp. 1068-1072; and for the years 1977-81, in *Congress and the Nation Vol. V*, pp. 1969-1078.

Armed Services

Defense and defense policy generally; aeronautical and space activities peculiar to or primarily associated with the development of weapons systems or military operations; maintenance and operation of the Panama Canal, including the Canal Zone; military research and development; national security aspects of nuclear energy; naval petroleum reserves (except Alaska); armed forces generally; Selective Service System; strategic and critical materials.

R 9 - D 8 *(97th Congress)*
R 10 - D 8 *(98th Congress)*

John Tower, Texas (1981-85)
John C. Stennis, Miss. (97th Congress)
Henry M. Jackson, Wash. (died Sept. 1, 1983)
Sam Nunn, Ga. (through 98th Congress)

Manpower and Personnel — Roger W. Jepsen, Iowa
Military Construction — Strom Thurmond, S.C.
Preparedness — Gordon J. Humphrey, N.H.
Sea Power and Force Projection — William S. Cohen, Maine
Strategic and Theater Nuclear Forces — John W. Warner, Va.
Tactical Warfare — Barry Goldwater, Ariz.

Banking, Housing and Urban Affairs

Banks, banking and financial institutions; price controls; deposit insurance; economic stabilization and growth; defense production; export and foreign trade promotion; export controls; federal monetary policy, including Federal Reserve System; financial aid to commerce and industry; issuance and redemption of notes; money and credit, including currency and coinage; nursing home construction; public and private housing, including veterans' housing; renegotiation of government contracts; urban development and mass transit; international economic policy.

R 8 - D 7 *(97th Congress)*
R 10 - D 8 *(98th Congress)*

Jake Garn, Utah (1981-85)
Harrison A. Williams Jr., N.J. (resigned March 11, 1982)
William Proxmire, Wis. (through 98th Congress)

Consumer Affairs — John H. Chafee, R.I. (97th Congress); Paula Hawkins, Fla. (98th Congress)
Economic Policy — William L. Armstrong, Colo. (97th Congress); Slade Gorton, Wash. (98th Congress)
Federal Credit Programs (98th Congress) — Paul S. Trible Jr., Va.
Financial Institutions — John Tower, Texas (97th Congress); William L. Armstrong, Colo. (98th Congress)
Housing and Urban Affairs — Richard G. Lugar, Ind. (97th Congress); John Tower, Texas (98th Congress)
Insurance (98th Congress) — Chic Hecht, Nev.
International Finance and Monetary Policy — John Heinz, Pa.
Rural Housing and Development — Harrison

"Jack" Schmitt, N.M. (97th Congress); Mack Mattingly, Ga. (98th Congress)
Securities — Alfonse M. D'Amato, N.Y.

Budget

Federal budget generally; concurrent budget resolutions; Congressional Budget Office.

R 12 - D 10

Pete V. Domenici, N.M. 1981-85
Ernest F. Hollings, S.C. (97th Congress)
Lawton Chiles, Fla. (98th Congress)

No standing subcommittees.

Commerce, Science and Transportation

Interstate commerce and transportation generally; Coast Guard; coastal zone management; communications; highway safety; inland waterways, except construction; marine fisheries; Merchant Marine and navigation; nonmilitary aeronautical and space sciences; oceans, weather and atmospheric activities, interoceanic canals generally; regulation of consumer products and services, science, engineering and technology research, development and policy; sports; standards and measurement; transportation and commerce aspects of Outer Continental Shelf lands.

R 9 - D 8

Bob Packwood, Ore. (1981-85)
Howard W. Cannon, Nev. (97th Congress)
Ernest F. Hollings, S.C. (98th Congress)

Aviation — Nancy Landon Kassebaum, Kan.
Business, Trade and Tourism — Larry Pressler, S.D.
Communications — Barry Goldwater, Ariz.
Consumer — Bob Kasten, Wis.
Merchant Marine — Slade Gorton, Wash. (97th Congress); Ted Stevens, Alaska (98th Congress)
National Ocean Policy Study (98th Congress) — Bob Packwood, Ore.
Science, Technology and Space — Harrison "Jack" Schmitt, N.M. (97th Congress); Slade Gorton, Wash. (98th Congress)
Surface Transportation — John C. Danforth, Mo.

Energy and Natural Resources

Energy policy, regulation, conservation, research and development; coal; energy related aspects of deepwater ports; hydroelectric power, irrigation and reclamation; mines, mining and minerals generally; national parks, recreation areas, wilderness areas, wild and scenic rivers, historic sites, military parks and battlefields; naval petroleum reserves in Alaska; nonmilitary development of nuclear energy; oil and gas production and distribution; pub-

lic lands and forests; solar energy systems; territorial possessions of the United States.

R 11 - D 9

James A. McClure, Idaho (1981-85)
Henry M. Jackson, Wash. (97th Congress)
J. Bennett Johnston, La. (98th Congress)

Energy and Mineral Resources — John W. Warner, Va.
Energy Conservation and Supply — Lowell P. Weicker Jr., Conn.
Energy Regulation — Gordon J. Humphrey, N.H. (97th Congress); Frank H. Murkowski, Alaska (98th Congress)
Energy Research and Development — Pete V. Domenici, N.M.
Public Lands and Reserved Water — Malcolm Wallop, Wyo.
Water and Power — Frank H. Murkowski, Alaska (97th Congress); Don Nickles, Okla. (98th Congress)

Environment and Public Works

Environmental policy, research and development; air water and noise pollution; construction and maintenance of highways; environmental aspects of Outer Continental Shelf lands; environmental effects of toxic substances, other than pesticides; fisheries and wildlife; flood control and improvements of rivers and harbors; nonmilitary environmental regulation and control of nuclear energy; ocean dumping; public buildings and grounds; public works, bridges and dams; regional economic development; solid waste disposal and recycling; water resources.

R 9 - D 7

Robert T. Stafford, Vt. (1981-85)
Jennings Randolph, W.Va.

Environmental Pollution — John H. Chafee, R.I.
Nuclear Regulation — Alan K. Simpson, Wyo.
Regional and Community Development — Frank H. Murkowski, Alaska (97th Congress); Gordon J. Humphrey, N.H. (98th Congress)
Toxic Substances and Environmental Oversight — Slade Gorton, Wash. (97th Congress); David Durenberger, Minn. (98th Congress)
Transportation — Steven D. Symms, Idaho
Water Resources — James Abdnor, S.D.

Finance

Revenue measures generally; taxes; tariffs and import quotas; foreign trade agreements; customs; revenue sharing; federal debt limit; Social Security; health programs financed by taxes or trust funds.

R 11 - D 9

Robert Dole, Kan. (1981-85)
Russell B. Long, La.

Economic Growth, Employment and Revenue Sharing — John Heinz, Pa.

Energy and Agricultural Taxation — Malcolm Wallop, Wyo.
Estate and Gift Taxation — Steven D. Symms, Idaho
Health — David Durenberger, Minn.
International Trade — John C. Danforth, Mo.
Oversight of the Internal Revenue Service — Charles E. Grassley, Iowa
Savings, Pensions and Investment Policy — John H. Chafee, R.I.
Social Security and Income Maintenance Programs — William L. Armstrong, Colo.
Taxation and Debt Management — Bob Packwood, Ore.

Foreign Relations

Relations of the United States with foreign nations generally; treaties; foreign economic, military, technical and humanitarian assistance; foreign loans; diplomatic service; International Red Cross; international aspects of nuclear energy; International Monetary Fund; intervention abroad and declarations of war; foreign trade; national security; oceans and international environmental and scientific affairs; protection of U.S. citizens abroad; United Nations; World Bank and other development assistance organizations.

R 9 - D 8

Charles H. Percy, Ill. (1981-85)
Claiborne Pell, R.I.

African Affairs — Nancy Landon Kassebaum, Kan.
Arms Control, Oceans and International Operations and Environment — Larry Pressler, S.D.
East Asian and Pacific Affairs — S.I. "Sam" Hayakawa, Calif. (97th Congress); Frank H. Murkowski, Alaska (98th Congress)
European Affairs — Richard G. Lugar, Ind.
International Economic Policy — Charles McC. Mathias Jr., Md.
Near Eastern and South Asian Affairs — Rudy Boschwitz, Minn.
Western Hemisphere Affairs — Jesse Helms, N.C.

Governmental Affairs

Budget and accounting measures; census and statistics; federal civil service; congressional organization; intergovernmental relations; government information; District of Columbia; organization and management of nuclear export policy; executive branch reorganization; Postal Service; efficiency, economy and effectiveness of government.

R 9 - D 8 *(97th Congress)*
R 10 - D 8 *(98th Congress)*

William V. Roth Jr., Del. (1981-85)
Thomas F. Eagleton, Mo.

Congressional Operations and Oversight (97th Congress) — Mack Mattingly, Ga.

Civil Service, Post Office and General Services — Ted Stevens, Alaska

Energy, Nuclear Proliferation and Government Processes — Charles H. Percy, Ill.

Federal Expenditures, Research and Rules (97th Congress) — John C. Danforth, Mo.

Governmental Efficiency and the District of Columbia — Charles McC. Mathias Jr., Md.

Information Management and Regulatory Affairs (98th Congress) — John C. Danforth, Mo.

Intergovernmental Relations — David Durenberger, Minn.

Oversight of Government Management — William S. Cohen, Maine

Permanent Subcommittee on Investigations — William V. Roth Jr., Del.

Judiciary

Civil and criminal judicial proceedings generally; penitentiaries; bankruptcy, mutiny, espionage and counterfeiting; civil liberties; constitutional amendments; apportionment of representatives; government information; immigration and naturalization; interstate compacts generally; claims against the United States; patents, copyrights and trademarks; monopolies and unlawful restraints of trade; holidays and celebrations.

R 10 - D 8

Strom Thurmond, S.C. (1981-85)
Joseph R. Biden Jr., Del.

Administrative Practice and Procedure (98th Congress) — Charles E. Grassley, Iowa

Agency Administration (97th Congress) — Charles E. Grassley, Iowa

Constitution — Orrin G. Hatch, Utah

Courts — Robert Dole, Kan.

Criminal Law — Charles McC. Mathias Jr., Md. (97th Congress); Paul Laxalt, Nev. (98th Congress)

Immigration and Refugee Policy — Alan K. Simpson, Wyo.

Juvenile Justice — Arlen Specter, Pa.

Patents, Copyrights and Trademarks (98th Congress) — Charles McC. Mathias Jr., Md.

Regulatory Reform (97th Congress) — Paul Laxalt, Nev.

Security and Terrorism — Jeremiah Denton, Ala.

Separation of Powers — John P. East, N.C.

Labor and Human Resources

Education, labor, health and public welfare generally; aging; arts and humanities; biomedical research and development; child labor; convict labor; American National Red Cross; equal employment opportunity; handicapped individuals; labor standards and statistics; mediation and arbitration of labor disputes; occupational safety and health; private pension plans; public health; railway labor and retirement; regulation of foreign laborers; student loans; wages and hours.

R 9 - D 7 *(97th Congress)*
R 10 - D 8 *(98th Congress)*

Orrin G. Hatch, Utah (1981-85)
Edward M. Kennedy, Mass.

Aging (98th Congress) — Charles E. Grassley, Iowa

Aging, Family and Human Services (97th Congress) — Jeremiah Denton, Ala.

Alcoholism and Drug Abuse — Gordon J. Humphrey, N.H.

Education (97th Congress) — Robert T. Stafford, Vt.

Education, Arts and the Humanities (98th Congress) — Robert T. Stafford, Vt.

Employment and Productivity — Dan Quayle, Ind.

Family and Human Services (98th Congress) — Jeremiah Denton, Ala.

Handicapped — Lowell P. Weicker Jr., Conn.

Investigations and General Oversight (97th Congress) — Paula Hawkins, Fla.

Labor — Don Nickles, Okla.

Rules and Administration

Senate administration generally; corrupt practices; qualifications of senators; contested elections; federal elections generally; Government Printing Office; *Congressional Record*; meetings of Congress and attendance of members; presidential succession; the Capitol, congressional office buildings, the Library of Congress, the Smithsonian Institution and the Botanic Gardens.

R 7 - D 5

Charles McC. Mathias Jr., Md. (1981-85)
Wendell H. Ford, Ky.

No standing subcommittees.

Select Ethics

Studies and investigates standards and conduct of Senate members and employees and may recommend remedial action.

R 3 - D 3

Malcolm Wallop, Wyo. (1981-83)
Ted Stevens, Alaska (1983-85)
Howell Heflin, Ala.

No standing subcommittees.

Select Indian Affairs

Problems and opportunities of Indians including Indian land management and trust responsibilities, education, health, special services, loan program and Indian claims against the United States.

R 4 - D 3

William S. Cohen, Maine (1981-83)
Mark Andrews, N.D. (1983-85)
John Melcher, Mont.

No standing subcommittees.

Select Intelligence

Legislative and budgetary authority over the Central Intelligence Agency, the Defense Intelligence Agency, the National Security Agency and intelligence activities of the Federal Bureau of Investigation and other components of the federal intelligence community.

R 8 - D 7

Barry Goldwater, Ariz. (1981-85)
Daniel Patrick Moynihan, N.Y.

Analysis and Production — Richard G. Lugar, Ind.
Budget — Malcolm Wallop, Wyo.
Collection and Foreign Operations — John H. Chafee, R.I.
Legislation and the Rights of Americans — Harrison "Jack" Schmitt, N.M. (97th Congress); David Durenberger, Minn. (98th Congress)

Small Business

Problems of small business; Small Business Administration.

R 9 - D 8 *(97th Congress)*
R 10 - D 9 *(98th Congress)*

Lowell P. Weicker Jr., Conn. (1981-85)
Sam Nunn, Ga.

Advocacy and the Future of Small Business (97th Congress) — S. I. "Sam" Hayakawa, Calif.
Capital Formation and Retention — Bob Packwood, Ore.
Entrepreneurship and Special Problems Facing Small Business (98th Congress) — Bob Kasten, Wis.
Export Promotion and Market Development — Rudy Boschwitz, Minn.
Government Procurement — Don Nickles, Okla.
Government Regulation and Paperwork — Orrin G. Hatch, Utah
Innovation and Technology — Warren B. Rudman, N.H.
Productivity and Competition — Slade Gorton, Wash.
Small Business: Family Farm (98th Congress) — Larry Pressler, S.D.
Urban and Rural Economic Development — Alfonse M. D'Amato, N.Y.

Special Aging

Problems and opportunities of older people including health, income, employment, housing and care and assistance. Reports findings and makes recommendations to the Senate, but cannot report legislation.

R 8 - D 7

John Heinz, Pa. (1981-85)

Lawton Chiles, Fla. (97th Congress)
John Glenn, Ohio (98th Congress)

No standing subcommittees.

Veterans' Affairs

Veterans' measures generally; compensation; armed forces life insurance; national cemeteries; pensions; readjustment benefits; veterans' hospitals, medical care and treatment; vocational rehabilitation and education.

R 7 - D 5

Alan K. Simpson, Wyo. (1981-85)
Alan Cranston, Calif.

No standing subcommittees.

Political Committees

Republican Policy Committee — John Tower, Texas
Republican Committee on Committees (makes Republican committee assignments) — Richard G. Lugar, Ind. (97th Congress); Nancy Landon Kassebaum, Kan. (98th Congress)
National Republican Senatorial Committee (campaign support committee for Republican senatorial candidates) — Bob Packwood, Ore. (97th Congress); Richard G. Lugar, Ind. (98th Congress)
Democratic Policy Committee (scheduling of legislation) — Robert C. Byrd, W.Va.
Democratic Legislative Review Committee (reviews legislative proposals, provides recommendations) — Dale Bumpers, Ark.
Democratic Steering Committee (makes Democratic committee assignments) — Robert C. Byrd, W.Va.
Democratic Senatorial Campaign Committee (campaign support for Democratic senatorial candidates) — Wendell H. Ford, Ky. (97th Congress); Lloyd Bentsen, Texas (98th Congress)

House Committees

Agriculture

Agriculture generally; production, marketing and stabilization of agricultural prices; animal industry and diseases of animals; crop insurance and soil conservation; dairy industry; farm credit and security; forestry in general; human nutrition; home economics; inspection of livestock and meat products; plant industry, soils and agricultural engineering; rural electrification; commodities exchanges; rural development.

D 24 - R 19 *(97th Congress)*
D 26 - R 15 *(98th Congress)*

E. "Kika" de la Garza, Texas (1981-85)
William C. Wampler, Va. (97th Congress)
Edward R. Madigan, Ill. (98th Congress)

Conservation, Credit and Rural Development — Ed Jones, Tenn.

Cotton, Rice and Sugar — David R. Bowen, Miss. (97th Congress); Jerry Huckaby, La. (98th Congress)

Department Operations, Research and Foreign Agriculture — George E. Brown Jr., Calif.

Domestic Marketing, Consumer Relations and Nutrition — Fred Richmond, N.Y. (resigned Aug. 25, 1982); Leon E. Panetta, Calif. (through 98th Congress)

Forests, Family Farms and Energy — James Weaver, Ore. (97th Congress); Charles Whitley, N.C. (98th Congress)

Livestock, Dairy and Poultry — Tom Harkin, Iowa

Tobacco and Peanuts — Charlie Rose, N.C.

Wheat, Soybeans and Feed Grains — Thomas S. Foley, Wash.

Appropriations

Appropriation of revenue for support of the federal government; rescissions of appropriations; transfers of unexpended balances; new spending authority under the Congressional Budget Act.

D 33 - R 22 *(97th Congress)*
D 36 - R 21 *(98th Congress)*

Jamie L. Whitten, Miss. (1978-85)
Silvio O. Conte, Mass.

Agriculture (97th Congress) — Jamie L. Whitten, Miss.

Agriculture, Rural Development and Related Agencies (98th Congress) — Jamie L. Whitten, Miss.

Commerce, Justice, State and Judiciary — Neal Smith, Iowa

Defense — Joseph P. Addabbo, N.Y.

District of Columbia — Julian C. Dixon, Calif.

Energy and Water (97th Congress) — Tom Bevill, Ala.

Energy and Water Development (98th Congress) — Tom Bevill, Ala.

Foreign Operations — Clarence D. Long, Md.

HUD - Independent Agencies — Edward P. Boland, Mass.

Interior — Sidney R. Yates, Ill.

Labor - HHS (97th Congress) — William H. Natcher, Ky.

Labor - Health and Human Services - Education (98th Congress) — William H. Natcher, Ky.

Legislative — Vic Fazio, Calif.

Military Construction — Bo Ginn, Ga. (97th Congress); W. G. "Bill" Hefner, N.C. (98th Congress)

Transportation — Adam Benjamin Jr., Ind. (died Sept. 7, 1982); William Lehman, Fla. (through 98th Congress)

Treasury - Postal Service (97th Congress) — Edward R. Roybal, Calif.

Treasury - Postal Service - General Government (98th Congress) — Edward R. Roybal, Calif.

Armed Services

Common defense generally; Department of Defense; ammunition depots; forts; arsenals; Army, Navy and Air Force reservations and establishments; naval petroleum and oil shale reserves; scientific research and development in support of the armed services; Selective Service System; strategic and critical materials; military applications of nuclear energy; soldiers' and sailors' homes.

D 25 - R 19 *(97th Congress)*
D 28 - R 16 *(98th Congress)*

Melvin Price, Ill. (1975-85)
William L. Dickinson, Ala.

Investigations — Richard C. White, Texas (97th Congress); Bill Nichols, Ala. (98th Congress)

Military Installations and Facilities — Jack Brinkley, Ga. (97th Congress); Ronald V. Dellums, Calif. (98th Congress)

Military Personnel and Compensation — Bill Nichols, Ala. (97th Congress); Les Aspin, Wis. (98th Congress)

Procurement and Military Nuclear Systems — Samuel S. Stratton, N.Y.

Readiness — Dan Daniel, Va.

Research and Development — Melvin Price, Ill.

Seapower and Strategic and Critical Materials — Charles E. Bennett, Fla.

Banking, Finance and Urban Affairs

Banks and banking including deposit insurance and federal monetary policy; money and credit; currency; issuance and redemption of notes; gold and silver; coinage; valuation and revaluation of the dollar; urban development; private and public housing; economic stabilization; defense production; renegotiation; price controls; international finance; financial aid to commerce and industry.

D 25 - R 19 *(97th Congress)*
D 30 - R 17 *(98th Congress)*

Fernand J. St Germain, R.I. (1981-85)
J. William Stanton, Ohio (97th Congress)
Chalmers P. Wylie, Ohio (98th Congress)

Consumer Affairs and Coinage — Frank Annunzio, Ill.

Domestic Monetary Policy — Walter E. Fauntroy, D.C.

Economic Stabilization — James J. Blanchard, Mich. (97th Congress); John J. LaFalce, N.Y. (98th Congress)

Financial Institutions Supervision, Regulation and Insurance — Fernand J. St Germain, R.I.

General Oversight and Renegotiation — Joseph G. Minish, N.J.

Housing and Community Development — Henry B. Gonzalez, Texas

International Development Institutions and Finance — Jerry M. Patterson, Calif.

International Trade, Investment and Monetary Policy — Stephen L. Neal, N.C.

Budget

Federal budget generally; concurrent budget resolutions; Congressional Budget Office.

D 18 - R 12 *(97th Congress)*
D 20 - R 11 *(98th Congress)*

James R. Jones, Okla. (1981-85)
Delbert L. Latta, Ohio

No standing subcommittees.

Task Forces

Budget Process (98th Congress) — Leon E. Panetta, Calif.
Capital Resources and Development (98th Congress) — Stephen J. Solarz, N.Y.
Economic Policy and Growth (98th Congress) — Les Aspin, Wis.
Economic Policy and Productivity (97th Congress) — David R. Obey, Wis.
Education and Employment (98th Congress) — Richard A. Gephardt, Mo.
Energy and Technology (98th Congress) — Timothy E. Wirth, Colo.
Energy and the Environment (97th Congress) — Timothy E. Wirth, Colo.
Enforcement, Credit and Multi-year Budgeting (97th Congress) — Norman Y. Mineta, Calif.
Entitlements, Uncontrollables and Indexing — Paul Simon, Ill. (97th Congress); Brian J. Donnelly, Mass. (98th Congress)
Federalism/State-Local Relations (98th Congress) — Bill Nelson, Fla.
Human Resources and Block Grants (97th Congress) — Richard A. Gephardt, Mo.
International Finance and Trade (98th Congress) — Mike Lowry, Wash.
National Security and Veterans (97th Congress) — Jim Mattox, Texas
Reconciliation (97th Congress) — Leon E. Panetta, Calif.
Tax Policy — Bill Nelson, Fla. (97th Congress); Thomas J. Downey, N.Y. (98th Congress)
Transportation, Research and Development, and Capital Resources (97th Congress) — Stephen J. Solarz, N.Y.

District of Columbia

Municipal affairs of the District of Columbia.

D 6 - R 3 *(97th Congress)*
D 7 - R 4 *(98th Congress)*

Ronald V. Dellums, Calif. (1979-85)
Stewart B. McKinney, Conn.

Fiscal Affairs and Health — Ronald V. Dellums,
Calif. (97th Congress); Walter E. Fauntroy, D.C. (98th Congress)
Government Operations and Metropolitan Affairs — William H. Gray III, Pa.
Judiciary and Education — Mervyn M. Dymally, Calif.

Education and Labor

Education and labor generally; child labor; convict labor; labor standards and statistics; mediation and arbitration of labor disputes; regulation of foreign laborers; school food programs; vocational rehabilitation; wages and hours; welfare of miners; work incentive programs; Indian education; juvenile delinquency; human services programs; Gallaudet College; Howard University.

D 19 - R 14 *(97th Congress)*
D 20 - R 11 *(98th Congress)*

Carl D. Perkins, Ky. (1967-84; died Aug. 3, 1984)
Augustus F. Hawkins, Calif. (through 98th Congress)
John M. Ashbrook, Ohio (died April 24, 1982)
John N. Erlenborn, Ill. (through 98th Congress)

Elementary, Secondary and Vocational Education — Carl D. Perkins, Ky. (died Aug. 3, 1984); William D. Ford, Mich. (acting chairman through 98th Congress)
Employment Opportunities — Augustus F. Hawkins, Calif.
Health and Safety — Joseph M. Gaydos, Pa.
Human Resources — Ike Andrews, N.C.
Labor-Management Relations — Phillip Burton, Calif. (died April 10, 1983); William L. Clay, Mo. (through 98th Congress)
Labor Standards — George Miller, Calif.
Postsecondary Education — Paul Simon, Ill.
Select Education — Austin J. Murphy, Pa.

Energy and Commerce

Interstate and foreign commerce generally; national energy policy generally; exploration, production, storage, supply, marketing, pricing and regulation of energy resources; nuclear energy; solar energy; energy conservation; regeneration and marketing of power; inland waterways; railroads and railway labor and retirement; communications generally; securities and exchanges; consumer affairs; travel and tourism; public health and quarantine; health care facilities; biomedical research and development.

D 24 - R 18 *(97th Congress)*
D 27 - R 15 *(98th Congress)*

John D. Dingell, Mich. (1981-85)
James T. Broyhill, N.C.

Commerce, Transportation and Tourism — James J. Florio, N.J.
Energy Conservation and Power — Richard L. Ottinger, N.Y.
Fossil and Synthetic Fuels — Philip R. Sharp, Ind.

Health and the Environment — Henry A. Waxman, Calif.

Oversight and Investigations — John D. Dingell, Mich.

Telecommunications, Consumer Protection and Finance — Timothy E. Wirth, Colo.

Foreign Affairs

Relations of the United States with foreign nations generally; foreign loans; international conferences and congresses; intervention abroad and declarations of war; diplomatic service; foreign trade; neutrality; protection of Americans abroad; Red Cross; United Nations; international economic policy; export controls including nonproliferation of nuclear technology and hardware; international commodity agreements; trading with the enemy; international financial monetary organizations.

D 21 - R 16 *(97th Congress)*
D 24 - R 13 *(98th Congress)*

Clement J. Zablocki, Wis. (1977-83; died Dec. 3, 1983)
Dante B. Fascell, Fla. (through 98th Congress)
William S. Broomfield, Mich.

Africa — Howard Wolpe, Mich.
Asian and Pacific Affairs — Stephen J. Solarz, N.Y.
Europe and the Middle East — Lee H. Hamilton, Ind.
Human Rights and International Organizations — Don Bonker, Wash. (97th Congress); Gus Yatron, Pa. (98th Congress)
Inter-American Affairs (97th Congress) — Michael D. Barnes, Md.
International Economic Policy and Trade — Jonathan B. Bingham, N.Y. (97th Congress); Don Bonker, Wash. (98th Congress)
International Operations — Dante B. Fascell, Fla. (through 1983); Dan Mica, Fla. (through 98th Congress)
International Security and Scientific Affairs — Clement J. Zablocki, Wis. (died Dec. 3, 1983); Dante B. Fascell, Fla. (through 98th Congress)
Western Hemisphere Affairs (98th Congress) — Michael D. Barnes, Md.

Government Operations

Budget and accounting measures; overall economy and efficiency in government including federal procurement; executive branch reorganization; general revenue sharing; intergovernmental relations; National Archives.

D 23 - R 17 *(97th Congress)*
D 25 - R 14 *(98th Congress)*

Jack Brooks, Texas (1975-85)
Frank Horton, N.Y.

Commerce, Consumer and Monetary Affairs — Benjamin S. Rosenthal, N.Y. (97th Congress); Doug Barnard Jr., Ga. (98th Congress)

Environment, Energy and Natural Resources — Toby Moffett, Conn. (97th Congress); Mike Synar, Okla. (98th Congress)
Government Activities and Transportation — John L. Burton (97th Congress); Cardiss Collins, Ill. (98th Congress)
Government Information and Individual Rights (97th Congress) — Glenn English, Okla.
Government Information, Justice and Agriculture (98th Congress) — Glenn English, Okla.
Intergovernmental Relations and Human Resources — L. H. Fountain, N.C. (97th Congress); Ted Weiss, N.Y. (98th Congress)
Legislation and National Security — Jack Brooks, Texas
Manpower and Housing — Cardiss Collins, Ill. (97th Congress); Barney Frank, Mass. (98th Congress)

House Administration

House administration generally; contested elections; federal elections generally; corrupt practices; qualifications of members of the House; *Congressional Record*; the Capitol; Library of Congress; Smithsonian Institution; Botanic Gardens.

D 11 - R 8 *(97th Congress)*
D 12 - R 7 *(98th Congress)*

Augustus F. Hawkins, Calif. (1981-84)
Frank Annunzio, Ill. (through 98th Congress)
Bill Frenzel, Minn.

Accounts — Frank Annunzio, Ill.
Contracts and Printing — Joseph M. Gaydos, Pa.
Office Systems — Robert H. Mollohan, W.Va. (97th Congress); Charlie Rose, N.C. (98th Congress)
Personnel and Police — Joseph G. Minish, N.J.
Services — Ed Jones, Tenn.

Policy Group

Information Computers (97th Congress) — Charlie Rose, N.C.

Task Forces

Committee Organization (97th Congress) — Augustus F. Hawkins, Calif.
Elections (98th Congress) — Al Swift, Wash.
Telephone Configuration (98th Congress) — Charlie Rose, N.C.

Interior and Insular Affairs

Public lands, parks and natural resources generally; Geological Survey; interstate water compacts; irrigation and reclamation; Indian affairs; minerals, mines and mining; petroleum conservation on public lands; regulation of domestic nuclear energy industry including waste disposal; territorial affairs of the United States.

R 23 - R 17 *(97th Congress)*
R 25 - R 14 *(98th Congress)*

Morris K. Udall, Ariz. (1977-85)
Manuel Lujan, N.M.

Energy and the Environment — Morris K. Udall, Ariz.
Insular Affairs — Antonio Borja Won Pat, Guam
Mines and Mining (97th Congress) — Jim Santini, Nev.
Mining, Forest Management and Bonneville Power Administration (98th Congress) — James Weaver, Ore.
Oversight and Investigations — Edward J. Markey, Mass.
Public Lands and National Parks — John F. Seiberling, Ohio
Water and Power (98th Congress) — Abraham Kazen Jr., Texas
Water and Power Resources (97th Congress) — Abraham Kazen Jr., Texas

Judiciary

Civil and criminal judicial proceedings generally; federal courts and judges; bankruptcy, mutiny, espionage and counterfeiting; civil liberties; constitutional amendments; immigration and naturalization; interstate compacts; claims against the United States; apportionment of representatives; meetings of Congress and attendance of members; penitentiaries; patents, copyrights and trademarks; presidential succession; monopolies and unlawful restraints of trade; internal security.

D 16 - R 12 *(97th Congress)*
D 20 - R 11 *(98th Congress)*

Peter W. Rodino Jr., N.J. (1973-85)
Robert McClory, Ill. (97th Congress)
Hamilton Fish Jr., N.Y. (98th Congress)

Administrative Law and Governmental Relations — George E. Danielson, Calif. (resigned March 9, 1982); Sam B. Hall Jr., Texas (through 98th Congress)
Civil and Constitutional Rights — Don Edwards, Calif.
Courts, Civil Liberties and Administration of Justice — Robert W. Kastenmeier, Wis.
Crime — William J. Hughes, N.J.
Criminal Justice — John Conyers Jr., Mich.
Immigration, Refugees and International Law — Romano L. Mazzoli, Ky.
Monopolies and Commercial Law — Peter W. Rodino Jr., N.J.

Merchant Marine and Fisheries

Merchant marine generally; oceanography and marine affairs including coastal zone management; Coast Guard; fisheries and wildlife; regulation of common carriers by water and inspection of merchant marine vessels, lights and signals, lifesaving equipment and fire protection; navigation; Panama Canal, Canal Zone and interoceanic canals generally; registration and licensing of vessels; rules and international arrangements to prevent collisions at sea; international fishing agreements; Coast Guard and Merchant Marine academies and state maritime academies.

D 20 - R 15 *(97th Congress)*
D 25 - R 14 *(98th Congress)*

Walter B. Jones, N.C. (1981-85)
Gene Snyder, Ky. (97th Congress)
Edwin B. Forsythe, N.J. (died March 29, 1984)
Joel Pritchard, Wash. (through 98th Congress)

Coast Guard and Navigation — Gerry E. Studds, Mass. (censured July 20, 1983; stripped of chairmanship); Walter B. Jones, N.C. (through 98th Congress)
Fisheries and Wildlife Conservation and the Environment — John B. Breaux, La.
Merchant Marine — Mario Biaggi, N.Y.
Oceanography — Norman E. D'Amours, N.H.
Panama Canal and the Outer Continental Shelf — Carroll Hubbard Jr., Ky.

Post Office and Civil Service

Postal and federal civil services; census and the collection of statistics generally; Hatch Act; holidays and celebrations.

D 15 - R 11 *(97th Congress)*
D 15 - R 9 *(98th Congress)*

William D. Ford, Mich. (1981-85)
Edwin J. Derwinski, Ill. (97th Congress)
Gene Taylor, Mo. (98th Congress)

Census and Population — Robert Garcia, N.Y.
Civil Service — Patricia Schroeder, Colo.
Compensation and Employee Benefits — Mary Rose Oakar, Ohio
Human Resources — Geraldine A. Ferraro, N.Y. (97th Congress); Donald J. Albosta, Mich. (98th Congress)
Investigations — William D. Ford, Mich.
Postal Operations and Services — William Clay, Mo.
Postal Personnel and Management — Mickey Leland, Texas

Public Works and Transportation

Flood control and improvement of rivers and harbors; construction and maintenance of roads; oil and other pollution of navigable waters; public buildings and grounds; public works for the benefit of navigation including bridges and dams; water power; transportation, except railroads; Botanic Gardens; Library of Congress; Smithsonian Institution.

R 25 - D 19 *(97th Congress)*
R 30 - R 18 *(98th Congress)*

James J. Howard, N.J. (1981-85)
Don H. Clausen, Calif. (97th Congress)
Gene Snyder, Ky. (98th Congress)

Aviation — Norman Y. Mineta, Calif.
Economic Development — James L. Oberstar, Minn.
Investigations and Oversight — Elliot H. Levitas, Ga.
Public Buildings and Grounds — John G. Fary, Ill. (97th Congress); Robert A. Young, Mo. (98th Congress)
Surface Transportation — Glenn M. Anderson, Calif.
Water Resources — Robert A. Roe, N.J.

Rules

Rules and order of business of the House; emergency waivers under the Congressional Budget Act of required reporting date for bills and resolutions authorizing new budget authority; recesses and final adjournment of Congress.

D 11 - R 5 *(97th Congress)*
D 9 - R 4 *(98th Congress)*

Richard Bolling, Mo. (1979-83)
Claude Pepper, Fla. (1983-85)
James H. Quillen, Tenn.

Legislative Process — Gillis W. Long, La.
Rules of the House — Joe Moakley, Mass.

Science and Technology

Scientific and astronautical research and development including resources, personnel, equipment and facilities; Bureau of Standards, standardization of weights and measures and the metric system; National Aeronautics and Space Administration; National Aeronautics and Space Council; National Science Foundation; outer space including exploration and control; science scholarships; federally owned or operated non-military energy laboratories; civil aviation research and development; energy research, development and demonstration (except nuclear research and development); National Weather Service.

R 23 - D 17 *(97th Congress)*
R 26 - R 15 *(98th Congress)*

Don Fuqua, Fla. (1979-85)
Larry Winn Jr., Kan.

Energy Development and Applications — Don Fuqua, Fla.
Energy Research and Production — Marilyn Lloyd Bouquard, Tenn.
Investigations and Oversight — Albert Gore Jr., Tenn.
Natural Resources, Agriculture Research and Environment — James H. Scheuer, N.Y.
Science, Research and Technology — Doug Walgren, Pa.
Space Science and Applications — Ronnie G. Flippo, Ala. (97th Congress); Harold L. Volkmer, Mo. (98th Congress)
Transportation, Aviation and Materials — Dan Glickman, Kan.

Select Aging

Problems of older Americans including income, housing, health, welfare, employment, education, recreation and participation in family and community life. Studies and reports findings to House, but cannot report legislation.

D 31 - R 23 *(97th Congress)*
D 38 - R 22 *(98th Congress)*

Claude Pepper, Fla. (1976-83)
Edward R. Roybal, Calif. (1983-85)
Matthew J. Rinaldo, N.J.

Health and Long-Term Care — Claude Pepper, Fla.
Housing and Consumer Interests — Edward R. Roybal, Calif. (97th Congress); Don Bonker, Wash. (98th Congress)
Human Services — Mario Biaggi, N.Y.
Retirement, Income and Employment — John L. Burton, Calif. (97th Congress); Edward R. Roybal, Calif. (98th Congress)

Select Children, Youth and Families

Problems of children, youth and families including income maintenance, health, nutrition, education, welfare, employment and recreation. Studies and reports findings to House, but cannot report legislation.

D 16 - R 9 *(98th Congress)*

George Miller, Calif. (1983-85)
Dan Marriott, Utah

Select Intelligence

Legislative and budgetary authority over the Central Intelligence Agency, the Defense Intelligence Agency, the National Security Agency, intelligence activities of the Federal Bureau of Investigation and other components of the federal intelligence community.

D 9 - R 5

Edward P. Boland, Mass. (1977-85)
J. Kenneth Robinson, Va.

Legislation — Romano L. Mazzoli, Ky.
Oversight and Evaluation — Charlie Rose, N.C. (97th Congress); Wyche Fowler Jr., Ga. (98th Congress)
Program and Budget Authorization — Edward P. Boland, Mass.

Select Narcotics Abuse and Control

Problems of narcotics, drug and polydrug abuse and control including opium and its derivatives, other narcotic

drugs, psychotropics and other controlled substances; trafficking, manufacturing and distribution; treatment, prevention and rehabilitation; narcotics-related violations of tax laws; international treaties and agreements relating to narcotics and drug abuse; role of organized crime in narcotics and drug abuse; abuse and control in the armed forces and in industry; criminal justice system and narcotic and drug law violations and crimes related to drug abuse. Studies and reports findings to House, but cannot report legislation.

D 11 - R 8 *(97th Congress)*
D 16 - R 9 *(98th Congress)*

Leo C. Zeferetti, N.Y. (1981-83)
Charles B. Rangel, N.Y. (1983-85)
Tom Railsback, Ill. (97th Congress)
Benjamin A. Gilman, N.Y. (98th Congress)

No standing subcommittees.

Small Business

Assistance to and protection of small business including financial aid; participation of small business enterprises in federal procurement and government contracts.

D 23 - R 17 *(97th Congress)*
D 26 - R 15 *(98th Congress)*

Parren J. Mitchell, Md. (1981-85)
Joseph M. McDade, Pa.

Antitrust and Restraint of Trade Activities Affecting Small Business — Thomas A. Luken, Ohio
Energy, Environment and Safety Issues Affecting Small Business — Berkley Bedell, Iowa (97th Congress); Ike Skelton, Mo. (98th Congress)
Export Opportunities and Special Small Business Problems — Andy Ireland, Fla. (switched to Republican Party July 5, 1984; stripped of chairmanship)
General Oversight (97th Congress) — John L. LaFalce, N.Y.
General Oversight and the Economy — Berkley Bedell, Iowa
SBA and SBIC Authority, Minority Enterprise and General Small Business Problems — Parren J. Mitchell, Md.
Tax, Access to Equity Capital and Business Opportunities — Henry J. Nowak, N.Y.

Standards of Official Conduct

Measures relating to the Code of Official Conduct; conduct of House members and employees; Ethics in Government Act.

D 6 - R 6

Louis Stokes, Ohio (1981-85)
Floyd Spence, S.C.

No standing subcommittees.

Veterans' Affairs

Veterans' measures generally; compensation, vocational rehabilitation and education of veterans; armed forces life insurance; pensions; readjustment benefits; veterans' hospitals, medical care and treatment.

D 17 - R 14 *(97th Congress)*
D 21 - R 12 *(98th Congress)*

G. V. "Sonny" Montgomery, Miss. (1981-85)
John Paul Hammerschmidt, Ark.

Compensation, Pension and Insurance — Sam B. Hall Jr., Texas (97th Congress); Douglas Applegate, Ohio (98th Congress)
Education, Training and Employment — Bob Edgar, Pa. (97th Congress); Marvin Leath, Texas (98th Congress)
Hospitals and Health Care — Ronald M. Mottl, Ohio (97th Congress); Bob Edgar, Pa. (98th Congress)
Housing and Memorial Affairs — Marvin Leath, Texas (97th Congress); Richard C. Shelby, Ala. (98th Congress)
Oversight and Investigations — G. V. "Sonny" Montgomery, Miss.

Ways and Means

Revenue measures generally; reciprocal trade agreements; customs, collection districts and ports of entry and delivery; bonded debt of the United States; deposit of public moneys; transportation of dutiable goods; tax exempt foundations and charitable trusts; Social Security.

D 23 - R 12

Dan Rostenkowski, Ill. (1981-85)
Barber B. Conable Jr., N.Y.

Health — Andrew Jacobs Jr., Ind.
Oversight — Charles B. Rangel, N.Y.
Public Assistance and Unemployment Compensation — Fortney H. "Pete" Stark, Calif. (97th Congress); Harold E. Ford, Tenn. (98th Congress)
Select Revenue Measures — William R. Cotter, Conn. (died Sept. 8, 1981); Fortney H. "Pete" Stark, Calif. (through 98th Congress)
Social Security — J. J. Pickle, Texas
Trade — Sam Gibbons, Fla.

Political Committees

Democratic Congressional Campaign Committee (campaign support committee for Democratic House candidates) — Tony Coelho, Calif. (97th Congress)
Democratic Personnel Committee (selects, appoints and supervises Democratic patronage positions) — Joe Moakley, Mass.
Democratic Steering and Policy Committee (scheduling of legislation and Democratic committee assignments) — Thomas P. O'Neill Jr., Mass.
Republican Committee on Committees (makes Republican committee assignments) — Robert H. Michel, Ill.

Republican Personnel Committee (selects, appoints and supervises Republican patronage positions) — John T. Myers, Ind.

Republican Policy Committee (advises on party action and policy) — Dick Cheney, Wyo.

National Republican Congressional Committee (campaign support for Republican House candidates) — Guy Vander Jagt, Mich.

Joint Committees

Economic

Studies and investigates all recommendations included in the president's annual Economic Report to Congress and reports findings and recommendations to the House and Senate.

Rep. Henry S. Reuss, D-Wis. (97th Congress)
Sen. Roger W. Jepsen, R-Iowa (98th Congress)

Library

Management and expansion of the Library of Congress; receipt of gifts for the benefit of the Library; development and maintenance of the Botanic Gardens; placement of statues and other works of art in the Capitol.

Rep. Augustus F. Hawkins, D-Calif. (97th Congress)
Sen. Charles McC. Mathias Jr., R-Md. (98th Congress)

Printing

Inefficiencies and waste in public printing, binding and distribution of government publications; federal paper procurement; executive branch department and agency printing plants; purchase of printing and binding equipment; Federal Printing Procurement Program; Depository Library Program; Government Printing Office; congressional publications including the *Congressional Record*.

Sen. Charles McC. Mathias Jr., R-Md. (97th Congress)
Rep. Augustus F. Hawkins, D-Calif. (98th Congress)

Taxation

Operation, effects and administration of the federal system of internal revenue taxes; measures and methods for simplification of taxes.

Rep. Dan Rostenkowski, D-Ill.

Post-Election Sessions

Congress has held seven post-election sessions since 1945.

1948. The 1948 post-election session of the 80th Congress lasted only two hours. Both chambers swore in new members, approved several minor resolutions and received last-minute reports from committees.

In addition to final floor action, several committees resumed work. The most active was the House Un-American Activities Committee, which continued its investigation of alleged communist espionage in the federal government.

1950. After the 1950 elections, President Harry S Truman sent a "must" agenda to the lame-duck session of the 81st Congress. The president's list included supplemental defense appropriations, an excess profits tax, aid to Yugoslavia, a three-month extension of federal rent controls and statehood for Hawaii and Alaska. During a marathon session that lasted until only a few hours before its successor took over, the 81st Congress acted on all of the president's legislative items except the statehood bills, which were blocked by a Senate filibuster.

1954. Only one chamber of the 83rd Congress convened after the 1954 elections. The Senate returned Nov. 8 to hold what has been called a "censure session," a continuing investigation into the conduct of Sen. Joseph R. McCarthy, R-Wis. (1947-57). By a 67-22 roll call the Senate Dec. 2 voted to "condemn" McCarthy for his behavior.

In other post-election floor action, the Senate passed a series of miscellaneous and administrative resolutions and swore in new members.

1970. President Richard M. Nixon criticized the lame-duck Congress as one that had "seemingly lost the capacity to decide and the will to act." Filibusters and intense controversy contributed to inaction on the president's request for trade legislation and welfare reform.

Congress nevertheless claimed some substantive results during the session, which ended Jan. 2, 1971. Several major appropriations bills were cleared for presidential signature. Congress also approved foreign aid to Cambodia, provided interim funding for the supersonic transport plane (SST) and repealed the Tonkin Gulf Resolution that had been used as a basis for American military involvement in Vietman.

1974. In a session that ran from Nov. 18 to Dec. 20, 1974, the 93rd Congress cleared several important bills for presidential signature, including a mass transit bill, a Labor-HEW appropriations bill and a foreign assistance package. A House-Senate conference committee reached agreement on a major strip-mining bill, but President Gerald R. Ford vetoed it.

Congress approved the nomination of Nelson A. Rockefeller as vice president. It also overrode presidential vetoes of two bills — one broadening the Freedom of Information Act, a second authorizing educational benefits for Korean War and Vietnam-era veterans.

1980. The lame-duck session of the 96th Congress was productive, at least until Dec. 5, the original adjournment

Year	Congress	Dates
1948	80th	Dec. 31, 1948 (2-hour session)
1950	81st	Nov. 27, 1950 — Jan. 2, 1951
1954	83rd	Nov. 8, 1954 — Dec. 2, 1954
1970	91st	Nov. 16, 1970 — Jan. 2, 1971 (Senate)
1974	93rd	Nov. 18, 1974 — Dec. 20, 1974
1980	96th	Nov. 12, 1980 — Dec. 16, 1980
1982	97th	Nov. 29, 1982 — Dec. 23, 1982 (Senate) Nov. 29, 1982 — Dec. 21, 1982 (House)

Recent Lame-Duck Sessions

date set by congressional leaders. By that date a budget had been approved, along with a budget reconciliation measure. Ten regular appropriations bills had cleared, though one subsequently was vetoed. Congress had approved two major environmental measures — an Alaskan lands bill and toxic waste "superfund" legislation — as well as a three-year extension of general revenue sharing.

After Dec. 5, however, the legislative pace slowed noticeably. Action on a continuing appropriations resolution for those departments and agencies whose regular funding had not been cleared was delayed, first by a filibuster on a fair housing bill and later by more than 100 "Christmas tree" amendments, including a $10,000-a-year pay raise for members. After the conference report failed in the Senate and twice was rewritten, the bill was shorn of virtually all its "ornaments" and finally cleared by both chambers on Dec. 16.

1982. Despite the reluctance of congressional leaders, President Reagan urged the convening of a post-election session at the end of the 97th Congress, principally to pass remaining appropriations bills.

Rising unemployment — and Democratic election gains in the House — made job creation efforts the focus of the lame-duck Congress, however. Overriding the objections of Republican conservatives, Congress passed Reagan-backed legislation raising the federal gasoline tax from 4 cents to 9 cents a gallon to pay for highway repairs and mass transit. Supporters said the legislation would help alleviate unemployment by creating 300,000 jobs.

Congress eventually cleared four additional appropria-

tions bills, packaging the remaining six in a continuing appropriations resolution that also included a pay raise for House members. Conferees dropped funding for emergency jobs programs to avert a threatened veto of the resolution.

The lame-duck session also was highlighted by Congress' refusal to fund production and procurement of the first five MX intercontinental missiles, the first time in recent history that either house of Congress had denied a president's request to fund production of a strategic weapon.

Senate Cloture Votes, 1917-84

The Senate's ultimate check on the filibuster is the provision for cloture, or limitation on debate, contained in Rule 22 of its Standing Rules. The original Rule 22 was adopted in 1917 following a furor over the "talking to death" of a proposal by President Woodrow Wilson for arming American merchant ships before the United States entered World War I. The new cloture rule required the votes of two-thirds of all the senators present and voting to invoke cloture. In 1949, during a parliamentary skirmish preceding scheduled consideration of a Fair Employment Practices Commission bill, the requirement was raised to two-thirds of the entire Senate membership.

A revision of the rule in 1959 provided for limitation of debate by a vote of two-thirds of the senators present and voting, two days after a cloture petition was submitted by 16 senators. If cloture was adopted by the Senate, further debate was limited to one hour for each senator on the bill itself and on all amendments affecting it. No new amendments could be offered except by unanimous consent.

Amendments that were not germane to the pending business and dilatory motions were out of order. The rule applied both to regular legislation and to motions to change the Standing Rules.

Rule 22 was revised significantly in 1975 by lowering the vote needed for cloture to three-fifths of the Senate membership (60, if there were no vacancies). That revision applied to any matter except proposed rules changes, for which the old requirement of a two-thirds majority of senators present and voting still applied.

In a further revision of the rule, the Senate in 1979 limited post-cloture delaying tactics by providing that once cloture was invoked, a final vote had to be taken after no more than 100 hours of debate. All time spent on quorum calls, roll-call votes and other parliamentary procedures was to be included in the 100-hour limit.

Following is a list of the 206 cloture votes taken between 1917, when Senate Rule 22 was adopted, and the end of 1984; 70 of the votes (in **bold type**) were successful.

Issue	Date	Vote	Yeas Needed
Versailles Treaty	Nov. 15, 1919	78-16	63
Emergency tariff	Feb. 2, 1921	36-35	48
Tariff bill	July 7, 1922	45-35	54
World Court	Jan. 25, 1926	68-26	63
Migratory birds	June 1, 1926	46-33	53
Branch banking	Feb. 15, 1927	65-18	56
Disabled officers	Feb. 26, 1927	51-36	58
Colorado River	Feb. 26, 1927	32-59	61
D.C. buildings	Feb. 28, 1927	52-31	56
Prohibition Bureau	Feb. 28, 1927	55-27	55
Banking Act	Jan. 19, 1933	58-30	59
Anti-lynching	Jan. 27, 1938	37-51	59
Anti-lynching	Feb. 16, 1938	42-46	59
Anti-poll tax	Nov. 23, 1942	37-41	52
Anti-poll tax	May 15, 1944	36-44	54
Fair Employment Practices Commission	Feb. 9, 1946	48-36	56
British loan	May 7, 1946	41-44	55
Labor disputes	May 25, 1946	3-77	54
Anti-poll tax	July 31, 1946	39-33	48
Fair Employment	May 19, 1950	52-32	64
Fair Employment	July 12, 1950	55-33	64
Atomic Energy Act	July 26, 1954	44-42	64
Civil Rights Act	March 10, 1960	42-53	64
Amend Rule 22	Sept. 19, 1961	37-43	54
Literacy tests	May 9, 1962	43-53	64
Literacy tests	May 14, 1962	42-52	63
Comsat Act	Aug. 14, 1962	63-27	60
Amend Rule 22	Feb. 7, 1963	54-42	64
Civil Rights Act	June 10, 1964	71-29	67
Legislative reapportionment	Sept. 10, 1964	30-63	62
Voting Rights Act	May 25, 1965	70-30	67
Right-to-work repeal	Oct. 11, 1965	45-47	62
Right-to-work repeal	Feb. 8, 1966	51-48	66
Right-to-work repeal	Feb. 10, 1966	50-49	66
Civil Rights Act	Sept. 14, 1966	54-42	64
Civil Rights Act	Sept. 19, 1966	52-41	62
D.C. Home Rule	Oct. 10, 1966	41-37	52
Amend Rule 22	Jan. 24, 1967	53-46	66
Open Housing	Feb. 20, 1968	55-37	62
Open Housing	Feb. 26, 1968	56-36	62
Open Housing	March 1, 1968	59-35	63
Open Housing	March 4, 1968	65-32	65
Fortas Nomination	Oct. 1, 1968	45-43	59
Amend Rule 22	Jan. 16, 1969	51-47	66
Amend Rule 22	Jan. 28, 1969	50-42	62
Electoral College	Sept. 17, 1970	54-36	60
Electoral College	Sept. 29, 1970	53-34	58
Supersonic transport	Dec. 19, 1970	43-48	61
Supersonic transport	Dec. 22, 1970	42-44	58
Amend Rule 22	Feb. 18, 1971	48-37	57
Amend Rule 22	Feb. 23, 1971	50-36	58
Amend Rule 22	March 2, 1971	48-36	56
Amend Rule 22	March 9, 1971	55-39	63
Military Draft	June 23, 1971	65-27	62
Lockheed Loan	July 26, 1971	42-47	60
Lockheed Loan	July 28, 1971	59-39	66
Lockheed Loan	July 30, 1971	53-37	60
Military Draft	Sept. 21, 1971	61-30	61
Rehnquist nomination	Dec. 10, 1971	52-42	63
Equal Job Opportunity	Feb. 1, 1972	48-37	57
Equal Job Opportunity	Feb. 3, 1972	53-35	59
Equal Job Opportunity	Feb. 22, 1972	71-23	63
U.S.-Soviet Arms Pact	Sept. 14, 1972	76-15	61
Consumer Agency	Sept. 29, 1972	47-29	51
Consumer Agency	Oct. 3, 1972	55-32	58
Consumer Agency	Oct. 5, 1972	52-30	55
School Busing	Oct. 10, 1972	45-37	55
School Busing	Oct. 11, 1972	49-39	59
School Busing	Oct. 12, 1972	49-38	58
Voter Registration	April 30, 1973	56-31	58
Voter Registration	May 3, 1973	60-34	63
Voter Registration	May 9, 1973	67-32	66
Public Campaign Financing	Dec. 2, 1973	47-33	54
Public Campaign Financing	Dec. 3, 1973	49-39	59
Rhodesian Chrome Ore	Dec. 11, 1973	59-35	63
Rhodesian Chrome Ore	Dec. 13, 1973	62-33	64
Legal Services Program	Dec. 13, 1973	60-36	64
Legal Services Program	Dec. 14, 1973	56-29	57

Appendix

Issue	Date	Vote	Yeas Needed
Rhodesian Chrome Ore	Dec. 18, 1973	63-26	60
Legal Services Program	Jan. 30, 1974	68-29	65
Genocide Treaty	Feb. 5, 1974	55-36	61
Genocide Treaty	Feb. 6, 1974	55-38	62
Government Pay Raise	March 6, 1974	67-31	66
Public Campaign Financing	April 4, 1974	60-36	64
Public Campaign Financing	April 9, 1974	64-30	63
Public Debt Ceiling	June 19, 1974	50-43	62
Public Debt Ceiling	June 19, 1974	45-48	62
Public Debt Ceiling	June 26, 1974	48-50	66
Consumer Agency	July 30, 1974	56-42	66
Consumer Agency	Aug. 1, 1974	59-39	66
Consumer Agency	Aug. 20, 1974	59-35	63
Consumer Agency	Sept. 19, 1974	64-34	66
Export-Import Bank	Dec. 3, 1974	51-39	60
Export-Import Bank	Dec. 4, 1974	48-44	62
Trade Reform	Dec. 13, 1974	71-19	60
Fiscal 1975 Supplemental Funds	Dec. 4, 1974	56-27	56
Export-Import Bank	Dec. 14, 1974	49-35	56
Export-Import Bank	Dec. 16, 1974	54-34	59
Social Services Programs	Dec. 17, 1974	70-23	62
Tax Law Changes	Dec. 17, 1974	67-25	62
Rail Reorganization Act	Feb. 26, 1975	86-8	63
Amend Rule 22	March 5, 1975	73-21	63
Amend Rule 22	March 7, 1975	73-21	63
Tax Reduction	March 20, 1975	59-38	60
Tax Reduction	March 21, 1975	83-13	60
Agency for Consumer Advocacy	May 13, 1975	71-27	60
Senate Staffing	June 11, 1975	77-19	64
New Hampshire Senate Seat	June 24, 1975	57-39	60
New Hampshire Senate Seat	June 25, 1975	56-41	60
New Hampshire Senate Seat	June 26, 1975	54-40	60
New Hampshire Senate Seat	July 8, 1975	57-38	60
New Hampshire Senate Seat	July 9, 1975	57-38	60
New Hampshire Senate Seat	July 10, 1975	54-38	60
Voting Rights Act	July 21, 1975	72-19	60
Voting Rights Act	July 23, 1975	76-20	60
Oil Price Decontrol	July 30, 1975	54-38	60
Labor-HEW Appropriations	Sept. 23, 1975	46-48	60
Labor-HEW Appropriations	Sept. 24, 1975	64-33	60
Common-Site Picketing	Nov. 11, 1975	66-30	60
Common-Site Picketing	Nov. 14, 1975	58-31	60
Common-Site Picketing	Nov. 18, 1975	62-37	60
Rail Reorganization	Dec. 4, 1975	61-27	60
New York City Aid	Dec. 5, 1975	70-27	60
Rice Production Act	Feb. 3, 1976	70-19	60
Antitrust Amendments	June 3, 1976	67-22	60
Antitrust Amendments	Aug. 31, 1976	63-27	60
Civil Rights Attorneys' Fees	Sept. 23, 1976	63-26	60
Draft Resisters Pardons	Jan. 24, 1977	53-43	60
Campaign Financing	July 29, 1977	49-45	60
Campaign Financing	Aug. 1, 1977	47-46	60
Campaign Financing	Aug. 2, 1977	52-46	60
Natural Gas Pricing	Sept. 26, 1977	77-17	60
Labor Law Revision	June 7, 1978	42-47	60
Labor Law Revision	June 8, 1978	49-41	60
Labor Law Revision	June 13, 1978	54-43	60
Labor Law Revision	June 14, 1978	58-41	60
Labor Law Revision	June 15, 1978	58-39	60
Labor Law Revision	June 22, 1978	53-45	60
Revenue Act of 1978	Oct. 9, 1978	62-28	60
Energy Taxes	Oct. 14, 1978	71-13	60
Windfall Profits Tax	Dec. 12, 1979	53-46	60
Windfall Profits Tax	Dec. 13, 1979	56-40	60
Windfall Profits Tax	Dec. 14, 1979	56-39	60
Windfall Profits Tax	Dec. 17, 1979	84-14	60
Lubbers Nomination	April 21, 1980	46-60	60
Lubbers Nomination	April 22, 1980	62-34	60
Rights of Institutionalized	April 28, 1980	44-39	60
Rights of Institutionalized	April 29, 1980	56-34	60
Rights of Institutionalized	April 30, 1980	53-35	60
Rights of Institutionalized	May 1, 1980	60-34	60
Bottlers' Antitrust Immunity	May 15, 1980	86-6	60
Draft Registration Funding	June 10, 1980	62-32	60
Zimmerman Nomination	Aug. 1, 1980	51-35	60
Zimmerman Nomination	Aug. 4, 1980	45-31	60
Zimmerman Nomination	Aug. 5, 1980	63-31	60
Alaska Lands	Aug. 18, 1980	63-25	60
Vessel Tonnage/Strip Mining	Aug. 21, 1980	61-32	60
Fair Housing Amendments	Dec. 3, 1980	51-39	60
Fair Housing Amendments	Dec. 4, 1980	62-32	60
Fair Housing Amendments	Dec. 9, 1980	54-43	60
Breyer Nomination	Dec. 9, 1980	68-28	60
Justice Department Authorization	July 10, 1981	38-48	60
Justice Department Authorization	July 13, 1981	54-32	60
Justice Department Authorization	July 29, 1981	59-37	60
Justice Department Authorization	Sept. 10, 1981	57-33	60
Justice Department Authorization	Sept. 16, 1981	61-36	60
Justice Department Authorization	Dec. 10, 1981	64-35	60
State, Justice, Commerce, Judiciary Appropriations	Dec. 11, 1981	59-35	60
Broadcast Senate Proceedings	April 20, 1982	47-51	60
Criminal Code Reform Act	April 27, 1982	45-46	60
Urgent Supplemental Appropriations, Fiscal 1982	May 27, 1982	95-2	60
Voting Rights Act	June 15, 1982	86-8	60
Debt Limit Increase	Sept. 9, 1982	41-47	60
Debt Limit Increase	Sept. 13, 1982	45-35	60
Debt Limit Increase	Sept. 15, 1982	50-44	60
Debt Limit Increase	Sept. 20, 1982	50-39	60
Debt Limit Increase	Sept. 21, 1982	53-47	60
Debt Limit Increase	Sept. 22, 1982	54-46	60
Debt Limit Increase	Sept. 23, 1982	53-45	60
Antitrust Equal Enforcement Act	Dec. 2, 1982	38-58	60
Antitrust Equal Enforcement Act	Dec. 2, 1982	44-51	60
Transportation Assistance Act	Dec. 13, 1982	75-13	60
Transportation Assistance Act	Dec. 16, 1982	48-50	60
Transportation Assistance Act	Dec. 16, 1982	5-93	60
Transportation Assistance Act	Dec. 19, 1982	89-5	60
Transportation Assistance Act	Dec. 20, 1982	87-8	60
Transportation Assistance Act	Dec. 23, 1982	81-5	60
Emergency Jobs Appropriations/ Interest Withholding	March 16, 1983	50-48	60
Emergency Jobs Appropriations/ Interest Withholding	March 16, 1983	59-39	60
International Trade and Investment/ Interest Withholding	April 19, 1983	34-53	60

Issue	Date	Vote	Yeas Needed	Issue	Date	Vote	Yeas Needed
International Trade and Investment/ Interest Withholding	April 19, 1983	39-59	60	Agriculture Appropriations, Fiscal 1985	Aug. 8, 1984	68-30	60
Defense Authorizations, 1984	July 21, 1983	55-41	60	Wilkinson Nomination	Aug. 9, 1984	65-32	60
Radio Broadcasting to Cuba	Aug. 3, 1983	62-33	60	**Financial Services** Competitive Equity Act	Sept. 10, 1984	89-3	60
National Gas Policy Act	Nov. 3, 1983	86-7	60	**Financial Services** Competitive Equity Act	Sept. 13, 1984	92-6	60
Capital Punishment	Feb. 9, 1984	65-26	60	**Broadcasting of Senate Procedures**	Sept. 18, 1984	73-26	60
Hydroelectric Power Plants	July 30, 1984	60-28	60	Broadcasting of Senate Procedures	Sept. 21, 1984	37-44	60
Wilkinson Nomination	July 31, 1984	57-39	60	**Surface Transportation and Uniform Relocation Assistance Act**	Sept. 24, 1984	70-12	60
Agriculture Appropriations, Fiscal 1985	Aug. 6, 1984	54-31	60	**Continuing Appropriations**	Sept. 29, 1984	92-4	60

Text of Court Opinions on Legislative Vetoes

In a landmark decision affecting the relative powers of the legislative and executive branches of government, the Supreme Court June 23, 1983, in a 7-2 ruling, declared the so-called "legislative veto" unconstitutional. The decision overturned a device that had been included in more than 200 laws beginning with Herbert Hoover's administration in 1932.

Historians and other experts on constitutional issues called the decision the most important constitutional ruling by the Court since its 1974 decision ordering President Richard M. Nixon to surrender subpoenaed White House tapes. Moreover, in his dissent, Justice Byron R. White wrote that the ruling "strikes down in one fell swoop provisions in more laws enacted by Congress than the Court has cumulatively invalidated in its history."

The broad ruling came in an obscure immigration case, Immigration and Naturalization Service v. Chadha. *The case had its beginnings in 1974 when a Kenyan who had overstayed his student visa won a decision from the Immigration and Naturalization Service (INS) suspending his deportation. The House of Representatives, exercising a legislative veto provision in the 1952 Immigration and Naturalization Act, vetoed that suspension. The student, Jagdish Rai Chadha, filed suit challenging the power of the House to take that action. Holding that the House had exceeded it constitutional powers, the 9th U.S. Circuit Court of Appeals agreed, and the Supreme Court, in its far reaching June 23 decision, upheld the ruling of the lower court.*

The following are excerpts from the Supreme Court's majority opinion striking down the legislative veto and from the dissenting opinion by Justice White. The majority opinion was written by Chief Justice Warren E. Burger on behalf of himself and Justices Harry A. Blackmun, William J. Brennan Jr., Thurgood Marshall, Sandra Day O'Connor and John Paul Stevens.

Nos. 80-1832, 80-2170 and 80-2171

_____

On appeal from the United States Court of Appeals for the Ninth Circuit:

Immigration and Naturalization
Service, Appellant
v.
Jagdish Rai Chadha et al.

On Writs of Certiorari to the United States Court of Appeals for the Ninth Circuit:

United States House of
Representatives, Petitioner
v.
Immigration and Naturalization
Service et al.

United States Senate, Petitioner
v.
Immigration and Naturalization
Service et al.

[June 23, 1983]

CHIEF JUSTICE BURGER delivered the opinion of the Court.

We granted certiorari in Nos. 80-2170 and 80-2171, and postponed consideration of the question of jurisdiction in No. 80-1832. Each presents a challenge to the constitutionality of the provision in §244(c)(2) of the Immigration and Nationality Act, 8 U.S.C. §1254(c)(2), authorizing one House of Congress, by resolution, to invalidate the decision of the Executive Branch, pursuant to authority delegated by Congress to the Attorney General of the United States, to allow a particular deportable alien to remain in the United States.

I

Chadha is an East Indian who was born in Kenya and holds a British passport. He was lawfully admitted to the United States in 1966 on a nonimmigrant student visa. His visa expired on June 30, 1972. On October 11, 1973, the District Director of the Immigration and Naturalization Service ordered Chadha to show cause why he should not be deported for having "remained in the United States for a longer time than permitted." Pursuant to §242(b) of the Immigration and Nationality Act (Act), 8 U.S.C. §1254(b), a deportation hearing was held before an immigration judge on January 11, 1974. Chadha conceded that he was deportable for overstaying his visa and the hearing was adjourned to enable him to file an application for suspension of deportation under §244(a)(1) of the Act, 8 U.S.C. §1254(a)(1). Section

244(a)(1) provides:

"(a) As hereinafter prescribed in this section, the Attorney General may, in his discretion, suspend deportation and adjust the status to that of an alien lawfully admitted for permanent residence, in the case of an alien who applies to the Attorney General for suspension of deportation and—

(1) is deportable under any law of the United States except the provisions specified in paragraph (2) of this subsection; has been physically present in the United States for a continuous period of not less than seven years immediately preceding the date of such application, and proves that during all of such period he was and is a person of good moral character; and is a person whose deportation would, in the opinion of the Attorney General, result in extreme hardship to the alien or to his spouse, parent, or child, who is a citizen of the United States or an alien lawfully admitted for permanent residence."

After Chadha submitted his application for suspension of deportation, the deportation hearing was resumed on February 7, 1974. On the basis of evidence adduced at the hearing, affidavits submitted with the application, and the results of a character investigation conducted by the INS, the immigration judge, on June 25, 1974, ordered that Chadha's deportation be suspended. The immigration judge found that Chadha met the requirements of §244(a)(1): he had resided continuously in the United States for over seven years, was of good moral character, and would suffer "extreme hardship" if deported.

Pursuant to §244(c)(1) of the Act, 8 U.S.C. §1254(c)(1), the immigration judge suspended Chadha's deportation and a report of the suspension was transmitted to Congress. Section 244(c)(1) provides:

"Upon application by any alien who is found by the Attorney General to meet the requirements of subsection (a) of this section the Attorney General may in his discretion suspend deportation of such alien. If the deportation of any alien is suspended under the provisions of this subsection, a complete and detailed statement of the facts and pertinent provisions of law in the case shall be reported to the Congress with the reasons for such suspension. Such reports shall be submitted on the first day of each calendar month in which Congress is in session."

Appendix

Once the Attorney General's recommendation for suspension of Chadha's deportation was conveyed to Congress, Congress had the power under §244(c)(2) of the Act, 8 U.S.C. §1254(c)(2), to veto the Attorney General's determination that Chadha should not be deported. Section 244(c)(2) provides:

"(2) In the case of an alien specified in paragraph (1) of subsection (a) of this subsection—

if during the session of the Congress at which a case is reported, or prior to the close of the session of the Congress next following the session at which a case is reported, either the Senate or the House of Representatives passes a resolution stating in substance that it does not favor the suspension of such deportation, the Attorney General shall thereupon deport such alien or authorize the alien's voluntary departure at his own expense under the order of deportation in the manner provided by law. If, within the time above specified, neither the Senate nor the House of Representatives shall pass such a resolution, the Attorney General shall cancel deportation proceedings."

The June 25, 1974, order of the immigration judge suspending Chadha's deportation remained outstanding as a valid order for a year and a half. For reasons not disclosed by the record, Congress did not exercise the veto authority reserved to it under §244(c)(2) until the first session of the 94th Congress. This was the final session in which Congress, pursuant to §244(c)(2), could act to veto the Attorney General's determination that Chadha should not be deported. The session ended on December 19, 1975. Absent Congressional action, Chadha's deportation proceedings would have been cancelled after this date and his status adjusted to that of a permanent resident alien.

On December 12, 1975, Representative Eilberg, Chairman of the Judiciary Subcommittee on Immigration, Citizenship, and International Law, introduced a resolution opposing "the granting of permanent residence in the United States to [six] aliens", including Chadha. The resolution was referred to the House Committee on the Judiciary. On December 16, 1975, the resolution was discharged from further consideration by the House Committee on the Judiciary and submitted to the House of Representatives for a vote. The resolution had not been printed and was not made available to other Members of the House prior to or at the time it was voted on. So far as the record before us shows, the House consideration of the resolution was based on ... Eilberg's statement ... that

"[i]t was the feeling of the committee, after reviewing 340 cases, that the aliens contained in the resolution

[Chadha and five others] did not meet these statutory requirements, particularly as it relates to hardship; and it is the opinion of the committee that their deportation should not be suspended."

The resolution was passed without debate or recorded vote. Since the House action was pursuant to §244(c)(2), the resolution was not treated as an Article I legislative act; it was not submitted to the Senate or presented to the President for his action.

After the House veto of the Attorney General's decision to allow Chadha to remain in the United States, the immigration judge reopened the deportation proceedings to implement the House order deporting Chadha. Chadha moved to terminate the proceedings on the ground that §244(c)(2) is unconstitutional. The immigration judge held that he had no authority to rule on the constitutional validity of §244(c)(2). On November 8, 1976, Chadha was ordered deported pursuant to the House action.

Chadha appealed the deportation order to the Board of Immigration Appeals again contending that §244(c)(2) is unconstitutional. The Board held that it had "no power to declare unconstitutional an act of Congress" and Chadha's appeal was dismissed.

Pursuant to §106(a) of the Act, 8 U.S.C. §1105a(a), Chadha filed a petition for review of the deportation order in the United States Court of Appeals for the Ninth Circuit. The Immigration and Naturalization Service agreed with Chadha's position before the Court of Appeals and joined him in arguing that §244(c)(2) is unconstitutional. In light of the importance of the question, the Court of Appeals invited both the Senate and the House of Representatives to file briefs *amici curiae*.

After full briefing and oral argument, the Court of Appeals held that the House was without constitutional authority to order Chadha's deportation; accordingly it directed the Attorney General "to cease and desist from taking any steps to deport this alien based upon the resolution enacted by the House of Representatives." *Chadha* v. *INS* (CA9 1980). The essence of its holding was that §244(c)(2) violates the constitutional doctrine of separation of powers.

We granted certiorari in Nos. 80-2170 and 80-2171, and postponed consideration of our jurisdiction over the appeal in No. 80-1832 ... (1981), and we now affirm....

II

[Section A Omitted]

B

Severability

Congress also contends that the provision for the one-House veto in §244(c)(2)

cannot be severed from §244. Congress argues that if the provision for the one-House veto is held unconstitutional, all of §244 must fall. If §244 in its entirety is violative of the Constitution, it follows that the Attorney General has no authority to suspend Chadha's deportation under §244(a)(1) and Chadha would be deported. From this, Congress argues that Chadha lacks standing to challenge the constitutionality of the one-House veto provision because he could receive no relief even if his constitutional challenge proves successful.

Only recently this Court reaffirmed that the invalid portions of a statute are to be severed "[u]nless it is evident that the Legislature would not have enacted those provisions which are within its power, independently of that which is not.'" *Buckley* v. *Valeo* (1976), quoting *Champlin Refining Co.* v. *Corporation Comm'n* (1932). Here, however, we need not embark on that elusive inquiry since Congress itself has provided the answer to the question of severability in §406 of the Immigration and Nationality Act, 8 U.S.C. §1101, which provides:

"If *any* particular provision of this act, or the application thereof to *any* person or circumstance, is held invalid, *the remainder of the Act and the application of such provision to other persons or circumstances shall not be affected thereby.*" (Emphasis added.)

This language is unambiguous and gives rise to a presumption that Congress did not intend the validity of the Act as a whole, or of any part of the Act, to depend upon whether the veto clause of §244(c)(2) was invalid. The one-House veto provision in §244(c)(2) is clearly a "particular provision" of the Act as that language is used in the severability clause. Congress clearly intended "the remainder of the Act" to stand if "any particular provision" were held invalid. Congress could not have more plainly authorized the presumption that the provision for a one-House veto in §244(c)(2) is severable from the remainder of §244 and the Act of which it is a part. See *Electric Bond & Share Co.* v. *SEC* (1938).

The presumption as to the severability of the one-House veto provision in §244(c)(2) is supported by the legislative history of §244. That section and its precursors supplanted the long established pattern of dealing with deportations like Chadha's on a case-by-case basis through private bills. Although it may be that Congress was reluctant to delegate final authority over cancellation of deportations, such reluctance is not sufficient to overcome the presumption of severability raised by §406.

The Immigration Act of 1924, Pub. L. No. 139, §14, 43 Stat. 153, 162, required the Secretary of Labor to deport any alien who entered or remained in the United States unlawfully. The only means by which a deportable alien could lawfully remain in

the United States was to have his status altered by a private bill enacted by both Houses and presented to the President pursuant to the procedures set out in Art. I, §7 of the Constitution. These private bills were found intolerable by Congress....

Congress first authorized the Attorney General to suspend the deportation of certain aliens in the Alien Registration Act of 1940, ch. 439, §20, 54 Stat. 671. That Act provided that an alien was to be deported, despite the Attorney General's decision to the contrary, if both Houses, by concurrent resolution, disapproved the suspension.

In 1948, Congress amended the act to broaden the category of aliens eligible for suspension of deportation. In addition, however, Congress limited the authority of the Attorney General to suspend deportations by providing that the Attorney General could not cancel a deportation unless both Houses affirmatively voted by concurrent resolution to *approve* the Attorney General's action....

The proposal to permit one House of Congress to veto the Attorney General's suspension of an alien's deportation was incorporated in the Immigration and Nationality Act of 1952.... Plainly, Congress' desire to retain a veto in this area cannot be considered in isolation but must be viewed in the context of Congress' irritation with the burden of private immigration bills. This legislative history is not sufficient to rebut the presumption of severability raised by §406 because there is insufficient evidence that Congress would have continued to subject itself to the onerous burdens of private bills had it known that §244(c)(2) would be held unconstitutional.

A provision is further presumed severable if what remains after severance "is fully operative as a law." *Champlin Refining Co.* v. *Corporation Comm'n.* There can be no doubt that §244 is "fully operative" and workable administrative machinery without the veto provision in §244(c)(2). Entirely independent of the one-House veto, the administrative process enacted by Congress authorizes the Attorney General to suspend an alien's deportation under §244(a). Congress' oversight of the exercise of this delegated authority is preserved since all such suspensions will continue to be reported to it under §244(c)(1). Absent the passage of a bill to the contrary, deportation proceedings will be cancelled when the period specified in §244(c)(2) has expired. Clearly, §244 survives as a workable administrative mechanism without the one-House veto....

[Sections C, D and E Omitted]

F

Case or Controversy

It is also contended that this is not a genuine controversy but "a friendly, non-adversary, proceeding," *Ashwander* v. *Tennessee Valley Authority* [1936] (Brandeis, J., concurring), upon which the Court

should not pass. This argument rests on the fact that Chadha and the INS take the same position on the constitutionality of the one-House veto. But it would be a curious result if, in the administration of justice, a person could be denied access to the courts because the Attorney General of the United States agreed with the legal arguments asserted by the individual.

A case or controversy is presented by this case. First, from the time of Congress' formal intervention, ... the concrete adverseness is beyond doubt. Congress is both a proper party to defend the constitutionality of §244(c)(2) and a proper petitioner under §1254(1). Second, prior to Congress' intervention, there was adequate Art. III adverseness even though the only parties were the INS and Chadha. We have already held that the INS's agreement with the Court of Appeals' decision that §244(c)(2) is unconstitutional does not affect that agency's "aggrieved" status for purposes of appealing that decision under 28 U.S.C. §1252. For similar reasons, the INS's agreement with Chadha's position does not alter the fact that the INS would have deported Chadha absent the Court of Appeals' judgment. We agree with the Court of Appeals that "Chadha has asserted a concrete controversy, and our decision will have real meaning: if we rule for Chadha, he will not be deported; if we uphold §244(c)(2), the INS will execute its order and deport him."

Of course, there may be prudential, as opposed to Art. III, concerns about sanctioning the adjudication of this case in the absence of any participant supporting the validity of §244(c)(2). The Court of Appeals properly dispelled any such concerns by inviting and accepting briefs from both Houses of Congress. We have long held that Congress is the proper party to defend the validity of a statute when an agency of government, as a defendant charged with enforcing the statute, agrees with plaintiffs that the statute is inapplicable or unconstitutional. See *Cheng Fan Kwok* v. *INS* [1968]; *United States* v. *Lovett* (1946).

G

Political Question

It is also argued that this case presents a nonjusticiable political question because Chadha is merely challenging Congress' authority under the Naturalization Clause, U.S. Const. art. I, §8, cl. 4, and the Necessary and Proper Clause, U.S. Const. art. I, §8, cl. 18. It is argued that Congress' Article I power "To establish a uniform Rule of Naturalization", combined with the Necessary and Proper Clause, grants it unreviewable authority over the regulation of aliens. The plenary authority of Congress over aliens under Art. I, §8, cl. 4 is not open to question, but what is challenged here is whether Congress has chosen a constitutionally permissible means of implementing that power. As we made clear in *Buckley* v. *Valeo* (1976), "Congress has

plenary authority in all cases in which it has substantive legislative jurisdiction, *M'Culloch* v. *Maryland* (1819), so long as the exercise of that authority does not offend some other constitutional restriction."

A brief review of those factors which may indicate the presence of a nonjusticiable political question satisfies us that our assertion of jurisdiction over this case does no violence to the political question doctrine. As identified in *Baker* v. *Carr* (1962), a political question may arise when any one of the following circumstances is present:

"a textually demonstrable constitutional commitment of the issue to a coordinate political department; or a lack of judicially discoverable and manageable standards for resolving it; or the impossibility of deciding without an initial policy determination of a kind clearly for nonjudicial discretion; or the impossibility of a court's undertaking independent resolution without expressing lack of the respect due coordinate branches of government; or an unusual need for unquestioning adherence to a political decision already made; or the potentiality of embarrassment from multifarious pronouncements by various departments on one question."

Congress apparently directs its assertion of nonjusticiability to the first of the *Baker* factors by asserting that Chadha's claim is "an assault on the legislative authority to enact Section 244(c)(2)." But if this turns the question into a political question virtually every challenge to the constitutionality of a statute would be a political question. Chadha indeed argues that one House of Congress cannot constitutionally veto the Attorney General's decision to allow him to remain in this country. No policy underlying the political question doctrine suggests that Congress or the executive, or both acting in concert and in compliance with Art. I, can decide the constitutionality of a statute; that is a decision for the courts.

Other *Baker* factors are likewise inapplicable to this case. As we discuss more fully below, Art. I provides the "judicially discoverable and manageable standards" of *Baker* for resolving the question presented by this case. Those standards forestall reliance by this Court on nonjudicial "policy determinations" or any showing of disrespect for a coordinate branch. Similarly, if Chadha's arguments are accepted, §244(c)(2) cannot stand, and, since the constitutionality of that statute is for this Court to resolve, there is no possibility of "multifarious pronouncements" on this question.

It is correct that this controversy may, in a sense, be termed "political." But the presence of constitutional issues with significant political overtones does not automatically invoke the political question doctrine. Resolution of litigation challenging

the constitutional authority of one of the three branches cannot be evaded by courts because the issues have political implications in the sense urged by Congress. *Marbury* v. *Madison* (1803), was also a "political" case, involving as it did claims under a judicial commission alleged to have been duly signed by the President but not delivered. But "courts cannot reject as 'no law suit' a bona fide controversy as to whether some action denominated 'political' exceeds constitutional authority." *Baker* v. *Carr*....

III

A

We turn now to the question whether action of one House of Congress under §244(c)(2) violates strictures of the Constitution. We begin, of course, with the presumption that the challenged statute is valid. Its wisdom is not the concern of the courts; if a challenged action does not violate the Constitution, it must be sustained:

> "Once the meaning of an enactment is discerned and its constitutionality determined, the judicial process comes to an end. We do not sit as a committee of review, nor are we vested with the power of veto." *Tennessee Valley Authority* v. *Hill (1978).*

By the same token, the fact that a given law or procedure is efficient, convenient, and useful in facilitating functions of government, standing alone, will not save it if it is contrary to the Constitution. Convenience and efficiency are not the primary objectives — or the hallmarks — of democratic government and our inquiry is sharpened rather than blunted by the fact that Congressional veto provisions are appearing with increasing frequency in statutes which delegate authority to executive and independent agencies....

JUSTICE WHITE undertakes to make a case for the proposition that the one-House veto is a useful "political invention," and we need not challenge that assertion. We can even concede this utilitarian argument although the long range political wisdom of this "invention" is arguable. It has been vigorously debated and it is instructive to compare the views of the protagonists.... But policy arguments supporting even useful "political inventions" are subject to the demands of the Constitution which defines powers and ... sets out just how those powers are to be exercised.

Explicit and unambiguous provisions of the Constitution prescribe and define the respective functions of the Congress and of the Executive in the legislative process. Since the precise terms of those familiar provisions are critical to the resolution of this case, we set them out verbatim. Art. I provides:

> "All legislative Powers herein granted shall be vested in a Congress of the

United States, which shall consist of a Senate *and* a House of Representatives." Art. I, §1. (Emphasis added). "Every Bill which shall have passed the House of Representatives *and* the Senate, *shall,* before it become a Law, be presented to the President of the United States; ..." Art. I, §7, cl. 2. (Emphasis added).

> "*Every* Order, Resolution, or Vote to which the Concurrence of the Senate and House of Representatives may be necessary (except on a question of Adjournment) *shall be* presented to the President of the United States; and before the Same shall take effect, *shall be* approved by him, or being disapproved by him, *shall be* repassed by two thirds of the Senate and House of Representatives, according to the Rules and Limitations prescribed in the Case of a Bill." Art. I, §7, cl. 3. (Emphasis added).

These provisions of Art. I are integral parts of the constitutional design for the separation of powers. We have recently noted that "[t]he principle of separation of powers was not simply an abstract generalization in the minds of the Framers: it was woven into the documents that they drafted in Philadelphia in the summer of 1787." *Buckley* v. *Valeo.* Just as we relied on the textual provision of Art. II, §2, to vindicate the principle of separation of powers in *Buckley,* we find that the purposes underlying the Presentment Clauses, Art. I, §7, cls. 2, 3, and the bicameral requirement of Art. I, §1 and §7, cl. 2, guide our resolution of the important question presented in this case. The very structure of the articles delegating and separating powers under Arts. I, II, and III exemplify the concept of separation of powers and we now turn to Art. I.

B

The Presentment Clauses

The records of the Constitutional Convention reveal that the requirement that all legislation be presented to the President before becoming law was uniformly accepted by the Framers. Presentment to the President and the Presidential veto were considered so imperative that the draftsmen took special pains to assure that these requirements could not be circumvented. During the final debate on Art. I, §7, cl. 2, James Madison expressed concern that it might easily be evaded by the simple expedient of calling a proposed law a "resolution" or "vote" rather than a "bill."

The decision to provide the President with a limited and qualified power to nullify proposed legislation by veto was based on the profound conviction of the Framers that the powers conferred on Congress were the powers to be most carefully circumscribed. It is beyond doubt that lawmaking was a power to be shared by both

Houses and the President. In The Federalist No. 73, Hamilton focused on the President's role in making laws:

> "If even no propensity had ever discovered itself in the legislative body to invade the rights of the Executive, the rules of just reasoning and theoretic propriety would of themselves teach us that the one ought not to be left to the mercy of the other, but ought to possess a constitutional and effectual power of self-defense." ...

The President's role in the lawmaking process also reflects the Framers' careful efforts to check whatever propensity a particular Congress might have to enact oppressive, improvident, or ill-considered measures. The President's veto role in the legislative process was described later during public debate on ratification:

> "It establishes a salutary check upon the legislative body, calculated to guard the community against the effects of faction, precipitancy, or of any impulse unfriendly to the public good which may happen to influence a majority of that body.... The primary inducement to conferring the power in question upon the Executive is to enable him to defend himself; the secondary one is to increase the chances in favor of the community against the passing of bad laws through haste, inadvertence, or design." The Federalist No. 73 (A. Hamilton).

See also *The Pocket Veto Case* (1929); *Myers* v. *United States* (1926). The Court also has observed that the Presentment Clauses serve the important purpose of assuring that a "national" perspective is grafted on the legislative process:

> "The President is a representative of the people just as the members of the Senate and of the House are, and it may be, at some times, on some subjects, that the President elected by all the people is rather more representative of them all than are the members of either body of the Legislature whose constituencies are local and not countrywide...." *Myers* v. *United States.*

C

Bicameralism

The bicameral requirement of Art. I, §§1, 7 was of scarcely less concern to the Framers than was the Presidential veto and indeed the two concepts are interdependent. By providing that no law could take effect without the concurrence of the prescribed majority of the Members of both Houses, the Framers reemphasized their belief, already remarked upon in connection with the Presentment Clauses, that legislation should not be enacted unless it

has been carefully and fully considered by the Nation's elected officials. In the Constitutional Convention debates on the need for a bicameral legislature, James Wilson, later to become a Justice of this Court, commented:

> "Despotism comes on mankind in different shapes. Sometimes in an Executive, sometimes in a military, one. Is there danger of a Legislative despotism? Theory & practice both proclaim it. If the Legislative authority be not restrained, there can be neither liberty nor stability; and it can only be restrained by dividing it within itself, into distinct and independent branches. In a single house there is no check, but the inadequate one, of the virtue & good sense of those who compose it."

Hamilton argued that a Congress comprised of a single House was antithetical to the very purposes of the Constitution. Were the Nation to adopt a Constitution providing for only one legislative organ, he warned:

> "we shall finally accumulate, in a single body, all the most important prerogatives of sovereignty, and thus entail upon our posterity one of the most execrable forms of government that human infatuation ever contrived. Thus we should create in reality that very tyranny which the adversaries of the new Constitution either are, or affect to be, solicitous to avert." The Federalist No. 22.

This view was rooted in a general skepticism regarding the fallibility of human nature later commented on by Joseph Story:

> "Public bodies, like private persons, are occasionally under the dominion of stong passions and excitements; impatient, irritable, and impetuous. . . . If [a legislature] feels no check but its own will, it rarely has the firmness to insist upon holding a question long enough under its own view, to see and mark it in all its bearings and relations to society."

These observations are consistent with what many of the Framers expressed, none more cogently than Hamilton . . .:

> "In republican government, the legislative authority necessarily predominates. The remedy for this inconveniency is to divide the legislature into different branches; and to render them, by different modes of election and different principles of action, as little connected with each other as the nature of their common functions and their common dependence on the society will admit." The Federalist No. 51. . . .

However familiar, it is useful to recall that apart from their fear that special interests could be favored at the expense of public needs, the Framers were also concerned, although not of one mind, over the apprehensions of the smaller states. Those states feared a commonality of interest among the larger states would work to their disadvantage; representatives of the larger states, on the other hand, were skeptical of a legislature that could pass laws favoring a minority of the people. It need hardly be repeated here that the Great Compromise, under which one House was viewed as representing the people and the other the states, allayed the fears of both the large and small states.

We see therefore that the Framers were acutely conscious that the bicameral requirement and the Presentment Clauses would serve essential constitutional functions. The President's participation in the legislative process was to protect the Executive Branch from Congress and to protect the whole people from improvident laws. The division of the Congress into two distinctive bodies assures that the legislative power would be exercised only after opportunity for full study and debate in separate settings. The President's unilateral veto power, in turn, was limited by the power of two thirds of both Houses of Congress to overrule a veto thereby precluding final arbitrary action of one person. It emerges clearly that the prescription for legislative action in Art. I, §§1, 7 represents the Framers' decision that the legislative power of the Federal government be exercised in accord with a single, finely wrought and exhaustively considered, procedure.

IV

The Constitution sought to divide the delegated powers of the new federal government into three defined categories, legislative, executive and judicial, to assure, as nearly as possible, that each Branch of government would confine itself to its assigned responsibility. The hydraulic pressure inherent within each of the separate branches to exceed the outer limits of its power, even to accomplish desirable objectives, must be resisted.

Although not "hermetically" sealed from one another, *Buckley* v. *Valeo*, the power delegated to the three Branches are functionally identifiable. When any Branch acts, it is presumptively exercising the power the Constitution has delegated to it. See *Hampton & Co.* v. *United States* (1928). When the Executive acts, it presumptively acts in an executive or administrative capacity as defined in Art. II. And when, as here, one House of Congress purports to act, it is presumptively acting within its assigned sphere.

Beginning with this presumption, we must nevertheless establish that the challenged action under §244(c)(2) is of the kind to which the procedural requirements of Art. I, §7 apply. Not every action taken by either House is subject to the bicameral-

ism and presentment requirements of Art. I. Whether actions taken by either House are, in law and fact, an exercise of legislative power depends not on their form but upon "whether they contain matter which is properly to be regarded as legislative in its character and effect."

Examination of the action taken here by one House pursuant to §244(c)(2) reveals that it was essentially legislative in purpose and effect. In purporting to exercise power defined in Art. I, §8, cl. 4 to "establish an uniform Rule of Naturalization," the House took action that had the purpose and effect of altering the legal rights, duties and relations of persons, including the Attorney General, Executive Branch officials and Chadha, all outside the legislative branch. Section 244(c)(2) purports to authorize one House of Congress to require the Attorney General to deport an individual alien whose deportation otherwise would be cancelled under §244. The one-House veto operated in this case to overrule the Attorney General and mandate Chadha's deportation; absent the House action, Chadha would remain in the United States. Congress has *acted* and its action has altered Chadha's status.

The legislative character of the one-House veto in this case is confirmed by the character of the Congressional action it supplants. Neither the House of Representatives nor the Senate contends that, absent the veto provision in §244(c)(2), either of them, or both of them acting together, could effectively require the Attorney General to deport an alien once the Attorney General, in the exercise of legislatively delegated authority, had determined the alien should remain in the United States. Without the challenged provision in §244(c)(2), this could have been achieved, if at all, only by legislation requiring deportation. Similarly, a veto by one House of Congress under §244(c)(2) cannot be justified as an attempt at amending the standards set out in §244(a)(1), or as a repeal of §244 as applied to Chadha. Amendment and repeal of statutes, no less than enactment, must conform with Art. I.

The nature of the decision implemented by the one-House veto in this case further manifests its legislative character. After long experience with the clumsy, time consuming private bill procedure, Congress made a deliberate choice to delegate to the Executive Branch, and specifically to the Attorney General, the authority to allow deportable aliens to remain in this country in certain specified circumstances. It is not disputed that this choice to delegate authority is precisely the kind of decision that can be implemented only in accordance with the procedures set out in Art. I. Disagreement with the Attorney General's decision on Chadha's deportation — that is, Congress' decision to deport Chadha — no less than Congress' original choice to delegate to the Attorney General the authority to make that decision, involves determinations of policy that Congress can implement in only one way; bicameral passage

Appendix

followed by presentment to the President. Congress must abide by its delegation of authority until that delegation is legislatively altered or revoked.

Finally, we see that when the Framers intended to authorize either House of Congress to act alone and outside of its prescribed bicameral legislative role, they narrowly and precisely defined the procedure for such action. There are but four provisions in the Constitution, explicit and unambiguous, by which one House may act alone with the unreviewable force of law, not subject to the President's veto:

(a) The House of Representatives alone was given the power to initiate impeachments. Art. I, §2, cl. 6;

(b) The Senate alone was given the power to conduct trials following impeachment on charges initiated by the House and to convict following trial. Art. I, §3, cl. 5;

(c) The Senate alone was given final unreviewable power to approve or to disapprove presidential appointments. Art. II, §2, cl. 2;

(d) The Senate alone was given unreviewable power to ratify treaties negotiated by the President. Art. II, §2, cl. 2.

Clearly, when the Draftsmen sought to confer special powers on one House, independent of the other House, or of the President, they did so in explicit, unambiguous terms. These carefully defined exceptions from presentment and bicameralism underscore the difference between the legislative functions of Congress and other unilateral but important and binding one-House acts provided for in the Constitution. These exceptions are narrow, explicit, and separately justified; none of them authorize the action challenged here. On the contrary, they provide further support for the conclusion that Congressional authority is not to be implied and for the conclusion that the veto provided for in §244(c)(2) is not authorized by the constitutional design of the powers of the Legislative Branch.

Since it is clear that the action by the House under §244(c)(2) was not within any of the express constitutional exceptions authorizing one House to act alone, and equally clear that it was an exercise of legislative power, that action was subject to the standards prescribed in Article I. The bicameral requirement, the Presentment Clauses, the President's veto, and Congress' power to override a veto were intended to erect enduring checks on each Branch and to protect the people from the improvident exercise of power by mandating certain prescribed steps. To preserve those checks, and maintain the separation of powers, the carefully defined limits on the power of each Branch must not be eroded. To accomplish what has been attempted by one House of Congress in this case requires action in conformity with the express procedures of the Constitution's prescription for legislative action: passage by a majority of both Houses and presentment to the President.

The veto authorized by §244(c)(2) doubtless has been in many respects a convenient shortcut; the "sharing" with the Executive by Congress of its authority over aliens in this manner is, on its face, an appealing compromise. In purely practical terms, it is obviously easier for action to be taken by one House without submission to the President; but it is crystal clear from the records of the Convention, contemporaneous writings and debates, that the Framers ranked other values higher than efficiency. The records of the Convention and debates in the States preceding ratification underscore the common desire to define and limit the exercise of the newly created federal powers affecting the states and the people. There is unmistakable expression of a determination that legislation by the national Congress be a step-by-step, deliberate and deliberative process.

The choices we discern as having been made in the Constitutional Convention impose burdens on governmental processes that often seem clumsy, inefficient, even unworkable, but those hard choices were consciously made by men who had lived under a form of government that permitted arbitrary governmental acts to go unchecked. There is no support in the Constitution or decisions of this Court for the proposition that the cumbersomeness and delays often encountered in complying with explicit Constitutional standards may be avoided, either by the Congress or by the President. See *Youngstown Sheet & Tube Co.* v. *Sawyer* (1952). With all the obvious flaws of delay, untidiness, and potential for abuse, we have not yet found a better way to preserve freedom than by making the exercise of power subject to the carefully crafted restraints spelled out in the Constitution.

V

We hold that the Congressional veto provision in §244(c)(2) is severable from the Act and that it is unconstitutional. Accordingly, the judgment of the Court of Appeals is

Affirmed.

JUSTICE POWELL, concurring in the judgment.

The Court's decision, based on the Presentment Clauses, Art. I, §7, cl. 2 and 3, apparently will invalidate every use of the legislative veto. The breadth of this holding gives one pause. Congress has included the veto in literally hundreds of statutes, dating back to the 1930s. Congress clearly views this procedure as essential to controlling the delegation of power to administrative agencies. One reasonably may disagree with Congress' assessment of the veto's utility, but the respect due its judgment as a coordinate branch of Government cautions that our holding should be no more extensive than necessary to decide this case. In my view, the case may be decided on a narrower ground. When Congress finds that a particular person does not satisfy the statutory criteria for permanent residence in this country it has assumed a judicial function in violation of the principle of separation of powers. Accordingly, I concur in the judgment. . . .

JUSTICE WHITE, dissenting.

Today the court not only invalidates §244(c)(2) of the Immigration and Nationality Act, but also sounds the death knell for nearly 200 other statutory provisions in which Congress has reserved a "legislative veto." For this reason, the Court's decision is of surpassing importance. And it is for this reason that the Court would have been well-advised to decide the case, if possible, on the narrower grounds of separation of powers, leaving for full consideration the constitutionality of other congressional review statutes operating on such varied matters as war powers and agency rulemaking, some of which concern the independent regulatory agencies.

The prominence of the legislative veto mechanism in our contemporary political system and its importance to Congress can hardly be overstated. It has become a central means by which Congress secures the accountability of executive and independent agencies. Without the legislative veto, Congress is faced with a Hobson's choice: either to refrain from delegating the necessary authority, leaving itself with a hopeless task of writing laws with the requisite specificity to cover endless special circumstances across the entire policy landscape, or in the alternative, to abdicate its lawmaking function to the executive branch and independent agencies. To choose the former leaves major national problems unresolved; to opt for the latter risks unaccountable policymaking by those not elected to fill that role. Accordingly, over the past five decades, the legislative veto has been placed in nearly 200 statutes. The device is known in every field of governmental concern: reorganization, budgets, foreign affairs, war powers, and regulation of trade, safety energy, the environment and the economy.

I

The legislative veto developed initially in response to the problems of reorganizing the sprawling government structure created in response to the Depression. The Reorganization Acts established the chief model for the legislative veto. When President Hoover requested authority to reorganize the government in 1929, he coupled his request that the "Congress be willing to delegate its authority over the problem (subject to defined principles) to the Executive" with a proposal for legislative review. He proposed that the Executive "should act upon approval of a joint committee of Congress or with the reservation of power of revision by Congress within some limited period adequate for its consideration." Congress followed President Hoover's suggestion and authorized reorganization subject to legislative review. Although the reorganization authority reenacted in 1933 did not contain a legislative

veto provision, the provision returned during the Roosevelt Administration and has since been renewed numerous times. Over the years, the provision was used extensively. Presidents submitted 115 reorganization plans to Congress of which 23 were disapproved by Congress pursuant to legislative veto provisions.

Shortly after adoption of the Reorganization Act of 1939, Congress and the President applied the legislative veto procedure to resolve the delegation problem for national security and foreign affairs. World War II occasioned the need to transfer greater authority to the President in these areas. The legislative veto offered the means by which Congress could confer additional authority while preserving its own constitutional role. During World War II, Congress enacted over thirty statutes conferring powers on the Executive with legislative veto provisions. President Roosevelt accepted the veto as the necessary price for obtaining exceptional authority.

Over the quarter century following World War II, Presidents continued to accept legislative vetoes by one or both Houses as constitutional, while regularly denouncing provisions by which Congressional committees reviewed Executive activity. The legislative veto balanced delegations of statutory authority in new areas of governmental involvement: the space program, international agreements on nuclear energy, tariff arrangements, and adjustment of federal pay rates.

During the 1970's the legislative veto was important in resolving a series of major constitutional disputes between the President and Congress over claims of the President to broad impoundment, war, and national emergency powers. The key provision of the War Powers Resolution, 50 U.S.C. §1544(c), authorizes the termination by concurrent resolution of the use of armed forces in hostilities. A similar measure resolved the problem posed by Presidential claims of inherent power to impound appropriations. In conference, a compromise was achieved under which permanent impoundments, termed "rescissions," would require approval through enactment of legislation. In contrast, temporary impoundments, or "deferrals," would become effective unless disapproved by one House. This compromise provided the President with flexibility, while preserving ultimate Congressional control over the budget. Although the War Powers Resolution was enacted over President Nixon's veto, the Impoundment Control Act was enacted with the President's approval. These statutes were followed by others resolving similar problems....

In the energy field, the legislative veto served to balance broad delegations in legislation emerging from the energy crisis of the 1970's. In the educational field, it was found that fragmented and narrow grant programs "inevitably lead to Executive-Legislative confrontations" because they inaptly limited the Commissioner of Education's authority. The response was to grant the Commissioner of Education rulemaking authority, subject to a legislative veto. In the trade regulation area, the veto preserved Congressional authority over the Federal Trade Commission's broad mandate to make rules to prevent businesses from engaging in "unfair or deceptive acts or practices in commerce."

Even this brief review suffices to demonstrate that the legislative veto is more than "efficient, convenient, and useful." It is an important if not indispensable political invention that allows the President and Congress to resolve major constitutional and policy differences, assures the accountability of independent regulatory agencies, and preserves Congress' control over lawmaking. Perhaps there are other means of accommodation and accountability, but the increasing reliance of Congress upon the legislative veto suggests that the alternatives to which Congress must now turn are not entirely satisfactory.

The history of the legislative veto also makes clear that it has not been a sword with which Congress has struck out to aggrandize itself at the expense of the other branches — the concerns of Madison and Hamilton. Rather, the veto has been a means of defense, a reservation of ultimate authority necessary if Congress is to fulfill its designated role under Article I as the nation's lawmaker. While the President has often objected to particular legislative vetoes, generally those left in the hands of congressional committees, the Executive has more often agreed to legislative review as the price for a broad delegation of authority. To be sure, the President may have preferred unrestricted power, but that could be precisely why Congress thought it essential to retain a check on the exercise of delegated authority.

II

For all these reasons, the apparent sweep of the Court's decision today is regrettable. The Court's Article I analysis appears to invalidate all legislative vetoes irrespective of form or subject. Because the legislative veto is commonly found as a check upon rulemaking by administrative agencies and upon broad-based policy decisions of the Executive Branch, it is particularly unfortunate that the Court reaches its decision in a case involving the exercise of a veto over deportation decisions regarding particular individuals. Courts should always be wary of striking statutes as unconstitutional; to strike an entire class of statutes based on consideration of a somewhat atypical and more-readily indictable exemplar of the class is irresponsible. It was for cases such as this one that Justice Brandeis wrote:

"The Court has frequently called attention to the 'great gravity and delicacy' of its function in passing upon the validity of an act of Congress.... The Court will not 'formulate a rule of constitutional law broader than is required by the precise facts to which it is to be applied.' *Liverpool, N.Y. & P.S.S. Co.* v. *Emigration Commissioners, supra.*" *Ashwander* v. *Tennessee Valley Authority* (1936) (concurring opinion).

Unfortunately, today's holding is not so limited.

If the legislative veto were as plainly unconstitutional as the Court strives to suggest, its broad ruling today would be more comprehensible. But, the constitutionality of the legislative veto is anything but clearcut. The issue divides scholars, courts, attorneys general, and the two other branches of the National Government. If the veto devices so flagrantly disregarded the requirements of Article I as the Court today suggests, I find it incomprehensible that Congress, whose members are bound by oath to uphold the Constitution, would have placed these mechanisms in nearly 200 separate laws over a period of 50 years.

The reality of the situation is that the constitutional question posed today is one of immense difficulty over which the executive and legislative branches — as well as scholars and judges — have understandably disagreed. That disagreement stems from the silence of the Constitution on the precise question: The Constitution does not directly authorize or prohibit the legislative veto. Thus, our task should be to determine whether the legislative veto is consistent with the purposes of Art. I and the principles of Separation of Powers which are reflected in that Article and throughout the Constitution. We should not find the lack of a specific constitutional authorization for the legislative veto surprising, and I would not infer disapproval of the mechanism from its absence. From the summer of 1787 to the present the government of the United States has become an endeavor far beyond the contemplation of the Framers. Only within the last half century has the complexity and size of the Federal Government's responsibilities grown so greatly that the Congress must rely on the legislative veto as the most effective if not the only means to insure their role as the nation's lawmakers. But the wisdom of the Framers was to anticipate that the nation would grow and new problems of governance would require different solutions. Accordingly, our Federal Government was intentionally chartered with the flexibility to respond to contemporary needs without losing sight of fundamental democratic principles....

This is the perspective from which we should approach the novel constitutional questions presented by the legislative veto. In my view, neither Article I of the Constitution nor the doctrine of separation of powers is violated by this mechanism by which our elected representatives preserve their voice in the governance of the nation.

III

The Court holds that the disapproval of a suspension of deportation by the resolution of one House of Congress is an exercise of legislative power without compliance with the prerequisites for lawmaking set forth in Art. I of the Constitution. Specifically, the Court maintains that the provisions of §244(c)(2) are inconsistent with the requirement of bicameral approval, implicit in Art. I, §1, and the requirement that all bills and resolutions that require the concurrence of both Houses be presented to the President, Art. I, §7, cl. 2 and 3.

I do not dispute the Court's truismatic exposition of these clauses. There is no question that a bill does not become a law until it is approved by both the House and the Senate, and presented to the President. Similarly, I would not hesitate to strike an action of Congress in the form of a concurrent resolution which constituted an exercise of original lawmaking authority. I agree with the court that the President's qualified veto power is a critical element in the distribution of powers under the Constitution, widely endorsed among the Framers, and intended to serve the President as a defense against legislative encroachment and to check the "passing of bad laws through haste, inadvertence, or design." The records of the Convention reveal that it is the first purpose which figured most prominently but I acknowledge the vitality of the second. I also agree that the bicameral approval required by Art. I, §§1, 7 "was of scarcely less concern to the Framers than was the Presidential veto" and that the need to divide and disperse legislative power figures significantly in our scheme of Government. All of this, the Third Part of the Court's opinion, is entirely unexceptionable.

It does not, however, answer the constitutional question before us. The power to exercise a legislative veto is not the power to write new law without bicameral approval or presidential consideration. The veto must be authorized by statute and may only negative [sic] what an Executive department or independent agency has proposed. On its face, the legislative veto no more allows one House of Congress to make law than does the presidential veto confer such power upon the President. . . .

A

. . . When the Convention did turn its attention to the scope of Congress' lawmaking power, the Framers were expansive. The Necessary and Proper Clause, Art. I, §8, cl. 18, vests Congress with the power "to make all laws which shall be necessary and proper for carrying into Execution the foregoing Powers [the enumerated powers of §8], and all other Powers vested by this Constitution in the government of the United States, or in any Department or Officer thereof." It is long-settled that Congress may "exercise its best judgment in the selection of measures, to carry into execution the constitutional powers of the government," and "avail itself of experience, to exercise its reason, and to accommodate its legislation to circumstances," *McCulloch* v. *Maryland* 420 (1819).

B

The Court heeded this counsel in approving the modern administrative state. The Court's holding today that all legislative-type action must be enacted through the lawmaking process ignores that legislative authority is routinely delegated to the Executive branch, to the independent regulatory agencies, and to private individuals and groups. . . .

The wisdom and the constitutionality of these broad delegations are matters that still have not been put to rest. But for present purposes, these cases establish that by virtue of congressinal delegation, legislative power can be exercised by independent agencies and Executive departments without the passage of new legislation. For some time, the sheer amount of law — the substantive rules that regulate private conduct and direct the operation of government — made by the agencies has far outnumbered the lawmaking engaged in by Congress through the traditional process. There is no question but that agency rulemaking is lawmaking in any functional or realistic sense of the term. . . .

If Congress may delegate lawmaking power to independent and executive agencies, it is most difficult to understand Article I as forbidding Congress from also reserving a check on legislative power for itself. Absent the veto, the agencies receiving delegations of legislative or quasi-legislative power may issue regulations having the force of law without bicameral approval and without the President's signature. It is thus not apparent why the reservation of a veto over the exercise of that legislative power must be subject to a more exacting test. In both cases, it is enough that the initial statutory authorizations comply with the Article I requirements. . . .

The Court's opinion in the present case comes closest to facing the reality of administrative lawmaking in considering the contention that the Attorney General's action in suspending deportation under §244 is itself a legislative act. The Court posits that the Attorney General is acting in an Article II enforcement capacity under §244. This characterization is at odds with *Mahler* v. *Eby* (1924), where the power conferred on the Executive to deport aliens was considered a delegation of legislative power. The Court suggests, however, that the Attorney General acts in an Article II capacity because "[t]he courts when a case or controversy arises, can always 'ascertain whether the will of Congress has been obeyed,' *Yakus* v. *United States* (1944), and can enforce adherence to statutory standards." This assumption is simply wrong, as the Court itself points out: "We are aware of no decision . . . where a federal court has reviewed a decision of the Attorney General suspending deportation of an alien pursuant to the standards set out in §244(a)(1). This is not surprising, given that no party to such action has either the motivation or the right to appeal from it." It is perhaps on the erroneous premise that judicial review may check abuses of the §244 power that the Court also submits that "The bicameral process is not necessary as a check on the Executive's administration of the laws because his administrative activity cannot reach beyond the limits of the statute that created it — a statute duly enacted pursuant to Article I."

More fundamentally, even if the Court correctly characterizes the Attorney General's authority under §244 as an Article II Executive power, the Court concedes that certain administrative agency action, such and recognizes that "[t]his Court has referred to agency activity as being 'quasi-legislative' in character. *Humphrey's Executor* v. *United States* (1935)." Such rules and adjudications by the agencies meet the Court's own definition of legislative action for they "alter[] the legal rights, duties, and relations of persons . . . outside the legislative branch" and involve "determinations of policy." Under the Court's analysis, the Executive Branch and the independent agencies may make rules with the effect of law while Congress, in whom the Framers confided the legislative power, Art. I, §1, may not exercise a veto which precludes such rules from having operative force. If the effective functioning of a complex modern government requires the delegation of vast authority which, by virtue of its breadth, is legislative or "quasi-legislative" in character, I cannot accept that Article I — which is, after all, the source of the non-delegation doctrine — should forbid Congress from qualifying that grant with a legislative veto.

C

The Court also takes no account of perhaps the most relevant consideration: However resolutions of disapproval under §244(c)(2) are formally characterized, in reality, a departure from the status quo occurs only upon the concurrence of opinion among the House, Senate, and President. Reservations of legislative authority to be exercised by Congress should be upheld if the exercise of such reserved authority is consistent with the distribution of and limits upon legislative power that Article I provides. . . .

[Section 1 Omitted]

2

The central concern of the presentation and bicameralism requirements of Article I is that when a departure from the

legal status quo is undertaken, it is done with the approval of the President and both Houses of Congress — or, in the event of a presidential veto, a two-thirds majority in both Houses. This interest is fully satisfied by the operation of §244(c)(2). The President's approval is found in the Attorney General's action in recommending to Congress that the deportation order for a given alien be suspended. The House and the Senate indicate their approval of the Executive's action by not passing a resolution of disapproval within the statutory period. Thus, a change in the legal status quo — the deportability of the alien — is consummated only with the approval of each of the three relevant actors. The disagreement of any one of the three maintains the alien's pre-existing status: the Executive may choose not to recommend suspension; the House and Senate may each veto the recommendation. The effect on the rights and obligations of the affected individuals and upon the legislative system is precisely the same as if a private bill were introduced but failed to receive the necessary approval. "The President and the two Houses enjoy exactly the same say in what the law is to be as would have been true for each without the presence of the one-House veto, and nothing in the law is changed absent the concurrence of the President and a majority in each House.". . .

This very construction of the Presentment Clauses which the Executive branch now rejects was the basis upon which the Executive Branch defended the constitutionality of the Reorganization Act, 5 U.S.C. §906(a) (1979), which provides that the President's proposed reorganization plans take effect only if not vetoed by either House. When the Department of Justice advised the Senate on the constitutionality of congressional review in reorganization legislation in 1949, it stated: "In this procedure there is no question involved of the Congress taking legislative action beyond its initial passage of the Reorganization Act." This also represents the position of the Attorney General more recently.

Thus understood, §244(c)(2) fully effectuates the purposes of the bicameralism and presentation requirements. I now briefly consider possible objections to the analysis.

First, it may be asserted that Chadha's status before legislative disapproval is one of nondeportation and that the exercise of the veto, unlike the failure of a private bill, works a change in the status quo. This position plainly ignores the statutory language. At no place in §244 has Congress delegated to the Attorney General any final power to determine which aliens shall be allowed to remain in the United States. Congress has retained the ultimate power to pass on such changes in deportable status. By its own terms, §244(a) states that whatever power the Attorney General has been delegated to suspend deportation and adjust status is to be exercisable only "as

hereinafter prescribed in this section." Subsection (c) is part of that section. A grant of "suspension" does not cancel the alien's deportation or adjust the alien's status to that of a permanent resident alien. A suspension order is merely a "deferment of deportation," *McGrath* v. *Kristensen* (1950), which can mature into a cancellation of deportation and adjustment of status only upon the approval of Congress — by way of silence — under §244(c)(2). Only then does the statute authorize the Attorney General to "cancel deportation proceedings" §244(c)(2), and "record the alien's lawful admission for permanent residence. . . ." §244(d). The Immigration and Naturalization Service's action, on behalf of the Attorney General, "cannot become effective without ratification by Congress." Until that ratification occurs, the executive's action is simply a recommendation that Congress finalize the suspension — in itself, it works no legal change. . . .

IV

The Court of Appeals struck §244(c)(2) as violative of the constitutional principle of separation of powers. It is true that the purpose of separating the authority of government is to prevent unnecessary and dangerous concentration of power in one branch. For that reason, the Framers saw fit to divide and balance the powers of government so that each branch would be checked by the others. Virtually every part of our constitutional system bears the mark of this judgment.

But the history of the separation of powers doctrine is also a history of accommodation and practicality. Apprehensions of an overly powerful branch have not led to undue prophylactic measures that handicap the effective working of the national government as a whole. The Constitution does not contemplate total separation of the three branches of Government. *Buckley* v. *Valeo* (1976). "[A] hermetic sealing off of the three branches of Government from one another would preclude the establishment of a Nation capable of governing itself effectively."

Our decisions reflect this judgment. As already noted, the Court, recognizing that modern government must address a formidable agenda of complex policy issues, countenanced the delegation of extensive legislative authority to executive and independent agencies. *[J. W.] Hampton & Co.* v. *United States* (1928). The separation of powers doctrine has heretofore led to the invalidation of government action only when the challenged action violated some express provision in the Constitution. In *Buckley* v. *Valeo* (1976) (per curiam) and *Myers* v. *United States* (1926), congressional action compromised the appointment power of the President. See also *Springer* v. *Philippine Islands* (1928). In *United States* v. *Klein* (1871), an Act of Congress was struck for encroaching upon judicial power, but the Court found that the Act also impinged upon the executive's

exclusive pardon power. Art II, §2. Because we must have a workable efficient government, this is as it should be.

This is the teaching of *Nixon* v. *Administrator of Gen. Servs.* (1977), which, in rejecting a separation of powers objection to a law requiring that the Administrator take custody of certain presidential papers, set forth a framework for evaluating such claims:

> "[I]n determining whether the Act disrupts the proper balance between the coordinate branches, the proper inquiry focuses on the extent to which it prevents the Executive Branch from accomplishing its constitutionally assigned functions. *United States* v. *Nixon.* Only where the potential for disruption is present must we then determine whether that impact is justified by an overriding need to promote objectives within the constitutional authority of Congress."

Section 244(c)(2) survives this test. The legislative veto provision does not "prevent the Executive Branch from accomplishing its constitutionally assigned functions." First, it is clear that the Executive branch has no "constitutionally assigned" function of suspending the deportation of aliens. " 'Over no conceivable subject is the legislative power of Congress more complete than it is over' the admission of aliens." *Kleindiest* v. *Mandel* (1972), quoting *Oceanic Steam Navigation Co.* v. *Stranahan* (1909). Nor can it said that the inherent function of the Executive Branch in executing the law is involved. *The Steel Seizure Case* resolved that the Article II mandate for the President to execute the law is a directive to enforce the law which Congress has written. *Youngstown Sheet & Tube Co.* v. *Sawyer* (1952). "The duty of the President to see that the laws be executed is a duty that does not go beyond the laws or require him to achieve more than Congress sees fit to leave within his power." *Myers* v. *United States* (Holmes, J., dissenting); (Brandeis, J. dissenting). Here, §244 grants the executive only a qualified suspension authority and it is only that authority which the President is constitutionally authorized to execute.

Moreover, the Court believes that the legislative veto we consider today is best characterized as an exercise of legislative or quasi-legislative authority. Under this characterization, the practice does not, even on the surface, constitute an infringement of executive or judicial prerogative. The Attorney General's suspension of deportation is equivalent to a proposal for legislation. The nature of the Attorney General's role as recommendatory is not altered because §244 provides for congressional action through disapproval rather than by ratification. In comparison to private bills, which must be initiated in the Congress and which allow a Presidential veto to be overriden by a two-thirds majority in both Houses of Congress, §244 aug-

ments rather than reduces the executive branch's authority. So understood, congressional review does not undermine ... the decisions of the Executive Branch.

Nor does §244 infringe on the judicial power, as JUSTICE POWELL would hold. Section 244 makes clear that Congress has reserved its own judgment as part of the statutory process. Congressional action does not substitute for judicial review of the Attorney General's decision. The Act provides for judicial review of the refusal of the Attorney General to suspend a deportation and to transmit a recommendation to Congress. *INS* v. *Wang*, (1981) (per curiam). But the courts have not been given the authority to review whether an alien should be given permanent status; review is limited to whether the Attorney General has properly applied the statutory standards for essentially denying the alien a recommendation that his deportable status be changed by the Congress. Moreover, there is no constitutional obligation to provide any judicial review whatever for a failure to suspend deportation. "The power of Congress, therefore, to expel, like the power to exclude aliens, or any specified class of aliens, from the country, may be exercised entirely through executive officers; or Congress may call in the aid of the judiciary to ascertain any contested facts on which an alien's right to be in the country has been made by Congress to depend." *Fong Yue Ting* v. *United States* (1893). See also *Tutun* v. *United States* (1926); *Ludecke* v. *Watkins* (1948); *Harisiades* v. *Shaughnessy* (1952).

I do not suggest that all legislative vetoes are necessarily consistent with separation of powers principles. A legislative check on an inherently executive function, for example that of initiating prosecutions, poses an entirely different question. But the legislative veto device here — and in many other settings — is far from an instance of legislative tyranny over the Executive. It is a necessary check on the unavoidably expanding power of the agencies, both executive and independent, as they engage in exercising authority delegated by Congress.

V

I regret that I am in disagreement with my colleagues on the fundamental questions that this case presents. But even more I regret the destructive scope of the Court's holding. It reflects a profoundly different conception of the Constitution than that held by the courts which sanctioned the modern administrative state. Today's decision strikes down in one fell swoop provisions in more laws enacted by Congress than the court has cumulatively invalidated in its history. I fear it will now be more difficult "to insure that the fundamental policy decisions in our society will be made not by an appointed official but by the body immediately responsible to the people," *Arizona* v. *California* (1963) (Harlan, J., dissenting). I must dissent.

Appendix 1
Statutes With
Provisions Authorizing
Congressional Review

This compilation, reprinted from the Brief for the United States Senate, identifies and describes briefly current statutory provisions for a legislative veto by one or both Houses of Congress. Statutory provisions for a veto by committees of the Congress and provisions which require legislation (i.e., passage of a joint resolution) are not included. The fifty-six statutes in the compilation (some of which contain more than one provision for legislative review) are divided into six broad categories: foreign affairs and national security, budget, international trade, energy, rulemaking and miscellaneous.

A
Foreign Affairs
and National Security

1. Act for International Development of 1961, Pub. L. No. 87-195, §617, 75 Stat. 424, 444, 22 U.S.C. 2367 (Funds made available for foreign assistance under the Act may be terminated by concurrent resolution).

2. War Powers Resolution, Pub. L. No. 93-148, §5, 87 Stat. 555, 556-557 (1973), 50 U.S.C. 1544 (Absent declaration of war, President may be directed by concurrent resolution to remove United States armed forces engaged in foreign hostilities).

3. Department of Defense Appropriation Authorization Act, 1974, Pub. L. No. 93-155, §807, 87 Stat. 605, 615 (1973), 50 U.S.C. 1431 (National defense contracts obligating the United States for any amount in excess of $25,000,000 may be disapproved by resolution of either House).

4. Department of Defense Appropriation Authorization Act, 1975, Pub. L. No. 93-365, §709(c), 88 Stat. 399, 408 (1974), 50 U.S.C. app. 2403-1(c) (Applications for export of defense goods, technology or techniques may be disapproved by concurrent resolution).

5. H. R. J. Res. 683, Pub. L. No. 94-110, §1, 89 Stat. 572 (1975), 22 U.S.C. 2441 note (Assignment of civilian personnel to Sinai may be disapproved by concurrent resolution).

6. International Development and Food Assistance Act of 1975, Pub. L. No. 94-161, §310, 89 Stat. 849, 860, 22 U.S.C. 2151n (Foreign assistance to countries not meeting human rights standards may be terminated by concurrent resolution).

7. International Security Assistance and Arms Control Act of 1976, Pub. L. No. 94-329, §211, 90 Stat. 729, 743, 22 U.S.C. 2776(b) (President's letter of offer to sell major defense equipment may be disapproved by concurrent resolution).

8. National Emergencies Act, Pub. L. No. 94-412, §202, 90 Stat. 1255 (1976), 50 U.S.C. 1622 (Presidentially declared national emergency may be terminated by concurrent resolution).

9. International Navigational Rules Act of 1977, Pub. L. No. 95-75, §3(d), 91 Stat. 308, 33 U.S.C. §1602(d) (Supp. III 1979) (Presidential proclamation of International Regulations for Preventing Collisions at Sea may be disapproved by concurrent resolution).

10. International Security Assistance Act of 1977, Pub. L. No. 95-92, §16, 91 Stat. 614, 622, 22 U.S.C. §2753(d)(2) Supp. III 1979) (President's proposed transfer of arms to a third country may be disapproved by concurrent resolution).

11. Act of December 8, 1977, Pub. L. No. 95-223, §207(2)(b), 91 Stat. 1625, 1628, 50 U.S.C. 1706(b) (Supp. III 1979) (Presidentially declared national emergency and exercise of conditional powers may be terminated by concurrent resolution).

12. Nuclear Non-Proliferation Act of 1978, Pub. L. No. 95-242, §§303, 304, 306, 307, 401, 92 Stat. 120, 130, 134, 137-38, 139, 144, 42 U.S.C. §§2160(f), 2155(b), 2157(b), 2153(d) (Supp. III 1979) (Cooperative agreements concerning storage and disposition of spent nuclear fuel, proposed export of nuclear facilities, materials or technology and proposed agreements for international cooperation in nuclear reactor development may be disapproved by concurrent resolution).

B
Budget

13. Congressional Budget and Impoundment Control Act of 1974, Pub. L. No. 93-344, §1013, 88 Stat. 297, 334-35, 31 U.S.C. 1403 (The proposed deferral of budget authority provided for a specific project or purpose may be disapproved by an impoundment resolution by either House).

C
International Trade

14. Trade Expansion Act of 1962, Pub. L. No. 87-794, §351, 76 Stat. 872, 899, 19 U.S.C. 1981(a) (Tariff or duty recommended by Tariff Commission may be imposed by concurrent resolution of approval).

15. Trade Act of 1974, Pub. L. No. 93-618, §§203(c), 302(b), 402(d), 407, 88 Stat. 1978, 2016, 2043, 2057-60, 2063-64, 19 U.S.C. 2253(c), 2412(b), 2432, 2434 (Proposed Presidential actions on import relief and actions concerning certain countries may be disapproved by concurrent resolution; various Presidential proposals for waiver extensions and for extension of nondiscriminatory treatment to products of foreign countries may be disapproved by simple (either House) or concurrent resolutions).

16. Export-Import Bank Amendments of 1974, Pub. L. No. 93-646, §8, 88 Stat. 2333, 2336, 12 U.S.C. 635e (Presidentially proposed limitation for exports to USSR in excess of $300,000,000 must be approved by concurrent resolution).

D
Energy

17. Act of November 16, 1973, Pub. L. No. 93-153, §101, 87 Stat. 576, 582, 30 U.S.C. 185(u) (Continuation of oil exports being made pursuant to President's finding that such exports are in the national interest may be disapproved by concurrent resolution).

18. Federal Nonnuclear Energy Research and Development Act of 1974, Pub. L. No. 93-577, §12, 88 Stat. 1878, 1892-1893, 42 U.S.C. 5911 (Rules or orders proposed by the President concerning allocation or acquisition of essential materials may be disapproved by resolution of either House).

19. Energy Policy and Conservation Act, Pub. L. No. 94-163, §551, 89 Stat. 871, 965 (1975), 42 U.S.C. 6421(c) (Certain Presidentially proposed "energy actions" involving fuel economy and pricing may be disapproved by resolution of either House).

20. Naval Petroleum Reserves Production Act of 1976, Pub. L. No. 94-258, §201, 90 Stat. 303, 309, 10 U.S.C. 7422(c)(2)(C) (President's extension of production period for naval petroleum reserves may be disapproved by resolution of either House).

21. Energy Conservation and Production Act, Pub. L. No. 94-385, §305, 90 Stat. 1125, 1148 (1976), 42 U.S.C. 6834 (Proposed sanctions involving federal assistance and the energy conservation performance standards for new buildings must be approved by resolution of both Houses).

22. Department of Energy Act of 1978 — Civilian Applications, Pub. L. No. 95-238, §§107, 207(b), 92 Stat. 47, 55, 70, 22 U.S.C. 3224a, 42 U.S.C. 5919(m) (Supp. III 1979) (International agreements and expenditures by Secretary of Energy of appropriations for foreign spent nuclear fuel storage must be approved by concurrent resolution, if not consented to by legislation;) (plans for such use of appropriated funds may be disapproved by either House;) (financing in excess of $50,000,000 for demonstration facilities must be approved by resolution in both Houses).

23. Outer Continental Shelf Lands Act Amendments of 1978, Pub. L. No. 95-372, §§205(a), 208, 92 Stat. 629, 641, 668, 43 U.S.C. §§1337(a), 1354(c) (Supp. III 1979) (Establishment by Secretary of Energy of oil and gas lease bidding system may be disapproved by resolution of either House;) (export of oil and gas may be disapproved by concurrent resolution).

24. Natural Gas Policy Act of 1978, Pub. L. No. 95-621, §§122(c)(1) and (2), 202(c), 206(d)(2), 507, 92 Stat. 3350, 3370, 3371, 3372, 3380, 3406, 15 U.S.C. 3332, 3342(c), 3346(d)(2), 3417 (Supp. III 1979) (Presidential reimposition of natural gas price controls may be disapproved by concurrent resolution;) (Congress may reimpose natural gas price controls by concurrent resolution;) (Federal Energy Regulatory Commission (FERC) amendment to pass through incremental costs of natural gas, and exemptions therefrom,

may be disapproved by resolution of either House;) (procedure for congressional review established).

25. Export Administration Act of 1979, Pub. L. No. 96-72, §7(d)(B), 7(g)(3), 93 Stat. 503, 518, 520, 50 U.S.C. app. 2406(d)(2)(B), 2406(g)(3) (Supp. III 1979) (President's proposal to domestically produce crude oil must be approved by concurrent resolution;) (action by Secretary of Commerce to prohibit or curtail export of agricultural commodities may be disapproved by concurrent resolution).

26. Energy Security Act, Pub. L. No. 96-294, §§104(b)(3), 104(e), 126(d)(2), 126(d)(3), 128, 129, 132(a)(3), 133(a)(3), 137(b)(5), 141(d), 179(a), 803, 94 Stat. 611, 618, 619, 620, 623-26, 628-29, 649, 650-52, 659, 660, 664, 666, 679, 776 (1980) (to be codified in 50 U.S.C. app. 2091-93, 2095, 2096, 2097, 42 U.S.C. 8722, 8724, 8725, 8732, 8733, 8737, 8741, 8779, 6240) (Loan guarantees by Departments of Defense, Energy and Commerce in excess of specified amounts may be disapproved by resolution of either House;) (President's proposal to provide loans or guarantees in excess of established amounts may be disapproved by resolution of either House;) (proposed award by President of individual contracts for purchase of more than 75,000 barrels per day of crude oil may be disapproved by resolution of either House;) (President's proposals to overcome energy shortage through synthetic fuels development, and individual contracts to purchase more than 75,000 barrels per day, including use of loans or guarantees, may be disapproved by resolution of either House;) (procedures for either House to disapprove proposals made under Act are established;) (request by Synthetic Fuels Corporation (SFC) for additional time to submit its comprehensive strategy may be disapproved by resolution of either House;) (proposed amendment to comprehensive strategy by SFC Board of Directors may be disapproved by concurrent resolution of either House or by failure of both Houses to pass concurrent resolution of approval;) (procedure for either House to disapprove certain proposed actions of SFC is established;) (procedure for both Houses to approve by concurrent resolution or either House to reject concurrent resolution for proposed amendments to comprehensive strategy of SFC is established;) (proposed loans and loan guarantees by SFC may be disapproved by resolution of either House;) (acquisition by SFC of a synthetic fuels project which is receiving financial assistance may be disapproved by resolution of either House;) (SFC contract renegotiations exceeding initial cost estimaes by 175% may be disapproved by resolution of either House;) (proposed financial assistance to synthetic fuel projects in Western Hemisphere outside United States may be disapproved by resolution of either House;) (President's request to suspend provisions requiring build up of reserves and limiting sale or disposal of certain crude oil reserves must be approved by resolution of both

Houses).

E
Rulemaking

27. Education Amendments of 1974, Pub. L. No. 93-380, §509, 88 Stat. 484, 567, 20 U.S.C. 1232(d)(1) (Department of Education regulations may be disapproved by concurrent resolution).

28. Federal Education Campaign Act Amendments of 1979, Pub. L. No. 96-187, §109, 93 Stat. 1339, 1364, 2 U.S.C. 438(d)(2) (Supp. III 1979) (Proposed rules and regulations of the Federal Election Commission may be disapproved by resolution of either House).

29. Act of January 2, 1975, Pub. L. No. 93-595, §2, 88 Stat. 1926, 1948, 28 U.S.C. 2076 (Proposed amendments by Supreme Court of Federal Rules of Evidence may be disapproved by resolution of either House).

30. Act of August 9, 1975, Pub. L. No. 94-88, §208, 89 Stat. 433, 436-37, 42 U.S.C. 602 note (Social Security standards proposed by Secretary of Health and Human Services may be disapproved by either House).

31. Airline Deregulation Act of 1978, Pub. L. No. 95-504, §43(f)(3), 92 Stat. 1705, 1752, 49 U.S.C. 1552(f) (Supp. III 1979) (Rules or regulations governing employee protection program may be disapproved by resolution of either House).

32. Education Amendments of 1978, Pub. L. No. 95-561, §§1138, 1212, 1409, 92 Stat. 2143, 2327, 2341, 2369, 25 U.S.C. 2018, 20 U.S.C. 1221-3(e) (Supp. III 1979) (Rules and regulations proposed under the Act may be disapproved by concurrent resolution).

33. Civil Rights of Institutionalized Persons Act, Pub. L. No. 96-247, §7(b)(1), 94 Stat. 349, 352-355, (1980) (to be codified in 42 U.S.C. 1997e) (Attorney General's proposed standards for resolution of grievances of adults confined in correctional facilities may be disapproved by resolution of either House).

34. Federal Trade Commission Improvements Act of 1980, Pub. L. No. 96-252, §21(a), 94 Stat. 374, 393 (to be codified in 15 U.S.C. 57a-1) (Federal Trade Commission rules may be disapproved by concurrent resolution).

35. Department of Education Organization Act, Pub. L. No. 96-88, §414(b), 93 Stat. 668, 685 (1979), 20 U.S.C. 3474 (Supp. III 1979) (Rules and regulations promulgated with respect to the various functions, programs and responsibilities transferred by this Act, may be disapproved by concurrent resolution).

36. Multiemployer Pension Plan Amendments Act of 1980, Pub. L. No. 96-364, §102, 94 Stat. 1208, 1213 (to be codified in 29 U.S.C. 1322a) (Schedules proposed by Pension Benefit Guaranty Corporation (PBGC) which requires an increase in premiums must be approved by concurrent resolution;) (revised premium schedules for voluntary supplemental coverage proposed by PBGC may be disap-

proved by concurrent resolution).

37. Farm Credit Act Amendments of 1980, Pub. L. No. 96-592, §508, 94 Stat. 3437, 3450, (to be codified in 12 U.S.C. 2121) (Certain Farm Credit Administration regulations or delayed by resolution of either House).

38. Comprehensive Environmental Response, Compensation, and Liability Act of 1980, Pub. L. No. 96-510, §305, 94 Stat. 2767, 2809 (to be codified in 42 U.S.C. 9655) (Environmental Protection Agency regulations concerning hazardous substances releases, liability and compensation may be disapproved by concurrent resolution or by the adoption of either House of a concurrent resolution which is not disapproved by the other House).

39. National Historic Preservation Act Amendments of 1980, Pub. L. No. 96-515, §501, 94 Stat. 2987, 3004 (to be codified in 16 U.S.C. 470w-6) (Regulation proposed by the Secretary of the Interior may be disapproved by concurrent resolution).

40. Coastal Zone Management Improvement Act of 1980, Pub. L. No. 96-464, §12, 94 Stat. 2060, 2067 (to be codified in 16 U.S.C. 1463a) (Rules proposed by the Secretary of Commerce may be disapproved by concurrent resolution).

41. Act of December 17, 1980, Pub. L. No. 96-539, §4, 94 Stat. 3194, 3195 (to be codified in 7 U.S.C. 136w) (Rules or regulations promulgated by the Administrator of the Environmental Protection Agency under the Federal Insecticide, Fungicide and Rodenticide Act may be disapproved by concurrent resolution).

42. Omnibus Budget Reconciliation Act of 1981, Pub. L. No. 97-35, §§533(a)(2), 1107(d), 1142, 1183(a)(2), 1207, 95 Stat. 357, 453, 626, 654, 659, 695, 718-20 (to be codified in 20 U.S.C. 1089, 23 U.S.C. 402(j), 45 U.S.C. 761, 767, 564(c)(3), 15 U.S.C. 2083, 1276, 1204) (Secretary of Education's schedule of expected family contributions for Pell Grant recipients may be disapproved by resolution of either House;) (rules promulgated by Secretary of Transportation for programs to reduce accidents, injuries and deaths may be disapproved by resolution of either House;) (Secretary of Transportation's plan for the sale of government's common stock in rail system may be disapproved by concurrent resolution;) (Secretary of Transportation's approval of freight transfer agreements may

be disapproved by resolution of either House;) (amendments to Amtrak's Route and Service Criteria may be disapproved by resolution of either House;) (Consumer Product Safety Commission regulations may be disapproved by concurrent resolution of both Houses, or by concurrent resolution of disapproval by either House if such resolution is not disapproved by the other House).

F
Miscellaneous

43. Federal Civil Defense Act of 1950, Pub. L. No. 81-920, §201, 64 Stat. 1245, 1248, 50 app. U.S.C. 2281(g) (Interstate civil defense compacts may be disapproved by concurrent resolution).

44. National Aeronautics and Space Act of 1958, Pub. L. No. 85-568, §302c, 72 Stat. 426, 433, 42 U.S.C. 2453 (President's transfer to National Air and Space Administration of functions of other departments and agencies may be disapproved by concurrent resolution).

45. Federal Pay Comparability Act of 1970, Pub. L. No. 91-656, §3, 84 Stat. 1946, 1949, 5 U.S.C. 5305 (President's alternative pay plan may be disapproved by resolution of either House).

46. Act of October 19, 1973, Pub. L. No. 93-134, §5, 87 Stat. 466, 468, 25 U.S.C. 1405 (Plan for use and distribution of funds paid in satisfaction of judgment of Indian Claims Commission or Court of Claims may be disapproved by resolution of either House).

47. Menominee Restoration Act, Pub. L. No. 93-197, §6, 87 Stat. 770, 773 (1973), 25 U.S.C. 903d(b) (Plan by Secretary of the Interior for assumption of the assets of the Menominee Indian corporation may be disapproved by resolution of either House).

48. District of Columbia Self-Government and Governmental Reorganization Act, Pub. L. No. 93-198, §§303, 602(c)(1) and (2), 87 Stat. 774, 784, 814 (1973) (District of Columbia Charter amendments ratified by electors must be approved by concurrent resolution;) (acts of District of Columbia Council may be disapproved by concurrent resolution;) (acts of District of Columbia Council under certain titles of D.C. Code may be disapproved by resolution of either House).

49. Act of December 31, 1975, Pub. L.

No. 94-200, §102, 89 Stat. 1124, 12 U.S.C. 461 note (Federal Reserve System Board of Governors may not eliminate or reduce interest rate differentials between banks insured by Federal Deposit Insurance Corporation and associations insured by Federal Savings and Loan Insurance Corporations without concurrent resolution of approval).

50. Veterans' Education and Employment Assistance Act of 1976, Pub. L. No. 94-502, §408, 90 Stat. 2383, 2397-98, 38 U.S.C. 1621 note (President's recommendation for continued enrollment period in Armed Forces educational assistance program may be disapproved by resolution of either House).

51. Federal Land Policy and Management Act of 1976, Pub. L. No. 94-579, §§203(c), 204(c)(1), 90 Stat. 2743, 2750, 2752, 43 U.S.C. 1713(c), 1714 (Sale of public lands in excess of two thousand five hundred acres and withdrawal of public lands aggregating five thousand acres or more may be disapproved by concurrent resolution).

52. Emergency Unemployment Compensation Extension Act of 1977, Pub. L. No. 95-19, §401, 91 Stat. 39, 45, 2 U.S.C. 359 (Supp. III 1979) (President's recommendations regarding rates of salary payment may be disapproved by resolution of either House).

53. Civil Service Reform Act of 1978, Pub. L. No. 95-454, §515, 92 Stat. 1111, 1179, 5 U.S.C. 3131 note (Supp. III 1979) (Continuation of Senior Executive Service may be disapproved by concurrent resolution).

54. Full Employment and Balanced Growth Act of 1978, Pub. L. No. 95-523, §304(b), 92 Stat. 1887, 1906, 31 U.S.C. 1322 (Supp. III 1979) (Presidential timetable for reducing unemployment may be superseded by concurrent resolution).

55. District of Columbia Retirement Reform Act, Pub. L. No. 96-122, §164, 93 Stat. 866, 891-92 (1979) (Required reports to Congress on the District of Columbia retirement program may be rejected by resolution of either House).

56. Act of August 29, 1980, Pub. L. No. 96-332, §2, 94 Stat. 1057, 1058 (to be codified in 16 U.S.C. 1432) (Designation of marine sanctuary by the Secretary of Commerce may be disapproved by concurrent resolution).

Congressional Reapportionment

Redistricting for the 1980s   *995*

Reapportionment History   *999*

Redistricting for the 1980s

Republicans were supposed to do well in the elections of 1982. A popular Republican president sat in the White House, the nation seemed to be taking a rightward political turn and the reapportionment mandated by the 1980 Census shifted a large number of U.S. House seats from the Democratic North to the more conservative Sun Belt.

It did not work out that way. With a substantial edge in the nation's state legislatures, particularly in those states that gained seats, Democrats were able to draw maps that helped them and hurt their opponents. After the 1982 elections, Democrats had won 26 additional seats in the House, including 10 of the seats created by redistricting.

But what might have a more lasting impact on the nation and its representative government was the new use to which the Supreme Court's edict of one-person, one-vote was put in the redistricting that followed the 1980 Census. In California, New Jersey and points between, Republicans and Democrats justified highly partisan remaps by demonstrating respect for the 1964 Supreme Court mandate that populations of congressional districts within states must be made as equal as possible. Other interests at stake in redistricting, such as the preservation of community boundaries and the grouping of constituencies with similar concerns, were brushed aside.

The Supreme Court itself seemed to approve this kind of partisan mapmaking. In June 1983 it overturned New Jersey's congressional district map on the ground that the population variations among the districts — the greatest of which was 0.69 percent — were too large and therefore unconstitutional. In its opinion the court ignored the fact that the map divided townships and cut up counties all across the state solely to give the Democrats a political advantage.

The Supreme Court had never addressed the constitutionality of districts that, while meeting the equal population test, nonetheless ensured the supremacy of the political party drawing the boundaries. But in a move that could affect future redistricting plans nationwide, the high court agreed in March 1985 to consider the constitutionality of "gerrymandering," the time-honored practice of drawing political boundary lines to the advantage of a particular party. The case, to be argued in the court's 1985-86 term, involved a 1981 Indiana state redistricting plan that a three-judge federal court panel found unconstitutional. The lower court said Indiana Republicans had rigged the state's legislative districts to their own advantage, depriving Democrats of the equal protection of the law. Democratic candidates for the state House received 51.9 percent

of the votes, and they ended up with only 43 percent of the seats. *(Reapportionment background, p. 999)*

1980 Reapportionment

The reapportionment and redistricting process began on New Year's Eve 1980 when the Census Bureau sent state population totals to President Jimmy Carter, along with a calculation of the size of each state's congressional delegation, beginning with the 1982 elections. In February 1981 the bureau began to release more detailed data breaking down the nation's population, in some cases to the city-block level. The bureau's maps took up 31,715 sheets. Texas alone was spread across more than 2,000 census map sheets.

The census figures themselves were not immune to challenge. In 1980 Detroit officials claimed that minorities in the city had been undercounted and argued that this would cost the city federal funds and congressional representation. (Many federal welfare programs use census figures to determine how much assistance each locality is entitled to receive.) A Michigan district court ordered the bureau to revise its national population figures upward to include blacks, Hispanics and others allegedly overlooked in the 1980 Census.

But in June 1981 the 6th U.S. Circuit Court of Appeals reversed that decision, stating that the claim was "based on a state of affairs not yet in existence and . . . so hypothetical in nature that it does not present a controversy capable of judicial resolution." The arguments used in the 1981 district court appeal dealt largely with the 1970 Census, in which the bureau's own research indicated census takers missed 2.5 percent of the population. More importantly, the bureau estimated it missed 7.7 percent of the nation's blacks, compared with only 1.9 percent of its whites. But the 1980 Census of these minority population counts unexpectedly turned out to be slightly higher than population estimates derived from demographic records, suggesting an apparent overcount rather than an undercount.

Nonetheless, the 1980 Census count confirmed that there was a dramatic decline in America's big-city population during the 1970s. Most central-city districts suffered severe shrinkage, and older suburban districts experienced slow growth, or none at all.

Meanwhile, there was substantial movement of the population from North to South and East to West. As a result, 17 House seats shifted from states in the Northeast and Midwest, the so-called Snow Belt, to those in the Sun

Belt states of the South and West. Florida was the biggest gainer, receiving four new seats. Texas picked up three additional seats; California two; and Arizona, Colorado, Nevada, New Mexico, Oregon, Tennessee, Utah and Washington one each.

New York, which lost almost 700,000 people in the 1970s, according to the census, was hit with a five-seat loss, the biggest one-time drop-off in House representation since New York and Virginia lost six seats each in 1840. Illinois, Ohio and Pennsylvania each lost two seats, while Indiana, Massachusetts, Michigan, Missouri, New Jersey and South Dakota lost one each.

Drawing the Lines

Only 44 states go through the redistricting process. The other six — Alaska, Delaware, North Dakota, South Dakota, Vermont and Wyoming — each have only one representative elected at large.

Anticipating the apparent gains the population shifts would give the GOP — and anxious to capitalize on them — the Republicans undertook a nationwide campaign to win control of more state legislatures in preparation for the critical 1981 redistricting process. They had only scattered success in the November 1980 elections. Democrats still controlled 28 of the nation's state legislatures, while the Republicans held only 15. (The remaining legislatures were divided, except for Nebraska, which has a unicameral, non-partisan Legislature.)

Despite this nationwide disadvantage, Republicans in individual states were able to hold their own. In Florida, for example, the Democratic Legislature drew only one new safe Democratic seat; the other three were expected to be competitive. In November 1982 the Democrats won two; the Republicans won the other two.

Partisan Maps. In several states where one or the other party was firmly in control, the redistricting process was overtly partisan. In Indiana the district map passed by the Republican-controlled Legislature April 30, 1981, was a textbook case of gerrymandering. Republicans drew the plan with the help of Market Opinion Research Corp.'s sophisticated computer system at a cost of more than $250,000. Its lines wove freely in and out of counties, concentrating Democratic voting strength into the districts of just three of the state's six Democratic incumbents and damaging the re-election prospects of the other three.

The state's Republicans made no apologies for their plan. As early as December 1980 they had made it clear they would take full advantage of their control of state government to secure a majority in Indiana's U.S. House delegation in the November 1982 elections. As it turned out, the lineup after the election was 5-5.

In California, Republicans sought to nullify redistricting plans drawn by the Democratic-controlled Legislature. California's plan, crafted by Democratic Rep. Phillip Burton, was designed to bring five more Democrats into the state's House delegation, which increased from 43 to 45 after the 1980 Census. Democrats in California held a 22-21 advantage in the 97th Congress. When Rep. William M. Thomas, R-Calif., called Burton's plan "an abomination," Burton countered that the Democrats had done only what Republicans had done in Indiana and were attempting to do in Washington and Colorado. California Republicans filed sufficient signatures to hold a referendum on the redistricting plan, and in June 1982 the state's voters rejected the map. However, six months earlier, the state

Supreme Court had ruled that the Burton plan would stay in effect for the 1982 elections regardless of the outcome of the referendum. A modified plan was drawn after the 1982 elections. Voters in November 1984 rejected an initiative to transfer redistricting authority from the Legislature and governor to a commission of retired appellate court judges.

Both the Indiana and California cases remained in the courts in 1985. In December 1984 a three-judge panel overruled the Indiana plan and ordered the state to come up with a new plan for the 1986 elections. The state appealed to the U.S. Supreme Court, which agreed early in 1985 to hear the case. At the same time the Supreme Court refused to hear a challenge brought by California Republicans to that state's redistricting plan, effectively returning the case for further state proceedings.

Court Plans. Sometimes, states cannot come up with a plan at all. This usually happens in states where control of the legislature is split between the parties, or where the governor's party does not control the state legislature. Philosophical or personal differences sometimes can interfere, even within parties. When deadlocks occur, the task of redistricting falls to the federal courts.

In Illinois, which lost two seats, no compromise could be reached between competing Democratic and Republican redistricting plans in 1981, and both parties filed suit in federal district court in Chicago. A three-judge panel, which included two judges with Republican backgrounds, heard the case and decided in favor of the Democratic plan. The Illinois Republicans' appeal to the U.S. Supreme Court was rejected.

A sharp drop in St. Louis' population cost Missouri one congressional seat. For most of 1981 it appeared that the problem might have to be solved by placing Democratic incumbents William L. Clay, a veteran black legislator, and Richard A. Gephardt, a "rising star," in the same district. The Democratic-dominated Legislature rejected this plan and failed to come up with another, leaving the decision up to a federal court panel. Much to the relief of the Democrats, the judicial plan penalized the Republicans, eliminating GOP Rep. Wendell Bailey's 8th District and forcing incumbent Republican Bill Emerson into a heavily Democratic district.

After Democratic Gov. Richard D. Lamm vetoed three redistricting maps passed by the Republican majority in Colorado's Legislature, a federal judge ordered Lamm and the legislative redistricting committee to negotiate. Talks in November 1981 failed to produce a compromise plan, so a federal court in Denver was given responsibility for drawing the district lines. The state gained one House seat, which Republicans easily won.

Minorities and Maps. Several states that managed to pass redistricting plans still had to clear another hurdle. Under the Voting Rights Act of 1965, the Justice Department had to approve redistricting plans in Alabama, Arizona, Georgia, Louisiana, Mississippi, South Carolina, Texas and Virginia, and parts of California, Colorado, Connecticut, Florida, Hawaii, Idaho, Maine, Massachusetts, Michigan, New Hampshire, New Mexico, New York, North Carolina and Oklahoma. The department could reject any redistricting plan in these states that diluted the voting strength or in any other way discriminated against blacks and other minorities.

This happened in several states in 1981. The North Carolina redistricting plan included a district that protected incumbent Democrat L. H. Fountain by curving around the heavily black community in Durham and the

Status of Redistricting

(As of March 25, 1985)

State	Redistricting Action
Alabama	Legislative plan enacted Aug. 18, 1981.
Arizona	Federal court approved legislative plan April 2, 1982.
Arkansas	Federal court plan enacted Feb. 25, 1982.
California	Voters rejected legislative plan, which was kept in place for 1982 elections. Modified plan drawn after 1982 elections. Supreme Court March 25, 1985, refused to hear challenge to plan, returning case for further state proceedings. Voters in November 1984 rejected move to transfer redistricting authority to commission of retired judges.
Colorado	Federal court plan enacted Jan. 28, 1982.
Connecticut	Special commission plan enacted Oct. 28, 1981.
Florida	Legislative plan enacted May 23, 1982.
Georgia	First plan voided by Justice Department. Second legislative plan enacted Aug. 8, 1982.
Hawaii	Federal court approved special commission plan May 5, 1982.
Idaho	Legislative plan enacted July 30, 1981.
Illinois	Federal court plan enacted Nov. 23, 1981.
Indiana	Legislative plan enacted May 5, 1981. Federal court panel overturned plan in December 1984. Supreme Court agreed March 25, 1985, to hear state appeal of lower court decision.
Iowa	Legislative plan enacted Aug. 20, 1981.
Kansas	Federal court plan enacted June 2, 1982.
Kentucky	Legislative plan enacted March 10, 1982.
Louisiana	Legislative plan approved Nov. 12, 1981. Two New Orleans districts voided by federal court Sept. 24, 1983. Legislature in December 1983 approved court-ordered plan.
Maine	Special commission plan enacted March 30, 1983.
Maryland	Special commission plan enacted April 9, 1982.
Massachusetts	Legislative plan enacted Dec. 16, 1981.
Michigan	Federal court plan enacted May 17, 1982.
Minnesota	Federal court plan enacted March 11, 1982.
Mississippi	First plan voided by Justice Department. Federal court enacted temporary plan June 9, 1982; court redistricting plan completed in January 1984.
Missouri	Federal court plan enacted Dec. 28, 1981.
Montana	Special commission plan enacted March 4, 1983.
Nebraska	Legislative plan enacted May 28, 1981.
Nevada	Legislative plan enacted June 3, 1981.
New Hampshire	Legislative plan enacted March 4, 1982.
New Jersey	Legislative plan, voided by federal court March 3, 1982, used for 1982 elections; Supreme Court upheld Republican-drafted plan June 4, 1984.
New Mexico	Legislative plan enacted Jan. 19, 1982.
New York	First plan voided by Justice Department. Second legislative plan enacted July 2, 1982.
North Carolina	First plan voided by Justice Department. Second legislative plan enacted Feb. 11, 1982.
Ohio	Legislative plan enacted March 25, 1982. Supreme Court June 4, 1984, affirmed lower court ruling that state must redraw congressional districts in 1985.
Oklahoma	Voters approved legislative plan Nov. 2, 1982.
Oregon	Legislative plan enacted Aug. 22, 1981.
Pennsylvania	Legislative plan enacted March 3, 1982.
Rhode Island	Legislative plan enacted April 9, 1982.
South Carolina	Federal court plan enacted March 8, 1982.
Tennessee	Legislative plan enacted June 17, 1981.
Texas	First plan voided by Justice Department Jan. 29, 1982. Federal court plan overturned by Supreme Court April 11, 1982. Second legislative plan enacted June 19, 1983.
Utah	Legislative plan enacted Nov. 11, 1981.
Virginia	Legislative plan enacted June 12, 1981.
Washington	Legislative plan voided in federal court Nov. 30, 1982. Special commission plan enacted March 29, 1983.
West Virginia	Legislative plan enacted Feb. 8, 1982.
Wisconsin	Legislative plan enacted March 25, 1982.

liberal university town of Chapel Hill. The Justice Department, in rejecting the plan, ruled on Dec. 8 that the "strangely irregular shape" of "Fountain's Fishhook" raised questions about the racial motivations of the state legislators. The legislators drew a second map, which put Durham County in Fountain's district. That map was approved, Fountain decided to retire, and a black came close to winning the Democratic nomination, winning 46 percent of the vote in a runoff.

In Georgia the Justice Department ruled that the Legislature improperly divided a "cohesive black community" in the Atlanta area between the 4th and 5th districts, reducing the chances that either would elect a black candidate to the House. Legislators then drew a plan that passed Justice Department review, but the elections for those two seats were postponed nearly a month to Nov. 30, 1982.

In Mississippi, Justice Department rejection of the legislative map resulted in creation of the state's first black-majority district since 1966. But the district was only 54 percent black, and civil rights leaders continued to pursue the matter in federal court. A court redistricting plan was completed in January 1984.

In Louisiana, blacks demanded creation of a black-majority district in New Orleans, a concept endorsed by both the state House and state Senate. Republican Gov. David C. Treen opposed the black-majority district because the resulting boundaries would have endangered the seat of GOP U.S. Rep. Bob Livingston, who represented the New Orleans suburbs. The governor prevailed upon legislators to approve a remap protecting incumbents, and Justice approved that map. Blacks then went to court, which threw out the New Orleans district lines Sept. 24, 1983. The Legislature approved a court-ordered plan later in the year.

Hispanics were the beneficiaries of Justice Department review in Texas. In January 1982 the department ruled that the map improperly diluted the Hispanic vote in two south Texas districts by making one of them 80 percent Hispanic and the other 52 percent Hispanic. A federal court subsequently drew a map redistributing the voters in those two districts, and Hispanics won both seats in 1982.

Bipartisan Commission Plans. A number of citizens' groups have argued that partisan redistricting should be ended. One method, promoted by Common Cause, would establish a commission composed of an equal number of appointees from each party, which would be expected to choose a non-partisan chairman. The commission then would have full authority to redistrict the state according to the latest census. Only two states — Hawaii and Montana — redistricted by using such a system. Both had only two districts. However, other states used a variant of the commission system and some resorted to it after their legislatures were unable to reach agreement on redistricting maps.

One hybrid form of the Common Cause plan was adopted by Iowa in 1980. In spite of their total control of state government, GOP legislators agreed to let the nonpartisan Legislative Service Bureau draw a plan, subject to the Legislature's approval. The bureau was instructed to follow objective criteria — population equality, compactness, contiguity, preservation of local boundaries — and to ignore partisan concerns or the wishes of incumbents.

The bureau's "non-partisan" plan, unveiled April 22, was a statistical beauty. The six districts were neat and compact, and they all followed county boundaries. None of the six varied in population from the state's ideal by more than 500 people.

But, to their surprise, two of the Republican incumbents found themselves living in the same district. The state Senate killed that plan. On its second try the bureau gave the two Republicans different districts but added a significant number of Democrats to one of them. Again the state Senate killed the plan. The third commission plan finally was approved even though the Republican legislators were not totally happy with it.

1982 Impact of Redistricting

After all the votes were counted in November 1982, the anticipated Republican windfall had turned into a rout. Republicans lost 26 seats in the House; their numbers fell from 192 to 166.

The Sun Belt proved the Republicans' greatest disappointment. The GOP had hoped to take a dozen of the seats shifted to the Sun Belt and far West states. But in the end Democrats won 10 of the 17.

Democrats also managed to sidestep the brunt of district losses in the Northeast and Midwest. In all, in the 10 Northern states that lost districts, Republicans came out 18 seats short of where they stood before the election.

In most of the 11 states that gained seats, the GOP seemed the natural beneficiary of demographic changes. All 11 were carried by Ronald Reagan in the 1980 presidential race and eight went for Republican Gerald R. Ford in 1976.

Nonetheless, legislatures or courts in six of the states drew new districts favoring or leaning to Democrats. And, contrary to prediction, not one of these new constituencies nominated a conservative Democrat. As a result, liberals, including four Hispanics, made up a large portion of the Sun Belt's House contingent in the 98th Congress.

Population and Politics

The most important story about the 1980 reapportionment and redistricting process might be how the "one-person, one-vote" principle came into increasing use as a means to further partisan gerrymandering.

When the Supreme Court handed down its *Wesberry v. Sanders* ruling in 1964, congressional districts in many states were malapportioned to favor rural interests over urban dwellers or to make nearly impossible the election of a black candidate to the House. In Georgia one district had more than three times as many people as another, and the Legislature had not redrawn district lines in more than 30 years.

Responding to court pressure, 39 states realigned district boundaries between 1964 and 1970. But because legislators were working from outdated 1960 Census figures, significant population inequalities among districts persisted. Meaningful implementation of the one-man, one-vote standard had to wait until publication of the 1970 Census figures. In 1972 voters elected representatives to the House from districts of nearly equal population for the first time in history.

At that time there still was lingering suspicion in many legislatures of the relatively new notion that one vote should have the same weight as another. Making district populations equal was seen by many legislators as a chore.

By 1982 that had changed. Legislators who were uncomfortable with one-man, one-vote rule were now eager to use it for partisan advantage. More than ever before, the dominant theme of redistricting was partisanship.

Reapportionment History

Reapportionment, the redistribution of the 435 seats in the U.S. House of Representatives among the states to reflect shifts in population, and redistricting, the redrawing of congressional district lines within each state, are among the most important processes in the U.S. political system. They help determine whether the House will be dominated by Democrats or Republicans, liberals or conservatives, and whether racial or ethnic minorities receive fair representation.

Reapportionment and redistricting occur every 10 years on the basis of the decennial population census. States whose populations grew quickly over the previous 10 years gain congressional seats, while those that lost population or grew much more slowly than the national average lose seats. The number of House delegates for the rest of the states remains the same.

The states that gain or lose seats must make extensive changes in their congressional maps. Even those states with stable delegations must make modifications that account for population shifts within their boundaries in accordance with Supreme Court "one-person, one-vote" rulings.

Despite their importance to the political process, reapportionment and redistricting draw little interest from the general public. This is ironic, wrote Andrea J. Wollock in the January 1982 issue of *State Legislatures*, because reapportionment is not only a "supremely important" political issue but also "a source of unsurpassed political drama and intrigue." Partisan interests are enhanced, personal ambitions of powerful politicians are furthered. Incumbents are protected or politically crippled. Tempers flare and fists fly, as they did during a redistricting debate in the Illinois Legislature in 1981.

Among the many unique features to emerge in the remarkable nation-creating endeavor of 1787 was a national legislative body whose membership was to be elected by the people and apportioned on the basis of population. In keeping with the nature of the Constitution, however, only fundamental rules and regulations were provided. How to interpret and implement the instructions contained in the document were left to future generations.

Within this flexible framework, many questions soon arose concerning the House of Representatives. How large was it to be? What mathematical formula was to be used in calculating the distribution of seats among the various states? Were the representatives to be elected at large or by districts? If by districts, what standards should be used in fixing their boundaries? The Congress and the courts have been wrestling with these questions for almost 200 years.

Until the mid-20th century, such questions generally remained in the hands of the legislators. But with growing concentration of the population in urban areas, variations in population among congressional districts became more pronounced. Efforts to persuade Congress to redress the grievance of heavily populated but under-represented areas proved unsuccessful. Rural legislators were so intent on preventing power from slipping out of their control that they managed to block reapportionment of the House following the census of 1920.

Not long afterward, litigants tried to persuade the Supreme Court to order the states to revise congressional district boundaries in line with population shifts. After initial failure, a breakthrough occurred in 1964 in the case of *Wesberry v. Sanders*. The court declared that the Constitution required that "as nearly as practicable, one man's vote in a congressional election is to be worth as much as another's."

In the years that followed the court repeatedly reaffirmed its "one-person, one-vote" requirement. In *Karcher v. Daggett* in 1983 the court held that no deviation from that principle was permissible unless the state proved that the population variation was necessary to achieve some legitimate goal. This ruling immediately drew fire from those who thought it would allow states to ignore several other traditional factors involved in redistricting — such as compactness of the district or integrity of county and city lines — in their quest for districts of precisely equal populations.

Early History

Modern legislative bodies are descended from the councils of feudal lords and gentry that medieval kings summoned for the purpose of raising revenues and armies. These councils did not represent a king's subjects in any modern sense. They represented certain groups of subjects, such as the nobility, the clergy, the landed gentry and town merchants. Representation was by interest groups and bore no relation to equal representation for equal numbers of people. In England, the king's council became Parliament, with the higher nobility and clergy making up the House of Lords and representatives of the gentry and merchants making up the House of Commons.

Beginning as little more than administrative and advi-

sory arms of the throne, royal councils in time developed into lawmaking bodies and acquired powers that eventually eclipsed those of the monarchs they served. The power struggle in England climaxed during the Cromwellian period when the king was executed and a "benevolent" dictatorship was set up under Oliver Cromwell. By 1800 Parliament was clearly the superior branch of government.

During the 18th and early 19th centuries, as the power of Parliament grew, the English became increasingly concerned about the "representativeness" of their system of apportionment. Newly developing industrial cities had no more representation in the House of Commons than small, almost-deserted country towns. Small constituencies were bought and sold. Men from these empty "rotten boroughs" often were sent to Parliament representing a single "patron" landowner or clique of wealthy men. It was not until the Reform Act of 1832 that Parliament curbed such excesses and turned toward a representative system based on population.

The growth of the powers of Parliament as well as the development of English ideas of representation during the 17th and 18th centuries had a profound effect on the colonists in America. Representative assemblies were unifying forces behind the breakaway of the colonies from England and the establishment of the newly independent country.

Colonists in America, generally modeling their legislatures after England's, used both population and land units as bases for apportionment. Patterns of early representation varied. "Nowhere did representation bear any uniform relation to the number of electors. Here and there the factor of size had been crudely recognized," Robert Luce pointed out in his book *Legislative Principles.*

In New England, the town usually was the basis for representation. In the Middle Atlantic region, the county frequently was used. Virginia used the county with additional representation for specified cities. In many areas, towns and counties were fairly equal in population. Thus territorial representation afforded roughly equal representation for equal numbers of people. Delaware's three counties, for example, were of almost equal population and had the same representation in the Legislature. But in Virginia the disparity was enormous (from 951 people in one county to 22,015 in another). Thomas Jefferson criticized the state's constitution on the ground that "among those who share the representation, the shares are unequal."

The Continental Congress, with representation from every colony, proclaimed in the Declaration of Independence in 1776 that governments derive "their just powers from the consent of the governed" and that "the right of representation in the legislature" is an "inestimable right" of the people. The Constitutional Convention of 1787 included representatives from all the states. However, in neither of these bodies were the state delegations or voting powers proportional to population.

Intentions of Founding Fathers

Andrew Hacker, in his book *Congressional Districting,* said that to understand what the framers of the Constitution had in mind when they drew up the section concerning the House of Representatives, it was necessary to study closely several sources: the Constitution itself, the recorded discussions and debates at the Constitutional Convention, *The Federalist Papers* (essays written by Alexander Hamilton, John Jay and James Madison in defense of the Constitution) and the deliberations of the states' ratifying con-

ventions.

The Constitution declares only that each state is to be allotted a certain number of representatives. It does not state specifically that congressional districts must be equal or nearly equal in population. Nor does it require specifically that a state create districts at all. However, it seems clear that the first clause of Article I, Section 2, providing that House members should be chosen "by the people of the several states," indicated that the House of Representatives, in contrast to the Senate, was to represent people rather than states. "It follows," Hacker wrote, "that if the states are to have equal representation in the upper chamber, then individuals are to be equally represented in the lower body."

The third clause of Article I, Section 2 provided that congressional apportionment among the states must be according to population. But Hacker argued that "there is little point in giving the states congressmen 'according to their respective numbers' if the states do not redistribute the members of their delegations on the same principle. For representatives are not the property of the states, as are the senators, but rather belong to the people who happen to reside within the boundaries of those states. Thus, each citizen has a claim to be regarded as a political unit equal in value to his neighbors." In this and similar ways, constitutional scholars have argued the case for single-member congressional districts deduced from the wording of the Constitution itself.

The issue of unequal representation arose only once during debate in the Constitutional Convention. The occasion was Madison's defense of Article I, Section 4 of the proposed Constitution, giving Congress the power to override state regulations on "the times . . . and manner" of holding elections for members of Congress. Madison's argument related to the fact that many state legislatures of the time were badly malapportioned: "The inequality of the representation in the legislatures of particular states would produce a like inequality in their representation in the national legislature, as it was presumable that the counties having the power in the former case would secure it to themselves in the latter."

The implication was that states would create congressional districts and that unequal districting was undesirable and should be prevented.

Madison made this interpretation even more clear in his contributions to *The Federalist Papers.* Arguing in favor of the relatively small size of the projected House of Representatives, he wrote in *No. 56:* "Divide the largest state into ten or twelve districts and it will be found that there will be no peculiar local interests . . . which will not be within the knowledge of the Representative of the district."

In the same paper, Madison said: "The Representatives of each state will not only bring with them a considerable knowledge of its laws, and a local knowledge of their respective districts, but will probably in all cases have been members, and may even at the very time be members, of the state legislature, where all the local information and interests of the state are assembled, and from whence they may easily be conveyed by a very few hands into the legislature of the United States." And, finally, in *Federalist Paper No. 57* Madison stated that ". . . each Representative of the United States will be elected by five or six thousand citizens." In making these arguments, Madison seems to have assumed that all or most representatives would be elected by districts rather than at large.

In the states' ratifying conventions, the grant to Con-

gress by Article I, Section 4 of ultimate jurisdiction over the "times, places and manner of holding elections" (except the places of choosing senators) held the attention of many delegates. There were differences over the merits of this section, but no justification of unequal districts was prominently used to attack the grant of power. Further evidence that individual districts were the intention of the Founding Fathers was given in the New York ratifying convention, when Alexander Hamilton said: "The natural and proper mode of holding elections will be to divide the state into districts in proportion to the number to be elected. This state will consequently be divided at first into six."

From his study of the sources relating to the question of congressional districting, Hacker concluded: "There is, then, a good deal of evidence that those who framed and ratified the Constitution intended that the House of Representatives have as its constituency a public in which the votes of all citizens were of equal weight.... The House of Representatives was designed to be a popular chamber, giving the same electoral power to all who had the vote. And the concern of Madison ... that districts be equal in size was an institutional step in the direction of securing this democratic principle."

Reapportionment of Seats

Article I, Section 2, Clause 3 of the Constitution laid down the basic rules for apportionment and reapportionment of seats in the House of Representatives: "Representatives ... shall be apportioned among the several States which may be included within this Union, according to their respective Numbers, which shall be determined by adding to the whole Number of free Persons, including those Bound to Service for a Term of Years, and excluding Indians not taxed, three-fifths of all other Persons. The actual Enumeration shall be made within three Years after the first Meeting of the Congress of the United States, and within every subsequent Term of Ten years, in such manner as they shall by Law direct. The number of Representatives shall not exceed one for every thirty Thousand, but each State shall have at least one Representative...."

The Constitution made the first apportionment, which was to remain in effect until the first census was taken. No reliable figures on the population were available at the time. The 13 states were allocated the following numbers of representatives: New Hampshire, three; Massachusetts, eight; Rhode Island and Providence Plantations, one; Connecticut, five; New York, six; New Jersey, four; Pennsylvania, eight; Delaware, one; Maryland, six; Virginia, 10; North Carolina, five; South Carolina, five; and Georgia, three. The apportionment of seats — 65 in all — thus mandated by the Constitution remained in effect during the 1st and 2nd Congresses (1789-93).

Apparently realizing that apportionment of the House was likely to become a major bone of contention, the 1st Congress submitted to the states a proposed constitutional amendment containing a formula to be used in future reapportionments. The amendment, which was not ratified, provided that following the taking of a decennial census there would be one representative for every 30,000 persons until the House membership reached 100, "after which the proportion shall be so regulated by Congress that there shall be not less than 100 representatives, nor less than one representative for every 40,000 persons, until the

number of representatives shall amount to 200, after which the proportion shall be so regulated by Congress, that there shall not be less than 200 representatives, nor more than one representative for every 50,000 persons."

First Apportionment by Congress

The states' refusal to ratify the reapportionment-formula amendment forced Congress to enact apportionment legislation after the first census was taken in 1790. The first apportionment bill was sent to the president on March 23, 1792. Washington sent the bill back to Congress without his signature — the first presidential veto.

The bill had incorporated the constitutional minimum of 30,000 as the size of each district. But the population of each state was not a simple multiple of 30,000. Significant fractions were left over when the number of people in each state was divided by 30,000. Thus, for example, Vermont was found to be entitled to 2.851 representatives, New Jersey to 5.98 and Virginia to 21.018. Therefore, a formula had to be found that would deal in the fairest possible manner with unavoidable variations from exact equality.

Accordingly, Congress proposed in the first apportionment bill to distribute the members on a fixed ratio of one representative for each 30,000 inhabitants, and give an additional member to each state with a fraction exceeding one-half. Washington's veto was based on the belief that eight states would receive more than one representative for each 30,000 persons under this formula.

A motion to override the veto was unsuccessful. A new bill meeting the president's objections was introduced April 9, 1792, and approved April 14. The act provided for a ratio of one member for every 33,000 inhabitants and fixed the exact number of representatives to which each state was entitled. The total membership of the House was to be 105. In dividing the population of the various states by 33,000, all remainders were to be disregarded. This was known as the method of rejected fractions; it was devised by Thomas Jefferson.

Reapportionment by Jefferson's Method

Jefferson's method of reapportionment resulted in great inequalities among districts. A Vermont district would contain 42,766 inhabitants, a New Jersey district 35,911 and a Virginia district only 33,187. Emphasis was placed on what was considered the ideal size of a congressional district rather than on what the size of the House ought to be. This method was in use until 1840.

The reapportionment act based on the census of 1800 continued the ratio of 33,000, which provided a House of 141 members. Debate on the third apportionment bill began in the House on Nov. 22, 1811, and the bill was sent to the president on Dec. 21. The ratio was fixed at 35,000, yielding a House of 181 members. Following the 1820 census, Congress approved an apportionment bill providing a ratio of 40,000 inhabitants per district. The sum of the quotas for the various states produced a House of 213 members.

The act of May 22, 1832, fixed the ratio at 47,700, resulting in a House of 240 members. Dissatisfaction with the method in use continued, and Daniel Webster launched a vigorous attack against it. He urged adoption of a method that would assign an additional representative to each state with a large fraction. His approach to the reapportionment process was outlined in a report he submitted to Congress in 1832: "The Constitution, therefore, must be understood not as enjoining an absolute relative equality — because

that would be demanding an impossibility — but as requiring of Congress to make the apportionment of Representatives among the several states according to their respective numbers, *as near as may be*. That which cannot be done perfectly must be done in a manner as near perfection as can be.... In such a case approximation becomes a rule."

Following the 1840 census, Congress adopted a reapportionment method similar to that advocated by Webster. The method fixed a ratio of one representative for every 70,680 persons. This figure was reached by deciding on a fixed size of the House in advance (223), dividing that figure into the total national "representative population" and using the result (70,680) as the fixed ratio. The population of each state was then divided by this ratio to find the number of its representatives and the states were assigned an additional representative for each fraction over one-half. Under this method the actual size of the House dropped.

The modified reapportionment formula adopted by Congress in 1842 was found to be more satisfactory than the previous method, but another change was made following the census of 1850. The new system was proposed by Rep. Samuel F. Vinton of Ohio and became known as the Vinton method.

Vinton Apportionment Formula

Under the Vinton formula, Congress first fixed the size of the House and then distributed the seats. The total qualifying population of the country was divided by the desired number of representatives, and the resulting number became the ratio of population to each representative. The population of each state was divided by this ratio and each state received the number of representatives equal to the whole number in the quotient for that state. Then, to reach the required size of the House, additional representatives were assigned based on the remaining fractions, beginning with the state having the largest fraction. This procedure differed from the 1842 method only in the last step, which assigned one representative to every state having a fraction larger than one-half.

Proponents of the Vinton method pointed out that it had the distinct advantage of making it possible to fix the size of the House in advance and to take into account at least the largest fractions. The concern of the House turned from the ideal size of a congressional district to the ideal size of the House itself.

Under the 1842 reapportionment formula, the exact size of the House could not be fixed in advance. If every state with a fraction over one-half were given an additional representative, the House might wind up with a few more or a few less than the desired number. However, under the Vinton method, only states with the largest fractions were given additional House members and only up to the desired total size of the House.

Reapportionments by Vinton Method

Six reapportionments were carried out under the Vinton method. The 1850 census Act contained three provisions not included in any previous law. First, it required reapportionment not only after the census of 1850 but also after all the subsequent censuses; second, it purported to fix the size of the House permanently at 233 members; and third, it provided in advance for an automatic apportionment by the secretary of the interior under the method prescribed in the act.

Following the census of 1860, according to the provisions of the act passed a decade before, an automatic reapportionment was to be carried out by the Interior Department. However, because the size of the House was to remain at the 1850 level, some states faced loss of representation and others would gain less than they expected. To avert that possibility, an act was approved March 4, 1862, increasing the size of the House to 241 and giving an extra representative to eight states — Illinois, Iowa, Kentucky, Minnesota, Ohio, Pennsylvania, Rhode Island and Vermont.

Apportionment legislation following the 1870 census contained several new provisions. The act of Feb. 2, 1872, fixed the size of the House at 283, with the proviso that the number should be increased if new states were admitted. A supplemental act of May 30, 1872, assigned one additional representative each to Alabama, Florida, Indiana, Louisiana, New Hampshire, New York, Pennsylvania, Tennessee and Vermont.

Another section of the 1872 act provided that no state should thereafter be admitted "without having the necessary population to entitle it to at least one representative fixed by this bill." That provision was found to be unenforceable because no Congress can bind a succeeding Congress. Moreover, no ratio was fixed by the act, although the basis on which the representatives were assigned was 131,425. In 1890 Idaho was admitted with a population of 84,385 and Wyoming with a population of 60,705.

With the Reconstruction era at its height in the South, the reapportionment legislation of 1872 reflected the desire of Congress to enforce Section 2 of the new 14th Amendment. That section attempted to protect the right of blacks to vote by providing for reduction of representation in the House of a state that interfered with the exercise of that right. The number of representatives of such a state was to be reduced in proportion to the number of inhabitants of voting age whose right to go to the polls was denied or abridged. The reapportionment bill repeated the language of the section, but it never was put into effect because of the difficulty of determining the exact number of persons whose right to vote was being abridged.

The reapportionment act of Feb. 25, 1882, provided for a House of 325 members, with additional members for any new states admitted to the Union. No new apportionment provisions were added. The acts of Feb. 7, 1891, and Jan. 16, 1901, were routine as far as apportionment was concerned. The 1891 measure provided for a House of 356 members, and the 1901 statute increased the number to 386.

Despite the apparent advantages of the Vinton method, certain difficulties revealed themselves as the formula was applied. Zechariah Chafee Jr. of the Harvard Law School summarized these problems in an article in the *Harvard Law Review* in 1929. The method, he pointed out, suffered from what he called the "Alabama paradox." Under that aberration, an increase in the total size of the House might be accompanied by an actual loss of a seat by some states, even though there had been no corresponding change in population. This phenomenon first appeared in tables prepared for Congress in 1881, which gave Alabama eight members in a House of 299 but only seven members in a House of 300. It could even happen that the state which lost a seat was the one state that had expanded in population, while all the others had fewer persons.

Chafee concluded from his study of the Vinton method: "Thus, it is unsatisfactory to fix the ratio of popu-

lation per Representative before seats are distributed. Either the size of the House comes out haphazard, or, if this be determined in advance, the absurdities of the 'Alabama paradox' vitiate the apportionment. Under present conditions, it is essential to determine the size of the House in advance; the problem thereafter is to distribute the required number of seats among the several states as nearly as possible in proportion to their respective populations so that no state is treated unfairly in comparison with any other state."

Maximum Membership of House

On Aug. 8, 1911, the membership of the House was fixed at 433. Provision was made in the reapportionment act of that date for the addition of one representative each from Arizona and New Mexico, which were expected to become states in the near future. Thus, the size of the House reached 435, where it has remained up to the present with the exception of a brief period (1959-63) when the admission of Alaska and Hawaii raised the total temporarily to 437.

Limiting the size of the House amounted to recognition that the body soon would expand to unmanageable proportions if Congress continued the practice of adding new seats every 10 years, to match population gains without depriving any state of its existing representation. Agreement on a fixed number made the task of reapportionment all the more difficult when the population not only increased but became much more mobile. Population shifts brought Congress up hard against the politically painful necessity of taking seats away from slow-growing states to give the fast-growing states adequate representation.

A new mathematical calculation was adopted for the reapportionment following the 1910 census. Devised by W. F. Willcox of Cornell University, the new system established a priority list that assigned seats progressively, beginning with the first seat above the constitutional minimum of at least one seat for each state. When there were 48 states, this method was used to assign the 49th member, the 50th member, and so on, until the agreed-upon size of the House was reached. The method was called major fractions and was used after the censuses of 1910, 1930 and 1940. There was no reapportionment after the 1920 census.

1920s Struggle

The results of the 14th decennial census were announced Dec. 17, 1920, just after the short session of the 66th Congress convened. The 1920 census showed that for the first time in history most Americans were urban residents. This came as a profound shock to persons accustomed to emphasizing the nation's rural traditions and the virtues of life on farms and in small towns. Rural legislators immediately mounted an attack on the census results and succeeded in postponing reapportionment legislation for almost a decade.

Thomas Jefferson once wrote: "Those who labor in the earth are the chosen people of God, if ever He had a chosen people, whose breasts He had made His peculiar deposit for substantial and genuine virtue. . . . The mobs of great cities add just as much to the support of pure government as sores do to the strength of the human body. . . . I think our governments will remain virtuous for many centuries as long as they are chiefly agricultural: and this shall be as long as there shall be vacant lands in any part of America. When they get piled up upon one another in large cities as in Europe, they will become corrupt as in Europe."

As their power waned throughout the latter part of the 19th century and the early part of the 20th, farmers and their spokesmen clung to the Jeffersonian belief that somehow they were more pure and virtuous than the growing number of urban residents. When finally faced with the fact that they were in the minority, these country residents put up a strong rear-guard action to prevent the inevitable shift of congressional districts to the cities.

Rural representatives insisted that, since the 1920 census was taken as of Jan. 1, the farm population had been under-counted. In support of this contention, they argued that many farm laborers were seasonally employed in the cities at that time of year. Furthermore, mid-winter road conditions probably had prevented enumerators from visiting many farms, they said; and other farmers were said to have been uncounted because they were absent on winter vacation trips. The change of the census date to Jan. 1 in 1920 had been made to conform to recommendations of the Agriculture Department, which had asserted that the census should be taken early in the year if an accurate statistical picture of farming conditions was desired.

Another point raised by rural legislators was that large numbers of unnaturalized aliens were congregated in Northern cities, with the result that these cities gained at the expense of constituencies made up mostly of citizens of the United States. Rep. Homer Hoch, R-Kan., submitted a table showing that, in a House of 435 representatives, exclusion from the census count of persons not naturalized would have altered the allocation of seats to 16 states. Southern and Western farming states would have retained the number of seats allocated to them in 1911 or would have gained, while Northern industrial states and California would have lost or at least would have gained fewer seats.

A constitutional amendment to exclude all aliens from the enumeration for purposes of reapportionment was proposed during the 70th Congress (1927-29) by Rep. Hoch, Sen. Arthur Capper, R-Kan., and others. During the Senate Commerce Committee's hearings on reapportionment, Sen. Frederick M. Sackett, R-Ky., and Sen. Lawrence D. Tyson, D-Tenn., said they too intended to propose amendments to the same effect. But nothing further came of the proposals.

Reapportionment Bills Opposed

The first bill to reapportion the House according to the 1920 census was drafted by the House Census Committee early in 1921. Proceeding on the principle that no state should have its representation reduced, the committee proposed to increase the total number of representatives from 435 to 483. But the House voted 267-76 to keep its membership at 435 and passed the bill so amended on Jan. 19, 1921. Eleven states would have lost seats and eight would have gained. The bill then was blocked by a Senate committee, where it died when the 66th Congress expired March 4, 1921.

Early in the 67th Congress, the House Census Committee again reported a bill, this time fixing the total membership at 460, an increase of 25. Two states — Maine and Massachusetts — would have lost one representative each and 16 states would have gained. On the House floor an unsuccessful attempt was made to fix the number at the existing 435, and the House sent the bill back to committee.

During the 68th Congress (1923-25), the House Census Committee failed to report any reapportionment bill, and

Congressional Apportionment, 1789-1980

Year of Census[1]

	1789†	1790	1800	1810	1820	1830	1840	1850	1860	1870	1880	1890	1900	1910	1930#	1940	1950	1960	1970	1980
Ala.				1*	3	5	7	7	6	8	8	9	9	10	9	9	9	8	7	7
Alaska																	1*	1	1	1
Ariz.														1*	1	2	2	3	4	5
Ark.						1*	1	2	3	4	5	6	7	7	7	7	6	4	4	4
Calif.							2*	2	3	4	6	7	8	11	20	23	30	38	43	45
Colo.										1*	1	2	3	4	4	4	4	4	5	6
Conn.	5	7	7	7	6	6	4	4	4	4	4	4	5	5	6	6	6	6	6	6
Del.	1	1	1	2	1	1	1	1	1	1	1	1	1	1	1	1	1	1	1	1
Fla.							1*	1	1	2	2	2	3	4	5	6	8	12	15	19
Ga.	3	2	4	6	7	9	8	8	7	9	10	11	11	12	10	10	10	10	10	10
Hawaii																	1*	2	2	2
Idaho											1*	1	1	2	2	2	2	2	2	2
Ill.				1*	1	3	7	9	14	19	20	22	25	27	27	26	25	24	24	22
Ind.				1*	3	7	10	11	11	13	13	13	13	13	12	11	11	11	11	10
Iowa							2*	2	6	9	11	11	11	11	9	8	8	7	6	6
Kan.									1	3	7	8	8	8	7	6	6	5	5	5
Ky.		2	6	10	12	13	10	10	9	10	11	11	11	11	9	9	8	7	7	7
La.				1*	3	3	4	4	5	6	6	6	7	8	8	8	8	8	8	8
Maine				7*	7	8	7	6	5	5	4	4	4	4	3	3	3	2	2	2
Md.	6	8	9	9	9	8	6	6	5	6	6	6	6	6	6	6	7	8	8	8
Mass.	8	14	17	13‡	13	12	10	11	10	11	12	13	14	16	15	14	14	12	12	11
Mich.						1*	3	4	6	9	11	12	12	13	17	17	18	19	19	18
Minn.								2*	2	3	5	7	9	10	9	9	9	8	8	8
Miss.				1*	1	2	4	5	5	6	7	7	8	8	7	7	6	5	5	5
Mo.					1	2	5	7	9	13	14	15	16	16	13	13	11	10	10	9
Mont.											1*	1	1	2	2	2	2	2	2	2
Neb.									1*	1	3	6	6	6	5	4	4	3	3	3
Nev.									1*	1	1	1	1	1	1	1	1	1	1	2
N.H.	3	4	5	6	6	5	4	3	3	3	2	2	2	2	2	2	2	2	2	2
N.J.	4	5	6	6	6	6	5	5	5	7	7	8	10	12	14	14	14	15	15	14
N.M.														1*	1	2	2	2	2	3
N.Y.	6	10	17	27	34	40	34	33	31	33	34	34	37	43	45	45	43	41	39	34
N.C.	5	10	12	13	13	13	9	8	7	8	9	9	10	10	11	12	12	11	11	11
N.D.											1*	1	2	3	2	2	2	2	1	1
Ohio			1*	6	14	19	21	21	19	20	21	21	21	22	24	23	23	24	23	21
Okla.														5*	8	9	8	6	6	6
Ore.									1*	1	1	2	2	3	3	4	4	4	4	5
Pa.	8	13	18	23	26	28	24	25	24	27	28	30	32	36	34	33	30	27	25	23
R.I.	1	2	2	2	2	2	2	2	2	2	2	2	2	3	2	2	2	2	2	2
S.C.	5	6	8	9	9	9	7	6	4	5	7	7	7	7	6	6	6	6	6	6
S.D.											2*	2	2	3	2	2	2	2	2	1
Tenn.		1	3	6	9	13	11	10	8	10	10	10	10	10	9	10	9	9	8	9
Texas							2*	2	4	6	11	13	16	18	21	21	22	23	24	27
Utah												1*	1	2	2	2	2	2	2	3
Vt.		2	4	6	5	5	4	3	3	3	2	2	2	2	1	1	1	1	1	1
Va.	10	19	22	23	22	21	15	13	11	9	10	10	10	10	9	9	10	10	10	10
Wash.											1*	2	3	5	6	6	7	7	7	8
W.Va.										3	4	4	5	6	6	6	6	5	4	4
Wis.							2*	3	6	8	9	10	11	11	10	10	10	10	9	9
Wyo.											1*	1	1	1	1	1	1	1	1	1
Total	65	106	142	186	213	242	232	237	243	293	332	357	391	435	435	435	437**	435	435	435

[1] Apportionment effective with congressional election two years after census.
† Constitution ratified. Original apportionment made in Constitution, pending first census.
# No apportionment was made in 1920.
* These figures are not based on any census, but indicate the provisional representation accorded newly admitted states by the Congress, pending the next census.
‡ Twenty members were assigned to Massachusetts, but seven of these were credited to Maine when that area became a state.
** Normally 435, but temporarily increased two seats by Congress when Alaska and Hawaii became states.

Source: *Biographical Directory of the American Congress* and Bureau of the Census

midway in the 69th Congress (1925-27) it became apparent that the committee would not produce a reapportionment measure. Accordingly, on April 8, 1926, Rep. Henry E. Barbour, R-Calif., moved that the committee be discharged from further consideration of a bill identical with that passed by the House in 1921 keeping the chamber's membership at 435.

Chairman Bertrand H. Snell, N.Y., of the House Rules Committee, representing the Republican leadership of the House, raised a point of order against Barbour's motion. The Speaker of the House, Nicholas Longworth, R-Ohio, pointed out that decisions of earlier Speakers tended to indicate that reapportionment had been considered a matter of "constitutional privilege" and that Rep. Barbour's motion must be held in order if these precedents were followed. But the Speaker said he doubted whether the precedents had been interpreted correctly. He therefore submitted to the House the question of whether the pending motion should be considered privileged. The House sustained the Rules Committee by voting 87-265 not to consider the question privileged.

Intervention by Coolidge

President Calvin Coolidge, who previously had made no reference to reapportionment in his communications to Congress, announced in January 1927 that he favored passage of a new apportionment bill during the short session of the 69th Congress, which would end in less than two months. The House Census Committee refused to act. Its chairman, Rep. E. Hart Fenn, R-Conn., therefore moved in the House on March 2, 1927, to suspend the rules and pass a bill he had introduced authorizing the secretary of commerce to reapportion the House immediately after the 1930 census. The motion was voted down 183-197.

The Fenn bill was rewritten early in the 70th Congress (1927-29) to give Congress itself a chance to act before the proposed reapportionment by the secretary of commerce should go into effect. The bill was submitted to the House, which on May 18, 1928, voted 186-165 to recommit it to the Census Committee. After minor changes, the Fenn bill was again reported to the House and was passed on Jan. 11, 1929. No record vote was taken on passage of the bill, but a motion to return it to the committee was rejected 134-227.

Four days later, the reapportionment bill was reported by the Senate Commerce Committee. Repeated efforts to bring it up for floor action ahead of other bills failed. Its supporters gave up the fight on Feb. 27, 1929 — five days before the end of the session, when it became evident that senators from states slated to lose representation were ready to carry on a filibuster that would have blocked not only reapportionment but all other measures.

Intervention by Hoover

As the date of the next census became imminent, President Herbert Hoover listed provision for the 1930 census and reapportionment as "matters of emergency legislation" that should be acted upon in the special session of the 71st Congress that was convened on April 15, 1929. In response to this urgent request, the Senate June 13 passed, 48-37, a combined census-reapportionment bill that had been approved by voice vote of the House two days earlier.

The 1929 law established a permanent system of reapportioning the 435 House seats following each census. It provided that immediately after the convening of the 71st Congress for its short session in December 1930, the president was to transmit to Congress a statement showing the population of each state together with an apportionment of representatives to each state based on the existing size of the House. Failing enactment of new apportionment legislation, that apportionment would go into effect without further action and would remain in effect for ensuing elections to the House of Representatives until another census had been taken and another reapportionment made.

Because two decades had passed between reapportionments, a greater shift than usual took place following the 1930 census. California's House delegation was almost doubled, rising from 11 to 20. Michigan gained four seats, Texas three, and New Jersey, New York and Ohio two each. Twenty-one states lost a total of 27 seats; Missouri lost three and Georgia, Iowa, Kentucky and Pennsylvania each lost two.

To test the fairness of two allocation methods — the familiar major fractions and the new equal proportions system — the 1929 act required the president to report the distribution of seats by both methods. But, pending legislation to the contrary, the method of major fractions was to be used.

The two methods gave an identical distribution of seats based on 1930 census figures. However, in 1940 the two methods gave different results: under major fractions, Michigan would have gained a seat lost by Arkansas; under equal proportions, there would have been no change in either state. The automatic reapportionment provisions of the 1929 act went into effect in January 1941. But the House Census Committee moved to reverse the result, favoring the certain Democratic seat in Arkansas over a possible Republican gain if the seat were shifted to Michigan. The Democratic-controlled Congress went along, adopting equal proportions as the method to be used in reapportionment calculations after the 1950 and subsequent censuses, and making this action retroactive to January 1941 to save Arkansas its seat.

While politics doubtless played a part in the timing of the action taken in 1941, the method of equal proportions had come to be accepted as the best available. It had been worked out by Edward V. Huntington of Harvard in 1921. At the request of the Speaker of the House, all known methods of apportionment were considered in 1929 by the National Academy of Sciences Committee on Apportionment. The committee expressed its preference for equal proportions.

Method of Equal Proportions

The method of equal proportions involves complicated mathematical calculations. In brief, each of the 50 states is initially assigned the one seat to which every state is entitled by the Constitution. Then "priority numbers" for states to receive second seats, third seats and so on are calculated by dividing the state's population by the square root of $n(n-1)$, where "n" is the number of seats for that state. The priority numbers are then lined up in order and the seats given to the states with priority numbers until 435 are awarded.

The method is designed to make the *proportional* difference between the average district size in any two states as small as possible. For instance, using 1980 census figures, if New Mexico got three seats and Indiana got 10, as occurred under the method of equal proportions, New Mexico would have an average district size of 433,323, and Indiana would have an average district size of 549,018. That makes Indiana's average district 27 percent larger than New Mexico's. On the other hand, if New Mexico got

two seats and Indiana got 11, as would have happened if the major fractions method had been used in 1980, New Mexico's average district of 649,984 would be 30 percent larger than Indiana's average of 499,107.

Two respected private statisticians, M. L. Balinski and H. P. Young, have argued that the equal proportions method has "cheated the larger states, and given undue representation to the smaller ones," in violation of the Supreme Court's one-person, one-vote rule. They have advocated a return to the Vinton method of apportionment. Such a bill was introduced in Congress in early 1981, but it received little attention and died at the end of the session.

Redistricting: Drawing the Lines

Although the Constitution contained provisions for the apportionment of U. S. House seats among the states, it was silent about how these members should be elected. From the beginning most states divided their territory into geographic districts, permitting only one member of Congress to be elected from each district.

But some states allowed would-be House members to run at large, with voters able to cast as many votes as there were seats to be filled. Still other states created what were known as multi-member districts; in these a single geographic unit would elect two or more members of the House. At various times, some states used combinations of these methods. For example, a state might elect 10 representatives from 10 individual districts and two at large.

In the first few elections to the House, New Hampshire, Pennsylvania, New Jersey and Georgia elected their representatives at large, as did Rhode Island and Delaware, the two states with only a single representative. Districts were used in Massachusetts, New York, Maryland, Virginia and South Carolina. In Connecticut, a preliminary election was held to nominate three times as many persons as the number of representatives to be chosen at large in the subsequent election. In 1840, 22 of the 31 states elected their representatives by districts. New Hampshire, New Jersey, Georgia, Alabama, Mississippi and Missouri, with a combined representation of 33 House seats, elected their representatives at large. Three states, Arkansas, Delaware and Florida, had only one representative each.

Those states that used congressional districts quickly developed what came to be known as the gerrymander. This was the practice of drawing district lines so as to maximize the advantage of a political party or interest group. The name originated from a salamander-shaped congressional district created by the Massachusetts Legislature in 1812 when Elbridge Gerry was governor. *(Box, p. 1007)*

Constant efforts had been made during the early 1800s to lay down national rules, by means of a constitutional amendment, for congressional districting. The first resolution proposing a mandatory division of each state into districts was introduced in Congress in 1800. In 1802 the legislatures of Vermont and North Carolina adopted resolutions in support of such action. From 1816 to 1826, 22 state resolutions were adopted proposing the election of representatives by districts.

In Congress, Sen. Mahlon Dickerson of New Jersey proposed such an amendment regularly almost every year from 1817 to 1826. It was adopted by the Senate three times, in 1819, 1820 and 1822, but each time it failed to reach a vote in the House.

Because most states accepted the principle of local representation, congressional efforts to pass a constitutional amendment were unsuccessful. Instead, a law was passed in 1842 that required continuous single-member congressional districts. That law required representatives to be "elected by districts composed of contiguous territory equal in number to the representatives to which said state may be entitled, no one district electing more than one Representative."

When President John Tyler signed the bill, he appended to it a memorandum voicing doubt as to the constitutionality of the districting provisions. The memorandum precipitated a minor constitutional crisis. The House, urged on by Rep. John Quincy Adams of Massachusetts, appointed a select committee to consider the action of the president. Chaired by the aging former president, the committee drew up a resolution protesting Tyler's action as "unwarranted by the Constitution and laws of the United States, injurious to the public interest, and of evil example for the future; and this House do hereby solemnly protest against the said act of the President and against its ever being repeated or adduced as a precedent hereafter." The House took no action on the resolution; several attempts to call it up under suspension of the rules failed to receive the necessary two-thirds vote.

Districting Legislation, 1850-1910

The districting provisions of the 1842 act were not repeated in the legislation that followed the 1850 census. But in 1862 an act separate from the reapportionment act revived the provisions of the act of 1842 requiring districts to be composed of contiguous territory.

The 1872 reapportionment act again repeated the districting provisions and went even further by adding that districts should contain "as nearly as practicable an equal number of inhabitants." Similar provisions were included in the acts of 1881 and 1891. In the act of Jan. 16, 1901, the words "compact territory" were added, and the clause then read "contiguous and compact territory and containing as nearly as practicable an equal number of inhabitants." This requirement appeared also in the legislation of Aug. 8, 1911. (The "contiguous and compact" provisions of the act subsequently lapsed and, as of mid-1985, had not been replaced.)

Several unsuccessful attempts were made to enforce redistricting provisions. Despite the districting requirements of the act of June 25, 1842, New Hampshire, Georgia, Mississippi and Missouri elected their representatives at large that autumn. When the House elected at that time convened for its first session on Dec. 4, 1843, objection was made to seating the representatives of the four states. The dispute was referred to the Committee on Elections. The majority report of the committee, submitted by its chairman, Rep. Stephen A. Douglas, D-Ill., asserted that the act of 1842 was not binding upon the states and that the representatives in question were entitled to their seats. An amendment to the majority report deleted all reference to the apportionment law. A minority report by Rep. Garrett Davis, Whig-Ky., contended that the members had not been elected according to the Constitution and the laws and were not entitled to their seats.

The matter was debated in the House Feb. 6-14, 1844. With the Democratic Party holding a majority of more than 60, and with 18 of the 21 challenged members being Democrats, the House decided to seat the members. However, by 1848 all four states had come around to electing their representatives by districts.

The next challenge a House representative encountered over federal districting laws occurred in 1901. A charge that the existing Kentucky redistricting law did not comply with the redistricting provision of the federal reapportionment law of Jan. 16, 1901, was leveled to prevent the seating of Rep. George G. Gilbert, D, of Kentucky's 8th District. The committee assigned to investigate the matter turned aside the challenge, asserting that the federal act was not binding on the states. The reasons given were practical and political:

"Your committee are therefore of opinion that a proper construction of the Constitution does not warrant the conclusion that by that instrument Congress is clothed with power to determine the boundaries of Congressional districts, or to revise the acts of a State Legislature in fixing such boundaries; and your committee is further of opinion that even if such power is to be implied from the language of the Constitution, it would be in the last degree unwise and intolerable that it should exercise it. To do so would be to put into the hands of Congress the ability to disfranchise, in effect, a large body of the electors. It would give Congress the power to apply to all the States, in favor of one party, a general system of gerrymandering. It is true that the same method is to a large degree resorted to by the several states, but the division of political power is so general and diverse that notwithstanding the inherent vice of the system of gerrymandering, some kind of equality of distribution results."

In 1908 the Virginia Legislature transferred Floyd County from the 5th District to the 6th District. As a result, the population of the 5th District was reduced from 175,579 to 160,191 and that of the 6th District was increased from 181,571 to 196,959. The average for the state was 185,418.

When the newly elected representative from the 5th District, Edward W. Saunders, D, was challenged by his opponent in the election, the majority of the congressional investigating committee upheld the challenge. They concluded that the Virginia law of 1908 was null and void because it did not conform with the federal law of Jan. 16, 1901, or with the constitution of Virginia, and that the district should be regarded as including the counties that were a part of it before enactment of the 1908 state legislation. In that case Saunders' opponent would have had a majority of the votes, so the committee recommended that he be seated. Thus, for the first time, it appeared that the districting legislation would be enforced, but the House did not take action on the committee's report and Saunders' challenger was not seated.

Court Action on Redistricting

After the long and desultory battle over reapportionment in the 1920s, those who were unhappy over the inaction of Congress and the state legislatures began taking their cases to court. At first, the protestors had no luck. But as the population disparity grew in both federal and state legislative districts and the Supreme Court began to show a tendency to intervene, the objectors were more successful.

Finally, in a series of decisions beginning with *Baker v. Carr* in 1962 (369 U.S. 186) the court exerted great influence over the redistricting process, ordering that congressional districts as well as state and local legislative districts be drawn so that their populations would be as nearly equal as possible.

Origins of the Gerrymander

The practice of "gerrymandering" — the excessive manipulation of the shape of a legislative district to benefit a certain incumbent or party — is probably as old as the republic, but the name originated in 1812.

In that year the Massachusetts Legislature carved out of Essex County a district that historian John Fiske said had a "dragonlike contour." When the painter Gilbert Stuart saw the misshapen district, he penciled in a head, wings and claws and exclaimed: "That will do for a salamander!" — to which editor Benjamin Russell replied: "Better say a Gerrymander!" — after Elbridge Gerry, then governor of Massachusetts.

Supreme Court's 1932 Decision

The 1962 ruling essentially reversed the direction the court had taken in 1932. *Wood v. Broom* (287 U.S. 1) was a case challenging the constitutionality of a Mississippi redistricting law. The question was whether the 1911 federal redistricting act — which required that districts be separate, compact, contiguous and equally populated and which had been neither specifically repealed not reaffirmed in the 1929 reapportionment act — was still in effect.

Speaking for the court, Chief Justice Charles Evans Hughes ruled that the 1911 act, in effect, had expired with the approval of the 1929 apportionment act and that the standards of the 1911 act therefore were no longer applicable. The court reversed the decision of a lower federal court, which had permanently enjoined elections under the new Mississippi redistricting act because it violated the standards of the 1911 act.

That the Supreme Court upheld a state law that failed to provide for districts of equal population was almost less important than the minority opinion that the court should not have heard the case. Four justices — Louis D. Brandeis, Harlan F. Stone, Owen J. Roberts and Benjamin N.

Cardozo — while concurring in the majority opinion, said they would have dismissed the Wood suit for "want of equity." The "want-of-equity" phrase in this context suggested a policy of judicial self-limitation with respect to the entire question of judicial involvement in essentially "political" questions.

'Political Thicket'

Not until 1946, in *Colegrove v. Green* (328 U.S. 549, 1946), did the court again rule in a significant case dealing with congressional redistricting. The case was brought by Kenneth Colegrove, a political science professor at Northwestern University, who alleged that Illinois' congressional districts — varying in size between 112,116 and 914,053 in population — were so unequal that they violated the 14th Amendment's guarantee of equal protection of the laws. A seven-man Supreme Court divided 4-3 in dismissing the suit.

Justice Felix Frankfurter gave the opinion of the court, speaking for himself and Justices Stanley F. Reed and Harold H. Burton. Frankfurter's opinion cited *Wood v. Broom* to indicate that Congress had deliberately removed the standard set by the 1911 act. "We also agree," he said, "with the four Justices [Brandeis, Stone, Roberts and Cardozo] who were of the opinion that the bill in *Wood v. Broom* should be 'dismissed for want of equity.'" The issue, Frankfurter said, was "of a peculiarly political nature and therefore not meant for judicial interpretation. . . . The short of it is that the Constitution has conferred upon Congress exclusive authority to secure fair representation by the states in the popular House and has left to that House determination whether states have fulfilled their responsibility. If Congress failed in exercising its powers, whereby standards of fairness are offended, the remedy lies ultimately with the people. . . . To sustain this action would cut very deep into the very being of Congress. Courts ought not to enter this political thicket. The remedy for unfairness in districting is to secure state legislatures that will apportion properly, or to invoke the ample powers of Congress." Frankfurter also said that the court could not affirmatively remap congressional districts and that elections at large would be politically undesirable.

Justice Hugo L. Black, joined by Justices William O. Douglas and Frank Murphy, in a dissenting opinion maintained that the district court did have jurisdiction over congressional redistricting. The three justices cited as evidence a section of the U.S. Code that allowed district courts to redress deprivations of constitutional rights occurring through action of the states. Black's opinion also rested on a previous case in which the court had indicated that federal constitutional questions, unless "frivolous," fall under the jurisdiction of the federal courts. Black asserted that the appellants had standing to sue and that the population disparities did violate the equal protection clause of the 14th Amendment.

With the court split 3-3 on whether the judiciary had or should exercise jurisdiction, Justice Wiley B. Rutledge cast the deciding vote in *Colegrove v. Green*. On the question of justiciability, Rutledge agreed with Black, Douglas and Murphy that the issue could be considered by the federal courts. Thus a majority of the court participating in the *Colegrove* case felt that congressional redistricting cases were justiciable.

Yet on the question of granting relief in this specific instance, Rutledge agreed with Frankfurter, Reed and Burton that the case should be dismissed. He pointed out that four of the nine justices in *Wood v. Broom* had felt that dismissal should be for want of equity. Rutledge saw a "want-of-equity" situation in *Colegrove v. Green* as well. "I think the gravity of the constitutional questions raised [are] so great, together with the possibility of collision [with the political departments of the government], that the admonition [against avoidable constitutional decision] is appropriate to be followed here," Rutledge said. Jurisdiction, he thought, should be exercised "only in the most compelling circumstances." He thought that "the shortness of time remaining [before the forthcoming election] makes it doubtful whether action could or would be taken in time to secure for petitioners the effective relief they seek." Rutledge warned that congressional elections at large would deprive citizens of representation by districts, "which the prevailing policy of Congress demands." In the case of at-large elections, he warned, "the cure sought may be worse than the disease." For all these reasons he concluded that the case was "one in which the Court may properly, and should, decline to exercise its jurisdiction."

Changing Views

In the ensuing years, law professors, political scientists and other commentators expressed growing criticism of the *Colegrove* doctrine and growing impatience with the Supreme Court's reluctance to intervene in redistricting disputes. At the same time, the membership of the court was changing, and the new members were more inclined toward judicial action on redistricting.

In the 1950s the court decided two cases that laid some groundwork for its subsequent reapportionment decisions. The first was *Brown v. Board of Education* (347 U.S. 483, 1954), the historic school desegregation case, in which the court decided that an individual citizen could assert a right to equal protection of the laws under the 14th Amendment, contrary to the "separate but equal" doctrine of public facilities for white and black citizens. Six years later, in *Gomillion v. Lightfoot* (364 U.S. 339, 1960), the court held that the Alabama Legislature could not draw the city limits of Tuskegee so as to exclude nearly every black vote. In his opinion, Justice Frankfurter drew a clear line between redistricting challenges based on the 14th Amendment, such as *Colegrove*, and 15th Amendment challenges to discriminatory redistricting as in *Gomillion*. But Justice Charles E. Whittaker said that the equal protection clause was the proper constitutional basis for the decision. One commentator later remarked that *Gomillion* amounted to a "dragon" in the "political thicket" of *Colegrove*.

By 1962 only three members of the *Colegrove* court remained: Justices Black and Douglas, dissenters in that case, and Justice Frankfurter, aging spokesman for restraint in the exercise of judicial power.

By then it was clear that malapportionment within the states no longer could be ignored. By 1960 not a single state legislative body existed in which there was not at least a 2-to-1 population disparity between the most and the least heavily populated districts. For example, the disparity was 242-1 in the Connecticut House, 223-1 in the Nevada Senate, 141-1 in the Rhode Island Senate and 9-1 in the Georgia Senate. Studies of the effective vote of large and small counties in state legislatures between 1910 and 1960 showed that the effective vote of the large counties had slipped while their percentage of the national population had more than doubled. The most lightly populated counties, on the other hand, advanced from a position of slight over-representation to one of extreme over-representation,

Malapportionment and Gerrymandering

The prevalence of malapportionment in the creation of U.S. congressional districts was, to many observers, one of the chief evils in the American system before the "one-person, one-vote" ruling by the Supreme Court in 1964. On Feb. 17 of that year, the court, in the case of *Wesberry v. Sanders*, declared that "as nearly as is practicable, one man's vote in a congressional election is to be worth as much as another's."

Malapportionment

Malapportionment occurred when districts of grossly unequal populations were created — either through actions of state legislatures in establishing new districts or, as was the more frequent practice in America, simply by failing to redistrict despite major population shifts.

Within a single state, populations in some congressional districts varied by as much as eight to one. Generally, growing urban areas were under-represented, to the advantage of rural areas.

Examples of great disparity in congressional district sizes in modern U.S. history included: New York (1930), 776,425 residents in the largest district and 90,671 in the smallest district; Ohio (1946), 698,650 and 163,561; Illinois (1946), 914,053 and 112,116; Arkansas (1946), 423,152 and 177,476; Texas (1962), 951,527 and 216,371; Michigan (1962), 802,994 and 177,431; Maryland (1962), 711,045 and 243,570; South Dakota (1962), 497,669 and 182,845.

The decennial census and ensuing reapportionment of House seats eventually forced redistricting in most states, although some resorted to the expedient of electing members at large (this occurred in Texas, Hawaii, Ohio, Michigan and Maryland in 1962) rather than face redrawing district lines.

A 1967 law (PL 90-196) banned at-large elections in states with more than one representative. However, that law has been interpreted variously by the states. And where divided states' legislatures have been unable to agree on a redistricting plan, the courts have had to impose their own plan.

Although sizes vary somewhat because of apportionment and inequalities that build between censuses, generally the districts start out nearly equal in population.

In their 1985 book, *Congress and Its Members*, political scientists Roger H. Davidson and Walter J. Oleszek noted:

> Population equality has thus been achieved at the expense of other goals. Parity in numbers of residents makes it hard to respect political divisions such as county lines. It also makes it hard to follow economic, social, or geographic boundaries. The congressional district, therefore, tends to be an artificial creation with little relationship to real communities of interest — economic or geographic or political. This heightens the congressional district's isolation, forcing candidates to forge

their own unique factions and alliances. It also aids incumbents, who have ways of reaching voters without relying on commercial communications media.

Gerrymandering

Gerrymandering was the name given to excessive manipulation of the shape of legislative districts to benefit a particular politician or political party. The gerrymander was named after Democrat Elbridge Gerry, the governor of Massachusetts in 1812 when the Legislature created a peculiar salamander-shaped district to benefit his party. *(Sketch of district, box, p. 1007)*

Unlike malapportionment, gerrymandering has not been prohibited by law. It still is used today by both political parties. In 1961 Republican legislators in New York created one gerrymander-like creature stretching across the greater part of upstate New York, his head hanging over Albany in the east and his tail reaching for Rochester in the west. Such salamander, tadpole and fishlike creatures sprang to life on the maps of New York City's boroughs. In North Carolina after the 1960 census, Democratic redistricters formed an almost perfect gerrymander shape to throw the state's sole Republican representative in with a strong Democratic opponent.

After the 1980 census, Democrats in control of California's Legislature drew a district in the San Francisco Bay area in which two segments were linked only by a body of water. New Jersey's map was a gerrymander that boasted some of the most bizarrely shaped districts in the nation. The Supreme Court threw those districts out in 1983 but on the grounds of population inequality, not because they were gerrymandered.

Davidson and Oleszek cite two kinds of gerrymandering: "packing" and "cracking." In the first case, a district line is drawn so as to encompass as many of one party's voters as possible, thus "packing" it with supporters. "Cracking" entails diluting one party's strength by dispersing it among two or more districts.

The intent of practically every gerrymander is political — to create a maximum number of districts that would elect the party candidates or types of candidates favored by the controlling group in the state legislature that did the redistricting, thus increasing, or maintaining, the political power of the already politically dominant group. Concluded Davidson and Oleszek:

> The long-range effects of gerrymanders are not easily measured.... Marginal or competitive districts (those where the winner gains less than 55 percent of the votes) are tougher for a party to capture and hold, but they have the advantage of yielding legislative seats with a modest number of voters (that is, a minimal winning coalition). Safe districts, while naturally preferred by the incumbents, can waste the majority party's votes by furnishing outsized victories.

holding almost twice as many seats as they would be entitled to by population size alone. Predictably, the rural-dominated state legislatures resisted every move toward reapportioning state legislative districts to reflect new population patterns.

Population imbalance among congressional districts was substantially lopsided but by no means so gross. In Texas the 1960 census showed the most heavily populated district had four times as many inhabitants as the most lightly populated. Arizona, Maryland and Ohio each had at least one district with three times as many inhabitants as the least populated. In most cases, rural areas benefited from the population imbalance in congressional districts. As a result of the postwar population movement out of central cities to the surrounding areas, the suburbs were the most under-represented.

Baker v. Carr

It was against this background that a group of Tennessee city dwellers successfully broke the longstanding precedent against federal court involvement in legislative apportionment problems. For more than half a century, since 1901, the Tennessee Legislature had refused to reapportion itself, even though a decennial reapportionment based on population was specifically required by the state's constitution. In the meantime, Tennessee's population had grown and shifted dramatically to urban areas. By 1960 the House legislative districts ranged from 3,454 to 36,031 in population, while the Senate districts ranged from 39,727 to 108,094. Appeals by urban residents to the rural-controlled Tennessee Legislature proved fruitless. A suit brought in the state courts to force reapportionment was rejected on grounds that the courts should stay out of legislative matters.

City dwellers then appealed to the federal courts, stating that they had no redress: the Legislature had refused to act for more than half a century, the state courts had refused to intervene and Tennessee had no referendum or initiative laws. They charged that there was "a debasement of their votes by virtue of the incorrect, obsolete and unconstitutional apportionment" to such an extent that they were being deprived of their right to "equal protection of the laws" under the 14th Amendment. (The 14th Amendment reads, in part: "No state shall . . . deny to any person within its jurisdiction the equal protection of the laws.")

The Supreme Court on March 26, 1962, handed down its historic decision in *Baker v. Carr*, ruling in favor of the Tennessee city dwellers by a 6-2 margin. In the majority opinion, Justice William J. Brennan Jr. emphasized that the federal judiciary had the power to review the apportionment of state legislatures under the 14th Amendment's equal protection clause. "The mere fact that a suit seeks protection as a political right," Brennan wrote, "does not mean that it presents a political question" that the courts should avoid.

In a vigorous dissent, Justice Frankfurter said the majority decision constituted "a massive repudiation of the experience of our whole past" and was an assertion of "destructively novel judicial power." He contended that the lack of any clear basis for relief "catapults the lower courts" into a "mathematical quagmire." Frankfurter insisted that "there is not under our Constitution a judicial remedy for every political mischief." Appeal for relief, he maintained, should not be made in the courts, but rather "to an informed civically militant electorate."

The court had abandoned the view that malapportionment questions were outside its competence. But it stopped there and in *Baker v. Carr* did not address the merits of the challenge to the legislative districts.

Gray v. Sanders

The one-person, one-vote rule was set out first by the court almost exactly one year after its decision in *Baker v. Carr*. But the case in which the announcement came did not involve congressional districts.

In the ruling in the case of *Gray v. Sanders*, the court found that Georgia's county-unit primary system for electing state officials — a system that weighted votes to give advantage to rural districts in statewide primary elections — denied voters equal protection of the laws.

All votes in a statewide election must have equal weight, held the court: "How then can one person be given twice or 10 times the voting power of another person in a statewide election merely because he lives in a rural area or because he lives in the smallest rural county? Once the geographical unit for which a representative is to be chosen is designated, all who participate in the election are to have an equal vote — whatever their race, whatever their sex, whatever their occupation, whatever their income, and wherever their home may be in that geographical unit. This is required by the Equal Protection Clause of the Fourteenth Amendment. The concept of 'we the people' under the Constitution visualizes no preferred class of voters but equality among those who meet the basic qualification. The idea that every voter is equal to every other voter in his State, when he casts his ballot in favor of one of several competing candidates, underlies many of our decisions. . . . The conception of political equality from the Declaration of Independence to Lincoln's Gettysburg Address, to the Fifteenth, Seventeenth, and Nineteenth Amendments can mean only one thing — one person, one vote."

The Rule Applied

The court's rulings in *Baker* and *Gray* concerned the equal weighting and counting of votes cast in state elections. In 1964, deciding the case of *Wesberry v. Sanders*, the court applied the one-person, one-vote principle to congressional districts and set equality as the standard for congressional redistricting.

Shortly after the *Baker* decision was handed down, James P. Wesberry Jr., an Atlanta resident and a member of the Georgia Senate, filed suit in federal court in Atlanta claiming that gross disparity in the population of Georgia's congressional districts violated 14th Amendment rights of equal protection of the laws. At the time, Georgia districts ranged in population from 272,154 in the rural 9th District in the northeastern part of the state to 823,860 in the 5th District in Atlanta and its suburbs. District lines had not been changed since 1931. The state's number of House seats remained the same in the interim, but Atlanta's district population — already high in 1931 compared with the others — had more than doubled in 30 years, making a 5th District vote worth about one-third that of a vote in the 9th.

On June 20, 1962, the three-judge federal court divided 2-1 in dismissing Wesberry's suit. The majority reasoned that the precedent of *Colegrove* still controlled in congressional district cases. The judges cautioned against federal judicial interference with Congress and against "depriving others of the right to vote" if the suit should result in at-large elections. They suggested that the Georgia Legislature (under court order to reapportion itself) or the U.S.

Congress might better provide relief. Wesberry then appealed to the Supreme Court, which heard arguments in the case in November 1963.

On Feb. 17, 1964, the Supreme Court ruled in the case of *Wesberry v. Sanders* (376 U.S. 1) that congressional districts must be substantially equal in population. The court, which upheld Wesberry's challenge by a 6-3 decision, based its ruling on the history and wording of Article I, Section 2 of the Constitution providing that representatives shall be apportioned among the states according to their respective numbers and be chosen by the people of the several states. This language, the court stated, meant that "as nearly as is practicable, one man's vote in a congressional election is to be worth as much as another's."

The majority opinion, written by Justice Black and supported by Chief Justice Earl Warren and Justices Brennan, Douglas, Arthur J. Goldberg and Byron R. White, said that, "While it may not be possible to draw congressional districts with mathematical precision, that is no excuse for ignoring our Constitution's plain objective of making equal representation for equal numbers of people the fundamental goal for the House of Representatives."

In a strongly worded dissent, Justice John M. Harlan asserted that the Constitution did not establish population as the only criterion of congressional districting and that the subject was left by the Constitution to the discretion of the states, subject only to the supervisory power of Congress. "The constitutional right which the court creates is manufactured out of whole cloth," Harlan concluded.

The *Wesberry* opinion established no precise standards for districting beyond declaring that districts must be as nearly equal in population "as is practicable." In his dissent, Harlan suggested that a disparity of more than 100,000 between a state's largest and smallest districts would "presumably" violate the equality standard enunciated by the majority. On that basis, Harlan estimated, the districts of 37 states with 398 representatives would be unconstitutional, "leaving a constitutional House of 37 members now sitting."

Neither did the court's decision make any reference to gerrymandering, since it discussed only the population, not the shape of districts. In a separate districting opinion handed down the same day as *Wesberry*, the court dismissed a challenge to congressional districts in New York City, which had been brought by voters who charged that Manhattan's "silk-stocking" 17th District had been gerrymandered to exclude blacks and Puerto Rican citizens.

Strict Equality

Five years elapsed between the court's admonition in *Wesberry v. Sanders* and the court's next application of constitutional standards to congressional districting.

In 1967 the court hinted at the strict stance it would adopt two years later. With two unsigned opinions, the court sent back to Indiana and Missouri for revision those two states' congressional redistricting plans because they allowed variations of as much as 20 percent from the average district population.

Two years later, Missouri's revised plan returned to the court for full review. With its decision in the case of *Kirkpatrick v. Preisler* (385 U.S. 450), the court by a 6-3 vote rejected the plan. It was unacceptable, held the majority, because it allowed a variation of as much as 3.1 percent from perfectly equal population districts.

The court thus made clear its strict application of "one person, one vote" to congressional redistricting. Minor deviations from the strict equal-population principle were permissible only when the state provided substantial evidence that the variation was unavoidable.

Writing for the court, Justice Brennan declared that there was no "fixed numerical or percentage population variance small enough to be considered *de minimis* and to satisfy without question the 'as nearly as practicable' standard." "Equal representation for equal numbers of people is a principle designed to prevent debasement of voting power and diminution of access to elected Representatives. Toleration of even small deviations detracts from these purposes," Brennan wrote.

The only permissible variances in population, the court ruled, were those that were unavoidable despite the effort to achieve absolute equality or those that could be legally justified. The variances in Missouri could have been avoided, the court said.

None of Missouri's arguments for the plan qualified as "legally acceptable" justifications. The court rejected the argument that population variance was necessary to allow representation of distinct interest groups. It said that acceptance of such variances to produce districts with specific interests was "antithetical" to the basic purpose of equal representation.

Justice Byron R. White dissented from the majority opinion, which he characterized as "an unduly rigid and unwarranted application of the Equal Protection Clause which will unnecessarily involve the courts in the abrasive task of drawing district lines." White added that some "acceptably small" population variance could be established. He indicated that considerations of existing political boundaries and geographical compactness could justify to him some variation from "absolute equality" of population.

Justice Harlan, joined by Justice Potter Stewart, objected that "whatever room remained under this Court's prior decisions for the free play of the political process in matters of reapportionment is now all but eliminated by today's Draconian judgments."

Practical Results

As a result of the court decisions of the 1960s, nearly every state was forced to redraw its congressional district lines — sometimes more than once. By the end of the decade, 39 of the 45 states with more than one representative had made the necessary adjustments.

However, the effect of the one-person, one-vote standard on congressional districts did not bring about immediate equality in districts in the years 1964-70. Most of the new districts were far from equal in population, because the only official population figures came from the 1960 census. Massive population shifts during the decade rendered most post-*Wesberry* efforts to achieve equality useless.

But following redistricting in 1971-72, based on the 1970 census, the result achieved was that House members elected in November 1972 to the 93rd Congress represented districts that differed only slightly in population from the state average. In 385 of the 435 districts, the district's variance was less than 1 percent from the state average district population.

By contrast, only nine of the districts in the 88th Congress (elected in 1962) deviated less than 1 percent from the state average; 81 were between 1 and 5 percent; 87 from 5 to 10 percent; and in 236 districts the deviation was 10 percent or greater. Twenty-two House members were

The Voting Rights Act

There is one form of gerrymandering that is expressly forbidden by law: redistricting for the purpose of racial discrimination. The Voting Rights Act of 1965, extended in 1970, 1975 and 1982, banned redistricting plans that diluted the voting strength of black communities. Other minorities, including Hispanics, Asian-Americans, American Indians and native Alaskans subsequently were brought under the protection of the law.

The law originally was aimed at those Southern states where blacks had long been targets of discrimination. At the time the original law was passed, racial redistricting was not a great problem since black voting strength was minimal. However, with the enhancement of registration and voting rights for blacks, lawmakers feared that affected states would, through gerrymandering, divide black communities among several congressional districts and lower the chances of electing black representatives. That concern resulted in Section Five, the pre-clearance provisions of the act under which nine states and parts of 13 others must receive Justice Department approval of their congressional redistricting plans.

The Voting Rights Act is widely considered the most effective civil rights measure ever enacted. The voter registration provisions have been the most successful. Black voter registration in Mississippi increased from 6.7 percent in 1964 to 67.4 percent in 1976. Black representation in state legislatures, which also come under the purview of the Voting Rights Act, increased substantially. But black congressional representation has not expanded as greatly. After the 1964 elections the nine states that now must clear entire state plans (Alabama, Alaska, Arizona, Georgia, Louisiana, Mississippi, South Carolina, Texas and Virginia) had 74 seats and no black congressmen. In 1985 they had 79 seats and just one black representative (Mickey Leland, D-Texas).

elected at large.

The Supreme Court made only one major ruling concerning congressional districts during the 1970s. On June 18, 1973, the court declared the Texas congressional districts, as redrawn in 1971, unconstitutional because of excessive population variance among districts. The variance between the largest and smallest districts was 4.9872 percent. The court returned the case to a three-judge federal panel, which adopted a new congressional district plan, effective Oct. 17, 1973.

Precise Equality

Almost exactly 10 years later, on June 22, 1983, the Supreme Court handed down another redistricting decision with sweeping implications. In a 5-4 decision, the court ruled in *Karcher v. Daggett* that states must adhere as closely as possible to the one-person, one-vote standard and bear the burden of proving that deviations from precise population equality were made in pursuit of a legitimate goal. The decision overturned New Jersey's congressional map because the variation between the most populated and the least populated districts was 0.69 percent.

Brennan, who wrote the court opinion in *Baker* and *Kirkpatrick*, also wrote the opinion in *Karcher*, contending that population differences between districts "could have been avoided or significantly reduced with a good-faith effort to achieve population equality."

"Adopting any standard other than population equality, using the best census data available, would subtly erode the Constitution's ideal of equal representation," Brennan wrote. "If state legislators knew that a certain *de minimis* level of population differences were acceptable, they would doubtless strive to achieve that level rather than equality. Furthermore, choosing a different standard would import a high degree of arbitrariness into the process of reviewing reapportionment plans. In this case, appellants argue that a maximum deviation of approximately 0.7 percent should be considered *de minimis*. If we accept that argument, how are we to regard deviations of 0.8 percent, 0.95 percent, 1.0 percent or 1.1 percent?... To accept the legitimacy of unjustified, though small population deviations in this case would mean to reject the basic premise of *Kirkpatrick* and *Wesberry*."

Brennan said that "any number of consistently applied legislative policies might justify" some population variation. These included "making districts compact, respecting municipal boundaries, preserving the cores of prior districts, and avoiding contests between incumbent Representatives." However, he cautioned, the state must show "with some specificity that a particular objective required the specific deviations in its plan, rather than simply relying on general assertions."

In his dissent Justice White criticized the majority for its "unreasonable insistence on an unattainable perfection in the equalizing of congressional districts." He warned that the decision would invite "further litigation of virtually every congressional redistricting plan in the nation"

The court did not address the underlying political issue in the New Jersey case, which was that its map had been drawn to serve Democratic interests. As a partisan gerrymander, the map had few peers, boasting some of the most oddly shaped districts in the country. One constituency, known as "the fishhook" by its detractors, twisted through central New Jersey's industrial landscape, picking up Democratic voters along the way. Another stretched from the suburbs of New York to the fringes of Trenton.

In separate dissents Justices Lewis F. Powell Jr. and John Paul Stevens broadly hinted that they were willing to hear constitutional challenges to instances of partisan gerrymandering. "A legislator cannot represent his constituents properly — nor can voters from a fragmented district exercise the ballot intelligently — when a voting district is nothing more than an artificial unit divorced from, and indeed often in conflict with, the various communities established in the State," wrote Powell.

Congress and Redistricting

Several attempts were made by Congress in the post-World War II period to enact new legislation on redistricting. Only one of these efforts was successful — enactment of a measure barring at-large elections in states with more than one representative.

On Jan. 9, 1951, President Harry S Truman, upon presentation of the official state population figures of the 1950 census, asked for changes in existing law to tighten federal control of state redistricting. Specifically, he asked for a ban on gerrymandering, an end to at-large seats in

states having more than one representative and a sharp reduction in the huge differences in size among congressional districts within most states.

On behalf of the administration, Emanuel Celler, D-N.Y., chairman of the House Judiciary Committee, introduced a bill to require compact and contiguous congressional districts that would not vary by more than 15 percent between districts within a state. The bill also eliminated at-large seats and made redistricting mandatory every 10 years in accordance with population changes. But the House Judiciary Committee took no action on the proposals.

Rep. Celler regularly introduced his bill throughout the 1950s and early 1960s, but it made no headway until the Supreme Court handed down the *Wesberry* decision in 1964. On June 24, 1964, a Celler bill was approved by a House Judiciary subcommittee. But the full committee did not act on the bill before adjournment of Congress.

On March 16, 1965, the House finally passed a redistricting bill. It established 15 percent as the maximum percentage by which a congressional district's population might deviate from the average size of the state's districts; prohibited at-large elections for any state with more than one House seat; required that districts be composed of "contiguous territory in as compact form as practicable," and forbade more than one redistricting of a state between decennial censuses. A major reason for House approval of Celler's bill appeared to be a desire to gain protection from court imposition of even more rigid criteria. But the measure encountered difficulties in the Senate Judiciary Committee. After considerable wrangling over its provisions, the committee voted to report the bill without precise agreement on its wording. No report was ever filed by the committee.

In 1967 a redistricting bill was passed by both the Senate and the House, but not in the same form. And the bill had a different purpose from that of previous bills dealing with the subject. Instead of trying to establish standards of fairness in drawing district lines, the chief purpose in 1967 was to prevent the courts from ordering redistricting of House seats or from ordering any state to hold elections at large — a procedure that many incumbent representatives feared — until after the House had been reapportioned on the basis of the 1970 census.

A combination of liberal Democrats and Republicans in the Senate managed to defeat the conference report Nov. 8, 1967, by a vote of 22-55. Liberals favored court action, which they believed would eliminate many conservative rural districts, while Republicans felt that redistricted areas, especially in the growing suburbs, would elect more Republicans than Democrats.

To avoid at-large elections, the Senate added a rider to a House-passed private bill. Under the rider, at-large elections of U.S. representatives were banned in all states entitled to more than one representative, with the exceptions of New Mexico and Hawaii. Those states had a tradition of electing their two representatives at large. Both of them, however, soon passed districting laws — New Mexico for the 1968 elections and Hawaii for 1970.

In 1971 Celler introduced a new version of his proposed redistricting legislation. Although the House Judiciary Committee reported the measure favorably, no further action was taken on the bill, and it died at the end of the 92nd Congress.

After the 1960 census, an attempt had been made to increase the size of the House to avoid some of the losses of seats that would otherwise be suffered by several states. By a vote of 12-14, the House Judiciary Committee on Sept. 9, 1961, rejected a motion to recommend enlarging the House to 453 seats. And by a vote of 14-15, the same committee rejected a bill reported by a subcommittee that would have increased the permanent size of the House to 438.

The Presidency

Reagan Appointments   1017
Presidential Vetoes   1031
Presidential Texts   1033

Reagan Appointments to Major Posts

Few of President Reagan's nominees to Cabinet, sub-Cabinet and other executive branch posts ran into serious opposition to their confirmation by the Senate. The Republican-dominated Senate gave rapid approval to his original Cabinet, overwhelmingly confirming within two days of his Jan. 20, 1981, inauguration all of the men he had chosen to head federal departments except Labor Secretary-designate Raymond J. Donovan. Allegations that Donovan had links to organized crime and labor racketeers held up his confirmation for several weeks, but he was confirmed Feb. 3. Later it was disclosed that the FBI had withheld damaging information from the Senate.

Two other Cabinet nominations — those of Alexander M. Haig Jr. to be secretary of state and James G. Watt to be interior secretary — caused more strife than Donovan's. Nonetheless both men were confirmed with little dissent. Although several senators expressed serious reservations about these and other nominations, they voted for confirmation, saying they felt Reagan was entitled to the Cabinet he wanted.

By the end of Reagan's first term, both Haig and Watt had left the Cabinet, and Donovan, who had been indicted on criminal charges, was on his way out. Three other members of Reagan's original Cabinet also left during Reagan's first term. *(Reagan Cabinet, box, p. 1019)*

In contrast to his first year in office, the president in 1982 began having difficulties in winning approval of his nominations for high-level executive branch positions. Opposition came chiefly from conservatives in his own party rather than from Democrats.

The conservative opposition was led by Sen. Jesse Helms, R-N.C. Helms' tactics often resulted in infighting between Senate factions over issues that had little to do with the nominees' qualifications. Helms and his colleagues used the nominations as a basis for challenging what they saw as the administration's abandonment of a sufficiently tough stance in arms talks with the Soviet Union.

Bipartisan opposition sidetracked other appointees, such as Reagan's nominees to the Legal Services Corporation. *(Box, p. 1028)*

Below are profiles of Cabinet members and others who served in key executive branch positions during the first Reagan administration, followed by brief accounts of major controversial nominations made from 1980 to 1984.

Cabinet, 1981-84

Agriculture

John R. Block, an Illinois farmer, was confirmed Jan. 22, 1981, as agriculture secretary by the Senate on a 98-0 vote. A 1957 graduate of the U.S. Military Academy at West Point, he left the Army in 1960 to take over his family's farm near Galesburg, Ill. He expanded it to 3,000 acres from 300, raised hogs and soybeans and was a former board member of the Illinois Farm Bureau.

When appointed in 1977 as director of the Illinois Department of Agriculture, Block was a strong advocate of revisions in Illinois' conservation law. He drew up a voluntary program that relied on financial incentives to reward farmers for protecting land from erosion.

Block played a major role in setting up a 1980 state conference on the problem of conversion of prime farm land to non-farm uses such as shopping centers or industrial development. He also pushed for development of state trade promotion offices abroad to act as "middlemen" for sales of Illinois farm products and the production of gasohol.

Major farm groups and the National Governors' Association (NGA) said Block had been unusually able and aggressive as Illinois agriculture director.

He was praised as an effective manager with experience in international trade and a good record on conservation and farm programs. Block had served on the NGA's committee on agriculture and agricultural export task force.

Food and nutrition groups, however, objected to Block. In testimony before Congress, Block had criticized Agriculture Department moves against the meat preservative sodium nitrite, which had been linked to cancer.

He also objected to controversial department dietary guidelines.

The Agriculture Department's stress on consumer issues under the Carter administration had been a sore point with many farmers. During the 1980 presidential campaign, Reagan objected to "unfounded attacks on nutritious, farm-produced foods unleashed by ... activists" in the Carter administration and promised to restore the department to "farmers and those who understand farming."

Attorney General

When **William French Smith** was nominated to head the Justice Department, he was a partner in the prestigious law firm of Gibson, Dunn and Crutcher, and Reagan's personal lawyer.

The Senate confirmed Smith as attorney general Jan. 22, 1981, on a 96-1 vote.

On Jan. 23, 1984, Smith made public plans to resign as attorney general and to return to his law practice. But he remained in office pending confirmation of his successor, presidential counselor Edwin Meese III. Meese was not confirmed until February 1985.

A Harvard law graduate, Smith primarily had been a labor lawyer, frequently negotiating for management in

labor disputes. He also had spent much time helping wealthy clients manage their finances. Reportedly, his advice helped make Reagan a millionaire.

In 1968 Gov. Reagan appointed Smith to the Board of Regents of the University of California. As a regent he opposed efforts to require the university to dispose of its holdings in companies doing business in South Africa. Smith said political motives should not influence investment decisions.

Smith helped lead efforts to fire black activist Angela Davis, an avowed communist, from the university faculty. He also supported the university's affirmative action plan that led to the controversial decision to reject white medical school applicant Allan Bakke in favor of less qualified blacks.

Commerce

The Senate confirmed **Malcolm Baldrige** as secretary of commerce on a 97-1 vote Jan. 22, 1981. A member of the Professional Rodeo Cowboys Association and a prize-winning steer roper, Baldrige was chairman of the board and chief executive officer of Scovill Inc. of Waterbury, Conn. Although not well known in Washington, D.C., he was widely respected in business circles and had strong Republican Party credentials.

In 1944 Baldrige graduated from Yale University. After serving in the Army during World War II, he joined Eastern Co. as foundry foreman, rising to president in 1960. He joined Scovill as executive vice president in 1962, becoming president and chief executive officer in 1963 and chairman and chief executive officer in 1969.

Baldrige was credited with launching Scovill, formerly a brass manufacturing concern, on an ambitious program of product expansion and diversification that transformed it into "a mini-conglomerate" with sales of $941.6 million in 1979, according to a Scovill board member. The manufacturing firm included such trade names as Hamilton Beach appliances and Yale locks.

A delegate to the Republican National Convention in 1968, 1972 and 1976, Baldrige was Connecticut co-chairman of United Citizens for Nixon-Agnew. He also was a member of the National Republican Finance Committee. In 1980 he was chairman of the Bush for President Committee in Connecticut, one of the few states that Bush won over Ronald Reagan.

Baldrige's father, H. Malcolm Baldrige, served in Congress as a Republican representative from Nebraska in 1931-33.

Defense

To run the Defense Department, Reagan chose a close adviser with diversified experience in high-level government administration. Two of the most prominent qualities of **Caspar W. Weinberger** were his reputed managerial prowess in a variety of roles and his loyalty to Reagan. The Senate confirmed Weinberger as defense secretary on Jan. 20, 1981, by a 97-2 vote.

Weinberger received his undergraduate and legal education at Harvard, served in the Army during World War II and began practicing law in San Francisco after the war.

He was a Republican member of the California Legislature from 1952 to 1958, then vice-chairman and chairman of the Republican state central committee from 1960 to 1964.

After Reagan's election as governor in 1966, Weinberger served as chairman of a state commission on governmental organization and economics (1967-68) and state finance director (1968-69). It was in this period that he acquired the nickname "Cap the Knife," a reference to his flair for budget cutting.

In January 1970 Weinberger became chairman of the Federal Trade Commission (FTC), then in turmoil from the just-ended chairmanship of Paul Rand Dixon. Weinberger won general acclaim for bringing harmony to the commission and became a favorite of liberals for staking out a more aggressively pro-consumer position than was being taken by the Nixon administration.

After less than six months at the FTC, Weinberger was tapped by Nixon as deputy director of the newly created Office of Management and Budget (OMB). Under OMB Director George P. Shultz, Weinberger directed the administration's budget process. Weinberger became OMB director in 1972 when Shultz became secretary of the Treasury.

During his OMB years Weinberger was a point man in Nixon's battle to establish the president's power to impound congressionally appropriated funds. Weinberger's tenure also coincided with the peak of domestic turmoil over the Vietnam War and the attendant pressure to cut the Pentagon budget.

When Weinberger became secretary of health, education and welfare (HEW) in January 1973, he was one of three domestic Cabinet officials who were simultaneously named White House counselors and who divided among themselves general oversight of the whole range of domestic policy. Other domestic Cabinet secretaries reported to the president through these super-secretaries.

Weinberger remained at HEW after Gerald R. Ford replaced Nixon in August 1974. In 1975 he followed his old superior Shultz to the Bechtel Corp., a San Francisco-based engineering and construction firm. Shultz had left Treasury for the firm in 1974. Weinberger joined the company as general counsel.

Education

T. H. Bell was confirmed as education secretary by the Senate 90-2 on Jan. 22, 1981. He became the second head of the department, which was established in 1980.

Just two days after President Reagan's landslide re-election victory Nov. 6, 1984, Bell became the first Cabinet member to announce he would not stay for a second Reagan term. Citing "personal reasons," Bell resigned effective Dec. 31. William J. Bennett, chairman of the National Endowment for the Humanities, was confirmed Feb. 6, 1985, to succeed him.

Unlike President Carter's choice to be the first education secretary, former California judge Shirley M. Hufstedler, who had virtually no experience in education, Bell had spent his entire career in the field.

He worked as a teacher, and later as a school superintendent, in public school systems in Idaho and Utah. From 1963 to 1970 he was Utah's superintendent of public instruction. After a short term as deputy commissioner in the U.S. Office of Education, he served as head of a school system near Salt Lake City for three years. From 1974 to 1976 he was U.S. education commissioner. He left that position to become Utah commissioner of higher education, the position he held when named by Reagan to be education secretary.

Education groups were pleased by the selection of a

Reagan Administration Cabinet

Following is a list of Cabinet officers who served in the Reagan administration from the time President Reagan took office on Jan. 20, 1981, through mid-1985.

Dates given are for actual service in office, which may vary from dates of confirmation by the Senate. *(Presidents and their Cabinets, 1933-80, Congress and the Nation Vol. V, p. 1111)*

Secretary of State

Alexander M. Haig Jr.—Jan. 21, 1981-July 16, 1982
George P. Shultz—July 16, 1982-

Secretary of the Treasury

Donald T. Regan—Jan. 22, 1981-Feb. 2, 1985
James A. Baker III—Feb. 4, 1985-

Secretary of Defense

Caspar W. Weinberger—Jan. 21, 1981-

Attorney General

William French Smith—Jan. 23, 1981-Feb. 22, 1985
Edwin Meese III—Feb. 25, 1985-

Secretary of the Interior

James G. Watt—Jan. 23, 1981-Nov. 8, 1983
William P. Clark—Nov. 21, 1983-Feb. 7, 1985
Donald P. Hodel—Feb. 7, 1985-

Secretary of Agriculture

John R. Block—Jan. 23, 1981-

Secretary of Commerce

Malcolm Baldrige—Jan. 23, 1981-

Secretary of Labor

Raymond J. Donovan—Feb. 4, 1981-March 15, 1985
William E. Brock III—April 29, 1985-

Secretary of Health and Human Services

Richard S. Schweiker—Jan. 22, 1981-Feb. 3, 1983
Margaret M. Heckler—March 9, 1983-

Secretary of Education

T. H. Bell—Jan. 23, 1981-Dec. 31, 1984
William J. Bennett—Feb. 6, 1985-

Secretary of Housing and Urban Development

Samuel R. Pierce Jr.—Jan. 23, 1981-

Secretary of Transportation

Drew Lewis—Jan. 22, 1981-Feb. 1, 1983
Elizabeth Hanford Dole—Feb. 7, 1983-

Secretary of Energy

James B. Edwards—Jan. 23, 1981-Nov. 5, 1982
Donald P. Hodel—Nov. 5, 1982-Feb. 7, 1985
John S. Herrington—Feb. 7, 1985-

---

fellow educator with long experience, detailed knowledge of education programs and a reputation as a competent administrator. Some lobbyists saw the choice as an indication that Reagan would abandon, or at least scale back, his campaign promise to abolish the Education Department.

Bell supported creation of the department, which was carved out of the old Department of Health, Education and Welfare (HEW). During his confirmation hearings before the Senate Labor and Human Resources Committee, Bell said he did not want to see a return to the days when education was a low-status part of the massive HEW.

Energy

The Senate confirmed **James B. Edwards** as energy secretary Jan. 22, 1981, on a 93-3 vote. Never intending to serve a full four-year term, Edwards resigned Nov. 5, 1982, to become president of the Medical University of South Carolina.

Shortly before being named energy secretary, Edwards said, "I'd like to go to Washington and close the Energy Department and work myself out of a job." Abolishing the department was an early Reagan campaign pledge.

Edwards was a fervent supporter of nuclear energy. He backed renewed commercial reprocessing of nuclear fuel, which had been banned by Presidents Ford and Carter. Reprocessing involved turning burned nuclear reactor fuel into fresh fuel, plutonium and highly radioactive liquid waste.

Environmental groups opposed Edwards because of his pro-nuclear position. During his confirmation hearings, Edwards maintained his support for reprocessing burned nuclear fuel, construction of breeder reactors and storage of nuclear waste in monitored vaults near the earth's surface. He also rejected the idea of giving states veto power over the location of nuclear waste dumps.

Edwards received a B.S. from the College of Charleston in 1950 and a D.M.D. from the University of Louisville School of Dentistry in 1955. He joined the U.S Maritime Service during World War II and served as a Navy dentist

Reagan's Judicial Appointments Begin ...

Through careful use of his power to appoint federal judges, President Reagan in his first term began an ideological transformation of the federal judiciary.

By the end of his second term it was anticipated that he would have selected a majority of the judges sitting on the federal district and appeals courts throughout the United States, completing a shift from a predominantly Democratic bench to a conservative Republican judiciary.

The Reagan administration, noted University of Massachusetts political science professor Sheldon Goldman, "has taken full advantage of the prerogatives of the presidency. They put on the bench ... people who are compatible with their ideology and political commitment.

"That was true of the Carter administration as well."

Administration officials were candid about their objectives in selecting new federal judges. Jonathan C. Rose, head of the Office of Legal Policy in the Justice Department, acknowledged that "philosophy certainly has been a factor with regard to our appointments."

"By and large, Carter tended to appoint people who have a very activist role in mind for the judiciary, who believe that judicial intervention can solve all manner of problems that might better be left to political intervention," Rose continued.

"The number of [Carter] appointments was so massive that we would have been derelict in our responsibility if we did not pay some attention to our obligation to try to produce some semblance of balance," he added.

The Reagan Record

In his first four years, Reagan named 167 federal judges, including Sandra Day O'Connor, whom he chose as the first woman member of the U.S. Supreme Court. *(O'Connor appointment, p. 712)*

Reagan named 130 federal district judges, men and women who handled civil and criminal cases every working day, cases that affect the everyday lives of citizens far more directly than do the cases before the Supreme Court.

Reagan placed 31 judges on the 12 regional appeals courts, the courts that review the rulings of the federal district judges. The majority of the decisions of these appeals courts are final; only a fraction are reviewed by the Supreme Court.

In addition, Reagan named two members of the new U.S. Court of Appeals for the Federal Circuit, which primarily hears patent and trademark cases, and three members of the U.S. Court of International Trade.

Conservative Choices

Although Reagan by the end of his first term had appointed one of every four sitting federal judges, he did not challenge the record set by his predecessor, President Jimmy Carter, who appointed more judges than any previous chief executive.

Carter, aided by 1978 legislation (PL 95-486) creating 152 new judicial posts, appointed 262 federal judges during his term. He did not appoint anyone to the Supreme Court, becoming the first full-term president in history to leave the White House with-

from 1955 to 1957. He remained in the Naval Reserve until 1967.

Associates credited Edwards with building his local Republican organization almost from the ground up. He was chairman of the Charleston County Republican Party from 1964 to 1969 and was the 1970 Republican chairman for the South Carolina's 1st Congressional District.

In 1971 Edwards ran for Congress and lost. In 1972 he was elected to the State Senate, and in 1974 became the South Carolina's first Republican governor since Reconstruction. In 1978, prohibited by law from seeking a second term, Edwards returned to his dental practice in Charleston.

Edwards strongly supported Reagan's 1976 bid for the Republican presidential nomination against President Gerald R. Ford. In the 1980 campaign, however, he initially backed John B. Connally. When Connally quit the race after losing the South Carolina primary, Edwards helped Reagan carry the state in the general election.

Donald P. Hodel succeeded Edwards as energy secretary Nov. 5, 1982. Hodel initially served on a recess appointment made while Congress was not in session; the Senate confirmed Hodel on Dec. 2, 1982, by an 86-8 vote.

After two years in the energy post, Hodel was confirmed on Feb. 6, 1985, as secretary of the interior by a 93-1 Senate vote. Hodel replaced William P. Clark, who had taken over as head of the department after Watt resigned under fire in October 1983. Hodel was replaced at Energy by John S. Herrington, White House personnel director. *(Details, p. 337)*

Hodel attended Harvard University and, after graduating from the University of Oregon law school in 1960, practiced law in Portland. From 1969 to 1977 he served as deputy administrator, and then administrator, of the Bonneville Power Administration.

In 1978 Hodel and his wife formed an energy consulting firm, Hodel and Associates Inc. He also was president of the National Electric Reliability Council, a national

... Ideological Shift in Federal Judiciary

out having that opportunity.

Most of Reagan's judicial appointees were wealthy, conservative, white Republican men. Only 17, including O'Connor, were women; only two were black, and eight were Hispanic. This was in sharp contrast to Carter's record, which included the appointment of 40 women judges, 38 blacks and 16 Hispanics, more than any other president.

However, despite the contrast, Reagan had still appointed more women and more Hispanic judges than any other president except Carter.

Reagan looked first of all for conservative nominees who endorsed a belief in judicial restraint, a view of the powers and the role of the federal courts as limited. Such ideological concerns were quite secondary for Carter, whose primary commitment was to enlarge the number of women and minority group members serving as judges.

A study of Reagan's first-term judicial appointments by Goldman pointed out that 98 percent of Reagan's nominees were white, 98 percent were Republican, and 92 per cent were male. In addition, Goldman reported, an unusually high percentage, 25 percent, were millionaires. By comparison, only 5 percent of Carter's appointees in his last two years were millionaires.

The Selection Process

Without fanfare, President Reagan early in his term abolished the nominating commissions President Carter had established to screen appeals court nominees. Reagan returned to the more traditional methods of selecting these candidates through con-

sultation with Republican members of Congress, party officials, interest groups and sitting federal judges.

Rose explained: "We looked at how the Carter Commissions operated and we were not happy with the results they produced," Rose said. "Carter was prepared to sacrifice quality and merit just to get a particular percentage of people on the bench."

Merit Ratings

The American Bar Association (ABA) has for more than three decades reviewed the qualifications of nominees for federal judgeships.

The ABA ratings provide the only constant in attempting to assess the quality of judicial nominations from administration to administration. Because of changes in the personnel of the ABA committee handing out these ratings — as well as changes in standards and philosophy over time — even use of these ratings is subject to criticism.

Of all Reagan's first-term nominees, 9.6 percent were found "exceptionally well qualified," while only 6.1 percent of Carter's nominees won this highest accolade. That difference evens out, however, when the 40.7 percent of Reagan nominees found "well qualified" are compared with the 49.6 percent of the Carter nominees given that rating.

Almost half of Reagan's nominees, 49.7 percent, won the minimal ABA rating of "qualified," which was given to 43.1 percent of Carter's choices. None of Reagan's selections were found unqualified, although 1.1 percent of Carter's received such an unfavorable rating.

---

organization of public and private electric systems dedicated to increasing the reliability and adequacy of power supplies. He had served on the Oregon Alternate Energy Development Commission.

Hodel served as under secretary of interior in 1981-82. As the No. 2 man at the department, he was responsible for carrying out the details of many of Secretary James G. Watt's programs.

Health and Human Services

The Senate confirmed **Richard S. Schweiker** as secretary of health and human services (HHS) on Jan. 21, 1981, by a 99-0 vote. After serving for two years in the post, Schweiker announced on Jan. 12, 1983, that he was resigning to become president of the American Council of Life Insurance, a trade and lobbying organization for life insurance companies.

Schweiker had served in the House representing Penn-

sylvania's 13th District from 1961 to 1969. He was elected in 1968 to the Senate and re-elected in 1974. As ranking Republican on the Senate Labor and Human Resources Committee and its Health Subcommittee, he had written and refined major health bills. He also was ranking member of the subcommittee on HHS appropriations.

Schweiker had been considered one of the most liberal Republicans in the Senate — a favorite of labor, a maverick in his party. He underwent an abrupt political conversion in 1976, however, following a losing campaign for vice president as Ronald Reagan's running mate.

For the most part, he no longer supported liberal causes or labor-backed issues. Schweiker made his conservative mark felt largely in the field of health policy. He fought effectively for less regulation and more private competition in the health care industry.

In December 1978 Schweiker announced plans to retire from the Senate at the end of the 96th Congress for personal reasons. Although some observers believed that

his alienation from organized labor had damaged him politically, others said his conservative shift would have helped rather than hurt him had he run for office again. In spite of the change in his voting pattern, he was still considered a moderate by most who knew him.

Before entering public life, Schweiker had served in the Navy, earned a degree from Pennsylvania State University, and worked for the family business, American Olean Tile Co.

Margaret M. Heckler was named Jan. 12, 1983, to succeed Schweiker as secretary of health and human services. Schweiker resigned to become president of the American Council of Life Insurance.

Former Rep. Heckler (1967-83), a moderate Republican who lost to liberal Barney Frank, D-Mass., in the November 1982 election, became the second woman in the Reagan administration to head a Cabinet department. The Senate on March 3 voted 82-3 to confirm the nomination. Elizabeth Hanford Dole had been confirmed as transportation secretary in February 1983.

In her first race for Congress in 1966, Heckler attracted national attention when she defeated Joseph W. Martin Jr., House Republican leader for two decades and the party's national chairman, in the GOP primary.

In Congress she pushed consumers', women's and Vietnam veterans' issues. When Reagan proposed eliminating veterans' storefront counseling centers, Heckler was one of his loudest critics. She energetically backed passage of the Equal Rights Amendment (ERA), later pushed extension of the deadline for ratification by the states, and fought unsuccessfully against dropping ERA from the Republican platform in 1980.

Like Schweiker, she opposed federal funding for abortion, a position that swung support of women's groups to Frank in the 1982 election.

Unlike Schweiker, she brought to office no notable expertise in the programs she would administer. During her eight terms in the House, Heckler served on the Agriculture, Banking, Government Operations, Science and Veterans' Affairs committees. She did not serve on panels with legislative responsibility for HHS programs. Her penchant for changing committee assignments kept her low on seniority lists except on Veterans' Affairs, where she was the second-ranking Republican.

In 1982 Heckler lost her congressional race in a newly drawn district that included about 70 percent of her old constituency.

Born Margaret Mary O'Shaughnessy in Flushing, N.Y., Heckler was the only child of Irish-Catholic immigrants. She graduated from Albertus Magnus College in 1953. After receiving a law degree from Boston College in 1956, she practiced law in Boston. Heckler was a Wellesley Town Meeting member from 1958 to 1966. She served on the Massachusetts Governor's Council from 1962 to 1966; she was the first woman elected to the council.

Housing and Urban Development

Samuel R. Pierce Jr., secretary of housing and urban development (HUD), made a habit of being "the first." Before he became Reagan's first and only black Cabinet member, Pierce broke barriers to become the first black named to a sub-Cabinet-level position in the Treasury Department, the first black to become a partner in a major New York law firm and the first black named to the board of directors of two major U.S. corporations.

A native New Yorker and lifelong Republican, Pierce never had any direct involvement in housing issues before being named HUD secretary. Supporters said his academic background, government experience and administrative abilities would serve him well in managing one of the largest federal agencies.

Pierce was not opposed by anyone on the Senate Banking Committee, which considered his nomination, or in the full Senate, which confirmed Pierce by a 98-0 vote on Jan. 22, 1981.

During his undergraduate days at Cornell University, Pierce was a star halfback on the football team and was elected to Phi Beta Kappa in his junior year. After time out for service in the Army during World War II, he received an A.B. from Cornell in 1947 and a J.D. from Cornell's law school in 1949. In 1952 he received a master's degree in tax law from New York University School of Law. He also did postgraduate study as a Ford Foundation Fellow at Yale Law School.

After finishing his education, Pierce served as assistant district attorney for New York County and later as assistant U.S. attorney for the Southern District of New York.

In 1955 he was named assistant under secretary of labor in the Eisenhower administration. He later became associate counsel and then counsel of the House Judiciary Antitrust Subcommittee.

Pierce returned to New York in 1957. Gov. Nelson A. Rockefeller named him to the Court of General Sessions, which later became part of the New York Supreme Court. When the post became elective, Pierce ran but was defeated by a Democrat.

In 1961 he joined the New York City labor law firm of Battle, Fowler, Stokes and Kheel. From 1970 to 1973 he served as general counsel of the Treasury Department in the Nixon administration.

Interior

Although his appointment was controversial, **James G. Watt** was confirmed as interior secretary 83-12 by the Senate on Jan. 22, 1981.

Watt resigned under congressional fire Oct. 9, 1983. He was succeeded by William P. Clark, longtime Reagan confidant and national security adviser. *(Details of Watt, Clark tenure, pp. 406, 474)*

Watt became interior secretary after a lifelong involvement with Western issues of land and water rights and came to Washington not as a stranger.

After finishing law school in 1962 at the University of Wyoming, Watt became legislative assistant and counsel to Sen. Milward L. Simpson, R-Wyo. (1962-67). In 1966 he joined the U.S. Chamber of Commerce, where he directed the natural resources section. From 1969 to 1972 he served in the Interior Department as deputy assistant secretary for water and power resources. He then served for three years as director of the Bureau of Outdoor Recreation, where he oversaw administration of the Land and Water Conservation Fund. He was vice chairman of the Federal Power Commission from 1975 to 1977, when he resigned to become president and chief legal officer of the Mountain States Legal Foundation.

Watt's nomination stirred up much controversy, primarily because of his work with the conservative law foundation. According to its literature, the Denver-based group

was a non-profit, tax-exempt organization dedicated to helping combat "excessive bureaucratic regulation and the stifling economic effects resulting from the actions of extreme environmentalist groups and no-growth advocates." Watt spent three years with the foundation and much of that time was used to challenge the Interior Department's methods of administering public lands.

William P. Clark was confirmed 71-18 by the Senate Nov. 18, 1983, to succeed Watt as secretary of the interior. On Jan. 1, 1985, Clark announced that he wanted to return to his California ranch after 18 years working in state and federal government at Reagan's behest.

Reagan's selection of Clark as interior secretary stunned most of official Washington. For the third time in his presidency, Reagan turned to the California attorney to fill a politically sensitive position. Reagan said he had "decided once again to turn to someone who has been a trouble-shooter and a result-oriented professional." He called Clark a "God-fearing Westerner, a fourth-generation rancher, a person I trust."

As with Clark's previous appointments as deputy secretary of state in 1981 and White House national security adviser in 1982, he lacked compelling credentials for the Interior slot, save two: He seemed to share Reagan's attitudes toward national policy and he enjoyed the president's full confidence.

Clark had been chief of staff during Reagan's first term as governor of California, by most accounts bringing managerial order to the administration. In 1969 Reagan appointed Clark to the first of several state judicial posts, culminating in a 1973 appointment to the state Supreme Court. Opponents of each judicial nomination often cited Clark's undistinguished academic career; he had no undergraduate degree and passed the state bar examination on his second try.

Clark's preference for the courtesy title "Judge" reflected not only his service on the California bench, but his avowed approach to formulating foreign policy. He had described that process using courtroom analogies — hearing out the experts and rendering a judgment.

While five environmental groups opposed Clark's nomination, two of the largest — the National Wildlife Federation and the National Audubon Society — withheld judgment. They said Clark had taken no positions on which they could base an assessment.

When Clark left the Interior Department, he was succeeded as secretary by Donald P. Hodel, who had served as secretary of energy since November 1982 and as under secretary of the interior under Watt in 1981-82.

Labor

Raymond J. Donovan resigned as secretary of labor March 15, 1985; he had been on leave without pay since October 1984. U.S. Trade Representative William E. Brock III was selected to replace Donovan.

The last member of Reagan's original Cabinet to win Senate approval, Donovan's confirmation was held up by Senate Labor and Human Resources Committee investigations into charges, made by an FBI informer, that Donovan and Schiavone Construction Co., a New Jersey firm Donovan had worked for since 1958, had provided illegal payoffs to corrupt union officials to maintain "labor peace." Other informants said the company had close ties with organized crime.

The Senate confirmed Donovan as labor secretary 80-17 on Feb. 3, 1981. Only Democrats voted against confirmation. It subsequently was disclosed that the FBI had damaging information that was provided to the White House but withheld from the Senate Labor Committee.

A three-judge federal court panel in Washington, D.C., on Dec. 29, 1981, appointed Leon Silverman as federal special prosecutor to investigate allegations of corruption against Donovan. The appointment of a special prosecutor had been requested by the labor secretary. Silverman announced Sept. 13, 1982, that his nine-month investigation had uncovered no evidence to warrant bringing charges against Donovan. *(Details, p. 656)*

In court documents made public Oct. 2, 1984, a Bronx County, N.Y., grand jury named Donovan in a 137-count indictment concerning financial dealings of the Schiavone Construction Co. while Donovan was the firm's executive vice president. The indictment accused Donovan and nine others of one count of grand larceny, 125 counts of falsifying business records and 11 counts of filing false documents in connection with a $186 million New York City subway-tunnel construction project for which Schiavone received a contract in 1978.

Donovan pleaded not guilty to the charges. Immediately after learning he had been named in the indictment, Donovan asked the president for a leave of absence without pay. Labor Under Secretary Ford B. Ford took over for him.

Donovan resigned as labor secretary after a New York Supreme Court judge refused to dismiss larceny and fraud charges against him.

Donovan received a B.A. from Notre Dame Seminary in New Orleans, La., in 1952. From 1953 to 1958 he worked for the American Insurance Co. in New Jersey. He left to join Schiavone as a shareholder and vice president. He became executive vice president in 1971.

He served as chairman of the 1980 Reagan-Bush campaign in New Jersey and was credited with rounding up blue-collar support that helped ensure Reagan's election victory in the state.

State

One of the most controversial members of President Reagan's original Cabinet was **Alexander M. Haig Jr.**, who served as secretary of state for the first 17 months of the Reagan administration. Haig resigned in a policy dispute on June 25, 1982. Reagan nominated George P. Shultz to succeed him. *(Details, p. 127)*

The Senate on Jan. 21, 1981, voted 93-6 to confirm Haig as secretary of state. The Senate Foreign Relations Committee had approved the nomination after five days of hearings in which the panel closely probed Haig's foreign policy views and expertise, questioned his morality and judgment, and tested the limits of his composure to a degree rare in Senate confirmation hearings.

Controversy centered on his actions as a White House aide in the Nixon administration. Haig was questioned about his role in requesting wiretaps on reporters and government officials in 1969-71; helping to devise President Nixon's Vietnam War policies; his activities during the final days of the Watergate scandal; and allegations that he had suggested to President Gerald R. Ford that he pardon Nixon.

A 1947 graduate of West Point, Haig served as an administrative assistant to Gen. Douglas MacArthur's dep-

uty chief of staff in occupied Japan in 1949. In 1951 he saw combat in several Korean War actions.

After various military assignments, Haig studied international relations at Georgetown University, earning an M.A. in 1961. He then worked in the Pentagon on European and Middle Eastern affairs and later became military assistant to Secretary of the Army — subsequently Deputy Secretary of Defense — Cyrus R. Vance.

Haig joined Henry A. Kissinger's National Security Council staff in 1969. As Kissinger's military adviser, Haig acted as liaison between the Pentagon and the State Department and screened all intelligence reports before they went to the president.

When Nixon aides H. R. Haldeman and John Erhlichman resigned from the White House in May 1973, Nixon selected Haig as his new chief of staff. Haig left the White House in 1974 when Ford appointed him commander of NATO. He retired from the Army in June 1979. He spent six months testing his chances for the 1980 Republican presidential nomination, but gave it up saying, "it would not be constructive for me to seek political office in 1980."

In December 1979 Haig was named president and chief operating officer of United Technologies Corp., a multinational aircraft manufacturer that was the third largest U.S. defense contractor in fiscal 1979.

George P. Shultz was serving as president of Bechtel Group Inc., a worldwide construction and engineering firm based in San Francisco, when President Reagan nominated him to succeed Haig as secretary of state. Shultz never received formal training in the diplomatic arts but had wide experience in foreign affairs.

The Senate confirmed Shultz as secretary of state 97-0 on July 15, 1982.

Shultz was an original member of President Nixon's Cabinet, serving as secretary of labor from January 1969 to June 1970, director of the Office of Management and Budget from June 1970 to May 1972, and secretary of the Treasury from May 1972 to April 1974.

At Treasury Shultz was the top U.S. official in trade matters. He represented the United States at meetings in Paris in March 1973 during an international monetary crisis. He was the chairman of Nixon's Council on Economic Policy, coordinating international economic policy.

As head of a U.S. East-West Trade Policy Committee, Shultz conducted the concluding stages of negotiations with the Soviet Union for a landmark trade agreement. In 1974 Shultz was a major opponent of the so-called Jackson-Vanik amendment to the 1974 Trade Act. The amendment prevented the granting of U.S. "most favored nation" trade status to the Soviet Union unless it allowed increased emigration of Jews.

Shultz had joined Bechtel in 1974. One of the firm's major clients was Saudi Arabia, and Shultz had developed a reputation for his expertise in Middle East affairs.

Shultz had served as an informal foreign policy adviser to Reagan and was mentioned prominently as a possible secretary of state when Reagan was making up his Cabinet after the 1980 election. He served as a campaign adviser on economics and was a member of the economic policy team during the transition period.

Transportation

President Reagan's first transportation secretary, **Drew Lewis**, was confirmed on a 98-0 vote by the Senate Jan. 22, 1981. Lewis resigned Feb. 1, 1983, to become chairman and chief executive officer of Warner Amex Cable Communications Inc., one of the nation's largest cable television companies. He was succeeded by Elizabeth Hanford Dole, assistant to President Reagan for public liaison.

Before entering the Cabinet, Lewis headed Lewis & Associates, a financial and management consulting firm in Plymouth Meeting, Pa. He served for 10 years as a trustee of the Reading Co., the holding company that operated the Reading Railroad, whose rail assets were folded into Conrail.

Lewis received a masters degree from Harvard Business School and did postgraduate work at the Massachusetts Institute of Technology.

In 1955 he went to work for a Philadelphia general contracting firm and held various positions responsible for construction supervision, cost control and other matters. He ended up as a member of the board of directors in 1960.

Lewis was a corporate vice president and assistant to the chairman of the National Gypsum Co., aiding in corporate development and acquisitions.

In 1969 he joined Simplex Wire and Cable Co. in Boston as president and chief executive officer, later assumed chairmanship of the board, and reorganized the company. And in 1970 Lewis became president and chief executive officer of Snelling and Snelling, a personnel agency.

Lewis was chairman of Richard S. Schweiker's successful congressional campaign in 1960 and chairman of his successful Senate campaign in 1968. Lewis was a local Republican leader as well as chairman of the state Republican Financial Committee from 1971 to 1973. He also had been a Republican National Committeeman from Pennsylvania.

Although he was successful in working for the candidacies of others, Lewis lost his only personal bid for public office in 1974 when he ran for governor of Pennsylvania.

As head of the Pennsylvania delegation at the 1976 GOP convention, Lewis supported Gerald R. Ford for president.

But he was one of the first establishment Republican leaders to back Reagan for the 1980 battle and became a trusted aide. Lewis managed Reagan's primary campaign in Pennsylvania and won him a majority of delegates even though Reagan lost the popular vote.

Lewis became an influential member of the Reagan transition team. He was a member of both the transition's executive advisory committee and the transition's transportation task force.

Elizabeth Hanford Dole, who succeeded Lewis, was confirmed 97-0 by the Senate Feb. 1, 1983, as secretary of transportation. Dole, married to Sen. Robert Dole, R-Kan., became the first woman in the Reagan administration to head a Cabinet department.

When Reagan announced Jan. 5 that he would nominate Dole, she was serving as his assistant for public liaison. She was reponsible for meeting with special interest groups, defusing criticism and building coalitions for administration concerns.

Members of Congress, congressional aides and lobbyists gave Dole high marks, describing her as extremely capable, hard-working, charming and a good politician. Although she did not have a background in transportation, they noted that Lewis, regarded as one of Reagan's most able Cabinet secretaries, also did not have much transpor-

tation experience.

As a member of the Federal Trade Commission from 1973 to 1979, Dole was known for her consumer orientation and a skepticism about the limits of government regulation. She resigned to work in her husband's unsuccessful presidential campaign. She later campaigned for Reagan and served as chairman of a task force on human services. Dole was deputy director of the White House Office of Consumer Affairs from 1971 to 1973 and executive director of a presidential consumer affairs commission from 1968 to 1971.

Dole received a B.A. in political science from Duke University in 1958. She went to Oxford University for postgraduate study and in 1960 completed work on an M.A. in education at Harvard University. In 1965 Dole graduated from Harvard Law School.

Treasury

President Reagan's first-term Treasury secretary, **Donald T. Regan**, was confirmed by the Senate on Jan. 21, 1981, by a 98-0 vote. The president announced on Jan. 8, 1985, that Regan and White House Chief of Staff James A. Baker III would trade jobs.

Regan had spent his entire career on Wall Street before joining the administration. He went to work for Merrill Lynch, Pierce, Fenner & Smith Inc. in 1946, after receiving his undergraduate degree from Harvard University and his law degree from the University of Pennsylvania and serving as a Marine in World War II.

At Merrill Lynch he worked his way up the corporate ladder, becoming president in 1968 and chairman in 1971 through what had been described as a combination of hard work, shrewdness and a tough disposition, which he attributed to his Marine training. As head of the investment firm, Regan became known as a maverick, developing Merrill Lynch into one of the largest and most innovative companies on Wall Street.

Although Regan was a member of such influential organizations as the Business Roundtable, the Committee for Economic Development and the Council on Foreign Relations, he had not been active in politics.

Other Key Positions

Central Intelligence Agency

After serving a brief stint as Reagan's 1980 campaign director, **William J. Casey** was named director of central intelligence. The nomination was confirmed by the Senate Jan. 27, 1981, by a 95-0 vote. *(Story, p. 141)*

Casey earned a B.A. degree from Fordham University in 1934 and a law degree for St. John's University Law School in 1937. He began practicing law the following year when he was admitted to the New York State Bar.

He was commissioned a lieutenant in the U.S. Navy when the war began in 1941 but poor eyesight confined him to a desk job in Washington. Through friends in legal circles, Casey connected with Maj. Gen. William J. "Wild Bill" Donovan, the Wall Street lawyer President Franklin D. Roosevelt tapped to form and run the Office of Strategic Services (OSS), the CIA's wartime predecessor. This led Casey into service in the OSS, working to infiltrate U.S. agents into Europe.

Casey left the OSS with a reputation as a forceful manager who could make tough decisions with speed and see that they were carried out.

He has been in and out of government service since World War II. In 1947-48 he was special counsel to the Senate Small Business Committee and later associate general counsel for the Marshall Plan.

He taught tax law at New York University between 1948 and 1962. In this period he wrote and published some 30 manuals for lawyers and executives.

Casey practiced law throughout his career, and among his partners was Leonard W. Hall, a legend in GOP circles in New York. Casey also was active in GOP politics. He worked for Thomas E. Dewey's 1940 and 1948 presidential bids. He ran a foreign policy group in Vice President Richard M. Nixon's 1960 presidential campaign.

In 1966 Casey ran unsuccessfully for the U.S. House. He worked again in 1968 for Nixon, who put him on the Advisory Committee on Arms Control and Disarmament in 1969.

President Nixon appointed Casey in 1971 to head the Securities and Exchange Commission (SEC), where he had a brush with scandal. It was disclosed that Robert Vesco had given the Nixon campaign a secret, $200,000 cash gift while under SEC investigation; Casey admitted meeting Vesco's lawyer the day the donation was made, but said he did not learn about the money until later.

He was named under secretary of state for economic affairs in 1973. In 1974-76 he served as president of the Export-Import Bank.

Office of Management and Budget

The Senate, by a vote of 93-0, confirmed **David A. Stockman** as director of the Office of Management and Budget (OMB) on Jan. 27, 1981. *(Box, p. 35)*

Born in Camp Hood, Texas, Stockman grew up in St. Joseph, Mich., where his father ran a fruit farm. He graduated from Michigan State University with a degree in American history and then enrolled in Harvard University's divinity school.

It was there that he came to the attention of Rep. John B. Anderson, R-Ill. (1961-81), who brought him to Washington in 1970 as his special assistant and two years later named him director of the Republican Conference, the policy-making committee of all House Republicans. During his tenure under Anderson, Stockman was known as a liberal party member.

In 1975 Stockman returned to Boston to study at Harvard's John F. Kennedy Institute of Politics. He left academia to run for Congress and won a seat representing the 4th District of Michigan with 61 percent of the vote. He was re-elected in 1978.

Despite his short tenure in the House, Stockman played a major role in the development of several pieces of key legislation: hospital cost containment, child health care, synthetic fuels and the Energy Mobilization Board.

Office of the U.S. Trade Representative

During Reagan's first term, **William E. Brock III** served as U.S. trade representative. His nomination was confirmed 99-0 by the Senate Jan. 21, 1981. Brock was confirmed as labor secretary April 26, 1985, succeeding Raymond J. Donovan who had resigned to stand trial on charges of larceny and fraud in New York. *(Donovan pro-*

file, p. 1023)

Brock graduated from Washington and Lee University in 1953. After a three-year stint in the Navy, he returned to work in his family's candy manufacturing business. He served in Congress as a representative from Tennessee in 1963-71. He was elected to the Senate in 1971, defeating Democratic incumbent Albert Gore. Brock lost his Senate seat in 1976 to Democrat Jim Sasser.

As chairman of the Republican National Committee from 1977 to 1981, Brock was praised for his organizing skills and for his efforts to broaden the party's base.

United Nations

In choosing **Jeane J. Kirkpatrick** as United Nations ambassador, Reagan delivered on promises to put at least one woman and one Democrat in his Cabinet. The appointment also reflected Reagan's vow to abandon Carter's policy of judging authoritarian U.S. allies on their human rights records rather than their anti-communism.

Kirkpatrick received undergraduate degrees from Stephens College in 1946 and Barnard College in 1948, then earned a master's degree in political science at Columbia University in 1950. She worked briefly as a research analyst at the State Department in the early 1950s and was a French government fellow at the Institut de Science Politique in Paris.

In 1955 she married and interrupted her career to raise three sons. In 1962 she began teaching part-time at Trinity College in Washington, D.C., and eventually completed her doctorate at Columbia in 1968, writing her dissertation on the Peronist movement in Argentina. She spoke French and Spanish and had given speeches overseas for the U.S. International Communication Agency.

Kirkpatrick joined the Georgetown University faculty in 1967 and became a resident scholar at the American Enterprise Institute, a Washington think tank, in 1977.

She also had been highly active in the Democratic Party, serving on various national party commissions. But her disillusionments with "McGovernism" in the 1970s led her to help found the Coalition for a Democratic Majority — a coalition of organized labor and "traditional liberals" such as Sen. Henry M. Jackson, D-Wash., who stressed American strength in foreign and defense policy as well as social welfare programs.

Kirkpatrick came to Reagan's attention in 1979 through an article she wrote for *Commentary* magazine called "Dictatorships and Double Standards." Soon after meeting Reagan, Kirkpatrick became a member of his foreign policy task force for the 1980 presidential campaign. She was unanimously confirmed by the Senate as U.N. ambassador Jan. 29, 1981.

In January 1985 Kirkpatrick announced her intention to resign the U.N. post. Although she had sought a high-level foreign policy job in the second Reagan administration, she apparently had not been offered the post she wanted. Kirkpatrick said she would return to her teaching post at Georgetown, where she would be free to "speak out clearly" on foreign policy matters. Saying she was "tired of swimming against the current of her own party," Kirkpatrick switched her party designation from Democrat to Republican in April 1985.

Kirkpatrick was succeeded at the U.N. by Vernon A. Walters, a retired Army lieutenant general who was a former deputy director of the CIA.

Council of Economic Advisers

Murray Weidenbaum was confirmed as chairman of the Council of Economic Advisers (CEA) on Feb. 24, 1981, by a 95-0 Senate vote. Weidenbaum resigned July 22, 1982, to return to his teaching post at Washington University in St. Louis, Mo.

At the time of his appointment to the CEA post, Weidenbaum was serving as director of the Center for the Study of American Business at Washington University. He had been a member of the faculty since 1964 and was chairman of the Department of Economics in 1966-69.

Weidenbaum served as assistant secretary of the Treasury for economic policy in 1969-71. In that post he became the first official to publicly recommend adoption of wage-price controls and was the administration's chief advocate for the general revenue sharing program.

From 1963 to 1964 Weidenbaum served as senior economist at the Stanford Research Institute; from 1958 to 1963 as corporate economist with the Boeing Co.; and from 1949 to 1957 as economist with the U.S Bureau of the Budget.

Weidenbaum received a B.A. from City College of New York, an M.A. from Columbia University and a Ph.D. from Princeton University.

He had served as an adjunct scholar for the American Enterprise Institute for Public Policy Research; member of the board of directors of the American Council for Capital Formation; and member of the Council on Foreign Relations. During the Reagan transition, Weidenbaum was chairman of the regulatory task force.

President Reagan chose **Martin S. Feldstein** to succeed Weidenbaum as chairman of the Council of Economic Advisers. Feldstein was confirmed Dec. 8 by a 77-18 vote, although he had been serving in the post since Sept. 8 on a recess appointment.

In order to assume the CEA post, Feldstein took a leave of absence from Harvard University, where he had been an economics professor since 1967. He also was serving as president of the National Bureau of Economic Research, which does independent economic research.

Feldstein received a B.A. from Harvard University and an M.A. and Ph.D. from Oxford University. He was a research fellow and lecturer at Nuffield College, Oxford University, from 1964 to 1967.

Feldstein resigned from the CEA effective July 10, 1984, to prepare for his return to Harvard University, which imposed a two-year limit on faculty members' leaves of absence. He also resumed the presidency of the National Bureau of Economic Research.

Treasury Under Secretary Beryl W. Sprinkel was confirmed April 17, 1985, to succeed Feldstein.

Federal Reserve Board

The Senate July 27, 1983, confirmed the nomination of **Paul A. Volcker** to a second four-year term as chairman of the Federal Reserve Board. Eight Republicans and eight Democrats opposed the nomination on the 84-16 vote.

Volcker began his second term Aug. 6. As chairman of the autonomous Federal Reserve, he had primary responsibility for guiding the nation's monetary policy. *(Details, p. 28)*

Volcker was originally appointed by Democratic President Carter in 1979. *(Congress and the Nation Vol. V, p. 961)*

Controversial Nominations

1981

F. Keith Adkinson. The Senate Commerce Committee Dec. 15 halted action on the nomination of Adkinson to the Federal Trade Commission after the ranking minority member, Sen. Howard W. Cannon, D-Nev., accused the nominee of lying about the details of his book and movie contract with a convicted felon who had provided testimony on organized crime to the panel.

Adkinson, a Washington lawyer, was national director of Democrats for Reagan-Bush during the 1980 campaign. Most of the controversy surrounding his nomination centered on allegations that he used his former position as a staff member of the Senate Permanent Subcommittee on Investigations to further his financial interests.

Cannon asked that the Commerce Committee meet in private to discuss confidential information. The committee rejected that request but then adjourned. Adkinson denied the allegation and charged Cannon with "gross abuse of his public office" for his accusations. On March 29, 1982, President Reagan withdrew the nomination upon Adkinson's request.

William M. Bell. Bell's nomination to head the Equal Employment Opportunity Commission led to the unusual situation of a black man being opposed by civil rights groups. Bell, a Detroit businessman, was an unsuccessful Republican candidate for the House in 1980.

Opposition to the nomination grew after an October hearing in which it was revealed that Bell had little experience in government, had never managed more than four employees and ran a job placement firm that had not found anyone a job in the preceding year.

When civil rights and women's groups announced their opposition to Bell, concern spread among Labor Committee members. Support was so weak that the administration asked the committee to postpone its vote on the nomination, which had been scheduled for Nov. 12. The nomination died at the end of the session.

Chester A. Crocker. Crocker's nomination to be assistant secretary of state for African affairs was opposed chiefly by Sen. Jesse Helms, R-N.C. Despite Helms' objections to Crocker's political and foreign policy views, the Foreign Relations Committee approved the nomination April 28. After the committee vote, Helms placed a "hold" on the nomination, delaying its passage onto the floor. After many behind-the-scenes negotiations, Helms agreed to drop his hold, and Crocker was confirmed by the full Senate 84-7 June 9.

John B. Crowell Jr. Crowell's nomination to be assistant secretary of agriculture for natural resources and environment sparked conflict-of-interest charges. Crowell was general counsel for the Louisiana-Pacific Corp., parent company of Ketchikan Pulp Co., an Alaskan subsidiary. On March 5, Ketchikan was found guilty of conspiring to fix prices and control the timber market in southeastern Alaska's Tongass National Forest.

Crowell denied any previous knowledge of the price-fixing and said he would not become involved in the department's handling of the Ketchikan case. The Senate Agriculture Committee approved Crowell's nomination April 1. But Democrats Edward M. Kennedy, Mass., and

Patrick J. Leahy, Vt., delayed floor action on the nomination, claiming that, despite his denials, they had new evidence that directly linked Crowell with the price-fixing activities. Kennedy and Leahy requested another hearing, but the Agriculture Committee refused. They then took their evidence to the full Senate. The nomination was confirmed 72-25 on May 20.

Anne M. Gorsuch (Burford). Gorsuch was confirmed May 5 as Environmental Protection Agency administrator by unanimous consent. Her nomination was widely opposed by environmental organizations, which charged that Gorsuch had neither an administrative background nor a history of concern for environmental protection.

Gorsuch, known as Anne M. Burford following her marriage, resigned under fire early in 1983. She was succeeded by William D. Ruckelshaus. *(Story, p. 454)*

Robert D. Hormats. Hormats' nomination to be assistant secretary of state for economic and business affairs was opposed by Sen. Jesse Helms, R-N.C., who felt that Hormats did not share Reagan's conservatism and would not carry out administration policies. Overriding Helms' objections, the Foreign Relations Committee voted April 28 to favorably report Hormats' nomination, which the full Senate subsequently confirmed.

C. Everett Koop. Several legal technicalities had to be cleared out of the way before the Senate could consider the nomination of Koop as surgeon general of the United States. Koop, a Philadelphia surgeon, was 64 years old and, under existing law, the surgeon general had to be under 64. The Senate added an amendment to a non-related House-passed bill eliminating the age requirement. The House eventually agreed to that rider, but House opponents of Koop then succeeded in adding language to other legislation requiring that the surgeon general have "specialized training or significant experience in public health programs," a qualification Koop's opponents said the surgeon could not meet. The Senate, however, confirmed Koop Nov. 16 by a 68-24 vote. *(Story, p. 531)*

Ernest W. Lefever. The Foreign Relations Committee June 5 rejected, 13-4, Lefever's nomination as assistant secretary of state for human rights. Lefever subsequently withdrew his name. It was the first time within memory that the committee had disapproved a presidential nominee.

Opponents questioned Lefever's commitment to human rights and its role in foreign policy. Lefever testified that he opposed cutting foreign aid assistance to nations whose governments violated human rights.

Lefever's credibility also was damaged by his testimony on the relationship between the Ethics and Public Policy Center, a non-profit think tank headed by Lefever, and the Nestlé Corp., a maker and exporter of infant formula. The foundation had received $25,000 from Nestlé and later reprinted and distributed an article favoring infant formula exports. Lefever denied any connection between the Nestlé donations and his foundation's position on the infant formula issue, but his disavowals were contradicted by a Nestlé official. Lefever's involvement in the issue was especially controversial because on May 21 the United States cast the lone dissenting vote against a World Health Organization code calling for a worldwide ban on advertising and promotion of baby formula because of its

Legal Services Corporation

Throughout his first term, President Reagan sought to abolish the Legal Services Corporation (LSC), which was established in 1974 to fund civil legal services for the poor. Congress consistently refused to go along, although it did reduce LSC funding and imposed new restrictions on the corporation's activities. *(Stories, pp. 677, 683, 695, 705)*

Reagan nominated to the board members he hoped would substantially restrict LSC operations. LSC lawyers, the agency's clients and its supporters in the legal community contended that by appointing members to the LSC governing board who were hostile to the corporation, Reagan tried to do by the backdoor what he could not accomplish through the front.

Not one board member nominated by Reagan between December 1981 and December 1984 was confirmed by the Senate, but those given recess appointments were able to sit until the end of the session of Congress following their appointments.

1981-82 Appointments. Reagan did not name anyone to the 11-member LSC board in the first 10 months of his administration. Then, in an effort to take control before the Carter administration's holdover board could approve the 1982 programs and grants, Reagan made seven recess appointments on Dec. 31, 1981. The new board members were William J. Olson, Howard H. Dana Jr., Marc Sandstrom, William F. Harvey, George E. Paras, Robert S. Stubbs II and David Satterfield.

While Congress was away for its 1982 election recess, Reagan Oct. 23 made two appointments to the board: Dan Rathbun and Frank Donatelli. The appointments gave acting Chairman William Harvey the full complement of 11 members prior to an Oct. 29 board meeting to select a new president of the corporation.

LSC President. A bipartisan group of 32 senators sent Reagan a letter Oct. 28 objecting to his making the recess appointments so close to the board meeting and in a manner that precluded Senate consideration of those appointments. The Senate could confirm or reject LSC nominees, but it had no power over the choice of a president, who actually ran the corporation.

The LSC voted to offer the presidency to Donald P. Bogard, an Indiana lawyer who had no poverty law experience and was director of litigation for Stokely Van Vamp Inc., a large food processing company in Indiana. He took over as LSC president Dec. 13, 1982, and eventually resigned the post effective Jan. 31, 1985.

Nominations Withdrawn. On Dec. 8, 1982, Reagan withdrew nine nominations to the board he had made earlier in the year: Olson, Dana, Harvey, Paras, Stubbs, Harold R. DeMoss Jr., Clarence V. McKee, Annie Laurie Slaughter and William L. Earl. The action came after 52 senators signed a letter saying they would not support three of Reagan's most conservative nominees — Olson, Harvey and Paras. The White House said some of the other six nominees were not "philosophically in tune" with administration policies. Eight of the nine nominations were before the Senate; the ninth, of Papas, had been held up in the Senate Labor and Human Resources Committee.

1983-84 Appointments. Four recess appointments were made by Reagan on Jan. 21, 1983: Milton M. Masson, Robert E. McCarthy, Donald E. Santarelli and E. Donald Shapiro. On Feb. 1 the White House received word that Shapiro, who had been under investigation on allegations of improperly enriching himself as dean of the New York Law School, declined to accept the appointment.

Reagan Oct. 7, 1983, announced his intention to nominate a full slate of LSC board members. They were Robert A. Valois, LeaAnne Bernstein, Claude G. Swafford, Paul B. Eaglin, Arnie Marie Gordon, Henry Chavira, Michael B. Wallace, William B. Durant III, Robert Francis Kane, Bernard M. Bloom and Pepe J. Mendez. Only eight nominations actually were submitted to the Senate, however. Gordon and Chevira withdrew from consideration; and Bloom's name was not submitted because his FBI background investigation was not available. The Senate did not complete action on the nominations.

Only four of the 11 slots for the LSC's board of directors — the minimum required to do business — were filled at the end of 1983. In addition to Masson, McCarthy and Santarelli, Reagan had appointed Ronald B. Frankum on Nov. 21, during a congressional recess.

Two additional recess appointments were made Jan. 21, 1984: Albert Angrisani and Peter Joseph Ferrara.

Reagan submitted 11 nominations to the Senate March 19, 1984. The nominees included Valois, Bernstein, Swafford, Wallace, Durant, Eaglin and Mendez, who previously had been nominated for LSC positions. Also nominated were Lorain Miller, Hortencia Benavides, Thomas F. Smegal Jr. and Basile Joseph Uddo.

Ten of the 11 nominees were approved by the Senate Labor Committee on May 2. Wallace's nomination was sent to the Senate without recommendation. The full Senate did not confirm any of the nominations before adjourning in October. All 11 nominees were given recess appointments Nov. 23.

The Senate confirmed the nominees June 12, 1985. James H. Wentzel, a Federal Trade Commission official, was chosen June 28 by the board to be LSC president.

adverse health implications in poor nations. *(Infant formula, p. 142)*

Myer Rashish. Rashish's nomination as assistant secretary of state for economic affairs was opposed by Sen. Jesse Helms, R-N.C. After the Foreign Relations Committee voted in favor of the nomination, Helms placed a "hold" on it. Helms relented after Rashish was recalled for a further hearing. The Senate confirmed the nomination June 11 by a 91-4 vote.

Warren Richardson. Nominated as assistant secretary of health and human services, Richardson withdrew in the face of charges that he was anti-Semitic. From 1969 to 1973, he had served as general counsel of the conservative Liberty Lobby, which frequently had been criticized for its racist and anti-Jewish sentiments. Richardson denied that he shared these views, but said "political realism" was forcing him to withdraw his name.

John R. Van de Water. On Nov. 19 the Labor Committee rejected, 8-8, the nomination of Van de Water for chairman of the National Labor Relations Board (NLRB). Van de Water was opposed by the AFL-CIO, which argued that he was an anti-labor partisan who could not serve as an impartial judge in settling labor-business disputes. A California labor lawyer, Van de Water advised companies on how to cope with unionization drives of their employees.

Lowell P. Weicker Jr., R-Conn., joined all committee Democrats in opposing Van de Water. Chairman Orrin G. Hatch, R-Utah, then tried unsuccessfully to have the nomination reported unfavorably. Senate Majority Leader Howard H. Baker Jr., R-Tenn., tried to discharge the committee from consideration of the nomination so it could be brought directly to the Senate floor. But his effort was blocked on the floor by an objection from Minority Leader Robert C. Byrd, D-W.Va.

Van de Water received an interim appointment as NLRB chairman in August while the Senate was in recess. Reagan resubmitted Van de Water's nomination to the Senate in February 1982. When Van de Water was named special assistant to the secretary of labor in November 1982, he resigned his post with the NLRB.

1982

Richard R. Burt. Burt's nomination as assistant secretary of state for European affairs threatened a conservative filibuster. Sen. Jesse Helms, R-N.C., objected to a 1979 story Burt wrote while reporting for *The New York Times*. In the article Burt used secret information on techniques for verifying Soviet compliance with SALT II. The nomination was blocked for months, but Burt had the support of Secretary of State George P. Shultz.

The Senate confirmed the nomination Feb. 16, 1983, by an 81-11 vote.

Robert T. Grey Jr. Opposition by Sen. Jesse Helms, R-N.C., and other conservatives killed Grey's nomination as deputy director of the Arms Control and Disarmament Agency. Helms opposed Grey's previous roles in nuclear arms control, and felt the nominee represented the administration's abandonment of a sufficiently tough stance on Soviet arms talks. The nomination was stalled in the Senate; Reagan withdrew the nomination on Jan. 4, 1983.

Rev. B. Sam Hart. President Reagan bowed to strong protests by civil rights groups Feb. 26 and withdrew his choice of Hart for a post on the six-member U.S. Civil Rights Commission. Hart, a black Philadelphia radio evangelist, had asked that his name be withdrawn.

Hart provoked controversy as soon as he was nominated. He said he opposed busing for school desegregation, the Equal Rights Amendment and the concept of homosexual rights.

Pennsylvania's two Republican senators, John Heinz and Arlen Specter, were unhappy with Reagan's choice. Both said they had not been consulted on the selection, and Heinz said he had strong reservations about Hart's qualifications. *(Story, p. 694)*

Norman Terrell. Conservatives in the Senate held up action on the nomination of Terrell as director of the Arm Control and Disarmament Agency's bureau of nuclear weapons control.

Terrell was controversial because of his role in nuclear arms control in previous administrations. Reagan withdrew the nomination Nov. 30.

1983

Kenneth L. Adelman. White House lobbying bore fruit April 14 when the Senate confirmed Adelman to head the Arms Control and Disarmament Agency by a 57-42 vote. The Foreign Relations Committee had reported the nomination unfavorably Feb. 24. Adelman, deputy ambassador to the United Nations, was named Jan. 12 to replace Eugene V. Rostow.

The three-month debate over the nomination was, in large part, a debate on Reagan's strategy for nuclear arms control. Opponents charged that Reagan had shown his indifference to arms control by naming a man without experience in or enthusiasm toward arms control. In addition, they said Adelman lacked the political status to be an effective advocate for arms control policies within the administration. *(Story, p. 233)*

Civil Rights Commission. Civil rights activists protested when Reagan announced May 26 that he was replacing three sitting members of the Civil Rights Commission with his own appointees. Reagan previously had appointed the chairman and vice chairman of the commission.

Opponents charged that Reagan's move undermined the commission's independence, and they set out to block the nominations.

After a six-month stalemate, Congress and the president agreed on compromise legislation reconstituting the commission and extending it for six years. The six-member presidentially appointed commission was to be replaced by an eight-member panel to be appointed half by the president and half by Congress. *(Story, p. 694)*

1984

Michael H. Armacost. The Senate by voice vote May 16 confirmed the nomination of Armacost as under secretary of state for political affairs, the No. 3 post at the State Department. The Senate Foreign Relations Committee had approved the nomination the day before; Sen. Jesse Helms, R-N.C., was the only committee member who did not vote. Helms had raised questions about Armacost's role in several Carter administration policy decisions affecting

Asia, but had said he was satisfied by Armacost's written responses to a series of questions.

Martha Seger. Seger, a finance professor at Central Michigan University, was named July 2 to the Federal Reserve Board on a controversial recess appointment that permitted her to serve, unconfirmed by the Senate, until the end of the 1985 session.

The Senate Banking Committee had approved the nomination June 28 on a 10-8 party-line vote, but committee Democrats had belittled her qualifications and vowed to continue their attack when the nomination reached the Senate floor. Reagan made the recess appointment after the committee vote, but before an important Federal Reserve meeting to set preliminary monetary growth targets for 1985.

By voice vote June 13, 1985, Seger was confirmed by the Senate for a term expiring in 1998.

J. Harvie Wilkinson. Wilkinson was confirmed Aug. 9 as a judge on the 4th U.S. Circuit Court of Appeals. The 58-39 vote came after the Senate voted to invoke cloture and cut off a filibuster against the nomination led by Sens. Edward M. Kennedy, D-Mass., and Howard M. Metzenbaum, D-Ohio. An earlier cloture motion had failed.

Kennedy and Metzenbaum contended that Wilkinson was not qualified for the post and that he waged an improper lobbying campaign to get an American Bar Association (ABA) committee to give him a "qualified" rating. The ABA panel regularly reviewed the qualifications of federal judicial appointments.

The Judiciary Committee approved the nomination 11-5 on March 15, but information subsequently surfaced suggesting that Wilkinson had encouraged the lobbying effort after learning that his nomination was in trouble with the ABA. At a Judiciary hearing Aug. 7, ABA committee Chairman Frederick B. Buesser Jr. said several panel members had complained about calls made on Wilkinson's behalf.

William A. Wilson. The Senate March 7 confirmed Wilson's nomination to be the first U.S. ambassador to the Vatican since 1867. Wilson, a Southern California rancher and land developer, had been President Reagan's personal envoy to the Vatican since February 1981. *(Story, p. 167)*

Leslie Lenkowsky. The Foreign Relations Committee May 15 killed the nomination of Lenkowsky to the No. 2 post at the U.S. Information Agency (USIA). A motion to report his nomination favorably failed 6-11.

The agency operated overseas cultural and exchange programs, among them an overseas speakers program. Questions about the speakers program arose early in the year in the wake of news reports that the agency was keeping a list of people it did not consider fit as speakers because of differences with the administration. Among the more than 90 individuals on the "blacklist" were presidential aspirant Sen. Gary Hart, D-Colo, civil rights activist Coretta Scott King and television journalist Walter Cronkite. During hearings, witnesses disagreed over Lenkowsky's knowledge of the list. Lenkowsky had been acting deputy direct of the agency since December 1983.

Presidential Vetoes, 1981-84

President Reagan vetoed 34 public bills during his first term in office. Reagan's predecessor, Democrat Jimmy Carter, vetoed 29 public bills during his four-year tenure. Reagan's immediate Republican predecessor, Gerald R. Ford, vetoed 61 bills during his two and one-half years in office.

Congress made seven veto override attempts in 1981-84; four were successful. Two vetoes were overridden in 1982, one in 1983 and one in 1984. Veto overrides require a two-thirds majority vote of both houses.

The record for veto overrides — 15 — was held by Andrew Johnson. Ford was second with 12 overrides.

Seventeen of Reagan's public bill vetoes were pocket vetoes. When Congress is in session, a bill becomes law without the president's signature if he does not act upon it within 10 days, excluding Sundays, from the time he receives it. But if Congress adjourns within that 10-day period, the bill is killed, or pocket-vetoed, without the president's signature.

In addition, Reagan vetoed five private bills during his first term. Four of the five were pocket-vetoed.

Following is a list of public and private bills vetoed by Reagan in 1981-84. Pocket-veto dates reflect dates of presidential memorandums of disapproval.

1981

1. H J Res 357 (Continuing Appropriations)
   Vetoed: Nov. 23, 1981
   No override attempt
   (Story, p. 45)
2. HR 4353 (Bankruptcy Fees on Lifetime Communities Inc.)
   Pocket-vetoed: Dec. 29, 1981
   (Story, p. 677)

1982

3. S 1503 (Standby Petroleum Allocation)
   Vetoed: March 20, 1982
   Senate sustained March 24: 58-36
   (Story, p. 376)
4. HR 5118 (Southern Arizona Water Rights Settlement Act)
   Vetoed: June 1, 1982
   No override attempt
   (Story, p. 435)
5. HR 5922 (Urgent Supplemental Appropriations, Fiscal 1982)
   Vetoed: June 24, 1982
   House sustained June 24: 253-151
   (Story, p. 50)
6. HR 6682 (Urgent Supplemental Appropriations, Fiscal 1982)
   Vetoed: June 25, 1982
   House sustained July 13: 242-169
   (Story, p. 50)
7. HR 6198 (Manufacturers Copyright Bill)
   Vetoed: July 8, 1982
   Veto overridden July 13
   House: 324-86, July 13
   Senate: 84-9, July 13
   (Story, p. 686)
8. HR 6863 (Supplemental Appropriations, Fiscal 1982)
   Vetoed: Aug. 28, 1982
   Veto overridden Sept. 10
   House: 301-117, Sept. 9
   Senate: 60-30, Sept. 10
   (Story, p. 50)
9. HR 1371 (Contract Disputes)
   Vetoed: Oct. 15, 1982
   No override attempt
   (Story, p. 781)
10. S 2577 (Environmental Research and Development)
    Vetoed: Oct. 22, 1982
    No override attempt
    (Story, p. 453)
11. S 2623 (Indian Controlled Community Colleges)
    Pocket-vetoed: Jan. 3, 1983
    (Story, p. 564)
12. HR 5858 (Private Bill for Relief of Certain Silver Dealers)
    Pocket-vetoed: Jan. 4, 1983
13. HR 7336 (Education Consolidation and Improvement Act Amendments)
    Pocket-vetoed: Jan. 12, 1983
    (Story, p. 564)
14. HR 9 (Florida Wilderness Act)
    Pocket-vetoed: Jan. 14, 1983
    (Story, p. 465)
15. HR 3963 (Anti-Crime Bill)
    Pocket-vetoed: Jan. 14, 1983
    (Story, p. 689)

1983

16. S 366 (Indian Claims Bill)
    Vetoed: April 5, 1983
    No override attempt
    (Story, p. 787)
17. S 973 (Tax Leasing Plan)
    Vetoed: June 17, 1983
    No override attempt
    (Story, p. 787)
18. HR 3564 (Feed Grains Bill)
    Vetoed: Aug. 12, 1983
    No override attempt
    (Story, p. 510)
19. H J Res 338 (Chicago School Desegregation)
    Vetoed: Aug. 13, 1983
    No override attempt
20. S J Res 149 (Dairy Assessment Delay Bill)
    Vetoed: Aug. 23, 1983
    No override attempt
    (Story, p. 505)

Appendix

21. HR 1062 (Oregon Land Transfer Bill)
    Vetoed: Oct. 19, 1983
    Veto overridden Oct. 25
    Senate: 95-0, Oct. 25
    House: 297-125, Oct. 25
    (Story, p. 476)
22. HR 4042 (El Salvador Certification)
    Pocket-vetoed: Nov. 30, 1983
    (Story, p. 165)

1984

23. S 684 (Water Resources Research)
    Vetoed: Feb. 21, 1984
    Veto overridden March 22
    Senate: 86-12, March 21
    House: 309-81, March 22
    (Story, p. 446)
24. S 2436 (Corporation for Public Broadcasting)
    Vetoed: Aug. 29, 1984
    No override attempt
    (Story, p. 282)
25. HR 1362 (Private Bill for Relief of Joseph Karel Hasek)
    Vetoed: Oct. 8, 1984
    No override attempt
26. S 1967 (Indian Affairs)
    Pocket-vetoed: Oct. 17, 1984
    (Story, p. 790)
27. HR 2859 (Private Bill for Relief of John Brizna Charles)
    Pocket-vetoed: Oct. 17, 1984

28. S 1097 (National Oceanic and Atmospheric Administration Research and Services Act)
    Pocket-vetoed: Oct. 19, 1984
    (Story, p. 790)
29. S 607 (Corporation for Public Broadcasting)
    Pocket-vetoed: Oct. 19, 1984
    (Story, p. 282)
30. S 2166 (Indian Health Care Improvement Act)
    Pocket-vetoed: Oct. 19, 1984
    (Story, p. 790)
31. HR 6248 (Armed Career Criminal Act of 1984)
    Pocket-vetoed: Oct. 19, 1984
32. HR 5172 (National Bureau of Standards Authorizations)
    Pocket-vetoed: Oct. 30, 1984
    (Story, p. 789)
33. S 540 (Health Research Extension Act of 1984)
    Pocket-vetoed: Oct. 30, 1984
    (Story, p. 550)
34. S 2574 (Public Health Service Act Amendments of 1984)
    Pocket-vetoed: Oct. 30, 1984
    (Story, p. 551)
35. HR 999 (American Conservation Corps Act of 1984)
    Pocket-vetoed: Oct. 30, 1984
    (Story, p. 671)
36. HR 5760 (Indian Affairs)
    Pocket-vetoed: Oct. 30, 1984
37. HR 723 (Private Bill for Relief of Marsha D. Christopher)
    Pocket-vetoed: Oct. 31, 1984
38. HR 452 (Private Bill for Relief of Jerome J. Hartmann and Rita J. Hartmann)
    Pocket-vetoed: Oct. 31, 1984
39. HR 5479 (Civil Actions and Procedures)
    Pocket-vetoed: Nov. 8, 1984
    (Story, p. 709)

President Carter's Fiscal 1982 Budget Message

Following is the text of President Carter's fiscal 1982 budget message sent to Congress Jan. 15, 1981.

TO THE CONGRESS OF
THE UNITED STATES:

My administration has faced a wide range of challenges at home and abroad, challenges stemming from our strengths, not our weaknesses: our strengths as a world leader, as a developed industrial nation, and as a heterogeneous democracy with high goals and great ambitions. Meeting these challenges satisfactorily requires that we establish priorities, recognizing the limits to even our Nation's enormous resources. We cannot do all that we wish at the same time. But we must provide for our security, establish the basis for a strong economy, protect the disadvantaged, build human and physical capital for the future, and safeguard this Nation's magnificent natural environment.

This budget provides for meeting these needs, while continuing a 4-year policy of prudence and restraint. While our budget deficits have been higher than I would have liked, their size has been determined for the most part by economic conditions. Even so, the trend has been downward. In 1976, the budget deficit equalled 4.0% of gross national product. This was reduced to 2.3% in the budget year that ended 3 months ago. The 1982 budget deficit is estimated to equal only 0.9% of gross national product.

The rate of growth in budget outlays has been held to a minimum. In spite of significant increases in indexed programs, outlays for nondefense programs — after adjusting for inflation — decrease slightly.

The 1982 budget calls for outlays of $739 billion, an increase of 1.0% when adjusted for inflation. Nondefense spending is projected to decline by 0.2% in real terms. The tax reductions I proposed as part of the economic revitalization program have been retained, but some have been delayed or phased in over a longer period in recognition of the continued high inflation rate. The budget deficit — which is now projected at $55.2 billion in 1981 — is estimated to decline to $27.5 billion in 1982.

In planning this budget, I have considered four major issues:

- What is the economic policy that will ensure prosperity for all while minimizing inflation?
- How much of our Nation's wealth should be used by the Federal Government?
- What are desirable spending proposals and strategies for defense, human resources, and investment?
- How can the management of Government be improved?

The Economy

During the last decade we withstood a series of economic shocks unprecedented in peacetime. The most dramatic of these were the explosive increases of OPEC oil prices. But we have also faced world commodity shortages, natural disasters, agricultural shortages, and major challenges to world peace and security. Our ability to deal with these shocks has been impaired by slower productivity growth and persistent, underlying inflationary forces built up over the past 15 years.

Nevertheless, the economy has proved remarkably resilient. Real output has grown at an average annual rate of 3% since I took office, and employment has grown by 2-1/2%. Nearly 8 million productive private sector jobs have been added to the economy. However, unacceptably high inflation remains our most difficult economic problem. This inflation requires that we hold down the growth of the budget to the maximum extent, while still meeting the demands of national security and human compassion. I have done so, as I did in my earlier budgets.

While budget restraint is essential to any appropriate economic policy, high inflation cannot be attributed solely to Government spending. The growth in budget outlays has been more the result of economic factors than the cause of them. For fiscal year 1981 alone, budget outlays must be increased by $9 billion over last year's estimate as a result of higher interest rates. Yet this increase results not only from inflation but from the monetary policies undertaken to combat it. Nearly $18 billion for 1981 reflects higher defense costs and higher automatic inflation adjustments than were anticipated a year ago.

We are now in the early stages of economic recovery following a short recession. Typically, post-recessionary periods have been marked by vigorous economic growth abetted by stimulative policies such as large tax cuts or spending programs. I am not recommending such actions, because persistent inflationary pressures dictate a restrained fiscal policy. However, I continue to recommend specific tax reductions that contribute directly to increased productivity and long-term growth.

The Size and Role of Government

We allocate about 23% of our Nation's output through the Federal budget. (Including all levels of government, the total government share of our gross national product is about one-third.) We must come close to matching Federal outlays with tax receipts if we are to avoid excessive and inflationary Federal borrowing. This means either controlling our appetite for spending or accepting the burden of higher taxes.

The growth of budget outlays is puzzling to many Americans, but it arises from valid social and national security concerns. Other developed countries face similar pressures. We face a threat to our security, as events in Afghanistan, the Middle East, and Eastern Europe make clear. We have a steadily aging population; as a result, the biggest single increase in the Federal budget is the rising cost of retirement programs, particularly social security. We must meet other important domestic needs: to assist the disadvantaged; to provide the capital needed by our cities and our transportation systems; to protect our environment; and to revitalize American industry.

I have been concerned with the proper role of the Federal Government in designing and providing such assistance. The Federal Government must not usurp functions that are best left to the private sector or to State and local governments. My administration has sought to make the proper assignments of responsibility, to resolve problems in the most efficient manner.

We have also recognized the need to simplify the system of Federal grants to State and local governments. Once again, I am proposing several grant consolidations in the 1982 budget, including a new proposal that would consolidate several highway programs. Previous consolidation proposals of my administration have been in the areas of youth training and employment, environment, energy conservation, airport development, and rehabilitation services. These consolidations are essential to improving our intergovernmental system. However, the Congress has so far agreed to consolidate only rehabilitation services grants. Therefore, I am proposing again the consolidations recommended earlier.

Appendix

Major Budget Priorities

Spending growth can be constrained; not easily, not quickly, but it is possible. My budget priorities have been established, once again, to achieve this goal in a responsible manner.

Three years ago, in my 1979 budget message, I outlined the following principles:

- The Nation's armed forces must always stand sufficiently strong to deter aggression and to assure our security.
- An effective national energy plan is essential to reduce our increasingly critical dependence upon diminishing supplies of oil and gas, to encourage conservation of scarce energy resources, to stimulate conversion to more abundant fuels, and to reduce our large trade deficit.
- The essential human needs of our citizens must be given high priority.
- The Federal Government must lead the way in investment in the Nation's technological future.
- The Federal Government has an obligation to nurture and protect our environment — the common resource, birthright, and sustenance of the American people.

My 1982 budget is again based on these principles.

Tax policy and economic revitalization. — I continue to believe that large inflationary individual income tax cuts are neither appropriate nor possible today, however popular they might appear in the short run. My economic revitalization program stresses tax reductions on a timetable that we can afford, and that will fight inflation by encouraging capital formation and increasing industrial productivity. This program stresses:

- simplification and liberalization of depreciation allowances;
- modification of the investment tax credit to encourage investment by temporarily depressed firms and by growing new firms;
- an income tax credit to offset increases in social security taxes;
- a liberalized earned income credit to also offset social security taxes and to encourage low-income earners to work;
- a working-spouse deduction to make more equitable the way working husbands and wives are taxed; and
- more favorable tax treatment for Americans in certain areas overseas to help American exports and strengthen the dollar.

Defense. — Maintaining a strong defense has been a primary objective of this administration. In order to meet the security needs of the Nation, real spending for defense increased in 1979 and 1980 by more than the 3% target I set at the NATO ministerial meeting in 1977. This real growth rate in defense spending has been maintained despite the adverse effects of higher than anticipated inflation, and restrained budgets.

To meet critical remaining needs, this budget includes a $6.3 billion supplemental request for 1981, largely for military pay increases and combat readiness. Together with congressional add-ons to my earlier 1981 request, this supplemental will increase defense programs almost 8% in real terms over 1980. For 1982 and beyond, the budget charts a course of sustained and balanced improvements in defense programs that will require real annual increases in funding of about 5% per year.

The budget request reflects a careful balance between the need to meet all critical defense needs, while maintaining fiscal restraint. There will be advocates for higher defense levels, but after careful review I do not believe that higher spending would add significantly to our national security. My budget already provides for the three major defense requirements:

- *Personnel recruitment and retention.* — Our armed forces can be no better than the quality of the people who serve in them. Accordingly, I recently approved the largest pay and benefits increase in history — a $4.5 billion compensation package that provides for an average compensation increase of 16%. This increase in base pay, plus better housing allowances, expanded enlistment and reenlistment bonuses, and special pay enhancements for submariners and other specialists, will help attract and retain highly qualified men and women.

- *Improving combat readiness.* — Increased compensation will be a key factor in overcoming key personnel shortages, which are the major source of readiness problems. In addition, there have been shortages in critical spare parts and, in a few cases, inadequate funds for training. The funds recommended by this budget should alleviate these problems.

- *Modernizing our forces.* — I also propose major investments to enhance substantially the capabilities of our forces: Strategic forces are being upgraded through continued procurement of Trident submarines and missiles, procurement of cruise missiles, modification of the B-52 bomber, and development of the MX missile. Army equipment, including tanks, armored vehicles, helicopters, and air defense and other missile systems, is being modernized. Fighter and attack planes are being added to Navy and Marine forces, and a continuing major shipbuilding program will add over 80 ships to our growing fleet between 1982 and 1986. The rapid deployment of our forces is being improved through the acquisition of more cargo ships and modification of airlift aircraft.

Foreign aid. — Foreign assistance remains crucial in achieving our country's international political and economic goals. From the start of my administration, I have stressed the need for substantial increases in assistance to friendly nations, many of whom are drastically harmed by constantly increasing oil prices and other external economic and security pressures. At the same time, I have insisted upon improved management of both our security and development assistance programs.

In the first 2 years of this administration, the Congress reduced my foreign aid requests but permitted some program growth. For the past 2 years, however, the Congress has failed to pass regular foreign aid appropriations. Assistance programs in 1981 are being funded under a continuing resolution that provides amounts slightly above the 1979 levels in nominal terms, and substantially below them in real terms.

I believe in the need for higher levels of aid to achieve foreign policy objectives, promote economic growth, and help needy people abroad. Foreign aid is not politically popular and represents an easy target for budget reduction. But it is not a wise one. For 1982, therefore, I am requesting a foreign assistance program level that is higher by 14% in real terms than the amount currently available for 1981. This request would reverse the recent real decline in aid and demonstrate that the United States retains its commitment to a world of politically stable and economically secure nations.

The bilateral development aid budget includes a U.S. response to the 1980 Venice Summit agreement that the major industrial countries should increase bilateral aid for food production, energy production and conservation, and family planning in the developing countries. Such an effort to increase the availability of resources on which the industrial countries depend will serve U.S. national security, and will stimulate additional actions by the private sector in the recipient countries. This U.S. effort is planned in the expectation that the other Summit countries will also increase aid in these sectors, in response to the Venice Summit agreement. We hope this initiative will lead to agreement on arrangements for increased consultation and cooperation among the major industrial countries providing increased bilateral aid to these three vital sectors.

Energy. — My administration, working with the Congress, has established fundamental new policies that will profoundly change the way the Nation produces and uses energy. They have already led to more domestic exploration and to substantial energy conservation. This energy program represents a major long-range national commitment to meeting one of our most pressing problems. It includes:

- Deregulation and decontrol of oil prices to be completed by October of this year.
- Establishment of the Synthetic Fuels Corporation, which will share with the private sector the risk in producing oil and natural gas substitutes that directly reduce U.S. oil imports.
- Support for energy research and development in technologies, such as solar and fusion energy, that the private sector would not finance.
- Development of the strategic petroleum reserve to reduce the impact of disruptions in world oil supplies.
- Energy conservation in public and nonprofit enterprises.
- Research on the environmental effects of energy production and use to assure that

adverse effects on environmental quality are minimized.

Continuation of a sound energy policy is essential to the Nation's well-being in the coming decades. Such a policy must include the pricing of energy at its true cost, mechanisms to stimulate conservation, incentives for the continued development of our own domestic sources of energy, encouragement for longer-run renewable forms of energy, and equity for all our citizens as we adjust to this new reality.

Basic science and space technology. — Basic research is essential to the long-term vitality of the Nation's economy. Because the benefits of such investments cannot be fully realized by individual companies, the Federal Government plays a key role in supporting such research.

My budgets have reversed a long period of decline in Federal support for basic research. The 1982 budget continues that policy by providing for 4% real growth in support for the conduct of basic research across all Federal agencies. The budget also provides for greater efforts to foster co-operation among government, business, and universities in research.

In addition, we have recognized the growing importance of improving scientific technology in the Nation's universities as critical to the advancement of science and to the training of scientific and engineering manpower.

My administration's comprehensive space policy encourages the practical, effective use of information obtained from orbiting satellites and the coordinated use of the Space Shuttle, now nearing completion. Successful resolution of development problems is expected to lead to the first manned orbital flight of the Shuttle in 1981.

With these increases, Federal support for basic research will have increased by almost 58% over 1978.

Social programs. — This budget supports my deep commitment to programs that help our citizens develop their full potential, and to programs assisting the poor, the unemployed, the elderly, and the sick.

The most extensive such programs are *social security* and *medicare*. Parts of this system are expected to experience short-run financing problems because higher than expected unemployment has decreased payroll taxes below previous forecasts, and high inflation has increased benefit payments. Therefore, the administration continues to urge the passage of legislation that would permit the three major social security trust funds to borrow from each other. In addition, it is essential that the Congress and the American people give early consideration to medium-term financing concerns.

The reports of the Commission on Pension Policy, which I established 2 years ago, and the National Commission on Social Security should stimulate constructive debate on these issues. These Commissions will complete their final reports during the coming months.

My administration has consistently maintained a strong commitment to remedying *youth unemployment* and the problems it causes. This budget includes an increase of $1.2 billion in 1982 and an additional increase of $0.8 billion in 1983 for the youth initiative I proposed last year. This initiative emphasizes the mastery of basic arithmetic and literacy skills, as well as the link between the classroom and the workplace.

The Job Corps would be continued at this year's level, serving twice as many youth as when my administration took office. In addition, my budget provides 240,000 public service jobs for low-income, long-term unemployed persons in 1982. This program is designed for the hard-core structurally unemployed, and includes substantial training in order to place men and women in permanent jobs. At the same time, the budget continues the countercyclical public service employment program through 1982 at the 100,000 level set by the Congress for 1981. The budget also provides a slight increase for the administration's private sector jobs initiative and essentially maintains the 1980 level of summer youth employment.

I am again proposing to augment medicaid with a *child health assurance* program effective by the end of 1982. This proposal, which the House of Representatives passed last year, would extend medicaid coverage to an additional 2 million children and pregnant women.

I am also proposing a number of changes in existing programs. For example, I am again proposing that retirement benefits for government employees be adjusted for inflation once, rather than twice, a year. This change would make these adjustments comparable to those for social security and most private sector automatic adjustment practices. The Congress approved a similar administration initiative last year for the food stamp program. This proposal would save $1.1 billion in 1982.

Benefits that are adjusted by statute for inflation will comprise nearly one-third of total Federal spending in 1981. During the last year, my administration has been assessing whether these adjustments are fair and equitable. We have concluded that the Consumer Price Index has several deficiencies as a measure of the true cost of living, particularly because of the manner in which it represents housing costs. I am therefore proposing, in this budget, that future benefits be based on an alternative, more representative index. The alternative index is already calculated and published by the Bureau of Labor Statistics. This proposal is designed to improve the technique of indexing these programs, not to reduce benefits. Therefore, no cost savings are assumed in the budget.

The budget also includes legislation to make unemployment benefits more nearly uniform among the States and to coordinate benefits more precisely with unemployment rates. Although this proposal would save about $2 billion in 1982 under the unemployment rates being projected for this budget, a slightly higher rate of unemployment would trigger extended benefits nationally. In such a case, unemployment benefits would be very close to those under current law. Even with the projected change, under current economic projections $1.5 billion would be paid in 1982 for extended benefits in States where the program is triggered.

I remain committed to a national health plan that would assure basic and catastrophic medical coverage for all Americans, as well as for prenatal and infant care. An estimated 22 million Americans lack any private or public health insurance coverage. Another 60 million people lack adequate basic coverage or protection against catastrophic medical expenses. Given the fact that adequate cost containment does not exist and the need for overall budgetary constraints, the budget does not include specific amounts for this plan. However, it is important that our Nation attempt to meet these needs and that the incentives in our health care system be restructured. A clear demonstration of success in restraining medical care costs is an essential prerequisite to the enactment of a national health plan.

My proposals to reform our welfare system should also be enacted as soon as possible. Such a program is essential to ensuring that no American goes hungry or lacks a reasonable income, and to provide needed fiscal relief to States, counties, and cities.

Improving Government Management

This budget reinforces my commitment to use resources not only wisely, but efficiently. During my administration we have:

- installed new Offices of Inspectors General in 15 major agencies to combat waste, fraud, and abuse;
- carried out a major Government-wide reform of the civil service system;
- reorganized important areas of the Federal Government, particularly those concerned with education and energy;
- reduced permanent Federal civilian employment by 45,000;
- achieved budgetary savings directly through improved cash management; and
- reduced paperwork and established a paperwork budget.

Such efforts to streamline the way the Government conducts its business are rarely dramatic. Improved efficiency is not the product of a simple sweeping reform but, rather, of diligent, persistent attention to many aspects of Federal program management.

One important aspect of improved management has been in the budget process itself. *Zero-base budgeting* is now an integral part of the decisionmaking system, providing a more systematic basis for mak-

ing decisions. We have also instituted a 3-year budget planning horizon so that the longer range consequences of short-term budget decisions are fully considered and understood.

In 1978 I made a major commitment to establish a system of controlling *Federal credit* since, in the past, the very large Federal loan guarantee programs had largely escaped the discipline of the budget process. This system is now in place.

I am gratified that the Congress has supported these efforts to improve budget control. Appropriations bills now include limits on many credit programs. The congressional budget resolutions place significantly greater emphasis on longer range budget trends and set overall credit targets.

While the credit control system provides a means of assessing and limiting Federal credit programs, I believe Federal credit programs have become unduly complex and pose an increasing threat to the effective and efficient operation of private capital markets. In particular, the Federal Financing Bank has become a major and rapidly growing source of off-budget funds for direct loans to a wide range of borrowers.

Therefore, I am recommending that a panel of outstanding financial and budget experts should be established to examine these issues. Such a panel should consider the treatment of credit activities in the budget, the adequacy of program administration, uniform rules and procedures for Federal credit programs, the role of the Federal Financing Bank, and the relationship of tax-exempt financing to overall credit and tax policies.

Conclusion

My budget recommendations reflect the major changes that have taken place in our country over recent decades. In 1950, social security and railroad retirement benefits accounted for less than 3% of budget outlays. Last year they accounted for more than one-fifth of the total. Mandatory outlays for entitlement programs, the levels of which are fixed by law, for interest on the public debt, and for payments under binding contracts account for three-fourths of total budget outlays. Because so much of the budget is committed under current law before either the President or the Congress begins the annual budget formulation process, controlling budget growth has been difficult, and the results uneven. It has been difficult because benefit payments and other legal obligations have too often been spared from annual budget scrutiny. The results have been uneven because budget restraint has fallen disproportionately on programs subject to the annual appropriations process.

My administration and the Congress began to redress this imbalance in the 1981 budget. The Congress passed, and I signed into law, a reconciliation bill that for the first time was used as a mechanism for changing a variety of entitlement and tax programs. I do not propose that we break faith with the American people by arbitrarily or unfairly reducing entitlement programs. However, these programs developed independently, and they should be made less duplicative, more consistent, and more equitable. The size of these programs, and our need for budget restraint, requires that we address these problems. I urge the Congress to build upon last year's experience and review all aspects of the budget with equal care.

The allocation of one-fifth of our Nation's resources through the Federal budget is a complex, difficult, and contentious process. Restraint on any program, small or large, is usually subject to heated debate. At a time when there is broad consensus that the size of the Federal budget is too large, we can no longer — as individuals or groups — make special pleas for exceptions to budget discipline. Too often we have taken the attitude that individual benefits or particular programs or specific tax measures are not large enough to require restraint. Too often we have taken the attitude that there must be alternative sources for reductions in programs that benefit our particular group. This attitude is in part responsible for the rapid budget growth we have experienced — and can no longer afford.

Given our Nation's needs and our economic constraints, my recommendations meet the fundamental demands of our society: a strong defense, adequate protection for the poor and the disadvantaged, support for our free enterprise economy, and investment in the Nation's future.

JIMMY CARTER

January 15, 1981

Ronald Reagan's First Inaugural Address

Following is the text of President Reagan's inaugural address as delivered Jan. 20, 1981.

To a few of us here today this is a solemn and most momentous occasion. And, yet, in the history of our nation it is a commonplace occurrence.

The orderly transfer of authority as called for in the Constitution routinely takes place as it has for almost two centuries and few of us stop to think how unique we really are. In the eyes of many in the world, this every-four-year ceremony we accept as normal is nothing less than a miracle.

Mr. President, I want our fellow citizens to know how much you did to carry on this tradition. By your gracious cooperation in the transition process you have shown a watching world that we are a united people pledged to maintaining a political system which guarantees individual liberty to a greater degree than any other, and I thank you and your people for all your help in maintaining the continuity which is the hallmark of our Republic.

Economic Affliction

The business of our nation goes forward. These United States are confronted with an economic affliction of great proportions. We suffer from the longest and one of the worst sustained inflations in our national history. It distorts our economic decisions, penalizes thrift and crushes the struggling young and the fixed-income elderly alike. It threatens to shatter the lives of millions of our people.

Idle industries have cast workers into unemployment, human misery and personal indignity. Those who do work are denied a fair return for their labor by a tax system which penalizes successful achievement and keeps us from maintaining full productivity.

But great as our tax burden is, it has not kept pace with public spending. For decades we have piled deficit upon deficit, mortgaging our future and our children's future for the temporary convenience of the present. To continue this long trend is to guarantee tremendous social, cultural, political, and economic upheavals.

You and I, as individuals, can, by borrowing, live beyond our means, but for only a limited period of time. Why should we think that collectively, as a nation, we are not bound by that same limitation? We must act today in order to preserve tomorrow. And let there be no misunderstanding — we are going to begin to act beginning today.

The economic ills we suffer have come upon us over several decades. They will not go away in days, weeks, or months, but they will go away. They will go away because we as Americans have the capacity now, as we have had in the past, to do

whatever needs to be done to preserve this last and greatest bastion of freedom.

Problem is Government

In this present crisis, government is not the solution to our problem. Government is the problem.

From time to time we have been tempted to believe that society has become too complex to be managed by self-rule, that government by an elite group is superior to government for, by and of the people. But, if no one among us is capable of governing himself, then who among us has the capacity to govern someone else.

All of us together — in and out of government — must bear the burden. The solutions we seek must be equitable with no one group singled out to pay a higher price.

We hear much of special interest groups, but our concern must be for a special interest group that has been too long neglected. It knows no sectional boundaries, crosses ethnic and racial divisions and political party lines. It is made up of men and women who raise our food, patrol our streets, man our mines and factories, teach our children, keep our homes and heal us when we're sick. Professionals, industrialists, shopkeepers, clerks, cabbies and truck drivers. They are, in short, "We the people," this breed called Americans.

Well, this administration's objective must be a healthy, vigorous, growing economy that provides equal opportunities for all Americans with no barriers born of bigotry or discrimination. Putting America back to work means putting all Americans back to work. Ending inflation means freeing all Americans from the terror of runaway living costs. All must share in the productive work of this "new beginning," and all must share in the bounty of a revived economy. With the idealism and fair play which are the core of our system and our strength, we can have a strong, prosperous America at peace with itself and the world.

So as we begin, let us take inventory. We are a nation that has a government — not the other way around. And this makes us special among the nations of the Earth. Our government has no power except that granted it by the people. It is time to check and reverse the growth of government which shows signs of having grown beyond the consent of the governed.

It is my intention to curb the size and influence of the Federal establishment and to demand recognition of the distinction between the powers granted to the Federal government and those reserved to the states or to the people. All of us need to be reminded that the Federal government did not create the states; the states created the Federal government.

Now so there will be no misunderstanding, it is not my intention to do away with government. It is rather to make it work — work with us, not over us; to stand by our side, not ride on our back. Government can and must provide opportunity, not smother it; foster productivity, not stifle it.

If we look to the answer as to why for so many years we achieved so much, prospered as no other people on earth, it was because here in this land we unleashed the energy and individual genius of man to a greater extent than had ever been done before. Freedom and the dignity of the individual have been more available and assured here than in any other place on earth. The price for this freedom at times has been high, but we have never been unwilling to pay that price.

It is no coincidence that our present troubles parallel and are proportionate [to] the intervention and intrusion in our lives that have resulted from unnecessary and excessive growth of government.

It is time for us to realize that we are too great a nation to limit ourselves to small dreams. We are not, as some would have us believe, doomed to an inevitable decline. I do not believe in a fate that will fall on us no matter what we do. I do believe in a fate that will fall on us if we do nothing.

Era of National Renewal

So, with all the creative energy at our command, let us begin an era of national renewal. Let us renew our determination, our courage, and our strength and let us renew our faith and our hope. We have every right to dream heroic dreams.

Those who say we are in a time when there are no heroes, they just don't know where to look. You can see heroes every day going in and out of factory gates. Others, a handful in number, produce food enough to feed all of us and much of the world beyond.

You meet heroes across a counter. And they're on both sides of that counter. There are entrepreneurs with faith in themselves and faith in an idea who create new jobs, new wealth and opportunity. They are individuals and families whose taxes support the government and whose voluntary gifts support church, charity, culture, art, and education. Their patriotism is quiet but deep. Their values sustain our national life.

Now, I have used the words "they" and "their" in speaking of these heroes. I could say "you" and "your" because I am addressing the heroes of whom I speak — you, the citizens of this blessed land. Your dreams, your hopes, your goals are going to be the dreams, the hopes and goals of this administration, so help me God.

We shall reflect the compassion that is so much a part of your makeup. How can we love our country and not love our countrymen? And loving them reach out a hand when they fall, heal them when they are sick and provide opportunity to make them self-sufficient so they will be equal in fact and not just in theory.

Can we solve the problems confronting us? Well, the answer is an unequivocal and emphatic yes. To paraphrase Winston Churchill, I did not take the oath I have just taken with the intention of presiding over the dissolution of the world's strongest economy.

In the days ahead I will propose removing the roadblocks that have slowed our economy and reduced productivity. Steps will be taken aimed at restoring the balance between the various levels of government. Progress may be slow — measured in inches and feet, not miles — but we will progress. It is time to reawaken this industrial giant, to get government back within its means, and to lighten our punitive tax burden. And these will be our first priorities, and on these principles, there will be no compromise.

Act Worthy of Ourselves

On the eve of our struggle for independence a man who might have been one of the greatest among the Founding Fathers, Dr. Joseph Warren, President of the Massachusetts Congress, said to his fellow Americans, "Our country is in danger, but not to be despaired of ... On you depend the fortunes of America. You are to decide the important question on which rests the happiness and liberty of millions yet unborn. Act worthy of yourselves."

Well, I believe we the Americans of today are ready to act worthy of ourselves, ready to do what must be done to ensure happiness and liberty for ourselves, our children, and our children's children.

And as we renew ourselves here in our own land, we will be seen as having greater strength throughout the world. We will again be the exemplar of freedom and a beacon of hope for those who do not now have freedom.

To those neighbors and allies who share our ideal of freedom, we will strengthen our historic ties and assure them of our support and firm commitment. We will match loyalty with loyalty. We will strive for mutually beneficial relations. We will not use our friendship to impose on their sovereignty, for our own sovereignty is not for sale.

As for the enemies of freedom, to those who are potential adversaries, they will be reminded that peace is the highest aspiration of the American people. We will negotiate for it, sacrifice for it; we will not surrender for it — now or ever.

Our forbearance should never be misunderstood. Our reluctance for conflict should not be misjudged as a failure of will. When action is required to preserve our national security, we will act. We will maintain sufficient strength to prevail if need be, knowing that if we do so we have the best chance of never having to use that strength.

Above all we must realize that no arsenal or no weapon in the arsenals of the world is so formidable as the will and moral courage of free men and women. It is a weapon our adversaries in today's world do not have. It is a weapon that we as Americans do have. Let that be understood by

those who practice terrorism and prey upon their neighbors.

Inaugural Day, Monuments

I am told that tens of thousands of prayer meetings are being held on this day. For that I am deeply grateful. We are a nation under God, and I believe God intended for us to be free. It would be fitting and good, I think, if each Inaugural Day in future years it should be a day of prayer.

This, as you've been told, is the first time in our history that this ceremony has been held on the West Front of the Capitol Building. Standing here, we face a magnificent vista, opening up on this city's special beauty and history. At the end of this open mall are those shrines to the giants on whose shoulders we stand.

Directly in front of me, the monument to a monumental man. George Washington, Father of our country. A man of humility who came to greatness reluctantly. He led America out of revolutionary victory into infant nationhood.

Off to one side, the stately memorial to Thomas Jefferson. The Declaration of Independence flames with his eloquence.

And then beyond the reflecting pool, the dignified columns of the Lincoln Memorial. Whoever would understand in his heart the meaning of America will find it in the life of Abraham Lincoln.

Beyond these monuments to heroism is the Potomac River, and on the far shore the sloping hills of Arlington National Cemetery with its row upon row of simple white markers bearing crosses or Stars of David. They add up to only a tiny fraction of the price that has been paid for our freedom.

Each one of those markers is a monument to the kind of hero I spoke of earlier. Their lives ended in places called Belleau Wood, The Argonne, Omaha Beach, Salerno and halfway round the world on Guadalcanal, Tarawa, Pork Chop Hill, The Chosin Reservoir, and in a hundred rice paddies and jungles of a place called Vietnam.

Under such a marker lies a young man — Martin Treptow — who left his job in a small town barber shop in 1917 to go to France with the famed Rainbow Division. There, on the Western front, he was killed trying to carry a message between battalions under heavy artillery fire.

We are told that on his body was found a diary. On the flyleaf under the heading, "My Pledge," he had written these words: "America must win this war. Therefore I will work, I will save, I will sacrifice, I will endure, I will fight cheerfully and do my utmost, as if the issue of the whole struggle depended on me alone."

The crisis we are facing today does not require of us the kind of sacrifice that Martin Treptow and so many thousands of others were called upon to make. It does, however, require our best effort, and our willingness to believe in ourselves and to believe in our capacity to perform great deeds; to believe that together and with God's help we can and will resolve the problems which confront us.

And after all, why shouldn't we believe that? We are Americans.

God bless you.

President Reagan's Economic Proposals

Following is the text of the address as delivered by President Reagan to a joint session of Congress on Feb. 18, 1981.

Mr. Speaker, Mr. President, distinguished Members of Congress, honored guests, and fellow citizens. Only a month ago, I was your guest in this historic building and I pledged to you my cooperation in doing what is right for this Nation that we all love so much.

I am here tonight to reaffirm that pledge and to ask that we share in restoring the promise that is offered to every citizen by this, the last, best hope of man on earth.

All of us are aware of the punishing inflation which has, for the first time in some 60 years, held to double digit figures for 2 years in a row. Interest rates have reached absurd levels of more than 20 percent and over 15 percent for those who would borrow to buy a home. All across this land one can see newly built homes standing vacant, unsold because of mortgage interest rates.

Almost eight million Americans are out of work. These are people who want to be productive. But as the months go by, despair dominates their lives. The threats of layoffs and unemployment hang over other millions, and all who work are frustrated by their inability to keep up with inflation.

One worker in a Midwest city put it to me this way: He said, "I'm bringing home more dollars than I thought I ever believed I could possibly earn, but I seem to be getting worse off." And he is. Not only have hourly earnings of the American worker, after adjusting for inflation, declined 5 percent over the past 5 years, but in these 5 years, Federal personal taxes for the average family increased 67 percent.

We can no longer procrastinate and hope that things will get better. They will not. Unless we act forcefully, and now, the economy will get worse.

National Debt

Can we who man the ship of state deny it is somewhat out of control? Our national debt is approaching $1 trillion. A few weeks ago I called such a figure — a trillion dollars — incomprehensible. I've been trying ever since to think of a way to illustrate how big a trillion is. The best I could come up with is that if you had a stack of $1,000 bills in your hand only four inches high you would be a millionaire. A trillion dollars would be a stack of $1,000 bills 67 miles high.

The interest on the public debt this year we know will be over $90 billion. And unless we change the proposed spending for the fiscal year beginning October 1, we'll add another almost $80 billion to the debt.

Adding to our troubles is a mass of regulations imposed on the shopkeeper, the farmer, the craftsman, professionals and major industry that is estimated to add $100 billion to the price of things we buy and it reduces our ability to produce. The rate of increase in American productivity, once one of the highest in the world, is among the lowest of all major industrial nations. Indeed, it has actually declined in the last 3 years.

I have painted a pretty grim picure but I think that I have painted it accurately. It is within our power to change this picture and we can act with hope. There is nothing wrong with our internal strengths. There has been no breakdown in the human, technological, and natural resources upon which the economy is built.

Four-Point Proposal

Based on this confidence in a system which has never failed us — but which we have failed through a lack of confidence, and sometimes through a belief that we could fine tune the economy and get a tune to our liking — I am proposing a comprehensive four-point program. Let me outline in detail some of the principal parts of this program. You will each be provided with a completely detailed copy of the entire program.

This plan is aimed at reducing the growth in Government spending and taxing, reforming and eliminating regulations which are unnecessary and unproductive or counterproductive, and encouraging a consistent monetary policy aimed at maintaining the value of the currency.

If enacted in full, this program can help America create 13 million new jobs,

nearly 3 million more than we would have without these measures. It will also help us gain control of inflation.

Tax Increase Rate Reduction

It is important to note that we are only reducing the rate of increase in taxing and spending. We are not attempting to cut either spending or taxing levels below that which we presently have. This plan will get our economy moving again, increase productivity growth, and thus create the jobs our people must have.

And I am asking that you join me in reducing direct Federal spending by $41.4 billion in fiscal year 1982, along with another $7.7 billion user fees and off-budget savings for a total savings of $49.1 billion.

This will still allow an increase of $40.8 billion over 1981 spending.

Full Funding for Truly Needy

I know that exaggerated and inaccurate stories about these cuts have disturbed many people, particularly those dependent on grant and benefit programs for their basic needs. Some of you have heard from constituents, I know, afraid that social security checks, for example, were going to be taken away from them. I regret the fear that these unfounded stories have caused and I welcome this opportunity to set things straight.

We will continue to fulfill the obligations that spring from our national conscience. Those who through no fault of their own must depend on the rest of us, the poverty stricken, the disabled, the elderly, all those with true need, can rest assured that the social safety net of programs they depend on are exempt from any cuts.

The full retirement benefits of the more than 31 million social security recipients will be continued along with an annual cost of living increase. Medicare will not be cut, nor will supplemental income for the blind, aged, and disabled, and funding will continue for veterans' pensions.

School breakfasts and lunches for the children of low income families will continue, as will nutrition and other special services for the aging. There will be no cut in Project Head Start or summer youth jobs.

All in all, nearly $216 billion worth of programs providing help for tens of millions of Americans — will be fully funded. But government will not continue to subsidize individuals or particular business interests where real need cannot be demonstrated.

And while we will reduce some subsidies to regional and local governments, we will at the same time convert a number of categorical grant programs into block grants to reduce wasteful administrative overhead and to give local government entities and States more flexibility and control. We call for an end to duplication in Federal programs and reform of those

which are not cost effective.

Restore Programs to States and Private Sector

Already, some have protested that there must be no reduction in aid to schools. Let me point out that Federal aid to education amounts to only eight percent of the total educational funding. For this eight percent the Federal Government has insisted on a tremendously disproportionate share of control over our schools. Whatever reductions we've proposed in that eight percent will amount to very little in the total cost of education. They will, however, restore more authority to States and local school districts.

Historically the American people have supported by voluntary contributions more artistic and cultural activities than all the other countries in the world put together. I wholeheartedly support this approach and believe that Americans will continue their generosity. Therefore, I am proposing a savings of $85 million in the Federal subsidies now going to the arts and humanities.

There are a number of subsidies to business and industry that I believe are unnecessary. Not because the activities being subsidized aren't of value but because the marketplace contains incentives enough to warrant continuing these activities without a government subsidy. One such subsidy is the Department of Energy's synthetic fuels program. We will continue support of research leading to development of new technologies and more independence from foreign oil, but we can save at least $3.2 billion by leaving to private industry the building of plants to make liquid or gas fuels from coal.

We are asking that another major industry, business subsidy I should say, the Export-Import Bank loan authority, be reduced by one-third in 1982. We are doing this because the primary beneficiaries of tax payer funds in this case are the exporting companies themselves — most of them profitable corporations.

High Cost of Borrowing

This brings me to a number of other lending programs in which Government makes low-interest loans. Some of them at an interest rate as low as 2 percent. What has not been very well understood is that the Treasury Department has no money of its own. It has to go into the private capital market and borrow the money. So in this time of excessive interest rates the government finds itself borrowing at an interest rate several times as high as the interest rate it gets back from those it lends the money to. This difference, of course, is paid by your constituents, the taxpayers. They get hit again if they try to borrow because Government borrowing contributes to raising all interest rates.

By terminating the Economic Development Administration we can save hundreds of millions of dollars in 1982 and

billions more over the next few years. There is a lack of consistent and convincing evidence that EDA and its Regional Commissions have been effective in creating new jobs. They have been effective in creating an array of planners, grantsmen and professional middlemen. We believe we can do better just by the expansion of the economy and the job creation which will come from our economic program.

Wefare and Unemployment Programs

The Food Stamp program will be restored to its original purpose, to assist those without resources to purchase sufficient nutritional food. We will, however, save $1.8 billion in fiscal year 1982 by removing from eligibility those who are not in real need or who are abusing the program.

Even with this reduction, the program will be budgeted for more than $10 billion.

We will tighten welfare and give more attention to outside sources of income when determining the amount of welfare an individual is allowed. This plus strong and effective work requirements will save $520 million in the next year.

I stated a moment ago our intention to keep the school breakfast and lunch programs for those in true need. But by cutting back on meals for children of families who can afford to pay, the savings will be $1.6 billion in fiscal year 1982.

Let me just touch on a few other areas which are typical of the kinds of reductions we have included in this economic package. The Trade Adjustment Assistance program provides benefits for workers who are unemployed when foreign imports reduce the market for various American products causing shutdown of plants and layoff of workers. The purpose is to help these workers find jobs in growing sectors of our economy. There is nothing wrong with that. But because these benefits are paid out on top of normal unemployment benefits, we wind up paying greater benefits to those who lose their jobs because of foreign competition than we do to their friends and neighbors who are laid off due to domestic competition. Anyone must agree that this is unfair. Putting these two programs on the same footing will save $1.15 billion in just 1 year.

Federal Regulation Burden

Earlier I made mention of changing categorical grants to States and local governments into block grants. We know, of course, that the categorical grant programs burden local and State governments with a mass of Federal regulations and Federal paperwork.

Ineffective targeting, wasteful administrative overhead — all can be eliminated by shifting the resources and decision-making authority to local and State government. This will also consolidate programs which are scattered throughout the Federal

bureaucracy, bringing government closer to the people and saving $23.9 billion over the next 5 years.

Our program for economic renewal deals with a number of programs which at present are not cost-effective. An example is Medicaid. Right now Washington provides the States with unlimited matching payments for their expenditures. At the same time we here in Washington pretty much dictate how the States are going to manage these programs. We want to put a cap on how much the Federal Government will contribute but at the same time allow the States much more flexibility in managing and structuring the programs. I know from our experience in California that such flexibility could have led to far more cost-effective reforms. This will bring a savings of $1 billion next year.

Space and Postal Agencies

The space program has been and is important to America and we plan to continue it. We believe, however, that a reordering of priorities to focus on the most important and cost-effective NASA programs can result in a savings of a quarter of a billion dollars.

Coming down from space to the mailbox — the Postal Service has been consistently unable to live within its operating budget. It is still dependent on large Federal subsidies. We propose reducing those subsidies by $632 million in 1982 to press the Postal Service into becoming more effective. In subsequent years, the savings will continue to add up.

The Economic Regulatory Administration in the Department of Energy has programs to force companies to convert to specific fuels. It has the authority to administer a gas rationing plan, and prior to decontrol it ran the oil price control program. With these and other regulations gone we can save several hundreds of millions of dollars over the next few years.

Defense Spending

I'm sure there is one department you've been waiting for me to mention, the Department of Defense. It is the only department in our entire program that will actually be increased over the present budgeted figure.

But even here there was no exemption. The Department of Defense came up with a number of cuts which reduced the budget increase needed to restore our military balance. These measures will save $2.9 billion in 1982 outlays and by 1986 a total of $28.2 billion will have been saved. Perhaps I should say will have been made available for the necessary things that we must do. The aim will be to provide the most effective defense for the lowest possible cost.

I believe that my duty as President requires that I recommend increases in defense spending over the coming years.

I know that you are aware but I think it bears saying again that since 1970, the

Soviet Union has invested $300 billion more in its military forces than we have. As a result of its massive military buildup, the Soviets have made a significant numerical advantage in strategic nuclear delivery systems, tactical aircraft, submarines, artillery and antiaircraft defense. To allow this imbalance to continue is a threat to our national security.

Notwithstanding our economic straits, making the financial changes beginning now is far less costly than waiting and having to attempt a crash program several years from now.

We remain committed to the goal of arms limitation through negotiation. I hope we can persuade our adversaries to come to realistic balanced and verifiable agreements.

But, as we negotiate, our security must be fully protected by a balanced and realistic defense program.

Let me say a word here about the general problem of waste and fraud in the Federal Government. One government estimate indicated that fraud alone may account for anywhere from 1 to 10 percent — as much as $25 billion — of Federal expenditures for social programs. If the tax dollars that are wasted or mismanaged are added to this fraud total, the staggering dimensions of this problem begin to emerge.

New Inspectors General

The Office of Management and Budget is now putting together an interagency task force to attack waste and fraud. We are also planning to appoint as Inspectors General highly trained professionals who will spare no effort to do this job.

No administration can promise to immediately stop a trend that has grown in recent years as quickly as Government expenditures themselves. But let me say this: waste and fraud in the Federal budget is exactly what I have called it before — an unrelenting national scandal — a scandal we are bound and determined to do something about.

Tax Proposals

Marching in lockstep with the whole program of reductions in spending is the equally important program of reduced tax rates. Both are essential if we are to have economic recovery. It's time to create new jobs. To build and rebuild industry, and to give the American people room to do what they do best. And that can only be done with a tax program which provides incentive to increase productivity for both workers and industry.

Our proposal is for a 10-percent across-the-board cut every year for three years in the tax rates for all individual income taxpayers, making a total cut in tax rates of 30 percent. This 3-year reduction will also apply to the tax on unearned income, leading toward an eventual elimination of the present differential between the

tax on earned and unearned income.

I would have hoped that we could be retroactive with this, but as it stands the effective starting date for these 10-percent personal income tax rate reductions will be called for as of July 1st of this year.

Again, let me remind you that while this 30 percent reduction will leave the taxpayers with $500 billion more in their pockets over the next five years, it's actually only a reduction in the tax increase already built into the system.

Unlike some past "tax reforms," this is not merely a shift of wealth between different sets of taxpayers. This proposal for an equal reduction in everyone's tax rates will expand our national prosperity, enlarge national incomes, and increase opportunities for all Americans.

Some will argue, I know, that reducing tax rates now will be inflationary. A solid body of economic experts does not agree. And tax cuts adopted over the past three-fourths of a century indicate these economic experts are right. They will not be inflationary. I have had advice that in 1985 our real production of goods and services will grow by 20 percent and will be $300 billion higher than it is today. The average worker's wage will rise (in real purchasing power) 8 percent, and this is in after-tax dollars and this, of course, is predicated on a complete program of tax cuts and spending reductions being implemented.

The other part of the tax package is aimed directly at providing business and industry with the capital needed to modernize and engage in more research and development. This will involve an increase in depreciation allowances, and this part of our tax proposal will be retroactive to January 1st.

The present depreciation system is obsolete, needlessly complex, and is economically counterproductive. Very simply, it bases the depreciation of plant, machinery, vehicles, and tools on their original cost with no recognition of how inflation has increased their replacement cost. We are proposing a much shorter write-off time than is presently allowed: a 5-year write-off for machinery; 3 years for vehicles and trucks; and a 10-year write-off for plant.

In fiscal year 1982 under this plan business would acquire nearly $10 billion for investment. By 1985 the figure would be nearly $45 billion. These changes are essential to provide the new investment which is needed to create millions of new jobs between now and 1985 and to make America competitive once again in the world market.

These won't be make-work jobs, they are productive jobs, jobs with a future.

I'm well aware that there are many other desirable and needed tax changes such as indexing the income tax brackets to protect taxpayers against inflation; the unjust discrimination against married couples if both are working and earning; tuition tax credits; the unfairness of the inheritance tax, especially to the family-owned farm and the family-owned business, and a num-

ber of others. But our program for economic recovery is so urgently needed to begin to bring down inflation that I am asking you to act on this plan first and with great urgency. Then I pledge I will join with you in seeking these additional tax changes at the earliest date possible.

Overregulation

American society experienced a virtual explosion in Government regulation during the past decade. Between 1970 and 1979, expenditures for the major regulatory agencies quadrupled, the number of pages published annually in the *Federal Register* nearly tripled, and the number of pages in the *Code of Federal Regulations* increased by nearly two-thirds.

The result has been higher prices, higher unemployment, and lower productivity growth. Overregulation causes small and independent businessmen and women, as well as large businesses, to defer or terminate plans for expansion, and since they are responsible for most of our new jobs, those new jobs just aren't created.

We have no intention of dismantling the regulatory agencies — especially those necessary to protect [the] environment and to ensure the public health and safety. However, we must come to grips with inefficient and burdensome regulations — eliminate those we can and reform the others.

I have asked Vice President Bush to head a Cabinet-level Task Force on Regulatory Relief. Second, I asked each member of my Cabinet to postpone the effective dates of the hundreds of regulations which have not yet been implemented. Third, in coordination with the task force, many of the agency heads have already taken prompt action to review and rescind existing burdensome regulations. Finally, just yesterday, I signed an executive order that for the first time provides for effective and coordinated management of the regulatory process.

Much has been accomplished, but it is only a beginning. We will eliminate those regulations that are unproductive and unnecessary by executive order, where possible, and cooperate fully with you on those that require legislation.

The final aspect of our plan requires a national monetary policy which does not allow money growth to increase consistently faster than the growth of goods and services. In order to curb inflation, we need to slow the growth in our money supply.

We fully recognize the independence of the Federal Reserve System and will do nothing to interfere with or undermine that independence. We will consult regularly with the Federal Reserve Board on all aspects of our economic program and will vigorously pursue budget policies that will make their job easier in reducing monetary growth.

A successful program to achieve stable and moderate growth patterns in the money supply will keep both inflation and interest rates down and restore vigor to our financial institutions and markets.

'Economic Recovery' Proposed

This, then, is our proposal. "America's New Beginning: A Program for Economic Recovery." I don't want it to be simply the plan of my Administration — I'm here tonight to ask you to join me in making it our plan. [Applause, members rising]

I should have arranged to quit right there.

Well, together we can embark on this road, not to make things easy, but to make things better.

Our social, political and cultural as well as our economic institutions can no longer absorb the repeated shocks that have been dealt them over the past decades.

Can we do the job? The answer is yes, but we must begin now.

We are in control here. There is nothing wrong with America that we can't fix. I'm sure there will be some who will raise the familiar old cry, "Don't touch my program — cut somewhere else."

I hope I've made it plain that our approach has been evenhanded; that only the programs for the truly deserving needy remain untouched.

The question is, are we simply going to go down the same path we've gone down before — carving out one special program here, another special program there. I don't think that is what the American people expect of us. More important, I don't think that is what they want. They are ready to return to the source of our strength.

The substance and prosperity of our Nation is built by wages brought home from the factories and the mills, the farms and the shops. They are the services provided in 10,000 corners of America; the interest on the thrift of our people and the returns for their risk-taking. The produc-

tion of America is the possession of those who build, serve, create and produce.

For too long now, we've removed from our people the decisions on how to dispose of what they created. We have strayed from first principles. We must alter our course.

The taxing power of government must be used to provide revenues for legitimate government purposes. It must not be used to regulate the economy or bring about social change. We've tried that and surely must be able to see it doesn't work.

Spending by Government must be limited to those functions which are the proper province of Government. We can no longer afford things simply because we think of them.

Next year we can reduce the budget by $41.4 billion, without harm to Government's legitimate purposes or to our responsibility to all who need our benevolence. This, plus the reduction in tax rates, will help bring an end to inflation.

In the health and social services area alone the plan we are proposing will substantially reduce the need for 465 pages of law, 1,400 pages of regulations, 5,000 Federal employees who presently administer 7,600 separate grants in about 25,000 separate locations. Over 7 million man and woman hours of work by State and local officials are required to fill out government forms.

I would direct a question to those who have indicated already an unwillingness to accept such a plan. Have they an alternative which offers a greater chance of balancing the budget, reducing and eliminating inflation, stimulating the creation of jobs, and reducing the tax burden? And if they haven't, are they suggesting we can continue on the present course without coming to a day of reckoning?

If we don't do this, inflation and the growing tax burden will put an end to everything we believe in and our dreams for the future. We don't have an option of living with inflation and its attendant tragedy, millions of productive people willing and able to work but unable to find a buyer for their work in the job market.

We have an alternative, and that is the program for economic recovery.

True, it will take time for the favorable effects of our proposal to be felt. So we must begin now.

The people are watching and waiting. They don't demand miracles. They do expect us to act. Let us act together.

Thank you and good night.

Reagan's Address on the Nation's Economy

Following is the text of President Reagan's Sept. 24, 1981, televised address to the nation reporting on the country's economic situation and re- *questing public support for further budget cuts and adjustments in Social Security payments.*

THE PRESIDENT: Good evening. Shortly after taking office I came before you to map out a four-part plan for national economic recovery: tax cuts to stimu-

late more growth and more jobs, spending cuts to put an end to continuing deficits and high inflation, regulatory relief to lift the heavy burden of government rules and paperwork, and, finally, a steady, consistent, monetary policy.

We've made strong, encouraging progress on all four fronts. The flood of new governmental regulations, for example, has been cut by more than a third. I was especially pleased when a bipartisan coalition of Republicans and Democrats enacted the biggest tax cuts and the greatest reduction in federal spending in our nation's history. Both will begin to take effect a week from today. These two bills would never have passed without your help. Your voices were heard in Washington and were heeded by those you've chosen to represent you in government. Yet, in recent weeks we've begun to hear a chorus of other voices protesting that we haven't had full economic recovery. These are the same voices that were raised against our program when it was first presented to Congress. Now that the first part of it has been passed, they declare it hasn't worked. Well, it hasn't. It doesn't start until a week from today.

Inflation Easing Up

There have been some bright spots in our economic performance these past few months. Inflation has fallen and pressures are easing on both food and fuel prices. More than a million more Americans are now at work than a year ago, and recently there has even been a small crack in interest rates. But let me be the first to say that our problems won't suddenly disappear next week, next month, or next year. We're just starting down a road that I believe will lead us out of the economic swamp we've been in for so long. It'll take time for the effect of the tax rate reductions to be felt in increased savings, productivity, and new jobs. It will also take time for the budget cuts to reduce the deficits which have brought us near runaway inflation and ruinous interest rates.

The important thing now is to hold to a firm, steady, course. Tonight I want to talk with you about the next steps that we must take on that course, additional reductions in federal spending that will help lower our interest rates, our inflation, and bring us closer to full economic recovery.

I know that high interest rates are punishing many of you, from the young family that wants to buy its first home to the farmer who needs a new truck or tractor. But all of us know that interest rates will only come down and stay down when government is no longer borrowing huge amounts of money to cover its deficits.

These deficits have been piling up every year and some people here in Washington just throw up their hands in despair. Maybe you'll remember that we were told in the spring of 1980 that the 1981 budget, the one we have now, would be balanced. Well, that budget, like so many in the past,

hemorrhaged badly and wound up in a sea of red ink.

More Cuts in Federal Spending

I have pledged that we shall not stand idly by and see that same thing happen again. When I presented our economic recovery program to Congress, I said we were aiming to cut the deficit steadily to reach a balance by 1984.

The budget bill that I signed this summer cut $35 billion from the 1982 budget and slowed the growth of spending by $130 billion over the next three years. We cut the government's rate of growth nearly in half.

Now we must move on to a second round of budget savings — to keep us on the road to a balanced budget.

Our immediate challenge is to hold down the deficit in the fiscal year that begins next week. A number of threats are now appearing that will drive the deficit upward if we fail to act. For example, in the euphoria just after our budget bill was approved this summer, we didn't point out immediately as we should that while we did get most of what we'd asked for, most isn't all. Some of the savings in our proposal were not approved; and since then, the Congress has taken actions that could add even more to the cost of government.

The result is that without further reductions, our deficit for 1982 will be increased by some $16 billion. The estimated deficit for '83 will be increased proportionately. And without further cuts, we can't achieve our goal of a balanced budget by 1984.

Now, it would be easy to sit back and say, "Well, it will take longer than we thought. We got most of what we proposed, so let's stop there." But that's not good enough.

Must 'Face Up' to Cuts

In meeting to discuss this problem a few days ago, Senator Pete Domenici of New Mexico, Chairman of the Senate Budget Committee, recalled the words of that great heavy-weight champion and great American Joe Louis just before he stepped into the ring against Billy Conn. There had been some speculation that Billy might be able to avoid Joe's lethal right hand. Joe said, "Well, he can run but he can't hide."

Senator Domenici said to me, "That's just what we're facing on runaway federal spending. We can try to run from it but we can't hide. We have to face up to it."

He's right, of course. In the last few decades we started down a road that led to a massive explosion in federal spending. It took about 170 years for the federal budget to reach $100 billion. That was in 1962. It took only eight years to reach the $200 billion mark and only five more to make it $300 billion. And in the next five we nearly doubled that.

It would be one thing if we'd been able to pay for all the things government de-

cided to do, but we've only balanced the budget once in the last 20 years.

$1 Trillion National Debt

In just the past decade, our national debt has more than doubled. And in the next few days it will pass the trillion dollar mark. One trillion dollars of debt — if we as a nation needed a warning, let that be it.

Our interest payments on the debt alone are now running more than $96 million a year. That's more than the total combined profits last year of the 500 biggest companies in the country; or to put it another way, Washington spends more on interest than on all of its education, nutrition and medical programs combined.

In the past, there have been several methods used to fund some of our social experiments. One was to take it away from national defense. From being the strongest nation on earth in the post World War II years, we've steadily declined, while the Soviet Union engaged in the most massive military buildup the world has ever seen.

Now, with all our economic problems, we're forced to try to catch up so that we can preserve the peace. Government's first responsibility is national security and we're determined to meet that responsibility. Indeed, we have no choice.

Well, what all of this is leading up to is — what do we plan to do? Last week I met with the Cabinet to take up this matter. I'm proud to say there was no hand-wringing, no pleading to avoid further budget cuts. We all agreed that the "tax and tax, spend and spend," policies of the past few decades lead only to economic disaster. Our government must return to the tradition of living within our means and must do it now. We asked ourselves two questions — and answered them: "If not us — who? If not now — when?"

Let me talk with you now about the specific ways that I believe we ought to achieve additional savings — savings of some $16 billion in 1982 and a total of $80 billion when spread over the next three years. I recognize that many in Congress may have other alternatives and I welcome a dialogue with them. But let there be no mistake: We have no choice but to continue down the road toward a balanced budget — a budget that will keep us strong at home and secure overseas. And let me be clear that this cannot be the last round of cuts. Holding down spending must be a continuing battle for several years to come.

Here is what I propose. First, I'm asking Congress to reduce the 1982 appropriation for most government agencies and programs by 12 percent. This will save $17.5 billion over the next several years. Absorbing these reductions will not be easy, but duplication, excess, waste and overhead is still far too great and can be trimmed further.

Defense Budget to be Cut

No one in the meeting asked to be

exempt from belt-tightening. Over the next three years, the increase we had originally planned in the defense budget will be cut by $13 billion. I'll confess, I was reluctant about this because of the long way we have to go before the dangerous window of vulnerability confronting us will be appreciably narrowed. But the Secretary of Defense assured me that he can meet our critical needs in spite of this cut.

Reduce Federal Staff

Second, to achieve further economies, we'll shrink the size of the non-defense payroll over the next three years by some 6½ percent, some 75,000 employees. Much of this will be attained by not replacing those who retire or leave. There will, however, be some reductions in force simply because we're reducing our administrative overhead. I intend to set the example here by reducing the size of the White House staff and the staff of the Executive Office of the President.

As a third step, we propose to dismantle two Cabinet departments, Energy and Education. Both secretaries are wholly in accord with this. Some of the activities in both of these departments will, of course, be continued either independently or in other areas of government. There's only one way to shrink the size and cost of big government and that is by eliminating agencies that are not needed and are getting in the way of a solution. Now, we don't need an Energy Department to solve our basic energy problem. As long as we let the forces of the marketplace work without undue interference, the ingenuity of consumers, business, producers and inventors will do that for us.

Similarly, education is the principal responsibility of local school systems, teachers, parents, citizen boards and state governments. By eliminating the department of education less than two years after it was created, we cannot only reduce the budget, but ensure that local needs and preferences rather than the wishes of Washington determine the education of our children. We also plan the elimination of a few smaller agencies and a number of boards and commissions, some of which have fallen into disuse or which are not being duplicated.

Loan Guarantee Reductions

Fourth, we intend to make reductions of some $20 billion in federal loan guarantees. These guarantees are not funds that the government spends directly. They're funds that are loaned in the private market and insured by government at subsidized rates. Federal loan guarantees have become a form of back door, uncontrolled borrowing that prevent many small businesses that aren't subsidized from obtaining financing of their own. They are also a major factor in driving up interest rates. It's time we brought this practice under control.

Welfare and Entitlement Reform

Fifth, I intend to forward to Congress this fall a new package of entitlement and welfare reform measures, outside Social Security, to save nearly $27 billion over the next three years. In the past two decades we've created hundreds of new programs to provide personal assistance. Many of these programs may have come from a good heart but not all have come from a clear head. And the costs have been staggering.

In 1955 these programs cost $8 billion. By 1965 the cost was $79 billion. Next year it will be $188 billion. Let there be no confusion on this score. Benefits for the needy will be protected, but the black market in food stamps must be stopped, the abuse and fraud by beneficiaries and providers alike cannot be tolerated, provision of school loans and meal subsidies to the affluent can no longer be afforded.

In California when I was Governor and embarked upon welfare reform, there were screams from those who claimed that we intended to victimize the needy. But in a little over three years we saved the taxpayer some $2 billion at the same time we were able to increase the grants for the deserving and truly needy by an average of more than 40 percent. It was the first cost of living increase they'd received in 13 years. I believe progress can also be made at the national level.

We can be compassionate about human needs without being complacent about budget extravagance.

Tax Reform

Sixth, I will soon urge Congress to enact new proposals to eliminate abuses and obsolete incentives in the tax code. The Treasury Department believes that the deficit can be reduced by $3.0 billion next year and $22 billion over the next three years with prompt enactment of these measures.

Now that we've provided the greatest incentives for saving, investment, work and productivity ever proposed, we must also ensure that taxes due the government are collected and that a fair share of the burden is borne by all.

Finally, I am renewing my plea to Congress to approve my proposals for user fees — proposals first suggested last spring, but which have been neglected since.

When the federal government provides a service directly to a particular industry or to a group of citizens, I believe that those who receive benefits should bear the cost. For example, this next year the federal government will spend $525 million to maintain river harbors, channels, locks, and dams for the barge and maritime industries. Yacht owners, commercial vessels and the airlines will receive services worth $2.8 billion from Uncle Sam.

My spring budget proposals included legislation that would authorize the federal government to recover a total of $980 million from the users of these services through fees. Now, that's only a third of the $3.3 billion it will cost the government to provide those same services.

None of these steps will be easy. We're going through a period of difficult and painful readjustment. I know that we're asking for sacrifices from virtually all of you. But there is no alternative. Some of those who oppose this plan have participated over the years in the extravagance that has brought us inflation, unemployment, high interest rates and an intolerable debt. I grant they were well intentioned but their costly reforms didn't eliminate poverty or raise welfare recipients from dependence to self-sufficiency, independence and dignity. Yet in their objections to what we've proposed they offer only what we know has been tried before and failed.

I believe we've chosen a path that leads to an America at work, to fiscal sanity, to lower taxes and less inflation. I believe our plan for recovery is sound and it will work.

Tonight I'm asking all of you who joined in this crusade to save our economy to help again. To let your representatives know that you'll support them in making the hard decisions to further reduce the cost and size of government.

Social Security

Now, if you'll permit me, I'd like to turn to another subject which I know has many of you very concerned and even frightened. This is an issue apart from the economic reform package that we've just been discussing, but I feel I must clear the air. There has been a great deal of misinformation and for that matter pure demagoguery on the subject of Social Security.

During the campaign I called attention to the fact that Social Security had both a short and a long range fiscal problem. I pledged my best to restore it to fiscal responsibility without in any way reducing or eliminating existing benefits for those now dependent on it.

To all of you listening and particularly those of you now receiving Social Security, I ask you to listen very carefully: First to what threatens the integrity of Social Security and then to a possible solution.

Some thirty years ago, there were 16 people working and paying the Social Security payroll tax for every one retiree. Today that ratio has changed to only 3.2 workers paying in for each beneficiary.

For many years we've known that an actuarial imbalance existed and that the program faced an unfunded liability of several trillion dollars.

Now, the short range problem is much closer than that. The Social Security retirement fund has been paying out billions of dollars more each year than it takes in and it could run out of money before the end of 1982 unless something is done.

Some of our critics claim new figures reveal a cushion of several billions of dollars which will carry the program beyond 1982. I'm sure it's only a coincidence that 1982 is an election year.

Appendix

The cushion they speak of is borrowing from the Medicare fund and the disability fund. Of course doing this would only postpone the day of reckoning. Alice Rivlin of the Congressional Budget Office told a congressional committee the day before yesterday that such borrowing might carry us to 1990, but then we'd face the same problem. And as she put it, we'd have to cut benefits or raise the payroll tax. Well, we're not going to cut benefits and the payroll tax is already being raised.

In 1977, Congress passed the largest tax increase in our history. It called for a payroll tax increase in January of 1982, another in 1985, and again in 1986 and in 1990.

When that law was passed we were told it made Social Security safe until the year 2030. But we're running out of money 48 years short of 2030.

For the nation's work force, the Social Security tax is already the biggest tax they pay. In 1935 we were told the tax would never be greater than 2% of the first $3,000 of earnings. It is presently 13.3% of the first $29,700 and the scheduled increases will take it to 15.3% of the first $60,600. And that's when Mrs. Rivlin says we would need an additional increase.

Some have suggested reducing benefits. Others propose an income tax on benefits, or that the retirement age should be moved back to age 68 and there are some who would simply fund Social Security out of general tax funds as welfare is funded. I believe there are better solutions. I am asking the Congress to restore the minimum benefit for current beneficiaries with low incomes. It was never our intention to take this support away from those who truly need it.

Possible Solutions

There is, however, a sizable percentage of recipients who are adequately provided for by pensions or other income and should not be added to the financial burden of Social Security.

The same situation prevails with regard to disability payments. No one will deny our obligation to those with legitimate claims. But there's widespread abuse of the system which should not be allowed to continue.

Since 1962, early retirement has been allowed at age 62 with 80 percent of full benefits. In our proposal we ask that early retirees in the future receive 55 percent of the total benefit, but, and this is most important, those early retirees would only have to work an additional 20 months to be eligible for the 80 percent payment. I don't believe very many of you were aware of that part of our proposal.

The only change we proposed for those already receiving Social Security had to do with the annual cost of living adjustment. Now, those adjustments are made on July 1st each year, a hangover from the days when the fiscal year began in July. We proposed a one-time delay in making that adjustment, postponing it for three months until October 1st. From then on it would continue to be made every 12 months. That one time delay would not lower your existing benefits but would, on the average, reduce your increase by about $86 one time next year.

By making these few changes, we would have solved the short and long range problems of Social Security funding once and for all. In addition, we could have cancelled the increases in the payroll tax by 1985. To a young person just starting in the work force, the savings from cancelling those increases would, on the average, amount to $33,000 by the time he or she reached retirement, and compound interest, add that, and it makes a tiny nest egg to add to the Social Security benefits.

However, let me point out, our feet were never imbedded in concrete on this proposal. We hoped it could be a starting point for a bipartisan solution to the problem. We were ready to listen to alternatives and other ideas which might improve on or replace our proposals. But, the majority leadership in the House of Representatives has refused to join in any such cooperative effort.

I therefore am asking, as I said, for restoration of the minimum benefit and for interfund borrowing as a temporary measure to give us time to seek a permanent solution. To remove Social Security once and for all from politics I am also asking Speaker Tip O'Neill of the House of Representatives and Majority Leader in the Senate Howard Baker to each appoint five members and I will appoint five to a task force which will review all the options and come up with a plan that assures the fiscal integrity of Social Security and that Social Security recipients will continue to receive their full benefits.

I cannot and will not stand by and see financial hardship imposed on the more than 36 million senior citizens who have worked and served this nation throughout their lives. They deserve better from us.

Well now, in conclusion, let me return to the principal purpose of this message, the budget and the imperative need for all of us to ask less of government, to help to return to spending no more than we take in, to end the deficits and bring down interest rates that otherwise can destroy what we've been building here for two centuries.

Requests Volunteer Help

I know that we're asking for economies in many areas and programs that were started with the best of intentions and the dedication to a worthwhile cause or purpose, but I know also that some of those programs have not succeeded in their purpose. Others have proven too costly, benefiting those who administer them rather than those who were the intended beneficiaries. This doesn't mean we should discontinue trying to help where help is needed. Government must continue to do its share. But I ask all of you, as private citizens, to join this effort too. As a people we have a proud tradition of generosity.

More than a century ago a Frenchman came to America and later wrote a book for his countrymen telling them what he had seen here. He told them that in America when a citizen saw a problem that needed solving he would cross the street and talk to a neighbor about it and the first thing you know a committee would be formed and before long the problem would be solved. And then he added, "You may not believe this, but not a single bureaucrat would ever have been involved." ... I believe the spirit of voluntarism still lives in America. We see examples of it on every hand, the community charity drive, support of hospitals and all manner of nonprofit institutions, the rallying around whenever disaster or tragedy strikes.

The truth is we've let government take away many things we once considered were really ours to do voluntarily out of the goodness of our hearts and a sense of community pride and neighborliness. I believe many of you want to do those things again, want to be involved if only someone will ask you or offer the opportunity. Well, we intend to make that offer.

We're launching a nationwide effort to encourage our citizens to join with us in finding where need exists and then to organize volunteer programs to meet that need. We've already set the wheels of such a volunteer effort in motion.

As Tom Paine said 200 years ago, "We have it within our power to begin the world over again."

What are we waiting for?

God bless you, and good night.

Reagan's Statement on Strategic Arms

Following is the text of President Reagan's Oct. 2, 1981, announcement of his strategic arms policy.

As President, it's my solemn duty to insure America's national security while vigorously pursuing every path to peace. Toward this end I've repeatedly pledged to halt the decline in America's military strength and restore that margin of safety needed for the protection of the American people and the maintenance of peace.

During the last several years a weakening in our security posture has been particularly noticeable in our strategic nuclear forces — the very foundation of our strategy for deterring foreign attacks.

A window of vulnerability is opening, one that would jeopardize not just our hopes for serious productive arms negotiations, but our hopes for peace and freedom. Shortly after taking office, I directed the Secretary of Defense to review our strategy for deterrence and to evaluate the adequacy of the forces now available for carrying out that strategy. He and his colleagues in consultation with many leaders outside the executive branch have done that job well. And after one of the most complex, thorough, and carefully conducted processes in memory, I am announcing today a plan to revitalize our strategic forces and maintain America's ability to keep the peace well into the next century.

Our plan is a comprehensive one. It will strengthen and modernize the strategic triad of land-based missiles, sea-based missiles and bombers. It will end longstanding delays in some of these programs and introduce new elements into others and just as important, it will improve communications and control systems that are vital to these strategic forces.

Three Objectives

This program will achieve three objectives. It will act as a deterrent against any Soviet actions directed against the American people or our allies. It will provide us with the capability to respond at reasonable cost and within adequate time to any further growth in Soviet forces. It will signal our resolve to maintain the strategic balance and this is the keystone to any genuine arms reduction agreement with the Soviets.

Let me point out here that this is a strategic program that America can afford. It fits within the revised fiscal guidelines for the Department of Defense that I announced last week. And during the next five years, the entire cost of maintaining and rebuilding our strategic forces will take less than 15 percent of our defense expenditures. This is considerably below the 20 percent of our defense budget spent on strategic arms during the 1960s when we constructed many of the forces that exist today. It is fair to say that this program will enable us to modernize our strategic forces, and at the same time meet our many other commitments as a nation.

Five Main Features

Now, let me outline the five main features of our program. First, I have directed the Secretary of Defense to revitalize our bomber forces by constructing and deploying some 100 B-1 bombers as soon as possible, while continuing to deploy cruise missiles on existing bombers.

We will also develop an advanced bomber with stealth characteristics for the 1990s.

Second, I have ordered the strengthening and expansion of our sea-based forces. We will continue the construction of Trident submarines at a steady rate. We will develop a larger and more accurate sea-based ballistic missile. We will also deploy nuclear cruise missiles in some existing submarines.

Third, I've ordered completion of the MX missiles. We have decided, however, not to deploy the MX in the racetrack shelters proposed by the previous administration or in any other scheme for multiple protective shelters. We will not deploy 20 missiles in 4600 holes nor will we deploy 100 missiles in 1000 holes.

We have concluded that these basing schemes would be just as vulnerable as the existing minuteman silos. The operative factor here is this: No matter how many shelters we might build, the Soviets can build more missiles, more quickly, and just as cheaply.

Instead, we will complete the MX missile which is much more powerful and accurate than our current minuteman missiles, and we will deploy a limited number of the MX missiles in existing silos as soon possible.

At the same time, we will pursue three promising long-term options for basing the MX missile and choose among them by 1984 so that we can proceed promptly with full deployment.

Fourth, I have directed the Secretary of Defense to strengthen and rebuild our communications and control system — a much neglected factor in our strategic deterrent. I consider this decision to improve our communications and control system as important as any of the other decisions announced today.

This system must be foolproof in case of any foreign attack. Finally, I have directed that we end our long neglect of strategic defenses. This will include cooperation with Canada on improving North American air surveillance in defense and as part of this effort I have also directed that we devote greater resources to improving our civil defenses.

This plan is balanced and carefully considered — a plan that will meet our vital security needs and strengthen our hopes to peace. It's my hope that this program will prevent our adversaries from making the mistake others have made and deeply regretted in the past. The mistake of underestimating the resolve and the will of the American people to keep their freedom and protect their homeland and their allies.

Now, I can only remain here for a few minutes. And I will do so for just a few questions that might deal with the statement or with policy. But for all the technical matters, I am going to turn you over to Secretary Cap Weinberger.

Questions from Reporters

Q: On that, would we be ready to use these new systems as bargaining chips in arms talks with the Soviets?

P: Well, I think everything having to do with arms, Helen, would have to be on the table.

Q: Mr. President, when exactly is the "window of vulnerability"? We heard yesterday the suggestion that it exists now. Earlier this morning a defense official indicated that it was not until '84 or '87. Are we facing it right now?

P: Well, I think in some areas we are, yes. I think the imbalance of forces, for example, in the Western front — in the NATO line, we are vastly outdistanced there. I think the fact that right now they have a superiority at sea.

Q: Mr. President, if there is or will be a "window of vulnerability", why is the MX any less vulnerable if it's in silos the location of which the Soviets presumably already know unless we were going to launch on their attack?

P: I don't know but what maybe you haven't gotten into the area that I'm going to turn over to the Secretary of Defense. I could say this. The plan also includes the hardening of silos so that they are protected against nuclear attack. Now, we know that is not permanent. We know that they can then improve their accuracy, their power, and their ability, but it would take them some time to do that and they would have to devote a decided effort to doing that.

Q: So this is a way then of buying time, is it?

P: In a way of narrowing that "window of vulnerability."

Q: Mr. President, some people already are saying that your decisions are based to a large extent on politics, domestic politics so let me ask you about two points. One, that you never considered the racetrack system because it was proposed by Jimmy Carter and you didn't want to have anything to do with something that he had

proposed. And, two, that you are not basing the MX in Utah and Nevada because of opposition from the Mormon church and your good friend Senator Paul Laxalt.

P: Sam, I can tell you now, no, the entire study of the basis for basing — I got tangled up there with two words that sounded so much alike — the MX missile was a very thorough study of all those proposals that had been made and, actually, I could refer you to the Town's Commission, their study and their report that we would not have an invulnerable missile basing by doing that. That all they would have to do is increase the number of targeted warheads on that particular area and take out the whole area. And, while it would force

them to build additional missiles, we would be just as vulnerable as we are in the present Minutemen.

Q: Laxalt didn't persuade you, sir?

P: No, no.

Q: Mr. President, your predecessor killed the B-1 manned bomber because he said it couldn't penetrate Soviet air defenses. The Soviets can make a lot of progress in radar between now and 1986. Can you guarantee that the B-1 could penetrate Soviet air defenses and is it the best plane as a cruise missile launch platform?

P: I think again — you are getting — I think that my few minutes are up and I am going to turn that question over to Cap. I know the answer to it, but I do believe that

you are getting in to the kind of questions that he is properly —

Q: Could you tell us why you decided to build the B-1 as opposed to your predecessors' decision not to build it? Do you think it can penetrate Soviet air space?

P: We have to have it because between the aging B-52 and the bomber we are developing, a newer bomber, there is too long a time gap in there. It would leave us a lengthy, vulnerable period. And the B-1 is designed not just to fill that gap, but it will then have a cruise missile-carrying capacity later in which it will still be worth the cost of building and worth having.

Now, I am going to turn it over to Cap here for the rest of the questions.

President Reagan's 1982 State of the Union Address

Following is the Congressional Record *text of President Reagan's State of the Union address to a joint session of Congress Jan. 26, 1982.*

THE PRESIDENT: Mr. Speaker, Mr. President, distinguished Members of the Congress, honored guests, and fellow citizens.

Today marks my first State of the Union address to you, a constitutional duty as old as our Republic itself.

President Washington began this tradition in 1790 after reminding the Nation that the destiny of self-government and the preservation of the sacred fire of liberty is "finally staked on the experiment entrusted to the hands of the American people." For our friends in the press, who place a high premium on accuracy, let me say: I did not actually hear George Washington say that, but it is a matter of historic record.

But from this podium, Winston Churchill asked the free world to stand together against the onslaught of aggression. Franklin Delano Roosevelt spoke of a day of infamy and summoned a nation to arms. Douglas MacArthur made an unforgettable farewell to a country he had loved and served so well. Dwight Eisenhower reminded us that peace was purchased only at the price of strength and John F. Kennedy spoke of the burden and glory that is freedom.

When I visited this Chamber last year as a newcomer to Washington, critical of past policies which I believe had failed, I proposed a new spirit of partnership between this Congress and this administration and between Washington and our State and local governments.

In forging this new partnership for America we could achieve the oldest hopes of our Republic — prosperity for our Nation, peace for the world, and the blessings of individual liberty for our children and, someday, for all of humanity.

It is my duty to report to you tonight on the progress that we have made in our relations with other nations, on the foundation we have carefully laid for our economic recovery and, finally, on a bold and spirited initiative that I believe can change the face of American Government and make it again the servant of the people.

The Economy — Past and Present

Seldom have the stakes been higher for America. What we do and say here will make all the difference to autoworkers in Detroit, lumberjacks in the Northwest, steelworkers in Steubenville who are in the unemployment lines, the black teenagers in Newark and Chicago, to hard-pressed farmers and small businessmen, and to millions of everyday Americans who harbor the simple wish of a safe and financially secure future for their children.

To understand the state of the Union, we must look not only at where we are and where we are going but where we have been. The situation at this time last year was truly ominous.

The last decade has seen a series of recessions. There was a recession in 1970, another in 1974, and again in the spring of 1980. Each time, unemployment increased and inflation soon turned up again. We coined the word "stagflation" to describe this.

Government's response to these recessions was to pump up the money supply and increase spending.

In the last 6 months of 1980, as an example, the money supply increased at the fastest rate in postwar history — 13 percent. Inflation remained in double digits and government spending increased at an annual rate of 17 percent. Interest rates reached a staggering 21½ percent. There were 8 million unemployed.

Late in 1981, we sank into the present recession, largely because continued high interest rates hurt the auto industry and construction. There was a drop in productivity and the already high unemployment increased.

This time, however, things are different. We have an economic program in place completely different from the artificial quick-fixes of the past. It calls for a reduction of the rate of increase in government spending, and already that rate has been cut nearly in half. But reduced spending alone is not enough. We have just implemented the first and smallest phase of a 3-year tax rate reduction plan designed to stimulate the economy and create jobs.

Already interest rates are down to 15¾ percent, but they must still go lower. Inflation is down from 12.4 to 8.9 percent, and for the month of December it was running at an annualized rate of 5.2 percent.

If we had not acted as we did, things would be far worse for all Americans than they are today. [Applause.]

Inflation, taxes and interest rates would all be higher.

An Era of American Renewal

A year ago, Americans' faith in their governmental process was steadily declining. Six out of ten Americans were saying they were pessimistic about their future.

A new kind of defeatism was heard. Some said our domestic problems were uncontrollable, that we had to learn to live with the seemingly endless cycle of high inflation and high unemployment.

There were also pessimistic predictions about the relationship between our administration and this Congress. It was said we could never work together. Well, those predictions were wrong.

The record is clear, and I believe history will remember this as an era of American renewal; remember this administration

as an administration of change, and remember this Congress as a Congress of destiny.

Together, we not only cut the increase in Government spending nearly in half, we brought about the largest tax reductions and the most sweeping changes in our tax structure since the beginning of this century. And because we indexed future taxes to the rate of inflation, we took away Government's built-in profit on inflation and its hidden incentive to grow larger at the expense of American workers.

Together, after 50 years of taking power away from the hands of the people in their States and local communities, we have started returning power and resources to them.

Together, we have cut the growth of new Federal regulations nearly in half. In 1981, there were 23,000 fewer pages in the *Federal Register*, which lists new regulations, than there were in 1980. [Applause.] By deregulating oil, we have come closer to achieving energy independence and helped bring down the costs of gasoline and heating fuel.

Together, we have created an effective Federal strike force to combat waste and fraud in Government. In just 6 months it has saved the taxpayers more than $2 billion — and it is only getting started.

Together, we have begun to mobilize the private sector — not to duplicate wasteful and discredited Government programs, but to bring thousands of Americans into a volunteer effort to help solve many of America's social problems.

Together, we have begun to restore that margin of military safety that insures peace. Our country's uniform is being worn once again with pride. [Applause.]

Together, we have made a New Beginning, but we have only begun.

Continued Recovery

No one pretends that the way ahead will be easy. In my Inaugural Address last year, I warned that the "ills we suffer have come upon us over several decades. They will not go away in days, weeks or months, but they will go away * * * because we as Americans have the capacity now, as we've had in the past, to do whatever needs to be done to preserve this last and greatest bastion of freedom." [Applause.]

The economy will face difficult moments in the months ahead. But, the program for economic recovery that is in place will pull the economy out of its slump and put us on the road to prosperity and stable growth by the latter half of this year.

That is why I can report to you tonight that in the near future the state of the Union and the economy will be better — much better — if we summon the strength to continue on the course we have charted.

And so the question: If the fundamentals are in place, what now?

Two things. First, we must understand what is happening at the moment to the economy. Our current problems are not the product of the recovery program that is only just now getting under way, as some would have you believe; they are the inheritance of decades of tax and tax, spend and spend.

Second, because our economic problems are deeply rooted and will not respond to quick political fixes we must stick to our carefully integrated plan for recovery. And that plan is based on four commonsense fundamentals: continued reduction of the growth in Federal spending; preserving the individual and business tax reductions that will stimulate saving and investment; removing unnecessary Federal regulations to spurt productivity; and maintaining a healthy dollar and a stable monetary policy — the latter a responsibility of the Federal Reserve System.

The only alternative being offered to this economic program is a return to the policies that gave us a trillion dollar debt, runaway inflation, runaway interest rates and unemployment.

The doubters would have us turn back the clock with tax increases that would offset the personal tax rate reductions already passed by this Congress.

Raise present taxes to cut future deficits, they tell us. Well, I don't believe we should buy that argument. There are too many imponderables for anyone to predict deficits or surpluses several years ahead with any degree of accuracy. The budget in place when I took office had been projected as balanced. It turned out to have one of the biggest deficits in history. Another example of the imponderables that can make deficit projections highly questionable: A change of only one percentage point in unemployment can alter a deficit up or down by some $25 billion.

As it now stands, our forecasts, which we are required by law to make will show major deficits, starting at less than $100 billion and declining, but still too high.

More important, we are making progress with the three keys to reducing deficits: economic growth, lower interest rates, and spending control. The policies we have in place will reduce the deficit steadily, surely and, in time, completely.

Taxes

Higher taxes would not mean lower deficits. If they did, how would we explain that tax revenues more than doubled just since 1976, yet in that same 6-year period we ran the largest series of deficits in our history? In 1980, tax revenues increased by $54 billion, and in 1980 we had one of our all-time biggest deficits.

Raising taxes won't balance the budget. It will encourage more Government spending and less private investment. Raising taxes will slow economic growth, reduce production, and destroy future jobs, making it more difficult for those without jobs to find them and more likely that those who now have jobs could lose them.

So I will not ask you to try to balance the budget on the backs of the American taxpayers. [Applause.]

I will seek no tax increases this year and I have no intention of retreating from our basic program of tax relief. [Applause.]

I promised the American people to bring their tax rates down and to keep them down, to provide them incentives to rebuild our economy, to save, to invest in America's future. I will stand by my word. Tonight I am urging the American people: Seize these new opportunities to produce, to save, to invest, and together we will make this economy a mighty engine of freedom, hope and prosperity again. [Applause.]

Federal Budget

Now, the budget deficit this year will exceed our earlier expectations. The recession did that. It lowered revenues and increased costs. To some extent, we are also victims of our own success. We have brought inflation down faster than we thought we could. [Applause.]

And in doing this, we have deprived Government of those hidden revenues that occur when inflation pushes people into higher income tax brackets. And the continued high interest rates last year cost the Government about $5 billion more than anticipated.

We must cut out more nonessential Government spending and root out more waste, and we will continue our efforts to reduce the number of employees in the Federal work force by 75,000.

The budget plan I submit to you on February 8 will realize major savings by dismantling the Departments of Energy and Education, and by eliminating ineffective subsidies for business. We will continue to redirect our resources to our two highest budget priorities — a strong national defense to keep America free and at peace, and a reliable safety net of social programs for those who have contributed and those who are in need.

Entitlement Programs

Contrary to some of the wild charges you may have heard, this Administration has not and will not turn its back on America's elderly or America's poor. [Applause.]

Under the new budget, funding for social insurance programs will be more than double the amount spent only 6 years ago.

But it would be foolish to pretend that these or any programs cannot be made more efficient and economical.

The entitlement programs that make up our safety net for the truly needy have worthy goals and many deserving recipients. We will protect them. But there is only one way to see to it that these programs really help those whom they were designed to help, and that is to bring their spiraling costs under control.

Today we face the absurd situation of a Federal budget with three-quarters of its expenditures routinely referred to as "uncontrollable" — and a large part of this goes to entitlement programs.

Committee after committee of this Congress has heard witness after witness describe many of these programs as poorly administered and rife with waste and fraud. Virtually every American who shops in a local supermarket is aware of the daily abuses that take place in the food stamp program — which has grown by 16,000 persons in the last 15 years. Another example is medicare and medicaid — programs with worthy goals but whose costs have increased from $11.2 billion to almost $60 billion, more than five times as much, in just 10 years.

Waste and fraud are serious problems. Back in 1980, Federal investigators testified before one of your committees that "corruption has permeated virtually every area of the Medicare and Medicaid health care industry." One official said many of the people who are cheating the system were "very confident that nothing was going to happen to them."

Well, something is going to happen. Not only the taxpayers are defrauded — the people with real dependency on these programs are deprived of what they need because available resources are going not to the needy but to the greedy.

The time has come to control the uncontrollable.

In August we made a start. I signed a bill to reduce the growth of these programs by $44 billion over the next 3 years, while at the same time preserving essential services for the truly needy. Shortly you will receive from me a message on further reforms we intend to install — some new, but others long recommended by your own congressional committees. I ask you to help make these savings for the American taxpayer.

The savings we propose in entitlement programs will total some $63 billion over 4 years and will, without affecting social security, go a long way toward bringing Federal spending under control.

But don't be fooled by those who proclaim that spending cuts will deprive the elderly, the needy and the helpless. The Federal Government will still subsidize 95 million meals every day. That is one out of seven of all the meals served in America. Head Start, senior nutrition programs, and child welfare programs will not be cut from the levels we proposed last year. More than one-half billion dollars has been proposed for minority business assistance. And research at the National Institutes of Health will be increased by over $100 million. While meeting all these needs, we intend to plug unwarranted tax loopholes and strengthen the law which requires all large corporations to pay a minimum tax. [Applause.]

I am confident the economic program we have put into operation will protect the needy while it triggers a recovery that will benefit all Americans. It will stimulate the economy, result in increased savings and provide capital for expansion, mortgages for homebuilding, and jobs for the unemployed.

The New Federalism

Now that the essentials of that program are in place, our next major undertaking must be a program, just as bold, just as innovative, to make government again accountable to the people, to make our system of federalism work again.

Our citizens feel they have lost control of even the most basic decisions made about the essential services of government, such as schools, welfare, roads, and even garbage collection. They are right.

A maze of interlocking jurisdictions and levels of government confronts average citizens in trying to solve even the simplest of problems. They do not know where to turn for answers, who to hold accountable, who to praise, who to blame, who to vote for or against.

The main reason for this is the overpowering growth of Federal grants-in-aid programs during the past few decades.

In 1960, the Federal Government had 132 categorical grant programs, costing $7 billion. When I took office, there were approximately 500, costing nearly $100 billion — 13 programs for energy conservation, 36 for pollution control, 66 for social services, 90 for education. And here, in the Congress, it takes at least 166 committees just to try to keep track of them.

You know and I know that neither the President nor the Congress can properly oversee this jungle of grants-in-aid; indeed, the growth of these grants has led to a distortion in the vital functions of government. As one Democratic Governor put it recently: The national government should be worrying about "arms controls, not potholes." [Applause.]

The growth in these Federal programs has, in the words of one intergovernmental commission, made the Federal Government "more pervasive, more intrusive, more unmanageable, more ineffective, more costly, and above all more unaccountable."

Let us solve this problem with a single bold stroke — the return of some $47 billion in Federal programs to State and local government, together with the means to finance them and a transition period of nearly 10 years to avoid unnecessary disruption.

I will shortly send the Congress a message describing this program. I want to emphasize, however, that its full details will have been worked out only after close consultation with congressional, State, and local officials.

Starting in fiscal 1984, the Federal Government will assume full responsibility for the cost of the rapidly growing medicaid program to go along with its existing responsibility for Medicare. As part of a financial equal swap, the States will simultaneously take full responsibility for aid to families with dependent children and food stamps. [Applause.]

This will make welfare less costly and more responsive to genuine need because it will be designed and administered closer to the grassroots and the people it serves.

In 1984, the Federal Government will apply the full proceeds from certain excise taxes to a grassroots trust fund that will belong, in fair shares, to the 50 States. The total amount flowing into this fund will be $28 billion a year.

Over the next four years, the States can use this money in either of two ways. If they want to continue receiving Federal grants in such areas as transportation, education and social services, they can use their trust fund money to pay for the grants or, to the extent they choose to forgo the Federal grant programs, they can use their trust fund money on their own, for those or other purposes. There will be a mandatory passthrough of part of these funds to local governments.

By 1988, the States will be in complete control of over 40 Federal grant programs. The trust fund will start to phase out, eventually to disappear, and the excise taxes will be turned over to the States. They can then preserve, lower or raise taxes on their own and fund and manage these programs as they see fit.

In a single stroke, we will be accomplishing a realignment that will end cumbersome administration and spiraling costs at the Federal level while we insure these programs will be more responsive to both the people they are meant to help and the people who pay for them.

Urban Enterprise Zones

Hand in hand with this program to strengthen the discretion and flexibility of State and local governments, we are proposing legislation for an experimental effort to improve and develop our depressed urban areas in the 1980's and 1990's. This legislation will permit States and localities to apply to the Federal Government for designation as urban enterprise zones. A broad range of special economic incentives in the zones will help attract new business, new jobs, new opportunity to America's inner cities and rural towns. Some will say our mission is to save free enterprise. I say we must free enterprise so that, together, we can save America. [Applause.]

Some will also say our States and local communities are not up to the challenge of a new and creative partnership. That might have been true 20 years ago before reforms like reapportionment and the Voting Rights Act, the 10-year extension of which I strongly support. It is no longer true today. This Administration has faith in State and local governments and the constitutional balance envisioned by the Founding Fathers. We also believe in the integrity, decency and sound good sense of grassroots Americans.

Private Sector Initiative Task Force

Our faith in the American people is reflected in another major endeavor. Our private sector initiatives task force is seeking out successful community models of

school, church, business, union, foundation and civic programs that help community needs. Such groups are almost invariably far more efficient that government in running social programs.

We are not asking them to replace discarded and often discredited Government programs dollar for dollar, service for service. We just want to help them perform the good works they choose, and help others to profit by their example. Three hundred eighty-five thousand corporations and private organizations are already working on social programs ranging from drug rehabilitation to job training, and thousands more Americans have written us asking how they can help. The volunteer spirit is still alive and well in America. [Applause.]

Other Concerns

Our Nation's long journey toward civil rights for all our citizens — once a source of discord, now a source of pride — must continue with no backsliding or slowing down. We must and shall see that those basic laws that guarantee equal rights are preserved and, when necessary, strengthened. Our concern for equal rights for women is firm and unshakable. We launched a new Task Force on Legal Equity for Women, and a Fifty-States Project that will examine State laws for discriminatory language. And for the first time in our history a woman sits on the highest court in the land. [Applause.]

So, too, the problem of crime — one as real and deadly serious as any in America today — demands that we seek transformation of our legal system, which overly protects the rights of criminals while it leaves society and the innocent victims of crime without justice.

We look forward to the enactment of a responsible Clean Air Act to increase jobs while continuing to improve the quality of our air. We are encouraged by the bipartisan initiative of the House and are hopeful of further progress as the Senate continues its deliberations.

Foreign Policy

So far I have concentrated largely on domestic matters. To view the state of the Union in perspective, we must not ignore the rest of the world. There is not time tonight for a lengthy treatment of foreign policy — a subject I intend to address in detail in the near future. A few words, however, are in order on the progress we have made over the past year re-establishing respect for our Nation around the globe and some of the challenges and goals we will approach in the year ahead.

At Ottawa and Cancún, I met with leaders of the major industrial powers and developing nations. Some of those I met were a little surprised that I did not apologize for America's wealth. Instead I spoke of the strength of the free marketplace system and how that system could help them realize their aspirations for economic development and political freedom. I believe lasting friendships were made and the foundation was laid for future cooperation.

In the vital region of the Caribbean Basin, we are developing a program of aid, trade and investment incentives to promote self-sustaining growth and a better, more secure life for our neighbors to the south. Toward those who would export terrorism and subversion in the Caribbean and elsewhere, especially Cuba and Libya, we will act with firmness.

Our foreign policy is a policy of strength, fairness and balance. By restoring America's military credibility, by pursuing peace at the negotiating table wherever both sides are willing to sit down in good faith, and by regaining the respect of America's allies and adversaries alike, we have strengthened our country's position as a force for peace and progress in the world.

Poland

When action is called for, we are taking it. Our sanctions against the military dictatorship that has attempted to crush human rights in Poland — and against the Soviet regime behind that military dictatorship — clearly demonstrated to the world that America will not conduct "business as usual" with the forces of oppression. [Applause.]

If the events in Poland continue to deteriorate, further measures will follow.

Let me also note that private American groups have taken the lead in making January 30 a day of solidarity with the people of Poland — so, too, the European Parliament has called for March 21 to be an international day of support for Afghanistan. I urge all peace-loving peoples to join together on those days, to raise their voices, to speak and pray for freedom.

National Security

Meantime, we are working for reduction of arms and military activities. As I announced in my address to the Nation last November 18, we have proposed to the Soviet Union a far-reaching agenda for mutual reduction of military forces and have already initiated negotiations with them in Geneva on intermediate range nuclear forces.

In these talks, it is essential that we negotiate from a position of strength. There must be a real incentive for the Soviets to take these talks seriously. This requires that we rebuild our defenses.

In the last decade, while we sought the moderation of Soviet power through a process of restraint and accommodation, the Soviets engaged in an unrelenting build-up of their military forces.

The protection of our national security has required that we undertake a substantial program to enhance our military forces.

We have not neglected to strengthen our traditional alliances in Europe and Asia, or to develop key relationships without partners in the Middle East and other countries.

Building a more peaceful world requires a sound strategy and the national resolve to back it up. When radical forces threaten our friends, when economic misfortune creates conditions of instability, when strategically vital parts of the world fall under the shadow of Soviet power, our response can make the difference between peaceful change or disorder and violence. That is why we have laid such stress not only on our own defense, but on our vital foreign assistance program. Your recent passage of the foreign assistance act sent a signal to the world that America will not shrink from making the investments necessary for both peace and security. Our foreign policy must be rooted in realism, not naivete or self-delusion.

A recognition of what the Soviet empire is about is the starting point. Winston Churchill, in negotiating with the Soviets, observed that they respect only strength and resolve in their dealings with other nations.

That is why we have moved to reconstruct our national defenses. We intend to keep the peace — we will also keep our freedom. [Applause.]

We have made pledges of a new frankness in our public statements and worldwide broadcasts. In the face of a climate of falsehood and misinformation, we have promised the world a season of truth — the truth of our great civilized ideas: individual liberty, representative government, the rule of law under God.

We have never needed walls or mine fields or barbwire to keep our people in. Nor do we declare martial law to keep our people from voting for the kind of government they want.

Everyday Heroes in America

Yes, we have our problems. Yes, we are in a time of recession. And it is true, there is no quick fix, as I said, to instantly end the tragic pain of unemployment. But we will end it. The process has already begun and we will see its effect as the year goes on.

We speak with pride and admiration of that little band of Americans who overcame insuperable odds to set this Nation on course 200 years ago. But our glory did not end with them — Americans ever since have emulated their deeds.

We don't have to turn to our history books for heroes. They are all around us. One who sits among you here tonight epitomized that heroism at the end of the longest imprisonment ever inflicted on men of our Armed Forces. Who will ever forget that night when we waited for television to bring us the scene of that first plane landing at Clark Field in the Philippines — bringing our POWs home? The plane door opened and Jeremiah Denton came slowly down the ramp. He caught sight of our flag, saluted, and said, "God bless America," and then thanked us for bringing him home. [Applause.]

Just 2 weeks ago, in the midst of a terrible tragedy on the Potomac, we saw

again the spirit of American heroism at its finest, the heroism of dedicated rescue workers saving crash victims from icy waters. We saw the heroism of one of our young Government employees, Lenny Skutnik, who, when he saw a woman lose her grip on the helicopter line, dived into the water and dragged her to safety. [Applause.]

And then there are countless quiet, everyday heroes of American life — parents who sacrifice long and hard so their children will know a better life than they have known; church and civic volunteers who help to feed, clothe, nurse and teach the needy; millions who have made our Nation, and our Nation's destiny, so very special —

unsung heroes who may not have realized their own dreams themselves but who then reinvest those dreams in their children.

Don't let anyone tell you that America's best days are behind her, that the American spirit has been vanquished. We have seen it triumph too often in our lives to stop believing in it now. [Applause.]

One hundred and twenty years ago, the greatest of all our Presidents delivered his second state of the Union message in this Chamber. "We cannot escape history," Abraham Lincoln warned. "We of this Congress and this administration will be remembered in spite of ourselves." The "trial through which we pass will light us down in honor or dishonor to the last generation."

That President and the Congress did not fail the American people. Together, they weathered the storm and preserved the Union.

Let it be said of us that we, too, did not fail; that we, too, worked together to bring America through difficult times. Let us so conduct ourselves that two centuries from now, another Congress and another President, meeting in this Chamber as we are meeting, will speak of us with pride, saying that we met the test and preserved for them in their day the sacred flame of liberty — this last, best hope of man on Earth.

God bless you, and thank you.
[Applause, the Members rising.]

President Reagan's Fiscal 1983 Budget Message

Following is the text of President Reagan's budget message to Congress Feb. 8, 1982.

TO THE CONGRESS OF
THE UNITED STATES:

One year ago, in my first address to the country, I went before the American people to report on the condition of our economy. It was not a happy occasion.

Inflation, interest, and unemployment rates were at painfully high levels, while real growth, job creation, new investment, personal savings, and productivity gains had virtually ceased. Our economy was staggering under the burden of excessive tax rates, double-digit inflation, runaway Government spending, counter-productive regulations, and uneven money supply growth. The economy, I declared, was in the "worst mess" in half a century.

To our great good fortune, there were many in the Congress who understood the nature of our difficulties and who rose with us to meet the challenge. Fundamental and long-overdue remedies were proposed and put in place. Together, we enacted the biggest spending and tax reductions in history. Counter-productive regulations have been swept away, and the Federal Reserve has taken action to bring excessive monetary growth under control.

The first year of the 97th Congress will be remembered for its decisive action to hold down spending and cut tax rates. Today, the question before us is whether the second year of this Congress will bring forward equal determination, courage, and wisdom. Clearly, there is a great deal more to be done.

Some seek instant relief from the economic problems we face. There is no such panacea. Our program began October 1, and it cannot solve in 4 months problems that have been building for more than 4 decades. All the quick fixes tried in the

past not only failed to solve but actually aggravated our economic difficulties. They simply ensured a new cycle of boom and bust, of exaggerated hopes and eventual disappointment.

We did not promise the American people a miracle. We did promise them progress, and progress they will get.

Our goal was and remains economic recovery — the return of non-inflationary and sustained prosperity. We seek a larger economic pie to provide all Americans more jobs, more after-tax income, and a better life. Quick fixes won't get us there.

What will get us there is firm resolve and unwavering adherence to the four fundamentals of our economic recovery program that I outlined to the Congress 1 year ago:

● Reducing personal and business taxes to stimulate saving, investment, work effort, and productivity.

● Reducing the growth of overall Federal spending by eliminating Federal activities that overstep the proper sphere of Federal Government responsibilities.

● Reducing the Federal regulatory burden in areas where the Federal Government intrudes unnecessarily into our private lives or interferes unnecessarily with the efficient conduct of private business or of State or local government.

● Supporting a moderate and steady monetary policy, to bring inflation under control.

At the same time, I have proposed strengthening the Nation's defenses, to restore our margin of safety and counter the Soviet military buildup.

Congressional response to these proposals has been positive and gratifying. While much remains to be done, we have made a good beginning.

The Nation's fiscal policy is now firmly embarked on a new, sound, and sustainable course. For the first time in 2 de-

cades, the destructive pattern of runaway spending, rising tax rates, and expanding budgetary commitments has been slowed, and with the cooperation of the Congress this year, will finally be broken.

● Where the growth rate of spending had soared to 17.4% in 1980, it is now declining dramatically — to 10.4% this year, and, under the budget I am submitting, to 4.5% next year.

● Where budget growth totaled $166 billion from 1979 to 1981, spending will rise by only 60% of that amount from 1981 to 1983, despite cost-of-living adjustments and the needed defense buildup.

● After having reached 23% of GNP in 1981, the Federal Government's claim on our economy will steadily recede — to 22% in 1983 and to below 20% by 1987.

● After a decade of tax-flation in which fiscal and monetary excess fueled the unrelenting rise of prices and the automatic increase of taxes, significant tax rate reductions have been enacted. A permanent safeguard against bracket creep and Government profiteering on inflation — income tax indexing — has also been created.

● Where Government had passively tolerated the swift, continuous growth of automatic entitlements and had actively shortchanged the national security, a long-overdue reordering of priorities has begun, entitlement growth is being checked, and the restoration of our defenses is underway.

This dramatic progress in reordering fiscal policy has been paralleled by a similar redirection of monetary policy. The excessive, unsustainable, and eventually ruinous growth of money and credit of the past decade has been curbed. The inflation spiral has been broken. The growth of prices is slowing down. Peoples' savings are beginning to flow out of unproductive speculation, tangible assets, and other inflation hedges back into the Nation's financial arteries where they will be available to power

The Budget Totals

(in billions of dollars)

	1981 Actual	1982 Estimate	1983 Estimate	1984 Estimate	1985 Estimate
Budget receipts	599.3	626.8	666.1	723.0	796.6
Budget outlays	657.2	725.3	757.6	805.9	868.5
Surplus or deficit (−)	−57.9	−98.6	−91.5	−82.9	−71.9
Budget authority	718.4	765.5	801.9	858.0	943.5

economic recovery, more jobs, and growing incomes and opportunities.

In short, we are putting the false prosperity of overspending, easy credit, depreciating money, and financial excess behind us. A solid foundation has been laid for a sound dollar, sustained real economic growth, lasting financial stability, and non-inflationary prosperity for all Americans.

We are also moving to shackle the regulatory juggernaut that burdened production, consumed jobs, and diminished productivity growth. During the past year no significant new regulatory statutes were enacted and few major new regulations were imposed. Additions to the *Federal Register* declined by 23,000 pages. Benefit-cost analysis was made mandatory for regulations. Dozens of existing regulations were reviewed, modified, or eliminated. Without taking into account billions of dollars of savings from regulations never formally proposed because of the changed climate our program has created, quantifiable one-time cost savings of over $3 billion and recurring annual savings of nearly $2 billion have been realized. And the effort has just begun.

A Year of Historic Achievement

These remarkable achievements are the cornerstones of our national economic recovery program. They far exceed anything that the skeptics and critics ever dreamed possible just 1 year ago. They occurred because the executive and legislative branches of our Government joined together to respond to the mandate of the American people and overcome the impediments that had paralyzed Washington for a decade. Together, we have launched a process of reform and change that can transform the course of events.

The Economic Recovery Tax Act of 1981 is the largest, most comprehensive, and most constructive tax bill ever adopted. With the cooperation of the Congress and support of the public, it was enacted in just 5 months. It addressed and substantially remedied most of the tax system's shortcomings and disincentives that had accumulated over decades — distortions that were imposing an increasingly

heavy toll on investment, economic growth, and job creation.

● The penalty tax rate on investment income has been eliminated. By dropping the top rate from 70 to 50%, the attractiveness of tax shelters will be reduced and the incentives for productive investment in stocks, bonds, new business ventures, and other financial assets will be increased. Our Nation's capital will again flow to the growth of business and jobs rather than to the vendors of protection from punitive taxation.

● Marginal tax rates have been significantly lowered for the first time in two decades. The 23% across-the-board rate reduction will mean $183 billion in lower taxes for individuals over the first 3 years. The financial reward for savings, work effort, and new production will stop diminishing and start rising once again.

● Powerful new incentives for savings have been established. Beginning this year, 50 million workers will be eligible for the first time to set aside tax-free up to $2,000 per year for Individual Retirement Accounts. The annual limit for existing Keogh and IRA investors will also be raised. By sharply altering the incentives for saving as opposed to consumption, a huge new flow of current income will be channeled toward restoring our productivity and lifting our national savings rate from last place in the industrial world.

● The taxation of phantom corporate profits has also been significantly curtailed. The new accelerated cost recovery system will shorten depreciation periods to 5 years for machinery and 15 years for structures. This will permit fuller recovery of asset costs, a more valid accounting of taxable profits, and a reasonable after-tax return on investments for the first time in years. By eliminating the drastic under-depreciation provided in previous tax law, after-tax business cash flow will be increased by $10½ billion this year and $211 billion over the next 6 years. This growing stream of funds for modernization, new machinery, new technology, new products, and new plants will revive our lagging productivity, restore our competitiveness in world markets, and spur the steady growth of jobs, production, and real incomes.

● The confiscatory taxing of estates and inheritances has been halted as well. By raising the exemption to $600,000, by lowering the rate to 50%, and by removing the limits on the marital deduction, 99.7% of all estates will eventually be exempt from estate taxation. Hard-working American farmers, small businessmen, investors, and workers can once again be confident that the sweat, sacrifices, and accumulations of a lifetime will belong to their heirs rather than their Government.

● Government profiteering on inflation has been abolished. Beginning in 1985, the individual income tax brackets, the zero-bracket amount, and the personal exemption will be corrected annually for inflation. Bracket creep will never again systematically plunder the rewards for production and effort. Government will never again use inflation to take a rising share of the peoples' income without a vote of their representatives.

The past year's achievements on spending control and the reestablishment of budgetary discipline are no less impressive than the sweeping tax changes. For the first time ever, the Congress activated its central budgetary machinery and overcame the spending impulses of its fragmented parts. The Omnibus Budget Reconciliation Act of 1981 was a watershed in fiscal history — a giant step toward the restoration of fiscal discipline. By the accounting of its own Congressional Budget Office, spending will be $35 billion lower this year and about $130 billion lower over the next 3 years due to just one bill passed in only 5 months after having been considered by 30 different committees, a bill that reduced, reformed or eliminated hundreds of programs. The growth of budgetary outlays is at last being brought in line with the growth of the tax base and the national income. Excess spending commitments, unnecessary programs and overlapping activities were meaningfully addressed in the Reconciliation Act for the first time in decades.

● As a result of congressional action in 1981, the growth of entitlements will be reduced by $41 billion during the next 3 years. For the first time, eligibility standards for food stamps and student loans have been tightened. Unemployment benefits have been targeted to States where they are needed. Subsidies for non-needy students have been reduced in the school lunch program. Abuses of the medicaid, nutrition, and AFDC programs have been curtailed, saving $14.4 billion over the next 3 years. Overly generous and unaffordable twice-a-year cost-of-living adjustments for Federal retirees have been eliminated. The "uncontrollables" are being brought under control, and benefits have been retargeted where they are most needed.

● Dozens of ineffective or counter-productive programs have been eliminated or reduced. The $4 billion make-work CETA public sector jobs program was abolished. Extravagant dairy subsidies have been cut substantially. The ineffective $700 million

Appendix

Economic Development Administration is being phased out. The Community Services Administration has been eliminated. An unnecessary $2 billion in Government subsidies for new energy supplies and technologies has been cut. The excessively-funded impact aid program was substantially scaled back. In short, a long-overdue housecleaning of excess budgetary commitments was accomplished.

● Inappropriate Federal subsidies have been withdrawn. Legislation to return Conrail to the private sector has been enacted. The National Consumer Cooperative Bank has been privatized. Subsidies to the auto industry for new technology demonstrations have been eliminated. Operating subsidies to local mass transit systems are being phased out. Subsidies to exporters have been sharply curtailed. Subsidized disaster loans to financially viable businesses have been eliminated.

● A major stride toward rationalizing the structure, reducing the cost, and increasing State and local flexibility in the Nation's $91 billion grant-in-aid system has been enacted. Fifty-seven narrow, redtape-ridden categorical grants programs have been replaced with 9 block grants. The pages of regulation imposed on State and local governments have been reduced from over 300 to 6, while the cost to the Federal budget has been reduced.

● Total funding for nondefense discretionary programs has been reduced. After continuous growth for two decades, the budget cost of these programs will actually decline from $137 billion in 1981 to $130 billion in 1982.

● An impressive start at reducing fraud, waste, abuse, and unnecessary Government overhead was made. The President's Council on Integrity and Efficiency, established to coordinate a Government-wide attack on fraud and waste, saved $2 billion in the last 6 months of 1981 alone. A comprehensive effort to collect $33 billion in delinquent debts has been launched and will recover $1.5 billion in 1982 and $4.0 billion in 1983. These estimates include recoveries of delinquent taxes due to the Internal Revenue Service. Federal nondefense employment has been reduced by 35,000 since January 1981. The cost of Government travel, publications, and consultants has been reduced substantially.

At the same time that the Congress joined in these long-overdue efforts to pare back the size of the Federal budget and slow its momentum of growth, it has fully supported our ambitious but essential plan to rebuild our national defense. A year ago every component of military strength was flashing warning lights of neglect, underinvestment, and deteriorating capability. Today, health is being restored.

● Pervasive deficiencies in readiness — including too many units not ready for combat, too many weapons systems out of commission, too few people with critical combat skills, and too few planes and ships fully capable of their missions — are being corrected. Funds for operations and main-

tenance, including training and aircraft flying hours, have been boosted. Backlogs of combat equipment needing repair are being eliminated. Adequate supplies of spare parts necessary to support high operating rates for training, as well as to provide war reserves, are being purchased.

● The serious inadequacy in pay and benefits that threatened the all-volunteer force, caused an exodus of skilled personnel, and sapped morale throughout the armed services has been corrected. Last year's 14.3% pay increase has improved recruit quality, boosted reenlistment rates, stopped the drain of critical skills, and contributed to the dramatic revival of morale in our military services. End-strength goals are now being exceeded. In addition, the percentage of recruits with higher test scores has risen in the past year.

● Critical investments in conventional and strategic force modernization are now moving rapidly forward. A new bomber for early deployment and an advanced (Stealth) bomber for the 1990's have been approved to retain our capability to penetrate Soviet air defenses. Development of a new, larger, and more accurate MX missile to preserve our land-based deterrent is proceeding. A 5-year shipbuilding program including 133 new ships and a total investment of $96 billion — double the 5-year program of the previous administration — has been launched. Rapid production of new combat systems including the M-1 Abrams tank, the AV-8B Marine Corps attack aircraft and the F/A-18 Navy tactical fighter have been approved. Improvements in our airlift and sealift forces to transport equipment and soldiers rapidly to counter military aggression anywhere in the world, are moving forward.

No Time to Retreat

These achievements of the first year truly constitute a new beginning. In every major dimension of national strength and well-being we have launched the redirection of policy that was so desperately needed and so long overdue. We are ending the destructive inflation and the financial disorder built up over a decade. We have removed the yoke of over-taxation from our workers and our business enterprises. We have begun to dismantle the regulatory straitjacket that impeded our commerce and sapped our prosperity. And we have reversed the dangerous erosion of our military capabilities.

The task before us now is a different one, but no less crucial. Our task is to persevere; to stay the course; to shun retreat; to weather the temporary dislocations and pressures that must inevitably accompany the restoration of national economic, fiscal, and military health.

The correction of previous fiscal and monetary excesses has come too late to avert an unwelcome, painful, albeit temporary business slump. In the months ahead there will be temptation to resort to pump-priming and spending stimulus programs.

Such efforts have failed in the past, are not needed now, and must be resisted at every turn. Our program for permanent economic recovery is already in place. Artificial stimulants will undermine that program, not reinforce it.

Likewise, previous excesses in money and credit growth have resulted in financial strain in many regions and sectors of our national economy. The adjustment to lower inflation and a more moderate money and credit policy did not come soon enough to avoid interest rates and unemployment far higher than we would like, and that we are working to reduce. But these effects are temporary. They cannot be remedied by a return to rapid, unsustainable expansion of Federal spending and money growth, which would drive inflation and interest rates to new highs. Our hard-won gains in reducing inflation must be preserved and extended — because permanent reduction of interest rates and unemployment is impossible if the fight against inflation is abandoned, just when it is being won.

Similarly, our budget deficits will be large because of the current recession, and because it is impossible in a short period of time to correct the mistakes of decades. But our incentive-minded tax policy and our security-based defense programs are right and necessary for long-run peace and prosperity, and must not be tampered with in a vain attempt to cure deficits in the short-run. The answer to deficits is economic growth and indefatigable efforts to control spending and borrowing. These principles we dare not abandon.

The Deficit Problem: Its Origins

Despite the new course we have charted and the gains we have achieved, the voices of doubt, retreat and rejection are beginning to rise. They conveniently forget that the present business slump was not caused by our program but is the result of the accumulated burdens of past policy errors, which we have taken action to redress. They fail to comprehend that our spending cuts and tax reductions were not designed to redistribute the output of a stagnant economy, but to revive the economy's growth and to increase its size — for the jobless as well as the affluent, for those who aspire to get ahead as well as those who have already arrived.

Increasingly, the larger budget deficits that we unavoidably face are offered as evidence that our entire course should be recharted. The matter of budget deficits, therefore, must be addressed squarely. We must fully comprehend why they have grown from our original projections, why they may remain with us for some time to come, what dangers they pose if not vigorously combatted and what steps we can and must take to steadily reduce their size and drain on our available savings.

Our original plan called for a balanced budget in 1984. Balance is no longer achievable in 1984, but the factors that

have postponed its realization are neither permanent nor cause for abandoning the goal of eventually living within our means.

In the near term, the most important setback to our budgetary timetable is the recession now underway. During 1982, receipts will decline by $31 billion and outlays rise by $8 billion due to the fall-off of business activity and the increase of unemployment-related payments. This factor alone accounts for nearly all of the difference between the $45 billion 1982 deficit we projected last year and our current estimate of $98.6 billion.

While the recession will end before this fiscal year is over, its budgetary impact will spill over for many years into the future. It will take time for the unemployment rate to come down and safety net payments to diminish. The growth of receipts will recover, but not at the levels previously projected. This will add billions to deficits for 1983 and 1984.

The second major factor widening the deficit projection is interest payments on our trillion dollar debt. Here we are being penalized doubly for the misguided policies of the past.

The discredited philosophy of spend and spend, borrow and borrow, saddled us with a permanent debt burden of staggering dimensions. This year's interest payment of $83 billion exceeds the size of the entire Federal budget as recently as 1958.

In addition, past fiscal, monetary, and credit excesses have resulted in temporarily high interest rates — rates that will come down, but only as inflation abates, private and public financing practices adjust, and long-term confidence rebuilds. Since market confidence has been so badly shaken by runaway inflation and interest rates in the past 3 years, it is apparent that interest rates over the next several years will fall less rapidly than we had originally anticipated. Between the huge inherited base of national debt, the high interest rates, and the large prospective additions to the national debt in the next several years, our total debt service costs will rise substantially.

Interest payments on the debt will exceed our original projections by $18 billion in 1982, $32 billion in 1983, and $182 billion over 1982-86 taken as a whole. The interest rate/debt service factor, then, constitutes a major source of the setback to our budget timetable. But let us be clear about its origins: it arises primarily from a legacy of past excesses, not from a shortfall in our current budget control effects, nor from a flaw in our overall program.

The third and most important factor contributing to the growth in deficit projections is quite simply the ironic by-product of our rapid and decisive success in bringing down the rate of inflation. Our economic forecast last February projected a 9.5% inflation rate in calendar year 1981 and a further decline to 7.7% in 1982. This projection was scorned by many as too rosy just 1 year ago. Yet the actual inflation rate in 1981 turned out to be lower than our

projection, and the inflation decline this year and next year almost certainly will exceed our earlier projections.

This is welcome news to every American and we have adjusted our inflation forecast accordingly. But lower rates of price increase also mean lower inflation components in wages and incomes and a reduced flow of inflation-swollen tax receipts to the Treasury.

This point is not merely academic. Over the next 5 years, our forecast projects a 9.9% average rate of growth in nominal GNP reflecting a steady fall of inflation to about 4½% by 1987. If nominal GNP growth were just 2% higher each year, reflecting a continuation of higher inflation, Federal receipts would be enlarged by the staggering sum of $353 billion over the 5 years. On paper, at least, the budget would be nearly balanced in 1987 rather than more than $50 billion in deficit.

But if the last decade offers any lesson, it is that we cannot inflate our way to budget balance. Indeed, every budget from 1975 forward projected a balanced budget 2 years into the future and growing surpluses in the out-years. Not one of these surpluses materialized for a very compelling reason: the monetary excesses needed to finance inflationary growth of wages and incomes are the enemy of savings, investment, real economic growth, and fundamental business confidence and financial stability. They lead to the kind of pervasive economic breakdown that we experienced during 1979-81 — a breakdown that swells Government spending, interrupts the flow of receipts, and causes prospective budgetary surpluses to vanish in a flow of red ink.

Thus, we cannot and will not pursue the will-o'-the-wisp of reflation nor the phantom of future budget surpluses premised on a continuance of high inflation.

Instead, we must recognize that for a period of time, success in our unyielding battle against inflation will appear to work against our goal of a balanced budget. Thus, while our current revenues will reflect the decline of inflation today, part of our current outlays will reflect the higher rates of inflation in years past. This is especially true in the case of some $249 billion in indexed programs. Generally, the inflation rate used to adjust indexed benefits lags a year or more behind the current payment period. During 1983, for example, an inflation rate of 6.5% is projected, but cost-of-living adjustments to social security and other program benefits will be 8.1% based largely on the actual inflation experience of 1981. Much the same is true of the $96.4 billion in debt service for 1983. Some part of that will reflect the higher cost of debt securities issued in 1980-82 when inflation and interest rates will have been higher than is now projected for 1983.

Thus, the conquest of inflation will contribute to budgetary imbalance for some years to come. But these deficits will prove manageable if we understand why we have them and redouble our efforts to re-

duce them.

The final factor contributing to the worsening of the deficit outlook is that all of the budget savings we had planned for last year were not actually achieved. Most importantly, our plan to ensure the short- and long-run solvency of social security was discarded by the Congress. In an effort to eliminate partisanship and facilitate movement toward a constructive solution, our reform proposal has been withdrawn in favor of a bipartisan commission charged with developing a plan to rescue the social security system by next fall. I am confident that the commission will do just that, but in the meanwhile our outlay projections must be increased by $6 billion in 1983 and $18 billion for 1987.

Likewise, the Congress failed to adopt all of the reforms we proposed for medicaid, guaranteed student loans, food stamps and other entitlements. Without further action, about $4 billion would be added to the 1983 deficit in these areas alone. While major and unprecedented action was taken to curb the growth of entitlements last year, the shortfall is still substantial. Entitlement reforms not acted upon by the Congress last year will add nearly $20 billion to the deficit over the next 3 years. When this is combined with substantial added outlays for farm subsidies and for discretionary programs that were not reformed, it is clear that the task of budget control is far from complete.

The Budget Deficit in Perspective

Taken together, the effects of recession, higher interest rates, declining inflation, and incomplete congressional action will mean high, continuing, and troublesome Federal budget deficits. Constant vigilance and relentless efforts to pare back future spending and borrowing will be imperative to ensure that they are not permitted to worsen and add further pressure to financial markets and interest rates.

Nevertheless, three features of these high deficit numbers must not be lost sight of even as we seek eventually to eliminate them.

First, even the 1982 deficit of $98.6 billion is not unprecedented in the context of a recession and recovery cycle. Relative to the present size of the U.S. economy, the budget deficit would have been $94 billion for 1975, followed by deficits of $139 billion, $91 billion and $97 billion in the next 3 years, respectively.

Second, these deficits reflect the excess spending commitments of past rather than new spending programs with potential to grow in the future. That means that by remaining firm in our efforts to reduce waste and excess, reform entitlements, reduce low priority spending, and gradually return domestic programs back to State and local governments, the gap between spending subject to firm fiscal discipline and revenues being lifted by steady economic expansion will gradually diminish.

Appendix

Finally, the share of GNP taken in taxes will be substantially lower and the incentives for savings markedly stronger. This expansion of the total savings supply will increase our capacity to absorb deficits and give us additional time to work toward their elimination.

$239 Billion Deficit Reduction Plan

The prospect of high deficits during the transition to strong economic growth and low inflation contains a profound warning: any relaxation of our budget control efforts, any backsliding to spending politics as usual, any retreat to time-worn excuses about "uncontrollables" — that results in spending growth significantly above our projections, will mean a serious threat to the progress of our entire economic recovery program. There is precious little margin for shirking or diluting the task the American people have charged us with. That task is nothing less than a constant, comprehensive, ceaseless search for ways to reduce the size of Government and the future growth of its spending.

The 1983 budget I am presenting to the Congress faithfully adheres to that mandate. If all proposed measures are adopted, the prospective deficit will be reduced by $56 billion next year, $84 billion in 1984, and $99 billion in 1985. In short, the budget this year represents much more than simply a tabulation of accounts or a compilation of spending decisions, large and small. Instead, it represents a far-reaching, resourceful, and integrated blueprint for reducing the prospective deficit by $239 billion over the next 3 years. It is a bold action plan that, if faithfully implemented, can cut the prospective deficits over that period by nearly 50%.

Our plan for deficit reduction consists of five parts. It addresses each area of the budget where actions to reduce the gap between spending and revenues are possible and desirable.

The first area concerns nonsocial security entitlements. Despite the heartening progress we made toward reform last year, the cost of these automatic spending programs will rise to $201 billion in 1983 without further action. This figure compares to only $119 billion in 1979.

Thus, our 1983 budget proposals continue the objective set out previously: to reduce the swift growth of automatic entitlements while preserving benefits for the truly needy. If acted upon fully by the Congress, these new reform measures will save $12 billion next year and $52 billion over the next 3 years. They include new steps to tighten eligibility, reduce errors and abuse and curtail unwarranted benefits in the welfare, medical, and nutrition programs. The explosive growth of medical programs — 16.7% per year since 1978 — will be contained with tighter reimbursement standards for providers, modest copayment requirements for medicaid beneficiaries, and, later in the year, a comprehensive

plan to reform the health care reimbursement system and provide new cost control incentives for all participants. We have also proposed measures to target guaranteed student loans better to those with financial need and to limit the cost growth of Federal military and civilian retirement programs.

Nevertheless, let me be clear on this point. Our administration has not and will not turn its back on our elderly or needy citizens. Under our new budget, funding for social insurance programs will be more than double the amount spent only 6 years ago. For example, the Federal Government will subsidize 95 million meals every day. That is one of every seven of all meals served in America. Headstart, senior nutrition programs, and child welfare programs will not be cut from the levels we proposed last year.

The second component of our deficit reduction plan covers domestic discretionary and other programs for purposes ranging from agricultural research to housing subsidies and manpower training. Our proposed savings here total $14 billion next year and $76 billion over the next 3 years.

These savings measures involve two essential principles. First, where programs are unnecessary, can be better targeted or can be significantly streamlined, we have proposed substantial reductions. Our proposals to convert the fragmented and wasteful CETA training program to a block grant, to target low-income energy assistance to the colder States where it is needed, to combine the WIC program with the child and maternal health block grant, and to further reduce subsidies to business for energy technology development and commercialization are all examples of this principle.

The other principle governing discretionary programs is that we have generally not provided inflation allowances for them. This will provide a powerful incentive to reduce overhead, waste, and low-priority activities and ensure that the money we spend for many worthwhile purposes in the areas of education, transportation, community development, and research is utilized in the most efficient and productive manner possible. Our deficit problem is simply too severe to permit business as usual to continue any longer.

The third component of the deficit reduction program involves user fees, or more appropriately, the recovery of costs borne by the taxpayers generally, but that predominantly benefit a limited group of businesses, communities or individuals. Total savings would amount to $2.5 billion in 1983 and $10 billion over the next 3 years.

While the Congress made great strides on most of our proposed budget cuts last year, the user fees proposals were a noticeable and disappointing departure from this pattern. The case for action now is even stronger than it was last year. With sacrifices required of almost every beneficiary of Federal programs, it is simply inexcusable and intolerable that yacht owners es-

cape without paying even a small part of the Coast Guard services; or that commercial and general aviation are not paying the cost of the air traffic control system that ensures their safety; or that ship and barge operators do not pay a fair share of the costs of waterways maintained by the Federal Government. Our user fee package corrects these and similar shortcomings in current budget policy and will contribute significantly toward reducing the deficit.

The fourth part of the plan is aimed at the executive branch and the most inexcusable of all forms of spending: lax management, the toleration of fraud and abuse, the failure to recover debts owed the Government or to dispose of properties it does not need, and outdated, inefficient, procurement practices.

Our fiscal plan has always assumed that our new management would take hold, and that savings would be possible in areas we have simply never looked at before. After 1 year, our new management team has indeed taken hold, the results to date have been impressive, and our plans for future savings are bold and far-reaching. All told, these efforts will reduce the budget deficit by $20 billion next year and $68 billion over the next 3 years.

We will collect the debts we are owed and the taxes we are due. New legislation will be needed in some cases, but much of these savings will flow from tighter, more aggressive management throughout executive branch agencies.

Likewise, we will move systematically to reduce the vast Federal holdings of surplus land and real property. It is estimated that the Federal Government owns approximately 775 million acres, and 405,000 buildings, covering about 2.6 billion square feet. Some of this real property is not in use and would be of greater value to society if transferred to the private sector. During the next 3 years we will save $9 billion by shedding these unnecessary properties while fully protecting and preserving our national parks, forests, wildernesses and scenic areas.

Our management efforts will also be directed toward the more cost-effective procurement of the goods and services required by the Federal Government. The changes we seek will increase competition for the Government's business, reduce and simplify paperwork and regulations, and develop better standards for our procurement processes and personnel. Over time these efforts will yield large outyear savings not included in the budget totals.

Finally, our emphasis thus far has been on reducing excessive tax rates and shrinking the Government's take from the paychecks of workers and the profits of business. On that principle we will not waver. But that does not mean unintended loopholes should go uncorrected, that obsolete tax incentives should be continued, or that profitable business should not contribute at least some minimum fair share to the cost of financing Government. Thus, our deficit reduction plan includes $34 billion

over the next 3 years in additional receipts from new initiatives in these areas.

About one-third of this total is attributable to our proposal to strengthen the minimum corporate tax, and a substantial share of the other tax revisions will also affect business. In every case, these measures involve the collection of a tax that is owed now or that was intended by the Congress, or elimination of incentives that are no longer needed due to the sweeping reform of business taxation contained in the Economic Recovery Act of 1981.

These new proposals will have no adverse impact on our economic recovery program, are fair and equitable, and will contribute significantly to the reduction of future deficits.

Continuing the Restoration of National Defense

Our 1983 budget plan continues the effort begun last year to strengthen our military posture in four primary areas: strategic forces, combat readiness, force mobility, and general purpose forces.

A thorough 8-month review of U.S. strategic forces and objectives preceded my decision this past October to strengthen our strategic forces. The review found that the relative imbalance with the Soviet Union will be at its worst in the mid-1980's and hence needs to be addressed quickly. It also concluded that the multiple protective structure basing proposal for MX did not provide long-term survivability since the Soviets could counter it (at about the same cost) by simply deploying more warheads.

In addition, our review pointed to serious deficiencies in force survivability, endurance, and the capability to exercise command and control during nuclear war. Current communications and warning systems were found to be vulnerable to severe disruption from an attack of very modest scale.

The 1983 budget funds programs to correct these deficiencies. The 1983 strategic program of $23.1 billion, an increase of $6.9 billion over 1982, provides for both near-term improvements and longer-term programs. These initiatives include:

● Early deployment of cruise missiles on existing bombers and attack submarines.

● Acquisition of a new bomber (the B-1B) and development of advanced technology (Stealth) bomber for deployment in the 1990's to provide a continued capability to penetrate Soviet defenses.

● Development and procurement of a new, larger, and more accurate land-based missile, the MX.

● Continued deployment of Trident ballistic missile submarines to strengthen the sea-based leg of our strategic deterrent.

Longer-term programs include: development of a survivable deployment plan for the MX missile, development of a new submarine-launched ballistic missile, continued improvements in the survivability of warning and communications systems, and improvements in strategic defenses

against both bomber and missile attacks.

The 1983 budget provides $114.3 billion in operations and military personnel costs, an increase of over $13 billion from the 1982 level to improve the combat readiness of our forces.

Today a major conflict involving the United States could occur without adequate time to upgrade U.S. force readiness. Our concerns with military readiness reflect both the long lead time required to procure sophisticated equipment (both parts and finished equipment) and past failures to provide adequate peacetime support for combat units. We cannot wait for a period of rising tensions before bringing forces up to combat readiness.

My program will continue to bolster combat readiness by increasing training, operating rates, and equipment support. There will be increased aircraft flying hours and supply inventories. In addition, backlogs of combat equipment and real property awaiting maintenance will be reduced. Also, the 1983 budget will provide levels of military compensation that will improve the readiness and capability of the All Volunteer Force.

Current U.S. mobility forces cannot move the required combat or combat support units fast enough to counter effectively military aggression in Europe, Korea or in the Southwest Asia/Persian Gulf region. For example, at present only a small light combat force could be moved rapidly to the Southwest Asia region. Major mobility shortages include wide-body military cargo aircraft; fast logistics ships; and prepositioned ships and associated support equipment. Elimination of these shortages is an essential first step toward improving U.S. military capability during the first 30 days after the beginning of a crisis.

The 1983 budget provides $4.4 billion for:

● Initial procurement of a fleet of improved C-5 cargo aircraft, and additional KC-10A tanker/cargo aircraft that will double our wide-bodied military airlift capability by the 1990's.

● Continued upgrading of existing C-5A aircraft to extend their effectiveness beyond the year 2000.

● Conversion of four additional fast logistic ships that will provide the capability to move heavy combat forces rapidly.

● Chartering a fleet of supply ships that can be stationed with equipment and supplies in Southwest Asia to reduce the time required for deployment of heavy forces.

In the last decade, the Soviet Union introduced large quantities of highly capable, new-generation tactical equipment including combat ships, tanks and aircraft, which must be countered by modernized U.S. forces. Also, the traditional U.S. superiority in system quality has been considerably narrowed, making Soviet quantitative advantages more serious. The Soviet military force buildup has increased the risk that they may rely on military power to support their foreign policy goals. For the U.S. to maintain, in concert with our

allies, sufficient conventional forces to deter potential aggression, our forces must be provided with adequate numbers of new, modern tactical equipment.

My 1983 budget includes $106.2 billion for general purpose forces (including both operations and investment), and $18 billion increase over 1982. A key initiative is an expanded shipbuilding program. The United States, dependent on open seas for commerce and military resupply, must have the naval capability to maintain control of vital sea lands. While our naval forces have declined from the mid-1960's, the Soviets have in existence or under construction eight new classes of submarines and eight new classes of major surface warships, including nuclear-powered cruisers and new aircraft carriers.

The budget provides an $18.6 billion shipbuilding program including full funding for two nuclear-powered aircraft carriers, to be constructed during 1983-87. Other ships included in my 1983 program are three large cruisers equipped with an advanced air defense system; two nuclear-powered attack submarines; two frigates for convoy protection and four mine countermeasure ships to improve fleet capability to operate in mined waters. My longer term objective is to increase the deployable battle force from 513 ships in 1982 to over 600 by the end of the decade.

In addition, the budget provides for increased production of ground and tactical air force weapons. Production rates will be increased for a variety of new systems such as the M-1 Abrams tank, light armored vehicles, and the AV-8B Marine corps attack aircraft.

All of this will be done with a major reform of the acquisition process and vastly improved management of defense operations, which will save $51 billion by 1987. In a continuing fight against fraud, waste, and inefficiency, the Secretary of Defense has appointed an Assistant for Review and Oversight and a Council on Integrity and Management Improvement.

Revitalization of American Federalism

The Constitution provides clear distinctions between the roles of the Federal Government and of the States and localities. In their wisdom, our founding fathers provided for considerable flexibility so that in following centuries these responsibilities could be adapted to new conditions. But in recent years we have not adapted well to new conditions. We have created confusion as to who is responsible for what. During the past 20 years, what had been a classic division of functions between the Federal Government and the States and localities has become a confused mess. Traditional understandings about the roles of each level of government have been violated.

Governments at all levels have had and will continue to face various problems. But, as Governor of California, I learned that a problem in one part of the country

does not automatically mean that we need a new Federal program in all 50 States. Yet that is what has happened.

In 1964, total Federal grants to State and local governments were $10 billion. By 1980, total Federal grants to States and localities exceeded $90 billion, meaning that 18% of Federal tax receipts were being passed through to States and localities for one reason or another. However, these funds were not passed through entirely benignly. Attached to them were Federal rules, mandates, and requirements. This massive Federal grantmaking system has distorted State and local decisions and usurped State and local functions.

I propose that over the coming years we clean up this mess. I am proposing a major effort to restore American federalism. This transition over nearly 10 years will give States and localities the time they need to plan for themselves when and how to meet State and local needs that are now being met with Federal Government funds. My proposal will also make available to the States and localities the tax resources that would otherwise fund these programs by the Federal Government.

In coming weeks, we will have intensive discussions with local and State officials, the Congress, and many others to hammer out a proposal I will soon send to the Congress. Essentially, I believe the Federal Government should assume full responsibility for the medicaid program which assures adequate health care for the poor. In contrast, financial assistance to the poor is a legitimate responsibility of States and localities. I am proposing, therefore, that the aid to families with dependent children (AFDC) and food stamp programs be turned over to the States. This swap will clarify responsibilities substantially because these programs will become the clear responsibility of one level of government or another. That responsibility is now mixed.

In addition, I propose that more than 40 current grant-in-aid programs costing the Federal Government about $30 billion a year be turned back to the States and localities, along with the funds to pay for them. During the period 1984-87, these programs will be funded by a specially designated set of taxes to be used exclusively for financing this transition program. These taxes will be deposited in a fund that will belong to the States. Each State will be able to make its own decision on how rapidly to phase out the turnback programs. This is because each State will have two options: it may use its share of the federalism trust fund to reimburse Federal agencies for continuing to carry out turnback programs, or it may ask that the programs be terminated and then use the funds directly for whatever purposes it desires.

Beginning in 1987, the federalism trust fund will gradually be dissolved and the tax sources themselves will be made available to the States.

The key to this program is that the States and localities make the critical choices. They have the time to make them in an orderly way. A major sorting out of Federal, State and local responsibilities will occur, and the Federal presence and intervention in State and local affairs will gradually diminish.

Conclusion

While some administration proposals have been turned down, turned aside, or compromised by the Congress, the overall assessment of the past year's action on the budget is heartening. Cooperation, support, goodwill, and a genuine sense of national purpose have enabled us to make significant progress in setting the Federal Government's affairs in order and America on the road to economic recovery.

I urge the Congress to approach the new, or renewed, proposals in this budget in the same spirit and with the same goodwill as it did my proposals of a year ago. Much has been accomplished. This budget proposes that more be done.

The proposals set forth in this budget will not be accepted readily. They are a second challenging installment of a politically difficult, yet necessary, program. In their specifics, these proposals will undoubtedly be altered by the Congress. The general direction we must travel, however, is clear. I urge the Congress to weigh these budget proposals thoughtfully, and to join me, and my administration, in a constructive effort to curb the growth of Federal spending and to provide for the Nation's security. We must, in the end, roll up our sleeves, face our responsibilities squarely, and persevere at the unending task of setting, and keeping, the Nation's affairs in order.

RONALD REAGAN
February 8, 1982

Reagan's Address on East-West Relations

Following is the White House text of President Reagan's May 9, 1982, speech as delivered at the Eureka College commencement ceremony, in Eureka, Ill.

THE PRESIDENT: Thank you very much. President Gilbert, Trustees, Administration, and Faculty, students and the friends of Eureka College and particularly those whose day this is — the graduating class of '82 — (applause) — Dan, you said the 25th and now the 50th. Do you mind if I try for the 75th? (Applause.)

But it goes without saying that this is a very special day for you who are graduating. Would you forgive me if I say it's a very special day for me also? Over the years since I sat where you, the graduating class of 1982, are now sitting, I've returned to the campus many times, always with great pleasure and warm nostalgia. Now, it just isn't true that I only came back this time to clean out my gym locker. (Laughter.)

On one of those occasions, as you've been told, I addressed the graduating class here, " 'neath the elms," and was awarded an honorary degree. At that time I informed those assembled that while I was grateful for the honor, it added to a feeling of guilt I've been nursing for 25 years, because I always figured that first degree they give me was honorary. (Laughter.)

Now, if it's true that tradition is the glue holding civilization together, then Eureka has made its contribution to that effort. Yes, it is a small college in a small community. It's no impersonal, assembly-line diploma mill. As the years pass, if you have let yourselves absorb the spirit and tradition of this place, you'll find the four years you've spent here living in your memory as a rich and important part of your life.

Oh, you'll have some regrets along with the happy memories. I let football and other extracurricular activities eat into my study time with the result that my grade average was closer to the C level required for eligibility than it was to straight A's. And even now I wonder what I might have accomplished if I'd studied harder. (Laughter.) (Applause.)

Now, I know there are differences between the Eureka College of 1932 and the Eureka of 1982, but I'm also sure that in many ways — important ways — Eureka remains the same. For one thing, it's impossible for you now to believe what I've said about things being the same. We who preceded you understand that very well, because when we were here we thought old grads who came back only after five years — not 50 — couldn't understand what our life was like and what had taken place and changed. So take my word for it. As the years go by, you'll be amazed at how fresh the memory of these years will remain in your mind; how easily you can relive the very emotions that you experienced.

The Class of '32 has no yearbook to record our final days on the campus. The Class of '33 didn't put out a *Prism* because of the hardships of that great Depression era. The faculty sometimes went for months on end without pay. And yet this school made it possible for young men and women, myself included, to get an education even though we were totally without funds, our families destitute victims of the Depression.

Yes, this place is deep in my heart. Everything that has been good in my life began here. (Applause.)

Graduation Day is called "Commencement" and properly so because it is both a recognition of completion and a beginning. And I would like, seriously, to talk to you about this new phase — the society in which you're now going to take your place as full-time participants. You're no longer observers. You will be called upon to make decisions and express your views on global events because those events will affect your lives.

I've spoken of similarities, and the 1980's like the 1930's may be one of those — a crucial juncture in history that will determine the direction of the future.

Meetings With European Leaders

In about a month I will meet in Europe with the leaders of nations who are our closest friends and allies. At Versailles, leaders of the industrial powers of the world will seek better ways to meet today's economic challenges. In Bonn, I will join my colleagues from the Atlantic Alliance nations to renew those ties which have been the foundation of Western, free-world defense for 37 years. There will also be meetings in Rome and London.

Now, these meetings are significant for a simple but very important reason. Our own nation's fate is directly linked to that of our sister democracies in Western Europe. The values for which America and all democratic nations stand represent the culmination of Western culture. Andrei Sakharov, the distinguished Nobel Laureate and courageous Soviet human rights advocate, has written in a message smuggled to freedom, "I believe in Western man. I have faith in his mind which is practical and efficient and, at the same time, aspires to great goals. I have faith in his good intentions and in his decisiveness."

This glorious tradition requires a partnership to preserve and protect it. Only as partners can we hope to achieve the goal of a peaceful community of nations. Only as partners can we defend the values of democracy and human dignity that we hold so dear.

East-West Relations

There is a single, major issue in our partnership which will underlie the discussions that I will have with the European leaders: the future of Western relations with the Soviet Union. How should we deal with the Soviet Union in the years ahead? What framework should guide our conduct and our policies toward it? And what can we realistically expect from a world power of such deep fears, hostilities, and external ambitions?

I believe the unity of the West is the foundation for any successful relationship with the East. Without Western unity, we'll squander our energies in bickering while the Soviets continue as they please. With unity, we have the strength to moderate Soviet behavior. We've done so in the past and we can do so again.

Our challenge is to establish a framework in which sound East-West relations will endure. I'm optimistic that we can build a more constructive relationship with the Soviet Union. To do so, however, we must understand the nature of the Soviet system and the lessons of the past.

The Soviet Union is a huge empire ruled by an elite that holds all power and all privilege. They hold it tightly because, as we've seen in Poland, they fear what might happen if even the smallest amount of control slips from their grasp. They fear the infectiousness of even a little freedom and because of this in many ways their system has failed. The Soviet empire is faltering because it is rigid — centralized control has destroyed incentives for innovation, efficiency and individual achievement. Spiritually, there is a sense of malaise and resentment.

But in the midst of social and economic problems, the Soviet dictatorship has forged the largest armed force in the world. It has done so by preempting the human needs of its people, and, in the end, this course will undermine the foundations of the Soviet system. Harry Truman was right when he said of the Soviets that, "When you try to conquer other people or extend yourself over vast areas you cannot win in the long run."

Yet Soviet aggressiveness has grown as Soviet military power has increased. To compensate, we must learn from the lessons of the past. When the West has stood unified and firm, the Soviet Union has taken heed. For 35 years Western Europe has lived free despite the shadow of Soviet military might. Through unity, you'll remember from your modern history courses, the West secured the withdrawal of occupation forces from Austria and the recognition of its rights in Berlin.

Other Western policies have not been successful. East-West trade was expanded in the hope of providing incentives for Soviet restraint, but the Soviets exploited the benefits of trade without moderating their behavior. Despite a decade of ambitious arms control efforts, the Soviet buildup continues. And despite its signature of the Helsinki agreements on human rights, the Soviet Union has not relaxed its hold on its own people or those of Western[1] Europe.

During the 1970's some of us forgot the warning of President Kennedy who said that the Soviets "have offered to trade us an apple for an orchard. We don't do that in this country." But we came perilously close to doing just that.

If East-West relations in the detente era in Europe have yielded disappointment, detente outside of Europe has yielded a severe disillusionment for those who expected a moderation of Soviet behavior. The Soviet Union continues to support Vietnam in its occupation of Kampuchea and its massive military presence in Laos. It is engaged in a war of aggression against Afghanistan. Soviet proxy forces have brought instability and conflict to Africa and Central America.

We are now approaching an extremely important phase in East-West relations as the current Soviet leadership is succeeded by a new generation. Both the current and the new Soviet leadership should realize aggressive policies will meet a firm Western response. On the other hand, a Soviet leadership devoted to improving its people's lives, rather than expanding its armed conquests, will find a sympathetic partner in the West. The West will respond with expanded trade and other forms of cooperation. But all of this depends on Soviet actions. Standing in the Athenian marketplace 2,000 years ago, Demosthenos said: "What sane man would let another man's words rather than his deeds proclaim who is at peace and who is at war with him?"

Policy for Peace

Peace is not the absence of conflict, but the ability to cope with conflict by peaceful means. I believe we can cope. I believe that the West can fashion a realistic, durable policy that will protect our interests and keep the peace, not just for this generation, but for your children and your grandchildren. (Applause.)

I believe such a policy consists of five points: military balance, economic security, regional stability, arms reductions, and dialogue. Now, these are the means by which we can seek peace with the Soviet Union in the years ahead. Today, I want to set this five-point program to guide the future of our East-West relations, set it out for all to hear and see.

Military Balance. First, a sound East-West military balance is absolutely essential. Last week NATO published a comprehensive comparison of its forces with those of the Warsaw Pact. Its message is clear. During the past decade, the Soviet Union has built up its forces across the board. During that same period, the defense expenditures of the United States declined in real terms. The United States has already undertaken steps to recover from that decade of neglect. And I should add that the expenditures of our European allies have increased slowly but steadily, something we often fail to recognize here at home.

Economic Security. The second point on which we must reach consensus with our allies deals with economic security. Consultations are under way among

Appendix

Western nations on the transfer of militarily significant technology and the extension of financial credits to the East as well as on the question of energy dependence on the East, that energy dependence of Europe. We recognize that some of our allies' economic requirements are distinct from our own. But the Soviets must not have access to Western technology with military applications, and we must not subsidize the Soviet economy. The Soviet Union must make the difficult choices brought on by its military budgets and economic shortcomings.

Regional Stability. The third element is regional stability with peaceful change. Last year in a speech in Philadelphia and in the Summit meetings at Cancún, I outlined the basic American plan to assist the developing world. These principles for economic development remain the foundation of our approach. They represent no threat to the Soviet Union. Yet in many areas of the developing world we find that Soviet arms and Soviet-supported troops are attempting to destabilize societies and extend Moscow's influence.

High on our agenda must be progress toward peace in Afghanistan. The United States is prepared to engage in a serious effort to negotiate an end to the conflict caused by the Soviet invasion of that country. We are ready to cooperate in an international effort to resolve this problem, to secure a full Soviet withdrawal from Afghanistan, and to ensure self-determination for the Afghan people.

In southern Africa, working closely with our Western allies and the African states, we've made real progress toward independence for Namibia. These negotiations, if successful, will result in peaceful and secure conditions throughout southern Africa. The simultaneous withdrawal of Cuban forces from Angola is essential to achieving Namibian independence, as well as creating long-range prospects for peace in the region.

Central America also has become a dangerous point of tension in East-West relations. The Soviet Union cannot escape responsibility for the violence and suffering in the region caused by its support for Cuban activities in Central America and its accelerated transfer of advanced military equipment to Cuba.

However, it was in Western Europe — or Eastern Europe, I should say — that the hopes of the 1970's were greatest, and it is there that they have been the most bitterly disappointed. There was hope that the people of Poland could develop a freer society. But the Soviet Union has refused to allow the people of Poland to decide their own fate, just as it refused to allow the people of Hungary to decide theirs in 1956, or the people of Czechoslovakia in 1968.

If martial law in Poland is lifted, if all the political prisoners are released, and if a dialogue is restored with the Solidarity Union, the United States is prepared to join in a program of economic support. Water cannons and clubs against the Polish people are hardly the kind of dialogue that gives us hope. It is up to the Soviets and their client regimes to show good faith by concrete actions.

Arms Reduction. The fourth point is arms reduction. I know that this weighs heavily on many of your minds. In our 1931 *Prism*, we quoted Carl Sandburg, who in his own beautiful way quoted the Mother Prairie, saying, "Have you seen a red sunset drip over one of my cornfields, the shore of night stars, the wave lines of dawn up a wheat valley?" What an idyllic scene that paints in our minds — and what a nightmarish prospect that a huge mushroom cloud might someday destroy such beauty. My duty as President is to ensure that the ultimate nightmare never occurs, that the prairies and the cities and the people who inhabit them remain free and untouched by nuclear conflict.

I wish more than anything there were a simple policy that would eliminate that nuclear danger. But there are only difficult policy choices through which we can achieve a stable nuclear balance at the lowest possible level.

I do not doubt that the Soviet people, and, yes, the Soviet leaders have an overriding interest in preventing the use of nuclear weapons. The Soviet Union within the memory of its leaders has known the devastation of total conventional war and knows that nuclear war would be even more calamitous. Yet, so far, the Soviet Union has used arms control negotiations primarily as an instrument to restrict U.S. defense programs and, in conjunction with their own arms buildup, a means to enhance Soviet power and prestige.

Unfortunately, for some time suspicions have grown that the Soviet Union has not been living up to its obligations under existing arms control treaties. There is conclusive evidence the Soviet Union has provided toxins to the Laotians and Vietnamese for use against defenseless villagers in Southeast Asia. And the Soviets themselves are employing chemical weapons on the freedom fighters in Afghanistan.

We must establish firm criteria for arms control in the 1980's if we're to secure genuine and lasting restraint on Soviet military programs throughout arms control. We must seek agreements which are verifiable, equitable, and militarily significant. Agreements that provide only the appearance of arms control breed dangerous illusions.

Last November, I committed the United States to seek significant reductions on nuclear and conventional forces. In Geneva, we have since proposed limits on U.S. and Soviet intermediate-range missiles, including the complete elimination of the most threatening systems on both sides.

In Vienna, we're negotiating, together with our allies, for reductions of conventional forces in Europe. In the 40-nation Committee on Disarmament, the United Nations[2] seeks a total ban on all chemical weapons.

Since the first days of my administration, we've been working on our approach to the crucial issue of strategic arms and the control and negotiations for control of those arms with the Soviet Union. The study and analysis required has been complex and difficult. It had to be undertaken deliberately, thoroughly, and correctly. We've laid a solid basis for these negotiations. We're consulting with Congressional leaders and with our allies, and we are now ready to proceed.

The main threat to peace posed by nuclear weapons today is the growing instability of the nuclear balance. This is due to the increasingly destructive potential of the massive Soviet buildup in its ballistic missile force.

Therefore, our goal is to enhance deterrence and achieve stability through significant reductions in the most destabilizing nuclear systems, ballistic missiles, and especially the giant intercontinental ballistic missiles, while maintaining a nuclear capability sufficient to deter conflict, to underwrite our national security and to meet our commitment to allies and friends.

For the immediate future, I'm asking my START, and START really means, we've given up on SALT, START means, "Strategic Arms Reduction Talks," and that negotiating team to propose to their Soviet counterparts a practical, phased reduction plan. The focus of our efforts will be, reduce significantly the most destabilizing systems, the ballistic missiles, the number of warheads they carry and their overall destructive potential.

At the first phase, or the end of the first phase of START, I expect ballistic missile warheads, the most serious threat we face, to be reduced to equal levels, equal ceilings, at least a third below the current levels. To enhance stability, I would ask that no more than half of those warheads be land-based. I hope that these warhead reductions as well as significant reductions in missiles themselves could be achieved as rapidly as possible.

In a second phase, we'll seek to achieve an equal ceiling on other elements of our strategic nuclear forces including limits on the ballistic missile throwweight at less than current American levels. In both phases, we shall insist on verification procedures to insure compliance with the agreement.

This, I might say, will be the twentieth time that we have sought such negotiations with the Soviet Union since World War II.

The monumental task of reducing and reshaping our strategic forces to enhance stability will take many years of concentrated effort. But I believe that it will be possible to reduce the risks of war by removing the instabilities that now exist and by dismantling the nuclear menace. (Applause.)

I have written to President Brezhnev and directed Secretary Haig to approach the Soviet government concerning the initiation of formal negotiations on the reduction of strategic nuclear arms, START, at

the earliest opportunity. We hope negotiations will begin by the end of June.

We will negotiate seriously, in good faith and carefully consider all proposals made by the Soviet Union. If they approach these negotiations in the same spirit, I'm confident that together we can achieve an agreement of enduring value that reduces the number of nuclear weapons, halts the growth in strategic forces and opens the way to even more far-reaching steps in the future. (Applause.)

I hope the Commencement today will also mark the commencement of a new era, in both senses of the word a new start toward a more peaceful and secure world.

Dialogue. The fifth and final point I propose for East-West relations is dialogue. I've always believed that people's problems can be solved when people talk to each other instead of about each other. And I've already expressed my own desire to meet with President Brezhnev in New York next month. If this can't be done, I'd hope we could arrange a future meeting where positive results can be anticipated. And when we sit down, I'll tell President Brezhnev that the United States is ready to build a new understanding based upon the principles I've outlined today. I'll tell him that his government and his people have nothing to fear from the United States. The free nations living at peace in the world community can vouch for the fact that we seek only harmony. And I'll ask President

Brezhnev why our two nations can't practice mutual restraint. Why can't our peoples enjoy the benefits that would flow from real cooperation? Why can't we reduce the number of horrendous weapons?

Perhaps I should also speak to him of this school and these graduates who are leaving it today — of your hopes for the future, of your deep desire for peace, and yet your strong commitment to defend your values if threatened. Perhaps if he someday could attend such a ceremony as this, he'd better understand America. In the only system he knows, you would be here by the decision of government and on this day the government representatives would be here telling most, if not all of you, where you were going to report to work tomorrow.

But as we go to Europe for the talks and as we proceed in the important challenges facing this country, I want you to know that I will be thinking of you and of Eureka and what you represent. In one of my yearbooks, I remember reading that, "The work of the prairie is to be the soil for the growth of a strong western culture." I believe Eureka is fulfilling that work. You, the members of the 1982 graduating class, are this year's harvest.

I spoke of the difference between our two countries. I try to follow the humor of the Russian people. We don't hear much about the Russian people. We hear about the Russian leaders. But you can learn a lot

because they do have a sense of humor and you can learn from the jokes they're telling. And one of the most recent jokes I found kind of — well, personally interesting. Maybe you might — tell you something about your country. The joke they tell is that an American and a Russian were arguing about the differences between our two countries. And the American said, "Look. In my country I can walk into the Oval Office, I can hit the desk with my fist, and say, 'President Reagan, I don't like the way you are governing the United States.'" And the Russian said, "I can do that." The American said, "What?" He says "I can walk into the Kremlin, into Brezhnev's office. I can pound Brezhnev's desk and I can say, 'Mr. President, I don't like the way Ronald Reagan is governing the United States.'" (Laughter.) (Applause.)

Eureka as an institution and you as individuals are sustaining the best of Western man's ideals. As a fellow graduate and in the office I hold, I'll do my best to uphold these same ideals. To the Class of '82, congratulations and God bless you. (Applause.)

[1] *The White House transcript indicated President Reagan intended to say "Eastern."*

[2] *The White House transcript indicated President Reagan intended to say "United States."*

President Reagan's 1983 State of the Union Address

Following is the Congressional Record *text of President Reagan's State of the Union address to a joint session of Congress Jan. 25, 1983.*

The PRESIDENT: Mr. Speaker, Mr. President, distinguished Members of the Congress, honored guests and fellow citizens: This solemn occasion marks the 196th time that a President of the United States has reported on the state of the Union since George Washington first did so in 1790. That is a lot of reports, but there is no shortage of new things to say about the state of the Union. The very key to our success has been our ability, foremost among nations, to preserve our lasting values by making change work for us rather than against us.

I would like to talk with you this evening about what we can do together — not as Republicans and Democrats, but as Americans — to make tomorrow's America happy and prosperous at home, strong and respected abroad, and at peace in the world.

As we gather here tonight, the state of our Union is strong, but our economy is

troubled. For too many of our fellow citizens — farmers, steel and auto workers, lumbermen, black teenagers, and working mothers — this is a painful period. We must all do everything in our power to bring their ordeal to an end. It has fallen to us, in our time, to undo damage that was a long time in the making, and to begin the hard but necessary task of building a better future for ourselves and our children.

We have a long way to go, but thanks to the courage, patience, and strength of our people, America is on the mend.

Let me give you just one important reason why I believe this — it involves many Members of this body.

Social Security Reform

Just 10 days ago, after months of debate and deadlock, the bipartisan Commission on Social Security accomplished the seemingly impossible.

Social security, as some of us had warned for so long, faced disaster. I, myself, have been talking about this problem for almost 30 years. As 1983 began, the system stood on the brink of bankruptcy, a double victim of our economic ills. First, a

decade of rampant inflation drained its reserves as we tried to protect beneficiaries from the spiraling cost of living. Then the recession and the sudden end of inflation withered the expanding wage base and increasing revenues the system needs to support the 36 million Americans who depend on it.

When the Speaker of the House, the Senate majority leader, and I formed the bipartisan Commission on Social Security, pundits and experts predicted that party divisions and conflicting interests would prevent the Commission from agreeing on a plan to save social security.

Well, sometimes, even here in Washington, the cynics are wrong. Through compromise and cooperation, the members of the Commission overcame their differences and achieved a fair, workable plan. They proved that, when it comes to the national welfare, Americans can still pull together for the common good.

Tonight, I am especially pleased to join with the Speaker and the Senate majority leader in urging the Congress to enact this plan by Easter.

There are elements in it, of course,

that none of us prefers, but taken together it forms a package that all of us can support. It asks for some sacrifice by all — the self-employed, beneficiaries, workers, Government employees, and the better-off among the retired — but it imposes an undue burden on none. And, in supporting it, we keep an important pledge to the American people: the integrity of the social security system will be preserved — and no one's payments will be reduced.

The Commission's plan will do the job. Indeed, it must do the job. We owe it to today's older Americans — and today's younger workers.

So, before we go any further, I ask you to join with me in saluting the members of the Commission who are here tonight, and Senate Majority Leader Howard Baker and Speaker Tip O'Neill, for a job well done.

Bipartisan Spirit

I hope and pray the bipartisan spirit that guided you in this endeavor will inspire all of us as we face the challenges of the year ahead.

Nearly half a century ago, in this Chamber, another American President, Franklin Delano Roosevelt, in his second state of the Union message, urged America to look to the future — to meet the challenge of change and the need for leadership that looks forward, not backward.

"Throughout the world," he said, "change is the order of the day. In every nation economic problems long in the making have brought crises of many kinds for which the masters of old practice and theory were unprepared."

He also reminded us that, "the future lies with those wise political leaders who realize that the great public is interested more in Government than in politics."

So, let us, in these next 2 years — men and women of both parties and every political shade — concentrate on the long-range, bipartisan responsibilities of Government, not the short-range or short-term temptations of partisan politics.

Economic Recovery

The problems we inherited were far worse than most inside and out of Government had expected; the recession was deeper than most inside and out of Government had predicted. Curing those problems has taken more time, and a higher toll, than any of us wanted. Unemployment is far too high. Projected Federal spending — if Government refuses to tighten its own belt — will also be far too high and could weaken and shorten the economic recovery now underway.

This recovery will bring with it a revival of economic confidence and spending for consumer items and capital goods — the stimulus we need to restart our stalled economic engines. The American people have already stepped up their rate of saving, assuring that the funds needed to modernize our factories and improve our technology will once again flow to business and industry.

The inflationary expectations that led to a 21½ percent interest prime rate and soaring mortgage rates 2 years ago are now reduced by almost half. Lenders have started to realize that double-digit inflation is no longer a way of life. So interest rates have tumbled, paving the way for recovery in vital industries like housing and autos.

The early evidence of that recovery has started coming in. Housing starts for the fourth quarter of 1982 were up 45 percent from a year ago. And housing permits — a sure indicator of future growth — were up a whopping 60 percent.

We are witnessing an upsurge of productivity and impressive evidence that American industry will once again become competitive in markets at home and abroad — insuring more jobs and better incomes for the Nation's workforce.

But our confidence must also be tempered by realism and patience. Quick fixes and artificial stimulants, repeatedly applied over decades, are what brought us the inflationary disorders that we have now paid such a heavy price to cure.

The permanent recovery in employment, production, and investment we seek will not come in a sharp, short spurt. It will build carefully and steadily in the months and years ahead.

In the meantime, the challenge of Government is to identify the things we can do now to ease this massive economic transition for the American people.

Federal Budget and Deficits

The Federal budget is both a symptom and a cause of our economic problems. Unless we reduce the dangerous growth rate in Government spending, we could face the prospect of sluggish economic growth into the indefinite future. Failure to cope with this problem now could mean as much as a trillion dollars more in national debt in the next 4 years alone. That would average $4,300 in additional debt for every man, woman, and child and baby in our Nation.

To assure a sustained recovery, we must continue getting runaway spending under control to bring those deficits down. If we do not, the recovery will be too short, unemployment will remain too high, and we will leave an unconscionable burden of national debt for our children. That we must not do.

Let us be clear about where the deficit problem comes from. Contrary to the drumbeat we have been hearing for the last few months, the deficits we face are not rooted in defense spending. Taken as a percentage of the gross national product, our defense spending happens to be only about four-fifths of what it was in 1970. Nor is the deficit, as some would have it, rooted in tax cuts. Even with our tax cuts, taxes as a fraction of gross national product remain about the same as they were in 1970.

The fact is, our deficits come from the uncontrolled growth of the budget for domestic spending. During the 1970s the share of our national income devoted to this domestic spending increased by more than 60 percent — from 10 cents out of every dollar produced by the American people to 16 cents. In spite of all our economies and efficiencies, and without adding any new programs, basic, necessary domestic spending provided for in this year's budget will grow to almost $1 trillion over the next 5 years.

The deficit problem is a clear and present danger to the basic health of our Republic. We need a plan to overcome this danger — a plan based on these principles.

It must be bipartisan. Conquering the deficits and putting the Government's house in order will require the best efforts of all of us.

It must be fair. Just as all will share in the benefits that will come from recovery, all would share fairly in the burden of transition.

It must be prudent. The strength of our national defense must be restored so that we can pursue prosperity in peace and freedom while maintaining our commitment to the truly needy.

And finally, it must be realistic. We cannot rely on hope alone.

Four-Part Plan for Recovery

With these guiding principles in mind, let me outline a four-part plan to increase economic growth and reduce deficits.

First, in my budget message, I will recommend a Federal spending freeze. I know this is strong medicine, but so far we have only cut the rate of increase in Federal spending. The Government has continued to spend more money each year, though not as much more as it did in the past. Taken as a whole, the budget I am proposing for the next fiscal year will increase no more than the rate of inflation — in other words, the Federal Government will hold the line on real spending. Now, that is far less than many American families have had to do in these difficult times.

I will request that the proposed 6-month freeze in cost-of-living adjustments recommended by the bipartisan Social Security Commission be applied to other Government-related retirement programs. I will also propose a 1-year freeze on a broad range of domestic spending programs, and for Federal civilian and military pay and pension programs.

Let me say right here, I am sorry, with regard to the military, in asking that of them because for so many years they have been so far behind and so low in reward for what the men and women in uniform are doing, but I am sure they will understand that this must be across the board and fair.

Second, I will ask Congress to adopt specific measures to control the growth of the so-called uncontrollable spending programs. These are the automatic spending programs, such as food stamps, that cannot be simply frozen — and that have grown by

over 400 percent since 1970. They are the largest, single cause of the built-in or structural deficit problem. Our standard here will be fairness — insuring that the taxpayers' hard-earned dollars go only to the truly needy; that none of them are turned away; but that fraud and waste are stamped out. And, I am sorry to say, there is a lot of it out there. In the food stamp program alone, last year we identified almost $1.1 billion in overpayments. The taxpayers are not the only victims of this kind of abuse; the truly needy suffer as funds intended for them are taken not by the needy but by the greedy. For everyone's sake, we must put .an end to such waste and corruption.

Third, I will adjust our program to restore America's defenses by proposing $55 billion in defense savings over the next 5 years. These are savings recommended to me by the Secretary of Defense, who has assured me they can be safely achieved and will not diminish our ability to negotiate arms reductions or endanger America's security. We will not gamble with our national survival.

Fourth, because we must insure reduction and eventual elimination of deficits over the next several years, I will propose a standby tax limited to no more than 1 percent of the gross national product to start in fiscal 1986. It would last no more than 3 years and it would start only if the Congress has first approved our spending freeze and budget control program. And there are several other conditions also that must be met, all of them in order for this program to be triggered. You could say that this is an insurance policy for the future, a remedy that will be at hand if needed, but only resorted to if absolutely necessary.

In the meantime, we will continue to study ways to simplify the Tax Code and make it more fair for all Americans. This is a goal that every American who has ever struggled with a tax form can understand.

At the same time, however, I will oppose any efforts to undo the basic tax reforms that we have already enacted — including the 10-percent tax break coming to taxpayers this July and the tax indexing which will protect all Americans from inflationary bracket creep in the years ahead.

Now, I realize that this four-part plan is easier to describe than it will be to enact. But the looming deficits that hang over us — and over America's future — must be reduced. The path I have outlined is fair, balanced, and realistic. If enacted, it will insure a steady decline in deficits, aiming toward a balanced budget by the end of the decade. It is the only path that will lead to a strong, sustained recovery.

Let us follow that path together.

Employment

No domestic challenge is more crucial than providing stable, permanent jobs for all Americans who want to work. The recovery program will provide jobs for most, but others will need special help and training for new skills. Shortly, I will submit to the Congress the Employment Act [of] 1983 designed to get at the special problems of the long-term unemployed as well as young people trying to enter the job market. I will propose extending unemployment benefits, including special incentives to employers who hire the long-term unemployed, providing programs for displaced workers, and helping federally funded and State-administered unemployment insurance programs to provide workers with training and relocation assistance. Finally, our proposal will include new incentives for summer youth employment to help young people get a start in the job market.

We must offer both short-term help and long-term help for our unemployed. I hope we can work together on this, as we did last year in enacting the landmark Job Training Partnership Act. Regulatory reform legislation, a responsible Clean Air Act, and passage of Enterprise Zone legislation will also create new incentives for jobs and opportunity.

Trade

One out of every five jobs in our country depends on trade. So, I will propose a broader strategy in the field of international trade — one that increases the openness of our trading system and is fairer to America's farmers and workers in the world marketplace. We must have adequate export financing to sell American products overseas. I will ask for new negotiating authority to remove barriers and get more of our products into foreign markets. We must strengthen the organization of our trade agencies and make changes in our domestic laws and international trade policy to promote free trade and the increased flow of American goods, services, and investments.

Our trade position can also be improved by making our port system more efficient. Better, more active harbors translate into stable jobs in our coalfields, railroads, trucking industry, and ports. After 2 years of debate, it is time for us to get together and enact a port modernization bill.

Education, training, and retraining are fundamental to our success, as are research, development, and productivity. Labor, management, and government at all levels can and must participate in improving these tools of growth. Tax policy, regulatory practices, and Government programs all need constant reevaluation in terms of our competitiveness. Every American has a role, and a stake, in international trade.

Education

We Americans are still the technological leaders in most fields. We must keep that edge, and to do so we need to begin renewing the basics — starting with our educational system. While we grew complacent, others have acted. Japan, with a population only about half the size of ours, graduates from its universities more engineers than we do. If a child does not receive adequate math and science teaching by the age of 16, he or she has lost the chance to be a scientist or an engineer.

We must join together — parents, teachers, grassroots groups, organized labor, and the business community — to revitalize American education by setting a standard of excellence.

In 1983, we seek four major education goals:

A quality education initiative to encourage a substantial upgrading of math and science instruction through block grants to the States.

Establishment of education savings accounts that will give middle and lower income families an incentive to save for their children's college education and, at the same time, encourage a real increase in savings for economic growth.

Passage of tuition tax credits for parents who want to send their children to private or religiously affiliated schools.

A constitutional amendment to permit voluntary school prayer; God should never have been expelled from America's classrooms in the first place.

Discrimination Against Women

Our commitment to fairness means that we must assure legal and economic equity for women, and eliminate, once and for all, all traces of unjust discrimination against women from the United States Code. We will not tolerate wage discrimination based on sex and we intend to strengthen enforcement of child support laws to insure that single parents, most of whom are women, do not suffer unfair financial hardship. We will also take action to remedy inequities in pensions. These initiatives will be joined by others to continue our efforts to promote equity for women.

Civil Rights Commission

Also in the area of fairness and equity, we will ask for extension of the Civil Rights Commission which is due to expire this year. The Commission is an important part of the ongoing struggle for justice in America, and we strongly support its reauthorization. Effective enforcement of our Nation's fair housing laws is also essential to ensuring equal opportunity. In the year ahead, we will work to strengthen enforcement of fair housing laws for all Americans.

Criminal Justice Reform

The time has also come for major reform of our criminal justice statutes and acceleration of the drive against organized crime and drug trafficking. It is high time that we make our cities safe again. This administration hereby declares an all-out war on big-time organized crime and the drug racketeers who are poisoning our young people. We will also implement rec-

ommendations of our Task Force on Victims of Crime, which will report to me this week.

Agriculture

American agriculture, the envy of the world, has been the victim of its own successes. With one farmer now producing enough food to feed himself and 77 other people, America is confronted with record surplus crops and commodity prices below the cost of production. We must strive, through innovations like the payment-in-kind "crop swap" approach, and an aggressive export policy, to restore health and vitality to rural America. Meanwhile, I have instructed the Department of Agriculture to work individually with farmers with debt problems to help them through these tough times.

Private Sector Initiatives Task Force

Over the past year, our Task Force on Private Sector Initiatives has successfully forged a working partnership involving leaders of business, labor, education, and government to address the training needs of American workers. Thanks to the task force, private sector initiatives are now underway in all 50 States of the Union and thousands of working people have been helped in making the shift from dead-end jobs and low-demand skills to the growth areas of high technology and the service economy. Additionally, a major effort will be focused on encouraging the expansion of private community child care. The new Advisory Council on Private Sector Initiatives will carry on and extend this vital work of encouraging private initiative in 1983.

Health Care

In the coming year we will also act to improve the quality of life for Americans by curbing the skyrocketing cost of health care that is becoming an unbearable financial burden for so many. And we will submit legislation to provide catastrophic illness insurance coverage for older Americans.

State and Local Governments

I will also shortly submit a comprehensive federalism proposal that will continue our efforts to restore to States and local governments their roles as dynamic laboratories of change in a creative society.

During the next several weeks, I will send to the Congress a series of detailed proposals on these and other topics and look forward to working with you on the development of these initiatives.

Pioneer Spirit

So far, now, I have concentrated mainly on the problems posed by the future. But in almost every home and work-place in America, we are already witnessing reason for great hope — the first flowering of the man-made miracles of high technology, a field pioneered and still led by our country.

To many of us now, computers, silicon chips, data processing, cybernetics, and all the other innovations of the dawning high technology age are as mystifying as the workings of the combustion engine must have been when that first Model T rattled down Main Street U.S.A.

But, as surely as America's pioneer spirit made us the industrial giant of the 20th century, the same pioneer spirit today is opening up another vast frontier of opportunity — the frontier of high technology. In conquering this frontier we cannot write off our traditional industries, but we must develop the skills and industries that will make us a pioneer of tomorrow. This administration is committed to keeping America the technological leader of the world now and into the 21st century.

America as World Leader

But let us turn briefly to the international arena. America's leadership role in the world came to us because of our own strength and because of the values which guide us as a society: Free elections, a free press, freedom of religious choice, free trade unions, and, above all, freedom for the individual and rejection of the arbitrary power of the State. These values are the bedrock of our strength. They unite us in a stewardship of peace and freedom with our allies and friends in NATO, in Asia, in Latin America and elsewhere. There are also the values which in the recent past some among us have begun to doubt and view with a cynical eye.

Fortunately, we and our allies have rediscovered the strength of our common democratic values. And we are applying them as the cornerstone of a comprehensive strategy for peace with freedom. In London last year, I announced the commitment of the United States to developing the infrastructure of democracy throughout the world. We intend to pursue this democratic initiative vigorously. The future belongs not to governments and ideologies which oppress their peoples but to democratic systems of self-government which encourage individual initiative and guarantee personal freedom.

But our strategy for peace with freedom must also be based on strength — economic strength and military strength. A strong American economy is essential to the well-being and security of our friends and allies. The restoration of a strong, healthy American economy has been and remains one of the central pillars of our foreign policy. The progress I have been able to report to you tonight will, I know, be as warmly welcomed by the rest of the world as it is by the American people.

We must also recognize that our own economic well-being is inextricably linked to the world economy. We export over 20 percent of our industrial production, and 40 percent of our farmland production is for export. We will continue to work closely with the industrialized democracies of Europe and Japan and with the International Monetary Fund to insure it has adequate resources to help bring the world economy back to strong, noninflationary growth. As the leader of the West and as a country that has become great and rich because of economic freedom, America must be an unrelenting advocate of free trade. As some nations are tempted to turn to protectionism, our strategy cannot be to follow them but to lead the way toward freer trade. To this end, in May of this year, America will host an economic summit meeting in Williamsburg, Va.

Defense Program

As we begin our third year, we have put in place a defense program that redeems the neglect of the past decade. We have developed a realistic military strategy to deter threats to peace and to protect freedom if deterrence fails. Our Armed Forces are finally properly paid, after years of neglect, are well trained, and becoming better equipped and supplied — and the American uniform is once again worn with pride. Most of the major systems needed for modernizing our defenses are already underway and we will be addressing one key system — the MX missile — in consultation with the Congress in a few months.

Foreign Policy

America's foreign policy is once again based on bipartisanship — on realism, strength, full partnership and consultation with our allies, and constructive negotiation with potential adversaries. From the Middle East to Southern Africa to Geneva, American diplomats are taking the initiative to make peace and lower arms levels. We should be proud of our role as peacemakers.

In the Middle East last year, the United States played the major role in ending the tragic fighting in Lebanon, and negotiated the withdrawal of the PLO from Beirut.

Last September, I outlined principles to carry on the peace process begun so promisingly at Camp David. All the people of the Middle East should know that, in the year ahead, we will not flag in our efforts to build on that foundation to bring them the blessings of peace.

In Central America and the Caribbean Basin, we are likewise engaged in a partnership for peace, prosperity, and democracy. Final passage of the remaining portions of our Caribbean Basin Initiative, which passed the House last year, is one of this administration's top legislative priorities for 1983.

The security and economic assistance policies of this administration, in Latin America and elsewhere, are based on realism and represent a critical investment in the future of the human race. This under-

taking is a joint responsibility of the executive and legislative branches, and I am counting on the cooperation and statesmanship of the Congress to help us meet this essential foreign policy goal.

U.S.-Soviet Relations

At the heart of our strategy for peace is our relationship with the Soviet Union.

The past year saw a change in Soviet leadership. We are prepared for a positive change in Soviet-American relations. But the Soviet Union must show, by deeds as well as words, a sincere commitment to respect the rights and sovereignty of the family of nations. Responsible members of the world community do not threaten or invade their neighbors and they restrain their allies from aggression.

For our part, we are vigorously pursuing arms reduction negotiations with the Soviet Union. Supported by our allies, we put forward draft agreements proposing significant weapons reductions to equal and verifiable lower levels. We insist on an equal balance of forces. And, given the overwhelming evidence of Soviet violations of international treaties concerning chemical and biological weapons, we also insist that any agreement we sign can and will be verifiable.

In the case of intermediate-range nuclear forces, we have proposed the complete elimination of the entire class of land-based missiles. We are also prepared to carefully explore serious Soviet proposals. At the same time, let me emphasize that allied steadfastness remains a key to achieving arms reductions.

With firmness and dedication, we will continue to negotiate. Deep down, the Soviets must know it is in their interests as well as ours to prevent a wasteful arms race. And once they recognize our unshakeable resolve to maintain adequate deterrence, they will have every reason to join us in the search for greater security and major arms reductions. When that moment comes — and I am confident that it will — we will have taken an important step toward a more peaceful future for all the world's people.

America's Noble Vision

A very wise man, Bernard Baruch, once said that America has never forgotten the nobler things that brought her into being and that light her path. Our country is a special place because we Americans have always been sustained, through good times and bad, by a noble vision — a vision not only of what the world around us is today, but what we, as a free people, can make it be tomorrow.

We are realists; we solve our problems instead of ignoring them, no matter how loud the chorus of despair around us.

But we are also idealists, for it was an ideal that brought our ancestors to these shores from every corner of the world.

Right now we need both realism and idealism. Millions of our neighbors are without work. It is up to us to see they are not without hope. This is a task for all of us. And may I say Americans have rallied to this cause, proving once again that we are the most generous people on Earth.

We who are in Government must take the lead in restoring the economy.

[Applause, the Members rising.]

The PRESIDENT. Here all that time I thought you were reading the paper. [Laughter.]

The single thing that can start the wheels of industry turning again is further reduction of interest rates. Just another one or two points can mean tens of thousands of jobs. Right now, with inflation as low as it is, 3.9 percent, there is room for interest rates to come down.

Only fear prevents their reduction. A lender, as we know, must charge an interest rate that recovers the depreciated value of the dollars loaned, and that depreciation is, of course, the amount of inflation. Today, interest rates are based on fear, fear that Government will resort to measures, as it has in the past, that will send inflation zooming again.

We who serve here in this Capital must erase that fear by making it absolutely clear that we will not stop fighting inflation; that, together, we will do only these things that will lead to lasting economic growth.

Yes, the problems confronting us are large and forbidding. And, certainly, no one can or should minimize the plight of millions of our friends and neighbors who are living in the bleak emptiness of unemployment. But we must and can give them good reason to be hopeful.

Back over the years, citizens like ourselves have gathered within these walls when our Nation was threatened; sometimes when its very existence was at stake. Always, with courage and commonsense, they met the crises of their time and lived to see a stronger, better, and more prosperous country.

The present situation is no worse and in fact is not as bad as some of those they faced. Time and again, they proved that there is nothing we Americans cannot achieve as free men and women.

Yes, we still have problems — plenty of them. But it is just plain wrong — unjust to our country and unjust to our people — to let those problems stand in the way of the most important truth of all: America is on the mend.

We owe it to the unfortunate to be aware of their plight and to help them in every way we can. No one can quarrel with that — we must and do have compassion for all the victims of this economic crisis. But the big story about America today is the way that millions of confident, caring people — those extraordinary "ordinary" Americans who never make the headlines and will never be interviewed — are laying the foundation, not just for recovery from our present problems, but for a better tomorrow for all our people.

From coast to coast, on the job and in classrooms and laboratories, at new construction sites and in churches and in community groups, neighbors are helping neighbors. And they have already begun the building, the research, the work, and the giving that will make our community great again.

I believe this because I believe in them — in the strength of their hearts and minds, in the commitment that each one of them brings to their daily lives, be they high or humble. The challenge for us in Government is to be worthy of them — to make Government a help, not a hinderance to our people in the challenging but promising days ahead.

If we do that, if we care what our children and our children's children will say of us, if we want them one day to be thankful for what we did here in these temples of freedom, we will work together to make America better for our having been here — not just in this year, or in this decade, but in the next century and beyond.

Thank you and God bless you.

[Applause, the Members rising.]

President Reagan's Fiscal 1984 Budget Message

Following is the text of President Reagan's budget message sent to Congress Jan. 31, 1983.

TO THE CONGRESS OF
THE UNITED STATES:

Two years ago, in my first address to the country, I went before the American people to report on the condition of our economy, which had suffered from many years of seriously misguided policies. I made a strong commitment to change the traditional shortsighted view that had previously been taken on economic priorities so that we could achieve our goal of long-term prosperity. I stated that we had a massive job before us.

Government spending was taking a rapidly increasing share of national income, burdensome Government regulation had stunted productivity increases, and ex-

cessive tax rates combined with erratic monetary policy resulted in serious disincentives to investment and long-term real economic growth. Inflation was at double-digit levels. Interest rates were at record highs. Real growth and job creation had ceased. New investment, productivity, and personal saving were stagnant. Our economy was in the worst mess in half a century.

To make matters worse, our military strength had been allowed to run down relative to the aggressively expanding military might of the Soviet Union. We were in serious danger of becoming powerless to deter or counter Soviet aggression around the world.

The economic program that I proposed at that time focused on long-range real growth. My tax proposals were designed to provide badly needed private incentives to stimulate saving and productive investment. I supported the Federal Reserve in its pursuit of sound monetary policy. I worked with the Congress to reverse the growth of Government programs that had become too large or outlasted their usefulness. I worked to eliminate or simplify unnecessary or burdensome regulations.

The unprecedented buildup of inflationary forces in the 1970's, however, exacerbated in severity and duration the economic downturn of recent years. One of the key detrimental forces has been the growing Federal budget. Despite our success in reducing the rate of growth of nondefense spending in the last two budgets, spending in 1983 will exceed 1981 levels by 21%, reflecting continued increases in basic entitlement programs, essential increases in defense spending, and rapid growth of interest costs.

Thus, the full effect of the changes we have made is taking time to develop. Overreactive short-term remedies are not the answer. What is essential now is that we continue to work together to rebuild this country — without losing sight of the four fundamentals of our economic program:

● Limiting tax burdens to the minimum levels necessary to finance essential Government services, thus maintaining incentives for saving, investment, work effort, productivity, and economic growth.

● Reducing the growth of overall Federal spending by eliminating Federal activities that overstep the proper sphere of Federal Government responsibilities and by restraining the growth of spending for other Federal activities.

● Reducing the Federal regulatory burden in areas where the Federal Government intrudes unnecessarily into our private lives or interferes unnecessarily with the efficient conduct of private business or of State or local government.

● Supporting a moderate and steady monetary policy, to bring inflation under control.

Two Years of Accomplishment

Over the past 2 years, dramatic improvements have been made in the way the Government affects our economy. The Congress joined with my administration in a cooperative and politically courageous effort to reverse a decade of runaway growth in spending and tax burdens, proliferation of unnecessary regulations and red tape, and erosion of our military strength.

Both the Omnibus Reconciliation Acts of 1981 and 1982 effected fundamental reforms in numerous Federal programs, and demonstrated a greatly heightened level of maturity and responsibility of the congressional budget process that has come to fruition with the help and support of this administration. Although I am disappointed that many administration spending-reduction proposals did not pass last year — which has resulted in higher deficits — I believe that the revitalized congressional budget process signifies a refreshing willingness on the part of the Congress to work with my administration to address squarely the many crucial, complex, and politically difficult budgetary dilemmas before us. The results have been impressive:

● Where the growth rate of spending was almost out of control at 17.4% a year in 1980, it is now declining dramatically — to 10.5% this year, and, with this budget, to 5.4% next year — which is no more than the projected rate of inflation; in effect, a comprehensive freeze on total Federal spending.

● Where spending growth totaled $220 billion from 1978 to 1981, a 48% increase, spending will rise by only 27% from 1981 to 1984, despite legislated cost-of-living adjustments and the needed defense buildup.

● For the first time since the Second World War, the Federal tax system has been fundamentally restructured. Income tax rates have been substantially reduced, greatly improving the climate for savings and investment. Excessive taxation of business income resulting from depreciation allowances rendered inadequate by inflation has been eliminated through depreciation reform. Tax loopholes have been closed, making the tax structure more equitable. Emphasis is shifting to financing programs through user fees commensurate with benefits and services provided.

● The excessive rates of growth of entitlement programs were curbed. Overly-broad eligibility criteria were tightened to limit benefit awards more to the truly needy, and eliminate or restrict unnecessary and costly payments of welfare-type benefits to those who are relatively well off and are, or ought to be, self-supporting. Overly-generous and unnecessarily frequent cost-of-living adjustments were pared back. Nonetheless, the growth of these programs has proven difficult to control and continues to be the primary cause of higher deficits.

● Limitation of Federal credit activity and off-budget spending is being achieved.

● The burgeoning growth of Federal regulations and red tape has been capped. The number of proposed new regulations has been reduced by one-third in the past 2 years. Unnecessary costs of Federal regulation to individuals, businesses, and State and local governments have been reduced by $6 billion in annual expenditures and $9 to $11 billion in capital costs. By the end of 1983, the time our citizens spend filling out Federal forms and reports will have been cut by over 300 million hours annually.

● Improvements in the management of Federal operations, such as better procedures for the collection of debts owed the Government and better cash-management practices, are being carried out. These improvements have helped reduce waste, fraud, and abuse in Government programs.

● And by the end of the 1982 fiscal year, the Federal nondefense workforce has been reduced by 91,300 employees since I took office.

During the past 2 years, we have also taken decisive measures to increase our military strength. At the same time, diplomatic approaches to increase our national security, such as arms reduction talks, have been vigorously pursued.

The improvement in our defense posture includes all of its major elements. Long-overdue modernization of our strategic forces is proceeding with new bomber-, submarine-, and land-based missile programs. Our conventional forces are also being modernized and strengthened, with new ships, tanks, and aircraft. Above all, successful recruiting and retention over the past 18 months have resulted in all of our armed services being more fully manned with capable, high-caliber men and women. The All Volunteer Force is now working well.

By any standards, these are accomplishments to be proud of. And I am proud of them. We have come far in restoring order to the chaos prevailing in our economy and Government affairs just 2 years ago.

This is not to say that we do not still face great problems such as excessive unemployment, slower than desired economic growth, and high deficits. During the past 2 years our Nation has labored to purge itself of the inflationary disease that for nearly two decades had progressively undermined the economy's ability to generate growth, capital formation, worker productivity incentives, and financial stability. Those inflationary fevers have largely subsided in the aftermath of my decision 2 years ago to redirect economic policy toward a more modest size and scope for the Federal Government, a series of tax rate reductions to reward productive investment and work effort, and a restrained monetary policy to sustain the purchasing power of individual savings and income.

Accompanying the marked progress in unwinding the damaging inflation spiral that plagued our Nation for so many years, financial markets in 1982 experienced their first sustained improvement in more than 5 years. Interest rates throughout the maturity spectrum declined substantially, and by yearend we can proudly report that key rates for home mortgages, consumer loans, and business investment were able to sus-

The Budget Totals

(in billions of dollars)

	1982 Actual	1983 Estimate	1984 Estimate	1985 Estimate	1986 Estimate
Budget receipts	617.8	597.5	659.7	724.3	841.9
Budget outlays	728.4	805.2	848.5	918.5	989.6
Surplus or deficit (—)	—110.6	—207.7	—188.8	—194.2	—147.7
Budget authority	779.9	847.4	900.1	997.4	1,079.6

tain their lower levels, indicating new confidence in administration policies and bringing much needed relief to the housing and auto industries, the farm community, and the export sector.

Inflationary pressures of the sort experienced during the past two decades extracted a heavy toll from our economy. We have learned that the problems we inherited were far worse than most inside and out of Government had expected; the recession was deeper and longer than most inside and out of Government had predicted. Curing these problems has taken more time and a higher toll than any of us wanted. Unemployment is far too high.

Fortunately, the long nightmare of runaway inflation is now behind us. Slowly, but steadily and unmistakably, our national economy is completing the transition from recession to recovery. The interaction of lower tax rates, reduced inflation, and falling interest rates has placed the consumer and the producer in a much strengthened position with respect to balance sheets, liquidity, after-tax income, and purchasing power.

There are numerous signs that the battered, sputtering inflation-warped economy that we found 2 years ago is on the mend, and that the dislocation and hardship we have suffered in the interim will prove to be a corrective interlude on the path of sustained recovery. But our confidence must also be tempered by realism and patience. Quick fixes and artificial stimulants, repeatedly applied over decades, are what brought on the inflationary disorders that we have now paid such a heavy price to cure.

In part as a result of the difficult period of disinflation, during the past year and one-half our projections of the Federal deficit have steadily risen. They have now reached very high levels, creating uncertainty in the financial markets and threatening to block the economic recovery ahead of us.

But before we consider what is to be done, we must review how we got here. And the truth is that as in the case of the social security fund, the looming gaps in our national budget are the consequence of both the inflation that got out of hand and the correctives that have been unavoidably applied to cure it.

During the 1970's, the share of our national income devoted to domestic programs and transfer payments soared by more than 50% — from 10 cents to 16 cents on every dollar produced by the American people. For a brief time, it appeared that we could afford all of this generosity because inflation badly misled us.

As inflation reached higher and higher peaks, the Treasury's coffers swelled from its take on inflated incomes and the upward creep of tax rates. For a time, we even financed our trillion dollar national debt on the cheap with interest rates that had not yet caught up with the spiraling inflation.

Meanwhile, defense spending grew at less than 60% of inflation, making room in the budget for extra domestic programs. The real purchasing power available to maintain our readiness, modernize our weapons, and maintain strategic nuclear safety declined by a startling 20%.

But it couldn't last — and it didn't. Today the Federal budget itself has become a major victim of the economic transition:

● The inflationary revenue windfall has dried up.

● Our staggering national debt until recently was being financed at the highest interest rates in peacetime history.

● The undelayable process of restoring our inflation-eroded military budgets and our decayed military strength has further strained our resources.

● Despite our great strides in reducing the spending growth over the last 2 years, the vast edifice of domestic programs remains significantly in place.

The social security system has also been a victim of our economic ills. First, the rampant inflation drained its reserves as Government tried to keep beneficiaries up with the spiraling cost of living that its own mistaken policies had created in the first place. Now the recessionary adjustments to disinflation have temporarily deprived it of the expanding wage base and growing revenues required to support commitments to the retired and disabled. As a result, for too long the specter of social security insolvency has haunted our Nation's elderly citizens and threatened to rupture the lifeline on which 36 million retired and disabled Americans depend.

But however obvious the threat of in-

solvency, one thing is certain: social security cannot and will not be allowed to fail the 36 million Americans who depend on it. With this commitment in mind, it is especially pleasing to me to join with the Speaker of the House and the Senate Majority Leader in urging the Congress to enact the bipartisan compromise plan developed by the National Commission on Social Security Reform.

There are elements in it that none of us prefers, but taken together it forms a package all of us can support. It asks for some sacrifice by all — the self-employed, beneficiaries, workers, new government employees, and the better-off among the retired — but it imposes an undue burden on none. And, in supporting it, we keep an important pledge to the American people: the integrity of the social security system will be preserved — and no one's payments will be reduced.

Toward Economic Recovery

To enhance prospects for sustained economic recovery and lower unemployment, I am proposing a sweeping set of fiscal policy changes designed to reduce substantially the mounting Federal deficits that threaten the renewal of economic growth. My plan is based on these principles.

It must be bipartisan. Overcoming the deficits and putting the Government's house in order will require the best efforts of all of us.

It must be fair. Just as all will share in the benefits that will come from recovery, all should share fairly in the burden of transition.

It must be prudent. The strength of our national defense must be restored so that we can pursue prosperity in peace and freedom, while maintaining our commitment to the truly needy.

Finally, it must be realistic. We cannot rely on hope alone.

With these guiding principles in mind, let me outline a four-part plan to increase economic growth and reduce deficits.

First, I am recommending a Federal spending freeze. I know this is strong medicine, but so far we have cut only the rate of increase in Federal spending. The Government has continued to spend more money each year, though not as much more as it did in the past. Taken as a whole, the budget I am proposing for the next fiscal year will increase no more than the rate of inflation — in other words, the Federal Government will hold the line on real spending. That is far less than many American families have had to do in these difficult times.

I will request that the proposed 6-month freeze in cost-of-living adjustments recommended by the bipartisan National Commission on Social Security Reform be applied to other Government benefit programs. I will also propose a 1-year freeze on a broad range of domestic spending programs, and for Federal civilian and military

Appendix

pay and pension programs.

Second, I will ask the Congress to adopt specific measures to control the growth of the so-called "uncontrollable" spending programs. These are the automatic spending programs, such as food stamps, that cannot be simply frozen — and that have grown by over 400% since 1970. They are the largest single cause of the built-in or "structural" deficit problem. Our standard here will be fairness — ensuring that the taxpayers' hard-earned dollars go only to the truly needy; that none of them is turned away; but that fraud and waste are stamped out. And, I am sorry to say, there is a lot of it out there. In the food stamp program alone, last year we identified almost $1.1 billion in overpayments. The taxpayers are not the only victims of this kind of abuse; the truly needy suffer, as funds intended for them are taken by the greedy. For everyone's sake, we must put an end to such waste and corruption.

Third, I will adjust our program to restore America's defenses by proposing $55 billion in defense savings over the next 5 years. These are savings recommended to me by the Secretary of Defense, who has assured me they can be safely achieved and will not diminish our ability to negotiate arms reductions or endanger America's security. We will not gamble with our national survival. As a percent of GNP, the level I am requesting for defense spending in 1984 is less than the United States spent during the decade of the 1960's. As a percent of the total Federal budget it is far less than was allocated for national defense in those years. We are 2 years into the program to re-arm America. Sustaining the momentum of this program is essential if we are to avoid slipping back into the inefficient and counterproductive pattern of wildly fluctuating defense spending levels.

Fourth, because we must ensure reduction and eventual elimination of deficits over the next several years, I will propose a stand-by tax limited to no more than 1% of the gross national product to start in fiscal year 1986. It would last no more than 3 years and would start *only* if the Congress has first approved our spending freeze and budget control program. You could say that this is an insurance policy for the future — a remedy that will be at hand if needed, but resorted to only if absolutely necessary.

In the meantime, we will continue to study ways to simplify the tax code and make it more fair for all Americans. This is a goal that every American who has ever struggled with a tax form can understand.

At the same time, however, I will oppose any efforts to undo the basic tax reforms we have already enacted — including the 10% tax break coming to taxpayers this July and the tax indexing that will protect all Americans from inflationary bracket creep in the years ahead.

This plan is urgently needed and is geared toward solving the problems of the growing deficits. But it naturally requires the cooperation of both branches of Government, both Houses, and both parties.

Thus, our plan is aimed at bridging the institutional, philosophical, and political differences that separate us — which are not as important as the overriding common objective of economic recovery and sustained prosperity for America.

After 2 years of reducing much of the overspending, we have now reached the bone in many places — programs where we will not propose further reductions. My administration will now work with the Congress in an effort to accommodate those special concerns of the legislative branch that have caused unnecessary strains in the past.

Thus, we will propose $3 billion more for education programs than was proposed last year, and almost $2 billion more for employment and training. Proposals for new rescissions of already-enacted budget authority will be held to an absolute minimum.

This budget process must be a two-way street, for the problem of large deficits is very real. Even when all reasonable measures are applied to the vast detail of the budget, the resulting deficits are large and progress toward reducing them slow. The political risks entailed in these deficit-containment measures are considerable. But the risk of doing nothing at all due to partisanship or legislative stalemate is much greater. I therefore urge the Congress to join with my administration behind this common-sense strategy.

Meeting — and Reshaping — Federal Responsibilities

My administration seeks to limit the size, intrusiveness, and cost of Federal activities as much as possible, and to achieve the needed increase in our defense capabilities in the most cost-effective manner possible. This does not mean that appropriate Federal responsibilities are being abandoned, neglected, or inadequately supported. Instead, ways are being found to streamline Federal activity, to limit it to those areas and responsibilities that are truly Federal in nature; to ensure that these appropriate Federal responsibilities are performed in the most cost-effective and efficient manner; and to aid State and local governments in carrying out their appropriate public responsibilities in a similarly cost-effective manner. The Nation must ask for no more publicly-provided services and benefits than the private sector can reasonably be asked to finance.

Education. One of the high priorities I have set for my administration is the return to a more appropriate role for the Federal Government in the Nation's education systems and policies. We have slowed the alarming rate of growth of Federal spending for education, an area that is rightfully and primarily a family and State and local government responsibility. From 1974 to 1981, Federal spending for education increased by 172%. From 1981 to 1982, however, outlays declined by more than $1 billion. My administration has accomplished a major consolidation of small

fragmented education programs into a flexible education block grant to States and localities. We have cut back on unnecessary regulation and Federal intrusion in local affairs.

The 1984 budget seeks to stabilize education spending, requesting $13.1 billion in budget authority for 1984. It reflects several important new initiatives to strengthen American education:

● Passing of tuition tax credits for parents who want to send their children to qualified private or religiously-affiliated schools.

● Establishing education savings accounts to give middle- and lower-income families an incentive to save for their children's college education and, at the same time, to encourage a real increase in savings for economic growth.

● Reorienting student aid programs to ensure that students and families meet their responsibilities for financing higher education, while making funds available across a wider spectrum of schools for the low-income students most in need.

● Allowing States or localities, if they so choose, to use their compensatory education funds to establish voucher programs to broaden family choice of effective schooling methods for educationally disadvantaged children.

● Helping States to train more mathematics and science teachers.

These initiatives represent the administration's continuing commitment to avoid improper Federal involvement in State, local, and family decisions, while preserving proper Federal support for key national policy goals such as supporting compensatory and handicapped education, facilitating access to higher education, and helping States improve science and mathematics education.

Research. My administration recognizes the Federal responsibility to maintain U.S. leadership in scientific research. Although support of basic scientific research represents a small share of the Federal budget, it is a vital investment in the Nation's future. Such research lays the foundation for a strong defense in the years to come, and for new technologies and industries that will help maintain our industrial competitiveness, create new jobs, and improve our quality of life. By carefully establishing budget priorities, my administration has been able to reinvigorate Federal support for basic scientific research. With my 1984 budget proposals, such support across the Government will have increased by more than 20% over the 1982 level.

Health care. A major problem for both individuals and the Federal Government in meeting health care needs is the rapid inflation of health care costs. The rate of increase in health care costs is excessive and undermines people's ability to purchase needed health care. Federal policies have contributed significantly to health care cost increases. The budget contains several major initiatives to reduce cost increases. We must eliminate the tax incentive for high-cost employee health in-

surance programs. Savings from medicare cost controls will be used to protect the aged from catastrophic hospital costs. Incentives will also be proposed to slow the growth of medicaid costs.

Agriculture. The administration seeks to move agricultural supply toward a better balance with demand by reducing farm production and Government program stocks. The budget proposes a four-part approach to solving the current surplus supply problem:

● establishing a payment-in-kind (PIK) program, under which farmers would receive surplus commodities now held for Federal loans, or owned by the Government, in return for reducing their production;

● freezing farm crop target prices at current levels;

● donating Government-held commodities through international humanitarian organizations for needy people around the world; and

● selling our agricultural produce abroad, both through commercial channels and through government negotiation.

Efforts are also continuing to identify surplus Federal land holdings for sale from those administered by the Departments of Agriculture and of the Interior. Planned sales total $500 million in 1984.

Transportation. In the transportation area, my administration has made major strides in implementing one of the fundamental principles in my program for economic recovery: having users pay for program costs that are clearly allocable to them. During the past year, I signed into law two administration-backed proposals to increase excise taxes on aviation and highway users and thereby provide funding needed to revitalize and modernize these important segments of the Nation's transportation system. The 1984 budget reflects the administration's continued commitment to the "users pay" principle by again proposing user fees for:

● construction and maintenance of deep-draft ports;

● the inland waterway system;

● selected direct Coast Guard services; and

● nautical and aviation maps and charts.

Recognizing the importance of our transportation system in maintaining and contributing to the Nation's economic and social well being, my administration secured passage of legislation designed to rebuild the Nation's highway and public transportation facilities. This legislation substantially increased funds available to the States and local communities to complete and repair the aging interstate highway system, to rehabilitate principal rural and urban highways and bridges, and to improve mass transit systems.

Fully capable ports and channels are essential to make U.S. coal exports competitive in world markets. My administration will work with the Congress to provide for timely and efficient port construction. We propose a system of user fees for existing

---

Impact of Stronger Economic Growth

● If the recovery of real GNP growth over the next 2 fiscal years is *about 1%* above our cautious projections, the deficit estimates would improve by an average of about $20 billion per year, and would result in lower deficits as follows:

	1984	1985	1986	1987	1988
Deficit (−) ($ billions)	−177	−177	−127	−119	−90

● An average real GNP growth rate *1.33%* higher each year over the next 6 years, compared to the prudent projections made in the 1984 budget, would result in a balanced budget by 1988. This is a "high growth" scenario but within the range of previous historical experience. My administration remains committed to the goal of a balanced budget and will propose additional policy actions, as needed, to achieve it.

---

port maintenance and new port construction. Local governments would be empowered to set up their own financing arrangements for the immediate construction of facilities in their areas.

Reducing the Federal presence in commercial transportation, currently regulated by the Interstate Commerce Commission, the Civil Aeronautics Board, and the Federal Maritime Commission, will improve the efficiency of the industry. To this end, my administration will seek further deregulation of trucking, airlines and ocean shipping. Experience since the adoption of initial transportation deregulation legislation has shown clearly that both consumers and industry benefit from reduced Federal involvement in these activities.

Energy. The administration has significantly reoriented the country's approach to energy matters in the past 2 years. Reliance on market forces — instead of Government regulation and massive, indiscriminate Federal spending — has resulted in greater energy production, more efficient use of energy, and more favorable energy prices. For example:

● The U.S. economy today is using 18% less energy to produce a dollar's worth of output than it did in 1973 when energy prices first began to rise.

● The price of heating oil and gasoline has actually fallen in real terms by 12% in the past 2 years — confounding past theories that insisted that these prices could only increase.

Federal energy programs and policies have been refocused and made more productive:

● Wasteful spending on large, unprofitable technology demonstrations has been curtailed.

● At the same time, spending has increased in areas where the Government has a key role to play — for example, in supporting long-term energy research.

● The strategic petroleum reserve has more than doubled in size over the past 2 years.

Criminal justice. My administration has also sought to strengthen the Federal criminal justice system by proposing major

legislative initiatives, such as bail for sentencing reform, by attacking drug trafficking and organized crime, and by achieving a better balance among law enforcement, prosecutorial, and correctional resources. Twelve regional task forces will focus on bringing to justice organized crime drug traffickers. The administration will strengthen efforts to identify, neutralize, and defeat foreign agents who pose a threat to the Nation.

International affairs. Our foreign policy is oriented toward maintaining peace through military strength and diplomatic negotiation; promoting market-oriented solutions to international economic problems; telling the story abroad of America's democratic, free-enterprise way of life; and increasing free trade in the world while assuring this country's equitable participation in that trade.

● The security assistance portion of the international affairs program has been increased to assist friendly governments facing threats from the Soviet Union, its surrogates, and from other radical regimes.

● Development aid emphasizes encouraging the private sectors of developing nations and increasing U.S. private sector involvement in foreign assistance.

● A major expansion of international broadcasting activities aimed primarily at communist countries is planned, and a new initiative will be undertaken to strengthen the infrastructure of democracy around the world.

● Special attention is being given to assuring adequate financing of U.S. exports while my administration seeks to obtain further reductions in the export subsidies of other governments.

My administration will submit to the Congress a proposal to increase the U.S. quota in the International Monetary Fund and the U.S. obligations under the IMF's General Arrangements to Borrow, as soon as negotiations on these issues are completed. This is necessary to ensure that the IMF has adequate resources to help bring the world economy back to strong, noninflationary growth.

Although now less than 2% of the bud-

get, international programs are critical to American world leadership and to the success of our foreign policy.

Minority-owned businesses. My administration will assist in the establishment or expansion of over 120,000 minority-owned businesses over the next 10 years. The Federal Government will procure an estimated $15 billion in goods and services from minority business during the 3-year period 1983-1985. It will make available approximately $1.5 billion in credit assistance and $300 million in technical assistance to promote minority business development during this period.

Civil service retirement. The 97th Congress made some improvements in the civil service retirement system. However, civil service retirement still has far more generous benefits and is much more costly than retirement programs in the private sector or in State and local governments. Accordingly, this budget proposes fundamental changes in civil service retirement designed to bring benefits into line with those offered in the private sector and reduce the cost of the system to affordable levels. Retirement benefit changes will be phased in over a period of years in order to avoid upsetting the plans of those at or near retirement.

Unemployment Demands Specific Attention

My administration seeks to provide appropriate assistance to the unemployed. There are three major groups who need help: the largest, those who are unemployed now but will find jobs readily as the economy improves; those whose jobs have permanently disappeared; and youth who have trouble finding their niche in the labor market.

Those in the first group need interim help because, historically, increases in jobs always lag in an economic recovery. Last year we provided a temporary program to give the long-term unemployed up to 16 added weeks of unemployment compensation, in addition to the up to 39 weeks available from our permanent unemployment insurance. This temporary program expires March 31, 1983. I propose to modify and extend the program for 6 more months, and provide an option for recipients to receive assistance in securing work through a system of tax credits to employers. This will give employers a significant incentive to hire the long-term unemployed, while workers will get full wages rather than the lower unemployment benefit.

Those whose jobs have permanently disappeared must be helped to find new long-term occupations. The Job Training Partnership Act, enacted last year, authorizes grants to States to help retrain such workers and assist them in locating and moving to new jobs. The Congress appropriated $25 million to start this new program in 1983. I am requesting $240 million to implement the program fully in 1984. In addition, I propose that the Federal unemployment law be changed to allow States to use a portion of the unemployment taxes they collect to provide such retraining and job search assistance to their unemployed workers. Regulatory reform and passage of enterprise zone legislation will also create new incentives for jobs and opportunity.

Those youth who have problems finding jobs after they leave school are often condemned to a lifetime of intermittent employment and low earnings. The new Job Training Partnership Act is designed to help disadvantaged youth acquire the basic skills potential employers look for when they hire. I am requesting $1.9 billion for the block grant to States under that Act. The States must use at least 40% of that for youth.

One of the problems hampering youth is inability to get meaningful work experience during school vacations. Such experience is invaluable to demonstrate their qualifications to potential permanent employers. The budget provides for 718,000 public summer job opportunities for disadvantaged youth. But we must also make it possible for youth to experience work in the private sector. The minimum wage law now frequently prevents this. Inexperienced youth cannot produce enough of value to make it worthwhile for employers to pay them the full minimum wage during short periods of employment. I therefore propose that the minimum wage for summer jobs for youth be reduced to $2.50 an hour. Limitation of the reduced minimum wage to the summer months will make it unlikely that employers will substitute youths for older workers.

I remain adamantly opposed to temporary make-work public jobs or public works as an attempted cure for non-youth unemployment. There are several reasons for this. The cost per "job" created is excessive; we cannot afford major new programs, particularly in our current budgetary straits; the actual number of new jobs "created" is minimal; the jobs created tend to be temporary and of a dead-end nature; and most such jobs do not materialize until after recovery is well underway.

Improving the Efficiency of Government

The proposed freeze on program funding levels will compel program managers in every agency of the Government to find more efficient ways of carrying out their programs. For too long, costs of Federal operations have been mounting unchecked.

Good management has not always been a priority of the executive branch. I have been correcting that situation.

My administration has redirected programs to improve their efficiency and to achieve cost savings Government-wide. My administration is committed to improving management and reducing fraud, waste, and abuse. The President's Council on Integrity and Efficiency (PCIE), made up of 18 Inspectors General, reported that almost $17 billion has been saved or put to better use in the past 2 years.

In 1982, I signed into law the Federal Managers' Financial Integrity Act. Under this Act, my Cabinet officers and other agency heads will report to me and the Congress annually on the status of their efforts to improve management controls that prevent fraud and mismanagement. A number of agencies have already begun to make significant improvements in this important area.

But the Government can go only so far with the seriously outdated and inefficient management/administrative systems that are currently in place. One-third of our large-scale computers, for example, are more than 10 years old. A comprehensive management improvement program was needed, so "Reform '88" was initiated. We intend to upgrade and modernize our administrative systems to make them more effective and efficient in carrying out the Government's business and serving the public.

We are already saving tax dollars by managing our almost $2 trillion yearly cash flow more effectively, collecting the Government's $250 billion of just debts, cutting Government administrative costs, modernizing Federal procurement systems, reducing internal regulations, controlling our office space and equipment more prudently, and streamlining the workforce in many departments and agencies. These cost-reduction efforts will continue.

Continuing Reform of Our Federal System

The overall efficiency of Government in the United States can also be improved by a more rational sorting out of governmental responsibilities among the various levels of government — Federal, State, and local — in our Federal system, and eliminating or limiting overlapping and duplication.

In 1981, the Congress responded to my proposals by consolidating 57 categorical programs into 9 block grants. In 1982, block grants were created for job training in the Jobs Training Partnership Act, and for urban mass transit in the Surface Transportation Act. The initiatives to be proposed this year will expand on these accomplishments.

Four new block grants will be proposed, with assured funding for major functions now addressed through categorical grants:

● A general Federal-State block grant covering approximately 15 categorical programs.

● A Federal-local block grant that would include the entitlement portion of the community development grant program and the general revenue sharing program.

● A transportation block grant.

● A rural housing block grant.

The administration is improving the management of intergovernmental assistance by providing State and local elected

officials with greater opportunity to express their views on proposed Federal development and assistance actions before final decisions are made. Under Executive Order 12372, Intergovernmental Review of Federal Programs, which I signed in July 1982, Federal agencies must consult with State and local elected officials early in the assistance decision process and make every effort to accommodate their views. The Order also encourages the simplification of State planning requirements imposed by Federal law, and allows for the substitution of State-developed plans for federally required State plans where statutes and regulations allow.

Through the President's Task Force on Regulatory Relief and the regulatory review process, the administration is eliminating and simplifying regulations affecting State and local governments that are burdensome, unnecessary, and counterproductive. These changes have improved local efficiency and accountability and reduced program costs. Twenty-five reviews were completed during the past 2 years by either the Task Force or by various Federal agencies. Available data indicate that regulatory relief actions will save State and local governments approximately $4 to $6 billion in initial costs, and an estimated $2 billion on an annual basis. My administration is also simplifying selected, generally applicable crosscutting requirements that are imposed on State and local governments as a condition of accepting financial assistance.

Federal Credit Programs: More Selective

The administration continues its strong commitment to control Federal credit assistance, which has serious effects on the Nation's financial markets. To this end, I propose a credit budget that reverses the accelerated rate of growth in direct and guaranteed lending by the Federal Government that occurred during the second half of the 1970's and the first years of the 1980's.

Federal intervention through guarantees and provision of direct lending misdirects investment and preempts capital that could be more efficiently used by unsubsidized, private borrowers. Because federally assisted borrowers are frequently less productive than private borrowers, large Federal credit demands must be reduced in order to improve prospects for economic growth.

Conclusion

The stage is set; a recovery to vigorous, sustainable, noninflationary economic growth is imminent. But given the underlying deterioration in the overall budget structure that has occurred over the past 2 years, only the most sweeping set of fiscal policy changes could help to reverse the trend and set the budget on a path that is consistent with long-term economic recovery.

If the challenge before us is great, so, too, are the opportunities. Let us work together to meet the challenge. If we fail, if we work at cross purposes, posterity will not forgive us for allowing this opportunity to slip away.

RONALD W. REAGAN
January 31, 1983

Reagan's Speech on Central America

Following is the Congressional Record *text of President Reagan's April 27, 1983, address on Central America as delivered before a joint session of Congress.*

THE PRESIDENT. Mr. Speaker, Mr. President, distinguished Members of the Congress, honored guests and my fellow Americans:

A number of times in the past years, Members of Congress and a President have come together in meetings like this to resolve a crisis. I have asked for this meeting in the hope that we can prevent one.

It would be hard to find many Americans who are not aware of our stake in the Middle East, the Persian Gulf, or the NATO line dividing the free world from the Communist bloc, and the same could be said for Asia. But in spite of, or maybe because of, a flurry of stories about places like Nicaragua and El Salvador and, yes, some concerted propaganda, many of us find it hard to believe we have a stake in problems involving those countries. Too many have thought of Central America as just a place way down below Mexico that cannot possibly constitute a threat to our well being.

That is why I have asked for this session. Central America's problems do directly affect the security and the well being of our own people. And Central America is much closer to the United States than many of the world trouble spots that concern us. As we work to restore our own economy, we cannot afford to lose sight of our neighbors to the south.

El Salvador is nearer to Texas than Texas is to Massachusetts. Nicaragua is just as close to Miami, San Antonio, San Diego, and Tucson as those cities are to Washington where we are gathered tonight.

But nearness on the map does not even begin to tell the strategic importance of Central America, bordering as it does on the Caribbean, our lifeline to the outside world. Two-thirds of all our foreign trade and petroleum pass through the Panama Canal and the Caribbean. In a European crisis at least half our supplies for NATO would go through these areas by sea. It is well to remember that in early 1942 a handful of Hitler's submarines sank more tonnage there than in all of the Atlantic Ocean. And they did this without a single naval base anywhere in the area.

Today the situation is different. Cuba is host to a Soviet combat brigade, a submarine base capable of servicing Soviet submarines, and military air bases visited regularly by Soviet military aircraft.

Because of its importance, the Caribbean Basin is a magnet for adventurism. We are all aware of the Libyan cargo planes refueling in Brazil a few days ago on their way to deliver medical supplies to Nicaragua. Brazilian authorities discovered the so-called supplies were actually munitions and prevented their delivery. You may remember that last month, speaking on national television I showed an aerial photo of an airfield being built in the Island of Grenada. Well, if that airfield had been completed those planes could have refueled there and completed their journey.

If the Nazis during World War II and the Soviets today could recognize the Caribbean and Central America as vital to our interests, should not we also?

El Salvador

For several years now, under two Administrations, the United States has been increasing its defense of freedom in the Caribbean Basin. And I can tell you tonight, democracy is beginning to take root in El Salvador, which until a short time ago knew only dictatorship. The new government is now delivering on its promises of democracy, reforms and free elections. It was not easy and there was resistance to many of the attempted reforms, with assassinations of some of the reformers. Guerrilla bands and urban terrorists were portrayed in a worldwide propaganda campaign as freedom fighters representative of the people. Ten days before I came into office, the guerrillas launched what they called a "final offensive" to overthrow the government. And their radio boasted that our new Administration would be too late to prevent their victory. Well, they learned that democracy cannot

1069

be so easily defeated.

President Carter did not hesitate. He authorized arms and munitions to El Salvador. The guerrilla offensive failed, but not America's will. Every President since this country assumed global responsibilities has known that those responsibilities could only be met if we pursued a bipartisan foreign policy.

As I said a moment ago, the Government of El Salvador has been keeping its promises, like the land reform program which is making thousands of farm tenants farm owners. In a little over 3 years, 20 percent of the arable land in El Salvador has been redistributed to more than 450,000 people. That is one in ten Salvadorans who have benefited directly from this program.

El Salvador has continued to strive toward an orderly and democratic society. The government promised free elections. On March 28th, little more than a year ago, after months of campaigning by a variety of candidates, the suffering people of El Salvador were offered a chance to vote — to choose the kind of government they wanted. Suddenly the so-called freedom fighters in the hills were exposed for what they really are: a small minority who want power for themselves and their backers, not democracy for the people. The guerrillas threatened death to anyone who voted. They destroyed hundreds of buses and trucks to keep the people from getting to the polling places. Their slogan was brutal: "Vote today, die tonight." But on election day, an unprecedented 80 percent of the electorate braved ambush and gunfire, and trudged for miles, many of them, to vote for freedom. That is truly fighting for freedom. We can never turn our backs on that.

Members of this Congress who went there as observers told me of a woman who was wounded by rifle fire on the way to the polls, who refused to leave the line to have her wound treated until after she had voted. Another woman had been told by the guerrillas that she would be killed when she returned from the polls, and she told the guerrillas, "You can kill me, you can kill my family, you can kill my neighbors; you can't kill us all." The real freedom fighters of El Salvador turned out to be the people of that country — the young, the old, the in-between — more than one million of them out of a population of less than five million. The world should respect this courage and not allow it to be belittled or forgotten. Again, I say in good conscience, we can never turn our backs on that.

The democratic political parties and factions in El Salvador are coming together around the common goal of seeking a political solution to their country's problems. New national elections will be held this year and they will be open to all political parties. The government has invited the guerrillas to participate in the election and is preparing an amnesty law. The people of El Salvador are earning their freedom and they deserve our moral and material support to protect it.

Yes, there are still major problems regarding human rights, the criminal justice system and violence against non-combatants and, like the rest of Central America, El Salvador also faces severe economic problems. But in addition to recession — depressed prices for major agricultural exports, El Salvador's economy is being deliberately sabotaged.

Tonight in El Salvador — because of ruthless guerrilla attacks — much of the fertile land cannot be cultivated, less than half the rolling stock of the railways remains operational, bridges, water facilities, telephone and electrical systems have been destroyed and damaged. In one 22-month period there were 5,000 disruptions of electrical power. One region was without electricity for a third of a year.

I think Secretary of State Shultz put it very well the other day: "Unable to win the free loyalty of El Salvador's people, the guerrillas," he said, "are deliberately and systematically depriving them of food, water, transportation, light, sanitation, and jobs. And these are the people who claim they want to help the common people."

They do not want elections because they know they would be defeated. But as the previous election showed the Salvadoran people's desire for democracy will not be defeated.

The guerrillas are not embattled peasants armed with muskets. They are professionals, sometimes with better training and weaponry than the government soldiers. The Salvadoran battalions that have received United States training have been conducting themselves well in the battlefield and with the civilian population. But so far we have only provided enough money to train 1 Salvadoran soldier out of 10, fewer than the number of guerrillas that are trained by Nicaragua and Cuba.

Nicaragua

And let me set the record straight on Nicaragua, a country next to El Salvador. In 1979 when the new government took over in Nicaragua, after a revolution which overthrew the authoritarian rule of Somoza, everyone hoped for the growth of democracy. We in the United States did too. By January of 1981, our emergency relief and recovery aid to Nicaragua totaled $118 million — more than provided by any other developed country. In fact, in the first 2 years of Sandinista rule, the United States directly or indirectly sent five times more aid to Nicaragua than it had in the 2 years prior to the revolution. Can anyone doubt the generosity and the good faith of the American people?

These were hardly the actions of a nation implacably hostile to Nicaragua. Yet the government of Nicaragua has treated us as an enemy. It has rejected our repeated peace efforts, it has broken its promises to us, to the Organization of American States and, most important of all, to the people of Nicaragua.

No sooner was victory achieved than a small clique ousted others who had been part of the revolution from having any voice in the government. Humberto Ortega, the Minister of Defense, declared Marxism-Leninism would be their guide, and so it is.

The government of Nicaragua has imposed a new dictatorship, it has refused to hold the elections it promised, it has seized control of most media and subjects all media to heavy prior censorship. It denied the bishops and priests of the Roman Catholic Church the right to say mass on radio during Holy Week, it insulted and mocked the Pope, it has driven the Miskito Indians from their homelands — burning their villages, destroying their crops, and forcing them into involuntary internment camps far from home; it has moved against the private sector and free labor unions; it condoned mob action against Nicaragua's independent human rights commission and drove the director of that commission into exile.

In short, after all of these acts of repression by the government, is it any wonder that oppositoin has formed? Contrary to propaganda, the opponents of the Sandinistas are not die-hard supporters of the previous Somoza regime. In fact, many are anti-Somoza heroes who fought beside the Sandinistas to bring down the Somoza government. Now they have been denied any part of a new government because they truly want a democracy for Nicaragua, and they still do. Others are Miskito Indians fighting for their homes, their lands and their lives.

The Sandinista revolution in Nicaragua turned out to be just an exchange of one set of autocratic rulers for another, and the people still had no freedom, no democratic rights, and more poverty. Even worse than its predecessor, it is helping Cuba and the Soviets to destabilize our hemisphere.

Meanwhile, the Government of El Salvador, making every effort to guarantee democracy, free labor unions, freedom of religion, and a free press, is under attack by guerrillas dedicated to the same philosophy that prevails in Nicaragua, Cuba and, yes, the Soviet Union.

Violence has been Nicaragua's most important export to the world. It is the ultimate in hypocrisy for the unelected Nicaraguan Government to charge that we seek their overthrow when they are doing everything they can to bring down the elected Government of El Salvador. The guerrilla attacks are directed from a headquarters in Managua, the capital of Nicaragua.

But let us be clear as the American attitude toward the Government of Nicaragua. We do not seek its overthrow. Our interest is to insure that it does not infect its neighbors through the export of subversion and violence. Our purpose, in conformity with American and international law, is to prevent the flow of arms to El Salvador, Honduras, Guatemala, and Costa Rica. We have attempted to have a dialogue with the Government of Nicaragua, but it persists in its efforts to spread violence.

We should not — and we will not —

protect the Nicaraguan Government from the anger of its own people. But we should, through diplomacy, offer an alternative. And, as Nicaragua ponders its options, we can and will — with all the resources of diplomacy — protect each country of Central America from the danger of war.

Even Costa Rica, Central America's oldest and strongest democracy, a government so peaceful it does not even have an army, is the object of bullying and threats from Nicaragua's dictators.

Nicaragua's neighbors know that Sandinista promises of peace, non-alliance, and non-intervention have not been kept. Some 36 new military bases have been built — there were only 13 during the Somoza years.

Nicaragua's new army numbers 25,000 men supported by a militia of 50,000. It is the largest army in Central America supplemented by 2,000 Cuban military and security advisers. It is equipped with the most modern weapons, dozens of Soviet-made tanks, 800 Soviet-bloc trucks, Soviet 152-MM howitzers, 100 anti-aircraft guns, plus planes and helicopters. There are additional thousands of civilian advisers from Cuba, the Soviet Union, East Germany, Libya, and the PLO. And we are attacked because we have 55 military trainers in El Salvador.

The goal of the professional guerrilla movements in Central America is as simple as it is sinister — to destabilize the entire region from the Panama Canal to Mexico. And if you doubt me on this point, just consider what Cayetano Carpio, the now-deceased Salvadoran guerrilla leader, said earlier this month. Carpio said that after El Salvador falls, El Salvador and Nicaragua would be "arm-in-arm and struggling for the total liberation of Central America."

Nicaragua's dictatorial junta, who themselves made war and won power operating from bases in Honduras and Costa Rica, like to pretend that they are today being attacked by forces based in Honduras. The fact is, it is Nicaragua's government that threatens Honduras, not the reverse.

It is Nicaragua who has moved heavy tanks close to the border, and Nicaragua who speaks of war. It was Nicaraguan radio that announced on April 8th the creation of a new, unified revolutionary coordinating board to push forward the Marxist struggle in Honduras.

Nicaragua, supported by weapons and military resources provided by the Communist bloc, represses its own people, refuses to make peace, and sponsors a guerrilla war against El Salvador.

President Truman's Message

President Truman's words are as apt today as they were in 1947, when he, too, spoke before a Joint Session of Congress:

At the present moment in world history nearly every nation must choose between alternative ways of life. The choice is not too often a free one.

One way of life is based upon the will of the majority, and is distinguished by free institutions, representative government, free elections, guarantees of individual liberty, freedom of speech and religion, and freedom from political oppression.

The second way of life is based upon the will of a minority forcibly imposed upon the majority. It relies upon terror and oppression, a controlled press and radio, fixed elections, and the suppression of personal freedoms.

I believe that it must be the policy of the United States to support free peoples who are resisting attempted subjugation by armed minorities or by outside pressures.

I believe that we must assist free peoples to work out their own destinies in their own way.

I believe that our help should be primarily through economic and financial aid which is essential to economic stability and orderly political processes.

...Collapse of free institutions and loss of independence would be disastrous not only for them but for the world. Discouragement and possibly failure would quickly be the lot of neighboring peoples striving to maintain their freedom and independence.

The countries of Central America are smaller than the nations that prompted President Truman's message. But the political and strategic stakes are the same. Will our response — economic, social, military — be as appropriate and successful as Mr. Truman's bold solutions to the problems of postwar Europe?

Some people have forgotten the successes of those years — and the decades of peace, prosperity, and freedom they secured.

Some people talk as though the United States were incapable of acting effectively in international affairs without risking war or damaging those we seek to help.

Are democracies required to remain passive while threats to their security and prosperity accumulate?

Must we just accept the destabilization of an entire region from the Panama Canal to Mexico on our southern border?

Must we sit by while independent nations of this hemisphere are integrated into the most aggressive empire the modern world has seen?

Must we wait while Central Americans are driven from their homes, like the more than four million who have sought refuge out of Afghanistan or the 1½ million who have fled Indochina or the more than one million Cubans who have fled Castro's Caribbean utopia? Must we, by default, leave the people of El Salvador no choice but to flee their homes, creating another tragic human exodus?

I do not believe there is a majority in the Congress or the country that counsels passivity, resignation, defeatism, in the face of this challenge to freedom and security in our own hemisphere.

I do not believe that a majority of the Congress or the country is prepared to stand by passively while the people of Central America are delivered to totalitarianism and we ourselves are left vulnerable to new dangers.

Only last week an official of the Soviet Union reiterated Brezhnev's threat to station nuclear missiles in this hemisphere — five minutes from the United States. Like an echo, Nicaragua's Commandate, Daniel Ortega, confirmed that, if asked, his country would consider accepting those missiles. I understand that today they may be having second thoughts.

Now, before I go any further, let me say to those who invoke the memory of Vietnam: There is no thought of sending American combat troops to Central America; they are not needed and, indeed, they have not been requested there. [Applause.]

All our neighbors ask of us is assistance in training and arms to protect themselves while they build a better, freer life.

We must continue to encourage peace among the nations of Central America. We must support the regional efforts now underway to promote solutions to regional problems.

We cannot be certain that the Marxist-Leninist bands who believe war is an instrument of politics will be readily discouraged. It is crucial that we not become discouraged before they do. Otherwise, the region's freedom will be lost and our security damaged in ways that can hardly be calculated.

If Central America were to fall, what would the consequences be for our position in Asia, Europe, and for alliances such as NATO? If the United States cannot respond to a threat near our own borders, why should Europeans or Asians believe that we are seriously concerned about threats to them? If the Soviets can assume that nothing short of an actual attack on the United States will provoke an American response, which ally, which friend, will trust us then?

The Congress shares both the power and the responsibility for our foreign policy.

Tonight, I ask you, the Congress, to join me in a bold, generous approach to the problems of peace and poverty, democracy and dictatorship in the region. Join me in a program that prevents Communists victory in the short run but goes beyond to produce for the deprived people of the area the reality of present progress and the promise of more to come.

Four Basic Goals in Central America

Let us lay the foundation for a bipartisan approach to sustain the independence and freedom of the countries of Central America. We in the Administration reach out to you in this spirit. We will pursue

four basic goals in Central America:

First: in response to decades of inequity and indifference, we will support democracy, reform and human freedom. This means using our assistance, our powers of persuasion and our legitimate "leverage" to bolster humane democratic systems where they already exist and to help countries on their way to that goal complete the process as quickly as human institutions can be changed. Elections — in El Salvador and also in Nicaragua — must be open to all, fair and safe. The international community must help. We will work at human rights problems, not walk away from them.

Second: In response to the challenge of world recession and, in the case of El Salvador, to the unrelenting campaign of economic sabotage by the guerrillas, we will support economic development. By a margin of two to one, our aid is economic now, not military. Seventy-seven cents out of every dollar we will spend in the area this year goes for food, fertilizers, and other essentials for economic growth and development. And our economic program goes beyond traditional aid: The Caribbean Basin Initiative introduced in the House earlier today will provide powerful trade and investment incentives to help these countries achieve self-sustaining economic growth without exporting United States jobs. Our goal must be to focus our immense and growing technology, to enhance health care, agriculture, industry, and to insure that we who inhabit this interdependent region come to know and understand each other better, retaining our diverse identities, respecting our diverse traditions and institutions.

Third: In response to the military challenge from Cuba and Nicaragua, to their deliberate use of force to spread tyranny, we will support the security of the region's threatened nations. We do not view security assistance as an end in itself, but as a shield for democratization, economic development and diplomacy. No amount of reform will bring peace so long as guerrillas believe they will win by force.

No amount of economic help will suffice if guerrilla units can destroy roads and bridges and power stations and crops again and again with impunity. But with better training and material help our neighbors can hold off the guerrillas and give democratic reform time to take root.

Fourth: We will support dialogue and negotiations both among the countries of the region and within each country. The terms and conditions of participation in elections are negotiable. Costa Rica is a shining example of democracy. Honduras has made the move from military rule to democratic government. Guatemala is pledged to the same course. The United States will work toward a political solution in Central America which will serve the interests of the democratic process.

Assurances

To support these diplomatic goals I offer these assurances:

The United States will support any agreement among Central American countries for the withdrawal — under fully verifiable and reciprocal conditions — of all foreign military and security advisors and troops.

We want to help opposition groups join the political process in all countries and compete by ballots instead of bullets.

We will support any verifiable reciprocal agreement among Central American countries on the renunciation of support for insurgencies on neighbors' territory.

And, finally, we desire to help Central America end its costly arms race, and will support any verifiable, reciprocal agreements on the non-importation of offensive weapons.

To move us toward these goals more rapidly I am tonight announcing my intention to name an Ambassador-at-Large as my special envoy to Central America. He or she will report to me through the Secretary of State. The Ambassador's responsibilities will be to lend United States support to the efforts of regional governments to bring peace to this troubled area and to work closely with the Congress to assure the fullest possible bipartisan coordination of our policies toward the region.

What I am asking for is prompt Congressional approval for the full reprogramming of funds for key current economic and security programs so that the people of Central America can hold the line against externally supported aggression.

In addition, I am asking for prompt action on the supplemental request in these same areas to carry us through the current fiscal year and for early and favorable Congressional action on my request for fiscal year 1984. And, finally, I am asking that the bipartisan consensus which last year acted on the trade and tax provisions of the Caribbean Basin Initiatives in the House again take the lead to move this vital proposal to the floor of both chambers. And, as I said before, the greatest share of these requests is targeted toward economic and humanitarian aid, not military.

What the administration is asking for on behalf of freedom in Central America is so small, so minimal, considering what is at stake. The total amount requested for aid to all of Central America in 1984 is about $600 million; that is less than one-tenth of what Americans will spend this year on coin-operated video games.

In summation, I say to you that tonight there can be no question: The national security of all the Americas is at stake in Central America. If we cannot defend ourselves there, we cannot expect to prevail elsewhere. Our credibility would collapse, our alliances would crumble, and the safety of our homeland would be put in jeopardy.

We have a vital interest, a moral duty, and a solemn responsibility.

This is not a partisan issue. It is a question of our meeting our moral responsibility to ourselves, our friends, and our posterity.

It is a duty that falls on all of us — the President, the Congress, and the people. We must perform it together. Who among us would wish to bear responsibility for failing to meet our shared obligation?

Thank you. God bless you and good night.

[Applause, the Members rising.]

President Reagan's 1984 State of the Union Address

Following is the Congressional Record *text of President Reagan's State of the Union address to a joint session of Congress Jan. 25, 1984.*

The PRESIDENT. Mr. Speaker, Mr. President, distinguished Members of the Congress, honored guests and fellow citizens. Once again, in keeping with time-honored tradition, I have come to report to you on the state of the Union. I am pleased to report that America is much improved, and there is good reason to believe that improvement will continue through the days to come.

You and I have had some honest and open differences in the year past. But they did not keep us from joining hands in bipartisan cooperation to stop a long decline that has drained this Nation's spirit and eroded its health. There is renewed energy and optimism throughout the land. America is back — standing tall, looking to the eighties with courage, confidence, and hope.

The problems we are overcoming are not the heritage of one person, party, or even one generation. It is just the tendency of government to grow, for practices and programs to become the nearest thing to eternal life we will ever see on this Earth. And there is always that well-intentioned chorus of voices saying, "with a little more power and a little more money, we could do so much for the people." For a time we forgot the American dream is not one of

making Government bigger; it is keeping faith with the mighty spirit of free people under God.

The Decade of the '80s

As we came to the decade of the eighties we faced the worst crisis in our postwar history. The seventies were years of rising problems and falling confidence. There was a feeling Government had grown beyond the consent of the governed. Families felt helpless in the face of mounting inflation and the indignity of taxes that reduced reward for hard work, thrift, and risk-taking. All this was overlaid by an ever-growing web of rules and regulations.

On the international scene, we had an uncomfortable feeling that we had lost the respect of friend and foe. Some questioned whether we had the will to defend peace and freedom.

But America is too great for small dreams. There was a hunger in the land for a spiritual revival, if you will, a crusade for renewal. The American people said: Let us look to the future with confidence, both at home and abroad. Let us give freedom a chance.

Americans were ready to make a new beginning, and together we have done it. We are confronting our problems one by one. Hope is alive tonight for millions of young families and senior citizens set free from unfair tax increases and crushing inflation. Inflation has been beaten down from 12.4 to 3.2 percent, and that is a great victory for all the people. The prime rate has been cut almost in half and we must work together to bring it down even more.

Together, we passed the first across-the-board tax reduction for everyone since the Kennedy tax cuts. Next year, tax rates will be indexed so inflation cannot push people into higher brackets when they get cost-of-living pay raises. Government must never again use inflation to profit at the people's expense.

Today, a working family earning $25,000, has $1,100 more in purchasing power than if tax and inflation rates were still at the 1980 levels. Real after-tax income increased 5 percent last year. And economic deregulation of key industries like transportation has offered more choices to consumers and new chances for entrepreneurs and protecting safety. Tonight, we can report and be proud of one of the best recoveries in decades. Send away the handwringers and the doubting Thomases. Hope is reborn for couples dreaming of owning homes, for risk-takers with vision to create tomorrow's opportunities.

The spirit of enterprise is sparked by the sunrise industries of high-tech, and by small business people with big ideas, people like Barbara Proctor, who rose from a ghetto to build a multimillion-dollar advertising agency in Chicago; and Carlos Perez, a Cuban refugee, who turned $27 and a dream into a successful importing business in Coral Gables, Fla.

People like these are heroes for the eighties. They helped 4 million Americans find jobs in 1983. More people are drawing paychecks tonight than ever before. And Congress helps — or progress helps everyone. Well, Congress does, too. In 1983, women filled 73 percent of all the new jobs in managerial, professional, and technical fields.

But we know that many of our fellow countrymen are still out of work, wondering what will come of their hopes and dreams. Can we love America and not reach out to tell them: You are not forgotten; we will not rest until each of you can reach as high as your God-given talents will take you.

The heart of America is strong; it is good and true. The cynics were wrong — America never was a sick society. We are seeing rededication to bedrock values of faith, family, work, neighborhood, peace and freedom — values that help bring us together as one people, from the youngest child to the most senior citizen.

The Congress deserves America's thanks for helping us restore pride and credibility to our military. And I hope that you are as proud as I am of the young men and women in uniform who have volunteered to man the ramparts in defense of freedom and whose dedication, valor, and skill increases so much our chance of living in a world at peace.

People everywhere hunger for peace and a better life. The tide of the future is a freedom tide, and our struggle for democracy cannot and will not be denied. This Nation champions peace that enshrines liberty, democratic rights, and dignity for every individual. America's new strength, confidence, and purpose are carrying hope and opportunity far from our shores. A world economic recovery is underway. It began here.

Four Goals to Keep America Free

We have journeyed far. But we have much farther to go. Franklin Roosevelt told us 50 years ago this month: "Civilization cannot go back; civilization must not stand still. We have undertaken new methods. It is our task to perfect, to improve, to alter when necessary, but in all cases to go forward."

It is time to move forward again, time for America to take freedom's next step. Let us unite tonight behind four great goals to keep America free, secure, and at peace in the eighties. Together:

We can ensure steady economic growth.

We can develop America's next frontier.

We can strengthen our traditional values.

And we can build a meaningful peace to protect our loved ones and this shining star of faith that has guided millions from tyranny to the safe harbor of freedom, progress, and hope.

Federal Deficits

Doing these things will open wider the gates of opportunity and provide greater security for all, with no barriers of bigotry or discrimination. The key to a dynamic decade is vigorous economic growth, our first great goal. We might well begin with common sense in Federal budgeting: Government spending no more than Government takes in.

We must bring Federal deficits down, but how we do that makes all the difference. We can begin by limiting the size and scope of Government. Under the leadership of Vice President Bush, we have reduced the growth of Federal regulations by more than 25 percent, and cut well over 300 million hours of Government-required paperwork each year. This will save the public more than $150 billion over the next 10 years.

The Grace Commission has given us some 2,500 recommendations for reducing wasteful spending, and they are being examined throughout the administration. Federal spending growth has been cut from 17.4 percent in 1980 to less than half of that today. And we have already achieved over $300 billion in budget savings for the period of 1982 to 1986. But that is only a little more than half of what we sought. Government is still spending too large a percentage of the total economy.

Now, some insist that any further budget savings must be obtained by reducing the portion spent on defense. This ignores the fact that national defense is solely the responsibility of the Federal Government. Indeed, it is its prime responsibility. And yet defense spending is less than a third of the total budget. During the years of President Kennedy, and in the years before that, defense was almost half the total budget. Then came several years in which our military capability was allowed to deteriorate to a very dangerous degree. We are just now restoring, through the essential modernization of our conventional and strategic forces, our capability to meet our present and future security needs. We dare not shirk our responsibility to keep America free, secure, and at peace.

The last decade saw domestic spending surge literally out of control. But the basis for such spending had been laid in previous years. A pattern of overspending has been in place for half a century. As the national debt grew, we were told not to worry, that we owed it to ourselves.

Now we know the deficits are a cause for worry. But there is a difference of opinion as to whether taxes should be increased, spending cut, or some of both. Fear is expressed that Government borrowing to fund the deficit could inhibit the economic recovery by taking capital needed for business and industrial expansion. I think that debate is missing an important point. Whether government borrows or increases taxes, it will be taking the same amount of money from the private sector and, either way, that is too much. Simple fairness dictates that Government must

not raise taxes on families struggling to pay their bills. The root of the problem is that Government's share is more than we can afford if we are to have a sound economy.

We must bring down the deficits to ensure continued economic growth. In the budget that I will submit on February 1, I will recommend measures that will reduce the deficit over the next 5 years. Many of these will be unfinished business from last year's budget. Some could be enacted quickly if we could join in a serious effort to address this problem. I spoke today with Speaker of the House O'Neill, Senate Majority Leader Baker, Senate Minority Leader Byrd and House Minority Leader Michel. I asked them if they would designate congressional representatives to meet with representatives of the administration to try to reach prompt agreement on a bipartisan deficit reduction plan. I know it will take a long hard struggle to agree on a full-scale plan. So what I have proposed is that we first see if we can agree on a downpayment.

Now, I believe there is basis for such an agreement, one that could reduce the deficits by about $100 billion over the next 3 years. We could focus on some of the less contentious spending cuts that are still pending before the Congress. These could be combined with measures to close certain tax loopholes, measures that the Treasury Department has previously said to be worthy of support. In addition, we could examine the possibility of achieving further outlay savings based on the work of the Grace Commission.

If the congressional leadership is willing, my representatives will be prepared to meet with theirs at the earliest possible time. I would hope the leadership might agree on an expedited timetable in which to develop and enact that downpayment.

But a downpayment alone is not enough to break us out of the deficit problem. It could help us start on the right path. Yet we must do more. So I propose that we begin exploring how together we can make structural reforms to curb the built-in growth of spending.

Budgeting Process

I also propose improvements in the budgeting process. Some 43 of our 50 states grant their Governors the right to veto individual items in appropriation bills without having to veto the entire bill. California is one of those 43 states. As Governor, I found this "line-item veto" was a powerful tool against wasteful or extravagant spending. It works in 43 states. Let us put it to work in Washington for all the people.

It would be most effective if done by constitutional amendment. The majority of Americans approve of such an amendment, just as they and I approve of an amendment mandating a balanced federal budget. Many states also have this protection in their constitutions.

To talk of meeting the present situation by increasing taxes is a Band-Aid solu-

tion which does nothing to cure an illness that has been coming on for half a century, to say nothing of the fact that it poses a real threat to economic recovery. Let us remember that a substantial amount of income tax is presently owed and not paid by people in the underground economy. It would be immoral to make those who are paying taxes pay more to compensate for those who are not paying their share.

Simplifying the Tax Code

There is a better way: Let us go forward with an historic reform for fairness, simplicity and incentives for growth. I am asking Secretary Don Regan for a plan for action to simplify the entire tax code so all taxpayers, big and small, are treated more fairly. And I believe such a plan could result in that "underground economy" being brought into the sunlight of honest tax compliance; and it could make the tax base broader so personal tax rates could come down, not go up. I have asked that specific recommendations, consistent with those objectives, be presented to me by December 1984. [Laughter.]

Space: The Next Frontier

Our second great goal is to build on America's pioneer spirit — I said something funny? I said this is America's next frontier, and that is to develop that frontier. A sparkling economy spurs initiative and ingenuity to create sunrise industries and make older ones more competitive.

Nowhere is this more important than our next frontier: Space. Nowhere do we so effectively demonstrate our technological leadership and ability to make life better on Earth. The Space Age is barely a quarter of a century old, but already we have pushed civilization forward with our advances in science and technology. Opportunities and jobs will multiply as we cross new thresholds of knowledge and reach deeper into the unknown.

Our progress in space, taking giant steps for all mankind, is a tribute to American teamwork and excellence. Our finest minds in government, industry, and academia have all pulled together, and we can be proud to say: We are first, we are the best, and we are so because we are free.

America has always been greatest when we dared to be great. We can reach for greatness again. We can follow our dreams to distant stars, living and working in space for peaceful, economic, and scientific gain. Tonight, I am directing NASA to develop a permanently manned space station and to do it within a decade.

A space station will permit quantum leaps in our research in science, communications, in metals and in lifesaving medicines which can be manufactured only in space. We want our friends to help us meet these challenges and share in their benefits. NASA will invite other countries to participate so we can strengthen peace, build prosperity, and expand freedom for

all who share our goals.

Just as the oceans opened up a new world for clipper ships and Yankee traders, space holds enormous potential for commerce today. The market for space transportation could surpass our capacity to develop it. Companies interested in putting payloads into space must have ready access to private-sector launch services. The Department of Transportation will help an expendable launch services industry to get off the ground. We will soon implement a number of executive initiatives, develop proposals to ease regulatory constraints, and, with NASA's help, promote private-sector investment in space.

The Environment

As we develop the frontier of space, let us remember our responsibility to preserve our older resources here on Earth. Preservation of our environment is not a liberal or conservative challenge. It is commonsense.

Though this is a time of budget constraints, I have requested for EPA one of the largest percentage budget increases of any agency. We will begin the long, necessary effort to clean up a productive, recreational area and a special national resource — the Chesapeake Bay.

To reduce the threat posed by abandoned hazardous waste dumps, EPA will spend $410 million, and I will request a supplemental increase of $50 million; and because the Superfund law expires in 1985, I have asked Bill Ruckelshaus to develop a proposal for its extension so there will be additional time to complete this important task.

On the question of acid rain, which concerns people in many areas of the United States and Canada, I am proposing a research program that doubles our current funding. And we will take additional action to restore our lakes and develop new technology to reduce pollution that causes acid rain.

We have greatly improved the conditions of our national resources. We will ask the Congress for $157 million beginning in 1985 to acquire new park and conservation lands. The Department of the Interior will encourage careful, selective exploration and production of our vital resources in an Exclusive Economic Zone within the 200-mile limit off our coasts — but with strict adherence to environmental laws and with fuller state and public participation.

Traditional Values

But our most precious resources, our greatest hope for the future, are the minds and hearts of our people, especially our children. We can help them build tomorrow by strengthening our community of shared values. This must be our third great goal. For us, faith, work, family, neighborhood, freedom and peace are not just words. They are expressions of what America means, definitions of what makes us a

good and loving people.

Education

Families stand at the center of our society. And every family has a personal stake in promoting excellence in education. Excellence does not begin in Washington. A 600-percent increase in Federal spending on education between 1960 and 1980 was accompanied by a steady decline in Scholastic Aptitude Test scores. Excellence must begin in our homes and neighborhood schools, where it is the responsibility of every parent and teacher and the right of every child.

Our children come first. And that is why I established a bipartisan National Commission on Excellence in Education, to help us chart a commonsense course for better education. Already, communities are implementing the Commission's recommendations. Schools are reporting progress in math and reading skills. But we must do more to restore discipline to schools; and we must encourage the teaching of new basics, reward teachers of merit, enforce tougher standards, and put our parents back in charge.

I will continue to press for tuition tax credits to expand opportunities for families, and to soften the double payment for those paying public school taxes and private school tuition. Our proposal would target assistance to low- and middle-income families. Just as more incentives are needed within our schools, greater competition is needed among our schools. Without standards and competition there can be no champions, no records broken, no excellence — in education or any other walk of life.

Prayer in School

And while I am on this subject, each day, your Members observe a 200-year-old tradition meant to signify America is one Nation under God. I must ask: If you can begin your day with a member of the clergy standing right here leading you in prayer, then why cannot freedom to acknowledge God be enjoyed again by children in every schoolroom across this land?

America was founded by people who believed that God was their rock of safety. He is ours. I recognize we must be cautious in claiming that God is on our side. But I think it is all right to keep asking if we are on His side.

Abortion

During our first 3 years, we have joined bipartisan efforts to restore protection of the law to unborn children. Now, I know this issue is very controversial. But unless and until it can be proven that an unborn child is not a living human being, can we justify assuming without proof that it is not? No one has yet offered such proof. Indeed, all the evidence is to the contrary. We should rise above bitterness and re-

proach. And if Americans could come together in a spirit of understanding and helping, then we could find positive solutions to the tragedy of abortion.

Crime

Economic recovery, better education, rededication to values all show the spirit or renewal gaining the upper hand. And all will improve family life in the 80's. But families need more. They need assurance that they and their loved ones can walk the streets of America without being afraid. Parents need to know their children will not be victims of child pornography and abduction. This year we will intensify our drive against these and other horrible crimes like sexual abuse and family violence. Already, our efforts to crack down on career criminals, organized crime, drug pushers, and to enforce tougher sentences and paroles are having effect. In 1982, the crime rate dropped by 4.3 percent, the biggest decline since 1972. Protecting victims is just as important as safeguarding the rights of defendants.

Creating Opportunities

Opportunities for all Americans will increase if we move forward on fair housing, and work to ensure women's rights, provide for equitable treatment in pension benefits and Individual Retirement Accounts, facilitate child care, and enforce delinquent parent support payments.

It is not just the home but the workplace and community that sustain our values and shape our future. So I ask your help in assisting more communities to break the bondage of dependency. Help us to free enterprise by permitting debate and voting "yes" on our proposal for enterprise zones in America. This has been before you for 2 years. Its passage can help high-unemployment areas by creating jobs and restoring neighborhoods.

A society bursting with opportunities, reaching for its future with confidence, sustained by faith, fair play, and a conviction that good and courageous people will flourish when they are free — these are the secrets of a strong and prosperous America, at peace with itself and the world.

Lasting and Meaningful Peace

A lasting and meaningful peace is our fourth great goal. It is our highest aspiration. And our record is clear: Americans resort to force only when we must. We have never been aggressors. We have always struggled to defend freedom and democracy.

We have no territorial ambitions. We occupy no countries. We build no walls to lock people in. Americans build the future. And our vision of a better life for farmers, merchants, and working people, from the Americas to Asia, begins with a simple premise: The future is best decided by ballots, not bullets.

Governments which rest upon the consent of the governed do not wage war on their neighbors. Only when people are given a personal stake in deciding their own destiny and benefitting from their own risks do they create societies that are prosperous, progressive, and free. Tonight, it is democracies that offer hope by feeding the hungry, prolonging life, and eliminating drudgery.

When it comes to keeping America strong, free and at peace, there should be no Republicans or Democrats, just patriotic Americans. We can decide the tough issues not by who is right, but by what is right.

Together, we can continue to advance our agenda for peace. We can:

Establish a more stable basis for peaceful relations with the Soviet Union;

Strengthen allied relationships across the board;

Achieve real and equitable reductions in the levels of nuclear arms;

Reinforce our peacemaking efforts in the Middle East, Central America, and Southern Africa;

Assist developing countries, particularly our neighbors in the Western Hemisphere; and

Assist in the development of democratic institutions throughout the world.

The wisdom of our bipartisan cooperation was seen in the work of the Scowcroft Commission, which strengthened our ability to deter war and protect peace. In that same spirit, I urge you to move forward with the Henry Jackson plan to implement the recommendations of the Bipartisan Commission on Central America.

Your joint resolution on the multinational peacekeeping force in Lebanon is also serving the cause of peace. We are making progress in Lebanon. For nearly 10 years the Lebanese have lived from tragedy to tragedy, with no hope for their future. Now the multinational peacekeeping force and our Marines are helping them to break their cycle of despair. There is hope for a free, independent, and sovereign Lebanon. We must have the courage to give peace a chance. And we must not be driven from our objectives for peace in Lebanon by state-sponsored terrorism. We have seen this ugly spectre in Beirut, Kuwait, and Rangoon. It demands international attention. I will forward shortly legislative proposals to help combat terrorism, and I will be seeking support from our allies for concerted action.

Our NATO Alliance is strong; 1983 was a banner year for political courage. And we have strengthened our partnerships and our friendships in the Far East. We are committed to dialogue, deterrence, and promoting prosperity. We will work with our trading partners for a new round of negotiations in support of freer world trade, greater competition, and more open markets.

A rebirth of bipartisan cooperation, of economic growth and military deterrence, and a growing spirit of unity among our

people at home and our allies abroad underline a fundamental and far-reaching change. The United States is safer, stronger, and more secure in 1984 than before. We can now move with confidence to seize the opportunities for peace — and we will.

Addressing the Soviet Union

Tonight I want to speak to the people of the Soviet Union to tell them: It is true that our governments have had serious differences. But our sons and daughters have never fought each other in war. And if we Americans have our way, they never will.

People of the Soviet Union, there is only one sane policy, for your country and mine, to preserve our civilization in this modern age: A nuclear war cannot be won and must never be fought. The only value in our two nations possessing nuclear weapons is to make sure they will never be used. But then would it not be better to do away with them entirely?

People of the Soviet: President Dwight Eisenhower, who fought by your side in World War II, said the essential struggle "is not merely man against man or nation against nation. It is man against war."

Americans are people of peace. If your government wants peace, there will be peace. We can come together in faith and friendship to build a safer and far better world for our children and our children's children. And the whole world will rejoice. That is my message to you.

American Heroes

Some days when life seems hard and we reach out for values to sustain us, or a friend to help us, we find a person who reminds us what it means to be Americans.

Sgt. Stephen Trujillo, a medic in the 2d Ranger Battalion, 75th Infantry, was in the first helicopter to land at the compound held by Cuban forces in Grenada. He saw three other helicopters crash. Despite the imminent explosion of the burning aircraft, he never hesitated. He ran across 25 yards of open terrain through enemy fire to rescue wounded soldiers. He directed two other medics, administered first aid, and returned again and again to the crash site to carry his wounded friends to safety.

Sergeant Trujillo, you and your fellow servicemen and women not only saved innocent lives, you set a nation free. You inspire us as a force for freedom, not for despotism, and yes, for peace, not conquest. God bless you.

And then there are unsung heroes. Single parents, couples, church and civic volunteers, their hearts carry without complaint the pains of family and community problems. They soothe our sorrow, heal our wounds, calm our fears, and share our joy.

A person like Father Ritter is always there. His Covenant House programs in New York and Houston provide shelter and help to thousands of frightened and abused children each year. The same is true of Dr. Charles Carson. Paralyzed in a plane crash, he still believed nothing is impossible. Today, in Minnesota, he works 80 hours a week without pay, helping pioneer the field of computer-controlled walking. He has given hope to 500,000 paralyzed Americans that someday they may walk again.

The Greatness of America

How can we not believe in the greatness of America? How can we not do what is right and needed to preserve this last best hope of man on Earth?

After all our struggles to restore America, to revive confidence in our country and hope for our future, after all our hard-won victories earned through the patience and courage of every citizen, we cannot, must not and will not turn back. We will finish our job. How could we do less? We are Americans.

Carl Sandburg said: I see America, not in the setting sun of a black night of despair * * *. I see America in the crimson light of a rising sun fresh from the burning, creative hand of God * * *. I see great days ahead for men and women of will and vision.

I have never felt more strongly that America's best days and democracy's best days lie ahead. We are a powerful force for good. With faith and courage, we can perform great deeds and take freedom's next step. And we will. We will carry on the traditions of a good and worthy people who have brought light where there was darkness, warmth where there was cold, medicine where there was disease, food where there was hunger, and peace where there was only bloodshed.

Let us be sure that those who come after will say of us in our time that in our time we did everything that could be done: We finished the race, we kept them free, we kept the faith.

Thank you very much, God bless you, and God bless America.

[Applause, the Members rising.]

President Reagan's Fiscal 1985 Budget Message

Following is the text of President Reagan's Feb. 1, 1984, budget message to Congress.

TO THE CONGRESS OF
THE UNITED STATES:

In the past year, the Nation's prospects have brightened considerably. The economy has grown strongly — beyond expectation. Inflation has been reduced to its lowest rate in 16 years. Unemployment has declined faster than at any other time in 30 years. We are well on our way to sustained long-term prosperity without runaway inflation.

Our national security is being restored. Our domestic programs are being streamlined to reflect more accurately the proper scope of Government responsibility and intervention in our lives. Government operations are being made more effective and efficient, as steps are taken to reduce costs.

These developments are the result of the program I proposed 3 years ago to correct the severe economic and political problems caused by previous short-sighted and misguided policies and priorities. That program focused on long-range real growth. My tax proposals were designed to provide badly needed incentives for saving and productive investment. I supported the Federal Reserve in its pursuit of sound monetary policy. I worked with the Congress to reverse the growth of Government programs that had become too large or had outlived their usefulness, and as a result, domestic programs, which had been growing rapidly for 3 decades, have finally been contained. I worked to eliminate or simplify unnecessary or burdensome regulations.

To the Nation's great good fortune, the preceding Congress appreciated the fundamental soundness of this program and joined with my administration in helping to make it a reality. Frequently, because of entrenched constituency special interests, the political risks involved in doing so were great. I thanked Members then, and continue to be grateful, for the crucial support my program received. The Nation is now beginning to reap the solid fruits of our joint perseverance and foresight.

The economy's response has fully vindicated my economic program. During the past 2 years the percentage rise in consumer price index has been no more than it was during the first 6 months of 1980. Economic recovery has been vigorous during the past year, with real GNP rising over 6% and industrial production by 16%. Unemployment, though still unacceptably high, has declined by a record 2½ percentage points in a single year. Capacity utilization in American plants has risen dramatically. Business investment in new plant and equipment has risen 11½% in the past year, in real terms. American productivity, stagnant from 1977 to 1981, climbed 3.7% between the third quarter of 1982 and the third quarter of 1983. Interest rates de-

clined substantially in mid-1982, followed by a major, sustained rally of the stock market that added half a trillion dollars to the net financial worth of American households. Real disposable personal income rose 5.1% in 1983. After a substantial decline, the U.S. dollar has rallied powerfully to its highest level in more than a decade.

We are not, however, out of the woods yet. Despite our success in reducing the rate of growth of nondefense spending in the last three budgets, spending in 1985 will exceed 1981 levels by 41%, reflecting continued increases in basic entitlement programs, essential increases in defense spending, and rapid growth of interest costs. Clearly, much remains to be done. The task of rebuilding our military forces to adequate levels must be carried to completion, and our commitment to provide economic and military support to small, poor nations that are struggling to preserve democracy must be honored. At the same time, further action is required to curb the size and growth of many programs and to achieve managerial efficiencies throughout Government, wherever the opportunity is present.

Three Years of Accomplishment

Last year, I reviewed the dramatic improvements during the preceding 2 years in Government operations, and in the way they affect the economy. I am happy to report that these improvements continued through a third year.

- Where the growth rate of spending was almost out of control at 17.4% a year in 1980, it will decline to 7.3% this year.
- Where spending grew 64% over the 4 years from 1977 to 1981, it will rise by only 41% over the 4-year period from 1981 to 1985, despite legislated cost-of-living adjustments and the needed defense buildup.
- The Federal tax system has been significantly restructured. Marginal income tax rates have been substantially reduced, greatly improving the climate for saving and investment. Depreciation reform has been enacted, restoring the value of depreciation allowances eroded by inflation. Tax loopholes have been closed, making the tax structure more equitable. Efforts have been made to shift to financing Government programs through user fees commensurate with benefits and services provided.
- Our military strength is being restored to more adequate levels.
- Domestic spending, which grew nearly 3-fold in real terms in a little more than 2 decades, will actually be lower this year than it was in 1981.
- The rapid growth of means-tested entitlement programs has been curbed. Eligibility criteria have been tightened to target benefits more to the truly needy, and significant steps have been taken to improve the efficiency and effectiveness of these programs. Unnecessarily frequent cost-of-living adjustments were pared back.
- The social security system has been rescued from the threat of insolvency raised by rampant inflation, excessive liberalizations, and lagging growth of its tax base.
- Unnecessary or excessive Federal credit activities have been eliminated or cut back. Improvements in the management and control of Federal credit activities are being pursued. The administration has supported the basic intent of proposed legislation that would move off-budget lending onto the unified budget, in order to provide better budgetary control over Federal lending.
- Proliferation of regulations and red tape has been stopped. The number of new Federal rules has fallen by over a quarter during the past three years, and hundreds of unnecessary old rules have been eliminated. For the first time, the *Federal Register* of new regulatory actions has grown shorter for three consecutive years; it is now one-third shorter than in 1980. Federal paperwork requirements have been cut by well over 300 million hours annually, and will be reduced even further in 1984. This has saved the American public over 150,000 work-years that had been spent every year filling out unnecessary Federal forms and reports. Our regulatory reform efforts to date will save individual citizens, businesses, and State and local governments over $150 billion over the next decade.
- Major management improvement initiatives are underway that will fundamentally change the way the Federal Government operates. The President's Council on Integrity and Efficiency has reported $31 billion in cost reductions or funds put to better use.
- The Federal nondefense work force has been reduced by 71,000 employees since I took office.

These are impressive accomplishments — accomplishments to be proud of and to build on. And together we can build on them. With this budget I call on all Members of the Congress once again for additional steps to ensure the firmness of our foundations and overcome the Nation's budget problem.

Maintaining Economic Recovery

Before us stands the prospect of an extended era of peace, prosperity, growth, and a rising standard of living for all Americans. What must we do to ensure that that promise shall be realized and enjoyed in the years to come? What must we do to ensure that the high price of adjustment to this new era paid by the Nation in recent years shall not have been paid in vain?

All signs point to continued strong economic growth, vigorous investment, and rising productivity, without renewed inflation — all but one. Only the threat of indefinitely prolonged high budget deficits threatens the continuation of sustained noninflationary growth and prosperity. It raises the specter of sharply higher interest rates, choked-off investment, renewed recession, and rising unemployment.

This specter must be laid to rest: just as fears of rampant inflation and its attendant evils are being laid to rest; just as fears of helplessness before growth in Soviet military might and all it threatens are being laid to rest; just as fears that the Nation's social security system would "go under" have been laid to rest. A number of actions will be required to lay it to rest. This budget requests these actions of Congress; it calls for measures to continue to curb the upward momentum of Federal spending and to increase Federal receipts. Other actions involve such fundamental reform of our fiscal procedures that they will require that the Constitution be amended.

Congress has each year enacted a portion of my budget proposals, while ignoring others for the time being. It is moving slowly, year by year, toward the full needed set of budget adjustments. I urge the Congress to enact this year not only the proposals contained in this budget, but also constitutional amendments providing for a line-item veto and for a balanced budget — rather than the fitful policy of enacting a half-hearted reform this year, another one next year, and so on.

Where Congress lacks the will to enforce upon itself the strict fiscal diet that is now necessary, it needs the help of the Executive Branch. We need a constitutional amendment granting the President power to veto individual items in appropriations bills. Forty-three of the fifty States give this authority to their governors. Congress has approved a line item veto for the District of Columbia, Puerto Rico, and the trust territories. It is now time for Congress to grant this same authority to the President. As Governor of California, I was able to use the line-item veto as a powerful tool against wasteful government spending. It works, and works well, in State government. Every number in this document bears testimony to the urgent need for the Federal Government to adopt this fundamental fiscal reform.

Let us also heed the people and finally support a constitutional amendment mandating balanced Federal budgets and spending limits. I encourage our citizens to keep working for this at the grassroots. If you want to make it happen, it will happen.

We must seek a bipartisan basis for fundamental reforms of Government spending programs. We need to reexamine just what, how, and how much the Federal Government should be doing — given our need for security and well-being and our desire to leave power and resources with the people. The President's Private Sector Survey on Cost Control (Grace Commis-

sion) has already come up with some interesting suggestions in this regard that, with the help of the Congress, will be adopted wherever possible.

To those who say we must raise taxes, I say wait. Tax increases pile unfair burdens on the people, hurt capital formation, and destroy incentives for growth. Tax cuts helped sustain the recovery, leading to faster growth and more jobs. Rather than risk sabotaging our future, let us go forward with an historic reform for fairness, simplicity, and growth. It is time to simplify the entire tax code so everyone is on equal footing.

The tax system must be made simpler and fairer; honest people should not pay for cheaters; the underground economy should come back into the sunlight; and everyone's tax rates should be reduced to spark more savings, investment, and incentives for work and economic growth. This is the blueprint for a brighter future and a fairer tax system. Therefore, I am directing the Department of the Treasury to complete a study with recommendations by the end of the year.

With these changes completed and the necessary fiscal tools in place, I am confident that we can devise a sweeping set of fiscal policy changes designed to reduce substantially the persistent Federal deficits that cloud our otherwise bright economic future. The plan must be based on these cardinal principles:

- It must be bipartisan. Overcoming the deficits and putting the Government's house in order will require everyone's best efforts.
- It must be fair. Just as all Americans will share in the benefits that are coming from recovery, all should share fairly in the burden of transition to a more limited role of Government in our society.
- It must be prudent. The strength of our national defense must be restored so that we can pursue prosperity in peace and freedom, while maintaining our commitment to the truly needy.
- Finally, it must be realistic. Government spending will not be curbed by wishful thinking.

In the meantime, the proposals in this budget provide important additional steps toward reducing the deficit.

Meeting Federal Responsibilities

My administration seeks to limit the size, intrusiveness, and cost of Federal activities as much as possible and to achieve the needed increase in our defense capabilities in the most cost-effective manner possible. This does not mean that appropriate Federal responsibilities are being abandoned, neglected, or inadequately supported. Instead, ways are being found to streamline Federal activity, to limit it to those areas and responsibilities that are truly Federal in nature; to ensure that

these appropriate Federal responsibilities are performed in the most cost-effective and efficient manner; and to aid State and local governments in carrying out their appropriate public responsibilities in a similarly cost-effective manner. The Nation must ask for no more publicly-provided services and benefits than the taxpayers can reasonably be asked to finance.

Education. I have devoted considerable time this year to the problems of our schools. The record of the last two decades is not good, though relieved in places by the efforts of many dedicated teachers, administrators, parents, and students. It has been extremely gratifying to observe the response all across the country to my call for a renewed commitment to educational excellence. Excellence in education will only happen when the States and school districts, parents and teachers, and our children devote themselves to the hard work necessary to achieve it. Federal money cannot buy educational excellence. It has not in the past and will not in the future. What we will do in this budget is seek resources to help the States plan and carry out education reforms. My budget includes $729 million, about 50% more than Congress appropriated for 1984, for the education block grant and discretionary fund. States and localities will receive this increase in resources and be able to use the funds for education reform without Federal prescription and interference.

The budget also provides for stabilizing funding for almost all major education State grant programs at the 1984 level and in the future allows room for modest growth for most of these programs.

Finally, the budget reflects continued support of several more important initiatives that will strengthen American education:

- Enactment of tuition tax credits for parents who send their children to qualified private or religiously-affiliated schools.
- Establishment of education savings accounts to give middle- and lower-income families an incentive to save for their children's college education and, at the same time, to encourage a real increase in saving for economic growth.
- Reorientation of student aid programs to ensure that students and families meet their responsibilities for financing higher education.
- Permission for States or localities, if they so choose, to use their compensatory education funds to establish voucher programs to broaden family choice of effective schooling methods for educationally disadvantaged children.
- Assistance to States to train more mathematics and science teachers.

Training and employment. While the economic forecast predicts continuing improvement in the economy and further steady declines in the unemployment rate,

I recognize that there are those who lack the skills to find and hold steady jobs. This is particularly true for some of our youth. In the past, Federal training and employment programs have not always helped these people gain the skills needed for success in the job market. Instead the Government spent precious tax dollars funding temporary, dead-end, make-work jobs that did little, if anything, to prepare these people for holding real jobs in the private sector. My administration worked with the Congress to change that. The Job Training Partnership Act, which I signed into law in 1982, involves private industry in the design and delivery of job training programs. Each year it will train 1.5 million disadvantaged adults and youths, dislocated workers, and welfare recipients in skills needed for private sector jobs. Additional work experience for over 700,000 disadvantaged youths will be provided during the summer months. What is needed now is not more Government programs, but removal of Government-created barriers that make it difficult for youths who want to work to find jobs. It has long been acknowledged that the minimum wage is a barrier to job finding for youths, especially minority youths, who lack skills. Therefore, I am again asking the Congress to authorize a wage of 75% of the minimum wage for youths newly hired for jobs during the summer months. This will let employers lower their costs to levels more in line with the skills youths possess, and it will help many young people find jobs and gain valuable work experience. The legislation I have proposed includes protections for adult workers.

Research. Recognizing the Federal responsibility to maintain and strengthen U.S. leadership in science and technology, the budget proposes further increases of more than 10% in Government-wide funding for basic research. The $8 billion planned for support of such research represents a relatively small share of the budget, but it is a critical investment in the Nation's future. Basic research lays the foundation for a strong defense in the years to come and for new technologies and industries that will maintain U.S. industrial leadership, create new jobs, and improve our quality of life.

Space. Our civilian space program has made remarkable progress in the past year. The space shuttle, the world's most advanced space transportation system, has made eight pathbreaking trips into space and is progressing rapidly towards achieving routine operational status.

We can now look forward confidently to the next major challenge in space — a space station. The space station, to be placed in permanent Earth orbit in the early 1990's, is intended to enhance the Nation's science and application programs, to help develop advanced technologies potentially useful to the economy, and to encourage greater commercial use of space. The budget provides planning money to initiate this program.

National defense. During the past 3 years, we have also taken decisive measures to increase our military strength to levels necessary to protect our Nation and our friends and allies around the world. At the same time, we have vigorously pursued diplomatic approaches, such as arms reduction talks, in an effort to ensure the principles of security and freedom for all.

The improvement in our defense posture has been across the board. Long-overdue modernization of our strategic forces is proceeding, while our conventional forces are also being modernized and strengthened. Successful recruiting and retention over the past 3 years have resulted in all of our armed services being more fully manned with capable, high-caliber men and women.

Energy. My administration has significantly reoriented the country's approach to energy matters toward reliance on market forces — instead of Government regulation and massive, indiscriminate Federal spending. This has resulted in greater energy production, more efficient use of energy, and more favorable energy prices. For example:

- The U.S. economy currently is using 30% less oil and gas per dollar's worth of output than it did 10 years ago when energy prices began to rise.
- Heating oil prices have been lower this past year than they were in January 1981, when I removed oil price controls. Gasoline prices have fallen to levels which, after adjustments for general inflation and sales taxes, are within 5% of those that prevailed in the U.S. in the 1950's.

Energy programs proposed in the budget are designed to complement market forces by focusing resources on limited but appropriate responsibilities of the Federal Government and by managing these programs well. Thus, for example, the budget proposes increased spending for basic and other long-term energy research. In addition, the administration continues its commitment to filling the strategic petroleum reserve. The reserve has more than tripled in size in the last three years.

Health care. Progress has been made in slowing the explosive growth of health costs. As part of the Social Security Amendments of 1983, Congress enacted the Administration's proposed fixed price prospective payment system for hospital care. This replaced the previous Medicare hospital reimbursement system under which hospitals were reimbursed for their costs. The new prospective payment system has altered incentives and should lessen the rate of increase in hospital costs.

Under the proposals in this budget, physicians will be asked to maintain present fee levels for medicare through the next fiscal year. Tax incentives prompting overly-costly employee health insurance benefits would be revised to make users and providers more sensitive to costs. Finally, resources for biomedical research will increase.

Transportation. My administration has sought to shift much of the costs of transportation from the general taxpayer to those who use transportation services and facilities. I signed into law several administration-backed proposals to increase excise taxes on aviation and highway users and thereby provide funding needed to revitalize and modernize these important segments of the Nation's transportation system. The proportion of the Department of Transportation's budget financed by user fees has risen from 49% in 1982 to 72% in 1985. The budget reflects the administration's continued commitment to the "users pay" principle by including receipts proposals for nautical and aviation aids, the inland waterway system, and construction and maintenance of deep-draft ports.

Recognizing the importance of safety in our transportation systems, the budget provides for significant improvements in this area. In addition, my administration secured passage of legislation designed to rebuild the Nation's highway and public transportation facilities. This legislation substantially increased funds available to the States and local communities to complete and repair the aging interstate highway system, to rehabilitate principal rural and urban highways and bridges, and to improve mass transit systems. The budget also provides for improvements in the safety of our transportation systems.

Improved ports and channels will help to make U.S. coal exports competitive in world markets. My administration will work with the Congress to provide for timely and efficient port construction. A system that recovers a significant portion of the cost of existing port maintenance and new port construction must be enacted prior to any new construction. In the last 3 years, my administration has sent several reasonable proposals to the Congress, and progress is being made. It is time for action on this important issue.

Reducing the Federal presence in commercial transportation, currently regulated by the Interstate Commerce Commission, the Civil Aeronautics Board, and the Federal Maritime Commission, will improve the efficiency of the industry. Authority for the Civil Aeronautics Board will expire next year, and its residual functions will be assumed by other agencies. The administration will continue to seek legislation to deregulate ocean shipping, and will propose legislation to deregulate oil pipelines and natural gas. Experience since the adoption of initial transportation deregulation legislation has shown clearly that both consumers and industry benefit from reduced Federal involvement in these activities.

Criminal justice. My administration has continued to strengthen the Federal criminal justice system by seeking major legislative changes in immigration policy, sentencing, and bail procedures, and by seeking increased funding for law enforcement activities. An additional organized

crime drug enforcement task force will be established in Florida, bringing the total number of task forces to 13. The budget proposes to bolster immigration control by strengthening border enforcement and improving the effectiveness of border inspection programs. Additional attorneys will be sought for the Internal Revenue Service and the Justice Department, underscoring my administration's determination to tackle the serious problem of tax protesters and evaders. The administration will enhance its efforts to identify, neutralize, and defeat foreign agents who pose a threat to the Nation.

International affairs. Our foreign policy is oriented toward maintaining peace through military strength and diplomatic negotiation; promoting market-oriented solutions to international economic problems; telling the story abroad of America's democratic, free-enterprise way of life; and reducing barriers to free trade both here and abroad.

- The security assistance portion of the international affairs program has been increased to assist friendly governments facing threats from the Soviet Union, its surrogates, and from other radical regimes.
- Development aid emphasizes encouraging the private sectors of developing nations and increasing U.S. private sector involvement in foreign assistance.
- The budget provides for continuing the major expansion of international broadcasting activities started last year. Television, exchanges of people, and other programs to improve communications with foreign countries are included.
- My administration will continue to work with the Congress to strengthen the management and coordination of the Government's international trade functions by consolidating them in a Department of International Trade and Industry.

The United States faces threats to its interests in many parts of the world. The Middle East, with its vital energy resources, is still in turmoil. In Central America, Marxist forces continue to threaten democratic governments, exploiting temporary economic dislocations and the continuing poverty of less developed countries. In Africa, the poorest nations of the world are facing the prospect of great privation, accentuated by drought. This budget addresses each of these concerns:

- It continues military and economic support for Israel and Egypt, with improved financial terms.
- It provides for a significant increase in assistance to Central America, the specific nature of which will be defined after our review of the recommendations of the National Bipartisan Commission on Central America.
- It provides special humanitarian

Appendix

aid to counter the immediate effects of African drought and proposes a longer-term program aimed at the root causes of Africa's economic problem.

Although now less than 2% of the budget, international programs are critical to American world leadership and to the success of our foreign policy.

Civil service retirement. There is growing recognition that civil service retirement has far more generous benefits and is much more costly than retirement programs in the private sector or in State and local governments. Accordingly, the administration continues its strong support of the civil service reform proposals advanced in last year's budget. In 1985, the administration will focus its legislative effort on three of those proposals, in modified form: cost-of-living adjustment (COLA) reform, a high 5-year salary average for the benefit formula, and increased employee and agency retirement contributions.

GI bill rate increase. The budget proposes legislation to provide a 15% increase in the rates of educational assistance and special training allowances to GI bill trainees and disabled veterans receiving vocational rehabilitation assistance, effective January 1985. The increase will offset increased costs since GI bill benefits were last raised in 1981. It will provide an increase in monthly education benefit checks to 544,000 veterans and their dependents and survivors.

Continuing Reform of Our Federal System

The overall efficiency of Government in the United States can also be improved by a more rational sorting out of governmental responsibilities among the various levels of government in our Federal system — Federal, State, and local — and by eliminating or limiting overlap and duplication.

In 1981, the Congress responded to my proposals by consolidating 57 categorical programs into nine block grants. In 1982, a block grant was created for job training in the Jobs Training Partnership Act.

The administration is improving the management of intergovernmental assistance by providing State and local elected officials with greater opportunity to express their views on proposed Federal development and assistance actions before final decisions are made. Under Executive Order 12372, Intergovernmental Review of Federal Programs, which I signed in July 1982, Federal agencies must consult with State and local elected officials early in the assistance decision process and make every effort to accommodate their views. The Order also encourages the simplification of State planning requirements imposed by Federal law, and allows for the substitution of State-developed plans for federally required State plans where statutes and regulations allow.

Controlling Federal Credit Programs

Federal credit in all its forms imposes costs on the U.S. economy that must be weighed against its benefits. Federal intervention through guarantees and direct loans may misdirect investment and pre-empt capital that could be used more efficiently by unsubsidized, private borrowers. Because federally assisted borrowers are frequently less productive than private borrowers, large Federal credit demands, and the degree of subsidy involved in Federal credit activity, must be reduced if we are to improve prospects for economic growth.

The administration continues its strong commitment to control Federal direct loans and loan guarantees. It has supported the basic intent of proposed legislation to move off-budget Federal lending into the unified budget. It seeks other basic reforms in the way in which direct loans and loan guarantees are presented and controlled.

In the coming year, my administration will issue a directive establishing Government-wide policies on credit. This directive will be both an explicit statement of the administration's goal in providing credit assistance and a means of controlling the manner in which that assistance is provided.

Regulatory Reform

Federal regulation grew explosively throughout the 1970's. Whether well or poorly designed, whether aimed at worthy or dubious objectives, these rules have one thing in common: they "tax" and "spend" billions of dollars entirely within the private sector of the economy, unconstrained by public budget or appropriations controls.

My administration has taken steps to correct this problem. Under Executive Order 12291, all Federal regulations must be reviewed by the Office of Management and Budget before being issued to determine whether their social benefits will exceed their social costs. As a result of this review process, we have reversed the rate of growth of Federal regulations. Hundreds of ill-conceived proposals have been screened out, and hundreds of existing rules have been stricken from the books because they were unnecessary or ineffective. Equally important, numerous existing regulations have been improved, and new rules have been made as cost-effective as possible within statutory limits. We are steadily winding down economic controls that regulate prices, form barriers to entry for new firms, and other anti-competitive regulations. At the same time we are increasing the effectiveness of our programs promoting health, safety, and environmental quality.

Our regulatory reform program has been open and public. New rules and changes to existing rules now require public notice and comment. My Executive Or-

der requires regulatory agencies to consider the interests of the general public as well as special interest groups in rulemaking proceedings. The Task Force on Regulatory Relief and the Office of Management and Budget have issued regular reports detailing the progress of regulatory reform efforts. *The Unified Agenda of Federal Regulations*, issued twice each year, describes all planned and pending regulatory changes in virtually all Federal agencies. The administration's *Regulatory Policy Guidelines*, published in August 1983, is the first comprehensive statement of regulatory policy ever to be issued.

I believe it is time the policies and procedures of Executive Order 12291 were enacted into law. Individual regulatory decisions will always be contentious and controversial, but surely we can all agree on the general need for regulatory reform. Making each Government rule as cost-effective as possible benefits everyone and strengthens the individual regulatory statutes. Regulation has become such an important role of the Federal Government that strong and balanced central oversight is becoming a necessity and a bi-partisan objective. The Laxalt-Leahy Regulatory Reform Act, which passed the Senate unanimously in 1982, would have accomplished this reform. I strongly urge the Congress to take up and pass similar legislation this year. In addition, my administration continues to support measures to deregulate financial institutions.

Improving the Efficiency of Government

It is important to continue to reduce the size of Government. It is equally important to use the remaining resources as efficiently and effectively as possible. My administration has begun to make great strides in doing exactly that.

During the past 3 years, we have initiated several Government-wide management improvement efforts under the guidance of the Cabinet Council on Management and Administration. They are:

—Reform 88;
—Personnel management reform;
—Federal field structure reform; and
—The President's Private Sector Survey on Cost Control.

These management improvement and cost reduction programs focus on 4 objectives:

—Reducing fraud, waste, and mismanagement;
—Improving agency operations;
—Developing streamlined Federal Government management systems; and
—Improving the delivery of services.

Reducing fraud, waste, and mismanagement. This objective seeks better use of appropriated dollars. The Presi-

dent's Council on Integrity and Efficiency (PCIE) was formed in early 1981 and is made up of 18 department and agency Inspectors General. They recently reported $8.4 billion in cost reductions or funds put to better use in the last 6 months of 1983 and a total of $31 billion since they were appointed. The PCIE is beginning to direct its efforts toward preventing problems before they occur, through improved technology and better audit processes, as described in their latest report.

The PCIE also found that enormous waste was occurring because the Federal Government had never established an effective cash management system — despite the fact that it handles almost a trillion dollars in cash annually. This is currently being corrected by installing sophisticated, up-to-date systems that the Department of the Treasury estimates could save as much as $3½ billion a year.

When my administration came to office we found delinquent debt owed the Government rising at a rate of over 40% per year — with a total debt outstanding of over $240 billion. After only 2 years' efforts, this annual growth rate has been reduced to 2%. A credit pre-screening system is now being put in place, and automated collection centers are being installed.

Federal procurement involves annual expenditures of $170 billion. Procurement was an overly complex process with only 50% of our contract dollars awarded under competitive bid. My administration has replaced three sets of regulations with one, and we are now setting up a new pro-competitive policy to cut costs.

We have extended our fight to reduce waste and mismanagement to a direct attack on that nemesis that has always characterized the Federal Government: red tape and paperwork. We have already reduced the paperwork burden placed on the private sector by the Federal Government by well over 300 million hours. In this current fiscal year we intend to reduce the burden by another 130 million hours.

Further savings and improvements are possible. The President's Private Sector Survey on Cost Control (Grace Commission) developed numerous recommendations for savings and cost avoidance. These recommendations range from reducing costs of Federal employee retirement programs to upgrading the Government's seriously outdated and inefficient management and administrative systems. I have already included many of these ideas in this budget

and will include more in future budgets. My administration will develop a tracking system to make sure they are carried out.

These are but a few of the efforts underway to make sure that appropriated funds go further and are used for the purposes for which they were intended.

Improving agency operations. I am directing Federal agencies to coordinate their administrative activities so that they reduce their current operating costs immediately, rather than wait for future improvements in systems and technologies. Savings resulting from these efforts are reflected in this budget. These efforts include: (1) consolidating headquarters and regional administrative services; (2) requiring service centers to meet minimum productivity standards for processing documents; (3) using private sector contractors to provide support services where appropriate and economical; (4) reducing Federal civilian employment by 75,000 by the beginning of 1985, reducing higher graded staff, and improving personnel planning; (5) reducing office space by 10%; (6) reducing printing plants by 25% and publications by 25%; and (7) eliminating the processing of documents altogether for most small agencies, by requiring them to obtain services from larger agencies that have efficient centers.

Developing streamlined Federal Government management systems. As we are reducing the size of Government and reducing fraud, waste, and abuse, we also need to change fundamentally the way the Federal Government is managed. When I came into office, we found that the Federal Government lacked a well-planned compatible management process, so we set about developing one. This effort involves five major projects: (1) planning and budgeting, (2) financial management and accounting, (3) personnel management and payroll, (4) personal and real property, and (5) automatic data processing and telecommunications management. Responsibilities and resources for the development of each of these management systems have been assigned to those agencies that have or are capable of developing the most advanced management system in each category. Without this effort, the Federal Government would continue to operate in an inefficient manner that does not serve our citizens well.

Improving the delivery of services. My administration is looking seriously at the way the delivery of Federal

services is handled across the country. The objective of this effort is to achieve improved service at lower cost, through improved technology and management techniques such as prescreening, computer matching, adjusted payment schedules, contractor and grantee performance incentives, and a streamlined field structure. All of these efforts are being planned and coordinated centrally as part of the budget process. The results of these efforts will be reported to the Congress together with resulting savings and proposals to upgrade management of the Federal Government.

Conclusion

Vigorous, noninflationary economic recovery is well underway. The long winter of transition from the misguided policies of the past, with their inflationary and growth-deadening side-effects, is now yielding to a new springtime of hope for America. The hope of continued recovery to long-term noninflationary prosperity can be realized if we are able to work together on further deficit reduction measures. Bold, vigorous fiscal policy action to break the momentum of entrenched spending programs, together with responsible and restrained monetary policy, is essential to keep the recovery on track; essential to the Nation's future economic health and vitality. Limited measures to increase receipts will also be necessary to make our tax system fairer and more efficient. But it is important — more than important, *crucial* — to get the mix of spending restraint and receipts increases right. There must be substantial reductions in spending and strictly limited increases in receipts.

I call urgently upon the Congress, therefore, to take the actions proposed in this budget. Far too much is at stake to permit casual dismissal of these essential belt-tightening measures. The Nation has paid a high price for the prospect of a secure, prosperous, noninflationary future; that prospect must not be sacrificed to a sense of complacency, to an expedient ducking of the issues.

With confidence in the ultimate beneficial effects of our actions, let us seize the high ground and secure, for ourselves and our posterity, a bright and prosperous future — a future in which the glory that was America is again restored.

RONALD W. REAGAN
February 1, 1984

Reagan's Report to Congress on ASAT Arms Control

Following are excerpts from the White House text of President Reagan's March 31, 1984, report to Congress regarding U.S. policy on antisatellite arms control.

PREFACE

The Congressional conference report for the Department of Defense Appropriations Act for the Fiscal Year ending September 30, 1984 states:

The conferees agree to provide $19,409,000 for advance procurement for the Antisatellite (ASAT) program as proposed by the Senate, instead of no funds as proposed by the House. However, the conferees direct that these

funds not be obligated or expended until 45 days following submission to the Congress of a comprehensive report on U.S. policy on arms control plans and objectives in the field of ASAT systems. In no event shall such report be submitted later than March 31, 1984. Such report should include specific steps the Administration contemplates undertaking, within the context of U.S.-Soviet negotiations, to seek a verifiable agreement with the Soviet Union to ban or strictly limit existing and future ASAT systems. The report should be unclassified, with classified addenda as required, and suitable for general release.

This report to Congress fulfills that requirement. It summarizes U.S. national security requirements pertaining to ASAT weaponry, and the problems and possibilities for ASAT arms control. The Report is in two versions, one is unclassified and the other, containing additional detail, is classified.

U.S. POLICY ON ASAT ARMS CONTROL

Overview

U.S. arms control policy must serve our fundamental national security objectives. In particular, arms control arrangements should reduce the risk of war (through measures which strengthen deterrence, increase confidence, and enhance strategic stability) or reduce the destructiveness of warfare. Arms control arrangements for space are desirable if they contribute to our overall deterrence posture and reduce the risk of conflict, not as ends in themselves. Similarly, possible limits or bans on anti-satellite (ASAT) arms must be judged not only in their ability to limit damage to space objects, but also in their contribution to achieving the basic objectives of arms control with respect to terrestrial conventional and nuclear conflict.

The U.S. National Space Policy, announced by the President July 4, 1982, is consistent with the long-standing U.S. approach to space arms control in previous agreements. It states:

"The United States will continue to study space arms control options. The United States will consider verifiable and equitable arms control measures that would ban or otherwise limit testing and deployment of specific weapons systems, should those measures be compatible with United States national security."

Guided by these criteria, the United States has been studying a range of possible options for space arms control with a view to possible negotiations with the Soviet Union and other nations, if such negotiations would serve U.S. interests. The United States is also prepared to examine space arms control issues in the Conference on Disarmament (CD). However, no arrangements or agreements beyond those already governing military activities in outer

space have been found to date that are judged to be in the overall interest of the United States and its Allies. The factors which impede the identification of effective ASAT arms control measures include significant difficulties of verification, diverse sources of threats to U.S. and Allied satellites and threats posed by Soviet targeting and reconnaissance satellites which undermine conventional and nuclear deterrence.

Notwithstanding these difficulties, the United States is continuing to study space arms control, in search of selected limits on specific types of space systems or activities in space which could satisfactorily deal with problems such as those described above. Until we have determined whether there are, in fact, practical solutions to these problems, we do not believe it would be productive to engage in formal international negotiations. The United States remains ready, however, to examine the problems and potential of space arms control at the Conference on Disarmament. . . .

Potential Benefits of Space Arms Control

. . . The spectrum of possible space arms control measures includes bans on specialized ASAT weapons and much less ambitious undertakings. To be acceptable any measure must be equitable, effectively verifiable and compatible with our national security. If any space arms control measures met these criteria, and were complied with, then they would have a number of potential benefits. For example, depending on the scope and effectiveness of an agreement, it might:

1. Limit specialized threats to satellites and constrain future threats to such key satellites as those for early warning. Such limitations on specialized threats to satellites, together with satellite survivability measures, could help preserve and enhance stability.

2. Raise the political threshold for attacks against satellites. Restricting threatening activity and/or prohibiting attacks on satellites would add to existing international law aimed at lowering the likelihood of conflict in space.

3. Meet some international concerns regarding the use of space for military purposes.

Problems Facing ASAT Arms Control

In addition to the potential benefits of space arms control, a balanced study of this topic must take into account a number of problems. . . .

Verification. Effective verification is fundamental to arms control. . . . The Congressional language mandating ASAT arms control efforts has been uniformly specific on the matter of verification: any ban on ASAT systems is to be verifiable.

. . . The open U.S. society makes the Soviet task of monitoring U.S. activities regarding arms control compliance a rela-

tively easy matter. In contrast, the closed Soviet society and the general Soviet tendency toward secrecy make U.S. monitoring and verification of compliance much more difficult. This problem is aggravated for ASAT systems because the satellites which serve U.S. and Allied security are few in number. Cheating on anti-satellite limitations, even on a small scale, could pose a disproportionate risk to the United States.

In this regard, the Soviets would have a far easier problem of verifying compliance with limitations on the U.S. ASAT system than we would have on the Soviet system. For example, a ban on all ASAT systems would require that the Soviet ASAT interceptor system be eliminated. The Soviet interceptor is relatively small and is launched by a type of space booster that the Soviets use for other space launch missions. It is not clear how many interceptors or boosters have been manufactured. The USSR could maintain a covert supply of interceptors which could be readied quickly for operational use, probably without risk of U.S. detection. Launch vehicles could be diverted from other missions to launch ASAT interceptors.

Verification problems apply to other aspects of space arms control as well. For instance, tests of a ground-based laser ASAT weapon could be concealed. In addition, determining with confidence whether an object hundreds of kilometers above the earth has been damaged could, in practice, be extremely difficult, and from what source it had been damaged could be extremely difficult or impossible. It may be difficult to determine whether a satellite has been damaged by electronic countermeasures. It is also difficult, or in some cases could be impossible, to determine whether an orbiting satellite contains a weapon.

Additional verification problems arise if ASAT testing is banned or limited. The wide variety of ASAT systems listed below in the discussion of problems of definition, and the fact that ASAT capabilities can be a by-product of systems developed for other missions, create problems of identifying what would be prohibited under testing limitations. The fact that ASAT capabilities are inherent in some systems developed for other missions or are amenable to undetected or surreptitious development makes it impossible to verify compliance with a truly comprehensive testing limitation that would eliminate tests of all methods of countering satellites. Test bans for a more limited class of ASAT systems may be verifiable, and these are being studied to determine if they are in our national interest. The breakout potential of that limited class of ASAT systems is very troublesome and creates doubt that limited test bans could be effective.

The difficult verification problems could, in some cases, be mitigated by future technological developments, or by cooperative measures contained in future arms control agreements. Such possibilities are

under study.

Breakout. Among the criteria which must be used in evaluating the implications for national security of any potential arms control measure is that of "breakout." This is the risk that a nation could gain a unilateral advantage if the agreement ceased to remain in force for any reason, for example through sudden abrogation, and obtain a head start in building or deploying a type of weapon which has been banned or severely limited. The importance of certain critical U.S. satellites, which are limited in numbers, could create an incentive for the Soviets to maintain a breakout capability.

Breakout potential could exist even if the Soviets, upon agreeing to a ban on ASAT systems, were to destroy all of their existing systems. The Soviets could retain the capability to redeploy quickly a system in which they would have confidence. If prior to the ban the United States had not tested its MV ASAT system, the Soviets alone would possess such proven technology. It might take the Soviets a year or less to deploy their system again.

Under a strict ASAT arms control regime, it is conceivable that the Soviets could change the basic character of their ASAT program. The USSR could have additional ASAT capability in equipment amenable to undetected or surreptitious development, which could be brought to operational status, or to a status that would permit rapid breakout. For example, any nation routinely conducting space rendezvous and docking operations, as the USSR does, could, under the guise of that activity, develop spacecraft equipped to maneuver into the path of, or detonate next to, another nation's spacecraft. Other types of systems amenable to such development include ballistic missiles with modified guidance software such as ICBMs, SLBMs and MRBMs, as well as space boosters with nuclear payloads. There is little reason to believe that the USSR would use any of these non-optimum capabilities in lieu of the system with known ASAT capabilities. However, a ban on the more readily identifiable ASAT systems could increase the likelihood that other systems would be covertly developed to have ASAT capability.

Disclosure of Information. While the difficult verification problems associated with ASAT arms control might be decreased with the establishment of cooperative measures, in some instances these measures could cause other problems. Information regarding certain U.S. space systems that are associated with national security is among the most sensitive information within the government. Cooperative measures with the objective of enhancing verification of an ASAT arms control agreement might require access to U.S. space systems that were alleged by the Soviets to have ASAT capabilities, and hence could create an unacceptable risk of compromising the protection of that information. Such measures could also have adverse effects on civil uses of space.

Definition. It is difficult to define what constitutes a space weapon for arms control purposes. There are technologies and systems designed for purposes other than ASAT, even some with little or no ASAT capabilities, which may be difficult to exclude from an ASAT definition. Likewise, there are technologies and systems which could have an ASAT application that might not be included in an ASAT definition.

The U.S. Congress has shown concern over space system survivability problems, especially in legislation which each chamber has passed relating the U.S. ASAT program to arms control. The Senate passed a measure to establish criteria governing the testing of ASAT warheads; in the deliberations over that provision, it was argued that "unless (ASAT) development is stopped, our most important and sensitive military satellites will be in jeopardy." The House of Representatives passed a measure deleting advanced procurement funds for the U.S. ASAT program; in those deliberations, it was argued "that the survival of current and projected U.S. space systems is vital to the national security of the United States." In keeping with those broadly-based satellite survivability concerns we need to recognize that "ASAT capability" relates to all systems capable of damaging, destroying or otherwise interrupting the functioning of satellites. Such systems include:

- maneuvering spacecraft (equipped to maneuver into the path of, or to detonate next to, another nation's spacecraft) such as the coorbital interceptor operationally deployed by the USSR.
- Direct ascent interceptors such as exo-atmospheric ABM missiles, ballistic missiles with modified guidance logic, space boosters carrying nuclear payloads, and homing vehicles such as the miniature vehicle system undergoing development by the United States.
- Directed energy weapons such as lasers and particle beams, (either ground-based or space-based, having sufficient power to damage satellites or their sensors.)
- Electronic countermeasures of sufficient power output to damage or interrupt satellite functions.
- Weapons which could be carried by manned space planes or orbital complexes.

Furthermore, problems of weapon definition are compounded because some non-weapon space systems, including civil and commercial systems, could have characteristics which would make it difficult to frame a definition to distinguish them from weapon systems. An effective space arms control measure should take into account weapon capabilities beyond those of specialized ASAT systems, and at the same time it must not unduly constrain the legitimate functions of non-weapon space systems.

In seeking ways to verify an ASAT weapon ban, the Administration has been confronted with critical definitional problems: (1) there are many different types of systems which could be used to destroy satellites; (2) in general, many activities related to space give rise to capabilities inherently useful for ASAT purposes, for example, the rendezvous and docking operations routinely conducted by the Soviets could be used to attempt to conceal development of one or more types of ASAT techniques, and (3) restricting the definition of what is an ASAT weapon could make an agreement easier to verify, but ineffective in achieving its purpose of protecting satellites. These definition problems interact with and compound the verification problems described above.

Vulnerability of Satellite Support Systems. ASAT arms control would not provide for survivability of all components of space systems. For example, attacks on other elements of a space system (e.g., ground stations, launch facilities, or communications links) may in some cases be easier and more effective than attacks on satellites themselves. Attacks on ground-based support systems can be carried out with strikes by conventional weapons, such as by cruise missiles with conventional warheads launched from ships or aircraft.

The Soviet Non-Weapon Military Space Threat. Examination of space arms control needs to include a discussion of the growing threat posed by present and projected Soviet space systems, which, while not weapons themselves, are designed to support directly the USSR's terrestrial forces in the event of a conflict. These include ocean reconnaissance satellites which use radar and electronic intelligence in efforts to provide targeting data to Soviet weapon platforms which can quickly attack U.S. and Allied surface fleets. In view of the fundamental importance of U.S. and Allied access to the seas in wartime, including for Allied reinforcement by sea, the protection of U.S. and Allied navies against such targeting is critical. Furthermore, as Soviet military space technology improves, the capabilities of Soviet satellites that can be used for targeting are likely to be enhanced and represent a greater threat to U.S. and Allied security. This point is explained at greater length below.

NATIONAL SECURITY CONSIDERATIONS REGARDING SPACE

Beyond the significant limitations inherent in space arms control discussed above, other national security interests must be taken into account. These would pertain even if verification were not so significant a concern.

Strengthening Deterrence

A fundamental purpose of defense and arms control policies is to maintain and strengthen deterrence, both conventional

and nuclear deterrence. ASAT limitations could, unfortunately, undermine deterrence in some instances.

Since the Soviet Union has an operational capability to destroy satellites while the United States does not, the current situation is destabilizing. If, for example, during a crisis or conflict, the Soviet Union were to destroy a U.S. satellite, the United States would lack the capability to respond in kind to avoid escalating the conflict. Thus, in present circumstances a U.S. capability to destroy satellites clearly responds to the need to deter such Soviet attacks on U.S. satellites in a crisis or conflict.

A comprehensive ASAT ban would afford a sanctuary to existing Soviet satellites designed to target U.S. naval and land conventional forces. The absence of a U.S. ASAT capability to prevent Soviet targeting aided by satellites could be seen by the Soviets as a substantial factor in their ability to attack U.S. and Allied forces and might offset Soviet concerns about the effectiveness of U.S. and Allied naval warfare capabilities. Uncertainty over their ability to employ satellites to target naval forces would decrease the Soviet perception of their chance for success, thereby adding to deterrence and stability. A U.S. ASAT capability would contribute to deterrence of conventional conflict.

For U.S. and Allied security, the United States must continue its efforts to protect against threatening satellites. ASAT capabilities complement the other measures that must be used throughout a conflict. To do otherwise would undermine both conventional and nuclear deterrence. (Further discussion of the above factors is provided in the classified version of this report.) . . .

Soviet Threats to U.S. Satellites

The current Soviet ASAT capabilities include an operational orbital interceptor system, ground-based test lasers with probable ASAT capabilities, and possibly, the nuclear-armed GALOSH ABM interceptors, and the technological capability to conduct electronic warfare against space systems.

The orbital interceptor must go into approximately the same orbit as its target and close at a specific velocity. There have been more than a dozen tests of the interceptor system, which we consider operational, including testing during a Soviet strategic forces exercise in 1982.

A Soviet high-altitude orbital interceptor capability is a possible threat, but we have no direct evidence of such a program by the Soviets, and we may not obtain such evidence before testing. Other techniques for accomplishing this objective may appear preferable to the Soviets. For example, they could also use their developing electronic warfare capabilities against high-altitude satellites. We cannot now say which, if any, such high-altitude capabilities may be developed by the USSR.

Continuing, or possible future, Soviet efforts that could produce ASAT systems include developments in directed energy weapons. We have indications that the Soviets are continuing development of ground-based lasers for ASAT applications. In addition, we believe the Soviets are conducting research and development in the area of space-based laser ASAT systems. We have, as yet, no evidence of Soviet programs to develop ASAT weapons based on particle beam technology.

(Additional data concerning Soviet threats to U.S. satellites are contained in the classified version of this report.) . . .

Utility of a U.S. ASAT Capability

The U.S. ASAT program is focused explicitly on those Soviet satellites which threaten U.S. and Allied terrestrial interests in time of war. All of these threatening Soviet satellites operate at low altitude. Without low altitude satellites to confirm detections of terrestrial targets, Soviet space-based targeting data would be significantly degraded. While the U.S. MV ASAT will be able to attack only a portion of the Soviet satellites, in doing so it would be able seriously to degrade the Soviet reconnaissance capability and thus serves U.S. deterrence objectives. It cannot and need not attack Soviet early warning satellites at high altitudes.

Because of their high launch rates and payload capacity, the Soviet space force has the inherent resiliency to make replacement of satellites a viable alternative (as long as ground facilities are intact). On-orbit spares, surge of launches in a crisis or prior to a hostility, and satellite replacement following ASAT attack are possible methods of replenishment. The U.S. program is structured to provide a number of readily available ASAT systems sufficient to counter expected Soviet surge and replenishment. . . .

Alternatives to Offset the Threat Posed by Soviet Satellites

U.S. force structure plans include a balanced package of complementary defensive measures. The capability to counter Soviet satellites is an important element of those plans. To the extent that we limit our capabilities to counter Soviet satellites, we tend to increase our need to augment our conventional forces to perform their terrestrial missions in the face of the Soviet threat from space, with attending costs.

To counter Soviet satellites by attacking their ground facilities would be an uncertain alternative to an ASAT capability and one which risked escalation of a conflict. A U.S. ASAT capability is a less risky and more effective and flexible way to deal militarily with the Soviet space-based threat.

The ASAT MV complements other protective measures which must be used throughout a conflict. These measures include communications and emissions security, evasive maneuvers and electronic countermeasures. These countermeasures are, however, reactive and cannot provide permanent protection. Moreover, they can impose sharp constraints on the operational effectiveness of U.S. forces in a conflict.

ARMS CONTROL PROSPECTS IN LIGHT OF POLICY AND NATIONAL SECURITY CONSIDERATIONS

The balance between the benefits and risks of ASAT arms control is quite sensitive. For example, there is a dilemma as to whether arms control restrictions that would constrain our ability to deal with Soviet targeting satellites, are in our national security interest. Our need to counter such Soviet satellites so as to support our terrestrial forces must be balanced against our interest in limiting threats to critical U.S. satellites. Our studies of possible ASAT arms control regimes are considering these concerns.

Soviet ASAT Arms Control Activities

Although the Soviets have periodically tested their operational ASAT interceptor, they regularly advance space arms control measures in international fora, without acknowledging their own ASAT capability. In their latest initiative last August, the Soviet Union submitted to the 38th United Nations General Assembly a draft treaty, the stated objectives of which are to prohibit testing and deployment of space-based weapons. It calls for elimination of existing ASAT systems, for a ban on the development of new ASAT weapons, and for a ban on attacks on satellites. The USSR also announced a "unilateral moratorium" on the launching of any type of ASAT weapon, to remain in effect as long as other countries refrain from putting into space ASAT weapons of any type.

U.S. Evaluation of Soviet Initiatives

The wording of these proposals had certain ambiguities and loopholes. For example, it would appear that the moratorium did not cover tests of ground-based systems, such as lasers. In any case, the Soviet moratorium appeared to be designed to block tests of the U.S. miniature vehicle ASAT interceptor, while allowing the USSR to maintain the world's only operational ASAT system. This is inconsistent with the USSR's profession "not to be the first to put into outer space any type of ASAT weapon."

The Soviet initiatives have fundamental shortcomings. Lack of effective verification is one of the major weaknesses of the draft treaty. It provides for national technical means of verification, but nothing beyond that. Indeed, the draft does not even prohibit actions that would impede

verification. In addition to the problem of verifying the elimination of the Soviet ASAT system, the draft treaty's proposal for a ban on destruction, damaging, and disruption of other states' space objects could also pose verification problems. The Soviet draft treaty is unclear with regard to Soviet targeting and reconnaissance satellites. The draft also does not deal with residual ASAT capabilities. For example, dismantling of the Soviet co-orbital ASAT system would still leave the USSR the option of using some of its Galosh ABM interceptor missiles in an antisatellite role. In addition, the draft treaty proposes that "piloted" spacecraft not be used for "military purposes." We strongly suspect that this provision is intended to constrain the use of the U.S. Space Transportation System (the Space Shuttle), which in the years ahead will serve as the primary U.S. launch system for national security as well as civil space missions. At the same time, the treaty would apparently not constrain the Soviet unpiloted space station.

Similarly, the possible motives behind the Soviet offer of a "moratorium" are suspect. In addition to their operational ASAT system the Soviets currently have other systems with ASAT capability. The Soviet moratorium deals only with their operational system, allowing the others to continue. For example, the Soviets could test ground-based lasers in an ASAT mode without violating their moratorium. Moreover, the Soviet offer came on the eve of the commencement of flight testing of the U.S. MV system. Thus, the timing suggests that the Soviet offer is designed to curtail the U.S. MV program and thereby leave the Soviet Union with a unilateral advantage in ASAT capability. Furthermore, a test moratorium would not necessarily cause their operational system to atrophy: after a hiatus of several years in ASAT testing, the Soviets were able to resume testing of their ASAT system without any apparent degradation in its performance. Programs in research and development pay a much higher price for a test moratorium. Even a short delay in the test program would delay the time that the U.S. ASAT could be operational. This would decrease the Soviet incentive to negotiate in good faith. (A full analysis of the Soviet draft treaty is provided in the classified version of this report.)

It appears that the Soviet objectives in their initiatives are to limit disproportionately the U.S. ASAT capability and to enhance the Soviet international image.

In sum, it appears that Soviet initiatives on ASAT arms control pose profound verification problems, as in the case of the Soviet treaty, or would leave the USSR with a destabilizing advantage, as in the case of both the treaty and the moratorium.

Multilateral Space Arms Control Activities

The United States has supported discussion of a broad range of questions on space arms control at the Conference on Disarmament (CD). The United States supported in 1983 the establishment of a CD Working Group on Outer Space. The United States does not favor having a working group undertake negotiations. Rather, we believe that a working group should address a broad range of space arms control issues, beginning with a thorough examination of the existing legal regime for space, before any conclusions can be drawn about negotiations which might be pursued in the CD. In 1983, the Soviets insisted that a working group on outer space in the CD be commissioned to begin negotiations. While the United States, our Allies, and the neutral and non-aligned nations of the CD all were ready to establish a working group without authority to negotiate, the Soviets blocked such action. The U.S. position this year in the CD is unchanged: the United States remains ready to proceed with a serious and responsible examination in the CD of space arms control.

Future Directions of ASAT Arms Control

U.S. space arms control policy seeks to reduce the risk of conflict and enhance strategic stability. Consistent with this purpose, the Administration has been evaluating a number of possible ASAT arms control options in light of whether they support our overall deterrence posture and are effectively verifiable. Despite efforts by this and the previous administration, no way has yet been found to design a comprehensive ASAT ban that meets these criteria.

The major problems for ASAT arms control discussed in detail in this report have hindered our efforts to develop effective arms control measures. In fact, it appears that the problems of verification tend to be greater the more comprehensive the limitation. Some less sweeping options under study would seek to limit or ban specific types of weapons systems. Since we must in any event be able to protect our satellites against threats that could be developed without our knowledge, there is a premium on finding ways to limit in arms control those ASAT systems that create the most difficult survivability problems. We are searching for limits on such systems which are effectively verifiable and which allow us to protect U.S. and Allied forces from threatening Soviet satellites, such as targeting satellites. Other options under examination would regulate certain threatening activities related to space.

The future of space arms control must also be considered in the broader context of U.S.-Soviet arms control relations. Soviet actions in other negotiating fora and Soviet actions with respect to compliance with existing arms control agreements must also be taken into account to determine the most appropriate course of action for the United States concerning arms control for outer space. In the meantime, the U.S. evaluation of possible future courses for ASAT arms control will be judged not simply in light of their ability to limit damage to space objects, but also in light of their contributions to the basic objectives of U.S. arms control policy with respect to terrestrial conventional and nuclear conflict.

The door is not closed to effective ASAT arms control measures. As noted earlier, the President has said that the United States will consider verifiable and equitable arms control measures that would ban or otherwise limit testing and deployment of specific weapons systems, should those measures be compatible with U.S. national security.

This remains the policy of the Administration. The active search for viable arms control opportunities in the ASAT area is continuing.

Political Charts

Winning Party in Presidential Races	*1089*
Presidential Elections, 1860-1984	*1090*
1980 Presidential Election	*1092*
1984 Presidential Election	*1093*
1984 Electoral Votes by States	*1094*
Republican Convention Balloting	*1095*
Democratic Convention Balloting	*1096*
Political Party Affiliations	*1098*
House Election Results, 1944-84	*1100*
House Seats and Electoral Votes	*1102*
97th Congress Special Elections	*1103*
1982 Election Results	*1104*
98th Congress Special Elections	*1113*
1984 Election Results	*1115*
Governors, 1980-84	*1122*

Victorious Party in Presidential Races, 1860-1984

No. of Times Parties Won

State	1860	1864	1868	1872	1876	1880	1884	1888	1892	1896	1900	1904	1908	1912	1916	1920	1924	1928	1932	1936	1940	1944	1948	1952	1956	1960	1964	1968	1972	1976	1980	1984	Dem.	Rep.	Other
Ala.	SD	[2]	R	R	D	D	D	D	D	D	D	D	D	D	D	D	D	D	D	D	D	D	SR	D	D[18]	D[19]	R	AI	R	D	R	R	22	6	3
Alaska																										R	D	R	R	R	R	R	1	6	0
Ariz.														D	D	R	R	R	D	D	D	D	D	R	R	R	R	R	R	R	R	R	7	12	0
Ark.	SD	[2]	R	[4]	D	D	D	D	D	D	D	D	D	D	D	D	D	D	D	D	D	D	D	D	D	D	D	AI	R	D	R	R	24	4	2
Calif.	R	R	R	R	R	R	D[6]	R	R	D[7]	R[12]	R	R	PR	D	R	R	R	D	D	D	D	D	R	R	R	D	R	R	R	R	R	9	22	1
Colo.					R	R	R	R	PP	D	D	R	D	D	D	R	R	R	D	D	R	R	D	R	R	R	D	R	R	R	R	R	9	18	1
Conn.	R	R	R	R	D	R	D	D	D	R	R	R	R	D	R	R	R	R	D	D	D	D	R	R	R	D	D	R	R	R	R	R	11	21	0
Del.	SD	D	D	R	D	D	D	R	D	R	R	R	R	D	R	R	R	R	D	D	D	D	R	R	R	D	D	R	R	D	R	R	14	17	1
D.C.																											D	D	D	D	D	D	6	0	0
Fla.	SD	[2]	R	R	R	D	D	D	D	D	D	D	D	D	D	D	D	R	D	D	D	D	D	R	R	R	D	R	R	D	R	R	19	11	1
Ga.	SD	[2]	D	D[5]	D	D	D	D	D	D	D	D	D	D	D	D	D	D	D	D	D	D	D	D	D	D	R	AI	R	D	D	R	26	3	2
Hawaii																										D	D	D	R	D	D	R	5	2	0
Idaho									PP	D	D	R	R	D	D	R	R	R	D	D	D	D	D	R	R	R	D	R	R	R	R	R	10	13	1
Ill.	R	R	R	R	R	R	R	R	D	R	R	R	R	D	R	R	R	R	D	D	D	D	D	R	R	D	D	R	R	R	R	R	9	23	0
Ind.	R	R	R	R	D	R	D	R	D	R	R	R	R	D	R	R	R	R	D	D	R	R	R	R	R	R	D	R	R	R	R	R	7	25	0
Iowa	R	R	R	R	R	R	R	R	R	R	R	R	R	D	R	R	R	R	D	D	R	R	D	R	R	R	D	R	R	R	R	R	5	27	0
Kan.		R	R	R	R	R	R	R	PP	D	R	R	R	D	D	R	R	R	D	D	R	R	R	R	R	R	D	R	R	R	R	R	6	24	1
Ky.	CU	D	D	D	D	D	D	D	D	D	R[13]	D	D	D	D	D	D	R	D	D	D	D	D	R	R	R	D	R	R	D	R	R	22	9	1
La.	SD	[2]	D	[4]	R	D	D	D	D	D	D	D	D	D	D	D	D	D	D	D	D	D	SR	D	R	D	R	AI	R	D	R	R	21	6	3
Maine	R	R	R	R	R	R	R	R	R	R	R	R	R	D	R	R	R	R	R	R	R	R	R	R	R	R	D	D	R	R	R	R	3	29	0
Md.	SD	R	D	R	D	D	D	R	D	R	R	D[14]	D[15]	D	D	R	R	R	D	D	D	D	R	R	R	D	D	D	R	D	R	R	20	11	1
Mass.	R	R	R	R	R	R	R	R	R	R	R	R	R	D	R	R	R	D	D	D	D	D	D	R	R	D	D	D	D	D	R	R	12	20	0
Mich.	R	R	R	R	R	R	R	R	R[8]	R	R	R	R	PR	R	R	R	R	D	D	D	R	R	R	R	D	D	D	R	R	R	R	6	25	1
Minn.	R	R	R	R	R	R	R	R	R	R	R	R	R	PR	R	R	R	R	D	D	D	D	D	R	R	D	D	D	R	D	D	D	11	20	1
Miss.	SD	[2]	[3]	R	D	D	D	D	D	D	D	D	D	D	D	D	D	D	D	D	D	D	SR	D	D	[20]	R	AI	R	D	R	R	21	5	3
Mo.	D	R	R	D	D	D	D	D	D	D	D	R	R	D	D	R	R	R	D	D	D	D	D	R	D	D	D	R	R	D	R	R	20	12	0
Mont.									R	D	D	R	R	D	D	R	R	R	D	D	D	D	D	R	R	R	D	R	R	R	R	R	10	14	0
Neb.			R	R	R	R	R	R	R	D	R	R	D	D	D	R	R	R	D	D	R	R	R	R	R	R	D	R	R	R	R	R	7	23	0
Nev.		R	R	R	R	D	R	R	PP	D	D	R	D	D	D	R	R	R	D	D	D	D	D	R	R	D	D	R	R	R	R	R	13	17	1
N.H.	R	R	R	R	R	R	R	R	R	R	R	R	R	D	D	R	R	R	R	D	D	D	R	R	R	R	D	R	R	R	R	R	6	26	0
N.J.	R[1]	D	D	R	D	D	D	D	D	R	R	R	R	D	R	R	R	R	D	D	D	D	R	R	R	D	D	R	R	R	R	R	14	18	0
N.M.														D	D	R	R	R	D	D	D	D	D	R	R	D	D	R	R	R	R	R	9	10	0
N.Y.	R	R	D	R	D	R	D	R	D	R	R	R	R	D	R	R	R	R	D	D	D	D	R	R	R	D	D	D	R	D	R	R	13	19	0
N.C.	SD	[2]	R	R	D	D	D	D	D	D	D	D	D	D	D	D	D	R	D	D	D	D	D	D	D	D	D	R[22]	R	D	R	R	23	7	1
N.D.									[9]	R	R	R	R	D	D	R	R	R	D	D	R	R	R	R	R	R	D	R	R	R	R	R	5	18	1
Ohio	R	R	R	R	R	R	R	R	R	R[10]	R	R	R	D	D	R	R	R	D	D	D	R	D	R	R	R	D	R	R	D	R	R	8	24	0
Okla.													D	D	D	R	D	R	D	D	D	D	D	R	R	R[21]	D	R	R	R	R	R	10	10	0
Ore.	R	R	D	R	R	R	R	R	R	R[11]	R	R	R	D	R	R	R	R	D	D	D	D	R	R	R	R	D	R	R	R	R	R	7	25	1
Pa.	R	R	R	R	R	R	R	R	R	R	R	R	R	PR	R	R	R	R	R	D	D	D	R	R	R	D	D	D	R	D	R	R	7	24	1
R.I.	R	R	R	R	R	R	R	R	R	R	R	R	R	D	R	R	R	D	D	D	D	D	D	R	R	D	D	D	R	D	D	R	12	20	0
S.C.	SD	[2]	R	R	R	D	D	D	D	D	D	D	D	D	D	D	D	D	D	D	D	D	SR	D	D	D	R	R	R	D	R	R	21	8	2
S.D.									R	D	R	R	R	PR	R	R	R	R	D	D	R	R	R	R	R	R	D	R	R	R	R	R	4	19	1
Tenn.	CU	[2]	R	D	D	D	D	D	D	D	D	D	D	D	D	R	D	R	D	D	D	D	D[17]	R	R	R	D	R	R	D	R	R	20	10	1
Texas	SD	[2]	[3]	D	D	D	D	D	D	D	D	D	D	D	D	D	D	R	D	D	D	D	D	R	R	D	D	D	R	D	R	R	23	6	0
Utah										D	R	R	R	R	D	R	R	R	D	D	D	D	D	R	R	R	D	R	R	R	R	R	8	15	0
Vt.	R	R	R	R	R	R	R	R	R	R	R	R	R	R	R	R	R	R	R	R	R	R	R	R	R	R	D	R	R	R	R	R	1	31	0
Va.	CU	[2]	[3]	R	D	D	D	D	D	D	D	D	D	D	D	D	D	R	D	D	D	D	D	R	R	R	D	R	R[23]	R	R	R	19	10	1
Wash.									R	D	R	R	R	PR	D	R	R	R	D	D	D	D	D	R	R	R	D	D	R	R[24]	R	R	9	14	0
W.Va.		R	R	D	D	D	D	D	D	R	R	R	R	D	R[16]	R	R	R	D	D	D	D	D	R	R	D	D	D	R	D	D	R	17	14	0
Wis.	R	R	R	R	R	R	R	R	D	R	R	R	R	D	R	R	PR	R	D	D	D	D	D	R	R	R	D	R	R	D	R	R	8	23	1
Wyo.									R	R	R	R	R	D	D	R	R	R	D	D	D	D	D	R	R	R	D	R	R	R	R	R	8	16	0
Winning Party	R	R	R	R	R	R	D	R	D	R	R	R	R	D	D	R	R	R	D	D	D	D	D	R	R	D	D	R	R	D	R	R	12	20	0

[1] Four electors voted Republican; three Democratic.
[2] Confederate States did not vote in 1864.
[3] Did not vote in 1868.
[4] Votes were not counted.
[5] Three votes for Greeley not counted.
[6] Five electors voted Democratic; one Republican.
[7] Eight electors voted Democratic; one Republican.
[8] Nine electors voted Republican; five Democratic.
[9] One vote each for Democratic, Republican and People's Party.
[10] Twenty-two electors voted Republican, one Democratic.
[11] Three electors voted Republican; one People's Party.
[12] Eight electors voted Republican; one Democratic.
[13] Twelve electors voted Republican; one Democratic.
[14] Seven electors voted Democratic; one Republican.
[15] Six electors voted Democratic; two Republican.
[16] Seven electors voted Republican; one Democratic.
[17] Eleven electors voted Democratic; one States' Rights.
[18] One elector voted for Walter Jones.
[19] Six of 11 electors voted for Harry F. Byrd.
[20] Eight independent electors voted for Byrd.
[21] One vote cast for Byrd.
[22] Twelve electors voted Republican; one American Independent.
[23] One elector voted Libertarian.
[24] One elector voted for Ronald Reagan.

With the exception of the District of Columbia, blanks indicate states not yet admitted to the Union. The District of Columbia received the presidential vote in 1961.

A — American Party
AI — American Independent Party
CU — Constitutional Union Party
D — Democratic Party
PP — People's Party
PR — Progressive (Bull Moose) Party
R — Republican Party
SD — Southern Democratic Party
SR — States' Rights Party

Summary of American...

YEAR	NO OF STATES	CANDIDATES		ELECTORAL VOTE		POPULAR VOTE	
		DEM.	GOP	DEM.	GOP	DEM.	GOP
1860(a)	33	Stephen A. Douglas Herschel V. Johnson	Abraham Lincoln Hannibal Hamlin	12 4%	180 59%	1,380,202 29.5%	1,865,908 39.8%
1864(b)	36	George B. McClellan George H. Pendleton	Abraham Lincoln Andrew Johnson	21 9%	212 91%	1,812,807 45.0%	2,218,388 55.0%
1868(c)	37	Horatio Seymour Francis P. Blair Jr.	Ulysses S. Grant Schuyler Colfax	80 27%	214 73%	2,708,744 47.3%	3,013,650 52.7%
1872(d)	37	Horace Greeley Benjamin Gratz Brown	Ulysses S. Grant Henry Wilson	(d)	286 78%	2,834,761 43.8%	3,598,235 55.6%
1876	38	Samuel J. Tilden Thomas A. Hendricks	Rutherford B. Hayes William A. Wheeler	184 50%	185 50%	4,288,546 51.0%	4,034,311 47.9%
1880	38	Winfield S. Hancock William H. English	James A. Garfield Chester A. Arthur	155 42%	214 58%	4,444,260 48.2%	4,446,158 48.3%
1884	38	Grover Cleveland Thomas A. Hendricks	James G. Blaine John A. Logan	219 55%	182 45%	4,874,621 48.5%	4,848,936 48.2%
1888	38	Grover Cleveland Allen G. Thurman	Benjamin Harrison Levi P. Morton	168 42%	233 58%	5,534,488 48.6%	5,443,892 47.8%
1892(e)	44	Grover Cleveland Adlai E. Stevenson	Benjamin Harrison Whitelaw Reid	277 62%	145 33%	5,551,883 46.1%	5,179,244 43.0%
1896	45	William J. Bryan Arthur Sewall	William McKinley Garret A. Hobart	176 39%	271 61%	6,511,495 46.7%	7,108,480 51.0%
1900	45	William J. Bryan Adlai E. Stevenson	William McKinley Theodore Roosevelt	155 35%	292 65%	6,358,345 45.5%	7,218,039 51.7%
1904	45	Alton B. Parker Henry G. Davis	Theodore Roosevelt Charles W. Fairbanks	140 29%	336 71%	5,028,898 37.6%	7,626,593 56.4%
1908	46	William J. Bryan John W. Kern	William H. Taft James S. Sherman	162 34%	321 66%	6,406,801 43.0%	7,676,258 51.6%
1912(f)	48	Woodrow Wilson Thomas R. Marshall	William H. Taft James S. Sherman	435 82%	8 2%	6,293,152 41.8%	3,486,333 23.2%
1916	48	Woodrow Wilson Thomas R. Marshall	Charles E. Hughes Charles W. Fairbanks	277 52%	254 48%	9,126,300 49.2%	8,546,789 46.1%
1920	48	James M. Cox Franklin D. Roosevelt	Warren G. Harding Calvin Coolidge	127 24%	404 76%	9,140,884 34.2%	16,133,314 60.3%
1924(g)	48	John W. Davis Charles W. Bryant	Calvin Coolidge Charles G. Dawes	136 26%	382 72%	8,386,169 28.8%	15,717,553 54.1%
1928	48	Alfred E. Smith Joseph T. Robinson	Herbert C. Hoover Charles Curtis	87 16%	444 84%	15,000,185 40.8%	21,411,991 58.2%
1932	48	Franklin D. Roosevelt John N. Garner	Herbert C. Hoover Charles Curtis	472 89%	59 11%	22,825,016 57.4%	15,758,397 39.6%
1936	48	Franklin D. Roosevelt John N. Garner	Alfred M. London Frank Knox	523 98%	8 2%	27,747,636 60.8%	16,679,543 36.5%
1940	48	Franklin D. Roosevelt Henry A. Wallace	Wendell L. Willkie Charles L. McNary	449 85%	82 15%	27,263,448 54.7%	22,336,260 44.8%
1944	48	Franklin D. Roosevelt Harry S Truman	Thomas E. Dewey John W. Bricker	432 81%	99 19%	25,611,936 53.4%	22,013,372 45.9%
1948(h)	48	Harry S Truman Alben W. Barkley	Thomas E. Dewey Earl Warren	303 57%	189 36%	24,105,587 49.5%	21,970,017 45.1%
1952	48	Adlai E. Stevenson John J. Sparkman	Dwight D. Eisenhower Richard M. Nixon	89 17%	442 83%	27,314,649 44.4%	33,936,137 55.1%
1956(i)	48	Adlai E. Stevenson Estes Kefauver	Dwight D. Eisenhower Richard M. Nixon	73 14%	457 86%	26,030,172 42.0%	35,585,245 57.4%
1960(j)	50	John F. Kennedy Lyndon B. Johnson	Richard M. Nixon Henry Cabot Lodge	303 56%	219 41%	34,221,344 49.7%	34,106,671 49.5%
1964	50*	Lyndon B. Johnson Hubert H. Humphrey	Barry Goldwater William E. Miller	486 90%	52 10%	43,126,584 61.1%	27,177,838 38.5%
1968(k)	50*	Hubert H. Humphrey Edmund S. Muskie	Richard M. Nixon Spiro T. Agnew	191 36%	301 56%	31,274,503 42.7%	31,785,148 43.4%

...Presidential Elections, 1860-1984

YEAR	NO OF STATES	CANDIDATES		ELECTORAL VOTE		POPULAR VOTE	
		DEM.	GOP	DEM.	GOP	DEM.	GOP
1972(l)	50*	George McGovern Sargent Shriver	Richard M. Nixon Spiro T. Agnew	17 3%	520 97%	29,171,791 37.5%	47,170,179 60.7%
1976(m)	50*	Jimmy Carter Walter F. Mondale	Gerald R. Ford Robert Dole	297 55%	240 45%	40,830,763 50.1%	39,147,793 48.0%
1980	50*	Jimmy Carter Walter F. Mondale	Ronald Reagan George Bush	49 9%	489 91%	35,483,883 41.0%	43,904,153 50.7%
1984	50*	Walter F. Mondale Geraldine Ferraro	Ronald Reagan George Bush	13 2%	525 98%	37,577,137 40.6%	54,455,074 58.8%

(a) 1860: John C. Breckinridge, Southern Democrat, polled 72 electoral votes. John Bell, Constitutional Union, polled 39 electoral votes.

(b) 1864: 81 electoral votes were not cast.

(c) 1868: 23 electoral votes were not cast.

(d) 1872: Horace Greeley died after election, 63 Democratic electoral votes were scattered, 17 were not voted.

(e) 1892: James B. Weaver, People's Party, polled 22 electoral votes.

(f) 1912: Theodore Roosevelt, Progressive Party, polled 86 electoral votes.

(g) 1924: Robert M. LaFollette, Progressive Party, polled 13 electoral votes.

(h) 1948: J. Strom Thurmond, States' Rights Party, polled 39 electoral votes.

(i) 1956: Walter B. Jones, Democrat, polled 1 electoral vote.

(j) 1960: Harry Flood Byrd, Democrat, polled 15 electoral votes.

(k) 1968: George C. Wallace, American Independent, polled 46 electoral votes.

(l) 1972: John Hospers, Libertarian Party, polled 1 electoral vote.

(m) 1976: Ronald Reagan, Republican, polled 1 electoral vote.

* Fifty states plus District of Columbia.

1980 Presidential Election

Total Popular Vote: 86,515,221
Reagan's Plurality: 8,420,270

STATE	RONALD REAGAN (Republican)		JIMMY CARTER (Democrat)		JOHN B. ANDERSON (Independent)		ED CLARK (Libertarian)		OTHER		PLURALITY
	Votes	%	Votes	%	Votes	%	Votes	%	Votes	%	
Alabama	654,192	48.8	636,730	47.5	16,481	1.2	13,318	1.0	21,208	1.6	17,462
Alaska	86,112	54.3	41,842	26.4	11,155	7.0	18,479	11.7	857	0.5	44,270
Arizona	529,688	60.6	246,843	28.2	76,952	8.8	18,784	2.2	1,678	0.2	282,845
Arkansas	403,164	48.1	398,041	47.5	22,468	2.7	8,970	1.1	4,939	0.6	5,123
California	4,524,858	52.7	3,083,661	35.9	739,833	8.6	148,434	1.7	90,277	1.1	1,441,197
Colorado	652,264	55.1	367,973	31.1	130,633	11.0	25,744	2.2	7,801	0.7	284,291
Connecticut	677,210	48.2	541,732	38.5	171,807	12.2	8,570	0.6	6,966	0.5	135,478
Delaware	111,252	47.2	105,754	44.8	16,288	6.9	1,974	0.8	632	0.3	5,498
D.C.	23,545	13.4	131,113	74.8	16,337	9.3	1,114	0.6	3,128	1.8	107,568
Florida	2,046,951	55.5	1,419,475	38.5	189,692	5.1	30,524	0.8	288	0.0	627,476
Georgia	654,168	41.0	890,733	55.8	36,055	2.3	15,627	1.0	112	0.0	236,565
Hawaii	130,112	42.9	135,879	44.8	32,021	10.6	3,269	1.1	2,006	0.7	5,767
Idaho	290,699	66.5	110,192	25.2	27,058	6.2	8,425	1.9	1,057	0.2	180,507
Illinois	2,358,049	49.6	1,981,413	41.7	346,754	7.3	38,939	0.8	24,566	0.5	376,636
Indiana	1,255,656	56.0	844,197	37.7	111,639	5.0	19,627	0.9	10,914	0.5	411,459
Iowa	676,026	51.3	508,672	38.6	115,633	8.8	13,123	1.0	4,207	0.3	167,354
Kansas	566,812	57.9	326,150	33.3	68,231	7.0	14,470	1.5	4,132	0.4	240,662
Kentucky	635,274	49.1	616,417	47.6	31,127	2.4	5,531	0.4	6,278	0.5	18,857
Louisiana	792,853	51.2	708,453	45.7	26,345	1.7	8,240	0.5	12,700	0.8	84,400
Maine	238,522	45.6	220,974	42.3	53,327	10.2	5,119	1.0	5,069	1.0	17,548
Maryland	680,606	44.2	726,161	47.1	119,537	7.8	14,192	0.9			45,555
Massachusetts	1,057,631	41.9	1,053,802	41.7	382,539	15.2	22,038	0.9	8,288	0.3	3,829
Michigan	1,915,225	49.0	1,661,532	42.5	275,223	7.0	41,597	1.1	16,148	0.4	253,693
Minnesota	873,268	42.6	954,174	46.5	174,990	8.5	31,592	1.5	17,956	0.9	80,906
Mississippi	441,089	49.4	429,281	48.1	12,036	1.3	5,465	0.6	4,749	0.5	11,808
Missouri	1,074,181	51.2	931,182	44.3	77,920	3.7	14,422	0.7	2,119	0.1	142,999
Montana	206,814	56.8	118,032	32.4	29,281	8.0	9,825	2.7			88,782
Nebraska	419,937	65.9	166,851	26.0	44,993	7.0	9,073	1.4			253,086
Nevada	155,017	62.5	66,666	26.9	17,651	7.1	4,358	1.8	4,193	1.7	88,351
New Hampshire	221,705	57.7	108,864	28.4	49,693	12.9	2,064	0.5	1,664	0.4	112,841
New Jersey	1,546,557	52.0	1,147,364	38.6	234,632	7.9	20,652	0.7	26,479	0.9	399,193
New Mexico	250,779	54.9	167,826	36.7	29,459	6.5	4,365	1.0	4,542	1.0	82,953
New York	2,893,831	46.7	2,728,372	44.0	467,801	7.5	52,648	0.8	59,307	1.0	165,459
North Carolina	915,018	49.3	875,635	47.2	52,800	2.8	9,677	0.5	2,703	0.1	39,383
North Dakota	193,695	64.2	79,189	26.3	23,640	7.8	3,743	1.2	1,278	0.4	114,506
Ohio	2,206,545	51.5	1,752,414	40.9	254,472	5.9	49,033	1.1	21,139	0.5	454,131
Oklahoma	695,570	60.5	402,026	35.0	38,284	3.3	13,828	1.2			293,544
Oregon	571,044	48.3	456,890	38.7	112,389	9.5	25,838	2.2	15,355	1.3	114,154
Pennsylvania	2,261,872	49.6	1,937,540	42.5	292,921	6.4	33,263	0.7	35,905	0.8	324,332
Rhode Island	154,793	37.2	198,342	47.7	59,819	14.4	2,458	0.6	660	0.2	43,549
South Carolina	441,841	49.4	430,385	48.1	14,153	1.6	5,139	0.6	2,553	0.3	11,456
South Dakota	198,343	60.5	103,855	31.7	21,431	6.5	3,824	1.2	250	0.1	94,488
Tennessee	787,761	48.7	783,051	48.4	35,991	2.2	7,116	0.4	3,697	0.2	4,710
Texas	2,510,705	55.3	1,881,147	41.4	111,613	2.5	37,643	0.8	528	0.0	629,558
Utah	439,687	72.8	124,266	20.6	30,284	5.0	7,226	1.2	2,759	0.5	315,421
Vermont	94,628	44.4	81,952	38.4	31,761	14.9	1,900	0.9	3,058	1.4	12,676
Virginia	989,609	53.0	752,174	40.3	95,418	5.1	12,821	0.7	16,010	0.9	237,435
Washington	865,244	49.7	650,193	37.3	185,073	10.6	29,213	1.7	12,671	0.7	215,051
West Virginia	334,206	45.3	367,462	49.8	31,691	4.3	4,356	0.6			33,256
Wisconsin	1,088,845	47.9	981,584	43.2	160,657	7.1	29,135	1.3	13,000	0.6	107,261
Wyoming	110,700	62.6	49,427	28.0	12,072	6.8	4,514	2.6			61,273
Totals	43,904,153	50.7	35,483,883	41.0	5,720,060	6.6	921,299	1.1	485,826	0.6	

1984 Presidential Election

Total Popular Vote: 92,652,793
Reagan's Plurality: 16,877,937

STATE	RONALD REAGAN (Republican) Votes	%	WALTER F. MONDALE (Democrat) Votes	%	DAVID BERGLAND (Libertarian) Votes	%	LYNDON H. LaROUCHE JR. (Independent) Votes	%	OTHER Votes	%	PLURALITY
Alabama	872,849	60.5	551,899	38.3	9,504	0.7			7,461	0.5	320,950
Alaska	138,377	66.6	62,007	29.9	6,378	3.1			843	0.4	76,370
Arizona	681,416	66.4	333,854	32.5	10,585	1.0			42	—	347,562
Arkansas	534,774	60.5	338,646	38.3	2,221	0.2	1,890	0.2	6,875	0.8	196,128
California	5,467,009	57.5	3,922,519	41.3	49,951	0.5			65,954	0.7	1,544,490
Colorado	821,817	63.4	454,975	35.1	11,257	0.9	4,662	0.4	2,669	0.2	366,842
Connecticut	890,877	60.7	569,597	38.8	204				6,222	0.4	321,280
Delaware	152,190	59.8	101,656	39.9	268	0.1			458	0.2	50,534
D.C.	29,009	13.7	180,408	85.4	279	0.1	127	0.1	1,465	0.7	151,399
Florida	2,730,350	65.3	1,448,816	34.7	754				131	—	1,281,534
Georgia	1,068,722	60.2	706,628	39.8	152		34		584	—	362,094
Hawaii	185,050	55.1	147,154	43.8	2,167	0.6	654	0.2	821	0.2	37,896
Idaho	297,523	72.4	108,510	26.4	2,823	0.7			2,288	0.6	189,013
Illinois	2,707,103	56.2	2,086,499	43.3	10,086	0.2			15,400	0.3	620,604
Indiana	1,377,230	61.7	841,481	37.7	6,741	0.3			7,617	0.3	535,749
Iowa	703,088	53.3	605,620	45.9	1,844	0.1	6,248	0.5	3,005	0.2	97,468
Kansas	677,296	66.3	333,149	32.6	3,329	0.3			8,217	0.8	344,147
Kentucky	821,702	60.0	539,539	39.4			1,776	0.1	6,328	0.5	282,163
Louisiana	1,037,299	60.8	651,586	38.2	1,876	0.1	3,552	0.2	12,509	0.7	385,713
Maine	336,500	60.8	214,515	38.8					2,129	0.4	121,985
Maryland	879,918	52.5	787,935	47.0	5,721	0.3			2,299	0.1	91,983
Massachusetts	1,310,936	51.2	1,239,606	48.4					8,911	0.3	71,330
Michigan	2,251,571	59.2	1,529,638	40.2	10,055	0.3	3,862	0.1	6,532	0.2	721,933
Minnesota	1,032,603	49.5	1,036,364	49.7	2,996	0.1	3,865	0.2	8,621	0.4	3,761
Mississippi	582,377	61.9	352,192	37.4	2,336	0.2	1,001	0.1	3,198	0.3	230,185
Missouri	1,274,188	60.0	848,583	40.0					12	—	425,605
Montana	232,450	60.5	146,742	38.2	5,185	1.3					85,708
Nebraska	460,054	70.6	187,866	28.8	2,079	0.3			2,091	0.3	272,188
Nevada	188,770	65.8	91,655	32.0	2,292	0.8			3,950	1.4	97,115
New Hampshire	267,050	68.6	120,347	30.9	735	0.2	467	0.1	418	0.1	146,703
New Jersey	1,933,630	60.1	1,261,323	39.2	6,416	0.2			16,493	0.5	672,307
New Mexico	307,101	59.7	201,769	39.2	4,459	0.8			1,041	0.2	508,870
New York	3,664,763	53.8	3,119,609	45.8	11,949	0.2			10,489	0.1	545,154
North Carolina	1,346,481	61.9	824,287	37.9	3,794	0.2			799	—	522,194
North Dakota	200,336	64.8	104,429	33.8	703	0.2	1,278	0.4	2,225	0.7	95,907
Ohio	2,678,560	58.9	1,825,440	40.1	5,886	0.1	10,693	0.2	27,040	0.6	853,120
Oklahoma	861,530	68.6	385,080	30.7	9,066	0.7					476,450
Oregon	685,700	55.9	536,479	43.7					4,348	0.3	149,221
Pennsylvania	2,584,323	53.3	2,228,131	46.0	6,982	0.1			25,467	0.5	356,192
Rhode Island	212,080	51.8	197,106	47.9	277	0.1			1,029	0.2	14,974
South Carolina	615,539	63.6	344,459	35.6	4,359	0.4			4,172	0.4	1271,080
South Dakota	200,267	63.0	116,113	36.5					1,487	0.5	84,154
Tennessee	990,212	57.8	711,714	41.6	3,072	0.2	1,852	0.1	5,144	0.3	278,498
Texas	3,433,428	63.6	1,949,276	36.1			14,613	0.3	254	—	1,484,152
Utah	469,105	74.5	155,369	24.7	2,477	0.4			2,735	0.4	313,736
Vermont	135,865	57.9	95,730	40.8	1,002	0.4	423	0.2	1,541	0.6	40,135
Virginia	1,337,078	62.3	796,250	37.1			13,307	0.6			540,828
Washington	1,051,670	56.2	807,352	42.9	8,844	0.5	4,712	0.6	11,332	0.6	244,318
West Virginia	405,483	54.7	328,125	44.3					2,134	0.2	77,358
Wisconsin	1,198,584	54.3	995,740	45.1	4,883	0.2	3,791	2.0	8,691	0.4	202,844
Wyoming	133,241	69.1	53,370	27.7	2,357	1.2					79,871
Totals	**54,455,074**	**58.77**	**37,577,137**	**40.56**	**228,314**	**.25**	**78,807**	**.08**	**241,261**	**.26**	

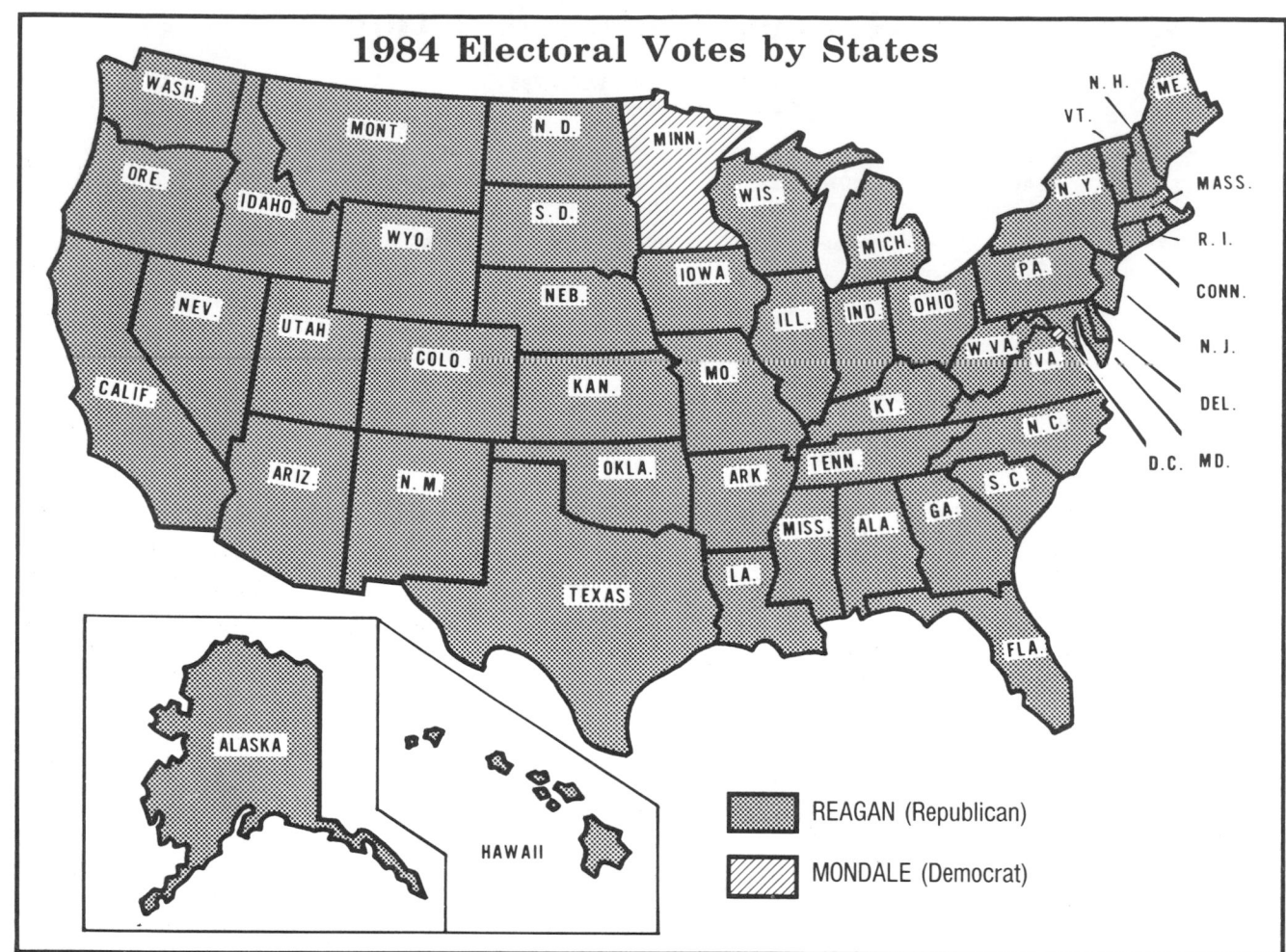

1984 Electoral Votes by States

REAGAN (Republican)

MONDALE (Democrat)

States	Electoral Votes	Reagan	Mondale	States	Electoral Votes	Reagan	Mondale
Alabama	(9)	9	—	Montana	(4)	4	—
Alaska	(3)	3	—	Nebraska	(5)	5	—
Arizona	(7)	7	—	Nevada	(4)	4	—
Arkansas	(6)	6	—	New Hampshire	(4)	4	—
California	(47)	47	—	New Jersey	(16)	16	—
Colorado	(8)	8	—	New Mexico	(5)	5	—
Connecticut	(8)	8	—	New York	(36)	36	—
Delaware	(3)	3	—	North Carolina	(13)	13	—
District of Columbia	(3)	—	3	North Dakota	(3)	3	—
Florida	(21)	21	—	Ohio	(23)	23	—
Georgia	(12)	12	—	Oklahoma	(8)	8	—
Hawaii	(4)	4	—	Oregon	(7)	7	—
Idaho	(4)	4	—	Pennsylvania	(25)	25	—
Illinois	(24)	24	—	Rhode Island	(4)	4	—
Indiana	(12)	12	—	South Carolina	(8)	8	—
Iowa	(8)	8	—	South Dakota	(3)	3	—
Kansas	(7)	7	—	Tennessee	(11)	11	—
Kentucky	(9)	9	—	Texas	(29)	29	—
Louisiana	(10)	10	—	Utah	(5)	5	—
Maine	(4)	4	—	Vermont	(3)	3	—
Maryland	(10)	10	—	Virginia	(12)	12	—
Massachusetts	(13)	13	—	Washington	(10)	10	—
Michigan	(20)	20	—	West Virginia	(6)	6	—
Minnesota	(10)	—	10	Wisconsin	(11)	11	—
Mississippi	(7)	7	—	Wyoming	(3)	3	—
Missouri	(11)	11	—	**Totals**	**(538)**	**525**	**13**

1984 Republican Convention Balloting
Presidential Candidate

Delegation	Total Votes	First Pres. Ballot[1] Reagan
Alabama	38	38
Alaska	18	18
Arizona	32	32
Arkansas	29	29
California	176	176
Colorado	35	35
Connecticut	35	35
Delaware	19	19
District of Columbia	14	14
Florida	82	82
Georgia	37	37
Guam	4	4
Hawaii	14	14
Idaho	21	21
Illinois	93	92
Indiana	52	52
Iowa	37	37
Kansas	32	32
Kentucky	37	37
Louisiana	41	41
Maine	20	20
Maryland	31	31
Massachusetts	52	52
Michigan	77	77
Minnesota	32	32
Mississippi	30	30
Missouri	47	47
Montana	20	20
Nebraska	24	24
Nevada	22	22
New Hampshire	22	22
New Jersey	64	64
New Mexico	24	24
New York	136	136
North Carolina	53	53
North Dakota	18	18
Ohio	89	89
Oklahoma	35	35
Oregon	32	32
Pennsylvania	98	97
Puerto Rico	14	14
Rhode Island	14	14
South Carolina	35	35
South Dakota	19	19
Tennessee	46	46
Texas	109	109
Utah	26	26
Vermont	19	19
Virginia	50	50
Virgin Islands	4	4
Washington	44	44
West Virginia	19	19
Wisconsin	46	46
Wyoming	18	18
Total	2,235	2,233

1. Not voting, 2.

1984 Democratic Convention Balloting
Presidential Candidate

Delegation	Total Votes	First Pres. Ballot[1]		
		Mondale	Hart	Jackson
Alabama	62	39	13	9
Alaska	14	9	4	1
Arizona	40	20	16	2
Arkansas	42	26	9	7
California	345	95	190	33
Colorado	51	1	42	1
Connecticut	60	23	36	1
Delaware	18	13	5	0
D.C.	19	5	—	14
Florida	143	82	55	3
Georgia	84	40	24	20
Hawaii	27	27	—	0
Idaho	22	10	12	0
Illinois	194	114	41	39
Indiana	88	42	38	8
Iowa	58	37	18	2
Kansas	44	25	16	3
Kentucky	63	51	5	7
Louisiana	69	26	19	24
Maine	27	13	13	0
Maryland	74	54	3	17
Massachusetts	116	59	49	5
Michigan	155	96	49	10
Minnesota	86	63	3	4
Mississippi	43	26	4	13
Missouri	86	55	14	16
Montana	25	11	13	1
Nebraska	30	12	17	1
Nevada	20	9	10	1
New Hampshire	22	12	10	0
New Jersey	122	115	—	7
New Mexico	28	13	13	2
New York	285	156	75	52
North Carolina	88	53	19	16
North Dakota	18	10	5	1
Ohio	175	84	80	11
Oklahoma	53	24	26	3
Oregon	50	16	31	2
Pennsylvania	195	177	—	18
Puerto Rico	53	53	—	0
Rhode Island	27	14	12	0
South Carolina	48	16	13	19
South Dakota	19	9	10	0
Tennessee	76	39	20	17
Texas	200	119	40	36
Utah	27	8	19	0
Vermont	17	5	8	3
Virginia	78	34	18	25
Washington	70	31	36	3
West Virginia	44	30	14	0
Wisconsin	89	58	25	6
Wyoming	15	7	7	0
Latin America	5	5	—	0
Democrats Abroad	5	3	1.5	0.5
Virgin Islands	6	4	—	2
American Samoa	6	6	—	0
Guam	7	7	—	0
Total	3,933	2,191	1,200.5	465.5

1. Other candidates: Thomas F. Eagleton, 18 (16 in Minnesota, 2 in North Dakota); George McGovern, 4 (3 in Massachusetts, 1 in Iowa); John Glenn, 2 (Texas); Joseph R. Biden Jr., 1 (Maine); Martha Kirkland, 1 (Alabama); not voting, 40 (27 in California, 7 in Connecticut, 2 in Arizona, 2 in Florida, 1 in Vermont, 1 in Wyoming); absent, 10.

1984 Democratic Convention Balloting Minority Planks

Delegation	Total Votes	No First Use of Nuclear Weapons			Defense Spending			Dual Primaries			Military Force Restrictions		
		Yea	Nay	Not Voting	Yea	Nay	Not Voting	Yea	Nay	Not Voting	Yea	Nay	Not Voting
Alabama	62	15	46	1	11	49	2	13	49	—	61	1	—
Alaska	14	7	7	—	1	13	—	2	12	—	13	1	—
Arizona	40	20	19	—	18	21	—	20	19	—	39	—	—
Arkansas	42	13	29	—	12	30	—	7	33	2	39	2	1
California	345	149	84	—	99	170	—	129	128	—	285	31	—
Colorado	51	31	16	4	5	45	1	26	24	1	51	—	—
Connecticut	60	28	24	8	32	27	1	27	33	—	60	—	—
Delaware	18	1	17	—	1	17	—	1	17	—	18	—	—
D.C.	19	15	4	—	17	2	—	14	5	—	6	12	—
Florida	143	47	76	20	42	81	20	27	110	6	95	25	23
Georgia	84	40	33	—	38	45	—	39	42	—	67	1	2
Hawaii	27	1	26	—	—	27	—	—	27	—	—	—	—
Idaho	22	9	—	—	10	11	—	9	13	—	22	—	—
Illinois	194	42	145	—	40	147	—	48	143	—	191	—	3
Indiana	88	31	46	—	18	64	—	23	64	—	88	—	—
Iowa	58	22	36	—	7	51	—	5	53	—	58	—	—
Kansas	44	14	29	1	6	38	—	10	34	—	44	—	—
Kentucky	63	14	48	—	10	52	—	15	47	—	55	8	—
Louisiana	69	24	32	—	30	39	—	44	22	—	44	22	—
Maine	27	7	16	—	3	23	—	10	16	—	23	1	—
Maryland	74	20	51	3	20	54	—	18	56	—	51	19	4
Massachusetts	116	89	24	—	69	43	1	82	31	1	112	—	—
Michigan	155	43	105	7	32	118	5	37	111	7	137	—	18
Minnesota	86	37	41	8	30	48	8	25	57	4	73	2	11
Mississippi	43	15	26	2	16	26	1	13	29	1	33	8	2
Missouri	86	20	62	4	22	62	2	24	61	1	70	—	16
Montana	25	8	15	2	4	21	—	5	20	—	25	—	—
Nebraska	30	2	25	3	2	25	3	10	17	3	24	—	6
Nevada	20	6	14	—	3	17	—	5	15	—	19	—	—
New Hampshire	22	10	12	—	5	17	—	1	21	—	22	—	—
New Jersey	122	9	113	—	9	113	—	7	115	—	116	6	—
New Mexico	28	7	19	2	2	26	—	3	25	—	27	1	—
New York	285	134	140	—	131	139	7	125	146	3	196	57	—
North Carolina	88	28	56	—	19	66	—	32	55	—	73	3	—
North Dakota	18	13	5	—	8	10	—	8	10	—	18	—	—
Ohio	175	71	103	—	47	122	6	40	133	2	173	—	2
Oklahoma	53	16	35	2	3	47	3	3	49	1	49	3	1
Oregon	50	32	13	5	26	21	3	24	24	2	49	—	1
Pennsylvania	195	42	153	—	39	156	—	53	142	—	195	—	—
Puerto Rico	53	—	53	—	—	53	—	—	53	—	10	43	—
Rhode Island	27	11	15	1	11	15	1	8	18	1	24	—	2
South Carolina	48	21	23	4	23	19	6	21	25	2	21	19	8
South Dakota	19	7	12	—	7	12	—	7	12	—	—	6	—
Tennessee	76	31	41	4	29	41	6	34	39	3	72	1	3
Texas	200	53	137	10	47	141	12	39	150	11	152	38	10
Utah	27	17	10	—	11	15	1	13	14	—	19	7	1
Vermont	17	11	4	—	10	4	—	10	4	—	12	3	—
Virginia	78	29	48	—	29	48	—	33	43	—	50	23	4
Washington	70	49	18	—	29	39	1	35	35	—	67	—	—
West Virginia	44	12	27	5	12	29	3	17	24	3	—	—	—
Wisconsin	89	28	45	16	26	57	6	31	54	4	83	6	—
Wyoming	15	2	12	—	2	12	—	13	1	—	13	1	—
Latin America	5	—	5	—	.5	4.5	—	—	5	—	5	—	—
Democrats Abroad	5	1.5	3.5	—	1.5	3.5	—	—	5	—	5	—	—
Virgin Islands	6	1.2	4.8	—	2.6	2.6	.6	1.2	4.8	—	4.8	1.2	—
American Samoa	6	—	6	—	—	6	—	—	6	—	6	—	—
Guam	7	—	7	—	—	7	—	7	—	—	7	—	—
Total	3,933	1,405.7	2,216.3	112	1,127.6	2,591.6	99.6	1,253.2	2,500.8	58	3,271.8	351.2	118

Political Party Affiliations in Congress...

(Letter symbols for political parties: Ad—Administration; AM—Anti-Masonic; C—Coalition; D—Democratic; DR—Democratic-Republican; F—Federalist; J—Jacksonian; NR—National Republican; Op—Opposition; R—Republican; U—Unionist; W—Whig. Figures are for the beginning of the first session of each Congress.)

Year	Congress	HOUSE Majority party	HOUSE Principal minority party	HOUSE Other (except vacancies)	SENATE Majority party	SENATE Principal minority party	SENATE Other (except vacancies)	President
1985-1987	99th	D-252	R-182	-	R-53	D-47	-	R (Reagan)
1983-1985	98th	D-269	R-165	-	R-54	D-46	-	R (Reagan)
1981-1983	97th	D-243	R-192	-	R-53	D-46	1	R (Reagan)
1979-1981	96th	D-276	R-157	-	D-58	R-41	1	D (Carter)
1977-1979	95th	D-292	R-143	-	D-61	R-38	1	D (Carter
1975-1977	94th	D-291	R-144	-	D-60	R-37	2	R (Ford)
1973-1975	93rd	D-239	R-192	1	D-56	R-42	2	R (Nixon-Ford)
1971-1973	92nd	D-254	R-180	-	D-54	R-44	2	R (Nixon)
1969-1971	91st	D-243	R-192	-	D-57	R-43	-	R (Nixon)
1967-1969	90th	D-247	R-187	-	D-64	R-36	-	D (L. Johnson)
1965-1967	89th	D-295	R-140	-	D-68	R-32	-	D (L. Johnson)
1963-1965	88th	D-258	R-177	-	D-67	R-33	-	D (L. Johnson) D (Kennedy)
1961-1963	87th	D-263	R-174	-	D-65	R-35	-	D (Kennedy)
1959-1961	86th	D-283	R-153	-	D-64	R-34	-	R (Eisenhower)
1957-1959	85th	D-233	R-200	-	D-49	R-47	-	R (Eisenhower)
1955-1957	84th	D-232	R-203	-	D-48	R-47	1	R (Eisenhower)
1953-1955	83rd	R-221	D-211	1	R-48	D-47	1	R (Eisenhower)
1951-1953	82nd	D-234	R-199	1	D-49	R-47	-	D (Truman)
1949-1951	81st	D-263	R-171	1	D-54	R-42	-	D (Truman)
1947-1949	80th	R-245	D-188	1	R-51	D-45	-	D (Truman)
1945-1947	79th	D-242	R-190	2	D-56	R-38	1	D (Truman)
1943-1945	78th	D-218	R-208	4	D-58	R-37	1	D (F. Roosevelt)
1941-1943	77th	D-268	R-162	5	D-66	R-28	2	D (F. Roosevelt)
1939-1941	76th	D-261	R-164	4	D-69	R-23	4	D (F. Roosevelt)
1937-1939	75th	D-331	R-89	13	D-76	R-16	4	D (F. Roosevelt)
1935-1937	74th	D-319	R-103	10	D-69	R-25	2	D (F. Roosevelt)
1933-1935	73rd	D-310	R-117	5	D-60	R-35	1	D (F. Roosevelt)
1931-1933	72nd	D-220	R-214	1	R-48	D-47	1	R (Hoover)
1929-1931	71st	R-267	D-167	1	R-56	D-39	1	R (Hoover)
1927-1929	70th	R-237	D-195	3	R-49	D-46	1	R (Coolidge)
1925-1927	69th	R-247	D-183	4	R-56	D-39	1	R (Coolidge)
1923-1925	68th	R-225	D-205	5	R-51	D-43	2	R (Coolidge)
1921-1923	67th	R-301	D-131	1	R-59	D-37	-	R (Harding)
1919-1921	66th	R-240	D-190	3	R-49	D-47	-	D (Wilson)
1917-1919	65th	D-216	R-210	6	D-53	R-42	-	D (Wilson)
1915-1917	64th	D-230	R-196	9	D-56	R-40	-	D (Wilson)
1913-1915	63rd	D-291	R-127	17	D-51	R-44	1	D (Wilson)
1911-1913	62nd	D-228	R-161	1	R-51	D-41	-	R (Taft)
1909-1911	61st	R-219	D-172	-	R-61	D-32	-	R (Taft)
1907-1909	60th	R-222	D-164	-	R-61	D-31	-	R (T. Roosevelt)
1905-1907	59th	R-250	D-136	-	R-57	D-33	-	R (T. Roosevelt)
1903-1905	58th	R-208	D-178	-	R-57	D-33	-	R (T. Roosevelt)
1901-1903	57th	R-197	D-151	9	R-55	D-31	4	R (T. Roosevelt) R (McKinley)
1899-1901	56th	R-185	D-163	9	R-53	D-26	8	R (McKinley)
1897-1899	55th	R-204	D-113	40	R-47	D-34	7	R (McKinley)
1895-1897	54th	R-244	D-105	7	R-43	D-39	6	D (Cleveland)
1893-1895	53rd	D-218	R-127	11	D-44	R-38	3	D (Cleveland)
1891-1893	52nd	D-235	R-88	9	R-47	D-39	2	R (B. Harrison)
1889-1891	51st	R-166	D-159	-	R-39	D-37	-	R (B. Harrison)
1887-1889	50th	D-169	R-152	4	R-39	D-37	-	D (Cleveland)
1885-1887	49th	D-183	R-140	2	R-43	D-34	-	D (Cleveland)
1883-1885	48th	D-197	R-118	10	R-38	D-36	2	R (Arthur)
1881-1883	47th	R-147	D-135	11	R-37	D-37	1	R (Arthur) R (Garfield)

...and the Presidency: 1789 to 1985

(Letter symbols for political parties: Ad—Administration; AM—Anti-Masonic; C—Coalition; D—Democratic; DR—Democratic-Republican; F—Federalist; J—Jacksonian; NR—National Republican; Op—Opposition; R—Republican; U—Unionist; W—Whig. Figures are for the beginning of the first session of each Congress.)

Year	Congress	HOUSE Majority party	HOUSE Principal minority party	HOUSE Other (except vacancies)	SENATE Majority party	SENATE Principal minority party	SENATE Other (except vacancies)	President
1879-1881	46th	D-149	R-130	14	D-42	R-33	1	R (Hayes)
1877-1879	45th	D-153	R-140	-	R-39	D-36	1	R (Hayes)
1875-1877	44th	D-169	R-109	14	R-45	D-29	2	R (Grant)
1873-1875	43rd	R-194	D-92	14	R-49	D-19	5	R (Grant)
1871-1873	42nd	R-134	D-104	5	R-52	D-17	5	R (Grant)
1869-1871	41st	R-149	D-63	-	R-56	D-11	-	R (Grant)
1867-1869	40th	R-143	D-49	-	R-42	D-11	-	R (A. Johnson)
1865-1867	39th	U-149	D-42	-	U-42	D-10	-	R (A. Johnson) R (Lincoln)
1863-1865	38th	R-102	D-75	9	R-36	D-9	5	R (Lincoln)
1861-1863	37th	R-105	D-43	30	R-31	D-10	8	R (Lincoln)
1859-1861	36th	R-114	D-92	31	D-36	R-26	4	D (Buchanan)
1857-1859	35th	D-118	R-92	26	D-36	R-20	8	D (Buchanan)
1855-1857	34th	R-108	D-83	43	D-40	R-15	5	D (Pierce)
1853-1855	33rd	D-159	W-71	4	D-38	W-22	2	D (Pierce)
1851-1853	32nd	D-140	W-88	5	D-35	W-24	3	W (Fillmore)
1849-1851	31st	D-112	W-109	9	D-35	W-25	2	W (Fillmore) W (Taylor)
1847-1849	30th	W-115	D-108	4	D-36	W-21	1	D (Polk)
1845-1847	29th	D-143	W-77	6	D-31	W-25	-	D (Polk)
1843-1845	28th	D-142	W-79	1	W-28	D-25	1	W (Tyler)
1841-1843	27th	W-133	D-102	6	W-28	D-22	2	W (Tyler) W (W. Harrison)
1839-1841	26th	D-124	W-118	-	D-28	W-22	-	D (Van Buren)
1837-1839	25th	D-108	W-107	24	D-30	W-18	4	D (Van Buren)
1835-1837	24th	D-145	W-98	-	D-27	W-25	-	D (Jackson)
1833-1835	23rd	D-147	AM-53	60	D-20	NR-20	8	D (Jackson)
1831-1833	22nd	D-141	NR-58	14	D-25	NR-21	2	D (Jackson)
1829-1831	21st	D-139	NR-74	-	D-26	NR-22	-	D (Jackson)
1827-1829	20th	J-119	Ad-94	-	J-28	Ad-20	-	C (John Q. Adams)
1825-1827	19th	Ad-105	J-97	-	Ad-26	J-20	-	C (John Q. Adams)
1823-1825	18th	DR-187	F-26	-	DR-44	F-4	-	DR (Monroe)
1821-1823	17th	DR-158	F-25	-	DR-44	F-4	-	DR (Monroe)
1819-1821	16th	DR-156	F-27	-	DR-35	F-7	-	DR (Monroe)
1817-1819	15th	DR-141	F-42	-	DR-34	F-10	-	DR (Monroe)
1815-1817	14th	DR-117	F-65	-	DR-25	F-11	-	DR (Madison)
1813-1815	13th	DR-112	F-68	-	DR-27	F-9	-	DR (Madison)
1811-1813	12th	DR-108	F-36	-	DR-30	F-6	-	DR (Madison)
1809-1811	11th	DR-94	F-48	-	DR-28	F-6	-	DR (Madison)
1807-1809	10th	DR-118	F-24	-	DR-28	F-6	-	DR (Jefferson)
1805-1807	9th	DR-116	F-25	-	DR-27	F-7	-	DR (Jefferson)
1803-1805	8th	DR-102	F-39	-	DR-25	F-9	-	DR (Jefferson)
1801-1803	7th	DR-69	F-36	-	DR-18	F-13	-	DR (Jefferson)
1799-1801	6th	F-64	DR-42	-	F-19	DR-13	vacancies	F (John Adams)
1797-1799	5th	F-58	DR-48	-	F-20	DR-12	-	F (John Adams)
1795-1797	4th	F-54	DR-52	-	F-19	DR-13	-	F (Washington)
1793-1795	3rd	DR-57	F-48	-	F-17	DR-13	-	F (Washington)
1791-1793	2nd	F-37	DR-33	-	F-16	DR-13	-	F (Washington)
1789-1791	1st	Ad-38	Op-26	-	Ad-17	Op-9	-	F (Washington)

Sources: U.S. Bureau of the Census. *Historical Statistics of the United States, Colonial Times to 1970.* Washington, D.C: Government Printing Office, 1975; U.S. Bureau of the Census. *Statistical Abstract of the United States, 1985.* Washington, D.C.: Government Printing Office, 1984; U.S. Congress. Joint Committee on Printing. *Official Congressional Directory.* Washington, D.C.: Government Printing Office, 1967- —.

Results of Elections in House...

	44	46	48	50	52	54	56	58	60	62	64	66	68	70	72	74	76	78	80	82	84
National Totals																					
Democrats	242	188	263	235	213	232	234	283	263	259	295	248	243	255	243	291	292	277	243[7]	269	253
Republicans	191	246	171	199	221	203	201	153	174	176	140	187	192	180	192	143	143	158	192	166	182
Alabama																					
Democrats	9	9	9	9	9	9	9	9	9	8[2]	3	5	5	5	4[2]	4	4	4	4	5	5
Republicans	0	0	0	0	0	0	0	0	0	0	5	3	3	3	3	3	3	3	3	2	2
Alaska																					
Democrats	—	—	—	—	—	—	—	1	1	1	1	0	0	1	1[4]	0	0	0	0	0	0
Republicans	—	—	—	—	—	—	—	0	0	0	0	1	1	0	0	1	1	1	1	1	1
Arizona																					
Democrats	2	2	2	2	1	1	1	1	1	2[1]	2	1	1	1	1[1]	1	2	2	2	2[1]	1
Republicans	0	0	0	0	1	1	1	1	1	1	1	2	2	2	3	3	2	2	2	3	4
Arkansas																					
Democrats	7	7	7	7	6	6	6	6	6	4[2]	4	3	3	3	3	3	3	2	2	2	3
Republicans	0	0	0	0	0	0	0	0	0	0	0	1	1	1	1	1	1	2	2	2	1
California																					
Democrats	16	9	10	10	11	11	13	16	16	25[1,4]	23	21	21	20	23[1]	28	29	26	22	28[1]	27
Republicans	7	14	13	13	19	19	17	14	13	15	17	17	18	20	15	14	17	21	17	17	18
Colorado																					
Democrats	0	1	3	2	2	2	2	3	2	2	4	3	3	2	2[1]	3	3	3	3	3[1]	2
Republicans	4	3	1	2	2	2	2	1	2	2	0	1	1	2	3	2	2	2	2	3	4
Connecticut																					
Democrats	4	0	3	2	1	1	0	6	4	5	6	5	4	4	3	4	4	5	4	4	3
Republicans	2	6	3	4	5	5	6	0	2	1	0	1	2	2	3	2	2	1	2	2	3
Delaware																					
Democrats	1	0	0	0	0	1	0	1	1	1	1	0	0	0	0	0	0	0	0	1	1
Republicans	0	1	1	1	1	0	1	0	0	0	0	1	1	1	1	1	1	1	1	0	0
Florida																					
Democrats	6	6	6	6	8	7	7	7	7	10[1]	10	9	9	9	11[1]	10	10	12	11	13[1]	12
Republicans	0	0	0	0	0	1	1	1	1	2	2	3	3	3	4	5	5	3	4	6	7
Georgia																					
Democrats	10	10	10	10	10	10	10	10	10	10	9	8	8	8	9	10	10	9	9	9	8
Republicans	0	0	0	0	0	0	0	0	0	0	1	2	2	2	1	0	0	1	1	1	2
Hawaii																					
Democrats	—	—	—	—	—	—	—	—	1	2[1]	2	2	2	2	2	2	2	2	2	2	2
Republicans	—	—	—	—	—	—	—	—	0	0	0	0	0	0	0	0	0	0	0	0	0
Idaho																					
Democrats	1	0	1	0	1	1	1	1	2	2	1	0	0	0	0	0	0	0	0	0	1
Republicans	1	2	1	2	1	1	1	1	0	0	1	2	2	2	2	2	2	2	2	2	1
Illinois																					
Democrats	11	6	12	8	9	12	11	14	14	12[2]	13	12	12	12	10	13	12	11	10	12[2]	13
Republicans	15	20	14	18	16	13	14	11	11	12	11	12	12	12	14	11	12	13	14	10	9
Indiana																					
Democrats	2	2	7	2	1	2	2	8	4[3]	4	6	5	4	5	4	9	8	7	6	5[2]	6[8]
Republicans	9	9	4	9	10	9	9	3	7	7	5	6	7	6	7	2	3	4	5	5	5
Iowa																					
Democrats	0	0	0	0	0	0	1	4	2	1[2]	6	2	2	2	3[2]	5	4	3	3	3	2
Republicans	8	8	8	8	8	8	7	4	6	6	1	5	5	5	3	1	2	3	3	3	4
Kansas																					
Democrats	0	0	0	0	1	0	1	3	1	0[2]	0	0	0	1	1	1	2	1	1	2	2
Republicans	6	6	6	6	5	6	5	3	5	5	5	5	5	4	4	4	3	4	4	3	3
Kentucky																					
Democrats	8	6	7	7	6	6	6	7	7	5[2]	6	4	4	5	5	5	5	4	4	4	4
Republicans	1	3	2	2	2	2	2	1	1	2	1	3	3	2	2	2	2	3	3	3	3
Louisiana																					
Democrats	8	8	8	8	8	8	8	8	8	8	8	8	8	8	7[4]	6[8]	6	5	6	6	6
Republicans	0	0	0	0	0	0	0	0	0	0	0	0	0	0	1	1	2	3	2	2	2
Maine																					
Democrats	0	0	0	0	0	0	1	2	0	0[2]	1	2	2	2	1	0	0	0	0	0	0
Republicans	3	3	3	3	3	3	2	1	3	2	1	0	0	0	1	2	2	2	2	2	2
Maryland																					
Democrats	5	4	4	3	3	4	4	7	6	6[1]	6	5	4	5	4	5	5	6	7	7	6
Republicans	1	2	2	3	4	3	3	0	1	2	2	3	4	3	4	3	3	2	1	1	2
Massachusetts																					
Democrats	4	5	6	6	6	7	7	8	8	7[2]	7	7	7	8	9[5]	10	10	10	10	10[2]	10
Republicans	10	9	8	8	8	7	7	6	6	5	5	5	5	4	3	2	2	2	2	1	1
Michigan																					
Democrats	6	3	5	5	5	7	6	7	7	8[1]	12	7	7	7	7	12	11	13	12	12[2]	11
Republicans	11	14	12	12	13	11	12	11	11	11	7	12	12	12	12	7	8	6	7	6	7
Minnesota																					
Democrats	2	1	4	4	4	5	5	4	3	4[2]	4	3	3	4	4	5	5	4	3	5	5
Republicans	7	8	5	5	5	4	4	5	6	4	4	5	5	4	4	3	3	4	5	3	3
Mississippi																					
Democrats	7	7	7	7	6	6	6	6	6	5[2]	4	5	5	5	3	3	3	3	3	3	3
Republicans	0	0	0	0	0	0	0	0	0	0	1	0	0	0	2	2	2	2	2	2	2
Missouri																					
Democrats	7	4	12	10	7	9	10	10	9	8[2]	8	8	9	9	9	9	8	8	6	6[2]	6
Republicans	6	9	1	3	4	2	1	1	2	2	2	2	1	1	1	1	2	2	4	3	3
Montana																					
Democrats	1	1	1	1	1	1	2	2	1	1	1	1	1	1	1	2	1	1	1	1	1
Republicans	1	1	1	1	1	1	0	0	1	1	1	1	1	1	1	0	1	1	1	1	1
Nebraska																					
Democrats	0	0	1	0	0	0	0	2	0	0[2]	1	0	0	0	0	1	1	0	0	0	0
Republicans	4	4	3	4	4	4	4	2	4	3	2	3	3	3	3	2	2	3	3	3	3

...of Representatives, 1944-1984

	44	46	48	50	52	54	56	58	60	62	64	66	68	70	72	74	76	78	80	82	84
National Totals																					
Democrats	242	188	263	235	213	232	234	283	263	259	295	248	243	255	243	291	292	277	243[7]	269	253
Republicans	191	246	171	199	221	203	201	153	174	176	140	187	192	180	192	143	143	158	192	166	182
Nevada																					
Democrats	1	0	1	1	0	0	1	1	1	1	1	1	1	1	0	1	1	1	1	1[1]	1
Republicans	0	1	0	0	1	1	0	0	0	0	0	0	0	0	1	0	0	0	0	0	1
New Hampshire																					
Democrats	0	0	0	0	0	0	0	0	0	0	1	0	0	0	0	1	1	1	1	1	0
Republicans	2	2	2	2	2	2	2	2	2	2	1	2	2	2	2	1	1	1	1	1	2
New Jersey																					
Democrats	2	2	5	5	5	6	4	5	6	7[1]	11	9	9	9	8	12	11	10	8	9[2]	8
Republicans	12	12	9	9	9	8	10	9	8	8	4	6	6	6	7	3	4	5	7	5	6
New Mexico																					
Democrats	2	2	2	2	2	2	2	2	2	2	2	2	0	1	1	1	1	1	0	1[1]	1
Republicans	0	0	0	0	0	0	0	0	0	0	0	0	2	1	1	1	1	1	2	2	2
New York																					
Democrats	22	16	24	23	16	17	17	19	22	20[2]	27	26	26	24	22[2]	27	28	26	22	20[2]	19
Republicans	22	28	20	22	27	26	26	24	21	21	14	15	15	17	17	12	11	13	17	14	15
North Carolina																					
Democrats	12	12	12	12	11	11	11	11	11	9[2]	9	8	7	7	7	9	9	9	7	9	6
Republicans	0	0	0	0	1	1	1	1	1	2	2	3	4	4	4	2	2	2	4	2	5
North Dakota																					
Democrats	0	0	0	0	0	0	0	1	0	0	1	0	0	1	0[2]	0	0	0	1	1	1
Republicans	2	2	2	2	2	2	2	1	2	2	1	2	2	1	1	1	1	1	0	0	0
Ohio																					
Democrats	6	4	12	7	6	6	6	9	7	6[1]	10	5	6	7	7[2]	8	10	10	11	10[2]	11
Republicans	17	19	11	15	16	17	17	14	16	18	14	19	18	17	16	15	13	13	12	11	10
Oklahoma																					
Democrats	6	6	8	6	5	5	5	5	5	5	5	4	4	4	5	6	5	5	5	5	5
Republicans	2	2	0	2	1	1	1	1	1	1	1	2	2	2	1	0	1	1	1	1	1
Oregon																					
Democrats	0	0	0	0	0	1	3	3	2	3	3	2	2	2	2	4	4	4	3	3[1]	3
Republicans	4	4	4	4	4	3	1	1	2	1	1	2	2	2	2	0	0	0	1	2	2
Pennsylvania																					
Democrats	15	5	16	13	11	14	13	16	14	13[2]	15	14	14	14	13[2]	14	17	15	13[7]	13[2]	13
Republicans	18	28	17	20	19	16	17	14	16	14	12	13	13	13	12	11	8	10	12	10	10
Rhode Island																					
Democrats	2	2	2	2	2	2	2	2	2	2	2	2	2	2	2	2	2	2	1	1	1
Republicans	0	0	0	0	0	0	0	0	0	0	0	0	0	0	0	0	0	0	1	1	1
South Carolina																					
Democrats	6	6	6	6	6	6	6	6	6	6	6	5	5	5	4	5	5	4	2	3	3
Republicans	0	0	0	0	0	0	0	0	0	0	0	1	1	1	2	1	1	2	4	3	3
South Dakota																					
Democrats	0	0	0	0	0	0	1	1	0	0	0	0	0	2	1	0	0	1	1	1[2]	1
Republicans	2	2	2	2	2	2	1	1	2	2	2	2	2	0	1	2	2	1	1	0	0
Tennessee																					
Democrats	8	8	8	8	7	7	7	7	7	6	6	5	5	5	3[2]	5	5	5	5	6[1]	6
Republicans	2	2	2	2	2	2	2	2	2	3	3	4	4	4	5	3	3	3	3	3	3
Texas																					
Democrats	21	21	21	21	22	21	21	21	21	21[1]	23	21	20	20	20[1]	21	22	20	19	22[1]	17
Republicans	0	0	0	0	0	1	1	1	1	2	0	2	3	3	4	3	2	4	5	5	10
Utah																					
Democrats	2	1	2	2	0	0	0	1	2	0	1	0	0	1	2	2	1	1	0	0[1]	0
Republicans	0	1	0	0	2	2	2	1	0	2	1	2	2	1	0	0	1	1	2	3	3
Vermont																					
Democrats	0	0	0	0	0	0	0	1	0	0	0	0	0	0	0	0	0	0	0	0	0
Republicans	1	1	1	1	1	1	1	0	1	1	1	1	1	1	1	1	1	1	1	1	1
Virginia																					
Democrats	9	9	9	9	7	8	8	8	8	8	8	6	5	4	3	5	4	4	1	4	4
Republicans	0	0	0	0	3	2	2	2	2	2	2	4	5	6	7	5	6	6	9	6	6
Washington																					
Democrats	4	1	2	2	1	1	1	1	2	1	5	5	5	6	6	6	6	6	5	5[1]	5
Republicans	2	5	4	4	6	6	6	6	5	6	2	2	2	1	1	1	1	1	2	3	3
West Virginia																					
Democrats	5	2	6	6	5	6	4	5	5	4[2]	4	4	5	5	4[2]	4	4	4	2	4	4
Republicans	1	4	0	0	1	0	2	1	1	1	1	1	0	0	0	0	0	0	0	2	0
Wisconsin																					
Democrats	2	0	2	1	1	3	3	5	4	4	5	3	3	5	5[2]	7	7	6	5	5	5
Republicans	7	10	8	9	9	7	7	5	6	6	5	7	7	5	4	2	2	3	4	4	4
Wyoming																					
Democrats	0	0	0	0	0	0	0	0	0	0	1	0	0	1	1	1	1	0	0	0	0
Republicans	1	1	1	1	1	1	1	1	1	1	0	1	1	0	0	0	0	1	1	1	1

1. State gained seats due to reapportionment.

2. State lost seats due to reapportionment.

3. Indiana 1960: Figures include final outcome of disputed election in 5th District where a Republican was at first certified the winner but the House decided to seat the Democrat. The 7-4 figure reflects the seating of the Democrat.

4. California 1962, Alaska and Louisiana 1972: Total includes one Democratic candidate who died before the election but his name remained on the ballot and he was re-elected. A special election was held the next year to fill the vacancy.

5. Massachusetts 1972: Democratic total includes Rep. Joe Moakley, elected as an Independent but served as a Democrat.

6. Louisiana 1974: One vacancy. There was no declared winner in the 6th District. A special election was held the next year to fill the vacancy.

7. Pennsylvania 1980: Includes Foglietta, Pa., elected as an Independant.

8. Indiana 1984: Figures include final outcome of disputed election in 8th District where a Republican was at first certified the winner but the House decided to seat the Democrat. The 6-5 figure reflects the seating of the Democrat.

Appendix

Distribution of House Seats and Electoral Votes

Based on Censuses of 1950, 1960, 1970 and 1980

	U.S. HOUSE SEATS							ELECTORAL VOTES			
	1953-1963	1960 Census Changes	1963-1973	1970 Census Changes	1973-1983	1980 Census Changes	1983-1985	1952, 1956, 1960	1964, 1968	1972, 1976, 1980	1984
Alabama	9	−1	8	−1	7	0	7	11	10	9	9
Alaska	1	—	1	—	1	0	1	3	3	3	3
Arizona	2	+1	3	+1	4	+1	5	4	5	6	7
Arkansas	6	−2	4	—	4	0	4	8	6	6	6
California	30	+8	38	+5	43	+2	45	32	40	45	47
Colorado	4	—	4	+1	5	+1	6	6	6	7	8
Connecticut	6	—	6	—	6	0	6	8	8	8	8
Delaware	1	—	1	—	1	0	1	3	3	3	3
District of Columbia	—	—	—	—	—	—	—	—	3	3	3
Florida	8	+4	12	+3	15	+4	19	10	14	17	21
Georgia	10	—	10	—	10	0	10	12	12	12	12
Hawaii	1	+1	2	—	2	0	2	3	4	4	4
Idaho	2	—	2	—	2	0	2	4	4	4	4
Illinois	25	−1	24	—	24	−2	22	27	26	26	24
Indiana	11	—	11	—	11	−1	10	13	13	13	12
Iowa	8	−1	7	−1	6	0	6	10	9	8	8
Kansas	6	−1	5	—	5	0	5	8	7	7	7
Kentucky	8	−1	7	—	7	0	7	10	9	9	9
Louisiana	8	—	8	—	8	0	8	10	10	10	10
Maine	3	−1	2	—	2	0	2	5	4	4	4
Maryland	7	+1	8	—	8	0	8	9	10	10	10
Massachusetts	14	−2	12	—	12	−1	11	16	14	14	13
Michigan	18	+1	19	—	19	−1	18	20	21	21	20
Minnesota	9	−1	8	—	8	0	8	11	10	10	10
Mississippi	6	−1	5	—	5	0	5	8	7	7	7
Missouri	11	−1	10	—	10	−1	9	13	12	12	11
Montana	2	—	2	—	2	0	2	4	4	4	4
Nebraska	4	−1	3	—	3	0	3	6	5	5	5
Nevada	1	—	1	—	1	+1	2	3	3	3	4
New Hampshire	2	—	2	—	2	0	2	4	4	4	4
New Jersey	14	+1	15	—	15	−1	14	16	17	17	16
New Mexico	2	—	2	—	2	+1	3	4	4	4	5
New York	43	−2	41	−2	39	−5	34	45	43	41	36
North Carolina	12	−1	11	—	11	0	11	14	13	13	13
North Dakota	2	—	2	−1	1	0	1	4	4	3	3
Ohio	23	+1	24	−1	23	−2	21	25	26	25	23
Oklahoma	6	—	6	—	6	0	6	8	8	8	8
Oregon	4	—	4	—	4	+1	5	6	6	6	7
Pennsylvania	30	−3	27	−2	25	−2	23	32	29	27	25
Rhode Island	2	—	2	—	2	0	2	4	4	4	4
South Carolina	6	—	6	—	6	0	6	8	8	8	8
South Dakota	2	—	2	—	2	−1	1	4	4	4	3
Tennessee	9	—	9	−1	8	+1	9	11	11	10	11
Texas	22	+1	23	+1	24	+3	27	24	25	26	29
Utah	2	—	2	—	2	+1	3	4	4	4	5
Vermont	1	—	1	—	1	0	1	3	3	3	3
Virginia	10	—	10	—	10	0	10	12	12	12	12
Washington	7	—	7	—	7	+1	8	9	9	9	10
West Virginia	6	−1	5	−1	4	0	4	8	7	6	6
Wisconsin	10	—	10	−1	9	0	9	12	12	11	11
Wyoming	1	—	1	—	1	0	1	3	3	3	3

97th Congress Special, 1981 Gubernatorial Returns

1981 Gubernatorial Elections

NEW JERSEY

	Vote Total	Percent
Thomas H. Kean (R)	1,145,999	49.5
James J. Florio (D)	1,144,202	49.4
Others	27,038	1.1

VIRGINIA

	Vote Total	Percent
Charles S. Robb (D)	760,357	53.5
J. Marshall Coleman (R)	659,398	46.4
Write-Ins	856	0.1

Special House Elections, 97th Congress

MICHIGAN — April 21, 1981

	Vote Total	Percent
Mark Siljander (R)	36,046	72.6
Johnie Rodebush (D)	12,461	25.1
Bette Irwin (LIBERT)	658	1.4
Robert Drenkhahn (AIP)	452	0.9

MARYLAND — May 19, 1981

	Vote Total	Percent
Steny H. Hoyer (D)	42,573	55.2
Audrey Scott (R)	33,708	43.5
Tom Mathers (LIBERT)	960	1.3

OHIO — June 25, 1981

	Vote Total	Percent
Michael Oxley (R)	41,987	50.2
Dale Locker (D)	41,646	49.8

MISSISSIPPI — July 7, 1981

	Vote Total	Percent
Wayne Dowdy (D)	55,656	50.4
Liles Williams (R)	54,744	49.6

PENNSYLVANIA — July 21, 1981

	Vote Total	Percent
Joseph F. Smith (R,I)	29,907	52.5
David B. Glancy (D)	24,390	42.8
Charles L. Duncan (CONSU)	2,283	4.0
David Dorn (LIBERT)	375	0.7

CONNECTICUT — Jan. 12, 1982

	Vote Total	Percent
Barbara B. Kennelly (D)	51,431	58.8
Ann P. Uccello (R)	36,085	41.2

OHIO — June 29, 1982

	Vote Total	Percent
Jean Ashbrook (R)	18,106	73.4
Jack Koelbl (D)	6,385	25.9

CALIFORNIA — July 13, 1982 (runoff)

	Vote Total	Percent
Matthew G. Martinez (D)	14,593	51.0
Ralph R. Ramirez (R)	14,043	49.0

NOTE: Katie Hall, D-Ill., was elected Nov. 2, 1982, to fill the remaining term of Adam Benjamin Jr., who died Sept. 4, and to the 98th Congress. *(See 1982 election returns for vote tally, p. 1104)*

Abbreviations

AIP	—American Independent Party
CONSU	—Consumer
D	—Democrat
I	—Independent
LIBERT	—Libertarian
R	—Republican

1982 Elections Returns for Governor, Senate and House

Following are final 1982 vote returns for the Senate, House and governorships, compiled by Congressional Quarterly from results furnished by the secretaries of state or election boards in the 50 states.

All candidates are included who were listed on the ballot. Due to the exclusion of scattered write-in votes from this chart and the results of rounding numbers in computing percentages, the totals do not always equal 100 percent. The box below shows party designation symbols.

   * indicates incumbents.

   X denotes unopposed candidates.

   - denotes minor parties for which the vote was not available.

ALABAMA

	Vote Total	Per-cent
Governor		
George C. Wallace (D)	650,538	57.6
Emory Folmar (R)	440,815	39.1
John Dyer (P)	4,364	0.4
Leo Suiter (C)	17,936	1.6
Henri Klingler (LIBERT)	7,671	0.7
John L. Jackson (NDPA)	4,693	0.4
Martin Boyers (S)	2,578	0.2
House		
1 Steve Gudac (D)	54,315	37.2
Jack Edwards (R)*	89,901	61.6
Bill Springer (LIBERT)	1,812	1.2
2 Billy Joe Camp (D)	81,904	49.6
William L. Dickinson (R)*	83,290	50.4
3 Bill Nichols (D)*	100,864	96.3
Richard Landers Jr. (LIBERT)	3,920	3.7
4 Tom Bevill (D)*	X	100.0
5 Ronnie G. Flippo (D)*	108,807	80.7
Leopold Yambrek (R)	24,593	18.2
Kenneth Ament (LIBERT)	1,474	1.1
6 Ben Erdreich (D)	88,029	53.2
Albert Lee Smith Jr. (R)*	76,726	46.4
Charles Ewing (LIBERT)	632	0.4
7 Richard C. Shelby (D)*	124,070	96.8
James Jones (LIBERT)	4,058	3.2

ALASKA

	Vote Total	Per-cent
Governor		
Bill Sheffield (D)	89,918	46.1
Tom Fink (R)	72,291	37.1
Joseph Vogler (AKI)	3,235	1.7
Richard L. Randolph (LIBERT)	29,067	14.9
House		
AL Dave Carlson (D)	52,011	28.7
Don Young (R)*	128,274	70.8

ARIZONA

	Vote Total	Per-cent
Governor		
Bruce Babbitt (D)*	453,795	62.5
Leo Corbet (R)	235,877	32.5
Sam Steiger (LIBERT)	36,649	5.0
Senator		
Dennis DeConcini (D)*	411,970	56.9
Pete Dunn (R)	291,749	40.3
Randall Clamons (LIBERT)	20,100	2.8
House		
1 William E. Hegarty (D)	41,261	30.5
John McCain (R)	89,116	65.9
Richard K. Dodge (LIBERT)	4,850	3.6
2 Morris K. Udall (D)*	73,468	70.9

	Vote Total	Per-cent
Roy B. Laos (R)	28,407	27.4
Jessica Sampson (YSA)	1,799	1.7
3 Pat Bosch (D)	58,644	36.7
Bob Stump (R)*	101,198	63.3
4 Wayne O. Earley (D)	44,182	30.4
Eldon Rudd (R)*	95,620	65.7
Richard A. Stauffer (LIBERT)	5,664	3.9
5 Jim McNulty (D)	82,938	49.7
Jim Kolbe (R)	80,531	48.3
Richard D. Auster (LIBERT)	3,332	2.0

ARKANSAS

	Vote Total	Per-cent
Governor		
Bill Clinton (D)	431,855	54.7
Frank D. White (R)*	357,496	45.3
House		
1 Bill Alexander (D)*	124,208	64.8
Chuck Banks (R)	67,427	35.2
2 Charles L. George (D)	82,913	46.1
Ed Bethune (R)*	96,775	53.9
3 Jim McDougal (D)	69,089	34.0
John Paul Hammerschmidt (R)*	133,909	66.0
4 Beryl Anthony Jr. (D)*	121,256	65.6
Bob Leslie (R)	63,661	34.4

Abbreviations for Party Designations

AD	—Anti-Drug	LIBERT	—Libertarian
AKI	—Alaskan Independence	LU	—Liberty Union
AM	—American	NA	—New Alliance
AMI	—American Independent	NDPA	—National Democratic Party of Alabama
BGG	—Bipartisan Good Government	NF	—Nuclear Freeze
C	—Conservative	NP	—Nonpartisan
CIT	—Citizens	NU	—New Union
COM	—Communist	P	—Prohibition
CONSU	—Consumers	PFP	—Peace and Freedom Party
CST	—Constitution	R	—Republican
D	—Democratic	RTL	—Right to Life
DFL	—Democratic Farmer-Labor	SOC	—Socialist
F LIBERT	—Free Libertarian	SOC LAB	—Socialist Labor
FP	—Free People's	SOC WORK	—Socialist Workers
I	—Independent	TAX	—Taxpayers
I-D	—Independent-Democrat	UN	—Unity
I-R	—Independent-Republican	WF	—World Federalist
JI	—Jeffersonian Independent	WL	—Workers League
L	—Liberal	YSA	—Young Socialist Alliance

	Vote Total	Per- cent

CALIFORNIA

Governor

Tom Bradley (D)	3,787,669	48.1
George Deukmejian (R)	3,881,014	49.3
James C. Griffin (AMI)	56,249	0.7
Dan P. Dougherty (LIBERT)	81,076	1.0
Elizabeth Martinez (PFP)	70,327	0.9

Senator

Edmund G. Brown Jr. (D)	3,494,968	44.8
Pete Wilson (R)	4,022,565	51.5
Theresa "Tena" Dietrich (AMI)	83,809	1.1
Joseph Fuhrig (LIBERT)	107,720	1.4
David Wald (PFP)	96,388	1.2

House

1 Douglas H. Bosco (D)	107,749	49.8
Don H. Clausen (R)*	102,043	47.2
David Redick (LIBERT)	6,374	3.0
2 John A. Newmeyer (D)	81,314	40.5
Gene Chappie (R)*	116,172	57.9
Howard Fegarsky (PFP)	3,126	1.6
3 Robert T. Matsui (D)*	194,680	89.6
Bruce A. Daniel (LIBERT)	16,222	7.5
John C. Reiger (PFP)	6,294	2.9
4 Vic Fazio (D)*	118,476	63.9
Roger B. Canfield (R)	67,047	36.1
5 Phillip Burton (D)*	103,268	57.9
Milton Marks (R)	72,139	40.5
Justin Raimondo (LIBERT)	2,904	1.6
6 Barbara Boxer (D)	96,379	52.4
Dennis McQuaid (R)	82,128	44.6
Howard C. Creighton (LIBERT)	3,191	1.7
Timothy-Allen Albertson (PFP)	2,366	1.3
7 George Miller (D)*	126,952	67.2
Paul E. Vallely (R)	56,960	30.2
Terry L. Wells (AMI)	2,205	1.2
Rich Newell (LIBERT)	2,752	1.4
8 Ronald V. Dellums (D)*	121,537	55.9
Claude B. Hutchison Jr. (R)	95,694	44.1
9 Fortney H. "Pete" Stark (D)*	104,393	60.7
Bill J. Kennedy (R)	67,702	39.3
10 Don Edwards (D)*	77,263	62.7
Bob Herriott (R)	41,506	33.7
Edmon V. Kaiser (AMI)	2,109	1.7
Dale Burrow (LIBERT)	2,403	1.9
11 Tom Lantos (D)*	109,812	57.1
Bill Royer (R)	76,462	39.7
Nicholas W. Kudrovzeff (AMI)	1,250	0.7
Chuck Olson (LIBERT)	2,920	1.5
Wilson Branch (PFP)	1,928	1.0
12 Emmett Lynch (D)	61,372	33.5
Ed Zschau (R)	115,365	63.0
Bill White (LIBERT)	6,471	3.5
13 Norman Y. Mineta (D)*	110,805	65.9
Tom Kelly (R)	52,806	31.4
Al Hinkle (LIBERT)	4,553	2.7
14 Baron Reed (D)	77,400	36.6
Norman D. Shumway (R)*	134,225	63.4
15 Tony Coelho (D)*	86,022	63.7
Ed Bates (R)	45,948	34.0
Stephen L. Gerringer (LIBERT)	3,073	2.3
16 Leon E. Panetta (D)*	142,630	85.4
G. Richard Arnold (R)	24,448	14.6
Anne Nixon Ball (R write-in)	—	—
17 Gene Tackett (D)	68,364	46.0

Charles Pashayan Jr. (R)*	80,271	54.0
18 Richard Lehman (D)	92,762	59.5
Adrian C. Fondse (R)	59,664	38.3
Marshall William Fritz (LIBERT)	3,501	2.2
19 Frank Frost (D)	66,042	35.8
Robert J. Lagomarsino (R)*	112,486	61.1
R. C. Gordon-McCutchan (LIBERT)	4,198	2.3
Charles J. Zekan (PFP)	1,520	0.8
20 Robert J. Bethea (D)	57,769	31.9
William M. Thomas (R)*	123,312	68.1
21 George Henry Margolis (D)	46,412	24.1
Bobbi Fiedler (R)*	138,474	71.8
Daniel Wiener (LIBERT)	7,881	4.1
22 Harvey L. Goldhammer (D)	46,521	23.5
Carlos J. Moorhead (R)*	145,831	73.6
Robert T. Gerringer (LIBERT)	5,870	2.9
23 Anthony C. Beilenson (D)*	120,788	59.6
David Armor (R)	82,031	40.4
24 Henry A. Waxman (D)*	88,516	65.0
Jerry Zerg (R)	42,133	31.0
Jeff Mandei (LIBERT)	5,420	4.0
25 Edward R. Roybal (D)*	71,106	85.5
Daniel John Gorham (LIBERT)	12,060	14.5
26 Howard L. Berman (D)	97,383	59.6
Hal Phillips (R)	66,070	40.4
27 Mel Levine (D)	108,347	59.5
Bart W. Christensen (R)	67,479	37.0
Zack Richardson (LIBERT)	6,391	3.5
28 Julian C. Dixon (D)*	103,469	78.9
David Goerz (R)	24,473	18.7
David W. Meleney (LIBERT)	3,210	2.4
29 Augustus F. Hawkins (D)*	97,028	79.8
Milton R. MacKaig (R)	24,568	20.2
30 Matthew G. "Marty" Martinez (D)*	60,905	53.9
John H. Rousselot (R)*	52,177	46.1
31 Mervyn M. Dymally (D)*	86,718	72.4
Henry C. Minturn (R)	33,043	27.6
32 Glenn M. Anderson (D)*	84,663	58.0
Brian Lungren (R)	57,863	39.6
Eugene E. Ruyle (PFP)	3,473	2.4
33 Paul Servelle (D)	55,514	32.2
David Dreier (R)*	112,362	65.2
Phillips P. Franklin (LIBERT)	2,251	1.3
James Michael Noonan (PFP)	2,223	1.3
34 Esteban Torres (D)	68,316	57.2
Paul R. Jackson (R)	51,026	42.8
35 Robert E. Erwin (D)	52,349	31.7
Jerry Lewis (R)*	112,786	68.3
36 George E. Brown Jr. (D)*	76,546	54.3
John Paul Stark (R)	64,361	45.7
37 Curtis P. "Sam" Cross (D)	68,510	38.5
Al McCandless (R)	105,065	59.1
Marc R. Wruple (LIBERT)	4,297	2.4
38 Jerry M. Patterson (D)*	73,914	52.4
William F. Dohr (R)	61,279	43.4
Anita K. Barr (LIBERT)	5,989	4.2
39 Frank G. Verges (D)	46,681	26.0
William E. Dannemeyer (R)*	129,539	72.2
Frank Boeheim (PFP)	3,152	1.8
40 Paul Haseman (D)	52,546	26.1
Robert E. Badham (R)*	144,228	71.5
Maxine Bell Quirk (PFP)	4,826	2.4
41 Tony Brandenburg (D)	58,677	28.8
Bill Lowery (R)*	140,130	68.9
Everett Hale (LIBERT)	4,654	2.3
42 James P. Spellman (D)	58,690	28.3

Dan Lungren (R)*	142,845	69.0
John S. Donohue (PFP)	5,514	2.7
43 Roy "Pat" Archer (D)	57,995	32.1
Johnnie R. Crean (R)	56,297	31.1
Ron Packard (R write-in)	66,444	36.8
44 Jim Bates (D)	78,474	65.0
Shirley M. Gissendanner (R)	38,447	31.8
Jim Conole (LIBERT)	3,904	3.2
45 Richard Hill (D)	50,148	29.2
Duncan L. Hunter (R)*	117,771	68.6
Jack R. Sanders (LIBERT)	3,839	2.2

COLORADO

Governor

Richard D. Lamm (D)*	627,960	65.7
John D. Fuhr (R)	302,740	31.7
Paul Grant (LIBERT)	19,349	2.0
Earl F. Dodge (P)	3,496	0.4
Alan Gummerson (SOC WORK)	2,476	0.2

House

1 Patricia Schroeder (D)*	94,969	60.3
Arch Decker (R)	59,009	37.4
Robin White (LIBERT)	3,619	2.3
2 Timothy E. Wirth (D)*	101,194	61.8
John C. Buechner (R)	59,580	36.4
Charles Jackson (LIBERT)	2,862	1.8
3 Ray Kogovsek (D)*	92,384	53.4
Tom Wiens (R)	77,409	44.8
Stormy Mon (LIBERT)	2,439	1.4
Henry John Olshaw (I)	656	0.4
4 Charles L. "Bud" Bishopp (D)	45,750	30.2
Hank Brown (R)*	105,550	69.8
5 Tom Cronin (D)	57,392	40.5
Ken Kramer (R)*	84,479	59.5
6 Steve Hogan (D)	56,598	35.6
Jack Swigert (R)†	98,909	62.1
J. Craig Green (LIBERT)	3,605	2.3

CONNECTICUT

Governor

William A. O'Neill (D)*	578,264	53.4
Lewis B. Rome (R)	497,773	45.9
Walter J. Gengarelly (LIBERT)	7,839	0.7

Senator

Toby Moffett (D)	499,146	46.1
Lowell P. Weicker Jr. (R)*	545,987	50.4
Lucien DiFazio (C)	30,212	2.8
James A. Lewis (LIBERT)	8,163	0.7

House

1 Barbara B. Kennelly (D)*	126,798	68.1
Herschel A. Klein (R)	58,075	31.2
Daniel Landerfen (LIBERT)	1,237	0.7
2 Sam Gejdenson (D)*	95,254	55.8
Tony Guglielmo (R)	74,294	43.5
Donald W. Wood (LIBERT)	1,255	0.7
3 Bruce A. Morrison (D)	90,638	50.0
Lawrence J. DeNardis (R)*	88,951	49.0
Joelle R. Fishman (COM)	696	0.4
Michael R. Cohen (LIBERT)	1,164	0.6
4 John A. Phillips (D)	71,110	42.9
Stewart B. McKinney (R)*	93,660	56.4
Lothar Frank (LIBERT)	1,127	0.7
5 William R. Ratchford (D)*	101,362	58.5
Neal B. Hanlon (R)	70,808	40.8
Jerry Brennan (LIBERT)	1,203	0.7

†Died Dec. 27.

	Vote Total	Percent
6 William E. Curry Jr. (D)	92,178	47.7
Nancy L. Johnson (R)	99,703	51.7
Monte Dunn (LIBERT)	1,091	0.6

DELAWARE

Senator

	Vote Total	Percent
David N. Levinson (D)	84,413	44.2
William V. Roth Jr. (R)*	105,357	55.2
Charles A. Baker (AM)	537	0.3
Lawrence D. Sullivan (LIBERT)	653	0.3

House

	Vote Total	Percent
AL Thomas R. Carper (D)	98,533	52.4
Thomas B. Evans Jr. (R)*	87,153	46.3
Mary D. Gise (AM)	1,109	0.6
David Nuttall (CIT)	558	0.3
Richard A. Cohen (LIBERT)	711	0.4

FLORIDA

Governor

	Vote Total	Percent
Robert Graham (D)*	1,739,553	64.7
L. A. "Skip" Bafalis (R)	949,023	35.3

Senator

	Vote Total	Percent
Lawton Chiles (D)*	1,636,857	61.7
Van Poole (R)	1,014,551	38.3

House

	Vote Total	Percent
1 Earl Hutto (D)*	82,482	74.5
J. Terry Bechtol (R)	28,285	25.5
2 Don Fuqua (D)*	79,096	61.7
Ron McNeil (R)	49,084	38.3
3 Charles E. Bennett (D)*	73,713	84.1
George Grimsley (R)	13,921	15.9
4 Bill Chappell Jr. (D)*	83,830	66.9
Larry Gaudet (R)	41,399	33.1
5 Dick Batchelor (D)	49,042	41.2
Bill McCollum (R)*	69,939	58.8
6 Kenneth H. "Buddy" MacKay (D)	85,799	61.3
Ed Havill (R)	54,058	38.7
7 Sam Gibbons (D)*	85,317	74.2
Ken Ayers (R)	29,624	25.8
8 C. W. Bill Young (R)*	X	100.0
9 George H. Sheldon (D)	90,673	48.8
Michael Bilirakis (R)	94,993	51.2
10 Andy Ireland (D)*	X	100.0
11 Bill Nelson (D)*	101,625	70.6
Joel Robinson (R)	42,323	29.4
12 Brad Culverhouse (D)	73,886	47.4
Tom Lewis (R)	81,864	52.6
13 Dana N. Stevens (D)	71,206	34.9
Connie Mack III (R)	132,906	65.1
14 Daniel A. Mica (D)*	128,627	73.0
Steve Mitchell (R)	47,542	27.0
15 Edward J. Stack (D)	67,058	42.9
E. Clay Shaw Jr. (R)*	89,128	57.1
16 Larry Smith (D)	91,869	67.9
Maurice Berkowitz (R)	43,343	32.1
17 William Lehman (D)*	X	100.0
18 Claude Pepper (D)*	72,137	71.2
Ricardo Nunez (R)	29,156	28.8
19 Dante B. Fascell (D)*	74,274	58.9
Glenn Rinker (R)	51,925	41.1

GEORGIA

Governor

	Vote Total	Percent
Joe Frank Harris (D)	734,090	62.8
Bob Bell (R)	434,496	37.2

House

	Vote Total	Percent
1 Lindsay Thomas (D)	65,625	64.1
Herb Jones (R)	36,799	35.9
2 Charles Hatcher (D)*	X	100.0
3 Richard Ray (D)	74,626	71.0
Tyron Elliott (R)	30,537	29.0
4 Elliott H. Levitas (D)*	38,758	65.5
Dick Winder (R)	20,418	34.5
5 Wyche Fowler Jr. (D)*	53,264	80.8
Paul Jones (R)	3,633	5.5
J. E. "Billy" McKinney (I)	9,049	13.7
6 Jim Wood (D)	50,459	44.7
Newt Gingrich (R)*	62,352	55.3
7 Larry P. McDonald (D)*	71,647	61.1
Dave Sellers (R)	45,569	38.9
8 J. Roy Rowland (D)	X	100.0
9 Ed Jenkins (D)*	86,514	77.0
Charles Sherwood (R)	25,907	23.0
10 Doug Barnard Jr. (D)*	X	100.0

HAWAII

Governor

	Vote Total	Percent
George Ariyoshi (D)*	141,043	45.2
D. G. Anderson (R)	81,507	26.2
Frank F. Fasi (I-D)	89,303	28.6

Senator

	Vote Total	Percent
Spark M. Matsunaga (D)*	245,386	80.1
Clarence J. Brown (R)	52,071	17.0
E. F. Bernier-Nachtwey (I-D)	8,953	2.9

House

	Vote Total	Percent
1 Cecil Heftel (D)*	134,779	89.9
Rockne H. Johnson (LIBERT)	15,128	10.1
2 Daniel K. Akaka (D)*	132,072	89.2
Amelia Oy Fritts (LIBERT)	6,856	4.6
Gregory B. Mills (NP)	9,080	6.2

IDAHO

Governor

	Vote Total	Percent
John V. Evans (D)*	165,365	50.6
Philip E. Batt (R)	161,157	49.4

House

	Vote Total	Percent
1 Larry LaRocco (D)	74,388	46.3
Larry E. Craig (R)*	86,277	53.7
2 Richard Stallings (D)	76,608	47.7
George Hansen (R)*	83,873	52.3

ILLINOIS

Governor

	Vote Total	Percent
Adlai E. Stevenson III (D)	1,811,027	49.3
James R. Thompson (R)*	1,816,101	49.4
Bea Armstrong (LIBERT)	24,417	0.7
John E. Roche (TAX)	22,001	0.6

House

	Vote Total	Percent
1 Harold Washington (D)*	172,641	97.3
Charles Allen Taliaferro (R)	4,820	2.7
2 Gus Savage (D)*	140,827	87.0
Kevin Walker Sparks (R)	20,670	12.8
Joseph Zvonkovach (write-in)	288	0.2
3 Marty Russo (D)*	137,391	74.0
Richard D. Murphy (R)	48,268	26.0
4 Michael A. Murer (D)	66,323	45.4
George M. O'Brien (R)*	79,842	54.6

	Vote Total	Percent
5 William O. Lipinski (D)	110,351	75.4
Daniel J. Partyka (R)	35,970	24.6
6 Leroy E. Kennel (D)	45,237	31.6
Henry J. Hyde (R)*	97,918	68.4
7 Cardiss Collins (D)*	133,978	86.5
Dansby Cheeks (R)	20,994	13.5
8 Dan Rostenkowski (D)*	124,318	83.4
Bonnie Hickey (R)	24,666	16.6
9 Sidney R. Yates (D)*	114,083	66.5
Catherine Bertini (R)	54,851	32.0
Sheila Jones (AD)	2,595	1.5
10 Eugenia S. Chapman (D)	63,115	41.0
John Edward Porter (R)*	90,750	59.0
11 Frank Annunzio (D)*	134,755	72.6
James F. Moynihan (R)	50,967	27.4
12 Daniel G. DeFosse (D)	40,108	30.7
Philip M. Crane (R)*	86,487	66.2
Joan T. Jarosz (LIBERT)	4,101	3.1
13 Robert Bily (D)	49,105	30.2
John N. Erlenborn (R)*	113,423	69.8
14 Dan McGrath (D)	53,914	35.4
Tom Corcoran (R)*	98,262	64.6
15 Tim L. Hall (D)	53,303	33.7
Edward R. Madigan (R)*	105,038	66.3
16 Carl R. Schwerdtfeger (D)	66,877	42.8
Lynn Martin (R)*	89,405	57.2
17 Lane Evans (D)	94,483	52.8
Kenneth G. McMillan (R)	84,347	47.2
18 G. Douglas Stephens (D)	91,281	48.4
Robert H. Michel (R)*	97,406	51.6
19 John Gwinn (D)	87,231	47.9
Daniel B. Crane (R)*	94,833	52.1
20 Richard J. Durbin (D)	100,758	50.4
Paul Findley (R)*	99,348	49.6
21 Melvin Price (D)*	89,500	63.6
Robert H. Gaffner (R)	46,764	33.3
Sandra L. Climaco (BGG)	4,344	3.1
22 Paul Simon (D)*	123,693	66.2
Peter G. Prineas (R)	63,279	33.8

INDIANA

Senator

	Vote Total	Percent
Floyd Fithian (D)	828,400	45.6
Richard G. Lugar (R)*	978,301	53.8
Raymond James (AM)	10,586	0.6

House

	Vote Total	Percent
1 Katie Hall (D)	89,369	56.9
Thomas H. Krieger (R)	66,921	42.6
Jesse Smith (SOC WORK)	806	0.5
2 Philip R. Sharp (D)*	107,298	56.2
Ralph W. Van Natta (R)	83,593	43.8
3 Richard C. Bodine (D)	83,046	48.8
John Hiler (R)*	86,958	51.2
4 Roger M. Miller (D)	60,054	35.1
Dan Coats (R)*	110,155	64.3
John B. Cameron (AM)	1,029	0.6
5 Allen B. Maxwell (D)	67,238	38.9
Elwood Hillis (R)*	105,469	61.1
6 George E. Grabianowski (D)	70,764	35.1
Dan Burton (R)	131,100	64.9
7 Stephen S. Bonney (D)	70,249	37.7
John T. Myers (R)*	115,884	62.3
8 Francis X. McCloskey (D)	100,592	51.4
Joel Deckard (R)*	94,127	48.1
Robert F. Arnove (CIT)	1,006	0.5
9 Lee H. Hamilton (D)*	121,094	67.1
Floyd E. Coates (R)	58,532	32.4
Stephen Arnold (CIT)	913	0.5
10 Andrew Jacobs Jr. (D)*	114,674	66.7

	Vote Total	Per-cent
Michael A. Carroll (R)	56,992	33.2
David W. Ellis (SOC WORK)	197	0.1

IOWA

Governor

	Vote Total	Per-cent
Roxanne Conlin (D)	483,291	46.5
Terry Branstad (R)	548,313	52.8
Marcia J. Farrington (LIBERT)	3,307	0.3
Jim Bittner (SOC)	2,767	0.3

House

		Vote Total	Per-cent
1	William E. Gluba (D)	61,734	40.8
	Jim Leach (R)*	89,585	59.2
2	Brent Appel (D)	69,539	41.1
	Tom Tauke (R)*	99,478	58.9
3	Lynn G. Cutler (D)	83,581	44.5
	Cooper Evans (R)*	104,072	55.5
4	Neal Smith (D)*	118,849	66.1
	Dave Readinger (R)	60,534	33.6
	Bill Douglas (SOC)	584	0.3
5	Tom Harkin (D)*	93,333	58.9
	Arlyn E. Danker (R)	65,200	41.1
6	Berkley Bedell (D)*	101,690	64.3
	Al Bremer (R)	56,487	35.7

KANSAS

Governor

	Vote Total	Per-cent
John Carlin (D)*	405,772	53.2
Sam Hardage (R)	339,356	44.4
Frank W. Shelton Jr. (AM)	6,136	0.8
James H. Ward (LIBERT)	7,595	1.0
Warren C. Martin (P)	4,404	0.6

House

		Vote Total	Per-cent
1	Kent Roth (D)	51,079	30.2
	Pat Roberts (R)*	115,749	68.4
	Kent Earnest (LIBERT)	2,305	1.4
2	Jim Slattery (D)	86,286	57.4
	Morris Kay (R)	63,942	42.6
3	William L. Kostar (D)	53,140	38.3
	Larry Winn Jr. (R)*	82,117	59.2
	Gene R. Blair (LIBERT)	3,439	2.5
4	Dan Glickman (D)*	107,326	73.9
	Gerald Caywood (R)	35,478	24.5
	Karl Peterjohn (LIBERT)	2,363	1.6
5	Lee Rowe (D)	47,676	31.1
	Bob Whittaker (R)*	103,551	67.6
	John L. Conger (LIBERT)	1,894	1.3

KENTUCKY

House

		Vote Total	Per-cent
1	Carroll Hubbard Jr. (D)*	X	100.0
2	William H. Natcher (D)*	49,571	73.8
	Mark T. Watson (R)	17,561	26.2
3	Romano L. Mazzoli (D)*	92,849	65.1
	Carl Brown (R)	45,900	32.2
	Dan Murray (LIBERT)	608	0.4
	Craig Honts (SOC)	400	0.3
	Norbert D. Leveronne (I)	2,840	2.0
4	Terry L. Mann (D)	61,937	45.3
	Gene Snyder (R)*	74,109	54.2
	Paul Thiel (LIBERT)	704	0.5
5	Doye Davenport (D)	28,285	34.8
	Harold Rogers (R)*	52,928	65.2
6	Don Mills (D)	49,836	41.4
	Larry J. Hopkins (R)*	68,418	56.8
	Ken Ashby (LIBERT)	1,185	1.0
	Don B. Pratt (I)	917	0.8

		Vote Total	Per-cent
7	Carl D. Perkins (D)*	82,463	79.4
	Tom Hamby (R)	21,436	20.6

LOUISIANA

House

		Vote Total	Per-cent
1	Bob Livingston (R)*	X	100.0
2	Lindy (Mrs. Hale) Boggs (D)*	X	100.0
3	W. J. "Billy" Tauzin (D)*	X	100.0
4	Buddy Roemer (D)*	X	100.0
5	Jerry Huckaby (D)*	X	100.0
6	Henson Moore (R)*	X	100.0
7	John B. Breaux (D)*	X	100.0
8	Gillis W. Long (D)*	X	100.0

MAINE

Governor

	Vote Total	Per-cent
Joseph E. Brennan (D)*	281,066	61.1
Charles L. Cragin (R)	172,949	37.6
J. Martin Bachon (I)	2,573	0.5
Vern Warren (I)	3,650	0.8

Senator

	Vote Total	Per-cent
George J. Mitchell (D)*	279,819	60.9
David F. Emery (R)	179,882	39.1

House

		Vote Total	Per-cent
1	John M. Kerry (D)	118,884	47.9
	John R. McKernan Jr. (R)	124,850	50.4
	Gregory J. Fleming (I)	4,221	1.7
2	James Patrick Dunleavy (D)	68,086	33.4
	Olympia J. Snowe (R)*	136,075	66.6

MARYLAND

Governor

	Vote Total	Per-cent
Harry R. Hughes (D)*	705,910	62.0
Robert A. Pascal (R)	432,826	38.0

Senator

	Vote Total	Per-cent
Paul S. Sarbanes (D)*	707,356	63.5
Lawrence J. Hogan (R)	407,334	36.5

House

		Vote Total	Per-cent
1	Roy Dyson (D)*	89,503	69.3
	C. A. Porter Hopkins (R)	39,656	30.7
2	Clarence D. Long (D)*	83,318	52.6
	Helen Delich Bentley (R)	75,062	47.4
3	Barbara A. Mikulski (D)*	110,042	74.2
	H. Robert Scherr (R)	38,259	25.8
4	Patricia O'Brien Aiken (D)	47,947	38.8
	Marjorie S. Holt (R)*	75,617	61.2
5	Steny H. Hoyer (D)*	83,937	79.6
	William P. Guthrie (R)	21,533	20.4
6	Beverly B. Byron (D)*	102,596	74.4
	Roscoe Bartlett (R)	35,321	25.6
7	Parren J. Mitchell (D)*	103,496	87.9
	M. Leonora Jones (R)	14,203	12.1
8	Michael D. Barnes (D)*	121,761	71.3
	Elizabeth W. Spencer (R)	48,910	28.7

MASSACHUSETTS

Governor

	Vote Total	Per-cent
Michael S. Dukakis (D)	1,219,109	59.4
John W. Sears (R)	749,679	36.6
Rebecca Shipman (LIBERT)	17,918	0.9
Frank Rich (I)	63,068	3.1

Senator

	Vote Total	Per-cent
Edward M. Kennedy (D)*	1,247,084	60.8
Raymond Shamie (R)	784,602	38.3

		Vote Total	Per-cent
	Howard Katz (LIBERT)	18,878	0.9

House

		Vote Total	Per-cent
1	Silvio O. Conte (R, D)*	X	100.0
2	Edward P. Boland (D)*	118,215	72.6
	Thomas P. Swank (R)	44,544	27.4
3	Joseph D. Early (D)*	X	100.0
4	Barney Frank (D)*	121,802	59.5
	Margaret M. Heckler (R)*	82,804	40.5
5	James M. Shannon (D)*	140,177	84.7
	Angelo Laudani (LIBERT)	25,224	15.2
6	Nicholas Mavroules (D)*	117,723	57.8
	Thomas H. Trimarco (R)	85,849	42.2
7	Edward J. Markey (D)*	151,305	77.8
	David Basile (R)	43,063	22.2
8	Thomas P. O'Neill Jr. (D)*	123,296	74.9
	Frank Luke McNamara Jr. (R)	41,370	25.1
9	Joe Moakley (D)*	102,665	64.1
	Deborah R. Cochran (R)	55,030	34.3
	Valerie Eckart (SOC WORK)	2,527	1.6
10	Gerry E. Studds (D)*	138,418	68.7
	John E. Conway (R)	63,014	31.3
11	Brian J. Donnelly (D)*	X	100.0

MICHIGAN

Governor

	Vote Total	Per-cent
James J. Blanchard (D)	1,561,291	51.4
Richard H. Headlee (R)	1,369,582	45.1
James Phillips (AMI)	7,356	0.2
Richard Jacobs (LIBERT)	15,603	0.5
Tim Crane (SOC WORK)	3,682	0.1
Martin McLaughlin (WL)	1,980	0.1
Robert Tisch (I)	80,288	2.6

Senator

	Vote Total	Per-cent
Donald W. Riegle Jr. (D)*	1,728,793	57.7
Philip E. Ruppe (R)	1,223,288	40.9
Daniel Eller (AMI)	12,660	0.4
Bette Erwin (LIBERT)	19,131	0.6
Steve Beumer (SOC WORK)	4,335	0.2
Helen Halyard (WL)	6,085	0.2

House

		Vote Total	Per-cent
1	John Conyers Jr. (D)*	125,517	96.7
	Bill Krebaum (LIBERT)	3,186	2.4
	Eddie Benjamin (WL)	1,140	0.9
2	George Wahr Sallade (D)	53,040	32.5
	Carl D. Pursell (R)*	106,960	65.4
	Barbara J. McKenna (LIBERT)	3,412	2.1
3	Howard Wolpe (D)*	96,842	56.3
	Richard L. Milliman (R)	73,315	42.6
	Lizzie M. Hudson (AMI)	693	0.4
	Robert S. Holderbaum (LIBERT)	1,111	0.7
4	David A. Masiokas (D)	56,877	38.8
	Mark Siljander (R)*	87,489	59.7
	Robert C. Drenkhahn (AMI)	690	0.5
	Richard Wagner (LIBERT)	1,544	1.0
5	Stephen V. Monsma (D)	87,229	46.9
	Harold S. Sawyer (R)*	98,650	53.1
6	Bob Carr (D)	84,778	51.4
	Jim Dunn (R)*	78,388	47.5
	James E. Hurrell (LIBERT)	1,818	1.1
7	Dale E. Kildee (D)*	118,538	75.4
	George R. Darrah (R)	36,303	23.1
	Dennis L. Berry (LIBERT)	1,842	1.2
	David Freund (WL)	568	0.3
8	Bob Traxler (D)*	113,515	91.0
	Sheila M. Hart (LIBERT)	11,219	9.0
9	Gerald D. Warner (D)	60,932	35.1

	Vote Total	Per-cent
Guy Vander Jagt (R)*	112,504	64.9
10 Don Albosta (D)*	102,048	60.1
Lawrence W. Reed (R)	66,080	39.0
William Spiers (LIBERT)	1,558	0.9
11 Kent Bourland (D)	69,181	39.5
Robert W. Davis (R)*	106,039	60.5
12 David E. Bonior (D)*	103,851	65.9
Ray Contesti (R)	52,312	33.2
Keith P. Edwards (LIBERT)	1,501	0.9
13 George W. Crockett Jr. (D)*	108,351	88.0
Letty Gupta (R)	13,732	11.1
Fred Mazelis (WL)	1,107	0.9
14 Dennis M. Hertel (D)*	116,421	95.0
Harold H. Dunn (LIBERT)	6,175	5.0
15 William D. Ford (D)*	94,950	72.8
Mitchell Moran (R)	33,904	26.0
Guy R. Collins (AMI)	1,555	1.2
16 John D. Dingell (D)*	114,006	73.7
David K. Haskins (R)	39,227	25.3
Susan Apstein (SOC WORK)	1,071	0.7
Paul Scherrer (WL)	450	0.3
17 Sander Levin (D)	116,901	66.6
Gerald E. Rosen (R)	55,620	31.7
Virginia L. Cropsey (LIBERT)	2,955	1.7
18 Allen J. Sipher (D)	46,545	25.7
William S. Broomfield (R)*	132,902	73.3
Joseph Cote (LIBERT)	1,813	1.0

MINNESOTA

Governor

	Vote Total	Per-cent
Rudy Perpich (DFL)	1,049,104	58.8
Wheelock Whitney (I-R)	711,796	39.9
Franklin H. Haws (LIBERT)	6,323	0.3
Kathy Wheeler (SOC WORK)	10,332	0.6
Tom McDonald (I)	7,984	0.4

Senator

	Vote Total	Per-cent
Mark Dayton (DFL)	840,401	46.6
David Durenberger (I-R)*	949,207	52.6
Fred G. Hewitt (LIBERT)	5,870	0.3
Jeffrey M. Miller (NU)	3,300	0.2
Bill Onasch (SOC WORK)	5,897	0.3

House

	Vote Total	Per-cent
1 Timothy J. Penny (DFL)	109,257	51.2
Tom Hagedorn (I-R)*	102,298	47.9
Clare H. Jarvis (LIBERT)	1,965	0.9
2 James W. Nichols (DFL)	103,243	45.5
Vin Weber (I-R)*	123,508	54.5
3 Joel Saliterman (DFL)	60,993	26.4
Bill Frenzel (I-R)*	166,891	72.1
Richard Laybourn (CIT)	3,427	1.5
4 Bruce F. Vento (DFL)*	153,494	73.2
Bill James (I-R)	56,248	26.8
5 Martin Olav Sabo (DFL)*	136,634	65.5
Keith W. Johnson (I-R)	61,184	29.4
Kathryn Anderson (CIT)	8,143	3.9
Thomas Wicklund (LIBERT)	2,491	1.2
6 Gerry Sikorski (DFL)	109,246	50.8
Arlen Erdahl (I-R)*	105,734	49.2
7 Gene Wenstrom (DFL)	107,062	49.7
Arlan Stangeland (I-R)*	108,254	50.3
8 James L. Oberstar (DFL)*	176,392	76.7
Marjory L. Luce (I-R)	53,467	23.3

MISSISSIPPI

Senator

	Vote Total	Per-cent
John C. Stennis (D)*	414,099	64.2
Haley Barbour (R)	230,927	35.8

House

	Vote Total	Per-cent
1 Jamie L. Whitten (D)*	79,726	70.9
Fran Fawcett (R)	32,750	29.1
2 Robert G. Clark (D)	71,536	48.4
Webb Franklin (R)	74,450	50.3
William V. Harris (I)	1,887	1.3
3 G. V. "Sonny" Montgomery (D)*	114,530	93.1
James Bradshaw (I)	8,519	6.9
4 Wayne Dowdy (D)*	79,977	52.6
Liles Williams (R)	69,469	45.6
Eddie L. McBride (I)	2,770	1.8
5 Arlon "Blackie" Coate (D)	22,634	21.5
Trent Lott (R)*	82,884	78.5

MISSOURI

Senator

	Vote Total	Per-cent
Harriett Woods (D)	758,629	49.1
John C. Danforth (R)*	784,876	50.9

House

	Vote Total	Per-cent
1 William Clay (D)*	102,656	66.1
William E. White (R)	52,599	33.9
2 Robert A. Young (D)*	100,770	56.5
Harold L. Dielmann (R)	77,433	43.5
3 Richard A. Gephardt (D)*	131,566	77.9
Richard Foristel (R)	37,388	22.1
4 Ike Skelton (D)*	96,388	54.8
Wendell Bailey (R)*	79,565	45.2
5 Alan Wheat (D)	96,059	57.9
John A. Sharp (R)	66,664	40.1
Kathie A. Fitzgerald (SOC WORK)	1,141	0.7
Alan H. Deright (I)	2,125	1.3
6 Jim Russell (D)	79,053	44.7
E. Thomas Coleman (R)*	97,993	55.3
7 David A. Geisler (D)	89,549	49.5
Gene Taylor (R)*	91,391	50.5
8 Jerry Ford (D)	76,413	46.9
Bill Emerson (R)*	86,493	53.1
9 Harold L. Volkmer (D)*	99,228	60.8
Larry E. Mead (R)	63,942	39.2

MONTANA

Senator

	Vote Total	Per-cent
John Melcher (D)*	174,861	54.4
Larry Williams (R)	133,789	41.7
Larry Dodge (LIBERT)	12,412	3.9

House

	Vote Total	Per-cent
1 Pat Williams (D)*	100,087	59.7
Bob Davies (R)	62,402	37.2
Don Doig (LIBERT)	5,113	3.1
2 Howard Lyman (D)	65,815	44.2
Ron Marlenee (R)*	79,968	53.7
Westley F. Deitchler (LIBERT)	3,154	2.1

NEBRASKA

Governor

	Vote Total	Per-cent
Bob Kerrey (D)	277,436	50.7
Charles Thone (R)*	270,203	49.3

Senator

	Vote Total	Per-cent
Edward Zorinsky (D)*	363,350	66.6
Jim Keck (R)	155,760	28.5
Virginia Walsh (I)	26,443	4.9

House

	Vote Total	Per-cent
1 Curt Donaldson (D)	45,676	24.9
Douglas K. Bereuter (R)*	137,675	75.1
2 Richard M. Fellman (D)	70,431	43.1
Hal Daub (R)*	92,639	56.7

	Vote Total	Per-cent
3 Virginia Smith (R)*	X	100.0

NEVADA

Governor

	Vote Total	Per-cent
Richard H. Bryan (D)	128,132	53.4
Robert F. List (R)*	100,104	41.8
Dan Becan (LIBERT)	4,621	1.9
None of the Above	6,894	2.9

Senator

	Vote Total	Per-cent
Howard W. Cannon (D)*	114,720	47.7
Chic Hecht (R)	120,377	50.1
None of the Above	5,297	2.2

House

	Vote Total	Per-cent
1 Harry Reid (D)	61,901	57.5
Peggy Cavnar (R)	45,675	42.5
2 Mary Gojack (D)	52,265	41.3
Barbara Vucanovich (R)	70,188	55.5
Teresa Vuceta (LIBERT)	4,043	3.2

NEW HAMPSHIRE

Governor

	Vote Total	Per-cent
Hugh Gallen (D)*	132,287	46.4
John H. Sununu (R)	147,774	51.9
Meldrim Thomson Jr. (I)	4,785	1.7

House

	Vote Total	Per-cent
1 Norman E. D'Amours (D)*	76,281	54.9
Robert C. Smith (R)	61,876	44.6
William C. Mackenzie (I)	752	0.5
2 Robert L. Dupay (D)	37,854	29.1
Judd Gregg (R)*	92,098	70.9

NEW JERSEY

Senator

	Vote Total	Per-cent
Frank R. Lautenberg (D)	1,117,549	50.9
Millicent Fenwick (R)	1,047,626	47.7
Henry Koch (LIBERT)	9,934	0.5
Julius Levin (SOC LAB)	5,580	0.3
Claire Moriarty (SOC WORK)	3,726	0.2
Robert T. Bastien (I)	2,955	0.1
Rose Zeidwerg Monyek (I)	1,830	0.1
Martin E. Wendelken (I)	4,745	0.2

House

	Vote Total	Per-cent
1 James J. Florio (D)*	110,570	73.3
John A. Dramesi (R)	39,501	26.2
Jerry Zeldin (LIBERT)	493	0.3
Patrick J. McCann (SOC LAB)	327	0.2
2 William J. Hughes (D)*	102,826	68.0
John J. Mahoney (R)	47,069	31.2
Bruce Powers (LIBERT)	1,233	0.8
3 James J. Howard (D)*	104,055	62.3
Marie Sheehan Muhler (R)	60,515	36.2
John Kinnevy III (CIT)	785	0.5
Lee A. Gesner Jr. (LIBERT)	701	0.4
Lawrence D. Erickson (SOC)	436	0.3
Joseph B. Hawley (I)	504	0.3
4 Joseph P. Merlino (D)	75,658	46.5
Christopher H. Smith (R)*	85,660	52.7
Bill Harris (LIBERT)	662	0.4
Eugene A. Creech (WF)	241	0.2
Paul B. Rizzo (I)	374	0.2
5 Fritz Cammerzell (D)	53,659	33.5
Marge Roukema (R)*	104,695	65.3
William J. Zelko Jr. (LIBERT)	2,004	1.2
6 Bernard J. Dwyer (D)*	100,418	68.1
Bertram L. Buckler (R)	46,093	31.3
Charles M. Hart (LIBERT)	920	0.6

		Vote Total	Per-cent
7	Adam K. Levin (D)	70,978	43.2
	Matthew J. Rinaldo (R)*	91,837	56.0
	Donald B. Siano (LIBERT)	1,294	0.8
8	Robert A. Roe (D)*	89,980	70.7
	Norm Robertson (R)	36,317	28.5
	Sidney J. Pope (LIBERT)	1,000	0.8
9	Robert G. Torricelli (D)	99,090	53.0
	Harold C. Hollenbeck (R)*	86,022	46.0
	Robert Shapiro (LIBERT)	1,767	1.0
10	Peter W. Rodino Jr. (D)*	76,684	82.6
	Timothy Lee Jr. (R)	14,551	15.7
	Katherine Florentine (LIBERT)	958	1.0
	Christine Keno (I)	659	0.7
11	Joseph G. Minish (D)*	105,607	64.3
	Rey Redington (R)	57,099	34.8
	Richard Roth (LIBERT)	1,531	0.9
12	Jeff Connor (D)	57,049	32.3
	Jim Courter (R)*	117,793	66.8
	Harold F. Leiendecker (LIBERT)	1,610	0.9
13	George Callas (D)	65,820	39.1
	Edwin B. Forsythe (R)*	100,061	59.5
	Paula Volpe (CIT)	955	0.6
	Don Smith (CST)	651	0.4
	Leonard T. Flynn (LIBERT)	769	0.4
14	Frank J. Guarini (D)*	94,021	74.3
	Charles J. Catrillo (R)	28,257	22.3
	Louis J. Sicilia (LIBERT)	471	0.4
	Kenneth Famularo (I)	921	0.7
	Jack Murphy (I)	1,704	1.3
	Herbert H. Shaw (I)	1,232	1.0

NEW MEXICO

Governor

	Vote Total	Per-cent
Toney Anaya (D)	215,840	53.0
John B. Irick (R)	191,626	47.0

Senator

	Vote Total	Per-cent
Jeff Bingaman (D)	217,682	53.8
Harrison "Jack" Schmitt (R)*	187,128	46.2

House

		Vote Total	Per-cent
1	Jan Alan Hartke (D)	67,534	47.6
	Manuel Lujan Jr. (R)*	74,459	52.4
2	Caleb Chandler (D)	50,599	41.6
	Joe Skeen (R)*	71,021	58.4
3	Bill Richardson (D)	84,669	64.5
	Marjorie Bell Chambers (R)	46,466	35.4
	David Arturo Fernandez (write-in)	158	0.1

NEW YORK

Governor

	Vote Total	Per-cent
Mario M. Cuomo (D, L)	2,675,213	50.9
Lew Lehrman (R, C, I)	2,494,827	47.5
John J. Northrup (F LIBERT)	16,913	0.3
Nancy Ross (NA)	5,277	0.1
Diane Wang (SOC WORK)	3,766	0.1
Robert J. Bohner (RTL)	52,356	1.0
Jane Benedict (UN)	6,353	0.1

Senator

	Vote Total	Per-cent
Daniel Patrick Moynihan (D,L)*	3,232,146	65.1
Florence Sullivan (R, C, RTL)	1,696,766	34.1
James J. McKeown (F LIBERT)	23,379	0.5
Steven Wattenmaker (SOC WORK)	15,206	0.3

House

		Vote Total	Per-cent
1	Ethan C. Eldon (D)	49,787	36.1

		Vote Total	Per-cent
	William Carney (R, C, RTL)*	88,234	63.9
2	Thomas J. Downey (D)*	80,951	63.9
	Paul G. Costello (R, C)	42,790	33.8
	Lewis VanDenEssen (RTL)	2,971	2.3
3	Robert J. Mrazek (D)	93,846	51.8
	John LeBoutillier (R, C)*	83,238	46.0
	Richard G. Bohner (RTL)	4,049	2.2
4	Robert P. Zimmerman (D, L)	63,390	36.3
	Norman F. Lent (R, C)*	105,241	60.4
	John J. Dunkle (RTL)	5,717	3.3
5	Arnold J. Miller (D, L)	67,002	38.8
	Raymond J. McGrath (R, C)*	100,485	58.1
	Thomas J. Boyle (RTL)	4,911	2.8
	Richard Horan (F LIBERT)	490	0.3
6	Joseph P. Addabbo (D, R, L)*	95,483	95.9
	Mark E. Scott (C)	4,074	4.1
7	Benjamin S. Rosenthal (D, L)*	84,013	77.2
	Albert Lemishow (R, C, RTL)	24,832	22.8
8	James H. Scheuer (D, L)*	91,830	89.5
	John T. Blume (C)	10,741	10.5
9	Geraldine A. Ferraro (D)*	75,286	73.2
	John J. Weigandt (R)	20,352	19.8
	Ralph G. Groves (C, RTL)	6,011	5.9
	Patricia A. Salargo (L)	1,171	1.1
10	Charles E. Schumer (D, L)*	89,852	79.2
	Stephen Marks (R, C)	21,726	19.1
	Alice J. Bertolotti (RTL)	1,873	1.7
11	Edolphus Towns (D)	39,357	83.7
	James W. Smith (R)	4,449	9.5
	Joseph N. O. Caesar (C, RTL)	1,357	2.9
	Patrick W. Giagnacova (L)	1,488	3.2
	Susan C. Zarate (SOC WORK)	359	0.7
12	Major R. Owens (D, L)	44,586	90.5
	David Katan Sr. (R)	3,215	6.5
	David E. Rosenstroch (C)	1,005	2.1
	Jahn-Clymer Francis (RTL)	453	0.9
13	Stephen J. Solarz (D, L)*	68,549	80.5
	Leon F. Nadrowski (R, RTL)	14,257	16.8
	James M. Gay (C)	2,324	2.7
14	Leo C. Zeferetti (D)*	51,728	42.9
	Guy V. Molinari (R, C, RTL)*	67,626	56.1
	Carl F. Grillo (L)	1,276	1.0
15	Betty G. Lall (D, L)	55,483	44.8
	Bill Green (R)*	66,262	53.6
	Henry Van Rossem (C)	1,953	1.6
16	Charles B. Rangel (D, R, L)*	76,626	97.5
	Michael T. Berns (C)	1,261	1.6
	Veronica Cruz (SOC WORK)	718	0.9
17	Ted Weiss (D, L)*	113,172	85.0
	Louis S. Antonelli (R, C, RTL)	19,928	15.0
18	Robert Garcia (D, R, L)*	57,009	98.9
	Rafael Perez (POPULAR)	655	1.1
19	Mario Biaggi (D, R, L, RTL)*	118,803	93.7
	Michael J. McSherry (C)	7,438	5.9
	Eva Chertov (SOC WORK)	584	0.4
20	Richard L. Ottinger (D)*	98,425	56.5
	Jon S. Fossel (R, C)	72,005	41.3
	Florence T. O'Grady (RTL)	3,798	2.2
21	J. Morgan Strong (D)	38,664	24.8
	Hamilton Fish Jr. (R, C)*	117,460	75.2
22	Peter A. Peyser (D)*	73,124	42.0
	Benjamin A. Gilman (R)*	92,266	52.9
	Charles C. Beck (C)	4,877	2.8
	Richard Bruno (RTL)	4,019	2.3
23	Samuel S. Stratton (D)*	164,427	76.1
	Frank Wicks (R, NF)	41,386	19.2
	Mark A. Dunlea (CIT)	1,119	0.5
	John G. Dow (L)	8,492	3.9
	Patricia A. Mayberry		

		Vote Total	Per-cent
	(SOC WORK)	659	0.3
24	Roy Esiason (D)	49,441	26.1
	Gerald B. H. Solomon (R, C, RTL)*	140,296	73.9
25	Anita Maxwell (D)	70,793	42.4
	Sherwood L. Boehlert (R)	93,071	55.8
	Donald J. Thomas (RTL)	2,963	1.8
26	David P. Landy (D)	43,208	28.4
	David O'B. Martin (R, C)*	108,962	71.6
27	Elaine Lytel (D, L)	79,209	44.2
	George C. Wortley (R)*	95,290	53.2
	Thomas M. Hunter (C)	2,783	1.5
	George Hyrcza (RTL)	1,904	1.1
28	Matthew F. McHugh (D, L)*	100,665	56.4
	David F. Crowley (R, C)	75,991	42.5
	Mark Masterson (RTL)	2,003	1.1
29	William C. Larsen (D)	47,463	30.2
	Frank Horton (R)*	104,412	66.4
	Edwin Lundberg (C)	5,370	3.4
30	Bill Benet (D)	48,764	27.9
	Barber B. Conable Jr. (R)*	119,105	68.2
	Richard G. Baxter (C)	3,853	2.2
	David J. Valone (RTL)	2,898	1.7
31	James A. Martin (D, L)	43,843	24.7
	Jack F. Kemp (R, C)*	133,462	75.3
32	John J. LaFalce (D, L)*	116,386	91.4
	Raymond R. Walker (R, C)	8,638	6.8
	Timothy J. Hubbard (RTL)	2,359	1.8
33	Henry J. Nowak (D, L)*	126,091	84.1
	Walter J. Pillich (R, C)	19,791	13.2
	James Gallagher (RTL)	4,095	2.7
34	Stanley N. Lundine (D)*	99,502	60.2
	James J. Snyder (R, C)	63,972	38.7
	Genevieve F. Ronan (RTL)	1,806	1.1

NORTH CAROLINA

House

		Vote Total	Per-cent
1	Walter B. Jones (D)*	79,954	81.3
	James F. McIntyre III (R)	17,478	17.8
	Bobby Yates Emory (LIBERT)	910	0.9
2	I. T. "Tim" Valentine Jr. (D)	59,617	53.5
	John W. Marin (R)	34,293	30.8
	Sue Lamm (LIBERT)	1,426	1.3
	H. M. Michaux Jr. (write-in)	15,990	14.4
3	Charles Whitley (D)*	68,936	63.5
	Eugene "Red" McDaniel (R)	39,046	36.0
	Marshall Sprague (LIBERT)	491	0.5
4	Ike Andrews (D)*	70,369	51.3
	William Cobey Jr. (R)	64,955	47.4
	Fritz Prochnaw (LIBERT)	1,720	1.3
5	Stephen L. Neal (D)*	87,819	60.3
	Anne Bagnal (R)	57,083	39.2
	Naudeen Beek (LIBERT)	631	0.4
	Merly Lynn Farber (SOC WORK)	174	0.1
6	Charles Robin Britt (D)	68,696	53.8
	Eugene Johnston (R)*	58,244	45.7
	J. Erik Christensen (LIBERT)	679	0.5
7	Charlie Rose (D)*	68,529	71.0
	Edward Johnson (R)	27,015	28.0
	Richard Hollenbeak (LIBERT)	990	1.0
8	W. G. "Bill" Hefner (D)*	71,691	57.4
	Harris D. Blake (R)	52,417	41.9
	Don Scoggins (LIBERT)	830	0.7
9	Preston Cornelius (D)	47,258	41.9
	James G. Martin (R)*	64,297	57.0
	David Braatz (LIBERT)	1,231	1.1
10	James T. Broyhill (R)*	80,904	92.7
	Jhon Rankin (LIBERT)	6,360	7.3

Appendix

	Vote Total	Per-cent
11 James McClure Clarke (D)	85,410	49.9
Bill Hendon (R)*	84,085	49.2
Linda Janka (LIBERT)	1,552	0.9

NORTH DAKOTA

Senator

Quentin N. Burdick (D)*	164,873	62.8
Gene Knorr (R)	89,304	34.0
Anna Bourgois (I)	8,288	3.2

House

AL Byron L. Dorgan (D)*	186,534	71.6
Kent H. Jones (R)	72,241	27.7
Don J. Klingensmith (P)	1,724	0.7

OHIO

Governor

Richard F. Celeste (D)	1,981,882	59.0
Clarence J. Brown (R)	1,303,962	38.9
Phyllis Goetz (LIBERT)	39,114	1.2
Kurt O. Landefeld (I)	14,279	0.4
Erwin J. Reupert (I)	17,484	0.5

Senator

Howard M. Metzenbaum (D)*	1,923,767	56.7
Paul E. Pfeifer (R)	1,396,790	41.1
Philip Herzing (LIBERT)	36,103	1.1
Alicia Merel (I)	38,803	1.1

House

1 Thomas A. Luken (D)*	99,143	63.5
John "Jake" Held (R)	52,658	33.7
James A. Berns (LIBERT)	4,386	2.8
2 William J. Luttmer (D)	53,169	34.2
Bill Gradison (R)*	97,434	62.7
Charles K. Shrout Jr. (LIBERT)	2,948	1.9
Joseph I. Lombardo (I)	1,827	1.2
3 Tony P. Hall (D)*	119,926	87.7
Kathryn E. Brown (LIBERT)	16,828	12.3
4 Robert W. Moon (D)	57,564	35.4
Michael G. Oxley (R)*	105,087	64.6
5 James R. Sherck (D)	70,120	44.8
Delbert L. Latta (R)*	86,450	55.2
6 Lynn Alan Grimshaw (D)	63,435	40.8
Bob McEwen (R)*	92,135	59.2
7 Roger D. Tackett (D)	65,543	42.0
Michael Dewine (R)	87,842	56.2
John B. Winer (LIBERT)	2,761	1.8
8 John W. Griffin (D)	49,877	33.6
Thomas N. Kindness (R)*	98,527	66.4
9 Marcy Kaptur (D)	95,162	57.9
Ed Weber (R)*	64,459	39.3
David Muir (LIBERT)	1,217	0.7
Susan A. Skinner (I)	1,785	1.1
James J. Somers (I)	1,594	1.0
10 John M. Buchanan (D)	57,983	36.7
Clarence E. Miller (R)*	100,044	63.3
11 Dennis E. Eckart (D)*	93,302	60.9
Glen W. Warner (R)	56,616	36.9
Jim Russell (LIBERT)	3,324	2.2
12 Bob Shamansky (D)*	82,753	47.3
John R. Kasich (R)	88,335	50.5
Russell A. Lewis (LIBERT)	3,939	2.2
13 Don J. Pease (D)*	92,296	61.2
Timothy Paul Martin (R)	53,376	35.4
James S. Patton (LIBERT)	5,053	3.4
14 John F. Seiberling (D)*	115,629	70.5

	Vote Total	Per-cent
Louis A. Mangels (R)	48,421	29.5
15 Greg Kostelac (D)	47,070	29.8
Chalmers P. Wylie (R)*	104,678	66.3
Steve Kender (LIBERT)	6,139	3.9
16 Jeffrey R. Orenstein (D)	57,386	34.2
Ralph Regula (R)*	110,485	65.8
17 George D. Tablack (D)	80,375	44.9
Lyle Williams (R)*	98,476	55.1
18 Douglas Applegate (D)*	X	100.0
19 Edward F. Feighan (D)	111,760	58.8
Richard G. Anter II (R)	72,682	38.3
Thomas Pekarek (LIBERT)	3,129	1.6
Kevin G. Killeen (I)	2,371	1.3
20 Mary Rose Oakar (D)*	133,603	85.6
Paris T. LeJeune (R)	17,675	11.3
Milton R. Norris (LIBERT)	2,844	1.8
Louise Haberbush (I)	1,930	1.3
21 Louis Stokes (D)*	132,544	86.1
Alan G. Shatteen (R)	21,332	13.9

OKLAHOMA

Governor

George Nigh (D)*	548,159	62.1
Tom Daxon (R)	332,207	37.6
Allah-U Akbar Allah-U Wahid (I)	2,764	0.3

House

1 James R. Jones (D)*	76,379	54.1
Richard C. Freeman (R)	64,704	45.9
2 Mike Synar (D)*	111,895	72.6
Lou Striegel (R)	42,298	27.4
3 Wes Watkins (D)*	121,670	82.2
Patrick K. Miller (R)	26,335	17.8
4 Dave McCurdy (D)*	84,205	65.0
Howard Rutledge (R)	44,351	34.3
Charles T. Emerson (I)	507	0.4
Marshall A. Luse (I)	441	0.3
5 Dan Lane (D)	42,453	28.9
Mickey Edwards (R)*	98,979	67.2
Paul E. Trent (I)	5,777	3.9
6 Glenn English (D)*	102,811	75.4
Ed Moore (R)	33,519	24.6

OREGON

Governor

Ted Kulongoski (D)	374,316	35.9
Victor G. Atiyeh (R)*	639,841	61.4
Paul J. Cleveland (LIBERT)	27,394	2.7

House

1 Les AuCoin (D)*	118,638	53.8
Bill Moshofsky (R)	101,720	46.2
2 Larryann Willis (D)	85,495	44.4
Bob Smith (R)	106,912	55.6
3 Ron Wyden (D)*	159,416	78.3
Thomas H. Phelan (R)	44,162	21.7
4 James Weaver (D)*	115,448	59.1
Ross Anthony (R)	80,054	40.9
5 J. Ruth McFarland (D)	98,952	48.8
Denny Smith (R)*	103,906	51.2

PENNSYLVANIA

Governor

Allen E. Ertel (D)	1,772,353	48.1
Richard L. Thornburgh (R)*	1,872,784	50.8
Lee Frissell (CONSU)	13,101	0.4

	Vote Total	Per-cent
Richard D. Fuerle (LIBERT)	10,252	0.3
Mark Zola (SOC WORK)	15,495	0.4

Senator

Cyril H. Wecht (D)	1,412,965	39.2
John Heinz (R)*	2,136,418	59.3
Liane Norman (CONSU)	16,530	0.5
Barbara I. Karkutt (LIBERT)	19,244	0.5
Kipp M. Dawson (SOC WORK)	18,951	0.5

House

1 Thomas M. Foglietta (D)*	103,626	72.3
Michael Marino (R)	38,155	26.6
Lisa Brannan (CONSU)	1,063	0.7
Ralph Mullinger (LIBERT)	572	0.4
2 William H. Gray III (D)*	120,744	76.1
William C. Saunders (LIBERT)	2,726	1.7
Milton Street (I)	35,205	22.2
3 Robert A. Borski (D)	97,161	50.1
Charles F. Dougherty (R)*	94,497	48.7
Carolyn Berger (CONSU)	980	0.5
Bruce Bishkin (LIBERT)	435	0.2
Mike Finley (SOC WORK)	881	0.5
4 Joseph P. Kolter (D)	100,481	60.1
Eugene V. Atkinson (R)*	64,539	38.6
Sam Blancato (CONSU)	2,082	1.3
5 Bob Burger (D)	44,170	32.8
Richard T. Schulze (R)*	90,648	67.2
6 Gus Yatron (D)*	108,230	72.0
Harry B. Martin (R)	42,155	28.0
7 Robert W. Edgar (D)*	105,775	55.4
Steve Joachim (R)	85,023	44.6
8 Peter H. Kostmayer (D)	83,242	50.3
Jim Coyne (R)*	80,928	48.9
Hans G. Schroeder (LIBERT)	483	0.3
Albert H. Reef (I)	882	0.5
9 Eugene J. Duncan (D)	49,583	34.9
Bud Shuster (R)*	92,322	65.1
10 Robert J. Rafalko (D)	49,868	32.5
Joseph M. McDade (R)*	103,617	67.5
11 Frank Harrison (D)	90,371	53.5
James L. Nelligan (R)*	78,485	46.5
12 John P. Murtha (D)*	96,369	61.1
William N. Tuscano (R)	54,212	34.4
Joseph E. Krill (I)	7,059	4.5
13 Martin J. Cunningham Jr. (D)	59,709	35.2
Lawrence Coughlin (R)*	109,198	64.3
Nicholas Kyodnieus (LIBERT)	917	0.5
14 William J. Coyne (D)*	120,980	74.9
John R. Clark (R)	32,780	20.3
Richard E. Calligiuri (LIBERT)	5,437	3.3
William R. Kalman (SOC WORK)	2,380	1.5
15 Richard J. Orloski (D)	58,002	42.2
Don Ritter (R)*	79,455	57.8
16 Jean D. Mowery (D)	37,364	28.7
Robert S. Walker (R)*	93,034	71.3
17 Larry J. Hochendoner (D)	61,974	42.4
George W. Gekas (R)	84,291	57.6
18 Doug Walgren (D)*	101,807	54.2
Ted Jacob (R)	84,428	45.0
William A. Lewis Jr. (LIBERT)	1,448	0.8
19 Larry Becker (D)	41,787	29.2
Bill Goodling (R)*	101,163	70.8
20 Joseph M. Gaydos (D)*	127,281	76.0
Terry T. Ray (R)	38,212	22.8
David L. Travis (LIBERT)	1,935	1.2
21 Anthony "Buzz" Andrezeski (D)	79,451	49.8
Thomas J. Ridge (R)	80,180	50.2
22 Austin J. Murphy (D)*	123,716	78.7

	Vote Total	Per-cent
Frank J. Paterra (R)	32,176	20.5
Deann Rathbun (SOC WORK)	1,323	0.8
23 Joseph J. Calla Jr. (D)	49,297	34.8
William F. Clinger Jr. (R)*	92,424	65.2

RHODE ISLAND

Governor

	Vote Total	Per-cent
J. Joseph Garrahy (D)*	247,208	73.3
Vincent Marzullo (R)	79,602	23.6
Hilary Salk (CIT)	7,033	2.1
Peter Van Daam (JI)	3,405	1.0

Senator

	Vote Total	Per-cent
Julius C. Michaelson (D)	167,283	48.8
John H. Chafee (R)*	175,495	51.2

House

	Vote Total	Per-cent
1 Fernand J. St Germain (D)*	97,254	60.7
Burton Stallwood (R)	61,253	38.3
Gertrude M. Jayne Fowler (I)	1,624	1.0
2 James V. Aukerman (D)	76,769	44.4
Claudine Schneider (R)*	96,282	55.6

SOUTH CAROLINA

Governor

	Vote Total	Per-cent
Richard Riley (D)*	468,819	69.8
William D. Workman Jr. (R)	202,806	30.2

House

	Vote Total	Per-cent
1 W. Mullins McLeod (D)	52,916	44.9
Thomas F. Hartnett (R)*	63,945	54.3
Walter Smith (LIBERT)	971	0.8
2 Ken Mosely (D)	50,749	41.5
Floyd Spence (R)*	71,569	58.5
3 Butler Derrick (D)*	77,125	90.4
Gordon T. Davis (LIBERT)	8,214	9.6
4 Marion E. Tyus (D)	40,394	36.7
Carroll A. Campbell Jr. (R)*	69,802	63.3
5 John Spratt (D)	69,345	67.6
John S. Wilkerson (R)	33,191	32.4
6 Robert M. Tallon Jr. (D)	62,582	52.5
John L. Napier (R)*	56,653	47.5

SOUTH DAKOTA

Governor

	Vote Total	Per-cent
Mike O'Connor (D)	81,136	29.1
William J. Janklow (R)*	197,426	70.9

House

	Vote Total	Per-cent
AL Thomas A. Daschle (D)*	142,122	51.6
Clint Roberts (R)*	133,530	48.4

TENNESSEE

Governor

	Vote Total	Per-cent
Randy Tyree (D)	500,937	40.4
Lamar Alexander (R)*	737,963	59.6

Senator

	Vote Total	Per-cent
Jim Sasser (D)*	780,113	61.9
Robin L. Beard (R)	479,642	38.1

House

	Vote Total	Per-cent
1 Jessie J. Cable (D)	27,580	22.8
James H. Quillen (R)*	89,497	74.1
James B. "Peppy" Fields (I)	3,778	3.1
2 John J. Duncan (R)*	X	100.0
3 Marilyn Lloyd Bouquard (D)*	84,967	61.8
Glen Byers (R)	49,885	36.3
Henry Ford Brock (I)	2,640	1.9

	Vote Total	Per-cent
4 Jim Cooper (D)	93,453	66.1
Cissy Baker (R)	47,865	33.9
5 Bill Boner (D)*	109,282	80.2
Laural Steinhice (R)	27,061	19.8
6 Albert Gore Jr. (D)*	X	100.0
7 Bob Clement (D)	72,359	49.5
Don Sundquist (R)	73,835	50.5
8 Ed Jones (D)*	93,945	74.9
Bruce Benson (R)	31,527	25.1
9 Harold E. Ford (D)*	112,143	72.4
Joe Crawford (R)	40,812	26.4
Isaac Richmond (I)	1,874	1.2

TEXAS

Governor

	Vote Total	Per-cent
Mark White (D)	1,697,870	53.2
William Clements (R)*	1,465,937	45.9
Bob Poteet (CIT)	8,065	0.3
David Hutzelman (LIBERT)	19,143	0.6

Senator

	Vote Total	Per-cent
Lloyd Bentsen (D)*	1,818,223	58.6
James M. Collins (R)	1,256,759	40.5
Lineaus Hooper Lorette (CIT)	4,564	0.1
John E. Ford (LIBERT)	23,494	0.8

House

	Vote Total	Per-cent
1 Sam B. Hall Jr. (D)*	100,685	97.5
John Traylor (LIBERT)	2,598	2.5
2 Charles Wilson (D)*	91,762	94.3
Ed Richbourg (LIBERT)	5,584	5.7
3 James L. McNees Jr. (D)	28,223	21.8
Steve Bartlett (R)	99,852	77.1
Jerry R. Williamson (LIBERT)	1,453	1.1
4 Ralph M. Hall (D)*	94,134	73.8
Peter J. Collumb (R)	32,221	25.3
Bruce liams (LIBERT)	1,141	0.9
5 John Bryant (D)	52,214	64.8
Joe Devaney (R)	27,121	33.7
John Richard Bridges (CIT)	459	0.6
Richard Squire (R)	732	0.9
6 Phil Gramm (D)*	91,546	94.5
Ron Hard (LIBERT)	5,288	5.5
7 Dennis Scoggins (D)	17,866	14.0
Bill Archer (R)*	108,718	85.0
Bill Ware (LIBERT)	1,338	1.0
8 Henry E. Allee (D)	38,041	42.6
Jack Fields (R)*	50,630	56.8
Mike Angwin (LIBERT)	547	0.6
9 Jack Brooks (D)*	78,965	67.6
John W. Lewis (R)	35,422	30.3
Dean Allen (LIBERT)	2,510	2.1
10 J. J. Pickle (D)*	121,030	90.1
Bradley Louis Rockwell (CIT)	4,511	3.4
William G. Kelsey (LIBERT)	8,735	6.5
11 Marvin Leath (D)*	83,236	96.4
Tom Kilbride (LIBERT)	3,136	3.6
12 Jim Wright (D)*	78,913	68.9
Jim Ryan (R)	34,879	30.5
Ed Olson (LIBERT)	743	0.6
13 Jack Hightower (D)*	86,376	63.6
Ron Slover (R)	47,877	35.2
Rod Collier (LIBERT)	1,567	1.2
14 Bill Patman (D)*	76,851	60.7
Joe Wyatt Jr. (R)	48,942	38.6
Glenn Rasmussen (LIBERT)	919	0.7
15 E. "Kika" de la Garza (D)*	76,544	95.7
Frank L. Jones III (LIBERT)	3,458	4.3
16 Ronald Coleman (D)	44,024	53.9
Pat B. Haggerty (R)	36,064	44.2

	Vote Total	Per-cent
Catherin A. McDivitt (LIBERT)	1,583	1.9
17 Charles W. Stenholm (D)*	109,359	97.1
James Cooley II (LIBERT)	3,271	2.9
18 Mickey Leland (D)*	68,014	82.6
C. Leon Pickett (R)	12,104	14.7
Thomas P. Bernhardt (LIBERT)	2,215	2.7
19 Kent Hance (D)*	89,702	81.6
E. L. Hicks (R)	19,062	17.3
Mike Read (LIBERT)	1,206	1.1
20 Henry B. Gonzalez (D)*	68,544	91.5
Roger V. Gary (LIBERT)	4,163	5.6
Benedict D. La Rosa (I)	2,213	2.9
21 Charles S. Stough (D)	35,112	24.6
Tom Loeffler (R)*	106,515	74.5
Jeffrey J. Brown (LIBERT)	1,243	0.9
22 Ron Paul (R)*	X	100.0
23 Abraham Kazen Jr. (D)*	51,690	55.3
Jeff Wentworth (R)	41,363	44.2
Parker Abell (LIBERT)	475	0.5
24 Martin Frost (D)*	63,857	72.8
Lucy P. Patterson (R)	22,798	26.1
David Guier (LIBERT)	998	1.1
25 Mike Andrews (D)	63,974	60.4
Mike Faubion (R)	40,112	37.9
Barbara Coldiron (CIT)	963	0.9
Jeff Calvert (LIBERT)	864	0.8
26 Tom Vandergriff (D)	69,782	50.1
Jim Bradshaw (R)	69,438	49.9
27 Solomon P. Ortiz (D)	66,604	64.0
Jason Luby (R)	35,209	33.8
Steven R. Roberts (LIBERT)	2,231	2.2

UTAH

Senator

	Vote Total	Per-cent
Ted Wilson (D)	219,482	41.3
Orrin G. Hatch (R)*	309,332	58.3
Lawrence R. Kauffman (AM)	953	0.2
George Mercier (LIBERT)	1,035	0.2

House

	Vote Total	Per-cent
1 A. Stephen Dirks (D)	66,006	37.2
James V. Hansen (R)*	111,416	62.8
2 Frances Farley (D)	78,981	46.2
Dan Marriott (R)*	92,109	53.8
3 Howard C. Nielson (R)	108,478	76.9
Henry A. Huish (I-D)	32,661	23.1

VERMONT

Governor

	Vote Total	Per-cent
Madeleine M. Kunin (D)	74,394	44.0
Richard A. Snelling (R)*	93,111	55.0
John L. Buttolph (LIBERT)	801	0.5
Richard F. Gottlieb (LU)	850	0.5

Senator

	Vote Total	Per-cent
James A. Guest (D)	79,340	47.2
Robert T. Stafford (R)*	84,449	50.3
Ion Laskaris (CIT)	897	0.5
Bo Adlerbert (LIBERT)	892	0.5
Jerry Levy (LU)	774	0.5
Michael Hackett (I)	1,463	0.9

House

	Vote Total	Per-cent
AL Mark A. Kaplan (D)	38,296	23.2
James M. Jeffords (R)*	114,191	69.2
Robin Lloyd (CIT)	6,409	3.9
George Trask (LIBERT)	1,407	0.9
Peter Diamondstone (LU)	2,794	1.7
Morris Earle (I)	1,733	1.1

Appendix

VIRGINIA

	Vote Total	Per-cent
Senator		
Richard J. Davis (D)	690,839	48.8
Paul S. Trible Jr. (R)	724,571	51.2
House		
1 John J. McGlennon (D)	62,379	43.7
Herbert H. Bateman (R)	76,926	53.9
2 G. William Whitehurst (R)*	X	100.0
3 John A. Waldrop Jr. (D)	63,946	40.8
Thomas J. Bliley Jr. (R)*	92,928	59.2
4 Norman Sisisky (D)	80,695	54.4
Robert W. Daniel Jr. (R)*	67,708	45.6
5 Dan Daniel (D)*	X	100.0
6 James R. Olin (D)	68,192	49.7
Kevin G. Miller (R)	66,537	48.5
Robert L. Fariss (I)	2,395	1.8
7 Lindsay G. Dorrier Jr. (D)	46,514	36.3
J. Kenneth Robinson (R)*	76,752	59.8
David J. Toscano (I)	4,950	3.9
8 Herbert E. Harris II (D)	68,071	48.6
Stan Parris (R)*	69,620	49.7
Austin W. Morrill Jr. (I)	2,373	1.7
9 Frederick C. Boucher (D)	76,205	50.4
William C. Wampler (R)*	75,082	49.6
10 Ira M. Lechner (D)	75,361	46.0
Frank R. Wolf (R)*	86,506	52.7
Scott R. Bowden (I)	2,162	1.3

WASHINGTON

	Vote Total	Per-cent
Senator		
Henry M. Jackson (D)*	943,655	68.9
Doug Jewett (R)	332,273	24.3
Jesse Chiang (I)	20,251	1.5
King Lysen (I)	72,297	5.3
House		
1 Brian Long (D)	59,444	32.4
Joel Pritchard (R)*	123,956	67.6
2 Al Swift (D)*	101,383	59.6
Joan Houchen (R)	68,622	40.4
3 Don Bonker (D)*	97,323	60.1
J. T. Quigg (R)	59,686	36.8
O'Dean Williamson (I)	5,049	3.1

	Vote Total	Per-cent
4 Charles D. Kilbury (D)	45,990	28.6
Sid Morrison (R)*	112,148	69.8
Michael Leroy Burns (FP)	2,530	1.6
5 Thomas S. Foley (D)*	109,549	64.3
John Sonneland (R)	60,816	35.7
6 Norman D. Dicks (D)*	89,985	62.5
Ted Haley (R)	47,720	33.2
Jayne H. Anderson (I)	6,193	4.3
7 Mike Lowry (D)*	126,313	70.9
Bob Dorse (R)	51,759	29.1
8 Beth Bland (D)	59,824	43.0
Rodney Chandler (R)	79,209	57.0

WEST VIRGINIA

	Vote Total	Per-cent
Senator		
Robert C. Byrd (D)*	387,170	68.5
Cleve Benedict (R)	173,910	30.8
William B. Hovland (SOC WORK)	4,234	0.7
House		
1 Alan B. Mollohan (D)	79,529	53.2
John F. McCuskey (R)	70,069	46.8
2 Harley O. Staggers Jr. (D)	87,904	64.0
J. D. Hinkle Jr. (R)	49,413	36.0
3 Bob Wise (D)	84,619	57.9
David Michael Staton (R)*	60,844	41.6
Adrienne Benjamin (SOC WORK)	787	0.5
4 Nick J. Rahall II (D)*	91,184	80.5
Homer L. Harris (R)	22,054	19.5

WISCONSIN

	Vote Total	Per-cent
Governor		
Anthony S. Earl (D)	896,812	56.8
Terry J. Kohler (R)	662,838	41.9
James P. Wickstrom (CST)	7,721	0.5
Larry Smiley (LIBERT)	9,734	0.6
Peter Seidman (I)	3,025	0.2
Senator		
William Proxmire (D)*	983,311	63.7
Scott McCallum (R)	527,355	34.1
Sanford G. Knapp (CST)	4,463	0.3

	Vote Total	Per-cent
George Liljenfeldt (LIBERT)	7,947	0.5
William Osborne Hart (I)	21,807	1.4
House		
1 Les Aspin (D)*	95,055	61.0
Peter N. Jannson (R)	59,309	38.1
Arthur F. Jackson (LIBERT)	1,438	0.9
2 Robert W. Kastenmeier (D)*	112,677	60.6
Jim Johnson (R)	71,989	38.7
David Beito (LIBERT)	1,368	0.7
3 Paul Offner (D)	75,132	42.8
Steve Gunderson (R)*	99,304	56.6
Kenneth P. Van Doren (LIBERT)	1,027	0.6
4 Clement J. Zablocki (D)*	129,557	94.5
John Gudenschwager (CST)	946	0.7
Nicholas P. Youngers (LIBERT)	4,064	3.0
John F. Baumgartner (I)	2,421	1.8
5 Jim Moody (D)	99,713	63.6
Rod K. Johnston (R)	54,826	34.9
William G. McCuen Jr. (LIBERT)	1,498	1.0
Walter G. Beach (I)	526	0.3
Cheryll Y. Hidalgo (I)	353	0.2
6 Gordon E. Loehr (D)	59,922	35.0
Thomas E. Petri (R)*	111,348	65.0
7 David R. Obey (D)*	122,124	68.0
Bernard A. Zimmerman (R)	57,535	32.0
8 Ruth C. Clusen (D)	74,436	42.0
Toby Roth (R)*	101,379	57.2
Anthony Theisen (LIBERT)	1,336	0.8
9 F. James Sensenbrenner Jr. (R)*	X	100.0

WYOMING

	Vote Total	Per-cent
Governor		
Ed Herschler (D)*	106,427	63.1
Warren A. Morton (R)	62,128	36.9
Senator		
Rodger McDaniel (D)	72,466	43.3
Malcolm Wallop (R)*	94,725	56.7
House		
AL Ted Hommel (D)	46,041	28.9
Dick Cheney (R)*	113,236	71.1

98th Congress Special, 1983 Gubernatorial Returns

1983 Gubernatorial Elections

LOUISIANA	Vote Total	Percent
Edwin W. Edwards (D)	1,006,561	62.3
David C. Treen (R)	588,508	36.4
Others	20,836	1.3

KENTUCKY		
Martha L. Collins (D)	561,674	54.5
Jim Bunning (R)	454,650	44.1
Nicholas McCubbin (I)	14,347	1.4

MISSISSIPPI	Vote Total	Percent
Bill Allain (D)	409,209	55.1
Leon Bramlett (R)	288,764	38.9
Charles Evers (I)	30,593	4.1
Billy Taylor (I)	7,869	1.0
Helen M. Williams (I)	6,302	.8

Special House Elections, 98th Congress

TEXAS — Feb. 12, 1983	Vote Total	Percent
Phil Gramm (R)	46,371	55.3
Dan Kubiak (D)	33,201	39.6
John Henry Faulk (D)	3,070	3.7
Bill Powers (D)	318	.4
Rex L. Carey (D)	268	.3
H. Martin Gibson	223	.3
George M. Chamberlain (D)	153	.2
Louis C. Davis (D)	84	.1
Joe R. English (D)	80	.1
Carl A. Nigliazzo (D)	78	.1
Joseph Agris (D)	59	.1

NEW YORK — March 1, 1983		
Gary L. Ackerman (D,L)	18,388	48.7
Albert Lemishow (R,C,QI)	8,331	22.1
Douglas F. Schoen (N)	5,997	15.9
Sheldon Leffler (I)	4,318	11.4
Unrecorded	690	1.8

COLORADO — March 29, 1983		
Daniel L. Schaefer (R)	49,816	63.3
Steve Hogan (D)	27,779	35.3
John Heckman (I)	1,112	1.4

CALIFORNIA — June 21, 1983		
Sala Burton (D)	44,790	56.9
Dunan Howard (R)	18,305	23.3
Richard Doyle (D)	6,582	8.4
Tom Spinosa (R)	2,933	3.7
Gary Arnold (R)	1,596	2.0
Tibor Uskert (D)	1,117	1.4
Bill Dunlap (R)	1,043	1.3
Evelyn Lance (D)	880	1.1
Michael Plunkett (D)	560	0.7
A. Paul Kangas (PFP)	448	0.6
Eric Garris (LIBERT)	408	0.5
Write-ins	6	—

ILLINOIS — Aug. 23, 1983	Vote Total	Percent
Charles A. Hayes (D)	39,623	93.7
Diane Preacely (R)	2,272	5.4
Ed Warren (I)	394	.9
Write-ins	2	—

GEORGIA — Nov. 8, 1983 (runoff)		
George W. "Buddy" Darden (D)	56,267	59.1
Kathryn McDonald (R)	38,949	40.9

WISCONSIN — April 3, 1984		
Gerald Kleczka (D)	76,384	65.0
Robert Nolan (R)	41,007	34.9

NOTE: H. James Saxton, R-N.J., was elected Nov. 6, 1984, to fill the remaining term of Edwin B. Forsythe, who died March 29, and to the 99th Congress. Carl C. "Chris" Perkins, D-Ky., was elected Now. 6, 1984, to fill the remaining term of Carl D. Perkins, who died Aug. 3, and to the 99th Congress. *(See 1984 election returns for vote tallies, p. 1115)*

Abbreviations

C	—Conservative
D	—Democrat
I	—Independent
L	—Liberal
LIBERT	—Libertarian
N	—Neighborhood
QI	—Queens Independent
R	—Republican
PFP	—Peace and Freedom

Special Senate Election, 98th Congress

WASHINGTON — Nov. 8, 1983

	Vote Total	Percent
Daniel J. Evans (R)	672,326	55.4
Mike Lowry (D)	540,981	44.6

1984 Elections Returns for Governor, Senate and House

Following are final official 1984 vote returns for the Senate, House and governorships compiled by Congressional Quarterly from figures supplied by each state's election agency. The box below shows party designation symbols. Because percentages are rounded, they do not all add to 100.

* indicates incumbents.

X denotes candidates without major-party opposition.

— denotes minor parties for which the vote was not available.

● result decided by U.S. House of Representatives.

ALABAMA

	Vote Total	Per-cent
Senate		
Howell Heflin (D)*	860,535	62.8
Albert Lee Smith Jr. (R)	498,508	36.3
S. D. "Yana" Davis (LIBERT)	12,191	0.9
Scattered write-ins	4	
House		
1 Sonny Callahan (R)	102,479	51.0
Frank McRight (D)	98,455	49.0
2 William L. Dickinson (R)*	118,153	60.3
Larry Lee (D)	75,506	38.6
Frank Tipler III (LIBERT)	2,156	1.1
3 Bill Nichols (D)*	120,357	96.2
Mark Thornton (LIBERT)	4,745	3.8
4 Tom Bevill (D)*	120,106	100.0
5 Ronnie G. Flippo (D)*	140,542	95.9
D. M. Samsil (LIBERT)	6,033	4.1
6 Ben Erdreich (D)*	130,973	59.6
J. T. "Jabo" Waggoner (R)	87,550	39.8
Steve Smith (LIBERT)	1,043	0.5
Mark Curtis (SOC WORK)	144	0.1
7 Richard C. Shelby (D)*	135,834	96.8
Charles A. Ewing (LIBERT)	4,498	3.2

ALASKA

Senate		
Ted Stevens (R)*	146,919	71.2
John E. Havelock (D)	58,804	28.5
Scattered write-ins	715	0.3
House		
AL Don Young (R)*	113,582	55.0
Pegge Begich (D)	86,052	41.7
Betty Breck (I)	6,508	3.2

ARIZONA

House		
1 John McCain (R)*	162,418	78.1
Harry W. Braun III (D)	45,609	21.9
2 Morris K. Udall (D)*	106,332	87.7
Lorenzo Torrez (I)	14,869	12.3
3 Bob Stump (R)*	156,686	71.8
Bob Schuster (D)	57,748	26.4
Lorraina M. Valencia (LIBERT)	3,894	1.8
4 Eldon Rudd (R)*	167,558	100.0
5 Jim Kolbe (R)	116,075	50.9
James F. McNulty Jr. (D)*	109,871	48.2
Herb Johnson (LIBERT)	1,992	0.9

ARKANSAS

Governor		
Bill Clinton (D)*	554,561	62.6
Woody Freeman (R)	331,987	37.4
Senate		
David Pryor (D)*	502,341	57.3
Ed Bethune (R)	373,615	42.7
House		
1 Bill Alexander (D)*	121,047	97.2
Peter Cochran (write-in)	3,481	2.8
2 Tommy F. Robinson (D)	103,165	47.1
Judy Petty (R)	90,841	41.5
Jim Taylor (I)	25,073	11.4
3 John Paul Hammerschmidt (R)*	X	X
4 Beryl Anthony Jr. (D)*	117,123	97.9
Roy Rood (write-in)	2,516	2.1

CALIFORNIA

House		
1 Douglas H. Bosco (D)*	157,037	62.3
David Redick (R)	95,186	37.7
2 Gene Chappie (R)*	158,679	69.5
Harry Cozad (D)	69,793	30.5
3 Robert T. Matsui (D)*	131,369	100.0
4 Vic Fazio (D)*	130,109	61.4
Roger Canfield (R)	77,773	36.7
Roger C. Pope (LIBERT)	4,039	1.9
5 Sala Burton (D)*	139,692	72.3
Tom Spinosa (R)	45,930	23.8
Joseph Fuhrig (LIBERT)	4,008	2.1
Henry Clark (PFP)	3,574	1.8
6 Barbara Boxer (D)*	162,511	68.0
Douglas Binderup (R)	71,011	29.7
Howard Creighton (LIBERT)	5,574	2.3
7 George Miller (D)*	158,306	66.7
Rosemary Thakar (R)	78,985	33.3
8 Ronald V. Dellums (D)*	144,316	60.3
Charles Connor (R)	94,907	39.7
9 Fortney H. "Pete" Stark (D)*	136,511	69.9
J. T. Eager Beaver (R)	51,399	26.3
Martha Fuhrig (LIBERT)	7,398	3.8
10 Don Edwards (D)*	102,469	62.4

Abbreviations for Party Designations

AE	—American Eagle		LAB F	—Labor and Farm
AM	—American		LU	—Liberty Union
AMI	—American Independent		NF	—Nuclear Freeze
C	—Conservative		NU	—New Union
CIT	—Citizens		P	—Prohibition
COM	—Communist		PFP	—Peace and Freedom
CST	—Constitution		POP	—Populist
CWP	—Communist Workers		POPU	—Popular
D	—Democratic		R	—Republican
DFL	—Democratic Farmer-Labor		RC	—Rainbow Coalition
I	—Independent		RP	—Rate Payers Against LILCO
IL	—Independent for LaRouche		RTL	—Right to Life
IP	—Independence		SOC	—Socialist
I-R	—Independent-Republican		SOC LAB	—Socialist Labor
IV	—Independent Vote		SOC WORK	—Socialist Workers
KP	—Key		TICP	—Tisch Independent Citizens
L	—Liberal		WL	—Workers League
LIBERT	—Libertarian		WWP	—Workers World

Robert P. Herriott (R)	56,256	34.3
Perr Cardestam (LIBERT)	2,789	1.7
Edmon V. Kaiser (AMI)	2,663	1.6
11 Tom Lantos (D)*	147,607	69.9
John J. Hickey (R)	59,625	28.3
Nicholas W. Kudrovzeff (AMI)	3,883	1.8
12 Ed Zschau (R)*	155,795	61.7
Martin Carnoy (D)	91,026	36.0
Bill White (LIBERT)	5,872	2.3
13 Norman Y. Mineta (D)*	139,851	65.2
John D. Williams (R)	70,666	33.0
John R. Redding (LIBERT)	3,836	1.8
14 Norman D. Shumway (R)*	179,238	73.3
Ruth "Paula" Carlson (D)	58,384	23.9
Fred W. Colburn (LIBERT)	6,850	2.8
15 Tony Coelho (D)*	109,590	65.5
Carol Harner (R)	54,730	32.7
Richard M. Harris (LIBERT)	3,086	1.8
16 Leon E. Panetta (D)*	153,377	70.8
Patricia Smith Ramsey (R)	60,065	27.7
Bill Anderson (LIBERT)	3,245	1.5
17 Charles Pashayan Jr. (R)*	128,802	72.5
Simon Lakritz (D)	48,888	27.5
18 Richard H. Lehman (D)*	128,186	67.3
Dale L. Ewen (R)	62,339	32.7
19 Robert J. Lagomarsino (R)*	153,187	67.3
James C. Carey Jr. (D)	70,278	30.9
Charles J. Zekan (PFP)	4,161	1.8
20 William M. Thomas (R)*	151,732	70.9
Mike LeSage (D)	62,307	29.1
21 Bobbi Fiedler (R)*	173,504	72.3
Charles Davis (D)	62,085	25.9
Robert T. Leet (LIBERT)	4,379	1.8
22 Carlos J. Moorhead (R)*	184,981	85.2
Michael B. Yauch (LIBERT)	32,036	14.8
23 Anthony C. Beilenson (D)*	140,461	61.6
Claude Parrish (R)	84,093	36.9
Larry Leathers (LIBERT)	3,580	1.5
24 Henry A. Waxman (D)*	97,340	63.4
Jerry Zerg (R)	51,010	33.2
James Green (PFP)	2,780	1.8
Tim Custer (LIBERT)	2,477	1.6
25 Edward R. Roybal (D)*	74,261	71.7
Roy D. "Bill" Bloxom (R)	24,963	24.1
Anthony G. Bajada (LIBERT)	4,370	4.2
26 Howard L. Berman (D)*	117,080	62.8
Miriam Ojeda (R)	69,372	37.2
27 Mel Levine (D)*	116,933	54.9
Robert B. Scribner (R)	88,896	41.8
Thomas L. O'Connor Jr. (PFP)	3,815	1.8
Jeff Avrech (LIBERT)	3,137	1.5
28 Julian C. Dixon (D)*	113,076	75.6
Beatrice M. Jett (R)	33,511	22.4
Don Federick (LIBERT)	2,930	2.0
29 Augustus F. Hawkins (D)*	108,777	86.6
Echo Y. Goto (R)	16,781	13.4
30 Matthew G. Martinez (D)*	64,378	51.8
Richard Gomez (R)	53,900	43.3
Houston A. Myers (AMI)	6,055	4.9
31 Mervyn M. Dymally (D)*	100,658	70.7
Henry C. Minturn (R)	41,691	29.3
32 Glenn M. Anderson (D)*	102,961	60.7
Roger E. Fiola (R)	62,176	36.6
Marc F. Denny (LIBERT)	2,517	1.5
Patrick J. McCoy (PFP)	2,051	1.2
33 David Dreier (R)*	147,363	70.6
Claire K. McDonald (D)	54,147	26.0
Gail Lightfoot (LIBERT)	4,738	2.3
Mike Noonan (PFP)	2,371	1.1
34 Esteban Edward Torres (D)*	87,060	59.8
Paul R. Jackson (R)	58,467	40.2
35 Jerry Lewis (R)*	176,477	85.5
Kevin Akin (PFP)	29,990	14.5
36 George E. Brown Jr. (D)*	104,438	56.6
John Paul Stark (R)	80,212	43.4
37 Al McCandless (R)*	149,955	63.6
David E. Skinner (D)	85,908	36.4
38 Bob Dornan (R)	86,545	53.2
Jerry M. Patterson (D)*	73,231	45.0
Michael S. Bright (PFP)	3,021	1.8
39 William E. Dannemeyer (R)*	175,788	76.2
Robert E. Ward (D)	54,889	23.8
40 Robert E. Badham (R)*	164,257	64.4
Carol Ann Bradford (D)	86,748	34.0
Maxine Bell Quirk (PFP)	3,969	1.6
41 Bill Lowery (R)*	161,068	63.4
Robert L. Simmons (D)	85,475	33.7
Sara Baase (LIBERT)	7,303	2.9
42 Dan Lungren (R)*	177,783	73.0
Mary Lou Brophy (D)	60,025	24.6
John S. Donohue (PFP)	5,811	2.4
43 Ron Packard (R)*	165,643	74.1
Lois E. Humphreys (D)	50,996	22.8
Phyllis Avery (LIBERT)	6,878	3.1
44 Jim Bates (D)*	99,378	69.7
Neill Campbell (R)	39,977	28.0
Jim Conole (LIBERT)	3,206	2.3
45 Duncan L. Hunter (R)*	149,011	75.1
David W. Guthrie (D)	45,325	22.9
Patrick Wright (LIBERT)	3,971	2.0

COLORADO

Senate

William L. Armstrong (R)*	833,821	64.2
Nancy Dick (D)	449,327	34.6
Craig Green (LIBERT)	11,077	0.9
Earl Higgerson (P)	1,376	0.3
David Martin (SOC WORK)	2,208	0.2

House

1 Patricia Schroeder (D)*	126,348	62.0
Mary Downs (R)	73,993	36.3
Kathy Emminizer (SOC WORK)	1,846	0.9
Dwight Filley (LIBERT)	1,686	0.8
2 Timothy E. Wirth (D)*	118,580	53.2
Michael J. Norton (R)	101,488	45.5
Jerry Van Sickle (LIBERT)	2,791	1.3
3 Mike Strang (R)	122,669	57.1
W Mitchell (D)	90,063	41.9
Robert Jalehka (LIBERT)	1,358	0.6
Henry John Olshaw (I)	880	0.4
4 Hank Brown (R)*	146,469	71.1
Mary Fagan Bates (D)	56,462	27.4
Randy Fitzgerald (LIBERT)	2,999	1.5
5 Ken Kramer (R)*	163,654	78.6
William Geffen (D)	44,588	21.4
6 Dan L. Schaefer (R)*	171,427	89.4
John Heckman (I)	20,333	10.6

CONNECTICUT

House

1 Barbara B. Kennelly (D)*	147,748	61.7
Herschel A. Klein (R)	90,823	37.9
Charles F. Sundblade (LIBERT)	791	0.3
2 Sam Gejdenson (D)*	124,110	54.4
Roberta F. Koontz (R)	103,119	45.2
Donald Wood (LIBERT)	1,024	0.4
3 Bruce A. Morrison (D)*	129,230	52.6
Lawrence J. DeNardis (R)	115,939	47.2
Michael R. Cohen (LIBERT)	426	0.2
James J. Valenti (I)	200	—
4 Stewart B. McKinney (R)*	165,644	70.4
John M. Ormon (D)	69,666	29.6
5 John G. Rowland (R)	130,700	54.3
William R. Ratchford (D)*	109,425	45.5
James P. Peron (LIBERT)	532	0.2
6 Nancy L. Johnson (R)*	155,422	64.0
Arthur H. House (D)	87,489	36.0

DELAWARE

Governor

Michael N. Castle (R)	135,250	55.5
William T. Quillen (D)	108,315	44.5

Senate

Joseph R. Biden Jr. (D)*	147,831	60.1
John M. Burris (R)	98,101	39.9

House

AL Thomas R. Carper (D)*	142,070	58.5
Elise R. W. du Pont (R)	100,650	41.4
G. Luther Etzel (LIBERT)	294	0.1

FLORIDA

House

1 Earl Hutto (D)*	X	X
2 Don Fuqua (D)*	X	X
3 Charles E. Bennett (D)*	X	X
4 Bill Chappell Jr. (D)*	134,694	64.8
Alton H. "Bill" Starling (R)	73,218	35.2
5 Bill McCollum (R)*	X	X
6 Buddy MacKay (D)*	167,409	99.3
7 Sam Gibbons (D)*	100,430	58.8
Michael N. Kavouklis (R)	70,280	41.2
8 C. W. Bill Young (R)*	184,553	80.3
Robert Kent (D)	45,393	19.7
9 Michael Bilirakis (R)*	191,343	78.6
Jack Wilson (R)	52,150	21.4
10 Andy Ireland (R)*	126,206	61.9
Patricia M. Glass (D)	77,635	38.1
11 Bill Nelson (D)*	145,764	60.5
Rob Quartel (R)	95,115	39.5
12 Tom Lewis (R)*	X	X
13 Connie Mack (R)*	X	X
14 Daniel A. Mica (D)*	153,935	55.4
Don Ross (R)	123,926	44.6
15 E. Clay Shaw Jr. (R)*	128,097	65.7
Bill Humphrey (D)	66,833	34.3
16 Larry Smith (D)*	108,410	56.4
Tom Bush (R)	83,903	43.6
17 William Lehman (D)*	X	X
18 Claude Pepper (D)*	76,404	60.5
Ricardo Nunez (R)	49,818	39.5
19 Dante B. Fascell (D)*	115,631	64.3
Bill Flanagan (R)	64,317	35.7

GEORGIA

Senate

Sam Nunn (D)*	1,344,104	79.9
Jon Michael Hicks (R)	337,196	20.1
Scattered write-ins	44	

House

1 Robert Lindsay Thomas (D)*	126,082	81.6
Erie Lee Downing (R)	28,460	18.4
2 Charles Hatcher (D)*	110,561	100.0
3 Richard Ray (D)*	111,061	81.4
Mitchell Cantu (R)	25,410	18.6
4 Pat Swindall (R)*	120,456	53.1
Elliott H. Levitas (D)	106,376	46.9
5 Wyche Fowler Jr. (D)*	151,233	100.0
6 Newt Gingrich (R)*	116,655	69.1
Gerald Johnson (D)	52,061	30.9
7 George "Buddy" Darden (D)*	106,586	55.2
William E. Bronson (R)	86,431	44.8
8 J. Roy Rowland (D)*	100,936	100.0
9 Ed Jenkins (D)*	109,422	67.5
Frank H. Cofer Jr. (R)	52,731	32.5
10 Doug Barnard Jr. (D)*	116,364	100.0

HAWAII

House
1 Cecil Heftel (D)*	114,884	82.7
Willard F. Beard (R)	20,608	14.8
Christopher Winter (LIBERT)	3,373	2.4
2 Daniel K. Akaka (D)*	112,377	82.2
A. D. Shipley (R)	20,000	14.6
Amelia Fritts (LIBERT)	4,364	3.2

IDAHO

Senate
James A. McClure (R)*	293,193	72.2
Peter M. Busch (D)	105,591	26.0
Donald B. Billings (LIBERT)	7,384	1.8

House
1 Larry E. Craig (R)*	139,085	68.6
Bill Hellar (D)	63,591	31.4
2 Richard H. Stallings (D)	101,287	50.0
George Hansen (R)*	101,117	50.0

ILLINOIS

Senate
Paul Simon (D)	2,397,303	50.1
Charles H. Percy (R)*	2,308,039	48.2
Steven I. Givot (LIBERT)	59,777	1.2
Marjorie H. Pries (CIT)	12,366	0.3
Nelson Gonzalez (SOC WORK)	4,913	0.1
Ishmael Flory (COM)	4,802	0.1
Scattered write-ins	273	

House
1 Charles A. Hayes (D)*	177,438	95.6
Eddie L. Warren (SOC WORK)	8,086	4.4
2 Gus Savage (D)*	155,349	83.0
Dale F. Harman (R)	31,865	17.0
3 Marty Russo (D)*	143,363	64.4
Richard D. Murphy (R)	79,218	35.6
4 George M. O'Brien (R)*	121,744	64.0
Dennis E. Marlow (D)	68,547	36.0
5 William O. Lipinski (D)*	106,597	63.6
John M. Paczkowski (R)	61,109	36.4
6 Henry J. Hyde (R)*	157,370	75.1
Robert H. Renshaw (D)	52,189	24.9
7 Cardiss Collins (D)*	135,493	78.4
James L. Bevel (R)	37,411	21.6
8 Dan Rostenkowski (D)*	114,385	71.3
Spiro F. Georgeson (R)	46,030	28.7
9 Sidney R. Yates (D)*	144,879	67.5
Herbert Sohn (R)	69,613	32.5
10 John Edward Porter (R)*	153,330	72.6
Ruth C. Braver (D)	57,809	27.4
11 Frank Annunzio (D)*	138,171	62.6
Charles J. Theusch (R)	82,518	37.4
12 Philip M. Crane (R)*	159,582	77.8
Edward J. LaFlamme (D)	45,537	22.2
13 Harris W. Fawell (R)	157,603	67.0
Michael J. Donohue (D)	77,623	33.0
14 John E. Grotberg (R)	135,967	62.2
Dan McGrath (D)	82,756	37.8
15 Edward R. Madigan (R)*	149,096	73.2
John M. Hoffman (D)	54,516	26.8
16 Lynn Martin (R)*	127,684	58.4
Carl R. Schwerdtfeger (D)	90,850	41.6
17 Lane Evans (D)*	128,273	56.7
Kenneth G. McMillan (R)	98,069	43.3
18 Robert H. Michel (R)*	136,183	61.0
Gerald A. Bradley (D)	86,884	38.9
19 Terry L. Bruce (D)	117,634	52.3
Daniel B. Crane (R)*	107,463	47.7
20 Richard J. Durbin (D)*	145,092	61.3
Richard G. Austin (R)	91,728	38.7
21 Melvin Price (D)*	127,046	60.2
Robert H. Gaffner (R)	84,148	39.8
22 Kenneth J. Gray (D)	116,952	50.3
Randy Patchett (R)	115,775	49.7

INDIANA

Governor
Robert D. Orr (R)*	1,146,497	52.2
W. Wayne Townsend (D)	1,036,832	47.2
Rockland Snyder (AM)	7,455	0.3
James A. Ridenour (LIBERT)	7,114	0.3

House
1 Peter J. Visclosky (D)	147,035	70.7
Joseph B. Grenchik (R)	59,986	28.8
James E. Willis (LIBERT)	943	0.5
2 Philip R. Sharp (D)*	118,965	53.4
Ken MacKenzie (R)	103,061	46.3
Cecil Bohanon (LIBERT)	637	0.3
3 John Hiler (R)*	115,139	52.4
Michael P. Barnes (D)	103,961	47.3
Robert A. Lutton (LIBERT)	652	0.3
4 Dan Coats (R)*	129,674	60.8
Michael H. Barnard (D)	82,053	38.5
John B. Cameron Jr. (AM)	858	0.4
Joseph F. Laiacona (LIBERT)	534	0.3
5 Elwood Hillis (R)*	143,560	67.9
Allen B. Maxwell (D)	66,631	31.5
David E. Osterfeld (LIBERT)	1,164	0.6
6 Dan Burton (R)*	178,814	72.7
Howard O. Campbell (D)	65,772	26.8
Linda Dilk (LIBERT)	1,278	0.5
7 John T. Myers (R)*	147,787	67.3
Arthur E. Smith (D)	69,097	31.5
Barbara L. J. Bourland (LIBERT)	2,810	1.3
● 8 Richard D. McIntyre (R)	116,641	49.8
Frank McCloskey (D)*	116,645	49.8
Michael J. Fallahay (LIBERT)	691	0.3
9 Lee H. Hamilton (D)*	137,018	65.1
Floyd E. Coates (R)	72,652	34.5
Douglas S. Boggs (LIBERT)	670	0.3
10 Andrew Jacobs Jr. (D)*	115,274	59.0
Joseph P. Watkins (R)	79,342	40.6
Bradford L. Warren (LIBERT)	877	0.4

IOWA

Senate
Tom Harkin (D)	716,883	55.5
Roger W. Jepsen (R)*	564,381	43.7
Garry DeYoung (I)	11,014	0.8
Scattered write-ins	422	

House
1 Jim Leach (R)*	131,182	66.8
Kevin Ready (D)	65,293	33.2
2 Tom Tauke (R)*	136,893	63.9
Joe Welsh (D)	77,335	36.1
3 Cooper Evans (R)*	133,737	60.7
Joe Johnston (D)	86,574	39.3
4 Neal Smith (D)*	136,922	60.7
Robert R. Lockard (R)	88,717	39.3
5 Jim Lightfoot (R)	104,632	50.8
Jerome D. Fitzgerald (D)	101,435	49.2
6 Berkley Bedell (D)*	127,706	62.0
Darrel Rensink (R)	78,182	38.0

KANSAS

Senate
Nancy Landon Kassebaum (R)*	757,402	76.0
James R. Maher (D)	211,664	21.2
Lucille Bieder (C)	9,380	0.9
Marian Ruck Jackson (AM)	6,918	0.7
Douglas N. Merritt (LIBERT)	6,755	0.7
Freda H. Steele (P)	4,610	0.5

House
1 Pat Roberts (R)*	159,931	76.0
Darrell Ringer (D)	49,015	23.3
Clement N. Scoggin (P)	1,816	0.9
2 Jim Slattery (D)*	112,263	60.0
Jim Van Slyke (R)	73,045	39.1
Kenneth C. Peterson Sr. (P)	1,744	0.9
3 Jan Meyers (R)	117,159	54.8
John E. Reardon (D)	85,441	39.9
John S. Ralph Jr. (I)	11,302	5.3
4 Dan Glickman (D)*	138,917	74.4
William V. Krause (R)	47,776	25.6
5 Bob Whittaker (R)*	144,075	73.5
John A. Barnes (D)	49,435	25.2
Vearl A. Bacon (P)	2,382	1.2

KENTUCKY

Senate
Mitch McConnell (R)	644,990	49.9
Walter D. Huddleston (D)*	639,721	49.5
Dave Welters (SOC WORK)	7,696	0.6

House
1 Carroll Hubbard Jr. (D)*	112,180	100.0
2 William H. Natcher (D)*	93,042	62.1
Timothy A. Morrison (R)	56,700	37.9
3 Romano L. Mazzoli (D)*	145,680	67.7
Suzanne M. Warner (R)	68,185	31.7
Peggy Kreiner (SOC WORK)	1,273	0.6
4 Gene Snyder (R)*	108,398	53.7
William P. Mulloy II (D)	93,640	46.3
5 Harold Rogers (R)*	125,164	75.9
Sherman W. McIntosh (D)	39,783	24.1
6 Larry J. Hopkins (R)*	126,525	71.4
Jerry Hammond (D)	49,657	28.0
Tony Suruda (LIBERT)	926	0.5
7 Carl C. Perkins (D)	122,679	73.7
Aubrey Russell (R)	43,890	26.3

LOUISIANA

Senate
J. Bennett Johnston (D)*	X	X

House
1 Bob Livingston (R)*	X	X
2 Lindy (Mrs. Hale) Boggs (D)*	X	X
3 W. J. "Billy" Tauzin (D)*	X	X
4 Buddy Roemer (D)*	X	X
5 Jerry Huckaby (D)*	X	X
6 W. Henson Moore (R)*	X	X
7 John B. Breaux (D)*	X	X
8 Gillis W. Long (D)*	X	X

MAINE

Senate
William S. Cohen (R)*	404,414	73.3
Elizabeth H. Mitchell (D)	142,626	25.9
P. Anne Stoddard (CST)	4,338	0.8
Scattered write-ins	28	

House
1 John R. McKernan Jr. (R)*	182,785	63.5
Barry J. Hobbins (D)	104,972	36.5
2 Olympia J. Snowe (R)*	192,166	75.7
Chipman C. Bull (D)	57,347	22.6
Kenneth E. Stoddard (CST)	4,242	1.7

MARYLAND

House
1 Roy Dyson (D)*	96,673	58.4
Harlan C. Williams (R)	68,865	41.6
2 Helen Delich Bentley (R)	111,517	51.4
Clarence D. Long (D)*	105,571	48.6
3 Barbara A. Mikulski (D)*	133,189	68.2
Ross Z. Pierpont (R)	59,493	30.5
Lawrence K. Freeman (I)	2,579	1.3

4 Marjorie S. Holt (R)*	114,430	66.2
Howard M. Greenebaum (D)	58,312	33.8
5 Steny H. Hoyer (D)*	116,310	72.2
John E. Ritchie (R)	44,839	27.8
6 Beverly B. Byron (D)*	123,383	65.1
Robin Ficker (R)	66,056	34.9
7 Parren J. Mitchell (D)*	139,488	100.0
8 Michael D. Barnes (D)*	181,947	71.5
Albert Ceccone (R)	70,715	27.8
Samuel K. Grove (LIBERT)	1,903	0.7

MASSACHUSETTS

Senate

John Kerry (D)	1,393,150	55.1
Raymond Shamie (R)	1,136,913	44.9
Scattered write-ins	408	

House

1 Silvio O. Conte (R)*	162,646	72.9
Mary L. Wentworth (D)	60,372	27.1
2 Edward P. Boland (D)*	132,693	68.7
Thomas P. Swank (R)	60,463	31.3
3 Joseph D. Early (D)*	148,461	67.4
Kenneth J. Redding (R)	71,765	32.6
4 Barney Frank (D)*	172,903	74.2
Jim Forte (R)	60,121	25.8
5 Chester G. Atkins (D)	120,008	53.4
Gregory S. Hyatt (R)	104,912	46.6
6 Nicholas Mavroules (D)*	168,662	70.4
Frederick S. Leber (R)	63,363	26.4
Donald P. Bachelder (RC)	7,615	3.2
7 Edward J. Markey (D)*	167,211	71.4
S. Lester Ralph (R)	66,930	28.6
8 Thomas P. O'Neill Jr. (D)*	179,617	91.8
Laura Ross (COM)	15,810	8.1
9 Joe Moakley (D)*	153,132	99.9
10 Gerry E. Studds (D)*	143,062	55.7
Lewis Crampton (R)	113,745	44.3
11 Brian J. Donnelly (D)*	172,010	100.0

MICHIGAN

Senate

Carl Levin (D)*	1,915,831	51.8
Jack Lousma (R)	1,745,302	47.2
Arthur R. Tisch (TICP)	22,882	0.6
Lynn Johnston (LIBERT)	7,786	0.2
Helen Meyers (SOC WORK)	2,686	0.1
William Roundtree (WWP)	2,279	0.1
Max Dean (I)	2,135	0.1
Samuel L. Webb (CWP)	1,196	
Fred Mazelis (WL)	818	
Scattered write-ins	23	

House

1 John Conyers Jr. (D)*	152,432	89.4
Edward J. Mack (R)	17,393	10.2
Andrew Pulley (SOC WORK)	685	0.4
2 Carl D. Pursell (R)*	140,688	68.6
Mike McCauley (D)	62,374	30.4
Greg Severance (TICP)	1,128	0.5
James L. Hudler (LIBERT)	937	0.5
3 Howard Wolpe (D)*	106,505	52.9
Jackie McGregor (R)	94,714	47.1
4 Mark D. Siljander (R)*	127,907	66.9
Charles S. Rodebaugh (D)	63,159	33.1
5 Paul B. Henry (R)	140,131	61.8
Gary J. McInerney (D)	85,232	37.6
Richard Whitelock (LIBERT)	1,312	0.6
6 Bob Carr (D)*	106,705	52.4
Tom Ritter (R)	95,113	46.7
Russel Severance (TICP)	936	0.5
James E. Hurrell (LIBERT)	773	0.4
7 Dale E. Kildee (D)*	145,070	93.1
Samuel Johnston (I)	10,663	6.8
8 Bob Traxler (D)*	126,161	64.4
John Heussner (R)	69,683	35.6

9 Guy Vander Jagt (R)*	150,885	70.9
John M. Senger (D)	61,233	28.8
Nicholas Hamilton (LIBERT)	680	0.3
10 Bill Schuette (R)	104,950	50.1
Donald J. Albosta (D)*	103,636	49.4
George Leef (LIBERT)	1,054	0.6
11 Robert W. Davis (R)*	126,992	58.6
Tom Stewart (D)	89,640	41.4
12 David E. Bonior (D)*	113,772	58.3
Eugene J. Tyza (R)	79,824	40.9
Keith P. Edwards (LIBERT)	1,388	0.7
13 George W. Crockett Jr. (D)*	132,222	86.6
Robert Murphy (R)	20,416	13.4
14 Dennis M. Hertel (D)*	113,610	59.1
John Lauve (R)	77,427	40.3
Virginia L. Cropsey (LIBERT)	1,105	0.6
15 William D. Ford (D)*	98,973	59.9
Gerald R. Carlson (R)	66,172	40.1
16 John D. Dingell (D)*	121,463	63.7
Frank Grzywacki (R)	68,116	35.7
Donald Kostyu (LIBERT)	1,042	0.5
17 Sander M. Levin (D)*	133,064	100.0
18 William S. Broomfield (R)*	186,505	79.4
Vivian H. Smargon (D)	46,191	19.7
Timothy O'Brien (LIBERT)	2,188	0.9

MINNESOTA

Senate

Rudy Boschwitz (I-R)*	1,199,926	58.1
Joan Anderson Growe (DFL)	852,844	41.3
Eleanor Garcia (SOC WORK)	5,351	0.3
Richard Putman (LIBERT)	4,653	0.2
Jeffrey N. Miller (NU)	3,129	0.2
Scattered write-ins	240	

House

1 Timothy J. Penny (DFL)*	140,095	57.0
Keith Spicer (I-R)	105,723	43.0
2 Vin Weber (I-R)*	153,308	63.1
Todd Lundquist (DFL)	89,770	36.9
3 Bill Frenzel (I-R)*	207,819	73.2
Dave Peterson (DFL)	76,132	26.8
4 Bruce F. Vento (DFL)*	167,678	73.5
Mary Jane Rachner (I-R)	57,450	25.2
Peter Brandli (SOC WORK)	2,919	1.3
5 Martin Olav Sabo (DFL)*	165,075	70.1
Richard D. Wieblen (I-R)	62,642	26.6
Kathryn Anderson (CIT)	7,725	3.3
6 Gerry Sikorski (DFL)*	154,603	60.5
Patrick Trueman (I-R)	101,058	39.5
7 Arlan Stangeland (I-R)*	135,087	57.0
Collin C. Peterson (DFL)	101,720	42.9
8 James L. Oberstar (DFL)*	165,727	67.2
Dave Rued (I-R)	79,181	32.1
David Salner (SOC WORK)	1,560	0.6

MISSISSIPPI

Senate

Thad Cochran (R)*	580,314	60.9
William F. Winter (D)	371,926	39.1

House

1 Jamie L. Whitten (D)*	136,530	88.4
John Hargett (I)	17,991	11.6
2 Webb Franklin (R)*	92,392	50.6
Robert G. Clark (D)	89,154	48.9
Hardy Caraway (I)	874	0.5
3 G. V. "Sonny" Montgomery (D)*	158,002	100.0
4 Wayne Dowdy (D)*	113,635	55.3
David Armstrong (R)	91,797	45.6
5 Trent Lott (R)*	142,637	84.7
Arlon "Blackie" Coate (D)	25,840	15.3

MISSOURI

Governor

John Ashcroft (R)	1,194,506	56.7
Kenneth J. Rothman (D)	913,700	43.3
Scattered write-ins	4	

House

1 William L. Clay (D)*	147,436	68.3
Eric Rathbone (R)	68,538	31.7
2 Robert A. Young (D)*	139,123	51.8
John Buechner (R)	127,710	47.5
Chad G. Colopy (LIBERT)	1,783	0.7
3 Richard A. Gephardt (D)*	193,537	100.0
4 Ike Skelton (D)*	150,624	66.9
Carl D. Russell (R)	74,434	33.1
5 Alan Wheat (D)*	150,675	66.0
Jim Kenworthy (R)	72,477	31.8
Mike Roberts (LIBERT)	5,068	2.2
6 E. Thomas Coleman (R)*	150,996	64.8
Kenneth C. Hensley (D)	81,917	35.2
7 Gene Taylor (R)*	164,586	69.6
Ken Young (D)	71,867	30.4
8 Bill Emerson (R)*	134,186	65.4
Bill Blue (D)	70,922	34.6
9 Harold L. Volkmer (D)*	123,588	52.9
Carrie Francke (R)	110,100	47.1

MONTANA

Governor

Ted Schwinden (D)*	266,578	70.3
Pat M. Goodover (R)	100,070	26.4
Larry Dodge (LIBERT)	12,322	3.3

Senate

Max Baucus (D)*	215,704	56.9
Chuck Cozzens (R)	154,308	40.7
Neil Halprin (LIBERT)	9,143	2.4

House

1 Pat Williams (D)*	126,998	65.6
Gary K. Carlson (R)	61,794	31.9
Royer G. Warren (LIBERT)	4,660	2.4
2 Ron Marlenee (R)*	116,932	65.9
Chet Blaylock (D)	60,445	34.1

NEBRASKA

Senate

J. James Exon (D)*	332,217	51.9
Nancy Hoch (R)	307,147	48.0
Scattered write-ins	304	

House

1 Doug Bereuter (R)*	158,836	74.1
Monica Bauer (D)	55,508	25.9
2 Hal Daub (R)*	139,384	64.9
Thomas F. Cavanaugh (D)	75,210	35.0
3 Virginia Smith (R)*	183,901	83.3
Tom Vickers (D)	36,899	16.7

NEVADA

House

1 Harry Reid (D)*	73,242	56.1
Peggy Cavnar (R)	55,391	42.4
Joe Morris (LIBERT)	1,885	1.4
2 Barbara F. Vucanovich (R)*	99,775	71.2
Andrew Barbano (D)	36,130	25.8
Dan Becan (LIBERT)	4,201	3.0

NEW HAMPSHIRE

Governor

John H. Sununu (R)*	256,571	66.8
Chris Spirou (D)	127,156	33.1
Scattered write-ins	180	

Senate

Gordon J. Humphrey (R)*	225,828	58.7
Norman E. D'Amours (D)	157,447	41.0

Saunder H. Primack (LIBERT)	1,094	0.3
Scattered write-ins	37	

House

1	Robert C. Smith (R)	111,627	58.6
	Dudley Dudley (D)	76,854	40.3
	John G. H. Muelhke Jr. (I)	1,435	0.8
	Arne B. Erickson (LIBERT)	570	0.3
2	Judd Gregg (R)*	138,975	76.2
	Larry Converse (D)	42,257	23.2
	Alan Groupe (LIBERT)	1,177	0.6

NEW JERSEY

Senate

Bill Bradley (D)*	1,986,644	64.2
Mary V. Mochary (R)	1,080,100	35.2
James T. Hagen (I)	10,409	0.3
Harold F. Leinendecker (LIBERT)	7,135	0.2
Julius Levin (SOC LAB)	6,053	0.2
Priscilla Schenk (SOC WORK)	3,224	0.1
Jasper C. Gould (I)	2,891	0.1

House

1	James J. Florio (D)*	152,125	71.9
	Frederick A. Busch Jr. (R)	58,800	27.8
	Jerry Zeldin (LIBERT)	786	0.4
2	William J. Hughes (D)*	132,841	63.2
	Raymond G. Massie (R)	77,231	36.7
3	James J. Howard (D)*	122,291	53.3
	Brian T. Kennedy (R)	105,028	45.8
	Frank Krushinski Jr. (I)	1,196	0.5
	Lawrence D. Erickson (I)	907	0.4
4	Christopher H. Smith (R)*	139,295	61.3
	James C. Hedden (D)	87,908	38.7
5	Marge Roukema (R)*	171,979	71.2
	Rose Brunetto (D)	69,666	28.8
6	Bernard J. Dwyer (D)*	118,532	55.9
	Dennis Adams (R)	90,862	42.8
	Stephen Friedlander (LIBERT)	2,686	1.3
7	Matthew J. Rinaldo (R)*	165,685	74.2
	John F. Feeley (D)	56,798	25.4
	Paul Nelson (LIBERT)	799	0.4
8	Robert A. Roe (D)*	118,793	62.7
	Marguerite A. Page (R)	69,973	36.9
	Daniel A. Maiullo Jr. (LIBERT)	629	0.3
9	Robert G. Torricelli (D)*	149,493	62.6
	Neil Romano (R)	89,166	37.4
10	Peter W. Rodino Jr. (D)*	111,244	83.7
	Howard E. Berkeley (R)	21,712	16.3
11	Dean A. Gallo (R)	133,662	55.8
	Joseph G. Minish (D)*	106,038	44.2
12	Jim Courter (R)*	148,042	65.0
	Peter Bearse (D)	78,167	34.3
	Joseph R. Kerr III (LIBERT)	1,624	0.7
13	H. James Saxton (R)	141,136	60.7
	James B. Smith (D)	89,307	38.4
	Don Smith (I)	1,516	0.7
	Bernardo S. Doganiero (SOC LAB)	524	0.2
14	Frank J. Guarini (D)*	115,117	65.7
	Edward T. Magee (R)	58,265	33.3
	Herbert H. Shaw (I)	1,835	1.0

NEW MEXICO

Senate

Pete V. Domenici (R)*	361,371	71.9
Judith A. Pratt (D)	141,253	28.1
Orlin G. Cole (write-in)	10	

House

1	Manuel Lujan Jr. (R)*	115,808	64.9
	Charles Ted Asbury (D)	60,598	34.0
	Steven P. Curtis (LIBERT)	1,936	1.1

2	Joe Skeen (R)*	116,006	74.3
	Peter R. York (D)	40,063	25.7
3	Bill Richardson (D)*	100,470	60.8
	Louis H. Gallegos (R)	62,351	37.7
	Shirley Jones (LIBERT)	2,388	1.4

NEW YORK

House

1	William Carney (R, C, RTL)*	107,029	53.1
	George J. Hochbrueckner (D, RP)	94,551	46.9
2	Thomas J. Downey (D, IP)*	97,648	54.7
	Paul Aniboli (R, C, RTL)	80,855	45.3
3	Robert J. Mrazek (D)*	120,191	51.0
	Robert P. Quinn (R, C)	112,909	47.9
	Elizabeth E. Capazzi (RTL)	2,651	1.1
4	Norman F. Lent (R, C)*	154,875	68.9
	Sheldon Engelhard (D, L)	65,678	29.2
	John J. Dunkle (RTL)	4,126	1.8
5	Raymond J. McGrath (R, C)*	138,560	62.4
	Michael d'Innocenzo (D, IV)	78,429	35.3
	Paul F. Callahan (RTL)	3,572	1.6
	Jack Olchin (L)	1,630	0.7
6	Joseph P. Addabbo (D, L)*	120,098	82.7
	Philip J. Veltre (R, C, RTL)	25,040	17.3
7	Gary L. Ackerman (D, L)*	97,674	69.3
	Gustave A. Reifenkugel (R, C)	43,370	30.7
8	James H. Scheuer (D, L)*	104,558	62.8
	Robert L. Brandofino (R, C)	62,015	37.2
9	Thomas J. Manton (D)	71,420	52.8
	Serphin R. Maltese (R, C, RTL)	63,910	47.2
10	Charles E. Schumer (D, L)*	115,867	72.4
	John H. Fox (R, C)	42,009	26.3
	Alfred F. Donohue Jr. (RTL)	2,116	1.3
11	Edolphus Towns (D, L)*	81,002	85.2
	Nathaniel Hendricks (R)	12,494	13.1
	Alfred Hamel (C)	1,568	1.6
12	Major R. Owens (D, L)*	82,047	90.5
	Joseph N. O. Caesar (R, C, RTL)	8,609	9.5
13	Stephen J. Solarz (D, L)*	82,610	65.9
	Lew Y. Levin (R, C, RTL)	42,737	34.1
14	Guy V. Molinari (R, C, RTL)*	117,041	70.2
	Kevin S. Sheehy (D)	49,776	29.8
15	Bill Green (R, I)*	107,644	56.1
	Andrew J. Stein (D, L)	84,404	43.9
16	Charles B. Rangel (D, R)*	117,759	97.0
	Michael T. Berns (C)	2,541	2.1
	Nan Bailey (SOC WORK)	1,098	0.9
17	Ted Weiss (D, L)*	162,489	81.5
	Kenneth Katzman (R)	33,316	16.7
	Leonard Steinman (C)	3,674	1.8
18	Robert Garcia (D, L)*	85,960	89.2
	Curtis Johnson (R)	8,970	9.3
	John W. Farrell (C)	1,398	1.5
19	Mario Biaggi (D, R, L, RTL)*	155,067	94.8
	Alice Farrell (C)	8,472	5.2
20	Joseph J. DioGuardi (R, C)	106,958	50.1
	Oren J. Teicher (D)	102,842	48.2
	Florence T. O'Grady (RTL)	3,549	1.7
21	Hamilton Fish Jr. (R, C, RTL)*	160,053	78.3
	Lawrence W. Grunberger (D)	44,274	21.7
22	Benjamin A. Gilman (R)*	144,278	68.5
	Bruce M. Levine (D, L)	57,934	27.5
	Robert DeMaggio (RTL)	8,274	3.9
23	Samuel S. Stratton (D)*	188,144	77.8
	Frank Wicks (R, NF)	53,060	21.9
	Richard Ariza (SOC WORK)	642	0.3
24	Gerald B. H. Solomon (R, C, RTL)*	164,019	73.2
	Edward J. Bloch (D)	60,188	26.8
25	Sherwood Boehlert (R)*	140,256	72.8
	James J. Ball (D)	52,434	27.2

26	David O'B. Martin (R, C)*	131,257	70.6
	Bernard J. Lammers (D)	54,663	29.4
27	George C. Wortley (R, C)*	122,215	56.6
	Thomas C. Buckel Jr. (D, L)	93,601	43.4
28	Matthew F. McHugh (D)*	123,334	56.6
	Constance E. Cook (R)	90,324	41.4
	Mark R. Masterson (RTL)	4,403	2.0
29	Frank Horton (R)*	138,362	69.6
	James R. Toole (D)	48,301	24.3
	James L. Hale (C)	7,957	4.0
	Donald M. Peters (RTL)	4,042	2.0
30	Fred J. Eckert (R, C, RTL)	119,844	54.4
	W. Douglas Call (D)	100,066	45.4
31	Jack F. Kemp (R, C, RTL)*	168,332	75.0
	Peter J. Martinelli (D, L)	56,156	25.0
32	John J. LaFalce (D, L)*	139,979	69.4
	Anthony J. Murty (R, C, RTL)	61,797	30.6
33	Henry J. Nowak (D, L)*	155,198	77.6
	David S. Lewandowski (R, C, RTL)	44,880	22.4
34	Stan Lundine (D)*	110,902	54.2
	Jill Houghton Emery (R, C)	91,016	44.5
	Carol L. Fisher (RTL)	2,560	1.3

NORTH CAROLINA

Governor

James G. Martin (R)	1,208,167	54.3
Rufus Edmisten (D)	1,011,209	45.4
H. Fritz Prochnow (LIBERT)	4,611	0.2
Gregory McCartan (SOC WORK)	2,740	0.1

Senate

Jesse Helms (R)*	1,156,768	51.7
James B. Hunt Jr. (D)	1,070,488	47.8
Bobby Yates Emory (LIBERT)	9,302	0.4
Kate Daher (SOC WORK)	2,493	0.1

House

1	Walter B. Jones (D)*	122,815	67.1
	Herbert W. Lee (R)	60,153	32.9
2	Tim Valentine (D)*	122,292	67.7
	Frank H. Hill (R)	58,312	32.3
3	Charles Whitley (D)*	100,185	64.1
	Danny G. Moody (R)	56,096	35.9
4	Bill Cobey (R)	117,436	50.6
	Ike Andrews (D)*	114,462	49.4
5	Stephen L. Neal (D)*	109,831	50.7
	Stuart Epperson (R)	106,599	49.3
6	Howard Coble (R)	102,925	50.6
	Robin Britt (D)*	100,263	49.3
	Meryl Lynn Farber (SOC WORK)	285	0.1
7	Charlie Rose (D)*	92,157	59.2
	S. Thomas Rhodes (R)	63,625	40.8
8	W. G. "Bill" Hefner (D)*	99,731	50.9
	Harris D. Blake (R)	96,354	49.1
9	J. Alex McMillan (R)	109,420	50.1
	D. G. Martin (D)	109,099	49.9
10	James T. Broyhill (R)*	142,873	73.4
	Ted A. Poovey (D)	51,860	26.6
11	Bill Hendon (R)	112,598	51.0
	James McClure Clarke (D)*	108,284	49.0

NORTH DAKOTA

Governor

George Sinner (D)	173,922	55.3
Allen I. Olson (R)*	140,460	47.7

House

AL	Byron L. Dorgan (D)*	242,968	78.7
	Lois Ivers Altenburg (R)	65,761	21.3

OHIO

House
1	Thomas A. Luken (D)*	121,577	55.1
	Norman A. Murdock (R)	88,859	40.3
	Kathleen M. Denny (I)	10,222	4.6
2	Bill Gradison (R)*	149,856	68.6
	Thomas D. Porter (D)	68,597	31.4
3	Tony P. Hall (D)*	151,398	100.0
4	Michael G. Oxley (R)*	162,199	77.5
	William O. Sutton (D)	47,018	22.5
5	Delbert L. Latta (R)*	132,582	62.7
	James R. Sherck (D)	78,809	37.3
6	Bob McEwen (R)*	150,101	74.0
	Bob Smith (D)	52,727	26.0
7	Michael DeWine (R)*	147,885	76.7
	Donald E. Scott (D)	40,621	21.1
	Elizabeth C. B. Hanna (write-in)	4,330	2.6
	Stephen Ogrod (write-in)	22	
8	Thomas N. Kindness (R)*	155,200	76.9
	John T. Francis (D)	46,673	23.1
9	Marcy Kaptur (D)*	117,985	54.9
	Frank Venner (R)	93,210	43.4
	Michael R. Nun (I)	2,255	1.1
	Elizabeth Lariscy (I)	1,459	0.7
10	Clarence E. Miller (R)*	149,337	73.0
	John M. Buchanan (D)	55,172	27.0
11	Dennis E. Eckart (D)*	133,096	66.8
	Dean Beagle (R)	66,278	33.2
12	John R. Kasich (R)*	148,899	69.5
	Richard Sloan (D)	65,215	30.5
13	Don J. Pease (D)*	131,923	66.4
	William G. Schaffner (R)	59,610	30.0
	James S. Patton (I)	7,223	3.6
14	John F. Seiberling (D)*	155,729	71.4
	Jean E. Bender (R)	62,366	28.6
15	Chalmers P. Wylie (R)*	148,311	71.6
	Duane Jager (D)	58,870	28.4
16	Ralph Regula (R)*	152,399	72.4
	James Gwin (D)	58,048	27.6
17	James A. Traficant Jr. (D)	123,014	53.3
	Lyle Williams (R)*	105,449	45.7
	Reynold J. Johnjulio (I)	2,198	1.0
18	Douglas Applegate (D)*	155,759	75.9
	Kenneth P. Burt Jr. (R)	49,356	24.1
19	Edward F. Feighan (D)*	139,605	55.2
	Matthew J. Hatchadorian (R)	107,957	42.7
	Arnold Gleisser (I)	5,277	2.1
20	Mary Rose Oakar (D)*	167,115	100.0
21	Louis Stokes (D)*	165,247	82.4
	Robert L. Woodall (R)	29,500	14.7
	Milton R. Norris (I)	4,363	2.2
	Omari Musa (I)	1,538	0.8

OKLAHOMA

Senate
	David L. Boren (D)*	906,131	75.6
	Will E. Crozier (R)	280,638	23.4
	Robert T. Murphy (LIBERT)	11,168	0.9

House
1	James R. Jones (D)*	113,919	52.2
	Frank Keating (R)	103,098	47.3
	D. Lynn Neal (LIBERT)	1,076	0.5
2	Mike Synar (D)*	148,124	74.1
	Gary K. Rice (R)	51,889	25.9
3	Wes Watkins (D)*	137,964	77.8
	Patrick K. Miller (R)	39,454	22.2
4	Dave McCurdy (D)*	109,447	63.6
	Jerry Smith (R)	60,844	35.4
	Gordon E. Mobley (LIBERT)	1,748	1.0
5	Mickey Edwards (R)*	135,167	75.6
	Allen Greeson (D)	39,089	21.9
	D. Frank Robinson (LIBERT)	4,470	2.5
6	Glenn English (D)*	96,994	58.9

	Craig Dodd (R)	67,601	41.1

OREGON

Senate
	Mark O. Hatfield (R)*	808,152	66.5
	Margie Hendriksen (D)	406,122	33.4
	Scattered write-ins	461	

House
1	Les AuCoin (D)*	138,393	53.1
	Bill Moshofsky (R)	122,247	46.9
2	Robert F. Smith (R)*	132,649	57.0
	Larryann C. Willis (D)	100,152	43.0
3	Ron Wyden (D)*	173,438	72.3
	Drew Davis (R)	66,394	27.7
4	James Weaver (D)*	134,190	58.2
	Bruce Long (R)	96,487	41.8
5	Denny Smith (R)*	130,424	54.5
	Ruth McFarland (D)	108,919	45.5

PENNSYLVANIA

House
1	Thomas M. Foglietta (D)*	148,123	74.9
	Carmine DiBiase (R)	49,559	25.1
2	William H. Gray III (D)*	200,484	91.0
	Ronald J. Sharper (R)	18,224	8.3
	Katherine L. Karlin (SOC WORK)	1,587	0.7
3	Robert A. Borski (D)*	152,598	63.9
	Flora L. Becker (R)	85,358	35.7
	John J. Hughes (I)	830	0.3
4	Joe Kolter (D)*	114,040	56.8
	James Kunder (R)	86,769	43.2
5	Richard T. Schulze (R)*	141,965	72.6
	Louis J. Fanti (D)	53,586	27.4
6	Gus Yatron (D)*	181,165	100.0
7	Bob Edgar (D)*	124,458	50.1
	Curt Weldon (R)	124,046	49.9
8	Peter H. Kostmayer (D)*	112,648	50.9
	David A. Christian (R)	108,696	49.1
9	Bud Shuster (R)*	118,437	66.5
	Nancy Kulp (D)	59,549	33.5
10	Joseph M. McDade (R)*	150,166	77.1
	Gene Basalyga (D)	44,571	22.9
11	Paul E. Kanjorski (D)	108,430	58.6
	Robert P. Hudock (R)	76,692	41.4
12	John P. Murtha (D)*	134,384	69.1
	Thomas J. Fullard III (R)	57,466	29.5
	Joseph E. Krill (AE)	2,664	1.4
13	Lawrence Coughlin (R)*	133,948	56.1
	Joseph M. Hoeffel (D)	104,756	43.9
14	William J. Coyne (D)*	163,818	76.6
	John Robert Clark (R)	42,616	19.9
	Richard E. Caligiuri (LIBERT)	6,699	3.1
	Alfred Duncan Jr. (SOC WORK)	664	0.3
15	Don Ritter (R)*	110,338	58.1
	Jane Wells-Schooley (D)	79,490	41.9
16	Robert S. Walker (R)*	138,477	77.8
	Martin L. Bard (D)	39,515	22.2
17	George W. Gekas (R)*	129,716	80.3
	Stephen A. Anderson (D)	31,770	19.7
18	Doug Walgren (D)*	149,628	62.7
	John G. Maxwell (R)	87,521	36.7
	Daniel M. Mulholland (LIBERT)	1,340	0.6
19	Bill Goodling (R)*	141,196	75.6
	F. John Rarig (D)	44,117	23.6
	Gary M. Shoemaker (LIBERT)	1,429	0.8
20	Joseph M. Gaydos (D)*	158,751	76.0
	Daniel Lloyd (R)	50,247	24.0
21	Tom Ridge (R)*	125,730	65.4
	James A. Young (D)	65,594	34.1
	Edward J. Hammer (I)	785	0.4
22	Austin J. Murphy (D)*	153,514	79.0
	Nancy S. Pryor (R)	39,752	20.4

	Clare M. Fraenzl (SOC WORK)	1,162	0.6
23	William F. Clinger Jr. (R)*	94,952	51.6
	Bill Wachob (D)	88,957	48.4

RHODE ISLAND

Governor
	Edward DiPrete (R)	245,059	60.0
	Anthony J. Solomon (D)	163,311	40.0
	Scattered write-ins	5	

Senate
	Claiborne Pell (D)*	286,780	72.6
	Barbara Leonard (R)	108,492	27.4
	Scattered write-ins	13	

House
1	Fernand J. St Germain (D)*	130,584	68.5
	Alfred Rego Jr. (R)	60,026	31.5
2	Claudine Schneider (R)*	135,161	67.7
	Richard Sinapi (D)	64,341	32.3

SOUTH CAROLINA

Senate
	Strom Thurmond (R)*	644,815	66.8
	Melvin Purvis Jr. (D)	306,982	31.8
	Stephen Davis (LIBERT)	13,333	1.4

House
1	Thomas F. Hartnett (R)*	103,288	61.7
	Ed Pendarvis (D)	64,022	38.3
2	Floyd Spence (R)*	108,085	62.1
	Ken Mosely (D)	63,932	36.7
	Cynthia E. Sullivan (LIBERT)	2,010	1.2
3	Butler Derrick (D)*	88,917	58.4
	Clarence E. Taylor (R)	61,739	40.6
	Robert Madden (LIBERT)	1,510	1.0
4	Carroll A. Campbell Jr. (R)*	105,139	63.9
	Jeff Smith (D)	57,854	35.2
	William Ray Pike (LIBERT)	1,431	0.9
5	John M. Spratt Jr. (D)*	98,513	96.3
	Dick Winchester (AM)	4,593	4.5
	Linda Blezins (LIBERT)	4,185	4.1
6	Robin Tallon (D)*	97,329	59.9
	Lois Eargle (R)	63,005	38.8
	Hugh Thompson (LIBERT)	2,050	1.3

SOUTH DAKOTA

Senate
	Larry Pressler (R)*	235,176	74.5
	George V. Cunningham (D)	80,537	25.5

House
AL	Thomas A. Daschle (D)*	181,401	57.4
	Dale Bell (R)	134,821	42.6

TENNESSEE

Senate
	Albert Gore Jr. (D)	1,000,607	60.7
	Victor Ashe (R)	557,016	33.8
	Ed McAteer (I)	87,234	5.3
	Khalil-Ullah Al-Muhaymin (I)	3,179	0.2
	Scattered write-ins	28	

House
1	James H. Quillen (R)*	113,407	100.0
2	John J. Duncan (R)*	132,604	77.3
	John F. Bowen (D)	38,846	22.7
3	Marilyn Lloyd (D)*	99,465	52.4
	John Davis (R)	90,216	47.6
4	Jim Cooper (D)*	93,848	75.2
	James Beau Seigneur (R)	31,011	24.8
5	Bill Boner (D)*	138,233	100.0
6	Bart Gordon (D)	103,989	62.8
	Joe Simpkins (R)	61,559	37.2
7	Don Sundquist (R)*	107,257	100.0
8	Ed Jones (D)*	118,653	100.0
9	Harold E. Ford (D)*	133,428	71.5
	William B. Thompson Jr. (R)	53,064	28.5

TEXAS

Senate

Phil Gramm (R)	3,111,348	58.5
Lloyd Doggett (D)	2,202,557	41.4
Scattered write-ins	273	

House

1	Sam B. Hall Jr. (D)*	139,829	100.0
2	Charles Wilson (D)*	113,225	59.3
	Louis Dugas Jr. (R)	77,842	40.7
3	Steve Bartlett (R)*	228,819	83.0
	Jim Westbrook (D)	46,890	17.0
4	Ralph M. Hall (D)*	120,749	58.0
	Thomas Blow (R)	87,553	42.0
5	John Bryant (D)*	94,391	100.0
6	Joe L. Barton (R)	131,482	56.6
	Dan Kubiak (D)	100,799	43.4
7	Bill Archer (R)*	213,480	86.7
	Billy Willibey (D)	32,835	13.3
8	Jack Fields (R)*	113,031	64.6
	Don Buford (D)	62,072	35.4
9	Jack Brooks (D)*	120,559	58.9
	Jim Mahan (R)	84,306	41.2
10	J. J. Pickle (D)*	186,447	99.8
11	Marvin Leath (D)*	112,940	100.0
12	Jim Wright (D)*	106,299	100.0
13	Beau Boulter (R)	107,600	53.0
	Jack Hightower (D)*	95,367	47.0
14	Mac Sweeney (R)	104,181	51.3
	Bill Patman (D)*	98,885	48.7
15	E. "Kika" de la Garza (D)*	104,863	100.0
16	Ronald D. Coleman (D)*	76,375	57.4
	Jack Hammond (R)	56,589	42.6
17	Charles W. Stenholm (D)*	143,012	100.0
18	Mickey Leland (D)*	109,626	78.8
	Glen E. Beaman (R)	26,400	19.0
	Jose Alvarado (I)	3,064	2.2
19	Larry Combest (R)	102,805	58.1
	Don R. Richards (D)	74,044	41.9
20	Henry B. Gonzalez (D)*	100,443	100.0
21	Tom Loeffler (R)*	199,909	80.6
	Joe Sullivan (D)	48,039	19.4
22	Thomas D. DeLay (R)	125,225	65.3
	Doug Williams (D)	66,495	34.7
23	Albert G. Bustamante (D)	95,721	100.0
24	Martin Frost (D)*	105,210	59.5
	Bob Burk (R)	71,703	40.5
25	Michael A. Andrews (D)*	113,946	64.0
	Jerry Patterson (R)	63,974	36.0
26	Dick Armey (R)	126,641	51.3
	Tom Vandergriff (D)*	120,451	48.7
27	Solomon P. Ortiz (D)*	105,516	63.6
	Richard Moore (R)	60,283	36.4

UTAH

Governor

Norman H. Bangerter (R)	351,792	55.9
Wayne Owens (D)	275,669	43.8
L. S. Brown (AM)	2,158	0.3

House

1	James V. Hansen (R)*	142,952	71.2
	Milton C. Abrams (D)	56,619	28.2
	Willy Marshall (LIBERT)	1,146	0.6
2	David S. Monson (R)	105,540	49.4
	Frances Farley (D)	105,044	49.1

Hugh Butler (LIBERT)	1,456	0.7
James Waters (I)	962	0.4
MaryEllen Gardner (AMER)	791	0.4

3	Howard C. Nielson (R)*	138,918	74.5
	Bruce R. Baird (D)	46,560	25.0
	D. W. Crosby (LIBERT)	1,094	0.6

VERMONT

Governor

Madeleine M. Kunin (D)	116,938	50.0
John J. Easton Jr. (R)	113,264	48.5
William Wicher (LIBERT)	1,904	0.8
Marian Wagner (CIT)	730	0.3
Richard Gottlieb (LU)	695	0.3
Scattered write-ins	222	0.1

House

AL	James M. Jeffords (R)*	148,025	65.4
	Anthony Pollina (D)	60,360	26.7
	James Hedbor (LIBERT)	9,359	4.1
	Peter Diamondstone (LU)	4,858	2.1
	Morris Earle (I)	3,313	1.5

VIRGINIA

Senate

John W. Warner (R)*	1,406,194	70.0
Edythe C. Harrison (D)	601,142	29.9
Scattered write-ins	151	

House

1	Herbert H. Bateman (R)*	118,085	59.1
	John McGlennon (D)	79,577	39.8
	E. J. Green (I)	2,154	1.1
2	G. William Whitehurst (R)*	136,632	99.8
3	Thomas J. Bliley Jr. (R)*	169,987	85.6
	Roger L. Coffey (I)	28,556	14.4
4	Norman Sisisky (D)*	120,093	99.9
5	Dan Daniel (D)*	117,738	100.0
6	James R. Olin (D)*	105,207	53.5
	Ray Garland (R)	91,344	46.5
7	D. French Slaughter Jr. (R)	109,110	56.5
	Lewis M. Costello (D)	77,624	40.2
	R. E. Frazier Sr. (I)	6,397	3.3
8	Stan Parris (R)*	125,015	55.8
	Richard L. Saslaw (D)	97,250	43.4
	Donald W. Carpenter (I)	1,814	0.8
9	Frederick C. Boucher (D)*	102,446	52.0
	Jefferson Stafford (R)	94,510	48.0
10	Frank R. Wolf (R)*	158,528	62.5
	John P. Flannery II (D)	95,074	37.5

WASHINGTON

Governor

Booth Gardner (D)	1,006,993	53.3
John Spellman (R)*	881,994	46.7

House

1	John R. Miller (R)	147,926	56.3
	Brock Evans (D)	115,001	43.7
2	Al Swift (D)*	142,065	58.6
	Jim Klauder (R)	93,472	38.6
	Gary Franco (POP)	6,855	2.8
3	Don Bonker (D)*	150,432	71.1
	Herb Elder (R)	61,219	28.9
4	Sid Morrison (R)*	150,322	76.1
	Mark Epperson (D)	47,158	23.9
5	Thomas S. Foley (D)*	154,988	69.7

	Jack Hebner (R)	67,438	30.3
6	Norman D. Dicks (D)*	124,367	66.1
	Mike Lonergan (R)	60,721	32.3
	Dan Blachly (LIBERT)	2,953	1.6
7	Mike Lowry (D)*	174,560	70.4
	Robert O. Dorse (R)	71,576	28.9
	Mark Manning (SOC WORK)	1,710	0.7
8	Rod Chandler (R)*	146,891	62.4
	Bob Lamson (D)	88,379	37.6

WEST VIRGINIA

Governor

Arch A. Moore Jr. (R)	394,937	53.3
Clyde M. See Jr. (D)	346,565	46.7

Senate

John D. Rockefeller IV (D)	374,233	51.8
John R. Raese (R)	344,680	47.7
Mary E. (Joan) Radin (SOC WORK)	3,299	0.5

House

1	Alan B. Mollohan (D)*	104,639	54.4
	James Altmeyer (R)	87,622	45.6
2	Harley O. Staggers Jr. (D)*	100,345	56.0
	Cleve Benedict (R)	78,936	44.0
3	Bob Wise (D)*	125,306	67.9
	Margaret Miller (R)	59,128	32.1
4	Nick J. Rahall II (D)*	98,919	66.7
	Jess T. Shumate (R)	49,474	33.3

WISCONSIN

House

1	Les Aspin (D)*	127,184	56.2
	Pete Jansson (R)	99,080	43.8
2	Robert W. Kastenmeier (D)*	159,987	63.6
	Albert E. Wiley Jr. (R)	91,345	36.3
3	Steve Gunderson (R)*	160,437	68.4
	Charles F. Dahl (D)	74,253	31.6
4	Gerald D. Kleczka (D)*	158,722	66.6
	Robert V. Nolan (R)	78,056	32.8
	K. Rick Kissell (LAB F)	1,427	0.6
5	Jim Moody (D)*	175,243	98.0
	William C. Breihan (SOC WORK)	3,364	1.9
6	Thomas E. Petri (R)*	170,271	75.8
	David L. Iaquinta (D)	54,266	24.2
7	David R. Obey (D)*	146,131	61.2
	Mark G. Michaelsen (R)	92,507	38.8
8	Toby Roth (R)*	161,005	67.9
	Paul Willems (D)	73,090	30.8
	Gary L. Barnes (LIBERT)	2,005	0.8
	Cornelius D. Van Handel (LAB F)	1,006	0.4
9	F. James Sensenbrenner Jr. (R)*	180,247	73.4
	John Krause (D)	64,157	26.1
	Stephen K. Hauser (CST)	1,306	0.5

WYOMING

Senate

Alan K. Simpson (R)*	146,373	78.3
Victor A. Ryan (D)	40,525	21.7

House

AL	Dick Cheney (R)*	138,234	73.6
	Hugh B. McFadden Jr. (D)	45,857	24.4
	Craig A. McCune (LIBERT)	3,813	2.0

Governors, 1981-84

Following is a list of governors who served during the period of President Reagan's first term, 1981-84. All governors serve four-year terms except those representing Arkansas, New Hampshire, Rhode Island and Vermont; they serve two-year terms. Party designation appears after the governor's name. D stands for Democrat; R, Republican. *(Governors, 1944-80, Congress and the Nation Vol. V, p. 1189)*

	Dates of Service
Alabama	
Forest "Bob" James (D)	1979-83
George C. Wallace (D)	1963-67, 1971-79, 1983-
Alaska	
Jay S. Hammond (R)	1974-82
Bill Sheffield (D)	1982-
Arizona	
Bruce Babbitt (D)	1978-
Arkansas	
Frank D. White (R)	1981-83
Bill Clinton (D)	1979-81, 1983-
California	
Edmund G. Brown Jr. (D)	1975-83
George Deukmejian (R)	1983-
Colorado	
Richard D. Lamm (D)	1975-
Connecticut	
William A. O'Neill (D)	1980-
Delaware	
Pierre S. DuPont IV (D)	1977-85
Florida	
Robert Graham (D)	1979-
Georgia	
George Busbee (D)	1975-83
Joe Frank Harris (D)	1983-
Hawaii	
George Ariyoshi (D)	1974-
Idaho	
John V. Evans (D)	1977-
Illinois	
James R. Thompson (R)	1977-
Indiana	
Robert D. Orr (D)	1981-
Iowa	
Robert Ray (D)	1969-83
Terry Branstad (R)	1983-

	Dates of Service
Kansas	
John Carlin (D)	1979-
Kentucky	
John Y. Brown Jr. (D)	1979-83
Martha Layne Collins (D)	1983-
Louisiana	
David C. Treen (R)	1980-84
Edwin W. Edwards (D)	1972-80, 1984-
Maine	
Joseph E. Brennan (D)	1979-
Maryland	
Harry R. Hughes (D)	1979-
Massachusetts	
Edward J. King (D)	1979-83
Michael S. Dukakis (D)	1975-79, 1983-
Michigan	
William G. Millikan (D)	1969-83
James J. Blanchard (D)	1983-
Minnesota	
Albert H. Quie (R)	1979-83
Rudy Perpich (D)	1976-79, 1983-
Mississippi	
William Winter (D)	1980-84
Bill Allain (D)	1984-
Missouri	
Christopher S. Bond (R)	1973-77, 1981-85
Montana	
Ted Schwinden (D)	1981-
Nebraska	
Charles Thone (R)	1979-83
Bob Kerrey (D)	1983-
Nevada	
Robert F. List (R)	1979-83
Richard H. Bryan (D)	1983-

Dates of Service

New Hampshire

Hugh Gallen (D)	1979-83
John H. Sununu (R)	1983-

New Jersey

Brendan T. Byrne (D)	1974-82
Thomas H. Kean (R)	1982-

New Mexico

Bruce King (D)	1971-75, 1979-83
Toney Anaya (D)	1983-

New York

Hugh L. Carey (D)	1975-83
Mario M. Cuomo (D)	1983-

North Carolina

James B. Hunt Jr. (D)	1977-85

North Dakota

Allen I. Olson (R)	1981-85

Ohio

James A. Rhodes (R)	1963-71, 1975-83
Richard F. Celeste (R)	1983-

Oklahoma

George P. Nigh (D)	1963, 1979-

Oregon

Victor Atiyeh (R)	1979-

Pennsylvania

Richard L. Thornburgh (R)	1979-

Rhode Island

J. Joseph Garrahy (D)	1977-85

South Carolina

Richard W. Riley (D)	1979-

South Dakota

William J. Janklow (R)	1979-

Tennessee

Lamar Alexander (R)	1979-

Texas

William Clements (R)	1979-83
Mark White (D)	1983-

Utah

Scott M. Matheson (D)	1977-85

Vermont

Richard A. Snelling (R)	1977-85

Virginia

John Dalton (R)	1978-82
Charles S. Robb (D)	1982-

Washington

John Spellman (R)	1981-85

West Virginia

John D. Rockefeller IV (D)	1977-85

Wisconsin

Lee Sherman Dreyfus (R)	1979-83
Anthony S. Earl (D)	1983-

Wyoming

Ed Herschler (D)	1975-

Index

Index

A

Abdnor, James (R-S.D.)
  water policy planning - 429
Abortion
  anti-abortion efforts - 52, 690-691 (box), 800
  constitutional amendment proposal - 675, 690-691
  federal funding ban - 540 (box), 690-691
  foreign aid funds ban - 136, 138
  Koop nomination - 531, 552
  O'Connor nomination - 712
  parental consent issue - 526, 553
  Supreme Court decisions - 675, 690, 691, 713, 725
  unisex insurance - 284
Abram, Morris - 694
Abrams, Elliott - 141
Abscam scandal - 800, 802, 804-809
Academy of Peace - 570
Accelerated Cost Recovery System - 66, 69
Acid rain
  Clean Air Act revision - 403, 405, 416, 417, 420-422
  striped bass conservation - 481
  water research - 446
Acquired immune deficiency syndrome (AIDS) - 542, 552
ACTION
  authorizations, appropriations - 602, 611
  Peace Corps independence - 136 (box)
Addabbo, Joseph P. (D-N.Y.)
  arms control talks - 209
  Pershing missiles - 229
Adelman, Kenneth L. - 233, 251, 1029
Adkinson, F. Keith - 1027
Administrative Procedures Act - 777-778
Adolescent Family Life Program - 540
Adolescents. *See Youth.*
Adoption Assistance and Child Welfare Act of 1980 - 553
Adult education - 556, 573-575, 577, 578
Advanced Ballistic Re-entry Vehicle (ABRV) - 218
Advanced Technology Foundation - 111, 119
Advertising
  cigarette warning labels - 543, 548-549
  infant formula marketing code - 142
  public broadcasting - 264
Advisory Commission on Conferences in Ocean Shipping - 319
Advisory Committee on Women Veterans - 619
Aegis missile defense system - 210, 219, 230, 234, 236, 240, 244
Aeroflot - 145
Aerojet-General Corp. - 455, 457
Aerospace Defense Command - 225
AFDC. *See Aid to Families with Dependent Children.*
Affirmative action
  cable TV deregulation - 280

Civil Rights Commission controversy - 694
  Supreme Court cases - 713, 726
Afghanistan
  aid for rebels - 126, 179
  Soviet chemical warfare - 219
AFL-CIO
  Democracy Program - 168
  domestic content bill - 102
  key issues - 645
  labor racketeering bill - 657
  oil allocation authority - 378
  pesticide law revision - 502
  rail strike, 1982 - 314
  synthetic fuel development - 398
Africa. *(See also names of specific countries.)*
  food aid - 178-179, 514
  foreign aid - 171, 173
  Reagan policy - 170
African art museum - 784
African Development Bank and Fund - 132, 154-155, 168, 173, 174
Age Discrimination in Employment Act - 609-610, 839
Aged persons. *(See also Medicaid, Medicare; Retirement and pensions; Social Security programs.)*
  air quality standards - 415
  dependent care tax credit - 697
  employment programs - 591, 594, 609-610, 658
  energy aid - 393
  food and nutrition programs - 585, 586, 593-594, 601, 609
  Foster Grandparents - 590, 611
  health education programs - 610
  housing assistance - 633, 637, 638
  HMO premiums - 532
  mental health programs - 524
  natural gas deregulation - 389
  Older Americans programs - 591, 593-594, 603, 609-610
  polling place access - 792-793
  Reagan's age - 846
  Supreme Court justices' ages - 711
  veterans geriatric research - 624
  VISTA volunteers - 610-611
  voter analysis, 1984 - 20
Agency for International Development (AID)
  abortion ban - 136
  Africa aid - 178
  African refugee assistance - 138
  authorizations, appropriations - 137, 148, 160, 173
  energy aid - 173
  small business research funds - 273
Agent Orange - 613, 615, 620-621
Aging Committee, Select (House)
  jurisdiction, leadership, subcommittees - 972
Aging Committee, Special (Senate)
  jurisdiction, leadership, subcommittees - 967
Agricultural aid programs. *(See also Farmers Home Administration; specific crops.)*
  commodity loans - 491, 495

  costs - 485, 486 (chart), 487, 489, 504, 513 (chart)
  deficiency payments - 491, 497, 511
  disaster loans - 495, 502, 507, 509, 514, 515, 516
  drought aid - 507, 509
  parity concept - 488, 491
  PIK program - 284, 485, 486, 491, 496, 498-499, 504, 508-509, 511, 514
  price supports - 487-493
  production control - 488, 492
  set asides - 491
  summaries - 491, 512
  target prices - 488, 489, 491, 504, 510-514
  user fees - 515-516
Agricultural interests, lobbying
  coal leasing moratorium - 353
  dairy program - 487
  domestic content bill - 102
  natural gas deregulation - 389
  oil allocation authority - 378
  omnibus farm bill - 487-489
  pesticide law revision - 501-502
  reclamation law revision - 431-433
Agricultural Stabilization and Conservation Service
  tobacco quotas - 498, 506
Agricultural trade
  Caribbean trade plan - 106-107
  commodities futures - 499-501
  contract sanctity - 108, 496, 499
  embargo aid - 487, 493, 495
  European subsidies - 103
  export aid - 496, 497, 511, 513, 514
  farm exports - 485, 486, 493
  international commodity prices - 97
  Soviet grain sales - 510 (box)
  tobacco imports - 505, 510, 512
Agriculture, Nutrition and Forestry Committee (Senate)
  jurisdiction, leadership, subcommittees - 611, 963
Agriculture and farming. *(See also Agricultural aid programs; Agricultural interests; Agricultural trade; Agriculture Department; Crop insurance; Food and nutrition; Irrigation; Migrant workers.)*
  acreage reduction - 492, 496-499, 508, 510, 511, 513
  chronology of action
    1981 - 487-495
    1982 - 496-503
    1983 - 503-511
    1984 - 511-516
  conservation - 493, 511
  farm debt - 485-486, 511
  drought aid for farmers - 507
  farm income - 485-486, 487, 490, 508, 513 (graph)
  guest workers - 692, 708
  legislative summary
    1981 - 6
    1982 - 8
  pest control - 492
  reclamation law revision - 431-433
  surplus production - 485-486, 496

Agriculture and Food Act of 1981 - 487-493
Agriculture Committee (House)
  jurisdiction, leadership, subcommittees - 611, 967-968
Agriculture Department (USDA). *(See also Food stamps; Forest Service, U.S.)*
  alcohol fuels program - 394-395, 503
  announcements timing - 510-511
  appropriations - 494
  dairy program - 505 (box), 507
  desalinization - 447
  endangered species - 477, 478
  farm credit - 512
  farm program estimates - 485-486, 487
  Farmers Home Administration loans - 502, 509
  firearms for Mexican border patrols - 503
  food aid programs - 598-601, 609
  grain inspection - 515
  grain reserves - 492
  housing programs - 635
  imputed interest - 80-81
  kitchen inspection - 516
  nutrition research - 612
  PIK program - 499, 508-509
  school lunch regulations - 591, 592
  Soviet grain embargo - 495
  target price freeze - 513
  tobacco program - 506, 507
A. H. Robins Co. - 285
Ahalt, J. Dawson - 504
AID. *See Agency for International Development.*
Aid to Families with Dependent Children (AFDC)
  background - 581
  benefit cuts - 58, 520, 582, 583, 586, 587, 596-597
  child support enforcement - 586, 605, 606
  eligibility requirements - 546, 547, 582, 587, 588, 611
  food stamp eligibility - 586, 596
  home health aid experiments - 647
  income accounting system - 588
  reform proposals - 603, 777
  vendor payments - 588
  work requirements - 520, 583, 586-588, 597
AIDS (acquired immune deficiency syndrome) - 542, 552
Air bags - 322
Air Force, U.S. *(See also Aircraft, military.)*
  appropriations - 214, 223, 246, 248
  Joint Chiefs reorganization plan - 224
  missiles - 218, 236
  planes - 208, 210, 212, 219, 230, 236, 244
  travel budget - 246
Air pollution. *(See also Acid rain.)*
  auto emissions - 422
  chronology of action
    1981-82 - 411-420
    1983-84 - 420-423
  Clean Air Act revisions - 408-409, 411-420

power plant conversion - 384
scrubbers - 422
Supreme Court decisions - 713
Air Transport Association - 696
Air transportation. *(See also Airports.)*
air traffic control - 290, 308-309
airline bankruptcy - 77
airline mergers - 310
aviation taxes - 72, 290
CAB consumer powers transfer - 325-326
cargo liability - 744
crash liability treaty (box) - 696
drug trafficking - 702
federal outlays (graph) - 290
insurance pact - 310
passenger miles (chart) - 313
terrorism penalties - 701
Aircraft, military. *(See also AWACS radar planes; B-1 bomber; Helicopters.)*
B-52 modernization - 211, 212, 221, 237, 244, 252
Backfire bomber - 250
F-16 fighters
deliveries to Israel - 193
sales to Pakistan - 133 (box)
Harriers - 221, 228, 236, 240
Lavi - 172-173
MiG fighters - 181, 182, 186
stealth bomber - 202, 208-210, 212, 218, 219, 226, 228, 229, 236, 237, 241, 244, 252
strategic minerals - 475
tactical fighters - 208, 210-212, 219, 221, 228, 230, 236, 240, 244
Taiwan sales (box) - 154
transport planes - 206, 210, 219, 221, 228
Aircraft carriers - 206, 207, 210, 218, 220, 221
Airport and Airway Trust Fund - 75-76, 290, 299, 308, 310
Airports
authorizations - 72
development aid - 290, 298-299
Alabama
highway aid - 307
revenue sharing - 117
school prayer decision - 676, 703
Tenn-Tom waterway - 433-435
voting rights action - 679, 680
Alaska. *(See also Indians and Alaskan natives.)*
food stamp program - 585
gas pipeline - 384-386
highway aid - 307
hospitals - 541
marine mammal protection - 479
offshore oil leases - 348, 349, 358, 359
oil and gas royalties - 344
oil export controls - 107
park lands - 463, 464
parks game hunting - 470, 474-475
revenue sharing - 117, 359
voting rights action - 679
wilderness areas - 343, 465, 466, 471
Alaska National Interest Lands Conservation Act - 475
Alaska Natural Gas Transportation Act - 385
Alaska Railroad - 314
Albosta, Donald J. (D-Mich.)
electoral defeat - 22
Alcohol, Drug Abuse and Mental Health Administration - 537
Alcohol fuel. *See Synthetic fuels.*
Alcoholic beverages
drunk boating fines - 328
drunk driving crackdown - 316-317
drunk driving debts - 705
export aid - 493
liquor taxes - 58, 81

minimum drinking age - 290, 306, 321-323
Virgin Islands rum industry - 106
wine tariffs - 109-111
Alcoholism
research, prevention, and treatment programs - 523-527, 537, 541-542, 551-552, 561, 618, 624, 774
Aleut tribe
fur seal harvest - 479, 481-482
Alexander, Bill (D-Ark.)
Reagan economic plan - 7
Alexander, Lamar - 12, 14
Aliens. *(See also Citizenship; Immigrants and immigration.)*
Chadha deportation case - 834
deportation, extradition - 677, 692
guest workers - 692, 708
radio licenses - 272
registration - 677
Supreme Court cases - 726-727
unemployment tax exemption - 665
Virgin Island status - 678, 688
All savers certificates - 66, 68, 70, 87
Allain, Bill - 14
Alleghany Corp. - 326-327
Allen, Richard V. - 142, 855
Allen J. Ellender Fellowship program - 570, 578-579
Alliance for Coal and Competitive Transportation - 315
Alzheimer's disease - 610
American Academy of Pediatrics - 546
American Association for the Advancement of Science
pesticide law revision - 502
American Association of Retired Persons - 320
American Bankers Association - 84, 89
American Baptist Churches - 255
American Bar Association
air crash liability treaty - 696
Legal Services Corp. - 677
American Bus Association - 311
American Civil Liberties Union
agent identity disclosure - 151
cable TV deregulation - 280
crime control package - 698
El Salvador human rights - 147, 186
extradition revision - 692
American Conservation Corps - 657, 667, 671
American Electronics Association - 273
American Enterprise Institute - 45, 67
American Farm Bureau Federation
dairy program - 504
pesticide law - 496, 502
American Hospital Association - 539
American Indians. *See Indians and Alaskan natives.*
American Institute of Architects - 815
American Israel Public Affairs Committee - 146
American Jewish Committee - 130
American Legion - 618
American Medical Association
FTC regulation of doctors - 274, 276-277, 538
handicapped infants - 607
heroin for cancer patients - 553
Medicare fee freeze - 57, 544-545
Medicare reform - 539
organ transplants - 549
American Newspaper Publishers Association - 271
American Political Science Association - 844
American Public Health Association - 531, 546
American Public Power Association - 370, 434
American Samoa - 535, 547

American School Food Service Association - 583
American Telephone & Telegraph Co. (AT&T)
deregulation - 261, 265, 270-272, 274
cable TV deregulation - 280
phone rate hike - 275, 278-279
Americas Watch - 186
Amnesty for illegal aliens - 676, 678, 692, 708
Amnesty International - 147, 186
Amoco. *See Standard Oil Co. of Indiana.*
Amtrak
authorizations - 289, 295-297, 320, 326
background - 292-293
board of directors - 296
commuter service transfer from Conrail - 291, 293, 294, 314
debt - 289, 326
"political" trains (box) - 296
rail strike, 1982 - 314
report and wait provision - 840
Amtrak Commuter Services Corp. - 294, 295
Amusement rides - 268, 285
Anadarko Basin - 384
Anderson, John B. - 21
Andrews, Ike (D-N.C.)
electoral defeat - 22
Andrews, Mark (R-N.D.)
budget - 59, 60
Garrison diversion - 444
hunger reports - 600
Andropov, Yuri V. - 126, 254, 854, 856
Andrus, Cecil D. - 342, 348, 352, 354, 404-406, 432, 472
Angola
foreign aid - 132-134, 176
Animals. *See Livestock and meat; Wildlife protection.*
Ansbach, West Germany - 248
Antarctica
criminal jurisdiction - 701
Anti-Ballistic Missile treaty - 240, 244, 252, 253
Antigua - 182
Anti-poverty programs. *See Community services; Economic Development Administration; Head Start; VISTA.*
Anti-satellite missile (ASAT)
arms control issues - 204, 234, 237, 240, 242-243
authorizations, appropriations - 229, 230, 236, 244-246
Langley base - 246, 248
Reagan message (text) - 1081-1085
testing limits - 234, 237, 240, 242-243 (box), 244, 245
Anti-Semitism
AWACS sale to Saudi Arabia - 130
Antitrust and competition
airline waivers - 325, 326
Alaska pipeline - 385
AT&T settlement - 261, 270-271
bus deregulation - 311, 312
coal leasing system - 353, 354, 357
coal slurry pipelines - 315, 320
damage limits for cities - 705-706
damages apportionment - 693
export trading companies - 101-102
foreign plaintiffs - 678, 688
FTC authorization - 277
joint research ventures - 706-707
maritime immunity - 290, 316-319, 324
oil industry exemptions - 376, 378-379, 381, 382, 390-391
Supreme Court cases - 741-743
trucking industry immunity - 321
weapons programs management - 203
Western Union international service - 265

American School Food Service Association - 583
Apache helicopters - 219, 221, 228, 230, 234, 237, 238
Apalachicola National Forest - 466
Apartheid - 105, 108
Appalachian Regional Commission - 44, 114, 115-116
Apple computers - 77
Appointments. *See Nominations and confirmations.*
Appropriations bills
limitation riders - 798
Appropriations Committee (House)
committee veto power - 839
jurisdiction, leadership, subcommittees - 128, 968
party ratios - 802
powers - 798
Appropriations Committee (Senate)
committee veto power - 839
jurisdiction, leadership, subcommittees - 128, 963
powers - 798
Aquatic Resources Trust Fund - 328
Arafat, Yasir - 195
Aransas National Wildlife Refuge - 482
Arapahoe Indians - 345
Archer, Bill (R-Texas)
Social Security reform - 659, 662
Architect of the Capitol
Capitol Hill development master plan (box) - 803
Senate television costs - 804
West Front restoration - 815
Archives. *(See also Records.)*
National Archives independence - 790
ARCO. *See Atlantic Richfield.*
Arctic research - 475
ARENA party - 187
Argentina
foreign aid authorization - 132-134, 160
international finance - 97
nuclear non-proliferation - 168
Arizona
highway aid - 307
Hoover Dam power pricing - 445-446
revenue sharing - 117
voting rights action - 679
wild and scenic rivers - 472-473
wilderness areas - 471, 472
Arkansas
highway aid - 307
revenue sharing - 117
wilderness areas - 471, 472
Arleigh Burke - 236
Armacost, Michael H. - 1030
Armed Resistance Unit - 813
Armed Services. *See Air Force; Army; Coast Guard; Defense Department; Marine Corps; Military pay and benefits; National Guard; Navy; Veterans affairs.*
Armed Services Committee (House)
jurisdiction, leadership, subcommittees - 968
Armed Services Committee (Senate)
jurisdiction, leadership, subcommittees - 964
Arms control. *(See also Missiles; Nuclear non-proliferation; Nuclear weapons; Plutonium production.)*
bargaining chip concept - 204, 209, 238, 244
build down approach - 231, 254, 257
compliance verification - 221-222, 255
destabilizing effect of weapons - 209, 222, 224, 227, 232, 234-235, 237, 242-244, 245, 250, 253
INF talks - 126, 209, 246, 251, 253, 254
"no first use" concept - 251

nuclear freeze movement - 217, 221-
222, 230-231, 235, 255-257
Reagan appointments - 233, 251
Reagan message (text) - 1045-1046
Reagan term overview - 4, 852-853
SALT II - 202, 221-222, 241, 249, 251,
253
Scowcroft panel recommendations -
226, 227 (box)
special report - 249-257
START - 251-257
test ban treaties - 241
throw weight concept - 254
U.S./Soviet arsenals - 203-204, 225,
234, 235, 250-251, 254
zero option plan - 251, 253, 256
**Arms Control and Disarmament
Agency** - 217, 224, 233, 249, 251
Arms Export Control Act - 154, 836
Arms sales
concessional loans - 170
foreign aid appropriations - 136
Guatemala aid block - 163
India - 153-154
Jordan - 124, 196
legislative veto - 124, 836
reporting thresholds - 132, 133, 135,
154, 836
Saudi Arabia - 129-131, 196
Special Defense Acquisition Fund - 135,
137
Taiwan (box) - 154
Armstrong, William L. (R-Colo.)
budget - 39, 53
congressional tax deductions - 829-830
Social Security reform - 662
sodbuster bill - 515
water policy planning - 431
Army, U.S.
Grenada invasion - 169, 183
Honduras construction - 176
Joint Chiefs reorganization plan - 224-
225
manpower ceiling - 208
military construction appropriations -
214, 223, 246-248
minority business aid - 276
modernization proposals - 202
pay scales - 214-215
Sinai peacekeeping force - 140-141
Army Corps of Engineers
cost sharing plan - 440-442
lakefront use - 438
payments in lieu of taxes - 469
water policy planning - 428-429
water projects authorizations, appro-
priations - 409, 433-435, 441, 443
Watt influence - 406
Arnett, Ray - 464
Arson - 685
Arthritis - 537, 543, 550-551
Asbestos - 571, 572, 575
Ashbrook, John M. (R-Ohio)
agent identity disclosure - 151
Ashe, Victor - 21
Asia. See names of specific countries.
Asian Development Bank and Fund -
132, 168, 174
Askew, Reubin - 17
Aspartame - 537
Aspin, Les (D-Wis.)
arms control - 204, 256
budget - 47
MX missile - 237-239
Aspinall, Wayne N. - 340, 429
**Assassinations and attempted assas-
sinations**
Gemayel - 191
Kennedy, John F. - 683
King - 786
Reagan - 127, 675, 683, 692, 698, 847
(box)

Sadat - 191, 195
U.S. presidents - 847
Assiniboine Indians - 792
**Associated General Contractors of
America** - 302
Association of American Railroads -
315, 433
**Association of Trial Lawyers of Amer-
ica** - 696
Athletics. See Sports and recreation.
Atkinson, Eugene V. (Pa.)
electoral defeat - 10
party shift - 799-800, 801
Atlantic Richfield - 385
**Atlantic States Marine Fisheries Com-
mission** - 481
Atomic energy. See Nuclear energy.
Atomic Energy Commission - 367
AuCoin, Les (D-Ore.)
MX missile - 239
offshore oil leases - 350
wilderness areas - 471
AuSable River - 473
Austin, Hudson - 182
Australia
arms sales review - 132, 135
tax indexing - 67
uranium exports - 369
Automobile industry. See also Gasoline;
Highways and roads; Traffic safety;
Trucks and trucking
air bag rule - 322, 713
air pollution issues - 411-423
auto theft bill - 323-324
Chrysler rescue (box) - 118
"domestic content" bill - 96, 99-100,
102, 104, 108-109, 645, 658
foreign imports - 99, 651, 654
FTC used car rule - 268, 273-274, 837
luxury car deductions - 81
odometer fraud bill - 285
passenger miles (chart) - 313
seat belt regulations - 290
AWACS radar planes
authorizations - 219
crew bonuses - 215
sales to Saudi Arabia - 126, 129-131,
193, 196, 836
Azores Islands - 213, 223

B

B-1 bomber
authorizations, appropriations - 206,
208, 209, 218, 219, 226, 228, 229,
237, 244
bases - 246
Reagan requests - 205, 220, 234, 235
role in U.S. arsenal - 202, 210, 212,
221-222, 225, 241, 252
Baby Doe. See Infants, medical neglect of
handicapped.
Bache Group Inc. - 83
Bahamas - 182
Baker, Howard H. Jr. (R-Tenn.)
access to schools for religious groups -
573
Adelman nomination - 231
aid to Nicaraguan rebels - 176
budget - 46, 54, 57, 60, 61
Casey, Hugel investigations - 141
Clinch River breeder reactor - 370,
371, 373
congressional pay - 822
defense spending - 234-235
farm target price freeze - 513
gas tax, highway bill - 303, 304
Grenada invasion - 169
hazardous waste controls - 458

Lebanon policy/war powers - 156-158
legislative veto - 837
MX missile - 239, 241
oil allocation authority - 378
retirement - 21, 812
Senate gym - 803
Senate leadership - 4, 5, 13, 17, 797,
798, 800, 801, 812, 816
Senate television - 800, 810-811, 816,
818
Social Security reform - 662
Voting Rights Act extension - 681
Williams resignation - 808
Baker, James A. III - 847
Balanced budget. See under Budget,
U.S.
Baldrige, Malcolm - 397, 1018
Baldwin-United Corp. - 83
Bank for Industrial Competitiveness -
111, 114, 119
Bank Holding Company Act of 1956 -
84, 92, 101
Bank of America - 385
BankAmerica Corp. - 83
Banking Act of 1933 - 88
**Banking, Finance and Urban Affairs
Committee (House)**
jurisdiction, leadership, subcommittees -
968-969
**Banking, Housing and Urban Affairs
Committee (Senate)**
jurisdiction, leadership, subcommittees -
964
Bankruptcy
administrative fees - 677-678
airlines - 77
courts reorganization - 692-693, 697,
698, 702, 704-705
Supreme Court cases - 314, 714, 744
**Bankruptcy Amendments and Federal
Judgeship Act of 1984** - 704-705
Bankruptcy Reform Act - 714
Banks and banking. (See also Credit
unions; Federal Deposit Insurance Corp.;
Federal Reserve Board; International
development banks; Savings and loan
associations.)
Alaska pipeline costs - 385
all savers plan - 87, 70
chronology of action on financial regulation
1981-82 - 87-90
1983-84 - 90-93
Consumer Co-op Bank - 268
export trading companies - 101-102
failures - 83
farm debt - 485-486, 491, 512
food stamp loss liability - 586
holding companies - 84, 88, 101
industry trends (graph) - 85
interest, dividend withholding - 75, 90-
92
international services - 84, 109
mortgage assumption plan - 634-635
regulation background (box) - 88
Rural Electrification loans - 514-515
solar bank - 394
South Africa loan ban - 108
Strategic Petroleum Reserve financing -
381
student loans - 559, 561, 566
Supreme Court cases - 743-744
Third World debt - 97-98, 104-105
Barbados - 182
Barnes, Michael (D-Md.)
pocket-veto power - 817
Barrack, Thomas J. - 707
Barrett, Laurence I. - 846
Barrier islands protection - 463, 467-
468
Battered wives - 607
Baucus, Max (D-Mont.)
antitrust damages - 693

Clean Air Act revision - 422
safe drinking water - 440
Baxter, William F. - 272
Beaverhead National Forest - 471
Bechtel Group - 127
Bedell, Berkley (D-Iowa)
farm budget cuts - 496
Beggs, James M. - 840
Begich, Nicholas J. - 804
Begin, Menachem
AWACS sale to Saudi Arabia - 129-
131
Golan Heights annexation - 141, 193
Iraq raid - 193
U.S. aid to Israel - 146
West Bank proposal - 194
Bekaa Valley, Lebanon - 191
Belgium
missile deployment - 232, 246, 255
Belize - 182
Bell, Terrel H. - 579, 558, 563, 1018-
1019
Bell, William M. - 1027
Bell Laboratories - 270, 272
Bennett, Charles E. (D-Fla.)
MX missile - 238-239
Bennett, William J. - 579
Bentsen, Lloyd (D-Texas)
Bush relationship - 854
disaster relief - 505
Bergland, Bob - 487
Bernhard, Prince - 100
Berry, Mary Frances - 694-695
Bethlehem Steel - 378
Better Government Association - 802
Bevill, Tom (D-Ala.)
Tenn-Tom waterway - 433
Biaggi, Mario (D-N.Y.)
ERA proposal - 682
Biden, Joseph R. (D-Del.)
budget - 59
Casey investigation - 142
Civil Rights Commission - 695
constitutional convention - 679
nuclear freeze - 257
Bilingual education - 569, 573-575, 577
Binary munitions. See Chemical and
biological weapons.
Bingaman, Jeff (D-N.M.)
election - 11
U.S. military facilities in Honduras - 247
Biomass fuels. See Synthetic fuels.
Birds
Matagorda Island accord - 482
wetlands protection - 480
Bishop, Maurice - 155, 169, 182
Black Bass Act of 1926 - 480
Black Lung Disability Trust Fund - 649-
650
Black Mesa Pipeline - 315, 320
Blackmun, Harry A.
appointment - 711-712
legislative veto - 835
Blacks
college endowment aid - 569
infant mortality - 546
Jackson presidential candidacy - 18
judicial appointments - 676
King statue in Capitol - 777, 784
members of Congress, 1974-85 (totals)
- 15 (box)
vote analysis, 1984 - 18, 20, 21, 23
voter registration (chart) - 680
Voting Rights Act extension - 680
Wheat election - 11
Blaize, Herbert - 183
Block, John R.
dairy programs - 504, 505
drought aid for farmers - 507
farm budget cuts - 496-497
farm loans - 512

farm programs - 485-486
omnibus farm bill - 488-490
PIK program - 498-499
profile - 1017
school lunch regulations - 592
Soviet grain sales - 510
target price freeze - 511
tobacco bill - 498
Block grants - 113, 519, 609, 771-772, 773-774
Blue Cross and Blue Shield - 521, 539
Board for International Broadcasting - 148, 149, 153, 166, 167
Board of Veterans Appeals - 623
Boats and boating
safety programs - 306, 307, 328
Bob Marshall wilderness area - 342
Bodega basin - 350
Boggs, Thomas Hale - 804
Boland, Edward P. (D-Mass.)
CIA in Nicaragua - 184
intelligence authorizations - 139
Nicaragua covert aid - 162, 163
Boll Weevils - 3, 6, 13, 37, 53, 68, 798, 800, 849
Bolling, Richard (D-Mo.)
budget reconciliation - 41
outside income limits - 823-824
Social Security benefits - 646
Bonds. See Stocks, bonds, and securities.
Bonker, Don (D-Wash.)
high-tech exports - 98
Bonneville Power Administration - 372, 337, 388, 434
Bookbinder, Hyman - 130
Boren, David L. (D-Okla.)
farm acreage reduction - 497
Boschwitz, Rudy (R-Minn.)
dairy price supports - 493
reelection - 21
Boulder Canyon Project Act of 1928 - 445
Bowen-McLaughlin-York Corp. - 153-154
Boxer, Barbara (D-Calif.)
Hoover Dam power pricing - 445
Bradley, Bill (D-N.J.)
agent identity disclosure - 140
international finance - 98
oil allocation authority - 376-378
Strategic Petroleum Reserve - 380
tax reform plan - 79
Three Mile Island cleanup - 370
Bradley, Tom - 12
Bradley troop carriers - 230, 234
Brady, James S. - 783, 847
Brady, Nicholas (R-N.J.) - 11
Brazil
international finance - 97
Breeder reactors. See under Nuclear energy.
Brennan, William J. Jr.
appointment - 711-712
legislative veto - 835
Brezhnev, Leonid - 126, 144, 249, 856
Bristol Bay - 358
Broadcasting. (See also Board for International Broadcasting; Federal Communications Commission; Public broadcasting; Radio; Television.)
coverage of House proceedings - 816, 818
coverage of Senate proceedings - 810-811, 818
deregulation - 273, 275, 281-282
fairness doctrine - 281
licenses - 263-264, 272-273
Supreme Court cases - 740
Brock, William E.
domestic content - 102
foreign trade targeting - 110
profile - 1025-1026

Soviet grain sales - 510
uranium imports - 369
Brooks, Jack (D-Texas)
transcript alterations - 814
Broomfield, William S. (R-Mich.)
AWACS sale to Saudi Arabia - 131
nuclear freeze resolution - 221, 256
Brother International Corp. - 142
Brotherhood of Locomotive Engineers - 290, 314
Brown, Charles - 270
Brown, Clarence J. (R-Ohio)
Alaska pipeline - 386
oil company mergers - 382
Brown, Edmund G. - 698, 845
Brown, Edmund G. Jr. - 11, 348, 349, 455
Brown, George E. Jr. (D-Calif.)
ASAT missile - 242-243
Clinch River breeder reactor - 373
Brown, Hank (R-Colo.)
African Development Fund - 155
Brown, Harold - 250
Brown, Lester O. - 814
Broyhill, James T. (R-N.C.)
Alaska pipeline - 386
Clean Air Act revisions - 417
Conrail sale proposal - 294, 328
nuclear power plant licensing - 368
nuclear waste disposal - 365
oil allocation authority - 378
Bruce, Terry L. - 23
Bryant, William B. - 806
Buckley, Esther Gonzalez-Arroyo - 694
Buckley, James L.
Board of International Broadcasting
salary - 153
F-16 sales to Pakistan - 133
Budget, U.S. (See also Taxes and taxation; Treasury, U.S.)
accounting practices
military aid change - 172
neutrality for Medicare expenditures - 540
off-budget for Strategic Petroleum Reserve - 379, 381, 393, 396
Social Security separation - 663
balanced budget plans - 30, 33, 37-38, 44, 47, 52, 679, 700 (box), 799
budget process - 5, 12, 32-35, 37, 41, 53, 54, 56, 59, 797-798
chronology of action
1981 - 37-45
1982 - 45-50
1983 - 50-56
1984 - 56-61
debt ceiling (box) - 42-43
defense spending summaries - 203 (graph), 207 (box), 234 (graph)
deficit projections - 28-29, 32, 33, 35, 37, 45-51, 54-56
deficit reduction
FY82 proposals - 37
FY84 proposals - 54-55
FY85 proposals - 56-60
Grace commission recommendations (box) - 791
pay-as-you-go plan - 47, 59
reconciliation cuts - 48-49, 51, 53
Rose Garden plan - 56, 59-61, 79
special reserve fund - 51
tax bills - 64, 77, 78
entitlement programs (box) - 38
legislative summary
1981 - 5-6
1982 - 8
1983 - 12-13
1984 - 16-17
presidential messages (text) - 1033-1036, 1050-1056, 1063-1069, 1076-1081

presidents, Congress and budget, 1980-85 (chart) - 36
Reagan term overview - 3-4, 848-850
reconciliation bill index to programs - 40
Budget Act. See Congressional Budget and Impoundment Control Act of 1974.
Budget Committee (House)
jurisdiction, leadership, subcommittees - 969
party ratios - 802
Budget Committee (Senate)
abolition proposal - 34
jurisdiction, leadership, subcommittees - 964
powers - 41
Buena Vista petroleum reserve - 346
Buffalo, N.Y.
education grants - 569
Buffalo Bill Dam - 432, 436
Bumpers, Dale (D-Ark.)
coal leasing - 351, 355, 356
Cuba resolution - 150
Pauley Group leases - 349
Bunzel, John - 694
Bureau of Indian Affairs (BIA)
block grant - 773
jurisdiction - 404
oil and gas leases - 344-345
schools - 576
Bureau of Justice Assistance - 700
Bureau of Land Management (BLM)
authorizations, appropriations - 463
coal leasing - 351-356
Oregon land tracts - 476
Outer Continental Shelf leases - 347
payments in lieu of taxes - 469
program diversity - 404
timber harvest - 473
watershed leasing - 351
wilderness areas - 339-344, 465
wildlife protection - 478-479
Bureau of Mines - 398, 404
Bureau of Outdoor Recreation - 463, 464
Bureau of Reclamation
dam repair funds - 438, 444
Hoover Dam - 445
payments in lieu of taxes - 469
reclamation law revision - 431-433
water policy planning - 428-430
water projects appropriations - 404, 409, 433-435, 441, 443
water projects cost sharing - 440-442
Burford, Anne M. (Gorsuch)
career - 403, 405, 406, 408, 454, 457, 460, 1027
clean air - 418, 419, 423
clean water - 439
contempt citation - 341, 449-452, 455
EPA appointments - 453
EPA operations - 403, 405, 408, 420
Superfund scandal - 405, 449-452, 454-457
Burford, Robert F. - 405, 406, 455
Burger, Warren E.
appointment - 711-712
executive privilege issue - 450
legislative veto - 835, 981
offshore leasing - 359
Supreme Court caseload - 714
Supreme Court police force - 683
Burlington Northern Co. - 469
Burt, Richard R. - 1029
Burton, Joseph R. - 805, 808
Burton, Phillip (D-Calif.)
California redistricting - 9
national park expansion - 464
national trails - 469
racketeering bill - 657
wilderness areas - 466, 471, 472

Bus industry
deregulation - 300, 310-314
passenger miles (chart) - 313
Bus Regulatory Reform Act of 1981 - 310-314
Bush, George
authority in Reagan assassination attempt - 847
banking deregulation - 84
biographical background (box) - 854-855
Clean Air Act revisions - 418-420
House campaigns, 1984 - 23
MX missile - 238-240
nerve gas funding - 228, 229
regulatory reform - 778
vice presidential candidacy - 19-20
Bush, Prescott - 854
Business and industry. (See also Advertising; Antitrust and competition; Business interests, lobbying; Business taxes; Commerce Department; Deregulation; Federal Trade Commission; Foreign trade; Hazardous wastes management; Patents and trademarks; Stocks, bonds and securities; names of specific industries.)
Alaska pipeline costs - 384-386
bankruptcy - 693, 702, 704-705
cash/credit card issues - 269, 284-285
energy aid - 590
contract sanctity - 108
corporate takeover reforms - 262, 283
environmental issues
Clean Air Act revision - 408-409, 411-421
environmental protection vs. economic growth issue - 405, 470
EPA relations - 408
illegal wildlife trade - 480
national parks protection - 467
seabed mining - 437
water pollution cleanup - 439
government assistance issues
Chrysler rescue (box) - 118
copyright "manufacturing clause" - 686
defense industries - 115, 116, 119
enterprise zones - 79, 119-120, 630, 639
industrial policy - 97, 111, 114, 119
minority firms program - 266
relocation aid - 787-788
strategic minerals - 475
timber contract relief - 473-474
health insurance plans - 534
information disclosure - 267-268, 779
insider securities trading - 276, 283
Job Training Partnership Act - 643, 655-656
joint research ventures - 706-707
product safety - 267-269
regulatory reform - 777-778
research funds - 266
science education - 565
Supreme Court cases - 741-748
vocational education committees - 578
Business interests, lobbying
Bildisco remedies - 704
Davis-Bacon Act exemption - 213
immigration reform - 692, 708
imputed interest - 80-81
noise control - 454
oil allocation authority - 378
pesticide law revision - 501-502
real estate depreciation - 79
tax cuts/increases - 37, 73
wilderness areas - 339-344, 470
Business taxes
carryovers - 69, 71
cruise convention deductions - 107, 76
depreciation - 32, 66, 68, 69, 74

employee plan contributions
  legal services - 70
  stock ownership - 68, 70, 82, 665
  welfare - 82
estimated tax liability - 74
export subsidies - 111-112
foreign payments deductions - 75, 81
foreign travel deductions - 76
fringe benefits - 82
golden parachutes - 81, 283
inventory liquidation - 76-77
investment tax credit - 74, 77
leasing provisions - 69, 73, 75, 81
lunch deductions - 73, 592
rate reductions - 70
research tax credit - 69
safe-harbor leases - 71, 75, 81
subchapter S taxation - 76
Supreme Court cases - 747-748
targeted jobs credit - 70, 76, 82, 672
Busing - 52, 565, 677, 693, 694, 708
(box), 800
"Buy America" provisions
  coal slurry pipelines - 315
  highway legislation - 315, 316
Byrd, Harry F. (I-Va.)
  retirement - 11
Byrd, Robert C. (D-W.Va.)
  acid rain - 481
  Capitol bomb explosion - 813
  Cardinal train (box) - 296
  industrial policy - 97
  Lebanon policy - 156-157
  Senate leadership - 5, 801, 812, 816
  Senate television - 810
  stealth bomber - 210
  Stonewall Jackson dam - 443
Byron, Beverly (D-Md.)
  ASAT missile - 243

C

CAB. See Civil Aeronautics Board.
Cabinet
  Department of International Industry
    and Trade proposal - 111
  Donovan indictment - 667, 846
  drug enforcement proposal - 689, 692,
    698, 699
  Meese confirmation wait - 707
  members (list) - 1019 (box)
  members' profiles - 1017-1025
  natural gas deregulation - 383
  protection of officers - 683
  Watt contempt resolution - 341
**Cabinet Council on Natural Resources
and Environment** - 334, 337, 406, 421,
428-429, 441, 475
**Cable Satellite Public Affairs Network
(C-SPAN)** - 816
Cable TV
  deregulation - 262, 274, 275, 279-281,
    703
  local rate authority - 272
  retransmissions - 694
  utility pole rates - 272
Calendar Wednesday - 799
Calero, Adolfo - 184, 185
Califano, Joseph A. Jr - 809-810, 814,
815
California
  Elk Hills petroleum reserve - 346-347
  forests - 473
  highway aid - 307
  Hoover Dam power pricing - 445-446
  offshore oil leases - 347-350, 357-359
  oil and gas royalties - 345
  reclamation law revision - 431-432
  revenue sharing - 117

voting rights action - 679
wild and scenic rivers - 472-473
wilderness areas - 465, 466, 470-472
Calkin, Brant - 341
Cambodia. See Kampuchea.
Camp David accords - 141, 193, 195
Canada
  acid rain - 417, 420-422
  Alaska pipeline - 385, 386
  fur seal harvest - 479
  Garrison Diversion project - 435, 443
  mineral leasing reciprocity - 341, 451-
    452
  uranium exports - 369
  U.S. maritime boundary treaty - 143-
    144
Cancer. *(See also Hazardous substances;
Radiation.)*
  Agent Orange exposure - 621
  cigarette warning labels - 548-549
  heroin use by patients - 553
  research and treatment - 541, 550
  risk statistics report - 537
  saccharin ban deferral - 530-531, 541
Cannon, Howard W. (D-Nev.)
  airport programs - 308
  electoral defeat - 11
  nuclear waste disposal - 365
Canyonlands National Park - 467
Cape Cod National Seashore - 463
Cape Hatteras National Seashore -
481
Capital punishment - 699, 708
Capitan Mountain wilderness area -
339, 342
Capitol Building, U.S.
  Architect's office - 803
  bomb explosion (box) - 813
  King statue - 777, 784
  master plan for development (box) -
    803
  West Front restoration - 815
Capitol Historical Society
  tax-exempt sales - 783
Capitol Police
  Capitol bomb explosion - 813
  drug investigations - 815
Cardinal (train) - 296
Caribbean countries. See also Cuba.
  Caribbean Basin Initiative - 91, 102,
    104, 106-107, 149, 181
  Grenada invasion - 155, 169, 182-184
  Radio Marti authorization - 166
Carlucci, Frank C. - 160, 851
**Carnegie Foundation for the Advance-
ment of Teaching** - 555, 570
Carruthers, Garrey E. - 352, 406
Carter, Jimmy
  agriculture policy - 488
  Alaska pipeline - 384-385
  arts, humanities endowments - 776
  defense policies
    arms control - 249-250, 255-256
    B-1 bomber - 252
    MX missile - 205, 218
    nuclear weapons - 138, 139, 215,
      241, 255-256
  budget - 36, 37, 201, 202, 207, mes-
    sage (text) 1033-1036
  congressional support - 853
  consumer affairs - 267
  economic policy - 3, 28, 30, 116
  election, 1980 - 19-21
  energy policy
    Clinch River breeder reactor - 370-
      372
    coal leasing program - 354
    Energy Department appointments -
      337
    natural gas regulation - 382, 388
    term overview - 333-334, 336, 393,
      397

nuclear power plant licensing - 367
nuclear waste disposal - 361-364
offshore oil leases - 348
oil and gas deregulation - 375-376
oil price decontrol - 377
power plant conversion - 383-384
Strategic Petroleum Reserve - 380
synthetic fuel - 398
environmental policy
  clean air - 412, 419
  payments in lieu of taxes - 469
  Superfund - 460
  water projects - 404, 428-430
  wilderness areas - 409, 466
ethics proposals - 684
federal pay - 214, 775, 823
foreign policy
  arms sales - 836
  Canada-U.S. maritime treaty - 143-
    144
  consulate closings - 149
  development banks - 129, 148
  human rights - 129, 141
  Soviet grain embargo - 487, 488,
    495
health policy - 524
housing authorization - 629
jobs programs - 653
judicial appointments - 676, 711, 1020-
  1021
labor support - 643
leadership style - 845
pocket-veto power - 817
tourism agency - 267
VISTA funding - 590
Carterfone decision - 271
Case, Francis - 388
Casey, William J.
  financial disclosure investigation - 141-
    142
  mining of Nicaraguan harbors - 184
  profile - 1025
  staff authorization - 152
Castro, Fidel
  Radio Marti authorization - 166
Catholic church and schools
  bishops on nuclear war - 255-256
  child health program - 540
  El Salvador human rights reports - 186
  tuition tax credit - 564
  U.S.-Vatican relations - 167
Catholic University - 694
Census Bureau
  poverty reports - 581, 599, 600, 603
  vote analysis - 16
Center for Excellence in Education -
605
Centers for Disease Control - 525, 542,
620, 621
Central America. *(See also Costa Rica;
El Salvador; Guatemala; Honduras; Kis-
singer commission; Nicaragua.)*
  Caribbean Basin Initiative - 102, 106-
    107, 149
  Common Market - 188
  Contadora group - 165, 185
  foreign aid - 170-172, 177-178, 240
  map - 183
  Radio Marti authorization - 166
  Reagan message (text) - 1069-1072
  Reagan policy overview - 4, 124-125
  special report - 181-189
  Stone mission - 165
  use of U.S. combat troops - 241, 245
**Central American Development Orga-
nization** - 188, 189
Central Arizona Project - 435-436
Central Intelligence Agency (CIA)
  agent identity disclosure - 151-152
  aid for Afghan rebels - 179
  authorization - 139-140, 152, 168
  Casey, Hugel investigations - 141-142

collection of foreign intelligence in U.S.
  - 140
drug enforcement policy board - 701
El Salvador role - 175, 187
Freedom of Information Act - 772, 776,
  788-789
Guatemala coup (1954) - 163
headquarters construction - 179
Nicaragua role - 125, 162-165, 171,
  176-177, 179, 182, 184, 838
protection of director - 683
USIA renaming - 149
Century 21 Real Estate Co. - 686
Chadha, Jagdish Rai - 834, 981
Chafee, John H. (R-R.I.)
  clean water bill - 439
  sewer grants - 427-428
  Tenn-Tom waterway - 435
Chamber of Commerce, U.S.
  Democracy Program - 168
  Watt address - 355
Chandler, Rod (R-Wash.)
  medical neglect of handicapped infants
    - 607
CHAP. See Child Health Assurance Pro-
gram.
Charles, Eugenia - 169, 183
Chase Manhattan Bank - 83, 92, 385
Cheese. See Dairy industry.
Chemical and biological weapons
  Air Force defenses - 248
  congressional refusal to authorize pro-
    duction - 201, 206, 211, 213, 217,
    218, 220, 223, 226, 228, 229
  Soviet stockpile and use - 204, 219
  study commission - 236
Chemical industry
  Agent Orange compensation - 613
  drug enforcement - 700
  EPA relations - 408
  patent extension - 693
  Superfund - 449-450, 459, 460
  toxic substances control - 453-454, 457
Chemical Manufacturers Association -
452
Cheney, Dick (R-Wyo.)
  House leadership - 5
  Reagan style - 845
  wilderness leasing - 342
Chernenko, Konstantin U. - 126
Chevron. See Standard Oil Co. of Cali-
fornia.
Child abuse
  child pornography - 697, 700-702
  medical neglect of handicapped infants
    - 553
  prevention and treatment programs -
    582, 591, 599, 606-608
**Child Abuse Prevention and Treat-
ment Act** - 607
**Child Health Assurance Program
(CHAP)** - 57, 522, 540, 543, 544, 546-
547, 582
Child nutrition and health. *(See also
Child Health Assurance Program; Maternal and child health; Women, Infants
and Children (WIC) program.)*
  emergency medical services - 552
  infant formula marketing code - 142-
    143, 149
  Medicaid assistance - 58, 535
  Reagan term overview - 582
  school lunch programs - 519, 520, 583,
    591-593, 601-602, 611-612
**Child Support Enforcement Amend-
ments of 1984** - 605-606
Children. *(See also Aid to Families with
Dependent Children; Child abuse; Child
nutrition and health; Day care programs;
Elementary and secondary education;
Family and marital issues; Infants;
Youth.)*

Amerasian immigration - 689
AID programs - 173
health programs - 57, 58, 525, 535, 552
mental health programs - 552
missing children - 686, 699, 700
Supreme Court cases - 727, 733-734
toy recalls - 285
welfare programs - 589
Children, Youth and Families Committee, Select (House)
jurisdiction, leadership, subcommittees - 972
Children's Defense Fund - 546
Chile
foreign aid - 132-134, 160
Chiles, Lawton (D-Fla.)
budget - 58, 60, 61
MX missile - 238-239
Senate leadership - 816
China, People's Republic of
trade status - 103, 107
U.S.-China communique (box) - 154
Chloracne - 615, 621
Choate, Pat - 302
Christopher, George - 845
Chronic Hazard Advisory Panels - 268
Chrysler Corp. (box) - 118
Church, Frank - 855
Churches. See Freedom of religion; Religion and religious organizations; Religious interests, lobbying.
Churchill, Winston - 144
CIA. See Central Intelligence Agency.
Cigarettes
fire-safe cigarettes - 285
taxes - 58, 76, 79, 549
warning labels - 543, 548-549
Circuit Court of Appeals
California wilderness areas - 466
disability review cases - 669
FTC funeral home rule - 277
legislative veto - 834
patent jurisdiction - 686-687
state tax exemption for congressmen - 823
Citibank - 385
Citicorp - 84, 92.
Cities. See Community development; State and local government.
Cities Service Co. - 341, 382
Citizen/Labor Energy Coalition - 389
Citizens band radio - 272
Citizenship
Amerasian immigration - 689
naturalization requirements - 677
Supreme Court cases - 727
Wallenberg honorary - 144
Citrus fruit - 99
Civil Aeronautics Board (CAB)
airline deregulation - 310
consumer powers transfer - 325-326
Civil defense
authorizations - 205, 206, 217-218
surplus federal property - 783
Civil rights. (See also Civil Rights Commission; Equal opportunity; Sex discrimination.)
Education Department reduced role proposal - 565
exclusionary rule - 709
habeas corpus claims - 699, 709
highway aid bill - 322
mail fraud bill - 780-781
Supreme Court cases - 725-741
Voting Rights Act extension - 680-681
Civil Rights Commission
authorization, appropriations - 678
Reagan policy overview - 848
restructuring - 676, 694-695, 1029
Civil rights interests, lobbying
broadcast deregulation - 281

Civil Rights Commission restructuring - 694-695
extradition revision - 692
immigration reform - 692
King holiday - 786
Voting Rights Act extension - 680
Civil service. See Federal employment.
Civil Service Reform Act - 775
Civil Service Retirement System - 661, 784
Civilian Conservation Corps - 671
Claims. (See also Foreign claims.)
air crash liability treaty - 696
federal employees - 689
Tris reimbursement - 688
Claims Court, U.S. - 686, 688
Clark, Robert G. - 11
Clark, William P. - 351
bishops on nuclear war - 256
environmental policy - 405
Interior career - 337, 407, 408
management style (box) - 474
mineral leasing - 351, 352, 356-358
national security adviser appointment - 142, 855
profile - 1023
water projects cost sharing - 441
Clark amendment - 134
Clausen, A. W. - 132
Clausen, Don H. (R-Calif.)
nuclear freeze movement - 256
offshore oil leases - 350
Claybrook, Joan - 322
Clayton Act - 693
Clean Air Act of 1970
effect on coal market - 353
revisions - 405, 408-409, 411-422
Clean Water Act of 1977 - 405, 409, 426, 439
Clean Water Action Project - 439
Clements, William - 12
Clinch River breeder reactor - 335, 336, 370-373, 395, 399-400
Close Up Foundation - 570, 578-579
Cloture. See Filibusters and cloture votes.
Coal industry
acid rain - 420-421
black lung trust fund - 649-650
Energy Department funds - 394
federal leasing program - 334, 351-357, 403, 406, 407, 838
power plant conversion - 383-384
rail strike, 1982 - 314
slurry pipelines - 315, 319-320
strip mining regulation - 468-469
synthetic fuels - 397-399
Tenn-Tom waterway - 433-434
wilderness leasing - 339
Coard, Bernard - 182
Coast Guard
authorizations - 300-301, 316, 328
oil spill liability - 437
retirement pay increases - 61
Coastal Barrier Resources System - 468
Coastal Zone Management Act of 1972 - 349, 358, 359
Cobalt - 475
Cobra helicopters - 228
Cocaine. See Drug trafficking.
Cochran, Thad (R-Miss.)
nuclear waste disposal - 365
payments in lieu of taxes - 469
re-election - 21
Coelho, Tony (D-Calif.)
dairy price supports - 494
MX missile - 239
wild and scenic rivers - 473
Cohen, William S. (R-Maine)
arms control - 257
MX deployment - 209, 210
nuclear freeze resolution - 231
COLAs. See Cost-of-living adjustments.

Colby, William E. - 855
Colleges. See Postsecondary education.
Collins, Martha Layne - 14
Colombia
Contadora group - 125, 165, 185
Colony oil shale project - 398
Colorado
coal leasing - 353, 356
highway aid - 307
oil shale - 398-399
revenue sharing - 117
voting rights action - 680
Colorado River - 409, 447
Commerce. (See also Agricultural trade; Banks and banking; Business and industry; Commerce Department; Consumer affairs; Federal Trade Commission; Foreign trade; Interstate Commerce Commission; Transportation.)
chronology of action
1981 - 263-269
1982 - 269-274
1983 - 274-278
1984 - 278-286
Commerce, Science and Transportation Committee (Senate)
jurisdiction, leadership, subcommittees - 964
Commerce Department. (See also Consumer Product Safety Commission; Economic Development Administration.)
appropriations - 264
economic development aid - 115
endangered species - 477, 478
Energy Department abolition proposal - 336, 397
energy technology trade - 111
export controls - 98, 101-102, 107-108
exports analysis - 664
fur seal harvest - 479, 481-482
marine mammal protection - 479, 481
marine sanctuaries - 438
maritime transfer - 299
Soviet economic sanctions - 145
striped bass conservation - 481
tourism in U.S. - 267
unfair foreign trade practices - 110
Commercial and Apartment Conservation Service - 400
Commission on Congressional Mailing Standards (House) - 826, 827, 831
Commission on Executive, Legislative and Judicial Salaries - 775, 823, 824, 827
Commission on Fair Market Policy for Federal Coal Leasing. See Linowes commission.
Commission on Fine Arts - 782
Commission on Fiscal Accountability of the Nation's Energy Resources - 345
Commission on the West Central Front of the United States Capitol - 803, 815
Committee for a Sane Nuclear Policy - 256
Committee on the Present Danger - 251
Commodity Control List - 107
Commodity Credit Corp.
dairy donations - 497
export aid - 497, 514
food aid for Africa - 178
food distribution - 599, 601
gasohol from grain surplus - 503
omnibus farm bill - 490, 493
PIK program - 499
Commodity Exchange Act - 283, 501
Commodity Futures Trading Commission - 283, 496, 499-501
Common Cause - 256, 707, 826, 829, 831

Communications Act of 1934 - 261, 265, 270, 271, 281
Communications and telecommunications. (See also Broadcasting; Federal Communications Commission; Telephone and telegraph companies.)
chronology of action
1981 - 263-269
1982 - 269-274
1983 - 274-278
1984 - 278-286
Reagan term overview - 261-262
Communications Satellite Corp. (COMSAT) - 786
Community action agencies - 590-591
Community development. (See also Housing; Welfare and social services.)
block grants - 113, 117, 590-591, 629-630, 631, 632, 634-636, 663-664, 774
Clean Air Act revision - 411-420
Economic Development Administration programs - 113-116, 118
enterprise zones - 79, 91, 115-116, 119-120
infrastructure maintenance - 115, 302 (box), 653, 793
Local Public Works program - 653
outlays (graph) - 630
neighborhood development - 632, 636
Phase II jobs plan - 664-665
sewer grants - 427
Community health programs - 524, 527, 551, 599, 602
Community Service Employment program - 610
Community services block grants - 520, 551, 590, 591, 599, 603-605, 773-774
Community Services Administration - 520, 582, 590, 773-774, 783
Comprehensive Employment and Training Act (CETA)
background - 653
expiration - 32, 643, 645, 648, 651, 655
youth employment programs - 648
Comprehensive Environmental Response, Liability and Compensation Act - 449-450, 460
Comprehensive Health Planning and Services Act - 774
Comptroller of the Currency - 84, 88, 92-93
Computers and computer systems
AT&T deregulation - 261, 270, 271
business, personal use - 81
computer education - 572
computer fraud - 701
school donations - 77
semiconductor chip piracy protection - 706
Soviet economic sanctions - 145
unauthorized access - 554, 699
Conable, Barber B. Jr. (R-N.Y.)
budget - 44
committee party ratios - 802
dairy program - 504, 505
disabled workers - 668
Superfund renewal - 461
Conference of Catholic Bishops - 255-256
Conference of Mayors, U.S. - 279-280, 600
Congregate Housing Services Program - 594, 637
Congress. (See also Congressional elections; Congressional ethics; Congressional-executive relations; Congressional pay and benefits; Congressional votes; House of Representatives, U.S.; Legislative veto; Senate, U.S.)
authorization, appropriation powers - 838

chaplains - 811-812
chronology of action
1981 - 801-804
1982 - 804-812
1983 - 812-816
1984 - 816-819
Grace commission criticism - 791
lame duck sessions - 9, 804, 828, 975-976
legislative process in brief - 873-876
legislative service organizations - 802
members
average age (chart) - 14
blacks, 1947-85 (totals) - 15 (box)
lists, 1981-85 - 953-961, 945-951
women, 1947-85 (totals) - 15 (box)
pages - 809-810, 813-814
party affiliations and presidency, 1789-1985 (chart) - 1098-1099
reports from agencies - 783
Supreme Court cases on powers - 761
Congress Watch - 386
Congressional Black Caucus - 47, 802
Congressional Budget and Impoundment Control Act of 1974 - 34 (box), 41, 51, 55, 56, 59-61, 684, 797
Congressional Budget Office
Amtrak estimates - 295
budget process study - 35
budget projections
FY82 - 41, 43
FY83 - 46, 48, 49
child nutrition program costs - 601
cost of legislation estimates - 777
debt service projections - 35
deficit reduction - 55
director - 67
disabled workers estimates - 668
education block grants - 560
energy programs estimates - 393, 397
entitlement study - 38
farm program estimates - 485, 486, 489, 496, 497
Grace commission analysis - 791
Hospital Insurance projections - 522
jobless health insurance - 542
mass transit estimates - 299
Medicare fund projections - 538, 539, 545
railroad retirement estimates - 666
social services block grants - 582
tax indexing estimates - 64
trade adjustment aid estimates - 665
veterans health care projections - 614
veterans job preference - 625
welfare programs estimates - 583, 586, 593
Congressional committees
franking privilege - 827
jurisdiction, leadership, subcommittees (tables) - 963-974
legislative veto - 833, 834, 838, 839, 840
party ratios - 798
posts of party switchers - 799-800
Congressional elections
campaign committees - 71
campaign spending - 21
disputed elections - 23
franking privilege - 827, 831-832
House
1982 - 9-11
1984 - 22-23
returns by state (lists)
1982 - 1104-1112
1984 - 1115-1121
Senate
1982 - 11-12
1984 - 21-22
special elections - 7, 9-11, 1103, 1113-1114
targeted Superfund grants - 457

Congressional ethics. *(See also Congressional pay.)*
Abscam scandal - 800, 802, 804-809
campaign contributions - 386
codes - 684
Crane sexual misconduct censure - 23, 813-814
drug use investigation - 815
Ferraro financial investigation - 818
Hansen financial conviction - 23, 818
Hatfield financial investigation - 818-819
Hinson resignation - 804
pages investigation - 809-810
Richmond resignation - 809
senators convicted in office (box) - 808
special-interest caucuses - 802
Studds sexual misconduct censure - 813-814
transcript alterations - 814-815
voting of members under investigation - 805 (box), 813
Williams resignation - 804-809, 819
Congressional-executive relations. *(See also Legislative veto.)*
budget process - 5, 34, 41, 53
Burford/Superfund controversy - 405, 449-452, 455-456
Civil Rights Commission controversy - 694
education regulations controversy - 563-564
foreign aid authorization process - 124, 128, 129, 132, 136-137, 146, 155-156, 161, 189
Fort Union coal leasing - 356
government reorganization authority - 790
Lebanon policy/war powers - 124, 156, 158, 192
pocket veto power (box) - 817
power rate study - 434
presidential support (box) - 853
Richmond plea bargain - 809
water policy planning - 428-430
Watergate legislative legacy - 684
Watt controversy - 405
White House lobbying
AWACS sale to Saudi Arabia - 129-131, 196
budget - 43
dairy price supports - 493
El Salvador aid - 155
MX missile - 238
NATO defense burden sharing - 247
nuclear freeze resolution - 256
oil allocation authority - 376-378
omnibus farm bill - 489
tax cut - 68
tax increases - 73
Congressional pay and benefits
chronology of action
1981 - 821-827
1982 - 827-830
1983 - 830-832
1984 - 832
day-care center - 815-816
expense allowances - 824-826, 829
franking privilege - 826-827, 831-832
outside income limits - 798 (box), 821-824, 827-831
pay raises - 61, 775, 792, 798 (box), 827-829, 830-832
procedures for raises - 821, 822, 824-825 (box)
salaries, 1789-1985 (chart) - 828
salary commission proposal - 832
Social Security coverage - 661, 831 (box)
tax deductions - 71, 821-823, 829-830
Congressional Quarterly
presidential support study (box) - 853

Congressional Research Service
electricity prices - 445
enterprise zones - 120
legislative veto - 837-840
poverty study - 581-582
Congressional Study Caucus - 802
Congressional votes. *(See also Filibusters and cloture votes.)*
key votes
1981 - 879-893
1982 - 895-909
1983 - 911-925
1984 - 927-941
recorded votes, statistics (box) - 10
Senate tie breakers - 228, 229, 238-240, 854
Connecticut
highway aid - 307
Indian lands claim - 787
revenue sharing - 117
wetlands protection - 481
Conoco Inc. - 382
Conover, C. Todd - 84, 92-93
Conrail
background (box) - 293-294
commuter lines transfer - 291, 293, 294, 314
major routes (map) - 327
rail strike, 1982 - 314
sale proposal - 289, 291-295, 326-328, 840
Conservation. *(See also Energy conservation; Soil conservation; Wildlife protection.)*
Canada-U.S. fishery treaty - 143-144
conflict with economic growth - 406
conservation corps proposal - 657, 667, 671
Interior Dept. programs (box) - 404
marine sanctuaries - 438
national park expansion - 463-465
Watt definition - 407
wetlands protection - 480-481
wild rivers protection - 472-473
wilderness areas - 465-467, 470-472
Conservative Democratic Forum - 800
Conservative Opportunity Society - 799
Constitution, U.S. *(See also Freedom of religion; Freedom of speech; Freedom of the press; Legislative veto.)*
bicentennial commission - 696
constitutional convention process - 52, 679, 709, 798
Eighth Amendment cases - 721-725
executive privilege
Gorsuch contempt citation - 450
Fifth Amendment cases - 717-719
First Amendment
agent identity disclosure - 151
school prayer decision - 703
Supreme Court cases - 714, 735-740
Fourth Amendment cases - 715-717
interstate commerce
banking regulation - 84
judicial independence
bankruptcy courts - 692, 702, 704, 714
origin of revenue bills - 72, 798
presidential succession (25th Amendment) - 847
proposed amendments
anti-abortion - 675, 690-691
balanced budget - 33, 52, 700 (box), 799
congressional salary commission - 832
equal rights - 682, 696-697
line-item veto - 33, 52
school prayer - 703
Sixth Amendment cases - 719-721
war powers
Lebanon policy - 156-157, 192, 836

Constitution, Virgin Islands - 777
Construction industry
mortgage aid bill - 633-634
public works jobs funding - 663-665
tax issues - 74
Consulate openings - 149
Consumer affairs. *(See also Advertising; Consumer interests, lobbying; Consumer product safety; Labeling and packaging.)*
air bag rule - 322
air crash liability - 696
Alaska pipeline costs - 384-386
bankruptcy court system - 704-705
cash discount/credit card bills - 269, 277, 284-285
chronology of action
1981 - 263-269
1982 - 269-274
1983 - 274-278
1984 - 278-286
Civil Aeronautics Board powers - 325-326
clean air - 409, 421
consumer education - 577
Co-op Bank - 268
dam repair cost sharing - 444
endangered species - 477
energy audits - 400
financial services - 83-84
FTC funeral home rule - 277
FTC regulation of doctors - 274
FTC used car rule - 268
generic drugs - 547-548
Hoover Dam power pricing - 445-446
natural gas prices - 388, 389
nuclear power costs - 367, 368, 374
oil price decontrol - 375-376
power rate study - 434
Reagan term overview - 262
Supreme Court cases - 728
telephone rates - 275, 278-279
Three Mile Island cleanup - 369-370
unisex insurance - 284
Consumer Federation of America - 284, 320
Consumer interests, lobbying
broadcast deregulation - 281
coal slurry pipelines - 315, 319-320
Consumer Product Safety Commission reauthorization - 267
credit card surcharge - 284-285
FTC used car rule - 274
maritime antitrust immunity - 317
natural gas deregulation - 382-383
omnibus farm bill - 487
Reagan term overview - 262
Consumer price index
trend, 1980-84 (graph) - 31
Consumer product safety. *(See also Hazardous substances.)*
amusement rides - 268, 285
anti-tampering law - 689, 696
boats - 328
chronic hazard advisory panels - 268
fire-safe cigarettes - 285
lawnmowers - 268
product liability insurance - 269, 285
tire defects - 317
toy recall - 285
Consumer Product Safety Commission - 262, 267-268, 277, 285, 688, 838, 839
Consumers Union of the U.S. - 274
Contadora group - 125, 165, 181, 185 (box)
Conte, Silvio O. (R-Mass.)
budget bill - 589
congressional income and taxes - 821, 830, 831
Garrison Diversion - 435, 443
synthetic fuels - 399

Continental Illinois Corp. - 83, 86
Contract sanctity - 108, 499
Contractors and consultants. *See Federal contractors and counsultants.*
Contractors Disputes Act - 781
Contras. *See Nicaragua.*
Coolidge, Calvin - 817
Cooperatives
   Co-op Bank - 268
   tobacco growers - 506
Coors, Joseph - 406
Copper - 99, 109-111
Copperhead artillery - 228, 230
Copyright
   cable TV transmissions - 694
   foreign trade issues - 106, 109, 110
   ''manufacturing clause'' - 686
   record and tape protection - 680, 686, 697, 707
   semiconductor chip protection - 706
   videorecorders - 744
Corcoran, Tom (R-Ill.)
   Alaska pipeline - 460
   oil allocation authority - 378
Corman, James C. - 286
Corn
   PIK program - 508
   price supports - 497
   target price freeze - 511-514
Corporation for Public Broadcasting - 264-265, 273, 275, 282-283, 714
Corps of Engineers. *See Army Corps of Engineers.*
Cosimo, Sicily - 246
Cosmetics
   anti-tampering law - 696
Cost-of-living adjustments (COLAs) - 774-775, 779-780
   congressional salaries - 821, 825, 831, 832
   federal retirement - 49-51, 55, 61, 217, 785
   Social Security reform - 38, 40, 646, 659, 660, 662-663, 670-671
   veterans disability benefits - 55, 616, 617, 620, 622-624
Costa Rica
   Contadora group talks - 185
   economy - 182
   foreign aid - 135, 138, 172
   Nicaraguan rebels - 184
Cotton
   inspection protection - 515-516
   PIK program - 508-509
   price supports - 489, 490, 510
   target price freeze - 511-514
Coughlin, Lawrence (R-Pa.)
   ASAT missile - 242
Council for a Livable World - 256
Council for Industrial Competitiveness - 111, 119
Council of Economic Advisers
   budget deficits - 45, 77
   export subsidies - 105
   farm program report - 504
   revenue projections - 64
Council on Environmental Quality (box) - 451
Countercyclical fiscal aid
   anti-recession aid - 113
   jobs programs - 652-653, 663-665
   outlays (graph) - 114
   special reserve fund - 51
Counterfeiting
   record and tape piracy - 680, 686
   trademarks - 699, 701
   Social Security cards - 647
Court of Appeals for the District of Columbia - 837
Court of Claims, U.S. - 686
Court of Customs and Patent Appeals, U.S. - 686

Court of Military Appeals - 695
Courter, Jim
   offshore oil leases - 350
Courts. *See Judiciary; Law profession and practice; Trial procedures.*
Covert Action Information Bulletin - 151
Cox, Archibald - 456
Coyne, Jim (R-Pa.)
   nuclear freeze movement - 256
Crane, Daniel B. (R-Ill.)
   sex scandal, censure - 23, 810, 812-814
Crane, Philip M. (R-Ill.)
   disabled workers - 668
   Social Security reform - 659
Cranston, Alan (D-Calif.)
   AWACS sale to Saudi Arabia - 131
   nuclear freeze movement - 257
   presidential candidacy - 17
   Reagan assassination attempt - 847
   Senate leadership - 5, 801, 812
   veterans' health - 621
   wilderness areas - 472
   Williams resignation - 808
Credit bureaus
   federal debt collection - 776-777, 780
Credit cards
   fraudulent use - 277, 284, 701
   surcharge ban - 269, 277, 284-285
Credit unions - 58, 87, 89
Crime and criminal justice. *(See also Ethics; Federal Bureau of Investigation; Judiciary; Law profession and practice; Prisons and prisoners; specific crimes.)*
   capital punishment - 699, 708
   chronology of action
      1981 - 677-680
      1982 - 680-694
      1983 - 694-698
      1984 - 698-709
   crime and riot insurance - 633
   criminal code revision - 678, 692, 697-701
   fine collection - 699, 702
   foreign police aid - 189
   forfeiture of profits - 699
   Freedom of Information Act exemptions - 776, 779, 789
   index totals, 1979-83 (graph) - 676
   law enforcement block grants - 773-774
   preventive detention - 692, 699
   repeat offenders - 689, 692, 701
   Supreme Court cases - 715-725
   undercover operations guidelines - 809
   victims compensation - 685, 699
   violent crime definition - 700
   witness protection - 685, 699, 700
Crime Victims Fund - 699
Crocker, Chester A. - 1027
Crop insurance - 491, 492, 495, 515
Cross-Florida Barge Canal - 442
Crowell, John B. Jr. - 405, 406, 409, 466, 473, 1027
Crude Oil Windfall Profit Tax Act - 77
Cruise missiles
   air launched (ALCMs) - 226, 229
   arms control issues - 209, 241, 249-251, 253-255
   ground launched (GLCMs)
      authorizations, appropriations - 209, 211, 212, 218, 221, 226, 228
      deployment - 232, 233, 237, 246-247, 250, 254-255
   sea launched (SLCMs) - 228, 241, 244
      battleship modernization - 206, 218, 228, 229, 236, 240
      Tomahawk - 228, 236, 244
   Soviet anti-ship - 210, 221, 236, 240
Cryptology - 140
Cuba
   Caribbean trade plan - 106

   Central America aid plan - 177
   Grenada invasion - 169
   Radio Marti - 149, 150, 166-167
   role in Central America - 124, 150, 162, 166, 177, 181-184, 188
   subversion resolution - 150
   travel ban - 713
Cuomo, Mario M. - 18
Currency
   dollar strength - 32, 97 (chart)
   gold standard proposal - 98
   illegal transactions - 700
   international markets - 95, 96
   krugerrand import ban - 108
   photographs - 714
   Special Drawing Rights - 104
Customs duties - 58, 791
Customs Service, U.S. - 111, 700
Cutler, M. Rupert - 466
Cyclosporine - 549-550
Cyprus
   foreign aid - 135, 138, 170, 173
Czechoslovakia
   missile deployment - 254
   World War II claims agreement - 142

D

Dairy industry
   cheese distribution - 599, 600
   contaminated milk - 490
   milk marketing orders - 741
   price supports - 49, 50, 487, 488, 490, 491, 493-497, 504-507
   UHT milk project - 514
Dalkon shield - 285
Dam, Kenneth W. - 182
D'Amato, Alfonse M. (R-N.Y.)
   Iran-Iraq war - 197
D'Amours, Norman E. (D-N.H.)
   offshore oil revenue - 350
Dams. *See Floods and flood control; Hydroelectric power; Irrigation.*
Danforth, John C. (R-Mo.)
   international economic reciprocity - 96
   offshore revenue sharing - 359
Danielson, George E. (D-Calif.) - 778
Dannemeyer, William E. (R-Calif.)
   budget plan - 47
   clean air sanctions - 423
   fetal research - 537
D'Aubuisson, Roberto - 125, 174, 187
Davidge, Ric - 464
Davis, Patti (Patricia Reagan) - 844
Davis, Richard J. - 11
Davis, W. Kenneth - 377
Davis-Bacon Act - 213, 304, 305, 637, 645, 791
Day-care programs
   adult programs - 619
   authorizations - 599, 604, 605
   block grant - 588-590
   child abuse prevention - 608
   demonstration project - 637
   food aid - 612
   latch key child aid - 609
   jobs funding - 663
   school lunch regulations - 592, 593
   Senate center - 815-816
   tax credit - 68, 69
Daylight Saving Time - 269, 277-278
Death penalty - 699, 708, 712
Deaver, Michael K. - 847
Defense. *(See also Aircraft, military; Arms control; Defense Department; Intelligence affairs; Joint Chiefs of Staff; Military pay and benefits; NATO; individual branches of the armed services.)*

   chronology of action
      1981 - 205-217
      1982 - 217-225
      1983 - 225-233
      1984 - 234-248
   computer fraud - 701
   defense budget summaries - 207 (box), 234 (graph)
   export controls - 98, 107-108
   ground combat forces - 206, 208, 210, 218-219, 236, 237, 244
   industry aid - 115, 116
   legislative summary
      1981 - 6
      1982 - 8
      1983 - 13-14
      1984 - 17
   legislative veto - 833
   manpower ceiling - 220, 245, 246
   military research - 205, 206, 209, 212, 235
   military vs. social spending issue - 3, 37, 46, 50, 56, 201, 202, 217
   Reagan term overview - 850-853
   strategic forces - 205-206, 210, 218, 236, 237
   strategic minerals - 475
   weapons vs. facilities issue - 224
Defense Authorization Act of 1984 - 790
Defense Department (DOD)
   aid for Afghan rebels - 179
   arms agency clearances - 224
   AWACS sale to Saudi Arabia - 129-131
   B-1 procurement goal - 237
   energy programs - 395
   equipment leases to foreign nations - 135
   export controls - 107-108
   Nicaragua covert aid - 165
   oil requirements - 346, 347
   Ras Banas base - 232
   report and wait provisions - 838
   role on CIA staff - 168
   small business research funds - 273
   space shuttle costs - 781
   technological edge - 98
   U.S. presence in Honduras - 176
   weapons waste scandals - 203
   wildlife protection - 477-479
Defense Industrial Base Revitalization Act - 116
Defense Intelligence Agency
   authorization - 152, 168
   civilian employees - 179
   insignia protection - 152
Defense Nuclear Agency - 621
Defense Production Act - 115, 116, 119, 217, 654
Deficit reduction. *See under Budget, U.S.*
Deficit Reduction Act of 1984 - 58, 78-82, 790
De la Garza, E. ''Kika'' (D-Texas)
   budget reconciliation - 494
   gasohol from grain surplus - 503
   omnibus farm bill - 488, 490
   welfare leadership - 611
De la Madrid, Miguel - 185
Delaware
   highway aid - 307
   revenue sharing - 117
Dellums, Ronald V. (D-Calif.)
   drug use investigation - 815
Democracy Program - 168
Democratic Caucus
   budget resolution - 53
   committee changes - 422, 800
Democratic Congressional Campaign Committee - 473
Democratic National Committee - 18

Democratic Party
congressional leadership and committees - 801-802, 812
convention, 1984 - 18-19, 792
convention balloting by state (chart) - 1096
Democracy Program - 168
platform, 1984 - 18, 711
platform minority plank balloting (chart) - 1097
primaries, 1984 - 17-18
Democratic Revolutionary Alliance - 184
Democratic Revolutionary Front - 166
Democratic Steering and Policy Committee - 800, 812
Democratic Task Force on Emergency Human Needs - 664
DeMuth, Christopher C. - 834
DeNardis, Lawrence J. (R-Conn.)
electoral defeat - 10
Denton, Jeremiah (R-Ala.)
Tenn-Tom waterway - 435
Deportation. See Aliens.
Depository Institutions Deregulation and Monetary Control Act - 87-90
Deregulation
airline - 310, 325
banking - 83-90
broadcasting - 261-262, 275, 281-282
bus industry - 290, 300, 310-314
cable TV - 262, 275, 279-281
Clean Air Act revision - 411-420
oil and gas industry - 333-336, 338, 375-390
Desegregation
busing - 52, 565, 677, 693, 694, 708 (box)
school aid - 556, 569, 571, 572
Supreme Court cases - 733-734
Destler, I. M. - 130
Destro, Robert - 694
Deukmejian, George - 12, 20, 23
Developing countries. (See also Foreign aid; International development banks.)
appropriations - 146, 148
exports - 109
infant formula marketing code - 142-143
seabed mining - 437
Third World debt - 97-98, 104-105, 335
Diablo Canyon nuclear power plant - 368
Dickey-Lincoln Dam - 438, 477-478
Dickinson, William L. (R-Ala.)
nuclear freeze resolution - 256
Dicks, Norman D. (D-Wash.)
ASAT missile - 242
Diego Garcia - 213, 214, 233
Dingell, John D. (D-Mich.)
auto theft bill - 324
broadcast deregulation - 282
Clean Air Act revisions - 411, 417-419
clean air sanctions moratorium - 422, 423
commodities futures trading - 500
Conrail sale proposal - 294
Gorsuch contempt citation/Superfund - 451
health block grants - 526
Hodel nomination - 337
natural gas deregulation - 389
oil company mergers - 382
phone rate hike - 278
Strategic Petroleum Reserve - 380
Superfund investigation - 455, 457
Watt contempt resolution - 341
Whoops rescue plan - 372
Dioxin - 456, 458, 459, 621
Disability Insurance Trust Fund - 645, 647, 658, 660, 663, 667-669

Disabled persons. (See also Handicapped persons.)
black lung trust fund - 649-650
food stamp eligibility - 585, 596
job services for developmentally disabled - 609
longshoremen's benefits - 657-658, 671
POW benefits - 616, 623
review process - 644
rights protection - 609
small business loans - 615
Social Security benefits - 647, 652, 656-657, 667-669
Spellman's House seat vacancy - 802, 804
SSI benefits - 58, 525, 535, 611
veterans' benefits - 59, 614, 616, 617, 620, 622-624
voting aid - 681
Disadvantaged. See Welfare and social services.
Disaster relief
African food aid - 178-179, 400, 514
African refugee assistance account - 138
crop insurance - 491, 492
drought aid for farmers (box) - 507
El Nino - 283
emergency loans - 502
farm loans - 55, 59, 61, 495, 509, 514-516
food distribution - 601
Italian earthquake - 138
outlays (graph) - 630
small business loans - 262, 265-266, 284
surplus corn sales - 505, 507, 508
Teton Dam damage - 444
Discharge petitions - 91, 799
Discrimination. See Civil rights; Racial discrimination; Sex discrimination.
Distilled Spirits Council of the United States - 323
District of Columbia
highway aid - 307
Home Rule Act - 793, 837, 839-840
revenue sharing - 117
sales taxes on Capitol souvenirs - 783
schools for congressional pages - 810, 814
District of Columbia Committee (House)
jursidiction, leadership, subcommittees - 969
Dixon, Alan J. (D-Ill.)
highway aid - 322
Doctors, medical. See Physicians.
DOD. See Defense Department.
Dodd, Christopher J. (D-Conn.)
child abuse prevention - 608
financial regulation - 92
Dole, Elizabeth Hanford
CAB consumer powers transfer - 325
Conrail sale proposal - 326-328
DOT leadership - 290
profile - 1024-1025
Dole, Robert (R-Kan.)
bankruptcy courts - 693
black lung trust fund - 650
budget - 54
business lunch deductions - 73
Civil Rights Commission - 695
congressional tax deductions - 822-823
deficit reduction - 55
disabled workers - 668
enterprise zones - 119
farm target price freeze - 513
food donation program - 601
food stamp program - 595
infant formula marketing code - 142
interest, dividend withholding - 91
Medicaid, Medicare - 528, 539

oil allocation authority - 378
omnibus farm bill - 488-490
Republican National Committee - 855
Senate leadership - 812, 816
Social Security - 661, 662, 785
social services block grant - 589
Soviet grain sales - 499
Strategic Petroleum Reserve - 380
tax bill - 79
tuition tax credit - 568
Voting Rights Act extension - 681
welfare leadership - 611
wife - 290
Domenici, Pete V. (R-N.M.)
budget - 38-39, 45, 53-54, 60
oil allocation authority - 378
pay raises - 61
sewer grants - 427
Strategic Petroleum Reserves - 381
tax indexing - 67
uranium industry regulations - 366, 368-369
Domestic International Sales Corporations - 81, 111-112
Domestic violence. See Family and marital issues.
Dominica - 182
Dominican Republic - 182
Donovan, Raymond J.
investigation/indictment - 643, 656 (box), 667, 682, 846
profile - 1023
Dorgan, Byron L. (D-N.D.)
Garrison diversion - 443
Dornan, Robert (R-Calif.)
House pay raise - 828
DOT. See Transportation Department.
Dowdy, Wayne (D-Miss.)
election - 7, 804
Downey, Thomas J. (D-N.Y.)
MX missile - 239
Down's syndrome - 607
Draft registration
continuation (box) - 218
Social Security registrants - 208
student aid eligibility (box) - 562
Supreme Court cases - 574, 714
Drayton, William - 408
Drug abuse
block grants - 523-527, 774
research institute - 537
treatment programs - 541-542, 551-552, 561, 618, 680, 689, 697, 702, 815
Drug Enforcement Administration - 699, 809
Drug industry. (See also Food and Drug Administration.)
anti-tampering act - 689, 696
black market diversions - 699, 701
generic drugs - 547-548
heroin for cancer patients - 553
immunosuppressive drugs - 549-550
orphan drug tax credits - 536, 552
patent protection - 678, 693, 696
tax shelter - 74
Drug trafficking
airplane use - 702
congressional drug use investigation - 815
congressional pages investigation - 810
Customs Service powers - 111
diversion of prescription drugs - 553, 699, 701
enforcement and penalties - 689, 692, 698-701, 854
firearms for Mexican border patrol - 503
international cooperation to prevent - 106, 168, 174
military justice coverage - 696
pharmacy robberies - 701

Richmond resignation - 809
Druse Moslem faction - 191
Drysdale Government Securities Group - 83
Duarte, José Napoleón - 125, 169, 171, 174, 182, 186, 187
Duck stamp revenues - 480-481
Duncan, Charles W. Jr. - 337
Durenberger, Dave (R-Minn.)
budget - 16
clean air enforcement - 422
clean water bill - 439
contract sanctity - 499
health leadership - 552
infant formula marketing code - 143
offshore revenue sharing - 359
oil allocation authority - 378
Medicare spending cuts - 533

E

E. I. du Pont de Nemours & Co. - 382
Eagleton, Thomas F. (D-Mo.)
anti-abortion amendment - 691
tobacco program - 489, 498
Williams resignation - 808
Earthquake
Hazards Reduction Act - 782, 788, 792
Italian relief - 138
East, John P. (R-N.C.)
anti-abortion proposal - 690-691
gas tax increase - 800
infant formula marketing code - 143
East Coast Fisheries Agreement - 143-144
East Germany
missile deployment - 254
Eckart, Dennis E. (D-Ohio)
acid rain - 422
nuclear non-proliferation - 138
safe drinking water - 440
Economic affairs. (See also Banks and banking; Budget, U.S.; Community development; Currency; Employment and unemployment; Enterprise zones; Federal Reserve Board; Foreign trade; Taxes and taxation.)
chronology of action on fiscal assistance
1981 - 115
1982 - 115-117
1983 - 117-119
1984 - 119-120
disposable income distribution - 519
economic indicators, 1981-84 (graphs) - 31
environmental program costs - 403, 405, 406, 411-420, 477-478
industrial policy - 96-97, 111, 114, 119
inflation - 27-32, 83-84, 521, 539
infrastructure maintenance - 115, 289, 302 (box), 653, 793
international factors - 32, 84, 95-98
legislative summary
1981 - 5-6
1982 - 8
1983 - 12
1984 - 16-17
Reagan message (text) - 1038-1044
Reagan term overview - 3-4, 33, 63-64, 843-844, 848-850
recession
agriculture effects - 485, 502, 509, 511
budget effects - 37, 46
countercyclical aid, jobs - 114, 652-653, 663-665
hunger, relief bills - 598-601, 611-612

onset - 32, 37, 65
recovery - 32, 54, 55
supply-side theory - 30, 33, 37, 45, 63, 848

Economic Committee (Joint)
jurisdiction, leadership, subcommittees - 974

Economic development (domestic). *See Community development.*

Economic development (foreign). *See Developing countries.*

Economic Development Administration
abolition proposal - 113-115, 630
authorizations, appropriations - 44, 115-116, 118
background - 115
jobs plan - 654
public works projects - 654

Economic Equity Act - 605

Economic Recovery Tax Act of 1981 - 65-71, 74, 77, 649

Economic Support Fund (ESF)
aid to Lebanon - 158
appropriations - 137, 148, 159-162, 170, 172, 173, 178
emergency aid - 135
Reagan Caribbean plan - 149

Economy, U.S. *See Economic affairs.*

Edgar, Bob (D-Pa.)
coal slurry pipelines - 315
dam repair cost sharing - 444
Tenn-Tom waterway - 433

Edge Act - 101

Edison Electric Institute - 370, 416

Education. *(See also Adult education; Education Department; Elementary and secondary education; Postsecondary education; Student aid; Teachers and teaching; Vocational education.)*
alien students - 677
block grants - 555, 773-774
budget targets - 39
chronology of action
1981 - 557-561
1982 - 561-565
1983 - 565-570
1984 - 570-580
health manpower programs - 530, 551
Reagan term overview - 520, 555-556
student anti-poverty projects - 611

Education Amendments of 1972 - 584, 708

Education and Labor Committee (House)
jurisdiction, leadership, subcommittees - 579, 611, 969

Education Commission of the States - 555

Education Consolidation and Improvement Act - 559-561, 564, 568

Education Department
abolition proposal - 520, 555, 556, 561, 565
appropriations - 555-556, 565, 568 (box), 589
asbestos in schools - 572
block grant guidelines - 561
college student aid rules - 558, 559
draft registration - 562, 574
impact aid - 575-576
Indian schools - 576
law education programs - 578-579
math/science education - 565, 571-572
migrant education - 569, 576
organization and procedures - 573
program regulations - 563-564
science education bill - 565
student aid eligibility - 566, 575, 576

Education of All Handicapped Children Act - 559, 560, 563, 567

Edwards, Edwin W. - 14

Edwards, Jack (R-Ala.)
arms control talks - 209

Edwards, James B.
Energy Department role - 334, 351-352
nuclear waste disposal - 363
oil allocation authority - 378
profile - 1019-1020

Eel River Basin - 350

EEOC. *See Equal Employment Opportunity Commission.*

Eggs - 507-508

Egypt
foreign aid - 134, 135, 137, 138, 146, 160, 161, 170, 171, 173
military facilities - 209, 211, 213, 223, 232
relations with Israel - 173, 195-196
Sadat assassination - 191

Eisenhower, Dwight D. - 19, 22, 388, 531, 694, 853

El Niño disaster aid - 283

El Salvador
Contadora group talks - 185
death squads - 125, 172, 174, 175, 177, 182, 188
Duarte election - 169, 174, 175
economy - 182
foreign aid
Caribbean Basin Initiative - 149
Central American aid plan - 177-178, 189
congressional conditions and limits
1981 - 133, 134, 135 (box), 186
1982 - 144
1983 - 159, 160, 165-166
1984 - 161, 169, 170, 172, 174-175, 839
1985 - 175
Reagan policy - 124-125, 129
totals, 1981-85 (box) - 186
human rights issues - 125, 135, 147, 165-166, 174-175, 177, 186-187
Kissinger commission report - 177-178, 188
land reform - 147, 161, 166, 172, 174, 182, 187
military training in Honduras - 176
murders of Americans - 161, 166, 172, 187
Nicaraguan aid to leftists - 123, 125, 162-164, 186
Reagan term overview - 856
Stone confirmation - 165
U.S. troops - 124, 237, 245

Elderly persons. *See Aged persons.*

Elections and politics. *(See also Congressional elections; Democratic party; Federal Election Commission; Gubernatorial elections; Presidential elections; Republican party.)*
polling place access - 792-793
Supreme Court cases - 740-741

Elections Campaign Amendments of 1974 - 684

Electric power. *See Utilities.*

Electronic publishing
AT&T deregulation - 271

Elementary and secondary education
bilingual education - 569, 574, 575, 577
block grants - 557, 559-561, 569
computer donations - 77
desegregation aid - 569, 571
disadvantaged children - 557, 559-561, 563-564
federal aid changes - 556, 568-569
handicapped children - 556, 557, 559, 560, 563, 567
impact aid - 556, 557, 559, 568-569, 573, 575-576
magnet schools - 556, 569, 571, 572
mainstreaming - 563
math/science education - 556, 565, 571-572, 782

private school aid - 561
Reagan term overview - 520
school improvement - 572, 577
schooling for congressional pages - 810, 814
tuition tax credit - 556, 561, 564, 567-568

Elementary and Secondary Education Act - 559-560

Elk Hills petroleum reserve - 346-347, 380

Ellender, Allen J. - 570, 578-579

Ellis, Richard H. - 252

Embassies and consulates. *See Foreign affairs.*

Emergency Home Purchase Assistance Act - 631, 633

Emergency Petroleum Allocation Act of 1973 - 375, 377, 378

Emergency preparedness. *(See also Civil defense; Disaster relief; Federal Emergency Management Agency.)*
energy outlays (graph) - 334

Emergency School Aid Act - 569, 571

Emery, David F. (R-Maine)
reclamation law revision - 432

Eminent domain principle
coal slurry pipelines - 315, 319-320

Emphysema - 549

Employee Retirement Income Security Act of 1974 (ERISA) - 77, 66, 670

Employment and unemployment. *(See also Disabled persons; Employment benefits and pay; Employment programs and job training; Federal employment; Labor and labor unions; Migrant workers; Occupational health and safety; Retirement and pensions; Social Security programs; Unemployment compensation.)*
Reagan term overview - 8, 32, 643-644, 645, 651, 659
trends, 1980-84 (graph) - 31

Employment benefits and pay. *(See also Disabled persons; Unemployment compensation.)*
airline employees benefits - 310
child support enforcement - 606
flexitime - 780
fringe benefits - 82
health insurance - 534, 538, 542-543
jury duty - 688
legal services plans - 70
sick pay - 647
stock ownership plans - 68, 70, 82
subminimum wage - 571, 645
Supreme Court cases - 731-733
welfare plans - 82

Employment programs and job training. *(See also Rehabilitation; Vocational education.)*
anti-recession jobs plan - 8, 32, 39, 46, 56, 113-114, 643, 651-654, 658-659, 663-665
auto domestic content bills - 108, 658
background - 653 (box), 774
CETA programs - 32, 648, 651, 653, 655
conservation corps - 657, 667, 671
dislocated workers - 656, 577
elderly programs - 591, 594, 609-610, 658
export subsidies - 105-106
gas tax, highway bill - 301, 643, 644
guest workers - 692, 708
housing industry recession - 633-634
illegal aliens - 676, 678, 692, 708
Job Training Partnership Act - 577, 643, 655-656
targeted jobs tax credit - 70, 76, 82, 672
trade adjustment aid - 100, 110, 645,

650-651, 658, 659, 665, 672
unemployment benefits - 72, 76, 645, 647-648, 654-655, 659, 665
veterans programs - 614, 617, 619-620, 624
welfare recipients - 586-588, 597

Endangered Species Act - 404, 477-479

Energy. *(See also Coal industry; Energy conservation; Energy Department; Natural gas; Nuclear energy; Oil industry; Solar energy; Synthetic fuels; Utilities.)*
chronology of action
1981-82 - 339-351, 361-371, 375-386, 393-397
1983-84 - 351-359, 371-374, 386-391, 397-400
federal outlays, 1976-85 (graph) - 334
foreign technology trade - 111
Linowes commission - 345
Supreme Court cases - 752-755

Energy Action - 385

Energy and Commerce Committee (House)
jurisdiction, leadership, subcommittees - 552, 969-970

Energy and Natural Resources Committee (Senate)
jurisdiction, leadership, subcommittees - 964-965

Energy conservation
building efficiency standards - 395
energy audits - 400
Energy Department programs - 336, 393-396, 400
federal outlays (graph) - 334
home weatherization - 393, 394, 396, 400
Hoover Dam power pricing - 445-446
oil price decontrol - 375-376
power plant conversion - 383-384
power rate study (box) - 434
Reagan administration de-emphasis - 333, 336
tax credit - 58, 80

Energy Department
abolition proposal - 334, 336, 337, 377, 393, 397
alcohol fuels program - 394-395
authorizations, appropriations - 393-397, 399-400, 434
breeder reactor programs - 370-371, 373, 400
Carter appointments - 351
coal leasing program - 354
conservation assistance - 400
gas price estimates - 382
home weatherization - 604, 605
naval petroleum reserves - 346-347
nuclear energy promotion - 337, 367
nuclear waste disposal - 336, 361-366, 467
nuclear weapons programs - 207, 215-216, 225, 235, 237, 240
power plant conversion - 384
Reagan appointments - 334, 337 (box)
solar research - 400
Strategic Petroleum Reserve - 379-382, 390
uranium imports - 369
Watt influence - 334, 406

Energy Independence Authority - 398

Energy Policy and Conservation Act of 1975 - 375, 376, 379, 380

Energy Research and Development Administration - 362, 367

Energy Research and Technology Administration - 397

Energy Security Act - 398, 833

Engineering and Science Manpower Act - 565

Enterprise zones - 79, 91, 115-117, 119-120, 630, 635, 639

Entitlement programs (box) - 38
Environment. (See also Air pollution;
Conservation; Environmental interests,
lobbying; Environmental Protection
Agency; Hazardous waste management;
Public lands; Water resources; Wilderness areas; Wildlife protection.)
chronology of action
1981-82 - 411-420, 425-438, 449-
454, 463-470, 477-480
1983-84 - 420-423, 438-447, 454-
461, 470-476, 480-482
Reagan term overview - 4
risk analysis - 454
Supreme Court cases - 752-755
**Environment and Public Works Com-
mittee (Senate)**
jurisdiction, leadership, subcommittees -
965
Environmental Defense Fund - 452
Environmental interests, lobbying
acid rain - 420-422
barrier islands protection - 467-468
Clean Air Act revision - 408-409, 411-
420
clean air sanctions - 423
clean water bills - 439, 440
Clinch River breeder reactor - 370-372
coal leasing program - 352-354, 356
coal slurry pipelines - 319-320
dam repair cost sharing - 444
endangered species - 477-478
Energy Department nominations - 337
EPA budget cuts - 455
Garrison Diversion project - 435, 443,
444
hazardous wastes disposal - 409, 452,
457-458
Interior Department programs - 404
national park expansion - 463
nuclear power plant licensing - 366-369
nuclear waste disposal - 361-364
ocean dumping - 436-437
offshore leases - 358
oil price decontrol - 375
Outer Continental Shelf leases - 347-
350
pesticide law - 496, 502, 509
Reagan opposition - 405
reclamation law revision - 431-432
sewer grants - 425
strategic minerals - 475
striped bass conservation - 481
Superfund renewal - 459-461
synthetic fuel development - 398
Tenn-Tom waterway - 433
timber harvest - 473
water policy planning - 429
water projects - 440, 503
Watt controversies - 406-407
wetland protection - 480-481
wild and scenic rivers - 472
wilderness areas - 339-344, 409, 465-
466, 470
Environmental Protection Agency. (See
also Hazardous waste management.)
authorizations, appropriations - 405,
439
Burford tenure - 408, 449-452, 454-
457
Clean Air Act revision - 411-420
clean air enforcement - 334, 421-423
clean drinking water enforcement - 440
clean water programs - 439
hazardous waste disposal - 403, 405,
409, 452-453, 457-459, 839
Lavelle tenure - 455, 457
noise control program - 454
ocean dumping - 436-437, 446
oversight hearings transcript alterations
- 814-815
pesticides - 501-502, 509

police powers - 458, 459
research funds - 453, 461
Ruckelshaus tenure - 405, 408, 454-457
school asbestos - 572
sewers - 302, 409, 425-428
Superfund controversy - 409, 449-452,
454-457, 459-461
uranium mine tailing standards - 369
Watt influence - 406
Environmental Study Caucus - 802
EPA. See Environmental Protection
Agency.
Episcopal Church - 255
**Equal Employment Opportunity Com-
mission**
authority transfer from Labor Depart-
ment - 839
Equal opportunity. (See also Affirmative
action; Desegregation; Sex discrimina-
tion.)
Supreme Court cases - 731-733
Equal Pay Act - 839
Equal Rights Amendment (ERA) - 682
(box), 696-697
Ertel, Allen E. (D-Pa.)
Three Mile Island cleanup - 370
Ethics and Public Policy Center - 141
Ethics Committee, Select (Senate)
franking privilege - 826, 827
jurisdiction, leadership, subcommittees -
966
Ethics in government. (See also Con-
gressional ethics; Medical ethics.)
Allen investigation - 142
bribery of foreign officials - 100
Burford investigation - 408
Casey, Hugel financial investigation -
141-142
Donovan investigation (box) - 656
FTC employees conflict of interest -
272-273
Lavelle indictment - 454-457
Legal Services Corp. consulting fees -
683
Meese investigation (box) - 707
Office of Government Ethics - 785-786
special prosecutor law - 681-683
Superfund scandal - 454-457, 459-461
Synthetic Fuels Corporation - 399
Watergate legislative legacy (box) -
684
Ethics in Government Act of 1978 -
682-684, 707, 785, 802, 818
Ethiopia
famine aid - 178
refugee aid - 149
European Community
agricultural subsidies - 103
Evans, Daniel J. (R-Wash.)
election - 14-15
Everglades National Park - 467
Executive branch. See Cabinet; Congressional-executive relations; Federal government (general); Legislative veto; Presidency; names of specific agencies and
departments.
**Executive Salary Cost-of-Living Adjust-
ment Act** - 825
Export Administration Act - 98, 100,
104, 107-109, 111, 145
Export-Import Bank
authorizations, appropriations - 104-
106, 136, 146, 160, 161, 171, 172
background - 105-106
Central America aid plan - 189
export trading companies - 101
Exports. See Agricultural trade; Foreign
trade.
Extradition. See Aliens.
Exxon - 385, 398

F

FAA. See Federal Aviation Administration.
Faden, Mike - 367
Fair Credit Reporting Act - 780
Falasha - 149
Fall, Albert B. - 346
Family and marital issues. (See also
Aid to Families with Dependent Children;
Military dependents; Pregnancy.)
adoption assistance - 589, 599, 607
child support enforcement - 586, 588,
597-598, 603, 605-606, 697
dependent care tax credit - 69, 697
domestic violence - 605-608
foregone interest - 82
former spouse benefits - 792
foster care - 77, 553, 606
marriage tax issues - 66, 68, 69, 70
Medicare for working aged - 545
pension reform - 667, 697
rent to relatives - 71
rights of parents - 733
Social Security benefits - 647
Farley, Frances - 23
Farm Credit Administration
Co-op Bank audit - 268
Farm Labor Contractor Registration Act
- 502
Farmers Home Administration (FmHA)
authorizations - 502, 509, 514
debt deferral - 509, 511, 512
disaster loans - 59, 61, 284
loan eligibility - 493, 515
loan programs - 491, 495, 509, 514,
516
Reagan proposals - 488, 512
rural housing assistance - 633, 634,
637
Farming. See Agriculture and farming.
FBI. See Federal Bureau of Investigation.
FCC. See Federal Communications Commission.
Federal Aviation Act of 1958 - 702
Federal Aviation Administration (FAA)
authorizations - 308, 310
modernization plan (box) - 309
Federal buildings - 467, 777
Federal Bureau of Investigation (FBI)
Abscam investigation - 800, 802, 804-
809
agent identity disclosure - 152
authorizations, appropriations - 140,
168, 676
crime statistics - 675
director's term - 684
hazardous waste controls - 458
missing children - 686
undercover operations guidelines - 804
Webster role - 687
**Federal Coal Leasing Amendments
Act of 1976** - 353
**Federal Communications Commission
(FCC)**
AT&T deregulation - 270
authorizations, appropriations - 263,
275-276
broadcasting deregulation - 261-262,
273, 281
cable TV deregulation - 279
international telecommunications deregulation - 265
licenses - 263-264, 272-273
phone rate hike - 275, 278-279
Radio Marti authorization - 167
regulations - 694
size reductions - 50
TV rerun rights - 275, 282
user fees - 263, 273

Federal contractors and consultants
arms sales - 153-154
Davis-Bacon Act - 213, 304, 305, 645,
637, 785
foreign aid projects - 173
health information - 538
interest collection veto - 781
minority firm program - 266
procurement costs and procedures - 58,
790
small business aid - 276
tax regulations - 75
timber industry bailout - 473-474
Federal Crop Insurance Corp. - 495
Federal Council on the Aging - 610
Federal courts. See Judiciary.
Federal debt. See Budget, U.S.
Federal Debt Collection Act - 787
Federal Deposit Insurance Corp. (FDIC)
Continental Illinois rescue - 83
farm debt - 486
problem list (graph) - 85
role in banking regulation - 84, 86, 87-
90
**Federal Election Campaign Act of
1971** - 684
**Federal Election Campaign Act
Amendments of 1976** - 821, 823, 829
Federal Election Commission - 684, 788
**Federal Emergency Management
Agency** - 328, 456
Federal employment. (See also Cost-of-
living adjustments; Office of Personnel
Management; Retirement and pensions.)
abortion funding ban - 691
Board for International Broadcasting
salaries - 153
CIA staffing and retirement - 140, 152
claims limit - 689
defense intelligence salaries - 179
flexitime - 780
food stamp eligibility - 596
former spouse benefits - 792
Grace commission on pensions - 791
grade reduction proposal - 791
hazardous duty pay for diplomats -
168
health benefits program - 528
high-level salaries - 821-822, 824-825,
827
impact aid - 557, 559, 573, 575-576
judges' salaries - 57, 58, 714, 762
Medicare coverage - 75, 533, 534, 784
National Guard torts - 677
outside pay exemption - 783
pay, pension increases - 49-51, 55, 61,
214, 219, 224, 228, 774-775, 779-
780, 785, 792
pay-for-performance plan - 787 (box),
792
Postal Service liabilities - 776
Social Security coverage - 661, 784-
785
Supreme Court decisions - 765-766
veterans' preference - 615, 625
whistleblowers - 792
Federal Energy Administration - 395
**Federal Energy Regulatory Commis-
sion** - 374, 383, 386, 387, 473, 837
Federal Financing Bank
Amtrak loans - 326
Export-Import Bank loans - 105
REA loans - 515
Federal government, general. (See also
Ethics in government; Federal contractors
and consultants; Federal employment;
Fraud, waste and abuse.)
chronology of action
1981 - 773-777
1982 - 777-784
1983 - 784-788
1984 - 788-793

cost estimates of legislation - 777
geographic distribution of funds - 783
paperwork reduction - 788
procurement costs - 790
Prompt Pay Act - 783
regulatory reform - 772
reorganization authority - 790, 839
reports to Congress - 783
savings from financial efficiency - 791
Supreme Court suits against U.S. - 767-768
surplus property donation - 694, 783
Federal Grain Inspection Service - 515
Federal Highway Administration - 302, 304, 306
Federal Home Loan Bank Board
background - 88
due-on-sale mortgages - 634
financial services regulation - 84, 87, 88
Federal Home Loan Mortgage Corp. (Freddie Mac)
due-on-sale mortgages - 634
tax status - 82
Federal Housing Administration (FHA)
HUD foreclosures on mortgages - 633
interest rates - 633
mortgage insurance - 49, 50, 635
Federal Industrial Mortgage Association - 111 119
Federal Insecticide, Fungicide and Rodenticide Act - 501, 509
Federal Insurance Contributions Act - 75, 534
Federal Land Policy and Management Act of 1976 - 342, 354, 356, 404
Federal lands. *See Public lands.*
Federal Maritime Commission
authorizations - 324-325
maritime antitrust immunity - 317-319
Federal National Mortgage Association (Fannie Mae) - 77
Federal Pay Comparability Act - 775, 780, 825
Federal Power Commission - 387-388, 406
Federal Privacy Act - 647
Federal Railroad Administration - 314, 326, 329
Federal Reserve Board
banking regulation - 84, 88, 92-93
budget coordination - 48, 54
commodities futures trading - 500, 501
credit card study - 284
domestic monetary policy - 28-29 (box), 32, 83, 95, 97, 664
export trading companies - 101
interest rates bill - 654
international currency market - 95
Federal Savings and Loan Insurance Corp. (FSLIC)
financial regulation - 87-90
Federal Service Impasses Panel - 780
Federal Tort Claims Act - 677
Federal Trade Commission (FTC)
antitrust authority - 706
authorizations, appropriations - 274, 276-277
CAB consumer powers - 325
cigarette warning labels - 549
funeral home rule - 277, 837
joint research ventures - 706
maritime antitrust immunity - 318, 319
Reagan term overview - 262
regulation of doctors - 274, 538
regulatory reform bill - 777-778
used car rule - 268, 273-274, 837
Federal Trade Commission Improvements Act - 837
Federal Unemployment Tax Act - 648, 665

Federal Water Pollution Control Act of 1972 - 425-427
Federation of American Hospitals - 539
Federation of American Scientists - 242
Feed. *See Grain.*
Feinberg, Alexander - 805
Feldstein, Martin S. - 77, 1026
Fenwick, Millicent (R-N.J.)
domestic content bill - 102
electoral defeat - 11
Fernandes, Ben - 19
Ferraro, Geraldine A. (D-N.Y.)
ethics investigation - 818
pension equity - 670
Superfund renewal - 459, 461
transport of radioactive material - 300
vice-presidential candidacy - 18-20
Fetal research - 537, 550
Fidelity Mortgage Investors - 678
Fields, Jack (R-Texas)
offshore revenue sharing - 359
Filibusters and cloture votes
antitrust damages - 693
budget - 61
busing - 677
constitutional convention procedures - 679
debt ceiling - 42
highway aid - 322
Hoover Dam power pricing - 445-446
list, 1917-84 - 977-979
maritime antitrust immunity - 318
Reagan term overview - 4, 800
school prayer - 572
Senate television - 810-811, 816
Voting Rights Act extension - 681
Finance Committee (Senate)
jurisdiction, leadership, subcommittees - 552, 611, 965
Findley, Paul (R-Ill.)
electoral defeat - 10
farm budget cuts - 496
tobacco bill - 498
Fire Administration, U.S. - 285
Fire prevention - 792
Firearms
CIA personnel - 140
food stamp investigators - 586
gun control/Reagan assassination attempt - 675
mandatory criminal sentences - 700
Mexican border patrol - 503
repeat offenders - 692, 701
Supreme Court police - 683
Fish and fisheries
bankruptcy - 704
barrier island jetties - 481
Canada-U.S. maritime treaty - 143-144
development funds - 307, 328
Everglades protection - 467
loan guarantees - 299
marine mammal protection - 479-480
offshore oil drilling - 347, 348, 350, 358
Sikes Act extension - 478-479
striped bass conservation - 481
tuna industry - 481
Fish and Wildlife Service - 404, 463, 480
Fisher, Louis - 839, 840
Flexitime - 780
Flood Control Act of 1944 - 435
Floods and flood control
barrier island development - 467, 468
dam repairs - 444-445
Garrison Diversion project - 435
Stonewall Jackson Dam - 443
Teton Dam disaster - 444
water policy planning - 430
water projects cost sharing - 441
WEB pipeline - 438
wild rivers protection - 472-473

Florennes, Belgium - 246
Florida
Cross-Florida Barge Canal - 442
ERA vote - 682
highway aid - 307
offshore leasing - 357-358
revenue sharing - 117
voting rights action - 679
wetlands protection - 480
wilderness areas - 465, 466, 471, 472
Florida National Scenic Trail - 469, 475
Florio, James J. (D-N.J.)
FTC authorization - 274
hazardous waste control - 457, 458
noise control - 454
Superfund renewal - 460-461
Fluoridation - 524, 552
Foley, Thomas S. (D-Wash.)
House leadership - 5, 801
omnibus farm bill - 489-490
Follow Through program - 556, 561, 605
Food and Drug Administration (FDA)
anti-tampering act - 689, 696
generic drugs - 547-548
orphan drugs - 536
saccharin ban - 530-531, 541, 838
Food and nutrition. *(See also Child nutrition and health programs; Food for Peace; Food stamps.)*
Africa aid - 178
Caribbean trade plan - 106-107
central kitchen inspections - 516
commodity distribution - 136, 178, 582, 586, 592-594, 598-601, 652
embargo ban - 100
food banks - 493
Older Americans program - 593-594, 609
omnibus farm bill - 493
Puerto Rico block grant - 585, 596, 773, 774
research - 612
saccharin ban deferral - 530-531, 541
UHT milk pilot project - 514
Food and Nutrition Service - 592
Food for Peace - 136, 179, 487, 493, 513, 514
Food Research and Action Center - 592, 600
Food stamps
authorizations - 489, 496, 583, 585, 594, 595, 598, 599, 602
background - 583-584
benefit cuts - 44, 48-50, 520, 582, 583-586, 611
eligibility requirements - 520, 582, 585, 596
firearms for investigators - 586
hunger task force recommendations - 600
inflation adjustments - 583-584
outlays - 520 (graph), 581
Puerto Rico block grant - 773, 774
Reagan New Federalism - 777
relation to housing aid - 635
violations - 586, 596
work requirements - 596
Forane - 696
Ford, Gerald R.
assassination attempt - 847
block grant proposals - 774
budget - 30
Bush appointments - 855
campaign, 1976 - 845
coal leasing - 353-354
countercyclical economic aid - 115, 653
Freedom of Information Act - 778
legislative veto - 836
naval petroleum reserves - 346
oil and gas decontrol - 375, 388
pocket-veto power - 817

Strategic Petroleum Reserve - 380
Ford, Wendell H. (D-Ky.)
nuclear power plants - 369
Senate television - 810
Ford, William D. (D-Mich.)
franking privilege - 831
Ford Motor Co. - 102
Foreign affairs. *(See also Arms control; Foreign aid; Foreign trade; Human rights; NATO; State Department; Travel and tourism; Treaties and international agreements; names of specific countries.)*
banking
export trading companies - 90
omnibus trade bill - 109
Third World debt - 97-98
U.S. international loans - 84
chronology of action
1981 - 129-144
1982 - 144-155
1983 - 155-169
1984 - 169-180
diplomatic service
consulate openings - 149
embassy security - 179
hazardous duty pay - 168
number and treatment of diplomats - 179
retirement pay - 61
international economic policy
chronology of action - 99-112
factors - 95-98
peso devaluation aid - 283, 284
law
antitrust suits - 678, 688
bribery of foreign officials - 100
extradition revision - 692
foreign records in U.S. trials - 699, 701
illegal currency transactions - 700
jurisdiction - 701
legislative summary
1981 - 6
1982 - 8
1983 - 13-14
1984 - 17
legislative veto - 833, 836 (box)
Reagan term overview - 853-857
taxation
Caribbean Basin Initiative - 106-107
income earned abroad - 81
shelters - 81
Foreign Affairs Committee (House)
jurisdiction, leadership, subcommittees - 128, 970
Foreign Agents Registration Act - 701
Foreign aid. *(See also Agency for International Development; International development banks; names of specific nations.)*
assessment (box) - 160
authorization procedure - 128, 155-156, 159, 170
authorizations, appropriations - 132-138, 145-146, 159-162, 170-174
barred nations - 138, 163, 174
Caribbean Basin Initiative - 149
Central America aid plan - 172, 177-178, 188-189
equipment leases - 135
Export-Import Bank tied aid - 106
food aid for Africa - 178-179
military vs. development aid issue - 128, 129, 132, 136-137, 145-146, 148, 155, 160, 161, 181
outlays, 1976-85 (graph) - 125
Reagan term overview - 128
Foreign claims
Army damage in Germany - 210
Czech settlement - 142
Supreme Court on Iran hostage agreement (box) - 143

Foreign Corrupt Practices Act of 1977 - 75, 100

Foreign Intelligence Advisory Board - 140

Foreign language education - 570-572, 580

Foreign Military Sales - 158, 159-162, 170, 172, 173

Foreign Relations Committee (Senate)
jurisdiction, leadership, subcommittees - 128, 965

Foreign Sales Corporations - 81, 111-112

Foreign Service - 61, 179

Foreign trade. *(See also Agricultural trade; Export-Import Bank; General Agreement on Tariffs and Trade; Ships and shipping; specific industries.)*
aid projects - 173
bribery of foreign officials - 100
Canadian, Mexican carriers - 311, 312
Caribbean trade plan - 102, 106-107, 149
Central American aid plan - 189
contract sanctity issue - 108
energy technology - 111
export controls - 98-100, 107-110
export subsidies - 81, 111-112
export trading companies - 90, 100-102
merchandise trade deficit - 32, 96 (chart)
military construction - 232
most-favored-nation designations - 103, 107, 836
nuclear technology - 138-139
omnibus trade bill - 109-111
overseas investment - 99
peso devaluation aid - 283, 284
product liability insurance - 269
protectionist issues
"Buy America" provisions - 305, 306, 315
copyright "manufacturing clause" - 686
domestic content bills - 96, 104, 108-109
reciprocity proposals - 96, 101-104, 108
textile labeling - 112
voluntary restraint concept - 96
Reagan philosophy - 95, 96
Soviet economic sanctions - 98, 100, 144-145
strategic minerals - 475
textile labeling - 548
trade adjustment aid - 100, 110, 643, 650-651, 658, 659, 665, 672
unfair practices - 96, 109-111

Forest industries
Farmers Home Administration loans - 514
housing construction - 633-634
timber harvest contracts - 405, 409, 470, 473-474
truck size limits - 308
wilderness areas - 465-466

Forest Service, U.S.
authorizations, appropriations - 463
Mount St. Helens monument - 469
national forests - 404, 469
timber harvest - 405, 473-474
watershed leasing - 350-351
Watt influence - 406, 407
wild and scenic rivers - 472, 473
wilderness areas - 339-344, 403, 409, 465-467, 470-472
wildlife protection - 478-479

Forsberg, Randall - 255, 256

Fort Belknap Indian Community - 792

Fort Lewis, Wash. - 247

Fort Union Basin - 352, 355

Fossil fuel research. *See Synthetic fuels.*

Foster, Jodie - 847

Foster Grandparents - 590, 611

Foundation for Educational Assistance - 565

France
agricultural subsidies - 103
arms control - 251, 253
arms sales to India - 153
international finance - 98
oil imports - 197
role in Lebanon - 126, 191, 192
Soviet economic sanctions - 145

Frank, Barney (D-Mass.)
1982 election - 10

Frankfurter, Felix - 782

Franking privilege - 826-827, 831-832

Franklin, Webb (R-Miss.)
1982 election - 11

Franklin Delano Roosevelt Memorial Commission - 782

Frankum, Ronald B. - 695

Fraud, waste and abuse in government programs
control bill - 783
CETA programs - 653
Economic Development Administration projects - 114
food stamp program - 583, 585, 586
Grace commission report - 791
longshoremen's disability benefits - 657-658, 671
Medicaid, Medicare claims - 529
National Public Radio - 275
New Deal jobs programs - 653
oil and gas royalties - 344-346
Pentagon overcharges - 203, 209
Powder River coal leases - 354-355
Reagan term overview - 771-772
summer feeding program - 592
Social Security disability benefits - 644, 647, 667-669
tax benefit leasing - 787
whistleblower awards - 792

Freedom of Information Act
commercial information - 268
Medicare review board exemption - 535-536
proposed changes - 772, 776, 778-779, 788-789
Supreme Court cases - 766

Freedom of religion
congressional chaplains - 811-812
school prayer - 703
Supreme Court decisions - 713

Freedom of speech
access to schools for religious groups - 573
agent identity disclosure - 151
Supreme Court cases - 735-738

Freedom of the press
agent identity disclosure - 151
AT&T in electronic publishing - 271
election projections - 285-286
Freedom of Information Act restrictions - 778-779, 788
UNESCO information order - 148
Supreme Court cases - 739

Freeze Voter '84 - 256

Frenzel, Bill (R-Minn.)
debt ceiling - 42
trade adjustment aid - 665
uranium imports - 369

Friedman, Milton - 32

Friends of the Earth - 256, 348, 405

FTC. *See Federal Trade Commission.*

Fuel Use Act of 1978 - 383-384

Fund for Assuring an Independent Retirement - 785

Funeral homes - 277, 837

Fur seal protection - 479 (box), 481-482

Futures Trading Act of 1982 - 499-501

G

GI Bill
background - 622
education loan limits - 616
expanded eligibility - 240, 563, 615, 620
revival proposal - 241, 580, 614, 616, 618, 620-622

Gabon
strategic minerals - 475

Gallatin National Forest - 471

Gallaudet College - 602

Gallen, Hugh - 12

Gallup Poll
crime survey - 675

Gambling taxes - 77

GAO. *See General Accounting Office.*

Garfield, James A. - 847

Garn, Jake (R-Utah)
banking regulation - 83, 87, 89-90, 92-93
congressional tax deductions - 830
high-tech exports - 98
housing authorization - 631, 635-636
Senate leadership - 5, 801, 812
tobacco program - 505

Garn-St Germain Depository Institutions Act - 90

Garrison Diversion project - 435, 443, 444

Gas. *See Natural gas.*

Gasohol. *See Synthetic fuels.*

Gasoline
average annual price (graph) - 335
excise taxes - 32, 76, 289-290, 301-307, 651, 652
lead additives - 408, 420, 456

GATT. *See General Agreement on Tariffs and Trade.*

Gaza - 195

Gemayel, Amin - 126, 192, 193

Gemayel, Bashir - 191

General Accounting Office (GAO)
arms sales amendments - 154
Capitol architect report - 803
coal leasing procedures - 352, 354-355
congressional pay raises - 828
Co-op Bank audit - 268
Grace commission analysis - 791
interest, dividend withholding - 91
maritime industry study - 318
military construction in Honduras - 176
national parks - 464
oil and gas royalties - 345
oil shortages report - 377, 379
pipeline safety recommendations - 328
sewer grants - 426
unemployment compensation report - 651
unisex insurance - 284
welfare report - 582
wilderness study - 340

General Agreement on Tariffs and Trade (GATT)
domestic content bills - 101, 102
Geneva talks (box) - 103
Polish obligations - 144

General Education Provisions Act - 564

General Motors - 378
auto theft bill - 324
domestic content bill - 102
rail strike - 314

General Public Utilities Corp. - 369-370

General Services Administration (GSA)
congressional furniture - 826

federal buildings policy - 777
Indian college construction - 569
National Archives independence - 790
presidential records - 683

General System of Preferences - 109-110

Generic drugs - 547-548

Genetic diseases - 525

Genocide treaty - 179-180

Geological Survey, U.S.
jurisdiction - 404
naval petroleum reserves - 346
oil and gas leases - 344-345

Georges Bank
offshore oil leases - 348, 358
U.S.-Canada maritime treaty - 143-144

Georgetown University
Ethics and Public Policy Center - 141

Georgia
highway aid - 307
revenue sharing - 117
voting rights action - 679, 680
wilderness areas - 471, 472

Gephardt, Richard A. (D-Mo.)
MX missile - 239
tax reform plan - 79

Gergen, David - 44

Geriatrics. *See Aged persons.*

Germany. *See East Germany; West Germany.*

Gerrymandering. *See House of Representatives, reapportionment.*

Gesell, Gerhard A. - 807

Getty Oil - 382, 390

Gibson, Dunn and Crutcher - 687

Gifford Pinchot National Forest - 469

Gingrich, Newt (R-Ga.)
House television/O'Neill confrontation - 17, 799, 816, 818
Studds, Crane censure - 814

Glass-Steagall Act - 88

Glenn, John R. (D-Ohio)
arms sales to India - 154
AWACS sale to Saudi Arabia - 130
GI Bill - 622
nuclear non-proliferation - 138
presidential candidacy - 17-18

Glossary of congressional terms - 861-871

Golan Heights
Israeli annexation - 141, 193-194

Gold standard - 98

Golden parachutes - 81, 283

Goldwater, Barry (R-Ariz.)
CIA mining of Nicaraguan harbors - 176
Helms amendments - 800
Reagan support, 1964 - 845, 846

Goldwater, Barry M. Jr. (R-Calif.)
drug use investigation - 815

Goodling, Bill (R-Pa.)
arms sales to India - 154
child nutrition programs - 601-602
omnibus education bill - 574

Goodyear - 378

Gore, Albert Jr. (D-Tenn.)
Gorsuch contempt citation/Superfund - 451
organ transplants - 550
Senate election - 21

Gorsuch, Anne M. *See Burford, Anne M. (Gorsuch).*

Gorton, Slade (R-Wash.)
budget - 54
EPA research veto - 453
watershed leasing - 351

Government. *See Federal government (general); State and local government.*

Government contractors. *See Federal contractors and consultants.*

Government employees. *See Federal employment.*

Government National Mortgage Association (GNMA)
authorizations - 631, 633
Government Operations Committee (House)
EPA hearings transcript alterations - 814-815
jurisdiction, leadership, subcommittees - 970
Governmental Affairs Committee (Senate)
jurisdiction, leadership, subcommittees - 965-966
waterfront racketeering investigation - 667
Governors. (See also Gubernatorial elections; National Governors' Conference.)
governors, 1981-84 (list) - 1122-1123
Grace, J. Peter - 772, 791
Grace commission - 58, 771, 772, 791
Gradison, Bill (R-Ohio)
campaign, 1984 - 13
Social Security reform - 660
tax indexing - 67
Grain. (See also Corn; Wheat.)
elevator bankruptcy - 687, 693, 704, 705
exports, embargo results - 100, 487, 488, 494, 495, 499
gasohol production - 503
inspection program - 515-516
price supports - 489, 490, 496, 510-511
reserves - 487, 488, 492
Soviet sales (box) - 510
Gramm, Phil (Texas)
budget - 39, 53
Budget Committee eviction - 799-800, 812
Clinch River breeder reactor - 373
domestic content bill - 102
hazardous waste disposal - 452
House rules changes - 813
IMF funding - 104-105
nuclear waste disposal - 365
oil allocation authority - 378
party switch - 14
Senate election - 21
Gramm-Latta budget plans - 39, 42-43
AFDC programs - 587
child nutrition programs - 592
housing - 631
social services - 589
Grant, J. B. - 502
Grapes - 109, 111, 503
Grassley, Charles E. (R-Iowa)
budget issues - 39, 53, 60
legislative veto - 837
Gray, Kenneth J. - 23
Great Bear wilderness area - 342
Great Britain
arms control - 251, 253
arms sales to India - 153
Lebanon peacekeeping force - 126
military construction - 248
missile deployment - 232, 246, 255
oil imports - 197
oil reserves - 338
Soviet economic sanctions - 145
tax treaty - 696
Greece
foreign aid - 134, 160, 162, 171, 173
military bases - 246
Green, Bill (R-N.Y.)
budget resolution - 53
Gorsuch contempt citation/Superfund - 451
Green River-Ham's Fork region - 354
Greene, Harold H. - 270-271
Greenham Common, U.K. - 245
Greenmail - 283
Greenspan, Alan - 660, 662

Gregg, Frank - 352, 354, 407
Grenada
foreign aid - 162
U.S. invasion - 4, 123, 155, 169, 181-184
Grey, Robert T. Jr. - 1029
Greyhound Lines Inc. - 311
Gromyko, Andrei - 257
Gros Ventre Indians - 792
Gross National Product (GNP)
trend, 1980-84 (graph) - 31
Guantanamo Naval Base
nuclear arms treaty - 139
Guaranteed Student Loan program - 556, 557-559, 561-563, 566, 566 (graph)
Guatemala
Contadora group talks - 185
foreign aid - 159, 160, 162, 163 (box), 171, 172, 182, 189
human rights issues - 182
Kissinger commission report - 177
Guayule rubber program - 513
Gubernatorial elections - 7, 12, 14, 23, 1103, 1113
returns by state (lists) - 1104-1112, 1115-1121
Guess, Francis F. - 694
Gulf of Mexico
offshore oil leases - 348, 358
Gulf Oil Co. - 349, 382, 390
Guns and gun control. See Firearms.
Guyana
Caribbean trade plan - 106
Grenada invasion - 182

H

Habib, Philip C. - 191
Hagedorn, Tom (R-Minn.)
Farmers Home Administration reauthorization - 502
Haig, Alexander M. Jr.
arms control - 251, 254
AWACS sale to Saudi Arabia - 131
Central America - 126
El Salvador aid - 186
foreign aid - 134, 137
nerve gas - 211
profile - 1023-1024
State Department tenure - 127, 142, 155, 194, 854-856
White House control remark - 127, 847
Haiti
foreign aid restrictions - 174
illegal aliens - 316
Halperin, Lawrence - 782
Hamilton, Lee H. (D-Ind.)
aid to Lebanon - 159
Hammer, Michael - 172
Hammond, Jay - 349
Handicapped persons. (See also Disabled persons.)
adoption aid - 607
airport access - 326
business loans - 283
congregate meals program - 594
education aid - 556, 557, 559, 560, 563, 567, 602
foster care income - 77
Head Start - 591
housing assistance - 632, 633, 637, 638
medical neglect of infants - 553, 582, 606-607
polling place access - 792-793
Supreme Court cases - 730
vocational rehabilitation - 82, 567, 576-578, 602-603, 608-609, 672
Hansen, George (R-Idaho)
electoral defeat - 23

ethics investigation - 818
Hansen, James V. (R-Utah)
parks protection - 475
Hardesty, Rex - 314
Harding, Warren G. - 346
Harkin, Tom (D-Iowa)
nuclear freeze movement - 256
outside income limits - 824
Senate election - 21
Harley-Davidson Motorcycle Co. - 454
Harris, James - 469
Harris poll on air quality - 418
Hart, B. Sam - 1029
Hart, Gary (D-Colo.)
arms control - 206
binary munitions - 219
Clean Air Act revisions - 418
industrial policy - 97
nuclear waste disposal - 363, 365, 368
presidential candidacy - 18
school lunch program - 592
Hart, Philip A. - 803
Hatch, Orrin G. (R-Utah)
abortion issues - 690-691
balanced budget amendment - 52
child care programs - 604
education leadership - 579
Equal Rights Amendment - 697
Freedom of Information Act restrictions - 779
generic drugs - 548
health block grants - 523, 526
health leadership - 552
health manpower programs - 530
rehabilitation aid - 567
saccharin ban deferral - 530-531, 541
welfare leadership - 611
Hatfield, Antoinette - 818-819
Hatfield, Mark O. (R-Ore.)
defense spending - 206, 209
draft registration - 208
ethics investigation - 818-819
jobs funding - 652
Lebanon policy/war powers - 157
Senate television - 818
timber contract relief - 473-474
water projects - 442
wilderness areas - 343, 472
Hawaii
education aid - 577
highway aid - 307
hospitals - 541
revenue sharing - 117
voting rights action - 679
Hawaii Prepaid Health Care Act - 77
Hawkins, Augustus F. (D-Calif.)
education leadership - 579
welfare leadership - 611
Hawkins, David - 418
Hawkins, Paula (R-Fla.)
dairy program - 497
Hayakawa, S. I. "Sam" (R-Calif.)
dairy program - 497
retirement - 11
wilderness areas - 342, 466
Hayden, Carl - 429
Hazardous Substance Response Trust Fund. See Superfund.
Hazardous substances. (See also Alcoholic beverages; Drug abuse; Hazardous waste management; Nuclear waste.)
Agent Orange - 613, 615, 620-621
air pollutants - 412, 413 (chart), 414, 417
aquifer protection - 440
asbestos in schools - 571, 572, 575
chronic hazard advisory panels - 268
cigarette warning labels - 543, 548-549
dioxin - 456, 458, 459
EPA authorizations - 453-454
extra military pay - 215

lead additives - 420
lead paint poisoning - 525
new drugs - 700
ocean dumping - 436
paraquat spraying of marijuana - 136
risk analysis - 454
saccharin ban deferral - 530-531, 541
sewer grants - 425-428
Tris - 688
Tylenol deaths - 542, 689, 696
Hazardous waste management. (See also Nuclear waste.)
Burford controversy - 449-452, 454-457
EPA disposal regulations - 409, 452-453, 457-459, 839
landfill dumping - 408
ocean dumping - 436-437
Superfund controversy - 449-452, 454-457, 459-461
transport regulations - 300, 328
victims compensation - 460
Hazardous Waste Treatment Council - 452-453
Head Start - 519, 561, 582, 590, 591, 603, 605
Health. (See also Drug industry; Child nutrition and health; Hazardous substances; Health and Human Services Department; Health insurance; Hospitals; Medicaid, Medicare; Mental health and illness; Nurses and nursing; Occupational health and safety; Physicians.)
abortion - 690, 691
AID programs - 173
block grants - 521, 522, 523-527, 773-774
chronic hazard advisory panels - 268
chronology of action
1981 - 523-532
1982 - 532-538
1983 - 538-543
1984 - 543-554
Clean Air Act revision - 411-420
community health programs - 524, 551, 599, 602
education programs - 524, 610
emergency care - 524
Food for Peace prerequisite - 136
home services - 524, 536-537, 663
manpower programs - 530
medical tax deductions - 75
outlays (graph) - 522
pesticide law revision - 501-502
planning programs - 521, 522, 523, 531-532, 537-538, 543
preventive services - 523, 524, 526, 538, 552, 553
primary care programs - 523, 525, 527, 551
public health emergencies - 542
Reagan term overview - 520-522
risk analysis - 454
safe drinking water - 440
Superfund cleanup - 449-452
tobacco bills - 498, 510
uranium mine standards - 369
Health and Human Services Department (HHS). (See also Food and Drug Administration; National Institutes of Health.)
abortion funding ban - 691
AFDC cuts - 586
appropriations - 589
cigarette warning labels - 549
community health centers - 525, 526
community services office - 590
day-care center standards - 608
disabled workers - 668, 669
domestic violence - 608
fire-safe cigarettes - 285
handicapped infants regulations - 607

Head Start - 591
health costs statistics - 521
health manpower programs - 530
home health aid experiments - 647
leadership - 552 (box), 611 (box)
links with HUD - 637
Medicaid, Medicare programs - 528,
    529, 533-536, 538-541, 545
nutrition research - 612
Older Americans programs - 609
organ transplants - 550
parental notification of abortion - 553
peer review organizations - 528, 533,
    536
poverty definition (box) - 587
radiation safety - 527
retirement age - 661, 663
Health Care Financing Administration
- 521
Health Education Assistance Loan program - 530
Health insurance - 75, 284, 521, 538,
542-543, 549, 665, 691
**Health maintenance organizations
(HMOs)** - 521, 522, 529, 532-534, 541,
551
Health Professions Student Loans - 530
Heart disease - 548-549
Hecht, Chic (R-Nev.)
election - 11
Heckler, Margaret M.
disabled workers - 668
electoral defeat - 10
Health and Human Services tenure -
    552, 611
health emergency fund - 542
Medicare fund projections - 522, 545
profile - 1022
Heflin, Howell (D-Ala.)
constitutional convention - 679
farm target price freeze - 513
Williams resignation - 805, 808
Heinz, John (R-Pa.)
energy conservation - 400
financial regulation - 92
high-tech exports - 99-100
Senate leadership - 801
Social Security - 657, 661
Three Mile Island cleanup - 370
Helicopters
anti-submarine - 210, 219, 221, 228,
    230, 240, 244
anti-tank - 206, 208, 210, 219, 221,
    234, 237, 244
carriers - 210, 228
transport - 208, 210
Hellfire missiles - 228
Helms, Jesse (R-N.C.)
abortion issues - 691, 800, 848
arms control - 852
Central America aid plan - 177
cigarette taxes - 79
dairy programs - 503, 505
farm programs - 485, 486
food donation program - 601
food stamps program - 583, 595, 602
gas tax, highway bill - 304, 800
genocide treaty - 180
hunger reports - 611-612
IMF funding - 104
King holiday - 786
Korean airliner downing - 169
omnibus farm bill - 488-490
PIK program - 498
re-election - 21
school prayer - 800
timber contract relief - 473
tobacco program - 503, 505
Voting Rights Act extension - 681
welfare leadership - 611
wilderness leasing - 342
Hemophilia - 525

Hendon, Bill (R-N.C.)
wilderness leasing - 343
**Heritage Conservation and Recreation
Service** - 464, 472
Heritage Foundation - 373
Heroin, for cancer patients - 553
Herrington, John S. - 337
Herschler, Ed - 467
Hesburgh, Theodore M. - 694
High schools. *See Elementary and secondary education.*
Higher education. *See Postsecondary education.*
Higher Education Act - 569
High-tech industries trade controls -
98, 99, 108-110
Highway Act of 1956 - 304
Highway Trust Fund - 297-298, 303-
306, 320-322
Highways. *(See also Traffic safety;
Trucks and trucking.)*
aid to states (chart) - 307
clean air enforcement - 422-423
economic development aid - 115-116
federal outlays (graph) - 290
gas tax, highway legislation - 32, 289,
    301-307, 651
infrastructure repairs (box) - 302
Interstate System - 297-298, 301-307,
    320
wilderness areas - 465-467
Hill, A. Alan - 451
Hill AFB, Utah - 223
Hinckley, John W. Jr. - 675, 692, 698,
847
Hinson, Jon C. (R-Miss.)
resignation - 804
Hispanics
Fernandes candidacy - 19
immigration reform - 692, 697, 708
judicial appointments - 676
voters - 20, 680
Historic preservation. *(See also Museums
and historic sites.)*
Capitol West Front restoration - 815
national parks - 463, 464, 476
rehabilitation tax credit - 69, 79, 80
Ho Chi Minh - 625
Hodel, Donald P.
acid rain - 420, 421, 456
career - 334, 337, 397, 408, 474,
    1020-1021
coal leasing - 357
nuclear waste disposal - 362
oil company mergers - 390
Holiday Inns - 378
Hollenbeck, Harold C. (R-N.J.)
electoral defeat - 10
Hollings, Ernest F. (D-S.C.)
air crash liability treaty - 696
AT&T deregulation - 271
B-1 bomber - 210
budget resolution - 53
energy efficiency standards - 395
presidential candidacy - 17
tax cut - 66
Holt, Cooper T. - 625
Homeless persons
food stamp eligibility - 612
HUD estimate - 629
runaway children - 700
shelter assistance - 637
Homes. *See Housing.*
Homestead Act of 1864 - 431
Homosexuality
congressional pages investigation - 809
Hinson resignation - 804
Studds censure - 814
Honduras
aid to Nicaraguan contras - 162, 182,
    184
Contadora group talks - 185

economy - 182
foreign aid - 160, 169, 172
Salvadoran military training - 176
U.S. military presence - 172, 176 (box),
    223, 233, 240, 241, 246-248
Honey - 516
Hong Kong
trade benefits - 110
Honoraria. *See Congressional pay and
benefits.*
Hoosier National Forest - 466
Hoover, Herbert - 833
Hoover, J. Edgar - 684
Hoover Dam - 409, 445-446
Hoover Institution - 694
Hopkins, Ed - 439
Hopkins, Harry - 653
Hormats, Robert D. - 1027
Horsepasture River - 473
Hospices - 533, 535, 542, 553
Hospital Insurance trust fund - 522,
538, 539, 544, 545, 645, 647, 658, 660,
663
Hospitals. *(See also Hospices.)*
abortion requirement - 691
costs - 521
health planning system - 531-532
heroin for cancer patients - 553
medical care of handicapped infants -
    607
Medicare payments - 522, 533, 534,
    538-541, 544, 545
military construction - 247
Public Health Service facilities - 520-
    522, 531
Veterans - 615, 617, 619
Hostages
airline hijacking penalties - 701
Iran release agreement - 3, 143 (box)
Houdaille Industries - 97
House Administration Committee
jurisdiction, leadership, subcommittees -
    970
House Democratic Caucus - 802
House of Representatives, U.S. *(See
also Congressional ethics; Congressional
pay and benefits; Congressional votes.)*
committees - 967-974
distribution of seats (chart) - 1102
election results, 1944-84 (chart) - 1100-
    1101
elections
    1982 midterm - 9-11
    1984 - 17, 22-23
leadership - 5 (chart), 801-802, 812-
    813, 973-974
membership (lists) - 946-948, 950-951
Office for the Bicentennial - 812
offices renovation - 803
origin of revenue bills - 798
reapportionment and redistricting - 4,
    9-10, 15, 995-998, 999-1013
rules changes - 798-799, 813
rules suspension - 696-697
session statistics (boxes) - 6, 8, 13, 16
Speaker's Commission on Pages - 810
Speaker's powers - 798
televised sessions - 17, 799, 816, 818
House Republican Study Committee -
802
House Un-American Activities Committee - 845
Housing. *(See also Housing assistance
and public housing; Mortgages and
home loans; Real estate industry and
taxes.)*
barrier island development - 467-468
chronology of action
    1981 - 631-633
    1982 - 633-635
    1983 - 635-638
    1984 - 638-639

construction industry - 473, 629
earthquake standards - 792
energy audits - 400
faculty - 82
insurance - 631, 633
Reagan term overview - 629-630
rent control - 631
Supreme Court on "testers" - 730
tax issues
    business use of home - 71
    energy tax credit - 69
    imputed interest - 80-82
    sale of residence - 69
    second homes - 71, 821-823
Housing and Community Development Amendments of 1981 - 631-633
Housing and Rural Recovery Act - 635-
638
Housing and Urban Development Department (HUD)
authorizations, appropriations - 634,
    635, 638
clean air laws - 412
Community Development block grants -
    636
energy aid - 394
energy efficiency standards - 395
flood insurance - 468
homeless persons estimate - 629
housing mix requirements - 632-633
links with Health and Human Services
    Department - 637
relocation expenses - 782
rent subsidies - 629
report and wait provisions - 838
solar bank - 394
Housing assistance and public housing. *(See also Community development;
Farmers Home Administration; Housing
and Urban Development Department;
Mortgages and home loans.)*
authorizations, appropriations - 105,
    631, 632, 637
counseling assistance - 633
elderly, handicapped assistance - 633
eligibility requirements - 631, 632
energy aid - 400, 603-605
"entitlement" communities - 632
home weatherization - 393, 394, 396,
    400, 590, 604, 605
Indian program - 632, 637
mobile homes - 633
mortgage revenue bonds - 82
outlays (graph) - 520
Reagan term overview - 582, 629-630
rehabilitation loans - 629, 632, 636,
    637
rent subsidies - 629, 631, 632, 634-638
rural programs - 633, 634, 637, 638
sewer grants - 439
urban homesteading - 632, 636
voucher plan - 629, 635, 638
How a bill becomes a law (chart) - 872
Howard, James J. (D-N.J.)
Gorsuch citation/Superfund - 450
minimum drinking age - 323
transport of radioactive material - 300
Howard University - 569, 578, 694
Howarth, James - 814
Huddleston, Walter D. (D-Ky.)
electoral defeat - 21
Hugel, Max C.
financial misconduct investigation - 141-
    142
Hulett, Stanley H. - 349
Human resources. *See Welfare and social services.*
Human rights
Argentina - 133, 134
Central America - 174, 181
Chile - 134
contract sanctity issue - 108

El Salvador - 125, 135, 147 (box), 165, 174, 186
Guatemala - 163, 182
Haiti - 174
Lefever nomination - 141
Nicaragua - 136, 184
Reagan term overview - 123-124, 856
Humphrey, Gordon J. (R-N.H.)
budget targets - 39
Clinch River breeder reactor - 373
re-election - 21
Hungary
trade status - 103, 107
Hunger - 598-600, 611-612
Hunger Committee, Select (Senate)
authorization - 612
Hunt, James B. Jr. - 21
Hunt, Reed O. - 88
Hunt banking commission - 88
Hunt silver crisis - 83
Hunter, Duncan (R-Calif.)
trade with Japan - 96
Hunting - 470, 474-475
Hussein, King - 124, 159, 195, 196-197
Hyde, Henry J. (R-Ill.)
abortion funding ban - 690, 691
Hydroelectric power. *(See also Utilities; Water projects.)*
dam repair funds (box) - 430
Grace commission recommendations - 791
Hoover Dam power pricing - 409, 445-446
power rate study - 434
water projects cost sharing - 441, 444
wild and scenic rivers - 472-473
Hypertension - 524, 552

I

Iacocca, Lee A. - 118
Ickes, Harold L. - 653
Idaho
ERA vote - 682
forests - 473
highway aid - 307
revenue sharing - 117
voting rights action - 679
wilderness leasing - 340
IEA. *See International Energy Agency.*
Ikle, Fred C. - 851
Illinois
ERA vote - 682
highway aid - 307, 322
revenue aid - 117
Illinois River - 473
IMF. *See International Monetary Fund.*
Immigrants and immigration. *(See also Aliens; Immigration and Naturalization Service; Refugees.)*
AFDC eligibility - 587
Amerasian children - 689
education aid - 561, 573, 576, 602
illegal aliens
amnesty - 676, 678, 692, 708
employment - 676, 678, 692, 708
firearms for Mexican border patrols - 503
from Haiti - 174, 316
Supreme Court cases - 726-727
reform proposals - 4, 678 (box), 692, 697, 698, 708
resettlement aid - 689, 697, 708
Immigration and Naturalization Act - 834
Immigration and Naturalization Service
Chadha case - 834, 981

undercover operations - 809
procedures - 677
Impact aid. *See Elementary and secondary education; Trade adjustment assistance.*
Imports. *See Foreign trade.*
Income taxes
capital gains - 66, 68, 69, 73, 79-81
charity deductions - 68, 69, 82
child care credit - 69, 697
child support enforcement - 605
commodity tax straddles - 70
cuts/increases - 65-67, 72-73, 77-79
earned income credit - 57, 79, 81
foreign income - 69, 81
fringe benefits - 70, 71, 82
income averaging - 81
inflation indexing - 65, 66, 67 (box), 68, 69
interest, dividend withholding - 73, 75, 78, 90-92
interest exclusion - 66, 70, 81
investment income - 69
marginal tax rate - 30, 66
marriage penalty - 66, 68, 69
medical deductions - 75
mileage deductions - 81
minimum tax - 73, 75
refund deductions for debts - 58, 791
residence issues - 69, 71, 80, 821, 822
restaurant tips - 73, 75
retirement plan deductions - 70, 75, 80
savings incentives - 30, 70
Social Security payroll taxes - 662
Subchapter S taxation - 76
tuition tax credit - 66, 78
Independence (ship) - 230, 236, 240
Independent Bankers Association - 486, 512
Independent Safety Board Act of 1974 - 300
Independent Truckers Association - 290
India
arms sales - 153-154
F-16 sales to Pakistan - 133
nuclear non-proliferation - 168
Indian Affairs Committee, Select (Senate)
jurisdiction, leadership, subcommittees - 966-967
Indian Claims Commission - 792
Indian Health Service - 531, 792
Indian Ocean
U.S. military presence - 207, 208, 211, 213, 233, 246
Indian Point nuclear project - 374
Indiana
highway aid - 307
revenue sharing - 117
wilderness areas - 465, 466
Indiana University - 605
Indians and Alaskan natives. *(See also Bureau of Indian Affairs.)*
abortion funding ban - 690
claims extension - 781
college construction - 564
Connecticut land claims veto - 787
conservation corps - 667, 671
economic development aid - 605, 790, 792
education aid - 573, 576, 577
food stamp eligibility - 586
fur seal harvest - 479, 481-482
Head Start - 591
housing programs - 632, 637
irrigation project veto - 790, 792
job training - 655, 656
nuclear waste disposal - 362, 364
oil and gas production, 1980-84 (chart) - 343
oil and gas royalties - 344-346

Reagan block grant proposal - 773
tribal colleges - 569
tribal tax breaks - 77
water rights - 432
Watt reservation remark - 407
Individual retirement accounts. *See IRAs.*
Industrial development bonds - 71, 76, 79, 80, 82
Industry. *See Business and industry.*
Infants
air quality standards - 415
formula marketing code - 141-143, 149
medical neglect of handicapped - 553, 606-607
mortality - 546, 600
Information Agency, U.S. (USIA)
authorization - 167
criticism from Democracy Program - 168
Radio Marti authorization - 166-167
renaming - 149
Inouye, Daniel K. (D-Hawaii)
aid to Israel - 146
Senate leadership - 5, 801, 812
Williams resignation - 808
Insanity. *See Mental health and illness.*
Institute for Peace - 579
Institute of Medicine - 550
Institute of Museum Services - 789
Insurance. *See also Health insurance; Medicaid, Medicare.*
airline pact - 310
barrier islands ban - 467, 468
export subsidies - 106
FHA premiums - 49, 50
financial services industry regulation - 84, 89, 92
life insurance taxation - 81
modco transfers - 74-75
overseas investment - 99
product liability - 269
Three Mile Island cleanup - 370
unisex premium computation - 284, 697
Intelligence affairs. *See also Central Intelligence Agency; Defense Intelligence Agency; Federal Bureau of Investigation.*
agent identity disclosure - 140, 151-152
authorizations - 139-140, 168, 179, 838
Casey, Hugel investigations - 141-142
executive order on collection in U.S. - 140
insignia protection - 140, 152
Nicaragua covert aid - 164-165, 229
Peace Corps independence - 136
protection of officials - 689
small business research funds - 273
Intelligence Authorization Act - 152
Intelligence Committee, Select (House)
jurisdiction, leadership, subcommittees - 972
Intelligence Committee, Select (Senate)
jurisdiction, leadership, subcommittees - 967
Intelligence Identities Protection Act - 151-152
Intelligence Oversight Board - 140
Interagency Task Force on Acid Precipitation - 421
Inter-American Development Bank - 132, 168, 174
Inter-American Foundation - 148
Interim Convention on Conservation of North Pacific Fur Seals - 479
Interior and Insular Affairs Committee (House)
jurisdiction, leadership, subcommittees - 970-971
Interior Department. *(See also Bureau of Indian Affairs; Bureau of Land Man-*

agement; Bureau of Mines; Bureau of Reclamation; National parks; Fish and Wildlife Service.)
appropriations - 399
barrier islands - 467-468, 481
coal leasing - 351-357
coal slurry pipelines - 320
Energy Department abolition proposal - 397
environmental programs - 404 (box), 405
Hoover Dam - 446
Indian claims - 781
offshore leases - 351-357, 358-359
oil and gas royalties - 344-346
Oregon land tracts - 476
Outer Continental Shelf leases - 347-350
Pauley Group leases - 349
strategic minerals - 475
stripmining regulation - 468-469
synthetic fuel research - 398
water projects - 428-431, 441, 446
watershed leasing - 350-351
Watt policies - 334, 405-408
wild and scenic rivers - 473
wilderness areas - 339-344, 465
wildlife protection - 477-479, 481
Intermediate-range nuclear forces (INF). *See Arms control.*
Internal Revenue Service (IRS)
business reporting - 71
child support enforcement - 588
congressional deductions - 71
disclosure of returns - 684
farm taxes - 508
federal debt collection - 780
fringe benefits - 82
imputed interest - 80-81
tax collection enforcement - 75, 91
tax rulings - 77
International affairs. *See Foreign affairs.*
International Atomic Energy Agency
U.S. withdrawal - 153
International Bank for Reconstruction and Development. *See World Bank.*
International Coffee Agreement - 665
International Communication Agency - 148, 149
International Court of Justice. *See World Court.*
International Development Association (IDA)
Africa aid - 173
authorizations, appropriations - 136-138, 148, 150, 159-162, 173-174
International development banks. *See also World Bank.*
authorizations, appropriations - 104, 131-132, 137, 138, 148, 150, 161-162, 168, 173-174
Caribbean Basin Initiative - 149
executive salaries - 138
International Emergency Economic Powers Act of 1977 - 111
International Energy Agency (IEA) - 376, 378-379, 381, 382, 390-391
International Free Raoul Wallenberg Committee - 144
International Industry and Trade Department - 111
International Military Education and Training - 161
International Monetary Fund (IMF)
authorizations, appropriations - 56, 93, 103-105, 168, 635
Reagan policy - 95-96
Third World debt - 97-98
International Telecommunications Union
Israeli membership - 153

International trade. *See Foreign trade.*
International Trade Commission, U.S. - 109, 512
Interstate Commerce Commission (ICC)
  bus industry deregulation - 311-314
  coal slurry pipelines - 320
  railroad accounting - 329
  report and wait provisions - 838
  size reduction - 50
Interstate Highway System
  authorizations - 290, 297-298, 301, 321-322
  gas tax, highway legislation - 301-307
  truck size limits - 324
Investments. *See Stocks, bonds and securities.*
Iodine 131 - 537
Iowa
  highway aid - 307
  revenue sharing - 117
Iowa (ship) - 206, 210, 211, 218-221
IRAs (individual retirement accounts) - 58, 68, 70, 80, 697
Iran
  hostage release - 3, 143 (box)
  oil production - 376, 380
  refugee aid - 149
  UN motion to expel Israel - 153
Iran-Iraq war - 191, 196-197, 338
Iraq
  foreign aid ban - 138
  Israeli reactor raid - 193
Irish Wilderness - 467
Irrigation projects
  dam repairs - 438
  desalinization - 446, 447
  Garrison diversion - 435, 441, 444
  Indian project veto - 790, 792
  reclamation law revision - 431-433
  water projects cost sharing - 441
  western water reclamation - 503
Isaac, William M. - 86
Islamic Revolutionary Movement - 192
Israel
  aid project contractors - 173
  AWACS sale to Saudi Arabia - 129-131, 193
  energy aid support - 173
  foreign aid - 134, 135, 137, 138, 146, 160, 161, 170-173, 194 (chart), 195
  Iraq raid - 193
  relations with Egypt - 173, 191, 195-196
  relations with U.S. - 193-195
  role in Lebanon - 123, 126, 158, 191-195
  Sinai peacekeeping force - 140-141
  trade talks - 109-110
  UN warning resolutions - 153
  West Bank issues - 146, 194
Italy
  foreign aid - 162
  Lebanon peacekeeping force - 126
  military construction - 246
  missile deployment - 232, 255
  Soviet economic sanctions - 145
Izaak Walton League - 475

J

Jackson, Andrew - 847
Jackson, Henry M. (D-Wash.)
  Alaska pipeline - 385-386
  death - 14
  Kissinger commission - 125

  nuclear power plant licensing - 368
  nuclear waste disposal - 362
  oil allocation authority - 377, 378
  power rate study - 434
  Strategic Petroleum Reserve - 381
  watershed leasing - 350-351
  wilderness leasing - 343
Jackson, Jesse - 18
Jackson, Thomas P. - 817
Jackson-Vanik trade act amendments - 107, 836
Jacobs, Andrew (D-Ind.)
  health leadership - 552
Jamaica - 182
Janklow, William J. - 12
Japan
  arms sales review - 132, 135
  auto exports - 99, 103, 651
  defense burden sharing - 153, 212, 213, 223, 232, 233, 241, 247
  domestic content bills - 101, 102, 108-109
  fur seal harvest - 479
  industrial and export policy - 96-97, 107, 114
  military facilities - 248
  nuclear technology - 138
  oil imports - 197, 335, 338
  trade reciprocity - 96, 102-103
Javits, Jacob K. - 30
Jeffords, James M. (R-Vt.)
  budget resolution - 53
  dairy price supports - 494
Jenrette, John W. - 806
Jepsen, Roger W. (R-Iowa)
  abortion issues - 691, 695
  electoral defeat - 21
  farm target price freeze - 513
  nuclear freeze movement - 256
Jews
  AWACS sale to Saudi Arabia - 129-131
  refugee aid in Israel - 148-149
  vote analysis, 1984 - 20
  Wallenberg citizenship - 144
Job Corps - 655, 656
Job safety. *See Occupational health and safety.*
Job training. *See Employment programs and job training; Rehabilitation; Vocational education.*
Job Training Partnership Act - 577, 643, 655-656
John Paul II, Pope - 167
John W. McCormack Institute of Public Affairs - 578
Johnson, Lyndon B. - 17, 27, 113, 115, 299, 463, 525, 581, 590, 774, 853
Johnson, Nancy L. (R-Conn.)
  election - 10
Johnston, J. Bennett (D-La.)
  energy aid formula - 604
  MX missile - 239
  natural gas deregulation - 383
  nuclear waste disposal - 364
  oil allocation authority - 377
  oil company mergers - 390
  Tenn-Tom waterway - 434-435
  timber contract relief - 474
Joint Chiefs of Staff - 224-225, 233, 245
Joint Logistics Planning Program - 196
Joint resolutions
  alternative to legislative veto - 837, 838
Jones, David C. - 225
Jones, Ed (D-Tenn.)
  conservation proposal - 513
  omnibus farm bill - 490
Jones, James R. (D-Okla.)
  budget issues - 12, 39-41, 45, 47, 48, 50, 59, 850

  jobs plan - 652
Jones, Walter B. (D-N.C.)
  barrier island jetties - 481
  Coast Guard authorizations - 316
  offshore oil revenue - 350
Jordan
  arms sales - 124, 196-197, 836
  foreign aid - 159, 170, 173
  West Bank, Palestinian issues - 194, 195
Jordan, Hamilton - 682
Judicial Conference, U.S. - 702, 704
Judiciary. *(See also Circuit Court of Appeals; Supreme Court.)*
  appeals court - 686-687
  bankruptcy courts - 692-693
  court appropriations - 676
  federal courts expansion - 698, 702, 704
  life tenure - 702, 704
  marshals - 688
  military justice revision - 695-696
  Reagan appointments - 676
  salaries of federal judges - 57, 58, 714, 824
  study commission - 693
  Supreme Court cases - 713, 762-765
Judiciary Committee (House)
  jurisdiction, leadership, subcommittees - 687, 971
Judiciary Committee (Senate)
  jurisdiction, leadership, subcommittees - 687, 966
Jupiter exploration - 776
Justice Assistance Act - 689
Justice Department. *(See also Federal Bureau of Investigation; Immigration and Naturalization Service.)*
  Abscam investigation - 815
  agent identity disclosure - 151
  Alaska pipeline - 385
  Allen investigation - 142
  anti-crime block grant - 700
  AT&T antitrust suit - 261, 265, 270
  authorizations, appropriations - 676, 677, 693, 698, 709
  Burford contempt citation - 408, 449-452, 455-457
  busing ban - 705
  CAB antitrust powers - 325
  civil rights in education - 565
  development organizations - 188
  drug enforcement - 692, 701
  Freedom of Information Act - 789
  hazardous waste controls - 455, 458, 459
  joint research ventures - 706
  maritime regulation - 319
  pocket-veto power - 817
  presidential disability - 847
  registration of foreign agents - 701
  special prosecutor law - 683
  state tax exemptions for congressmen - 823
  Supreme Court role - 713
  Voting Rights Act enforcement (chart) - 679, 681
  wilderness leasing - 342

K

Kahn, Alfred - 30
Kaiser, Frederick M. - 837, 838
Kampuchea
  Amerasian immigration - 689
Kansas
  highway aid - 307
  revenue sharing - 117

Kasich, John R. (R-Ohio)
  election - 10
Kassebaum, Nancy Landon (R-Kans.)
  air crash liability treaty - 696
  budget resolution - 60
  natural gas deregulation - 383, 389
Kasten, Robert W. (R-Wis.)
  aid to Israel - 146
  noise control - 454
Kaufman, Frank A. - 823
Kazen, Abraham Jr. (D-Texas)
  dam repairs - 426
Kean, Thomas H. - 7
Kefauver, Estes - 547
Kelly, Richard - 802, 806
Kemp, Jack F. (R-N.Y.)
  House leadership - 5
  international finance - 98
  Republican convention - 20
  tax increase bill - 72
  tax reduction - 30, 65-66
Kemp-Roth tax plan - 63
Kennedy, Edward M. (D-Mass.)
  aid to Nicaraguan rebels - 176
  criminal code bill - 698
  El Salvador aid - 175
  energy efficiency standards - 395
  famine aid - 178
  health block grants - 526
  health leadership - 552
  health manpower programs - 530
  infant formula marketing code - 142
  jobs plan - 652
  judiciary leadership - 687
  nuclear freeze resolution - 231
  pocket-veto power - 817
  saccharin ban deferral - 530-531
  sex discrimination in education - 561
Kennedy, John F. - 463, 653, 683, 847
Kennelly, Barbara B. (D-Conn.) - 18
Kentucky
  highway aid - 307
  revenue sharing - 117
Kenya
  U.S. use of military facilities - 209, 213
Keogh plans - 68, 70, 75
Kerry, John F. - 22
Key votes
  1981 - 879-893
  1982 - 895-909
  1983 - 911-925
  1984 - 927-941
Keynes, John Maynard - 27
Keynesian economic theory - 27-28, 30, 32
Kidnapping - 683, 700
King, Martin Luther Jr.
  birthday holiday - 772, 786
  Capitol statue - 777, 784
Kings Bay, Ga., Trident base - 213, 246
Kirkland, Lane - 645, 662
Kirkpatrick, Jeane J. - 19, 20, 183, 856, 1026
Kissinger, Henry A. - 125, 177-178, 181, 188
Kissinger commission (National Bipartisan Commission on Central America) - 125, 171, 172, 177-178, 181, 188-189
Knights of Columbus - 256
Koch, Edward I. - 116
Kolter, Joseph P. (D-Pa.)
  electoral defeat - 10
Koop, C. Everett - 531, 552, 1027
Korean Air Lines - 155, 169
Kostmayer, Peter H. (D-Pa.)
  MX missile - 239
Kraft, Timothy - 682
Kristol, Irving - 30
Krugerrands - 108
Kvitsinsky, Yuli A. - 251

L

La Cieba air base - 233
Labeling and packaging
  anti-tampering bill - 689, 696
  cigarette warnings - 543, 548-549
  saccharin - 838
  textiles - 112, 548
Labor and Human Resources Committee (Senate)
  jurisdiction, leadership, subcommittees - 552, 579, 611, 966
Labor and labor unions. (See also AFL-CIO; Employment and unemployment; Labor Department; Labor interests, lobbying; names of specific unions.)
  AFDC benefit ban for strikers - 588
  bus deregulation - 311-312
  chronology of action
    1981 - 645-651
    1982 - 651-658
    1983 - 658-667
    1984 - 667-672
  Davis-Bacon Act - 213, 304, 305, 645
  decline of influence - 643
  food stamp ban for strikers - 583-585, 596
  racketeering - 657-658, 666-667, 700
  rail strike, 1982 - 290, 314
  railroad retirement system - 648-649
  Reagan Hollywood background - 844-845
  Supreme Court cases - 748-752
  transportation industry strikes - 290
  vocational education committees - 578
  vote analysis, 1984 - 20, 643, 645
Labor Department
  appropriations - 589
  authority transfer to EEOC - 839
  black lung trust fund - 650
  Conrail sale proposal - 295
  copyright "manufacturing clause" - 686
  disability compensation - 671
  Donovan investigation - 656
  emergency jobs proposal - 652
  employment for elderly - 594, 609
  inflation rate estimate - 521
  job training programs - 655
  migrant farm worker protection - 503
  Overseas Private Investment Corp. - 99
  unemployment statistics - 652
  veterans programs - 617, 620
Labor interests, lobbying
  Alaska pipeline - 385
  bankrupt companies - 702, 704, 705
  Bildisco remedies - 702
  broadcast deregulation - 578
  Clean Air Act revision - 411, 417, 421
  coal slurry pipelines - 315, 320
  Conrail sale proposal - 291-295
  copyright "manufacturing clause" - 686
  domestic content bills - 96
  federal pay-for-performance plan - 787
  immigration reform - 692
  natural gas deregulation - 389
  oil allocation authority - 378
  oil price decontrol - 376
Labor Management Racketeering Act - 666
Labor-Management Relations Act of 1947 - 666
Labor-Management Reporting and Disclosure Act of 1959 - 666
Labor Racketeering Act - 657
Lacey Act of 1900 - 480
Laghi, Pio - 167
Lajes AFB - 213, 223
Lance, Bert - 18

Land and land use. See Agriculture and farming; Irrigation; Property rights; Public lands; Soil Conservation.
Land and Water Conservation Fund - 463-465, 481
Land Is for People - 432
Landrum-Griffin Act - 666
Landsat - 781, 789
Lang, Daniel L. - 315
Langley AFB, Va. - 246, 248
Lanham Trademark Act - 686
Lantos, Annette - 144
Lantos, Tom (D-Calif.)
  Wallenberg citizenship - 144
Laos
  Amerasian immigration - 689
Lasers
  copperhead artillery shells - 228, 230
  isotope separation - 216
  space weaponry - 206, 208, 226, 237, 251
Latin America. (See also Central America; specific countries.)
  nuclear arms treaty - 139
  Radio Marti authorization - 166
LATIRN - 221
Latta, Delbert L. (R-Ohio) (See also Gramm-Latta.)
  budget issues - 39, 44, 48
  farm budget cuts - 496
Lautenberg, Frank R. (D-N.J.)
  election - 11
  minimum drinking age - 323
  phone rate hike - 279
Lavelle, Rita M. - 455, 456, 460
Lavi - 172-173
Law enforcement. See Crime and criminal justice.
Law Enforcement Assistance Administration (LEAA)
  demise - 676, 685 (box)
  replacement grants - 689, 697
Law of the Sea treaty - 437, 696
Law profession and practice. (See also Legal Services Corp.; Trial procedures.)
  attorneys' fees - 688, 699, 701, 709, 727
  education programs - 570, 578-579
  legal services plans - 70, 82
  National Guard torts - 677
  pretrial services - 684
  special prosecutors - 681-683
Lawn mowers - 268
Laws. (See also State and local government.)
  public law statistics - 6, 8, 11 (box)
Laxalt, Paul (R-Nev.)
  Reagan nomination, 1984 - 20
  water projects cost sharing - 441
LEAA. See Law Enforcement Assistance Administration.
Lead
  deposits in wilderness areas - 467
  gasoline additives - 408, 456
  paint poisoning - 525
Leadership Conference on Civil Rights - 680, 695
Leahy, Patrick J. (D-Vt.)
  legislative veto - 837
  U.S. role in Lebanon - 192
Leather products - 106-107
Lebanese Emergency Assistance Act of 1983 - 158
Lebanon
  aid project contractors - 173
  foreign aid - 135-136, 158-159, 170
  Israeli/Syrian role - 123, 126, 146, 156-158, 191-195
  Reagan policy overview - 4, 846
  U.S. embassy bombing - 158, 179, 191
  U.S. military role - 126, 155, 156-159, 169, 191-193, 229, 836

Lederer, Raymond F. (D-Pa.)
  Abscam investigation - 802, 806-807, 809
Lee, Rex E. - 834
Lefever, Ernest W. - 129, 141, 1027, 1029
Legal Services Corp.
  abolition proposal - 676, 687
  authorizations, appropriations - 677, 683, 695, 705
  Reagan appointments - 695, 1028 (box)
Legislative process
  brief summary - 873-876
  glossary of congressional terms - 861-871
  how a bill becomes a law (chart) - 872
Legislative veto
  arms sales - 124, 132
  AWACS sale to Saudi Arabia - 129
  Caribbean trade plan - 107
  college student aid - 558
  congressional alternatives - 799, 839-840
  Conrail sale proposal - 294, 327-328
  consumer product safety - 262, 267, 277
  District of Columbia statutes - 793
  Education Department rules - 563-564
  foreign policy uses - 833, 836 (box)
  FTC authorization - 276
  FTC funeral home rule - 837
  FTC used car rule - 268, 273-274, 837
  government reorganization - 790
  impoundment provisions of budget act - 34
  natural gas deregulation - 837
  regulatory reform bill - 777-778
  Romania trade status - 103, 107
  special report - 833-840
  statutes authorizing congressional review - 990-992
  Supreme Court decision overturning - 4, 14, 713-714, 799 (box), 833-837, 981-992 (text)
  varieties - 834 (box), 837
  wilderness leasing - 342
Lehman, John F. Jr. - 851
Leland, Mickey (D-Texas)
  hunger committee - 612
Lenkowsky, Leslie - 1030
Lent, Norman F. (R-N.Y.)
  transport of radioactive material - 300
Lesher, William G. - 489
Letelier, Orlando - 134
Levin, Carl (D-Mich.)
  Japanese defense spending - 153
  jobs programs - 664
  legislative veto - 837
Levitas, Elliott H. (D-Ga.)
  Consumer Product Safety Commission authorization - 839
  electoral defeat - 22
  Gorsuch citation/Superfund - 450, 455-457
  hazardous waste management - 453, 458, 460
  legislative veto - 837
  nuclear freeze resolution - 231
Lewis, Arthur D. - 311
Lewis, Drew
  bus deregulation - 312
  Conrail sale proposal - 291, 327
  DOT leadership - 290
  gas tax, highway legislation - 302, 303
  maritime transfer - 299
  profile - 1024
Library Committee (Joint)
  jurisdiction, leadership, subcommittees - 974
Library of Congress. (See also Congres-

sional Research Service.)
  building construction - 803
Library Services and Construction Act - 578
Libraries
  aid authorizations - 578
  presidential libraries - 793
  record copyrights - 707
Libya
  foreign aid ban - 138
Lincoln, Abraham - 847
Line-item veto - 52, 578, 791
Linowes, David F. - 345, 352, 355
Linowes commission - 352, 355-357
Liquor. See Alcoholic beverages.
Literacy
  adult education - 574, 575
  Food for Peace prerequisite - 136
  library programs - 578
  voter tests - 680
Livestock and meat
  Caribbean exports - 106
  dairy program effects - 505, 507
  drought aid - 503
  firearms for Mexican border patrols - 503
  silage loans - 513, 514
  wilderness grazing - 340
LoADs missile defense - 219
Lobbies and lobbying. See Agricultural interests; Business interests; Congressional-executive relations; Environmental interests; Labor interests; Religious interests; names of specific lobbying organizations.
Local Public Works program - 630 (graph), 653
Locker, Dale - 7
Lockheed Aircraft Corp. - 100, 118
Logging. See Forest industries.
Long, Clarence D. (D-Md.)
  electoral defeat - 22
  Stone confirmation - 165
  U.S. role in Lebanon - 229
Long, Gillis W. (D-La.)
  House leadership - 5, 801
Long, Russell B. (D-La.)
  congressional tax deductions - 822, 830
  disabled workers - 668
  interest, dividend withholding - 91
  Medicaid, AFDC spending - 597
  Senate television - 810-811
  Social Security issues - 657, 661, 785
  tax indexing - 67
Long Island Lighting Company - 373
Longshoremen - 657-658, 666, 671, 752
Lott, Trent (R-Miss.)
  Clinch River breeder reactor - 373
  dairy program - 504
  enterprise zones - 119
  franking privilege - 831
  House leadership - 5, 812
  oil allocation authority - 378
Louisiana
  highway aid - 307
  offshore leasing - 358
  revenue sharing - 117, 359
  Strategic Petroleum Reserve - 379-382
  voting rights action - 679, 680
  wetlands protection - 480, 481
Louisiana-Pacific Corp. - 406, 409, 466, 473
Love Canal - 449, 452
Lowry, Mike (D-Wash.)
  electoral defeat - 15
  MX missile - 239
Lugar, Richard G. (R-Ind.)
  commodity futures trading - 499
  mortgage aid bill - 633-634
  Senate leadership - 812
  U.S.-Vatican relations - 167

Lujan, Manuel (R-N.M.)
  payments in lieu of taxes - 469
  wilderness leasing - 339, 342
Luken, Thomas A. (D-Ohio)
  acid rain - 422
Lumber. *See Forest industries.*
Lusinchi, Jaime - 185
Lyng, Richard E. - 489

M

MacGuigan, Mark - 144
MacKay, Buddy (D-Fla.)
  budget resolution - 59
Madigan, Edward R. (R-Ill.)
  health planning - 537-538
Madison, James - 817
Magana, Alvaro - 147, 186
Magnet schools - 556, 569, 571, 572
Mail fraud - 787
Maine
  highway aid - 307
  offshore leasing - 359
  revenue sharing - 117
  voting rights action - 679
Manatt, Charles T. - 18
Manhattan Project - 436-437
Mankiewicz, Frank - 275
Mann, Thomas E. - 844
Marathon Oil Co. - 382
March for Life - 690
Marcos, Ferdinand E. - 174
Marijuana. *(See also Drug trafficking.)*
  paraquat spraying - 136
Marine Corps, U.S.
  aircraft - 207, 221, 226, 230, 236
  Grenada invasion - 169, 183
  Joint Chiefs reorganization plan - 224
  Lebanon role
    deployment - 155-159, 191-192
    headquarters attack - 126, 155, 156, 191, 192, 229
    peacekeeping force - 124, 126, 144, 191
    pullout - 156, 169, 191-193
  Nicaragua, 1930s - 181
  Reagan buildup proposal - 202
Marine Mammal Protection Act of 1972 - 479-481
Marine Protection, Research and Sanctuaries Act - 436, 438, 446
Maritime Administration - 291, 299, 324-325
Maritime affairs. *See Ships and shipping.*
Maritime Boundary Settlement Treaty - 143-144
Mark Twain National Forest - 466
Markey, Edward J. (D-Mass.)
  nuclear power plant licensing - 368
  nuclear waste disposal - 365
  Pershing missile deployment - 253
Marks, Marc L. (R-Pa.)
  retirement - 11
Maronite Christian faction - 192
Marriott, Dan (R-Utah)
  retirement - 23
Marriott, J. Willard Jr. - 326-327
Marshall, Thurgood
  appointment - 711-712
  legislative veto - 835
Marshals
  service of process - 688
Marti, José - 149, 150, 167
Martin, D. G. - 23
Martin, David O'B. (R-N.Y.)
  Clean Air Act revision - 423
Maryland
  highway aid - 307
  revenue sharing - 117

state tax exemptions for congressmen - 823
Mashantucket Pequot Indian tribe - 787
Mass transit
  authorizations - 299-300
  block grants - 306
  federal outlays (graph) - 290
  financing - 71
  gas tax, highway bill - 32, 289-290, 301-307, 651
  highway aid bill - 322
Massachusetts
  highway aid - 307
  offshore oil leases - 348, 357-359
  revenue sharing - 117
  voting rights action - 679
Masson, Milton - 695
Matagorda Island - 482
Maternal and child health
  anti-recession relief - 599
  authorizations - 525, 546, 547
  block grants - 523, 527, 774
Maternal and Child Health and Crippled Children's Services Act - 525
Mathematics education - 570-572
Mathias, Charles McC. Jr. (R-Md.)
  Abscam investigation - 809
  Lebanon policy/war powers - 157
  Senate television - 810
Mattingly, Mack (R-Ga.)
  Williams resignation - 805
Mauritania
  famine aid - 178
Mavroules, Nicholas (D-Mass.)
  MX missiles - 238-239
Mazzoli, Romano L. (D-Ky.)
  immigration reform - 692
McCarran-Walter Act - 692
McCarthy, Robert E. - 695
McCloskey, Frank (D-Ind.)
  disputed election - 23
McClure, James A. (R-Idaho)
  Alaska pipeline - 385
  antitrust exemption for IEA participants - 379
  Clinch River breeder reactor - 373
  coal leasing - 351
  dam repairs - 444, 445
  Energy Department abolition proposal - 397
  Energy Department appropriations - 396
  energy preparedness - 390
  natural gas deregulation - 383, 389
  nuclear waste disposal - 364, 365
  offshore leasing - 358
  oil allocation authority - 338, 376-378
  oil and gas royalties - 345-346
  oil price decontrol - 376
  power rate study - 434
  public land policy - 405
  Senate leadership - 5, 801, 812
  Strategic Petroleum Reserve - 379-382
  water policy planning - 431
  Whoops rescue plan - 371
  wilderness areas - 339-340, 343, 344, 409, 466, 470
McConnell, Mitch - 21
McCormack, John W. - 578
McCurdy, Dave (D-Okla.)
  ASAT missile - 243
McDade, Joseph R. (R-Pa.)
  offshore oil leases - 358
McDonald, Larry P. (D-Ga.)
  House rules changes - 813
  Korean airliner downing - 169
  nuclear non-proliferation - 139
McFadden Act - 88
McGovern, George - 18, 21, 612
McHugh, Matthew F. (D-N.Y.)
  ASAT missile - 242

McIntyre, Richard D. - 23
McKean, John R. - 707
McKernan, John R. Jr. (R-Maine)
  election, 1982 - 10
McKinley, William - 847
McMillan, J. Alex - 23
McNamara, Robert S. - 132
Medfly - 492
Medicaid, Medicare. *See also Child Health Assurance Program.*
  abortion funding ban - 690
  background (box) - 535
  benefits cuts - 519, 520
  committee jurisdiction - 552
  coverage for disabled persons - 657
  coverage of federal employees - 75, 784
  eligibility - 605, 611
  funding cuts - 44, 47-49, 55-58, 523, 527-529, 532-536, 597, 598 (box)
  health insurance for unemployed - 542-543
  hospice payments - 542, 553
  hospital payments reform - 538-541
  organ transplants - 549-550
  outlays (graph) - 522, 644
  physicians fees - 80, 544-546
  Professional Standards Review Organizations - 521, 523, 529, 533, 535-536
  Provider Reimbursement Review Boards - 535-536
  Reagan term overview - 519-522, 777
  tax bill - 72, 79
Medical care. *See Health.*
Medical ethics. *(See also Abortion.)*
  heroin for cancer patients - 553
  neglect of handicapped infants - 553, 607
  NIH research - 550, 551
  organ transplants - 549-550
Medical records - 554
Medical schools - 530, 677
Meese, Edwin III
  background - 687
  draft registration - 218
  nomination investigation - 707 (box), 846
  Reagan assassination attempt - 847
Meese, Ursula - 707
Mejia Victores, Oscar - 163
Melcher, John (D-Mont.)
  dairy price supports - 494
  farm target price freeze - 513
  imputed interest - 80-81
  oil and gas royalties - 346
  school lunch regulations - 592
  wilderness leasing - 344
Memorial Sloan-Kettering Cancer Center - 554
Mental health and illness
  block grants - 523, 524, 526-527, 537, 774
  disabled workers - 669
  insanity defense - 675, 692, 698-700
  POW benefits - 616, 623
  research, treatment programs - 551-552
  Supreme Court cases - 733
  veterans services - 619, 623
Mental Health Systems Act of 1980 - 524
Mental retardation. *See Handicapped persons.*
Merchant marine. *See Ships and shipping.*
Merchant Marine and Fisheries Committee (House)
  jurisdiction, leadership, subcommittees - 971
Merit Systems Protection Board - 686
Merrill Lynch - 84

Metcalf, Lee - 471
Metzenbaum, Howard M. (D-Ohio)
  Alaska pipeline - 385, 386
  Alaska pipeline - 314
  antitrust damages - 693
  cable TV deregulation - 280
  dam repairs - 444, 445
  generic drugs - 548
  Hoover Dam power pricing - 445-446
  maritime antitrust immunity - 316-318
  maritime subsidies - 316
  Meese investigation - 707
  oil allocation authority - 378
  oil company mergers - 390
  oil industry antitrust exemptions - 379, 390, 391
  oil price decontrol - 376
  reclamation law revision - 432
  Rural Electrification loans - 514
  timber contract relief - 473-474
  tobacco program - 505
  Whoops rescue plan - 372
Mexico
  Colorado River salinity control - 447
  Contadora group - 125, 165, 185
  firearms for U.S. border patrol - 503
  international finance - 97
  oil exports - 335
  U.S. guest worker program - 678
Michel, Robert H. (R-Ill.)
  budget issues - 47
  clean air sanctions - 423
  dairy program - 504, 505
  election, 1982 - 11
  GOP stategy - 797
  House leadership - 5, 7, 798, 801-802, 812
  IMF funding - 105
  MX missile - 238
  nuclear freeze resolution - 222
  Studds, Crane censure - 814
Michigan
  highway aid - 307
  revenue sharing - 117
  voting rights action - 679
  wild and scenic rivers - 472, 473
Middle East. *(See also Persian Gulf; Rapid Deployment Force; names of specific countries.)*
  map - 193
  nuclear non-proliferation - 139
  oil reserves - 338
  special report - 191-197
  U.S. foreign aid - 172-173
  U.S. policy - 127, 169
  U.S. military capability - 211, 213, 246
  western oil imports - 376-377
Migrant and Seasonal Agricultural Worker Protection Act - 502-503
Migrant workers
  block grant - 773
  community services program - 591
  education aid - 576
  food stamp eligibility - 596
  health centers - 523, 526, 551, 599
  job training - 655, 656
  pesticide law revision - 502
  preschool education - 564, 569
  protection bill - 502-503, 658
Migratory Bird Conservation Act of 1929 - 480
Migratory Bird Hunting Stamp Act of 1934 - 480
Military affairs. *See Defense.*
Military aid. *See Foreign aid.*
Military Airlift Command - 225
Military and Civilian Employees Claims Act - 689
Military Assistance Program (MAP)
  authorizations, appropriations - 134-135, 137, 159-162, 171, 172

Military dependents
abortion funding ban - 690
AFDC eligibility - 597
child support enforcement - 597
facilities construction - 224, 232, 246
impact aid (box) - 560
medical program - 618
Military justice system - 695-696
Military pay and benefits. *See also GI Bill; Veterans affairs.*
burial benefits - 616, 617
Coast Guard authorizations - 316
cost-of-living adjustments - 775
double-dipping - 779
increases and bonuses - 211, 214-215, 224, 228, 240, 244-245
report and wait provisions - 840
retirement benefits - 49-50, 57, 58, 61
survivor benefit plan - 216-217
unemployment benefits - 648, 655
Milk. *See Dairy industry.*
Miller, George (D-Calif.)
budget plan - 47, 59
oil and gas royalties - 345, 346
Miller, James C. III - 834
Mineral Leasing Act of 1920 - 340, 344, 350, 353, 359
Mineral resources. *(See also Mines and mining; specific minerals.)*
chronology of action
1981-82 - 339-351
1983-84 - 351-359
government title - 352-353
Interior Department programs - 404
seabed mining - 437
wilderness areas - 465-466
Minerals Management Services - 344-346, 404
Mines and mining
mine drainage research - 446
seabed mining - 437
strategic minerals - 475
wilderness areas - 340, 409, 465, 471
Mineta, Norman Y. (D-Calif.)
Gorsuch citation/Superfund - 451
Mining Law of 1872 - 340
Minish, Joseph G. (D-N.J.)
electoral defeat - 22
Minnesota
highway aid - 307
revenue sharing - 117
tuition tax deductions - 568
Minority Enterprise Small Business Investment Corporations - 283
Minority groups. *(See also Affirmative action; Blacks; Hispanics; Indians and Alaskan natives; Jews; Women.)*
aid for elderly - 610
business firms - 262, 266, 276, 283
FCC license preference - 272
judicial appointments - 676
medical school aid - 530
vote analysis, 1984 - 20-21
Voting Rights Act extension - 680
Misawa air base - 232, 233
Miskito Indians - 185
Missiles. *(See also Aegis missile defense; Anti-satellite missile; Arms control; Cruise missiles; MX missile; Pershing missiles; Space weaponry; Trident missiles.)*
air-to-air - 240, 244
anti-aircraft - 226, 228, 230, 237, 244
anti-ballistic missile defense - 206, 208, 217-219, 226
anti-tank - 221, 228, 230, 237, 244
Lance - 215
Midgetman - 227, 229, 236, 237, 244, 252
Minuteman - 205, 206, 209, 210, 227, 231, 252, 254
Patriot - 221, 244
Phoenix - 240

Scowcroft commission recommendations - 226, 227 (box)
SLBMs - 250, 252, 254
Soviet ICBMs - 201, 203-204, 221, 222, 227, 229, 231, 235, 237, 238, 250, 251, 254
Soviet IRBMs - 249-251, 253, 254
Stinger - 196, 221, 836
warheads
ABRV - 218
anti-tank - 228
Mark 12As - 205, 206, 208, 210, 218
MARV - 236
MIRVs - 227, 229, 249, 252
neutron bomb - 215-216, 255
Missing children - 686, 699, 700
Mississippi
highway aid - 307
revenue sharing - 117
Tenn-Tom waterway - 433-435
voting rights action - 679, 680
wilderness areas - 471, 472
Missouri
highway aid - 307
revenue sharing - 117
wilderness areas - 465, 466, 471, 472
Missouri (ship) - 218, 236, 240, 244
Mitchell, George J. (D-Maine)
Clean Air Act revisions - 419
Lebanon policy/war powers - 157
Mitchell, John H. - 808
Moakley, Joe (D-Mass.)
ASAT missile - 242-243
legislative veto - 837
Mobil Oil Corp. - 382, 390
Mobile homes - 633
Moffett, Toby (D-Conn.)
election, 1982 - 10
EPA operations - 408, 420
nuclear power plant licensing - 368
transcript alterations - 814
Molinari, Guy V. (R-N.Y.)
hazardous waste disposal - 453
Molloy, James T. - 810
Mondale, Walter F.
arms control - 257
environmentalist support - 405
industrial policy - 97
National Education Association support - 579
presidential campaign, 1984 - 17-21
tax policy - 64, 78
Monetary policy. *See Federal Reserve.*
Monetarism - 30, 32
Money market deposit accounts - 90
Money market funds - 83-84, 87, 89
Monongahela National Forest - 466
Monson, David S. - 23
Montana
coal leasing - 352, 353, 355-357
highway aid - 307
Indian programs - 792
revenue sharing - 117
wilderness areas - 341-342, 465-467, 471
Montgomery, G. V. "Sonny" (D-Miss.)
veterans leadership - 623
Montreal Protocols - 696
Moon, criminal jurisdiction - 701
Moorhead, Carlos J. (R-Calif.)
nuclear power plant licensing - 368
Moran, Donald W. - 587
Morgan Guaranty & Trust - 385
Morocco
U.S. use of military facilities - 233
Mortgage revenue bonds - 638
Mortgages and home loans. *(See also Farmers Home Administration; Federal Home Loan Bank Board; Federal Home Loan Mortgage Association; Federal Housing Administration.)*

due on sale clauses - 90, 634-635
emergency aid for unemployed - 620, 638
foreclosure on subsidized properties - 633
FHA insurance premiums - 49, 50, 635
FHA interest rate - 633
GNMA purchase authorization - 631, 633
holders rights - 733
mortgage-backed securities - 93, 638-639
mortgage money supply - 638
subsidy bill - 631, 633-634
VA graduated payments - 616
VA guaranty entitlement - 623
VA user fees - 50, 59, 618
Morton, Rogers C. B. - 353
Most-favored-nation designations - 103, 107, 836
Mothers Against Drunk Drivers (MADD) - 323
Motor Carriers Act - 311
Motor Vehicle Theft Law Enforcement Act of 1984 - 323-324
Motorcycles - 96, 454
Mount Baker-Snoqualmie National Forest - 351
Mount St. Helens National Volcanic Monument - 469
Mountain States Legal Foundation - 352, 406
Moynihan, Daniel Patrick (D-N.Y.)
dairy program - 504-505
executive order on intelligence collection - 140
nuclear emergency planning - 374
sewer grants - 427
Social Security issues - 646, 661
Tenn-Tom waterway - 434
Mozambique
famine aid - 178
Mubarak, Hosni - 195
Muller, Robert E. - 625
Murkowski, Frank H. (R-Alaska)
Alaska pipeline - 385
Murphy, John M. - 806, 807
Murray, Jon Garth - 811
Murtha, John P. (D-Pa.)
Abscam investigation - 802, 806, 807
outside income limits - 823
Museums and historic sites
Institute of Museum Services - 789
King statue - 777, 784
presidential libraries - 789
Roosevelt memorial - 782-783
Smithsonian art museums - 784
Truman home - 476
Music industry
record copyrights - 697
Mutual Development and Security Administration - 160
MX missiles
arms control issues - 202, 204, 208, 221-222, 225-229, 235, 238, 249, 250, 252, 254, 257
basing plans - 205, 207, 208, 210-212, 214, 218, 220, 223, 226, 227, 231-232, 248, 252
development authorizations - 206, 208, 209, 211, 212, 221, 228
LoADS defense system - 219
production authorizations - 60, 217, 219, 220, 228, 229, 234-240, 244, 245
Scowcroft panel recommendations - 226, 227 (box)
warheads - 205, 218, 226
Myers, John T. (R-Ind.)
congressional tax deductions - 830
Myers, Michael "Ozzie" - 806, 814

N

Nader, Ralph
Alaska pipeline - 386
Namibia
Angola aid authorization - 134
Narcotics. *See Drug abuse; Drug trafficking; Heroin.*
Narcotics Abuse and Control Committee, Select (House)
jurisdiction, leadership, subcommittees - 972-973
Natchez Trace National Scenic Trail - 469, 475-476
Nation at Risk - 555
National Academy of Sciences
drinking water pollution - 440
health studies - 550, 552
speed limit study - 306
National Advisory Committee on Education of Handicapped Children - 567
National Advisory Committee on Oceans and Administration - 457
National Advisory Committee on Women's Educational Programs - 576
National Aeronautics and Space Administration (NASA)
appropriations/legislative veto - 840
authorizations - 776, 781, 786, 789
weather satellites - 786
National Agricultural Chemicals Association - 502
National Archives and Records Administration - 790
National Assessment of Educational Progress - 573, 576, 578
National Association of Broadcasters - 282
National Association of Counties - 600
National Association of Evangelicals - 256, 257
National Association of Letter Carriers - 785
National Association of Manufacturers - 183
National Association of State Departments of Agriculture - 502
National Audubon Society - 407
National Automobile Dealers Association - 285
National Bipartisan Commission on Central America. *See Kissinger commission.*
National Bureau of Standards - 788
National Bus Traffic Association - 311
National Cable Television Association - 279, 280
National Cancer Institute - 553
National Center for Education Statistics - 556, 573, 575, 576, 578
National Center for Research in Vocational Education - 578
National Clean Air Coalition - 418
National Coal Association - 468
National Coalition Against the Misuse of Pesticides - 502
National Coalition for Peace Through Strength - 257
National Commission for Employment Policy - 655, 656
National Commission on Air Quality - 416, 418
National Commission on Excellence in Education - 555, 565, 570
National Commission on Innovation and Productivity - 708
National Commission on Reform of Criminal Laws - 698

National Commission on Social Security Reform - 644, 645, 652, 658, 659, 660, 662 (box)
National Commission on Space - 789
National Committee on the Treatment of Intractable Pain - 553
National Conciliation Party - 187
National Conference of Catholic Bishops - 690
National Consumer Cooperative Bank - 262, 268
National Council on Vocational Education - 578
National Critical Materials Council - 475
National Defense Education Act - 555
National Defense Reserve Fleet - 325
National Direct Student Loans - 558
National Driver Register - 316
National Drug Enforcement Policy Board - 701
National Education Association (NEA)
   school improvement aid - 579
   software profits - 577
   support for Mondale - 579
National Endowment for Democracy - 167-168
National Endowment for the Arts - 776, 789
National Endowment for the Humanities - 776, 789
National Environmental Policy Act of 1969 - 451
National Environmental Protection Act - 404
National forests. *See Forest Service, U.S.*
National Futures Association - 499-501
National Gas Act of 1938 - 387
National Governors' Association
   food assistance programs - 600, 772
   oil allocation authority - 378
National Guard
   education benefits - 622
   private party fighting ban - 245
   tort claims coverage - 677
National Health Service Corps - 530, 551
National Highway Traffic Safety Administration
   air bag rule - 322
   authorizations, appropriations - 300, 306, 317
   defective tires - 317
   odometer fraud estimate - 285
   speed limit enforcement - 300, 306
National Information and Resource Clearing House for the Aging - 594
National Inholders Association - 464
National Institute of Mental Health - 551
National Institute on Alcohol Abuse and Alcoholism - 537, 542, 551
National Institute on Drug Abuse - 537, 542, 551
National Institutes of Health (NIH)
   authorization - 537, 543, 550-551
   orphan drugs - 536
   public health emergencies - 542
National League of Cities - 272, 279, 280
National Nuclear Freeze Campaign - 257
National Oceanic and Atmospheric Association (NOAA)
   authorization - 782, 790
   Landsat program - 781
   seabed mining - 437
National Organization for Women - 531
National Park Service
   land acquisition - 463-465
   mission - 404

park protection - 467
wild and scenic rivers - 472
National parks. *(See also National Park Service.)*
   Alaskan game hunting - 474-475
   Clean Air Act revision - 412-413, 416
   expansion - 463-465
   inholders - 464
   jobs funding - 663
   mineral leasing - 340
   overuse - 467
   payments in lieu of taxes - 469
   protection - 467, 470, 475
   repairs - 467
   Truman home - 476
   Watt policies - 403, 407
   wild and scenic rivers - 472
National Parks and Conservation Association - 475
National Petroleum Reserve - 344
National Public Radio - 275
National Recreational Boating Safety and Facilities Improvement Fund - 306
National Republican Congressional Committee - 816
National Republican Senatorial Committee - 812
National Rifle Association - 475
National Right to Life Committee - 690
National Science Board - 555
National Science Foundation
   authorization - 776, 782, 786
   educational summit - 570
   math-science education - 565, 571-572
National Sea Grant College Program - 350
National security. *See Defense.*
National security adviser - 142
National Security Agency
   authorization - 152, 168
   cryptology program - 140
National Security Council - 847
National Taxpayers Union - 52, 272, 435
National Technical Institute for the Deaf - 602
National Telecommunications and Information Administration - 264
National Trails System - 469-470, 475-476
National Transportation Safety Board - 300, 310, 321
National Trust for Historic Preservation - 815
National Wetlands Inventory Project - 480
National wilderness preserves. *See Wilderness areas.*
National Wildlife Federation - 407, 436, 469, 475
National wildlife refuges. *See Wildlife protection.*
National Women's Political Caucus - 682
Native Americans. *See Indians and Alaskan natives.*
NATO. *See North Atlantic Treaty Organization.*
Natural gas
   Alaska pipeline - 384-386
   deregulation - 333, 335-336, 375, 382-383, 387-390, 837
   federal oil and gas production, 1980-84 (chart) - 343
   federal oil and gas royalties - 344-346
   offshore leasing - 357-358
   Outer Continental Shelf leases - 347-350, 358-359
   Overthrust Belt reserves - 339
   pipeline safety programs - 301
   power plant conversion - 383-384

"take or pay" contracts - 382-383
watershed leasing - 350-351
Watt leasing policies - 403, 407
wilderness leasing - 339-344
Natural Gas Policy Act of 1978 - 335-336, 375, 382, 387-388, 837
Natural resources. *See Environment.*
Natural Resources Defense Council - 420
Naval aircraft - 208, 210, 228, 230, 236, 244
Naval ships. *(See also Submarines.)*
   Aegis defense system - 210, 219, 230, 234, 236, 240, 244
   amphibians - 208, 210, 221, 230, 240
   authorizations - 206, 210, 212, 219, 221, 236, 244
   carriers - 206-208, 210, 215, 218-220, 234, 240
   ship modernization - 206, 208, 210, 212, 218, 236, 240, 244
Navy, U.S. *(See also Naval aircraft; Naval ships; Submarines.)*
   Joint Chiefs reorganization plan - 224
   military facilities in Greece - 246
   ocean dumping - 436-437
   pay scales - 214, 215
   petroleum reserves - 346-347
   Reagan buildup plan - 202, 205-207, 218, 226, 234
   shipyard subsidies - 325
Neas, Ralph G. - 695
Nebraska
   ERA vote - 682
   highway aid - 307
   legislative chaplains - 811-812
   revenue sharing - 117
Neighborhood development. *See Community development.*
Neighborhood Reinvestment Corp. - 632, 636
Nelson, Bill (D-Fla.)
   budget resolution - 59
Nerve gas. *See Chemical and biological weapons.*
Nestlé Corp. - 141
Net Worth Guarantee Act - 89
Netherlands
   bribery of foreign officials - 100
   missile deployment - 232, 246-247, 255
Neutron bomb - 215-216, 255
Nevada
   highway aid - 307
   Hoover Dam power pricing - 445-446
   MX missile deployment - 212
   nuclear test exposure screening - 550
   revenue sharing - 117
   trademark modification ruling - 686
New Federalism - 113, 117, 289-290, 519, 521, 771-772, 774 (box), 777
New Hampshire
   highway aid - 307
   revenue sharing - 117
   voting rights action - 679
   wilderness areas - 471, 472
New Jersey
   highway aid - 307
   offshore oil leases - 347-350, 359
   revenue sharing - 117
New Jersey (ship) - 206, 208, 210-212, 218
New Mexico
   coal leasing - 353
   highway aid - 307
   revenue sharing - 117
   uranium industry - 366, 369
   voting rights action - 679
   wilderness areas - 471-472
New York Central Railroad - 292
New York City
   fiscal recovery (box) - 116
   sewage dumping - 446

transport of radioactive material - 300
New York State
   highway aid - 307
   nuclear power plants - 373, 374
   offshore leasing - 359
   revenue sharing - 117
   voting rights action - 679
New Zealand
   arms sales review - 132, 135
Newark, Ohio, military base - 223
Newberry, Truman H. - 808
News media. *See Broadcasting; Freedom of the press; Print media and publishing.*
Nicaragua
   aid to contras
      congressional opposition - 124, 229, 241, 245
      1983 suspension votes, action - 125, 155, 162-165, 170, 183
      1984 cutoff - 125, 169, 171-172, 175-177, 184-186
   CIA assassination manual - 176
   CIA role - 162-165, 171, 176-177, 179, 182, 184-185, 836, 838
   Contadora group - 185
   expulsion of diplomats - 164
   foreign aid to Sandinistas - 124, 136, 181-182
   harbor mining - 125, 176, 182, 184
   Kissinger commission report - 177, 188
   Reagan term overview - 123-125, 181-182, 856
   role in El Salvador - 123, 125, 162, 184
   use of U.S. combat troops - 237, 245
   World Court case (box) - 187
Nicaraguan Democratic Force - 184, 185
Nickles, Don (R-Okla.)
   longshoremen's compensation - 671
   oil allocation authority - 377
Nimmo, Robert P. - 623
Niskanen, William A. - 45, 434
Nitze, Paul H. - 251
Nixon, Richard M.
   block grant proposals - 774
   breeder reactors - 371
   Bush appointments - 855
   civil rights appointments - 694
   Clean Air Act - 412
   economic development aid - 115
   election, 1972 - 17, 22
   executive privilege issue - 450
   jobs programs - 115, 653
   naval petroleum reserves - 346
   oil allocation authority - 377
   oil and gas price controls - 334, 375, 388
   Peace Corps - 136
   pocket-veto power - 817
   presidential immunity - 714
   presidential records law - 683
   revenue sharing - 117
   Vietnam war/legislative veto - 833, 836
   water pollution act - 425
   Watergate legislative legacy - 684
NOAA. *See National Oceanic and Atmospheric Administration.*
Noise control - 297, 310, 454
Noise Control Act of 1972 - 454
Nominations and confirmations
   appointments to major posts - 1017-1026
   arms control posts - 233, 251
   Civil Rights Commission - 694, 848
   congressional, of bankruptcy judges - 704
   controversial nominations - 846, 1027-1030
   Energy Department officials (box) - 337

environmental posts - 406, 408, 455, 456, 464, 469, 470, 474
health posts - 552
judicial appointments - 676, 692, 711, 712, 1020-1021 (box)
law enforcement posts (box) - 687
Legal Services Corp. - 683, 695, 705, 1028
Meese financial associates - 707
Pentagon posts - 851
recess appointments - 705
State Department posts - 855-856
Norfolk Southern Corp. - 289, 326-327
Norman, David L. - 804
North American Wildlife and Natural Resources Conference - 407
North Atlantic Treaty Organization (NATO)
arms control - 251, 253
arms sales review - 132, 135
claims against U.S. - 210
decoupling strategy - 250
defense burden sharing - 212, 213, 220, 222, 223, 232-233, 241, 245-248, 250
export control coordination - 107
missile deployment - 232, 246, 250
nerve gas policy - 211
Soviet economic sanctions - 103
Spanish membership - 155
North Carolina
barrier islands - 480, 481
ERA vote - 682
highway aid - 307
offshore leasing - 359
revenue sharing - 117
voting rights action - 679
wilderness areas - 471, 472
North Dakota
coal leasing - 355
Garrison Diversion project - 435
highway aid - 307
revenue sharing - 117
water projects - 443, 444
North Korea
arms to Grenada - 183
North Sea oil reserves - 338
North Slope oil and gas reserves - 344, 346
North Umpqua River - 473
Northern Mariana Islands - 547
Northwest Energy Co. - 385
NOW accounts - 87
Nuclear energy. (See also Nuclear power plants; Nuclear Regulatory Commission; Nuclear waste.)
chronology of action
1981-82 - 361-371
1983-84 - 371-374
breeder reactors - 138, 370-373, 393, 395, 399-400
Energy Department programs - 334, 336, 337, 393-395
gas-cooled reactors - 394, 395
industry troubles - 334, 336
inertial confinement fission - 216
NRC background - 367
Nuclear non-proliferation. (See also Arms control.)
foreign aid authorization - 136
resolutions - 138-139
State Department authorization - 168
Symington waiver for Pakistan - 134
theft of materials - 685-686
Nuclear Non-proliferation Act - 139, 836
Nuclear power plants. (See also Nuclear waste.)
evacuation planning - 373, 374
interim licensing - 366-369, 373-374
Three Mile Island cleanup - 336, 369-370

Washington system default - 336, 371, 372
Nuclear Regulatory Commission
authorization - 366-369, 373-374
background - 367
Clinch River breeder reactor - 372
nuclear power plant licensing - 336, 366-369, 371, 373-374
nuclear waste disposal - 362-364, 366
report and wait provisions - 838
Nuclear waste. (See also Plutonium production.)
away-from-reactor storage - 362-365
comprehensive disposal plan - 336, 361-366
laser isotope separation - 216
monitored, retrievable storage - 363, 365, 366
ocean dumping - 436-437
pilot plant - 216
transport of radioactive material - 300
Utah proposal - 467
Waste Isolation Pilot Plant (WIPP) - 362, 364
Nuclear weapons. (See also Arms control; Missiles; Nuclear non-proliferation; Radiation.)
breeder reactors - 370-371
contract sanctity issue - 108
Cuba resolution - 150
Energy Department programs - 215-216, 225, 237, 240, 393, 397
freeze movement - 217, 221-222, 230-231, 255-257, 852
Latin American treaty ban - 139
Reagan modernization plan - 202
spent fuel - 361-366, 368, 369
test ban treaties - 241
Nuclear Weapons Freeze Campaign - 256
"Nuclear winter" - 244, 255
Nunn, Sam (D-Ga.)
arms control - 204, 257
ASAT missile - 243
B-1 bomber - 252
defense burden sharing - 241, 247
labor racketeering bill - 657
migrant farm worker protection - 502-503
military pay - 214
MX deployment - 209, 210
Nurses and nursing
education - 530, 537, 551
institute veto - 543, 550-551
shortage in VA hospitals - 617
Nursing homes
Medicare coverage - 522, 535, 541, 546, 547
veterans - 615, 619
Nutrition. See Food and nutrition; Child nutrition and health.

O

Oahe irrigation project - 438
Oakar, Mary Rose (D-Ohio)
budget amendment - 47
Oberdorfer, Louis F. - 356, 807, 811
Oberstar, James L. (D-Minn.)
Caribbean trade plan - 106
Obey, David R. (D-Wis.)
budget issues - 39, 47
Obscenity and pornography
child pornography - 697, 700-702
obscene phone messages - 275-276
Stewart definition - 712
Ocala National Forest - 466
Occidental Petroleum - 382

Occupational health and safety. (See also Hazardous substances; Radiation.)
disability compensation - 671
migrant worker protection - 502-503
pesticide law revision - 502
Supreme Court cases - 751
Oceans. (See also Fish and fisheries; Outer Continental Shelf.)
barrier islands - 467-468, 481
energy research - 299, 394, 395
marine mammal protection - 479-481
NOAA authorization - 782
seabed mining - 437
waste dumping - 436-437, 446-447
O'Connor, John Jay III - 712
O'Connor, Sandra Day
abortion - 675
appointment - 676
legislative veto - 835
offshore leasing/state powers - 358-359
Office of Drug Abuse Policy - 699
Office of Economic Opportunity - 590
Office of Export Administration - 107
Office of Federal Procurement Policy - 786-787, 790
Office of Government Ethics - 684, 785
Office of Juvenile Justice and Delinquency Prevention - 700
Office of Management and Budget (OMB)
agency reports to Congress - 783
budget projections - 39, 45, 61
commodities futures trading - 499
drinking water bill - 430
drug enforcement policy board - 701
EPA programs - 408, 461
farm programs - 485
Freedom of Information Act administration - 789
geographic distribution of federal funds - 783
poverty definition - 587
power rate study - 434
procurement policy office - 786-787, 790
regulatory reform - 778
risk analysis - 454
security clearances - 224
stockpile silver sales - 216
transportation needs - 302
water projects cost sharing - 441
water research - 446
Office of Personnel Management
ethics office - 785-786
former spouse benefits - 792
pay-for-performance plan (box) - 787
retirement benefits - 784
Veterans Administration staffing - 619
Office of Refugee Programs
appropriations - 138
Office of Self-Help Development and Technical Assistance - 268
Office of Surface Mining - 404, 406, 468-469
Office of Technology Assessment
biomedical ethics - 551
oil report - 338
Superfund renewal - 460
Office of the Comptroller of the Currency - 88
Office of Water Research and Technology - 429-431
Ogallala Aquifer - 447
O'Hair, Madalyn Murray - 811
Ohio
highway aid - 307
revenue sharing - 117
Oil industry
Alaskan crude export controls - 107
allocation authority - 336, 338, 376-378

antitrust exemption for IEA participants - 378-379, 390-391
Canada-U.S. maritime treaty - 143-144
Caribbean exports - 106-107
drilling boom/bust - 335
energy aid funds - 400
energy crisis of 1970s - 333
exploration areas (map) - 348
federal oil and gas production, 1980-84 (chart) - 343
federal oil and gas royalties - 344-346
import fees - 51
mergers - 335, 382, 390
oil shale research - 394
Outer Continental Shelf leases - 347-350, 357-359
overcharges - 396, 603, 604
Penn Square bank collapse - 84
Persian Gulf security - 191, 197
price decontrol - 375-376
prospects - 338
Soviet economic sanctions - 144-145
spill liability - 437-438
stripper wells - 68, 70
Superfund - 449, 459, 460
synthetic fuel prospects - 397-399
tax shelter - 74, 77
U.S. consumption, 1973-84 (graph) - 335
U.S. imports - 333, 335, 338
U.S. production - 333, 338
watershed leasing - 350-351
Watt leasing policies - 403, 406, 407
wetlands protection - 480-481
wilderness leasing - 339-344
windfall profits tax - 66, 68, 70, 76, 81, 333, 375-376
world petroleum market - 335, 336, 376-379
Oil reserves. (See also Strategic Petroleum Reserve.)
allocation authority - 376-378
federal oil and gas royalties - 344
naval petroleum reserves - 346-347
oil company mergers - 382
oil shale reserves - 346
prospects - 338
Prudhoe Bay fields - 76, 384-386
Rocky Mountain Overthrust Belt - 339, 340, 342, 407
Oklahoma
highway aid - 307
revenue sharing - 117
voting rights action - 679
Okun, Arthur M. - 29
Old Age and Survivors Insurance Fund - 644, 645-647, 658, 659, 660, 663
Older Americans Act programs - 591, 593-594, 603, 609-610
Olmer, Lionel H. - 98
Olson, James E. - 272
Olympic Games commemorative coins - 783
Oman
military facilities - 209, 213, 233, 246, 248
OMB. See Office of Management and Budget.
Omnibus Crime Control and Safe Streets Act - 698, 774
Omnibus Reconciliation Act of 1981 - 40, 41
Omnibus Reconciliation Act of 1982 - 48-50
O'Neill, Thomas P. Jr. (D-Mass.)
budget issues - 46, 49, 60
congressional pages investigation - 810
defense spending - 234-235
deficit reduction - 55
Equal Rights Amendment - 696-697
foreign aid - 170
highway aid - 300, 322

House leadership - 5, 13, 17, 800, 801, 812, 849
House pay raise - 828
House television/Gingrich confrontation - 799, 816-818
immigration reform - 697, 708
Lebanon policy/war powers - 126, 156-157, 192
MX missile - 238-239, 241
natural gas deregulation - 387, 389-390
nuclear freeze resolution - 231
partisanship - 798
Reagan economic policies - 850
Reagan political style - 846
Social Security issues - 33, 35, 46, 660, 662
Studds, Crane censure - 814
tax bills - 3, 68, 72, 77
wilderness leasing - 342
O'Neill irrigation project - 435
OPEC. See Organization of Petroleum Exporting Countries.
Opp, Jeffrey - 809
ORDEN - 147
Oregon
forests - 473, 474
highway aid - 307
land tract veto override - 476
offshore leasing - 358
revenue sharing - 117
wild and scenic rivers - 472-473
wilderness areas - 465-467, 470-472
Oregon Inlet - 481
Organ transplants - 549-550
Organization of American States (OAS)
Nicaraguan aid 136, 165
Reagan Caribbean plan - 149, 181
role in U.S. Cuba policy - 150
Organization of Eastern Caribbean States - 169, 182
Organization of Petroleum Exporting Countries (OPEC) - 197, 333, 335, 338
U.S. oil imports, 1973-84 (graph) - 335
Organized crime. See Crime and criminal justice.
Organized labor. See Labor and labor unions.
Oriental art museum - 784
Oriskany - 206-208, 211, 212
Orphan drugs - 532, 536, 552
Orphan Products Board - 536
Ortega, Daniel - 185
Osceola National Forest - 465, 466
Ottinger, Richard C. (D-N.Y.)
Alaska pipeline - 386
nuclear power plant licensing - 368
nuclear waste disposal - 365
solar energy research - 336, 399
Outdoor Recreation Resources Review Commission - 463
Outer Continental Shelf
gas decontrol - 387
oil leasing - 334, 344, 347-350, 357-358, 404
revenues for park expansion - 463-465
Supreme court decision - 358-359
Outer Continental Shelf Lands Act - 347, 348, 358
Overseas Private Investment Corp. - 99
Owyhee River - 473
Oxley, Michael (R-Ohio)
election - 7

P

Packwood, Bob (R-Ore.)
airport programs - 308
Amtrak authorizations - 295-297

AWACS sale to Saudi Arabia - 131
broadcast freedom bill - 281
phone rate hike - 279
Senate leadership - 801, 812
trucking industry antitrust immunity - 321
Page Board - 810
Pahlavi, Mohammed Reza - 197
Pakistan
aid for Afghan rebels - 179
arms embargo - 153
drug traffic - 168
F-16 sales (box) - 133
foreign aid - 132-135, 138
Palestine Liberation Organization (PLO) - 126, 148, 173, 191, 193-196
Palestinians - 126, 191, 194
Palm oil - 99
Palmerola, Honduras - 246
Panama
Contadora group - 125, 165, 185
Panetta, Leon E. (D-Calif.)
budget issues - 39-40, 44
food donation program - 600, 601
Papago Indians - 432, 435-436
Paperwork Reduction Act of 1980 - 788
Paraguay
foreign aid - 160
Paraquat - 136
Parents. See Family and marital issues.
Parks. See National parks; Sports and recreation.
Parties, political. See Democratic Party; Republican Party.
Partnership taxation - 82
Passport fees - 149
Patent and Trademark Office - 686, 708
Patents and trademarks
appeals court - 678
aspartame - 537
counterfeiting prohibition - 699, 701
foreign trade issues - 110
generic drugs - 547-548
generic trademarks - 706
intelligence service insignia - 140, 152
law extensions and changes - 686, 693, 696, 708
orphan drugs - 536
Supreme Court cases - 745, 748
trademark amendments - 686
user fees - 686
Patterson, Jerry M. (D-Calif.)
African Development Fund - 155
electoral defeat - 22
Pauken, Thomas W. - 136
Paul, Ron (R-Texas)
nuclear non-proliferation - 139
Pauley Group (box) - 349
Pauley Petroleum Inc. - 349
Payment-in-kind (PIK) program - 61, 491, 496, 498-499, 507-509
Pea Island National Wildlife Refuge - 481
Peace Corps
abortion funding ban - 690
agency independence - 136
Peace institute - 570, 579
Peace PAC - 256
Peanuts
price supports - 487-489, 492
Pearlman, Mark - 172
Pearson, James B. - 34, 813
Pease, Donald (D-Ohio)
trade with Japan - 96
Pell, Claiborne (D-R.I.)
arms control - 257
AWACS sale to Saudi Arabia - 130
fur seal treaty - 479
Pell grants - 556, 557-559, 561-563, 566, 575, 576, 618

Pendleton, Clarence M. - 694
Penn Central Railroad - 291-293
Penn Square Bank - 83, 84, 86
Penner, Rudolph G. - 67
Pennsylvania
highway aid - 307
revenue sharing - 117
Three Mile Island cleanup - 369-370
wilderness areas - 471, 472
Pennsylvania Railroad - 292
Pensions. See Retirement and pensions.
Pentagon. See Defense Department.
Pepper, Claude (D-Fla.)
Rules Committee chair - 812
Social Security reform - 659, 660, 662
Pequot Indians - 787
Percy, Charles H. (R-Ill.)
arms control - 256
Cuba resolution - 150
electoral defeat - 21
foreign aid - 133, 161
highway aid - 322
Lebanon policy/war powers - 156-157
Tenn-Tom waterway - 434
Peres, Shimon - 194
Perkins, Carl D. (D-Ky.)
access to schools for religious groups - 573
budget reconciliation - 42
child nutrition programs - 601
education leadership - 579
teacher scholarships - 579
welfare leadership - 611
Perle, Richard N. - 98, 851
Pershing missiles
arms control issues 204, 209, 249-257
authorizations, appropriations - 218-220, 226, 228, 229, 244
deployment - 209, 228, 232, 237, 246, 250, 253, 254
Persian Gulf
oil supply security - 191, 197
U.S. military capability - 197, 206, 207, 209, 212, 213, 218, 223, 232-233
Pesticides and pest control
law revision - 496, 501-502
program funding - 509
tobacco imports - 505
Petri, Thomas E. (R-Wis.)
water project cost sharing - 442
Petroleum. See Oil industry.
Petroleum Overcharge Restitution Fund - 604
Pfaelzer, Mariana - 349
Phalange faction - 193
Pharmaceutical Manufacturers Association - 547
Pharmaceuticals. See Drug industry.
Philippines
foreign aid - 174
Phosphate mining - 465, 471
Photovoltaics - 111
Physicians
abortion issues - 690-691
disabled workers - 671
education - 530, 551
FTC regulation - 274, 276-277, 538
heroin for cancer patients - 553
medical neglect of handicapped infants - 553, 606-607
Medicare payments - 57, 58, 533, 535-536, 544-546
Pick-Sloan Plan - 435, 438
Pickle, J. J. (D-Texas)
railroad retirement - 666
Social Security reform - 659, 661
Pierce, Samuel R. - 1022
PIK. See Payment-in-kind program.
Pipelines
Alaska pipeline - 384-386
coal slurry - 315, 319-320
natural gas pricing - 382-383, 387-389

safety programs - 301, 314, 318
Siberian pipeline - 98, 103, 126, 127
take or pay contracts - 388, 389
trans-African - 819
WEB pipeline - 438
Planned Parenthood - 531
Plutonium production
nuclear waste reprocessing - 138, 216, 336, 337, 361, 363, 366, 369
breeder reactors - 138, 370-372
Pocket-veto power (boxes) - 799, 817
Pocket vetoes - 165, 282, 564, 671, 698, 709, 788-790, 792
Point Arena basin - 350
Poisons. See Hazardous substances; Pesticides.
Poland
economic sanctions - 98, 144-145
export controls - 100
foreign aid - 135, 138
Police and law enforcement. See Capitol Police; Crime and criminal justice; Federal Bureau of Investigation; Secret Service.
Political parties. See Democratic Party; Republican Party.
Politics. See Elections and politics.
Pollution. (See also Air pollution; Hazardous waste management; Waste disposal and treatment; Water pollution.)
chronology of action
1981-82 - 449-454
1983-84 - 454-461
equipment loans - 283, 284
Pornography. See Obscenity and pornography.
Porphyria cutanea tarda - 621
Ports. See Ships and shipping.
Portugal
Azores air base - 213, 223
Post Office and Civil Service Committee (House)
jurisdiction, leadership, subcommittees - 971
Postal Service, U.S.
authorizations - 775-776
congressional frank - 826-827
mail fraud - 780-781, 787
Postal Telegraph and Cable Corp. - 265
Postsecondary education. (See also Adult education; Student aid; Vocational education.)
endowment aid - 569, 579
enrollment - 561
high-tech training - 116
Indian colleges - 569
Indian graduate fellowships - 576
library projects - 578
merit scholarships - 605
small business research funds - 273
teachers - 572, 579
water research institutes - 446
work-study program - 563
Potomac Heritage National Scenic Trail - 469, 475
Poverty. (See also Welfare and social services.)
official definition - 581-582, 587 (box)
rate reports - 598-600, 603
Powder River Basin
coal leasing - 352, 354-355
Powell, Lewis F.
appointment - 711-712
legislative veto - 835
offshore leasing - 359
Pratt, George C. - 806, 808
Pratt, Richard T.
banking deregulation - 84, 87
Pregnancy. (See also Abortion.)
adolescent pregnancy - 525-527, 540, 552-553

AFDC benefits - 588

Child Health Assurance Program - 540, 546-547

cigarette warning labels - 549

family planning - 173, 523, 526, 773

fetal research - 550, 551

unisex insurance - 284

World Health Organization funding ban - 138

Preschool education. See Head Start.

Presidency. (See also Congressional-executive relations; Reagan, Ronald.)

assassination attempts - 847

candidates and vote summary, 1860-1984 (charts) - 1089-1091

distribution of electoral vote (chart) - 1102

executive orders

foreign intelligence in U.S. - 140

regulatory reform - 778

executive privilege issue

Gorsuch contempt citation/Superfund - 449-452, 455-456

Watt papers controversy (box) - 341

party affiliations in Congress, 1789-1985 (chart) - 1098-1099

presidential immunity - 714

presidential records law - 683

protection of aides - 683

reorganization authority - 790, 839

Supreme Court cases of powers of president - 761

White House aides outside pay - 785-786

Presidential election, 1984

arms control issue - 201-202, 257

convention funding - 792

debates - 20

Democratic convention - 18-19

Democratic primaries - 17-18

electoral vote by state (chart) - 1094

landslide background (chart) - 22

popular vote by state (chart) - 1093

Republican convention - 19-20

Republican primaries - 19

social safety net issue - 581-582, 603

tax policy issue - 63-64, 78

vote analysis - 19 (chart), 20-21, 645

Presidential libraries - 793

Presidential messages (texts) - 1033-1085

President's Commission on Financial Structure and Regulation - 88

President's Commission on Strategic Forces. See Scowcroft missile panel.

President's Council on Environmental Quality - 351

President's Private Sector Survey on Cost Control (Grace commission) - 58, 791 (box)

President's Task Force on Food Assistance - 600

Press issues. See Freedom of the press.

Pressler, Larry (R-S.D.)

satellite protection - 224, 243

Preventive detention - 692, 699

Preventive health services - 523, 524, 526, 538

Pribiloff Islands - 479, 481-482

Price-fixing. See Antitrust and competition.

Price supports. See Agricultural aid programs.

Primary care block grant - 774

Print media and publishing. (See also Freedom of the press.)

AT&T deregulation - 271

copyright "manufacturing clause" - 686

Printing Committee (Joint)

jurisdiction, leadership, subcommittees - 974

Prisoners of war

veterans benefits - 616, 623

Prisons and prisoners. (See also Trial procedures.)

contraband - 699

drug monitoring programs - 689, 697, 702

education aid - 577

escape - 699

habeas corpus claims - 699, 709

jobs programs - 672

preventive detention - 692, 699

repeat offenders - 689, 692, 701

Senate subpoena power - 802

Social Security fraud - 647

Supreme Court cases - 721-723, 730-731

Pritchard, Joel (R-Wash.)

MX missile - 238

Tenn-Tom waterway - 433

Privacy Act

federal debt collection exemption - 780

relation to Freedom of Information Act - 789

waiver for prisoners - 647

Privacy rights. (See also Privacy Act.)

abortion issues - 690

cable TV deregulation - 280-281

computer fraud - 701

medical records - 554

Private and parochial schools. (See also Tuition tax credit.)

federal aid - 561

Supreme Court decisions - 713

Private Industry Councils - 655

Professional Air Traffic Controllers Organization - 290, 309

Professional Standards Review Organization - 521, 523, 529, 533, 535-536

Project Democracy - 167

Property rights. (See also Real estate.)

Indian land claims - 787

national park land acquisition - 464

Oregon land tracts - 476

Supreme Court cases - 745

Provider Reimbursement Review Boards - 535-536

Proxmire, William (D-Wis.)

congressional pay and tax deductions - 822, 829-830

debt ceiling filibuster - 42

noise control - 454

nuclear waste disposal - 364, 365

Senate gym - 803

synthetic fuels - 399

Whoops rescue plan - 372

Prudhoe Bay oil and gas reserves - 76, 338, 384-386

Pryor, David (D-Ark.)

farm target price freeze - 513

Public assistance. See Welfare and social services.

Public broadcasting

advertising - 264

Corporation for Public Broadcasting vetoes - 282-283

editorials - 714

funding - 262, 264-265, 273, 275-276

Public debt. See Budget, U.S.

Public health. See Health.

Public Health Service - 520-522, 523, 531, 550, 552

Public Health Service Act - 525, 540

Public housing. See Housing assistance and public housing.

Public lands

chronology of action

1981-82 - 463-470

1983-84 - 470-476

coal leasing - 334, 352-353

conservation corps - 667, 671

Matagorda Island accord - 482

naval petroleum reserves - 346-347

oil and gas production, 1980-84 (chart) - 343

oil and gas royalties - 344-346

Outer Continental Shelf leases - 347-350

reclamation law background - 431-432

watershed leasing - 350-352

wetlands protection - 480-481

wilderness leasing - 339-344

wildlife protection - 478-479

Public laws (statistics) - 6, 8, 11 (box)

Public schools. See Elementary and secondary education.

Public Telecommunications Facilities Program - 282

Public utilities. See Utilities.

Public Works Administration - 653

Public Works and Transportation Committee (House)

jurisdiction, leadership, subcommittees - 971-972

Public Works and Economic Development Act of 1965 - 115

Puerto Rico

Caribbean trade plan - 107

cruise regulations - 329

food stamp program - 595

health aid - 547

highway aid - 307

liquor taxes - 58

nuclear arms treaty - 139

nutrition block grant - 585, 596, 773, 774

veterans medical care - 618

Pursell, Carl D. (R-Mich.)

budget bill - 589

Q

Quadrennial review commission. See Commission on Executive, Legislative and Judicial Salaries.

Quayle, Dan (R-Ind.)

budget resolution - 53

Senate committee changes - 813

Queen, Richard I. - 143

R

Rabbinical Assembly - 255

Racial discrimination

IMF funding - 105

Supreme Court decisions - 713

tuition tax credit - 568

Voting Rights Act extension - 680-681

Radiation

cancer risk report - 537

fallout from nuclear tests - 537, 550, 605

medical care for exposed veterans - 615, 619, 620

safety programs - 526, 527

Radio. (See also Broadcasting.)

broadcast licenses - 263-264, 272

deregulation bill - 273

public broadcasting ads - 264

submarine communication - 244

Radio Free Europe - 149, 153

Radio Liberty - 149, 153

Radio Marti - 149, 150, 166-167

Radio Shack - 98

Railpax. See Amtrak.

Railroad Accounting Principles Board - 326, 329

Railroad Retirement System - 70, 648-649, 666, 791

Railroad Unemployment Compensation - 666

Railroads

Alaska railroad transfer - 314

Amtrak authorizations - 295-297, 320

coal slurry pipeline opposition - 315, 319-320

Conrail sale proposal - 291-295, 326-328

federal outlays (graph) - 290

noise control - 454

passenger miles (chart) - 313

"political" trains (box) - 296

strike, 1982 - 290, 314

Supreme Court cases - 745

Tenn-Tom waterway - 432, 435

Railway Association, U.S. (USRA)

Alaska railroad - 314

authorization - 326

Conrail sale proposal -291-295

Ramirez, Blandina Cardenas - 694-695

Rand Corp. - 309

Randolph, Jennings (D-W.Va.)

acid rain - 422

Appalachian Regional Commission - 115

peace institute - 579

radiation protection - 526

retirement - 21

Superfund renewal - 461

Rape

crisis centers - 524

prevention and treatment - 552, 553

Rapid Deployment Force - 206, 207, 209, 210, 212-214, 218, 223, 246

RARE. See Roadless Area Review and Evaluation.

Ras Banas military base - 211, 213, 214, 223, 232

Rashish, Myer - 1029

Rat control - 552

Ratchford, William R. (D-Conn.)

synthetic fuels - 399

Reagan, John - 844

Reagan, Maureen - 844

Reagan, Michael - 844

Reagan, Nancy Davis - 20, 590, 844

Reagan, Nellie Wilson - 844

Reagan, Patricia (Patti Davis) - 844

Reagan, Ronald. (See also Congressional-executive relations; Nominations and confirmations; Presidency.)

abortion - 540, 691, 848

agriculture

budget cuts - 496-497

dairy program - 487, 488, 491, 493-497, 503, 505

farm debt aid - 512

migrant worker protection - 502-503

omnibus farm bill - 487-490

payment-in-kind (PIK) bills - 498-499, 508

Soviet grain embargo and sales - 487, 488, 494, 495, 510

tobacco program - 503

assassination attempt - 675, 683, 692, 698, 845, 847 (box)

biographical background (box) - 844-845

budget

administration proposals - 37-39, 44-46, 50-51, 56, 797

balanced budget amendment - 52

budget messages

FY1983 - 1050-1056

FY1984 - 1063-1069

FY1985 - 1076-1081

budgets (chart) - 36

debt ceiling requests - 41-42

deficit reduction - 37, 55-57

line-item veto amendment - 52
lobbying - 43, 44, 56-57
social program spending (box) - 589
supplemental appropriations vetoes - 50, 149, 150, 562, 830
term overview - 33, 34
business and industry
bankruptcy bill veto - 677-678
copyright "manufacturing clause" veto - 686
oil and gas deregulation - 375-386
Papago water rights - 436
robotics veto - 789
school tax leasing veto - 787
small business loans - 265-266, 615
small business research funds - 273
strategic minerals - 475
timber contract relief - 473
veterans loans - 615
Civil Rights Commission - 676, 694-695, 848
Coast Guard - 316
commerce and consumer affairs
Alaska pipeline - 384-386
Consumer Product Safety Commission reauthorization - 267
Co-op Bank - 268
public broadcasting - 264-265, 282-283
TV rerun rights - 282
crime and law enforcement
child pornography - 702
crime control package - 698
drug enforcement department veto - 689, 692, 698
Legal Services Corp. - 683, 695, 705
defense
arms control strategy - 201-204, 206, 209, 221-222, 225, 228-229, 231, 249-257, 852-853
ASAT message (text) - 1081-1085
budget requests - 201-203, 207 (box), 217, 225, 233-234
buildup policy - 201-203, 205, 208, 214, 217, 220, 225, 228, 234
draft registration - 218
military construction appropriations - 212-214
military pay - 211, 214
national security adviser - 142
MX missile - 207, 209, 212-213, 218, 220, 235, 238-239
naval forces - 205, 207, 211, 218, 234
neutron bombs - 215
policy overview - 850-853
Star Wars - 245
strategic arms statement (text) - 1045-1046
strategic minerals - 475
economic affairs
block grants/revenue sharing - 4, 113, 519, 771-772, 773-774, 777
development aid - 113-114, 115-116
economic messages (text) - 1038-1044
enterprise zones - 113, 117, 119-120, 630, 635, 639
free-market philosophy - 27, 28, 30, 95-96, 113, 291, 333-338, 375, 488, 629, 651, 789, 843-844, 848-850
international issues - 95-98, 103, 104, 131-132, 148
tax cuts - 30, 32, 33, 63-64, 65-68, 77-78
tax increases - 32, 72-76, 78-82, 798
education
access to schools for religious groups - 572-573
bilingual education - 575
block grants - 557, 559-561
budget cuts - 565

college student aid cuts - 557-559
education amendments veto - 564
Education Department abolition proposal - 565
impact aid - 575
Indian colleges veto - 564
term overview - 555-556
tuition tax credit - 564, 566, 567
elections and politics
campaign, 1984 - 17, 19-21, 855
farm states tour - 512
network election projections - 286
personal popularity - 4
political philosophy - 846, 847
energy
Alaska pipeline - 384-386
coal slurry pipelines - 315
Energy Department administration - 334, 337, 393-397
energy preparedness - 390
mineral leasing - 339-344, 347-350
nuclear energy - 361-373, 393, 394, 395
oil allocation authority - 338, 376-378, 391
oil and gas deregulation - 334, 375-376, 382-383, 387-390
Rural Electrification loans - 515
solar energy development - 394, 395
Strategic Petroleum Reserve - 379-383
synthetic fuels - 398-400
environment
acid rain - 420, 421
Clean Air Act revision - 405, 411-420
economic growth priority - 403, 405, 421
EPA budget and program cuts - 405, 409, 451, 461
EPA research funds veto - 453
Florida wilderness area veto - 465, 466
noise control - 454
relations with environmental groups - 405
sewer grants - 425-428, 439
Superfund controversy - 449-452, 455-456, 459-460
timber contract relief - 473
water research veto - 446
water projects - 428-429, 436, 441-442
foreign affairs
Africa policy - 170, 171, 179
arms sales - 154, 836
AWACS sales to Saudi Arabia - 129-131, 196, 836
Canada-U.S. maritime boundary treaty - 143-144
Central America message (text) - 1069-1072
Central America policy - 123-125, 177-178, 181-182, 188-189
China-U.S. communique - 154
consulate openings - 149
Cuba resolution - 150
El Salvador aid - 124-125, 147, 165-166, 174-175, 186-188, 817, 856
embassy security - 179
F-16 sales to Pakistan - 133
foreign aid requests - 123, 128, 132, 136-138, 159-162, 170-174, 853-857
genocide treaty - 179
Grenada invasion - 123, 169, 183
Guatemala aid block - 163
human rights policy - 123-124, 141, 856
infant formula resolution - 142-143
Iranian hostage release agreement - 143
Israeli relations - 146, 193-195

Lebanon policies - 123, 126, 155-159, 191-193, 846
nuclear non-proliferation - 138-139
Nicaragua policy - 124-125, 162-165, 175-177, 184-186, 856
Persian Gulf security - 197
U.S.-Soviet relations - 4, 126, 201-202, 856, 1056-1057 (message text)
foreign trade
Caribbean Basin Initiative - 102, 104, 106-107, 149, 181
domestic content bill - 108
export trading companies - 101
Romania status - 103, 107
Soviet Union - 98, 100, 144-145
steel imports - 109-110
general government
attorney fees veto - 709
arts, humanities endowments - 776
Bureau of Standards funding veto - 788
contractors interest veto - 781
federal pay proposal - 775, 779-780, 785, 823
Freedom of Information Act - 778-779, 788-789
Indian land claims vetos - 787, 792
King holiday - 786
Oregon land tracts veto - 476
payments in lieu of taxes - 469
regulatory reform - 777-778
space programs and satellites - 786, 789
health
arthritis institute veto - 550
block grants - 523-527
health planning systems - 532
health professions veto - 551
Indian programs veto - 792
manpower programs - 530
Medicaid, Medicare - 527-529, 532-536, 538, 544, 545
term overview - 521-522
housing
block grants - 631
funding cuts - 629
mortgage aid veto - 629, 633-634
voucher plan - 629, 634-638
immigration reform - 678 (box), 708
intelligence affairs - 140
labor
conservation corps veto - 671
Donovan investigation - 656
elderly jobs program veto - 658
jobs programs - 32, 114, 643-644, 651, 652, 655, 659, 663-664
legislative victories - 645
strikes - 290
leadership style - 844-846
legislative veto - 833-834, 840
presidential messages (texts)
inaugural address - 1036-1038
State of the Union address
1982 - 1046-1050
1983 - 1059-1063
1984 - 1072-1076
school prayer - 572, 846, 848
Social Security - 38, 645-647, 658, 660, 670
transportation
aviation taxes - 290, 308
highways - 289-290, 297-298, 301-307
maritime affairs - 299, 315-316, 325
mass transit programs - 289-290, 299-300
minimum drinking age - 290, 321, 323
railroads - 289, 295, 314, 327
speed limit enforcement - 300
veterans affairs - 615, 618, 618
Voting Rights Act extension - 676

welfare and social services
Aid to Families with Dependent Children - 586, 596-598
energy aid - 604
food stamps cuts - 584, 594-596
hunger reports - 599, 600, 612
nutrition programs - 585, 591-593
social program spending - 37-38, 583, 586, 589 (box)
term overview - 519-520, 580-581
VISTA funding - 590
workfare proposal - 583, 586
Reagan, Ronald Jr. - 844
Real estate industry and taxes
construction deductions - 74
depreciation - 79, 82
financial diversification - 84
mortgage assumption laws - 634-635
rehabilitation tax credit - 69, 74, 79, 80
trademark modification - 686
Reclamation Act - 431-432, 444
Reclamation Safety of Dams Act - 430
Reconciliation. *See under Budget, U.S.*
Reconstruction Finance Corp. - 97
Records. *(See also Archives.)*
EPA oversight hearings transcript alterations - 814-815
false ID - 647, 689
foreign, in U.S. trials - 699, 701
Freedom of Information Act overhaul plan - 788-789
medical, access to - 554
presidential records law - 683
Records (musical)
copyright protection - 680, 686, 707
Recreation. *See Sports and recreation.*
Reforestation Trust Fund - 307
Refugees. *(See also Immigrants and immigration.)*
AID African assistance account - 138
child education - 561
resettlement aid in Israel - 148-149
resettlement aid in U.S. - 689, 697, 708
Regan, Donald T.
banking deregulation - 84
deficit reduction - 55
profile - 1025
revenue sharing - 117
tax plans - 65, 849
Regional development. *See Community development.*
Regula, Ralph (R-Ohio)
Japanese defense spending - 213
Regulatory agencies
legislative veto - 834, 837
reform bill - 772, 776-778
reform task force - 854
Supreme Court cases - 745-746
Regulatory Reform Act - 778
Rehabilitation
job services for developmentally disabled - 609
vocational aid for handicapped - 82, 567, 576-578, 602-603, 608-609, 672
Rehabilitation Act - 566, 567, 608-609
Rehnquist, William H.
appointment - 711-712
Chadha case/legislative veto - 835, 837
offshore leasing - 359
Religion and religious organizations.
(See also Freedom of religion; Religious interests, lobbying.)
access to school facilities - 571-573, 703
church payroll taxes - 82
school prayer - 572, 703 (box)
Religious interests, lobbying
broadcast deregulation - 281
extradition revision - 692
Lefever nomination - 141
nuclear freeze - 255-256
Vatican-U.S. relations - 167

Voting Rights Act extension - 680
Relocation aid - 787-788
Rent control - 631
Rent subsidies. *See under Housing assistance.*
Report and wait provisions - 837, 838, 840
Republican Congressional Campaign Committee
IMF funding - 105
Republican National Committee - 694
tax increases - 73
Republican Party
congressional leadership and committees - 801-802, 812
convention, 1984 - 19-20, 792
convention balloting by state (chart) - 1095
Democracy Program - 168
platform, 1984 - 19-20
primaries, 1984 - 19
Republican Study Committee - 816
Reserve Officer Training Corps - 215, 623
Reserves, petroleum. *See Oil reserves.*
Residential Conservation Service - 400
Resource Conservation and Recovery Act of 1976 - 409, 449, 452, 454, 457-460
Restaurant industry - 73, 75
Retarded persons. *See Handicapped persons.*
Retirement and pensions. *(See also Social Security programs.)*
age issues - 610, 659-661, 670
CIA benefit plan - 152
civil service/Social Security comparison (box) - 784
corporate plans - 75
federal benefits - 49-51, 55, 61, 217, 774-775, 779-780
IRAs - 58, 68, 70, 80
Keogh plans - 68, 70, 75
military annuity plan - 216-217
railroad retirement system - 70, 648-649, 666
Reagan term overview - 644
sex discrimination - 667, 669-670
Supreme Court cases - 744-745
tax issues - 65, 68
unisex insurance - 284
Retirement Equity Act - 667, 669-670
Revenue Act of 1978 - 65
Revenue sharing
block grants history (box) - 774
distributed funds (chart) - 117
offshore oil royalties - 350, 359
outlays (graph) - 114
program extension - 113, 117-118
Reagan plans - 113, 519, 521, 771-772, 777
Rhode Island
highway aid - 307
revenue sharing - 117
Rhodes, John J. (R-Ariz.)
House leadership - 801
Ribicoff, Abraham - 34, 813
Rice
payment-in-kind program - 508
price supports - 489, 490, 492, 497
target price freeze - 511-514
Richardson, Warren - 1029
Richmond, Fred (D-N.Y.)
resignation - 804, 809
Ridge, Thomas J. (R-Pa.)
election - 11
Right of association cases - 738
Rinaldo, Matthew J. (R-N.J.)
budget resolution - 53
Rios Montt, Efrain - 163
Riot insurance - 633

Rivers and waterways. *(See also Water projects.)*
Colorado River salinity - 447
Cross-Florida Barge Canal - 442
Tennessee-Tombigbee - 433-435, 443
preservation - 472-473
Roadless Area Review and Evaluation - 342, 344, 409, 466, 471
Roads. *See Highways and roads.*
Robb, Charles S. - 7
Robelo Callejas, Alfonso - 184
Robotics - 789
Rock Island Railroad - 301, 314, 714
Rockefeller, John D. "Jay" IV - 21-22
Rockefeller, Nelson A. - 398
Rocky Mountain Overthrust Belt - 339, 340, 342, 384
Rodent control - 524
Rodino, Peter W. (D-N.J.)
Judiciary Committee - 687
legislative veto - 837
Roe, Robert A. (D-N.J.)
clean water bill - 439
sewer grants - 427
water projects cost sharing - 441-442
Romania
trade status - 103, 107
Romero, Oscar - 188
Roosevelt, Franklin D. - 88, 782-783
Roosevelt, Theodore - 346, 431
Rose, Charlie (D-N.C.)
tobacco program - 497-498, 510
Rose Garden budget plan - 56, 59-61, 79
Rostenkowski, Dan (D-Ill.)
capital gains taxes - 79-80
Caribbean trade plan - 102, 106
congressional tax deductions - 821
deficit reduction - 55
enterprise zones - 79
interest, dividend withholding - 91
Medicare reform - 539
Social Security reform - 659
tax reduction - 65, 68, 849
tuition tax credit - 568
unemployment benefits - 654
welfare benefits - 611
Rostow, Eugene V. - 231, 251
Roth, William V. Jr. (R-Del.)
Lebanon policy/war powers - 157
tax reduction - 63, 65-66
Rothschild, Edwin - 385
Rousselot, John (R-Calif.)
budget plan - 47
Rowny, Edward L. - 251
Rubber industry
domestic content bill - 108
guayule - 513
Ruckelshaus, Jill - 694
Ruckelshaus, William D.
acid rain - 420, 421
EPA tenure - 405, 408, 454-457
Superfund - 449, 460
Rudman, Warren B. (R-N.H.)
antitrust damages - 693
dairy program - 505
oil company mergers - 390
Rules and Administration Committee (Senate)
jurisdiction, leadership, subcommittees - 966
Rules Committee (House)
jurisdiction, leadership, subcommittees - 972
party ratios - 802
Runaway and Homeless Youth Act of 1974 - 700
Rural affairs. *See Agriculture and farming; Community development; Farmers Home Administration.*
Rural Electrification Administration (REA)

authorization - 495
loan repayments - 514-515
Reagan economic message - 488
Rural Housing Preservation Grants - 637-638
Rural Telephone Bank - 493
Russo, Marty (D-Ill.)
MX missile - 239

S

Saccharin - 530-531, 541, 838
Sadat, Anwar - 191, 195
Safe Drinking Water Act of 1974 - 409, 440
Safety. *See Air transportation; Consumer product safety; Hazardous substances; Occupational safety and health; Traffic safety.*
Sagan, Carl - 255
Sahel Development Fund - 173
Sakhalin Island
Korean airliner downing - 169
Salazar, Lucia - 184
SALT II. *See Strategic Arms Limitation Treaty.*
Salt River dams - 444
Saltonstall-Kennedy fund - 307
Saltzman, Murray - 694-695
San Juan Basin - 471
San Lorenzo, Honduras - 246
Sandinistas - 181-182, 184-186
Sandino, Augusto - 181
SANE - 256
Santa Cruz Basin - 350
Santa Maria Basin - 348-350, 358-359
Santa Mercedes - 325
Santarelli, Donald E. - 695
Sasser, Jim (D-Tenn.)
power rate study - 434
Satellites. *(See also Anti-satellite missile.)*
launch licenses - 789
NOAA authorization - 781
sales - 786, 789
user fees - 781
weather - 786
Saudi Arabia
arms sales - 196, 197, 836
AWACS planes sales - 126, 129-131, 836
oil production - 380
Save EPA Committee - 408
Savings and loan associations
all savers certificates - 87
financial services industry problems - 83-87
Garn-St Germain act - 87-90
industry trends (graph) - 85
regulation - 92-93
Sawhill, John C. - 398
Sawyer, Harold S. (R-Mich.)
hazardous waste management - 460
Scapegoat wilderness area - 342
Scheuer, James H. (D-N.Y.)
EPA research funds - 453, 461
Schiavone Construction Co. - 656
Schlafly, Phyllis - 682
Schlesinger, James R. - 337, 367
Schmitt, Harrison "Jack" (R-N.M.)
electoral defeat - 11
Schmults, Edward C. - 838
Schneider, Claudine (R-R.I.)
budget resolution - 53
Clinch River breeder reactor - 373
Scholarships. *See Student aid.*
School meals. *See Child nutrition and health.*
School prayer
constitutional amendment - 675-676,

703 (box), 800
omnibus education bill - 572 (box), 573-575
Supreme Court decisions - 712
Schools. *(See also Elementary and secondary education.)*
access for religious groups - 572-573, 703
asbestos removal - 571, 572, 575
day-care programs - 608
repair plans - 664-665
tax leasing veto - 787
Schroeder, Patricia (D-Colo.)
congressional tax deductions - 830
Reagan style - 846
Schroeder, Victor A. - 399
Schulze, Richard T. (R-Pa.)
Social Security reform - 659
Schweiker, Richard S.
campaign, 1976 - 845
disabled workers - 668
Health and Human Services tenure - 552, 611
health emergency fund - 542
profile - 1021-1022
saccharin ban deferral - 531
Science and technology. *(See also National Academy of Sciences; National Science Foundation; Office of Technology Assessment.)*
education - 565, 570-572, 782
EPA research veto - 453
industrial policy - 111
joint research ventures - 706-707
marine research - 350
nuclear technology proliferation - 138
robotics research - 789
small business research funds - 273
space weaponry - 242
pesticide law revision - 501-502
Soviet economic sanctions - 145
Science and Technology Committee (House)
jurisdiction, leadership, subcommittees - 972
Scowcroft, Brent - 204, 226, 227, 250
Scowcroft missile panel - 204, 226, 227 (box), 250, 252
Seafirst Corp. - 83
Sears, Roebuck - 84
Seattle, Wash.
watershed leasing - 350-351
Secret Service
Capitol security - 813
Freedom of Information Act restrictions - 779
protection of public officials - 683
Reagan assassination attempt - 847
spending limits - 683, 793
Securities and Exchange Commission (SEC)
bribery of foreign officials - 100
commodities futures trading - 500-501
corporate takeover reforms - 282
insider trading curbs - 262, 276, 283
Thompson investigation - 399
Securities companies. *See Stocks, bonds, and securities.*
Seger, Martha - 1030
Seiberling, John F. (D-Ohio)
Alaska pipeline - 386
ASAT missile - 242
barrier island jetties - 481
national parks protection - 467, 475
wilderness areas - 339, 342-343, 409, 470-472
Seismology
earthquake prediction - 782
exploration technology - 340, 342-344
Selective Service System - 208, 562 (box)

Semiconductor chips
copyright protection - 706
Senate, U.S. *(See also Congressional ethics; Congressional pay and benefits; Congressional votes; Filibusters and cloture votes; Nominations and confirmations.)*
committees - 963-967
elections
1982 midterm - 11-12
1983 - 17, 21-22
Hart office building - 803
Historical Office - 812
leadership - 5 (chart), 801, 812, 967
membership (lists) - 945, 948, 949
operations study - 800, 813
senatorial courtesy - 797, 800
session statistics (boxes) - 6, 8, 13, 16
subpoena power (box) - 802
televised sessions - 810-811, 818
treaty powers - 696
Senate Democratic Conference
social security benefits - 646
Senior Executive Service - 775
Senior Reserve Officer Training Corps - 623
Separation of church and state. *See Freedom of religion.*
Separation of powers. *See Congressional-executive relations; Legislative veto.*
Sergeant York tanks - 230, 237
Sewers. *See Waste disposal.*
Sex discrimination. *(See also Affirmative action.)*
education - 561, 570, 576, 580
insurance - 284, 697
pension equity - 667, 669-670
Supreme Court decisions - 708, 734-735, 713
Shamansky, Bob (D-Ohio)
electoral defeat - 10
tobacco bill - 498
Shamir, Yitzhak - 146, 194
Sharp, John A. - 11
Sharp, Philip R. (D-Ind.)
Alaska pipeline - 386
natural gas deregulation - 389
oil allocation authority - 377-378
oil company mergers - 382
Strategic Petroleum Reserve - 381
Shaw, E. Clay (R-Fla.)
Cross-Florida Barge Canal - 442
Shaw, Luther W. - 502
Sheffield, Bill - 12, 349
Shelby, Richard C. (D-Ala.)
acid rain - 422
Shenandoah (train) - 296
Shipping Act of 1916 - 316, 317
Shipping Act of 1984 - 317-319, 324
Ships and shipping. *(See also Naval ships.)*
antitrust immunity - 290, 316-319, 324
cruise ship conventions - 76
domestic content bill - 102
federal outlays (graph) - 290
illegal aliens - 678
maritime administration transfer - 299
maritime authorizations - 320
maritime subsidies - 290, 299, 316, 325
medical care for seamen - 523, 531, 535
port development - 442
port user fees - 315-316, 791
Puerto Rico cruises - 329
Supreme Court cases - 747, 752
Shipyard Incentive Program - 325
Shlaudeman, Harry W. - 165
Shopping centers
tenant bankruptcy - 693, 704, 705
Shoreham nuclear power plant - 373
Shoshone Indians - 345

Shultz, George P.
acid rain - 421
arms control - 233, 257
Contadora group - 185
El Salvador rights report - 166
foreign aid commission - 160
Lebanese hostilities - 156
Middle East policies - 194
profile - 1024
Soviet economic sanctions - 145
State Department tenure - 127, 155, 855-856
use of military force - 123
Shuster, E. G. "Bud" (R-Pa.)
coal slurry pipelines - 315
Sicily
missile deployment - 246
Sickle cell disease - 537
Sierra Club - 341, 405, 407, 466
Sikes Act - 478-479
Silver
defense stockpile - 216
market forces/bank losses - 83
Silverman, Leon - 656
Simon, Paul (D-Ill.)
Senate victory - 21, 23
Simpson, Alan K. (R-Wyo.)
GI bill proposal - 618
gas tax increase - 800
nuclear emergency planning - 374
nuclear power plant licensing - 368
nuclear waste disposal - 363, 365
Rural Electrification loans - 514
safe drinking water - 440
veterans health - 621, 623
water policy planning - 431
Simpson, Milward L. - 406
Sinai peacekeeping force - 140-141
Sjoblom, Glen - 437
Small business. *(See also Small Business Administration.)*
accounting - 69-70
defense production stimulus - 116
depreciation - 69, 81
Export-Import Bank loans - 106
export trading companies - 101
government contract aid - 276, 790
hazardous waste control - 452, 457, 458
imputed interest - 80-81
peso devaluation aid - 61
overseas investment - 99
relocation aid - 782, 787-788
research funds - 266, 273
shareholder size - 69
tax help - 68
trade adjustment aid - 650-651
veterans loans - 615
Small Business Act of 1953 - 276
Small Business Administration
authorizations - 265-266, 283-284
disaster loans - 59, 61, 516
minority programs - 266, 276
Reagan term overview - 262
research programs - 273
Tris reimbursement - 688
Small Business Committee (House)
jurisdiction, leadership, subcommittees - 973
Small Business Committee (Senate)
jurisdiction, leadership, subcommittees - 967
Small Business Investment Corporations - 283
Smith, Denny (R-Ore.)
wilderness areas - 471, 472
Smith, Mary Louise - 694
Smith, Robert F. (R-Ore.)
wilderness areas - 471, 472
Smith, William French
background - 687
LEAA shutdown - 685

legislative veto - 833-834
Meese investigation - 707
profile - 1017-1018
wilderness leasing - 342
Smith-Hughes Act of 1917 - 577
Smithsonian Institution - 784
Snelling, Richard A. - 23
Snowmobiles - 465
Social Security Act - 588, 589, 665
Social Security Administration
disabled workers - 668
Social Security programs. *(See also Cost-of-living adjustments; Disability Insurance Trust Fund; Hospital Insurance Trust Fund; Medicaid, Medicare; National Commission on Social Security Reform; Old Age and Survivors Trust Fund; Railroad Retirement System; Supplemental Security Income.)*
benefit limits proposals - 33, 35, 38, 40, 46, 47, 519, 556, 662, 670-671
chronology of rescue efforts (box) - 660
coverage of church employees - 82
coverage of congressmen (box) - 831
coverage of federal employees - 784-785, 661
death payments - 646
disability benefits - 644, 647, 652, 656-657, 667-669
financing reform - 4, 643, 644, 645-647, 652, 658, 658-663
minimum benefits - 44, 646-647
outlays (graphs) - 520, 644
retirement age - 659-661, 663
Supreme Court cases - 766-767
tax increases - 65, 78, 662
taxation of benefits - 80, 586, 662
Social services. *See Welfare and social services.*
Society of Professional Journalists - 151
Society of Separationists - 811
Sohio. *See Standard Oil Co. of Ohio.*
Soil conservation
omnibus farm bill - 493
sodbuster bill - 511, 513, 515
Soil Conservation Service
water policy planning - 428, 429
water projects - 441
Solar energy
Energy Department programs - 334, 336, 393-395
research funding - 399-400
technology trade - 111
Solar Energy and Conservation Bank - 394
Solarz, Stephen J. (D-N.Y.)
nuclear freeze resolution - 256
Solicitor general - 713
Solid Waste Disposal Act - 452
Solidarity
Polish economic sanctions - 98, 144-145
Soldiers of fortune - 245
Solomon, Gerald B. (R-N.Y.)
dam repair funds - 430, 444
Somalia
foreign aid - 134, 159
refugees - 149
U.S. use of military facilities - 209, 213
Sombrotto, Vincent - 785
Somoza, Anastasio - 181, 183
South Africa
investment ban - 108
Lefever nomination - 141
nuclear non-proliferation - 168
strategic minerals - 475
South Asia
nuclear non-proliferation - 139
South Carolina
highway aid - 307
revenue sharing - 117
voting rights action - 679, 680
South Dakota
B-1 bomber bases - 246

financial institutions regulation - 84, 92
highway aid - 307
revenue sharing - 117
voting rights action - 679
WEB pipeline - 438
South Korea
Amerasian immigration - 689
military facilities - 248
trade benefits - 110
South Yemen
foreign aid ban - 138
Southeast Asia
Amerasian immigration - 689
chemical warfare - 219
Soviet Purchasing Commission - 145
Soviet Union. *(See also Arms control.)*
Afghanistan invasion - 133, 179, 219
arms sales to India - 153
Central America aid plan - 177
chemical warfare - 219
Cuba resolutions - 150
economic sanctions - 98, 107, 126, 127, 144-145
fur seal harvest - 479
grain embargo - 107, 487, 488, 494, 495
grain sales - 499, 510 (box)
immigration to Israel - 148
Korean airliner downing - 155, 169, 225, 228, 254, 856
Reagan policy overview - 856
role in Central America - 124, 162, 177, 181-183, 188
role in Lebanon - 192
U.S. high-tech exports - 99-100, 144
Wallenberg whereabouts - 144
Soybeans
price supports - 492
Soviet grain sales - 510
Space programs
satellites - 781, 786, 789
shuttle - 776, 781
space station - 789
Space weaponry - 242, 244, 245, 851
ASAT missile - 204, 229, 230, 234, 236, 237, 240, 242-243 (box), 244-246
laser research - 206, 208, 226, 237, 251
Strategic Defense Initiative - 202, 206, 235, 237, 240, 242, 253
Spain
NATO entry - 155
Special Defense Acquisition Fund - 135, 137
Special Drawing Rights - 104, 105
Special orders - 799
Special Situation Group - 854
Specter, Arlen (R-Pa.)
Civil Rights Commission - 695
congressional tax deductions - 830
Speedy Trial Act - 684
Spellman, Gladys N. (D-Md.)
seat vacancy - 802, 804
Spent fuel management. *See Nuclear waste.*
Sports and recreation
Alaska parks hunting - 470, 474-475
amusement rides - 268, 285
boating, fishing taxes - 328
national parks - 463-465, 469-470
offshore oil leasing - 358
water projects - 441
wetlands protection - 480-481
wild and scenic rivers - 472-473
wilderness areas - 339, 465
SSI. *See Supplemental Security Income.*
St. George Basin - 358
St. George's Medical College - 183
St Germain, Fernand J. (D-R.I.) *(See also Garn-St Germain Act.)*

financial institution regulation - 83, 87, 89-90, 92-93

housing authorization - 635-636

IMF funding - 105

St. Joe Minerals Corp. - 341

St. Lucia - 183

St. Vincent - 183

Stafford, Robert T. (R-Vt.)

Clean Air Act revision - 411, 419, 422

EPA research veto - 453

health block grants - 526

health manpower programs - 530

nuclear waste disposal - 364

sewer grants - 427

Superfund renewal - 461

Staggers, Harley O. (D-W.Va.)

Shenandoah (train) - 296

Stallings, Richard - 23

Standard Oil Co. of California - 346-347, 349, 382, 390

Standard Oil Co. of Indiana - 349

Standard Oil Co. of Ohio - 385

Standards of Official Conduct Committee (House)

jurisdiction, leadership, subcommittees - 973

Star Wars. *See Space weaponry.*

Stark, Fortney H. "Pete" (D-Calif.)

PIK tax change - 508

START. *See Strategic Arms Reduction Talks.*

Stassen, Harold E. - 19

State and local government

abortion statutes - 690-691

commerce and consumer affairs

cable TV regulation - 262, 272, 274, 275, 279-281

Co-op Bank tax exemption - 268

product liability insurance - 269, 285

crime and law enforcement

anti-crime aid - 675, 685, 689, 697, 700

antitrust damages - 705-706

habeas corpus claims - 699

missing children - 686

State Justice Institute - 693, 706

Supreme Court cases - 755-761

trademarks - 686

victims assistance - 699

voting rights action - 679

economic affairs

banking - 84, 89-90, 92

block grants - 773-774, 777

bond issues - 76, 80, 82, 92

Chrysler rescue - 118

cost estimates of legislation - 777

enterprise zones - 119-120

infrastructure repairs - 302

mortgage assumption plan - 634-635

payments in lieu of taxes - 469

revenue sharing - 113, 117-118, 630, 772 (graph)

surplus federal property donations - 694, 783

tax exemption for congressmen - 823

education

access to schools for religious groups - 573

education block grants - 559-561, 571, 572

education regulations - 563, 564

equipment purchases - 576, 577

handicapped education - 567

Reagan term overview - 555-556

school prayer - 676

vocational education - 576-578

elections and politics

governors, 1981-84 (list) - 1122-1123

gubernatorial elections - 7, 12, 14, 23, 1103-1121

legislative elections - 12, 23-24

legislators' tax deductions - 71

polling place access - 792-793

Republican gains - 4

energy

conservation programs - 393-394, 400

mineral leasing - 344, 347-350, 352-354, 358-359

nuclear emergency planning - 374

nuclear waste disposal - 361-366

synthetic fuel development - 398

environment

air pollution - 411-422

coal slurry pipelines - 315

hazardous waste management - 458, 459

noise control - 454

park development - 463-465

pesticide law revision - 502

sewer grants - 425-428

strip mining regulation - 468-469

water resources - 409, 429, 430, 435, 439-442, 444, 446, 447

wildlife preservation - 478-479, 482

health

health programs - 523, 531-532, 546, 551, 552

Medicaid, Medicare - 528-529, 532-536, 541, 553

medical neglect of handicapped infants - 553

housing - 636, 638

labor

disabled workers - 668

job programs - 647, 655-656, 664

unemployment compensation - 647-648, 654

nuclear freeze movement - 256

transportation

bus deregulation - 310-314

drunk drivers - 316-317, 322-323

highway aid - 297-298, 303-305, 307 (chart), 321-322

port user fees - 315-316

Reagan term overview - 289-290

truck size limits - 317-318

welfare

AFDC administration - 586-588, 597-598

child abuse prevention - 608

child nutrition programs - 593

child support enforcement - 606

food stamp administration - 594-596

hunger task force recommendations - 600

Older Americans programs - 593-594

Reagan term overview - 519, 771-772

refugee resettlement - 689

social services block grants - 588-591

work requirements - 583, 596

State Department. *(See also Agency for International Development.)*

agricultural export contract sanctity - 499

aid to Israel - 146

aid to Turkey - 171

arms agency clearances - 224

arms sales to India - 154

authorization - 143, 148-149, 167-168

Canadian mineral leases - 341

Cuba resolution - 150

Czech claims agreement - 142

drug enforcement - 692, 701

El Salvador human rights reports - 166, 174

F-16 deliveries to Israel - 193

farm export embargoes - 496

foreign mission staff requirements - 179

Guatemala aid block - 163

hazardous duty pay - 168

Lefever nomination - 141

Nicaraguan World Court case - 187

Reagan appointments - 127 (box), 155 (box), 855-856

Soviet economic sanctions - 145

U.S. withdrawal from UNESCO - 148

State Justice Institute - 706

State of the Union addresses (text) - 1046-1050, 1059-1063, 1072-1076

Steel Caucus - 802

Steel Corp., U.S.

Marathon acquisition - 382

Steel industry

Clean Air Act revision - 411-420

domestic content bill - 108

import controls - 109-110, 111, 119

Stein, Jacob A. - 707, 846

Stennis, John C. (D-Miss.)

nuclear waste disposal - 365

Tenn-Tom waterway - 433-435

Stephens, G. Douglas - 11

Stevens, John Paul

appointment - 711-712

legislative veto - 835

school prayer - 703

Stevens, Ted (R-Alaska)

Alaska pipeline - 385-386

Alaska railroad - 314

battleship modernization - 211, 229

congressional pay and tax deductions - 822, 827, 829-830

defense spending - 209

franking privilege - 826

1981 congressional session - 7

Senate leadership - 5, 801, 812

Social Security coverage for federal employees - 785

Williams campaign funds investigation - 819

Stevenson, Adlai E. III - 12

Stewart, Potter

retirement - 711, 712

Stockholm International Peace Research Institute - 255

Stockman, David A.

acid rain - 420, 421

Amtrak authorizations - 295-297

budget issues - 30, 39, 41, 53

child nutrition programs - 601

Clean Air Act revision - 417

Clinch River breeder reactor - 370, 373

defense spending - 202, 851

environmental programs - 408, 456

farm target price freeze - 513

food donation program - 601

food stamp program - 612

hunger reports - 600

offshore revenue sharing - 359

omnibus farm bill - 487

poverty rate - 581

profile - 1025

Reagan economic plan - 45

synthetic fuels - 399

timber contract relief - 474

water projects cost sharing - 442

Stocks, bonds, and securities. *(See also Securities and Exchange Commission.)*

commodities futures trading - 68, 70, 499-501

corporate takeover reforms - 283

employee stock ownership plans - 70, 82, 665

Hugel misconduct investigation - 142

"incentive" options - 70

industrial development bonds - 71, 76, 79, 80, 82

insider trading curbs - 262, 276, 283

mortgage market - 638-639

mortgage revenue bonds - 82, 91, 638

municipal revenue bonds - 92

New York City fiscal recovery - 116

option straddles - 81

repurchase agreements - 705

securities companies regulation - 83-84, 87-90, 92-93

Supreme Court cases - 746-747

tax law changes - 76, 82

U.S. savings bonds - 48, 49

Wall Street reactions - 32, 44, 65

Washington Public Power Supply System default - 336, 371, 372

Stokes, Louis (D-Ohio)

Studds, Crane censure - 814

Stone, Richard B. - 165

Stonewall Jackson dam - 443

Stop ERA - 682

Strategic Air Command - 225, 252

Strategic Arms Limitation Treaty (SALT II) - 202, 221-222, 241, 249

Strategic Arms Reduction Talks (START) - 221-222, 229, 251-257

Strategic Defense Initiative - 202, 206, 235, 237, 240, 242, 253

Strategic Petroleum Reserve

fill rate - 338, 379-382, 390, 791

off-budget accounting - 379, 381, 393, 396

oil allocation authority - 375-377

relation to Elk Hill reserves - 347

site map - 380

status and value - 338

test sale proposal - 390

Stratton, Samuel S. (D-N.Y.)

nuclear waste disposal - 363, 369

U.S. role in Lebanon - 229

Street people. *See Homeless persons.*

Stringfellow Acid Pits - 455, 457

Strip mining - 354, 404, 406, 468-469

Studds, Gerry E. (D-Mass.)

sex scandal/censure - 810, 812-814

Student aid

college aid - 557-559, 561-563, 565

draft registration compliance - 562 (box), 574

eligibility rules - 557-559, 562, 566, 575 (box)

employer-provided aid - 82

food stamp eligibility - 596

guaranteed loans, 1973-84 (graph) - 566

health professions - 530

Indian fellowships - 576

Latin American scholarships - 189

loan consolidation - 562, 563

loan repayments - 58, 559, 566, 791

military recruits - 241, 244-245

Reagan term overview - 520, 555-556

veterans - 240, 562, 563, 580, 618, 621-622

work-study program - 602

Student Loan Marketing Association (Sallie Mae) - 559, 562, 563, 566, 567

Stump, Bob (R-Ariz.)

election, 1982 - 11

party shift - 801, 812

Subchapter S taxation - 76

Submarines

communications - 237, 244

crew bonuses - 215

Los Angeles class - 208, 220, 221, 228, 230, 236, 240, 244

Los Angeles class follow-on - 236, 240

ocean dumping - 436-437

SLBMs - 203, 250, 252, 254

Trident launchers

authorizations - 206, 207, 217-221, 226, 228-230, 236, 244

components - 206, 230

Kings Bay base - 213, 246

Submerged Lands Act of 1953 - 347

Subways. *See Mass transit.*

Sudan

famine aid - 178

foreign aid - 134, 138, 160

Sudden Infant Death Syndrome - 525
Sugar
Caribbean exports - 106, 149
overseas investments - 99
price supports - 487, 488, 492
Sununu, John - 12
Superfund - 409, 449-452, 454-457, 459-461
Superior Oil Co. - 382
Supplemental Security Income (SSI)
benefits - 519, 582, 585, 597, 598, 602, 663
disabled children - 525, 535
eligibility requirements - 58, 611, 646
energy aid - 590
income accounting system - 588
Supreme Court. (See also Supreme Court cases.)
abortion decisions - 540, 675, 690, 691
agent identity disclosure - 151
air bag rule - 322
antitrust damages - 693
bankruptcy courts - 692-693, 698, 702, 714
budget ruling - 51
cable TV deregulation - 279, 280
Clean Air Act - 413, 420
coal leasing system - 357
congressional contempt power - 452
death penalty - 712
disabled workers - 669, 671
draft registration/student aid - 562 (box), 574 (box)
exclusionary rule - 709
franking privilege - 826, 831-832
Iran hostage release agreement (box) - 143
jurisdiction and workload - 693, 695-696, 713, 714
labor contracts of bankrupt companies - 702
legislative veto decision - 799 (box), 833-840, 981-992 (text)
justices
list, 1981-84 - 711-712
salaries - 714
Marathon Oil merger - 382
mortgage assumption laws - 634
Nixon tapes - 450
O'Connor appointment - 676, 711, 712
offshore leases - 352, 358-359
overview, 1981-84 - 711-714
pocket-veto power - 799 (box), 817
police force - 683
presidential immunity - 714
protection of justices - 683
redistricting - 15
Rock Island Railroad bankruptcy - 314
school prayer - 574, 703
sex discrimination in education - 570, 580, 708
student aid/draft registration - 562 (box), 574 (box)
truck size limits - 324
tuition tax deductions - 568
voting rights - 680
Supreme Court Building - 803
Supreme Court cases
Abrams v. Martin - 723
Akron Center for Reproductive Health v. City of Akron - 725
Albernaz v. United States - 718
Alessi v. Raybestos-Manhattan - 749
Alfred L. Snapp & Co. v. Puerto Rico - 755-756
Allen v. McCurry - 762
Allen v. Wright - 735
Allstate Insurance Co. v. Hague - 758
Aloha Airlines v. Director of Taxation of Hawaii - 748
Aluminum Company of America v.

Central Lincoln Peoples Utility District - 755
American Bank & Trust Co. v. Dallas County - 760
American Broadcasting Cos. v. Federal Communications Commission - 740
American Broadcasting Cos. v. WNCN Listeners Guild - 740
American Express v. Koerner - 728
American Iron and Steel Institute v. Natural Resources Defense Council - 755
American Medical Association v. Federal Trade Commission - 745
American Paper Institute v. American Electric Power Service Corp. - 754
American Society of Mechanical Engineers v. Hydrolevel Corp. - 742
American Textile Manufacturers Institute v. Donovan - 751
American Tobacco Co. v. Patterson - 731-732
Amoco Production Co. v. Jicarilla Apache Tribe - 747
Anderson v. Celebrezze - 738
Anderson Bros. Ford and Ford Motor Credit v. Valencia - 728
Arizona v. California - 761
Arizona v. Manypenny - 763
Arizona v. Maricopa County Medical Society - 742
Arizona v. Rumsey - 719
Arizona v. San Carlos Apache Tribe - 758
Arizona Electric Power Cooperative v. Mid-Louisiana Gas - 754
Arizona Governing Committee for Tax Annuity and Deferred Compensation Plans v. Norris - 734-735
Arkansas Electric Cooperative Corp. v. Arkansas Public Service Commission - 754
Arkansas Louisiana Gas Co. v. Hall - 753
Armco v. Hardesty - 760
Army and Air Force Exchange Service v. Sheehan - 763
ASARCO v. Idaho State Tax Commission - 759
Ashcroft v. Planned Parenthood - 691, 725
Associated General Contractors of California v. California State Council of Carpenters - 742
Bacchus Imports v. Dias - 760
Badaracco v. Commissioner of Internal Revenue - 748
Baldrige v. Shapiro - 766
Ball v. James - 740
Baltimore Gas and Electric Co. v. Natural Resources Defense Council - 754
BankAmerica Corp. v. United States - 743
Barclay v. Florida - 722
Barefoot v. Estelle - 722
Barrentine v. Arkansas-Best Freight System - 748
Bearden v. Georgia - 724
Beecher v. Boston NAACP - 726
Belknap v. Hale - 751
Bell v. New Jersey - 756
Bell v. United States - 724
Beltran v. Myers - 766
Berkemer v. McCarty - 718
Bernal v. Fainter - 726
Bill Johnson's Restaurants v. National Labor Relations Board - 750
Block v. Community Nutrition Institute - 741
Block v. Neal - 767
Block v. North Dakota - 754
Block v. Rutherford - 731

Blue Shield of Virginia v. McCready - 742
Blum v. Bacon - 767
Blum v. Stenson - 727
Blum v. Yaretsky - 728
Board of Education, Island Trees Union Free School District v. Pico - 736
Board of Education of Henrick Hudson Central School District v. Rowley - 730
Board of Education of Paris Union School District v. Vail - 729
Board of Governors of the Federal Reserve System v. Investment Company Institute - 743
Bob Jones University v. United States - 735
Bolger v. Youngs Drug Products Corp. - 737
Bose Corp. v. Consumers Union of the United States - 739
Boston Firefighters v. Boston NAACP - 726
Boston Police Patrolmen's Association v. Castro - 726
Bowen v. U.S. Postal Service - 750
Bowsher v. Merck & Co. - 768
Bread Political Action Committee v. Federal Election Commission - 741
Briscoe v. LaHue - 728-729
Brown v. Hartlage - 736
Brown v. Hotel & Restaurant Employees and Bartenders Union - 756
Brown v. Socialist Workers '74 Campaign Committee (Ohio) - 738
Brown v. Thompson - 740
Buczynski v. General Motors - 749
Bullington v. Missouri - 718
Bureau of Alcohol, Tobacco and Firearms v. Federal Labor Relations Authority - 751
Burlington Northern v. United States - 745
Burnett v. Grattan - 733
Bush v. Lucas - 737
Cabell v. Chavez-Salido - 726
Calder v. Jones - 739
California v. Arizona and the United States - 760
California v. Grace Brethren Church - 764
California v. Ramos - 723
California v. Secretary of the Interior - 754
California v. Sierra Club - 752
California v. Trombetta - 724
California ex rel. State Lands Commission v. United States - 760-761
California Medical Association v. Federal Election Commission - 735-736
Capital Cities Cable v. Crisp - 758
Carson v. American Brands - 762
Carter v. Kentucky - 717
CBS v. Federal Communications Commission - 740
Chandler v. Florida - 723
Chappell v. Wallace - 729
Chardon v. Soto - 729
Charles D. Bonanno Linen Service v. National Labor Relations Board - 748
Chevron USA v. Natural Resources Defense Council - 755
Chicago and North Western Transportation Co. v. Kalo Brick & Tile Co. - 745
Citizens Against Rent Control/Coalition for Fair Housing v. City of Berkeley - 736
City of Akron v. Akron Center for Reproductive Health - 691, 725
City of Lockhart, Texas v. United States - 741
City of Los Angeles v. Lyons - 764

City of Memphis v. Greene - 727-728
City of Mesquite v. Aladdin's Castle - 727
City of Milwaukee v. Illinois and Michigan - 752
City of Mobile v. Bolden - 680, 681
City of New York v. National Sea Clammers Association - 753
City of Newport v. Fact Concerts - 765
City of Port Arthur, Texas v. United States - 741
City of Revere v. Massachusetts General Hospital - 756
Clark v. Community for Creative Non-Violence - 737-738
Clayton v. United Auto Workers - 749
Clayton Brokerage Co. v. Leist - 746
Clements v. Fashing - 755
Cole v. Georgia - 720
Colorado v. New Mexico - 761
Colorado v. Nunez - 716-717
Commissioner of Internal Revenue v. Engle - 748
Commissioner of Internal Revenue v. Portland Cement Company of Utah - 747
Commissioner of Internal Revenue v. Tufts - 748
Commissioners and Mental Health/Mental Retardation Administrators for Bucks County v. Halderman - 733
Common Cause v. Schmitt - 736
Common Cause v. William F. Bolger - 831
Commonwealth Edison Co. v. Montana - 759
Community Communications Co. v. City of Boulder, Colo. - 706, 742
Community Television of Southern California v. Gottfried - 730
Complete Auto Transit v. Reis - 749
Connecticut v. Johnson - 719-720
Connecticut v. Teal - 732
Connecticut Board of Pardons v. Dumschat - 723
Connick v. Myers - 737
Consolidated Rail Corp. v. Darrone - 730
Consumer Alert v. State Farm - 746
Container Corporation of America v. Franchise Tax Board - 760
Cooper v. Federal Reserve Bank of Richmond - 733
Copperweld Corp. v. Independence Tube Corp. - 743
Cory v. White - 755
County of Washington v. Gunther - 734
Crawford v. Board of Education of Los Angeles - 734
Crown, Cork & Seal v. Parker - 732
Cuyler v. Adams - 730-731
Daily Income Fund v. Fox - 746-747
Dames & Moore v. Regan - 761
Davis v. Scherer - 729
Delaware State College v. Ricks - 762
DelCostello v. International Brotherhood of Teamsters - 750-751
Deleet Merchandising Corp. v. United States - 748
Delta Air Lines v. August - 762
Democratic Party of the United States v. LaFollette - 738
Dennis v. Sparks - 765
Department of Transportation v. State Farm - 746
Diamond v. Diehr - 745
Dickerson v. New Banner Institute - 724
Dickman v. Commissioner of Internal Revenue - 748
Diedrich v. Commissioner of Internal Revenue - 747

Director, Office of Workers' Compensation Programs v. Perini North River Associates - 752

Dirks v. Securities and Exchange Commission - 746

District of Columbia Court of Appeals v. Feldman - 764

Dixson v. United States - 725

Doe v. Bolton - 690

Donovan v. Dewey - 751

Donovan v. Lone Steer - 751

Eddings v. Oklahoma - 722

Edgar v. MITE Corp. - 757

Edward J. Bartolo Corp. v. National Labor Relations Board - 751

Edwards v. Arizona - 721

Ellis v. Brotherhood of Railway, Airline and Steamship Clerks - 751

Energy Reserves Group v. Kansas Power & Light Co. - 753

Engle v. Isaac - 763

Enmund v. Florida - 722

Environmental Protection Agency v. National Crushed Stone Association - 752

Environmental Protection Agency v. National Sea Clammers Association - 753

Environmental Protection Agency v. Natural Resources Defense Council - 755

Equal Employment Opportunity Commission v. Associated Dry Goods Corp. - 731

Equal Employment Opportunity Commission v. Shell Oil Co. - 732

Equal Employment Opportunity Commission v. Wyoming - 756

Escambia County, Fla. v. McMillan - 741

Escondido Mutual Water Co. v. La Jolla, Rincon, San Pasqual, Pauma and Pala Bands of Mission Indians - 755

Estelle v. Smith - 721

Exchange Oil and Gas Corp. v. Eagerton - 760

Exxon Corp. v. Eagerton - 760

Fair Assessment in Real Estate Association v. McNary - 763

Falls City Industries v. Vanco Beverage - 742

Farmar v. United States - 748

Federal Bureau of Investigation v. Abramson - 766

Federal Communications Commission v. Gottfried - 730

Federal Communications Commission v. ITT World Communications - 768

Federal Communications Commission v. League of Women Voters of California - 738

Federal Communications Commission v. WNCN Listeners Guild - 740

Federal Election Commission v. Americans for Change - 736

Federal Election Commission v. Democratic Senatorial Campaign Committee - 741

Federal Election Commission v. National Right to Work Committee - 741

Federal Energy Regulatory Commission v. American Electric Power Service Corp. - 754

Federal Energy Regulatory Commission v. Mid-Louisiana Gas Co. - 754

Federal Energy Regulatory Commission v. Mississippi - 753

Federal Trade Commission v. Standard Oil Company of California - 762

Federal Trade Commission v. Grolier - 766

Federated Department Stores v. Moitie - 763

Fedorenko v. United States - 727

Fidelity Federal Savings & Loan Association v. de la Cuesta - 743

Finley v. Murray - 765

Finnegan v. Leu - 749

Firefighters v. Stotts - 726

Firestone Tire & Rubber Co. v. Risjord - 762

First National City Bank v. Banco para el Comercio Exterior de Cuba - 743

First National Maintenance Corp. v. National Labor Relations Board - 749

Flanagan v. United States - 721

Florida v. Casal - 716

Florida v. Royer - 715

Florida Department of State v. Treasure Salvors - 756

Flynt v. Ohio - 735

Ford Motor Co. v. Equal Employment Opportunity Commission - 732

Foremost Industries v. Richardson - 764

Franchise Tax Board of California v. Construction Laborers Vacation Trust for Southern California - 764

Franchise Tax Board of California v. U.S. Postal Service - 766

Franklin Mint Corp. v. Trans World Airlines - 744

Furniture & Piano Moving, Furniture Store Drivers, Helpers, Warehousemen & Packers v. Crowley - 751

F. W. Woolworth Co. v. Taxation and Revenue Department of New Mexico - 759

G. D. Searle & Co. v. Cohn - 755

General Building Contractors Association v. Pennsylvania - 728

General Motors Corp. v. Devex Corp. - 745

General Telephone Company of the Southwest v. Falcon - 732

Gillette Co. v. Miner - 758

Globe Newspaper Co. v. Superior Court - 739-740

Goldsboro Christian Schools v. United States - 735

Grace Brethren Church v. United States - 764

Greene v. Lindsey - 735

Griffin v. Oceanic Contractors - 747

Grove City College v. Bell - 570, 580, 708, 735

Guardians Association v. Civil Service Commission of New York - 732

Gulf Offshore Co. v. Mobil Oil Corp. - 763

Gulf Oil Co. v. Bernard - 763

H. A. Artists v. Actors' Equity - 741-742

H. L. v. Matheson - 725

Haig v. Agee - 151, 736

Haring v. Prosise - 729

Harlow v. Fitzgerald - 765

Harris v. McRae - 690

Hartzell Propeller v. Reyno - 763

Hathorn v. Lovorn - 740

Havens Realty Corp. v. Coleman - 730

Hawaii Housing Authority v. Midkiff - 757

Hayfield Northern Railroad Co. v. Chicago & Northwestern Transportation Co. - 756

Heckler v. Campbell - 767

Heckler v. Community Health Services of Crawford County - 767

Heckler v. Day - 767

Heckler v. Edwards - 765

Heckler v. Mathews - 767

Heckler v. Ringer - 767

Heffron v. International Society for Krishna Consciousness - 738

Heinhold Commodities v. Leist - 746

Helicopteros Nacionales de Colombia v. Hall - 759

Hendricks County Rural Electric Membership Corp. v. National Labor Relations Board - 748

Hensley v. Eckerhart - 729

Herman & MacLean v. Huddleston - 746

Herweg v. Ray - 767

Hewitt v. Helms - 731

Hillsboro National Bank v. Commissioner of Internal Revenue - 747

Hinton v. United States - 725

Hishon v. King & Spalding - 735

Hobby v. United States - 724

Hodel v. Indiana - 753

Hodel v. Virginia Surface Mining and Reclamation Association - 752-753

Hoover v. Ronwin - 757

Hopper v. Evans - 722

Howe v. Smith - 731

Huddleston v. Herman & MacLean - 746

Hudson v. Louisiana - 718

Hudson v. Palmer - 717

Idaho v. Oregon and Washington - 761

Illinois v. Abbott & Associates - 743

Illinois v. Andreas - 716

Illinois v. Gates - 716

Illinois v. Lafayette - 716

Immigration and Naturalization Service v. Chadha - 714, 762, 833-840, 981-992 (text)

Immigration and Naturalization Service v. Delgado - 717

Immigration and Naturalization Service v. Lopez-Mendoza - 727

Immigration and Naturalization Service v. Phinpathya - 726

Immigration and Naturalization Service v. Stevic - 726

Imperial County v. Munoz - 762

In re R. M. J. - 736

Independent Federation of Flight Attendants v. TWA - 731

Insilco Broadcasting Corp. v. WNCN Listeners Guild - 740

Insurance Corp. of Ireland v. Compagnie des Bauxites de Guinea - 763

International Longshoremen's Association v. Allied International - 748

Interstate Commerce Commission v. American Trucking Association - 746

Inwood Laboratories v. Ives Laboratories - 748

Irving Independent School District v. Tatro - 730

Jackson Transit Authority v. Amalgamated Transit Union - 750

Jacksonville Bulk Terminals v. International Longshoremen's Association - 750

James v. Kentucky - 720

Jefferson County Pharmaceutical Association v. Abbott Laboratories - 742

Jefferson Parish Hospital District v. Hyde - 743

Jewett v. Commissioner of Internal Revenue - 747

Jim McNeff v. Todd - 750

Joint Meeting of Essex and Union Counties v. National Sea Clammers Association - 753

Jones v. Barnes - 721

Jones v. Helms - 730

Jones v. United States - 723

Jones & Laughlin Steel Corp. v. Pfiefer - 752

J. Truett Payne Co. v. Chrysler Motors Corp. - 745

Justices of Boston Municipal Court v. Lydon - 719

Kaiser Steel Corp. v. Mullins - 742

Karcher v. Daggett - 15, 740

Kassel v. Consolidated Freight Ways Corp. - 757

Keeton v. Hustler Magazine - 739

Kenai Peninsular Borough v. Alaska - 752

Kern County Water Agency v. Sierra Club - 752

Kirby Forest Industries v. United States - 745

Kirchberg v. Feenstra - 734

Kissinger v. Halperin - 765

Koehler v. Engle - 720

Kolender v. Lawson - 727

Kosak v. United States - 768

Kremer v. Chemical Construction Co. - 732

Kush v. Rutledge - 729

Landon v. Plasencia - 726

Lane v. Williams - 763

Larkin v. Grendel's Den - 739

Larson v. Valente - 738-739

Lassiter v. Department of Social Services of Durham County - 733

Lehman v. Lycoming County Children's Services Agency - 764

Lehman v. Nakshian - 731

Lehr v. Robertson - 727

Limbach v. Hooven & Allison - 748

Little v. Streater - 733

Local 926, International Union of Operating Engineers v. Jones - 758

Lockheed Aircraft Corp. v. United States - 767

Logan v. Zimmerman Brush Co. - 731

Loretto v. Teleprompter Manhattan CATV Corp. - 757

Los Angeles City Council v. Taxpayers for Vincent - 737

Louisiana v. Mississippi - 761

Lugar v. Edmondson Oil Co. - 728

Lynch v. Donnelly - 739

Mabry v. Johnson - 725

Maine v. Thornton - 717

Marine Bank v. Weaver - 746

Marsh v. Chambers - 739, 811-812

Marshall v. Lonberger - 753

Martinez v. Bynum - 756

Maryland v. Louisiana - 759

Massachusetts v. New Hampshire - 755

Massachusetts v. Sheppard - 717

Mayor of Philadelphia v. Halderman - 733

McCain v. Lybrand - 741

McCarty v. McCarty - 745

McDaniel v. Sanchez - 740

McDonald v. City of West Branch, Mich. - 729

McDonough Power Equipment v. Greenwood - 765

McElroy v. United States - 724

McKaskle v. Wiggins - 721

McNichols v. Baldrige - 766

Memphis Bank & Trust Co. v. Garner - 759-760

Mennonite Board of Missions v. Adams - 733

Merck & Co. v. Bowsher - 768

Merrill Lynch, Pierce, Fenner and Smith v. Curan - 746

Merrion v. Jicarilla Apache Tribe - 747

Metromedia v. City of San Diego - 736

Metropolitan Edison Co. v. National Labor Relations Board - 750

Metropolitan Edison Co. v. People Against Nuclear Energy - 753

Michael M. v. Superior Court of Sonoma County - 734

Michigan v. Clifford - 716

Michigan v. Long - 716

Michigan v. Mid-Louisiana Gas Co. - 754

Michigan v. Summers - 715

Michigan Canners & Freezers Association v. Agricultural Marketing and Bargaining Board - 756

Middlesex County Ethics Committee v. Garden State Bar Association - 764

Middlesex County Sewerage Authority v. National Sea Clammers Association - 753

Migra v. Warren City School District Board of Education - 756

Mills v. Habluetzel - 727

Mills v. Rogers - 733

Minneapolis Star & Tribune Co. v. Minnesota Commissioner of Revenue - 739

Minnesota v. Murphy - 718

Minnesota State Board for Community Colleges v. Knight - 737

Minnick v. California Department of Corrections - 726

Mississippi University for Women v. Hogan - 734

Missouri v. Hunter - 719

Monroe v. Standard Oil Co. - 735

Monsanto v. Spray-Rite Service Corp. - 743

Montana v. Northern Cheyenne Tribe - 758

Montana v. United States - 755

Morris v. Slappy - 721

Morrison-Knudsen Construction Co. v. Director, Office of Workers' Compensation Programs - 752

Moses H. Cone Memorial Hospital v. Mercury Construction Corp. - 764

Motor Vehicle Manufacturers Association of the United States v. State Farm Mutual Automobile Insurance Co. - 746

Mueller v. Allen - 739

Murphy v. Hunt - 723

NAACP v. Claiborne Hardware Co. - 736-737

National Association of Broadcasters v. WNCN Listeners Guild - 740

National Association of Greeting Card Publishers v. U.S. Postal Service - 768

National Broadcasting Co. v. Federal Communications Commission - 740

National Collegiate Athletic Association v. Board of Regents of the University of Oklahoma - 743

National Cotton Council v. Donovan - 751

National Gerimedical Hospital and Gerontology Center v. Blue Cross of Kansas City - 742

National Labor Relations Board v. Amax Coal Co. - 749

National Labor Relations Board v. Bildisco - 702, 744

National Labor Relations Board v. City Disposal Systems - 751

National Labor Relations Board v. Hendricks County Rural Electric Membership Corp. - 749

National Labor Relations Board v. Transportation Management Corp. - 751

National Republican Senatorial Committee v. Democratic Senatorial Campaign Committee - 741

Nevada v. United States - 754

New England Power Co. v. New Hampshire - 755

New Mexico v. Mescalero Apache Tribe - 756

New York v. Belton - 715

New York v. Ferber - 736

New York v. Quarles - 718

New York v. Uplinger - 725

New York Mercantile Exchange v. Leist - 746

Newport News Shipbuilding & Dry Dock Co. v. Equal Employment Opportunity Commission - 734

Nix v. Williams - 721

Nixon v. Fitzgerald - 765

Norfolk Redevelopment and Housing Authority v. C & P Telephone Co. - 746

North Dakota v. United States - 753

North Haven Board of Education v. Bell - 734

Northern Pipeline Construction Co. v. Marathon Pipeline Co. - 692, 702, 744

Northwest Airlines v. Transport Workers Union of America - 731

O'Dell v. Espinoza - 728

Ohio v. Johnson - 719

Olim v. Wakinekona - 731

Oliver v. United States - 717

Oregon v. Bradshaw - 721

Oregon v. Kennedy - 719

Oregon-Columbia Chapter, Associated General Contractors of America v. National Labor Relations Board - 749-750

Pacific Gas & Electric Co. v. State Energy Resources Conservation and Development Commission - 753-754

Pacific Northwest Chapter of the Associated Builders & Contractors v. National Labor Relations Board - 749-750

Pallas Shipping Agency v. Duris 752

Palmore v. Sidoti - 730

Paratt v. Taylor - 728

Patsy v. Board of Regents of the State of Florida - 728

Patton v. Yount - 720

Pennhurst Parents-Staff Association v. Halderman - 733

Pennhurst State School and Hospital v. Halderman - 733, 765

Pennsylvania Association for Retarded Citizens v. Pennhurst State School - 733

Pension Benefit Guaranty Corp. v. R. A. Gray & Co. - 744-745

Perry Education Association v. Perry Local Educators' Association - 737

Pfizer v. Government of India - 678, 688

Philko Aviation v. Shacket - 758

Pickett v. Brown - 727

Pillsbury Co. v. Conboy - 717-718

Piper Aircraft Co. v. Reyno - 763

Planned Parenthood v. Ashcroft - 691, 725

Plumbers and Pipefitters, AFL-CIO v. Local 334 - 749

Plyler v. Doe - 726

Polk County v. Dodson - 765

Pond v. Walden - 757

Potomac Electric Power Co. v. Director, Office of Workers' Compensation Programs - 752

Press-Enterprise Co. v. Superior Court of California - 740

Princeton University v. Schmid - 736

Prosser's Moving & Storage Co. v. Robbins - 744

Public Service Commission of New York v. Mid-Louisiana Gas Co. - 754

Pulley v. Harris - 723

Pulliam v. Allen - 757

Pullman-Standard v. Swint - 732

Pyramid Lake Paiute Tribe of Indians v.

Truckee-Carson Irrigation District - 754

Railway Labor Executives' Association v. Gibbons - 744

Ralston v. Robinson - 724

Ramah Navajo School Board v. Bureau of Revenue of New Mexico - 759

Reed v. Ross - 720

Regan v. Taxation with Representation of Washington - 737

Regan v. Time - 739

Regan v. Wald - 761

Rendell-Baker v. Kohn - 728

Rhodes v. Chapman - 721-722

Rice v. Norman Williams Co. - 757

Rice v. Rehner - 758

Richardson v. United States - 719

Ridgway v. Ridgway - 758

Rivera-Rodriguez v. Popular Democratic Party - 741

Robbins v. California - 715

Roberts v. New Hampshire - 755

Roberts v. U.S. Jaycees - 738

Rodriguez v. Compass Shipping Co. - 747

Roe v. Wade - 690, 691

Rogers v. Lodge - 740-741

Rosales-Lopez v. United States - 719

Rose v. Lundy - 763

Rosewell v. Lasalle National Bank - 759

Rostker v. Goldberg - 734

Rowan Cos. v. United States - 747

Rubin v. United States - 746

Ruckelshaus v. Monsanto Co. - 745

Ruckelshaus v. Sierra Club - 754

Russello v. United States - 724

San Diego Gas & Electric Co. v. City of San Diego 745

Santosky v. Kramer - 733

Schad v. Borough of Mount Ephraim - 735

Schall v. Martin - 723

Schneider Moving & Storage Co. v. Robbins - 744

Schweiker v. Gray Panthers - 766

Schweiker v. Hogan - 767

Schweiker v. McClure - 767

Schweiker v. Wilson - 730

Scindia Steam Navigation Co. v. De Los Santos - 747

Seattle Times Co. v. Rhinehart - 739

Secretary of State of Maryland v. Munson - 737

Secretary of the Interior v. California - 358, 754

Securities and Exchange Commission v. O'Brien - 747

Securities Industry Association v. Board of Governors of the Federal Reserve System - 743-744

Segura v. United States - 717

Selective Service System v. Minnesota Public Interest Group - 762

Shaw v. Delta Air Lines - 758

Shepard v. National Labor Relations Board - 750

Silkwood v. Kerr-McGee Corp. - 754

Simopoulos v. Virginia - 691, 725

Smith v. Phillips - 719

Smith v. Robinson - 730

Smith v. Wade - 729

Solem v. Bartlett - 758

Solem v. Helm - 722

Solem v. Stumes - 721

Sony Corporation of America v. Universal Studios - 744

South Carolina v. Regan - 760

South-Central Timber Development v. Wunnicke - 758

South Dakota v. Neville - 718

Southern Pacific Transportation Co. v. Commercial Metals Co. - 746

Southland Corp. v. Keating - 756

Spaziano v. Florida - 723

Sporhase v. Nebraska - 757

State of Minnesota v. Clover Leaf Creamery - 757

Steadman v. Securities and Exchange Commission - 746

Steagald v. United States - 715

St. Martin Evangelical Lutheran Church and Northwestern Lutheran Academy v. State of South Dakota - 738

Strickland v. Washington - 721

Sumitomo Shoji America v. Avagliano - 732

Summa Corp. v. California - 757

Summit Valley Industries v. United Brotherhood of Carpenters & Joiners - 750

Summitt v. Sowders - 723

Sumner v. Mata - 762

Sure Tan v. National Labor Relations Board - 726-727

Taxation with Representation of Washington v. Regan - 737

Taylor v. Alabama - 715

Tennessee v. Arkansas - 760

Texaco v. Short - 757

Texas v. Brown - 715-716

Texas v. Certain Named and Unnamed Undocumented Alien Children - 726

Texas v. New Mexico - 761

Texas Department of Community Affairs v. Burdine - 731

Texas Industries v. Radcliff Materials - 741

Thigpen v. Roberts - 724

Thomas v. Review Board of the Indiana Employment Security Division - 738

Three Affiliated Tribes of the Fort Berthold Reservation v. World Engineering - 759

Tibbs v. Florida - 719

Toll v. Moreno - 726

Tower v. Glover - 729

Trans World Airlines v. Franklin Mint Corp. - 744

Truckee-Carson Irrigation District v. United States - 754

Tuten v. United States - 724

Underwriters National Assurance Co. v. North Carolina Life & Health Insurance Guaranty Association - 758

Union Labor Life Insurance v. Pireno - 742

United Brotherhood of Carpenters & Joiners v. Scott - 729

United Building and Construction Trades Council of Camden County v. Mayor and Council of City of Camden - 757

United Mine Workers of America Health and Retirement Funds v. Robinson - 748

United Parcel Service v. Mitchell - 748-749

United Parcel Service v. U.S. Postal Service - 768

United States v. Arthur Young & Co. - 748

United States v. Baggot - 764

United States v. Bliss Dairy - 747

United States v. Clark - 766

United States v. Cortez - 715

United States v. Cronic - 721

United States v. DiFrancesco - 718

United States v. Doer - 718

United States v. $8,850 in U.S. Currency - 728

United States v. Erika - 767

United States v. Frady - 763

United States v. Generix Drug Corp. - 746

United States v. Goodwin - 723
United States v. Gouveia - 721
United States v. Grace - 737
United States v. Grace Brethren Church - 764
United States v. Hastings - 718
United States v. Jacobsen - 717
United States v. Johnson - 715
United States v. Karo - 717
United States v. Knotts - 715
United States v. Lee - 767
United States v. Leon - 709, 717
United States v. Lorenzetti - 766
United States v. Louisiana - 760
United States v. MacDonald - 719
United States v. Maine - 760
United States v. Mendoza - 764
United States v. Mitchell - 767
United States v. Morrison - 720
United States v. Morton - 766
United States v. New Mexico - 759
United States v. One Assortment of 89 Firearms - 725
United States v. Place - 716
United States v. Ptasynski - 748
United States v. Rodgers - 725, 735
United States v. Ross - 715
United States v. Rylander - 747-748
United States v. Security Industrial Bank - 744
United States v. Sells Engineering - 764
United States v. Stauffer Chemical Co. - 765
United States v. Swank - 747
United States v. Turkette - 724
United States v. Valenzuela-Bernal - 723
United States v. VARIG Airlines - 768
United States v. Villamonte-Marquez - 716
United States v. Vogel Fertilizer Co. - 747
United States v. Weber Aircraft Corp. - 766
United States v. Whiting Pools Inc. - 744
United States v. Will - 761-762
United States v. Yermian - 725
United States House of Representatives v. Chadha - 762
United States Railroad Retirement Board v. Fritz - 729-730
United States Senate v. Chadha - 762
United Steelworkers of America v. Flowers - 751
United Steelworkers of America v. Sadlowski - 750
United Steelworkers of America v. Swint - 732
United Transportation Union v. Long Island Rail Road Co. - 755
Universities Research Association v. Coutu - 748
University of Texas v. Camenisch - 730
Upjohn Co. v. United States - 720
U.S. Department of State v. Washington Post - 766
U.S. Industries/Federal Sheet Metal v. Director, Office of Workers' Compensation Programs - 752
U.S. Nuclear Regulatory Commission v. People Against Nuclear Energy - 753
U.S. Postal Service v. Council of Greenburgh Civic Association - 735
U.S. Postal Service Board of Governors v. Aikens - 732
Valley Forge Christian College v. Americans United for Separation of Church and State - 738
Velde v. National Black Police Association - 766
Verlinder v. Central Bank of Nigeria - 764

Village of Hoffman Estates v. Flipside - 755
Virginia Surface Mining and Reclamation Association v. Hodel - 752-753
Wallace v. Jaffree - 703
Waller v. Georgia - 720
Washington v. Chrisman - 715
Washington v. Seattle School District No. 2 - 733-734
Washington v. United States - 760
Washington Metropolitan Transit Authority v. Johnson - 752
Wasman v. United States - 724
Watkins v. Sowders - 723
Watt v. Alaska - 752
Watt v. Energy Action Educational Foundation - 753
Watt v. Western Nuclear Inc. - 754
Weaver v. Graham - 731
Webb v. Webb - 760
Webb's Fabulous Pharmacies v. Beckwith - 745
Weinberger v. Catholic Action of Hawaii/Peace Education Project - 753
Weinberger v. Romero-Barcelo - 753
Weinberger v. Rossi - 761
Welsh v. Wisconsin - 717
Western and Southern Life Insurance Co. v. State Board of Equalization of California - 759
Western Oil and Gas Association v. California - 754
Westinghouse Electric Corp. v. Tully - 748
Westinghouse Electric Corp. v. Vaughn - 733
White v. Massachusetts Council of Construction Employers - 756
White v. New Hampshire Department of Employment Security - 763
Widmar v. Vincent - 703, 738
Williams v. United States - 724
Woelke & Romero Framing v. National Labor Relations Board - 749-750
Wood v. Georgia - 720
W. R. Grace & Co. v. United Rubber, Cork, Linoleum and Plastic Workers - 750
Xerox Corp. v. County of Harris, Texas - 758
Youngberg v. Romero - 733
Zant v. Stephens - 722
Zipes v. TWA - 731
Zobel v. Williams - 727
Surface Transportation Assistance Act of 1982 - 290, 321
Surgeon general - 531, 549, 552
Surinam
Caribbean trade plan - 106
Survivor Benefit Plan - 216-217
Suzuki, Zenko - 153
Swigert, Jack - 9
Symington amendment - 134
Symms, Steven D. (R-Idaho)
budget targets - 39
Clean Air Act revisions - 419
Cuba resolution - 150
infant formula marketing code - 143
safe drinking water - 440
Social Security reform - 661
Synar, Mike (D-Okla.)
MX missile - 239
Synthetic fuels
alcohol fuels subsidy program - 394-395, 495
coal leasing - 352
fossil fuel research - 396, 400
funding cuts - 393, 397-399
gas tax exemption - 306
grain surplus conversion - 503
prospects - 398-399
Synthetic Fuels Corp. - 59, 394, 397-399

Synthetic Liquids Fuel Act - 398
Syria
economic aid ban - 135, 162
role in Lebanon - 123, 156-158, 191-193

T

Tacoma, Wash.
watershed leasing - 350-351
Taft, Robert A. - 846
Taft, William Howard - 346
Taft-Hartley Act - 666, 700
Taiwan
arms sales reduction (box) - 154
trade benefits - 110
Taiwan Relations Act - 154
Talbott, Strobe - 257
Talladega National Forest - 466
Tanks
authorizations, appropriations - 206, 208, 210, 212, 218-219, 221, 228, 230, 234, 236, 237
DIVAD - 244
Tapes
record and tape piracy - 680, 686
Task Force on Regulatory Relief - 419-420
Tauke, Tom (R-Iowa)
broadcast deregulation - 282
phone rate hike - 279
Tauzin, W. J. "Billy" (D-La.)
broadcast deregulation - 282
Tax Equity and Fiscal Responsibility Act of 1982 - 48, 49, 72-77, 90, 540
Tax Reform Act of 1976 - 65, 71, 684
Taxation Committee (Joint)
congressional tax deductions - 821
jurisdiction, leadership, subcommittees - 974
tax study - 66, 68
Taxes. (See also Business taxes; Income taxes; Internal Revenue Service; Real estate industry and taxes.)
aviation - 75-76, 290, 308
benefits leasing - 787
chronology of action
1981 - 65-71
1982 - 72-77
1983 - 77-78
1984 - 78-82
collection compliance - 75, 90-91
deficit contingency plan - 50, 51
disclosure of returns - 58, 684
energy issues - 58, 70, 74, 80, 333
enterprise zones - 79, 119-120, 635
estate and gift - 66, 68, 70, 81
excise taxes
boat fuel and fishing equipment - 328
cigarette - 58, 76, 79, 549
gasoline - 32, 63, 76, 289-290, 301-307
liquor - 58, 81
telephone - 71, 76, 81
exemptions
mortgage revenue bonds - 638
state tax, for congressmen - 823
federal payments in lieu of taxes - 469
imputed interest - 80-82
inflation indexing - 32, 63, 64, 65-69
investment credit to Caribbean nations - 149
orphan drug development credit - 536
partnerships - 82
payment-in-kind income - 508
Reagan tax plans - 30, 32, 37-38, 44, 45, 51, 57, 65-66, 72, 77-79, 798, 848-850

revenue effect of changes - 32, 67, 71 (chart), 74 (chart)
Supreme Court cases - 735, 759-760
Treasury reform plan - 64, 78-79
tuition tax credit - 66, 561, 564, 567-568
Teachers and teaching
faculty housing - 82
math-science education - 565, 571-572
research and training - 556, 605
scholarships - 579, 605
U.S. territories - 573
Teamsters Union - 643, 657
Teapot Dome petroleum reserve - 346-347
Technology. See Science and technology.
Telecommunications. See Communications and telecommunications.
Telecommunications Research and Action Council - 281
Telephone and telegraph companies
accounting systems - 263-264
AT&T deregulation - 261, 265, 270-272
excise taxes - 71, 76, 81
international Western Union service - 265
obscene messages - 275-276
rate hike - 275, 278-279
Rural Electrification loans - 514-515
Television. (See also Broadcasting; Cable TV.)
broadcast licenses - 263-264
deregulation bill - 273
election projections - 285-286
nuclear war programs - 255
public broadcasting ads - 264
Reagan's mastery of - 3, 27, 844
rerun rights - 262, 275, 282, 694
Tellico Dam - 477
Tennessee
highway aid - 307
ERA vote - 682
revenue sharing - 117
wilderness areas - 443, 471, 472
Tennessee-Tombigbee Waterway - 433-435
Tennessee Valley Authority
Clinch River reactor - 372
power rate study (box) - 434
water policy planning - 429
Terrell, Norman - 1029
Territories, U.S.
teacher training - 573, 576
Terrorism
Capitol bomb explosion - 813
Chile aid authorization - 134
contract sanctity issue - 108
crime control package - 701
El Salvador - 175
embassy security - 179, 191, 192
FBI authorization - 140
Freedom of Information Act restrictions - 776, 779
Nicaraguan aid authorization - 136, 165
Reagan policies - 123
theft of nuclear materials - 685-686
U.S. PLO policy - 173
warhead safety - 215
Teton Dam - 444
Texaco - 382, 390
Texas
B-1 bomber bases - 246
highway aid - 307
Matagorda Island accord - 482
offshore leasing - 358
revenue sharing - 117
Strategic Petroleum Reserve - 379-382
voting rights action - 679
wetlands protection - 480
wilderness areas - 471, 472

Textile industry
Caribbean imports - 106-107, 149
labeling - 112, 548
Tris reimbursement - 678, 688
Thailand
Amerasian immigration - 689
drug traffic - 168
Theft
nuclear materials - 685-686
Third World. See Developing countries.
Thomas, Edwin - 707
Thomas, Lee M. - 408, 456
Thompson, Frank Jr. - 806, 807
Thompson, James R. - 12
Thompson, Victor M. - 399
Three Mile Island
accident - 336, 366, 367, 368
cleanup plan - 369-370
Thriftway Co. - 420
Thornburgh, Richard L. - 370
Thurmond, Strom (R-S.C.)
antitrust damages - 693
balanced budget amendment - 52
Judiciary Committee - 687
nuclear waste disposal - 365
Senate leadership - 5, 801
Tris reimbursement - 688
Voting Rights Act extension - 681
Tidal Basin
FDR memorial - 782-783
Timber industry. See Forest industries.
**Times Beach, Mo., dioxin contamina-
tion** - 456, 458
Tlatelolco treaty - 139
Tobacco. (See also Cigarettes.)
imports - 512
price supports - 488, 489, 492, 496-
498, 504-507, 509-510
quota costs, levies (box) - 506
Tobacco Institute - 285
Tomahawk missile - 228, 236, 244
Tower, John (R-Texas)
AWACS sale to Saudi Arabia - 131
budget resolution - 60
housing authorization - 635
impact aid - 560
Joint Chiefs reorganization plan - 224
MX missile - 239
nuclear waste disposal - 363, 364
retirement - 21
Senate leadership - 801
Toxic substances. See Hazardous substances.
Toxic Substances Control Act of 1976 -
453
Trade, foreign. See Foreign trade.
Trade Act of 1974 - 107, 110, 651, 665
Trade Adjustment Assistance Act -
110, 643, 649-650, 658
Trademarks. See Patents and trademarks.
Traffic safety
air bag rule - 322
authorizations - 300, 306
child restraints - 323
drunken driving legislation - 306, 316-
317
minimum drinking age - 290, 322-323
seat belt regulation - 290
speed limit enforcement - 300, 306
tire defects - 317
truck size limits - 324
Trailways Inc. - 311
Trains. See Railroads.
Transportation. (See also Air transportation; Automobile industry; Highways and
roads; Railroads; Ships and
shipping; Transportation Department;
Trucks and trucking.)
block grants history - 774
bus deregulation - 290, 300, 310-314

chronology of action
1981 - 291-301
1982 - 301-317
1983 - 317-321
1984 - 321-329
federal outlays, 1981-84 (chart) - 329
satellite launch licenses - 789
Tennessee-Tombigbee waterway - 433-
435
Transportation Assistance Act of 1982
- 301-307, 652
Transportation Department (DOT)
air bag rule - 322
Amtrak background - 293
Amtrak funding - 326
Conrail sale proposal - 294-295, 326-
328, 840
consumer activities - 325-326
hazardous materials shipments - 328
highway estimates - 321
infrastructure repairs - 302
Interstate completion - 297-298
leadership - 290
maritime affairs - 299, 319, 320, 324
pipeline safety - 328
railroad safety regulations - 329
report and wait provisions - 838
Safety Board appropriations - 300
satellite launch licenses - 789
seat belt regulation - 290
transport of radioactive material - 300
truck size limits - 324
Travel and Tourism Administration -
267
Travel and tourism industry
cruise convention deductions - 76
foreign tourists in U.S. - 266-267
offshore oil leases - 348, 350
passport fees - 149
Puerto Rico cruises - 329
Travis AFB, Calif. - 247
Treasury, U.S. (See also Budget, U.S.;
Taxes and taxation; Treasury Department.)
borrowing
debt ceiling - 42-43
interest rate on bills - 31 (graph), 32,
35, 40, 49, 76
loans
Aquatic Resources Trust Fund - 328
black lung trust fund - 650
civil service retirement system - 784
Co-op Bank stock - 268
Export-Import Bank - 105
railroad retirement system - 649
Rural Electrification Administration -
514
Social Security trust funds - 659-660,
662-663
revenues
budget receipts (graph) - 64
customs duties - 58, 791
debt collection - 58, 776-777, 780,
787, 791
duck stamp receipts - 480-481
military annuity enrollment - 216-217
mineral leases - 344, 346, 347, 349-
351, 359
oil and gas royalties (chart) - 345
Olympic coins - 783
overseas private investment - 99
park user fees - 469-470
patent fees - 686
power sales - 337, 434, 445-446
railroad retirement - 665
student loan repayments - 58, 791
timber contracts - 473
Watt land sale plan - 407
Treasury Department. (See also Customs Service, U.S.; Internal Revenue Service.)
bank regulation - 84, 88, 89, 105

commodities futures trading - 501
congressional tax regulations - 821-823
contract tax regulations - 75
contractors' claims for interest - 781
Crime Victims Fund - 699
debt collection - 58, 791
development banks report - 128
drug enforcement - 692, 701
faculty housing regulations - 82
foreign trade - 664
international currency market - 95, 98
tax compliance - 90-91
tax cut estimates - 66
tax reform plan - 64, 78-79
Treaties and international agreements
air crash liability (box) - 696
Alaska pipeline - 385
Anti-Ballistic Missile - 240, 244, 252,
253
British tax treaty - 696
Camp David accords - 141, 193, 195
Canada-U.S. maritime boundary - 143-
144
China-U.S. communique (box) - 154
Czech claims agreement - 142
domestic content bills - 102
fur seal harvest limit - 479
genocide outlawing - 179-180
Iran hostage release (box) - 143
Law of the Sea - 437, 696
nuclear test bans - 241
prohibition of nuclear weapons in Latin
America - 139
SALT II - 201, 221-222, 241, 249
theft of nuclear materials - 685
Treen, David C. - 14
Trial procedures. (See also Law profession and practice.)
charge of juveniles - 700
exclusionary rule - 699, 709, 713
expedited treatment - 706
fine imposition - 702
foreign business records - 699
habeas corpus claims - 699
insanity defense - 675, 692, 699-700
juror compensation - 688
mandatory sentences - 689, 692, 700
pretrial services - 678, 685
Senate subpoena powers (box) - 802
sentencing guidelines - 699
service of process - 688, 735
Supreme Court cases - 719-721
wiretap issues - 693, 700
**Tribally Controlled Community Col-
leges Act** - 564
Trible, Paul S. (R-Va.)
election - 11
product liability - 285
Trident missiles. (See also Submarines.)
production authorizations - 206, 221,
226, 228
role in nuclear arsenal - 202, 222, 234
Trident II development authorizations -
226, 228-230, 235, 236, 237, 244
Trinidad and Tobago - 182
Tris - 678, 688
Trowbridge, Alexander - 662
Trucks and trucking
antitrust immunity - 321
bus deregulation - 310-314
noise control - 454
size limits - 41, 301, 305, 307-308, 324
taxes - 81, 301, 303
trucker strike - 290
Truman, Bess - 476
Truman, Harry S - 476, 847
Tsakos, Basil A. - 818-819
Tsongas, Paul E. (D-Mass.)
ASAT missile tests - 242-243
congressional tax deductions - 830
energy conservation - 400
PIK bills - 498

retirement - 22
Tuberculosis control - 552
Tucson, Ariz.
Papago water rights - 432, 435-436
Tuition tax credit - 66, 556, 561, 564,
567-568, 713
Tunisia
foreign aid - 135, 138
Tuolumne River - 472-473
Turkey
aid project contractors - 173
foreign aid - 134, 135, 160, 162, 170,
171, 173
U.S. use of airfields - 232, 233, 248
Twentieth Century Fund - 555
Tylenol - 542, 689, 696

U

Udall, Morris K. (D-Ariz.)
Alaska pipeline - 386
coal leasing - 355
coal slurry pipelines - 315
dam repairs - 444
environmental programs - 405
Hodel nomination - 337
Hoover Dam power pricing - 445
nuclear power plant licensing - 368,
369
nuclear waste disposal - 364, 365
oil and gas royalties - 346
Papago water rights - 435-436
reclamation law revision - 432
wilderness leasing - 339
U.K. See Great Britain.
Ullman, Al - 286
U.N. See United Nations.
Unemployment compensation
AFDC eligibility - 585
benefit increases - 72, 643, 654-655,
665
eligibility - 647-648
food aid for unemployed - 598-601
income tax threshold - 76
mortgage aid for unemployed - 638,
620
outlays (graph) - 520
payroll deductions - 76
supplemental federal benefits - 659,
684
UNESCO. See United Nations Educational, Scientific and Cultural Organization.
UNICEF. See United Nations International
Children's Emergency Fund.
Uniform Code of Military Justice - 695-
696
Uniform Relocation Act - 782, 787
**Union of American Hebrew Congrega-
tions** - 255
Union of Concerned Scientists - 242,
253, 367
Union Oil Co. - 399
Unions. See Labor and labor unions.
Unitarian Universalist Association -
255
United American Bank - 83
United Auto Workers
auto imports - 651, 654
Chrysler rescue - 118
domestic content bill - 101, 102, 645,
658
United Methodist Church - 255
United Nations (UN)
authorizations, appropriations - 135,
136, 138, 148, 168
genocide treaty - 179-180

Grenada resolution - 183
Nicaraguan World Court case - 187
nuclear freeze movement - 256
seabed mining - 437
Security Council
Golan Heights annexation - 141
Nicaragua - 184
U.S. Lebanon policy - 158
warning on Israel - 153
United Nations Educational, Scientific and Cultural Organization (UNESCO)
press order - 148
U.S. withdrawal - 148
United Nations International Children's Emergency Fund (UNICEF)
authorizations, appropriations - 136, 138
United Presbyterian Church - 255
United Steel Workers
Clean Air Act revision - 417
steel import limits - 645
Universities. See Postsecondary education.
University of Georgia - 578
University of Hartford - 578
University of Kansas - 578
University of Massachusetts at Boston - 578
University of Utah - 605
Uranium industry
enrichment technology - 138
mine tailings - 366-367
import curbs - 368-369
Urban affairs. See Community development; State and local government.
Urban Development Action Grants - 113, 629-630, 631, 632, 634, 636
Urban Education Foundation of Pennsylvania - 579
Urban homesteading - 632, 636
Urban Institute - 302
Reagan policies effect study - 64, 519, 556, 582
Urban parks - 463, 464
Uruguay
foreign aid - 160
U.S. See inversion of name of agency or organization; e.g., Information Agency, U.S.; Steel Corp., U.S.
U.S.S.R. See Soviet Union.
Utah
coal leasing - 353
highway aid - 307
MX deployment - 212
nuclear waste disposal - 467
nuclear tests fallout - 605
oil shales - 398
revenue sharing - 117
wilderness areas - 339, 340, 471, 472
Utilities. (See also Natural gas; Nuclear power plants; Telephone and telegraph companies; Tennessee Valley Authority.)
acid rain - 420-422
Clean Air Act revision - 411-420
coal slurry pipelines - 315, 319-320
energy audits - 400
Grace commission power recommendation - 791
Hoover Dam power pricing - 445-446
oil allocation authority - 378
plant construction costs - 336, 374
power plant conversion - 383-384
power rate study - 434
relocation aid - 746
Rural Electrification debt - 514-515
Three Mile Island cleanup plan - 369-370
Washington state default - 337, 372
water projects cost sharing - 441
Western coal users - 353
wild and scenic rivers - 472-473

V

VA. See Veterans Administration.
Van Cleave, William R. - 850, 851
Van de Water, John R. - 1029
Vander Jagt, Guy (R-Mich.)
political ads - 816, 818
Vatican
U.S. diplomatic relations (box) - 167
Venereal disease control - 523, 526, 552
Venezuela
Contadora group - 125, 165, 185
international finance - 97
oil exports - 335
Vento, Bruce F. (D-Mich.)
water projects costs - 435
Verde River - 473
Vermont
highway aid - 307
revenue sharing - 117
wilderness areas - 471, 472
Veterans Administration (VA)
Advisory Committee on Former Prisoners of War - 616
Advisory Committee on Women Veterans - 619
Agent Orange compensation - 613, 615, 620-621
alcohol, drug treatment programs - 618, 624
burial benefits - 616, 617
business loans - 615
education programs - 614, 617
health program projections - 614
hospitals - 615, 617-619, 624
jobs programs - 617
leadership - 623
mortgage aid - 50, 59, 616, 618, 620, 623, 638
Veterans affairs. (See also GI Bill; Veterans Administration; Vietnam veterans.)
authorizations, appropriations (chart) - 614
budget cuts - 39, 48-50
chronology of action
1981 - 615-616
1982 - 617-618
1983 - 618-620
1984 - 620-625
civil service job preference - 615, 625
dental benefits - 616
disability benefits - 615-617, 620, 622-624
food stamp eligibility - 596
job training - 619-620, 624, 655, 665
medical care for radiation exposure - 615, 619, 620
Pell grant eligibility - 562, 563, 618
Reagan term overview - 613-614
Supreme Court cases - 735
Veterans' Affairs Committee (House)
jurisdiction, leadership, subcommittees - 623, 973
Veterans' Affairs Committee (Senate)
jurisdiction, leadership, subcommittees - 623, 967
Veterans of Foreign Wars - 618, 625
Vetoes. (See also Legislative veto; Line-item veto; Pocket vetoes.)
arthritis institute - 550
attorney fees - 709
bankruptcy bill - 677-678
copyright "manufacturing clause" - 686
budget resolution - 45
Bureau of Standards funding - 788, 789
conservation corps - 671

Corporation for Public Broadcasting - 282-283
dairy assessments (box) - 505
drug enforcement department - 689, 692, 698
education amendments - 564
El Salvador aid requirements - 165
EPA research funds - 453
federal contractors interest collection - 781
Florida wilderness area - 465, 466
health professions aid - 551
housing/congressional pay - 830
Indian colleges - 564
Indian health programs - 792
Indian land claims - 787, 792
jobs for elderly - 658
mortgage aid - 629, 633-634
oil allocation authority - 338, 376-378
Oregon land tracts - 476
Papago water rights - 436
presidential vetos, 1981-84 (list) - 1031-1032
school tax leasing - 787
supplemental appropriations bills - 50, 149, 150, 566, 830
water research - 446
Vice-presidency. (See also Bush, George.)
authority in presidential disability - 847
protection of aides - 683
Senate tie votes - 228, 229, 238-240, 854
Viera, José Rodolfo - 172
Vietnam
Amerasian immigration - 689
Vietnam veterans
Agent Orange compensation - 613, 615, 620-621
education benefits - 240, 617, 623
GI Bill benefits - 621-622
health programs - 624
job programs - 82, 619-620, 672
readjustment counseling - 613, 615, 618-619
Vietnam Veterans of America - 625
Vilseck military base - 222-223
Virgin Islands
Caribbean trade plan - 107
constitution - 777
education aid - 573, 576
health assistance - 547
nuclear arms treaty - 139
status of aliens - 678, 688
tax issues - 77
veterans medical care - 618
Virginia
highway aid - 307
revenue sharing - 117
voting rights action - 679, 680
wilderness areas - 471, 472
VISTA. See Volunteers in Service to America.
Vocational education - 116, 556, 574, 576-578
Vocational Education Act of 1963 - 576, 577
Vocational rehabilitation programs - 591, 602-603, 608-609, 623-624, 647
Voice of America - 166-167
Volcker, Paul A.
anti-inflation policy - 28-29
deficits - 32
financial regulation - 84-86, 93
international currency market - 95
profile - 1026
Volunteers in Service to America (VISTA)
authorizations, appropriations - 582, 590, 591, 598, 602, 610-611
Voting. See Congressional votes; Elections and politics.

Voting Rights Act
background (box) - 1012
extension - 4, 676-678, 680-681
Justice Department action (chart) - 679
Supreme Court cases - 740-741

W

Wages and salaries. See Congressional pay and benefits; Employment benefits and pay; Federal employment; Military pay and benefits.
Waggonner, Joe D.
Social Security reform - 662
Walco National Corp. - 809
Walesa, Lech - 144
Walker, Robert S. (R-Pa.)
House television - 816
outside income limits - 823
transcript alterations - 815
Wallace, Henry A. - 485
Wallenberg, Raoul - 144
Wallop, Malcolm (R-Wyo.)
Pauley Group leases - 349
water policy planning - 431
Watt support - 407
wetlands protection - 481
wilderness areas - 341, 467
Williams resignation - 805
Walters, Harry N. - 623
War Powers Resolution of 1973
background - 156, 684, 836
Cuba resolution - 150
effect of legislative veto - 836, 839
Grenada invasion - 169, 183
U.S. Lebanon policy - 124, 144, 155-159, 191-192, 836
Warner, John (R-Va.)
ASAT missile - 243
Warner Amex Cable Communications - 290
Warren AFB, Wyo. - 246, 248, 252
Warsaw Pact forces - 237
Washington
forests - 473, 474
highway aid - 307
Mount St. Helens monument - 469
revenue sharing - 117
watershed leasing - 350-351
wilderness areas - 471, 472
Washington, D.C. See District of Columbia.
Washington, George - 451
Washington Public Power Supply Service (WPPSS) - 336, 337, 371, 372 (box)
Washington Workshops Foundation - 570
Waste. See Fraud, waste and abuse in government programs.
Waste disposal and treatment. (See also Hazardous waste management; Nuclear waste.)
Farmers Home Administration loans - 495
ocean dumping - 436, 446-447
sewer grants - 405, 409, 425-428, 439
sewer studies - 302
Waste Isolation Pilot Plant - 216
Water and Environmental Quality Improvement Act of 1970 - 451
Water pollution
clean water bills - 439
federal programs - 409
ocean dumping - 436-437
safe drinking water - 52
sewer grants - 425-428
striped bass conservation - 481
Water Pollution Control Act of 1972 - 439

Water projects. *(See also Floods and flood control; Irrigation.)*
appropriations - 433-435
Carter hit list - 404
cost sharing plan - 440-442
dam repair funds - 438
deauthorizations - 438
Farmers Home Administration loans - 495
policy planning - 428-431
Reagan term action - 409
WEB pipeline - 438

Water resources. *(See also Oceans; Rivers; Water pollution.)*
chronology of action - 425-438
coal slurry pipelines - 315, 320
groundwater management - 409, 440, 447
hazardous waste control - 459, 460
marine sanctuaries - 438
policy planning - 428-431
reclamation law revision - 436
salinity control - 446, 447
watershed oil and gas leases - 350-351
Western reclamation projects - 503
wild and scenic rivers - 472-473

Water Resources Council - 428-431, 442

Water Resources Planning Act of 1965 - 429

Water Resources Research Act of 1964 - 429

Water transportation. *See Rivers and waterways; Ships and shipping.*

Watergate scandals
legislative aftermath (box) - 684
special prosecutors - 681-683

Watt, James G.
career history - 351, 355-356, 406-407, 464
coal leasing - 351-357, 838
contempt resolution - 341 (box), 451-452
controversial style - 403, 405-407, 474, 846
endangered species - 477-478
energy policy role - 334, 337, 397, 406
environmental policy role - 403, 404, 409
lands policy - 405-408
Linowes commission - 352, 355-357
national parks - 463-465, 467
offshore leasing - 357, 358
oil and gas royalties - 344-346
Outer Continental Shelf leases - 347-350
profile - 1022-1023
reclamation law revision - 431
strip mining regulation - 468-469
water policy planning - 428-431
watershed leasing - 351
wild rivers - 472
wilderness leasing - 339-344

Waxman, Henry A. (D-Calif.)
acid rain - 421
Clean Air Act revisions - 411, 418-419, 422
clean air sanctions moratorium - 423
Consumer Product Safety Commission authorization - 277, 839
environmental programs - 405
generic drugs - 548
health leadership - 552
saccharin ban deferral - 531
safe drinking water - 440

Ways and Means Committee (House)
jurisdiction, leadership, subcommittees - 552, 611, 973
party ratios - 802

Weapons. *See Arms control; Arms sales; Chemical and biological weapons; Firearms; Nuclear weapons; Space weaponry.*

Weather satellites - 786
Weaver, James (D-Ore.)
Oregon land tracts - 476
timber contracts - 473
wilderness areas - 471
Weber, Vin (R-Minn.)
Clinch River breeder reactor - 373
Webster, William - 687
Wednesday Group - 302
Weicker, Lowell P. Jr. (R-Conn.)
budget targets - 39
Education Department regulations - 563
health block grants - 526
health manpower programs - 530
Lebanon policy/war powers - 157
Weidenbaum, Murray - 1026
Weinberger, Caspar W.
bombers - 212
career and reputation - 127, 155, 217, 847, 851
defense budget - 53, 201, 202
military pay - 214
MX deployment - 212
nerve gas - 211
neutron bomb - 215
profile - 1018
use of military force - 123
Weinstein, Jack B. - 809
Weiss, Ted (D-N.Y.)
revenue sharing - 118
Welfare and social services. *(See also Aid to Families with Dependent Children; Child nutrition and health programs; Community services block grants; Food stamps; Handicapped persons; Health; Housing assistance.)*
budget cuts - 37-38, 58
chronology of action
1981 - 583-594
1982 - 594-598
1983 - 598-603
1984 - 603-612
definition of poverty (box) - 587
employee benefit plans - 82
energy assistance - 588-590, 603-605
food distribution program - 599-601
jobs programs - 599, 655-656, 672
leadership (box) - 611
legislative summary
1981 - 6-7
means tests - 791
Medicare provisions - 541
organ transplant aid - 549-550
outlays for income security (graph) - 520
Pribilof Island programs - 482
Reagan term overview - 519-520, 581-582, 777
social program spending - 589 (box), 598, 602 (box), 603-605
social services block grant - 588-590
workfare proposal - 583, 586, 596, 597

West Germany
arms sales to India - 153
claims against U.S. - 210
defense burden sharing - 222-223, 247, 248
military base improvements - 222-223, 230
missile deployment - 204, 228, 232, 255
oil imports - 197
Soviet economic sanctions - 145
West Potomac Park - 782
West Virginia
highway aid - 307
revenue sharing - 117
water projects - 443
wilderness areas - 465, 466
Western Electric - 270, 272

Western Union - 265
Wetlands protection - 480-482
Wetlands Conservation Fund - 480
Wetlands Loan Act of 1961 - 480
Weyerhaeuser Co. - 456, 469
Whales - 348
Wheat
food aid for Africa - 178
PIK program - 499, 508
price supports - 489, 490, 496, 497, 510-511
reserve - 178, 601
target price freeze - 511-514
Wheat, Alan (D-Mo.)
election - 11
Wheeler, Burton K. - 805
Whistleblower awards - 792
White, Byron R.
appointment - 711-712
assault on - 683
legislative veto - 835, 837, 981
offshore leasing - 359
White, Frank D. - 12
White, George M. - 803, 810, 815
White House. *See Congressional-executive relations; Presidency.*
White House Office of Cabinet Affairs - 791
White House Office of Science and Technology
risk analysis - 454
Whitten, Jamie L. (D-Miss.)
congressional tax deductions - 821-822
jobs funding - 652
Lebanon policy/war powers - 157
WIC. *See Women, Infants and Children program.*
Wild and Scenic Rivers Act of 1968 - 472
Wild and Scenic Rivers System - 470, 472-473
Wildcat River - 473
Wilderness Act of 1964 - 339, 340, 465, 470
Wilderness areas
Clean Air Act revision - 412-413, 416
mineral leasing - 334, 339-344
preservation - 407, 409, 463, 465-467, 470-472
Wilderness Society - 341, 407, 466, 475
Wildflecken military base - 222
Wildlife protection
Alaska parks hunting - 470, 474-475
chronology of action
1981-82 - 477-480
1983-84 - 480-482
coal leasing program - 354
Endangered Species Act - 477-478
fur seal treaty (box) - 479
Garrison diversion project - 371, 443, 444
grizzly bear habitat - 341-342
illegal trade - 480
Interior Department programs - 403, 404
marine mammals - 348, 479-480, 481
Matagorda Island accord - 482
payments in lieu of taxes - 469
Pribilof seal harvest - 481-482
Sikes Act extension - 478-479
striped bass conservation - 481
water projects - 440
Watt policies - 403
wilderness areas - 465
Wilkinson, J. Harvie - 1030
Williams, Harrison A. Jr. (D-N.J.)
investigation/resignation - 11, 800, 802, 804-809, 819
Williams, Leroy - 809
Williams, Pat (D-Mont.)
wilderness leasing - 342

Wilson, Charles (D-Texas)
drug use investigation - 815
Wilson, Charles H. - 814
Wilson, Kathy - 682
Wilson, Pete (R-Calif.)
election - 11
wilderness areas - 472
Wilson, William A. - 167, 1030
Wilson, Woodrow - 346
Wind River Reservation - 345
Windfall profits tax - 66, 68, 70, 76, 81, 375-376
Windmills - 111, 394, 395
Wine - 109-111
Winter, William - 21
Wirth, Timothy E. (D-Colo.)
AT&T deregulation - 261, 270-272
auto theft bill - 324
broadcast deregulation - 281-282
industrial policy - 97
oil allocation authority - 378
phone rate hike - 279
Wisconsin
highway aid - 307
revenue sharing - 117
wilderness areas - 471, 472
Wise, Bob (D-W.Va.)
Stonewall Jackson dam - 443
Woensdrecht, Netherlands - 246
Women. *(See also Abortion; Family and marital issues; Maternal and child health; Pregnancy; Sex discrimination; Women, Infants and Children (WIC) program.)*
Advisory Committee on Women Veterans - 619
domestic violence - 607, 608
economic equity issues - 582, 605, 697
Equal Rights Amendment - 682 (box), 696-697
Ferraro candidacy - 18-19
jobs programs - 663
judicial appointments - 676
Medicaid coverage - 57, 58
members of Congress, 1947-85 (totals) - 15 (box)
O'Connor appointment - 711
pension plans - 644, 697
rape crisis centers - 524
substance abuse treatment programs - 552
UN Decade for Women - 136, 138
vocational training - 577, 578
vote analysis, 1984 - 20-21
Women, Infants and Children (WIC) program
anti-recession relief bill - 599
authorization - 582, 612
commodity distribution - 586
spending ceiling - 592
Women's Educational Equity Act - 561, 573-577, 773
Wool - 490
Work and working conditions. *See Employment benefits and pay.*
Work Incentive program - 597
Works Progress Administration (WPA) - 653
World Bank. *(See also International Development Association.)*
authorizations, appropriations - 131-132, 148, 159, 161-162, 173-174
Central American economies - 182
IDA appropriations - 137
Reagan Caribbean plan - 149
Reagan policies - 95-96, 128
U.S. contributions limit (box) - 150
World Court
Canada-U.S. maritime arbitration - 143-144
Nicaraguan case against U.S. - 184, 187 (box)
World Food Program - 136

World Health Organization
    infant formula marketing code - 142-143, 149
    reproduction program funding ban - 138
Wright, Jim (D-Texas)
    Alaska pipeline - 386
    clean air sanctions - 423
    education-social welfare spending - 602
    foreign aid - 170
    House leadership - 5, 801, 812
    jobs plan - 652
    poverty definition - 587
    synthetic fuels - 399
Wyden, Ron (D-Ore.)
    energy technology trade - 111
    wilderness areas - 471
Wylie, Chalmers P. (R-Ohio)
    IMF funding - 105
Wyman, Jane - 844

Wyoming
    coal leasing program - 352, 353
    highway aid - 307
    oil shales - 398
    revenue sharing - 117
    voting rights action - 679
    wilderness areas - 339, 340, 465-467, 471-472

Y

Yarborough, Ralph - 854
Yates, Sidney R. (D-Ill.)
    coal leasing - 355, 357
    environmental programs - 405
    offshore leasing - 357-358
    wilderness leasing - 339, 343
Yellow Pages - 270-271

Yellowstone National Park - 463, 467
Young, C. W. "Bill" (R-Fla.)
    Nicaragua covert aid - 162
Young, Don (R-Alaska)
    wilderness leasing - 342, 343
Young Adult Conservation Corps - 657
Youth. *(See also Children; Elementary and secondary education; Postsecondary education.)*
    adolescent pregnancy - 525-527, 540, 552-553, 691
    deliquency prevention - 700
    job training programs - 82, 519, 553, 648, 655, 667, 671, 672
    mental health services - 552
    minimum drinking age - 290, 321-323
    pension plan participation - 670
    subminimum wage - 645, 571
    vote analysis, 1984 - 20
Youth Conservation Corps - 648, 657

Z

Zablocki, Clement J. (D-Wis.)
    arms sales to India - 154
    AWACS sales to Saudi Arabia - 131
    binary munitions - 219
    foreign aid - 160, 161
    Lebanon policy/war powers - 156-157, 192
    Nicaragua covert aid - 163
    nuclear freeze resolution - 230, 256
Zaire
    cobalt production - 475
    foreign aid - 159, 173
ZIP code
    9-digit plan - 775
Zorinsky, Edward (D-Neb.)
    Lebanon policy/war powers - 157
    radio board salaries - 153
Zschau, Ed (R-Calif.)
    high-tech exports - 98